ISBN 978-1-5281-4062-1
PIBN 10924157

1 MONTH OF
FREE
READING

at

www.ForgottenBooks.com

By purchasing this book you are
eligible for one month membership to
ForgottenBooks.com, giving you
unlimited access to our entire
collection of over 1,000,000 titles via
our web site and mobile apps.

To claim your free month visit:

www.forgottenbooks.com/free924157

English
Français
Deutsche
Italiano
Español
Português

www.forgottenbooks.com

Mythology Photography **Fiction**
Fishing Christianity **Art** Cooking
Essays Buddhism Freemasonry
Medicine **Biology** Music **Ancient
Egypt** Evolution Carpentry Physics
Dance Geology **Mathematics** Fitness
Shakespeare **Folklore** Yoga Marketing
Confidence Immortality Biographies
Poetry **Psychology** Witchcraft
Electronics Chemistry History **Law**
Accounting **Philosophy** Anthropology
Alchemy Drama Quantum Mechanics
Atheism Sexual Health **Ancient History**
Entrepreneurship Languages Sport
Paleontology Needlework Islam
Metaphysics Investment Archaeology
Parenting Statistics Criminology
Motivational

APPLETONS'

ANNUAL CYCLOPÆDIA

AND

REGISTER OF IMPORTANT EVENTS

OF THE YEAR

1888.

EMBRACING POLITICAL, MILITARY, AND ECCLESIASTICAL AFFAIRS; PUBLIC
DOCUMENTS; BIOGRAPHY, STATISTICS, COMMERCE, FINANCE, LITERATURE, SCIENCE, AGRICULTURE, AND MECHANICAL INDUSTRY.

NEW SE

NEW YORK:
D. APPLETON AND COMPANY,
1, 3, AND 5 BOND STREET.
1889.

APPLETONS'

ANNUAL CYCLOPÆDIA

AND

REGISTER OF IMPORTANT EVENTS

OF THE YEAR

1888.

EMBRACING POLITICAL, MILITARY, AND ECCLESIASTICAL AFFAIRS; PUBLIC
DOCUMENTS; BIOGRAPHY, STATISTICS, COMMERCE, FINANCE, LITERA-
TURE, SCIENCE, AGRICULTURE, AND MECHANICAL INDUSTRY.

NEW SERIES, VOL. XIII.

WHOLE SERIES, VOL. XXVIII.

NEW YORK:
D. APPLETON AND COMPANY,
1, 3, AND 5 BOND STREET.
1889.

PREFACE.

The year 1888 was notable in the United States for elections that changed the political complexion of two branches of the National Government, and in Europe for the death of two emperors of Germany. Under the title "United States, Presidential Elections in," the reader will find in this volume a condensed compilation, by counties, of the figures of the last five presidential elections, more conveniently arranged for comparison than such figures ever have been before. In the articles "Harrison," "Morton," and "United States," the other facts of the canvass are set forth. The changes in Germany may be found under that title and in the articles on the three emperors—"Wilhelm I," "Friedrich III," and "Wilhelm II." Other movements, political and military, are recorded in the articles "Abyssinia," "Afghanistan," "Great Britain," "France," "Samoa," and "Zanzibar," the article on Samoa being accompanied by a new map, which shows the harbor secured for the United States. Besides the public works described in the article "Engineering," a most important one is set forth under "Nicaragua," where the reader will find the latest facts about what now appears to be the most feasible plan for a ship-canal between the two oceans, illustrated by a colored bird's-eye view. The "Financial Review" furnishes the usual fine summary of the year's transactions, and the increase of our material prosperity may be further noted in the articles on the separate States and Territories, and in that entitled "Cities, American, Recent Growth of," continued from the two preceding volumes. The most noted deaths of the year, in the United States, were those of Gen. Sheridan and Chief-Justice Waite, on whom the reader will find articles, as well as on their successors, Gen. Schofield and Chief-Justice Fuller, the last-named illustrated by a portrait on steel. Among the other losses of eminent citizens may be noted the Hon. Roscoe Conkling, who was a victim of the March blizzard; the venerable A. Bronson Alcott and his daughter Louisa; Asa Gray, the botanist; Mrs. Lozier, the physician; Seth Green, the pioneer pisciculturist; and Richard A. Proctor, the scientist. The Obituaries, both American and Foreign, will be found to cover a wide range.

Among the special and timely articles are those on "Absentee," "Agnostic," "Atlantic Ocean Hydrography," "Burial Laws," "Balance of Power," "Beds, Folding," "Boats, Collapsable," "Charity Organization," "Camps for Boys," "Co-operation," "Cremation, Progress of," "Congress, Contested Elections in,"

"Diplomats, Dismission of," "Epidemics," "Government Departments," "House-Boats," "Immigration," "King's Daughters," "Lands, Public," "Mining Laws," "Mars, Recent Studies of," "Petroleum," "Sunday Legislation," "Teachers' Associations," and the "United States Navy." Most of these articles are furnished by experts, among whom are Prof. Herbert B. Adams, Willard Parker Butler, Prof. Stephen F. Peckham, Prof. John K. Rees, and Lieut. Raymond P. Rodgers, U. S. N.

Instead of one colored illustration, this year the volume has four—the bird's-eye view of the proposed Nicaragua Canal, and maps of the Territories (soon to be States) of Montana, Washington, and the Dakotas, though the congressional action in regard to these Territories took place in 1889. The three steel portraits include the new President and Chief-Justice of the United States and the young Emperor of Germany. Among the other illustrations of special interest are the new bridge over Harlem river, the moving of Brighton Beach Hotel, the appearance of New York streets after the great blizzard, the Eiffel Tower, the Lick Observatory, the maps of Southern Africa and the Samoan Islands, the new United States cruisers, the series showing evolution of the railway-car, the map of Mars as seen through the great telescope, and the numerous fine portraits in the text, including those of Vice-President Morton and Gen. Schofield.

NEW YORK, *April 6, 1889.*

CONTRIBUTORS.

Among the Contributors to this Volume of the "Annual Cyclopædia" are the following:

Herbert B. Adams, Ph. D.,
Professor in Johns Hopkins University.
CO-OPERATION.

Jerome Allen, Ph. D.,
Editor of the School Journal.
TEACHERS' ASSOCIATIONS.

Marcus Benjamin,
Fellow of the London Chemical Society.
GRAY, ASA,
PHARMACY,
PROCTOR, RICHARD ANTHONY,
and other articles.

J. H. A. Bone,
Editor of the Cleveland (O.) Plaindealer.
OHIO.

Arthur E. Bostwick, Ph. D.
IDENTIFICATION, PERSONAL.

Charles B. Boyle.
MARS, RECENT STUDIES OF.

Samuel M. Brickner.
DISSECTING.

Miss Nellie Brightman.
ELY,
PORT ARTHUR,
and other articles on new cities.

Willard Parker Butler.
MINING LAW IN THE UNITED STATES.

Mrs. Isa Carrington Cabell.
ARNOLD, MATTHEW.

Milo D. Campbell,
Gov. Luce's private secretary.
MICHIGAN.

Thomas Campbell-Copeland.
UNITED STATES, PRESIDENTIAL ELECTIONS IN.

James P. Carey,
Financial Editor of the Journal of Commerce.
FINANCIAL REVIEW OF 1888.

John D. Champlin, Jr.,
Editor of Cyclopædia of Painters and Paintings.
FINE ARTS IN 1888.

Henry Dalby,
Editor of the Montreal Star.
CANADIAN ARTICLES.

Maurice F. Egan,
Professor in Notre Dame University.
ROMAN CATHOLIC CHURCH.

Rev. William E. Griffis, D. D.,
Author of "The Mikado's Empire."
JAPAN.

George J. Hagar,
Of Newark (N. J.) Public Library.
ARTICLES IN AMERICAN OBITUARIES.

Mrs. Louise S. Houghton.
CHARITY ORGANIZATION.

Frank Huntington, Ph. D.
ABYSSINIA,
BULGARIA,
GERMANY,
and other articles.

Ernest Ingersoll,
Author of "The Crest of the Continent."
CALGARY,
VANCOUVER,
and other articles on new cities.

Abram S. Isaacs, Ph. D.,
Editor of the Jewish Messenger.
JEWS.

Arthur S. Jennings.
BRICKWORK.

Mrs. Helen Kendrick Johnson.
HARRISON, BENJAMIN,
and other articles.

Charles Kirchhoff.
CENTRAL AND SOUTH AMERICAN ARTICLES.

William H. Larrabee.
BAPTISTS,
BUDDHISM,
MOHAMMEDANS,
and other articles.

Albert H. Lewis, D. D.,
Author of "A History of Sunday Legislation."
SUNDAY LEGISLATION.

Frederick Leuthner.
LABRADOR (AND MAP).

William F. MacLennan,
Of U. S. Treasury Department.
UNITED STATES, FINANCES OF THE.

Frederick G. Mather.
ANTI-POVERTY SOCIETY,
IMMIGRATION,
and other articles.

Miss Bessie B. Nicholls.
GOVERNMENT DEPARTMENTS,
LANDS, PUBLIC.
and other articles.

Col. Charles Ledyard Norton.
CAR-BUILDING,
CORDAGE,
ENGINEERING,
and other articles.

Rev. S. E. Ochsenford.
LUTHERANS.

Prof. Stephen F. Peckham,
Chemist to the Geological Survey of Minnesota.
PETROLEUM.

Prof. John K. Rees,
Director of the Observatory of Columbia College.
ASTRONOMICAL PROGRESS AND DISCOVERY.

Lieut. Raymond P. Rodgers, U. S. N.
UNITED STATES NAVY.

Miss Esther Singleton.
ALCOTT, AMOS BRONSON AND LOUISA MAY.

T. O'Conor Sloane, Ph. D.
ASSOCIATIONS FOR ADVANCEMENT OF SCIENCE,
PATENTS.

William Christopher Smith.
ARTICLES ON THE STATES AND TERRITORIES.

Rev. J. A. Spencer, D. D.
LITERATURE, CONTINENTAL,
PROTESTANT EPISCOPAL CHURCH.

Parker Syms, M. D.
SURGERY.

Robert K. Turnbull.
BOXING.

Arthur Dudley Vinton.
BURIAL, LAW OF,
EPIDEMICS,
and other articles.

Louis von Eltz.
MUSIC, PROGRESS OF, IN 1888.

William J. Youmans, M. D.,
Editor of the Popular Science Monthly.
CHEMISTRY,
METALLURGY,
METEOROLOGY,
PHYSIOLOGY.

ILLUSTRATIONS.

PORTRAITS ON STEEL.

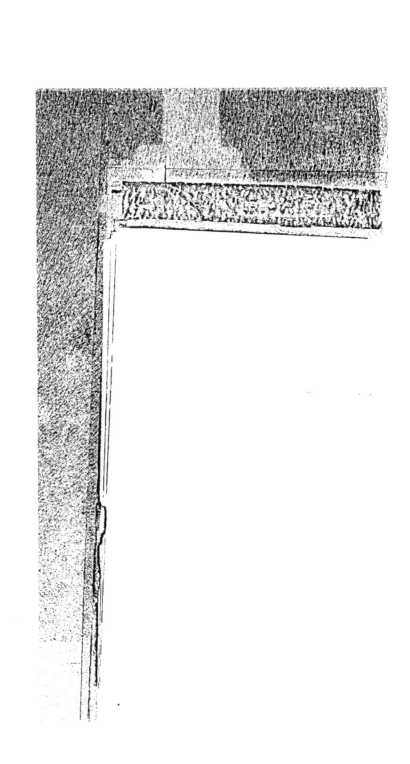

THE
ANNUAL CYCLOPÆDIA.

A

ABSENTEE. This term, with its natural derivatives, *absenteeism, absenteeship*, etc., has become somewhat conspicuous in contemporary literature, and is generally regarded as of recent origin. But it has a very respectable antiquity, dating back at least to 1537, when the so-called Absentee Parliament was held at Dublin, Ireland (Act of Absentees 28 Henry VIII, chapter 3). Of Henry VIII, Camden says (1605), that he "enriched himselfe by the spoyles of Abbays . . . and absenties in Ireland." Swift, in the "Argument against Bishops" (1761), says, "The farmer would be screwed up to the utmost penny by the agents and stewards of absentees." In the present century the term is used so commonly that citations are unnecessary, and those that have been given are quoted merely to show that the original meaning has survived the changes of centuries. Absenteeism is not peculiar to Ireland. History abounds with "absentee kings" as well as landlords. "The Norwegians," says the historian Freeman, in his "Norman Conquest," "preferred a foreign and absentee king," and Wallace ("Russia") refers to the "prevailing absenteeism among the landlords."

In general the term carries with it an intimation of reproach. Its simple meaning is —one who habitually or systematically stays away from home ; the attainder of reproach is derived from the assumption that any one who derives his income from investments on property in one country, and spends it in another, necessarily impoverishes the land from which his income is derived. The case of Ireland is the most noteworthy of any for the consideration of American readers, inasmuch as absenteeism is more general there than among any other English-speaking people, and to it has been ascribed a great part of the ills to which the Irish peasantry have fallen heir. In any argument in favor of home residence, however, it is necessary to assume that the personal presence, influence, and example of the landlords would be upon the whole beneficial. In

point of fact, Ireland is probably quite as well off with a considerable fraction of her landed gentry beyond the seas as she would be if they remained persistently at home.

In 1672 Sir William Petty estimated that one fourth of the personal property in Ireland belonged to absentees, and Prior in his list published in 1729 reckoned their income at £350,000. In 1769 the estimated income of the absentees was £581,700, and Swift in his time declared that one third of the rental of Ireland was spent in England. Absenteeism, according to the best authorities, continued to increase until the peace of 1816, when it began to diminish. Returns presented to Parliament in 1872 showed that 25·5 per cent. of Irish soil was owned by absentee proprietors, and 26 per cent. by proprietors who, though resident in Ireland, did not live upon their own premises. Prior to these returns a large number of estates had been impoverished by idle and extravagant squireens, and in 1848 and 1849 laws were passed facilitating the sale of encumbered estates, which has continued up to the present time, and has upon the whole reduced the average of absenteeism by subdividing the large estates and combining the small ones so that the present tendency is toward properties of moderate size.

Many historians, however, hold that while Ireland had her own Parliament the local nobility and gentry lived largely on their estates in summer but passed the winter in Dublin, thus spending their incomes among their own tenantry, or at least favoring the local circulation of ready money. With the union of Ireland with Great Britain (1801) London naturally became the political metropolis common to both countries. Moreover, the agrarian disturbances rendered residences so uncomfortable and dangerous that a large number of landed proprietors removed their families to the Continent and rarely visited Ireland.

The absentees have not lacked defenders, who hold that absence has no injurious effect

under modern systems of financial exchange.
Thus an Irish landlord living in France receives
his rental through bills of exchange, not in bullion, and these bills represent in the end the
value of exports from the United Kingdom into
France; otherwise, the remittance could not be
made. While the absentee therefore consumes
French goods for the most part, he aids in
creating a demand for a corresponding amount
of British goods, so that his tenants are benefited as much as if he had remained at home.
It must be confessed that this argument is not
altogether satisfactory from a practical and
common-sense stand-point, but it served its
purpose in its day. The fact is that the legitimate profits made by the tradespeople and
others patronized by the absentee accumulate
in and about his foreign residence, whereas,
if he had remained at home the benefit would
have accrued to his own dependents, and the
wealth of his native land would have been correspondingly augmented. A just conclusion
would seem to be, then, that while absenteeism
does entail a certain loss upon the home property, the loss is not fairly represented by the
gross income derived from the estates. There
are numerous channels through which partial
compensations return to the source whence
the income is derived.

Granting a good disposition on the part of
the land-holder, it is no doubt desirable to reduce absenteeism everywhere to its lowest
terms, especially in a country where there is
practically no middle class, as is measurably
true of Ireland. The disposition to relegate
the duty of supervision to an overseer or agent
is always objectionable, since too often such
agents are not on good terms with the tenants
and strive only to increase their own percentages while securing as large returns as possible
for their principals.

In free countries enforced residence is of
course out of the question, but where the laws
are just and properly administered there is
little danger that absenteeism will be sufficiently general to affect the welfare of the community. Where it has through past mismanagement become a crying evil, the remedy lies
in the slow result of reformatory measures rather than in any arbitrary or revolutionary proceedings.

ABYSSINIA, a monarchy in Eastern Africa.
The ruler is King John or Johannis, who is
usually spoken of by his title of Negus. The
territory directly subject to him is about 130,-
000 square miles in extent, with a population
of not more than 2,000,000 souls. It consists
of a high plateau, of the average elevation of
7,000 feet above the sea, which is nearly surrounded by the low-lying provinces of the
Soudan. The tributary kingdom of Shoa has
an area of 16,000 square miles, and is much
more fertile and populous than Abyssinia proper, containing 1,500,000 inhabitants. The King
of Shoa has recently occupied Harrar, which
extends to the southwest, south, and east of

Abyssinia, with an area of 700,000 square miles,
peopled by Gallas, Somalis, and other tribes,
which are practically independent.

The Army. — The military forces are commanded by Ras or generals, who are at the
same time governors of provinces. The most
powerful general is Ras Aloula, ruler of the
northern part of the kingdom, who invaded the
Soudan and fought a battle with Osman Digma,
and afterward attacked the Italians when they
attempted to establish posts in the hills back
of Massowah. His army numbers about 50,000
infantry and 8,000 horse, and is armed with
18,000 Remington rifles that were captured
from the Egyptians, and 500 Wetterli rifles
from the Italians at Dogali. The army of the
Negus is of the same strength in point of
numbers, but has only 10,000 rifles. Another
army in the west consists of 20,000 warlike
troops with 4,000 rifles, and finds employment
in guarding against incursions of the Soudanese. King Menelek, of Shoa, with his subordinate Ras Diurgué, has a force of 80,000 infantry with 50,000 rifles, besides a large body
of cavalry, making a total force to resist invasion of over 200,000 men, one third of whom
are armed with breach-loaders, and the rest
with muskets and spears. The artillery consists of 40 pieces, 30 Krupps having been taken
from the Egyptians, besides machine-guns.

The Difficulty with the Italians. — The Abyssinians are Christians, and their archbishop,
called the Abuna, is selected and ordained by
the Coptic Patriarch at Alexandria. This circumstance and the former possession by the
Egyptian Government of the port of Massowah,
which gives the Abyssinians their only access
to the sea, gave rise to frequent contentions
between the Negus and the Egyptian Government. When the Soudan was evacuated, the
British Government promised freedom of trade
through this port in return for Abyssinian aid
in extricating the garrisons of Kassala and other
posts in the Soudan. The Italians, who in 1885
established themselves in Massowah and on
the adjacent coast, with the acquiescence of
Great Britain, were not bound by this guarantee. The Negus suspected an intention on
the part of the Italians to conquer and colonize
his territory, and resented restrictions that
they imposed on trade.

The English Mission. — The almost complete
annihilation of a detachment of 540 Italian
troops in the vicinity of Dogali in January,
1887, by Ras Aloula, who nearly surrounded
them with 20,000 men, led the Italian Government to determine on a regular war. In the
hope of averting this, the British Government
to which the Negus had appealed in his difficulties with the Italians, endeavored to inter-
cede, sending Mr. Portal and Major Beech as
envoys to the Negus in November, 1887. The
conditions on which Mr. Portal was authorized
to offer peace were the acknowledgment of the
Italian occupation of Saati, the cession of a
part of the Bogos country, the conclusion of

a treaty of amity and commerce, and an apology for the attack at Dogali. On arriving at Asmara, the headquarters of Ras Aloula, Mr. Portal and his companions were made prisoners, and after many days' detention were sent on in search of the Negus, who was moving from place to place. At last they overtook him on December 5, and were well received, but accomplished nothing in the way of peace negotiations. They left him at Chelicot on December 5, and returned with letters to the Queen of England.

The Italians at Massowah.—By the beginning of 1888 the Italians had erected strong fortifications to guard against attacks either from the land or from the sea. The town of Massowah, which originally belonged to Turkey, and was annexed by Egypt in 1866, is built on a coral island, about two thirds of a mile in length, in the Bay of Arkiko, and has but one road connecting it with the mainland. The Italians have their arsenal at Abd-el-Kader, on a promontory to the north. The army headquarters were at Fort Monkullo, four miles inland. A railroad which ran from Arkiko in the south along the coast to the arsenal, and thence to Monkullo, was extended in February to Dogali and Saati, the terminus being fifteen miles from Massowah. This line of communications was rendered impregnable, and constituted a strong base for operations in the interior. The regular garrison, or special African corps, forms a part of the permanent army of Italy, consisting in 1888 of 238 officers and 4,772 men. It is recruited by voluntary enlistment from all the regiments of the army. A soldier enlists in this service for the term of three years, and receives a special bounty. This body was supplemented by an expeditionary force that was sent from Italy in the autumn of 1887, consisting of 480 officers, 10,500 men, and 1,800 horse. There were besides 2,000 native irregulars under the chief Debeb. The commander-in-chief of the forces was Lieut.-Gen. Asinari di San Marzano. The commandant at Massowah was Maj.-Gen Saletta. The brigade composed of the African corps, under Maj.-Gen.Gené, and another brigade, under Maj.-Gen. Cagni, were encamped in the beginning of February not far from Saati. A brigade, under Gen. Baldissera was stationed in the north at Singes, where a strong fort was built on the road to Keren, while the fourth brigade, under Maj.-Gen. Lauza, was posted at Arkiko. The fortress and field artillery consisted of 160 pieces.

The Advance of the Negus.—While the Italians were making their position secure around Massowah, the Negus refrained from attacking them, expecting that the large re-enforcements from Italy would attempt to avenge Dogali by marching into his country. There he was well prepared for them. Ras Aloula's army was not far back on the edge of the plateau at Ghinda and Asmara, which places were strongly fortified. In the latter part of February King

John joined Ras Aloula at Asmara, and finding the Italian fortifications completed, concluded that it would be unsafe to attack them. The Italians having made their base secure and perfected their commissary system, sent out flying parties for the purpose of learning the country and of provoking the enemy to advance. Ras Aloula pushed out his outposts, and there were several skirmishes, the Abyssinians invariably retreating. Colonel Vigono, the Italian chief of staff, made an excursion to the Agametta plateau in quest of a suitable position for summer quarters, though there was no intention of advancing beyond Saati before another season. By March the wells were partly dried up and the Abyssinians had drained the country of supplies. The army began to diminish, many parties deserting and going back to their homes. Ras Aloula remained with a part of his forces till June, and then left for his own province.

Mission to Shoa.—There were rumors of a rupture between King Menelek and the Negus, and the Italians, who were aware of the ambitious desire of the King of Shoa to overthrow Johannis and assume the title of Negus, sent Dr. Ragazzi in March to Shoa, by sea, with presents and offers of an alliance. But nothing was accomplished by this mission.

Peace Negotiations.—Overtures for peace were opened by the Negus on March 20, with a message to a native chief who was friendly to the Italians. Gen. San Marzano sent word that if the Negus wished to treat for peace, he must address himself to the commander-in-chief. On the 28th an Abyssinian officer brought a letter from Johannis asking for peace, in which he alluded to the ancient friendship between himself and the King of Italy, and expressed regret for the course taken by Ras Aloula. On March 30 two Abyssinian chiefs were sent by King Johannis, who was then at Saberguma, about ten miles south of Santi, to Gen. San Marzano to continue the negotiations. The Negus marshaled at that point a formidable army, either for the purpose of attacking, or as a military demonstration. On instructions received by telegraph from the Italian Government the Negus was offered peace on condition (1) that he should acknowledge the Italian occupation of Santi; (2) that he should not oppose the occupation of other points where the troops could spend the hot season; (3) that he should guarantee the safety of the tribes that had sought Italian protection. On the 31st the Negus replied that he could not accept the conditions, and on April 2 he retired from Saberguma with his forces, which were estimated at 90,000 men. In April the Italian expeditionary force returned to Italy.

Defeat of Italian Troops.—Debeb, a native chief who for a time served with the Italians as a mercenary, deserted them with his followers in March, and engaged in plundering the region around Massowah. On July 31 the Italian commander-in-chief sent against him 600

Bashi-Bazouks, under five European officers, and Adem Aga, a native ally, who enlisted 200 Assaortins on the way. The latter sent information to Debeb during the march, and the Italian captain, posting the rest of his force around the village of Saganeiti, where Debeb was with 700 men, half of them armed with muskets, entered the place with 100 Bashi-Bazouks, and drove the Abyssinians out of a fort, which he then occupied. The Assaortins went over to the enemy during the fight, and the Italian irregulars fled from the fort in disorder. Those outside were panic-stricken, and the entire force was routed, with a loss of 350 men. The Italian officers, with the few who stood by them, fell fighting, and the rest were killed in flight. Before the occurrence of this reverse, Maj.-Gen. Baldissera had relieved Gen. San Marzano in the command of the Italian forces in Africa. The chieftain Debeb was a relative of the Negus, whose favor he regained with the Italian rifles with which his force of scouts were armed when they deserted with their leader to the Abyssinians. His raids during July in the Habash country, lying between the mountains and the Red Sea, grew so bold that he plundered the neighborhood of Arkiko, four miles from Massowah, before the punitive expedition was undertaken. The principal sufferers were the Assaortins, which tribe was under Italian protection. The Italian commander-in-chief hoped by the expedition to Saganeiti to encourage the revolt of the petty chiefs of the province of Tigré, who had thrown off the authority of the Negus when he withdrew his troops to meet the dervishes. Capt. Cornacchia, commanding the expedition, had orders to surprise Saganeiti by a forced march, but to withdraw if he found that the enemy knew of his approach. He failed to observe his orders as to speed and secrecy, and when he reached Saganeiti, which is seventy-five miles distant from Massowah, he allowed himself to be ambushed in the village, which had the appearance of being deserted when his force first entered.

Diplomatic Difficulties.—The military governor of Massowah on May 30 imposed a tax on real-estate proprietors and traders for streets and lights, and on June 1 a license-tax on dealers in liquors and food. French and Greek merchants refused to pay these taxes. In the summer, the French Government, which has regarded with jealousy Italy's occupation of Massowah, put forward the claim that the capitulations existed there, as in other Eastern countries, and that Italy was debarred from imposing taxes and exercising criminal jurisdiction as regards French citizens and protégés without the consent of France. Signor Crispi denied that the capitulations had existed there under Turkish and Egyptian rule, declared that if they had they were extinguished by Italian occupation, and asserted that, even if they still were in force, foreigners would be subject to municipal taxation, as in Bulgaria,

Cyprus, Egypt, and Turkey. In a second note he explained that the judicial system at Massowah was the same as at Tadjurah and Zeilah, declared that the occupation of Massowah fulfilled the conditions laid down in the general act of the Berlin Conference, and characterized the objections of France in the following vigorous words:

It is not from Turkey that complaints and objections reach us, but, as is always the case, from France, who has succeeded in attracting Greece into the orbit of her demands: from France, who would appear to regard the pacific progress of Italy as tending to diminish her own power, as if the African continent did not afford ample scope to the legitimate activity and civilizing ambition of all the powers.

The Greek Government at first supported the protests of France, but was brought to accept the Italian view. The Italian foreign minister characterized the course of the French Government with a severity of language not usual in diplomatic intercourse, because it seemed actuated by a meddlesome desire to interfere, since there were only two French traders in Massowah, and the capitulations had been invoked by the French consul in behalf of Greeks, who were claimed to be French protégés. After the exchange of views between the Italian and Greek Cabinets, the merchants paid their taxes, but before that occurred several had been arrested, and some of them banished as rebels. M. Goblet, in August, replied to the Italian note in a circular, insisting that France had always regarded Massowah as Egyptian and Turkish territory. France was the only power having a vice-consul there, and he had received his exequatur from the Porte. Italy had for a long time disclaimed the idea of permanent occupation, and had failed to fulfill the requirements of the Berlin Convention of 1885, by not notifying the fact of taking possession to the powers, so that they might have an opportunity to make objections. The French minister denied that the capitulations could be set aside without the consent of the powers interested, and pointed out that, in other cases, as in those of Tunis, Bosnia, and Cyprus, the power taking possession had been able to produce a treaty concluded with the protected or sovereign government. He concluded by saying that if Europe assented to the Italian procedure the French Government would take note that henceforward the capitulations disappear without negotiation and without accord of the powers wherever a European administration is established.

This discussion gave Turkey an opportunity to renew her claim of suzerainty over the western coast of the Red Sea. The Porte dispatched a circular note to the powers, declaring the Italian occupation of Massowah to be a violation of treaties, and denying that the mention of its possessions on the Arabian coast only in the Suez Canal convention implies a renunciation of its sovereignty over the Soudan. Russia, as well as France, joined in the diplomatic protest of the Porte. Germany, Great

Britain, Austria-Hungary, and Spain declared the capitulations inapplicable to Massowah.

Annexation of Zulla.—One of the grounds for French remonstrances against the Italian policy in Africa was that France had some vague claims under old treaties to portions of the coast south of Massowah that Italy in 1888 added to her possessions. Italian irregulars occupied Zulla, which was nominally still subject to Egypt, and in like manner established themselves at Dissé and Adulis. In the beginning of August the Italian flag was unfurled at Zulla, and a protectorate was formally proclaimed over the district. The Italian Government, in a note to the signatories of the general act of the Berlin Conference, notified them of its action, which it declared to be only an official confirmation of a previously existing fact, and a step that was taken in compliance with the demands of the local sheikhs. The Italian flag was raised also at Adulis and Dissé.

ADVENTISTS, SEVENTH-DAY. The statistics of the Seventh-Day Adventist Church, as given in the "Year-Book" for 1888, show that it consists of thirty conferences, with the Australian, British, Central American, General Southern, New Zealand, Pacific Islands, South African, and South American missions. They returned, in all, 227 ministers, 182 licentiates, 889 churches, and 25,841 members. The whole amount of tithes received during the year was $172,721. The General Conference Association is a body which has been incorporated under the laws of the State of Michigan to act as the business and financial agent of the General Conference. It will guard the financial interests of the General Conference, and is expected to furnish provisions for the care of the property, deeds, bequests, and wills that may accrue to that body, and to keep its accounts. The object of the association is in its constitution declared to be to diffuse moral and religious knowledge and instruction by means of publishing-houses for such purpose, publications therefrom, missionaries, missionary agencies, and other appropriate and available instrumentalities and methods. Being wholly benevolent, charitable, and philanthropic in its character, the payment of dividends on any of its funds is prohibited, and its property may only be used for carrying into effect the legitimate ends and aims of its being. As reported to the General Conference the receipts of the Tract and Missionary Society for the year 1887 were $10,181, and the expenditures, $3,118. Besides missionary labor in the United States and other countries, tracts and publications had been sent by the society to South and West Africa, British and Dutch Guiana, Brazil, the West Indies, British Honduras, several places in Russia, some of the islands of the Pacific Ocean, to different points in the Southern States, and to city missions under the control of the General Conference. The society at its annual meeting recommended the circulation of a particular newspaper, the purpose of which is to oppose the "National Reform"

movement for the incorporation of a recognition of the Christian religion into the Constitution of the United States. The International Sabbath-school Association returned an income of $6,446, and expenditures of $6,038. Provisions were made at its annual meeting for the preparation of series of lessons for the years 1888-'89 on Old Testament history, "The United States in Prophecy," "The Third Angel's Message," on the leading doctrines of the Bible "for the use of those newly come to the faith," and, for little children, on the life of Christ, with special lessons on "God's Love to Man" for the camp-meeting Sabbath-schools.

The receipts of the Central Publishing Association had been $412,416. The Pacific Publishing Association returned property and assets to the value of $246,949.

The accounts of the Education Society were balanced at $86,664, and its assets were valued at $58,017. The organization of departments of manual training in the schools of the denomination was approved; and the preparation of a pamphlet was directed to explain the purpose and nature of that branch of instruction.

The Health and Temperance Association had enjoyed a large increase of activity. The Rural Health Retreat Association reported a fund amounting to $21,372.

General Conference.—The General Conference of Seventh-Day Adventists met in its twenty-sixth annual session at Oakland, Cal., Nov. 13, 1887. Elder George I. Butler presided. The conference in Norway was admitted, constituting the third conference in the Scandinavian field. The conference lately organized in West Virginia was received. The president made an address in which he spoke of the work of the denomination as advancing, notwithstanding increasing opposition. Remarkable success had attended the movements in Holland, and fields were opening, besides the United States, in South Africa, South America, and the West Indies. Immediate acts of prosecution against members for violation of the Sunday laws of some of the States had been restrained, so that none were now embarassed by them, but the current in favor of making those laws more stringent was increasing, and greater difficulties in that direction were to be anticipated. Delegates from foreign fields reported concerning the condition of their work; from the Scandinavian countries that there were in Denmark, 9, in Norway, 4, and in Sweden, 10 churches, with an aggregate membership of 810 in the three conferences. It had been difficult to furnish from the office of publication books enough to meet the demands of canvassers. The work in this branch was self-sustaining. The mission in England had been in progress for about nine years, and now returned four churches and about 185 members. In Australia there were three churches and 150 observers of the seventh day. The plan of holding mission schools in Central Europe, Scandinavia, and Great Britain for the purpose of educating canvassers and colporteurs was approved by the conference. The subject of securing a ship for missionary work among the islands of the sea was favorably considered, but postponed on account of the lack of funds available for the purpose, and was referred to a committee, which was authorized to receive gifts during the year and report to the next general conference. A week of prayer was appointed, to be observed from December 17 to December 25, and a programme of subjects for each day's services was arranged. A committee was appointed to which were referred all questions growing out of prosecutions under the Sunday laws of the States against seventh-day observers; and it was authorized to prepare a statement properly defining the position which Sabbath-keepers should occupy in the various contingencies which may arise under the enforcement of those laws. Further resolutions were adopted on this subject, declaring that

Whereas, The teachings of Christ entirely divorce the church and the state; and, *Whereas,* The state has no right to legislate in matters pertaining to religious institutions, and Sunday is only a religious institution; therefore, *Resolved,* That we as a people do oppose by all consistent means the enactment of Sunday laws where they do not exist, and oppose the repeal of exemption clauses in Sunday laws where they do exist; that we recommend that a pamphlet be prepared (1) showing the true relation which should exist between the church and the state; (2) exposing the organized efforts now being made to unite church and state by changing the Constitution of our country; (3) showing the real effect of unmodified Sunday laws in places where they have been in force; and that said pamphlet be placed in the hands of all legislative bodies where efforts are or shall be made to secure the enactment of Sunday laws.

Whereas, To quietly and peaceably do our work six days in the week, as well as to keep the seventh day as the Sabbath of the Lord, is duty toward God, and an inalienable right, and that with which the state can of right have nothing to do; therefore, *Resolved,* That there is no obligation resting upon any observer of the seventh day to obey any law prohibiting labor on the first day of the week, commonly called Sunday. That while asserting this right, and while practicing the principle avowed in this resolution of working the six working-days, the resolution is not to be so construed as either to sanction or approve any arrogance on the part of any, or any action purposely intended to offend or impose upon the religious convictions or practice of any person who observes the first day of the week. *Whereas,* we deem it essential to the proper work of the third angel's message that the true relation existing between the church and the state, and the relation that exists between what men owe to God and what they owe to civil government should be understood; therefore, *Resolved,* That we recommend that this subject be made a part of the regular course of Bible study in all our colleges: and that special attention be given to it by our ministers in the field.

Resolutions were adopted declaring that

Whereas, Our Saviour has laid down the one sole ground on which parties once married can be divorced; and, *Whereas,* The practices of society have become most deplorable in this respect, as seen in the prevalence of unscriptural divorces; therefore, *Resolved,* That we express our deprecation of this great evil, and instruct our ministers not to unite in marriage any parties so divorced; and that we exhort our own people, when about to contract matrimonial alliances, to bear in mind, and give due weight to the injunction of the apostle, "only in the Lord."

The fifth annual session of the European Council was held at Moss, Norway, June 14 to 21, 1887. Action was taken with reference to colportage; to the translation into different languages and publication of books; to the conduct of mission journals; and to the education of missionaries.

AFGHANISTAN, a monarchy in Central Asia, lying between the Punjaub and Beluchistan on the south and Russian-Turkestan on the north, with Persia on the west. The ruler is the Ameer of Cabul, Abdurrahman Khan, who has striven with some success to consolidate his authority over the semi-independent tribes that owe him allegiance, but by the imposition of taxes provoked a revolt among the Ghilzais, who are the most numerous and warlike tribe of his immediate subjects.

Internal Disorders.—The Ameer was not able to re-establish his authority over the tribes that rebelled against taxation in 1887. One of his generals, Gholam Hyder Orakzai, led an army consisting of six regiments of infantry, four squadrons of cavalry, and an artillery force of thirteen guns against the rebels in the Ghuzni district during the winter, and succeeded in inflicting some punishment on them and in restoring order for the time being. In January Abdurrahman went to Jelalabad with a force of 12,000 men for the purpose of reducing to submission the Shinwarri, Teerah, and other insurgent tribes of northeastern Afghanistan. His commander-in-chief, Gholam Hyder Khan Charkhi, had already been operating in that country and entered into negotiations with the Shinwarris.

Mistrusting the vigilance or fidelity of the Persian authorities who had once let Ayub Khan, the Afghan pretender, escape from his retreat at Meshed, and allowed him to carry on a correspondence with the rebels, the British Government persuaded the Shah to deliver him over into its custody. He left Meshed in January, and was taken to India, and securely interned at Rawul Pindi.

In the summer Ishak Khan, the Governor of Afghan-Turkistan, showed signs of insubordination. He is a cousin of Abdurrahman, being the son of Azim Khan, who was Ameer of Cabul for a few months in 1867, and was overthrown by Shere Ali. Ishak Khan was Abdurrahman's companion in exile, and has always professed subservience to his cousin, yet he has long been suspected of aspiring to the throne. He has discharged the duties of his post with ability and diligence for eight years, and in his own province he has contributed to the success of Abdurrahman's project of uniting the several parts of Afghanistan into a single realm, and has enabled the Ameer to draw some of his best troops from the Uzbecks of Turkistan. The province has been subdued by Ishak's unassisted efforts, and the Ameer has never ventured to interfere with his administration.

The Russo-Afghan Boundary.—The joint Anglo-Russian Boundary Commission completed the last stage of the boundary delimitation before the end of January, 1888, and dispatched the final protocol with maps of the frontier on February 4. The English commissioners, Maj. Peacocke and Capt. Yate, then returned to England over the Trans-Caspian Railway and through Russia.

The Central Asian Railway.—The Russo-Bokharan Railway, which was completed as far as Chardjui in 1887, was extended through Bokhara to the terminus at Samarcand, and opened with festivities in July, 1888. Gen. Annenkoff, who projected and directed the construction of the road, has been appointed chief director for two years, and has the disposal of 4,500,000 rubles, which is less than half the sum that the Department of the Imperial Control has decided to be requisite to finish the work, but more by 1,500,000 rubles than the general has declared to be sufficient. The total cost of the line has been 43,000,000 rubles. The whole length of the railway from the Caspian to Samarcand is 1,345 versts, or about 900 miles. The section from Kizil Arvat was begun seven and a half years before the completion of the work, but the whole line east of that place was built in three years, and the section from the Oxus to Samarcand, a distance of 346 versts, or 230 miles, was rushed through in six months. The cost of this section is officially stated at 7,198,000 rubles. The journey between St. Petersburg and Samarcand will not take more than ten days, after the railroad is in proper working-order.

Annexation of Pishin to British India.—By virtue of the treaty made by the Ameer Yakub Khan at Gandamak on May 26, 1879, the districts of Pishin and Sibi were assigned to the British Government for temporary occupation and administration. The revenues beyond what was necessary for the expenses of civil administration were to be paid over to the Ameer. After the abdication of Yakub Khan these districts remained in British occupation, whereas the Kunam valley was evacuated by the British troops in 1880, and handed over to the independent control of the Tussi. On the completion of the Sibi-Pishin Railway in 1887 the occupied districts were formally incorporated in the Indian Empire, and placed under the administration of the chief commissioner of British Beluchistan.

AGNOSTIC. Although directly derived from the Greek ἄγνωστος (unknown, unknowing, unknowable), this word in its Anglicized form is not found in any of the standard dictionaries prior to 1869. Richard Holt Hutton is responsible for the statement that it was suggested by Prof. Thomas Henry Huxley at a social assemblage held shortly before the formation of the subsequently famous Metaphysical Society.

To Huxley in turn it was suggested by St. Paul's reference to the altar raised in honor of "the unknown God." An agnostic is one who holds that everything beyond the material is unknown and probably unknowable. In his view the whole visible and calculable universe is material in greater or less degree, and therefore to some extent knowable, but the unseen world and the Supreme Being are beyond human perceptions and therefore unknowable.

The "Spectator" of Jan. 29, 1870, said of Prof. Huxley: "He is a great and even severe agnostic, who goes about exhorting all men to know how little they know." Again, in 1871, Mr. Hutton writes: "They themselves (the agnostics) vehemently dispute the term (atheism) and usually prefer to describe their state of mind as a sort of know-nothingism or agnosticism or belief in an unknown and unknowable God."

In 1874 St. George Mivart ("Essay on Religion") refers to the agnostics as "Our modern sophists . . . who deny that we have any knowledge save of phenomena." "Nicknames," says the "Spectator" of June 11, 1876, "are given by opponents, but agnostic was the name demanded by Prof. Huxley for those who disclaimed atheism, and believed with him in an 'unknown and unknowable' God, or in other words that the ultimate origin of all things must be some cause unknown and unknowable."

Principal Tulloch in an essay on agnosticism in the "Scotsman" of Nov. 18, 1876, said: "The same agnostic principle which prevailed in our schools of philosophy had extended itself to religion and theology. Beyond what man can know by his senses, or feel by his higher affections, nothing, as was alleged, could be truly known."

Conder, in "The Basis of Faith" (1877), wrote: "But there is nothing *per se* irrational in contending that the evidences of theism are inconclusive, that its doctrines are unintelligible, or that it fails to account for the facts of the universe or is irreconcilable with them. To express this kind of polemic against religious faith, the term agnosticism has been adopted."

Dr. James McCosh in an essay on "Agnosticism as developed in Huxley's 'Hume'" ("Popular Science Monthly," August, 1879), writes: "I am showing that the system is false and thus leads to prejudicial consequences—false to our nature, false to the ends of our being."

In 1880 (June 26), the "Saturday Review" printed the definition so widely quoted by the orthodox press: "In nine cases out of ten, agnosticism is but old atheism 'writ large.'"

Sir George Birdwood ("Industrial Arts of India," 1880) said: "The agnostic teaching of the Sankhya school is the common basis of all systems of Indian philosophy."

James Anthony Froude, in his "Life of Carlyle" (1882), writes: "He once said to me that the agnostic doctrines were to appearance like the finest flour, from which you might expect the most excellent bread; but when you came to feed on it you found it was powdered glass, and you had been eating the deadliest poison."

These are but a few of the examples that abound in contemporary literature. For Prof. Huxley's own views, the reader is referred to his works, especially such essays and chapters as are semi-religious or speculative. While Prof. Huxley is, as has been seen, popularly and no doubt rightly credited with having originated the term agnostic, in its modern acceptation, he is by no means the founder of the school that holds to a belief solely in material things. The Grecian sophists, and probably more anciently still the various Chinese and Oriental schools, taught and teach similar theories. In more recent times Descartes, Kant, David Hume, John Stuart Mill, and others have followed out trains of thought more or less identical, but all suggestive, whether just or not, of atheism. With Huxley the repudiation of atheism was strongly emphasized, but his orthodox opponents have never been willing to admit that he and his contemporaries succeeded in freeing themselves from the implied charge. As popularly phrased by the "Saturday Review," it is held to be "atheism writ large"; and yet, when candidly examined, the agnostic creed can hardly be distinguished from those of the more liberal Christian sects. It is an accepted principle of law that a court may properly decide as to the scope of its own jurisdiction, and a school of religion or philosophy should in like manner, and in good faith be permitted to interpret its own belief. While repudiating the charge of atheism, the agnostics have frankly admitted their inability to define or individualize their conception of a deity. Perhaps it is not unnatural that those sects which accept the teachings of the Old and the New Testament, in this regard, should consider non-acceptance as equivalent to atheism. Some of the more important of the essays bearing upon this subject are as follows: "Agnosticism," sermons delivered in St. Peter's, Cranley Gardens, by the Rev. A. W. Momerie, (Edinburgh and London, 1887); "Agnosticism and Women," "Nineteenth Century," vol. vii, by B. Lathbury; "Agnosticism and Women," a reply, "Nineteenth Century," vol. vii, by J. H. Clapperton; "Confessions of an Agnostic," "North American Review"; "The Assumptious of Agnostics," "Fortnightly Review," vol. xlii, by St. George Mivart; "An Agnostic's Apology," "Fortnightly Review," vol. xix, by Leslie Stephen; "Variety as an Aim in Nature," "Contemporary Review," November, 1871, by the Duke of Argyle.

ALABAMA. State Government.—The following were the State officers during the year: Governor, Thomas Seay, Democrat; Secretary of State, C. C. Langdon; Treasurer, Frederick H. Smith, succeeded by John L. Cobbs; Auditor, Malcolm C. Burke, succeeded by Cyrus D. Hogue; Attorney-General, Thomas N. McClellan; Superintendent of Public Instruction,

Solomon Palmer; Commissioner of Agriculture, Rufus F. Kolb; Railroad Commissioners, Henry R. Shorter, Levi W. Lawler, W. C. Tunstall; Chief-Justice of the Supreme Court, George W. Stone; Associate Justices, David Clopton and H. M. Somerville.

Finances.—The balance in the treasury on Oct. 1, 1887, was $276,488.82, and on the same date in 1888 it was $555,587.87. During the year, in accordance with a law passed by the last Legislature, the entire school-fund, hitherto retained in the counties and disbursed there, was paid into the State treasury. Of this fund, there was in the treasury at the latter date $181,301.21; leaving the actual balance for general purposes, after deducting this and other special funds, $316,916.39. The bonded debt of the State remains the same as in 1887. An act of the last Legislature providing for refunding the 6-per-cent. bonds amounting to $954,000 into 3½-per-cents. has not yet been complied with by the Governor, as the former bonds are not redeemable till 1890, and he asks an extension of his power till that time. The tax valuation of the State in 1886 was $173,808,-097; in 1887, $214,925,869. And for the present year about $223,000,000.

Education.—The report of the State Superintendent of Education for the year ending Sept. 30, 1887, presents the following statistics: Outside of the cities and special school districts, 3,658 schools for white pupils and 1,925 for colored pupils were maintained; the total number of pupils enrolled in the former being 153,304, and in the latter 98,396. The average daily attendance was 93,723 in the white schools, and 63,995 in the colored. During this time the total number of white children within school age was 272,730; of colored children, 212,821. There were 2,413 male teachers in the white schools and 1,237 female; 1,264 colored male teachers and 569 female. The average length of the school year was only 70.5 days, a decrease of over sixteen days from figures of the previous year, due to the omission of returns from the city and special district schools in this report. The total sum available to the State for school purposes during the year was $515,989.95, and the expenditures amounted to $527,319.88, necessitating the use of a portion of the unexpended balance of former years. The schools of the State stand in urgent need of stronger financial support. For several years the school fund has been increased but slightly, while the school population has been steadily growing in numbers, being 32,614 greater at the close of the school year in 1887 than in the previous year. The per capita disbursement by the State in 1887, being about seventy cents, is less than in many of the Southern States.

The Convict System.—The contracts under which the convicts sentenced to the State Penitentiary had been previously employed, expired by their terms on the first of January, and, in accordance with the law, proposals were issued for a new lease, which was awarded to the East Tennessee Coal, Iron, and Railroad Company. The convicts are to be employed in the Pratt coal-mines, near Birmingham, where the company agrees to build prisons and to maintain schools for the benefit of the convicts. Female convicts are exempted from this lease, and also all those who by reason of age, infirmity, or physical defect, were unable to perform hard labor. The class of convicts last described are gathered at the walls of the old Penitentiary at Wetumpka, and are engaged in such employments as are suited to their condition.

" In accepting this proposal," remarks the Governor in his last message to the Legislature, " whereby the continuance of the present lease system in Alabama appears to be fixed for a term of ten years, I do not intend to give the sanction of my judgment to the perpetuation of the lease system. I thought, however, and still think, considering the state of our finances, which does not yet justify an entire disregard of pecuniary considerations, and considering also the characteristics of those who constitute very largely the criminal class, that the lease system could not at present be dispensed with."

Railroads.—The report of the railroad commissioners for this year shows that there are 3,205 miles of railroad, including branches and sidings, in the State. During the year, 530 miles of new railroad were constructed, indicating an unusually rapid development.

Yellow Fever.—Great alarm was felt throughout the State, in the latter part of September, over reports of the existence of yellow fever in several localities. These reports proved unfounded, except in regard to Decatur, where, about September 20, several well-defined cases appeared. The disease soon became epidemic, and all who were able to leave the city, at once fled, leaving scarcely 500 persons remaining out of a population of several thousand. Quarantine regulations were enforced against the city, and the regular course of business was suspended. Although the epidemic was at no time violent, one or more new cases appeared almost daily for about two months, when the frosts of the latter part of November put an end to the scourge. The total number of cases reported up to November 1, was 123, of which 30 terminated fatally. The cases reported in November increase these figures but slightly. Contributions were received from several Northern cities in aid of the sufferers. Sporadic cases among refugees from Decatur occurred in other parts of the State, but there was no epidemic.

Decisions.—A decision of the State Supreme Court was rendered in March, declaring unconstitutional the act of the last General Assembly making appropriations for the establishment and support of a State University for colored people. The act provides that the sums appropriated shall be taken from that part of the common-school fund set apart for the education of the colored race in Alabama. The opinion holds that this university is not a part of the common-school system of the State within the meaning of the Constitution, and that the act under consideration, in declaring that the sum appropriated shall be taken from that portion of the common-school fund given to the colored race destroys the equality of the apportionment of that fund between the white and colored races required by the Constitution.

Earlier in the year another act of the same General Assembly, requiring locomotive engineers to obtain a license from the State, was passed upon by the United States Supreme Court and upheld. It was urged that the act, when enforced against engineers running into the State from outside points, became in effect a regulation of interstate commerce, and, therefore, unconstitutional, but the court refused to consider it as such.

In October the same court decided that the law prohibiting the employment of color-blind persons by railroads and requiring all railroad employés to have their sight tested by a board of experts was not a regulation of interstate commerce.

Political.—The first State Convention of the Labor party, which assembled at Montgomery on March 22, was the earliest political movement of the year. The delegates voted to present no separate State ticket, but advised that Labor candidates for the Legislature and for Congress be presented in the several districts. A platform was adopted, of which the following is the more important portion:

We favor such legislation as may lead to reduce the hours of labor; to prohibit the competition of convict labor with honest industry; to secure the sanitary inspection of tenements, factories, and mines; to compel corporations to pay their employés in lawful money of the United States at intervals of not longer than two weeks; and to put a stop to the abuse of conspiracy laws.

We also aim at the ultimate and complete ownership and control by the Government of all railroads, telegraph and telephone lines within its jurisdiction. We would have the General Government issue all moneys without the intervention of banks, and postal savings-banks added to the postal system. We also desire to simplify the procedure of our courts and diminish the expenses of legal proceedings, that the poor may be placed on equality with the rich, and the long delays which now result in scandalous miscarriages of justice may be prevented.

And since the ballot is the only means by which in our republic the redress of political and social grievances is to be sought, we especially and emphatically declare for the adoption of what is known as the " Australian system " of voting, in order that the effectual secrecy of the ballot and the relief of candidates for public office from the heavy expenses now imposed upon them may prevent bribery and intimidation, do away with practical discrimination in favor of the rich and unscrupulous, and lessen the pernicious influences of money in politics.

The Prohibitionists met in convention at Decatur on April 18, and made the following nominations: Governor, J. C. Orr; Secretary of State, L. C. Coulson; Attorney-General, Peter Finley; Auditor, M. C. Wade; Treasurer,

N. F. Thompson; Superintendent of Education, M. C. Denson.

A platform was adopted demanding, in addition to prohibition, national aid to education, a residence of twenty-one years by foreigners before voting, better election laws, and the abolition of the internal-revenue system.

On May 9 the Democratic Convention met at Montgomery, and nominated the following candidates: Governor, Thomas Seay; Secretary of State, C. C. Langdon; Treasurer, John L. Cobbs; Auditor, Cyrus D. Hogue; Attorney-General, Thomas N. McClellan; Superintendent of Education, Solomon Palmer.

Brief resolutions were adopted as follow :

That the firmness, ability, and statesmanship displayed by President Cleveland in the administration of his high office entitle him to the confidence and support of his fellow-citizens. That we indorse and approve his administration, and especially his action and efforts to make a reform and reduction of the tariff, and we believe that the interests of the country demand his re-election, and to that end our delegates to the National Convention are hereby instructed to vote for his nomination.

That we are unalterably opposed to the present war tariff. We demand reform of the tariff and a reduction of the surplus in the Treasury by a reduciton of tariff taxation.

That we indorse the administration of Gov. Seav, which has been so eminently satisfactory to the whole people of Alabama.

That we favor a liberal appropriation for public schools, in order that the means of acquiring a knowledge of the rudiments of education may be afforded to every child in the State.

That we favor the encouragement of immigration to this State, and to that end we recommend such wise and judicious legislation by the General Assembly as will best accomplish that result.

The Republican State Convention met at Montgomery, May 16, and nominated the following ticket: Governor, W. T. Ewing; Secretary of State, J. J. Woodall; Auditor, R. S. Heflin; Attorney-General, George H. Craig; Treasurer, Sam T. Fowler: Superintendent of Education, J. M. Clark. This ticket was considerably changed before the election, Robert P. Baker being the candidate for Secretary of State, Napoleon B. Mardis for Attorney-General, and Lemuel J. Standifer for Superintendent of Education. The following resolutions were passed:

That while we depreciate all sectional issues and wish for harmony between all the citizens of our great country, we demand as the legal and constitutional right of the people that the exercise of the right of suffrage shall be full and untrammeled, and that the ballot shall be counted and returned as cast in all sections of this great republic, and to help secure this end we favor a national law to regulate the election of members of Congress and Presidential electors, and demand that the election laws of Alabama be so amended as to hinder fraud and not encourage it.

That we condemn President Cleveland's tariff message and the Mills tariff bill as tending toward free trade and to the destruction of American industries and to the degradation of American labor to the servile condition of European labor, and we favor liberal protection to all American industries and labor.

That we condemn Senator Morgan's declaration that the vast mineral wealth of Alabama is a "doubtful blessing," because it tends to increase the laboring-man's wages, as hostile to labor, which is the great foundation of human progress and wealth.

That we favor national aid for the education of the children of the republic, and therefore indorse the Blair Bill.

That we favor civil-service reform, and condemn President Cleveland's wholesale removal from office for party reasons, while professing to be in favor of civil-service reform.

That we favor the entire abolition of the internal-revenue system.

That we oppose, now as heretofore, the present convict system of Alabama as brutal, and because it brings convict labor into competition with honest free labor.

At the election, August 6, the Democratic ticket received its usual large majority. The Legislature elected is overwhelmingly Democratic, 32 out of 33 Senators and 91 out of 100 members of the House being Democratic. An amendment to the State Constitution, designed to reduce the amount of local and special legislation demanded at each legislative session, failed of adoption, receiving fewer than 50,000 votes out of a total poll of over 180,000. At the November election a Democratic delegation to the national House of Representatives was chosen. The Democratic presidential ticket received 117,310 votes; the Republican, 57,197; the Prohibition, 583.

ALCOTT, AMOS BRONSON, educator, born in Wolcott, Conn., Nov. 29, 1799; died in Boston, Mass., March 4, 1888. The family arms was granted to Thomas Alcocke in 1616, and the first of the name appearing in English history is John Alcocke, who, after receiving the degree of doctor of divinity at Cambridge, became Bishop of Ely, and was preferred Lord-

AMOS BRONSON ALCOTT.

Chancellor of England by Henry VII. He transformed the old nunnery of St. Radigund in Cambridge to a new college called Jesus. Alcocke was "given to learning and piety from childhood, growing from grace to grace, so that in his age were none in England higher for holiness." Thomas and George Alcocke came to New England with Winthrop's company in

1630, and the descendant of the former, Capt. John, who held a commission from his kinsman Gov. Trumbull, lived on his father's estate, "Spindle Hill," where his grandson, Amos Bronson, the son of Joseph Chatfield and Anna Bronson Alcox, was born. "My father was skilful in handicraft, and in these arts I inherited some portion of his skill, and early learned the use of his tools," wrote Mr. Alcott in his diary, when describing his life in the primitive days of New England. In 1814 he entered Silas Hoadley's clock-factory in Plymouth, and at the age of sixteen began to peddle books about the country. In 1818 he sailed to Norfolk, Va., where he hoped to engage in teaching, but, failing in this, he bought silk and trinkets and made a peddling tour in the adjacent counties, where he enjoyed the hospitality of the planters, who, astonished at the intellectual conversation of this literary Autolycus, received him as a guest. He spent the winter of 1822 in peddling among the Quakers of North Carolina, but abandoned this life in 1823, and began to teach. He soon established an infant-school in Boston, which immediately attracted attention from the unique conversational method of his teaching; but this was in advance of the time, and he was denounced by the press and forced to retire. He then removed to Concord, Mass., where he devoted himself to the study of natural theology and reform in civil and social institutions, education, and diet, and frequently appeared on the lecture platform, where his originality made him attractive. In 1830 he married Miss Abby May, a descendant of the Quincy and Sewall families, and removed to Germantown, Pa., but in 1834 he returned to Boston, and reopened his school, which he continued for several years. His system was to direct his pupils to self-analysis and self-education, foreing them to contemplate the spirit as it unveiled within themselves, and to investigate all subjects from an original standpoint. A journal of the school, kept by one of his pupils, Elizabeth P. Peabody, was published under the title of "A Record of Mr. Alcott's School" (Boston, 1834; 3d ed., 1874). The school suggested to his daughter that of "Plumfield," which is described in "Little Men."

At the invitation of James P. Greaves, of London, the friend and fellow-laborer of Pestalozzi in Switzerland, Mr. Alcott went to England in 1843, and Mr. Greaves having died in the mean time, Mr. Alcott was cordially received by his friends, who gave the name Alcott Hall to their school in Ham, near London. On his return he was accompanied by Charles Lane and H. G. Wright, with whom he endeavored to establish the "Fruitlands," in Harvard, Mass., an attempt to form a community upon a philosophical basis, which was soon abandoned. After living for a while in Boston, Mr. Alcott returned to Concord, where his life was that of a peripatetic philosopher. For forty years he was the friend and compan-

ion of Emerson, who described him to Carlyle as "a majestic soul, with whom conversation is possible." He frequently gave "conversations" in cities and villages, on divinity, ethics, dietetics, and other subjects. These gradually became formal, and were continued for nearly fifty years. They have been thus described: "He sits at a table or desk, and after his auditors have assembled begins to talk on some scientific subject mentioned beforehand. He continues this for one hour exactly—his watch lying before him—in a fragmentary, rambling manner, and concludes with some such phrase as 'The spirit of conversation is constrained tonight,' 'Absolute freedom is essential to the freedom of the soul,' 'Thought can not be controlled.' Then he stops, and the next evening begins with another theme, treats it in the same desultory way, and ends with similar utterances."

The opening of the Concord School of Philosophy, in 1878, gave him new intellectual strength, and he was prominent in its proceedings. The last years of his life were spent with his daughter Louisa, in Boston. He was the intimate friend of Channing, Hawthorne, Garrison, Phillips, Emerson, and Thoreau. The latter describes him as "One of the last philosophers—Connecticut gave him to the world; he peddled first her wares, afterward, as he declares, her brains. These he peddles still, bearing for fruit his brain only, like the nut its kernel. His words and attitude always suppose a better state of things than other men are acquainted with, and he will be the last man to be disappointed as the ages revolve. He has no venture in the present. . . . A true friend of man, almost the only friend of human progress, with his hospitable intellect he embraces children, beggars, insane, and scholars, and entertains the thought of all, adding to it commonly some breadth and elegance. Whichever way we turned, it seemed that the heavens and the earth had met together since he enhanced the beauty of the landscape. I do not see how he can ever die; Nature can not spare him."

Besides numerous contributions to periodical literature, including papers entitled "Orphic Sayings" in "The Dial" (Boston, 1839-'42), he wrote "Conversations with Children on the Gospels" (2 vols., Boston, 1836); "Tablets" (1868); "Concord Days" (1872); "Table-Talk" (1877); "Sonnets and Canzonets" (1882); and "The New Connecticut," an autobiographical poem, edited by Franklin B. Sanborn (Boston, 1887).

His daughter, **LOUISA MAY**, author, born in Germantown, Pa., Nov. 29, 1832; died in Boston, Mass., March 6, 1888, was educated by her father. Her first literary attempt, "An Address to a Robin," was made at the age of eight, and she soon began to write stories. In 1848 she wrote her first book, "Flower-Fables," for Ellen Emerson, but this made no impression on its publication in 1855. In 1851 she published in "Gleason's Pictorial" a romantic story, for which she received five dollars. Mr. Alcott never achieved worldly success, and, as the family were in straitened circumstances about this time, she engaged in teaching in Boston, where she took a "little trunk filled with the plainest clothes of her own making and twenty dollars that she had earned in

LOUISA MAY ALCOTT.

writing." At one time she aspired to become an actress, and had perfected her arrangements for a first appearance, but was prevented by her friends. She occasionally appeared in amateur performances, and wrote a farce entitled "Ned Batchelder's Adventures," which was produced at the Howard Athenæum. She also wrote a romantic drama, "The Rival Prima Donna," the manuscript of which she recalled and destroyed on hearing of dissension among the actors regarding the arrangement of the cast. In December, 1862, she entered into Government service as a hospital nurse, and was stationed in the Georgetown Hospital, near Washington, D. C., until prostrated by typhoid fever, from the effects of which she never recovered. In 1865 she visited Europe as a traveling-companion, and soon after her return to Boston published "Little Women," which pictured her home life, and brought her fame and fortune. This was received with such favor that when "Little Men" was issued the publishers received advance orders for 50,-000 copies. Miss Alcott addressed herself to children, and no author's name is more endeared to the young than hers. Although there is little in her writing that is not drawn from personal experience, this is so colored by her imagination, and so strong through her sympathy with life, that her books represent the universal world of childhood and youth. But while they are characterized by humor, cheerfulness, good morals, and natural action, their healthfulness may be somewhat questionable on account of the sentimentality that is woven into her work and breaks the natural grace of childhood by introducing the romantic element, and a hint of self-importance and independence that tends to create a restless and rebellious spirit. She devoted herself to the care of her father, and in "death they were not divided." The sale of "Little Women" has reached 250,000; that of all her works together, over 800,000. Her publications are: "Flower-Fables" (Boston, 1855); "The Rose Family" (1864); "Moods" (1865; revised ed., 1881); "Little Women" (1868); "Hospital Sketches" (1869); "An Old-Fashioned Girl" (1869); "Little Men" (1871); "Aunt Jo's Scrap-Bag," a series containing "Cupid and Chow-Chow," "My Girls," "Jimmy's Cruise in the Pinafore," and "An Old-Fashioned Thanksgiving" (1871-'82); "Work, a Story of Experience" (1873); "Eight Cousins" (1874); "Rose in Bloom" (1876); "Silver Pitchers" (1876); "Under the Lilacs" (1878); "Jack and Jill" (1880); "Proverb Stories" (1882); "Spinning-Wheel Stories" (1884); and the first of a new series, "Lulu's Library" (1885).

ANGLICAN CHURCHES. General Statistics.—The "Year-Book" of the Church of England for 1888 shows that the gross amount of money raised voluntarily and expended in 1886 on the building and restoration of churches, the endowment of benefices, the erection of parsonages, and the provision of burial grounds, while it was considerably less than in 1884, exceeded £1,000,000; and of this sum £53,000 were raised in the four Welsh dioceses. The details of this particular branch of church effort as carried out at Bristol and Plymouth are recorded for the first time in the present volume. They show that while the population of Bristol has increased by nearly 55 per cent. the net gain in church accommodation has been 70 per cent., while the whole expenditure upon church extension has been more than £500,000. A similar work has been going on in the three towns of Plymouth, Devonport, and Stonehouse, at a gross expenditure of £131,000. Nearly £500,000 (£445,398) were raised during twelve years for founding the six new sees of Truro, St. Albans, Liverpool, Southwell, and Wakefield; £50,000 in six years to complete the Bishop of Rochester's "ten churches scheme." The "Universities and Public Schools Missions" for the supply of destitute places in the large towns and parochial missions for the laity have increased steadily. Activity in work for the promotion of temperance, for the rescue of the victims of vice, and for reform, has gone on with growing activity. The statistics of ordinations show that during fourteen years 10,020 persons had been admitted to the order of deacons; and of these admissions, the annual average for the former half of the period was 660, and for the latter half, 770. The statistics of confirmations show that while the average number annually for the nine years ending with 1883 was 166,000, the average for the succeeding three years was nearly

204,000. During 1886, 77 new churches were built, and 185 restored, raising the number of new churches, between 1877 and 1886, to 809, and of restored churches to 2,572. Under the Church Buildings Acts 838 new parishes or districts were constituted beween 1868 and 1880. The number of permanent mission buildings other than parish and district churches is given as 4,717, with accommodation for 843,272 persons. Confirmations were held during 1887 at 2,361 centers; the whole number of persons confirmed being 213,638. The voluntary contributions toward the maintenance of Church schools between 1884 and 1886 were given as £1,755,958 ; the contributions between 1873 and 1887 to the "Hospital Sunday" collections as £727,250, the whole number of collections being 33,134. It was claimed that during the twenty-five years, 1860–'84, Churchmen voluntarily contributed £528,653 for the education of ministerial candidates, £35,175,000 for church building and restoration, £7,496,478 for home missions, £10,100,000 for foreign missions, £22,421,542 for educational work, mainly elementary, £3,818,200 for charitable work (distinctively Church of England), and £2,103,-364 for clergy charities, making a total of £81,-573,237, Contributions to parochial purposes, unsectarian societies, and middle-class schools are not included in the estimate.

Missionary Societies.—The annual meeting of the Church Missionary Society was held May 1. Sir John Kennaway presided. The total receipts of the society for the year had been £221,330, but they had not covered the expenditure, and there remained a debt of £9,000 to be cleared off; and to meet the demands of various funds, the incomeof the preceding year must be exceeded by £37,000. Forty-three candidates for missionary work, twelve of whom were women, had been received during the year. A resolution was passed approving the action of the Executive Committee in calling for picked men to work among Mohammedans.

The income of the Church Zenana Missionary Society was returned at £23,268. The society includes 900 associations and more than 500 working parties laboring in support of the mission. From the missions—in West Africa, East and Central Africa, Egypt and Arabia, Palestine, Persia and' Bagdad, India, Ceylon, Mauritius, China, Japan, New Zealand, Northwest America, and the North Pacific—were returned 280 stations, 247 foreign and 265 native ordained men, 62 European and 3,534 native lay and female workers, 44,115 communicants, and 1,859 schools, with 71,814 pupils. The native contributions had amounted to £15,142.

The annual public meeting of the Society for the Propagation of the Gospel in Foreign Parts was held in London, July 10. The meeting was distinguished by the presence of many of the bishops who had come to attend the Lambeth Conference. The Archbishop of Canterbury presided. The secretary's report showed that the number of ordained missionaries, including nine bishops, on the society's list at that time, was 596, viz., in Asia, 187; in Africa, 139 ; in Australia and the Pacific, 17 ; in North America, 183 ; in the West Indies, 33 ; and in Europe, 37. Of them, 114 were natives laboring in Asia, and 19 in Africa. There were also in the various missions of the society about 2,000 catechists and lay teachers, mostly natives, and more than 400 students in the society's colleges. Papers were read and remarks made in reference to various aspects of the missionary work in their several fields of labor by the Bishops of Calcutta ("Provincial and Diocesan Organization in India"), Japan, Rangoon, North China, Cape Town, Zululand, Equatorial Africa, Sydney, Fredericton, Missouri, North Dakota, and Guiana, and the Archdeacon of Gibraltar. A paper by the Rev. R. R. Winter, of Delhi, on "Woman's Work in Missions," was read by the secretary.

At a meeting of the Board of Missions of the Province of Canterbury, held July 21, the Archbishop of Canterbury, presiding, said that the board did not seek to work as a new missionary society, or wish to collect money; but that it desired to bring before the Church the necessity of doing a great deal more for missions than was being done at present, and to give proper information to the vast numbers of persons who knew nothing of the missions or of the immensity of the interests centered in them. Several of the American and colonial bishops spoke of the condition and requirements of missionary interests in different parts of the world, and of the importance of giving greater unity to the missionary work. A resolution was adopted assuring the bishops of the various dioceses and missionary jurisdictions abroad of the desire of the board "to aid them in the work of extending the Master's kingdom."

Free and Open Church Association.—It was reported at the annual meeting of this society, in March, that the council had decided to issue an address calling upon the people to defend the Church by uniting in a great effort to get rid of the pew system. The Bishop of Rochester had written that the church which "blandly encouraged her wealthy children to build stately churches for their own enjoyment," leaving the poor to worship in a cold school-room, "forfeited her claim to be the church of the nation."

The Church House.—A plan for the establishment, in London, by a company, of a "Church House," to serve as an informal "headquarters" for the adherents of the Anglican churches, their societies and associations, and as a place of deposit for archives, libraries, and collections, took form in July. The final report of the Executive Committee, which had been appointed by the movers of the project to consider the subject, was presented to the General Committee June 7. A charter of incorporation had been granted for the enterprise on the 23d of February. The receipts in its behalf up to June 30 had amounted to £45,853, while a balance of £2,681 was remaining at the banker's, besides investments and deposits to the sum of £35,868. The total liabilities incurred and to be incurred in the purchase of the site—which is on the south side of Dean's Yard—amounted to £42,-431, for the provision of which the resources of the corporation were amply sufficient. The Archbishop of Canterbury, speaking on the adoption of the report, remarked on the practical value of the scheme, which would provide a house not only useful as a place of business for the Church of England in England, but also as a general meeting-point and rallying-ground for the Anglican communion throughout the world. He was anxious that a good reference library should be formed as soon as possible. A full collection of reports of church work in all parts of the world was needed. Valuable contributions concerning the transactions of the American Church Conventions had already been received from the Bishops of Iowa and Albany. Formal possession was taken of the site on the 21st of July, when the first annual meeting of the corporation was held, and suitable action was taken for accepting the property. The purpose of the scheme was defined to be for facilitating intercommunion among the churches throughout the world. The buildings already on the ground will be occupied for the present, and the erection of others or of better ones will be left to the future, as the means and needs of the enterprise may be developed.

Church of England Temperance Society.—A breakfast was given by the Council and Executive of this association, July 11, to the bishops attending the Lambeth Conference, for purposes of consultations respecting the progress of the society; the movement against the liquor traffic among the native races; and methods by which the organization of the society abroad might be accelerated and made more effective. The Bishop of London presided. A letter was read from the Bishop of New York representing that great benefit had been derived in America from the influence of the society. Resolutions were adopted declaring that the importation of spirituous liquors from England and other countries was having a disastrous effect upon native races in the colonies and dependencies of the British Empire, and recommending the formation of diocesan branches of the society. The resolutions were supported by the Bishops of Sydney, Cork, Pennsylvania, Huron, Colombo, and Zululand, and the Bishop Coadjutor of Antigua. The Bishop of Sydney declared that it was absolutely impossible to exaggerate the utterly disastrous effect which the traffic in spirituous liquors was exercising everywhere.

Powers of the Archbishop.—The case of Read and others *vs.* the Archbishop of Canterbury, involving an appeal of four members of the Church of England resident in the diocese of Lincoln against the refusal of the Archbishop of Canterbury of their request to cite the Bishop of Lincoln to answer allegations of offense in matters of ritual, was decided by the Judicial Committee of the Privy Council, Aug. 3, after an *ex-parte* hearing. The Bishop of Lincoln was charged by the petitioners with having offended in respect to the celebration of the Communion by using lighted candles on the Communion-table when they were not required for the purpose of giving light; by making at the same service and when pronouncing the benediction, the sign of the cross; by standing while reading the prayer of consecration with his back to the people; and by deviating in no fewer than ten ways from the ceremony prescribed by the Book of Common Prayer. The petitioners prayed the archbishop to cite the inculpated bishop to answer these charges, referring as precedents for the exercise of this power to the case of "Lucy *vs.* the Bishop of St. Davids" (1695), and of the Bishop of Cloghan, which was cited in 1822 by the Archbishop of Armagh. The archbishop replied that, "Considering the fact that in the course of 300 years since the Reformation, there is no other precedent" (than the Bishop of St. David's case), "and considering the political and other exceptional circumstances under which this particular case was decided," he objected to acting without instruction from a court of competent jurisdiction. The decision of the Judicial Committee was to the effect that their lordships were of the opinion that the archbishop had jurisdiction in the case. They were also of the opinion that the abstaining of the archbishop from entertaining the suit was a matter of appeal to Her Majesty. They desired to express no opinion whatever whether the archbishop had or had not a discretion whether he would issue the citation. They would humbly advise Her Majesty to remit the case to the archbishop, to be dealt with according to law. The decision is considered an important one, in that it establishes the right of the archbishop to call bishops to account.

Water in the Communion Service.—A case was heard before the Court of Arches of the Province of Canterbury, February 14, in which the Rev. S. J. Hawkes, of Pontebury, diocese of Hereford, was charged with having administered to communicants water instead of wine at the celebration of the holy communion. The defendant admitted that he had used water on the occasion, as charged, but pleaded that he had intended no offense against the rubrics. He had not been aware beforehand that there was to be a communion service. Finding no wine in the flagon, he in his surprise ordered the clerk to get something. The clerk had brought water, and he had used it without thinking to examine it. Lord Penzance, in giving his decision, while admitting the defendant's excuses, thought that he had erred in judgment; he should have made an explanation or dismissed the congregation, and postponed the service. The court would do no more than admonish the defendant against a repetition of the offense, and condemn him in the costs. The conduct of the minister in instituting the proceedings was, however, justified. Such a departure from the order of proceedings in the celebration of the holy communion was no light matter. The rubrics of the Prayer-Book were not merely directory, but were in their smallest incidents nothing less than positive commands of law, strictly to be followed and faithfully obeyed. So serious a departure as this case disclosed could not be passed over, in the opinion of the court, without ecclesiastical censure, except at the risk of implying that the breach of them was venial, trivial, or unimportant.

The Convocations.—Both houses of the Convocation of Canterbury met for the dispatch of business, Feb. 29. The archbishop exhibited to their lordships of the upper house letters patent, dated Sept. 16, 1887, conveying the royal assent to the newly amended canons as to the hours of marriage, agreed to by both houses, and gave notice that it was necessary that the two houses should meet together, in order that the new and amended canons might be made, promulgated, and executed. The ceremonial of summoning and receiving the lower house, in full official form, was then performed for the first time, it was said, since 1603. The archbishop read, in Latin and English, the new enactments which brought the law of the Church into harmony with the law of the land, after which the document of assent was signed by the archbishop and bishops, and by the prolocutor, deans, archdeacons, and proctors of the lower house. A resolution of the lower house relating to the election of incumbents by parishioners in cases where the living is vested in the parishioners, was amended and approved. It recommends the insertion of a clause in the Church Patronage Bill providing for the selection of a permanent committee by the parishioners, through which the election shall be conducted. A petition was presented from the Lord's Day Observance Society on the subject of the relaxation of Sunday observance, which appeared to have increased of late years, and to the great increase of Sunday labor; to which the house responded that it deemed it its duty "to appeal to the clergy, to all instructors of the young, and to all who exercise influence over their fellowmen, not to suffer this Church and country to lose the priceless benefits of the rest and sanctity of the Lord's Day. Its reasonable and religious observation is for the moral, physical, and spiritual health of all ranks of the population, and to it our national well-being has been largely due." Sympathy was expressed with the clergy in the difficulties to which they were subjected in the collection of tithes, and the efforts of the house were pledged in favor of measures for remedying them. The president (archbishop) was requested to appoint a committee to consider the question of an increase of the episcopate. A desire was expressed to

have an opportunity of considering the details of certain proposed bills dealing with the ecclesiastical courts before they are settled in the parliamentary committees.

The lower house, recognizing the urgent need of an increase of the clergy, declared by resolution "that it will welcome the accession of duly qualified persons possessed of independent means who will offer themselves for the work of deacons; but that it deprecates any alteration of the law and of the ancient usages of the Church which would involve the relaxation of the solemn obligations of holy orders." The governmental measure for the restriction of the opium trade with China by giving control of the matter for a period to the Chinese authorities was approved, and the hope was expressed that measures would be taken to prevent the importation of opium into Burmah, and that the Government might see its way clear to "bring about the final extinction of the Bengal monopoly." A further development was suggested of parochial guilds, in which, the house declared, might be discerned a wide possibility of increased spiritual good, both in town and country parishes.

The Convocation assembled again April 24. A report was presented in the upper house from a joint committee of the two houses on the relations of the Convocations of the Northern and Southern Provinces, the consideration of which was deferred. A motion was carried for the appointment of a joint committee to report as to any new organization required to enable the Church to reach the classes of the population now outside of religious organizations. Satisfaction was expressed at the unanimous passage of the House of Commons of the resolution of Mr. McArthur in regard to the traffic in drink with native races. The bishops acted favorably upon an *articulus cleri* of the lower house respecting the exclusion of the clergy from the county councils proposed to be erected under the new Local Government Bill, asking them to take steps to obtain such alteration in the measure as would prevent such exclusion. The lower house having, without instruction from the upper house, acted upon motions suggesting additions to the Church Catechism, dealing with questions of doctrine concerning which the Episcopate claimed the exclusive right of origination, a resolution was passed by the upper house, declaring itself unable to consider the action in question, because it could not regard it "as regular and desirable that synodical validity should be given to formularies professing to set forth the doctrines of the Church for the drawing up and circulation of which the consent of the president had not been applied for and obtained." A report was made in the House of Laymen recommending an increase of the Episcopate, and the adoption, as far as possible, of county boundaries as the bases of the boundaries of dioceses. Concerning the principles which should regulate a system of pensions for disabled or aged clergy, the house expressed the opinion that "a considerable portion of the fund should be provided by the laity, or by non-beneficiaries; that every clergyman, in order to become eligible for a pension, should be expected to contribute an adequate amount to the pension fund; that the pension should be free from seizure by creditors; and that the age at which, as a general rule, the pensions should commence, should be sixty-five." The house approved the purpose of the Tithe Rent-charge Recovery Bill as a measure for facilitating the collection and recovery of the charge in question.

The Convocation of York met for the dispatch of business April 17. The archbishop, in his opening address, remarking upon differences that had occurred between the two houses at previous sessions, said that the present position of the Convocation had occasioned much anxious thought with him, and that he feared that the two houses would not be able to coöperate in the future. The prolocutor of the lower house (the Dean of York) regarded these remarks as a reflection upon his official course, and offered his resignation, which was accepted. The Rev. Chancellor Espin, D. D., was chosen prolocutor. Resolutions were adopted in the upper house urging the need of the Church for legislation on the ecclesiastical courts, and, without committing itself to the approval of particular recommendations, indicating the report of the Royal Commission, dated July 13, 1883, as the suitable basis of such legislation.

The Lambeth Conference.—The third Lambeth Conference of Bishops of the Anglican Communion—often designated the "Pan-Anglican Conference"—was opened June 30. While the idea of holding a conference of this kind had been frequently mentioned before, the proposition for the first assemblage took serious form in the Canadian Provincial Synod of 1865, which unanimously resolved to urge upon the Archbishop and Convocation of Canterbury that some means should be adopted "by which the members of our Anglican Communion in all quarters of the world should have a share in the deliberations for her welfare, and be permitted to have a representation in one general council of her members gathered from every land." This appeal, it is said, was prompted by the condition of affairs then existing in South Africa, in view of the pronunciation of a sentence of deposition against Bishop Colenso. In compliance with the request, which was seconded by the Convocation of Canterbury, the archbishop issued in February, 1867, an invitation to all the bishops in communion with the Church of England, 144 in number, to meet for purposes of Christian sympathy and mutual counsel on matters affecting the welfare of the Church at home and abroad; explaining, at the same time, that the meeting would not be competent to make declarations or lay down definitions on points of doctrine, but would tend to promote unity of faith and to bind the bodies represented "in straiter bonds of peace and brotherly charity." Seventy-six bishops responded to this invitation, while the bishops and Archbishop of the Province of York declined to join in the movement. The conference met on the 24th of September, 1867. Its time was largely occupied with discussions of the affairs of the South African churches, while several questions were submitted to committees to be reported upon by them to a meeting of the bishops then remaining in England, in the following December. The second conference was called, again at the suggestion of the Canadian Synod, in July, 1877, and, the bishops of the province of York having concluded to take part in it, was attended by 100 bishops. It met on the 29th of June, and adjourned on the 27th of July, 1878. The subjects discussed regarded "The best mode of maintaining union among the various branches of the Anglican Communion"; "Voluntary boards of arbitration for churches to which such an arrangement may be applicable"; "The relations to each other of missionary bishops and of missionaries in various branches of the Anglican Communion acting in the same country"; "The position of Anglican chaplains and chaplaincies on the Continent of Europe and elsewhere"; "Modern forms of infidelity and the best means of dealing with them"; and "The condition, progress, and needs of the various churches of the Anglican Communion." The reports on these subjects, as adopted by the Conference, were incorporated as a whole in a combined "letter," and put forth to the world in the name of the hundred bishops assembled; which letter was also published in Latin and Greek translations.

The following invitation to the Conference of 1888 was sent out to 209 bishops:

LAMBETH PALACE, *Nov.* 9, 1887.

RIGHT REVEREND AND DEAR BROTHER:

I am now able to send you definite information with regard to the Conference of Bishops of the Anglican Communion to be held at Lambeth, if God permit, in the summer of next year.

In accordance with the precept of 1878, it has been arranged that the Conference shall assemble on Thursday, July 3, 1888. After four days' session there will be an adjournment, in order that the various committees appointed by the Conference may have opportunity for deliberation. The Conference will reassemble on Monday, July 23, or Tuesday, July 24, and will conclude its session on Friday, July 27.

Information as to the services to be held in connection with the Conference, and other particulars, will be made public as the time draws near.

I have received valuable suggestions from my episcopal brethren in all parts of the world as to the objects upon which it is thought desirable that we should deliberate. These suggestions have been carefully weighed by myself and by the bishops who have been good enough to co-operate with me in making the preliminary arrangements, and the following are the subjects definitely selected for discussion:

1. The Church's Practical Work in Relation to, (a) Intemperance; (b) Purity; (c) Care of emigrants; and, (d) Socialism.

2. Definite Teaching of the Faith to Various Classes, and the Means thereto.

3. The Anglican Communion in Relation to the Eastern Churches, to the Scandinavian and other Reformed Churches, to the Old Catholics, and others.
4. Polygamy of Heathen Converts. Divorce.
5. Authoritative Standards of Doctrine and Worship.
6. Mutual Relations of Dioceses and Branches of the Anglican Communion.

May I venture again to invite your earnest prayer that the Divine Head of the Church may be pleased to prosper with his blessing this our endeavor to promote his glory and the advancement of his kingdom upon the earth.

I remain, your faithful brother in Christ,
EDW. CANTUAR.

The Conference was attended by 145 prelates, representing the Church as follows: The Archbishop of Canterbury and 33 bishops of the province of Canterbury; the Archbishop of York and 11 bishops of the province of York; the Archbishops of Armagh and Dublin and 9 Irish bishops; the Bishop of Minnesota (representing the Presiding Bishop of the United States) and 28 American bishops; the Metropolitan of Fredericton and 8 Canadian bishops; the Metropolitan of Calcutta and 4 Indian bishops; the Metropolitan of Sydney and 3 Australian bishops; 4 bishops from New Zealand; 6 from South Africa; 4 from the Canadian Territories, and the remainder, missionary bishops, including the Bishop of Gibraltar and the Bishop in Jerusalem and the East, who exercise chorepiscopal functions. The Bishop of Gloucester and Bristol acted as Episcopal Secretary; the Dean of Windsor as General Secretary; and the Archdeacon of Maidstone as Assistant Secretary. The Archbishop of Canterbury presided.

The preliminary meetings of the Conference included a service in Canterbury Cathedral on June 30, and a service in Westminster Abbey, with sermon by the Archbishop of Canterbury. The Conference was opened on the 3d of July. The sermon was preached by the Bishop of Minnesota, and bore reference to the importance of unity in the Church, the hindrances to it, and the possibility of a comprehensive union. The business meetings were opened with an address by the Archbishop of Canterbury, in the course of which the various subjects that would be submitted for discussion were referred to. The subject of "Definite Teaching of the Faith to Various Classes, and the Means thereto," was then discussed in private, the opening speeches being by the Bishops of London, Maine, and Carlisle.

The subject of the second day's discussion was "The Anglican Communion in Relation to the Eastern Churches, to the Scandinavian and other Reformed Churches, to the Old Catholics and others," and was introduced by the Archbishop of Dublin. The Bishop of Winchester spoke on the point of intercommunion; the Bishop of Gibraltar gave an account of his interviews with Eastern prelates, and of the state of feeling on the Continent toward the English Church; and the Bishop of Lichfield related the result of his and the Bishop of
VOL. XXVIII.—2 A

Salisbury's visit to the Old Catholics, in 1887. (See "Annual Cyclopedia" for 1887, article OLD CATHOLICS.)

On the third day the subject of "Authoritative Standards of Doctrine and Worship" was introduced by the Bishop of Sydney, and spoken to by the Bishops of Aberdeen, Western New York, and Australia. The Bishop of Salisbury suggested that very large powers should be conferred on future Lambeth Conferences. The "Mutual Relations of Dioceses and Branches of the Anglican Communion" was discussed by the Bishops of Cape Town, Brechin, and Derry. A petition from the English Church Union, urging resistance to any tampering with the law of marriage, the concerting of measures for securing the celebration of the Holy Communion in all churches on Sundays and holy days, for the reservation of the sacrament, and for the better observance of days of abstinence, was laid on the table.

On the fourth day, "The Church's Practical Work in Relation to (a) Intemperance; (b) Purity; (c) Care of Emigrants; and (d) Socialism," was considered, the several departments of the subject being introduced by (a) the Bishop of London; (b) the Bishops of Durham and Calcutta; (c) the Bishops of Liverpool and Quebec; and (d) the Bishops of Manchester and Mississippi.

The Conference then adjourned till July 23, to give place to the meetings of the committees appointed to consider the subjects referred to them.

The closing service of the Conference was held July 28, in St. Paul's Cathedral, where a sermon was preached by the Archbishop of York.

The results of the deliberations of the Conference, which were published immediately after its adjournment, include an encyclical letter, addressed to "The Faithful in Christ Jesus"; the resolutions formally adopted; and reports of committees accepted but not adopted by the Conference. While the encyclical letter is official and the resolutions are given as formal utterances of the Conference, it was avowed that the reports should be taken to represent its mind only in so far as they were reaffirmed or adopted in the resolutions; but they were printed in the belief that they would offer "fruitful matter for consideration." At the head of the questions which had engaged attention, the letter placed that of the duty of the Church in the promotion of temperance and purity. While the evil effects of intemperance could hardly be exaggerated and total abstinence was highly valued as a means to an end, the language was discountenanced "which condemns the use of wine as wrong in itself independently of its effects on ourselves or on others," and the practice of substituting some other liquid in the celebration of Holy Communion was disapproved. A general action of all Christian people—nothing short of which would avail—was invited to arrest the evil of impurity, by raising the tone of public opinion and stamping out ignoble and corrupt traditions. The sanctity of marriage was compromised by increasing facilities for divorce, respecting which the Church should insist upon adherence to the precept of Christ. "The polygamous alliances of heathen races are allowed on all hands to be condemned by the law of Christ; but they present many practical problems which have been solved in various ways in the past. . . . While we have refrained from offering advice on minor points, leaving these to be settled by the local authorities of the Church, we have laid down some broad lines on which alone we consider that the missionary may safely act. Our first care has been to maintain and protect the Christian conception of marriage, believing that any immediate and rapid successes which might otherwise have been secured in the mission field would be dearly purchased by any lowering or confusion of this idea." The growing laxity in the observance of Sunday as a day of rest, of worship, and of religious teaching, was deprecated. The importance of the attitude of the Church toward the social problems of the day was urged; and its duties in this category were to be discharged by faithfully inculcating the definite truths of the faith as the basis of all moral teaching: particularly by a more constant supervision of, and a more sustained interest on the part of the clergy in the work done in Sunday-schools; by encouraging the study of Holy Scripture; by cautious and discreet treatment of doubts arising from the misapprehension of the due relations between science and revelation — respecting which, "where minds have been disquieted by scientific discovery or assertion, great care should be taken not to extinguish the elements of faith, but rather to direct the thinker to the realization of the fact that such discoveries elucidate the action of laws which, rightly conceived, tend to the higher appreciation of the glorious work of the Creator, upheld by the word of his power"; and by similar caution in the treatment of questions respecting inspiration. A reference to questions in the mutual relations of dioceses and branches of the communion between which cases of friction may arise, was followed by a definition of the attitude of the Anglican Communion toward the religious bodies now separated from it, which, it was declared:

Would appear to be this: We hold ourselves in readiness to enter into brotherly conference with any of those who may desire intercommunion with us in a more or less perfect form. We lay down conditions on which such intercommunion is, in our opinion, and according to our conviction, possible. For, however we may long to embrace those now alienated from us, so that the ideal of the one flock under the one shepherd may be realized, we must not be unfaithful stewards of the great deposit intrusted to us. We can not desert our position either as to faith or discipline. That concord would, in our judgment, be neither true nor desirable which should be produced by such a surrender. But we gladly and thankfully recognize the real religious work which is carried on by Christian bodies not of our communion. We can not close our eyes to the visible blessing which has been vouchsafed to their labors for Christ's sake. Let us not be misunderstood on this point. We are not insensible to the strong ties, the rooted convictions, which attach them to their present position. These we respect, as we wish that on our side our own principles and feelings may be respected. Competent observers, indeed, assert that not in England only, but in all parts of the world, there is a real yearning for unity—that men's hearts are moved more than heretofore toward Christian fellowship. May the spirit of love move over the troubled waters of religious difference.

With respect to the Scandinavian Church, the seeking of fuller knowledge and the interchange of friendly intercourse was recommended as preliminary to the promotion of closer relations. Though it was not believed that the time had come for any direct connection with the Old Catholic or other Continental movements toward reformation, the possibility of an ultimate formal alliance with some of them was hoped for. While there were no doctrinal bars to communion with the Eastern Churches such as existed in the Roman Catholic Church, and while all Episcopal intrusions within their jurisdiction and all schemes of proselytizing were to be avoided, it was only right, the letter declares,

That our real claims and position as a historical Church should be set before a people who are very distrustful of novelty, especially in religion, and who appreciate the history of Catholic antiquity. Help should be given toward the education of the clergy, and, in more destitute communities, extended to schools for general instruction.

While it was considered desirable that the standards, as repeatedly defined and as reiterated in the letter, should be set before the foreign churches in their purity and simplicity:

A certain liberty of treatment must be extended to the cases of native and growing churches, on which it would be unreasonable to impose, as conditions of communion, the whole of the thirty-nine articles, colored as they are in language and form by the peculiar circumstances under which they were originally drawn up. On the other hand, it would be impossible for us to share with them in the matter of holy orders as in complete intercommunion, without satisfactory evidence that they hold the same form of doctrine as ourselves. It ought not to be difficult, much less impossible, to formulate articles in accordance with our own standards of doctrine and worship, the acceptance of which should be required of all ordained in such churches.

The resolutions formally adopted by the Conference are in general harmony with the precepts set forth in the encyclical letter. Besides approving, in general terms, the positions assumed in the several reports, they give more formal and detailed expressions concerning some of the questions considered in them. They declare that "the use of unfermented juice of the grape, or any liquid other than true wine in the administration of the cup in Holy Communion, is unwarranted by the example of our Lord, and is an unauthorized departure from the custom of the Catholic Church"; that the Church can not recognize divorce except in the case of fornication or adultery, or sanction the marriage of a person divorced, contrary to this law, during the life of the other party; that the guilty party, in case of a divorce for fornication or adultery, can in no case during the life of the other party be regarded as a fit recipient of the blessing of the Church on marriage, but that the privileges of the Church should not be refused to innocent parties thus married under civil sanction; that persons living in polygamy should not be admitted to baptism, but that they be accepted as candidates and kept under Christian instruction until such time as they shall be in a position to accept the law of Christ; while the wives of polygamists may be admitted to baptism, but it must be left to the local authorities of the Church to decide under what circumstances they may be baptized. The growing laxity in the observance of the Lord's Day, and especially the increasing practice of making it a day of secular enjoyment, are deprecated, and it is resolved "that the most careful regard should be had to the danger of any encroachment upon the rest which, on this day, is the right of the working-classes as well as of their employers." The opinion of the Conference was expressed that no particular portion of the Church should undertake revision of the Book of Common Prayer without serious consideration of the possible effect of such action on other branches of the Church. The following articles were suggested as supplying a basis on which approach may be made toward "home reunion":

The Holy Scriptures of the Old and New Testaments as "containing all things necessary to salvation," and as being the rule and ultimate standard of faith; the Apostles' Creed as the baptismal symbol, and the Nicene Creed as the sufficient statement of the Christian faith; the two sacraments ordained by Christ himself—baptism and the Supper of the Lord—ministered with unfailing use of Christ's words of institution, and of the elements ordained by him; the historic episcopate, locally adapted in the methods of its administration to the varying needs of the nations and peoples called of God into the unity of his Church.

The Conference requested the constituted authorities of the various branches of the communion:

Acting, so far as may be, in concert with one another, to make it known that they hold themselves in readiness to enter into brotherly conference (such as that which has already been proposed by the Church in the United States of America) with the representatives of other Christian communions in the English-speaking races, in order to consider what steps can be taken either toward separate reunion, or toward such relations as may prepare the way for fuller organic unity hereafter.

With expressions of sympathy and fraternal interest toward the Scandinavian Church, the Old Catholic Church of Holland, the Old Catholic Community of Germany, the "Christian Catholic Church" in Switzerland, the Old Catholics in Austria, and the Reformers in Italy, France, Spain, and Portugal, the Conference, "without desiring to interfere with the

rights of bishops of the Catholic Church to interpose in cases of extreme necessity," deprecated any action that does not regard primitive and established principles of jurisdiction and the interests of the whole Anglican Communion. The question of relations with the Moravian Church was remitted to a committee and to the Archbishop of Canterbury. Hope was expressed that the barriers to fuller communion with the Eastern Churches and jurisdictions might, in course of time, be removed by further intercourse and extended enlightenment. The Archbishop of Canterbury was requested to consider whether it is desirable to revise the English version of the Nicene Creed and the *Quicunque Vult* (Athanasian Creed). Lastly it was resolved:

That, as regards newly constituted churches, especially in non-Christian lands, it should be a condition of the recognition of them as in complete intercommunion with us, and especially of their receiving from us episcopal succession, that we should first receive from them satisfactory evidence that they hold substantially the same doctrine as our own, and that their clergy subscribe articles in accordance with the express statements of our own standards of doctrine and worship; but that they should not necessarily be bound to accept in their entirety the thirty-nine Articles of Religion.

Church Congress.—The twenty-eighth Church Congress met at Manchester, October 1. The Bishop of Manchester presided, and the opening sermon was preached by the Archbishop of York. The president, in opening the discussions, spoke of the value of the Congress as an instrument for creating enlightened public opinion; in which, by bringing men of different opinions together, and giving them equal opportunities to present their views, it had advantages over the press. On the subject, "To what Extent should Results of Historical and Scientific Criticisms, especially the Old Testament, be recognized in Sermons and Teachings," the Rev. J. M. Wilson declared that the clergy must tell the truth, and the whole truth; the Dean of Peterborough sought a definition of the results of criticism; and the president considered the introduction of difficult questions of criticism into the ordinary teachings of the pulpit very undesirable. In the discussion of the question, "How to supply the Defects of the Parochial System by Means of Evangelizing Work," the Rev. W. Carlisle, founder of the Church Army, described the working methods of that organization. Other subjects discussed, with the principal speakers upon them, were: "The Church in Wales (Mr. J. Dilwyn Llewellen, on "Tithes," the Dean of St. Asaph, on "The Work of the Church"); "The Duty of the Church to Seamen" (on which persons particularly interested in mission work among seamen gave the results of their experience and observations); "Positivism; its Truths and Fallacies" (the Rev. W. Cunningham, the Rev. C. L. Engstrom, and Mr. A. J. Balfour); "The Needs of Human Nature, and their Supply in Christianity" (the Archbishop of York and Mr. A. Balfour); "Gambling and Betting" (the Rev. Nigel Madan, Prebendary Grier, the Dean of Rochester, and the Rev. Charles Goldney); "The Foreign Missions of the Church of England and the Protestant Episcopal Church of the United States of America" (Rev. F. H. Cox, on "Missions to English-Speaking People," Rev. Dr. Coddington on "Missions to Savages," the Rev. R. Bruce on "Missions to Colonial Lands," and a number of the colonial bishops); "Atheism" (Mr. R. H. Hutton); "Agnosticism" (the Rev. H. Wace, D. D., and "Pessimism" (the Rev. A. W. Momerie); "Temperance; the Demoralization of Uncivilized Races by the Drink-Traffic" (Dr. J. Grant Mills, the Hon. T. W. Pelham, Sir Charles Warren); "Disposal of the Dead" (F. Seymour Harlen, the Rev. H. R. Haweis, Mr. A. Sington, and the Bishop of Nottingham); "The Sunday-school System in its Relation to the Church" (Canon Elwyn, Canon Trotter, the Rev. J. W. Gedge, and Mr. J. Palmer); "Social Purity" (the Bishop of Newcastle, Mr. G. S. S. Vidal, and G. B Morgan, D. D.); "Hindrances to Church Work and Progress" (the Bishops of Carlisle and Wakefield and Archbishop Farrar); "Adaptation of the Prayer-Book to Modern Needs" (Canon Meyrick, Archdeacon Norris, Dr. Lumby, of Cambridge, and the Bishops of Sydney, Jamaica, and Grahamstown); "Maintenance of Voluntary Schools; Should the Education in them be Free and Religious?" (Prebendary Roe, the Rev. Dr. Cox, Canon Gregory, and Mr. J. Talbot); "The Bearing of Democracy on Church Life and Work" (Rev. C. W. Stubbs, Rev. Llewellen Davis, Mr. T. Hughes, Q. C., and Archdeacon Watkins); "Lay Representation in Church Councils and Statutory Parochial Councils" (Lord Egerton, of Patton, Canon Fremantle, and Mr. R. D. Uslin); "Free and Open Churches, Reserved Seats, and their Influence on Attendance" (Prebendary Hannah, the Earl of Carnarvon, Earl Nelson, and the Rev. H. D. Burton); "The Various Phases of Christian Service—Worship, Almsgiving, Work, and Home Life" (Canon Furse, the Bishop of Wakefield, Canons Hoare and Jelf, and the Bishops of Glasgow and Galloway, and of Mississippi); "Church Finance" (Rev. W. A. Whitworth, Mr. Stanley Leighton, M. P., and Mr. H. C. Richmond); "Eschatology" (Canon Luckock, Archdeacon Farrar, Rev. C. H. Waller, and Rev. Sir George W. Cox); "Increase of the Episcopate;" "The Desirableness of Reviving the Common Religious Life of Men" (the Dean of Lincoln); and "Lay Help." At "Workingmen's Meetings," held in the evenings during the session, the subjects were presented, in popular addresses, of "The Needs of Human Nature, and their Supply in Christianity" (the Archbishop of York and Mr. A. J. Balfour); "Hindrances to Church Work and Progress" (the Bishops of Carlisle and Wakefield and Archdeacon Far-

rar); "Competition, Co-operation, and Over-Population" (the Bishop of Bedford, Hon. and Rev. A. T. Lyttleton, Archdeacon Farrar, and Prof. Symes); and "the Several Aspects of the Question of Sunday Observance," including the questions of the closing of public houses, the opening of libraries and museums, and Sunday recreation and traveling (Sir W. Houldsworth, M. P., Canon McCormick, and the Bishop of Newcastle).

The Irish Synod.—The General Synod of the Episcopal Church in Ireland met in Dublin in April. The report of the representative body said that the total assets of the Church at the close of 1887 amounted to £7,313,838. The total contributions received during the year footed up to £136,963. The total expenditure for the year had been £438,848. About £12,000 had been received by the treasurers of the "Victoria Jubilee Fund" for the education of the sons and daughters of the clergy. About £3,300 had been received for the purchase of the palace at Armagh, as a residence for the primate.

ANTI-POVERTY SOCIETY, an organization that grew out of the candidacy of Henry George for Mayor of New York city in November, 1886. The number of votes polled for Mr. George on that occasion was a surprise to politicians, and the result was accepted by the members of the United Labor party, whose candidate Mr. George was, as an indication that they should push forward their peculiar doctrines by other means and in other fields. On the 26th of March, 1887, a few men assembled in the city of New York and organized the Anti-Poverty Society, with the following brief declaration: "Believing that the time has come for an active warfare against the conditions that, in spite of the advance in the powers of production, condemn so many to degrading poverty, and foster vice, crime, and greed, the undersigned associate themselves together in an organization to be known as the Anti-Poverty Society. The object of the society is to spread, by such peaceable and lawful means as may be found most desirable and efficient, a knowledge of the truth that God has made ample provision for the needs of all men during their residence upon earth, and that poverty is the result of the human laws that allow individuals to claim as private property that which the Creator has provided for the use of all." The presidency was accepted by Dr. Edward McGlynn, who had become prominent by his connection with the candidacy of Mr. George. A high authority from within the society declares that its indications are "to do God's work. We band ourselves together to do the work of God; to rouse the essentially religious sentiment in men and women, which looks to the helping of suffering. We want to do what churches and creeds can not do—abolish poverty altogether; to secure to each son of God, as he comes into the world, a full share of God's natural bounties, an equal right in all the advantages and fruits of civilization and progress, a fair chance to develop all his powers." Still another authority defines the scope of the organization as follows: "The poverty that we would abolish arises from the inability to get work, or from the low wages that are paid for work. The inability to get work arises from the lamentable fact that, in most countries—in most civilized countries especially, and in those countries that have attained to the highest civilization and have the densest population, which is an immense factor in high civilization—the general bounties of Nature are appropriated as private property by a few, by a class, and the masses are literally deprived of their divine inheritance; and so, instead of having the equal right to get at the general bounties of Nature, and thus fulfill the duty as well as exercise the right of supporting themselves and their families—the same equal chances that every other man in the world may have—they have to go cringing and begging of the few, who are the unjust monopolists of the generous bounties of God, for the boon to labor. They have to crave as a blessing the chance to get work; and where there is an unseemly competition—a scramble like that of brute beasts at the trough—it rests with the monopolists to give the work to the one that will content himself with the least and the poorest fare of all—to the one that will consent to live and reproduce his species with the least proportion of the products of his labor." It has been said that the society leans somewhat to the side of the Anarchists, and this might seem to have some foundation from the recent remarks of Dr. McGlynn, who said: "Killing for political purposes is to be considered as something totally different from the crime of murder. If I should happen to read in to-morrow's papers that the Czar had been killed, I wouldn't put any crape on my hat. Without discussing whether, in moral casuistry, it is lawful to kill the Czar, still I must acknowledge the grand and noble character of the men who think it their duty to do their best to kill him. These heroic men feel that they are doing the noblest and holiest thing they could do for their country in trying to kill the Czar." It was expected that the society would be in such shape as to make its influence felt in the November canvass of 1887 in the State of New York, when the Secretary of State and other State officers were to be elected. Mr. George was nominated for Secretary of State, but he polled scarcely any more votes in the whole State than he had polled for Mayor of New York in 1886. Whatever political influence and strength remained to the United Labor party and the Anti-Poverty Society was apparently thrown for their candidate for Mayor of New York in 1888, who received fewer than 10,000 votes, against 68,000 for George as Mayor in 1886, and 70,000 for George as Secretary of State in 1887.

ARCHÆOLOGY. (American.) Glacial Man in America.—The evidences of the existence of man in America in the Glacial epoch have been summed up by Prof. F. W. Putnam, in the Boston Society of Natural History, and Dr. C. C. Abbott, in the American Association for the Advancement of Science. They include the palæolithic implements which Dr. Abbott has found from time to time since 1876 in the gravels of the Delaware valley, near Trenton, N. J., with parts of two skulls. The formation in which these relics occur is declared glacial by Prof. Cook, State Geologist; it is referred by Mr. W. J. McGee, of the United States Geological Survey, to the southernmost extension of the overwash gravels from the terminal moraine formed during the latter epoch of cold of the Quaternary; and is pronounced by the Rev. G. Frederic Wright, who has examined the terminal moraine of the great glacier from New Jersey westward, across Ohio, to be the direct result of the melting of the glaciers as they retired northward. Dr. Metz, of Madisonville, Ohio, found a chipped implement in the gravel at that place, eight feet below the surface, in 1885, and another at about thirty feet below the surface, in a similar deposit on the Little Miami river, opposite Loveland, in 1887, both in a formation unquestionably glacial. Miss Franc E. Babbitt reported to the American Association, in 1888, concerning the finding of implements and fragments of chipped quartz at Little Falls, Minn., where they occurred in a well-defined thin layer in the modified drift forming the glacial flood-plain of the Mississippi river. Specimens of all these findings were compared by Prof. Putnam with specimens from Abbeville and St. Acheul, France, and with an English specimen from the collection of Mr. John Evans, and were found to bear similiar marks of human workmanship, so evident and so uniform in their character as to leave the supposition of their having been results of accident out of the question. They were, however, made from different materials: those from Trenton being, with four exceptions, of argillite; the two from Ohio, one of black chert and the other from a hard, dark pebble, not yet identified; and those from Little Falls, of quartz. Each of these materials was the one suitable for the purpose most easily obtained at the place where it was in use. These implements and the European specimens together show, Prof. Putnam remarks in his review, "that man in this early period of his existence had learned to fashion the best available material, be it flint, argillite, quartz, chert, or other rocks, into implements and weapons suitable to his requirements"; and "that his requirements were about the same on both sides of the Atlantic, when he was living under conditions of climate and environment which must have been very nearly alike on both continents, and when such animals as the mammoth and the mastodon, with others now extinct, were his companions." Evidences of later oc-

cupancy, perhaps by the descendants of palæolithic man, have been found by Mr. Hilborn T.
Cresson, in traces of pile-structures in the alluvial deposits at Naaman's Creek, in Delaware.
At two of the structures, or "stations," only
argillite implements were found, many as rude
as some of the palæolithic types, with a large
number of long, slender spear-points of that
material. In a third station, these forms are
mixed with implements of quartz, jasper, and
other silicious material, with traces of rude
pottery. All these discoveries, according to
Prof. Putnam, show that man had occupied a
portion of North America, from the Mississippi
river to the Atlantic Ocean, at a time when
the northern part of the United States was
covered with ice, and that at that early period
he must have been contemporaneous with the
mastodon and mammoth. "When we compare the facts now known from the eastern
side of the continent," Prof. Putnam continues, "with those of the western side, they
seem to force us to accept a far longer occupation by man of the western coast than
of the eastern; for not only on the western
side of the continent have his remains been
found in zoölogical beds unquestionably earlier
than the gravels of the Mississippi, Ohio, and
Delaware valleys, but he had at that time
reached a degree of development equal to that
of the inhabitants of California at the time of
European contact, so far as the character of
the stone mortars, chipped and polished stone
implements, and shell-beads found in the auriferous gravels can tell the story."

The Construction of a Mound.—A careful examination has been made by Mr. Gerard Fowke
of one of the mounds in Pike County, Ohio,
in order to ascertain the exact method of its
construction. The presence of holes showing
traces in the shape of the dark mold resulting
from the decay of wood of its having contained
posts, and arranged in a regular order, indicated that the mound was built upon the site
of a house. A trench had been dug outside
of the house, possibly for drainage. Near the
middle of the house, which measured about
forty feet from side to side, there had been a
large fire, from which the ashes had been removed to an ash-bed, which was elliptical,
and measured thirteen feet from east to west
and five feet from north to south. Near
the center of it was a hole a foot deep and
ten inches across, filled with clean white
ashes, in which was a little charcoal packed
very hard. At one end of the ash-bed, and
continuous with it, though not apparently a
part of it, was a mass of burned animal bones,
in equal pieces, ashes, and charcoal. After
the fire had burned down, a grave had been
dug at the middle of the house, ten feet long
from east to west, a little more than six
feet broad, and fourteen inches deep, having
straight sides slanting inward, with rounded
corners. Ashes had been thinly sprinkled on
the bottom and a single thickness of bark laid

upon them, while the sides had been lined
with wood or bark from two to four inches
thick. Two bodies had been placed side by
side in the grave, both extended at full length
on their backs with their heads directly west.
The space within the grave on one side of the
skeletons had been covered with ashes that
had been removed from the fire, the thickness
of the deposit increasing from a mere streak at
the feet to six inches at the head, and extending across the grave nearly in contact with
the companion head. The earth removed from
the grave was thrown around on every side so
as to leave the bodies in a hole nearly two feet
deep. No trace appears of any protecting
material having been laid over the bodies.
They were covered with a black, sandy earth,
which had been packed so firmly that it required a pick to loosen it, reached beyond the
grave on every side, and was about five and a
half feet high. No remains were found in the
mound above the grave of the posts which had
probably once stood there. The author assumes that the great fire near the middle of
the house had been made from the timbers
composing it; that the upper timbers had been
torn down, and the posts cut off at the surface.
For the purpose of covering the grave, sand
was brought from a ridge a short distance
away. There was no stratification. Earth
had been piled up first around the black mass,
forming the grave-mound, and then different
parties had deposited their loads at convenient places, until the mound assumed its final
conical arrangement. The lenticular masses
through almost the whole mound showed that
the earth had been carried in skins or small
baskets. The completed mound was thirteen
feet high and about one hundred feet in diameter. Three other skeletons were found within
it, two on the original surface of the ground,
and one two feet and a half above it. The
bones were covered with a dull-red substance,
showing a waxy texture under the knife-blade,
from which it is supposed that the flesh was
removed before burial. No relics were found
with any of the skeletons.

The Great Serpent Mound.—With the aid of a
committee of ladies of Boston, who secured
subscriptions for the purpose of nearly $6,000,
Prof. Putnam, of the Peabody Museum of
Archæology, purchased for that institution, in
June, 1887, sixty acres of ground, including the
"Great Serpent Mound," in Adams County,
Ohio, and it was converted into an inclosed
park. The mound was restored, so far as was
practicable, by replacing the earth and other
material that had been plowed or washed or
carried away. Trees foreign to the spot are
to be removed, and replaced with those that
are indigenous, so as to make the park an *ar-
boretum* of native trees. As described by
Prof. Putnam, in the American Association of
1888, the length of the serpent from tip to tip
is about 1,000 feet, and the length, including
convolutions, 1,415 feet. The builders appear to

have leveled a ledge of rock before constructing the embankment. Frequent fires seem to have burned during the construction; and in one place so many people had been gathered that the clay was beaten like a floor. The spot has since become covered by a foot of soil. In the center of the elliptical mound that formed the reptile's head was once a pile of stones that had been brought up from the creek; they had been blackened by long-continued fires. No sign was observed that the serpentine embankment was ever used for burial purposes, but an oval mound was found near by in which nine skeletons were discovered—one of them so near the surface that a plow had broken down the stones that formed the coffin and carried away a part of the pelvis. Seven feet below the surface, and lying transversely under the first skeleton, was another resting on a stone floor, over which huge stones had been so piled that the bones were crushed almost to dust. Underneath the stone floor was a stratum several feet thick of black ashes, evidently of burned corn, in which lay a skeleton over six feet in length and of massive proportions.

Origin of the Ohio Mounds.—The evidence obtained through the explorations of the United States Bureau of Ethnology are regarded by Dr. Cyrus Thomas as indicating that the typical ancient works in Ohio—the circles and squares, and other works of that type, together with the mounds pertaining to them, or appearing to be built by the same people—were constructed by the ancestors of the Cherokees. Another class of structures—walls, inclosures, and defensive works in the northern part of the State, and also in eastern Michigan—are attributed to some branch of the Iroquois or Huron-Iroquois stock; the box-shaped stone graves, to the Delawares and Shawnees. Certain stone mounds and mounds containing stone vaults or graves of a peculiar type, indicating "a savage life, and fierce warfare with beasts of prey," are difficult to account for, and are probably the work of a tribe that has become extinct. The effigy-mounds, of which only a few are known in Ohio, but which are compared with similar works in Wisconsin and with the bird-effigies of Georgia, also "present a problem difficult to solve." Fortifications of the type of which Fort Ancient is an example are attributed to the Cherokees; while the work named presents some indications of the influence of the white man. "Omitting the last from the list," says Dr. Thomas, "there remains clear and satisfactory evidence that the ancient works of the State are due to at least six different tribes."

The Rev. S. D. Peet finds in some peculiar features of the earth-works of the Scioto valley, evidences of the existence of a clan-system among the builders. Among these features is the formation in circles and squares of areas varying from twenty-seven to fifty acres. Such works are generally regarded as village-sites, and are accompanied by fortifications and signal-mounds on the neighboring hills, with covered or walled ways to the river-bank. In some cases there are graded roads through the terraces to the inclosures, as at Newark, Piketon, and Marietta. The villages are situated at intervals, showing that the people dwelt in different centers, and there are very few works between these centers.

Against the supposition that the mound-builders of these villages were the Cherokees, Dr. Peet argues that these works are entirely different from those found in Tennessee, southern Kentucky, and northern Georgia, the habitat of the Cherokees in historic times; and the relics found in the Cherokee country differ from those in the Ohio mounds. The works in the Cherokee country are large rectangular inclosures without circles, while many of the pipes called duck-pipes are found there. There are very few pipes with curved stems, and none of the variety of sculptured animal figures seen on the Ohio pipes; and no effigies of any kind, which are common in Ohio, and more common in Wisconsin, are to be seen in Tennessee.

Preservation of Ancient Monuments.—The committee of the American Association for the Advancement of Science for the preservation of archæological remains on public lands reported to the Buffalo meeting of the Association that it would be well if the following remains of early America could be preserved: Chaco Cañon, from the forks of Escavoda Cañon, for a distance of eight miles up, also one mile back from the brink of the cañon walls on each side; Cañon de Chelly, Cañon del Muerto, Walnut Cañon, the ruin on Fossil creek on the east branch of the Rio Verde and about fifteen miles south of Camp Verde military reservation; the ruin in Mancos Cañon, the round towers situated on the flat valleys of the lower Mancos; the cavate lodges on the cinder-cone about eight miles east of Flagstaff, Arizona Territory. Besides these groups of ruins and dwellings, there are isolated remains in the territories of New Mexico, Arizona, and Utah, numbering over forty, which demand preservation. The Pueblos, which are not in treaty reservations or grants, and the old Mandan and Arickaree village on the Fort Berthold Indian reservation, Dakota Territory, to be preserved when they shall cease to be inhabited by Indians.

The committee has caused a bill to be introduced in Congress providing for a reservation in New Mexico for the purpose of archæological study.

Peruvian.—A Peruvian object, of a unique character and hitherto undescribed, in the Ethnographical Museum of the Trocadero, in Paris, has been brought to notice by Dr. Vernenu in "La Nature." It is a hollowed cylinder, of a substance resembling bronze, bearing various ornaments upon its circumference and its upper rim. and measuring sixty millimetres in length and twenty-five millimetres in interior diameter. It is marked on the outside by two parallel series of double spirals running in the general direction of its length in such a manner as to form four figures resembling the letter S. Twelve rings, solid with the vessel itself, are evenly disposed in rows of four. Those of the first row are exactly above those of the third, while those of the second row occupy an intermediate position. Movable rings, having spherical swellings in the lower part, are hung upon the fixed rings of the upper row in such a way that they strike the

TINTINNABULUM FOUND IN PERU.

vessel when it is shaken. On the flat rim at the top of the vessel are two groups of two human figures each, facing each other, and representing the same scene. In each of them a repulsive-looking man stands in the attitude of being about to strike with his hatchet a second personage, whom he is holding down. The features and appearance of the four figures and the hatchets bear a distinctly Peruvian stamp. The relic is supposed to be a *tintinnabulum*, or little bell, like those borne on the ends of staffs by Buddhist mendicants in the East, with which they seek to attract the attention of persons from whom they ask alms.

England.—The British Act for the Preservation of Ancient Monuments has been in force for five years; but, according to Lieut.-Gen. Pitt-Rivers, who is intrusted with its administration, only one owner has voluntarily offered any monument to be put under it. All had to be sought out and asked to accept the act, and

the larger number of the owners of scheduled monuments refused. Those who refused generally did so, however, on the ground that they wished to remain responsible for their own monuments; and very little damage to prehistoric works is going on at present. Public opinion has done more for their preservation than any act of Parliament could do.

Old Roman Wall of London.—A part of the old Roman wall of London has been discovered under the site that has been obtained for the new North Post-Office. The upper part of the wall only was broken down, while the rest is in almost perfect condition, with its masonry sharp and true. One hundred feet of the structure have been cleared and exposed to view. It is constructed with facing-courses of stone— Reigate or "rag"—with red tile, and grouted core. A fragment of a similar structure of genuine Roman work also exists, or did exist, in the cellars on Tower Hill.

Old Roman Baths at Bath.—Traces of the old Roman baths at Bath were first noticed in 1755. Further discoveries of remains were made in 1871. The properties covering the ruins were obtained by the corporation of Bath, and some of the works were opened to public view in 1883. One of the most important of them is 81 feet long and 38 feet wide; and is situated in the center of a hall 110 feet long and 68 feet 6 inches wide, which was formerly roofed with a vault supported by pilasters and arches, and is divided into three aisles, the middle one of which covered the bath. The pedestals and lower parts of some of the pilasters are still standing, and the steps going down into the bath are well preserved. Behind the pilasters, in the side-aisles, which were decorated with sculpture, was a promenade gallery. The floor of this hall was twenty feet below the level of the neighboring modern street. Another spacious apartment had two sudatories, or sweating-rooms, with a fireplace between them and fines to heat them. The circular bath, which is shown in the illustration, has been discovered recently. It appears to have been once lined with lead. These structures were an object of special attention to the British Association, which met in Bath, in September, 1888, and the members of that body devoted an afternoon to visiting and inspecting them. The members assembled around the great oval bath and in it, while the mayor of the city gave an account of the work of opening up the ruins, their character, and the degree of Roman civilization of which they gave evidence. After the Romans left Britain, the baths seem to have been allowed to fall into ruins, for a teal's egg had been found in them, and the common bracken had sprung up. New baths have been built upon the foundations of some of these structures.

Celtic Earthworks in Hampshire.—As many as forty Celtic earthworks are described by Mr. T. W. Shore as remaining in Hampshire, England, in a state of preservation more or less complete. They are of various kinds and shapes, and where they inclose areas and form the so-called camps they are of very different dimensions. Most of them are hill-fortresses, but there are also marsh and peninsular fortresses, and one example exists of a small former insular refuge. The present surroundings of these earthworks are of service in assisting to determine their original uses, for, although the woodland features may have changed, the geological conditions are the same as in Celtic times. The camps could hardly have been permanently inhabited sites, for few traces of dwellings or articles of domestic use have been found within them, and from these and other circumstances they appear to have been strongholds for defense in case of attack. If this is allowed, then these areas must have had a distinct relationship to the number of people required for their defense and to the population and their capital or the number of cattle they were intended to shelter. With these data we may draw approximately accurate inferences respecting the location and density of the Celtic population at the time of their construction.

Roman.—In the course of the excavations of the German Institute in the Forum, adjoining the temple of Julius, foundations solidly and well built in travertine have been discovered, which Prof. Richter has identified with the Arch of Augustus. The arch appears to have been one of three piers, like the arches of Severus and Constantine, the middle passage being fourteen feet wide.

Remains of an Archaic Civilization.—Excavations have been made at the site of the ancient Sybaris for the sake of recovering the ruins of the Grecian city that was destroyed five centuries before Christ. Ruins attributable to such a city have not yet been found, but a necropolis has been discovered in the neighborhood which indicates that there existed there previous to the Greek period a more ancient city, the remains of which bear evidence of an archaic civilization precisely corresponding with that, specimens of which have been found at Vetulonia, Civita Castellana, Corneto, and various points in other parts of the peninsula, and in some details with the finds in the lacustrine deposits of the northern provinces. Among the most striking specimens of ancient archaic art, are the cinerary urns of the hut type, such as have been found on the Alban mountains under two strata of volcanic deposits, and which, with the well-tombs, are characteristic features at Corneto (or Tarquinia). The urns are vessels of the rudest forms of pottery, hand-made and half-baked; and with them in one of the well tombs at Corneto were found bronze helmets of most skillful fabric and swords of bronze or iron; and in some of the tombs copies of the helmets in clay, made for covers to the round urns, a use to which the original helmets seem to have been put

ROMAN BATH, AT BATH, ENGLAND.

after the death of their owner. In the same necropolis with these are found the "corridor" tombs and "chambers," the latest and best known form of the Etruscan tomb, the paintings on some of which at Corneto form a series coming down to Roman times. Conflicting views have been expressed concerning the origin of these objects. Helbig believes that they are all Etruscan, and represent only different phases of Etruscan civilization; and while to a certain extent there were overlappings in the method of disposing of the dead, there was in no case a break, such as would be caused by the intrusion of a strange race introducing new arts. The bronze arms and implements he considers of Phœnician and Carthaginian origin, of date not earlier than 900 B. C., or about the period of the entry of the Etruscans into Italy. Their identity with the relics found at Sybaris, which the Etruscans did not reach, and with articles in the lake-dwellings, which are supposed to be of much earlier date, are cited as militating against this view. Fiorelli and some other Italian archæologists maintain that they are relics of a primitive Italic civilization anterior to the Etruscan, and cite the community of the articles from such widely separated localities in support of their view. Gamurrini would identify them with a Pelasgic civilization.

A Ruined Bath.—A bath has been opened at Ostia, under the direction of Prof. Lanciani, which seems to have been struck by some disaster—perhaps an earthquake—while in full use, and to have been completely buried. The statues found there are broken as if by a fall on them of the masonry from above, and have been split vertically, while the fragments have been scattered to some distance from their bases.

Situlæ, or Lot-Vases.—Excavations at various places in Upper Italy have brought to light a number of vessels of the class called situlæ (or vases for the purpose of the lot), bearing peculiar decorations. One found at the Villa Benvenuti, near Este, is 12¼ inches high, and is composed of two plates of bronze riveted together. It widens from the base in a curved shape to near the top, and terminates in a restricted neck and overhanging lip. Elaborate decorations are worked in three zones, toward the upper part of the vessel. A specimen from the tombs at the Certosa Bologna, is decorated in four zones, the lowest of which is composed of animals natural and winged, and the others are occupied respectively with military, religious, and pastoral subjects. Another situla at Bologna has three zones. Bronze specimens of allied character with these have been found at Castelvetro, Modena, and in Tyrol, but the more important specimens are from Cisalpine Gaul, or the immediately adjacent territory. The date of these works is uncertain, but Italian archæologists assign them to the latter half of the fifth century before Christ.

Greece. The Hellenic Society.—The Hellenic Society (London) has been active in connection with schemes of exploration, among which were the organization of the excavations undertaken in Cyprus, to be carried out by the director and students of the British School at Athens, and assistance to explorations in Asia Minor, which were conducted by Prof. Ramsay and Mr. Theodore Bent. Accounts of the work in which it had a part were given in the "Journal of Hellenic Discoveries." Special mention was made, in the report of the discoveries on the Acropolis at Athens, of the excavation by the German Institute of a temple of the Kabeiroi near Thebes; and of the excavations of the American School at Dionusos, to the northeast of Pentelicus, which had been identified as the center of worship of the deme of Icaria. Foundations of two shrines, of Apollo and of Dionysus, had been found, and some sculptured remains of high importance.

Discoveries in the Acropolis at Athens.—Among the objects disclosed by the excavations on the Acropolis is a head, one of the most ancient sculptures ever found upon that site, carved in Poros stone, and retaining a rich and brilliant coloring. The hair and beard are painted blue and the face red; and the pupils of the eyes are delineated with the chisel as well as painted in. The head appears to be that of a triton, the rest of the body of which, in the form of a serpent ending in the tail of a fish, was found near the same place. At a later date were found a leaden vessel, quite shapeless through oxidation, and a portion of the torso of a statue of Hercules in Poros stone, half life-size.

Mr. Carl D. Buck, of the American School at Athens, has described in the "American Journal of Archæology" certain inscriptions, found on the Acropolis in December, 1887, of the fourth century before Christ, which record the dedication of vessels—apparently by freedmen who had been acquitted of the charge of violating the conditions of their emancipation.

Excavations at Sicyon.—The excavations carried on by the American School of Classical Studies on the site of ancient Sicyon in December, 1887, and January, 1888, were made mostly in the theatre. The orchestra was laid bare, and work was done in other parts of the building. Two drains were found. The sculptures include a marble hand grasping what might be the hilt of a sword, being a fragment of a statue of which no other part has been discovered; and a marble head and the torso to which it belongs, separated, appertaining to a statue representing a Dionysus "of youthful and girlish aspect" which was thought to belong to the Alexandrian epoch. This statue is the first considerable example of Sicyonian sculpture found on the old site. The main portion of the orchestra, like the theatre at Epidaurus, has no flooring other than hard earth. About thirty copper coins were found, part of them Sicyonian, and the remainder Roman. An inscription found in a village near the site consists of seven names, one of which contains the old Sicyonian form of Σ (χ). Its date may possibly be as early as 450 B. C.

Icaria.—In the course of the investigations begun by the American School at Icaria, the Pythian or Temple of Apollo was discovered, with a relief representing Apollo with long curls seated on the *omphalos*, holding a mass of twigs in one hand, and a patera in the other. Behind him stands a woman, while in front is an altar with an adorant. Another relief represents Apollo playing on the lyre. A large platform of marble, a marble-seat, some bases, and two walls, one of which makes a curve as if it might inclose the dancing-ground of a theatre, were also found.

Discoveries at Cephissus and Dionysos.—In their excavations at Cephissus, the American School discovered the head of a colossal male statue, a *basso rilievo* representing a warrior, a torso of a statue without a head, and many inscriptions.

Investigations at the spot known as Dionyso? have brought to light fragments of draped statues of an archaic epoch supposed to belong to Dionysus; the torso of an undraped statue; the bearded head of a man, also attributed to Dionysus and referred to the sixth century, before Christ; and a headless *stela*, like the *stela* of Aristion which is to be seen in Athens. Many of these objects were found in the walls of a half-ruined chapel standing on the spot and evidently built of old materials. The excavations have also laid bare a portion of the wall of the *peribolos* of the temple, and the bases of some votive offerings.

Statuettes at Tanagra.—At Tanagra has been found the tomb of a child, within which were thirteen statuettes of the same subject, representing a nude man pressing to his bosom with his left hand a cock. Several terra-cotta vases were found in the same place, of diverse forms, and for the most part ornamented with flowers (*anthemia*). One of the statuettes found at the same time represents a woman standing; another, an old woman with a babe in her arms; another, a youth standing clad in a chiton, with a purse in his right hand, and a chlamys hanging from his left arm. Others represent women seated, two naked children seated, a naked child squatting on its heels, three men seated, and one man standing.

The Temple of Aphrodite at Cerigo.—A report on the remains of the ancient temple of Aphrodite in Cerigo has been made by Dr. Schliemann to the Berlin Society of Anthropologists. The site is identical with that of the Church of the Holy Kosmos; and the stones of the ancient sanctuary almost sufficed for the erection of the church. The temple was a closed structure made of tufa-stone, with two rows of Doric columns, four on each side, of extremely archaic style. They are still preserved in the church, with their capital and ornaments; but only two of them, as well as the base of a column, are *in situ*. On a hill-top in the neighborhood are remains of Cyclopean fortifications, which Dr. Schliemann thinks, from the character of the potsherds found, can not be older than the seventh century before Christ.

The Rock-Cut Tombs of Mycenæ.—The excavations at Mycenæ continue to reveal fresh tombs, so that the extent of the necropolis can not yet be inferred. It appears, however, that all the land surrounding the ancient city, except where it was unsuitable, was used for burial. The tombs are on the slope of the hill, and consist of one or two chambers, which are reached by passages either horizontal or having a downward inclination, sometimes more than 20 metres long and 2 or 2½ metres broad. The chambers are 35 or 40 square metres in area, and constructed with great care. They appear to have been family vaults, and to have their doors and passages carefully hidden, to protect them against spoliation. The skeletons are imperfectly preserved, and seem to have been disturbed whenever fresh interments were made; they were simply laid out at full length, or placed in a sitting posture. The tombs are ascribed to an earlier date than the Homeric age, and even to a time as far back as 2000 B. C. They have yielded some objects that had not been found in other tombs of the same date—such as bronze mirrors, small knives that served as scissors, and razors, which are now shown to have been in use even in those early times. The most abundant

articles are beads that belonged to necklaces. They vary in shape, and are chiefly of glass; but some are of stone as large as a franc-piece, and engraved on one side with pictures of animals; and some are of onyx or natural crystal. A silver vase in the shape of a *phiale*, 0·18 metre in diameter, and having one handle, is adorned on the outer side of its rim with faces of men in gold, and a golden ornament under each. The character of the articles is described as mostly Eastern.

A Theatre and Temple at Mantineia.—The excavations made during 1887 and 1888 by the French Archæological School at Mantineia began with the clearing of the theatre, which was built of the common stone of the district, and presents some peculiar features. While parts of the building are so ruined that their ancient form can not be reconstructed, the conduits by which the rain-water was carried off are in comparatively good preservation. Near this building are the foundations of a temple, which may be the temple to Hera spoken of by Pausanias; but no inscription has been found by which to determine to whom it was dedicated. This foundation and the remains of the temple are both very near the surface of the soil. A large semicircular building, of which about a metre in height of the walls is left, gave the inscription Κύκλος ὁ πρὸς τὸ γυμνάσιον. In front and alongside of it were large double *stoai* which may have formed part of the gymnasium. The wall of the circuit of the town, in a fair state of preservation to the height of a metre or more, is built of large polygonal stones, and is 20 stadia in perimeter; more than a hundred of its towers are preserved. The roads mentioned by Pausanias as named after the respective towns have been discovered. Among the less massive relics are the pieces of sculpture by Praxiteles recorded by Pausanias as being in the temple of Leto, including on one pedestal a representation of the muses and of Marsyas playing on the flute; a number of inscriptions, one of which records the name of the great general Philopœmen; some terra-cotta tablets, which are supposed to have been theatre-tickets; and votive tablets. The stones of the ancient city have been liberally used in the construction of the houses of the modern town; and some of the most interesting objects were found walled in within the sanctuary of the Byzantine church.

Cyprus. Temple of Aphrodite at Old Paphos.—A "Cyprus Exploration Fund" has been formed, under the auspices of the Society for the Promotion of Hellenic studies, to carry out on the island of Cyprus the same kind of work of identification and recovery of remains of antiquity that has been successfully accomplished in Palestine, Asia Minor, and Egypt. It is under the care of a special committee of persons interested in archæological research. Permission was obtained from the authorities to excavate at Kouklia, on the site of the ancient Paphos, and operations were begun there in

December, 1887, under the supervision of Mr. Ernest A. Gardener. Excavations were also made in January, 1888, by Mr. M. R. James at the hill Leontari Vouno, Nikosia, in the course of which were discovered traces of early houses and walls, deep cuttings in the rock, a massive fort, primitive walls mixed with early pottery and other objects pointing to a remote period, and archaic tombs. In the tombs were found about two hundred vases, with fragments of pottery and broken articles of bronze, lead, and copper.

The temple of Aphrodite, at old Paphos, was cleared out, and a large portion of the walls was laid bare. The majority of the walls were found to belong to the restoration of the temple made by Tiberius; but the Romans appear to have made changes in the orientation of the parts of the structure that they touched, so that difficulty was met in tracing an accurate plan of the work. The plan of the temple falls into two main divisions—the south wing, standing detached, and a quadrilateral, containing various halls and inclosures. The south wing appears to be the earliest part of the building of which any traces remain. It consists of a large hall or court, bounded on the west by a wall of massive blocks. Between this court and the great quadrangle are remains of some irregular chambers and some pier bases, which may have been part of a triple avenue leading to the court. The rest of the site is occupied by buildings of later construction, of which, beginning at the south, the first to attract attention is a great hall or stoa, with a row of columns down the center. The construction is Roman, but it probably retains the general character of earlier buildings ; and of such earlier chambers sufficient traces remain to allow of a fairly accurate restoration. A considerable number of inscriptions, a marble head of Eros, said to be "a valuable acquisition to the treasures of Greek art," fragments of bronze and terra-cotta, a fine bronze-gilt pin, and a crystal cylinder belonging to a scepter, were found in the temple. Among the inscriptions in the Cypriot syllabary was a tablet containing a letter from Antiochus to Ptolemy Alexander, a tablet bearing a list of contributors to a feast called the Elaichristion, and a tablet bearing an elegiac inscription recording that at the suggestion of King Nikokles the town was fortified. Most of the inscriptions were on the pedestals of statues dedicated in the temple in Ptolemaic times, which confer much light on the constitution of Cyprus during that period. Some very interesting objects were found in the tombs of various periods that lie below the temple on the slope toward the sea. A third work of excavation was carried on at Anargeth, which was identified as the site of an ancient village, probably called Melantha, where Apollo was worshiped under the title of Opaon.

Perforated Monoliths.—Some curious perforated stones—monoliths—near Anoyra, in the Lima-

sol district, have been examined by Dr. F. H. Guillemard. They are similar to two monoliths at Kuklia, which are described by Cesnola, and have been regarded as Phœnician, and, perhaps, Phallic. Twenty-seven such stones have been found at Anoyra, all of a hard limestone. They are usually two feet in depth, and from ·2 feet 5 inches to 4 feet 3 inches in width, while the hole is generally about 9 inches wide, and from 2½ to 4 feet high. The height above ground ranges from 6 to 10 feet. These stones are believed by Dr. Guillemard, from their situation and accompaniments, to have been parts of mills or of olive-presses. Others believe that though they may have been adapted and utilized for such purposes as these, they were originally Phœnician, or prehistoric, and Phallic.

Ancient Sites in Asia Minor.—Mr. J. T. Bent, giving an account to the British Association of some discoveries that he had made in Asia Minor, said that during a cruise along the south coast of that country, he had found the sites of three ancient towns and identified them by inscriptions. In one place were thirty-three inscriptions, many of them of great local interest, introducing a doctor, Aristobulus by name, who is mentioned by Galen, and numerous consuls and pro-consuls of Rome, who ruled there. Local offices and dignitaries, family names and customs, are referred to in all these inscriptions. At about five miles from Lydæ, inland, the author discovered the ruins of a fortress buried in a thick forest overlooking a lake, and identified the place from inscriptions as Lissa.

Egypt Exploration Fund.—The Egypt Exploration Fund, in acknowledgment of liberal contributions to its resources (which amount to fully one half of its fund) from the United States, has authorized the presentation to the Museum of Fine Arts, in Boston, of a selection of Greek antiquities from Naucratis and of Egyptian antiquities from Nebesheh, the city of Onias, and Bubastis, and of a statue of heroic size of Rameses II.

The work of the fund for 1888 was begun by Mr. F. Llewellen Griffith on the mounds of Kûm abû Billû, at Tarrâneh, on the western edge of the delta. The site is supposed to represent an ancient city named Terenuthis. The remains yielded little that was of interest, and the work was discontinued.

Hyksos Monuments at Bubastis.—The excavations on the site of the great temple of Bubastis were resumed on the 23d of February, 1888, by Mr. Edouard Naville, with Mr. F. Llewellen Griffith, Count d'Hulst, and the Rev. Mr. MacGregor. The two pits formed in 1887 were thrown into one, and the ground was cleared from east to west, following the axis of the temple till the whole width of the building was laid bare. Among the discoveries were a third hall built by Osorkon I, of red granite lined with sculptured slabs ; the remains of a colonnade ; a monolithic shrine in red granite ; two statues of an officer named Amenophis, inscribed with the cartouches of Amenophis III, and the torso of a woman of the same epoch ; traces of Amenophis IV (or Khu-en-Aten) in the shape of the name of that king's patron deity. The results of the investigations brought up the number of the names of the kings who had left traces of their work here to twenty-two, beginning with Pepi Merira, of the sixth dynasty, including Usertesen III, of the twelfth dynasty, and ending with Nectanebo.

Evidences associating the site with the rule of the Hyksos kings were found in the shape of an architrave sculptured with the cartouch of Apepi, and the remains of three statues of this period. One of these was headless, but was seated upon a throne, with cartouches and standard, giving the family name, the throne name, and the "banner" name of the king in a perfect state of preservation. This is the first instance in which a Hyksos statue has been found with a legible inscription. The inscriptions read as follows: "The divine Horus who embraces the lands, the good god Userenra, the son of Ra, Raian, loving his *Ka*, everliving." This name, Raian, is new to the Egyptian monuments, although it suggests a curious coincidence with an Arab tradition of the going of Joseph to Egypt, which, as given by Mas'údi, relates that "the Hamites who peopled Egypt had been for some time ruled over by women, in consequence of which kings from all quarters were lusting after their land. An Amelekite king named al-Walid invaded it from Syria and established his rule there. After him came his son, Rayyán ibu al-Walid, in whose time Joseph was brought to Egypt."

Mr. Petrie has adduced reasons, from the readings on two cylinders bearing the titles of this king, for supposing that the name should be read Khian rather than Raian, and that this makes his connection with the Rayan of Arab tradition almost impossible. The Rev. Henry George Tomkins, however, has suggested that "if we must read Khian, the name may still be intended by the ΙΑΝΝΑΣ of Manetho, with rough breathing." and adds "that in this case we may find for the first time traces of a Hyksos proper name in northern Syria; for Assur-nazirpal received tribute from Khaian or Khindani 'on the further bank of the Euphrates,' that is, on the western side, south of the junction of the Khabûr. And Shalmaneser took tribute of Khaian, the son of Gabas, in northern Syria toward the west. There are local traces of such a name, especially the ancient ruins and great tanks of Khurbet Haiyan, east of Bethel, which have been thought to mark the site of the important Canaanite city Ai or Hai."

Mr. F. Llewellen Griffith has compared the prenomen of the king as given on this statue —Ra-suser-n—with the name inscribed in imperfect characters in the cartouch of a black granite lion from Bagdad, in the British Museum, which presents some resemblance to it.

This lion is one of a class of sphinxes in black granite that have been found at several sites in Lower Egypt, and are assigned to a period previous to the eighteenth dynasty.

Portraits of the Greco-Roman Period.—Mr. Petrie placed on exhibition in London the objects that he recovered in the exploration of a vast cemetery, which he found near the pyramid containing the tomb of Amenemhat III. The cemetery proved to be one of the Ptolemaic and Roman epochs, and furnished many new facts respecting the dress, mode of burial, etc., of the Hellenized and Romanized Egyptians of the three or four centuries before and after the Christian era. The mummies of two or three earlier centuries had gilt sculptured head-pieces, and those dating from about A. D. 150 had portraits inserted in the place of the head. These portraits, of which there were more than thirty, were painted, apparently in colored wax, upon very thin wooden panels, and are preserved in all their freshness. Many of them are said to be wonderfully expressive ; one, representing the face of a man of mature age, "is modeled with singular force and skill," and four are "excellent portraits" of ladies. These heads were slipped into the mummy-case, and it appears to have been the custom to keep the mummy, thus adorned, for several years in the house of the family. An important fragment of papyrus, containing a transcript of a part of the second book of tho Iliad, beautifully written, is included in the collection, and with it is the skull of the owner, a lady, with shreds of her hair twisted over it.

The Pyramid and Statues of Lake Mœris.—The researches of Mr. W. M. Flinders Petrie in the Fayoum have brought to light what are supposed to be the remains of the structures described by Herodotus as two pyramids crowned with colossal statues standing in the midst of Lake Mœris. At Beyahmu, a village about four miles north of Medinet-el-Fayoum, ruins destitute of inscriptions and called *Kursi Far'un*, or Pharaoh's chair, had been already remarked and described by Ebers as resembling dilapidated altars rising above other fragments of solid masonry. Ebers had also suggested a connection between these objects and the pyramids of Herodotus. Mr. Petrie found that they were, in fact, two piles of masonry standing on two stone platforms, at the corner of one of which was an angular block of some sloping structure, like the corner of a pyramid. The piles of rubbish in which the ruins were half imbedded, were found to contain a vast number of fragments of limestone, red granite, and a hard and highly polished yellow quartzite sandstone. A search among these fragments soon brought out scraps of hieroglyphic inscription, a morsel of bass-relief paneling, and a royal oval containing the name of Amenemhat III—the Mœris of Herodotus. As the search was continued, numerous chips were found containing bits of detail, or wrought in the likeness of the undulating surface of the human body, scraps of ornamentation such as are carved on the thrones of the colossi of the period of the twelfth dynasty, and, finally, a polished sandstone nose measuring eleven and a half inches in width. From this feature, Mr. Petrie estimates that the statue, when perfect, must have been about thirty-five feet high. The masses of fragments about the other altar give hope that similar remains of a second statue may be found there. The pedestals are twenty-two feet high. Supposing the statues to have been set upon a base three feet high, the total elevation of the figures above the ground is estimated to have been sixty feet. Each pedestal appears to have been surrounded by an open court, walled around to about the height of the base of the statue. As these walls inclined inward, like the sides of pyloons and pyramids, the effect when viewed from a distance would be precisely that of a truncated pyramid surmounted by a seated statue. The exaggerations by Herodotus of the heights of the monuments—which he gave as "fifty fathoms above the surface of the water, and extending as far beneath "—as well as of the size of Lake Mœris, are ascribed to his having visited the country during the inundation, and to his having been misled by his guides, who were probably no more trustworthy than the dragomans of the present day.

Mr. Cope Whitehouse, on the other hand, who has made a survey of the depression called the Raian basin, to the south and west of the Fayoum, believes that he has found there the site of an ancient lake that was ample and deep enough to answer the description given by Herodotus as of Lake Mœris. It is described as being forty miles long, twenty miles wide, and more than two hundred and fifty feet deep, and connected with two other depressions, one of which is represented by the Birket-al-Keroun, and the other is the Gharaq basin. The Birket is fed by the canal called the Bahr Jusuf, which runs almost parallel with the river from Osioot, till it finds a pass through the hills and enters the Fayoum. After emerging from the pass it divides into four branches, running in different directions toward the Birket or different parts of the depression. A fifth channel may also be traced. Within the depression, near the northwestern edge, is a hill called Grande Butte, or Haram by the Egyptians, which may be the island described by Herodotus.

Documents in the Babylonian Language.—A large number of clay tablets and fragments of tablets inscribed with cuneiform characters have been discovered among the ruins of Tel-el-Amarna, in Upper Egypt, the site of the capital built by Amenophis IV, or Khu-en-Aten. They were discovered in the tomb of a royal scribe, and consist largely of letters and dispatches sent by the kings and governors of Palestine, Syria, Mesopotamia, and Babylonia, to Amenophis III and IV; and a note in hieratic on one of them says that a large portion of them had been

transferred from Thebes to the new capital of Khu-en-Aten, along with the rest of the royal archives. Palestine was held at the time by Egyptian garrisons, and the representatives of the Egyptian Government appear to have been active in sending home news about all that was going on. Among the cities of Palestine from which letters were dispatched were Byblas, Smyrna, Akko or Acre, Megiddo, and Ashkelon; and reference is made in one of the letters to a coalition, at the head of which was the king of Gath.

About three fourths of the whole number of the tablets have been deposited in the Royal Museum of Berlin and the British Museum. Among those in the Berlin collection are letters and dispatches from Tushratta, King of Mitanni; Burraburriyash, King of Karaduiyash; and other kings of parts of Mesopotamia. The fact is established in them that Tushratta was the father-in-law of Amenophis III, thus confirming the representations on the scarabei of that king, that he married a Mesopotamian woman. Among the eighty-five tablets acquired by the British Museum are several of considerable importance for the study of the relations which existed between the kings of Mesopotamia and Egypt. A dispatch from Tushratta to Amenophis III refers to a treaty which existed between the father of the former and Amenophis, and conveys proposals for a marriage between his great-nephew and the daughter of the Egyptian king. A dispatch from Burraburriyash to Amenophis IV, besides allusions to a treaty, mentions exchanges of gifts. Letters from the king of a country called Alashiva also mention gifts and negotiations, and ask for the return of the property of a subject of Alashiya who had died in Egypt leaving his family in the former country. Other dispatches are from Tushratta to the wife of Amenophis III, the greatly beloved Ti of the Egyptian monuments, who appears to have been the daughter of Tushratta, in which the proposed alliance of his great-nephew with Amenophis's daughter is again mentioned. Mr. A. H. Sayce has found in one of the inscriptions a mention of a *targumanam* or dragoman having been sent with a letter, giving the first example of the use of this word.

Memphis Colossi of Rameses II.—Major Arthur Bagnold described before the Society of Biblical Archæology, at its February meeting, the raising of the pair of colossal statues of Rameses II, at Memphis, which are mentioned by Herodotus and Diodorus as having stood in front of the temple of Ptah. One of them had been partly brought to light by Sloane and Caviglia, and Hekekian Bey once began to dig around it; and a cast of its face was in the British Museum. The colossus was raised by the aid of hydraulic apparatus, propped up, photographed, and then laid upon its back, in the position which it had before occupied. It is thought to have been about thirty-five feet high, but was broken off at the knees, and the feet could not be found. It is admirably carved, and the face of the king is nearly perfect.

Tombs at Siout.—The rock-cut tombs of Siout, ancient Lycopolis, have been re-examined by Mr. F. Llewellen Griffith, who made careful transcripts of all the extant inscriptions. Mr. Griffith determined the date of the great tomb known as Stahl-Antar, having found that it was excavated in the reign of Usertesen I. of the twelfth dynasty. He also discovered that the upper ranges of tombs in the same cliff belong to the hitherto unrepresented dynasties of Herecleopolis (the ninth and tenth dynasties of Manetho).

Book of the Dead — Ani Papyrus.—A hieroglyphic papyrus containing a recension of the Book of the Dead, which was written for the royal scribe Ani, in the early part of the nineteenth dynasty, has been acquired for the British Museum. It is in excellent preservation, and, except for the absence of a character here and there, is complete, and contains some vignettes of rare beauty. The fact that it contains a chapter, the one hundred and seventy-fifth, which has not been found complete anywhere else, gives it an extraordinary value.

Early Christian Sculptures.—Many specimens of early Christian sculptures from Egypt show traces of the ancient pagan styles, and of the adaptation of them to the purposes of the Christian faith. In a very primitive presentation of the Virgin and Child, with a figure dressed in a dalmatica standing before them, from the Fayoum, the two principal figures are entirely nude, and are described as simply reproducing the well-known group in Egyptian art, of Isis suckling Horus; even the chair in which the Virgin is seated is of the same fashion as the chairs of the twenty-sixth or earlier dynasties. In a representation of a saint standing in a niche, the colonnettes are designed after columns of purely Egyptian temples. A bass-relief of St. George slaying the dragon has its counterpart in figures of Horus slaying Set. In a collection of Coptic textiles centaurs, sirens, cupids, and other fabulous figures from the pagan mythology appear as common ornaments. Of this character are a composition of the Triumph of Bacchus in the Museum of Lyons, and three embroidered pieces at South Kensington containing half-length figures of Apollo, Hermes, and Hercules, with their names inscribed on the background. In an *alto-rilievo* representing Christ and his apostles, also from Akhmin, and assigned to the period of Theodosius II or Marcian, the figures are arranged, standing in line, without attempt at artistic grouping, dressed in the style of Roman sculpture, and separated by a simple ornamental motive. Each of the heads is surrounded by a nimbus, that of our Lord being distinguished by a cross inside of the circle. These various objects combine, in the view of those who have examined them, to illustrate the artistic activity of the period forming the link between ancient and modern art.

Palestine. The Pool of Bethesda.—The Palestine Exploration Fund has announced the discovery by Herr Conrad Schick, near the Church of St. Anne, Jerusalem, of what may in all probability be identified with the Pool of Bethesda. An apparently uninterrupted chain of evidence from A. D. 333 to the year 1180 speaks of the *Probatica piscina* as near the church of St. Anne. The place spoken of is said by the earliest writers to have formerly had five porches, then in ruins. Recently the Algerian monks laid bare a large tank or cistern cut in the rock to the depth of thirty feet, lying nearly under a later building, a church with an apse at the east end. The cistern is 55 feet long from east to west, and 12½ feet in breadth from north to south. A flight of 24 steps leads down into the pool from the eastern scarp of rock. This pool was not, however, large enough to supply the first requisite for the Pool of Bethesda—that it should be possible to have five porches; but Sir Charles Wilson had pointed out that this condition could be fulfilled if there were a twin pool lying by the side of this one, so that the two pools could have one portico on each of the four sides, and one between them on the wall of separation. Such a pool has been since discovered by Herr Schick. It is 60 feet long, and of the same breadth with the first pool. The pool is therefore concluded to be undoubtedly the one pointed out by the writers as the *Piscina Probatica ;* and it affords ample room for the five porches spoken of in the Gospel, as well as for the five porticoes—which were probably the same—which are spoken of by the "Bordeaux Pilgrim" as being then there in ruins.

The Walls of Jerusalem.—The topography of ancient Jerusalem has been difficult to make out, and the site of the sepulchre of the kings of Judah remains unknown. But the problem has been simplified by recent excavations, the bearing of which was explained in the British Association by Mr. George St. Clair. We now for the first time know the contours of the rock and the features of hill and valley before the 80 feet of *débris* began to accumulate. The Akra of the Maccabees being defined, it is seen how, by the recorded filling up of the Asmonean valley, the two parts of the Lower City became joined into one crescent, lying with its concave side toward the Upper City, according to the description of Josephus. The investigations of Sir Charles Warren show that the temple must be placed on the summit of Moriah, with Solomon's palace southeast of it, leaving a vacant square of 300 feet where now we have the southwest quarter of the Haram area. From the southeast quarter of the Haram inclosure extends the wall of Ophel, discovered by Warren, running 76 feet to the south, then bending toward the southwest. Further, it is found that from the Gate of the Chain, in the west wall of the Haram inclosure, a causeway, with complicated structures, extends westward toward the Jaffa Gate. Having this groundwork, we may proceed to place the walls. The third wall, built by Agrippa, does not concern us. The site of the second wall has been partly fixed by Herr Conrad Schick. The first wall was the wall of the Upper City. On the northern side it ran from the Jaffa Gate to the Haram wall. The uncertainty has been about its southern portion. The investigations of the author have led him to adopt a line that corresponds in detail with the descriptions in the Book of Nehemiah. Taking Nehemiah's night survey, then the consecutive allotments of work assigned to those who repaired the walls, and, thirdly, the points successively reached and passed by the processionists when the walls were dedicated, it is shown that every mention of a gate or a tower, the number and order of the salient and re-entering angles, and every other note of locality, exactly agree with the course of the walls as suggested. This course, moreover, involves the least possible variation from the present line of walls, and that more in the way of addition than of deviation. The hypothesis commending itself as true by corresponding minutely with Nehemiah's description, by tallying exactly with other Biblical references, and by meeting all the other requirements of the case, it has the important practical bearing that it indicates the site of the royal sepulchres, of the stairs of the City of David, of "the gate between the two walls," etc., and shows that Zion was the eastern hill.

Hittite. Characteristic Figures of the Inscriptions.—In a course of lectures at the British Muse-

the peoples of the country of the Khatti mentioned on the Assyrian monuments. Some of the personages among the representatives of the Hittites on Egyptian monuments, and also figures of persons in authority found at Jerablus, or Carchemish, are represented with the "pigtail," while other figures are in long hair without this style of dress. This would indicate—supposing the mass of the population to have been Semitic or of allied race—that there was in some of the cities at least, a ruling stock of another race, which may have been Tartar. On the opposite sides of the walls of the great chasm of Bogaz Keui are processions, one of male the other of female figures which meet at the head of the ravine, where a gigantic male figure, standing on the bent-down heads of two persons with long robes, and a female figure standing on some animal and wearing a mural crown are presenting floral symbols in which is a form like that of the mandragora or mandrake, to each other. The figures in the female procession, each bearing what resembles an unstrung bow, remind the observer of the Amazons; and it is a striking fact that Bogaz Keui is not far from the place, by the river Thermodon, to which the Greeks assigned the Amazons. If the story of the Amazons was purely legendary, these sculptures might be regarded as showing that it was believed in in what might be regarded as their own country. A seal lately obtained from Yusgat, now in the British Museum, is considered to cast some light on the nature of the Hittite inscriptions. It is circular and contains solar, devo-

CENTRAL BASS-RELIEF AT BOGAZ KEUI.

um, Mr. Thomas Tyler expressed it as the currently received opinion that there probably never was a Hittite empire in such a sense as the word empire now suggests. The view that the nation consisted of independent states or cities, which formed federations under pressure of the necessities of war is apparently confirmed by the expression, "King of the Hittites," used in the Old Testament. These peoples are to be identified with the Khita of the Egyptians and

tional, and symbolical designs, with a male figure bringing tribute or a present, and a female making obeisance to a king sitting on a throne, behind whom are other figures symbolical, perhaps, of the spoils of war or the hunt. The design is analogous to a portion of the doorway inscription from Jerablus, in which oxen, asses, and other valuable possessions, the spoils of war, are presented to a king wearing a pigtail and a conical cap. A quadrangular seal from Tarsus, engraved on five faces, bears on one face two figures presenting a floral symbol resembling the mandrake, while of seven other principal figures, two, one having the head of a hawk, wear the pigtail. All the figures have the toes turned up, as in what are called the Hittite boots. Figures also occur resembling the *crux ansata*, or symbol of life, of the Egyptian monuments.

The Stela of Fassiller.—Mr. Sterrett, of the American School at Athens, describes the discovery at Fassiller, not far from the site of Lystra, in Isauria, of a monument of the same class of the sculptures at Bogaz Keui, Euyûk, and Giaur Kalesi. It is an immense monolithic *stela*, now lying on its back, and contains the figures of two men and two lions in very high relief. Occupying the center of the stone, at the bottom, is an erect human figure, clothed in a gown draping the whole of it, to the ground. The hands are clasped on the breast, with the chin touching them. The head-dress seems to be a helmet: its mouth is open; its ears and eyes are very large. On either side of this figure stands a lion, full face, about as tall as the man without his crested helmet, and with the legs not divided; that is, the curvatures alone are indicated, while the mass of stone between the legs has not been dug away. Above the human figure is a second figure of a man striding forward, his left foot, which is in front, supporting his whole weight. This foot rests on the top of the crest of the helmet of the lower figure; but the feet are not chiseled out, or even indicated. The legs are merely straight lines. The right hand is raised, and holds a round object, with something projecting from it vertically on one side, while a large object is held under the left arm. This object reaches to the feet, but diminishes in size and relief, till at the foot the relief is very slight. On the head is a grand tiara, with four divisions or bosses. The whole height of the *stela* is 7·23 metres; width at bottom, 2·75 metres: thickness at top, 0·32 metre. A circular seal having a string-hole, was engraved on one of the two convex sides with a human figure having an ox's head and wearing the boots with turned up toes, and with a design on the other side that could not be made out.

Babylonia. Babylonian Exploration Fund of Philadelphia.—An exploring party has been sent out to Babylonia under the auspices of the Babylonian Exploration Fund of Philadelphia, and sailed from New York on the 23d of June. It consists of Dr. John P. Peters, director, with his assistant, Mr. J. D. Prince; Dr. Hilprecht, of the University of Pennsylvania, and Dr. Harper, of Yale, Assyriologists; Mr. P. H. Field, architect; and Mr. J. H. Haynes, photographer. Arrangements were made for carrying on the work for one year, its continuance to depend upon the success achieved during that time. The Babylonian Exploration Fund was organized in Philadelphia, in November, 1887, under the presidency of Dr. Pepper, Provost of the University of Pennsylvania, and

obtains its funds through the subscriptions of citizens.

The Temple at Sippara.—In describing the temple that Mr. Rassam has discovered at Aboo Hubba, the site of the ancient Sippara, or Sepharvaim, Mr. W. St. Chad Boscawen has pointed out the close resemblance that it presented to the Jewish temple. Its internal arrangements and even the names of the different portions were identical with those of the Jewish temple. The Holy Place (*hekal*) was separated from the Holy of Holies (*parrako*) by a veil. In the civil portions of the temple a close parallel was presented to those of the Mohammedan mosque. The temple was the treasury; it was also the school, and, like the mosque, was supported by a glebe or *wakuf* . estates and a regular tithe. Several thousand tablets had been discovered by Mr. Rassam in the treasury of the temple, covering a period extending from the fall of Nineveh, 625 B. C., until the time of Alexander the Great. These archives throw much light upon all branches of Babylonian social customs, and make possible a restoration of the life of the people in the by-gone past with the fullest detail. Among the tablets is one recording the payment of the tithes by the *major domo* of Belshazzar, and a list of the dues paid by the prince himself in behalf of himself and his father. The date of the reign of the older Sargon, as given on the cylinder of Nabonidus which was recovered in this temple (about 3800 B. C.), may be regarded as correct. The historical statements on the same cylinder are in all other particulars accurate. Among the other inscriptions found on this site, were some cylinders recording the restoration of the great canal known as the Nahr Malka by Khammurabi, who reigned about 2200 B. C. These inscriptions, coupled with others written nearly fifteen centuries later by Nabopolassar, show that during that long interval the Euphrates had shifted its course to the west. In Sargon's time (3800 B. C.) the river no doubt flowed close to the walls of Sippara, but in 2200 B. C. it had removed so far west that a canal had to be cut to connect the city with the river, and in 550 B. C. this canal had to be still further prolonged to meet the still receding river. These facts afford evidence of the antiquity of the city.

Africa. The Caves of the Troglodytes. — The caves of the troglodytes, near Ain Tarsil, about three days' ride southwest of the city of Morocco, have been visited and partly explored by a correspondent of the London "Times." They had been previously visited by Balanza and Sir Joseph Hooker, who mention them but did not explore them. They are situated in a narrow gorge, or cañon, the cliffs of which rise almost perpendicularly from a deep valley, and are cut in the solid rock at a considerable height from the ground. In some places they are in single tiers, and in other places in two or three tiers, one above the other, and ordinarily inaccessible, except by ropes and ladders. The entrances to the caves vary from 3½ to 4½ feet in height, are about 8 feet broad, and give access to rooms of comfortable size, furnished with windows, which were in some cases connected with other smaller rooms, also furnished with windows. The appearance of the caves is hardly consistent with the conception of the troglodytes as savages, which has been drawn from Hanno's account of them. For these abodes show signs of great labor, and indicate that their builders, in making the floors and ceilings perfectly smooth, and putting more than one window in the same room if it was a large one, had ideas of care and comfort.

Russia. The Tomb of a Scythian King.—Interesting and important discoveries have been made in the exploration by the Russian Imperial Archæological Commission of the mounds of that district of the western Caucasus which is traversed by the river Kuban. One of the most important of them—the Great Kurgan near Krymskaia—consists of three chambers, extending through a length of 67 feet. The walls are of massive, well-hewed slabs of stone, stuccoed and frescoed, and the floor, of stone slabs, is laid in cement. The first of these chambers contained numerous archæological relics of earthenware, silver, engraved beads, remains of an iron wheel and of two horses, and the skeleton of a young woman of high rank, with a triangular golden plate bearing figures in relief, which formed part of her tiara, and other personal ornaments of gold. The second room contained a few relics. In the third, or principal room, was a skeleton, which is presumed to be of a Scythian king, having around its neck a thick golden unclosed hoop, bearing figures at the ends; near it a golden plate, which was probably part of head-dress, and around it silver drinking-horns and drinking-cups, a silver quiver overlaid with gold and adorned with figures, copper arrows, and iron spear-points. Remains of rotten boards and nails indicated that both bodies had been inclosed in coffins. The relics are assigned to a date not much later than the Christian era, and are believed to represent an age of Scythian arts and customs of which little has hitherto been known.

ARGENTINE REPUBLIC, an independent republic of South America. (For details of area, population, etc., see "Annual Cyclopædia" for 1883.)

Government.—The President is Dr. Juarez Celman, whose term of office will expire on Oct. 12, 1892; the Vice-President is Dr. Carlos Pellegrini. The Cabinet was composed of the following ministers: Interior, Dr. Eduardo Wilde; Foreign Affairs, N. Q. Costa; Finance, Dr. W. Pacheco; Justice, Dr. F. Posse; War and Navy, Gen. E. Racedo. The Argentine Minister at Washington is Don Vicente G. Quesada, and the Consul at New York, Señor Adolfo G. Calvo. The American Minister at Buenos Ayres is Bayless W. Hanna, and the Consul, Edward L. Baker.

Finances.—On March 31, 1888, the foreign indebtedness of the republic amounted to $92,-427,000; the domestic debt, at the same date, amounted to $47,000,000; total, $139,427,000. The provinces have besides a foreign debt of $88,219,611, and a domestic debt of $25,000,-000. The income in 1887 was $58,135,000, and the expenditure, $50,019,000.

The law making the authorized note-circulation of banks a legal tender will expire on Jan. 9, 1889, when it will forcibly have to be renewed. On June 15, 1888, the Government had in circulation $6,000,000 of fractional paper money. In 1887 the gold premium at Buenos Ayres averaged 35¼ per cent., as compared with 38¾ in 1886, and 37 in 1885. Early in May, 1888, the Government held $77,000,-000 gold coin, ready to moderate the premium. A bridle has been put on wild stock speculation by limiting the delivery of stocks on time sales to thirty days. Since 1880 the Argentine Government, provinces, railroads, etc., have contracted loans to the amount of $305,-810,000; out of this amount only $43,080,000 went toward canceling matured bonds. Several new loans were negotiated in Europe during 1888; one for £7,000,000 for the conversion of outstanding Government bonds from 6 per cent. interest to 4½ per cent.; £2,000,000 in behalf of the city of Buenos Ayres; £2,000,-000, city of Rosario; £2,000,000, province of Córdoba; £1,000,000, province of Santa Fé; £600,000, province of Tucuman; province of Mendoza, £1,000,000; province of San Juan, £1,000,000; province of Entre-Rios, £1,200,-000; and, province of Corrientes, £1,000,000; together, £21,200,000. The bank of the province of Buenos Ayres also floated a $20,000,000 loan in Germany. During 1887 the national bank increased its capital by $12,000,000, and the following banks were founded: The German and Rio de la Plata Bank, capital on shares, $2,000,000; the French Bank, $2,000,000; the new Italian Bank, $2,000,000; the Argentine People's Bank, $1,000,000; and the Buenos Ayres People's Bank, $3,000,000; the Banco de Córdoba increasing its capital $500,000.

On June 15, 1888, the total note circulation of banks was $87,925,000. On June 15, 1887, it was $79,000,000. The banking and currency of the Argentine Republic have been in an extremely unsettled condition for several years. A resolute attempt to put them upon a better basis was made in the law of Nov. 3, 1887, which made banking practically free, and provided a national currency guaranteed by national bonds bearing 4½ per cent. interest in gold. These bonds are delivered to any banking institution that submits to the required Government inspection, for 85 per cent. of their par value, and may be deposited as security for an issue of bills up to the face value of the bonds.

Army and Navy.—The army of the republic exclusive of the National Guard, according to official returns of June, 1887, was 6,256 strong, comprising 2,945 infantry, 2,571 cavalry, and 740 artillery. The National Guard was 400,-000 strong.

The navy consists of 38 vessels, mounting 73 guns, of a total tonnage of 16,612, with 13,055 indicated horse-power, and manned by 1,966 sailors. There are three iron-clads, four cruisers, four gun-boats, seven torpedo-boats, four steam transports, and sixteen smaller steam and sailing craft.

Railroads.—The lines in operation in the summer of 1887 were as follow:

	Length in kilometres.
Government lines	1,374
Lines belonging to the province of Buenos Ayres	989
Lines belonging to the province of Santa Fé	293
Lines belonging to the province of Entre-Rios	286
Private lines	3,701
Total	**6,648**

There were in course of construction 1,651 kilometres, to which will be added 7,925 kilometres of new lines, at a total cost of £58,500,000, on which the Government has undertaken to guarantee 5 per cent. interest, with the exception of the Formosa-Tarija line, on whose cost only 4½ per cent. is to be guaranteed. The Argentine railroad system forwarded in 1887 7,657,406 passengers, and 3,705,876 tons of merchandise. The gross earnings were $23,805,722, and the running expenses $13,177,772 leaving net earnings to the amount of $10,627,950. During 1886 and 1887, concessions were granted for the building of 17 lines of railway; in 1888 there were 84 applications for concessions to construct new lines.

In 1888, 200 kilometres of tramway, out of a total of 600 kilometres to be constructed in the immediate vicinity of Buenos Ayres, were in working order.

Telegraphs.—The lines in operation in 1887 were owned and operated as follows:

LINES.	LENGTH IN KILOMETRES.			Offices.	Employés.
	Miles.	Wire.	Cable.		
State lines	18,017	30,668	78	407	1,305
Private lines	5,164	12,135	63	261	352
Total	**23,181**	**42,803**	**141**	**668**	**1,657**

There were added to the Argentine telegraph system in 1887, 3,400 kilometres of line, and 4,000 kilometres were repaired. There were in course of construction 850 kilometres of state lines. The number of private telegrams sent was 651,280; Government messages 85,049. The receipts rose from $271,441 to $337,497; the expenses amounted to $515,425.

Postal Service.—The number of post-offices in 1887 was 672. The number of letters handled in 1886 was 24,362,842, of which 1,188,361 were Government dispatches, and 3,494,564 foreign letters; newspapers, 19,993,-472, of which 2,185,324 were foreign.

New Steamer Lines.—A contract was made in January, between the Government of the Argentine Republic and Robert P. Houston, of England, by which the latter agrees to construct ten steamers, of at least 4,000 tons burden and a speed of 16 knots an hour, to ply between the north of Europe and the ports of the Argentine Republic, and four steam-launches for emigrant service in Europe. Also four steamers to ply between the United States and the ports of the Argentine Republic. The principal conditions of the agreement are the following: The Government of the Argentine Republic guarantees a loan of 5 per cent. per annum on £1,250,000 for the European service, and 5 per cent. per annum on £360,000 for the United States line. The contractor for the European service agrees that these steamers shall always fly the flag of the Argentine Republic, and that, in case of war, the Government shall have the option to buy them at a sum not greater than their original cost. Exceptionally good accommodations are to be provided for emigrants.

In case the revenues of the contracting company exceed five per cent., it will refund to the Government from this excess the sums it has received as guarantees, and in case the revenues reach ten per cent., the excess is to be divided between the Government and the company. The guarantee terminates at the end of eighteen years. It is stipulated that in going from Europe the steamers must not call at any port except Montevideo and places where it is customary to take coal; but on the return trip they may call at any port. One of the steamers must arrive in the Argentine Republic at least once a week. Passenger and freight rates are to be fixed by agreement between the Government and the company. The company also agrees to furnish each steamer with a refrigerator capable of holding at least 3,000 dressed sheep or an equivalent amount of beef. The service is to begin in February, 1889, and by the following November all the steamers must be running.

The United States service will be performed under similar conditions, except that no refrigerators are to be placed on these vessels.

Commerce.—In 1886 there entered Argentine ports 4,727 sailing-vessels, with a joint tonnage of 764,238 tons, and 6,288 steamers registering 2,751,052 tons. In 1887 the increase in the arrivals was 4,000 vessels, with a total tonnage of 1,000,000.

The foreign trade of the Argentine Republic for six years has been:

YEARS.	Imports.	Exports.
1882	$61,246,000	$60,389,000
1883	80,435,000	60,207,000
1884	94,056,000	68,029,000
1885	92,221,000	83,879,000
1886	97,658,000	69,584,000
1887	116,292,000	83,827,000

The revenue collected from customs was $44,114,000 in 1887, an increase of thirty per cent. over 1886.

The Argentine foreign trade was distributed in 1886 as follows (in thousands of dollars):

COUNTRIES.	Import.	Export.
England	38,432	10,071
France	17,002	22,342
Belgium	7,821	10,924
Germany	8,044	6,951
Italy	4,647	2,476
Spain	3,717	1,166
Holland	780	...
United States	7,643	3,580
Brazil	28.9	1,943
Uruguay	6,417	2,767
Chili	68	2,819
Paraguay	1,413	419
West Indies	20	1,184
Other countries	4,845	3,742
Total	97,658	69,884

The Argentine Republic is rapidly advancing toward the position of an important grain-exporting country. Immense tracts of pasture are being converted into farmland. A few years ago not sufficient wheat was raised to supply the home market. The number of reapers imported into the country last year was 1,429. The chief exports of Argentine products in 1887 were: Indian corn, 361,000 tons; wheat, 233,000 tons; linseed, 81,000 tons; jerked beef, 19,800 tons; wool, 240,000,000 pounds (against 290,000,000 in 1886); sheepskins, 67,000,000 pounds; cattle, 110,000 head.

The American trade with the Argentine Republic is shown in the following table:

YEARS.	Import into the United States.	Domestic exports to the Argentine Republic.
1885	$4,775,616	$3,984,190
1886	4,854,890	5,020,885
1887	4,977,013	5,911,027

Beginning with the year 1888, the export duty on wool and all products emanating from stock-raising has been abolished. An octroi, or consumption-tax, is charged on all goods leaving the bonded warehouses for local consumption, but from this tax several articles are exempted, paying from 2 to 60 per cent. import duty. The free list remained the same as in 1887. A French syndicate has conceived the plan of organizing a service of tug-boats, vessels through the Straits of Magellan, between the Atlantic and the Pacific, the toll to be twenty cents a ton. Chili would have to give its consent, and has been applied to.

Education.—There are 3,000 schools and educational establishments in the republic, attended by 230,000 pupils.

Immigration. — The number of immigrants landed in 1887 was 120,842, in 574 steamers, as compared with 93,116 in 1886. During the first six months of 1888 there arrived 63,503 immigrants. During the six years, from 1882 to 1887, both inclusive, 515,220 immigrants landed.

During the summer of 1888 the Government sent to Europe the General Commissioner of Immigration, Don Samuel Navarro, to make arrangements for advancing passage-money to desirable individuals from the north of Europe wishing to emigrate to the republic, under provisions of the law of November, 1887, to be repaid in three equal yearly installments; the first, one year after arrival.

Colonization.—A colonization society has been formed in Brussels, Belgium, for the settlement and exploitation of 40,000 hectares of land granted by the Argentine Government for the purpose to Florimond van Varenbergh, the capital being fixed at 2,500,000 francs, and the charter of the company extending over twenty years. The site is on the Atlantic, on the peninsula of Valdez, and the colony is to be called " New Flanders." The *concessionnaire* has bound himself to introduce there 125 Belgian families of farmers Another colonization company was formed at Corrientes, " La Colonizadora de Corrientes," with a capital of $1,000,000.

The Government has made the following land grants during seven consecutive years: In 1881, 40,000 hectares; in 1882, 20,000; in 1883, 120,000; in 1884, 40,000; in 1885, 182,000; in 1886, 907,000; and in 1887, 4,369,000, together, 5,678,000 hectares. During the first four months of 1888 the total land sales amounted to 2,752,818 hectares, sold for $23,851,495.

Exploring Expeditions.—The Geographical Institute of Buenos Ayres, under Government aid, has undertaken to explore southern Patagonia. Don Augustin del Castillo, captain of a frigate, who explored that part of the country before, was to command the expedition, which sailed for the Gallegos islands, and was to penetrate, if possible, beyond Lago Argentino to Lagos Viedna and San Martin, returning by the Rio Negro; also to determine the precise boundaries between the republic and Chili.

Another expedition, having for its object the exploration of the eastern slopes of the Cordillera from Mendoza to the Rio Negro, left on Dec. 1, 1888, undertaken by Dr. Frederick Kurtz, Professor of Botany at the University of Córdoba, and Dr. William Bodenbender, of the Palæontological Museum of that city. The expense is defrayed by the Geographical Institute of Buenos Ayres, and by the National Academy of Sciences at Córdoba jointly.

Permanent Exhibition.—The President has issued a decree creating a permanent exhibition of Argentine products at Buenos Ayres.

Cattle.—The slaughterings at the *saladeros* for exportation of salted hides in the valley of the Rio de la Plata were as follows:

PLACES.	1887.	1886.	1885.
Buenos Ayres	61,000	152,000	246,500
Montevideo	180,000	314,000	256,500
On the rivers	581,000	744,000	755,000
Rio Grande	420,000	341,000	385,000
Total	1,242,000	1,581,000	1,643,000

The slaughtering operations for the season of 1888 were 763,900 head of cattle in the Argentine Republic, and on the banks of rivers, 452,-250 in Uruguay, and 396,000 in Rio Grande, constituting a total of 1,622,150 head.

Harbor Improvements.—The Argentine Congress approved Engineer Manero's plans, and voted $10,000,000 for the construction of a new port, the work on which is begun, and will consist first, of a canal 328 feet wide and 21 feet deep below low-water level, prolonging the Balisas river for the entrance of large ships; a basin of the same depth will be constructed for vessels remaining but a short time, and four other docks or basins also of the same depth, whose wharves will have a total length of 26½ feet; finally, a maritime basin of equal depth, and 4,692 feet long will be made. All the masonry will be of asphaltum blocks and brick. Separate storehouses will be built for imported goods and goods to be exported, which will o:cupy a total area of 3,280 feet by 164 feet, and have a capacity of 10,963.900 cubic feet. All the wharves will be provided with loading and unloading appliances.

Waterworks.—On June 23, 1888, the Government accepted the propositions of Messrs. Samuel B. Hale & Co., to complete the waterworks of the city, which will involve an outlay of $21,000,000. The toll per house per month is to be $6.

Viticulture.—The area under culture with vines in 1887, was about 2,700 hectares of 2½ acres; and the wine-production amounted to about 6,000,000 gallons, worth $1,500,000. The vine-growing is chiefly in the province of San Juan, which produces grapes enough to make 250,000 hectolitres of wine. One wine-making establishment—that of Marenco and Ceresoto—exports 25,000 hectolitres annually, its cellars, factories, etc., covering a space of 30,000 square yards, and occupying, during vintage-time, between 350 and 500 operatives. There are several similar concerns in the province, which exports 80,000 hectolitres per annum. The vines cultivated are Monas, Mollat, and Uva de Viña; Bordeaux vines have also been procured from Chili, the wine therefrom resembling Burgundy more than Bordeaux.

Quarantine.—In August, 1888, the governments of the Argentine Republic, Uruguay, and Brazil concluded a convention regulating uniformly among them the rules that henceforth are to be observed respecting quarantine as between them and as regards other nations, together with the sanitary inspection service.

The Falkland Islands.—The Argentine Republic has renewed its claim to the Falkland Islands, now held by Great Britain. These islands are in the South Atlantic Ocean, between 51° and 53° south latitude, and between 57° and 62° west longitude. They consist of the East Falkland, area 3,000 square miles; the West Falkland, 2,300 square miles; and about one hundred small islands with an area of nearly 1,200 square miles. Mount Adam, the highest ground in the colony, rises 2,315 feet above the sea. The Falkland Islands were discovered by Davis in 1592, and visited by Hawkins in 1594. In 1763 they were taken possession of by France; subsequently they were held by the Spaniards until 1771, when they were for a time abandoned, and the sovereignty of them was given up to Great Britain. In 1833 they were taken possession of by the British Government for the protection of the whale-fishery. In 1884 the population was 1,640. The revenue in 1885 was £10,438, and the expenditure £7,598; the imports in the same year amounted to £48,314, and the exports to £97,846.

ARIZONA. Territorial Government.—The following were the Territorial officers during the year: Governor, C. Meyer Zulick; Secretary, James A. Bayard; Treasurer, C. B. Foster; Auditor, John J. Hawkins; Attorney-General, Briggs Goodrich, who died in June, and was succeeded by John A. Rush, by appointment of the Governor; Superintendent of Public Instruction, Charles M. Strauss; Commissioner of Immigration, Cameron H. King, succeeded by Thomas E. Farrish; Chief-Justice of the Supreme Court, James H. Wright; Associate Justices, William W. Porter and William H. Barnes.

Finances.—The debt of the Territory is now somewhat over $600,000. Of this sum, $350,-000 had been funded into bonds by the Legislatures previous to 1887, and the Legislature of that year provided for the funding of $200,-000 additional by the issue of bonds to that amount. These bonds were sold at par in the following November to the Bank of Arizona. The same Legislature raised the interest on Territorial warrants from eight to ten per cent., and increased the poll-tax from $2.00 to $2.50. The assessed valuation of the Territory in 1887 was $26,313,500. For 1888 there has been a gain of $1,000,000 in Maricopa County, and $500,000 in Yavapai County alone.

Education.—The school system is not yet effective in drawing a proper proportion of the youth of the Territory into the public schools. The average daily attendance during the scholastic year ending in 1885 was but 3,226, although there were 10,219 children of school age in the Territory. That is, only 31 children out of every 100 attended school during that year, although the total expenditures for public schools amounted to $138,164.83. For the year ending in 1886 the showing is but little better, as the Territory disbursed $135,-030 with the result of securing an average attendance of 35 out of each 100 children. The reports for 1887–'88 indicate improvement, but there is still an evident need of a compulsory school law.

Land Claims.—On this subject, the Governor says, in his annual report: "Surveyor-General Hise, in his recent report to the Land Department, says there are Spanish and Mexican private land claims pending in his office covering 5,195,348 acres. The early settlement of these grants is in every way desirable, in order that such claims, if any there be, as are just may be confirmed, and such as are fraudulent may be rejected, and the honest settler who in good faith located upon and paid the Government for his land may peacefully enjoy the same. The proposition before Congress to transfer these claims to a special court created for this purpose, if passed, or any transfer of the settlement of these claims from the Interior Department and Congress to the judicial arm of the Government, can not fail to work incalculable hardship to our settlers, and consequent damage to the Territory."

Irrigation.—It is claimed that in the past few years over $2,500,000 have been expended in Arizona in the construction of irrigating-canals, and that in the next year at least $1,500,000 more will be expended. Great activity and enterprise is being shown throughout the entire southern portion of the Territory in locating water-rights, taking out canals, and reclaiming desert lands. The most extensive and successful irrigating canals are to be found in the Salt River valley, where canals over 200 miles in length and reclaiming about 225,000 acres are now in operation, and nearly 100 miles more are in process of construction. In Pinal County, along Gila river, canals designed to reclaim over 200,000 acres are being constructed. In the counties of Pima, Cochise, Graham, and Yuma, the reclamation of land is not so extensive, but beginnings have been made. On the Little Colorado and its tributaries, in the county of Apache, about 20,000 acres are under cultivation, while in the Verde valley, Yavapai County, about 2,500 acres have been restored.

Stock-Raising.—The following is the number of cattle and their assessed value for 1888, in the various counties, as returned to the Territorial auditor.

COUNTIES.	Number.	Value.
Apache	65,472	$666,551 87
Cochise	78,294	782,940 00
Gila	19,974	201,196 00
Graham	45,541	455,410 00
Mohave	20,752	254,212 00
Pinal	31,460	314,814 00
Yavapai	141,174	1,694,088 00
Yuma	8,340	85,411 00
Maricopa	12,698	168,898 00
Total	418,715	$5,582,515 87

To this total should be added Pima County, with 94,735 cattle, valued at $1,012,290.

Mining.—The product of gold and silver for Arizona in 1887 is reported by Wells, Fargo, & Co. at $5,771,555, a slight decrease from the previous year. In November, 1887, a vein of gold of exceptional richness was discovered by two miners in Yavapai County, on Hassayampa river, about twelve miles from Prescott. Over $10,000 were taken from this mine in a few weeks, and an organization of capitalists was soon made to develop the property, which is called the Howard mine.

Railroads.—For 1888 the total number of miles of railroad assessed in the Territory was 1,053·41, valued at $7,317,930.57, a slight increase in the total assessment over the preceding year. No new lines have been constructed during the year. The Territory needs a greater number of north-and-south lines meeting the two great trunk lines passing through the Territory east and west. The following shows the details of the assessment for the year: Atlantic and Pacific, 893·41 miles, assessed at $7,282.03 per mile; total valuation, $2,862,136. Arizona Mineral Belt, 30 miles, at $5,706.33 per mile; total, $171,-190. Arizona Narrow-Gauge, 10 miles, at $5,200 per mile; total, $52,000. Arizona and New Mexico, 41 miles, at $4,502.22 per mile; total, $184,591.13. Maricopa and Phœnix, 34·45 miles, at $7,000 per mile; total, $354,650. Prescott and Arizona Central, 73·8 miles, at $5,151.62 per mile; total, $377,613.75. Southern Pacific, 383 miles, at $7,500 per mile; total, $2,872,500.

Political.—The Democratic Territorial Convention met at Tucson on September 5, and renominated as delegate to Congress, Marcus A. Smith. Candidates for the Territorial Assembly were also nominated. The convention took an unusual position in refusing, by a vote of 30 to 34, to pass a resolution approving the national and the Territorial administration. Two weeks later the Republican Territorial Convention met at the same place, and nominated Thomas F. Wilson for Delegate, together with a ticket for the Legislature. Resolutions were adopted accepting the national platform, condemning the Democratic administration in the nation and Territory, and embracing also the following:

We condemn the pernicious practice of the present Administration in appointing men who are not only non-residents, but who are total strangers to the great natural, mineral, agricultural, and other resources of the Territories, as well as the important function and duties of the high offices whereof they are incumbent; and in this connection we respectfully invite attention to the custom at the present observed (we believe heretofore unheard of in America) of creating a horde of spies, ferrets, and blackmailing emissaries called "special agents," who, under cover of law and the pay and support of the Government, make it their business to obstruct and retard the honest settler and miner from developing our great resources and filling this Territory with thrifty and happy homes. This system now in vogue in Arizona is equalled in iniquity, if at all, only by the British plan of espionage in Ireland.

We demand the removal of the Apache Indians from the Territory.

It is the duty of Congress to appropriate sufficient money to construct reservoirs for water-storage in this Territory and for the development of artesian water, the benefits of which would enhance all values and bring to the treasury fourfold return.

At the November election the Democratic ticket was successful by about the usual majority, and a majority of the Democratic candidates for the Legislature were elected.

ARKANSAS. State Government.—The following were the State officers during the year: Governor, Simon P. Hughes, Democrat; Secretary of State, Elias B. Moore; Treasurer, William E. Woodruff; Auditor, William R. Miller; Attorney-General, Daniel W. Jones; State Land Commissioner, Paul M. Cobbs; Superintendent of Public instruction, Wood E. Thompson; Chief-Justice of the Supreme Court, Sterling R. Cockrill; Associate Justices, William W. Smith and Burrill B. Battle.

Mining Excitement.—The State Geologist, in a letter to the Governor, in August, says:

There has long been a popular belief that gold and silver existed in paying quantities in the State of Arkansas. During the last few years, notably since 1885, a great many people have become excited upon the subject of the occurrence of the precious metals about Hot Springs, and through the country west of there. This excitement culminated in 1887–'88. In some portions of the State it reached such a pitch that almost every man abandoned his usual occupation to stake off claims and turn miner. Every unfamiliar rock was regarded as a valuable ore or an "indication" of something, and these delusions have been kept alive by assayers, some of whom were, perhaps, sincere, but some of them certainly fraudulent. These same assayers and their dupes have been so successful that they induced capitalists and business men, both in and out of the State, and especially the visitors to the Hot Springs, to believe in the value of the region for mining purposes to such an extent that during the last two and a half years companies have been incorporated under the laws of Arkansas with a total capital stock of more than $111,000,000 for the purpose of working the supposed gold and silver mines and ores of the State.

After a careful assay of ores from all the so-called mines, the geologist fails to find more than two silver deposits that could by any possibility be successfully worked. Of the alleged gold-mines he says: "It is very doubtful whether a single one of them has ever legitimately returned a single ounce of gold. . . . The future of Arkansas, as a mining State, must depend upon her coal, iron, manganese, antimony, and possibly zinc, lead, and graphite. In these, and in oil-stone, marble, chalk, marl, and building-stone she is rich. The geology of the State is not favorable for the production or mining of the precious metals."

Immigration.—The natural resources of Arkansas have long failed of development, from lack of population, but the necessity of attracting immigrants to the State has not until recently been recognized. Early this year, a call was issued by the Governor for a State Convention to consider means of attracting settlers. This convention met at Little Rock, on January 31, and provided for a bureau of immigration, to be maintained by subscriptions secured by a canvass of each county. It also recommended to the next General Assembly the establishment of a State board of immigration. The necessity of such a board was afterward discussed and urged by the various political parties, in convention and during the political canvass.

Convicts.—The evils of the convict lease system received a fresh illustration during the year in the treatment of prisoners at Coal Hill Camp, in Johnson County, where a large number of convicts were employed in the coal-mines. An inspection made in March by the State Penitentiary Commissioners revealed the fact that the convicts had been worked beyond the prescribed number of hours, had not been sufficiently fed or clothed or lodged, had been worked when physically unable, and had been in charge of brutal keepers, whose punishments had caused death to some and severe torture to many others. The convicts at this camp were ordered back by the Governor to the State Penitentiary, the warden of which was summarily removed for negligence or criminal conduct in permitting such abuses. The immediate overseer of the camp escaped punishment by fleeing the State.

Political.—The first political convention of the year met at Little Rock on April 30, being held under the auspices of the Union Labor party. This convention nominated the following ticket: Governor, C. M. Norwood; Secretary of State, G. W. Terry; Auditor, A. W. Bird; Attorney-General, W. J. Duval; Chief-Justice of the Supreme Court, O. D. Scott; Superintendent of Public Instruction, B. P. Baker; State Land Commissioner, R. H. Morehead. No nomination was made for the office of State Treasurer. Resolutions were adopted as follow:

We favor such legislation as will secure the reforms demanded by the Agricultural Wheel, the National Farmers' Alliance, and the Knights of Labor.

We pledge ourselves to do our utmost to enforce:
1. Taxation of all lands held for speculative purposes at their full value.
2. A strict execution of the election laws and such legislation as will secure a free ballot and a fair count.
3. The consolidation of the elections, State and national.
4. A change in the convict system, the abolition of the contract system, and the working of the convicts within the walls of the Penitentiary at Little Rock.
5. A road-tax and a reduction of days for road-working.
6. A public-school system that will educate all the people, and we favor national aid to education.
7. A law regulating mining and proper ventilation for same.
8. Laws subjecting trusts, railroads, and other corporations to State control.
"We favor the establishment of a labor and agricultural bureau."

This ticket relied for its support primarily upon the labor organizations, especially those of the farmers, of which the Agricultural Wheel is the most considerable in the State. It was greatly strengthened, however, by the decision of the Republicans to support it. A convention of Republicans, held in May, elected delegates to the National Republican Convention, but intrusted the selection of a State ticket to the State Executive Committee, which announced the adoption of the Union Labor ticket early in July.

The Democratic State Convention met at Little Rock on May 31. For more than two months previous, aspirants for the gubernatorial nomination had been engaged in a thorough canvass of the State, two or more of them generally appearing upon the same platform in joint debate. The principal objection to Gov. Hughes, who was a candidate for renomination, rested upon the fact that a third term in that office would be contrary to precedent and would establish an undesirable practice. It was also claimed that the abuses existing in the penal institutions of the State were due in some measure to the Governor's neglect to examine their management properly. The other candidates before the people were John G. Fletcher, J. P. Eagle, W. M. Fishback, and E. W. Rector. The first ballot in the convention showed that no one had obtained a majority of the delegates, although the temper of the convention was evidently opposed to a third term. Gov. Hughes received 122 votes; Fletcher, 113; Eagle, 97; Fishback, 96; Rector, 25. A session of four days and 126 ballots were required before a choice was made. The nominee, J. P. Eagle, received on the final ballot 248 votes, against 201 votes for Gov. Hughes. Other nominees of the convention were as follow: Secretary of State, B. B. Chism; Auditor, W. S. Dunlop; Treasurer, William E. Woodruff; Chief-Justice of the Supreme Court, Sterling R. Cockrill; Attorney-General, William E. Atkinson; Superintendent of Public Instruction, Wood E. Thompson; State Land Commissioner, Paul M. Cobbs.

The platform approves the national Administration, the tariff message of the President, and the Mills Bill, reiterates the doctrine of State rights, and continues as follows:

We favor liberal appropriations by Congress for the improvement of our waterways, to the end that commerce may be facilitated and rates of transportation regulated and cheapened, by bringing them into competition with those artificial avenues of traffic whose natural tendency is toward monopoly and extortion.

We point with pride to the successful administration of State affairs by the Democratic party and the results that prove its wisdom and patriotism—to wit: The rate of taxation reduced from seven to five mills, the marvelous increase of material wealth of the State, which was greatly enhanced by the passage of laws which subjected the property of wealthy corporations to the payment of an equitable proportion of the cost of their own protection, on a basis of fairness to themselves and justice to the people; the liberal encouragement and fostering care extended to the cause of public education; the founding and sustaining on a basis of broad liberality the various charitable institutions of the State; and the payment of so much of the just debt of the State as has already been accomplished, with the promise of its entire satisfaction at no distant day.

We indorse the action of the Legislature of 1887 in providing for a geological survey of the State, and favor the establishment by the next Legislature of a bureau of agriculture, manufacture, mining, and immigration.

We favor a system of liberal enactment for the encouragement of railroads and manufacturing establishments, but are opposed to any exemption in their favor from the burdens of taxation, which can not be extended alike to all tax-payers and citizens.

We indorse the united efforts of liberal-minded citizens of the State, regardless of political affiliations, to organize and build up a State bureau of immigration, and hereby second their invitation, extended to all earnest, honest, and intelligent people everywhere, regardless of political opinion or religious belief, to make their homes in Arkansas, where a cordial welcome from the people will be extended to them, and a variety of undeveloped resources, unexcelled by any equal area on the globe, promises a generous reward for industrious labor.

The financial embarrassment of the State having been safely and certainly relieved, we favor such modifications of the convict system of the State as can be effected, to the end that the State shall assume the complete control and responsibility for their maintenance; that their labor may not be brought into open and direct competition with the honest and voluntary labor of the people, and on such a reformatory basis that novices in crime may not be subjected to the baneful influences of contact and association with hardened criminals.

We congratulate the people upon the growth of personal temperance throughout the State, and are in favor of the strict enforcement of the laws now in our statutes restricting the illicit sale of intoxicating liquors, believing that it affords a striking example of the beneficent effects of the principle of local self-government.

On July 4 the Prohibitionists of the State met and adopted the following resolutions:

We congratulate the friends of prohibition in Arkansas on the good they have accomplished in the contest with the liquor traffic, as is evidenced by the fact that at least one half of the State to-day stands redeemed from the presence of the saloon, and nearly one half of our voters have been educated up to the point where they will, under our local-option laws, vote against license.

That the friends of prohibition feel thankful to the past Legislatures for the passage of our local-option law, by and through which so much good has been done to our people and damage to the whisky traffic; and they would suggest that if said laws were amended in some particulars they would be more efficient, and we would request said amendments be made by the next Legislature.

That notwithstanding we are now in full accord with the national Prohibition party, and will put electors in the field, yet we will not nominate candidates for the various State offices, but will do all we can to advance the cause of temperance on the one hand and break down the liquor traffic on the other, by local option and such other means as we may be able in a lawful way to command.

At the election on September 3, owing in part to Democratic dissensions growing out of the heated contest for the nomination, the Democratic majority was more than 2,000 fewer than in 1886. Eagle received 99,214 votes, and Norwood 84,233; a Democratic majority of 14,981. These figures do not include the votes of nine townships of Pulaski County, the poll-books for which were stolen from the County Clerk's office after the election. The Legislature chosen was overwhelmingly Democratic, the minority consisting in part of Republicans and in part of Union Labor representatives. At the same election the question of calling a convention to frame a new Constitution was voted upon. Returns from all but three counties gave 41,818 votes in favor of the convention, and 90,780 against it. The November election resulted in favor of the Democratic national ticket.

ARNOLD, MATTHEW, English critic, born in Laleham, near Staines, England, Dec. 24, 1822; died in Liverpool, England, April 15, 1888. He was the eldest son of Dr. Thomas Arnold, author of a "A History of Rome," who became master of Rugby School in 1827, and there introduced new methods of discipline and instruction that created an epoch in the educational history of England. The son, after spending some years in a private school, was sent to Winchester College for a year in order to become familiar with the traditional system of English public schools. He then entered Rugby in 1837, and in 1841 came out near the head of the school, having in 1840 won a scholarship at Balliol College, Oxford. His audacious wit and brilliant conversation won the admiration of his fellow-students. Under the

MATTHEW ARNOLD.

despotic but practical mastership of Dr. Jenkins, Balliol had become the hardest working college at Oxford; but, says Andrew Lang, "the Oxford of Mr. Arnold's undergraduate years was very much what Oxford had always been, a place for boating, cricket, and lounging." In his poem entitled "The Gipsy Scholar," he has embalmed the memories of those pleasant days. While he was at Balliol, Oxford was stirred with theological discussion. John Henry Newman was in the fullness of his popularity, and Arnold's intimate friend, Arthur Hugh Clough "took these things too hardly for his happiness." Mr. Arnold won a scholarship for proficiency in Latin the first year, and gained the Newdigate prize with an essay on "Cromwell" in the second, but obtained only a second class at graduation. In 1845 he was elected a fellow of Oriel College. His friendship with Arthur Hugh Clough of the same college is embalmed in the elegiac poem of "Thyrsis." Not desiring to take holy orders or to follow the life of a college tutor, he became private secretary of Lord Lansdowne, a leader of the Whigs, in 1847. In 1848 he published under

his initial "A.," a volume called "The Strayed Reveler, and other Poems," which shows his inherited love of Greek sentiment and form, and his early devotion to Wordsworth. These poems include "The Forsaken Merman," the exquisite pagan poem "Resignation," and "The Sick King of Bokhara," an admirable picture of Eastern life in Central Asia. Three years later, in 1851, after teaching at Rugby as assistant master for a short time, he married a daughter of Justice Weightman, and was appointed to the office of lay inspector of schools, with supervision over the schools of the British and Foreign School Society, representing the Nonconformists. The laborious duties of a school inspector were the regular occupation of his life, and only ceased two or three years before he died. Many of his reports are preserved in the annual Blue Book issued by the Committee of the Council on Education. In these he urged, with the force of his epigrammatic and luminous style, the elevation of elementary education by such steps as existing conditions and the example of more progressive countries showed to be practicable. In 1859 he was sent to the Continent as foreign assistant commissioner to study the French, German, and Dutch systems of primary education. Eventually William E. Forster, who married Arnold's elder sister, framed a measure that established a much more rational, complete, and effective system of elementary instruction. In 1865 Mr. Arnold went on another official tour to examine into the state of secondary education abroad. His observations were embodied in "Schools and Universities on the Continent," which appeared in 1867. From that time he was possessed with the idea that the lack of organized middle-class education, such as exists in Germany and France, and the consequent ignorance of art, languages, and literature, and indifference to their refining influences, were the explanation of the dullness, vacuity, sordid instincts, blind prejudices, and moral obtuseness that characterize the middle classes of English society. He made it his task to hold up for reprobation the faults he grouped under the name of "Philistinism," and to prove that it can be remedied by wider and better education. Five years after the publication of his first volume of poems, which were remarkable for classic finish, and therefore unattractive to the general public, he issued a second under the title of "Empedocles on Etna, and other Poems," but, soon becoming dissatisfied with the leading poem, he suppressed almost the whole edition. In 1854 he published under his name a volume containing some poems that were new and some that had appeared in the former collections, and this was followed soon afterward by another volume. These established his reputation among scholars, and in 1857 he was called to the chair of Poetry at Oxford. In 1858 appeared a tragedy after Greek models, named "Merope," which of itself was not so well received as was the remarkable essay on the principles of criticism that formed the preface. His last appearance as a poet is in "New Poems" (1867); but this is a misnomer, for, like most of his volumes, it is full of reprinted pieces. "Empedocles" is restored in its entirety, but the most remarkable additions are "Thyrsis," "The Terrace at Berne," "Dover Beach," the stanzas on Obermann, and those from the "Grande Chartrense." In two small volumes entitled "Lectures on translating Homer" and "Last Words," he argued the adaptability of the hexameter to the English language. His "Essays in Criticism," which first appeared in 1865, have had a broadening and elevating effect on the writing of reviews and throughout the range of modern English literature. "Study of Celtic Literature" appeared in 1867. His lectures gave to the Oxford professorship of Poetry an importance that it never had attained before. He was re-elected at the end of five years, but was compelled by the statute to retire on the conclusion of his second term, and when subsequently solicited to become a candidate again, he invariably declined, recoiling from the contest that would arise from clerical opposition caused by his writings. Assuming that historical and philological criticism had unsettled much that formed the accepted body of Christian belief, and perceiving that Christianity was losing its hold on some classes of society, he gave his mind to the consideration of what is permanent, spiritual, and ennobling in religion, with the view of presenting a purified and rational form of faith that would command the acceptance of the callous and the skeptical. Ten or twelve years after he had broached the subject in a magazine, he published a volume containing his conclusions under the title of "Literature and Dogma." This was supplemented by a review of criticisms upon it, entitled "God and the Bible," and in 1877 by "Last Essays on Church and Religion." His "Complete Poems" were published in two volumes in 1876, and, with the addition of more recent verses, in three volumes in 1885. Among his books not already mentioned are "Culture and Anarchy" (1869); St. Paul and Protestautism," with an essay on "Puritanism and the Church of England" (1870); "Friendship's Garland," a witty and amusing satire (1871); "Higher Schools and Universities in Germany" (1875); "Isaiah, XL, L, XVI, with the Shorter Prophesies allied to it, edited with Notes" (1875); a selected edition of Johnson's "Lives of the Poets" with Macaulay's "Life of Samuel Johnson" (1878); and "Mixed Essays" (1879). He was an industrious writer for current literature, and few first-rate English magazines failed to number him among their contributors. His visits to the United States were made in 1883 and in 1886, during both of which tours he lectured in most of the larger cities. His last collected essays were "American Lectures" (1887); and his last paper was "Civilization in the United States," a widely read and much quoted article, in which he severely criticises

American habits, manners, literature, morals, and general want of interest to the traveler. "The man that introduced the useful adaptation 'Philistine,'" says Augustine Birrell, "could have little sympathy with Democracy."

ASSOCIATIONS FOR THE ADVANCEMENT OF SCIENCE. American.—The thirty-seventh annual meeting of the American Association for the Advancement of Science was held at Cleveland, Ohio. The Central High School building was devoted to the sessions. The meeting began on Aug. 15, and adjourned Aug. 22, 1888. The following were the officers of the meeting: President, John W. Powell, of Washington, D. C.; Vice-Presidents: Section A, Mathematics and Astronomy, Ormond Stone, of the University of Virginia, Va.; Section B, Physics, Albert A. Michelson, of Cleveland, Ohio; Section C, Chemistry, Charles E. Munroe, of Newport, R. I.; Section D, Mechanical Science and Engineering, Calvin M. Woodward, of St. Louis, Mo.; Section E, Geology and Geography, George H. Cook, of New Brunswick, N. J.; Section F, Biology, Charles V. Riley, of Washington, D. C.; Section H, Anthropology, Charles C. Abbott, of Trenton, N. J.; Section I, Economic Science and Statistics, Charles W. Smiley, of Washington, D. C. Secretaries: Section A, C. L. Doolittle, of Bethlehem, Pa.; Section B, Alex. Macfarlane, of Austin, Tex.; Section C, William L. Dudley, of Nashville, Tenn.; Section D, Arthur Beardsley, of Swarthmore, Pa.; Section E, John C. Branner, of Little Rock, Ark.; Section F, Bernhard E. Fernow, of Washington, D. C.; Section H, Frank Baker, of Washington, D. C.; Section I, Charles S. Hill, of Washington, D. C. Permanent Secretary, Frederick W. Putnam, of Cambridge, Mass.; General Secretary, Julius Pohlman, of Buffalo, N. Y.; Secretary of the Council, C. Leo Mees, of Columbus, Ohio; Treasurer, William Lilly, of Mauch Chunk, Pa.

Proceedings.—The meeting was called to order by the retiring president, Samuel P. Langley, who resigned the chair to John W. Powell, the president-elect. After the usual courtesies from the city and a brief address by the president, the meeting organized, and the sections took possession of the rooms assigned them. In the afternoon the several vice-presidents delivered their addresses before their respective sections, and in the evening the retiring president, Samuel P. Langley, gave his address.

Sections.—In the mathematical section about twenty-one papers were read touching on the problems of astronomy and theory of physical instruments as well as pure mathematics. Ormond Stone's address was "On the Motions of the Solar System." William Harkness gave an account of the instruments and processes employed by the United States Transit of Venus Commission to determine the solar parallax from photographs of the transit of Venus in Dec., 1882. Asaph Hall's paper "On the Supposed Canals on the Surface of the Planet Mars" was devoted to the so-called "Canals of Mars," whose existence the paper tended to throw into discredit.

The physical section was well represented. The address by Albert A. Michelson was devoted to a consideration of the problems in relation to light-waves. A report on the teaching of physics was presented on behalf of a committee by Thomas C. Mendenhall. It took full cognizance of the increased knowledge of teachers and their consequent adaptability for more advanced work in the elementary schools. For the latter experimental work was recommended. For college courses three hours a week during the junior year was suggested as a minimum. The report elicited considerable discussion. W. Le Conte Stevens's paper on "The Qualities of Musical Sounds" was of much interest as asserting that difference of phase among the components of a sound affected its quality. Edward L. Nichols and W. S. Franklin described some experiments they had made to determine the velocity of the electric current. Although their method would have detected a current of one thousand million metres a second, it gave only negative results, tending to prove that the velocity sought was in excess of this amount. Edward P. Howland read a practical paper on instantaneous photography, treating of the necessary conditions for its success. He recommended as an illuminant a mixture of sulphur and magnesium. He gave an interesting lecture, with experiments, on the same subject.

The chemical section was largely occupied with a discussion of methods of water analysis. A committee handed in its report, stating the progress made, and was continued. "The Presence and Significance of Ammonia in Potable Waters" was admirably treated by E. S. H. Bailey. Albert W. Smith spoke on the subject of water and water-supply, with special reference to Cleveland; while the brines from the gas-wells near the same city were discussed by Charles F. Mabery and Herbert H. Dow. A paper of great interest was presented by William P. Mason, of the Rensselaer Polytechnic Institute, on "Fatal Poisoning by Carbon Monoxide." It described the fatal accidents due to an escape of fuel-gas at Troy, N. Y., on Jan. 6, 1887. Three deaths and a number of cases of serious illness resulted. The autopsies disclosed nothing abnormal except the vivid redness of the tissues and blood. The latter showed absorption bands due to the carbon monoxide, and a specimen was exhibited that still showed the characteristic color and absorption spectrum. In the discussion that this paper elicited, William S. Dudley spoke of cigarette-smoking, and traced its evil effects to the inhalation of the products of combustion containing carbon monoxide. The products from one and one fourth cigarette killed a mouse, and its death was found to be due to this gas and not to nicotine or any other alkaloid. The vice-president's address in this section, by Charles E. Munroe, presented the advanced views of chemistry, as developed by the labors of Mendelejeff and those who have followed in his steps in their endeavors to systematize chemistry. The title of the address was "Some Phases in the Progress of Chemistry." The committee on indexing chemical literature presented its sixth report.

The section of mechanical science and engineering was somewhat delayed in its work by the absence of its vice-president, Calvin M. Woodward, but Charles H. J. Woodbury, of Boston, Mass., was elected to fill his place. The Nicaragua and the Panama canals both were subjects of papers, the former being treated of by Robert E. Peary, the latter by Wolfred Nelson. "The Influence of Aluminium upon Cast-iron," as in the well-known "mitis castings," was the subject of a paper by William J. Keep, and a discussion by William J. Keep, Charles F. Mabery, and L. D. Vorce. The first-named read a paper detailing its beneficial effects upon stove-castings, and gave the foundation for the debate alluded to. The quality of the castings, it was shown, was in every way improved by the addition of small amounts of the metal in question. By repeated remeltings of a given sample, followed by a coresponding series of analyses, it was shown that the aluminium remained in the metal, and did not, practically speaking, disappear to any extent. Much of its influence on the final castings was due to the fact that it kept the carbon in the graphitic form, precluding the possibility of white iron.

In the geological and geographical section a number of interesting papers on geological subjects were read, but geography was omitted from the programme. A large number of speakers gave the results of their observations and studies. George H. Cook, the vice-president, in his address, spoke on the "International geological congress, and our part in it as American geologists." He gave briefly the history of the congress and its efforts to settle upon fixed systems of nomenclature, and colors for indicating different formations on geological maps. He made the plea that the American workers should be more actively represented, and that names less local, geographical, and strange, should be adopted for different formations. The labors of John S. Newberry, as usual, were represented by several papers, one on the oil-fields of Colorado, and others on palæontological subjects. Sources of oil and gas recently discovered in Ohio, Kentucky, and Indiana, were described by Edward Orton. A new form of geological map was exhibited by J. T. B. Ives. It consists of a series of colored pasteboards, each of which represents a geological system, the most recent rocks forming the highest layer. Where rocks of a given system do not exist they are cut out of the pasteboard representing them. Then by placing these different layers one upon the other a geological map is produced, valuable for purposes of instruction.

The proceedings of the biological section were, perhaps, as a whole, of less interest than usual. Charles V. Riley, the vice-president of the section, in his address, spoke on the causes of variation in organic forms, giving some of the most advanced points yet touched on by the evolutionary philosophy. A number of papers were strictly monographs of primarily technical interest. Edward P. Howland touched the more practical aspect of the subject in his paper on anæsthesia. He described remarkable results in prolonged insensibility produced by a mixture of nitrous oxide and oxygen administered in compression chambers. There seemed to be hardly any limit, comparatively, to the time a patient could be kept safely in the anæsthetic condition by the system he described.

The section of anthropology was crowded with interesting matter. This section is a strong feature of the meetings, and is said to have shown a distinct advance this year. Daniel G. Brinton, in his paper entitled "On the Alleged Mongolian Affinities of the American Race," strongly argued against the tenet held by so many that the Chinese and the American aborigines are of common stock. He stated that in true racial characteristics they widely differ, and that the obliquity of the eyes is rather an accidental than a family feature. Horatio Hale read two papers—one upon "The Aryan Race, its Origin and Character," devoted to proving the Asiatic origin of the Aryan family; the other, "An International Language." The second attracted much attention. He strongly upheld the importance of discussing the requisites of such a language, and devoted much time to showing the insufficiency of Volapük. As a sequence to this paper, a resolution was passed by the council, authorizing the appointment of a committee to attend any congress meeting for the consideration of an international language. The committee consisted of Messrs. Hale, Henshaw, and McFarland. Other features of this section's work were Frederick W. Putnam's illustrated paper on the "Serpent Mound," and the work done there during the last year in connection with its preservation and the explorations about it; Otis T. Mason's lecture on "Woman's Share in Primitive Industry," which was also illustrated by lantern projections; and Garrick Mallery's report on "Algonkin Pictographs." Charles C. Abbott's address was a summary of the evidence of the antiquity of man in eastern North America, showing that pre-glacial man is no longer a question but an established fact.

The committee appointed to memorialize the United States Congress on the subject of the preservation of archæologic remains upon public domain handed in its report, naming numerous remains of the early inhabitants of the continent which should be kept from destruction.

The section of economic science and statistics was favored with unusually interesting papers. Charles W. Smiley's address was of re-markable interest. It was entitled "Altruism considered Economically." The necessity for governmental supervision over the forests of this country was the subject of a paper by Bernhard E. Fernow. He placed the value of the forests annually destroyed at from ten to twenty million dollars. Industrial training was brought before the section by Mrs. Laura O. Talbot, and her paper elicited a good discussion on the subject. Edward Atkinson's paper on "The Uses and Abuses of Statistics," showed how inexperienced persons may be misled in attempting to draw conclusions from statistics. He maintained that a strictly metallic currency was needed for the world, eliciting a strong remonstrance from Edward Daniels. The latter subsequently read a paper on "Our Monetary System," presenting views in favor of a paper currency. A carefully prepared and elaborate paper on this subject was by Edward H. Ammidown, upon "Suggestions for Legislation on the Currency." Wilbur O. Atwater, treating of the "Food-supply of the Future," predicted an increased production based on the discoveries of science. The decay of American ship-building was considered by Charles S. Hill. He demanded governmental fostering of shipping and ship-building. The Nicaragua Canal was also the subject of a report by Henry C. Taylor and of a paper by Lieut. Robert E. Peary.

Address of Retiring President.—The retiring president, Prof. Samuel P. Langley, devoted his address to "The History of a Scientific Doctrine." It treated of the subject of radiant energy, and eloquently depicted the struggles of past generations of scientific workers performed in quest of the laws and causes of light and heat. He showed how persistently the old caloric or substantial theory of light had overshadowed physical science, and how recently it had been disposed of. He stated that Science was not infallible, "that her truths are put forward by her as provisional only, and that her most faithful children are welcome to disprove them." He indicated one great problem waiting solution—the relation between temperature and radiation.

Several public lectures were given, among which was one by the president, John W. Powell, on "Competition as a Factor in Human Progress." He drew an important distinction between the actual laws of human progress and the doctrine of the survival of the fittest. Evolution, he declared, was barred from human progress—in its march the fittest did not always survive—the mind was advancing in some senses at the expense of the body. The struggle for existence is transferred from man to the works of his own hand. The beneficence of the process together with the speaker's own confidence in the love and charity of his fellow-men were well depicted. Thomas C. Mendenhall lectured on "Japanese Magic Mirrors." These lectures were complimentary to the citizens of Cincinnati.

Attendance.—The attendance of members at the meeting as registered was 342. One hundred and ninety-four papers were read in the several sections. The usual receptions were tendered by citizens. The members visited various localities of interest, and had an enjoyable excursion on the lake.

Appropriations.—The income of the research fund for the past year was granted to Frederick W. Putnam for the furtherance of his archæological explorations in relation to the Serpent Mound in Ohio.

Meeting of 1889.—The next meeting is to be held at Toronto, Can., under the following officers: President, Thomas C. Mendenhall, of Terre Haute, Ind.; Vice-Presidents: Mathematics and Astronomy, Robert S. Woodward, of Washington, D. C.; Physics, Henry S. Carhart, of Ann Arbor, Mich.; Chemistry, William L. Dudley, of Nashville, Tenn.; Mechanical Science and Engineering, Arthur Beardsley, of Swarthmore, Pa.; Geology and Geography, Charles A. White, of Washington, D. C.; Biology, George L. Goodale, of Cambridge, Mass.; Anthropology, Garrick Mallery, of Washington, D. C.; Economic Science and Statistics, Charles S. Hill, of Washington, D. C. Permanent Secretary, Frederick W. Putnam, of Cambridge, Mass.; General Secretary, C. Leo Mees, of Terre Haute, Ind.; Secretary of Council, Frank Baker, of Washington, D. C. Secretaries of sections: Mathematics and Astronomy, George C. Comstock, of Madison, Wis.; Physics, Edward L. Nichols, of Ithaca, N. Y.; Chemistry, Edward Hart, of Easton, Pa.; Mechanical Science and Engineering, James E. Denton, of Hoboken, N. J.; Geology and Geography, John C. Branner, of Little Rock, Ark.; Biology, Amos W. Butler, of Brookville, Ind.; Anthropology, William M. Beauchamp, of Baldwinsville. N. Y.; Economic Science and Statistics, John R. Dodge, of Washington, D. C.; Treasurer, William Lilly, of Mauch Chunk, Pa.

British.—The British Association for the Advancement of Science held its fifty-eighth annual meeting at Bath, beginning, Sept. 3, 1888. Twenty-four years have elapsed since this city was the scene of its labors. The list of presidents is as follows: President of the Association, Sir Frederick J. Bramwell; Section Presidents: Mathematics and Physics, Prof. George F. Fitzgerald; Chemistry, Prof. William A. Tilden; Geology, Prof. William Boyd Dawkins; Biology, Prof. William T. Thistleton Dyer; Geography, Sir Charles Wilson; Statistics, Lord Brannwell; Mechanics, William H. Preece; Anthropology, Gen. Pitt-Rivers. The city of Bath possessing no public hall. a temporary building was erected at a cost of £700 to provide a reception-room and offices.

General Meeting.—The first general meeting was held on Wednesday, September 6, at 8 P. M. Sir Henry E. Roscoe, the retiring president, resigned his chair to the president-elect, Sir Frederick J. Bramwell. Prof. Roscoe intro-

duced his successor by a few happily chosen words, alluding to Sir Charles Lyell, president at the former Bath meeting of 1864, stating that pure science was honored in Prof. Lyell, while in the election of Sir Frederick J. Bramwell a tribute is paid to applied science.

President's Address.—The president's address began with a review of the work of old time engineers, who developed prime movers, and brought the story down to the present day. He spoke of the increased perfection of the modern steam-engine, but reminded his hearers of his own prophecy made at the York meeting, that the steam-engine would in the next century be a thing of the past. He then cited gas, naphtha, and caloric engines to prove that the direction of engineering progress had been correctly indicated by him. The effect of the "next to nothing" in engineering practice was then developed. He cited the effect of minute impurities upon metals, of the importance of the introduction of precisely the right amount of air into steam-boiler and other furnaces to secure economy of fuel, and of the effect of alloys upon metals even when in minute proportions. The influence of the "little" was well illustrated in gun-practice where the difference of density of the air above and below a projectile is supposed to cause its lateral deviation. He also cited the fact that a projectile fired due north, a distance of twelve miles in one minute, would deviate from the meridian 200 feet. The tenor of the latter portion of the address was the importance of minute accuracy in engineering practice.

Sections.—*Mathematical and Physical Science.*—Prof. Fitzgerald, elected as substitute for Prof. Schuster, began his address by a tribute of regret for the loss of Prof. Schuster as president, who was too ill to attend the meeting. His address was devoted to the exposition of J. Clerk Maxwell's theory that electro-magnetic phenomena are due to an intervening medium. "The year 1888," he affirms, "will ever be memorable as the year in which this great question has been experimentally decided by Hertz, in Germany, and I hope, by others in England." The intervening medium, he stated, has been decided to exist. Prof. Hertz produced rapidly alternating currents of such frequency that their wave-length was about two metres, giving 100,000,000 vibrations per second. With these he detected phases of interference corresponding with those of light-waves. Thus we seemed to be approaching a theory of the structure of the ether.

Chemical Science.—Prof. Tilden devoted himself to the subject of the teaching of chemistry. He advocated a better system, a higher grade of teachers, and less hours of labor for them, in order that they might have time to keep abreast of the age by reading. He said that it took longer than it did formerly to make a chemist. as more was expected of him; he had to be almost polytechnical in his education.

Geology.—Prof. Dawkins spoke of the advances in this science, more especially as regarding the filling up of former gaps in the sequence of animal and plant forms and types. He insisted that the Darwinian theory was receiving additional confirmation. Treating of the question of time in geology, he stated his belief that all attempts to express geologic time in terms of years were failures.

Biology.—Prof. Thistleton Dyer began by alluding to the loss biological science had sustained in the deaths of the great botanists Asa Gray and Anton De Bary. He then spoke of the outlook presented by the world for the development of systematic botany. London, he said, possessed the best facilities for the work. England, the United States, and Russia were the most active in the prosecution of the laborious task. He pleaded for more workers and for increased accuracy in nomenclature. After reviewing the work done in different portions of the globe, and describing the areas covered by different investigators, he spoke of the Darwinian theory. Prof. Weisman's theory of the continuity of the germ-plasm and the increased difficulty it might throw on the acceptance of the Darwinian hypothesis were spoken of, and the recent school of the new Lamarckism was described. The speaker's tendency was to adhere to Darwin, yet it is interesting to note how in the present day of discussions Darwin's own doubts are so clearly brought forward. This is very noticeable in Prof. Thistleton Dyer's address. Physiological botany, putrefaction, and bacterial inoculation for disease were finally treated in some detail. The address was long and very able.

Geography.—Col. Wilson reviewed the history of commerce and the various centers and paths which it had chosen in the past. The influence of the Suez Canal was considered, and the immense importance it had given to England in the world of commerce was explained. For the Panama Canal the speaker predicted far less important changes and results. African geography and the retardation of the development of the continent by its deadly climates were, in conclusion, touched upon.

Mechanical Science.—Mr. Preece, in his address, described the development of practical electricity. He spoke of Prof. Oliver Lodge's brilliant experiments in electrostatic discharge, and noted the discussion which was to take place upon the subject of lightning-conductors. The history of the telegraph and its most recent improvements and achievements were next in order. One hundred and ten thousand miles of cable have been laid by English ships, and £40,000,000 have been invested in the same by English capitalists. Thirty-seven ships are maintained to carry on repairs and lay new cables. In 1875 it was thought wonderful to transmit 80 words a minute to Ireland, while now 461 words a minute can be sent. The economic features of electric lighting and the history of its development, the

transmission of energy by electricity, and other practical applications were described. Finally, the distinction was drawn between the physicist's and engineer's conceptions of electricity, the first treating it as a form of matter, the latter as a form of energy.

Attendance, etc.—The attendance at the meeting was nearly 2,000. Public lectures, excursions to points of interest, and exhibitions by Col. Gouraud and Mr. Henry Edmunds, of the phonograph and graphophone, were features of the occasion. The president for 1889 was announced as Prof. William Henry Flower.

Appropriations.—The grants for scientific research, divided among all the sections, aggregate £1,645.

ASTRONOMICAL PROGRESS AND DISCOVERY.

Instruments.—The Royal Observatory of Greenwich, England, has had constructed a new personal-equation machine, to be used with the transit-circle. An object-glass 7¼ inches in aperture, is fastened in front of the object-glass of the transit-circle telescope, when this telescope is made horizontal and pointed north. In the focus of the outer lens (51 feet away) is placed the vertical plate of the personal-equation machine. This plate can be made to show an artificial star or sun. The plate is moved by suitable apparatus at any desired speed, and the star's transit is observed over the wires in the transit circle. The true times of transit over the wires are registered automatically by means of contacts between two sets of platinum studs, properly constructed and adjusted. The special point aimed at in this instrument was to reproduce the same conditions as when the heavenly bodies were observed with the transit circle. The results obtained are said to be very satisfactory.

In the June, 1888, number of the "Monthly Notices of the Royal Astronomical Society," Sir Howard Grubb describes a new arrangement of electrical control for driving-clocks of equatorials. The apparatus was devised for the stellar photographic instrument of the Mexican (Chapultepec) Observatory. The novel part of the apparatus is the governor. In this particular governor he uses, instead of the ordinary balls, a brass ring loaded with lead and cut into eight segments : and in addition to gravity, springs are applied, one to each segment, tending to supplement the force of gravity. By this arrangement the speed of the governor may be increased from 90 to 135 revolutions. A number of ingenious devices are employed for controlling the motion, deteeting the errors, and correcting them.

The new heliometer mounted at the Cape Observatory by Dr. Gill, employs electric illumination only for all the scales, circles, etc. Accumulators were first used, the charging being done by Grove batteries; but this was found to be so troublesome, dirty, and expensive, that they now employ a dynamo run by a steam-engine.

Herr E. V. Gothard, in the "Zeitschrift für

Instrumentenkunde," describes a simple apparatus, which he has devised for the purpose of registering the readings of the wedge photometer without disturbing the condition of the eye by bringing up a light to read the micrometer-head.

Herr Repsold has recently proposed a partially automatic method of recording transits. The transit is mounted so as to be virtually an equatorial, with a small motion only in hour-angle near the meridian. A star just before transit is brought into the center of the field of view, and the driving-clock started, so that the star remains steadily in the same part of the field, and its position in the field may be observed with the right-ascension micrometer. Meanwhile the telescope is following the star up to the meridian, and on reaching the meridian the clock-work is automatically disconnected and a record made on the chronograph sheet.

United States Naval Observatory.—Prof. William Harkness, of the executive committee of the Transit-of-Venus Commission, has given the preliminary results of the work of that commission, which are detailed elsewhere. The great equatorial has been used in observations on the fainter satellites and double stars. The transit-circle work has been continued, as in previous years, and comets and asteroids

known as the Henry Draper Memorial has been much extended. The second annual report of the director on this work, shows that two telescopes are kept at work at the observatory, photographing stellar spectra every clear night. Four assistants are required in making the pictures, and five are employed for measurements and reductions. The report gives the mode of testing the sensitive plates. Mrs. Draper has sent to the observatory the 15- and 28-inch reflectors constructed by Dr. Draper, which are used in the above-mentioned work. In continuation of the work of examining high altitudes for the purpose of testing their suitability for astronomical purposes, Prof. Todd, of Amherst, tested some high points in Japan, whither he had gone to observe the eclipse of August, 1887. His report is favorable.

In Parts 3, 4, and 5 of vol. xviii of the "Annals" are described Mr. Parkhurst's photometric measures of the asteroids, observations made during the total lunar eclipse of Jan. 28, 1888, the photographic search for a lunar satellite, and Mr. W. H. Pickering's observations of the total solar eclipse of Aug. 29, 1886.

Yale College Observatory.—Dr. Elkin's report for 1887–'88 has been published. Heliometer observations on the parallaxes of the ten first-magnitude stars are completed. His results are as follow:

STAR.	Parallax.	Probable error.	No. of comparison-stars.	No. of observations.	Proper motion.
α Tauri (Aldebaran)............................	+ 0·116″	± 0·029″	6	64	0·202″
α Aurigæ (Capella)............................	+ 0·107	047	2	16	0·442
α Orionis (Rigel).............................	− 0·009	049	2	16	0·022
α Canis Minoris (Procyon)....................	+ 0·266	047	2	16	1·257
β Geminorum (Pollux)...................	+ 0·063	047	2	16	0·628
α Leonis (Regulus)	+ 0·093	018	4	15	0·255
α Boötis (Arcturus)...........................	+ 0·018	022	10	89	2·287
α Lyræ (Vega)....................	+ 0·064	045	2	80	0·844
α Aquilæ (Altair).............................	+ 0·199	047	4	16	0·647
α Cygni (Arided).....	− 0·042	047	4	16	0·010

and star occultations by the moon, and observations of stars for the Yarnall Catalogue have been kept up. Prof. Eastman began his zone work with the transit circle about October 1st.

Capt. R. L. Phythian has replaced Commander Brown as Superintendent of this observatory.

A circular "Relating to the Construction of a New Naval Observatory" has been issued by the Navy Department. The plans of the proposed observatory have been completed. It will be on Government property, at Georgetown Heights, Washington, D. C., and will comprise nine buildings. 1, the main building, 69×307 feet, which will contain the transit-room, library, etc.; 2, the great equatorial building, 46×72 feet; 3, the clock-room, 18×20 feet; 4 and 5, observers' rooms, each 18×20 feet; 6 and 7, east transit-circle building and west transit-circle building, each 30×40 feet; 8, prime vertical building, 18 × 20; 9, boiler-house, 45×54.

Harvard College Observatory.—Through the continued liberality of Mrs. Draper, the work

The value for α Canis Minoris (Procyon) above given agrees well with the mean of the values found by Auwers and Wagner. Struve found for α Aquilæ (Altair) a value of +0·181″, and Hall's value for α Tauri (Aldebaran) was +0·102″. O. Struve obtained very different parallaxes for Aldebaran and Capella, and the seven independent determinations of parallax of α Lyræ which have previously been made, agree fairly well in assigning to it a parallax of about +0·17″. Dr. Elkin is now engaged on a triangulation of the regions near the pole, to get fundamental places of twenty-four stars; and in connection with Dr. Gill (at the Cape of Good Hope) he will this winter observe the opposition of Iris for the determination of solar parallax.

Lick Observatory.—The Lick Observatory was formally transferred by the trustees to the regents of the University of California on June 1, 1888. Of the $750,000 left by Mr. Lick for the purpose of building the observatory and purchasing instruments, all has been expended except, it is said, about $90,000. This is the nucleus of a fund the interest of which is to pay for the care and use of the observatory and instruments. The University of California is making efforts to increase this maintenance fund to $1,000,000. The observatory has recently issued the first volume of its publications. The contents of the volume are Mr. Lick's deeds of trust; Prof. Newcomb's report on glass for objectives; report of Mr. Burnham's work at Mount Hamilton in testing the climate for double-star work in 1879 and again in 1881; descriptions of the buildings and instruments; an account of the engineering and building at Mount Hamilton in 1880–'85; observations of the transits of Mercury in 1881, and of Venus in 1882; geological reports; meteorological observations, 1880–'85; reduction-tables for Lick Observatory.

instruments. (See "Annual Cyclopædia" for 1885, page 54.)

New American Observatories.—The Denver University Observatory, of Colorado, is to be provided with new observatory buildings and a new refracting telescope with 20-inch object-glass. The telescope is to be mounted 5,000 feet above sea-level, or 800 feet higher than the great Lick telescope. Mr. H. B. Chamberlain, of Denver, is the donor.

The Dearborn Observatory, of Chicago, is being removed to Evanston (within a few miles of Chicago). It will be placed on a site 250 feet from Lake Michigan. It is expected that the 18½-inch equatorial will be remounted in its new home in January, 1889.

Foreign Observatories.—The report of the Pulkowa Observatory for 1887 says that the 30-

LICK OBSERVATORY.

Mr. Keeler has recently shown that the seeing in winter is not especially better at the observatory than at lower elevations. At other times "the secret of the steady seeing at Mount Hamilton lies in the coast fogs. These roll in from the sea every afternoon in the summer, rising from 1,500 to 2,000 feet. They cover the hot valley, and keep the radiation from it shut in. There are no fogs in day-time, and few in winter."

The complete instrumental equipment of the observatory is as follows: equatorials of 36, 12, and 6½ inches aperture. a 4-inch comet-seeker, photoheliograph, 6-inch meridian circle, declinograph, 4-inch transit and zenith telescope combined, 2-inch universal instrument, three chronographs, five independent clocks, besides controlled clocks and chronometers, minor astronomical and a good set of meteorological

inch refractor was employed by Dr. Hermann Struve in measuring those of Burnham's double stars which are only seldom measurable with the old 15-inch, together with other stars of which measures are scarce, making a working catalogue of 750 stars. Observations were also made of the fainter satellites of Saturn, and of that of Neptune. Ludwig Struve has calculated the constant of precession and the motion of the solar system in space. He obtained values not greatly different from those previously calculated.

The Royal Observatory, Greenwich, is to have a new 28-inch refractor. The glass disks have been cast by Messrs. Chance, and the lenses will be made by Sir Howard Grubb.

At the Oxford Observatory Prof. Pritchard examined for the Photographic Committee of the Royal Society two silver-on-glass mirrors of the same aperture, but of different focal lengths. He found that mirrors, particularly those of short focal length, are comparatively unsuitable for the photographic work of charting the heavens.

At the Paris Observatory M. Loewy's new method for determining aberration and refraction is being used. The brothers Henry have continued their magnificent work in celestial photography, having taken seventy-four plates of different parts of the sky in 1887. The report of the director, Admiral Mouchez, contains an engraving of the Pleiades made up from three of the Henry protographs.

Astronomical Photography.—Prof. Pritchard, of Oxford Observatory, was encouraged by his success in determining from photographic plates the parallaxes of the components of 61 Cygni, to discuss the parallaxes of μ Cassiopeiæ and the pole-star. His equatorial he improved, and on each of fifty-three nights four plates were taken of μ Cassiopeiæ. The exposures varied from five to ten minutes. About three per cent. of the plates were injured or unsuitable for measurement. He took two impressions on the same plate, slightly moved in position. Two comparison-stars were used. The resulting parallaxes were:

From star (A) $\pi = 0.0501'' \pm 0.027''$.
"   "   (B) $\pi = 0.0211 \pm 0.0235$.

An investigation of the results obtained by using only a few selected plates of 61 Cygni and μ Cassiopeiæ has led Prof. Pritchard to give up the laborious method used in the case of 61 Cygni, and hereafter to limit the observations to five nights in each of the four periods of the year indicated by the position of the parallactic ellipse. He hopes in this way to determine in one year the parallaxes of fifteen stars. He plans to apply this method systematically to all stars between the magnitudes 1·5 to 2·5 which are well visible at Oxford. From a discussion of the approximate parallaxes that he expects to obtain, Prof. Pritchard hopes to infer some important cosmical relations. The result of his approximate determination of the parallax of Polaris is $\pi = 0.052'$. A mean of all the determinations of preceding observers is, according to Maxwell Hall, $\pi = 0.043'$. From six months' observations, Prof. Pritchard has obtained the following provisional parallaxes:

α Cassiopeiæ, 0·072″ ± 0·042″.
β Cassiopeiæ, 0·157 ± 0·039.
γ Cassiopeiæ, 0·050 ± 0·047.

Isaac Roberts has taken photographs of the ring nebulæ in the Lyre (57 M. Lyræ), the dumb-bell nebulæ (27 M. Vulpeculæ), and the fine, globular star-cluster (13 M. Herculis). In the first the ring was well shown, also the central star and nebulous matter in the interior, but there was no evidence of resolvability. The photographs seem to confirm the suspicion that the central star is variable. Photographs of the star-cluster showed prominent features not noticed by Sir J. Herschel and

the Earl of Ross. All these photographs were enlarged from three to twenty-five times. Mr. Roberts calls attention to the important fact that, owing to different causes, which are not easily discernible, but may be atmospheric, chemical, and mechanical, the same area in the heavens will show, on the same exposure with similar plates, with apparently the same clearness of sky, surprising differences in the number of stars. He finds, on comparing MM. Henry's plate of the stars in Cygnus taken in 1885, with those taken by himself in 1886 and in 1887, that the number of stars in the Henry plate is 3,124; in his plate of 1886, 5,023; and in his plate of 1887, 16,206; the exposure in each case was sixty minutes. The brothers Henry have succeeded in taking a photograph of the Pleiades after an exposure of four hours, which shows very much more nebulous matter than their well-known photograph taken last year. The negative shows stars down to the seventeenth magnitude.

Photographic Chart of the Heavens.—Dr. Gill, at the Cape of Good Hope, is pushing this work in its preliminary stages with great energy. The photographic instrument is kept at work by two observers from evening twilight until dawn. The reduction of the plates from south polar distance 0° to 12·5° has been completed, and measurements are proceeding to south polar distance—30°. Derby dry plates were used with half-hour exposures, instead of an hour as previously. Dr. Gill, in a paper published by the International Committee for the Photographic Charting of the Heavens, proposes the establishment of a central bureau consisting of chief, assistants, secretaries, and a staff of measurers and computers to take the photographs and measure them and make a catalogue, the work to go on for twenty-five years. at a cost of $50,000 per annum. This would require the cataloguing of 2,000,000 stars. Some astronomers object to this work as being unnecessary. It is expected that a considerable number of observatories in Europe and America will begin work on the photographic chart in 1889.

Solar Parallax.—Prof. William Harkness, in No. 182 of the "Astronomical Journal," gives an abstract of his paper, read before the A. A. A. S. "On the Value of the Solar Parallax deducible from American Photographs of the Last Transit of Venus." In this paper an account was given of the instruments and processes employed by the United States Transit of Venus Commission in determining the parallax of Venus from photographs of the transit of Venus which occurred in December, 1882. Let π be the solar parallax, and δA and δD, respectively, the corrections to the right ascensions and declinations of Venus given by Hill's tables of that planet. Then, on the assumption that Hansen's tables of the sun are correct, there resulted from measurements of the distances between the centers of the Sun and Venus, made upon 1,475 photographs, taken respectively at Washington, D. C.; Cedar Keys, Fla.; San Antonio, Tex.; Cerro Roblero, N. M.; Wellington, South Africa; Santa Cruz, Patagonia; Santiago, Chili; Auckland, New Zealand; Princeton, N. J.; and the Lick Observatory, Cal. :

$$\pi = \quad 8\cdot847'' \pm 0\ 013''$$
$$\delta A = +\ 2\cdot893$$
$$\delta D = +\ 1\ 254$$

and the corresponding mean distance from the earth to the sun is 92,385,000 miles, with a probable error of only 125,000 miles. These numbers are doubtless close approximations to the results that will be obtained from the complete discussion of all the photographs; but they can not be regarded as final, for several reasons, chief among which is the fact that the reduction of the position-angles of Venus relatively to the Sun's center is still unfinished. When these angles are combined with the distances, it is likely that the probable error of the parallax will be somewhat reduced. The photographs taken at Lick Observatory seem to indicate that for altitudes 4,000 feet above sea-level, the values of the refraction given by the tables in general use are somewhat too large. Prof. L. Cruls has published the results of the Brazilian observations of the transit of Venus made at three stations, St. Thomas (Antilles), Pernambuco, and Punta-Arenas. The final result for parallax is $\pi = 8\cdot808''$. This curiously coincides exactly with the result of the English observations, taking the lowest probable result.

Eclipses of the Moon.—Two interesting total eclipses of the moon occurred in 1888. The first on January 28, and the second at midnight, July 22. The moon rose eclipsed on January 28, but was beautifully visible on July 22. Observers of the eclipse of January 28 report a remarkable contrast between the visibility of the eclipsed moon on that occasion and in October, 1884. The moon at the latter date was scarcely visible, while at the former it shone with a light that was plainly visible. Prof. Filopanti, of Bologna, thinks that the red color during the total eclipse arose in part from a phosphorescent quality of the exposed lunar surface. To astronomers these two eclipses of the moon were especially interesting as affording opportunity for the observation of the occultations of faint stars by the moon. Dr. Döllen, of the Pulkowa Observatory, Russia, prepared lists of stars to be occulted by the moon, and sent them to many observatories in Europe and the United States, with the request that the times of disappearance and reappearance be noted and forwarded to him. He reports that he has obtained in this way observations of 783 phenomena (396 disappearances and 387 reappearances), made at fifty-five different places. The places of observation are so favorably situated that he considers there is ample material for calculating the place, the diameter, and possibly the ellipticity and the parallax of the moon. For the parallax and distance of the moon he has bases of 90° in latitude and 150° in longitude.

Asteroids.—The small planet Istria (183) was rediscovered by Palisa, April 7, 1888. Of the first 250 of the planets, 238 have been observed at second opposition. Only two of the exceptions are between numbers 200 and 250. Since the article in the "Annual Cyclopædia" for 1887 was written, No. 268 has been named Adorea; 269 has not been named, and 270 has been styled Anahita. The opposition in longitude of Sappho (80) occurred April 12, 1888. Observations were made by many astronomers to determine the correction to the elements of the planet's orbit. In August and September, 1889, this planet will make a near approach to the earth, on account of the eccentricity of its orbit and the commensurability of its period with that of the earth. Observations of this planet will be taken in 1889 to determine the value of solar parallax. Prof. C. H. F. Peters gives the following results of some of his photometrical work on the small planets :

	Volume in millions of cubic kilometres.
Vesta, 6·5 magnitude	32·2
Ceres, 7·7 "	21·8
Pallas, 8·6 "	6·4
Hygeia	4·3
Eunomia	4·3
Juno	3·7
Hebe	2·4
Iris	2·4
Psyche	2·1
Lutetia	1·9

The total volume of the ten largest asteroids, therefore, is 81·5 millions of cubic kilometres; that of the first seventy, Prof. Peters found to be 127·74; and as the volume of the earth is 1,082,841 millions of cubic kilometres, the combined volumes of the first seventy asteroids is to that of the earth as 1 to 7,862.

Prof. Daniel Kirkwood has published recently an exceedingly interesting work of sixty pages on "The Asteroids or Minor Planets between Mars and Jupiter." This gives, among other items of interest, the asteroids in the order of discovery, to and including No. 271, the elements of the asteroids, theories in regard to the origin of asteroids, etc. The following asteroids have been discovered since the table in the "Annual Cyclopædia" for 1887 was prepared :

No.	Name.	Discoverer.	No. of discovery.	Date of discovery.
271	Penthesilea	Dr. Knorre, at Berlin.	4	Oct. 13, 1887
272	Antonia	M. Charlois, at Nice	2	Feb. 4, 1888
273	Atropos	Herr Palisa, at Vienna	61	March 8
274	Philagoria	" " "	62	April 3
275	Sapientia	" " "	63	April 15
276	Adelheid	" " "	64	April 17
277		M. Charlois	3	May 3
278	Paulina	Herr Palisa	65	May 16
279		" "	66	Oct. 25
280		" "	67	Oct. 31

Comets.—Six comets were discovered in 1888 up to November 1. Comet I was discovered early in the morning of February 19, by Mr. Sawerthal as he was returning from the photographic observatory of the Royal Observatory at the Cape of Good Hope. He noticed with the naked eye a suspicious object, which, on investigation with the opera-glass, proved to be a comet. The observations of various observers show that the comet was well defined, the tail being distinctly visible to

It has been suggested that there were three tails. In May the appearance of the comet was said to be similar to that of Encke's comet (Dec. 2, 1871), as drawn by Prof. Hall. A sudden increase in brightness is reported to have occurred about May 23. The spectrum obtained was faint, but fairly broad, continu-

LICK OBSERVATORY—PIER OF THE GREAT TELESCOPE.
Mr. Lick's tomb is in the base of the pier.

the naked eye, and estimated in April to be nearly 5° in length. The nucleus was seen elongated by many ; others report a complete separation into two portions. The duplicity of the nucleus was confirmed by observations made by Barnard, at Lick Observatory. The separation of the two portions was estimated by C. B. Hill to be about equal to 3″ of arc. Observers report the tail very bright along the central axis, and much fainter on either side.

ous, and crossed by three faint bands, corresponding to the well-known carbon-bands characteristic of cometary spectra in general.

Comet II is the twenty-fifth reappearance of the Encke comet, the period of which is 3·3 years. It was detected on the evening of July 8, by John Tebbutt, at Windsor, New South Wales. Its position had been predicted by Drs. Backlund and Seraphimoff, and it was found almost exactly in the place assigned.

In a 4½-inch telescope it appeared as a small, bright, nebulous star, without a nucleus. It was moving rapidly both east and south. This comet was originally discovered on Nov. 26, 1818, by the astronomer Pons, at Marseilles. It was then visible for seven weeks. Prof. Encke, of Berlin, subjected the observations to a careful investigation, and showed that the orbit was elliptical, with a period of about three and one third years. He identified the comet with the comets of 1786 I, 1795, and 1805, and predicted its return. His calculations were almost exactly fulfilled. Ordinarily it appears to have no tail. In 1848 it had two, one about 1° in length directed from the sun, and the other a little shorter, and turned toward it. At perihelion the comet passes within the orbit of Mercury, and at aphelion its distance from the sun is about equal to that of Jupiter. Investigations of the motions of this comet show that its period is steadily diminishing by about two and a half hours in every revolution. Encke's theory was that the comet, in moving through space, met with a resistance from some rare medium, which was not able to impede the greater masses of the planets. Many astronomers are inclined to doubt the existence of a resisting medium; but lately, Dr. Backlund, the Swedish astronomer, from an examination of the observations of the comet between 1871 and 1881, concludes that there is a retardation, although the amount is less than that assigned by Encke. No other comet seems to be retarded, so that if we accept the theory of a resisting medium we must imagine that it does not extend very far from the sun. The investigations of Mr. Sherman seem to point in the same direction as those of Dr. Backlund.

Comet III was discovered by W. R. Brooks, of Geneva, N. Y., August 7. On August 10, Prof. Boss reported the comet as small and condensed, and showing, with low powers, as a star of the ninth magnitude. It had a short tail with an estimated length of 10′, and of the same breadth as the head. It had already passed perihelion when discovered, and was rapidly diminishing in brightness. It was thought that observations might be made up to the October moon.

Comet IV was found at Nice Observatory on August 9. The ephemeris shows that the comet is slightly increasing in brightness. This comet is one of the short-period comets. Its last appearance was in 1880; its period is 7·4 years. The present is its seventh appearance. This comet was first discovered by M. Faye, at the Paris Observatory, on Nov. 22, 1843. It had a bright nucleus and short tail, but was not visible to the naked eye. Leverrier investigated its orbit, and predicted its return to perihelion on April 3, 1851. It returned within a day of the time predicted. Its perihelion distance is about 100,000,000 miles, and its aphelion distance about 500,000,000 miles.

Comet V was discovered on September 2, by E. E. Barnard, at the Lick Observatory. It was described as circular, 1′ in diameter, eleventh magnitude, with a well-defined nucleus. No decided motion was observed in twenty minutes. Prof. Boss calculated the provisional elements given in the table, which show that the theoretical brightness at perihelion would be about seventy times the brightness at discovery. The same observer furnishes the following notes:

September 5. The comet has a soft but condensed light. The coma is somewhat less than 30″ in diameter, and symmetrical. The condensation is very uniform toward the center, without a distinct nucleus Under illumination the central parts—some 5″ in diameter—appear as a star of 11·5 magnitude.

September 6. There is a very small nucleus of about the thirteenth magnitude.

September 10. The nebulosity is elliptical, with axes of about 40″ and 60″ respectively. Nuclear condensation well marked, and is, perhaps, 10″ south of the center of the nebulous mass.

Comet VI was discovered by E. E. Barnard, at Lick Observatory, October 31. He describes it as having no tail, a strong central condensation, of the eleventh magnitude, or fainter; the nebulosity was 1′ in mean diameter, and was much elongated.

We give the approximate elements of these comets in the following table:

Designation.	Gr. M. T. Perihelion passage.	☊	ω	*i*	Log. *q*.	Discovery.	Synonym.	Remarks.
1888, I....	1888, March, 16·96	245° 30′	350° 49′	42° 17′	9·84450	Feb. 18, Sawerthal..	Comet *a*, 1888	
II...	1888, June, 28	334° 39′		12° 53′	9 5852	July 8, Tebbutt.....	*b*,	Encke's.
III..	1888, July, 30·25	101° 6′	57° 49′	74° 4′	9·95424	Aug. 7. Brooks	*c*,	
IV..	1888, Aug., 20	209° 40′		11° 22′	0·240	Aug. 9. Nice Obs'y..	*d*,	Faye's.
V...	1888, Dec., 10·41	8° 28′	357° 46′	165° 7′	0·12668	Sept. 2, Barnard....	*e*,	
VI..	1888, Sept., 9·45	137° 52′	267° 10′	45° 53′	0·04984	Oct. 31, Barnard ...	*f*,	

W. F. Denning says that fourteen comets were discovered between 1827 and 1836, while between 1877 and 1886 forty-nine were discovered. In seven years E. E. Barnard and W. R. Brooks have discovered twenty comets—ten apiece—and to the end of 1887 they had received $2,700 in prizes. In the September number of "The Observatory," T. W. Backhouse gives the following interesting table in regard to naked-eye comets seen since 1881:

COMET.	First seen with naked eye.	Duration of naked-eye visibility.	Greatest length of tail.
1881, *b* (Great)..........	1881, June 29.	89 days	20½°
1881, *c* (Schaberle's)....	1881, July 27..	82 "	10½
1882, *a* (Wells's)........	1882, May 11..	24 "	1
1882 (Great)..........	1882, Oct. 1...	133 "	23
1883, *b* (Pons-Brooks's).	1883, Nov. 19..	70 "	6½
1885, *d* (Fabry's)	1886, March 29	29 "	·88
1886, *f* (Barnard's)	1886, Nov. 9..	49 "	27½
1888, *a* (Sawerthal's)....	1888, April 7..	87 "	5½

Double and Binary Stars.—J. E. Gore gives in the "Monthly Notices of the Royal Astronomical Society" for December, 1887, formulæ for the rectangular co-ordinates of the double star Σ 1847, and gives the proper motion of the star as 0·1053" per annum in the direction of position angle 114·1°. The following table gives:

The 36-inch equatorial of Lick Observatory shows, "at a little less than one fifth of the width of the ring from its outer edge, a fine but distinct dark line, a mere spider's thread, which could be traced along the ring nearly to a point opposite the limb of the planet. This line marked the beginning of a dark shade,

STAR.		ρ Eridani.	λ Ophiuchi.	70 (ρ) Ophiuchi.	Σ 3121.
Time of periastron	T	1823·55	1787·9	1807·65	1878·52
Position of node	Ω	135° 0' (1870)	105·5° (1900)	120° 5' (1850)	......
Position of periastron	λ	240° 0'	152·5°	171° 45'	......
Inclination	γ	88° 31'	88·1°	56° 25'	......
Eccentricity	e	0·674	0·4424	0·4912	0·80868
Semi-axis major	a	6·96"	1·53"	4·50"	0·6725"
Mean motion	μ	− 1·19°	+0·9638°	− 4·098°	......
Period in years	P	302·37	87·5	87·84	84·65
Computer		J. E. Gore.	S. Glasenapp.	J. E. Gore.	M. Celoria.

The Sun.—The minimum period for sun-spot occurrence was prolonged during the first four months of 1887. There was a sudden slight increase in the number of spots in the beginning of May, 1887. In the present eleven-year period two minima have occurred: one, from Sept. 22 to Dec. 8, 1886, and the other from January to May, 1887. Including both of these periods in the same minimum, by neglecting the interruptions at the close of 1886, then the whole minimum period includes 222 days, and the date of the minimum may be given approximately as Jan. 10, 1887. This does not refer to the absolute minimum for this eleven-year period. On Oct. 28, 1887, some faculæ, attached to a group of faint spots, are reported to have become on a sudden intensely bright, and faded again as quickly. No other change of importance occurred in the spots themselves, or in their neighborhood. Within three minutes both faculæ and spots had entirely disappeared. The magnetic instruments indicated no disturbance. There were many days in 1887 when the sun was without spots, but very rarely were faculæ entirely absent.

Saturn.— Many skilful observers, among whom may be mentioned M. Trouvelot, Dr. Terby, and Mr. Elger, consider that the rings of Saturn are not stable, but are subject to continual changes. Dark masses have been observed on ring C, indentations have been seen on its inner edge, and other noticeable appearances recorded. Some astronomers have been inclined to consider that these appearances have no real existence, but that they are due to bad seeing, distorting eye-pieces, etc. Prof. Hall, in using the great Washington glass, was, we think, unable to see some of the markings drawn on the rings by Trouvelot in his well-known picture of Saturn, as seen with a 26-inch instrument. Mr. Keeler, of Lick Observatory, in the February number of the "Sidereal Messenger," in speaking of the distortion of Saturn's shadow, drawn by Trouvelot, says he had often noticed the distortion "when observing with the 12-inch equatorial, with a low power on a poor night; but it always disappeared on employing a sufficiently high power, or with improvement in the definition."

which extended inward, diminishing in intensity, nearly to the great black division. At its inner edge the ring was of nearly the same brightness as outside the fine division. No other markings were visible."

In the supplements to the "Pulkowa Observations," Prof. H. Struve discusses his own observations made with the 15-inch refractor in 1884–'86 on Iapetus, Titan, Rhea, and Dione, with a view to correcting the elements of these satellites and also of determining the mass and ellipticity of Saturn. Herr Struve's value of the mass of Saturn agrees closely with Bessel's, being 1 ÷ 3,498; the sun being unity.

G. W. Hill, in the "Astronomical Journal," of July 12, 1888, discusses the motion of Hyperion and the mass of Titan. He points out the errors in the calculations of several computers, and gives as his value of the mass of Titan 1 ÷ 4,714, the mass of the planet being unity.

Mars.—Prof. Schiaparelli's observations on Mars, made during the opposition of 1881–'82, have been published. His new map agrees in general with that drawn in 1879. There are some noticeable differences, however, these being in a region seen by a number of observers to undergo changes. The main interest of this memoir centers in the full account of the "remarkable duplication of many of the canals." Thirty duplications are recorded between December, 1881, and February, 1882. The author thinks the phenomenon is periodic, and he concludes that duplication is connected with a period corresponding to the tropical year of Mars, and depending on the martial seasons. The tendency to duplication is pointed out as showing itself in other regions of Mars. Other observers have noted this tendency. Schiaparelli thinks it impossible to deny the reality of the duplications, however difficult of explanation they may be. E. W. Maunder, in the September number of "The Observatory," in discussing Schiaparelli's observations, remarks that "it seems impossible to accept this as a description of a real objective change taking place upon the actual surface of the planet, though as a record of a subjective appearance it must be unhesitatingly received. Prof.

Schiaparelli's advantages in the way of keen and trained eye-sight, and telescopic and atmospheric definition are beyond challenge. Hitherto the puzzle has received no satisfactory solution, for Mr. Proctor's suggestion that the canals are rivers is quite irreconcilable with the account Prof. Schiaparelli has given of the

The Chief Meteor-Showers. — W. F. Denning gives, in the January, 1888, number of "Monthly Notices of the Royal Astronomical Society," a list of the chief meteor-showers, derived from his observations made during the past fifteen years, the positions being corrected for precession, and brought up to 1890.

NAME OF SHOWER.	Duration.	Date of maximum.	Radiant point.		Sun's longitude.
1. Quadrantids.............	December 28–January 4......	January 2.....	$a = 229\cdot 8^\circ$	$\delta = + 52\cdot 5$	$281\cdot 6^\circ$
2. Lyrids................	April 16–22................	April 20.......	$269\cdot 7$	$+ 82\cdot 5$	$31\cdot 3$
3. η Aquarids.............	April 30–May 6	May 6 ...... ,	$337\cdot 6$	$- 2\cdot 1$	$46\cdot 3$
4. δ Aquarids.............	July 23–August 25..........	July 28	$339\cdot 4$	$- 11\cdot 6$	$125\cdot 6$
5. Perseids...............	July 11–August 22..........	August 11...	$45\cdot 9$	$+ 56\cdot 9$	$138\cdot 5$
6. Orionids................	October 9–29...............	October 18 ...	$92\cdot 1$	$+ 15\cdot 5$	$205\cdot 9$
7. Leonids................	November 9–17	November 13...	$150\cdot 0$	$+ 22\cdot 9$	$231\cdot 5$
8. Andromedes............	November 25–30..............	November 27...	$25\cdot 3$	$+ 43\cdot 8$	$245\cdot 8$
9. Geminids...............	December 1–14	December 10...	$108\cdot 1$	$+ 82\cdot 6$	$259\cdot 5$

NOTES.—2. Probably moving in orbit of Comet I, 1861. 8. Have orbital resemblance to Halley's comet. 5. Obvious displacement of radiant point from night to night. May have some connection with Comet III, 1862. 6. Radiant shows no displacement. 7. Observed from earliest times. Seen by Humboldt, 1799. Magnificent return in 1888, and splendid shower in 1866. Very meager during the last fifteen years. These meteors form a complete ellipse, and the earth meets a few at every passage through the node. But the meteors are nearly all massed in the neighborhood of their parent, Comet I, 1866. It is supposed that there are minor groups of meteors pursuing the same orbit; if so, we may have a revival of this display in 1888, for on the night of Nov. 12, 1822, shooting-stars, mingled with balls of fire, were seen in vast numbers at Potsdam, by Klöden. 8. Observed in 1798. Recurred in 1838. Very brilliant showers, Nov. 27, 1872, and 1885. It is uncertain whether this group forms an unbroken stream or not. Returns of the showers should be looked for in 1892 and 1898.

appearances he has observed. But it is quite likely that Proctor's further suggestion that they are 'optical products,' neither objective realities nor optical illusions, but phenomena of diffraction, may prove more satisfactory. Further observations are urgently desired to test the point—observations not confined to two or three favorable nights near opposition, but begun early and ended late, and carried on with the most persistent continuity."

In the "Astronomical Journal" for August, 1888, Prof. Asaph Hall, of Washington, D. C., says he made very careful observations of Mars during June, 1888. These were begun in the twilight, and were continued for eighteen nights, but he was unable to see anything like the regular canals drawn by the European observers. The only remarkable change he noticed was the diminution in the size of the white spot at the south pole of the planet. These observations were made with the great 26-inch instrument.

In the "Astronomical Journal" for September, Prof. Holden, of Lick Observatory, gives a series of drawings of Mars, as seen with the great 36 inch Lick telescope. He reports that they have seen none of the canals double, although many of the more important have been sketched as broad bands covering the spaces on Schiaparelli's map that are occupied by pairs of canals. The observations also fail to discover any important changes in the continent Libya, which had been reported as submerged.

Jupiter.—A remnant of the great red spot is still to be observed in the planet's southern hemisphere. This "rosy cloud" was first figured and described by Prof. C. W. Pritchett, of Morrison Observatory, Glasgow, Missouri, on July 9, 1878. The persistency of the spot has led some observers to consider that they were looking at the solid body of the planet through a hole, as it were, in Jupiter's clouds.

Mr. Denning gives some interesting data as to heights of fire-balls and shooting-stars. Eighty fire-balls, between 1865 and 1887, gave an average height at beginning of 69·2 miles, and 30·2 miles at end of flight. Comparing these heights with the heights of meteors (nearly all shooting-stars of the first magnitude or fainter), he gives the following table:

AUTHORITY.	No. of Meteors.	Height at beginning.	Height at ending.
E. Heis.	271	76·9 miles.	50·1 miles.
A. S. Herschel.. ..	86	79·5 "	53·8 "
T. H. Waller	48	81·4 "	52·4 "
W. F. Denning*....	18	80·0 "	54·2 "

* Stars seen in 1887.

A careful discussion of the various records gives the following mean relative heights:

	At beginning.	At ending.	At middle course.
Fire-balls.........	69 miles.	30 miles.	49·5 miles.
Shooting-stars.....	80 "	54 "	67·0 "

It is supposed that telescopic meteors are at still greater elevations than the brighter forms of these bodies.

Meteorites. — In April, 1888, Prof. H. A. Newton read before the National Academy of Sciences a paper "Upon the Relation which the Former Orbits of those Meteorites that are in our Collections, and that were seen to fall, had to the Earth's Orbit." His studies led him to adopt three propositions: 1. The meteorites that we have in our cabinets, which were seen to fall, were originally (as a class, and with few exceptions), moving about the sun in orbits that had inclinations less than 90°; that is, their motions were direct, not retrograde. 2. Either the stones that are moving in the solar system across the earth's orbit move in general in direct orbits; or else, for some reason, the stones that move in retrograde orbits do not in general come through the air to the ground. 3. The perihelion-distances of nearly all the orbits in which these stones move were not less than 0·5 nor more than 1·0 time the earth's radius. The author assumes as fully proved the connection of comets with meteors, and considers therefore that the meteorites have velocities relative to the sun not greater than 1·414 nor less than 1·244 time the earth's velocity in its orbit (earth's orbital velocity 18·38 miles a second).

Mr. Lockyer, in his paper read before the Royal Society, Nov. 17, 1887, gives the result of his experiments on meteorites. He examined meteoritic spectra under various conditions, particularly that of feeble temperature. He found it possible to obtain from meteorites spectra that showed the most peculiar features of almost every variety of spectrum—solar, star, nebular, and cometary. "In the spectra of nebulæ, for instance, seven lines have been detected, of which three were traced to hydrogen, three to low-temperature magnesium, and the seventh, which has not yet been traced to its originating element, has been given by the glow from the Dhurmsala metecrite. The most characteristic nebular line was identified with the low-temperature fluting of magnesium, and the unusual spectrum obtained from the comets of 1866 and 1867 was ascribed to the same cause. The changes observed in the spectrum of the great comet of 1882 were such as would correspond to the changes induced by the change of temperature in the spectrum of a meteorite; and the changes in the spectrum of Nova Cygni, and the bright lines in such a star as R. Geminorum received a similar explanation; while a very full, in parts almost perfect, reproduction of a considerable portion of the solar spectrum has been obtained by taking a composite photograph of the arc spectrum of several stony meteorites, taken at random between iron meteoric poles. These and similar observations have led Mr. Lockyer to regard all self-luminous bodies in the celestial spaces as composed of meteorites, or masses of meteoritic vapor produced by heat brought about by condensation of meteor-swarms due to gravity, so that the existing distinction between star, comets, and nebulæ rests on no physical basis. All alike are meteoritic in origin, the differences between them depending upon differences in temperature, and in the closeness of the component meteorites to one another. *Novæ* (new stars that blaze forth suddenly) are explained as produced by the clash of meteor-streams, and most variable stars are regarded as uncondensed meteor-streams. Stars with spectra like that of Alpha Orionis (Rigel) are considered not as true suns, but as mere clouds of incandescent stones; probably the first stage of meteoritic condensation. Stars with spectra of the first and second type represent the condensed swarm in its hottest stages, while spectra of Secchi's fourth type indicate an advanced stage of cooling." Objection has been

raised to Mr. Lockyer's hypothesis by M. Stanislas Meunier. He contends that the only conclusion we are as yet entitled to draw from the spectroscopic researches on meteorites is, that they are composed of the same original matter as other celestial bodies.

The Observatory of Milan has published Part II, No. VII, of its observations. This last number contains a catalogue which is supplementary to two preceding ones. The first (1874) contained the observed paths of 7,152 meteors seen in 1872; the second (1882) contained 7,602 meteors, and the present publication contains 9,627 meteors.

Solar Physics.—The experiments of Prof John Trowbridge and C. C. Hutchins lead them to conclude that there is unmistakable evidence of the existence of carbon vapor in the sun, and that at the point of the sun's atmosphere where the carbon is volatilized the temperature of the sun approximates to that of the voltaic arc. An exceedingly valuable contribution to science has been made by C. C. Hutchins and E. L. Holden in regard to the meaning of the lines in the solar spectrum. They say that "The dispersion given by the apparatus in the order of spectrum in which we work is such that a single wave-length occupies on the negative a space of 1·12 millimetres. This makes the distance between lines D_1 and D_2 6·7 millimetres. We are convinced that there is much in the whole matter of coincidences of metallic and solar lines that needs re-examination; that something more than the mere coincidences of two or three lines out of many is necessary to establish even the probability of the presence of a metal in the sun." They have examined some of the doubtful elements in the list given by Prof. Young in his book on "The Sun," and find the evidence as follows: For cadmium, there were two perfect coincidences; for lead, cerium, molybdenum, uranium, vanadium, there was no good evidence in favor of their existence in the sun. Among the metals whose existence in the solar atmosphere has seemed probable, their experiments seem to show that bismuth and silver were present, but that tin, potassium, and lithium were doubtful. They also furnish evidence of the existence of platinum in the sun, claiming that between wave-lengths 4,250 and 4,950 to find 64 lines of platinum, 16 of which agree with solar lines.

Henry Crew has made some observations with the spectroscope on the period of the rotation of the sun. He obtained, for the mean equatorial velocity, 2·437 miles a second, which corresponds to a true period of rotation of 25·88 days. Mr. Crew thinks that, while the sun-spot layer (or photosphere, if they be the same) is accelerated in the neighborhood of the equator, the layer, which by its absorption gives rise to the Fraunhofer lines, tends to lag behind, having here a smaller angular velocity than in higher latitudes. Comparing the year 1886 with 1887, observers report that the average height of both the chromosphere and prominences has been constant. The prominences had decreased in number. The heights of the largest prominences were much diminished. Some preliminary investigations in regard to the surface-currents of the sun seem to indicate: 1. That the direction at the poles is generally vertical to the limb; 2. That there is a decided current crossing the equator, sometimes in a northerly, and at other times in the southerly direction; 3. That changes of direction occur most frequently in mid latitudes.

Spectroscopy.—Prof. Grünwald, of Prague, has propounded a theory, according to which the wave-lengths of the lines due to a certain element in a given compound are to the wave-lengths due to that same element, when the first compound is combined with some further body, as the volume the element occupies in the first case is to the volume it occupies in the second. Examining the low temperature spectrum of hydrogen, he finds that the wave-lengths of its several lines are just double those of the lines of the water spectrum, line for line. Similar, but less simple relationships are given for other spectra, and Prof. Grünwald concludes from them that hydrogen and oxygen are compound bodies, and are dissociated in the sun. Hydrogen is inferred to have a composition of the form A_4b; of which the supposed element A is associated with the line of the corona 1474 K; and b with the 'helium' line D_3. Louis Bell, Fellow of Johns Hopkins University, has given, in the "American Journal of Science," a paper describing his careful determination of the wave-lengths of the D_1 line of sodium. The result is to increase slightly Thalen's correction of Ångström's value, the wave-length finally adopted being 5,896·08 tenth-metres. Prof. Rowland has followed this with a table of the relative wave-lengths of about 450 standard lines, based upon the above determination, and designed to be used in connection with his photographic map of the normal spectrum. R. Copeland considers that he has discovered a line in the spectrum of the Great Nebula of Orion corresponding to the place of D_3. He remarks that "the occurrence of this line in the spectrum of a nebula is of great interest, as affording another connecting link between gaseous nebulæ and the sun and stars with bright-line spectra, especially with that remarkable class of stars of which the first examples were detected by MM. Wolf and Rayet in the constellation of Cygnus." The Astronomer Royal of England, at the January, 1888, meeting of the Royal Astronomical Society, called special attention to two points of interest in the spectroscopic determinations of the motions of stars in the line of sight. One point referred to the motion of Sirius. This star has shown a complete reversal of motion since Dr. Huggins's first results. In 1868, Dr. Huggins found the motion to be 29 miles a second receding from the earth; in 1872, 18 to 22 miles a second. The Greenwich observations in 1875–'76, showed a mo-

tion of 24 miles a second. Subsequent years gave the following result: 1876–'77, 12 miles; 1877–'78, 23 miles; 1879–'80, 15 miles; 1880–'81, 11 miles; 1881–'82, 2 miles; thus showing a decreasing recessional motion. In 1882–'83 the motion was 5 miles a second, approaching the earth; 1883–84, 19 miles, approaching 1884–'85, 23 miles, approaching; 1885–'86, 24 miles, approaching; 1886–'87, 1 mile approaching; and for the year 1887, 6 miles receding. These results are to be accepted with great caution, as astronomers are not yet fully satisfied that an apparent change in the displacement of the F. line indicates a real motion in the line of sight. The change of motion indicated by the above figures is very much larger than any that would appear probable from the known motion of Sirius in its orbit. The second point of interest referred to the orbital motion of Algol. The spectroscopic observations seem to show that this interesting variable is revolving about a primary, and that the system to which it belongs is, as a whole, approaching the earth. Further observations are necessary to establish anything definite. Prof. H. C. Vogel, in a communication to the Royal Prussian Academy, says that photography has been successfully employed to overcome the effect of atmospheric tremors, so noticeable in spectroscopic work investigating stellar motions. The time of exposure employed is from half an hour to two hours.

The Constant of Aberration.—Prof. Hall has published the results of his reduction of the observations made in the years 1862–'67 upon a Lyræ by Profs. Hubbard, Newcomb, Harkness, and himself, with the prime - vertical transit-instrument of the Naval Observatory, for the purpose of determining the constants of nutation and aberration. He obtained as the most probable value of the constant of aberration, $20·4542'' \pm 0·0144''$. This, with Michelson and Newcomb's determination of the velocity of light, gives for the solar parallax a value of $8·810'' \pm 0·0062''$.

Resisting Medium.—Freiherr v. Haerdtl, a pupil of Oppolzer, lately read a paper at Kiel University on the periodic comet of Winnecke. He found no indication of any influence on the comet's motion due to a resisting medium. On the other hand, O. T. Sherman considers that the variations in the motion of Encke's comet, other than those produced by planetary attraction, are caused "by a resisting medium connected with the sun, and disturbed by those forces which produce and are produced by sunspots." He considers "that the zodiacal light is intimately connected with these disturbing forces, being in fact a locus of condensation of matter driven from the sun similarly to the tail of a comet from the nucleus, and after condensation again precipitated upon the solar surface."

Catalogues.—Le Verrier, on becoming Director of the Paris Observatory in 1854, planned to reobserve Lalande's catalogue of 47,390 stars. He considered it necessary to make three observations in right ascension, and three in declination. Up to 1879 only about one third of the observations had been made. The annual number of observations was about 7,000. Since 1879 the instruments have been increased by the Bischoffsheim meridian circle, and the director, Admiral Mouchez has augmented the observing-staff. During the past eight years the number of observations for the catalogue has amounted to about 27,500. The first installment of this valuable catalogue has been published in two volumes, one devoted to the catalogue, and the other to the individual observations. The stars are in the first six hours of right ascension, observed during the years 1837 to 1881. It contains 7,245 stars, and represents 80,000 observations in both elements. The introductory chapters contain a comparison of the Paris Catalogue with Auwer's re-reduction of Bradley. M. Bossert furnishes a valuable investigation of the proper motions of 374 stars in the catalogue, and supplies a long list of errors in Lalande.

In the Dunsink Catalogue of 1,012 southern stars, by Rambaut, most of the stars are between 2° and 23° south declination. The observations were made between November, 1882, and September, 1885, and are of stars which needed reobservation.

The second part of the eighth volume of the O'Gyalla Catalogue has been recently published. This catalogue briefly indicates the character of the spectrum of each star observed in the zone selected, which lies between the equator and the 15th parallel of south declination. The publication is intended as a continuation of the spectroscopic study of the northern heavens projected some years ago by Prof. Vogel and Dr. Dunér. The faintest stars observed are of the 7½ magnitude. The third volume of the Potsdam "Observations" gave the first installment of the survey, the number of stars being 4,051, lying in the zone between 20° north and 1° south declination. The O'Gyalla Catalogue contains 2,022 stars. The spectra show that types I a and II a are most frequent. Only three cases of III b are given.

The ninth volume of the "Observations" has also been issued and contains those observations made in 1886. Dr. Konkoly describes instruments and methods. Spectrum-photometry of thirty-four fixed stars and of the planets Mars, Jupiter, and Saturn is the most original of the work. Some nebulæ and comets, and some special stars, were examined photometrically or with the spectroscope. Many notes in regard to the appearance of the solar surface on each day of the observation, and a table of positions of sun-spots for 1886, are given. A large number of meteor observations and a list of radiants completes the volume.

Volume xlix, Part I, of the "Memoirs of the Royal Astronomical Society" contains Dr. Dreyer's new general catalogue of 7,840 nebulæ and clusters of stars, being the catalogue of the late Sir John F. W. Herschel, revised, corrected and enlarged. The Council of the Royal Astronomical Society has printed an additional 225 copies of this catalogue, on account of its value to astronomers. It is supposed to give the records of all nebulæ of which the places have been published up to December, 1887.

A. M. W. Downing, in the May, 1888, "Monthly Notices of the Royal Astronomical Society," gives the positions for 1,750, and proper motions for 154 stars south of 29° south declination. This catalogue is deduced from a revision of Powalky's "Reduction of the Star-places of Lacaille's 'Astronomiæ Fundamenta.'"

Dr. Peters, of Hamilton College, Clinton, N. Y., has undertaken to collate all available existing manuscripts of Ptolemy's catalogue, for which purpose he has visited the principal libraries of Europe and has the assistance of Mr. Knobel of England.

Pulkowa Observatory has published the catalogue for 1865 of the principal stars to the fourth magnitude, as far as 15° south declination. This catalogue re-examines the stars in the old catalogue for the epoch of 1845.

J. G. Porter has published the result of two and a half years' work with the three-inch transit. The catalogue contains 4,050 stars between 18° 50' and 22° 20' south declination. Most of the stars down to the 8 5 magnitude have been observed, as well as some fainter ones. The proper motions of 75 stars are given in the appendix.

S. C. Chandler has published a valuable catalogue of variable stars, in Nos. 179 and 180 of the "Astronomical Journal." The catalogue has been printed separately for distribution. The author says: "Thirteen years have passed since the appearance of Schönfeld's Second Catalogue of variable stars. A work that shall represent the knowledge of to day as that did the knowledge of its date, is an urgent need of this branch of astronomy." This preliminary catalogue is issued in hopes of supplying that need. A great deal of care has been given to its preparation. The catalogue shows that of the 225 stars comprised in it, 160 are distinctly periodic; 12 belong to the so-called *Novæ*. Of the periodic variables, Mr. Chandler has been able to assign both maximum and minimum epochs for 63 stars; maximum epochs alone for 82; minimum epochs alone, for 14, 9 of these being of the Algol type. The elements of 124 stars are the results of Mr. Chandler's own investigations; for 22 he has adopted those of Schönfeld, and for 14 those of Argelander, Gould, Parkhurst, and others, after independent examination had shown that the data at hand would not give essentially improved values. He has added to the catalogue an arbitrary estimate of the color or redness of many of the stars. The catalogue also contains a list of some of the doubtful cases of variables.

Polaris.—T. H. Safford gives the year 2102 A. D. as the time of nearest approach of Polaris to the north pole, when the declination will be 89° 32′ 23.″ The star, he says, will reach 89° about the year 1944, and be for about 300 years within a degree of the pole.

Medals.—The gold medal of the Royal Astronomical Society of England was awarded on Feb. 10, 1888, to Prof. Arthur Auwers, for his re-reduction of Bradley's observations. At the April meeting of the National Academy of Sciences of the United States, the Draper Astronomical Medal was presented to Prof. Edward C. Pickering, Director of the Harvard College Observatory. At the same meeting the Lawrence Smith Medal for original work on the subject of Meteorites, was awarded to Prof. Hubert A. Newton, of Yale College, New Haven, Mass.

Bibliography.—A large number of valuable papers have been printed in the serial publications devoted to astronomical knowledge, and during the year the following books have been published: "The Asteroids or Minor Planets between Mars and Jupiter," by Daniel Kirkwood; "Movements of the Earth," by J. Norman Lockyer; "Old and New Astronomy," several parts, by Richard A. Proctor; "Astronomy for Amateurs," by Thomas W. Oliver; "The New Astronomy," by Samuel P. Langley. "A Text-book on Astronomy," by Prof. Charles A. Young. The Smithsonian Institution has published a "Bibliography of Astronomy for the year 1887," by William C. Winlock, of the U. S. Naval Observatory at Washington, D. C.

Messrs. Chandler and Ritchie have published the new "Science Observer Code," to be used in the telegraphic distribution of announcements of discovery and of positions from Oct. 1, 1888.

ATLANTIC OCEAN, HYDROGRAPHY OF. Rapid progress has been made of late years in the acquirement of knowledge concerning the sea and its phenomena. Especially is this true of the great ocean subdivision known as the "North Atlantic." With its dependent gulfs and seas, this ocean covers an area of something like 18,000,000 square miles, about one eighth of the total sea-surface of the globe. Commercially its importance largely exceeds that of all other oceans. Lying as it does between the great civilized continents, Europe on the east and America on the west, its commerce is as a hundred to one when compared with that of larger and more remote seas. For this reason it has been more thoroughly explored than any other ocean-tract, and its phenomena of tides and currents, winds and temperatures, depths and shallows, are better known.

The Hydrographic Office of the United States Navy has always been in the front rank of investigation. Struggling from the first with meager appropriations, it has nevertheless contributed its full share to the world's knowledge of this great highway of civilization.

Among the most creditable of its recent undertakings is the publication of monthly pilot-charts, showing not only the meteorological conditions that may be looked for with reasonable certainty, and the more or less regular variations of currents, but all the obstacles, floating wrecks and the like, of which any trustworthy intelligence can be obtained. To these are added what may be termed the eccentricities of natural phenomena, such as cyclones, water-spouts, the appearance of whales, etc. The course taken by all exceptionally severe storms is noted, and, as the charts are of a convenient size (24 x 30), they can be easily kept for reference in a drawer or in a portfolio, and thus afford a highly valuable record of the sea and its mysteries, for the benefit of navigators.

A single instance may be cited: The collision between the steamers "Thingvalla" and "Geiser" is among the most startling of recent disasters. If the captains of those vessels had followed, even approximately, the courses plotted for transatlantic steamers on the pilot-chart for August, both vessels might have been still afloat, and the hundred and more persons that went down with the sinking ship might yet have been alive.

The monthly issue of the pilot-chart is on "Mercator's projection," so called, and includes the whole area between the sixtieth parallel of north latitude and the equator. The preparation of each edition involves three printings, namely, the "base," the "blue data," and the "red data."

I. The base may be termed the *constant* of the chart. It is printed with black ink, and includes only the permanent features of sea and shore. Coast-lines, islands, and the like, are clearly marked, also the general set of currents, the compass-card, explanatory tables, storm-cards, etc. The parallels of latitude and longitude divide the whole into squares of ten degrees on a side, and these again are subdivided into what are known as "ocean-squares," of five degrees each. To avoid confusion of lines, these smaller squares are not shown, but they are easily plotted by quartering the large parallelograms.

II. The "blue data," which are printed directly over and upon the permanent data, consist mainly of a meteorological forecast for the month following the date of issue. There are also included the principal sailing-routes and steamship-routes recommended for the month. These routes vary from month to month, according to well-established laws. Thus, in the summer months, the probable southern limit of icebergs is tolerably well known, and the steamer-routes are carried well southward of the danger-line. So in regard to the ordinary sailing-routes, it is probable that any vessel following the sailing directions of the pilot-chart will shorten her voyage by days or hours, according to the length of the trip. These sailing-routes are plotted from the logs and special reports of vessels, which have been accumulating in the Hydrographic Office since its establishment in 1829. The charts and circulars of information are sent free to masters of vessels, who, in return, are generally ready and glad to furnish special reports. In this way it has been possible to gather trustworthy details concerning almost every "ocean-square" in the North Atlantic. Some of the squares are, of course, more frequently crossed by vessels than others, and the average direction and force of the wind in these squares can be stated with reasonable certainty for every month in the year. A simple and ingenious system of symbols has been adopted for the charts, whereby the meteorological probabilities may be forecast for a given square by any one who takes the trouble to look. Of course, the forecasts are not absolutely certain of realization, but the chances are that they will not be far out of the way. The map on this page is a portion of the pilot-chart for different prevailing winds. The lines of long dashes show the course of recent storms, and the short ones the drift of derelict vessels with the dates when reported.

III. The "red data" embrace the very latest information that has been gleaned from all possible trustworthy sources up to the hour of going to press. The printed information covers the land-spaces of the chart, and includes a list of all recent changes of lights, buoys, beacons, etc., condensed special reports of noteworthy events, accounts of extraordinary storms, dangerous obstructions, and barometric comparisons. The symbolic data, also printed in red ink, show where drifting wrecks were last seen, and mark the erratic courses that they have followed as they have been encountered from time to time by different vessels. In like manner, water-spouts, drifting buoys, floating logs, and everything that is dangerous to navi-

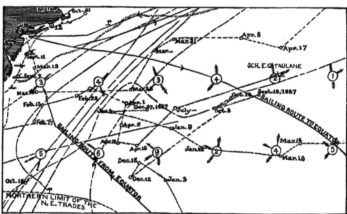

PILOT-CHART FOR OCTOBER, 1888.

October, 1888, lying eastward of New York. For typographical reasons the different colors of the data are not shown, but some idea of the completeness of the information is afforded. Each of the small circles with divergent arrows represents an ocean-square. The numeral within the circle represents the percentage of calms; 7, for instance, indicates that there are seven chances in one hundred that calms will be encountered. The arrows fly with the wind, showing its direction, and they indicate the direction of the prevailing winds. The small cross-bars show the average force of the wind, according to Beaufort's scale—the standard commonly used by seamen. Thus, four cross-bars indicate 4 of Beaufort's scale, namely, a "whole-sail" breeze, as it is called. The various lengths of the arrows indicate the greater or lesser frequency of the gation, finds a place on the pilot-chart, which may very probably serve as a warning to save life and property.

One of the most remarkable cases recorded on the charts is that of the extraordinarily named American schooner "Twenty-one Friends." She was abandoned at sea, and first reported as a derelict, March 24, 1885, about 160 miles off the mouth of Chesapeake Bay. The Gulf Stream carried her east-north-east about 2,130 miles, where she was reported in August. Thence she drifted easterly and southeasterly, and was last reported, Dec. 5, 1885, in the Bay of Biscay, having drifted 3,525 miles in eight months and ten days. During her wanderings, which were largely in the most frequented part of the ocean, she was reported twenty-two times, and the number of vessels that passed near her without seeing her can of course never be known. The dotted red line that represents her course on the pilot-chart is only one of many that cross and re-cross one another in all directions.

Wide as the ocean is, not a year passes without mysterious disappearances. Many of them are doubtless due to collisions with "derelicts," as they are termed by the Hydro-graphic Office, or with some of the many other drifting obstacles recorded by the "red data" of the pilot-charts.

The headquarters of the Hydrographic Office are in Washington, but the branch-office in New York, under the management of Lieut. V. N. Cottman, U. S. N., bears a most im-portant part in the active work of the bureau. This office occupies by courtesy a corner of the Maritime Exchange, situated on the lower floor of the great Produce Exchange building. Perhaps no better place could be found to keep the bureau in touch with the great ship-ping interests of the world. To the Maritime Exchange almost every ship-owner, captain, and underwriter goes on business or to give and receive information, and in this way many valuable facts are secured at the latest possible moment before going to press. It is some-what humiliating that such an important and beneficent Government work should be carried on in such narrow quarters; but, on the other hand, it is a high compliment to its usefulness that a great business organization like the Maritime Exchange should freely make room for it, where space is cramped at best, and where every square foot has a money value.

The official records show that during the year 6,739 vessels were visited; nautical infor-mation was furnished to 88,345 masters of ves-sels and others; 10,397 pilot-charts were gra-tuitously distributed, and 3,601 special detailed reports on the subject of marine meteorology were forwarded for use in the preparation of the pilot-charts.

The practical value of the branch-offices has led to their establishment in other seaports, and they are now in operation at Baltimore, Boston, New Orleans, New York, Philadelphia, and San Francisco. Every year there are be-tween 5,000 and 6,000 lives lost at sea, and, while with the increase of commerce this average is not unlikely to be maintained, the Hydrographic Office is engaged in a noble work in reducing the chances of disaster.

The popular notion that sailing-vessels are being driven from the seas by steam compe-tition is said by good authority to be erroneous. The sailing-tonnage of the world is, and prob-ably always will be, nearly or quite double that of steam. It is not generally realized that, in spite of the long period of depression to which the American merchant marine has been subjected in consequence of the war for seces-sion and because of congressional indifference, the tonnage of the United States is second only to that of Great Britain, and nearly double that of any other nation.

The publication of the pilot-charts was begun in December, 1884, and they have made their way by mere force of merit into the chart-rooms of all nations. The co-operation of the Signal Service and of the Naval Bureau was cordially given, and merchant-captains were quick to recognize the value of the undertaking, and became at once willing contributors to the stock of general information.

None of the other maritime nations have as yet attempted to follow the example of the United States in the issue of pilot-charts. That they will sooner or later do so is to be expected, but at present the United States Hydrographic Office may be pardoned for a reasonable degree of pride in its unique and original work.

AUSTRALIA, a continent surrounded by the Pacific Ocean, forming a part of the British Empire. The areas of the colonies occupying the Australian continent, with that of the neighboring island of Tasmania and the colony of Fiji, and their estimated population at the close of 1886, are as follows:

COLONIES.	Area.	Population.
New South Wales	310,700	1,001,996
Victoria.................	87,884	1,008,048
South Australia..........	903,425	312,758
Queensland	668,497	342,614
Tasmania	26,375	137,811
Fiji.....................	7,740	126,010
Total................	2,004,621	2,923,732

The estimated population of Australia and Tasmania on Jan. 1, 1888, was 2,943,364. In the whole of Australia the number of persons to the square mile is less than one. In Vic-toria it is 11·79; in New South Wales, 3·37; in Tasmania, 5·40. The total excess of arrivals over departures by sea for the whole of Aus-tralasia (including New Zealand) in 1887, was 64,856, showing a decrease as compared with the previous year of 5,671. The excess was greatest in New South Wales, where it was 23,516, whereas in South Australia the depart-ures exceeded the arrivals by 2,384. At the present rate of increase the population of the Australian colonies in the year 1900 will be 5,000,000.

The aggregate revenue of the Australasian colonies in 1885 was £23,750,000, and the aggregate expenditure, £25,250,000. In twelve years the revenue had increased 94 per cent., while the population had increased 54 per cent. The total debt was £70,250,000, or £23 3s. 9d. per head of population. Between 1851 and 1886 the value of the gold mined in all the colonies was £324,000,000, of which Victoria produced £217,000,000.

Agriculture.—The census tables show that 31 per cent. of the people of Australasia from whom statistics could be collected (about 40 per cent.), are engaged in agricultural occupa-tions, while 31 per cent. follow manufacturing and mining, 10 per cent. are employed in trade and transportation, 17 per cent. in professional occupations, and 11 per cent. as laborers. Of the last category a large percentage are employed in field-labor, while the inhabitants of the remote districts, concerning whom there are no returns, make the ratio of agricultural producers much larger than appears in the statistics. All the colonies have pre-emption laws to attract agricultural colonists, but most of them have been late in introducing the system in a practical shape, and slow in improving their first illiberal regulations, owing to the antagonistic interests and influence of the wool-growers. There is an apparent profit to the state in this policy, for while a large income is flowing into the exchequer from pastoral leases, the selling value of the public lands is constantly rising. Public men have recently, however, become impressed with the shortsightedness of a policy that has retarded the growth of the colonies, and with the liberalization of the land laws the democratic sentiment grows stronger and the money-power of the lease-holders is losing control over the policy of the Government. The graziers are nevertheless able, by fictitious entries and by the actual use of force, to keep settlers out of lands that are by law open to them. The laws of New South Wales provide for the selection of farms of 640 acres or less at the price of 20s. an acre, to be paid for by installments of 1s. an acre, interest being charged at the rate of 4 per cent.; also of grazing-farms of 2,560 acres, which, like the agricultural homesteads, must be fenced. Victoria allows deferred payments of 1s. an acre per annum on 320 acres at the same uniform price, on condition that improvements costing 20s. an acre shall be made on the land. South Australia sells to homesteaders a maximum area of 1,000 acres at the same price and terms of payment, requiring 10s. worth of improvements. Queensland grants homesteads of 160 acres for only 2s. 6d. an acre, payable at the rate of 6d. annually, if 7s. 6d. worth of improvements are made, and permits other selections of from 320 to 1,280 acres at no fixed rate of payment, but on the condition of improvements of the value of 10s. to the acre. South Australia and Western Australia each fix the maximum size of the settler's holding at 1,000 acres, the price being in the former 20s., and in the latter 10s, payable in twenty annual installments, each colony requiring improvements of 10s. an acre, while in Western Australia the land must in addition be fenced. In Tasmania settlers can take up 320 acres at 20s., paying 2s. a year without further conditions. The privilege of selecting land in this colony was taken away from fresh immigrants, whether they have paid their passages or have been aided by the Government, by an act that went into force in 1888.

The number of acres that had been sold up to the beginning of 1887, and the area that was not yet alienated in the several colonies, were as follows:

COLONIES.	Total taken up.	Remaining in crown.
Victoria..................	22,459,388	83,756,377
New South Wales.......	41,255,464	156,556,586
Queensland.............	10,995,374	416,667,956
South Australia.........	11,278,944	566,918,056
Western Australia.......	2,155,895	622,482,905
Total.................	88,205,060	1,796,856,860
Tasmania................	4,513,454	12,866,546
Grand total.........	92,718,514	1,808,723,406

Of the total area now cultivated in the Australian colonies 3,697,954 acres are devoted to wheat, yielding 45,541,592 bushels, of which about 9,000,000 bushels were available for export in 1886. Since then the home requirements have gained on production, leaving a smaller surplus.

The increase of live stock is shown by the following figures:

STOCK.	1870.	1884.
Horses..............	797,800	1,304,285
Cattle..............	4,712,918	8,464,370
Sheep..............	51,294,241	75,626,404
Pigs................	694,848	1,108,940

In 1872 the exports of wool from all these colonies amounted to 181,459,780 pounds, and in 1885 to 404,088,149 pounds. In 1886, however, owing to the damage by rabbits, the total production was only 398,541,828 pounds, the average per sheep being 4·62 pounds, and the total value, £16,218,846. The average value was 9¾d. a pound, and the total represented £4 16s. 4d. a head of the population.

The Rabbit Pest.—About twenty years ago the colonists of Australia and New Zealand, having grown prosperous during the period when the civil war had stopped the production of wool in the United States and caused the price to rise, began to found societies of acclimatization for the introduction and breeding of hares and rabbits, in order to enjoy the sports to which they had been accustomed in England. Every land-owner became anxious to secure ground-game on his own estate. Their satisfaction at finding the soil and climate adapted for the animals was of short duration; for at the rate of ten litters a year, instead of four and six, as in England, with no natural enemies to keep down their numbers, the rabbits, which grew to enormous size, in a few years began to affect seriously the sheep-industry and check agricultural operations. They consumed the herbage up to the doors of the farm-houses, destroyed orchards and vegetable gardens, caused the abandonment of land that had produced thirty bushels of wheat and sixty of barley to the acre, and ate the grass down to the roots, turning to desert immense tracts of pasture, and driving both sheep and farmers from entire sections of the country. Wealthy proprietors, after spending large sums in the effort to exterminate the vermin, ended by abandoning their estates. Shooting, trapping, hunting with ferrets, and poisoning with arsenic, strychnia, and phosphorus, destroyed them by millions, yet checked but slightly their multiplication. Wire-fences were early tried to confine them within bounds, but they burrowed beneath the in-closures without difficulty. Since then, how-ever, rabbit-proof fences have been devised, yet in some localities they have learned to leap over fences that were considered a per-fect barrier. The Government of New South Wales, for the purpose of protecting the popu-lous districts of the eastern division, proposes to build a wire fence, 400 to 500 miles long, from Albury to the borders of Queensland, at an estimated cost of £770,000. The Parliament of that colony offered a bonus of sixpence for every rabbit killed, and the payments under the act have increased in rapid progression, the sum called for in 1886 being £146,000, in 1887 about £250,000, and in 1888 it was cal-culated to amount to £500,000. The same Government has now offered a reward of £25,-000 to any person who shall invent an effect-ive process for the extermination of rabbits that shall not be injurious in its operation to horses, sheep, or other domestic animals. The inventor must demonstrate the efficacy of his method or process, which must be one that is yet unknown in the colony, at his own expense, and will receive the prize after a year's trial. Pasteur, who discovered remedies for the silk-worm disease and cattle-disease, communicated to the agents-general in London a method that he had already tried with success in France. This is to produce an epidemic of chicken-cholera, a disease that is very infec-tious and fatal among rabbits, though harmless to other animals, except poultry. In the spring of 1888 a party of French and English scien-tists went to Australia, taking with them infu-sions containing the microbes of this disease, with the intention of introducing the infection among the rabbits of various localities by lay-ing before them contaminated food, after which it was expected to spread spontaneously.

The Federal Council.—The British Parliament in 1885 authorized the formation of a council of the colonies, to meet at least once every two years for discussion and united action on matters of common Australian interest. The second meeting of the council was held at Ho-bart, Tasmania, the regular place for assem-bling, in January, 1888, terminating a three-days' session on the 19th. New Zealand, South Australia, and New South Wales had not joined the confederation, and the repre-sentatives of the other colonies discussed the means of inducing them to take part in the councils.

The New Hebrides.—The anxiety of the Aus-tralians on account of the French occupation of the New Hebrides islands abated when the French Government set a date for the with-drawal of the military force. A convention for a joint naval commission was signed on Nov. 16, 1887, and the French agreed to evacu-ate the islands within four months from that date. On Jan. 26, 1888, the English and French representatives signed at Paris a dec-laration defining the functions and powers of the Anglo-French Naval Commission, and es-tablishing regulations for its guidance. The commission consists of a president and two British and two French naval officers. It is charged with the maintenance of order and the protection of the lives and property of British and French citizens in the New Hebri-des. The presidency of the commission shall be held in alternate months by the command-ers-in-chief of the British and French naval forces present in the group. The regulations provide that in the event of a disturbance of peace and good order in any part of the New Hebrides where British or French subjects are found, or in case of danger menacing their lives or property, the commission shall forth-with meet and take measures for repressing disturbance or protecting the interests endan-gered, but not resorting to military force un-less its employment is considered indispensa-ble. If a military or naval force lands, it must not remain longer than is deemed necessary by the commission. In a sudden emergency the British and French naval commanders nearest the scene of action may take measures for the protection of persons or property of either nationality, in concert if possible, or separately when only one force is near the dis-turbed locality; but they must at once report to the senior officers, who shall communicate the report to each other, and immediately summon the commission. The commission has no power to interfere in disputes concerning title to land or to dispossess either natives or foreigners of lands that they hold in posses-sion, but it is charged with the police duties of stopping the slave-trade with the Kanakas and of preventing acts of piracy. The last of the French troops left the New Hebrides on March 15.

The Chinese Question.—Anticipations of an in-crease of Chinese laborers and of the effect of their competition on the condition of the white laboring class, have produced an exciting po-litical and international question in the Aus-tralian colonies. Two high commissioners, accredited by the Chinese Government, visited Australia in May, 1887, with the objects of learning the manner in which their country-men were treated and of advancing commercial relations between the two countries. They found little to complain of in the treatment of the Chinese, but questioned the rightful-ness of restrictions on immigration that have recently been introduced, especially the head-tax that is imposed in the various colonies. The Chinese ambassador in London, on Dec. 12, 1887, asked the explanation of this ex-ceptional legislation, and objected to it as a violation of treaty obligations. Chinese com-petition is most severe on the tropical northern shores of Australia, especially in the Northern

Territory of South Australia. The white residents of the territory in the spring of 1888 addressed a memorial to the Governments of New South Wales, Victoria, and Queensland, urging restrictive measures, in which they blamed their own Government for introducing the evil by importing Chinese laborers for the gold-mines at public expense, and afterward allowing them to squat on Government lands, to bid for Government contracts, and to vote as rate-payers. From that district they had advanced inland by way of Roper and McArthur rivers into Queensland and the South Australian ruby-fields. The Governor resident at Port Darwin in the beginning of April advised the authorities in Adelaide of information that had come to him, according to which vessels sailing under the Chinese flag were preparing to land a great number of Chinamen to work the ruby-mines. The Government has hitherto encouraged the immigration of Chinese into the territory, because they alone have developed the agricultural resources of the land, and are almost the only laborers who will long remain and work in the mines. Without them it would not have been possible to build the Port Darwin Railroad, which is expected to make the territory prosperous and self-supporting. There are at present 6,000 Chinese in the Northern Territory and only 600 Europeans. There is a regulation limiting the Chinese to a distance of 1,000 miles inland, but the South Australian Government proposes now to adopt in respect to the Northern Territory the same restrictions on immigration that prevail in the rest of Australia. The Chinese question is treated by Australian politicians as a workingman's question, although the workingmen there, unlike those of California, have not yet felt the direct competition of Chinamen in the trades, save in furniture-making, which the Chinese have learned and pursue on their own account. They have been very successful as gardeners, and have taught the English colonists many improvements in the cultivation of fruits and vegetables. The large cities are entirely supplied with such produce from their gardens. Once before, when the Chinese, who began to come in 1851, increased from 2,000 in 1854 to 42,000 in 1859, Victoria imposed a capitation tax on immigrants, which had the effect of reducing the Chinese population to 20,000 by 1863, when the poll-tax was removed. The first of the more recent measures was passed in 1881 in consequence of the action of the authorities of Western Australia, who were about to import Chinese laborers. The Chinese evaded the tax by procuring letters of naturalization, which their countrymen in Victoria began to take out in unusual numbers. While only 91 letters had been issued to Chinese during the eleven years preceding, there were 317 naturalizations in 1882, and the number increased to 1,178 in 1885. The arrivals by sea had fallen on the imposition of the head-tax from 1,348 in 1881 to 327 in 1882, and then increased at almost the same rate at which naturalization papers were taken out, until they reached 1,108 in 1886. In 1885 additional precautions were taken in connection with the forms of naturalization, in order to prevent fraudulent personation, and there was an increase of 438 in the number of arrivals in 1886 over the previous year, because the papers that had been purchased from Chinese residents in the colony would not be thereafter available. By the laws of Victoria and New South Wales, a poll-tax of £10 is payable on every Chinese immigrant, for which the master of the vessel is responsible, and no vessel is allowed to bring more than one immigrant for each 100 tons. Queensland collects a tax of £30 on each Chinaman landed, and limits the number that can be brought in a vessel to one for each fifty registered tons. Tasmania has adopted the restrictions that prevail in Victoria and New South Wales, and requires vaccination, as does South Australia, which, except for the Northern Territory, imposes a poll-tax of £10, but allows a passenger for every ten tons. In all cases Chinamen who are naturalized British subjects are exempt from the operation of the acts. In New Zealand an act was passed in 1882 restricting the immigration of any person born of Chinese parents, but this law has not received the approval of the home Government, and is inoperative. The number of Chinese in all the Australian colonies does not exceed 51,000, and is smaller than it was before the yield of gold began to fall off. Instead of increasing, the Chinese population is said to have diminished of recent years at the rate of 3 per cent. per annum. Living in compact colonies, they are conspicuous in the towns, though forming a very small fraction of the population. The only districts outside of the Northern Territory of South Australia where they outnumber the white population are the mining-camps and plantations of the torrid part of Queensland, where they have been introduced as laborers.

The question raised in the letter of Lew-ta-Ien, the Chinese Minister, was submitted to the premiers of the different colonies by Lord Salisbury. Sir Henry Parkes, replying for New South Wales, and D. Gillies for Victoria, urged the home Government to make a treaty similar to that which was being negotiated between China and the United States. Public meetings were held in the two colonies, much political feeling was aroused on the subject, street demonstrations took place, anti-Chinese riots were threatened, and, finally, the executives manifested their energy by prohibiting the landing of Chinamen and sending about four hundred back to China. The New Zealand Government, in order to accomplish the same object, declared all the ports of China to be infected districts. In the middle of May a severer Chinese restriction bill was introduced as a Government measure in the New South Wales Parliament, and passed the House of Assembly at once. It was made operative from the beginning of that month, and contained no exception in favor of immigrants who were then on the seas or in Australian ports. The act was virtually prohibitive, restricting the number of passengers to one for every 300 tons of the vessel carrying them, and raising the poll-tax to £100. Chinese were allowed to trade only in certain districts, and only five in each district. Naturalization of Chinese was forbidden. No Chinamen could mine without authority, and all must take out licenses annually to be allowed to reside in the colony. The Legislative Council refused to suspend the rules to hurry the passing of the bill, and meanwhile the supreme court granted writs of *habeas corpus* for the release of fifty Chinamen who were detained in Sydney Harbor, declaring their detention illegal. Two amendments of the Legislative Council, one keeping open the Supreme Court to persons who have claims for indemnity, and the other striking out the clause limiting the Chinese to certain areas and occupations, which latter was drawn in imitation of the existing regulations for foreigners in China, were accepted by the Assembly; and, when the Council stood firm, others were adopted by the Government, and finally accepted by the house, removing the features of the bill that were most flagrantly in contravention of the treaties, but not mitigating its severity as a restrictive measure. An intercolonial conference on the subject of restriction was held at Sydney. Its conclusions were embodied in the bill that was introduced in the Victorian Parliament, which opened its sessions on June 21.

The right of domicile of Chinamen in British dominions rests not merely on international law and the comity of nations, but on the first article of the treaty of Nankin, signed Aug. 29, 1842, which provides that there shall be peace and friendship between the sovereigns of Great Britain and China and between their respective subjects, " who shall enjoy full security and protection for their persons and property within the dominions of the other." This treaty was renewed by the one signed at Tientsin on June 26, 1858. The Pekin Convention of 1860 provides that Chinese in choosing to take service in British colonies are at liberty to enter into engagements and take passage in British vessels at the open ports, and that the Chinese authorities shall, in concert with the diplomatic representative of Great Britain, frame regulations for the protection of emigrants sailing from the open ports.

· · **Traffic in Arms with the Pacific Islanders.**—Great Britain has for three or four years been attempting to induce other nations to enter into an agreement prohibiting the sale of fire-arms and powder and of alcoholic liquors in the western Pacific. The consequences of supplying the natives with arms of precision are described in a blue-book on the subject. In some of the islands the people kill each other in family and tribal feuds. The effect on the relations of the natives with whites is pointed out by Bishop Selwyn, of Melanesia, in a letter to the Colonial Office. Any outrage committed by a white man is sure to be avenged by a volley fired at the next boat's crew, and then a man-of-war is sent to punish the islanders, and a party landed, often in the face of a heavy fire, thus " exposing valuable lives for the most trivial of causes." Recently the boats of the "Eliza Mary" were fired on from the New Hebrides, the natives mistaking the English vessel for the "Tongatabu," a labor vessel flying the German flag, which had recruited laborers for Samoa under the pretense that they were for Queensland.

Without waiting for a convention, the governments of Queensland and Fiji in 1884 prohibited the sale of fire-arms to natives. But these regulations are evaded by the labor agents who find that guns and powder are the only price that will gain laborers for the sugar-plantations. When an international agreement was proposed, France at once signified her willingness to enter into the compact if the other powers should do likewise. Germany returned no answer to the proposal. The United States declined to accede to the proposed regulations. Mr. Bayard in his reply recognized their general propriety and the responsibility of conducting such traffic under proper and careful restrictions, while signifying the intention of the Government of the United States for the present " to restrain its action to the employment, in the direction of the suggested arrangement, of a sound discretion in permitting traffic between its own citizens in the articles referred to and the natives of the western Pacific islands."

New South Wales.—The oldest of the Australian colonies has been self-governing since 1855. The present Governor is Lord Carrington, who entered on the office in December, 1885. The present ministry, which was constituted on Jan. 19, 1887, is composed of the following members: Premier and Colonial Secretary, Sir Henry Parkes; Colonial Treasurer, John Fitzgerald Burns; Minister for Lands, Thomas Garrett; Minister for Works, John Sutherland; Attorney-General, Bernhard Ringrose Wise, who received his appointment on May 27, 1887; Minister for Public Instruction, James Inglis; Minister for Justice, William Clarke; Postmaster-General, C. J. Roberts; Minister for Mines, Francis Abigail; President of the Executive Council, Julian Emmanuel Salomons, who represents the Government in the Legislative Council, but holds no portfolio.

The revenue in 1886 amounted to £7,594,300, of which £2,389,138 were derived from the state railways, £2,068,571 from customs, and £1,643,955 from the public lands, the sales amounting to £1,206,438. The revenue has increased from £22 per head of population in 1871 to £39 in 1886. The total expenditure in

000. Woolen-mills are not profitable in either colony, and recently the Victorian Parliament has added 5 per cent. to the duty on woolens, which was before 15 to 20 per cent.

There were 1,890 miles of railway in operation in 1886, which had been built at a total cost of £24,962,972. The earnings for the year were £2,160,070, and the expenses, £1,492,992. The telegraphs had 20,797 miles of wire, constructed at a cost of £666,028.

Rich silver-mines have been discovered near the border of South Australia in a district called Broken Hills. The ore-deposits extend over more than twenty miles, and many companies have been formed and mines opened. The report of a week's run of the principal mine in March, 1888, showed 1,709 tons of ore treated, and 73,659 ounces of silver extracted.

Victoria.—The Constitution was granted in 1854. Unlike New South Wales, which enjoys universal suffrage, Victoria limits the privilege of voting by a property qualification. The Governor is Sir Henry Brougham Loch, who was appointed on April 10, 1884. Sir William Foster Stawell was appointed Lieutenant-Governor on Nov. 6, 1886, and in the event of the death or absence from the colony of the Governor will assume the administration of the Government. The Cabinet is made up as follows: Premier, Minister of Mines, and Minister of Railways, Duncan Gillies; Chief Secretary and Commissioner of Water-Supply, Alfred Deakin; Attorney-General, H. J. Wrixon; Commissioner of Public Works, J. Nimmo; Minister of Justice, Henry Cuthbert; Commissioner of Trade and Customs, W. F. Walker; Commissioner of Crown Lands and Survey, J. L. Dow; Minister of Public Instruction, Charles H. Pearson; Minister of Defense, Sir James Lorimer; Postmaster-General, F. T. Derham; Ministers having portfolios with no offices attached, James Bell and D. M. Davies.

The public revenue for the year that ended June 30, 1887, was £6,733,867; the expenditure, £6,665,863. The yield of customs duties was £2,132,361; the income from railways, £2,453,345; from posts and telegraphs, £418,295; from crown lands, £587,100. The interest and expenses of the debt absorbed £1,272,591 of the total expenditure; the working expenses of the railroads were £1,364,400, of other public works £887,827, and of the postal and telegraph service £578,451; the cost of public instruction, £670,856. The revenue for the fiscal year 1887–'88 is estimated at £7,444,000, and the revenue £6,906,000. The public debt in June, 1887, amounted to £33,119,164, of which £25,404,847 were raised to build railroads, £5,004,791 for irrigation works, £1,105,557 for school-buildings, and £1,603,969 for other public works. Interest is at the average rate of 4½ per cent.

The estimated population on Jan. 1, 1888, was 1,036,118, having increased from 862,346 in 1881. The number of births in 1886 was 30,824; deaths, 14,952; marriages, 7,737. The death-rate in 1887 was 15·70 per 1,000. The excess of births over deaths in that year was only 6·4 per cent. Immigration has declined since the withdrawal of the aid given by the colony before 1874. In 1886 there arrived by sea 93,404 persons, against 76,976 in 1885, and departed 68,102, against 61,994. About half of the population live in towns. The capital, Melbourne, contained 390,000 inhabitants in 1887.

The imports in 1886 were £18,530,575, which was about the average value for five years; but the exports fell off from £15,551,758 in 1885 to £11,795,321 in 1886. The imports of wool amounted to £2,331,599, and the exports to £4,999,662; imports of timber, £1,170,539; of woolens, 892,868; of cottons, £1,027,674. The exports of gold were £1,954,326. The quantity of wool shipped to Great Britain was 93,889,887 pounds.

The state railroads in June, 1887, had a total length of 1,880 miles, besides 316 miles in course of construction. The cost of the lines was £26,479,206. The receipts in the year 1886-'87 were £2,453,087; the expenses, £1,427,116. There were 4,094 miles of telegraph lines, with 10,111 miles of wire at the close of 1886.

South Australia.—According to a law that went into force in 1881 the Legislative Council consists of twenty-four members, of whom eight retire every three years, and are replaced by new members, two from each of the four districts, who are voted for on one ticket by the whole colony. The House of Assembly numbers fifty-one members, who are chosen by universal suffrage.

The Governor is Sir William F. C. Robinson, who was appointed in February, 1883. The heads of the six ministerial departments are as follow: Premier and Treasurer, Thomas Playford, Chief Secretary, James Gordon Ramsay; Attorney-General, Charles Camden Kingston; Commissioner of Crown Lands, Jenkins Coles; Commissioner of Public Works, Alfred Catt; Minister of Education, Joseph Colin Francis Johnson.

The revenue in 1887 was £1,869,942; the expenditure, £2,165,245. The public debt, all of which was raised for public works, amounted, on Dec. 31, 1887, to £19,168,500.

The population on Dec. 31, 1886, was estimated at 312,758, comprising 162,980 males and 149.778 females. The number of births registered in 1886 was 11,177; deaths, 4,234; marriages, 1,976. The number of immigrants was 17,623; of emigrants, 25,231. At the end of 1887 the population was computed at 312,421, showing a loss of 337. The population of the Northern Territory is not included in these estimates. The death-rate in 1887 was 12·62 per 1,000.

The value of imports in 1886 was £4,852,750; of exports, £4,489,008. The exports of wool were valued at £1,955,207; of wheat and flour, £626,610; of copper and copper-ore, £230,868.

The mileage of railways in December, 1886, was 1,381. There were 417 miles in progress. The length of telegraph lines was 5,459 miles; since the length of wire·, 10,310 miles.

Queensland.—The Constitution dates from 1859, when the colony was separated from New South Wales. The members of the upper house are nominated for life; those of the popular branch are elected by restricted suffrage. The Governor, Sir Anthony Musgrave, was appointed in April, 1883. The composition of the ministry is as follows: Premier, Chief Secretary, and Vice-President of the Executive Council, Sir Samuel Walker Griffith, who is also Colonial Treasurer; Postmaster-General, Walter Horatio Wilson; Attorney-General, Arthur Rutledge; Secretary for Mines and Public Works, William Oswald Hodgkinson; Colonial Secretary and Secretary for Public Instruction, Berkeley Basil Moreton; Secretary for Public Lands, Henry Jordan; without portfolio, Sir James Francis Garrick.

On May 1, 1886, the colony contained 322,853 inhabitants, of whom 190.344 were males and 132,509 females. There were 10,500 Chinese and 10,165 Polynesians in the total, which does not include the aborigines, numbering about 12,000. The increase since the census of 1881 was 109,328, equal to 51·20 per cent. The estimated population on June 30, 1887, was 354,596. According to the census of 1886, 55,890 persons were engaged in agriculture, 51,489 in industries, 7,040 in professional pursuits, 19,790 in commerce, and 171,163 were wives, children, and domestic servants. The number of births in 1886 was 12,582; deaths, 5,575; marriages, 2,785. The population of Queensland on Jan. 1, 1888, was computed to be 366.940. The death-rate for 1887 was 14·56 per 1,000. The average density of population in 1884 was 0·478 per square mile, that in the northern division of 255,400 square miles being 0·24, in the central division of 223,341 square miles 0·17, and in the southern division of 189,751 square miles 1·16. The northern division contained 52,339 inhabitants, the central, 38,821, and the southern, 221,693.

The total value of imports in 1886 was £6,103,227; the value of exports, £4,933,970, of which sum £1,413,908 represent wool, and £855,510 sugar. Other exported products, besides gold, are hides. tin, preserved meat, silver-ore, and pearl-shell. There were 54,010 acres under sugar-cane in 1886, and of this area 34,657 acres yielded 58,545 tons of sugar valued at £1,125,284.

At the end of 1886 there were 1,555 miles of railway completed and 637 miles under construction. Their capital cost was £10,716,352; the receipts in 1886 were £640,845, and the running expenses £476,966.

The length of telegraph lines was 8,225 miles, with 14,443 miles of wire.

Western Australia.—The Government is administered by a Governor assisted by a Legislative Council, one third of its members being appointees of the Crown. The present Governor is Sir Frederick Napier Broome, who has held the post since December, 1882. The revenue in 1886 was £388,564, and the expenditure, £394,675. The revenue for 1887 was estimated at £404,190 and the expenditure at £478,189.

The population is growing rapidly by immigration. The number of inhabitants, exclusive of aborigines, was estimated at 39,584 at the end of 1886. There were 2,346 natives in service with colonists in 1881. The number of births in 1885 was 1,466; of deaths, 806. During that year 5,615 persons arrived in the colony, and 1,877 departed. On Jan. 1, 1888, there was a population of 142,488 in the colony, according to official statistics. The rate of deaths during the previous year had been 17·11 per 1,000.

The imports in 1886 were valued at £758,012; the exports at £630,393. The chief exports are wool and lead-ore. There were 202 miles of railroad in operation at the end of 1886 and 299 miles were building. The telegraph lines of the colony had a total length of 2,405 miles.

Tasmania.—The Constitution was first adopted in 1871, and amended in 1885. The Parliament consists of a Legislative Council of 18 members, elected by land-owners and the educated classes, and a House of Assembly of double that number, elected under a property qualification. The Governor is Sir Robert G. C. Hamilton, who was appointed in January, 1887. The Cabinet is composed of the following ministers: Premier and Chief Secretary, Philip Oakley Fysh; Treasurer, Bolton Stafford Bird; Attorney-General, Andrew Inglis Clark; Minister of Lands and Works, Edward Nicholas Coventry Braddon.

The area of Tasmania, which was formerly known as Van Diemen's Land, is 26,215 square miles, and the estimated population in December, 1886, was 137.211. The aborigines are entirely extinct. The number of births in 1886 was 4,627; deaths, 1,976; marriages, 985. There were 16.399 immigrants and 14,630 emigrants. On Jan. 1. 1888, the island contained 142,478 inhabitants. The deaths registered in 1887 were at the rate of 15·45 per 1,000.

The imports in 1886 were valued at £1,756,567 and the exports at £1,331,540. The chief articles of export are tin, wool, preserved and fresh fruits, gold, timber, hides, and bark.

The railroad mileage in 1886 was 303, while 138 miles were in course of construction in 1887. There were 1,772 miles of telegraph lines and 2,353 of wire at the end of 1886.

Fiji.—British sovereignty was proclaimed on Oct. 10, 1874. The colony is administered as a Crown dependency by a Governor who is also High Commissioner for the Western Pacific. The present Governor is Sir John Bates Thurston. Fourteen of the sixteen provinces are ruled by native chiefs. The colony consists of a group of islands, of which there are eighty that are inhabited, the largest being Viti Levu, with an area of 4,250 square miles, and the next largest Vanua Levu, which is 2,600 square miles in extent. The island of Rotumah was annexed in December, 1880. The native Fijians are Methodists in religion, except one twelfth who are Roman Catholics. The population of the colony in 1886 was 124,742, and consisted of 2,105 Europeans, 832 half-castes; 6,146 Indian coolies; 3,075 Polynesian indentured laborers; 110,037 Fijians, 2,321 natives of Rotumah, and 226 others. Among the Fijians there were 3,991 births and 4.908 deaths in 1886, and among Europeans, 77 births and 45 deaths.

The revenue in 1886 was £64,574 and the expenditure £78,133. The imports amounted to £230,629 and the exports to £283,496. The chief commercial products are sugar, copra, and bananas. The yield of sugar in 1886 was 11,716 tons grown on 10,543 acres, while 18,128 acres are devoted to cocoanuts.

AUSTRIA-HUNGARY, a dual monarchy in central Europe, composed of the empire of Austria, often called Austria proper, and otherwise known as the Cisleithan Monarchy, and the Kingdom of Hungary, called sometimes the Transleithan Monarchy, as the river Leis divides the two territories, and sometimes the dominions of the crown of St. Stephen. Austria is composed of numerous semi-autonomous states, and the provinces of Croatia and Slavonia, which form an integral part of the Hungarian Monarchy, possess in common a separate diet. The two monarchies alike owe allegiance to the House of Hapsburg, the head of which is Emperor of Austria and King of Hungary. They have a common army, with separate militia systems for the defense of their own borders, a single navy, and also a common diplomatic service, and they are united further in a customs union. The common ministry which looks after affairs of imperial concern is responsible to delegations from the two parliaments, which meet annually in separate halls, discussing all questions apart, but voting as one body in case of disagreement. Each delegation consists of 60 members. of whom 20 are chosen from the upper and 40 from the lower house of the respective legislatures.

The reigning monarch is Josef I, born Aug. 18. 1830, who was proclaimed Emperor of Austria on Dec. 2. 1848, and crowned King of Hungary on June 8, 1867, after the ancient Constitution was restored. The Crown-Prince is the Archduke Rudolf, born Aug. 21, 1858.

The Ministry of Foreign Affairs for the whole monarchy has been directed by Count G. Kálnoky de Köröspatak since Nov. 21, 1881. Lieutenant Field-Marshal Count Bylandt-Rheydt, who had been Minister of War since June 21, 1876, resigned on account of illness in March, 1888, and was succeeded by General Baron Bauer, previously commander of the Vienna corps. The Common Minister of Finance is Benjamin de Kállaky, who was appointed on June 4, 1882.

Area and Population.—The population of the Austro-Hungarian Empire on Dec. 31, 1886, was estimated to be 39,640,834. The population of Austria proper was 23,070,688, and that of Hungary 16,570,146. In Austria there were 11.188,462 males and 11.882,226 females in 1885; in Hungary at the time of the census of 1880 the males numbered 7,702,810 and the females 7,939,192.

The number of births in Austria proper in 1886 was 876,063; deaths, 678,458; marriages, 180,191; excess of births over deaths, 197,605. The births in Hungary in 1885 numbered 737,-110; deaths, 522,650; marriages, 165,169; excess of births over deaths, 214,460. Vienna contained in 1887, with its suburbs, 1,270,000 inhabitants, while Buda-Pesth, the capital of Hungary, had in 1886 a population of 422.557. That of Prague, the chief city of Bohemia, had at the last census 162,323; the sea-port Trieste, 144,844; Lemberg, 109,746.

The Occupied Provinces.—The area and the population in 1885 of the Turkish provinces of Bosnia and Herzegovina, the area of Novi-Bazar, which the Congress of Berlin likewise gave over to the military occupation of Austria-Hungary, though the civil administration was reserved for Turkey, and its population according to the enumeration of 1879, are shown in the following table:

PROVINCES.	Area in square miles.	Population.
Bosnia	16.200	187,574
Herzegovina	3.540	1,148,517
Novi-Bazar	3,522	168,000
Total	23,262	1,504,091

Of the inhabitants of Bosnia and Herzegovina 492,710 are Musselmans, 571,250 Orthodox Greeks, 265,788 Roman Catholics, and 5,805 Jews. There has been an increase of about 44,000 in the Mohammedan population since 1879. The Austrian military organization and obligatory service has, with some modifications, been extended to Bosnia and Herzegovina.

Commerce.—The total value of the exports of Austria-Hungary in 1886 was 698,632,273 florins, against 672,083,194 florins in 1885. The value of the imports in 1885 was 557,948,324 florins. The value of grain, pulse, and flour exported in 1886 was 95,445,185 florins; timber, 57,570,588 florins; sugar, 49,119,976 florins; instruments, watches, etc., 48,311,398 florins; wool and woolen manufactures, 47,-361,901 florins; live animals. 47,277,808 florins; animal products, 33,799,970 florins; beverages, 29,284,292 florins; fruit, nuts, hops, etc., 25,657,334 florins; leather and leather manufactures, 25,127,130 florins; glass and glass-wares, 19,446,478 florins; fuel, 19,324,-155 florins; flax, hemp, and other fibers, 19,-127,006 florins; wood and bone manufactures, 18,186,692 florins; cotton manufactures, 15,-184,411 florins; minerals, 12,839,295 florins; paper and paper manufactures, 11,914,262 florins; iron and iron manufactures, 10,546,811 florins; tobacco, 7,625,530 florins.

The value of the precious metals exported in 1886 was 1,797,057 florins, while the imports were 12,282,529 florins.

The following table exhibits the movement of imports in 1885, and of exports in 1886 across the frontiers of contiguous countries and by sea-ports:

COUNTRIES.	Imports.	Exports.
Germany	337,495.617	397,282,570
Trieste	87,881.560	99,763,181
Roumania	40.047.638	84,370,591
Flume and other ports	81,748,124	45,672.479
Russia	21,390,116	20,549,044
Italy	19,176,409	42,424,557
Servia	14,162,174	18,378,699
Switzerland	6,477,370	39,436,413
Montenegro	285,004	72,425
Turkey	284,312	687,814
Total	557,948,324	698,632,273

In Austria the area sown to wheat in 1885 was 1,194,059 hectares, yielding 17,015,680 hectolitres; 2,000,971 hectares were under rye, producing 27,984,480 hectolitres; 1,166,416 hectares under barley, producing 18,344,870 hectolitres; 1,829.047 hectares under oats; producing 33,389,650 hectolitres; 367,657 hectares under corn, producing 7,008,060 hectolitres. Vineyards covered 228,949 hectares. There is a considerable export of wine and barley, and in some years of wheat.

The agricultural returns of Hungary for 1886 give 4,070,360 hectares as the area devoted to wheat and rye, and the yield as 51,850,560 hectolitres. The crop of barley on 1,044,219 hectares was 13,343,882 hectolitres. Corn was cultivated on 1,914,159 hectares, and the crop amounted to 29,767, 527 hectolitres. Vineyards covered 363,562 hectares, and the value of the wine produced was 40,691,000 florins. There are large exports of horses, cattle, and sheep from both Austria and Hungary.

Railroads.—The railroads of Austria had a total length of 13,618 kilometres or 8,512 miles on Jan. 1, 1887. There were 3,596 kilometres of state lines, besides 84 kilometres that are worked by companies, 1.590 kilometres belonging to companies that are worked by the Government, and 8,348 kilometres owned and operated by private corporations. Hungary had 9,352 kilometres or 5,843 miles, making the total mileage for the empire 14,355. The state lines in Hungary had a total length of 4,243 kilometres and the lines of companies were 5,109 kilometres in length, including 402 kilometres that were operated in connection with the Government railroads.

The Post-Office.—The number of letters and postal cards carried in the Austrian mails in 1886 was 408,475,000; patterns and printed matter, 56.337,000; newspapers, 90,112,800. The receipts amounted to 26,367.103 florins, and the expenses to 22,619,102 florins.

The number of letters that passed through the Hungarian post-office in 1885 was 117,953,-000, inclusive of post-cards; patterns and printed inclosures, 17,756,000; newspapers, 47,031,000. The receipts were 10.281,768 florins, and the expenses 8,543.492 florins.

Telegraphs.—Austria had 24,442 miles of line and 64,050 miles of wire in 1886, and Hungary 11,215 miles of line and 41,520 miles of wire. There were 2,000 miles of line in Bosnia and Herzegovina. The number. of messages transmitted by the Austrian telegraphs in 1885 was 6,701,899. In Hungary 6,009,596 messages were dispatched in 1886.

Navigation.—The number of vessels entered at the port of Trieste in 1885 was 6,971, of 1,267,946 tons; cleared, 6,932, of 1.264,051 tons. The number entered at all Austro-Hungarian ports was 63,681, of 7,705,202 tons; the number cleared was 63,502, of 7,697,560 tons. Of the vessels 80 per cent. and of the tonnage 87 per cent. were Austrian. The mercantile marine consisted in 1886 of 61 ocean steamers, of 69,452 tons. 82 coasting steamers, of 14,491 tons, and 9,225 sailing-vessels of all kinds, of 228,044 tons.

The Army.—The active army and its reserve are under the control of the Imperial authorities, whereas the Landwehr and the Landsturm that has been recently organized under the law of 1886 are controlled by the ministry of national defense of each monarchy. The legal period of military service for every able-bodied man in the empire, except those who are exempt on account of family conditions, is three years with the colors, though the actual term is usually much shorter. The annual recruit is about 94,000 men. After completing the period of active service at twenty-three, they are liable for service in the reserves till the age of thirty, and then pass into the Landwehr for two years, and after that are enrolled in the Landsturm for ten years longer.

The standing army in 1887 numbered 267,-179 men. Its war strength was 805,904. The Austrian Landwehr numbered 152,632 men; the Hungarian Honved, 167,369; the Austrian Landsturm, 228,876; the Hungarian Landsturm, 212,246; the gendarmerie, 6,164; making the total military strength of the empire 1,573,191 men. exclusive of officers, who number 17,867 in time of peace, and 32,785 in war. The number of horses is 50,362 in peace, and 211,462 in war; the number of field-guns, 816 in peace, and 1,748 in war.

One full corps was armed with the new repeating rifle by the beginning of 1888, and in January the reservists were called out to be drilled in its use.

The Navy.—The iron-clad navy in 1887 consisted of 12 vessels. There were in process of construction the "Kronprinz Erzherzog Rudolf," a barbette turret-ship, 12 inches of armor, and the "Stephanie," a barbette belted ship of 5,100 tons, with 9-inch plates, and engines of from 8,000 to 11,000 horse-power.

There were 10 unarmored cruisers, 2 classed as frigates and 8 as corvettes, 6 torpedo-vessels, 16 coast-guards, 2 river monitors, and 38 torpedo-boats.

Common Finances.—The expenditure for the whole monarchy in 1887 was 123,855,414 florins, as compared with 119,724,748 florins in 1886. The budget estimates for 1888 make the expenditure for the common affairs of the monarchy 134,480,397 florins, of which 41,-510,397 florins are covered by the surplus revenue from customs and 90,149,426 florins are the contributions from the Austrian and Hungarian treasuries, the remainder being the receipts of the various ministries. The expenditure of the ministry of Foreign Affairs is estimated at 3,859,100 florins; expenditure on the army, 117,162,360 florins, of which 18,-619,775 florins are for extraordinary purposes; expenditure on the navy, 11,323,224 florins, including 2,145,147 florins of extraordinary expenditure; expenses of the Board of Control, 129,153 florins.

For the administration of the occupied provinces of Bosnia and Herzegovina in 1888 the expenditure was estimated at 9,076,218 florins, and the revenue at 9.147,189 florins. The cost of the army of occupation is placed at 4,424,-000 florins.

The Triple Alliance. — The defensive alliance between Austria and Germany was negotiated at Gastein and Vienna after the Berlin Congress by Prince Bismarck in consequence of the unfriendly attitude of Russia. Italy subsequently joined the league, and after its renewal in February, 1887, on the arrangement of details at the interviews between Prince Bismarck and Count Kálnoky and Signor Crispi at Friedrichsruh in September, the terms of the original Austro-German treaty of alliance were for the first time published to the world. The new treaty, except in minor particulars in respect to the military forces to be maintained and the conditions of mobilization, is officially declared to be identical with the other. The agreement is generally understood to be that if either Austria or Germany, without being the aggressor, is attacked by Russia, the combined military forces of the two empires will move against that power; if France should attack either Germany or Italy, she would be opposed by both those powers acting in common; and if France and Russia should combine to assail one or more of the allied powers, the entire military and naval strength of the league would be called into immediate action. The original treaty between the two emperors contained three clauses. The first binds each power to assist the other with its entire military force in case either should be attacked by Russia, the second engages each to observe an attitude of benevolent neutrality if its ally should be attacked by a power other than Russia, but to co-operate with its full military strength and only conclude a peace in common if Russia should join the attacking power either by active aggressions or by military measures involving menace. The third clause provides that the treaty should be kept secret, and only be communicated to a third power by mutual agreement, and contains an agreement that the Emperor Alexander should be informed, in case the Russian armaments assumed a menacing character, that an attack against one would be considered as directed against both.

The animosity of the Russian press against the Germans was rekindled by the publication of the part of the treaty that was directed against Russia. The Russian Government had been informed of the terms of the alliance some time before. The movement of Russian cavalry and other troops toward the German and Austrian frontiers had already begun, and there was a general expectation that war would break out in the spring. The Austrian delegations voted a large credit, and the cantonments of troops on the Galician border were soon more than equal to the Russian force, except in cavalry. The fortresses were strengthened, and 200,000 huts were built to quarter the soldiers along the frontier.

The coolness existing in the latter part of 1887 between Russia and Germany, and the menacing concentration of Russian troops on the Polish frontiers, were partly the result of an intrigue which was attributed, but not actually traced, to Orleanists, who desired to embroil Germany and France, and nearly succeeded in their purpose. The Czar came into possession of a letter of the date of Aug. 27, 1887, bearing the supposed signature of Prince Ferdinand of Bulgaria, addressed to the Countess of Flanders, and imploring her to induce her brother, the King of Roumania, and the King of the Belgians to use their influence, the one with the Czar and the other at the Austrian court, on his behalf. He would not, it is said in the letter, have accepted the Bulgarian throne except for the secret encouragement of Germany, and as a proof of this a document was inclosed under the same cover which was in the hand-writing of Prince Reuss, the German ambassador at Vienna, but unsigned. This conveyed assurances that if the Prince should decide to take possession of the throne of Bulgaria, Germany was not in the position at the moment to lend any official aid or encouragement, but that, however hostile the political acts of the German Government might appear, the time would come when it would reveal its secret sentiments and extend its open support. In a second letter to the Countess of Flanders complaint is made of the changed attitude of Germany, but in a third the Prince is made to say that, subsequent to the meetings at Friedrichsruh with Kálnoky and Crispi, Prince Bismarck had given him renewed assurances. The misunderstanding occasioned by this correspondence was dispelled when the Czar passed through Berlin in November, 1887, and stopped to pay his respects to his uncle,

the Emperor Wilhelm, after having declined a ceremonious interview at Stettin in September. Being brought face to face with the German Chancellor, he openly charged him with duplicity in encouraging Ferdinand's course secretly while officially condemning it as a contravention of the treaty of Berlin. Bismarck declared the communication purporting to have come from Prince Reuss to be a forgery, and on inquiry it turned out that the entire correspondence was fictitious. The concentration of Russian troops did not immediately cease after the exposure of the forged documents, but there was soon an abatement of activity, first on the part of Russia, and then on the part of Austria, so that the Government did not deem it necessary to call the delegations together to ask of them an additional credit. The assurance of the Czar that the military movements had no aggressive purpose did more than anything else to quiet the war alarm. Prince Bismarck, in a speech in the Reichstag, on the German army bill, delivered February 6, spoke of the fears that had arisen during the past year as having more reference to Russia than to France, and reviewed the situation and the relations between Germany and Russia. He expressed no fear on account of the massing of Russian troops on the German and Austrian frontiers, which he explained by saying, "I conclude that the Russian Cabinet has arrived at the conviction, which is probably well founded, that in the next European crisis that may take place, the weight of Russia's voice in the diplomatic Areopagus of Europe will be the heavier the further Russia has moved her troops toward the western frontier."

M. Tisza, in answer to an interpellation, said, on January 28, that Russia, in pursuance of a plan of military reorganization, had effected a large displacement of troops toward the Austrian frontier, which compelled Austria-Hungary to take measures for her protection.

Austria.—The present Austrian Cabinet, which was first constituted on Aug. 19, 1879, is composed of the following ministers: Minister of the Interior, Count Edward Taafe; Minister of Public Instruction and Ecclesiastical Affairs, Dr. Paul Gautsch von Frankenthurn, appointed Nov. 6, 1885; Minister of Finance, Dr. J. Dunajewski; Minister of Agriculture, Count Julius Falkenhayn; Minister of Commerce and National Economy, Marquis von Bacquehem, appointed July 28, 1886; Minister of Landesvertheidigung, or National Defense, Major-General Count S. von Welsersheimb; Minister of Justice, A. Prazak; without portfolio, F. Ziemialkowski.

The Reichsrath is composed of a House of Lords, consisting of hereditary peers, princes of the Church, and life-members, and an Elective Chamber, consisting at present of 353 deputies, representing towns, chambers of commerce and industry, and rural districts. The consent of the Reichsrath is necessary for all

Fejérváry; Ministry near the King's Person,
Baron Béla Orezy; Ministry of the Interior,
Baron Béla Orezy *ad interim*; Ministry of Education and Public Worship, Dr. August Tre-
fort; Ministry of Justice, Theophile Fabiny,
appointed May 17, 1886; Ministry of Communications and Public Works. Gabriel de Baross,
appointed Dec. 21, 1886; Ministry of Agriculture, Commerce, and Industry, Count Paul Scé-
chényi; Ministry for Croatia and Slavonia,
Coloman de Bedekovich.

The Hungarian Parliament consists of the
House of Magnates and the House of Representatives. The former was reformed in 1885,
and now comprises 51 ecclesiastical representatives, 50 life-peers, 16 state dignitaries and
judges who have seats by virtue of their offices,
20 archdukes, and 286 hereditary peers. The
representatives in the lower house are not
chosen by separate classes and voted for indirectly, as in Austria, but are elected by the direct vote of all male citizens over twenty years
of age who are possessed of a low property
qualification or belong to the educated class.

Revenue and Expenditure. — The Hungarian
budgets uniformly present a deficit, and in
some years the expenditures very largely exceed the revenue. The receipts of the treasury
for 1888 are estimated at 326,641,987 florins,
the ordinary receipts being 319,899,999 florins,
and the transitory revenue 6,741,988 florins.
About one fourth of the revenue is derived
from direct taxes on land, buildings, and incomes, and one fourth from excise and customs
duties and monopolies.

The total expenditure for 1888 is estimated
at 345,037,108 florins, of which 321,072,608
florins constitute the ordinary expenditures of
the Government, 2,267,426 florins are transitory expenditures, 13,771,079 florins are investments, and 7,925,995 florins are extraordinary common expenditures. The ordinary expenditures under the chief heads are as follow:
National debt, 115,599,408 florins; Ministry of
Finance, 56,594,439 florins; state raiways, 26,-
463,380 florins; quota of ordinary common expenditures, 21,770,061 florins; Ministry of Communications and Public Works, 14,249,038 florins; Ministry of Justice, 11,972,024 florins;
debts of guaranteed railroads taken over by the
state, 11,724,285 florins; Ministry of the Interior, 11,440,926 florins; Ministry of Agriculture, Industry, and Commerce, 10,897,823 florins; Ministry of National Defense, 8,484,547
florins; Ministry of Instruction and Worship,
6,591,340 florins; administration of Croatia,
6,054,134 florins; pensions, 5,314,701 florins.

The annual deficits since 1867 have accumulated into a debt that is nearly double the
special debt of Austria. It amounted in 1886
to 1,342,380,381 florins, while Hungary's share
of the common debt was 248,000,000 florins
more, the total charge absorbing 37 per cent.
of the revenue. The excessive expenditures
have been caused by the construction of railroads faster than the traffic warranted.

B

BALANCE OF POWER. In the modern European acceptation of the term, the balance of power is a mutual understanding among sovereign states that no one state may interfere with the independence of any other state. In this may perhaps be found the germ of that congress of nations to which many thoughtful minds look forward as the ultimate arbiter that shall render possible the disarmament of Europe. Neither the phrase itself nor the idea from which it springs, is of recent origin. The small states of ancient Greece combined first against the threatening domination of Athens and afterward against that of Sparta. More recently Europe, with show of systematic organization, combined to resist the aggressions of Spain, then against France, and still more recently against Russia. Most of the wars resulting from these combinations have probably tended to the establishment of international law and to the advancement of human liberty. Upon the whole, while the balance of power has perpetuated in Europe some of the relics of mediæval barbarism, it has tended to preserve a certain international equilibrium, which has probably prevented many wars, and has certainly preserved the autonomy of many of the lesser powers.

Conspicuous among the advocates of the balance of power is the Chevalier Friedrich Von Gentz (1764–1832). As head secretary at the Congress of Vienna and at the Conference of Ministers at Paris in 1815, he had abundant opportunities to study the opinions of leading European diplomatists. In 1806, while Europe was well-nigh subjugated by Napoleon, he published "Fragments upon the Balance of Power in Europe." He defines the term as "a constitution subsisting between neighboring states more or less connected with one another, by virtue of which no one among them can injure the independence or essential rights of another, without meeting with effectual resistance on some side, and consequently exposing itself to danger." His fundamental propositions are: 1. No state must ever become so powerful as to coerce all the rest; 2. Every state that infringes the conditions is liable to be coerced by the others; 3. The fear of coercion should keep all within the bounds of moderation; 4. A state that attains a degree of power adequate to defy the union should be treated as a common enemy.

Ferdinand III, Emperor of Germany is believed to have conceived the idea of a European Congress in 1640, with a view to terminating the Thirty Years' War and reconciling the hostile interests of church and state. After protracted negotiations the Congress of Münster or Westphalia assembled (July, 1643), the Catholics and Protestants being represented by their respective delegates, while France, Sweden, Venice, and the Pope were represented as mediators by embassadors. The negotiations extended over a period of five years, for it was not until October, 1648, that the treaty was signed. It is remarkable that such apparently hopeless differences could be reconciled at all, but the Treaty of Westphalia proved to be for Europe almost what Magna Charta was to England. It was in effect the first official recognition of interdependent rights among rival European interests. In other words, it inaugurated a balance of power. France and Sweden were appointed mediators, with the right of intervention in case of need to uphold the provisions of the treaty, and the hostile religious sects within the borders of Germany were guaranteed independence, while they were bound over to keep the peace. To Cardinal Mazarin was due the main feature of this compact, and although the unity and autonomy of Germany were injuriously curtailed, and French aggression was proportionately encouraged, the treaty was substantially recognized and enforced down to the time of the French Revolution.

Nevertheless, peace was not secured to Europe by the treaty. The ambitions of Louis XIV led to minor wars of conquest, and finally to a disastrous attempt at the forcible annexation of Spain, with a view to uniting the two kingdoms under Bourbon rule. The crisis had been foreseen, and an attempt was made to preserve the balance of power by an equable partition of the Spanish dominions. Such an arrangement was not at all to the taste of the aggressive Louis XIV, who, as has indeed been the case with almost all monarchs in all time, did not hesitate to break through such a flimsy barrier as a mere parchment treaty. His attempt to place his grandson upon the Spanish throne revived the question of the balance of power. It was evident that the union of France and Spain would be fatal to the existing schemes of dependence and independence. Among the disastrous consequences anticipated was the restoration of the Stuarts in England and the inevitable ascendency of Catholics all over Europe. England, Austria, and Holland, therefore, the three great Protestant powers of the period, with others of the lesser states, formed a coalition against Louis, and the war continued until 1715, when under the Treaty of Utrecht the relations of all the European states were carefully readjusted, Philip V retaining the Spanish crown, and every precaution being taken to prevent a possible union of France and Spain under one sovereign, since such a union would at once destroy the equilibrium. Although these elaborate provisions failed effectually to dissociate the two branches of the house of Bourbon, and although the Treaty of Utrecht was obnoxious to England, the peace of Europe was secured for thirty years.

Until about the beginning of the nineteenth century, Russia was substantially ignored by the European family of states. France, Spain, Sweden, Austria, and Holland, with occasional intervention on the part of Great Britain, had preserved such an equilibrium as seemed good to them, and none of the smaller states had been arbitrarily absorbed by their more powerful neighbors. During these years, Peter and Catherine of Russia had developed the resources of their empire, and Frederick II had raised Prussia from a subordinate to an independent place. Conquests of the great maritime powers had extended colonization to Asia and India. The United States of America had secured independence, and Poland had been forcibly partitioned by Russia, Austria, and Prussia. The partition of Poland (1772) was but the first of a series of events that culminated in the French Revolution. It was the first deliberate and gross violation of the system of treaties based upon that of Westphalia, and with the French Revolution all pretense of preserving the balance of power on its old lines was abandoned. Small states were overpowered and annexed, and Europe saw her ancient boundaries shifted to meet the new conditions.

To thoughtful observers, like the Chevalier Gentz, and to the leading statesmen of the period, including those of Great Britain, the temporary nature of then existing conditions seemed evident. The meteoric career of Napoleon, even when he might almost have written himself the ruler of Europe, did not mislead these master-minds. They steadily held that lasting peace could be regained only through the restoration of national rights, and that this could only be effected by combining against the common enemy. After many discouraging failures, a coalition was at last formed, resulting in the overthrow of Napoleon.

The Congress of Vienna met in November, 1814, and remained in session until June, 1815. Here, for the first time, the most powerful and distinguished of living sovereigns and statesmen met, prepared to make mutual concessions, with a view to a lasting peace. Even France, whose ambition had plunged Europe into prolonged war, was admitted an equal to the council, M. Talleyrand representing her interests. In the then existing condition of European affairs, certain relics of mediævalism survived, and certain provisions that afterward proved insupportable were embodied in the treaty.

The fact that all the contracting parties were more or less dissatisfied with the results of its deliberations, goes far to show that selfish interests were in general overruled. In point of fact, the treaties then signed were observed in the main for the better part of half a century. They survived the revolution of 1848, and though modified in some quarters, and even abrogated in others, they may be said to have survived in many of their main features until the great German wars of 1866 and 1870.

At Vienna, in 1815, the first international constitution was framed, defining the boundaries of European states, all the contracting parties agreeing thereto, guaranteeing the independence of the small principalities and free cities, as well as incorporating in its provisions the Constitution of the German Confederation. Every state in Europe had the right to appeal to the rest in case of infringement, and it seemed, for a time, as though the foundations had been laid for permanent peace. In the course of time several appeals were made to the high contracting parties, and many international disagreements were averted by the wise measures adopted in conferences convened under the provisions of the treaty. Thus was inaugurated the nearest approach to an actual balance of power, and during the long period of general peace that followed, the European world certainly made rapid progress in the direction of universal amity.

But with advancing years, complications were developed; there were wheels within wheels. Such compacts can only be maintained while all parties are measurably satisfied with the working of the system, and the northern powers formed what was known as a Holy Alliance among themselves, otherwise an alliance offensive and defensive, unifying their interests and binding themselves to act together in all emergencies. It was held, and not without reason, that under the Treaty of Vienna, the allied powers could interfere arbitrarily in the internal affairs of states, on the ground that the peace of Europe was endangered thereby. Conferences were held at Aix-la-Chapelle (1818), Carlsbad (1819), and Troppeau (1820), and restrictive measures were adopted, which were obnoxious to some of the treaty powers. At Verona, in 1822, the Duke of Wellington, as the representative of Great Britain, declared that his Government could no longer countenance the actions of an alliance that interfered so intimately with the internal affairs of individual states. England preferred isolation to any such tyrannical combination. Thus was inaugurated the principle of non-intervention, on the strength of which England, in 1852, declined to act with Prussia in preventing the Napoleonic restoration in France. On the same ground, England joined France in protesting against the invasion of Schleswig, and opposed alone the annexation to France of Savoy and Nice. The traditions of Vienna were thus gradually ignored, and had become practically a dead letter when, in 1863, Napoleon III proposed a new congress for the readjustment of the balance of power. The proposition was rejected, largely through the refusal of England to participate.

In spite of the still subsisting guarantees of the powers, Denmark was compelled to surrender her choicest provinces in the Schleswig-Holstein campaign—a federal execution, as it was called, by the German powers, and in 1866 Austria was driven from the confederation in a startlingly energetic incursion by the Prussians. This was the first war of any magnitude undertaken in defiance of possible interference under the compact of Vienna, and the humiliation of France followed as a natural consequence four years later. Taking advantage of the crisis in Western Europe, Russia abrogated the pledges made at the end of the Crimean war, and thus passed away almost the last vestige of the Treaty of Vienna.

At the present time no open alliances can be said to exist among any of the European nations. The balance of power, as it was understood in 1815 and the following years, has disappeared, though its influence is no doubt still indirectly felt. The autonomy of Switzerland and Belgium would probably be defended by a general alliance, should it be seriously threatened, but the main idea of all the great powers at present is to make an efficient soldier of every able-bodied man. To all appearance, the military power of the German Empire far exceeds that of any other single state, a condition of affairs wholly at variance with the principles laid down at Vienna, but against which no power on earth is at present entitled to remonstrate.

That a third step toward permanent peace and possible disarmament will ere long be taken, may probably be counted upon with some degree of confidence, and if the lessons taught by Westphalia and Vienna are permitted to have their due effect, the third general congress may effect still more lasting and beneficial results.

BAPTISTS. The "American Baptist Year-Book" for 1888 gives statistics of the Baptist churches in the United States, of which the following is a summary: Number of associations, 1,231; of ordained ministers, 20,477; of churches, 31,891; of members, 2,917,315; of Sunday-schools, 15,447, with 116,453 officers and teachers, and 1,126,405 pupils; number of additions by baptism during the year, 158,373. Amount of contributions: for salaries and expenses, $5,849,756; for missions, $905,673; for miscellaneous purposes, $1,961,332. Value of church property, $48,568,686. In all North America, including the United States, Canada, Mexico, the West Indies, etc., are returned 1,305 associations, 32,861 churches, 21,071 ministers, 3,031,845 members, and 165,835 baptisms; in South America (Brazil), 6 churches, 14 ministers, 175 members, and 30 baptisms; in Europe, 80 associations, 3,506 churches, 2,592 ministers, 387,645 members, and 6,013 baptisms; in Asia, 8 associations, 718 churches, 558 ministers, 68,618 members, and 3,287 bap-

tisms; in Africa, 3 associations, 88 churches, 85 ministers, 3,247 members, and 142 baptisms; in Australia, 6 associations, 175 churches, 131 ministers, and 15,189 members; total for the world, 1.402 associations, 37,354 churches, 24,451 ministers, 3,506,719 members, and 175,-307 baptisms.

Of the Baptist educational institutions in the United States, seven theological institutions return 48 instructors and 579 pupils; 30 universities and colleges, 255 instructors and 4,012 pupils, of whom 687 were preparing for the ministry; 30 seminaries for the education of young women exclusively, 276 instructors and 3,597 pupils; 42 seminaries and academies for young men and for pupils of both sexes, 232 instructors and 4,125 pupils, of whom 237 were preparing for the ministry; and 19 institutions for the colored race and Indians, 157 instructors and 5,408 pupils, 342 of whom were preparing for the ministry. The total value of the grounds and buildings of these 128 institutions was $9,118,096; and the amount of their endowments, so far as was reported, was $8,763,385. Twelve Baptist homes, ministers' homes, and orphanages, with a total valuation of $553,000 of property, had the care of 626 inmates. Four of them possessed endowments to the amount of $92,792.

I. American Baptist Societies.—The statistics of the women's Baptist societies for 1887 were as follow: Woman's Baptist Foreign Mission Society (Boston); receipts, $64,668. The society sustained 29 missionaries and 102 schools, in which 3,428 pupils were enrolled; Woman's Baptist Foreign Missionary Society of the West (Chicago); receipts, $32,114; missionaries supported, 24; Women's Baptist Home Mission Society (Chicago); receipts $35,691; missionaries (in the United States and Mexico), including Bible women and helpers, 71. The society sustains a training-school at Chicago, from which 11 pupils had been graduated; Woman's American Baptist Home Mission Society (Boston); receipts, $23,573. It supports teachers at schools in the United States, Indian Territory, Mexico, and Alaska.

The tenth annual meeting of the Woman's American Baptist Home Missionary Society, the object of which is the education of women and children among the freed people, Indians, and immigrants, was held in Worcester, Mass., in May. The receipts had been $30,805, and the expenditures $26,935.

Publication Society.—The sixty-fourth annual meeting of the American Baptist Publication Society was held in Washington, D. C., May 18. The Hon. Samuel Crozer presided. The total receipts of the society for the year in all of its departments had been $582,491. A reserved fund for the purchase of machinery and enlargement of business had been set aside from the profits of the book department during previous years, which now amounted to $87,463. The cash receipts in the book department had been $449,882, and the entire business done by it, including sales on credit, amounted to $502,702. One hundred and twelve new publications had been added to the list, and 29,307,797 copies of all publications—books, pamphlets, tracts, and periodicals, new and old—had been printed : of these, 28,115.225 were "graded helps" and papers for Sunday-schools. The receipts in the missionary department, including the balance on hand at the beginning of the year, had been $105,190. Eighty-seven missionaries had been employed in the United States, two in Germany and Sweden, and five special missionaries—native Armenians — in the Turkish empire. These returned 42 churches constituted, 299 Sunday-schools organized, and 934 persons baptized. The receipts for Bible work had been $29,439, while $21,482 had been expended for the purchase of Scriptures and for appropriations of Scriptures for the Missionary Union and the Southern Baptist Convention.

Home Mission Society.—The fifty-sixth annual meeting of the American Baptist Home Mission Society was held in Washington, D. C., May 16. The Hon. C. W. Kingsley presided. The total receipts during the year had been $351,596. Among the matters of special note which had marked the year's history of the society were mentioned in the report, the completion and occupancy of the mission headquarters in the city of Mexico and the enlargement of the work in that republic; the completion of a subscription of $15,000 for Chinese mission headquarters in San Francisco, and the purchase of a site on which a building is being erected; the securing of a larger amount thrn usual for church-edifice work; the appointment of an additional superintendent of missions for a new Western district, and of a district secretary for the Southern States; the beginning of mission work among the Poles and Bohemians in the United States; and the adoption of a new school for Indians in the Indian Territory. Missionary operations had been conducted in 45 States and Territories, and in Ontario, Manitoba, British Columbia, Alaska, and three Mexican states. The whole number of laborers employed had been 743. French missionaries had labored in 6 States; Scandinavian in 16 States and Territories; and German in 18 States and Territories, Ontario, and Manitoba; 161 persons had labored among the foreign population, and 217 missionaries and teachers among the colored people, Indians, and Mexicans; 1,594 churches and out-stations, returning 30,974 members, had been supplied; 2,886 members had been received by baptism; 137 churches had been organized; and 734 Sunday-schools, returning 47,410 attendants, had been under care. In the church-edifice department, 88 churches had been aided by gifts or loans, or both; the aggregate amount of gifts being $32,737, and of loans, $20,510. With the aid of these sums, property valued at about $200,000,000 had been secured to the denomination. Thirty-

three churches had paid off their loans; 232 loans were outstanding; and the whole number of churches aided by gifts and loans had been 931. The amount of the loan fund was $120,555; and the receipts for the Benevolent Fund had been $45,305. The schools included 12 incorporated and 6 unincorporated institutions, in which 137 teachers had been engaged and 3,741 pupils enrolled; 17 colored schools returned 115 teachers, 14 of whom were colored, with 2,995 pupils, 318 of whom were studying for the ministry, 980 preparing for teachers, and 36 medical students. Industrial education had been systematically imparted at 8 institutions, and more or less attention given to it at the others. The three schools for the Indians in the Indian Territory returned 232 pupils. The Indian University, near Muscogee, had 86 students enrolled. The third school, a new one for the society, was at Sa-sak-wa, in the Seminole nation. Six schools, with an aggregate enrollment of 250 pupils, were conducted in Mexico.

Missionary Union.—The seventy-fourth annual meeting of the American Baptist Missionary Union was held in Washington, D. C., beginning May 21. The Hon. George A. Pillsbury, of Minnesota, presided. The receipts of the year, from all sources and for all purposes, had been $411,385; the appropriations for current expenses had been $390,586; and $20,550 had been added to annuity funds and permanent accounts. A committee which had been appointed at the previous annual meeting to consider and report upon the advisability of accepting from the Publication Society the Baptist missionary work which had been begun in Turkey reported a unanimous agreement of its members that it could not recommend acceptance. "The claims of other fields, in still more pressing need, and brighter still in promise," it represented, "are more, far more, than enough to employ the utmost resources at the command of the Missionary Union." A communication was ordered made to the officers of the Congo Free State expressing the conviction of the members of the Union that the welfare and spiritual prospects, and even the continued existence, of the native population of that state require immediate suppression of the traffic in intoxicating liquors within its borders; and a request to be addressed to the Government of the United States to use its influence to secure the same result in the Congo Free State, other parts of Africa, and the West Pacific islands. A recommendation was made that a fund of $100,000, to be called the "Judson Centenary Fund," be raised by individual subscriptions of not less than $1,000 each, to be expended in sustaining the foreign missions. From the missions to the heathen—the Burmese, Karen, Shan, Kachin, Chin, Assamese, Garo, Naga, Telugu, Chinese, Japan, and Congo missions—were returned 67 stations, 881 out-stations, 262 missionaries, 826 native preachers, 98 Bible-women, and 257 other native helpers

—in all 1,443 missionary laborers, 642 church-es with 61,062 members, 252 Sunday-schools with 7,311 pupils, 754 schools with 702 native teachers and 17,504 pupils, and 562 churches and chapels. The total of contributions for churches, schools, and general purposes, was $44,583; value of missionary property, $19,852. From the European missions—in Sweden, Ger-many, Russia, Denmark, France, and Spain—were returned 161 ordained and 307 unordained preachers, 654 churches, and 66,146 members. The whole number of baptisms during the year was 10,602—5,532 in the European, and 5,070 in the heathen missions. In the special work of translation, revision, and printing of Scriptures, the revision of the Shan New Tes-tament had been completed, and a new edition partly stereotyped, while the Old Testament was ready for printing. The Sgau Karen Old Testament was under final revision and prepara-tion. A new and revised edition of the Bur-man Bible was going through the press. The translation of the Old Testament into Assamese was nearly done, and the New Testament was under revision. Translations of the New Tes-tament into the Lhota Naga and Angami Naga dialects had been begun. Several missionaries were engaged in translating the New Testa-ment into different languages of the Congo. The Rev. R. H. Ferguson had been commis-sioned to reduce the Kachin language to writ-ing, with a view to the translation of the Bible into it. The missions in Russia are among nominally Lutheran populations of Germanic origin—as the Letts and Esthonians—the churches among whom were gathered mostly by agents of the German Committee of the Union.

Southern Baptist Convention.—The Southern Baptist Convention met at Richmond, Va., May 11, 745 delegates being present. The convention is composed of delegates—laymen and ministers—from each Southern State. It is purely a missionary body, having no eccle-siastical jurisdiction or control of the churches, and does its work through the Foreign Mis-sion Board, which has its office at Rich-mond, and the Home Mission Board, having offices at Atlanta, Ga. The former president of the convention, the Rev. P. H. Mell, D.D., Chancellor of the University of Georgia, who had presided over the meetings for fifteen years in succession, had died during the year. The Rev. James P. Boyce, D.D., President of the Southern Baptist Theological Seminary, was chosen president. The Home Mission Board had received during the year $48,023, while $41,154 had been raised for the same purposes by co-operative bodies (State and local boards). It had employed 287 missionaries, occupied 1,114 churches and stations, and returned 4,857 persons baptized, 431 Sunday-schools organized, with 17,240 teachers and pupils, 306 churches constituted, and 64 houses of worship built at a cost of $54,068. The board had sustained a mission in Cuba, in which, in a little more than two years since the first church was or-ganized, 1,100 persons had been baptized, 17 missionaries were employed, 9 native preachers had been engaged, 6 churches and 19 stations had been established, and $4,640 had been contributed by the people in one year. The Foreign Mission Board had been incorporated. It returned an income of $86,385, and had expended $82,775. Its missions were in Mexi-co, Brazil, Italy, West Africa, and northern, central, and southern China. The women's missionary societies had contributed $18,000 in aid of the work. The various committee reports on missionary work urged enlargement of foreign mission enterprises, enforced the im-portance of labors among the colored people of the South, and commended the work among the Germans, Chinese, and other foreigners in the United States, and especially that in Cuba. A collection of $3,600 was taken for sending additional missionaries to Mexico. The two boards were instructed to appoint a committee to confer with a committee representing the Northern Baptist societies, "not with a view to organic union," but to consider what can be done to adjust their several fields and agencies, so as not to have conflict of agencies. The in-vested funds of the Theological Seminary were shown to amount to $315,000, and the real es-tate to $200,000. The classes included 157 stu-dents.

German Baptists.—The German Baptists of the United States are organized into five confer-ences — the Eastern, Central, Northwestern, Southwestern, and Texas Conferences. These conferences returned in 1887, 13,187 members, 930 baptisms, and $127,742 of contributions for missionary and other purposes.

Colored Baptists.—The Colored Baptists of the United States are organized in three societies. The Baptist African Missionary Convention of the Western States and Territories (formerly the Baptist General Association of the Western States and Territories), formed in 1873, is in-terested in mission work in Africa, where it has a mission at Mukimvika, on the Congo. The fourteenth annual meeting, held in 1887, was attended by representatives of churches and associations from Illinois, Iowa, Kansas, Missouri, Nebraska, and Indiana. The society co-operates with the American Baptist Mis-sionary Union.

The Baptist Foreign Missionary Convention of the United States, organized in 1880, at its meeting in 1887 returned its receipts at $4,069, and its expenditures at $4,018. Ten States were represented in the roll of its members. It has a mission among the Vey tribe on the borders of Liberia.

The American National Baptist Convention was formed in 1886. The corresponding sec-retary, Rev. Richard de Baptiste, who had spent two years in gathering the general sta-tistics of the colored Baptists, reported in 1887 that 26 institutions of learning were pro-vided for them, with which were connected

152 teachers, and 3,609 pupils; that there were 19,375 volumes in the libraries of 17 of these institutions, and that the total value of 23 of the institutions was $1,072,140. The religious statistics of these people were as follow: number of district associations, 300; of churches, 10,068; of ordained ministers, 6,605; of members, 1,155,486; of Sunday-schools, 3,304; with 10,718 officers and teachers, and 194,492 pupils; number of baptisms last reported, 48,-212; value of contributions—for salaries and expenses, $230,445; for missions, $23,253; for education and other objects, $47,900. Forty journals are edited and controlled by colored Baptists.

The meetings of all of these societies for 1888 were held in succession at Nashville, Tenn., beginning on the 18th of September. They were followed by a special meeting of the American Baptist Home Mission Society to consider its work among the colored people. At a united session of the African Missionary Convention of the Western States and Territories and the Foreign Missionary Convention, a plan was reported for the unification of the foreign missionary work of the two bodies, and for co-operation with the Missionary Union. It provided for the formation of a new society, to be known as the American Baptist Foreign Mission Convention, into which the existing foreign missionary societies should be merged; and for co-operation with the Missionary Union on a plan which should allow the independence of each society while securing mutual consultation and assistance. The plan received favorable consideration, and was referred to the Executive Board of the societies and churches for discussion during the year. At the meetings of the National Convention and the Home Mission Society, papers and addresses were presented respecting the common objects in which the two bodies were interested. A resolution was adopted by the former body pledging co-operation with the American Baptist Home Mission Society in its work for the colored people.

II. Free-Will Baptist Church.—The statistics of this church, as tabulated in the "Free-Will Baptist Register and Year-Book" for 1888, give the footings: Number of yearly meetings, 48; of quarterly meetings, 183; of churches, 1,531; of ordained ministers, 1,314; of licensed preachers, 167; of members, 82,686. The latest general statistics of other liberal Baptist bodies, similar in faith and practice to the Free-Will Baptists, are those given in the "Liberal Baptist Year-Book" for 1884, and are summarized as follows: Original Free-Will Baptists of North Carolina, 8,232; other Free-Will Baptist Associations in the United States (besides those affiliated with the Free-Will Baptist Church), 4,958; General Baptists, 13,-225; Separate Baptists, 6,329; United Baptists, 1,400; Church of God, 40,000 (see "Church of God" in another part of this

article); Free Christian Baptists of New Brunswick, 10,777; Free Baptists of Nova Scotia, 3,415; making, with the members of the Free-Will Baptist Church, 171,022 of similar faith.

The educational institutions of the Free-Will Baptist Church include Hillsdale (Mich.), Bates (Lewiston, Maine), Rio Grande (Gallia County, Ohio), Storer (Harper's Ferry, W. Va.); Ridgeville (Ind.), and West Virginia (Flemington, Taylor County) colleges, and six preparatory seminaries. The reports of the benevolent societies are for 1887. The receipts of the Education Society were $3,600; and the total amount of its three invested funds was $9,908. The receipts of the Home Mission Society were $8,108; its permanent fund amounted to $11,-125. The sum of $5,667 had been raised and expended for home missionary work by five yearly meetings and the Central Association. The society sustained missions at Cairo, Ill., Lincoln, Neb., Oakland, Cal., Worcester, Mass., Harper's Ferry, W. Va. (with Storer College), and in the Western States. The church at Hampton, Va., had become self-supporting. The receipts of the Foreign Missionary Society were $15,244; the amount of its Permanent fund was $10,103; of its Bible-school fund, $18,-360; and of the Bible-school hall fund, $63. Its missions, which are in Bengal and Orissa, India, returned 24 missionaries; 578 communicants, with 37 additions by baptism; 2,672 Sunday-school pupils; and a native Christian community of 1,229 persons. In the day and other schools were 3,628 pupils, of whom 407 were classed as "Christian," 1,481 as "Hindu," 118 as "Mohammedan," and 1,622 as "Santal."

III. The Brethren, or Tunkers.—The annual meeting of the Brethren, or Tunkers, was held in North Manchester, Ind., in May. The convention declared against the wearing of mustaches and the trimming of hair by barbers; cautioned members in respect to taking oaths; and warned members living in Western States against writing flattering reports concerning their crops and financial success unless they were sustained by facts. It also reaffirmed its previous declarations against the use of tobacco; decided that applicants for membership should promise to refrain from the habit; and directed that ministers who chew or smoke should not be allowed to assist in church adjudications. An arrangement was made for giving help to poor congregations in Denmark and Sweden.

IV. Church of God.—The distinctive doctrines of the Church of God, as given in brief in its "Year-Book" for 1888, are:

That the believers in any given locality, according to the divine order, are to constitute one body; that the division of believers into sects and parties, under human names and creeds, is contrary to the spirit and letter of the New Testament Scriptures, and constitutes the most powerful barrier to the success of Christianity.

That the believers of any given community, organized into one body, constitute God's household or family, and therefore should, according to the teachings of the New Testament Scriptures, be known by the name of "Church of God."

That the Scriptures, without note or comment, constitute a sufficient rule of faith and practice; that creeds and confessions of faith tend to divisions and sects among believers.

That there are three ordinances of a representative character, equally binding upon all believers, namely: immersion in water in the name of the Father, the Son, and the Holy Ghost; the washing of the saints' feet (see Christ's example, precept, and promise); and the eating of bread and drinking of wine in commemoration of the sufferings and death of Jesus.

The "Year-Book" gives the statistics of sixteen annual elderships, as follow:

ELDERSHIPS.	When organised.	No. of ministers.	No. of members.
East Pennsylvania	1830	77	5,778
Ohio	1836	56	4,000
West Pennsylvania	1844	36	2,000
Indiana	1846	32	1,200
Iowa	1848	23	1,000
Illinois	1853	40	1,600
Michigan	1850	22	400
German	1854	5	200
Southern Indiana	1857	16	1,900
Texas, Arkansas, and Indian Territory	1857	27	*900
Kansas	1871	27	700
Maryland and Virginia	1872	17	950
Nebraska	1875	20	500
Maine	1878	20	1,100
West Virginia	1884	20	1,000
Missouri	1871	12	425
Total	....	450	28,688

* Including 424 Indians.

The total number of members, including 6,000 scattered, is estimated to be not less than 29,683. S. M. Smucker, LL. D., estimates it at 30,000

The educational institutions are Findlay College, Findlay, Ohio, incorporated in 1882, opened for students in 1886, and now returning a faculty of 13 members and upward of 170 students; and Barkleyville Academy, Barkleyville, Venango County, Pa., chartered in 1884, having property valued at $6,000, and returning an average attendance of about fifty pupils. The periodicals of the church include a weekly general religious newspaper and two Sunday-school journals. The Central Book Store was established in 1885, and balanced its accounts on the 30th of April, 1887, at $20,-657. The General Missionary Society was organized in 1845, and has conducted successful missions in different parts of the United States. The missions among the Cherokee Indians in the Indian Territory return 424 members, 9 organized churches, 4 Sunday-schools, 10 preachers, 12 preaching appointments, and 2 meeting-houses, with a third in building. The subject of establishing a foreign mission has been considered by the General Eldership, but nothing definite has yet been accomplished in the matter. A fund has been accumulated by voluntary contributions from the Annual Elderships, of more than $600.

The general and highest legislative and judicatory body of the Church is the General Eldership, which meets every three years. The next meeting will be held at North Bend, Iowa, in June, 1890.

Baptist Congress.—The seventh annual Baptist Congress was held in Richmond, Va., Dec. 4, 5, and 6. The Hon. J. L. M. Curry presided. The purpose of the meeting was exclusively the discussion of the questions laid down in the programme, with entire freedom in the expression of opinion. The first topic to be considered was "Education," respecting which papers were read on "How far shall the State Educate?" by Prof. B. Puryear, "Common vs. Parochial Schools," by the Rev. P. S. Moxom and by the Rev. Walter Rauschenbusch; and the discussion was continued by the Rev. Norman Fox, D. D., Prof. W. C. Wilkinson, and Prof. E. H. Johnson. The subject of "Temperance" was discussed in papers on "High License," by the Rev. Wayland Hoyt, D. D., and "Prohibition," by the Rev. H. A. Delano, who was supported by other speakers. Other topics discussed were "A National Divorce Law," by the Hon. A. S. Bacon and the Rev. Norman Fox, D. D.; "The Limits of Immigration," by the Hon. J. G. Sawyer, Rev. H. A. Delano, Rev. L. W. Crandall, Rev. George E. Horr, Jr., Hon. E. N. Blake, F. M. Ellis, D. D., H. McDonald, D. D., and other speakers; "Romanism: its Relation to Scientific Thought," by A. J. Rowland, D. D.; "Its Political Aspects," H. McDonald, D. D., and others; "Mohammedan Propagandism," by the Rev. F. S. Dobbins, Norman Fox, D. D., and other speakers; "Christian Science," Rev. G. E. Horr, Jr., W. E. Hatcher, D. D., and Dr. T. T. Eaton; and "The Purity of the Church—Terms of Admission," by E. T. Hiscox, D. D., and "Nature and Discipline," by F. M. Ellis, D. D., and W. W. Boyd, D. D.

V. Baptists in Great Britain and Ireland.—The "Baptist Handbook" for 1888 gives the following statistics of the Baptist churches in the United Kingdom: Number of churches, 2,764; of chapels, 3,701, containing 1,198,027 sittings; of members, 304,385; of Sunday-school teachers, 46,786; of Sunday-school pupils, 458,200; of local preachers, 4,118; of pastors in charge, 1,860. It was estimated that the churches from which no returns had been received would add 10,000 to the list of members.

Baptist Union of England and Wales.—The annual spring meeting of the Baptist Union of England and Wales was opened April 23 with an address by the Rev. Dr. Clifford on the general subject of the condition of the faith. Particular interest was attached to the question of the relations of the Union with the Rev. C. H. Spurgeon, who had withdrawn from connection with it (see "Annual Cyclopædia" for 1887), because he regarded its practice as too tolerant of persons holding and teaching doctrines of questionable orthodoxy. The Council of the Union, a kind of executive committee, consisting of one hundred members, had, in December, 1887, appointed a committee to visit Mr. Spurgeon, and "deliberate with him as to how the unity of our denomination in true love and good works may best be maintained." This committee reported to a subsequent meeting of council, Jan. 18, 1888, that Mr. Spurgeon had declined to discuss the question of his action toward the Union, and that he could not see his way clear to withdraw his resignation; but that he had furnished a statement embodying the following conditions:

In answer to the question what I would advise as likely to promote permanent union in truth, love, and good works? I should answer: (1) Let the Union have a simple basis of Bible truths; these are usually described as "evangelical doctrines." (2) I know of no better summary of these than that adopted by the Evangelical Alliance, and subscribed by members of so many religious communities for several years. The exact words need not be used of course, but that formula indicates the run of truth which is most generally followed among us, and should be so followed.

He had, however, declared that he would not undertake, on these conditions being complied with by the Union, to rejoin it, but would await results. The question was again considered at subsequent meetings of the council, and a declaration was adopted which was intended to define the attitude of the Union in relation to the questions at issue, in terms that would be acceptable to Mr. Spurgeon. This declaration was brought before the Union at the present meeting, and after discussion and the consideration of amendments, was adopted in the following terms:

That while expressly disavowing any power to control belief or restrict inquiry, yet, in view of the uneasiness produced in the churches by recent discussions, and to show our agreement with one another and with our fellow-Christians on the great truths of the Gospel, the council deem it right to say: Baptized into the name of the Father, and of the Son, and of the Holy Ghost, we have avowed repentance toward God and faith in the Lord Jesus Christ the very elements of a new life; as in the supper we avow our union with one another while partaking of the symbol of the body of our Lord broken for us, and of the blood shed for the remission of sins.

The Union, therefore, is an association of churches and ministers professing not only to believe the facts and doctrines of the Gospel, but to have undergone the spiritual change expressed or implied in them. This change is the fundamental principle of our church life.

The following facts and doctrines are commonly believed by the churches of the Union: The divine inspiration and authority of the Holy Scriptures as the supreme and sufficient rule of our faith and practice and the right and duty of individual judgment in the interpretation of it; the fallen and sinful state of man; the Deity, the incarnation, the resurrection of the Lord Jesus Christ, and his sacrificial and mediatorial work; justification by faith—a faith that works by love and produces holiness; the work of the Holy Spirit in the conversion of sinners and in the sanctification of all who believe; the resurrection and the judgment at the last day, with the eternal blessedness of the righteous and the eternal punishment of the wicked.

As an historical fact, the last half of this statement has generally been accepted by the great majority of the Union in the usual sense; but from the first, some, while reverently accepting all divine teaching, have accepted other interpretations, which seem to them consistent with it, and the Union have had no difficulty in working with them.

This action was not accepted by Mr. Spurgeon, who declared himself "one outside of the Union," and having no right to have anything further to do with its creeds or its declarations. "All has been done that can be done," he said, "and yet without violence we can not unite; let us not attempt it any more; but each one go his own way in quiet, each striving honestly for that which he believes to be the revealed truth of God. I could have wished that instead of saving the Union, or even purifying it, the more prominent thought had been to conform everything to the word of the Lord."

The Irish department of the British and Irish Home Mission was transferred to an executive committee in Ireland. Resolutions were adopted declaring that the question of disestablishment in Wales was ripe for settlement, and ought to be no longer postponed; and deprecating any further extension of state aid to denominational schools.

The autumnal meetings of the Union were held at Huddersfield, beginning October 1. Dr. Clifford presided. The report on the funds in connection with the Union showed that the whole amount invested up to the close of the last year was £116,554, showing an increase of about £3,000. Annuities amounting to £5,216 were paid every year. The Augmentation fund was £500 short, and the Education fund required increasing. A minute was adopted renewing the protests of the Union against the maintenance by the state of "the system of sectarian elementary schools," and reiterating the declaration that "a really national system of undenominational day-schools can alone supply the educational needs of the country without violating the rights of conscience." Meetings were held in behalf of the Baptist Foreign Missions and of the British and Irish Home Missions; and prepared papers were read and addresses delivered on various subjects of denominational interest.

Baptist Missionary Society.—The annual meeting of the Baptist Missionary Society was held April 24. Mr C. Townsend, J. P., of Bristol, presided. The income of the society had been £61,341, showing an increase from the previous year of £2,938: yet the balance-sheet exhibited a debt of £5,859, which had been caused by increased expenditure. This would, however, probably be extinguished by the proceeds of legacies which would not have to go to the reserve fund. The publication of Mr. Bentley's "Grammar and Dictionary of the Congo Language" was mentioned as an event of much importance. The use of the steamer "Peace" for the purpose of Mr. Stanley's expedition to relieve Emin Pasha (contrary to the policy of the society not to participate in enterprises that might have a military aspect) was shown in the report to have been unavoidable, because the suffering followers of the explorer had to be got out of the country. An offer of £15,000 had been made by Mr. Arthrington, of Leeds, to the society, in conjunction with two other missionary societies, for the purpose of carrying the Gospel to the tribes on the banks of the Amazon and its tributaries; but its acceptance would have involved heavy and permanent additional expenditure, and it had, therefore, been declined.

The income of the Baptist Zenana Mission in India had been £6,586. A deficit of £288 was returned.

The Bible Translation Society had published, or assisted to publish, new versions of the Bible or parts of the Bible translated by Baptist missionaries in fourteen languages of India, China, Japan, Ceylon, and West Africa. Its receipts for the past year had been £2,817. The chief items reported in the expenditure were grants of £1,600 to the Baptist Missionary Society for translations, £300 to the "Mission Press" at Calcutta, and £250 to colporteurs in India.

Baptist Union of Wales.—The statistics of the Baptist Union of Wales, reported at its meeting in August (held in Cardigan), showed that the number of churches and mission-stations had increased from 663 in 1872 to 797, and the Sunday pupils from 61,167 to 100,-330. Five thousand four hundred and forty-eight persons had been baptized during the year. Resolutions were passed concerning Welsh "legislative needs" (of which disestablishment was declared to be one), condemning the recommendations of the Royal Commission on Education, and approving the society for the utilization of the Welsh language.

VI. General Baptist Association.—The one hundred and nineteenth meeting of the General Baptist Association of the New Connection was held in Derby in April. The Rev. W. H. Tetley presided. The summary of the statistics of membership showed that the total number of additions by baptism during the year had been 2,236, and the net gain of members 113. The report of the building fund showed that its capital amounted to £6,332 and its receipts for the year had been £1,399, while loans had been made to the amount of £850. Since the fund was instituted more than £18,-000 had been granted in loans to the churches. The receipts for foreign missions were £8,107. The debt of the fund (£800) was reduced by £700. Action was taken in favor of an Association book fund.

BAZAINE, FRANÇOIS ACHILLE, French general, born in Versailles, Feb. 13, 1811; died in Madrid, Spain, Sept. 23, 1888. He was the son of a French officer, and after leaving the École Polytechnique he joined the Foreign Legion in 1831, and served five years in Africa, rising to the grade of first lieutenant, and winning the cross of the Legion of Honor on the field of battle. He went to Spain in 1837, and fought in two hard campaigns against the Carlists, returning to Algeria as captain in 1839. He

saw much fighting during the next nine years, and when the Foreign Legion, organized as a brigade of infantry, was sent to the East in 1854, he was appointed to the command. He greatly distinguished himself before Sebastopol, and after its capture was named military governor of the place, and promoted to be general

FRANÇOIS ACHILLE BAZAINE.

of division. In the Italian campaign of 1859, he commanded a division in the attack on Melegnano, where he was wounded, and in the battle of Solferino he took a conspicuous part. He was given a high command in the French expedition against Mexico, distinguished himself by brilliant and energetic tactics, and on the recall of Marshal Forey in 1863 succeeded as commander-in-chief. He received the Grand Cross of the Legion of Honor, having been made a commander in 1856, and in September, 1864, he was promoted Marshal of France. His vigorous aggressive strategy drove President Juarez into a corner of the country. The fortress of Oajaca surrendered in February, 1865, the garrison of 7,000 men laying down their arms. He also organized a barbarous but effective system of guerilla warfare. Bazaine married a wealthy Mexican lady, and soon afterward misunderstandings arose between him and the Emperor Maximilian, who suspected the French general of lukewarmness in his cause, when fortune began to turn in favor of Juarez, owing, as Bazaine alleged, to the obstinate resistance of the Mexicans and the policy of the United States. Napoleon sent orders for the ultimate withdrawal of the French troops, and when Bazaine was suspected of a design to make himself emperor instead of Maximilian, he dispatched Gen. Castelnau to arrange the evacuation.

Finally, at a council of Mexican notables, Bazaine declared the maintenance of the empire impossible, and on March 12, 1867, having retreated to Vera Cruz, he embarked with all his forces for France. On his arrival he was greeted with a storm of reproaches. He nevertheless retained the confidence of Napoleon III, and was made a senator and intrusted with the command of the corps stationed at Nancy, and in October, 1869, was given the chief command of the Imperial Guard.

When the Franco-Prussian War began, Bazaine had command of the Third Corps. He might have supported Gen. Frossard at Forbach, but would not move without orders. On Aug. 13, 1870, he took command of the Army of the Rhine, with which he checked Gen. Steinmetz at Berny on the following day, allowing Napoleon and his staff to retreat in safety. He retired on Metz, perhaps in order to detain the enemy until MacMahon's army was formed at Châlons. If he had ordered the Imperial Guards to support Canrobert at Gravelotte, the Germans might have been driven into a retreat, instead of forcing him to retire into the citadel of Metz. His army was the only compact force that remained after the surrender of Marshals Lebœuf and Canrobert and the capture of the Emperor. The garrison made many brave sorties, but each party was beaten back. After fruitless efforts to obtain better terms, the commandant signed a capitulation on Oct. 27, 1870, before a single shot of the enemy had fallen within the walls of the fortress, in accordance with which his command of 173,000 men marched out without their arms. His declaration that his army was vanquished by famine was contradicted by witnesses, who said that there was food, and that the men had in their knapsacks six days' rations. Accusations of treachery resounded on every side. It was discovered on investigation that he had held communication with Bismarck through a go-between named Regnier, and after learning the pretended determination of the Germans not to treat on any terms with the Government of National Defense, had allowed himself to be duped into inactivity and finally into a surrender by Bismarck, who suggested that far better conditions of peace would be granted if he kept his army intact in order to support a serious Government with which Germany could negotiate. Thus the wily diplomatist held out the hope of the restoration of the empire with German aid. After his return from captivity Bazaine published a book entitled "L'Armée du Rhin," in which he avowed that he felt no obligation to obey the Government of National Defense after the downfall of the empire, and considered himself justified in acting independently. It was not till then that he was cited to appear in August, 1871, before the Committee of Military Investigation of the National Assembly at Versailles. He offered himself for trial by court-martial without awaiting the report. He

was not arraigned till Oct. 6, 1873. The Duc d'Aumale presided over the tribunal. The marshal, who wore his full uniform and the decorations of the Legion of Honor, in reply to the charges of military incapacity in letting himself be blockaded in Metz by a force not much superior and in capitulating, and of treasonable correspondence with the enemy with the object of making himself independent of the Government of National Defense, he said that the motto of "honor and country" that he bore on his breast had been his for the forty years that he had served France, at Metz as well as elsewhere. He was found guilty (1) of having capitulated before the enemy in the open field; (2) of having agreed to terms making his command lay down their arms; (3) of having entered into negotiations with the enemy before doing all that duty and honor demanded; (4) of having surrendered a fortified place that was intrusted to him to defend. He was condemned on December 10 to death and military degradation, but in compliance with the unanimous recommendation of his judges, President MacMahon commuted the sentence to twenty years' seclusion. He was incarcerated in Fort Sainte Marguerite, near Cannes, on December 26. In the following August he lowered himself from a window by a rope into a boat, on which he made his escape to a ship lying off the island, and reached Italy. From there he went to Cologne, and to England, and finally he took up his residence in Madrid. In September, 1874, he published in the New York "Herald" a defense of his conduct during the war, to which Prince Friedrich Karl bore honorable testimony, and in 1883 he went over the ground again in a volume.

BEDS, FOLDING. Bedsteads so contrived that they can be folded into a more or less compact form are to be found in all civilized and, perhaps, in some uncivilized lands, and are of almost as many different patterns as are the tables and chairs that keep them company. Goldsmith's familiar lines in the "Deserted Village" are more than a century old:

> The chest contrived a double debt to pay,
> A bed by night, a chest of draws by day,

and they go to show that folding beds were not uncommon at that time. In 1888 about forty patents were issued in the United States bearing upon such articles of furniture, and a visit to any industrial exhibition or large furniture establishment affords abundant evidence that the supply keeps well up with the demand. This is largely due no doubt to the crowding of population in the large cities. Where a family occupies a flat or "apartments," the question of space becomes very important, and where a single person occupies a room, perhaps a small one, his comfort is greatly enhanced by being able to double the floor-space by disposing of the bed during the day-time.

To begin with the simpler and least expensive forms of folding beds, it may be said that ingenious mechanics not infrequently provide themselves with convenient devices of this character without calling upon the furniture-dealer.

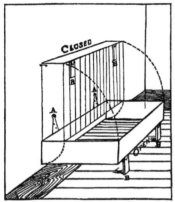

One of the simplest possible is shown in Fig. 1. It is a shallow oblong box with the bottom preferably of slats and the sides and ends deep enough to receive the mattress and coverings that are to be used. This depth should exceed the thickness of the mattress by three or four inches. Diagonal braces may be placed at the corners to prevent the racking unavoidable in raising and lowering. One side of the box is attached to the wall by means of strong iron hinges (A A) which should be screwed to the studs if the wall is of lath and plaster, or otherwise secured so as to bear the strain. To the other side of the box, legs (B B) are attached, also by hinges, so that they lie flat against the slats when the bed is raised to its day-time place and secured by hooks against the wall. To keep coverings and mattress from falling against the wall when the bed is lowered, bands of some suitable material are used.

The same general principle may be employed with any of the light cots kept by dealers, but in this case the wall-hinges must be attached to projections bearing them out from the wall so that there will be room for mattress, covering, etc., between wall and slats. It will naturally occur to any one with an eye to decorative effects, that a curtain hung over this somewhat unsightly object when it is hooked up, will effectually conceal it, and it may, with the exercise of a little taste, be made really ornamental.

The occupant of a narrow hall bedroom in New York requiring more space and a table, had recourse to the device shown in Fig. 2. The bedstead was one of the light cots referred to above. Fixing two stout screw-eyes (C C) in the studding at the head of the bed, he lashed the head-piece loosely to them, so that the lashings should serve as hinges. To the foot of the bed he attached a line and passed the free end through a pulley (D) fixed near the ceiling. It was an easy matter, the bedding being properly lashed, to hoist the whole affair until it rested flat against the wall as shown in the figure. For additional security, the long slack of the hoisting-line was passed around outside the bed and made fast to two hooks about seven feet from the floor. The upper pair of legs was either folded down as shown or opened and used as a shelf. A drawing-board placed upon the lower pair of legs, as shown in the engraving at E, converted them into a very passable substitute for a table. Recently some inventor has hit upon the same idea, and has patented it with some improvements and elaborations.

On yachts and other small vessels folding bunks are sometimes provided for the crew by stretching stout canvas across a rectangular iron frame and hinging the frame to the lining of the vessel. In this case the outer side of the frame is supported by hooks attached to lines depending from the deck-beams. When not in use, the frames are folded up flat against the side of the vessel, and occupy scarcely any room at all.

The next step in elaboration is the "mantel-bed," so called, which is to be found at the dealers' in several forms. Substantially, it is similar to those at first described, except that it is independent of the wall, having a wood-work frame or box into which it is folded when not in use. It is, moreover, so hung that the operations of lifting and lowering are more easily performed than where the weight is not distributed or counterbalanced. When not in use, cur-

tains sliding on rods are drawn in front of the whole structure, and the top may even be used as a shelf or mantel. Ingenious self-acting attachments adjust the legs of the bedstead, so that they open or shut as the bed is lowered or raised.

A slightly more complicated form of the mantel-bed is similar in structure, save that it folds endwise, involving a joint midway of the mattress and side-pieces.

The bedsteads thus far described are quite moderate in price, and are coming into use very extensively. They are better in many respects than the more costly kinds, since the open structure admits free circulation of air through and about the mattress and coverings while they are not in use. The more elaborate and ornamental folding beds, "cabinet-beds," as they are sometimes called, are manufactured in a great variety of styles, and are very complete and ingenious in all their appointments.

Figs. 3 and 4 show one of the direct-acting kind, where the bed is wheeled outward before being lowered from its upright position. The raising and lowering are usually facilitated by counter-weights, springs, or pulleys concealed in the casing. For low-ceiled rooms cabinet-beds are made which fold in the middle, instead of being raised bodily. These, however, project farther into the room when folded, and in them it is impracticable to use the "wire mattresses" as generally furnished to the trade.

Cabinet or furniture bedsteads are often only ornamental coverings for the bedding, but many of them include also a wardrobe, with drawers, or, if desired, a washstand, mirror, and the like, all very compact and convenient. These beds stand with the side to the wall when in use, or with the foot to the wall if preferred. That is to say, the wardrobe part is swung or pulled out toward the middle of the room, and the bed is then lowered. This is hardly an objection, since the whole structure is mounted on easily-rolling castors, and can be removed with very little exertion. Figs. 3 and 4 show one of these combination

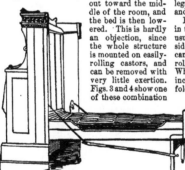

FIG. 3.—CABINET-BED—SIDE.

beds in front and side elevation. When not in use, it is a handsome piece of furniture, and to a casual observer suggests nothing more than an ordinary wardrobe and bureau. Another class of folding-beds includes those in-tended for use in camps or wherever easy transportation is essential. The common type of cot with a canvas support for the mattress and

FIG. 4.—CABINET-BED—END.

coverings is so well known that it does not require illustration. In effect it is precisely like the one shown in Fig. 5, except that the legs can not be folded parallel to the side-pieces, and it lacks the long braces marked A A.

Fig. 5 shows one of the best camp-beds in the market. The legs turn on a bolt in the usual manner at B, but are so attached to the side-rails, by means of an iron fixture, that they can be folded parallel to the side-rails, and rolled up in the canvas as shown at C. When open for use, the bed is six feet three inches long and twenty-nine inches wide; folded it forms a roll about six inches in diameter one way and four inches the other way. The weight is fifteen pounds.

A camp-bed somewhat more elaborate in construction than that shown in the illustration has semi-cylindrical side-rails of wood. They are made of three-ply veneering similar to the chair-seats commonly in use, except that they are not perforated. To these the canvas stretcher is firmly tacked, and within them are simple iron fixtures to serve as braces for the legs. All the attachments are laid within the hollow semi-cylinders when the bed is to be folded, and then the canvas is rolled and packed between the two, which, when strapped together, form a handsome varnished cylindrical box less than four inches in diameter, and weighing altogether eleven pounds.

Many varieties of camp-beds are manufactured which fold much more compactly than those here described, some of them within the dimensions of a moderate sized valise. These may all be classed as were modifications of the cots described. Taking Fig. 5, for instance, cutting the side-rails into four pieces, and fur-

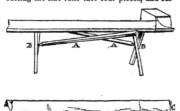

FIG. 5.—CAMP-BED.

nishing each section with independent sets of legs, it is evident that the whole could be rolled up in a more compact form than that shown. The weight, however, is naturally increased, and the trouble of taking apart and putting together is considerably greater. Where space for transportation is to be considered, some of these more compact devices are very convenient.

BELGIUM, a monarchy in western Europe. It was formerly a part of the Netherlands, but seceded and formed itself into an independent state in 1830. Prince Leopold of Saxe-Coburg-Gotha was elected king by a National Congress in the following year. His son, Leopold II, the present King of the Belgians, succeeded to the throne on Dec. 10, 1865, at the age of thirty. The law-making power is vested in two chambers, called the Senate and the Chamber of Representatives, both of which are elective. The members of the Cabinet, who assumed office on Oct. 26, 1884, are as follow: President of the Council and Minister of Finance, A. Beernaert; Minister of Justice, J. Lejeune; Minister of the Interior and of Public Instruction, J. Devolder; Minister of War, Gen. C. Pontus; Minister of Railways, Posts, and Telegraphs, J. H. P. Vandenpeereboom; Minister for Foreign Affairs, Prince de Chimay; Minister of Agriculture, Industry, and Public Works, the Chevalier A. de Moreau.

Area and Population.—The area of the kingdom is 29,455 square kilometres, or 11,373 square miles. The estimated population on Dec. 31, 1886, was 5,909,975, comprising 2,-951,300 males and 2,958,675 females. Between 1880 and 1886 the rate of increase was 1·14 per cent. per annum. According to the census of 1880 there were 2,237,867 Belgians speaking French only, and 2,479,747 speaking Flemish only, while 41,046 could speak only German, and 471,872 spoke at least two of these languages.

All the people of the kingdom are professing Catholics except some 15,000 who are Protestants and 3,000 Jews. Education is backward, but is gradually becoming diffused under a law making elementary education more general than it formerly was. Universal education is one of the demands of the Liberals, but the party in power opposes it, and is sustained by a decided majority of the electors, composed of the wealthy class and constituting only one tenth of the adult male population. The budget of 1888 allots 1,613,620 francs for superior education, 3,747,490 francs for intermediate education, and 10,167,774 francs for primary education. Of the total population over fifteen years of age in 1880 the proportion who could not read nor write was 42 per cent., whereas between the ages of seven and fifteen it was only 29·4 per cent.

The number of births in 1886 was 166,451; of deaths, 116,264; of marriages, 39,642; excess of births over deaths, 50,187. The number of emigrants in 1886 was 17,029, which was less by 2,775 than the number of immigrants. The population of the principal cities on Jan. 1, 1887, was as follows: Brussels, with suburbs, 425,204; Antwerp, 204,498; Ghent, 145,424; Liège, 137,559.

Revenue and Expenditure.—The ordinary budget for many years has almost invariably shown a deficit. In 1885, when an extraordinary expenditure of 44,974,750 francs was contemplated in the estimates, with an estimated extraordinary revenue of only 6,159,884 francs, the ordinary budget was revised so that there remained a small surplus. In the following year, instead of the expected surplus of 3,000,-000 francs, there was an actual deficit of more than that amount. In 1887 the revenue fell below the expenditure nearly 2,500,000 francs. The estimates for 1888 make the total ordinary revenue 313,641,559 francs, and the ordinary expenditure 307,743,123 francs. The income from property taxes is estimated at 23,883,100 francs; from personal taxes, 19,232,000 francs; from trade licenses, 6,580,000 francs; from customs, 24,682,600 francs; from excise, 39,-775,500 francs; from registration duties, 23,-860,000 francs; from succession duties, 19,-420,000 francs; from stamp duties, 6,820,000 francs; from railways, 114,500,000 francs; from telegraphs, 3,103,700 francs; from the post-office, 9,421,300 francs; from navigation dues, 4,280,000 francs; from the national bank and amortization funds, 11,493,100 francs; from domains and forests, 1,300,000 francs; from other sources, 5,290,259 francs.

The expenditure for interest on the public debt amounts to 96,102,231 francs; civil list and dotations, 4,568,675 francs; for expenses of the Ministry of Justice, 15,426,361 francs : of the Ministry of Foreign Affairs, 2,377,020 francs; of the Ministry of the Interior and Public Instruction, 21,829,764 francs; of the

Ministry of Public Works, 16,712,281 francs; of the Ministry of Railways, Posts, and Telegraphs, 83,850,116 francs; of the Ministry of War, 46,003,270 francs; of the Ministry of Finance, 15,290,905 francs; of the gendarmerie, 3,946,000 francs; repayments and other expenditures, 1,636,500 francs.

The national debt, including the capitalized value of annuities amounting to 30,106,000 francs, exceeds 2,500,000.000 francs. The funded debt consists of 219,959,633 francs of 2½-per-cent. bonds, 519,859,000 francs of 3-per-cents., and 1,185,509,458 of 3½-per-cents. The credit of the Government, notwithstanding its large and gradually increasing debt, is so good that the 3½-per-cent. bonds stand at 2 per cent. above par in the market.

The Post-Office.—The number of letters that passed through the Belgian post-office in 1886 was 90,744,556, not reckoning 14,123,401 official letters; the number of postal cards, 26,568,401; printed inclosures, 55,268,000; newspapers, 94,394,000. The receipts during 1886 amounted to 14,806,595 francs, and the expenditure to 8,893,171 francs.

The Army.—The army budget for 1888 fixes the peace effective at the following figures:

TROOPS.	Officers.	Rank and file	Total.
Infantry	1,187	32,495	34,882
Cavalry	356	5,506	5,562
Artillery	447	7,081	8,188
Engineers	90	1,479	1,569
Gendarmerie	58	2,080	2,138
Train	453	1,350	1,802
Total	3,315	50,571	53,836

The staff, numbering 125 officers, and 772 officers of the medical corps, are not included in this statement. The number of horses is 8,900; of guns, 200. The war-strength of the army is 120,000 men, 13,800 horses, and 240 guns. There is besides a civic guard, which in 1887 numbered 41,222 men.

An extensive plan for fortifying the line of the Meuse was adopted in 1887, but the Government has resolved for the present to direct its efforts chiefly to extending and arming the fortifications at Liége and Namur. These two fortresses will absorb all the army at its present strength, except the troops that are required to garrison Brussels and the central citadel at Antwerp. The Ministry of War has obtained a credit of 60,000,000 francs for the purchase of modern ordnance of large caliber. The works at Liége, when extended to the adjacent heights, are considered sufficient to arrest the passage of a German army up the Meuse valley. Namur on the French side is not so strong a position, and only guards one of the routes from France, while that by way of Mons and Charleroi is left open. Contracts have been awarded for the construction of twenty-one metallic forts along the Meuse, which will strengthen the defenses against a German invasion. They will consist of cupolas and will be completed by the end of 1890.

Commerce and Industry.—The returns for the general commerce of 1886 give the value of the imports as 2,662,715,581 francs, and of the exports as 2,512,122,555 francs. The imports for home consumption amounted to 1,335,049,000 francs, and the exports of Belgian produce to 1,181,974,000 francs. The imports of breadstuffs were valued at 205,069,000 francs; the exports at 54,514,000 francs; imports of textile materials, 177,211,000 francs; exports, 98,154,000 francs; imports of yarns, 27,121,000 francs; exports, 136,261,000 francs; imports of tissues, 31,546,000 francs; exports, 67,238,000 francs; imports of live animals, 72,047,000 francs; exports, 34,641,000 francs; imports of hides and skins, 79,926,000 francs; exports, 69,929,000 francs; imports of chemicals, 52,669,000 francs; exports, 18,551,000 francs; imports of timber, 50,972,000 francs; of metals, 29,866,000 francs; of oils, 21,022,000 francs; exports of iron, wrought and unwrought, 54,118,000 francs; of machinery, 50,813,000 francs; of coal, 50,127,000 francs; of glass, 48,940,000 francs; of sugar, 32,567,000 francs; of paper, 23,614,000 francs; of steel, 17,672,000 francs; of arms, 13,127,000 francs. The export of sugar in 1885 exceeded the import by 53,000 metric tons. The product of pig and wrought iron in 1885 was 1,182,125 tons, and in 1886 it was 1,167,132 tons.

The share of France in the import trade of 1886 was 251,031,092 francs, and in the export trade, 329,580,022 francs. Great Britain furnished 172,324,410 francs of the imports, and took 236,416,435 francs of the exports. The imports from the Netherlands were larger, amounting to 199,841,114 francs, while the United States came next after England with 160,394,949 francs of imports, Germany following with 151,941,981 francs, and then Russia with 74,224,681 francs, the Argentine Republic with 59,981,433 francs, Sweden and Norway with 37,941,106 francs, Roumania with 31,307,880 francs, Peru with 29,840,208 francs, Brazil with 21,346,203 francs, and Uruguay with 17,574,454 francs. The third largest consumer of Belgian products was Germany, the exports to that country amounting to 195,790,476 francs. The Netherlands took 175,417,466 francs. The exports to other countries were small in comparison, 40,647,175 francs going to the United States, 34,064,322 francs to Italy, and 29,457,862 francs to Switzerland, after which come Spain, the Argentine Republic, Brazil, Turkey, and Russia.

Navigation.—In 1886 the number of vessels entered at Belgian ports was 6,216, of 4,094,026 tons, of which 3,367, with a total tonnage of 2,351,344, were British. The number cleared was 6,206, of 4,060,901 tons. The commercial marine in 1887 numbered 67 vessels, of 86,837 tons, of which 55 vessels, of 81,285 tons, were steamers. There were 342 fishing vessels, of 12.009 tons.

Railroads.—The lines worked by the state

had a length of 3,175 kilometres, and the lines worked by companies were 1,246 kilometres in length on Jan. 1, 1887, making a total of 4,421 kilometres, or 2,763 miles. The receipts of the state railroads in 1886 were 117,918,-879 francs, and the expenses 66,241,271 francs. On the lines of the companies the receipts were 35,144,278 francs, and the expenses 19,-213,485 francs. The capital expended by the Government in building railroads was 929,-697,462 francs up to the end of 1885, while railroads that had been purchased were paid for in annuities representing 319,798,631 francs of additional capital.

Telegraphs.—The number of dispatches, private and official, in 1886 was 6,798,108. The length of lines on Jan. 1, 1887, was 3.800 miles, with 17,900 miles of wire. The receipts for 1886 were 2,868,650 francs, and the expenses, 3,679,250 francs.

Elections.—The biennial elections for one half of the seats in the Chamber, and the quadrennial elections for the renewal of one half of the Senate were held on June 12, 1888. The Conservatives, who in the last Chamber numbered 96 against 42 Liberals, and in the Senate 42 against 27, were successful, owing to the defection of the Radicals who had previously supported Liberal candidates. In the new Chamber there are 98 Conservatives and 40 Liberals, and in the Senate 51 Conservatives and 18 Liberals.

The Language Question.—The Flemings have recently raised the language question by organizing a party to secure for their mother-tongue the equality that the Constitution guarantees. Until Hendrik Conscience demonstrated the literary capabilities of Flemish, and appealed to race pride in his historical and satirical passages, the Flemings were content to see the French employed almost exclusively in official intercourse, in the courts, and in the army, and even cultivated it themselves in their commercial and social relations. When their national spirit was finally aroused, the adoption of French as the language of instruction in the Royal Athenæum, which was opened at Antwerp in 1886, gave occasion for its manifestation in a storm of indignation that compelled the Government to alter its decision. In the summer of 1887 the King was almost mobbed for delivering a French oration at the dedication of statues to Flemish heroes in Bruges. The inequalities of which the Flemings complain are that no official is appointed to a post in southern Belgium without being conversant with French, whereas there are thousands in Flanders who know no Flemish; that French is the language of public boards and assemblies and of the army; and, notably, that it is used in military and criminal courts in Flanders, even when the accused person speaks only Flemish. The knowledge of French has long been a prerequisite for an appointment in the army. Deputy Coremans, of Antwerp, introduced a bill requiring candidates for commissions to be examined in both languages, and the Government adopted the measure, which simply carries out a provision of the Constitution. Its practical effect would be to exclude Walloons from officers' posts, and after it had been passed by a large majority, the Government was induced by popular clamor to recede from the constitutional position and support a substitute measure, which merely recommended the study of Flemish. By this action the ministry offended not only the Flemish Liberals, but the Clericals, who had been its firm supporters.

Foreign Relations.—The Belgium scheme of fortification aroused the jealousy of the German Government, which endeavored in 1888, with partial success, to force Belgium into a military alliance and secure an understanding by which the fortress of Liége and the railroads will be handed over to the Germans in the event of another French war. King Leopold's sympathies are supposed to be with Germany by reason of family ties and dynastic traditions, while the present Clerical-Conservative ministry is suspected of the same partiality or, at any rate, of antagonism to the ruling powers in France. The prevailing sentiment among the people, however, leans toward France. The Liberal party and the entire Walloon population of the south are warm friends of the republic, while the Flemings are indifferent. By manifesting a desire to exert diplomatic pressure on Belgium, the German Government aroused the anti-German feeling of the country; but since England has refused to renew her pledges in regard to defending the neutrality of Belgium, and is even partly committed to the anti-French alliance, the Belgian Government may be constrained to meet the wishes of Germany. Early in 1888 the German minister made complaints respecting attacks on the German Government by a portion of the Belgian press. This was hardly done with a view to the immediate abatement of the offense, because the Belgian press is the freest in Europe. The Liberal organs assail the King and his Cabinet with the full liberty that the Constitution accords, and if they use the same license in speaking of German policy the Ultramontane journals denounce the French authorities in terms as immoderate. These representations regarding the press led up to others relative to the French control of the Nord Belge Railroad, which the German Government complained gave an unfair strategical advantage to France, although the railroad from Verviers to the German frontier was in German hands and the entire network of the Duchy of Luxembourg was worked by the imperial railroad administration of Alsace-Loraine. Finally came the overtures with regard to the occupation of Belgian fortresses by Prussian troops in case France should begin a war against Germany. The French sympathies of the people, especially of the Walloons, who are not only allied to the French in blood and language, but are grateful to them for their aid in the struggle for Belgian independence, is manifested on every occasion, The Socialists, for instance, when forbidden to bear the red flag in their processions, carry the French colors in its stead, and journalists and politicians of Liberal views express distrust and alarm at the aims of Germany. King Leopold is the special object of Radical and Republican attacks on account of his suspected predilections. When he visited Louvière in the summer a mob of 25,000 workingmen gathered in the streets, shouting "Down with the German!"

Adjustment of the Netherlands Boundary.—By the treaty of November, 1842, and the boundary convention of August, 1843, the rectification of the frontier between Belgium and Holland was left for amicable settlement between the two countries. A convention was made on Jan. 5, 1888, with reference to the exchange of some villages on the frontier, and also relative to the boundary, which was fixed in the canal of Terneuzen. The communes of Baarle and Hertog, in North Brabant, were transferred to the Netherlands, because it was impossible to enforce customs regulations within them, and the situation had created difficulties for both governments.

International Congresses.—An international industrial exhibition at Brussels was opened on June 7, 1888. It attracted many exhibitors from England, France, and other countries.

An International Congress of Commercial Law met at Brussels, on September 30, to elaborate a project of international legislation in the matter of bills of exchange and maritime law in conformity with the principles approved at the former session at Antwerp in 1885.

An international conference having for its object the co-operation of the principal states in collecting and publishing information regarding their customs tariffs was held at Brussels in March, and adjourned for six months after adopting a draft convention, which it was expected the governments would accept. The co-operation of customs officials in compiling such information not only will save merchants from trouble and losses resulting from ignorance and misunderstanding, but may lead to the removal of anomalies in the various tariffs.

Offices have been established by the Belgian Government for the purpose of supplying persons intending to emigrate with information of use to them that can be obtained through the diplomatic and consular agents.

BETTING. The modern practices of betting, in their various forms, especially among people who speak the English tongue, are so popular and so dangerously demoralizing that their reasonable restriction has become one of the legislative problems of the day. The practice is as old as the race, and, like gambling for stakes and the use of intoxicants, is so common to mankind in general that its complete suppression can hardly be looked for while human nature remains as it is.

None of the lexicographers have discovered or devised a satisfactory derivative origin for the word "bet." A bet may be defined as a sum of money or its equivalent promised by one person to another if some doubtful question is decided in a specified way. The possible variations upon this simple statement of the case are nearly infinite; the bet may be made between two persons only on even terms, or between any number of persons on uneven terms. It may rest upon the result of a single event or upon the combined result of any number of events. In short, it offers all the unhealthful excitement of gambling, without the formalities that usually surround the card-table.

Betting has, until within a generation, been more common among the upper classes, so called, in Great Britain than among the corresponding classes in America. This is largely due to the influence of New-England schools and churches where it was taught that all betting was not only dishonest and dishonorable, but sinful as well. That these teachings had, and still have, a powerful restraining influence is not to be questioned, but it is equally indisputable that the habit of betting on all manner of events is rapidly gaining ground in all classes of society.

Probably there was never before so much betting on the result of an election as during the presidential canvass of 1888. It was estimated that in the city of New York alone something like $2,000,000 changed hands within a few days. Syndicates were formed by the different parties for the placing of bets. In many instances odds were given and the money placed in the hands of a stake-holder. One somewhat notorious person in New York is reported to have had nearly $70,000 in current funds in his possession.

All this is contrary to law, and the vote of any person having a bet that might influence that vote may be challenged. In most of the States there are statutes more or less rigorous against betting in various forms, but it may be said that in general nobody minds them, and pool-selling, book-making, and betting on horse-racing, boat-racing, ball-matches, and the like, goes on without apparent let or hinderance. In the United States, laws against betting have been so long in existence that their inefficiency has for the most part failed to excite comment.

In Great Britain there has been comparatively recent legislation, which has an interesting bearing on the question. While it is manifestly impossible to enforce a law prohibiting private bets between individuals, however objectionable such bets may be, it is certainly within the legitimate province of legislation to make it dangerous for designing persons to ply their trade in a public way.

In Great Britain the evils of betting have been recognized in the statutes at least since Queen Anne's time, when if any one gained a bet of more than ten pounds the loser was entitled to recover the amount if he had paid it, and if he did not do so within three months, any one might sue him for three times the amount, with costs. This act was long a dead letter, but was unearthed for some purpose in 1844, and subsequently annulled by the Gaming Act (8 and 9 Vict.). Unfortunately as it seems, the annulment of this act was closely coincident with an enormous increase in betting on horse-races. "List shops" were opened, where any one could stake money in advance on any horse, and so many acts of dishonesty were perpetrated that the Betting Houses Act (16 and 17 Vict.) was introduced by Sir Alexander Cockburn, afterward Lord Chief-Justice of England, and by him carried successfully through Parliament. This act suppressed all permanent places kept expressly for betting purposes, the object being to remove obtrusive temptation from the daily walks of the multitude, who were the easiest prey of swindlers. The act applied only to England, and one result was that Scotland soon became a headquarters for the professional swindlers of the United Kingdom. In due time, however, the provisions of the act were extended to Scotland, and the evils arising from established and permanent betting-places were largely diminished. This act, carefully prepared by George Anderson, of Glasgow, went into effect in July, 1874, upon which the Scottish betting-agents closed their establishments and moved to Boulogne, where a thriving business was carried on by mail and otherwise, until the evil results became so manifest that the French Government in turn interfered, and the agents were driven to new devices. So successful are they, however, in evading the law, that it is estimated that about £5,000,000 changes hands every year on the results of horse-racing alone. In England, legislation appears to discriminate between what is termed "ready-money" betting and betting on credit, the former being made illegal, while the latter is not so specified. One result has been that among the poorer classes small clubs have been formed, where betting is carried on upon credit, just as it is among the wealthy at their palatial club-houses. Bets of honor, these are called, and when a "gentleman" or a "nobleman" loses, he will go to any extreme to meet his obligations on the Monday following; repeatedly have men mortgaged their lands and pawned their wives' jewels in order to escape the disgrace that would follow the non-payment of such an obligation. It has therefore been held that it would be better, if possible, to place restrictions upon betting on credit, rather than upon betting with ready money, since the credit system permits the bettor to incur any number of liabilities for almost any period of time, in advance. He loses, let us say, on the first event, but hope bids him strain every nerve to meet his obligations, for may he not win on the second? If all betting transactions involved cash

in hand and a stake-holder, it would seem that the incitement to great sacrifices of real property under stress of emergency would be largely wanting.

It is a noteworthy feature of betting transactions that no legal documents or contracts are in use. Millions of dollars and hundreds of thousands of pounds change hands every year on the strength of a memorandum penciled in a note-book at the time of making the bet. All betting is conducted, as the phrase goes, "upon honor," and, considering the magnitude of the transactions, it is certainly remarkable how few are the failures to pay.

Whether it is possible wholly or even partially to restrict betting, is a question that can be argued on both sides, with little hope of settlement. That the practice is demoralizing in the extreme is unquestionable.

A professional sharper is said to have summarized the case as follows, when asked how he made his calling pay: "It follows by a law of Nature," said he. "We are told that there is a child born into this world every second, and therefore there must be a daily addition of more than five millions to the population of the globe. Now, the deuce is in it if, with this continual rising of fresh spooneys to the surface of society, I can not come across as many as will serve my turn."

It is this class of professional sharpers that is most harmful to the community, and any reasonable legislation looking to restraining their proceedings would be welcomed by all the law-abiding classes. The making of private bets can probably be prevented or restrained only by promoting a sentiment against it; but it would seem possible and desirable to prohibit public betting, and especially to render betting on elections dangerous as well as disreputable.

The talk of racing and betting men abounds in slang phrases, many of which, as used in England, are not understood by Americans. As they are frequently encountered in English novels, a few definitions are appended. A "dollar," in betting parlance, means five shillings; a "quid" is a pound sterling; "fivers" and "tenners" are respectively five- and ten-pound notes; a "pony" is twenty-five pounds; a "century" is one hundred pounds; and a "monkey" is five hundred pounds; a "thou" is the recognized abbreviation of thousand. "A stiff 'un" or a "dead 'un" is a horse that has been entered for a race, but will not compete; "skinning the lamb" means that the book-maker has not bet against the winning horse. "Hedging," in its simplest meaning, implies that a bettor having made his bet, becomes fearful of losing, and bets the other way, so as to make the accounts balance as nearly as may be. A more elaborate definition is given as follows by an English writer: "Suppose that a betting man backs a particular horse for a certain race before the entries are due, and that the horse is entered, favorably weighted, and accepts—it is pretty certain to come to shorter odds than it was backed for. After its owner has accepted, it may be assumed that the price will not be more than fifty to one, which the maker of the bet will lay to the same person, so that he may himself stand to win fifty pounds to nothing! That is hedging." Further, if the horse becomes a favorite, and attains the price of say ten to one, the bettor may lay off or hedge twenty-five pounds more, in which case he is said to "stand on velvet." In other words, he is sure to win in any event, hence the turf proverb, "No bet is good until it is well hedged to."

BÉZIQUE (bay-zeek), a game with cards. Sometimes it is spelled *bazique.* The word seems to be naturally derived from the Spanish *besico,* a little kiss, in allusion to the distinctive feature of the game, as hereinafter described, namely the "marriage" of the queen and the knave. Murray gives it as a corruption of the French, *besigue,* a game at cards. Bézique, in its present form, is a revival, with modifications, or perhaps a combination of several old games possessing certain features in common. Chief among these is "marriage," and among the others are "brusquembille," "l'homme de bron," "briscan" or "brisque," and "cinq cents." "Brisque" bears the closest likeness to bézique, and is, in fact, nearly identical save that it is played with a double pack and with certain features rendered necessary by the introduction of additional cards. The following rules and directions govern the game in America, and are substantially identical with those accepted elsewhere. They are, in the main, rules as laid down by "Cavendish" (Henry Jones), the recognized English authority on the game:

In bézique two packs of ordinary playing cards are used, but before shuffling all cards below the denomination of seven are rejected, as in euchre, and the remaining 64 cards (32 in each pack) are cut as usual. The game may be played by two, three, or four persons.

Two-handed Bézique. The dealer deals eight cards to himself and his adversary as follows: three to his adversary, three to himself, then two to each, and again three to each.

The cards rank as follow: Ace, ten, king, queen, knave, nine, eight, seven. In case of ties the leader wins. Trumps win other suits.

The objects of the play are: 1. To promote in the hand various combinations of cards which, when *declared,* entitle the holder to certain scores as given in the table; 2. To win aces and tens; 3. To win the so-called last trick.

After dealing, the cards remaining undealt are called the "stock." They are laid on the table a little to one side, and the top card is turned up for trumps, and laid near the stock, and the stock cards are slightly spread so that they can be readily taken by the players as the game proceeds.

The non-dealer plays any card out of his hand. The dealer plays a card to it, the two constituting a "trick." He need not follow suit, nor play a card that wins the trick. He wins the trick by playing a higher card or trumps it (which he may do, although holding in his hand a card of the suit led), he has to lead. Whoever wins the trick has the next lead; but, before playing, each player draws one card from the stock, the winner of the trick drawing the top card, the other player the card next it; by this means the number of the cards in each hand is restored to eight, as at first. This alternate playing a card and drawing a card continues till all the stock, including the trump card (generally exchanged for the seven), which is taken up last, is exhausted. The rules of play then are as hereinafter prescribed. The tricks are left face upward on the table until the end of the hand; they have no value except for the aces and tens that they contain.

Declaring.—A "declaration" can only be made by a player immediately after winning a trick, and before drawing a card from the stock. The declaration is effected by placing the declared cards face upward on the table, where they remain. Though left on the table, they still form part of the hand, and can be played to a trick just the same as if they had not been declared. Each score is marked at the time of declaring.

Players are not bound to declare unless they like, although they may win a trick and hold scoring cards.

A card can not be played to a trick and be declared at the same time.

It is optional to declare or exchange the seven of trumps after winning a trick with some other card. When declared the seven need not be shown unless asked for. When exchanged the seven is put in the place of the turn-up card, and the turn-up is taken into the player's hand. The card taken in exchange for the seven can not be declared until the player exchanging has won another trick.

Any number of combinations may be declared to one trick, provided the same card is not used twice over. Thus, a player having declared four kings, and holding two or three queens matching as to suit may, after winning another trick, marry them all at the same time. But, if a player holds king and queen of spades, and knave of diamonds, he must not put down the three cards to score marriage and bézique. He must first score one combination, say bézique; then, after winning another trick, he may place the king on the table and score marriage.

In declaring fresh combinations one or more cards of the fresh combination must proceed from the part of the hand held up. For instance: a player having sequence in trumps should first declare marriage in trumps, and then, having won another trick, he can declare the sequence by adding the sequence cards. If he incautiously shows the sequence first, he can not afterward score marriage of the king and queen on the table.

The same card can be declared more than once, provided the combination in which it afterward appears is of a different class. Thus: suppose spades are trumps, the queen of spades can be declared in marriage of trumps, in sequence, and in four queens; but a king or queen once married can not be married again, nor can a card having taken part in a set of four take part in another set of four, to make four aces, kings, queens, or knaves; nor can one bézique card be substituted for another to form a second single bézique.

Table of Bézique Scores.—Each seven of trumps, declared or exchanged, counts 10; king and queen of any suit (marriage), when declared, count 20; king and queen of trumps (royal marriage), when declared, count 40; queen of spades and knave of diamonds (called bézique), when declared, count 40; queen of spades and knave of diamonds, declared twice in one deal by the same player (called double bézique), count 500.

The above score is in addition to the forty, if, perhaps, already scored for single bézique.

In order to entitle to double bézique, all four cards must be on the table at the same time, and unplayed to a trick. If all four are declared together, only 500 can be scored, and not 540.

Any four aces, whether duplicates or not, when declared, count 100; any four kings, whether duplicates or not, when declared, count 80; any four queens, whether duplicates or not, when declared, count 60; any four knaves, whether duplicates or not, when declared, count 40; sequence of best five trumps, when declared, counts 250. The best five trumps are ace, ten, king, queen, and knave. If a player has already declared a royal marriage (40 points) he can subsequently declare a trump sequence (250 points); but, if the sequence be declared first, it precludes the subsequent declaration of the royal marriage with the same cards. Each ace or ten taken or saved in trick counts ten. The winner of a trick containing an ace or ten at once adds ten to his score; if the trick consists of two aces or tens, or one of each, he adds twenty.

Sometimes aces and tens are not scored till the end of the hand. In this case, each time an ace or ten is played the winner of the trick takes up the cards on the table, and turns them face downward in front of himself; and when all the cards have been played, each player looks through his cards to ascertain how many aces and tens it contains. When near the end of the game, if scoring in this way, it occasionally happens that both sides can score out. This being so, some players deduct the number of aces and tens held by one from those held by the other, and only allow the majority of aces and tens to reckon. Other players, when near the end, count the aces and tens in their tricks at once if it makes count. Thus: being 960, and having four aces and tens in the tricks, the player would at once call game. Others, again, give precedence in scoring aces and tens to the player who wins the last trick. But the best and simplest method is to mark each ace and ten as the score accrues, not only at the end, but all through the game, as is done in the case of other scores.

The winner of the last trick counts ten.

The Last Eight Tricks.—The last two cards of the stock are taken, one by each player, as before, the loser of the last trick taking the turn-up or seven, as the case may be. When the stock is exhausted no further declarations can be made. Then all cards on the table that have been exposed in declaring are taken up by the player to whom they belong, and the play of the last eight tricks commences. The winner of the previous trick now leads; the second player must follow suit if he can, and must win the trick if he can. If he holds a trump, and is not able to follow suit, he must win the trick by trumping. The winner of the trick leads to the next. The tricks are still only valuable for the aces and tens they may contain.

The winner of the last trick scores ten points.

Mode of Scoring.—A numbered dial with hand, or a bézique-board and pegs, or counters, may be used. The last plan is to be preferred. Eleven counters are required by each player, one marking 500, four each marking 100, one marking 50, and five each marking 10. The counters are placed to the left of the player, and when used to score are transferred to his right. This system of marking shows at a glance not only how many each player has scored, but, by looking to his left, how many he is playing for. This is often important when near the end of the game.

The game is usually played 1,000 up. If one player scores 1,000 before his adversary obtains 500, the game counts double. A *partie* is the best three games out of five, reckoning a double as two games.

Hints to Beginners.—The first difficulty in playing to the tricks is to decide what cards to throw away and what cards to retain, so as to do the least harm to your chance of scoring.

1. It is, if anything, disadvantageous to get the lead unless you have something to declare. Therefore, when a card (not an ace or a ten) is led, do not take it, but throw away a losing card. (See 5 and 12.)

2. The cards that can be spared without loss are sevens, eights, and nines, as they form no part of any of the scoring combinations. (But see 7.)

3. After these, the least injurious cards to part with

are knaves (except the bézique knave and the knave of trumps).

4. It is better, when in difficulties, to lead a ten or an ace, as a rule, than a king or queen, though there are many exceptions. Aces count a hundred, kings only eighty, and queens only sixty; but kings and queens can marry and aces can not. And, as a rule, if you play for four aces, you have to sacrifice some other combination, and having shown four aces, you are pretty sure to lose some of them in the tricks. Remember that every ace or ten lost to you makes a difference of twenty in the score.

5. It is seldom advisable to go for four aces unless you happen to hold three, and are in no difficulty. Ra make tricks with the aces when opportunity offer

6. If driven to lead an ace or a ten, and your adversary does not take the trick, it is often good play to lead another next time.

7. Do not part with small trumps if it can be helped. The seven, eight, and nine of trumps should be kept to trump aces or tens led. If possible keep one small trump in hand to get the lead with when you want to declare.

8. Do not part with trump sequence cards. Even if you have a duplicate card of the trump sequence you should not play it until near the end of the hand, as playing it shows your opponent that you have a duplicate. This frees his hand, as he need no longer keep sequence cards. Armed with this knowledge, he will trump every ace and ten you subsequently lead.

9. Until near the end of the hand, do not part with bézique cards, even after declaring bézique. By so doing you give up all chance of double bézique, the score for which is very high. Having declared bézique, and holding or drawing another bézique card, sacrifice everything, even sequence cards if necessary, for the chance of double bézique.

10. Having a choice between playing a possible scoring card from your hand, or a small trump from your hand, or a card that you have declared, as a rule play the declared card, so as not to expose your hand.

11. Avoid showing your adversary, by what you declare, that he can not make the trump sequence or double bézique. By keeping him in the dark you hamper his game, and as a likely consequence may save some of your tens or aces from being taken by him. For example, (hearts being trumps) suppose early in the hand you hold four queens, viz., two queens of hearts and two queens of spades. It is much better to sacrifice, or, at all events, to postpone scoring, sixty, and not to declare these, than to let your adversary know that he can not make sequence or bézique. (Compare 8.)

12. Whenever your adversary leads a card (not the ace) of a suit of which you hold the ten, take the trick with the ten. This rule does not apply to trumps, as in that suit you require the ten to form part of your sequence.

13. When there are only two cards left in the stock, win the trick if possible. It is the last chance to declare, and it also prevents your adversary from declaring anything more that hand.

14. Toward the end of the hand run your eye over the cards your adversary has on the table, and play accordingly. For example: suppose your opponent has an ace on the table, and you hold a card of that suit, throw away that card that you may be able to trump the ace in the play of the last eight tricks.

15. In playing the last eight tricks your only object should be to save your aces or tens and to win those of the adversary.

16. It is of more importance to win aces and tens than at first sight appears. It is very captivating to sacrifice a number of small scores for the chance of obtaining a large one, and very agreeable when such play succeeds. But it is the practice of experienced players to make sure of a number of small scores. They say

that a player who habitually wins the most aces and tens will come off winner in the long run.

17. Endeavor to remember in what suits the aces and tens have been played; and, in leading small cards, choose those suits of which the most aces and tens are out. By this means you diminish your opponent's chance of making aces and tens.

18. Similarly, after your adversary has declared aces, avoid leading cards which he can win with those aces.

19. Again, in discarding small cards, retain those which are least likely to be taken by aces and tens.

20. By carefully watching your adversary's play you can judge to a great extent what cards he has in hand, and what combinations he is going for. Thus: if he declares a marriage, and discards the king, but retains the queen, he is probably going for queens; if he shows another marriage, and discards another king, the inference is strengthened. With attention and experience it is surprising how much may be inferred as to your adversary's game, and your own line of play is thereby materially directed.

Rules and Penalties of Bézique.—1. The highest deals. In cutting, the cards rank as in playing.

2. The players deal alternately throughout the game.

3. If the dealer gives his adversary or himself too few cards, the number must be completed from the stock. The non-dealer, not having looked at his cards, may, if he prefers it, have a fresh deal. (See also Rule 8.)

4. If the dealer gives his adversary too many cards, the player having too many must not draw until his number is reduced to seven. If the dealer gives himself too many cards, the non-dealer may draw the surplus cards, and add them to the stock. But if the dealer, having too many cards, looks at his hand, he is liable to Rule 9.

5. If a card is exposed in dealing, the adversary has the option of a fresh deal.

6. If a player draws out of his turn, and the adversary follows the draw, there is no penalty. If the adversary discovers the error before drawing he may add twenty to his score, or deduct twenty from that of the other player.

7. If the first player, when drawing, lifts two cards instead of one, the adversary may have them both turned face upward, and then choose which he will take. If the second player lifts two cards, the adversary has a right to see the one improperly lifted, and at the next draw the two cards are turned face upward, and the player not in fault may choose which he will take.

8. If a player plays with seven cards in his hand, the adversary may add twenty to his own score, or deduct twenty from that of the other player. On discovery of the error, the player with a card short must take two cards at his next draw instead of one.

9. If both players draw a second time before playing, there is no penalty. But, if at any time during the play of the hand one player discovers the other to have nine cards, himself holding but eight, he may add 200 to his own score, or deduct 200 from that of the other player. The player having nine cards must play to the next trick without drawing.

10. If a player at two-handed bézique shows a card on the table in error, there is no penalty, as he can not possibly derive any benefit from exposing his hand.

11. If a player at three or four handed bézique shows a card on the table in error, he must leave it on the table, and he can not declare anything in combination with it.

12. If a player at two-handed bézique leads out of turn, there is no penalty. If the adversary follows, the error can not be rectified.

13. If a player at three or four handed bézique leads out of turn, he must leave the exposed card on the table, and he can not declare anything in combi-

nation with it. If all the players follow to a lead out of turn there is no penalty, and the error can not be rectified.

14. The cards played must not be searched.

15. If a player revokes in the last eight tricks, or does not win the card led, if able, all aces and tens in the last eight tricks are scored by the adversary.

16. An erroneous score, if proved, may be corrected at any time during the hand. An omission to score, if proved, can be rectified at any time during the hand.

Triple, or Three-Handed Bézique.—When playing three-handed bézique, three packs are employed, and all play against each other, as in three-handed euchre.

The dealer deals to his left, and the eldest hand has the lead. The players deal in rotation.

Triple bézique counts 1,500, and all the cards of triple bézique must be on the table at the same time. The game is usually 2,000 up.

In playing the last eight tricks, the third hand, if unable to follow suit, nor to win the trick by trumping, may play any card he pleases.

In other respects, the method of playing is the same as in the two-handed game.

Four-Handed Bézique.—When playing four-handed bézique, four packs of cards are employed. The players may all play against each other, or with partners. When playing with partners, the partners are cut for, two highest against two lowest, and sit opposite to each other, as when playing whist.

Triple bézique counts 1.500, and all the cards of triple bézique must be on the table at the same time, but the béziques may be declared from the hand of either partner. A player may declare when he or his partner takes a trick. In playing the last eight tricks, the winner of the previous trick plays with his left-hand opponent; these two play their cards against each other, and score the aces and tens, and then the other two similarly play their cards. The game is usually 2,000. One player scores for himself and partner.

Bézique Panache.—In the game so called, the four aces, four kings, four queens, four knaves, must be, in order to count, composed of spades, diamonds, hearts and clubs; thus an eighty of kings, composed of two kings of spades, one of hearts, and one of diamonds, does not form a combination; and, in like manner with queens and knaves. This game ought to be the object of special agreement.

Bézique without a Trump.—This is played as the ordinary game, except that no card is turned to make a trump, but the trump is decided by the first marriage which is declared. For example: you or your adversary declare a marriage in clubs, then clubs become trumps, and so on with the other suits.

The five highest trumps, orscore of 250, can not be declared until after the first marriage has been declared. The seven of trumps in this game does not count ten points. The béziques, four kings, four queens, etc., are counted the same as in bézique when the trump is turned, and can be declared before the trump is determined. It is the same with the other cards which form combinations; their value remains the same as in the ordinary game of bézique.

Polish Bézique (sometimes called "Open Bézique," or "Fildniski") differs in many particulars from the ordinary game. When a scoring card is played, the winner of the trick places its face upward before him (the same rule applies in the case of two scoring cards to a trick) forming rows of aces, kings, queens, knaves, and trump tens. These are called "open cards." Cards of the same denomination are placed overlapping one another lengthwise, from the player toward his opposite, to economize space. When a scoring card is placed among the open cards, all the sevens, eights, nines, and plain suit tens in the tricks are turned down. Open cards can not be played a second time, and can only be used in declaring. Whether so used or not they remain face upward on the table until the end of the hand including the last eight tricks. A player can declare after winning a trick and before drawing again when the trick won contains one or more cards which, added to his open cards, complete any combination that scores. Every declaration must include a card played to the last trick won. Aces and tens must be scored as soon as won, and not at the end of the hand. The seven of trumps can be exchanged by the winner of the trick containing it ; and if the turn-up card is one that can be used in declaring, it becomes an open card when exchanged. The seven of trumps, when not exchanged, is scored for by the player winning the trick containing it.

" Compound declarations " are allowed, that is, cards added to the open cards can be used at once (without waiting to win another trick), in as many combinations of different classes as they will form with the winner's open cards. Thus, suppose A has three open kings and wins a trick containing a king ; before drawing again he places the fourth king with the other three and scores 80 for kings. This is a simple declaration. But if the card led was the open queen of trumps and A won it with the king, and he has the following named open cards : three kings three queens, and ace, ten, and knave of trumps, he at once declares royal marriage (40) ; four kings (80) ; four queens (60) ; and sequence (250), and he scores altogether 430.

Or, if ace of spades is turned up, and ace of hearts is led, the second player has two open aces and wins the ace of hearts with the seven of trumps, and exchanges. He scores 10 for the exchange, 10 for the ace of hearts, 10 for the ace of spades, adds the aces to his open cards, and scores 100 for aces—130 in all. If a declaration or part of a declaration is omitted, and the winner of the trick draws again, he can not amend his score.

A second declaration can not be made of a card already declared in the same class. For instance, a queen once married can not be married again, and a fifth king added to four already declared, does not entitle to another score for kings.

It must be kept in mind that no declaration can be effected by means of cards in hand. Thus B, having three open queens and a queen in hand, can not add his open cards to his hand. He must win another trick containing a queen when he can declare queens. Declarations continue during the play of the last eight tricks exactly as during the play of the other cards.

The game is 2,000 up. It is desirable after each deal to shuffle thoroughly ; otherwise, a number of small cards will run together in the stock and detract from the interest of the game. It is also well to follow the rules for ordinary bézique respecting changes of cards ; otherwise, the scores of one may run very high and the other very low, thus impairing the interest of the game. The lead is even more disadvantageous than in common bézique. It is important not to lead anything that can be won by ordinary bézique cards. It is often desirable to win with a high card, though able to win with a low one ; thus, having king and nine of a suit of which the eight is led, if you win the trick you should take it with the king. It is not so important to win aces and tens, especially the latter, as in ordinary bézique. A difficult point in the game is to decide whether to win tricks with sequence cards, on the chance of eventually scoring sequence, or to reserve trumps for the last eight tricks. As a rule, if the hand is well advanced, and you are badly off for trumps, win tricks with sequence cards, and especially if you have duplicate sequence cards make them both. If badly off in trumps toward the end of the hand, and your adversary may win double bézique, keep in hand an ace or ten of the bézique suits, since when it comes to the last eight tricks, where suit must be followed, you may prevent the score of double bézique.

Grand or Chinese Bézique.—This is played like ordinary bézique, except that four packs are shuffled together and used as one, and nine cards are dealt to the players, three at a time to each. When a combination is declared and one of the cards composing it is played away, another declaration may be completed (after winning a trick) with the same cards. For instance, C declares four aces, and uses one to win a trick, or throws one away. He has a fifth ace in his hand, and wins a trick ; he can add to it the three remaining declared aces and score four aces again, and so on. Marriages can be declared over and over again ; thus king and queen of hearts are declared, and the player draws another king of hearts. He plays the declared king and wins the trick. He can then marry the queen again. This is sometimes objected to, on the ground of alleged bigamy, but if permitted only after the declared king is played—that is to say, removed from the sphere of active life—his queen may properly be regarded as a widow, free to marry again.

Bézique follows the same rule, if, for instance, a knave is played away, another knave makes another bézique, and so with double and triple bézique, if the former declared cards which remain unplayed can be matched from cards in hand to make the required combinations. Sequence can be declared over and over again, and compound declarations made among the declared cards are now generally allowed. The sevens of trumps do not count, nor does the last trick, unless by special agreement among the players. The game is 3,000 up. The points for the players to aim at are to declare four aces or sequence, which can then be declared over and over again, if fresh aces or sequence cards are taken into the hand (the duplicate sequence cards being first played away). With fair probability of sequence, everything else, including even aces or chance of double bézique, should be sacrificed.

BIBLE SOCIETIES. American.—The seventy-second annual meeting of the American Bible Society was held May 10. The Hon. E. L. Fancher presided. The cash receipts of the society for the year for general purposes had been $557,340, in addition to which $4,971 had been received to be permanently invested. The cash disbursements for general purposes had been $506,453. The funds held in trust, of which only the income is available, amounted to $347,721, and had yielded during the year $13,662. The investments for general purposes amounted to $204,561, and had returned an income of $10,282. More than two hundred volumes had been added to the library, two thirds of the number being copies of the Scriptures in various languages, some of them representing work done in ancient times. Progress was reported on translations of the Scriptures into Spanish, Modern Syriac, popular Japanese, and Telugu. Preparatory to printing an edition in ancient Armenian, a committee of scholars in Constantinople had been invited to give counsel in respect to doubtful readings. The Muskokee version was under examination with reference to corrections for a new edition. Translations into the Indian languages of Mexico were desired, but could not be undertaken for the want of a competent translator. Progress had been made with the version for the Laos people. The question of a version into the easy Wenli of China was under advisement. Versions in other Chinese dialects were undergoing revision. The whole number of issues during the year at home and in foreign coun-. tries had been 1,504,647 copies. In the missionary and benevolent work of the society, 387 Bible distributors were employed in foreign lands, and 126 colporteurs in the United States. The general re-supply of the United States, which had been in progress for six years, was now drawing to a close. So far, it had resulted in the visitation of 5,001,844 families, 607,009 of whom were found without the Scriptures; and the supply of 427,346 families and 243,764 individuals in addition. Amendments to the charter of the society had been procured, enlarging its powers to take and hold real estate by bequest or devise, which had previously been limited by the condition that the property be alienated within three years; and giving it authority to receive gifts and bequests in trust.

British and Foreign.—The annual meeting of the British and Foreign Bible Society was held in London, May 2. Lord Harrowby presided. The gross income of the society for the year had been £250,382, and the expenditure £224,823. As more than £100,000, however, of the total income was merely the price paid for the books sold, the net income had really been only £147,000. The whole number of Bibles and parts thereof issued had been 4,206,032, or 273,354 more than in the previous year. The money received was spent on foreign agencies, on auxiliaries abroad, and on kindred societies. The agents had charge of the depots, superintended the colporteurs, watched the passing through the press of the Bibles in the native languages of foreign countries, and sold the Scriptures—all with the object of promoting as far as possible the putting of the Bible into every man's hand. Speakers at the anniversary dwelt upon the benefits realized in missionary lands from furnishing converts with the Scriptures in their own tongues.

BOATS, COLLAPSABLE. Scientifically constructed boats capable of being folded or collapsed into comparatively small space are a modern invention. If we ignore the rude barbaric contrivances made of the inflated skin of animals and which were merely rafts or floats, it may fairly be said the existing type of folding boat came into being without passing through the usual protracted stages of development. The inventor is the Rev. E. L. Berthon, an English clergyman, and to him belongs the credit of having first conceived, and subsequently worked out the problem.

In June, 1849, the "Orion," a favorite passenger-steamer plying between Liverpool and Glasgow, ran upon a sunken rock off Port Patrick within two or three hundred yards of the shore. The accident was the result of inexcusable carelessness, as the weather was clear and the sea calm. The ship hung for a few minutes upon the rock, and then slid off into deep water, sinking at once and carrying with her about 200 persons of whom 150 were drowned. Only one of her boats was safely launched, and that was captured by the sailors and firemen. The

others were swamped by the rush of terrified passengers. Among the saved was a clergyman, a friend of Mr. Berthon, who wrote and published an account of his experiences. Knowing Mr. Berthon as a good draughtsman, he asked him to prepare some illustrations for the book, and while making the drawings the idea of a collapsable boat came into his mind.

Then followed the usual difficulties that beset inventors. For a quarter of a century he fought the battle single-handed. In his own words: "Nothing but faith and confidence in the invention which a higher power put into my mind, and a sense of certainty that some day it would prevail, carried me through. And now I am thankful to say that these boats are to be found in all parts of the world. They have been adopted by the Admiralty and by the India Board, and though, as hitherto, ship-owners stand off as being free from all responsibility with regard to the lives of their crews and passengers so long as they act up to a most defective law, I may confidently assert that the day is not far distant when this system of supplementary boats will be general."

The inventor's description of the boat is as follows: "Imagine a long melon cut into thin slices" (evidently the rind alone is meant), "their shape will be more or less lenticular. Now suppose these to be jointed together at each

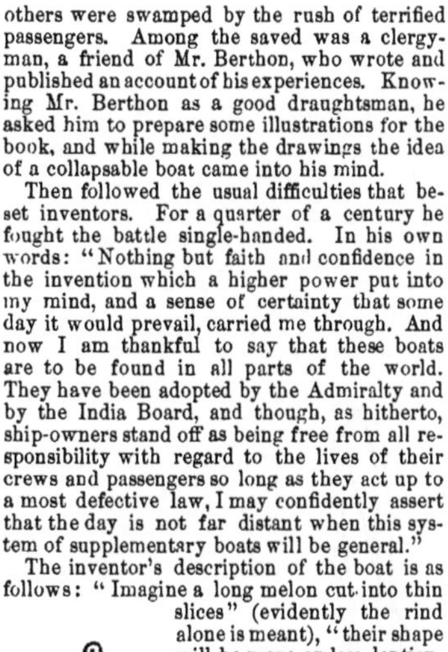

FIG. 1.—BERTHON FOLDING-BOAT, MIDSHIP SECTIONS.

1, Boat collapsed against bulwarks. 2, Same boat expanded automatically, on letting go the gripes, showing arrangement of thwarts, bottom boards, and gunwale struts. *a a*, Strong canvas cover, protecting the boat when collapsed against the bulwarks. *a b*, Chainwale of wood, to which cover is attached. The shaded spaces are eight air-cells between the skins, all separate and water-tight.

end so as to lie flat side by side, like the leaves of a shut book, or to take any other positions radiating from a central line. Now if a certain number of such segments, properly placed at certain distances, are connected together by some flexible material on their outer edges, and made water-tight, the structure becomes a boat, but having as yet only one skin, it would only float so long as that skin is not pierced. But now let us suppose another skin to be applied to the inner edges of these lenticular segments and made water-tight, not merely is there a boat within a boat, but the spaces between the segments, being all separate and distinct, an injury to one does not affect the rest."

In fact the structure forms a true life-boat amply provided with water-tight compartments, and capable of anything that an ordinary boat can do, except that its canvas skin is more easily pierced than the wood or iron of which boats are usually constructed. So long as the Berthon boat is properly handled and kept in open water, she is as safe as any other boat of her size.

Fig. 1 is a sectional view of a boat folded and open as explained in the context. Fig. 2 shows a fully equipped boat at the davits with the temporary canvas covering partly removed to show the profile of the

lenticular segments heretofore described) which are hinged to the stem and stern posts. When collapsed these timbers fall down on either side of the keelson in vertical and parallel planes, and when opened they assume such positions as to form the skeleton of the boat, extending the two canvas skins as described.

Experiments were at first made with India-rubber, but while it served admirably when new it was found that it would not stand exposure to changes of climate, and this failure led the British Admiralty to condemn the boat as a failure. Years elapsed before they could be induced to reconsider their availability when covered with canvas. The canvas as now prepared is saturated with boiled oil and litharge, and in every ten pounds is dissolved one pound of yellow soap. This keeps the fabric soft and pliable, and at the same time increases its strength. Boats thus constructed have been in use for from four to eight years, and are to all appearance as serviceable as they ever were.

FIG. 2.—BERTHON FOLDING-BOAT. SHEER PLAN.

folded boat. One very important feature of these boats is that they open themselves automatically as soon as the weight comes on the falls. There is therefore nothing to be done but to swing the boat clear of the chain-wale and lower away. Of course the same difficulties in taking the water are present as in the case of ordinary boats.

The materials used in construction are mainly wood and canvas. The longitudinal timbers are preferably strips of American elm, steamed and bent in a mold, and riveted together with copper. The stem and stern posts are attached to the keelson, and on each side are four longitudinally curved timbers (A A A, Fig. 1) (the

In practical service these boats collapse into about one fifth of the space occupied by an ordinary boat. They may be laid one on top of another, stowed below decks, or, which is by far the best plan, lashed along outside the bulwarks as shown in Fig. 2. It is said that the frames are strong enough to sustain the full complement of passengers at the davits, but lowering a crowded boat into the water is extremely dangerous and, as with all boats, it is best to allow the crew only on board.

The Berthon boats are built of all sizes, from the light, single-handed canoe, easily folded and carried under the arm, to the large life-boat, 40 feet long by 13½ feet beam. Boats of this latter size are in use in the British navy. They weigh about fifty-five hundred pounds, and collapse to 2½ feet. A wooden boat of like dimensions weighs more than twice as

Fig. 3.—Douglass Folding-Boat.

much. Such a boat will carry eight horses, and a heavy field-gun with its gunners, besides the regular crew of oarsmen. The boat is beached, broadside on, and one of her gunwales is lowered till it is nearly on a level with the bottom-boards. Then the horses are led off without difficulty, as they are generally very glad to step or jump over the gunwale for the sake of getting on shore. Of course, with such a freight as here specified, extra floor-boards are necessary to guard against restive horses.

The importance of such boats for military and naval purposes, and for hunting and exploring expeditions, is self evident, but of far greater consequence is their use for life-saving on board our great passenger-steamers, as well as on the huge troop-ships used by European powers. These vessels often carry nearly or quite two thousand souls, and their full complement of non-collapsable boats is capable of carrying only about six hundred, even under the most favorable circumstances. With the great passenger-steamers the case is hardly any better. They all of them carry more of the ordinary type of boat than they are by law required to carry, but the supply is far short of the necessity, and lack of room prohibits the transportation of more boats. Probably it is not desirable that the use of ordinary boats by vessels either of the merchant service or of the navy should be altogether abandoned. A fair supply should always be at hand, but a supplementary supply of collapsable boats is a necessity, and should be required by law, now that their practical utility has been proved. It is satisfactory to notice that the great transatlantic steamship lines have anticipated legislative action in this respect, and all the best ships are now equipped with collapsable boats. The "City of New York," the latest accession to

the transatlantic passenger fleet, has thirty large boats, capable of carrying every soul on board under ordinary conditions. Sixteen of these are non-collapsable, ten are "Chambers's patent unsinkable, semi-collapsable boats," and four are Berthon boats.

The Chambers boats mentioned are shallow boats fitted with washboards, which increase the height of the sides and the consequent carrying capacity of the boat. They are stowed one on top of another, three occupying the space of an ordinary boat. When raised into position, the washboards lock themselves in place. These boats are provided with forty air-tight compartments, and the bottom is so arranged that it serves as a life-raft in case of accident. Under the seats are lockers for provisions, etc.

Another folding boat known as the Douglass model is largely used in this country. It is based on the Berthon principle in so far as concerns its folding longitudinal timbers, but it is much lighter, and is intended mainly for the use of sportsmen. It is not a life-boat, having only one skin, and no water-tight compartments.

With each boat stout curved transverse ribs are provided which are easily adjusted and sprung into place when the boat is expanded, keeping the whole structure firmly stretched. External strips of hard wood protect the canvas from wear and tear, and add to its strength. (See Fig. 3.) The seats and floor-boards are seen folded in the illustration, with the stout ribs that keep the frame expanded when in use.

Still another type of folding boat collapses endwise like an accordion, the bent ribs pressing inward against one another toward the midship section. When expanded these boats are stiffened by a jointed or hinged timber fastened along the bottom for a keelson or backbone. In transportation these boats take

Fig. 4.—Osgood Folding-Boat.

up very little room, as it is possible to stow them in a bag or a box no bigger than a moderate-sized trunk. The one shown in Fig. 4 is known as the Osgood folding boat. The box in which, with all its attachments, it is packed for transportation, measures thirty-eight inches by seventeen inches, by eighteen inches deep. The oars, paddles, etc., are jointed for ease of packing. The weight of a twelve-foot boat is from twenty-five to fifty pounds, according to the completeness of its equipment.

At the Glasgow International Exhibition in 1888, was exhibited the Shepard collapsable life-boat which has several distinctive features. (Fig. 5.) The transverse timbers work on

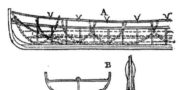

FIG. 5.—SHEPARD COLLAPSABLE LIFE-BOAT.
A, Sheer plan, collapsed. B, Cross-section, expanded and collapsed.

a swivel attached to the keelson. When the boat is expanded their upper ends lock to the inwales, and are firmly held in position. When stowed these ribs are turned, as shown by the dotted lines at A, so that they overlap one another in a plane nearly identical with that of the keelson and end posts. The other dotted lines show bottom-boards, etc. At B is represented the midship section as it appears when expanded and when folded.

These boats have been adopted by some of the transatlantic steamship lines.

BOLIVIA, an independent republic of South America. (For details relating to area, territorial divisions, population, etc., see "Annual Cyclopædia" for 1883 and 1886).

Government.—The President of the republic is Don Aniceto Arce, whose term of office will expire on Aug. 1, 1892. His Cabinet is composed of the following ministers: Foreign Affairs, Señor Velarde; Finances and Interior, Don Telmo Ichazo; War, General Cabrera. Bolivia is not represented by a minister at Washington, nor are the United States at present represented at La Paz, except by Samuel S. Carlisle, American Consul-General. The Bolivian Consul-General at New York is Don Melchor Obarrio.

Army.—The strength of the regular army is 3,031 rank and file, the number of officers being 367.

Finances.—The foreign debt has been reduced to $826,000, $2,280,000 having been paid during the past four years in settlement of Chili's claims arising from the war on the Pacific. The home debt amounts to $2,500,000. The budget for 1887-'88 estimates the income at $3,665,790, and the outlay at $4,599,225. In

order to increase the revenue it is proposed to raise the duties and the liquor-tax and the tax on patents. The exportation of national coin will continue to be prohibited until apprehensions of a monetary crisis shall be allayed. The by-laws of the new "Banco de la Paz" have been approved. Congress had voted $10,000 toward defraying Bolivia's representation at the Paris Exhibition of 1889, but the Government finding that the amount would not suffice to do so with dignity, a bill increasing it has been submitted. The sum of $300,000 has been voted toward additional mint machinery at Potosi.

Treaties.—An understanding has been arrived at between Bolivia and the Argentine Republic, fixing the boundary between them in the Chaco in a preliminary manner; a commission was to convene in November to determine the frontier line definitively. Negotiations with Brazil about a treaty of commerce, amity, and navigation were still pending; it will embrace an understanding facilitating the Madeira Mamoné Railroad scheme. The treaty of commerce with Peru is to be revised and completed; the boundary treaty with Paraguay is to become a subject of negotiations without further delay. Bolivia has engaged to send delegates to the Congress about to meet at Montevideo for the purpose of laying down rules for private international rights. A treaty of commerce and amity mutually guaranteeing literary and artistic right has been concluded with France and signed.

Railroads.—An English company has been formed in London for the purpose of building a line of railway from Arica to Bolivia in conjunction with the present owners and shareholders of the Arica and Tacna Railroad, with a capital of £2,000,000. The parties chiefly interested in this new enterprise are Messrs. Clark Brothers, who have built railways in the Argentine Republic, Richard Campbell, the Australian Bank in London, and Mr. John Meiggs. The new line is to reach La Paz via Tacna and Corocoro. The Huanchaca Company has resolved to build, with its own funds and without interest guarantee, a railroad and telegraph line from Oruro to the Bolivian frontier.

Telegraphs.—A new telegraph line is in course of construction between Tupiza and Tariza. As it will be connected with the Huanchaca Mining Company's private line, it will insure rapid communication with Mallendo and Europe. The project of an international telegraph bureau has, therefore, been submitted to Congress by the Government.

Public Works.—In July Don Cristian Suarez Arana arrived at Puerto Pacheco after having accomplished the junction between the road that leads from Isozog to Las Salinas and the wagon-road opened in that direction from Puerto Pacheco, thus establishing direct communication with the Paraguay river. The two departments more directly benefited are Chuquisaca and Santa Cruz. The settlements of agriculturists in the Chaco will be greatly benefited by this, as it will have a tendency to attract immigration toward this region, one of the most fertile of South America. In the Bolivian mining regions new wagon-roads have also been authorized by Congress.

Electric Light.—Not only is La Paz to be traversed by tramway-lines, but the electric light has been universally introduced.

Exploring Expedition.—In January Baron de la Rivière arrived at Chililaya, Bolivia, after having passed nearly a year on the Tipuani river, an affluent of the Mapiri. He had been on a gold-hunting expedition among the districts which gave the ancient Peruvians all their gold. The baron speaks highly of the abundance of gold, but declares the climate to be of the worst description, and the region to be infested with vermin and deadly animals. He started into the forests with over two hundred men. Of this number only a very few have returned with him. The others succumbed to fevers, snake bites, and like evils.

Cinchona-bark.—The shipments abroad of Bolivian cinchona-bark have been steadily on the increase in 1888, not only cultivated but wild grown, thus more than compensating for the falling off from the island of Ceylon, which latter exported from October 1 to September 20, 11,632, 251 pounds, as compared with 13,-921,109 in 1886–'87, and 15,226,152 in 1885–'86· The cultivated Bolivian bark has, in 1888, been exported not only in flat pieces, but also in the shape of tubes, and is still highly esteemed on account of its large quinine contents. Meanwhile, Peruvian cinchona planters assert that, at ruling prices abroad, their industry has ceased to be profitable; but, as stated, this does not deter them from exporting more than ever. A recent report by a gentleman named Van Lon, who resides in Batavia, indicates that there is likely to be a further heavy increase in the production of Java, not only on account of the enlarged acreage of trees that has been planted, but because it is found that the new growth is capable of producing bark that will yield 18 per cent. of alkaloid. It is stated that there are 12,000 acres under cultivation in Java, which, at 800 trees per acre, would give about 10,-000,000 trees, which, at 1½ pound a tree (the Indian average), would yield 15,000,000 pounds, spread over six years. While the supply from Bolivia and Java thus promises to be abundant enough, the Government of India has published for the information of the public, through the Bulletin of the Royal Gardens, Kew, some particulars of the new process of extracting quinine from the cinchona-bark by means of oil. By the aid of this process, perfected lately by Mr. Gamme, it is found possible to utilize the calisaya or yellow bark variety, and to extract from it the whole of its quinine in a form indistinguishable chemically or physically from the best brands of European manufacture, and this so cheaply that not merely in times like the present of depressed markets, but at all periods, it will not cost the Government more than twenty-five rupees per pound. Should all the expectations which this important discovery has awakened be realized, it is believed that it will lead to the substitution of Indian-manufactured quinine for the febrifuge in the hospitals and dispensaries of India, and, as a necessary consequence, to the substitution of yellow bark for red bark in the Sikkim plantations.

Indian Troubles.—In May another rising of Indians occurred in the province of Sicasica, some eight thousand of them being in arms, and threatening to massacre all the whites. They were commanded by a chief of the name of Villca; but the cavalry garrisoned at Ayoayo was hurried on to suppress the revolt, which was quelled and the ringleaders imprisoned.

River Navigation.—The Bolivian Government has granted to Mr. John L. Thorndike the exclusive privilege for ten years of steam navigation between the Desaguadero river and Lake Poopó, all material which he will require for his enterprise to be admitted duty free. Since the Peruvian Government has seized the railroads of the Mollendo-Arequipa-Puno lines of Peru their administration has become so bad that Bolivian merchants who had been availing themselves of these lines in connection with Lake Titicaca for the transportation of their goods, have been compelled to return to the Arica-Tacna outlet, and this in spite of the fact that from Tacna the goods have to be forwarded on mules' backs, and that at Arica the goods have to pay storage and harbor expenses, which are not charged at Mollendo. While this is the case, the Bolivian Government has ordered the organization of custom-houses at the Mollendo Agency, at Puerto Perez or La Paz and the remaining ports of Lake Titicaca, in conformity with an understanding arrived at with Peru, and in conformity with the law of July 16, 1885, regulating the general customs' service.

Bolivia at the Barcelona Exhibition.—The Huanchaca Mining Company has made a magnificent display of its rich copper ores and blende, and the Bolivian firm of Artola Brothers, of Bolivian embroideries, textile fabrics, seeds, feathers, skins, chocolate, and small figures of whites and Indians dressed in the costumes of the country, together with a thousand curiosities, all together giving a high idea of Bolivia's resources and its manual and artistic skill highly creditable to the South American inland republic.

BORNEO, the largest of the Malaysian islands, having a length of 850 miles and a breadth of 600 miles. Its area is about 270,-000 square miles. The Dutch claim suzerain rights over the greater part of the island, comprising the entire region south of the native state of Sarawak, which has long been administered by Englishmen, and the territory belonging to the Sultan of Sulu. In 1881 the British North Borneo Company was chartered in England, and took possession of the northern end of the island, by virtue of a grant from the Sultan of Sulu. Commercial stations were established, and a civil administration was organized by 1883, when the revenue collected amounted to $50,738, while the expenditure amounted to five times that sum. The area of British North Borneo, as the new state was called, is 31,106 square miles. Its population is 150,000. The principal products are beeswax, edible birds'-nests, camphor, cocoanuts, coffee, dammar, fruits, salt fish, guttapercha, hides, India-rubber, elephants' tusks, cattle, pepper, rattans, rice, sago, seeds, pearls, sharks' fins, tortoise and other shells, tobacco, trepang, cedar, and many kinds of cabinet-woods. The imports increased from $429,000 in 1883 to $535,000 in 1887, and the exports from $159,000 to $535,000. The climate is temperate, and agricultural colonies have been founded, the sales of land up to the end of 1887 having been 120,000 acres. There are plantations of sugar, coffee, pepper, and other tropical products. The soil has been found to be remarkably good for tobacco-culture, and, in the first three months of 1888, applications were made for 158,335 acres more. Borneo tobacco now competes successfully with that grown in Sumatra. There are five companies engaged in planting tobacco. The revenue now exceeds the expenditures, not reckoning the proceeds of land sales, which are treated as capital. The revenue is derived from duties on opium, salt, tobacco, and spirits, export duties, fees, and rents. Stations were first founded at Sandakam, Papar, Kiminas, Gaya, Kudat, and Silam, on the coast, and, as soon as land was cleared at those points, immigrants began to arrive, and the Dyaks of the interior brought in their produce to sell. A police force was recruited from Malays and Dyaks, Sulu Islanders, Nubians and Somalis from Africa, and Sikhs from India. Tribal feuds and head-hunting forays are now of rare occurrence. In 1884 the territory was enlarged by the additional grant of Dent Land in the south. The country enjoys the advantages of settled government under a system of laws copied from the code of India. There are offices, barracks, hospitals, jails, and wharves at all the stations. Explorations recently made in the interior have resulted in the discovery of alluvial gold in paying quantities on the Segama river, and of coal-beds in the southern province, but only the agricultural wealth of the country has thus far been developed. The forests produce some of the finest woods that are known, among them the valuable bilian-tree, and there is already a considerable export of timber to China. The British Government in the beginning refused to extend political protection to the North Borneo Company, as there was at that time a prejudice against the annexation of new countries. New possessions have since been added to the British Empire in many parts of the world, and the Government has at length decided to declare a protectorate over British North Borneo, Sarawak, and the large native state of Brunei.

BOXING. Individual prowess is a large factor in the survival of the fittest. Man is no exception. From the beginning the praises of the man of speed, of muscle, of skill in the use of nature's weapons have been sculptured and sung. To acquire physical superiority has been the study of ages. The ancients paid great honor to the runner, the dumb-bell lifter, or any other specialist; but they outdid themselves when it came to the winner of the *pancratium*, a combination of boxing and wrestling, kicking, biting, gouging, and choking, beside which the contests of the modern prize-ring under what are known as the London rules are a parlor amusement.

To become a clever boxer is now the study of many people who a few years ago would have considered it degrading to be seen in the street with a pugilist. Books on this subject are being rapidly placed on the market, and schools of self-defense are opening all over the country. To be a fairly good boxer is soon to be a requisite in more than one occupation. The police of at least one American city (Pittsburg) are being instructed in the art of boxing at the expense of the tax-payers, and it is expected that when the force is composed entirely of proficient boxers the use of the club and pistol will almost entirely cease.

Boxing as it is now known, outside of those old-time brutalities with the cestus (a sort of brass knuckles), is about three hundred years old. It came into prominence first in England. The old English idea of boxing—to call it an art as it was then seems ludicrous—was but little better than that of the ancient Greeks and Romans. In olden times in England two so-called boxers entered a ring to settle the question which had the greater brute strength, courage, wind, and endurance. There was not the slightest question of brains in the battle. Soon a man came forward who was able by a show of agility to make up for his lack of size in a fight with one of these old-time giants; and then came a fighter like Tom Crib, who introduced the famous "milling on the retreat" tactics, and it became possible for a man like Tom Spring, who was not much more than medium sized (a middle-weight) and, a few years afterward, for Tom Sayers, almost a small man, to beat all the heavy-weights in England and hold the championship belt. When such results became possible, boxing might be said to have really become a science.

Since the time when only giants could be victorious pugilists this science has undergone more than one revolution. Once the two fighters stood toe to toe, and to retreat, to go down, to manœuvre in any way, was disgraceful. Once men used the left hand as a shield and the right as a mace. Then the right hand became the shield and the left the weapon of offense. In the time of Heenan and Sayers, the English fighters depended mainly upon the right; but Heenan showed them the superiority of the left. For years it was said that only a "yokel" hit with his right fist, or struck a swinging blow. John L. Sullivan, the mightiest pugilist of the age, who brought the business of pugilism from the gutter to a profession almost as well-paying as base-ball-playing or riding running horses, revolutionized all that, developed the blow on the point of the jaw, and with swinging, round-arm blows of his terrible right, incased though it was in a boxing-glove, mowed down opponents who trusted to their knowledge and practice of boxing to defeat him. Possibly some of Sullivan's triumphs are explained by the facts that he came out at a time when pugilism was at a low ebb and good big men were scarce, and that he met his opponents under Marquis of Queensberry rules instead of under the rules of the London Prize-Ring, which would have suited many of them far better. Sullivan's battle with Charles Mitchell, under the London rules, in France, in March, 1888, resulted in a draw after a protracted encounter. A man, Sullivan's inferior in weight by forty pounds, facing him in a bare-knuckle fight for hours, has done much to change the popular idea of scientific boxing. A few years ago it was all right-hand swinging blows, and decisive battles in very short time; now it is more caution, more careful hitting, and mostly with the left hand, the right being saved, as before Sullivan's advent, for the *coup de grâce.* Sullivan took boxing to one extreme, to win or lose in short order by one decisive hit on a tender spot, the point of the jaw. Mitchell has turned back the tide by his long, waiting tactics; while another man, Jack Dempsey, the wonderful middle-weight, has been a sort of balance-wheel.

Even before the idea had been broached of using the legs in a prize-fight, or the rules allowed it, there was some knowledge of the most vulnerable spots for blows. The pit of the stomach, called "the mark," was one of these, and a severe blow on this spot was very telling. Other points of attack were the butt of the ear or on the jugular vein; the temples, the eyes, the throat, just over the heart, and on the short ribs. The extreme sensitiveness of the pit of the stomach and the chin was left for John L. Sullivan to demonstrate. The "big fellow," as his admirers delighted to call him, while sitting in a surgeon's chair having the arm that he broke over Patsy Cardiff's head reset, told the writer of this article that he discovered his famous "knock-out" blow partly by accident and partly from reading the works of a famous English novelist. Sullivan said he knocked men out of time in the beginning of his career by delivering a swinging right-hand blow on

the neck on the jugular vein. But he soon found the full-arm swinging blow as dangerous to his own hand and forearm as to his opponent's circulation, so he changed the full-arm swing to a half-arm one, and tried to deliver the blow on the jaw-bone instead of on the neck, as it was equally effective and less likely to be fatal. However little future boxers may value Sullivan's round-arm delivery, they can not fail to give him credit for centralizing his fire and for pointing out a supremely vulnerable spot.

Preliminary Points.—Gentlemen want to learn, not the tricks of the ring, but the simple points of scientific pugilism. The first thing in boxing is to learn to double the fist correctly, "make up a bunch of fives," as it is called in ring-parlance. Not one man in a thousand can do this, not because there is anything difficult about it, but because so few will make the attempt naturally. A novice is sure to protrude the middle, or second finger, thinking he is making a very formidable weapon of his hand, when in reality he is only increasing his chances for that curse of boxing —broken hand-bones. At best, ninety-nine amateurs in a hundred double up the fist squarely, that is, with the first and second fingers closed tightly and the third and fourth loosely folded. This makes another ugly-looking but very ineffective weapon, sure to be injured at the first good blow. To double the fist correctly, open out all the fingers and the thumb to the widest stretch, then close naturally. The backs of the big knuckles, the only ones that should ever strike on an opponent, will be found to have formed an arch when the hand is tightly closed. In fighting or boxing the hands should be held loosely, half open, all the muscles and those of the forearms relaxed, till the moment of delivery, when the fist should be most tightly closed. No one can practice throwing a base-ball without learning how thoroughly interdependent the muscles are. The wisdom of resting the hands by giving them perfect freedom while not actually delivering a blow has been illustrated by many great boxers. Those masters, Jem Mace and Joe Coburn, always manœuvred in the ring with hands as open as if they were about to wrestle, not to strike with the fists. Indeed, the wonderful Gypsy's commonest trick in a ring was hitching up his waist-band, wiping his hands on his fighting-breeches, or rubbing them together. Dominick McCaffrey, in his easy forty-minute victory over Golden, in their skin-tight glove contest, was doing with his hands a great deal of the time the practice that a school-girl does with her fingers in order to be able to stretch an octave. Jem Carney, in the light-weight championship battle with Jack McAuliffe, used the same method of keeping his hands fit for their work. For boxing-practice with ordinary gloves the hands do not need the hardening the pugilists give theirs before a matched battle; but no blow in boxing should be delivered with the hand or glove open. A light blow should be given in showing a friend a move, not by slapping, tapping, or "flicking," but by accurate gauging of the time and distance. When an amateur can deliver a light blow with a closed hand delicately, he is becoming artistic. They say that Mace could knock down an ox or simply touch the powder on a lady's face with a blow from his clinched hand. The story may have just a flavor of the trip-hammer-and-watch-crystal tale about it, but Mace certainly was a wonderful artist. Pugilists harden their hands in different ways. The change from the bare-knuckle fighting of olden times to the dog-skin-glove battles of recent years does away with much disagreeable and tiresome work in this direction. Good, hard rubbing is one of the best things in the world to harden the flesh and bones of the hand. Alcohol, lemon-juice, rock-salt, gunpowder, saltpeter dilute, tannin, and alum are some of the washes used. Jem Carney, the English light-weight champion, used to whet his hands over a smooth plank for hours a day during his training, slapping the backs of his hands back and forth over the wood as a man straps a razor. As, in spite of all precaution, a carelessly delivered upper-cut, a blow on an opponent's head, or a failure when very tired to have the hands as well closed as they should be, is always liable to injure the hand, it might not be out of the way to mention a simple remedy, of which few surgeons are apt to think. It will do away with what most fighters' hands have, unsightly bunches from the broken bones not having been properly set. A silver dollar inserted under the bandage over the broken bone will press the ends in together so tightly as to heal them most completely and without a bunch. A wooden dollar would answer just as well.

How to Stand.—A good position in boxing is very important. The approved position is with the body erect, weight between the legs, the left being advanced in front of the right. The toes of the left foot are turned *in*, those of the right foot *out*. The rule among the eleverest of the professionals is "On the flat of the left; on the ball of the right." The right leg need *not* be behind the other in a line running from the heel of the right foot through the ball to the heel of the left, as has sometimes been taught. It would require a tight-rope walker's balancing powers to stand with one foot exactly behind the other in delivering a blow, though the right will greatly second the effort if it is pretty nearly behind the left. The right leg should be slightly bent at the knee, the left held straight but not stiff. Just how far apart the feet should be kept, is another matter of individual practice, influenced also by each one's height and build. The most convenient distance between the feet is generally about half the ordinary step. It would tire anybody but a statue to keep

this or any one position long, and the muscles of the legs and body are rested by stepping about. In walking about an attempt should be made to keep the left foot a little in advance of the right, and be ready to fly into the attitude in no time. Proficiency in leg-work, which is most important, can only be acquired by long practice and natural aptitude. Some boxing-teachers tell pupils to stand with the left or advanced foot turned *out*. This is contrary to the whole theory and practice of boxing, which simply tries to make the most of nature's laws in every instance. The very important thing about a position is the advantage it gives to get quickly backward or forward and to second the delivery of blows. Let any one when standing perfectly still with his left foot advanced and the toes turned well *out*, try to spring backward or forward; then try it with the toes turned *in*. All pedestrians, sprinters, six-day runners, and heel-and-toe walkers progress with feet either held perfectly straight or with the toes turned a trifle in. The child of nature, the American Indian, travels in the same way, and so do most mail-carriers and policemen. The variety of positions in which to do good and effective boxing is as great as is the number of boxers. Every man selects that attitude best suited to his height, reach, length of leg, and tactics. To stand well up, so as to take full advantage of the height, is generally considered wise, some men even standing on the toes. This is seemingly a very tiresome attitude, yet it is one that Tom Sayers frequently assumed. A man's position, however, must be governed by other considerations than a sole wish to stand as tall as possible. Any one that has ever tried to hit a punching-bag knows that force is gained for the blows, even if speed is lost, by assuming a stooping attitude.

The Arms.—The left arm should be held out perhaps a little farther than elbow-distance from the body, with the hand held so that the thumb is uppermost. The left arm in position should form an obtuse angle. The right arm should be thrown across the body, with the hand held in the neighborhood of the left nipple, or over the pit of the stomach, as individual practice finds it more effectual to hold a high or a low guard. Holding a low guard renders "stopping" less speedy, but "cross countering" more forcible. The right arm, if held for a high guard, should form an acute angle; if for a low guard, a right angle. The elbow, it is now determined, should be held close to the body. There are no prominent pugilists who now attempt guarding with the elbow to any extent. As with the legs, the arms are not held rigidly in their positions. In fact, some of the most successful boxers seldom stand on guard as they are pictured. The right hand should not be too strictly confined to the position described, but it can not be allowed as much latitude as the left, which is the offensive member. The right is at once the buckler and the reserve force of the body. Its duties are to "stop" the incoming left of an opponent, or to "cross-counter" his deliveries.

Why the left and not the right foot and arm are advanced in scientific boxing, is the first thing that a beginner, who always wants to stand right foot and right hand foremost, asks to know. The left arm, side, and leg are held in front of the right for two reasons. First, an opportunity is given by bringing the left arm out in advance of the right to infliot punishment as well as to guard it. The only use that a novice makes of his left is to guard with it, using his right entirely for offensive work. The left is not in general use as the right hand is, and but for this getting it into a position where a little blow, and a half-pushing blow at that, from it tells, no amount of practice could enable a man to do much with it. It takes a left-handed man to throw a stone well with the left hand, and he can not use his right. No right-handed man can hit in the same manner with his left that he can with his right. But with practice he can hit a good left-handed blow in a little different manner. Think of the amount of practice it takes for a person used to driving a nail with the right hand to become able to drive the nail with the hammer held in his left hand! But with a hammer-head only, and with a different kind of blow, he can drive a nail with the left hand quite well.

The holding of the left arm and leg in advance of the right is a wonderfully clever yet simple way of making boxers ambidextrous. The plan does not render the left as handy as the right, but it enables it to hit a different kind of blow, which is almost if not quite as effective as the sledge-hammer smash of the right. The second reason is, that the right, the most accomplished hand, is made to do guard and reserve if not skirmish duty. It is always more important to defend than to offend, and at the same time the right is "stopping" an opponent's blows, its hitting strength is being kept in reserve for a heavy blow on jaw or ribs when the opportunity comes.

To Hit, and not be Hit.—To learn hitting out, stand up before an eight or ten pound punching-bag in the attitude described; draw the left arm and shoulder back so that the arm forms a slightly acute angle with the fist or gloved hand opposite the side or short ribs and the left shoulder twisted back, the right shoulder, of course, coming forward in accommodation and the right fist or glove moving from its position over the mark or the left nipple up almost upon the left shoulder. The bag should always be used to learn hitting, as a beginner feels more confidence than in practicing on an opponent. When drawn or twisted back as far as possible without straining clinch the left hand as tightly as possible, and suddenly shoot it forward, or "lead" at the bag as hard as possible, helping the force of the blow by drawing back the right arm and right side of the body and stepping in with the left foot. In delivering the blow, be sure

to have the hand in a natural position—that is, with the thumb on top, not on the outside of the closed fist. Strike forward as far and as straight as possible. The bag, if light, should be swinging freely, and it should be struck, "met," as it is coming toward the hitter. A heavy bag should never be hit except when it is swinging from the striker. The left-hand blow is not hit as the blow with the right is, but is a sort of quick, half-push—a "jab" or a "prop" it is called in ring-parlance. No blows with the right hand should be struck during the early practice, but every effort should be made to acquire dexterity, force, and speed in delivery with the left. It is not the few hard hits with this hand that tell so much as the many light blows for which no return blow or counter is taken. After some confidence has been acquired by bag-work, practice with an opponent should be begun. Always try to land the blows squarely on his face or body. To "stop" an opponent's blows and never to get hit, is even more important than effective hitting. It tires more to strike than to stop; therefore, if two men were to meet, one of whom was a perfect stopper though he could hit scarcely at all, and the other could not "stop" blows, the good stopper would win. Very few of the present-day boxers excel as stoppers. None can come near the excellence of that wonderful ex-champion of the light-weights, Billy Edwards, who in his day worsted all who came before him, regardless of difference in size and weight. To stop well requires much practice and good hard work with as many different kinds of hitters as possible. As the left-hand blow of an opponent is coming in for the face, the right, which has been lying across the breast, should be suddenly raised, the palm turning outward as it meets the incoming punch. The blow should be stopped in such a way as to have the forearm or wrist of the striker land on the tightened muscles of the forearm of the stopper. It is hard to clinch the hand too tightly or "stop" too forcibly. A few good hard stops will sometimes so hurt an adversary's arm as to render him most cautious about "leading." Do not attempt to throw off the blow; the best way is merely to stop it. Always keep the right elbow as low, near the ribs, as possible.

There is a left-hand lead for the body as well as for the head. The point of attack on the body is the pit of the stomach or "mark." To hit the "mark" effectively, the hand should be turned so that the back or large knuckles are on top and the thumb on the inside. The weight should greatly assist this blow. The stop or guard for the body lead is with the right, but struck downward instead of upward. Much stopping is very trying to the arms. Tom Sayers's right forearm was as much injured as if it were broken, if it was not broken, in the battle with John C. Heenan, stopping the Troy giant's terrific left-handers. Few fighters emerge from a battle without forearms black and blue from wrist to elbow from stopping their opponents' blows.

Dodging and Countering.—As a rest and as one of the easiest ways of inculcating use of the straight counter the teacher of one of the best boxing-schools in this country always takes up the "slipping" or dodging of the left-hand lead as soon as his pupils can show fair proficiency in hitting and stopping. Dodging and countering the left lead is performed by throwing the face suddenly toward the right shoulder as the left lead is about to land on nose, mouth, or eye, the head being at the same time dodged slightly forward and a little toward the right, the left hand being simultaneously sent in on the opponent's face. The beauty of this blow is its ease of delivery and the combination of muscles which aid its force. A boxer can hardly be so tired that he can not use this method of punishing an opponent, and in many a prolonged contest has it secured the victory. Variety may be given this manœuvre by occasionally making the counter do on an opponent's body.

The greatest exercise movements in boxing are the straight counters. The straight or left-hand counters are made on face and body just as the left leads are, only, instead of the blows being made when an opponent is on guard, they are delivered in response to his leads. To straight counter: The moment an opponent leads, stop his left with the right, and simultaneously, or a fraction of a second later, as individual practice finds best, let go the left forcibly on face or body.

As almost everybody is so much in need of left-hand development and practice, the best boxing-teachers instruct in the feints with the left in an effort to make the left the offensive one before any attempt is made to teach the offensive use of the right hand.

A feint is a make-believe. It may consist of a pronounced false movement with the fist or glove, but a scowl, a clinching of the teeth, a stamp of the foot might serve. A clever feinter so manages it that he gets an opponent nervous —"rattled"— off his balance — with arms in a position impossible to be serviceable in guarding, while he himself is drawn back in a perfect attitude for a tremendous blow which he lets go at exactly the right moment. Feints may be made with the left for the face followed by a blow for the features, or on the body followed by a body-punch, or a body-feint may be followed by a face-blow or *vice versa*. A left-hand feint may be followed with a blow of the right hand or the opposite, or a half-dozen feints may be made before any real attempt is made to plant a hit.

The Right Hand.—Not till familiarity with the use of the left has been acquired should any effort be made at right-hand delivery. The great right-hand blow is called the cross-counter. All but direct right-hand leads, and they are very seldom made by experts, are modifications or complications of the cross-counter

principle. John L. Sullivan's early work was successfully done by the full-arm swinging cross-counter, which he modified, after a few broken hands, to a half-arm swinging blow. There are two good ways of striking the cross-counter. One way, the first to be described, has the advantage in speed and handiness of delivery, but the second method is considered the safer. That is, there is less danger of being severely countered in return.

When boxing with an opponent for practice, have him lead with the left for the face. Instead of stopping the blow with the right forearm, as before treated, or dodging it by throwing the face toward the right shoulder, throw the face just a trifle toward the left shoulder and, without turning so much as to take the eye from the hitter's face, rise as much as possible on the ball of the right foot, and try to hit him with the right on the jaw, or on the neck close under the ear, by throwing the right hand and arm over, "*across*" the incoming left, which should slide harmlessly over the cross-counterer's right shoulder. A little practice will show just how to turn the hand slightly so as to land on the jaw or neck with the clinched knuckles of the third and fourth fingers. This is one of the prettiest, most scientific, and severest punishing blows in the whole science of boxing. The cross-counter may be guarded by throwing the right hand up to the base of the ear, catching the counter in the palm and throwing it off. It may also be avoided by ducking. To duck the cross-counter, throw the head straight down as the blow is near its destination, and bring it up on the outside of the blow, which, of course, has just missed. Perhaps the best way is to dodge it. In dodging turn the face to the right as the left lead is delivered; this will present the back of the head for the receipt of the cross-counter, and make an opponent liable to break his hand. Variety is sometimes given to the cross-counter by aiming at the short ribs instead of the jaw. This is called the low cross-counter. To strike the old fashioned or safe cross-counter, dodge the left lead as if to make the dodge and left counter, but come up quickly close beside the antagonist and deliver the right like lightning on jaw or neck. It should always be remembered that landing a good straight left-hand blow on an opponent's nose or chin will prevent his effectively "crossing" that blow at least. Another stop for the cross-counter, especially when an opponent is much addicted to its use, is to land a few solid left-handers on his right shoulder. This will temporarily paralyze his right delivery.

Ultra-Scientific Work.—Good head-work generalship and ducking and dodging are very essential; ability to manœuvre the feet is, if anything, more important. Only long practice will tell an individual how much ducking he can do with safety, and it is best to rely on ducking only as a resort in a tight pinch. Properly balanced on the feet, and well practiced in getting backward or forward and breaking ground to the side, is generally easier and safer than ducking in close quarters, which frequently compels one to lose sight of his opponent.

A boxer who battles on the defensive, depending only on straight counters or the old-fashioned cross-counters, a good stopper and ducker, and well up in leg-work, will bother a much heavier man, no matter how expert.

As the Marquis of Queensberry's rules for boxing-matches are understood in this country, there is very little chance for an in-fighter, but it is one of the great things in boxing. Especially is in-fighting valuable in an unexpected encounter. The principal point about in-fighting is to keep both hands at work. In an unexpected fracas let the opponent do all the hugging and struggling; keep the left going straight in his face and at the body-mark, and half swing the right on neck, jaw, and short ribs.

A very expert blow which few, even of the professionals, have mastered, is the draw and counter for the cross-counter. The enemy's fire, the right cross-counter, is drawn by a clever feint with the left. His cross-counter is stopped with the left, and the movement of the body, which aids in stopping his right with the left, helps in sending a tremendous right into his jaw.

Another clever move is the inside right. Few of the most expert use it, but it is a very effective blow. The inside right is used instead of the cross-counter by stopping a left lead with the right, making the movement of body for the stop aid in getting the right into position and delivering a counter with it on the jaw, but inside instead of outside and across the arm that led.

Upper cutting is sometimes effective, but is always so dangerous to whomsoever attempts it that many boxers do not attempt it at all. The upper cut is a counter. It should only be used after careful illustration by a good teacher. The blow should never be employed except when an opponent comes in head down.

BRAZIL. (For details relating to area, territorial divisions, population, etc., see "Annual Cyclopædia," for 1884.)

Government.—The Emperor is Dom Pedro II, born Dec. 2, 1825. He returned from Europe on August 23 with his health restored. His Cabinet is composed of the following ministers: President of the Council of Ministers and Minister of Finance, Senator João Alfredo Correa d'Oliveira; Minister of the Interior, Deputy José Fernandes da Costa Pereira, Jr.; Minister of Justice, Deputy Dr. Antonio Ferreira Vianna; Minister of Foreign Affairs, Senator Antonio da Silva Prado; Navy, Senator Luiz Antonio Viera da Silva; War, Senator Thomaz José Coelho de Almeida; Agriculture, Deputy Rodrigo Augusto da Silva. The Brazilian Minister at Washington is Dr. João Arthuro de Louza Correia. The Consul-General of Brazil at New York is Dr. Salvador Mendonça. The American Minister at Rio de Janeiro is Thomas J. Jarvis; the Consul-General, H. Clay Armstrong.

Finances.—The Sterling debt of Brazil amounted, on March 31, 1888, to £29,000,000, and the home debt to 437,306,700 milreis. The paper money in circulation on April 30, 1888, consisted of treasury notes to the amount of 188,861,263 milreis; notes of the Bank of Brazil, 15,276,850; notes of the Bank of Bahia, 975,550 milreis; notes of the Bank of Maranhão 166,700. The treasury notes form part of the home debt referred to. The budget for 1889 estimates the ordinary expenditure at 188,108,671 milreis; the outlay authorized for 1888 had been 141,230,103 milreis; the income in 1889 is estimated at 140,000,000 milreis, as compared with 138,395,000 authorized for 1888.

Brazilian finances have been gradually improving, as the diminished deficits of 1886 and 1887 show. During seven consecutive years the deficits, reduced to sterling money, have been: 1881, £1,294,000; 1882, £1,185,000; 1883, £2,784,000; 1884, £2.679,000; 1885, £3,947,000; 1886, £2,863,000; and 1887, £2,302,000. The deficits in 1886 and 1887 chiefly arose from railroads and other public works. The deficit for 1888, it is believed, will not exceed £1,300,000. The floating debt is $4,656,000. The paying of wages to the freedmen will require an extensive circulation of additional silver coin to the amount of about $7,000,000, for which the equivalent in treasury notes of 500 to 2,000 reis will be withdrawn. This amount of silver will have to be bought in the open market.

Army.—The actual strength of the Brazilian army is 1,520 officers and 13,528 men; in the event of war it may be raised to 30,000. There is also a gendarmerie in actual service of 6,847 men, 1,008 of whom are at Rio. After the new census shall have been taken, the National Guard, at present dissolved, will be reorganized. The Comblain carbine, now in use in the Brazilian army, will soon be replaced by another weapon, while the artillery is to receive Bange field-pieces.

Navy.—The naval forces of the empire were composed in 1888 of nine iron-clads, six cruisers, a mixed school corvette, a paddle-wheel steamer for artillery practice, four *patachos* or light school craft; five torpedo-boats of the first class; three third-class torpedo-boats; 15 gun-boats, 7 of which have paddle-wheels, 4 are wooden with screw, and 4 steel with screw; two steam-transports, and eleven steam-launches. The two new gun-boats have received their armament, and there were on the stocks, in a forward state of construction, two other gun-boats—all of them steel. The Brazilian fleet mounts 134 rifled Whitworth and Armstrong guns, 94 Nordenfeld *mitrailleuses*, 11 rapid-fire Nordenfeld guns, 4 Hotchkiss revolving guns, and 11 smooth-bore pieces. The collective horse-power is 19,329, and the tonnage, 40,252. It is manned by 4,272 sailors and officers.

Postal Service.—The report of the postmaster-general, dated Dec. 31, 1887, shows that there were then in operation 1,963 post-offices, of which 553 were in the province of Minas-Geraes, and 11 in that of Goyaz. The total receipts for the second half of 1886 and the whole of 1887, were 3,064,281 milreis, and the expenses 3,324,783, the deficit not exceeding 260,501, which is trifling considering the size of the country and the moderate rate of postage. Three provinces had a surplus. Money orders were paid to the amount of 1,712,204 milreis. The number of letters handled in the foreign mails was 4,012,879, distributed as follows: Portugal, 1,131,500; France, 673,452; England, 634,580; Germany, 554,320; Italy, 373,158; United States, 213,837; Rio de la Plata, 140,278; Spain, 97,117; Belgium, 44,-623; other countries, 140,010. The number of foreign letters exceeded those of 1886 by 226,917. The home mails forwarded 12,042,-998 letters and 27,271,139 newspapers.

Telegraphs.—In July, 1888, there were in operation 10,633 kilometres of Government telegraphs, with 18,403 kilometres of wire, connecting 170 offices. The service includes 48 kilometres of cable, the bulk of which is in the Bay of Rio.

Commerce.—The development in Brazil's foreign commerce during the quinquennial period 1882-'83 to 1886-'87 is shown in the ensuing tables, reduced to *contos*, or thousands of milreis:

YEARS.	Import.	Export.	Total trade.
1882-'83	190,264	197,088	387,297
1883-'84	194,432	216,014	410,446
1884-'85	178,431	226,270	404,701
1885-'86	197,502	194,962	392,464
1886-'87	209,407	263,520	472,927
Total	970,036	1,097,799	2,067,835

On examining the amounts exported of each of the nine principal products shipped, it will be found that for the last two fiscal years the figures were as follow: Coffee, 326,186 tons in 1885-'86, and 364,409 tons in 1886-'87; sugar, respectively, 112,399 and 226,010; cotton, 15,054 and 23,280; India-rubber, 8,150 and 14,083; tobacco, 25,904 and 22,988; hides, 16,768 and 12,975; cocoa, 4,188 and 3,566; Brazil-nuts, 5,564 and 5,692; and rum, 570,372 litres against 562,661. During the five years named, the export of diamonds reached altogether the value of 2,438,000 milreis, and that of gold bullion and dust 6,573,000 milreis. Coffee shipments from the ports of Rio de Janeiro and Santos were as follow, during the twelve months from July 1 to June 30:

DESTINATION.	1887-'88.	1886-'87.
	Bags.	Bags.
To Europe	1,312,784	3,110,472
To the United States	1,764,581	2,648,006
To other countries	117,773	135,229
Total	3,195,138	5,893,707

The sugar and cotton exportations from Pernambuco have been as follow:

YEARS.	Sugar.	Cotton.
	Tons.	Bales.
1886	106,797	125,244
1887	145,055	248,700
1888	177,818	269,396

The export of hides from Rio Grande do Sul in 1887 was 856,111, compared with 758,522 in 1886.

The American trade with Brazil exhibits these figures:

FISCAL YEAR.	From the United States to Brazil.	From Brazil to the United States.
1885	$7,258,085	$45,263,660
1886	6,480,738	41,907,532
1887	5,071,656	52,958,176
1888	7,063,892	53,710,284

The maritime movement at Rio in 1887 was as follows: Sea-going vessels entered, 1,102; sailed, 824; coastwise crafts entered, 1,203; sailed, 1,511. The nationality of vessels entered at Santos in 1887 was: Brazilian, 263; British, 129; German, 102; French, 58; other flags, 274; total, 826.

Railroads.—During the summer of 1888 the Minister of Public Works submitted his report to Parliament. The past thirty years have endowed the country with 8,402 kilometres of railway, the system being as follows: Government lines, 2,013 kilometres; lines on whose capital the Government has guaranteed interest, 2,585; provincial lines, 95; lines on which provinces have either guaranteed the interest or paid subsidies, 1,552; lines on which neither interest has been guaranteed nor subsidies granted, 2,157; total, 8,402. There will consequently be in operation in two years something like 13,000 kilometres of railway. The lines guaranteed by the state represent a capital of 143,322,128 milreis, or £16,125,352.

River Navigation.—Navigation on the central artery of communication, the São Francisco, is unencumbered for a distance of 1,500 kilometres, and, after the railways starting from Pernambuco and Bahia shall connect with it, the products of the interior of Minas-Geraes will have an outlet toward the sea. The rivers Tieté and Piracicaba in the province of São Paulo are already made navigable, completing communication in the eastern portion of the province, and soon the Mogiana Company will render navigable the rivers Mogy-Guassú, Pardo, and Rio Grande, assisted by the Western Minas Railroad Company.

Harbor Improvements.—Notable progress has been made in improving the harbors of Marauhão and Ceará, and proposals have been made to the Government to put in better condition that of Pernambuco. A wharf of considerable length is to be built at Santos; the entry to the port of Rio Grande, continually obstructed by quicksands, is also to be deepened.

Austrian Steamer Lines.—The speculators for a rise in wheat at New York and Chicago ran up that cereal to such a point in 1888 and thereby enhanced the price of flour so much that Hungarian flour has sold more advantageously than ever at Rio, giving rise to regular steamship lines from Trieste and Fiume direct to Rio. The magnitude of this flour interest in Brazil will be best understood by referring to the amounts shipped thither from the United States in the past sixteen years, aggregating 9,462,648 barrels, there being a 21-per-cent. increase during the past eight years, as compared with the shipments of the preceding eight years.

Emancipation.—Prior to the resignation of the Cotegipe Cabinet, in March, abolitionists were still exposed to persecution at the hands of the men in power ; but José de Patrocinio and Senators Joaquin Nabuco, Dantas, Prado, and João Alfredo have persevered undaunted in their endeavors to bring about the immediate abolition of slavery. The bill passed both houses on May 13, the recommendation of the new Cabinet and the law was signed the same day by the Princess-Regent, and promulgated. Full returns had at last been obtained of the slave registration of March 30, 1887. The total number was 723,419, of the declared value of 485,225,212 milreis. It was estimated, however, that emancipations and deaths had reduced this number to 600,000. The entire bill, as framed by Senator Prado, consisted of five brief articles, as follows: I. Declaring free, from date of the law, all slaves in the empire ; II. Relieving from further service the free-born children of slave mothers; III. Localizing the new freedmen within their county for two years; IV. Empowering the Executive to issue the necessary regulations; V. Revoking all contrary provisions.

Judging from experience in other countries where slavery has been suddenly abolished, there was some apprehension that it would be difficult to secure the coffee-crop, then in its prime, and get it properly prepared for market. The freedmen have worked steadily, and there has been no disorder. The crop has come in a little more slowly, and is, perhaps, a little less carefully prepared. The planters have been sullen, but resigned. The rise in coffee in the past few years has benefited the planters. Sugar has also advanced considerably, and the central sugar-house system had prepared this branch of industry for the inevitable event for years past. The "Centro da Industria e do Commercio do Assucar," an association of sugar-planters and exporters, is actively at work to introduce the diffusion process of extracting the sugar from the canes, instead of the almost antiquated centrifugal system, together with the latest and most approved American and European methods and machinery, and a more rational system of cane cultivation.

Immigration.—The number of immigrants landed at Rio in 1887 was 31,310, 17,115 of them being Italians, 10,205 Portuguese, 717 Germans, and 274 Austrians. There also arrived at Rio 4,134 in transit for Santos and 405 for São Francisco, constituting a total of 35,849 immigrants as compared with 25,741 in 1886 and 30,135 in 1885. Adding to the landings at Rio the direct arrivals of immigrants at outports, 20,151, the aggregate gain of population in 1887 was 56,000. The Provincial Assembly of São Paulo has passed a law authorizing extension of aid to immigrants from abroad, to the number of 100,000 per annum, for five consecutive years, while the province of Minas-Geraes has contracted for 30,000, to be procured during a twelvemonth.

Industries.—Great enterprise and activity were displayed in many localities to foster and create a variety of industries. A firm in São Paulo has begun to turn out an article of wax matches, competing with the imported Swedish. Sulphuric acid is being manufactured from Sicilian brimstone, both in the province of São Paulo and at Rio. Rio and Porto Alegre have each a glass-factory, and at Rio Grande do Sul artificial guano is made. There is also a glue-factory. Tanneries are numerous, using the valuable domestic materials that abound. At Rio there are refineries of cotton-seed oil and castor-oil. The Government has three powder-mills, but gunpowder for hunting and mining is still imported. At Macacos, near Rio, dynamite is manufactured. Soap of all grades is made at São Paulo, Porto Alegre, Pelotas, and Rio. Composition and stearine candles, vying with the best European and American makes, are turned out at Rio and Pelotas. Brazilian vegetable wax—*carnauba*—is used for a similar purpose, and seems to have a promising future.

Most of the cotton-weaving factories in Brazil do their own dyeing. At São Paulo calico-printing is carried on successfully. At Rio Grande do Sul there is a large woolen factory connected with a dyeing establishment. Steam sugar-refineries are in operation at Rio, Bahia, Taubaté, and Rio Grande do Sul. Several rectifying distilleries exist at Rio. Artificial wines, liquors, and cognacs, are chiefly made at Rio. There are many breweries, and some Brazilian beers have been awarded a premium in Europe, having stood the trip across the Atlantic admirably.

At Itú, in the province of São Paulo, a paper-mill is to be equipped and one at Maranhão. Creditable paper-hangings are printed at Rio on imported rolls.

There were in operation, on Jan. 1, 1888, 36 central sugar-houses, the Government guaranteeing the interest on 35 of them. Nearly all of the machinery was imported from France. Since Jan. 1, 1888, all machinery and tools intended to be used for manufacturing have been admitted duty free.

Viticulture.—In 1887 the province of São Paulo produced 5,000 hectolitres of wine, selling the red wines at 100 to 125 francs the hectolitre, and the white wines at 150 to 200. The Government has ordered for gratuitous distribution in Brazil 8,000 stalks of vines from France, and as many from Spain and Portugal, Madeira, and the Azores. The native vine, indigenous to the province of Matto-Grosso, *Vitis sycoïdes*, will also be widely distributed. At Pará a wine is made from fresh cocoa beans and pulp declared by travelers to be delicious and refreshing.

Exploring Expeditions.—The second Xingú expedition, under the command of Dr. von den Steinen, which in 1887 explored the interior of Matto-Grosso, returned to Cujaba early in 1888, the result being the discovery of a great Carib nation in the center of South America, the Bacairi and Nahugua, and the discovery of the Camayura and Auite tribes of Indians, who speak the ancient Tupi language, and whose weapons are slings. The tributary of the Xingú, the Culnene, was thoroughly explored.

Toward the close of 1887, Col. Labre, after ascending the Madeira river as far as Bolivia, descended the Rio Madre de Dios at a point where it is joined by the Rio Acre or Aquiry, thus proving that communication between the Amazon and Bolivia is comparatively easy without undergoing all the trouble caused by the Beni rapids. This discovery seems to open up a great future for that region.

BRICKWORK. The construction of buildings in brick is a very ancient art. The fire-resisting qualities and remarkable durability of the material have contributed to make it the most popular of all building materials. In recent years there has been a rapid advance in the art of making bricks, which has, in a measure, revolutionized the construction of brick buildings. The shape was, until recently, to a great extent limited to the simple parallelopiped; but bricks are now produced in a great variety of forms and in different colors. Thus there are bricks formed so that when laid side by side they produce a continuous molding, either horizontally, as in the case of a string-course or plinth, or vertically, as in jambs of door and window openings. Bricks are also made in

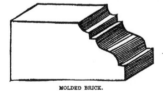

MOLDED BRICK.

wedge-shapes for arches, and of other forms for the construction of pavements, curbs, sills, cornices, copings, etc. The form of brick in which the surface is ornamented is coming more into use every day, although this descrip-

tion of ornament is often made of terra cotta. The architect has thus at his command means of producing effects that were not previously within his reach. Although the architectural effect is satisfactory, the construction of brickwork,

MOLDED BRICK FOR DOOR-JAMB.

in regard to strength, is open to improvement. The common custom is to employ face-bricks of a superior quality to those on the interior of the wall, and this is an obstacle to good construction, as such bricks are almost invariably larger than the commoner varieties, and hence can not be properly bonded in or tied together. Even a graver error, which, in the United States, is almost universal, is that of using what is known as "running bond." Formerly the practice was to build brickwork in one of the systems known respectively as English and Flemish bond, and the ancient brick buildings in Europe are all of this construction. In recent years the running

MOLDED BRICK FOR PIERS.

bond has, in our country, almost entirely taken their place. In English bond, the bricks are laid with their long and short sides (technically termed stretchers and headers) parallel to the length of the wall in alternate courses, while in Flemish bond they are laid alternately headers and stretchers in each course. Both systems have the advantage of forming "bond," or, by the arrangement, lapping the bricks to produce a solid mass. The construction of running bond will depend upon whether the wall is exterior or interior. If the latter, the bricks will all be laid stretchers—that is, with the long side parallel to the side of the wall, except in every fifth or seventh course, when they will be laid headers. When the wall is exterior, all the bricks on the face are laid stretchers, bonding being obtained by laying the back bricks in every fifth or seventh course diagonally, and cutting off the corners of the face-bricks at these points, in order to permit their introduction. The objection to this form of construction is that, as headers are introduced in only one course out of five, the remainder of the wall is unconnected, except by the mortar, and thus the principle upon which correct bonding is based, that no two mortar-joints should come under one another, is violated.

The strength of a wall depends, to a great extent, upon the quality of the mortar em-

ORNAMENTAL BRICK.

ployed. To make good mortar, clean, sharp sand is required, and a lime having no inconsiderable hydraulic qualities. These are mixed in the proportion of about one of lime to four of sand, with no more water than is necessary to moisten the whole of the parts

ORNAMENTAL BRICK.

and allow of the mixture's being thoroughly worked. The custom in many parts of the country is very common of using lime that is but little better than pure chalk. Such lime is not at all suitable, and not a few of the building accidents that have occurred from weak

ORNAMENTAL BRICK.

brickwork may be directly attributed to the bad quality of the mortar by reason of the employment of chalk lime.

The foundations of a building are obviously important. In localities where stone abounds, they are often constructed in what is known as rough or random rubble, which consists of rough pieces of stone laid, without dressing, in such a way as to produce the best bond possible under the circumstances. Examples

EXTERIOR WALL IN RUNNING BOND.

of this system of the construction of foundation are found in nearly all buildings of New York city, formed of the gneiss rock of which Manhattan Island is mainly composed. Brick is a good material for foundations, and, if it is well burned, the moisture has no effect upon it. Where brick is employed for foundations, it is usual to form footings. These consist of widely

INTERIOR WALL IN RUNNING BOND.

spread courses, diminished by offsets equal to half the thickness of a brick till the width of the wall is reached. In good construction, every brick in the footings is laid a header where possible, while all stretchers necessitated by the width of the course are placed in the interior of the wall. The brick or stone footings may either be built upon the soil or

FOUNDATION OF HOLLOW WALL.

upon a bed of concrete, depending upon the nature of the soil. Where hard rock or gravel is found on the site of a building, footings may be laid directly upon it, but otherwise the use of concrete is advisable. Concrete for this purpose is composed of lime or cement mixed with sand and ballast. In heavy work, Portland or Rosendale cement is generally preferred.

Bricks being absorbent, the moisture from the ground will frequently rise by capillary attraction. To prevent this, damp courses are

SILVERLOCK'S HOLLOW BOND.

employed. These consist of a layer of some material impervious to moisture, which is laid immediately above the ground-line. Asphalt, sheet-lead, slate, and Portland cement are among the materials employed for the purpose. To prevent the penetration of water into the interior of a building, it is frequently advisable to construct an area-wall around the entire site, at a distance from the main walls of the building of about three inches. Such walls are built wholly below the ground, and are finished on top with a course of molded bricks. With the same object, the main walls of isolated buildings are sometimes constructed with a cavity in the interior, which not only effectually prevents the dampness from penetrating into the building, but also assists in rendering it warmer in winter and cooler in summer. Such walls, known by the general term of "hollow walls," are constructed of two casings about two inches apart, such casings being connected by the insertion of iron or brick ties every two or three feet. The ties are always formed in such a manner as to prevent the passing of moisture across them. At the bottom of the cavity in these walls is a gutter connected with the drain, and any water that finds its way through the outer casing is conducted away.

Hollow bond, as distinguished from hollow walls, is used in some parts of the country for the erection of small buildings, fence-walls, and in other positions where but little strength is required. There are two methods of constructing such walls, known respectively as Silverlock's and Dearne's, and both of these systems are limited in their application to walls of the thickness of a single brick. In Silverlock's bond the bricks are all laid on edge, stretcher and header alternately in each course, producing an appearance somewhat similar to that of Flemish bond in solid brick-work. Dearne's plan is to lay the bricks all headers and flat in one course, and all stretchers on edge in the other. The only advantage of hollow bond is the saving in material. Besides these bonds or systems of laying the bricks, there are others in common use. Diagonal bond is sometimes employed

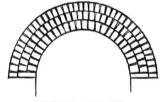

SEMICIRCULAR ROUGH ARCH.

in executing thick walls for heavy buildings. On the exterior it is similar to English bond; but on the interior the bricks are laid diagonally, with the object of obtaining a better bond. For the purpose of tying together the component parts of brick walls of all kinds, hoop-iron bond is sometimes employed. In England its use is common, but in the United States it is not employed to any great extent. The hoop-iron is laid in between the mortar-joints, in every fifth or seventh course, and is lapped at all corners and joints. To prevent oxidization the iron is often covered with

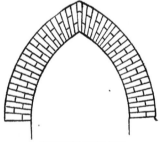

EQUILATERAL GAUGED ARCH.

tar, or is galvanized. Sometimes it has jagged edges to give it a better hold on the mortar.

The construction of arches in brick may be divided into two distinct classes: 1. Those known as gauged, in which each brick is cut or gauged to a wedge shape in order to produce a parallel mortar-joint, and in which the ends are curved to conform to the curve of the arch; 2. Those known as rough arches, in which the bricks are laid without cutting. In the latter case, the difference in the lengths of the curves, that is, of the intrados and the extrados of the arch, is reached by the formation of wedge-shaped mortar-joints. Gauged arches are formed of specially made bricks, in which a proportion of sand has been used to render them friable, and the cutting is effected by means of a coarse-toothed saw, the exact shape being obtained by rubbing the sides on a stone, to the form of a template. This is

INVERTED ARCH.

often done by the bricklayer on the job, but more frequently in the brickmaker's yard, from detail drawings furnished him by the architect. The names by which arches are known, unlike most of the technicalities of the building-trade, are substantially identical throughout the country. They are taken in nearly every case from the curves to which they are formed. Thus we have semi or semicircular, segmental, elliptical, and cycloidal arches. Among pointed arches there is the equilateral, which comprises two arcs struck from the abutments. The inverted arch is always segmental, and is struck upside down, for the purpose of distributing the weight of the superincumbent building over the space intervening between two piers. Flat arches are useful over horizontal window and door heads, and are usually formed with the camber or curve on the intrados.

The manner in which the exterior joints of brickwork are finished varies considerably in different parts of the country and in different

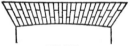

FLAT ARCH.

kinds of work. In interior walls the joint is "struck," that is, finished by drawing the trowel along it to render it smooth. Where the same wall is plastered, the mortar is left rough so as to form a key for the plaster. In exterior walls the mortar-joints, as a rule, are finished level with the bricks, and the whole surface is painted with two or three coats of oil-paint. The mortar-joints are thus hidden. A small brush guided by a straight edge and dipped in white paint is used to paint in the mortar-joints at the proper distance apart.

BUDDHISM. An analysis of Southern Buddhism, which has been published by the Bishop of Colombo, embodies the results of twelve years' observation of the system in Ceylon and first-hand studies of the sacred books. The author draws a general distinction between the traditional school of interpretation, as it is known to Singalese scholars, and that to which Europeans incline. "The Singalese tradition, if it differs, differs always in the direction of a meaning more puerile, more wooden, less Christian," although the higher meaning may in some cases be acknowledged by the Buddhist interpreter.

Numerical estimates of Buddhist adherents are of no value, because Buddhism, unlike other religions, does not claim exclusive possession of the ground. It is a parasitic religion, ready to thrive where it can, without displacing or excluding another with which it comes in contact. While a Christian or a Mohammedan or a Hindoo can be that only, a Buddhist can also be a Confucianist or a Taoist or both, and to a great extent a Hindoo or planet-worshiper. In Ceylon, the statues of Hindoo deities are found in the precincts of the Buddhist *viharas;* on the Buddhist festivals, Buddhists visit Hindoo and Buddhist temples alike; when Buddhists are sick the Hindoo or the devil-priest meets the Buddhist monk at the door without offense. "What is most practically the refuge of a Ceylon Buddhist is not anything truly Buddhistic, but the system of astrology, charm, devil-dancing, and other low superstitions." It is these, and not the doctrines of the Tripitaka or any rule of self-sacrifice, that the Buddhist has to abandon when he becomes a Christian.

Buddhism is a system of precepts or a method of escape from evil, which is discovered and lost again and again in successive ages. The precepts are held to be unchangeable, but become lost sight of till a new Buddha appears, who revives the knowledge of them for the benefit of his age. All the Buddhas of the successive ages—the term "ages" being taken in an infinite sense—"do and say exactly the same things; they are born in the same family, leave home at the same hour of the night, throw their bowls into the same stream, and so on." The Buddha of the present age is Gautama.

There is not the slightest hint that the truth came by revelation from any person superior to the Buddha, or that the Buddha is in any sense God. But, if it be asked whether Buddhists believe the Buddha to be a mere man, or to be the Supreme Being, the question can not be answered in one word. Buddhism does not possess the idea of distinct grades of being, permanently separated from one another. To Buddhism all life is one. He who was a god may now be a brute, and afterward may be a man. The difference is not one of indelible character, but of stage. But of all beings, a Buddha has reached the highest stage. He is, therefore, the supreme being, but the phrases in which this dogma is expressed do not imply anything like what we mean by God. The Buddha attained a position higher—not in dominion, but in enlightenment—than those of the highest deities known to Buddhism, Indra and Maha Brahmá; in fact, he is represented as having passed through the stages of being both, on his way to his final birth, as a Buddha.

The sources of information respecting Gautama are, on the one hand, the Tripitaka, or threefold collection of sacred books, which form the canon of Southern Buddhism, and may be spoken of as the books of 250 B. C.; and, on the other hand, the biographies of Buddha, that of Asvaghosha, which is attributed to the first century, A. D, that which bears the name of Buddhagosha, which may belong to the fifth century, A. D., and the Lalita Vistára, or "beautiful, detailed narrative," of uncertain date, but between the first and sixth centuries. The last works are the chief source of Arnold's "Light of Asia," while the books of 250 B. C. are the source of the lives given by Rhys Davids in the Hibbert Lectures, and Dr. Oldenberg in his "Buddha."

Evidence exists as to the prevalence as far back as about 250 B. C., of Buddha's teaching and of some of the sermons and traditions, carved on the rocks or on pillars, in different parts of India, in the form of edicts of Asoka under the name of Devánampiyo Piyadasi. Their date is established by the mention of contemporary Greek kings, and they are accredited in the Singalese chronicle, the Mahar-ranso. In comparison with whatever historical matter is incorporated in the Tripitaka, the sources of information of the other class are untrustworthy. Whatever is included in them and not in the Tripitaka that must naturally have been inserted there if it had been believed, can be regarded as of later fabrication. Of this character are most of the points of the biographies that bear any reference to Christianity. Singalese chronicles go much further back than 250 B. C., and with the same circumstantiality. They give lists of kings who preceded Asoka, and lists of monks who were leaders of Buddhist congregations from Gautama's time till then. It would be unreasonable to refuse all credit to the earlier part of these chronicles. It is hardly possible to distrust them so far as to doubt that the sacred books, substantially as we have them, existed a hundred years earlier.

In the Pitaka substantial facts are chronicled correctly, but adorned, not overlaid, with fictitious and often absurd circumstances. The falsehood in the stories does not seriously interfere with the truth; it falls off directly the story is handled. The incredible elements of the Pitaka life of Gautama are mostly of this nature. They belong to what is little else than a conventional mode of narration; they are little more than the epithets that we used to select, without thought of truth or falsehood, from our *Gradus*, to adorn the plain substantives of our originals. The separation of the history from them requires no exercise of the critical faculty, and gives no room for arbitrary decisions.

The resultant biography of Gautama shows nothing supernatural and nothing that in those days was strange. Many high-born persons went through renunciations similar to his, and bore among their adherents the title of Buddhas. A like course was prescribed in the laws of Menu as a regular part of a Brahman's life. Gautama is not recorded as having performed any act of conspicuous or extraordinary goodness or self-sacrifice in his historical life; but he attributed to himself these and all sorts of noble actions in former births. Most probably his career was as nearly as possible that of an ordinary, devoted teacher, and he was distinguished, not by strange acts, but by a strange degree of sympathy, insight, and constructive ability.

The historical treatment of the life of Gautama shows nearly all the parts of his biography that are relied on as parallel to Christian history to belong to the unhistorical Lalita Vistára and the other later books. Whether these northern biographies borrowed from Christianity, is an interesting question that depends on the date of Asvaghosha—which some put as early as 70 B. C., some as late as 70 A. D.; on the veracity of the early Christian traditions as to the travels of the apostles; and on the degree of intercourse between Kaniska's Indian court and the western countries. But even were all admitted, the resemblances to Christianity are small and few. In the historical narration there are, to the author's view, only two points that bear resemblance to anything in the life of Christ. One is the visit of the old sage, who, after the birth of Gautama, predicted that he would be a Buddha, and rejoiced to have seen him; but this story is wanting in some of the important features of the similar incident in the life of Christ; and, moreover, it only corresponds with the common Indian custom of getting a sage to visit the infant and pronounce his horoscope. The other is the so-called temptation of Buddha by Mara; but in this case the attempt is very different from that which was made upon Christ by Satan, and is an inevitable incident of the story.

Other apparent instances are fictitious. By a multitude of little parodies, nearly all of them misleading, a total impression is conveyed which is very far removed from the truth. Likenesses to Christianity, and most touching ones, there are; but they are generally in the expression of man's weakness and need, not in the method of meeting it.

The Nirvána of the books and of present Ceylonese conviction is the state in which there is not left any capacity for re-birth. This state, which sees final death within reach, might be called the potentiality of final Nirvána; and it is inaccurately imagined to be happiness to have attained that potential stage, and to know that one has no more births before him. The attainment of Nirvána, thus inaccurately thought of, is possible in life; its final achievement, in the last death, is Paranirvána.

In practice, the Ceylon Buddhist among the masses is both better and worse than his creed. Better because, instead of a distant Nirvána, or a series of births, he has before him the next birth only, which he thinks will be in heaven if he is good, in hell if he is bad; because he calls on God in times of distress, and has a sort of faith in the one creator, whom his priests would teach him to deny. Worse because his real refuge is neither Buddha nor his books, nor his order, but devils and devil-priests and charms and astrology and every form of groveling superstition.

BULGARIA, a principality in eastern Europe that was set apart from the Turkish Empire and given an independent government by the Treaty of Berlin, signed July 13, 1878. Eastern Roumelia was at the same time constituted an autonomous province of Turkey, remaining under the direct political and military authority of the Sultan. The governor-general was to be nominated for the term of five years by the Sultan, who must select a Christian, and submit his choice to the approval of all the treaty powers. The Sultan was given the right, which he has never exercised, to erect fortifications on the land and sea frontiers of Eastern Roumelia, and to maintain Ottoman troops there. The Roumelians were to preserve internal order by means of a gendarmerie, assisted by a local militia, but, in case of a disturbance of the peace within or without, the governor-general could call in Turkish troops. The treaty arrangements were overturned by a revolution that occurred on Sept. 17, 1885, when the governor-general was deposed, and the union of Eastern Roumelia with Bulgaria was proclaimed. Prince Alexander of Bulgaria assumed the administration of the province, and the Eastern Roumelians and Bulgarians joined in repelling the Servian invasion, for which the union of the two provinces gave occasion. The signatory powers held a conference in Constantinople, and as the result of their deliberations the Sultan issued a firman on April 6, 1886, in which he recognized the change in the *status quo* by confiding the government to Prince Alexander and by agreeing to a modification of the organic statute, at the same time. reclaiming certain districts of Kirjali and twenty villages in Rhoupchous or the Rhodope, which are peopled almost entirely by Mussulmans. A commission was appointed to revise the organic statute in order to bring it into harmony with the changed conditions, chiefly by transferring the administration of the customs to the Bulgarian Government and amending the Turkish tribute. The proceedings of this Turco-Bulgarian commission were not completed, owing to the revolution of Aug. 20, 1886, which resulted in the abdication of Prince Alexander. The annual tribute to Turkey, which was fixed by the organic statute at 245,000 pounds Turkish, the Provincial Assembly arbitrarily reduced to 185,000 pounds, including

the customs equivalent, and after the revolution of September, 1885, no part of it was paid till 1888. Bulgaria has undertaken to pay the debt of Eastern Roumelia to the Porte, which at the beginning of 1880 amounted to 743,532 Turkish pounds, according to the modified estimate of the Provincial Assembly, and to 1,082,542 Turkish pounds, if the original sum is maintained.

The council of ministers was composed in 1888 as follows: Prime Minister and Minister of the Interior, Stambuloff; Minister of Foreign Affairs and of Public Worship, Dr. Stransky; Minister of Finance, Natchevich; Minister of War, Colonel Mutknroff; Minister of Justice, Stoiloff; Minister of Public Instruction, Zivkoff. This ministry was constituted from elements of both the Liberal and Conservative parties on Aug. 31, 1887, after Prince Ferdinand's assumption of authority. It contained the three regents, Stambuloff, Mutkuroff, and Zivkoff, who had exercised the powers of government during the latter period of the interregnum, Zivkoff having succeeded Karaveloff after the latter's arrest for complicity in the military insurrection of February, 1887.

The present Prince of Bulgaria is Ferdinand, Duke of Saxe-Coburg, the youngest son of Augustus, the Duke of Saxe-Coburg, and the Princess Clementine, of Bourbon-Orleans, daughter of Louis Philippe, King of the French. Ferdinand, born Feb. 26, 1861, was elected prince by the unanimous vote of the National Assembly on July 7, 1887, in succession to Prince Alexander, who abdicated on Sept. 7, 1886. He assumed the government on Aug. 8, 1887. The treaty powers have not ratified his election, and none of them have yet formally recognized his government.

The National Assembly of Bulgaria under the Constitution of 1879 consists of a single chamber, the members of which are elected by universal suffrage, in the proportion of one to every ten thousand inhabitants, for three years. The prince may dissolve the Assembly, but must order new elections within four months.

Commerce.—The people of both provinces pursue agriculture almost exclusively, and grain is the chief product and article of export. Sheep are kept in large numbers, and there is a considerable household manufacture of woolen cloth and braid in Eastern Roumelia. There is an export trade in timber from the mountains. Wine and raki, tobacco, and silk cocoons are among the other products of this province. The imports of Bulgaria for 1884 were valued at 46,351.280 leii or francs, and the exports at 48,867,237 leii. In 1885 the trade of Eastern Roumelia is included from the 1st of November in the returns, which give the imports as 38.843,517 leii, and the exports as 42,017,984 leii. In 1886 the value of imports was 61,687,169 leii, and of exports 37,768,679 leii. The imports from Austria-Hungary were 16,481,598 leii in value; from

Great Britain, 15,829,805 leï; from Turkey, 12,899,346 leii. The exports to Turkey were valued at 16,958,508 leii; to France, 9,327,-563 leii; to Great Britain, 4,585,685 leii. The share of Eastern Roumelia in the total imports was 15,860,000 leii, and in the exports 11,186,-750 leii.

Finances.—The budget for 1887 makes the revenue 47,218,266 leii or francs, and the expenditure 47,374,414 leii. The estimates for 1888 fix the receipts at 53,708,046 leii, and the disbursements, at 69,047,770 leii. The chief branches of expenditure are: War, 23,223,340 leii; Interior, 7,513,694 leii; the debt, 6,373,438 leii; Finance Department, 5,763,112 leii; Public Works, 5,114,484 leii. In December, 1887, the Sobranje authorized a loan of 50,000,000 leii, of which 19,000,000 leii were to be applied to the construction of the Zaribrod-Sofia-Vakarel railroad, the same sum to the purchase of the Varna line, 2,000,000 leii to discharging the debts of Prince Alexander, and the remainder to army equipments. The Government was not successful in placing this loan. It undertook to pay 140,000 Turkish liras as the amount of the Eastern Roumelian tribute to the Porte, with 21,000 liras per annum on account of arrears, and in 1888 made the first payments. The quota of the Turkish debt to be borne by the principality of Bulgaria was left to be settled by agreement between the signatories of the Berlin Treaty, but the powers have not yet fixed any sum.

The Bulgarian Government in the latter part of 1887 reduced the tariff on goods coming from Turkey, and entered into an understanding with the Porte, which made a like concession. In 1888 the Turkish Government, in its desire to please Russia, adopted various harassing regulations, refusing to recognize Bulgarian postage-stamps or Bulgarian passports, and levying a duty of 8 per cent. on imports from Bulgaria. Bulgaria retaliated in May by placing the same duty on Turkish goods, until finally Turkey reduced its duty to 1 per cent. An order of the Bulgarian Government doubling the duty on Russian spirits in July provoked a remonstrance from the German consul at Sofia, who has charge of Russian interests until diplomatic intercourse with Russia shall be resumed.

The Army.—Universal obligatory military service has been adopted. The army consists of 12 regiments of infantry, 3 of cavalry, 3 of artillery, with 24 field-guns and 2 mountain-guns, and 7 companies of pioneers. The peace effective is 29,000 men, and the war strength 100,000 men. The South Bulgarian contingent in time of war is 26,000 men. The infantry, who are well drilled, are armed with Martini rifles. The Government, in 1888, purchased 15,000,000 cartridges in Belgium, prosecuted works of fortification at Varna, Bourgas, and other points, and prepared vigorously for war, which, Prince Ferdinand predicted in a speech that made a sensation throughout Europe in

the opening months of the year, was near at hand, and would find him ready to die for Bulgarian liberty.

Area and Population.—The area of the principality of Bulgaria is 24,360 square miles, and its population, according to a census that was taken in 1881, is 2,007,919, consisting of 1,027,-803 males and 980,116 females. Eastern Roumelia or South Bulgaria, as it has been officially called by the Bulgarians since the union, has an area of 13,500 square miles, and contained on Jan. 13, 1885, when the last census was taken, 975,050 inhabitants. The Christian Bulgarians numbered 681,734; Turks and Moslem Bulgarians, 200,498; Greeks, 53,028; gypsies, 27,190; Jews, 6,982; Armenians, 1,865; foreigners, 3,733. The retrocession to Turkey of the canton of Kirjali, and of twenty Mussulman villages of the Rhodope in accordance with the Turco-Bulgarian arrangement of April 6, 1886, that was concluded on the recommendation of the Constantinople conference, reduced the Mussulman population by 40,000, and emigration has diminished further the number of Mohammedans. The capital of United Bulgaria is Sofia, Philippopolis, the former seat of the Eastern Roumelian Government having been reduced to a prefecture. Sofia has 20,501 inhabitants; Philippopolis, 33,442; Rustchuk, 26,163; Varna, 24,555; Shumla, 23,093.

The Diplomatic Situation.—In October, 1887, M. Nelidoff, the Russian ambassador at Constantinople, suggested to the Porte that the Sultan should order Prince Ferdinand to leave Bulgaria, and that Russian and Turkish commissioners should be sent to govern the principality for four months, choosing a new Cabinet, dissolving the Chamber, and ordering the election, at the end of three months, of a new assembly, to which should be submitted the choice of two candidates that Russia would nominate for prince. The incident of the forged documents supervened (see AUSTRIA-HUNGARY), and after the explanations between the Czar and Bismarck the German Government repeated its declarations regarding the illegality of Prince Ferdinand's position and its acquiescence in the restoration by peaceable and diplomatic means of Russia's influence in Bulgaria as it existed before the dismissal of the Russian Minister of War and the Russian officers of the Bulgarian army. Germany supported the Russian demand that the Sultan should declare Ferdinand a usurper, but Austria would not join in any declaration on the subject.

Revolutionary Raid at Bourgas.—Russian diplomatic activity was accompanied, as usual, by an attempt to incite insurrection in Bulgaria. Capt. Nabokoff, a Russian, who had been condemned to death for participation in the rebellion that had been effected at Bourgas in 1886 under cover of two Russian gunboats, but who had been set free on being claimed as a Russian subject, was the leader of the new attempt, and behind him was the chief of the

Bulgarian Russophiles, Zankoff, who was in exile at Constantinople, while his coadjutors were three cashiered officers of the Bulgarian army, and Andre Kappe, a Montenegrin. Money was supplied by the Slav committees in Moscow and Odessa. They recruited a band of over one hundred Montenegrin mercenaries, and chartered a Greek vessel at the Turkish port of Vasiliko to convey the party to Kustenje, pretending that they were emigrants. When near the village of Keupruli, on the Roumelian coast of the Black Sea, near Bourgas, they compelled the master of the vessel to set them on shore. They tried to incite the Roumeliotes to join them, but without success. The Prince of Montenegro had tardily telegraphed a warning of the plot to the Porte, yet the Bulgarian authorities received notice from Constantinople in time to intercept the revolutionists before they reached Bourgas. The Bulgarian troops nearly surrounded them, and killed eighteen, while many were taken prisoners, including Kappe, only about twenty making their escape into Turkish territory, where they were arrested by the Ottoman authorities. Capt. Nabokoff and Capt. Boyanoff, a notorious Bulgarian revolutionist, were among the slain. Among the documents captured were letters implicating Zankoff, Hitrovo, the Russian minister at Bucharest, the city attorney of Odessa, and a Montenegrin priest named Kapitchich, who had a hand in the abduction of Prince Alexander. Three other bands were organized in Montenegro for the descent on Bourgas, but the Turkish Government arrested some of the enrolled men, and prevented their embarking. A Russian war-vessel appeared off Bourgas at the moment when the attempt to surprise the place by night was to be made, and vanished after its failure. These events took place in the beginning of January.

Russian Proposals.—The Porte, which had recalled Riza Bey, its commissioner in Bulgaria, on the arrival of Prince Ferdinand, decided in January to send again a representative to Sofia, and appointed Kiazim Bey its commissioner. M. Nelidoff thereupon threatened to leave Constantinople, and the appointment was canceled. Under Russian pressure the Turkish authorities also released the Montenegrins who had taken part in the Bourgas affair. In February, Count Schouvaloff, the Russian ambassador at Berlin, explained the Russian position to the German Chancellor, and as a result of the *pourparlers*, a telegram was sent from the Russian Foreign Office, asking the powers to declare illegal the presence of Prince Ferdinand of Coburg in Bulgaria and at the head of the Bulgarian Government, and to communicate that declaration to Turkey, and request Turkey to notify it to the usurping prince. This was followed by a note explaining the consequences of such action, which would be that the Bulgarian ministry would drive Prince Ferdinand from Bulgaria, and convoke an elective assembly under the supervision of the representatives of the powers; the assembly would send a deputation to the Czar in acknowledgment of Russia's services in liberating Bulgaria; the Czar, content with this act of satisfaction, would renounce the idea of having a civil or military representative in the future Government; and all the powers would accept any prince that the assembly would choose comformably to the stipulations of the Treaty of Berlin. Russia, after an interchange of views with all the cabinets, communicated the suggestion to the Porte, and was supported in identical notes by Germany and France, while England, Austria, and Italy sent separate communications of negative import. After receiving a second, more emphatic note from Russia, and one still more urgent from Germany, the Grand Vizier laid the matter before the council of ministers, and in pursuance of an *iradé* sent a dispatch to M. Stambuloff on March 5, which ran as follows:

On the arrival of Prince Ferdinand of Coburg in Bulgaria, I declared to His Highness in a telegram of August 22, 1887, that as his election by the National Bulgarian Assembly had not received the assent of all the signatory powers of the Berlin Treaty, and as that election had not been sanctioned by the Sublime Porte, his presence in Bulgaria was contrary to the Berlin Treaty and was illegal.

To-day I have to declare to the Bulgarian Government that in the view of the Imperial Government his position remains the same—that is to say, the presence of Prince Ferdinand at the head of the principality is illegal and contrary to the Treaty of Berlin.

The effect of this declaration was to rouse into activity all the elements in Bulgaria that were hostile to Prince Ferdinand or to independence. Clement, Metropolitan of Tirnova, was dismissed for insulting the prince. Revolutionary bands made incursions from Macedonia and Servia, but were promptly met by soldiery. Opposition journals called on Prince Ferdinand to resign, and anti-national cliques were busy in the army. Manifestations of a revolutionary spirit had been made easy by the action of Prince Ferdinand's Government in abolishing the press censorship before the close of 1887, and in restoring to their rank in the army many officers who had participated in the deposition of Prince Alexander and other Russian plots. Ferdinand, however, effectually counteracted these symptoms of restlessness by making a tour of the towns, in all of which he was received with demonstrations of loyalty that proved in the eyes of Europe the attachment of the mass of the Bulgarian people to their *de facto* prince as the embodiment of a stable government and of national independence.

Cabinet Crisis.—In the spring, Major Popoff, who had done more than any one else to defeat the Russian revolutionary conspiracy in the time of the regency, was arrested, with four other officers, on the charge of malversation of public money. A discrepancy of 7,000 francs was discovered in the regimental accounts. For this his subordinates were chargeable, and no suspicion of dishonesty could rest on the patriotic soldier who had refused Gen. Kaulbars's offered bribe of 200,000 rubles to deliver Sofia over to the revolutionists in November, 1886. But he had offended Stambuloff, who was jealous of his influence with the prince, and therefore a court-martial cashiered him and condemned him to four years' imprisonment. Col. Nicolaieff, president of the court-martial, publicly declared that the trial was unfairly conducted, and on the strength of this opinion Natchevich and Stoiloff, the Conservative members of the Cabinet, urged the prince to quash the sentence or order a re-trial. Stambuloff threatened to resign if this advice were followed. On June 12, Stoiloff and Natchevich tendered their resignations. When apprised of their action, Stambuloff sent to the prince the resignations of himself and his Liberal colleagues. A compromise was effected, in accordance with which Prince Ferdinand, on June 28, remitted the penalty of imprisonment. The majority of the officers of the army were incensed at the result of the trial, and some of them entered into a plot to rescue him from prison, and seize Stambuloff and the other Liberal ministers. Five officers were arrested as ringleaders. Another dispute occurred between the Conservative members of the Cabinet and Stambuloff on account of attacks on the former in the Liberal press, and they again handed in their resignations, but the prince brought about an accommodation.

The Servian Frontier Rectification.—The dispute in regard to the possession of a tract of pasture lands in the Bregovo district, which was one of the causes of the Servo-Bulgarian war, was finally settled in July, 1888, in accordance with the agreement arrived at between the two governments, by a mixed commission sitting at Negotina. The difference between the two countries arose from the fact of the frontier line having become changed through the deviation from its former course of the Timok river. The question was settled by a mutual exchange of land. The Porte raised an objection to the direct negotiations with Servia in the first place, and now protested against the cession of Bulgarian territory without the previous consent of the suzerain power. This protest was simply intended as a formal assertion of reserved rights, and after explanations had been offered by the Bulgarian Government it was withdrawn. In September, when negotiations were opened for the conclusion of a commercial treaty between Bulgaria and Servia, Turkey put forth more emphatically a claim to participation in the treaty, requesting that the Servian Government should recognize the Turkish minister resident at Belgrade as the first Turco-Bulgarian plenipotentiary. But Servia consented to treat with Bulgaria alone.

The Eastern Railways.—From the time when rail connection between Europe and the Bosporus was first contemplated, the project has passed through many vicissitudes. The statesmen who governed Turkey in the reigns of Abdul Medjid and Abdul Aziz planned a junction with the Austrian *réseau,* while Gen. Ignatieff, through palace influences and diplomatic chicanery, sought to shape a scheme to join the projected railways of European Turkey with those of Russia. For ten years or more the political troubles of the Porte prevented any step being taken. At length, in 1868, contracts were awarded to the Belgian Van der Elst, and when he failed, the Vienna banker Hirsch obtained a new concession, contracting to build a line from Constantinople to the Austrian frontier near Agram, with four branches running to the Ægean Sea from Adrianople, to Salonica from Pristina, to the Black Sea, and into Servia, the total net being 2,500 kilometres. On the security of a subvention of 14,000 francs per kilometre per annum for ninety-nine years, Hirsch obtained subscriptions for 1,980,000 bonds of 400 francs each, which were rendered attractive by the feature of lottery drawings. When the South Austrian Railroad Company declined to assume the contract for working the lines at a stipulated rental of 8,000 francs per kilometre per annum, Hirsch, with the aid of Parisian financiers, founded a French company for the purpose, called the Société d'Exploitation des Chemins de Fer Orientaux, which has since changed its domicile to Austria. Ignatieff, in 1872, after Mahmoud Pasha had become foreign minister, succeeded in having the whole plan changed. The Austrian and Servian junctions were abandoned, and the length of the line was reduced to 1,280 kilometres, running to Bellova, to connect with the Roumanian and Russian lines by means of the Varna-Rustchuk line. A part of the money that was subscribed for the abandoned portions was paid to Hirsch as compensation for the change of contract, none of it being returned to the bondholders. Austrian and English diplomacy was set in motion to induce the Porte to extend the Bellova line to Nish in order to join it with a projected line through Servia, and in 1875 Turkey and Austria entered into a mutual engagement to construct railroads to Nish on the one part, and to Belgrade on the other, before the end of 1879. Then came the bankruptcy of the Turkish treasury, the Servian war, the Bulgarian rebellion, and the Russo-Turkish War, all of which events had their origin in the conflict. The Treaty of Berlin settled the question in the Austrian sense, and restored the main features of the original Hirsch project. Servia and Bulgaria were bound to build the sections of the lines lying within their respective territories. Russian diplomacy endeavored still to defeat the arrangement by bringing pressure on Prince Alexander to grant a concession to Russian contractors for a line from Sofia to Rustchuk, relying on Russian influence over the new principality to postpone indefinitely the construction of the line from Vakarel to Zaribrod enjoined by the Treaty of Berlin. The Bulgarian ministers steadfastly resisted the Russian demand, which was renewed and urged in many forms, and thus began the friction between Russia and Bulgaria. Russian influences at Sofia and Constantinople were strong enough, however, to delay the meeting of the *Conférence à Quatre*, which was announced for the early months of 1881, until 1883, and when the convention was finally drawn up the Bulgarian delegates were deterred from signing it until the Russian clique at Sofia concluded that further opposition was useless. Then a scheme to obtain the contract for Russian engineers was tried, but Karaveloff outwitted Kojander, the Russian diplomatic agent, and secured it for a Bulgarian syndicate. The coolness that arose on this account between the Russian representative and the Bulgarian Prime Minister, who was refused admittance to the Russian agency, excited the resentment of the latter, and brought him into the condition of mind to prepare the revolution in Eastern Roumelia in the following year, which led to the complete estrangement of Russia.

By the convention concluded at the *Conférence à Quatre*, in 1883, Austria, Bulgaria, Servia, and Turkey agreed among themselves to build railroads connecting the European system with Constantinople and Salonica. The two lines were to be completed and opened for traffic in the summer of 1886. Austria built the section from Budapesth to Belgrade and opened it in September, 1884. Servia plunged into debt in order to fulfill her part promptly, and had the roads running southward to the Turkish frontier and eastward to the Bulgarian frontier ready for operation before Bulgaria and Turkey had fairly begun their continuations. Bulgaria was the slowest in performing her part of the engagement, and aroused the anger of the Servians, who were the readier on this account to begin the campaign against Bulgaria that placed it out of her power to complete her section of the Constantinople line within the time set. Turkey was not much behind Bulgaria in finishing the junction lines. The Salonica railroad was joined to the Servian branch from Belgrade in 1887, yet could not be opened under the provision of the convention before the route to Constantinople. It was, however, officially opened on May 18. The passage from Vienna to Salonica takes thirty-five hours.

The Bulgarian section has been built with domestic capital and native labor at the low cost, for a mountain railroad, of 200,000 francs per mile. The total cost, amounting to 17,000,000 francs, inclusive of rolling-stock, has been defrayed from the ordinary revenues of the principality, 3,500,000 francs being still due to the contractors. The length is 114 kilometres, or 72 miles. The road was ready to go into operation in July. From Vakarel to Bellova the line had already been built by the Société des Raccordements, and was the property of the Porte, subject to a mortgage to the construction company. By the terms of the original contract the Porte was under obligations to give the working of both the Macedonian line and the Bulgarian junction road to the Société d'Exploitation des Chemins de Fer Orientaux, but it had long before quarreled with Baron Hirsch, and would have no further dealings with his company. It offered the contract for the Bellova road to the Société, which, possessing no rolling-stock, sublet it to the contractor working the Servian railroads. The Bulgarian Government applied for permission to operate the junction line, and received no reply, as Russian influences were predominant in Constantinople. The Turkish Government also refused to conclude a postal convention in regard to Eastern Roumelian letters until Bulgaria threatened to use the Austrian post-office in Constantinople, and on July 12 the Turkish authorities consented to accept them when bearing Bulgarian stamps.

The Bulgarian railroad was opened with festivities on the 12th of August, and the first through train that passed over the international route entered Constantinople on the morning of the 14th. The trip from Vienna to Constantinople takes less than forty-eight hours. The Bulgarian line had been open for internal traffic from July 5.

Brigandage.—The Bulgarian Government had a serious grievance against the Turkish authorities in the fact of their supineness in regard to the operations of Macedonian brigands who made incursions into Bulgaria from the Balkan mountains, and when safe on Turkish soil again made no pretense of concealing themselves or their business, but openly established their arsenals in the villages. On July 8, a band of fifty brigands from the Rhodope descended on Bellova, and carried off two railroad officials, Austrian citizens named Ländler and Binderby. They gave notice that their prisoners would be released on the payment of a ransom of 3,300 Turkish pounds into the hands of a Greek named Illiopulos, the consular agent of his Government at Tatar-Bazardjik. The diplomatic agents of England, Austria, Italy, Servia, and Roumania demanded of Stambuloff that he should take steps to secure the release of the captives, which he finally accomplished at the end of five weeks by the payment of the stipulated ransom. Other acts of brigandage led to fresh representations. Sometimes the robbers assumed the character of partisans of Russia, whose object was to drive Prince Ferdinand from the throne. Their bands were composed of Macedonians, Montenegrins, and Bulgarian refugees. Their chief lurking-place was in the Rhodope mountains. The Bulgarian Government redoubled its efforts to repress the evil, and through its remonstrances obtained the co-operation of the Ottoman authorities. The district around Sofia was infested with robbers, and was scoured with gendarmes, who captured some. A band was surrounded by troops near the Macedonian frontier, and fourteen were captured and straightway hanged.

Seizure of the Bellova Railroad.—On July 15 the Bulgarian Government, alleging the necessity to guard the line in consequence of the attack of brigands on the station at Bellova, took possession of the Bellova - Vakarel Railroad. The *concessionaires* of the Porte had already been refused permission to operate the line, on the ground that a Bulgarian law forbade a foreign company from working a line over Bulgarian territory without special permission, which the Government could not see its way to accord. The Porte appealed to the organic statutes of Eastern Roumelia, but the Bulgarian Government refused to recognize this as being longer in force after the Tophané convention and the retrocession of the Rhodope villages. Finally, in order to clear away the complications arising from illegalities on its own side, the Porte decided to turn over the administration of both the Bulgarian junction and the Vranja-Uskub line to Baron Hirsch. The Sofia Government still insisted on a preferential right to work the Eastern Roumelian section in connection with the rest of the Bulgarian line, to the advantage of both the international and the local service, and offered to assume all responsibilities for the operation, the interest on the bonds, and the purchase of the road. A truce was agreed to, whereby the Oriental Railway Company assumed the administration of the Constantinople line, and provisionally of the Bulgarian junction line. When Baron Hirsch's company attempted to take over also the Vranja-Uskub line difficulties were invented, and the Franco-Servian company was left in possession. The Bulgarian Government arranged through an English syndicate to purchase the Varna-Rustchuk Railroad, with the proceeds of an issue of bonds, the total sum amounting to nearly 47,000,000 francs. The road, which continues temporarily its mail and through passenger service, was transferred to the Government administration on August 26. A new line, 200 kilometres long, passing through Rasgrad and Tirnova, and joining the southern railway, is determined upon.

BURIAL, LAW OF. The due protection of the dead engaged the earnest attention of the great law-givers of the polished nations of antiquity. The laws of the Greeks carefully guarded the private rights of individuals in their places of interment, and a similar spirit shows forth in the clear intelligence and high refinement of Roman jurisprudence. Upon the common law of England (from which the large body of American jurisprudence is deduced) the Roman civilization, laws, usages, arts, and manners must have left a deep impression, have become intermixed and incorporated with Saxon laws and usages, and constituted the body of the ancient common law. For about four hundred years England, under the name of Britain, formed a part of the Roman Empire; and there is no reason to believe that, when the Roman domination came to an end, the Romanized Britons abandoned with political allegiance the civilization and jurisprudence they had so long enjoyed; still less that they would seek or desire in any way to withdraw from the sepulchres and graves of their dead the protection that those laws had so fully afforded. On the contrary, it is distinctly shown by Scandinavian historians that the partially civilized Saxons had been specially taught to reverence their places of burial. Nor do we find in the history of the occasional inroads of the Danes any evidence that these invaders obliterated in the slightest degree the reverential usages in the matter of the dead coming down from the Romans or from Odin. The early laws of that rude people, carefully collected in the twelfth century by the learned antiquarian, Saxo Grammaticus, speak with abhorrence of those who insult the ashes of the dead, not only denouncing death upon the "*alieni corruptor cineris,*" but condemning the body of the offender to lie forever unburied and unhonored. The law of the Franks (near neighbors of the Saxons) not only banished from society him who dug up a dead body for plunder, but prohibited any one from relieving his wants until the relatives of the deceased consented to his readmission to society, thus distinctly recognizing the peculiar and personal interest of the relatives in the remains. Nor was the right to protect the dead abrogated by the Norman Conquest. It is true that the swarm of Roman Catholic ecclesiastics that poured into England with the Conqueror exerted themselves actively and indefatigably to monopolize for the Church the temporal authority over the bodies of the dead, and finally succeeded in ingrafting upon English common law that curious and subtle distinction which still exists in Great Britain and her colonies, viz., that the heir can invoke the civil courts to protect (or give compensation for an injury to) the monument, coffin, or grave-clothes of his ancestor, while the ecclesiastical authorities alone have the right of property in the remains and the disposal of the body of the dead person. This distinction has never been fully recognized by common law in the United States; and because the American and English cases differ on this point, it is necessary that the student of the law of burial should acquaint himself with the history of burial law as above briefly recounted. When the United States adopted the English common law as the law of the land, they eliminated from it the ecclesiastical element, and thus the right to protect the bodies of the dead reverted to those who had previously possessed it. But to this day the taint of ecclesiastical interference in civil affairs is observed in some States. Thus, it has been held that neither the heir nor the executor nor administrator could maintain an action at common law for the personal mutilation of a corpse placed upon a railroad track and run over by a train, whether such mutilation was accidental or intentional; but in nearly every State the common law has been abrogated or supplemented by statutes, making it both a civil and criminal offense to mutilate the body or disturb the dust of a dead person. It is worthy of remark that, while the law has in many instances recognized the right of individuals, by will or by contract during life, to dispose of their bodies after death, it has never yet recognized any right of the heir or the executor to dispose of the cadaver for any purpose except that of burial—for example, neither the heir nor the executor has the right to sell the dead body to a medical college for dissection.

The duty of burial lies primarily upon the executor or administrator, but the rule involves only so much of the idea of property in the remains as is necessary to enable him to do his duty; and, when the burial is over, the right of the executor ceases, except in case of an improper interference with the cadaver, the grave, the coffin, or the grave-clothes. In the absence of any testamentary provision, the husband has the right to designate the place of burial of his deceased wife; but, after the body has been once buried, any further disposition of the remains belongs to the next of kin. A similar right to control the burial-place of a deceased husband rests with the wife; and it has even been held that a widow who had ordered the funeral of her husband was liable for the cost thereof, although she was an infant at the time, the expense being deemed necessary. Either wife or husband can be compelled to perform the duty of burial or adopt the alternative of renouncing the right; but the method and place of burial are

in their discretion if they choose, subject only to such considerations of public policy as would prevent indecency, impropriety, or danger to the living. The children of a deceased person possess, next in order, according to the priority of their ages, the right to bury their parent, together with the additional right to remove or protect the remains. If there be no children, then the next of kin possess the right; but, if the next of kin be of an equal degree of relationship to the deceased, but divided in opinion, the courts may determine, by evidence of the wishes and mode of life of the deceased, the method and proper place of burial. In case the deceased dies away from home and friends, the stranger in whose house the body is may cause it to be buried, and pay the expense out of the effects of the deceased, or have a primary claim upon the decedent's estate. And, in case the relatives are unable or unwilling to bury the dead body, the public authorities must perform the interment.

As has been previously mentioned, there is no property in a corpse; it can not be retained by creditors, nor attached for non-payment of debts; it is not an export nor an import, and can not be taxed as such. Yet the common law is not without remedies to protect graves. A suit for trespass can be maintained by the owner of the land or person having charge or custody of it against any person disturbing a grave; the party who has caused the burial, or the next of kin, can bring an action for any injury done to the monument, the coffin, or the grave-clothes, and equity may be invoked to protect a grave from desecration. But, while these are the common-law remedies, the statutes of nearly all the States of the Union have created additional protections and remedies, making the disturbance of the dead a criminal offense, and severely punishing the desecration of graves.

C

CALIFORNIA. State Government.—The following were the State officers at the beginning of the year: Governor, R. W. Waterman, Republican, elected Lieutenant-Governor, but acting as Governor since the death of Governor Bartlett in 1887; Secretary of State, W. C. Hendricks, Democrat; Treasurer, Adam Herold, Democrat; Comptroller, J. P. Dunn, Democrat; Attorney-General, G. A. Johnson Democrat; Surveyor-General, Theodore Reichert, Republican; Superintendent of Public Instruction. Ira G. Hoitt, Republican; State Engineer, William H, Hall, Democrat; Railroad Commissioners, A. Abbott, P. J. White, J. W. Rea; Chief-Justice of the Supreme Court, Niles Searls; Associate Justices, E. W. McKinstry, J. D. Thornton, J. R. Sharpstein, Jackson Temple, T. B. McFarland, A. Van R. Patterson.

Valuations.—For 1887 the total assumed valuation of the State was $908,119,480, and for 1888, before revision by the State Board of Equalization, $1,083,333,328, an increase in one year of $175,213,848. Fresno County leads with an increase of $21,649,564, followed by San Francisco with $20,974,905; San Diego, $19,127,914; Santa Clara, $15,428.412; Los Angeles, $12,678,218; and Tulare, $9,360,958. The total valuation of San Francisco County is $272,711,006.

Decisions.—On April 30 the Supreme Court of the United States rendered a final decision adverse to the State in the celebrated tax suits brought to recover State and county taxes assessed upon the principal railroads within its jurisdiction. The defenses set up by the defendant companies were, first, alleged discrimination against the companies contrary to the fourteenth amendment of the Constitution in disallowing a deduction for mortgages, which is allowed to all other citizens; second, that the assessors included property which, by the State Constitution, the State Board of Equalization had no right to assess, but which was assessable and actually assessed by county boards; third, that assessments in some of the cases included franchises granted to the company by Congress, such as that of constructing railroads in the United States' Territories as well as in the State. The Circuit Court found these defenses to be true in points of fact, and the Supreme Court without expressing any opinion on the first ground of defense, based on the fourteenth amendment, sustains the other grounds and affirms the judgments of the Circuit Court. The decision conforms to the former decision of the Court made two years ago, in reference to similar taxes on some of the same roads, the only new point being the illegality of taxing franchises granted to the company by Congress. The judgments of the Circuit Court in all cases are affirmed.

This decision covers suits brought by the State against the Central Pacific Railroad Company, Southern Pacific Railroad Company, Northern Railway Company, and California Pacific Railroad Company.

On May 31, in the case of the Turlock Irrigation Company *vs.* Williams, the State Supreme Court rendered a decision of great importance, upholding the constitutionality of the Wright irrigation law passed by the last Legislature. Extensive irrigation has been hitherto impossible in the State by reason of the decision of the same court, that riparian owners had a right to the natural and undiminished flow of the stream as against all other persons. As any act of the Legislature giving to other individuals or private corporations rights in the stream would be unconstitutional, the Wright law created public irrigation districts, provided for their organization, and then declared that the use of water required by such districts for irrigation, together with rights of way and other property necessary for them *should be a public use*, and that private rights and property should be condemned and taken for such use. The court decided that such districts were in effect public corporations, and their right to take or condemn private property was constitutional. The court say:

The districts, when organized as provided in the act under discussion, have all the elements of corporations formed to accomplish a public use and purpose, according to the rules of law laid down in Hagar *vs.* Supervisors of Yolo County. Such a general scheme, by which immigration may be stimulated, the taxable property increased, the relative burdens of taxation upon the whole people decreased, and the comfort and advantage of many thriving communities subserved, would seem to redound to the common advantage of all the people of the State to a greater or less extent. It is true that incidentally private persons and private property may be benefited, but the main plan of the Legislature, viz., the general welfare of the whole people, inseparably bound up with the interests of those living in sections which are dry and unproductive without irrigation, is plain to be seen pervading the whole of the act in question. If the use for which property is taken be to satisfy a great public want or public exigency, it is a *public use* within the meaning of the Constitution, and the State is not limited to any given mode of applying that property to satisfy the want or meet the exigency.

Another decision of this year declares the act of 1880, providing for the protection of lands from overflow, to be unconstitutional in that it permits the levy of assessments upon land-owners without giving them notice or allowing them a hearing thereon, providing also for a summary mode of collection without a suit at which the tax-payer could be heard.

Industrial.—The total wheat product of the State for 1887 is estimated at 874,000 tons of 2,000 pounds each, distributed among the counties as follows:

COUNTIES.	Tons.	COUNTIES.	Tons.
Alameda	25,000	San Luis Obispo	40,000
Butte	70,000	Santa Barbara	20,000
Colusa	80,000	Santa Clara	10,000
Contra Costa	30,000	Santa Cruz	10,000
Fresno	50,000	Shasta	5,000
Kern	30,000	Siskiyou	5,000
Lake	4,000	Solano	30,000
Los Angeles	30,000	Sonoma	15,000
Mendocino	5,000	Stanislaus	50,000
Merced	50,000	Sutter	50,000
Monterey	30,000	Tehama	40,000
Napa	5,000	Tulare	50,000
Placer	15,000	Ventura	10,000
Sacramento	20,000	Yolo	50,000
San Bernardino	5,000	Yuba	15,000
San Diego	15,000		
San Joaquin	60,000	Total	874,000

While the eastern and northern counties of the Sacramento valley show an increased yield over 1886, there is a decrease in the San Joaquin and Santa Clara valleys and in the southern counties. The total product is nearly 200,000 tons less than in 1886.

The production of wool for 1887 is placed at 31,564,231 pounds or about 7,000,000 pounds less than in the previous year. Revised estimates give as the production for 1884, 37,415,330 pounds; for 1885, 36,561,390 pounds, and for 1886, 38,500,160 pounds.

The raisin industry is in a flourishing condition, the product for 1887 being 800,000 boxes or 1,600,000 pounds, an increase of nearly 100,000 boxes in one year. Nearly one half of this total comes from Fresno County, which a few years ago was considered a barren plain, but which has proved to be admirably adapted to this industry.

Other dried fruits were produced in the State as follow:

	Pounds.		Pounds.
Prunes	1,825,000	Figs, sun-dried	90,000
Apples, sun-dried	750,000	Apples, evaporated	550,000
Peaches, sun-dried	1,750,000	Apricots, evapo-	
Plums, sun-dried	450,000	rated	3,000,000
Pears, sun-dried	40,000	Apricots, bleach'd	
Grapes, sun-dried	600,000	Peaches, evaporat-	
Apricots, sun-dried	200,000	ed, peeled	500,000
Nectarines, sun-dried	100,000	Peaches, evaporat-	
		ed, unpeeled	750,000

There were also produced 1,090,000 pounds of honey extracted, 250,000 pounds of honey in the comb, and 25,000 pounds of beeswax.

There was an estimated yield of 1,500.000, pounds of walnuts, 500,000 pounds of almonds, and 250,000 pounds of peanuts.

The vintage of 1887 yielded 13,900,000 gallons distributed among the counties as follows: Napa, 2,700,000; Sonoma, 1,500,000; Santa Clara and Santa Cruz, 2,220,000; Alameda and Colusa, 1,000,000; Fresno, 2,000,000; Los Angeles and south, 2,000,000; Sacramento and north, 1,000,000; other counties, 1,500,000.

The total acreage of vines in the State is estimated at 150,000 acres, of which about 100,000 acres are in bearing.

Chinese Immigration.—The number of Chinese arriving and departing through the port of San Francisco during the period from 1852 to Nov. 17, 1880, the date at which the restriction act went into effect, was 253,035 and 123,061 respectively.

From Nov. 17, 1880, to Aug. 5, 1882:
Arrivals	45,665
Departures	13,414

From Aug. 5, 1882, to Dec. 31, 1885:
Arrivals	18,709
Departures	40,221

For the year ending Dec. 31, 1886:
Arrivals	6.714
Departures	12,267

For the year ending Dec. 31, 1887:
Arrivals	11,572
Departures	9,919

The collector of the port says: "Our Chinese population, notwithstanding the statistics indicate an excess of departures over arrivals since Aug. 5, 1882, in fact shows no diminution, being recruited through the underground viaducts, across the borders from British Columbia and Mexico."

Political.—The only State officer to be regularly elected this year was a Chief-Justice of the Supreme Court. The Prohibitionists nominated their candidate, Robert Thompson, on April 4, at a convention which also chose delegates to the National Prohibition Convention. The Democrats on May 17 nominated Niles Searls, also at a convention for selecting delegates to the National Convention and presidential electors. The Democratic platform adopted at this time indorses the administration of President Cleveland, favors tariff reform, free coinage of gold and silver, the election of United States Senators by a direct vote of the people, and the establishment of a system of postal telegraphy by the Government. The following portion relates to State issues:

Resolved, That we favor the enacting of such measures as shall place our various industries on an equality before the law in the use and distribution of the waters of the streams of this State for irrigation, mining, milling, and other beneficial purposes.

We commend the action of our Democratic State officials in pressing the California tax cases toward ultimate decisions, and hope this most important issue will not be permitted to rest without final adjudication upon its merits. We once more condemn the acts of those corporations which have persistently refused to pay their lawful portion of the public revenue. This failure to respond to a just demand has seriously contracted the public-school fund, and must render our educational system less effective, until collection is enforced, or the honest tax-payer is compelled to contrib-

ute beyond his proportionate share. The Republican party, ever sincere in its professions, has finally disavowed all intention to resist the demands of its corporate masters. It refuses to stigmatize their encroachments or to question their misconduct, but, on the contrary, as the action of its late State Convention demonstrates, yields ready compliance to their dictation. While fully appreciating the benefits of organized capital, we declare that the protection of those privileges which our Constitution declares are the common heritage, is paramount to the increase of individual wealth.

Resolved, We believe that the public should be protected from the great non-tax-paying trusts and corporations which now challenge the authority of the Government. The Democratic party was founded to maintain the interests and liberties of the people. It alone is competent to resist those encroachments which imperil the safety of the State. The Republican party, while professing to be the friend of labor, has demonstrated by its uniform action that its tendencies are toward the creation of monopolies and trusts, through whose instrumentality alone it hopes to perpetuate its existence. The Democartic party emanated from the people. Its aim has always been to care for the weak and to be just to the strong. While it is ever ready to promote industries and to stimulate enterprise, it never will permit wealth to shirk its rightful obligations or to impose upon poverty the expenses of a Government formed for the benefit of all.

No nomination was made by the Republicans at their State Convention in May, which was merely preliminary to the National Convention, but a second convention was held in August for that purpose and for the purpose of nominating presidential electors. Before this date the resignation of Judge McKinstry created a second vacancy on the Supreme Bench to be filled by popular election. The convention nominated W. H. Beatty, formerly Chief-Justice of the Supreme Court of Oregon, to be Chief-Justice and S. D. Works to succeed Judge McKinstry. The following platform, prepared by an indorsement of the work of the National Convention, was adopted:

Resolved, That we declare that the welfare of California demands, and the dignity of labor and the interests of capital require, the maintenance by the National Government of the American system of a tariff for protection, under this policy which has been constantly supported by the Republican party since its foundation. . . . We arraign the Democratic party of California for supporting the national Democratic party, which stands upon a platform that declares for British free trade as promulgated by the Mills Bill, and view with alarm this assault upon our American labor. We insist that the success of this British policy would destroy the growing industries of our commonwealth, especially the grape, raisin, nut, wool, lumber, borax, lead, quicksilver, sugar, beet, and cereal industries; also our manufacturing interests, and would reduce the wages of our workingmen to starvation point; and we further believe that the legitimate efforts of organized labor to protect itself against cheap and contract labor. is a direct step toward the perpetuation of the American protective tariff system sustained by the Republican party; also, that proper apprenticeship laws should be adopted.

Resolved, We pledge to the American people, and especially the people of California, that our candidates for Congress, if elected, will sustain the protective policy of the Republican party, and will oppose the British and Solid South policy of the Democratic party; that our American industries shall be protected for the benefit of the American people, and that American labor shall be fostered and protected as against the competition of foreign labor; we denounce as un-

American and contrary to the best interests of the Republican party the cheap-labor policy of the Democratic Solid South of to-day, as we did the slave-labor policy of the Democratic Solid South of 1861; and we declare that the one was, and the other if permitted to continue will be, destructive to the best interests of the laboring-classes of this republic.

Resolved, That the purity of the ballot is the pillar of the State, and the denial of a free ballot to the humblest American citizen, whatever his color or race, imperils the liberties of the people; we therefore denounce as dangerous to our country the Democratic policy of the Solid South in depriving the colored people living there of their right to vote. A government based upon frauds committed against the elective franchise can not long survive.

Resolved, That a financial policy whereby both gold and silver shall form the basis of circulation, whether the money used by the people be coin or in certificates redeemable in coin, or both, as convenience may require, is imperatively demanded.

Resolved, That we commend our Representatives in Congress for their efforts in behalf of restrictive Chinese legislation, thus redeeming the pledges of the party made for them, and renew our determination to make such restriction effective, and in every way to prevent the competition of Chinese with American labor. We thank the Republican National Convention for its emphatic declaration on the subject, and we have implicit faith that the Republican party of the nation will protect us in all our industries against the Chinese.

On August 10 the State committee of the American party adopted the Republican ticket as their own. On the following day the Democratic State committee added the name of Jeremiah F. Sullivan to their ticket as the successor of Judge McKinstry. Some doubt was felt in the early stages of the campaign as to the ability of the Republicans to carry the State on account of the failure of the National Convention to nominate James G. Blaine, the choice of Californian Republicans for President, and the hostile record of Harrison, the nominee, toward Chinese exclusion. These factors did not, however, prove influential with the voters, and at the November election the Republicans obtained a strong plurality on both the State and National ticket, electing a Congressional delegation of the same complexion as in the preceding Congress. The official vote for President will be found in the article entitled "United States."

San Francisco.—During 1887 the bank exchanges for the city reached the amount of $828,427,816.35, an increase of $186,206,425.14, or 22 per cent. This shows San Francisco to be the sixth city of the Union in the volume of banking business. In round numbers the exports amounted to $33,000,000, against $35,000,000 for 1886, showing an apparent decrease of about $2,000,000.

The imports for the year reached $41,780,943, against $36,048,621 for 1886, showing an increase of $5,732,322. The customs receipts were $6,742,078.41, against $5,855,619.93 for 1886, an increase of $886,458.48. Despite the fact that two transcontinental railway lines have been completed to the Pacific Ocean on the north and one on the south, San Francisco remains the great port of entry for teas and silks.

CAMPS FOR BOYS. Summer camps of a social, or at least of a non-military character, have long been a distinctive feature of American rural life. They are a natural outgrowth of the Methodist camp-meeting, which, in its turn, was but an organized development of a life common to all the pioneer settlers of the continent. The idea has developed in many different directions. In the older States, the canvas tents of the early camp-meeting have been superseded by permanent structures, as at Cottage City, Mass., and Ocean Grove, N. J. The educational purpose in connection with such gatherings found its first successful realization at Chautauqua, and there are now several similar organizations in various parts of the country. Among the most commendable of these annual encampments are those intended for the benefit of boys, and incidentally for the convenience and necessities of their parents and guardians. Such camps are of comparatively recent origin, the oldest of which an authentic account is at hand having been opened for its first season in 1885. But long before this, encampments formed a more or less regular feature of the summer term in many schools, that at West Point, established as a regular part of the course in 1816, being, no doubt, the first of its kind in the country. It is certain that as early as 1860 Mr. Gunn, principal of the famous "Gunnery," as his school was called, in Litchfield, Conn., used to take his pupils into camp among the beautiful Berkshire hills, and about twenty-five years ago William T. Adams ("Oliver Optic"), in a story for boys, entitled "In School and Out," introduced an episode of camp-life. Mr. Adams informs us that the whole passage is imaginary, and that he had never heard of such an enterprise on the part of any school.

The instances cited differ from modern camps for boys in that they are either undertaken for recreation alone or form a part of the regular curriculum. The modern camp, on the contrary, is an independent affair, existing for its own purposes and having a definite object in view, namely, the care and government, with or without instruction, of a number of boys. With a great many parents and guardians the long summer vacation presents numerous perplexing questions, and in many cases it is difficult to provide adequate amusement and recreation coupled with reasonable supervision and restraint. The summer camp is designed to meet these requirements. It removes its members from the undesirable influences of cities and hotels; it provides them sufficient amusement and employment, and while affording plenty of fun and exercise in the open air, reduces to a minimum their opportunities for getting into mischief, and renders it quite impossible for them, in the exuberance of their youthful spirits to become, even unconsciously, a source of annoyance to their elders.

The selection of a site for a camp is of prime importance. It should be far enough away from other habitations to secure immunity from too frequent visitors, and yet it should be near enough to hotel accommodations to enable anxious mothers to visit their sons without too much trouble and delay. It should be so far away from shops and other village attractions that applications for leave to go to town will not be made for trivial reasons. The location should be, if possible, on a sandy or gravely formation with sufficient slope—preferably to the south or southwest—to insure good drainage. Pure and abundant drinking-water is essential, and a large body of water, a lake rather than a river, is quite as necessary. The ordinary forest growth of a mountain region is desirable in the immediate vicinity. Spruce, hemlock, pine, and cedar do not generally grow where there are natural malarial conditions, and judicious thinning out will let in enough sunlight to dissipate too dense a shade.

In the matter of shelter, there is a wide diversity of practice. Some of the camps have substantially built log-cabins, others rely upon tents, others upon regular frame buildings, and still others use portable houses, such as were described in the "Annual Cyclopædia" for 1886. In all cases there should be some substantial shelter within reach, available for general purposes at all times and for social resort and refuge in case of prolonged storms.

For many reasons, tents are to be preferred for quarters. The best is the ordinary army regulation wall - tent costing, with a fly or double roof-covering, about twenty-five dollars. Such a tent affords ample quarters for two, and may be made to accommodate four, but this is not desirable. When properly set up and cared for, a tent is proof against the heaviest rain and will stand against any wind of ordinary violence.

One obvious advantage in the use of tents or of easily portable houses is, that they are exposed to the elements only during the period when actually in use. When the summer is over, they are securely stored, and they are as good as ever when the next season opens.

Where permanent structures are used the tendency is naturally toward greater luxury than is compatible with true camp - life, and the health of pupils is not unlikely to suffer in consequence. Colds are almost unknown among soldiers in the field; but in barracks or permanent quarters they are by no means exempt. Floors should be provided for all tents. If made in panels—say two panels to each tent —they can be easily removed and stacked for the winter.

The mess-hall, as it may be called for lack of a better name, need be nothing more than a stout frame building, thoroughly weather-proof and capable of withstanding any wind. Two rooms are desirable—a dining - room and a sitting-room—but it is possible to make one room answer for both purposes. The mess-hall should be raised well clear of the ground, so that wind and weather can sweep underneath during the winter months. In the case of an established camp, where a large part of the equipment is necessarily left on the ground, some permanent custodian is indispensable, for even in the wilderness valuable property may prove tempting to maurauders.

The daily routine of the camp must depend largely upon circumstances, which differ more or less in all cases. There should, however, be regular hours for rising, for meals, and for retiring, as well as for the study-hour, if there is one. In a general way, the daily calls of a military camp may be followed, beginning with reveille and ending with tattoo and taps. If possible, a bugle should be used, but, if not, a whistle is a fairly good substitute. Different calls may be devised for the different offices of the day. The use of some such instrument in preference to a bell, a gong, or a tin horn, is, of course, simply sentimental, but discordant noises seem sadly out of place amid sylvan surroundings. Immediately after reveille, blankets and bedding should, in pleasant weather, be hung out to air, and all hands fall in for police duty, sweeping out tents, and, in general, putting the camp to rights for the day. At a suitable interval after breakfast, an hour or so may be set apart for study; but study from books is properly subordinated to the study of nature, to learning the thousand useful things incident to a self-reliant life in the open air. The successful management of such a camp calls for a combination of qualities by no means common. The superintendent should, in the first place, be thoroughly in sympathy with boys, otherwise he can not enter into the spirit of the situation. He must possess that quality of moral force which commands ready obedience and is capable of enforcing authority. He must, moreover, be a good "all-round" athlete, familiar with boats, a good swimmer, handy with tools, and even capable of teaching a boy to mend his own clothes or repair a damaged tent.

The object of a summer camp is not instruction in the ordinary lines of learning. It is designed to develop the individual resources, to cultivate helpfulness, and enable a boy, should he ever be left figuratively or actually upon a desert island, to make the best of the situation. As little restraint as possible is exercised, but gentlemanly manners are at all times required, and more attention is paid to the manly qualities of truthfulness, honor, and mutual helpfulness than to the learning of schools. The following is an extract from the circular of one of the most successful of existing camps, indicating the outfit required for each pupil:

Three suits of underclothing suitable for summer.
Three suits of pajamas simply made.
The usual toilet-articles.
An *old* thick overcoat, an *old* jacket, a colored flannel shirt, and a pair of slippers will be found serviceable.
One Norfolk jacket, with two stout pairs of knee-trousers.

Four pairs of corduroy stockings.
Two flannel shirts.
One pair of swimming-trunks.
One worsted belt.
One cap, or light felt hat.
One pair of heavy all-wool camp-blankets, gray.
Three pairs of rubber-soled gymnasium shoes.
One pair of stout leather boots.
One pair of rubber boots.
One rubber coat.
No fire-arms will be allowed.

Each boy will be allowed twenty-five cents a week for personal expenses while in camp; it is requested that no other money be furnished to any boy for use during the summer. Necessary additional expenses will be paid by the camp, and an account will be sent to parents.

There will be two terms, the first beginning near the end of June and ending about the beginning of August, and the second beginning early in August and ending early in September.

The fees for the two terms will be $150; for one term, $85.

CANADA, DOMINION OF. See DOMINION OF CANADA.

CAPE COLONY, a British colony in South Africa, the form of government of which was established on March 11, 1853. British Caffraria was incorporated in the colony in 1865, and responsible government was established in 1872. The executive authority is vested in the Governor, assisted by an Executive Council appointed by the Crown. The legislative power rests with a Legislative Council of 22 members, elected for seven years, presided over *ex-officio* by the Chief-Justice, and a House of Assembly of 74 members, elected for five years. On Sept. 1, 1887 an act took effect giving the Transkeian territories representation in the Legislative Council, and two members in the House of Assembly. The Governor of the Cape of Good Hope is Sir Hercules George Robert Robinson, appointed in 1880. He is also commander-in-chief of the forces within the colony, and High Commissioner for South Africa. The Governor is assisted in his administration by a ministry of five members.

Area and Population.—The area of Cape Colony is 213,636 square miles, including 14,230 square miles in the Transkeian territory. The estimated population of the colony and its dependencies in 1885 was 1,252,347. The total white population is estimated at 300,000. The capital of the colony, Cape Town, had a population of 60,000 in 1886. Kimberley had a population of 25,000, and Port Elizabeth, a population of 18,000, in the same year. During 1886, 4,731 marriages were registered in the colony. Assisted immigration was stopped in 1886. The number of emigrants sent out by the emigration agent in London between 1873 and 1885 was 23,337, the greatest number in any single year being 4,645 in 1882. Basutoland, with an area of 168,000 square miles and 168,000 inhabitants, of whom only 400 are whites, a rich grain-producing district, is administered by a resident commissioner under the High Commissioner for South Africa. Bechuanaland, 180,000 square miles in extent, with a Caffre population of

478,000, and Pondoland, with 200,000 inhabitants, are British protectorates. The Pondos have as yet refused to receive a resident commissioner.

Finances.—The revenue for the year 1888 is estimated at £3,451,000, and the expenditure at £3,110,000. Of the total revenue of the colony, one third is derived from customs, and one third from railways. One third of the expenditure is for the public debt, and one fifth for railways. On Jan. 1, 1887, the colony had a public debt of £21,171,854, besides £1,289,439 raised for guaranteed companies. Colonial paper money has been issued to the amount of £2,360,000.

Commerce.—The total value of imports for 1886 was £3,799,261, and of exports, including specie and diamonds, £7,306,588. For the year 1887 the exports were £7,535,037. The value of the wool exported in 1886, was £1,580,432; ostrich-feathers, £546,280; hides and skins, £397,091; copper-ore, £559,328; Angora hair, £232,134; wine, £23,426; diamonds, £3,504,756. In 1887 the export of diamonds was 3,598,930 carats, valued at £4,240,000.

The number of vessels entered and cleared at the ports of the colony in 1886 was 3,555, having a tonnage of 5,549,217.

The number of miles of state railroads in the colony at the end of 1886 was 1,599; the gross earnings were £1,048,686, and expenses, £646,715. The capital expended on railways to the end of 1886 has been £14,130,616. The net earnings, which averaged 2¼ per cent. for the two years preceding, were 4₁⁰/₁₀ per cent. in 1887.

The revenue from the postal service amounted in 1886 to £125,634, and the expenditure to £183,057. The number of letters carried during the year was 6,529,874, and of newspapers, 8,151,885.

The total length of the telegraph lines in the colony at the end of 1886 was 4,329 miles. During the year, 770,500 messages were sent.

Naval Defenses.—The colonial and imperial Governments are jointly fortifying the harbor of Table Bay, the Cape Government providing the labor. Works at Simon's Bay have been built by the British Government.

Natal.—The colony of Natal was separated from the Cape of Good Hope in 1856. The Governor is assisted by an Executive Council, composed of the chief functionaries, and a Legislative Council made up to seven appointed and twenty-three elected members. The present Governor is Sir Arthur Elibank Havelock, who was appointed to the post in October, 1885. The revenue in 1886 was £600,177, and the expenditure £717,414. In 1887 the revenue rose to £816,680, while the expenditure was £689,325. The public debt at the end of 1887 was £4,035,126.

The area of the colony is 21,150 square miles, and the population, as returned in 1886, is 442,697. Between 1878 and 1884, when assisted immigration ceased, 4,526 immigrants

CENTRAL & SOUTHERN
AFRICA

SCALE OF MILES
0 100 200 300 400 500

were brought into the colony at Government expense. The white population at the end of 1887 was 35,866. There were 32,312 Indian coolies. One quarter of these are indentured to the planters for a term of five years. The free Indians compete with white mechanics and clerks, and the further importation of indentured laborers, who, after the expiration of their term of servitude enter the field of white labor, meets with strong popular opposition. The native population was 408,922, but of this number more than 225,000 live on reservations, and the colonists are anxious to remove them to Zululand.

The total trade by sea in 1887 amounted to £3,333,000, against £2,333,000 in 1886. The chief exports are wool, sugar, hides, corn, and recently gold, of which £120,021 were exported in eleven months of 1887. A large part of the commerce consists of transit trade with the interior.

Railroads to the Orange Free State and the Transvaal borders were authorized by the Legislative Council in March, 1888, and a loan of £1,500,000 has been raised for the purpose. The development of the railroads to within a short distance of the frontier has assisted the improvement of the trade of Natal, which has greatly increased since the gold discoveries in the Transvaal. The railroad mileage at the close of 1887 was 217, against 195 in 1886.

South African Customs and Railway Union.—A conference of the South African states and colonies to consider the question of railway extension into the republics and an agreement with regard to customs and the collection of duties, which it would necessitate, was called at the initiative of the English, who had neglected the matter of railroad communication with the Orange Free State and the Transvaal until the construction of the Delagoa Bay Railroad threatened to divert the trade of those states and of the central parts of South Africa. Delegates from Cape Colony, Natal, and the Orange Free State met at the conference, which concluded its sessions on Feb. 18, 1888. The South African Republic, which had carried through the Delagoa Bay project in spite of British discouragement, was not represented. The conference agreed on the principle of a uniform scheme of tariffs for the four members of the proposed Zollverein. The duties would be collected at the seaboard by Cape and Natal officials, and the colonial governments would retain one quarter to cover the cost of collection, harbor works, and postal and cable subsidies, paying three quarters into the treasury of the Orange Free State or the Transvaal Republic according to the destination of the goods. To carry out this arrangement, it would be necessary for the Transvaal to enter into a similar agreement with Portugal by which the same rates of duty should be levied on imports brought over the Delagoa Bay Railroad, or, in case the South African Republic declined to enter the union or to impose a duty on goods

entering by way of Delagoa Bay, the Orange Free State must impose duties at its Vaal frontier which shall be equal to the appointed tariff less the Portuguese transit duties. Imports destined for the crown colonies of Basutoland and British Bechuanaland would be subjected to the same maritime duties, and their governments would, like the republics, receive three fourths of the sums collected. A uniform tariff of 12 per cent. was proposed, of which 3 per cent. would be retained as the transit charge. Sir Gordon Sprigg, the Cape minister, who presided, suggested that if the republics both declined to enter into the arrangement, the British Government might agree with the Portuguese Government on a uniform tariff, the British and Portuguese colonial authorities retaining part as transit charges, and paying the difference to the Dutch republics or to inland merchants in the form of a rebate. The conference agreed on specific duties on guns, spirits, tea, coffee, and tobacco; on a free list comprising fence-wire, machinery, railroad materials, printers' material, and pig iron; on a 10-per-cent. rate for agricultural implements, vehicles, and iron manufactures; and on a general tariff of 12 per cent. on all other articles. Between the colonies and states composing the union free trade shall exist, except in spirits and sugar.

Cape Colony agreed to extend its railroad lines to the Orange river near Colesberg, there to join lines that the Orange Free State promised to build northeastward through Blomfontein to Harrismith, and thence through the coal and gold fields to the Vaal river. At Harrismith an extension of the Natal system will join the line.

In Natal, where the existing tariff is 7 per cent., as against 15 per cent. in Cape Colony, there was much opposition to the customs union. President Krüger, of the South African Republic, expressed himself as desirous for free trade with the Free State and the colonies, but his Government was precluded from entering the customs union by a customs treaty with Belgium and an agreement with the Netherlands South African Railway Company permitting goods to be imported by way of the Delagoa Bay Railroad free of duty. The railroad proposals were carried in the Free State Volksraad after a long discussion, by the casting vote of the President, and in the last days of May a large majority agreed to the customs union with the English colonies. During the session a resolution was passed also in favor of federal union with the Transvaal. The Cape Legislative Council in August rejected the proposition of a customs union, after it had been approved by the Assembly. The Transvaal Government agreed to admit imports from the colonies at the same rates as on the Portuguese frontier, and to cancel the concession to the Dutch and German railroad company, remitting duties on freight, on obtaining a pledge from the British Government that it would not acquire the Delagoa Bay Railroad, which has been built from Lorenzo Marquez as far as the hills bordering the Northern Transvaal territory, and is to be carried across these and extended to Pretoria. The right of Portugal to the country of the Maputos south of Delagoa Bay having been established by arbitration, the Queen of Amatongaland early in 1888 acknowledged the sovereignty of the King of Portugal over this part of her territory. The Cape Parliament authorized the extension of the railways from Colesberg to the Orange river and from Kimberley to the Vaal river. As soon as Parliament was prorogued, on Aug. 17, the Government called a special session to reconsider the customs union tariff bill, and both branches passed it, in order to avert a Cabinet crisis.

Zululand.—On May 14, 1887, Zululand was annexed to the British Empire by proclamation. Mr. Osborn, the resident commissioner and chief magistrate of the new possession under Sir Arthur Havelock, gathered such of the Zulus as would accept his invitation at Nkonjeni on July 7, where he hoisted the British flag and read the proclamation. Usibepu, the most powerful of the chiefs among whom the British had partitioned the country after the deposition of King Cetewayo, who had been permitted to retain his territory in the northeast on the king's restoration, was beaten by the Usutus, or Zulus, who were attached to the dynasty, under Cetewayo's son, Dinizulu, and was driven into the Zulu Reserve. After the annexation, as soon as laws and regulations had been made for the territory, the British made preparations to restore their ally and his followers to the lands from which they had been expelled, but deferred their intention when Dinizulu and Umyamyana made preparations to drive out the renegades again. Dinizulu retired into the New Republic, but came back after vainly imploring the Boers to join him in an attack on the British and their Zulu allies, and became involved in a quarrel with another chief. Both were summoned before the special commissioner to have their differences settled. Dinizulu was at first contumacious, but on Nov. 14, 1887, they both appeared and were ordered each to pay a fine of cattle. At the end of that month Usibepu and Sokwetyata, another chief who had fled into the Reserve, were restored. In January, 1888, Usibepu attacked a kraal belonging to some of Dinizulu's people, seized their cattle, and drove the Usutus off the land. Dinizulu again went to the New Republic to ask the assistance of the Boers. While he was absent, in April, some police who attempted to make arrests at the kraal of Undabuko, his uncle, were forcibly ejected. In May Dinizulu fell upon the chief Humelane and recaptured stolen cattle. The Zululand police, with an escort of dragoons, proceeded to execute warrants of arrest against him and other chiefs. Dinizulu and Undabuko collected their followers at Ceza, in the ex-

treme northwest, and compelled the British force to retreat after sharp fighting, in June. Zulus who were loyal to their king, Dinizulu, then rose in rebellion in all parts of the country. Store-keepers in different parts of Zululand were murdered, and natives who were friendly to the English were plundered. On June 23 the Usutus attacked Usibepu, who had raised an impi at the call of Governor Havelock, and routed his force inflicting heavy losses. Usibepu fled, with the police at Ivuna, who were also attacked. The English raised levies of natives in Basutoland and the Reserve, and • sent them under European leaders to quell the rebellion, while troops were moved forward from Durban to the frontier, and from Cape Town to Durban, and re-enforcements were even sent from England and Egypt. Lieut.-Gen. Smyth, commanding the British forces in South Africa, went to Zululand to direct operations. A body of troops, native levies, and police advanced from Nkojeni against the Usutus under a brother of Cetewayo named Tshingana, at Hlopekulu, near White Umvolosi river, and defeated them, after six hours' fighting, on July 2, losing two white officers and a large number of natives. Usutu chiefs looted Sokwetyata's cattle and attacked the magistrate of Inkhandla district. In the beginning of July Somkeli and his vassals rose in the Umvolosi district against Mr. Pretorius, the sub-commissioner, and other chiefs on the coast near San Lucia joined the rebellion. Before marching upon Ceza, where Dinizulu had been joined by his loyal subjects from all parts of Zululand, and had a force of 4,000 warriors, Gen. Smith sent an expedition to the Umvolosi. Somkeli surrendered voluntarily, and ordered his under chiefs to desist from hostilities. Other columns dispersed the minor insurgent forces in the south and east of Zululand. The general waited for levies of Zulus and Basutos, but these never came except in small numbers. Sir Arthur Havelock did not share the current opinion as to Dinizulu's guilt, and was anxious to save the Zulus from a war of extermination, and hence arose the usual differences between the civil and the military authorities. The only considerable native force that was raised was John Dunn's impi, numbering over 1,500 warriors, which took part in the reduction of Somkeli near San Lucia. The British forces, numbering about 2,000 British regulars, besides police, Natal volunteers, and native levies, began to move on Ceza in the early part of August, establishing military stations at various points. Dinizulu and Undabuko, whose followers had dwindled to 1,000 men through hunger and cold, fled into the Transvaal. The Zulus several times attacked the British posts and flying columns, and raided the friendly natives in the Reserve. Usibepu, the prime mover of the troubles, was supported, if not instigated, by the Natal colonists and officials, who have shown uniform hostility to the royal family of Zululand, and a determination to uproot the loyal attachment of the Zulu Caffres to their hereditary kings. The murders and robberies of the English *protégé* first drove Dinizulu and his starving followers to acts of retaliation. Usibepu's people also invaded Swaziland, and killed men and women on the pretence that the Swazis had helped Cetewayo. The revolt of Somkele was due to an unjustifiable attack by Usibepu, who had been admonished to keep quiet by the British authorities. Dinizulu gave himself up in September to the Transvaal authorities on a promise that he should not be surrendered to the English, who willingly acquiesced in an arrangement that relieved them of the responsibility of putting him on trial for his life. Undabuko made his escape into Amatongaland, but afterward delivered himself up to the civil authorities at Nkojeni. The British Government announced the intention of maintaining Zululand as a permanent possession. Gen. Smyth, who arrived at Nkojeni on August 1, left Zululand in the beginning of September, leaving an army of occupation consisting of 1,500 troops.

The New Republic.—After Cetewayo was allowed to return to Zululand, Usibepu made war on him and compelled him to take refuge in the Zulu Reserve, where he died. His people, the Usutus, under Undabuko and Dinizulu, obtained the assistance of Transvaal Boers by ceding to them the third part of Zululand, and defeated Usibepu, who in his turn fled into the Reserve. The Boers formed the New Republic of Western Zululand on the lands that had been sold to them, and acquired others on the sea-shore. The British, in response to an appeal from the Usutus themselves, interfered, and induced the Boers to give up the latter, except such as were actually occupied, and to forego their claim to a protectorate over the whole of Zululand, by conceding their right to the territory of Western Zululand, and formally recognizing the New Republic. In October, 1887, a treaty of union was concluded between the South African Republic, formerly called the Transvaal, and the New Republic of Western Zululand. The treaty was ratified by the Volksraad of the South African Republic when it met in May, 1888, and also by that of the New Republic in June, subject to the approval of the British Imperial Government, in accordance with the treaty concluded after the Transvaal war, which placed the foreign relations of the republic under the suzerain control of Great Britain. Gen. Joubert and another commissioner were sent from Pretoria to take over the government of the New Republic, and when the reorganization was effected Lucas Meyer, the former President, was left at the head of the administration, with the title of Border Commissioner.

Boer Invasion of Khama's Territory.—The territory lying between the Macloutsie and Shashi rivers has for some time been the subject of dispute between Khama, the chief of the Ba-

mangwatos, and Lobengula, king of Matabeleland. The Transvaal Boers, in order to forestall the English, who, having ousted the Dutch from Bechuanaland, apportioned the best farming-lands among immigrants of British birth, made a ferry across the Crocodile river, just below the mouth of the Macloutsie, with the object of taking possession of the disputed tract under grants that had been issued to Boer citizens some time before. A Transvaal Boer named Grobelaar, in July, 1888, went with an escort as special envoy of the Transvaal Government to Lobengula. When the Boers were returning through the debatable ground, in order to cross by the ferry, Chief Khama forbade them the right of passage, and when Khama sent some men to stop them, the Boers took away their guns. A stronger party was sent to retake them, and this was fired upon, but Khama's people returned the fire, and charged on the Boers, who fled after two of them had been killed and the commander and another wounded. The scene of the fight was on land that has been in dispute between Khama and Lobengula, and lies just within the British protectorate. The High Commissioner asked for explanations from the Transvaal Government, which had nominated Grobelaar an envoy to Lobengula. Khama collected a force of 3,000 men armed with rifles, besides 300 horsemen with Martini-Henry breech-loaders, and was joined by a band of British border police. A force of Transvaal Boers was encamped on the opposite bank of Crocodile river, in readiness for action, while the matter was being investigated by commissioners of the British and the Transvaal Governments. Gen. P. J. Joubert and H. Pretorius were the representatives sent from the Transvaal to co-operate with Sir Sidney Shepard, the administrator of Bechuanaland, in an inquiry into the facts. The incident led to the important intimation being made by Sir Hercules Robinson, under instructions from the British Government, to the President of the South African Republic, that the Matabele, Mashona, and Makalaka territories, and the northern part of Khama's territory, as far as the Zambezi, are solely within the sphere of British influence. Lobengula, the Matabele king, concluded a treaty with England in April, by which he bound himself to refrain from entering into any correspondence or treaty with any foreign state or power to sell or cede any portion of his dominions, including the tributary territories of Mashona, Maka, and Malaka, without the previous consent of the British High Commissioner. The Transvaal Republic was cut off by this treaty from any extension northward, except with the sanction of the British. The Boer Government therefore sent Commander Grobelaar to Lobengula to remind him of a previous treaty that he had made with the Transvaal, but the chief of Matabeleland refused to discuss the subject. Grobelaar died of his wounds two weeks after the affray with Khama's men. Another fight took place between Mokhuchwane, the headman who had stopped Grobelaar, and two traders named Francis and Chapman who attempted to cross by the same ferry. At the request of President Paul Krüger, of the South African Republic, the British Imperial authorities, in the summer of 1887, modified the original proclamation of the protectorate up to 22d parallel of latitude, by fixing an eastern limit at the longitude of the mouth of the Macloutsie. The Boers claimed not only the right to the route through the disputed territory and grants of land within it, but also a protectorate over Matabeleland, by virtue of a treaty that they made with Moselekatze, the grandfather of Lobengula.

German Colonization and British Expansion.—The British port of Walfisch Bay is the only good harbor on the entire seaboard of German Southwest Africa, extending through twelve degrees of latitude, and it gives access to the two principal rivers running through Damaraland and Namaqualand. The bay of Angra Pequeña in the south has disappointed the expectations of the Germans, while Porto do Ilheo or Sandwich Haven is small and threatened with obstruction by sand. The Germans are indignant that Great Britain should desire to retain this *enclare*, only twenty-five square miles in extent, which is absolutely useless since the German annexation of the country. The English Government might be willing to exchange it for Togoland, which is a similar source of annoyance in the midst of British possessions on the Gold Coast, but fears the dissatisfaction of the Cape Colonists. In April, 1888, Nama robbers made an attack on the little English settlement, which was only saved from massacre by the timely dispatch of troops from Cape Colony. The Cape Government complained to the German Governor that the protectorate had not been made effective. After the withdrawal of British protection, which was likewise only nominal, and was formally renounced in 1880 by the English Government, Germany proclaimed a protectorate over Damaraland, or as the Germans sometimes call it Hereroland, comprising the region between the Orange and the Cunene rivers, by virtue of a treaty made with the head-chief Maherero by the Lüderitz Company, which had undertaken to work the abandoned copper mines. The enterprise proved unprofitable, as it had before in the hands of the English, on account of the cost of carrying the ore to the coast, and the company failed in its duty to maintain order, and afforded no protection to the disappointed Hereros, whose herds of cattle suffered, as before, from the black-mailing incursions of the vengeful Nama Hottentots, once the masters of the whole country, but now confined to their robber-nests in the mountains of southwestern Hereroland. Anarchy and disorder reached such a degree that in 1887 German officials were repeatedly attacked and the horses and cattle of the imperial commissary were stolen. The new Boer republic of Upingtonia in the

northeastern part of the German possessions, toward Ovamboland, was brought to the verge of dissolution by attacks of the Zwartboy Hottentots and fights with Bushmen. Discoveries of paying gold-quartz in Hereroland are likely to revive the fortunes of the earliest, but most neglected, of the German colonial possessions, and may induce the German Colonization Society for Southwest Africa, which has succeeded the Lüderitz corporation, to give the promised police protection. An Englishman named Stevens, when leaving the copper mine back of Walfisch Bay in 1857, took with him a fragment of rock of curious appearance. Many years afterward he went to live with his sons, who were gold-miners in Australia. On seeing auriferous quartz he was struck by its resemblance to his specimen, which was produced, and was found on analysis to be a rich piece of gold ore. After his death two of his sons, with two companions, went to Walfisch Bay to prospect, arriving in October, 1887. They obtained permission from the German authorities, who placed little faith in their story or in their prospects of success, since several expeditions of scientific geologists had failed to make any promising discovery. These practical miners, nevertheless, found paying rock within a few weeks. The richest vein is on an island in Swakop river near Walfisch Bay. The natives as soon as they saw what was wanted brought sacks of gold quartz to Stevens from various quarters, showing that there are extensive gold fields. In quality the ores are said to compare favorably with those of the best Californian or Australian workings. The Australians were employed at first by the Colonial Society, but since March, 1888, their operations have been conducted for the account of a branch syndicate that has the monopoly of the gold mines. The German Colonial Society for Southwest Africa has recently designated only the northern part of its possessions, extending from Swakop river to the Portuguese boundary at the Cunene, as German Damaraland, while the region between Swakop and Orange rivers is officially known as German Namaland. The German protectorate includes some fertile land in the north, resembling the neighboring Portuguese possessions. The greater part of the country, however, is only fit for grazing, and is so poorly watered that the herds of its 200,-000 inhabitants, scattered over 290,000 square miles of territory, find only a scanty herbage. There is a small export trade in cattle, but the commerce is much smaller than formerly. The German West African Company is an enterprise distinct from the colonization society that succeeded Lüderitz, and has for its object the development of trade with the interior. The English Government, by the occupation of Bechuanaland, had driven a wedge between the German possessions and the Transvaal, and by the annexation of San Lucia Bay and the extension of its suzerainty over Amatongaland, had shut out German influence from the east coast. The region south of the upper and middle Zambesi was still considered a prospective field for German enterprise and a path by which Germany might in the future reach the Boers whom the hated English have walled in from the outside world. The Delagoa Bay Railroad is, indeed, a German enterprise, but British influence is predominant at Lisbon, and Delagoa Bay territory is likely soon to become English by purchase. The British announcement that the entire region south of the Zambesi, as far west as the actual bounds of Damaraland, is within the sphere of British interests was intended to warn the Germans away from the rich but undeveloped commercial field of central South Africa, and to hem in the independent Boers on the north side also. England bound herself by a memorandum agreement not to extend her dominion westward beyond the 20th meridian. She now asserts her ultimate claim to the whole interior east of this line. A mere announcement does not accomplish that object except in respect to the Transvaal Republic, which dare not now officially organize annexations northward. But while the Germans are dreaming of commercial routes across the Kalahari desert, the English are extending the Northern Cape Railroad to the Vaal river, and soon English companies will be working the gold-bearing ledges that are known to exist in Khama's kingdom and Mashonaland, where many locate the gold-mines of ancient Ophir. Two syndicates obtained conflicting mining rights in the disputed tract between the two kingdoms, one of them from Khama and the other from Lobengula, but on the advice of Sir Theophilus Shepstone both concessions were canceled. The influx of English capital and settlers into the Transvaal gold-fields promises in time to give the Anglo-Saxon race the same social and political ascendancy in the Boer republic that they have at the Cape. Gold exists in South Africa only in lodes of rock, and must be worked with steam machinery and expensive stamps. The emigration is therefore not of the adventurous and migrating kind that is attracted by alluvial washings, but consists of skilled laborers who will be permanent residents unless the seams give out. The Transvaal authorities maintain good order, and in return the mine-owners willingly pay special taxes, and not only support the greatly increased expenses of Government, but fill to overflowing the treasury of the republic, which a few years ago was bankrupt, owing to the aversion of the Boers to paying any taxes at all. The British are desirous of using the Zambesi as a route to the central parts of South Africa, but are hindered by the tolls and import duties exacted by the Portuguese Government.

CAR-BUILDING. Fifty years ago a few wheelwrights and carriage-makers were experimentally engaged in adapting the four-wheeled road-wagon of the period for use on a tramway. There was no "car-building industry" in existence. To-day more than 15,000 men earn their bread by constructing railway-carriages of various kinds, and 500,000 earn their living through the management of the carriages after they are built. There were then in service a few tram-cars of comparatively rude construction, drawn by horses for the most part, and designed for the transportation of passengers or freight over short distances. Now it is estimated that there are in use about 78,000 cars, of all descriptions, drawn by nearly 30,000 locomotive-engines, over 150,600 miles of track. These figures are substantially from Poor's "Manual of Railroads," the accepted authority on the subject. There are about 140 car-building establishments in operation in the United States, and not only do these turn out cars for ordinary passenger traffic and for miscellaneous freight and merchandise, but they build vestibule and palace "coaches," restaurant or buffet cars, observation cars, mail, express, refrigerating, and milk cars, menagerie and circus cars, and cars for the different kinds of live-stock. Some of these latter are so complete in their special appointments that they are not inaptly termed "palace-cars" after their kind, the latest addition to the list being a "palace-car for hens," designed for the conveyance of from 3,500 to 4,500 live fowl, in comparative luxury. This car is described as two feet higher than the ordinary freight-car; it has two aisles, one longitudinal the other transverse. It is partitioned off into 116 compartments, each four feet square. Food is carried beneath the car, and water in a tank on top; the supply being sufficient for a full load for a journey of 2,000 miles. The "Car-Builder's Dictionary" specifies regular car-types as follows:

Baggage-car, boarding-car, box-car, buffet-car, caboose or conductor's car, cattle or stock car, coal-car, derrick-car, drawing-room car, drop-bottom car, dump-car, express-car, flat or platform car, gondola-car, hand-car, hay-car, hopper-bottom car, horse-car, hotel-car, inspection-car, lodging-car, mail-car, milk-car, oil-car, ore-car, palace-car, passenger-car, pay-car, post-office car, push-car, postal-car, refrigerator-car, restaurant-car, sleeping-car, sweeping-car, tank-car, tip-car, tool or wrecking car, three-wheeled hand-car.

This list is confessedly incomplete, for new devices are continually added to meet the demands of the time.

J. E. Watkins, of the National Museum in Washington, in his reports on the Department of Transportation, gives a history of car-building, which places its origin at the beginning of the century, when active brains in this country and in England perceived the advantages of tramways for the transit of wheels. In 1812 John Stevens published a pamphlet explaining the advantages of railway travel, and expressed the belief that passengers might by this means be carried at the rate of one hundred miles an hour. The highest speed yet attained does not fully realize this dream, but it would be rash to say that such a feat will never be accomplished. About 1819 Benjamin Dearborn, of Boston, petitioned Congress in regard to wheeled-carriages for the conveyance of mails and passengers " with such celerity as had never before been accomplished, and with complete security from robbery on the highway." His memorial points to the sleeping-car and the train-restaurant as among the possibilities of the future. But Congress was indifferent then, as now, to matters outside of practical politics, and the committee to whom the matter was referred never saw fit to rescue it from oblivion.

In the mean time the problem had been successfully solved on the Stockton and Darlington Railway in England, and in 1825 William Strickland was sent abroad in the interest of the Pennsylvania Society for the Promotion of Internal Improvement. As a result of his reports on English railways, private enterprise took courage in America. The first cars here, as in England, were constructed for tramway service. They were in connection with the granite-quarries at Quincy, Mass., and in Delaware County, Pa., in 1826; and in 1827 a coal-road nine miles long was opened from the Mauch Chunk mines to Lehigh river. The rolling-stock of these early roads was the work of wagon-builders, whose purpose was merely to mount stout boxes upon wheels suitable for running upon rails. The complicated problems of oscillating trucks and passing curves at high speed came in later.

The early annals of car-building are necessarily somewhat incomplete. One of the first references to the infant industry is found in the Philadelphia "American Daily Advertiser," under date of Nov. 26, 1832. It describes the trial trip of the locomotive built by M. W. Baldwin, of that city:

It gives us pleasure to state that the locomotive engine built by our townsman, M. W. Baldwin, for the Philadelphia, Germantown, and Norristown Railroad Company, has proved highly successful. In the presence of a number of gentlemen of science and information on such subjects, the engine was yesterday placed on the road for the first time. All her parts had been previously highly polished and fitted together in Mr. Baldwin's factory. She was taken totally apart on Tuesday and removed to the company's depot, and yesterday morning she was completely put together, ready for travel. After the regular passenger-cars had arrived from Germantown in the afternoon, the tracks being clear, preparation was made for her starting. The placing the fire in the furnace and raising the steam occupied twenty minutes. The engine (with her tender) moved from the depot in beautiful style, working with great ease and uniformity. She proceeded about one half a mile beyond the Union Tavern at the township line, and returned immediately, a distance of six miles, at a speed of about twenty-eight miles to the hour. Her speed having to be greatly slackened at all road-crossings, and it being after dark, but a portion of her power was used.

It is needless to say that the spectators were delighted. From this experiment there is every reason to believe that this engine will draw thirty tons gross, at an average speed of forty miles to the hour, on a level road. The chief superiority of this engine over any of the English ones, now consists in the light

VOL. XXVIII.—9 A

weight—which is but between four and five tons—her small bulk, and the simplicity of her working machinery. We rejoice at the result of this experiment, as it conclusively proves that Philadelphia, always famous for the skill of her mechanics, is enabled to produce steam-engines for railroads, combining so many superior qualities as to warrant the belief that her mechanics will hereafter supply nearly all the public works of this description in the country, and by our superiority in the adaptation of this motive power, as we have hitherto in navigation, perhaps supply England herself. By the company's advertisement in to-day's paper, it will be seen that this engine will take her place regularly on the road this day.

Cars are here mentioned, incidentally as it were, in connection with the new locomotive, but the citation proves that the "regular passenger-cars" were already familiar to the public. Other early allusions are somewhat uncertain as to date. About 1830 "Peter Parley" wrote:

Now, in order to carry on all this business more easily, the people are building what is called a railroad. This consists of iron bars laid along the ground, and made fast, so that carriages with small wheels may run along upon them with facility. In this way, one horse will be able to draw as much as ten horses on a common road. A part of this railroad is already done, and, if you choose to take a ride upon it, you can do so. You will mount a car something like a stage, and then you will be drawn along by two horses, at the rate of twelve miles an hour.

Such was the beginning of the Baltimore and Ohio Railroad, now known so familiarly to millions of people that it is called the " B. & O." for short. Its construction was begun in 1828, and the first section of fifteen miles was ready for traffic in May, 1830. Fig. 2 is the sketch, probably somewhat fanciful, that accompanied Peter Parley's description.

In November, 1832, an advertisement appeared in Philadelphia papers in the interest of the Philadelphia, Germantown, and Norristown Railroad, in which, after the schedule of trains, was the following paragraph:

Passengers wishing to take a short excursion will find this a very pleasant one. The scenery along the road is very beautiful, and at Germantown Mr. Wunder's hotel is fitted up in a style that will render comfort on a warm day, as refreshments of the best quality and in abundance will be constantly on hand; and persons wishing to take a walk in the fields will find the scenery on the Wissahickon very romantic and beautiful, and but a few minutes' walk from the railroad.

The firm of Kimball & Davenport, of Cambridgeport, Mass., was probably the first in the United States to take up car-building on a large scale. They entered upon the business in 1834, and for twenty-two years were among the leading establishments in that branch of industry. Charles Davenport was the active member of the concern. He delivered his first passenger-car to the Boston and Worcester Railroad in the spring of 1835. It was a departure from the English coach-body pattern, though it retained the side doors. The seats all faced one way, which necessitated turning the car at the end of the route. Mr. Davenport soon devised reversible seats, but did not patent them, and

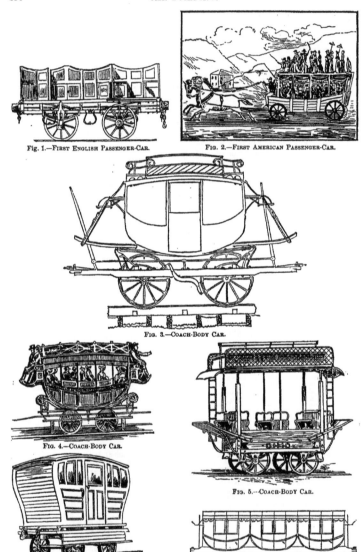

Fig. 1.—First English Passenger-Car.

Fig. 2.—First American Passenger-Car.

Fig. 3.—Coach-Body Car.

Fig. 4.—Coach-Body Car.

Fig. 5.—Coach-Body Car.

Fig. 6.—Davis's Drawing for Car.

Fig. 7.—First Plan of Long Car.

FIG. 8.—FIRST CAR WITH RAISED ROOF.

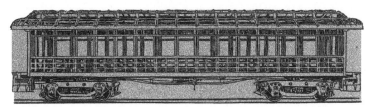

FIG. 9.—FRAME OF MODERN PASSENGER-CAR.

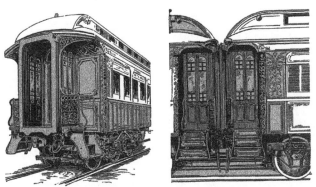

FIGS. 10 AND 11.—PARLOR-CARS IN VESTIBULE TRAIN.

they presently became public property. He patented and used a buffer coupling arrangement, with double-acting draw-springs. In 1838 he built the first eight-wheel passenger-car, with seats for sixty persons, and to his enterprise and ingenuity were largely due many of the improvements in car-building that were made prior to the civil war.

The managers of the Delaware Car-Works, of Wilmington, have kindly furnished from their files the following account of the oldest passenger-car now in use, "Morris Run, No. 1," constructed for the Tioga Railroad Company, and delivered complete, according to contract, the 10th of September, 1840. This may be taken as representing the best type of passenger-car then constructed:

This car has been in continuous service from that date up to the present time. It was placed on exhibition at the Chicago Exposition of Railway Appliances, held in 1883, as an illustration of the durability of passenger-coaches when constructed of the best materials, as well as to furnish an historically interesting and instructive comparison between the earliest and later types of railway-carriages. This car was constructed upon an order for "one first-class passenger-car," to be finished in every respect in a "highly modern" manner, with all the latest improvements. It was styled in the contract "An eight-wheeled passenger and ladies' accommodation car," and was intended to excel anything of the kind then running in the country. Although at this late day we can scarcely realize the actual state of things as they then existed, owing to the vast improvement which has taken place since, it is fair to assume that the car "Morris Run, No. 1," when it left the shop did equal and perhaps excel its kind in beauty of finish, in comfort of appointments, and in excellence of arrangements. Its extreme age and the fact of its still remaining in service after the lapse of almost half a century, attest beyond question the thoroughness of its construction and the quality of the materials used.

The general dimensions of the car were as follow: Thirty-two feet in length of frame; 8 feet 6 inches in width of frame; 6 feet 4 inches in height from floor to ceiling (no raised floor). For this "eight-wheeled ladies' car," built with continuous framing, solid bracing, double uprights, stationary sash, Venetian blinds, and dead-light neatly trimmed, the price charged was $2,000, delivered free on board of a vessel at the wharf of the builders. It may be added that for some heavy wrought-iron brace-rods, studs, and bolts, thought necessary for extra strength in the bodies, an additional sum of $40 was afterward allowed, bringing up the price to $2,040. This figure, however interesting it may be in the light of modern comparisons, when the cost of a first-class passenger-car ranges, depending upon the details of the finish and fittings, anywhere from $4,200 to $5,500, must not be considered as a wholly trustworthy basis of relative costs in labor and materials in those early days compared with the present costs for the same structure. We must bear in mind the various improvements that have since entered into the construction of a car as elements of increased expense, such as the monitor roof with its glazed deck-sash; the decorated head-lining or ceiling; the patent couplers, buffers, etc., with wider and heavier platforms, built as a part of the car-floor framing; the elaborate chandeliers, bracket-fixtures, trimmings, basket-racks, and hardware generally, as well as the compartment conveniences, such as closets, wash-stands, water-coolers, etc., that go toward completing a modern coach. The single item of trucks alone has been developed in the direction of safety, elegance, and durability far beyond the dreams of inventors in 1836.

The patent lead-lined anti-friction journal-bearings, the patent oil-boxes, springs, equalizing devices, improved body-bolt bearings, with collateral safeguards in the way of safety and check-chains, the air-brakes, and iron truck-framing—all these contribute nowadays not only to the superiority of the car, but to its greater cost, to say nothing of the use of refined steel for the axles, springs, etc., and the complex and numerous patented designs of the modern wheel itself. The matter of upholstery and decoration inside and out, the use of hard woods highly polished, the ornate carving upon the paneling inside, the patented designs of seat-frames, the expensive method of heating, the improved style of glazing and ornamentation—these likewise form a part of the modern car, and must be counted as elements in any comparison of the old with the new.

It will readily be seen, therefore, that at $2,040, with the cheaper labor and material of those days, and eliminating the many sources of expense incurred at present in car-building, the "Morris Run No. 1" was a fair specimen of the best class of coach that it was possible to turn out at that time. The windows of this car had the peculiarity of being glazed in solid, without any sash (presumably on account of the early fear lest, if the windows were opened, accidents would be sure to follow), and the wooden panels forming the sides of the car were made to open by sliding the lower half up inside of the upper half. These panel-openings were very narrow, and were intended for ventilation rather than for sight. As may be imagined, this gave the car a very odd appearance upon the outside. Yet it was by no means a bad idea, since, in the first days of railroading, before the passengers had become accustomed to the novelty of this rapid form of locomotion, and equally familiar with the dangers of sight-seeing through the side-openings while in motion, it proved a source of safety, which should at least entitle it to our lenient criticism.

The car had no raised roof, the upper boarding being laid on flat from end to end, and extending somewhat beyond the body for protection to passengers while alighting. Just when this feature of hoods was adopted it is difficult to say—in fact, the whole design of the "Morris Run No. 1" was a total departure from the then old-fashioned standards of railway-carriages in use abroad and copied in this country. The latter were simply the ancient form of swinging stage-coach bodies, placed on long frame-trucks in sets of three, with side-openings in the shape of the primitive coach-doors, a horizontal plank for the side-step, and with a single pair of open-spoke iron wheels under each coach-body. At the ends were great cog-brakes extending to the brakeman's seat upon the top of the coach, from which position he could see the signals of the driver, and be governed accordingly.

Four-wheeled passenger cars were used at this time, and the body was suspended upon leather thorough-braces, similar to the old-fashioned Concord coaches. The seats were placed around on the inside, so that the passengers were facing each other. A double row of seats was placed upon the top of the cars also, where the passengers sat back to back. When collecting fares, the conductor did not enter the cars for that purpose, but passed around on the outside upon a foot-board. There were no brakes, either on the engine or on the cars; consequently the train had to be stopped by reversing the engine. Sometimes the eccentrics would catch on the center, so as not to revolve, in which case the engine could only be started by some application of mechanical force.

The wood-working tools consisted of but two or three machines, the perfected machines of those days consisting of a circular saw and Daniel's planer, which could plane but half a car-sill at one motion, the piece being taken out and reversed after each motion, and a very limited assortment of other primitive appliances of a like degree of adaptability. Now, the labor-saving machines could be enumerated by the score, and the Daniel's planer has been supplanted by a powerful machine, planing all four sides at once, while machines for mortising square holes, for carving, for scraping lumber, so that it does not have to be treated with sand-paper, and numerous other inventions have added to the car-builders' facilities.

The shops at this period were constructed to take cars not over forty feet long, as their standard length was but thirty-nine feet, while nowadays they are often nearly double this length; so that with each decade, as railroad-building has increased and travel became more general, the equipment was made correspondingly larger and stronger and more comfortable, until to-day the finest day-coaches rival the best parlor-cars in all essentials for the comfort of travelers, being equipped with lavatories, hot-water and steam-heating apparatus, gas, electric lights, and luxurious upholstery, while every year additional appliances are introduced for comfort and safety.

Referring to the illustrations in detail: Fig. 1 shows what is believed to be the first rail-car ever constructed exclusively for passengers. It was designed by George Stephenson for the Stockton and Darlington Railway (England) in 1825, and for several years such cars were in use on that road, especially in summer. They were without roofs and were designed only for fair-weather service. Fig. 2 has been already referred to. Figures 3, 4, and 5 are types of what may be termed the "coach-body car." Fig. 5 represents a car imported from England for use on the Albion Railroad in Nova Scotia, where it was in service for several years. It had seats for only four passengers. Fig. 6 is the side elevation in detail of a coach-body car, a working plan in fact for the guidance of the builders, and as such is no doubt the most accurate representation in existence of this type. The original drawing was made in 1831 by John B. Davis, a resident engineer, and is certified by James Goold, then, and for years afterward, a builder of cars and carriages in Albany, N. Y.

It soon occurred to American builders that it would be a distinct gain to reduce the number of wheels and increase the carrying capacity by uniting several of these coach-bodies, as in Fig. 7; and it is curious to note that the curved body-lines are still retained by modern English builders, while American builders early discarded them for straight frames, which are obviously superior constructionally to the curved type. In Fig. 8 is shown what was probably the first car constructed with a raised roof, designed to afford more head-room, and to bring the center of gravity as near the ground as possible. The end compartments contained toilet arrangements and a refreshment-room or bar. The passengers sat back to back, facing outward along a longitudinal partition. This particular car was called the "Victory," and the design was patented by Richard Imlay. It was in use on the Germantown Railroad in 1836, and was undoubtedly the pioneer of the "monitor" roofs. The increased length and weight of cars led to the invention of the "bogie" or eight-wheeled truck, which is generally regarded as an American invention, but which Mr. Watkins finds described in an English pamphlet, by Thomas Tredgold, as early as

1827. He is unable to learn, however, that it came into favor in England before 1860, while it was in general use on the Baltimore and Ohio Railroad as early as 1835. Fig. 9 shows the ordinary first-class passenger car in frame and complete, substantially as used at present on all American railroads.

The now familiar type of car-wheels was not reached without a vast expenditure of time and money. At first they were made with detached spokes, but the advantage of solid iron plates was soon recognized, and for many years chilled cast-iron wheels were used almost exclusively on American roads. The improved methods of making steel have rendered it possible to use a stronger, lighter, and more durable material, and wrought-iron wheels, with steel tires, are now largely employed. For sleeping-cars, wheels constructed partly of paper are extensively used. A disk four inches thick is formed by gluing together numerous sheets of specially prepared paper-board. These are dried under heavy pressure and fitted around a cast-iron hub, which is provided with a flange. The circumference of the disk is trimmed in a turning-lathe to fit the steel tire, and finally two thin wrought-iron plates are placed on either side of the paper disk, and the whole is fastened together with twenty-five or thirty small iron bolts. Wheels constructed on this plan are peculiarly "easy riders," the weight falling on the edges of the combined sheets of paper-board, which insures an exceptionally even distribution of strains.

Palace, parlor, and special or private cars are the latest development of American ingenuity. In perfection of construction and equipment they far exceed anything of the kind built abroad, and have to a considerable extent found favor on transatlantic lines. The very latest improvement is the "vestibuled train" whereby several parlor or other of the costlier kinds of cars are coupled together, forming in effect one continuous vehicle, dust, smoke, and cinders being wholly excluded and a supply of pure, fresh air admitted at the forward end. The flat frame, marked A, is attached to a hood of flexible material folded so as to expand and contract like the bellows of an accordion. When two vestibuled cars are coupled, as in Fig. 11, the frames are locked together, and the hoods are kept extended by powerful springs, so that the whole train is homogeneous.

The dimensions, cost, etc., of the ordinary types of cars, as at present used on American railroads, are as follow:

CLASS.	Length.	Weight.	Price.
	Feet.	Pounds.	
Platform or flat car..	34	16,000 to 19,000	$280
Freight or box car ..	34	22,000 to 27,000	550
Refrigerator-car ...	30 to 34	28,000 to 34,000	800 to 1,100
Passenger-car	50 to 52	45,000 to 60,000	4,400 to 5,000
Drawing-room car..	50 to 65	70,000 to 80,000	10,000 to 20,000
Sleeping-car........	50 to 70	60,000 to 90,000	12,000 to 20,000
Street-car..........	16	5,000 to 6,000	800 to 1,200

CHARITY ORGANIZATION, the banding together of all benevolent agencies, municipal, institutional, and private, for the better administration of charity and for a study of the causes and cure of pauperism. (For a full definition of charity organization and a history of the New York City Charity Organization Society, see "Annual Cyclopædia" for 1885.) The fundamental idea of charity organization is that pauperism is a disease of the body politic and must be dealt with on scientific principles; that all the problems of modern social, industrial, and political life affect the great question of pauperism; and that experience teaches that its scientific solution is possible. Charity organization has elevated to a profession the practical dealing with this problem.

Aims.—It is a false idea that the aim of charity organization is to relieve the rich from imposture. Its aim is rather to enlist the rich in an attempt to change the conditions of distress. The warfare that in its preventive work it wages against imposture is for the sake, not of the rich, but of the poor, because of the demoralizing effect upon character of successful imposture, because of the check upon liberality, and because money given to fraudulent cases is so much diverted from the truly needy. Saving money to the country is not the object, but an incident of its work.

Methods.—The methods of charity organization are of two kinds—preventive and constructive. The former includes the detection and suppression of frauds, a search into the causes of the poverty of individuals, and the securing of adequate and suitable relief where relief is needed. For these purposes it makes use of investigation, registration, conference, and co-operation, acting on the principle that the organization of charitable work is the most effectual means of preventing poverty, as the organization of labor is an efficient means of increasing wealth. On this principle it is an agency for the collection and diffusion of intelligence, its business being not to distribute alms, but to show those individuals, churches, societies, and public authorities who do, how to make the most of their bounty. It is not a relieving agency; it discovers difficulties, and society finds the means of meeting them. In constructive work it includes both the rich and the poor, aiming to educate both classes in their relative duties, to break down class prejudices, and to build up the character of the poor. The first of these objects it seeks to attain through direct teaching in churches, in educational institutions, and through the press; the second by establishing friendships between individuals of both classes through its system of friendly visiting; and the third by the personal influence of the friendly visitor, educating the poor in courage and hope, in providence and skill, and by bringing reformatory influences to bear. In recommending individuals for relief, the question is never, Is he worthy? but, Will relief make him better?

The preventive work of organized charity includes, in Syracuse a Society for the Prevention of Cruelty to Children; in Philadelphia an excursion fund for women with infants or sick children; in Buffalo, Brooklyn, and Orange, N. J., day nurseries; in Wilmington, Del., the regular visitation of the almshouse and of the Boys' Reform-School. Five cities maintain labor-bureaus or work-exchanges, five have wood-yards, seven have wayfarers' lodges or friendly inns, nine provide sewing for women, three have laundries, and a fourth—New York—is taking steps toward opening one. Indianapolis has free baths, and makes a special feature of Thanksgiving dinners and Christmas work, associating together individuals and families of the rich and poor by these means. Baltimore, in connection with its friendly inn and provident wood-yard, also maintains two workshops where the old and feeble are provided with employment suited to their condition. In New York a committee of legal protection has been formed to protect the poor against oppression or imposture. Its mere existence has proved largely preventive. In the past year it has given counsel in four cases and active assistance in three. Attempts to impose upon respectable workingwomen were also exposed by New York and Baltimore acting in co-operation, and the offenders were brought to justice. New York publishes in its "Monthly Bulletin," a cautionary list of fraudulent societies or of individuals fraudulently soliciting aid. It also examines sensational appeals sent to newspapers, and exposes those that have no good claim upon public sympathy.

Beggars.—In view of the danger now threatening society, of a caste of confirmed paupers, the charity organization societies of the large cities are making strenuous efforts to break up the practice of street-begging, and with measurable success. The New York society, through its special agent, last year procured the arrest of 117 beggars, 115 of whom were committed, and 2 discharged with reprimand; 270 were warned, counseled, assisted, and directed. The results upon the practice of street-begging are very marked.

Central Registration.—In 1886 the co-operation of the various charity organization societies of the country was made more perfect by a system of central registration at Buffalo. This system is of the greatest benefit in tracing frauds and in diffusing intelligence. It includes, besides the registration of hundreds of thousands of investigated cases, a plan for a telegraphic code, a plan to secure uniform statistics, a plan for introducing teaching of charity-organization subjects into high-schools and colleges, and the preparation of a primer of organized charity for educational purposes.

Education.—Buffalo has for two years made charity organization a subject of study in its high-school. Johns Hopkins University has established a course of lectures on the subject, Harvard and Cornell Universities and the

Union Theological Seminary of New York have included some of the literature of charities in their courses of reading. A digest of practical suggestions for treatment of various forms of distress and misfortune has recently been prepared by the central committee of the New York society and sent to every charity organization society in the United States and Great Britain for suggestion and amendment, in the hope thus to supply the English-speaking world with "a code that shall be at least the basis of a benign, intelligent, and helpful system of charitable therapeutics." A body of legal suggestions has been prepared by lawyers of ability and published in a hand-book for friendly visitors. The district conferences are also a valuable means of practical education.

The mere existence of charity organization is an education of the public in true philanthropy. Charity without alms was a surprise. The proof that it could exist was a powerful means of educating public opinion and tends to reconcile class with class.

The constructive work of charity organization is chiefly in education of the poor. There is nothing in the system to encourage in the poor a distaste to earning a living. It continually builds up a sense of the honorable nature of labor and of the dishonor of accepting unnecessary alms. Association with the friendly visitor raises the standard of ideas of comfort and dignity, and gives new courage, hope, and strength of character, while the visitor also imparts direct instruction in thrift, neatness, and the care of children. Technical education is given by some societies. Two have kitchen-gardens, two have cooking-schools, five have sewing-schools. Other educational methods are a night-school for boys in Buffalo and a girls' club and reading-room in New Brunswick, N. J. The various provident schemes are an education in self-denial, frugality, and forethought.

Provident Schemes.—Indianapolis has a Dime Savings and Loan Association, with 166 depositors holding 456 shares of $25 each. Newburg and Castleton (Staten Island), N. Y., and Newport, R. I., have savings societies, the latter admirably successful and peculiarly needed from the anomalous nature of social conditions there. Five cities have coal savings societies, and Philadelphia has a well-managed loan relief. The office is in the building of a manufacturer, and all appearance of charity is thus removed. Security is insisted upon, and a special feature is that, when possible, it is the personal guarantee of a friend in the borrower's own circle, who thus has a personal interest in his sobriety and industry. All legal forms are carefully insisted upon and regular payments enforced. The educational value of this system has been found very great. New York has just inaugurated with good promise a system of stamps for penny savings.

Friendly Visitors.—As a collation of the fig-ures of the various societies shows that the ratio of cases lifted from dependence to self-support is in direct proportion to the number of friendly visitors employed, the supreme importance of this branch of the work becomes evident. The total number reported last year from 34 societies, representing 65 per cent. of the whole number, and 88 per cent. of the population in their fields of work, was 3,560, or about one for 2,292 of the estimated paupers in these fields. Of the actual cases treated, this number of visitors is as 1 to 164 families. To provide uniformly at the rate of 1 to 5 families, the rate actually existing in Boston, 103,750 would be needed, or 1 volunteer worker out of every 16 families of the 52 cities under consideration. New York has 180 volunteer visitors. Among the friendly visitors of Boston are 40 college-students.

Legislation.—Besides the regular business of investigation, registration, visiting, exposure of frauds, direction of charitable effort, promotion of co-operation, and education, much effort has been given to both preventive and constructive work in the way of procuring a better legislation. The first, and in many respects the most important law procured by charity organization was that secured in New Haven in 1880, regulating the sale and use of intoxicating liquors, which is still the best in force in the country. In 1883, through its efforts, Massachusetts passed a law for bringing children of worthless parents before the courts and giving them into proper guardianship. In 1886, charity organization in various cities memorialized Congress in favor of postal savings-banks. The memorial was unfavorably reported, but the effort is laid aside temporarily only. In 1887, Boston, after three years of continuous effort, succeeded in getting a law prohibiting begging and peddling by children. In 1886, the Committee on Mendicancy of New York procured amendments to the State penal code to include stale beer dives in the category of disorderly houses. It also, in 1887, secured legislation which passed both Houses unanimously, defining more clearly who are vagrants, lengthening the terms of commitment with a view to a more reformatory discipline, and making more futile the pretexts by which professional beggars legalize their traffic; but Gov. Hill withheld his signature. It also attempted, in connection with charity organization in other cities and with the State Charities Aid Association, to procure postal savings-banks, but without success. They secured a bill for municipal lodging-houses, but it has remained a dead letter, the Board of Estimate and Appropriation persistently refusing the $23,000 asked for by the city. In October, 1888, a special committee of charity organization was appointed to take it up. In 1886 the Charity Organization Society of New Haven procured a local ordinance suppressing low variety theatres. In 1887 a bill was secured in Pennsylvania providing a system of wayfarers' lodges, and they are now in operation. The same year Baltimore tried to procure an amendment to the law forbidding street-begging, was unsuccessful, and is continuing the fight. New York is now attempting to secure longer sentences for drunkenness and vagrancy; and efforts are being made, and will be continued at Washington, to carry out the views of the combined societies with regard to immigration.

When charity organization does not procure legislation directly, it does it indirectly by constant agitation of certain topics, and by educating the popular mind as to the precise nature of legislation needed. In general, it may be said that the legislation most needed is that of such a character as to render criminal legislation unnecessary.

Order.—In 1881 the Executive Committee of the Boston Charity Organization Society called the attention of the police commissioners to the lack of interest in enforcing the license, screen, and Sunday laws, and the laws forbidding the selling of liquor to minors and habitual drunkards, or to be drunk on the premises. After two years of agitation, they were measurably successful.

Statistics.—Charity organization was instituted in London in 1869; in America (in Buffalo, N. Y.), in 1878. There are now 82 affiliated societies in Great Britain, 93 in Europe, Asia, Africa, and Australia, and 65 in the United States, with correspondents for co-operation in investigation or aid in 85 towns or villages, where no society exists. It is estimated that 1 in 125 of the whole population belongs to the dependent classes, is either a pauper or a criminal or dependent on them, The urban pauperism of the country is as 1 to 16 ; 62·5 per cent., or five eighths of the pauperism within the bounds of the thirty-four larger societies, or one sixth of the entire pauperism of the United States, has been investigated and registered.

Co-operation.—Charity organization, in the various towns and cities where it exists, has obtained the co-operation of 66 per cent. of voluntary out-door charities, of 69 per cent. of indoor institutional relief, of 80 per cent. of the boards that distribute relief from taxation, of 45 per cent. of the churches, and of 50 per cent. of private beneficence. These figures represent co-operation promised and available, rather than actually and fully used. Its benefits are to a large degree mutual.

Results.—In Elberfeld, Germany, charity organization has reduced pauperism 78 per cent. in fifteen years; in London, 30 per cent. in ten years; in Buffalo, 37 per cent. in ten years. In many cities it has entirely done away with public out-door relief. In Cincinnati there was a decrease in one year of 16 per cent. of pauperism; in the smaller towns and cities the result is more marked. In New York, in five years, 4,548 families have been made self-supporting who were previously chronic depend-

ents. The results for law and order are very evident in some of the smaller towns, notably, in Newport, R. I., and Castleton, Staten Island. In the large towns they are not yet visible.

Conclusions.—From the tabulation of statistics collected in the thirty-two larger towns, it is conclusively shown that from 40 to 53 per cent. of all applicants for charity need employment rather than relief; that from 16 to 23 per cent. need police discipline; and that from 31 to 37 per cent., or one third of the whole number, need material assistance. In other words, two thirds of the real or simulated destitution of the country could be wiped out by a more perfect adjustment of supply and demand for labor, and by a more efficient administration of the laws. The fact that the best successes of charity organization are in the small towns, shows that the cure of pauperism is a question not of alms, nor of a redistribution of wealth, but of neighborhood.

The value of the statistics collected and tabulated, and of the conclusions drawn from them, is evident. The aid that co-operative study and experiment by so large a body of experts lend, to the student of social questions, can hardly be overestimated. The financial economy of the work is excelled only by its moral economy. Edward Atkinson's estimate of the value to the community of a single man converted from pauperism to self-support, shows a gain to New York city alone of $1,819,200 in the past year. This amount, compared with the $30,-000 that the organization cost, gives but a faint idea of the gain to society. Among its moral benefits are the uplifting of character, the inspiring of confidence between class and class, and the holding of public officials, such as boards of health and inspectors of buildings, to their duties.

Charity organization is steadily growing in favor, but is not yet sufficiently understood and trusted either by rich or by poor. An attempt made in New York in the spring of 1888 to bring it into disrepute as "a device of capital, not to save the poor, but to save itself—a class-movement, a conspiracy against the interests of labor," brought forward a large number of new adherents, but doubtless was not without its effect upon the minds of the lower classes.

Bibliography.—Chicago publishes a monthly bulletin, "The Council," a series of useful monographs upon topics connected with the work. "The Monthly Register," of Philadelphia, is a medium of communication between twenty-four of the societies. "Lend a Hand," a monthly magazine, devoted to philanthropy, gives much space to it, and publishes monthly lists of reports, essays, and books on kindred subjects. London publishes a "Charity Organization Review"; New York, a "Monthly Bulletin" for the information of members, a "Directory of Charities," a "Handbook for Visitors," and various miscellaneous papers. Baltimore and Boston publish "Directories of

Charities," and Boston, besides issuing valuable tracts, publishes a "Select List" of books and papers on charitable work, to be found in the Boston Public Library and elsewhere. All the larger towns publish annual reports. The American Social Science Association Report, No. 12, contains valuable monographs on charity organization, and there are very many scattered through various State reports, which are lost, except to limited circles. The valuable pamphlet, "Notes on the Literature of Charities," by Prof. Herbert Adams, issued by Johns Hopkins University, is the best guide to the study of this subject.

CHEMISTRY. Chemical Philosophy.—Pursuing his researches into the nature and origin of the elements, Mr. William Crookes applies the term meta-elements to designate such substances as have been revealed in his own experiments and those of Krüss and Nilson in the rare earths, the chemical differences between which are so faint as to render it doubtful whether they are to be classed as separate elements or modified forms of the same element. Among such bodies are those into which yttrium, erbium, samarium, etc., probably split up. When the only perceptible chemical difference is, say, an almost imperceptible tendency for the one body to precipitate before the other, or when the chemical differences reach the vanishing-point while well-marked physical differences still remain, the problem is an embarrassing one. Seven classes of such cases that have occurred in the author's experiments are described. If we multiply the elements in accordance with these shades of differences we are liable to come in conflict with the periodic theory, which "has received such abundant verification that we can not lightly accept any interpretation of phenomena which fails to be in accordance with it." To meet this difficulty he applies the hypothesis already suggested in his British Association address on the "Genesis of the Elements" (see "Annual Cyclopædia" for 1886), that the atoms are not necessarily all absolutely alike among themselves; but that the smallest ponderable quantity of any element "is an assemblage of ultimate atoms almost infinitely more like each other than they are like the atoms of any other approximating element"; and that the atomic weight ascribed to the substance "merely represents a mean value around which the actual weights of the individual atoms of the element range within certain limits."

A theory of the form and action of the atoms of carbon, suggested to Professors Victor Meyer and Riecke by experiments in diversion of the four valencies from their positions, supposes that the atom is a sphere surrounded by an ether-shell, and that it is itself the carrier of the specific affinity, while the surface of the ethereal envelope is the seat of the valencies. Each valency is conditioned by the existence of two opposite electrified poles, forming a system

called a di-pole. The middle point of the line joining each pair of poles remaining always in the surface of the envelope, but freely movable in it, the di-pole would be able to rotate freely around this central point. The atom being supposed to possess a greater attraction for the positive than for the negative ends of the di-poles, the positive ends would turn toward its center, while the valencies of the same atom would repel each other, and take up their positions at the corners of the tetrahedron, from which, however, they can be deflected.

The theory of valency as upheld by Helmholtz, with its classification of the elements as monads, dyads, triads, etc., according to the number of definite, or atomic charges of electricity which are associated with them, is called in question by Prof. Henry Armstrong, who advances in its place what he terms a theory of "residual affinity." He would define a molecular compound as one formed by the coalescence of two or more molecules, unattended by redistribution of the constituent radicles, and in which the integrant molecules are united by residual affinities. In other words, the unit charge must be capable in certain cases of promoting the association, not merely of two, but of at least three atoms. After explaining his theory in some of its details, with graphic illustrations, the author adds that if his contention is correct that residual affinity plays a far more important part than has hitherto been supposed, and that it must be taken into account in all discussions on valency, "it follows of necessity that our views regarding the constitution of the majority of compounds at present rest upon a most uncertain basis. . . . The properties of compounds being demonstrably dependent on the intra-molecular conditions, it is difficult for a chemist to resist the feeling that the peculiarities manifested by the different elements are also very probably the outcome of differences in structure. . . . There appears to be an increasing weight of evidence to favor the assumption that the influence exercised by compounds in cases of chemical change is local in its origin; that it is exercised more by a particular constituent or constituents—in particular directions, in fact—than by the molecule as a whole."

A relation has been discovered by Dr. C. Bender to exist between certain physical constants and chemical valency. On mixing two chemically inactive salt solutions, the density, expansion, and electrical resistance of the mixture generally diverge very considerably from the arithmetical mean of those of the constituents. But Dr. Bender finds it possible to prepare "corresponding" solutions, which, on mixing, shall not exhibit such divergence, and further, the strengths of those "corresponding" solutions expressed in gramme-molecules per litre bear extremely simple relations to each other. For example, with respect to density and expansion, a solution of sodium chloride containing one gramme-molecule per litre of water at 15° C. corresponds with a solution of potassium chloride also containing a gramme-molecule, or a barium-chloride solution containing half a gramme-molecule, barium being divalent; corresponding with these are also a solution of ammonium chloride containing $\frac{4}{4}$ gramme-molecule, and a lithium-chloride solution in which $\frac{3}{3}$ gramme-molecule is dissolved in a litre of water. With respect to electrical conductivity, the following also correspond: Solutions of NaCl, LiCl, and $\frac{1}{4}$ (BaCl$_2$), each containing n gramme-molecules; and of KCl and NH$_4$Cl, each containing $\frac{4}{4}$ n gramme-molecules per litre.

Chemical Physics.—A close relation has been found by Carnelly and Thomson to exist between the solubility and the fusibility of isomeric carbon compounds. Pictet had observed that the lower the melting-point of a solid, the longer are the oscillations of its molecules, so that the product of the melting-point, measured from the absolute zero, by the oscillation, is constant. Hence, the author's reason, of two isomers, the one with the lower melting-point will, at any temperature below this point, have its molecules moving with oscillations of greater amplitude than the one with the higher melting-point; and being in less stable condition, they will be more readily separated from their fellows. Solution also being a sort of loosening process to the molecules, should follow a similar rule. Hence, it is concluded, the order of fusibility is the order of solubility; and in any series of isomeric acids, not only is the order of solubility of the acids themselves the same as the order of fusibility, but the same order of solubility extends to all the salts of these several acids. The authors find that for any series of isomeric compounds the order of solubility is the same whatever be the nature of the solvent; and that the ratio of the solubilities of the two isomerides in any given solvent is very nearly constant, and is therefore independent of the nature of the solvent.

In his earlier experiments on the union of bodies by pressure (see "Annual Cyclopædia" for 1883), Spring made use of simple substances; in his later work compound bodies are used. Mixtures of dry, pure, precipitated barium sulphate and sodium carbonate were subjected to the influence of a pressure of six thousand atmospheres under various conditions of temperature and duration of contact. It was found that the amount of barium carbonate produced by this action increases with the number of times the mixture is compressed. After a single compression the amount was about one per cent. If the solid block produced by this compression is ground into fine bits and again subjected to the same pressure, and the process repeated a second time, about five per cent. of the barium carbonate results. A sixth compression yielded nine per cent. of the product. If the little blocks produced by one, three, and six compressions are left to themselves for some days

and then examined, it is found that, up to a certain limit, reached in about fourteen days, the amount of barium carbonate formed increases with the length of time during which the blocks have been exposed. When the reactions are reversed—that is, when sodium sulphate and barium carbonate are mixed and subjected to pressure, a part of the barium carbonate, increasing with repetitions of the pressure, passes over into the sulphate. The author regards it as established that matter assumes under pressure a condition relative to the volume it is obliged to occupy; and that for the solid state, as for the gaseous, there is a critical temperature, above or below which changes by simple pressure are no longer possible.

Heating a platinum wire nearly to melting in an atmosphere of chlorine, W. R. Hodgkinson observed that the walls of the glass vessel were covered with a yellow deposit that proved to be platinous chloride, while the less heated part of the wire was incrusted with fine long crystals of platinum, and a lambent flame was seen playing about the wire. With bromine instead of chlorine, less of the salt was formed, but the flame was more pronounced; with chloride of bromine, both phenomena were intensified; with iodine the action was weak; but with chlorine and iodine it was very vigorous. With phosphoric chloride, the phosphorus united with the platinum and melted it; and with silicon fluoride the wire was covered with crystals supposed to be of silicon.

The cause of the ejection of solid particles from platinum and palladium when glowing under the influence of the electric current, with formation of incrustations upon the glass tube surrounding the wire, has been investigated by Dr. Alfred Berliner. It proves to be produced by the escape of gases occluded within the metal, carrying off particles of the substance with them.

The vapor-density of sulphur has been redetermined by Dr. Biltz. Previous experiments made at a limited range of temperature not far from its boiling-point, indicated a composition of this element of six atoms to the molecule. The later experiments by Dr. Church, now confirmed by Dr. Biltz, made at higher temperatures and showing a regular decrease of vapor-density as the temperature rises, give the normal constitution of two atoms to the molecule, which is reached at 860° C., as alone standing the test of intervals of temperature.

Experiments upon the vapor-density of ferric chloride by Drs. Grünewald and Victor Meyer for the purpose of determining its molecular formula, give as a result FeCl$_3$ as the true symbol, instead of Fe$_2$Cl$_6$. The result brings the formula of this salt into harmony with those of the corresponding salts of aluminum, AlCl$_3$, and Indium, InCl$_3$. It follows that the former view as to the tetrad nature of iron must be laid aside.

Thomson and Threlfal have found that on

passing electric sparks through nitrogen contained in a tube at a pressure of less than 0·8 of an inch of mercury, a very slow, permanent diminution of the volume of the nitrogen occurs. If the tube is heated at 100° C. for several hours, the original volume is regained.

New Substances.—A curious compound of arsenious iodide with the hexiodide of sulphur has been obtained by Dr. Schneider, of Berlin. It appears in a dark-gray mass of homogeneous hard and brittle crystals, which yield a reddish-brown powder on pulverization. They can not be preserved in the air, losing all their iodine in twenty-four hours, but can be kept in sealed tubes for any length of time. The compound is of peculiar interest on account of its bearing upon the theory of affinities. The hexiodide of sulphur affords the only known instance in which the supposed six combining bonds or affinities of sulphur are satisfied by monad atoms; and the natural supposition that it would be eminently "saturated" is overthrown by this revelation of its capacity to enter into new compounds.

The compound KF,3HF has been prepared by M. Moissen by combining potassium fluoride and hydrofluoric acid in suitable proportions, avoiding any sudden rise of temperature. On cooling the solution to −23° C., crystals separated. The crystals are extremely deliquescent, are decomposed by water into the free acid and potassium fluoride, and dissolve in water with production of the most intense cold. If they are suddenly heated with crystalline silicon, the mass becomes incandescent, and a violent disengagement of silicon tetrafluoride gas occurs.

While experimenting on the production of gelatinous gun-cotton, F. Nettlewood obtained, by the nitration of alginic acid, a body sufficiently elastic on compression but not explosive, which gave a brown color when dissolved in water in alkaline solution. The original color of the nitro-alginic acid was bright yellow, and it was insoluble in water. Unmordanted cotton gave a fine Bismarck-brown color, which was fast to soap, more so than many aniline colors, and equaling chrysoidine. Mordanting with alumina or tartar-emetic did not increase the fastness or the depth of the color. The depth of shade was considerable, and could be worked to a great intensity. In an acid solution the dye failed to attach itself to the fiber, ammonia being the best alkali.

A large number of new aromatic fluorine substitution products have been prepared by Drs. Wallech and Hensler, the properties of which point to some interesting conclusions regarding the physical nature of fluorine itself. It is found that in all cases the specific gravity of a compound is raised by the introduction of fluorine instead of hydrogen, while on the other hand the substitution of fluorine is found to have a remarkably small effect in raising the boiling-point. A still more interesting fact is that the difference between the boiling-points of corresponding iodine and bromine substitu-

tion products, and again between those of bromine and chlorine is smaller than that between the substitution derivatives of chlorine and fluorine. While this difference of boiling-points between corresponding bromides and chlorides amounts to from 20° to 23° C., that between chlorides and fluorides approaches 40° C. This fact, coupled with the small influence which the substitution of fluorine exerts upon the boiling-point, indicates the probability that the boiling-point of free fluorine itself lies very much below that of chlorine (−33·5° C.), and that fluorine much more nearly approaches the volatility of hydrogen. Indeed, it appears likely that fluorine is one of the so-called permanent gases, and might form a worthy object for the attention of those who have been successful in forcing the other "permanent" gases to reveal their boiling-points. Under all circumstances fluorine attaches itself to carbon with far greater tenacity than any of the other halogens.

Several compounds of silicon tetrafluoride with organic derivatives of ammonia, similar to the body 2N, H_2SiF_4, have been formed by Messrs. Comey and Loring Jackson, of Harvard. One of two compounds with aniline formed by them is remarkable for being insoluble in the usual organic solvents, only alcohol slowly acting upon it with decomposition. Brought in contact with water it is at once decomposed, with deposition of silicic acid; the solution, on evaporation, yields pearly tabular crystals of aniline fluosilicate. aniline fluoride remaining dissolved. Another aniline compound was formed as a white powder, decomposing when warm or when treated with water, and even spontaneously on keeping.

A new base. theophylline, has been discovered by Dr. Kossel in tea, which, while an isomer of theobromine, differs very materially from it in physical and certain chemical properties. Theophylline forms a well-crystallized series of salts with the mineral acids, and with platinum, gold, and mercury chlorides, and, like theobromine, yields with silver nitrate a silver substitution compound, which is readily soluble in nitric acid.

A new base and its series of salts, belonging to the group known as "platinum bases," have been obtained by Dr. Heinrich Alexander, of Königsberg. The base has the composition $Pt(OH)_2$, $4NH_2O$, and may be considered as the hydroxylamine-platinum compound corresponding to the free base of the green salt of Magnus. The chloride of the series had been already prepared by Lossen. The free base is precipitated from this salt on the addition of stronger bases, and is perfectly stable in the air, extremely insoluble in water and alcohol, and behaves like a true metallic hydroxide. The sulphate, phosphate, oxalate, and two interesting isomeric salts, have been obtained.

A new series of isomorphous double chlorides of the metals of the iron and alkali groups have been prepared by Dr. Neumann. The general formula of the system is $4RCl\ M_2Cl_6 + 2H_2O$, where R may represent any member of the group of alkali metals, and M either iron, chromium, or aluminum. Magnesium and beryllium are also included in the series, $2MgCl_2$ or $2BeCl_2$ replacing $4RCl$. They all crystallize in forms belonging most probably to the regular system, generally in octahedrons or rhombic dodecahedrons, with the exhibition of characteristic and brilliant colors.

Pure trichloride of nitrogen has been prepared by Dr. Gattermann, of Göttingen. As usually made, the substance is rather a varying mixture of several chlorides than homogeneous. The author's process consisted in washing the crude product, which was as richly chlorinated as possible, with water till all the sal-ammoniac was removed, draining it, and leading it over a rapid stream of chlorine. The success of the operations, which were performed without accident, was ascribed to the fact that they were performed on dull wintry days, when the sun's actinism was very low. But at last, in about the thirtieth preparation, the oil exploded with its usual detonation. At the same moment, Dr. Gattermann noticed that the sun had broken through the clouds, and was shining upon his apparatus. The apparently spontaneous explosions seem, therefore, to be due to the violent dissociation of the chloride by the wave-motion of light. It was found that the burning of a piece of magnesium ribbon near the oil was as effective as sunlight in producing the explosion. The temperature of dissociation of the compound was determined to be about 95° C.

The allotropic amorphous modification of antimony, signalized by M. Gore, and resulting from the decomposition of antimony chloride, bromide, or iodide by the battery, has been obtained by P. Hérard. The author heated antimony to dull redness in a current of nitrogen, and observed a development of grayish vapors which condensed in a gray powder on the sides of the glass tube in which the apparatus terminates. This powder consists of minute globules united like the amorphous arsenic of Bettendorff; it contains 98·7 per cent. of antimony. Its specific gravity at 0° is 6·22, while that of crystalline antimony varies, according to Isidore Pierre, from 6·725 to 6·737. Amorphous antimony melts at 614° C., while crystalline antimony melts at 440° C.

Three new chlorine compounds of titanium have been obtained by Drs. Koenig and Van der Pfordten, of Munich. They may be considered as chlorine derivatives of titanic acid, $Ti(OH)_4$, and form the only complete series of such compounds with which we are as yet acquainted in inorganic chemistry.

E. A. Schneider has obtained a compound of manganese sesquioxide with cupric oxide, and has thereby formed a new illustration of the properties which indicate an analogy on the one hand between the manganese oxide and the sesquioxides of iron, chromium, and aluminum, and on the other hand, between the oxides of copper, silver, and mercury, and those of the alkali metals. The experiment also confirms the arrangement in Mendelejeff's classification of the elements by which manganese occupies the place between chromium and iron.

Four new zinc titanates have been obtained by Lucien Levy by melting titanic acid with mixtures of zinc and potassium sulphates. At dull redness the product is always the sesquibasic titanate. At bright redness it is one of the three others, according to the proportion of flux.

Three new sulpho-chlorides of mercury have been isolated by Drs. Poleck and Goercki, of Breslau. The peculiar changes of color which occur when a solution of mercuric chloride is precipitated by sulphureted hydrogen gas—from white to yellow, orange, brownish red, and black, are produced by different degrees of combination of the chloride and sulphur, forming different substances, of which the first had been already shown by Rose to be $2HgS$, $HgCl_2$. The present authors have, by careful manipulation, succeeded in securing other compounds—$3HgS$, $HgCl_2$, $4HgS$, $HgCl_2$, and $5HgS$, $HgCl_2$, while the final product is the sulphide of mercury, HgS, itself. In each case the filtrate was found to be free from quicksilver and chlorine, proving that the extra molecule of the chloride had in each case combined. These sulpho-chlorides are very stable, perfectly insoluble in water, insoluble in hydrochloric and nitric acids, but soluble in *aqua regia*.

A tetrasulphide of benzine has been prepared pure, by Dr. Otto, of Brunswick. It appears when phenyl-disulphide, prepared by passing sulphureted hydrogen gas through an alcoholic solution of benzine-sulphuric acid, is allowed to stand, when the liquid separates into monoclinic crystals of sulphur and a yellow oil. The yellow oil consists of a phenyl-tetrasulphide $(C_6H_5)_2S_3$, which at the ordinary temperature is a very viscid, heavy, highly refracting oil with an unpleasant odor. It is a comparatively stable compound, but on warming with colorless ammonium sulphide is reduced to disulphide. According to Klason, phenyl-tetrasulphide is also the product of the action of dichloride of sulphur, S_2Cl_2, upon thiophenol, $C_6H_5.SH$, the mercaptan of the benzine series, and Otto shows that this is really the case.

A new gas, of the composition PSF_3, and possessing some remarkable properties, has been discovered by Prof. Thorpe and Mr. J. W. Rodger. It is called thiophosphoryl fluoride. Various methods of preparing it are given. It is spontaneously inflammable, and burns with a greenish-yellow flame tipped at the apex with blue. It is readily decomposed by the electric spark with deposition of sulphur; is slowly dissolved by water; and is somewhat soluble in ether, but not in alcohol and benzine. It can be reduced to a liquid by means of Cailletet's apparatus.

To the gaseous hydrates already known, M. Villard has added analogous hydrates of methane, ethane, ethylene, acetylene, and protoxide of nitrogen. They are generally less soluble and less easily liquefied than those previously obtained, and are decomposable at the respective temperatures of 21·5°, 12°, 18·5°, 14°, and 12°, all C. It is shown in the case of methane and ethylene that a gas may form a hydrate above its critical temperature of liquefaction, and that these two gases have a critical temperature of decomposition considerably higher than the others.

The gas, allene, the isomer of allylene, the second member of the acetylene series of hydrocarbons, has been obtained pure and examined by MM. Gustavson and Demjanoff, of Moscow. It is very different in some of its properties from ordinary allylene, yet is represented by the same empirical formula, C_2H_4. It is obtained from the action of zinc-dust upon an alcoholic solution of dibrom-propylene. It is colorless, has a peculiar smell, and burns with a smoky flame. Unlike allylene, it yields no precipitate with ammoniacal copper or silver solutions, but gives white precipitates with aqueous solutions of mercury salts.

A sodium salt of zincic acid has been isolated in the crystalline state by M. Comey, and Loring Jackson, of Harvard University. On shaking with alcohol a concentrated solution of zinc or zinc oxide in soda, the mixture separated on standing into two layers, a heavier aqueous and a lighter alcoholic layer. The heavier layer, being washed with alcohol solidified with a mass of white crystals, while the alcohol washings, on standing, deposited long white crystals, which when purified and analyzed, gave their composition as 2 NaHZn$O_2 + 7H_2O$, or 2Zn(OH)(ONa) + 7H_2O. Hence this new salt may be regarded as hydrated sodium zincate. It is soluble in water and alcohol holding soda in solution, but is decomposed both by pure water and alcohol.

Some new salts of camphoric acid have been described by J. H. Manning and G. W. Edwards. Manning found that manganese camphorate, $MnC_{10}H_{14}O_4$, was precipitated from a mixture of potassium camphorate and manganese sulphate heated on the water-bath. It is white. Chromium camphorate, Cr_2 ($C_{10}H_{14}O_4$)_3, was obtained as a bluish-green precipitate from a mixture of potassium camphorate and solution of chromium sulphate. Ferric camphorate, probably a subcamphorate, resulted from the precipitation of a strong solution of ferric chloride with potassium camphorate. It had a yellowish color and was insoluble in water, and gave on drying at 100° a buff-yellow powder. A white heavy precipitate of mercuric camphorate, $Hg_2 C_{10}H_{14}O_4$, was formed on adding potassium camphorate to a concentrated solution of mercuric chloride.

A new tetrahydric alcohol, $C_{10}H_{20}O_4$, belonging to the series $C_nH_{2n}O_4$, has been synthetically prepared in the laboratory of M. Friedel, by M. Combes. It is the first tetrahydric alcohol which has been prepared by direct synthesis, and is one of the results of the application by M. Combes of the aluminum chloride reaction of MM. Freidel and Crafts to the fatty series.

A substance having all the appearance of silk is prepared by M. de Chardonnet by the addition to an etherized solution of nitrated cellulose of a solution of perchloride of tin, and to this mixture a little of a solution of tannic acid in alcohol. A fine stream of this liquid, under water acidulated with nitric acid, becomes consistent, and may be drawn out, dried, and wound. It is gray or black in aspect, supple, transparent, cylindrical, or flattened, of silky aspect and touch, and breaks under a weight of twenty-five kilogrammes the square millimetre. The fiber burns without the flame being propagated; is unattackable by acids and alkalies of mean concentration, by hot or cold water, alcohol, or ether, but is dissolved in etherized alcohol and acetic ether.

Saccharine is a coal-tar product which was discovered in 1879 by Ira Remsen and C. Fahlberg, and is distinguished by the intensity of its sweetness, which is rated at two hundred and fifty times that of cane-sugar. It is prepared by a long and complicated process, and has a composition which is represented by the formula $C_7H_5SO_3$. It is a white powder, or appears crystallized in short, thick prisms, has an odor of bitter almonds, is hardly soluble in cold water, more so in boiling water, and quite soluble in alcohol and ether, and has an acid reaction. When mixed in solutions or used as a sweetening, it is hardly distinguishable to ordinary human tastes from sugar; but it has been observed that insects are not attracted to it, and some insects avoid it. It is a strong antiseptic, and does not perceptibly interfere with digestive action, except in an acid medium, when its antiseptic power is greatly weakened, and digestion is retarded. It is not eliminated by the salivary or the mammary glands, but is carried away in the urine. It has been used to some extent as an emollient in diabetes and intestinal affections, and to prevent the absorption of the ptomaines of the blood, but its value for these purposes has not been settled. No use has been found for it in ordinary economy, except to assist in adulterations.

On completing the filtration of a solution of pig-iron in hydrochloric acid, P. W. Shimer observed a minute residue in the beaker. It was a gritty substance, with a steel-gray color and metallic luster. Under the microscope it appeared to be made up of opaque cubical crystals and fragments of the same color and luster. The material had a specific gravity of 5·10, and was insoluble in hydrochloric, but readily soluble in nitric acid. Upon analysis it was found to consist of about 88 per cent. of a titanium carbide, in which titanium and carbon are present in very nearly the exact proportion of their atomic weights.

The only compounds formed by the union of metallic bases with benzine-sulphonic acid, prepared and analyzed previous to the experiments of T. H. Norton and T. W. Schmidt, were the barium, copper, zinc, and silver salts. The authors have increased this number by the addition of the cadmium, manganese, nickel, cobalt, and mercurous salts.

New Processes.—A new method of preparing silicon, and recent researches respecting its allotropic modifications are reported by H. N. Warren. The element is prepared from bars of silicon eisen, by dissolving away the iron connected with the positive wire in dilute sulphuric acid, and treating the solid residue, heated to redness, with a stream of carbonic anhydride, and subsequently heating in contact with zinc. On dissolving the zinc away, the silicon separated in a crystalline condition. A further quantity was simultaneously converted into graphitoid silicon by fusing at a full white heat in contact with aluminum and parting by means of acid. The three modifications of silicon may be converted by suitable means from the crystalline to the graphitoid, and even to the amorphous, or *vice versa*.

The following means for determining the quantity of morphine in opium has been awarded by the Austrian Pharmaceutical Society the prize offered for a simple method sufficiently accurate to meet the practical need: Five grammes of the opium powder are macerated in a small flask, with 75cc of lime-water, for twelve hours, with frequent shaking. This is then filtered through a plaited filter. To 60cc. of the filtrate, corresponding to 4 grammes of opium, which is brought into a weighed flask of such a size as to be nearly filled by the ether and ammonia, there are added 15cc. of ether and 4cc. of normal ammonia. The flask is then well corked, and the contents are mixed by gentle agitation. The flask is then set aside for from six to eight hours, the temperature being kept at from 10° C. to 15° C. At the end of that time the ethereal layer is removed, 5cc. of fresh ether are added, and the flask is gently shaken. The ether is again removed, and finally the crystals of morphine, which have separated, are collected on a small plaited filter. The crystals which remain in the flask are washed with 5cc. of distilled water. This wash-water is brought on the filter, and finally the flask and also the filter and its contents are dried at 100° C. The crystals on the filter are transferred to the flask, and this is then dried until a constant weight is obtained. The morphine thus produced is pure, and dissolves completely, though slowly, in 100 parts of saturated lime-water. The principles of treatment are the same for opium extract and opium tincture.

A method for detecting by the magnet adulterations of nickel and some other metals has been described by T. B. Warren. Two samples of nickel tubes having been carelessly mixed and the magnet applied to them, they were found to be unequally attracted by the magnet, and were finally re-sorted by this test and re-separated into the original lots. Differences in the appearances of the two lots could be detected only on a close examination. Portions of the metal were alloyed with tin, arsenic, and antimony separately, and this had a decided effect on their magnetic polarity. Cobalt is similarly affected when alloyed with paramagnetic metals.

A process for the determination of tannin by means of diluted lead acetate, employed by M. Villon, depends upon the fact that that salt precipitates tannin and not gallic acid and its allies. Tannin liquors and lead liquors are prepared (the latter containing a proportion of sodium acetate with the lead acetate); measured portions of them are left in contact for five minutes and then filtered; and the specific gravities of the lead acetate, the tannin liquor, and the filtered mixture, are severally taken, all at the same temperature; and from these the proportion of tannin is calculated.

A method for extracting the alkaloids of cinchona-bark with cold oil has been used in the Government factory at Sikkim with most satisfactory results. By it all the quinine is separated as against only about half by the process formerly used, and the quality of the product is unimpaired.

A basic process for iron described by W. Hutchinson as used in South Staffordshire, differs from the ordinary basic process in that the converting is conducted in two stages. 1, desiliconizing the metal in an acid-lined converter; and, 2, dephosphorizing in a converter with a basic lining.

A method is described by F. A. Gooch for the separation of sodium and potassium from lithium by the action of amyl alcohol on the chlorides. It is also applied to the separation of the same metals from magnesium and calcium.

In experiments made by W. H. Greene to ascertain whether mercury can be purified by distillation, or whether foreign metals are vaporized with it, twelve distillations were made of mercury which had been mixed with bismuth, lead, tin, sodium, and copper. The retorts contained no residue of mercury and the distilled mercury was pure.

Hasebroek proposes as a delicate test for bismuth the addition of hydrogen peroxide made alkaline with potassium or sodium hydrate to bismuth subnitrate, which, on heating, from white becomes brownish yellow with the evolution of oxygen.

The investigations of Christopher Rawson of the various methods of estimating indigotin show that indigo, when finely pulverized, is completely dissolved by sulphuric acid, at from 90° to 95° C., in one hour. The permanganate method affords a quick and ready means for the approximate valuation of indigoes, but the results obtained are sometimes too high. The method of precipitation with sodium chloride and titration with potassium permanganate gives results which, for all practical purposes, are trustworthy.

The accuracy of the soda-lime process for determining nitrogen having been questioned, W. O. Atwater and C. D. Woods have given attention to the methods of manipulation and the sources of error and ways of avoiding them, and have been convinced that when rightly managed it gives excellent results. At the same time they decline to say that they regard the soda-lime method as entirely reliable, even for protein compounds, unless all needed precautions are observed.

To detect and measure magnetic susceptibility in substances which show no evidence of magnetism under the usual processes, Mr. T. B. Warren places a weight of the substance experimented upon in the pan of a chemical balance which is adjusted to the magnetic meridian; equilibrium having been made, a magnet is placed directly under the scale-pan, when, if the substance is paramagnetic or positive, the pan will be drawn down. The weights that have to be added to restore equilibrium give the measure of the susceptibility of the substance in hand. Diamagnetic or negative substances are also attracted under the same condition, instead of being repelled, as might be supposed; and the author infers from this that magnetic repulsion, in a positive sense, does not exist. To measure magnetic permeability, a plate of the metal or stratum of the liquid is inserted between the magnet and some iron-filings. When the plate is removed, the magnet is attracted to within a fixed distance of the filings, and the weight required to produce equilibrium is noted, the plate is then inserted, and the diminished attraction is again noted. The difference in weight is due to the arrest of magnetic influence by the interposed layer.

Sulphuric acid and naphthalamine hydrochloride have been found by C. E. Howard to be most delicate and satisfactory reagents for detecting the presence of nitrogenous and chloride impurities in drinking-water. Water but slightly tainted with nitrous acid only gives a very faint pink on application of these tests. In proportion as the contamination is greater, the coloration is more intense, until a deep carmine is produced. The reagents for chlorides, the presence of considerable quantities of which may indicate contamination by animal excreta, are nitric acid and silver nitrate. They produce in water containing chlorides a white precipitate of silver chloride, the exhibition of which rises from a mere opalescence when the quantity of chloride is slight to a distinct deposit when the contamination is considerable.

Chemistry of the Arts. — W. N. Hartley has shown that light may effect changes in organic coloring substances in other ways than by promoting oxidation or reduction, thus: The color of an organic substance is an effect of its highly complex structure, notwithstanding the fact that its composition may be simple enough. It may consist, for instance, of but three or four elements—carbon, hydrogen, and oxygen, with, perhaps, nitrogen—but the number of atoms necessary to produce the smallest particle or molecule of color is large; and every color depends upon the way in which the atoms are arranged in the molecule. The shifting of a single atom will cause a brilliant color to become colorless. The effect of light on such substances is variable; sometimes the change induced is oxidation; it is sometimes a molecular change, or the rearrangement of the atoms in the molecule. Light may also be capable of resolving a complex substance into two or more simpler substances. The color of a substance depends upon the rate of vibration of its molecules. The more brilliant the light the more ample are the vibrations. It is easy, then, to understand how a light of great brilliancy may throw a colored molecule into such a state of intense vibration that the molecule will fall to pieces. The complex and unstable compound is resolved into two or more simple and colorless bodies. Unstable colors are also liable to be changed by oxygen, which is never excluded from framed pictures; moisture, which is used in the mounting of pictures, and is in the air; and acidity, which exists to a greater or less extent in all towns where coal is burned, and which is sometimes a property of the paper on which drawings are made. All preparations of lead are sensitive to impurities of the air, and should never be used in works of art; and of mercury, only pure cinnabar or vermillion. Acidity may be partly remedied by washing the paper in a slightly alkaline solution, or by using weak borax-water in applying the pigments. Of the various colors, the yellows and crimson are most affected by sunlight, and blue and gray tints by an impure atmosphere. The difference in the effect of direct sunlight and diffused daylight upon colors is very great. In the latter the prevailing rays are the yellow ones, while the violet and ultra-violet rays, which are so active in direct sunlight, are absent. Diffused light sufficient for the exhibition of pictures is forty times weaker than average direct sunlight, or four hundred times weaker than that of summer.

In a paper read at the British Association on "The Action of Light on Water-colors," Dr. Arthur Richardson named cadmium yellow, cadmium orange, king's yellow, and indigo, as colors which bleach by oxidation under the combined influence of light, air, and moisture, but are permanent in an atmosphere of carbon dioxide or in dry air. A second group of colors on which light exerts a reducing action, which is independent of air, and in some cases takes place in the absence of moisture, includes Prussian blue, vermillion, lakes, gamboge, etc. Prussian blue fades in moist air; much more rapidly in an atmosphere of carbonic dioxide; but is permanent in dry air. Mixed with cadmium yellow, Prussian blue gave a green which was very sensitive to light if moisture was present, but was permanent in dry air. Vermillion was shown to fade in dry and moist air, also in an inert atmosphere like carbon dioxide. With cadmium yellow an oxide was formed which blackened in moist air in a few hours, though in dry air light was without action on it. The author condemns as unsafe those pigments which fade in dry air, and shows that the greater number of paints are stable in sunlight, provided moisture is absent.

When petroleum is stored in lead-lined tanks, the lead is rapidly corroded, with the formation of a heavy, brownish-colored powder. This powder has been found to consist of a carbonate and hydrated oxide of lead and a small quantity of valerate of lead; the brownish color is due to organic matter. The hypothesis that the white lead, of which the powder practically consists, and a paraffin, is formed by the action of an oxidizing agent and a small quantity of valeric acid present in the petroleum on the lead, is supported by experiments made by William Fox.

H. Le Chatelier has found that hydrated cements treated with a large excess of water give up not only the lime present as hydrate, but also, in time and after treatment with fresh quantities of water, they surrender nearly all the lime in combination. Slow-setting cements contain much calcium hydrate; quick-setting cements, very little.

Analytical Chemistry.—In the analysis of milk as recommended by the Association of Official Agricultural Chemists, the butter is estimated by drying on the water-bath for thirty minutes, or by drying with powdered asbestos for two hours at 100° C. For casein, the milk is digested with H_2SO_4, or the dried residue is rubbed up and transferred to the soda-lime combustion tube, or is transferred to a digestion flask, and the casein estimated by the method of Kjeldahl. For the estimation of the fat, a strip of blotting or filtering paper is saturated with a measured quantity of milk, and dried, after which the fat is extracted from it; or the milk is dehydrated by means of anhydrous sulphate of copper; the fat is extracted by means of the low-boiling products of petroleum; the butter is saponified with solution of potassium hydroxide in alcohol, and the excess of the alkali is determined by means of a solution of hydrochloric acid. In Babcock's method for estimating water in fat, the milk is placed in ignited asbestos, and subjected, at 100° C., to a slow current of dry air till the water is expelled. The tube containing the solids from this operation is placed in an extraction apparatus, and exhausted in the usual way. In Prof. Macfarlane's method the milk is absorbed in asbestos fiber in a tube,

which is then exposed, to dry it, for ten or twelve hours at a temperature of 90° C. The tube is then exhausted with petroleum ether, dried, cooled, and weighed. The loss represents the butter fat. For sugar, the milk, its specific gravity having been determined, is treated with mercuric nitrate or mercuric iodide solution for precipitation of albumen, shaken, filtered, and subjected to polariscopic examination. For the estimation of ash, the milk, treated with nitric acid, is dried and burned at a low red heat till the ash is free from carbon.

In the analysis of butter, a portion of the sample, taken from the inside of the mass, is placed on a slide, treated with a drop of pure sweet-oil, and examined with a microscope and with polarized light and the selenite plate. Pure butter will show neither crystals nor a particolored field with selenite, while other fats, melted and cooled and mixed with butter, will usually present crystals and variegated colors. The specific gravity and the melting-point are determined with apparatus prepared for that purpose. Volatile and soluble acids are estimated by processes requiring considerable manipulation. The amount of water is ascertained by heating at 105° C. for two hours in a flat-bottomed platinum dish full of sand. Salt is volumetrically ascertained by adding hot water, waiting till the melted fat has all collected on the top, and running the water, without any of the fat, into an Erlenmayer flask. The salt is also determined in the filtrate by means of solution of silver nitrate. The methods of estimating curd depend on the principle of drying a weighed portion and extracting the fat with ether or petroleum. The residual mass is then weighed, and the curd determined by loss or ignition. In Babcock's method for the determination of casein, dried butter is treated with light petroleum till all fat is removed. The residue is then ignited with soda-lime or treated by the Kjedahl method.

For the determination of traces of arsenic in tissues, yarns, and paper-hangings, R. Fresenius and E. Hintz digest the chopped tissue with hydrochloric acid for one hour; add solution of ferrous chloride, and heat till the excess of hydrochloric acid has passed off, and then boil till the distillation is stopped by frothing. More than two thirds of the liquid in the retort could generally be distilled over. A second distillation with hydrochloric acid is effected, and the sulphureted hydrogen treatment is applied. After elimination of organic matter, the precipitate is filtered, treated with bromo-hydrochloric acid and ferrous chloride, and distilled. Treatment with sulphureted hydrogen gives arsenic trisulphide.

The state of combination in which quicksilver is dissolved in natural waters has been studied by G. F. Becker in the course of his investigations of the quicksilver deposits of the Pacific slope. Pyrite or marcasite almost invariably accompanies cinnabar; gold is associated with it in a considerable number of cases; copper sulphides or sulpho-salts not infrequently; and sulphides of arsenic and antimony and zinc-blende sometimes. The waters of Steamboat Springs are now depositing gold, probably in the metallic state; sulphides of arsenic, antimony, and mercury; sulphides or sulpho-salts of silver, lead, copper, and zinc; iron oxide and possibly iron sulphides; manganese, nickel, and cobalt compounds, with a variety of earthy minerals. The sulphides most abundant in the deposits are found in solution in the water itself, while the other metallic compounds occur in deposits from springs now active or which have been active within a few years. These springs are thus adding to the ore-deposit of the locality, which has been worked for quicksilver in former years. There is reason to suppose that deposition is also in progress at Sulphur Springs. Experiments were made to determine the conditions of solubility and of precipitation of quicksilver and the other metallic constituents of the deposits in the various earthy salts or mixtures of them, held in the waters. They showed that there is a series of compounds of mercury of the form HgSnNaS, one or other of which is soluble in aqueous solutions of caustic soda, sodic sulphhydrate, or sodic sulphide, and apparently also in pure water, at various temperatures. These solutions subsist, to a greater or less extent, in the presence of sodic carbonates, borates, and chlorides. There is strong evidence that the waters of Steamboat Springs contain mercury in the same form, if indeed they do not still carry it in solution. Bisulphide of iron, gold, and zinc-blende form double sulphides with sodium, which appear to be analogous with that of mercury. Copper gives a double sulphide, but combines more readily with sodic sulphhydrate than with the simple sulphide. All of the soluble sulpho-salts may exist in the presence of sodic carbonates. Mercuric sulphide is readily precipitated from these solutions, by cooling, by dilution, and by other conditions that may be brought about among the substances existing in the solutions.

In examining olive-oil for mixture of lard oil, Mr. T. B. Warren confirms the presence of poppy-oil by passing ozone into the mixture, when a black product will be obtained by $S.Cl_2$, and the viscosity will be increased. The lard-oil may be removed by boiling the coagulum in a moderately strong alkaline solution. The remaining mass is washed and treated for the estimation of the iodine absorptions, when, knowing the iodine absorption of the mixture and the proportion of it due to the recovered lard-oil, we have the difference corresponding to the olive and poppy oils. If we know that two oils only are present, and we know the iodine absorption of each, we have no difficulty in fixing on the quantities of each necessary to correspond with the determination.

The composition of the persulphide of hydro-

gen has been determined by Dr. Rebs, of Jena, to be H_2S_5. It is a bright-yellow, mobile, transparent oil, possessing an odor peculiar to itself. When dry it may be preserved in a closed tube without decomposition, but in contact with water it breaks up rapidly, with evolution of sulphureted hydrogen and separation of sulphur.

A new method of testing alcoholic liquors, discovered by Prof. Schwartz, consists in determining the specific gravity and the index of refraction of the substance under examination.

Mr. Thomas Turner has experimented upon the value of the sulphuric-acid method for estimating silicon in iron and steel, and has compared it with the *aqua-regia* method. His conclusions are, that with cast-irons of specially good quality the silicon can be correctly estimated by evaporation with dilute sulphuric acid; with phosphoric irons the residue obtained, though white, is often impure, and should be further treated in order to obtain accurate results; with phosphoric irons containing titanium, the silica is contaminated with iron, with titanic oxide, and phosphoric acid. The residue may be very nearly white and still contain 20 per cent. of substances other than silica; on treatment with *aqua regia*, the color of the residue is usually an indication of its purity.

Chemical Synthesis. — Dr. E. H. Keiser has effected a synthesis of water, in which a known weight of oxygen in the form of copper oxide has been made to combine with an actually weighed quantity of hydrogen. The weighing of the hydrogen was accurately effected by causing it to be occluded in palladium, whereby a compound was formed which is stable at ordinary temperatures, but gives out its hydrogen when heated. A new determination of the atomic weight of oxygen by this process gives it as slightly lower than 15·96 and more nearly 15·87.

Drs. Emil Fischer and Tafel have succeeded in artificially preparing glucose directly from glycerin. The glycerin was oxidized by means of soda and bromine to aldehyde, and this was subjected to a subsequent condensation by means of alkalies. The synthesis had been previously effected by decomposition of acrolein dibromide with baryta water, but the new method is a far easier one.

Bernthsen and Semper have produced by artificial synthesis the substance nucine, or juglon, which appears in the form of needle-shaped crystals upon the outer coatings of walnuts, and which has been found in the expressed juice of the same.

The synthesis of crystalline dicalcium arseniate, or pharmacolite, has been effected by M. Dufet through the slow interdiffusion of solutions of nitrate of lime and di-sodium arseniate. The gradual precipitation thus brought about resulted in the formation of a group of crystals exactly resembling those of pharmacolite-monoclinic prisms of a pearly luster and frequently possessing a pink tint. The chemical analysis of the crystals led to the formula $HCaAsO_4 + 2H_2O$; and the substance thus becomes chemically as well as physically isomorphous with brushite, the corresponding phosphate of calcium, $HCaPO_4 + 2H_2O$.

Atomic Weights.—The following new method for the determination of the atomic weight of oxygen was described by W. A. Noyes at the American Association:

The apparatus to be used consists of a U-tube, filled with copper oxides, to one side of which is attached a tube with a capacity of about 20 cc., and to the other side a three-way stop-cock. The U-tube is first exhausted and weighed; it is then heated, and pure hydrogen is passed in. The hydrogen is converted into water, which then condenses in the tube on the opposite side from the stop-cock. The gain in weight of the apparatus gives the weight of the hydrogen. After weighing, the gases remaining in the apparatus are pumped out and analyzed. The water is also expelled, and from the loss in weight of the apparatus the weight of oxygen is determined. The advantages of the method are: The weight of the hydrogen is determined directly; the weight of the oxygen is also found directly and independently of the weight of the hydrogen; each is weighed in a vacuum, and the usual correction of the weights to a vacuum becomes unnecessary; impurities in the hydrogen, and especially any nitrogen which it contains, will be detected and the amount determined; finally, no error can result from incomplete combustion of the hydrogen.

In the report of the Committee on Electrolysis of the British Association, a direct determination of the ratio between the atomic weight of copper and that of silver, based upon the electrolytic experiments of W. N. Shaw, is made to give $Ag:Cu = 17:10$; whence the atomic weight of copper is made 63·833, or, corrected, 63·360. This value being different from that ordinarily received, a direct determination was made, at the request of Prof. J. P. Cooke, by T. W. Richards. This experimenter deduced an atomic weight for copper of 63·44, which, although it does not exactly coincide with Shaw's results, is nearer to them than the old accepted value of 63·17.

The atomic weight of didymium, freed from all other allied metals known at that time, was determined by Cleve, in 1874, as 147. After the discovery of samarium as an accompaniment to didymium, and under evidence that it was present in the sample examined by him, the author made a new determination of the atomic weight of didymium, freed from samarium, as 142·3.

With the atomic weight 198·6, osmium has formed a notable exception to the periodic law, standing at the opposite end of the platinum group from where its other properties would place it. The atomic weight of this metal has now been redetermined by Prof. Seubert by means of the analysis of the pure double chlorides of osmium with ammonium and potassium, and is fixed at 191·1. This gives to it its proper place in the periodic classification, as before iridium.

Considering that it is desirable that all determinations of atomic weights should be connected as directly as possible with hydrogen, J. W. Mallet describes a method by which this may be done in the case of gold. A known weight of zinc is dissolved in dilute sulphuric acid, and the hydrogen evolved is measured. A solution of bromide or chloride of gold is then treated with zinc more than sufficient to precipitate the whole of the gold, the residual zinc being determined by the hydrogen evolved on treatment with sulphuric acid. The difference in volume of hydrogen obtained gives a direct means of calculating the atomic weight of gold.

Chemistry of Plants.—Helen C. De S. Abbott is convinced that a similarity of one or more chemical constituents is to be found in all plants which have reached the same stage of evolution—that there is a development in chemical constitution, closely connected with their morphological evolution, which plants pass through—and hence that chemical character, as indicating the height of the plant in the scale of progression, is essentially appropriate for a basis of classification. Some one compound, as saponin, will be found with similar botanical characters in plants of distinct genera and families on the same plane of evolution or development. Chemical constituents of plants are found in varying quantities during stated periods of the year. Certain compounds present at one stage of growth are absent at another. Different parts of plants may contain distinct compounds; whether any of the constituents found in plants are, as has been said, the result of destructive metabolism, and of no further use in its economy, or not, it is a significant fact that certain cells, tissues, or organs peculiar to a plant secrete or excrete compounds peculiar to them which are to be found in one family, or in species which are closely allied.

The chemistry of the onion as a field-crop has been studied by R. W. E. McIvor, in Australia. The soil in which the plant is grown is a chocolate loam of basaltic origin containing in a virgin state sometimes as much as 0·28 per cent. of nitrogen and 0·20 per cent. of phosphoric acid extractable by hydrochloric acid. While non-nitrogenous guanos and superphosphates have in a few instances slightly increased the crop, it has been found that manures containing nitrogen in the form of sulphate of ammonia or as a constituent of blood-guano produce more satisfactory results. The liberal use of superphosphate mixed with sulphate of ammonia has invariably proved more beneficial on the poorer land than superphosphate alone. The largest returns, however, have resulted from the joint use of a fertilizer composed of the sulphates of ammonia and potash and superphosphate. The farmers are of opinion that onions produced by the aid of purely chemical manures keep in good condition for a longer period than those obtained from ground which is naturally "forcing," or which has been recently manured with rich farmyard manure. It seems fairly clear to the author that the onion, "in common with other crops," depends upon the soil for its supplies of nitrogen. The mean composition of air-dried onions growing on unmanured land was found to be:

Water	894·8
Combustible matter (N = 2·87)	101·0
Ash	4·2
Total	1,000·0

The total nitrogen and mean composition of ash show that an average crop of, say, eight tons will remove from an acre:

	Lbs.		Lbs.
N....	42·48	P_2O_5	10·88
K_2O	29·86	Cl............ ..	0·80
Na_2O	1·88	SO_3................	22·90
CaO................	6·52	SiO_2	1·72
MgO................	2·70		
Fe_2O_3	0·80	Total	119·54

The total sulphur in air-dried onions was found to average 0·051 per cent.

The presence of aluminum was supposed to be peculiar to Lycopodium among plants; but Prof. Church has found traces of it in the ashes of many other plants. It occurs in all the species of Lycopodium which were examined, except those which are of epiphytic habit, but not in the allied genus *Selaginella ;* and in the ashes of some—but not all—tree-ferns in large proportions.

Domestic Chemistry.—The results of observations of the effect of free carbonic acid in potable water on leaden pipes have been summarized by E. Reichardt. Only water containing free carbonic acid has been found to attack the pipes. The view that lead pipes conducting such water become incrusted gradually, and thereby capable of resisting corrosion, has not been proved. Except with hard waters holding much lime, no deposit has been observed, even after years of use. Mountain springs do not usually contain more than enough free carbonic acid to dissolve the monocarbonate of lime present, hardly enough to form bicarbonate; but sometimes waters holding much lime in solution have more. Experiments thus far show that these spring-waters do not attack lead in more than the most minute degree. River-waters more frequently contain free carbonic acid than spring-waters, but in far smaller quantity. It has thus far been found that waters containing bicarbonates do not attack lead, and even free carbonic acid, in small quantities, is without effect in the presence of much lime and magnesia. But the less mineral matter a water contains, or the "softer" it is, the more readily is lead dissolved. Distilled or carbonic-acid-free water dissolves lead slowly with separation of oxyhydrate; distilled water holding carbonic acid in solution dissolves lead in much larger quantity, with a separation of basic lead carbonate, which can be very complete. Water to be conducted through lead pipes should, under all circumstances, be examined for free carbonic acid and the amount determined. Its action on lead plates should also be noted.

In the experiments of J. H. Long, made in July and August, 1886, to determine the rate of oxidation or destruction of the sewage of the city of Chicago, which is carried through the Illinois and Michigan Canal to the Illinois river, examinations were made of the dilute sewage at the point (Bridgeport) where it is pumped into the canal, and of specimens of the water taken on the same day at stations selected at intervals through a distance of 159 miles, in which a total descent of 1,467 feet occurs. The conditions of the tests were variously complicated at the several stations, so that no absolute result was possible; but the experiment as a whole was interpreted as showing "in a fair and unmistakable way the general fact of the gradual purification of a highly contaminated water by what may be broadly termed oxidation "; and importance is claimed for the investigations "as showing pretty fully the rate at which a city's sewage is destroyed under certain conditions of temperature, dilution, and velocity of flow." Investigations were also made in the succeeding winter—December, January, and February—to ascertain the effect of cold. The results were marked by perplexing irregularities, but tended to show a slow rate of change at that season.

Prof. Atwater has published some of the results of his analyses of the flesh of American fishes in tables which give severally the proximate ingredients, as directly determined, of the flesh, and of the water-free substance of the flesh; the percentages of phosphoric acid, sulphuric acid, and chlorine in the flesh; classification of fish by percentages of flesh, chiefly muscular tissue, in the entire body; classification by proportions of water-free substance in the flesh; classification by proportions of fat in the flesh; composition of water-free substance in flesh of preserved fish; composition of flesh in preserved fish; and composition, including both flesh and refuse. Other analyses have been reported—of cod by Prof. Chittenden, and of menhaden by Prof. G. H. Cook; comparisons of the groupings made by the author according to the percentages of the different classes of constituents with the classification by families as practiced by ichthyologists, show no very definite connection between the two. In the analyses of preserved fishes, the replacement of the water in the flesh by salt is remarked upon as a matter of physiological interest.

As a simple and inexpensive freezing-mixture, J. A. Bachman has used the spent nitro-sulphuric-acid mixture which had been employed in a Grove battery, with snow. At temperatures of about zero Centigrade, this acid, with various proportions of snow, gave a fall of from thirty to thirty-two degrees of temperature, or nearly the same as that obtained when simple hydrochloric acid is employed. As there was so little difference in the result when the snow was used within considerably wide limits of proportion, it was found most satisfactory to mix the snow with the acid until it reached the consistency of a thin mush, dispensing with weighing. The temperature obtained when the snow is wet is almost as low as when it is dry, which is not the case when hydrochloric acid alone is used. When working at a temperature near zero, the spent acids answered as well as, if not better than, hydrochloric acid; but when endeavoring to obtain lower temperatures than —30° C. by previously cooling the acid, better results were obtained with hydrochloric acid.

Out of a large number of chemical compounds experimented upon, Prof. William Thomson has found that those having the most remarkable antiseptic properties are the compounds of fluorine, hydrofluoric acid, the acid and neutral fluorides of sodium, potassium, and ammonium, and the fluo-silicates of those bases. Of these, sodium fluo-silicate is perhaps the best suited for an antiseptic. It is not poisonous, possesses no smell, and is sparingly soluble in water. It has only a very slightly saline taste, and may therefore be employed in preserving food without communicating any taste to it. A saturated solution containing 0·61 per cent. of the salt is not irritating to wounds, while it possesses great antiseptic power for animal tissues.

The value of phosphorus pentoxide as a disinfectant has been measured by Dr. Kinyoun, in experiments on cultivations of the microorganisms of anthrax, yellow fever (Finlay), typhoid fever, Asiatic cholera, and cholera nostras, the nutrient medium being agaragar. The cultivations were divided into series according to the way they were covered. The result of the experiments was the conclusion that this substance is a surface disinfectant only, having little, if any, penetrating power, and is wholly unfit for fumigation and disinfection where penetration is desirable; and that its limited scope of usefulness is altogether met in the use of bichloride of mercury.

P. Bockairy, in testing butter, substitutes toluene for benzine. The test-tube is heated to 50° C., and shaken up so as to mix the two liquids. If the sample is a fat, turbidity immediately occurs, but if it is butter, even if mixed with fat, the two liquids mingle without turbidity. The purity of the butter is determined by keeping the test-tube for half an hour in water at 40° C. If the butter is pure, there is no turbidity, but if it contains a foreign fat, turbidity at once appears, and ultimately a precipitate.

From examinations of certain waters—one of them being a "mineral" water free from all possible sources of contamination—Prof. E. H. S. Bailey has been led to consider that free ammonia may be sometimes a natural constituent, and not indicative of any pollution, of the water.

Apparatus.—For preserving constant the vacuum employed in fractional distillation, Godefroy uses two vertical tubes united at their lower ends by a fine tube, of which, when they are not in use, one, A, is entirely filled with mercury, while the other, B, contains more or less mercury, according to the vacuum desired. The tubes are so adjusted that as soon, on making the exhaust, as the pressure in B is less than will support the mercury column in A, this column falls, and the mercury rises in B till it cuts off the outlets connecting with the exhaust.

A new form of apparatus for fractional distillation, by Dr. J. Tcherniac, in the technical transformation of ammonium sulpho-cyanide into calcium sulpho-cyanide, is described by T. H. Norton and A. H. Otten. The novel feature is the introduction of a device called a *déverseur*, to prevent the frothing accompanying the rapid distillation of the ammoniacal liquor.

Edward Hart has devised a simple apparatus, such as can be made by an amateur glassblower, for fractional distillation. The principle of it is the familiar one of the "dephlegmator." The bent tube is so adjusted that the condensed portion runs down and passes around its inside at each bend, while the vapor passes upward through the ring of descending liquid.

In an apparatus by Ramsey and Young for determining vapor-densities of solids and liquids, a test-tube, having inserted from its top a thermometer with its bulb covered with cotton, is put in communication with a Sprengel pump. The apparatus having been cooled and exhausted, the liquid to be examined is allowed to trickle down the thermometer and moisten the cotton. The stream of liquid having been cut off, the pressure and temperature are noted as soon as they become constant. Air is then admitted, and a second reading of pressure and temperature is taken. If the experiment is made with a solid, the bulb of the thermometer is previously covered with it by dipping into the melted substance.

An improved form of apparatus for gas analysis described by J. T. Willard is essentially a combination of Elliott's and Frankland's apparatus for the analysis of gases incident to water analysis, with important modifications and additions. It was designed for use with mercury, but admits the employment of water.

In W. Thomson's improved form of Lewis Thomson's instrument for determining the calorimetric value of fuels and organic compounds, the substance is burned in a stream of oxygen instead of with potassium chloride.

A new apparatus for condensing gases by contact with liquids, described by Prof. Lunge, consists of a series of perforated plates made of stone-ware, arranged in column. The gases as they rise are brought into immediate contact with an extensive plane surface of the absorbing liquid.

An electrolytic method for liquefying gases is employed by H. N. Warren, which is described as being better adapted than the usual method, when a compound gas, like HCl, is required.

In Knublauch's improved form of apparatus for the determination of sulphur in coal-gas, a metallic holder is filled with gas, and water is turned on. The gas, together with five or six times its volume of air, is drawn into a combustion tube and over heated asbestos. The sulphur products are absorbed in a solution of potassium carbonate.

Improvements in apparatus for rapid gas analysis by Dr. Arthur H. Elliott consist in reducing the length of the tubes by enlarging the upper portion of the bulbs, and by substituting a solution of bromine in potassic bromide for the liquid element to absorb illuminants.

For the generation of sulphureted hydrogen or hydrogen gas, J. H. J. Dagger uses a glass vessel containing hydrochloric acid, which is connected from its lower tubulure, by means of a flexible tube, with the generator, and the two vessels, supported by wooden forks, are arranged at different heights and fixed to the side of the H_2S cupboard. The lower part of the generator is filled to about half an inch above the end of the acid-tube with pieces of glass or glass marbles; above this layer is the iron sulphide or the zinc, as the case may be, in small pieces. The flow of gas can be stopped or regulated by altering the levels.

An adjustment of the Reichard's aspirator has been applied by Prof. LeR. C. Cooley as part of an apparatus for removing noxious vapors in the evaporation of corrosive liquids.

To obviate the liability to accident from the bumping that follows an explosion in Liebig's trough, Arthur Michael places an India-rubber plug on the bottom of the trough, and holds the eudiometer firmly down upon it.

An apparatus has been devised by Thomas C. Van Nûys for the estimation of carbonic acid by means of barium hydrate, the chief purpose of which is to afford means for preventing the contact of external air containing carbonic acid with the barium hydrate when triturated with oxalic acid or when filtered and washed.

Mr. Fletcher, of Warrington, has introduced a tubing made of two layers of India-rubber with soft tin-foil vulcanized between, which is said to be gas-tight under any pressure, and free from smell after long-continued use, while it retains the flexibility and elasticity of an ordinary rubber tube.

Nickel has been found by Prof. Dittmar to be a most durable material for making basins in which to conduct operations with aqueous caustic alkalies.

In an apparatus described by G. H. Bailey for maintaining constant temperatures up to 500° C., the substance to be heated is placed in a glass tube, together with the bulb of an air-thermometer, and these are inclosed in a wider tube resting on the iron casing of a furnace. The air-thermometer serves to measure the temperature, and is connected with a gas-regulator, by which means the temperature may be kept constant at any desired degree.

A source of error in experiments, due to the formation of carbonic dioxide by the action of ozone on the cork stoppers, and India-rubber connectors of the apparatus, has been detected by Kieser and F. H. Storer, of Bussey Institute. H. Karsten had also observed that such connectors are liable to oxidation, even in mere air and at ordinary temperatures. He found the yield of carbonic acid increased fourfold when non-nitrogenized substances were exposed to air ozonized by phosphorus instead of to ordinary atmospheric air.

Miscellaneous.—The address of Prof. Tilden, as vice-president for 1888 of the chemical section of the British Association, was devoted largely to the subject of chemistry teaching, which, in spite of the great advance of the science, was still hampered, he said, by the ignorance and indifference of the public. One man is required to teach college classes, both elementary and advanced, in pure and applied chemistry, inorganic and òrganic, theoretical and practical. "This is a kind of thing which kills specialism, and without specialists we can have not only no advance, but no efficient teaching of more than rudiments. That teachers ought to engage in research at all is by no means clear to the public and to those representatives of the public who are charged with the administration of the new institutions. . . . A popular mistake consists in regarding a professor as a living embodiment of science—complete, infallible, mysterious; whereas in truth he is, or ought to be, only a senior student who devotes the greater part of his time to extending and consolidating his own knowledge for the benefit of those who come to learn of him, not only what lies within the boundaries of the known, but how to penetrate into the far greater region of the unknown. Moreover, the man who has no intellectual independence, and simply accepts other people's views without challenge, is pretty certain to make the stock of knowledge with which he sets out in life do service to the end." The little demand among schoolmasters for high attainments in chemistry, the indifference of manufacturers who, when they want chemical assistance, instead of employing trained chemists are often satisfied with the services of boys "who have been to an evening class for a year or two," and the difficulty of finding a satisfactory career in connection with chemistry, are assigned as other reasons for the lack of attention to the efficient teaching of the science. The disposition to encourage young chemists to engage in investigation and attack difficult problems, may be carried too far. "Already we are in danger of losing the art of accurate analysis. One constantly meets with young chemists who are ready enough to discuss the constitution of benzine, but can not make a reliable combustion. And, according to my own experience, attempts at research among inexperienced chemists become abortive more frequently in consequence of deficient analytical skill than from any other cause."

An unnecessary amount of time is often spent on qualitative mineral analysis, while an acquaintance with the properties of common and important carbon compounds ought to be acquired at an early stage. Quantitative work—serious work, in which good methods are used and every effort made to secure accuracy—might with advantage be taken up much sooner than usual. One of the best means of preparing for original research is to select suitable memoirs, and to work conscientiously through the preparations and analyses described. "When chemistry is taught, not with professional or technical objects in view, but for the sake of educational effects, as an ingredient in a liberal education, the primary object is to make the student observe and think. But with young students it is very important to proceed slowly, for chemistry is really a very difficult subject at first."

Concerning the constitution of meteorites, Prof. Lockyer names fourteen elements which occur most constantly in such bodies, and eleven others which occur less frequently or in smaller quantities. Of them, only hydrogen, nitrogen, and carbon occur in an elementary condition. Hydrogen and nitrogen are asserted to be occluded as gases by the stones. Carbon exists in the forms of graphite and the diamond. The proportion of compound substances known on the earth that are found on meteorites is smaller, many terrestrially common ones being absent. Thus, free quartz has not been found in any meteors. Many of the meteoric chemical combinations, on the other hand, are unknown to terrestrial mineralogy. A compound of carbon with hydrogen and oxygen exists as a white or yellowish crystallizable matter, soluble in ether and partly so in alcohol, and exhibiting the characters and the composition of one or more hydrocarbonaceous bodies with high-melting points. Various alloys of nickel and iron occur, with which magnesium is always associated, the four principal of which have respectively six, ten, fourteen, and sixteen equivalents of iron to one of nickel. Among other minerals are Lawrencite, protochloride of iron; Maskelynite, with the composition of labradorite; and silica (as asmanite). Among the compounds identical in composition and crystallographic character with minerals found on our globe, are magnetic pyrites, magnetite, chromite, and the following silicates: olivine varieties, enstatite and bronzite, diopside and augite, anorthite and labradorite, and breunerite. The oxides of carbon have been detected in many meteorites, where they are assumed to have been occluded. When the meteoric substance is heated and examined with the spectroscope, the most volatile elements appear first, and so on in regular order, and this without regard to the proportions in which they are respectively present.

The blackening of silver chloride under exposure to light has been accounted for in various ways. Some chemists attribute it to a reduction of the chloride to metallic silver, while others believe that a subchloride is formed. Experiments by Spencer B. Newberry support the former view. The salt was exposed under water with frequent stirring to expose fresh surfaces to the light, and constant circulation of air resulted—in each case under two distinct processes of separation—in the production of metallic silver.

The differentiation of yeast is presented by Mr. C. G. Matthews, of Burton-on-Trent, as an exceedingly interesting field for experiment, in which may be found some of the causes of yeast deterioration. There are many species of *saccharomyces*, and of so nearly equal vitality, that a variety of ferments are often present in what the brewer may regard as a pure yeast. Variations in the character of a fermentable liquid tending to the nourishment of certain ferments, rather than others, may determine the growth of a majority of one species, especially in the case of spontaneous fermentations. A natural selection has doubtless taken place in the case of brewer's yeast, which may be regarded as an educated and modified form from spontaneous or air-sowed fermentation; and all ordinary yeasts contain a preponderating quantity of this selected form. It is not until an abnormal percentage of some other kind appears that its presence is demonstrable, though some time before this the yeast may have exhibited peculiarities in its action. Hayduck has traced a connection between the amount of nitrogen yeast contains and its fermentative capacity, and has found that an increased nitrogen percentage is accompanied, as a rule, by increased fermentative power; but that after a certain limit, the latter diminishes. Yeast takes up nitrogen in proportion to the amount of that constituent existing in the wort, and will take up more at a higher than at a lower temperature. If quick yeast be carried through consecutive worts of high gravity, a marked deterioration ensues—owing, doubtless, to a repleted state of the ferment. It has become so rich in protoplasmic constituents that saccharine solutions no longer exert their normal stimulating effect, and it is quite possible that in addition the cells are alcoholized or partially asphyxiated. Such deteriorated yeast may be restored to activity by fermentation in a comparatively weak wort, and it is a fair reasoning that the surplus constituents are passed into new cells without drawing entirely on the cell-forming constituents of the wort. The visible deterioration of yeast by the accession of bacteria is a matter of high importance. All through the process air-borne germs are being conveyed into the products, and when the opportunity arrives they take effect, and this opportunity occurs when the vitality of the yeast has been lowered; for a healthy fermentation precludes their development. Bacteria then may be reasonably regarded as both cause and effect in yeast degeneration.

CHILI, an independent republic of South America. (For details relating to area, see "Annual Cyclopædia" for 1884.) Final returns of the census of Nov. 26, 1885, showed the population at the time to have been 2,527,-320, exclusive of 50,000 wild Indians, and including 51,882 foreigners.

Government.—The President is Don Manuel Balmaceda, whose term of office will expire on Sept. 18, 1891. The Cabinet was composed in 1888 of the following Ministers: Foreign Affairs, Don Demetrio Lastavria; Interior, Don Pedro Lucio Cuadra; Treasury, Don Enrique S. San Fuente; Industries and Public Works, Don Vicente Davilla Larrain; War and Navy, Don Evaristo Sanchez Fontenilla; and Justice, Señor F. Puga Borne. The Chilian Minister to the United States is Don Domingo Gana. The Consul-General in New York is Don Federico A. Beelen; the Consul-General for California, Nevada, and Oregon, resident at San Francisco, is Don Juan de la Cruz Cerda. The United States Minister to Chili is William R. Roberts; the American Consul at Valparaiso is James W. Romeyn.

Army.—The strength of the permanent army was fixed by law of Dec. 30, 1887, at 5,385, consisting of two regiments of artillery; one battalion of sappers; eight of foot, and three regiments of horse, to be added to which there is a coast artillery force of 500; constituting in the aggregate 5,885 men, commanded by 932 officers. The military school is attended by 115 cadets. The National Guard, organized under provisions of the law of Sept. 26, 1882, is composed of 90 corps, numbering in the aggregate 48,674 file.

Navy.—In conformity with the provisions of the law of Dec. 30, 1887, there were in active service in 1888 two frigates and one monitor, all armored vessels; three corvettes; three cruisers; two gun-boats; one transport; four "escampavías," and eleven torpedo-boats, out of thirty-one vessels composing the Chilian fleet, with a joint tonnage of 17,495. The navy was commanded by 55 officers; there were 239 surgeons, pilots, and apprentices on board, and 1,988 sailors and marines. The naval school at Valparaiso was attended by 70 cadets.

Public Works.—In April the work connecting Lake Vichuquen with the ocean was begun. This work will result in the formation of a strong military port.

Finances.—The foreign indebtedness of Chili consisted, on Jan. 1, 1888, of the following outstanding bonds: 3-per-cent. loan of 1843, $533,000; 4½-per-cent. loan of 1885, $4,024,-000; 4½-per-cent. loan of 1886, $30,050,000; and 4½-per-cent. nitrate certificates, $5,830,-003; constituting a total of $40,437,005, money chiefly expended in the construction of Government lines of railway; consequently, Chili has something to show for what she owes abroad. The home debt was contracted partially during the war of independence, in part also for the building of railroads, and finally

during the war with Spain and the one with Peru and Bolivia; 3 and 7 per cent. bonds were issued, and since 1837 the latter have gradually been reduced through the operations of the sinking-fund; of these bonds, there were outstanding, on Dec. 31, 1887, $6,543,-900; furthermore, $16,965,756. for which there exists no sinking-fund, and, finally, there are $24,887,916 paper money, the internal debt thus reaching, in the aggregate, the sum of $48,397,572, on Dec. 31, 1887, as compared with $49,917,637 on Dec. 31, 1886; which at the time included $26,687,916 paper money; of which, consequently, during the twelve-month, $1,800,000 had been withdrawn from circulation and destroyed.

The actual income in 1887 was $45,888,953, as compared with $17,000,000 in 1877, and $9,000,000 in 1866, whereas the actual outlay in 1887 was only $37,113,408 for ordinary and extraordinary expenditures; so that a surplus resulted of $8,775,545. On Dec. 31, 1887, the Chilian treasury held in cash the sum of $21,-277,710, without counting the bar-silver retained as reserve to secure the note circulation, and without the $2,298,754 of capital and interest which Peru was then still owing Chili. The budget for 1889 estimates the revenue at $46,000,000, and the expenditure at $53,000,000, the deficit to arise from railroads which the Government intends building, in conformity with the authority obtained from Congress under date of Jan. 20, 1888.

The Council of State sanctioned the plan authorizing the President to spend the sum of $1,204,000 for the purpose of canceling the county debts of the republic with the exception of those of Valparaiso and Santiago.

On Aug. 7, 1888, the contract terminated which gave to certain banks the privilege of issuing bank-notes; there were in all eighteen banks enjoying the advantage named, and on a cash capital of $23,111,887, their circulation amounted to $16,061,262. The three leading banks circulating notes, comprised in the above sum, are the Banco Nacional, with a capital of $6,000,000, and a circulation of $4,500,456; the Banco de Valparaiso, capital $5,125,000, issue $4,098,312; and the Banco de Santiago, capital $4,000,000, issue 2,673,600. The Government intends to decree in the future the free issue of bank-notes under the proviso of the guarantees stipulated by section 7 of the law of March 14, 1887.

Charitable Institutions, etc.—The Government paid subsidies to hospitals, lazarettos, vaccination offices, and to the fire departments, to the amount of $650,600, distributed among 225 establishments. The police was subsidized by $471.900. For 1888 there had been set aside for the benefit of all the institutions named $1,196,140.

Cholera.—Between Dec. 25, 1887, and Feb. 3, 1888, there were in Valparaiso alone 4,500 cases of cholera, 1,357 proving fatal; the epidemic disappeared gradually with the advent of cool weather, but during the first fortnight in March, there were still 201 cases of which 77 resulted in death.

Postal Service.—The number of post-offices in operation in 1887 was 481, dispatching during the year 37,308,210 items of mail-matter. The number of ordinary letters handled in the mails in 1886 was 14,299,883; registered letters, 125,902; sample packages, 39,639; judicial notifications, 15,392; Government messages, 703,255; and newspapers, 20,124,139; together, 35,308,210, dispatched in 1886. The receipts in 1887 were $483,439, nearly balancing the expenses. Postal money-orders were paid out in 1886 to the amount of $1,633,322. The Government paid subsidies to ocean steamers for carrying the correspondence in 1886 to the extent of $223,880.

Railroads.—The Chilian railroad system, on Dec. 31, 1887, consisted in in the first place of Government lines:

	Length in kilometres.
Santiago to Valparaiso	187
Branch line, Las Vegas to Santa Rosa	45
Santiago to Maule and San Fernando to Palmilla, branch line	304
Santiago to Concepcion	413
Angol to Traiguen	72
Renacio to Victoria	75
Total	1,096

Next of private lines:

	Kilometres.
Arica to Tacna	63
Pisagua to Tres Marias	106
Iquique to Virginia	194
Patillos to Salitreras del Sur	93
Mejillones to Cerro Gordo	29
Antofagasta to Ascotan	297
Taltal to Refresco	52
Chanaral to Las Animas	60
Caldera to Copiapó	242
Carrizal Bajo to Cerro Blanco	81
Coquimbo to La Serena	15
Ovalle to Panulcillo	123
Serena to Rivadavia	78
Tongoy to Tamaya	55
Laraquete to Maquegua	40
Total	1,558

The Government lines projected, toward the cost of which Congress voted in 1888 the sum of £3,517,000, or its equivalent, were:

	Kilometres.
Victoria to Valdivia	403
Coihué to Mulchen	43
Concepcion to Cañete	160
Tomé to Cauquenes	200
Talca to Constitucion	85
Palmilla to Pichilemu	45
Pelequen to Peumo	35
Santiago to Melipilla	59
Santiago to Peñon	27
Calera to Cabildo	76
Vilos to Salamanca	128
Ovalle to San Marcos	60
Guasco to Vallenar	43
Total	1,369

Other Means of Internal Transportation.—In the cities of Santiago and Valparaiso there are comfortable tramway lines; in the former a distance of 60 kilometres, in the latter of 10. There are tramways, moreover, at Concepcion, Copiapó, Chillan, Limache, Rengo, Quillota, San Felipe, Santa Rosa, Serena, and Talca. There are besides in the country about 800 wagon-roads measuring 66,000 kilometres in length, and 2,000 ordinary roads of a total length of 40,000 kilometres. Seventy-eight water-courses are navigable a distance of over 4,800 kilometres.

Telegraphs.—The Government owns nearly all the telegraph lines in operation, there being 150 offices in 1886, increased to 170 in 1887. The length of line was 10,300 kilometres, and of wire 12,148, the entire cost of which has only been $844,325. There were sent 419,777 private telegrams in 1886, bringing $121,248, and 112,819 Government messages charged $80,476. Private lines exist between Santiago and Valparaiso, Arica and Tacna, Santa Rosa de Los Andes and the Argentine Republic, and a cable runs along the coast. Concessions have been granted to build additional private lines between Arica and Tacna, Serena and Coquimbo, Santiago and the Condes mines, and Concepcion and Talcalguano. Telephone lines are in operation at Santiago, Valparaiso, and in other cities.

Commerce.—The foreign-trade movement in Chili has been as follows:

ITEMS.	1886.	1887.
Import	$47,101,350	$48,680,969
Increase		1,529,512
Export.		
Products of the mines	40,264,340	49,449,015
Agricultural products	9,710,747	9,369,247
Manufactures	66,521	46,081
Sundry merchandise	107,891	46,655
Gold coin	644,416	817,485
Re-export	446,734	821,475
Total	$51,240,149	$59,549,958
Increase		8,309,809

Chili produced in 1887 29,150 tons of fine copper, compared with 35,000 in 1886; the export during the first nine months of 1888 was 23,675 tons fine, against 22,990 during the corresponding period of the previous year.

The Chilian exportation of nitrate of soda has been as follows:

DESTINATION.	1885.	1886.	1887.
	Quintals.	Quintals.	Quintals.
To Northern Europe	8,554,087	7,950,452	13,851,720
To the Mediterranean	41,930	163,092	237,875
To the United States on the Atlantic	827,296	1,436,189	1,532,026
To the United States on the Pacific	77,712	255,505	229,946
Total	9,501,625	9,805,238	15,351,567

The American trade with Chili exhibits these figures:

FISCAL YEAR.	Imports from Chili into the United States.	Domestic exports from the United States to Chili.
1883	$485,584	$2,887,551
1884	537,986	3,286,945
1885	604,525	2,192,672
1886	1,182,845	1,973,548
1887	2,868,283	2,062,507
1888	2,894,520	2,423,308

General Production.—The "Sinopsis Estadistica," Santiago, 1887, sums up the productive activity of the republic in the following words: "Agriculture, in its main branches, produces annually, on the average, 7,000,000 hectolitres of wheat, 3,000,000 hectolitres of barley and other cereals, and a proportionate amount of vegetables and fruit peculiar to the temperate zone. In 1886 the country exported over 1,300,000 hectolitres of wheat in the grain and in the form of flour, and 266,800 litres of wines. Cattle production amounts to 500,000 head per annum, and that of sheep and goats to 2,000,000 on an average. The mineral branch turns out some 25,000 to 40,000 tons of copper, 160,000 kilogrammes of silver, 10,000,000 tons of coal, over 15,500,000 quintals of nitrate of soda, large amounts of manganese, and for the working of metals, etc., there are in operation foundries and machinery of the first class. Manufacturing furnishes an ample supply of ordinary commodities. There are a great many flour-mills and other factories. A large sugar-refinery is in operation at Viña del Mar, near Valparaiso, while at Santiago there is a wool-weaving establishment producing fine cloths, etc., and smaller ones are to be met with in the interior, as well as other industries. Exclusive privileges are granted to newly invented industries foreign to the country, and a good many such are in course of exploitation."

Merchant Marine.—There were afloat under the Chilian flag on March 15, 1887, 37 steamers with a joint tonnage of 18,769; 7 ships with 7,866 tons; 91 barks with 45,989 tons; 5 brigs with 1,514 tons; 8 schooner-brigs with 2,295 tons; 12 schooners with 1,225 tons; and 19 sloops with 1,058; together, 179 vessels with 78,716 tons. Two new steamers and 16 sailing-vessels were registered during a twelve-month, while 2 steamers and 10 sailing-vessels were either sold or wrecked. The maritime movement in 1886 was, vessels entered, 9,568, with a joint tonnage of 8,081,229, and 9,654 sailed, measuring jointly 8,368,887 tons, bringing 47,167 passengers and taking away 41,032, so that 6,135 remained in port.

Education.—The Chilian university at Santiago is called the "Instituto Nacional." In 1886 422 students attended the lectures on law and political science; 290 on medical science; 122 on pharmacy; 30 on physics and mathematics; and 104 cultivated the fine arts—i.e., drawing, painting, sculpture, and architecture; total number of students, 968. Four hundred and five diplomas were granted. The lyceums in the provinces, of which there are twenty-two, were attended by 3,892 pupils in the same year, so that altogether 4,860 youths were receiving a higher degree of education, and for 1888 Congress set aside a subsidy of $829,694 for the same purpose. The free schools numbered 862, with 78,810 pupils, the average attendance being 47,780; there are besides normal schools; and for all public schools Congress voted a subsidy of $1,406,000 for 1888; adding thereto salaries of professors, teachers, pensions, and money spent on new school - buildings and

libraries, Chili spent in a single year on education $4,957,437.

Newspapers.—The number of periodical publications throughout the country in 1888 was 130; 30 in Santiago, 15 in Valparaiso, 5 in Iquique, 4 each in Concepcion, Copiapó, Curicó, Serena, and Talca, 3 each in Ancud, Angeles, Cauquenes, Chillan, San Cárlos, San Felipe, Vallenar, and Freirina, and 2 each in Ligua, Melipilla, Osorno, Pisagua, Quillota, Quirihue, Rancagua, and San Fernando—one in nearly every chief town of a department.

CHINA, an empire in eastern Asia. The Tsait'ien or Emperor, Hwangti, born in 1871, succeeded to the throne by proclamation, Jan. 22, 1875, on the death of the Emperor T'ung-chi. He is the ninth Emperor of China of the Tartar dynasty of Ts'ing. During his infancy the affairs of the Government were directed by the Empress Dowager, widow of the Emperor Hienfung, in concert with Prince Ch'un, father of the present Emperor. On becoming of age, Feb. 7, 1887, the young Emperor assumed the government of his dominions though the Empress Regent still exercised the royal prerogative to a certain extent till July, 1888, when she retired from active state duties. The administration of the Government is under the direction of the Neiko or ministers of state, four in number, two Tartars and two Chinese, with two assistants from the Han-lin or Great College. Seven boards assist the ministers in the administration of the empire. In addition, there is a board of public censors, independent of the Government, consisting of from 40 to 50 members, under two presidents, one of Tartar and the other of Chinese birth. Any member of this board is privileged to present remonstrances to the Emperor, and one censor must be present at the meetings of any of the Government boards.

Area and Population.—The total area of China and its dependencies is 4.179,559 square miles, with a population of 404,180,000, not including Corea. In the latter part of 1886 there were 7,695 foreigners resident in the open ports, of whom 3,438 were British, 777 Japanese, 741 Americans, 629 Germans, 471 Frenchmen, and 319 Spaniards. More than half of the foreigners reside in Shanghai.

Finances.—As the receipts of the Government from internal sources are not made public, the amount of revenue can only be estimated. The ordinary revenue was estimated in 1886 at 66,400,000 haikwan taels, or about $80,344,000, derived from the following sources: Land-tax, payable in money, 20,000,000 taels; rice tribute, 2,800,000 taels; salt-taxes, 9,600,000 taels; maritime customs, 15,000,000 taels; native customs, maritime and inland, and inland levy on foreign opium, 6,000,000 taels; transit levy on miscellaneous goods and opium, foreign and native, 11,000,000 taels; licenses, 2,000,000 taels. The receipts from foreign customs amounted in 1886 to 15,144,678 taels. The customs duties fall more upon exports than imports. The main expenditure is for the maintenance of the army, which is estimated to cost 60,000,000 taels per annum. The total external debt was estimated at $25,000,000 in 1887. A preliminary agreement was made with an American syndicate, contracting for the minting of money, and granting concessions for banking, negotiating loans, building and operating railroads, and opening and working mines. Revelations regarding the character of the intermediary, a Polish adventurer, and the opposition of British and German rivals of the *concessionaires*, led the Tsungli-Yamen to reject the arrangement. The Chinese Government subsequently obtained from an English manufacturer the machinery and dies for coining new copper cash, which will be composed of less brittle metal than those now in circulation, and also silver taels or dollars, and 50, 20, and 10 cent pieces.

The Army.—The army consists in time of peace of about 250,000 men, and this number can be increased to about 850,000 in time of war. Most of the troops are armed with either Mauser or Remington rifles, and the Government possesses a good supply of Krupp 8-centimetre field-cannon. Large quantities of foreignmade arms have been purchased, and the arsenals of China, under foreign supervision, are beginning to turn out both arms and ammunition. Besides the Chinese and Manchu militias, each province possesses a regular army of enlisted troops under the command of its viceroy. The army of Pechili, which served as a model for the rest, has been instructed by European officers, and is well armed and uniformed. Fears of Russian aggression in the west and on the side of Corea have led to the reorganization of the army of Manchuria. There are 30,000 troops constantly under arms, including 15,000 from the Pechili army, which form a nucleus. The total military strength of the three districts into which Manchuria is divided is from 250,000 to 300,000 men. There are breech-loading rifles provided for about one third of them, while the others are armed in part with muskets. The cavalry carry Winchester or Remington repeating-rifles. The Russian Ussuri frontier is fortified, and the towns of Kirin and Ningati are girdled with forts, some of which are strengthened by steel plates. There is a line of telegraph from Pekin to Aigun on the Amoor river. The administration of the Ili territory was reorganized in June, 1888. The soldiers receive good pay and food unless they are defrauded by their officers. The garrison at Umritsi, which had not been paid for six months, formed a plot in June to murder Liu Tsin Tan, their commander-in-chief and the governor of the new dominion. They laid a mine of powder under his residence, but the plot was divulged just before the time for its execution, and the chief conspirators, numbering thirty men and officers, were cruelly put to death. The Central Government seeks to make the military organization a means of settling the thinly peopled expanse of Manchuria and Mongolia, and apportions lands among the soldiers. This policy is followed not only for the purpose of raising a more effectual bulwark against Russian encroachments, but also to relieve the congested parts of China, and create a field for colonization where the Chinese emigrants will escape the hostile edicts and oppressive regulations that are driving them back from foreign shores. The Bannermen, or Manchu soldiery, number 90,000 or 100,000 at Pekin, where they form an imperial guard to protect the dynasty against external or internal foes, while 20,000 more are distributed among the chief cities of China. They are not pure Tartars, because there are not more than 1,000,000 people of unmixed Manchu blood among the 23,000,000 now inhabiting Manchuria, where a reserve army of 183,000 Bannermen is kept up.

The Navy.—The iron-clad navy in 1887 consisted of two powerful armored ships, built in Germany, of 7,335 tons displacement, 6,000 horse-power, and a speed of 14½ knots. Each is protected by 14-inch armor, and carries four 12-inch Krupp breech-loading guns in two barbette towers, *en échelon*, protected by 12-inch armor; one armored cruiser, built in Germany, of 2,300 tons displacement, carrying two 8-inch Krupp guns, *en barbette*, protected by 10-inch armor, and one 6-inch Krupp; two unarmored steel cruisers of 2,200 tons displacement, carrying two 8-inch Armstrong guns, besides 40-pounders and machine-guns; two unarmored steel cruisers, of 1,400 tons displacement, each carrying two 25-ton Armstrong guns and four 40-pounders; twelve gunboats, each mounting a single heavy gun; two strongly armed corvettes, built at Stettin; and two fast armored cruisers, built in 1887 by Sir William Armstrong. The squadrons of Foochow, Shanghai, and Canton include between forty and fifty unarmored cruisers, corvettes, sloops, and gunboats. One cruiser of 2,150 tons displacement and 2,400 horse-power has been built in China, and others are in course of construction. There are also several swift torpedo-boats.

Commerce.—The total value of imports amounted in 1886 to 87,479,323 haikwan taels, or $105,849,980, and the total exports during the same year to 77,206,568 haikwan taels, equal to $93,419,947. The chief imports and exports, and their values for 1886, are as follow:

IMPORTS.	Haikwan taels.	IMPORTS.	Haikwan taels.
Opium	24,988,561	Coal	1,798,956
Cotton goods.....	29,049,658	Oil	2,215,027
Raw cotton.....	825,624	Seaweed. shell-fish,	
Woolen goods	5,630,948	etc..............	2,192,052
Metals	5,319,102		

EXPORTS.	Haikwan taels.	EXPORTS.	Haikwan taels.
Tea.............	33,504,820	Hides	996,247
Silk.............	28,834,843	Paper, tinfoil, etc....	678,583
Sugar...........	1,688,403	Clothing.............	948,523
Straw braid	2,089,185		

During 1886 the principal countries participated in the trade with China as follows, the values being given in haikwan taels:

COUNTRIES.	Imports from—	Exports to—	Total trade.
Great Britain	22,084,756	19,745,694	41,780,447
Hong-Kong................	34,889,671	22,552,676	57,442,347
India	16,980,035	531,601	17,511,636
United States............	4,647,383	9,685,691	14,333,024
Continent of Europe (without Russia)............	2,749,083	11,928,404	14,677,487
Japan	5,691,489	1,222,086	6,913,525
Russia (in Europe and Asia)................	202,918	7,039,332	7,242,250

There were exported in 1886, 295,639,300 pounds of tea, of which 126,604,950 pounds went to Great Britain, 768,856 pounds to Russia, 40,591,750 pounds to the United States, 20,733,000 pounds to Hong-Kong, and 17,120,666 pounds to Australia.

The reports of the Imperial Maritime Customs for 1887 show an increase of 6,000 piculs in the imports of opium, the total being 73,877 piculs (1 picul=133⅓ pounds). This does not denote an increased consumption of Indian opium, but is probably due to placing the junk-trade between the Continent and the ports of Hong-Kong and Macao, from which smuggling was formerly encouraged, under the control of the Chinese customs authorities by an arrangement with the British and Portuguese governments. In 1887 the system of paying a fixed duty to the customs authorities in lieu of *likin* and of admitting opium in bond first went into operation. The sum collected as prepaid *likin* duties by the customs department was for the year 4,645,843 taels. In spite of the opium convention, the use of Indian opium is steadily growing less. Only the wealthy or old people, unaccustomed to the flavor of the native-grown drug, will pay the higher price of Patna opium. The difference of quality is disappearing with the introduction of improved methods of cultivation, and already opium is grown in Honan that is almost as good as that of Patna, and costs $40 less per picul. Practically all the prepared opium contains a considerable admixture of the Chinese product.

The Chinese have taken largely to importing cotton-yarn instead of the finished goods. The yarn-trade has increased from 108,360 piculs in 1878 to 523,114 piculs in 1887, the value being 12,547,653 taels, or more than one third of the entire value of the cotton goods imported. The yarn of Bombay is preferred to that of Manchester. The imports of iron and steel have fallen off, and the import of kerosene-oil shows a remarkable decrease—from 23,038,101 gallons in 1886 to 12,015,135 gallons in 1887, which is probably due to the discouragement of its use by the authorities because of the many fires it has caused. The export of silk in 1887 was 56,000 piculs, or about the same quantity as in the preceding year, with an increase of five per cent. in prices. The exports of silk-cocoons and manufactured silks were greater than in 1886. The exports of straw braid, which is the staple of the trade of Tientsin and Chefoo,

have increased from 25,930 piculs in 1877 to 150,952 piculs, valued at about $4,500,000 in 1887. The tea-trade has suffered from the competition of the Indian product, which is sold for a third less in the London market. The Chinese Government in 1887 asked the opinion of the Foochow Chamber of Commerce as to the cause of the decadence of the tea-trade. The report represents that the tea-growers have grown negligent in their methods of cultivation, no longer ditching or manuring or pruning or planting new shrubs, and that they strip the leaves four or five times a year, instead of three times, as formerly. The leaves are full of dust and stalks, and are too dry to admit of sufficient firing. The sophistication and adulteration practiced by the tea-guilds lowers the quality of the product still further. The dust and stalks have caused the markets of the Continent of Europe to slip away, and now Australia and Canada prefer the more carefully cultivated teas of Ceylon. The decline of the tea-trade in 1886, which caused the alarm of the Government, became more marked in 1887, the quantity diminishing 5 per cent., while there was a fall in value of 12 per cent.

Navigation.—During 1886, 28,244 vessels, of 21,755,460 tons, were entered and cleared at Chinese ports, of which 23,262 were steamers, of 20,619,615 tons. Of the total number, 16,193, of 14,006,720 tons, were British; 7,852, of 5,374,821 tons, Chinese; 2,702, of 1,499,296 tons, German; 413, of 143,799 tons, American; 380, of 270,002 tons, Japanese; and 123, of 158,400 tons, French.

The tonnage of 1887 was 22,199,661, the largest ever known. Of this, 14,171,810 tons, or about two thirds, were British; 5,670,123 tons, or one fourth, Chinese; 1,480,083 tons, or one sixteenth, German; 306,169 tons were Japanese; 130,890 tons were French; and 66,539 tons were American.

Railroads and Telegraphs.—A small railway from Tongsan, at the Kai-ping mines, to Yung-chong, in the province of Chihli, was originally built for the conveyance of coal. It has obtained a considerable passenger-traffic also, declared a 6-per-cent. dividend on its paid-up capital for 1887, and in 1888 was extended to Tientsin. Another railroad extending from Kai-ping to Petang is in course of construction. In 1884 there were 3,089 miles of telegraph lines and 5,482 miles of wire in operation.

Navigation of the Upper Yangtse.—The English inserted in the treaty relative to the open ports a clause opening Chung-King also to foreign trade as soon as steamers could be made to ascend so far. The last open port on the Yangtse Kiang at present is Ichang, 1,000 miles from the sea. Chung-King, the commercial emporium of the wealthy province of Szechuen, which has a population of 70,000,000, is 500 miles higher, while between them is a series of rapids, where the river passes through a narrow, rocky chasm.

Junks are dragged by men up-stream along the bank, and descend by shooting the rapids. An Englishman named Archibald Little formed a company and built a steamer of special design. When he was ready to make the experimental trip, he applied for permission through the British minister. The Imperial Government advised with the chief provincial officials, who raised objections, both real and fanciful, and pleaded at least for delay, which was granted. Aside from the danger of collision with junks when the steamer is working its way up the swift current, there was a probability that the boating population of Chung-King would attack the steamer and crew in order to discourage the competition of a line of steamboats.

Trade Regulations.—The English Government in the late opium convention obtained the consent of the Government of Pekin to a provision admitting opium free to all parts of the empire without its being subjected to transit dues on the payment of 80 taels a chest at the port of entry in addition to the customs duty. This drug is now the only commodity that circulates throughout China free from the *likin* taxes that are levied by the local authorities on goods passing by road, river, or canal through their several jurisdictions. The *likin* was originally a war tax imposed by the provinces to raise means for the purpose of suppressing the Taiping rebellion. The stations are so near together that the price of goods carried far into the interior is many times enhanced, and transportation is delayed to a corresponding extent. Native traders, who compound the taxes with corrupt officials, have an advantage over foreigners. A clause in the opium convention provides for the commutation of the *likin* tax by the payment to the imperial revenue officers of a tax equal to half of the duty. This secures a transit pass that carries goods through all the *likin* barriers to the place of destination. The British merchants, on securing this concession, were confident of being able to compete successfully with the French in the provinces of Yunnan, Quangsi, and Quangtung. According to the report of the British consul at Pakhoi, however, it has proved illusive as a means of stimulating trade, because, when the goods reach the declared market they are subjected there to a tax approximating the sum of the *likin* taxes they would otherwise have to pay. The Provincial Government at Canton argues that there are no treaty restrictions against taxing Chinese and property in their possession. The principle here involved was a subject of discussion in connection with the trade of the treaty ports, until it was settled by the Chefoo Convention that the local authorities have a right to impose *likin* in the open ports outside the limits of the foreign settlements.

The Chinese Government has decided to introduce the system of bonded warehouses. A beginning was made in Shanghai on Jan. 1, 1888. The privilege of warehousing bonded goods was restricted to the China Merchants' Steam Navigation Company, a corporation composed entirely of mandarins and other Chinese. The British merchants of Shanghai raised an outcry against this arrangement, and blamed their Government for not interfering to obtain for them a share in the privilege. They charged the German minister, Herr von Brandt, with bringing about the monopoly for the purpose of injuring them, and declared that the warehouses having the right of storing goods in bond would gain all other business, and that the rows of warehouses and miles of wharves that they had constructed would be deserted. Herr von Brandt explained that the Chinese Government wished to test the system before establishing it permanently, and therefore restricted it to the wharves of the native company, and would not listen to a proposition to admit all warehouses that offered sufficient guarantees.

The Condition of Chinese Abroad.—In August, 1886, three high officials were sent abroad as an imperial commission to inquire into the treatment and condition of Chinese emigrants in foreign countries. They first visited Manila, in the Philippine Islands, where the Chinese complained bitterly of the wrongs they received at the hands of the Spaniards, and begged for the appointment of consular agents to protect them. Although they are plundered with impunity by lawless individuals and subjected to extortionate taxes by the authorities, yet their community of 50,000 souls is thriving. At Singapore the Chinese number 150,000, and are the richest of all the inhabitants, owning four fifths of the land and much commercial capital. The British Government has recently consented to the appointment of a Chinese consul, but he has no jurisdiction over the laborers passing through the port in great numbers. These are looked after by a British registrar-general, who does not prevent the perpetration of gross frauds by the labor companies. In Malacca and Penang they found the Chinese prosperous in business. There are 100,000 Chinamen in Perak and Selangore, mostly engaged in mining tin, several of whom are millionaires. The 30,000 Chinese residents in Rangoon are many of them merchants dealing in rice and in precious stones. In Sumatra there are large numbers of Chinese laborers employed on the tobacco plantations. Those who are saving do well, but the majority are addicted to gambling, and in this they are encouraged by the overseers, who keep those who fall in debt at work beyond the legal term, because they are ignorant of their right to return home at the end of three years. The Dutch authorities promised to have this righted. In Batavia the Chinese are heavily taxed, and gambling is common. In other Dutch colonies, containing more than 200,000 Chinese immigrants, they are treated "most outrageously" by the authorities. In Australia, the Chinese, who, on landing, are subjected to a tax of from

£10 to £30, prayed that measures for their protection might be taken. The commissioners reported that there were several millions of Chinamen doing business as merchants or working as laborers in foreign countries. In some ports emigration is increasing, and the Chinese merchants are thriving. Their prosperity has excited the jealousy of the peoples among which they dwell, and caused hostile measures to be adopted by foreign governments. The Dutch authorities have been endeavoring to expel them from their colonies, and collisions between the Chinese and natives are of frequent occurrence. If steps are not taken to render the residence of the Chinese abroad more secure and peaceful, the commissioners fear that they will all flock home. They view with dread the prospect of this sudden influx of population in the overcrowded districts of the sea-coast. After placing their report in the hands of Chan Chih-tung, the Viceroy of Canton, they set out, in September, 1887, on a journey to Borneo to study the condition of their countrymen in British North Borneo, Sarawak, and the Dutch possessions. The viceroy, in forwarding their report to Pekin, accompanied it with a memorial in which he recommended the appointment of consuls to look after the interests of Chinese subjects in foreign lands. He suggested that consuls-general should be maintained in Manila, in some of the Dutch colonies, in Sydney, and in Singapore. So important did he consider the matter of appointing a consul-general to Manila that he obtained the consent of the Government of Madrid, but this was withdrawn when the colonial authorities objected. The treaties of 1857, that give European governments the right to maintain consuls in China, do not accord reciprocal rights to the Chinese Government. The omission is simply due to the heedlessness of the Chinese negotiators, who had no thought when the instruments were drawn up that China would ever want to send officials abroad. The number of Chinese emigrants who sailed from Hong-Kong during 1887 was 82,897, being 18,000 more than in the previous year. About half of the increase was due to a larger emigration to the Straits Settlements, while 5,000 more emigrants than in 1886 were destined for the United States, and 3,500 more for the Australian colonies.

Inundation in Honan.—One of the periodical floods that have caused the Hoang-Ho, or Yellow river to be known as "China's Sorrow," occurred in the autumn of 1887. This river, rising in the mountains of Thibet, and descending with great rapidity from the Mongolian plateau, washing down great quantities of the loose, fine, yellow earth called loess, has changed its course in the flat coast region nine times within the historical period. In 1852, having for five hundred years poured its great volume of water into the Yellow Sea south of the promontory of Shantung, it burst its northern bank near Kaifeng-fu, the capital of the

province of Honan, where it enters the great eastern plain, and cut a new bed through the northern part of Shantung into the Gulf of Pechili. In 1887 this process was reversed. After an unusually rainy September the stream broke through the southern embankment at Cheng-chow, forty miles above Kaifeng-fu, on the 28th of that month. Where the first breach occurred 5,000 men, who were strengthening the levee, were drowned, and at another spot nearly 4,000 laborers were swept away. The bed of the river was several feet above the surface of the land. When the gap attained a breadth of 1,200 yards, the river deserted its bed. The overflow confined itself at first to the channel of the Lu-Chia river, but soon flooded the Chungnou district, destroying 100 villages and inundating the lands of 300 more. Several of the suburbs of the great commercial city of Chusien-Chen were swept away, and the elevated situation of the main town alone saved it from destruction. The flood spread over a low, thickly populated district, beginning 70 miles south of Kaifeng-fu, submerging 1,500 villages, and when it reached the valley of the Huai-Ho, the destruction of life and property was still greater. Many walled cities were depopulated and virtually destroyed. There were between one and two millions of persons drowned, and some say as many as seven millions. The most careful estimate makes the number of those who lost their lives 1,600,000, and of those who were left homeless and destitute 5,000,000. Millions of those left without shelter or means of life, perished of famine and cold. The Emperor and Empress contributed largely from their private fortunes to relieve the distress, and the Government did everything within its power, beginning by ordering 32,000,000 pounds of rice from Central China destined for Pekin, to be taken at once to the inundated district. The guilds co-operated with the mandarins in distributing relief. The river, if left to itself, would probably have formed a channel very nearly along its ancient bed. The Government ordered the breach to be closed as soon as the waters subsided, appropriating $2,500,000 for the purpose. When the work was begun in the spring the people of Honan destroyed material that was sent to mend the dikes, because they wished to have the river run in its new bed. and not return to their province. The soldiers and workmen who were sent to stay the progress of the flood or to repair the damage were sometimes surprised by a fresh overflow, and in one instance nearly 5,000 soldiers were drowned together. The waters of the river spread over a district 7,500 square miles in extent in a series of lakes. The cities of Chin-chow, Wei-shi, Tsung-mow, Yen-lin, Fu-kao, Shiva, Cheng-chow, Taikang, Taiping, and Ying-chow were submerged, and all but the northern part of Chow-kia-kow. The waters found an outlet through the Huai-Ho into the Hongtsze Lake, flooding a wide district in the province of Nganwhei, and a part of the overflow reached the sea, six months after the first catastrophe, a long distance south of the ancient mouth of the Hoang-Ho, while the main volume entered the Great Canal near the Hongtsze Lake, and flowed through it into the Yangtse-Kiang. When all efforts that were made in the winter to stop the breach proved useless, the Government set a force of 60,000 men at work to dig a deep canal for the purpose of tapping the river above Cheng-chow, and leading it into its regular channel at a point below the gap. The barriers that were interposed to confine the river to its bed at Cheng-chow were all swept away by the midsummer freshet caused by melting snows. After the expenditure of over $10,000,000 with no satisfactory result, the Emperor de-graded the two high officials who had charge of the work of restoration, and sent them to Manchuria to work on the military roads. There were damaging floods in the province of Manchuria in the autumn of 1888. Moukden, the capital, was inundated, and all the crops in the neighboring district were destroyed. Extending over the country, the floods caused wide-spread misery, and at last reached the port of Newchang, where the foreign quarter was submerged.

Earthquake in Yunnan.—A destructive earth-quake visited the province of Yunnan late in December, 1887, laying the capital and other towns in ruins. The shocks lasted four days. There were 5,000 persons killed by the falling of houses in the capital district. At Lainon the destruction was almost as great. Farther north, at Lo-chan, 10,000 persons lost their lives, and the aspect of the country was changed by the sinking of tracts of land and the forma-tion of lakes in their place.

CITIES, AMERICAN, RECENT GROWTH OF. Anniston, a city of Calhoun County, Alabama, in the northeastern part of the State, on the main line of the East Tennessee, Virginia, and Georgia Railroad, at the crossing of the Georgia Pacific, 60 miles from Birmingham, and 100 from Atlanta, Ga. It has a population of 12,-000, which is twice what it had one year ago. It lies in the heart of the great iron region of the South. The ore is mined in open cut, without tunneling or underground delving, and the supply seems inexhaustible. A hill, or rather mountain-side, of iron within the corpo-rate limits of the town has been dug from for upward of ten years, with scarcely perceptible results. The hills that surround the town are largely of iron-ore. The Coosa and Cahaba coal-fields, affording the best of coking-coal, are within 25 and 45 miles, and vast forests supply timber at convenient distance. Lime-stone abounds. There was a furnace here dur-ing the civil war to supply iron to the Confed-erate Government; but it was destroyed by the national troops in 1865. The site, with the main deposits of iron-ore, was purchased by a private citizen eighteen years ago, and in 1872 the Woodstock Iron Company was organ-ized, owning more than 40,000 acres. Messrs. Noble and Tyler were at its head, and the town is named for Mrs. Tyler, "Annie's Town." Prior to 1883 no land was sold. The city was surveyed and laid out, drainage-system per-fected, streets macadamized, buildings, church-es, stores, and school-houses erected, and rail-road connections secured, entailing not one dollar of debt upon the inhabitants, who num-bered at that date 4,000. It is lighted by electricity and gas, and has two daily papers, and five miles of street-railway. It is 800 feet above sea-level, and one of the highest points accessible to railroads in the State. Pure water is supplied by an artesian well, forced to a res-ervoir one mile distant at an elevation of 236 feet. A pressure of 100 pounds to the inch renders fire-hydrants sufficient, without steam-engines. Four hundred houses were completed within the first six months of 1888. Anniston owns 30,000 acres of coal-land, and 75,000 acres of brown and red hematite iron-ore. Its capital is upward of $10,000,000—more than that of the whole State in 1880. It employs 6,000 workingmen, to whom $60,000 are paid, weekly, in wages. Four charcoal-furnaces are in operation, with an annual capacity of 50,-000 tons of car-iron. Two of these were built in 1873 and 1879, and have never known a cold day except for repairs. Two coke-furnaces, to have an annual capacity of 100,000 tons of pig-iron each, are being completed this year. The largest pipe-works in the United States, with a daily output of 200 tons of finished pipe, are in course of construction. The United States Rolling Stock Company has a plant of $1,000,-000 in Anniston, having purchased the car and car-wheel works and car-axle forge of the town. The daily capacity is twenty-five cars. Anniston has the only steel-blomary in the South, and the largest cotton-mill in the State, producing 115,000 yards a week of sheetings and shirtings. Goods have this year been ex-ported to Shanghai, China. There is a cotton-compress with a daily capacity of 1,000 bales. There are two foundries, a rolling-mill, machine-shops, boiler and sheet-iron works, planing-mills, and fire-brick works, a horse-shoe man-ufacturing company, and factories of stoves, agricultural implements, and ice. There are four railroads, two of which are operated and owned by the citizens, viz.: The Anniston and Atlantic, connecting with the Georgia Central at Sylacauga, and the Anniston and Cincin-nati, connecting with the Cincinnati Great Southern at Atalla. The latter has been com-pleted this year, and cost $1,000,000. The yearly tonnage of the three railroads, in full operation, is 118,765 gross tons. Competitive freight rates are the right of Anniston by lo-cation. New Orleans is 14 hours distant; Cincinnati, 17; Washington, 26. There are three banks, one National, capital and surplus $300,000; one State, and one savings, capital of each, $100,000. There are churches of all denominations, and a new school-building, Anniston being a separate school-district. Two pay-schools, for boys and girls, stone structures, are the gift to the town of Mr. Noble.

Birmingham, a city of Jefferson County, Ala., 50 miles north of the center of the State, 100 miles from Montgomery, 349 miles from New Orleans, and 1,017 miles from New York. It was founded in 1871 by the Elyton Land Company, owning 4,150 acres, with capital of $200,-000. Its altitude above sea-level is 602 feet. The population in 1880 was 4,500; in 1885, 21,347; in 1886, 30,000; in October, 1887, 41,725; in October, 1888, it was estimated at 50,000. About 40 per cent. are colored. Surrounding villages, sustained by the city, make the population of the district between 65,000 and 70,000. The taxable valuation of property in 1881 was $2,953,375.37; in 1887, $33,019,-485; increase in the county during the same period, over $26,000,000. The sales of the Land Company for the year 1885-'86 were $2,250,000; for the first three weeks in August, 1887, $1,000,000. The debt of the city is $355,000. Iron is the prominent industry. Ore is supplied by Red mountain, six miles distant, estimated to contain 500,000,000,000 tons. The thickness of beds on an average is 22 feet, and the impurities are of lime, assisting fluxing. Limestone lies in the valley. Coal is also distant six miles, in the Warrior field, the largest in the State. One million tons of coke are required yearly by the district. The cost of manufacturing pig-iron is $9 a ton. There are 21 furnaces, the first of which, within corporate limits, went into blast in 1880. The daily output is 2,073 tons. Six trunk railroads enter the city, which has a Union passenger depot, and others are in course of construction. There are numerous branch, belt, and short mineral roads. Competitive rates lower the cost of transportation. There are 66 miles of street-railway, in horse-car and dummy lines, electric-lights and gas-works, 4 daily and 11 weekly newspapers, and 37 churches. There are 11 banks, possessing aggregate capital, surplus, and undivided profit of $2,750,000, with deposits amounting to $2,500,000. Education is under the control of a board of commissioners. There are 34 public schools in 8 buildings, a college, an academy, and numerous private schools. The drainage is not completed; but the Waring system has been adopted, and from seven to eight miles of sewers are constructed yearly. The water-supply is also insufficient; $500,000 have been appropriated for enlargement of works, and it is proposed to tunnel Red mountain to the Cahaba river, eight miles distant. An abundant supply will result, with pressure almost sufficient to dispense with fire-engines. An appropriation of $300,000 for a Government edifice has been recently made by Congress. The manufactures, which are shipped throughout the United States and to Canada and Mexico, and exported to Europe, are of iron, steel, and wood, lumber being derived from virgin forests. In addition to the larger industries—iron-works, foundries, machine and car shops, rolling and planing mills, etc.—are bridge and bolt, iron-roofing, tool, tack, furniture, stove, soap, carriage and wagon, and clothing factories, brick and fire-brick works, breweries, steam-bottling works, and a cotton-compress. The total number of employés is 22,010; yearly wages and salaries, $10,010,892. The annual volume of business is $56,000,000. Convict labor is employed in the mines. The climate is healthful. There are three summer-resorts and seventeen hotels.

Bowling Green, the county-seat of Wood County, Ohio, in the great northwestern Ohio natural-gas and oil field, 20 miles south of Toledo, on the Toledo, Columbus, and Southern Railway. The population in 1885 was 2,000; at present it is 4,000. Gas was found in 1885, and 21 wells have been drilled, averaging in depth 1,100 feet, and varying in flow from 1,000,000 to 5,000,000 cubic feet a day. The formation is: Drift, 10 feet; limestones, 400; shales, 680; Trenton, 20. As a rule, gas is found in the Trenton rock at a depth of 10 feet, the volume being determined by the porosity. About 40 wells are scattered over Wood County, yielding, at a low estimate, 160,000,000 cubic feet daily. The field is divided, Bowling Green occupying the center of the larger area. Oil was discovered in 1886. The county owns 104 wells, producing daily 10,400 barrels; and 9 miles from the city, at Cygnet, is the tank-farm, of 50 tanks, holding 35,000 barrels each, from which oil is pumped to refineries distant 45 miles. The capacity of the pipe-line is 8,000 barrels daily, and extensions to Chicago and Toledo are proposed. The depth of the wells is from 1,175 to 2,000 feet, and from 35 to 50 feet in the Trenton sandstone. The pool is estimated to contain 60 square miles, and 100,000 acres of land in the county are under lease for gas and oil purposes. The town is on a limestone ridge, and lime, burned by gas in four patent kilns, is sold below competition by that made with coal and wood fuel. Glass-sand abounds, and there are four glass-factories, employing 500 hands. The quality of the glass, it is claimed, is improved by gas-burning. There are 2 planing-mills, and a rolling-mill is being constructed. Incubators, also, are heated by gas. There are 5 newspapers (1 in the German language), 2 banks (both private), with aggregate deposits of $300,000; total capital, surplus, and deposits, over $1,000,000. Four hundred residences and several business blocks were constructed in 1887. Water-works are projected, costing from $50,000 to $75,000. The drainage is good, and the streets are wide. Two railroad lines secure outlets to the Great Lakes and trunk lines, and competing rates reduce freight. Additional facilities will be added by a branch road that has been surveyed through the town. The county fair-ground covers 57 acres. The surrounding farms are of rich, black soil, needing no fertilizing.

Calgary, an incorporated city of 2,500 inhabitants, in the province of Alberta, Canada. It is near the confluence of the Bow and Elbow rivers, within sight of the Rocky Mountains, and just outside of their eastern foot-hills. It is nearly north of Fort Benton, Montana, distant from that point about 200 miles, and has an altitude of 3,388 feet above the sea. This is the point where the Canadian Pacific Railway enters the Rocky Mountains, and it is the center of a vast cattle and sheep grazing region, of which Calgary is the supplying point and headquarters. The city is well built, the excellent stone of the neighborhood being largely employed in its structures. Several handsome churches and commodious school-houses have been erected, and the appearance of the town is far in advance of what would be expected of its recent origin and rapid growth. A public water-system, good drainage, electric street-lighting, police and fire departments, and other modern appurtenances of city organization, testify to its alertness. The banks are especially noteworthy for their strength and business facilities. This is one of the headquarters of the mounted police, and a center of Indian trading; there are also Dominion and railway land-agencies here. A railway is about to be built north and south from Calgary, to connect it with the coal region of Lethbridge, the ranching country around Edmonton, and other districts now reached by stages. The surrounding region is rapidly undergoing development, by means of irrigation, in grazing and farming industries, while new mines are constantly opening in the mountains. All this is of advantage to Calgary, which has the same situation relative to the mountain border of Canada that Denver has in relation to Colorado.

Canton, Stark County, Ohio, 60 miles from Cleveland. The population in 1870 was 8,660; in 1880, 12,258; in 1888, estimated at 30,000. Manufactures are the prominent interest, and include: Mowers and reapers, thrashing-machines, farm implements, safes, hay-racks, hay-tedders, sulky and hand plows, reaper-knives and sections, steel cutlery, saddlery, hardware, feed-cutters, horse-powers, mining and milling machinery, street-lamps, glass, iron bridges, springs, saws, iron roofing, hay-carriers, castings, stoves, steam-boilers and engines, stoneware, brick, flour, carriages, wooden articles, printing-presses, drilling-machines, tin and wooden pumps, doors, blinds and sash, feed-mills, flouring machinery, bells, lawn-rakes, post-hole diggers, house furniture, carpets, glass oil-tanks, hay-forks, bee-hives, paper boxes, faucets, surgical chairs, toilet and laundry soaps, brooms, woolen goods and yarns, blank-books, baking-powder, mattresses, extension ladders, hardware, novelties, files, revolving book and dry-goods cases, roasted coffees, watches, watch-cases, and railway signals. The capital invested is $10,000,000, and the yearly p o c amount to $13,000,000. Six thousand workingmen are employed. The machinery manufactured is shipped to Europe, North and South America, Australia, and elsewhere. The Buckeye Works—capital, $1,500,-000—employ 900 hands, and have a capacity of 15,000 harvesting-machines and 2,000 thrashers. Four mills consume daily 2,500 bushels of wheat. The county is, save one, the largest producer of wheat in the State, averaging yearly 1,286,410 bushels. Coal-fields underlie it. Forty large mines are worked, with a daily output of 6,000 tons, some of which are within a mile of the city. Two hundred others are operated by farmers. Cheap fuel and free sites for factories induce location. Clay for pottery, sewer-pipes, and brick abounds, with building and limestone and black-band ore. There are 5 railroads, with unlimited connections. Canton is lighted by gas, electricity, and gasoline. There are 3 daily newspapers (one in German), 6 banks (of which two are National), a street-railroad system, and a dummy-line of two miles, water-works of the Holly system, owned by the city, so that no tax is paid for water, and a drainage system of storm-water sewerage. There are 17 churches, a central high-school costing $99,600, 7 ward and 4 relief public-school buildings, and 2 parochial schools, 1 opera-house, 6 modern hotels, a public library, 2 tabernacles, public halls, a paid fire department, with electric-alarm system, telegraph facilities, and telephone communication to a distance of 75 miles. It has a free mail-delivery. The summer-resorts are numerous. There is a new post-office building and an Odd Fellows Hall. A United States Signal Service station is located here.

Chattanooga, Hamilton County, Tenn., at the foot of Lookout mountain, on Tennessee river, six miles from the southern boundary of the State. Chattanooga was founded in 1836, and first known as Ross's Landing, from the name of the Cherokee chief. It was incorporated in 1852. The population in 1860 was 2,545; in 1870, 6,091; in 1880, 12,879; in 1887, 36,903; and in 1888 it is estimated at 50,000. During the civil war it was an important strategic point, and a famous battle was fought near it. Thirteen thousand National soldiers are buried in the cemetery. Chattanooga is on the great natural highway through the mountains, and was the focus of interstate wagon-roads in days gone by. It is 195 miles above Mussel Shoals, and on the completion of engineering works at that point, will possess valuable facilities for river transportation. It is only thirty-four miles farther from the Gulf by water than Cincinnati. The iron industry has progressed for twelve years. Four furnaces are in blast within the city limits, and it is the financial distributing-point for a dozen more in the district. The coal-mining plants, from which the supplies of fuel are drawn, number twenty-two, with a total output in 1886 of

1.200,000 gross tons. It is the first point in the South where the manufacture of Bessemer steel was attempted. The daily capacity of the Roane works is 250 tons of rails of this steel. Nine lines of railroad enter Chattanooga, formed by four trunk, and one independent system. There is also a narrow-gauge line to the top of Lookout Mountain, costing $150,000; an incline to that point, costing $75.000; and another to Mission Ridge, costing $25,000. A belt road of 30 miles runs 128 passenger and 500 freight cars daily. Truck-farming is a profitable industry. During the year 30,000,-000 feet of lumber, 1,000,000 bushels of grain, 200,000 tons of iron-ore, and from 5,000 to 10,-000 bales of cotton, with farm produce, are floated to the city from upper points. There are three daily and six weekly newspapers, electric and gas light companies, water-works, five banks (three of which are National), with total capital, surplus, etc., of $1,360,000, a public school attendance of 6,000, in addition to numerous private schools, and two universities. The sewerage system has cost $150,000. There are twenty miles of street-railway, and an electric line is building. The city contains an opera house and twelve hotels. The tax-valnation in 1880 was $3,294,992; in 1885, $6,480,-960; in 1888, $12,323,000. The sales of real estate during the year 1886 were $3,028,125; in 1887, $13,264,505. The city debt is $206,-000. The manufacturing establishments in 1885 numbered 99. At present there are 152, 132 of which employ steam-power. The capital invested is $8,711,700; hands employed, 8,432; yearly wages, $3,332,900; products, $10,655,000. There are eight foundries and machine-shops, as many factories of agricultural implements, two cotton-compresses, two steam-boiler shops, three rolling-mills, ten planing and eight saw mills, two stove works, two large tanneries, extensive pipe works, six brass and seven brick works, factories of springs, carriages and wagons, scales, boxes, tacks, soap, candy, cane mills, wire nails, cigars, furniture, fertilizers, galvanized and architectural iron, artificial stone, powder, dynamite, and many small industries. Chattanooga has twenty-five churches, independent of those of the colored population. Many of these are handsome buildings. The post-office and customs house is a fine edifice. Chattanooga is a United States Signal Service station.

Cheyenne, a city, capital of Wyoming Territory and county-seat of Laramie County. Cheyenne was first settled in 1867; its population, as given by the census returns of 1880, was 3,456; but in 1887 it was estimated at 10,000. It lies at the base of the Rocky-Mountains, about forty miles from the western line of Nebraska, and about twelve miles north of Colorado, and is on the line of the Union Pacific Railway, 516 miles west of Omaha, and at the junction of the Denver Pacific, Colorado Central, and Cheyenne and Northern railways. It is proposed to extend the last road as far north

as the line of the British possessions. Another road soon to be completed, the Cheyenne and Burlington, a branch of the Burlington and Missouri system, will add another to the city's facilities for communication. The assessed valuation of real estate in 1886 was $2,208,-457; the total amount of real and personal property was $2,675,000. It is understood that the assessment-roll represents only about one third of the actual value of the property. In 1887 there was an increase of about half a million dollars, the amounts aggregating $3,253,-000. A large portion of the personal property in the city and county consists of live-stock, the principal source of wealth; in 1886 this interest in the county was assessed at a value of $4,481,194. Cheyenne is, moreover, the supply-point for a great stock-raising territory, many of the largest owners of ranches having their homes in the city. The manufactures, though a secondary interest, are increasing. There are two saddle and harness establishments, a carriage and wagon factory, a planing-mill and wood-work factory, two bookbinderies, two breweries, and two cigar-factories. The total value of manufactures for 1886 was about $500,000. The Union Pacific Railway employs several hundred men in its machine and car-repairing shops. The Cheyenne and Burlington is also to have a shop there very soon. The tax-levy for 1887 was eight and three fourth mills, divided as follows: general revenue, five and a half mills; streets and alleys, one and one quarter mill; bonds of 1875, one half mill; bonds of 1882, one mill; bonds of 1884, one half mill. The water-works, owned by the city, were constructed at a cost of about $150,000. The source of supply is 127 feet higher than the city, and the gravitation affords sufficient force for all domestic and manufacturing purposes. The water comes from Crow Creek, the source of supply to Lakes Absaracca and Mahpealutah, the city owning 160 acres of land, controlling one mile of water on Crow Creek, 480 acres partly covered by Lake Mahpealutah, and 160 partly covered by Lake Absaracca. The system includes sixty fire-hydrants and steam-pumping machinery, on the line of the main pipe, for extinguishment of fires. It is estimated that with an increase of storage-basins the present system would supply a population of 50,000. The city has the best modern system of sewerage, an alarm-system fire department; telephone communication, gas and electric lighting, and a street-railway. By act of the Legislature of 1886, an appropriation of $150,000 was made for a Territorial Capitol to be completed in two years. There are five banks with capital aggregating more than $1,000,000. and average deposits of over $3,000,000. Three daily and three weekly newspapers are issued. The Union Pacific Railway has built here one of its finest depots, at an expense of over $100,000, and that of the Cheyenne and Burlington was erected at a cost of about $90,000. Other noteworthy buildings are 8 churches, 4 public schools with property valued at $75,000; a convent school that cost $50,000; a county hospital, $35,000; an opera-house, $40,000; and a club-house, $30,000. The Young Men's Christian Association has a membership of about 300, and an income of more than $3.000. It has a fine hall, a gymnasium, and a free reading-room. The county library, containing nearly 2,000 volumes, is open to the public. Three-quarters of a mile northwest of the city are the grounds of the Territorial Fair Association, containing 80 acres of land, and furnished with suitable buildings and a fine race-track. Fort Russell three miles west, has recently been enlarged at a cost of $150,000, and is a permanent military post, the largest in the department of the Platte. Twenty miles northwest of the city is the Silver Crown Mining District, the development of which was begun in 1886. Several mines are now in operation that will yield over fifty dollars to the ton. A smelter having a capacity of thirty tons a day has been erected there, and a concentrator, and about one hundred men are engaged in the mines. Several of the mines are more than one hundred feet deep, and it is the opinion of mineralogists who have looked into the matter that richer gold and silver ore will be reached at a greater depth.

Council Bluffs, the largest and oldest town in western Iowa, with a population of 35,000. Council Bluffs (a name given by the Indians), began as an Indian trading-post, and then became a settlement of the Mormons after they removed from Nauvoo, Ill., in 1846. When the California gold discoveries sent emigration westward this place became one of the main starting-points for overland travel. It is at the foot of and upon the bluffs forming the eastern margin of the bottom-lands bordering the Missouri, and is connected with Omaha, Neb., immediately opposite, by a railway-bridge, and a wagon-bridge across which street cars will presently be run by electric motors. The business and a large part of the best residence part of the town is upon the level expanse at the foot of the bluffs; but many fine streets run into the beautiful ravines that indent the highlands; and upon their wooded crest is an extensive public park, the cemeteries, and the reservoir of the water-system, supplied by pumping (through settling-basins) from Missouri river. The city hall and court-house, the Federal building, and the high-school, are stately edifices. Just outside of town is a State institution for the instruction and care of deaf-mutes which has 375 pupils. The city is well paved, sewered, and policed. It is lighted with gas, but the incandescent system of electric lighting is extensively used. There are some exceedingly handsome churches and society halls, and a public library of 7,500 volumes is well patronized. There are three daily newspapers and several weeklies. As a railway

focus, Council Bluffs has long been eminent. This is the eastern terminus of the Union Pacific system, and a western terminus of the Northwestern, Burlington, Milwaukee and St. Paul, Rock Island, Wabash, and Illinois Central systems, from Chicago, while other railways lead north to Sioux City and St. Paul, and south to the cities along Missouri river. All this centers in one great station. These railway facilities make the city a flourishing business point, the wholesale and jobbing trade amounting in 1887 to $33,000,000, of which one third was in agricultural implements alone—an item in which Council Bluffs is exceeded only by Kansas City. Manufacturing is not so forward, the combined products amounting to $4,000,000 a year. Several railroads have extensive repair-shops here, and one corn-cannery employs 400 men. Wagons and carriages form another leading object of manufacture. The public schools are well managed and numerous, and the Roman Catholic Church supports two academies; but there are no special institutions of higher learning. The healthfulness of the town is high, and many persons doing business in Omaha prefer to make their residence here. A few miles below the city a lake-like lagoon from the Missouri forms a summer pleasure-place, where hotels have been built, and boating and fishing attract excursionists.

Decatur, Morgan County, Ala., 25 miles from the northern boundary, on Tennessee river, at intersection of the East Tennessee, Virginia and Georgia and the Louisville and Nashville railroads. It is on the water-shed between the Gulf of Mexico and Ohio river, has an altitude of 600 feet, and enjoys all advantages of the valley of the Tennessee. It is in the cereal belt, producing grains, blue grass, clover, etc., a cotton region, and tobacco-growing country, and the mineral resources are also unlimited, including coal and iron in close proximity, while timber of best quality abounds. Limestone, asphalt, building-stone, granite and marble, manganese, glass-sand, and brick-clay are available. The town was devastated during the civil war. On Jan. 11, 1887—the date of organization of the Land Improvement and Furnace Company with 5,600 acres of town, 50,000 acres of mineral lands, and $400,000 capital—it contained fewer than 1,500 inhabitants. In one year, $900,000 had been expended in improvements, including industries; and the population in July, 1888, was 7,500. It has a street-railway, an electric-light and telephone company, 1 daily and 3 weekly newspapers, a water-works system costing $200,000, and 2 banks (one National), with capital of $100,000 each. It was surveyed by a landscape engineer, and the sewerage is of the Waring system. Freight rates are competitive. Other railroad lines, in addition to the two trunk systems, are projected and constructing. Navigation of the river is dependent on completion of the works at Mussel Shoals.

The schools are private. Industries completed or begun include a 70-ton charcoal iron-furnace, costing $100,000; a charcoal company's plant of $120,000; a bridge and construction company, $100,000; oak extract works, $60,000; a horseshoe-nail factory, $100,000; boiler and engine works, $100,000; a $1,000,000 plant of the United States Rolling Stock Company; car-construction and repair-shops, $300,000; a car-wheel foundry, $60,000; an ice factory, $10,000; a cotton-compress, $75,000; a furniture, sash, door, and blind factory, 6 brickyards, large lumber-yards and mills, and an artificial stone company. The daily output of 3 band saws is 60,000 feet of lumber, and of 1 circular saw, 15,000, while 2,500,000 shingles are handled yearly by the latter company. A steamboat is owned and operated in the business. An opera-house and business blocks are building. Two thousand residences and cottages have been erected. The "Tavern" cost $140,000.

Durham, Wake County, North Carolina, 25 miles from Raleigh, on the North Carolina Railroad; population, nearly 8,000. It owes its prosperity to a single world-famed industry. Prior to the civil war, tobacco was manufactured in one small factory, which fell into the hands of the National army, pending negotiations for surrender by Gen. Johnston, in 1865. Orders received for the product of this establishment, after the disbandment of the armies, gave an impetus of growth to the town, which now has business connections all over the world. The largest granulated smoking-tobacco factory in the world, with a capacity of 10,000,000 pounds yearly, is here. It has a larger payroll than any other manufacturing establishment in the State. Cigarettes are the specialty of another company, and 254,133,333 were shipped during 1886. The increase for the month of July over the same month for the year previous was 20,895,140. There are more than a dozen factories of tobacco and snuff. The tobacco-boxes are made here. A cotton-mill, of 8,568 spindles and 200 looms, produces 9,000 yards of cloth a day, the bulk of which is made into tobacco-bags. There is also a bobbin and shuttle mill, with a capacity of 90,000 pieces a week, for cotton, woolen, silk, jute, flax, and woolen mills. A tobacco-cure company makes three forms of medicaments, and a fertilizer company uses tobacco-dust as a basis. The sales of tobacco in a year from a single warehouse amounted to 8,330,000 pounds. The amount paid for stamps on tobacco, from the figures of the Internal-Revenue Office, in six years and nine months, was $37,878,212.83. The streets are paved with stone, there are electric lights and water-works, eleven churches, two newspapers, and a graded-school building erected at a cost of $6,500, which accommodates 500 pupils. There are also two female seminaries.

Eau Claire, a city, county-seat of Eau Claire County, Wis., at the confluence of Chippewa and Eau Claire rivers. It is 321 miles northwest of Chicago, and 84 miles east of St. Paul. The population in 1880 was 10,118, according to the United States census; in 1885 it was 21,668, according to the State census; and it is now estimated at 25,000. The Chicago, St. Paul, Minneapolis and Omaha Railroad, the Chicago, Milwaukee and St. Paul Railroad, and the Wisconsin Central Line, with branches extending in various directions, including those of the pine, hard wood, and mineral regions of the north. The chief water-power is supplied by the dam across Chippewa river, giving eighteen feet head, while the dam on Eau Claire river supplies the linen and other mills. These rivers, spanned by ten bridges, are thickly lined with manufacturing establishments, including a dozen large saw-mills, a sash-and-door factory, a linen-mill, a furniture factory, a refrigerator factory, two foundries, and a factory of electrical machinery and appliances. The following statement exhibits the principal statistics for 1888: Assessed value of property, $5,404,487.89; bonded debt, $195,000; school census, 4,401; men employed in saw-mills, etc., 1,572; amount of lumber sawed, 182,000,000 feet; lath sawed, 62,000,000; shingles sawed, 82,000,000; paper made, 2,621,000 pounds; value of lumber, lath, and shingles, $2,541,000; value of sash, doors, and blinds made, $333,000; value of paper and pulp made, $140,000. Eau Claire is one of the largest lumber manufacturing cities in the United States. It manufactures annually 300,000,000 feet of lumber. It has 25 miles of water-mains with 320 hydrants, 2 electric-light companies with circuits 41 miles long, an electric fire-alarm system, 4½ miles of street-railway, 3 public parks, a sewage system, paved streets, an opera-house built at a cost of $60,000, with a seating capacity of 1,200, beautiful residences and churches, 2 daily newspapers, a female academy, a free public library, a fine race-track, and an agricultural exposition building. It has telephonic connections with all the neighboring towns. A noted characteristic of this climate is its pure, dry atmosphere, which is favorable to those afflicted with pulmonary troubles. The Chippewa is one of the largest rivers in the State, and its great valley, with its numerous streams, proffers an accessible supply of timber, consisting of maple, oak, birch, elm, hemlock, and bass-wood. For the encouragement of new manufacturing enterprises, a bonus of $100 is offered for each operative who shall be regularly and steadily employed in any legitimate manufacturing enterprise. This policy, during this the first year of the experiment, has secured the establishment of four large enterprises in Eau Claire.

Ely, a town in northern Minnesota, organized in 1886 by the Ely Mining Company, population about 1,000. It contains the Chandler iron mine, which is in process of development to a width of 130 feet, length 1,000 feet, with from one to eight feet of stripping. Over 300 men are employed, and 1,000 tons of ore are shipped daily on 50 cars each of 20 tons capacity. The ore, a hard hematite, assays 68 per cent. metallic iron, and is low in phosphorus. It has a saw-mill producing 30,000 feet of lumber daily, principally used in the construction of the Chandler and other mines. The first ore train entered this town Aug. 15, 1888, and through trains between this point and Duluth, Minn., were put on the Duluth and Iron Range Railroad Aug. 21, 1888.

Fort Wayne, the county-seat of Allen County, Ind., on St. Mary's river, in the northeastern part of the State. It originated in a fort built in 1794 by Gen. Anthony Wayne. The inhabitants in 1828 numbered 500; in 1840, 1,200; in 1860, 10,319; in 1880, 25,760; in 1888, estimated at 40,000. The first city charter was granted in 1839. On July 4, 1843, the Wabash and Erie Canal was opened. Nine railway lines pass through the city. Improved farms and forests of hard-wood timber surround the city. Within thirty-five miles are 23 stave and bolt factories; the annual output of each is from 500,000 to 13,000,000 staves and headings. There are 4 banks, 5 daily newspapers, 10 miles of street-railway, a public and a Catholic library, Young Men's Christian Association reading-rooms, and churches of all denominations. There are fine Catholic church, school, and hospital buildings. Their library cost $65,000, exclusive of books, and contains 5,000 volumes. The First Presbyterian, recently erected, cost $90,000. There are 12 public-school buildings. The system was established in 1853, and reorganized in 1873. The attendance is 3,500 pupils. There are several institutions for higher education, notably Methodist and Lutheran. There are forty miles of water-main, supplying water for domestic purposes and fire protection. Forty-two thousand dollars were expended in improvements of sewerage during 1887, and $77,000 on streets and side-walks. There are two opera-houses, a Masonic Temple, and an academy of music. The new Government building, a handsome structure, cost $200,000. The city is lighted by electricity. The manufacturing industries include the shops of the Pennsylvania Railway Company, the White wheel-works, employing 130 hands, with monthly wages of $4,000; a walnut-lumber firm employing 200 men and manufacturing 6,000,000 feet of walnut alone yearly; a company manufacturing gas-work machinery and apparatus, a brass-foundry, two large breweries, wagon and pulley works, handle-factories, grain-elevator, woodworking and mill machinery, iron-works, lumber yards and mills, and coffee, spice, baking-powder, and flouring mills.

Glenwood Springs, an incorporated town in Garfield County, Col., at the western base of the main range of the Rocky Mountains, where the Roaring Fork enters Grand river. Its growth, previous to getting railroad connection with Denver, was very slow, but since the autumn of 1887 the population has increased to 3,000. This is due to the advantageous situation of the town as the supplying-point of the Grand River valley; and to the presence there of remarkable thermal springs, in the utilization of which a large capital is being invested. The advantage of situation consists in its being at the convergence of three main valleys along which will naturally flow the products of mines and ranches, and currents of travel. Two railways, the Colorado Midland and the Grand River branch of the Denver and Rio Grande, now terminate at Glenwood, but both are to be extended westerly The Burlington and other routes have been surveyed through this point, which thus bids fair to become a railway center, and consequently a point of commercial supremacy. This part of the State abounds in coal, both anthracitic and bituminous. The former is of excellent quality, and from the latter superior coke is made. About 15,000 acres of coal-lands were taken up in this district previous to 1887, for which the Government was paid nearly $204,000. Many mines and coking-ovens have already been opened by corporations, and preparations are making for others. Much of this product is directly tributary to Glenwood. Immense bodies of hematite and magnetic iron ore occur in the mountains, at places easily accessible; while lime, fire-clay, and other furnace ingredients abound. Hence it is expected that smelting-furnaces and iron-mills will be erected at Glenwood within a short time, to which could be most cheaply brought (as it is all down grade) the silver and lead ores mined in the high ranges eastward and southward, while branch railroads about to be constructed will add to the list of mines tributary to this new town. There is little room for agriculture in the immediate vicinity, but farther down Grand river lies an extensive ranching and cattle-grazing district, which will sell and buy from this market the moment that railway connection is established. The thermal springs here are of remarkable size and power. They gush out in many places along Grand river, just below the picturesque cañon at the mouth of which the town is built. The principal one is in the edge of the city, and has a basin sixty feet in diameter. The overflow of this is conducted into an oval pool, floored and walled in with concrete and masonry, which is nine hundred and sixty feet in length. Beside this great pool elaborate bath-houses, parlors, amusement-rooms, etc., have been built, in which all modern appliances are employed, and in connection with which a large hotel and sanitarium are in process of erection. These buildings are steam-heated, lighted by electricity, and surrounded by ornamental grounds. The temperature of the waters at their exit is 126° Fahr.; and some springs arise inside small caves which are filled with steam, forming natural vapor-baths. The water is clear, and not unpleasant in taste or smell when hot and fresh. They contain an unusual quantity of solid ingredients, such as salts of soda, magnesia, iron, and lime, with sulphur and carbonic acid, and are believed to possess remedial qualities of a high order. The altitude of the locality is 5,200 feet, and the air and water of that purity to be expected among the mountains. The town is well built, and contains school-houses, churches, and business blocks that would do credit to a far older and more populous place. There are three newspapers, two of which are dailies; two banks, with a capital of $100,000 each; and two large hotels. Water is supplied by a gravity system from a mountain brook; and the streets and most of the larger business-houses and dwellings are lighted by electricity.

Hastings.—the county-seat of Adams County, in the southern central part of Nebraska, on the Chicago, Burlington, and Quincy Railroad, 180 miles west of Omaha. This city has grown up during the past ten years with phenomenal strength and vigor. It has a population of 12,000, and, besides the main line of the Burlington system, has branches of the Union Pacific (St. Joseph and Grand Island Railroad), the Missouri Pacific, and the Northwestern (Frémont, Elkhorn, and Missouri Valley Railroad). Other railroads are surveyed to reach this point. The surrounding country is fertile and well settled. Corn is the principal crop, but the rearing of live-stock is an equally important industry. The city is solidly built, in its business part, while its more scattered residence portion possesses many handsome houses. The principal streets are paved and sewered, and the whole city is lighted by gas and electricity. Twenty miles of horse-car tracks have been laid. There are two daily newspapers, a board of trade, several banks, a powerful loan-and-investment association, and considerable wholesale business. In addition to the public schools, which occupy large brick buildings, there is here the nucleus of a university in Hastings College, an institution under the control of the Presbyterians, which is well endowed and offers a full course of collegiate instruction. This school admits both sexes to equal privileges, and has about two hundred students. All the leading religious denominations have churches, and the Young Men's Christian Association, the Masonic, and other societies, maintain their organizations. There is a large and handsome opera-house.

Hutchinson, a city, the county-seat of Reno County, Kansas, on Arkansas river, at the point first reached by the Atchison, Topeka, and Santa Fé Railroad. The population, by official census returns, has increased more than 10,000 in three years. It was founded in 1872 by Clinton C. Hutchinson, and all deeds to town lots contained forfeiture clauses prohibiting the sale of intoxicating liquors and keeping of

gambling resorts. The first newspaper was published in 1872, and 5,000 copies were printed and sent East as advertisements. At the same date a population of 600 incurred a debt of $100,000 for public improvements. Four bridges (one 1,680 feet long) and a court-house were built. The growth was slow and substantial, and proportioned to the settlement of the county, a rich agricultural region. There are two other lines of railroad, and two more are approaching. Hutchinson has twelve salt companies. A recent drill for natural gas resulted in the discovery, at a depth of 425 feet, of a salt-deposit from 300 to 320 feet thick, and 10 miles square. Salt is brought to the surface by saturation of water in wells, which is pumped to large tanks and evaporated. The tanks present a curious appearance, owing to crystallization of salt through the leaks. The ground beneath often resembles snow-drifts. The aggregate capacity of the works in operation is 5,700 barrels of salt a day. The freight on lumber for the year was $150,000; on coal, $150,000; and on building-stone, $100,000. The business-houses are of brick and stone—131 of these and 1,380 dwelling-houses were constructed during the year past. Hutchinson is fast becoming a meat-packing center and manufacturing point. The capacity of a meat-packing establishment in operation is 2,000 hogs a day. A contract was signed at Chicago, in September, 1888, for the erection of a large lard-refinery and cotton-seed-oil factory and a pork-packing house. The buildings and plants will cost $500,000. A stock-yard and salt company has paid $98,000 for grounds, and it is contemplated that $500,000 will be invested. The city is lighted by gas and electricity, has water-works, street-car lines, a daily newspaper, telephone facilities, and comfortable hotels. The schools are excellent; the churches numerous and well supported. There is a handsome Masonic Temple.

Jacksonville, Duval County, Florida, a commercial city and winter resort, on St. John's river, 15 miles from the ocean, in the northeastern part of the State. The population is 25,000. During the winter season from 60,000 to 70,000 visitors register at twenty hotels, in addition to others in boarding-houses. It is lighted by gas and electricity, has street-railways, daily newspapers, telegraph, ocean and domestic, and telephone facilities; 2 National, 3 private, and 2 savings banks; 8 miles of cast-iron water-main, with water-supply from artesian wells, and 9 miles of terra-cotta sewers. The sanitation is elaborate, but during the year there were 4,711 cases of yellow fever, and 412 deaths. The tide rises three feet in the river. The city has an ocean port, the harbor being improved by jetties at the mouth of the river, in operation since 1879. There is a foreign and coastwise commerce. The river traffic has decreased of late years, by reason of increase of railroads, of seven of which Jacksonville is the terminus. The total

2,208 miles in the State are tributary to the city. It is a center of fruit-packing and shipping. A company has been organized for orange-auction and forwarding. The leading jobbing business is the wholesale grain and feed trade. There are 90 wholesale establishments and 500 retail, which employ nearly 5,000 hands. The amount of business capital in both branches is $20,000,000. A cotton-house, with gin and press, is being erected, and the city will eventually become a cotton-center. There is a direct line of steamships to New York. A new charter has recently been granted, by which the corporate limits are extended. The public schools number eleven, white and colored, with an attendance of 2,254 pupils. The value of school property is $70,-500. There are also private, art, and music schools, and a Young Men's Christian Association. The streets are paved, and there are shelled roads. It has lumber-mills, cigar-factories, a brush-factory, boiler and machine shops, founderies, marine railways, jewelry and curio, carriage and wagon, and ice factories, a coffee and spice mill, binderies, and other manufacturing industries.

Lincoln.—The capital of Nebraska, in Kent County, 65 miles southwest of Omaha; population, 35,000. There is no river here, or natural site for a town; but the place was chosen to be the capital when it was a mere cross-road because of its central position in what then constituted the population of Nebraska. The State became owner of the town-site, and sold nearly $400,000 worth of lots within a few years, so rapidly did people assemble and property appreciate. Lincoln is now the railroad-center of the State. The Burlington route's trains enter and leave over six different lines; the Union Pacific has lines both north and south; the Elkhorn route comes in by two lines, and the Missouri Pacific by one. At least 1,000 men are employed here by the railways alone. Partly as cause, partly as effect of these railroad facilities, an enormous wholesale and jobbing trade has arisen. The sales of groceries amount to $4,000,000 annually. Agricultural implements, cigars and tobacco, dry goods, drugs, and liquors follow, augmenting the wholesale business to $12,000,000 annually, making it a serious competitor in trade with Omaha, St. Joseph, and Kansas City. As a grain-market Lincoln is important. Her merchants own seventy-five elevators in all parts of the State, and handle three fourths of the cereal-crop of Nebraska—i. e., from fifteen to twenty million bushels of corn and small grains. Ten Eastern grain-dealers maintain buyers here. Live-stock forms another element of prosperity. Three quarters of the total shipment of beef and swine from the State passes through Lincoln, and is quartered in her immense stock-yards. Two pork-packing houses represent, combined, a plant of $200,000, and can pack 5,000 hogs a day; a

beef-packing house is soon to be built. Factories of several kinds are rising. The brick-and-tile works employ 150 men the year round, and can make 50,000 common bricks and 12,000 pressed bricks daily, besides all sorts of tiles. The Lincoln canning-factory is capable of packing a million cans of vegetables and 2,000 barrels of vinegar in a year. In all, 70 factories are now counted in the city, whose combined product amounts to $8,000,000 annually. As the capital of the State the city has many public institutions, some of which are imposingly housed. The new Capitol is a stately edifice, after the style of the Capitol at Washington, built of white limestone from the bluffs of Platte river, and capped by a dome rising 200 feet above the trees of the park in which it stands. The interior is handsomely finished, and the whole building cost $500,000. Three miles southward is the State Insane Asylum, and the Penitentiary stands in another suburb. The post-office and other Federal offices occupy a large and ugly structure on the public square, and a county court-house is soon to be built at a cost of $200,000. Lincoln derives a large part of its distinction from its institutions of learning. Here is the State University, occupying a group of large buildings in shaded grounds, which form a park in the midst of the town. These grounds were reserved by the State, and the main building was erected in 1870, at a cost of $140,-000, out of funds accruing from the sale of city lots. Since then other buildings have been added, laboratories furnished, etc., until now this university is one of the best equipped in the West. It is under a board of regents, and will ultimately embrace an academic course, an industrial college, and colleges of medicine, law, and the fine arts, to which will be added special advanced courses; only the first two are organized, as yet, under sixteen professors and several instructors. A preparatory school is attached, and the tendency of the curriculum is toward modern and practical requirements, rather than toward classical training. This appears in the prominence given to the Industrial College, which offers two courses, leading to the degrees of bachelor of agriculture and bachelor of civil engineering. An experimental farm is carried on by the State in connection with this college. In 1887-'88 this university had 400 students. It is free to residents of Nebraska, and receives, without further examination, the graduates of about twenty accredited high-schools in State. Besides this, the Methodist Church opened in September, 1888, the Wesleyan University. It occupies a building costing $70,000, three miles from the center of the city, and owns 240 acres of gift-land. This school is designed to be a university, and among its foremost departments will be a polytechnic school. A third university, just founded, is under the care of the Campbellite Church; and the Roman Catholics support a convent school having 150 pupils. Business colleges and a complete system of public schools are to be added to this remarkable list of educational facilities. The State Library has 30,000 volumes, and is especially rich in law-books. The society of Lincoln is of an intelligence and culture unusual in towns so far west, and the wealth is considerable. The city is therefore well kept and handsome. All of the principal streets are well shaded and paved, and street-cars run in every direction. Gas and elictricity light the streets and houses. Many examples of modern architecture, commercial and domestic, adorn the town, and some of the churches are costly and handsome.

Mobile, the only seaport of Alabama, on Mobile river, at the head of Mobile Bay, 24 miles from the Gulf of Mexico. The population in 1880 was 29,132; in 1888 it was estimated at 40,000. The Government has appropriated $250,000 for improvement of the harbor, where deep water is needed. At present vessels of 15½ feet are floated. During the year 138 vessels entered the port, with a tonnage of 128,250 tons. It is the outlet of 2,000 miles of navigable rivers. passing through rich agricultural, iron, and coal regions, and it is important as a coal port. The trade in coal for the year was 39,433 tons, of which 648 were imported. Next to New Orleans it was the largest cotton-receiving market of the South prior to the civil war, the average annual exports for five years being 632,308 bales. The receipts (which have been greatly diminished by increase of railroads and construction of interior compressors) for the year 1886–'87 were 216,142 bales. Timber has largely replaced the cotton interest; the shipments, foreign and coastwise, reach yearly 30,000,000 feet. From 150,000 to 200,000 pieces of white-oak for wine-barrel staves are shipped yearly, bringing from $120 to $150 a thousand: and the Seaboard Oil-Refining Company, of New York, has its staves for oil-barrels manufactured here. Cypress shingles are a leading industry; 130,000,000 were the combined product of eight mills in 1887. The dust, composed of long, stringy particles, is used in constructing roads through the marshes by which the city is surrounded, forming an elastic, soundless road-bed. The wool trade is increasing, and the sales of rosin and turpentine during the year reached 132,092 and 28,725 barrels respectively. Truck-farming in the suburbs began in 1879, and is a profitable investment. The value of the crop of the past year was $294,971. There are five railroads, one recently completed to Birmingham, and a steamboat trade with Montgomery. There is a line of steamers to Liverpool, England, and one to New York. Water-works costing $500.000 have been recently constructed, and $240.000 were expended on new wharves during 1887. There are 5 banks, 9 insurance companies, 34 churches, 1 daily and several weekly newspapers, 4 orphan asylums, a United

States marine hospital, a Jesuit college, academies, and numerous private schools. The High-School, for colored children, is a large building. There are electric and gas works. Mobile has the only American Anti-Friction-Metal Company, with a daily output of 5,000 pounds, tan-yards, paper and wooden box, barrel, harness, saddlery, wagon, and other factories, and cotton-mills in operation and constructing. African Village, a few miles distant, contains all survivors of the last slave-ship that entered Mobile Bay (in 1859), the majority of whom were freed by the emancipation proclamation before being sold. Many of the older ones speak their native tongue.

Montgomery, a city, the capital of Alabama, in the county of the same name, on bluffs of the Alabama river. 400 miles above Mobile Bay and 40 miles below the junction of the Coosa and Tallapoosa rivers. The population in 1880 was 16,713; in 1886, nearly 30,000. Navigation is open all the year. The city lies in the prairie belt, between the northern and southern pine regions, and its resources are in agriculture, mineral development, and yellow pine and hard woods. It was incorporated in 1837, and made the capital ten years later. Since 1880 it has enjoyed a "boom," and shares in the prosperity of Birmingham and other mineral districts. During this period, over 2,500 dwellings were built and occupied within its limits. About twenty-five per cent. of the inhabitants are engaged in manufactures. From 120,000 to 140,000 bales of cotton are handled yearly. There are 7 large storage warehouses, with capacity of 73,-500 bales, 2 compresses, and 4 ginneries. There are 3 railroads, with lines in six directions. The bulk of river trade is controlled by a city steamboat company, giving bills of lading to New York and Liverpool, *via* Mobile. The total tonnage yearly of all freight is 500,000 tons. A narrow-gauge railroad of fifty miles, southeast to the timber district, has been constructed. The total capital invested in business for 1887, was $15,595,000, and the annual volume of business was $30,185,000. The grocery trade reaches $7,000,000, and the dry-goods trade $3,000.000 yearly. The city is lighted by gas and electricity, and has an electric railway of fifteen miles. Power is applied overhead. Water-works supply 5,000,-000 gallons of artesian water, and the drainage is perfect. There are 5 banks (2 National), 3 daily newspapers, 2 theatres, 7 hotels, 1 infirmary, and 9 churches for whites. There are 5 public-school buildings (3 white and 2 colored), a business college, and private schools. A State University has been recently founded. Two land companies have parks at Riverside and Highland Hill, the former a manufacturing suburb, the latter a place of public resort. Land is given to manufactures, which include an iron furnace. foundries, and machine and car shops, and boiler-works, cotton, cotton-seed-oil, flouring and wood-working mills, brick-yards, carriage and wagon, ice, candy, soap, fertilizer, cigar, paper-box, vinegar, cracker, and sausage factories, a plant for distilling alcohol from smoke. and an oil-refinery. The Capitol building was erected in 1851, on a site reserved by the founder in 1817 for the anticipated purpose. The United States Post-Office (which cost $130,000) and city buildings are handsome.

Montpelier, Indiana, 38 miles south of Fort Wayne, on the main line of the Fort Wayne, Cincinnati, and Louisville Railway; population estimated at 1,000. The town is on an elevated plateau, by the Salamonie river. Three gas-wells are in operation, flowing millions of cubic feet a day. The town is thoroughly piped, and by means of pipe-lines could easily furnish gas to many other towns and cities of northern Indiana. Petroleum exists also in a field 20 miles in length. A well within the corporate limits flows 100 barrels in twenty-four hours, with double capacity by pumping. Building-stone and limestone abound. There is a large quarry, with latest improvements in steam machinery, electric blasting, etc., where 25 cars can be loaded daily. The timber-supply is very large. Glass-sand of superior quality is found in close proximity. The drainage is excellent, and the water-supply abundant. There are 4 churches, a Citizens' Bank, with assets of $297,000, two hotels, and good schools. A large bending-works has been erected. Free gas and free land are offered as inducements to manufacturers. Rail connection with the great trunk lines is made.

Muncie, a city of Indiana, the county-seat of Delaware County, on an elevated plateau above White river, east of the center of the State. The population in 1880 was 5,263 ; in 1888 it was estimated at 14,000. It is surrounded by a thriving farming community. Natural gas was discovered in 1886, and twenty wells are in operation, averaging 915 feet in depth, with a total capacity of 90,000,000 cubic feet in twenty-four hours. The gas is of excellent quality, dry, and free from sulphur. The Trenton rock, which here reaches its highest point, with a downward trend to east and west, is struck at 75 feet above sea-level, and is drilled to a depth of 30 feet. Muncie has three competing trunk lines of railroad, affording access to markets in all directions. The electric lights, in addition to gas, are of two systems. There are 12 churches, 3 daily newspapers, a library, 4 banks (one of which is National), 4 brick school-buildings, valued at $100,000, with a regular attendance of 1,300 pupils. The water-works have a pumping capacity of 2,500,000 gallons a day. Water for manufacturing is supplied by the river and Buck creek, and is offered free, as are gas and land, to induce location. There are five miles of sewers, telegraph and telephone facilities, and a paid fire department, with electric alarm. Muncie has a board of trade. Establishments located or contracted for are: A bending-works; a

jute-bagging factory, with capacity of 20,000 yards a day, employing 200 hands; machine-shops; a saw-mill; bridge and wood-carving companies; a straw-pulp, a paper, 3 glass, and a rubber works; skewer, duster, handle, wheel-furnishing and heading factories; flour-mills; elevators; and minor industries. About 2,000 hands are employed. The court-house, recently completed, is a handsome structure, costing $250,000. There is an opera-house and a free mail-delivery.

New Orleans, a city and port of entry of Louisiana, on Mississippi river, 105 miles from its mouth. During the winter there is an influx of from 20,000 to 40,000 visitors. The population in 1870 was 191,413, of whom 142,293 were whites; in 1880, 216,090 (whites, 158,367); in 1887, 246,950 (whites, 202,800). The debt of the city, Sept. 1, 1888, was $17,491,546.58. This amount does not include the Gaines judgment, on appeal, for $1,925,667.82. New Orleans is the largest cotton-receiving market in America, and the largest in the world, with the exception of Liverpool. But the percentage of the total crop received has fallen behind, owing to the large overland movement from the interior. Its cotton exchange was established in 1870. The receipts for the year 1887-'88 were 1,912,228 bales, averaging $46.25 a bale, out of a total crop of 6,928,245 bales. The largest receipts were in 1861, viz., 2,255,448 bales. The largest since the war were in 1882-'83, viz., 1,999,598 bales. The exports for the year 1887-'88 were 1,550,994 bales, valued at $71,844,280. In 1880 there were nineteen establishments for cotton-compressing. Prior to 1880 there were but two through railroads. At present there are six trunk lines, constructed in consequence of the completion of the jetties in Mississippi river in 1879, assuring deep water and an ocean terminus at New Orleans. The freight of these for the year ending Aug. 31, 1888, was 2,568,624,551 pounds forwarded, and 2,992,532,335 pounds received. The tonnage of two canals for the year, of 5,978 vessels, was 105,441 tons. There are numerous canals for drainage. The height of ante-bellum prosperity was reached by New Orleans in 1860. Only produce of the lower Mississippi valley was exported. At present the tonnage of the port is greater than ever, and the amount of commerce is much larger. The character of the imports and exports is completely changed. The greatest advance of late years, and the most promising field of the future, lies in coal and iron from Southern districts in course of development; in lumber from Southern forests; in the wool and hide trade of Texas and Mexico; in various Mexican produce; and in wool, fruits, and other products of California and the Pacific coast. The foreign imports include tea, silk, Japan ware, kari gum, Alaskan furs, whale-oil, spermaceti, walrus ivory, cochineal, balsam, orchilla, rubber, jalap, sponges, mohair, etc. The ocean traffic with New York has been extended, and vast additions are made to the usual cargoes of cotton, sugar, molasses, and rice to that port. Raw material is returned manufactured, and large imports are received through New York. The average yearly receipts of wool are 30,000,000 pounds, the immense wool trade of Texas passing through the port; and of hides, upward of 12,000,000 pounds. The trade in tropical fruits of Central and South America, originated a few years ago, has increased with steady growth, and is now the largest single item of foreign importation; 50,000 bunches of bananas were imported in 1880. For the past year 2,500,000 bunches were imported, against 1,421,145 bunches in 1887; and 6,000,000 cocoa-nuts, against 2,449,915 of the year previous. The grain trade with the interior is fluctuating. The total value of domestic produce received by river, lake, and rail for the year ending Aug. 31, 1888, was $168,474,393. By United States Custom-House statement, the imports of foreign goods for 1888 were $11,558,562; exports, $80,698,062; customs receipts, $2,791,984. The foreign exports for the year were $504,808; transshipments to Mexico, $2,085,957; imported commodities entered without appraisement for transportation to interior points, $2,756,858. The number of vessels clearing the port for the year ending July 31 was 1,031, with a tonnage of 1,150,430 tons, and 1,060 vessels entered, of 1,151,715 tons. The number of vessels belonging to the port at same date were 437; gross tonnage, 50,350. The manufactures have largely increased, outstripping the commerce. The capital invested in 1870 was $5,429,140; in 1880, $8,565,303; in 1888, $21,667,670. In 1880 there were 915 establishments, against 2,185 at present; and 4.411 hands were employed, against 23,865 to-day, of whom 6,270 are women. The yearly wages are $8,242,599, slightly less than the entire capital in 1880. The products are valued at $41,508,546. Raw material of all kinds is in close proximity, and transportation to factory and market is cheap. Exemption from taxation and license was secured for ten years by the Constitution of 1879, extended in April last for a similar period. The principal advance has been in the manufacture of boots and shoes, of which there are 226 establishments; in men's clothing, manufacture of jeans having been recently introduced; in foundries and machine-shops, which supply most of the machinery for Southern cotton, rice, and sugar mills; in lumber, malt liquors, artificial ice, and fertilizers; in rice-cleaning and polishing and sugar-refining. Hawaiian sugar is imported for this purpose in addition to Cuban. There are two large refineries and a sugar exchange. The tobacco production has doubled. For 55 establishments in 1830 there are at present 188, and 33,120,667 cigars and 33,888,245 cigarettes were manufactured during the year, while 1,683,638 pounds of manufactured tobacco, 141,916 of perique, and 37,824 of snuffs complete the output. There is also in-

crease in manufacture of cotton goods. Other industries include artificial limbs and flowers, bags, bagging, boxes, bricks, brooms and brushes, canned goods, carriages and wagons, cars, cisterns (a local industry), confectionery, coffins, corks, corsets, cotton-seed oil, china, cordials and sirups, distillation of pine, drugs, dyes, flags, food, furniture, hardware, hairwork, glycerine, hammocks, hosiery, moss, mattresses, mineral waters, perfumeries, pottery, saddles and harness, safes, soap, sails, shot, trunks, tinware, and vinegar. The clearings of 14 banks (8 National, with capital of $2,925,000, and one a United States depositary) for the year ending August 31 were $448,016,066, an increase of $41,447,618 over those of 1887. The balances are $52,970,305. The insurance companies number 16, and there is a State lottery with a capital of $1.000,000. There are 6 street-railroads and 7 daily newspapers, 1 in the French and 1 in the German language. In 1884 the churches, including colored, numbered 171. Public schools were established in 1840. The attendance is large. Among other educational institutions are Tulane University, the Jesuit College, and the Ursuline Convent. There are 17 public parks. Hospitals, asylums, and infirmaries are numerous. Architecture, for which the city was never noted, has recently progressed. Drinking-water is obtained from cisterns, and there are water-works from the river. An artesian well, owned by an ice-factory, yields 150,000 gallons from a depth of 600 feet. The Custom-House, next to the Capitol and Treasury at Washington, is the largest public building in the United States. Two opera-houses (one French) and numerous theatres and clubs provide amusement during the season from January to May. A cotton exposition was held in 1884–'85, toward which Congress appropriated $1,365,000, with $300,000 for exhibit. (See "Annual Cyclopædia" for 1884, page 573.)

Ogden, Weber County, Utah, at the foot-hills of the Wasatch mountains, near Great Salt Lake, at the junction of Weber and Ogden rivers. It has a population of nearly 9,000. It is the center of five leading trunk lines of railroad, receiving (on a basis of the first four months of the year), 19,278,000 pounds of freight, and forwarding 8,268,000 pounds. The revenue to the railroads is $368,386.68. Other roads are building, contracted for by Ogden citizens. It is known as "Junction City." The streets are wide, and there is natural sewerage, with running water on both sides of the sidewalks. Water is supplied by mountain springs and streams. The town is lighted by electricity, and there are street-cars, telephones, etc. The productions of the region include iron, which abounds in brown and purple hematite ores, cost of delivery, $1.50 to $2 a ton; wool; salt, evaporated naturally from the lake; lime, in mountain deposits; building-stone; and coal. Coke is furnished by gas-works. Ogden possesses valuable water-power.

The fall in Ogden cañon is 550 feet in five miles. The motors of an electric-light company, a powder-mill, and several flouring-mills are run by this power. There are, in addition, a woolen-mill, and cigar, knitting, and canning factories. Fine fruit is grown in the surrounding country. The educational and religious advantages are good. The Central School is a handsome building, and there is a fine hotel.

Port Arthur, a city in the province of Ontario, Canada, population 6,000, situated on the west side of Thunder Bay, at the head of Canadian navigation on Lake Superior, and 60 miles west of the Nipigon river. In 1800 it was a terminal point of the Hudson Bay Fur Company, and in 1872 it was named Prince Arthur's Landing in honor of Prince Arthur, then a resident of Canada. It has public and private schools of the highest grade, a court-house, a town-hall, board of trade, registry, port, and inland-revenue offices. It has two banks, brick blocks valued at $300,000, and first-class hotels. There is a fine harbor in which the Government has constructed 2,000 feet of a breakwater at a cost of $150,000, the entire projected length being about a mile. Within the harbor lines are 2,500 yards of docks. It is located on the Canadian Pacific Railway line, and is a terminus for both the eastern and Lake Superior division and the western or prairie division. Its grain-elevators have a capacity of 2,000,000 bushels. In the vicinity are extensive quarries of marble and limestone suitable for building purposes, and inexhaustible quantities of brown and red sandstone, slate, and granite. Silver and gold mines, discovered in 1883, are located forty miles southwest of the town. An unlimited extent of mining land may be purchased from the Crown at $2 per acre. It is the center of exploring and prospecting parties. The mining districts are known as the Beaver and the Silver Mountain, the former employing 48 men. The tunnel of the Silver Mountain mine is 1,400 feet in length, and the shaft is 400 feet deep. The value of real estate in 1887 was $1,250,000. It has steamboat connection with Fort Williams four times a day. Twenty-five miles distant are the Kakabeka Falls on the Kaminiotiquia river, a celebrated resort for tourists. A daily paper, the "Port Arthur Daily Sentinel," is published, and a daily steamboat line runs to Duluth, connecting with the trains of the Canadian Pacific Railway.

Providence, one of the capitals of Rhode Island, at head of Narragansett Bay, 34 miles from the ocean, was founded by Roger Williams in 1636. Seventy years later the population was 1,500. In 1832, when incorporated, it had 18,000 inhabitants; in 1870, 68,904; in 1880, 104,857; in 1887, 122,050. The manufacture of cotton was introduced in 1793, and of woolen goods a few years later. The number of establishments in the State in 1885, of which Providence was the natural headquarters, was: Of cotton, 90, capital $21,-

150,000, product, $21,770,000; of wool, 34, capital $8,560,000, product $18,980,000. Other manufactures are gymnastic apparatus and jewelry which is one of the most extensive industries. There is a large British hosiery mill and colony. Notwithstanding its location, Providence has no foreign commerce. There is a line of steamships to New York and Boston, and the city is the terminus of a Baltimore line of coast steamers connecting at Baltimore and Norfolk with railroad and other steamboat lines. There are local lines to shore resorts, which are numerous. The streets are narrow but remarkably clean. To Sept. 30, 1884, the water-works had cost $6,491,167.60, and the sewerage, $1,685,214. At the same date there were 86 churches; 1 high, 11 grammar, 38 intermediate, and 43 primary schools, costing yearly $252,326; and 14 lines of horse-car railways. Among the public buildings may be mentioned the State-House (built in 1759), the Friends' Meeting-House (in 1727), the Board of Trade (erected as a market in 1773), the First Baptist Church (in 1775), and University Hall (in 1770). The city hall cost $1,500,000. The Narragansett Hotel, completed in 1878, is eight stories high; its cost was $1,000,000. It is of pressed brick, and can accommodate 400 guests. The Masonic Hall, Butler Exchange, Arcade, library, and court-house, are some handsome specimens of modern architecture. The State Prison is at Providence, and there are numerous hospitals and asylums. Roger Williams Park contains 100 acres. The Washington Insurance Company, organized in 1799, has extended its business largely of late years. The new Catholic cathedral and opera-house are fine edifices.

Quincy.—A city of Adams County, Ill. The population in 1880 was 27,268, but there was an increase of 30 per cent. by 1887, and it is believed that the census of 1890 will show 40,000. This is due to an awakening of enterprise on the part of the citizens. Previous to 1885 trade was stagnant, manufactures were depressed, property was low in value, taxes were high, the city was deep in litigation and debt, and everybody was discouraged. "Then some of the patriotic citizens who had hitherto held aloof from local affairs began the work of restoration and redemption. The lawsuits were compromised, the debt was funded, streets were improved, water, gas, and electric lights were provided, and municipal enterprise awakened the people. . . . The citizens began to realize the enormous natural advantages of their situation, and to seek the trade of the million or more people who live within 75 miles of her court-house. Capital appeared from its hiding-places, labor flocked in to take advantage of high wages, manufacturing establishments sprung up like magic, real estate rose in value, extensive building operations began, and everybody prospered." The number and beauty of the public buildings that now grace this town are remarkable—a fact partly due to the stores of excellent brick-clay and architectural stone in the immediate neighborhood. These include a new Federal building, a new city hall, and a new county court-house, all of noble and costly proportions. The State of Illinois has just completed here the erection and installment of a soldiers' home, which occupies spacious ornamental grounds on the edge of the city, and shelters nearly six hundred veterans of the civil war. This home is arranged upon the cottage-plan, squads of forty-five or fifty dwelling in detached houses, but all assembling for meals, for amusement, for public entertainments, Sunday worship, etc., in the large central building. The buildings all differ in materials and design, so that the architectural effect is varied and pleasing. There are a hospital, dairy, railway station, etc. This was the first of the State institutions of this kind; but Iowa, Michigan, and some other States have followed the example. The latest new public building is the handsome public library. This faces the city park, has a frontage of 100 feet and capacity for 100,000 volumes. It was built by popular subscription, and is well supported. Besides the book-shelves, the building contains reading-rooms, study-rooms, etc. Quincy takes great interest in intellectual and literary matters, and supports many reading-circles and literary and self-improvement societies.

Raleigh, the capital of North Carolina, in Wake County, near the center of the State. The population in 1870 was 7,900; in 1880, 9,265; in 1887, 14,000. It is lighted by electricity, has a street-railway, and has contracted for water-works and an improved sewerage system. The mechanical industries are carshops, with capacity of ten cars a day, two clothing-factories, a cotton-seed-oil mill, a manufacturing company to make shuttle-blocks for cotton-mills and grind phosphates, an ice-factory, an iron-foundry, and a shoe-factory, with minor establishments. A good business is done in cotton; from 50,000 to 75,000 bales are handled yearly. Here is a white marble post-office, which cost $355,000, and a new brick school-house, which accommodates 700 pupils. The Capitol building, a massive, domed structure of gray granite, is at the junction of four avenues. The State Penitentiary, costing upward of $1,000,000, for which $75,000 was appropriated yearly for ten years by the Legislature, is a model institution. It contains within stone walls the low log structure first used for penal purposes by the State. One of the State insane asylums, of which there are three (two colored and one white), is on the outskirts; and institutions for the deaf, dumb, and blind are located in or near the city. A fine geological museum is in the Agricultural Department. The attendance on the public schools reaches 2,000 pupils. In addition, there are a Baptist and an Episcopal school for girls, a boys' academy, and other private schools. Wake Forest,

a Baptist College, and the University of North Carolina, at Chapel Hill, are distant a few miles. There are a university, a normal, and a medical school for colored students. The first and last of these are supported by philanthropic donations, and conducted by the Baptist Home Missionary Society. Together they occupy six buildings, on a campus of twelve acres, and have 450 students. The departments are industrial, normal, academic, theological, and legal. Shade-trees of elm, oak, and magnolia and flowering gardens for nine months in the year, are a feature of the city.

Santa Fé, the capital of New Mexico Territory, 20 miles from Rio Grande river, in a basin surrounded by mountains, 7,300 feet above the sea. The population in 1850 was 4,846; in 1888 it was estimated at 7,000. Seventy per cent. are Mexicans. The climate is delightful. The temperature is remarkably even. A sanitarium, with capacity of 640,000 cubic feet, for Eastern invalids, has been established, the only one within the Territory. There is also a hospital for Territorial patients, with air-space capacity of 288,000 cubic feet. The city is very old. In 1541 it was in existence as a "pueblo" of the Indians, and contained 15,000 souls. It became the capital of the Territory after occupation by the Spaniards, the present executive mansion having been erected at this time and known as the "Adobe Palace." It is one story high, with walls five feet thick. It is the only town in New Mexico with competitive railroad lines. Two roads are completed, and seven others projected to pass through, or with the city as objective point. Ten million pounds of wool are shipped yearly. A peculiar herb, "aurole," adapted for washing wool, which imparts a fine, soft gloss, abounds. Agricultural land surrounds the town, of which a large part is owned by the Government, and is subject to entry. There is a land-office. The rain-fall in 1881 was 21 inches, and it has since increased steadily. The county has produced more from mines than perhaps the whole Territory outside. The gold in placers of the Ortiz grant alone, of 60,000 acres, is estimated at from $100,000,000 to $150,000,000. The mine was once worked by 10,000 Spaniards. On expulsion of the latter in 1680, all mines were filled up by the natives, and churches and mining archives destroyed. Their return was permitted in 1705, under promise to discontinue mining forever. Copper, silver, lead, and zinc are also found. There are 20,000 acres of coking, bituminous coal, and 8,000 acres of anthracite. Nearly every religious sect is represented in Santa Fé. The cathedral, when completed, will cost $400,000. The first Protestant church was built in 1855. The oldest church in the United States—that of San Miguel—founded in 1550, was rebuilt in 1710. It is of adobe. The total value of public buildings is $1,250,000. There are three public schools, the University of Mexico (with an Indian department), a Catholic college and orphans' school, a Presbyterian academy, the Ramona School for Indian girls, costing $65,-000, and a Catholic school for Indian boys. A daily newspaper is published, and there are two national banks, capital of each, $150,000. The Capitol, erected at a cost of $200,000, and Territorial Penitentiary, $150,000, are fine buildings. Adobe, or sun-dried earth, unburned, with or without straw, is the leading material for residences. Santa Fé has a planing-mill, a cracker-factory, and a brewery. Pottery is manufactured by the Indians.

Saratoga Springs, a watering-place of New York, 36 miles north of Albany, in Saratoga County, near the center of the State. The resident population is estimated at 12,000. There are upward of 40 mineral springs, with various medicinal properties. The principal are the Vichy, discovered in 1872, by drilling 180 feet. Water is forced to the surface by natural pressure of carbonic-acid gas. It is alkaline, rather than salt. There are a magnetic spring and baths near old High Rock. The Geyser, spouting 25 feet, was discovered in 1870. Others are the Congress and Columbia, in Congress Spring Park; the Hathorn, Empire, High Rock, Excelsior, Star, Champion, Hamilton, Washington, White Sulphur, etc. The tract was owned by Iroquois Indians of the Mohawk tribe, and was a favorite hunting-ground. The value of the springs was known to the Mohawks, Oneidas, Onondagas, Senecas, and Cayugas, who resorted to them. The Saratoga patent was sold to citizens of Albany in 1684. High Rock Spring was first visited by white men in 1767, when a wounded English baronet was restored to health. A settlement was made here in 1773. The present town was founded in 1819, and made a post-office in 1826. There are six mammoth hotels and numerous others, affording accommodations for from 15,000 to 20,000 visitors. The season is from July 10 to September 1. The architecture is varied, and the gardens and grounds extensive and beautiful. The attractions beside the springs are parks, drives, the lake, the race-course, and club-house. The Association for Racing was organized in 1864, and a charter was obtained in 1865. The town has one national bank, with a capital of $125,000 and equal surplus. The town-hall was erected at a cost of $130,000. The New York Central and the Delaware, Lackawanna, and Western are the principal railroads.

Tower, a town in northern Minnesota, incorporated in 1884, is situated in a region of valuable timber-land on the south shore of Lake Vermilion; population 5,000. It is one and one half mile from Tower mines, for which its provision-stores furnish supplies, no general store being located in the mining district, which has a population of over 1,000 men, the majority of them householders. It has five churches, two graded schools, the First National Bank of Tower, capital $50,000, a

cold-storage warehouse capable of keeping two car-loads at the freezing-point, a brick-yard which turns out 20,000 bricks a day, a lumber company, the output of whose mills in 1888 was 10,000,000 logs, large shipments being made to Duluth, Two Harbors, and Ely, and ninety cars being used for the business in one month. There are two saw-mills with a capacity of about 80,000 feet of lumber daily, and a prominent social organization called the Skandinavian Society. Fine brick-clay is found in the vicinity, and east of the town is Burntside Lake, a popular camping-ground. The Minnesota Iron Company, Charlemagne Tower, of Philadelphia, president, employs 1,400 men, and holds 8,000 acres of land, covering the larger portion of the iron deposits in that district, extending to the shores of Lake Vermilion, and including the present site of Tower city and beyond its limits eastward for a distance of 75 miles. The ore is found in two lenses averaging 60 feet wide at an altitude of 1,000 feet above Lake Superior, and 1,600 feet above the ocean-level. The first ore was taken out in 1884, immediately subsequent to the completion of the railroad from Tower to Two Harbors in the spring of that year. The first shipments of ore, amounting to 64,000 tons, were made by railroad July 3, 1884. In 1886 the output reached 304,000 tons, and would make over 150,000 tons of rails, the Minnesota Iron Company contributing one tenth of the entire iron product of the Lake Superior region. The ore is principally celebrated for the small proportion of phosphorus contained in it, on account of which it is sought by manufacturers of Bessemer steel, who pronounce it the purest magnetic ore known. It assays as high as 68 per cent. of metallic iron and ·055 of phosphorus. The veins of ore average from 16 to 160 feet in width, and the ore belt is from 6 to 10 miles wide. This mining region is regarded as virtually one great deposit of iron ore extending through the range of hills overlooking Lake Vermilion. In 1887 the output was over 450,000 tons. There are nine pits each furnished with the latest and most approved appliances for excavating, hoisting, and transferring to the ore cars. The pits bear the names of the promoters of the enterprise. The Stuntz pit is from 20 to 60 feet 40 feet. At a depth of 60 feet the ore was brought through a tunnel to be hoisted to the railroad cars. The Stone pit, one eighth of a mile west of the Stuntz, is worked in three slopes, the width of the deposit varying from 25 to 125 feet, the deepest point below the surface being 100 feet. The mine cars are hoisted directly from this pit by powerful drums. The Ely pit, directly west of the Stone and adjoining it, when opened for a distance of 200 feet, showed a vein of good ore at the second level 129 feet wide. It is now 400 feet long, 50 feet deep, and from 20 to 120 feet in width. In the vicinity are two air-compressors for working powder-drills, two engines and drums for hoisting purposes, and electric-light machinery consisting of 2 dynamos of 20 lights each, lighting pits, trestles, and docks. Two gangs of miners are worked, one by night and one by day, throughout the year. The number of men employed in the pits is about 1,100; the wages each month amount to about $55,000. Tower pit No. 1 at a depth of 100 feet when opened for a distance of 250 feet on the length of vein showed good ore at one point over 155 feet in width. The ore of Tower pit No. 2 showed clean for 400 feet, with an average width of 100 feet in ore. The shaft in this deposit is 60 feet deep, the ore being taken through a tunnel from the bottom of the shaft to the railroad cars by an endless rope attached to 9 cars with a capacity of 2 tons each. The Breitung pit, where a diamond-drill is in operation, lies south of the Tower, and is from 10 to 40 feet wide by 100 feet long and 50 feet deep. The North Lee has been opened 200 feet in length by 50 feet in depth, and from 30 to 40 feet in width, a shaft having been sunk 50 feet below the bottom from which drifts are being run. The South Lee shows a vein 20 feet wide exposed for about 100 feet in length. The pits of this company are all comprised in the length of one mile. The ore bed is blasted with dynamite cartridges containing about 50 per cent. of nitro-glycerine, the blasts being discharged every six hours. The product of these mines, 4,000 tons of ore daily, is shipped to steel-works in Pittsburg and Chicago, and supplies furnaces in Duluth, Buffalo, Troy, Toledo, Ashtabula, Cleveland, Erie, Scranton, and other cities. The Minnesota Iron Company have expended in the building and equipment of the railroad and ore docks, and in the development of the mines not less than $4,000,000. New receiving ore docks have been built by the company in Cleveland the present year (1888), bringing the ore into direct competition with foreign ores. An immense body of iron ore of a high grade has been discovered this year in section 19, by the Minnesota Exploration Company. Four miles from Tower is the Union mine, the property of which extends along the range for the distance of about a mile. The post-office of Tower mines is called Soudan. Tower is connected with Two Harbors by a railroad 68 miles in length, constructed in 1884, and extended to Duluth in 1887, connecting the mines with the capital of the State by rail via that city. The Duluth and Iron Range Railroad is equipped with upward of 350 double eight-wheel ore cars with a capacity of 24 gross tons each—the Minnesota Iron Company alone getting out the present year 180 cars of ore daily—and 17 large consolidated locomotives, which haul from 450 to 500 tons to a train. The railroad passes through spruce and tamarack swamps to Two Harbors and through miles of otherwise unbroken wilderness. The substructure across the swamps where it was said a railroad never could be built is a cordu-

roy three feet thick, supporting stone ballast over which from 2,000 to 3,000 gross tons of ore are transported daily during the shipping season. In the stock piles nine cubic feet of ore will weigh one gross ton. The grades are very steep, and over $100,000 is to be expended in lowering them. This will admit of an increase in the length of the ore-trains. Nearly half a million tons of ore have been shipped over the road the present season. From Two Harbors to Duluth, Minn., the line passes along the shore of Lake Superior, opening up a region of several thousand square miles abounding in wealth. It is estimated that there are 1,500,000,000 feet of pine lumber in the vicinity which can be easily reached. A popular division of the railroad is the Lester Park Short Line. Lake Vermilion, on which the town lies, is 35 miles in length, and contains 371 islands. Its shores are irregular, and bordered with a forest of pines alternating with hills covered with verdure and wild flowers which overlook the Tower mines and the adjoining town. From Jasper's Peak there is a fine view of the Indian reservation on an island in the most picturesque portion of the lake, which the inhabitants still navigate in birch-bark canoes, sometimes formed of one piece of bark weighing 25 pounds. It abounds with fish, and in the woods on its banks are large and small game. A little steamer takes pleasure parties across its waters, which at sunset are of the color of vermilion.

A range of hills, bordering the southern shore of the lake, embraces some of the richest and most extensive deposits of iron ore in the world, discovered in 1880 by George C. Stone, of Duluth, Minn., and scientifically explored by Prof. Chester, of Hamilton College, the work of collecting the specimens employing two summers, and that of examination one winter.

Two Harbors, a town in northern Minnesota, on the shores of Agate Bay, 27 miles north of Duluth, population about 400. It is a popular pleasure-resort, has first-class hotels, a brick machine-shop, car-shop, foundry, round-house for locomotives, and an ore pier extending 600 feet into the bay, provided with 130 pockets, each with a capacity of 110 tons, making the dock-storage 14,300 tons. The docks of the Duluth and Iron Range Railroad received, in 1888, 30,000 tons of coal. The first cargo of iron ore from the Tower mines was shipped from the ore docks on Aug. 19, 1884, the shipments amounting that year to 62,124 tons. In 1885 the shipments reached 225,484 tons; in 1886, 300,000 tons; in 1887, 400,000 tons. In 1888, for the season to August 20, the shipments of iron ore were 185,000 tons as against 191,000 tons for 1887 to that date, and 185,000 tons for 1886 to the same day. Four acres of dock property are owned by the Elys to be used for shipping granite. An appropriation of $10,000 has been made by the Government for a light-house. The town has a building association and has had a rapid growth. A steamboat runs daily to Duluth, and a large fleet of vessels is employed during the season along the lake-shore in trade or in pleasure excursions to that city, to Isle Royale, celebrated for its brook-trout fishing, and to the Apostle Islands. Within two miles of the town valuable copper mines are in process of development. It is proposed to inclose the bay by means of two breakwaters, one of which is partly finished, four hundred feet of it having been built at a cost of $20,683; the entire cost is estimated at $77,500. The bay is of vast importance to the iron interest, as the port is the place of shipment of ore from the great Vermilion mines at Tower and Ely. In 1886 an appropriation of $22,500 was made by the Government for its improvement.

Vancouver, a seaport of recent origin on the coast of the mainland of British Columbia. It stands upon a gentle slope bordering English Bay and Coal Harbor, near the entrance of Burrard Inlet, an arm of the sea deeply indenting the mountainous coast, and furnishing safe anchorage for vessels of the deepest draught. The shore was covered with forests of trees, whose average height exceeded 200 feet, until 1885, when it was definitely settled that here should be built the terminus of the Canadian Pacific Railway. A town was then surveyed, systematic clearing began, and a settlement sprang up with great rapidity, anticipating the railway. A year later fire swept away the town, which has been rebuilt in a much more substantial manner, most of the business center being of brick or stone and exhibiting many fine structures. The terminal facilities of the railway and connecting steamship lines are extensive and complete, and the commerce is very large. A line of steamers plies between here and Yokohama and Hong-kong, under the flag of the Canadian Pacific Steamship Company, at intervals of about three weeks; and coast lines of steamers run daily to Victoria and the Puget Sound ports, and less frequently to San Francisco and Sitka. There is a large foreign trade by sailing-vessels, also, in lumber, squared timber, and merchandise, while the fishing interest is becoming profitable. An important jobbing and wholesale trade is carried on with interior towns and northerly coast-points; and the manufacture of spars and ship-timber, from the gigantic Douglas fir of the region, together with lumber and dressed articles, such as doors, sash, blinds, and cabinet-stuff, employs hundreds of workmen. All this has come into existence since the last census, and no precise figures are available. The town is now a city in organization and appearance. Its population approaches 6,000, and includes many persons of wealth, whose homes are costly and filled with modern appointments. A magnificent hotel is operated by the railway company, and the many opportunities for enjoyment and sport, the mild climate and wonderfully picturesque surroundings, attract tourists and sportsmen. The city is lighted by gas and electricity, has public water-works, a uniformed police, and a paid fire department, hospitals, and public schools.

Victoria, a seaport at the southern extremity of Vancouver Island. It is the capital and largest city of British Columbia. It began forty years ago as a trading-station and *entrepôt* of the Hudson Bay Company. When the gold discoveries upon the upper Fraser river caused a rush to British Columbia, in 1858-'62, Victoria suddenly attained a population of 30,000, and it passed through a feverish season of business and inflated property-valuation. With the decline of the gold excitement this dwindled, but under the recent development of the province, due to the completion of the Canadian Pacific Railway and the growth of Alaska on the one hand, and the neighboring region around Puget Sound on the other, Victoria has advanced to a present population of 12,000. It has a beautiful site, and its mild climate is healthful, closely resembling that of the Devonshire coast of England. Beaconhill Park, overlooking the Straits of Fuca and the Olympic mountains, the beautiful grounds of Government House, and many fine suburban drives, make the place one of the most interesting in Canada. Three miles westward is the harbor and naval station of Esquimault (pronounced Es-kwi-malt), which is the rendezvous of the British Pacific squadron. Here has just been completed a graving-dock costing $450,000. Here and at Victoria English people and manners predominate, and the atmosphere of the place is in marked contrast to that of the American Pacific coast towns. Victoria has an immense shipping interest, and does a large business in naval supplies, general merchandise, coal, timber, and fish. The transpacific steamships from Vancouver to China and Japan touch here. A regular line plies weekly between Victoria and San Francisco, and fortnightly to Alaska. Daily steamers run to Vancouver, New Westminster, and the ports on Puget Sound. A railway runs thence up the eastern coast of the island to Nanaimo, where vast deposits of coal are mined, and agricultural and forest products are made available in large quantities. Victoria is growing steadily, and replacing the earlier structures with handsome and commodious business blocks. Banking, postal, and telegraphic facilities are of the best order. In addition to public schools, there are several private academies, and churches of every denomination. The Chinese, among whom are many wealthy merchants and contractors, form a large element in the population, but have not yet aroused that antagonism which meets them in the United States.

Winnipeg, the capital of Manitoba and commercial center of western Canada. It has a population of 30,000, and an assessment value of $40,000,000. This city stands in the center of vast prairies, on the bank of Red river, at the mouth of the Assiniboine, its principal tributary from the west. Both these streams are navigable by steamboats, though this method of transportation has been almost entirely superseded by railroads. Before 1870 the place was hardly more than a fortified post of the Hudson Bay Company, known as Fort Garry, the center of a small farming and hunting community of people, mostly half-breeds, called the Red River Colony. An insurrection among these led to the dispatch of an army thither, which made its way through the wilderness from Fort William, on Lake Superior, and subdued the malcontents. This was in 1870. The exploration and advertisement of the value of the region led to emigration there immediately afterward, and the people soon demanded railroad connection with the east. In 1879 a road was completed up the Red river, to connect with a line to St. Paul; and in 1883 the Government line, now incorporated with the Canadian Pacific, was opened between Winnipeg and Port Arthur, on Thunder Bay, the nearest harbor on the north shore of Lake Superior. Under this impetus, and because of a great influx of settlers upon the free prairies of Manitoba and westward, the city grew with extraordinary rapidity, and public and private enterprises were undertaken upon an immense scale. A second railroad to the United States was built, several local lines were constructed, and the Canadian Pacific pushed westward, reaching and crossing the Rocky mountains in 1885. Then came a succession of bad crops, a second insurrection of the half-breeds of the Northwest Territories, and a consequent cessation of immigration. Under this stress, Winnipeg's inflated prosperity collapsed, and a time of great discouragement and hardship ensued. From this it has now recovered, and business, re-established on a firmer foundation, is steadily advancing. "Notwithstanding all you have been told about it, you can hardly be prepared to find the frontier trading-post of yesterday transformed into a city of 30,000 inhabitants, with miles of imposing structures, hotels, stores, banks, and theatres, with beautiful churches, schools, and colleges, with tasteful and even splendid residences, with immense mills and many manufactories, with a far-reaching trade, and with all the evidences of wealth, comfort, and cultivation to be found in cities of a century's growth. . . . Situated just where the forests end and the vast prairies begin, with thousands of miles of river [boat] navigation to the north, south, and west, and with railways radiating in every direction, Winnipeg has become the commercial focus of the Canadian Northwest. . . . From there the wants of the people in the West are supplied, and this way come the products of their fields, while from the far north are brought furs in great variety." The buildings of the Provincial Government are commodious, but have little architectural pretension. They stand upon the bank of the Assiniboine, and are surrounded by growing trees. Opposite Winnipeg is the suburb St. Boniface, the seat of a Roman Catholic archbishop, where are convents, academies, and a theological school. The climate in Winnipeg is much like that of Minnesota, though rather more severe in winter. It is, however, healthful for most persons, and its winter rigors do not interfere with either business or pleasure.

COLOMBIA, an independent republic of South America. (For details relating to area, population, etc., see "Annual Cyclopædia" for 1886 and 1887.)

Government.—The President is Dr. Rafael Nuñez, whose term of office will expire on Aug. 6, 1892. His Cabinet is formed of the following ministers: Of Government, Don Domingo Ospina Camacho; Foreign Affairs, Don Vicente Restrepo; Finance, Don Felipe Paul; War, Gen. Antonio B. Cuervo; Education, Don Jesus Casas Rojas; Treasury, Don Cárlos Martinez Silva; Public Works, Gen. Rafael Reyes. The office of Vice-President has been abolished for the term of the present administration, and Gen. Eliseo Payan put on the retired list and pensioned.

The United States Minister at Bogotá is Dabney H. Maury, and the Colombian Minister at Washington is Don José Marcelino Hurtado. The Colombian Consul at New York is Don Climaco Calderon. The American Consul-General at Bogotá is John G. Walker; the Consul at Carthagena, William B. McMaster; at Colon-Aspinwall, Victor Vifquain; at Medellin, William Gordon; and the Consul-General at Panama, Thomas Adamson.

Finance.—The statement submitted to Congress for the fiscal year 1888 by the Minister of Finance shows that to the external debt of £1,913,000, mostly held in England, there has to be added £806,000 accumulated interest. The internal funded debt amounts to $5,087,000, while the floating debt, which consists of numerous commitments to railway and other enterprises, amounts to $24,568,000. The total internal debt reaches, therefore, the sum of $29,605,000. In addition, there is an issue of inconvertible paper money amounting to $10,130,000. The revenue for the ensuing fiscal year is estimated at $18,173,700, and the expenditure at $23,852,800, showing a deficit of $5,679,100.

The gross amount of duties collected at the Colombian custom-houses in 1887 was $4,795,263, the expenses were $300,951, leaving the treasury $4,494,312 net proceeds. The custom-house at Barranquilla collected $3,098,000; that at Carthagena, $906,000; Cúenta, $327,000; Buenaventura, $263,000, and Tumaco, $75,000; none of the other custom-houses collected over $50,000. By decree of June 13, the duties to be collected at Cúcuta, in the interior, on imports has been fixed at 25 per cent. to date from August 14.

Army.—The strength of the Federal army on a peace footing, for 1889 and 1890, has been fixed at 5,500 men, with their officers; in war-time the States are bound to furnish a contingent of one per cent. of the population.

Commerce.—The following tabular statement shows Colombian trade with some of the leading commercial countries:

EXPORTS.

YEAR.	United States.	England.	France.
1881	$5,991,890	$6,677,505	$5,016,006
1882	4,961,470	5,452,281	5,893,696
1883	5,171,455	3,509,798	4,188,836
1884	3,591,843	2,108,588	4,238,606
1885	2,342,077	1,154,042	3,491,071

IMPORTS.

YEAR.	United States.	England.	France.
1881	$5,389,138	$5,909,776	$6,214,345
1882	6,408,346	5,296,660	5,959,346
1883	6,868,971	6,099,414	5,954,352
1884	6,381,821	5,944,571	7,169,408
1885	5,589,369	3,881,964	6,067,603

The United States' trade with Colombia in two years has been:

FISCAL YEAR.	Import.	Domestic export to Colombia.
1887	$3,950,958	$5,978,965
1888	4,393,258	4,923,259

Railroads.—At the annual election of directors of the Panama Railroad Company, held in New York on March 26, the president, J. G. McCullough, resigned, and his successor, Gen. John Newton, was installed. The former remarked on the occasion: "The road was bought in 1881 at $290 net per share. Dividends as high as 10, 12, 16, 20, and 24 per cent. on the capital stock of $7,000,000 have been paid. For the past year a little less than 9 per cent. was earned, and 6 per cent. was paid in January, leaving $660,000 in the treasury. The company to-day has no floating debt, and there is not a suit against it pending in the United States. The physical condition of the property is about perfect. Since the riots and fires of 1885 the stations have been rebuilt of corrugated iron, and the equipment of rolling-stock is ample."

In March a railroad company, limited, was incorporated in London with a share capital of £172,000 for the purpose of purchasing and operating the El Dorado-Honda Railroad.

In May a Franco-Belgian company was formed with a capital of 2,500,000 francs, 2,400,000 francs paid in, for the purpose of obtaining concessions for railways in Colombia, and building and operating them.

Simultaneously the National Government of Colombia approved the contract entered into by the State of Antioquia with O. S. Brown for the continuation and completion of the railroad between Puerto Barrio and Medellin, the capital necessary being $6,000,000.

Steamer Lines.—Negotiations have been opened between the Government of the State of Panama and the Pacific Steam Navigation Company for the extension of its line to the northern sections of Panama by the establishment of a tri-monthly service of light-draught steamers to run between Panama and Puerto Pedregal, in the province of Chiriqui, and the port of Sona, in the province of Veragua, a subsidy to be paid the company of $700 for each round trip.

In April the steamer "Flamborough" left Colon for Kingston, Jamaica, being the pioneer ship of a new line between Colon, Jamaica, and Hayti.

In August it transpired that the West India Lloyd Steamship Company had given orders to build six steamers for the purpose of more rapidly transporting tropical fruits to New York and England. To this end, two of the steamers will ply between New Orleans and Savanilla, touching at intermediate ports and connecting at Trujillo with two other vessels of the line, which will run between New York and Livingston, Guatemala, Nassau, Jamaica, Trujillo, and the Island of Inagua, the nearest of the West Indian Islands to New York and Great Britain. The two largest and finest steamers will ply between London and Colon, touching at Plymouth, the Azores, and Jamaica, and connecting with the New York steamers at Inagua.

Telegraphs.—On February 15 Bogotá was united with Quito, the capital of Ecuador, by telegraph, and in June with Carthagena; at the same time telegraphic communication was established between Panama, Barranquilla, Carthagena, and Santa Marta, and a telephone company was making arrangements for establishing communication by telephone between Panama and Colon.

In October the Panama Railroad Company was authorized by the Government to send public messages over the wires of its line between Panama and Colon till the Government shall have constructed its own line.

Wagon-Road.—In May the government of the State of Bolivar opened the wagon-road from Tolú to Sincelejo. This road was built to bring the rich region of Sábanas, Bolivar, in closer communication with the coast.

Mineral Resources.—Colombia contains numerous gold and silver bearing zones, and iron and copper, lead, zinc, antimony, arsenic, and cinnabar are to be found among the metals, while salt-beds abound, and sulphur, kaolin, and fire-clay are to be found. Cundinamarca and Boyacá are comparatively poor in gold and silver bearing lands if we except the Ariari and Guguaqui gold-beds, the silver-bearing copper-lodes of Tosca, the gold veins of Villa de Leiva and Loatá, and the gold washings in the beds of the Guataque and Cocuy. In the eastern ridge of the Cordillera, which separates Pamplona from Bucaramanga and covering a space of over fifty kilometres, the primitive formations are interspersed by gold and silver bearing ledges. Under the Spanish rule these reefs were worked. The wealth obtained from them is a matter of history, while a visit to-day to those localities affords proof of the vast amount of labor that was expended to cut mountain - tunnels yet to be seen, some of which are from 50 to 500 metres in length. These main tunnels, opened in former days, measure about ten kilometres, and when one remembers that the rock cut through is granite and that the means of working were of a most primitive nature, it becomes evident that only rich returns would repay the labor required to overcome such obstacles. At Baya and Vetas thin quartz lodes are found. Here the richest leads are situated either horizontally or perpendicularly, a fact with which the old miners were well acquainted, as is proved by the manner in which they followed the lodes. These Baya and Vetas mines, or "Pamplona" mines, were abandoned after the declaration of independence, and although we know from periodical inspection that they contain great wealth, they are not worked any more than are the numerous reefs that are everywhere observable, which have never yet been touched by the miner's pick. In this region there is the old Santa Catalina mine, which was worked by an English company up to 1850 and abandoned as unprofitable simply because the process of amalgamation was defective, and not from the absence of good metal. The company had also at that time to contend against the decree that was issued prohibiting the exportation of the precious metals. At no great distance from Baya and Vetas rich gold washings have been formed by volcanic action and the wear and tear of ages and climatic influences on the sides of the mountains. Here the gold is found in a *detritus* composed of quartz, gneiss, mica, and iron; and from the beds of the Ematá and Giron, which wash through this formation, gold has been found for centuries. In the Bucaramanga gold washings the precious metal is found principally in scale and seldom as dust or nuggets, and it is owing to miners not having noted this fact that they have lost through defective apparatus the gold that otherwise would have well repaid them for their labors. The gold-washing machinery of to-day would save every grain that was then lost. Its quality is the best known, showing only ·02 of silver to ·98 pure gold. There are furthermore the Goajira and Rio Hacha alluvial deposits, the Tiqui quartz reefs, and the Porcé Sinú, San Jorge, and Uré sands. The reason of the failure of the Sinú company is clearly explained by the fact that the apparatus was inappropriate for working the kind of gold-ore that is found there. In Antioquia the Porcé and Neelin rivers may be mentioned as rich in gold for a distance extending over twenty-three leagues in length by fifteen leagues in breadth, and here a cubic metre of earth has produced one pound in weight of gold, while at Dos Bocas on one occasion one pound in weight of gold was obtained from only fifteen pounds of sand.

VOL. XXVIII.—12 A

The Panama Canal.—Two important events have occurred in the history of the Panama Canal since the last annual meeting was held in Paris on July 21, 1887—-the change of the canal from one at the sea-level to one with locks, and the issuing of a loan. M. Ferdinand de Lesseps, president of the canal company, and the board of managers during the latter part of 1887 came to the conclusion that a total change of system had become imperative, if the canal was to be dug within a reasonable time, thereby keeping the expense of accomplishing the work within certain limits. A contract was consequently made on Dec. 10, 1887, with M. Gustave Eiffel, an engineer of note, constructor of the gigantic tower for the Paris Exhibition of 1889, who undertook to construct such locks as the company would approve, on his submission of plans, with their working machinery, and to do such excavation and like work as may be necessary for the work of construction. It was expected that ten locks would be required; still the company reserved the right to postpone its decision as to the number of locks till April, 1889, allowing to M. Eiffel an extension of time for the completion of the two upper locks if the decision thereupon be not announced by Jan. 1, 1889. M. Eiffel engages to finish all the work stipulated for by June 30, 1890. His contract does not include the control of the Chagres river, nor any part of the canal work not immediately connected with the building of the locks and their operation when completed. Allowances of 33,200,000 francs were made M. Eiffel to enable him to get into a position to build the first four locks, 6,000,000 francs, however, being applicable to the second four. An extraordinary meeting of shareholders was held at Paris in March, and on this occasion M. de Lesseps said : "The direction of the canal with locks does not differ from the direction of the sea-level canal. This canal will have, in all its length, in each lock the same width and depth of water as the final canal. The largest vessels—those 150 metres long, and having a draught of 8 metres—will be able to pass in 1890 from one ocean to another. All our efforts are concentrated on the necessity of opening the canal for universal navigation with the greatest rapidity by absolutely sure means. After the inauguration, the yield of the transit taxes alone being 125,218,750 francs and all the expenses 103,926,260 francs, there will be a margin in round numbers of 21,000,000 francs to be distributed among the shareholders after deducting the reserve funds and the tenure to the Colombian Government." Over 1,000 shareholders were in attendance at the meeting ; M. de Lesseps's report was unanimously approved, together with the resolution to make a loan of 340,000,000 francs. The report estimated the amount requisite for finishing the canal at 654,000,000 francs, 254,000,000 being necessary to pay for excavation, 125,000,000 for locks and masonry,

15,000,000 for reservoirs for the feeding of the upper portion of the canal, 50,000,000 for material, and 210,000,000 for the covering of general expenses and the interest on bonds and shares. The French Chamber of Deputies passed the Panama Canal Lottery Loan Bill without Government guarantee early in May, and the Senate in June. The bill provided for the issue of 600,000,000 francs in bonds, the numbers to be drawn after the manner of a lottery twice a year, and the winners to receive premiums of various amounts. It also provided 20 per cent., or 120,000,000 francs, to be set aside in French *rentes* for the payment of prizes, and to serve as a sinking-fund. On June 27, 360,000,000 francs, being half the amount authorized, were offered for subscription with a lottery scheme including three annual prizes of 500,000 francs each, and three of 250,000 francs; furthermore six of 100,000 francs, there being six drawings per annum, distributing altogether 3,390,000 francs yearly till the year 1913, beginning with which 2,200,000 francs per annum will be drawn for in four drawings and embracing two prizes of 500,000 francs each, two of 250,000 and four of 100,000, the minor lots ranging between 1,000 and 10,000 francs. Bonds were issued having a face value of 400 francs, payable by lots or at 400 francs within 99 years by a special deposit of French *rentes*, and offered at 360 francs, bearing 15 francs per annum interest. Out of the 2,000,000 bonds offered, 860,000 were sold. At the first drawing the large prizes were taken by bonds that had not been sold, to the great disappointment of subscribers, the company therefore decided that at the October drawing all the prizes should be given to the 860,000 bonds that had been sold; it was compelled to take this course by the dissatisfaction of the bond-holders.

At the time of making the contract with M. Eiffel, the plan of eight locks was adopted. On their departure from the Atlantic Ocean the vessels would at first encounter two locks of 8 metres fall each, subsequently two of 11 metres each, the length of the lock-chambers being 180 metres. Hence the altitude overcome would be 38 metres. The difference between the .latter and the total height of the mountain-range was to be overcome by excavations. On the west side three locks of 11 metres fall were to be built and one of 8 metres fall. The difference of 3 metres is necessary on account of the lower level of the Pacific Ocean at low tide. Subsequently, in May, it was deemed advisable to modify the plan by building ten locks instead of the eight alluded to, lock 1 to be located at Bohio Soldado; 2, at San Pablo; 3, at Matachin; 4, at Obispo; 5, at Emperador—all on the Atlantic side; 6, at Cucaracha; 7 and 8, at Paraiso; 9, at Pedro Miguel; and 10, at Miraflores—all on the Pacific side. There are to be three locks of 11 metres fall, and two locks of 8 metres fall on each end of the canal—that is, on the Atlantic and Pacific sides of the center of the canal.

The canal, through its entire length, is to have the same depth as the eventual sea-level canal, but through the adoption of the canal with locks, the excavation yet to be done is limited to from 34,000,000 to 40,000,000 cubic metres. But the construction of the locks alone will not suffice; the main point is the feeding of those works. For the latter purpose embankments have to be made in connection with the rivers Chagres, Obispo, and Rio Grande, the former of which alone is capable of furnishing per second 10 cubic metres of water, which it is estimated would suffice for the passage through the locks of ten vessels, of a joint tonnage of 20,000, per diem. The total amount of excavation actually accomplished in 1886 had been 11,727,000 cubic metres; during the first nine months of 1887 it was 9,877,000.

In August 250,000 hectares of land in Colombia were transferred to the canal company under the contract made by the company with the Government. Nathan Appleton, who was sent by the United States Government as a delegate to the international congress held in Paris, in 1879, to decide as to the route that should be adopted, and has been connected with the enterprise from its beginning, being asked his opinion about the change of plan, said the adoption of the lock system was the only thing that remained to assure success.

The Panama Canal Company, late in November, resolved to offer for public subscription on December 10 the 1,140,000 unsold lottery bonds; but the shares declined so rapidly that it became evident the subscription would result in failure. M. de Lesseps and his colleagues resigned, and at their request the Tribunal of the Seine appointed Messrs. Hue, Bandelot, and De Normandie to settle the company's affairs. On December 6 the company's shares had dropped to 175, and on December 17 they fell to 93·75 francs, recovering 12 francs next day.

Ice Monoply at Panama.—On March 1 the sole right to manufacture, import, and sell ice in the Department of Panama was sold at Bogotá, at the Ministry of the Treasury, the buyers to pay $45.000 a year in advance for the privilege, in silver coin of 0·835 fineness. The exclusive privilege thus granted runs fifteen years, but work must begin in ten months. At the expiration of the concession the manufactories will become Government property.

Registration of Companies.—The following law was signed by President Nuñez on May 25:

ARTICLE I. All firms or companies formed outside of Colombia, which carry on a permanent business within its territory, shall register their deeds of partnership or charters in the notary's office of the district where they intend doing business.

ART. II. Such companies or firms will not be considered to have been legally established, nor will they be able to claim the protection of the law, if they have not previously been duly legalized by the Executive. For this reason those companies or firms will be considered to have been dissolved which, up to the present date, have not been legalized in the manner herein provided or do not obtain such legalization within six months from date.

ART. III. All firms and companies shall have a duly legalized representative, with a fixed place of abode.

ART. IV. Should any company not appoint a representative, then the President of the republic will appoint some one to represent the company, and such nominee will enjoy the rights and privileges appertaining to the place when filled by any one appointed by the firm or company.

ART. V. The present law in no way affects the Panama Interoceanic Canal Company, which will continue to be ruled solely by the existing treaties and contracts.

Foreign Relations.—The message of President Nuñez, delivered at the opening of Congress on July 20, said: "An extradition treaty has been signed with the United States; it had been rendered necessary by the exceptional state of affairs that now exists on the Isthmus of Panama in consequence of the extraordinary influx of foreigners to the Isthmus. The Cerruti question was submitted to arbitration, and was decided by the Government of Spain, which will also decide on the boundary question now pending with Venezuela. Until that decision is reached, Venezuela and Colombia will respect the *status quo* which has existed up to date. The boundary question with Costa Rica will also be decided by Spain, and thus a possible conflict between the two countries prevented. On Sept. 7, 1887, the Government declared its intention to abrogate clauses 10, 11, and 23 of the commercial treaty with Ecuador, the abrogation to take effect July 7, 1888, when those clauses providing for mutual concessions to imported produce of the two countries will become void."

The Extradition Treaty.—The extradition treaty referred to in President Nuñez's message was signed in Bogotá May 7 last by Señor Vicente Restrepo, Minister of Foreign Affairs of Colombia, and John G. Walker, *Chargé d'Affaires* of the United States, and received the sanction of the National Legislative Council on May 25.

which is stipulated in the request for his extradition. Article VII provides that if the accused is not proved guilty within three months he shall be set at liberty. Article X says that neither of the contracting parties undertakes to hand over its own citizens for trial by the other. By Article XI the fact that the accused may be liable to other charges shall not be held to debar him from extradition. One year's notice of the annulment of the convention must be given.

COLORADO. State Government.—The following were the State officers during the year: Governor, Alva Adams, Democrat; Lieutenant-Governor, Norman H. Meldrum, Republican; Secretary of State, James Rice, Republican; Treasurer, Peter W. Breene, Republican; Auditor, Darwin P. Kingsley, Republican; Attorney-General, Alvin Marsh, Republican; Superintendent of Public Instruction, Leonidas S. Cornell, Republican; Railroad Commissioner, A. D. Wilson; Chief-Justice of the Supreme Court, William E. Beck; Associate Justices, Joseph C. Helm and S. H. Elbert, who resigned in August. Gov. Adams appointed M. B. Gerry to hold the place made vacant by Judge Elbert until a successor should be elected in November, when Victor A. Elliot was chosen. At the same election Charles D. Hayt was chosen to succeed Chief-Justice Beck at the close of his term.

Population.—By the census of 1880 the number of people in the State was 194,327; in 1885 there were, according to the State census of that year, 243,910 people. Upon the basis of the school census of this year, it is estimated that there were 850,000 people in the State at the date of the census in April.

Education.—The following statistics, compiled by the Superintendent of Education, indicate the growth of the public schools during the past two years:

ITEMS.	1887.	1888.	Increase.
Number of districts...............................	779	990	211
Total school population...........................	65,216	76,212	11,229
Enrolled in high-school's..........................	1,180	1,158	23
Enrolled in graded schools........................	24,471	27,986	3,515
Enrolled in ungraded schools......................	17,800	21,606	4,806
Enrolled in public schools........................	42,901	50,745	7,844
Average daily attendance..........................	27,147	31,516	4,369
Number of school-houses..........................	686	820	184
Value of property................................	$2,492,701	$3,286,021	$745,820
Expended for buildings, sites, and furniture......	$193,287 89	$306,771 16	$118,483 27
Total expenditures...............................	$565,025 76	$1,152,411 78	$287,388 02
Expenditure per capita of school population.......	$13 26	$15 12	$1 96
Expenditure per capita of enrollment.............	$20 16	$22 71	$2 75

It provides for the extradition of persons accused of murder or attempt at murder, of counterfeiting, forgery, fraudulent disposal of public funds, robbery, burglary, where attended with violent entry of a public or private place, perjury or subornation of perjury, rape, arson, piracy, the destruction of railroads, tramways, or any construction the injury of which would involve danger to life. Article V provides that no one accused of political crimes shall be handed over on any other charge than that

The Capitol.—The Legislature of 1885 passed an act providing for the erection of a State capitol building at Denver, and creating a board of capitol managers to superintend the work. A contract was made by the board for constructing the foundation, and in July the work under this contract was substantially completed. Preparations were made during the latter part of the year for beginning the superstructure, which is to be largely of sandstone from quarries at Gunnison.

Railroads.—The following statistics show the mileage of railroads in the State in November:

	Miles.
Denver and Rio Grande	1,487
Union Pacific	1,272
Atchison, Topeka, and Santa Fé	471
Burlington and Missouri	345
Colorado Midland	250
Missouri Pacific	175
Denver, Texas, and Gulf	147
Denver, Utah, and Pacific	65
Denver and Santa Fé	6
Chicago, Rock Island, and Pacific (estimated)	250
Total	4,513

The Denver, Texas, and Gulf Road to Fort Worth, Tex., was completed early in the year, giving direct communication from Denver to the Gulf of Mexico. If the Federal Government can be induced to construct a suitable harbor on the coast, this line will prove of great value in the development of Colorado. Another road, completed later in the year, was the Rock Island and Pacific, to Colorado Springs. Various branch lines were also in process of construction.

Stock-Raising.—In Colorado, as in other parts of the Western plains, the cattle industry is gradually changing in character and methods. A Colorado journal says: "The plains in the eastern part of the State which, less than a dozen years ago, were covered with cattle, are being rapidly settled and only the poorest range is left. A striking illustration of this fact is found in Pueblo County. The range cattle are being shipped out of that section of the country, some to the ranges in the western part of the State and some east to Kansas and Nebraska. It is only a question of time when the ranges in the western part of the State will be settled also, and the herds compelled to move again. But it will only be changing the business from the control of a few into the control of many. There are large portions of the mountainous parts of the State that will be utilized as ranges, but they will accommodate a comparatively small number of cattle. The system will be entirely changed, and while the altitude in many parts of the State will prevent the raising of corn in such abundance as in Kansas and Nebraska, other fodder can be raised in as great abundance and so much cheaper that Colorado cattle-raisers can compete with those of any other portion of the country. That this can be done in Eagle County has been demonstrated, and land which, a few years ago, was deemed worthless for farming, because of the altitude, is now yielding large profits."

The Utes.—The people of the State have long desired to rid themselves of the presence of these Indians, who have several times threatened the public safety. By an early treaty with the United States, they were separated into three reservations, known as the White River, Uncompaghre, and Southern Ute reservations. In 1879, when the Meeker massacre occurred, the Government made a new treaty, which resulted in the removal of the White River and Uncompaghre Utes to the Uintah Reservation in Utah. But the refusal of Colorow and his band to remain in Uintah, and their annual return to Colorado for fishing and hunting, finally led to trouble with his band last year, when they were driven back to Utah by the Colorado State troops.

As a consequence of this disturbance, and through the efforts of Colorado citizens, a bill was passed by Congress this year, providing for a commission to treat with the Southern Utes, the only remaining band in the State, and to procure their removal to southern Utah. The commissioners appointed in July under this act were T. C. Childs, of Washington, R. B. Weaver, of Arkansas, and J. Montgomery Smith, of Wisconsin. They reached the Ute reservation in August and spent several months in negotiation, during which, with several Ute leaders, they visited southern Utah with a view of selecting the proposed reservation. They were finally successful in the object of their mission, the Indians having consented to the removal. A tract of about 1,190,000 acres will be thereby opened to settlers in the State.

Insurance.—The sixth annual report of the Insurance Commissioner, for the year ending in May, estimates that new risks were taken during the year against fire amounting to $50,619,776, and upon life amounting to over $8,000,000. This business was done almost entirely by outside companies. "The record heretofore made by Colorado companies," says the commissioner, "has been indifferent, and in some cases positively bad. There has been bad faith in many of them from their very inception."

The Deep-Water Harbor Convention.—Early in July a convention, composed chiefly of Texans, with a few representatives from Colorado and Kansas, was held at Fort Worth, Tex., for the purpose of promoting a movement to secure a deep-water harbor on the Gulf coast. The convention adopted resolutions of which the following is an extract:

It is the sense of the convention that the commercial, agricultural, mining, and stock-raising interests, not only of Texas, but of all the territory north and west thereof, as well as the commerce and trade of the United States with other countries, demand a first-class port on the coast of Texas.

This convention believes that such a port ought to be selected by a board of competent engineers appointed by the United States Government.

The remainder of the resolutions urge upon Senators and Representatives in Congress the need of appropriations for this work. It was also voted to recommend a second convention to be held in Denver at an early date, which should include representatives from all the States and Territories west of the Mississippi. Pursuant to a proclamation by Gov. Adams, this convention assembled at Denver on August 28, and remained in session several days. Delegates were present from nearly all the States and Territories embraced in the call, except from the Pacific States. Gov. Thayer, of

Nebraska, was chosen permanent chairman, and ways and means of securing the objects of the meeting were discussed at length. A difference of opinion prevailed as to whether Galveston or some other port on the coast should be designated for improvement. Two reports were submitted by the committee on resolutions, of which the majority report, recommending no particular harbor, was adopted.

On October 17 a committee appointed by the convention met at Dallas, Tex., adopted a draft of a bill to be presented to Congress, and took measures to secure its early consideration by that body.

Political.—Both the Union Labor party and the Prohibition party met in State convention at Denver on September 1. A conference committee was selected by each convention to agree upon a fusion ticket, but the refusal of the Union Labor men to ratify the ticket so agreed upon, brought the plan to naught. The Union Labor men nominated a State ticket headed by De La Martyr.

The Prohibition nominees were: For Governor, W. C. Stover ; Lieutenant - Governor, Warren R. Fowler; Secretary of State, W. W. Waters; Treasurer, Harry G. Schoock; Auditor, W. A. Rice: Attorney-General, J. H. Boughton; Superintendent of Schools, J. A. Smith; Supreme Court Judge (long term), A. W. Brazee; Supreme Court Judge (short term), D. E. McCaskell; Regents of the State University, Isaac T. Keator, D. W. Robbins.

On September 4 the Republican State Convention met in Denver. There were five candidates for the gubernatorial nomination, each having upon the first formal ballot the following support: David H. Moore, 131 votes; Job A Cooper, 122; Ex-Senator H. A. W. Tabor, 186; Wolfe Londoner, 34: Lieutenant-Governor Meldrum, 74. On the fifth ballot Job A. Cooper was nominated. The remainder of the ticket was completed as follows: For Lieutenant-Governor, William G. Smith ; Secretary of State, James Rice; Treasurer, W. H. Brisbane; Auditor, Louis B. Schwanbeck; Attorney-General, Samuel W. Jones; Superintendent of Public Instruction, Fred Dick; Regents of the State University, Charles R. Dudley, S. A. Giffin; Supreme Court Judges (long term), Charles D. Hayt; (short term), Victor A. Elliott.

Resolutions were adopted ratifying the work of the National Convention and favoring liberal pensions, anti-Chinese legislation, a fair ballot, and free coinage of silver. On State questions the platform declares as follows:

We favor fair but stringent legislation respecting the railways in the State. We declare that pools, rebates, and all discriminations should be prohibited, and the prohibition rigidly enforced by heavy penalties. We also demand legislation that will prevent the charging of exorbitant rates. We also demand legislation prohibiting all officers, judicial, legislative, and executive, from accepting, directly or indirectly, railway-passes or free tickets.

We also declare in favor of stringent State and national legislation prohibiting trusts and combinations of every kind and nature.

While we uphold the National Government in all its endeavors to preserve the public domain for the benefit of honest settlers, we must earnestly condemn the course pursued by the present Administration in its wholesale attempt to cancel and annul pre-emption and homestead entries at the instance of land-agents, thereby tyrannically and dishonestly taking from poor but honest settlers their money and homes.

That the Legislature enact laws providing for the protection of the health and safety of those engaged in mining and other hazardous occupations.

That the lien-law of the State be so amended as to secure to the laborer wages earned by him, and prevent his being defrauded of them by dishonest practices at the hands of unscrupulous persons.

We favor a liberal appropriation by the State Legislature for the purposes of inducing immigration and advertising the resources of the State.

We urge our congressional delegation to continue their efforts to secure all legislation necessary to perfect a system of reservoirs in the Rocky Mountains for irrigation purposes.

A resolution was also passed urging such legislation as would permit the surplus of $1,000,-000 of current funds in the State treasury to be applied in payment of the State debt.

The Democratic State Convention assembled at Denver on September 19, and nominated the following ticket without a contest: For Governor, Thomas M. Patterson; Lieutenant-Governor, John A. Porter; Treasurer, Amos G. Henderson; Secretary of State, W. R. Earhart; Auditor, Leopold Meyer; Attorney - General, J. M. Abbott; Superintendent of Public Instruction, J. A. Hough; Regents of the University, F. A. Chavez, Charles Ambrook; Judges of the Supreme Bench (long term), M. B. Gerry; (short term), A. J. Rising.

The platform ratifies the acts of the National Convention, favors free coinage of silver, denounces trusts, and discusses State questions at length as follows:

We demand that all reservation of public lands in Colorado not absolutely necessary for the uses of the Government shall be thrown open for occupation and settlement; and we pledge ourselves to the people to use all available means to secure that end and to secure to all *bona-fide* settlers now on said reservations their rights.

The existing laws of the United States with regard to the public timber domain are emphatically condemned, and we charge the Republican party with responsibility for the same. By these laws, as construed and enforced by the courts, railway companies are given unlimited and unrestricted right to denude the public domain of its best timber, while the privileges given to private citizens with regard to taking timber for necessary purposes are so restricted as to practically deny them its use.

We deplore the evils of alien landlordism everywhere, and especially sympathize with those on the borders of our State who are suffering from its pernicious effects, and we demand the enactment of such Federal and State legislation as will give relief to our suffering fellow-citizens and prevent its further extension. We favor the passage of a law establishing a board of mediation and arbitration, with power to inquire into and adjust all disputes arising between employer and employé, to be created as is provided by the laws of the State of New York on that subject, and embodying the recommendations of President Cleveland to Congress on April 22, 1886.

We demand that the funds of the State Treasury, instead of being used to create p   e for the Treasurer's office, shall be placed at interest, under regulations and safeguard to be provided by law, whereby such interests shall be added to such funds and become a part thereof, and we pledge all of our candidates for the Legislature to the enactment of such a law.

Being opposed to all unnecessary taxation, either direct or indirect, we repudiate the proposed amendment to our State Constitution, which is intended to increase the rate of State taxation, and call upon the people to aid us in defeating it. The proposed increase results from Republican extravagance, continued by that party in disregard of its pledges, the expenses and appropriations for the last General Assembly having been above $500,000 for each of the years 1887-'88, exclusive of appropriations for the capitol building.

We again denounce the payment of county, precinct, and court officers by a system of exorbitant fees, and again demand that their compensation shall be fixed by salary and paid at stated intervals.

We favor the passage of a law concerning elections which shall embody the best features of the Californian and Australian systems.

We reiterate the sentiments of our past platforms concerning the necessity of legislation which will more effectually regulate and restrain all lines of transportation, rebates, overcharges, discriminations against individuals and localities, fictitious capitalization, and disregard of constitutional checks, which will continue until such legislation and the establishment of a board of commissioners, with ample power to inquire into and correct abuses and to fix and enforce uniform maximum rates for freight and passenger traffic, and we pledge all our candidates on the State and legislative ticket to its enactment. We propose no legislation that can affect the rights of railway companies, to cripple or injure them, but we insist that the rights of individuals and localities must be protected and preserved. We denounce the majority of the Senate of the last General Assembly which defeated the will of the people by preventing such legislation, and we commend the House of Representatives for its gallant but ineffectual effort to protect and secure the rights of the people.

We heartily indorse the proceedings of the late Interstate Deep-Water Harbor Convention of Denver, and pledge the nominee of this convention for Congress to do all in his power, if elected, to secure the establishment of ample harbor facilities on the Texas coast.

The necessity of a reservoir system, by means of which our surplus waters can be stored and utilized for agricultural and kindred purposes, is constantly increasing, and we promise to labor for the ultimate accomplishment of this object.

We believe in the encouragement of free and intelligent immigration to this State, and favor the passage of a law creating a bureau of immigration to be composed of the Executive Department without additional salary.

Foreign contract labor and Chinese immigration are the product of Republican administrations. We denounce them both, and earnestly recommend the enactment of such further legislation as is essential for their complete destruction.

We are opposed to the further sale of our school-lands, and demand an investigation of the manner in which said lands have heretofore been disposed of.

After an energetic canvass, the Republican State and national ticket was successful in the November election, by pluralities ranging from 10,000 to 14,000. Only one of the forty-two counties in the State returned a Democratic plurality. A Republican Congressman was elected, and the next Legislature will be Republican. The people voted at the same election upon the question whether the rate of taxation

for State purposes for 1889 and 1890 should be increased from four to five mills, and also upon two amendments to the State Constitution—one permitting county indebtedness within certain limits, the other modifying the clause forbidding a State debt, and especially providing that a loan of $600,000 may be contracted to meet obligations of the State outstanding on Dec. 31, 1888. All of these propositions were defeated.

CONGO FREE STATE, a country in equatorial Africa, constituted by the general act of the Congo Conference, which was signed at Berlin, Feb. 26, 1885. The boundaries of the state were defined by conventions made by the International Association of the Congo with Germany on Nov. 8, 1884, with Great Britain on Dec. 16, 1884, with the Netherlands on Dec. 27, 1884, with France on Feb. 5, 1885, and with Portugal on Feb. 14, 1885. The powers reserve for a period of twenty years the right of deciding whether freedom of entry shall be maintained or not. The navigation of the Congo is placed under an International Commission representing all the powers signing the act. By a vote of the Belgian Legislature, April 28 and 30, 1885, the Free State was placed under the sovereignty of King Leopold II individually, the Belgian Government having no power or responsibility in relation to it.

The Governor-General is M. Ledeganck, under whom are chiefs of provinces and other officials. There are four administrative divisions or provinces: the Lower Congo, Livingston Falls and the Pool, the district between the Pool and the equator, and the Upper Congo. The principal stations occupied are Banana, Boma, Matadi, Lukunga, Leopoldville, Bangala, Stanley Falls, and Luluabourg. Stanley Falls, which had been abandoned in consequence of Arab attacks, was reoccupied in 1888 by officers of the Free State. Tippoo Tib, who has been the most prosperous of the Arab slave raiders in this region, having his seat at Nyangwe, had for some time previous acted as temporary chief of the station, and received a salary for maintaining order. The Central Government at Brussels consists of the King of the Belgians, and three heads of Departments—Foreign Affairs and Justice, Finance, and the Interior.

Area and Population.—The state includes a small section on the north bank of the Congo, from its mouth to Manyanga, French territory intervening between this last station and the mouth of the Likona, whence the boundary extends northward to 4° north latitude, eastward to 30° east longitude, southward to Lake Bangweolo, 12° south latitude, westward to 24° eats longitude, northward to 6° south latitude, then westward to the south bank of the Congo at Nokki. The area of the Free State is estimated at 1,056,200 square miles, with a population of about 27,000,000. There is an army of 2,000 native Africans.

Finances.—The revenue is derived from a subsidy granted by the King of the Belgians. The expenditures are estimated at $350,000.

Commerce.—The chief articles of export are palm-oil, ivory, India-rubber, coffee, gum copal, peanuts, orchil, and cam-wood. The principal imports are cotton cloth, gunpowder, spirits, and tobacco. The rubber exported in 1887 was valued at 2,000,000 francs; ivory, 1,500,000 francs; coffee, 1,497,000 francs; peanuts, 701,870 francs; palm-oil, 648,560 francs. The total exports were about 7,000,000 francs, and the imports of equal value. By a decree that was published in November, 1888, the transport and sale of firearms and ammunition is prohibited on the Upper Congo and its tributaries. The survey for a railroad from the coast to Stanley Pool has been completed. The line is to run from Matadi to Stanley Pool, 350 kilometres, starting at a level of 7 metres above the sea, and gradually rising to 60 metres.

The French Possessions.—The French acquisitions in the Congo region, about 250,000 square miles in extent, have not yet been commercially developed. The frontier question between France and the Free State was finally settled in the summer of 1888 by the evacuation of the post of Kundja that the French occupied on Ubangi river.

CONGREGATIONALISTS. Statistics.—The following is a summary of the statistics of the Congregational churches in the United States, as they are given in the "Congregational Year-Book" for 1888. The additions, removals, and gains cover a period extending in several of the States to two years, and in others to various fractional parts of more than one year:

Churches, whole number.........................	4,404
Members, whole number.........................	457,584
Members added on confession	41,156
Members, gain (actual, comparing totals)........	21,205
Baptisms, adult	20,123
Baptisms, infant	11,966
Families reported...........................	268,775
Sunday-schools, members	551,691
Sunday-schools, gain in members...	29,704
Sunday-schools, average attendance............	324,719
Sunday-schools, united with the Church from	18,399
Sunday-schools, benevolent contributions of......	$162,012

BENEVOLENT CONTRIBUTIONS OF THE CHURCHES.

For the Year 1887 only	$2,095,485
Of which for foreign missions.................. ...	319,404
Of which for education........................	221,237
Of which for church building	122,590
Of which for home missions	436,577
Of which for A. M. A	151,608
Of which for Sunday-schools	24,996
Of which for New West	43,960
Of which for ministerial aid	9,133
Of which for other objects	737,731
Legacies paid	329,663
Home expenditures...........................	5,078,950
Home expenditures, increase................	1,169,755

The seven theological seminaries of Andover, Bangor, Chicago, Hartford, Oberlin, Pacific, and Yale, returned in all 46 professors, 21 instructors or lecturers, 23 advanced or graduate students, and 420 undergraduate students.

The American Congregational Association has for its object to preserve, improve, and promote the best use of the Congregational Library; to care for the Congregational House (in Boston), and remove the incumbrances upon it; and to further the general interests of Congregationalism. It owns the Congregational House, which is valued at about $425,000 and is liable in funded obligations of $184,500. The Library includes 34,000 volumes and more than 140,000 pamphlets, and is housed in a fire-proof structure.

Educational Societies.—The receipts of the American College and Education Society for the year ending April 30, 1887, were $57,994. Two hundred and ninety-one students were assisted during the year, and 7,287 since 1816. In both departments, of aid to colleges and assistance to students fitting for the ministry, the society had a large agency in social organization throughout the West.

The New West Education Commission seeks to promote Christian civilization in Utah and adjacent States and Territories by the education of children and youth and other kindred agencies. Its total income for the year ending July 1, 1887, was $61,318, or $3,956 more than the receipts of any previous year; and its indebtedness was returned at $10,000, $5,000 having been paid off during the year. It had sustained 28 schools of all grades, with which 59 teachers and 2,383 pupils were connected. It had erected four new buildings and had made additions to two others, at a total cost of $30,475.

American Congregational Union.—The thirty-fourth annual meeting of the American Congregational Union was held in New York city, January 12. The Rev. Dr. William M. Taylor presided. The date of closing the financial year having been changed from April 30 to December 31, the report was for only eight months. The total receipts for this term had been $81,200, which, with $48,394 in the treasury on May 1, appropriated but not called for, made the total available resources for the year 1887 $129,584. The total expenditures for eight months had been $85,081; and there remained in the treasury, mostly of moneys appropriated but not paid, $129,595. Grants of $45,008 had been made to 59 churches, and loans of $13,650 to 17 churches, 3 churches receiving both grants and loans; 35 parsonages had been added, at an average cost to the Union of $347, making a total of 140 parsonages completed under the auspices of the Union, while 19 more were in building. The report of the treasurer showed that $102,223 had been contributed back by the churches that had been aided by the Union during its career, and $76,704 had been returned on loans, insurance on buildings burned, and houses sold. It was thus shown that "the only difference between a loan and a grant is the time allowed for payment." All aid from the Union is in the form of temporary relief. The aided churches reported additions by profession of 8,213 members.

American Home Missionary Society. — The sixty-second annual meeting of the American Home Missionary Society was held at Saratoga Springs, N. Y., June 5. The Rev. Dr. Julius H. Seelye presided. The entire resources of the society for the year had been $550,886, and the whole amount paid to missionaries had been $511,641. There were still due to missionaries for labor performed $1,559, and the appropriations already made and daily becoming due amounted to $78,395, making the total amount of pledges $79,955. Twenty State organizations of women, with 1,100 local auxiliaries, were co-operating with the society. Fifteen hundred and eighty-four ministers had been employed during the year, or some part of it, in the supply of 3.084 congregations, of whom five had preached to colored people, and 144 in foreign languages, viz., to Welsh, German, Scandinavian, Bohemian, Spanish, Chinese, Indian, French, and Mexican congregations. These missionaries reported that 130 churches had been organized, and 59 had become self-supporting; that 116 houses of worship had been completed, 15 chapels built, 33 parsonages provided, and 6,310 members had been added on confession of faith during the year. Eighty-seven persons connected with the missionary churches were preparing for the ministry. The number of Sunday-schools under the care of the missionaries was 2,205, and with these were connected about 130,000 pupils. Two hundred and eighty-eight new schools had been organized. The contributions to benevolent objects reported by 786 missionaries amounted to $35,641.

American Missionary Association. — The forty-seventh annual meeting of the American Missionary Association was held in Providence, R. I., beginning October 25. The Rev. William M. Taylor, D. D., presided. The total receipts, including the balance from the previous year, had been $328,147, and the expenditures had been $328,788. The whole number of schools sustained by the association was 93, 20 of which were normal schools. It was estimated that of the 15,000 negro teachers in the South, educating 800,000 pupils, 13,500 had become teachers from missionary schools, and more than 7,000 of them from the schools of this association. The normal schools are situated at Wilmington, N. C., Charleston and Greenwood, S. C., Atlanta, Macon, Savannah, Thomasville, and McIntosh, Ga., Mobile, Athens, and Marion, Ala., Memphis, Jonesboro', Grand View, and Pleasant Hill, Tenn., Lexington and Williamsburg, Ky., Santee Agency, Neb., and Oahe and Fort Berthold, Dakota. The association provides also the teaching-force at the Ramona Indian school, Santa Fé, New Mexico, and normal departments were connected with six of the colleges. Four new churches had been organized during the year. The following are the statistics of the schools, exclusive of the normal schools, and of church work:

SCHOOLS.

ITEMS.	In the South.	Indian schools.	Total.
Number of schools...............	58	18	76
Number of instructors..........	266	50	316
Number of pupils................	9,896	580	10,476
Theological students............	87	..	87
Law students	73	..	73
College students	68	..	68
Preparatory-college students	165	..	165
Normal students................	836	10	846
Grammar-grade students	1,996	48	2,089
Intermediate-grade students	2,998	108	3,106
Primary pupils..................	3,881	419	4,250

There are, in addition, 17 Chinese schools on the Pacific coast, with 39 teachers.

CHURCH WORK.

ITEMS.	In the South.	Indian schools.	Total.
Number of churches.............	131	5	186
Number of missionaries.........	102	13	115
Number of church-members.....	8,065	397	8,452
Added by profession of faith.....	721	80	730
Scholars in Sunday-schools......	16,023	1,091	17,114

Thirteen woman's State organizations were co-operating with the association. A gift of one million dollars to the work of the association, from Daniel Hand, of Clinton, Conn., was announced and acknowledged with an expression of thanks. The fitness of the colored people of America to carry on missionary work in Africa was discussed affirmatively by the Rev. Dr. Strieby, secretary of the association, in a paper on "American Freedmen and African Colonization." Among the other papers read was one on "The Hopefulness of Indian Missions," by Secretary Beard.

American Board. — The seventy-ninth annual meeting of the American Board of Commissioners for Foreign Missions was held at Cleveland, Ohio, beginning October 2. The Rev. Richard S. Storrs, D. D., presided, and was re-elected president for the ensuing year. The receipts of the year from gifts had been $394,568, being $27,610 more than the like receipts of the previous year, and $9,687 more than the average for the past five years. Of this amount $152,510 had been contributed through the four Woman's Boards (Woman's Board of Missions, Woman's Board of the Interior, Woman's Board of the Pacific, and Woman's Board of the Pacific Isles). The receipts from legacies had been $146,853. Adding to these two classes of receipts the income from permanent funds, $11,258, the total income of the society for the year had been $552,179, or $73,785 more than the total income of the previous year. The sum of $62,500 had been appropriated from the "Swett fund," which had been set apart to meet special calls, chiefly for use in China and Japan, and $51,082 from the "Otis bequest," set apart for new missions, for the work in West Central and East Central Africa, Hong-Kong, northern Japan, and North Mexico. The total expenditures, including these appropriations, had been $666,-

399. There had also been received and expended for the relief of suffering, occasioned chiefly by famine in central Turkey, $31,695. The following is the General Summary of the Missions of the Board in Asia Minor, China, Africa, the Pacific Islands, Mexico, Spain, Austria, European Turkey, India, Ceylon, and Japan:

GENERAL SUMMARY, 1887-1888.

Missions	22
Stations	90
Out-stations	960
Places for stated preaching	1,126
Average congregations	61,188
Adherents	100,914
Ordained missionaries (11 being physicians)	167
Physicians not ordained	12
Other male assistants	11
Women	282
Whole number of laborers sent from this country	472
Native pastors	166
Other native helpers	1,969 2,135
Whole number of laborers	2,607
Pages printed	18,650,000
Churches	336
Church-members	30,546
Added during the year	4,388
Whole number from the first, as nearly as can be learned	105,477
Theological seminaries and station-classes	17
Pupils	251
Colleges and high-schools	59
Boarding-schools for girls	50
Common schools	592
Whole number under instruction	42,733
Native contributions	$124,274

Among the incidents showing advance in the various mission fields were the gradual elevation of the standards in the theological seminaries at Marsovan, Harpoot, and Marash, Asiatic Turkey, for adaptation to the growing needs of the field and to the better class of candidates furnished by the colleges; the proclamations that had been issued in many provinces of China describing the missionaries as teachers of virtue, and their influence as helpful to the state, and enjoining upon the people to refrain from violence and live with them as hosts and guests; the restoration of the rights of the missionaries in Micronesia, which had been disturbed by the Spanish occupation—while the German occupation of the Marshall Islands had but slightly affected the condition of the work there; the dedication of a church at Sofia, Bulgaria; and the discussion of a proposition for a union of the Congregational and Presbyterian churches in Japan. The Home for missionary children at Auburndale, Mass., had a fund of $18,500, and had accommodated several missionary families for longer or shorter periods, as well as missionary children not otherwise provided for.

A report from the committee on the codification of the rules and by-laws of the board, which had been appointed in the preceding year, was received and adopted. Included in it were various propositions of amendments, which were arranged in two classes: first, such as were necessary to make the by-laws conform to law and usage; and, second, such as experience had indicated for convenient working. Among those of the latter class

were one making the number of corporate members 250 instead of "200 active members," and striking out the word "active"; one making all nominations, except the appointment of the nominating committee, subject to the approval of the board; and others, fixing the number of members of the Prudential Committee at ten; designating three corresponding and recording, and assistant recording secretaries, instead of "secretaries" simply; providing for the appointment by the Prudential Committee of an editorial secretary; and changing the number of corporate members who may demand a special meeting from seven to twenty-five. A committee of fifteen was appointed

To consider the relation of the board to the churches and individuals who make the board their missionary agent, and the expediency, in view of the facts which they may ascertain, of securing a closer union between them, and especially including the subject of the selection of corporate members, and that this committee be instructed to report such action, if any, as they may deem wise in this direction, at a subsequent annual meeting of the board.

Ordination of William H. Noyes, and the Doctrine of Future Probation.—The points of doctrine involved in what is called the "Andover Case" (see "Annual Cyclopædia" for 1886 and 1887, article "Congregationalists") was again made a subject of public attention in October by the action of a council held with the Berkeley Street Church, Boston, in ordaining the Rev. William H. Noyes to be a missionary. Mr. Noyes was one of the young men who had offered their services to the American Board in 1886, and had been rejected on account of his views respecting "future probation." Twenty-two churches were invited to participate in the council that was called to deliberate on the subject of the ordination, four of which failed to respond. The council met October 22, and was presided over by the Rev. Joseph T. Duryea, D. D. After the council had decided, in the face of adverse motions made by opponents of the contemplated measure, to proceed with the business for which it had been called, Mr. Noyes offered a statement of belief, in which he said respecting "future probation":

Regarding future things, I believe that the supreme fact revealed is the coming of our Lord Jesus Christ in glory to the judgment. Christ's judgment will not be arbitrary, but in righteousness, according to his Gospel. This judgment, I believe, is final. The wicked shall forever depart from God, but the righteous shall forever live with God. I believe that we shall all stand before the judgment-seat of God and each one of us shall give an account of himself to God, whose servant each one is, and before whom each standeth or falleth. Of the intermediate state I hold no positive doctrine. I do not know what effect physical death will have upon character. What I dread for my fellow-men is spiritual death. The spirit of God will not strive with men forever. Then woe is me if I preach not the Gospel at once. With the gospel message I believe there go decisive opportunity and obligation to repent. We simply should so present his message that men will be saved by it and not lost. Those who do not hear the message in this life, I trustfully leave with God. I do not claim to know God's method of dealing with them, but I do not refuse to think of them. I entertain in their behalf what I conceive to be a reasonable hope that somehow, before their destinies are fixed, there shall be revealed to them the love of God in Christ Jesus. In this, as in other questions in which God has given no decisive answer, I merely claim the liberty of the Gospel.

In reply to the questioning by members of the council, he said that his faith was more vital to him now than when he offered himself to the board, but that he had not intentionally changed the form of his expression of belief regarding future probation. He had intended to convey the same impression to the board as now. He had found the doctrine neither taught nor forbidden in the Scriptures. The council expressed its satisfaction with the examination, and advised the Berkeley Street Church to endeavor to secure an arrangement by which he could work under the same direction as the other missionaries of the Congregational churches; and that, in case such an arrangement could not be made, the church itself assume the responsibility of his direction and support. Mr. Noyes was then ordained. Application was afterward made to the Prudential Committee of the American Board to accept the candidate as a missionary to Japan. This the committee declined to do in a letter in which its own action and the action of the American Board at the annual meetings in 1886 and 1887 approving its course were reviewed. Respecting the present situation of the case, the committee had hoped, when the new application was presented, that experience and further study had so far modified Mr. Noyes's previously expressed views, that he could withdraw his former statements, and so express himself that he could be approved without violation of the instructions of the board. But in this particular it had been disappointed. Had he been able to withdraw or modify his statements previously made, his case might possibly be considered simply on the basis of a new statement. But he had repeatedly assured the committee in conference that he had not consciously altered his opinions or his expression of them. All of his statements taken together made it plain that he was to be included among those candidates "who accept, under some form of statement, the hypothesis of a probation after death," and in relation to whom the board had given instructions adverse to their appointment. The committee had therefore voted:

That inasmuch as the Rev. William H. Noyes declines to withdraw the statements made by him to the committee at the time of his previous applications for appointment which favor the hypothesis of a probation after death—this hypothesis being, as he there states, "in harmony with Scripture," and one which "honors Christ in giving completeness to his work," and which is to him "a necessary corollary" to a belief in the universality of the atonement; and inasmuch as he has now emphatically stated to the committee that he knows of no change in his feelings or his expression of them, nor in his position, since he first presented them to the Prudential Committee in

1866, except that his faith has become "more vital"; therefore, in accordance with the instructions given to the committee by the board at its annual meeting in 1886, which were reaffirmed with emphasis in 1887, when this particular case was under review, the committee has no option but to decline to appoint the applicant so long as he holds these views.

Congregational Union of England and Wales.— The Congregational Union of England and Wales met in London, May 7. The Rev. Dr. Bruce presided, and the Rev. Griffith John was chosen president for the ensuing year. The financial statement showed that the income of the Union for the year had been £10,122, and the expenditure, £11,092. The secretary's report represented that the proposed conference between the Congregational and Baptist churches had been postponed, but not without hope that the aim of preventing denominational overlapping would presently be accomplished. The decision of the Tooting case in favor of the Congregationalists was mentioned, with an expression of regret that such a cause of contention with the Presbyterians should have existed. A plan had been prepared for the celebration of the bicentenary of the revolution of 1688, with addresses and lectures, and by making the subject a special feature of the autumnal meetings of the body. The proposed celebration was approved of by the Union. The formation of church-guilds had been encouraged. Measures had been taken for the Union becoming its own publisher of books, etc. The committee had supported the bill for legalization of marriage with a deceased wife's sister; had abstained from taking action in reference to the early closing bill; had arranged for presentation to the Union of a memorial of the Band of Hope Union, in reference to the use of non-alcoholic liquors at the sacrament; and had devised plans by which the time of the Union should not be so much encroached on as heretofore by deputations. They had not acceded to Rev. Foster Lepine's suggestion that arrangements should be made by which party politics would be avoided at the representative meetings of the Union. The Jubilee fund had been closed with total receipts recorded at £434,470, and total disbursements at £248,875. The Welsh churches had raised £100,000 for the extinction of debts, and £93,236 had been contributed toward metropolitan church extension. The working expenses of the scheme for seven years had amounted to £2,201, no part of which had come out of the contributions. A protest was adopted against the management of Halloway College, an institution, it was held, which, while the founder had intended it should be undenominational, appeared to have fallen too much under the influence of the established Church. A letter of commendation was ordered sent to the Australian and Canadian churches. A resolution was adopted protesting against fresh legislation which should provide for supporting denominational schools out of the rates.

The receipts of the Church Aid Society had been £38,712, and its expenditures about £30,000. It had aided during the year 1,101 congregations, under the care of 474 pastors and 109 missionaries.

The thirty-fourth annual meeting of the English Congregational Chapel Building Society was held in Bristol, April 10. The total resources for the year had been £7,258. The payments had been £4,241. The total receipts from the beginning of the society's operations had been £173,855, and the disbursements £165,811.

London Missionary Society.—The annual meeting of the London Missionary Society was held May 10. Lord Brassey presided. The income of the society had been £125,000, and its expenditures, £128,000. The 184 men and women missionaries were aided in their work by 1,500 native pastors and 5,000 native preachers. Progress was reported of the missions in China, India, Madagascar, where, notwithstanding a critical stage had been reached, there were signs of advance, and a concentration of missionaries near the capital was needed; South Africa, where the conditions were not encouraging; New Guinea, where advance was making; and Samoa, where the society had 27,000 adherents, who built their own churches, supported their own pastors, and contributed £1,000 a year to the parent society.

Autumnal Meeting of the Union.—The Congregational Union met in its autumnal session at Nottingham, October 9. The Rev. Dr. Robert Bruce presided, and spoke in his opening address in criticism of the proposals in the educational report of the Royal Commissioners. A resolution was adopted disapproving the policy embodied in the recommendations of the majority of the commission, as distinctly reactionary in character, and thereby confirming the forebodings which the Union had expressed at its meeting in May. Objection was made in particular to the proposed appropriation of local rates to schools under private management, and to the removal of restrictions on sectarian teaching; and the opinion expressed in former resolutions was reiterated, that no system of education will be satisfactory under which national funds are appropriated to schools or training-colleges which are under the control of denominational managers. Papers were read on "The Work of Congregational Churches in England—in Villages," by the Rev. A. D. Phillips; "in Urban Congregations," by the Rev. H. H. Huffodine; "Among the Working-Classes in Towns," Rev. F. W. Neuland; "Church Extension in Large and Growing Centers," Mr. W. H. Conyers; "Efforts among Special Classes, such as Canalmen and Navvies," Rev. T. Gascoigne; "The Need of a System of Christian Economics," Rev. F. W. Stead; "Pentateuchal Criticism," Prof. O. C. Whitehouse; and on other subjects of interest to the churches. A public meeting was held in celebration of the revolution of 1688. The consideration of a resolution denouncing the coercive policy of the Government in Ireland was declined by the assembly as such; but opportunity was given at adjournment for holding a special meeting of ministers and delegates to entertain it. The resolution as adopted by this meeting placed its action on the ground that the question was one of national righteousness "far away from and above every question of party and politics.". Seventy-five ministers and delegates protested against the suspension of the sessions for holding this meeting. It was shown at a meeting in behalf of the Irish Evangelical Society that there are 27 Congregational churches in Ireland, 9 of which are self-supporting, with 85 out-stations, 17 ministers, 24 lay preachers, one evangelist, 2,636 adherents, and more than a thousand pupils in Sunday-schools.

The Tooting Case.—The "Tooting case," the decision of which in favor of the Congregationalists is mentioned in the account of the proceedings of the Congregrational Union, arose from a controversy with the Presbyterian Church respecting the title to the old meeting-house at Tooting-Graveney, which had been put in trust by Emma Mills in 1786, as a "place for Protestant Dissenters of the Presbyterian or Independent denomination." The place had been used under this trust till 1879 as an Independent chapel. In that year a resolution was passed by the congregation, at the request of the pastor, to apply for admission to the Presbyterian Church. The application was granted by the Presbyterian Synod, and a representative of the Presbyterian Church of England was delegated to preside over a meeting of the society. Suit was brought in behalf of the Congregationalists to test the title to the meeting-house. The decision of the court was given in March. It declared the action by which the transfer to the Presbyterian Church was made to be invalid—first, for want of unanimity in the application by the congregation, the presence of one dissentionist when the vote was taken showing that it was opposed; and, second, because the affiliation of the society with the English Presbyterian Church as now constituted must be regarded as in contravention of the original trust. Although "Presbyterians" are mentioned in the deed, the present rules of the Presbyterian Church as contained in the "Book of Order," are quite inconsistent with the Independency of 1786; for, the court declared, Independency consists in each particular church "standing alone" and being "self-governed"; while the "Book of Order" is directly contrary to that position. The decision was applied only to the external relations of the Church, and was not held to affect either the title of the pastor or the right of the existing congregation to regulate its own internal affairs in its own way.

CONGRESS OF THE UNITED STATES. The Fiftieth Congress assembled for its first session Dec. 5, 1887. It was composed as follows:

SENATE.

President, John J. Ingalls.
Secretary, Anson G. McCook.

Alabama.
1889. John T. Morgan, D.
1891. James L. Pugh, D.

Arkansas.
1889. James H. Berry, D.
1891. James K. Jones, D.

California.
1891. Leland Stanford, R.
1893. George Hearst, D.

Colorado.
1889. Thomas M. Bowen, R.
1891. Henry M. Teller, R.

Connecticut.
1891. Orville H. Platt, R.
1893. Joseph R. Hawley, R.

Delaware.
1889. Eli Saulsbury, D.
1893. George Gray, D.

Florida.
1891. Wilkinson Call, D.
1893. Samuel Pasco, D.

Georgia.
1889. Alfred H. Colquitt, D.
1891. Joseph E. Brown, D.

Illinois.
1889. Shelby M. Cullom, R.
1891. Charles B. Farwell, R.

Indiana.
1891. Daniel W. Voorhees, D.
1893. David Turpie, D.

Iowa.
1889. James F. Wilson, R.
1891. William B. Allison, R.

Kansas.
1889. Preston B. Plumb, R.
1891. John J. Ingalls, R.

Kentucky.
1889. James B. Beck, D.
1891. J. C. S. Blackburn, D.

Louisiana.
1889. Randall L. Gibson, D.
1891. James B. Eustis, D.

Maine.
1889. William P. Frye, R.
1893. Eugene Hale, R.

Maryland.
1891. Ephraim K. Wilson, D.
1893. Arthur P. Gorman, D.

Massachusetts.
1889. George F. Hoar, R.
1893. Henry L. Dawes, R.

Michigan.
1889. Thomas W. Palmer, R.
1893. F. B. Stockbridge, R.

Minnesota.
1889. Dwight M. Sabin, R.
1893. Cushman K. Davis, R.

Mississippi.
1889. E. C. Walthall, D.
1893. James Z. George, D.

Missouri.
1891. George G. Vest, D.
1893. Francis M. Cockrell, D.

Nebraska.
1889. C. F. Manderson, R.
1893. A. S. Paddock, R.

Nevada.
1891. John P. Jones, R.
1893. William M. Stewart, R.

New Hampshire.
1889. Wm. E. Chandler, R.
1891. Henry W. Blair, R.

New Jersey.
1889. John R. McPherson, D.
1893. Rufus Blodgett, D.

New York.
1891. William M. Evarts, R.
1893. Frank Hiscock, R.

North Carolina.
1889. Matt. W. Ransom, D.
1891. Zebulon B. Vance, D.

Ohio.
1891. Henry B. Payne, D.
1893. John Sherman, R.

Oregon.
1889. Joseph N. Dolph, R.
1891. John H. Mitchell, R.

Pennsylvania.
1891. J. D. Cameron, R.
1893. Matthew S. Quay, R.

Rhode Island.
1889. Jonathan Chace, R.
1893. Nelson W. Aldrich, R.

South Carolina.
1889. Matthew C. Butler, D.
1891. Wade Hampton, D.

Tennessee.
1889. Isham G. Harris, D.
1893. William B. Bate, D.

Texas.
1889. Richard Coke, D.
1893. John H. Reagan, D.

Vermont.
1891. Justin S. Morrill, R.
1893. G. F. Edmunds, R.

Virginia.
1889. H. H. Riddleberger, R.
1893. John W. Daniel, D.

West Virginia.
1889. John E. Kenna, D.
1893. C. J. Faulkner, D.[1]

Wisconsin.
1891. John C. Spooner, R.
1893. Philetus Sawyer, R.

Whole number of Senators, 76. Republicans, 39, and Democrats, 37.

---

[1] Seat contested by Daniel B. Lucas, Dem., who was appointed by the Governor of West Virginia.

HOUSE OF REPRESENTATIVES.

Alabama.
James T. Jones, D.
H. A. Herbert, D.
William C. Oates, D.
A. C. Davidson, D.
James E. Cobb, D.
J. H. Bankhead, D.
W. H. Forney, D.
Joseph Wheeler, D.

Arkansas.
Poindexter Dunn, D.
C. R. Breckenridge, D.
Thomas C. McRae, D.
John H. Rogers, D.
Samuel W. Peel, D.

California.
T. L. Thompson, D.
Marion Biggs, D.
Joseph McKenna, R.
W. W. Morrow, R.
Charles N. Felton, R.
William Vandever, R.

Colorado.
George G. Symes, R.

Connecticut.
Robert J. Vance, D.
Carlos French, D.
Charles A. Russell, R.
Miles T. Granger, D.

Delaware.
J. B. Pennington, D.

Florida.
R. H. M. Davidson, D.
Charles Dougherty, D.

Georgia.
T. M. Norwood, D.
H. G. Turner, D.
Charles F. Crisp, D.
Thomas M. Grimes, D.
John D. Stewart, D.
James H. Blount, D.
J. C. Clements, D.
H. H. Carlton, D.
A. D. Candler, D.
George T. Barnes, D.

Illinois.
R. W. Dunham, R.
Frank Lawler, D.
William E. Mason, R.
George E. Adams, R.
A. J. Hopkins, R.
Robert R. Hitt, R.
T. J. Henderson, R.
Ralph Plumb, R.
L. E. Payson, R.
Philip S. Post, R.
William H. Gest, R.
G. A. Anderson, D.
W. M. Springer, D.
J. H. Rowell, R.
J. G. Cannon, R.
Silas Z. Landes, D.
Edward Lane, D.
Jehu Baker, R.
R. W. Townshend, D.
John R. Thomas, R.

Indiana.
Alvin P. Hovey, R.
John H. O'Neall, D.
J. G. Howard, D.
William S. Holman, D.
C. C. Matson, D.
T. M. Browne, R.
William D. Bynum, D.
James T. Johnson, R.
J. B. Cheadle, R.
William D. Owen, R.
George W. Steele, R.
James B. White, R.
Benjamin F. Shively, D.

Iowa.
John H. Gear, R.
Walter I. Hayes, D.
D. B. Henderson, R.
William E. Fuller, R.
Daniel Kerr, R.
J. B. Weaver, D. G. B.
E. H. Conger, R.
A. R. Anderson, Ind.
Joseph Lyman, R.
A. J. Holmes, R.
Isaac S. Struble, R.

Kansas.
E. N. Morrill, R.
E. H. Funston, R.
B. W. Perkins, R.
Thomas Ryan, R.
J. A. Anderson, R.
E. J. Turner, R.
Samuel R. Peters, R.

Kentucky.
John H. Gear, R.
Polk Laffoon, D.
W. G. Hunter, R.
A. B. Montgomery, D.
Asher G. Caruth, D.
John G. Carlisle, D.
Wm. C. P. Breckinridge, D.
J. B. McCreary, D.
George M. Thomas, R.
W. B. Taulbee, D.
H. F. Finley, R.

Louisiana.
T. S. Wilkinson, D.
M. D. Lagan, D.
Edward J. Gay, D.
N. C. Blanchard, D.
C. Newton, D.
S. M. Robertson, D.

Maine.
Thomas B. Reed, R.
N. Dingley, Jr., R.
Seth L. Milliken, R.
C. A. Boutelle, R.

Maryland.
Charles H. Gibson, D.
Frank T. Shaw, D.
Harry W. Rusk, D.
Isidor Rayner, D.
Barnes Compton, D.
L. E. McComas, R.

Massachusetts.

Robert T. Davis, R.
John D. Long, R.
Leopold Morse, D.
Patrick A. Collins, D.
E. D. Hayden, R.
Henry C. Lodge, R.

W. Cogswell, R.
C. H. Allen, R.
E. Burnett, D.
John E. Russell, D.
W. Whiting. R.
F. W. Rockwell, R.

J. Logan Chipman. D.
Edward P. Allen, R.
James O'Donnell, R.
Julius C. Burrows, R.
Melborne H. Ford, D.
Mark S. Brewer, R.

Michigan.

J. E. Whiting. D.
T. E. Tarsney, D.
B. M. Cutcheon, R.
S. O. Fisher. D.
Seth C. Moffatt, R.[1]

Thomas Wilson, D.
John Lind. R.
John L. McDonald, D.

Minnesota.

Edmund Rice, D.
Knute Nelson. R.

John M. Allen, D.
J. B. Morgan, D.
T. C. Catchings, D.
F. G. Barry, D.

Mississippi.

C. L. Anderson, D.
T. R. Stockdale. D.
C. E. Hooker, D.

William H. Hatch, D.
C. H. Mansur, D.
A. M. Dockery, D.
James N. Burns, D.
William Warner, R.
John T. Heard, D.
John E. Hutton, D.

Missouri.

John J. O'Neill. D.
John M. Glover, D.
M. L. Clardy. D.
R. P. Bland. D.
William J. Stone, D.
W. H. Wade, R.
James P. Walker, D.

John A. McShane, D.
James Laird, R.

Nebraska.

G. W. E. Dorsey, R.

Nevada.

W. Woodburn, R.

New Hampshire.

L. F. McKinney, D.

J. H. Gallinger, R.

New Jersey.

George Hires. R.
J. Buchanan, R.
John Kean. Jr. R.
J. N. Pidcock, D.

W. W. Phelps, R.
H. Lehlbach. R.
William McAdoo, D.

New York.

Perry Belmont, D.
F. Campbell, D.
S. V. White, R.
P. P. Mahoney, D.
A. M. Bliss, D.
A. J. Cummings, D.
L. S. Bryce, D.
T. J. Campbell, D.
S. S. Cox, D.
F. B. Spinola, D.
T. A. Merriam, D.
W. B. Cockran, D.
A. P. Fitch. R.
W. G. Stahlnecker, D.
Henry Bacon, D.
J. H. Ketcham, R.
S. T. Hopkins, R.

E. W. Greenman. D.
Charles Tracey, D.
George West. R.
J. H. Moffit, R.
A. X. Parker, R.
J. S. Sherman, R.
David Wilbur, R.
James J. Belden, R.
Milton Delano, R.
N. W. Nutting, R.
T. S. Flood. R.
Ira Davenport, R.
C. S. Baker. R.
J. G. Sawyer. R.
J. M. Farquhar, R.
J. B. Weber, R.
W. G. Laidlaw, R.

North Carolina.

L. C. Latham, D.
F. M. Simmons, D.
C. W. McClammy, D.
John Nichols, Ind.
J. M. Brower, R.

A. M. Rowland. D.
J. S. Henderson, D.
W. H. H. Cowles. D.
T. D. Johnston, D.

Ohio.

Benjamin Butterworth, R.
Charles E. Brown, R.
E. S. Williams. R.
S. S. Yoder. D.
George E. Seney, D.
M. M. Boothman. R.
James E. Campbell, D.
Robert P. Kennedy, R.
William C. Cooper, R.
Jacob Romeis, R.
A. C. Thompson, R.

Jacob J. Pugsley. R.
Joseph H. Outhwaite, D.
Charles P. Wickham, R.
C. H. Grosvenor, R.
Beriah Wilkins, D.
Joseph D. Taylor, R.
William McKinley, Jr., R.
Ezra B. Taylor, R.
George W. Crouse. R.
Martin A. Foran, D.

Oregon.

Binger Herman, R.

Pennsylvania.

H. H. Bingham, R.
Charles O'Neill, R.
Samuel J. Randall, D.
William D. Kelley, R.
Alfred C. Harmer, R.
S. Darlington. R.
R. M. Yardley, R.
D. Ermentrout, D.
John A. Hiestand. R.
William H. Sowden, D.
C. R. Buckalew, D.
John Lynch, D.
Charles N. Brumm, R.
Franklin Bound, R.

F. C. Bunnell, R.
H. C. McCormick, R.
Edward Scull. R.
L. E. Atkinson. R.
Levi Maish, D.
John Patton. R.
W. McCullogh, D.
John Dalzell. R.
Thomas N. Bayne, R.
O. L. Jackson, R.
James T. Maffitt, R.
Norman Hall, D.
William L. Scott. D.
E. S. Osborne (at large), R.

Rhode Island.

Henry J. Spooner, R.

Warren O. Arnold, R.

South Carolina.

Samuel Dibble, D.
George D. Tillman. D.
James S. Cothran, D.
William H. Perry, D.

John J. Hemphill, D.
George W. Dargan, D.
William Elliott, D.

Tennessee.

Roderick R. Butler. R.
Leonidas C. Houk, R.
John R. Neal. D.
Benton McMillin, D.
James D. Richardson, D.

Joseph E. Washington, D.
Wash. C. Whitthorne, D.
Benj. A. Enloe, D.
Peter T. Glass, D.
James Phelan, D.

Texas.

Charles Stewart. D.
William H. Martin, D.
C. Buckley Kilgore, D.
David B. Culberson, D.
Silas Hare, D.
Joseph Abott, D.

William H. Crain, D.
Lytton W. Moore, D.
Roger Q. Mills, D.
Joseph D. Sayers, D.
Sam'l W. T. Lanham, D.

Vermont.

John W. Stewart, R.

William W. Grout, R.

Virginia.

Thos. H. B. Browne. R.
George E. Bowden, R.
George D. Wise, D.
William F. Gaines, R.
John R. Brown, R.

Samuel I. Hopkins, Ind.
Charles T. O'Ferrall, D.
W. H. Fitz Lee, D.
Henry Bowen, R.
Jacob Yost, R.

West Virginia.

Nathan Goff. R.
William L. Wilson, D.

Charles P. Snyder. D.
Charles E. Hogg. D.

Wisconsin.

Lucien B. Caswell. R.
Richard Guenther. R.
Robert M. La Follette, R.
Henry Smith, Ind.
Thomas B. Hudd, D.

Charles B. Clark, R.
Ormsby B. Thomas, R.
Nils P. Haugen, R.
Isaac Stephenson, R.

The whole number of Representatives is 325, of whom 163 are Democrats, 152 Republicans, 2 Labor, 2 Independents, and 1 Greenbacker.

DELEGATES FROM THE TERRITORIES.

Arizona—Marcus A. Smith. D.
Dakota—Oscar S. Gifford. R.
Idaho—Fred. S. Dubois. R.
Montana—Joseph K. Toole, D.
New Mexico—Anthony Joseph, D.
Utah—J. T. Caine, (People's Ticket).
Washington—Charles S. Voorhees, D.
Wyoming—Joseph M. Carey, R.

John D. Ingalls, of Kansas, was President *pro tempore* of the Senate; Anson G. McCook, Secretary; William P. Canaday, Sergeant-at-arms; J. G. Butler, Chaplain; and James W. Allen, Postmaster.

The House organized by electing John G. Carlisle, of Kentucky, Speaker, by the following vote: John G. Carlisle, 163; Thomas B. Reed, of Maine, 147; C. N. Brumm, of Pennsylvania, 2.

---

[1] Seth C. Moffatt, of the 11th Michigan district, died Dec. 22, 1887, and Henry W. Seymour (R.), was elected to fill the vacancy.

In the course of his address, on taking the Speaker's chair, Mr. Carlisle said:

"Gentlemen, there has scarcely ever been a time in our history when the continued prosperity of the country depended so largely upon legislation in Congress as now, for the reason that the dangers which at this time threaten the commercial and industrial interests of the people are the direct results of laws which Congress alone can modify or repeal. Neither the Executive Department of the General Government nor the local authorities of the several States can deal effectively with the situation which now confronts us. Whatever is done must be done here ; and if nothing is done the responsibility must rest here.

"It must be evident to every one who has taken even a partial view of public affairs that the time has now come when a revision of our revenue laws and a reduction of taxation are absolutely necessary in order to prevent a large and dangerous accumulation of money in the Treasury. Whether this ought or ought not to have been done heretofore is a question which it would be useless now to discuss. It is sufficient for us to know that the financial condition of the Government and the private business of the people alike demand the prompt consideration of these subjects and a speedy enactment of some substantial measure of relief.

"Unfortunately, gentlemen, we are menaced by dangers from opposite directions. While a policy of non-action must inevitably, sooner or later, result in serious injury to the country, we can not be unmindful of the fact that hasty and inconsiderate legislation upon subjects more or less affecting great financial and industrial interests might produce, temporarily at least, disturbances and embarrassments which a wise and prudent course would entirely avoid. Investments made and labor employed in the numerous and valuable industries which have grown up under our present system of taxation ought not to be rudely disturbed by sudden and radical changes in the policy to which they have adjusted themselves, but the just demands of an overtaxed people and the obvious requirements of the financial situation can not be entirely ignored without seriously imperiling much greater and more widely extended interests than any that could possibly be injuriously affected by a moderate and reasonable reduction of duties.

"No part of our people are more immediately and vitally interested in the continuance of financial prosperity than those who labor for wages: for upon them and their families must always fall the first and most disastrous consequences of a monetary crisis; and they, too, are always the last to realize the benefit resulting from a return to prosperous times. Their wages are the first to fall when a crisis comes, and the last to rise when it passes away. Our effort should be to afford the necessary relief to all without injury to the interests of any; and it seems to me that course of legislation should be pursued which will guarantee the laboring-people of the country against the paralyzing effects of a general and prolonged financial depression, and at the same time not interfere with their steady employment, or deprive them of any part of the just rewards of their toil. If this can be done—and I believe it can, if our deliberations are conducted with the wisdom and patriotism which the gravity of the situation demands—this Congress will have cause to congratulate itself upon an achievement which promises peace and prosperity to the country for many years to come."

The following officers of the House were chosen: Chaplain, Rev. W. H. Milburn ; Chief Clerk, Thomas O. Towles; Sergeant-at-Arms, John P. Leedom ; Postmaster, Lycurgus Dalton; Doorkeeper, A. B. Hurt.

The President's Message.—Dec. 6, 1887, the President's Message was sent in. It was as follows:

To the Congress of the United States :

You are confronted at the threshold of your legislative duties with a condition of the national finances which imperatively demands immediate and careful consideration. The amount of money annually exacted through the operation of present laws from the industries and necessities of the people largely exceeds the sum necessary to meet the expenses of the Government.

When we consider that the theory of our institutions guarantees to every citizen the full enjoyment of all the fruits of his industry and enterprise, with only such deduction as may be his share toward the careful and economical maintenance of the Government which protects him, it is plain that the exaction of more than this is indefensible extortion and a culpable betrayal of American fairness and justice. This wrong, inflicted upon those who bear the burden of national taxation, like other wrongs, multiplies a brood of evil consequences. The public Treasury, which should only exist as a conduit conveying the people's tribute to its legitimate objects of expenditure, becomes a hoarding place for money needlessly withdrawn from trade and the people's use, thus crippling our national energies, suspending our country's development, preventing investment in productive enterprise, threatening financial disturbance, and inviting schemes of public plunder.

This condition of our Treasury is not altogether new; and it has more than once of late been submitted to the people's representatives in the Congress, who alone can apply a remedy. And yet the situation still continues, with aggravated incidents, more than ever presaging financial convulsion and widespread disaster. It will not do to neglect this situation because its dangers are not now palpably imminent and apparent. They exist none the less certainly, and await the unforeseen and unexpected occasion when suddenly they will be precipitated upon us.

On the 30th day of June, 1885, the excess of revenues over public expenditures after complying with the annual requirement of the sinking-fund act was $17,859,735.84. During the year ended June 30, 1886, such excess amounted to $49,405,545.20, and during the year ended June 30, 1887, it reached the sum of $55,567,849.54. The annual contributions to the sinking fund during the three years above specified, amounting in the aggregate to $138,058,320.94 and deducted from the surplus as stated, were made by calling in for that purpose outstanding three-per-cent. bonds of the Government. During the six months prior to June 30, 1887, the surplus revenue had grown so large by repeated accumulation and it was feared the withdrawal of this great sum of money needed by the people would so affect the business of the country, that the sum of $79,864,100 of such surplus was applied to the payment of the principal and interest of the three-per-cent. bonds still outstanding, and which were then payable at the option of the Government.

The precarious condition of financial affairs among the people still needing relief, immediately after the 30th day of June, 1887, the remainder of the three-per-cent. bonds then outstanding, amounting with principal and interest to the sum of $18,877,500, were called in and applied to the sinking-fund contribution for the current fiscal year. Notwithstanding these operations of the Treasury Department, representations of distress in business circles not only continued but increased, and absolute peril seemed at hand. In these circumstances the contribution to the sinking fund for the current fiscal year was at once completed by the expenditure of $27,684,283.55 in the purchase of Government bonds not yet due, bearing four and four and one half per cent. interest, the premium paid thereon averaging about twenty-four per cent. for the former and eight per cent. for the latter.

In addition to this the interest accruing during the current year upon the outstanding bonded indebtedness of the Government was to some extent anticipated, and banks selected as depositories of public money were permitted to somewhat increase their deposits.

While the expedients thus employed, to release to the people the money lying idle in the Treasury, served to avert immediate danger, our surplus revenues have continued to accumulate, the excess for the present year amounting on the 1st day of December to $55,258,701.19, and estimated to reach the sum of $113,000,000 on the 30th day of June next, at which date it is expected that this sum, added to prior accumulations, will swell the surplus in the Treasury to $140,-000,000.

There seems to be no assurance that, with such a withdrawal from use of the people's circulating medium, our business community may not in the near future be subjected to the same distress which was quite lately produced from the same cause. And while the functions of our national Treasury should be few and simple, and while its best condition would be reached, I believe, by its entire disconnection with private business interests, yet when, by a perversion of its purposes, it idly holds money uselessly subtracted from the channels of trade, there seems to be reason for the claim that some legitimate means should be devised by the Government to restore in an emergency, without waste or extravagance, such money to its place among the people.

If such an emergency arises there now exists no clear and undoubted Executive power of relief. Heretofore the redemption of three-per-cent. bonds, which were payable at the option of the Government, has afforded a means for the disbursement of the excess of our revenues; but these bonds have all been retired, and there are no bonds outstanding the payment of which we have the right to insist upon. The contribution to the sinking fund which furnishes the occasion for expenditure in the purchase of bonds has been already made for the current year, so that there is no outlet in that direction.

In the present state of legislation the only pretense of any existing Executive power to restore, at this time, any part of our surplus revenues to the people by its expenditure, consists in the supposition that the Secretary of the Treasury may enter the market and purchase the bonds of the Government not yet due, at a rate of premium to be agreed upon. The only provision of law from which such a power could be derived is found in an appropriation bill passed a number of years ago; and it is subject to the suspicion that it was intended as temporary and limited in its application, instead of conferring a continuing discretion and authority. No condition ought to exist which would justify the grant of power to a single official, upon his judgment of its necessity, to with-

hold from or release to the business of the people, in an unusual manner, money held in the Treasury, and thus affect, at his will, the financial situation of the country; and if it is deemed wise to lodge in the Secretary of the Treasury the authority in the present juncture to purchase bonds, it should be plainly vested, and provided as far as possible, with such checks and limitations as will define this official's right and discretion, and at the same time relieve him from undue responsibility.

In considering the question of purchasing bonds as a means of restoring to circulation the surplus money accumulating in the Treasury, it should be borne in mind that premiums must, of course, be paid upon such purchase, that there may be a large part of these bonds held as investments which can not be purchased at any price, and that combinations among holders, who are willing to sell, may unreasonably enhance the cost of such bonds to the Government.

It has been suggested that the present bonded debt might be refunded at a less rate of interest, and the difference between the old and new security paid in cash, thus finding use for the surplus in the Treasury. The success of this plan, it is apparent, must depend upon the volition of the holders of the present bonds; and it is not entirely certain that the inducement which must be offered them would result in more financial benefit to the Government than the purchase of bonds, while the latter proposition would reduce the principal of the debt by actual payment, instead of extending it.

The proposition to deposit the money held by the Government in banks throughout the country, for use by the people, is, it seems to me, exceedingly objectionable in principle, as establishing too close a relationship between the operations of the Government Treasury and the business of the country, and too extensive a commingling of their money, thus fostering an unnatural reliance in private business upon public funds. If this scheme should be adopted it should only be done as a temporary expedient to meet an urgent necessity. Legislative and Executive effort should generally be in the opposite direction, and should have a tendency to divorce, as much and as fast as can safely be done, the Treasury Department from private enterprise.

Of course it is not expected that unnecessary and extravagant appropriations will be made for the purpose of avoiding the accumulation of an excess of revenue. Such expenditure, besides the demoralization of all just conceptions of public duty which it entails, stimulates a habit of reckless improvidence not in the least consistent with the mission of our people or the high and beneficent purposes of our Government.

I have deemed it my duty to thus bring to the knowledge of my countrymen, as well as to the attention of their representatives charged with the responsibility of legislative relief, the gravity of our financial situation. The failure of the Congress heretofore to provide against the dangers which it was quite evident the very nature of the difficulty must necessarily produce, caused a condition of financial distress and apprehension since your last adjournment, which taxed to the utmost all the authority and expedients within Executive control; and these appear now to be exhausted. If disaster results from the continued inaction of Congress, the responsibility must rest where it belongs.

Though the situation thus far considered is fraught with danger which should be fully realized, and though it presents features of wrong to the people as well as peril to the country, it is but a result growing out of a perfectly palpable and apparent cause, constantly reproducing the same alarming circumstances —a congested national Treasury and a depleted monetary condition in the business of the country. It need hardly be stated that while the present situation demands a remedy, we can only be saved from a like predicament in the future by the removal of its cause.

Our scheme of taxation, by means of which this needless surplus is taken from the people and put into the public Treasury, consists of a tariff or duty levied upon importations from abroad, and internal revenue taxes levied upon the consumption of tobacco and spirituous and malt liquors. It must be conceded that none of the things subjected to internal revenue taxation are, strictly speaking, necessaries; there appears to be no just complaint of this taxation by the consumers of these articles, and there seems to be nothing so well able to bear the burden without hardship to any portion of the people.

But our present tariff laws, the vicious, inequitable, and illogical source of unnecessary taxation, ought to be at once revised and amended. These laws, as their primary and plain effect, raise the price to consumers of all articles imported and subject to duty, by precisely the sum paid for such duties. Thus the amount of the duty measures the tax paid by those who purchase for use these imported articles. Many of these things, however, are raised or manufactured in our own country, and the duties now levied upon foreign goods and products are called protection to these home manufactures, because they render it possible for those of our people who are manufacturers to make these taxed articles and sell them for a price equal to that demanded for the imported goods that have paid customs duty. So it happens that while comparatively a few use the imported articles, millions of our people, who never used and never saw any of the foreign products, purchase and use things of the same kind made in this country, and pay therefor nearly or quite the same enhanced price which the duty adds to the imported articles. Those who buy imports pay the duty charged thereon into the public Treasury, but the great majority of our citizens, who buy domestic articles of the same class, pay a sum at least approximately equal to this duty to the home manufacturer. This reference to the operation of our tariff laws is not made by way of instruction, but in order that we may be constantly reminded of the manner in which they impose a burden upon those who consume domestic products as well as those who consume imported articles, and thus create a tax upon all our people.

It is not proposed to entirely relieve the country of this taxation. It must be extensively continued as the source of the Government's income; and in a readjustment of our tariff the interests of American labor engaged in manufacture should be carefully considered, as well as the preservation of our manufacturers. It may be called protection, or by any other name, but relief from the hardships and dangers of our present tariff laws, should be devised with especial precaution against imperiling the existence of our manufacturing interests. But this existence should not mean a condition which, without regard to the public welfare or a national exigency, must always insure the realization of immense profits instead of moderately profitable returns. As the volume and diversity of our national activities increase, new recruits are added to those who desire a continuation of the advantages which they conceive the present system of tariff taxation directly affords them. So stubbornly have all efforts to reform the present condition been resisted by those of our fellow-citizens thus engaged, that they can hardly complain of the suspicion, entertained to a certain extent, that there exists an organized combination all along the line to maintain their advantage.

We are in the midst of centennial celebrations, and with becoming pride we rejoice in American skill and ingenuity, in American energy and enterprise, and in the wonderful natural advantages and resources developed by a century's national growth. Yet when an attempt is made to justify a scheme which permits a tax to be laid upon every consumer in the land for the benefit of our manufacturers, quite beyond a reasonable demand for governmental regard, it suits the purposes of advocacy to call our manufactures infant industries, still needing the highest and greatest degree of favor and fostering care that can be wrung from Federal legislation.

It is also said that the increase in the price of domestic manufactures resulting from the present tariff is necessary in order that higher wages may be paid to our workingmen employed in manufactories, than are paid for what is called the pauper labor of Europe. All will acknowledge the force of an argument which involves the welfare and liberal compensation of our laboring-people. Our labor is honorable in the eyes of every American citizen; and as it lies at the foundation of our development and progress, it is entitled, without affectation or hypocrisy, to the utmost regard. The standard of our laborers' life should not be measured by that of any other country less favored, and they are entitled to their full share of all our advantages.

By the last census it is made to appear that of the 17,392,099 of our population engaged in all kinds of industries 7,670,493 are employed in agriculture,- 4,074,238 in professional and personal service (2,934,- 876 of whom are domestic servants and laborers), while 1,810,256 are employed in trade and transportation, and 3,837,112 are classed as employed in manufacturing and mining.

For present purposes, however, the last number given should be considerably reduced. Without attempting to enumerate all, it will be conceded that there should be deducted from those which it includes 375,143 carpenters and joiners, 285,401 milliners, dressmakers, and seamstresses, 172,726 blacksmiths, 133,756 tailors and tailoresses, 102,473 masons, 76,- 241 butchers, 41,309 bakers, 22,083 plasterers, and 4,891 engaged in manufacturing agricultural implements, amounting in the aggregate to 1,214,023, leaving 2,623,069 persons employed in such manufacturing industries as are claimed to be benefited by a high tariff.

To these the appeal is made to save their employment and maintain their wages by resisting a change. There should be no disposition to answer such suggestions by the allegation that they are in a minority among those who labor, and therefore should forego an advantage, in the interest of low prices for the majority; their compensation, as it may be affected by the operation of tariff laws, should at all times be scrupulously kept in view; and yet with slight reflection they will not overlook the fact that they are consumers with the rest; that they, too, have their own wants and those of their families to supply from their earnings, and that the price of the necessaries of life, as well as the amount of the wages, will regulate the measure of their welfare and comfort.

But the reduction of taxation demanded should be so measured as not to necessitate or justify either the loss of employment by the workingman nor the lessening of his wages; and the profits still remaining to the manufacturer, after a necessary readjustment, should furnish no excuse for the sacrifice of the interests of his employés either in their opportunity to work or in the diminution of their compensation. Nor can the worker in manufactures fail to understand that while a high tariff is claimed to be necessary to allow the payment of remunerative wages, it certainly results in a very large increase in the price of nearly all sorts of manufactures, which, in almost countless forms, he needs for the use of himself and his family. He receives at the desk of his employer his wages, and perhaps before he reaches his home is obliged, in a purchase for family use of an article which embraces his own labor, to return in the payment of the increase in price which the tariff permits, the hard-earned compensation of many days of toil.

The farmer and the agriculturist who manufacture nothing, but who pay the increased price which the tariff imposes, upon every agricultural implement, upon all he wears, and upon all he uses and owns, except the increase of his flocks and herds and such things as his husbandry produces from the soil, is invited to aid in maintaining the present situation; and he is told that a high duty on imported wool is necessary for the benefit of those who have sheep to shear, in order that the price of their wool may be increased. They of course are not reminded that the farmer who has no sheep is by this scheme obliged, in his purchases of clothing and woolen goods, to pay a tribute to his fellow-farmer as well as to the manufacturer and merchant; nor is any mention made of the fact that the sheep-owners themselves and their households must wear clothing and use other articles manufactured from the wool they sell at tariff prices, and thus as consumers must return their share of this increased price to the tradesman.

I think it may be fairly assumed that a large proportion of the sheep owned by the farmers throughout the country are found in small flocks numbering from twenty-five to fifty. The duty on the grade of imported wool which these sheep yield, is ten cents each pound if of the value of thirty cents or less, and twelve cents if of the value of more than thirty cents. If the liberal estimate of six pounds be allowed for each fleece, the duty thereon would be sixty or seventy-two cents, and this may be taken as the utmost enhancement of its price to the farmer by reason of this duty. Eighteen dollars would thus represent the increased price of the wool from twenty-five sheep and thirty-six dollars that from the wool of fifty sheep; and at present values this addition would amount to about one third of its price. If upon its sale the farmer receives this or a less tariff profit, the wool leaves his hands charged with precisely that sum, which in all its changes will adhere to it, until it reaches the consumer. When manufactured into cloth and other goods and material for use, its cost is not only increased to the extent of the farmer's tariff profit, but a further sum has been added for the benefit of the manufacturer under the operation of other tariff laws. In the mean time the day arrives when the farmer finds it necessary to purchase woolen goods and material to clothe himself and family for the winter. When he faces the tradesman for that purpose he discovers that he is obliged not only to return in the way of increased prices, his tariff profit on the wool he sold, and which then perhaps lies before him in manufactured form, but that he must add a considerable sum thereto to meet a further increase in cost caused by a tariff duty on the manufacture. Thus in the end he is aroused to the fact that he has paid upon a moderate purchase, as a result of the tariff scheme, which, when he sold his wool seemed so profitable, an increase in price more than sufficient to sweep away all the tariff profit he received upon the wool he produced and sold.

When the number of farmers engaged in woolraising is compared with all the farmers in the country, and the small opinion they bear to our population is considered, by which it is made apparent that, in the case of a large part of those who own sheep, the benefit of the present tariff on wool is illusory; and, above all, when it must be conceded that the increase of the cost of living caused by such tariff, becomes a burden upon those with moderate means and the poor, the employed and unemployed, the sick and well, and the young and old, and that it constitutes a tax which, with relentless grasp, is fastened upon the clothing of every man, woman, and child in the land, reasons are suggested why the removal or reduction of this duty should be included in a revision of our tariff laws.

In speaking of the increased cost to the consumer of our home manufactures, resulting from a duty laid upon imported articles of the same description, the fact is not overlooked that competition among our domestic producers sometimes has the effect of keeping the price of their products below the highest limit allowed by such duty. But it is notorious that this competition is too often strangled by combinations quite prevalent at this time, and frequently called trusts, which have for their object the regulation of the supply and price of commodities made and sold

by members of the combination. The people can hardly hope for any consideration in the operation of these selfish schemes.

If, however, in the absence of such combination, a healthy and free competition reduces the price of any particular dutiable article of home production, below the limit which it might otherwise reach under our tariff laws, and if, with such reduced price, its manufacture continues to thrive, it is entirely evident that one thing has been discovered which should be carefully scrutinized in an effort to reduce taxation.

The necessity of combination to maintain the price of any commodity to the tariff point, furnishes proof that some one is willing to accept lower prices for such commodity, and that such prices are remunerative; and lower prices produced by competition prove the same thing. Thus where either of these conditions exists a case would seem to be presented for an easy reduction of taxation.

The considerations which have been presented touching our tariff laws are intended only to enforce an earnest recommendation that the surplus revenues of the Government be peremptorily reduced by the reduction of our customs duties, and, at the same time, to emphasize a suggestion that in accomplishing this purpose, we may discharge a double duty to our people by granting to them a measure of relief from tariff taxation in quarters where it is most needed and from sources where it can be most fairly and justly accorded.

Nor can the presentation made of such considerations be, with any degree of fairness, regarded as evidence of unfriendliness toward our manufacturing interests, or of any lack of appreciation of their value and importance.

These interests constitute a leading and most substantial element of our national greatness and furnish the proud proof of our country's progress. But if in the emergency that presses upon us our manufacturers are asked to surrender something for the public good and to avert disaster, their patriotism, as well as a grateful recognition of advantages already afforded, should lead them to willing co-operation. No demand is made that they shall forego all the benefits of governmental regard; but they can not fail to be admonished of their duty, as well as their enlightened self-interest and safety, when they are reminded of the fact that financial panic and collapse, to which the present condition tends, afford no greater shelter or protection to our manufactures than to our other important enterprises. Opportunity for safe, careful, and deliberate reform is now offered; and none of us should be unmindful of a time when an abused and irritated people, heedless of those who have resisted timely and reasonable relief, may insist upon a radical and sweeping rectification of their wrongs.

The difficulty attending a wise and fair revision of our tariff laws is not underestimated. It will require on the part of the Congress great labor and care, and especially a broad and national contemplation of the subject, and a patriotic disregard of such local and selfish claims as are unreasonable and reckless of the welfare of the entire country.

Under our present laws more than four thousand articles are subject to duty. Many of these do not in any way compete with our own manufactures, and many are hardly worth attention as subjects of revenue. A considerable reduction can be made in the aggregate, by adding them to the free list. The taxation of luxuries presents no features of hardship; but the necessaries of life used and consumed by all the people, the duty upon which adds to the cost of living in every home, should be greatly cheapened.

The radical reduction of the duties imposed on raw material used in manufactures, or its free importation, is of course an important factor in any effort to reduce the price of these necessaries; it would not only relieve them from the increased cost caused by the tariff on such material, but the manufactured product being thus cheapened, that part of the tariff now laid upon such product as a compensation to our manufacturers for the present price of raw material could be accordingly modified. Such reduction, or free importation, would serve, beside, to largely reduce the revenue. It is not apparent how such a change could have any injurious effect upon our manufacturers. On the contrary it would appear to give them a better chance in foreign markets with the manufacturers of other countries, who cheapen their wares by free material. Thus our people might have the opportunity of extending their sales beyond the limits of home consumption, saving them from the depression, interruption to business, and loss caused by a glutted domestic market and affording their employés more certain and steady labor with its resulting quiet and contentment.

The question thus imperatively presented for solution should be approached in a spirit higher than partisanship and considered in the light of that regard for patriotic duty which should characterize the action of those intrusted with the weal of a confiding people. But the obligation to declared party policy and principle is not wanting to urge prompt and effective action. Both great political parties now represented in the Government have by repeated and authoritative declarations condemned the condition of our laws which permits the collection from the people of unnecessary revenue, and have in the most solemn manner, promised its correction, and neither as citizens nor partisans are our countrymen in a mood to condone the deliberate violation of these pledges.

Our progress toward a wise conclusion will not be improved by dwelling upon the theories of protection and free trade. This savors too much of bandying epithets.

It is a condition which confronts us—not a theory. Relief from this condition may involve a slight reduction of the advantages which we award our home productions, but the entire withdrawal of such advantages should not be contemplated. The question of free trade is absolutely irrelevant; and the persistent claim, made in certain quarters, that all efforts to relieve the people from unjust and unnecessary taxation are schemes of so called "Free Traders" is mischievous and far removed from any consideration for the public good. The simple and plain duty which we owe the people is to reduce taxation to the necessary expenses of an economical operation of the Government, and to restore to the business of the country the money which we hold in the Treasury through the perversion of governmental powers. These things can and should be done with safety to all our industries, without danger to the opportunity for remunerative labor which our workingmen have, and with benefit to them and all our people, by cheapening their means of subsistence and increasing the measure of their comforts.

The Constitution provides that the President "shall from time to time give to the Congress information of the state of the Union." It has been the custom of the Executive, in compliance with this provision, to annually exhibit to the Congress, at the opening of its session, the general condition of the country, and to detail with some particularity the operation of the different Executive Departments. It would be especially agreeable to follow this course at the present time and to call attention to the valuable accomplishments of these departments during the fiscal year. But I am so much impressed with the paramount importance of the subject to which this communication has thus far been devoted, that I shall forego the addition of any other topic, and only urge upon your immediate consideration the "state of the Union" as shown in the present condition of our Treasury and our general fiscal situation, upon which every element of our safety and prosperity depends.

The reports of the heads of departments, which will be submitted, contain full and explicit information touching the transaction of the business intrusted to them, and such recommendations relating to legislation in the public interest as they deem advisable. I ask for these reports and recommendations the deliberate examination and action of the legislative branch of the Government. There are other subjects not embraced in the departmental reports demanding legislative consideration and which I should be glad to submit. Some of them, however, have been earnestly presented in previous messages, and as to them I beg leave to repeat prior recommendations.

As the law makes no provision for any report from the Department of State a brief history of the transactions of that important department together with other matters which it may hereafter be deemed essential to commend to the attention of Congress, may furnish the occasion for a future communication.

Washington, Dec. 6, 1887.   Grover Cleveland.

Revenue Reform.—The great question of the session was revenue reform, as the Democratic majority of the House of Representatives undertook to carry out the policy outlined in the President's message. For this purpose the Democratic members of the Ways and Means Committee set to work and drafted the Mills Bill, so called after the chairman of the committee, Roger Q. Mills, of Texas. April 2, 1888, that gentleman reported this measure as one "to reduce taxation, and simplify the laws in relation to the collection of revenue"; and it was referred to the committee of the whole, and ordered to be printed with the accompanying majority report and the minority report submitted by Mr. McKinley, of Ohio. The bill was taken up for discussion April 17, and the debate was opened by Mr. Mills in support of the measure and Mr. Kelley, of Pennsylvania, in opposition to it. On May 19 the general debate was closed with speeches by Speaker Carlisle and Mr. Reed, of Maine; on May 31 the debate under the five-minute rule was begun, and July 19 it closed. Mr. Springer, of Illinois, on that occasion said: "The debate on the pending bill began on the 17th day of April last; since that time the committee has been occupied in general debate twenty-three day and eight evening sessions. There were consumed in the general debate one hundred and eleven hours and fifty-four minutes—fifty-six hours and eighteen minutes by Democrats, and fifty-five hours and thirty-six minutes by Republicans or those opposed to the bill. In all, one hundred and fifty-one speeches were made during the general debate on this bill. The debate upon the bill by paragraphs began May 31, since which time there have been occupied twenty-eight days, or one hundred and twenty-eight hours and ten minutes, including the time that will be consumed to-day. The whole number of days devoted to the debate and consideration of the bill has been fifty-one, and the number of hours two hundred and forty. This debate will perhaps be known as the most remarkable that ever occurred in our parliamentary history. It has awakened an interest not only throughout the length and breadth of our own country, but throughout the civilized world; and henceforth, as long as our Government shall endure, it shall be known as 'The Great Tariff Debate of 1888.'"

In his opening speech, Mr. Mills urged a reduction of the revenue on the ground that it exceeds the needs of the Government, and is produced by a system of taxation adopted to meet the emergencies of the civil war: "Mr. Chairman, during our late civil war the expenditures required by an enormous military establishment made it necessary that the burdens of taxation should be laid heavily in all directions authorized by the Constitution. The internal-revenue and direct taxes were called into requisition to supplement the revenues arising from customs, to aid the Treasury to respond to the heavy demands which were being daily made upon it. The duties on imports were raised from an average on dutiable goods of 18·84 per cent. in 1861 to an average of 40·29 per cent. on dutiable goods during the five years from 1862 to 1866, inclusive. This was recognized at the time as an exceptionally heavy burden. It was stated by the distinguished gentleman who then presented to the House the bill so largely increasing the duties, and which to-day bears his honored name, that it was demanded by the exigencies of war, and must cease on the return of peace. In his own words, he said: 'This is intended as a war measure, a temporary measure, and we must as such give it our support.' More than twenty years have elapsed since the war ended. A generation has passed away and a new generation has appeared on the stage since peace has returned to bless our common country; but these war taxes still remain; and they are heavier to-day than they were on an average during the five years of the existence of hostilities. The average rate of duty during the last five years, from 1883 to 1887, inclusive, on dutiable goods amounts to 44·51 per cent., and during the last year the average is 47·10 per cent. Instead of the rate of taxation being reduced to meet the wants of an efficient administration of government in time of peace, it continues to grow and fill the coffers of the Government with money not required for public purposes, and which rightfully should remain in the pockets of the people."

But, in the opinion of Mr. Mills, excessive taxation is not the greatest evil of the existing tariff: "The greatest evil that is inflicted by it is in the destruction of the values of our exports. Remember that the great body of our exports are agricultural products. It has been so through our whole history. From 75 to over 80 per cent. of the exports of this country year by year are agricultural products. Cotton is first, then bread-stuffs, pork, beef, butter, cheese, lard. These are the things that keep up our foreign trade, and when you put on or keep on such duties as we have now—war duties which were regarded as so enormous even in the very midst of hostilities that they were declared to be temporary—when you put on or retain those duties, they limit and prohibit importation and that limits or prohibits exportation. It takes two to make a trade. All the commerce of all the countries of the world is carried on by an exchange of commodities — commodities going from the country where they are produced at the least cost to seek a market in those countries where they can either not be produced at all or where they can be produced only at the highest cost of production. We are the great agricultural country of the world, and we have been feeding the people of Europe, and the people of Europe have got to give us in exchange the products of their labor in their shops; and when we put on excessive duties for the purpose of prohibiting the importations of their goods, as a necessary result we put an excessive duty upon the exportation of our own agricultural products. And what does that do? It throws our surplus products upon our own markets at home, which become glutted and oversupplied, and prices go down. So it is with the people of Europe who are manufacturing and producing things that we can not produce, but which we want. Their products are thrown upon their home markets, which are glutted and oversupplied, and their prices likewise go down. And whenever, from any cause, prices start up in Europe, our tariff being levied mainly by specific duties upon quantity, not upon value, the tariff goes down, and then we see large importation and, as a result, large exportation. Then we see a rise in agricultural products; then we see the circulation of money all through the whole of our industrial system; we see our people going to work, our manufactories starting up, and prosperity in every part of the land."

Mr. Mills also argued that the protective system, while of advantage to particular manufacturers, tends to cripple our production: "We are the greatest agricultural people in the world. We exceed all others in the products of manufacture, but we export next to nothing of our product. Why should we not export the three hundred and seventy-five millions of cotton goods which England is now exporting? She buys her cotton from us, pays the cost of transportation to her factories, makes the goods, and sends them all over the world. That trade, at least the most of it, is ours whenever we get ready to take it. Why should we not make and send out the hundred millions of woolen goods which she is annually exporting? We have the advantage of her in almost everything except cost of materials. Why should we not make and export the hundred millions of iron and steel which she is making and sending away annually? There is no reason except that high tariffs and trusts and combinations are in our way, and they muster all their forces to prevent us from taking the place which our advantages entitle us to take. We are the greatest people in the world. We have the highest standard of civilization; we have the highest and best diffusion of knowledge among our people. We utilize the power of machinery more than any people in the world. We produce by our labor more than any people in the world. We have everything to command success in any contest over any rival. We are the first cotton-producing country. We have wool, flax, hemp; our country is full of coal and ores and lumber, and yet with all these advantages over all others we have pursued a suicidal policy of protection, which has closed the markets of the world against us; and not content to stop here, we have plundered the great body of our agricultural people out of a large part of their wealth. We must make a departure. Instead of laying the burdens of taxation upon the necessaries of life, instead of destroying our foreign commerce, we should encourage it as we would encourage our home commerce. We should remove every unnecessary burden. We should lay taxes to obtain revenue, but not restrict importation. We should place every material of manufacture on the free list, start up our fires, put our wheels in motion, and put all our people to work at good wages."

After arguing that it is increased production that makes cheap goods and high wages, Mr. Mills said, in regard to the effect of the existing tariff on labor: "I have taken from the first annual report of the Commissioner of Labor and the report of the census on wages some figures given by manufacturers themselves of the total cost of the product and the labor cost of the articles they are making. I have put the tariff duty by the side of them to show whether in the little reductions we are asking in this bill we have gone beyond that pledge we as a party have made that we would not reduce taxation so low as to injure our laborers, or as not to cover the difference in cost of labor between American and foreign products. This will show, and I ask your attention to it, that the tariff is not intended to and does not benefit labor, It will show that the benefit of the tariff never passes beyond the pocket of the manufacturer, and to the pockets of his workmen.

"I find in this report one pair of five-pound blankets. The whole cost, as stated by the manufacturer, is $2.51. The labor cost be paid for making them is 35 cents. The present tariff is $1.90. Now, here is $1.55 in this tariff over and above the entire labor cost of these blankets. Why did not that manufacturer go and give that money to the laborer? He is able to do it. Here is a tariff that gives him $1.90 on that pair of blankets for the benefit of his laborer, but notwithstanding that the tariff was imposed for the benefit of American labor and to preserve high wages, every dollar of that tariff went into the manufacturer's pocket. The poor fellow who made the blankets got 35 cents and the manufacturer kept the $1.90.

"Here is one yard of flannel, weighing four ounces; it cost 18 cents, of which the laborer got 3 cents; the tariff on it is 8 cents. How is it that the whole 8 cents did not get into the pockets of the laborer? Is it not strange that those who made the tariff and fastened upon the people these war rates in a time of profound peace, and who are now constantly assailing the Democratic party because it is untrue to the workingman, did not make some provision by which the generous bounty they gave should reach the pocket of him for whom they said it was intended? They charge that we are trying to strike down the labor of the country. Why do they not see that the money they are taking out of the hard earnings of the people is delivered in good faith to the workman? One yard of cassimere, weighing 16 ounces, cost $1.38; the labor cost is 29 cents; the tariff duty is 80 cents. One pound of sewing-silk costs $5.66; the cost for labor is 85 cents; the tariff is $1.69. One gallon of linseed-oil costs 46 cents; the labor cost is 2 cents; the tariff cost is 25 cents. One ton of bar-iron costs $31; the labor cost is $10; the tariff fixes several rates for bar-iron. I give the lowest rate, $17.92. One ton of foundry pig-iron costs $11; the labor costs $1.64; the tariff is $6.72."

After continuing the discussion of this point in detail, Mr. Mills said: "Now, Mr. Chairman, I have gone through with a number of articles taken from these official reports made by the manufacturers themselves, and I have shown that the tariff was not framed for the benefit of the laborer, or that if it was so intended by those who framed it, the benefit never reaches the laborer, not a dollar of it. The working-people are hired in the market at the lowest rates at which their services can be had, and all the 'boodle' that has been granted by these tariff bills goes into the pockets of the manufacturers. It builds up palaces; it concentrates wealth; it makes great and powerful magnates; but it distributes none of its beneficence in the homes of our laboring poor."

As to the spirit of the protective system which is sometimes called the American policy, Mr. Mills said: "I repel it, sir; it is not American. It is the reverse of American. That policy is American which clings most closely to the fundamental idea that underlies our institutions and upon which the whole superstructure of our Government is erected, and that idea is freedom—freedom secured by the guarantees of government; freedom to think, to speak, to write; freedom to go where we please, select our own occupations; freedom to labor when we please and where we please; freedom to receive and enjoy all the results of our labor; freedom to sell our products, and freedom to buy the products of others, and freedom to markets for the products of our labor, without which the freedom of labor is restricted and denied; freedom from restraints in working and marketing the products of our toil, except such as may be necessary in the interest of the Government; freedom from all unnecessary burdens; freedom from all exactions upon the citizen except such as may be necessary to support an honest, efficient, and economical administration of the Government that guarantees him protection to 'life, liberty, and the pursuit of happiness'; freedom from all taxation except that which is levied for the support of the Government; freedom from taxation levied for the purpose of enriching favored classes by the spoliation and plunder of the people; freedom from all systems of taxation that do not fall with 'equal and exact justice upon all'—that do not raise the revenues of government in the way that is least burdensome to the people and with the least possible disturbance to their business. That, sir, is the American policy."

Mr. McKinley, of Ohio, who spoke May 18, conceded the necessity of reducing the revenue of the Government, but denied that the reduction should be made, as proposed in the Mills Bill. He said: "It will be freely confessed by our political opponents that this bill is but the beginning of a tariff policy marked out by the President, and is a partial response only to his message, to be followed up with additional legislation until our system of taxation shall be brought back to the ancient landmarks of the Democratic party, to a purely revenue basis; that is, that the tariff or duty put upon foreign importations shall hereafter look to revenue and revenue only, and discard all other considerations.

"This brings us face to face, therefore, with the two opposing systems, that of a revenue as distinguished from a protective tariff, and upon their respective merits they must stand or fall. Now, what are they? First, what is a revenue tariff? Upon what principle does it rest?. It is a tariff or tax placed upon such articles of foreign production imported here as will produce the largest revenue with the smallest tax.

"To secure larger revenue from lower duties necessitates largely increased importations, and if these compete with domestic products the latter must be diminished or find other and distant and I may say impossible markets or get out of the way altogether. A genuine revenue tariff imposes no tax upon foreign importations the like of which are produced at home, or. if produced at home, in quantities not capable of supplying the home consumption, in which case it may be truthfully said the tax is added to the foreign cost and is paid by the consumer.

"A revenue tariff seeks out those articles which domestic production can not supply, or only inadequately supply, and which the wants of our people demand, and imposes the duty upon them, and permits as far as possible the competing foreign product to be imported free of duty. This principle is made conspicuous in the bill under consideration; for example, wool, a competing foreign product, which our own flock-masters can fully supply for domestic wants, is put upon the free list, while sugar, with a home product of only one eleventh of the home consumption, is left dutiable.

"What is a protective tariff? It is a tariff upon foreign imports so adjusted as to secure the necessary revenue, and judiciously imposed upon those foreign products the like of which are produced at home or the like of which we are capable of producing at home. It imposes the duty upon the competing foreign product; it makes it bear the burden or duty, and, as far as possible, luxuries only excepted, permits the non-competing foreign product to come in free of duty. Articles of common use, comfort, and necessity which we can not produce here it sends to the people untaxed and free from custom-house exactions. Tea, coffee, spices, and drugs are such articles, and under our system are upon the free list. It says to our foreign competitor, if you want to bring your merchandise here, your farm products here, your coal and iron ore, your wool, your salt, your pottery, your glass, your cottons and woolens, and sell alongside of our producers in our markets, we will make your product bear a duty; in effect, pay for the privilege of doing it. Our kind of a tariff makes the competing foreign article carry the burden, draw the load, supply the revenue; and in performing this essential. office it encourages at the same time our own industries and protects our own people in their chosen employments. That is the mission and purpose of a protective tariff. That is what we mean to maintain, and any measure which will destroy it we shall firmly resist, and if beaten on this floor we will appeal from your decision to the people, before whom parties and policies must at last be tried. We have free trade among ourselves throughout thirty-eight States and the Territories and among sixty millions of people. Absolute freedom of exchange within our own borders and among our own citizens is the law of the republic. Reasonable taxation and restraint upon those without is the dictate of enlightened patriotism and the doctrine of the Republican party. Free trade in the United States is founded upon a community of equalities and reciprocities. It is like the unrestrained freedom and reciprocal relations and obligations of a family. Here we are one country, one language, one allegiance, one standard of citizenship, one flag, one Constitution, one nation, one destiny. It is otherwise with foreign nations, each a separate organism, a distinct and independent political society organized for its own, to protect its own, and work out its own destiny. We deny to those foreign nations free trade with us upon equal terms with our own producers. The foreign producer has no right or claim to equality with our own. He is not amenable to our laws. There are resting upon him none of the obligations of citizenship. He pays no taxes. He performs no civil duties; is subject to no demands for military service. He is exempt from State, county, and municipal obligations. He contributes nothing to the support, the progress, and glory of the nation. Why should he enjoy unrestrained equal privileges and profits in our markets with our producers, our labor, and our tax-payers? Let the gentleman who follows me answer. We put a burden upon his productions, we discriminate against his merchandise, because he is alien to us and our interests, and we do it to protect our own, defend our own, preserve our own, who are always with us in adversity and prosperity, in sympathy and purpose, and, if necessary, in sacrifice. That is the principle which governs us. I submit it is a patriotic and righteous one. In our own country, each citizen competing with the other in free and unresentful rivalry, while with the rest of the world all are united and together in resisting outside competition as we would foreign interference."

Mr. McKinley denied that the Mills Bill, though it professed to aim at a reduction of the revenue, would have that result so far as its tariff changes were concerned : "Take from this bill its internal-revenue features, its reduction of twenty-four and a half million dollars from tobacco and from special licenses to dealers in spirits and tobacco, eliminate these from the bill, and you will not secure a dollar of reduction to the Treasury under its operation. Your $27,000,000 of proposed reduction by the free list will be more than offset by the increased revenues which shall come from your lower duties; and I venture the prediction here to-day that if this bill should become a law, at the end of the fiscal year 1889 the dutiable list under it will carry more money into the Treasury than is carried into the Treasury under the present law, because with every reduction of duties upon foreign imports you stimulate and increase foreign importations; and to the extent that you increase foreign importations, to that extent you increase the revenue."

Mr. McKinley criticised certain inconsistencies in the details of the bill, and then denounced one of the main features of it: "Now, there is one leading feature of this bill, which is not by any means the most objectionable feature, but which, if it stood alone, ought to defeat this entire measure; and that is the introduction of the ad-valorem system of assessment to take the place of the specific system now generally in force. You all know the difference between the ad-valorem system and the specific mode of levying duties. One is based upon value, the other upon quantity. One is based upon the foreign value, difficult of ascertainment, resting on the judgment of experts, all the time offering a bribe to undervaluation; the other rests upon quantity, fixed and well known the world over, always determinable and always uniform. The one is assessed by the yard-stick, the ton, and the pound-weight of commerce, and the other is assessed by the foreign value, fixed by the for-

eign importer or his agent in New York or elsewhere; fixed by the producer, fixed by anybody at any price to escape the payment of full duties."

Of the value of a home market and the diffusion of profits under a protective system, Mr. McKinley said : "Why, the establishment of a furnace or factory or mill in any neighborhood has the effect at once to enhance the value of all property and all values for miles surrounding it. They produce increased activity. The farmer has a better and a nearer market for his products. The merchant, the butcher, the grocer, have an increased trade. The carpenter is in greater demand; he is called upon to build more houses. Every branch of trade, every avenue of labor, will feel almost immediately the energizing influence of a new industry. The truck-farm is in demand; the perishable products, the fruits, the vegetables, which in many cases will not bear exportation, and for which a foreign market is too distant to be available, find a constant and ready demand at good paying prices. What the agriculturist of this country wants more than anything else, after he has gathered his crop, are consumers —consumers at home, men who do not produce what they eat, who must purchase all they consume; men who are engaged in manufacturing, in mining, in cotton-spinning, in the potteries, and in the thousands of productive industries which command all their time and energy, and whose employments do not admit of their producing their own food. The agriculturist further wants these consumers near and convenient to his field of supply."

After arguing that a protective system maintains high wages for the laborer, Mr. McKinley asserted that it also tends to reduce prices of commodities, and he illustrated his position as follows: "Blankets are numbered according to grade and according to weight. There are several grades of five-pound blankets numbered 1, 2, 3, 4, and 5. A No. 1 five-pound blanket made in the city of Philadelphia sells for $1.72. The labor represented in the blanket is 87½ cents; the duty is $1.02. Of a scarlet blanket, five pounds, the price is $2.27; the labor is 87½ cents; the duty is $3.17. Of the white all-wool Falls of Schuylkill blanket, the price is $3.62; the labor, $1.05; the duty, $2.60. Of the Gold-Medal blanket the price is $4.53; the labor, $1.05; the duty, $3.50.

"Now, Mr. Chairman, if the duty was added to the cost, what would the American manufacturers get for these blankets? They should get for the first blanket $2.74. How much do they get? They get only $1.72. They should get for the second blanket, duty added, $3.77. How much do they get? They get $2.27. They should get for the third $5.12. How much do they get? They get $3.17. They should get, duty added, for the fourth class $6.22. How much do they get? They get $4.35. They should get, duty added, for the highest grade $8.03. How much do they get? They get $4.05.

"Now, Mr. Chairman, what did these same blankets cost in 1860 under a revenue tariff, under the free-trade domination of this country by the Democratic party? What did we pay for the same blankets that year, as contrasted with what we pay now? The blanket that sells to-day for $1.02 sold in 1860 for $2. The blanket that sells now for $1.45 sold in 1860 for $2.50. The blanket that sells now for $1.31 sold in 1860 for $2.25. The blanket that sells now for $1.90 sold in 1860 for $3.50. The blanket that sells now for $2.58 sold for $3.75 in 1860. The blanket that sells now for $4.35 sold for $7.50 in 1860. The blanket that sells for $5.85 now sold for $10 in 1860. The blanket that sells now for $6.80 sold for $13 in 1860."

After appealing to the experience of the country in support of a protective system, and citing its prosperity as a result of such a system, Mr. McKinley said: "Who is objecting to our protective system? From what quarter does the complaint come? Not from the enterprising American citizen; not from the manufacturer; not from the laborer, whose wages it improves; not from the consumer, for he is fully satisfied, because under it he buys a cheaper and a better product than he did under the other system; not from the farmer, for he finds among the employés of the protected industries his best and most reliable customers; not from the merchant or the tradesman, for every hive of industry increases the number of his customers and enlarges the volume of his trade. Few, indeed, have been the petitions presented to this House asking for any reduction of duties upon imports. None, that I have seen or heard of, and I have watched with the deepest interest the number and character of these petitions that I might gather from them the drift of public sentiment—I say I have seen none asking for the passage of this bill, or for any such departure from the fiscal policy of the Government so long recognized and followed, while against this legislation there has been no limit to petitions, memorials, prayers, and protests, from producer and consumer alike.

"This measure is not called for by the people; it is not an American measure; it is inspired by importers and foreign producers, most of them aliens, who want to diminish our trade and increase their own; who want to decrease our prosperity and augment theirs, and who have no interest in this country except what they can make out of it. To this is added the influence of the professors in some of our institutions of learning, who teach the science contained in books and not that of practical business. I would rather have my political economy founded upon the every-day experience of the puddler or the potter than the learning of the professor, the farmer and factory hand than the college faculty. Then there is another class who want protective tariffs overthrown. They are the men of independent wealth, with settled and steady incomes, who want everything cheap but currency; the value of everything clipped but coin—cheap labor but dear money. These are the elements which are arrayed against us."

Mr. Randall, in a speech delivered May 18, advocated reducing the revenue by a repeal of the internal-revenue taxes: "These taxes have always been the last to be levied and the first to be repealed when no longer needed. It was the boast of Jefferson that he had given the death-blow to the excise tax, 'that most vexatious of all taxes,' at the commencement of his administration; and among other things for which he received the thanks of the Legislature of his native State on his retirement from office was for 'internal taxes abolished.'

"The first tax also to be repealed after the war of 1812 was the excise tax, which was recommended by Madison, and was the first law enacted under the administration of Monroe.

"The Democratic Convention of 1884 declared that 'the system of direct taxation known as the internal revenue is a 'war tax,' and this declaration, taken in connection with other declarations in the platform which I will quote further on, clearly establishes the fact that the opinion of the convention was that the internal-revenue 'war' taxes should first go, and should all go whenever a sufficient sum was realized from custom-house taxes to meet the expenses of the Government, economically administered. We are practically in such condition now, and a true response to these instructions warrants the repeal of the internal laws to the extent the bill proposes.

"I favor now, as I have always done, a total repeal of the internal-revenue taxation. In the bill which I introduced I proposed to sweep all these taxes off the statute-book except fifty cents on whisky, and I would transfer the collection of that tax to the customs officials, if, upon examination and reflection, it was found to be practicable."

Mr. Randall argued that the amount of protective duty is not added to the price paid by a consumer for an article except in cases where home production can not supply the market and so let competition fix prices; he held, too, that a tariff tax is not a bounty paid by one class to another, as there is an equalization of profits among all who partake of the benefits of an industrial system; and he argued against the notion that farmers could sell their products in dear markets and buy commodities in cheap ones under a free-trade system: "If the farmer ceases to buy the products of the manufacturers, he will certainly cease to sell to them, and must sell his products in the market where he buys what he consumes himself. Suppose last year we had manufactured a thousand millions' worth less than we did and had gone abroad for these products, expecting to pay for them with agricultural products; could a thousand millions more of agricultural products have been sold abroad at the price such products brought here? We sold all the wheat and corn and meat products that Europe would take at the prices that prevailed. Who can tell at what prices Europe would have taken even five hundred millions or one hundred millions more of our agricultural products than she did take? The mere statement of the proposition is enough to disclose the error on which it is founded, and shows the importance of uniting manufactures with agriculture, or, as Jefferson states it, putting the manufacturer by the side of the farmer. In fact, both must, in our country, depend almost exclusively on our home market. It is folly, if not a crime, to attempt a change in these respects. It would bring ruin and bankruptcy without the possibility of having such a result accomplished. The greater the diversity of industries in any country, the greater the wealth-producing power of the people, and the more there is for labor and capital to divide, and the more independent that country becomes."

Mr. Randall criticised the Mills Bill severely in detail. He said: "Notwithstanding these facts, we have before us the bill of the committee, which is not in any proper sense a revision of the tariff, but consists of amendments constituting, I might say, a patchwork upon the existing law, perpetuating and multiplying its numerous infirmities of phraseology; its ambiguities and inequalities, which have perplexed and vexed the executive officers in its administration, have been the subject of volumes of Treasury decisions year by year, and have embroiled the Government and merchants in untold litigation, making it necessary to create new courts for the special trial of customs cases, which are increasing in number month by month, and involve unknown millions of demands upon the Government—a constant menace to the Treasury. Not only have the committee ignored the recommendations of Secretaries Manning and Fairchild and of the customs officers at the various ports for the adoption of specific duties, but have actually, in a large number of cases, substituted ad-valorem rates for existing specific duties, thus showing preference for a system which has been abandoned by all the civilized commercial nations on the globe, and which has been characterized as a system under 'which thieves prosper and honest traders are driven out of business.'

" A declared purpose of this bill is to secure ' free raw materials, to stimulate manufactures.' In execution of this idea the bill places on the free list a large number of articles which are really articles of manufacture, such as salt, sawed and dressed lumber, laths and shingles, hackled and dressed flax, burlaps, machinery, terne or galvanized plates, glue, glycerine, soap, certain proprietary articles, extracts of hemlock, oils of various kinds, including hemp-seed and rape-seed, olive and fish oils, refined sulphur, various coal-tar prep-

arations, earth-paints, distilled oils, alkalies, and various other chemical compounds; various manufactured mineral substances, prepared China clay, quicksilver, bricks of all kinds except fire-brick, prepared meats, lime, plaster of Paris, ground and calcined, various prepared drugs and chemicals, and many other articles of like character. These constitute the products of large and useful industries throughout the United States, in which many millions of capital are invested and employing many thousands of working people.

" At the same time the bill leaves or puts upon the dutiable lists such articles as lead ore, iron ore, zinc ores, nickel ore, and coal, which might be called raw materials, if that term can be properly applied to anything involving the expenditure of labor in its production. Further than this, the bill not only makes the so-called ' raw materials' free, such, for example, as flax, jute, hemp, hemp-seed and rape-seed, crude borax, opium, and hair of animals, but places on the free-list the manufactured products of these materials, namely, burlaps (for bagging, etc.), hemp-seed and rape-seed oil, boracic acid, codein and other salts and compounds of opium, and curled hair for mattresses, etc. Thus the manufacture of such articles is made impossible in this country, except by reducing American labor to a worse condition than that of labor in Europe. It goes even further, and places or leaves dutiable certain so-called raw materials, as, for example, iron ore, lead, coal, paper, paints, caustic soda and other alkalies, and sulphate of ammonia, while placing on the free list articles made from these materials, such as hoop-iron and cotton-ties, iron or steel sheets or plates or taggers iron coated with tin or lead, known as tin-plates, terne-plates, and taggers tin, sulphate of iron or copperas, machinery, books and pamphlets, paintings, soap, and alum. In other words, the bill leaves or makes dutiable the raw material and puts on the free list the article manufactured from it, thus not only placing an insurmountable barrier in the way of making such articles here, but actually protecting the foreign manufacturer and laborer against our own, and imposing for their benefit a burden upon the consumer in this country.

" Again, the bill places lower rates on some manufactured articles than on the materials used in making them, as, for instance, manufactures of paper, 15 per cent., and the paper to produce it at 25 per cent.

" It leaves an internal-revenue tax of more than 300 per cent. on alcohol used in the arts, amounting, according to a fair estimate, to as much as the entire amount of duty collected on raw wool, which alcohol enters as a material in a vast number of important and needful articles, which the committee have either made free or have so reduced the rates thereon that the duty would be less than the tax on the alcohol consumed in their manufacture.

" In some cases the difference between the

duty imposed by the bill on the so-called raw materials and the articles made from them is so small as to destroy these industries, except upon the condition of leveling the wages of home labor to that of Europe.

"In a large number of articles throughout the schedules not already named, the reductions proposed by the bill are so large that the effect must be to destroy or restrict home production and increase enormously foreign importations, thus largely increasing customs revenue instead of reducing it.

"It is claimed by the committee that the bill will reduce the customs revenue about $54,000,000. On the contrary, I assert that it is fair to estimate that its effect would be to largely increase the revenue instead of reducing it; while the amount of material wealth it would destroy is incalculable.

"Those supporting the bill hold themselves out as the champions of the farmer while they take from him the protective duties on his wool, hemp, flaxseed, meats, milk, fruits, vegetables, and seeds. And what do they give him in return?

"They profess to give the manufacturer better rates than they now have. If this be so, how is the farmer to be benefited, or where does he get his compensation for the loss of his protective duties?

"Much has been said about removing taxes upon 'necessaries,' and imposing them upon 'luxuries.' What does this bill propose in that direction? It gives free olive-oil to the epicure, and taxes castor-oil 97 per cent.; it gives free tin-plate to the Standard Oil Company, and to the great meat-canning monopolies, and imposes a duty of 100 per cent. on rice; it gives the sugar trust free bone-black, and proposes prohibitory duties on grocery grades of sugar; it gives free license to the tobacco-manufacturer while retaining prohibitive duties on manufactured tobacco; it imposes a duty of 40 per cent. on the 'poor man's blanket' and only 30 per cent. on the Axminster carpet of the rich. It admits free of duty fine animals imported by the gentlemen of the turf, and makes free the paintings and the statuary of the railway millionaire and the coal baron."

Mr. Reed, of Maine, in closing the debate on the Republican side, May 19, said: "The revenue-reform argument is either a false pretense or covers the whole ground. Protection is either in its essence a benefit or a curse. You can not dilute a curse and make it a blessing. Ratsbane and water are no more food than ratsbane pure. Incidental protection is a sham. Tariff for revenue only goes down before the same arguments which are used against protection.

"If protection be a tax for manufacturers' benefit then it is the same tax if it be the result of even a revenue tariff. Incidental protection is of all the most inexcusable. It is an accident which ought to be avoided like a railway disaster. If when you take one dollar from the citizen for the Treasury and four for the manufacturer, is it any the less robbery that you call it a revenue tariff?

"If you gentlemen on the other side believe what you say, you ought to be as furious against the rapine and plunder of the Mills Bill as you profess to be against those of the present law."

In answer to the argument that protection increases the price of articles consumed by the amount of duty, Mr. Reed said: "Why do men with such beliefs so plain, and so distinct, hesitate to do their duty? It is because every wind that blows, every sight that strikes their eyes, every sound that resounds in their ears, shows the folly of their theories, the absurdity of their logic. What use is it to tell the people. of this empire that they have been robbed and plundered one thousand millions of dollars every year, during the very time when over 3,500 miles of distance cities have been springing up like magic, richer in a decade than the Old World cities have grown in centuries; when 120,000 miles of railroad have been built, which compress the broad expanse of a continent into a week of time; when the commerce of its inland lakes has grown to rival the commerce between the two worlds; when from every land under the sun the emigrants have been flocking to its happy shores, drawn there by the peace and prosperity which shine on all its borders and sweep from circumference to center. There are no eyes so dull that can not see the ever-rising glories of this republic except those which are bandaged by the prejudices of long ago."

In vindication of the theory of protection, he argued: "Man derives his greatest power from his association with other men, his union with his fellows. Whoever considers the human being as a creature alone, by himself, isolated and separated, and tries to comprehend mankind by mathematically adding these atoms together, has utterly failed to comprehend the human race and its tremendous mission.

"Sixty millions even of such creatures without association are only so many beasts that perish. But sixty millions of men welded together by national brotherhood, each supporting, sustaining, and buttressing the other, are the sure conquerors of all those mighty powers of nature which alone constitute the wealth of this world. The great blunder of the Herr Professor of political economy is that he treats human beings as if every man were so many foot-pounds, such and such a fraction of a horse-power. All the soul of man he leaves out.

"Think for a moment of the foundation principles involved in this question, which I now ask, Where does wealth come from? It comes from the power of man to let loose and yet guide those elemental forces the energy of which is infinite. It comes from the power of man to force the earth to give her increase, to hold in the bellying sail the passing breeze, to harness the tumbling waterfall, to dam up the great rivers, to put bits in the teeth of the lightning. Foot-pounds and fractions of a horse-power will never do this. It takes brains and the union of foot-pounds and fractions of a horse-power working harmoniously together.

"For a nation to get out of itself or out of the earth all the wealth there is in both, it is not necessary for the nation to buy cheap or sell dear. That concerns individuals alone. What concerns the nation is how to utilize all the work there is in men, both of muscle and brain, of body and of soul, in the great enterprise of setting in motion the ever-gratuitous forces of nature.

"There is only one way to get the best work out of men, and that is to give each the work he can do best. You can only accomplish this by diversifying industry. To diversify industry completely in a country such as ours there is but one way given under Heaven among men. To enable the American people themselves to supply all their wants, you must give and assure to the American people the American markets. What does this phrase mean in practical life? It means that we, the nation, say to capital, 'Embark yourself in the manufacture of such and such articles and you shall have a market to the extent of the wants of the American people.'

"Capital then says to labor, 'Go with me into this new field, all of you who like this work best, and we will share the results.' Then begins a new industry. Multiply this by hundreds and you have a community where every man honestly minded will get what on the whole suits him best, and the nation will get the greatest amount of work from the greatest number."

Maintaining that the protective tariffs of the world have really cheapened production, Mr. Reed said: "Tariff taxes! How men like to fool themselves with phrases! Because the taxing power is used not only for revenue but as the barrier, and taxes are odious, therefore the barrier must be odious also. How can taxes produce? This is only mere word-trifling. Can you keep cattle out of the cornfield by sticking wood into the ground? Yes, if you make a fence.

"Do you mean to tell me, said the wise bumpkin to the engineer on the banks of the Merrimac, do you mean to tell me that you can make that stream useful by putting rocks into it? Yes, said the engineer, as he proceeded to build his dam and set in motion the water-wheels of mighty Lowell."

Alluding to the promise held out by free trade for a share in the business of the markets of the world, Mr. Reed said: "To hear these rhetoricians declaim, you would imagine the markets of the world a vast vacuum, waiting till now for American goods to break through, rush in, and fill the yearning void. Will your goods go to Austria, to Italy, Germany, Russia, or France? Around all these benighted countries are the 'Chinese' walls of tariff taxes. Britain herself is protected by vast capital, accumulated through ages, the spoils of her own and other lands, by a trade system as powerful as it is relentless. All these nations will contest with you the other countries which they already overflow.

"Does your mouth water over the prospect? What market do you give up for all this? Where is the best market in the world? Where the people have the most money to spend. Where have the people the most money to spend? Right here in the United States of America after twenty-seven years of protectionist rule. And you are asked to give up such a market for the markets of the world! Why, the history of such a transaction was told twenty-four hundred years ago. It is a classic. You will find it in the works of Æsop, the fabulist.

"Once there was a dog. He was a nice little dog. Nothing the matter with him except a few foolish free-trade ideas in his head. He was trotting along happy as the day, for he had in his mouth a nice shoulder of succulent mutton. By and by he came to a stream bridged by a plank. He trotted along, and, looking over the side of the plank, he saw the markets of the world and dived for them. A minute after he was crawling up the bank the wettest, the sickest, the nastiest, the most muttonless dog that ever swam ashore!"

Mr. Carlisle, of Kentucky, in closing the debate on the Democratic side, May 19, dwelt on the financial condition of the country: "It appears from the last official statement that there was in the Treasury at the close of the last month, including subsidiary and minor coins, the sum of $136,143,357.95 over and above all the current liabilities of the Government. This was $56,676,662.65 more than the surplus on hand on the 1st day of December, 1887, and shows that there has been since that date an average monthly increase of $11,-335,332.15. The surplus accumulation each month under the existing system of taxation is more than the total cost of the Government during the first two years of Washington's administration, while the aggregate sum is considerably in excess of the whole expenditure of the Government during the first eighteen years of its existence under the Constitution, including civil and miscellaneous expenses, war, navy, Indians, pensions, and interest on the public debt.

"Every dollar of this enormous sum has been taken by law from the productive industries and commercial pursuits of the people at a time when it was sorely needed for the successful prosecution of their business and under circumstances which afford no excuse whatever for the exaction. There is not a monarchical government in the world, however absolute its form or however arbitrary its power, that would dare to extort such a tribute from its subjects in excess of the proper requirements of the public service; and the question which Congress is now compelled to determine is whether such a policy can be longer continued here in this country, where the people are supposed to govern in their own right and in their own interest."

In reference to the efforts made by the Treasury Department to employ the surplus on hand, Mr. Carlisle said: "On the 17th day of last month the Secretary of the Treasury, in pursuance of authority conferred upon him by the law of March, 1881, as interpreted by the two Houses of Congress, issued a circular inviting proposals for the sale of bonds to the Government. The first purchase was made under this invitation on the 18th day of April, and between that date and the close of business yesterday, a period of one month, he has purchased on account of the Government four-per-cent. bonds to the amount of $13,456,500, upon which interest had accrued at the date of the purchase to the amount of $53,172.07. For these bonds he was compelled to pay the sum of $17,046,136.06, which was $3,536,464 more than the principal and accrued interest, or a premium of 26¼ per cent. During the same time and under the same authority he purchased 4½-per-cent. bonds to the amount of $12,404,450, upon which interest had accrued to the amount of $108,086.55. For these bonds he paid the sum of $13,379,188.37, which was $866,652.37 in excess of the principal and interest. The premium paid upon this class of bonds was nearly seven per cent.

"This is the situation into which the Government has been forced by the failure of Congress in past years to make provision for a reduction of taxation. Millions of dollars which ought to have remained in the hands of the people who earned the money by their labor and by their skill in the prosecution of business have been taken away from them by law to be paid out to the bondholders in excess of their legal demands against the Government. And, sir, if the present Congress shall adjourn without applying a remedy, this unjust process must go on for an indefinite length of time. In the presence of such a situation we can not afford to quarrel about trivial details. A reduction of the revenue—not by increasing taxation, as some propose, but by diminishing taxation in such manner as will afford the largest measure of relief to the people and their industries— should be the great and controlling object to which everything else should be subordinated. I do not mean that every interest, however small and insignificant, should not be carefully considered in a friendly spirit, but I do mean that the general interests of the many should not be subordinated to the special interests of the few."

In reference to the theoretical question underlying the issue of tariff reduction, Mr. Carlisle said: "Although the question now presented is purely a practical one, it necessarily involves, to some extent, a discussion of the conflicting theories of taxation which have divided the people of this country ever since the organization of the Government. There is a fundamental and irreconcilable difference of opinion between those who believe that the power of taxation should be used for public purposes only, and that the burdens of taxation should be equally distributed among all the people according to their ability to bear them, and those who believe that it is the right and duty of the Government to promote certain private enterprises and increase the profits of those engaged in them by the imposition of higher rates than are necessary to raise revenue for the proper administration of public affairs; and so long as this difference exists, or at least so long as the policy of the Government is not permanently settled and acquiesced in, these conflicting opinions will continue to embarrass the representatives of the people in their efforts either to increase or reduce taxation.

"While no man in public life would venture to advocate excessive taxation merely for the purpose of raising excessive revenue, many will advocate it, or at least excuse it, when the rates are so adjusted or the objects of taxation are so selected as to secure advantages, or supposed advantages, to some parts of the country or to some classes of industries over other parts and other classes; and this, Mr. Chairman, is the sole cause of the difficulties we are now encountering in our efforts to relieve the people and reduce the surplus. It is the sole cause of the unfortunate delay that has already occurred in the revision of our revenue laws, and if the pending bill shall be defeated and disaster in any form shall come upon the country by reason of overtaxation and an accumulation of money in the Treasury, this unjust feature in our present system will be responsible for it.

"Whenever an attempt is made to emancipate labor from the servitude which an unequal system of taxation imposes upon it, whenever it is proposed to secure as far as possible to each individual citizen the full fruits of his own earnings, subject only to the actual necessities of the Government, and whenever a measure is presented for the removal of unnecessary restrictions from domestic industries and international commerce, so as to permit freer production and freer exchanges, the alarm is sounded and all the cohorts of monopoly are assembled to bear their heralds proclaim the immediate and irretrievable ruin of the country."

Mr. Carlisle cited cases in which business prosperity had followed tariff reduction; and conceding that a general movement toward higher wages and lower prices for manufactures had prevailed for years here and elsewhere, he held that the result was due to other causes than protection in cases where it accompanied protection: "Mr. Chairman, it has been stubbornly contended all through this debate that high rates of duty upon imported goods are beneficial to the great body of consumers, because such duties, instead of increasing the price of the domestic articles of the same kind, actually reduce the prices. If this be true, all the other arguments in support of the existing system are not only superfluous, but manifestly unsound. The proposition that a high tariff enables the producer to pay higher wages for his labor, and the proposition that it also reduces the prices of the articles he has to sell, which are the products of that labor, are utterly inconsistent with each other, and no ingenuity of the casuist can possibly reconcile them. Labor is paid out of its own product, and unless that product can be sold for a price. which will enable the employer to realize a reasonable profit and pay the established rates of wages, the business must cease or the rates of wages must be reduced. When the price of the finished product is reduced by reason of the increased efficiency of labor, or by reason of the reduced cost of the raw material, the employer may continue to pay the same or even a higher rate of wages and still make his usual profits. But the tariff neither increases the efficiency of labor nor reduces the cost of the raw material.

"I do not deny that prices have greatly fallen during the last fifty years, not only in this country, but all over the civilized world—in free-trade countries as well as in protectionist countries. Nor do I deny that during the same time the general tendency has been toward an increase in the rates of wages; and this is true also of all civilized countries, free-trade and protection alike. It is not possible for me now to enumerate, much less discuss, all the causes that have contributed to these results. One of the most efficient causes, in fact the most efficient cause, is the combination of skilled labor with machinery in the production of commodities. The introduction and use of improved machinery has wrought a complete revolution in nearly all our manufacturing industries, and in many cases has enabled one man to do the work which it required one hundred men to do before. Here is a statement furnished by the United States Commissioner of Labor to the chairman of the Committee on Ways and Means, showing the value of the product of a week's labor in spinning cotton yarn by hand and the value of the product of a week's labor combined with machinery in the same industry: In 1813, one man working sixty hours by hand could turn out three pounds of cotton yarn, worth $2.25, or seventy-five cents per pound; now the same man, if he were living, could turn out in sixty hours with the use of machinery 3,000 pounds of cotton yarn of the same character, worth $450, or fifteen cents per pound. The cotton-spinner now receives as wages for his week's work more than three times as much as the

total value of the product of a week's work, including the value of the material, in 1813; and yet labor is far cheaper to the employer now than it was then. Although the employer now receives only one fifth as much per pound for his cotton yarn as he did in 1813, he realizes from the sale of the products of a week's labor just two hundred times as much as he did then.

"I have also a statement prepared by the same official, showing the relative production and value of product of a weaver using hand and power machinery, from which it appears that a weaver by hand turned out in seventy-two hours in 1813 45 yards of cotton goods (shirting), worth $17.91, while a weaver now, using machinery, turns out in sixty hours 1,440 yards, worth $108. Substantially the same exhibit could be made in regard to a very large number of our manufacturing industries.

"It is strange, Mr. Chairman, in view of these facts, that the prices of manufactured goods have fallen or that the wages of the laborers who produce them have risen? Is it not, on the contrary, remarkable that there has not been a greater fall in prices and a greater increase in wages? Undoubtedly there would have been a greater reduction in prices and a greater increase in wages if there had been a wider market for the products and a lower cost for the material.

"The tremendous productive forces at work all over the world in these modern times, and the small cost of manual labor in comparison with the value of the products of these combined forces, can not be realized from any general statement upon the subject. In order to form some idea of the magnitude of these natural and mechanical forces, and the efficiency of manual labor and skill when connected with them, let us look at the situation in six of our own manufacturing industries. In the manufacture of cotton goods. woolen goods, iron and steel, sawed lumber, paper, and in our flouring and grist mills, there were employed, according to the latest statistics, 517,299 persons, not all men, but many of them women and children. This labor was supplemented by steam and water power equal to 2,496,299 horse-power. This is equal to the power of 14,977,794 men; and thus we find that a little over 517,000 persons of all ages and sexes are performing, in connection with steam and water power, the work of 15,495,093 adult and healthy men.

"The railroad, the steam-vessel, the telegraph, the improved facilities for the conduct of financial transactions, and many other conveniences introduced into our modern systems of production and distribution and exchange have all contributed their share toward the reduction of prices, and it would be interesting to inquire what their influence has been, but I can not pursue this particular subject further without occupying too much time."

Touching upon the necessity for foreign markets for our agricultural products, Mr. Carlisle said: "Of course our home market has been constantly improving, and under any system of taxation will continue to improve to a greater or less extent with the increase of population and wealth, the extension of the use of machinery, which reduces the cost of production, and the multiplication of facilities for communication and transportation, which reduces the cost of distribution. But how long, Mr. Chairman, are our farmers to be compelled to pay tribute to other industries and wait for the creation of a home market that will take all their own products at fair prices? Among our greatest agricultural products are wheat and cotton. They constitute the main reliance of millions of our people for a profitable use of their lands, and many hundred million dollars are invested in the soil and buildings and machinery devoted to their production. Taking the average crop of wheat in this country for several years past, and assuming that there shall be no increase whatever in production, and that the domestic consumption per capita shall remain just at what it now is, there would still be no sufficient home market for this great agricultural staple until our population had reached nearly one hundred million.

"The official statistics of the domestic production, exportation, and home consumption of raw cotton show that it would require three times as much machinery and three times as many operatives as we now have to convert this material into commercial fabrics here at home; in other words, we are now compelled to export two thirds of our product to be manufactured in foreign countries, while one third only is manufactured at home by all the machinery and labor now employed. In 1880 there were $219,505,000 invested in cotton manufactures, and there were employed in that industry 172,554 hands. To work up our present production of raw cotton would require an investment in this manufacture of $660,000,000 and the employment of 517,662 hands. If we have been more than one hundred years, with the time the present high tariffs, in so developing our cotton manufactures as to enable them to take one third of our product at European prices, how many more centuries will be required to enable them to consume the whole product at prices fixed by competition here at home? When gentlemen have solved this problem to the satisfaction of the American cotton-grower, he may be able to listen with patience to the arguments by which they attempt to convince him of the immense advantages of a home market that will never exist. What is to be done with these great agricultural products, and with many others which are now exported, while the farmers are waiting for the home market which the advocates of restrictive legislation have been promising them for so many years? Are the farmers and planters of the North and South to abandon their wheat and cotton lands or cultivate crops not suited to their soil or climate while gentlemen are making experiments to ascertain whether or not a home market may not be created by legislation? No, sir. No matter what gentlemen may predict or what they may promise, these great industries must go on, and the American farmer must sell his products in any market he can reach and at any price he can get."

It would be impossible to follow the whole course of the debate or to take up the discussion of particular points; but these extracts from the speeches of acknowledged leaders may serve to indicate the general character of the arguments. The Mills Bill passed the House of Representatives, July 21, by the following vote:

YEAS—Abbott, Allen of Mississippi, Anderson of Iowa, Anderson of Mississippi, Anderson of Illinois, Bacon, Bankhead, Barnes, Barry, Biggs, Blanchard, Bland, Blount, Breckinridge of Arkansas, Breckinridge of Kentucky, Brower, Bryce, Buckalew, Burnes, Burnett, Bynum, F. Campbell of New York, Campbell of Ohio, T. J. Campbell of New York, Candler, Carlton, Caruth, Catchings, Chipman, Clardy, Clements, Cobb, Cockran, Collins, Compton, Cothran, Cowles, Cox, Crain, Crisp, Culberson, Cummings, Dargan, Davidson of Alabama, Davidson of Florida, Dibble, Dockery, Dougherty, Dunn, Elliott, Enloe, Ermentrout, Fisher, Fitch, Ford, Forney, French, Gay, Gibson, Glass, Grimes, Hall, Hare, Hatch, Hayes, Heard, Hemphill, Henderson of North Carolina, Herbert, Holman, Hooker, Hopkins of Virginia, Howard, Hudd, Hutton, Johnston of North Carolina, Jones, Kilgore, Laffoon, Lagan, Landes, Lane, Lanham, Latham, Lawler, Lee, Lynch, Macdonald, Mahoney, Maish, Mansur, Martin, Matson, McAdoo, McClammy, McCreary, McKinney, McMillin, McRae, McShane, Mills, Montgomery, Moore, Morgan, Morse, Neal, Nelson, Newton, Norwood, Oates, O'Ferrall, O'Neall of Indiana, O'Neill of Missouri, Outhwaite, Peel, Penington, Phelan, Pidcock, Rayner, Rice, Richardson, Robertson, Rogers, Rowland, Russell of Massachusetts, Rusk, Sayers, Scott, Seney, Shaw, Shively, Simmons, Smith, Snyder, Spinola, Springer, Stahlnecker, Stewart of Texas, Stewart of Georgia, Stockdale, Stone of Kentucky, Stone of Missouri, Tarsney, Taulbee, Thompson of California, Tillman, Tracey, Townshend, Turner of Georgia, Vance, Walker, Washington, Weaver, Wheeler, Whitthorne, Wilkins, Wilkinson, Wilson of Minnesota, Wilson of West Virginia, Wise, Yoder, Carlisle, Speaker—162.

NAYS—Adams, Allen of Massachusetts, Allen of Michigan, Anderson of Kansas, Arnold, Atkinson, Baker of New York, Baker of Illinois, Bayne, Belden, Bingham, Bliss, Boothman, Bound, Boutelle, Bowen, Bowen, Brewer, T. H. B. Browne of Virginia, Brown of Ohio, J. R. Brown of Virginia, Brumm, Buchanan, Bunnell, Burrows, Butler, Butterworth, Cannon, Caswell, Cheadle, Clark, Cogswell, Conger, Cooper, Crouse, Cutcheon, Dalzell, Darlington, Davis, De Lano, Dingley, Dorsey, Dunham, Farquhar, Felton, Finley, Flood, Fuller, Funston, Gaines, Gallinger, Gear, Gest, Goff, Greenman, Grosvenor, Grout, Guenther, Hartner, Haugen, Hayden, Henderson of Iowa, Henderson of Illinois, Hermann, Hires, Hitt, Holmes, Hopkins of Illinois, Hopkins of New York, Houk, Hovey, Hunter, Jackson, Johnston of Indiana, Kean, Kelley, Kennedy, Kerr, Ketcham, La Follette, Laidlaw, Laird, Lehlbach, Lind, Lodge, Long, Lyman, Mason, McComas, McCormick, McCullogh, McKenna, McKinley, Merriman, Milliken, Moffitt, Morrill, Morrow, Nichols, Nutting, O'Donnell, O'Neill of Pennsylvania, Osborne, Owen, Parker, Patton, Payson, Perkins, Peters, Phelps, Plumb, Post, Pugsley, Reed, Rockwell, Romeis, Rowell, Russell of Connecticut, Ryan, Sawyer, Scull, Seymour, Sherman, Sowden, Steele, Stephenson, Stewart of Vermont, Struble, Symes, E. B. Taylor of Ohio, J. D. Taylor of Ohio, Thomas of Kentucky, Thomas of Illinois, Thomas of Wisconsin, Thompson of Ohio, Turner of Kansas, Vandever, Wade, Warner, Weber, West, White of Indiana, White of New York, Whiting of Massachusetts, Wickham, Wilber, Williams, Yardley, Yost—149.

NOT VOTING—Belmont, Browne of Indiana, Davenport, Foran, Glover, Granger, Hiestand, Hogg, Moffatt, Perry, Randall, Spooner, Whiting of Michigan, Woodburn—14.

The only Republicans who voted for the bill were Brower of North Carolina, Fitch of New York, and Nelson of Minnesota. The only Democrats who voted against it were Bliss, Greenman, and Merriman of New York, and Sowden of Pennsylvania. Randall of Pennsylvania was paired against the bill with a Democrat who favored it.

The text of the Mills Bill, which formed the main issue in the Presidential canvass, is given as a matter of record:

Be it enacted, etc., That on and after the 1st day of October, 1888, the following articles mentioned in this section, when imported, shall be exempt from duty:

Timber, hewed and sawed, and timber used for spars and in building wharves.

Timber squared or sided.

Wood unmanufactured, not specially enumerated or provided for.

Sawed boards, planks, deals, and all other articles of sawed lumber.

Hubs for wheels, posts, last-blocks, wagon-blocks, oar-blocks, gun-blocks, heading-blocks, and all like blocks or sticks, rough, hewed, or sawed only.

Staves of wood.

Pickets and palings.

Laths.

Shingles.

Clapboards, pine or spruce.

Logs.

Provided, That if any export duty is laid upon the above-mentioned articles, or either of them, by any country whence imported, all said articles imported from said country shall be subject to duty as now provided by law.

Salt, in bags, sacks, barrels, or other packages, or in bulk, when imported from any country which does not charge an import duty upon salt exported from the United States.

Flax straw.

Flax, not hackled or dressed.

Tow of flax, or hemp.

Hemp, manila, and other like substitutes for hemp.

Jute-butts.

Jute.

Sunn, sisal-grass, and other vegetable fibers.

Burlaps, not exceeding 60 inches in width, of flax, jute, or hemp, or of which flax, jute, or hemp, or either of them, shall be the component material of chief value.

Bags of jute for grain.

Machinery designed for the conversion of jute or jute-butts into cotton-bagging, to wit, cards, roving-frames, winding-frames, and softeners.

Iron or steel sheets, or plates, or taggers iron, coated with tin or lead, or with a mixture of which these metals is a component part, by the dipping or any other process, and commercially known as tin-plates, terne-plates, and taggers tin.

Beeswax.

Glycerine, crude, brown, or yellow, of the specific gravity of 1·25 or less at a temperature of 60° Fahr., not purified by refining or distilling.

Phosphorus.

Soap-stocks, fit only for use as such.

Soap, hard and soft, all which are not otherwise specially enumerated or provided for.

Sheep-dip.

Extract of hemlock, and other bark used for tanning.

Indigo, extracts of, and carmined.

Iodine, resublimed.

Oil, croton.

Hemp-seed and rape-seed oil.

Petroleum.

Alumina—alum, patent alum, alum substitute, sulphate of alumina, and aluminous cake, and alum in crystals or ground.

All imitations of natural mineral waters, and all artificial mineral waters.

Baryta, sulphate of, or barytes, unmanufactured.

Boracic acid, borate of lime, and borax.

Copper, sulphate of, or blue vitriol.

Iron, sulphate of, or copperas.

Potash, crude, carbonate of, or fused, and caustic potash.

Chlorate of potash and nitrate of potash, or salt-peter crude.

Sulphate of potash.

Sulphate of soda, known as salt-cake, crude or refine , or niter-cake, crude or refined, and Glauber's-saltd

Nitrate of soda.

Sulphur, refined, in rolls.

Wood-tar.

Coal-tar, crude.

Aniline oil and its homologues.

Coal-tar, products of, such as naphtha, benzine, benzole, dead oil, and pitch.

All preparations of coal-tar not colors or dyes, and not acids of colors and dyes.

Log-wood and other dyewoods, extracts and decoctions of.

Alizarine, natural or artificial.

Spirits of turpentine.

Ocher and ochery earths, umber and umber earths.

Olive-oil, salad-oil, cottonseed-oil, whale-oil, seal-oil and neat's-foot oil.

All barks, beans, berries, balsams, buds, bulbs, bulbous roots, and excrescences, such as nut-galls, fruits, flowers, dried fibers, grains, gums, and gum-resins, herbs, leaves, lichens, mosses, nuts, roots, and stems, vegetables, seeds, and seeds of morbid growth, weeds, woods used expressly for dyeing, and dried insects, any of the foregoing which are not edible and not specially enumerated or provided for.

All non-dutiable crude minerals, but which have been advanced in value or condition by refining or grinding, or by other process of manufacture, not specially enumerated or provided for.

All earths or clays unwrought or unmanufactured.

Glass plates or disks unwrought, for use in the manufacture of optical instruments, spectacles, and eyeglasses.

Opium, crude and not adulterated, containing 9 per cent. and over of morphia, for medicinal purposes.

Iron and steel cotton ties for hoops, for baling or other purposes, not thinner than No. 20 wire gauge.

Needles, sewing, darning, knitting, and all others not specially enumerated or provided for in this act.

Copper, imported in the form of ores, regulus of, and black or coarse copper and copper cement, old copper fit only for remanufacture.

Antimony, as regulus or metal.

Quicksilver.

Chromate of iron or chromic ore.

Mineral substances in a crude state and metals unwrought not specially enumerated or provided for.

Brick, other than fire-brick.

German looking-glass plates, made of blown glass and silvered.

Vegetables in all their natural state or in salt or brine, not specially enumerated or provided for.

Chicory-root, ground or unground, burned or prepared.

Acorns and dandelion-root, raw or prepared, and all other articles used, or intended to be used, as coffee or substitutes therefor, not specially enumerated or provided for.

Cocoa, prepared or manufactured.

Dates.

Currants, Zante or other.

Fi s.

Meats, game and poultry.

Milk, fresh.

Egg-yolks.

Beans, pease, and split pease.

Bibles, books, and pamphlets, printed in other languages than English, and books and pamphlets and all publications of foreign governments, and publications of foreign societies, historical or scientific, printed for gratuitous distribution.

Bristles.

Bulbs and bulbous roots, not medicinal.

Feathers of all kinds, crude or not dressed, colored, or manufactured.

Finishing powder.

Grease.

Grindstones, finished or unfinished.

Curled hair, for beds or mattresses.

Human hair, raw, uncleaned and not drawn.

Hemp and rape seed, and other oil-seeds of like character.

Garden seeds.

Osier or willow, prepared for basket-makers' use.

Broom-corn.

Brush-wood.

Rags, of whatever material composed.

Rattans and reeds, manufactured but not made up into finished articles.

Stones, manufactured or undressed, freestone, granite, sandstone, and all building or monumental stone.

All strings of gut or any other like material.

Tallow.

Waste, all not specially enumerated or provided for.

Sec. 2. That on the 1st day of October, 1888, in lieu of the duties heretofore imposed on the articles hereinafter mentioned, there shall be levied, collected, and paid the following rates of duty on said articles severally:

Glycerine, refined, 3 cents per pound.

Acid, acetic, acetous, or pyroligneous acid, exceeding the specific gravity of 1.047, 5 cents per pound.

Castor beans or seeds, 25 cents per bushel of 50 pounds.

Castor-oil, 40 cents per gallon.

Flaxseed or linseed oil, 15 cents per gallon.

Licorice, paste or rolls, 5 cents per pound.

Licorice-juice, 35 per cent. ad valorem.

Baryta, sulphate of, or barytes, manufactured, one eighth of 1 cent per pound.

Chromate of potash, 2½ cents per pound.

Bichromate of potash, 2½ cents per pound.

Acetate of lead, brown, 2 cents per pound.

Acetate of lead, white, 3 cents pe pound.

White lead, when dry or in pulp, or when ground or mixed in oil, 2 cents per pound.

Orange mineral, and red lead, 1½ cent per pound.

Litharge, 1½ cent per pound.

Nitrate of lead, 2 cents per pound.

Magnesia, medicinal, carbonate of, 3 cents per pound.

Magnesia, calcined, 7 cents per pound.

Magnesia, sulphate of, or Epsom salts, one fourth of 1 cent per pound.

Prussiate of potash, red, 7 cents per pound.

Prussiate of potash, yellow, 3 cents per pound.

Nitrate of potash, refined, or refined saltpeter, 1 cent per pound.

Sal-soda, or soda crystals, one eighth of 1 cent per pound.

Bicarbonate of or supercarbonate of soda, and saleratus, calcined or pearlash, three-fourths of 1 cent per pound.

Hydrate or caustic soda, one half of 1 cent per pound.

Soda silicate or other alkaline silicate, one fourth of 1 cent per pound.

Sulphur, sublimed or flowers of, $12 per ton.

Ultramarine, 3 cents per pound.

Paris green, 12½ per cent. ad valorem.

Colors and paints, including lakes, whether dry or mixed, or ground with water or oil, not specially enumerated or provided for, 20 per cent. ad valorem.

Zinc, oxide of, when dry, 1 cent per pound; when ground in oil, 1½ cent per pound.

All medicinal preparations known as cerates, conserves, decoctions, emulsions, extracts, solid or fluid, infusions, juices, liniments, lozenges, mixtures, mucilages, ointments, oleo-resins, pills, plasters, powders, resins, suppositories, sirups, vinegars, and waters, of any of which alcohol is not a component part, which are not specially enumerated or provided for, 20 per cent. ad valorem.

All ground or   e e spices not specially enumerated or provided for, 3 cents per pound.

Proprietary preparations, to wit: All cosmetics, pills, powders, troches or lozenges, sirups, cordials, bitters, anodynes, tonics, plasters, liniments, salves, ointments, pastes, drops, waters, essences, spirits, oils, or preparations or compositions recommended to the public as proprietary articles or prepared according to some private formula as remedies or specifics for any disease or diseases or affections affecting the human or animal body, including all toilet preparations whatever used as applications to the hair, mouth, teeth, or skin, not specially enumerated or provided for, 30 per cent. ad valorem.

Morphia or morphine and all salts thereof, 50 cents per ounce.

Acid, tannic or tannin, 50 cents per pound.

China, porcelain, parian, and bisque, earthen, stone, or crockery ware composed of carthy or mineral substance, including plaques, ornaments, charms, vases, and statuettes, painted, printed, enameled, or gilded, or otherwise decorated in any manner, 50 per cent. ad valorem.

China, porcelain, parian, and bisque ware not decorated in any manner, 40 per cent. ad valorem.

White granite, common ware, plain white or cream-colored, lustered or printed under glaze in a single color; sponged, dipped, or edged ware, 35 per cent. ad valorem.

Brown earthenware, common stoneware, gas-retorts, and roofing-tiles, not specially enumerated or provided for, and not decorated in any manner, 20 per cent. ad valorem.

All other earthen, stone, and crockery ware, white, colored, or bisque, composed of earthy or mineral substances, not specially enumerated or provided for in this act, and not decorated in any manner, 35 per cent. ad valorem.

Paving-tiles, not encaustic, 20 per cent. ad valorem.

Encaustic tiles, not glazed or enameled, 30 per cent. ad valorem.

All glazed or enameled tiles, 40 per cent. ad valorem.

Slates, slate-pencils, slate chimney-pieces, mantels, slabs for tables, and all other manufactures of slate, 20 per cent. ad valorem.

Green and colored glass bottles, vials, demijohns, and carboys (covered or uncovered), pickle or preserve jars, and other plain, molded, or pressed green and colored bottle-glass, not cut, engraved, or painted, and not specially enumerated or provided for, 1 cent per pound; if filled, and not otherwise provided for, and the contents are subject to an ad valorem duty, or to a rate of duty based on their value, the value of such bottles, vials, or other vessels shall be added to the value of the contents for the ascertainment of the dutiable value of the latter; but if filled and not otherwise provided for, and the contents are not subject to an ad valorem duty or to a rate of duty based on their value, they shall pay a duty of 1 cent per pound in addition to the duty, if any, on their contents.

Cylinder and crown glass, polished, above 24 by 30 inches square and not exceeding 24 by 60 inches square, 20 cents per square foot; all above that 30 cents per square foot.

Unpolished cylinder, crown, and common window-glass, not exceeding 10 by 15 inches square, 1¼ cent per pound; above that, and not exceeding 16 by 24 inches square 1¾ cents per pound; above that, and not exceeding 24 by 30 inches square, 2 cents per pound; all above that 2¼ cents per pound: *Provided*, That unpolished cylinder, crown, and common window-glass, imported in boxes containing 50 square feet as nearly as sizes will permit, now known and commercially designated as 50 feet of glass, single thick and weighing not to exceed 55 pounds of glass per box, shall be entered and computed as 50 pounds of glass only; and that said kinds of glass imported in boxes containing, as nearly as sizes will permit, 50 feet of glass, now known and commercially designated as 50 feet of glass, double thick and not exceeding 90 pounds in weight, shall be entered and computed as 80 pounds of glass only; but in all other cases the duty shall be computed according to the actual weight of glass.

Cast polished plate-glass, silvered, or looking-glass plates, above 24 by 30 inches square and not exceeding 24 by 60 inches square, 25 cents per square foot; all above that, 45 cents per square foot.

Porcelain and Bohemian glass, chemical glassware, paluted glassware, stained glass, and all other manufactures of glass, or of which glass shall be the component material of chief value, not specially enumerated or provided for, 40 per cent. ad valorem.

Iron in pigs, iron kentledge, $6 per ton.

Iron railway bars, weighing more than 25 pounds to the yard, $11 per ton.

Steel railway bars and railway bars made in part of steel, weighing more than 25 pounds to the yard, $11 per ton.

Bar-iron, rolled or hammered, comprising flats not less than 1 inch wide nor less than three eighths of 1 inch thick, seven tenths of 1 cent per pound; comprising round iron not less than three fourths of 1 inch in diameter, and square iron not less than three fourths of 1 inch square, and flats less than 1 inch wide or less than three eighths of 1 inch thick, round iron less than three fourths of 1 inch and not less than seven sixteenths of 1 inch in diameter, and square iron less than three fourths of 1 inch square, 1 cent per pound: *Provided*, That all iron in slabs, blooms, loops, or other forms less finished than iron in bars, and more advanced than pig-iron, except castings, shall be rated as iron in bars, and pay a duty accordingly; and none of the above iron shall pay a less rate of duty than 35 per cent. ad valorem: *Provided further*, That all iron bars, blooms, billets, or sizes or shapes of any kind, in the manufacture of which charcoal is used as fuel, shall be subject to a duty of not less than $20 per ton.

Iron or steel T-rails, weighing not over 25 pounds to the a , $14 per ton; iron or steel flat rails, punched, $45 per ton.

Round iron, in coils or rods, less than seven sixtenths of 1 inch in diameter, and bars or shapes of rolled iron, not specially enumerated or provided for, 1 cent per pound.

Iron or steel, flat with longitudinal ribs, for the manufacture of fencing, four tenths of 1 cent per pound.

Sheet-iron, common or black, thinner than 1 inch and not thinner than No. 20 wire gauge, 1 cent per pound; thinner than No. 20 wire gauge and not thinner than No. 25 wire gauge, one and one tenth of 1 per cent per pound; thinner than No. 25 wire gauge and not thinner than No. 29 wire gauge, one and one fourth of 1 cent per pound; thinner than No. 29 wire gauge, and all iron commercially known as common or black taggers iron, whether put up in boxes or bundles or not, 30 per cent. ad valorem: *Provided*, That on all such iron and steel sheets or plates aforesaid, excepting on what are known commercially as tin-plates, terne-plates, and taggers tin, when galvanized or coated with zinc or spelter, or other metals, or any alloy of those metals, one fourth of 1 cent per pound additional when not thinner than No. 20 wire gauge; thinner than No. 20 wire gauge and not thinner than No. 25 wire gauge, one half cent per pound additional, and when thinner than No. 25 wire gauge, three fourths of 1 cent per pound additional.

Hoop or band or scroll or other iron, 8 inches or less in width, and not thinner than No. 10 wire gauge, 1 cent per pound; thinner than No. 10 wire gauge and not thinner than No. 20 wire gauge, 1·1 cent per pound; thinner than No. 20 wire gauge, 1·3 cent per pound: *Provided*, That all articles not specially enumerated or provided for, whether wholly or partly manufactured, made from sheet, plate, hoop, band, or scroll iron herein provided for, or of which such sheet, plate, hoop, band, or scroll iron shall be the material of chief value, shall pay one fourth of 1 cent per pound more duty than that imposed on the iron from which they are made, or which shall be such material of chief value.

Cast-iron pipe, six tenths of 1 cent per pound.

Cut nails and spikes, of iron or steel, 1 cent per pound.

Cut tacks, brads, or sprigs, 35 per cent. ad valorem.

Iron or steel railway fish-plates or splice-bars, eight tenths of 1 cent per pound.

Wrought-iron or steel spikes, nuts, and washers, and horse, mule, or ox shoes, 1½ cent per pound.

Anvils, anchors, or parts thereof, mill-irons and mill-cranks, of wrought-iron, and wrought-iron for ships, and forgings of iron and steel, for vessels, steam-engines, and locomotives, or parts thereof, weighing each 25 pounds or more, 1½ cent per pound.

Iron or steel rivets, bolts, with or without threads or nuts, or bolt-blanks, and finished hinges or hinge-blanks, 1½ cent per pound.

Iron or steel blacksmiths' hammers and sledges, track-tools, wedges, and crowbars, 1½ cent per pound.

Iron or steel axles, parts thereof, axle-bars, axle-blanks, or forgings for axles, without reference to the stage or state of manufacture, 1½ cent per pound.

Horseshoe-nails, hob-nails, and wire nails, and all other wrought-iron or steel nails, not specially enumerated or provided for, 2½ cents per pound.

Boiler-tubes or other tubes or flues or stays, of wrought-iron or steel, 1½ cent per pound.

Chain or chains, of all kinds, made of iron or steel, less than three fourths of 1 inch in diameter, 1½ cent per pound; less than three fourths of 1 inch and not less than three eighths of 1 inch in diameter, 1½ cent per pound; less than three eighths of 1 inch in diameter, 2 cents per pound.

Hand, back, and all other saws, not specially enumerated or provided for, 30 per cent. ad valorem.

Files, file-blanks, rasps, and floats of all cuts and kinds, 35 per cent. ad valorem.

Iron or steel beams, girders, joists, angles, channels, car-truck channels, TT columns and posts, or parts or sections of columns and posts, deck and bulb beams, and building forms, together with all other structural shapes of iron or steel, six tenths of 1 cent per pound.

Steel wheels and steel-tired wheels for railway purposes, whether wholly or partly finished, and iron or steel locomotive, car, and other railway tires, or parts thereof, wholly or partly manufactured, 2 cents per pound; iron or steel ingots, cogged ingots, blooms or blanks for the same without regard to the degree of manufacture, 1½ cent per pound.

Iron and steel wire and iron and steel wire galvanized, and all manufactures of iron and steel wire and of iron and steel wire galvanized shall pay the duties now provided by law: *Provided*, That no such duty shall be in excess of 60 per cent. ad valorem.

Clippings from new copper, fit only for manufacture, 1 cent per pound.

Copper in plates, bars, ingots, Chili or other pigs, and in other forms, not manufactured, 2 cents per pound ; in rolled plates, called braziers' copper, sheets, rods, pipes, and copper bottoms, 30 per cent. ad valorem.

Lead-ore and lead-dross, three fourths of 1 cent per ound.

p Lead, in pigs and bars, molten and old refuse lead run into blocks, and bars and old scrap lead fit only to be remanufactured, 1¼ cent per pound. Lead in sheets, pipes, or shot, 2¼ cents per pound.

Sheathing or yellow metal, 30 per cent. ad valorem.

Nickel, in ore or matte, 10 cents per pound on the nickel contained therein.

Zinc-ores, 20 per cent. ad valorem.

Zinc-spelter, or tutenegue, in blocks or pigs, and old worn-out zinc fit only to be remanufactured, 1¼ cent per pound ; zinc, spelter, or tutenegue, in sheets, 2 cents per pound.

Hollowware, coated, glazed, or tinned, 2¼ cents per pound.

Needles for knitting and sewing-machines, 20 per cent. ad valorem.

Pens, metallic, 35 per cent. ad valorem.

Type metal, 15 per cent. ad valorem.

New type for printing, 15 per cent. ad valorem.

Manufactures, articles, or wares, not specially enumerated or provided for, composed wholly or in part of copper, 35 per cent. ad valorem ; manufactures, articles, or wares, not specially enumerated or provided for, composed of iron, steel, lead, nickel, pewter, tin, zinc, gold, silver, platinum, or any other metal, or of which any of the foregoing metals may be the component material of chief value, and whether partly or wholly manufactured, 40 per cent. ad valorem.

Cabinet and house furniture of wood, finished, 30 per cent. ad valorem.

Manufactures of cedar wood, granadilla, ebony, mahogany, rosewood, and satinwood, 30 per cent. ad valorem.

Manufactures of wood, or of which wood is the chief component part, not specially enumerated or provided for, 30 per cent. ad valorem.

All sugars not above No. 13 Dutch standard in color shall pay duty on their polariscopic test as follows, namely :

All sugars not above No. 13 Dutch standard in color, all tank-bottoms, sirups of cane-juice or of beet-juice, melada, concentrated melada, concrete and concentrated molasses, testing by the polariscope not above seventy-five degrees, shall pay a duty of 1·15 cent per pound, and for every additional degree or fraction of a degree shown by the polariscopic test they shall pay thirty-two thousandths of 1 cent per pound additional.

All sugars above No. 13 Dutch standard in color shall be classified by the Dutch standard of color, and pay duty as follows, namely :

All sugars above No. 13 and not above No. 16 Dutch standard, 2·20 cents per pound.

All sugars above No. 16 and not above No. 20 Dutch standard. 2·40 cents per pound.

All sugars above No. 20 Dutch standard, 2·80 cents per pound.

Molasses testing not above fifty-six degrees by the polariscope shall pay a duty of 2⅜ cents per gallon ; molasses testing above fifty-six degrees shall pay a duty of 6 cents per gallon : Provided, That if an export duty shall hereafter be laid upon sugar or molasses by any country whence the same may be imported, such sugar or molasses so imported shall be subject to duty as provided by law at the date of the passage of this act.

Sugar-candy, not colored, 5 cents per pound.

All other confectionery, 40 per cent. ad valorem.

Potato or corn starch, rice-starch, and other starch, 1 cent per pound.

Rice, cleaned, 2 cents per pound ; uncleaned, or rice free of the outer hull and still having the inner cuticle on, 1½ cent per pound.

Rice-flour and rice-meal, 15 per cent. ad valorem.

Paddy, or rice having the outer hull on, 1 cent per pound.

Raisins, 1½ cent per pound.

Peanuts or ground-beans, three fourths of 1 cent per pound : shelled, 1 cent per pound.

Mustard, ground or preserved, in bottles or otherwise, 6 cents per pound.

Cotton thread, yarn, warps, or warp yarn, whether single or advanced beyond the condition of single by twisting two or more single yarns together, whether on beams or in bundles, skeins, or cops, or in any other form, valued at not exceeding 40 cents per pound, 35 per cent. ad valorem ; valued at over 40 cents per pound, 40 per cent. ad valorem.

On all cotton cloth, 40 per cent. ad valorem.

Spool-thread of cotton, 40 per cent. ad valorem.

Flax, hackled, known as dressed line, $10 per ton.

Brown and bleached linens, ducks, canvas, paddings, cot-bottoms, diapers, crash, huckabacks, handkerchiefs, lawns, or other manufactures of flax, jute, or hemp, or of which flax, jute, or hemp shall be the component material of chief value, not specially enumerated or provided for, 25 per cent. ad valorem : Provided, That cuffs, collars, shirts, and other manufactures of wearing apparel, made in whole or in part of linen, and not otherwise provided for, and hydraulic hose, 35 per cent. ad valorem.

Flax, hemp, and jute yarns, and all twines of hemp, jute, jute-butts, sunn, sisal-grass, ramie, and China-grass, 15 per cent. ad valorem.

Flax or linen thread, twine, and packed thread and all manufactures of flax, or of which flax shall be the component material of chief value, not specially enumerated or provided for, 25 per cent. ad valorem.

Oil-cloth foundations or floor-cloth canvas or burlaps, exceeding 60 inches in width, made of flax, jute, or hemp, or of which flax, jute, or hemp, or either of them, shall be the component material of chief value, 25 per cent. ad valorem.

Oil-cloths for floors, stamped, painted, or printed, and on all other oil-cloth (except silk oil-cloth), and on water-proof cloth, not otherwise provided for, 25 per cent. ad valorem.

Gunny-cloth, not bagging, 15 per cent. ad valorem.

Bags and bagging, and like manufactures, not specially enumerated or provided for, including bagging for cotton composed wholly or in part of flax, hemp, jute, gunny-cloth, gunny-bags, or other material, three eighths of 1 cent per pound.

Tarred cables or cordage, 25 per cent. ad valorem.

Untarred manila cordage, 25 per cent. ad valorem.

All other untarred cordage, 25 per cent. ad valorem.

Seines and seine and gilling twine, 25 per cent. ad valorem.

Sail-duck, or canvas for sails, 25 per cent. ad valorem. Russia and other sheetings of flax or hemp, brown or white, 25 per cent. ad valorem. All other manufactures of hemp or manila, or of which hemp or manila shall be a component material of chief value, not specially enumerated or provided for, 25 per cent. ad valorem.

Grass-cloth and other manufactures of jute, ramie, China and sisal-grass, not specially enumerated or provided for, 25 per cent. ad valorem : Provided, That as to jute, jute-butts, sunn, and sisal-grass, and manufactures thereof, except burlaps, not exceeding sixty inches in width, this act shall take effect Jan. 1, 1889 ; and as to flax, hemp, manila, and other like substitutes for hemp, and the manufactures thereof, upon July 1, 1889.

Sec. 3. On and after Oct. 1, 1888, there shall be admitted, when imported, free of duty : All wools, hair of the alpaca, goat, and other like animals. Wools on the skin. Woolen rags, shoddy, mungo, waste, and flocks.

And on and after Jan. 1, 1889, in lieu of the duties

heretofore imposed on the articles hereinafter mentioned in this section, there shall be levied, collected, and paid the following rates of duty on said articles severally: Woolen and worsted cloths, shawls, and all manufactures of wool of every description, made wholly or in part of wool or worsted, not specially enumerated or provided for, 40 per cent. ad valorem.

Flannels, blankets, hats of wool, knit goods, and all goods made on knitting-frames, balmorals, woolen and worsted yarns, and all manufactures of every description, composed wholly or in part of wool or worsted, the hair of the alpaca, goat, or other animals, not specially enumerated or provided for, 40 per cent. ad valorem : *Provided,* That from and after the passage of this act, and until the 1st day of October, 1888, the Secretary of the Treasury be, and he is hereby, authorized and directed to classify as woolen cloth all imports of worsted cloth, whether known under the name of worsted cloth or under the name of "worsteds" or "diagonals," or otherwise.

Bunting, 40 per cent. ad valorem. Women's and children's dress-goods, coat-linings, Italian cloths, and goods of like description, composed in part of wool, worsted, the hair of the alpaca, goat, or other animals, 40 per cent. ad valorem.

Clothing, ready-made, and wearing apparel of every description, not specially enumerated or provided for, and balmoral skirts and skirting, and goods of similar description or used for like purposes, composed wholly or in part of wool, worsted, the hair of the alpaca, goat, or other animals, made up or manufactured wholly or in part by the tailor, seamstress, or manufacturer, except knit goods, 45 per cent. ad valorem.

Cloaks, dolmans, jackets, talmas, ulsters, or other outside garments for ladies' and children's apparel, and goods of similar description or used for like purposes, composed wholly or in part of wool, worsted, the hair of the alpaca, goat, or other animals, made up or manufactured wholly or in part by the tailor, seamstress, or manufacturer (except knit goods), 45 per cent. ad valorem.

Webbings, gorings, suspenders, braces, beltings, bindings, braids, galloons, fringes, gimps, cords, cords and tassels, dress-trimmings, head-nets, buttons, or barrel buttons, or buttons of other forms for tassels or ornaments wrought by hand or braided by machinery, made of wool, worsted, the hair of the alpaca, goat, or other animals, or of which wool, worsted, the hair of the alpaca, goat, or other animals is a component material, 50 per cent. ad valorem.

Hemp and jute carpeting 6 cents per square yard.

Floor-matting and floor-mats exclusively of vegetable substances 20 per cent. ad valorem.

"All other carpets and carpetings, druggets, bockings, mats, rugs, screens, covers, hassocks, bed-sides of wool, flax, cotton or parts of either or other material, 40 per cent. ad valorem."

Endless belts or felts for paper or printing machines, 30 per cent. ad valorem.

Sec. 4. That on and after the 1st day of October, 1888, in lieu of the duties heretofore imposed on the articles hereinafter mentioned, there shall be levied, collected, and paid the following rates of duty on said articles severally :

Paper, sized or glued, suitable only for printing paper, 15 per cent. ad valorem.

Printing paper, unsized, used for books and newspapers exclusively, 12 per cent. ad valorem.

Paper boxes, and all other fancy boxes, not otherwise provided for, 25 per cent. ad valorem.

Paper envelopes, 20 per cent. ad valorem.

Paper hangings, and paper for screens or fire-boards, surface-coated paper, and all manufactures of which surface-coated paper is a component material not otherwise provided for, and card-board, paper antiquarian, demy, drawing, elephant, foolscap, imperial, letter, note, and all other paper not specially enumerated or provided for, 25 per cent. ad valorem.

Beads and bead ornaments of all kinds, except amber, 40 per cent. ad valorem.

Blacking of all kinds, 20 per cent. ad valorem.

Bonnets, hats, and hoods for men, women, and children, composed of hair, whalebone, or any vegetable material, and not specially enumerated or provided for, 30 per cent. ad valorem.

Brooms of all kinds, 20 per cent. ad valorem.

Brushes of all kinds, 20 per cent. ad valorem.

Canes and sticks, for walking, finished, 20 per cent. ad valorem.

Card clothing, 20 cents per square foot ; when manufactured from tempered steel wire, 40 cents per square foot.

Carriages, and parts of, not specially enumerated or provided for, 30 per cent. ad valorem.

Dolls and toys, 30 per cent. ad valorem.

Fans of all kinds, except palm-leaf fans, of whatever material composed, 30 per cent. ad valorem.

Feathers of all kinds, when dressed, colored, or manufactured, including dressed and finished birds and artificial and ornamental feathers and flowers, or parts thereof, of whatever material composed, not specially enumerated or provided for, 35 per cent. ad valorem.

Friction and lucifer matches of all descriptions, 25 per cent. ad valorem.

Gloves of all descriptions, wholly or partially manufactured, 40 per cent. ad valorem: *Provided,* That gloves made of silk taffeta shall be taxed 50 per cent. ad valorem.

Gun wads of all descriptions, 25 per cent. ad valorem.

Gutta-percha, manufactured, and all articles of hard rubber not specially enumerated or, provided for, 30 per cent. ad valorem.

Hair, human, if clean or drawn, but not manufactured, 20 per cent. ad valorem.

Bracelets, braids, chains, rings, curls, and ringlets composed of hair, or of which hair is the component material of chief value, and all manufactures of human hair, 25 per cent. ad valorem.

Hats, materials for: Braids, plaits, flats, willow sheets and squares, fit only for use in making or ornamenting hats, bonnets, and hoods, composed of straw, chip, grass, palm-leaf, willow, hair, whalebone, or any vegetable material, not specially enumerated or provided for, 20 per cent. ad valorem.

Hat-bodies of cotton, 30 per cent. ad valorem.

Hatters' plush, composed of silk or of silk and cotton, 15 per cent. ad valorem.

Inks of all kinds, and ink-powders, 20 per cent. ad valorem.

Japanned ware of all kinds not specially enumerated or provided for, 30 per cent. ad valorem.

Kaolin, crude, $1 per ton.

China clay or wrought kaolin, $2 per ton.

Marble of all kinds, in block, rough, or squared, 40 cents per cubic foot.

Marble, sawed, dressed, or otherwise, including marble slabs and marble paving-tiles, 85 cents per cubic foot.

All manufactures of marble not specially enumerated or provided for, 30 per cent. ad valorem.

Papier-maché, manufactures, articles, and wares of, 25 per cent. ad valorem.

Percussion caps, 30 per cent. ad valorem.

Philosophical apparatus and instruments, 25 per cent. ad valorem.

Umbrella and parasol ribs, and stretcher frames, tips, runners, handles, or other parts thereof, when made in whole or chief part of iron, steel, or any other metal, 30 per cent. ad valorem ; umbrellas, parasols, and shades, when covered with silk or alpaca, 50 per cent. ad valorem ; all other umbrellas, 30 per cent. ad valorem.

Watches, watch-cases, watch-movements, parts of watches, watch-glasses, and watch-keys, whether separately packed or otherwise, and watch materials not specially enumerated or provided for in this act, 25 per cent. ad valorem.

Webbing, composed of cotton, flax, or a mixture of

these materials, not specially enumerated or provided for in this act, 30 per cent. ad valorem.

SEC. 5. That the following amendments to and provisions for existing laws shall take effect on and after the passage and approval of this act:

Section 6 of the act of March 3, 1883, entitled "An act to reduce internal-revenue taxation, and for other purposes," providing a substitute for title 33 of the Revised Statutes of the United States, is hereby amended as to certain of the sections and parts of sections or schedules in such substituted title so that they shall be as follows, respectively:

"SEC. 2,499. Each and every imported article not enumerated or provided for in any schedule in this title, which is similar, either in material, quality, textures, or the use to which it may be applied, to any article enumerated in this title as chargeable with duty, shall pay the same rate of duty which is levied on the enumerated article which it most resembles in any of the particulars before mentioned; and if any non-enumerated article equally resembles two or more enumerated articles on which different rates of duty are chargeable, there shall be levied on such non-enumerated article the same rate of duty as is chargeable on the article which it resembles paying the highest rate of duty; and on articles, not otherwise provided for, manufactured from two or more materials, the duty shall be assessed at the rate at which the dutiable component material of chief value may be chargeable; and the words 'component material of chief value,' whenever used in this title, shall be held to mean that dutiable component material which shall exceed in value any other single component material found in the article; and the value of each component material shall be determined by the ascertained value of such material in its last form and condition before it became a component material of such article. If two or more rates of duty shall be applicable to any imported article, it shall pay duty at the highest of such rates: Provided, That any non-enumerated article similar in material and quality and texture and the use to which it may be applied to any article on the free list, and in the manufacture of which no dutiable materials are used, shall be free of duty."

SEC. 2,502. Schedule A—Chemical products.—By striking out from this schedule the words "distilled spirits containing 50 per cent. of anhydrous alcohol, $1 per gallon"; also, by striking out the words "alcohol containing 94 per cent. anhydrous alcohol, $2 per gallon."

THE FREE LIST.

SEC. 2,503. By striking out the clause in this section commencing with the words "articles the growth, produce, and manufacture of the United States," and inserting in lieu thereof the following:

"Articles the growth, produce, and manufacture of the United States, when returned after having been exported without having been advanced in value by any process of manufacture or by labor thereon; casks, barrels, carboys, bags, and other vessels of American manufacture exported filled with American products, or exported empty and returned filled with foreign products, including shooks when returned as barrels or boxes; but proof of the identity of such articles shall be made under general regulations to be prescribed by the Secretary of the Treasury; and if any of such articles are subject to internal tax at the time of exportation, such tax shall be proved to have been paid before exportation, and not refunded: Provided, That this clause shall not include any article upon which an allowance of drawback has been made, the reimportation of which is hereby prohibited except upon payment of duties equal to the drawbacks allowed."

The clause relating to "wearing apparel," etc. (tariff, pa agra 815), is hereby amended so that it shall read as follpirs:

"Wearing apparel, implements, instruments, and tools of trade, occupation, or employment, professional books, and other personal effects (not merchandise)

of persons arriving in the United States, not exceeding in value $500, and not intended for the use of any other person or persons, nor for sale; but this exemption shall not be construed to include machinery or other articles imported for use in any manufacturing establishment or for sale: Provided, however, That the limitation in value above specified shall not apply to wearing apparel and other personal effects which may have been taken from the United States to foreign countries by the persons returning therefrom; and such last-named articles shall, upon production of evidence satisfactory to the collector or officer acting as such that they have been previously exported from the United States by such persons, and have not been advanced in value or improved in condition by any process of manufacture or labor thereon since so exported, be exempt from the payment of duty: And provided further, That all articles of foreign production or manufacture which may have been once imported into the United States and subjected to the payment of duty, upon reimportation, if not improved in condition, except by repairs, by any means, since their exportation from the United States, be entitled to exemption from duty upon their identity being established, under such rules and regulations as may be prescribed by the Secretary of the Treasury.

"Theatrical scenery and actors' and actresses' wardrobes brought by theatrical managers and professional actors and actresses arriving from abroad for their temporary use in the United States; works of art, drawings, engravings, photographic pictures, and philosophical and scientific apparatus brought by professional artists, lecturers, or scientists arriving from abroad for use by them temporarily for exhibition and in illustration, promotion, and encouragement of art, science, or industry in the United States; and wearing apparel and other personal effects of tourists from abroad visiting the United States shall be admitted to free entry under such regulations as the Secretary of the Treasury may prescribe; and bonds shall be given, whenever required by the Secretary of the Treasury, for the payment to the United States of such duties as may be imposed by law upon any and all such articles as shall not be exported within six months after such importation: Provided, however, That the Secretary of the Treasury may, in his discretion, extend such period for a further term of six months in cases where application therefor shall be made.

"Wearing apparel, old and worn, not exceeding $100 in value, upon production of evidence satisfactory to the collector and naval officer (if any) that the same has been donated and imported in good faith for the relief or aid of indigent or needy persons residing in the United States, and not for sale."

SEC. 6. That section 7 of the act approved March 3, 1883, entitled "An act to reduce internal-revenue taxation, and for other purposes," is hereby amended so that it shall read as follows:

"Whenever imported merchandise is subject to an ad valorem rate of duty, or to a duty based upon or regulated in any manner by the value thereof, the duty shall be assessed upon the actual market value or wholesale price of such merchandise, at the time of exportation to the United States, in the principal markets of the country from whence imported, and in the condition in which such merchandise is there bought and sold for exportation to the United States or consigned to the United States for sale, including the value of all cartons, cases, crates, boxes, sacks, and coverings of any kind, and all other costs, charges, and expenses incident to placing the merchandise in condition packed, ready for shipment to the United States: Provided, That if there be used for covering or holding imported merchandise, whether dutiable or free, any material or article, other than the ordinary, usual, and necessary coverings used for covering or holding such merchandise, duty shall be levied and collected thereon at the rate to which such material or article would be subject if imported separately" : *Provided, further,* That so much of the foregoing as relates to boxes, sacks, or coverings shall not apply to boxes, sacks, or such other boxing or covering as may be the usual and necessary covering for machinery or parts thereof.

Sec. 7. That section 8 of the act of March 3, 1883, entitled "An act to reduce internal-revenue taxation, and for other purposes," amending section 2,841 of the Revised Statutes of the United States, is hereby further amended so that said section of the Revised Statutes shall be as follows :

"Sec. 2841. Whenever merchandise imported into the United States is entered by invoice, one of the following declarations, according to the nature of the case, shall be filed with the collector of the port, at the time of entry, by the owner, importer, consignee, or agent; which declaration so filed shall be duly signed by the owner, importer, consignee, or agent, before the collector, or before a notary public or other officer duly authorized by law to administer oaths and take acknowledgments, who may be designated by the Secretary of the Treasury to receive such declarations and to certify to the identity of the persons making them ; and every officer so designated shall file with the collector of the port a copy of his official signature and seal : *Provided,* That if any of the invoices or bills of lading of any merchandise imported in any one vessel, which should otherwise be embraced in said entry, have not been received at the date of the entry, the declaration may state the fact, and thereupon such merchandise of which the invoices or bills of lading are not produced shall not be included in such entry, but may be entered subsequently.

"Declaration of consignee, importer, or agent.

"I, ——, do solemnly and truly declare that the invoice and bill of lading now presented by me to the collector of —— are the true and only invoice and bill of lading by me received of all the goods, wares, and merchandise imported in the ——, whereof —— is master, from ——, for account of any person whomsoever for whom I am authorized to enter the same ; that the said invoice and bill of lading are in the state in which they were actually received by me, and that I do not know nor believe in the existence of any other invoice or bill of lading of the said goods, wares, and merchandise; that the entry now delivered to the collector contains a just and true account of the said goods, wares, and merchandise, according to the said invoice and bill of lading ; that nothing has been, on my part, nor to my knowledge on the part of any other person, concealed or suppressed, whereby the United States may be defrauded of any part of the duty lawfully due on the said goods, wares, and merchandise ; that the said invoice and the declaration therein are in all respects true, and were made by the person by whom the same purports to have been made ; and that if at any time hereafter I discover any error in the said invoice, or in the account now rendered of the said goods, wares, and merchandise, or receive any other invoice of the same, I will immediately make the same known to the collector of this district. And I do further solemnly and truly declare that to the best of my knowledge and belief [insert the name and residence of the owner or owners] is [or are] the owner [or owners] of the goods, wares, and merchandise mentioned in the annexed entry ; that the invoice now produced by me exhibits the actual cost [if purchased] or the actual market value or wholesale price [if otherwise obtained], at the time of exportation in the principal markets of the country where procured, of the said goods, wares, and merchandise, including the value of all cartons, cases, crates, boxes, sacks, and covering of any kind, and all other costs, charges, and expenses incident to placing said goods, wares, and merchandise in condition packed ready for shipment to the United States, and no other or different discount, bounty, or drawback, but such as has been actually allowed on the same."

"Declaration of owner in cases where merchandise has been actually purchased.

"I ——, do solemnly and truly declare that the entry now delivered by me to the collector of —— contains a just and true account of all the goods, wares, and merchandise imported by or consigned to me, in the ——, whereof —— is master, from ——; that the invoice and entry which I now produce contain a just and faithful account of the actual cost of the said goods, wares, and merchandise, including the value of all cartons, cases, crates, boxes, sacks, and coverings of any kind, and all other costs, charges, and expenses incident to placing said goods, wares, and merchandise in condition packed, ready for shipment to the United States, and no other discount, drawback, or bounty but such as has been actually allowed on the same ; that I do not know nor believe in the existence of any invoice or bill of lading other than those now produced by me, and that they are in the state in which I actually received them. And I further solemnly and truly declare that I have not in the said entry or invoice concealed or suppressed anything whereby the United States may be defrauded of any part of the duty lawfully due on the said goods, wares, and merchandise; that the said invoice and the declaration thereon are in all respects true, and were made by the person by whom the same purports to have been made ; and that if at any time hereafter I discover any error in the said invoice or in the account now produced of the said goods, wares, and merchandise, or receive any other invoice of the same, I will immediately make the same known to the collector of this district."

"Declaration of manufacturer or owner in cases where merchandise has not been actually purchased.

"I, ——, do solemnly and truly declare that the entry now delivered by me to the collector of —— contains a just and true account of all the goods, wares, and merchandise imported by or consigned to me in the ——, whereof —— is master, from —— ; that the said goods, wares, and merchandise were not actually bought by me, or by my agent, in the ordinary mode of bargain and sale, but that nevertheless the invoice which I now produce contains a just and faithful valuation of the same, at their actual market value or wholesale price at the time of exportation, in the principal markets of the country where procured for my account [or for account of myself or partners] ; that the said invoice contains also a just and faithful account of all the cost of finishing said goods, wares, and merchandise to their present condition, including the value of all cartons, cases, crates, boxes, sacks, and coverings of any kind, and all other costs and charges incident to placing said goods, wares, and merchandise in condition packed, ready for shipment to the United States, and no other discount, drawback, or bounty but such as has been actually allowed on the said goods, wares, and merchandise; and the said invoice and the declaration thereon are in all respects true, and were made by the pe o by whom the same purports to have been made *that* I do not know nor believe in the existence of any invoice or bill of lading other than those now produced by me, and that they are in the state in which I actually received them. And I do further solemnly and truly declare that I have not in the said entry or invoice concealed or suppressed anything whereby the United States may be defrauded of any part of the duty lawfully due on the said goods, wares, and merchandise ; and that if at any time hereafter I discover any error in the said invoice, or in the account now produced of the said goods, wares, and merchandise, or receive any other invoice of the same, I will immediately make the same known to the collector of this district."

Sec. 8. That any person who shall knowingly make any false or untrue statement in the declarations provided for in the preceding section, or shall aid or procure the making of any such false statement as to any matter material thereto, shall, on conviction thereof, be punished by a fine of not exceeding $5,000, or by imprisonment at hard labor not more than three years, or both, within the discretion of the court: *Provided*, That nothing in this section shall be construed to relieve imported merchandise from forfeiture for any cause elsewhere provided by law.

Sec. 9. That sections 2970 and 2983 of the Revised Statutes of the United States are hereby amended so that the same shall be, respectively, as follows:

"Sec. 2970. Any merchandise deposited in bond in any public or private bonded warehouse may be withdrawn for consumption within three years from the date of original importation, on payment of the duties and charges to which it may be subject by law at the time of such withdrawal: *Provided*, That nothing herein shall affect or impair existing provisions of law in regard to the disposal of perishable or explosive articles."

"Sec. 2983. In no case shall there be any abatement of the duties or allowance made for any injury, damage, or deterioration sustained by any merchandise while deposited in any public or private bonded warehouse: *Provided*, That the duty assessed on merchandise withdrawn from any such warehouse shall be assessed on the quantity withdrawn therefrom at the time of such withdrawal; but no greater allowance for leakage or evaporation of wines, liquors, and distilled spirits shall be made than is or may be allowed by law on domestic spirits or wines in bond: *And provided further*, That nothing in this section as amended shall restrict or in any way affect the liability of the proprietors of bonded warehouses on their bonds: *And provided further*, That nothing herein shall restrain or limit the exercise of the authority conferred on the Secretary of the Treasury by section 2964 of the Revised Statutes."

Sec. 10. That sections 2803 and 3058 of the Revised Statutes be amended to read as follows:

"Sec. 2803. Any baggage or personal effects arriving in the United States in transit to any foreign country may be delivered by the parties having it in charge to the collector of the proper district, to be by him retained, without the payment or exaction of any import duty, or to be forwarded by such collector to the collector of the port of departure, and to be delivered to such parties on their departure for their foreign destination, under such rules, regulations, and fees as the Secretary of the Treasury may prescribe."

"Sec. 3058. All merchandise imported into the United States shall, for the purpose of this title, be deemed and held to be the property of the person to whom the merchandise may be consigned; but the holder of any bill of lading consigned to order and properly indorsed shall be deemed the consignee thereof; and in case of the abandonment of any merchandise to the underwriters, the latter may be recognised as the consignee."

Sec. 11. That authority is hereby given to the Secretary of the Treasury, in his discretion to dispense whenever expedient with the triplicate invoices and consular certificates now required by sections 2853, 2854, 2855 of the Revised Statutes of the United States; and triplicate invoices and consular certificates shall in no case be required when the value of the merchandise shipped by any one consignor, in any one vessel, at one and the same time does not exceed $100; and the Secretary of the Treasury, with the concurrence of the Secretary of State, is hereby authorized to make such general regulations in regard to invoices and consular certificates as in his judgment the public interest may require.

Sec. 12. That all fees exacted and oaths administered by officers of the customs, under or by virtue of existing laws of the United States, upon the entry of imported goods and the passing thereof through the customs, and also upon all entries of domestic goods, wares, and merchandise for exportation, be, and the same are hereby, abolished; and in case of entry of merchandise for exportation, a declaration, in lieu of an oath, shall be filed, in such form and under such regulations as may be prescribed by the Secretary of the Treasury; and the penalties for false statements in such declaration provided in the fourth section of this act shall be applicable to declarations made under this section: *Provided*, That where such fees, under existing laws, constitute, in whole or in part, the compensation of any officer, such officer shall receive, from and after the passage of this act, a fixed sum for each year equal to the amount which he would have been entitled to receive as fees for such services.

Sec. 13. That section 2900 of the Revised Statutes be, and hereby is, amended so as to read as follows:

"Sec. 2900. The owner, consignee, or agent of any imported merchandise which has been actually purchased may at the time, and not afterward, when he shall make and verify his written entry of his merchandise, make such addition in the entry to the cost or value given in the invoice, or *pro forma* invoice, or statement in form of an invoice, which he shall produce with his entry, as in his opinion may raise the same to the actual market value or wholesale price of such merchandise, at the period of exportation to the United States, in the principal markets of the country from which the same has been imported; and the collector within whose district any merchandise, whether the same has been actually purchased or procured otherwise than by purchase, may be imported or entered, shall cause such actual market value or wholesale price thereof to be appraised; and if such appraised value shall exceed by 10 per cent. or more the entered value, then, in addition to the duties imposed by law on the same, there shall be levied and collected a duty of 20 per cent. ad valorem on such appraised value. The duty shall not, however, be assessed upon an amount less than the invoice or entered value, except as elsewhere especially provided in this act.

Sec. 14. That all invoices of imported merchandise shall, at or before the shipment of the merchandise, be produced to the consul, vice-consul or commercial agent of the United States of the consular district from which the merchandise is imported to the United States, and if there be no consul, vice-consul, or commercial agent for said district, then said invoices shall be produced to the consul, vice-consul, or commercial agent of the district nearest thereto, and shall have indorsed thereon, when so produced, a declaration signed by the purchaser, manufacturer, owner, or agent, setting forth that the invoice is in all respects correct and true; that it contains, if the merchandise was obtained by purchase, a true and full statement of the time when, and the place where the same was purchased, and the actual cost thereof and of all charges thereon; and that no discounts, bounties, or drawbacks are contained in the invoice but such as have actually been allowed thereon; and when obtained in any other manner than by purchase, the actual market value or wholesale price thereof at the time of exportation to the United States in the principal markets of the country from whence exported; and that no different invoice of the merchandise mentioned in the invoice so produced, has been or will be furnished to any one. If the merchandise was actually purchased, the declaration shall also contain a statement that the currency in which such invoice is made out is the currency which was actually paid for the merchandise by the purchaser.

Sec. 15. That section 2,931 of the Revised Statutes be, and hereby is, amended so as to read as follows:

"Sec. 2,931. The decision of the collector of customs or officer acting as such at the port of importation and entry, as to the rate and amount of duties to be paid on any merchandise, and the dutiable costs and charges thereon, shall be final and conclusive against all persons interested in such merchandise unless the owner, importer, consignee, or agent of the merchandise, shall, within ten days after and not on any day before the ascertainment and liquidation of the duties by the proper officers of the customs, as well in cases of merchandise entered in bond as for consumption, give notice in writing to the collector if dissatisfied with the aforesaid decision, setting forth therein, distinctly and specifically, and in respect to each entry, the reasons of his objection thereto, and shall also, within thirty days after the date of such ascertainment and liquidation, appeal therefrom to the Secretary of the Treasury, who, on receiving such appeal, shall forthwith call upon the collector for a report thereon; and the collector shall thereupon, if he adheres to his decision, set forth, specifically and in detail, to the Secretary, the reasons therefor; and the decision of the Secretary on such appeal shall be final and conclusive, and such merchandise, or costs and charges, shall be liable to duty accordingly, unless suit shall be brought, within ninety days after the decision of the Secretary of the Treasury on such appeal, for any duties which shall have been paid before the date of such decision on such merchandise, or costs any charges, or within ninety days after the payment of duties paid after the decision of the Secretary. No suit shall be begun or maintained for the recovery of any duties alleged to have been erroneously or illegally exacted, until the decision of the Secretary of the Treasury shall have been first had on such appeal, unless the decision of the Secretary shall be delayed more than ninety days from the date of such appeal. And when a suit shall be brought by the United States to recover the additional duties found due on any ascertainment and liquidation thereof, and not paid, the defendant or defendants shall not be permitted to set up any plea or matter in defense excepting such as shall have been set forth in a protest and appeal made as herein prescribed."

SEC. 16. That the section of the Revised Statutes numbered 3,012 shall be, and hereby is amended by adding at the end of said section the following words:

"And there shall be attached to the said bill of particulars, when served as aforesaid, a copy of each and every such protest or notice of dissatisfaction, and of every appeal relied upon by the plaintiff or plaintiffs in said suit; and the said bill of particulars shall declare the date of liquidation; and a bill of particulars, having been served as aforesaid, shall not thereafter be amended by the plaintiff, or by the court on the plaintiff's motion, so as to increase the total sum claimed therein as having been exacted in excess."

SEC. 17. That no suit which by this act, or by any law of the United States is permitted to be begun against a collector of customs to recover money alleged to have been illegally exacted by him on imported merchandise, shall hereafter be begun or maintained in any court of any State of the United States, but each and every such suit shall be begun in the circuit court of the United States for the district in which such alleged illegal action shall have been made.

SEC. 18. That section 3,012½ of the Revised Statutes shall be, and hereby is, amended so as to read as follows:

"Whenever it shall be shown to the satisfaction of the Secretary of the Treasury (first) that, in any case of unascertained or estimated duties, more money has been paid to or deposited with a collector of customs than the law required to be paid or deposited; and also (second) whenever the Secretary of the Treasury shall have decided, on an appeal to him as herein provided, that more money has been paid to or deposited with a collector of customs than the law required; and also (third) whenever any judgment shall have been recovered and entered, in any court of the United States, against a collector of customs, for duties illegally exacted by him on imported merchandise, and a certificate of probable cause shall have been entered in said suit, in compliance with the provisions and requirements of section 989 of the Revised Statutes, from which judgment the Attorney-General shall certify, in conformity with the act of March 3, 1875 (Chapter CXXXVI), that no appeal or writ of error will be taken by the United States, and from which judgment the Secretary of the Treasury shall also be satisfied that no such appeal or writ of error ought to be taken; and also (fourth) whenever any suit or suits have been begun against a collector of customs to recover money exacted by him and paid under protest, and an appeal, as required by law, and a bill of particulars has been served therein on the defendant or his attorney, as required by law, and when by the legal effect of any judgment of a court of the United States, satisfactory to the Attorney-General and the Secretary of the Treasury as aforesaid, the said exaction of such duties shall have been declared illegal, and protests, appeals, and bills of particulars have been made according to the law in force at the time of importation, and the proper officers of the customs shall, under the instructions of the Secretary of the Treasury, have reliquidated the entries covered, by said suit or suits, and bill or bills of particulars, according to the principles and rules of law prescribed by said judgment, and the district attorney appearing of record for the defendant shall certify that such suits have been discontinued, the Secretary of the Treasury shall, in each and all of the before-mentioned cases, always excepting judgments or 'judgment cases' in suits commonly known as 'charges and commission' suits, which last named shall only be paid in pursuance of a specific appropriation therefor, draw his warrant upon the Treasurer in favor of the person or persons entitled to the overpayment, or the sum expressed in said judgment, or the sum thus found due on reliquidation of the entries in discontinued suits, including costs payable by law, directing the Treasurer to refund and pay the same out of any money in the Treasury not otherwise appropriated. The necessary moneys therefor are hereby appropriated, and this appropriation shall be deemed a permanent indefinite appropriation."

SEC. 19. That section 2,927 of the Revised Statutes is hereby amended by the addition of the following words thereto:

"No allowances for damages to goods, wares, and merchandise imported into the United States shall hereafter be made in the estimation and liquidation of duties thereon; but the importer thereof may abandon to the Government all or any portion of goods, wares, and merchandise included in any invoice, and be relieved from the payment of the duties on the portion so abandoned: *Provided*, That the portion so abandoned shall amount to 10 per cent. or over of the total value of the invoice."

SEC. 20. That any person who shall give or offer to give or promise to give, excepting for such duties or fees as have been levied or required according to the forms of law, any money or thing of value, directly or indirectly, to any officer or servant of the customs or of the United States, in connection with or pertaining to the importation, or appraisement, or entry, or examination, or inspection of goods, wares, or merchandise, including herein any baggage, or of the liquidation of the entry thereof, shall, on conviction thereof, be fined not less than $100 nor more than $5,000, or be imprisoned at hard labor not more than two years, or both, at the discretion of the court; and evidence of such giving or offering or promising to give satisfactory to the court in which such trial is had, shall be regarded as *prima facie* evidence that such giving or offering or promising was contrary to law, and shall put upon the accused the burden of proving that such act was innocent and not done with an unlawful intention.

SEC. 21. That any officer or servant of the customs or of the United States who shall, excepting for lawful duties or fees, demand, exact, or receive from any person, directly or indirectly, any money or thing of value in connection with or pertaining to the importation, appraisement, entry, examination, or inspection of goods, wares, or merchandise, including herein any baggage or liquidation of the entry thereof, shall, on conviction thereof, be fined not less than $100 nor more than $5,000, or be imprisoned at hard labor not more than two years, or both, at the discretion of the court; and evidence of such demanding, exacting, or receiving satisfactory to the court in which such trial is had, shall be *prima facie* evidence that such demanding, exacting, or receiving was contrary to law, and shall put upon the accused the burden of proving that such act was innocent and not with an unlawful intention.

SEC. 22. That section 2,864 of the Revised Statutes be, and hereby is, amended so as to read as follows:

"SEC. 2,864. That any owner, importer, consignee, agent, or other person who shall, with intent to defraud the revenue, make or attempt to make any entry of imported merchandise by means of any fraudulent or false invoice, affidavit, letter, or paper, or by means of any false statement, written or verbal, or who shall be guilty of any willful act or omission by means whereof the United States shall be deprived of the lawful duties, or any portion thereof, accruing upon the merchandise, or any portion thereof, embraced or referred to in such invoice, affidavit, letter, paper, or statement, or affected by such act or omission, shall for each offense be fined in any sum not exceeding $5,000 nor less than $50, or be imprisoned for any time not exceeding two years, or both; and, in addition to such fine, such merchandise, or the value thereof, shall be forfeited, which forfeiture shall only apply to the whole of the merchandise, or the value thereof, in the case or package containing the particular article or articles of merchandise to which such fraud or alleged fraud relates; and anything contained in any act which provides for the forfeiture or confiscation of an entire invoice in consequence of any item or items contained in the same being undervalued be, and the same is hereby, repealed."

SEC. 23. That all imported goods, wares, and merchandise which may be in the public stores or bonded warehouses or on shipboard within the limits of any port of entry, or remaining in the customs offices, on the day and year when this act, or any provision thereof, shall go into effect, except as otherwise provided in this act, shall be subject to no other duty, upon the entry thereof for consumption, than if the same were imported respectively after that day; and all goods, wares, and merchandise remaining in bonded warehouses on the day and year this act, or any provision thereof, shall take effect, and upon which the duties shall have been paid, shall be entitled to a refund of the difference between the amount of duties paid and the amount of duties said goods, wares, and merchandise would be subject to if the same were imported respectively after that date.

SEC. 24. That sections 3,011 and 3,013 of the Revised Statutes be, and hereby are, repealed as to all importations made after the date of this act.

SEC. 25. That on and after the 1st day of October, 1888, all taxes on manufactured chewing-tobacco, smoking-tobacco and snuff, all special taxes upon manufacturers of and dealers in said articles, and all taxes upon wholesale and retail dealers in leaf-tobacco be, and are hereby repealed: *Provided*, That there shall be allowed a drawback or rebate of the full amount of tax on all orignal and unbroken factory packages of smoking and manufactured tobacco and snuff held by manufacturers, factors, jobbers, or dealers on said 1st day of October, if claim therefore shall be presented to the Commissioner of Internal Revenue prior to the 1st day of January, 1889, and not otherwise. No claim shall be allowed and no drawback shall be paid for an amount less than five dollars, and all sums required to satisfy claims under this act shall be paid out of any money in the Treasury not otherwise appropriated. It shall be the duty of the Commissioner of Internal Revenue, with the approval of the Secretary of the Treasury, to adopt such rules and regulations, and to prescribe and furnish such blanks and forms as may be necessary to carry this section into effect.

SEC. 26. That on and after the 1st day of October, 1888, manufacturers of cigars shall each pay a special

tax of three dollars annually, and dealers in tobacco shall each pay a special tax of one dollar annually. Every person whose business it is to sell or offer for sale cigars, cheroots, or cigarettes shall, on and after the 1st day of Oct., 1888, be regarded as a dealer in tobacco, and the payment of any other special tax shall not relieve any person who sells cigars, cheroots, or cigarettes from the payment of this tax: *Provided*, That no manufacturer of cigars, cheroots, or cigarettes shall be required to pay a special tax as a dealer in tobacco, as above defined, for selling his own products at the place of manufacture: *Provided*, That the bond required to be given in conformity with the provisions of title 35 of the Revised Statutes of the United States, by every person engaging in the manufacture of cigars in the internal-revenue districts of the United States, shall be in such penal sum as the collector of internal revenue may require, not less than $100, with an addition of $10 for each person proposed to be employed by such person in making cigars.

SEC. 27. That the sum of $20,000, or so much thereof as may be necessary, be, and the same is hereby appropriated, out of any money in the Treasury not otherwise appropriated. for the alteration of dies, plates, and stamps, for furnishing blanks and forms, and for such other expenses as shall be incident to the collection of special taxes at the reduced rates provided in this act.

SEC. 28. That section 3361 of the Revised Statutes of the United States, and all laws and parts of laws which impose restrictions upon the sale of leaf-tobacco, be, and are hereby, repealed.

SEC. 29. That whenever in any statute denouncing any violation of the internal-revenue laws as a felony, crime, or misdemeanor, there is prescribed in such statute a minimum punishment, less than which minimum no fine, penalty, imprisonment, or punishment is authorized to be imposed, every such minimum punishment is hereby abolished; and the court or Judge in every such case shall have discretion to impose any fine, penalty, imprisonment, or punishment not exceeding the limit authorized by such statute, whether such fine, penalty, imprisonment, or punishment be less or greater than the said minimum so prescribed.

SEC. 30. That no warrant, in any case under the internal-revenue laws, shall be issued upon an affidavit making charges upon information and belief, unless such affidavit is made by a collector or deputy collector of internal revenue or by a revenue agent; and, with the exception aforesaid, no warrant shall be issued except upon a sworn complaint, setting forth the facts constituting the offense and alleging them to be within the personal knowledge of the affiant. And the United States shall not be liable to pay any fees to marshals, clerks, commissioners, or other officers for any warrant issued or arrest made in prosecutions under the internal-revenue laws, unless there be a conviction or the prosecution has been approved, either before or after such arrest, by the attorney of the United States for the district where the offense is alleged to have been committed, or unless the prosecution was commenced by information or indictment.

SEC. 31. That whenever a warrant shall be issued by a commissioner or other judicial officer having jurisdiction for the arrest of any person charged with a criminal offense, such warrant, accompanied by the affidavit on which the same was issued, shall be returnable before some judicial officer named in section 1,014 of the Revised Statutes residing in the county of arrest, or if there be no such judicial officer in that county, before some such judicial officer residing in another county nearest to the place of arrest; and the judicial officer, before whom the warrant is made returnable as herein provided, shall have exclusive authority to make the preliminary examination of every person arrested as aforesaid, and to discharge him, admit him to bail, or commit him to prison, as the case may require: *Provided*, That this section shall not apply to the Indian Territory.

Sec. 32. That the circuit courts of the United States, and the district courts or judges thereof exercising circuit-court powers, and the district courts of the Territories, are authorized to appoint, in different parts of the several districts in which said courts are held, as many discreet persons to become commissioners of the circuit courts as may be deemed necessary; and said courts, or the judges thereof, shall have authority to remove at pleasure any commissioners heretofore or hereafter appointed in said districts.

Sec. 33. That the Commissioner of Internal Revenue, with the approval of the Secretary of the Treasury, may compromise any civil or criminal case, and may reduce or remit any fine, penalty, forfeiture, or assessment under the internal-revenue laws.

Sec. 34. That section 3,176 of the Revised Statutes be amended so as to read as follows.

"Sec. 3,176. The collector or any deputy collector in any district shall enter into and upon the premises, if it be necessary, of any e son therein who has taxable property and who refuses or neglects to render any return or list required, or who renders a false or fraudulent return or list, and make, according to the best information which he can obtain, including that derived from the evidence elicited by the examination of the collector, and on his own view and information, such list or return, according to the form proscribed, of the objects liable to tax owned or possessed or under the care or management of such person, and the Commissioner of Internal Revenue shall assess the tax thereon, including the amount, if any, due for special tax, and a penalty of 25 per cent., and he may add to such tax interest at the rate of 10 per cent. per annum thereon from and after the date when such tax became due and payable. The interest so added to the tax shall be collected at the same time and in the same manner as the tax. And the list or return so made and subscribed by such collector or deputy collector shall be deemed good and sufficient for all legal purposes."

Sec. 35. That nothing in this act shall in any way change or impair the force or effect of any treaty between the United States and any other government, or any laws passed in pursuance of or for the execution of any such treaty, so long as such treaty shall remain in force in respect of the subjects embraced in this act; but whenever any such treaty, so far as the same respects said subjects, shall expire or be otherwise terminated, the provisions of this act shall be in force in all respects in the same manner and to the same extent as if no such treaty had existed at the time of the passage hereof.

Sec. 36. That section 3,255 of the Revised Statutes of the United States be amended by striking out all after said number and substituting therefor the following:

"And the Commissioner of Internal Revenue, with the approval of the Secretary of the Treasury, may exempt distillers of brandy made exclusively from apples, peaches, grapes, or other fruits from any provision of this title relating to the manufacture of spirits, except as to the tax thereon, when in his judgment it may seem expedient to do so.

"The Secretary of the Treasury may exempt all distilleries which mash less than twenty-five bushels of grain per day from the operations of the provisions of this title relating to the manufacture of spirits, except as to the payment of the tax, which said tax shall then be levied and collected on the capacity of said distilleries; and said distilleries may, at the discretion of said Secretary, then be run and operated without store-keepers or 'store-keepers and gaugers.' And the Commissioner of Internal Revenue, with the approval of said Secretary, may establish special warehouses in which he may authorize to be deposited the product of any number of said distilleries to be designated by him, and in which any distiller operating any such distillery may deposit his product, which, when so deposited, shall be subject to all the laws and regulations as to bonds, tax, removals, and

otherwise as other warehouses. The Commissioner of Internal Revenue, with the approval of the Secretary of the Treasury, is hereby authorized and directed to make such rules and regulations as may be necessary to carry out the provisions of this section: *Provided*, That such regulations shall be adopted as will require that all the spirits manufactured shall be subject to the payment of the tax according to law."

Sec. 37. That the provisions of an act entitled "An act relating to the production of fruit brandy, and to punish frauds connected with the same," approved March 3, 1877, be extended and made applicable to brandy distilled from apples or peaches, or from any other fruit the brandy distilled from which is not now required, or hereafter shall not be required, to be deposited in a distillery warehouse: *Provided*, That each of the warehouses established under said act, or which may hereafter be established, shall be in charge either of a store-keeper or a store-keeper and gauger, at the discretion of the Commissioner of Internal Revenue.

Sec. 38. That section 3332 of the Revised Statutes, and the supplement thereto, shall be amended so that said section shall read as follows:

"When a judgment of forfeiture, in any case of seizure, is recovered against any distillery used or fit for use in the production of distilled spirits, because no bond has been given, or against any distillery used or fit for use in the production of spirits, having a registered producing capacity of less than one hundred and fifty gallons a day, every still, doubler, worm, worm-tub, mash-tub, and fermenting-tub therein shall be sold, as in case of other forfeited property, without being mutilated or destroyed. And in case of seizure of a still, doubler, worm, worm-tub, fermenting-tub, mash-tub, or other distilling apparatus of any kind whatsoever, for any offense involving forfeiture of the same, it shall be the duty of the seizing officer to remove the same from the place where seized to a place of safe storage; and said property so seized shall be sold as provided by law, but without being mutilated or destroyed."

Sec. 39. That whenever it shall be made to appear to the United States court or judge having jurisdiction that the health or life of any person imprisoned for any offense, in a county jail or elsewhere, is endangered by close confinement, the said court or judge is hereby authorized to make such order and provision for the comfort and well-being of the person so imprisoned as shall be deemed reasonable and proper.

Sec. 40. That all clauses of section 3244 of the Revised Statutes, and all laws amendatory thereof, and all other laws which impose any special taxes upon manufacturers of stills, retail dealers in liquors, and retail dealers in malt liquors, are hereby repealed.

Sec. 41. That this act is intended and shall be construed as an act supplementary and amendatory to existing laws, and the rates of duty and modification of clauses, provisions, and sections as herein specifically made are intended and shall be construed as a repeal of all clauses, provisions, and sections in conflict herewith, but as to all clauses, provisions, and sections in existing laws not herein specifically changed, modified, or amended the rates of duty now existing shall be and remain in full force and effect. This act shall be in force from and after Oct. 1, 1888, except as herein otherwise provided.

This measure was referred in the Senate to the Finance Committee, and the Republican majority of that committee prepared a substitute which they reported by way of amendment October 3. The matter was taken up October 8, and Mr. Allison, of Iowa, made the opening speech in explanation of the Senate bill; but it was not very earnestly discussed, and no attempt was made to push it to a vote before adjournment. The Senate measure aimed at a reduction of reducing the revenue to the extent of from $65,000,000 to $73,000,000; it dealt with all the schedules of the tariff and was avowedly a revision of the customs duties with the purpose of maintaining their protective features though it is not in all respects consistent with that purpose. The heaviest reduction was on internal-revenue taxation, tobacco being made free and the tax on alcohol used in the arts being reduced. The great reduction proposed in the customs duties was the cutting down of the tariff on sugar about one half. Some articles were put on the free list, reducing the estimated revenue still further; but in nearly all the schedules the proposed changes might be expected to increase rather than diminish duties collected. To put the distinction broadly, the Senate bill increased the internal-revenue reduction provided for in the Mills Bill and made the tariff reduction mainly in the duties on sugar and molasses which the Mills Bill had touched but lightly.

The Fisheries Treaty.—Another important matter dealt with was the fisheries treaty sent to the Senate by the President, Feb. 20, 1888. It was negotiated by Thomas F. Bayard, Secretary of State, William L. Putnam, of Maine, and James B. Angell, of Michigan, on the part of the United States, and Joseph Chamberlain, L. S. Sackville West, and Charles Tupper on the part of Great Britain, and was designed to settle "the interpretation of the convention of Oct. 20, 1818," concerning which much controversy had arisen with the Canadian authorities after the termination, June 30, 1885, of the fisheries articles of the treaty of 1871. The proposed treaty was signed at Washington, Febuary 15, and the President in his message transmitting the document to the Senate for consideration, said: "I am given to understand that the other governments concerned in this treaty will, within a few days, in accordance with their methods of conducting public business, submit said treaty to their respective legislatures, when it will be at once published to the world. In view of such action it appears to be advisable that, by publication here, early and full knowledge of all that has been done in the premises should be afforded to our people. It would also seem to be useful to inform the popular mind concerning the history of the long-continued disputes growing out of the subject embraced in the treaty and to satisfy the public interest touching the same, as well as to acquaint our people with the present status of the questions involved, and to give them the exact terms of the proposed adjustment, in place of the exaggerated and imaginative statements which will otherwise reach them. I therefore beg leave respectfully to suggest that said treaty and all such correspondence, messages, and documents relating to the same as may be deemed important to accomplish these purposes be at once made public by the order of your honorable body." This was considered

a sort of challenge to the Senate, and it was promptly accepted by that body. The treaty, contrary to the usual custom, was at once published, and after May 28 it was debated in open session. It is as follows:

Whereas differences have arisen concerning the interpretation of Article I of the Convention of Oct. 20, 1818, the United States of America and Her Majesty the Queen of the United Kingdom of Great Britain and Ireland, being mutually desirous of removing all causes of misunderstanding in relation thereto and of promoting friendly intercourse and good neighborhood between the United States and the possessions of Her Majesty in North America, have resolved to conclude a treaty to that end, and have named as their plenipotentiaries—that is to say:

The President of the United States, Thomas F. Bayard, Secretary of State; William L. Putnam, of Maine; and James B. Angell, of Michigan;

And Her Majesty the Queen of the United Kingdom of Great Britain and Ireland, the Right Hon. Joseph Chamberlain, M. P.; the Hon. Sir Lionel Sackville Sackville West, K. C. M. G. Her Britannic Majesty's Envoy Extraordinary and Minister Plenipotentiary to the United States of America; and Sir Charles Tupper, G. C. M. G., C. B., Minister of Finance of the Dominion of Canada:

Who, having communicated to each other their respective full powers, found in good and due form, have agreed upon the following articles:

Article I. The high contracting parties agree to appoint a mixed commission to delimit, in the manner provided in this treaty, the British waters, bays, creeks, and harbor of the coast of Canada and of Newfoundland, as to which the United States, by Article I of the convention of Oct. 20, 1818, between the United States and Great Britain, renounced forever any liberty to take, dry, or cure fish.

Art. II. The commission shall consist of two commissioners to be named by Her Britannic Majesty and of two commissioners to be named by the President of the United States, without delay, after the exchange of ratifications of this treaty.

The commission shall meet and complete the delimitation as soon as possible thereafter.

In case of the death, absence, or incapacity of any commissioner, or in the event of any commissioner omitting or ceasing to act as such, the President of the United States or Her Britannic Majesty, respectively, shall forthwith name another person to act as commissioner instead of the commissioner originally named.

Art. III. The delimitation referred to in Article I of this treaty shall be marked upon British admiralty charts by a series of lines regularly numbered and duly described. The charts so marked shall, on the termination of the work of the commission be signed by the commissioners in quadruplicate; one copy whereof shall be delivered to the Secretary of State of the United States and three copies to Her Majesty's Government. The delimitation shall be made in the following manner, and shall be accepted by both the high contracting parties as applicable for all purposes under Article I of the convention of Oct. 20, 1818, between the United States and Great Britain.

The three marine miles mentioned in Article I of the convention of Oct. 20, 1818, shall be measured seaward from low-water mark; but at every bay, creek, or harbor, not otherwise specially provided for in this treaty, such three marine miles shall be measured seaward from a straight line drawn across the bay, creek, or harbor, in the part nearest the entrance at the first point where the width does not exceed ten marine miles.

Art. IV. At or near the following bays the limits of exclusion under Article I of the convention of Oct. 20, 1818, at points more than three marine miles from low-water mark, shall be established by the following lines, namely:

At the Baie des Chaleurs the line from the light at Birch Point, on Miscou Island, to Macquereau Point light; at the Bay of Miramichi, the line from the light at Point Escuminac to the light on the eastern point of Tabisintac Gulley; at Egmont Bay, in Prince Edward Island, the line from the light at Cape Egmont to the light at West Point; and off St. Ann's Bay, in the province of Nova Scotia, the line from Cape Smoke to the light at Point Aconi.

At Fortune Bay, in Newfoundland, the line from Connaigre Head to the light on the southeasterly end of Brunet Island, thence to Fortune Head; at Sir Charles Hamilton Sound, the line from the southeast point of Cape Fogo to White Island, thence to the north end of Peckford Island, and from the south end of Peckford Island to the east headland of Ragged Harbor.

At or near the following bays the limits of exclusion shall be three marine miles seaward from the following lines, namely:

At or near Barrington Bay, in Nova Scotia, the line from the light on Stoddard Island to the light on the south point of Cape Sable, thence to the light at Baccaro Point; at Chedabucto and St. Peter's Bays, the line from Cranberry Island light to Green Island light, thence to Point Rouge; at Mira Bay, the line from the light on the east point of Scatari Island to the northeasterly point of Cape Morien; and at Placentia Bay, in Newfoundland, the line from Latine Point, on the eastern mainland shore, to the most southerly point of Red Island, thence by the most southerly point of Merasheen Island to the mainland.

Long Island and Bryer Island, at St. Mary's Bay, in Nova Scotia, shall, for the purpose of delimitation, be taken as the coasts of such bay.

Art. V. Nothing in this treaty shall be construed to include within the common waters any such interior portions of any bays, creeks, or harbors as can not be reached from the sea without passing within the three marine miles mentioned in Article I of the convention of Oct. 20, 1818.

Art. VI. The commissioners shall from time to time report to each of the high contracting parties, such lines as they may have agreed upon, numbered, described, and marked as herein provided, with quadruplicate charts thereof; which lines so reported shall forthwith from time to time be simultaneously proclaimed by the high contracting parties, and be binding after two months from such proclamation.

Art. VII. Any disagreement of the commissioners shall forthwith be referred to an umpire selected by the Secretary of State of the United States and Her Britannic Majesty's minister at Washington; and his decision shall be final.

Art. VIII. Each of the high contracting parties shall pay its own commissioners and officers. All other expenses jointly incurred in connection with the performance of the work, including compensation to the umpire, shall be paid by the high contracting parties in equal moieties.

Art. IX. Nothing in this treaty shall interrupt or affect the free navigation of the Strait of Canso by fishing-vessels of the United States.

Art. X. United States fishing-vessels entering the bays or harbors referred to in Article I of this treaty shall conform to harbor regulations common to them and to fishing-vessels of Canada or of Newfoundland.

They need not report, enter, or clear, when putting into such bays or harbors for shelter or repairing damages, nor when putting into the same, outside the limits of established ports of entry, for the purpose of purchasing wood or of obtaining water; except that any such vessel remaining more than twenty-four hours, exclusive of Sundays and legal holidays, within any such port, or communicating with the shore therein, may be required to report, enter, or clear; and no vessel shall be excused hereby from giving due information to boarding officers.

They shall not be liable in any such bays or harbors for compulsory pilotage; nor, when therein for the purpose of shelter, of repairing damages, of purchasing wood, or of obtaining water, shall they be liable for harbor dues, tonnage dues, buoy dues, light dues, or other similar dues; but this enumeration shall not permit other charges inconsistent with the enjoyment of the liberties reserved or secured by the convention of Oct. 20, 1818.

Art. XI. United States fishing-vessels entering the ports, bays, and harbors of the eastern or northeastern coasts of Canada or of the coasts of Newfoundland under stress of weather or other casualty may unload, reload, transship, or sell, subject to customs laws and regulations, all fish on board, when such unloading, transshipment, or sale is made necessary as incidental to repairs, and may replenish outfits, provisions, and supplies damaged or lost by disaster; and in case of death or sickness, shall be allowed all needful facilities, including the shipping of crews.

Licenses to purchase in established ports of entry of the aforesaid coasts of Canada or of Newfoundland, for the homeward voyage, such provisions and supplies as are ordinarily sold to trading-vessels, shall be granted to United States fishing-vessels in such ports, promptly upon application and without charge; and such vessels, having obtained licenses in the manner aforesaid, shall also be accorded upon all occasions such facilities for the purchase of casual or needful provisions and supplies as are ordinarily granted to the trading-vessels; but such provisions or supplies shall not be obtained by barter, nor purchased for re-sale or traffic.

Art. XII. Fishing-vessels of Canada and Newfoundland shall have on the Atlantic coast of the United States all the privileges reserved and secured by this treaty to United States fishing-vessels in the aforesaid waters of Canada and Newfoundland.

Art. XIII. The Secretary of the Treasury of the United States shall make regulations providing for the conspicuous exhibition by every United States fishing-vessel, of its official number on each bow; and any vessel required by law to have an official number, and failing to comply with such regulations, shall not be entitled to the licenses provided for in this treaty.

Such regulations shall be communicated to Her Majesty's Government previously to their taking effect.

Art. XIV. The penalties for unlawfully fishing in the waters, bays, creeks, and harbors, referred to in Article I of this treaty, may extend to forfeiture of the boat or vessel and appurtenances, and also of the supplies and cargo aboard when the offense was committed; and for preparing in such waters to unlawfully fish therein penalties shall be fixed by the court, not to exceed those for unlawfully fishing; and for any other violation of the laws of Great Britain, Canada, or Newfoundland relating to the right of fishery in such waters, bays, creeks, or harbors, penalties shall be fixed by the court, not exceeding in all $3 for every ton of the boat or vessel concerned. The boat or vessel may be holden for such penalties and forfeitures.

The proceedings shall be summary and as inexpensive as practicable. The trial (except on appeal) shall be at the place of detention, unless the judge shall, on request of the defense, order it to be held at some other place adjudged by him more convenient. Security for costs shall not be required of the defense, except when bail is offered. Reasonable bail shall be accepted. There shall be proper appeals available to the defense only; and the evidence at the trial may be used on appeal.

Judgments of forfeiture shall be reviewed by the Governor-General of Canada, in council, or the Governor, in council, of Newfoundland, before the same are executed.

Art. XV. Whenever the United States shall remove the duty from fish-oil, whale-oil, seal-oil, and fish of all kinds (except fish p ese e in oil), being the produce of fisheries carried on by the fishermen of Canada and Newfoundland, including Labrador, as well as from the usual and necessary casks, barrels, kegs, cans, and other usual and necessary coverings containing the products above mentioned, the like products, being the produce of fisheries carried on by the fishermen of the United States, as well as the usual and necessary coverings of the same, as above described, shall be admitted free of duty into the Dominion of Canada and Newfoundland.

And upon such removal of duties, and while the aforesaid articles are allowed to be brought into the United States by British subjects, without duty being reimposed thereon, the privilege of entering the ports, bays, and harbors of the aforesaid coasts of Canada and Newfoundland shall be accorded to United States fishing-vessels by annual licenses, free of charge, for the following purposes, namely:

1. The purchase of provisions, bait, ice, seines, lines, and all other supplies and outfits;

2. Transshipment of catch, for transport by any means of conveyance;

3. Shipping of crews.

Supplies shall not be obtained by barter, but bait may be so obtained.

The like privileges shall be continued or given to fishing-vessels of Canada and of Newfoundland on the Atlantic coasts of the United States.

Art. XVI. This treaty shall be ratified by the President of the United States, by and with the advice and consent of the Senate; and by Her Britannic Majesty, having received the assent of the Parliament of Canada and of the Legislature of Newfoundland; and the ratifications shall be exchanged at Washington as soon as possible.

In faith whereof we, the respective plenipotentiaries, have signed this treaty, and have hereunto affixed our seals.

Done in duplicate at Washington this 15th day of February, in the year of our Lord 1888.

PROTOCOL.

The treaty having been signed, the British plenipotentiaries desire to state that they have been considering the position which will be created by the immediate commencement of the fishing season before the treaty can possibly be ratified by the Senate of the United States, by the Parliament of Canada, and the Legislature of Newfoundland.

In the absence of such ratification the old conditions which have given rise to so much friction and irritation might be revived, and might interfere with the unprejudiced consideration of the treaty by the legislative bodies concerned.

Under these circumstances, and with the further object of affording evidence of their anxious desire to promote good feeling and to remove all possible subjects of controversy, the British plenipotentiaries are ready to make the following temporary arrangement for a period not exceeding two years, in order to afford a *modus vivendi* pending the ratification of the treaty.

1. For a period not exceeding two years from the present date, the privilege of entering the bays and harbors of the Atlantic coasts of Canada and Newfoundland shall be granted to United States fishing-vessels by annual licenses at a fee of $1.50 per ton for the following purposes:

The purchase of bait, ice, seines, lines, and all other supplies and outfits.

Transshipment of catch and shipping of crews.

2. If, during the continuance of this arrangement, the United States should remove the duties on fish, fish-oil, whale- and seal-oil (and their coverings, packages, etc.), the said licenses shall be issued free of charge.

3. United States fishing-vessels entering the bays and harbors of the Atlantic coasts of Canada or of Newfoundland for any of the four purposes mentioned in Article I of the convention of Oct. 20, 1818, and not remaining therein more than twenty-four hours, shall not be required to enter or clear at the custom-house, providing that they do not communicate with the shore.

4. Forfeiture to be exacted only for the offenses of fishing or preparing to fish in territorial waters.

5. This arrangement to take effect as soon as the necessary measures can be completed by the colonial authorities.
    J. CHAMBERLAIN.
    L. S. SACKVILLE WEST.
    CHARLES TUPPER.
WASHINGTON, *Feb.* 15, 1888.

PROTOCOL.

The American plenipotentiaries, having received the communication of the British plenipotentiaries of this date conveying their plan for the administration to be observed by the Governments of Canada and Newfoundland in respect of the fisheries during the period which may be requisite for the consideration by the Senate of the treaty this day signed, and the enactment of the legislation by the respective Governments therein proposed, desire to express their satisfaction with this manifestation of an intention on the part of the British plenipotentiaries, by the means referred to, to maintain the relations of good neighborhood between the British possessions in North America and the United States; and they will convey the communication of the British plenipotentiaries to the President of the United States, with a recommendation that the same may be by him made known to the Senate for its information, together with the treaty, when the latter is submitted to that body for ratification.
    T. F. BAYARD.
    JAMES B ANGELL.
    WILLIAM L. PUTNAM.

WASHINGTON, *Feb.* 15, 1888.

In his speech in criticism of the treaty, May 29, Mr. Frye, of Maine, said of the delimitation articles: "The first eight articles relate entirely to delimitation. Who asked for delimitation? Who entered complaint that the fishermen in the northeast could not tell where the three-mile shore-line was, or where bays six miles wide at their mouths were? Did this commission ever hear of any complaint? I am aware, sir, that Great Britain, about 1823, in the pursuit of her aggressiveness toward us, declared that these bays were to be measured from headland to headland. But I am equally aware that in less than six months after that claim was made she sent instructions to the colonial officers not to enforce it, and for the whole seventy years it never has been enforced, except in two instances, that of the 'Argus' and the 'Washington.' The 'Washington' was seized in 1843 in the Bay of Fundy fishing outside of the three-mile shore-line. I am equally well aware that subsequently, when we made claim, and on the seizure of the 'Argus,' the two seizures, the whole matter was referred to arbitrators; and that after hearing they determined that neither the 'Argus' nor the 'Washington,' was within British waters. In other words, they determined that the claim made by Great Britain was not sustained by the law or by the treaties, and that this three-mile shore-line and six-mile bay were to control."

Of the ninth and tenth articles, he said: "And the President of the United States congratulates us in his message that at last the Strait of Canso is free and open. Why, sir, it never was closed in the history of the world, and no nation ever dared to close it, and no nation ever dreamed of closing it. It lies on this map here. It is the highway between the Gulf of St. Lawrence and the Atlantic Ocean. We have the right secured to us since 1783, ours to-day, around the Magdalen Islands, rights on the easterly shores of the gulf, and certainly we have rights in the broad Atlantic Ocean, and this strait is the open highway connecting our rights in the ocean and our rights in the bay. I say it never was closed, and no one ever dreamed of closing it.

"When a United States fishing-vessel, under the Treaty of 1818, puts into a harbor or bay for shelter she need not report and enter! Is not that an immense privilege to be granted to us? There can not be found in the history of any civilized maritime nation in the whole world an instance where a vessel putting in for shelter was compelled to report and enter. No vessel is compelled to report and enter until she communicates with the shore, until she lands a man or a cargo or goes to the shore to buy or to ship or do something of that kind."

Of the thirteenth article, Mr. Frye said: "We determine by law how our vessels shall be recognized ourselves. We give to one vessel a register, to another an enrollment, to another a license, and it is our privilege to give to the registered vessel a license or an enrollment, and to the licensed vessel a register, and no nation has the right to say to us you can not do this thing. It is a matter for us to determine for ourselves; and yet these commissioners in this treaty have surrendered that right and have declared that our fishing-vessels shall be known by a great mark on the bow which can be seen at a distance, pursued and harassed if you do not give them free fish. It was a shame for our commissioners to do that thing."

To the fourteenth article he also took exception: "Article XIV contains all the legal amenities which have been commended to us. I wish to call the attention of Senators to them and see how they like them. The article provides that where a United States fishing-vessel is fishing within the three-mile shore-limit the only penalty shall be forfeiture of the vessel and her cargo. They shall not hang the captain nor crucify the men. The 'Highland Light,' the only vessel in the last two years taken for violating the law and fishing within the three-mile shore-line, was tried and condemned; and what did she do? She caught enough mackerel within the three-mile shore-line for a breakfast for the crew, and to-day she is a Canadian cruiser. So the first amenity under the treaty is that if one of our fishermen worth about $10,000, with a cargo worth perhaps $3,000 more, is caught within these delimited waters—the Bay of Chaleur, Fortune Bay, or any ten-mile bay—catching mackerel enough for the crew's breakfast, the crime shall not be punished by any greater penalty

than the forfeiture of the $10,000 vessel and the $3,000 cargo. This is an amenity of the law. No wonder that the President and Secretary Bayard commend it!"

In commenting on the fifteenth article, he said: "Mr. President, we do not acquire commercial privileges by this treaty unless we buy them. Now this is a complete surrender of the position which we have occupied for more than fifty years. We claimed these privileges and these rights. We have insisted upon their enjoyment. We have enjoyed them up to two years ago; and now here is a treaty which admits that Canada's refusal has been right and that we have been wrong; which admits, if we desire to enjoy these privileges, we must buy them of Canada instead of claiming them under the laws of Great Britain and of the United States."

Mr. Gray, of Delaware, said, June 11, in vindication of the treaty: "Now, what has been accomplished by this treaty for the fishermen? In the first place, we have surrendered no doctrine as to jurisdictional waters which it was important to the United States to maintain. So far as area goes we have conceded less of our contention than Great Britain has of hers, and nothing of any value has been conceded by us. For uncertain, vague, and disputed lines of exclusion there is given reasonable, certain, and easily ascertained lines, marked by definite and prominent landmarks. The headland dispute is forever disposed of, and in our favor.

"And, excepting two or three of the bays delineated, all other bays over ten miles wide are conceded, a concession never before made. Compare these practical results with the impossible as well as impolitic course recommended by the majority, of insisting upon a barren recognition of the right to fish in all bays not less than six miles wide, after seventy years of fruitless demand or silent acquiescence.

"What comment is necessary on the statement of the majority report on page 20, that we have given up to the British these great bodies of water, meaning the delimited bays, and that we, by this treaty, 'cede to Great Britain complete dominion over these numerous and for fishing purposes the most valuable of the bays along the coast of British North America'? We never had the right, except perhaps by an intermittent sufferance, to cast a seine or wet a line in any of these waters. The right to exclude us was always maintained, and it is misleading to say, as the majority report does on page 18, that from the time of the seizure of the 'Washington' to the present no case of seizure for fishing in these bays has come to the notice of the committee. Nearly all the time from the case of the 'Washington' down to the present has been covered by the two treaties of reciprocity, and in the intervals uncovered by the permission which those treaties gave to the fishermen of the United States to fish in all British-American waters the cases of fishermen warned off from these bays were numerous and of constant occurrence.

"Mr. President, the majority report, and likewise the Senator from Maine, are so furious and so illogical in their assaults on this treaty that they even find fault with the ninth article, which declares 'that nothing in this treaty shall interrupt or affect the free navigation of the Strait of Canso by fishing-vessels of the United States.' And yet it is a fact that though this provision was meant among other things to prevent any inference of exclusion from the delimitation of Chedabucto Bay, it does for the first time in our history absolutely dispose of the pretensions of the colonial authorities to control as against our vessels the right of transit through this strait or gut of Canso.

"And now with reference to the privileges in addition to those secured by Article X. Article XI provides for every facility that a fishing-vessel may require in the ports of the Dominion except the purchase of distinctively fishing outfits. Thus commercial rights, so called, are secured to fishing-vessels which practically are the same as are secured to trading-vessels by the arrangement of 1830; and the restriction in the proviso to the first article of the convention of 1818 of the right of entry into bays, harbors, etc., to the four purposes of shelter, repairing damages, purchasing wood, and obtaining water is almost abrogated, as all these additional purposes for which entry may be made into ports are made lawful. Let us examine this important article more closely, because the majority report of the committee distinctly denies its efficiency to produce the results claimed for it by the President. To properly understand what this article means and what we have secured by it, it is necessary to consider just what the claim or contention of Canada was and has always been as to rights of our fishermen under the convention of 1818. The first article of that convention, after the clause in which the United States renounce forever any liberty heretofore enjoyed or claimed by the inhabitants thereof to take, dry, or cure fish on or within three marine miles of any of the coasts, bays, creeks, or harbors of His Britannic Majesty's dominions in America not included within the conceded limits, contains the following proviso, which has been repeated so often, *usque ad nauseam:*

Provided, however, That the American fishermen shall be permitted to enter such bays or harbors for the purpose of shelter and of repairing damages therein, of purchasing wood, and of obtaining water, and for no other purpose whatever. But they shall be under such restrictions as may be necessary to prevent their taking, drying, or curing fish therein, or in any other manner whatever abusing the privileges hereby reserved to them.

"There has always been the claim on the part of the provinces and Great Britain that this language, plainly and literally interpreted, excluded American fishermen from entering all colonial bays and harbors for any other purpose than the four purposes mentioned in the proviso, and that claim and contention has never been successfully controverted by the United States. This would give them the right to exclude the visits of fishermen to colonial ports for commercial purposes, so they have always contended, though they have not at all times exercised the right claimed. And so true it is that American fishermen have for many years, notably during the time the reciprocity treaties of 1854 and 1871 were in force and during the period of licenses from 1866 to 1870, in all a period of thirty years, as well as imperfectly and intermittently before 1854, enjoyed the privilege of buying bait and supplies and of transshipping their cargoes of fish. But their right to do these things was not admitted to exist under the convention of 1818, nor do I know that it was ever claimed as a right under that convention by the United States. That paragraph provides for and secures to the fishing-vessels of the United States every right of hospitality that they can reasonably demand. I know the Senator from Maine and the Senator from Massachusetts think that rights of hospitality ought not to be the subject of treaty stipulation, but that is not the practice in negotiations between countries, and I submit to the Senate that where the extent to which hospitality has been extended or ought to be extended, has ever come into question or doubt, it is a matter of the greatest importance and of the greatest advantage to those who are affected by it that that extent should be definitely fixed by conventional obligation."

Of the general scope and result of the treaty, Mr. Gray said: "Now, what is the position of Canada under this treaty? Is it a fair and just one for her to assume, and one which it is right and just for us to concede? I declare that it is both, and no fair man, it seems to me, can say otherwise. She has conceded nearly all that we have any right in fairness to ask. We have no right to demand that while we shut her out of our markets, she should give up without reserve every advantage that she possesses by reason of her geographical position and proximity to the great fishing-banks off her coasts, and that we shall make her harbors our basis of fishing operations while we refuse to share with her any advantages that we possess. I repeat, she has given us nearly everything we ask and more than we had the right to demand."

August 8, Mr. Evarts, of New York, said of the spirit in which the Canadians have acted: "I understand that the system of worrying was always brought into play whenever we asserted our right in fishing, and they asserted their contravention of it, in order to bring us to a departure from the fishing interests to the trading and commercial interests. There never has been a doubt of it. Whenever this irritation and teasing in the interests of trade induced the governments to try experiments of reciprocal interchange, then this resort merged the causes of irritation, and any adjudications or determinations were also merged therein for the time. This process, this method of the provinces, is an impetration upon us in the absence of logic. As Hudibras says, it works—

> "'Not by force of carnal reason,
> But indefatigable teasing.'

" And it has been very successful. You can tease a great and powerful and neighboring nation with prosperity open all around it. When we are brought into a critical period of resisting rights, then, under the anomalous condition by which England, in its relation to its provinces, has always undertaken to treat with us, as it were, *per interpositam personam*, it is left for the provinces to make trouble, to make complaints, to make the teasing and the imputations, and then they say to the Canadians, in effect, ' Well, we can not back you up in these methods, but we will let you run along if you can prevail on your great neighbor to give what you seek,' and that is, reciprocity and a free market."

He denied the necessity of a treaty of the kind under consideration: " We are constitutionally in our habits repugnant to treaties. No good comes of encroaching upon our customs laws and duties by entangling treaties— none whatever. Let us govern, let Great Britain govern, let every other nation govern its own interior arrangements of trade. Let it mark its own hospitalities. Let it mark its own duties. Let it mark its own deference to the rights of others. We will do the same for ourselves, too. That is the way to conduct politically these relations of commerce, of hospitality, of deference, of self-respect, of impartial treatment.

"That is the great subject outside of the fishery, but when this prevalent and extending hospitality of trade has reached everything except our fishing-vessels and our fishermen, when it has included and embraced every fishing-vessel and every fisherman of Great Britain in this extension of commercial reciprocity and commercial hospitality, it is said that by virtue of the clauses of the Treaty of 1818 and the Treaty of 1783 we have covenanted forever that fishermen are outside of progressive hospitality, pretending that covenant proscription for this gallant and favored pursuit and all who pursue it can not be ameliorated. They would say that when all others may warm themselves in the hospitality that is wide open to commerce all over these shores, with the United States to everybody else, we have covenanted our fishermen to be outside of that progress, and we must submit to it.

"The covenant was not of proscription, not of exclusion. All commercial relations excluded everything but the fishermen, and they were expressly allowed what was meant to be, and what should have been, insisted upon from the beginning, hospitality to them according

to the whole reach that they needed or desired *qua* fishermen.

" The difficulty was that they were not so much afraid that these fishing-vessels and fishermen would have the means of buying there. There was nothing to sell nor anybody to sell to them for the most part, and there was no local interest to exclude a traffic that would bring money for what they had to sell. The trouble was that the imperial power excluded all importation, and that these fishing-vessels, having this hospitality as extensive as their fishing needs, should not, in the refusal of all other commercial admission, be the means of smuggling and bringing there to sell tobacco or spirits or any of those items that the United Kingdom intended to preserve for revenue purposes.

" Senators will understand what a difference there was between fishing facilities and commercial traffic. All these shores were only occupied and defended for fishing purposes. If they let the fishermen, with any allowance of trade, come in, then where are their customhouses, where are their revenue officers, where is their possible means by which they can keep us from smuggling and encroaching upon the revenues and breaking over the colonial policy of Great Britain?

" Obedience on our part was rightfully claimed upon this reason and was properly yielded by us. All we wanted was hospitality in our fishing interests. The interdict of trade was universal and inexorable, and there was no ground for an exception in favor of the fishermen. But when the interdict of trade was withdrawn and trade rushed in, when you invite it everywhere and have your customhouses and your revenue system and want to make revenue out of it, why can not a fishing-vessel, with 'touch-and-trade' privileges from its government, trade like the rest? We give this facility on our shores everywhere to foreign fishermen under similar circumstances.

" That is the proper situation of whether or not we should be satisfied with these restrictions, these proscriptions, these oppressions, these harassing and insolent exclusions, under a covenant, it is said, that should inexorably ostracize our fishermen when the ports were opened to everybody else."

August 21, Mr. Morgan, of Alabama, said of the danger of leaving open the questions settled by the treaty : " So these vain fulminations of this eminent committee who think, as it appears from their utterances, that they have their grasp upon the President of the United States to compel him to do obedience to their will, and who think that by their supplications directed to the British throne they can mitigate and assuage the conduct of Queen Victoria with respect to our fisheries and our fishermen are harmless. These gentlemen can fulminate their idle bulls against the President and against the policy involved in this treaty, they can accept uncertainty and darkness in the place of light, insecurity in place of the firm rock upon which this treaty would place the rights of the American people, they can create agitation in the land, but, sir, the people of the United States are revolting against these high assumptions on the part of this committee. They are revolting against the idea that the Senate of the United States, that can not declare war of its own motion and by its own resolution, should put this country in a category where war is one of the dismal prospects of the near future in the contemplation of many men who are as firm in their integrity, as bold in their defense of right as any on that side, and who, perhaps, are just as fearless of the results of war as any who have declaimed against this treaty on that side. It does not shame us or alarm us to look the truth in the face, and to be willing to admit and act upon whatever we know to be true.

" The Senate to-day forces the people of the United States into rough and immediate contact with the most dangerous question that can possibly be stated, and that under the depressing influence and shadow of a report which is brought in here by the Committee on Foreign Relations that is intended and well calculated to prevent the British Government from doing anything further in respect of negotiation with us, except merely to find out what we mean by these declarations. I repeat the remark I sometimes have had occasion to make in this debate, that if this were the action of the British Parliament, and if a treaty that we had approved or were willing to approve had been laid before that Parliament by the Queen, and if it had been debated as it has been debated here, and if a committee of the House of Commons had made the same report that we make here in respect of the American people, if they had charged us with outrageous, willful violations of a treaty, if they had declared that the time for negotiation with us in respect of this matter had passed and that this was not a fit subject of negotiation, I can not be so mistaken in American opinion as not to feel entirely warranted in saying before the Senate to-day we would accept that as a challenge to war.

" Now, how they may accept it is not for me to say or even to conjecture, for I know not. I trust in God that the events which seem to lie before us, which will repeat those wrongs of the past as well as cause others of the same nature that are to come, about which we have had so much trouble, may not be of such an aggravated character as to force these two great and magnificent peoples into collision with each other about so small a matter as the duty on salt fish. I trust so.

" Will that side of the chamber pardon me for saying, however, that when you have gone to that extent, and when these calamities occur and these trials are pressing on our country, her interests, her feelings, her sensibilities, shall all be ours, and we will march breast to breast with you with the same alacrity as if

we had never divided in opinion with you on this question or any other, and what the majority shall decree to be the will of the American people in respect to these controversies in the future shall be our will? With one united voice we will go into any contest that may arise, Mr. President, notwithstanding all the sneers and slurs, the contumely and contempt that have been thrown upon the gentlemen on this side of this chamber because of their connection with the late rebellion and their advocacy of this treaty. We shall prove just as true as you are to the flag of the American Union. We will spend our money just as freely as you do and more freely than many of you have done. We have shed our blood where some of you have not dared to shed it in times that have passed, and you will find the old spirit animating the Southern Democracy. You will find that the man who can lead the American hosts to victory in the contests you may bring about and the wars you may provoke will receive from the united Democracy of the country that sort of support and love and affectionate reverence which our fathers bestowed upon Andrew Jackson, and which will cling to his memory in Democratic hearts in the South while time itself shall last, if this shall still be a nation."

August 21, the Senate refused to ratify the proposed treaty by the following vote:

Yeas—Bate, Beck, Berry, Blackburn, Blodgett, Brown, Cockrell, Coke, Colquitt, Daniel, Faulkner, George, Gorman, Gray, Hampton, Harris, Jones of Arkansas, McPherson, Morgan, Pasco, Payne, Pugh, Ransom, Reagan, Vest, Walthall, Wilson of Maryland—27.

Nays—Aldrich, Allison, Blair, Chace, Chandler, Dawes, Dolph, Edmunds, Evarts, Farwell, Frye, Hale, Hawley, Hiscock, Hoar, Ingalls, Jones of Nevada, Manderson, Mitchell, Platt, Plumb, Quay, Sabin, Sawyer, Sherman, Spooner, Stewart, Stockbridge, Teller, Wilson of Iowa—30.

Absent—Bowen, Butler, Call, Cameron, Cullom, Davis, Eustis, Gibson, Hearst, Kenna, Morrill, Paddock, Palmer, Riddleberger, Saulsbury, Stanford, Turpie, Vance, Voorhees—19.

August 23, the President sent to the Senate the following message, asking for fuller power to undertake retaliation in case harsh measures should become necessary in consequence of the rejection of the fisheries treaty:

To the Congress:

The rejection by the Senate of the treaty lately negotiated for the settlement and adjustment of the differences existing between the United States and Great Britain concerning the rights and privileges of American fishermen in the ports and waters of British North America, seems to justify a survey of the condition to which the pending question is thus remitted.

The treaty upon this subject concluded in 1818, through disagreements as to the meaning of its terms, has been a fruitful source of irritation and trouble. Our citizens engaged in fishing enterprises in waters adjacent to Canada have been subjected to numerous vexatious interferences and annoyances; their vessels have been seized upon pretexts which appeared to be entirely inadmissible, and they have been otherwise treated by the Canadian authorities and officials in a manner inexcusably harsh and oppressive.

This conduct has been justified by Great Britain

and Canada by the claim that the Treaty of 1818 permitted it, and upon the ground that it was necessary to the proper protection of Canadian interests. We deny that treaty agreements justify these acts, and we further maintain that, aside from any treaty restraints, of disputed interpretation, the relative positions of the United States and Canada as near neighbors, the growth of our joint commerce, the development and prosperity of both countries, which amicable relations surely guarantee, and, above all, the liberality always extended by the United States to the people of Canada, furnish motives for kindness and consideration higher and better than treaty covenants.

While keenly sensitive to all that was exasperating in the condition, and by no means indisposed to support the just complaints of our injured citizens, I still deemed it my duty for the preservation of the important American interests, which were directly involved, and in view of all the details of the situation, to attempt by negotiation to remedy existing wrongs, and to finally terminate by a fair and just treaty these ever-recurring causes of difficulty.

I fully believe that the treaty just rejected by the Senate was well suited to the exigency, and that its provisions were adequate for our security in the future from vexatious incidents and for the promotion of friendly neighborhood and intimacy, without sacrificing in the least our national pride or dignity.

I am quite conscious that neither my opinion of the value of the rejected treaty nor the motives which prompted its negotiation are of importance in the light of the judgment of the Senate thereupon. But it is of importance to note that this treaty has been rejected without any apparent disposition on the part of the Senate to alter or amend its provisions, and with the evident intention, not wanting expression, that no negotiation should at present be concluded touching the matter at issue.

The co-operation necessary for the adjustment of the long-standing national differences with which we have to deal, by methods of conference and agreement, having thus been declined, I am by no means disposed to abandon the interests and the rights of our people in the premises or to neglect their grievances, and I therefore turn to the contemplation of a plan of retaliation as a mode, which still remains, of treating the situation.

I am not unmindful of the gravity of the responsibility assumed in adopting this line of conduct, nor do I fail in the least to appreciate its serious consequences. It will be impossible to injure our Canadian neighbors by retaliatory measures without inflicting some damage upon our own citizens. This results from our proximity, our community of interests, and the inevitable commingling of the business enterprises which have been developed by mutual activity.

Plainly stated, the policy of national retaliation manifestly embraces the infliction of the greatest harm upon those who have injured us, with the least possible damage to ourselves. There is also an evident propriety, as well as an invitation to moral support, found in visiting upon the offending party the same measure or kind of treatment of which we complain, and, as far as possible, within the same lines. And, above all things, the plan of retaliation if entered upon should be thorough and vigorous.

These considerations lead me at this time to invoke the aid and counsel of the Congress and its support in such a further grant of power as seems to me necessary and desirable to render effective the policy I have indicated.

The Congress has already passed a law, which received Executive assent on the 3d day of March, 1887, providing that in case American fishing-vessels being or visiting in the waters or at any of the ports of the British dominions of North America, should be or were lately had been deprived of the rights to which they were entitled by treaty or law, or if they were denied certain other privileges therein specified, or vexed and harassed in the enjoyment of the same, the President

might deny to vessels and their masters and crews of the British dominions of North America any entrance into the waters, ports, or harbors of the United States, and also deny entry into any port or place of the United States of any product of said dominions, or other goods coming from said dominions to the United States.

While I shall not hesitate upon proper occasion to enforce this act, it would seem to be unnecessary to suggest that if such enforcement is limited in such a manner as shall result in the least possible injury to our own people, the effect would probably be entirely inadequate to the accomplishment of the purpose desired.

I deem it my duty, therefore, to call the attention of the Congress to certain particulars in the action of the authorities of the Dominion of Canada, in addition to the general allegations already made, which appear to be in such marked contrast to the liberal and friendly disposition of our country as in my opinion to call for such legislation as will, upon the principles already stated, properly supplement the power to inaugurate retaliation already vested in the Executive.

Actuated by the generous and neighborly spirit which has characterized our legislation, our tariff laws have, since 1866, been so far waved in favor of Canada as to allow free of duty the transit across the territory of the United States of property arriving at our ports and destined to Canada, or exported from Canada to other foreign countries.

When the Treaty of Washington was negotiated in 1871, between the United States and Great Britain, having for its object very largely the modification of the Treaty of 1818, the privileges above referred to were made reciprocal and given in return by Canada to the United States, in the following language, contained in the twenty-ninth article of said treaty:

"It is agreed, that for the term of years mentioned in Article XXXIII of this treaty, goods, wares, or merchandise arriving at the ports of New York, Boston, and Portland, and any other ports in the United States, which have been or may from time to time be specially designated by the President of the United States, and destined for Her Britannic Majesty's possessions in North America, may be entered at the proper custom-house and conveyed in transit, without the payment of duties, through the territory of the United States, under such rules, regulations, and conditions for the protection of the revenue as the Government of the United States may from time to time prescribe; and under like rules, regulations, and conditions, goods, wares, or merchandise may be conveyed in transit without the payment of duties from such possessions through the territory of the United States, for export from the said ports of the United States.

"It is further agreed that, for the like period, goods, wares, or merchandise arriving at any of the ports of Her Britannic Majesty's possessions in North America, and destined for the United States, may be entered at the proper custom-house and conveyed in transit, without the payment of duties, through the said possessions under such rules and regulations and conditions for the protection of the revenue as the government of the said possessions may from time to time prescribe; and under like rules and regulations and conditions, goods, wares, or merchandise may be conveyed in transit, without payment of duties, from the United States through the said possessions to other places in the United States, or for export from ports in the said possessions."

In the year 1886 notice was received by the representatives of our Government that our fishermen would no longer be allowed to ship their fish in bond and free of duty through Canadian territory to this country, and ever since that time such shipment has been denied.

The privilege of such shipment which had been extended to our fishermen was a most important one, allowing them to spend the time upon the fishing-grounds, which would otherwise be devoted to a voyage home with their catch, and doubling their opportunities for profitably prosecuting their vocation. In forbidding the transit of the catch of our fishermen over their territory in bond and free of duty the Canadian authorities deprived us of the only facility dependent upon their concession, and for which we could supply no substitute.

The value to the Dominion of Canada of the privilege of transit for their exports and imports across our territory and to and from our ports, though great in every aspect, will be better appreciated when it is remembered that for a considerable portion of each year the St. Lawrence river, which constitutes the direct avenue of foreign commerce leading to Canada, is closed by ice.

During the last six years the imports and exports of British Canadian provinces carried across our territory, under the privileges granted by our laws, amounted in value to about $470,000,000, nearly all of which were goods dutiable under our tariff laws, by far the larger part of this traffic consisting of exchanges of goods between Great Britain and her American provinces brought to and carried from our ports in their own vessels.

The treaty stipulation entered into by our Government was in harmony with laws which were then on our statute-book, and are still in force.

I recommend immediate legislative action conferring upon the Executive the power to suspend by proclamation the operation of all laws and regulations permitting the transit of goods, wares, and merchandise in bond across or over the territory of the United States to or from Canada.

There need be no hesitation in suspending these laws arising from the supposition that their continuation is secured by treaty obligations, for it seems quite plain that Article XXIX of the treaty of 1871, which was the only article incorporating such laws, terminated on the 1st day of July, 1885.

The article itself declares that its provisions shall be in force "for the term of years mentioned in Article XXXIII of this treaty." Turning to Article XXXIII we find no mention of the twenty-ninth article, but only a provision that Articles XVIII to XXV, inclusive, and Article XXX shall take effect as soon as the laws required to carry them into operation shall be passed by the legislative bodies of the different countries concerned, and that "they shall remain in force for the period of ten years from the date at which they may come into operation, and further until the expiration of two years after either of the high contracting parties shall have given notice to the other of its wish to terminate the same."

I am of the opinion that the "term of years mentioned in Article XXXIII," referred to in Article XXIX as the limit of its duration, means the period during which Articles XVIII to XXV, inclusive, and Article XXX, commonly called the "fishery articles," should continue in force under the language of said Article XXXIII.

That the joint high commissioners who negotiated the treaty so understood and intended the phrase is certain, for in a statement containing an account of their negotiations, prepared under their supervision and approved by them, we find the following entry on the subject: "The transit question was discussed, and it was agreed that any settlement that might be made should include a reciprocal arrangement in that respect for the period for which the fishery articles should be in force."

In addition to this very satisfactory evidence supporting this construction of the language of Article XXIX, it will be found that the law passed by Congress to carry the treaty into effect furnishes conclusive proof of the correctness of such construction.

This law was passed March 1, 1873, and is entitled "An act to carry into effect the provisions of the treaty between the United States and Great Britain,

signed in the city of Washington the 8th day of May, 1871, relating to the fisheries." After providing, in its first and second sections, for putting in operation Articles XVIII to XXV, inclusive, and Article XXX of the treaty, the third section is devoted to Article XXIX, as follows: "Sec. 3. That from the date of the President's proclamation authorized by the first section of this act, and so long as the Articles XVIII to XXV, inclusive, and Article XXX of said treaty shall remain in force according to the terms and conditions of Article XXXIII of said treaty, all goods, wares, and merchandise arriving," etc., etc., following in the remainder or the section the precise words of the stipulation on the part of the United States as contained in Article XXIX, which I have already fully quoted.

Here, then, is a distinct enactment of the Congress limiting the duration of this article of the treaty to the time that Articles XVIII to XXV, inclusive, and Article XXX should continue in force. That in fixing such limitations it but gave the meaning of the treaty itself, is indicated by the fact that its purpose is declared to be to carry into effect the provisions of the treaty, and by the further fact that this law appears to have been submitted before the promulgation of the treaty, to certain members of the Joint High Commission, representing both countries, and met with no objections or dissent.

There appearing to be no conflict or inconsistency between the treaty and the act of the Congress last cited, it is not necessary to invoke the well-settled principle that in case of such conflict the statute governs the question.

In any event, and whether the law of 1873 construes the treaty or governs it, section 29 of such treaty, I have no doubt, terminated with the proceedings taken by our Government to terminate Articles XVIII to XXV, inclusive, and Article XXX of the treaty. These proceedings had their inception in a joint resolution of Congress passed May 3, 1883, declaring that in the judgment of Congress these articles ought to be terminated, and directing the President to give the notice to the Government of Great Britain provided for in Article XXXIII of the treaty. Such notice having been given two years prior to the 1st day of July, 1885, the articles mentioned were absolutely terminated on the last-named day, and with them Article XXIX was also terminated.

If by any language used in the joint resolution it was intended to relieve section 3 of the act of 1873 embodying Article XXIX of the treaty from its own limitations, or to save the article itself, I am entirely satisfied that the intention miscarried.

But statutes granting to the people of Canada the valuable privileges of transit for their goods from our ports and over our soil, which had been passed prior to the making of the treaty of 1871 and independently of it, remained in force; and ever since the abrogation of the treaty, and notwithstanding the refusal of Canada to permit our fishermen to send their fish to their home market through her territory in bond, the people of that Dominion have enjoyed without diminution the advantages of our liberal and generous laws.

Without basing our complaint upon a violation of treaty obligations, it is nevertheless true that such a refusal of transit and the other injurious acts which have been recited constitute a provoking insistance upon rights neither mitigated by the amenities of national intercourse nor modified by the recognition of our liberality and generous considerations. The history of events connected with this subject makes it manifest that the Canadian Government can if so disposed administer its laws and protect the interests of its people without manifestation of unfriendliness and without the unneighborly treatment of our fishing-vessels of which we have justly complained; and whatever is done on our part should be done in the hope that the disposition of the Canadian Government may remove the occasion of a resort to the additional executive power now sought through legislative action.

I am satisfied that upon the principles which should govern retaliation our intercourse and relations with the Dominion of Canada furnish no better opportunity for its application than is suggested by the conditions herein presented; and that it could not be more effectively inaugurated than under the power of suspension recommended.

While I have expressed my clear conviction upon the question of the continuance of section 29 of the treaty of 1871, I, of course, fully concede the power and the duty of the Congress in contemplating legislative action to construe the terms of any treaty stipulation which might upon any possible consideration of good faith limit such action; and likewise the peculiar propriety in the case here presented of its interpretation of its own language as contained in the laws of 1873, putting in operation said treaty, and of 1883 directing the termination thereof; and if in the deliberate judgment of Congress any restraint to the proposed legislation exists it is to be hoped that the expediency of its early removal will be recognized.

I desire also to call the attention of the Congress to another subject involving such wrongs and unfair treatment to our citizens as, in my opinion, require prompt action.

The navigation of the Great Lakes and the immense business and carrying trade growing out of the same, have been treated broadly and liberally by the United States Government, and made free to all mankind, while Canadian railroads and navigation companies share in our country's transportation upon terms as favorable as are accorded to our own citizens.

The canals and other public works built and maintained by the Government along the line of the lakes are made free to all.

In contrast to this condition, and evincing a narrow and ungenerous commercial spirit, every lock and canal which is a public work of the Dominion of Canada is subject to tolls and charges.

By Article XXVII of the treaty of 1871 provision was made to secure to the citizens of the United States the use of the Welland, St. Lawrence, and other canals in the Dominion of Canada, on terms of equality with the inhabitants of the Dominion, and to also secure to the subjects of Great Britain the use of the St. Clair Flats Canal on terms of equality with the inhabitants of the United States.

The equality with the inhabitants of the Dominion which we were promised in the use of the canals of Canada did not secure to us freedom from tolls in their navigation, but we had a right to expect that we, being Americans and interested in American commerce, would be no more burdened in regard to the same than Canadians engaged in their own trade; and the whole spirit of the concession made was, or should have been, that merchandise and property transported to an American market through these canals should not be enhanced in its cost by tolls many times higher than such as were carried to an adjoining Canadian market. All our citizens, producers and consumers, as well as vessel owners, were to enjoy the equality promised.

And yet evidence has for some time been before the Congress, furnished by the Secretary of the Treasury, showing that while the tolls charged in the first instance are the same to all, such vessels and cargoes as are destined to certain Canadian ports are allowed a refund of nearly the entire tolls, while those bound for American ports are not allowed any such advantage.

To promise equality and then in practice make it conditional upon our vessels doing Canadian business instead of their own is to fulfill a promise with the shadow of performance.

I recommend that such legislative action be taken as will give Canadian vessels navigating our canals, and their cargoes, precisely the advantages granted to

our vessels and cargoes upon Canadian canals, and that the same be measured by exactly the same rule of discrimination.

The course which I have outlined, and the recommendations made, relate to the honor and dignity of our country, and the protection and preservation of the rights and interests of all our people. A government does but half its duty when it protects its citizens at home and permits them to be imposed upon and humiliated by the unfair and overreaching disposition of other nations. If we invite our people to rely upon arrangements made for their benefit abroad, we should see to it that they are not deceived; and if we are generous and liberal to a neighboring country, our people should reap the advantage of it by a return of liberality and generosity.

These are subjects which partisanship should not disturb or confuse. Let us survey the ground calmly and moderately, and, having put aside other means of settlement, if we enter upon the policy of retaliation, let us pursue it firmly, with a determination only to subserve the interests of our people, and maintain the high standard and the becoming pride of American citizenship.   GROVER CLEVELAND.

EXECUTIVE MANSION, *Aug.* 23, 1888.

After the reading of this message in the House of Representatives, a bill such as the President asked for was introduced; on August 30 it was amended and reported favorably from the committee to which it was referred; and on September 8 it was passed. But the Senate took no action on the measure, the majority holding that the retaliatory law of 1887, which the President had not used, gave him ample power in the premises. Mr. Sherman, of Ohio, submitted a resolution for an investigation of the relations of the United States and Canada, with a view to establishing closer relations, but the subject remained undecided at the close of the session.

Chinese Exclusion.—On March 1, 1888, the Senate passed a resolution asking the President to negotiate a treaty with China, providing that no Chinese laborer shall enter the United States. This treaty was negotiated and transmitted to the Senate, March 17. That body amended it by adding a provision that Chinese laborers formerly in this country but now absent should be excluded, whether holding certificates to that effect or not. The treaty was then approved, and a measure passed to carry it into effect, which was signed September 13. On September 3, after a rumor that the Chinese authorities had refused to ratify the treaty, Mr. Scott, of Pennsylvania, brought forward the following bill in the House of Representatives

A supplement to an act entitled "An act to execute certain treaty stipulations relating to Chinese," approved the 6th day of May, 1882.

Be it enacted, etc., That from and after the passage of this act, it shall be unlawful for any Chinese laborer who shall at any time heretofore have been or may now or hereafter be a resident within the United States, and who shall have departed or shall depart therefrom, and shall not have returned before the passage of this act, to return to or remain in the United States.

SEC. 2. That no certificates of identity provided for in the fourth or fifth sections of the act to which this is a supplement shall hereafter be issued; and every certificate heretofore issued in pursuance thereof is hereby declared void and of no effect; and the Chinese laborer claiming admission by virtue thereof shall not be permitted to enter the United States.

Sec. 3. That all the duties prescribed, liabilities, penalties, and forfeitures imposed, and the powers conferred, by the second, tenth, eleventh, and twelfth sections of the act to which this is a supplement are hereby extended and made applicable to the provisions of this act.

Sec. 4. That all such part or parts of the act to which this is a supplement as are inconsistent herewith are hereby repealed.

In explanation of his measure, Mr. Scott said: "I desire to call attention to what this bill proposes to do. Under sections 4 and 5 of the statute of 1882, enacted in conformity with the treaty of 1880, it was provided that a Chinaman then a resident of the United States might, under certain conditions, leave the United States, go to China, and return, but was to do so under a certificate issued by the authority of our Government certifying his identity and that he was a resident of the United States. Under this authority, which our treaty stipulations under the treaty of 1880 did not require us to give, a Chinaman could take his certificate and return to China; and as the truth is a merchantable commodity from a Chinese point of view, those certificates were, in many instances, sold to Chinamen, who had never been in this country, who took them and came to the United States in violation of the law. When a Chinaman reached the port of San Francisco the duty of the collector of the port under the law was to determine his identity; and when the collector by positive evidence knew that the Chinaman offering the certificate was not the person to whom it had been originally issued, the collector at once required such Chinaman to leave the country. But it was just here that the United States courts came in and upon habeas-corpus proceedings declared, in many instances, that the Chinaman offering the certificate was the original owner. By this process, Chinese laborers by the thousands have been permitted to come to the United States fraudulently under certificates which had never been issued to them."

The measure was at once passed without a division, and sent to the Senate. In that body it was discussed at some length and passed September 7, by a vote of 37 to 3, there being 36 Senators absent. Those voting in the negative were Brown, Hoar, and Wilson, of Iowa.

September 10, Mr. Sherman, of Ohio, on a motion to reconsider the passage of the bill, said: "Mr. President, having already early in this debate expressed my strong desire to vote for the exclusion of Chinese laborers from this country, and believing that this bill if it stood alone, without any connection with the treaty with China recently pending in the Senate, would be a wise bill, I yet appeal to Senators on both sides of the chamber, for considerations of national honor which ought always first to be heeded on any question that is presented to us, that they allow the bill to stand in its present position until we can ascertain whether or not the treaty now pending between the two nations will be ratified. That is my only desire. If this bill is allowed to remain in its present position and it shall turn out that this treaty will not be ratified and that the Chinese Government has taken ground against the ratification of the treaty, then I should be willing to vote and I would vote with pleasure for the passage of this bill; but pending that question I submit as a matter of national honor whether it is right and proper for us to seek to nullify a treaty that is now being considered by a friendly nation, a treaty that has been ratified by this body, to which we have committed ourselves in every possible way—whether it is right at this stage of the proceedings to proceed to nullify and abrogate not only all existing treaties with China, but the treaty at present pending between these two nations? I frankly say that if our position were reversed, and Great Britain were thus to act toward the American people, I would without hesitation vote for a declaration of non-intercourse or war.

"It is a departure from all the usages of civilized nations. It is a departure from all considerations of national honor. No man believes that the House of Representatives would have passed this bill except upon the supposition that the treaty had been rejected by China. It was understood in that House at the time it was passed that the Chinese Government had refused to ratify the treaty, or it would not have passed. I can assume that but for that supposed fact the bill could not have passed the House of Representatives. It came to us here; and but for the general idea that the treaty had been rejected by China the bill would surely have been referred to the Committee on Foreign Relations and taken the ordinary course prescribed by our rules for the consideration of public measures. There is no doubt about that.

"Early in the debate I said that my action and my neglect to make the ordinary motion to refer the bill to the Committee on Foreign Relations was based on the idea that I then assumed to be accurate and correct, that the President of the United States had information that this treaty would not be ratified, and therefore that the Congress of the United States would be at liberty to proceed upon that basis. Proceeding upon that basis I was willing that Congress should by law put an end to this whole system of Chinese immigration.

"But since that time the condition has changed. We are informed officially by the President of the United States that this treaty is still under consideration. We are informed from other sources, of which there can be no question, that the Chinese minister is now on his way to this country for the purpose of either conveying to us intelligence that it has been ratified or that it has not been ratified."

The motion to reconsider was lost by a vote of 20 to 21, September 17, and a resolution to withhold the measure from the House was offered by Mr. Edmunds, of Vermont, but not until it had passed beyond control of the Senate and into the hands of the House Committee on Foreign Relations. The committee delayed sending the bill to the President until news came that the Chinese Government had refused to ratify the treaty, and the President signed the measure October 1.

To the Congress:

I have this day approved House bill No. 11,336, supplementary to an act entitled "An act to execute certain treaty stipulations relating to Chinese," approved the 6th day of May, 1882.

It seems to me that some suggestions and recommendations may properly accompany my approval of this bill.

Its object is to more effectually accomplish by legislation the exclusion from this country of Chinese laborers.

The experiment of blending the social habits and mutual race idiosyncrasies of the Chinese laboring classes with those of the great body of the people of the United States has been proved by the experience of twenty years, and ever since the Burlingame treaty of 1868, to be in every sense unwise, impolitic, and injurious to both nations. With the lapse of time the necessity for its abandonment has grown in force, until those having in charge the government of the respective countries have resolved to modify and sufficiently abrogate all those features of prior conventional arrangements which permitted the coming of Chinese laborers to the United States.

In modification of prior conventions, the treaty of November 17, 1880, was concluded, whereby, in the first article thereof, it was agreed that the United States should at will regulate, limit, or suspend the coming of Chinese laborers to the United States, but not absolutely prohibit it; and under this article an act of Congress, approved May 6, 1882 (see volume 22, page 58, Statutes at Large), and amended July 5, 1884 (volume 23, page 115, Statutes at Large), suspended for ten years the coming of Chinese laborers to the United States, and regulated the going and coming of such Chinese laborers as were at that time in the United States.

It was, however, soon made evident that the mercenary greed of the parties who were trading in the labor of this class of the Chinese population was proving too strong for the just execution of the law, and that the virtual defeat of the object and intent of both law and treaty was being fraudulently accomplished by false pretense and perjury, contrary to the expressed will of both governments.

To such an extent has the successful violation of the treaty and the laws enacted for its execution progressed, that the courts in the Pacific States have been for some time past overwhelmed by the examination of cases of Chinese laborers who are charged with having entered our ports under fraudulent certificates of return or seek to establish by perjury the claim of prior residence.

Such demonstration of the inoperative and inefficient condition of the treaty and law has produced deep-seated and increasing discontent among the people of the United States, and especially with those resident on the Pacific coast. This has induced me to omit no effort to find an effectual remedy for the evils complained of and to answer the earnest popular demand for the absolute exclusion of Chinese laborers having objects and purposes unlike our own and wholly disconnected with American citizenship.

Aided by the presence in this country of able and intelligent diplomatic and consular officers of the Chinese Government and the representations made from time to time by our minister in China under the instructions of the Department of State, the actual condition of public sentiment and the status of affairs in the United States has been fully made known to the Government of China.

The necessity for remedy has been fully appreciated by that Government, and in August, 1886, our minister at Pekin received from the Chinese Foreign Office a communication announcing that China, of her own accord, proposed to establish a system of strict and absolute prohibition of her laborers, under heavy penalties, from coming to the United States, and likewise to prohibit the return to the United States of any Chinese laborer who had at any time gone back to China "in order" (in the words of the communication) "that the Chinese laborers may gradually be reduced in number and causes of danger averted and lives preserved."

This view of the Chinese Government, so completely in harmony with that of the United States, was by my direction speedily formulated in a treaty draught between the two nations, embodying the propositions so presented by the Chinese Foreign Office.

The deliberations, frequent oral discussions, and correspondence on the general questions that ensued, have been fully communicated by me to the Senate at the present session, and, as contained in Senate Executive Document O, parts 1 and 2, and in Senate Executive Document No. 272, may be properly referred to as containing a complete history of the transaction.

It is thus easy to learn how the joint desires and unequivocal mutual understanding of the two governments were brought into articulated form in the treaty, which, after a mutual exhibition of plenary powers from the respective governments, was signed and concluded by the plenipotentiaries of the United States and China at this capital on March 12 last.

Being submitted for the advice and consent of the Senate, its confirmation, on the 7th day of May last, was accompanied by two amendments, which that body ingrafted upon it.

On the 12th day of the same month the Chinese minister, who was the plenipotentiary of his Government in the negotiation and the conclusion of the treaty, in a note to the Secretary of State, gave his approval to these amendments, "as they did not alter the terms of the treaty," and the amendments were at once telegraphed to China, whither the original treaty had previously been sent immediately after its signature on March 12.

On the 13th day of last month I approved Senate bill No. 3304 "to prohibit the coming of Chinese laborers to the United States." This bill was intended to supplement the treaty, and was approved in the confident anticipation of an early exchange of ratifications of the treaty and its amendments and the proclamation of the same, upon which event the legislation so approved was by its terms to take effect.

No information of any definite action upon the treaty by the Chinese Government was received until the 21st ultimo—the day the bill which I have just approved was presented to me—when a telegram from our minister at Pekin to the Secretary of State announced the refusal of the Chinese Government to exchange ratifications of the treaty unless further discussion should be had with a view to shorten the period stipulated in the treaty for the exclusion of Chinese laborers, and to change the conditions agreed on, which should entitle any Chinese laborer who might go back to China to return again to the United States.

By a note from the *chargé-d'affaires ad interim* of China to the Secretary of State, received on the evening of the 25th ultimo (a copy of which is herewith transmitted, together with the reply thereto), a third amendment is proposed, whereby the certificate, under which any departing Chinese laborer alleging the possession of property in the United States would be enabled to return to this country, should be granted by the Chinese consul instead of the United States collector, as had been provided in the treaty.

The obvious and necessary effect of this last proposition would be practically to place the execution of the treaty beyond the control of the United States.

Article I of the treaty proposed to be so materially altered, had, in the course of the negotiations, been settled in acquiescence with the request of the Chinese plenipotentiary, and to his expressed satisfaction.

In 1886, as appears in the documents heretofore referred to, the Chinese Foreign Office had formally proposed to our minister strict exclusion of Chinese laborers from the United States without limitation; and had otherwise and more definitely stated that no term whatever for exclusion was necessary, for the reason that China would of itself take steps to prevent its laborers from coming to the United States.

In the course of negotiations that followed, suggestions from the same quarter led to the insertion in behalf of the United States of a term of "thirty years," and this term, upon the representations of the Chinese plenipotentiary, was reduced to "twenty years," and finally so agreed upon.

Article II was wholly of Chinese origination, and to that alone owes its presence in the treaty.

And it is here pertinent to remark that everywhere in the United States laws for the collection of debts are equally available to all creditors without respect to race, sex, nationality, or place of residence, and equally with the citizens or subjects of the most favored nations and with the citizens of the United States recovery can be had in any court of justice in the United States by a subject of China, whether of the laboring or any other class.

No disability accrues from non-residence of a plaintiff, whose claim can be enforced in the usual way by him or his assignee or attorney in our courts of justice.

In this respect it can not be alleged that there exists the slightest discrimination against Chinese subjects, and it is a notable fact that large trading-firms and companies and individual merchants and traders of that nation are profitably established at numerous points throughout the Union, in whose hands every claim transmitted by an absent Chinaman of a just and lawful nature could be completely enforced.

The admitted and paramount right and duty of every government to exclude from its borders all elements of foreign population which for any reason retard its prosperity or are detrimental to the moral and physical health of its people, must be regarded as a recognized canon of international law and intercourse. China herself has not dissented from this doctrine, but has, by the expressions to which I have referred, led us confidently to rely upon such action on her part in co-operation with us as would enforce the exclusion of Chinese laborers from our country.

This co-operation has not, however, been accorded us. Thus from the unexpected and disappointing refusal of the Chinese Government to confirm the acts of its authorized agent and to carry into effect an international agreement, the main feature of which was voluntarily presented by that Government for our acceptance, and which had been the subject of long and careful deliberation, an emergency has arisen in which the Government of the United States is called upon to act in self-defense by the exercise of its legislative power. I can not but regard the expressed demand on the part of China for a re-examination and renewed discussion of the topics so completely covered by mutual treaty stipulations as an indefinite postponement and practical abandonment of the objects we have in view, to which the Government of China may justly be considered as pledged.

The facts and circumstances which I have narrated lead me, in the performance of what seems to me to be my official duty, to join the Congress in dealing legislatively with the question of the exclusion of Chinese laborers, in lieu of further attempts to adjust it by international agreement.

But while thus exercising our undoubted right in the interests of our people and for the general welfare of our country, justice and fairness seem to require that some provision should be made by act or joint resolution, under which such Chinese laborers as shall actually have embarked on their return to the United States before the passage of the law this day approved, and are now on their way, may be permitted to land provided they have duly and lawfully obtained and shall present certificates heretofore issued permitting them to return in accordance with the provisions of existing law.

Nor should our recourse to legislative measures of exclusion cause us to retire from the offer we have made to indemnify such Chinese subjects as have suffered damage through violence in the remote and comparatively unsettled portions of our country at the hands of lawless men. Therefore I recommend that, without acknowledging legal liability therefor, but because it was stipulated in the treaty which has failed to take effect, and in a spirit of humanity befitting our nation, there be appropriated the sum of $276,619.75, payable to the Chinese minister at this capital on behalf of his Government as full indemnity for all losses and injuries sustained by Chinese subjects in the manner and under the circumstances mentioned.   GROVER CLEVELAND.

EXECUTIVE MANSION, Oct. 1, 1888.

The Direct-Tax Bill.—The liveliest episode of the session was the struggle in the House of Representatives over the bill to pay back the direct tax levied by the Government in 1861 and only partially collected. It was passed by the Senate, Jan. 18, 1888, as follows:

Be it enacted, etc., That it shall be the duty of the Secretary of the Treasury to credit to each State and Territory of the United States and the District of Columbia a sum equal to all collections made from said States and Territories and the District of Columbia, or from any of the citizens or inhabitants thereof, or other persons, under the act of Congress, approved Aug. 5, 1861, and the amendatory acts thereto.

SEC. 2. That all moneys still due to the United States on the quota of direct tax apportioned by section 8 of the act of Congress approved Aug. 5, 1861, are hereby remitted and relinquished.

SEC. 3. That there is hereby appropriated, out of any money in the Treasury not otherwise appropriated, such sums as may be necessary to reimburse each State, Territory, and the District of Columbia for all money found due to them under the provisions of this act; and the Treasurer of the United States is hereby directed to pay the same to the governors of the States and Territories and to the commissioners of the District of Columbia: *Provided,* That where the sums, or any part thereof, credited to any State, Territory, or the District of Columbia, have been collected by the United States from the citizens or inhabitants thereof, or any other person, either directly or by sale of property, such sums shall be held in trust by such State, Territory, or the District of Columbia for the benefit of those persons or inhabitants from whom they were collected, or their legal representatives: *And provided further,* That no part of the money collected from individuals and to be held in trust as aforesaid shall be retained by the United States as a set-off against any indebtedness alleged to exist against the State, Territory, or District of Columbia in which such tax was collected: *And provided further,* That no pa   of the money hereby appropriated shall be paid out by the governor of any State or Territory, or any other person, to any attorney or agent under any contract for services now existing or heretofore made between the representative of any State or Territory and any attorney or agent. All claims under the trust hereby created shall be filed with the governor of such State or Territory and the commissioners of the District of Columbia, respectively, within six years next after the passage of this act, and all claims not so filed shall be forever barred, and the money attributable thereto shall belong to such State, Territory, or the District of Columbia, respectively, as the case may be.

Only ten Senators voted against the measure, and there were men of both parties in favor of it and opposed to it. The most important amendment offered was the following, proposed by Mr. Vance, of North Carolina:

SEC —. That the Secretary of the Treasury be, and he is hereby, authorized and directed to credit and pay to each State a sum equal to the amounts collected therein respectively as a tax or duty on raw cotton, under the provisions of the act approved July 1, 1862, and the supplemental and amendatory acts thereto, which sums, when so credited and paid, shall be accepted and held by the States in trust, first, for such of the producers who paid said tax or duty, or their legal representatives, as may make claim to and prove their identity, and the amount of taxes paid, in two years after the passage of this act, and, second, the remainder, if any, to be held and used only as a permanent free-school fund: *Provided*, That where cotton was produced in one State, and, under permit from the Government of the United States, shipped to another State, and the taxes thereon collected in the latter State, then the amount of all such taxes shall be paid to the State in which the cotton was produced.

SEC. —. That there is hereby appropriated, out of any money in the Treasury not otherwise appropriated, such sums as may be necessary to carry out the provisions of this act; *Provided*, That any State accepting the trust hereby created is prohibited from paying any part of the funds received to any person, syndicate, or corporation except the producers who paid the taxes on cotton grown by them or their legal representatives; and in no case shall the payment be made to an assignee of such claim.

This amendment was rejected by the following vote:

YEAS—Bate, Berry, Butler, Call, Coke, Daniel, George, Harris, Jones, of Arkansas, Pugh, Quay, Ransom, Reagan, Vance, Walthall, Wilson of Maryland—16.

NAYS—Aldrich, Allison, Beck, Blair, Blodgett, Brown, Cameron, Chase, Chandler, Cockrell, Cullom, Davis, Dawes, Dolph, Evarts, Farwell, Faulkner, Frye, Gorman, Hale, Hawley, Hiscock, Hoar, Ingalls, McPherson, Manderson, Mitchell, Morgan, Paddock, Palmer, Payne, Platt, Plumb, Sabin, Saulsbury, Sawyer, Sherman, Spooner, Stanford, Stewart, Stockbridge, Teller, Turpie, Vest, Voorhees, Wilson of Iowa—46.

ABSENT—Blackburn, Bowen, Colquitt, Edmunds, Eustis, Gibson, Gray, Hampton, Hearst, Jones of Nevada, Kenna, Morrill, Pasco, Riddleberger—14.

Some of the Senators who opposed the amendment were in favor of refunding the cotton-tax, and their position was explained by Mr. Voorhees, of Indiana, who said: "I appeal to the Senators who think as I do on the subject of the cotton-tax not to encumber the original bill with the amendment which is proposed. That defeats the whole concern. At the proper time and under proper circumstances nobody will go further or consider more favorably the proposition embraced in the amendment than I will.

"The question is not always, Mr. President, what is just, but what is practicable and attainable. Let us take the good we can, which is within our reach, and then grasp after more

hereafter, if a hereafter on that subject should come.

"I look upon the bill as presented here as a practical measure, settling and closing up a difficult subject, one that has embarrassed the Treasury in its accounts, and one which has worked inequality, irregularity, and injustice to many States.

"I desire to say this much because I rank myself one of those who think that the cotton-tax was a measure perhaps of oppression and injustice. I do not intend that my vote against this amendment shall be misunderstood as unfriendly to relief on that point, but I should look upon my vote for that amendment now as a vote against this bill, which I heartily concur in."

The measure was reported to the House of Representatives by the Finance Committee, April 3, with two amendments, one inserting "by set-off or otherwise," in the first section after the word "collections," and the other cutting off the final proviso. The case against the bill was presented by Mr. Oates, of Alabama: "The bill before the committee provides for the refunding or repaying in part to the States and Territories and to the District of Columbia, and in part to the individuals from whom it was collected, the direct tax levied under the act of Aug. 1, 1861. A provision in a general revenue bill passed at that time levied for the exigencies of the war which was then impending twenty million dollars annually and apportioned it among the States, Territories, and the District of Columbia according to their respective populations. There were supplementary acts subsequently passed, but these related only to the States then in insurrection or rebellion.

"This law could not, owing to the existence of actual war, be enforced in the Southern States. These supplemental acts contained much harsher provisions for their enforcement than the original act contained. It is a most singular fact, I will remark in passing, that although this law laid this tax annually, there never was any attempt made to collect it except for the first year, and yet, so far as I have been able to find, that law is yet unrepealed. So uneven was it in its operation and contrary to what the people had been accustomed to, I suppose, was the consideration which caused its non enforcement, notwithstanding it was a constitutional enactment.

"The collections of this tax in the loyal or Northern States and Territories, with, I believe, a single exception, were made through the States and Territories and the District of Columbia. They availed themselves of the provision in the act allowing 15 per cent. to be retained out of the collections by all States and Territories which assumed its payment. I believe Delaware was the only exception. All the others assumed and paid, with the exception named, and the Territories of Utah and New Mexico, the amount of the assess·

ment apportioned to their populations respectively. The Territory of Washington never paid in full, but all others of the Union States and Territories assumed and paid the tax, mark you, not as States and Territories, but they collected it from the people, and for the employment of their machinery in collecting this money from the people they retained 15 per cent. of the collections, which aggregated $2.250,000. And, gentlemen, it was asserted here yesterday, that this bill carried $15,000,-000 only. If you will examine it you will find that it covers the whole field, including the 15 per cent. deduction, and that it aggregates $17,500,000.

"In the Southern States it could not at the time be enforced, but as the Union arms conquered that territory collectors of this tax followed and collected by assessment and sale in many cases, and in many others by receiving in money directly from the property owner the amount of assessments against his property. There were many irregularities in some of the conquered districts in the matter of the assessments and collections. A notable instance was that in South Carolina, where the entire town of Beaufort was sold after the notice of sale had been misdescribed so far as the property was concerned, the notice given being of a misleading character, and thus the property was thereby sacrificed and the owners robbed of their homes.

"After the war the process of enforced collection in the Southern States continued. Greater progress was made in some localities, as in Louisiana, South Carolina, and Virginia, than in others; but in none, save the State of Louisiana, were the collections completed and the sum raised which had been assessed to them.

"After the war, in view of the condition of affairs in the South the industries of the people completely revolutionized, everything out of joint, the people broken down in fortune and prostrated—the Congress from time to time passed acts delaying and postponing the collection of this tax in those States; the last of which was passed in 1868 and extended the time to the 1st day of January, 1869, since which for a period of twenty years no effort whatever has been made to collect a dollar of this tax.

"The aggregate of collections is about $17,-500,000, which leaves uncollected $2,500,000 only in round numbers, or one eighth of the original assessment. And this alone is the pretext upon which the passage of this bill is urged—because only one eighth of that tax remains uncollected and which has been allowed to sleep for twenty years, it is now made the pretext for bringing forth this bill to deplete the Treasury of $17,500,000 in the interest of those who desire to get rid of the surplus in the Treasury otherwise than by reducing the taxation which now burdens the people and cripples our national prosperity.

Other gigantic schemes of misappropriation are to follow if this be successful."

Mr. Wheeler, of Alabama, criticised the measure as essentially unfair: "The effect of the cotton-tax law would be to pay money back to those from whom it was wrongfully taken. It would be very difficult, if not impossible, to return the money to those by whom the direct tax was actually paid, under the bill now being considered, as most of the $17,000,000 was paid by the States. Again, those States whose population and wealth have increased since 1861 would be losers, while a State which has not been so fortunate would gain if the direct tax were refunded. In discussing the equity of questions like these we must assume that the $17,000,000 proposed to be paid must be collected in some way from the people, and we must further assume that States pay taxes, substantially, in proportion to their population and wealth. Proceeding under these assumptions, Maine, for instance (if we except Vermont), has changed less than any State, her population being about 3 per cent. greater than in 1860, while the population of Nebraska has increased about 3,000 per cent. Again, the assessed value of property in Maine has increased about 72 per cent., while in Nebraska the increase in the assessed value of property has been more than 3,500 per cent., now surpassing Maine in both wealth and population. Nebraska's part of the direct tax was $19,312, while that of Maine was $420,826. Maine would get twenty dollars for every one received by Nebraska, and yet the amount Nebraska would have to pay to make up the $17,000,000 would exceed that which would be contributed by Maine."

The argument for this bill was put by Mr. Buchanan, of New Jersey, as follows: "Although this tax was an annual tax, no attempt was made to levy or collect it beyond the first year. Other means of raising money were found, and this tax, so unequal in its operation, paid only by the loyal States, or enforced by seizure and sale in conquered territory, already impoverished by the misfortunes of war, was abandoned. By a report from Ros. A. Fish, assistant register of the Treasury, dated March 22, 1886, the amount levied upon the several States, the per cent. allowed for collection, the amount collected in each instance, and the balance remaining due, as appears by the books of the Treasury up to that date, is shown.

"By this report it will be observed that $2,640,314.49 remains uncollected from fourteen States and Territories, that $17,359,685.51 was paid by the States and Territories; and of these twenty-nine, each paid in full. This table is the strongest argument which can be presented, showing the inequalities of this collection. For instance, while Alabama's quota was $529,313.33, she still owes $511,028.30; Wisconsin's quota was $519,688.67; she has paid it all. Tennessee's quota was $669,498;

she still owes $277,493.52. Indiana's quota was $904,875.33. It was paid. Mississippi's quota was $413,084.67; she still owes $302,046.21. New Jersey's quota was $450,134; and every cent of it has been paid. To make things equal, this tax should be collected from each State by collection, set-off, or otherwise, shall be credited to such State; second, that all moneys still due shall be remitted and relinquished; third, that the sums collected from each State shall be returned to it absolutely where the State paid it as a State, and where it was collected by the Government of individuals in a State, in trust, to repay to such individuals.

"If the collection of this tax is not to be completed—and no one advocates that nor claims that it is needed—no fairer way, in my judgment, of correcting this inequality can be devised than the provision made by the bill before us.

"Bitterly as this measure is being fought, even this falls short of doing exact justice. Many of the States which assumed and paid this tax borrowed the money with which they paid it, and in some instances such States have paid interest on this money so borrowed from them until the present. My own State paid (with the 15 per cent. allowance) $450,134. She paid that money in 1861, now nearly twenty-seven years ago. She issued bonds for her war debt. Many of those bonds bore 7 per cent. interest. But if we reckon interest on $450,134 for twenty-five years at 6 per cent. we have the sum of $675,201 for interest alone, which my State should be repaid to put her upon an equality with Utah, which paid nothing, or with Alabama, which has paid next to nothing.

"Mr. Chairman, there is no 'section' in this measure. There is no politics in it. There is one simple, straightforward proposition to do justice to all, so far as the principal paid is concerned, and I am amazed at the fierce opposition it encounters."

Under the leadership of Mr. Oates, a number of Southern Representatives united in filibustering to prevent the passage of the bill, and they succeeded in preventing the transaction of other business and the adjournment of the House from April 4 to April 12; so that the legislative day, Wednesday, April 4, 1888, lasted 192 hours, though the House took several recesses, and was not therefore continuously in session during that time. The deadlock was finally broken under an agreement made at a caucus of the Democratic Representatives that the measure should be taken up Thursday, Dec. 6, 1888, and put to a final vote Tuesday, December 11, the Northern Democrats who had been urgent for its passage yielding so far to Southern Democrats as to agree to its postponement for the session. On the day set, the house passed the measure.

Postal Matters.—A bill relating to permissible marks in printing and writing upon second, third, and fourth class matter was passed by the House Jan. 13, 1888, and by the Senate January 17, and duly approved by the President. It is as follows:

Be it enacted, etc., That mailable matter of the second class shall contain no writing, print, or sign thereon or therein in addition to the original print, except as herein provided, to wit, the name and address of the person to whom the matter shall be sent; index-figures of subscription book, either printed or written; the printed title of the publication and the place of its publication; the printed or written name and address, without addition of advertisement, of the publisher or sender, or both, and written or printed words or figures, or both, indicating the date on which the subscription to such matter will end; the correction of any typographical error; a mark, except by written or printed words, to designate a word or passage to which it is desired to call attention; the words "sample copy," when the matter is sent as such; the words "marked copy," when the matter contains a marked item or article; and publishers or news-agents may inclose in their publications bills, receipts, and orders for subscription thereto, but the same shall be in such form as to convey no other information than the name, place of publication, subscription price of the publication to which they refer, and the subscription due thereon. Upon matter of the third class, upon the wrapper or envelope inclosing the same, or the tag or label attached thereto, the sender may write his own name, occupation, and residence or business address, preceded by the word "from," and may make marks other than by written or printed words to call attention to any word or passage in the text, and may correct any typographical errors. There may be placed upon the blank leaves or cover of any book or printed matter of the third class a simple manuscript dedication or inscription not of the nature of a personal correspondence. Upon the wrapper or envelope of third-class matter or the tag or label attached thereto may be printed any matter mailable as third class, but there must be left on the address-side a space sufficient for a legible address and necessary stamps. With a package of fourth-class matter, prepaid at the proper rate for that class, the sender may inclose any mailable third-class matter, and may write upon the wrapper or cover thereof, or tag or label accompanying the same, his name, occupation, residence, or business address, preceded by the word "from," and any marks, numbers, names, or letters for purpose of description, or may print thereon the same, and any printed matter not in the nature of a personal correspondence, but there must be left on the address side or face of the package a space sufficient for a legible address and necessary stamps. In all cases directions for transit, delivery, forwarding, or return shall be deemed part of the address, and the Postmaster-General shall prescribe suitable regulations for carrying this section into effect.

Sec. 2. That matter of the second, third, or fourth class containing any writing or printing in addition to the original matter, other than as authorized in the preceding section, shall not be admitted to the mails, nor delivered, except upon payment of postage for matter of the first class, deducting therefrom any amount which may have been prepaid by stamps affixed, unless by direction of the Postmaster-General such postage shall be remitted; and any person who shall knowingly conceal or inclose any matter of a higher class in that of a lower class, and deposit or cause the same to be deposited for conveyance by mail, at a less rate than would be charged for both such higher and lower class matter, shall for every such offense be liable to a penalty of $10.

The House, on Feb. 2, 1888, passed the following measure in regard to books as second-class matter:

A bill to amend section 14 of the act approved March 3, 1879, entitled "An act making appropriations for the service of the Post-Office Department for the fiscal year ending June 30, 1880, and for other purposes," and relating to second-class mail-matter.

Be it enacted by the Senate and House of Representatives of the United States of America in Congress assembled. That the fourteenth section of the act approved March 3, 1879, entitled "An act making appropriations for the service of the Post-Office Department for the fiscal year ending June 30, 1880, and for other purposes," be, and the same is hereby, amended by adding to the proviso thereof, and at the end of said section, the following words, namely:

"And that no publications, that are but books or reprints of books, whether they be issued complete or in parts, bound or unbound, or in series, or whether sold by subscription or otherwise, shall be admitted to the mails as second-class matter."

Nothing further was done with this measure; but a bill was passed amending the act excluding offensive matter from the mails, and another amending the act authorizing the Postmaster-General to adjust claims of postmasters for losses by fire, etc. An act was passed also limiting the work of letter-carriers to eight hours a day.

Telegraph Affairs.—On Feb. 9, 1888, the Committee of the House on Post-Offices and Post-roads reported an act supplementary to the act of July 1, 1862, entitled "An act to aid in the construction of a railroad and telegraph line from the Missouri river to the Pacific Ocean, and to secure to the Government the use of the same for postal, military, and other purposes." The evil which this measure was designed to remedy was described as follows in the report of the majority of the committee: "The House of Representatives, by resolution adopted Feb. 26, 1886, empowered the Committee on Post-Offices and Post-roads to ascertain and report whether 'additional legislation is needed to prevent a monopoly of telegraphic facilities; to secure to the Southern, Western, and Pacific States the benefits of competition between the telegraph companies; and to protect the people of the United States against unreasonable charges for telegraphic services;' and to carry out the purposes of the inquiry authorized the committee to send for and examine persons, books, and papers, administer oaths to witnesses, and employ a stenographer. Pursuant to the terms of the resolution the committee heard statements and examined witnesses with a view of ascertaining especially the relations of the land-grant railroads and telegraphic lines to the lines of other telegraph companies, to the public, and to the Government. As a result of their investigations the conclusion was reached that the Pacific railroads had not complied with the requirements of the acts under which they were incorporated, for the reason that, instead of constructing, maintaining, and operating a telegraph line, they had divested themselves of this obligation by contracting with the Western Union Telegraph Company to perform the service."

The two leading sections of the act were as follows:

1. That all railroad and telegraph companies to which the United States has granted any subsidy in lands or bonds or loan of credit for the construction of either railroad or telegraph lines, which, by the acts incorporating them, or by any act amendatory or supplementary thereto, are required to construct, maintain, or operate telegraph lines, and all companies engaged in operating said railroads or telegraph lines shall forthwith and henceforward, by and through their own respective corporative officers and employés, construct, maintain, and operate for railroad, governmental, commercial, and all other purposes, telegraph lines, and exercise by themselves alone all the telegraph franchises conferred upon them and obligations assumed by them under the acts making the grants as aforesaid.

2. That whenever any telegraph company which shall have accepted the provisions of title 65 of the Revised Statutes shall extend its line to any station or office of a telegraph line belonging to any one of said railroad or telegraph companies, referred to in the first section of this act, said telegraph company so extending its line shall have the right and said railroad or telegraph company shall allow the line of said telegraph company so extending its line to connect with the telegraph line of said railroad or telegraph company to which it is extended at the place where their lines may meet, for the prompt and convenient interchange of telegraph business between said companies; and such railroad and telegraph companies, referred to in the first section of this act, shall so operate their respective telegraph lines as to afford equal facilities to all, without discrimination in favor of or against any person, company, or corporation whatever, and shall receive, deliver, and exchange business with connecting telegraph lines on equal terms, and affording equal facilities, and without discrimination for or against any one of such connecting lines; and such exchange of business shall be on terms just and equitable.

The remaining provisions were merely to furnish the necessary machinery for enforcing the requirements of these sections, and to invest the Interstate Commerce Commission with the authority and charge them with the duty of seeing the law carried out. The measure passed the House March 3, and subsequently passed the Senate and received the President's signature.

The Senate passed a bill putting all telegraph lines running from one State to another under the supervision of the Interstate Commerce Commission; but the House failed to act on it before adjournment. In that body the minority of the Committee on Commerce reported in favor of such a measure March 20, but the majority reported in favor of a bill establishing a postal telegraph system, formulating the following conclusions:

1. That the time has arrived when the Government should construct and operate a postal-telegraph system as a branch of its postal service.
2. That the service will undoubtedly be self-supporting.

3. That the Government has the right to build and operate telegraph lines under the jurisdiction of its Post-Office Department.

4. That public opinion will not permit, and good faith and justice do not require, the purchase by the Government of the property and franchises of the Western Union Telegraph Company.

Pensions.—On March 8, 1888, the Senate passed a dependent pension bill, but it failed to get through the House. A measure pensioning prisoners taken by the Confederates during the civil war also failed. An act was passed, however, and approved, providing that pensions hereafter granted to widows of soldiers of the war of the rebellion shall begin at the date of the death of their husbands, not from the date of filing claims. A bill was passed and approved increasing to $30 a month the pension for total deafness, and likewise an act enabling certain volunteer soldiers denied the $100 bounty under the act of 1872 to receive the benefit of that act; and also a measure providing for the payment of $100 a year for each inmate in State and Territorial soldiers' homes. Special pension bills were passed in favor of Mrs. Logan and Mrs. Blair, but the bill in favor of Mrs. Sheridan failed to get through the House of Representatives. In all, 638 private pension bills were passed, of which 569 became laws with the President's signature, and 69 became laws without it.

Miscellaneous.—On May 29, 1888, both Houses passed and the President approved a bill reviving the grade of General of the Army, so that Gen. Sheridan, then in imminent danger of death, might be appointed.

On May 10, 1888, the Senate passed, after discussion for more than three weeks, a bill forfeiting all lands heretofore granted to any State or corporation to aid in the construction of a railroad which lands are opposite to and conterminous with the portion of any such railroad not now completed and in operation. In the House of Representatives the majority of the Committee on Public Lands reported a substitute for the Senate bill, which was debated July 5 and passed July 6. The House bill provided for the forfeiture of lands lying along the sections of subsidized railroads not completed within the time specified in the grant, and the clashing of these two measures prevented decisive action.

On May 9, 1888, the Senate passed an international copyright bill, but the House failed to act on it.

On May 21, 1888, the House of Representatives passed a bill making the Department of Agriculture an Executive department the head of which shall be a Cabinet officer; and September 21, the Senate passed the measure with an amendment cutting out the provision of the House bill transferring the Signal Service from the War Department to that newly created. So the bill fell by the way.

Early in the session the President sent a message to Congress recommending the creation of a national board of arbitration, and

April 18, 1888, the House of Representatives passed a measure carrying out the Executive recommendations; but it was not reached in the Senate.

The Blair educational bill was discussed at length, and passed the Senate Feb. 15, 1888, by a vote of 39 to 29; but it was not brought up in the House.

In his third annual message the President expressed a doubt as to authority to purchase bonds over and above the requirements of the sinking-fund, though the authority had been given in a clause in an appropriation bill, June 30, 1882. On April 5, 1888, the Senate passed a resolution declaring that such purchase of bonds is lawful, and April 16, the House passed a resolution to the same effect.

On March 21, 1888, the House passed a bill to establish a Department of Labor to be under control of a Commissioner of Labor. May 22, the Senate amended and passed the measure; and May 31, both Houses agreed to accept the report of a conference committee. The bill was approved by the President; and it merely reorganized the existing Bureau of Labor Statistics.

On March 19, 1888, the House of Representatives passed a measure authorizing the Secretary of the Treasury to issue silver certificates in denominations of twenty-five, fifteen, and ten cents; but the Senate failed to take up the measure.

On April 19, 1888, the Senate passed a bill admitting South Dakota into the Union; but it failed in the House, and so no action was taken on measures for the admission of other new States. The bill for organizing the Territory of Oklahoma also failed.

The House of Representatives made careful investigations of immigration and of trusts and combinations; but reached no result in legislation on either subject.

A bill was passed authorizing the President to arrange a conference between the nations of Central America, South America, and the West Indies for the establishment of international arbitration and the promotion of commerce.

Measures were adopted appropriating money for a gun-factory and for several new ships of war.

A bill was passed making certain judgments and decrees in Federal courts liens on property throughout the State in which the court is held.

Congress provided for an international conference to secure greater safety for life and property at sea; for twenty-seven new public buildings; for an investigation by the Geological Survey of means of storing water in arid regions; for representation at the expositions in Paris, Brussels, Barcelona, and Melbourne.

Measures not already mentioned that failed to become laws were the bill to quiet the title of settlers on the Des Moines river lands; the bill raising the salary of district judges; the bill for the repeal of the pre-emption and timber-culture laws, and the amendment of the homestead law; the Pacific Railroad funding bill; the bill for the forfeiture of the Northern Pacific grant; the bill to incorporate the Nicaragua Canal Company; the bill to pay losses of depositors in the Freedmen's Bank; the bill for the erection of coast defenses; the bill for the taking of the next census; the bill for the inspection of meat for export.

CONGRESS OF THE UNITED STATES, CONTESTED ELECTIONS IN THE. In this article are summarized all the principal contested elections that have occurred in Congress since the adoption of the Federal Constitution. It is the usage of the House of Representatives to refer all cases of contested seats to the Committee on Elections. The duty of that committee is to examine and report its opinion upon such matters as shall be referred to it by the House; but such opinion, though clothed with a certain authority, is not conclusive upon the House; it may be overruled, and not unfrequently is. The usage of the committee is, after an examination into the facts of the case, to elaborate a report in which these facts are set forth with accuracy; from this statement of fact to deduce the reasons for supporting the one or the other candidate; and to report its opinion to the House, both at length and in the form of a condensed resolution. It is upon this resolution, and not upon the reasons or arguments of the committee, that the House acts, and whether they have or have not concurred with the committee in their views of each case, will not appear as a matter of record on their journals, which will only show that they have concurred with it in the final result. Yet if the House do not dissent from the conclusion of the committee, they may, in general, be presumed to have sanctioned the process of reasoning by which that conclusion was attained.

The Qualifications of Senators of the United States will be found in the Constitution, Article I, section 3; and of Representatives, in Article I, section 2. The debates on amendments originally proposed to be made to the Constitution, in regard to the power of Congress over the subject of elections of members of Congress, will be found in "Lloyd's Debates," vol. ii, p. 244, *et seq.* The original papers and documents of Congress, or the greater portion of them, from the First to the Sixth Congress, were destroyed by the English with the Capitol in 1814, and among other important papers those relating to contested elections were consumed. "Lloyd's Debates" and the newspapers of the day, however, afford us general information of the transactions recorded in the missing documents. But Congress has frequently ordered or authorized the collection and publication, by the public printer, of proceedings in contested elections, either singly or in groups; and such publications are authoritative and should be consulted by the student.

CONTESTANTS.	Congress.	Year.	
Abbott vs. Frost	44th	1876	House.
Abbott vs. Vance	....	....	.....
Abbott, Joseph C	42d	1872	Senate.
Acklen vs. Darrall	45th	1877	House.
Adams vs. Wilson	18th	1823	House.
Allen, Thomas	23d	1833	House.
Anderson vs. Chrisman	36th	1860	House.
Anderson vs. Reed	47th	1882	House.
Archer vs. Allen	34th	1855	House.
Aycrigg vs. Dickerson	26th	1840	House.
Bailey, John	18th	1824	House.
Baldwin vs. Trowbridge	39th	1865	House.
Ball, M. D.	47th	1882	House.
Barnes vs. Adams	41st	1869	House.
Barney vs. McCreery	10th	1807	House.
Baskin vs. Cannon	43d	1875	House.
Bassett vs. Bayly	13th	1814	House.
Baxter vs. Brouis	....	....	.....
Beach, G. F.	37th	1862	House.
Beard vs. Corker	41st	1871	House.
Beck, James B.	40th	1867	House.
Bell vs. Snyder	42d	1873	House.
Bennet vs. Chapman	34th	1855	House.
Biddle vs. Richard	18th	1824	House.
Biddle vs. Wing	19th	1826	House.
Birch vs. King	38th	1863	House.
Birch vs. Van Horn	40th	1867	House.
Bisbee vs. Hull	46th	1879	Senate.
Bisbee vs. Finley	47th	1882	House.
Blair vs. Barrett	36th	1860	House.
Blakey vs. Golladay	40th	1867	House.
Blodgett vs. Norwood	42d	1871	Senate.
Bogy, Lewis V	42d	1873	Senate.
Boles vs. Edwards	42d	1871	House.
Bonzano, N F.	38th	1865	House.
Botkin vs. Maginnis	48th	1884	House.
Botts vs. Jones	25th	1843	House.
Bowden vs. De Large	42d	1872	House.
Boyd vs. Kelso	31th	1866	House.
Boyden vs. Shober	41st	1870	House.
Boyton vs. Loring	46th	1879	House.
Bradley vs. Slemons	46th	1879	House.
Breaux vs. Darrall	44th	1875	House.
Bright, Jesse D	35th	1858	Senate.
Bromberg vs. Haralson	44th	1876	House.
Brooks vs. Davis	35th	1857	House.
Brown, John Young	40th	1867	House.
Bruce vs. Loan	38th	1863	House.
Burleigh vs. Armstrong	42d	1872	House.
Burns vs. Young	43d	1872	House.
Butler, M. C	46th	1879	Senate.
Buttz vs. Mackey	44th	1876	House
Byington vs. Vandever	37th	1861	House.
Cabell vs. Brockenbrough	29th	1846	House.
Caldwell, Alexander	42d	1873	Senate.
Campbell vs. Weaver	49th	1886	House.
Campbell, Lewis D	42d	1872	House.
Campbell vs. Morey	48th	1884	House.
Cannon, George Q	43d	1875	House.
Cannon, George Q	47th	1882	House.
Carpenter, C. C	46th	1881	House.
Carrigan vs. Thayer	38th	1863	House.
Cavanagh, James M	36th	1868	House.
Cessna vs. Meyers	42d	1871	House.
Chalmers vs. Manning	48th	1884	House.
Chapman vs. Ferguson	35th	1857	House.
Chaves vs. Clever	40th	1867	House.
Chrisman vs. Anderson	36th	1860	House.
Christy vs. Wimpy	41th	1869	House.
Clarke, W. T	42d	1871	House.
Clarke vs. Hall	34th	1856	House.
Connor vs. Cain	45th	1878	House.
Cooke vs. Cutts	47th	1882	Senate.
Corbin, David T	45th	1879	House.
Covode vs. Foster	41st	1869	House.
Cox vs. Strait	44th	1876	House.
Craige vs. Shelley	48th	1884	House.
Culpeper, John	10th	1807	House.
Curtin vs. Yocum	46th	1879	House.
Cutter, R. King	38th	1865	House.
Daily vs. Estabrook	36th	1860	House.
Darrall vs. Bailey	41st	1868	House.
Dean vs. Field	45th	1877	House.
Delano vs. Morgan	40th	1867	House.
Dodge vs. Brooks	39th	1865	House.
Donnelly vs. Washburn	46th	1879	House.
Doty vs. Jones	25th	1838	House.
Draper vs. Johnson	22d	1882	House.
Duffy vs. Mason	46th	1879	House.
Easton vs. Scott	14th	1816	House.

CONTESTANTS.	Congress.	Year.	
Eggleston vs. Struder	41st	1869	House.
English vs. Peelle	45th	1884	House.
Eustis, James B.	44th	1876	Senate.
Fabre vs. Eustis	34th	1855	House.
Farlee vs. Runk	29th	1845	House.
Fenn vs. Bennett	44th	1876	House.
Field, A. P.	38th	1864	House.
Finley vs. Bisbee	45th	1877	House.
Finley vs. Walls	44th	1876	House.
Fitch, Graham N.	35th	1858	Senate.
Flanders, Benjamin F.	37th	1863	House.
Follett vs. Delano	39th	1864	House.
Foster, Charles H	37th	1862	House.
Foster vs. Covode	41st	1869	House.
Foster vs. Pigott	37th	1863	House.
Fouke, P. B.	34th	1855	House.
Frost vs. Metcalfe.	45th	1878	House.
Fuller vs. Dawson	39th	1864	House.
Gallatin, Albert	3d	1794	Senate.
Garrison vs. Mayo	45th	1884	House.
Gause vs. Hodges	43d	1873	House.
Gibson vs. Sheldon	43d	1873	House.
Giddings vs Clarke	42d	1872	House.
Goggin vs. Gilmer.	28th	1843	House.
Gooding vs. Wilson	42d	1871	House.
Grafton vs. Conner	41st	1870	House.
Graham vs. Newland	24th	1836	House.
Grover, Asa P.	40th	1867	House.
Gunter vs. Wilshire	43d	1874	House.
Hahn, Michael	37th	1863	House.
Halsted vs. Cooper	26th	1840	House.
Hammond vs. Herrick	15th	1818	House.
Haralson, Jere	46th	1880	House.
Haralson vs. Shelley	45th	1877	House.
Harrison vs. Davis	36th	1860	House.
Hawkins, Alvin	37th	1863	House.
Hillyer vs. McIntyre	42d	1871	House.
Hogan vs. Pile	40th	1866	House.
Hoge vs. Reed	41st	1868	House.
Holmes, J. C.	46th	1880	House.
Holmes vs. Sapp	46th	1879	House.
Howard vs. Cooper	36th	1860	House.
Hurd vs. Romeis	49th	1886	House.
Hunt vs. Chilcott	40th	1867	House.
Hunt vs. Menard	40th	1869	House.
Hunt vs. Sheldon	41st	1869	House.
Jacks, T. M.	38th	1865	House.
Jayne vs. Todd	38th	1864	House.
Johnson, J. M.	38th	1865	House.
Jones, Thomas L	40th	1867	House.
Jones vs. Mann	40th	1868	House.
Kelly vs. Harris	13th	1814	House.
Key, Philip B	10th	1807	House.
Kidd vs. Steele	49th	1886	House.
Kingsbury vs. Fuller	35th	1858	House.
Kline vs. Meyers	38th	1863	House.
Kline vs. Verree	37th	1871	House.
Knott, J. Proctor	40th	1867	House.
Knox vs. Blair	38th	1863	House.
Koontz vs. Coffroth	39th	1866	House.
Lamar vs. King	47th	1882	House.
Lamar vs. Gallegos	33d	1854	House.
Lawrence vs. Sypher	43d	1874	House.
Lee vs Rainey	42d	1876	House.
Leftwich vs. Smith	41st	1870	House.
Le Moyne vs. Farwell	44th	1875	House.
Leverson vs. Felton	49th	1886	House.
Levy, David	27th	1841	House.
Lindsay vs. Scott	38th	1863	House.
Littell vs. Robbins	31st	1850	House.
Lowe, F. F	37th	1862	House.
Lowe vs. Wheeler	47th	1882	House.
Lowell, Joshua A.	27th	1842	House
Lynch vs. Chalmers	47th	1882	House.
McCabe vs. Orth	46th	1880	House.
McCloud, John B	37th	1863	House.
McDowell vs. George	47th	1882	House.
McGrorty vs. Hooper	40th	1867	House.
McHenry vs. Yeaman	38th	1863	House.
McKay, Matter of	49th	1886	House.
McKee vs. Young	40th	1867	House.
McKenzie vs Braxton	42d	1871	House.
McKenzie vs Kitchen	37th	1863	House.
Mackey vs O'Conner	46th	1879	House.
McKissick vs. Wallace	42d	1872	House.
McLean vs. Broadhead	48th	1884	House.
McMullen, W. L	42d	1873	House.
Mabson vs Oates	47th	1882	House.
Mann, W. D.	38th	1875	House.
Manzanares vs. Luna	48th	1884	House.

CONTESTANTS.	Congress.	Year.	
Martin, B. F	43d	1874	House.
Massey vs. Wise	48th	1884	House.
Maxwell vs. Cannon	43d	1874	House.
Maxwell vs. Ryall	26th	1840	House.
Mead, Cowles.	9th	1805	House.
Merchant et al. vs. Ackien	46th	1880	House.
Merriam vs Henley	49th	1886	House.
Misserry, William S	31st	1851	House.
Milliken vs. Fuller	34th	1855	House.
Monroe vs. Jackson	30th	1848	House.
Moore vs. Letcher	23d	1834	House.
Morton vs. Daily	37th	1872	House.
Myers vs. Moffett	41st	1869	House.
Naylor vs. Ingersoll	26th	1840	House.
Newsman vs. Ryan	41st	1869	House.
Niblack vs. Walls	42d	1872	House.
Norris vs. Handley	42d	1871	House.
Nutting vs. Reilly	45th	1871	House.
O'Ferrall vs. Paul	48th	1884	House.
O'Hara vs. Kitchin	46th	1881	House.
Otero vs. Gallegos	34th	1856	House.
Patterson, John J	42d	1873	Senate.
Patterson vs. Belford	45th	1877	House.
Patterson vs. Morrow	40th	1886	House.
Perkins, Jared	31st	1851	House.
Phelps, V. W	35th	1858	House.
Pigott vs Foster	47th	1863	House.
Pinchback, P. B.	43d	1873	Senate.
Pratt vs. Goode	44th	1875	House.
Pomeroy, T. C.	42d	1872	Senate.
Pool vs Skinner	48th	1884	House.
Porterfield vs McCoy	14th	1816	House.
Potter vs. Robbins	28d	1834	Senate.
Powell vs. Butler	40th	1867	House.
Prentiss vs. Ward	25th	1838	House.
Preston vs. Harris	36th	1860	House.
Price vs. McClurg	38th	1863	House.
Ramsay vs. Smith	1st	1789	House.
Randolph vs. Jennings	11th	1809	House.
Ray vs. McMillan	43d	1874	Senate.
Read vs. Cosden	17th	1822	House.
Reading vs Taylor	41st	1870	House.
Redstone, A. E.	50th	1888	House.
Reeder vs. Whitfield	34th	1856	House.
Reid vs. George	41st	1870	House.
Reid vs. Julian	41st	1860	House.
Richardson vs. Rainey	45th	1877	House.
Robbins, Asher	28d	1884	Senate.
Rodgers, John B	37th	1863	House.
Sapp, W. F.	46th	1881	House.
Segar, Joseph E.	37th	1862	House.
Sessingham vs. Frost.	47th	1882	House.
Sheafe vs. Tillman	41st	1870	House.
Sheridan vs. Pinchback	43d	1874	House.
Shiel vs. Thayer	37th	1861	House.
Shields vs. Van Horn	41st	1869	House.
Sleeper vs. Rice	38th	1863	House.
Sloan vs. Rawles	43d	1873	House.
Smalls vs. Tillman	47th	1882	House.
Smith, Charles	38th	1865	House.
Smith vs. Brown	40th	1868	House.
Smith vs. Robertson	47th	1882	House.
Spalding, Thomas	9th	1805	House.
Spencer vs. Morey	44th	1876	House.
Spink vs. Armstrong	42d	1870	House.
Spofford vs. Kellogg	46th	1877	House.
Stanton vs Lane	37th	1861	House.
Stewart vs. Phelps	40th	1867	House.
Stolband vs. Robertson	47th	1882	House.
Stovall vs. Cabell	47th	1882	House.
Strobach vs. Herbert	47th	1882	House.
Strotton vs. Vroom	26th	1840	House.
Switzler vs. Anderson	40th	1866	House.
Switzler vs. Dyer	41st	1867	House.
Symes vs. Trimble	40th	1867	House.
Sypher vs. St. Martin	41st	1863	House.
Taliaferro vs. Reading	12th	1811	House.
Taylor vs. Reading	41st	1869	House.
Thobe vs. Carlisle	50th	1888	House.
Thomas vs. Arnell	39th	1866	House.
Thomas vs. Davis	43d	1873	House.
Thompson, William	31st	1850	House.
Tift vs. Whitely	41st	1871	House.
Tillman vs. Smalls	45th	1877	House.
Todd vs. Jayne	38th	1864	House.
Trimble, Lawrence	40th	1867	House.
Tucker vs. Booker	41st	1870	House.
Turner vs. Baylies	11th	1809	House.
Turney vs. Marshal	34th	1855	House.
Vallandigham vs. Campbell	35th	1857	House.

CONTESTANTS	Congress.	Year.	
Van Wyck *vs.* Greene............	41st	1863	House.
Wallace *vs.* McKinley	48th	1884	House.
Wallace *vs.* Simpson	41st	1868	House.
Washburn *vs.* Voorhees	39th	1865	House.
Whittlesey *vs.* McKenzie	41st	1870	House.
Whitmore *vs.* Herndon.....	42d	1872	House.
Whyte *vs.* Harris	35th	1857	House.
Wigginton *vs.* Pacheco	45th	1877	House.
Williams *vs.* Bowers	13th	1813	House.
Williamson *vs.* Sickles	36th	1860	House.
Willoughby *vs.* Smith	14th	1815	House.
Wilson, Benjamin....	43d	1874	House.
Wilson *vs.* Carpenter............	46th	1879	House.
Wing, W. W....................	87th	1868	House.
Witherspoon *vs.* Davidson........	47th	1882	House.
Wright *vs.* Fisher...............	21st	1880	House.
Wool *vs.* Peters	48th	1884	House.
Wright *vs.* Fuller	32d	1852	House.
Yates *vs.* Martin	46th	1880	House.
Young, John D	40th	1867	House.
Yulee *vs.* Mallory...............	82d	1871	Senate.
Ziegler *vs.* Rice	41st	1869	House.

CONKLING, ROSCOE, an American statesman, born in Albany, N. Y., Oct. 30, 1829 ; died in New York city, April 18, 1888. His father, Alfred (1789–1874), was a member of Congress from 1821 to 1823, judge of the United States District Court for the Northern District of New York from 1825 to 1852, and minister to Mexico from 1852 to 1853. After receiving an academic education, Roscoe studied law under his father, and in 1846 entered the office of Spencer & Kernan in Utica. In 1850, on the resignation of the District Attorney of Oneida County, he was appointed by the Governor for the remainder of the term. In the same year he was admitted to the bar, and in 1858 elected Mayor of Utica. At the end of his term there was a tie between the two candidates for election, in consequence of which Mr. Conkling continued in the office another term. He was elected to Congress in 1858 as a Republican, and re-elected in 1860. He was again a candidate in 1862, but was defeated by Francis Kernan; but in 1864 he was once more opposed to Mr. Kernan, and was elected. He was returned for Congress a fourth time in 1866, but did not take his seat for that term, having been chosen United States Senator in January, 1867, an office which he held continuously till 1881. His term of service in the two houses, therefore, covered the most critical period in the recent history of this country —the exciting years just before and during the civil war, and the reconstruction period immediately following. His first work in the House was as a member of the Committee on the District of Columbia, of which he afterward became chairman. He was also a member of the Committee of Ways and Means and of the special Reconstruction Committee of Fifteen. His first important speech was in favor of the fourteenth amendment to the national Constitution. He early took an assured position in the House, made many vigorous speeches, and showed the qualifications for leadership that appeared so prominently in his later career. He was an active supporter of the policy of Lincoln's administration in the conduct of the

war, attacked the generalship of McClellan, and opposed Spaulding's legal-tender act. After the war he took an active part in the legislation connected with the reconstruction of the Southern States, was opposed to President Johnson's policy, and helped to pass the Civil Rights Bill over his veto. In the Senate he was a member of the Judiciary Committee from the first, was connected with nearly all the leading committees, and chairman of those on commerce and revision of the laws. During the administration of President Grant, Mr. Conkling had much to do with shaping the policy of the Government toward the Southern States. He was a zealous supporter of the President, and soon became the recognized leader of that section of the party which favored his renomination. In the National Republican Convention of 1876 Mr. Conkling was the candidate favored for the nomination by the majority of the New York delegation, and received ninety-three votes; but, in consequence of the opposition of the minority under the leadership of George William Curtis, the New York ballot was transferred to Mr. Hayes. In the proceedings growing out of the disputed election that followed, Mr. Conkling took a leading part. He was a member of the committee that framed the Electoral-Commission

ROSCOE CONKLING.

bill, and advocated it in an able speech in the Senate, taking the ground that the question of the commission's jurisdiction should be left to that body itself. His absence from the Senate when the vote was taken on the Louisiana decision of the commission, was caused by his absence from the city. In 1880 Senator Conkling strongly advocated the election of Gen. Grant for a third term. About this time the division of the Republican party into two factions, popularly called "Stalwarts" and "Half-breeds," became more marked, and their opposition more pronounced. Mr. Conkling and

Mr. Blaine were recognized as the leaders of the factions. The personal enmity between them is said to have dated from a bitter controversy over a bill introduced into Congress by Mr. Conkling in 1866 providing for the reorganization of the army of the United States and looking to the abolition of the Provost-Marshal Bureau. The Half-breeds triumphed in the nominating convention of 1880, and Mr. Garfield was elected. When he took his seat in March, 1881, Mr. Conkling and his colleague, Thomas C. Platt, claimed the right to control the Federal appointments in their State. When the President appointed William H. Robertson, an opponent of Mr. Conkling, to the collectorship of the port of New York, the latter opposed his confirmation, asserting that he should have been consulted in the matter, in accordance with pledges made to him by the President. Mr. Garfield then withdrew all other nominations to New York offices, leaving that for the collectorship to be acted upon separately. Not being able to defeat the confirmation, Mr. Conkling and Mr. Platt resigned from the Senate and returned home in order to appeal to the people of New York, through the State Legislature, to vindicate them and rebuke the President by their prompt re-election. After a long and exciting contest, the matter was decided against them by the election as Senators of Warner Miller and Elbridge G. Latham. The latter received 61 votes to 28 for Mr. Conkling. Mr. Conkling sent the following letter to his supporters:

The heroic constancy of the Spartan band which so long stood for principle and truth has my deepest gratitude and admiration. Borne down by forbidden and abhorrent forces and agencies which never before had sway in the Republican party, the memory of their courage and manhood will long live in the highest honor. The near future will vindicate their wisdom and crown them with approval. Please ask them all for me to receive my most grateful acknowledgments.   ROSCOE CONKLING.

Returning to private life, Mr. Conkling resumed the practice of law, settling in New York city. In 1882 President Arthur sent his name to the Senate for a place on the bench of the United States Supreme Court, in place of Ward Hunt, but Mr. Conkling declined. During his residence in New York he was engaged in many important cases, and the fortune of $200,000 that he left at his death was accumulated during those six years. In 1885–'86 he was counsel of the State Senate Investigating Committee appointed for the purpose of examining into the alleged fraud and bribery in the grant of the Broadway horse-railroad franchise by the Board of Aldermen in 1884. After the taking of testimony, which lasted about three months, Mr. Conkling and Clarence A. Seward made an argument, which resulted in the repeal of the Broadway Railroad charter. Mr. Conkling appeared for the Central Pacific Railway in several suits, and he wrote an opinion for this road in answer to the charges contained in the report of an investigating

commission. He appeared for the Commercial Telegraph Company in its suit against the New York Stock Exchange and the Gold and Stock Ticker Company; was connected with the suit brought by the Bankers and Merchants' Telegraph Company against the Western Union, and was engaged in the Stewart will contest. In 1885 he spent three months in Europe. In the great storm of March 12, 1888, in New York (known as "the blizzard"), he walked from his Wall Street office to his club, near Twenty-third Street, and from the effects of this exposure, added to those of a cold contracted at a hearing in the Stewart will case, he never recovered, the disease taking the form of an abscess at the base of the brain. Mr. Conkling received the degree of LL. D. from Madison University in 1877. His wife, a sister of Horatio Seymour, and his only child, a daughter, survived him.

CONNECTICUT. State Government.—The following were the State officers during the year: Governor, Phineas C. Lounsbury, Republican; Lieutenant-Governor, James L. Howard; Secretary of State, Leverett M. Hubbard; Treasurer, Alexander Warner; Comptroller, Thomas Clark; Secretary of the State Board of Education, Charles D. Hine; Insurance Commissioner, Orsamus R. Fyler; Railroad Commissioners, George M. Woodruff, W. H. Haywood, William O. Seymour; Chief-Justice of the Supreme Court, John D. Park; Associate Justices, Elisha Carpenter, Dwight W. Pardee, Dwight Loomis, and Sidney B. Beardsley.

Finances.—The balance in the State treasury on July 1, 1886, was $230,442.48. During the biennial period since that date the total receipts, including $1,034,808.08 from a sale of new State bonds authorized by the Refunding act of 1887 were $4,958,973.06, and the expenditures, including $1,030,000 paid for bonds redeemed, $4,437,716.51, leaving a balance on June 30, 1888, of $751,699.03. Some of the items of expenditure are given in the following table:

ITEMS.	Ending June 30, 1887.	Ending June 30, 1888.
Sessions of the General Assembly	$110,129 39	$427 00
Judicial expenses	262,995 22	280,539 90
Board of prisoners in county jails	78,281 15	89,785 81
State Normal School	24,177 41	18,341 38
Common schools	236,328 40	237,224 50
State prison	104,112 63	198,082 68
State Reform School	56,666 24	85,325 43
Humane institutions	140,617 08	143,258 35
Sick and wounded soldiers	60,002 80	43,963 23
National Guard	167,592 95	153,907 00

The largest sources of revenue for 1887 were from State tax collected by the towns, $698,-355.22; from tax on insurance companies, $230,074.87; from savings-banks, $211,393.72; from railroads, $567,571.99; military commutation taxes, $103,045. For 1888 the receipts were $437,157.23 from the State tax; $231,-775.63 from insurance companies; $223,985.70

from savings-banks; $641.724.79 from railroads; and $109,055.40 from the military commutation taxes. A reduction of the State tax rate from 2 to 1¼ mills caused the decreased revenue from the State tax in the latter year.

The funded debt of the State on the first day of July, 1886, was $4,271,200. In accordance with the Refunding act of 1887, the 5-per-cent. bonds of 1877, amounting to $1,030,-000, were redeemed during that year and $1,000,000 of bonds bearing 3½ per cent. interest were issued. The debt, thus reduced by $30,000 and by $600 of other bonds redeemed, stood as follows on June 30, 1888:

Issue of 1865, unredeemed	$600
Issue of March 19, 1882, payable in 1903..........	500,000
Issue of April 4, 1888, payable in 1908............	1,000,000
Issue of March 10, etc., 1885, payable in 1910	1,740,000
Issue of May 18, 1887, payable in 1897............	1,000,000
Total.................	$4,240,600

Later in 1888 the Treasurer, exercising his power to redeem at any time the issue of 1887, called in $500,000 of that loan, paying for it out of the large surplus in the treasury.

The telegraph companies in the State refused during the year to pay the full tax assessed on their gross earnings in the State, and there is a controversy as to the constitutionality of the gross-earnings law except when applied to business of the companies done wholly within the State. The companies claim that the tax is a regulation of interstate commerce when imposed upon their revenue derived from messages coming in or going out of the State. The Western Union Company has paid for 1888 a tax of $715.14. If a tax is due on the total receipts it would amount to $3,389.48. No legal measures to collect the balance claimed by the State have been taken.

Education.—The amount of the school fund held by the State for the benefit of the common schools, on June 30, was $2,019,572.40. From the income of this, the sum of $116,119 was distributed in 1888 for the support of schools. This was about 75 cents for each child, the number of school-children enumerated in 1888 being 154,532. The income distributed in 1887 was $114,945, and the number of children of school age 153,260. For the school year 1886–'87 the following statistics are compiled: Public-school districts, 1,424; number of public schools, 1,628; number of school-houses, 1,655; average length of school year, in days, 180·18; graded schools, 361; evening schools, 26; estimated value of school property, $5,739,895.01; number of pupils enrolled, 125,794; number of pupils in private schools, 15,953; number of children in no school, 20,821; average wages of male teachers per month, $68.82; average wages of female teachers per month, $38.50. The total amount raised from all sources for support of the public schools in 1886–'87 was $1,793,369.19, and the expenditures were $1,768,371.06.

The State Normal School at New Britain is in a flourishing condition, having graduated in 1887 the largest class (62) in its history of thirty-five years. The total attendance at the school for the year was 292, or 26 larger than in any previous year. Additions and improvements in the school-building have recently been made out of a legislative appropriation in 1886.

In September, 1887, the first text-book ever published by the State was issued and distributed to the various schools. This was a small treatise, authorized by the Legislature of 1886, upon physiology and hygiene, especially with reference to the effect of alcoholic liquors on the human system.

Under the child-labor law of 1886, forbidding the employment of children under thirteen years of age in factories, etc., a total of 1,173 children had been discharged by employers up to September, 1887, but no perceptible increase of school attendance resulted therefrom. By an act of 1887, the authorities charged with enforcing the law were also given power to place in school any children found by them unlawfully employed.

Insurance.—Four new life-insurance companies were licensed in 1887 to do business in the State, and two ceased to exist. The six standard Connecticut companies increased their assets during the year by $2,769,263 and their liabilities, except capital, by $2,236,160. Four life associations conducted on the assessment plan had insurance of $63,402,500 in force Dec. 31, 1887, of which $13,160,250 was written during the year. They paid losses of $657,593. The single accident company, the Travelers', received $2,102,258 in premiums and paid $948,-760 for losses. Of the 113 companies engaged in fire insurance, ten stock and sixteen mutual companies are Connecticut corporations. The assets of these stock companies increased from $26,317.436 in 1886 to $26,989,632 in 1887, and the liabilities, including capital, scrip, and special funds from $18,574.374 to $19,621,398. The Connecticut stock companies now have a surplus of $18,318,324 as regards policy-holders and the mutual companies, $1,103,520.

Banks.—The number of savings-banks in the State at the beginning of the year was eighty-five, having assets valued at $107,896,912, and a surplus of $3,514,772. The deposits had increased during the year preceding by $4,765,-113.87, making a total amount of $102,189,-934.72. The number of depositors had increased 11,527, showing that the increase of deposits is not due to an accumulation of interest credited to depositors' accounts.

There were also eight State banks with assets of $4,563,914.74, total surplus, $512,109.92; and eight trust and loan companies with assets of $4,430,445.08, surplus, $295,414.81.

The number of national banks in the State at the beginning of the year was eighty-three, having an aggregate capital of $24,505,410. The surplus fund of these banks amounts to $6,908,034.74, and they hold as undivided profits $1,937,197.33. Their outstanding circulation, in common with all of the country, has suffered a reduction of several millions, the amount now being $8,698,693. They hold as individual deposits $24,478,665.09, and their total liabilities reach the sum of $70,295,835.20.

There have been but two failures among the national banks of the State, the first of which, the First National of Bethel, paid in full. The latest is the failure of the Stafford National, of Stafford Springs.

Since the origination of the national banking system, ninety-six banks have been organized in Connecticut, but thirteen have ceased to exist. During the year two national banks, representing a capital of $102,450, were closed, and two, representing a capital of $200,000, were organized. The circulation of the closed banks outstanding amounts to $50,169; and the circulation issued to the new beginners is $45,000.

Railroads.—In 1887, the railroad mileage of the State was increased by the construction of 11·6 miles of new road by the Meriden and Waterbury Company, making the total mileage in January of this year 1,159 miles. Upon the subject of abolishing grade-crossings, the Railroad Commissioners report that, during 1887, 41 petitions involving 70 crossings were presented to the board, all of them from the Consolidated Railroad. Over 60 hearings were given on these petitions, and orders made for the abrogation of 32 crossings on terms favorable to the respective towns interested. Thirty-seven petitions were pending at the end of the year, but the danger of a wholesale removal of grade-crossings, feared at one time during that year, has been averted by the conservative course of the board.

Militia.—The last report of the Adjutant-General shows the total strength of the militia, according to the last muster, to be 2,513 officers and men. The number of men in the State liable to military duty is 82,591.

Charities.—At the State Hospital for the Insane there were, on June 30, 568 male and 724 female patients; a total of 1,292. This is an increase of 146 patients in two years. Between June 30 and the end of the year there was an unusually large number of admissions, bringing the total nearly up to 1,400, the limit to the capacity of the hospital. The trustees report the institution to be in a highly satisfactory condition; they oppose any further additions to the buildings, as there are already as many patients as can be satisfactorily managed at one institution.

The Putnam Statue.—By a vote of the State Legislature in 1886, a commission was created and the sum of $10,000 appropriated for the purpose of erecting a suitable monument to Gen. Israel Putnam, of Revolutionary fame, who was a native of the State. Pursuant to this act, an equestrian statue was erected over the remains of Gen. Putnam at Brooklyn, a small town in Windham County, and on June 14 of this year, the unveiling and presentation ceremonies took place. Governor Lounsbury, in behalf of the State, accepted the memorial

from the commissioners, a commemorative address was made by Henry C. Robinson, of Hartford, and other appropriate exercises were held. The State thus rescues from neglect the resting place of one of its distinguished sons.

Political.—The Prohibition State Convention, held at Hartford on August 1, placed in nomination the following ticket: For Governor, Hiram Camp; Lieutenant-Governor, Nathan Babcock; Secretary of State, Theodore I. Pease; Treasurer, George W. Kies; Comptroller, Edward Manchester.

The usual declarations in favor of prohibition were adopted, together with the following:

That the Sabbath should be preserved and defended as a civil institution without oppressing any who religiously observe the same on any other day of the week.

That a uniform system of laws concerning marriage and divorce and social purity should be adopted.

That the immigration of paupers and convicts should be prohibited.

That the purity and freedom of suffrage should be provided for by the adoption of the so-called Australian system of voting by secret ballot, and that only citizens of the United States should be allowed to vote in any State.

The combinations of foreign syndicates or native capitalists to control the production and sale of necessary products or to monopolize great tracts of land should be forbidden.

On August 14 the Republicans met in convention at Hartford, and nominated the following candidates without a contest: For Governor, Morgan G. Bulkeley; Lieutenant-Governor, Samuel E. Merwin; Secretary of State, R. Jay Walsh; Treasurer, E. S. Henry; Comptroller, John B. Wright. The platform, omitting some unimportant features, is as follows:

We approve the declaration of principles contained in the platform of the Republican party, adopted at Chicago.

We are hostile to the theories of free trade and to the Democratic idea of a "tariff for revenue only."

We believe that the unexampled prosperity of this country and the elevated condition of our people are due chiefly to the policy of protection which has been adopted and continued by the Republican party, and we therefore favor such tariff laws as will in the future protect American labor and industries against the ruinous competition of the underpaid labor of foreign countries.

In this State the Republican party has put in operation the existing law restraining the sale of intoxicating liquors. That law recognizes our ancient theories of local self-government and places it in the power of every town to prohibit the sale of intoxicating liquors within its limits. We favor the principles of that law and pledge ourselves to such additional legislation as may from time to time be found necessary to suppress the evils of intemperance.

We favor such legislation as will provide for the compulsory secrecy of the ballot, and secure free suffrage and an honest counting of ballots throughout the country.

We recognize the services and sacrifices of the veteran soldiers and sailors of the republic and favor liberal pension legislation in their behalf.

The nominees of the Democratic State Convention held in New Haven on September 4, were: for Governor, Luzon B. Morris; Lieutenant-Governor, John S. Kirkham; Secretary of State, Henry A. Bishop; Treasurer, J. Griffin Martin; Comptroller, Nicholas Staub. The platform approves the national ticket and platform, the tariff-reform message of the President, the Mills Bill, and the fisheries treaty, as well as the administration of President Cleveland in general. Upon State questions it says:

The Democratic party again renews its demand for that privilege to which every voter is entitled, the secret ballot. Freemen will not readily accept the recent promise of the party that has in the Legislature repeatedly set aside their hopes, and defeated this important measure of protection against intimidation.

We emphatically protest against the policy of extending to partisan boards, for party purposes, the authority to issue and control liquor-licenses. These boards, in justice to the people, should be non-partisan—not, as now, mere political machines used for the success of the Republican party. Too frequently the test of an applicant's fitness for license is measured by the benefit to be derived by the party which controls the boards.

A fair choice of the voters of Connecticut expressed through the ballot-boxes, in the election of State officers, should be respected in Connecticut as it is in thirty-four States of this Union. Our Constitution should be reformed and admit of an election of Governor and other State officers by a plurality of votes, as presidential electors are chosen in every State, so that a candidate lacking more than 9,000 votes of a majority, and more than 1,800 votes of the number received by his opponent, may not be treated as duly elected, and inaugurated.

There was also a Labor ticket in the field, headed by A. F. Andrews. At the November election Morris (Democrat), received 75,074 votes for Governor; Bulkeley (Republican), 73,659; Camp (Prohibition), 4,631; and Andrews (Labor), 273 votes. Although the Democratic ticket received a plurality of 11,415 votes, it did not obtain a majority over all, which is necessary under the State Constitution for an election. The decision is therefore thrown upon the next Legislature, whose members were chosen at the same November election. This legislature will consist of 17 Republicans and 7 Democrats in the Senate, and 152 Republicans and 96 Democrats in the House, with 1 Independent. The Republican ticket will therefore be chosen. The vote for President was as follows: Harrison, 74,584; Cleveland, 74,920; Fisk, 4,234; Labor ticket, 240. The Congressional delegation stands 3 Republicans to one Democrat, against 3 Democrats and one Republican in the last Congress.

CO-OPERATION. Each country has its special form of co-operative effort. In Germany it is the credit-unions, sometimes called the peoples' banks. These societies numbered 1,910 in 1883, and, in connection with nearly as many more co-operative societies of various kinds, had 1,200,000 members, with $50,000,000 share capital and $122,500,000 borrowed capital, and did a yearly business of $500,000,000. The credit-unions resemble joint-stock companies, having among others the important additional features that the stock may be paid for in small regular payments, that every stockholder is liable for the entire debts of the bank as in a simple partnership, and that the money gathered from the stock and from funds borrowed by the unions is loaned to their members at 6 to 10 per cent. interest. This not only encourages saving, but enables a poor but bright mechanic to obtain at reasonable interest money with which to begin business. These credit-unions, which were founded by Dr. Schulze, of Delitzsch, Saxony, in 1850, have also grown to large proportions in Austria, 1,129 such unions, or 74 5 per cent. of all the co-operative societies of that country in 1881 being of this nature.

In France, although many distributive societies are reported, and in Paris over seventy workingmen's co-operative societies are engaged in production, mostly on a small scale, the greatest success has been in profit-sharing, wherein the proprietors of a large manufactory, shop, railroad, or insurance company, give their employés, in addition to wages at market prices, a percentage of the net profits. Only a few of those that have tried it have abandoned the plan, which arouses the workman's zeal and increases his efficiency in such a degree as to restore to the managers, it is believed, a full equivalent for the dividend. Of the 98 firms in Europe, since grown to 104, which in 1883 thus shared profits with their help, 49 were in France, 18 in Germany, 12 in Switzerland, and 8 in England. Twenty-three had begun prior to 1870, and 33 more prior to 1880.

In England the greatest success has been in distributive co-operation or store-keeping on the so-called Rochdale plan, to be briefly described below, which was brought to public notice by the Rochdale pioneers in 1844. At the end of 1887 there were in England and Scotland 1,348 such retail co-operative stores, with 858,237 members, £8,461,888 share capital, £968,175 loan capital, sales in 1887 of £22,343,651, and a net profit of £2,940,337. There were also 15 supply associations, selling at little above cost, with 63,841 members, £642,360 share and loan capital, and a trade of £2,754,264. There were also an English and a Scotch wholesale society, with a share and loan capital of £1,120,874 and sales of £7,274,494 to the retail societies. The 1,432 co-operative societies of all kinds in Great Britain reported at the last Co-operative Congress in 1888 had a membership in 1887 of 945,619, a share capital of £10,012,048, sales of £34,189,715, and profits of £3,193,178. The growth has been steady for a long time. To the surprise of all, 721 of 1,255 societies in Great Britain reporting in 1887 gave credit.

At the twentieth annual Co-operative Congress in England in 1888, 67 productive societies were also reported, with 22,480 members, £651,369 shares, and £207,718 loan capital, a business of £1,574,145, and net profits of £59,500. There are no returns of the methods of dividing profits, but this defect will be remedied this year. It is known that most of the societies give no share of their profits to non-stockholding workmen; but the demand on the part of co-operators is rapidly growing. Of the 77 productive societies that had been in business or were just beginning in England, Wales, and Scotland at the close of 1887, 17 were in cotton, linen, silk, and wool, 12 in leather, 10 in metal, 9 in flour, 6 in farming, 4 in printing, and 19 in as many different kinds of manufacturing.

If the announced aims of the leaders of co-operation in England are realized in any such degree in the next twenty-five years as they have been in the past twenty-five, we may look for a great growth of that for which previous success has prepared the way, namely, co-operative production, wherein labor shall share in the profits of manufacturing, and, through the organization of consumers already secured to the extent of over 800,000 families, shall be able to deal a serious blow at the sweating system and other devices of those employers who, in the rage to produce more cheaply than their rivals, offer their employés ruinously low wages or unhealthful conditions of employment.

The great success in the United States has been in building and loan associations, which are as distinctively American as the credit-unions are German. Still, there are some successful and now rapidly growing stores, and these as the simplest and historically the earliest form of co-operation in this country may be first considered.

Distributive Co-operation.—The co-operative store, and much later the factory, were introduced and fostered for a long period by organizations of workingmen. Most of these organizations have given place to others having different objects, until to-day nearly all successful co-operative enterprises are carried on independently of any organization and even of each other. The first attempts at co-operation between 1847 and 1859 were made in New England by the New England Protective Union. Nearly all failed after a time, from lack of the co-operative spirit and from ignorance of the best methods. In trying to sell for cost, as did these union stores, the average manager is usually confronted with a deficit at the end of each year because of unexpected but inevitable depreciation of goods and from other losses. The bitter rivalry of private stores is also aroused. The latter will sell some staple article even below cost, and, by widely advertising this particular article, will draw off the trade of unthinking men from the co-operative store, which may, on the whole, be selling cheaper.

The next attempt at co-operation was made by the Patrons of Husbandry, known also as Grangers, and in the South recently as "The Wheel." (See "Annual Cyclopædia" for 1886, page 42.) This is often associated exclusively with the celebrated granger legislation against the abuses of the railroads, but in reality it has accomplished a great deal for its members in education upon practical farm topics and in many other ways, not the least of which has been the result of its co-operative features. These features have been in part represented by purchasing agencies, which bought machinery, groceries, and dry goods for the farmers or sold their products in the large cities on orders from the local unions. Still more important and common has been the concentration of all the trade of the members of a local grange or even of a State grange on a strictly cash basis at such wholesale dealers and manufacturers as would sell at the lowest prices all things needed on the farm and in the home. In hundreds of cases, too, grange stores have been established on the faulty plan just described of the old union stores—that is, selling at or near cost. Some of these stores continue prosperous, as at Torrington and Lebanon, Conn., but most have failed from the same ignorance of approved methods, from inability to find managers who possessed the knowledge lacking in the members, and from the same absence of the co-operative spirit which caused the downfall of the union stores. Yet, aside from the great educational value even of failure, these grange stores, as well as the methods of concentrating trade upon establishments that would give special discounts, have been a great help to the farmer in forcing down in private stores the general level of prices, which in the seventies were often exorbitantly high.

To the now extinct order of the Sovereigns of Industry belongs the credit of having propagated extensively in this country the best methods of distributive co-operation embodied in the Rochdale plan. The essential superiority of this plan over others lies in its provision that goods shall be sold at regular retail prices, and any profits above what is sufficient for a reserve fund and interest on capital are paid to customers annually or semi-annually, in proportion to their trade for the period, though stockholders may receive a larger per cent. of dividend on their trade than outsiders. The other provisions, such as shares of small value, limitation of the number that one can hold, and the allowance of but one vote to a stockholder independent of his shares, are common to other systems. This is the plan on which most of the English and permanently successful American stores have been managed since it was introduced in England by the Rochdale Pioneers in 1844, and brought to general attention in this country thirty years later by the Sovereigns of Industry.

The latter organization, founded by William H. Earle, of Worcester, Mass., in 1874, devoted most of its strength during its six years' life to the spread of distributive co-operation. For two years paid lecturers, well acquainted with the most approved methods of co-operation, were kept in the field to organize local councils and help them to establish stores in the right way. In 1875 the 310 councils reporting at the annual meeting of the order returned a membership of 27,984. Of these the majority went no further than to obtain discounts at private stores, and many stopped with merely the educational features; but in 1877, 94 councils, having a membership of 7,273, reported an average capital in their stores of $884, and a total business of $1,089,372, at an average saving to the members of 14 per cent., or an aggregate profit of $152,512, equal to a saving of $21 to every man and woman belonging to those councils. But the organization had its birth at the worst time for success in the past twenty-five years. It was during the prolonged financial depression following 1873, when thousands who had joined the order could not get work and felt obliged to resort to private stores that would trust. Then, too, the growth had been too rapid to permit of wise management; the knowledge of English methods was too little diffused at the start, and especially were there too few possessed of actual experience in the Rochdale stores who could be made managers of the new enterprises. Fortunately, all these difficulties time and education may remove, in fact are already removing, as appears from the considerable number of successful stores to be found in New England, New Jersey, Kansas, Texas, and in a less degree in some other sections and States. Several of the largest of existing stores are survivals of the Sovereign enterprises.

In 1866 there were 53 co-operative stores in New England, with an aggregate trade of $2,000,000 and a capital of about $210,000. In Texas there were 155 co-operative stores, all connected with a central association con-

amounted to $296,576.12 in merchandise and 8,757 bales of cotton, an increase of over $100,000 during the year. Ten-per-cent. dividends were paid on stock, and the remaining two thirds of the $16,320.33 were in part placed in the contingent fund and in part divided among the 602 association and individual stockholders. The entire number of stockholders of the central and subordinate associations exceeds 6,000.

Next in size is the Johnson County Co-operative Association, of Olathe, Kansas, which has been in business since July, 1876, on the Rochdale plan of dividends on trade. Its sales in 1887 amounted to $245,000 and its capital to $66,000, if the surplus of $16,000 be included.

The Philadelphia Industrial Co-operative Association, began in 1874 on the Rochdale plan, reported a trade in 1886 of $171,278.04, divided as follows: Groceries, $123,636.16; meat, $19,772.11; dry goods, $8,908.33; boots and shoes, $13,499.94; coal, $5,461.50; total, $171,278.04. The capital, in the hands of 2,355 members, and invested in a central and three branch stores, amounted to $40,000.

At Allegan, Mich., is a co-operative store with $30,000 capital and a trade in 1887 of $165,384.09, which sells everything at 4 per cent. above total cost, and keeps down expenses to 4.1 per cent. of the trade. This is the best showing made by any co-operative store as far as known in the United States.

Among the other large and vigorously growing co-operative stores of the country should be mentioned the ten next in size to the four already considered. For convenience, the entire fourteen are included in this table:

No.	NAME.	Location.	Trade in 1887.	Capital.
1..	Texas Co-operative Association	Galveston, Tex.	Over $600,000	$63,585
2..	Johnson County Co-operative Association	Olathe, Kan.	245,000	66,000
3..	Philadelphia Industrial Co-operative Association	Philadelphia, Pa	171,278*	40,000
4..	Allegan Co-operative Association	Allegan, Mich	165,384	30,000
5..	Beverly Co-operative Association	Beverly, Mass.	124,901*	7,000
6..	Trenton Co-operative Society	Trenton, N. J	98,000	9,819
7..	Arlington Co-operative Association	Lawrence, Mass	97,909	19,190
8..	Sovereigns Trading Company	New Britain, Conn	90,000	17,500
9..	Sovereigns Co-operative Association	Webster, Mass	76,500	5,000
10..	Industrial Co-operative Association	New Bedford, Mass	74,000	13,013
11..	Riverside Co-operative Association	Maynard, Mass	62,684	19,532
12..	Hammonton Fruit-Growers' Union	Hammonton, N. J	60,044	17,121
13..	Progressive Co-operative Association	Worcester, Mass	41,897	4,981
14..	New Brunswick Co-operative Society	New Brunswick, N. J	26,487	8,223

All but Nos. 1, 4, 5, and 12 are on the Rochdale plan.
* In 1886.

ducted by the Patrons of Husbandry; the total capital of these stores in 1885 was returned at $744,500, and the trade was $1,977,579.90. The central association, called the Texas Co-operative Association Patrons of Husbandry, whose headquarters are at Galveston, reported at the tenth annual meeting, in July, 1888, a capital of $63,835, owned by 226 co-operative associations and 376 individuals, in all parts of the State. Each branch association trades and divides the profits on its own account. The trade of this central association

In order to determine the growth of co-operation in 1887 over that in 1886, when full returns from most of our co-operative enterprises were secured, circular letters were sent to the largest of these. Only two (and those were small enterprises) are known to have failed—namely, an old store at Seneca Falls, N. Y., which committed the fatal mistake of selling on trust, and a new, poorly managed enterprise in Buffalo, N. Y. These failures are more than offset by the rapidly growing trade of several new stores, one of which—the Phillipsburg

Co-operative Store No. 1, of Phillipsburg, N. J.—reported a trade of $32,983 in 1887. Of the twenty stores, including twelve of the fourteen given in the table above, which made complete returns, only five reported a decrease in trade. Excluding the large Texas store, lest its size and success overbalance the rest, the business of the other nineteen amounted to $1,290,550, being an increase in one year of 24 per cent. If we include the Texas stores, the remaining thirty-nine in New England—which did business amounting to more than $1,000,000 in 1886—and the twenty to·thirty other successful stores in the country, we may safely estimate the entire distributive co-operation in the United States in 1887 at between $5,000,000 and $6,000,000. This is not a large sum in comparison with the figures in Great Britain; but, if the present rate of growth of 24 per cent. a year continues, co-operative distribution will soon assume an important position in our industrial life.

It is the common opinion that the price of goods to the consumer is raised by the retailer from 30 to 100 per cent. over the wholesale price. This is completely disproved, as far as co-operative stores are concerned (and other stores rarely charge over 5 to 10 per cent. more), by statistics, gathered by the writer, of ten large and successful co-operative stores, of which five are in Massachusetts, two in New Jersey, two in Pennsylvania, and one in New York. In these ten stores, which sold groceries and in some cases meat, and in 1886 did a business of $420,494.20, the retail price was only 17·27 per cent. above the wholesale. The expenses for wages, rent, teams, freight from the wholesaler, depreciation of stock, insurance, ice, water-rent, taxes, stationery, and all other incidental running expenses, exclusive of interest on capital, amounted to 12·74 per cent. of the cost price, or nearly three fourths of the entire increase in price. Interest at 5 per cent. on the capital employed, which was returned as $66,242 actually paid in, aside from surplus, would be $3,312.10; this is almost 1 per cent. of the wholesale price, leaving only an average of 3·6 per cent. on the wholesaler's price that can be credited to profits, and which admitted in these stores of an average dividend of not quite 4·5 per cent. on the retail price.

The greatest cause of disaster in most co-operative stores that fail, next to trusting, lies in a high ratio of expense to trade. In eleven successful co-operative stores especially studied with regard to this point, the average percentage of running expenses to trade was only 7·7, and in no case did it reach 10. Few stores can succeed whose running expenses are allowed to equal 10 per cent. of the trade. Lavish expenditure for rent, teams, numerous employés, and a "stylish" appearance, wrecks many a co-operative enterprise. The idea of co-operation is substance rather than shadow—the best and purest goods—not display. One of the greatest savings of co-operation comes from the fact that costly plate-glass show-windows, location on a main street, employés enough to be able to wait at once on all customers in the busiest hours of the day, and teams to carry home every small article, are not necessary to attract custom. If such be necessary, the first steps in co-operation have not yet been taken. A good, clean, wholesome store, in a convenient location, and one or two teams to deliver heavy goods, are, of course, requisite. But where a market is already secured among those banded together in a co-operative experiment, the need of the expensive means of advertising just referred to should no longer be felt. The very essence of co-operative distribution is the dispensing with the wastes of competitive business.

Productive Co-operation.—This is the ideal of all thinking co-operators, and the goal toward which their efforts are directed. But few steps toward it have been taken. The idea of its advocates is that the workmen in our manufacturing establishments should save money enough to establish factories of their own; should have the requisite knowledge of human nature to select able foremen and superintendents; and sufficient moral fiber to co-operate cheerfully and submit to the rigid discipline necessary in a successful manufacturing enterprise. The first requisite, capital, is more easily secured through the issue of stock in shares of $5 to $25 each than are the other conditions. But the few marked successes chronicled below indicate that the prospects of success are not as chimerical as has been supposed, and that, especially in enterprises like the making of barrels, boots and shoes, hats, watch-cases, and iron castings, where the zeal and efficiency of the workman count for more relatively to the capital and service of the manager than in other kinds of manufacturing, a considerable growth of co-operation may fairly be expected within the next twenty years. Through ignorance of men and methods, and lack of the moral qualities necessary to prevent all serious jealousies and dissensions, the vast majority of wage-earners are at present unfitted for productive co-operation.

The greatest success in this country is that of the co-operative coopers of Minneapolis. The oldest of the eight co-operative shops of that city, known as the Co-operative Barrel Manufacturing Company, was begun in 1874, and now has assets of $45,000, owned in equal amounts, as the constitution requires, by each of its ninety stockholders. Only one who is a journeyman cooper, and known to be of good moral character, can become a stockholder. If he is unable to pay the full value of a share at once, an assessment of from $3 to $5 is paid from his weekly wages, when the shop is running full time. Five per cent. interest is given on stock. The men work by the piece, and divide among themselves, according to their work, all the ordinary gains or losses of the business. But gains or losses coming from fire, from non-paying creditors, from changes in the value of real estate held, from the work of hired help, or from outside ventures undertaken by the association, are apportioned according to the stock—that is, equally among all the members.

These eight companies, employing about two thirds of the 600 coopers in Minneapolis, are all organized on the same basis, and have been uniformly successful, having a steady local demand for their products from the largest flouring-mills in the world, and, excepting one defalcation of a few hundred dollars, have lost nothing of the several million dollars that during the past fourteen years have passed through the hands of their more than fifty treasurers. Owing to less need of expensive foremen, merely to see that they attend to their work, and owing further to their readiness, when forced by competition, to work on half-wages rather than stop, these coopers are recognized as able to undersell any private shops in the city; but the latter are sustained by some of the millers to guard against any possible combination to raise prices among the co-operative companies. The effects of this form of organization upon the morality and thrift of the men are extraordinary. Most of the coopers are now strictly temperate, and they are worth, in a large majority of cases, from $2,000 to $4,000 each. The average wealth of the 90 members of the oldest company is at least $3,500. There is also a successful co-operative cooper-shop at Dundas, Minn., and one at Milwaukee. In the latter city is a flourishing co-operative association of plumbers which is increasing its capital in 1888 to $50,000. In 1886, the date of the latest full returns at hand, the business amounted to over $70,000, and included three fourths of all the journeyman-plumbers in the city. By dispensing with most of the foremen, these co-operators save nearly one third in the cost of plumbing. Profits have been largely divided on the basis of wages, but a part has gone to increase the capital. In 1886, the plumbers of New York city tried to organize co-operatively, and, according to one of their leaders, who has fallen heir to the business they were fast building up, they would have attained as great success as in Milwaukee, if they had only had the patience to wait a little longer and to work in harmony. At Lynn, Mass., is a co-operative shoe-factory, the Lynn Knights of Labor Co-operative Boot and Shoe Company, established in 1886, which is doing a successful and rapidly growing business with a capital of $8,000. After paying 5 per cent. interest on capital, and devoting 10 per cent. of the profits to a sinking fund, and as much more to a co-operative fund to assist other co-operative enterprises, the remaining profits are divided equally between capital and labor. Each workman gets his share of the labor dividend, in proportion to his wages.

Most of the other co-operative manufacturing companies, give no dividends to labor as such, but the stock is in many hands, and the stockholder has but one vote. The following are the most successful, and from their history of five to twenty-one years, give evidence of reasonable stability: Stoneham Co-operative Shoe Company, Stoneham, Mass.; Wakefield Co-operative Shoe Company, Wakefield, Mass.; Kingston Co-operative Foundry Company, Kingston, Mass.; Leonard Co-operative Foundry Company, Taunton, Mass.; Somerset Co-operative Foundry Company, Somerset, Mass.; East Templeton Co-operative Chair Company, East Templeton, Mass. These six companies, with a capital of $125,000, do a business of about $500,000. Outside of Eastern Massachusetts the most successful are the Solidarity Watch Case Company, in Hope Street, Brooklyn, with 110 employés and $67,000 capital, in 1887; the Fulton County Co-operative Leather, Glove, and Mitten Manufacturing Association, of Johnstown, N. Y.; the Co-operative Collar and Cuff Company, of Troy, N. Y., with a capital of $15,000, and business of nearly $40,000, in 1888; and the St. Louis Furniture-Workers' Association. The sales of this latter in 1887—nine years after beginning business—were $116,520, and the wages paid, mostly to stockholders, were $43,421.

Co-operative Building and Loan Associations.—By far the most important and successful form of co-operation in the United States is that of the Co-operative Building and Loan Association, sometimes called merely building association, or, as in Massachusetts, the co-operative bank. Beginning about fifty years ago in Philadelphia, and attaining to strength there in the decade of 1850–1860, they have been spreading rapidly since 1875 in Pennsylvania, New Jersey, Massachusetts, Western New York, Ohio, Illinois, Minnesota, and many other Western States, and are now reaching into the South. The capital of the co-operative bank is limited to $1,000,000, in shares whose full value is $200 each. The shares are not paid for at once, or within a short time of beginning business, as is usual with corporations, but are paid at the rate of one dollar a month, a new series of shares being issued semi-annually and annually. This would require two hundred months, or sixteen years and two thirds for the payment of a share, but for another feature of the system. The money accruing to the treasury from these monthly payments, and from all other sources, is loaned every month to such of the shareholders as offer the highest premium. The profits from these loans and premiums furnish the dividends, which usually amount to between six and seven per cent. Every one can borrow for aid in building or buying a home, to the amount of the par value of his share, but no more. As security he must offer his shares and such other property as may appear to the directors sufficient. They will lend nearly up to the full market value of such security, while the savings-banks are only allowed to lend to the extent of 60 per cent. of the assessed value of the real-estate security. It may be asked how a poor man who has not real estate can borrow, even of a co-operative bank? The answer is, if he wishes to buy an estate he can borrow of the bank the greater part of the needed purchase money, and give as security therefor a mortgage of the property at the time he receives his deed therefor. Of course the bank can not furnish the whole amount of the purchase-money. But if one has a very little money and will subscribe to, say five shares, he can borrow $1,000. A man can thus build a house, mortgaging it as security to the co-operative bank. The would-be borrowers, as has been said, bid for the privilege. Premiums range from five to fifty cents a share, but rarely over twenty-five cents for any length of time. The by-laws of the co-operative banks usually require the successful bidder for a loan to pay one month's interest and premium immediately. If a loan is not approved, a month's interest and premium are forfeited. Successful bidders can always obtain shares for their loan. If one borrow $2,000 at fifteen cents premium a share (the average amount now prevailing in Massachusetts), he is subject to three monthly charges: First, a payment of ten dollars on his ten shares, which he had first to take before borrowing; second, a payment of one dollar and a half as a premium; and, third, a payment for interest, which, on $2,000, at 6 per cent. (the usual rate), is $10. In all, then, he pays $21.50 a month, until his shares mature in about eleven years, when the bank will hold his note for $2,000, and he will hold shares worth $2,000. The two accounts are canceled, and thus for a little more than the expense of rent in the mean time a man finds himself owner of a comfortable home.

Any one with sufficient security—which, as it observed, most workmen have not—might borrow the $2,000 of a savings-bank, pay 6 per cent. interest, the usual charge on such loans, or $1,320 during the eleven years, and then pay the debt, making $3,320. The same sum borrowed of a co-operative bank will involve a payment during the one hundred and thirty-two months, at $21.50 a month, of $2,835, besides the loss of, perhaps, $400 more in compound interest to the close of the eleven years on these payments. Two things are to be said: First, it is not always necessary in Massachusetts, where money is more plenty than in the West, for one to pay a fifteen cent premium for a very long time. Whenever the borrower finds it possible to bid off $2,000 for a lower premium, say five cents, he may do so, and with this loan pay off his other, borrowed at a higher rate, for one can repay his loan at any time, retaining his shares or not, as he chooses. The only charges are, that the borrower must pay double interest and premium for one month, and have a new mortgage made and the old one discharged. In some States, and occasionally in Massachusetts, the loans are bid off at so high a premium that the actual payments, reckoning compound interest on them, are more than would be necessary if the money were borrowed from an ordinary savings-bank. But it may still be said that, human nature being as it is, scarcely one man in a thousand will make provision by constant voluntary monthly deposits in a savings-bank to repay his $2,000 mortgage at the end of the eleven years. This is the real justification for the existence of the co-operative banks. Their shareholders feel compelled to make their regular monthly payments. Before the man is aware of it, he has paid for his home and acquired the valuable habit of saving. The results are in every sense satisfactory, six to seven per cent. dividends being generally made. Again, these banks enable the depositors, who are in most cases wage-earners, to use their own deposits, whereas the money deposited in the savings-banks in Massachusetts—$300,000,-000 in 1886—supplies the capital of the great employers of industry, and thus does not so directly promote the co-operative ideal — a larger share by the workmen in the profits of industry. In addition to nearly all the advantages of the justly famous postal savings-banks of Europe, the co-operative banks give much higher interest and keep the deposits for actual use among the lenders of the immediate neighborhood. By the Massachusetts law at least twenty-five persons must be associated together for organizing such a corporation, and no person can hold more than twenty-five shares, of the ultimate value of $200 each, in one corporation. No member can have more than one vote. A member may at any time, on thirty days' notice, withdraw any shares not pledged as security for loans, after paying any fines that may be due. By so doing he loses such portion of the profits as was previously credited to the share, and must bear such a proportion of any unadjusted loss as the by-laws may determine.

In most of the older building associations in the Middle and Western States the premiums are not paid monthly, but are deducted in a lump sum from the face of the loan to the borrower. For example, if a man, in order to borrow $1,000, offers ten per cent. premium, instead of receiving the $1,000 and paying monthly ten per cent. in addition to the monthly payments of one dollar a share, he will in many banks receive $900, but must take five $200 shares as security on which five dollars a month and interest on the $900 are paid. The Massachusetts plan, often called the installment plan, is now being adopted with increasing frequency by the new companies, and is simpler, and, many claim, more just to the borrower. Money is worth more and premiums much higher in Chicago and St. Paul than in Boston. Indeed, they seem unreasonably high, bringing in from fifteen to twenty per cent. profit to the depositors.

In the fifty-one co-operative banks of Massachusetts in 1887, the assets were $4,211,948 to the credit of 20,755 depositors, and 3,797 persons representing nearly 20,000 souls had borrowed this sum for aid in erecting homes. The growth has been over twenty per cent. almost from the opening of the first co-operative bank in that State in 1877. Premiums are low in Massachusetts, but the returns to depositors average fully six per cent. The first series of the first bank matured in 1888, after just eleven years. The payment of $132 in monthly installments of one dollar thus enabled depositors to draw out at the end of the time an increase equal to five per cent. (of the entire $132) from the beginning. In October, 1886, there were 37.730 depositors and 8,562 borrowers in the 151 building associations of New Jersey, the assets of which were $9,300,705. In Hamilton County, Ohio, in which Cincinnati is situated, there were in 1888 340 associations with 60,000 shareholders and $15,000,000 assets. The weekly deposit was $167,000, and three fourths of all the mortgages recorded in the county are through these building associations. In 1886 there were eight of these associations in Minneapolis and forty in St. Paul. All were successful, and in fact not a single failure in the past five years has come to my notice, though a few must have occurred; the percentage of success is certainly higher than in most forms of private business. In Buffalo, N. Y., great good has been done by these wonderful promoters of thrift, and hundreds are the homes that the wage-earners of that city have obtained by their means. This might be said of hundreds of other cities and towns in this country.

But the greatest results are naturally to be found in Pennsylvania, and especially in Philadelphia, the birth place of the movement. In 1886 there were over 90,000 shareholders and 15,000 borrowers of the 400 building associations in Philadelphia. The assets of 120 were nearly $8,749,339.17. It is safe to say that in the more than 1,200 co-operative building associations of the State there are over $50,000,000 assets owned by nearly a quarter of a million depositors, and borrowed by over 40,000 families representing 200,000 persons, who are thus enabled to build and pay for homes which, without these invaluable banks, they would have been forced to rent.

Only one thing seems needed to secure their safe as well as rapid growth. The Massachusetts legislation, which carefully provides against recognized dangers in management and which requires full reports, as in the case of the no more complicated or important savings-banks, should be every where adopted; although a few minor changes would be needed to provide for those associations already doing business on systems different from that prescribed in Massachusetts. All new associations might be required to conform to the Massachusetts plan. Reports to the bank commissioners of each State should be required for subsequent publication. If this be done, the future of this peculiarly American form of co-operation will

be secured. But if such legislation is not speedily had in some States the collapse of many associations will surely follow, and work great hardship to thousands.

Co-operation is so useful in diffusing a knowledge of business methods, in giving the discontented masses an insight into the difficulties that capitalists as well as laborers must endure, and, finally, when successful, in elevating the condition of all participants, that the present needless obstacle of defective legislation in the way of successful co-operation should be speedily removed. Only Massachusetts has as yet made much progress in this direction, and she has not gone far enough. As in savings-banks and building associations, the State should prescribe methods of procedure.

Bibliography.—See Annual Reports of the British Co-operative Congresses, and the English Parliamentary Report in 1886, on Co-operation in Europe; Report for 1886 of the Massachusetts Bureau of Labor Statistics; the "Westminster Review" for October, 1885; "Workingmen Co-operators," by Acland and Jones; "History of Co-operation," by Holyoake; "Co-operation in the United States," edited by Profs. H. B. Adams and R. T. Ely, of Baltimore, and written in 1886 and 1887 by five graduates of the Johns Hopkins University, who divided the field among them; and the Massachusetts Labor Bureau Report for 1886 and the New Jersey Reports for 1886 and 1887.

CORDAGE. Twisted fibers of any material, when less than one inch in circumference, are known as cords, twines, threads, strings, yarns, lines, and the like. When several of these are twisted or laid together, forming a line more than one inch in circumference, it is called a rope. In the trade and with sailors, the size of a rope is always designated by the measure of its circumference; with landsmen and non-experts, it is designated by the diameter. It is easier and more accurate to measure the circumference than to measure the diameter, owing to the depressions between the strands; hence the former method is preferable, and in this article, when the size of a rope is mentioned, it will be understood that the circumference is meant. In modern practice, vegetable fiber, iron or steel wire, and, to a limited extent, animal fibers are used in the manufacture of rope. In commercial parlance, many substances are called "hemp" which are not really the product of that plant. Thus "manila hemp" is from a species of banana. Sisal hemp is from the leaves of the Central American agave, etc. The following list describes many of these substances in detail, but the word hemp must be taken in a commercial sense, as usage has in many cases decreed its application to fibers that merely resemble those of the true hemp.

Coir is the outer fibrous covering of the cocoa-nut. It is less used for cordage than formerly when rope cables were more commonly employed, but its lightness gives it certain advantages over hemp and manila. A rope made from this material will float almost like cork, and when used as a cable ascends in a rising curve from the anchor to the surface of the water, instead of forming a dependent or sinking curve, as is the case with less buoyant material. Fresh water rots it, but salt water appears to have a preservative effect. It is still largely used by native sailors in the Indian Ocean. In preparing it for manufacture, the husks are soaked for some time in water and then beaten to separate the fibers from the dust with which they are surrounded.

Cotton is much used for the smaller ropes, rarely larger than three or four inches in circumference. It is comparatively weak, and retains moisture to an extent that renders it liable to rot. But it is easy to handle, is much used under cover, and to some extent on ship-board when not likely to be subjected to severe strains.

Hemp (*Cannabis sativa*) of the common commercial variety may be regarded as the rope-maker's staple. Asia is the native habitat of the plant, but it is now extensively cultivated all over Europe, and to a considerable extent in America. The plant usually matures at a height of eight or ten feet, but has been known to grow as high as seventeen feet. The stems are dried, beaten, and crushed in a hemp-mill, and then subjected to fermentation in water or moisture, and afterward beaten with mallets or passed through a machine called a "break." The fibers are separated from the bark and other waste substances, and are then hackled or combed into hanks or skeins, and packed in bundles of about 200 pounds each, for shipment. Good hemp-fiber is yellowish-green, smooth, glossy, and without odor. Russian and Italian hemp are considered the best for the general purposes of rope-making. American hemp is dark-gray, and, while strong, will not stand the weather so well as the European varieties.

Hair is readily made into ropes by the ordinary processes of manufacture. It is used to some extent for lariats or tether ropes, and for various parts of harnesses and bridles, usually in sparsely settled or uncivilized countries.

Jute is prepared from the fibers of *corchorus olitorus* and *corchorus capsularus*. The cordage is very inferior in quality, and is only used when strength and durability are of no account. The main use of the fiber is in coarse textile fabrics, such as bagging, and floor-cloths.

Leather or Hide.—The hide is cut into strips when green, and laid up by hand or by machinery into small rope. It is used sparingly on board ship, where its toughness enables it to stand friction better than hemp, but it is only about one third as strong. It is also used for lariats or lassos.

Manila (*Musa textilis*) is chiefly grown in the Phillipine Islands, and derives its commercial name from the capital town. It is often called "Manila hemp," but is, in reality, derived from the stalk of a species of banana. Rope made from this substance is more buoyant than common hemp; is more pliable, causes less friction, and endures moisture better. Its strength, when new, is about equal to that of hemp. It is very extensively used by American rope-makers, and has largely taken the place of common hemp for maritime purposes.

Moss.—The long moss that grows on trees in the Southern United States is often made up into coarse rope for various uses, mainly in sparsely settled regions, where it is difficult or impossible to procure the commercial article. It is, of course, merely a make-shift, as it possesses neither strength nor durability.

Phormium Hemp is derived from the leaves of the *Phormium tenax* of New Zealand, a plant allied to the lily family. The leaves grow to a length of nine feet in their native habitat. When the fibers are carefully selected, the product is second only to manila for beauty and strength. During the civil war in America it came largely into use, mainly as an adulterant of manila, and the inferior quality of cordage thus produced is said to have brought the material into discredit.

Silk has, at times, been made into ropes of great beauty and strength, but their cost is so great that they are merely articles of curiosity or luxury.

Sisal, also called "sisal hemp," is the fiber of a plant closely allied to the American aloe or century-plant. The commercial name refers rather to the product than to the plant that yields it. The fibers of the various agaves are extracted from the thick leaves by pounding. They are most familiar in the "grass" hammocks commonly sold in the shops.

Sunn Hemp (*Crotolaria juncea*), known also as Bengal hemp. It is grown in many different provinces of Hindustan and in the Sunda Islands. The best comes from Comercolly, and is very strong, white, and durable. It is the product of a papilionaceous plant allied to the pea family.

The whole art of cordage-making rests upon the mechanical principle that causes two or more single hair-like fibers, when twisted and laid side by side, to wind around each other on being released. The familiar device of twisting a piece of cord, doubling it upon itself, and then allowing the two parallel parts to relieve their unnatural torsion by twisting

FIG. 1.—AN EGYPTIAN ROPE-WALK, 1500 B. C.

around each other, exhibits the fundamental principle of the rope-maker's art. Long experiment has established to a nicety the exact degree of torsion necessary to secure the best results with the different fibers in use. If the fibers or any of them are twisted too much, the finished rope is weakened, and has a tendency to kink; if too little twist is given, the rope is "dead," and the fibers do not properly combine their strength.

Fig. 1 is copied from a tomb at Thebes, of the time of Thothmes III, the Pharoah of the Exodus. It represents the interior of a rope-maker's shop, and cleverly indicates the material used (leather) by showing the hide of an animal, presumably a goat, and two coils of thongs cut from the hide and ready for laying up into rope. The Egyptian rope-makers worked in couples. One sat on a stool and payed out the yarns, while the other, with a belt about his waist, walked backward, twisting as he went, and regulated the tension by his weight. The yarns were made fast to a swivel-hook, which in turn was attached to the belt, and a weighted lever or twister enabled him to apply the necessary force of torsion. Hemp, papyrus-fiber, palm-fiber, and hair were also used by the Egyptians and by other nations of antiquity in rope-making.

The initial factor in modern rope-making, shown in Fig. 2, is known as the "rope-maker's

winch." Such machines are often carried on shipboard. With an ordinary winch, about fifteen inches in diameter, it is possible to make good two-inch rope. A is the plan of the cogged wheels, B is a "loper," or swivel-hook, to which the farther ends of the yarns are attached. C is the winch complete and in service, and D is the "top"—a conical piece of hard wood scored at the sides, so that it can be grasped by the hand without checking the passage of the strands. Four hooks are provided, so that either three-stranded or four-stranded rope can be made, and the central hook is used upon occasion for giving an extra twist to large rope —"hardening it up," as the sailor's phrase goes, a service for which the small hooks are not strong enough. One revolution of the large wheel gives nine turns to each of the small ones and their respective hooks.

The winch is generally used to make over old junk into serviceable stuff. In this case, one end of the length of junk is attached to the loper, and the other end is untwisted sufficiently to allow the separate strands to be attached to the winch-hooks and insert the top. By turning the crank in the required direction it is evident that the twist will be removed simultaneously from the rope and from the separate strands that compose it. By reversing the motion of the crank the rope can be again laid up as it was before, or fresh yarns can be substituted when required, and the junk made over into serviceable rope. When new rope is to be made, fresh yarns are attached to the winch-hooks, the other ends being made fast to the loper, and the crank is turned until a sufficient tension is imparted to the separate strands. The top is then inserted between the strands near the loper, and the crank is turned in the opposite direction. This permits the strands to twist around one another, the process being followed up and regulated by a man who holds the top. When four-stranded rope is handled, the heart, or core, passes through a central hole in the top and is attached to the large central hook of the winch.

Such is the simplest process of rope-making by machinery, but it is largely a hand process requiring at least one man at the crank, one or two at the top to overhaul the separating or uniting strands, and a third or fourth at the loper to regulate the strain upon the entire length of rope. In manufacturing rope on a large scale, far greater rapidity of action is essential, and further combinations of machinery are necessary.

The process with hemp is taken as the standard. When the bales are opened the fibers are found somewhat loosely folded in large hanks or bundles looking like masses of flaxen hair. These are hackled (sometimes spelled "heckled") or combed out to remove the dust, woody fiber, and the like. The hand-hackle is a board set at a steep incline, and having at its upper end a row of strong sharp steel hooks. The hackler throws the end of the bunch of hemp against these hooks, which engage it and hold it firmly, while with a coarse comb he straightens out the fibers and with a sharp knife cuts away foreign substances. Machinery has been invented that does away with hand-hackling. When the first hackling is done by hand, the hemp is then thrown into a box and subjected to a further hackling process by machinery. This is effected first by a "spreader," a sort of endless comb formed by steel teeth about three inches long set in an endless band, which revolves over drums. The hemp is fed to the spreader at one end and is gathered into a loose strand called a "sliver" at the other end. Thence it passes over "drawing-boards," not unlike the spreaders in construction, but which move faster, reduce the size of the sliver, arrange the fibers that compose it smoothly side by side, and deliver it at last in a continuous band, which falls naturally into coils in a box as it leaves the machine. When the box is full, the sliver is severed and the box is wheeled away to the this way is commonly known as "patent cordage" as distinguished from the old-fashioned irregularly laid varieties.

The bobbin-stand and the perforated plates just described are at one end of the "rope-walk," a name appropriately derived from the

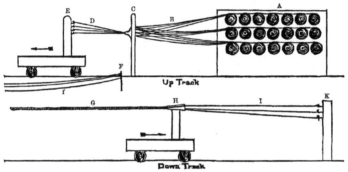

FIG. 3.—A ROPE-WALK.

A, bobbin-frame; B, yarns leading from the bobbins; C, a row of perforated plates (see also Fig. 4); D, strands or readies; E, winch, similar to C, Fig. 2; F, a fixed pin, to which the readies (f) are attached when hard twisted. The car moves with the arrow. K, point of attachment for the readies when about to be laid up; I, readies reaching from end to end of the walk; H, the top (see also D, Fig. 2); G is the finished rope. The car moves with the arrow.

"spinner," where it is again passed over toothed brands, which further reduce it, and suffer it, when it contains the proper number of fibers, to enter a tube, on emerging from which it receives a twist to the right and is at once converted into yarn and wound upon large spools or bobbins ready to be sent to the rope-walk or the machine-room. In the former case they are set upon a frame as at A, Fig. 3.

At this point one of the chief differences between old and new methods comes in. Hand-made rope assembles the yarns in a strand, but a yarn that begins on the outside of a strand may find its way to the inside and out again, thus varying the strain to which it may be subjected. In modern machinery the yarns, B, are led from the bobbins through holes in circular plates at C, Fig. 3, and shown in detail in Fig. 4. The holes, made large enough to permit the free passage of the yarns, are bored in concentric circles as shown. Through them the yarns pass to a tube the exact size of the required strand, and then receive the twist from left to right that lays them together in their permanent relation (D, Fig. 3). Obviously the yarns that pass through the outer circles of holes will remain on the outside of the strand, and in like manner each of the concentric circles of perforations delivers its own layer of yarns, so that each yarn has its place marked out for it through the entire length of the strand. Rope that is made in

methods followed by the rope-makers of antiquity, as seen on the sculptured tombs of Thebes. Rope-walks are often 1,000 to 2,000 feet long. The one at the Charlestown (Mass.) Navy-Yard is 1,360 feet long, and in them the best cordage is always made. Devices for dispensing with the "walk" are used, but their product, until recently, was, in technical parlance, "dead" as compared with the product of the rope-walk. An expert recog-

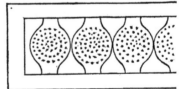

FIG. 4.—PERFORATED PLATES.

nizes machine-made rope in an instant, even without touching it, but there is no recognized difference in the market price.

After passing through the plates and tubes just described, the strands are attached to swivel-hooks on a frame similar to the rope-maker's winch previously described, but in this case mounted on a car (E, Fig. 3), and the ends are drawn away by machinery down the rope-walk, the hooks revolving at a furious rate, while a skilled workman superintends the process as the work progresses. In a word, the "winch" in a rope-factory is mounted on a tram-car, while the bobbin-frame remains stationary.

As many strands can be twisted at a time as there are hooks on the winch, and their length is only limited by the length of the rope-walk. When the car reaches the end of the walk the strands, or as they are now called the "readies," are removed from the hooks and fastened to stationary hooks or pegs. At the same time the yarns are cut at the other end of the walk, and there also the ends of the readies are made fast, and the long, hard-twisted strands lie side by side, reaching from end to end of the rope-walk.

In large factories the walks are equipped with double tracks, one of them devoted to the final laying up of the rope. For this purpose a car is fitted with a standard, which supports a "top" like that shown in Fig. 1. When it is desired to lay up a rope, the readies are shifted to the other track, and inserted in the scores of the top as seen at D, in Fig. 2, and at H, in Fig. 3; the ends of the strands are released and, aided by machinery which propels the car, the strands begin to twist firmly around one another. The car, as it advances about as fast as a man can walk, leaves a perfect rope behind it (as at G, Fig. 3), which when finished

independently of the other (see arrows near A A A, Fig. 5). At the same time all three of the bobbins are geared to a large outer frame, F F F, that revolves in a contrary direction as indicated by the large arrow. In practice this large frame stands facing toward C. It is here shown at right angles to its proper position, to simplify the drawing.

When set in motion the action of the machine is perplexing to the eye, and it is scarcely possible to follow its movements. The strands B B B are led from the flying bobbins to a tube the size of the required rope, and the reversed motion of the large frame, F F F, gives the necessary twist to the combining strands just as they enter the tube C. From the other end of the tube they emerge in the form of a rope or cable (D), of any desired size, according to the size of the machine. This is carried directly to a reel (E), and is coiled up ready for shipment. The largest rope-machines are not more than thirty feet long—a great saving in space when compared with the 1,000 feet or more occupied by a rope-walk. Moreover, machine-made rope can be produced of any desired length: 3,000 feet is not uncommon for drilling cables, whereas the product of a rope-walk must frequently be spliced. John Good has invented a machine that does the spinning and laying at one operation.

Fig. 6 shows the different kinds of cordage

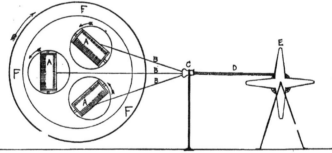

FIG. 5.—A ROPE-MAKING MACHINE.

A, A, A, bobbins carrying twisted readies, and so geared that they can revolve end over end with the arrows; F, F, F, a large frame supporting the bobbin-frames, and geared so as to revolve with large arrow; B, B, B, readies receiving a double twist from the reversed action of the bobbin-frames; C, forming-tube; D, finished rope; E, reel.

is as long as the walk itself, less what is taken up by the twist of the strands.

The machine process of rope-making is more difficult to describe, owing to the complicated operations involved. In Fig. 5, let A A A represent large bobbins or spools filled with readies or twisted strands. These are mounted on axles set in frames, which have other axles or gimbals of their own, so that while the strands are being reeled off from the bobbins, the bobbins in turn can revolve end over end, each

in common use. A is *right-handed*, or *plain laid* rope—the ordinary rope of commerce —having three strands. B is four-stranded or shroud-laid rope, also right-handed. The fifth strand marked *a* is the heart of soft stuff, and is necessary in rope of this character because four strands can not be laid up together without leaving a vacant space in the middle. C is *cable-laid* or *hawser-laid* rope, composed of three plain laid ropes, and therefore left-handed, since the completed rope must have a twist contrary to its own strands (the strands in this case being right-handed, three stranded

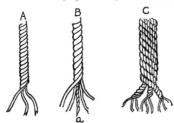

FIG. 6.—THE LAY OF CORDAGE.

rope). This kind of rope requires an extra twist to harden it and render it impervious to water, but this detracts from the strength of the fiber; besides, it stretches considerably under strain. Plain laid rope, moreover, contains more yarns than hawser-laid. Their relative strength is as 8·7 to 6. A new process gives a cord substitute for binding-wire, used by farmers, of which $11,000,000 worth was used in the United States in 1888.

About $25,000,000 are invested in the manufacture of cordage in the United States. About 8,250 spindles are in use, including those used for rope and twine. The consumption of hemp is 104,000,000 pounds annually, representing an equal weight of the finished product. It is impossible to ascertain even approximately the relative proportions of the different sizes and qualities.

White rope.—This term is commonly applied to all rope made of untarred hemp. It is the strongest cordage adapted to ordinary use.

Back-handed Rope.—In this the strands are given the same twist as the yarns, right-handed that is. Of course this must be a forced process, since they tend to twist together left-handed. When closed, therefore, they form a left-handed rope. It is more pliable than the plain laid and is less likely to kink.

Four varieties of hard-service rope are used in the United States Navy, namely, hemp, manila, hide, and wire. The sizes furnished in the equipment of a man-of-war range from 1¼ inch (15 thread) to 10 inches inclusive.

A rope-yarn of medium size should sustain a weight of 100 pounds, but owing to unavoidable inequalities in distributing strains the strength of a finished rope can not be fairly estimated by multiplying the number of yarns by 100. The difference in the average strength of a yarn differs with the size of the rope, thus in a 1¼-inch rope the strength for each yarn may be estimated at 104 pounds, while in a 12-inch rope it is equal only to 76 pounds.

The navy rules for ascertaining the breaking strain of Government rope are as follow:

White rope or *untarred hemp.* Multiply the square of the circumference in inches by 1371·4.

Tarred hemp. Use 1044·9 as the multiplier.
Manila rope. Use 783·7 as the multiplier.
The answers will nearly equal the breaking-strain in pounds.
Iron-wire rope. Multiply the weight in pounds per fathom (6 feet) by 4480.
Steel-wire rope. Use 7098 as the multiplier. The answers will be in pounds as before.

The square of half the circumference gives the breaking-strain of inferior plain laid rope in tons. This is a safe rule and easy to remember; but no cordage should be subjected to a strain of more than one third its estimated strength.

To ascertain the weight of common plain laid, tarred rope, multiply the square of the circumference by the length in fathoms, and divide by 4·24. The answer will be in pounds.

COREA, a monarchy in eastern Asia. The reigning monarch, Li-Hi, succeeded King Shoal Shing in 1864. The Government is an hereditary monarchy of an absolute type, modeled on that of China. No important step is taken in the affairs of Corea without the consent of the Chinese Government. The suzerainty of China has been acknowledged by Corea since the seventeenth century, and the dependent relation is stated in the Chinese-Corean frontier trade regulations. The revenue is principally paid in grain, and depends upon the state of the harvests. In 1886 the customs duties amounted to $160,278, and they were estimated to exceed $200,000 in 1887. There is a standing army of about 2,000 officers and men, constituting a royal guard, who are armed mostly with breech-loading rifles.

Area and Population.—The estimated area is 82,000 square miles, with a population of 10,-528,937, of whom 5,312,323 are males, and 5,216,614 females. The capital, Seoul, has about 250,000 inhabitants. In 1887 there were about 3,700 foreign residents in Corea, consisting of 3,000 Japanese, 600 Chinese, and 100 others, mainly Germans, Americans, British, French, and Russians. The language of the country is intermediate between Mongolo-Tartar and Japanese.

Commerce.—The values of the imports and exports for three years were as follow:

YEAR.	Imports.	Exports.
1884	$968,408	$444,629
1885	1,651,562	388,023
1886	2,474,158	504,225

The principal imports in 1886 were cotton goods of the value of $1,300,613; metals, chiefly copper, $64,718; rice, $586,543; silk, 25,-318; dyes and colors, $38,660; kerosene-oil, $20,207. Rice is not usually an article of import, but the deficiency caused by a bad harvest in 1885 had to be supplied from abroad. The leading exports were cowhides, of the value of $382,066, and beans, valued at $51,733. The Government has a monopoly of the product of ginseng, which is exported overland to China to the value of $400,000 annually. The chief agricultural products are rice, millet, beans, and jute. Japan controls the greater part of the foreign trade, and in 1886 imported into Corea goods of the value of $2,020,630; the exports from Corea to Japan during the same year were valued at $488,041. Gold to the amount of $500,000 was exported from Corea in 1886.

In 1886, 557 vessels, of 161,900 tons, entered the open ports of Jenchuan, Fusan, and Yuen-san from foreign countries; while 560 vessels, of 162,435 tons, cleared the ports.

The trade-returns for 1887 show a substantial improvement. The total value of imports at the open ports was $2,815,441, in which cotton goods figured for $1,884,497. The exports amounted to $804,996. Cowhides usually constitute two thirds of the exports, but in this year the export of beans was greatest in value.

Foreign Relations.—The suzerain rights of China over Corea were suffered to fall into abeyance until the danger of a Russian annexation of the northern part of the kingdom, for the sake of having a winter port on the Pacific, excited alarm both in China and in Japan. The Chinese Government, on this account, determined on a more visible display of the relations of sovereign and vassal. The King of Corea, on the contrary, was filled with a desire to show his independence of China, being influenced in his decision by his ambitious queen, who was made the victim of allurements held out by intriguing foreign representatives in Seoul. Since the retirement of Herr von Möllendorff, the King's adviser in foreign affairs has been an American named Denny. During the past five years China has acted on many occasions as a suzerain power. When an insurrection occurred in Corea, which was the outcome of a plot to place the country under Russian protection, the capital was occupied by Chinese troops, and Corean statesmen were imprisoned and banished by the Chinese authorities. The King has often applied to the Chinese Government to perform acts that he would have no hesitation in deciding on for himself if he were independent. Yet, in his foreign relations, encouraged by foreign advisers and borne out by treaties made with the sanction of China, but in which no mention is made of Chinese suzerainty, he determined to act as an independent sovereign by sending envoys abroad. He accredited a minister to the United States and another to the principal European capitals. The former arrived at Washington toward the end of 1887, and, after a long delay, was formally received by the President. After investing his representatives with the rank of ministers plenipotentiary, and notifying the foreign representatives at Seoul, the King sent a memorial to Li Hung Chang, in which he acknowledged his vassalage and justified his course in giving his envoys plenipotentiary rank with the argument that high officials from a weak state will receive equal consideration with inferior ones from a powerful nation, adding the comment that Corea was nearly as large and strong as

Japan, the significance of which is found in the fact that Japan was formerly considered a vassal of China. Li Hung Chang objected to giving the Corean envoys the same rank as Chinese representatives abroad, but withdrew his objections on the conditions that the Corean envoys, on arriving at the foreign capitals, should report to the Chinese ministers, and be introduced by them to the foreign ministers of the countries to which they were accredited; that the Chinese minister should take precedence of the Corean minister on public occasions; and that the Corean ministers should consult with the Chinese ministers on all questions of importance. The King accepted these conditions. When the Corean envoy, Pak Ding-Yang, reached Washington, he was confronted with the difficulty, which Li Hung Chang had not taken into consideration in his arrangement, that a diplomatic representative of a vassal state, subject to the guidance of the envoy of the suzerain power, has no standing in Western diplomacy. He accordingly, perhaps not without the foreknowledge of his Government, obtained his reception at Washington without the intervention of the Chinese representative. The Chinese Foreign Office thereupon demanded explanations from the Corean King, and received the assurance that the envoy had exceeded his instructions.

Outbreak in Seoul.—A fanatical outbreak of the population of the capital against foreigners occurred in the early summer. It was caused by Chinamen who spread a report that American missionaries kidnapped Corean children and boiled them in order to obtain a preparation that is used in making photographs. The authorities in Seoul took steps to protect the missionaries before the disturbance occurred; but nine Corean officials who were suspected of being engaged in the sale of children to foreigners were seized by the mob and decapitated in the streets. In response to telegrams from the foreign representatives at Seoul, American, French, and Russian gun-boats at the port of Chemulpo, forty miles distant, sent landing parties, numbering about one hundred marines altogether, for the protection of their countrymen, and on the following morning a force arrived from a Japanese vessel.

COSTA RICA, one of the five Central American republics. The area is estimated at 19,980 square miles, and on Dec. 31, 1886, the population was 196,280.

Government.—The President of the republic since March 12, 1885, is Don Bernardo Soto, whose Cabinet is composed of the following ministers: Foreign Affairs, Don Miguel J. Jimenez; Finance and Commerce, Don Mauro Fernandez; Interior, Public Works, Justice, Public Worship, and Charity, Don José Astua Aguilar; and War, Don Rodulfo Soto. The Costa-Rican Minister at Washington is Don Pedro Pérez Zeledón. The United States Minister to the five Central American republics, resident at Guatemala, is H. C. Hall. The

Costa-Rican Consul-General at New York is Don José M. Muñoz; at San Francisco, Don Teodoro Lemmen Meyer. The American Consul at San José is J. Richard Wingfield.

Army.—The strength of the permanent army has been reduced to 1,000 men for 1888, to be increased to 5,000 in the event of civil disturbances, and, in case of war, it is to be raised numerically according to the exigencies of the case. The citizens capable of bearing arms are 23,838 between the ages of eighteen and thirty-five; 7,986 between thirty-six and fifty; and 8,414 over fifty, constituting a reserve of 40,238 men.

Finances.—The Government during the fiscal year 1887-'88 succeeded in paying off the entire consolidated home debt of $3,000,000, while punctually paying the interest on the floating debt, and withdrawing and destroying $25,000 of paper money quarterly. The budget for 1888-'89 estimates the outlay at $3,480,-922, and the income at $3,494,743, the actual revenue collected in 1887-'88 having been $3,447,380. The public indebtedness will stand on March 31, 1889, as follows: Five-percent. sterling debt, £2,000,000; paper money in circulation, $844,943; due Union Bank, $300,000; Consolidated Church and University funds, $346,124. The payment of interest on these amounts will involve an outlay of $758,-150, and $100,000 will be applied to the canceling of paper money. The latter will all be withdrawn and destroyed in eight years and a half. Toward the eventual paying off of the sterling debt the Government will use the 60,000 ordinary shares that will be turned over to it in conformity with the agreement relating to the construction of the railroad and conversion of the debt; furthermore, the proceeds of one third of 800,000 acres of land recently pledged to the River Plate Trust Company of London will be used for the same purpose. Meanwhile, the Union Bank has been authorized to issue bank-notes to the extent of four times its cash capital, under the proviso of maintaining a metallic reserve of one quarter of its note circulation.

Education.—In the normal section of the Superior Young Ladies' College at San José there were granted in 1888 forty scholarships, 20 of these being awarded, beside gratuitous instruction, a pension of $15 a month and 20 instruction without pension. Congress, during the summer of 1888, voted $300,000 for the building of public school-houses and the further development of gratuitous instruction.

Commerce.—The imports into Costa Rica in 1887 reached a total of $5,601,225, England contributing $1,771,466; Germany, $815,729; France, $612,076; Spain, $32,750; Italy, $4,608; Belgium, $997; the United States, $1,440,729; Colombia, $798,665 ($798,665 of the latter amount being coin); Ecuador, $21,741; and Central America, $101,644. On the other hand, the exports amounted to $6,236,563, of which $5,235,865 represented

coffee; $669,544, bananas; $75,113, hides; $30,728, India-rubber; $20,032, mother-of-pearl; $68,972, sundry merchandise; and $68,972, coin. The increase in exports over those of 1886 was $3,010,756, chiefly due to the rise in coffee which brought as much as $20 per quintal free on board. Of bananas the amount shipped exceeded that of the previous year by $172,789.

The American trade was as follows:

FISCAL YEAR.	Import into the United States.	Domestic export to Costa Rica.
1888	$1,608,979	$1,064,549
1887	1,409,516	708,030
1886	898,045	548,215

Coffee-Planting.—The coffee of Costa Rica is highly appreciated both in the United States and in Europe, on account of its fine qualities and exquisite aroma; consequently, it commands a high price. Intending settlers on the coffee-lands of Costa Rica are warned not to buy the land necessary for a plantation wholly with borrowed capital, the interest rate on the spot being too high. They ought to possess money enough to pay cash for at least two thirds of the land. The net returns from a well-managed coffee-estate average about twelve per cent. per annum. The cost of a coffee-plantation depends in the first place on the quality of the soil, and next on whether it is situated in the vicinity of a large town. Cultivated coffee-land is worth from $110 to $335 an acre. The crops are very irregular; an abundant yield is the next year usually followed by a poor one; the third year it will prove tolerably good, and the fourth again an ample one. The newly planted shrubs will be in bearing at the end of four years. When the coffee-bean begins to form, plenty of rain is welcome, and but moderate sunshine. If blossoming be not soon succeeded by rains, the young berry will shrivel under a tropical sun. The annual coffee-product of Costa Rica varies between 10,000 and 15,000 tons.

Telegraphs.—The Government resolved in August to construct lines of telegraph to connect Liberia, Nicoya, and Santa Cruz with the system now in operation.

Railroads.—On October 16, the shareholders of Costa Rican railroads met in London. The lines acquired by purchase from the concessionaire, Mr. Keith, are the one from Puerto Limon to Carillo, 71 miles, and one from Cartago to Alaguela, via San José. Work is proceeding rapidly on the line that is to connect Cartago with Reventazon, 3,400 workmen being employed. The Costa Rican system now in course of completion is all the more important as it will form another link of communication between the Atlantic and the Pacific. The company received a subsidy in the form of 800,000 acres of Government lands. The Government has ordered the building of a national wagon-road between Esparta and Bagaces.

Steamer Lines.—During the year, the Government made a contract with the Hamburg-American line. and another with the Spanish Transatlantic line, to touch once a month at Port Limon. The contracts with the Marqués de Campos and with Don Rafael Montúfar were forfeited for not complying with engagements in time.

Colonization.—A contract has been made by the Government with Eric Guido Gaertner to go to the United States and Europe and form colonizing companies for the settlement of desirable immigrants on the agricultural and mineral lands of the republic.

Exploration.—Another scientific exploration of the volcano Irazu was resolved upon by the Government during the spring, and H. Pittier, an American topographic engineer, was intrusted with the task. The exploration was made to the satisfaction of the Government, and valuable facts in connection with this mountain were ascertained. It was shown that its altitude is 1,411 metres, and not 1,503, as the first measurement had erroneously fixed it. The volcano has three craters, the most recently formed of which dates from the eruption of 1723. Mr. Fittier deplored the barbarous destruction of the magnificent forest that covered the flanks of this gigantic cone, and urges the Government to prevent the devastation from becoming complete.

Central American Union Movement.—On July 6 President Soto issued a decree advocating the assembling of a Central American diet for the purpose of planning the re-establishment of a union of the five republics, pending which Costa Rican citizenship was extended to the citizens of Guatemala, Honduras, Salvador, and Nicaragua. This initiative on the part of Costa Rica having met with a cordial response, the diet, which was composed of one representative from each of the five republics, met at San José on September 15, and Don Ricardo Jimenez, the representative of Costa Rica, was elected chairman.

American Arbitration.—On March 24 President Cleveland announced his decision on the disputed questions between Costa Rica and Nicaragua, in which he said:

The functions of arbitrator having been conferred upon the President of the United States by virtue of a treaty signed at the city of Guatemala on the 24th day of December, 1886, between the republics of Costa Rica and Nicaragua, whereby it was agreed that the question pending between the contracting governments in regard to the validity of their treaty of limits of the 15th day of April, 1858, should be submitted to the arbitration of the President of the United States of America ; that, if the arbitrator's award should determine that the treaty was valid, the same award should also declare whether Costa Rica has the right of navigation of the river San Juan with vessels of war or of the revenue service, and other points. And the arbitrator, having delegated his powers to the Hon. George L. Rives, Assistant Secretary of State, who, after examining and considering the said allegations, documents, and answers, has made his report in writing thereon to the arbitrator.

Now, therefore, I, Grover Cleveland, President of the United States of America, do hereby make the following decision and award:

1. The above-mentioned treaty of limits, signed on the 15th day of April, 1858, is valid.

2. The republic of Costa Rica under said treaty, and the stipulations contained in the sixth article thereof, has not the right of navigation of the river San Juan with vessels of war ; but she may navigate said river with such vessels of the revenue service as may be related to and connected with her enjoyment of the "purposes of commerce" accorded to her in said article, or as may be necessary to the protection of said enjoyment.

Retaliation.—On September 17 the Secretary of the Treasury at Washington issued the following circular in regard to discriminating dues on Costa Rican vessels:

This department is informed through the Department of State that various lines of foreign and Costa Rican vessels plying between Costa Rica and New York, New Orleans, and other ports in the United States, as well as between Costa Rica and European ports, are allowed in Costa Rica a rebate of five per cent. of the customs duties and also certain privileges as to port charges. Such rebate is not conceded to vessels of the United States. The cargoes of Costa Rican vessels entering the United States, therefore, will be subjected to the discriminating duties levied by section 2,501, Revised Statutes, as embodied in the act of March 3, 1883. Officers of the customs will take action accordingly.

CREMATION, PROGRESS OF. The argument that Sir Henry Thompson published in 1874 (see "Annual Cyclopedia" for 1876, p. 216) in favor of cremation as a method of disposing of the dead, although it was urged principally upon sanitary grounds, was shocking to a considerable part of the public. Many persons regarded it as a covert attack upon Christianity. Yet the thought was not new, for it had been broached in Italy in 1866; Gorini and Pollini had published the results of experiments in cremation in 1872, and a model furnace, illustrating the practicability of the process, had been shown by Prof. Brunetti, of Padua, at the Vienna Exhibition of 1873. The Cremation Society of England was formed, in 1879, for the purpose of obtaining information on the subject, and adopting the best method of performing the process as soon as that could be determined. Legal opinions having been obtained to the effect that this method of disposing of human bodies was not illegal, provided no nuisance was occasioned by it, an arrangement was made with one of the London cemeteries for the erection of a crematory on its grounds. The execution of this contract was forbidden by the Bishop of Rochester, and then an independent property was obtained at Woking, and a Gorini furnace was erected upon it, in which it was proved by experiment, in 1879, that a complete combustion of an adult human body could be effected in about an hour, without causing any smoke or effluvia, and with the reduction of every particle of organic matter to a pure, white, dry ash. Human cremations had already taken place abroad, by Brunetti in 1869 and 1870; at Dresden and Breslau (the latter in a Siemens apparatus, with gas) in 1874;

two at Milan, in close receptacles, with gas, in 1876; and two in 1877. The Cremation Society of Milan, established in 1876, and having now two Gorini furnaces, had, on the 31st of December, 1886, cremated 463 bodies. Similar buildings to that of the Milan Society, but on a smaller scale, have been constructed at Lodi, Cremona, Brescia, Padua, Varese, and in the Campo Varano Cemetery at Rome, at the last of which 123 cremations were performed between April, 1883, and the 31st of December, 1886. The whole number of cremations in Italy till the last date was 787. The only place in Germany where the process is regularly performed is Gotha, where the first human body was reduced in a building constructed, with permission of the Government, in December, 1878, and 473 reductions had taken place on the 31st of October, 1887. Cremation societies have been formed in Denmark, Belgium, Switzerland, Holland, Sweden, and Norway, and at several places in the United States. A bill to establish and regulate cremation was approved by the Legislative Council of New South Wales in 1886, but failed to pass the House of Assembly. A spacious crematory at Père la Chaise, Paris, was first used on the 22d of October, 1887. The English society's crematory went into operation in 1884, after a judgment had been obtained from Mr. Justice Stephen that this mode of disposing of the dead is legal, provided no nuisance is incurred; and thirteen cremations had taken place in it at the end of November, 1887. According to Sir Henry Thompson, "the complete incineration is accomplished" (in the Gorini furnace) "without escape of smoke or other offensive product, and with extreme ease and rapidity. The ashes, which weigh about three pounds, are placed at the disposal of the friends, and are removed; or, if desired, they may be restored at once to the soil, being now perfectly innocuous, if that mode of dealing with them is preferred. One friend of the deceased is always invited to be present." To prevent the process being abused by people desiring to conceal evidences of poisoning, it is insisted that, in all cases where the cause of disease is in doubt, an autopsy shall be made. If this is objected to by the family of the deceased, the doubtful case is avoided. The friends of cremation profess to desire that, in all legislation that may be sought authorizing the process, the most effective safeguards that can be devised shall be provided against an irregular use of it.

A congress of friends of cremation was held in Vienna, in September, at which reports were made showing that about fifty furnaces had been erected in different countries, of which twenty were in Italy, one in Germany, one in England, one in Switzerland, one in France, and the rest in the United States. According to a paper read by Mr. C. K. Remington in the American Association (Cleveland meeting,

1888), crematories are in operation near nine cities of the Union, viz.: Washington, Lancaster, Pittsburg, and Philadelphia, Pa.; Brooklyn, and Buffalo, N. Y.; Detroit, Mich.; St. Louis, Mo.; Los Angeles, Cal.; and in many other places cremation societies have been established for a considerable time. The crematory at Buffalo is supplied with a Venini furnace, by which a body can be reduced, without offensive results, in an hour and a half or less. The apparatus was inspected with much interest by members of the American Association in 1886; and among the results of the visit were the formation of several cremation societies and the erection, in one or two instances, of crematories. The religious prejudices that at first existed against this method seem to be passing away. The Bishop of Manchester, in a sermon delivered in April, 1888, said that if there is anything in Paul's doctrine of the resurrection bearing upon the subject, he thought that "it indicates that of the two modes proposed, cremation is the more Christian."

CUBA, an island in the West Indies, belonging to Spain. (For statistics of area, population, etc., see "Annual Cyclopædia" for 1883.)

Army.—The Commander-in-Chief and Captain-General of the island is Don Sabas Marin. The strength of the Spanish forces in Cuba in 1888 was 20,000. The principal features of the proposed military reforms in Spain and her colonies comprise compulsory service for every born or naturalized Spaniard who has attained twenty years of age. There is to be no exemption, either in time of peace or in war, except for physical infirmity. The duration of service will be twelve years in the peninsula and eight in the colonies. Three years will be passed in actual service, four in the first reserve, and five in the second reserve, the last class being only liable to be called out one month in each year in time of peace. No pecuniary redemption will be permitted, except for an exchange from colonial to home service.

Finance.—The Cuban budget for 1888-'89 estimates the outlay at $25,614,494, and the income at $25,622,968. The actual receipts in 1886-'87 prove to have been $24,352,489 instead of $25,994,725 as had been estimated, while the actual expenses were $26,444,641 instead of $25,959,735 as estimated. During the first six months of the fiscal year 1887-'88 the actual receipts were $9,959,126 as compared with the estimated, $10,389,203; on the other hand, the expenses did not exceed $8,904,751 instead of reaching the estimate, $11,378,648.

In October proposals were made to the Colonial Minister of Spain for a conversion of the bonded debt of the island and its floating indebtedness, the whole aggregating the equivalent of £25,000,000. These propositions came simultaneously from Spanish and foreign banking institutions. The conversion would chiefly bear on the 620,000,000 francs of the loan of 1886, the interest and sinking-fund charge of which would be reduced from $6\frac{1}{8}$ per cent. to $4\frac{3}{8}$ per cent. yearly, while the time the new bonds would have to run would be extended to seventy-five years instead of the present fifty years.

In June, 1888, the excise duty on fresh meat had produced since its establishment, three years previously, $118,187 to municipalities, and $899,133 to the treasury.

Railroads.—During the spring important sums were subscribed at Puerto Principe for the construction of a narrow-gauge railroad from that city to Santa Cruz del Sur. Simultaneously it was decided to extend the Caibarien and Sancti Spiritus railroad to Santa Clara, with a new branch line from Placetas to Hernandez.

Telegraphs.—In August a cable was laid between Cuba and Hayti, connecting Cuba with Puerto Plata, Santo Domingo, Curaçoa, and Venezuela.

Telephones.—By a decree of May 12, the Queen-Regent of Spain set forth the conditions upon which telephone enterprise may be undertaken in Cuba, Porto Rico, and the Philippine archipelago. The state is to receive at least six per cent. of the gross receipts. The concessions are to last twenty years, at the end of which period everything passes to the state. The telephones, as regards taxes, way-leaves, and hours of service, are to be on the same footing as state departments. The *concessionnaires* will have to guarantee the service, and erect offices open to the public. The maximum charge for places situated within municipal boundaries is $102. This charge is increased to $204 for flats, and $333 for hotels, clubs, etc. An additional $1.50 may be charged for every 100 metres outside the municipal boundaries.

New Ports.—The port of Mariel was made a port of entry in March; it is believed that this port will have a most prosperous future. A railway will eventually connect it with the Western Railroad *via* Guanajay. Asphaltum is found in the neighborhood of Mariel, and it is expected that a good export trade can be established therein to the United States. Another new port soon to be made a port of entry is San Cayetano, near the town of Esperanza.

Commerce.—The American trade with Cuba is shown in the following table:

FISCAL YEAR.	Import from Cuba into the United States.	Domestic export from the United States to Cuba.	Total trade.
1883	$65,544,534	$14,567,918	$80,112,452
1884	57,181,497	10,562,880	67,744,377
1885	42,306,093	8,719,195	51,025,288
1886	51,110,780	10,020,879	61,131,659
1887	49,515,434	10,138,930	59,654,364
1888	49,319,087	9,724,124	59,043,211

Sugar and Molasses Production.—The following tabular statement shows the amounts of sugar and molasses produced in the island during the last decade:

YEARS.	Sugar.	Molasses.	Together.
	Tons.	Tons.	Tons.
1879	570,225	146,341	716,566
1880	530,189	114,223	644,482
1881	693,764	96,747	790,511
1882	595,837	134,224	727,061
1883	460,397	100,292	560,689
1884	558,987	115,552	674,539
1885	631,967	146,984	778,951
1886	731,723	187,064	918,787
1887	646,578	153,015	799,593
1888	623,017	148,577	771,594
Total	6,042,684	1,340,019	7,382,703

On comparing the total amount of sugar and molasses produced during the quinquennium 1879–'83 with that of the last quinquennium, 1884–'88, an increase of 504,225 tons will be found to result in the latter, or about 15 per cent.

During crop-time, in 1888, field-hands were scarce, and commanded without difficulty $20 wages a month and found.

Average prices paid for sugar at Havana, in rials, gold:

GRADES.	Crop of 1888.	Crop of 1887.
Special sorts, No. 12, suitable for Spain.	$6\frac{1}{4}$	$5\frac{7}{8}$
Clayed, No. 12, current quality	6·31$\frac{1}{4}$	$5\frac{3}{4}$
Centrifugals, polarization, $\frac{96}{97}$	5·87$\frac{1}{2}$	$4\frac{3}{4}$
Muscovadoes, polarization, $\frac{88}{89}$	4.69	$3\frac{9}{16}$
Molasses sugars, polarization, $\frac{88}{89}$	4·68$\frac{3}{4}$	$3\frac{5}{16}$

The cheapened production through improved processes and perfected machinery, together with the higher prices realized, materially assisted in placing sugar-planting in Cuba once more on a basis of moderate prosperity, despite the still heavy taxes and the abolition of the "patronato."

Mining.—According to the official statistics, the mineral production of Cuba during the year 1886 was 2,066 tons of asphaltum, 112,755 tons of iron-ore, 40 tons of manganese-ore, and 45 tons of copper-ore. The exports during the same year were 112,755 tons of iron-ore to the United States, 1,403 tons of asphaltum to the United States and England, 45 tons of copper-ore to England, and 40 tons of manganese to the United States.

In May, 1888, a royal order was published dividing Cuba into two mineral districts, the eastern district being composed of the provinces of Santiago de Cuba and Puerto Principe, and the western district of the provinces of Havana, Santa Clara, Matanzas, and Pinar del Rio, each district to be placed in charge of a special mine-inspector. Among the mines for which at the same time titles were granted by the Government were two quicksilver-mines, covering an area of 27 hectares, and one for antimony, covering 60 hectares. The Government declared it was willing to offer all the advantages possible with a view to developing the country, but that there would be a difficulty from insufficiency of labor for working on a large scale—a difficulty which, however, could easily be surmounted by importing miners from Spain or elsewhere. In June an American company acquired in the province of Santiago de Cuba the ownership of several manganese-mines. The contract provided for the payment of $1 United States gold for each ton of ore exported, the number of tons to be exported not to exceed 21,000 yearly, and the export dues to be paid quarterly in the sum of $5,250, whether the maximum quantity be exported or not. The copper-mines of San Fernando and the Santa Rosa Company at Santa Clara exported some copper through the port of Cienfuegos about the same time; they begin to be worked ona large scale.

The Cuban Bessemer Iron Ore range is of considerable interest in connection with the American Juragua Iron Company, the joint property of the Bethlehem Iron Company and the Pennsylvania Steel Company. In a recently published description of the locality the Sigua or Arroyo de la Plata mines are specially referred to. One of the six Sigua properties is described as showing outcrops varying from 150 to 450 feet in width, with a very large amount of ore in sight. They are located about four miles back of the Carribean Sea, about twenty-two miles by road from the Bay of Santiago de Cuba. The Government employs all means in its power to encourage and promote the mining industry in the island of Cuba. Mining companies are, by a special law, exempted for a period of twenty years from all taxation, and for a period of seven years from import duties on all materials, machinery, etc., for use in the construction and operation of mining works. These exemptions cover railway, harbor, and all other works belonging to mining companies. Labor is easily obtainable at the rate of eighty cents a day, and under proper management is very efficient. The climate in the hills where these mines are situated is healthful.

Up to the middle of June, 1888, there had been registered 300 mines, to work which a concession had been applied for in the province of Santiago de Cuba, namely: iron, 103; manganese, 37; copper, 151; silver, 2; gold, 3; sulphate of zinc, 3; lead, 1; antimony, 1; and coal, 1. One of the gold-mines is near the village of Jiguaní, on the bank of the river of the same name. A fair quantity of gold is said to be in the bed of the stream, and a joint-stock company was organized to work this mine. Favorable accounts were also received from the San Anastasio gold-mine at Guaracabulla, near Placetas, Santa Clara.

New Textile Fiber.—Don Leopoldo del Castillo, of Puerto Principe, has introduced a new fiber, that of the quimbombó plant, indigenous to the locality and island, growing spontaneously in all sorts of soil throughout the year, and furnishing a soft, white fiber of great strength, considered superior to flax. Good progress has also been made with ramie culture at Guines.

General Condition.—The stringent measures taken in August, 1887, by Captain-General Marin for the purpose of purifying the customs service at Havana, have produced tangible results in the shape of larger revenue from that source ever since. In April, brigandage and kidnaping had assumed such proportions that the Captain-General issued a decree declaring martial law in five provinces containing one hundred cities, towns, and villages. In one instance a wealthy merchant, Señor Galindez, was kidnaped and not released till his ransom of $40,000 had been paid. Incendiary fires on the sugar-estates, leading to heavy losses from the destruction of standing canes, were also of frequent occurrence during a season of drought in the spring. The measures alluded to, which were adopted by the Captain-General to suppress crime throughout Cuba, proved most beneficial in their results. The robber bands were broken up completely, and fugitive members were captured daily, among others, one of the band that had carried off Señor Galindez. Among other inflictions the island was subject to, Havana was visited by small-pox, of which there were 2,000 cases in December, 1887, and January and February, 1888, 580 proving fatal; later it spread to Cienfuegos and Manzanillo with less violence. The yellow fever made its appearance in September at Santo Espiritu and Paredes, decimating chiefly the Spanish troops stationed in those localities, with a few cases at Santiago. On September 4 and 5 a most destructive cyclone swept the island. Its disastrous effects were felt the whole length of Cuba. Its greatest violence spent itself in the province of Santa Clara. This cyclone was as disastrous as that which occurred in 1883. The destruction of property on shore and along the coast in harbors and bights was counted by millions, the loss of life at the same time reaching 1,000. The Captain-General left immediately on a tour of inspection in the devastated districts, but after visiting Matanzas and Cárdenas was suddenly recalled to Havana by the alarm felt in the latter city on account of the numerous strikes occurring in various trades, the movement being the result of the cigarmakers' strike. The authorities were resolved to take the severest measures to prevent a disturbance; but good order prevailed, the cigarmakers' strike, having kept at one time 8,000 operators out of employment, ending early in October. At 4 A. M., on July 2, a severe shock of earthquake was experienced at Baracoa and vicinity; the damage to property was considerable, but there was no loss of life. In September, in the district of Roque springs that had been dry for a long time were again flowing, partially submerging some estates, their reappearance exciting general alarm throughout the district.

American Consular Service.—The Consul-General at Havana is Ramon O. Williams; the Consul at Matanzas, Frank H. Pierce; · at Santiago, Otto E. Reimer; at Cienfuegos, Henry A. Ehninger.

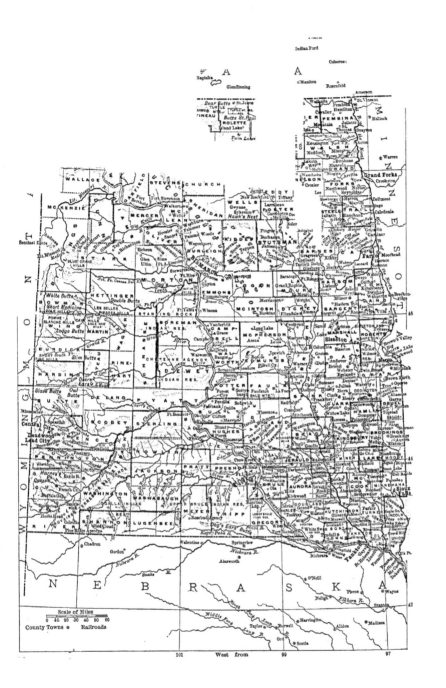

Modus Vivendi Treaty.—On Jan. 12, 1888, the Madrid Government "Gaceta" published the text of the agreement between Spain and the United States for the prolongation until June 30 of the suspension of differential dues upon vessels and cargoes from either, in connection with the colonial trade. Dating from July, the arrangement was prolonged pending the conclusion of a more ample treaty, the agreement to be liable to termination on two months' notice being given by either side.

Canada and Cuba.—Toward the middle of November a report was received from Ottawa, Ontario, that Sir Charles Tupper was actively engaged in negotiating a treaty of commerce between the Dominion of Canada and Spain, Sir Charles proposing to secure for Canadian products the advantages in Cuba and Porto Rico that were granted to the United States by the treaty rejected in 1885.

It was agreed in that treaty, negotiated by President Arthur in 1884, that the United States should admit duty free or with certain scheduled duties all the so-scheduled articles that were the products of the Spanish Isles, Cuba, and Porto Rico; and that Spain should grant similar privileges in those isles to all products of the United States.

Among the articles to be admitted free of duty into the United States were horses, cocoa, coffee, fresh fruits, hemp, flax, hides, palm-oil, sugars not above No. 16 Dutch standard, molasses, woods, sponges, guano, and coin. On cigars and cigarettes the duty was to be 12½ per cent. ad valorem; fine tobacco, with stems, 37 cents a pound; without stems 50 cents a pound; other tobacco, 17½ cents a pound; snuff, 25 cents a pound; tobacco manufactured, 20 cents a pound; not manufactured, 15 cents a pound.

Among the articles to be admitted free of duty into the Spanish Isles from the United States were beer, fresh meats, bacon, fish, grain and other cereals except rice, flour of cereals except rice, lard, cheese, cattle, sheep and hogs, clay, tiles, bricks, minerals, useful tools, agricultural implements, crude petroleum, tar, pitch, resin, coal, seeds, building-stones, ice, cast-iron in pigs, cast-iron in tubes, malleable iron and steel, wire, nails, screws, wrought-iron tubes, substances used in chemical industries, drugs.

The report alluded to added that hopes were entertained in Canada of building up an extensive trade in the Spanish West Indies for Canadian products. The Canadian Government had, indeed, been engaged for a year or two in trying to secure the West India trade for that country, but till then with seemingly little success.

D

DAKOTA. Territorial Government.—The following were the Territorial officers during the year: Governor, Louis K. Church; Secretary, M. L. McCormack; Treasurer, —— Lawler; Auditor, James A. Ward; Chairman of the Board of Education, Eugene A. Dye; Attorney-General, C. F. Templeton, succeeded by T. C. Skinner; Commissioner of Immigration, P. F. McClure; Chief-Justice of the Supreme Court, Bartlett Tripp; Associate Justices, Charles M. Thomas, William H. Francis, succeeded by Roderick Rose, William B. McConnell, Cornelius S. Palmer, succeeded by John W. Carland, James Spencer. By act of Congress of this year two new judicial districts were created. Over these the President late in the year appointed Attorney-General Templeton and Louis W. Crofoot as associate justices.

Finances.—The Territorial debt has not been increased during the year, the treasury being more than able to meet demands upon it. The total receipts for the year ending September 30 were $532,766.51, while the expenditures for the same time were but $488,109.21. The annual interest on the debt is $56,026.50.

Population.—According to estimates of the Commissioner of Immigration, the population of the Territory on the last day of June, 1887, was 568,477, and at the same date this year 630,823, a gain of 62,346. This estimate does not include Indians or Government officials and others upon the reservations, who would increase the total to 700,000. The proportion of the foreign-born element is about one in three of the population. A majority of the settlers of foreign nativity are Scandinavians; next come Germans, Canadians, Irish, and Russians in the order mentioned. There is scarcely a foreign country unrepresented among the inhabitants of the Territory.

The total of lands newly filed on and purchased by immigrants for settlement for the year ending June 30, 1888, approximates 2,500,000 acres, or 3,900 square miles, an area twice that of the State of Delaware. There still remains an area of over 22,000,000 acres open for settlers, outside of the 27,000,000 acres now comprised in the Indian reservations.

Assessments.—The total value of property in the Territory, as shown by the assessment roll for 1888 amounts to $161,420,974.80, an increase of nearly $4,500,000 over 1887. As 4,300 miles of railroad and other property in the Territory belonging to railroads, with a valuation of over $40,000,000, is not assessed and forms no part of this valuation (railroads being taxed upon their gross earnings), and as property is usually assessed at from half to two thirds of its actual value, it is a moderate estimate to place the actual property value of the

Territory at $320,000,000. The following table shows some details of the assessment:

PROPERTY ASSESSED.	Number.	Value.
Acres of land	28,832,816	$91,875,720
Town lots		26,125,555
Horses	268,410	12,120,346
Mules	16,057	522,772
Cattle	597,808	7,634,548
Sheep	152,896	207,790
Swine	174,026	446,811
Property invested in merchandise.	....	6,571,007
Carriages, etc	....	2,250,964

The total tax levy for the year was 3 mills on the dollar.

Education.—There are two systems of common schools in the Territory. Fifteen counties are operated under a district system, by which the people retain the burden of administration in their own hands or delegate it to a school board of three members in each school district, who are chosen annually. Seventy-one counties are operated under a township system, in which the chief authority is vested in a township school board made up of directors, one from each school district of the township, elected annually by the people. Besides these, the city and graded schools are operated under general and special laws, while the various State institutions for higher and special education are operated under special acts, and, as a rule, are independent of the general system of schools.

The University of Dakota, at Vermilion, has 20 instructors, and an attendance of more than 300 pupils. During the year a dormitory for young women and an east wing to the main building were constructed, at a cost of $25,000. The University of North Dakota, of more recent origin, has instructed 98 pupils during the past school year, an increase of 23 over the preceding year. A dormitory building, for which the Legislature of 1887 appropriated $20,000, was completed and occupied early in 1888. The university buildings sustained considerable damage through a storm, in June, 1887. At the Agricultural College, in Brookings, 228 pupils were enrolled during the school year, and in June the first class was graduated. A dormitory for women was erected during the year out of the appropriation by the last Legislature for that purpose. The Normal School at Madison had about 150 students during the year, and that at Spearfish 104. Appropriations by the last Legislature enabled additions to be made to the school-buildings at both of these institutions. The Legislature also made an appropriation for paying the tuition of classes of teachers or intending teachers in several of the denominational and private schools of the Territory, thus enabling many teachers to improve themselves without the expense of a long journey. The law provided that ten of these institutions may be designated by the Territorial board of education, and each may have a class of from ten to twenty-five members, whose tuition will be paid by the Territory upon order from the Territorial board, at the rate of $1 a week. During the year eight institutions have had classes on these conditions. A total sum of $3,906.22 has been paid these schools for this work.

The School of Mines, at Rapid City, created by the Legislature of 1885, completed its first year in June, having enrolled 48 students. The corps of instruction embraces four professors and two assistants. This school is also charged with the duty of surveying and investigating the mineral resources of the Territory, especially in the Black Hills, and during the year it published a valuable report upon the tin-deposits in that region.

Charities and Prisons.—The Hospital for the Insane at Yankton secured an appropriation of $92,500 from the last Legislature, for the purpose of enlarging its capacity by the construction of two additional wings to the main building. But charges of irregularity were made against the trustees of the institution; the Governor, in September, 1887, after an examination by the Public Examiner, suspended from their duties a majority of the members of the board, and, after further examinations, on November 2 removed the members so suspended for official misconduct and neglect of duty. As the remainder of the board then resigned, the Governor appointed an entirely new board of five members, who proceeded to construct the additions. In consequence of this difficulty the work was scarcely completed at the close of the present year. The removed members of the Board of Trustees took legal proceedings to test the power of the Governor to make such removals, but the decision was adverse to them. The number of patients at this hospital during the year was nearly 200. At the North Dakota Hospital there were 178, an increase of 31 over the previous year. At the School for Deaf Mutes, at Sioux Falls, there were 44 pupils during the year, which is the largest attendance in its history. A workshop and other buildings have been constructed.

The Penitentiary at Sioux Falls contained 92 convicts on July 1, an increase of 10 in one year. The total number confined during the year was 128. Since December, 1882, the date of its opening, the institution has received 325 prisoners, and released 233. At the Bismarck Penitentiary there were about 50 prisoners on July 1. Extensions have been made to the prison-building by the construction of a south wing. By an act of the last Legislature $30,000 was appropriated for buildings for a reform school at Plankinton, and this sum was expended in constructing and furnishing a building of four stories, with out-buildings, which were ready for occupancy in August. Up to October 1, however, no persons had been placed under the care of the institution.

Railroad Construction.—The total railroad mileage in the Territory on January 1 was 4,207 miles. There were completed, or to be completed during the building season of 1888, the following lines: From Watertown to Huron, 72 miles, on the Duluth, Watertown and Pacific Railway; from Willmar, Minn., to Sioux Falls, 23 miles, on the Duluth and Willmar Railway; from Cherokee, Iowa, to Sioux Falls, 16 miles, on the Illinois Central Railway; and 15 miles on the St. Paul, Minneapolis and Manitoba Railway, making a total of 4,333 miles. Activity in railroad construction was not so marked as in the year immediately preceding.

Agriculture.—Farming is the chief industry of the Territory, and the growing of wheat has been the leading occupation. Wheat is grown at a minimum cost, which varies from 24 cents a bushel on the bonanza farms of the Red River valley (where the large area tilled and the employment of special machinery result in more than the usual economy) to 36 cents a bushel, the average cost on farms of ordinary size.

The following statistics for 1887 show the production and acreage of wheat and other cereals for that season (one county excepted):

CEREALS.	Acres.	Bushels.
Wheat	3,818,754	62,558,499
Corn	608,807	24,511,726
Oats	1,172,289	43,267,478
Rye	17,559	816,556
Barley	235,155	6,400,568
Buckwheat	5,749	97,280
Flax	412,741	3,910,944

Indians.—There has been no serious disturbances at the various Indian agencies during the year, and the Indians were reported to be making progress in farming in nearly every case. The Sisseton agency reported about 1,500 Indians, the Cheyenne River agency 2,925, the Crow Creek and Lower Brulé about 2,500, the Pine Ridge 5,609, the Standing Rock 4,385, the Rosebud 7,404, and the Yankton 1,837. Two other agencies, the Fort Berthold and Devil's Lake, have about 4,000.

An act of Congress was passed in May designed to meet the wishes of Dakota citizens for diminishing the size of the great Sioux reservation and opening the region to settlers. By the terms of the act, about half of the reservation, or over 10,000,000 acres, was to be purchased by the Government at fifty cents an acre, and the remaining portion was to be divided into five distinct reservations. A commission was created to secure the assent of the Indians to this proposal, and the President appointed R. H. Pratt, Judge Wright, and William Cleveland, as such commissioners. During August, September, and October, conferences were held by these commissioners with the various Sioux tribes at the agencies; but it was found impossible to secure the assent of three fourths of the whole tribe, which, by the terms of the act, was necessary to make it operative. In fact, very few of the Indians assented to its provision, the great majority demanding $1.25 an acre for their land. Some of the Sioux chiefs went to Washington, and

there held conferences with the Secretary of the Interior, but no agreement was reached.

Local Option.—The constitutionality of the local-option law of 1887 was passed upon by the Territorial Supreme Court in February, and its validity as a police regulation was sustained. The court says that, as the States under their Constitutions are considered to have power to pass such laws, so "the organic act of the Territory is so far a constitution in character, and the temporary government thereby created is so far sovereign that it has the power to enact any and all laws in the nature of police regulations not in conflict with the statutes and Constitution of the United States; that police regulations are necessarily local, and could not well be exercised by Congress over all its outlying territory; that it intended to, and must necessarily have placed somewhere outside of Congress, but subject to its ultimate control, the power of regulating the affairs of municipal concern."

Another act of the same year, authorizing township bonds in payment for the construction of public artesian wells, was declared invalid, by the same court, later in the year.

Taxation of Railroads.—The Governor says, in his annual report: "In 1879 the Legislature passed an act providing for the taxing of railroads under the gross-earnings system. I quote the following from section 24: 'The percentage of gross earnings hereinbefore specified to be paid shall be in lieu of all other taxation of the road-bed, etc., used in or incident to the operation of such railroad. All property of railroads not above enumerated, subject to taxation, shall be treated in all respects, in regard to assessment, equalization, and taxation, the same as similar property belonging to individuals, whether said lands are received from the General Government or from other sources.' In 1883 the Legislature passed another act providing for the collection of taxes on railroad property. The following is a part of section 1 of said chapter: 'In lieu of any and all other taxes upon any railroads, except railroads operated by horse-power, within this Territory, or upon the equipment, appurtenances, or appendages thereof, or upon any other property situated in this Territory belonging to the corporation owning or operating such railroads, or upon the capital stock or business transaction of such railroad company, there shall hereafter be paid into the treasury of this Territory a percentage of all the gross earnings of the corporation,' etc. As the law stood prior to 1883, it is plain that the Legislature intended to exempt from the ordinary and usual method of taxation only such property as was actually used in or necessarily incident to the operation of the roads. Whether said chapter goes further and exempts more property than is used in and incident to the operation of the roads, is a disputed question between the officers of the Territory and the railroad companies. In 1880 the officers of

DAKOTA.

the county of Traill assessed and levied taxes for that year upon lands granted to the Northern Pacific Railroad Company for the purpose of aiding in the construction of said road, said lands not being a part of the road-bed or any way used for railway purposes. The county treasurer proceeded to advertise said lands for sale for non-payment of taxes. An application was made to the Territorial District Court to enjoin the collection of such taxes. On appeal, the Supreme Court of the Territory gave judgment for the defendant. Appeal was taken to the Supreme Court of the United States, and the decree of the Supreme Court of the Territory of Dakota was reversed, with directions to cause a decree to be entered perpetually enjoining the treasurer of Traill County from any further proceeding to collect the taxes, the court holding that the provisions in the act of July 17, 1870—that the lands granted to the Northern Pacific Railroad Company by the act of July 2, 1864, shall not be conveyed to the company or any party entitled thereto ' until there shall be first paid into the Treasury of the United States the cost of surveying, selecting, and conveying the same by the company to party in interest '—exempt these lands from State or Territorial taxation until such payment is made into the Treasury. That ' the Northern Pacific Railroad Company has acquired no equitable interest in the lands so granted to it by reason of completing its road and thus earning the granted lands which are subject to State or Territorial taxation before such payment is made into the Treasury of the United States.' The doctrine promulgated by the Supreme Court in this case was set aside by act of Congress approved July 10, 1886. Accordingly, the Territorial officers caused the surveyed lands belonging to the Northern Pacific Railroad Company to be assessed both in 1887 and 1888. The company has not paid the taxes, and the validity of the tax has not been passed upon by the courts."

Another question has been in dispute as to the validity of a gross-earnings tax. The same company, having rendered its returns of gross earnings for 1886, was taxed by the Territory thereon $76,000, half of which became payable on or before Feb. 15, 1887, and the other half on or before Aug. 15, 1887. After paying the first installment, the company refused to pay that which became due August 15, and, for the purpose of satisfying the tax, the Territorial treasurer distrained a large amount of rolling-stock. The corporation brought suit to prevent the sale, and obtained from the District Court a permanent injunction restraining it. The company in its complaint showed that the tax upon its earnings, local within the Territory, would not for the year exceed $12,000, and the suit was maintained on the grounds that the tax upon all the earnings not local within the Territory was a tax upon interstate commerce and void, and the company having already paid more than the whole tax on local

earnings for the year, no more could be collected. The case was taken to the Supreme Court of the Territory, and the decision of the District Court affirmed.

Section 1925 of the Revised Statutes of the United States provides as follows: "In addition to the restrictions upon the legislative power of the Territories contained in the preceding chapter, section 1925, the legislative assemblies of Colorado, Dakota, and Wyoming shall not pass any law impairing the rights of private property or make any discrimination in taxing different kinds of property, but all property subject to taxation shall be taxed in proportion to its value." The question then arises as to whether the gross-earnings law is not in conflict with this section of the Revised Statutes. This question was not raised in the late suit to enforce collections under the gross-earnings law. The Northern Pacific Railroad Company, during 1888, paid about $10,000 tax under the gross-earnings law. As under its charter the road-bed of the Northern Pacific Railroad Company and all necessary property appurtenant thereto are exempt from taxation, it follows, if the gross-earnings law is invalid, that the company will escape all taxation.

Division and Statehood.—During the year there was much agitation and discussion throughout the Territory on these two subjects, in the course of which the various bills pending before Congress were thoroughly canvassed. On February 29 an address was issued to the people by the Division and Statehood Committee, appointed by the Huron Convention of July, 1887, urging the people, in making their political nominations, to select only pronounced divisionists, and exhorting the press to maintain an earnest advocacy of the division cause. Later in the year this committee called a general convention, to meet at Huron on July 10 and 11, in the interest of division, and, following this on the 12th, separate conventions of the various professions and of farmers and business men for the same purpose. These conventions met and adopted resolutions favoring division. The various party conventions also generally adopted division resolutions, and nominated candidates favorable to division. The result of the general election in November rendered an early admission of the Territory probable, and consequently gave renewed vigor to discussion of the division question. North Dakota had hitherto been considered hostile to the plan of admission as two States; but with the approach of the actual fact of admission there seems to have been a weakening of this sentiment. While it had hitherto been scarcely possible to bring together a convention of divisionists in North Dakota, such a meeting was held at Watertown on December 5. This convention resolved:

That we favor the division of North Dakota Territory on the seventh standard parallel, and the immediate admission of the northern portion into the Union of States.

That we are emphatically in favor of the name of North Dakota for the proposed new State.

That the Fiftieth Congress should provide for the admission of North Dakota.

That in case the Fiftieth Congress fails to provide for the admission of North Dakota as a State, we earnestly request the President-elect to call a special session of the Fifty-first Congress for that purpose.

· That the Eighteenth Legislative Assembly of North Dakota Territory is urged to provide at the earliest practicable moment after its meeting in January, 1889, for a constitutional convention for North Dakota.

That South Dakota, Montana, and Washington are respectfully invited to co-operate with North Dakota in this movement for admission.

Political.—On June 27 the Prohibitionists of the Territory met in convention at Redfield, and nominated S. H. Crammer for delegate to Congress. The Democratic Convention was held at Jamestown on July 11, and nominated J. W. Harden. The Republican Convention assembled at Watertown on August 23, and was in session three days before nominating a candidate. On the seventeenth ballot George A. Mathews received a majority over delegate Gifford, who had been the leading candidate through nearly all the balloting.. The following are some of the resolutions adopted:

The Republicans of North and South Dakota, in convention assembled, hereby publish and declare: That the present Democratic Administration at Washington, emulating the present Tory Administration in the government of Ireland, has maintained and exercised a tyranny over this Territory, unjust, unwarranted, and subversive of the principles of the founders of the republic, in denying admission into the Union of the States, for the sole and only reason that a majority of our people differ with the Administration upon the political issues of the day.

That we arraign the present Governor of this Territory for prostituting his high office to personal and ambitious ends and purposes; that he maintains a perfect indifference to the wants of the people whom he rules; that he encourages large and unwise appropriations; that he threatens to veto measures unless the Legislature shall be subservient to his will; that his appointees in many cases are men who have no qualifications for office, but are his personal retainers, supported at the public expense.

That by every precedent established in the history of the admission of new States into the Union, by the rights guaranteed under the Constitution and the laws of the United States, it is the duty of Congress to admit both North and South Dakota into the sisterhood of States; and the refusal by a Democratic House to so admit us is a violation of the duties and obligations of its members, and we hereby reiterate our unalterable opposition to admission as a whole.

A revision of the tariff was favored, and the President was denounced for his pension vetoes.

A second Democratic convention, composed of delegates belonging to the faction hostile to Gov. Church, and representing twenty-three counties of North Dakota, was held at Grand Forks on September 21, at which W. R. Bierly was nominated for delegate. The platform adopted claims that it is necessary for all of the Territory lying north of the north line of the State of South Dakota to elect a delegate to the United States Congress; demands Statehood for North Dakota by the next Congress;

the election of a Legislature pledged to abolish the railroad commission, and the abolition of all Territorial laws enlarging the appointing powers of any and all Federal officers; the speedy opening of Indian reservations; the passage of an act of Congress permitting county commissioners to lease school lands at a fair rental prior to Statehood; the speedy improvement of the rivers of North Dakota and Minnesota; and the erection of safeguards in insurance of stock, grain, implements, growing crops, etc.

At the November election Mathews received 70,215 votes, Harden 40,846, and Bierly 1.753. The Republican candidate obtained a plurality of 9,509 in North Dakota, and 19,860 in South Dakota. The next Legislature will consist of 19 Republicans and 5 Democrats and Independents in the council, and 42 Republicans and 6 Democrats and Independents in the House. The presence of two Democratic candidates in the contest was the result of hostility between two factions of the party, led respectively by Gov. Church and M. H. Day. The first open rupture between these leaders occurred at Watertown, in May, when a Democratic convention met to choose delegates to the National Convention. The Day faction, being in the minority, refused to join with the Church delegates, but held a convention of its own, selected its delegates to the National Convention, and appointed a committee to secure evidence to impeach Gov. Church. But the delegates from the Church convention were admitted to the National Convention. Later in the year the committee of the Day convention published a series of charges against the Governor, his political activity being the chief cause of complaint.

DELAWARE. State Government.—The following were the State officers during the year: Governor, Benjamin T. Biggs, Democrat; Secretary of State, John P. Saulsbury; Treasurer, William Herbert; Auditor, John H. Boyce; Attorney-General, John Biggs; Chief-Justice of the Supreme Court, Joseph P. Comegys: Associate-Justices, Ignatius C. Grubb, John W. Houston, John H. Paynter; Chancellor, Willard Saulsbury.

Finances.—The Treasurer's report presents the following summary of State finances for the year ending Jan. 1, 1888: Balance in treasury at the close of the fiscal year, Dec. 31, 1886, $29,849.08; receipts during the year, $493,576.58: total, $523,425.66. Paid out during the year, $478,632.18; balance, Dec. 31, 1887, $44,793.48. In addition to the balance of the general fund, there was due from the late Breakwater and Frankford Railroad Company, now consolidated with the Delaware, Maryland and Virginia Railroad Company, interest to July 1, 1882, amounting to $38,866.66. The largest regular receipts were, from tax on railroads, $62,594.79; from clerks of the peace for licenses, $54,232.70; and from sale of school-books, $5,640.98.

The expenditures include $16,467.12 for the judiciary, $12,588.24 for the National Guard, $17,850 for interest on State bonds, $25,000 for free schools; $6,000 for colored schools; $10,403 to members of the General Assembly, and $13,078.08 for allowances made by the General Assembly. The bonded debt at the beginning of the year was $824,750; against which the State holds the general-fund investments given above, so that the actual debt is only $151,700.

Militia.—During 1887 the State militia was considerably strengthened and more fully equipped, with the aid of money coming from the General Government, and of an appropriation of $2,000 by the Legislature. At the beginning of the year the force consisted of but 312 men, partially uniformed; at the close of the year there were 560, fully equipped.

Education.—At a meeting of the Trustees of the Delaware State College, held in March, the contest over the resignation of President Caldwell, postponed from the previous July meeting, was ended by the president's voluntarily asking for his release, in order to accept another place. Action upon the resignations of the professors was indefinitely postponed, except in the case of one *bona fide* resignation. The president reported that, for the year beginning in September, 1887, there were but 17 pupils in actual attendance, of whom only one paid tuition. Since its reorganization, in 1870, when it was placed under State control, the institution has had 236 male students, or an average of 13 a year. At no time has the study of agriculture and mechanic arts been the leading object of the college, as required by law. More than one hundred students have been graduated in the scientific, academic, and other courses, and thus far not one in the agricultural course.

A tempory president was elected from the Board of Trustees, which also appointed a committee to secure for the college the appropriation made by Congress for the establishment of agricultural-experiment stations in the various States. Some efforts had previously been made by the trustees to obtain this appropriation, but the Federal authorities expressed doubts whether the college could be considered an agricultural college, to which alone by the statute the donation could be made. Later in the year, however, the appropriation was secured.

Wilmington.—An election for mayor and other city officers was held on June 2, at which the Democrats carried their usual majorities except on the vote for mayor. Great dissatisfaction with the Democratic nominee existed in his own party, in consequence of which the Republican candidate, Albert Harrington, obtained a majority of 776 votes, running over 1,000 votes ahead of his ticket in a total poll of 6,588.

Political.—The only State officers to be chosen this year were three State senators and the lower house of the Legislature entire. Nominations for these offices were made in county conventions, but State conventions were necessary to select candidates for presidential electors and for a member of Congress. The Democrats met at Dover, on August 28, and unanimously renominated Congressman Penington, and selected an electoral ticket. Resolutions were adopted approving the work of the St. Louis Convention and the administration of President Cleveland, and continuing as follows:

We approve the administration of the Governor and other State officers, and in State affairs we advocate the continuance of the simple, honest, and economical administration of affairs which has always characterized the rule of the Democratic party; and as true Democrats we recognize and obey the popular will, as evidenced by the special election held last November, and declare ourselves in favor of accomplishing the reforms long conceded, by all parties in the State, to be demanded by popular sentiment, through the medium of a constitutional convention to be provided for at as early a day as in the judgment of the Legislature, acting for itself as a co-ordinate branch of the State government, it may be properly and constitutionally done.

The Republican State Convention, held at Dover, on September 2, nominated for Congress Charles H. Treat, selected an electoral ticket, and passed the usual resolutions in support of the national platform and ticket. On State issues the platform reaffirmed the following declarations, made at the preliminary State Convention on May 17, which chose delegates to the Chicago Convention:

The free and untrammeled suffrage which lies at the foundation of the institutions of the republic has been overthrown in this State since the enactment of the disfranchising laws of 1873. This flagrant denial of citizenship to a large portion of the people who are not the owners of property has produced a fruitful crop of dishonesty and jobbery in the management of State, county, and municipal affairs, while the assessors of the city of Wilmington and the levy court of New Castle County, in openly and boldly refusing to place upon the assessment lists over two thousand citizens whose right to qualify to vote was undisputed, have placed themselves before the public as breakers of the law, and are deserving of the execration of all good citizens.

We renew the demand heretofore reiterated by the Republican party, for the speediest calling of a convention to revise the Constitution of this State, and urge upon the voters that no one should be sent to the next Legislature known to be opposed to this measure of reform.

We recognize the fact that the saloon has become a potent element in the politics of the State, and is being used to influence and control the action of the people in the exercise of their political rights; and as the question of licensing houses for the sale of intoxicating drinks involves the moral as it does the political rights of the people, we believe it to be the duty of the Legislature to enact laws that will make effective their will in this respect. We, therefore, declare ourselves in favor of a law embracing the principle of local option, and providing for high license when granted.

We approve of the recent act of the Legislature in securing to the city of Wilmington honest elections through the operations of a registry law, and declare ourselves in favor of similar legislation by extending the same principles to all State and county elections.

To which the later convention added the following:

We believe that the will of the people is supreme in making or amending the fundamental law of the State, and that no convention should be called for that purpose but by the authority of the people; and it is the sense of this body that the large majority of votes cast for a convention at the special election held the first Tuesday of November, 1887, is the proper evidence of the will of the people in this matter, and should be accepted by the General Assembly as full authority for passing an act, at its next session, calling a convention and providing for the election of delegates thereto at as early a period as practicable.

A Prohibition ticket was also in the field, headed by Charles E. Register for Congress. At the November election, Mr. Cleveland received 16,414 votes; Gen. Harrison, 12,973; Mr. Fisk, 400. Congressman Penington was re-elected by a majority equal to that for the Democratic electoral ticket; but, while the Democrats carried the State, their candidates for the Legislature in Kent and Sussex Counties were unexpectedly defeated. Two of the three senators elected, and 14 of the 21 representatives, were Republicans. This result gives the Republicans a majority of 2 on joint ballot in the next Legislature (Senate, 7 Democrats, 2 Republicans; House, 7 Democrats, 14 Republicans), and insures the election of a Republican successor to United States Senator Eli Saulsbury. This overturn was the result of an attempt to defeat the re-election of Senator Saulsbury, made by certain members of his own party. At the primaries in Kent and elsewhere the anti-Saulsbury faction succeeded in nominating candidates favorable to James L. Wolcott, the leader of that faction; and the followers of Saulsbury retaliated at the polls by voting for the Republican candidates.

Elections.—The Governor says, in his message to the Legislature:

The use of money at elections everywhere is alarmingly on the increase. That use has in this State become so great as to call forth a protest by all who favor the purity of the ballot. The present law upon the statute-book does not seem to meet the present needs, and the enforcement of its provisions is practically a dead letter. I deem it my duty to call your attention to the wholesale bribery which has become a main feature in elections, and urge upon you the necessity of prompt action in the matter. So unblushing has the practice become, that the votes of men are openly bartered for and secured. I would suggest that you take into consideration the enactment of a law governing the holding of all primary elections in this State. There is at present no statute regulating the same, excepting one relating to the primary elections in New Castle County.

Constitutional Convention.—The Republican party, by its platform declarations of this year, committed itself to calling a constitutional convention, although at the election of last year the vote in favor of such convention did not quite reach the figures required for such an act by the existing Constitution. In view of the success of the Republicans in the election, the Governor cautions the Legislature as follows:

By an act passed at the last session of the General Assembly, a special election was held on the day there-in specified. At that election the number of votes cast for a convention is by many held under the provisions of the Constitution to be insufficient to authorize you to call the same, or make provisions for its calling. You will at the outset be confronted with the grave question, whether or not you, as legislators, have authority under the provisions of Article IX to call a convention upon the basis of the vote cast as aforesaid. No rash measures should be resorted to. It is better to make haste slowly in securing that which is deemed necessary, and which the increase of population and needs of the State may require, than it would be to attempt to secure it by means seemingly at least revolutionary.

DENMARK, a constitutional monarchy in Northern Europe. The King, Christian IX, born April 8, 1818, succeeded to the throne Nov. 15, 1863. He is a member of the house of Schleswig-Holstein-Sonderburg-Glücksburg, and was appointed to the succession of the crown of Denmark by the treaty of London of May 8, 1852, and by the Danish law of succession of July 31, 1853. The Constitution of Denmark is embodied in a charter, according to which the executive power is vested in the King and his ministers, and the right of making and amending laws in the Rigsdag or Diet, acting in conjunction with the King. The Rigsdag comprises the Landsthing and the Folkething or House of Commons. The former consists of 66 members, of whom 12 are appointed for life by the Crown from among the actual or former representatives of the kingdom, and 54 are elected indirectly by the people for a term of eight years. The Folkething consists of 102 members elected by universal suffrage for a term of three years in the proportion of one member for every 16,000 inhabitants. The Landsthing, besides its legislative functions, appoints from its midst every four years the assistant judges of the Rigsret, who with the ordinary members of the Höiesteret, form the highest appellate court, and can alone try parliamentary impeachments.

The ministry or Statsraadet consists at present of the following seven members: Jacob Brœnnum Scavenius Estrup, President of the Council and Minister of Finance; H. G. Ingerslev, Minister of the Interior; J. M. V. Nellemann, Minister of Justice and for Iceland; Otto Ditlev, Baron Rosenœrn-Lehn, Minister of Foreign Affairs; Col. J. J. Bahnsen, Minister of War; Commander N. F. Ravn, Minister of Marine; J. F. Scavenius, Minister of Public Education and Ecclesiastical Affairs.

Area and Population.—The area of Denmark and its dependencies is 14,124 square miles, and the estimated population on Jan. 1, 1886, was 2,108,000. The increase in the population has averaged 10·29 per cent. in the towns and 5·99 per cent. in the country districts during the past fifteen years. The population of Copenhagen in 1886 was 285,700. The average emigration for the ten years preceding 1887 was nearly 6,000 per annum. Nearly all the emigrants settled in the United States. Between 1851 and 1878 about 20,000 Danes joined the Mormon community in Utah. The conversions have since been fewer in each succeeding year. In 1887 only 120 Danes were baptized into the Mormon Church.

The Army.—The total peace strength of the army in 1887 was 335 officers and 16,318 men. The war strength is about 50,000 officers and men, exclusive of the extra reserve force of 14,000 officers and men, which is only called out in emergencies.

The Navy.—At the end of 1887 the Danish navy consisted of 33 steamers, of which 9 were armor-clad ships. The others were 1 cruiser frigate, 2 cruiser corvettes, 4 third-class cruisers, 8 gun-boats, 4 school-ships, and 5 survey vessels. The "Tordenskjöld" is the largest torpedo-vessel in the Baltic. She is protected with deck-armor and a belt of cork, and carries a 14-inch Krupp-breech-loader in a thickly plated barbette tower, and two torpedo-launches, besides appliances for shooting Whitehead torpedoes. Denmark has a fleet of 14 torpedo-boats, and is building 20 more.

Finances.—The estimated revenue for the year ending March 31, 1889, is 53,799,872 kroner, or $14,465,189, derived from the following sources: Domains, 832,674 kroner; interest of reserve fund, railway surplus, etc., 4,363,385 kroner; direct taxes, 9,576,600 kroner; stamp duty, 2,755,000 kroner; duty on inheritance and transfer of property, 1,954,000 kroner; law fees, 2,114,400 kroner; custom-house duties, excise on distilleries, etc., 27,527,400 kroner; lottery, 900,000 kroner; revenue from the Faroe Islands, 63,278 kroner; revenue from sinking-fund, deposits, and pension funds, 2,223,285 kroner; miscellaneous receipts, 1,489,850 kroner. The total expenditure for the same year is estimated at 55,879,705 kroner, or $15,024,831, apportioned as follows: Civil list and appanages, 1,223,744 kroner; Rigsdag and Council of State, 306,616 kroner; interest and other expenses of the national debt, 7,176,940 kroner; pensions, 3,463,265 kroner; Ministry of Foreign Affairs, 386,456 kroner; Ministry of the Interior, 2,851,530 kroner; Ministry of Justice, 3,207,657 kroner; Ministry of Public Worship and Education, 1,973,440 kroner; Ministry of War, 10,386,617 kroner; Ministry of the Navy, 6,599,766 kroner; Ministry of Finance, 3,166,472 kroner; Ministry for Iceland, 99,964 kroner; extraordinary state expenditure, 8,370,898 kroner; public works, 6,666,840 kroner. A reserve fund that is maintained to afford means at the disposal of the Government in the event of sudden emergencies amounted, in 1887, to 27,870,000 kroner. The public debt, on March 31, 1888, was 193,017,689 kroner. The foreign debt was 13,319,666 kroner in 1887. The expenditure for the public debt in 1887 was 7,176,940 kroner.

Commerce.—The total value of the imports for the year 1885 was 249,223,711 kroner, or $67,013,483, and of the exports, 162,261,370 kroner, or $43,630,276. The commerce was divided among the different classes of goods in 1885 as follows:

CLASSES.	Imports.	Exports.
	Kroner.	Kroner.
Food-stuffs	84,500,000	113,200,000
Textiles and clothing	41,700,000	5,700,000
Other articles of consumption	21,900,000	4,600,000
Raw materials	85,600,000	28,200,000
Tools and plant	15,500,000	10,600,000

The principal articles of import and their values in 1885 were as follow: Textiles, 36,612,490 kroner; cereals and flour, 32,895,982 kroner; metal manufactures, 20,671,807 kroner; timber and manufactures of, 19,198,917 kroner; coal, 14,730,383 kroner; linseed, colza, etc., 11,757,705 kroner; stones, 8,254,454 kroner; coffee, 6,972,216 kroner; sugar, 6,165,220 kroner; tobacco, 5,295,029 kroner. The chief exports and their values in 1884 were as follow: Cattle and other animals, 38,240,830 kroner; butter, 30,398,629 kroner; hams, etc., 13,173,076 kroner; hides, 7,618,645 kroner; wheat-flour, 7,266,648 kroner; barley, 6,563,253 kroner; fish, 6,218,853 kroner; eggs, 3,359,893 kroner; woolen goods, 3,349,555 kroner. The trade of Denmark with the principal commercial countries is shown in the following table, which gives the values in kroner.

COUNTRIES.	Imports from —	Exports to —
Germany	93,570,417	52,236,823
United Kingdom	54,170,549	62,803,154
Sweden and Norway	42,024,975	32,502,376
United States	15,834,916	2,180,023
Rest of America	1,294,888	14,408
Russia	11,025,965	2,214,876
Holland	6,819,428	628,755
France	5,524,600	1,910,495
Belgium	4,990,124	1,323,179
Danish colonies	4,143,972	4,198,155
Spain	1,574,565	120,696
Asia	521,373	843,144

Of the total area of Denmark, 80 per cent. is productive. The leading crops are rye, barley, oats, and wheat. The total value of the agricultural product in 1883 was 298,407,276 kroner. In 1885 15,448 cattle were imported and 98,807 exported.

The export of butter is chiefly to Great Britain. Oleomargarine is also exported. A law to regulate its manufacture and sale was passed on April 1, 1885, and renewed in March, 1888. By a narrow majority, the Folkething refused to forbid the coloring of artificial butter or the mixing of artificial with natural butter, as demanded by the Government, but agreed to restrictions whereby a fixed scale of colors must be used and not more than 50 per cent. of butter may be mixed with imitations. The Government was given discretionary power to prohibit the exportation of butterine. This question for the first time in many years brought a part of the Opposition to the support of the Government, and caused members of the Conservative party to vote with the Opposition. The country is suffering from an economical depression, which especially affects the agricultural class, comprising two thirds of the population. The constitutional struggle has hitherto prevented the people from dividing into a land party and a town party, but the present parties seem to be tired of their interminable contest, and the vote on the new oleomargarine bill indicates a tendency toward the same political grouping of interests that prevails in Sweden. The increase in German import duties has nearly closed one of the main outlets for important agricultural products, and more recently Sweden has raised her tariff and thus shut off another large market for Danish exports. The constitutional crisis has prevented the conclusion of treaties of commerce and navigation for the extension of foreign markets, and even the renewal of treaties that have expired, like the one with Spain. The Danes are troubled about the injury to their commerce and shipping interests that the German North Sea canal is expected to cause. Some propose a rival canal across Jutland, connecting the Cattegat with the North Sea; others have revived the old idea of a Scandinavian customs union; and many statesmen of both parties think that a good part of the North Sea trade can be preserved to Denmark by establishing a free port at Copenhagen besides the customs port. For the examination of this last mentioned project both houses of the Rigsdag have voted considerable sums of money, and the Government has appointed a commission to take the subject in charge.

The Constitutional Crisis.—The chronic conflict between the Executive and the Folkething over military and naval appropriations was renewed when the Government brought in the budget in January, 1888. When the struggle began, on the accession of the Estrup ministry in 1876 and the first presentation of the fortification scheme, the people sustained the position taken by the lower house by electing a Liberal majority of two thirds. After repeated dissolutions, the Liberals have retained their preponderance, numbering 75 in the present Folkething, against 27 Conservatives. At first all the ministers were taken from the Landsthing. Later, three of the seven were chosen from among the Conservative members of the representative chamber. The budget of 1889 was amended by the committee of the Folkething, to which it was referred, and early in March was passed in the modified form by a vote of 78 to 10, with 13 abstentions. The budget committee of the Landsthing restored the army appropriations and the items of the provisional budget of the previous year that the lower house had stricken out. A joint committee of both Houses was unable to frame a budget that was satisfactory to the Folkething, which, moreover, stood out against the fortification project that was again presented by the Government. For this the sum of 1,387,112 kroner had been raised by voluntary contributions before April 1, when the King closed the session and again decreed a provisional budget. The Government bases its action on an article of the Constitution that authorizes the promulgation of provisional laws in

cases of urgent necessity; and the Höiesteret decided, when the question was brought up in a private suit, that the provisional decrees are constitutional unless they are rejected by both branches of the Legislature. Legislation by Executive edicts has not been confined to the ordinary finance law, but the criminal and press laws have been modified by provisional laws, which the Folkething has subsequently rejected, while the Landsthing, without expressly ratifying them, has refrained from adverse action. The Rigsret, which is alone competent to decide constitutional questions, has not yet passed upon their validity. The Minister of War announced, after the rejection of the project for fortifying Constantinople on the land side, that the work would nevertheless be begun, and that the Government would obtain the money where it could find it. This project has been before Parliament for fifteen years. Some of the military authorities, as well as the majority of the Folkething, condemn the plan, because it transcends the financial abilities of the country, and it would take nearly the whole Danish army to man the fortress, leaving three quarters of the country defenseless.

From both parties proposals have gone forth for the cessation of the long dead-lock. Before the reassembling of the Parliament on October 1, party caucuses were held to consider the basis of a compromise. The Government has promised the associated labor organizations to bring in measures for the establishment of superannuation and invalid insurance funds, and is disposed to follow the German scheme of social legislation as a means of counteracting socialism, which is spreading among the trade-unions. The majority of the agricultural labor-unions of Zealand in 1888 united formally with the Social Democratic party, while the minority set up a political programme embracing superannuation pensions for laborers, abolition of indirect taxes and duties on necessaries, secrecy of elections, and improvement of the common schools. The Social Democrats demand woman suffrage also. The Liberal Opposition in the Folkething is divided into groups, called the People's party, the Left, the Progressives, the Liberalists, the Constitutional Defense Association, and the Democrats. All except Berg's diminished following are in favor of co-operating with the Conservatives in productive legislation. Only ten members of the Folkething still support the former leader of the Liberal party in his demand for ministerial responsibility to Parliament and the selection of the Cabinet from the majority. Some of the present leaders of the Opposition are ex-Ministers Klein and Krieger, who, with other Moderate Liberals, left the Ministerial party in 1887. The Liberals have recently conceded the complete legislative equality of both houses of the Rigsdag and the right of the King to appoint counselors of his own selection.

Foreign Relations.—The sum of the external aspirations of the Danish people is comprised in their hope of the restoration of North Schleswig, embracing the part north of Flensburg and Tondern, and including those towns. The Treaty of Prague contains a promise that this district would either be restored to Denmark or its inhabitants would be allowed to decide by a vote whether they should be Danes or Germans. The present Government, by its fortification scheme and in its general policy, betrays antagonism toward Germany. The majority of the people, however, see no escape from commercial and political dependence on their powerful neighbor, and deem a friendly and conciliatory policy a necessity. A small party of old Danes are still filled with hatred for their former foes. The young German Emperor endeavored to win good opinions in Denmark by sending objects from the royal collections to an international exhibition that was held at Copenhagen in the summer of 1888, and thus encouraging German manufacturers to take part. In the latter part of July he visited the Danish capital. While he was driving with King Christian, the crowds of Germans on the streets raised cheers in their own language, and many Danes hurrahed, while others hissed.

Iceland.—The chief of the dependencies of Denmark is Iceland, which has an area of 39,756 square miles, and in 1880 had a population of 72,445. It has its own constitution and administration under a charter dated Jan. 5, 1874. The legislative power is vested in the Althing, consisting of 36 members, of whom 30 are elected by popular suffrage, and 6 are nominated by the Crown. At the head of the administration is a minister who is nominated by the Crown, and is responsible to the Althing. The highest local authority is the Governor or Stiftamtmand. There are also three amtmands for the western, northern, and eastern districts of Iceland.

Colonies.—The Danish colonies of the greatest commercial importance are in the West Indies, and consist of the islands of St. Croix, St. Thomas, and St. John. The inhabitants are engaged in the cultivation of the sugar-cane, and export from 12,000,000 to 16,000,000 pounds of raw sugar, and about 1,000,000 gallons of rum annually. The colonists of St. Croix have determined to relieve themselves of the burden of the military force quartered upon them by the Danish Government, which absorbs $75,000, or half the revenue of the island. The colonial council has adopted a resolution, in spite of the objections of the Governor, in favor of replacing the Danish military with a police force that will cost only $32,000 per annum. The imports from Greenland to Denmark in 1885 amounted to 511,069 kroner, and the exports from Denmark to Greenland to 619,513 kroner.

DIPLOMATES, DISMISSION OF. More than one diplomate has been requested by the United States to leave her boundaries, or has been recalled by the power from which he was accredited. The first foreign diplomate to render himself obnoxious to the United States was citizen Genet (sometimes also spelled Genest), Minister from France. During Washington's second term it became known that a diplomatic envoy had been commissioned by the new French Republic, and was on his way to America. The President had been advised by his Cabinet to receive him at once upon his arrival, but neither Washington nor his advisers had any idea that the chief object of the new mission would be to break up the policy of neutrality just formally proclaimed. There was in the United States at this time a popular sentiment in favor of France, and this sentiment had in the Cabinet of Washington an earnest sympathizer in the person of Thomas Jefferson.

Though honestly in favor of preserving neutrality as long as possible, Mr. Jefferson held doubts, and not without reason, of our ability to preserve it against the feebly disguised ill-will of Great Britain; and in the event of a rupture with that country his judgment was by no means adverse to a close union with France. Mr. Genet, when accredited to the United States, was yet quite a young man, not more than twenty-seven years of age. He had been well trained, and through the influence of his sisters, who were in the household of Queen Marie Antoinette, had entered the diplomatic service at St. Petersburg, but he had imbibed such heated revolutionary sentiments that, at the breaking out of the French Revolution the Russian Government seized the first opportunity to furnish him his passports to return to Paris. This event probably recommended him to the extremists in France, and particularly pointed him out as a suitable agent to serve their objects in republican America.

In the year 1793, to go as Mr. Genet did from Paris to Philadelphia by way of Charleston, S. C., was not less out of the way than it would be now to go from here to London by way of Rio Janeiro. There could have been but one object in journeying thus—that was to try the temper of the populace before going to the Government. If such was the case, nothing could have been more satisfactory to Mr. Genet. He was received at Charleston with great attention, and his progress through the country to Philadelphia was a continued ovation.

Mr. Genet was neither crafty, cool, nor insincere, and the incense offered him completely turned his head. He began at once to deal out commissions to fit out privateers and to enlist officers and men for the French naval service.

President Washington received him with all proper courtesy, and Mr. Jefferson for a moment seemed to have cherished visions of international amity; but they were both rudely wakened from their repose by the complaints of the British minister, Mr. Hammond, remonstrating against the capture of British vessels by ships fitted out from United States ports under the authority of this new envoy. So outrageous became the actions of Mr. Genet, and so offensive was his mode of treating the Government, that he speedily forfeited the friendship of Mr. Jefferson, and fell in the popular esteem faster than he had ever risen, and ultimately was deposed in disgrace at the request of President Washington. He had, however, in the mean time married a daughter of Governor Clinton, of New York, and he remained here some years after being deposed from his place as minister.

In Jefferson's administration there was a good deal of trouble with a Spanish minister, Mr. Carlos de Yruga. For some interference, the President requested his recall, and the Spanish Government promptly recalled him and sent another minister to take his place. But he, too, had married an American woman, Miss McKean, of Philadelphia, and as a deposed minister he remained, rendering himself, however, so obnoxious to the Government that President Jefferson requested him to leave the country. He replied that he received instructions from his King, and not from the President. John Quincy Adams, then in Congress, introduced a bill empowering the President to convey out of the country any minister who remained after his recall and after reasonable notice to leave. This action of Congress was reported to the Spanish Government, and resulted in a peremptory demand for him to return, which he reluctantly obeyed.

Mr. Madison's administration was not free from like trouble. The English minister, Mr. Jackson, representing George III, rendered himself so objectionable by outrageous interference in our affairs that his recall was demanded after a very brief stay.

The next dismissed minister was Nicholas Poussin, who represented France. His offense was an insolent criticism of an action taken by the Department of State on some French claim while Gen. Taylor was President and John M. Clayton Secretary of State. His dismissal was very summary. His passports were sent to him in reply to his insolent communication to the Department of State.

Sir John F. Crampton was the next minister dismissed. He had for some years most acceptably represented England at Washington, but, as he broke the provisions of international law by recruiting here for the British army during the Crimean War, his recall was requested.

Then came the Catacazy sensation. He succeeded Mr. Stockl as Minister from Russia. He brought with him his wife, and her beauty rendered her so conspicuous that unpleasant memories were awakened of her previous residence in and about Washington before she had become Madame Catacazy, and Mrs. Fish, wife of the Secretary of State, refused to receive her. The minister's position was not agreeable, and, as he was very far from being an agreeable person, he soon got into trouble, and eventually the minister and his surroundings became so objectionable that President Grant requested his recall.

The latest diplomate in difficulty was Lord Sackville West, the British minister. Up to the date of his blunder he had been one of the most popular of foreign ministers. About the end of October, 1888, he received a letter from one Charles F. Murchison, who represented himself as a naturalized citizen of English birth, and asked advice as to the party for which he should vote. The British Minister replied to this letter, and advised his correspondent to vote for Grover Cleveland and the Democratic party, as favorable to England. This letter of Murchison's was generally conceded to be a trap set to embarrass the British Minister, whose recall was at once requested. The request not being promptly complied with, the Department of State, on the 30th of October, sent Lord Sackville his passports. The incident, happening during a presidential canvass, created much excitement.

DISASTERS IN 1888. Trustworthy records of disasters are always difficult of access. First reports almost invariably place the losses, whether of life or property, at a higher figure than the facts justify; and the final authentic reports are published, if at all, only in local journals or in court records, where they are practically inaccessible for general reference. The following list is necessarily taken from many different, and often contradictory sources of information. As a rule, no accidents are noted that involve the loss of fewer than three lives. A vast majority of the accidental deaths that occur take place by ones and twos, and are so numerous that space can not be spared to record them. In most cases, it has been possible to give a trustworthy monthly summary of the deaths and injuries caused by railroad accidents, the records of these being more fully collated and compared than any other class of accidents.

January 4. Fire: $200,000 worth of property destroyed in Los Angeles, Cal.

5. Railway: broken trestle on the Canadian Pacific Railway, 6 killed. Fire: storehouse in United States Navy-Yard, Brooklyn, loss $200,000. Railway: landslide near Eggleston Springs, Va., train derailed, 3 killed, 1 injured.

7. Fire: in Chicago, Ill., loss $500,000. Heavy losses also in Louisa Court-House, W. Va.

9. Railway: collision near Edson, Wyoming, 2 killed, 10 injured.

10. Railway: broken wheel near Haverhill, Mass., 9 killed, 13 injured (5 fatally).

11. Earthquake shocks in Canada.

12. Earthquakes in South Carolina and Georgia. Blizzard in Dakota, many lives lost. Fire: exhibition building in Columbus, Ohio, 300 valuable dogs killed. Panic in a town in the Tyrol, 8 lives lost.

13. Fire in Indianapolis, loss $1,000,000 (estimated). Blizzard in the Northwest, many lives lost by exposure.

14. Fire: railway buildings burned at Fort Worth, Tex., loss, $100,000.

15. Railway: collision near Ottumwa, Iowa, 3 killed, 1 injured.

17. Railway: broken rail near Bluffton, Ohio, train derailed, 1 killed, 8 injured.

19. Blizzard in the Northwest, accompanied with much suffering and loss.

21. Fire in Montreal, loss $300,000.

23. Fire in Philadelphia, estimated loss $1,000,000. Railway: train derailed at high speed on a curve near Baxterville, N. Y., 16 injured.

24. Explosion in Wellington colliery, Victoria, B. C., 80 lives lost. Railway: broken rail near Bluffton, Ohio, 1 killed, 9 injured.

29. Railway: defective switch near Cary, Miss., 3 killed.

30. Fire in New York city, estimated loss $2,000,-000.

Railway: summary for the month, total number of accidents 239, 67 killed, 228 injured.

February 1. Shipwreck: British bark Abercorn off coast of Washington Territory, 20 lives lost. Earthquake in Vermont. Fire in Buffalo, N. Y., estimated loss $1,000,000.

9. Railway: broken wheel near Clontarf, Minn., train derailed, 14 injured.

, 10. Explosion: powder - mill near Wapwallopen, Pa., 4 killed, 20 injured.

13. Explosion and fire from the upsetting of a kerosene lamp at Silverbrook, Pa., 6 lives lost.

15. Tornado at Mount Vernon, Ill., the town nearly destroyed, 39 killed, 125 injured, much property damaged.

16. Explosion: in a coal-mine near Kaiserlautern, Bavaria, 40 killed.

24. Railway: collision near Colton, Neb., 2 killed, 10 injured.

25. Drowned: several thousand workmen engaged in repairing the levees of the Yellow river, China.

27. Explosion: steam ferry-boat near South Vallejo, Cal., 20 lives lost.

Railway: summary for the month, total number of accidents 174, killed 28, injured 164.

March 2. Shipwreck: French schooner Fleur de la Mer, off Cayenne, 60 lives lost.

3. Hurricane in Madagascar, 11 vessels wrecked, 20 lives lost.

9. Fire: office of the "Evening Union" burned at Springfield, Mass., 6 lives lost.

12. Storm in the North Atlantic States, commonly known as the "Blizzard," about 70 lives lost, many vessels wrecked and railway traffic suspended for several days. Railway: train derailed, 3 killed, 3 injured.

16. Railway: train derailed by snow near Sharon, N. Y., 4 killed, 4 injured.

17. Railway train derailed and bridge broken near Blackshear, Ga., 27 killed, 35 injured. News of an earthquake in China; many thousand lives lost.

20. Fire: the Baquet Theatre at Oporto, Portugal, more than 100 lives lost.

22. Railway: train derailed near Oswego, Ore., 12 injured.

29. Explosion in a mine near Rich Hill, Mo., 5 killed, 23 injured.

Railway: summary for the month, total number of accidents 172, killed 85, injured 211.

April 1. Fire: Amphitheatre at Zelaya, Mex., 18 lives lost, many injured.

2. Shipwreck: bark Princess, off Caminha, Portugal, 23 lives lost.

5. Railway: bridge carried away near New Hampton, Iowa, 6 killed, 20 injured.

6. Railway: train derailed near Rockingham, Vt., 2 killed, 5 injured.

7. Shipwreck: loss reported of steamer Rio Janeiro with 120 passengers.

13. Railway: train derailed near King's, Ala., 4 killed, 10 injured.

15. Railway: collision near West Philadelphia, Pa., 1 killed, 22 injured.

16. Tornado: Dacca, India, more than 100 killed, more than 1,000 injured. Shipwreck: collision, steamers Werra and Biela off Deal, England, 10 lives lost.

19. Explosion: colliery at Workington, England; 22 lives lost.

28. Railway: train derailed near Portville, N. Y., 20 injured.

29. Shipwreck: collision, ship Smyrna and steamer Moto, off Isle of Wight, 13 lives lost.

30. Shipwreck: French fishing-fleet reported caught in a gale off Iceland, 137 lives lost. Floods: much damage in New England and in Minnesota and Wisconsin. Shipwreck: steamship Queen of the Pacific sunk at Port Harford, Cal.

Railway: summary for the month, number of accidents 136, killed 42, injured 191.

May 6. Railway: car loaded with dynamite exploded by collision at Locust Gap, Pa., 17 dwelling-houses wrecked, 8 killed, 25 injured. Shipwreck: American steamship Eureka sunk by collision with British steamship Benison off Cape Henlopen.

7. Hailstorms: Delhi and Moradabad, India, about 150 lives lost.

10. Explosion of gas: St. Paul's Cathedral, Buffalo, destroyed. Falling rocks in a mine in Saxony, 18 killed.

12. Floods: much damage in Iowa and Illinois.

13. Lightning: oil-tanks exploded at Oil City, Pa., a great fire ensues, endangering the town.

14. Railway: collision near Fountain, Col., fire and explosion of a powder-car followed, 4 killed, 20 injured.

15. Railway: collision, Moscow and Kursk Railway in Russia, 11 lives lost; train derailed near Salida, Col., 13 injured.

17. Explosion: 8,000 pounds of powder and 125 pounds of dynamite near Stockton, N. J., 1 killed, 6 injured.

20. Floods (see May 12): the overflow of the Mississippi begins to subside, after having done immense damage.

21. Floods in Mesopotamia, 500 lives lost (estimated).

23. Railway: two trains derailed almost simultaneously from parallel and adjacent bridges near Cameron, Iowa, 4 killed, 2 injured.

30. Railway: collision near Bordeaux, Wyoming, 3 killed, 6 injured.

Railway: summary for May, total number of accidents 144, killed 43, injured 158.

June 1. Explosion: steam-boiler at Wyandotte, Mich., 3 killed.

4. Railway: collision near Tampico, Mex., 18 killed, 41 injured. Fire: Mundine Hotel burned in Rockdale, Tex., 11 lives lost.

7. Storms in New England and Canada, losses of life and property.

13. Shipwreck: loss of a German steamer with 1,100 pilgrims on board.

14. Railway: train derailed near Braddock, Kan., 15 injured.

18. Floods: Leon river, Mex., much property destroyed, more than a thousand lives lost.

19. Railway: train derailed near Pope's Head Run, Va., 4 killed, 5 injured. Fire: steamer Nord burned at Kiel, 8 lives lost.

24. Drowned: steam-launch capsizes in Passaic river, 6 lives lost (five women).

26. Railway: collision near Cable City, Pa., 6 killed 4 injured.

27. Railway: train derailed near Tenessa, Ala., 4 killed, 6 injured.

30. Floods: (reported) Canton river, China, 2,000 lives lost (estimated).

Railway: summary for the month, total number of accidents 143, killed 40, injured 125.

July 5. Tornado at New Brunswick, N. J., 1 life lost, several injured, and many buildings damaged.

6. Railway collision near Nanticoke, Pa., 30 injured. Explosion: steam-boiler in Pittsburg, Pa., 3 killed, several injured.

7. Fire: farm-house burned near Sault St. Marie, Mich., 4 lives lost.

9. Earthquake in Maryland.

10. Heavy rains destroy much property in the Mississippi and Ohio valleys.

11. Fire: diamond-mine at Kimberly, South Africa, 224 lives lost; at Alpena, Mich., 1,300 people rendered homeless.

12. Railway: broken bridge near Orange Court-House, Va., 10 killed; derailment and broken trestle near Orange Court-House, Va., 9 killed, 22 injured. Floods: in Pennsylvania, much damage done.

13. Shipwreck: British ship Star of Greece, off Adelaide, Australia, 17 lives lost.

15. Volcanic eruption in Japan, 500 lives lost (estimated); violent storms in the northern United States.

17. Railway: collision near Oxmoor, Ala., 2 killed, 8 injured.

19. Storm: Wheeling, W. Va., and vicinity, 23 lives lost.

20. Explosion on board a tug-boat near Westport, Ind., 7 lives lost.

July 30. Volcanic eruption reported in Philippine Islands, 100 lives lost (estimated).

Railway: summary for the month, total number of accidents 157, killed 60, injured 169.

August 1. Railway: collision at Olive Hill, Ky., 3 killed, 3 injured.

3. Fire: New York city, 20 lives lost.

8. Railway: train derailed near Morgantown, Ind., 18 injured. Fire: New York City, 4 lives lost.

9. Fire: at Chattanooga, Tenn., 5 lives lost. Yacht upset on the Delaware river near Pennsville, N. J., 5 women drowned.

10. Yellow fever becomes epidemic at Jacksonville, Fla.

11. Flood: reservoir bursts in Valparaiso, Chili, 50 lives lost.

13. Railway: landslide near Shohola, Pa., wreck took fire, 1 killed, 33 injured.

14. Shipwreck: collision off Nova Scotia, steamers Thingvalla and Geiser, the latter sank, 117 lives lost.

21. Floods: great damage in Louisiana and on the upper Ohio.

22. Shipwreck: collision off San Francisco, steamers City of Chester and Oceanic, 20 lives lost. Boiler explosion at Necnab, Wis., 14 killed, 9 injured. Tornado in the vicinity of Still Pond, Md., and in Delaware, 11 lives lost.

26. Railway: train derailed near Fort Buford, Dak., 5 injured (3 fatally).

27. Railway: collision near Krum, Iowa, 3 killed, 4 injured. Shipwreck: Norwegian steamer Bratsberg on Cape Balance, Gulf of St. Lawrence, 15 lives lost. Fire in Hamburg, 6 lives lost.

31. Shipwreck: collision, steamers Snaresbrook and Cairo, off Tarifa, Spain, 11 lives lost. Waterspout near Little Rock, Ark., 7 lives lost.

Railway: summary for the month, total number of accidents 222, killed 56, injured 202.

September 1. Oil-tank bursts near Findlay, Ohio, fire ensues, 3 lives lost.

2. Fire in Baltimore, Md., 7 lives lost. Platform falls at a religious meeting in Belgium, 3 killed, many injured.

4. Landslide, Monroe, N. H., 5 killed.

5. Railway: collision in France, 9 killed, 13 injured.

9. Railway: collision near Waynesville, Ohio, circus train run into by freight train, 5 killed, 22 injured, cause, fog. Fire in San Francisco, estimated loss, $1,000,000. Destructive floods in Spain.

10. Railway: collision, excursion train run into by freight train, Rittman, Ohio, 4 killed, 25 injured. Disastrous floods in Mexico.

11. Explosion in a Montana mine, 9 killed, 6 injured. Destructive floods in Georgia. Severe earthquake shocks in Greece.

12. Railway: train derailed by cattle near Pocatello, Idaho, 3 killed, 11 injured. Cyclone in Mexico.

13. Shipwreck: collision, Steamers Sud America

and La France off Canary Islands, 40 lives lost (reported). Cyclone: Cuba, 1,000 lives lost (estimated). Volcanic eruption and floods in the Philippine Islands, several hundred lives reported lost.

14. Railway: derailment, collision, and explosion, two trains wrecked near Ankenytown, Ohio, 3 killed, 36 injured (several fatally). Destructive floods in the Carolinas.

17. Floods: Tyrol, Switzerland, 28 lives lost (estimated).

19. Railway: collision near East Winona, Wis., 18 injured; accident in Hanover, 4 soldiers killed, many injured. Fire in Queensland, alleged loss, $2,000,000.

26. Fire: prairie fires consume many houses and hundreds of acres of grain in Dakota. Destructive storm on the North Atlantic coast.

27. Fire in Kronstadt, 14 lives lost.

29. Destructive hurricane in the West Indies.

Railway: summary for the month, total number of accidents 128, killed 46, injured 228.

October 2. Severe storm on the Great Lakes, several lives lost, and many wrecks.

5. Shipwreck: French fishing-bark Madeline run down by steamship Queen. 21 lives lost.

6. Railway: collision near Dickerson's Station, Md., 3 killed, 6 injured.

7. Platform gives way at a church celebration in Reading Pa., 158 injured.

10. Railway: collision, excursion train, near Mud Run, Pa., 63 killed, 23 injured; Amphitheatre Falls at Quincey, Ill., 300 injured.

16. Railway: collision near Tamanend Switch, Pa., 10 killed, 23 injured.

17. Explosion and wreck: steamer Ville de Calais, 25 lives lost.

19. Railway: train derailed owing to a misplaced switch near Washington, Pa., 2 killed, 23 injured.

27. Railway: train derailed near Alexander City, Ala., 2 killed, 10 injured.

29. Railway: collision near Pulaski, Ky., 3 killed, several injured.

Railway: summary for the month, total number of accidents 146, killed 120, injured 223.

November 2. Explosion: a thrashing-machine in Bucks County, Pa., 6 killed.

3. Explosion in a coal-mine in Aveyron, France, 80 killed.

4. Railway: collision near Marshall, Tex., 3 killed; 2 injured; train derailed near Vicksburg, Miss., 3 killed, 2 injured. Fire: at Godfrey, Ill., young ladies' seminary burned, loss $250,000. Explosion in a mine in Clinton County, Pa., 17 killed. Shipwreck: steamer Saxmundian off Cowes, 22 lives lost.

6. Explosion: in a mine near Frontenac, Kan., 39 killed.

7. Shipwreck: steam ferry-boat sunk near Calcutta, 60 lives lost.

9. Fire: at Rochester, N. Y., 33 lives lost. Explosion: in a mine near Pittsburg, Kan., 150 killed.

10. Shipwreck: collision off New York, steamer Iberia sunk by the Umbria.

12. Railway: collision near Rock Station, Wyoming, 2 killed, 10 injured.

14. Explosion: fire-damp in a mine near Dour, Belgium, 32 lives lost. Railway: collision near Valley Falls, W. Va., 5 killed, 4 injured.

16. Shipwreck: steamer off the coast of India, supposed loss of 900 lives. Destructive storms on the coast of Great Britain.

20. Explosion: steam-boiler in Montana, 4 killed, 4 injured.

23. Fire: business part of Eureka Springs, Ark., estimated loss $200,000.

24. Fire: Judson Female College, Madison, Ala.

26. Railway: collision near Husted, Col., wreck caught fire, 2 killed, 4 injured.

27. Wreck: a life-boat upsets off the English coast, 12 lives lost.

30. Fire: in Calumet and Hecla mine, Michigan, 8 lives lost.

Railway: summary for the month, total number of accidents 145, killed 38, injured 179.

December 5. Railway: collision near Detroit, 10 injured (5 fatally).

6. Shipwreck: British steamer Hartlepoole, at Egersund, Norway, 17 lives lost.

8. Fire: steam ferry-boat Maryland, with a number of passenger cars on board, burned at New York.

11. Explosion in a grain-mill at Chicago, 3 killed, several injured.

12. Fire: Chicago Opera House partly burned, loss $50,000.

13. Explosion of a gun on a French man-of-war, 6 killed.

19. Destructive storm in eastern Canada.

23. Fire: steamboat Kate Adams burned on the Mississippi, between 30 and 40 lives lost.

24. Fire: steamboat John J. Hanna burned near Plaquemine, on the lower Mississippi, more than 30 lives lost. Explosion of powder at Mount Pleasant, Ohio, 1 killed, many injured.

25. Fires: at Marblehead, Mass., and at Cincinnati, Ohio, estimated losses $800,000 and $200,000 respectively.

28. Explosion of a shell at Messina, Sicily, 16 soldiers killed. Earthquake shock felt in England.

30. Fire: steamer Bristol burned at her wharf, Newport, R. I.

Railway: summary of the month, total number of accidents 142, killed 37, injured 163.

DISCIPLES OF CHRIST. The "Year-Book" of the Disciples of Christ for 1888 gives the number of churches as 6,437, with 620,000 communicants; and of Sunday-schools as 4,500, with which are connected 33,340 officers and teachers, and 318,000 pupils. The number of preachers is 3,262; value of church property, $10,368,361. The estimated annual increase of members is 47,600. Twenty-nine institutions of learning—including 5 universities, 19 colleges, and 5 institutes—are represented in the "Year-Book"; besides which several are mentioned from which no report had been received. The Annual Missionary Conventions of the Disciples of Christ, including the conventions of the General Christian Missionary Society, the Foreign Christian Missionary Society, and the Christian Woman's Board of Missions, were held in Springfield, Ohio, October 23 to 26. The first of these bodies promotes the extension and work of domestic missions and church extension in the United States and Territories, and besides applying its own special funds and directing its own working organization, co-operates with the various State boards, which represent in the aggregate a scale of operations much larger than its own. Its receipts for the year had been $28,384, besides which it had a balance from the previous year of $1,371. Its expenditures had been $25,766. The receipts for the church extension fund had been $7,028 in cash and $20,321 in pledges. Pledges were also made during the meeting of the convention to the amount of $60,281. Loans are made from the fund for no longer period than five years, for no larger an amount than $500, to churches whose building shall not cost more than $5,000. It was decided to establish a branch Board of Church Extension at Kansas City, Mo. The society had employed during the year 35 laborers, under whose efforts 107 churches had been visited and assisted, 51 new and unorganized places visited, 10 churches organized, and 308 persons baptized.

The State boards had altogether employed in 1887, 200 missionaries, who had organized 123 churches, assisted 63 places in building, visited and assisted 1,878 churches, visited 326 new and unorganized places, and who returned 8,970 baptisms.

A committee that had been appointed in the previous year to confer with a committee of the Free-Will Baptist Church with reference to union, reported that union would involve four fundamental points: The adoption of a name honoring Christ as the sole head of the Church; the creed basis that Jesus Christ is the Son of God; conformity of the work to the model of the New Testament; and recognition of the independence of the congregations in local affairs. The committee recommended co-operative local union, so far as practicable, to begin at once. A committee was appointed to continue the correspondence.

The income of the Foreign Christian Missionary Society for the year had been $62,767. The receipts had increased regularly each year, except one, from the first, and the increase in the last six years had been fivefold. The society sustained 24 mission stations in England, Scandinavia, Turkey, India, Japan, and China, with which were connected 37 missionaries and 22 helpers, 2,473 converts, 2,689 children in Sunday-schools, and 380 in day-schools, and in which 798 additions of members were returned.

The Christian Woman's Board of Missions comprised 1,161 auxiliary societies in the local churches, having 14,000 members, and had received, in contributions obtained by their assistance, $22,334. It sustained home missions, a mission in India, and missions in Jamaica, which last returned 17 stations, 1,251 members, and 700 pupils in the schools. The children's bands, of which there were 415, 117 having been organized during the year, had contributed $4,068 to the funds of the society.

DISSECTION, an operation by which the different parts of a body are exposed for study of their structure and arrangement. Various names are given to dissection, depending upon the purpose and the organ concerned in the operation. Osteotomy has for its purpose the exposure of bones; neurotomy, the laying bare of nerves; angiotomy, the exhibition of blood-vessels; and desmotomy, the disclosure of ligaments. The history of dissection is blended with that of anatomy. Its value in the study of medicine was recognized by the ancients, and five centuries before the Christian era Democritus and Hippocrates are said to have examined the bodies of the inferior animals. Aristotle, Syennesis of Cyprus, and Diogenes of Appollonia are among the eminent men of science who dissected the lower animals for anatomical purposes. Alexandria was the seat of the first dissection of the human body.

Through the liberality of the Ptolemies, dissection became a regular part of the study of medicine. Herophilus and Erisistratus here became eminent as the first human anatomists; and the latter is reported to have been so zealous in his pursuit that he dissected not only the dead body, but the living as well. Of him Tertullian writes: "He was a butcher, who dissected six hundred men to discover nature, and hated man to learn the structure of his frame." Alexandria became the medical center of the world, and Galen is said to have traveled thither from Pergamus to see a skeleton. With the dark ages, came a decline in the study of medicine. The Mohammedans, into whose hands Alexandria had passed, forbade dissection, since it was inhibited by the Koran. Abdallatiff was the only exception to this rule, and was obliged to study the bones of the body in cemeteries. The cremation of the corpse in Rome prevented the practice of dissection in that city, and Marius and Galen were content to dissect apes.

In 1315, Mondini dissected two female subjects in the University of Bologna, and dissected and demonstrated one in the following year. He was followed by Leonardo da Vinci, Matthew de Gradibus, Achillini, and Gabriel de Zerbis, all of whom dissected the human body, privately and publicly. Jacobus Sylvius taught in Paris in the sixteenth century, demonstrating his lectures on the lower animals. The greatest practical anatomist of early modern times, however, was Andrew Vesalius, who freed the medical world from the authority of Galen's ape anatomy, and was the founder of a new school, that which prevails at the present day. His investigations on the human cadaver gave a new impetus to the study of anatomy, and it was only the dearth of bodies and the lingering prejudice against dissection that restrained the enthusiasm of his many followers. Such names as Eustachius, Fallopius, Arantius, Variolus, and Vidius, multiply with the beginnings of the new science.

Even at this time, when dissection was frequently carried on by the teachers of anatomy, it was never practiced by medical students. In the progress of time, however, practical anatomy gained in favor, and the thousands of students from all parts of Europe who attended the Italian schools of medical learning, carried their enthusiasm back to their native lands. Public feeling on the subject did not diminish, however, and was wrought still higher by repeated grave-robberies, especially in England. Recognizing the necessity of laws to govern dissection, Henry VIII, in 1540, granted to the College of Surgeons and Barbers four felons annually for dissection; and, in 1565, Queen Elizabeth gave the same privilege to the College of Physicians. These are the first two instances in history of legislation on this troublesome subject. General dissection did not flourish yet, and as late as the middle of the eighteenth century, a fine was imposed for dis-

secting outside of Barber-Surgeon's Hall. William Hunter was the first to overstep these limits, and, following his example, hundreds of men in the profession had their private dissecting-rooms. In 1752, George II decreed that all murderers executed in London and Westminster should be delivered to the medical schools. Executions were not numerous enough to supply the needs of the colleges, and a class of men arose, known as resurrectionists, who rifled the grave-yards, and who multiplied so rapidly that in 1828 there were over one hundred regular resurrectionists in London. The evil grew so monstrous that in 1829 Parliament appointed a committee to frame a law that would remedy existing troubles and provide an adequate supply for the medical schools. This committee called in as witnesses most of the eminent anatomists of the United Kingdom, and the testimony of Sir Astley Cooper is interesting for its incidental statement of the value of dissection: "Without dissection there can be no anatomy, and anatomy is our polar star; for without anatomy a surgeon can do nothing, certainly nothing well. . . . I would not remain in a room with a man who attempted to perform an operation in surgery who was unacquainted with anatomy; he can not mangle the living if he has not operated on the dead." The committee recommended that "all persons throughout the kingdom, of every rank and degree, who die without kindred or friends, or who are unclaimed by kindred or friends within a certain period, be appropriated to dissection, the body after dissection being buried with funeral rites." Three years later the Warburton anatomy act was passed, which practically embodies these suggestions, and which governs the disposition of the unclaimed dead in the United Kingdom at the present day. As a preamble the bill has the following paragraph:

Whereas, A knowledge of the causes of diseases, and methods for treating and curing them, can not be acquired without anatomical examination; and *whereas,* crimes are committed to secure bodies, which are not numerous enough, for the prevention of such crimes and for the protection of the study of anatomy it shall be legal for the Secretary of State and the Chief Secretary of Ireland to grant a license to practice anatomy to any professor or teacher of anatomy, medicine, or surgery.

Inspectors of schools of anatomy are provided for, whose duties consist in keeping as full returns as possible of subjects dissected, and who are required to see that the law is rigidly enforced. Executed murderers are exempt from dissection under this act. According to a law passed by Parliament in 1871, a body must be interred within two months after it has been secured, except when it is obtained in October, when six months are allowed.

In the United States, the first law on the subject of dissection was passed by New York State in 1789. A more comprehensive law was enacted in 1854, which, with its various amendments, stands to-day as follows:

It shall be lawful for the governors, keepers, wardens, managers, and persons having lawful control and management of all public hospitals, prisons, almshouses, asylums, morgues, and other public receptacles for deceased persons, to deliver, under the conditions hereinafter mentioned and in proportion to the number of matriculated students, the bodies of deceased persons therein to the professors and trustees in all the medical colleges of the State authorized by law to confer the degree of doctor of medicine. And it shall be lawful for said professors and teachers to receive such bodies and use them for the purposes of medical study. Medical colleges which desire to avail themselves of the provisions of this act, shall notify said governors, keepers, wardens, and managers of public hospitals, penitentiaries, almshouses, asylums, morgues, and other public receptacles for the bodies of deceased persons in the counties where the colleges are situated, and in counties adjacent thereto, of such desire, and it shall be obligatory upon said governors, keepers, wardens, and managers to notify the proper officers of said medical colleges whenever there are dead bodies in their possession that come under the provisions of this act, and to deliver said bodies to said colleges on their application : *Provided, however*, That such remains shall not have been desired for interment by any relative or friend of such deceased person within forty-eight hours after death : *Provided, also*, That the remains of no persons who may be known to have relatives or friends shall be so delivered or received without the assent of such relatives or friends : *And provided*, That the remains of no person detained for debt, or a witness, or on suspicion of a crime, or of any traveler, or of any person who shall have expressed a desire in his or her last illness that his or her body be interred, shall be delivered or received as aforesaid, but shall be buried in the usual manner : *And provided, also*, That in case the remains of any person so delivered or received shall be subsequently claimed by any relative or friend, it shall be given up to said relative or friend for interment ; and it shall be the duty of said professors and teachers to dispose of said remains in accordance with the instruction of the Board of Health in said localities where such medical colleges are situated, after the remains have served the purpose of study aforesaid. And for any neglect or violation of the provisions of this act, the party so neglecting shall forfeit and pay a penalty of not less than twenty five dollars, nor more than fifty dollars, to be sued for and recovered by the health-officer of said cities and places for the benefit of their department.

Twenty-three other States of the Union have declared dissection to be legal : Alabama, Arkansas, California, Colorado, Connecticut, Georgia, Illinois, Indiana, Iowa, Kansas, Maine, Massachusetts, Michigan, Minnesota, Missouri, Nebraska, New Hampshire, New Jersey, Ohio, Pennsylvania, Tennessee, Vermont, and Wisconsin. In all these States the law is similar in its conditions and provisions to that of New York. Most of the States have also declared disinterment of bodies to be a misdemeanor, while some States have made no provision but the gallows for the supply of bodies for the dissecting-room. The tendency at the present day, however, is strongly toward liberal laws.

In Paris and Vienna all bodies from the public hospitals and workhouses are given to the medical schools. In Göttingen the supply is maintained by the dead from the public institutions, and by the poor that are supported at the expense of the state. The same conditions exist throughout Germany. Holland supplies its medical colleges in a similar manner, imposing but few restrictions. The dissection-laws of Canada, similar to those in the United States, were modeled after the English.

The facilities for dissection at the present day are vast improvements upon those of forty years ago. The instruments are finely made and adjusted. The soap-stone or granite slab has replaced the wooden plank on which the cadaver was laid, and the architecture and ventilation of the dissecting-room are now such as to lend a cheerful aspect to the otherwise gloomy atmosphere. A large sky-light usually covers the room, which is without windows and is lighted at night by electric lamps. Cleanliness abounds, and no unnecessary parts of a body are left in the room. The danger from dissection wounds is greatly diminished by the use of collodion, carbolated vaseline, carbolic acid, and kindred antiseptics, which are used by the students while they are at work.

The difficulty of making the vessels stand out distinctly was early recognized by anatomists. In the sixteenth and seventeenth centuries, air, water, ink, milk, and various colored fluids were used. It soon became evident that some substance must be employed that would harden in the vessels after injection, and suet and wax were next called into requisition. Improvement followed improvement, and injections of plaster of Paris, rubber, glue, and ether found adherents. But none of these methods would do for prolonged dissection, and, until the introduction of alcohol, this was almost impossible. At the present day, arseniate of soda is almost universally used : but chloride of zinc, common salt, hyposulphite of soda, and acetate of alumina still find favor. The usual method of injection is, to sever the common carotid artery near the root of the neck, and attach the peripheral end to the syringe. A pasty mass of a saturated solution of arseniate of soda and plaster of Paris is then prepared, and is forced through the arteries at short intervals of time, so as not to rupture any of the more delicate vessels. The preparation is usually tinted with some aniline dye. When the veins are injected for any purpose, a blue color is used. About three quarts of the mixture suffices for the average body. For courses in operative surgery, and for lectures on the various systems, as the vascular, nervous, and muscular, other methods are employed, sometimes more complicated than that described. In Berlin, Vienna, Paris, and Heidelberg, where the supply of bodies from the various sources exceeds the demand, no body is allowed in the dissecting-room over seven days, and no injections or antiseptic preparations are made use of. See Hyrtl's "Lehrbuch der Anatomie des Menschen" (8th ed., Vienna, 1863) ; "The Gold-headed Cane"; William Hunter's Introductory Lectures ; and W. W. Keen's "Early History of Practical Anatomy" (Philadelphia, 1874).

DOMINION OF CANADA. The year 1888 was marked by an unusual number of changes in the Government of the Dominion. Lord Lansdowne's term of office as Governor-General expired, and he was appointed Viceroy of India, leaving Canada in May. (For biographical sketch and portrait of Lord Lansdowne, see the "Annual Cyclopædia" for 1883, page 468.) He was succeeded at Ottawa by Lord Stanley of Preston, who on June 11 issued the proclama-

LORD STANLEY OF PRESTON.

The Right Hon. Sir Frederick Arthur Stanley, Baron Stanley, of Preston, P. C., G. C. B., was born in 1841, and in 1864 married Constance, eldest daughter of the Earl of Clarendon. He was created a peer in 1886, and was appointed Governor-General of Canada in 1888. He has represented Preston and North Lancashire in the House of Commons, and has held office in the Imperial Government successively as a Lord of the Admiralty, Financial Secretary for War, Financial Secretary to the Treasury, Secretary of State for War, Colonial Secretary, and President of the Board of Trade. He served in the Grenadier Guards from 1858 till 1865, and was gazetted lieutenant and captain in 1862. He is brother and heir presumptive of the present Earl of Derby. Lord Stanley of Preston is a conservative in politics.

tion announcing his appointment to the Governor-Generalship. The death of the Hon. Thomas White, Minister of the Interior, deprived the Dominion Cabinet of one of its ablest and most respected members. Mr. White was succeeded in the ministry by the Hon. Edgar Dewdney, who retired from the Lieutenant-Governorship of the Northwest Territories. Sir Charles Tupper resigned the portfolio of Minister of Finance to return to London as High Commissioner for Canada, and was succeeded by the Hon. G. E. Foster, Minister of Marine and Fisheries. The Hon. Charles Tupper (son of Sir Charles) entered the Cabinet as Minister of Marine and Fisheries. The Hon. A. W. McLelan, Postmaster-General, accepted the Lieutenant-Governorship of Nova Scotia, and his portfolio fell to the Hon. John Haggart. The Hon. J. B. Plumb, Speaker of the Senate, died during the session of Parliament on March 12.

Parliament.—Twenty-four by-elections took place during the year, but without effecting any material change in the balance of parties heretofore existing in the House of Commons. Parliament met on February 23, and was prorogued on May 22.

Parliament was opened on February 24 by Lord Lansdowne, who delivered the following speech from the throne

Honorable Gentlemen of the Senate:
Gentlemen of the House of Commons:

It affords me much gratification to meet you once more at the commencement of the parliamentary session, and to congratulate you upon the general prosperity of the country. Although the labors of the husbandman have not been rewarded in some portions of the Dominion by an adequate return, the harvest of last year has on the whole been plenteous, while in Manitoba and the Northwest Territories it was one of remarkable abundance.

The negotiations between her Majesty's Government and that of the United States for the adjustment of what is known as "The Fishery Question" have, I am pleased to inform you, resulted in a treaty which will, I venture to hope, be considered by you as honorable and satisfactory to both nations. The treaty, with the papers and correspondence relating thereto, will be laid before you, and you will be invited to adopt a measure to give effect to its provisions.

The extension and development of our system of railways have not only rendered necessary additional safeguards for life and property, but have given greater frequency to questions in which the interests of rival companies are found to be in conflict, and to require authoritative adjustment. As further legislation appears to be needed for these purposes, a measure will be submitted to you for the consolidation and improvement of "the Railway act."

Experience having shown that amendments are required to make the provisions of the act respecting Elections of the Members of the House of Commons more effective and more convenient in their operation, you will be asked to consider a measure for the amendment of that statute. The act respecting Controverted Elections may likewise require attention with a view to the removal of certain questions of interpretation which have arisen and which should be set at rest. My Government has availed itself of the opportunity afforded by the recess to consider the numerous suggestions which have been made for improving the details of the Act respecting the Election Franchise, and a measure will be submitted to you for the purpose of simplifying the law and greatly lessening the cost of its operation.

The growth of the Northwest Territories renders expedient an improvement in the system of government and legislation affecting these portions of the Dominion, and a bill for that purpose will be laid before you. A bill will be submitted to you to make a larger portion of the modern laws of England applicable to the Province of Manitoba and to the Northwest Territories in regard to matters which are within the control of the Parliament of Canada, but which have not as yet been made the subject of Canadian legislation.

Among other measures, bills will be presented to you relating to the judiciary, to the Civil-Service act, and to the audit of the public accounts.

Gentlemen of the House of Commons:

The accounts for the past year will be laid before you as well as the estimates for the ensuing year. They have been prepared with a due regard to economy and the requirements of the public service.

Honorable Gentlemen of the Senate:
Gentlemen of the House of Commons:

I commend these important subjects and all matters affecting the public interests which may be brought before you to your best consideration, and I feel assured that you will address yourselves to them with earnestness and assiduity.

The Budget.—Sir Charles Tupper, Minister of Finance, in moving the House into Committee of Ways and Means, on April 27, said that the revenue of the Dominion for the year ending June 30, 1887, amounted to $35,754,993, an increase of $454,993 over the estimate. The actual expenditure was $35,657,860, an excess of $57,860 over the estimates, thus leaving a surplus in place of the expected deficit. He estimated the revenue for the year 1887-'88 at $36,900,000, and the expenditure at about $37,-000,000, the estimates to be laid before Parliament amounting to $35,421,440.22: and the supplementary estimates would include amounts for mail subsidies and steamship subventions. He said the Dominion had incurred a debt of £1,000,000 in England for. temporary accommodation. Since May last the country had experienced a certain amount of financial stringency, and one of the results had been that three banks had ceased to transact business. The past summer was one of unusual beat and drought in the province of Ontario, and the harvest was not up to the average. The same cause had operated against the extensive lumber industry, and on account of the lowness of the water, timber that had been cut and lay in the streams could not be made marketable. This had caused a certain drain on the resources of the banks, in order that the legitimate requirements of those engaged in the industry should be provided for. But against this they had occasion to be gratified by the splendid harvest in Manitoba and the Northwest. Still it must be borne in mind that we were going ahead rather too quickly. In our cities, and especially in Toronto, there had been a certain amount of speculation in real estate. In the end, the short crop in Ontario and these other attendant circumstances, would prove a blessing in disguise by the curtailment of importations. However, by the exercise of economy and prudence, Canada would soon recover from the present stringency, her trade being sound at the core, and would soon return to its normal condition. At the beginning of the fiscal year the Government, chiefly in deference to the banking community, lowered the limit of deposits in the savings-banks, and fixed the amount to be received from any depositor to be $300 in any one year, and $1,000 in all. Originally, the savings-bank deposits were unlimited; a reduction was then made to $10,000, and afterward this was again brought down to $3,000; now the limit is $1,000. The effect on the Government savings-bank deposits had been that some of the larger deposits held by the Government had been withdrawn, and had gone to swell the general business of the country by transfers to the banks where higher rates of interest were offered. The million pounds sterling borrowed in England represented an amount that was expected to have been received from Canadian depositors, the capital expenditure of the country having had to be met out of ordinary revenue.

With regard to the working of the iron and steel tariff, the trade retuns showed that the average duty levied by the United States on imports of iron and steel for the year ending June 30, 1887, was 41 per cent. ad valorem; the average rate for the same articles imported into Canada for the nine months ending March 31, under the new tariff, was 23½ per cent. ad valorem. Comparing the United States customs tariff on all goods imported for home consumption with the Canadian tariff on similar imports, the trade returns show this result for the year ended June 30, 1887: Average rate on United States imports, 31½ per cent. ad valorem. Average rate on Canadian imports, 21½ per cent. ad valorem. Comparing dutiable articles under the United States customs tariff with the same articles under the Canadian tariff, the trade returns for 1886-'87 show the average duty on United States imports for home consumption to be 47 per cent. ad valorem against an average of 28¾ per cent. ad valorem on Canadian imports for the same period. Under the Mills Bill the average customs rates on dutiable articles, based on United States imports for home consumption for 1886-'87, is estimated to be 43½ per cent. ad valorem, while under the amended Canadian tariff for the nine months ended March 31, 1888, the average customs rates on dutiable articles entered for home consumption has been 31¾ per cent. ad valorem. The effect of the tariff on the market prices had been to make a small increase, but not to the full extent of the increased duty. He took, by way of illustration, the value of warrants in Glasgow, that being the best gauge of the general level of the iron market, and as at Glasgow prices were pretty even during February and December, 1887. Taking pig-iron, the price in Canada was only from $1 to $1.25 per gross ton higher in December than in February, 1887, while the additional duty, which took effect July 1, was $2.24 per gross ton, indicating that the foreign maker, carriers, and importers, etc., had made a concession of about $1 to $1.25 per ton to retain the trade. In other words, the consumer paid fully one half the amount of duty contributed to the revenue. As to bar-iron, the price was as follows: In February, 1887, $1.60 to $1.65 per 100 pounds; in December, 1887, $1.85 to $1.90 per 100 pounds, showing an advance of only 25 cents per 100 pounds, while the extra duty was 45 cents per 100 pounds. As to cast-iron water-pipes, the contract prices for the corporation of Montreal averaged as follows: For 1885, $18.50 per gross ton; for 1886, $26.21 per gross ton; for 1887, $33.14 per gross ton; for 1888, only $32.10 per gross ton; although the increase in duty has been $8 per ton. The Montreal water-pipes for 1888, above referred to, are to be made in Canada from Canadian ore. The increase of price over the average for 1885-'86 is thus about half the increase in duty.

After referring in detail to the effect of the tariff in promoting the exploration of new fields in the iron industry, and to the improved business of the old iron and steel industries, Sir Charles took up the question of trade with the West Indies. This trade, on the whole, had been good; the price of Canadian fish in the West Indies had been satisfactory to fishermen and merchant shippers. An important factor in this trade was the return cargoes of sugar and the recent change in the sugar duties. Putting the same duty upon all sugars for refining, according to their polariscopic test, had had the effect of encouraging the importation of West Indian sugar, especially into Nova Scotia. In 1878 the total value of imports entered for consumption from all the West Indies was $1,181,728, and in 1886 this had increased to $3,249,642.

Passing to the cotton industry, there are now about 60,000 bales of raw cotton, in value about $3,000,000, used annually in the Dominion, being an increase in ten years of nearly 50,000 bales. In the Dominion there are now about half a million spindles, employing about 9,000 hands, with an invested capital of about $8,000,000. To show how steadily interprovincial trade has developed in Canada, returns furnished by the Intercolonial Railway show that the following movements took place in 1878 and in 1887 in passengers and articles carried both ways:

ITEMS.	1878.	1887.
Flour, barrels..............	687,778	758,480
Grain, bushels.............	331,170	1,016,834
Live-stock, number.........	46,498	80,782
Lumber, feet	56,600,000	161,100,000
Manufactures, tons........	140,858	
Other articles (not including fire-wood), tons..........	230,741	520,000
Total freight, tons..........	522,710	1,131,834
Passengers, number........	618,957	940,144

In both years flour, live-stock, and lumber were local, as distinguished from through freight for export. As regards grain, there were 440,454 bushels local freight in 1887, against 331,470 in 1878. The total increase of freight in 1887, as compared with 1878, was 608,000 tons; and, speaking of the proportions between local and through freight, the general manager says that the increase is about equally divided. This would give an increase of local traffic equal to over 300,000 tons in 1887, as compared with 1878, or an increase of 57 per cent. The increase in the movement of passengers was indicative also of increased interprovincial trade. Taking some of the articles carried westward, the growth of this trade he regarded as indicated by the quantity of coal yearly transported by rail from Nova Scotia. For the several years from 1879 to 1886 the following quantities were carried west by the Intercolonial Railway: 1879, 570 tons; 1880, 10,246 tons; 1881, 30,629 tons; 1882, 35,089 tons; 1883, 54,891 tons; 1884, 112,898 tons; 1885, 165,791 tons; 1886, 175,512 tons.

Sir Charles submitted to Parliament a series of tables showing comparative statistics for each year since confederation. The Canada

Federal gross debt, with assets, for years ended 30th June was as follows:

YEARS.	Gross Debt.	Assets.
1867 (Confederation created).......	$93,046,051	$17,317,410
1868............................	96,896,666	21,189,581
1869 (Better terms to Nova Scotia).	112,361,998	36,502,679
1870 (Manitoba created a Province, debt $472,090).................	115,993,706	37,753,964
1871 (British Columbia admitted, debt $1,666,200)................	115,492,682	37,786,165
1872............................	122,400,179	40,213,107
1873 (Prince Edward Island admitted, debt 4,927,060).............	129,743,482	29,894,970
1874............................	141,163,551	32,835,586
1875............................	151,663,401	35,655,028
1876 (Intercolonial Railway opened)	161,204,687	36,653,173
1877............................	174,675,884	41,440,525
1878............................	174,957,268	34,595,199
1879............................	179,483,871	36,498,683
1880 (Intercolonial Railway finished)	194,634,440	42,182,552
1881 (C. P. R. begun).............	199,861,587	44,465,757
1882............................	205,365,251	51,708,601
1883............................	202,159,104	48,692,389
1884 (Provincial debts assumed, $7,172,297)...................	242,482,416	60,320,505
1885 (C. P. R. finished, last spike Nov. 7).......................	264,703,607	68,295,915
1886 (Temporary loan to C. P. R. of $20,000,000. Manitoba debt assumed, $8,317,226)..........	273,164,841	50,003,234
1887 ($10,189,521 added to debt, being purchase-money of 6,793,014 acres of land from C. P. R.)......	273,187,626	45,873,611

Canada taxation, being customs and excise duties collected, during years ended 30th June:

YEARS.	Excise.	Customs.
1868.....................	$3,602,588	$8,578,880
1869.....................	2,710,028	8,272,580
1870.....................	3,619,622	9,334,213
1871.....................	4,295,945	11,841,104
1872.....................	4,735,652	12,787,982
1873.....................	4,460,682	12,954,164
1874.....................	5,594,904	14,925,193
1875.....................	5,069,687	15,351,011
1876.....................	5,563,487	12,523,588
1877.....................	4,941,898	12,546,988
1878.....................	4,858,672	12,782,524
1879.....................	5,890,768	12,900,659
1880.....................	4,282,427	14,071,843
1881.....................	5,343,022	18,406,092
1882.....................	5,884,860	21,581,570
1883.....................	6,260,116	23,009,582
1884.....................	5,459,809	20,028,890
1885.....................	6,449,102	18,985,428
1886.....................	5,552,905	19,373,552
1887.....................	6,308,201	22,378,801

Canada imports for home consumption, divided into free and dutiable, during years ended 30th June:

YEARS.	Dutiable.	Free.
1868.................	$43,655,696	$28,829,610
1869.................	41,009,342	26,332,928
1870.................	45,127,422	26,110,181
1871.................	60,094,862	26,553,180
1872.................	68,545,718	39,163,898
1873.................	71,409,196	56,105,398
1874.................	76,235,858	51,168,316
1875.................	78,141,482	41,477,229
1876.................	60,243,846	34,489,572
1877.................	60,919,960	35,380,523
1878.................	59,776,589	31,422,983
1879.................	55,430,012	24,911,596
1880.................	54,182,967	17,599,352
1881.................	71,620,725	19,990,879
1882.................	85,757,483	26,591,494
1883.................	91,588,839	31,548,660
1884.................	50,010,498	28,170,148
1885.................	78,269,618	29,440,401
1886.................	70,658,819	28,943,875
1887.................	78,120,679	27,518,749

Imports of iron and steel and manufactures thereof into the Dominion for home consumption for years:

1868.	$6,555,365	1878.............	$9,398,306
1869.............	7,355,780	1879.............	7,962,295
1870.............	7,750,567	1880.............	10,128,660
1871.............	10,808,645	1881.............	12,955,855
1872.............	15,918,179	1882.............	17,499,488
1873.............	25,435,020	1883.............	20,089,274
1874.............	20,790,387	1884.............	14,790,727
1875.............	18,199,198	1885.............	11,415,718
1876.............	12,965,117	1886.............	11,058,365
1877.............	11,082,321	1887.............	18,595,046

Relative value of ten principal exports (home production) from Dominion of Canada, fiscal year 1887:

Wood and manufactures	$21,166,580	Fish.............	$6,875,810
		Furs and hides...	2,329,918
Grains, barley, pease, and flour,	16,001,897	Eggs.............	1,825,559
		Coal.............	1,522,272
Animals.........	10,461,442	Meats	1,094,076
Cheese	7,103,978	Gold	1,017,401

The number of post-offices in the successive years has been as follow: In 1868, 3,638; in 1869, 3,756; in 1870, 3,820; in 1871, 3,943; in 1872, 4,135; in 1873, 4,518; in 1874, 4,706; in 1875, 4,892; in 1876, 5,015; in 1877, 5,161; in 1878, 5,378; in 1879, 5,696; in 1880, 5,773; in 1881, 5,935; in 1882, 6,171; in 1883, 6,395; in 1884, 6,837; in 1885, 7,084; in 1886, 7,295; in 1887, 7,534.

The postal revenue in 1868 was $1,024,710; and the expenditure, $1,053.570. In 1887 the revenue was $2,603,256, and the expenditure, $3,458,101.

The total Canadian debt payable in London, July 1, 1887, was as follows:

Rate of Interest.		Amount.
3½ per cent............................		$24,383,833
4 "	....	140,836,599
5 "	....	2,433,333
6 "	....	4,052,473
Total...............		$171,675,736
Interest paid.......................		$6,850,745

Other statistical tables were submitted, similar to those presented at the previous session, and published in the "Annual Cyclopædia" for 1887, which contained statistics from 1868 to 1886. The figures for 1887 are as follow:

Deposits by the people in the chartered banks of Canada, $107,154,483.

Deposits in the savings-banks, $50,944,785.

Discounts given by the chartered banks, $169,357,-325.

Total exports of Canada, $89,515,811.

Shipping employed, not including coasting-vessels, 14,317,099 tons register.

Coasting-trade tonnage employed, 17,513,677 tons register.

Railway, mileage, in Canada, 12,292.

Life insurance in Canada, net amount in force, $191,566,168.

Fire insurance in Canada, amount at risk in 1887, $633,523,697; in 1886 (omitted last session), $586,-733,022.

Business failures in Canada, $16,311,745.

After referring to the failure of Erastus Wiman's attempt to promote unrestricted reciprocity sentiment in Canada, and deprecating the idea of driving the protected industries into the United States, Sir Charles said:

I have used a strong term; I have said this scheme of unrestricted reciprocity is a folly, a mad folly; and I say so for this reason, that if every man in this House was of opinion that Canada should commit suicide, as it would have to do by adopting unrestricted reciprocity—I say if that was the position of every man of both sides of the House, we would have no more chance of obtaining unrestricted reciprocity with the United States than we would have of dictating to the Imperial Parliament who should advise Her Majesty's ministers. Not a bit more. I can scarcely find any simile or language that would show the helplessness and the utter futility of adopting such a policy. This subject has been discussed now for many months, it has been put forth in the most captivating form by the ablest men on the opposite side of the House, both in this House and abroad through the country, and they have found papers so wanting in information and so blindly subservient to party influences as to advocate their scheme—and what has been the result? Why, point me to a paper in the United States, Republican or Democratic, Mugwump or anything else—show me a single paper possessing the slightest influence in that country that would ever give support to a scheme which would take away the barriers between the trade of Canada and the trade of the United States, and leave Canada free to admit the products of England.

Sir, we have the most abundant evidence that it is only necessary for us to have confidence in ourselves, and to devote ourselves unsparingly in the future to the great task of developing the inexhaustible resources of this country. Then, whenever the time comes that we shall have the management of these matters entirely in our own hands, we shall be able to enter upon even terms into negotiations with other countries for the extension of our commercial relations. I say, sir, that we not only have the advantage of this great domain, with its inexhaustible resources, but we have over us the flag of the mightiest empire in the world, and under its ægis we can go forth with greater confidence than any man can possess, representing a community of only five millions of people, we can go forth knowing that in the remotest section of the world that flag is waving over our heads, that there are behind us an army, a navy, and a moral force of a great empire that will give Canada all the protection that she can desire. Sir, under these circumstances, to throw away our birthright for a mess of pottage, to go looking for commercial reciprocity with a foreign country—even if we could obtain it, I say a policy of that kind would be, in my opinion, to make us forget what Canadians never will forget, the gratitude they owe to the great empire of which we form a part, and the duty of building up on this northern portion of the continent of America, a power to which every Canadian will feel proud to belong.

Unrestricted Reciprocity.—The principal debate of the session was on the question of unrestricted reciprocity between Canada and the United States.

Sir Richard Cartwright (Liberal) moved, on March 14:

That it is highly desirable that the largest possible freedom of commercial intercourse should obtain between the Dominion of Canada and the United States, and that it is expedient that all articles manufactured in, or the natural products of either of the said countries should be admitted free of duty into the ports of the other (articles subject to duties of excise or of internal revenue alone excepted). That it is further expedient that the Government of the Dominion should take steps at an early date to ascertain on what terms and conditions arrangements can be effected with the United States for the purpose of securing full and unrestricted reciprocity of trade therewith.

Hon. Mr. Foster (Minister of Marine and Fisheries) moved in amendment:

That Canada in the future, as in the past, is desirous of cultivating and extending trade relations with the United States in so far as they may not conflict with the policy of fostering the various interests and industries of the Dominion which was adopted in 1879 and has since received in so marked a manner the sanction and approval of its people.

Mr. Jones of Halifax (Liberal) moved an amendment:

That in any arrangement between Canada and the United States providing for the free importation into each country of the natural and manufactured productions of the other, it is highly desirable that it should be provided that during the continuance of any such arrangement the coasting-trade of Canada and of the United States should be thrown open to vessels of both countries on a footing of complete reciprocal equality, and that vessels of all kinds built in the United States or Canada may be owned and sailed by the citizens of the other and be entitled to registry in either country and to all the benefits thereto appertaining.

Sir Richard Cartwright, in supporting his motion, said:

"I will take two facts alone, which appear to me, and I think will appear to this House, to be of very great importance in this connection; and of which I have here as absolute evidence as it is possible for any man to have. I will take the movement of the population in this country in the last quarter of a century, beginning in the year 1861 and going down to the year 1886, which is the last moment for which I have absolutely accurate statistical information. What are these facts? Sir, they are facts which I state with pain. But I say that we have here incontestable evidence that in these twenty-five years, one in every four of the native - born population of Canada has been compelled to seek a home in a foreign country, and that of all the immigrants whom we have imported at great cost, three out of four have been compelled to follow in the track of that fraction of the native-born population.

"The formal reports of the United States show that in the year 1860 there were 249.000 men of Canadian birth in the United States; that in ten years they had grown to 490,000 souls, and that in 1880, there were 707,000 Canadians in the United States. It must be remembered that by no means represents the total exodus of our people, because, when you come to deal with such large numbers as these, you must allow for the death rate which prevailed in the twenty years from 1860 to 1880. That death-rate, after careful examination, I believe to have been about 74,000 in the first decade, and 120,000 in the second, in all equal to 194,000. It is clear, therefore, that between 1860 and 1880, for some cause or other, which it is not my present purpose to analyze, at least 650,000 Canadians found homes in the United States.

"Apply another test. If you choose to turn to the report of Trade and Navigation, which the Minister of Customs with commendable promptitude has laid on the table, there you will find evidence which ought to convince this House that within the last fourteen or fifteen years, although there has been a considerable increase of population—but far inferior to that we ought to have had—there has been, and it is a noteworthy fact, a very large reduction in the total volume of trade. Here is the honorable gentleman's own blue book laid within these last few days on the table of the House, and from that I see that in 1873, fifteen years ago, the total volume of trade was $217,500,-000, with a population of 3,750,000; that, to-day, with a population which honorable gentlemen opposite estimate, though incorrectly, at 4,800,-000, our total volume of trade and exports is $202,000,000, being $15,000,000 less than it was fifteen years ago, although we have 1,000,-000 people or thereabout more. Apply another test. I find in 1873 the average per head of exports and imports amounted to $58 odd; according to the honorable gentleman's own statement, the average per head of exports and imports to-day is $41.50.

In twenty years the Government have trebled our debt, in twenty years they have trebled our taxes, and when the budget comes to be brought down I think the House will find that the liabilities of the people of this country are very far indeed from being fully discharged or measured even by our present enormous debt. Again I say for the moment I suspend my remarks on their failure to create an important interprovincial trade. That is a question which requires a little more discussion than it suits me to give it at the moment; and here again I ask my friends from the maritime provinces, when the time comes, to contribute for the information of the House their views as to the success which has attended our efforts to create a trade in that direction. Nor will I dwell just now further on the lamentable failure after the expenditure of over $100,000,000 of public money, to produce or obtain any adequate settlement of the Northwest. But I will say a word or two as to the utter failure to obtain any adequate return from our great public works. The public accounts are here, and those public accounts show that the people of Canada have expended well nigh $200,000,000 in the construction of railways and canals and divers other improvements. Time was when we hoped those would give us something like an adequate return, directly or indirectly, but the time has now arrived when we find these expectations very bitterly disappointed. How now stands the case? I take the public accounts for 1887, and I find, all told, a charge of $3,970,000 for the expenses of operating those public works, and that is the nominal charge. The real charge, if our accounts were kept as any other country on earth would keep them, would be nearer $4,500,000, or, at all events, $4,250,000 than $3,970,000. What do we get as a return? We get a total income of $3,270,000. Not only do we not receive one farthing of interest on the outlay of $200,000,000, but there is a dead annual loss of $700,000 a year, not to speak of the various important items which under our most vicious system of book-keeping are charged to capital account.

"What possible available remedies are there for such a state of things? So far as I can see, these remedies are four. In the first place, I think that a very great improvement might be made by reforming our present most oppressive and unjust system of taxation. I say that an immense improvement might be made by so revising our Constitution in the manner which we have pressed from this side of the House time and again, and in the manner which we have seen our friends—not our friends but the friends of the Government—in conference assembled have lately likewise proposed; and by so altering the Constitution that this tyrannical conduct on the part of the Federal authorities toward the rights and privileges of the local legislatures should be put an end to forever. On the other hand, that which is equally important is that this system of bribes, and all those frequent and incessant forays, by various provincial governments on the Dominion treasury, whenever they have been extravagant and got into a scrape, may likewise be put a stop to; and for a third remedy, sir, that this most mischievous railway monopoly which has barred our progress up to the present time, and which has barred the settlement and prosperity of northwestern Manitoba, should likewise be put an end to. But most of all and most important of all, do I believe would be the success in the obtaining of the proposition which I ask the Government to try and obtain in the resolution now in your hands, the obtaining of perfect free trade with the people of the United States. I say, sir, that that is worth all the rest. Give us that, and railway monopolies will cease to vex and harass you; give us that, and the Federal relations will speedily adjust themselves as Federal relations ought to do and as Federal relations were intended to do; give us that, and the sting would be taken out of those tariff combines, more particularly if the United States, as there is now a good hope that it will do, proceeds to emancipate itself from the trade fetters it most foolishly put on. It may be said that this is a heroic remedy. Well, all I can say is that if it be, never in the history of this country, at any rate, was a heroic remedy more needed.

"I contend that for almost everything our farmers have to sell the United States, if only we had free and unrestricted trade with them, would afford us absolutely the best market; and I contend further that, besides being the best market, it is literally the only market for a great many important articles which we produce. See, in spite of all artificial obstacles, how huge a percentage of the total volume of our trade is the volume of our trade with the United States. Out of a total volume of trade of $202,-000,000, the United States supply the trade of

$83,000,000. Out of $81,000,000 of exports of our own produce, we sell to the United States, or sold last year over $36,000,000, or very nearly half. Out of a total of goods entered for consumption of $105,000,000, we bought $45,000,000 from the United States. We find that, of 18,779 horses which we sold, the United States bought 18,215. We find that, of 443,000 sheep, the United States bought from us 363,000. We find that, of 116,000 cattle, in spite of all tariff restrictions, they bought from us 45,000 head. Of $107,000 worth of poultry, the United States bought $99,000 worth. Of about $2,000,000 worth of eggs—$1,825,000, to be accurate—the United States bought all. Of $593,000 worth of hides, the United States bought $413,000 worth. Of 527,000 tons of coal, the United States bought 404,000. Of 140,000 tons of gypsum, the United States bought all. Of iron-ore, the United States bought all. Of salt, all that we sold the United States bought from us. Of stone and marble, all that we sold the United States bought from us. In spite of fishery disputes, and taxes I suppose, of $6,875,000 worth of fish that we sold, the United States was our best customer and bought $2,717,000 worth. Of $20,485,000 worth of lumber, the United States bought as nearly as possible half, $9,353,-000 worth. Of 1,416,000 pounds of wool, the United States bought 1,300,000 pounds. Of 9,456,000 bushels of barley, the United States again bought all. Of $743,000 worth of hay, the United States bought $670,000. Of $439,-000 worth of potatoes, the United States bought $328,000. Of $83,000 worth of general vegetables, they bought $75,000 worth. Of $254,-000 worth of miscellaneous agricultural products, the United States bought $249,000 worth, without speaking of innumerable smaller articles, such as apples, flax, and a great variety of other things; and, if the duties were once removed, no one who has ever been in Manitoba and the Northwest but knows that the United States would become by all odds our best customer for a great deal of our high-class wheat. Why, in the mere article of manufactures, the United States, out of a total of $3,079,000, bought $1,289,000 worth, and of miscellaneous articles the United States bought $569,000 worth out of a total of $644,-000. There are two things to which I want to call the attention of all the members of this House. One is that, for very obvious reasons, our exports to the United States are largely undervalued. They do not at all fairly represent the amount we sell. So long as they maintain a high tariff, it is the obvious interest of every Canadian seller to underestimate the value of the articles he has to sell, and, as every one knows, the thing is habitually and constantly done. In another respect it is very important that the House should know that in the case of an enormous number of the articles to which I have called specific attention, there is room for well-nigh unlimited expansion. Given free trade, given unrestricted intercourse, and that trade might assume nearly unlimited proportions in regard to a great many of these articles.

"It has been made a grave ground, it has been attempted to be set up as an insuperable ground of objection, that, when you propose to enter into a treaty for unrestricted trade with the United States, you must thereby, of necessity, discriminate against English manufactures and the manufactures of all other countries except the United States. Now, that is true. I admit that. More than that, I will admit that, *prima facie*, what we propose to-day is a very unusual thing. I will admit— I am in nowise disposed to shrink from any argument which can be fairly advanced—I admit frankly that, when a semi-dependent state, when a colony proposes in one breath to tax the goods of the parent state and admit the goods of a foreign state free, while at the same time the parent state admits our goods and the goods of other countries free, and the foreign state taxes those goods very heavily, it is a very unusual thing indeed. I grant that it is clean against all formulas. I do not deny that. I admit that it appears to be reversing the action of one hundred years ago when England lost half of this continent because she endeavored to tax their goods without giving them representation, and I admit that we are going a little far in taxing her goods and not the goods of the people of the United States. I grant that this needs explanation, and I am prepared to say that I can give a full explanation why in the interests of England itself this thing should be done. I think I have stated the case as strongly as honorable gentlemen can well desire. Now, let us first of all look at the material results which will flow to England should this discrimination take place, and here let me say, what is obvious to every one who has given the subject a second thought, that, in our peculiar geographical position toward the United States, it is perfectly apparent that we can not hope to gain free intercourse and unrestricted reciprocity with them without discriminating against the goods of other countries, unless and until the United States are prepared to go in for free trade with all the world, in which case our proposition would not be necessary. The thing, I grant, is of the essence of the bargain. I am not in the least degree desirous of concealing that fact, but, so far as the material side is concerned, the practical results of assimilating our tariff in certain points to the American tariff as against England have been immensely and, I suspect, purposely exaggerated. In the first place, the House ought to remember that at this very day our tariff is pretty nearly as hostile to English manufactures as that of the United States. Then it is well to bear in mind that, the tariff to the contrary notwithstanding, England has always managed to carry on a large trade with the United States, and especially with the northern portion of it. There can be no doubt, I think, that if we succeed in getting unrestricted trade we shall become much richer, and if we become much richer there is no doubt that we shall buy a much larger quantity of English goods than we do at present, though perhaps not in the same line. I believe that the result of England giving us a free hand in this matter would be simply to make some little alteration in the character but not in the quantity of the goods she sells.

"I do not say, and it is false to assert that I have ever said, that Canada has not made any progress during the past twenty years. I admit considerable progress has been made in certain directions. But what I contend for now is this, that the progress has been partial, inadequate, far below what the natural resources of our country would warrant. It is also far below what we made ourselves in the twenty years before 1861, and infinitely below what the United States made in the first twenty years of their existence, when their population was equal to ours. I am quite willing to grant that a few towns have grown and prospered within the past few years, but I say it was none the less true that over many wide areas of this country our population is stationary and even retrograde. It is none the less true that from one end of Canada to the other, the value of farm lands is less to-day than it was six, seven, or eight years ago; it is none the less true that the value of farm products is enormously lowered, and that our farmers are exposed to a far more intense competition than they hitherto experienced. Great new forces are coming into existence, the full effect of which we are only beginning to feel. There is danger lest Canada, so far as regards our native-born population, should sink into a mere residuum, a country from which the best and most intelligent of our people are fleeing, not by hundreds or by thousands, but by millions. Then as to foreign immigrants, if these statistics can be relied upon, it is clear that we are becoming a mere dumping-ground for the refuse of those whom we import into this country. No one supposed, when we came together in this Confederation, stretching over half a continent, that we were to remain semi-dependent forever. We are growing in stature, not as fast as honorable gentlemen say, but still we are growing, and we are entitled to a larger measure of responsibilities and to a larger measure of rights. One thing is clear, that every one, as I have said, who thinks twice on the subject knows and feels that things are not satisfactory for us in many ways. I see no way of our becoming a valuable member of a British federation save only on one consideration, and that is that you broaden your base and take care that you unite yourselves with the United States in the bonds of a firm and friendly alliance which is not likely to be broken, and there is no way in which that is more likely to be done than by greatly increasing and promoting the trade between the two countries."

Hon. Wilfrid Laurier (leader of the Opposition), in supporting Sir Richard Cartwright's motion, said :

"The national policy has not developed our native industry, and has not created the home market for our agricultural products, as we were promised. But the necessity of widening the area of our trade and commerce is so great that we have been looking around in this direction and in the other direction to find new outlets and new channels for our trade. In the debate on the address during the present session, the mover of the address told us with pride that the Government had sent a commissioner to Australia in order to obtain the trade of that country ; he told us that they had opened communication with the Argentine Republic in order to establish a trade with that country. What will come of these efforts ? What has come of all similar efforts ? What has come of our sending commissioners to Brazil, to the West Indies, and to Spain ? Nothing, for the very obvious reason that, burdened as we are by our protective tariff, we can not meet free-trade England in those markets ; so that the conclusion is inevitable that all the efforts we have made so far to develop our trade and commerce, and to broaden their area, ever since 1867, have been a succession of failures. We are a colony of England, it is true ; but we are a colony not by force but by choice ; and if we are a colony to-day, it is because we are convinced that at the present day our colonial independence is quite compatible with all kinds of national advancement and material prosperity. If you on the other side pretend that our colonial relation curtails and limits our possibilities, that England would allow us to reach a certain altitude and not go higher, I say you slander England ; and if any man were to rise on the other side and tell us that England would be jealous at whatever we could do to improve our condition, I would say that man does not know England ; he mistakes the England of to-day for the England of one hundred years ago. I commend to the consideration of these fervent loyalists on the other side, whose mouths are ever full of the word loyalty, the following words spoken by Lord Palmerston twenty years ago in reference to the British North American provinces : ' If these provinces felt themselves strong enough to stand upon their own ground, and if they desire no longer to maintain their connection with us, we should say, " God speed you, and give you the means to maintain yourselves as a nation ! " ' These are the sentiments of British statesmen. They tell us that whenever we want our political liberty, we are free to have it. But what we ask is not political independence ; we want to keep the flag of England over our heads ; but we affirm that we are economically independent as we are legislatively independent. Colonies have interests in common with the mother-land, but colonies have interests of their own also ; and to-day we levy a heavy toll on all imports from Great Britain. We have done that not only for the sake of collecting revenue, but also for the purpose of protection, to enable us to manufacture ourselves what we had formerly purchased from England, and to that extent to destroy British trade. There was a time when this would not have been tolerated ; there was a time when England would have disallowed such a policy ; but now we adopt it as a matter of course ; now our policy is never questioned — why ? Because England has long ago admitted the principle that colonies have interests of their own, and that it is within their right and power to develop and foster and promote those interests, even to the point of clashing with British interests."

Hon. Mr. Chapleau (Secretary of State), in supporting Mr. Foster's amendment, said :

" On some abstract questions men can dictate to the people, they can state certain opinions and impose them on the people ; but on a question of policy like this it is the voice of the people that decides ; and the voice of the people is against you. Your statistics may be good, and you may be able to make them prove anything you want, but the only statistics I want are statistics of the sentiments and feelings of the people ; and those are against you. The people themselves have their say, and in discussing questions of this kind abstract theories of men have no influence over them. Free trade is in the hearts of the people of England ; and why ? Because in England after long years, I might say, after centuries, of well-digested, of well-guided, of well-applied protection, the manufacturing genius of the English people has acquired a perfection that can not be surpassed or equaled. Manufacturers in England challenge and defy all competition, and in a country like England, where the largest possibilities of production have been attained, cheap living is the desideratum of the working-classes. Free trade is in the hearts of the people of England, whatever might be the difficulties which at the present moment it might entail on the financial condition of the country. On the other hand, protection is in the hearts of the people of the United States ; and why ? Is it because the genius for manufacturing industries has not developed there ? It has to an immense extent ; it has so much that American manufacturers are the rivals of Great Britain in almost all the markets of the world. Why is protection still in the hearts of the people of the United States ? It is, and will be so long as there is a productive South, an extensive West, affording opportunities for the activity and intelligence of the sons of workingmen to progress under the protective policy which has done great benefit in the past. But it is still more in the hearts of the people of the United States, because the structure they have built necessarily requires further time to become consolidated so as to be able to defy the world. Again, why is it in the hearts of the people of the United States? It is because, in their view of developing manufacturing industries, they look to this northern part of the continent as being very soon or in the future, or in the near future, to become one of the accessories of the great republic, not by war, not by coercion, but by the good policy they have impressed upon the minds of their people and which our Government are trying to impress on the minds of the people of this country. Should we not pursue the same course, should we not build up our own prosperity, our own national spirit, and our own nation? We are doing it."

On April 6 the House divided on Mr. Jones's amendment to the amendment, which was negatived by yeas, 67; nays, 124. Hon. Mr. Foster's amendment was carried on the same division reversed.

Partial Reciprocity.—On March 28, the Hon. Peter Mitchell, one of the opponents of the Government, called attention to complaints made in Washington of bad faith on the part of the Dominion Government, in failing to carry out the terms of what is known as the "standing-offer clause" of the customs act of 1879, which reads as follows:

Any or all of the following things, that is to say, animals of all kinds, green fruit, hay, straw, bran, seeds of all kinds, vegetables (including potatoes and other roots), plants, trees, and shrubs, coal and coke, salt, hops, wheat, pease and beans, barley, rye, oats, Indian corn, buckwheat, and all other grain, flour of wheat and flour of rye, Indian meal and oatmeal and flour and meal of any other grain, butter, cheese, fish (salted or smoked), lard, tallow, meats (fresh, salted, or smoked), and lumber, may be imported into Canada free of duty, or at a less rate of duty than is provided by this act, upon the proclamation of the Governor in Council, which may be issued whenever it appears to his satisfaction that similar articles from Canada may be imported into the United States free of duty, or at a rate of duty not exceeding that payable on the same under such proclamation when imported into Canada.

Certain of these articles have been put upon the free list by Congress, but the Canadian Government has failed to reciprocate in accordance with the terms of the clause. Sir John Macdonald insisted that the clause was permissive and not obligatory, and that the Canadian free list was much more liberal than the American free list. The Premier also took the ground that it was not in the interest of certain classes of Canadians to put the clause into operation. On April 4, the debate being resumed, Sir Charles Tupper declared the policy of the Government to be to obtain a free interchange of the natural products of the two countries, and said that all the articles to which the attention of the Government had been drawn by the United States Government as having been placed on the American free list would be put upon the Canadian free list.

An act was passed repealing section 9 of the customs act, and substituting the following clause:

Any or all of the following things, that is to say, animals of all kinds, hay, straw, vegetables (including potatoes and other roots), salt, pease, beans, barley, malt, rye, oats, buckwheat, flour of rye, oatmeal, buckwheat-flour, butter, cheese, fish of all kinds, fish-oil, products of fish and of all other creatures living in the water, fresh meats, poultry, stone or marble in its crude or unwrought state, lime, gypsum or plaster of Paris (ground, unground, or calcined), hewed or wrought or unwrought burr and grindstones, and timber and lumber of all kinds unmanufactured in in whole or in part, including shingles, clapboards, and wood-pulp, may be imported into Canada free of duty, or at a less rate of duty than is provided for by any act at the time in force, upon proclamation of the Governor-General, which may be issued whenever it appears to his satisfaction that similar articles from Canada may be imported into the United States free of duty, or at a rate of duty not exceeding that payable on the same under such proclamation when imported into Canada.

Bucket-Shop Gambling.—One of the most interesting acts passed at this session was that introduced by the Hon. Senator Abbott, a member of the Government and Mayor of Montreal, respecting "Gaming in Stocks and Merchandise." Great efforts were made in behalf of certain "bucket-shops" to defeat this measure, and it was claimed that the proverbial coach-and-four could be driven through this, or indeed any act that might be framed for the suppression of what is commonly called "bucket-shop" gambling. But several convictions were secured under the act. The penalty prescribed is imprisonment for any term not exceeding five years, and a fine not exceeding $500.

Temperance.—On motion to go into supply, Hon. Mr. Mills (Liberal) moved an amendment:

That, in the opinion of this House, it is the duty of the ministry to submit to Parliament a measure embracing such provisions as will remove all legal impediments to the efficient working of the Canada Temperance Act.

Sir John Macdonald denied the existence of any impediment to the workings of the act. The object of the motion was simply to force the Government to adopt a policy on the temperance question. This the Government, as a Government, has always declined to do, members of the Cabinet voting, according to their individual inclinations, for or against temperance legislation. The amendment was negatived by 57 yeas to 109 nays.

Ship-Channel.—The progress of the port of Montreal has been seriously hampered by the heavy tonnage-dues levied on shipping by the Harbor Commission to meet the interest on the amount advanced by the Dominion Government for the widening and deepening of the ship-channel in Lake St. Peter and the river St. Lawrence between Montreal and Quebec. This year the Government agreed to assume the debt, and an act was passed releasing the Harbor Commission from the obligation to pay either interest or principal of the debt, and authorizing the Government to expend in completing the channel any sums remaining unexpended of those authorized to be advanced to the Harbor Commission for the work. The condition on which the debt is assumed is, that hereafter no tonnage-dues are to be levied upon shipping at the port of Montreal.

A similar act was passed making the graving-dock at Lévis, opposite Quebec, a public work, and assuming the debt of the Quebec Harbor Commission.

Public Acts.—The following public acts, which are not referred to in detail, were passed :

Authorizing a loan of $25,000,000, to pay the floating debt and to carry on public works.

Granting certain railway subsidies.

Extending the time for the completion of the Chignecto Marine Transport Railway.

Imposing regulations on the Auditor-General.

Restricting the rate of interest payable in the Post-Office and Government savings-banks to a maximum of 4 per cent., the actual rate to be prescribed from time to time by the Governor-General in Council.

Continuing the existing voters-lists until the completion of the revision in 1889 under the Electoral-Franchise act.

Providing for the holding of elections in the Northwest Territories on the same day as in other parts of Canada.

Providing rules for civil-service examinations, and for inquiries as to irregularities at examinations.

Providing for the employment of clerks in the office of the High Commissioner.

Making regulations for the Department of Public Printing and Stationery.

Authorizing the appointment of a Deputy Commissioner of Patents.

Providing for a Legislature for the Northwest Territories.

Amending the Territories Real Property act.

Vesting certain powers in the crofters' colonization commissioners to be appointed.

Amending the Indian act.

To regulate the licensing of international and inter-provincial ferries.

Amending the adulteration act.

Amending the weights-and-measures act as regards the contents of packages of salt. Every barrel of salt offered for sale to contain 280 pounds of salt, and to have the gross and net weight permanently marked on the barrel.

Amending the steamboat-inspection act.

Amending the banking act by providing that whenever a person granting a warehouse receipt or bill of lading, and carrying on certain businesses, is also the owner of the goods mentioned in the receipt, such receipt and the right and title of the bank to the goods shall be as valid as though the person making the receipt and the owner of the goods were different persons.

Authorizing any insurance company incorporated by the Legislature of the late Province of Canada, or by any of the Provincial Legislatures, to avail itself of the provisions of the Insurance act.

Assenting to the Treaty of Washington, 1888.

Ratifying the International Convention for the Preservation of Submarine Telegraph Cables.

To remove doubts respecting the laws of England, as they existed on July, 15, 1870, being in force in Manitoba.

Respecting defective letters patent.

To amend the Supreme and Exchequer Courts act.

To authorize the appointment of a new puisne judge at Montreal or Quebec.

To extend the jurisdiction of the Maritime Court of Ontario.

Prohibiting the advertising of counterfeit money.

Enacting that there shall be no appeal in criminal cases to any court in the United Kingdom.

Providing that publishers and editors shall only be tried for libel in the provinces in which they reside or publish their papers.

Amending the Summary Convictions act.

Amending the act respecting Punishments, Pardons, and the Commutation of Sentences.

Amending the Dominion Elections act.

Imposing new customs regulations.

Altering excise duties.

The railway act.

Ratifying an agreement between the Government and the Canadian Pacific Railway Company, by which the latter relinquishes its monopoly privileges in Manitoba, and the Government guarantees the interest on the company's bonds at 3½ per cent. to the extent of fifteen million dollars.

Two acts amending the Canada Temperance act.

Imposing severe penalties for the use of fraudulent marks on merchandise, imitation of trade-marks, etc.

The St. Lawrence Canals.—In 1816 a joint commission of both Houses of Parliament of Upper Canada reported on the subject of connecting Lake Erie and Lake Ontario. In 1821 a commission was appointed to consider the subject, and two years later it reported in favor of constructing the Welland Canal of such dimensions as would accommodate the class of vessels then navigating the lakes. The result of this report was the incorporation of the Welland Canal Company, which proposed to establish the necessary communication by a canal and railway. The work was begun in 1825 (the year in which the Erie Canal was finished and opened), and was completed in 1829. In that year two schooners, one of eighty-five tons, ascended the canal from Lake Ontario to the Welland river. Subsequently the main line of the canal was extended over the Welland river to Port Colborne. In 1851 the Government approved this project and granted a loan of $200,000 ; and the work was completed in 1853. In 1873 a new enlargement was begun, making the locks 270 feet long, 45 feet wide, and 12 feet deep. From Allanburg to Port Dalhousie, 11 miles, a new canal was built ; and since that time the old canal, although kept in repair and well maintained, has been chiefly used as a water-power. But even with 12 feet of water the canal was not deep enough. Grain-laden vessels at Port Colborne had to lighter much of their cargoes to the Welland Railroad, which hauled the grain to Port Dalhousie, where it was again loaded, and the cost of this lighterage was a great drain on the income of the canal. It was decided to give the canal for its entire length a draught of 14 feet, not by dredging, but by building up the locks and banks 30 inches higher. Up to the time this work was begun the Welland Canal had cost about $18,000,000. The total expenditures upon this canal down to June 30, 1887 (when the enlargement had been completed), were $23,062,615. As soon as the latest improvements had been made, it was apparent that the vast expenditure on the Welland Canal must remain of little direct benefit until the St. Lawrence canals were made of corresponding capacity. There has been no profit in carrying grain to Kingston for transshipment to Montreal by the barge lines. The cost of handling at

Kingston, and transshipment, practically destroyed the natural advantages of the Canadian route. But the appropriation now made by the Canadian Government to deepen the St. Lawrence canals to fourteen feet will enable the majority of lake vessels to engage cargoes at Duluth, Chicago, or other ports of the upper lakes, and bring their loads through to Montreal or the Atlantic Ocean without breaking cargo. Therefore, the Government of the Dominion of Canada began the work of deepening what are known as the St. Lawrence canals, or the artificial ways that make navigation possible around the rapids and shallow waters that abound in the St. Lawrence river between Ogdensburg and Montreal. In 1841, when the system of canals between Montreal and Lake Ontario was designed, it was in contemplation to afford a depth, at all stages of the St. Lawrence waters, of nine feet. But the St. Lawrence, from various causes, is subject to fluctuations, the extent of which it was impossible, when those canals were constructed, to arrive at with precision, and the observations and experience of subsequent years have shown that while the intermediate river reaches at all times afford ample depth for vessels of nine feet draught, in the canals themselves, at certain periods of low water, this depth can not be maintained, the bottom not having been sunk enough. In 1871 it was decided to enlarge the canals on the St. Lawrence route, so as to afford a navigable depth of twelve feet throughout. Subsequently it was decided that the depth should ultimately be increased so as to accommodate vessels of fourteen feet draught; and accordingly in the scheme of enlargement that has so far been carried out, a channel in the canals is provided for vessels drawing twelve feet only, while all permanent structures, locks, bridges, etc., are being built of such proportions as to accommodate vessels of fourteen feet draught, the locks being 270 feet long between the gates, and 45 feet in width, with a clear depth of 14 feet of water on the sills. The lower of the St. Lawrence canals is the Lachine. This canal extends from Montreal to the village of Lachine, overcoming the Lachine Rapids, the first of the series of rapids that bars the ascent of the river. The full scheme for the enlargement of this, in common with the other canals of the St. Lawrence, contemplated affording a navigable depth of fourteen feet throughout; but the improvement immediately in view was only intended to furnish a navigable depth of twelve feet in the canal proper; and accordingly on the reaches between Lachine and Côte St. Paul, between Côte St. Paul and St. Gabriel, and between St. Gabriel and Wellington Basin. the channel has been adapted to navigation by vessels of twelve feet draught only. All permanent works on the canal have been built to afford a navigable depth of fourteen feet. The total rise of lockage is 45 feet, and the number of locks is five. The Beauharnois

Canal, which is the next in order up the stream, begins on the south side of the St. Lawrence, 15¼ miles from the head of the Lachine Canal. It connects Lakes St. Louis and St. Francis, and passes the three rapids known respectively as the Cascades, the Cedars, and the Coteau. The locks are 200 feet by 45 feet. The total rise is 82½ feet; and the number of locks is nine. The depth of water on the sills is 12 feet. Nothing has been done toward the enlargement of the canal. Still proceeding up the channel of the river from the head of the Beauharnois to the foot of the Cornwall Canal, there is a navigable stretch through Lake St. Francis of 32¾ miles. The Cornwall Canal extends past the Long Sault Rapids. Two locks at the new lower entrance (taking the place of three on the old line), were in constant use during the season of navigation. The dimensions of the new locks are those of the general enlargement scheme. The basin between these two locks is 825 feet long. Of the four locks still to be dealt with, one is already under contract, together with works for the improvement of the upper entrance, and arrangements are being made for further works either on the summit level or above the town of Cornwall. The proposed channel will be sunk to such depth as to admit of the passage of vessels of fourteen feet draught. The total rise is 48 feet. The highest grade of canals is known by the name of Williamsburg; which includes the Farran's Point, Rapide Plat, and Galops Canals. Much trouble has been experienced in this group of canals, owing to low water. The Farran's Point Canal is three quarters of a mile long, with one lock, the navigable depth being nine feet. No work has been done at this point. The Rapide Plat Canal is 4 miles long, with two locks, each 200 feet by 45. The total rise is 11½ feet and the depth of water on the sills is nine feet. One of the two new locks is practically completed, giving a depth for navigation of fourteen feet. The new works include the enlargement of the channel above and for some distance below the present guard-lock at the head of the canal, and the construction of a new lock and a supply-weir in connection with the old lock. The bottom of the channel, for a distance of about one thousand feet below, and out into deep water, above the lock, about seven hundred feet, will be excavated to afford a navigable depth of fourteen feet. The Galops Canal enables vessels to overcome the rapids at Pointe Aux Iroquois, Pointe Cardinal, and the Galops. The work under contract is the excavation and deepening of a channel at the upper end leading to deep water, so as to give a depth available for vessels of fourteen feet draught. The work is practically completed, and access to this canal is found to be greatly facilitated. Preparations are being made with a view to extend the fourteen-foot navigation down to deep water below the rapids, and to place a guard-lock at that point.

The Galops Rapids, about seven miles below Prescott, the most shallow of the three passed by the Galops Canal, are being improved by certain works of sub-marine blasting and dredging, begun in 1880. These consist of the excavation of a straight channel through the rapids, 3,300 feet long, 200 feet wide, and of such depth as to afford safe passage at low water to vessels of fourteen feet draught. This implies affording a depth of seventeen feet of water. The whole of the work of drilling and blasting is completed, but the broken rock has to be removed by the dredging-machine, and this work is in progress. It is one of considerable difficulty, owing to the rapidity of the current and the necessity of avoiding interruption to navigation. Above the Galops Rapids there is unobstructed navigation to the foot of the Welland Canal at the head of Lake Ontario. Much anxiety has been expressed at the various ports on Lake Ontario, over the fact that such an increased volume of water would pass over the Galops Rapids, owing to the heavy blasting at that point, and also through the enlarged St. Lawrence canals. Should the quantity of water be largely increased, it is thought that the depth in the several ports of Lake Ontario may be considerably reduced, to the great injury of the respective cities belonging to such ports. As a part of the scheme for enlarging the waterways through Canada, the great work of deepening the channel of the St. Lawrence river, from Montreal to Quebec, was completed in 1888. This work was first agitated over sixty years ago, and was begun in 1844; and the result is that where there was formerly only eleven feet of water there is now twenty-seven and a half feet, and large ocean steamers can enter the docks at Montreal, six hundred miles from the mouth of the St. Lawrence. There are now twenty-two lines of ocean steamers that sail to and from Montreal. Engineers say that the commerce of a port increases according to the cube of the increase in the depth of the channel, and statistics show that this law of increase has been fulfilled at Montreal as the channel has been gradually deepened. Some idea of the magnitude of the work which has been done can be gained from the fact that in Lake St. Peter, eight million cubic yards of clay were removed, an amount of excavating equal to what was done in building eight hundred miles of the Canadian Pacific Railroad. In some places solid rock has been "scooped out" to a depth of several feet, and altogether it was quite fitting that the engineers in charge, and the Montreal, Provincial, and Dominion governments should rejoice together over what has been accomplished. Montreal now has a population of 250,000, and with her deep-water outlet on the one side, and the Canadian Pacific Railroad on the other, she looks hopefully to the future, and pictures for herself a day when she shall have many times her present population and commerce.

E

ECUADOR, an independent republic in South America, covering an area on the mainland of 643,295 square kilometres, while the Galápagos Islands measure 7,643 square kilometres. According to the census taken in 1885, the population was distributed as follows:

PROVINCES.	Inhabitants.	Capitals.	Inhabitants.
Carchi	23,388	Tulcan	4,000
Imbabura	56,476	Ibarra..........	10,000
Pichincha	187,844	Quito	80,030
Leon..............	80,028	Latacunga......	15,000
Tungurahua	79,526	Ambato........	12,000
Chimborazo	90,782	Riobamba	18,000
Bolivar...........	31,327	Guaranda	6,000
Rios	32,041	Babahoyo	5,000
Oriente	15,850	......	.....
Guayas	95,640	Guayaquil......	40,000
Manabi	64,284	Portoviejo......	10,000
Esmeraldas	11,146	Esmeraldas	3,000
Oro	21,606	Machala........	5,000
Azogues..........	43,265	Azogues	4,000
Azuay............	104,369	Cuenca..........	30,000
Loja	60,880	Loja	10,000
Galápagos........	204	......	....
Total	1,004,651		252,000

The population given in detail above does not include the wild Indians of the eastern provinces and eastern slopes of the Andes, supposed to number in the aggregate some 600,000 souls.

Government.—The President is Dr. Antonio Flores, whose term of office will expire on June 30, 1892. His Cabinet was composed as follows: Interior and Foreign Affairs, Gen. Don Francisco J. Salazar; Public Instruction, Worship, and Charity, Don Elias Laso; Finance, Don José Toribio Noboa; War and Navy, Gen. Sáenz. The Consul of Ecuador at Washington is the Marquis de Chambrun; the Consul-General at New York, Don Domingo L. Ruiz; and the Consul at Philadelphia, Edward Shippen. The American Consul-General at Guayaquil is Owen McGarr.

Finances.—According to the statement made by the Minister of Finance, the indebtedness was $13,196,095 capital and $1,152,487 interest due thereon on June 10, 1887, constituting an aggregate debt of $14,348,582. This includes the sterling debt, the principal of which is £1,824,000, and the accumulated unpaid interest was £373,920 on June 10, 1888, thus increasing the amount due in Europe to £2,197,-920. This sterling debt had its origin at the time Colombia was dissolved into three independent states, viz., New Granada (now called Colombia), Venezuela, and Ecuador, in 1830, and represents the portion of the old Colomhian debt assumed by Ecuador. Up to the year 1867 the interest was regularly paid on it, but since then it is in default, although the bondholders were content to receive only 1 per cent. per annum till the customs receipts at Guayaquil should begin to exceed $400,000 per annum, 25 per cent. of the surplus to go toward increasing the interest till it reached 6 per cent. Although since the pacification of the country the customs receipts at Guayaquil have swelled to an amount warranting 4½ per cent. per annum on the sterling debt, this clause of the engagement has not been enforced hitherto, for political reasons; but since the accession to power of Dr. Antonio Flores, the new President, matters are taking a turn more favorable to the bondholders. Thus the Executive issued, under date of September 10, a decree inviting the council of foreign bondholders to appoint a commissioner with full power to negotiate with the Government a reorganization of the debt on a mutually acceptable basis. The outstanding internal and external indebtedness is trifling, considering the resources of the country, which requires the carrying out of public works, notably railroads, all of which would be facilitated by an upright, prompt financial policy. In response to the decree named, the council of bondholders in London will delegate one of its members to go to Quito and arrange matters if possible. The actual income of the state in 1886 was $5,107,992, and sufficed to meet the outlay.

In April, 1888, the Bank of Ecuador advanced the Government $900,000 at 9 per cent. interest per annum, the net income of the Guayaquil custom-house being pledged. Banks are in a flourishing condition. Thus, the Bank of Ecuador declared 20 per cent. dividend in 1886 and in 1887, the International Bank respectively 10 and 12 per cent., the Anglo-Equatorian 8 and 12, and the Banco Hipotecario 15¼ and 16 per cent.

Army.—The strength of the regular army in 1888 was 4,730 file, 3,320 thereof being foot, 1,060 artillery, and 350 horse; there being four battalions of infantry, two companies of artillery, and one regiment of cavalry, all fully armed and equipped, and the arsenals at Guayaquil and Quito well stocked with ammunition and everything necessary, in addition to which there were ordered from the United States 700 Remington rifles, and 100,000 cartridges. The National Guard was composed, in 1888, of 76 battalions, 68 being foot, 2 artillery, and 6 horse, completely organized.

Navy.—In 1887 Ecuador had only two men-of-war, the "Cotopaxi" and the "Nueve de Julio"; both are steamers, the former having cost £11,500, and the latter £19,300. They are new, unexceptionable in every respect. In January, 1888, the new gun-boat "Tunguráhua" arrived from England.

Treaty.—Prior to his return from Europe Dr. Antonio Flores, then President-elect of Ecuador, but at the time still minister at Paris, negotiated a new treaty of commerce and navigation between his country and France, together with a consular convention, to take the place of the treaty concluded at Quito on June 6, 1843. The new treaty is to remain operative to February, 1892, and the consular convention for ten years, dating from May 12, 1888, when both agreements were signed. A separate agreement covered literary, artistic, and industrial property, guaranteeing it to citizens of either country.

Railroads.—On March 27, 1888, a company was incorporated at Guayaquil, having for its object the construction of railroads and other public works in the republic. It acquired by purchase from the original contractor, Mark J. Kelly, the control over the Yaguachi-Duran railway, then about finished, together with that of the line from Yaguachi to Chimbo, and the one from Chimbo to Sibambe, both in course of construction. The company will issue 8-per-cent. bonds, the interest to be paid out of the salt monopoly secured, the first bond issue being subscribed for beforehand.

Commerce.—The exports in 1886 amounted to $8,014,409, including $403,988 specie and bullion, and 37,172,576 pounds of cocoa, worth $6,505,201; 2,973,346 pounds of coffee, worth $321,121; India - rubber, $282,897; hides, $280,055; vegetable ivory, $89,020; straw hats, $23,680, the rest being made up by oranges, pine-apples, and quinine-bark. The American trade presents the following figures:

FISCAL YEAR.	Import into the United States.	Domestic export to Ecuador.
1887	$1,131,169	$1,049,852
1888	1,118,627	810,567

The number of vessels that entered Ecuadorian ports in 1886 was 376, of which 185 entered at Guayaquil alone (117 thereof being steamers), without counting small coasters.

Partial Tariff Modifications.—Dating from Jan. 1, 1888, the following changes in the rates of import duties became operative: Almanacho and green plants to enter duty free: an additional cent per kilogramme to be laid on potatoes, rice, large stoneware vessels, timber, and lumber; two cents additional per kilogramme on soda for washing, hand-pumps, iron and steel rails and sleepers, iron tubes less than 0·12 metre in diameter if forming part of machinery, dye-woods, printing-paper; ten cents per kilogramme: crude stearine, fancy water-mugs, twine for sewing bags, marble; fifty cents per kilogramme: imitation silver or gold plated jewelry, hats, caps; one dollar per kilogramme: all other jewelry.

Cocoa.—There arrived at Guayaquil from the interior for shipment abroad, in 1887, 334,267 quintals of cocoa, against 384,752 in 1886; 244,724 in 1885, and 176,955 in 1884. From Jan. 1 to Oct. 23, 1888, 254,000 quintals were received at Guayaquil, against 305,000 in 1887.

Ivory-Nuts.—There had been shipped abroad from Guayaquil, in 1887, 258,125 quintals of ivory-nuts, against 197,808 in 1886, 169,000 in 1885, and 107,759 in 1884.

Earthquakes.—On September 25 a sharp shock of earthquake was felt at Elena at eight o'clock in the evening, and simultaneously at Guayaquil, lasting about two minutes. The shocks were followed by flashes of lightning. At that time of year lightning has been unknown heretofore in the localities named. Another very heavy shock was experienced at Guayaquil on November 16, at twenty-five minutes to three P. M.; the people fled from their houses thoroughly panic-stricken.

Benedictine Monks for Ecuador.—On July 20 seven Benedictines from St. Mary's Abbey, Newark, N. J., left New York for Ecuador, to establish a church in the republic. Three of them were Americans and four Germans, the latter, however, being citizens of the United States. They took with them a large quantity of the most improved farm and garden implements, the whole forming three wagonloads of cases, more machinery and tools to be sent for as the occasion may demand. They emigrated to Ecuador at the solicitation of the bishop of that country.

EGYPT, a principality in Northern Africa, tributary to Turkey. The reigning sovereign, called the Khedive, is Mohammed Tewfik, born Nov. 19, 1852, who succeeded to the throne on the abdication of his father, the Khedive Ismail, June 26, 1879. He is the sixth ruler of the dynasty of Mehemet Ali, who was appointed Governor of Egypt in 1806. The administration of Egypt is carried on by native ministers, subject to the rulings of the Khedive, and under the supervision of England. There is a legislative council of thirty members, of whom sixteen are elected and fourteen appointed by the Khedive, but it has only advisory powers.

Area and Population.—The area of Egypt proper, the southern boundary of which was provisionally fixed at Wady Halfa, about 800 miles south of Cairo, in January, 1887, is estimated at 11,000 square miles. The country is divided into El Said or Upper Egypt and Masr-el-Bahri or Lower Egypt. The population in 1882 was 6,806,381, composed of 6,715,495 Egyptians and 90,886 foreigners. Of the Egyptians, 6,469,-716 had fixed abodes and 245,779 were nomads. The bulk of the foreigners are Greeks, Italians, French, Austrians, English, and Germans. Ninety per cent. of the foreign population reside in Lower Egypt. The average annual increase in the population since 1846 has been 1·25 per cent. The inhabitable land in Egypt comprises 6,216,530 acres, of which 3,745,971 acres are in Lower and 2,470,559 acres in Upper Egypt.

Commerce.—The total exterior commerce of Egypt for 1886 amounted to 17,977,851 Egyptian pounds, in which sum the imports are represented by 7,848,231 pounds, and the exports by 10,129,620 pounds. The imports of specie for the same year were 1,838,797 pounds, and the exports, 2,972,520 pounds. The commer-

cial intercourse with different foreign countries for 1886 was as follows, the value being given in Egyptian pounds (£E1=$5):

COUNTRIES.	Exports to—	Imports from—	Total.
Great Britain	6,413.209	3,068,680	9,481,899
Turkey	865,250	1,303,442	1,668,692
France and Algeria	906,767	883,010	1,789,777
Austria	598,048	909,528	1,507,576
Italy	591,762	270,438	862,200
Russia	1,045,520	445,369	1,490,889
India, China, etc	8,363	491,059	499,422
Greece	37,412	90,046	127,458
America	21,356	62,565	83,921
Other countries	141,873	324,144	466,017
Total	10,129,620	7,848,281	17,977,851

The values of the principal articles of commerce for the year 1886 were, in Egyptian pounds, as follow:

EXPORTS.	Values.	IMPORTS.	Values.
Cotton	7,120,812	Cotton goods	1,472,276
Cotton-seed	1,251,943	Coal	864,286
Beans	467,952	Clothing	1,045,000
Wheat	78,912	Indigo	180,160
Sugar	453,817	Timber	320,000
Lentils	18,428	Wines and spirits.	363,114
Skins	116,553	Coffee	175,086
Rice	108,803	Tobacco	246,858
Gum	14,850	Refined sugar	112,921
Maize	1,865	Machinery	132,003
Wool	65,568	Wheat	205,110

The increase in the tobacco receipts for the year 1886 was £80,000, due to the introduction of Greek tobacco under the new commercial treaty.

The decrease in the value of the imports for 1886 from those of 1885, was 1,140,811 Egyptian pounds, and the decrease in the value of the exports was 1,295,350 pounds.

Agriculture.—The report of the statistical bureau in Cairo for 1887 makes the cultivated area 4,961,462 feddans, showing an increase of 247,056 feddans in three years. The area planted to cotton was 874,645 feddans in 1886, 865,-526 in 1887, and 1,057,513 in 1888. The cotton product in 1887 was 3,025,965 cantars, or 378,245,000 pounds. The cultivation of cotton is extending rapidly in Upper Egypt, where the fellahs find it a more profitable crop, and one requiring less care and outlay, than sugar-cane. The cultivation of bersim, a kind of clover, occupied 941,222 feddans in 1888, and there were 617,605 feddans in Lower and 623,495 in Upper Egypt under wheat. Although sugar culture is declining, the product in 1887 was 1,090,-424 cantars, worth 573,859 Egyptian pounds, inclusive of the rum and molasses products. The chief crops of lesser importance are beans, lentils, Indian corn, oats, rice, and durra. The farm animals have greatly decreased, owing to contagious diseases and the impoverishment of the people. There are at present, to every 100 feddans or acres, 9 buffaloes, 5 animals of other kinds, including camels, horses, asses, mules, and cattle, and 20 sheep.

Railways, Telegraphs, and Posts.—In 1886 there were 900 miles of railway in operation. The telegraph lines belonging to the Government at the end of 1887 had a total length of 3,172 miles. The Government has established a telephone line 140 miles long, extending from Cairo to the petroleum-wells on the Red Sea, consisting of a bare iron wire, running along the sand without poles or insulators.

The post-office carried 7,620,000 inland and 5,075,000 foreign letters during 1886. In 1887 the number of internal letters was 8,174,000, and the total correspondence 12,916,000.

The Suez Canal.—The number of vessels that passed through the Suez Canal in 1886 was 3,100, with a gross tonnage of 8,183,313. Of these 2,331, of 6,254,417 tons, were British; 227, of 699,194 tons, French; 161, of 314,715 tons, German; 127, of 312,964 tons, Dutch; 77, of 191,333 tons, Austrian; 69, of 184,960 tons, Italian; 25, of 88,076 tons, Spanish; 24, of 58,288 tons, Russian; 28, of 47,991 tons, Norwegian; 6, of 3,363 tons, Turkish; 4, of 3,056 tons, Egyptian; and 1, of 1,292 tons, Belgian. The deepening of the canal to 8½ metres has been completed.

The gross receipts of the company in 1886 were £2,241,095, as compared with £2,601,998 in 1885; £2,576,083 in 1884; £2,645,506 in 1883; and £2,536,343 in 1882. The net profits in 1885 were £1,361,150, yielding a dividend to the shareholders, after providing for the sinking-fund, of 17·08 per cent. The statutes provide that of all net earnings over 5 per cent., 71 per cent. shall go to the general shareholders, 15 per cent. to the Egyptian Government, 10 per cent. to the founders' shares, 2 per cent. to the employés, and 2 per cent. to the managing directors. Of the 395,840 shares that were issued, 176,602 were taken by the Khedive of Egypt, and were by him transferred to the British Government in 1875 for the sum of £3,976,582. The dividends on these shares up to the year 1894 he had already alienated, signing them over to the Suez Canal Company. The share capital of the canal amounts to 197,-920,000 francs, and the bonded debt of various descriptions to 177.292,426 francs.

A convention defining the status of the Suez Canal was arranged in the early part of 1888 between Great Britain, France, and Turkey, and agreed to by all the powers. Turkey obtained modifications giving her the presidency at the annual meetings and permitting the transportation at all times of troops to the eastern shore of the Red Sea. When the time came to ratify the convention, the Porte asked permission to add an explanatory protocol denying the view expressed by the Italian Government as to its bearing on the dispute between Turkey and Italy with regard to Massowah and other Italian posts on the African Red Sea coast, but the powers would not assent to the Turkish view. The convention was finally signed at the Porte on October 29. The first three articles are devoted to the subjects of the neutrality of the canal and the security of the works and material of the company, and

the next four to the position of belligerents in the canal and its ports of access. The canal is declared free for the transportation of war material and the passage of ships of war in war times as well as in times of peace. The eighth article specifies the duties of foreign diplomatic agents in Egypt, and confers on the Porte the presidency at the annual meetings. The ninth and tenth articles establish the responsibility of the Khedive, and define the conditions under which he will have to appeal to the the Sultan and the right of Turkey to provide for the defense of the eastern coast of the Red Sea. The next three articles sanction the territorial rights of Turkey and the sovereign prerogatives of the Sultan and of the Khedive outside of the obligations of the treaty. The remaining articles declare that the treaty is not limited to the duration of the Suez Canal concessions, and provide for the exchange of ratifications within a month of the date of signature.

Finance.—The English have been unable to ingraft on Egypt the Indian methods of administration, and have been compelled to abandon their efforts to govern the people in their own way. Their general direction of the internal policy of the Central Government has resulted in important reforms, yet these have failed to win the affection of the people, and have been attended with increased burdens. English reformers have improved the irrigation works, abolished the *corvée*, reformed the prisons, and to a large extent done away with arbitrary imprisonment and the use of the kourbash, and have introduced ameliorations in the railroad service and throughout the judicial and civil administration; and yet anarchy and impoverishment are worse than ever before, and the financial situation is still critical, although there has been an improvement of public credit, as compared with the period of bankruptcy and disorganization that followed the burning of Alexandria and the British war of occupation. During 1882 and 1883 a floating debt of nearly £6,000,000 was contracted. The debt in 1884 stood at £101,000,000. Since then it has grown to £103,028,000, but nearly the whole of the increase was still available in the beginning of 1888, when there remained unexpended of the international loan £1,251,000, with a cash reserve of £415,000 in the coffers of the Caisse de la Dette, and £76,000 of cash in the Government treasury. Excepting more rigorous exactions of the land or irrigation taxes, the only increase of taxation in four years have been taxes on Europeans previously exempt and an increase in the tobacco duties. The annual interest on the debt, amounting to £4,250,000, has been paid without any deduction from the coupon. The interest payable abroad, with the Turkish tribute of nearly £700,000, makes a sum of £4,750,000 that the country has to provide annually to meet foreign claims. The average gross value of the exports of cotton, sugar, beans, and wheat between 1880 and 1884 was £11,367,000 per annum, not counting the war year of 1882. In 1885 and 1886, owing to a fall in prices, the value was only £9,986,-500 per annum.

The accounts of the treasury are full of arbitrary changes, adopted for the purpose of showing each year a favorable result. The revenue for 1887 is given as £8,010,749, against £7,896,654 in 1886, and £7,980,233 in 1885. The expenditure is said to have amounted to £7,987,067, against £8,039,980 in 1886, and £7,834,379 in 1885. This shows a surplus of £23,682 in 1887, as compared with a deficit of £143,326 in 1886, and a surplus of £145,854 in 1885. The deficit in 1886 is accounted for by the expenditure for *corvée* abolition and diminished railroad receipts. There were, however, in that year extraordinary and non-recurring receipts, under a new law granting perpetual exemption from military service, amounting to £249,900, whereas the payments for temporary exemption in the previous year were only £17,300. The revenue for 1885 was swelled to a nearly equal amount by abnormal railroad receipts paid for the transportation of English troops. The *corvée* charge was continued in 1887; but the deficit was changed into a surplus by manipulation of the accounts in transferring the estimated deficit in the receipts of the domains and Daira administrations, which is £140,000 and the salaries of employés of the Government for the last month of the year, amounting to £200,000, to the budget of 1888. This jugglery was necessary to avoid a deficit, notwithstanding the new tax on foreigners, which yielded £65,000, and that on tobacco-culture, producing £8,000. The revenue from direct taxes in 1887 was £5,468,981; from indirect taxes, £1,545,950; from remunerative administrations, £884,095; and from other sources, £111,773. The receipts from the land-tax in 1887 show a slight increase, owing to an extension of the cultivated area. In years of a good Nile a continued improvement can be counted on in the future, owing to the public works that the English have constructed. But in 1888 they have had, for the first time, to confront a situation caused by a bad Nile and, at the same time, an increase in military expenditures, due to their selfish and mistaken policy on the Red Sea coast.

The expenditure for 1887 under the different heads was as follows: Debt and tribute, £4,899,220; civil list and pensions, £701,318; remunerative expenditure, £698,275; public security, £652,843; administration, £753,219. Under the head of remunerative expenditure is included the item of £32,374 for the fruitless search for petroleum on the coast of the Red Sea, in which enterprise the Government has sunk £169,164 altogether. A comparison with former years shows some saving in administrative expenses, due to economies, and a reduction in the civil list and pensions, owing to the commutation of pensions.

The budget estimates for 1888 make the net revenue £8,126,661, and the expenditure £8,102,661. A reduction in the price of military exemption was expected to increase the revenue from this source by £150,000. The troubles in the Soudan have led to an increase in the army and gendarmerie, which had been reduced in order to lighten the expenses. The final estimate of the results of the low Nile is that 260,000 acres between Cairo and Assouan will be thrown out of cultivation, causing a loss of revenue for 1889 of £300,000. The loss to the country will amount to more than £1,000,000.

The Egyptian convention placed to the credit of the Government, to be expended for certain specified extraordinary purposes, the sum of £10,129,074, being the proceeds of the international guaranteed loan of £9,000,000 and of the sales of Government lands and old material and the recovery of arrears. Of this total, £4,143,956 were paid out for Alexandria indemnities, £100,000 for a court-house and custom-house, and £78,118 for the emission of the loan. Of £2,757,000 that were appropriated to covering past deficits, there remained £73,680 unexpended at the close of 1887. Of £1,000,000 that were assigned to the Soudan to meet the cost of evacuation, there had been paid out £884,182, and out of an equal sum set aside for irrigation works the expenditures had been £479,715. Of the fund assigned to the commutation of pensions, only £41,162 remained, so that the saving in the ordinary budget under this head ceased with 1887. The total balance remaining from the extraordinary fund was £1,250,945, including £500,000 that is held as a reserve for general treasury purposes. Of the balance, £740,165 was actually disposable, the remainder consisting of public lands that had not yet been sold. The charges upon the revenue on account of debts of all descriptions are estimated for 1888 at £4,306,000, divided as follows: New guaranteed loan, redeemable by a fixed annuity, £307,000; privileged debt, bearing 5 per cent. interest, £1,087,000; 4 per cent. interest on the unified debt, £2,184,000; estimated deficit of interest on the domains and Daira Sanieh loans, £350,000; interest payable to England on Suez Canal shares, £194,000; payment to Daira Sanieh loan commissioners, £34,000; Moukabala annuity, £50,000. In 1888 a new 4½-per-cent. loan was contracted for the conversion of the Daira Sanieh debt, and the further commutation of pensions by the sale of land belonging to the Daira and the domains.

The Government made in 1888 a settlement of the ex-Khedive Ismail's claims, which have been presented annually since the English occupation, but were never before examined or adjudicated upon. He claimed that the International Commission of Inquiry had taken land that he had never conceded, and also the stock and crops on the domains, which had never been accounted for to him, and that the indemnity of £260,000 a year that he had been promised had never been paid. He reckoned his total claim on the Egyptian Government at about £5,000,000.

The Government made a settlement with him and his sons, by which the portion of the civil list payable to the family, amounting at their estimate to £116,000 was capitalized at fourteen years' purchase, and paid over in the form of 32,000 acres to be selected from the domain lands, valued at £1,630,000. The Egyptian Government claimed that the pensions paid to the princes ceased at their deaths, and in agreeing to convert them into property it conceded Ismail's claim to dispose of his civil list on his death. In lieu of other claims that he had brought he agreed to accept £100,000 in cash, while the Government restored the two palaces in Cairo that formerly belonged to him and the one in Constantinople, which he has made his residence.

Irrigation Works.—The most important work done by English engineers in Egypt is the completion of the barrage, which is a great weir extending across both branches of the Nile. It was begun by French engineers, but abandoned as useless. As soon as it was constructed, Sir Colin Moncrieff determined to utilize it, in the face of the criticisms of English as well as of French engineers. During the first six months of 1887 the Rosetta aqueduct was completed. Next in importance to the barrage is the Canal Tewfiki, which will be opened in 1889. Starting from the apex of the delta, it runs east of the eastern branch to the sea. Irrigating siphons, regulating bridges and locks, distributing sluices, and drainage canals have been constructed within the delta and on both sides of the river. Drainage is at present a greater *desideratum* in Lower Egypt than water-supply. The Mahmoudieh Canal, which supplies Alexandria with water and furnishes water communication between the port and the river, has been dredged. Improved irrigation and the reclamation of submerged lands have caused an extension of cotton cultivation in the Fayoum district. A beginning has been made of cotton-planting in the province of Beni Souef, and in that and the neighboring provinces of Assiout, Minieh, and Girgeh the cleaning of the Ibrahimish Canal and other works have increased the production of sugar by one third.

The expenditure of Sir Colin Moncrieff's department in 1887 was 800,356 Egyptian pounds, of which one half was spent on new works and one half in repairing and maintaining the old. Of the total sum, 213,726 Egyptian pounds came from the ordinary budget, 349,023 pounds from a fund of one million pounds sterling that was raised for public works, and 237,607 pounds from a special fund applicable to the abolition of the *corvée*. The most beneficial reform of the British administration has been the substitution of free for forced labor on the canals. Under the old system men were compelled to leave their homes, often when their labor was most needed for their crops, and made to work at mending the canals in the most inefficient and wasteful manner. If they brought no tools, they were made to dredge out the mud with their bare hands. Their families brought them food, carrying it sometimes a great distance. In 1883 there were 202.650 men thus employed for one hundred days each. In 1884 the number was reduced to 165,000. In 1885 there were 125,936 men employed at forced labor, while 116,535 Egyptian pounds were paid for substituted hired labor. In 1886 the *corvée* laborers numbered 95,093, and 265,066 Egyptian pounds were expended on paid labor. In 1887 the number of fellaheen called out for the *corvée* was reduced to 87,120, and the cost of substituted free labor was 233,561 Egyptian pounds.

The Ministry of Nubar Pasha.—In 1884 Sherif Pasha resigned the post of Prime Minister because he was unable to approve the policy of evacuating the Soudan, on which the British Government insisted. Riaz Pasha, the ex-Premier, a Mohammedan of Turkish origin, who was greatly respected by the Egyptians for patriotism and integrity, declined the office because he held the same views. Nubar Pasha, an Armenian Christian of European education, though equally convinced of the folly of abandoning the Soudan, accepted the post, and was supposed to be a willing instrument of English policy. He was not popular, but was known as a statesman of great experience and ability. He applied himself to the task of smoothing the way for the English projects, and opposed only those that were totally impracticable. When Sir Colin Scott Moncrieff had built the barrage and cleaned out the canals, he proposed that his engineers should direct the irrigation, as well as provide the water, assuming that the provincial officials were all corrupt. Nubar Pasha, however, insisted on preserving the power of the mudirs, who were the visible representatives of authority. With less success, he opposed the sweeping changes that Clifford Lloyd introduced in the Interior Department. Under the old system the mudirs exercised and abused the right to arrest and transport without trial persons suspected of crime. During the former ministry of Riaz Pasha, 1,300 suspicious persons were sent to work in the quarries. Local sheikhs procured the imprisonment of their enemies or of individuals who would ray money to regain their liberty. Yet, when Clifford Lloyd emptied the prisons, setting free thousands of prisoners, some of whom had been detained six years without trial. and placed the prison system and the power of commitment under the direction of English officials, charging police officers with the executive functions of the mudirs, the prestige of the latter was destroyed, and brigandage and crimes of violence became so rife that Nubar's views were finally accepted, and the old system was re-established, with safeguards against abuses. The power to arrest "suspects" was restored to the mudirs, but arrested persons could only be committed to prison after a judicial examination before a court consisting of the mudir, a judge, a representative of the Interior Department, and two or three sheikhs of the province. When the English determined on abolishing the *corvée*, the Public Works and Finance departments both suggested the imposition of a water-tax for the purpose; but Nubar Pasha pointed out that the Khedive Ismail had raised the taxes ten per cent. on the ground of increased irrigation, and that the peasantry would not submit to an arbitrary increase, because they look upon the tax as an equivalent for the water furnished. The Egyptian Convention set free an annual sum of £450,000 for the reduction of the land-tax, which the Finance Ministry wished to apply to taxes that could not be collected, while Sir Colin S. Moncrieff needed as much for the abolition of forced labor. At Nubar's suggestion, the amount was divided, £250,000 a year being applied to a gradual abolition of the *corvée*, and £200,000 to offset taxes that could not be collected.

To provide means for their projected reforms, or to escape from the danger of a default of interest, the English were always ready to increase the land-tax or resort to new imposts, notwithstanding the evident signs of overtaxation and impoverishment. Nubar Pasha resisted this destructive policy, and suggested economy of expenditure and the extension of the taxable area by bringing fresh lands under culture as the best means of preserving the financial equilibrium. He instituted a finance committee to examine every proposed change that involved increased expenditure. To promote the second object he gave away large tracts of uncultivated public land, with exemption from taxes for three, six, or ten years. To supply with water 250,-000 feddans that were thus taken up, the Nubarieh Canal was built by a private company. Nubar's efforts to keep down expenses and simplify the administration finally brought him into collision with Sir Evelyn Baring in the summer of 1887, and from that time their relations were never cordial. The Prime Minister objected, not so much to the employment of Europeans in the Government departments as to the complication of the administrative machinery by the creation of new departments, bureaus, sections, and subsections. In a report that was signed by Sir Edgar Vincent, Sir Colin Scott Moncrieff, Yakub Artin Pasha, and Blum Pasha on May 24. 1888, the Prime Minister was charged with having obstructed many economies that the financial authorities had proposed. Later, the question of reforming the *octroi* administration came up. Nubar Pasha, following a report of Yakub Artin Pasha, proposed that the *octrois* and the indirect taxes should be placed under the direction of the Ministry of Finance instead of being administered by a separate department. The

change would necessitate the abolition of a post held by a Frenchman, and M. d'Aubigné, the French agent, therefore objected. The Khedive then called upon Nubar Pasha to withdraw his recommendation, and he obeyed, but at the same time called his master's attention to the hostile report, and asked the Khedive either to defend his minister or allow him to reply to his accusers. The Khedive made no reply, and Nubar went on to say that he stood between two fires, and had been made the scapegoat of both the native party and the English, and concluded with the words, "I owe too much to your Highness ever to resign, but it is within your Highness's power to dismiss me when you will." On the following day, June 8, his dismissal was published. This action was taken by the Khedive without consultation with Sir Evelyn Baring, who was absent at Cairo.

The New Ministry.—Tewfik Pasha not only dismissed his Cabinet, but summoned Riaz Pasha to form a new one, without consulting with his English advisers. He had not shown such independence before since the beginning of the English occupation. His choice of a new minister was generally interpreted as a triumph of the anti-English party and of Ghazi Mukhtar Pasha, the Turkish commissioner, whose recall the English had been unable to bring about, and who exercised an unwelcome influence and authority in the country, which grew stronger with every fresh blunder committed by the English administrators. Mukhtar had two months before predicted the very date of the fall of Nubar. He conferred with the Khedive on the evening of the dismissal, received an ovation on the streets when returning from the palace, and Riaz consulted him before accepting office and making up the new Cabinet. The Turkish Government had, since the early period of Mukhtar's residence in Egypt, maintained a diplomatic attitude of observation till January, 1888, when it instructed its commissioner to warn the Egyptian Government against entering into commercial treaties with foreign powers, as instanced by the tobacco convention with Greece to the prejudice of Turkish produce, and to admonish the Khedive against overstepping the firmans in respect to overtaxation of his people. On the removal of Nubar Pasha, Sir Evelyn Baring hastened to Alexandria. He did not attempt to alter the composition of the new Cabinet, except to secure the withdrawal of Omar Lutfi's name as Minister of War and the transfer of Ali Mubarek Pasha, who had been offered the post of Minister of Public Works. The Cabinet was finally constituted as follows: Riaz Pasha, President of the Council, Minister of the Interior, and Minister of Finance; Fakri Pasha, Minister of Justice; Zulfikar Pasha, Minister for Foreign Affairs; Mustapha Fehmi Pasha, Minister of War; Zeki Pasha, Minister of Public Works; Ali Mubarek Pasha, Minister of Public Instruction.

Fighting in the Soudan.—In September, 1886, after the Egyptians had taken Tamai, Osman Digma retired from the neighborhood of Suakin. The Governor-General of the Red Sea Littoral then urged the friendly tribe of Amharas to capture Tokar, and refused to let them trade until they had accomplished that task. They made the attempt, and so harassed the tribes of the neighborhood that the latter called upon Osman Digma to return from Kassala and drive away their persecutors. He came with a considerable army, and after inflicting punishment on the Amharas, laid regular siege to Suakin in the beginning of January, 1888. On the night of the 2d the Arabs began to fire on the redoubts, but were dispersed by shots from the gun-boats in the harbor. The Amharas and other friendly natives, with freed slaves and deserters from Osman Digma's forces, attacked the enemy, with varying success. On January 17 a party of these allies advanced against Osman Digma's camp at Handoub, while Col. Kitchener, the Governor-General of the Red Sea Coast, followed with the regular cavalry. The camp was surprised and captured, but the enemy retook it from the rear, and received Col. Kitchener's force, as it came up to join in the pursuit, with a hot fire, wounding him and another English officer. The garrison of Suakin was compelled to take the offensive, because the "rebels" or "dervishes" had pushed their trenches close under the walls and fired frequently on the forts, and had succeeded in driving off cattle from under the protection of the guns. A large number of slaves that Osman Digma had collected to export to Arabia were released by the expedition to Handoub, and about 180 of his followers were killed. He retired northward with more than 2,000 men, and attacked and defeated the Amhara tribe at Darah. Soon the rebels returned to Handoub, and resumed plundering. On March 4 they took a position in force in an abandoned fort, and opened fire on one of the chief redoubts. A detachment of Egyptian troops was beaten back by a furious countercharge of Baggara horsemen, who were armed only with spears. Among the killed was Col. Tapp, one of the principal English officers. The enemy, whose losses were severe, abandoned their intrenchments. The dervishes also gave trouble in Upper Egypt by raiding the country between Wady Halfa and Assouan, which necessitated the strengthening of the frontier force. On April 27 Osman Digma was joined by Abu Girgeh, with 3,000 Baggara warriors. The railroad between Suakin and Handoub, had been torn up to build a stockade at Handoub, but the prospect of capturing Suakin was diminishing as the English completed their fortifications. A high stone wall with bastions mounted with heavy cannon was surrounded with a chain of detached forts that were provided with Krupp and Gardner guns and with electric lights, and connected with a railroad for the rapid transference of troops from point to point. The English opened negotiations with Osman Digma and Abu Girgeh, who expressed a willingness to allow trade, but declared that they would attack every armed force that they found in the country. Egyptian steamers and coastguard dhows that patrolled the coast were unable to stop the slave and contraband trade with Jeddah, yet the hostile Arabs effectually blockaded the trade that was begun under English protection at Agig. Rumors that arrived from Khartoum indicated that the Mahdi's successor, the Khalifa Abdullah, lived in fear of his enemies, and that dissensions had sprung up among his supporters. In February Osman Janoo, one of his emirs, was defeated by Zaid, a slave of the Sultan of Darfour; but the Mahdist forces put down the rebellion two months later, and sent the Sultan's head to Khartoum. Another uprising between Suakin and Berber was likewise suppressed. Slatin Bey, one of the European prisoners at Khartoum was subjected to ignominious treatment.

The former Governor of Bahr-el-Ghazelle, Lupton Bey, an English officer, who was held as a prisoner by the Khalifa, and whose technical knowledge was made use of in the arsenal, died at Khartoum in July.

In June rumors reached Europe from Khartoum and other parts of the Soudan of the victorious march of a "white pasha," who had entered the province of Bahr-el-Ghazelle at the head of a large military force and established his rule over a wide region. He was at first supposed to be Henry M. Stanley, and afterward seemed more likely to be Emin Bey retreating from the Equatorial Province. The Khalifa sent a large force to Fashoda against the stranger. This and two later expeditions returned unsuccessful. At Gallabat the Soudanese gained a signal victory over the Abyssinians in July. The fighting near Wady Halfa continued during the summer. On August 27 a force of 600 dervishes drove 250 Egyptian soldiers out of Fort Khormoussa, but the position was regained by Col. Wodehouse, who sent a re-enforcement of 150 Soudanese, supported by a gun-boat. On September 17 the besiegers of Suakin took up a position within a thousand yards of the outer forts, where they strongly intrenched themselves. They enlarged and strengthened their position, where about 1,500 men were posted, supported by a large force in the wood near by. On September 25 they made an attack on one of the forts. They accomplished their object in closely investing the town, which was to cut off the water-supply. Some of their shells fell inside the town, but on September 30, after mining to within 500 yards of the Water Fort in preparation for an assault, tkey were driven from the nearer trenches by a heavy fire from the forts and a war-vessel.

Col. Kitchener, by maintaining the embargo on trade and fomenting war between the friendly tribes and the rebels, was directly responsible for the renewal of disturbances in the Suakin district. He aggravated the situation by encouraging and subsidizing predatory raids against hostile tribes and sending piratical expeditions down the coast. The naval force was employed in maintaining the trade blockade. Several vessels were captured when landing goods. Permission was given in December, 1887, to the friendly inhabitants of Agig to trade with foreign merchants under stringent restrictions and Government supervision; but the Governor was soon afterward displaced and a personal enemy of Osman Digma appointed, which led to the blockade of the roads by the latter. Col. Kitchener's policy of denying trade, which was generally condemned in England and finally resulted in his transfer to the appointment of Adjutant-General of the Egyptian Army, was adopted for the purpose of coercing the Mahdists to remove their own fanatical inhibition of commerce with infidels. The export of gum arabic from Suakin in 1879 amounted to 207,084 Egyptian pounds, and coffee from Abyssinia and ivory were exported to the amount of 20,000 Egyptian pounds each. The Mahdi prohibited the gathering of the gum of Kordofan, and for five years there has been little trade with the interior. The Mahdist government is based on ascetic religious principles, and, where the authority of the Khalifa is supreme, the possession of riches is discouraged, half of each man's property is counted as belonging to state, and enjoyment of luxuries or display of wealth is treated as a crime. The coast Arabs, on the other hand, are eager traders, and, by holding out the promise of trade as a reward, the Governor-General expected to gain their loyalty and the sooner open up the trade in gum and other valuable products of the Soudan; but, instead of that, he only brought back the miseries of war and stimulated the clandestine exchange of slaves for arms and ammunition. His troublesome restrictions and irritating policy sent many recruits to Osman Digma's banner even from the friendly Amhara tribes. The English officers affect a stringent military régime because they hope thereby to succeed to the authority of the Mahdi throughout the Soudan. The power exercised by the Khalifa over the remotest tribes of the desert is attributed to the fear of the black regiments that were enrolled and drilled by Gordon Pasha and of the Baggaras and other fierce tribes from beyond the Nile and also to the exaction of hostages.

The rebel forces that laid close siege to the town in September were those commanded by Abu Girgeh. Shells were cast within the Water Fort every night, and some burst in the town. On October 30 the enemy attempted to storm that fort, but were driven back by a heavy fire from the guns of the forts and ships. Gen. Grenfell, the commander-in-chief, arrived in the beginning of November with re-enforcements. On the 8th he led out the mounted infantry and horse artillery and made an unsuccessful attempt to enfilade the enemy's trenches. As the result of this reconnoissance he returned to Cairo to dispatch re-enforcements, for he found the enemy strongly intrenched and well supplied with cavalry, infantry, and six rifled guns firing Armstrong shells, which were served with remarkable skill.

The military situation on the Nile was equally critical. The Egyptian garrisons were re-enforced; but the raids of the enemy grew bolder and more frequent, and in the beginning of November their commander at Dongola, Walad-el-Njunni, was engaged in collecting an army for the invasion of Upper Egypt. The Egyptian Government decided to increase the army by 2,000 men, costing £51.000 per annum.

The Equatorial Provinces. — The position of Emin Pasha at Wadelai after the abandonment of the Soudan was entirely analogous to that of Gen. Gordon at Khartoum, and Emin, who had been made Governor of the Equatorial Provinces by Gordon, was as determined as his chief to maintain the government that he had established, although retreat was open to him by way of Zanzibar. He has kept together a well-organized army of blacks and aided in preserving peace and order, for which services the inhabitants paid the taxes that were necessary to support his command long after they had thrown off the absolute authority that he had exercised when the power and prestige of the Khedive's Government stood behind him; and, when support was withheld, he sustained his troops by means of a trade in ivory through Uganda and by planting cotton. In letters that from time to time reached Europe, he expressed the hope that Great Britain would send an expedition to annex the rich country that he had saved from anarchy. When his position began to be precarious, Henry M. Stanley started up the Congo with a relief expedition that was fitted out under the auspices of the British East African Association, a rival to the similarly named German organization. Tippoo Tib, an Arab slave-dealer, who maintains a strong military organization in the region of the Upper Congo, promised to assist the expedition. (See EMIN PASHA.)

On April 4 Emin Pasha received a message from the Khalifa, ordering him to surrender and to disband his troops. A few weeks later his scouts on the Nile beyond Lado reported that an army was approaching. Emin Pasha then determined to advance with the bulk of his troops in order to surprise the enemy, and defeat him by a sudden blow, if possible, for money and provisions were lacking for a regular campaign. The army sent against Emin Pasha was said to be 4,000 strong, and to be ascending the Nile in four steamers and many boats. In the south, Kabrega, King of Unyoro, had been beaten by the ferocious young King of the Waganda, who now held both shores of Albert Nyanza. Emin had lived on nominally good terms with M'tesa, the late King of Uganda, whereas his son and successor, Myanga, was avowedly hostile. This war between the two powerful neighboring kingdoms in the south interrupted Emin's communications with Zanzibar, and cut off the shortest route by which a relief expedition could reach him from the Congo. When it seemed certain that Stanley's purpose of succoring Emin Pasha had miscarried, Major Barttelot, his lieutenant, who had remained in charge of the supplies in camp at Yambuga, on the Aruwimi, in May, 1888, set out in search of his chief at the head of 100 Soudanese soldiers that were left by Stanley, and 640 Zanzibari and Manyema bearers that Tippoo Tib raised for him. The latter proved unruly, and Barttelot employed harsh means to reduce them to obedience, but before he had gone far the Manyema bearers mutinied against his severe punishments, and assassinated the leader. The second in command, J. S. Jameson, returned to organize another expedition, but was stricken with a fatal fever. After the failure of these expeditions, Dr. Carl Peters and other persons interested in German colonial enterprises in East Africa obtained subscriptions of 1,000,000 marks for an expedition to rescue Emin Pasha, who is a German by birth, and was known as Dr. Schnitzer before he received his title in the Egyptian service, under the conduct of Dr. Peters, Lieut. Wissmann, and Herr Junker. The object of the enterprise was more plainly political than was that of the disastrous English expeditions. The route chosen runs for 1,500 kilometres, or more than three quarters of the distance, through territory over which Germany claims jurisdiction. From Mutansige, where the German possessions end, to Wadelai, the distance in a straight line is only 400 kilometres. The plan was to establish permanent stations along the route. The expedition was delayed by the troubles that occurred in the German possessions (see ZANZIBAR).

EMIN PASHA. The close of the year 1888 leaves the fate of Emin Pasha and of his rescuer, Henry M. Stanley, involved in mystery, while during its course but few, and for the most part unauthentic, tidings have been received from either. That the expedition was successful in arriving at its point of destination is proved by the official report received on December 23, from the Congo Free State, of the return of Stanley to Aruwimi river, in company with Emin, in August of the present year; but when the meeting took place, and whether the presence of one or both on the Congo in that month conflicts with the assertion of Osman Digma at Suakin, December 14, that Emin Pasha with a white traveler, who had been sent to his rescue, surrendered to the troops of the Khalifa on October 11, is matter of conjecture. The strongest proof of the latter story is the accompanying copy of a letter, recognized by Gen. Grenfell as the one written by himself for the Khedive of Egypt, which was forwarded to

Emin by Stanley; but whether the letter was taken from Emin himself or from Stanley, or was captured from some runner, it is impossible to determine.

Stanley (see "Annual Cyclopædia" for 1887, page 250) left Bolombo, May 11, 1887. It is known that he encountered great hardships in arriving at this point, 892 miles from the Atlantic. Scarcity of provisions, difficulties of obtaining transportation, and obstructions on the route, rendered it, in his own words, "a period of great anxiety; and whether we shall be able to tide over, without breach of order, I know not." After he passed Bolombo the conditions improved, the natives were more friendly, and sufficient rations were obtained. On June 18 the mouth of the Aruwimi river was reached, and a camp established, which Stanley left on the 23d with an advance-guard, and instructions that the porters promised by Tippoo Tib should follow with stores. A note was received from him, July 2, which is thus far the last direct communication, and all knowledge of his movements and whereabouts has since been derived from rumor alone. Explorers have been almost unanimous in opinion as to his safety. Stories have been afloat of a mysterious white pasha carrying all before him in the Bahrel Ghazel district, supposed to be Stanley, or, perhaps, Emin; and Arabs arriving at Kinshassa at one time said that Stanley had been wounded in a fight with natives, and that half of his escort had deserted. The first intelligence of import was received from couriers from Tabora, reaching Zanzibar on Nov. 1, 1888. Their tidings were a year old, but they reported that at the close of November, 1887, detachments of Arabs trading from Tabora in the regions between Lakes Albert Nyanza and Muta Nzige encountered the rear-guard of Stanley's expedition at a point west of the Albert Nyanza, and southeast of Sanga. Stanley himself was not seen, being two days in advance, but tales of hardships endured on the way were told by this party of thirty. There had been fighting with the natives for provisions, one of the white men of the party had died, forty had been drowned in crossing a great river, and Stanley with others had been ill with fever. This had delayed the march, already slow, three weeks. The total force, deducting all losses, was estimated by the Arabs at 250, but they were believed to be able to accomplish the journey. The northeasterly direction of the line of march had been abandoned to avoid the swamps, and Stanley was then proceeding north, intending to strike afterward to the east toward Wadelai, distant, it was estimated, a journey of forty or fifty days.

The reports of combats with the natives are substantiated by accounts from reconnoitring parties from the Aruwimi camp, who passed quantities of bones, supposed to be those of victims fallen in battles between the expedition and native tribes, and also by dispatches from Emin, dated at the beginning of 1888. Emin was at that time in difficult straits, owing to the non-arrival of the promised stores, and had received reports of Stanley, stripped of men and supplies, hemmed in between the Maboda country and the Albert Nyanza, as also of his change of march in an unknown direction, owing to conflicts with the Matongora and Mino tribes. Advices from Emin, bearing date September and November, 1887, gave no tidings whatever of Stanley, though he himself headed in November a reconnoitring party to find him. In a letter to Dr. Felkin, published in the "Scotchman" of April 11, which bore date Sept. 3, 1887, in allusion to the Congo route, Emin said: "I know the almost impassable swamps, the number of rivers with floating vegetation, from personal observation, and I know well enough the difficulties which a traveler will have to surmount in marching from the Congo here." And yet this route through unexplored territory was deemed safer by the explorer than the more direct one through hostile Uganda.

Whether, as was asserted by Mr. Jameson, second to Maj. Barttelot in command, Tippoo Tib awaited news of the arrival of the advance-guard before sending carriers, or it arose from remissness in fulfilling his contract, a whole year was consumed in collecting the porters, who finally did not reach the appointed number. The severity of Maj. Barttelot had been severely commented on; officers and men were alike dissatisfied. Tippoo, it is said, vainly remonstrated against his treatment of the men. On June 10 he left the camp with a force of 22 Soudanese, 110 Zanzibaris, and 430 Manyemas, under command of a native Arab chief, Muni Somai. His intention, expressed in a letter to Mr. Mackinnon, was to follow Stanley, and, if possible, to find him, and, failing this, to reach Emin Pasha; and, if further search by them both were deemed futile, to place his forces at Emin's disposal. On July 19 he was assassinated by the Manyema force, who deserted, and on return to camp, Maj. Jameson proceeded to Stanley Falls, to organize another expedition. But his death at Bangala, August 17, put an end to all hopes of the kind. Capt. Van Gèle, a Belgian officer of the Congo, denies that Tippoo Tib was accessory to the death of Barttelot, and that chief, who was absent on an exploring party with Lieut. Baert, Belgian resident at Stanley Falls, south of Kassongo, expressed great regret, declaring he would have given half his fortune to avert the catastrophe, and repeated that he had warned Maj. Barttelot. These details are all that so far has been learned of the relief expedition. Maj. Bonny is in command of the Aruwimi camp, and it is said he was lately reached by a rumor that Stanley was proceeding at the back of the great oil rivers, under the British flag, and that the natives were friendly.

As regards Emin and his companion, Casati, who was left in November, 1886, with a detachment of soldiers at Unyoro, letters to Capt. Camperio from the latter, of date Sept. 1 and 24, 1887, say that he had been taken prisoner by King Traxiore, whom he finally persuaded to become friendly to Emin, and who eventually charged him with a mission to negotiate an alliance. Emin's position in the beginning of April was reported hazardous. Two native messengers, who had been delayed by capture by Ugarda tribes, said, on August 1, at Zanzibar, that a summons to surrender had been received from the Mahdi at Khartoum, threatening attack, as also a letter from Sufton Bey (which Emin considered a forgery), urging assent to the surrender, in order to avert a massacre of Europeans at Khartoum and Wadelai. Outposts confirmed reports of the Mahdi's advance, alleging appearance of armed vessels at the confluence of the Nile and Sobat, and Emin had decided to advance with the bulk of his troops by the left bank of the Nile, and endeavor to surprise the Mahdi, compensating for lack of provisions by the rapidity of his attack. He was sorely troubled by the non-arrival of Stanley. Provisions were scarce, and the troops beginning to become discouraged. There have been reports of the arrival of Stanley at Wadelai early in January and of the concerted action of him and Emin, but these are denied.

In reply to a request of Gen. Grenfell for news of Stanley, Osman Digma furnished at Suakin the news received in a letter from the Khalifa Abdulla, of the surrender of Emin and a white traveler in chains by the officers and troops of the former to Oman Saleh, commanding a steamer expedition to the equator, which reached Lado on October 11. Oman Saleh found a quantity of feathers and ivory. He reported that a white traveler sent to Emin, named Stanley, brought orders from the Khedive to accompany him, offering the remainder of the force the option of going to Cairo or remaining. They refused to enter Turkish service, and welcomed Oman. Another traveler had visited Emin and was gone, but he was making search for him. In proof of the capture, Osman Digma sent Snider cartridges, alleged to have been taken from Emin, and Dr. Junker says that Emin was provided with Snider arms. But the date on these was twenty years old, and the weight of evidence lies with the letter of the Khedive, the existence of which, being a state secret, is with difficulty explained, and renders it impossible to regard the whole as a stratagem to secure the surrender of Suakin in exchange for the lives of the white prisoners. If Stanley returned alone to Bongala, as is said in advices of December 21, leaving Emin in possession of plentiful stores of ivory, with numerous oxen, and in health but for a slight affection of the eyes, he may have escaped the fate of Emin, should the latter prove indeed a captive.

A second expedition for the relief of Emin has been for some time under discussion at Berlin, to be commanded by Lieut. Wissman, and it is expected to set out in February, 1889.

The delay is partly due to the impossibility of obtaining the passage of the East African bill by the Reichstag before that date. The expedition is advocated by the German Government as assisting the anti-slavery operations in Africa.

A letter written by Mr. Stanley reached Brussels on January 16. It was dated at Boma of Bonalya Muretia, August 17, and was addressed to Tippoo Tib. He says: "I reached here this morning with 130 Wangwana, 3 soldiers, and 66 natives belonging to Emin Pasha. It is now eighty-two days since I left Emin Pasha on the Nyanza. I only lost three men all the way. Two were drowned, and the other decamped. I found the white men who were looking for Emin Pasha quite well. The other white man, Cassati, is also well. Emin Pasha has ivory in abundance, thousands of cattle and sheep, goats and fowls, and food of all kinds. I found him a very good and kind man. He gave all our white and black men numbers of things. His liberality could not be excelled. His soldiers blessed our black men for their kindness in coming so far to show them the way. Many of them were ready to follow me out of the country, but I asked them to stay quiet a few months, that I might return and fetch the other men and goods left at Yambunga. If you go with me it is well; I leave it to you. I will stay here ten days, and will then proceed slowly. I will move hence to Big Island, two hours' march from here above this place. There there are plenty of houses, and plenty of food for the men. Whatever you have to say to me, my ears will be open with a good heart as it has always been toward you. Therefore if you come, come quickly, for on the eleventh morning from this I shall move on. All my white men are well, but I left them all behind except my servant William, who is with me."

ENGINEERING. Bridge over Harlem River.—The insignificant estuary that separates Manhattan Island from the mainland promises to become in itself a compendium of bridge architecture. It is already crossed by numerous structures representing nearly all the types of bridge-building, from solid masonry to finest steel. The latest addition, as shown in Fig. 1, is a good specimen of modern engineering. It crosses the river at 181st Street.

The banks at this point are quite high and precipitous, those on the island or west shore rising directly from the water, while those on

Fig. 1.—New Bridge over Harlem River.

the mainland are now separated from the water by flats on which are wharves, railway tracks, etc. The new bridge is for a highway.

The structure is combined masonry, steel, and wrought-iron, carrying foot and road-ways. The approaches are each 660 feet long, and the remaining 1,060 feet—the bridge proper—consists of two steel arches and a central stone pier. The carriage-way is 50 feet wide, with a 15-foot side-walk on either hand. The carriage-way is laid with granite blocks, and is 151 feet above the river. The intrados of the arch is 133 feet above the river.

One of the most interesting engineering features of the structure is the bearing of the arch ribs, as illustrated in Fig. 2. At the end of each rib the top and bottom chords converge, and a second bearing or bed is formed, which receives the projecting surface of the pin, a free space being left between the skewback bearing and terminal of the rib. Thus a sort of hinge-joint is formed that secures a true thrust undisturbed by varying load or by changes of temperature. As the rib can oscillate freely in such a

FIG. 2.—PIVOT-BEARING AND SKEWBACK, HARLEM BRIDGE.

bearing, no destructive strain is possible. Each rib thus ends, constructionally speaking, in a sort of point. As a concession to the public the general lines of the rib are carried out as shown in outline, but these outlined parts do none of the work. It is rather a pity that these superfluous plates were added. They detract from the character of the structure, and the public should be educated up to such devices. With an extreme range of temperature, a rise and fall of the crown of the arch through a space of three inches may occur, and many times this amount is provided for by the pivotal bearing.

Each arch consists of six ribs thus constructed and supported. They are spaced laterally 14 feet from center to center. Their rise is 90 feet. They are connected by bracing that

has two distinct functions, namely, wind bracing, in the line of upper and lower flanges or chords of the ribs; and sway bracing, which extends from rib to rib at each junction of the voussoirs or panels. From the upper surfaces of the arch rise vertical columns, upon which rest the cross floor-beams. These columns are 15 feet from center to center, and they determine the varying length of the rib panels, already alluded to, as each column starts from the termination of a joint between the voussoirs. The two main arches, one spanning the river, the other the railroads, stree's, and low ground on the east bank, are identical in construction. They contain about 7,500 tons of iron and steel.

The skewbacks, pins, and bearings are of forged steel. The arch-ribs are of steel. Both open-hearth and Bessemer steel are used, but the tests call for an ultimate tensile strength of 62,000 to 70,000 pounds to the square inch, an elastic limit of not less than 32,000 pounds, with a minimum elongation of 18 per cent. The bracing, vertical posts, and floor-beams are of wrought-iron. Most of the riveting is done by machine, air riveters being used for work *in situ*. Before being riveted together, all abutting surfaces were painted. Rivets of seven-eighths-inch diameter are used throughout. William R. Hutton is the chief-engineer, with Theodore Cooper as assistant.

Pontoon Bridge at Nebraska City.—Pontoon bridges are generally used for temporary purposes, but there are some notable exceptions. At Nebraska City the Missouri river has two arms, and the main branch has a very swift current, often bearing large quantities of driftwood. The lesser arm is crossed by a permanent crib-work, 1,050 feet long. The pontoon section is 1,074 feet long. A central span of 528 feet is closed by two swinging sections, which form a V-shaped junction, with the angle pointing down stream. When it is desired to open the draw, the fasts at the apex are cast off, and the two halves at once swing apart, the current doing all the work. The operation of closing is also aided by the current, and the whole, it is said, can be effected by one man. The floats are constructed so that the ordinary "flood trash" of the river is carried under them by the force of the current. The constructing engineer was Colonel S. N. Stewart, of Philadelphia, and the success of the bridge has been such that others are already proposed for the great Western rivers. The cost of the structure was $18,000, and it was built in a surprisingly short time.

Just above the pontoon is a second bridge, built for the use of the railroads. This also is a recently completed structure. It was built by the Union Bridge Works, and is of steel throughout. The caissons were sunk in December, 1887, and January and February, 1888. The first piece of metal was put in position February 13, and on June 8 the last piece was in place. The through spans are 400 feet, the deck span 325 feet long. The entire length of the bridge is 1,128 feet, and its weight is 1,489 tons. The stone piers are 85 feet high, and are 18 by 46 feet at the base.

The Arthur Kill Bridge.—The history of this bridge involves some interesting problems in law as well as in mechanics. Arthur, or more properly Authur (that is "farther") Kill is a tidal river separating Staten Island, N. Y., from New Jersey. It is, therefore, an interstate bridge, and the sanction of the General Government had to be secured for its erection. The Secretary of War held the plans under consideration for nine months, and finally approved them without modification. Then followed an injunction procured by the State of New Jersey, which checked the work for six months longer, and was finally disposed of by Justice Bradley, of the United States Circuit Court, who decided against the injunction, holding that Congress had the right to regulate interstate commerce even though the States themselves were opposed to its action.

The great importance of securing railroad communication with the mainland is obvious at a glance, since the shores of Staten Island are admirably adapted for purposes of commerce. Five or ten miles of additional wharfage will be opened on New York harbor, and the facilities of shipment will thus be very largely increased. The bridge was authorized by act of Congress of 16 June, 1886, and two years were allowed for its completion. On 13 June, 1888, the great draw was pronounced in working order. The bridge is owned by an independent organization, the Staten Island Rapid Transit Company, and is open to the use of all railroads on payment of the regular tolls. This removes it from the suspicion of monopoly, since it is practically a public highway. The Kills at this point are about 600 feet wide for navigable purposes, and the entire length of the bridge, exclusive of approaches, is 800 feet. It consists of two shore-spans of 150 feet each, covered by fixed trusses, and two draw-spans of 206 and 204 feet each in the clear. The draw-bridge is the largest now in existence, the total length being 500 feet, but it can be opened or closed in about two minutes. The lower chords of the draw-trusses are 30 feet above mean high water. The iron work was pushed with great rapidity, and under apprehensions at times of delay on account of strikes. In four weeks the draw-span was put together. Two weeks more were required for the adjustment of the machinery. The draw contains 656 tons, and each of the approaches contains 85 tons of metal. The total cost of the bridge was $450,000. The iron work was supplied by the Kingston Bridge Company, and Charles Ackenheil was the superintending engineer. In modern engineering works, especially where they are pushed forward with rapidity, there is often a culpable carelessness. The Arthur Kill bridge was completed without any fatal accident.

Bridge at Benares, India.—An important link in the Indian system of railroads was finished and opened for traffic early in February. The structure is named for Lord Dufferin, Viceroy of India, who took part in the opening ceremonies. The bridge was constructed for the Oudh and Rohilcund Railway Company, under the superintendence of H. B. Hedersedt, chief engineer, and F. T. G. Walton, executive engineer. The river Ganges at this point is more than 3,000 feet wide, and the total length of the bridge is 3,568 feet. The work has been more than eight years under construction. The shifting sand-bed and the rapid current, with great fluctuations in the depth of water, have presented obstacles to rapid work. The main stream is crossed by seven spans of iron girders of 356 feet, each supported on brick piers. But less than half the brickwork of these great piers is visible, no less than 120 feet of the masonry being below water, and 82 feet representing foundations carried into the sandy bed of the river, which here, in the rainy season, has a depth of 92 feet, with a velocity of 20 feet a second. The total cost of the bridge, not including the approaches, was about $3,000,000. Since 1881 Mr. Walton has had the personal superintendence of the work, and his services were recognized by the Empress, who created him a Commander of the Indian Empire. The city of Benares is one of the most important, historically and commercially, in India, and is regarded as sacred by the Hindus. The opening of direct railroad communication with the sea-coast will vastly increase its commercial facilities, and will no doubt radically change its character before many years.

Foot-Bridge, River Ouse.—The city of Bedford, England, lies on the north side of the river Ouse, about forty-five miles from its mouth. The corporation of the city acquired land on the south side of the stream for a public recreation-ground, and it became necessary to span the river with a foot-bridge of such construction that it would not obstruct the view, for public gardens already existed on the north side of the stream. It was deemed necessary also to insist upon a clear waterway of fifteen feet in mid-channel. There was practically no place for abutments. The conditions were met by means of the double arch shown in the illustration, the upper one consisting of two arched ribs by which the lower arch bearing the footway is supported. The clear span is 100 feet, and the footway is 7 feet wide. The arched ribs each consist of four angles 4 inches by 3 inches by $\frac{7}{16}$ inch, braced together by angle irons 3 inches by 3 inches by $\frac{5}{16}$ inch and 2½ inches by 2½ inches by $\frac{7}{16}$ inch, and flat bars 3 inches by $\frac{5}{16}$ inch, and 2½ inches by $\frac{5}{16}$ inch; the ribs are 1 foot 6 inches deep by 1 foot wide at the center, increasing in width to the abutments, where they are also splayed out horizontally to withstand the wind pressure. The suspension rods are $\frac{3}{4}$ inch diameter attached to the vertical members of the rib by 1-inch pins at intervals of 5 feet, and to the angle-iron stringer beams, which carry the roadway. The roadway consists of corrugated flooring plates ¼ inch thick, 3 inches deep, and 1 foot pitch. The plates are covered with concrete of cement and granite chippings, and

On the 8th of July took place the official ceremonies attending the opening of this magnificent work near St. Omer on the Neuf-Fossé Canal, which connects the ports of Calais, Gravelines, and Dunkerque with the canal system to

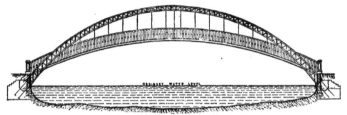

Fig. 3.—Foot-Bridge over the River Ouse.

as the first part of the roadway is necessarily rather steep, it is stepped out into 2-feet-6-inches treads, with a 3-inch rise. The stringer beams, to which the flooring plates are riveted, are of angle irons 6 inches by 3 inches by ¼ inch, bent to a radius of 114 feet, having a versed sine of 11 feet 6 inches; and an ornamental rolled iron is riveted to each with countersunk rivets. Two ornamental cast-iron pillars are fixed at each approach, and termi-

the southward. It was begun by Louis XIV, and all the barge traffic from the ports in the vicinity of Calais, are obliged to pass through this section on their way to Paris or Lisle. The annual traffic amounts to 800,000 tons, and will become greater with increased facilities. Hitherto the change of level at Les Fontinettes has been overcome by means of locks, and boats were often detained for several days awaiting their turn. While contemplating the construc-

Fig. 4.—Hydraulic Canal Lift at Les Fontinettes, France.

nate the hand railing. The total weight of the iron work in this remarkable structure, including the flooring plates, bolts, ornamental pillars, etc., is less than 28½ tons. The bridge was designed by John J. Webster, and was erected under his superintendence.

tion of a second series of locks, the attention of the administration was directed to a hydraulic canal lift that had been constructed on the Trent and Mersey Canal in England. The result was that a contract was made with Messrs. Clark and Cail, an English firm, for the construction of a lift at Les Fontinettes. A prospective view of the completed work is given in the illustration. It consists of two immense troughs of plate-iron—sections of the canal, they may be termed—capable of receiving and floating boats of 300 tons. Each of these troughs rests upon the head of a piston, which works in the cylinder of a hydraulic press. These presses are in deep wells sunk between the towers in the foreground. The presses are connected by a pipe with a sliding valve, and when this is open a hydrostatic balance is established. If one of the troughs is more heavily loaded than the other, it descends and forces the other to ascend, and the preponderance of lifting force may be turned one way or the other by the usual hydrostatic appliances. The stroke of the pistons is equal to the difference between the water-levels, about forty-three feet. The weight of a trough or "lock-chamber," as they are technically called, is 800 tons when full of water.

Supposing the two lock-chambers to be in position, one at the upper and the other at the lower level: if the communicating valve is opened the upper chamber will descend, and the lower one will rise, and after a few oscillations they will stop midway *in equilibrio.* To prevent this, the upper chamber is supercharged with a weight of water equal to that contained in a press, so that it continues its motion until it reaches the lower level of the canal. Thus each chamber in alternation lifts the other with the least possible waste of water. The chambers are metallic frames constructed according to the accepted rules of resistances. The presses are the largest in existence, 55 feet high and 6½ feet in diameter, and calculated to resist an internal pressure of 27 atmospheres. There were no precedents, as smaller cast-iron presses had collapsed under less strain. It was therefore decided to use rolled-steel rings superposed and set in a groove to prevent lateral movement. To secure absolute tightness the compound cylinder thus formed was lined with copper in a single sheet $\frac{1}{16}$ of an inch thick. An experimental section constructed on this principle sustained a pressure of 175 atmospheres without distortion.

The passage of a boat, which formerly required two hours, is now effected in three minutes. The apparatus is the largest of the kind in existence, and reflects much credit upon Mr. A. Barbet, the engineer of the contracting establishment. A similar lift has more recently been completed in Belgium.

Docks at Havre.—The Bellot Basin, the latest artificial improvement to the important French port of Havre, is constructed upon made land southward of the Tancarville Canal. It is bounded on the south by a masonry dike 3,280 feet in length and a stockade 1,790 feet in extent. Its total length, including that of the entrance-lock, is 3,762 feet. Its two divisions are known as the east and west docks, which are of unequal length, but of a uniform width of 720 feet. The total area of the dock is 253,460 square yards. The entrance-lock is 98 feet wide and is provided with tide-gates, the leaves of which are of rolled iron, 54 feet wide and 36 feet high, arranged with air and water chambers, so that the weight upon the hinges can be varied between the extremes of 25 tons and 155 tons. The sluiceways, also 98 feet wide, are spanned by revolving bridges operated by powerful hydraulic machinery, as are also the gates, sluiceways, and capstans of the whole basin.

The construction of the beton work was very difficult, owing to the exposed nature of the shore, liable to be swept by severe storms. The excavations had to be kept dry by pumping at every rise of the tide, and in some cases the pumps had to be hoisted as the tide rose. The blocks used for the foundations were 22 feet wide by 33 feet long, each with a central aperture, to allow excavation from within the block. Thirty days were allowed for the setting of the beton. When the masonry was complete the central space was filled in with beton. A barge carrying a boiler, which furnished steam for the pumping machinery, was moored between two of the blocks, so that the pumping was effected with great rapidity. By this process 87 blocks were sunk, representing 1,575,000 cubic feet.

Double-ender Screw Ferry-Boat.—The use of the double-ender paddle-wheel ferry-boat has been carried to greater perfection in America than elsewhere. Indeed, it is only recently that they have been at all used abroad. A new type of boat has recently been launched at Newburg, N. Y., for use on the New York and Hoboken Ferry. She is a double-ender, with a screw at each end. The shaft runs the entire length of the boat, and the screws always rotate together, being incapable of independent movement.

Many advantages are claimed for this system. All the machinery is below decks, enlarging the deck-room about 20 per cent. The absence of paddle-wheels, of course, largely increases the cabin-room. The engines are of the ordinary triple-expansion type, but the crank-pins are of uniform diameter, because the engine will be worked in one direction quite as much as in the other. For the same reason the screw-propeller blades have both faces alike, since they will be required to work both ways. One of the obstacles to ferry-boat navigation is the liability of the slips to become filled with ice. Ordinary tug-boats have been found very effectual in clearing the slips by simply revolving their screws. Paddle-wheels have merely a surface effect. It is thought, therefore, that the new type of boat will be able to clear ferry-slips of ice with great ease. It has been suggested by Capt. Zalinsky, inventor of the dynamite gun, that the ordinary type of ferry-boat could be easily made available for harbor defense by mounting pneumatic guns upon them. It is evident that a vessel of the type of the "Bergen," as the new boat is named, would have many advantages over side-wheelers for war service, since her screws and the most vulnerable parts of her machinery are under water. The "Bergen's" builders are Thomas C. Marvel & Sons, of Newburg, N. Y.

Ferry at Greenwich, England.—More than two centuries and a half have passed since a ferry was first established at Greenwich, on the Thames, below London, but no attempt has been made until the present year to introduce modern methods. The peculiar difficulties of the situation include a sloping river-bottom and a tidal rise and fall of 20 feet. At high water, therefore. the boat can land at the bulk-head line, but at low tide she can not approach it within three or four times her length. To overcome this, an inclined railway, 348 feet long, has been laid on the bottom, the whole securely bedded in concrete. Up and down this incline a landing-stage is moved by means of suitable machinery, and two platforms are made to travel back and forth between the landward side of the stage and the wharf, whatever the distance may be. "On each side of the river," says London "Engineering," in a detailed description of this ferry, "close behind the abutment, two cast-iron cylinders are sunk close to each other to a depth of 145 feet below the level of the roadway. The cylinders are 10 feet diameter on top, increasing in size by varying cones to 11 feet 6 inches in diameter at the bottom. The metal varies in thickness from $\frac{7}{8}$ inch to $1\frac{1}{8}$ inch. The contractor for this work, with fine old English crusted conservatism, is doing the sinking of the cylinders with divers, so that it is at once evident that speed of sinking and cost are matters of comparatively small importance.

"The cylinders are for the purpose of wells, in which weights will be worked to act as counterpoises to the traveling carriages and landing-stage. Sufficient engine-power has been provided to overcome the inertia in moving these platforms, and also any additional weight of traffic which they may carry. As the slope on which they travel is 1 in 10, one tenth of the weight in the wells will balance that of the platforms and landing-stage."

It seems well nigh incredible that such primitive methods of propulsion should be used in the greatest capital of the world, and there is no obvious reason why the double-ended American ferry-boat system should not have been used to advantage in dredged ferry-slips, instead of the comparatively complicated stages and platforms here described.

Moving the Brighton-Beach Hotel.—During the winter of 1887-'88 the ocean made such encroachments along the beach of Coney Island that the foundations of the Brighton-Beach Hotel were undermined and the entire basement story was washed away. The most approved devices were tried in vain to prevent the inroads of the sea, and the hotel proprietors finally decided to move the building back

six hundred feet to a place of safety, a work of no small magnitude, since the building, a wooden structure, was 465 feet long, 150 feet deep, and three stories high. The estimated weight was 5,000 tons. The contract was awarded to B. C. Miller & Son, of Brooklyn, who agreed to do the work for $12,000.

The first operation was to lay twenty-four parallel tracks underneath the building and extending landward about three hundred feet. A mile and a half of rails and 10,000 ties were used, the ties resting upon planks. The building was then jacked up, and 112 ordinary platform cars, hired for the purpose, were rolled under the building, having transverse timbers laid across them for the sills to rest upon. A twenty-foot section of the hotel was raised enough to admit the passage of the cars with an inch or two to spare, and when the car was in place the section was lowered, care being taken to adjust the bearing so as to secure as even a distribution of weight as possible. The cars were jacked apart before the weight was allowed to settle upon them. Heavy tackle-blocks and falls were next attached to the twenty-four lines of cars upon which the bridge finally rested, and the running parts were attached, as shown in the illustration, to locomotives, some of the falls crossing one another, so that each gang of locomotives had its pulling-strain distributed over more than half of the building.

On April 3 the ropes were tightened for the first time, and the building was moved a short distance without difficulty. The next day, with four locomotives, it was moved to the end of the rails. The track already passed over was then taken up and moved in front of the locomotives and the rest of the journey completed without the least difficulty. Probably it is the most considerable feat of house-moving ever undertaken.

Harbor Improvement.—Commercially speaking, one of the most important works recently undertaken by the United States Government is the deepening of the channel in New York harbor. In view of the greater length and deeper draft of ocean steamers, it has become necessary to deepen the channels, and at the same time to straighten them, because quick turns are impossible for very long ships. Large steamers are obliged to fix their hours of sailing so as to reach the bar at high tide, and inward bound vessels are frequently obliged to anchor outside and wait for high water. In 1884 an appropriation of $200,000 was made by Congress for the improvement of Gedney's channel, and Col. G. L. Gillespie, of the United States Corps of Engineers, was directed to make a survey with a view to determining the best course of procedure. The result of careful soundings showed that no shoaling whatever had taken place since the first accurate coast survey of 1835, a channel twenty-three feet deep having been maintained by the natural scour of the tides. It was held, therefore, that

Fig. 5.—Moving Brighton-Beach Hotel.

the natural forces were adequate only to maintaining this depth, and that a greater depth could be secured only by contracting the tidal prism. To effect this, it was recommended that a dike be built from near Coney Island in a southwesterly direction toward Sandy Hook. Such a dike would close two of the least used channels, but would increase the natural scour of the Main and Swash channels and would presumably deepen them to thirty feet at mean low water.

The appropriation, however, was specifically for the deepening of Gedney's channel,

wheels near the deck. The scoop is lowered to the bottom, where it runs on wheels. The steel connecting pipe contains a ball-and-socket joint, and includes also a short length of heavy India-rubber pipe re-enforced with steel bands, in order to prevent breakage when the vessel is rolling or pitching in a seaway. By means of a steam jet connected with the top of the centrifugal pump, a vacuum is produced within the pump and pipe, under the effects of which vacuum water rises through the pipes until the pump-chamber is completely filled. Then, on starting the pump and opening the outlet

FIG. 6.—BOAT AT WORK DEEPENING CHANNEL IN NEW YORK HARBOR, WITH DRAWINGS OF DREDGES.

and hydraulic excavators were employed, which worked by means of centrifugal pumps and deepened the channel two feet over a width of 1,000 feet. In 1886 a further appropriation of $750,000 was granted for the general improvement of the harbor, and as this was insufficient for the proposed dike it was decided to continue dredging operations.

The contract was awarded to the Joseph Edwards Dredging Company. The vessels employed under this system are propellers, fitted with centrifugal pumps and dredging scoops. Each vessel is divided by bulkheads into tanks for the reception of the dredged material. In the bottom of the tanks are valves operated by

valve hitherto closed, it at once begins to draw up material. At the upper surface of the scoop, a foot above the bottom of the channel, a water-valve is arranged, which may be opened or closed by means of a small rope or lanyard. This is done from the deck of the propeller, and regulates the proportions of water and solid material. The operative can tell by the sound of the pump whether it is receiving too much or too little solid material, and sets the valve accordingly. When at work, the boat steams ahead at a rate not to exceed two miles an hour, dragging the scoops slowly over the bottom. The pumps are driven as fast as possible, as it is found that their efficiency is cu-

mulative in proportion to the speed, that is,
ten strokes in a given time will do more than
twice as much work as five strokes in the same
time. The boats are very wide, so that the
rolling is slight, and the suction pipes are attached amidships, so that they are but little
affected by the pitching.

At the close of the season a nearly uniform
depth of 26 feet had been secured in a channel
about 600 feet wide. Three dredgers similar
to the one described were kept constantly at
work, their total daily capacity being 6,500
cubic yards of solid matter. All the material
is taken out to sea and dumped in not less than
14 fathoms of water.

Thus far observations have shown that instead of shoaling during the winter, the dredged
out channels are slightly deepened by the
storms of winter, and there is some reason for
hoping that the dike may not, after all, prove
to be necessary.

Lumber-Raft.—The launching of a great lumber-raft, and its dispersion while *en route* to
New York, in 1887, were recorded in the "Annual Cyclopædia" for that year (page 257). The
projectors of the enterprise were not discouraged by failure, but began preparations for a
repetition of the experiment on a still larger
scale. The port of Joggins, on the Bay of Fundy, was as before selected for the building and
launching, and the experience gained in former
attempts was utilized to the best advantage.
The construction was begun in March, and
finished about the 1st of July in anticipation
of the high spring tides of that month. The
logs were laid together in a great cradle constructed for the purpose. A massive chain-
cable ran longitudinally through the center.
Its links were 11 inches long and 7 inches wide
and 1¼ inch thick. At distances of 10 feet
radial chains diverged from this central cable
and were clamped to cross-pieces on the outside of the raft. At intervals between the
cross-chains, the raft was bound by girths of
wire rope. It is evident that when towed by
means of a line attached to the central cable
the tendency of the stress must be to bind
the whole together in a solid mass.

The raft was cylindrical, with the ends ta-
pered. It was 595 feet long and 150 feet in
girth at the midship section. It contained
22,000 logs averaging 40 feet in length, and
the total weight was estimated at 10,000 to
15,000 tons. The expected high tide came on
July 25, submerging the seaward end of the
raft as it lay upon the ways.

The raft slid into the water as soon as the
blocks were knocked away. When the enormous weight and dimensions of the mass are
taken into the account, it is highly creditable
to the designer, Hugh R. Robertson, an old
lumberman, that the launch was effected with
such perfect success. The "Great Eastern,"
it will be remembered, was only launched after three months of hard work and after the
resources of English engineers had been well

VOL. XXVIII.—20 A

FIG. 7.—THE GREAT TIMBER-RAFT.

nigh exhausted. She exceeded the raft in length by less than 100 feet.

Two powerful sea-going tugs, the "Underwriter" and the "Ocean King," undertook the work of towing the raft to New York, which was effected, without accident or material delay, in 11 days, a distance of 700 miles. Heavy

Erie Basin where, after being visited by thousands, it was broken up and the logs disposed of at an alleged profit of $10,000 to $12,000. It is understood that the success of the scheme has been the death-blow to further enterprises of the same kind, for the general lumber-shipping interests would be so seriously injured, and the danger to navigation is so great in case the raft breaks up at sea, that the Dominion authorities will not permit similar undertakings in the future.

Hoisting-Shears.—With the increased size and weight of machinery and naval equipment, it has become necessary largely to improve the appliances for handling them. On one of the moles of the National Dock at Marseilles, France, a powerful set of shears was erected early in the year, under contract for the Marseilles Chamber of Commerce, by the Compagnie de Fives-Lille. The conditions called for variable powers of 25, 75, and 120 tons, to be obtained at will, with a proportional output of water for hydraulic pressure, and the load had to be lifted 22 feet above the quay and carried horizontally from 28 feet beyond the edge to 16 feet in the rear, so that the load might be taken from a ship and deposited upon a truck, and *vice versa*. It is believed that direct hydraulic action for very heavy weights is now achieved for the first time. In the large apparatus constructed by Sir William Armstrong, the lifting power only was employed, the shifting process being effected through independent mechanism.

FIG. 8.—120-TON SHEARS, AT THE FORT OF MARSEILLES.

seas were encountered off Cape Cod, and the plank sheathing on the bow was carried away. The raft was anchored for a few hours in Vineyard Haven, while the tugs procured supplies. The inside course was followed through Long Island Sound. Five tugs were necessary to bring the raft through the tortuous channels of Hell Gate and the East river and into the

Technically, the apparatus is of the type known as the oscillating tripod. It consists of two lateral iron-plate uprights, (Fig. 8), resting upon the wharf wall, and of a beam, jointed to them above and connected below with the head of the piston of a hydraulic press. This latter rests upon an iron-plate frame, bolted to masonry. The piston pulls the beam toward it when it descends, and carries along in the same motion the shears, as well as the load suspended from their point of junction, and the load is thus carried to a distance of 16 feet from the edge of the wharf in order to be placed upon a car. Conversely, if the piston rises, it pushes before it the entire framework, as well as the lifting apparatus, so that the latter can be lowered on a line 28 feet beyond the face of the wharf.

The lifting apparatus consists likewise of a hydraulic press suspended from the summit of the tripod; but, in order to prevent the joints of the cylinder from working under the action of the load, which would tend to open them and cause leakages, it is not suspended from the exact axis of the junction of the shears. The cylinder rests directly upon a huge stirrup 45 feet in length, the arms alone of which are affixed to the axis, through a Cardan joint. Under such circumstances, the stress of the load carried by the piston-rod is exerted solely upon the branches of the stirrup, and the sides of the cylinder work only under the pressure of the motive water. The latter is introduced

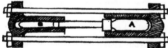

FIG. 9.—AUTOMATIC MULTIPLIER (WITH SHEARS).

at the base of the press, through a valve operated at will by a man who stands upon a platform arranged for the purpose.

In order to produce the three powers of 25, 75, and 120 tons called for by the specifications, and at the same time expend in each case a corresponding quantity of water under pressure, it is of course necessary to cause the pressure of the motive water to vary in proportion. This result is reached by calculating the diameter of the two cylinders so as to obtain the mean power of 75 tons, in making the water of the general conduit act directly under

the normal pressure of 50 atmospheres. For the powers of 25 and 120 tons, use is made of an automatic multiplier, which consists of two cylinders arranged end to end, in which move pistons A and B (Fig. 9) of different diameters. When it is a question of lifting 120 tons, the water at 50 atmospheres actuates the piston A, and B forces water into the lifting cylinder under a largely increased pressure. If the load to be lifted is but 25 tons, the water at 50 atmospheres actuates the piston B, and A forces the water into the same cylinder at a much lower pressure. The same operations are effected in the other cylinder when the extreme loads of 25 and 120 tons are moved. The shears are likewise provided with a hydraulic cylinder (Fig. 8), placed on the back of the beam, and serving through a cable, to bring the piston of the large cylinder to the end of its upward stroke, and for certain accessory work. Finally, the apparatus as a whole is completed by an accumulator containing in reserve a large part of the water necessary for each operation.

Steamships.—A noteworthy step in the development of steam navigation is found in the sister-ships, the "City of New York" and the "City of Paris." The first of these was in active service during the summer, and the last was nearly ready for her trial trip at the end of the year. Not only are these vessels larger than any other of the Atlantic liners, but the twin-screw principle receives in them its first trial on a large scale for the merchant service.

The builders are Messrs. James and George Thompson, of Clydebank, near Glasgow, who have turned out many of the finest vessels afloat. The particulars of the design were left to them, the only conditions specified by the Inman Company being that the vessels were to be unsinkable, as comfortable as any hotel, and as swift as possible consistently with the conditions first named. The following table shows at once the dimensions of these latest additions to the fleet, and the development of first-class passenger steamers since the earliest days of regular transatlantic steam navigation:

TABLE GIVING CHIEF DIMENSIONS OF NOTABLE ATLANTIC LINERS.

STEAMERS.	Built.	Tons.	Length.	Beam.	Depth.	Proportion of beam to length.	Proportion of depth to length.
			ft. in.	ft. in.	ft. in.		
*Great Western	1835	1,340	212 4	35·4	23·2	5.99	9·15
*Great Britain	1841-'43	3,500	274·2	48·2	31 5	5·68	8·70
†City of Glasgow	1850	1,600	227	32	24	7·09	9·45
†Britannic	1874	5,004	455	46	34	9 89	13 88
†City of Berlin	1875	5,491	488	44	36½	11·90	13·46
†Gallia	1879	4,509	430	44	36	9·77	11·94
†Arizona	1879	5,147	450	45 2	37½	9·96	12·40
‡Servia	1881	7,392	515	52	40½	9·90	12·62
‡Alaska	1881	6,932	500	50	39 7	10·0	12·63
†City of Rome	1881	8,141	546	52	54 ½	10·5	9·29
‡Aurania	1882	7,269	470	57	39	8 24	12·05
‡Oregon	1883	7,375	500	54	37 ½	9·25	12·57
‡America	1884	6,500	482	51	37½	8·47	11·52
‡Umbria and Etruria	1884	7,718	501·6	57·2	38·2	8·75	13·13
‡Saile	1885	5,381	455	48	36 3	9·47	12·55
‡Laha	1887	5,661	465	49	36½	9·48	12·68
‡City of New York and City of Paris	1888	10,500	560	63	43	8·89	13·02

NOTE.—Those marked * were built of wood, † of iron, and ‡ of steel.

Throughout, the vessels were constructed under the surveillance of Lloyd's agents, and according to the best-approved plans of modern marine architecture. When nearly ready for launching, 7,000 tons of material had gone to the construction of each ship; the heaviest steel castings for the hulls being the stern-posts (26 tons each), and the heaviest for the engines (50 tons). The steel was all subjected to an anti-corrosive process.

The hull of each vessel is divided by permanent transverse bulkheads into fifteen watertight compartments, including three for boilers and two for machinery, the latter being separated by a longitudinal bulkhead. The doors in the bulkheads are on the upper deck far above the load-water-line, it being determined not to trust to the doors being promptly shut in case of danger. None of the compartments exceeds 35 feet long, and the quantity of water they hold to load-water-line is 1,250 tons, or to upper deck, 2,250 tons. Even were two or three filled, the flotation of the vessel would not be placed in danger, and her buoyancy could easily be trimmed. As an additional precaution, the vessel has two bottoms, the space between them being four feet. They serve a double purpose, for not only will the existence of an inner bottom make it certain that no part of the ship will be flooded by a fracture of the external bottom, but the space can be utilized for carrying water-ballast, to the extent of 1,600 tons, for adding to the stability or altering the trim of the ship. The stability of the vessels is further secured by "rolling chambers," similar to those that have been successfully tried on several modern war-vessels. The chambers in this case are 35 feet long, and extend athwart ship. When partially filled with water, the greatest weight is naturally at the lowermost side, and tends to keep that side down when the ship rolls in the opposite direction. It can not, however, keep it down altogether, and a considerable portion of the water finds its way across the chamber before the return roll takes place. Thus there is a constant tendency of the water toward the side that is about to roll upward, and the weight being shifted just at the critical moment, the equilibrium of the ship is partially preserved, and the uncomfortable rolling motion is largely diminished.

One feature, which adds greatly to the luxuriousness of the appointments, is the arrangement of the main saloon, which, instead of being of the proportions ordinarily dictated by the space between decks, is carried up through three of the five decks, having an arched roof 22 feet high, 53 feet long, and 25 feet wide.

The steering-apparatus has been designed specially with a view to the use of the vessels as armed cruisers in case of war. The plan of the rudder with one of the twin screws is given in Fig. 10. The rudders have a superficial area of 250 square feet, larger than has been adopted for the largest war-vessels, and

the power of the hydraulic steering machinery will be appreciated when it is known that the rudder can be crowded hard over when the ship is going full speed ahead. Of course, this implies a tremendous strain upon all the parts.

FIG. 10.—TWIN SCREW ON STEAMER.

The steering is effected by a small tiller, that being regarded as more certain of adjustment than the ordinary wheel. The illustration (Fig. 10) sufficiently shows the position of one of the twin screws, its mate, of course, being in position on the other side of the stern-post. The machinery in each vessel consists of two sets of engines of the three-crank, triple-expansion type. Each set of engines is capable of driving the vessel at a good rate of speed should the other engines break down.

The full complement of passengers and crew is in round numbers 2,000 souls, and the total amount of deck area is about 150,000 square feet. Duplicate electric-light systems are carried to all parts of the ship.

In actual performance the "City of New York" is said to have fully equaled the expectations of her builders, though she has not yet "broken the record" in running time. She encountered several very severe storms, however, and behaved admirably.

A Large Gas-Holder.—A conspicuous object to passengers on the East river, N. Y., is the large tank recently constructed for the Consolidated Gas Company of New York during the summer of 1888. The engineering difficulties were considerable, since the available land was "made ground" composed of city dumpings, and below this was quicksand. The usual subterranean brick tank was dispensed with, as being too expensive, and an iron tank was substituted, resting on the surface of the ground. To prepare for this, a circle of heavy piles was driven, corresponding with the diameter of the tank, and the inclosed space was filled with concrete to a thickness of two feet. On this the bottom plates of the tank were laid. The tank is of wrought-iron. The plates at the lowest course are $\frac{7}{8}$ inch thick, and are laid double, so as to give $1\frac{3}{4}$ inch thickness of metal. The plates are arranged to break joints. Where two plates abut, a strap of iron with six rows of rivets is carried over the joint. For each of these butt joints there is one strap, either inside or outside the tank, according to the locality of the joint. As the sides rise they diminish in thickness. The tank is 192 feet in diameter and 42 feet 9 inches deep. A box girder is carried round the top of the tank, and upon this rest the 24 standards that serve as guides for the holders. These are made of channel bars, and are tied together with lattice girders in several courses. The holder is in three sections, each about 41 feet high, and the general construction is similar to that ordinarily followed in similar work. The frame-work rises about 150 feet above the street-level, and the capacity of the holder is 3,250,000 cubic feet. The inlet and outlet pipes are 30 inches in diameter.

The Transcaspian Railway. — To American engineers the length of time consumed in constructing this line of railway seems excessive in view of recent achievements on the Western Continent, but the East moves more slowly than the West, and very probably the obstacles to more rapid construction were insurmountable. At all events, it has taken about seven and a half years to complete the 900 miles destined primarily to facilitate Russian military communication with the Central Asian provinces, and, secondarily, to open up those regions to commerce. The construction has been almost wholly under the supervision of General

laid in three years, some of the secrets of rapid track-laying having been learned in the mean time. When the line is in complete working order, the estimated schedule time is ten days from St. Petersburg to Samarcand. Through passengers to Central Asia will travel by rail as far as the foot of the Caucasus mountains, thence cross the range by carriage road, over 150 miles, thence by rail to Baku on the western shore of the Caspian Sea. Ouzoun Ada, the western terminus of the Transcaspian Railway, is reached by steamer, and thence the line runs direct to Samarcand. The engineering difficulties were comparatively trifling. Three rivers had to be bridged, namely, the Tejend, the Murghab, and the Oxus or Amoo Darya. The bridge across the last named stream is of considerable size. Some difficulty was experienced with the shifting sands of the desert, but a preventive and restrictive agent was found in the shrub "saxaul," which flourishes with nothing better than sand to grow upon, and eventually forms an effectual barrier. Certain parts of the route, it was found, were liable to sudden floods, but a system of conduits was constructed, which proved effectual. For the rest, the way was for the most part a dead level, and called for none of the ingenuity wherein engineers delight.

The line has been constructed at a very low cost, owing to the cheapness of native labor— about $14,000 a mile. General Annenkoff had a special two-storied living-car constructed, containing all the equipment necessary to comfort-

FIG. 11.—THE EIFFEL TOWER.

Annenkoff. The line passes through some of the most inhospitable desert regions of the earth. The progress of the work was comparatively slow at first, and the major part of the line eastward from Kizil Arvat has been

able existence, and in this he and his staff kept constantly near the track-layers. It is not probable that the line will prove attractive to tourists, since the scenery is monotonous in the extreme, and the romance of Eastern travel largely disappears when the railroad takes the place of the caravan; but as a stimulant to native industries it must in the course of time prove highly effective. The line was formally opened on the anniversary of the Czar's coronation, May 27, 1888.

The Eiffel Tower.—This superb work was so nearly complete at the end of the year that its construction may be regarded as an accomplished fact. As a feature of the great Paris Exposition of 1889, it is certain to attract a large share of attention. The illustration is from a perspective drawing made by M. Hanin, of Paris, with a view to representing the tower exactly as it will look when finished. Photographs will of course distort the proportions even under the most favorable conditions. On December 31 the structure was about 800 feet high. The total height is to be 984 feet. It is intended merely as an ornamental observatory, though some important scientific observations may be made from its summit. The progress during the latter part of the work averaged 36 feet a week. In comparison with the Eiffel Tower, the heights of other lofty structures are of interest. Washington Monument, 555 feet; Cologne Cathedral, 512 feet; Strasburg Cathedral, 466 feet; St. Stephens, Vienna, 443 feet; St. Peter's, 433 feet; St. Paul's, 404 feet.

The Garabit Viaduct.—Among engineers M. Eiffel's reputation will gain more from the viaduct near Garabit, France, than from the Paris tower. The central arch of the viaduct is 540 feet span, and rests upon two large piers, the metallic part of which is 195 feet high. The total weight of the arch is 2,608,540 pounds. Cables were, of course, used to support the two parts of the arch. M. Eiffel found by experiment that an increase of half an inch in the length of the cables increased the tension 2,200 pounds. By introducing a half-inch wedge under the end of one of the cables, the neighboring cables were decreased in tension 2,200 pounds, distributed over the other cables as a whole. These latter, therefore, were contracted to an extent corresponding to such diminution of tension, and they consequently raised the arch. The totalization of the slight liftings due to the repetition of this manœuvre on each of the cables finally effected a general lifting of four inches. When it was desired to lower the arch, the operation was just the contrary, that is to say, the wedges were removed in succession.

After the two halves of the arch had been brought so close together that there was room only for the insertion of the center-piece, the process of keying was begun. As the two halves had, during the mounting, been held a little above their final position, there was a few inches more space between them than was necessary for the insertion of the key, and it was only necessary to remove progressively a few wedges to bring the parts into contact. This operation was effected with such pre-

cision that the key of the extrados was driven home with a few blows of the hammer, a wonderful instance of accurate calculation, considering the enormous size of the parts.

In April, before the viaduct was opened for travel, two tests were made, one with a sta-

FIG. 12.—HANDHOLE DISTRIBUTION, BROADWAY, NEAR EXCHANGE PLACE.
Showing trench, manhole, handholes, distributing duct, and service-pipe.

tionary load of 405 tons, and the same load moving. The deflection in the first instance was 0·27 inch, and in the second 0·46 inch.

Subways for Electric Wires.—The multiplication of overhead electric wires in the streets is so

FIG. 13.—MANHOLE. METHOD OF HANDLING CABLES.

objectionable that measures have been taken in most of the world's great cities to place

them underground. According to the report of Dr. Schuyler S. Wheeler, of the New York Board of Electrical Control, New York has 4,453 miles of underground wires; Paris, 4,100; Brooklyn, 2,100; Chicago, 200; Boston, 400; and Pittsburg, 1,000. These figures probably considerably understate the mileage in operation at the end of 1888, but they are the latest available for the foreign cities. New York city has been to a more serious extent the victim of overhead wires than any other large city, and all sorts of devices, legal and otherwise, were resorted to in order that no change should be made. After long delays, laws were passed sufficiently stringent to compel the laying of subways, and the capacity of subway construction now finished is given by the report as about 34,665 miles.

About 600 patents and plans relating to underground systems for wires were examined before a final decision was reached. It appeared that no system as yet devised could be regarded as wholly satisfactory, the nature of electricity being such that where wires are bunched or even near one another they suffer mutually from what is known to electricians as "induction," the result being a loss of efficiency.

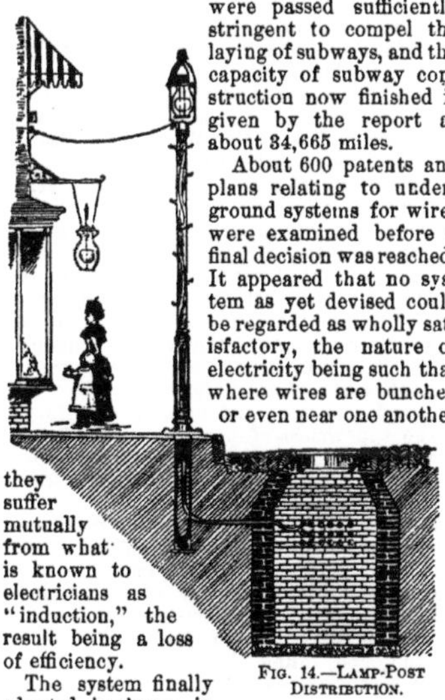

FIG. 14.—LAMP-POST DISTRIBUTION.

The system finally adopted is shown in the illustrations. Fig. 12 shows a conduit with its pipes partially covered in. On top of the main conduit is shown a section of the Edison incandescent illuminating system. Fig. 13 shows the interior of a manhole, and Fig. 14 the lamp-post adopted by the board with the store and house connections. The pipes are of iron four inches in diameter and in lengths of twenty feet. They are laid in hydraulic concrete to secure insulation, and the wires separately insulated are passed through them by means of a jointed rod, such as is used by chimney-sweepers, and may be taken out for examination or repair.

Railway Tunnels in Russia.—It is worthy of remark that, notwithstanding the very great extent of the Russian Empire, but few tunnels have had to be excavated for its railroads. Till recently tunnels have been used only in the Polish provinces and the Ural; now the tunnels of the Caucasus may be added to the list. The Novorossisk branch of the Caucasus Railroad passes through two tunnels, the longer of which is 1,338 metres, and the shorter 365 metres in length. The Souram Tunnel of the Baku-Batoum Railway, which was opened on the 31st of October, is the largest tunnel in Russia, being 4·4 kilometres, or a mile and three quarters long. By its means the steep grades of the Souram Pass are avoided, and the petroleum trains, which formerly had to be divided at this point, are now able to pass to the Black Sea unbroken.

EPIDEMICS. At certain periods in the history of mankind certain diseases have attained such force as to affect large areas of territory and kill great numbers of men; and have then been known as epidemics. It is the design of this article to sketch the general history of the greatest of these epidemics.

The Black-Death.—One of the most memorable of the epidemics of the middle ages was a great pestilence in the fourteenth century, which devastated Asia, Europe, and Africa. It was an Oriental plague, marked by inflammatory boils and tumors of the glands, such as break out in no other febrile disease. On account of these boils and from the black spots (indicative of putrid decomposition) which appeared upon the skin, it has been generally called the black-death. The symptoms were many, though not all were found in every case. Tumors and abscesses were found on the arms and thighs of those affected, and smaller boils on all parts of the body; black spots broke out on all parts of the skin, either single, united, or confluent. Symptoms of cephalic affection were frequent; many patients became stupefied, and fell into a deep sleep, losing also their speech from palsy of the tongue; others remained sleepless, without rest. The fauces and tongue were black, and as if suffused with blood. No beverage would assuage the burning thirst. Contagion was evident, for attendants caught the disease from their relatives and friends. But still deeper sufferings were connected with this pestilence: the organs of respiration were seized with a putrid inflammation, blood was expectorated, and the breath diffused a pestiferous odor. The plague spread with the greater fury, as it communicated from the sick to the healthy; contact with the clothes or other articles which had been used by the infected induced the disease, and even the breath of the sick, who expectorated blood, caused a contagion far and near. As it advanced, not only men, but animals also fell sick and expired.

In England the plague first broke out in the county of Dorset, whence it advanced through the counties of Devon and Somerset to Bristol, and thence reached Gloucester, Oxford, and London. Probably few places escaped, perhaps not any, for the annals of contemporaries report that throughout the land only a tenth part of the inhabitants remained alive. From

England the contagion was carried by a ship to Norway, where the plague broke out in its most frightful form, with vomiting of blood, and in the whole country spared not one third. The sailors found no refuge on their ships, and vessels were often seen drifting on shore, whose crews had perished to the last man.

It is hard to measure the mortality of the black-death; some numerical statements are not, indeed wanting, but they are scarcely credible when we consider the civilization or lack of civilization of the fourteenth century. Rudeness was general. Witches and heretics were burned alive; wild passions, severity, and cruelty everywhere predominated. Human life was but little regarded. Cairo lost daily, when the plague was raging with its greatest violence, from 10,000 to 15,000. In China more than thirteen millions are said to have died. India was almost wholly depopulated. Tartary and the Tartar kingdom of Kaptschak, Mesopotamia, Syria, Armenia, were covered with dead bodies. Cyprus lost almost all its inhabitants, and ships without crews were seen driving about the Mediterranean, spreading the plague where they went ashore. It was reported to Pope Clement, at Avignon, that throughout the East (probably excepting China) 23,840,000 people had fallen victims to the plague. In Venice 100,000 died, and in London at least the same number, while 124,434 Franciscan friars died in Germany. In Avignon the Pope found it necessary to consecrate the Rhone, that bodies might be thrown into the river without delay. In Vienna, where for some time twelve hundred inhabitants died daily, the interment of corpses in the church-yards and within the churches was prohibited, and the dead were arranged in layers by thousands in large pits outside the city, as had been already done at Cairo and Paris and London. The palace and the cot alike felt the fury of the plague. One king, two queens (Alonso XI; Johanna, Queen of Navarre, daughter of Louis X; and Johanna of Burgundy, wife of King Philip de Valois), one bishop, and great numbers of other distinguished persons fell victims to it. The whole period of time during which the black plague raged with destructive violence in Europe was (with the exception of Russia, where it did not break out until 1351) from 1347 to 1350; from this latter date to 1383 there were various pestilences, bad enough indeed, but not so violent as the black-death.

Ireland was much less heavily visited than England, and the disease seems scarcely to have reached the mountainous regions of that land; and Scotland, too, would perhaps have remained free from it, had not the Scotch availed themselves of the discomfiture of the English to make an irruption into England, which terminated in the destruction of their army by the plague and the sword, and the extension of the pestilence through those who escaped over the whole country.

In Sweden two princes died (Haken and Knut, half-brothers of King Magnus), and in Westgothland alone 466 priests. The inhabitants of Iceland and Greenland found in the coldness of their inhospitable climes no protection against this enemy which invaded them. In Denmark and Norway the people were so occupied with their own misery that the accustomed voyages to Greenland ceased, and at the same time great icebergs formed on the coast of East Greenland, and no mortal from that time, even to the present day, has seen that shore or the former dwellers thereon.

It may be assumed that Europe lost by the black-death twenty-five million people, or about one fourth of her inhabitants. That her nations could overcome, as quickly as they did, this terrible loss, without retrograding more than they did, is a most convincing proof of the indestructibility of human society as a whole.

The Dancing Mania.—The effects of the black-death had not yet subsided, and the graves of millions of its victims were scarcely green, when a strange delusion arose. It was a convulsion that in the most extraordinary manner infuriated the human frame and excited the astonishment of contemporaries for more than two centuries. It was called in some portions of Europe the Dance of St. John, or of St. Vitus, on account of the strange leaps by which it was characterized and which gave to those affected, while performing their wild dance and screaming and foaming with fury, all the appearance of persons possessed. It did not remain confined to particular localities, but was propagated by the sight of the sufferers over the whole of Europe.

As early as 1374 assemblages of men and women were seen at Aix-la-Chapelle who had come out from Germany, and, united by one common delusion, exhibited to the public, both in the streets and in the churches, a strange spectacle. They formed circles, hand in hand, and, losing all control over their senses, continued, regardless of the by-standers, dancing for hours together in wild delirium, until at length they fell to the ground in a state of exhaustion. Then they complained of extreme oppression, and groaned as if in the agonies of death, until cloths were bound tightly around their waists, when they recovered and remained free from complaint until the next attack. This practice of swathing was resorted to on account of the tympany that followed these spasmodic ravings; but the by-standers frequently relieved patients in a less artificial manner by thumping and trampling upon the parts affected. While dancing, they neither saw nor heard, being insensible to external impressions through the senses, but were haunted by visions, their fancies conjuring up spirits, whose names they shrieked out, and some of them afterward asserted they felt as if they had been immersed in a stream of blood, which obliged them to leap so high. Others during the paroxysm saw the heavens open and the saints and Virgin Mary, according as the religious notions of the age were strangely and variously reflected in their imaginations. When the disease was completely developed, the attack began with epileptic convulsions. Those affected fell senseless, panting and laboring for breath. They foamed at the mouth, and, suddenly springing up, began their dance with strange contortions.

It was but a few months ere this disease had spread from Aix-la-Chapelle, where it appeared in July, over the neighboring Netherlands. In Liege, Utrecht, Tongres, and many other towns the dancers appeard with garlands in their hair and their waists girt with cloth bandages, that they might, as soon as the paroxysm was over, receive immediate relief from the attack of tympany. This bandage, by the insertion of a stick, easily twisted tight. Many, however, obtained more relief from kicks and blows, which they found numbers of persons ready to administer, for wherever the dancers appeared the people assembled in crowds to gratify their curiosity with the frightful spectacle. Peasants left their plows, mechanics their workshops, housewives their domestic duties, to join in the wild revels. Girls and boys quitted their parents, and servants their masters, to amuse themselves at the dances of those possessed, and greedily imbibed the poison of mental aberration.

The priests and the authorities took an interest in the afflicted, who were numbered by thousands. They divided them into separate parties, to each of which they appointed responsible superintendents to protect them, and so sent them on pilgrimages to chapels and shrines, principally to those of St. Vitus, near Zabern and Rotestrué, where priests were in attendance to work upon the misguided minds, and where it is probable that many were, through the influence of devotion, cured of this lamentable affliction. Yet in most cases music afforded the sufferers relief. At the sound of the flute or zithern they awoke from their lethargy, opened their eyes, and moving slowly at first, according to the measure of the music, were, as the time quickened, gradually hurried on to a most passionate dance. Throughout the summer season cities and villages resounded with the notes of musical instruments, and patients were everywhere met with who looked upon dancing as their only remedy.

There were more ancient dancing plagues. In the year 1237 upward of a hundred children were said to have been seized suddenly at Erfurt, and to have proceeded dancing and jumping along the road to Arnstadt. When they arrived at that place they fell exhausted to the ground, and, according to an old chronicle, many of them, after they were taken home to their parents, died, and the rest remained affected to the end of their lives with a permanent tremor. Another occurrence is related to have taken place at the Mosel bridge at Utrecht in 1278, when two hundred fanatics began to dance, and would not desist when a priest passed by carrying the host to a person who was sick, upon which, as if in punishment, the bridge gave way and they were all drowned. A similar event is also said to have occurred as early as the year 1027. Eighteen peasants are said to have disturbed divine service on Christmas eve, by dancing and brawling in the churchyard, whereupon the priest inflicted a curse upon them that they should dance and scream a whole year without ceasing.

The Sweating-Sickness.—After the fate of England had been decided by the Battle of Bosworth, on Aug. 22, 1485, the joy of the nation was clouded by a strange disease, which, following in the rear of Henry's victorious army, spread in a few weeks from the distant mountains of Wales to the metropolis of the empire. It was a violent inflammatory fever, which, after a short rigor, prostrated the powers as by a blow, and amid painful oppression of the stomach, headache, and lethargic stupor, suffused the whole body with a fetid perspiration. All this took place in a few hours, and the crisis was always over within the space of a day and a night. The internal heat that the patient suffered was intolerable, yet every refrigerant was certain death. At first the new foe was scarcely heeded; citizens and peasants went in joyful procession to meet the victorious army, for the nation, after its many years of civil war, looked forward to happier days of peace. Very shortly, however, after the King's entry into the capital on the 28th of August, the sweating-sickness, as the disease was called, began its ravages among the dense population of the city. Two lord mayors and six aldermen died within one week; many who had been in perfect health at night were on the following morning numbered with the dead. The disease for the most part marked for its victims robust and vigorous men, and, as many noble families lost their chiefs, extensive commercial houses their principals, and wards their guardians, the festivities were soon changed into mourning and grief. By the end of the year the disease had spread over the whole of England. Many persons of rank, of the ecclesiastic and civil classes, became its victims, and great was the consternation when it broke out in Oxford. Professors and students fled in all directions, but death overtook many of them, and the university was deserted for six weeks. The accounts that have been handed down are very imperfect, but we may infer from the general grief and anxiety, that the loss of life was very considerable.

In the summer of 1506 the sweating-sickness visited England for a second time. The renewed eruption of the epidemic was not on this occasion connected with any important occurrence, so that contemporaries have not even mentioned the month when it began; and in the autumn it disappeared.

A third time, in 1517, the sweating-sickness broke out, and was so violent and rapid in its course that it carried off those who were attacked in two or three hours, so that the first shivering fit was regarded as the commencement of certain death. Among the poorer classes the deaths were innumerable, and no precautions averted death from the houses of the rich. This time the sweating-sickness lasted six months, and reached its height about six weeks after its first appearance.

But a heavier affliction was in store. In May, 1528, the sweating-sickness again broke out in England, and fourteen months later brought a scene of horror upon all the nations of Northern Europe scarcely equaled during any other epidemic. It appeared at once with the same intensity it had shown before, was ushered in by no previous indications, and between health and death there lay but a brief term of five or six hours. Once or twice again this fearful epidemic visited localities in Europe, but by the autumn of 1551 it had vanished from the earth.

Yellow Fever.—The New World has contributed its quota to the epidemic diseases that afflict humanity. There is reason to believe that yellow fever existed among the native tribes of Central America and the West Indies for many years prior to the discoveries of Columbus, while it is certain that before that date it was unknown in Europe, and probably unknown in Asia and Africa. The history of general literature, and especially of medical science, from 1492 till a comparatively recent period is not only scanty but almost buried under a mass of illiteracy and quackery. It is therefore hard to find trustworthy records of the appearance of yellow fever until within the last century or century and a half. There is, however, reason to suspect that the Spaniards in San Domingo suffered from yellow fever during the first year (1493) they passed on that island; it is more certain that they did suffer in 1494, the year that is usually given as the first when white men were attacked with the disease.

The scanty and unsatisfactory records for the one hundred and forty-four years from 1493 to 1635 justify the belief that not fewer than nineteen yellow-fever epidemics occurred in Santo Domingo, Porto Rico, and the Isthmus of Darien, while it is probable that Mexico has yearly suffered from the disease since the foundation of Vera Cruz in 1519.

One of the curious and ridiculous theories at one time believed by the credulous attributed the yellow fever to the importation of slaves from Africa. The first three hundred Africans were brought to Cuba in 1521 or 1523, and during the succeeding two hundred and forty-two years about 60,000 more were imported; but after 1763 the importation increased so enormously that in 1774 Cuba had a colored population of 75,180. In 1762 Havana was besieged, captured, and held by a force of 30,000 English soldiers and sailors. During that year the disease claimed many victims, and was prob-

ably for the first time carried by invalid officers or men into Great Britain, so that it is not surprising that many historians should have erred in saying that the disease first appeared in this year; yet there are ample proofs that it was an epidemic in Havana the year previous (1761).

From 1635 the historical record of the visitations of yellow fever becomes more and more authentic, and no doubt is entertained that the first European settlers in Guadeloupe, in 1635, suffered severely. During the ensuing one hundred and twenty-eight years, from 1635 to 1762, history records 208 invasions of yellow fever in eighty-six of these years in 43 different localities. Among these there were in what are now the United States, from 1691 or 1693 (when Boston was invaded by yellow fever—its first positive appearance in this country) to 1762, not fewer than 44 epidemics in 12 different places.

It is contended by some authorities that epidemics of yellow fever are not indigenous to the United States, but due wholly to importation from foreign lands, such as the West Indies, and notably from Cuba, between which and the United States about 2,000 vessels ply annually, carrying goods amounting to more than seventy million dollars.

Thus, in Florida there has never been an epidemic of yellow fever that could not be demonstrably traced to direct importation from abroad. The epidemic of 1841, at St. Augustine, was imported from Havana; that of 1822, at Pensacola, from the same place; that of 1825, at Pensacola, from the West Indies; that of 1834, at Pensacola, was imported in war-vessels; that of 1839, at St. Augustine, was carried thither from Charleston, S. C.; that of 1839, at Pensacola, was carried from Mobile and New Orleans; that of 1841, at St. Augustine, was imported from Havana; those of 1842, 1843, 1844, 1845, 1846, and 1847, at Pensacola, were imported in war-vessels; those of 1862 and 1865, at Key West, were imported from Havana; that of 1867, at Pensacola, was imported from Jamaica; that of 1869, at Key West, was imported from Cuba; that of 1871, at Cedar Keys and Tampa, from Havana; those of 1873 and 1874, at Pensacola, from Havana, as was also the scourge that devastated the little seaport town of Fernandina in 1877, and the more recent epidemic of 1888.

The following is a statement of the principal localities in the United States where yellow fever has appeared, with their elevations above sea-level, dates of beginning and suspension of the disease, and mortality when known:

Alabama.—Blakely, 25 feet, 1822. Cahawba, 175 feet, 1821. Citronelle, 65 feet, 1853. Demopolis, 125 feet, 1853. Dog River Factory, 30 feet, 1853. Fort Claiborne, 75 feet, from July 4 to Dec. 1, 1819. Fort Morgan Island, 20 feet, Aug. 13, 1867. Fort St. Stephen, 75 feet, July 4 to Dec. 1, 1819. Hollywood, 75 feet, 1853. Mobile, 20 feet, 1705; 1765; 1766; 1819; 1821; 1822; 1824; 1825; 1827; 1828; Sept. 14, 1829, mortality 130; Sept. 10, 1837, mortality 850; 1838;

Aug. 11 to Oct. 20, 1839, mortality 650; 1841; Aug. 20, 1842, mortality 60; Aug. 18 to Nov. 5, 1843, mortality 240; 1844; 1847, mortality 76; 1848, mortality 75; 1849, mortality 50; 1851; July 13 to Nov. 1, 1853, mortality 1,151; 1854; Sept. to Nov., 1855, mortality 30; 1858; Aug. 13, 1867; Sept. 4 to Nov. 10, 1873, mortality 102. Montgomery, Sept. to Nov., 1853, mortality 35; Sept. to Nov., 1854, mortality 45; Aug. 22 to Nov. 19, 1870; Aug. 21 to Nov. 29, 1873, mortality 27. Pollard, 60 feet, 1873. Selma, 200 feet, 1824; Sept. 17 to Nov. 13, 1853, mortality 32; 1854; 1855.

Arkansas.—Spring Hill, 50 feet, 1853. Columbia, 135 feet, June, 1853. Fort Smith, 460 feet, 1823. Grand Lake, 130 feet, 1853. Little Rock, 350 feet, 1873. Napoleon, 142 feet, 1853.

Connecticut.—Chatham, 200 feet, Aug. 29, 1796. Hartford, 60 feet, 1798; 1800. Knowles Landing, 25 feet, Aug., 1796, mortality 9. Middletown, 40 feet, June, 1820. New Haven, 35 feet, 1743; 1794; 1803; 1804; 1805; 1819. New London, 25 feet, Aug. 26 to Nov., 1798, mortality 81. Norwalk, 25 feet, 1798. Stamford, 20 feet, 1745. Stonington, 20 feet, 1798.

Delaware.—Christiana, 20 feet, 1798. Duck Creek, 20 feet, 1798. Newcastle, 25 feet, 1798. Wilmington, 45 feet, 1798, mortality 250; 1802, mortality 86.

Florida.—Apalachicola, 15 feet, 1826. Cedar Keys, 15 feet, 1871. Gainesville, 160 feet, Aug., 1871. Jacksonville, 14 feet, 1857. Key West, 15 feet, 1824; 1829; June, 1841, mortality 26; Aug., 1853, mortality 112; 1854; June 20 to Oct., 1862, mortality 71; 1864; 1865; 1867; 1869. Milton, 20 feet, 1853. Pensacola, 15 feet, 1764; 1765, mortality 125; 1811; Aug. to Oct. 10, 1822, mortality 257; 1825; 1827; 1834; 1839; 1841; 1843; 1844; 1845; 1846; 1847; 1848; July 9, 1853; 1854; 1858; Aug. 25, 1863; July 24, 1867, mortality 34; Aug. 6, 1873, mortality 61; 1874. St. Augustine, 10 feet, 1807; Aug., 1821, mortality 140; 1838; Aug. 15, 1839; 1841, mortality 26. St. Joseph's, 15 feet, 1841. Suwanee, 50 feet, 1836. Tampa, 20 feet, 1839; Sept., 1853; 1871. Tortugas, 12 feet, 1862, mortality 4; July 4, 1867, mortality 38. Pensacola Bay, Aug. 14 to Nov. 19, 1873, 62.

Georgia.—Augusta, 185 feet, 1839; 1854. Bainbridge, 120 feet, 1873. Columbus, 185½, mortality, 3. St. Mary's, 15 feet, Sept. 5 to Oct., 1808, mortality 84. Savannah, 30 feet, 1807; 1808; 1819; 1820; 1827; 1852, mortality 19; 1853; Aug. 5, 1854, mortality 580; 1858.

Illinois.—Cairo, 322 feet, Sept. 1 to Sept. 25, 1873, mortality 17.

Kentucky.—Louisville, 450 feet, Sept. 22 to Oct. 15, 1873, mortality 5.

Louisiana.—Alexandria, 75 feet, 1819; 1822; 1827; 1831; 1837; 1839; 1847; 1853; 1854; Sept. 13, 1855. Algiers, 10 feet, 1847; 1853; 1858. Ascension, 25 feet, 1823. Baton Rouge, 50 feet, 1817; 1819; 1822, mortality, 60; 1827; 1829; 1837; Oct., 1843; 1847; 1853. Bay of St. Louis, 10 feet, Aug., 1820. Bayou Sara, 75 feet, 1847; 1853. Burat Settlement, 10 feet, Sept. 22, 1854. Carrollton, 15 feet, 1847; May 18, 1855. Centreville, 20 feet, Sept. 18 to Nov. 18, 1853; Sept. to Oct., 1855. Clinton, 85 feet, Sept. 1 to Dec., 1853, mortality, 75. Cloutierville, 175 feet, Aug. 14 to Dec. 14, 1853; 1854. Covington, 25 feet, 1847. Donaldsonville, 30 feet, 1828; 1830, mortality, 30. Franklin, 15 feet, Oct. 19 to Nov. 24, 1853; 1854. Gretna, 1858. Iberville, 28 feet, (dates not recorded.) Jeannerretta, 15 feet, Oct. 7, 1854. Jesuits Bend, 10 feet, Sept. 12, 1854. La Fayette, 12 feet. June 22, 1847. Lake Providence, 100 feet, 1853. Mandeville, 15 feet, 1847. McDonoughville, 1858. Natchitoches, 180 feet, 1839. New Iberia, 20 feet, 1839; 1867; 1870. New Orleans, 10 feet, 1796; 1791; 1794; 1795; 1796; 1797; 1799; 1800; 1801; 1802; 1804; 1809; 1811; 1812; June 18 to Dec., 1817, mortality 800; 1818, mortality 115; July 1, 1819, mortality 2,190; July, 1820; Sept. 1, 1822, mortality 239; Aug. 23, 1823; Aug. 4, 1824, mortality, 108; June 23, 1825, mortality, 49; May 18, 1826, mortality 5; July 19, 1827, mortality, 109; June 18, 1828, mortality 130;

May 23, 1829, mortality 215; July 15, 1830, mortality 117; June 9, 1831, mortality 2; Aug. 15, 1832, mortality 18; July 12, 1833, mortality, 210; Aug. 28, 1834, mortality 95; Aug. 23, 1835, mortality 284; Aug. 24, 1836, mortality 5; July 24, 1837, mortality 442; Aug. 25, 1838, mortality 17; July 23, 1839, mortality 452; July 25, 1840, mortality 5; July 27, 1841, mortality 594; July 30, 1842, mortality 211; July 5, 1843, mortality 487; July to Sept., 1844, mortality 148; 1845, mortality 2; Aug. to Oct., 1846, mortality 160; Aug. to Dec., 1847, mortality 2,259; June to Nov., 1848, mortality 850; Aug. to Dec., 1849, mortality 737; July to Oct., 1850, mortality 102; 1851, mortality 16; July to Dec., 1852, mortality 415; May to Dec., 1853, mortality 7,970; July to Dec., 1854, mortality 2,423; June to Dec., 1855, mortality 2,670; Aug. to Nov., 1856, mortality 74; June to Dec., 1857, mortality 199; June to Oct. 10, 1858, mortality 3,889; 1862; 1863; 1864; June 10 to Dec. 22, 1867, mortality 3,063; May 16 to Dec., 1870, mortality 587; Aug. 4 to Oct., 1871, mortality 55; Aug. 28 to Nov. 30, 1872, mortality 225; July 4 to Nov. 18, 1873, mortality 225. Opelousas, 60 feet, 1829; Oct. 20 to Nov., 1837; Aug. to Nov., 1839; 1842; 1853; 1867. Pattersonville, 20 feet, Aug. 8 to Dec., 1853, mortality 45; Sept., 1854; Sept., 1855. Plaquemine, 6 feet, 1837; 1839; 1847; Sept. to Oct., 1853; 1858. Point a la Hache, 8 feet, Oct., 1854. Port Barre, 1870; Port Hudson, 75 feet, 1839; Oct. 13, 1841; 1843. St. Francisville, 80 feet, 1811. West Feliciana Parish, 1817; 1819; 1823; 1827; Sept. 22, 1829; Aug. 28, 1839; Aug. 28, 1833; 1839; 1843; 1846; 1848; 1853. St. John Baptiste, 20 feet, 1853. St. Martinsville, 20 feet, 1839. St. Mary's Parish, 15 feet, Sept. to Oct., 1854; Shreveport, 220 feet, Sept. to Dec., 1853; Aug. 12 to Nov. 10, 1873, mortality 1,759. Thibodeaux, 15 feet, 1853, mortality 160; Sept. 12 to Oct., 1854. Trenton, 80 feet, 1853. Trinity, 175 feet, Aug. to Oct., 1865. Vidalia, 175 feet, Aug., 1853. Ville Platte, 50 feet, 1870. Washington, 65 feet, 1837; 1839; 1852; Aug. 15, 1853; 1854; 1867.

Maryland.—Baltimore, 60 feet, 1794; 1795; Aug. to Nov., 1797; 1798; 1799; 1800; 1801; 1802; 1805; July 21 to Oct. 30, 1819; 1820; 1821; 1822; 1868. West River, 15 feet (dates not recorded.)

Massachusetts.—Boston, 45 feet, 1691; 1693; 1795; 1796; 1798, mortality, 200; 1800; 1802, mortality, 60; 1805; 1819; 1858. Holliston, 75 feet, 1741, mortality, 15. Nantucket, 20 feet, 1741, mortality 259. New Bedford, 25 feet, 1800; 1801. Newburyport, 20 feet, 1796. Salem, 20 feet, 1798.

Mississippi.—Biloxi, 10 feet, 1702; 1839; 1847; 1852; 1858. Brandon, 300 feet, Sept. 15, 1853; Sept. 23 to Nov. 18, 1854. Canton, 320 feet, 1853. Clinton, 175 feet, Aug. 28 to Oct., 1853. Cooper's Wells, 275 feet, Aug. 23, 1855, mortality 13. Grand Gulf, 200 feet, 1853. Greenwood, 140 feet, 1853. Jackson, 275 feet, 1853; 1854. Natchez, 150 feet, Sept. to Nov. 9, 1817, mortality 9; Sept. to Dec., 1819, mortality 180; Aug. 10 to Oct. 18, 1823, mortality 312; Aug. 20 to Nov. 1, 1825, mortality 150; 1827; Sept. 1 to Nov. 1829, mortality 90; Sept. 8 to Nov. 25, 1837, mortality 250; Sept. to Nov. 1839, mortality 235; 1844; June to Nov. 1848; July 17, 1853; 1855; 1858. Pascagoula, 10 feet, 1847; 1853. Pass Christian, 15 feet, 1847; 1853; 1855; 1858. Petit Gulf Hills, 200 feet, 1853. Port Gibson, 200 feet, 1853. Rodney, 175 feet, 1829; Sept. 6, 1843; 1847; 1853. Shieldsborough, 10 feet, Aug. 20, 1820; Aug. 5, 1829; 1839. Vicksburg, 175 feet, 1839; Sept. to Oct., 1841; 1847; 1858; 1871. Washington, 175 feet, Aug. to Nov., 1825, mortality 52. Whitzell's Landing, 125 feet, 1817. Woodville, 100 feet, 1844; 1852; Aug. 9, 1853; Sept., 1855; 1858. Yazoo City, 140 feet, Sept. 1, 1853.

Missouri.—St. Louis, 475 feet, 1854; Aug. 14, 1855. New Design, 420 feet, 1797, mortality 57.

New Hampshire.—Portsmouth, 40 feet, Aug. to Oct. 1798, mortality 100.

New Jersey.—Bridgeton, 50 feet, 1798. Gloucester City, 20 feet, 1805. Perth Amboy, 20 feet, 1811, mortality 5. Port Elizabeth, 20 feet, Aug. 9 to Sept.; 1798. Woodbury, 1798.

New York.—Albany, 85 feet, Aug., 1746, mortality 45; 1798. Bay Ridge, 20 feet, July 13, 1856. Brooklyn, 40 feet, July to Sept., 1809, mortality 40; 1823; July 14, 1856. Catskill, 50 feet, 1743; 1794; Aug. 10 to Sept. 28, 1803, mortality 8. Governor's Island, 25 feet, July 29, 1856; Sept. to Oct. 26, 1870, mortality 49. Gowanus, 15 feet, 1856. Greenfield, 150 feet, 1798; Huntington, 20 feet, 1795; 1798. New York city, 35 feet, 1668; 1702, mortality 570; 1732; 1741; 1742; 1743, mortality 217; 1745; 1747; 1748; 1762; 1790; Aug. to Oct. 15, 1791; 1792; 1793; 1794; July 19, 1795, mortality 730; 1796; 1797; Aug. to Nov., 1798, mortality, 2,080; July to Nov., 1799, mortality 76; Sept. to Oct. 14, 1800, mortality 21; Sept. to Oct., 1801, mortality 16; 1802, mortality 2; July 18 to Oct., 1803, mortality 700; June to Oct., 1805, mortality 340; June to Nov., 1806; 1807, mortality 3; 1808, mortality 1; 1809, mortality 2; 1810, mortality 1; 1815, mortality 7; 1816; 1817, mortality 4; 1818, mortality 4; Aug., 1829, mortality 37; 1820, mortality 2; 1821, mortality 18; July 10 to Nov. 5, 1822, mortality 230; 1823, mortality 5; 1824, mortality 8; 1825, mortality 1; 1826, mortality 2; 1827, mortality 4; 1828; 1829; 1830, mortality 1; 1832, mortality 1; 1833, mortality 2, 1834, mortality 1; 1835, mortality 2; 1838, mortality 8; 1839, mortality 9; 1843, mortality 5; 1844, mortality 4; 1848; 1847; Aug. 12, 1848, mortality 12; 1852, mortality 1; 1853, mortality 14; 1854, mortality 20; 1855, mortality 5; 1872; May 23 to Oct., 30, 1873, mortality 19. Queensborough, 1801. Red Hook, 30 feet, 1856. Staten Island, 20 feet, Aug. 23, 1848; July 14 to Oct. 28, 1856, mortality 25. West Neck, 18 feet, 1795. West Point, 25 feet, 1804. Yellow Hook, 20 feet, 1856.

North Carolina.—Beaufort, 8 feet, 1854; Sept. 24 to Nov. 17, 1864, mortality 68; 1871. Smithville, 15 feet, 1862. Washington, 35 feet, 1800. Wilmington, 25 feet, 1796; 1800, Aug. 9, 1821; Aug. 6 to Nov. 27, 1862, mortality 446.

Ohio.—Cincinnati, 550 feet, 1871; 1873, Gallipolis, 520 feet, 1796.

Pennsylvania.—Bald Eagle Valley, 550 feet, 1799. Chester, 25 feet, 1798, mortality 50. Chester County, 1805. Kensington, 15 feet, 1793; Lisburn, 250 feet, Aug., 1803. Marcus Hook, 15 feet, 1798. Nitany, 550 feet, 1799. Philadelphia, 35 feet, 1695; Aug. 1, 1699, mortality 220; 1732; 1741, mortality 250; 1742; 1743; 1744; 1747; Aug. to Nov., 1762; 1791; Aug. 15 to Dec., 1793, mortality 4,041; 1794; 1796; Aug. 1 to Oct. 15, 1797, mortality, 1,300; Aug. 1 to Nov. 1, 1798, mortality 3,500; July to Nov., 1799, mortality 1,000; 1800; 1801; 1802, mortality 307; 1803, mortality 195; 1805, mortality 400; 1807, mortality 3; 1809; 1810, mortality 3; 1811, mortality 5; 1813, mortality 6; 1814, mortality 7; 1815, mortality 2; 1816, mortality 2; 1819, mortality 13; July 24, 1820, mortality 83; July 19 to Oct., 1853, mortality 128; 1854; June 29, 1870, mortality 18. Southwalk, 20 feet, 1793.

Rhode Island.—Block Island, 20 feet, June to Dec., 1801. Bristol, 20 feet, 1795; 1796; 1797. Newport, 20 feet, 1806. Providence, 35 feet, 1794; 1795, mortality 45; Aug. 13, 1797, mortality 45; 1800; July 19 to Aug., 1805. Westerly, 25 feet, 1798; 1805.

South Carolina.—Charleston, 10 feet, 1699; 1703; 1728; May to Oct., 1732, mortality 12 daily; 1734; 1739; 1745; 1748; 1753; 1755; 1761; 1762; 1768; 1770; 1792; 1794; 1795; 1796; 1797; 1798, mortality 239; 1800, mortality 184; 1802, mortality 96; 1803; 1804, mortality 148; 1805; 1807, mortality 162; 1812; July to Nov., 1817, mortality 272; Aug. to Oct., 1819, mortality 177; June to Aug., 1822, mortality 2; Aug. to Nov., 1824, mortality 235; Aug. to Sept., 1825, mortality 2; Aug. to Nov., 1827, mortality 64; Aug. to Sept., 1828, mortality 26; Sept. to Nov., 1830, mortality 30; Aug. to Oct., 1834, mortality 49; Aug. to Sept., 1835, mortality 25; Aug. to Nov., 1838, mortality 351; June to Oct., 1839, mor-

tality 134; Aug. to Oct., 1840, mortality 22; 1843; Aug. to Nov., 1849, mortality 125; Aug. to Nov., 1852, mortality 310; Aug. to Nov., 1854, mortality 627; Aug. to Nov., 1856, mortality 211; Sept. to Nov., 1857, mortality 13; July to Dec., 1858, mortality 717; 1862; 1864; July 19 to Nov., 1871, mortality 213. Beaufort, 10 feet, Aug. 6 to Nov. 21, 1871, mortality 7. Columbia, 200 feet, 1854. Fort Moultrie, 15 feet, 1852; Aug. 15, 1858. Georgetown, 10 feet, Aug. 20 to Oct. 28, 1854. Hilton Head, 10 feet, Sept. 8 to Oct. 25, 1862. Mount Pleasant, 10 feet, 1817; 1848; 1852; 1854; 1856; 1857.

Tennessee.—Memphis, 260 feet, 1853; 1855; 1866; Sept. 14 to Nov. 9, 1873, mortality 1,244.

Texas.—Alleyton, 250 feet, Sept. 4 to Dec., 1867, mortality 45. Anderson, 200 feet, 1867. Austin, 450 feet, 1867. Bastrop, 260 feet, 1867. Beaumont, 50 feet, 1863. Belleville, 180 feet, 1855. Brazoria, 20 feet, 1859. Brenham, 350 feet, Aug. 11 to Oct. 31, 1867, mortality 120. Brownsville, 25 feet, Sept. 23 to Dec. 23, 1853, mortality 50; Aug. to Nov., 1858, mortality 41; 1862. Calvert, 325 feet, Oct. 12, 1867, to Jan. 10, 1868, mortality 250; 1873. Chapel Hill, 200 feet, Aug. 6 to Dec., 1867, mortality 123. Columbus, 250 feet, 1873. Columbia, 25 feet, 1833, mortality 132. Corsicana, 425 feet, 1873. Corpus Christi, 15 feet, 1862; Aug., 1867; 1873. Cypress City, 60 feet, 1858; 1859. Danville, 160 feet, 1867. Edinburg, 100 feet, July, 1859, mortality 13. Goliad, 50 feet, July 12, 1867, mortality 23. Galveston, 5 feet, Sept. 30 to Oct. 11, 1839, mortality 250; July 5, 1844, mortality 400; Oct. 1 to Nov. 25, 1847, mortality 200; Aug. 16 to Nov. 28, 1853, mortality 536; Aug. 9 to Nov. 5, 1854, mortality 404; Aug. 27 to Nov. 14, 1858, mortality 344; Sept. 27 to Nov. 30, 1859, mortality 182; Sept. 1 to Nov. 20, 1864, mortality 259; 1866; June 26 to Nov., 1867, mortality 1,150. Harrisburg, 55 feet, 1867. Hempstead, 166 feet, 1859; Aug. 9, to Nov. 26, 1867, mortality 151. Hockley, 50 feet, 1853. Houston, 37 feet, 1839; 1844; 1847; 1848; 1853; 1854; 1858; 1859; 1864; 1870. Huntsville, 200 feet, Aug. 9 to Oct. 19, 1867, mortality 130. Independence, 250 feet, 1867. Indianola, 10 feet, Sept., 1852; 1853; 1858; 1859; 1862; June 20, 1867, mortality 80. La Grange, 450 feet, Aug. to Nov., 1857, mortality 200. Liberty, 40 feet, 1867. Liverpool, 25 feet, Aug., 1853, mortality 4. Matagorda, 15 feet, 1862, mortality 120; 1863. Millican, 300 feet, 1864; Oct. 15 to Nov. 12, 1867, mortality 4. Montgomery, 180 feet, 1859. Navasota, 200 feet, Aug. 12 to Dec., 1867, mortality 154. Oldtown, 20 feet, Oct. 13, 1867. Port Lavaca, 15 feet, July 3 to Oct., 1867. Richmond, 125 feet, 1853; 1859. Rio Grande City, 200 feet, 1867, mortality 150. Sabine City, 10 feet, July to Oct. 1, 1863, mortality 14. Saluria, 10 feet, 1853. Sugarland, 100 feet, 1859. Victoria, 50 feet, Aug. 1 to Dec. 25, 1867, mortality 200.

Virginia.—Alexandria, 25 feet, Aug. 1, 1803, mortality 200. City Point, 15 feet, 1798. Gosport, 20 feet, 1855. Hampton Roads, 1869. Norfolk, 20 feet, 1747; 1794; 1795; 1796; 1797; 1798; 1799. July 26 to Oct. 30, 1800, mortality 250; 1801; 1802; 1803; 1804; 1805; Aug. 1, 1821; Sept. 1, 1826; 1845; Aug. 7, 1852; Oct. to Nov. 2, 1854, mortality 3; June 30 to Oct., 1855, mortality 1,807. Petersburg, 20 feet, 1798. Portsmouth, 20 feet, 1852; 1854; Aug. 1 to Oct., 1855, mortality 1,000. Richmond, 50 feet, 1806. Scotts Creek, 15 feet, June 29, 1855. Winchester, 700 feet, July, 1804.

The yellow-fever epidemic of 1888 was confined to Florida and parts of Alabama and Georgia. It began in August and ended about November; the mortality, all told, being probably not more than one thousand.

It will be apparent from these statistics that the methods of recording the rise, progress, duration, and extent of epidemic diseases are as yet by no means perfect. The historian and the physician alike meet with this obstacle in their researches. A wise and enlightened public opinion, recognizing the advantage of close observation and of permanent record, may in the future remove this obstacle and governmental records afford the student more facts and therefore more facilities to learn aright.

Small-pox.—Small-pox is not indigenous to either Europe or America. Into the former continent it was introduced, by the Saracens, from Africa, about 622 and 710 A. D. Its early history is shrouded in obscurity. Of its origin we know nothing, but we do know now that it never occurs save as a consequence of infection conveyed from one person to another.

On its first introduction it ravaged Spain, then spread over Europe, sparing, however, for a time such isolated countries as Denmark, where it did not appear until 1527. It was carried to the West Indies in 1517, and reached Mexico in 1520 and Brazil in 1563. Farther north it first appeared in Maryland, having been brought there by an English ship in the early part of the seventeenth century. Thence it spread rapidly through Virginia, the Carolinas, New England, and other portions of the colonies.

The epidemic force of small-pox was, however, broken by the discoveries of inoculation and vaccination. Lady Mary Wortley Montague introduced inoculation for the small-pox from Turkey, her son having been successfully inoculated in 1718. She was allowed by way of experiment to inoculate seven convicts who, on recovery, were pardoned. A small-pox hospital was opened in London in 1746, but inoculation had not been universally adopted when Jenner, in 1796, discovered the safe and sure method of vaccination with the *pus* from cow-pox. The last notable visitation of small-pox began in 1870, running over all of Europe and America, and abating in 1873.

Cholera.—After the discovery of vaccination by Jenner had quelled the ravages of small-pox, Europe enjoyed comparative immunity from epidemics until the appearance of a new pestilence (the cholera) before unheard of there. Long known in India, this disease first began to attract the attention of Europeans in 1817. So slow, so steady, so even in its progress is the march of cholera, that it has been said to average the daily journey of a man.

In the month of August, 1817, cholera broke out in India in two separate places, viz., at Chittagong and Jessore. In 1818 it attacked Calcutta and invaded Hindustan. Ceylon and Malacca, Burmah and Sumatra, were attacked the following year. Java, Borneo, and the Philippines were attacked in 1820, and in 1821 Persia, Syria, and China. Not until 1823 did the cholera reach the frontier of Europe, where it finally spent its strength along the shores of the Caspian Sea.

A short respite followed this first invasion, and the plague slept until 1829; but in this fatal year it moved from Persia to Bokhara, Tartary, the shores of the Caspian Sea, ravaged Siberia, and even penetrated into Russia. In 1830 the plague desolated the empire of the Czar, entering Moscow on the 20th of September. The ravages were frightful. In two months 4,385 persons died. Still creeping slowly westward, in August, 1831, the plague invaded Prussia and Austria, slaying 1,400 in Berlin and 2,000 in Vienna. From these points it spread widely. The Baltic provinces suffered first, after which, leaping the North Sea, it entered Great Britain, and on Jan. 27, 1832, broke out in Edinburgh, and on February 10 in London.

This epidemic seems to have entered France from England. On the 15th of March, 1832, it was at Calais, and on the 28th of the same month at Paris, whence it extended to Holland, and in 1833 to Portugal. Spain suffered in 1834. The mortality was very great. During the six months that the cholera raged in Paris it found 18,406 victims out of a total population of 645,693, or 23 deaths for 1,000 of inhabitants. Switzerland alone of all the nations escaped its visitations.

On June 8, 1832, the cholera made its first appearance in Quebec, Canada, having undoubtedly been transmitted from Great Britain. Thence it spread rapidly over the American continent.

The second visitation of cholera was no less deadly than the first. From 1837 to 1847 Europe had been free from it, but India had suffered during the entire decade. In 1845, however, the plague appeared in Tartary and a few months later in Persia, whence it spread rapidly to Egypt *via* Bagdad and Mecca. In 1847 it had reached the shores of the Caspian Sea, and in the autumn of the same year appeared almost simultaneously in Moscow and Constantinople. Not until early in 1848 did it appear in St. Petersburg, but very quickly afterward it was found in Poland, Holland, France, Belgium, and England. From France the epidemic spread to Italy (Switzerland being again spared) and to the Mediterranean nations. It reached the United States in 1849, ravaging various portions of the country from May to November, and was particularly severe in the Mississippi valley.

The third visitation of cholera differed from the two preceding, in that it did not start from India, but originated in the Baltic states, appearing at Copenhagen in July and August, 1853. Upon this occasion the spread of the plague was unusually rapid, and nearly all of Europe was visited by it before the end of the year. By July, 1854. it had made its appearance in Northern Africa and Western Asia. It raged with violence among the armies in the Crimea.

The fourth and last epidemic came from the East, reaching Europe through Persia, Mecca, Suez, and Egypt, and entering France through the port of Marseilles, in June, 1865. It ravaged Europe until 1867, when it disappeared. The epidemic reached the United States in 1865, and was most severe in the West, especially at Chicago, St. Louis, and Nashville. The mortality in the East was comparatively light, the deaths in New York being 583, and in Brooklyn 573. An epidemic of cholera visited the Mississippi valley in 1873.

EVANGELICAL ASSOCIATION. The "Family Christian Almanac" of the Evangelical Association gives statistics of that body for 1888, of which the following is a summary: Number of conferences (including those of Germany, Switzerland, and the Japan mission), 26; whole number of members, 141,853; number of baptisms—2,560 of adults and 9,528 of infants; of itinerant preachers, 1,159; of local preachers, 647; of churches, 1,916, having a total probable value of $4,561,862; probable value of parsonages, $723,251; amount of collections for the Missionary Society, $107,511; for the Sunday-school and Tract Union, $2,671; for the Orphan Home, $4,614; for "Conference Claimants" (worn-out ministers and the widows and children of deceased ministers), $7,051; number of Sunday-schools, 2,404, with 29,910 officers and teachers, and 165,255 pupils; number of catechetical classes, 723, with 9,358 catechumens.

EVENTS OF 1888. The year was, upon the whole, remarkable for an absence of conspicuously noteworthy events. The general election in the United States, resulting in a peaceful revolution in political affairs, was the most important to Americans; while to Europeans, the sickness and death of the two German Emperors was for months the principal subject of interest. The wars that have been waged have been in remote corners of the earth, and most of the victories that have been gained have been in the way of scientific or commercial progress.

January 1. Grand Pontifical high mass celebrated in St. Peter's, Rome, in honor of the Pope's Jubilee—the fiftieth anniversary of his consecration as a priest.
5. Committees announced in the House of Representatives by Speaker Carlisle. France: Senatorial elections; the Republicans lost three seats.
8. Completion of the Mexican International Railway. Lucius Q. C. Lamar resigns the Secretaryship of the Interior to accept a seat in the United States Supreme Court.
11. Kentucky: J. B. Beck re-elected to the United States Senate.
12. Gen. E. S. Bragg nominated to be United States Minister to Mexico; confirmed by the Senate. The Senate confirms the following nominations: Don M. Dickinson to be Postmaster-General, William F. Vilas to be Secretary of the Interior.
16. L. Q. C. Lamar confirmed by the Senate as Associate Justice of the Supreme Court.
17. The President transmitted to Congress the reports of the Pacific Railway Commission. Mississippi: E. C. Walthall re-elected United States Senator.
19. The Senate ratified the extradition treaty with the Netherlands, and confirms the appointment of Eugene Semple to be Governor of Washington Territory.
25. Iowa: J. F. Wilson re-elected United States Senator from Iowa.

27. House of Representatives passes the Deficiency Appropriation bill as amended by the Senate (approved February 7).
February 3. Austria-Germany: Treaty of alliance officially announced.
6. Germany: Prince Bismarck explains to the Reichstag the nature of the Austro-Germanic alliance. Sweden: A new Cabinet formed, with M. Bildt as president.
8. Germany: The Reichstag passes a new military loan bill, authorizing an army of about 700,000 men and appropriating 280,000,000 marks for the purpose.
9. England: Opening of Parliament.
15. Fishery commissioners for the United States, Canada, and Great Britain sign an international treaty at Washington. The Senate passes a bill to aid in the establishment and temporary support of public schools.
17. Germany: The Reichstag continues the anti-socialist law for two years.
29. The House passes a bill authorizing the Secretary of the Treasury to apply the Treasury surplus to the purchase of United States bonds. New Jersey: County Option High License bill passed by the Assembly over the Governor's veto; Senate concurs March 6. The Senate passes a bill to provide for the compulsory education of Indian children.
March 8. The House passes the Military and Postal Telegraph bill.
4. Egypt: The British-Egyptian garrison of Suakin repulses an attack of the Arabs.
8. The Senate passes the Dependent Pensions bill.
16. Germany: Obsequies of the late Emperor at Charlottenburg.
17. France: Gen. Boulanger deprived of his command.
19. England and Wales: Local Government bill introduced in the House of Commons. The United States Supreme Court confirms the Bell Telephone patent.
22. Both houses of Congress adopt the Urgent Deficiencies bill (approved April 2).
24. Costa Rica-Nicaragua: The President of the United States announced his decision as arbitrator.
27. France: Gen. Boulanger placed on the retired list.
29. New York: The Assembly passes the Crosby High License bill.
30. Brazil: A new ministry formed, with Señor Alfredo as Premier and Minister of Finance.
31. Spain: Trial by jury approved by the Senate. Ecuador: Gen. Antonio Flores elected President (see June 10). Roumania: A new Cabinet formed, with M. Rosetti as Premier.
April 1. The Mills Tariff bill introduced in the House of Representatives.
4. France: A new ministry formed, with M. Floquet as president. Rhode Island: Royal C. Taft elected Governor.
5. The Senate passes Bond Purchase bill with amendments.
15. France: Gen. Boulanger elected to the Chamber of Deputies from the Department du Nord by more than 60,000 majority.
16. House of Representatives passes resolution to purchase United States bonds with Treasury surplus.
17. Francis Tillon Nicholls (Democrat) elected Governor of Louisiana, 85,786 majority. State election in Louisiana.
18. Bill to legalize marriage with deceased wife's sister, passed by English House of Commons. The Pope confirms the declaration of the Supreme Congregation of the Holy Roman and Universal Inquisition, condemning the use of means known as "the plan of campaign" and "boycotting" in contests between landlords and tenants in Ireland (see April 20).
19. Senate pa   bill for the admission of Dakota as a State, and   the organization of Lincoln as a Territory.
20. Papal circular condemning "boycotting," etc., issued to Irish bishops (see April 18).

26. Crosby High License bill passed by New York State Senate (see May 9).

28. France: Chamber of Deputies passes Panama Lottery Loan bill (see June 5). The United States gun-boat Yorktown and the dynamite cruiser Vesuvius launched at Philadelphia.

30. Irish Land Commission bill passed by English House of Commons. Melville Weston Fuller, of Illinois, nominated by the President for Chief-Justice of the Supreme Court of the United States.

May 1. New York: General Conference of the Methodist Episcopal Church opens.

3. New York: Ballot Reform bill passed by State Assembly (see May 10).

8. New York: Bill to provide for the execution of murderers by electricity passed by the Senate.

9. New York: Crosby High License bill vetoed by Governor Hill.

10. New York: Ballot Reform bill passed by the Senate.

13. Brazil: Bill to abolish slavery approved by the Regent.

15. Conventions representing United Labor and Union Labor, met in Cincinnati, Ohio; representing Equal Rights, in Des Moines, Iowa.

17. Great Britain: Irish Catholic members formally deny the right of the Holy See to interfere in Irish politics. United States: The Senate passes Pension Appropriation bill (see June 7).

22. The Senate passes bill to establish a Department of Labor (see June 13).

23. Louisiana: Randall L. Gibson (Democrat) elected United States Senator.

24. United States: House of Representatives passes Post Office Appropriation bill (see June 14).

27. Central Asia: First train passes over the railway to Samarcand. Ireland: The National League confirm the action of their representatives in Parliament (see May 17).

30. Prohibition party: National Convention opened at Indianapolis, Ind.

31. Ballot Reform bill passed by the Legislature of Massachusetts. Canada: Lord Stanley succeeds Lord Lansdowne as Governor-General.

June 1. Philip H. Sheridan appointed General of the United States Army in accordance with a special act of Congress. The Senate confirms Robert B. Roosevelt as Minister to the Netherlands, and confirms Philip H. Sheridan as General of the Army. France: The Chamber of Deputies rejects Gen. Boulanger's motion of urgency on revising the Constitution and dissolving the Chambers. New York: Governor Hill signs the bill for executions by electricity. Oregon: Election carried by Republicans, 7,408 plurality.

5. The Democratic National Convention meets at St. Louis. France: The Senate passes the Panama Lottery Loan bill (see April 28).

6. Grover Cleveland renominated by the Democrats for President of the United States.

7. Allen G. Thurman nominated for Vice-President by the Democrats. Pension Appropriation bill approved by the President (see May 17).

10. Ecuador: Gen. Antonio Flores inaugurated as President.

11. New York: Governor Hill vetoes the Ballot **Reform bill.**

12. Rhode Island: Jonathan Chace elected United States Senator.

13. Bill establishing a Department of Labor approved by the President (see May 22).

14. The Senate passes Post-Office Appropriation bill (see May 24).

15. Germany: The Emperor Friedrich Wilhelm died. William II succeeds to the imperial throne.

18. Germany: Obsequies of the late Emperor Frederick III, at Potsdam.

19. Republican National Convention meets in Chicago (see June 25).

22. The House passes the Naval Appropriation bill and the Sundry Civil Appropriation bill.

24. Ireland: A papal encyclical reiterated the former decree against boycotting and the plan of campaign.

25. Benjamin Harrison, of Indiana, and Levi P. Morton, of New York, respectively nominated by the Republicans for President and Vice-President of the United States.

27. The House of Representatives passes United States Public Land bill.

July 2. The Senate passes the River and Harbor Appropriation bill. Reunion of Federal and Confederate veterans at Gettysburg—twenty-fifth anniversary of the battle.

3. Prussia: Herr Herrfurth appointed Vice-President of the Ministerial Council and Minister of the Interior.

9. Mexico: Gen. Porfirio Diaz re-elected President.

11. United States: Census bill passed by the House.

12. Diplomatic and Consular Appropriation bill signed by the President. France: The Chamber of Deputies rejects Gen. Boulanger's motion for dissolution; a vote of censure passed upon Boulanger.

13. France: A duel with swords between the Prime Minister and Gen. Boulanger, the latter wounded.

19. Africa: Major Edmund M. Barttelot, Stanley's chief lieutenant in the expedition for the relief of Emin Pasha, was murdered by natives. Italy: The Chamber of Deputies passes an Electoral Reform bill.

20. United States: The Senate confirms Melville W. Fuller to be Chief-Justice of the Supreme Court, the vote stood 41 to 20.

21. The Mills Tariff bill passes the House of Representatives, 162 to 149. The Senate passes Freedmen's Savings and Trust bill.

23. France: Gen. Boulanger defeated in an election for member of the Chamber of Deputies (see August 19.)

25. United States Senate passes Naval Appropriation bill.

26. United States Senate passes Army Appropriation bill.

27. England: The Local Government bill passed its third reading in the House of Commons.

30. Venezuela: Dr. Juan Pablo Rojas Paul assumes the presidency.

31. Italy takes formal possession of Massowah and the adjoining territory.

August 1. The Senate passes Sundry Civil Appropriation bill.

5. Gen. Philip H. Sheridan died, at Nonquit, Mass.

6. A train runs from London to Edinburgh, 400 miles, in seven hours and twenty-five minutes, including stoppages.

8. The Senate passes bill to prohibit the immigration of Chinese laborers. England: The Parnell Commission bill passed its third reading in the House of Commons.

10. Hayti: Louis Étienne Felicité Salomon abdicated the presidency, a war of factions followed.

13. Germany: Count Von Moltke placed on the retired list of the army; Gen. Van Waldersée succeeds him as Chief of Staff. United States: The River and Harbor bill became a law without the President's signature.

14. Gen. J. M. Schofield succeeds to the command of the army of the United States, vice Sheridan deceased.

15. The American party met in convention at Washington and nominated Gen. James L. Curtis, of New York, for President, and James L. Grier, of Tennessee, for Vice-President.

18. Prussia: Karl Heinrich von Bötticher appointed Vice-President of the Prussian Ministerial Council.

19. France: Gen. Boulanger re-elected as a member of the Chamber of Deputies.

21. United States Senate rejects the fisheries treaty by a vote of 30 to 27.

23. The President in a message asks for enlarged powers under the retaliation act.

29. Hanover: Rudolph von Bennigsen, leader of the National Liberal party, appointed Governor.

81. China refuses to ratify the treaty restricting immigration to the United States. Alabama: Thomas Seay (Democrat) re-elected Governor by about 75,000 plurality.

September 8. Arkansas: James P. Eagle (Democrat) elected Governor by 14,981 majority.

4. Vermont: W. P. Dillingham (Republican) elected Governor by 27,647 majority.

8. The House of Representatives passes the bill carrying out the President's recommendations regarding the fisheries. John L. M. Curry resigns the post of minister to Spain.

9. The President formally accepts the Democratic nomination for re-election.

10. Maine: Edwin C. Burleigh (Republican) elected Governor by 18,495 plurality.

11. Benjamin Harrison formally accepts the Republican nomination for President. The Grand Army of the Republic meets at Columbus, Ohio.

13. Chinese laborer's immigration bill approved by the President.

14. The Senate passes bill regulating the arbitration of differences between railroads.

22. China rejects the immigration treaty.

24. India: The British contingent gained a decisive victory over the Thibetans at Jalapla Pass.

October 1. The President signs the bill excluding the Chinese from the United States. Confirmations by the Senate: Lambert W. Tree, of Illinois, to be minister to Russia, and John G. Parkhurst, of Michigan, to be minister to Belgium.

6. The steel cruiser Baltimore launched at Philadelphia.

7. France: Concessions of territory announced from the King of Annam.

8. Melville W. Fuller takes the oath as Chief-Justice of the Supreme Court.

9. The Senate: John H. Oberly, of Illinois, confirmed as Commissioner of Indian Affairs. Chicago: Strike of 2,000 car-drivers. Congress passes supplementary legislation as to counting the presidential vote.

12. Germany-Italy: Emperor William visits Rome.

15. France: The Chamber of Deputies reassembles, and M. Floquet introduces his bill to revise the Constitution.

17. Hayti: Gen. Francois Dennis Legitime elected President. Subsequently his election was disputed, and a war of factions followed, lasting until after the end of the year.

20. New York city: Fifteenth annual meeting of the National Women's Temperance Union. Daniel Hand, of Clinton, Conn., gives the American Missionary Association $1,000,000 for the education of Southern negroes. The General Deficiency bill approved by the President. Congress adjourns after the longest continuous session on record.

22. The Supreme Court affirms the constitutionality of the law against liquor-selling in Iowa, and of an Alabama law prescribing tests for color-blindness among railroad employés.

23. Scotland: The Parnell libel case against the "London Times," opens at Edinburgh.

27. Hayti: The American steamer Haytien Republic, siezed by the local authorities for alleged blockade-running.

80. Lord Sackville-West, the British minister resident at Washington, officially notified that he is no longer acceptable as a diplomatic representative, on the ground that he had criticised the action of the United States Government.

November 6. Benjamin Harrison, the Republican candidate, elected President.

9. Africa: The Mahdi with a large army is reported to have attacked and captured the town of Wadai.

10. Europe: An agreement is announced among the great powers to exterminate the African slave trade.

13. The Knights of Labor open their eleventh annual meeting at Indianapolis.

14. Brooklyn, N. Y.: Strike of car-drivers, three city lines "tied up" (strike ends November 16).

19. The Empress-Dowager of Germany (widow of Frederick), visits England. American steamer Haytien Republic confiscated at Port-au-Prince, despite the protest of the American minister.

23. Knights of Labor re-elect Mr. Powderly as grand master workman.

24. The United States steamship Boston reaches New York from Port-au-Prince, with yellow fever on board. Several deaths, including the surgeon, occur.

27. Florida: For the first time in 112 days there are no new cases of yellow fever and no deaths in Jacksonville.

29. England: The Ashebourne Extension bill passes the House of Commons.

December 2. France: Great popular demonstration in Paris in honor of Baudin.

8. The Fiftieth Congress begins its second session.

5. The American Forestry Congress meets in Atlanta, Ga.

7. Maryland: A formidable resistance to legal authority begins among the oyster-dredgers of Chesapeake Bay.

8. Alabama: Serious lynching riot, and loss of life at Birmingham.

11. The First National Sabbath Convention meets at Washington.

12. United States steamers Galena and Yantic sail for Hayti to demand the release of an American passenger steamer. The House of Representatives passes the Direct Tax bill, 178 to 96.

13. Africa: Dispatches reach the coast declaring that Stanley and Emin Pasha are prisoners to the Mahdi.

14. France: A bill introduced in the Chamber of Deputies giving the Panama Canal Company more time to fill its contract. South Carolina: The State Assembly favorably reports an educational qualification for voters.

17. Mississippi: Conflict between whites and negroes at Wahalak.

18. New York city: A new wing of the Metropolitan Museum of Art is opened with imposing ceremonies.

20. Congress adjourns till Jan. 2, 1889. Egypt: Engagement between the British and Egyptian garrison of Suakin, and a besieging force of Arabs, the latter defeated with heavy loss.

21. Africa: Dispatches to date of August 17 agree that Stanley and Emin Bey are safe and at liberty. United States: Both houses of Congress adjourn for the holidays.

23. Hayti: The confiscated American steamer Haytien Republic surrendered to the United States vessels sent to Port-au-Prince to secure her release.

24. Great Britain: Parliament adjourns till Jan. 31, 1889.

F

FINANCIAL REVIEW OF 1888. This year was a remarkable one in very many respects. Two Emperors of Germany died within an interval of but little more than three months; yet these events and the succession of the youthful Emperor William III resulted in no political friction and in no financial disturbance. At all the great European monetary centers there was a demand for gold with which to supply the requirements of the Argentine Republic and of Russia, but with such care was this conducted that no legitimate business interests directly suffered. At home there was an unusually excited presidential canvass which resulted in a radical change in the administration; yet while the campaign was most hotly conducted there was no interruption to business, and although the question of the tariff was directly involved, manufacturing of goods likely to be affected was only partially checked. A fall in the market value of silver to the lowest price on record did not arouse apprehensions in the public mind concerning the stability of our currency, although the vaults of the Treasury were full to overflowing of the coined dollars, and the only effect produced by the decline in silver was temporarily to limit the output at the mines. While gold was at intervals exported to Europe none went forward as an exchange operation, the shipments being wholly made on special order. Speculators manipulated the cotton market in August and forced the price so high that the staple was imported from Liverpool at a profit, and, in October wheat was advanced to figures which, could the grain have been obtained abroad, would have justified its importation. The country had a fairly good crop of winter wheat and there was a partial failure of spring sowed grain, the former maturing under very favorable conditions, while the latter was blighted by unprecedentedly early frosts, yet the corn-crop escaped injury. Early in the spring the East was visited by the most severe storm of snow experienced in many years, while at the same time mild weather prevailed in the extreme Northwest, and when the wheat in that section was being blasted by frost the temperature was genial at all other points in the country. While the great transportation lines were so crowded with business that the rolling stock was insufficient for the traffic a war of rates was inaugurated by one of the most conservatively managed roads in the East, resulting not only in demoralization of tariffs but in unsettling confidence in the market value of our stocks at home and abroad. Executive officers of railroad corporations, responsible for millions of share and bond property, permitted their subordinates to aid in depreciating its value by frequently and persistently cutting

passenger and freight rates, and mismanagement of these roads finally became so atrocious that bankers representing large interests here and abroad were called upon to interfere and demand a reformation. The country was generally prosperous; farmers received good prices for their crops; manufacturers realized fair profits while labor was suitably rewarded; merchants in almost every section had reason to be satisfied with the results of the year's business, and losses through failures in trade were comparatively limited. But while the industrial and mercantile classes enjoyed a good degree of prosperity many of those who depend upon the proceeds of investments for support were harrassed by the fear of loss if they did not actually suffer from reduction of revenue caused by smaller dividends from share properties.

At the opening of the year the Bank of England had a stock of £20,164,214 bullion, 38 per cent. of reserve to liabilities, and a 4 per cent. minimum rate of discount. The highest stock of bullion during the year was £23,460,624, March 21, and then the proportion of reserve was 44¼, and the bank-rate 2 per cent. By December 6 the bullion had been drawn down to £18,303,473, the bank minimum had ruled at 5 per cent. since October 3, although for several weeks the open market discount rate was only 2¾ per cent., and the bank had advanced the price of gold bars to the highest figures, 77 shillings 10½ pence, in order to check withdrawals of bullion for export. When the year opened the Bank of France had £44,033,104 gold. The highest for the year was £45,438,652, and the lowest £40,663,432, November 29. On January 7 the estimated amount of gold in the Bank of Germany was £25,986,000. The greatest sum was £33,732,000, June 23, but by the beginning of November this had dwindled to £28,563,000. Comparing the highest and the lowest amounts of bullion in each of the three banks, it is seen that there was a loss of £5,157,151 by the Bank of England, £4,775,220 by that of France, and £5,169,000 by that of Germany. The shipments from this country to Great Britain were about £2.250,000, and to Germany £2,900,000, and all this gold was drawn for indirect shipment to South America. The bankers in London and Berlin who had contracted to supply the Argentine Republic kept the open markets of the principal European centers bare of gold during the greater part of the year, but how much was thus obtained it is impossible to say. The movement to South America was doubtless nearly equal to three fourths the aggregate of all the withdrawals from the European banks and from New York, or not far from £14,000,000, the remainder going to Russia, which took £5,000,000, and Holland, £1,000,000. The Argentine loan, negotiated early in the year in England and Germany was for the purpose of enabling the free banking system of that country to be carried into effect. This law provided for the issue of notes of banks against a 4½-per-cent. Government stock for which payment could be made only in gold, which metal was required to be lodged in the National Bank until January 1, 1890, after which it might be used by the Government for the redemption of a portion of the foreign debt. After the drain of gold from London and other European centers had become so great as to absorb the open market supply, a resort was had to the banks for further amounts, and then it was that the official discount rates began to be disturbed. Almost simultaneously, early in October, the rates at the Banks of England and France were advanced, the former to 5 and the latter to 4½ per cent., and at the same time there was an unexpected shipment of £500,000 in Bank of England notes to Russia, supposed to be for the purpose of holding in lieu of gold against a new issue of rubles. The condition of the European markets became so strained by reason of this movement to South America and to Russia, that the bankers negotiating with the Argentine Republic notified that Government that further shipments thither would endanger the success of the loan, and thereupon the banking law was amended so as to permit the gold held by the National Bank to be released. This temporarily relieved the pressure, and the gold thereafter sent to South America was ordered out from New York by London and German bankers. Toward the end of November a London and Paris syndicate negotiated a £20,000,000 conversion loan for the Russian Government, and this tended to keep the rates for money high at all the European centers for the remainder of the year.

Among the important events of the year was the successive defeat of various labor organizations. The determined stand taken by the Philadelphia and Reading managers in January resulted in the abandonment by the Knights of Labor in the mining regions of all efforts to dictate the policy of the company, and this also caused the ending of the miners' strike in the Lehigh valley region. The next movement of importance was that of the engineers on the

were more clearly manifested this year, and at the annual convention in November the official report showed a decrease of 300,000 in membership during the year, and only 259,518 on the rolls. The losses were heaviest in the Eastern States and in the large cities. The treasurer's report showed that the receipts were not sufficient to meet the expenses, and retrenchment became necessary.

The silver question was rarely discussed during the year. The United States Treasurer and the Secretary of the Treasury both suggested to Congress the advisability of suspending coinage of the standard dollar and the keeping of the purchases of silver bullion in the form of ingots, but no action was taken by Congress on the suggestion. The order of the Secretary of the Treasury directing that checks, drawn against deposits of gold by the banks in the Sub-Treasury, be received for duties at the New York Custom-House went into effect July 1, and it not only proved of great convenience to the mercantile public, but it tended to lessen the demand for currency, including silver certificates.

The following tabular survey of the economical conditions and results of 1888 contrasted with these of the preceding year is from the " Commercial and Financial Chronicle " :

ECONOMICAL CONDITIONS AND RESULTS.	1887.	1888.
Coin and currency in the United States, November 1......	$1,678,009,959	$1,694,771,688
Bank clearings in the United States...................	51,050,705,285	49,097,528,591
Business failures.............	167,560,944	123,829,973
Imports of merchandise	708,818,473	725,224,183
Exports of merchandise	715,301,044	691,766,462
Gross earnings, 108 railroads..	874,569,365	856,626,292
Railroad construction, miles...	18,080	7,000
Wheat raised, bushels........	456,329,000	414,868,000
Corn raised, bushels..........	1,456,161,000	1,987,790,000
Cotton raised, bales..........	7,017,707	6,900,000
Pig-iron produced, gross tons.	6,417,148	6,499,739
Steel rails, Bessemer, net tons.	2,290,197	1,528,057
Anthracite coal, gross tons....	34,641,017	38,145,718
Petroleum (runs), production, barrels............	21,819,027	16,095,448
Immigration into the United States......	510,058	518,515

The prices of leading staples on or about Jan. 1, 1889, compared with prices at the same date in 1888 and 1887, were as follows:

PRICES OF LEADING STAPLES.	1887.	1888.	1889.
Cotton, middling uplands, per pound......	9 $\frac{7}{16}$	10 $\frac{1}{16}$	9¼
Wool, American XX, per pound............	39	37	38
Iron, American pig No. 1, per ton.........	$20 00 to $21 00	$21 00 to $21 50	$18 00 to $18 50
Steel rails at mills, per ton..............	$36 00 to $37 00	$32 00 to $33 00	$28 00
Wheat, No. 2 red winter, per bushel......	98½	92	$1 01½
Corn, Western mixed No. 2, per bushel......	48½	68	46
Pork, mess, per barrel...................	$12 25 to $12 75	$15 50 to $16 00	$14 00 to $14 25

Chicago, Burlington and Quincy. The defeat of the Brotherhood of Locomotive Engineers was a severe blow to the organization, and one from which it did not recover. The indications of disintegration of the order of Knights of Labor which were visible at the close of last year

Manufacturing Industries.—With the exception of the strike of the miners in the Schuylkill and Lehigh valley coal regions, early in 1888, and some smaller troubles of this character in other branches of business, at intervals during the year, producers and manufacturers were comparatively undisturbed by the demands of labor organizations. The fact was early recognized that Congress would make an attempt to revise the tariff, and the uncertainty which existed regarding the final action of that body upon this subject induced manufacturers of articles likely to be affected by changes in the tariff to restrict their operations and to confine the production so far as was possible to current needs. It was not until after the presidential election that there was any important activity in manufacturing of goods, and then only in woolens. The production of cottons was large and the mills generally did a profitable business. The output of pig-iron was about 6 per cent. below the large production of 1887, and the decrease was most marked in Bessemer pig. The manufacture of structural iron and steel, however, was greater than in 1887 or in 1886. The product of the Tennessee and Alabama iron-manufacturing districts was a striking feature, as also was the new process of the petroleum jet blast for the manufacture of iron and steel, which, it was claimed, would greatly reduce the cost of production. The output of anthracite coal was the largest on record, and schedule prices were generally well maintained until December, when decreased consumption and an accumulation of stocks caused a slight reduction.

The Money Market.—Money on call, represented by bankers' balances, ranged from 10 to 1 per cent. during the year. The 6 and 7 per cent. rates were in January, on March 2, and on October 3, due, on the last named day, to large withdrawals for the West and also by the customary demand for settlements. In the last two weeks of December, 8 per cent. was recorded, and on the last day of the year money loaned at 10 per cent., but then the demand came from belated borrowers in the absence of representatives of lenders. Scarcely anything was done in time-loans in stock collateral until toward the close of January when there were a few transactions at 4½ per cent. for six months and 4 for sixty days. Rates grew easier early in February and contracts were made at 3 per cent. for sixty days to four months, and 4 for six months, but toward the close of February rates were firmer at 4 to 5 per cent. for ninety days to four months and 5 to 5½ for six months, the expectation then being that bank reserves would be materially reduced by Treasury operations. These rates ruled quite uniformly throughout March, becoming slightly easier toward the close, but early in April, under the influence of offerings of foreign money on call and on time, rates fell to 3 to 3½ per cent. for sixty days to four months and 4½ to 5 for six months to the end of the year. After the Secretary of the Treasury commenced to buy bonds, thus insuring ease in money, the offerings were liberal but the demand was not urgent, borrowers being satisfied that they could procure all needed accom-

modation in the call-loan branch of the market, where the rate gradually fell to an average of 2 per cent. In May the exports of gold encouraged lenders to hope that they could do better later in the season than by offering money at the then low rates, and many of them withheld their offerings on time and employed their funds in the call-loan market, but the demand was comparatively insignificant and the smaller supply had no effect upon rates. Early in June time-loans were quoted at 2½ per cent. for ninety days, 3 for four months, and 3½ for the remainder of the year, and toward the middle of the month the rate was 2 per cent. for sixty days. In July some foreign money was placed for about four months' time at 1½ to 2½ per cent. on strictly prime collateral, and this forced domestic lenders out of the market temporarily. By the close of the month, however, quotations were 2½ to 3 per cent. for sixty days, 3 for ninety days; 3½ for four months, and 4 to 4½ for four to six months. Early in August there was a slight advance in the call-loan rate, due to withdrawals of funds for the West, but before the close quotations fell off again, influenced by the light inquiry for time-loans which caused lenders to employ their money on call. Then quotations were 2½ to 3 per cent. for sixty to ninety days; 3 to 3½ for ninety days to four months; and 3½ to 4½ for four to six months. By the middle of September rates were 5 per cent. for four, five, and six months, but very little was done and there was then an impression that rates would become still easier by reason of a return of funds from the West. During the first few days in October call-loans advanced to 7 per cent., partly in consequence of withdrawals for the monthly settlements, but mainly because of a drain of money to the West, it being attracted thither by the wild speculation in wheat. Time-loans were then quoted at 4½ to 5 per cent. for four, five, and six months, but they were not in demand, and toward the close of the month, under the influence of offerings by bankers with foreign connections, the rate fell to 3 to 3½ per cent. for the remainder of the year and 4 to 5 for four, five, and six months. Call money had by this time gradually declined to an average of 2 per cent. Early in November many of the banks and trust companies, finding time-loans unremunerative and commercial paper scarce, bought freely of railroad mortgages taking anything that would yield above 4 per cent., but later in the month there was a good inquiry from almost every quarter for time-loans, based upon the expectation of an active demand for money for manufacturing and business enterprises, and rates moved up to 3½ per cent. for sixty days; 4 for ninety days to four months; and 4½ to 5 for four to six months. Call money ranged from 4 to 2 per cent. In December lending on time was practically confined to a few of the city trust companies and to out-of-town institutions and the demand was not very urgent until toward the close when there was a good inquiry for loans for sixty days at 4 per cent. Rates early in the month were 3 to 3½ per cent for sixty days, 3½ to 4 for sixty days to four months, and 4½ to 5 for four to six months. After the middle of the month bank reserves fell off, three of the largest city institutions held nearly the whole of the surplus reported by all the banks, call-money ruled at an average of about 5 per cent., and the supply came chiefly from bankers having balances and a few trust companies.

Early in the year mercantile paper was in abundant supply. Rates were 5 to 5½ per cent. for sixty to ninety day indorsed bills receivable in the beginning of January, gradually falling, under the influence of a better demand, to 4¾ to 5 by the end of the month. In February the range was from 4½ to 5, and in March paper sold less freely with rates up to 5 to 5½ per cent. by the close. In April the supply was small, but the demand was good, and rates were 4¾ to 5½ per cent. In May quotations fell off to 4 to 4½, and in June, influenced by more urgency in the inquiry, rates declined to 3½ to 4 per cent., recovering in the next month to 4 to 4½, and in August to 4½ to 5. In September paper was abundant, but none of the banks were buying, and consequently rates advanced to 5½ to 6; but in October the demand improved, and quotations fell to 4¾ to 5, dropping the next month to 4 per cent. In December the inquiry grew light toward the close, and the quotation was 5½ per cent.

It will be seen by the above that at no time during the year was there any real scarcity of money, and borrowers on call, on time, and on commercial paper found a comparatively liberal supply offering. The New York associated banks held at the beginning of the year $103,653,200 gold and legal-tender notes, consisting of $75,235,400 of the former and $28,417,800 of the latter. By the end of March the gold had been reduced to $71,351,300, but under the influence of bond purchases and other accumulations from Treasury operations, this item was carried to $93,694,200 by July 14, and then, by reason of the demand for the interior for crop purposes, it fell to $78,862,400 by September 8, rising to $94,281,300, the maximum of the year, by October 20, showing the effect of large bond purchases and the return movement from the interior. The legal-tender maximum for the year was recorded August 4. Then the drain to the West and South caused a decline to the minimum of $26,700,900 by November 10. Deposits

were $371,305,900, the minimum of the year, January 7, and the maximum, $421,884,300, was reached October 20, meanwhile falling from $418,234,000, July 14, to $406,309,100, September 22. Loans and discounts were at the minimum, $354,767,900, January 21, and at the maximum, $397,243,200, October 13. The surplus reserve was $10,826,725 at the opening of the year, rising to $23,258,825 by January 28, falling to $8,620,875 April 7, recovering to $28,463,700, the maximum, July 16, declining to $10,314,550 October 13, sharply reacting to $16,901,025 October 20, and then gradually falling to $6,281,350 December 29.

The Secretary of the Treasury, with a view to the relief of the money market, and in order to distribute the Treasury holdings of cash, decided early in the year further to increase the number of designated depositories, and, in pursuance of this policy, the amount of money on deposit with national banks throughout the country was increased from $52,109,918, January 1, to $61,921,294 by May 1. Then followed a gradual reduction to $59,091,239 by September 1, and afterward, in consequence of the surrender of bonds for the security of deposits, the amount was reduced to $51,925,078, December 1, and at the end of the year the public money held by the designated depositories was $52,390,154. Under the authority of the act of October, 1882, reaffirmed April 17, the Secretary of the Treasury on April 23 commenced purchasing 4 and 4½ per cent. United States bonds, continuing to do so to the end of the year, with the exception that on October 10, after taking $51,394,200, purchases of the 4-per-cents. were suspended, and thereafter buying was confined to the 4½s. The bond-purchases at the end of the year amounted to $101,715,500, and the sum paid therefor, including premiums, was $120,254,940. The bonds came chiefly from New York and vicinity, and payments for the same were made through the banks in this section of the country, thus largely accounting for the increase of cash and of reserves in our banks. But to the extent that these bonds were held by the Treasury as security for circulation, the amount distributed to the banks was only 10 per cent. of the par value and the premiums. The high price which the bonds commanded in the market by reason of the Treasury purchases induced liberal surrenders of circulation after the beginning of September, but these were confined by law to $3,000,000 per month.

Appended is the New York Clearing-House statement of totals at the beginning of each quarter of 1888 and at the end of the year:

DATE.	Loans.	Specie.	Circulation.	Deposits.	Legal tenders.
January 7	$360,070,500	$75,235,400	$8,089,900	$371,305,900	$28,417,800
March 31	368,582,000	71,351,300	7,602,700	378,318,900	31,124,000
June 30	377,085,800	90,707,100	7,627,500	408,880,700	33,192,500
September 29	390,707,800	85,326,400	6,589,000	408,714,900	31,609,500
December 29	388,798,700	76,521,300	4,862,800	400,314,600	29,588,700

The condition of the New York Clearing-House banks, the rates for money, exchange, and silver, and prices for United States bonds on or about Jan. 1, 1889, compared with the preceding two years, are shown in the following summary:

BANK RETURNS, ETC.	1887.	1888.	1889.
NEW YORK CITY BANKS:			
Loans and discounts	$348,687,500	$356,540,000	$358,798,700
Specie	82,718,100	71,139,300	76,521,800
Circulation	7,911,500	8,077,300	4,862,300
Net deposits	359,268,600	359,350,800	400,814,600
Legal tenders	19,370,400	27,259,800	29,838,700
Required reserve	89,817,150	89,839,950	100,078,650
Reserve held	102,088,500	98,399,100	106,360,000
Surplus reserve	$12,271,350	$8,559,150	$6,281,350
MONEY, EXCHANGE, SILVER:			
Call-loans	4 @ 8	5 @ 6	4 @ 7
Prime paper, 60 days	5 @ 6½	6 @ 6½	5 @ 5½
Silver in London, per ounce	46¼ d.	44 7/16 d.	42¼ d.
Prime sterling bills, 60 days	4 81½	4 83½	4 85
UNITED STATES BONDS:			
6s, currency, 1898	131¾	125	127½
4½s of 1891, coupon	110¼	108¼	108½
4s of 1907, coupon	127⅛	126¼	126½

Foreign Exchange.—The imports of merchandise for 1888 were $16,405,675 above those for 1887, and the exports of domestic and foreign merchandise for the same time were $23,534,582 less. The excess of merchandise imports over exports for the year was $33,457,691, against $6,482,566 exports over imports in 1887. There was an excess of $37,199,619 exports over imports of specie and bullion in 1888, against $24,872,499 imports over exports in 1887. The excess of exports over imports of merchandise and specie in 1888 was $3,741,928, against $18,389,933 imports over exports in 1887.

Foreign exchange was strong early in January in consequence of a scarcity of commercial bills, and the low rates for discounts in London encouraged purchases of long sterling. Toward the middle of the month offerings of maturing drafts and a reduction in the Bank of England minimum to three per cent. from four caused a decline in sight bills, and the tone of the market was heavy at the close of the month. At the beginning of February there was a fall of one cent per pound sterling, mainly due to the offerings of bills against new securities placed abroad, and it was estimated that over $30,000,000 railroad bonds had been so disposed of since the commencement of the year, money in Europe being cheap—1⅝ to 1½ in London for sixty days' to three months' bank bills, 2¼ to 2¾ in the open market at Paris, and 1⅝ to 1¾ at Berlin. By the middle of the month, however, the tone grew firmer in consequence of a scarcity of bills, although there was a reduction in the Bank of England minimum to 2½ per cent., and in the rate of the Bank of France to the same figure. Toward the end of the month and early in March there was a further advance in sterling, due to a limited supply of commercial bills and to a demand to remit for stocks sold for European account, confidence abroad in American securities being unsettled by the strike on the Chicago, Burlington and Quincy, and by the unfavorable traffic returns of the Erie and of the Reading. About the middle of March the Bank of England minimum was reduced to 2 per cent., but this had no particular effect upon exchange, which became easier, mainly because of offerings of bills drawn against purchases of stocks for European account. The first shipment of gold, $300,000, was made March 29, but this went out on special order, and not as the result of an exchange operation. Early in April the rates fell off because of continued offerings of bankers' bills, although commercial sterling continued scarce, but before the close of the month there was an upward reaction, partly due to dearer money in London, which early in May caused an advance in the Bank of England minimum to 3 per cent. There were other shipments of gold May 9, May 12, and during the week ending May 26, but these were also sent on special order, and indirectly to the Argentine Republic, London bankers then being engaged in supplying demands for that country, which gradually grew urgent. At no time during the month were the rates of sterling high enough to justify gold exports as an exchange operation. The Bank of England reduced its minimum rate to 2½ per cent. June 6. The bills drawn against the negotiation of the Baltimore and Ohio, the Reading, and a Canadian loan gradually came upon the market in June, but additional shipments of gold were made, also on special order. The rates fell off in July, but gold continued to go forward in response to an apparent determination by the managers of the Imperial Bank of Germany still further to augment its supplies of the metal. Toward the close of the month exports of grain were liberal, and these furnished a better supply of commercial bills, and there were also offerings of drafts in anticipation of the movement of cotton. The pressure of this exchange caused a further decline in rates early in August, but the tone soon grew firmer under the influence of dearer money in London and an advance in the Bank of England minimum to 3 per cent. On the 9th the corner in August deliveries of cotton not only stopped the export of that staple but it caused the import of cotton from Liverpool, to the value of about $500,000, thus affecting commercial bills. In September the market was in an anomalous condition. Rates were near the gold exporting point, because commercial bills were small in volume, the supply being limited in consequence of the scarcity of freight-room which prevented free shipments of staples. Discounts were so high in London that bankers did not care to anticipate a decline in the exchange market by making speculative sales. Sterling was directly affected on the 13th by an advance in the Bank of England minimum to 4 per cent., and a rise in the Bank of France to 3½. Toward the end of the month rates were very firm, and on October 4 the Bank of England minimum was further advanced to 5 per cent., the Bank of France to 4½, and that of Germany to 4, forcing a rise in sight sterling very near to the gold exporting point, and on the 9th $500,000 was sent to London on special order. The speculation in wheat stopped exports, and the cotton movement was late, so that the supply of commercial bills was insignificant. About the middle of the month sterling fell off on a better offering of bankers' bills and a lighter demand, and by the close the tone was decidedly easier, there then being a greater supply of cotton drafts and cheaper money in London, due to the temporary suspension of gold exports to South America. In November commercial and bankers' bills were scarce, there was a demand to cover speculative sales, and rates were firm throughout the month. Toward the close about $5,000,000 gold went to London and Germany, wholly on special order. In December the tone of the market was firm for short bills and easy for long, in consequence of dearer discounts in London, and during the second week some bankers advanced short drafts to a price very near the gold exporting point, but no gold was sent as an exchange operation, although about $3,000,000 went to Germany and $2,000,000 to London on special order. In the third week the exchange market was quiet and firm, and $1,000,000 gold went to Berlin. For the remainder of the month the tone was barely steady, but without any alteration in nominal rates. None of the gold sent abroad this year—$11,252,962 to London and $14,514,467 to Berlin—went forward as an exchange operation. The metal was first attracted to Great Britain by a desire on the part of the bankers—who were under engagement to supply the Argentine Republic —to avoid disturbing the London money market by drawing from the Bank of England. On October 9 the news of the shipment hence of $500,000 tended immediately to ease the open market discount rate in London. The exports to that center in November and De-

cember were made because the bankers above referred to, being parties to the negotiation of the Russian conversion loan of £20,000,000, were willing to pay a premium for bar-gold amounting to about one half to one quarter of a penny per ounce below the price demanded by the Bank of England. The movement to Germany in the summer was, as stated above, due to efforts of the Imperial Bank to augment its stock of this metal, and, having obtained a supply, the bank sought to retain it by advancing its rate of discount, and December 6 this rate moved up to 4½ per cent., thus aiding in attracting further amounts from London and New York.

Railroads.—The majority of managers of railroads of the country claimed, in those of the annual reports which at the end of the year were made public, that their properties had felt the effect of the fourth and fifth sections of the Interstate Commerce Act, and particularly of the latter, which prohibits pooling, more severely than they did during that portion of the previous year in which the act was in operation, for the reason that the competition from new lines was great, and also because agreements for the maintenance of rates were not generally regarded. The Eastern trunk lines suffered to some extent from the aggressive course pursued by the Canadian roads, but the old established routes felt the influence of competition by more recently established trunk lines and their connections, to which differentials had to be given, and these rates were by no means uniformly maintained. In the Northwest the old roads were called upon to meet the competition of newly organized lines which waged a guerilla warfare to get business, and succeeded in keeping rates in an unsettled state throughout nearly the whole of the year. In the Southwest rates were forced to low points by excessive competition and the aggressive course of the Missouri Pacific, and the result was reductions of dividends to points never before reached in the history of the roads. Southern lines enjoyed a greater degree of prosperity by reason of an increase of traffic and comparative immunity from competition, but some of the Eastern roads suffered severely during the year, although mainly from local influences. One feature was the action of the Iowa railroad commissioners in formulating a new distance tariff of rates for roads in that State far below those previously ruling. This action was resisted by the companies, and on application to Judge Brewer, of the United States Supreme Court, an injunction was granted, July 26, restraining the commissioners from enforcing the new tariff, the judge taking the ground that rates must be reasonable and just, and sufficiently high to enable the roads to meet expenses and fixed charges and leave something for the stockholders. The manner in which the railroad commissioners prepared their tariff was made the subject of a judicial investigation by State

Judge Fairall, and irregularities were disclosed sufficient to induce him also to enjoin the execution of the tariff. These decisions served to influence the commissioners of other Western States to be more conservative in their action, and complaints of injustice were confined to the Iowa commissioners. The course taken by the directors of the Chicago, Milwaukee and St. Paul in passing the dividend on the common stock and reducing it on the preferred September 12, aroused the European stockholders of the company to that extent that they almost unanimously agreed to deposit their holdings with a prominent London banking-house with a view to securing united action for self-protection against what they regarded as reckless management on the part of the directors. Subsequently, October 18, the Atchison, Topeka and Santa Fé managers themselves invited the co-operation of an American banking-house with European connections with a view to giving assurance to stock and other security holders that the financial affairs of the company would be conservatively administered. During November a plan was made public for the organization of a railroad clearing-house, intended primarily to embrace only the Southwestern roads. But the scheme was afterward made to include all lines running northwest, west, and southwest of Chicago and St. Louis. In the shape in which it was presented it provoked the opposition of some of the Granger roads, and this led to important modifications. The consideration of the plan was subsequently deferred, and early in December, in response to a general demand for the adoption of some measures which would result in ending the rate wars and in restoring and maintaining tariffs, conferences were held in Chicago by some of the Western railroad managers, which were attended by Commissioners Cooley and Morrison of the Interstate Commission, and the fact was then disclosed that the unsettled condition of the passenger business resulted mainly from the issue of tickets to brokers who were allowed an excessive commission, which course was decided, by Messrs. Cooley and Morrison, to be in violation of law. Revelations of the methods pursued by some railroad officials for the purpose of evading the Interstate Act called forth the expression by the commissioners of a determination to punish such violations of the law as could be proved, and public feeling became aroused to such an extent that a demand was made for radical reforms in railroad management. During the third week in December there was a conference in New York between the presidents of the leading Western roads and bankers with European connections, which resulted in an agreement being made to restore and maintain rates, and to limit the authority of subordinates to change the tariff. Petitions were in circulation at the close of the year for the modification of the Interstate Act, but the commissioners were understood to be opposed to any essential change in the law, and it was regarded as probable that nothing would be done at that session of Congress. The South Carolina Legislature amended the State law so as to restore the power of the railroad commission to regulate rates of freight and passenger transportation. Among the prominent events of the year were the placing of the Missouri, Kansas and Texas in the hands of receivers; the completion of the reorganization of the Philadelphia and Reading, the Texas and Pacific, and the Chesapeake and Ohio; the financial embarrassments of the Atchison, Topeka and Santa Fé, resulting from the Chicago extension and the railroad war in the Southwest; the purchase by Mr. Gould of a control of the St. Louis, Arkansas and Texas; the placing of the Minneapolis and St. Louis in the hands of a receiver; the changes in the management of the Baltimore and Ohio; and the lease by the Louisville, New Albany and Chicago of the Louisville Southern, giving it connection with Chattanooga and the South. Railroad construction was active early in the year, and the new mileage for 1888 was about 7,000 miles, which, at $20,000 per mile for road and equipment, would call for an outlay of about $140,000,000. The following shows gross and net earnings of the principal trunk roads, the reports, except for the Pennsylvania, being made for fiscal years, and the returns of the New York Central including the operation of the West Shore leased line:

ROADS.	1882-'83.	1883-'84.	1884-'85.	1885-'86.	1886-'87.	1887-'88.
PENNSYLVANIA:						
Gross earnings	$51,089,252	$48,566,918	$43,615,084	$50,879,077	$55,671,313	$58,172,068
Net earnings	19,336,102	18,089,902	16,135,269	17,759,482	18,584,728	18,840,925
NEW YORK CENTRAL:						
Gross earnings	33,770,912	28,142,669	24,429,441	30,506,361	85,297,055	36,182,920
Net earnings	13,020,127	10,299,356	8,110,069	11,595,934	12,918,432	8,872,299
ERIE:						
Gross earnings	22,802,246	21,687,485	18,984,573	22,500,046	24,210,353	24,582,519
Net earnings	7,357,663	5,279,358	4,587,056	6,111,408	6,819,685	6,829,350
BALTIMORE AND OHIO:						
Gross earnings	19,787,887	19,486,697	16,616,642	18,422,488	20,659,036	20,358,492
Net earnings	8,705,828	7,760,300	5,643,057	6,986,695	6,538,905	6,152,980

The Crops.—The wheat-crop for the season of 1888, as reported by the Department of Agriculture, was 414,868,000 bushels, while that of corn was 1,987,790,000, or about the largest on record. Good authorities claim that the cotton crop will be not far from 6,900,000 bales. Conditions for winter wheat were unfavorable throughout the entire season, and the average was uniformly low, but the harvest was better than was expected, the average yield being about twelve bushels to the acre. Spring sowed wheat started in good condition, and the highest average was in July. During the following month there was a material reduction, and in September there came frosts in the extreme Northwest which caused irreparable damage in some sections, the extent of which was not fully revealed until after the harvest. Corn planting was delayed in the northern portion of the belt by reason of low temperature, but favoring suns and rain aided in a rapid development of the plant, and the condition was high during the entire season with the exception of Kansas where hot winds and local droughts did some damage. The crop was gathered under very favorable circumstances, and the bulk of it was out of the way of frost before the advent of freezing temperature. The oat crop was unprecedented, being estimated at about 707,737,000 bushels, that of barley at 50,000,000, and that of rye at 25,000,000 bushels. Cotton was late in coming to maturity by reason of heavy rains during September. The indications early in the season pointed to deficient crops of wheat in all the importing countries of Europe, and this news stimulated a prompt movement of the grain to market, and our farmers generally obtained good prices for their product. Toward the close of September speculative manipulation, based upon evidence of a shortage in the crop of spring sowed grain carried the price to two dollars for the options of that month and correspondingly affected the price for later deliveries. This checked exports and caused a sharp advance in the price of flour. Of the 3,568,650 bushels of wheat exported during October only 303,-300 went from the Atlantic ports, the remainder being shipped from San Francisco and other Pacific ports from whence the exports for the corresponding month in 1887, were only 668,-654 bushels. Of the 2,733,694 bushels of wheat exported in November, 2,382,522 were shipped from the Pacific coast. For six months ending December 31, exports of wheat were 28,220,770 bushels, of which 17,584,316 went from California and Oregon, against 44,679,666, of which 10,340,417 from the Pacific ports, for the same time in 1887. Wheat-flour exports for six months this year were 4,843,790 barrels against 6,235,926 for the corresponding period in 1887.

Taking the prices in the New York market on or about January 1 in each year and the total yield for the previous season, we have the following approximate results:

THE CROPS.	Yield.	Price.	Value.
1887.			
Wheat, bushels.......	456,329,000	$0 92	$419,822,680
Corn, bushels	1,456,161,000	63	917,281,430
Cotton, bales	7,017,707	10 7⁄16	359,763,397
1888.			
Wheat, bushels.......	414,868,000	1 01½	421,091,020
Corn, bushels.........	1,987,790,000	46	914,388,400
Cotton, bales.........	6,900,000	9¼	380,006,250

The Stock-Market for 1888.—During the whole of April and July, the greater part of January, June, August, and September, and the latter portion of December, the stock-market was strong, while in March, May, November, and October it was weak, and in February the tendency was generally downward. The declines were at intervals arrested and the current of prices changed by favorable news, manipulation of specialties, and the temporary removal of causes of depression. The cutting of rates by Western, Northwestern, and Southwestern roads continued almost without interruption from the beginning to the end of the year, and the lower revenues resulting therefrom compelled a reduction of dividends to such an extent that, in one case—that of the St. Paul—the European stockholders were induced to unite for self-protection, and in December prominent banking-houses, who represented large investment interests here and abroad, felt called upon to interfere and insist upon the ending of the disastrous rate-war. Through their influence a pledge to restore tariffs was obtained, and the railroad situation improved toward the close of the year. While the principal transportation lines were unfavorably influenced by rate-wars, the stocks of the coal companies reflected the harmonious management of this important interest, and the market-values of these properties almost uniformly improved. There was a more confident feeling at the opening of January regarding the immediate future. This was based upon the expectation of continued ease in money and upon the conviction that the public would soon come into the market, first as purchasers of bonds and then of stocks. There was a good demand from investors at home and abroad for railroad mortgages during the greater part of the month, but it was not until the third week that the inquiry for stocks grew important. Then the market became active, and it continued strong to the close. Reading was unfavorably influenced early in the month by the strike of miners in the Schuylkill region of Pennsylvania, these men demanding an advance in wages and insisting upon the reinstatement of train employés who had been discharged for cause. This strike resulted in a virtual suspension of mining by the Reading during the entire month, but the other coal companies were not unfavorably affected, because the demand for coal was in excess of the supply. Later in the month the very encouraging annual reports of the Delaware, Lackawanna and Western and of the Delaware and Hudson stimulated good buying of these properties. Cutting of rates by some of the Granger roads encouraged attacks by the bears early in the month, and later there was an assault upon Reading and the Gould specialties, but the short interest was so largely increased by these speculative sales that the bull party were enabled to turn the market upward during the third week in the month, the properties which were most largely oversold were sharply advanced, and the tone was strong to the end of the month. In February the course of prices was downward, influenced by vigorous cutting of rates by roads in the Northwest, which soon involved all the Granger lines, and, toward the close of the month, by the strike of the engineers on the Chicago, Burlington and Quincy, caused by the refusal of a demand for increased wages, and also by the adherence of the company to its rule for a classification of engineers according to length of service and the character of the work they performed. Early in the first week of the month the pacific tenor of a speech by Prince Bismarck before the German Parliament had a stimulating effect upon the European markets, and the improvement there was reflected in our own. This was followed by selling some of the trunk-line stocks on the theory that the fight between the Granger roads would involve Eastern connections, but subsequently the action of the trunk-line executive committee in settling export rates and ignoring cuts by Western lines tended to bring about a reaction. During the second week the Granger war was less vigorously prosecuted, and the strike of the miners in the Schuylkill region was practically ended. This news aided in a decided recovery. The movement was irregular, although generally upward, in the third week, but during the closing days of the month the engineers' strike, selling of stocks for European account, and bearish demonstrations caused the market to close heavy. Rate-cutting was vigorously prosecuted by Western roads during March, until near the end, when there was an agreement to restore rates; but while the war was in progress the stocks of the Granger roads were more or less unsettled. Reading was unfavorably affected early in the month by decreased net earnings for January. The striking engineers of the Chicago, Burlington and Quincy were warring against the road in every conceivable manner, endeavoring to prevent its successful operation with non-union engineers, and rumors that other Western lines would be involved had a depressing effect. The embargo upon business in this section, and the suspension of trading on the stock-exchange, resulting from the blizzard of March 12, did not immediately unfavorably influence the market, for as soon as business was resumed purchases of stocks for European account carried prices sharply upward, but toward the close of that week news of the strike on the Atchison, Topeka and Santa Fé, the men sympathizing with the engineers of the Chicago, Burlington and Quincy, and rumors of similar trouble on the Union Pacific, brought about a downward reaction. Then followed a recovery, assisted by the declaration that the strike on the Chicago, Burlington and Quincy was practically ended, the company securing a full complement of new men, and also by the agreement of West-

ern roads to cease cutting and to restore rates; but before the close of that week Missouri Pacific fell heavily on a rumor, subsequently confirmed, that the dividend would be reduced. During the last week of the month Reading was attacked on the news that the statement for February would show a large loss in net earnings, and the market was more or less unsettled to the close in consequence of bearish attacks and disquieting rumors regarding the railroad situation in the West. The strike on the Chicago, Burlington and Quincy was officially declared off April 4, the attempt to induce the switchmen at Chicago to assist the engineers by refusing to handle freight of the company having failed, and this was the first signal defeat of the Brotherhood of Engineers since the strike of 1877. Another important event affecting the stock-market was the action of Congress on the Bond Purchase measure, which was immediately followed by an order by the Secretary of the Treasury directing purchases of 4 and 4½ per cent. bonds; and another event was the breaking of the deadlock in the House of Representatives over the Direct Tax Refund Bill, that body having been in continuous session for nine days, thereby obstructing important legislation. The movement in stocks was a little feverish during the first few days of the month owing to disquieting rumors from the West, but it soon felt the influence of the ending of the Chicago, Burlington and Quincy strike and of the other events above noted, and there was a substantial recovery in the market, which continued, almost uninterruptedly, to the close, large purchases of bonds by the Secretary of the Treasury after the 23d almost daily stimulating an advance. The rise in some of the properties was so rapid during April, that in May realizing sales and bearish attacks were invited, and the tendency of the market was downward. The course of prices was, however, only gradually changed. In the first week of the month the bears sought to force declines, but their efforts appeared to be resisted by purchases for European and domestic account. The Northern Pacifics were favorably affected by reports of negotiations for the purchase of a large tract of land; and Missouri Pacific and the other Gould specialties advanced in consequence of speculative manipulation. The bears first attacked New England, Reading, and Union Pacific. Then advantage was taken of unfavorable weather for the crops to assail the Grangers. The decline was checked on the 16th by the news of the prompt taking in London of the Baltimore and Ohio loan for $10,000,000, and this indicated the favorable reception of the Reading loan when that should be offered, but in the following week gold exports to Germany on special order were large, the liquidation of the pools in Reading, St. Paul, and New England was discovered, and persistent attacks by the bears carried prices downward until the 25th, when news that a syndicate had bought $24,-686,000 of the Reading 4-per-cents, and $11,-946,880 of the first preference incomes caused a rise in that stock in which the whole market sympathized. During the last few days of the month, however, the bears renewed their attacks upon the market, assailing Missouri Pacific, New England, Reading, and St. Paul, and the fall in these made the movement more or less unsettled to the close. Stocks were unfavorably affected during June by the prolonged discussion of the tariff bill in the House; by the action of the Iowa railroad commissioners in promulgating rates below those formerly ruling; by cuts by the trunk lines; and by reduced dividends on some of the principal Western roads. One prominent event was the placing of the Reading 4-per-cent. fifty-year loan in London and New York, and another was the purchase by the Pullman of the Baltimore and Ohio palace-car outfit. The course of the market was irregularly downward until about the middle of the second week, when there was a reaction, due to a covering of short contracts, and prices were not affected by the news, on the 15th, of the death of the Emperor Frederick, of Germany, as the foreign markets were not in the least influenced thereby. During the third week the tendency was generally upward, and the existence of a large short interest not only aided in sustaining prices, but it encouraged the bulls to advance some of their specialties. The market gradually improved in tone and in activity during July. Crop-prospects were excellent; the Iowa railroad managers were looking for a favorable decision in their suit before the United States Court to restrain the Iowa railroad commissioners from enforcing the new distance tariff of rates, and there was good buying of stocks for European account. The Grangers, the coal-shares, the Gould specialties, and the Northern Pacific properties, took the lead early in the month. Then came a rise in Western Union, based upon the favorable outlook for the ending of the cable-rate war, and later there was an advance in Louisville and Nashville, encouraged by the expectation that a stock dividend would soon be declared. New York and New England and American cotton-seed oil certificates were the favorites with speculators in this class of stocks, and Delaware, Lackawanna and Western and Delaware and Hudson were directly affected by the improved prospects of the coal-trade. Toward the close of the month the Grangers were favorably influenced by the decision of Judge Brewer in the Iowa railroad cases, and thereafter for the remainder of the month the market was active and strong. In the first few days of August the leaders were New England, Lake Shore, Western Union, Reading, the other coal properties, and Union Pacific. The Grangers were favorably affected by news from the crops, and soon after the opening of the month one feature was a well-sustained specu-lative movement in Delaware, Lackawanna and Western. During the first week there was a sharp fall in Central New Jersey, caused by the marketing of a block of stock owned by the Lehigh Valley, but when this was disposed of there was a rapid recovery. The tendency of the market was downward in the second week, the bulls among the traders having sold their stocks, and the bears being encouraged to indulge in raids. The Grangers were affected by news of frosts, and there was some selling of St. Paul in expectation of reduced dividends. Early in the following week there was a manipulated advance in the last-named stock, the coal-shares were pushed upward, and later the Vanderbilt specialities took the lead, followed by the Northern Pacifics and the Oregons, the two latter being affected by the news that the remainder of the Northern Pacific third mortgage had been sold to a Frankfort syndicate. Toward the close of this week the Grangers fell off in consequence of cutting of rates, and the Canadian stocks were unfavorably affected by the message of the President on the relations of this country with Canada. During the last week in the month there was a further advance in Delaware, Lackawanna and Western, and in the other coal-shares, in the Northern Pacifics, and in the Oregons, and later in the Grangers, which were influenced by the decision of State Judge Fairall in the Iowa railroad cases, he restraining the commissioners from putting into effect the new tariff. The market closed strong. European purchases of stocks, manipulation of leading Granger and coal properties, based upon a prosperous crop and coal season, and liberal buying of stocks by domestic investors and speculators caused prices to rise rapidly during the early part of September. Then followed a sharp fall in St. Paul, due to the passing of the dividend on the common stock, succeeded by as rapid a rise on news that the foreign stockholders had combined for mutual protection against the management, and one prominent feature thereafter was a well-sustained advance in New England. The market was generally strong to the close. One feature toward the end of the month was a heavy fall in Hocking Valley on the news that the arbitrators in the suit against J. S. Burke had decided against the company. Considering the fact that the news was unfavorable early in October, stocks held up remarkably well. There were unsettled grain-markets resulting from the wheat deal at Chicago, a good inquiry for money for the West, a suspension on the 10th of purchases of 4-per-cents. by the Secretary of the Treasury, the financial embarrassment of the Atchison, Topeka and Santa Fé, and liquidation by some of the pools in the specialities. Early in the second week the bears indulged in frequent raids, but the effect of these was to some extent counteracted by manipulation of New York and New England, the Grangers, Union Pacific, and Reading, and also by liberal purchases of bonds by the Secretary of the Treasury. Toward the end of the week an unsettled market in Boston. due to a further fall in Atchison, Topeka and Santa Fé, affected the speculation here, but supporting orders caused the market to close strong. During the third week it was announced that the financial embarrassments of the Atchison, Topeka and Sante Fé had been relieved by the issue of three-year notes for $7,000,000. secured by a short second mortgage, but this had only a temporary effect upon the stock, which steadily declined, unfavorably influencing New England and nearly all properties owned in or managed from Boston. An abstract of the annual report of the Missouri Pacific making unsatisfactory disclosures caused a sharp fall in that property, and about the only strong stocks during the remainder of the week were the Vanderbilt specialties, Union Pacific, Richmond Terminal, and the East Tennessees, the two latter being affected by the lease by the former of the East Tennessee, Virginia, and Georgia. In the early part of the last week of the month one feature was a fall in Reading incomes, caused by doubts as to the ability of the company to meet the interest, and this decline affected the stock. Another feature was a further fall in Atchison, Topeka and Santa Fé on the publication of the annual report. Then came a rise in the Gould specialties, assisted by a rumor, which was subsequently denied, that Mr. Gould had obtained control of the Atchison, Topeka and Sante Fé, and this was followed by an advance in New England, American cotton-seed oil, and in other low-priced specialties. There was a fairly strong tone to the market during the first few days of November, and a very confident feeling that no matter what was the result of the presidential election there would be a more active speculation. On the day following the election the market opened very strong, but there was an immediate selling movement, mainly due to realizations, assisted by rumors of rate troubles on the trunk lines, and the tendency was generally downward for the remainder of the week. On the following Monday the announcement was made that the New York Central had ordered a reduction of one third in the rates for west bound business, the excuse being that some of the other lines were getting traffic by cutting rates. This caused free selling of all the trunk-line stocks, confidence in the future of the market was unsettled, the bears were encouraged to raid leading properties, and the tendency was downward for the remainder of the week and until about the middle of the following week, when news that the Southwestern troubles were likely soon to be adjusted and that negotiations had been opened for settlement of the trunk-line differences started a covering of short contracts which carried the market upward. Then came news of large withdrawals of gold on special order for Berlin and

London, and this again encouraged attacks by the bears, but later the declaration of the usual dividends on the Chicago and Northwestern and a confirmation of reports that an agreement had been made to restore rates among the Southwestern roads brought about a recovery, and the market closed strong for all except New England, which was freely sold in consequence of the closing of the transfer books, thus setting at rest rumors that there would be a contest for control. The tendency was generally downward for the remainder of the month, with a sharp fall in Rock Island as the feature during the last week, but the trunk lines were inclined to improve on news that a partial agreement had been made to restore rates on west bound business. In December the course of this market was generally downward until toward the close. During the first week Atchison, Topeka and Santa Fé and Missouri Pacific were unsettled and lower, and the last-named stock sold at the lowest figures recorded since 1884. but there was subsequently a recovery on the announcement that at a meeting of the executive committee an order had been issued to take no more business except at remunerative rates, it then appearing that the tariff had been cut about 40 per cent. on some classes below the published schedule. Toward the close of the week the whole market advanced on news that rates would be restored on the 17th on the trunk lines. In the second week the tone was generally stronger under the lead of the coal-shares, and it was also favorably influenced by the declaration of the usual quarterly dividend on Missouri Pacific. Rock Island was, however, freely sold at intervals in expectation that the dividend would be reduced. During the third week the market was favorably affected by united efforts on the part of Western railroad managers to put an end to the demoralization which existed in that section and in the Southwest. Agreements were formulated and generally signed to restore rates on freight on January 1, and to prevent further cuts in passenger tariffs by withdrawing tickets in the hands of brokers. Toward the close of the week an important conference was held in New York, at which were present the presidents of all Western lines, except the Chicago and Alton, and representatives of three leading banking-houses with foreign connections, and at this meeting it was agreed that the rates then ordered restored should be maintained. This action was regarded as definitely settling the railroad situation, the market responded in a very decided rise, which was assisted by a manipulated advance in Delaware, Lackawanna and Western, and the tone was strong at the close of that week. The declaration of a 1-per-cent. quarterly dividend on Rock Island caused a further fall in that stock to the lowest figures since 1877, but it subsequently reacted. Early in the last week of the month the market was favorably influenced by the declaration of the dividends on the Vanderbilt specialties, and by a further improvement in the Western railroad situation; but it was a little irregular after Wednesday in consequence of active money, although the tone was generally strong to the close. Total sales of all stocks for the year 1888 were 65,179,206 shares against 85,-291,028 in 1887; 100,802,050 in 1886; 93,184,-478 in 1885; 95,416,368 in 1884; 96,037,905 in 1883; 113,720,665 in 1882; 113,392,685 in 1881; and 97,919,099 in 1880. The transactions in Government bonds at the New York Stock Exchange in 1888 were $6,573,700, and in railroad and miscellaneous bonds, $345,214,-057. The following table shows quotations of leading stocks at the beginning of January, 1887, 1888, and 1889:

LEADING STOCKS.	1887.	1888.	1889.
New York Central	118½	107½	108
Erie	84½	28⅛	27¼
Lake Shore	90½	94¼	104⅛
Michigan Central	98½	87½	87⅜
Rock Island	120¼	112½	97
Illinois Central	138	118¼	115
Northwest, common	115¼	107½	108¼
St. Paul, common	90½	75⅝	64
Dela., Lackawanna and Western	136¾	129¼	144¾
Central New Jersey	55⅝	75	95½

The following table shows the highest and lowest prices of a few of the speculative stocks in 1888 and the highest in 1887:

SPECULATIVE AND OTHER SHARES.	1887.	1888.	
	Highest.	Highest.	Lowest.
Canadian Pacific	68⅜	62½	51½
Canada Southern	64⅝	57⅛	45¼
Central New Jersey	86½	95½	73¼
Central Pacific	48⅜	87⅛	26¼
Chattanooga	88½	85½	71
Cleveland, Col., C., and Ind	68	65	42½
Consolidated Gas	89	83¼	68⅛
Delaware and Hudson	106¼	134	103
Dela., Lackawanna and Western	189¼	145½	128¼
Erie	85¼	80½	22¾
Hocking Valley	89½	86¼	17
Lake Shore	98½	104⅛	85½
Louisville and Nashville	70½	64½	50¾
Manhattan Elevated Consol	161½	98¼	77½
Michigan Central	95¼	92½	72
Missouri, Kansas, and Texas	84½	18⅛	10
Missouri Pacific	112	80½	66½
New York Central	114¾	111	102½
New York and New England	66	53½	29½
Northwestern	127¾	116	102½
Northern Pacific	84¼	29½	19½
Northern Pacific, preferred	63¼	64	42½
Omaha	54½	42½	81½
Omaha, preferred	118¼	110½	93
Oregon Transcontinental	85¼	82	17½
Pacific Mail	58⅜	40¼	28½
Reading	71½	54⅞	44⅜
Richmond Terminal	58	29½	19
Rock Island	140⅞	114¼	94⅞
St Paul	95	78	59½
Texas and Pacific	85¼	26⅜	18⅜
Union Pacific	68¼	66¼	48
Western Union	81⅞	86½	70¼

FINE ARTS IN 1888. Under this title are treated the principal art events of the past year, ending with December, 1888, including especially the great exhibitions in Europe and the United States, the sales and acquisitions of works of art, and the erection of public statues and monuments.

Paris: Salon.—The exhibition (May 1 to June 30) comprised 5,523 numbers (selected from 7,640 presented), classified as follows: Paintings, 2,586; cartoons, water-colors, pastels, porcelain pictures, etc., 1,119 sculpture, 1,059; engraving in medals and precious stones, 57; architecture, 180; engraving, 522.

Section of painting: Medal of honor awarded to Édouard Detaille by 108 votes against 96 to Benjamin-Constant. First-class medals: Paul Louis Delance, Nils Forsberg. Second-class medals: Gustave Édouard Le Sénéchal, Gaston Latouche, Auguste Joseph Truphème, Nicolas Berthon, Aimé Perret, Louis Victor Watelin, Louis Le Poittevin, Arsène Rivey, Paul Leroy, Auguste Flameng, Georges Callot, Maurice Jeannin. Third-class medals: Édouard Grandjean, Jean Brunet, Joseph Aubert, Abel Boyer, Léon Boudot, Émile Isenbart, Amand Laroche, Léon Richet, Franc Lamy, Alexis Vollon, Alfred Smith, Daniel Ridgway Knight, Théophile Henri Décanis, Walter Gay, Jacques Louis Odier, Guignon, Adrien Jourdeuil, William Henry Howe, Paul Lecomte, Eugène Dauphin, Étienne Tournès, Paul Schmitt, J. Gari Melchers, John Lavery, Eugène Laurent Vail, Michel Matins, Henry Mosler, Aymar Pezant, François Sallé, Gotthardt Kuehl, Karl Cartier, Johannes Grimelund, Mlle. Maximilienne Guyon.

Section of sculpture: Medal of honor awarded to Jean Turcan, by 98 out of 168 votes. No first-class medal awarded. Second-class medals: Henri Louis Levasseur, Eugène Quinton, Camille Lefèvre, Louis Joseph Enderlin, Joseph Gardet, Pierre Barbaroux. Third-class medals: Louis Dominique Mathet, Louis Auguste Baralis, Léon Kinsburger, Ringel d'Illzach, Hippolyte Peyrol, Léon Pilet, Charles Jacquot, Louis Holweck, Eugène Robert, Paul François Choppin, François Pompon, Christian Erickson.

Section of engraving: Medal of honor awarded to Edmond Hédouin, by 99 votes against 60 to Achille Jacquet. No first-class medal awarded. Second-class medals: Léon Boisson (line engraving), Auguste Hilaire Laveillé (wood). Third-class medals: Messrs. Eugène Fornet, Ricardo de los Rios, Paul Émile Leterrier, Claude Faivre, and Mme. Marie Louveau-Rouveyre (etching); Charles Théodore Deblois (line); Hippolyte Constant Dutheil, Théodore Delangle, Jean Baptiste Guillaume, Claude Faivre (wood); Georges William Thornley, Hippolyte Fanchon (lithography).

Section of architecture: Medal of honor awarded to Henri Adolphe Deglane, unanimously. First-class medal: Charles Louis Girault. Second-class medals: Jean Hardion, Gabriel Ruprich-Robert, Jean Bréasson, Gaston Redon, Charles Georges Roussi. Third-class medals: Émile Jay, Arsène Pierre Lafargue, Eugène Rigault, Paul Laffollye, Édouard Michel Lewicki, Augustin Salleron.

Édouard Detaille, to whom was awarded the medal of honor, exhibited an enormous landscape crowded with figures, entitled "Le Rêve," which must rank as his masterpiece. It represents a plain just after dawn, with gently rising land occupied by a host of French infantry bivouacking on the heather, among white bowlders and wild flowers, with sentinels guarding piled arms and watch-fires with drifting smoke. Above, in a cloudy sky tinged with rosy light, is a vision of innumerable soldiers of the First Empire, infantry, cavalry, and artillery, with eagles and shot-torn banners, moving eastward in noiseless array.

Benjamin-Constant, who stood next to Detaille in the contest for the medal of honor, was represented by a huge decorative triptych, entitled "L'Académie de Paris, les Lettres, les Sciences," destined for the Salle du Conseil, in the Sorbonne. In the middle division, seated in a semi-circle of columns, are the rector and elders of the Academy, (all portraits), in modern costumes under amber, red, black, and violet gowns. In "Les Lettres" a muse in green and black is addressing the muses of lyric poetry, history, and tragedy, grouped on a marble bench in a splendid portico. In "Les Sciences" are figures typifying astronomy, engineering, etc., one of whom is instructing a workman. The work is distinguished, like all the artist's pictures, for vivid coloring and rich imagination.

Paul Louis Delance, first-class medalist, illustrated on another huge canvas "La Légende de Saint-Denis." In a landscape of ancient Paris and its environs, with a summer atmosphere and sky, the saint, who has been decapitated, walks to the resting-place which bears his own name, carrying his own head, his shoulders and bleeding neck being decorated with a gilded nimbus. The peasants, who are startled at meeting the apparition, are full of spirit, and a kneeling woman is very pathetic. Notwithstanding the incongruous subject, the artist has made a noble picture, striking in massing and coloring.

An enormous composition of nude figures, more than life-size, is Albert Maignan's "Les Voix du Tocsin." A great bell, hung in a lofty tower, is rung by the hands of spirits who, swinging in the air, tug at the ropes with might and main. Other demons hover around the clanging bell, while a third set scream, shout, and weep as they fly out from beneath it. Below is a conflagration with ruddy glare and drifting smoke. The conception is poetical, and the draughtmanship and coloring excellent.

Opposite it hung "L'Enlèvement de Proserpine," by Ulpiano Checa, a pupil of the Academy of Madrid. Though somewhat theatrical in parts, the four black horses of Pluto, with breath of smoke and eyes of fire, are notable for excellent painting and good foreshortening.

Bouguereau's "Premier Deuil" represents Adam and Eve mourning over the corpse of Abel. Adam, seated, holding across his knees the body of his son, stoops to kiss the head of Eve who, kneeling by his side, weeps with hands clasped to her face. The figures, life-size, are magnificent studies of the nude, so colorless as to look like sculptures, but full of dignity, grace, and feeling. Another contribution by this master, entitled "Baigneuse," is a life-size, full-length, nude figure of a beautiful young girl, drying one foot on a rock while steadying herself by holding a hanging bough.

"Esclaves à Vendre," by Gustave Boulanger, represents slaves exposed for sale in Rome. A Gallic maiden, nude, with a wooden label fastened about her neck, leans wearily against the wall, while a huge Numidian, with impassive features, his arms embracing his knees, squats on the ground beside her.

Jules Lefebvre's "L'Orpheline" shows a nobly-painted church interior, with an old woman in cloak and hood kneeling in prayer in one of the pews, and a pale child clad in mourning seated beside her, looking outward with sorrowful eyes, as if in a dream. It is a pathetic work, of masterly execution.

"La Naissance de Benjamin," by Émile Lévy, is an interior with small, full-length figures. A pallid mother lies on a couch covered with white bed-linen, while an attendant, holding the child poised on one hand, turns toward her, and other women stand around. It is all a broad, massive composition, of delicate and harmonious tone.

Jules Breton's "Jeunes Filles se rendant à la Procession" is a village scene with a procession of peasant girls, such as he loves to paint.

Lhermitte's "Le Repos," shows a group of reapers, more robust and real than Breton's peasants, and firmly and broadly treated.

Philippe Roll's "Manda Lamétrie, Fermière," a milkmaid with filled pail, standing beside a cow, in an atmosphere of light and sunshine, is a remarkable work, with reminiscences of Bastien-Lepage.

"The Communion," of Henry Lerolle, is a large canvas, with life-size figures of women in brown, gray, and black dresses, listening to a priest addressing the communicants kneeling at the altar-rail of a vast church. It is in the simple, flat tones characteristic of the painter, so noticeable in his earlier work, "Jeune Fille chantant dans une Église," now in the Metropolitan Museum, New York.

Henner is represented by a Saint Sébastien, a nearly life-size corpse lying among rocks, with three women, one of whom is drawing an arrow from the body; and by a portrait, a girl with heavy masses of red hair flowing over her bosom, which is partly draped with a light-blue robe falling from the shoulders.

Hébert's "Aux Héros sans Gloire," a mournful woman with impassive features and dark eyes set in an olive face, her unbound black tresses crowned with laurel, sits in a mysterious half-gloom—the genius of heroic Death. She wears a purple robe bound with a black girdle, and leans with one arm on a marble urn, while a wreath of convolvulus drops from her hand.

Pictures exhibited by American artists: J. C. Arter, "Interieur-Picardie"; Edmond Aubrey-Hunt, "Honfleur"; Henry Bacon, "Construction d'un Bateau"; William Baird, "La Seine";

Ellen K. Baker, "Rêverie" and "Un Nourrisson"; Edward H. Barnard, Portrait; Henry Bisbing, "La Sieste sur le Rivage—Hollande" and "Un Coin de la Ferme—Normandie"; Sadie Blackstone (Canada), "Senlisse—Vallée de Chevreuse"; Carl Blenner, Portrait; Émile Boggio (Venezuela), "Lecture"; Frank M. Boggs "Harfleur" and "Le Havre"; Dwight F. Boyden, "La Route de Lafaux" and "L'Antonine"; Amanda Brewster, Portraits (2); Frederick A. Bridgman, "Dans une Villa de Campagne—Alger" and "Soit d'Été—Alger"; Blair Bruce (Canada), "Le Fantôme de la Neige"; Edgar Cameron, "Dans l'Atelier"; Kate Augusta Karl, "Le Choix d'une Romance"; Leslie G. Cauldwell, Portrait; Francis B. Chadwick, "La Mère Rabicotte"; Murray Clinton-Smith "Dans les Marais de Criquebœuf"; Maximilien Colin, "Atelier de Dames"; Irving Conse, "Fleur de Prison"; L. H. Coyner, "Nature Mort"; Alger Currier, "Déesse" and "A la santé!"; Ralph Curtis, "Carmen"; George D. Monfried, "Chemin en Cerdagne" and "Église d'Angoustrine"; Wilder Darling, "La Première Visite de la Grand'mère"; Charles H. Davis, "Un Soir d'Hiver" and "Avril"; Louis Paul Dessar, "L'Orphelin"; Henry Patrice Dillon, "Mort de Paul Bert"; William L. Dodge, "David"; Pauline Dohn, "Tête d'Enfant"; J. D. P. Douglas, "Brutalité"; Julie Dunn, "Automne"; Frank Duveneck, Portrait; José Thomas Errazuris (Chili), "Sur les Dunes" and Portrait; Charles S. Forbes, Portrait; Jesse Leach France, "Marée Basse—Bretagne"; Elizabeth Jane Gardner, "Deux Mères de Famille"; Walter Gay, "Le Bénédicité" and "Un Asile"; Rosalie Gill, Portrait; Abbott Graves, "Pivoines"; Clifford Grayson, "Étude"; Eleanor Greatorex, "Pasqua Fiorita—Florence"; Kathleen Greatorex, "Les Fleurs du Vent—Florence"; R. Hewett Green, "Marchande de Fleurs"; Charlotte Gore Greenough, "Entrée de la Château de la Grand' Cour, près Dinan"; Edward Grenet, "Ballade à la Lune"; Peter Alfred Gross, "Place de la Fontaine, à Liverdun," and "Liverdun sur la Moselle"; Philip L. Hale, "Petite Fille aux Chrysanthèmes"; Alexauder Harrison, "Marée Haute"; Birge Harrison, "Départ du Mayflower"; A. Butler Harrison, "La Lande"; Herman Hartwich, "Le Sieste"; Childe Hassam, "Jour du Grand Prix"; Herman G. Herkomer, Portrait; Bertha Hewit, "Les Sœurs"; George Hitchcock, "L'Annonciation"; S. Francis Holman, Portrait; Samuel Isham, Portrait; Louisa Rogers Jewett, Portrait; John Kavanagh, "Le Maitre d'École de Village" and Portrait; Anna Elizabeth Klumpke, "Á la Buanderie" and Portrait; Daniel Ridgway Knight, "L'Appel au Passeur"; Eugene Armand La Chaise, Portrait; Lucy Lee Robbins, "Nonchalance" and Portrait; Pedro Francisco Lira (Chili), "Femme Chilienne Vouée à Notre-Dame-de-Merci" and "Raccommodeuse Chilienne"; Eurilda Loomis, "Vie Rustique—Picardie"; Francis W. Loring, "Le Pont à Chioggia"; Albert Lynch (Peru), "L'Hiver"

and "Sortie de Bal"; Walter Mac Ewen, "Une Histoire de Revenant"; Ernest L. Major, Sainte-Geneviève"; William L. Marcy, Portrait; Arthur F. Matthews, "Pandore" and "En Hollande"; J. G. Melchers, "Les Pilotes"; Willard Leroy Metcalf, "Marché de 'Kousse Kousse' à Tunis"; Arturo Michelena (Venezuela), "Charité" and "Étude"; Henry Mosler, "La Captive Blanche" and "Fête de la Moisson"; Albert H. Munsell, "Navire Droit Devant"; Carl Newman, "Une Religieuse"; Elizabeth Nourse, "Une Mère!"; Stephen Hills Parker, "Pandore"; Charles Sprague Pearce, "La Rentrée du Troupeau"; Clinton Peters, Portrait; William L. Picknell, "Novembre—Solitude"; J. A. Prichard, "La Prière"; Robert L. Reid, "La Fuite en Egypte"; Charles S. Reinhart, "L'Attente des Absents" and "La Marée Montante"; Theodore Robinson, "Un Apprenti Forgeron"; Pedro Rodriguez-Flyel (Venezuela), "La Fête d'une Jenue Mère" and Portrait; Cristobal Rojas (Venezuela), "Première Communion" and "Vente par Autorité de Justice"; Julius Rolshoven, "Hamlet"; Andre Santa-Maria (Colombia), "Un Refuge"; Frank Scott, "Retour de la Pêche"; Robert V. V. Sewell, Portrait; Edward E. Simmons, "Le Fils du Charpentier" and "Mère et Enfant"; Marie Simpson, "Le Déjeuner du Pauvre"; Eduard Sivori (Buenos Ayres), "La Mort d'un Paysan" and "Sans Famille"; Frank Otis Small, "Ramsès et sa Fille jouant aux Échecs"; William J. Smedley, "Le Bateau du Père"; Ellen Starbuck, Portrait; Julius L. Stewart, Portrait; Frank W. Stokes, "Les Orphelines" and "Un Bon Sermon"; George M. Stone, Portrait; Charles H. Strickland, Portrait; Elizabeth Strong, "Les Orphelines"; Frances Hunt Throop, "Le Réveil"; Georgette Timpkin, "La Moisson"; Gaylord S. Truesdell, "Le Berger et Son Troupeau"; Miss Sydney Tully (Canada), "Étude"; Miss Jessie B. Tuttle, "Un Coin de Village"; Alfredo Valenzuela-Puelma (Chili), Portrait; Pierre L. L. Vautheir (Brazil), "Le Port de Rouen"; Robert W. Vonnoh, Portrait; Lionel Walden, "Sur la Tamise"; Charles T. Webber, Portraits (2); Cecilia E. Wentworth, Portrait; Ogden Wood, "Dans les Dunes"; Percy Woodcock (Canada), "Fin du Jour."

The Salon receipts for the season were 400,-000 francs, which leaves, after deducting 240,-000 francs for expenses, 160,000 francs to be added to the invested capital of the Société des Artistes Français. As this amounted last year to 747,429 francs, the Société now has a capital of more than 900,000 francs, for the advancement of the arts and to the aid of unfortunate artists.

Paris: Miscellaneous.—The National Museums of France—the Louvre, the Luxembourg, Versailles, and Saint-Germain—and all objects of art in state buildings are, by a decree of last September, placed under one director, appointed by the President of the republic on the nomination of the Minister of Instruction. His official quarters will be in the Louvre.

A gallery of portraits of artists, painted mostly by themselves, similar to that of the Uffizi, Florence, was opened in the Pavillon Denou, at the Louvre, in February. It constitutes already a very valuable collection, made up of works from Versailles, the Louvre, the Luxembourg, the École des Beaux-Arts, and other public galleries.

The Académie des Beaux-Arts, section of painting, elected as a member, in place of Gustave Boulanger, deceased, Gustave Moreau, by 19 votes, against 10 for Jules Lefebvre, 5 for Jean Jacques Henner, and 1 for Émile Lévy.

The École des Beaux-Arts has had under instruction during the past year 1,220 pupils, of whom 600 were in the architecture classes, while only about 400 were students of painting. During the same time the Royal Academy of London had only about 200 pupils.

The sale of the Goldschmidt collection in Paris, in May, produced in the aggregate 1,067,-094 francs, of which the fifty-three pictures by modern masters brought 795,570 francs. Among the best prices obtained, were: Troyon, "Vallée de la Toucque," 175,000 francs, bought by M. Bischofsheim ; "La Barrière," 101,000 francs ; "L'Abreuvoir," 35,000 francs ; "Chèvres et Roses," 16,000 francs. Delacroix: "Côtes du Maroc," 30,000 francs ; "Herminie et les Vergers," 25,400 francs ; "Christ en Croix," 15,600 francs ; "Enlèvement de Rebecca," 29,-100 francs ; "Joueurs d'Échecs, 12,200 francs ; "Cavalier Grec," 9,200 francs. Dupré: "Moulin à Vent," 20,100 francs ; "Sous Bois," 16,710. Théodor Rousseau : "La Rivière," 25,000 francs ; "Fôret de Fontainebleau," 7,000 francs. Décamps: "Une Cour de Ferme," 30,400 francs ; "Paysan Italien," 12,000 francs ; "La Porchère," 19,200 francs ; "Boule Dogue et Terrier," 16,000 francs (Louvre). Meissonier: "Le Docteur," 17,000 francs. Ziem: "Vue de Venise," 26,000 francs. Géricault : "Amazone," 8,500 francs.

The collection of Comte Duchatel, ancient and modern pictures, sold in Paris, May 14, brought 176,250 francs. The highest prices realized were: Jules Breton, "Les Vendanges à Château-Lagrange," 29,100 francs ; Meissonier, "Un Poète," 40,000 francs ; Ruysdael, "Cascade," 30,000 francs ; Van der Heyden, "Eglise et Place de Ville," (Holland), 19,500 francs.

The Poidatz collection, sold in Paris in March, produced in the aggregate 116,000 francs. Daubigny's "Pont de Mantes" and Millet's "Tonte des Moutons" (sheep-shearing) brought each 13,000 francs.

The Gellinard collection, sold March 19, produced 199,916 francs. Corot's "Diana and Nymphs" brought 12,000 francs, and his "Martyrdom of St. Sebastian," 15,000 francs.

The sale of the works of the late Gustave Guillaumet, painter, in Paris, realized 265,000 francs. His work entitled "Le Désert," was presented by the family to the state.

A monument to Gambetta, a pedestal of stone crowned by a group in bronze, representing a young woman seated on a winged lion—symbolizing "Triumphant Democracy"—with other symbolic groups at the base, was unveiled, July 13, in the Place du Carrousel, Paris. It is the work of MM. Boileau, architect, and Aubé, sculptor, and was erected by subscription.

A bronze statue of Shakespeare, by Paul Fournier, presented to the city of Paris by William Knighton, was unveiled, October 14, at the intersection of the Boulevard Haussmann and the Avenue de Messine. The figure is three metres and four metres and fifty centimetres.

London: Royal Academy.—The nineteenth winter exhibition was devoted, as usual, to works of the old masters and deceased British artists, gathered from public and private collections, with the additional attraction of a collection of sculpture and Renaissance bronzes and medals. Only about 160 pictures were shown, but among them were Titian's "Europa"; Ribera's "St. Jerome praying in the Desert"; Velasquez's "Femme à l'Éventail" and "Don Balthazar Carlos"; Claude's "Europa" and "Enchanted Castle"; and several Rembrandts and Vandykes. There were also examples of Hobbema, Ruysdael, Jan Steen, Hals, and Van de Velde, and of Reynolds, Gainsborough, and others of the British school.

The one hundred and twentieth annual exhibition opened in May with 2,077 numbers, selected from nearly 6,000 contributions, including oil-paintings, water-colors, works in black and white, architectural drawings, and sculptures. The total attendance during the season was 356,118 ; total receipts, £23,346 ; total value of works sold, £21,599.

Of first importance among the pictures exhibited is Sir Frederick Leighton's "Captive Andromache," a decorative work measuring seven feet by fourteen, illustrating the passage in the Iliad where Hector tells of his prevision of her fate, when she shall have fallen into the hands of the Greeks. The scene represents the farmyard of Pyrrhus, in Thessaly, with buildings on the left ; on the right is a fountain pouring from a lion's head in the wall into a marble basin, and between them a long vista of trees and meadows, with an intensely blue sky laden with white thunder-clouds. In the middle, Andromache, clad in black, forms one of a company of women slaves who, at decline of day, have gathered at the fountain. Standing with her chin resting in one hand, while the other sustains her elbow, she is half-aroused from her sorrowful memories by the gambols of an infant, the center of a group in the foreground at the right. Near the front three stalwart peasants look toward her as they walk quickly past, and at the left, behind Andromache, are children and another group of damsels. It shows all of Sir Frederick's peculiarities, and is marked by fine drawing, learned conventionalism, painstaking care, and grace, but is rather an elaborate bas-relief than a scene of life.

Alma-Tadema's "Roses of Heliogabalus" illustrates one of the boyish pranks of the emperor of nineteen, who has overwhelmed his guests at a banquet by a shower of roses which slaves have been heaping on the velarium overhead as the feast proceeded. Heliogabalus, his lentil-shaped eyes suggesting his Syrian origin, reclines, partly covered with a mantle of cloth of gold, on a silver couch, holding near his lips a cylix, from which he delays to drink, as he watches the struggles of his guests. In technical skill and in richness of color the painter has never excelled this work, but its want of composition leads one to regret that so much labor has been spent on such a subject.

Sir John Millais's "Cairnleeth Moss, Birnam" ($4\frac{1}{2} \times 7$ feet), may serve as a companion-piece to "Over the Hills and Far Away." All the foreground is marsh with clumps of moss and rushes mirrored in tinted pools; in the middistance is meadow-land with a dark belt of pines, and in the background rugged hills. His "Murthly Moss, Perthshire" (5 feet square), represents Murthly Castle at Christmas-eve, 1887, with the warm light of late afternoon on the snow, over which crows are skimming.

Solomon J. Solomon's "Niobe," one of the successes of the year, depicts the anguish-stricken mother standing upon a flight of steps, convulsively clinging to the dead body of one of her children, with the dead and dying forms of the others around her. The work is full of strength and vigor, and suggestive of a brilliant future for the artist.

Orchardson's "Her Mother's Voice" represents a middle-aged widow listening to his daughter as she sings, attended by her lover.

The exhibition was strong in portraits and in landscapes, but want of space will not permit their enumeration.

The new associates elected by the Royal Academy are: W. B. Richmond, Onslow Ford, and Arthur Blomfield.

The pictures purchased for the Chantry Bequest are: Vicat Cole's "Pool of London"; W. Logsdail's "St. Martin's-in-the-Fields"; Adrian Stokes's "Upland and Sky"; and Frank Bramley's "A Hopeless Dawn."

London: Grosvenor Gallery.—The winter exhibition, called "A Century of British Art," consisted of pictures by British painters between 1737 and 1837, among them being Hogarth, Reynolds, Gainsborough, Lawrence, Mulready, Wilkie, Ramsay, Raeburn, Opie, Constable, Calicott, Bonington, Collins, Linnell, and Wilson. Hogarth was represented by twenty-five canvases, comprising "Garrick as Richard III," "Garrick and his Wife," "Peg Woffington," "The Lady's Last Stake," and "Monamy showing a Picture."

The twelfth summer exhibition of the Grosvenor Gallery, opened as usual in May, was chiefly noteworthy for the absence of contributions by many artists whose names have heretofore been the fortune of the enterprise.

Among the more conspicuous pictures were: Jacomb Hood's "Triumph of Spring," John Reid's "Smugglers," Arthur Hacker's "By the Waters of Babylon," and W. F. Britten's "Noble Family of Huguenot Refugees shipwrecked on the Suffolk Coast." One of the best portraits as well as one of the best pictures in the exhibition was E. F. Gregory's "Miss Mabel Galloway," a young girl in crimson, seated at a table amid elaborately-painted accessories. Briton Riviere's "Adonis's Farewell," is really a painting of dogs. McWhirter, Philip R. Morris, Henry Moore, Keeley Hallswell, W. J. Hennessey, Mark Fisher, Ernest Parton, and other well-known names, were represented by landscapes and sea-pieces.

London: New Gallery.—This gallery opened in May, in Regent Street, under the management of Comyns Carr and C. E. Hallé, was the result of troubles in the Grosvenor Gallery management, which led to the secession of a number of painters, among them Alma-Tadema, Burne-Jones, W. B. Richmond, Hubert Herkomer, Holman Hunt, George F. Watts, and Prof. Legros.

Among the most noteworthy contributions are three by Burne-Jones who, though elected an associate of the Royal Academy in 1885, seems to prefer to exhibit elsewhere. The first of these, called "The Rock of Doom," is a nude full-length standing Andromeda, chained to the rock in the sea, just discovered by the winged-sandaled Perseus, who is soon to deliver her. "The Doom fulfilled" is the sequel, showing the hero, encircled by the coils of the slimy sea-monster, wielding his Hermes-given sword with fatal effect. "The Tower of Brass," a tall canvas (7 feet 5 inches × 3 feet 10 inches) hanging between these two, represents the story of Danaë, who, in a crimson robe over a violet dress, stands watching the building of King Acrisius's brazen tower.

Alma-Tadema sent six works, two portraits, a study, a sketch for the "Heliogabalus" in the Royal Academy, a small canvas entitled "Venus and Mars," and another called "He loves me, he loves me not," representing a girl on a green couch beneath a window, picking the petals of a flower, while another languidly watches her.

"The Angel of Death," by G. F. Watts, represents a figure with dark-gray wings, in a gray-green robe and white headdress, soothing a sleeping babe as she gently draws it toward herself.

Hubert Herkomer, W. B. Richmond, and Frank Holl contributed portraits; Sir John Everett Millais, two works, entitled "Forlorn" and "The Last Rose of Summer," both female figures; Prof. Legros, a "Dead Christ" and "Femmes en Prière"; C. E. Hallé, a "Paolo and Francesca"; and J. R. Weguelin, a canvas, 4 × 9 feet, representing "Bacchus and the Choir of Nymphs," reclining on the seashore.

London: Miscellaneous.—At the sale of the pictures of Charles Waring, deceased, held in London, April 28, the following prices were obtained: Munkacsy, "Christ before Pilate" (original study for the large picture), 900 guineas. Constant Troyon. "The Ferry," 8,500 guineas; "Harrowing," 1,330 guineas; "The Watering Place," 560 guineas. Among pictures of various owners, sold at the same time, were: D. G. Rossetti, "Proserpina," 710 guineas; "Vision of Fiammetta," 1,150 guineas. Rosa Bonheur, "Labourages Nivernais" (replica of picture in Luxembourg), 4,200 guineas. Turner, "Burning of Houses of Parliament in 1834," 1,500 guineas. Thomas Faed, "Reading the Bible," 1,750 guineas. Hook, "Gold of the Sea," 1,640 guineas.

The Marton Hall collection of seventy-one pictures, formed by the late H. W. F. Bolckow, M. P., sold May 5, brought in the aggregate £71,387. Among them were: Rosa Bonheur, "Return from Pasture" (1862), 2,050 guineas; "Deer crossing Rocks in Forest of Fontainebleau" (1865), 1,740 guineas; "Denizens of the Highlands" (1857), 5,550 guineas. Constant Troyon, "The Water-Cart" (bought from the artist for £40), 2,000 guineas (Agnew). Meissonier, "Refreshment" (1865), 1,970 guineas. Landseer, "Braemar" (1857), 4,950 guineas (Agnew); "Intruding Puppies" (1821), 1,000 guineas (Colnaghi); "Taking a Buck," 1,950 guineas. Millais, "Northwest Passage" (1874), 4,000 guineas (Agnew). Turner, "Old London Bridge," 2,800 guineas (Colnaghi). W. Müller, "Ancient Tombs and Dwellings in Lycia" (1844), 3,750 guineas. F. Goodall, "Subsiding of the Nile" (1873), 1,450 guineas. David Cox, "Counting the Flock" (1852), 1,980 guineas; "Driving Home the Flock," 1,300 guineas. William Collins, "The Skittle Players" (1832), 1,510 guineas. Thomas Faed, "The Silken Gown," 1,450 guineas; "Baith Faither and Mither," 1,350 guineas.

The Gatton Park collection, formed by Lord Monson early in the present century, sold May 12, contained twenty-one pictures, which brought £11,439. Among them were: Leonardo da Vinci (or Cesare da Cesto), "Vierge au bas-relief" (bought from Woodburn at 4,000 guineas), 2,100 guineas (Davis). Nicolas Maas (or Karl Fabritius), "The Card Players," 1,310 guineas (National Gallery). Sir Joshua Reynolds, "Pick-a-back" (Mrs. Payne Gallwey and her son), 4,100 guineas (Agnew). At the same time were sold: Gainsborough, "Hon. Mrs. Henry Fane" (1778; sold last year for 4,850 guineas), 2,900 guineas (Davis); "Elizabeth, Duchess of Grafton," 970 guineas. Romney, "Lady Hamilton reading the 'Gazette' of one of Nelson's Victories," 1,250 guineas (Agnew).

Collection of the late T. Walker, sold June 2: David Cox, "Collecting the Flock," 2,250 guineas. John Linnell, "Hampstead Heath," 1,510 guineas. Carl Müller, "Bay of Naples," 1,500 guineas; "Salmon Traps on the Llede" (1862), 1,500 guineas. William Collins, "Barmouth Sands" (1835), 1,000 guineas. Patrick

Nasmyth, "View in Hampshire" (1826), 1,010 guineas. Rosa Bonheur, "Spanish Muleteers crossing the Pyrenees" (1857), 3,600 guineas (Agnew); "Brittany Shepherds" (1854), 1,000 guineas. Landseer, "The Hunted Stag" (1859), 2,850 guineas.

At the sale of the Marquis of Exeter, June 7 and 8, thirty-nine pictures brought £9,224. Among them were: Jan Van Eyck, "Madonna with St. Margaret" (1426), 2,500 guineas (Murray). On the same day was sold a Rubens, "Portrait of the Artist and his Wife," from Packington Hall collection, for 2,500 guineas (Agnew).

Alma-Tadema's "Vintage Festival" has been purchased for the Melbourne (Australia) museum.

Lord Lansdowne's "Cuyp" and his two Rembrandt's, "Portrait of a Lady" and "Portrait of the Painter," have been sold to Sir Edward Guinness for £50,000.

A statue of Sir Bartle Frere, by Brock, has been erected on the Thames Embankment. Statues of Gen. Gordon, by Stuart Burnett, and one of William Wallace, by G. Stevenson, have been unveiled at Aberdeen.

Glasgow.—The International Exhibition was formally opened on the 8th of May by the Prince and Princess of Wales. There were ten fine-art galleries, of which two were devoted to loan pictures in oil by British artists; one by sale pictures in oil by British artists; one by loan pictures and one by sale pictures in oil by foreign artists; two by water-colors; one by sculpture; and two by architecture and photography. The exhibits numbered nearly 2,700.

Stratford-on-Avon.—A monument to Shakespeare was unveiled in September. It is a bronze statue of the poet seated, reading a book, on a granite pedestal, at the angles of which are bronze figures of Hamlet, representing philosophy; Falstaff, comedy; Prince Hal, history; and Lady Macbeth, tragedy.

Brussels.—"L'Homme à la Houe" ("The Man with a Hoe"), Millet's celebrated picture, has been sold to M. Van den Eynde, for 84,000 francs. It was bought at the Salon of 1863, by M. Blanc, for 1,500 francs; was afterward in the Defoer collection, Paris, at the sale of which it brought 59,000 francs.

Copenhagen.—The exhibition illustrating the art, industries, and natural products of Denmark, Sweden, and Norway, and of the art-industries of foreign nations, was held in the Tivoli Gardens. Of foreign countries, Russia and France were best represented; Germany and Italy also made a good show.

Dresden.—The first large exhibition of paintings in water-color opened in Germany, held last winter, proved a great success.

Munich.—The collection of Count Salm Reifferscheid, sold in September, realized 334,980 marks. Some of the best prices obtained were: Andreas Achenbach, "A Valley," 27,100 marks; "Château on the Rhine," 13,000

marks; " Chestnut Forest," 9.800 marks. Constant Troyon, " Passing Cattle," 22,700 marks. Benjamin Vautier, " The Burial," 13,500 marks.

United States: Exhibitions, etc.—The National Academy of Design, New York, held its sixty-third annual exhibition, April 2 to May 12, with 598 entries. The sales amounted to $22,000, for eighty-four works.

The Clarke prize for the best figure composition was awarded to H. Siddons Mowbray for his " Evening Breeze." The first Hallgarten prize, $300, was given to G. De Forest Brush, for " The Sculptor and the King "; the second, $200, to H. R. Poore, for " Fox Hounds "; the third, $100, to Charles C. Curran, for " A Breezy Day." The Norman W. Dodge prize, $300, for the best picture painted in the United States by a woman, was awarded to Mrs. Amanda B. Sewell, for her " Portrait of Dora Wheeler."

At the annual meeting of the National Academy, held in April, the officers elected were: Daniel Huntington, president; T. W. Wood, vice-president; T. Addison Richards, corresponding secretary; Albert Jones, treasurer. The following were elected academicians: E. H. Blashfield, T. W. Dewing, Walter Shirlaw. Associate academicians: George De Forest Brush, Charles C. Curran, Will H. Low, H. Siddons Mowbray, H. R. Poore, Augustus St. Gaudens, Olin L. Warner, Robert Blum, William M. Chase, Robert C. Minor.

The seventh annual autumn exhibition was held November 19 to December 15.

At the fourth annual Prize Fund Exhibition of the American Art Association, held in New York in May, the catalogue contained 338 numbers, including pictures and sculpture. But one prize, of $2,000, was awarded to J. Alden Weir, for his " Idle Hours," a large *genre* picture which is to go to the Metropolitan Museum. Four gold medals of $100 each were given as follows: Charles Henry Eaton, best landscape; J. C. Nicoll, best marine, "The Sea "; Percy Moran, best figure composition, "The Forgotten Strain "; O. E. Dallin, best statue, "The Indian Hunter."

The Society of American Artists held its tenth annual exhibition at the Yandell Gallery, New York, April 7 to May 5. The Seward Webb prize for the best landscape painted by an American artist under forty years of age, was awarded to J. H. Twachtman, for his " Windmills."

An exhibition of historical portraits, most of them of Philadelphia social celebrities, at the Philadelphia Academy of Fine Arts, which closed January 15, contained about 500 works. Several were attributed to Lely and Kneller; others were by Hesselius, Robert Feke, Sully, Gilbert Stuart, the Peales, Otis, and Neagle.

The American Water-Color Society's twenty-first annual exhibition was held in New York, January 30 to February 25. Two prizes, of $300 each, one given by Mrs. Frank Leslie, for the best figure or still-life; the other by W. T. Evans, for the best landscape or marine painted in this country by an American painter, were awarded, February 18, by vote of the members. The first was awarded to J. Alden Weir, for his " Preparing for Christmas "; the second to Horatio Walker, for his " Landscape with Pigs." The amount of sales was $24,000.

The Philadelphia Academy of Fine Arts held its fifty-eighth annual exhibition, February 16 to March 29. The first Tappan prize ($200) was awarded to Benjamin Fox, for his picture entitled " Sympathy "; the second Tappan prize ($100) to M. H. Bancroft, for " Bad News." The gold medal was given to Charles S. Reinhart, for " Washed Ashore ": the silver medal to Howard R. Butler, for " La Récolte des Vareches " (Salon, 1886).

The most important art sale of the year was that of the Albert Spencer collection, on the evening of February 28, at Chickering Hall, New York. The sixty-eight pictures sold for $284,025. The prices of some of the best works were as follow: Troyon, " Drove of Cattle and Sheep," $26,000 (S. P. Avery). Jules Breton, " Le Soir," $20,500 (Mrs. W. B. Ogden). Gérôme, " Serpent Charmer," $19,500. Delacroix, " Entombment," $10,600; " Tiger drinking," $6,100. J. F. Millet, " The Gleaners," $10,400; " Peasant Woman and Child," $3,500; " Diana Reposing," $2,500; " Shepherdess," $7,500; " Sleeping Woman," $2,500. Meissonier, " Standard Bearer of the Flemish Civic Guard," $9,200; " A Musician," $8,800. Corot, " Morning," $8,400; " Farm at Toulon," $7,000. Daubigny, " Midsummer—Edge of a Pond," $8,650. Rousseau, Theodore, " Sunset," $7,300; " Autumn Evening," $6,100; " Sunset in a Wood," $5,000; " Ravines of Apremont," $4,300; " Cottage at Berri," $5,200; " Plains of Barbizon," $1,850; " Lone Tree in Autumn," $1,200. Fromentin, " Arab Falconer," $6,500; " Arab Women," $6,400; " Horse-Trading in the Desert," $2,550; " Boar Hunt," $3,800; " The Fire," $1,050. Diaz, " In the Woods," $5,900; " Assumption," $2,650; " Passing Storm," $4,100; " Clearing in the Forest," $4,700. Isabey, " Fête at Hôtel Rambouillet," $4,600. Schreyer, " Advance Guard," $5,000.

A collection of water-colors by W. Hamilton Gibson, and of oils by Kruseman Van Elten, exhibited at the American Art Galleries from March 13, was sold March 19. The former brought $12,259; the latter, $8,032.

The Edward Kearney and Jordan L. Mott collections, exhibited at the American Art Galleries, were sold March 28 and 29, 130 pictures bringing $130,590. Among the best prices obtained were: Rosa Bonheur, " Deer in the Forest," $5,500; Bouguereau, " Resting," $4,800; Gérôme, " Circassian Slave," $4,800; Schreyer, " Teamster in the Marshes of the Danube," $4,000.

The Christian H. Wolff collection, exhibited at the American Art Galleries, New York, from March 26 to April 2, was sold for about $27,000.

The Edward F. Rook collection, sold April 5, consisted of American and European pictures, among the latter being specimens of Schreyer, Moreau, Madrazo, Hamon, Villejas, Berne-Bellecour, and Lenort. Eighty-three pictures brought $20,715.

The Godfrey Mannheimer collection of seventy-four minor pictures, by good masters, was sold, April 12, for $48,780. Knaus's "Blacksmith Shop" brought $7,000.

The collection of Henry F. Chapman, Jr., sold April 12, consisted chiefly of good examples of the French schools. Lerolle's "End of the Day" brought $3,500; Dupré's "Summer Day," $3,225; Rousseau's "Sunshine through Clouds," $2,500; a drawing by Millet, $3,000. The sale brought in the aggregate $74,395.

The collection of Herman Herzog, a German-American painter, residing in Philadelphia, consisting of 226 of his own works, landscapes and marines, sold April 25–27, brought $16,515.

The R. S. Clark collection, and other pictures, sixty-three in all, were sold May 3 and 4, and brought in the aggregate $39,866. The highest price was $3,400 for Schreyer's "Wallachian Teamsters resting."

The Boston Art Club's thirty-seventh exhibition, (January 13 to February 11), consisted chiefly of portraits and landscapes.

The studio properties of Léon y Escosura, with many pictures by himself, and some attributed "old masters," sold at the Buchen Art Galleries, New York, brought in the aggregate $116,667. Forty-one pictures by the artist sold for $29,145; the "old masters" for $21,117. "St. George and the Dragon," attributed to Raphael, was withdrawn for want of an $8,000 bid.

Among the pictures exhibited in New York during the past year were twenty-one large canvases by the French painter Paul Philippoteaux, illustrative of the civil war and of Gen. Grant's career; "The Right of Way," and several cattle pieces, by Mrs. Emily J. Lakey, a pupil of Van Marcke; about a hundred pictures by the Russian painter Vassili Verestchagin, chiefly of subjects connected with the Russo-Turkish War and the Indian mutiny, and of scenes in Turkistan (previously exhibited in Vienna, Paris, London, and other European cities). Delacroix's "Les Convulsionnaires de Tanger" (*Salon*, 1888), was exhibited by Knoedler & Co., and sold to W. T. Walters, Baltimore. Munkacsy's "Christ on Calvary," exhibited in New York last year, has been bought by John Wannamaker, Philadelphia, for more than $100,000.

A bronze statue of Garibaldi, by Giovanni Turini, was unveiled, June 4, in Washington Square, New York. The figure is 8 feet 10 inches high, and stands on a granite pedestal 14 feet 6 inches high. It was erected by popular subscription by Italian residents at a cost of $10,000.

A bronze equestrian statue, heroic size, of Gen. Israel Putnam, was unveiled at Brooklyn, Conn., June 14.

A bronze statue of Josiah Bartlett, the first signer of the Declaration of Independence, the work of Karl Gerhardt, was dedicated July 4, at Amesbury, Mass.

The monument to Francis Scott Key, author of the "Star Spangled Banner," the gift of the late James Lick, was unveiled, July 4, at San Francisco. It is of bronze, executed in Rome by W. W. Story.

A statue of Sergeant William Jasper, the hero of Fort Moultrie in the Revolutionary War, the work of Alexander Doyle, was unveiled, February 22, at Savannah, Ga.

Among many statues and monuments erected at Gettysburg during the year was a bronze figure of heroic size, of Gen. Warren, by Karl Gerhardt.

A statue of Richard Stockton, in marble, and of Gen. Philip Kearney, in bronze, were placed, August 21, by the State of New Jersey, in the old Hall of Representatives, Washington.

A bronze statue of William H. Seward was erected at Auburn, N. Y., in October. It is by Walter G. Robinson.

A bronze statue of Longfellow, by Franklin Simmons, was unveiled at Portland, Me., September 29.

FLORIDA. State Government.—The following were the State officers during the year: Governor, Edward A. Perry, Democrat; Lieutenant-Governor, Milton H. Mabry; Secretary of State, John L. Crawford; Treasurer, Edward S. Crill; Comptroller, William D. Barnes; Attorney-General, Charles M. Cooper; Superintendent of Public Instruction, Albert J. Russell: Commissioner of Lands and Immigration, Charles L. Mitchell; Chief-Justice of the Supreme Court, Augustus E. Maxwell; Associate Justices, George P. Raney and R. B. Van Valkenburgh, who died on August 1, and was succeeded by H. L. Mitchell by appointment of the Governor. He had already been nominated to succeed Judge Van Valkenburgh, by the Democratic State Convention held in May, and was elected in November.

Finances.—At the beginning of 1887 there was a balance in the State treasury of $255,-894.63. The receipts during the year from all sources were $535,871.65, and the expenditures $681,120.26, leaving a balance of $110,646.02 at the close of the year. The largest receipts were from the license tax, $130,420.28, and the State tax on property, $228,638.07. The expenditures include $149,470.43 for jurors and witnesses, $79,954, for interest on the public debt, $70,000 for legislative expenses, $34,531.-10 for care of the insane, $36,639 for judicial salaries, and $21,875 for executive salaries.

There was no change in the State debt during the year, but about $10,000 of State bonds representing the debt were added to the sinking-fund, and the same amount to the school fund. The amount of State bonds held by individuals was thus reduced from $430,700 at the beginning of 1887, to $411,300 at the close. The assessed valuation of the State for 1887 was $86,265,662, against $76,611,409 for 1886.

Education.—The following statistics exhibit the condition of the public schools during the school year 1886–'87:

Whole number of schools, 2,103 ; increase over the year 1835–'86, 184. Total enrollment, 82,453 ; average daily attendance, 51,059 ; increase in daily attendance over 1885–'86, 6,246 ; number of white teachers employed, 1,739 ; number of colored teachers employed, 579 ; total amount of funds expended from all sources for school purposes and raised by the State and counties, $449, 299.15 ; number of white schools operated, 1,590 ; number of colored schools operated, 513 ; value of school property owned by the State and counties, and used in the school work, $521,500.

The State normal colleges for each race, established by the last Legislature, were organized and opened in October, 1887, at the beginning of the school year. The one for white students, at De Funiak Springs, had matriculated fifty students during the first three months ; the one for colored students, at Tallabassee, received forty students during the same time. In both of these colleges tuition is entirely free. The State also supports a flourishing agricultural college and an institute for blind and deaf mute children, in which there were twenty at the beginning of the year.

Immigration.—The people of the State have formed a State Immigration Association, to aid the State Immigration Commissioner in his work. This association holds annual meetings and elects executive officers for the year. A large meeting was held at Jacksonville in May.

Yellow Fever.—Isolated cases of yellow fever in a mild form appear to have been found at Tampa as early as the autumn of 1887. The disease survived the winter and spring at that place, and, early in the latter season, the cases becoming known to Surgeon-General Hamilton of the Marine Hospital corps, he notified Gov. Perry of the fact, and also publicly announced the existence of the disease in the State. But no heed was paid to this warning, no quarantine regulations adopted, and the statement was generally discredited. Meanwhile, during the early summer, one or more cases were always to be found at Tampa, and before August 1 the disease had appeared at Plant City, Manatee, Palmetto, and other small places in the State. There were, however, only a few patients at each place, and the facts were kept from the public prints. The first case came to Jacksonville from one of these infected localities in the last week of July; but it was not until about August 8 that public announcement of the existence of several cases in the city was made. In a few days more the disease had become epidemic, twenty-six cases appearing before August 15. About this time reports from Manatee showing that there had been twenty-three cases at that place, from Palmetto showing a number of cases, and from other places, were published. There was great excitement throughout the State, and many people living at points not

threatened, believing that the epidemic would cover the whole State, fled to the North. Jacksonville in a few days lost nearly half of its population of 30,000, and business was almost entirely suspended. An executive committee of the citizens was chosen to aid the city authorities in suppressing or controlling the epidemic, diseased persons were isolated at a hospital outside the city, infected buildings were burned, cannon were fired, a refugee camp was established, and other measures were adopted for relief. Nearly all important centers in the South quarantined against the city, and enforced their regulations strictly. Up to and including Saturday, August 18, 33 cases were reported in the city, and 5 deaths. From this time, in spite of repressive measures, the epidemic obtained a firmer hold, the number of cases reported each day rapidly increasing. Up to and including August 25 there were 91 cases and 12 deaths reported, and to September 1, 234 cases and 32 deaths. On August 28 the General Government, through the Marine Hospital service, took more open and direct control of quarantine regulations than before, by means of an order of Surgeon-General Hamilton establishing a refugee camp, to be known as Camp Perry, at which all persons from the city should be detained ten days before going to a temporary camp at Waycross, Ga., from which they might proceed northward. No trains were allowed to run from the city, except to Camp Perry, and a rigid inspection and fumigation of the mails and baggage was required. A second temporary camp at Live Oaks was established, and those at Dupont and on the Chattachoochee river discontinued. These regulations called forth a protest from the citizens, who at a public meeting on August 31 passed resolutions denouncing the action of the Surgeon-General. The latter, in a public letter, justified his course and refused to recede. Hitherto offers of assistance from outside sources had been refused ; but as the infected area and the number of cases increased, the citizens found themselves no longer able to meet the exigency, and on September 5 the city authorities issued a call for pecuniary or other assistance. This was promptly and generously responded to, especially in the Northern cities. Before October 1 more than $200,000 had been sent to the unfortunate city. The progress of the epidemic after September·1 is shown by the following figures: Cases up to and including September 8, 555, deaths 66 ; September 15, cases 921, deaths 117 ; September 22, cases 1,878, deaths 212 ; September 29, cases 2,547, deaths 248 ; October 6, cases 3,118, deaths 282 ; October 13, cases 3,526, deaths 311 ; October 20, cases 3,767, deaths 327 ; October 27, cases 4,043, deaths 345 ; November, 3, cases 4,266, deaths 361 ; November 10, cases 4,469, deaths 384 ; November 17, cases 4,601, deaths 392 ; November 24, cases 4,674, deaths 407 ; December 1, cases 4,697, deaths 410 ; December 8, cases 4,704, deaths

412. Few if any cases occurred after the last date, and by December 15 refugees began to return to the city. Several well-known men had fallen victims to the disease, and the loss to the business and material growth of the city was severe.

Outside of Jacksonville cases of the fever were reported, about September 7, at McClenny, about thirty miles west of the city, where a number of deaths occurred. Ten days later, cases were found at Gainesville, and soon afterward the presence of the fever was acknowledged at Fernandina, from which place the infection had been brought to Gainesville. There seem to have been cases at Fernandina several weeks before this time. Late in the month, Sanderson was added to the list of infected places. In the latter part of October it was reported that the fever had existed at Enterprise for several months, and that 16 cases and 2 deaths had occurred.

At all these places the epidemic raged until the last of November, when hard frosts stayed its progress, although some cases occurred after that date, especially at Jacksonville. Up to December 1 there had been at Fernandina about 1,200 cases and 38 deaths; at McClenny, over 200 cases and 22 deaths; at Sanderson, about 35 cases and 2 deaths; at Gainesville, nearly 100 cases and about 12 deaths; at Palmetto, about 45 cases; at Enterprise, about 30 cases and 4 deaths. Quarantine restrictions were removed at Fernandina on December 1.

Political.—The election of 1888 was the first under the new Constitution. Aside from the presidential contest, there was to be chosen a full set of State officers, including three judges of the Supreme Court, that body being chosen for the first time by popular election. The Democratic State Convention met at St. Augustine, on May 29, and was in session four days. There were four candidates for the gubernatorial nomination: Gen. Robert Bullock, Francis P. Fleming, Robert W. Davis, and J. G. Speer. After about twenty ballots the last two-named withdrew, but a choice was not reached until the fortieth ballot, when Fleming was declared the nominee. The ticket was completed as follows: For Secretary of State, John L. Crawford; for Comptroller, William D. Barnes; for Treasurer, Frank J. Pons; for Attorney-General, William B. Lamar; for Superintendent of Public Instruction, Albert J. Russell; for Commissioner of Immigration, Lucius B. Wombwell; for Justices of the Supreme Court, A. E. Maxwell, George P. Raney, and H. L. Mitchell. The following are among the resolutions adopted:

That we advocate a liberal policy on the part of the General Government in the matter of public improvements, and hold that the South has a right to demand this until her waterways and harbors are adjusted to the needs of commerce to the same extent as other sections of the country.

That it is the duty of the State to educate its children, and that we favor the maintenance of the present liberal provisions for our system of public schools.

That the remarkable and steady growth of our population, and the enormous flow of capital seeking permanent investment in our State, is a noteworthy indication of the prosperity of the State, and that we invite worthy and industrious people from all quarters to come and settle among us, with the confident assurance of a friendly welcome, and an equal opportunity; and we heartily approve the recent establishment of a State Immigration Association, and pledge it our cordial sympathy and earnest support in its efforts to people our State with honest citizens, no matter whence they come.

That the nominee of this convention for Governor, by the acceptance of the nomination, stands pledged to regard the recommendation of the different counties of this State as expressed by the Democrats of the several counties through their party organization for that most vital and important of all positions, their county commissioners.

President Cleveland's efforts in behalf of tariff reform and civil service reform were approved, and delegates to the St. Louis convention, who were chosen at the same time, were instructed to vote for his renomination.

The Republican convention was held at Ocala, on July 31. The following ticket was nominated: For Governor, V. J. Shipman; Secretary of State, Henry W. Chandler; Attorney-General, John Eagan; Comptroller, C. W. Lewis; State Treasurer, Walter Bishop; Superintendent of Public Instruction, J. K. Rainey; Commissioner of Agriculture, John P. Apthorp; Supreme Court Judges, E. M. Randall, J. H. Goss, Charles Swayne.

The platform adopted contains the following resolutions upon State questions:

That we heartily favor a protective duty on oranges, lemons, pineapples, vegetables, tobacco, wool, lumber, cotton, sugar, rice, and other products of our State, that shall enable our farmers to compete against the underpaid and degraded labor of Egypt, Italy, Spain, Bermuda, and other foreign countries.

That the laws for the assessment and collection of revenue are unequal in application, and utterly unfitted to meet the wants of a growing and prosperous State. We favor a thorough revision of the whole system, so that the burdens of taxation shall be lightened, equalized, and brought into harmony with our advancing civilization.

That we favor the repeal of our present road law, compelling as it does the poor settler to labor six days every spring and fall on the public roads, while the non-resident, though he may own his millions of acres, is exempt; and we demand the enactment of a law providing for the maintenance of the road out of the funds raised by general taxation.

That we favor the public-school system, which is the offspring of the Republican party, and express our belief that it can be best nourished and perfected by its natural parent.

That the Republican party cordially sympathizes with all wise and well-directed efforts for the promotion of temperance and morality, and we indorse the principles of local option, now embodied in the Constitution of the State.

That, true to the spirit of retrogression, which characterizes the Democratic party, it has discontinued the Bureau of Immigration, which, under a Republican administration, had turned into our State a tide of immigration that brought millions of wealth within our border, and changed forests into fruitful fields.

That the Farmers' Alliance, Farmers' Union, State Horticultural Society, Sub-Tropical Exposition, and labor organizations have our full and hearty sympathy and support.

That we denounce the present Democratic Railroad

Commission. Its halting inefficiency has annoyed and exasperated the transportation companies, and utterly failed to accomplish the reform for which it was created.

That we are uncompromisingly in favor of free speech and the unrestricted right of all citizens to lawfully meet and consult together upon the political questions of the day.

That we recognize in the State militia our necessary and sole protection in times of possible riot and disorder, and that we favor liberal appropriations for its support and maintenance, and a hearty spirit of aid and sympathy on the part of the State government.

That in the counties of Madison, Jefferson, Gadsden, and Jackson we recognize a condition of anarchy and defiance of the laws of our State for the protection of the citizen in his constitutional rights, in that the citizens of those counties are prevented by intimidation and force from holding lawful assemblies, casting a ballot representing their honest convictions, and having the same fairly counted; and that we call the attention of our State authorities to this fact, and demand of them the faithful execution of their trust as a government of the whole people of the State.

The Prohibitionists held a State convention at Orlando in September, and nominated presidential electors, but voted not to present a State ticket. The canvass, which promised to be of exceptional interest, lost in a large degree its importance when the yellow-fever epidemic appeared in the State. Yet the total vote polled at the election in November was larger than in any previous election. Mr. Cleveland received 39,561 votes; Harrison, 26,657; and Fisk, 423 votes. For Governor, Fleming received 40,255 votes, and Shipman 26,485. All the Democratic candidates on the State ticket were elected, and also two Democratic Congressmen. But few Republicans were elected to the Legislature.

FRANCE, a republic in western Europe. The present form of government was proclaimed Sept. 4, 1871. The executive authority is vested in the President of the republic, and the legislative power in an assembly of two houses—the Senate and the Chamber of Deputies. The Senate is composed of 300 members, elected for nine years. They are divided into three classes, one class retiring by rotation every three years. The Chamber of Deputies is composed of 584 members, one to every 70,-000 inhabitants, elected by universal suffrage under the *scrutin de liste*, which was adopted on June 16, 1885. The term of service is four years. In 1885 there were 10,181,095 electors, of whom 7,896,100 voted in the election of that year. The senators receive a salary of 15,000 francs, and the deputies 9,000 francs per annum. The President is elected for a term of seven years by a majority of votes of the Senate and Chamber of Deputies united in a National Assembly. He receives a salary of 600,000 francs, with 600,000 francs additional for expenses. The Senate and Chamber of Deputies meet every year on the second Tuesday in January, and must remain in session at least five months.

The President of the republic is Marie-François Sadi Carnot, elected Dec. 3, 1887. (For biography and portrait, see "Annual Cyclo-

pædia" for 1887.) The President, in the exercise of his executive functions, makes his decisions in accordance with the advice of his ministers, who are responsible to the Legislature. The first Cabinet after the accession of President Carnot was formed on Dec. 12, 1887, and consisted of the following members: President of the Council, Minister of Finance, and Minister of Posts and Telegraphs, Pierre Emmanuel Tirard; Minister of Foreign Affairs, Léopold Émile Flourens; Minister of the Interior, Jean Marie Ferdinand Sarrien; Minister of Public Instruction, Worship, and Fine Arts, Étienne Léopold Faye; Minister of Justice, C. A. Fallières; Minister of War, Gen. Logerot; Minister of Marine and the Colonies, François C. de Mahy, who retired, and was succeeded on Jan. 5, 1888, by Vice-Admiral Krantz; Minister of Commerce and Industry, Auguste Lucien Dautresme; Minister of Public Works, Émile Loubet; Minister of Agriculture, François Viette.

Area and Population.—The area of France is 528,572 square kilometres, or 204,177 square miles. The population on May 30, 1886, was 38,218,903, or 187 to the square mile. France is divided into 87 departments, subdivided into 362 arrondissements, containing 2,871 cantons and 36,121 communes. The number of the communes is constantly increasing.

The number of marriages in 1886 was 283,-193; of births, 912,782; of deaths, 860,222. The excess of births over deaths was 52,560, as compared with 85,464 in 1885, 78,974 in 1884, 96,803 in 1883, 97,027 in 1882, 108,229 in 1881, 61,840 in 1880, 96,667 in 1879, 98,175 in 1878, and 142,620 in 1877. In Bouches-du-Rhône there were 3,114 more deaths than births in 1886; in Manche, 2,302; in Calvados, 1,946; in Eure, 1,897; in Orne, 1,863; in Seine-et-Oise, 1,823; in Rhône, 1,779. In 37 departments altogether there was a surplus of 36,139 deaths, while in the remainder the births exceeded the deaths by 88,699.

The census of 1886 included 1,126,531 foreigners who were resident in France. The foreigners in 1881 numbered 1,001,090, as compared with 801,754 in 1876. The number of Belgians was 432,265; of Italians, 240,733, against 165,313 in 1876; of Germans, 81,986, against 59,028; of Spaniards, 73,781; of Swiss, 66,281; of British and Irish, 37,006; of Dutch, 21,232; of Austro-Hungarians, 12,090; of Russians and Poles, 10,489; of Americans, including South Americans, 9,816. On Oct. 2, 1888, in response to a demand from the working-people, who considered themselves injured by the free ingress of foreign competitors, and as a rejoinder to recent regulations of the German authorities respecting the presence of foreigners in Alsace-Lorraine, the Government issued a decree imposing onerous conditions on the residence of citizens of foreign states in France. The statistics published by the Ministry of Commerce in connection with this decree show that, whereas the foreigners domiciled in France constituted little more than 1 per cent. of the population in 1851, the proportion was more than double in 1876, rising to 2⅓ per cent. in 1881, and in 1886 to 3 per cent. The number of Italians in 1886 was 264,568, having quadrupled in 55 years. In the department of Bouches-du-Rhône they form a twelfth part of the population, numbering 70,088, while in the Maritime Alps, the department that has Nice for its chief place, there are 39,165, and in Paris 28,351. The total number of Belgians is 482,261, of whom 298,991 reside in the department of the Nord, where they constitute one eighteenth of the whole population. The number of Germans is more than 100,000, but before the war there were double that number. Nearly one third of them are in Paris. The Spaniards and Portuguese have nearly trebled since 1851, numbering now 80,842, nearly all of whom are found in the departments north of the Pyrenees and south of the Garonne. The Swiss number 78,584, of whom 27,233 inhabit the department of the Seine. The number of Dutch is 37,149, of whom more than half live in Paris. The English, Scotch, and Irish number 36,134, and of these 14,701 live in Paris. The number of natives of North and South America is only 10,253, of whom 6,915 are in Paris. These figures include persons born on French soil who have acquired citizenship in foreign countries, constituting about one fourth of the total, but not naturalized French citizens, who number 103,886, whereas in 1872 there were only 15,303 naturalized Frenchmen.

The decree of the President of the republic requires every foreigner settling in France or making a prolonged stay to make a declaration within fifteen days of his arrival at the *mairie* of the commune where he intends to fix his residence, or at the prefecture, if it is in Paris or Lyons, setting forth (1) his name and those of his father and mother, (2) his nationality, (3) the place and date of his birth, (4) the place of his last domicile, (5) his profession or means of subsistence, (6) the names and nationality of his wife and minor children, in case they accompany him. When the domiciled foreigner changes his residence to another commune, he must there make a similar declaration before the *maire*. Foreigners residing in France at the time when the decree was published were required to comply with its provisions within thirty days. A supplementary decree extended the period to Jan. 1, 1889. Infractions of the regulations prescribed in the decree are punishable with police penalties, without prejudice to the right of expulsion, which can be exercised by the Minister of the Interior by virtue of the law of Dec. 2, 1849.

Religion and Education.—In the census of 1881, 78·50 per cent. of the population, or 29,201,703 persons, belonged to the Roman Catholic Church; 1·8 per cent., or 692,800, were Prot-

estants; 53,436 were Jews; and 7,684,906 persons refused to state their religious belief. All religions are equal by law, and state allowances are granted to those sects whose adherents number more than 100,000. In the budget of 1888, the sum of 45,743,563 francs was devoted to these allowances, distributed as follow: Roman Catholics, 43,503,723 francs; Protestants, 1,551,600 francs; Jews, 180,900 francs; Mussulmans, 216,340 francs; administration, etc., 291,000 francs.

Public education is under the supervision of the Central Government. In 1885-'86 there were 85,887 elementary schools, 63,207 of which were lay schools, and 22,680, clerical schools; 70,313 were public and the rest private schools. The total number of pupils was 6,274,563, of whom 4,988,758 were educated in the public schools. The number of teachers in the elementary schools was 135,216 in 1886—88,668 in the lay, and 46,548 in the clerical schools. In November, 1884, there were 381 secondary schools, with 98,495 pupils. There were 87 normal schools for males and 75 for females in 1886. Education is provided for adult males in 6,667 communes, and for adult females in 1,135 communes, the total number of pupils in 1885-'86 being 167,798 males and 30,036 females. The number of graduates at the state universities in 1884 was 12,195. In that year 8,307 students were in attendance at the faculty or University of Paris. There are also numerous technical, industrial, and other special schools. In the budget of 1886-'87, the total sum devoted to educational purposes was 94,497,000 francs, of which sum 81,460,000 francs were for primary and 13,037,000 francs for intermediate education. For the 16 schools of letters and philosophy, 14 of law, and 6 of medicine, the sum of 11,709,214 francs was assigned in the budget. The state faculties of theology were abolished in 1885. The Protestant faculties at Montauban and Paris have, however, been continued by annual votes of the Chambers, because they are the only legal training-colleges for the pastors of the two Protestant state churches, whereas the Catholic faculties were not recognized by the bishops as training-schools for priests.

Commerce and Industry.—The total special commerce of France in 1887 amounted to 7.590,546,000 francs, of which 4,270,772,000 francs represent imports, and 3,319,774,000 francs, exports. The most important class of commodities is that of alimentary substances, comprising wines, cereals, fruits, animals, coffee, sugar, etc., which were imported to the amount of 1,600,387,000 francs, and exported to the amount of 721,175,000 francs. Of raw products, including wool, raw silk, oils, skins and hides, cotton, and lumber, the imports were valued at 1.998,836,000 francs, and the exports at 717,387,000 francs. Of manufactured articles, including woolen, silk, and cotton goods, leather and leather goods, machinery, metal goods, arms, etc., the imports were 552,091,000 francs, and the exports 1,693,567,-000 francs. Of miscellaneous products, the value of the imports was 119,458,000 francs, and that of the exports, 187,645,000 francs. In the total foreign commerce of France for 1886, amounting to 7,456,900,000 francs, exclusive of specie, the imports amounted to 4,208,100,000 francs. and the exports to 3,248,-800,000 francs. The imports of coin and bullion were valued at 443,517,878 francs, and the exports at 333,262,342 francs. The transit trade amounted to 585,000,000 francs in 1886.

The trade of France with other countries in 1886 was, in millions of francs, as follows:

COUNTRIES.	Imports from—	Exports to—
Great Britain	525	855
Belgium	419	443
Spain	398	178
Germany	335	207
Italy	300	192
United States	293	289
Argentine Republic	228	110
British India	192	8
Russia	170	19
Turkey	124	46
Algeria	124	189
China	119	4
Switzerland	103	210
Austria	107	14
Portugal	74	23
Brazil	52	57

The number of silk-culturists in 1887 was 136,388, against 136,706 in 1886. In 1886 there was imported into France 154,994,874 kilogrammes of sugar, while the home manufactured sugar amounted to 412,161,821 kilogrammes. The product of wheat in 1886 was 290,000,000 bushels, and in 1887 it was 322,-000,000 bushels. The yield of wine in 1886 was 692,584,728 gallons; in 1887, 536,000,000 gallons. In 1887 232,800,000 gallons of wine were imported, and 48,114,000 gallons exported. In 1886 the live-stock in France included 2,911,-392 horses, 13,104,970 cattle, 22,616,547 sheep, 1,483,000 goats, and 5,681,088 swine. The number of persons who were gaining their livelihood by agriculture in 1882 was 6,913,000, which was four per cent. less, as compared with the total population, than in 1862. The total number of agricultural holdings was 5,-672,007, of which 2,167,667 were under 2½ acres, 2,635,030 between 1 and 25 acres, 783,-641 from 25 to 125 acres, 56,866 from 125 to 250 acres, 20,644 from 250 to 500 acres, 7,942 from 500 to 1,250 acres, and only 217 larger than 1,250 acres. The number of owners of land was 4,835,246, which was 405,269 less than in 1862, a part of the decrease being accounted for by the transfer of Alsace-Lorraine, with 187,000 land-owners to Germany. Nearly 80 per cent. of the cultivators are owners of their farms, 14 per cent. are tenants, and 6 per cent. are *metayers*, dividing the profits with the landlord, who furnishes the land and the capital. The number of proprietors had increased, and the number of tenants and *metayers* had decreased in twenty years.

Navigation.—In 1886, 100,796 vessels of all descriptions were entered at French ports, having an aggregate tonnage of 18,490,692. Of this number, 79,112, of 9,994,889 tons, sailed under the French flag. The number of vessels cleared during the same year was 102,386, of 19,023,334 tons, of which 80,151, of 10,368,362 tons, sailed under the French flag.

In 1885 there were engaged in the French fisheries 85,915 men, with 23,877 vessels. The value of the fishery product was 51,469,080 francs. In January, 1887, the mercantile navy consisted of 14,100 sailing-vessels and 951 steamers. The sailing-vessels had a tonnage of 492,-807, and their crews numbered 74,129 men. The steamers had an aggregate burden of 500,-484 tons, and employed 12,790 men.

Railroads.—The railroads of France in January, 1888, had a total length of 32,248 kilometres. The state is the owner of only 2,597 kilometres, and does not operate more than half of its lines. The receipts of all the railroads in 1887 were 1,021,424,230 francs, against 1,007,137,227 francs in 1886. The gross receipts of the state lines are estimated at 30,-084,000 francs, and the expenses at 25,203,000 francs. During the fiscal year 1887-'88 the Government built 791 kilometres of additional railroads.

Telegraph and Postal Service.—On Jan. 1, 1885, there were 86,868 kilometres of telegraph lines, with 258,202 kilometres of wire. In 1885 were sent 23,091,360 telegraph messages, 21,150,444 of which were inland, and 1,940,916 foreign.

The number of letters and postal cards forwarded in 1885 was 679,145,983; of journals, 413,981,338; of samples, circulars, etc., 433,-024,173.

The postal and telegraph receipts in 1885 were 166,578,653 francs, and the expenses 184,-424,235 francs. The telegraphs have been worked at a loss to the treasury ever since the Government telegraph service was established in 1851.

Finances.—The estimated revenue for the year 1887 was 3,134,336,415 francs, and the expenditure 3,133,731,289 francs. The budget for 1888, presented in February, 1887, calculated the ordinary revenue at 3,253,583,183 francs, derived from the following sources: Indirect taxes, domains, and state monopolies, 2,778,-829,689 francs; direct taxes, 474,753,494 francs. The estimated ordinary expenditure is 3,253,-104,738 francs, the principal heads being: Ministry of War, 694,934,530 francs; Ministry of Marine, 219,883,311 francs; Ministry of Public Instruction, 133,048,190 francs; Ministry of Public Works, 176,046,604 francs; other ministries, 256,822,445 francs; expenditure on the public debt, 1,337,275,671 francs; administration and salaries of the President, senators, and deputies, 345,860,097 francs. The extraordinary expenditures, balanced by receipts from special sources, were 473,605,131 francs for the home office, treasury, and other special votes, and 83,796,200 francs for special state expenses.

Of this latter amount 32,870,000 francs went to the account of state railways, 13,064,700 francs for naval invalids, 9,307,500 francs for the national printing-office, 16,867,100 francs for the legion of honor, and 9,221,600 francs for the savings-bank. In June, 1887, the budget for 1888 was cut down by 182,205,000 francs, leaving the corrected expenditure, ordinary and extraordinary, 3,628,301,069 francs.

The total consolidated debt of France amounted in 1888 to 23,728,096,228 francs, the interest upon which is 826,241,131 francs annually, divided as follows: 3-per-cent. *rente*, 482,934,-911 francs; 4-per-cent. *rente*, 446,096 francs; 4½-per-cent. *rente*, 305,426,874 francs. The redeemable debt, life annuities, and other engagements of the treasury swell the capital of the debt to about 32,500,000,000 francs. All the communes and departments of France have their own budgets and debts. The total communal receipts in 1887 were 470,133,297 francs and the departmental receipts, 97,236,261 francs. In the budget of the city of Paris for 1888 the revenue and expenditure were made to balance at 304,169,794 francs. The principal source of revenue of Paris is from the *droits d'octroi* or tolls on articles of consumption, estimated to amount to 137,738,200 francs in 1888. The interest and sinking-fund of the municipal debt, amounted to 106,139,058 francs in 1888.

In order to sustain the increased expenditure of the Government in recent years the import duties have been made much higher than they were formerly, the stamp duties have been raised, and taxes on sugar, wine, and salt, and that on railroad transportation, have been increased. On March 13, 1888, the Chamber decided to take away the privilege that wine and apple growers have enjoyed of distilling spirits from their own produce free of duty. The imposition of new duties on live animals caused a large falling off in the cattle imports in 1887, while the import of fresh meat increased. The duty on wheat was raised in March, 1885, and again on April 1, 1887, causing a considerable advance in the price of bread. In September, 1888, the bakers at St. Ouen and St. Denis refused to make bread at the prices fixed by the municipal authorities, and the Cabinet met to consider the question of suspending the grain duties, as it is empowered to do when the price of bread rises to a point threatening the food-supply of the people. One effect of the high duty on wheat was that Belgian bread was imported and sold in Paris in large quantities.

The Army.—The peace strength of the French army in 1888 was 499,789 officers and men, and 118,927 horses. This does not include the gendarmerie and the Garde Républicaine, which together amount to 25,922 officers and men. With these included, the effective, deducting the number absent on sick-leave and furloughs, was 465,588. The nominal force provided for in the budget for 1888 was divided as follows:

CLASSES OF TROOPS.	Officers and men.
Staff	3,999
Schools	3,037
Administrative and medical	3,293
Infantry	306,937
Infantry, administrative	16,105
Cavalry	70,324
Artillery	73,221
Engineers	10,930
Train	11,840
Gendarmerie	22,725
Garde Républicaine	3,200
Total	525,711

The territorial army numbers 37,000 officers and 579,000 men. The total war force of France is about 3,750,000 men, of which number 2,500,000 have received some military instruction. The expenditure for the army in 1888 was 694,934,530 francs.

The Navy.—The effective navy in 1888 consisted of 393 vessels, comprising 17 line-of-battle ironclads, 9 ironclad cruisers, 10 ironclad *guarda costas*, 4 ironclad gun-boats, 9 battery cruisers, 9 first-class cruisers, 15 of the second, and 18 of the third class, 2 torpedo cruisers, 14 avisos of the first, 26 of the second, and 6 of the third class, 13 transport avisos, 6 torpedo avisos, 20 gun-boats, 40 sloop gun-boats, 10 sea-going torpedo-boats, 72 first-class and 41 second-class torpedo-boats for coast defense, 5 pontoons, 25 transports, and 22 sailing-vessels. The "Caïman" and the "Terrible," sister-ships to the "Indomptable," belted ships with 19¾ inches of compound armor at the water-line, carrying 75-ton guns mounted *en barbette* in two fixed towers, are practically completed, and the "Requin" is approaching completion. The "Admiral Baudin," a monster ironclad of 11,200 tons displacement with 21¾-inch plates at the water-line, armed with three 60-ton and twelve smaller guns, and the "Formidable," a sister-ship, were completed in 1888. The "Hoche" and the "Neptune," of 10,500 tons, and the "Marceau," a heavily armored steel cruiser with four barbette towers, having three full decks, and fitted with four torpedo tubes, will be ready for service by 1890. Two first-class ironclad squadron vessels, four first-class ironclad gun-boats, four armored gun-boats of the second class, two battery cruisers, two torpedo cruisers, eleven cruisers of various classes, and a large number of first-class torpedo-boats are in different stages of construction. Another first-class ironclad and two torpedo dispatch-boats will be begun in 1889. Before the end of that year one first-class and four third-class cruisers will be finished, and three first-class, one third-class, and the two torpedo cruisers are expected to be done the year after. The expenditure on the navy set down in the budget for 1888 is 219,883,311 francs. The valuation of the fleet given in the budget is 502,000,000 francs.

Fall of the Tirard Ministry.—The Cabinet was overturned on March 30 by a vote of 268 to 234 on a motion of M. Laguerre, leader of Gen. Boulanger's faction, which numbered only 13 in the Chamber, in favor of the revision of the Constitution. Royalists and Bonapartists supported the motion from their different standpoints, and were joined by the followers of M. Clémenceau, now an opponent of his cousin Boulanger, whom he first lifted into power, yet committed to the principle of revision. The changes of Government have invariably been produced in recent years by such a temporary combination of the greater part of both the Royalist parties with the Radicals for the sake of overturning an Opportunist Ministry, or with the Opportunists in order to oust one that is dominated by the Advanced Left. The Chamber in 1888 was divided into seventeen separate factions, viz., the Legitimists, whose Pretender is Don Carlos or Don Jaime; the Fusion Legitimists, under the Duc de la Rochefoucauld; the Philippists, who have accepted the manifesto of the Comte de Paris; the Compromise Royalists, represented by Baron de Mackan and M. Piou; the Victorian Bonapartists; the Jeromist Bonapartists; the Bonapartists pure and simple; the Left Center, led by M. Ribaud; the Opportunists, whose leader was Jules Ferry; the Advanced Left, under M. Brisson and M. Goblet; the Radicals, under M. Floquet and M. Clémenceau; the Extreme Radicals, of whom M. Millerand was the chief; the Old Convention School, led by M. Madier de Montjau; the Possiblists, under M. Basly and M. Camélinat; the Boulangists, who had a spokesman in M. Laguerre; the Rational Radicals, led by M. Maret; and the Anarchists, who had now an able representative in Parliament, Félix Pyat, elected by the great constituency of the Bouches-du-Rhône.

The Floquet Cabinet.—The President of the Chamber, M. Floquet, who had undertaken to form a cabinet in May, 1887, but had failed, again accepted the task when called upon by President Carnot. He was then thought to be a stumbling-block in the way of the coveted alliance with Russia, because he once shouted *Vive la Pologne* in the presence of the Czar Alexander II, but a show of courtesy by Baron Mohrenheim, the Russian minister, had removed that disqualification. The list was not completed till April 3, as M. Loubet, who agreed to retain the portfolio of Public Works, and M. Ricard, who accepted that of Justice, found that they could not agree to the revision paragraph of the ministerial declaration, and withdrew. As finally constituted, the Cabinet was composed as follows: President of the Council and Minister of the Interior, Charles Floquet; Minister of War, Charles de Freycinet; Minister of Foreign Affairs, M. René Goblet; Minister of Marine and the Colonies, Admiral Krantz; Minister of Finance, Posts and Telegraphs, M. Peytral; Minister of Public Instruction, Fine Arts, and Worship, Edouard Lockroy; Minister of Public Works, M. Deluns-Montaud; Minister of Justice, M. Ferrouillat; Minister of Commerce and Industry, Pierre Legrand; Minister of Agriculture, François Viette.

The Premier was an advocate in Paris and a prominent Republican during the empire, joined the Commune, was a deputy in 1871, resigned when unable to effect a reconciliation between the Government and the Commune, became president of the Municipal Council, re-entered the Chamber in 1876, and acted with the Extreme Left; was appointed Prefect of the Seine by Gambetta in 1882, and worked in complete harmony with the Municipality until he was compelled to resign because of his sympathy with the autonomist demands of the Parisians, was elected a deputy in October, 1882, and was chosen President of the Chamber when M. Brisson became Premier in 1885. He presided over the Chamber with dignity and impartiality, rebuking the Radicals for wishing to oppress their colleagues when they moved to hold a session on Good Friday, and openly condemning the vote in favor of revision. The Cabinet was one of the Radical Left, to which group MM. Floquet, De Freycinet, Goblet, Lockroy, and Viette belonged, while M. Peytral was a member of the Extreme Left, and recently the sponsor of Félix Pyat before the electors of Marseilles, who returned that Socialist to the Chamber by a large majority. The other three civilian members were Moderate Liberals. The War Ministry was given to M. de Freycinet because he had always coveted that portfolio, having held it in the Provisional Government of 1870, and having fallen out with Gambetta because it was refused him by the latter. The selection of a civilian, and especially a statesman so volatile and fond of innovation, was viewed with distrust, as was also the appointment to the Foreign Office of M. Goblet, who when Premier had joined Gen. Boulanger in a plan for a military demonstration in connection with the Schnaebele affair, which was vetoed by President Grévy.

"Republican concentration" was the watchword of the new Government. The ministerial declaration was non-committal in regard to the questions of separation of church and state, Paris self-government, and the progressive income tax; and in regard to constitutional revision the Government asked to be intrusted with the duty of indicating the propitious moment to begin a work of such importance, which was destined to place the political organization in complete harmony with republican principles. A bill was promised with reference to associations as a preliminary to the definite regulation of the relations of church and state. Among the financial measures to be considered, was a scheme for remodeling the liquor and the succession duties. The bills to augment the military forces, that had passed the Chamber and were to be considered by the Senate, were described as a means of securing the respect due to the nation, and as a guarantee for the maintenance of peace, calculated to prepare conditions favorable to the celebration of the centenary of 1789.

Proceedings of the Chambers.—In the first ballot for a President of the Chamber to succeed M. Floquet, M. Brisson received the most votes, the others being divided between M. Clémenceau, leader of the Extreme Left, and M. Andrieux, ex-Prefect of Police. The latter withdrew, and M. Clémenceau led on the second ballot. On the following morning, when the voting was resumed, the Moderates put forward M. Méline, ex-Minister of Agriculture and leader of the Protectionists, as their candidate, but M. Brisson refused to retire, which made the vote a tie between Méline and Clémenceau, giving the election to the former by right of seniority in age.

When Parliament re-assembled after the Easter holidays, M. Floquet said that the Government desired strength to deal with pretenders, whether draping themselves in the flag or speaking in plebiscitary enigmas, and on being challenged to say whether revision, that is, the Radical scheme of the election of the Senate by universal suffrage, were postponed indefinitely, asked the Chamber to wait until the call for revision ceased to be a Royalist snare or a cloak for conspiring dictators. The order of the day was then carried by 379 to 177 votes.

The sugar bounties, which transfer to the coffers of the sugar manufactures from 70,000,-000 to 90,000.000 francs annually that are raised by general taxation and make French sugar three times as dear in France as in England, were reduced by a bill that passed the Senate on July 17. The surtax of forty francs on foreign alcohol was continued for an indefinite period. In the discussion of a bill to exact compensation for accidents to workmen it was proposed that the family of a foreign workman should not be entitled to compensation from employers in case of death by accident unless resident in France, until it was pointed out that this would make the labor of foreigners more desirable to employers. A bill was passed regulating the employment of women and children in factories.

The ministerial budget scheme was rejected by the budget committee, the majority of the members being Moderate Republicans, owing to the practice of the Reactionaries of aiding in the election of a committee hostile to the Government of the day. The Government proposed an increase of 60,000,000 francs in the ordinary expenditure for 1889, and of 90,000,000 francs in special military and naval expenditure. M. Peytral expected an increase of 12,000,000 francs in the revenue through the Universal Exposition and 25,000,000 francs from the readjustment of the sugar duties. The deficit he proposed to cover by issuing treasury bonds for 100,000,000 francs.

The Government was censured by the Senate on July 1 for not dismissing the *mairie* of Carcassonne, who had been convicted of an election fraud that was intended, not to alter the result, but to save the necessity of a second ballot. Appealing to the Chamber, the ministers obtained a vote of confidence, which was passed by 326 votes against 173. Charges against the monks of a reformatory at Citeaux led to the passing of a bill to suppress all male religious orders, which was defeated in the Senate. It was decided to improve the naval defenses of Brest and Cherbourg. The army bill, reducing the term of military service to three years, while making the obligation universal, including seminarists and students of the liberal professions, who have, however, to serve only one year with the colors, has been before the Chambers for several years, and has been remodeled by different ministers of war. In 1888 it finally passed the Senate.

The session closed in the middle of July, and the new session opened on October 15. M. Floquet presented his revision proposals, which did not involve the abolition of the Senate, but restricted its control over legislation to the right of remonstrance and postponement, and did not touch the presidential power, which the extreme Radicals wished to do away with altogether.

The revision scheme proposes that one third both of the Senate and the Chamber shall retire every second year, the two sets of elections being held simultaneously. Between the Radical demand of direct election of senators and the present system a compromise is made by having the delegates nominated by the communes, instead of by the municipalities, which is indirect election in two degrees, in the place of three. It proposes that the Council of State shall be nominated partly by Parliament and partly by chambers of commerce and trade-unions. It is to be given a consultative voice in legislation from a judicial point of view, and be divided into technical sections, qualified to advise on questions affecting labor, commerce, agriculture, and the arts. The council shall frame bills at the instance of the Government, and its commissaries will take part in their discussion in Parliament. Bills will be first introduced in the Chamber, and after it has passed them the Senate will have only a suspensive veto, leaving the question to be decided by the next biennial election. The Senate can send back to the Chamber amendments to the budget, but the vote of the Chamber on these shall be final. The power of the President and the Senate to dissolve the Chamber is to be abolished. The stability of ministries, of which there had been twenty-three since the foundation of the republic. was promoted by providing that they can only be removed by the President after a formal vote of want of confidence.

Boulangism.—When Gen. Boulanger was presented for the first time as a candidate for the Chamber in four departments, Gen. Logerot, Minister of War, sought an interview with him, and, after receiving his positive denial that he had taken any part in the election manœuvres, told him to return to Clermont, the headquarters of the army corps that he commanded, and take care that his name should not be improperly used by his friends in the future. Not many days afterward he broke his parole by going to Paris in disguise, where he was recognized by an army officer, and on investigation it was found that he had personally directed the electioneering campaign by means of cipher telegrams. For these acts he was relieved of his command and placed in non-activity, called before a court-martial, consisting of five generals, on March 26, 1888. This was the signal for demonstrations for and against Boulanger, and, while his trial was pending, he was a candidate at Marseilles, receiving a small vote, and in Aisne, where he headed the poll in the primary elections, although as an officer in active service he was ineligible, and then withdrew in favor of one of his partisans. He defended himself before the military court by saying that he came to Paris to visit his sick wife and denying his participation in the electoral canvass; but when confronted with the telegraphic dispatches, he made no answer. The court voted unanimously against him, and President Carnot signed the decree placing him on the retired list. Freed thus of the restraints imposed by his military duties, he openly took the field as a candidate for the department of the Nord with an address in which he accused the Chamber of suppressing the defenses of the nation, and the Senate of checking every reform, and his judges of condemning him for reasons which they dared not avow. His condemnation gave him a greater prominence than he had before. The antagonists of the third republic—Imperialists, Clericals, Royalists, and many extreme Radicals and Socialists—supported him, openly or secretly, as the representative of dissatisfaction with the existing order of things and with the men who controlled the policy of the nation. His popularity rested chiefly on the military reforms that he had effected as Minister of War. He was regarded among the common soldiers and the peasantry as the creator of an army that was capable, or soon would be, of avenging Sedan, and in his speeches he hinted vaguely at war. The rural voters, who formerly adhered to the empire, at the beck of Bonapartist leaders, now turned to Boulanger as the embodiment of the idea of personal government, which is strong among the French peasantry. Boulanger called himself a democratic Republican, although his political friends and financial supporters were Bonapartists; and, in his demand for a revision of the Constitution, he hinted at a system resembling that of the United States, in which the President should be chosen by a plébiscite, and the ministers be responsible to him, and not to Parliament. The Monarchist and Socialist factions that constituted his party each hoped to shape the changes after their own ideas. He was elected by a majority of 100,000 in the Nord, where Bonapartists and

Republican extremists are strong. He was elected in the Dordogne also, but took his seat as deputy for the Nord department. The programme on which he was elected, chiefly by Bonapartist votes, was dissolution, revision, and a constituent assembly. He made his appearance in the Chamber on June 4, and arraigned parliamentarism, characterizing cabinets as servile tools of selfish coalitions, and the President as a mere log. Expressing a Platonic belief in the Radical plan of abolishing both the Senate and the presidency, he proposed as a practical solution the election of the Senate by universal suffrage, the submission of laws to a referendum, and the election of the President directly by the people, who desired to have a visible head of the Government. Then a national policy would take the place of intrigue, and France would enter on the condition of having fixed and regular governments. M. Floquet in his reply described the scheme as veiled Cæsarism, and alluded to one of Boulanger's manifestoes, in which he said that the people must be cared for like a child.

On July 12 Gen. Boulanger appeared in the Chamber again, in order to bring forward a motion for the dissolution of the Chamber, supporting it in a speech denunciatory of the existing Chamber and of the Government. The Prime Minister replied in caustic terms, describing him as one who, having passed from vestibules into antechambers, yet had the effrontery to insult tried Republicans, the least of whom had done the republic more good than he could do it harm; whereupon Gen. Boulanger declared that M. Floquet had "impudently lied" in speaking of him as a frequenter of antechambers, and announced that he resigned his seat, his letter of resignation being already in the speaker's hands. His purpose was to obtain another election from the people. He at once presented himself as a candidate to fill a vacancy in the representation of the Ardèche, but was defeated, as was his nominee, Paul Déroulède, the apostle of revenge, in the Charente. His revision scheme was presented, and referred to the committee on revision that had been appointed at the beginning of the new ministry. During the five months of the existence of his party of National Protest, which was amply supplied with Bonapartist funds, he had received in the various by-elections fully half a million votes. The insult to the Premier resulted, as was expected, in a duel. Gen. Boulanger's seconds were M. Laisant and Count Dillon; M. Floquet's were MM. Clémenceau and Georges Périn. The insulted party chose swords as the weapons. They met on the following morning. Gen. Boulanger showed a determination to make the duel fatal, rushing into close quarters with impetuosity, and, after the interchange of slight wounds on both sides, M. Floquet, in parrying a thrust, pierced him in the throat, inflicting a severe wound close to the carotid artery. The result was humiliating to the soldier, particularly so because M. Floquet had the reputation of not knowing how to handle a sword, and had not practiced for twenty years till the preceding winter, when he fenced for the benefit of his health. On August 19 he was a candidate in elections that were held in the department of the Nord, where his majority was only 27,000, in the Charente-Inférieure, where he received 57,000 votes to 42,000, and in the Somme, where he had 76,000 votes to 41,000 for his Republican opponent.

After this electoral triumph, which caused much alarm throughout Europe, Gen. Boulanger disappeared, and traveled *incognito* in foreign lands, not returning till October. On the 24th of that month he appeared before the revision committee of the Chamber, having two days before taken his seat as a member for the department of the Somme. He said that he would leave the question of revision to be decided entirely by the Constituent Assembly, and declined to give his own views further than that he desired an Executive that should not be responsible to the Legislature. There was a renewal of disquieting popular agitation. Collisions took place at political meetings between Boulangists and anti-Boulangists, and on October 30 the Government ordered the police to seize pictures that were sold in the streets representing Gen. Boulanger driving out the deputies from the Chamber, and portraits, likewise in uniform, of the Comte de Paris and Prince Victor Bonaparte.

Strikes and the Closure of the Labor Exchange.— The Bourse du Travail in Paris is a large hall for the use of workingmen's associations and unions, and was built with municipal subventions. The majority of the Syndical Chambers, which have their offices there, belong to the Possiblist party, which aims at gradual social revolution by constitutional and peaceable means, while some are Anarchists, others are Blanquists, and some style themselves Independent, and show revolutionary tendencies. One of the objects of the central labor hall was to maintain an open register where employers could find workmen at the different trades without the intervention of the employment bureaus, which charge fees that are often exorbitant. This feature was not sufficiently developed, because hirers of labor persisted in patronizing the private agencies. In the summer of 1888 the war of class interests broke out in a series of strikes in Paris, which were instigated mostly by the leaders of the revolutionary minority. The specter of labor politics has influenced the selection of cabinets by the Presidents who preceded M. Carnot, and was one cause of their instability, for they have usually been chosen from among the discredited leaders of the Opportunist minority, the Floquet Cabinet being the first that approximates the center of gravity of the Republican party. The labor disturbances of the year began at the annual celebration of the Com-

munist insurrection at the cemetery of Père Lachaise on May 27. Some of the extreme Socialists, under the lead of Henri Rochefort and the "Intransigeant" newspaper, had attached themselves to the Boulangist movement. A large section of the Possiblists, led by Citizen Joffrin, had joined a Society of the Rights of Man hostile to Boulanger, which had been founded by MM. Clémenceau and Ranc, and had for its ostensible object the defense of the republic against attempts at reaction or dictatorship. Orators from these groups, as well as Blanquists and Anarchists, made speeches over the graves of Communards. As a Boulangist wreath was being deposited at the foot of the wall where the defenders of the Commune were shot down by the Versaillais troops, an Anarchist named Lucas, who had recently been tried for an attempt on the life of Louise Michel at a public meeting in Havre, fired with a revolver at the bearer, whose name was Rouillon, wounding two Blanquists in the crowd. A fight ensued between Anarchists and Communists, which was stopped by the police. On July 25 a general strike of the laborers in the building trades began in Paris, throwing out of employment a great number of other workmen of the class most addicted to Anarchist sentiments. The strike originated among the laborers employed at the Exhibition works on the Champs de Mars, who demanded 60 centimes an hour, the price established by the Municipal Council for the public works of the city, instead of 45 or 50 centimes, that the contractors were paying. Men throughout Paris who continued at work were compelled by the strikers to throw down their tools. Most of the strikers were Belgians, Italians, and Germans. The police, assisted by the military, attempted to prevent disturbance and illegal interference with workmen, and many strikers were arrested, but let go. The Municipal Council rejected, by 40 to 28 votes, a proposition of M. Vaillant to aid the strikers with money. By July 31, the number of workmen on strike who had inscribed their names at the Syndical Chamber was 9,812. The carters joined the strike in the beginning of August. M. Floquet received a deputation of strikers, and announced that the Government would permit no interference with combinations to strike nor intimidation of laborers who wished to work. Strikes were threatened by the carpenters and in other trades where wages were lower than the municipal tariff. The agitation and strikes spread to the provinces. Disturbances were made by strikers at Amiens, who sacked and burned a velvet-factory and fought the police behind barricades. At Bességes the miners struck for an advance of 50 per cent. At Calais demonstrations of the unemployed were accompanied by violence. The upsetting of carts and taking away of tools went on in Paris, and the public prosecutor could find no law directed against such offenses. The hair-dressers, coffee-house waiters, cooks, and dairymen took revenge on the employment agents by destroying their signs and windows. The funeral, on August 8, of Gen. Eudes, ex-Communard and leader of the Blanquists, who fell dead while addressing a meeting of strikers, gave rise to two serious affrays with the police, who captured some red flags that were unfurled in the procession after a struggle, and, after a bomb was thrown, charged on a mob, making arrests, and repeated the charge when the crowd besieged and stoned the police station, cutting with their swords, not only Anarchist rioters, but many spectators, even women and children. The funeral procession was to have started from the Bourse du Travail, but in compliance with a clamor for the closing of this rallying-place, where strikers had been encouraged and inflamed by many violent speeches, the Government had decided to take possession of the hall, and this morning sent troops to stop all the approaches. On August 13 the joiners, and afterward the cabinet-makers struck in sympathy with the laborers. The fund that was raised for the strikers having given out, at the end of twenty-five days, when many families were suffering from hunger, the strike was abandoned, and the 3,000 laborers who still held out returned to work. The workmen employed on the Eiffel tower, the swaying of which created alarm as to its security, also struck, and did not resume till an increase was granted. Strikers at the coal-mines at Treuil attacked miners who continued at work on September 26, and fought desperately with the police who interfered.

The Wilson Case.—Daniel Wilson, ex-President Grévy's son-in-law, who was charged with complicity in the swindling operations of Mme. Ratazzi and others who had been convicted or were on trial for obtaining money on the pretense of procuring decorations, was convicted by the Correctional Tribunal on March 1, and sentenced to two years' imprisonment and a fine of 3,000 francs. It was proved that he had promised the Cross of the Legion of Honor for a bribe, and his counsel argued that this was not obtaining money on false pretenses because he really possessed influence. The Court of Appeals adopted that view, and quashed the conviction.

Foreign Relations.—The adoption of vexatious passport regulations by the German Government for the purpose of making the entrance into Alsace-Lorraine difficult to Frenchmen caused much irritation in France, and led to retaliatory restrictions. The regulations were contained in an administrative decree that was published in May ordering that every foreigner arriving in Alsace-Lorraine by the French frontier, whether he is simply passing through the country or desires to reside there, must have a passport furnished by his Government or its diplomatic representatives, bearing the *visa* of the German embassy in Paris. The *visa*, the expense of which is fixed in all cases at twelve francs fifty centimes, must be renewed every year. Every Frenchman who remains more than twenty-four hours in the commune of Alsace-Lorraine, arriving by any of the frontiers, must make a declaration of residence and establish his identity by a passport viséed by the German embassador at Paris, which formality will entitle him to remain eight weeks, at the end of which he must obtain permission to prolong his stay from the president of the district. Before giving his *visa* in such cases the embassy must make inquiries of the provincial authorities whether there are any objections to the sojourn of the person seeking permission.

The regulations proved an annoyance, not only to Frenchmen, but to travelers of all nationalities who enter Germany through Alsace-Lorraine, many of whom were stopped at the frontier because their passports had not received the requisite *visa* of the German embassador. Some of the German travelers were roughly treated by the exasperated inhabitants of the French border districts which led to attacks in the German official press denouncing France as a "savage country," and calling on other nations to adopt toward her the policy that they pursue in regard to uncivilized countries. On June 20 two French newspaper correspondents were expelled from Berlin for writing and telegraphing to Paris matter that was insulting to high personages.

The jealousy that has existed between France and Italy since the occupation of Tunis, becoming a settled condition on the entrance of Italy into the Austro-German alliance, the terms of the Triple Alliance were made known to the world in the beginning of 1888, while French and Italian plenipotentiaries were engaged in the negotiation of a new commercial treaty to end the war of tariffs which added to the causes of tension. The sensitiveness shown in the negotiations prevented a satisfactory conclusion by mutual concessions, and in January the negotiations were interrupted, to be resumed again in June.

In the summer arose the incident of the refusal of French subjects and *protégés* to pay communal taxes at Massowah on the advice of the French Government, and the resulting correspondence in regard to the capitulations (see ABYSSINIA). M. Goblet's note was couched in calm diplomatic language, and the heated and provocative tone in which Signor Crispi replied and his visit about the same time at Friedrichsruhe gave rise to a suspicion of German promptings. "The powers, having before them all the details of the discussion," said the Italian minister in his reply of August 13 to M. Goblet's second note, "will know which side is in the wrong—whether it is the power which enforces respect for the law assuring public order or whether it is the one which excites a peaceful population to disregard the law and to defy the authority of the established Government." Italy was technically in the wrong in treating the capitulations as having lapsed before a formal notification to the powers of the taking possession of Massowah, in compliance with the Congo treaty that was made at Berlin in 1885, and in his first circular Signor Crispi made such notification. This was treated by the French Government in the further correspondence as only a preliminary to negotiations respecting the abolition of the capitulations by consent of the powers.

The Hungarian Premier, M. Tisza, in announcing in May that the Hungarian Government would not take no official part in the French Exhibition of 1889, as he had already declared a year before, but would discourage Hungarians from exhibiting, based the decision on the ground that the French Government would not or could not protect foreigners from violence. His utterances on this subject in the Hungarian Chamber conveyed an admonition that the days of Hungarian sympathy for France were over in a tone so provocative that explanations were asked.

Colonies.—The colonial possessions and protectorates of France have a total area of 2,267,034 square kilometres, with a population of 26,003,995. The following table shows the area and population of the colonies and protectorates, according to the latest estimates and returns:

POSSESSIONS.	Square kilometres.	Population.
Asia :		
Possessions in India..........	509	275,261
Cochin-China ,.............	59,458	1,792,738
French Tonquin	90,000	9,000,000
Africa :		
Algeria......................	667,000	3,817,465
Senegambia..................	250,000(?)	183,237
Gaboon and Gold Coast........	180,000(?)	186,133(?)
Congo region	480,000(?)	500,000(?)
Réunion	2,512	179,639
Sta. Marie	830	7,634
Nossi Bé and Mayotte....		21,348
Obock......................	10,000	22,370
America :		
Guiana	121,413	26,502
Guadeloupe	1,869	181,098
Martinique..................	987	169,232
St. Pierre and Miquelon	235	6,300
Oceania :		
New Caledonia	19,823	56,468
Marquesas Islands	1,244	5,776
Tahiti and Moorea............	1,179	10,639
Tabuai and Raivavai	209	665
Tuamotu, Gambier, and Rapa islands	1,000	8,500
Total colonies	1,788,263	16,439,995
Protectorates :		
Tunis	118,000	2,000,000
Annam	275,300	6,000,000
Cambodia....................	83,860	1,500,000
Comoros......................	1,606	53,000
Total	478,766	9,553,000
Grand total	2,267,034	26,003,995

The budget for 1888 estimates 41,841,331 francs for the colonies, including 2,500,000 francs for New Caledonia, 6,333,000 francs for Senegambia, 3,000,000 francs for Cochin-China, and 3,250,000 francs for Annam.

By a decree that was issued on Oct. 17, 1887, the whole of the possessions of France in Indo-China, comprising Cochin-China, Tonquin, Annam, and Cambodia, were united under one civil governor-general of Indo-China, with a lieutenant-governor in Cochin-China, a resident-general in Tonquin and Annam, and a resident-general in Cambodia. M. Constans, previously resident at Hanoi, was nominated Governor-General, but in the beginning of September, 1888, he was dismissed in consequence of a dispute between himself and the under-secretary for the colonies, and M. Richaud, his chief subordinate, was appointed to succeed him. The revenue of French Indo-China for 1888 was estimated at $13,656,000, and the expenditure at $18,756,126. The estimated revenue of Annam and Tonquin for 1887–'88 was 44,860,000 francs, and the expenditure 44,758,230 francs. The expenses of the annexation and Government of Tonquin up to the end of 1887 were 299,000,000 francs. For 1888 the ministry asked for $20,000,000 francs, and was almost defeated by the vote of the Chamber on February 13. The number of troops maintained in Indo-China is still nearly 14,000. There are moreover 18,000 native troops. The King of Annam has ceded to France the towns of Haiphong, Hanoi, and Tourane, and the country around them, and has decreed that French property shall be subject to French laws in Tonquin and the free ports, and that Frenchmen may acquire property in any part of his kingdom, subject to the laws of Annam. Rebellion against French authority, or "piracy," as it is called, is still rife in Tonquin, and the conquerors have resorted to the plan of imposing heavy fines on villages that are suspected of aiding or harboring pirates, and distributing one half of the proceeds among villages distinguished for loyalty, while the remainder is employed in maintaining and improving the Tonquinese militia, which has been reorganized under the name of the civil native guard, and is no longer trusted to oppose the rebel bands, but is employed for police duties only. In October, 1888, the former King of Annam, who, with his minister Thuyet, kept up a vigorous resistance after his capital had been captured and another king installed, was made a prisoner by French troops, Thuyet being slain. For protecive and fiscal purposes, the French general tariff was put in force in Indo-China on July 1, 1887. Although it increased the revenue, the change did not stimulate the importation of French goods, and the effect on commerce and production was very unfavorable.

The Senegambian possessions have been extended in the past four years, either by treaties with native chiefs or by simple assumption of dominion, until they include the whole of the upper Niger as far as the great falls east of Timbuctoo. The territory claimed by France embraces all the country behind British Gambia and Portuguese Senegambia and half of the region inclosed in the great bend of the Niger. Between Sierra Leone and Portuguese Senegambia the French have a strip of coast. Their possessions in this region are about 130,000 square miles in extent, not counting the indefinite claims to the east of the Niger. The trade of Senegambia, which is almost exclusively with France, now amounts to 50,000,000 francs per annum, equally divided between imports and exports. On the Guinea coast France claims about 10,000 square miles behind the stations of Grand Bassam, Assinie, Grand Popo, Porto Novo, and Kotonere, from which an export trade in cabinet-woods and palm-oil is carried on. The exports from Porto Novo alone are estimated at 1,000,000 francs a year, and the imports at an equal amount. The practice of claiming the entire interior back of occupied sections of the coast has led to a rivalry between the French, whose coast line faces the west, except the limited establishments on the Ivory and Gold Coasts, and the British, whose possessions on the Guinea coast, if extended into the interior, will cut off the French from the regions lying behind Senegambia, which they claim to include in their sphere of influence, and over a part of which they assert, but have not yet exercised, a protectorate. In this race the British have at present the advantage in their possession of the water-way of the Niger.

The activity of the English on the Niger impelled the French to push more vigorously the project of extending their Senegambian provinces so as to embrace the upper Niger and Timbuctoo. When this scheme was first entertained several expeditions were sent from St. Louis to penetrate to the Niger, and 50 miles were built of a railroad that was to extend from Medina, on the middle Senegal, to Bamakou, on the upper Niger, a distance of over 300 miles. After sinking much capital and losing many lives in fights with the natives' and by the diseases of the climate, the work was stopped. In 1887 Lieut. Caron descended the Niger in a gun-boat from Sansanding to Timbuctoo, where he was inhospitably received. This is the precursor of other expeditions, which will result in the annexation of Timbuctoo, an important trading-center, but not the only town in the western Soudan in which a caravan trade is carried on with the north. The work on the Senegal railroad is to be resumed, and the project has been revived of extending it through the Sahara so as to connect Senegambia with Algeria.

The French have lately been busy in extending their influence over the tribes of the interior behind the Gold Coast. One of the chiefs near Lagos was seized and transported by the British for listening to overtures of French officers, one of whom subsequently visited Abeokuta, a populous town in the kingdom of Agbas, and made a treaty with several native chiefs, which, except for the active measures that were taken by the British, would have resulted in closing the roads to Lagos and diverting the entire trade of the river Ogoun to Porto Novo.

The French possessions in the Gaboon and Congo regions have expanded greatly since 1884, until now the French Congo, the Ogowé, and the Gaboon colonies have an area of 238,000 square miles that is conceded to France, while her sphere of influence on the north of the Congo reaches at present over at least 160,000 square miles more. The entire basin of the Ogowé, and the Kwilu with its stations were conceded by the Berlin Conference, while her claim to the interior as far as the Mobangi, which has been identified as the Wellé, comprising the entire north bank of the river until it cuts the 4th parallel of north latitude, has been virtually admitted. The commercial value of these acquisitions has been very slight up to the present time. The entire trade of the Gaboon is estimated not to exceed 10,000,000 francs per annum. The total trade of the French dominions in Africa amounts to about 500,000,000 francs. Including Algeria and Tunis, about 700,000 square miles, or nearly one sixteenth of the entire surface of Africa, are subject to France, with a population of between 7,000,000 and 10,000,000 souls.

The Marquesas Islands have been a French protectorate since 1841. In September, 1888, the French flag was hoisted and the islands were taken possession of after severe fighting between French marines and the natives.

The New Hebrides convention released France from an engagement, made in 1847, not to annex Raiatea, Borabora, and Huahine, called the Isles sous le Vent or the Leeward Islands, of the Society Archipelago. In 1878 the French took possession of the principal one of the group, Raiatea, and since then the French flag has floated over the island, but only through the sufferance of Great Britain, and, by virtue of a convention that had to be renewed annually, only for six months of each year. The English and German residents, hoping still to induce the British Government to revoke its decision by fomenting native opposition to the French occupation, stirred up a rebellion against King Tamatoa, the ruler who enjoyed French protection. After failing to intimidate the rebels with cannon shots, the officer in command of the naval force on Dec. 17, 1887 issued an ultimatum calling on the inhabitants to submit to Tamatoa, and on the refusal of several chiefs the gun-boat "Scorpion" bombarded their villages and landed troops. On March 16, the French flag was raised on all the islands. Five days after the annexation of Huahine the natives hostile to French rule attacked a patrol, killing an officer and two sailors. The disturbance was quelled, and did not recur. In June the hostile natives of Raiatea sent a demand that the French should evacuate the island, to which the naval commander replied by landing a company of marines and a cannon.

The Wallis Islands, lying midway between Samoa and Fiji, were declared a French protectorate on Dec. 31, 1887. French influences became predominant half a century ago, but regard for British susceptibilities prevented annexation at that time. Unea, the principal island, is only 7 miles long, but contains 4,000 inhabitants, belonging to the finest of the Pacific races, a large majority of whom, including Amélie, their Queen, are Catholics.

Algeria.—The Governor-General of Algeria is Louis Tirman, appointed Nov. 26, 1881.

In the census of 1886, the population was 3,817,465, exclusive of wandering Arab tribes, occupying an area of 122,867 square miles. Of the total population the department of Algiers contained 1,380,541, Constantine 1,566,419, and Oran 869,505. To the above must be added the Algerian Sahara, with an estimated area of 135,000 square miles, and an estimated population of 50,000. In 1886, of the total population, 261,591 were of French origin, 42,744 naturalized Jews, 3,274,354 French indigenous subjects, 5,055 Tunisians, and 233,721 foreigners, including Spaniards, Italians, Anglo-Maltese, and Germans. The population of the city of Algiers in 1886 was 71,199; of Oran, 58,545; of Constantine, 36,536.

The total expenditure of the Government for 1887 was 120,340,256 francs, the cost of the civil government being 39,205,285 francs; special services, 6,127,206 francs; military services, 54,048,968 francs; extraordinary expenses, 20,958,797 francs; colonization, 2,815,000 francs. The revenue for the same year was 43,734,303 francs. The number of troops in Algeria was 54,000.

The imports in 1886 amounted to 242,274,279 francs, of which 189,175,785 francs came from France, and 53,098,494 from other countries. The exports were 182,255,122 francs, 125,587,932 francs to France and 56,667,191 francs to other countries.

The lines of railway open for traffic in 1887 were 1,290 miles in length. The receipts in 1886 amounted to 21,174,400 francs.

Wine-growing is an industry of increasing importance. The area planted in vineyards in 1887 was 190,000 acres, yielding 2,000,000 hectolitres of wine. The product of the older vineyards compares favorably with the best French wines. The phylloxera has appeared, but has been kept in check by stringent measures of protection. The colonization of Algeria has increased rapidly since 1871, when 10,500 refugees from Alsace-Lorraine were granted lands and the means of beginning as agriculturists. During the past eleven years 8,000 families have been settled under favorable conditions on lands that were taken from the Arabs in consequence of revolts, at a cost to the Government of 15,000,000 francs, not reckoning the value of the land. Grasshoppers did much damage to the growing crops in 1887, and in 1888 swarms of crickets devastated many localities.

Tunis.—The principality of Tunis has not been formally annexed, but is under the regency of France. The ruling Bey is Sidi Ali, born Oct. 5, 1817, who succeeded his brother, Sidi Mohamed-es-Sadok, Oct. 28, 1882. The French Resident-General, M. Massicault, practically administers the government of the country under the Bureau des Affaires Tunisiennes of the French Foreign Office.

The area is about 42,000 square miles, and the estimated population is 2,100,000, of which number 2,028,000 are Mohammedans, 45,000 Jews, 25,100 Roman Catholics, 400 Greek Catholics, and 100 Protestants. The capital city, Tunis, has a population of about 145,000.

The estimated revenue for 1887-'88 was 21,806,531 francs, which was balanced by the expenditure. The main sources of revenue are as follow: Direct taxes, 7,454,562 francs; monopolies, 4,355,625 francs; customs, 2,020,000 francs. The charges for civil government that are borne by France do not exceed 150,000 francs per annum. In 1886, 5,752 vessels, of 1,301,695 tons, entered, and 5,592 vessels, of 1,292,275 tons, cleared the ports of Tunis. The principal articles of export are olive-oil, wheat, barley, sponges, and woolen goods. The imports are cotton goods, coffee, sugar, spirits, silks, etc. Tunis had 256 miles of railway and 2,000 miles of telegraph in operation in 1885.

Since Tunis was made a French protectorate European farms have become numerous, the cultivation of the vine has been introduced and is extending, foreign commerce has doubled, banks have been established, and public works have been constructed, though without undue haste. Much attention is given to the conservation and improvement of native industries, and some new branches have been introduced. There has been much progress in education, primary schools having been established in all parts of the country, and supplied with teachers from a normal college in Tunis. The Government has given care to the preservation and encouragement to the study of the ancient monuments that are scattered through the country, and has founded libraries and museums. In 1888 the first steps were taken toward the establishment of a uniform system of education, such as exists in France; but the Italians, who have schools in which their language is taught and formerly received concessions and encouragement from the Bey, objected to having the continuance or the character of these schools depend on the will of French officials. They therefore invoked the capitulations, which were originally designed for the protection of subjects of the Christian powers of Europe against arbitrary acts of Mussulman governments. The French Government, while insisting that the capitulations were still operative at Massowah, denied the Italian contention that they were in force in Tunis. The Italian residents in Tunis objected especially to the new school-regulations that the Bey had issued, introducing the inspection of schools by French officials, and the Italian school-masters, under the instructions of the Consul-General, refused admittance to the Bey's inspectors. The powers, which had sustained Italy in the Massowah question, because in that port the authority of the former Mohammedan Government had been openly superseded, as in Cyprus and Bosnia, joined in the Italian protest in respect to Tunis, because, although the authority of France is supreme, she has only accepted a protectorate, and ostensibly maintains the rule of the Bey.

The Panama Canal.—The affairs of the Panama Canal Company reached a crisis in December, 1888. The technical committee of the Paris Congress of 1879 estimated the total cost of a sea-level canal of 73 kilometres at 1,200,000,000 francs, of which 1,070,000,000 francs would be for tunnel construction. The company has had to contend with difficulties from the beginning. The first attempt to float the shares failed, and on the second attempt the subscription was barely covered. The issues of obligations have never more than partially succeeded. The company has labored under the disadvantage of having to pay 5-per cent. dividends out of the capital. The engineering difficulties were greatly underestimated; the disadvantages of the deadly climate, for instance, were not sufficiently taken into account. The company had money enough to begin work in 1881, and by 1888 had 11,000 men employed. After three years, only 119,-000,000 tons of the estimated 3,500,000,000 tons of excavation had been removed. Many millions have been spent in constructing a dam, more than a mile long and 140 feet high, across the Chagres valley, in order to prevent the river in times of flood from sweeping away the canal works; but this dam is still far from being completed. The company had expended 1,400,000,000 francs by 1888. After repeated appeals, the French Chamber was induced to authorize a lottery loan on June 8, 1888, but the subscriptions were disappointing. The company sold only 850 of these bonds; yet to make good its promise as to prizes it was compelled, under the law, to invest 100,000,000 francs in *rentes*. A final effort was made to raise a new loan. It was announced that unless 400,000 obligations were taken up the subscription would be null and void. Only 125,000 were subscribed, and on December 14 the company suspended payments. The Chamber refused to authorize the company to defer payments for three months. M. de Lesseps said that the canal could be finished by 1891, not on the level plan but with locks, and that 357,000,000 francs of additional capital would be required. It was proposed to form a new company to complete the work, which should assume the capital obligations of the old company, but pay no interest on the existing bonds and shares until it can be defrayed out of the profits of the canal. M. de Lesseps and his

colleagues resigned their posts as administrators of the company on December 14, whereupon the Tribunal of the Seine appointed judicial liquidators.

FRIEDRICH WILHELM NICOLAUS KARL, eighth King of Prussia and second Emperor of Germany, born in Potsdam, Prussia, Oct. 18, 1831; died there, June 15, 1888. He was the only son of Emperor Wilhelm I of Germany, who at the time his son was born was Prince Wilhelm of Hohenzollern, second son of King Friedrich Wilhelm III of Prussia. The birth of the prince was the occasion of general rejoicing throughout Prussia, as the succession to the crown devolved upon the issue of Prince Wilhelm; the Crown-Prince, afterward Friedrich Wilhelm IV, being childless. His mother, Augusta, daughter of the Grand Duke Karl Friedrich of Saxe-Weimar, a woman of rare attainments, devoted her whole time and energy to his education. Col. von Unruh was appointed his military instructor, and on his tenth birthday the prince officially entered the army as second lieutenant of the First Regiment of the Guards. The first tutor of the young prince, the Rev. W. Godet, was succeeded in 1844 by Dr. Ernst Curtius, the Greek historian, who directed his studies till 1850. According to a custom of the Hohenzollern family, which requires every prince to learn a trade, Prince Friederich, at the age of fourteen, chose that of a printer, and, in Hoenels' royal printing-office at Berlin, attained such proficiency that, in setting up the type for a book in German, Greek, and Latin, one of the oldest compositors had difficulty in keeping pace with him. Much of his time between 1841 and 1846 was spent in traveling throughout Germany. In 1846 he entered the University of Bonn, the favorite educational institution of German princes. He spent four semesters at the university, engaged in the study of history, civil and criminal law, and kindred sciences. His vacations were spent in pedestrian tours and in the study of the architecture of Cologne, Aix-la-Chapelle, and other German cities. At the university he was highly popular, in spite of the fact that the name of Prussian was then a rebuke in the Rhineland province. On May 3, 1849, he entered the First Foot Guards. The year 1850 was spent in traveling through Switzerland, the Tyrol, the north of Italy, and the south of France. The opening of the London Industrial Exhibition of 1851 took him to England for the first time, where he became acquainted with his future bride, the Princess Victoria, then a girl of eleven years. On his return to Berlin he was promoted to the rank of captain in the Guards, and the following year he accompanied the Emperor Nicholas of Russia back to St. Petersburg, where he was appointed colonel of a Russian regiment. He studied the practical workings of administrative law under Herr Flottwell president of the province of Brandenburg, and the art and tactics of war under Von Moltke. Toward the close of 1853 he went to Italy, where he spent four months in the company of painters, sculptors, archæologists, and statesmen, and first met Pope Pius IX, for whom he always retained a feeling of veneration.

He was now ordered to serve with the dragoons, and his commander, Col. von Griesheim, was instructed to subject him to the actual labors and duties of a soldier's life. In 1854 he was appointed a member of a commission to test the Minié rifle, and shortly afterward he was nominated to the command of the Second Landwehr Guards.

In 1855 Col. von Moltke became adjutant to the prince, who had attained the rank of colonel, and in September of that year, in company with Moltke, he visited England, and before his return he became betrothed to the princess royal. In May, 1856, he again visited England, and in August of this year went to Moscow as the representative of the Prussian royal house at the coronation of the Emperor Alexander II. The following December, on returning from a visit to England, he visited Paris for the first time. The Empress Eugenie, in a letter to a friend, described the prince as tall and handsome, slim and fair, and commented: "They are an imposing race, these Germans. Louis calls them the race of the future. But we have not come to that."

He married Princess Victoria on Jan. 25, 1858. On becoming Crown-Prince, when his father succeeded to the throne of Prussia on the death of King Friedrich Wilhelm IV, he was sworn in a member of the King's Council, and was appointed on the commission for the reorganization of the army. After the dissolution of the Chamber of Deputies and the abolition of the liberty of the press in 1863, the Crown-Prince protested against the methods of the Bismarck ministry, which he declared to be "both illegal and injurious to the state and the dynasty." The King demanded a retraction of his sentiments on pain of being recalled to Berlin and deprived of his military command. The prince replied that he could not retract his speech, that he was ready, if required, to lay down his commission in the army and resign his seat in the Council of State, saying, "If I am not allowed to speak my mind, I must naturally wish to dissever myself entirely from the sphere of politics."

Domestic legislation in Prussia was overshadowed in 1864 by a war with Denmark, arising out of the disputed succession to the duchies of Schleswig and Holstein. The Crown-Prince had at this time attained the rank of lieutenant-general in the army without having ever seen a battle, but the outbreak of the Danish war sent him to the field of real warfare as an officer on the staff of Field-Marshal Wrangel. He was engaged at the battle of Düppel, and in the subsequent operations of the Prussian and Austrian forces in the brief campaign that resulted in the defeat of Denmark, displaying courage and energy, and on

his return to Berlin he was nominated to the general command of the Second Army Corps.

In the war with Austria Prince Friederich was placed in command of the Second Army Corps, forming the left wing of the force in Silesia. He was also appointed general of infantry and military governor of Silesia during the continuance of hostilities. The Second Army Corps was intended to play a secondary part, but when Saxony was occupied without opposition, and the armies were concentrated for the invasion of Bohemia, the burden on the Crown-Prince's shoulders was largely increased. By three days' fighting he successfully carried his army from the frontier to the Elbe, defeating four of the six army corps opposed to him. He fought spirited engagements at Trautenau and Nachod, coming up to the latter place at a critical moment in support of Gen. Steinmetz. Fighting continued until June 29, when the prince with his army took possession of Skalitz. During this brief campaign, the soldiers under the Crown-Prince had captured five colors, two standards, twenty guns, and 8,000 prisoners. The great battle of Sadowa or Königgrätz was fought on July 3, 1866. The opportune arrival of the Crown Prince with his army, which was fifteen miles away at the beginning of the engagement, gave the victory to the Prussians after one of the most sanguinary battles of modern times. For this victory the prince received the Order of Merit on the field of battle, and shortly after the close of the war was appointed president of a military commission to analyze and formulate the experiences of the war. The prince described his recollections of the war in a privately printed work entitled "Erinnerungen aus dem Kriege."

In October, 1869, the Crown-Prince, accompanied by Prince Ludwig of Hesse, journeyed by way of Vienna, Venice, Athens, and Constantinople to Egypt, to attend the opening of the Suez Canal.

The outbreak of the Franco-Prussian war in 1870, found the Crown-Prince in command of one of the three divisions of the German army, consisting of the armies of Bavaria, Würtemberg, and Baden, and the Fifth, Sixth, and Eleventh North German Corps, numbering in all about 200,000 men. The first military triumph of the war was his victory on Aug. 4, 1870, over a portion of Marshal MacMahon's forces stationed at Weissenbourg. Alsace was now open to the prince, the roads to Strasburg and Bitsch were seized, and in his further advance toward the passes of the Vosges he encountered the main body of the army of MacMahon at Wörth. This battle, which lasted fifteen hours, terminated in a decisive victory for the prince, the French losses being 10,000 killed or wounded, and 6,000 prisoners. By the 11th of August, the Crown-Prince had crossed the Vosges and occupied the town of Nancy. He detached the Baden division of his army, which captured Hagenau, and besieged Strasburg. The Castle of Lichtenburg was taken by the Würtemberg division, and Pfalsburg was invested by the Bavarians. After the battles of Mars-le-Tour and Gravelotte, between Prince Friedrich Karl and Marshal Bazaine, the Crown-Prince began his march toward Paris, and laid siege to the fortresses of Toule and Verdun, and finally reached Chalons. MacMahon now endeavored to make a circuit to the north, and by forced marches to reach and relieve Metz in an attack upon Friedrich Karl. The Crown-Prince set out in pursuit, and although MacMahon had four days' start, he was overtaken at the fortified town of Sedan, which he had occupied with 110,000 men and 230 guns. The joint forces of the Crown-Prince and Prince Friedrich Karl surrounded him with an army of 250,000 men and 800 guns, and on September 1 the battle took place which resulted in the defeat of the French forces, and the capture of the Emperor Napoleon III. The Crown-Prince now pushed rapidly on to Paris, and on September 19 his army occupied Versailles, and laid siege to the capital. From this time until the termination of the siege, the prince personally directed the operations around the city, including the repulse of the French under Gen. Vinoy, on September 30. In recognition of the victories that he had gained at Weissenbourg, Wörth, and Sedan, the King raised him to the rank of field-marshal, which was the first instance of that rank being conferred on a prince of the reigning family. On March 7, 1871, after the conclusion of peace, the prince issued his farewell manifesto to his soldiers of the Third Army Corps, and rejoining the Emperor at Nancy, returned to Berlin in a blaze of triumph. On arriving there he was decorated by the Emperor with the grand cross of the Iron Cross.

"Unser Fritz," as he was affectionately called, returned unquestionably the most popular commander of the war. He was the idol of his soldiers, and his subsequent triumphant reception in South Germany, as Inspector-General of the Fourth German Army Corps, proved how complete was the union between the north and the south, which his military achievements had helped to bring about.

The Crown-Prince manifested keen interest in the development of Germany, and in scientific, industrial, and patriotic undertakings, the Kaiser-Wilhelm-Stiftung for invalid soldiers, and the excavations at Olympia, being notable instances of his activity. On various occasions he accompanied or represented his father, as at the opening of the Vienna Exhibition in 1873 and the funeral of Victor Emmanuel at Rome in 1878, and visited Sweden and Denmark in 1873, St. Petersburg in 1875, and Holland and Belgium in 1876–'77. When the Emperor was wounded by Nobling in 1878, the prince was recalled from England to carry on the Government.

The conflict between Prussia and the Vatican was pending, and in a letter to the Pope the Crown-Prince thus emphatically expressed himself: "To the suggestion in your holiness's letter that the laws of Prussia should be so modified as to accord with the statutes of the Roman Church, no Prussian monarch could listen for a moment. The independence of the monarchy, which, as a patriot and my father's heir, I am bound to maintain, would at once be compromised if its freedom of legislation were subordinated to any external power." During his temporary occupancy of the throne he was called upon to sign the death-warrant of the young Anarchist, Hoedel, who had made an attempt upon the Emperor's life in May, 1878, and it is said that he went through days of mental agony before he felt himself sufficiently steeled to put his name to the warrant. The Treaty of Berlin was ratified by the Crown-Prince in his capacity as deputy Emperor.

The Emperor Alexander II of Russia was assassinated in 1881, and it devolved upon the Crown-Prince to represent Prussia at the funeral in St. Petersburg. Anxiety was felt in Germany for his safety, in consequence of the threats of the Nihilists, and the Emperor, when pressed to prevent his son visiting Russia, replied, "*Cest notre métier.*"

After an extended tour through western Europe, the Crown-Prince visited Rome in January, 1884, where, in an audience with the Pope, the differences still existing between the empire and the Vatican were amicably discussed. He was present at the Jubilee of Queen Victoria's reign, in London, in June, 1887.

The disease that eventually proved fatal to the Crown-Prince was first noticed in January, 1887, as an inflammatory affection of the throat, accompanied by a cough and slight hoarseness. These symptoms refusing to yield to ordinary treatment, and the appearance of a small growth upon the left vocal chord, aroused in the minds of the attending physicians the suspicion that the disease was malignant. No change in his condition resulted from a long sojourn at Ems, and in May several German specialists, in consultation, decided that the prince was suffering from cancer of the larynx, and that an immediate operation for its extirpation was imperative. Before resorting to such extreme measures, it was thought advisable to get the opinion of some other specialist, and Dr. Morell Mackenzie was summoned from London for a consultation with Profs. Gerhardt, Von Bergmann, and Tobold, and Drs. Von Lauer, Wegner, and Schrader. As the result of his examination, Dr. Mackenzie claimed that, although the growth might possibly be cancerous, the symptoms did not warrant a positive diagnosis, and he consequently declined to give an opinion as to the exact nature of the disease until a portion of the growth had been submitted to microscopical examination. He accordingly removed, on May 21, a portion of the diseased tissue, which was sent to Prof. Virchow for examination. The result failed to reveal any evidences of cancer in the growth, and Dr. Mackenzie advised against the radical operation proposed by the German surgeons, favoring intra-laryngeal rather than extra-laryngeal treatment. The case having been placed entirely under his care, Dr. Mackenzie proceeded to remove the growth by means of forceps especially devised for the purpose. The portions of the tumor removed at each operation were sent to Prof. Virchow for microscopical examination, but no evidences of cancer were found in any of them. In July Dr. Mackenzie reported that the growth had been entirely removed from the left vocal chord. However, it soon reappeared and, despite all treatment, gradually increased in size. For several months after the prince's return from the Queen's Jubilee there was very little change in his condition, but while he was at San Remo, in November, the disease suddenly assumed a more serious phase, and Dr. Mackenzie was summoned from London. The growth was found to be very much increased in size, and other portions of the larynx had become involved, but hopes were still entertained that the condition would ultimately disappear under appropriate treatment. Contrary to these expectations, the tumor continued to increase in size, and by the beginning of the following February, it had become so large as to encroach considerably upon the air-passages, and seriously impede respiration. The imminent danger of suffocation rendered the operation of tracheotomy necessary. The operation was performed on Feb. 9, 1888, by Dr. Bramman, Prof. Bergmann's assistant. The beneficial results of the operation were immediately apparent in the improvement in respiration, which was now accomplished through a silver tracheotomy tube, inserted into the wind-pipe through an opening in the neck. For several weeks after the operation there was a slight improvement in the patient's condition. On March 4, a portion of necrosed tissue, which had come away through the tracheotomy tube, was examined microscopically by Prof. Waldeyer, who found the first distinct evidences of the presence of cancer.

The death of Emperor William I, on March 9, made the Crown-Prince King of Prussia and Emperor of Germany under the title of Friedrich III. On the 10th he left San Remo for Berlin, and on his arrival was published, simultaneously with his proclamation to the people, a letter to Prince Bismarck warmly acknowledging the services of the Chancellor during the reign of the late Emperor. Among the first acts of the new Emperor's reign were the promotion of General von Blumenthal to the rank of field-marshal, and the conferring of the order of the Black Eagle on Dr. Friedburg, the Russian Minister of Justice, a Jew by descent. His proclamation of an amnesty decree for political offenses was hailed as a concession to Liberal sentiment. Early in his reign the inundations in the eastern and north-

ern portions of Germany aroused his sympathies, and he sent the Empress to inspect the relief measures instituted at Posen.

A fortnight had hardly elapsed after his accesion to the throne before an unfavorable change took place in the progress of his disease, and on March 21 he issued a decree, addressed to the Crown-Prince, expressing the wish that the latter should make himself conversant with the affairs of state. The prince was accordingly intrusted with the preparation and discharge of such business as the Emperor assigned to him, and empowered to affix all necessary signatures without obtaining special authorization.

A serious difficulty arose between the Emperor and Empress and Prince Bismarck, regarding the contemplated marriage between the Princess Victoria and Prince Alexander of Battenburg, ex-Prince of Bulgaria. Prince Bismarck threatened to resign, and the projected alliance was abandoned.

About the 16th of April the Emperor's condition became critical, bronchitis having supervened, but he improved in condition, and on June 1 he left Charlottenburg for Potsdam. A few days later a ministerial crisis arose in consequence of the disinclination of the Emperor to give his assent to the quinquennial election bill adopted by the Prussian Diet. The official publication of the bill was followed by the resignation of Herr von Puttkamer, the Minister of the Interior and Vice-President of the Ministerial Council.

Abscesses began to form in the Emperor's neck, in the neighborhood of the wound made in performing the operation of tracheotomy, and the patient experienced great difficulty in swallowing, and grew rapidly weaker. The cancer was extending, and already the whole of the larynx was involved, and the surrounding organs were invaded to such an extent that an opening appeared between the trachea and the œsophagus, permitting food to escape through the tracheotomy tube. Artificial feeding had to be resorted to, but the efforts of the physicians to relieve his condition were of no avail, and on June 15 the German nation was called upon, a second time in a little more than three months, to mourn the death of their sovereign.

Emperor Friedrich III was succeeded on the throne by his eldest son, Friedrich Wilhelm, born Jan. 27, 1859, who reigns under the title of Emperor William II of Germany. The other surviving children are Princess Charlotte, born July 24, 1860; Prince Heinrich, born May 20, 1862; Princess Victoria, born April 12, 1866; Princess Sophie Dorothea, born June 14, 1870; and Princess Margarethe, born April 22, 1872.

After the death of the Emperor the Government published the official reports of the German doctors who were in attendance upon him, and in this report Sir Morell Mackenzie was censured both for his opposition to the operation of extirpation of the larynx, as proposed by the German physicians at the beginning of the disease, and for his treatment of the case after it had been placed under his care. Not long afterward the Scotch specialist published a book entitled "The Fatal Illness of Frederick the Noble" (London, 1888), in which he answered the charges made against him by the Germans, and in his turn made serious accusations against them, alleging that the diseased growth may have been benign in the beginning, and cancer have been induced by frequent electro-cauterization before he took the case, and that death was hastened by the clumsy recklessness of Dr. von Bergmann, who made a false passage in inserting a tracheotomy tube. For a portrait of the Emperor Friedrich Wilhelm, see "Annual Cyclopædia" for 1887, frontispiece.

FRIENDS. The number of members of the Society of Friends in America, as computed by C. W. Pritchard, editor of the "Christian Worker," from the minutes of the yearly meetings for 1887, is 72,968. This shows an increase in two years of 3,493, of which the yearly meetings west of the Alleghany Mountains are credited with 3,271, and the Eastern yearly meetings with 222.

Standards of Faith.—Although the Society of Friends has, as a body, refused to adopt a formal creed, its standards of faith are well defined and frequently promulgated. Its doctrines are illustrated in the writings of Robert Barclay, George Fox, William Penn, and other early Friends; and for more than two hundred years the yearly meetings of the Society have added what has seemed to be needed, in the way of exhortation, reproof, and elucidation. The views of American Friends who most closely adhere to the primitive features of belief and practice are expressed, with statements of the principles and arguments on which they are based, in epistles and special declarations that have been issued from time to time by the Philadelphia Yearly Meeting.

Orthodox Divisions.—Mention has been made in previous volumes of the "Annual Cyclopædia" of the growth of divisions among Friends respecting doctrines and forms of worship, and particularly respecting the tolerance of certain outward forms of ritual, such as vocal prayer, singing, baptism, and the observance of the Lord's Supper, against which the earlier Friends bore testimony. The origin of these divisions may be traced back to the year 1830, when doctrinal views were first preached and published in England by members of the Society tending to exalt the sacrifice of the cross rather than the inward work of the Holy Spirit, as the chief element of the covenant of salvation. A small separation took place in England on account of these preachings; and the doctrines spreading to America, the Philadelphia Yearly Meeting, in 1836, remonstrated with the London Yearly Meeting upon the subject. In 1843, the Philadelphia Yearly Meeting issued a pamphlet entitled "The Ancient Testimony of the Society of Friends, commonly called Quakers, respecting some of their Christian Doctrines and Practices." It contained extracts from the declarations and writings of the earlier Friends, concerning the one true God, divine revelation, the fallen state of man, the universality of the light of Christ, the Holy Scriptures, justification, baptism and the Supper, divine worship, ministry, prayer, war, slavery, trade and lying, and parents and children, and urged that those testimonies be maintained. In 1845, the advocates of the later views had obtained the preponderance in the New England Yearly Meeting, and it was divided. In 1836 the Ohio Yearly Meeting invited the attention of the London Yearly Meeting to the agitation, and urged it to take action for the removal of the "cause of complaint." That meeting failing to respond satisfactorily to its request, the Ohio Yearly Meeting, though not without objection, adopted a pamphlet that had been issued in the previous year by the Philadelphia Yearly Meeting—corresponding in spirit with the "Ancient Testimony" already mentioned—entitled "An Appeal for the Ancient Testimony of the Society of Friends," together with the testimony that had been adopted in 1830 by the eight yearly meetings then existing in America. The Ohio Yearly Meeting was divided in 1854, the party adhering to the old order retaining about two thirds of the members. Upon the reception of the usual epistle from this body, the Indiana Yearly Meeting declined to correspond with it, and gave its fellowship to the other meeting bearing the same name. The latter is the body which has been described in previous volumes of the "Annual Cyclopædia" as the Ohio Yearly Meeting, and which, in 1878, changed its discipline in regard to marriage and other subjects, and refused in 1885 and 1886 to reaffirm the testimony of the society against the outward rites of baptism and the Lord's Supper. Divisions have also taken place in Western, Canada, Kansas, and Iowa Yearly Meetings, one branch of each of which, together with the Philadelphia Yearly Meeting, where no separation has occurred, are in unison in support of the ancient order. None of these conservative meetings took part in the General Conference of Friends that was held in Richmond, Ind., in 1887.

These divisions are in no way related to the separation that resulted about 1822 from the preaching of Elias Hicks.

Doctrinal Statements. — The declaration of faith that was adopted by the General Conference of Friends that was held in Richmond, Indiana, in September, 1887 (see "Annual Cyclopædia" for 1887), was considered, but not approved, in the Dublin and London Yearly Meetings. The Dublin Yearly Meeting adopted a minute declaring that it did not see its way formally to adopt the declaration; but was willing to receive it as a valuable outcome of the conference. The minute of the London

Bell   S Hollyer

D. APPLETON & Cº

Yearly Meeting, which was adopted at the close of a long discussion, after expressing the cordial esteem of English Friends for their American brethren, and conveying to them a fresh message of love and encouragement, reaffirmed in general terms the belief of the society in the fundamental and scriptural principles of the Gospel of Christ, but with respect to this particular article, recorded that " this meeting refrains from expressing any judgment on the contents of the declaration now produced."

The following statement of the doctrine of justification by faith and regeneration, and on the beginning of salvation, has been adopted by the Indiana Yearly Meeting, with the reservation that it is not intended to cover the whole ground of belief on any other point :

By repentance toward God and faith toward our Lord Jesus Christ, the sinner experiences justification. This is pardon, forgiveness, remission, absolution for his past transgressions. By faith in the atoning blood of Christ shed on Calvary, the guilt of his sins is taken away, and their legal penalties remitted. He experiences conversion. This implies a change of heart and becoming a new creature in Christ Jesus. He experiences regeneration—a new birth, a new life in his soul, a being born again of the incorruptible seed. He experiences adoption ; he becomes a son. He experiences the witness of the Spirit, and cries, Abba, Father ! and then Christ does dwell in his heart by faith. Sanctification begins contemporaneously with and as soon as a man is justified. 'Therefore being justified by faith, we have peace with God through our Lord Jesus Christ : by whom, also, we have access by faith into this grace wherein we stand, and rejoice in hope of the glory of God.'

Missions.—The Indiana Yearly Meeting has adopted a proposition for the formation of a "Board of American Friends' Foreign Missions," to exercise for the present advisory functions, while it is left optional with existing associations of men and women Friends whether they shall surrender the control of their work to it ; the board not to be organized till six yearly meetings have agreed to unite in it.

Several American Friends' Women's Societies for Missionary Work have been established within recent years. The first was formed in connection with the Western Yearly Meeting, in 1881. Others have been organized, in connection with the Philadelphia Yearly Meeting, in 1882; Iowa, 1883 ; Indiana, 1883 ; New England, 1884 ; Ohio, 1884 ; Canada, 1885 ; North Carolina, 1885; Kansas, 1885; and New York, 1887. College Societies have been formed at Earlham College, Indiana, and Wilmington College, Ohio. In 1886 these societies had 3,892 members, and had raised $27,840. The "Friends' Missionary Advocate " is published in their interest, at Chicago.

The American Indian Missions are under the control of an associated committee, which returned a total of 383 members in the meetings of the Indian Territory, showing a net increase for the year of forty-six. There are also stations among the Mexican Kickapoos and Iowas. White's Manual Labor School, in Indiana, occupying an estate of 760 acres, is well supplied with buildings and mechanical shops, and re-

turned in 1888 an enrollment of 85 pupils, more than half of whom were professed Christians. Three day-schools in the Indian Territory had 64 pupils. Other schools, wholly or partly under the care of individual yearly meetings, were maintained among the Eastern Cherokees in North Carolina, at Tunessassa, N. Y., and at Douglass Island, Alaska ; having a total enrollment of 344 pupils. The expenditures of Friends during the year for Indian education, including buildings, had been $9,222.

The mission in Mexico returns 42 members admitted, and a total enrollment of 127 pupils in the schools. Schools for boys are sustained at Matamoras and Victoria ; for girls at Victoria and Quintero ; and a boys' and girls' school at Santa Barbara.

A mission conference of Friends was held in London, in April. Mr. Samuel Southall, of Leeds, occupied the chair. It appeared from the reports that the society is indirectly represented in Japan by four or five members. Mechanical and religious labor are carried on in South Africa by Mr. Elbert Clarke. A number of missionaries are at work in India, and a favorable opening was recognized in Burmah. Two missionary Friends are laboring in China. In Madagascar, Friends have many thousand native Christians under their care. The results of effort among Syrians have not been wholly satisfactory. The results of home mission work were encouraging.

The Friends' Missionary Station at Constantinople was established in 1881, and is carried on in harmony with the work of the American Board. A meeting was organized in 1883, with twenty men and women as members. The mission has an estate valued at $8,000, at Stamboul, with a dispensary, which is resorted to by Moslems and Armenians. An industrial school is carried on at Bahjijig, sixty miles from Constantinople, with which thirty pupils are connected.

FULLER, MELVILLE WESTON, eighth Chief-Justice of the Supreme Court of the United States, born in Augusta, Me., Feb. 11, 1833. He was graduated at Bowdoin College, Maine, in 1853, studied law in Bangor with his uncle, George M. Weston, and then at Harvard Law School, and began practice in 1855 in his native city. There he was an associate editor of the "Age," served as President of the Common Council, and became City Attorney in 1856. He resigned that office in June of the same year and removed to Chicago, Ill., where he was in practice for thirty-two years. He rose to the highest rank in his profession, and was concerned in many important cases, among which were the National Bank tax - cases, one of which was the first that was argued before Chief-Justice Waite, the Cheney ecclesiastical case, the South Park Commissioners' cases, and the Lake Front case. He was a member of the Illinois Constitutional Convention of 1862, and in 1863-'65 of the lower house of the Legislature, where he was a leader of one branch of the Democratic party. He was a delegate to the Democratic National Conventions of 1864, 1872, 1876, and 1880. On April 30, 1888, he was nominated by President Cleveland to be Chief-Justice of the United States, and on July 20 he was confirmed by the Senate. On October 8 he took the oath of office and entered upon his duties. Judge Fuller is, with one exception, the youngest member of the Supreme Court. He has attained reputation as a public speaker. Among his addresses are one welcoming Stephen A. Douglas to Chicago in 1860, and one on Sidney Breese, which is prefixed to Judge Breese's "Early History of Illinois" (1884). The degree of LL.D. was conferred upon him by the Northwestern University and by Bowdoin College in 1888.

G

GEORGIA. State Government.—The following were the State officers during the year: Governor, John B. Gordon, Democrat; Secretary of State, Nathan C. Barnett; Treasurer, R. U. Hardeman; Comptroller-General, William A. Wright; Attorney-General, Clifford Anderson; Commissioner of Agriculture, J. T. Henderson; State School Commissioner, James S. Hook; Railroad Commissioners, Alexander S. Irwin, C. Wallace, L. N. Trammell; Chief-Justice of the Supreme Court, L. E. Bleckley; Associate Justices, M. H. Blandford and T. J. Simmons.

Finances.—For the two years ending on September 30 the report of the State Treasurer is as follows: Balance in the treasury on Sept. 30, 1886, $250,927.96; receipts during the subsequent year, $1,682,652.89; disbursements during the same time, $1,583,818.47; balance on Sept. 30, 1887, $349,762.38; receipts during the subsequent year, $1,900,692.21; disbursements in the same time, $2,019,103.07; balance on Sept. 30, 1888, $231,351.52. The State receives $300,000 each year for rental of the Western and Atlantic Railroad, and $25,000 from hire of convicts, in addition to the amounts raised by State taxation.

The bonded debt of the State bearing interest on Sept. 30, 1887, was as follows: Bonds of 1884, interest 4½ per cent., $3,392,000; bonds of 1877, interest 6 per cent., $2,141,000; bonds of 1870, interest 7 per cent., $2,098,000; bonds of 1872, interest 7 per cent., $307,500; bonds of 1876, interest 7 per cent., $542,000; obligations to the State University, $255,000: total, $8,735,500. To this should be added $91,040 of non-interest-bearing bonds not canceled, but of which $74,235 were canceled during the present year, leaving the total debt on September 30, $8,752,305. The issue of 1877 will become due on Jan. 1, 1889, and for the purpose of meeting this obligation the Legislature of 1887 authorized the issuance of $1,900,000 of new bonds at a rate to be fixed by the Governor. During the present year a sale of these at 4½ per cent. interest was negotiated at a premium of 4½ per cent. This is the highest price ever paid for bonds issued by the State, and indicates an increased confidence in its credit. On October, 1890, 'the bonds of 1870 will mature, and it will devolve upon the Legislature chosen this year to provide for their payment.

Provision was made by the Legislature of 1887 for gradually reducing the debt by creating a sinking-fund for the years 1887 and 1888 and for the years 1897 to 1915, inclusive, thus carrying into effect the clause of the State Constitution requiring that $100,000 should be raised each year by taxation, and held as a sinking-fund, for the payment of State bonds.

Assessments.—The total assessed valuation of property for 1888 was $357,167,458, of which $29,304,127 was the valuation of railroad property. The valuation for 1887 was $341,504,921, of which $24,899,592 was railroad property. The following table gives some details of the assessment of 1888 compared with that of 1879:

PROPERTY TAXED.	1879.	1888.
Improved lands	$88,629,168	$107,733,644
City and town property	49,007,286	84,921,108
Live-stock	21,017,684	25,745,018
Farm implements	2,971,372	5,040,475
Household furniture	9,156,404	13,632,614
Cotton manufactories	1,640,000	8,088,167
Iron works	295,640	580,801
Invested in mining	97,580	197,549
Bank stock	4,667,567	7,609,855
Money, solvent notes, etc	26,513,005	34,715,451
Merchandise	12,012,755	18,657,759

The valuation of property held by colored persons has risen from $5,182,398 in 1879 to $9,631,271 in 1888.

Education.—The following statistics of the public schools for the school-year 1887 were compiled and published during 1888: Schools for white pupils, 5,083; schools for colored pupils, 2,512; schools established under local laws, 201; enrollment of white pupils, 208,865; enrollment of colored pupils, 133,429; total, 342,394; average attendance, 226,290.

During 1888 a census of persons within school-age was taken, showing 292,624 white and 267,657 colored children, or a total of 560,281. Of the total, 61 per cent. were enrolled as school-attendants during 1887, but only 41 per cent. were in regular attendance. The average length of the school-year is not over three months. During 1887 the sum of $493,509.52 was raised by the State for the schools, and $302,477.74 by city and county taxation.

An act to establish a technological school, as a branch of the State University, and forming one of its departments for the education and training of students in the industrial and mechanical arts was approved on Oct. 13, 1885. Pursuant to this act a commission, charged with the duty, selected a site in the city of Atlanta and erected suitable buildings at a cost of $101,062.98. These were transferred to the State by the commission in October, 1888, when the first school-year began. The institution opened under favorable conditions, 113 students being enrolled before the close of 1888.

Charities.—The State Lunatic Asylum is the largest and most expensive charity of the State. On Oct. 1, 1887, it contained 910 white and 385 colored patients, a total of 1,295. This total had increased on Oct. 1, 1888, to 1,386, of whom 980 were white and 406 colored patients. The cost of supporting the institution is about $180,000 per annum.

The Georgia Academy for the Blind had 91 pupils in attendance during the year, 78 white and 13 colored. The expenses of the institution were $17,580.62 for the year. The institution for the Deaf and Dumb has an average attendance of nearly 100 pupils. For 1887 the disbursements for this charity amounted to $18,226.32; for 1888, $16,315.96.

Penitentiary.—There were on Oct. 1, 1886, in the different convict camps, 1,526 prisoners, of whom 1,377 were colored and 149 white persons. At the same date in 1888 there were 1,537 prisoners, 1,388 colored and 149 white. During the two years there were 81 deaths, or 3¼ per cent. of the total number on the rolls. This rate of mortality could hardly happen under any other than the convict-lease system.

The State Capitol.—Up to October 24 of this year the total sum expended by the Capitol commissioners upon the new Capitol building was $851,064.75. The contract for its construction calls for an expenditure of $862,756.75. The structure was completed, according to the contract, at the end of the year, and is an imposing work well suited to the needs of the State. No debt was incurred in its erection, the requisite funds being obtained by the levy of a special tax.

Railroad Commission.—The Governor says in his message in November: "The Railroad Commission has grown in importance with the enormous development of the railroad system of the State. It has been uniformly conservative in its policy and cautious in its action upon the very delicate questions and sensitive interests with which it has to deal. The result is that the commission has grown in the confidence of the people and in the respect of the corporations.

"The Supreme Court of the United States, on the 29th of October last, in the case of the Georgia Railroad and Banking Company *vs.* James M. Smith, *et al.*, affirmed the decision of the court below. This decision is in effect an affirmance of the right of the Railroad Commission to fix rates for the Georgia Railroad and Banking Company, as for any person or company or corporation which does business as a common carrier in this State, and finally disposes of a litigation which has been pending in the courts for several years."

The State Railroad.—The report of the committee appointed by the Legislature of 1887 to appraise the Western and Atlantic Railroad, preparatory to making some disposition of it at the end of the present lease in 1890, was completed and published in August. The road is about 137 miles in length, running from Augusta to Chattanooga, Tenn. The committee estimates its present value, including rolling-stock, stations, etc., at $6,064,139.06. During the eighteen years that the present lessees have held it, betterments have been made by them upon it to the value of $750,889.74, as estimated by the committee. For these betterments the lessees demand compensation. The general condition of the road is pronounced by the committee to be good. At the session of the Legislature in November, several plans, both for the sale and lease of the road, were fully discussed in committee, and two reports made to the House. The sentiment was generally opposed to a sale of the property, but the matter went over to the next session for determination.

Confederate Soldiers.—Under the act of 1879, and acts amendatory thereto, bounties were paid triennially to soldiers who had suffered amputation of a limb or limbs on account of injuries received in the service of the Confederate States. The sum thus paid from the treasury of the State amounted in 1879 to $69,870; in 1883 to $61,605; and in 1886 to $57,650. The act approved Oct. 24, 1887, provides small annual bounties for a number of classes of disabled Confederate soldiers who were not included in the benefits of the act of 1879. The purpose of this act was to embrace and relieve all who had been permanently disabled by wounds or disease in the Confederate service. From the large number of applications filed under this law, nearly eleven hundred were allowed; the payments made up to and including Nov. 2, 1888, amounting in the aggregate to $27,525. The beneficiaries under this act will be increased in 1889, without change in the law, by the number of those who have been recognized as entitled under the act of 1879, and may be still living and resident in the State of Georgia; and $65,000 is estimated as the amount that must be paid to them.

Prohibition.—During the year there has been an evident reaction from the prohibition movement of the two years preceding. Under the local-option law all but 38 of the 138 counties of the State had declared for prohibition before the last of September, 1887. Before the close of 1888, however, the number of "wet" counties had increased to 64.

Legislative Session.—The Legislature elected in October met on November 7, and remained in session till December 22, adjourning on that day to meet on the first Wednesday of July following. It elected T. J. Simmons to be

Judge of the Supreme Court, and United States Senator Colquitt to be his own successor in the United States Senate. There was no opposition to either candidate. The appropriation bill and the tax bill were the most important measures passed. Unusual liberality was shown in these toward the educational interests of the State. The Technological School recently established obtained an appropriation of $18,000; the branch colleges belonging to the State University received a separate appropriation for the first time, and an additional tax of one half of one per cent. for 1889, and of 1 per cent. for 1890 was voted for the public schools. The annual session of these schools may now be lengthened from three months to four months in 1889 and five months in 1890, and a corresponding increase in their efficiency is expected. The act of Congress providing for establishing agricultural experiment stations in the various States was accepted, but instead of establishing such a station in connection with an agricultural college, as required by the terms of the act, the Legislature appropriated $5,000, in addition to the sum payable to the State under the act, for the construction of a new State institution to be located by a board of commissioners. The sum of $85,000 was appropriated as the final payment for the construction of the new Capitol, and $92,000 for furnishing it and for ornamenting the grounds. Provision was also made for an additional sinking-fund to meet the State debt when it shall become payable. It was made unlawful for corporations or other employers to pay their employés in checks or orders payable in merchandise at the employer's store; all such notes or checks must be redeemable in cash. Banks and building associations were relieved from the double taxation heretofore imposed upon them.

Political.—The Democratic State Convention met at Atlanta on August 8, and renominated Governor Gordon, Secretary Barnett, Treasurer Hardeman, Comptroller Wright, and Attorney-General Anderson. It adopted the following resolutions:

We heartily indorse the platform of principles adopted by the Democratic National Convention at St. Louis this present year, and the nominations of Grover Cleveland and Allen G. Thurman as candidates upon the principles embodied in it. Federal taxation can only be rightfully imposed to provide for the necessary and proper purposes of the General Government economically administered. Luxuries should not be unbridled in order that necessities may be burdened. We indorse the platform of the National Democracy of 1888, and the recent message of the President as the proper construction of the platform of 1884, advanced to the conditions of 1888.

The Democracy of Georgia deplore the spirit of sectionalism which seems still to animate the passions of the leaders of the Republican party and some of their misguided followers. We seek a manly fraternity among all the States and peoples of the United States, and declare that the only enemies of perpetual American concord are those Republicans who insist upon reviving and maintaining the passions of past conflicts, terminated forever and honorably adjusted. Let others deal in post-mortem feuds. "We face

the rising and not the setting sun," and invite all men who love liberty regulated by law to unite with us in efforts after the highest progress of our State and common country. We denounce the Republican party as having been the worst and most destructive enemy of our State.

With no grudge against the policy or the people who preserved the Union, we hail with pleasure the accession to Democratic ranks of those Republicans who abandoned that party when convinced that it had ceased to struggle to perpetuate the Union, and had left for its mission only the tasks of keeping alive feuds and oppressing the poor, and who have joined the party which opposes legislation for favored classes and propounds a policy for the general good.

There was no opposition ticket, and at the election in October Governor Gordon received the entire vote cast. A State Legislature was elected at the same time, composed almost entirely of Democrats. The people also voted upon a constitutional amendment proposed by the last Legislature, increasing the number of Supreme Court judges from three to five. This was defeated by a vote of 37,638 votes in favor, to 46,720 against, four counties not reporting. At the November election, Cleveland received — according to unofficial returns — 100,472 votes; Harrison, 40,443 votes; and Fisk, 1,802 votes. An unbroken Democratic delegation to Congress was chosen.

GERMANY, an empire in Central Europe, consisting of a confederation of twenty-six states, united under the Constitution of the German Empire, which went into force on May 4, 1871. At the beginning of 1888 the reigning sovereign was Emperor Wilhelm I, born March 22, 1797, who was proclaimed the first German Emperor at Versailles, Jan. 18, 1871, and died March 9, 1888. He was succeeded by his eldest and only surviving son, Friedrich, born Oct. 18, 1831, who at the time of his accession to the throne was suffering from what proved to be cancer of the larynx, and died, after a reign of three months, June 15, 1888. (See FRIEDRICH WILHELM.) His eldest son, the present Emperor, Wilhelm II, was born Jan. 27, 1859. The heir-apparent is Friedrich Wilhelm, born May 6, 1882.

The legislative functions of the empire are vested in two bodies of representatives of the people: the Bundesrath or Federal Council, composed of 62 members, appointed each year by the individual states that they represent; and the Reichstag, or Diet of the Realm, numbering 397 members, elected for a term of three years by universal suffrage. There are 9,769,-802 electors, constituting 20·9 per cent. of the population. In the general election of 1887, 7,540,938, or 77·5 per cent. of the electors voted. Both the Bundesrath and the Reichstag meet in annual session. The members of the Reichstag are elected from 397 districts, of which 21 consist wholly of towns, 93 of districts each containing a town of at least 20,000 inhabitants, and 283 of districts without any large towns. In 252 districts the majority of the population is Protestant. The Bundesrath is presided over by the Chancellor of the Empire. The President of the Reichstag is elected by the deputies.

Area and Population.—The area of Germany is 211,196 square miles, and its population, on Dec. 1, 1885, was 46,855.704, of whom 22,933,664 were males, and 23,922,040 females. The average density of the population was 221 per square mile. There were 5,378,077 inhabited houses, and 9,999,558 households in 1885. The bulk of the population is Teutonic, but there were 3,205,000 non-Germanic inhabitants, including 2,454,000 Slavs; 2,800,000 Walloons and French; 150,000 Lithuanians; 140,000 Danes; and 140,000 Wends, Moravians, and Bohemians. In 1886, 76,687 persons emigrated from the German Empire by way of the German ports and Antwerp, 41,898 of whom were males, and 34,789 females; there were 10,609 families, comprising 38,950 persons. Of the emigrants in 1886, Prussia sent 50,461; Bavaria, 8,068; Würtemberg, 3,717; Baden, 2,833; Saxony, 2,388; Hesse, 1,725; Mecklenburg-Schwerin, 1,262; Hamburg, 1,675; Oldenburg, 990; Bremen, 883; and Alsace-Lorraine, 602. The United States received 72,403; Brazil, 2,045; British North America, 330; other American countries, 1,068; Africa, 191; Asia, 116; and Australia, 534. In addition to the above total, 3,188 Germans left the empire by way of Rotterdam, Amsterdam, and Havre in 1886. The number of emigrants from the empire in 1887 was 99,712. On Dec. 1, 1886, there were 372,792 foreigners in Germany.

Commerce and Industry.—The total export trade of the empire in 1887 was valued at 3,269,900,-675 marks, against 3,127,655,275 marks in 1886. The imports amounted to 3,268,517,950 marks in 1887, and to 3,018,475,350 marks in 1886.

Protective duties on grain and cattle were imposed in 1879, which had the effect of increasing the receipts of the treasury from the duties on cereals from 14,300,000 to 30,600,000 marks, and from the cattle duties from 1,021,-500 to 4,590,750 marks. Nevertheless, they had failed to protect German agriculture from the competition of foreign countries where production is much cheaper. The duties were raised in 1885 still higher, but without producing the desired effect. Wheat, instead of rising, fell to a price unknown for a century. The Central Council of Agriculture, therefore, called for a further measure to preserve the agricultural interests of Germany, both large and small, from the ruin with which they were menaced. The Government proposed to double the existing duties, but the Reichstag, in the measure that was finally passed, slightly reduced this proposal. The new tariff fixes the duty on wheat and rye at about 40 cents a bushel; on oats and malt, 31 cents; on barley, 18 cents; on buckwheat, legumes, and Indiancorn, 16 cents. Farinaceous preparations pay duties from 30 to 50 per cent. higher than formerly.

In 1886–'87 there was under cultivation a total area of 64,989,560 acres. The leading agricultural products were, wheat, 2,933,065 tons, produced from 4,791,583 acres; rye, 6,702,134 tons, from 14,596,255 acres; barley, 2,570,921 tons, from 4,328,600 acres; oats, 5,341,483 tons, from 9,615,337 acres; potatoes, 27,657,340 tons, from 7,289,367 acres; clover, hay, etc., 28,242,253 tons, from 21,367,500 acres; wines, 33,066,594 gallons, from 300,752 acres; tobacco, 81,166,000 pounds, from 49,000 acres. The product of raw and refined sugar was 1,418,900 tons. The total value of the mineral products in 1886 was 463,000,000 marks. The value of the coal raised was 300,-727,000 marks; lignite, 40,270,000 marks; iron-ore, 29,642,000 marks; zinc-ore, 7,722,000 marks; lead-ore, 15,919,000 marks; copper-ore, 14,415,000 marks; silver and gold, 3,977,-000 marks; mineral salts, 13,427,000 marks; other salts, 35,024,000 marks. In 1886 the value of the pig-iron produced in Germany was 140,383,000 marks, 229 furnaces being in operation. The finished iron was valued at 418,-727,000 marks, and the total value of the productions of foundries of all kinds was 690,000,-000 marks. In the manufacture of iron 200,000 men are employed.

Navigation.—In 1887 the mercantile navy comprised 694 steamers, of 453,914 tons, and 3,327 sailing-vessels, of 830,789 tons, making a total of 4,021 vessels, of 1,284,703 tons. Of these, 2,518 vessels, of 412,417 tons, belonged to Prussian ports. The total number of sailors employed in the merchant service in 1887 was 39,021. The movement of shipping at all German ports in 1886 was as follows:

VESSELS.	With cargoes.	Tonnage.	In ballast.	Tonnage.	Total No.	Total tonnage.
Entered...	49,819	9,423,304	9,485	869,109	59,304	10,292,413
Cleared...	44,791	7,688,540	14,445	2,655,881	59,286	10,339,421

Of the total tonnage entered and cleared 10,-263,013 tons were under the German and 5,751,954 tons under the British flag.

Railroads.—The total length of the railroads open to traffic in 1887 was 24,197 miles, of which 21,112 miles belonged to the state. The Government is rapidly acquiring all the remaining lines now owned and operated by private companies. The total amount expended in the construction of German railways to the end of 1886 was 9,472,606,000 marks. The receipts for 1886 were 998,693,000 marks, and the expenses 574,975,000 marks, showing a net profit of 4·42 per cent. on the capital.

Telegraphs and Postal Service.—At the end of 1886 the length of telegraph lines in the empire was 53,874 miles, having 191,272 miles of wire. The number of messages during the year was 20,510,294, of which 14,568,346 were internal.

The receipts of the post-office during 1886–'87, amounted to 202,346,932 marks, and the expenditure to 175.676,000 marks. There were 18,688 post-offices, employing 97,863 persons, at the end of 1886. During the year there were transmitted 858,587,550 letters, 261,056,660 post-cards, 20,187,170 patterns,

245,618,370 stamped wrappers, 578,611,143 journals, and 180,492,148 registered packets and money-orders of the total declared value of 18,116,304,652 marks.

Education.—Elementary education is general and compulsory throughout Germany. In 1886 only 1·06 per cent. of the recruits of the army could neither read nor write. Among 169,240 recruits, which was the number that entered the army in 1887, there were 163,203 who had received an education in Germany, 4,822 were educated in some foreign language, and 1,215 could neither read nor write. In 1881 there were 57,000 elementary schools, with 7,100,000 pupils, in Germany. In 1885 there were 347 normal schools, with 26,281 pupils; 858 gymnasia, with 186,766 students; and 270 Realschulen, with 49,196 students. In addition there were, in 1887, 9 technical high-schools, with 3,985 students; and 4,346 industrial and special schools. There are 21 universities in Germany, with the following numbers of instructors and matriculated students in 1887–'88:

UNIVERSITIES.	Professors and teachers	STUDENTS.				
		Theology.	Juris-prudence.	Medicina.	Philosophy.	Total.
Berlin	292	669	1,006	1,140	1,839	4,654
Bonn	143	259	273	371	497	1,400
Breslau	134	347	217	390	452	1,406
Erlangen	61	370	119	262	114	865
Freiburg	83	124	287	479	307	1,197
Giessen	59	99	147	141	143	530
Göttingen	121	255	181	248	424	1,108
Greifswald	80	383	74	528	130	1,115
Halle	114	610	127	330	462	1,529
Heidelberg	106	85	290	240	323	938
Jena	92	154	166	213	185	718
Kiel	84	71	40	292	164	567
Königsberg	98	248	114	270	232	859
Leipsic	186	698	685	713	940	3,081
Marburg	84	256	114	360	279	1,009
Munich	170	187	1,261	1,211	558	8,167
Münster	42	344			170	514
Rostock	39	74	42	121	106	343
Strassburg	105	95	189	221	802	807
Tübingen	87	623	392	272	173	1,464
Wurzburg	66	163	281	899	160	1,458
Total	2,251	6,053	5,935	8,701	7,965	28,674

In fourteen of the universities the faculties are Protestant; in four, viz., Freiburg, Münich, Münster, and Wurzburg, they are Catholic; and in three, viz., Bonn, Breslau, and Tubingen, they are mixed Protestant and Catholic.

The Army.—The peace strength of the German army in 1887–'88 was 18,936 officers, 471,007 rank and file, 90,492 horses, and 1,374 guns. The new army law of March 11, 1887, renewed the Septennate, which is to continue in force till March 31, 1894, and added 50,000 soldiers to the regular military establishment, fixing the peace strength of the army at 468,409 rank and file, and 23,991 officers, surgeons, paymasters, etc. The war strength of the army is 1,567,600 officers and men, 312,730 horses, and 2,958 guns. To these numbers may be added the Landsturm and one-year volunteers, together numbering 1,082,400 officers and men, and the untrained men capable of serving in the army, numbering 3,020,000,

making the total available force in time of war 5,670,000 officers and men. The railway and telegraph service in time of war numbers 1,238 officers, 7,000 men, and 5,400 horses.

The Prussian contingent of the German army had a peace strength in 1887–'88 of 361,902 officers and men.

The empire is divided into nine fortress districts, in which there are 17 fortified places of the first class and 26 other fortresses.

In the session of 1887–'88 the Government introduced an army reorganization bill for increasing the fighting strength of the nation in war time by 700,000 men or more. The Reichstag passed the bill on the third reading without much opposition, on Feb. 8, 1888, and approved a money bill to provide 281,550,536 marks for carrying it into execution, authorizing a loan of 278,335,562 marks, while the Federal governments furnished the remainder in matricular contributions. The new army law extends the period of service in the Landwehr, and provides for arming and equipping both the Landwehr and Landsturm forces, and for supplying them with barracks, artillery, munitions, and other necessary war materials. The organization of the Landwehr into regiments and battalions is to be replaced by a territorial division into infantry brigade districts, and the subdivision of these into battalion districts, which will be extended to Würtemberg and Bavaria.

When the Crown-Prince Friedrich became Emperor, he announced in a rescript, dated March 26, 1888, that, like his father, he should devote his immediate and unremitting attention to the army, and gave notice of intended changes in drill tactics, made necessary by the introduction of improved infantry weapons, which rendered expedient more thorough individual drilling and stricter training in discipline under fire. In order to enable the army to give attention to these matters, he suggested the discontinuance of the system of formation in triple ranks, which is never used in war. Wilhelm II, on September 9, published an order directing that, in grateful remembrance of his father, the new infantry drill regulations should be put in force. The German infantry wear lighter helmets than formerly, and no longer march with their overcoats coiled round the back and chest, but strap them to their knapsacks, in the French fashion. The cuirassiers have laid aside the cuirass, and are now armed with the lance, like the uhlans, and the same weapon is being adopted for the hussars. The new magazine rifles of the infantry are fitted with small knife-like bayonets. In the autumn manœuvres a captive balloon was used for observations.

Gen. Field-Marshal Count von Moltke, Chief of the General Staff of the German Army since Sept. 18, 1858, on August 3 asked the Emperor to relieve him of his post and permit him to spend the remainder of his days in rural retirement, saying that, at his great age, he is no longer able to mount a horse. In the letter accepting his resignation, and in an ordinance, dated August 10, relieving him of his former post and appointing him to the presidency of the National Defense Commission, which was filled by the Emperor Friedrich when Crown Prince, Wilhelm II eulogized the services of the retiring strategist, who had attained the age of nearly eighty-eight years. The Emperor appointed as Marshal von Moltke's successor Gen. Count von Waldersee, who was born in 1832, first served on the general staff in 1866, was made a colonel for his services in the Franco-Prussian War, and was appointed quartermaster-general in 1882, in connection with which post he has acted as deputy chief of the general staff and aide-de-camp general to the Emperor.

The Navy.—The naval forces of the Empire in 1887 consisted of 105 vessels of an aggregate displacement of 201,521 tons, mounting 605 guns. The ironclad navy comprises 8 frigates, 5 corvettes, and 14 gun-boats, 11 of which are built on the same model, and armed each with a single 36-ton gun. Among the unarmored vessels are the cruisers "Zieten," "Hohenzollern," "Pfeil," and "Blitz," which are built for offensive ocean warfare, and are capable of steaming 16 miles an hour. The number of first and second class torpedo-boats that were completed was 110, and others were building. The larger vessels in course of construction on Jan. 1, 1888, were two frigate cruisers, of 4,800 tons, the "Prinzessin Wilhelm" and "Irene"; three corvettes, the "Eber," "Schwalbe," and "B"; a transport, the "Ersatz Eider"; and two dispatch-boats, "Wacht" and "Ersatz Pommerania." The last named was completed in July. The *personnel* of the navy on Jan. 1, 1888, consisted of 7 admirals; 800 officers, including engineers and surgeons; and 14,437 non-commissioned officers, marines, and sailors. Germany has three ports of war, viz., Kiel and Dantzic on the Baltic, and Wilhelmshaven on the North Sea. In the naval manœuvres the last-named port was subjected to a sham attack, which was repelled in a way to prove in the view of the umpires that the place is impregnable. In a similar attack on the harbor of Kiel, a new method of attacking hostile craft and exploding submarine mines was tried by swimmers in inflated rubber suits, who were sent out with explosives from vessels.

Lieut.-Gen. von Caprivi, who succeeded Herr von Stosch as Chief of the German Admiralty in 1883, besides completing the construction of the torpedo-flotilla, and building several fast cruisers, formed a training squadron, which is an admirable school for sailors, introduced a system that enables Germany to put ships in commission with great promptitude, organized a cruising squadron that has been the chief instrument in the formation of the German colonial empire, and raised the entire fleet to such a degree of effectiveness that no accidents and failures, such as marked the British and French evolutions in the summer of 1888, occurred during the manœuvres of the German squadron. When Wilhelm II succeeded to the throne, the project of a further development of the ironclad navy by adding to the number of armored battle-ships and replacing with modern vessels those of obsolete types came into favor, and Gen. von Caprivi, who had given his attention chiefly to coast defenses and unarmored fast cruisers, retired from the naval office, to be succeeded by Vice-Admiral Count von Monts, who has undertaken to build up a navy that shall be superior to that of any of the second-rate naval powers, not even excepting Italy, for offensive as well defensive purposes. Of the thirteen squadron ironclads afloat in 1888, only the broadside frigate "König Wilhelm," the central-battery ships the "Kaiser" and "Deutschland," and the corvette "Oldenburg" are regarded as satisfactory by naval critics. The four corvette cruisers, of the "Sachsen" type, having only deck-armor at the ends, are considered weak. The broadside ship "Hansa," with six-inch armor, was removed from the navy list in 1888, and two others, the "Kronprinz" and "Friedrich Karl" are to go out of commission as soon as more modern ironclads can be built to take their places. The class of corvette cruiser now approved of, which was under construction in the beginning of 1888, is a vessel of from 3,000 to 4,000 tons displacement, with a complete belt of armor at the water-line, carrying a few heavy guns in a thickly armored central battery. It is proposed to construct ten such vessels altogether, of which five are to be begun immediately. For the defense of the North Sea and Baltic Ship-canal twelve gun-boats are to be constructed of similar design to the existing ones, but larger. In the naval budget estimates for 1889–'90 the Government proposes the expenditure, in the space of six years, of 116,800,000 marks on the construction of 28 new vessels, 4 of which will be first-class ironclads of the latest design, costing 9,300,000 marks each; 9 will be coastguard ironclads; 7 are to be protected cruiser corvettes, costing 5,500,000 marks each; and of the others 4 will be unprotected cruisers, 2 avisos, and 2 torpedo division boats.

The Baltic and North Sea Ship-canal, which is intended primarily for strategical purposes, will facilitate navigation and commerce in this part of Europe and alter the course of trade in favor of Germany. The canal will run from Holtenau, in the Gulf of Kiel, in a southwesterly direction, by way of Rendsburg, to a point on the Elbe below Hamburg, about half-way between Brunsbüttel and St. Margarethan. Its length will be 61 miles; its breadth at the surface of the water 196 feet, and at bottom 84 feet; and its depth 27 feet. There will be one lock at each end. The work will be completed by 1895. Dantzic is to be converted into a second-class naval station to counterbalance the one that Russia has created at Libau, and for the defense of the southern end of the canal Brunsbüttel is to be fortified likewise. It is intended in the future to extend the ship-canal from the Elbe across the northern part of Hanover to the Jade on which Wilhelmshaven is situated, which will enable ships of war to pass between that port and Kiel without going to sea, and afford means of communication between all the German naval ports even if an enemy held entire command of the German Ocean.

The Ministry.—The Imperial Secretaries of State do not form a cabinet, but act independently of each other and under the supervision of the Chancellor, Prince Bismarck-Schönhausen. The departments are filled as follows: Ministry for Foreign affairs, Count Herbert von Bismarck; Imperial Home Office, Herr von Bötticher, who is also the Representative of the Chancellor; Imperial Admiralty, Count von Monts; Imperial Ministry of Justice, Dr. von Schelling; Imperial Treasury, Dr. Jacobi; Imperial Post-office, Dr. Stephan; Imperial Railroad Bureau, Herr Maybach; Imperial Exchequer, Herr von Stünzer; Bureau of the Imperial Invalid Fund, Dr. Michaelis.

The Prussian Ministry of State consisted in the beginning of 1888 of the following members: President of the Council, Minister of Foreign Affairs, and Minister of Commerce and Industry, Prince Otto von Bismarck-Schönhausen; Vice-President of the Council of Ministers and Minister of the Interior, Robert Victor von Puttkamer; Minister of State and Secretary of State for the Interior, Herr von Bötticher; Minister of War, Gen. Bronsart von Schellendorf; Minister of Public Works, Dr. August von Maybach; Minister of Agriculture, Domains, and Forests, Dr. Robert Lucius; Minister of Justice, Dr. Friedberg; Minister of Public Worship, Education, and Medical Affairs, Herr von Gossler; Minister of Finance, Herr Scholz.

Finances.—The budget for the year ending March 31, 1889, estimates the receipts of the German Empire at 921,689,140 marks, derived from the following sources:

SOURCES OF REVENUE.	Marks.
Customs and excise duties	498,360,610
Stamps	27,655,000
Posts and telegraphs	80,064,098
Printing-office	1,086,090
Railways	18,284,100
Imperial bank	1,741,500
Departmental receipts	9,848,758
Interest of invalid fund	26,359,414
Interest of imperial funds	948,000
Extraordinary receipts	99,676,566
Federal contributions	212,670,009
Total	921,689,140

The estimated ordinary expenditure is 771,961,-697 marks. The following are the principal items: Expenditure for the army, 362,465,016 marks; navy, 35,900,751 marks; imperial treasury, 271,266,326 marks; interest on the national debt, 27,803,000 marks; pension fund, 28,717,888 marks; invalid fund, 26,359,414 marks. The estimated extraordinary expendi-

ture includes a deficit of 22,157,246 marks in the finances of 1886–'87; 77,267,954 marks of expenditure for military purposes; 12,920,318 marks for the navy, and 17,880,750 marks for the interior. The Federal contributions toward the revenue of 1887–'88 were 186,937,-315 marks.

The total funded debt was estimated to be 576,372,000 marks on Oct. 1, 1887. The whole debt bears interest at 4 per cent. There was also an unfunded debt of 138,868,475 marks on April 1, 1887. As an offset to the public debt there are several invested funds, amounting to 666,241,100 marks. These include the invalid fund, the fortification fund, the parliamentary-buildings fund, and the war treasure of 120,000,000 marks.

The Reign of Friedrich I.—While the Emperor Wilhelm I was gradually sinking under the infirmities of old age, the Crown-Prince Friedrich Wilhelm was seized with the disease of which he eventually died. The physicans declared it to be cancer, and if their verdict had been accepted the Crown-Prince would have been precluded from the exercise of the royal and imperial prerogatives on the death of his father, according to the Prussian family law, which provides for a regency in case the successor to the throne is suffering from an incurable malady. Prince Friedrich was an opponent of the system of absolutism and military rule that was cultivated by his father and Prince Bismarck, and a sympathizer with the advocates of parliamentary government and of personal liberty, but after some unavailing conflicts with the Chancellor he had not raised his voice in public affairs for many years. The old Emperor endeavored to persuade the Crown-Prince to abdicate his right of succession to the powers of royalty by nominating as regent his son, Prince Friedrich Wilhelm, who was on bad terms with both his parents, but was a favorite of his grandfather, whose military and monarchical ideas of government he shared. The Crown-Princess Victoria would have been cut off, not only from the dignity of Empress-Consort during her husband's reign, but from the privileges and allowances of Empress-Dowager after his death. She had averted the legal disqualification of the prince for the succession by having the case committed to the English specialist in throat-diseases, Dr. Morell Mackenzie, who asserted that there were no symptoms of cancer. In order to remove him from the influences of his family she now went with him to San Remo, by the advice of Dr. Mackenzie, who declared the climate of Berlin to be too harsh. After the death of his father he returned from Italy to assume the government under the titles of Emperor Friedrich I of Germany and King Friedrich III of Prussia. Arriving in Berlin on March 12, he issued a proclamation to the people, giving praise to his father for the great achievements of his reign and to the people for the sacrifices that made them possible. He promised to devote all his efforts to carrying on the work of making Germany a shield of peace and attending to the welfare of the country, in agreement with the Federated Governments and with the constitutional organs of the empire and of Prussia. The proclamation was accompanied with a rescript to the Chancellor, in which he foreshadowed the policy that he was determined to follow. The Constitution and laws of the empire and of Prussia should, above all, be based on the reverence and the conscience of the nation, and therefore frequent changes in Government institutions and the laws are to be avoided. In the empire the constitutional rights of the Federated Governments are to be faithfully respected, as well as those of the Reichstag, but from both a like respect for the rights of the Emperor is due. New requirements of the nation, as they arise, must be satisfied. The army and navy should be kept up to the highest perfection in training and organization. The programme embraced the continuance of social legislation, the admission of a wider class to the advantages of superior education, religious toleration and equal protection for all confessions, the discouragement of private and the checking of public extravagance, the reduction of the number of civil officials so as to allow an increase of salaries, the control of municipal taxation, and the encouragement of art and science. Friedrich's deliverance was greeted in liberal circles as the presage of a new political era. On March 21 the Emperor issued a decree empowering the Crown-Prince to act in his place and to sign documents whenever he should be unable to attend to business. On March 31 an imperial proclamation of amnesty extended full pardon to all persons who had been sentenced in Prussia for *lèse majesté*, insulting members of the royal family, offenses connected with the exercise of political rights, resisting the authorities or disturbing public order, and offenses against the press laws. Military offenses were also amnestied by an imperial decree, dated April 19, granting a free pardon to soldiers and sailors who had been sentenced for resisting officers of the law or violating public order, to those undergoing disciplinary punishment, and to those who had been found guilty of absenting themselves without leave or of deserting for the first time, provided that no charge of conspiracy was made out against them. Another decree set at liberty all who had been convicted of political offenses in Alsace-Lorraine, including infractions of the special laws of the Reichsland regarding publications, seditious cries, and prohibited banners and emblems. This and other conciliatory acts and expressions went further than anything that had occurred since the war to disarm the feeling of revenge in France, where Friedrich was remembered as the most chivalrous and considerate commander among the conquerors. Among his other acts of government may be mentioned directions to rebuild the Dom-Kirche in Berlin, making it a memorial cathedral of the Evangelical Church; the conferring of titles of honor on many dignitaries, parliamentarians, and industrialists; the abolition of expensive and irrational military exercises, signs, and distinctions; and the furtherance of the scheme of insurance for aged and invalid laborers, which became law while he was Emperor. When Posen was devastated by an inundation he gave 50,000 marks from his private purse for the sufferers, while the Empress Victoria, leaving his sick-bed, visited the flooded district and inspected the arrangements for relief. The Emperor labored to discharge his official duties, notwithstanding his bodily distress and weakness, but a relapse compelled him to delegate one part of his functions, having to do with military affairs, to his son, whom he had previously empowered by a rescript that was published on March 23 to consider and settle such matters of Government as the Emperor should refer to him and append his signature to state papers as the Emperor's substitute without special order, as it was the Emperor's wish that the Crown-Prince should make himself acquainted with affairs of state by taking an immediate part therein.

Differences between the Emperor and the Imperial Chancellor, if they had not yet arisen, were inevitable, owing to the great diversity of their political opinions, although the Emperor took every occasion to express his regard for Prince Bismarck and to treat him as indispensable. About the end of March the Chancellor was informed at a conference with the Emperor at Charlottenburg, the castle which he made his residence, that the Emperor intended within a few days to summon Prince Alexander of Battenberg, ex-Prince of Bulgaria, whose brother had married the Empress's sister, to Berlin, in order to confer on him the order of the Iron Cross, assign him to the command of an army corps, and raise him to the dignity of Fürst, as preliminaries to his formal betrothal to the Princess Victoria. This princess, the eldest unmarried daughter of the Emperor, who was not quite twenty-two years old, had formed an attachment for Alexander before he was called to the Bulgarian throne; but the Emperor Wilhelm disapproved a union between them, and had exacted from him a promise that he would not press his suit. The Chancellor, when he heard of the intended marriage, protested against it as a step of grave political moment, which would be likely to disturb the external relations of Germany and lead to difficulties with Russia, in view of the prince's continued candidacy for the Bulgarian throne, his pledges to the Bulgarian people, and his connection with their anti-Russian aspirations. The Empress, who had firmly set her mind on securing her daughter's happiness, angrily resented the Chancellor's interference in what she regarded as a private family matter, although the Emperor was inclined to defer to the statesman's objections and give up, or at least postpone, the intended alliance. Prince Bismarck presented his reasons in a written memorial and announced the intention of laying down his office if the Empress did not abandon her design. In Russia the intended marriage seemed to be regarded with indifference or even as a way of eliminating Prince Alexander from the Bulgarian complications, since it would not be fitting for a son-in-law of the German Emperor to become a vassal of the Sultan, nor would he be considered an acceptable candidate for the throne of the principality in view of the article of the Berlin Treaty excluding all members of reigning dynasties. Yet Prince Bismarck held firmly to his opinions, while the Empress seemed equally determined. They had several interviews, Prince Alexander's visit to Berlin being put off several times meanwhile. The Chancellor crisis, as it was called, lasted more than a week, and ended with the sacrifice of the marriage project to state reasons and the continuance of Prince Bismarck in office. Prince Henry, of Prussia, the younger son of the Emperor, married his cousin, the Princess Irene, of Hesse, in May; and in the beginning of September the Princess Sophie, Victoria's younger sister, was betrothed to Constantine, the Crown-Prince of Greece.

Shortly before the Emperor's death another ministerial crisis arose that gave proof of the strength of his reformatory purposes. The law of the Reichstag making the duration of parliaments five years instead of three was promptly signed by him; but when a bill of identical provisions in reference to the period of the Prussian Diet was brought to him, he withheld it for further consideration and returned it to the Vice-President of the Ministry of State, Robert Victor von Puttkamer, on the following day, May 27, with his signature attached, and an accompanying letter, saying he expected that in the future the freedom of elections would not be impaired by the interposition of official influence. Minister von Puttkamer, an extreme Conservative, whose interpretation of the remarkable rescript of Jan. 4, 1882, declaring that officials were bound by their oaths to promote the policy of the Government at elections had earned for him the nickname of "electoral patronage chief," answered the Emperor by referring to this command of his predecessor and to the electoral laws, which impose but slight restraints on official activity at elections. The Emperor declared that the law should not be published till he received the required assurance, and this the Prussian Minister of the Interior considered to be equivalent to his dismissal. He accordingly tendered his resignation, which was forthwith accepted. Prince Bismarck manifested surprise at the retirement of his colleague, and exhibited his regret in an ostentatious manner. The National Liberals were disappointed at the fact that the successor of Herr von Puttkamer

was not chosen from their ranks, and as soon as Herr Herrfurth, under-secretary in the Interior Department, was nominated, they threatened to dissolve the "cartel" or electoral alliance with the Conservatives which was called into existence by Prince Bismarck's appeal to the nation after the rejection of the army bill and the dissolution of Parliament. Herr von Puttkamer was succeeded as Vice-President of the Prussian Ministry by Herr von Bötticher, Secretary of State for the Interior, who received the appointment in August.

The Emperor Friedrich's Diary.—In the latter part of September the "Deutsche Rundschau" magazine, published extracts from the diary of the Emperor Friedrich covering the period of the French war. The editor accompanied the publication with a note to the effect that the extracts were received from a person to whom the late Emperor had communicated the diary, or portions of it, with permission to publish it when three months had passed after his death. The diary shows that Friedrich had pressed for the immediate mobilization of the whole army and navy as soon as Count Bismarck informed him that the negotiations with France in regard to the candidacy of Prince Hohenzollern for the Spanish throne had broken down and that war was inevitable. At the close of the war, when the question of German union came up, it was Friedrich who from the beginning urged the creation of the empire, while the King was very reluctant to take such a step until he was persuaded by the Crown-Prince and the Grand Duke of Baden. Bismarck said he feared that the proclamation of the empire would cause Bavaria and Würtemberg to join their fortunes with the Austrian Empire, and wished to leave the question to be solved by time. He seems to have resented the interposition of the prince in the political question, even going to the length of threatening to resign, while seeking to bring about the result at which Friedrich aimed at his own time and in his own way, having the demand proceed from the Reichstag instead of from the allied German princes; but he finally deferred to the prince's views, supported by those of the heads of the states of Baden, Oldenburg, Weimar, and Coburg, and composed the letter which the King of Bavaria was induced to accept as his own, inviting King Wilhelm to assume the imperial crown. When the matter was finally settled, the Crown-Prince wrote with elation of the realization of long-deferred hopes of the German people and of the dreams of German poets, and regarded it as the result of his own persevering efforts. When the title of "German Emperor" was fixed upon, since the Bavarian plenipotentiaries objected to that of "Emperor of Germany," which was proposed by the Crown-Prince, the King said: "My son is devoted with his whole soul to the new order of things, while I care not a straw about it, and only cling to Prussia."

The Emperor Friedrich had at different times had copies taken of parts of his diary. The original was found at San Remo after his departure, and was forwarded to his wife, in whose possession it remained after his death. The new Emperor and Prince Bismarck were angry at the divulging of the extracts that appeared in the "Rundschau," the authenticity of which was called in question by the chancellor, who declared that the historical statements were untrue, saying, in a report to the Emperor Wilhelm, that his father, the author of the diary, was not allowed to be made privy to the political negotiations in France, for fear that he would betray the confidence reposed in him to the English court. In this report he gave his opinion that the diary in the form in which it was published was a forgery, and recommended that the author should be criminally prosecuted on the charge of libeling the memory of the Emperor Friedrich in declaring him capable of menacing Bavaria and Würtemberg with threats of war to compel them to enter the empire and in ascribing to the Prussian Government intentions such as were involved in the statement of the diary that the Chancellor threatened as soon as the French war was over to combat the doctrine of Papal infallibility. In replying to a passage representing him as returning to Varzin on July 13, 1870, under the impression that peace was secured, the Chancellor exhibits his attitude during the negotiations over the Hohenzollern candidature for the Spanish throne in a new light by saying that, far from considering peace secured, he was convinced that war was necessary, and that he intended to resign his ministry and to return to Varzin if the King's reluctance to engage in war had led to a peaceful conclusion of the diplomatic controversy. In accordance with the Chancellor's suggestion, the Minister of Justice instituted criminal proceedings. The unsold numbers of the magazine were confiscated by the Government, and Prof. Geffcken, who furnished the diary for publication, was arrested on the charge of either calumnious attacks on the memory of the dead or of divulging state secrets. In his examination by the judicial authorities he repeated the statement that he had received the diary from the Emperor, but the authorities in their inquiries acted on the suspicion that the Empress Victoria had procured the publication. She was called upon, but refused to deliver the original diary into the custody of the state to be placed in the Prussian archives.

The Accession of William II.—The young Crown-Prince during his father's brief reign held little communication with his parents, and maintained a rival court in Berlin, consorting with reactionary politicians and military men, and evincing in toasts and speeches a dislike for his father's pacific and progressive policy. His first act after the death of Friedrich was to issue two striking addresses, one to the army and one to the navy. In the former he said

that he assumed the place to which he was called with unshakable confidence, because he was aware of the enthusiastic feeling of honor and duty that his predecessors had implanted in the army. The attachment between the army and the monarchs of the Hohenzollern dynasty had grown stronger with each generation. "Thus," he continued, "we belong to each other, I and the army. Thus were we born for each other. And firmly and inseparably will we hold together, whether God's will gives us peace or storm." A proclamation to the Prussian people was issued on June 18, in which he promised to be a just and mild prince, to foster piety and the fear of God, to protect peace, to promote the welfare of the country, and to be a helper of the poor and the oppressed, and a true guardian of the right, counting on the fidelity of his people, who have always stood faithfully by their king, in good and in evil days.

The ceremony of opening the Reichstag in the Old Palace at Berlin on June 25, on which occasion he was attended by most of the sovereign princes of Germany and by the dignitaries of the empire, was a pageant of unexampled splendor. Two days later he took the oath on the Prussian Constitution before both houses of the Diet with a pomp and circumstance that were equally impressive and spectacular. The father had chosen to reign under the name with which he was originally christened and by which he was best known throughout his life. The son, who also bore the double name of Friedrich Wilhelm, discarded the first part in order to follow the royal style of his grandfather, whose example he continually extolled, and which, he said in his speech from the throne, he was resolved to follow, striving to assure the military and political safety of the empire abroad and watching over the execution of the laws at home. He adopted the first Wilhelm's economical policy as his own in regard to affording to the working population, in conformity with Christian morality, such protection as legislative measures can give to the weak and distressed in the struggle for existence, and in this way seeking to equalize unhealthy social contrasts; but all efforts having an aim or tendency to undermine public order be considered it necessary to suppress. His foreign policy he declared to be to maintain peace with every one, as far as lies in his power, and not to use the strength obtained through the new military law for aggressive purposes, for Germany needs no fresh military glory nor conquests since she has won by fighting the right to exist as a united and independent nation.

In his opening speech the Emperor spoke of the existing arrangements with Austria-Hungary and Italy as permitting him to cultivate his personal friendship for the Emperor of Russia and the peaceful relations that have existed with the neighboring Russian Empire for a hundred years. On July 13 he set out from Potsdam on a visit to his friend and relative the Czar. He embarked at Kiel in the royal steam-yacht "Hohenzollern," which was escorted by an ironclad squadron under the command of his brother, Prince Henry. He was met at sea by the Russian Emperor, taken to St. Petersburg on the yacht "Alexandria," and there entertained with a military spectacle and other pageants. From there he went to Stockholm, arriving on July 26, and, after exchanging courtesies with King Oscar, sailed two days later for Copenhagen, where he was the guest of the King of Denmark for a few hours, and returned to Germany after an absence of eighteen days. He next manifested his perfect confidence in Prince Bismarck by paying him a visit at Friedrichsruhe. On August 16 the Emperor delivered a speech at a dinner of officers of the Third Army Corps, in which he denied the imputation that his father was willing to relinquish a part of the conquered territory as the price of disarmament and lasting peace, and said that in the army there is but one opinion, and that is "that we would leave our entire eighteen army corps and 42,000,000 inhabitants lying 'on the field rather than abandon one single stone of what we have won."

After the trial evolutions of the fleet and the autumnal manœuvres of the army, which were arranged on an unprecedented scale, the young Kaiser carried out his intention of visiting his allies, the sovereigns of Austria-Hungary and Italy. On September 25 he set out on his tour, first visiting the German courts of Detmold, Stuttgart, and Munich, and on October 3 arrived at Vienna, where he was received with festivities, and afterward spent some time in a hunting trip with the Emperor Franz Josef. His visit at the Quirinal with King Umberto occurred in October. On the 12th he was the guest of Pope Leo at the Vatican, after which he inspected a parade of the Italian military, and on the 21st arrived again in Germany.

The Emperor was offended at the comments and insinuations of the Liberal press touching the friction and conflicting purposes which the question of the Battenberg marriage, the controversy between the doctors in regard to the treatment of his father's disease, and the proceedings in relation to the publication of Friedrich's diary proved to have existed between members of the royal family and to be still existent between himself and his mother. At last he complained of the attitude of the press in a reply to an address of the municipal authorities of Berlin that he made to the burgomaster. That official resented the inference that any part of the newspaper press was subject to his direction, and the papers vindicated themselves with unwonted boldness. The Liberal and the Conservative papers at first disputed as to which had given offense, the most indiscreet revelations regarding the royal family having appeared in the semi-official journals. An official announcement made it clear

that it was the language of the Liberal press to which the Emperor objected, especially to comparisons between himself and his father. The Liberal journals criticised his desire to suppress the side of the controversy that was unfavorable to himself, while giving free scope to comparisons that were unfavorable to his father's memory, and declared that the independent press of Berlin would "defend its independence against the municipal authorities as well as against every one else who threatens it," and that it would "render unto the Kaiser the things that are his, and also unto the free Constitution what belongs to it."

On November 22 the Emperor opened the Reichstag with great pomp of rank, uniform, and military display. In the speech from the throne he announced a measure relating to co-operative societies and the completion of the legislation for the insurance of aged and ailing laborers. He expressed satisfaction at the signs of sympathy and attachment that had been shown to him and to the idea of the German Empire that he represented by the princes and peoples of the Federated States. The alliance with Austria and Italy he declared to have no other object but peace. "To plunge Germany needlessly into the horrors of war, even if it were a victorious one," he said, "I should find inconsistent with my belief as a Christian and with my duties as Emperor toward the German people. Filled with this conviction, I thought it meet, soon after ascending the throne, to visit in person, not only my allies in the empire, but also the monarchs who are my neighbors and friends, and to confer with them regarding the task of securing peace and prosperity for our peoples. The confidence that was shown in me and my policy warrants me in hoping that I and my allies and friends will, with God's help, succeed in maintaining the peace of Europe."

The Anti-Socialist Law.—The repressive law against Socialists and Anarchists was originally passed in 1878 for a limited period, and has been periodically renewed without material alteration, sometimes for two, and sometimes for three years. In January, 1888, the Government proposed not only that it should be re-enacted for a period of five years, but that the penal provisions should be strengthened. The punishment for printing or circulating forbidden publications was to be increased from six to twelve months' imprisonment, together with a fine of 1,000 marks, and in other cases the penalties were rendered more severe. Certain classes of offenders would be liable, not only to be expelled from their ordinary domicile, as under the old act, but to be banished from the empire altogether, and deprived of their rights of citizenship. The bulk of the Clerical party, under the lead of Dr. Windhorst, demanded the mitigation, instead of the accentuation, of the act, and were seconded by the Liberalists. The National Liberals declined to prolong the act for more than two years, and even the National Conservative party objected to the expatriation clauses. The measure, at the end of a long and animated discussion, was referred to a committee of twenty-eight members, and as altered in their hands and finally passed by the House and signed by the Emperor Friedrich, it is simply a continuance of the act as it stood before for two more years from the autumn of 1888.

Insurance of Workingmen.—The last installment of the scheme of insurance against the worst consequences of poverty, which was foreshadowed in the imperial message of Nov. 17, 1884, is the bill making provision for work-people incapacitated by age or chronic ailments, which was elaborated by the Federal Council in the summer of 1888. The measure provides for compulsory insurance, the funds for which are raised in three parts, one of them being contributed by the Imperial Government by means of assessment, one part by employers, and the third part by the laborers themselves, the men paying in 21 pfennige, or about 5 cents weekly, and the women 14 pfennige. Every man who becomes invalided will receive a pension of 120 marks, and every woman 80 marks. The pension for superannuated working-people begins at the age of seventy-one, with an allowance of 180 marks. No contributions are exacted during the periods when men are required to perform military service.

The first part of Bismarck's scheme of state socialism was the sick-insurance law that was enacted in 1883, which compels the workman to insure himself against sickness by contributing to a fund insuring him medical care and medicines from the beginning of his sickness, and half-wages for thirteen weeks. At the end of this time he falls a charge on another fund, which is raised from employers under the law that was passed in 1884 for insuring against accidents. The first accident-insurance act was a tentative measure, and was made to apply only to those trades and occupations in which accidents are most frequent. It was extended in 1885 to a much larger class, and made to cover also workingmen employed by the Government in the railway, postal, telegraph, and naval and military administrations. By a supplementary act that was passed in 1887, and went into operation on Jan. 1, 1888, accident insurance was extended further to all persons engaged in marine occupations, with the exception of fishermen and those employed on small craft, who are to be dealt with in a later act. The accident-insurance fund is raised by compulsory assessments on employers, who are grouped for the purpose into associations, according to employments and locality, and these are divided into sections. Exclusive of the one that was created for the execution of the marine-insurance act, there are sixty-two associations in Germany, which are, to a large extent, self-governing, drawing up their own statutes and regulations,

and managing their own finances. They were divided in 1886 into 366 sections. The association of marine employers is divided into six sections. The Government control is exercised through the Imperial Insurance Department, which initiates the organization of the associations, supervises their administration, approves their statutes, divides such of them as become unmanageable, and acts as a last court of appeal in disputes on the subject of the payment of insurance that arise between the employers and the employed. This supervising board, which is an organ of the state, consists, in part, of permanent members, who are appointed by the Emperor, and, in part, of delegates of the employers and the workingmen, who are elected for four years. The insurance indemnities to be paid out of the fund consist of the expenses of the cure in cases of disablement, where there is no legal obligation on others to bear them; of a fixed allowance during the disablement; and of an allowance to the family in case of death. The allowance in each case is calculated according to a scale based on the annual wages. The assessments are made by specially appointed committees or by the boards themselves. Each section has an arbitration committee, which is presided over by an official, while the assessors are elected representatives of the employers and the employed. The members of the association must provide the expenses of administration and accumulate a reserve fund. The share of each member of the association depends on the number of workmen that he employs, and is subject to increase if the employment is especially dangerous. The indemnities are paid by post-office orders. The associations are required to consult with the workmen in drawing up regulations for the avoidance of accidents, and to see that these are enforced, which, of course, is in the interest of members of the association, the amount of whose assessments depends on the frequency of accidents.

The boards of the sixty-two trade associations organized under the insurance law that was in force in 1886 contained 742 members, and the 366 sectional boards were composed of 2,356 members. There were 6,501 officers, 39 salaried inspecting agents, 404 arbitration courts, and 2,445 representatives of the workmen. The number of business establishments was 269,174; the number of work-people insured, 3,473,435; and the total amount of annual wages on which the indemnities were calculated was 2,276,250,000 marks, or $543,157,000. The total amount of indemnities paid out during 1886 was 1,736,500 marks; the cost of administration was 2,374,000 marks; and the cost of investigating accidents, fixing indemnities, arbitrating, and taking precautions against accidents was 282,000 marks. A reserve of 5,516,000 marks was formed, and, including this, the total expenditure was 10,521,500 marks, while the total receipts were 12,646,000 marks. Including employés of the state, the total number of workmen insured was 3,725,313. There were 100,159 accidents during the year, of which 2,716 were fatal, requiring 5,935 indemnities to be paid to widows, orphans, and other relatives of the deceased. The total expenditure was about 72 cents per head of the persons insured, and $1.15 on every $250 of wages; but, deducting the costs of institution and the contributions to the reserve fund, the expenditure was 18 cents per capita and 48 cents on every $250 of wages paid. The cost of administration largely exceeded the amount of indemnities paid, but the expense will be less disproportionate after the system is established, and will be partly covered by the interest on the reserve fund. This part of the expenditure is large because the associations have to see to the prevention of accidents and the investigation of their nature and causes, not merely to pay indemnities. The amount paid in indemnities will increase from year to year as new annual allowances are made to injured men and their families, while the cost of administration will remain stationary, or, perhaps, decrease, and therefore the report is considered to be, under all the circumstances, a favorable showing.

The Incorporation of Hamburg and Bremen.—The two chief seaports of Germany remained till 1888 outside the customs boundary of the Zollverein, which had, however, absorbed the territorial districts and some of the populous suburbs of the old Hanse towns. In October these cities gave up their ancient privileges as free ports and entered the Zollverein, thus rendering complete the policy of the commercial union of the German states, which was initiated by Prussia sixty years before political union was achieved. Their claim to remain free ports was conceded in 1868, and was ratified in the Imperial Constitution of 1871, although the privilege was in the case of Hamburg restricted to the city and port, and withdrawn from the rest of the state, which extends to the mouth of the Elbe, embracing 160 square miles. It was arranged that the two Hanse towns should remain outside the common customs boundary until they should themselves demand admittance. In 1880 the German Government brought pressure to bear to secure the inclusion of Hamburg in the customs league, which was desirable to Germany for political reasons, and still more for commercial reasons, because the 7,000 ships entering the port every year and taking cargoes to the most remote countries of the world, carried, besides German goods, large quantities of the manufactures of England and other countries, which the Chancellor desired to see displaced by German products. A project of union was negotiated on May 25, 1881, subject to the approval of the Hamburg Legislature. There was much opposition among the citizens, but the Senate agreed to the treaty, which it thought would be beneficial to the commerce of the port. The House of Burgesses could not accept that view,

but ratified the convention on being appealed to for the sacrifice of private and local advantage in the interest of national prosperity. The conditions of trade had so changed, however, as to make the isolation for which Hamburg had stood out less desirable to preserve than it was when the city entered the empire. Formerly Hamburg merchants had to depend on British products, for there were but few German manufactures, but in recent years many of the manufactured articles that are in most demand in neutral markets are produced in Germany more cheaply than in Great Britain. The growth in the trade of the port for the past ten years has been twice as great in German as it has in British manufactures. The German Chancellor, under these circumstances, could exact the acquiescence of the most unwilling of the burghers by threatening so to build up and favor Altona and Glücksburg that the German trade would leave Hamburg, and pass through those ports. A small area on the north bank of the Elbe, with the small islands opposite, was still reserved, and the space was subsequently extended, yet it only affords room for mooring vessels to the wharves, and for the erection of warehouses that simply correspond to the bonded warehouses of every customs port. In order to carry into effect the resolution of the Hamburg Government, of June 15, 1881, to enter the German customs union, time was required to build warehouses and make quays in that part of the city that is still free from customs, in order that the important transit and shipping trade might not be lost. It was therefore decided that the resolution should not go into effect till October, 1888. The seven years have been employed in making a great transformation, widening canals, building docks and quays, and erecting in the place of the poor buildings that formerly stood near the water blocks of warehouses that are as large and fine as can be found in any seaport. The cost of the improvements has been about 160,000,000 marks, one fourth of which was defrayed by the Imperial Government. The bill to incorporate Hamburg in the customs union was passed in 1882 by the Reichstag, notwithstanding the vehement opposition of the free-traders in that assembly. The city of Bremen was in like manner induced to join the Zollverein, and the German authorities began the collection of customs duties in both places on the same day, Oct. 17, 1888. A great number of officials visited the citizens and received their declarations as to the possession of dutiable goods. A reasonable amount was allowed to go free, but on all other goods liable to pay duty the back duties were levied, which were turned into the treasury of the Hamburg state, while all duties accruing subsequent to the formal incorporation into the Zollverein belong to the treasury of the empire, in consideration of which Hamburg is relieved from the annual military subsidy of 5,000,000 marks that she has paid heretofore. The part of the city on the left bank of the

Elbe, for which the free-port privileges are retained, was made into an island by digging a broad canal. Ships are permitted to pass from the sea into this free port without customs inspection, and the supervision between it and the customs-union territory is left to Hamburg officials. No bridges are allowed to be made between the free-port part of the town and other parts, nor will any one be permitted to reside within the district that remains open to free trade. The city of Hamburg has till now retained the system of taxation that was prevalent in the middle ages, but before the incorporation in the Zollverein all the old excise duties were abolished, and its fiscal conditions were assimilated to those of the rest of the empire.

The Prussian Elections.—After it had passed the bill making the electoral period five years, the Prussian Diet was dissolved, and new elections were held in October. In the new quinquennial the Government majority, as made up of the "Cartel Brothers," or union of the Conservatives and National Liberals, was strengthened, and if on any question this alliance should be broken, the Government can obtain a strong working majority, as it has in former parliaments, by attracting the support of the Clericals. The United Conservatives elected 199 deputies, losing one seat, while the National Liberals increased their representation from 72 to 87. The Clericals elected 97 members, the same number as in 1885. The Poles kept their 15 and the Danes their 2 seats; but the Guelphs lost a seat, electing only a single member, and the Independents decreased from 5 to 3. The Feisinnige or Liberalist party lost 11 seats to the National Liberals, electing 29 members, against 40 in the last Diet.

Foreign Relations.—On Feb. 6, 1888, Prince Bismarck reviewed the political situation in a great speech that he made in the Reichstag in connection with the loan bill to provide the money for adding 700,000 men to the fighting force of the empire. France, he said, looked less explosive than it had a year before, for the election of a pacific President and the appointment of a ministry composed of men who subordinated their plans to the peace of Europe were favorable signs that the French Government did not wish to plunge its hand into Pandora's box. The apprehensions that had arisen, which had been encouraged in order to further the passage of the military bill, were caused by the massing of Russian troops near the German and Austrian frontiers. In demanding the money for arming and equipping the Landwehr the Government had made the most of this menacing movement of troops, and encouraged the warlike attitude of the German press. Now that the passage of the bill was certain, the Chancellor sought to calm the public mind, saying that he was convinced that the dislocation of troops proceeded from no intention to fall upon Germany unawares, because in his recent interview with the Czar he had been

assured that no such purpose was contemplated. In explaining the causes that led to the alliance with Austria, he ironically declared that at the Berlin Congress he had acted almost like a third plenipotentiary of Russia in his desire to serve that power, but that his intentions were misinterpreted by the Russian press, and a controversy regarding the course of German diplomacy arose, which led to "complete threats of war from the most competent quarter." Hence he negotiated at Gastein and Vienna the treaty of alliance. "We shall sue for love no longer," he said, "either in France or Russia. The Russian press and Russian public opinion have shown to the door an old, powerful, and trustworthy friend, and we shall not seek to push our way in again. We have tried to re-establish our old intimate relations, but we shall run after no one." He conceded, to the dismay of the Austrians and especially of the Hungarians, the right of domination that Russia claimed in Bulgaria, and said that it was no concern of Germany's if Russia should restore by force the supremacy that she exercised before 1885. In any case, he was convinced that "the tiny province between the Balkans and the Danube is not an object of sufficient importance to involve Europe in a war extending from Moscow to the Pyrenees and from the North Sea to Palermo, of which no mortal can foresee the results, and yet at its close the combatants would scarcely know why they had fought at all." He was not alarmed at exhibitions of Russian hatred, "for no wars are waged for mere hatred." He did not believe that Russia would attack Germany, even if she became involved in a war with France; but, if a war with Russia should break out, no French Government could be strong enough to restrain the French people from a war against Germany. The new military bill enables Germany to place an army of 1,000,000 men on each frontier. "When we undertake a war," said the Chancellor, "it must be a people's war, which all approve. If we are attacked, then the *furor Teutonicus* will flame out, and against that no one can make head." He concluded with the proud boast, "We Germans fear God, and nothing else in the world."

The Austrian Government gave no indication of willingness to permit Russia to regain by an armed intervention the supremacy in Bulgaria that Russian arrogance and intrigue had lost, and Tisza, in the Hungarian Chamber, intimated the contrary. The German Kaiser, by visiting the Czar before going to the Austrian and Italian courts, showed a desire to conciliate Russia, which was partly due to his personal friendship for Alexander III. In August, Crispi, the Italian Premier, had an interview with Prince Bismarck at Friedrichsruhe, and stopped at Vienna to confer with Count Kálnoky, who also had his annual meeting with the German Chancellor.

Besides the passport regulations for Alsace-Lorraine nothing occurred to cause ill-feeling between France and Germany. An Alsatian Government clerk named Dietz was tried, with his wife, for selling information to the French authorities regarding the German railroads in Alsace-Lorraine, and was sentenced to a long term of imprisonment. In November a German ex-officer, who was settled in France as a teacher of languages, was arrested in the act of mailing a Lebel cartridge. These and other spy incidents caused less stir than the expulsion from Prussia, on November 17, of two French journalists, named Latapieh and D'Oriot, for publishing obnoxious statements concerning members of the royal family.

Colonial Possessions.—Germany had no dependencies beyond the seas before 1884. Since that date she has established protectorates over extensive regions in Africa and many islands in the Pacific Ocean. In 1884, Togoland, on the Slave Coast of West Africa, with Porto Seguro and Little Popo, in all about 400 square miles, with 40,000 inhabitants and a trade of $1,200,000 a year, was annexed, and in the same year the German flag was raised over the Cameroon region, extending for 300 miles along the coast, from Rio del Rey on the north to the River Campo on the south, and into the interior to 15° of east longitude, comprising 120,000 square miles. The exports of Cameroons, consisting mainly of oils, are valued at $3,750,000 per annum. Damaraland and Namaqualand, in South Africa, were taken under German protection between 1884 and 1886, embracing a territory of 230,000 square miles, with 200,000 native inhabitants (see CAPE COLONY).

In East Africa the territory acquired by the German East African Society in Usagora and the neighboring districts, comprising 20,700 square miles, was made a German protectorate in 1885 by the *Schutzbrief*, or protecting charter of the Emperor. In the same year Wituland, 5,200 square miles in extent, was added; and in 1886, by virtue of an agreement with Great Britain and Zanzibar, the German Government established a protectorate over 122,800 square miles of territory in East Africa. The German acquisitions extend from Kilimanjaro mountain on the north to the River Rovuma in the south. The total area in Africa that has been brought under German domination is about 740,000 square miles, not including 200,000 square miles in East Africa, over which German traders claim to have secured territorial rights, comprising the districts of Khutu, Usambara, Pare, Ugono, Arusha, Djagga, Usavamo, Ulena, Wamatshonde, Mahenge Magindo, Girijania, Sabaki, the Galla country, and Ukamba Gasi. The districts that were included in the protectorate before 1888 are Usagara, Ukami, Nguru, and Usegua. The entire region embraced in the German sphere of influence has a coast line stretching from Cape Delgado in 11° of south latitude to the harbor of Wanga in 4° 30″, and extends inland to the great lakes. In accordance with a treaty made with the Sultan of Zanzibar on April 28, 1888, the German East African Company has acquired a fifty-years' lease of the entire strip of coast, with rights to all duties and tolls, whereas previously the possessions of the company were cut off from the sea, and it had only a concurrent right to use the two harbors of Dar-es-Salam and Pangani. The region south of Tana is inhabited by the peaceful Suaheli tribes, while north of that river, in the Galla country and on the Somali coast, dwell the warlike and predatory Galla and Somali tribes. The little sultanate of Witu, which lies immediately north of the Tana, is administered by a company connected with the German Colonial Association. The territory that came under German dominion by arrangement with Great Britain is bounded by a line passing from Witu to Fungasombo, and Mknumbi, and then running to the ocean, which it strikes at a point between the mouths of Mknumbi and Osi rivers. The boundary on the other side ascends the Osi as far as Kau, and then the river Magogoni to its source, whence it follows a straight line to Witu. The soil is fruitful and well-watered, and on the coast are several good harbors. The Germans expect to find a rich field of commerce in Somaliland. The country produces gum-arabic, frankincense, myrrh, and other aromatic resins and herbs, coffee of the finest quality, honey and wax, ostrich-feathers, ivory, dye-woods, pharmaceutical plants, cloves, cocoanuts, sesame, earth-nuts, palm-oil, and gum copal, and on the plateau that forms the interior the Bedonins and pastoral Somali tribes raise herds of camels that they count by thousands, as well as sheep and goats, cattle, and asses in vast numbers, and all ride Arab horses of purest race. There is now a large export of cattle, hides, and butter. In the Suaheli country the Germans have experimented in the cultivation of cotton, tobacco, sugar, which is already raised and manufactured by the Arabs, vanilla, pepper, nutmeg, and indigo. The result of the trials in tobacco-culture has encouraged them to undertake planting on a large scale. The specimens of cotton proved fair in quality, and much is expected from the cultivation of coffee in a country that is the natural habitat of the plant. The German East African Plantation Society has 62,000 acres planted, and has adopted a system of modified slavery, contracting with Indian traders, who furnish gangs of 150 negroes for terms of two years, the contractors feeding, housing, and overseeing the laborers.

The northern part of southeastern New Guinea, lying between Humboldt Bay and Huon Gulf, with an area of 70,300 square miles and an estimated population of 109,000 souls, was made a German possession during 1885 and 1886, and given the name of Kaiser Wilhelm's Land. New Britain and other islands lying between 141° and 154° of east longitude and between 8° of south latitude and the equator, having a land surface of 18,150 square miles and 188,000 inhabitants, were annexed in 1885, and called Bismarck Archipelago. In 1886 were added the islands of Bougainville, Choiseul, Isabel, and others in the northern part of the Solomon group, with an area of 8,500 square miles and a population of 80,000 persons. The acquisitions of 1885 included some of the Marshall Islands, having an area of 42 square miles and about 10,000 inhabitants. The Providence and Crow groups have also become German territory. In the summer of 1888 the natives for the first time attacked German officials in the Bismarck Archipelago. Kaiser Wilhelm's Land is the field of operations for a trading and colonization society called the New Guinea Company, which has stations on the coast at Finsch-Haven and Constantine and Hatzfeld. harbors. There is much land that is considered suitable for settlement by Europeans and adapted for the cultivation of tobacco and food-plants, but no progress has yet been made in colonization. The islands of the Bismarck Archipelago produce copral, or dried cocoanut, of which 1,500 tons were exported in 1885, mother-of-pearl, and trepang. A plantation at Blanche Bay is producing cotton of the Sea Island variety. In New Guinea there have been several collisions with the natives, who have no rifles, but use the spear and the bow with dexterity. The first serious fight occurred in December, 1886, in Huon Gulf, where a boat from the "Samoa" gun-boat was attacked, which led to the burning of their village. The same punishment befell the assailants who killed some Malay laborers on a plantation at Hatzfeld harbor in July, 1887.

GILCHRIST, ROBERT, an American lawyer, born in Jersey City, N. J., Aug. 21, 1825; died there, July 6, 1888. He had a liberal education at private schools, studied jurisprudence, in 1847 was admitted to the bar of New Jersey, and practiced his profession till the time of his death. He was a counselor of the Supreme Court of the United States, and was a member of the Assembly of New Jersey in 1859. In 1861 he enlisted, in response to the first call by the State for troops, and went to the front as captain in the Second New Jersey Volunteers. Until the close of the war he adhered to the Republican party, but he left that party on the question of the reconstruction of the Southern States, and in 1866 was nominated for Congress on the Democratic ticket. In 1869 he was appointed Attorney-General for the unexpired part of the official term vacated by the resignation of Hon. George M. Robeson, and in 1873 was reappointed for a full term. In 1875 he was presented as a candidate for the office of United States Senator. In 1873 he was appointed one of the commissioners to revise the Constitution of the State of New Jersey, but resigned before that work was completed; and, likewise, his obligations to important professional engagements required him to decline an appointment as a justice of the Supreme Court, as also the office of Chief-Justice of New Jersey. Mr.

Gilchrist was endowed with a bold will and intrepid moral courage; he was faithful, just, generous, and notably non-partisan. His knowledge of the principles of jurisprudence, especially of constitutional law, was erudite and accurate and profound, and few have been engaged in a greater number of celebrated

ROBERT GILCHRIST.

causes. As Attorney-General his services were acknowledged to be valuable. His interpretation of the fifteenth amendment peaceably secured the right of negro suffrage in New Jersey, and he was the author of the Riparian Rights act, and was the counsel for the State in the suit to test the constitutionality of that statute. From this source the fund for the maintenance of the public schools of New Jersey is chiefly derived. In his private practice his thoroughness and attention to minute detail made him exceptionally successful. His skill and courage secured to the United States the half-million dollars left by Joseph L. Lewis to be applied to the payment of the national debt, and he brilliantly won many other important suits. Mr. Gilchrist was not only an able counselor in many matters relating to the most difficult portions of law-practice, but was an effective orator before a jury. He continned to pursue his profession until the last year of his life.

GOVERNMENT DEPARTMENTS AT WASHINGTON. The administration of the United States Government is conducted by the President through nine departments, the heads of which are appointed by him, and, with two exceptions, constitute his Cabinet of advisers. These Departments are the State, Treasury, War, Navy, Interior, Post-Office, Justice, Agriculture, and Labor. The respective Secretaries of State, Treasury, War, Navy, and Interior, and the Postmaster and Attorney Generals, receive an annual salary of $8.000; the Commissioners of Agriculture and Labor, $5,000. Public business in these departments is transacted between the hours of 9 A. M. and 4 P. M. Until 2 P. M. the buildings are open to visitors, but 'at that hour they are closed to all but official employés. An annual report to Congress, in detail, is made by each head of a department, giving the expenditure of its contingent fund, together with the number and name of all employés and the salaries paid to each. The total number of persons employed in the several branches of the civil service is 132,072; total number in the departments at Washington, 3,433.

State Department.—This occupies the south pavilion of the State, War, and Navy Department Building, on Seventeenth Street, south of Pennsylvania Avenue and immediately west of the Executive house. The structure is in the style of the Italian Renaissance, and consists of three harmonious buildings, with connecting wings. This department was established July 27, 1789, under the name of Department of Foreign Affairs, its secretary bearing the same title. On Sept. 15, 1789, it received its present denomination, its duties being also extended. The total number of employés of this department is 1,345; in department proper, 78. All diplomatic intercourse of the United States with foreign powers is conducted by the Secretary of State, who instructs and corresponds with all ministers and consuls and negotiates with foreign ministers. He holds the first rank among members of the Cabinet, and, by act of Jan. 19, 1886, is designated to succeed to the presidency in the event of a vacancy in both Executive offices. He is custodian of the Great Seal of the United States, and affixes it to documents and commissions. He also preserves the originals of treaties and of all laws and resolutions of Congress, and directs their publication, with amendments to the Constitution and proclamations of admission of new States into the Union. He grants and issues passports, and makes annual report to Congress of commercial information received from diplomatic and consular sources. There is an assistant secretary, salary, $4,500; a second assistant secretary, salary, $3,500; and a third assistant secretary, salary, $3,500. There are six bureaus, the chiefs of which receive $2,100 yearly, viz.: Bureau of Indexes and Archives; Diplomatic Bureau, in three divisions (total number employed in diplomatic service abroad, 63); Consular Bureau, in three divisions (same countries allotted to each as in Diplomatic Bureau—total number employed in consular service abroad, 1,204); Bureaus of Accounts, of Rolls and Library, and of Statistics. The appropriation for the diplomatic and consular service for the year 1888 was $1,429,942.44.

Treasury Department.—The building is of Ionic architecture, at Fifteenth Street and Pennsylvania Avenue, 582 × 300 feet. This department has existed since Feb. 11, 1776, under a resolution of the First Congress of Delegates, assembled in Carpenter's Hall, Philadelphia,

providing for a committee of five to superintend finances. The Treasury was successively extended until on Sept. 2, 1789, it was organized as a department. Subsequent additions have been made to its officers. The total number employed in the Treasury service is 15,228; in the department proper, 2,477. The duties of the Secretary of the Treasury embrace the collection and disbursement of the national revenues, plans for the improvement of which he devises, and the support of the public credit. He annually submits to Congress estimates and accounts of expenditures of appropriations, warrants for payment of which are issued by him, as also for the covering in of funds. He also superintends the coinage and printing of money, the construction of public buildings, the administration of the Coast and Geodetic Survey, life-saving, lighthouse, revenue-cutter, steamboat inspection, and marine hospital branches of the public service, and collection of statistics. There are two assistant secretaries, with annual salaries of $4,000. The office work is in 10 divisions, viz.: warrants, estimates, and appropriations; appointments; customs; public moneys; loans and currency; mercantile marine and internal revenue; revenue marine; stationary, printing, and blanks; captured property, claims and lands; mails and files and special agents. The following are the principal officers of the Treasury:

First Comptroller.—Office established Sept. 2, 1789. Countersigns all warrants issued by the secretary, and receives accounts from First and Fifth Auditors (with exception of customs returns), and from the Commissioner of the General Land-Office; revises them, and certifies balances. Salary, $5,000.

Second Comptroller. — Office established March 3, 1817. Revises accounts from Second, Third, and Fourth Auditors. Salary, $5,000.

Commissioner of Customs, more properly Third Comptroller.—Office created March 3, 1849. Certifies accounts of receipts in general from customs, and disbursements for collection of them, also for revenue-cutter, life-saving, and shipping services, seal-fisheries in Alaska, lighthouses, marine hospitals, etc. Commissions customs officers, approves bonds, files oaths, etc. Salary, $4,000. The total number employed in collection of customs is 4,356; in the revenue marine, 997.

Six Auditors, salary $3,600 per annum each, receive all accounts of Government expenses, which they certify in following order:

First Auditor.—All accounts accruing in the Treasury (except those of internal revenue), including contingent expenses of Congress, Judiciary, etc. The work of the office is in 5 divisions, viz: customs; judiciary; public debt; warehouse and bond; miscellaneous. Office established Sept, 2, 1789.

Second Auditor.—Accounts in part of War Department, for pay of army, back pay and bounty, Soldiers' Home, and various military institutions, expenses relating to Indians, etc.

All clothing accounts of the army are adjusted finally, also property accounts ot Indian agents. Office established March 3, 1817.

Third Auditor.—Remaining accounts of the War Department, army pension, Military Academy, horse claims, claims miscellaneous, etc. Office established, March 3, 1817.

Fourth Auditor.—Accounts of the navy, including pay, pensions, and prize-money. Office established March 3, 1817.

Fifth Auditor.—Accounts of the State Department and internal revenue, census, Smithsonian Institution, National Museum, etc. Office established March 3, 1817.

Sixth Auditor, in the Post-Office Department building. Adjusts finally all accounts for postal service, subject to appeal to the First Comptroller. Collects debts, etc., of the Post-Office Department. Office established July 2, 1836.

Treasurer of the United States.—Office established Sept. 2, 1789. In charge of all public moneys on deposit in the Treasury at Washington, in nine sub-treasuries at Boston, New York, Philadelphia, Baltimore, New Orleans, San Francisco, St. Louis, Chicago, and Cincinnati, and in the national bank United States depositaries. Pays the interest on the public debt and salaries of members of the House of Representatives. Trustee of bonds for national bank circulation and custodian of Indian trust fund bonds. Salary, $6,000.

Register of the Treasury.—Office established Sept. 2, 1789. Official book-keeper of the United States. Prepares an annual statement to Congress of all receipts and disbursements of public funds, signs and issues all bonds, and registers warrants. Salary, $4,000.

Comptroller of the Currency.—Office established June 3, 1864. Under direction of the secretary, he controls the national banks. The number of these is 294. Salary, $5,000.

Solicitor.—Chief law-officer of the Treasury, with special cognizance of revenue frauds. Approves bonds, etc. Salary, $4,000.

Commissioner of Internal Revenue.—Office established July 1, 1862. Duties, assessment and collection of internal taxes, preparation of instructions and stamps. The work of the office is in 8 divisions, viz., appointments, law, tobacco, accounts, distilled spirits, stamps, assessments, revenue agents. Salary, $6,000. The total number employed in the service is 3,218. A laboratory, with chemist and microscopist, for tests of oleomargarine, under the act of 1886, is attached to this bureau.

Director of the Mint.—Salary, $4,500. The total number of employés in the 3 mints and 6 assay offices in the United States is 948. The amount of silver required to be coined monthly, by act of Feb. 28, 1878, is $2,000,000.

Supervising Architect of Treasury.—Office established 1853. Salary, $4,500. The total number employed on public buildings is 655.

Commissioner of Navigation.—Salary, $3,600. Number of employés, 46.

Superintendent of the Life-Saving Service.—Service reorganized June 18, 1878. Salary, $4,000. The number of life-saving stations is 213; of employés, 242.

Superintendent of Steamboat Inspection.—Salary, $3,500. He presides at meetings of Board of Supervising Inspectors on the third Wednesday in January. The number of employés is 164.

Supervising Surgeon-General of Marine Hospital Service.—Instituted 1799; office, No. 1421 G Street, N. W. Salary, $4,000. The number of employés is 406.

Light-House Board.—Organized Aug. 31, 1862; employs 1,321 persons. The following bureaus occupy separate buildings, viz.:

Bureau of Engraving and Printing, corner Fourteenth and B Streets, S. W. The number of employés is 895. The number of sheets of securities produced in 1888 was 38,038,939; cost, $948.819.29. The chief of the bureau has a salary of $4,000.

Bureau of Statistics, No. 407 Fifteenth Street, N. W. The number of employés is 35. The chief of the bureau has a salary of $3,000. It furnishes annual reports on commerce and navigation, internal commerce, annual statistical abstract, quarterly reports on commerce, navigation, and immigration, monthly statement of imports and exports, reports on total values of foreign commerce and immigration, of exports of breadstuffs, of provisions, of petroleum and cotton.

Coast and Geodetic Survey.—Building south of the Capitol. Reorganized April 29, 1843. The superintendent's salary is $6,000. Besides annual reports to Congress, it publishes maps and charts of our coasts and harbors, books of sailing-directions, and annual tide-tables. The number of employés is 173.

War Department.—Established Aug. 7, 1789; occupies the north wing of the State, War, and Navy Department Building. The total number in the service, including the army of the United State, Signal Corps, etc., is 31,958; in the department proper, 1,536. All duties of the military service, purchase of supplies, transportation, etc., devolve upon the Secretary of War, who is also invested with affairs of a civil nature. He provides for the taking of meteorological observations, arranges the course of studies at the Military Academy, supervises the work and expenditures of the engineer corps, and purchases real-estate for national cemeteries. He controls the appropriation of the Mississippi River Commission, and directs the construction of piers or cribs by owners of saw-mills, the removal of sunken vessels obstructing navigation, etc., and regulates bids for contracts. The headquarters of the army are in the War Department. The standing army of the United States numbers 27,159 men. The army appropriation for the fiscal year 1888 was $23,724,718.69. Salary of the general, $13,500. Chiefs of bureaus of

War Department have the rank of brigadier-general. Salary, $5,500. They are:

Adjutant-General, has 5 assistants. Promulgates orders of the President and the general of the army, conducts correspondence, has charge of enlistment, recruiting service and muster-rolls, and general discipline. Office force, 590; staff corps, 17.

Inspector-General, has one assistant. Reports upon *personnel* and material of the army, inspects posts, stations, depots, etc., and accounts of disbursing officers. Force of office, 5; staff corps, 7; detailed officers of the line, 4.

Quartermaster-General, has 5 assistants. Provides transportation, quarters, clothing, etc., for the army. In charge of national cemeteries. Force of office, 164; staff corps, 61. Number of civilian employés at military departments outside of Washington, 1,563.

Commissary-General, has 2 assistants. In charge of Subsistence Department. Force of office, 40; staff corps, 26.

Surgeon-General, has 6 assistants. Force of office, 437; staff corps, 195. Number of civilian employés in various places, 313.

Paymaster-General, has 1 assistant. Pays the army. Force of office, 48; staff corps, 48. Number of army paymasters, rank of major, 42.

Chief of Engineers, has 3 assistants. Has direction of all fortifications, survey, and improvements of rivers and harbors, engineers' work in the field, bridges, etc. Force of office, 64; staff corps, 109; engineer battalion, 450.

Chief of Ordinance, has 3 assistants. In care of arsenals, artillery service, and all weapons and munitions of war. Force of office, 40; staff corps. 59.

Judge-Advocate-General, has 1 assistant. He is chief of the Bureau of Military Justice. Force of office, 13; staff corps. 8.

Chief Signal Officer. Superintends Signal Service. Number of stations, 182; force of office, 227; staff corps, 17; signal corps of the army, 487. The first systematic synchronous meteorie reports were taken in the United States Nov. 1, 1870. Cautionary signals on the Atlantic and Gulf coast were established in October, 1871.

Office of Publication of War Records, corner of G and Twentieth Streets, N. W. Force of office, 26.

The Army Medical Library and Museum, in the National Museum, employs 46 persons.

The appropriation for the Military Academy at West Point, N. Y., for 1888, was $419,936.93.

Navy Department.—Established April 30, 1798. It occupies the south half of the east connecting wing of the State, War, and Navy Department Building. Total number in service, including United States Navy and Marine Corps, 15,429; in the department proper, 257. The Secretary of the Navy has general direction of the construction, equipment, manning, armament, and employment of all vessels of war of the United States. The office of the Admiral of the Navy is in Washington; salary, 13,000. The total number on the active list of the navy is 9,006; on the active list of the Marine Corps, 1,992. The total number of pay-clerks, cadets, etc., at navy yards and stations is 3,770. The navy appropriation for the fiscal year 1888 was $25,767,848.19. The following are the bureaus, organized in 1862, the chiefs of which receive salaries of $5,000: Bureau of Yards and Docks; Navigation (the judge-advocate-general—salary, $4,500—is attached to this bureau); Ordnance; Equipment and Recruiting; Provisions and Clothing; Medicine and Surgery; Construction and Repair; Steam-Engineering. There are also the Naval Observatory at Washington, Twenty-third and E Streets, N. W., ; superintendent's salary, $5,000. Hydrographic Office, hydrographer's salary, $3,000. Office of the Nautical Almanac, superintendent's salary, $3,500.

Interior Department.—Established March 3, 1849, occupies the building known as the Patent-Office, covering two squares between Seventh and Ninth and F and G Streets, N.W.; style, Doric. The total number employed in the service is 9,154; number appointed by the President and secretary, 3,600. The legal organization of the department places under the supervision of the Secretary of the Interior all business of public lands and surveys, Indians, pensions, patents, railroads, education, the commissions of inter-state commerce and the United States Pacific Railway, the architect of the Capitol, and certain hospitals in the District of Columbia. He has also the direction of the census, and is invested with certain powers and duties in the Territories. There are two assistant secretaries; salary, $4,000 each. The following officers are heads of bureaus:

Commissioner of Patents, salary, $5,000, has 1 assistant. Prior to the organization of the Interior Department, patents were issued by the Secretaries of State and War and the Attorney-General. The number of employés is 578. The receipts of the office in six months ending June 30, 1888, were $508,091.26.

Commissioner of Pensions, salary $5,000, has 2 deputies and 1 medical referee. Office established March 2, 1833, under the Secretary of War; transferred to the Interior Department March 3, 1849. The Pension building is in Judiciary Square. The number of employés is 1,554; number of pension agencies, 18; appropriation for 1888, $83,152,500.

Commissioner of the General Land-Office (in the Patent-Office building), salary $4,000, has 1 assistant; office established April 25, 1812, in the Treasury Department. The number of employés is 468. The Land-Office audits its own accounts. The number of land-offices, is 111; surveyor-generals, 15.

Commissioner of Indian Affairs (Second National Bank building, Seventh Street, N. W.), salary 4,000; has 1 assistant. Office established July 9, 1832. The number of employés is 101; Indian agents, 60; Indian appropriation for the fiscal year 1888, $5,226,897.66.

Commissioner of Education (corner of G and Eighth Streets, N. W.), salary, $3,000. Bureau established March 2, 1867. The number of employés is 41.

Commissioner of Railroads (corner G and Eighth Streets, N. W.), salary, $4,500. Bureau established June 19, 1878. The force of the office is 7.

Director of the Geological Survey (Hooe Building, F Street, N. W.), salary $6,000. Office established March 3, 1879. The number of employés is 240.

Interstate Commerce Commission (Sun Building, F Street, N. W.), appointed Feb. 4. 1887. The number of Pacific Railway commissioners is three.

The officers in the District of Columbia under the Interior Department, are: Recorder of Deeds, Register of Wills, and Inspector of Gas-Meters.

Post-Office Department, established, temporarily, Sept. 22, 1789, and permanently, May 8, 1794. Occupies the Post-Office building, covering one square between Seventh and Eighth and E and F Streets, N. W. Style, Corinthian. The number of employés in the department and postal service is 94,386; in the department proper, 600. The appropriation for the fiscal year 1888, was $55,694,650.15. The Postmaster-General appoints all officers and employés of the department, with the exception of his three assistants, and all postmasters in the United States at a salary less than $1,000. He makes postal treaties, awards contracts, and directs the foreign and domestic mail service.

First Assistant Postmaster-General, salary, $4,000. In charge of Appointment Office, with 5 divisions.

Second Assistant Postmaster-General, salary, $4,000. In charge of Contract Office, with 3 divisions.

Third Assistant Postmaster-General, salary, $4,000. In charge of Finance Office, with 4 divisions.

The other officers of the Post-Office Department are:

Superintendent of Foreign Mails (corner Eighth and E Streets, N. W.), salary $3,000.

Superintendent of the Money Order System, (corner of Eighth and E streets, N. W.), salary, $3,500. Work of office in 6 divisions,

Superintendent of Dead-Letter Office.—The number of employés is 110, and the work of the office is in 6 divisions. The number of pieces of mail matter treated in the office during the year 1887 was 5,578,965.

The number of postmasters in the United States is 54,774; assistant postmasters, 384. The number of employés in Railway Mail Service, is 4,760. The number of pieces of mail matter handled by them in 1887 was 5,851,394,-057. There are foreign agencies of the Post-Office Department at Shanghai and Panama, in charge of the consuls-general.

Department of Justice.—Established June 22 1870. Opposite Treasury building, on Pennsylvania Avenue. The office of Attorney-General was created Sept. 24, 1789. The total number employed in the service is 1,800; in the department proper, 89. The Attorney-General, as chief law-officer of the Government, furnishes advice and opinions to the President and heads of Executive departments upon all legal questions referred to him; represents the United States in the Supreme Court, the Court of Claims, and any other court, when deemed necessary; supervises and directs United States attorneys and marshals in the several judicial districts of the States and Territories, and provides special counsel for the United States when required by any department. His assistants are: Solicitor-General, salary, $7,000; two Assistant Attorney-Generals, salaries, $5,000. The law-officers of the Executive Department, allowed by the act of 1870, are the Solicitor of the Treasury, salary, $4,500; Solicitor of Internal Revenue, salary, $4,500; Assistant Attorney-General for Department of the Interior, salary, $5,000; Assistant Attorney-General for Post-Office Department, salary. $4,000; Naval Solicitor, salary, ——; Examiner of Claims, State Department. salary, $3,500.

The number of United States district attorneys is 70; number of assistants, 65; number of special assistants, 39; number of United States marshals, 70; number of deputies, etc., 1,467.

Department of Agriculture, South Washington, opposite Thirteenth Street; established May 15, 1862. The first distribution of rare grains, seeds, plants, etc., under the Commissioner of Patents, was made on July 4, 1836; the first propagating garden established in 1858. The number of employés is 408. The appropriation for the department for the fiscal year 1888, was $1,028,730. The duty of the Commissioner of Agriculture is to acquire and diffuse among the people of the United States useful information connected with agriculture, and to procure, propagate, and distribute new and valuable seeds and plants. The following are the principal officers: Chief of Bureau of Animal Industry, bureau established May 29, 1884, for investigation of diseases among animals. Entomologist, investigates insect-ravages; section of silk-culture established 1884. Botanist, section of vegetable pathology established July 1, 1886. Chemist, analyzes butter, soils, fertilizers, etc.; experiments in manufacture of sugar. Microscopist, for this and other departments. Statistician, collects statistics from domestic and foreign sources. The number of State agents is 23; 1 in England. The divisions are: Forestry, ornithology, pomology, seeds, propagating garden, library.

Department of Labor, Kellogg Building, No. 1416 F Street, N. W. By act of June 13, 1888, the Bureau of Labor of the Interior Department, established June 27, 1884, was erected into a department, "the general design and duties of which shall be to acquire and diffuse among the people of the United States useful information on subjects connected with labor, in the most general and comprehensive sense of that word, and especially upon its relations to capital, hours of labor, the earnings of la-boring men and women, and the means of pro-moting their material, social, intellectual, and moral prosperity." Until the complete organi-zation of the department has been effected, the condition of the bureau remains the same. The number of employés under the legal or-ganization is 64.

Closely connected with the above-named departments are:

The United States Civil-Service Commission.—Offi-ces in City Hall building; established Jan. 16, 1883, "to regulate and improve the civil-serv-ice of the United States." The commissioners receive salaries of $3,500 each; the Chief Ex-aminer, $3,000. Examinations are held for places in the departmental, customs, and postal services in every State and Territory of the Union.

Government Printing - Office.—This establish-ment is at the corner of North Capitol and H Streets, Washington. The total number of employés is 2,038. The Public Printer has a salary of $4,500.

One officer of the Department of Justice, and one medical officer from the army, navy, and Marine Hospital Service, respectively, are de-tailed to the National Board of Health, estab-lished March 3, 1879.

GRAY, ASA, botanist, born in Paris, N. Y., Nov. 18, 1810; died in Cambridge, Mass., Jan. 30, 1888. He was descended from a Scotch-Irish family, who emigrated to this country in the early part of the last century, and in 1795 his grandfather settled in the Sauquoit val-ley. When a boy he fed the bark-mill and drove the horse of his father's tannery; but, as he showed a greater fondness for study than for farm-work, his father sent him to the Clinton Grammar School. In 1825 he entered Fairfield Academy, where he spent four years, and his first interest in botany was aroused by reading on that subject in Brewster's "Edin-burgh Encyclopædia." A story is told of his eager watching for the first spring beauty in the spring of 1828, which, by the aid of Amos Eaton's "Manual of Botany," he found to be the *Claytonia Virginica*. Owing to the wishes of his father, and probably his own inclina-tion, he entered himself as a student at the Medical College of the Western District of New York in Fairfield, Herkimer County, and in 1831 he was graduated at that institution. The sessions were short, and the remainder of his time was spent in study with physicians in the vicinity. His leisure was occupied in gathering an herbarium, and he began a cor-respondence with Dr. Lewis C. Beck and Dr. John Torrey, who aided him in the determina-

tion of his plants. He never entered upon the practice of medicine, but, on receiving his de-gree, became instructor in chemistry, mineral-ogy, and botany in Bartlett's High School in Utica, N. Y., where he was an instructor from 1831 till 1835. In 1832 he gave a course of lectures on botany at the Fairfield Medical School, and in 1834 he delivered a course on mineralogy and botany at Hamilton College, Clinton, N. Y. During the year 1833–'34, he was assistant to John Torrey, then Pro-

ASA GRAY.

fessor of Chemistry and Botany at the Col-lege of Physicians and Surgeons in New York city, but that institution could not afford to retain his services, and in 1836, through the efforts of Dr. Torrey, he was made curator of the New York Lyceum of Natural History. Dr. Gray's earliest papers in botany—"A Monograph of the North American Rhyncosporæ" and "A Notice of Some New, Rare, or Otherwise Interesting Plants from the Northern and Western Por-tions of the State of New York"—were read before the Lyceum in December, 1834, and in 1836 his first text-book, "Elements of Botany," was published in New York. This volume, with various revisions, was widely adopted in schools and academies, and for a long time was almost the only text-book on botany in popular use.

In 1836 Dr. Gray was appointed botanist of the exploring expedition to the South Pacific, under Capt. Charles Wilkes, but, owing to the delay in the starting of the expedition, he re-signed that place in 1838. Meanwhile, he be-came actively associated with Dr. Torrey in the preparation of the "Flora of North Ameri-ca," Parts I and II of the first volume of which were issued in July and October, 1838; and in November of that year he sailed for Europe to consult the various herbaria that contained large numbers of American plants made by foreign collectors. He visited England, Scot-land, France, Germany, Switzerland, Italy, and

Austria, and met all of the eminent botanists of the day, forming life-long friendships with some of them. In 1838 he was chosen Professor of Botany and Zoölogy in the University of Michigan, but he never filled that chair, although his name heads the list of the faculty; and in 1842 he resigned that appointment to accept the Fisher chair of Natural History in Harvard University, which place he held until his death. On his return from Europe, he pushed to rapid completion Parts III and IV of the "Flora," which were issued in June, 1840, and completed Volume I. Of Volume II, he issued Part I in May, 1841, and Part II in April, 1842, while Part III was not published until February, 1843, when he had settled in Cambridge. His energies were thereafter for a time most closely directed to his duties at Harvard, where the botanical department of that university was practically created by him. On his accession there no herbarium was in existence; there was no library, and only one insignificant greenhouse in a garden that was all confusion, containing only a few plants of value. He soon brought together an herbarium and library, and arranged the garden systematically; but his collection of plants shortly overran his house and was in every room. Dreading their destruction by fire, he offered to present his collections to Harvard on condition that a suitable building be erected for them, and accordingly, in 1864, through the liberality of Nathaniel Thayer, of Boston, a brick building was provided for their reception. At that time (November, 1864), the herbarium contained at least 200,000 specimens, and the library had about 2,200 volumes, and when Dr. Gray died the herbarium had nearly doubled in size, and become by far the largest and most valuable of its kind in America. The library, at the same time, was roughly estimated to contain something over five thousand volumes and three thousand pamphlets. The botanic garden was also improved during his administration by the addition of several greenhouses, in which were cultivated a choice selection of exotics, and the garden itself contained good representatives of the temperate regions, the collection of the *Compositæ* being especially important. His work as a teacher continued until the close of his life, and under his immediate instruction have been at one period or another nearly all of those who have since aided in the development of botanical studies in the United States. Dr. Gray was relieved from the active duties of his chair in 1872 by the appointment of Prof. George L. Goodale to be his associate, and in 1873 he was still further relieved by the call of Prof. Charles S. Sargent to the care of the botanic garden, while in 1874 Dr. Sereno Watson became curator of the herbarium.

Dr. Gray's scientific work began at a time when the old artificial systems of botany were giving way to the natural system, and with Dr. Torrey he was among the first to attempt the classification of species on the natural basis of affinity. After the publication of the two volumes of the "Flora of North America," which brought it down to the end of the *Compositæ*, the accumulation of fresh material had so increased that to finish the great undertaking would require an appendix larger than the original. In 1873 he again took up this work, and published Part II of Volume II on the *Gamopetalæ* in "The Synoptical Flora of North America" (New York, 1878). He issued Part II of Volume I—the *Caprifoliaceæ compositæ*—in 1884, and his last labors, just before his death, were on the grape-vines of North America. The valuable acquisitions of the National Government exploring expeditions were referred to him, and the results are to be found in numerous memoirs published in the official reports and as separate monographs. The most important of these are "Plantæ Lindheimerianæ," an account of plants collected in Western Texas by Ferdinand Lindheimer (Boston, 1849-'50); "Plantæ Fendlerianæ Novi Mexicanæ," a description of plants collected in New Mexico by August Fendler (1849); "Plantæ Wrightianæ Texano-Neo Mexicanæ," describing the extensive collections made by Charles Wright (Washington, 1852-'53); "Plantæ Novæ Thurberianæ," being those gathered by George Thurber, botanist to the Mexican Boundary Survey (Boston, 1854); "Genera Floræ Americæ Boreali Orientalis Illustrata" (New York, 1848-'49); and a report on the botanical specimens brought back by Capt. Charles Wilkes (1854). He also reported on the plants collected in Japan by the Perry expedition in 1856, and, in one of his more important papers upon "The Botany of Japan" (1859), based upon the collection made by Charles Wright, of the Rogers Exploring Expedition, he demonstrated the close relationship between the floras of Japan and Eastern North America. Dr. Gray's relation to Darwinism was important. Although a man of the deepest religious convictions, and thoroughly imbued with a firm belief in a divine Creator, he declared, "I am scientifically, and in my own fashion, a Darwinian, philosophically a convinced theist, and religiously an acceptor of the 'creed' commonly known as the 'Nicene' as the exponent of the Christian faith." It was largely through his efforts that Darwin's "Origin of Species" was published in America, and graceful tributes to his influence are rendered by Darwin in his "Life and Letters." Dr. Gray's literary works consist of collections of papers variously published and of lectures, notably a series before the Divinity School of Yale in 1880. They are "A Free Examination of Darwin's Treatise on the 'Origin of Species,' and of its American Reviewers" (Cambridge, 1861); "Darwiniana: Essays and Reviews pertaining to Darwinism" (New York, 1876); and "Natural Science and Religion" (1880). The degree of A. M. was given him in 1844 by Harvard, while that of LL. D. came to him from Hamilton in 1864, from Harvard in 1875, and from McGill in 1884. In 1887, on the occasion of his last vísit to Europe, he was everywhere received with distinguished honors. Cambridge gave him the degree of Dr. Sc, Edinburgh gave him her LL. D., and Oxford her D. C. L. In 1874, he was appointed a regent of the Smithsonian Institution, succeeding Louis Agassiz in that office. He was elected a fellow of the American Academy of Arts and Sciences in 1841, was its president in 1863-'73, and in 1871 presided over the American Association for the Advancement of Science, delivering his retiring address at the Dubuque meeting on "Sequoia and its History." Dr. Gray was one of the original members of the National Academy of Sciences, but afterward passed to the grade of honorary membership. Besides his connection with societies in this country, he was either corresponding or honorary member of the Linnean Society and the Royal Society in London, and of the Academies of Sciences in Berlin, Munich, Paris, St. Petersburg, Stockholm, and Upsala. He was a large contributor to periodical literature, and his separate papers include nearly two hundred titles. For many years he was one of the editors of the "American Journal of Science," and his "Botanical Contributions" were long published in the "Proceedings of the American Academy of Sciences and Arts." He also wrote biographical sketches of many who have achieved eminence in science; of these the more important American subjects were Jacob Bigelow, George Engelmann, Joseph Henry, Thomas P. James, John A. Lowell, William B. Sullivant, John Torrey, and Jeffries Wyman. On his desk at the time of his death was left the unfinished necrology for 1887 of botanists. Dr. Gray's series of text-books are used throughout the United States, and have passed through many editions. They include "Elements of Botany" (New York, 1836), republished as "Botanical Text-Book" (1853), and now called "Structural and Systematic Botany" (1858); "Manual of the Botany of the Northern United States" (Cambridge, 1848; 5th ed., New York, 1867); "First Lessons in Botany and Vegetable Physiology" (New York, 1857); "Botany for Young People and Common Schools," comprising "How Plants Grow" (1858) and "How Plants Behave" (1872); "Field, Forest, and Garden Botany" (1868), which has been bound with the "First Lessons in Botany" under the title "School- and Field-Book of Botany" (1875); "Structural Botany or Organography, with Basis of Morphology" (1879), being the first volume of the series called "Gray's Botanical Text-Book" and "Elements of Botany" (1887), which is a revision of the "First Lessons in Botany." The funeral services were held on February 2 in Appleton Chapel of Harvard, and his remains were buried in Mount Auburn Cemetery. Of the several memoirs

of his life, that by Walter Deane (with portrait), in the "Bulletin of the Torrey Botanical Club" for March, 1888, and that by William G. Farlow, in the "Memorial of Asa Gray," issued by the American Academy of Arts and Sciences" (Cambridge, 1888), are the most important. See also a "List of the Writings of Dr. Asa Gray, chronologically arranged," with index, in the "American Journal of Science" for September and October, 1888.

GREAT BRITAIN AND IRELAND, UNITED KINGDOM OF, a monarchy in western Europe. The reigning sovereign is Victoria I, Queen of Great Britain and Ireland and Empress of India, who was born on May 24, 1819, and succeeded to the throne on June 20, 1837. The heir-apparent is Albert Edward, Prince of Wales, born Nov. 9, 1841, and the next in succession is his eldest son, Albert Victor, born Jan. 8, 1864.

The legislative power is vested in the House of Lords and House of Commons, constituting together the Parliament of the British Empire, which holds annual sessions, usually lasting from the middle of February to the end of August. The House of Lords, in the session of 1887, consisted of 560 members, made up of 5 peers of the blood royal, 2 archbishops, 22 dukes, 20 marquises, 120 earls, 29 viscounts, 24 bishops, 294 barons, 16 Scottish representative peers, and 28 Irish representative peers. Twelve new peerages were created in 1887. The reform bill of 1884, with the redistribution-of-seats act of 1885, fixed the number of seats in the House of Commons at 670, of which England and Wales fill 495, Ireland 103, and Scotland 72.

The total number of registered electors in 1887 was 5,848,173, of whom 4,492,875 belonged to England and Wales, 779,389 to Ireland, and 575,909 to Scotland. The county electors in England and Wales numbered 2,582,610; in Ireland, 662,741; and in Scotland, 326,055. The borough electors numbered 1,895,440 in England and Wales, 112,556 in Ireland, and 235,450 in Scotland. The university constituencies furnished 14,825 electors in England and Wales, 4,092 in Ireland, and 14,404 in Scotland. The members of Parliament receive no compensation.

Most of the members of the present Cabinet were appointed on Aug. 3, 1886. It is composed as follows: Prime Minister and Secretary of State for Foreign Affairs, the Marquis of Salisbury; Lord High Chancellor, Lord Halsbury, formerly Sir Hardinge S. Giffard; Lord President of the Council, Viscount Cranbrook, formerly Gathorne Hardy; Chancellor of the Exchequer, George Joachim Goschen; Secretary of State for the Home Department, Henry Matthews; Secretary of State for War, Edward Stanhope; First Lord of the Treasury, William Henry Smith; Secretary of State for the Colonies, Sir Henry Thurstan Holland; Secretary of State for India, Viscount Cross, formerly Sir Richard Cross; First Lord of the Admiralty,

Lord George Hamilton; Lord Chancellor of Ireland, Lord Ashbourne, formerly Edward Gibson; Chief Secretary to the Lord Lieutenant of Ireland, Arthur J. Balfour; Chancellor of the Duchy of Lancaster, Lord John Manners; President of the Board of Trade, Lord Stanley; Lord Privy Seal, Earl Cadogan; President of the Local Government Board, Charles Thomas Ritchie; Minister without portfolio, Sir Michael Hicks-Beach.

Area and Population.—The area of the United Kingdom is 120,832 square miles, with an estimated population in 1887 of 37,091,564, exclusive of the army, navy, and merchant seamen abroad. At the census of 1881 the population was 35,241,482—17,254,109 males and 17,987,373 females. The total area of the British Empire is 8,981,130 square miles, and the population is estimated at 310,735,840 persons. In 1886 there were in the United Kingdom 1,145,070 births, 697,990 deaths, and 240,869 marriages. The number of marriages in Ireland in 1887 was 20,945, against 20,594 in 1886; the births 112,400, against 113,927; the deaths 88,585, against 87,292. The total number of emigrants from the United Kingdom was 396,702 in 1887, of whom 281,487 were natives of Great Britain and Ireland. The immigrants numbered 119,013, of whom 85,475 were natives of the British Islands. Of the emigrants 296,881 went to the United States, 44,424 to British North America, and 35,282 to Australasia. In 1886 there were 63,135 emigrants from Ireland. Emigration from the United Kingdom, especially to the United States, is found to increase whenever the general prospects of trade improve. From the maximum of 413,288 in 1882 emigration declined to 264,385 in 1885, and then showed a large increase in 1886 and a further increase in 1887. The British and Irish emigrants of 1887 exceeded the number of any previous year since the nationalities began to be distinguished except 1883. The proportion of emigration to population was ·76 per cent, which was less than in 1882 and 1883, when it was ·79 and ·90 per cent, respectively, but was greater than in any other year since 1854. The net emigration was 196,012 in 1887, as compared with 152,882 in 1886, and 122,176 in 1885. The Irish percentage in the aggregate emigration since 1853 is 41, the Scotch 10. Of the 4,222,377 emigrants to the United States from the United Kingdom during 35 years, 2,165,532 were Irish. In the same period 647,974 went to British North America from the United Kingdom, but the Irish contributed only 168,349 to the total; of 1,228,176 emigrants to Australasia from 1853 to 1887, the Irish contingent was 283,331; and of 271,600 who went to all other places, 19,639 were Irish. Of the Irish emigrants of 1887 no less than 87·6 per cent. were bound for the United States.

The population of the chief cities of the United Kingdom in 1887, computed by the Registrar-General, was as follows: London, 4,215,192; Glasgow, 674,095; Liverpool, 592,991; Birmingham, 441,095; Manchester, 377,529; Dublin, 353,082; Leeds, 345,080; Sheffield, 316,288; Edinburgh, 236,002; Bristol, 223,695; Bradford, 224,507; Nottingham, 224,230; Salford, 218,658; Belfast, 208,122; Hull, 196,855; Newcastle-on-Tyne, 157,048. The most densely populated cities are Liverpool, with 114 persons to the acre; Manchester, with 88; Glasgow, with 86; London, with 56; Plymouth and Birmingham, with 53; Bolton and Brighton, with 47; and Leicester, with 45.

Religion.—The Protestant Episcopal is the established religion of the United Kingdom, though all forms of religious observance are freely tolerated. The Established Church numbered 13,500,000 members in England and Wales in 1883, 76,939 in Scotland in 1884, and 620,000 in Ireland in 1888. There are 2 archbishops and 31 bishops in England. In 1882 the Church of England possessed 14,573 churches and chapels, and in 1881 there were 24,000 clergymen of all grades. The total annual income of the various cathedral establishments and benefices of the Church is estimated at £10,000,000. The Church of Scotland is organized on the Presbyterian system of government, in which the clergymen are all equal. There are in all 84 presbyteries grouped into 16 synods, divided into 1,320 parishes, with 1,625 churches and chapels, and 1,700 clergymen in 1887. In 1886 there were 571,029 members or communicants. The Church of Ireland in 1888 had 2 archbishops, 11 bishops, 1,750 clergymen, 1,500 churches, and 620,000 members. The Roman Catholics in 1887 numbered 1,354,000 in England and Wales, with 2,314 priests and 1,304 churches. In Scotland there were 326,000 members, 334 priests, and 327 churches. In Ireland in 1881 the Roman Catholic population was 3,960,891. The Presbyterian Dissenters from the Church of Scotland had 1,180 ministers, 1,118 churches, and 331,055 members in 1887. The United Presbyterian Church of Scotland in 1886 had 620 ministers, 565 churches, and 182,063 members. In 1883 the Jewish population of Great Britain was estimated at 70,000, of whom 40,000 resided in London.

Education.—A royal commission on education that was appointed in 1886 made its final report in June, 1888. The commission recommended that school accommodations should be provided for one sixth of the population, and that that should be the proportion of daily attendance. The minimum space for each child in school buildings should be ten square feet. A supply of secondary schools should be organized adequate for the wants of the whole country, and promising children of poor parents should be enabled to take advantage of them. The classification of instruction and of Government examinations should be more elastic, as the present methods lead to cramming and overpressure. The parliamentary grant, which is distributed on the principle of payment by results, the commission do not propose to abolish, but the income of the school should not be wholly dependent thereon, and the results ought to be more thoroughly tested, since under the present system the children lose with extraordinary rapidity the knowledge that has been so laboriously and expensively imparted to them. In view of the fact that the training of teachers is now mainly conducted in denominational colleges, the minority of the commission proposed that secular normal colleges should be established on a large scale by the state, while the majority thought that such schools should be at first of an experimental character, and that they should depend on private liberality. The minority thought that Sunday-schools could relieve the day-schools of a large part of the religious and moral instruction, but the majority reported in favor of compulsory religious instruction. The commissioners were unanimous in recommending that the minimum age at which a child can be taken from school and sent to work should be eleven, instead of ten, as under the act of 1876, and that attendance at school for half the time should be required for two years longer. They concurred, too, in the opinion that the process of recovering fines for non-attendance by distress, instead of by commitment, has encouraged parents to defy the law. They recommend, in the place of a uniform curriculum for all schools that is only adapted for the largest and best equipped, a simplified standard for the small village schools. Reading-books should be increased, and prepared with the aim of infusing in the minds of the scholars a confirmed taste for reading, for the gratification of which school libraries should be provided; drawing should be taught as an aid to instruction in writing; and the teaching of arithmetic should not be confined to dry exercises in numbers, but ought to show the applications of the science. The commission recommended the extension and improvement of instruction in English, history, geography, and elementary science. Singing should be taught by note, as well as by ear. Boys and girls should receive some physical training, and the girls receive instruction, in addition to their needlework, in practical cookery and elementary physiology. The commissioners recommended the introduction of manual and technical training in the elementary schools, but were not in agreement as to the method and extent. The number of schools inspected in 1886 was 19,022 in England and Wales, as compared with 18,895 in 1885, and 3,092 in Scotland, as compared with 3,081. The average attendance was 3,438,425 in England and Wales and 476,890 in Scotland in 1886. There were 89,180 teachers in England and Wales, and 11,389 in Scotland. Of the schools in England and Wales, 4,402 were directly under school-boards; 11,798 were connected with the National Society or Church of England; 554 were Wesleyan; 882 were Roman Catholic, and 1,387 were undenominational,

or conducted under the auspices of other societies. In Scotland there were 2,569 public schools, 96 connected with the Church of Scotland, and 154 Roman Catholic, and 273 belonging to other religious bodies or undenominational. There were 41 training colleges, with 3,259 students, in England and Wales in 1886, and in Scotland 7, with 859 students. In Ireland the number of national schools in operation in 1886 was 8,024, with 490,484 children in average attendance. The English schools in 1886 received £2,866,700 in annual grants from Parliament, and £3,960,489 from endowments, school fees, local rates, and voluntary subscriptions; the annual grants for primary schools in Scotland amounted to £419,217, and the income from other sources was £594,161; in Ireland £851,973 of annual grants were supplemented by £84,837 from other sources. The education estimates for England and Wales for 1888–'89 are £3,576,077. The increase in the number of children enrolled in in 1887 was 129,000, and the increase in daily attendance over the preceding year was 89,000. The number on the school registers amounts to 16·41 per cent., or nearly one sixth of the population, having increased from 7·08 per cent. in 1869. The average cost of maintenance for each scholar in daily attendance is £2 14s. 11½d. in the board schools, and £1 16s. 4½d. in the voluntary schools.

Commerce and Industry.—The total value of imports in 1887 was £361,935,006, against £349,863,472 in 1886, and £370,967,955 in 1885. The exports of British produce in 1887 had a total value of £221,398,440, against £212,434,754 in 1886, and £213,044,500 in 1885. The exports of foreign and colonial produce amounted to £59,106,598 in 1887, against £56,234,263 in 1886, and £57,359,194 in 1885. The imports of gold bullion and specie in 1887 were £9,939,934 and the exports £9,323,614, as compared with £13,392,256 of imports and £13,783,706 of exports in 1886, and £13,376,561 of imports, and £11,930,818 of exports in 1885. The imports in 1887 were divided among the different classes of commodities as follows: Articles of food and drink, £148,860,404; tobacco, £3,409,267; metals, £16,618,148; chemicals and dyes, £7,728,884; oils, £6,088,246; raw materials, £111,963,919; manufactured articles, £54,134,820; miscellaneous, £13,131,318. The exports of domestic products were divided as follows: Articles of food and drink, £10,093,317; raw materials, £12,753,980; textile fabrics and thread, £108,060,714; metals, raw and worked, £34,930,183; machinery, £11,145,745; apparel, etc., £10,227,990; chemicals and drugs, £7,028,392; all other manufactured or partly manufactured, £27,158,119. The quantity of grain and flour imported *per capita*, in 1886, was 185·76 pounds, as compared with 155·85 pounds in 1869; the quantity of sugar, 65·96 pounds, as compared with 42·56 pounds; of butter, 7·17 pounds, as compared with 4·52 pounds; of bacon and hams, 11·95 pounds, as compared with 2·68 pounds; of cheese, 5·14 pounds, as compared with 3·52 pounds. The import of wheat in 1887 was 11,156,930 quarters, against 14,192,000 quarters in 1885, 7,131,-100 in 1870, and 5,343,800 in 1866. Of the import of 1887, 6,100,000 quarters came from the United States, 1,418,000 quarters from India, 660,800 quarters from Canada, 224,500 quarters from Australasia, 922,130 quarters from Russia, 367,710 quarters from Chili, and 258,620 quarters from Germany.

The chief articles of import and their values in 1887 were as follow: Grain and flour, £47,-819,927; raw cotton, £39,897,316; wool, £24,-280,593; metals, £16,618,148; sugar, £16,412,-734; wood and timber, £11,989,159; butter and oleomargarine, £11,886,717; silk manufactures, £10,373,166; tea, £9,858,083; bacon and hams, £8,629,941; flax, hemp, and jute, £8,554,322; chemicals, £7,728,884; seeds, £6,-961,940; animals, £6,149,066. The following were the largest exports: Cotton manufactures, £70,956,769; iron and steel manufactures, £25,000,356; woolen and worsted manufactures, £24,138,407; machinery, £11,145,745; linen, jute manufactures, and apparel, £10,-227,990; coal, £10,176,402.

The area under cultivation in England in 1887 was 32,597,398 acres, or 80 per cent. of the total area; 4,721,823 acres, or 60 per cent. in Wales; 20,819,947 acres, or 74 per cent., in Ireland; and 19,466,978 acres, or 28·8 per cent., in Scotland. The wheat-crop of Great Britain in 1887 was 74,322,747 bushels, as compared with 61,467,898 bushels in 1886. The yield per acre was 32·07 bushels, against 26·89 bushels in the preceding year, and against a normal average of 28·80 bushels. The acreage under wheat was 1·37 per cent. greater than in 1886. The barley-crop was 65,300,994 bushels in 1887, as compared with 72,090,269 bushels in 1886; the aggregate yield of oats was 107,283,392 bushels, against 116,596,481 bushels; the produce of potatoes was 3,564,-894 tons, against 3,167,763 tons; the crop of turnips was 19,747,726 tons, against 29,982,940 tons. In Ireland there was likewise an increase in the wheat and potato crops, and a falling off in barley, oats, and turnips, owing, as in England, to the dry spring and summer.

The live-stock in 1887 comprised 1,936,925 horses, 10,639,960 cattle, 29,401,750 sheep, and 3,720,957 swine.

The product of the fisheries in 1887 was valued at £4,104,445 in England, £1,396,963 in Scotland, and £648,000 in Ireland. The total number of men employed was 125,764, with 32,189 boats.

The total value of the mineral products of the United Kingdom in 1886 was £55,010,241. There were mined during the year 157,518,482 tons of coal, valued at £38,145,930; and 4,967,-574 tons of iron-ore, valued at £11,259,834. The number of persons engaged in mining in 1886 was 561,092, of whom 448,657 worked underground. The export of coal was 23,283,389

tons. France received of this 4,081,343 tons, valued at £1,635,581; Germany, 2,857,819 tons, valued at £1,009,560; Italy, 2,852,204 tons, valued at £1,101,698. The total consumption of iron-ore in the United Kingdom during 1886 was 17,336,000 tons. There were 399 blast-furnaces in operation, and 6,566,451 tons of pig-iron and 2,541,928 tons of steel were manufactured.

In 1886, 1,715,044,800 pounds of cotton were imported, of which 1,517,186,720 pounds were retained for home consumption. Wool was imported to the extent of 596,470,995 pounds, and 312,006,380 pounds were exported. There were 7,465 factories in the United Kingdom in 1885, employing 1,034,911 hands, 406,320 males and 629,248 females. The children employed in the factories numbered 43,308 males and 48,-503 females.

Navigation.—In 1886 the mercantile marine of Great Britain was composed of 17,917 vessels of all kinds, of 7,134,269 tons, employing 204,584 men. They were divided as follows: Engaged in foreign trade—3,018 steam-vessels, of 3,491,330 tons, employing 97,602 men; 2,923 sailing-vessels, of 2,526,117 tons, with crews of 50,590 men; engaged in home trade, 1,667 steam-vessels, of 300,598, tons, with 18,062 men and 9,626 sailing-vessels, of 646,697 tons, with 32,696 men; engaged in both home and foreign traffic, 235 steam-vessels, of 110,091 tons, and 3,485 men; and 448 sailing-vessels, of 59,436 tons, and 2,129 men. During 1886 there were built and registered in the United Kingdom, 308 steamers, of 154,638 tons, and 363 sailing-vessels, of 138,362 tons. At the end of 1886, the total number of vessels of all kinds registered as belonging to the United Kingdom was 22,815, with a tonnage of 7,927,818, a decrease of 68,227 tons from the preceding year. The total tonnage of vessels of all kinds which entered and cleared the ports of the United Kingdom during 1886 was 62,841,077, of which 46,078,299 tons were under the British flag, and 16,762,778 under foreign flags. The main part of the foreign tonnage was divided among the chief trading countries as follows; Norway, 3,848,860; Germany, 3,535,926; France, 1,782,752; Denmark, 1,463,-675; Sweden, 1,386,076; Holland, 1,486,970; Spain, 952,066; Italy, 537,845; Belgium, 620,-726; Russia, 429,616; United States, 392,268; Austria, 112,492.

The Post-Office and Telegraphs.—The number of post-offices in the United Kingdom on March 31, 1887, was 17,191. The permanent staff of the post-ofhee was composed of 50,033 males and 3,767 females. The total number of letters sent in 1887 was 1,460,000,000; post-cards, 180,000,000; newspapers, 151,000,000; parcels and book-packets, 402,000,000. Foreign money orders were issued to the number of 10,813,034, valued at £25,354.601. The inland money orders numbered 9,762,562, valued at £22,262,708. There were 31,605,984 postal orders sent, valued at £12,958,940. During the year ending March 31, 1888, there were delivered in the United Kingdom 1,512,200,000 letters, 188,800,000 post-cards, 389,500,000 books and circulars, 152,300,000 newspapers, and 36,732,000 parcels. There were 8,351 post-office savings-banks in 1886, with 3,731,421 open accounts, amounting to £50,874,330. The deposits made in 1886 were £15,696,852, against £15,034,694 in 1885. There were 3,643,161 open accounts in England and Wales, 139,681 in Scotland, and 158,848 in Ireland on Dec. 31, 1887. The total amount standing to the credit of all open accounts was £53,974,065. The regulations of the savings-banks, which were twenty-seven years old, were amended by an act of Parliament which went into force in 1888. The main purpose of the act was originally to increase the limit of deposits allowed in a single year from £30 to £50; yet this provision was abandoned on account of the opposition of the banking element in the House of Commons. The transfer of deposits from the name of one depositor to that of another is made easier, restrictions on payments to creditors, assignees, or relatives of deceased depositors are removed, and the general indemnity enjoyed by the post-office authorities is modified and the Post-master General made liable for payments made to the wrong person in cases of fraud in which the depositor is not implicated. Another act of Parliament passed during the session does practically abolish the limit of £30, for it permits a depositor who has reached that limit to have the whole or a part of the £30 to be invested in consols, which pay 3 per cent. interest, whereas the savings-banks give only 2½ per cent. The depositor is not allowed, however, to invest more than £100 in any one year or £300 in all. The author of the bill hopes that it will lead to millions of people becoming interested in Government securities, as in France, instead of the few thousands who are now holders of consols.

The revenue from the post-office in 1886–'87 was £10,715,976; expenditure, £8,201,343.

On April 1, 1887, there were 29,895 miles of telegraph lines in operation in the United Kingdom, with 173,539 miles of wire. The revenue for 1886–'87 was £1,855,686, and the expenditure £1,939,768, showing a deficit of £84,082. The total number of messages sent was 50,243,639—42,320,185 in England and Wales, 5,106,774 in Scotland, and 2,816,680 in Ireland.

Railways.—The total length of railroads open for traffic in the British Empire in 1886 was 55,599 miles, of which the United Kingdom had 19,332 miles; India, 13,390 miles; Canada, 11,523 miles; Australia, 8,891 miles; Cape Colony and Natal, 1,995 miles; other colonies, 468 miles. The 19,332 miles of railroad in the United Kingdom in 1886, carried 725,584,390 passengers; the total receipts for the year were £69,591,953, and at the end of the year the paid up capital was £828,344,254. In 1887 the new capital invested was £17,628,000, making the total capital at the end of that year £845,-

972,000. The freight receipts for the year showed a considerable improvement, and the passenger receipts were also larger, enabling the companies to pay an average dividend of over 4 per cent., whereas in 1886 it was below 4 per cent. The first and second class passenger receipts have steadily decreased for ten years, while third-class travel has increased. The gross receipts of the railroads in 1887 were £70,900,000.

The Army.—The army estimates for 1887–'88 called for an expenditure of £18,393,900 to provide for an effective of 149,391 men of all ranks, exclusive of the force maintained in India. In the beginning of 1887 the total strength of the regular army was 208,357 officers and men, of whom 73,215 were in England, 3,730 in Scotland, 25,252 in Ireland, 9,289 in Egypt, 70,790 in India, 24,889 in the colonies, and 1,192 on passage. The force in the United Kingdom was 102,197, while the troops stationed abroad numbered 186,160. The number of horses was 24,242, and the number of field-cannon 624. The total military strength of the nation in 1877–'88, according to the returns of the various forces, was 679,522 men of all ranks, comprised of 138,765 men on the regular establishment at home and in the colonies, 52,000 in the first class of the army reserve, 5,300 men in the second class, 141,438 militia, 14,405 yeomanry, 255,923 volunteers, and 71,691 regular troops in India.

The War Office has settled on the pattern of a magazine rifle, with which the regular troops are to be furnished. The artillery has been provided with a new twelve-pounder field-gun, and a large number of machine-guns are to be issued. The national defense bill, which was enacted in the session of 1888, gives the Government larger and more stringent powers over the volunteer organizations, especially in regard to their mobilization, and also in regard to the mobilization of the militia in public emergencies. A sensation was caused in December, 1888, by the peremptory disbandment of the Ancient and Honorable Artillery Company of the City of London, which refused to be treated on the same same footing as the ordinary militia, and would not submit to the regulations issued by the War Office to secure discipline and efficiency.

The Navy.—The naval estimates for the year 1888–'89 call for an expenditure of £12,082,800, an increase of £506,000 over the estimates for 1887–'88. This increase is more than accounted for by the vote of £1,863,500 for naval armaments, an item that formerly appeared in the army estimates. Attached to the navy are 62,400 officers and men, against 62,500 in 1887–'88. The government of the navy is in the hands of the Board of Admiralty, in which the First Lord, who is a member of the Cabinet, has supreme authority. In December, 1887, there were 400 vessels of all kinds in commission in the British navy, besides 106 engaged in harbor service. The armored fleet numbers 48 vessels. In the British navy there are five vessels capable of steaming at a speed greater than 20 knots an hour, and 37 capable of making between 15 and 20 knots.

The vessels in process of construction were the "Blake" and "Blenheim," each of 9,000 tons displacement, which are designed for a maximum speed of 22 knots; the "Vulcan," which is calculated to attain 20 knots; and seven small vessels of about the same speed. The armament of the navy in 1887-'88 included 1,281 breech-loading cannon, 790 quick-firing guns, and 1,818 torpedoes. In 1888-'89 £2,669,089 are to be expended on new vessels, hulls, and machinery. The hull of the "Sans Pareil," a sister ship to the "Victoria," which was launched in April, was completed in September, 1888. She has a displacement of 10,-470 tons, armor 16 and 18 inches thick, a single turret constructed of compound 18-inch plates, mounting a 10-ton gun, and coal space for a voyage of 7,000 miles at 10 knots, while her maximum speed is 17 knots. The "Medea" and the "Medusa," the first of five twin-screw second-class cruisers of identical build, were launched in the summer, and the "Melpomene" in September. Of 2,800 tons displacement, they have engines of 9,000 horse-power, capable of giving a speed of 20 knots, and will be armed with five breech-loading guns of 6-inch caliber, besides quick-firing and machine-guns and torpedo tubes. They have no side-armor, depending on the position of their vital parts, their speed, and the ease with which their guns can be manipulated.

The Admiralty are spending £750,000 on ships and guns for the special squadron in Australasia, which is to be maintained by joint contributions of the Imperial and the Colonial governments. During the years 1887-'88 there were 18 vessels completed and made ready for commission, with an aggregate of 64,650 tons, of which 41,000 tons are iron-clads; and in 1888-'89 the new vessels number 29, of 100,-000 tons, of which 60,000 tons are iron-clads. The programme laid down by Lord North-brook in 1885 has been completed in three years, instead of in five, as was calculated. The "Nile" and the "Trafalgar," the heaviest ships ever built in England, were launched within two years after their keels were laid, and were nearly completed in 1888. The policy of completing as rapidly as possible the ships that are begun is pursued, but the efforts of the Admiralty have been hampered through the slowness of the War Office in supplying guns. There were eight finished iron-clads in 1888 that were useless for lack of ordnance.

Naval manœuvres were conducted in the summer of 1888 on a scale of unprecedented magnitude. A supposititious hostile fleet, consisting of 9 armored and 12 unarmored vessels and 12 torpedo-boats, under the command of Admiral Sir George Tryon, was blockaded in the two Irish ports of Berehaven and Lough Swilly by a fleet of 13 armored and 13 unar-mored vessels and 12 torpedo-boats, command-ed by Admiral Baird. Mimic war was de-clared on July 23. The passage of the fleets to their rendezvous revealed the unseaworthi-ness both of the torpedo-boats and the torpedo-catchers. On August 2 a cruiser escaped un-observed from Lough Swilly; on the following night the "Warspite," a powerful steel-clad cruiser, the "Iris," and the "Severn" passed by the blockading squadron at Berehaven in spite of electric lights and rockets; and on the night of the 4th three other vessels ran the blockade at Lough Swilly. Some of the es-caped vessels attacked Aberdeen, Leith, and Edinburgh, and preyed on the commercial shipping, and when Admiral Baird sailed in pursuit Sir George Tryon went to Liverpool and took possession of the harbor and the iron-clad left to defend it, while another squadron levied tribute on the ports of the east coast of England. The experiments demonstrated the difficulty of sealing up a hostile fleet as power-ful as that of France in its own harbors with the present naval force of Great Britain, and led to the conclusion that in the event of war with a first-class naval power the entire coast and all the commerce of England except what is in the mouth of the Thames would be at the mercy of the enemy's fleet.

Finances.—For the year ending March 31, 1888, the revenue was £88,135,000, and the expenditure, £87,846,295. The principal items of expenditure were as follow: Charges on the consolidated fund, £27,928,000; expenses of the army, £18,393,900; of the navy, £12,261,-508; collection of customs and of inland rev-enue, £2,715,727; post-office, £5,420,770; tele-graph service, £1,950,248; packet service, £699,341. The treasury receipts for the year ending March 31, 1887, were £138,364,759, and the issues, £132,414,652, leaving a balance of £5,950,107. Of the total receipts from cus-toms in 1887, amounting to £20,312,886, the amount realized from tobacco, tea, spirits, and wines was £19,334,193, leaving less than a million pounds for the other articles on the list. During the ten years from 1878 to 1887, the total expenditure of the Government ex-ceeded the total revenue by £9,102,135. On March 31, 1887, the national debt was £736,-278,688, divided as follow: Funded debt, £637,-637.640; terminable annuities, £81,123,148; unfunded debt, £17,517,900. The annual charges on the debt are £27,958,023. A treas-ury minute of May 25, 1887, proposes, by a permanent annual charge of £26,000,000 to re-deem the funded debt in about fifty-six years. A large scheme of conversion was successfully carried out by Chancellor of the Exchequer Goschen in April, 1888. The new 3-per-cent. stock, amounting to £166,000,000, which was redeemable without notice was exchanged for 2¾-per-cent. consols, and consols and reduced 3-per-cents. were converted into the same stock, the holders, who were entitled to a year's notice, being induced to take it by a bonus of ¼ of 1 per cent. and the continuance of the old rate of interest for another year. The scheme effects a yearly saving on the charge of the public debt of £1,400,000 from the beginning of 1889 and of double that sum from 1903, when the rate of interest will descend to 2½ per cent., which is guaranteed for twenty years thereafter. The holders of £514,-000,000 out of £558,000,000 3-per-cent. stocks of all descriptions accepted the arrangement, and the Chancellor of the Exchequer was authorized to pay off the remainder during 1889. The new stock, which acquired the market name of "Goschen's," stood for some time above par. A similar scheme of conversion was contemplated by Mr. Gladstone, when at the head of the Treasury, and was attempted by Mr. Childers without success.

In the budget for 1888-'89 the Chancellor of the Exchequer looked for a surplus on existing taxation of £2,377,000 ; but he had to make provision for the promised contribution in aid of the rates for the new system of local self-government. Grants from the Imperial Exchequer to the local bodies, amounting to £2,600,000 were to be withdrawn, but permanent resources estimated to bring in £5,-500,000 annually were promised instead, consisting mainly of license duties, some at present operative and others to be afterward created, and, in addition, the Central Government was to pay over to the county council one half the total receipts from the probate duties. But the withdrawal of the control of public-houses from the county councils, and other important changes in the local government bill, necessitated considerable modification of this financial scheme.

The immediate obligation on the Chancellor of the Exchequer to facilitate the changes in local government was met by a grant of one third of the probate duty, distributed in England and Wales according to the amount of indoor pauperism, which, with the abolition of the hawkers' duty, the readjustment of the carriage duty, and the relief from income-tax of lands returning no agricultural profit, reduced the surplus by nearly £1,500,000. On the other hand, the withdrawal of local grants was to come into operation at once, though to a limited extent, the succession duty was increased by ¼ per cent. in the case of lineal succession and 1½ per cent. for heirs by collateral descent, heavier taxation was exacted from the Stock Exchange in the form of an additional stamp on contract notes, a transfer duty on securities to bearer, and a registration duty on limited liability companies. and an import duty of 5s. a dozen was laid on bottled wines. Thus Mr. Goschen reconstructed a surplus of £1,762,-000, which enabled him to reduce the income-tax from 7d. to 6d. in the pound. The proposed duty on bottled wines was modified so that it falls only on expensive champagnes, while in compensation the hawkers' duty was not abolished, but reduced one half.

The Parliamentary Session.—The third session of the present Parliament was opened by Royal Commission on February 9. In the Queen's speech mention was made of the completed Anglo-Russian demarkation of the Afghan boundary, the unsuccessful mission to the King of Abyssinia to dissuade him from engaging in war with Italy, the pending fisheries negotiations at Washington, the arrangement concluded with France for the regulation of the Suez Canal, the New Hebrides convention with the same power, and the sugar-bounty conference in London. The House of Commons was asked to consider estimates for improvements in the defense of the ports and coaling-stations and for providing a special squadron for the protection of Australasian commerce, the cost of which would be borne partially by the colonies. The result of measures passed at the cost of great labor in the preceding session for the benefit of Ireland was said to be a diminution of agrarian crime and the abatement of the power of coercive conspiracies. New measures tending to develop the resources of Ireland and to facilitate an increase in the number of proprietors of the soil were promised. The principal measure in the legislative programme was the reform of local government in England, including the adjustment of the relations between local and imperial finance and the mitigation of the burdens resting on the rate-payers. Other legislative proposals relate to cheapening land transfers, the collection of tithe rent-charge, the promotion of technical education, the prevention of preferences in railway rates on foreign and domestic produce, the remedying of abuses in the formation of limited liability companies, and the amendment of the law as to the liability of employers in case of accidents; also bills for improving Scottish universities and regulating borough police in Scotland, and proposals for diminishing the cost of private bill legislation. The debate on the address was over on February 23. Mr. Parnell's motion denouncing the administration of the crimes act, in the discussion of which Mr. Gladstone inveighed against the "cruel, wanton, and disgraceful bloodshed" committed by the Irish constabulary at Mitchelstown, and declared exultantly that the Government had been unable to put down either the National League or the Plan of Campaign, was lost by a vote of 317 against 229. Mr. Shaw-Lefevre offered an amendment demanding the wiping out of arrears and the prevention of evictions, which was rejected by a majority of 261 against 186. The revision of the procedure rules was the first work undertaken after the address was voted, and changes of considerable importance were carried almost without resistance. The hour of meeting on ordinary days was altered from 4 o'clock to 3 o'clock, and it was arranged that, while the sittings were to end normally at 1 o'clock, opposed business should not be taken without special permission after midnight. The closure rule was made more stringent, the numbers of the majority required to put it in force being reduced from 200 to 100. When this proposal was put to the vote, the dissentients mustered only 134 against 256. The Government was also supported by large majorities in the proposals to strengthen the rules against disorderly conduct, irrelevance, repetition, dilatory motions for adjournment, and vexatious divisions. The revival of the standing committees provisionally appointed in 1883 led to a proposition from the Home Rulers for constituting the representatives of Scotland and Wales respectively standing committees for dealing with Scotch and Welsh bills. The revised rules were made standing orders on the 7th of March.

The resignation of Lord Charles Beresford, Junior Naval Lord of the Admiralty, shortly before the meeting of Parliament, weakened the party in power, which had lately lost seats to the Gladstonian Liberals in by-elections. He resigned because the First Lord, after agreeing to the creation of a regular naval intelligence department, nullified the measure by reducing the pay of the officers detailed for this service. In common with other naval men, Lord Charles Beresford considered the system of administration of the navy wasteful and inefficient, and held that in technical matters like this it should be made the duty of the civilian who is now the sole autocrat of the navy to be guided by the opinion of the naval authorities. Later in the year, Lord Wolseley, who testified before a royal commission that the defenses of the country were in an unsatisfactory condition, repeated his assertions in public, and was taken to task by the Prime Minister; whereupon he brought the matter forward again in the House of Lords, reasserting that the demands of military and naval men did not receive proper attention. The Government, although the financial situation was critical, could not withstand the assaults of the military and naval experts. Both the War Office and Admiralty promised amendment, and eventually large expenditures were proposed.

A bill to reorganize the Irish Land Commission met with little favor in any quarter. A bankruptcy bill for Ireland became law, but the opposition of the Parnellites and Liberals caused the abandonment of Mr. Balfour's measure for the arterial drainage of the basins of the rivers Bann, Barrow, and Shannon.

The Local Government Act.—The government of counties in England and Wales is entirely reconstituted by the new act, which was signed on August 13, and the functions of the governing bodies have been much enlarged. A great part of the powers of the justices of Quarter Sessions is transferred to a county council, which consists of county councilors, elected for three years by the freeholders, and county aldermen, elected by the councilors. The council has power to levy and expend all rates, borrow money, pass the accounts of the county treasurer, license houses for music and danc-

ing and race-courses, establish and direct lunatic asylums for paupers, establish and maintain reformatory and industrial schools, erect and repair bridges, keep the highways in repair, fix the fees of inspectors and analysts, appoint the county treasurer, county surveyor, public analysts, and coroners and health officers, and determine their salaries, divide the county into polling districts for parliamentary elections, execute laws relating to contagious diseases of animals, destructive insects, the pollution of rivers, the keeping and sale of explosives, fish conservancy, wild birds, weights and measures, and gas-meters, assess damages for riots, and provide for the registration of scientific societies, places of worship, charitable gifts, and loan societies. Appeals against the amount of rates in any locality can be made to the Quarter Sessions. The county council and the Quarter Sessions have joint control over the police. The Local Government Board can at any time confer new powers on the county councils. The receipts from local taxation licenses are to be paid over to the county councils, and the Government is empowered to transfer to them the authority to levy these duties. The county councils also have the disposal of 40 per cent. of the receipts from probate duties, but are required to pay school fees for pauper children, half the salaries of health officers, the maintenance of pauper lunatics, half the cost of the police, etc. Any of the powers of the county council, except that of raising money by taxation or loan, may be delegated to committees. Boroughs containing a population in June, 1888, of over 50,000 were created by the act into administrative counties, and are called county boroughs. In these, however, the mayor, aldermen, and burgesses, who occupy the place of the chairman, aldermen, and county councilors of other counties, do not have the appointment of county officers, but can appoint the coroner when his district does not extend beyond the borough limits. The power of dividing the county into election districts and some other rights of the county council are withheld. A borough with 10,000 inhabitants or upward retains its municipal administrations, but is assessable by the county council, like the rest of the county in which it lies. In the case of boroughs of fewer than 10,000 inhabitants having their separate courts of quarter sessions, the county council assumes the administration in regard to lunatic asylums, reform schools, coroners, and some other matters, and in all boroughs of fewer than 10,000 inhabitants the control of the police, the appointment of analysts, and the execution of the laws relating to contagious diseases of animals, weights and measures, and gas-meters is transferred to the county council.

The metropolis is created into an administrative county, in which the sheriff and the justices of the peace and of quarter sessions are appointed by the Crown. The city of London loses the privilege of electing the sheriff of

Middlesex, and the powers and duties of the Court of Quarter Sessions and justices of the city are divided between the Court of Common Council and the county council. The Metropolitan Board of Works is extinguished, and all its great powers and responsibilities devolve on the county council of London, which also has charge of reformatory schools, industrial schools, pauper lunatic asylums, and the licensing of places for music and dancing, and of racecourses within ten miles of Charing Cross, extermination of cattle-disease, prevention of fires, inspection of food, regulation of the storage of explosives and petroleum, and matters connected with tramways, railways, and gas and water supply, besides the assessment and levying of county rates. The commissioners of sewers remain the sanitary authority, and in other matters of local management no change is made in the government of the city, while in other parts of the metropolis the vestries and district boards will still have the direction of branch sewers, street-cleaning, lighting, paving, and the abatement of nuisances, until by a future enactment these powers are transferred to district councils elected by a body of electors corresponding to the burgesses of a municipal borough. The county council of London consists of nineteen aldermen, chosen at a special meeting of the council, and one hundred and eighteen councilors, or double the number of parliamentary representatives, who are elected, like these, by direct suffrage, whereas under the old system the rate-payers elected the vestrymen, the vestry the members of the district board, and each district board a member of the Metropolitan Board of Works. The Metropolitan Board of Works had recently been the subject of an investigation by a royal commission, and the revelations of bribery and corruption insured a smooth passage for the London clauses of the bill. In the elections for the county council, even members of the Metropolitan Board of Works against whom no charges had been brought shared the disgrace and discredit attaching to the old body through the actions of the culpable members, and were invariably defeated.

The Government intended to combine the reform of local government with temperance reform by conferring on the county councils the power to license public-houses and to abrogate licenses, thus introducing the principle of local option. The Liberals approved this part of the bill, but opposed the proposition to compensate liquor-sellers whose licenses should be taken away. On this question some of the supporters of the Government in Parliament took the side of the Opposition, and in some of the parliamentary elections many votes were lost. The ministry could not strike out the compensation clause without sacrificing the powerful support of the licensed victualers, and therefore abandoned the main part of the intended reform, and restricted the judicial powers of the county council in this matter

to the granting of music and dancing licenses. The elections for the county councils were appointed for January, 1889, and the new bodies enter on their functions on April 1, 1889.

The Adjourned Session.—The House of Commons was occupied with the local government bill and the bill for the investigation of charges and allegations against members of Parliament till the usual time for separation. The railway rates bill, which was introduced in the House of Lords, re-establishes the railway commission on a new basis, compels companies to frame a classified schedule of charges, and prohibits undue preference in freight rates. When the local government bill had finally passed through all the stages, and the tithe rent-charge bill, which was finally abandoned, the employers' liability bill, which with many others was also thrown over, and other measures had been discussed and some progress made with the budget, the House adjourned on August 13 to meet again on November 6 in order to finish the votes in supply and other necessary business. The proposed employers' liability act was not pressed because Mr. Broadhurst and other workingmen representatives declared that it was worthless. The old act was therefore continued. The determination of the Parnellites and Gladstonians to bring forward the arrears question and expose the cruelties and abuses of coercion was the main cause of the extraordinary length of the session. The questions raised in Mr. Morley's vote of censure, which was rejected in the latter part of June by a majority of 93, were gone over again in the debate on the estimates for the Irish administration. Mr. Labouchere, who was one of the most pertinacious assailants of the ministry, about three weeks before the close of the session moved the adjournment of the House in order to call attention ironically to the unsatisfactory state of public business. A libel law amendment bill, introduced by Sir Algernon Borthwick, removes some of the hardships to which owners of newspapers are subjected by vexatious prosecution on account of statements that have been published in good faith. Mr. Bradlaugh's parliamentary oaths bill was a compromise with the ministry, and provides that members who desire to affirm in lieu of an oath must state beforehand that they either have no religious belief, or that their belief forbids them to take an oath. Mr. Morley and some of the extreme Radicals objected to this proviso, and Dr. Hunter and Mr. Picton joined with the ultra-Conservatives in an unsuccessful effort to defeat the bill. Sir Edward Watkins's channel tunnel scheme was again defeated. A large majority voted against an early closing bill introduced by Sir John Lubbock. A merchant shipping bill presented by Lord Onslow and a bill offered by the Lord Chancellor for consolidating the mortmain acts were passed without opposition, as were also Lord Herschell's bill to exempt tools and bedding from the law of distress and Mr. Stanhope's bill to facilitate the sale of glebe lands. Parliament was not prorogued till December 24.

Proposed Reforms in the Constitution of the House of Lords.—After the defeat of the motion of Lord Rosebery for a committee to inquire into the constitution of the House of Lords with a view to extensive reforms, Lord Dunraven presented a bill which was withdrawn after eliciting from the Government a promise to introduce at some future time a measure for facilitating the entrance of life peers into the House, and before the end of the session he brought in a tentative bill, which, however, found little support, and was not carried beyond a second reading. The Prime Minister also approved the proposition to give the Upper House the power that the House of Commons already possessed of expelling unworthy members. Lord Cadogan proposed a committee which should not only revise the standing orders and strike out such obsolete rules as that requiring the members of the House of Commons to stand uncovered while the Lords sit covered in joint session, but should also elaborate substantial changes in the constitution—such as making the age of entrance twenty-five instead of twenty-one years, disqualifying peers who do not attend the sittings of the House, increasing the number required for a quorum, which is at present three, and allowing peers to resign their seats.

Resignation of Sir Charles Warren.—In the autumn of 1888 a series of ghastly murders took place in London and its environs, at intervals usually of a few days, most of them in the densely populated Whitechapel district. The seven victims were all women of degraded lives, and their bodies were mutilated in a manner indicating that the murders were all the work of a single hand. The popular indignation at the inefficiency of the police was great, its chief objects being the Home Secretary, Henry Matthews, and the Chief Commissioner of the Police, Sir Charles Warren, who had distinguished himself as the leader of the Bechuanaland expedition, was afterward a commander of constabulary in Ireland, and was then placed at the head of the Metropolitan police, in which capacity he rendered himself obnoxious to the London democracy by taking vigorous measures to prevent a meeting of the unemployed in Trafalgar Square. He had differences with the Secretary of the Home Department because Sub-Commissioner Monro, who had charge of the detective force, consulted directly with the Secretary, and tendered his resignation, but withdrew it when Mr. Monro himself resigned. Mr. Matthews continued, however, to advise with the latter regarding criminal matters and the re-organization of the detective bureau. When accused of incompetency because the police failed to catch the Whitechapel murderer, Sir Charles Warren defended himself in a magazine article explaining that he was in no wise responsible for the organization or discipline of the detective force.

Secretary Matthews reprimanded him for publishing matter relating to the police, which was forbidden by a regulation issued from the Home Office. Warren replied that the Metropolitan police is governed by statute, and denied the authority of the Home Secretary to regulate the force, at the same time again offering his resignation, which was accepted on November 10.

The Sweating System.—A select committee of the House of Lords was appointed to inquire into the sweating system at the East End of London, and the scope of the inquiry was afterward extended to embrace the whole country. Many employers made concessions to their work-people as soon as the investigation was set on foot. The sweating system in its narrower sense is understood as meaning the employment of labor by sub-contractors, who, being without capital or commercial standing, can practice impositions on their employés with impunity. In a larger sense it is taken to comprehend all the methods by which, in house-labor, piece-work, and other forms of employment not protected by the regulations of trade unions or the factory acts, the hours of work are lengthened, the rate of production stimulated, and wages cut down to a minimum. The sub-contractors in the clothing industry of the East End of London are accustomed to hire unskilled hands at a shilling a day for sixteen hours' work, and women receive only seven shillings a dozen for finishing trousers, each pair taking four hours to finish. The merchants in clothing, furniture, shoes, and other articles produced with a considerable subdivision of labor make arrangements for their supply with contractors, who sometimes furnish the materials, and sometimes receive all or part of them from the merchants. The contractors have the articles made, either complete or in parts, by sub-contractors, who carry on the manufacture in their own houses or in ill-ventilated workshops, training children, youths, women, and foreign immigrants to perform each one some minute part of the process. In so far as women and children are employed, these sweaters' dens come within the purview of the factory and workshop act of 1878. There are, however, such legal formalities required to be gone through with before an inspector can gain entrance that when he arrives all evidence of evasions of the law can be removed. Many of the contracting tailors, shoemakers, and cigarmakers are Jews, and to some extent, though not as often as was supposed, their victims are immigrant Jews from the east of Europe. One effect of the subdivision of labor incident to the contract system by which the large retailers of London obtain their stock of goods is that the skilled tailors, shoemakers, and other tradesmen have been forced by the competition of sweaters to emigrate to other places, and the apprenticeship system has disappeared. The laborers that become skilled only in some single mechanical manipulation are not only reduced to starvation wages, but when change of fashion or trade depression throws them out of work, they are less able to turn to other employments than they would be if they had learned their trade in all its branches.

Tithe Agitation in Wales.—The land troubles in Wales chiefly took the form of resistance to the tithe rent-charge, of which the Established Church and the English universities are the beneficiaries. The great majority of the Welsh are Nonconformists, and in many parts of the country the churches are empty, and the Establishment is a heavy and a useless burden for the people, who, as was the case in Ireland, have to support in addition their separate religious institutions. The present agitation is for a commutation of the tithes in view of the fall in the prices of agricultural produce, with the ultimate aim of the disestablishment of the Church of England in Wales and complete relief from the tribute exacted of the Welsh for a religion the English have vainly sought to impose on them, most of the ministers of which are strangers to the people and their language. A Welsh Land League was formed, and the farmers banded together to compel the Church Commissioners to resort to legal compulsion to collect the tithes. The latter attached cattle and movables in distraint proceedings, but wherever the law officers appeared they were confronted by crowds of farmers with stout sticks, and in the few cases in which property was seized there were disturbances, as at Meifod, Whitland, and Brynterifife.

Gold-Mining in Wales.—Gold has recently been discovered in certain parts of Wales, associated with silver, in ledges that are as rich as are found in California and Australia. The claim of the Crown to all precious metals found is a serious hindrance to mining in the United Kingdom. Alluvial gold was discovered in the south of Ireland during the political disturbances in the latter part of the last century, and many hundreds of men and women flocked to the locality and washed out gold-dust and nuggets deposited in the stream beds; but the military drove them away, and the Government asserted its right to the gold, and for some time guarded the field, which has not been worked to this day. One of the Welsh mines was opened in 1887 at great expense, and when a large amount of gold had been extracted and the value of the mine was confirmed, the Government interposed, demanding a royalty of one thirtieth of the product from the landholder, who had already leased the mining rights for thirty years for one fortieth royalty. The lessee found that he had no redress when his employés stole the gold, because, if the Crown did not assert its right to the property, it belonged to nobody.

The Crofters.—The Lewis island in the Hebrides was the scene of a deer raid, forcible seizures of lands, and collisions with the military and police toward the end of 1887. The land belongs to Lady Matheson. One half of the surface has been leased to strangers as a deer-forest, and one half of the remainder converted into sheep-farms. There is consequently much overcrowding, and the crofters and cottars have to pay twenty and thirty shillings rent an acre for land that is so poor that no one would take it at any price if it were in England. The herring-fishery enabled them to pay the rent till this failed, leaving them destitute. Commissioners appointed to inquire into the condition of the people found them suffering already for lack of food, and threatened with starvation. The population of the island was 25,487 in 1881. Sentences were passed at Edinburgh, on February 3, upon sixteen prisoners concerned in disturbances, who were condemned to from nine to fifteen months' imprisonment. The Crofters Commission, empowered by act of Parliament to revise rents in the Highlands, reduced rents on the island of Sanday nearly 49 per cent. and canceled 81 per cent. of the arrears. On other estates the reductions were from 30 to 60 per cent., and arrears were wiped out to the extent of from 40 to 80 per cent. On the estate of the Duke of Argyll, who participated in the newspaper controversy over the crofter question, the rents were largely reduced.

The Plan of Campaign.—The Plan of Campaign in Ireland was organized in 1886, and was sustained and encouraged by the members of the National League chiefly on the Luggacurren, Mitchelstown, Ponsonby, O'Grady, Brooke, and Leader estates. In each case the tenants, after presenting their demands regarding a reduction of rent, the amount of back-rent they are willing to pay, and other conditions, if they meet with a refusal, place the sum that they consider due in a common purse, which is committed to the custody of a trustee, usually either a politician or a priest. The trustee notifies his willingness to settle with the landlord on the terms that have been concerted, expressing the determination otherwise to use the fund in defending the tenants against evictions or vexatious legal proceedings, and in supporting the evicted. The landlords formed a corporation or league for the purpose of combating the Plan of Campaign, by advancing money to embarrassed landlords and working vacant farms from which the tenants had been evicted. They also organized a subsidiary emergency committee, which undertook to furnish tenants or caretakers for evicted farms, and sheriffs' deputies to enforce writs of ejectment. In some cases new tenants were imported from the Protestant districts.

The tenants on Lord Lansdowne's property at Luggacurren demanded a reduction of 20 per cent. The holders of 34 of the best farms, together with 20 sub-tenants, were evicted, and were maintained by the league in wooden huts, while their land was worked for the landlord by the Land Corporation. No tenants could be found willing to take the vacant farms, and a large force of emergency men and police was kept on the estate in order to defend the property. Two of the tenants who joined the Plan of Campaign accepted the landlord's terms, and paid their rent and costs, thereby forfeiting the sum they had paid into the "war chest." The leader of the Plan of Campaign on the estate, Mr. Kilbride, who was one of the principal tenants and the companion of William O'Brien on an oratorical tour in Canada and the United States, was elected member of Parliament for South Kerry, and took his seat at the beginning of the session of 1888. On June 21 negotiations for a settlement on the basis of the sale of the farms to the tenants under the Land Purchase Act, on condition of their paying a year's rent, which was half the arrears, were begun between Father Dempsey in behalf of the tenants and Townsend Trench, Lord Lansdowne's agent, and were continued during the landlord's visit to his estate, but were suddenly broken off after he left in August.

On the Ponsonby estate at Youghal the tenants, acting under the advice of Dr. Tanner and Mr. Lane, Irish members of Parliament, asked a reduction of 25 per cent. on judicial rents, which was more than double the average reduction that was subsequently made in cases adjudicated by the Land Commission. Evictions were carried out against eight tenants, but after desperate riots, in which the police killed a man named Hanlon with a bayonet, the authorities contented themselves with holding the rest of the tenants in a state of siege.

The tenants on the O'Grady estate at Herbertstown demanded an abatement of 40 per cent., while the landlord offered 15 per cent. The principal farms were taken possession of by the authorities. Thomas Moroney, a tenant, was committed to jail for contempt of court, because he concealed his assets, in bankruptcy proceedings to which he was subjected.

On Lady Kingston's Mitchelstown estate the Plan of Campaign was adopted in December, 1886, when the tenants demanded an abatement of 20 per cent. The farmers and the shopkeepers in the town disposed of all their movable property, and business remained at a standstill till a settlement was effected in 1888, based on the decisions of the Land Commissioners, who made an average reduction of 20½ per cent. in the rents. The owner's husband and agent, Mr. Webber, agreed to apply the same rate of reduction to arrears due to March, 1887, and to reinstate evicted tenants and forgive them all costs, that they might have their rents fixed by the Land Commission.

The Plan of Campaign was adopted on Murray Stewart's estate, near Glenties, the tenants demanding 33 per cent. reduction in January, 1888, although the Land Commission had only granted 15 per cent. reduction in the same locality.

The Plan of Campaign was a failure on the property of the Skinner's Company; yet it was successful on Lord Dillon's estate, where the demands of the tenants were granted after a struggle, during which Major Neild was fatally assaulted by the tenants and their friends, who mistook him for a process-server.

The evictions that attracted most attention in 1888 were those on Lord Massarene's estate. The agent had recommended in 1886, after the heavy fall in prices, an abatement of 15 per cent. on judicial, or 20 per cent. on non-judicial rents, but Lord Massarene refused to accept his advice, though all the other landlords that he represented had followed his suggestions, and employed other agents, whom he instructed to adopt every means to break up the combination that was formed among the greater part of the tenants to secure a reduction of 20 per cent. on judicial, and 25 per cent. on non-judicial rents. After the Plan of Campaign had been in operation on the estate for eighteen months, the Land Commissioners in numerous cases made the reductions in the rents, averaging 22½ per cent., or only 2½ per cent. less than the tenants demanded. Then the landlord offered to compromise, but excepted three of the tenants, whom he considered to be leaders of the resistance, and his proposition was therefore rejected by the tenants as a body. The Protestant tenants had not joined the combination, having received an abatement. The agents instituted proceedings whereby ten of the tenants were evicted, and some of them prosecuted for resistance.

Landlord Leader of the Curass estate refused an abatement of 25 per cent. He evicted eight tenants in February, 1887, who were housed and fed by their friends. The whole district rose against the landlord, who was unable to cultivate his own farm of 3,000 acres, as his laborers left, and no smith, butcher, or other tradesman would do any work for him. When some of the tenants showed an inclination to come to terms, they were visited by moonlighters and beaten, and one man named Curtin was shot and wounded. Proceedings were taken under the crimes act, and several persons were convicted of boycotting Leader. On Sept. 5, 1888, Mr. Leader suddenly appeared on the estate, with 20 bailiffs and 100 police, and evicted 5 tenants, some of whom had barricaded their houses, and threw stones, and poured boiling water on the heads of the police.

On Lord Clanricarde's estate a demand was made for an abatement of 40 per cent. The feeling against the landlord was exceptionally bitter, and the conflict was carried on without mercy on either side. Houses were burned and blown up, woods set on fire, crops and cattle destroyed, telegraph wires cut, roads torn up and blockaded, and eight persons killed. Here and nearly everywhere the campaigners held their ground at the opening of the season of 1888, and in some cases they had gained their point, so that Mr. Gladstone could boast that the plan of campaign was " entire, successful, and triumphant."

On the Coolgreany estate in County Wexford, near the border of County Wicklow, there were eighty tenants, and of these all but ten were evicted. One of these, John Kinsella, took refuge on the farm of a man named Kavanagh, and some days afterward 18 emergency men with Freeman, the bailiff of the estate, made a raid for cattle on this farm. They were warned by the police that the intended seizure was illegal. Kavanagh, Kinsella, and many others of the evicted tenants were in the court-yard, and as the emergency men came up Kavanagh raised a pitchfork in a threatening manner. Upon that Freeman stepped forward, and, taking aim with a pistol, shot Kinsella dead, after which the emergency men entered the yard and drove off the cattle. One of the policemen went before the magistrate, Lord Courtown, to report the murder, but he refused to issue a warrant. At the inquest five witnesses swore to the killing of Kinsella by Freeman, and yet, when the matter was presented to the grand jury, that body ignored the bill. An indictment against Freeman was nevertheless tried, but the prosecuting attorney seemed to act in collusion with the defense, a pistol was produced as Freeman's which the bullet did not fit, the judge instructed the jury that Freeman did not fire the shot, and no steps were taken to find out who else could have been the murderer. The landlord of Coolgreany, Mr. Brooke, gained a victory by compelling the managers of the Plan to pull down the comfortable houses that had been erected for the evicted tenants in order to prevent their seizure for rent.

The Plan of Campaign was adopted on the Vandeleur estate in West Clare more recently than in the other cases. The reduction asked was 25 per cent. on judicial, and 35 per cent. on non-judicial rents. Several of the tenants went before the land court in 1888 and obtained reductions averaging 32½ per cent. The rents had been raised 25 per cent. in 1874, out of revenge, it is said, for the landlord's defeat as a parliamentary candidate, and a considerable rent was exacted even for bog-land that the tenants had reclaimed. The tenants had taken the land originally in the wild state, and had brought it under cultivation and made all the improvements. The Plan of Campaign was adopted in the beginning of 1887, when 300 tenants put their money into the "war chest," 100 others joined the combination, and 120 were not admitted because they were insolvent and unable to pay their rent into the fund. The agent negotiated with the nine parish priests on the estate, headed by the Rev. Dr. M. Dinan, who insisted on the original demand. Proceedings were taken against 85 tenants, and writs of ejectment were procured in 24 cases, and carried out in July, 1888. The alarm was sounded with the church bells at the approach of the evicting party, and the people cut all the bridges on the road to Kilrush. A force of 200 police and military was employed to carry out the executions, who effected an entrance into the barricaded houses by means of a battering-ram, and were received with showers of missiles and boiling water. The men who defended the houses were threatened with rifles if they would not come out, many were badly beaten with clubs, and the furniture in the houses was destroyed by the police. After the evictions the houses were demolished.

The Papal Rescript.—Since the nomination of Archbishop Walsh to the Irish primacy the hierarchy as well as the local clergy have been practically unanimous in the National cause, which Cardinal Manning and many of the English Catholic clergy embraced with Mr. Gladstone and his party. The Catholic landlord class, headed by the Duke of Norfolk, on the other hand, redoubled their efforts to secure the Church's condemnation of the Irish movement, especially the agrarian phase. The Duke of Norfolk was sent as the representative of the Catholic Union on the occasion of the Pope's sacerdotal jubilee. In January Pope Leo, in replying to some Irish pilgrims, said that no occasion can arise when public benefit can come from the violation of justice, which is the foundation of order and the common good. The view indicated by this pronouncement was called in question by Archbishop Walsh on the authority of private declarations of the Pope. On April 18, however, the Pope formally condemned the Plan of Campaign and boycotting, in an edict addressed to the Irish clergy, which was the result of the mission of Monsignor Persico to Ireland, and of the deliberations of the Congregation of the Inquisition on his report. The grounds of the condemnation are that it is unlawful to break a voluntary contract that has been freely made between landlord and tenant; that the land law has opened the courts to tenants who think that they have entered into inequitable contracts, although of their own free will; and that the funds collected for the prosecution of the Plan of Campaign are in many cases extorted from the contributors. Boycotting is declared to be opposed to the principles both of justice and of charity when it is used against people who are willing to pay a fair rent or who are desirous of exercising the legal right to take vacant farms. The Irish clergy and laity are advised and exhorted not to transgress the bounds of Christian charity and of justice while endeavoring to secure a remedy for the distress of the people.

Mr. Dillon, Mr. O'Brien, and other leaders in the Plan of Campaign raised their voices to protest against the conclusions of this decree even before it was circulated in Ireland, dwelling especially on the point that the contracts between landlords and tenants are far from being voluntary on the part of the latter. It failed of the effect that the Tories expected, and even the clergy largely disregarded the command, while the Irish leaders vehemently protested against the Papal interposition in politics. The

Irish bishops held a theological conference regarding the interpretation of the rescript, and refrained from promulgating it till they had learned from the Pope whether the condemnation was to be understood as conditional, limited by the reasons given by Cardinal Monaco for the prohibition of the Plan of Campaign. The answer came that it was absolute.

A meeting of Irish members of Parliament to protest against the Papal rescript was followed on May 20 by a popular assemblage in Hyde Park, London, which numbered 6,000. Similar demonstrations took place all over Ireland. The Bishop of Limerick, Dr. O'Dwyer, was the only prelate who gave full effect to the Papal admonition in a pastoral letter, and vigorously denounced the agitation that was carried on by Roman Catholics against their Holy Father, the Pope. In his and some other dioceses the parish priests refrained from taking an open part in the meetings, yet even then they sent letters of regret expressive of sympathy. The feeling of the subordinate clergy was so rebellious that a schism was feared if the Vatican adhered to the position it had taken. The branches of the league and public boards throughout the country protested against the intervention of the Pope, a council of laymen that met in Dublin condemned the decree, and even bishops showed opposition and explained away its plain intent. The Pope listened to the remonstrances of the Irish hierarchy and the arguments of Archbishop Walsh, who visited Rome, and, without retracting his theological position regarding property rights and the binding force of contracts, while declaring his condemnation of boycotting and the Plan of Campaign to be unqualified and final, he was satisfied to see his decree become what the Irish politicians threatened to make it, a dead letter, and sent explanations which modified its application. At a meeting of the archbishops and bishops that was held at Conliffe College on May 30 resolutions were unanimously adopted declaring that the decree was intended to affect the domain of morals alone, and saying that assurances had just been received from the Pope displaying deep and paternal interest in the temporal welfare of the country, and showing that, so far from intending to injure the National movement, it was his intention to remove things that he feared might in the long run prove obstacles to its advancement. The resolutions conveyed a warning to the people against the use of hasty or irreverent language with reference to the Sovereign Pontiff or the sacred congregations, and a reminder to the leaders of the National movement that the Roman Pontiff has an inalienable and divine right to speak with authority on questions appertaining to faith and morals, which was accompanied with an expression of lasting gratitude to the Nationalist leaders for their services to religion and morality. This, the first formal acceptance by the prelates of the Pontifical injunction, beginning with the deprecatory announcement that it was given "in obedience to the commands of the Holy See," was praised by the Nationalist press for its "eloquent silence" in making no mention of the Plan of Campaign or boycotting.

At a general meeting of the archbishops and bishops, held in the College of Maynooth on June 27 and 28, the following statement was adopted: (1) The demand of the agricultural tenants in the matter of rent is in substance for the establishment of an impartial public tribunal to adjudicate between landlord and tenant. They do not claim the right to fix the rent themselves, but object to its being determined by the arbitrary will of the landlord. (2) The principle that tenants should be protected by law against exorbitant rents and eviction has been recognized by the British Parliament in the land act of 1881 and subsequent statutes. (3) The tenants ask the effective application of this principle and the removal of obstacles that have been allowed to remain, even where the right to have a fair rent fixed has been conferred by act of Parliament. (4) The most serious of these obstacles is the accumulation of arrears from exorbitant rents, which the courts have no power to reduce. The heavy indebtedness of tenants puts it in the power of harsh landlords to use the threat of eviction as a means of keeping back their tenants from applying to the Land Commission to have their rents adjusted. (5) Thousands of tenants have been deprived of the right of recourse to the courts and their legal status as tenants by having had notices of eviction served upon them. (6) No difficulty exists in providing a remedy. There is already an act in operation in Scotland applicable to arrears, under which rents have been judicially reduced 30 per cent. and arrears no less than 61 per cent., but Parliament has refused to extend the operation of the act to Ireland. (7) Unless Parliament at once applies some effective measure for the protection of Irish tenants from oppressive exactions and arbitrary eviction, consequences disastrous to public order and to the safety of the people must ensue.

Archbishop Walsh, in an address to the dean and chapter of his diocese in the early part of July, described the results of his interviews with Pope Leo, whom he had fully informed of the claims and aspirations of the Irish in regard both to national autonomy and the redress of agrarian grievances, and said that the people of Ireland may count on the entire sympathy of the Vatican on every legitimate effort, and that the foolish fiction that recent legislation has done justice to the people or to the tenants finds no footing there. The Pope, in July, addressed an encyclical letter to the Irish bishops, in which he condemned the conduct of the men who put themselves forward to upset his authority and the duties of religion. The priests absented themselves from public meetings in behalf of the Plan of Campaign only for a few weeks. After the return of Archbishop Walsh from Rome they took as active a part as ever in the meetings.

Arrest of Members of Parliament.—In January, 1888, Mr. Cox, member of Parliament for East Clare, was sentenced to four months' imprisonment for a speech inciting his hearers to join the league, and accusing the Government of driving the Irish people to commit outrages. Commoners Pyne and Gilhooly were committed to jail about the beginning of the parliamentary session. English Gladstonians were inclined to go into Ireland and defy the Government on the crimes act into operation against them, but concluded to leave the agitation in the hands of Irishmen. John Morley and the Marquis of Ripon made a political tour in Ireland in January in order to manifest the sympathy of the English Liberal party. In April, John Dillon and William O'Brien went over from London with the express purpose of braving the Government by taking an active part in the Plan of Campaign, and of convening meetings in proclaimed districts. Mr. Dillon met the tenants of Lord Massarene's estate at Tullyallen, and delivered a speech intended to counteract the effect produced by the act of the tenant that had first been evicted in October, 1887, who had redeemed his farm, saying that the sympathies of Englishmen did not go with men who went cringing to their landlords. For this speech he was arrested, and tried at Mill, County Louth, and was sentenced on May 10 to six months' imprisonment for taking part in an illegal conspiracy to induce tenants not to pay and with having taken part in an unlawful assembly in a proclaimed district. He was the sixteenth member of Parliament who, up to that time, had been sentenced under the crimes act. On September 18 he was unconditionally released by order of the Lord Lieutenant, because the rigors of confinement had seriously impaired his health. William O'Brien and others were brought to trial at Loughrea on April 19, on the charge of having attempted to hold an illegal meeting on the 8th of the same month. The crimes act was applied with severity to boycotters. Persons were sentenced to three and four months' imprisonment with no further proof of conspiracy than that they had individually refused to sell their merchandise or services to members of the constabulary force, even when the latter had made a demand for things with which they were already plentifully supplied, for the sole purpose of procuring evidence and making arrests. One of the anomalies of the administration of the act was the increase of sentences by county courts on appeal from the courts of summary jurisdiction. One of many instances was that of Mr. Blane, a member of Parliament, whose sentence the Appellate Court raised from four to six months, adding the penalty of hard labor.

Thomas Condon, member of Parliament, was imprisoned two weeks in May in Cork jail for advocating the Plan of Campaign, and on his release was tried and sentenced to a month's confinement for conspiring, with others, to induce certain persons not to pay a levy of £1,000 that the grand jury of Cork County ordered to be paid as compensation to Constable Leahy, who was injured by the crowd in the Mitchelstown riots. J. O'Brien, member of Parliament, after undergoing a sentence of four months in Tullamore jail, was taken at its expiration to Kilkenny, to pass through a second term of imprisonment of the same length. James O'Kelly was arrested in London, on July 24, when leaving the Houses of Parliament, and was tried at Boyle on the charge of inciting his constituents not to give evidence under the "Star Chamber" clauses of the crimes act, and sentenced on August 10 to imprisonment for four months. John E. Redmond, member of Parliament, with Edward Walsh, proprietor of the "Wexford People" newspaper, was tried and convicted of using intimidating language in reference to a landlord at Scarawalsh, a proclaimed district, in saying that the landlord would find no tenants for a farm from which he had evicted the occupier, and that he could not afford to arouse the ill-will of the people among whom he lived. Mr. Redmond was confined in Tullamore jail five weeks, regaining his liberty on October 30. William Redmond was present at some evictions at Coolroe, where the bailiffs were resisted desperately and several constables assaulted. He was tried for inciting people to obstruct officers of the law in the discharge of their duties, and was sentenced to prison for three months. Mr. Sheehan, member of Parliament for East Kerry, was committed to Tralee prison for a month in November, having been convicted of using threatening and abusive language to the district inspector of the constabulary. Near the end of the year, Edward Harrington was condemned to six months' imprisonment in Tullamore jail for publishing in his paper, the "Kerry Sentinel," reports of the meetings of suppressed branches of the National League. A question of privilege was raised in Parliament, near the close of the session, in the case of Mr. Sheehan, on whom a summons was served by an Irish policeman within the precincts of the House of Commons.

The Plan of Campaign was not defeated by the imprisonment of Irish members, and after the Mandeville inquest the Government relaxed the severities to which the prisoners were subjected, and embraced the first pretext they could find for releasing the leaders. They were scornfully dared, across the benches of Parliament, to apply the crimes act to Roman Catholic priests, and visit them with the indignities of prison garb, association with felons, oakum-picking, and stone-breaking. Many of the landlords who attempted to fight the Plan of Campaign were glad to accept in the end the terms offered, and receive their rent from the trustees of the Plan. Among these were Lord Dillon, Lord Westmeath, and Lord De Freyne. The Marquis of Conyngham, Mr. Murphy, the landlord of Gweedore, and others, dismissed their agents and compromised with their tenants. It was impossible to find tenants for evicted farms, and toward the close of the year 5,000 farms were vacant.

The Death of John Mandeville.—Mr. Mandeville, an Irish member of Parliament, was taken to Cork jail with William O'Brien in 1887, and transferred with him to Tullamore jail. He struggled against being clothed in prison dress, though less pertinaciously than O'Brien, and resisted being placed in companionship with criminals and the performance of menial prison work. In consequence he was subjected frequently during his confinement to disciplinary punishment; and as he was a man of remarkable strength and vigor, the officials were more severe and merciless with him than with his fellow-prisoner. The punishment-cell, where his bed was a bare plank, was so chill and damp that his throat became sore, and continued so during the whole time he was in prison. When placed on punishment-diet he was unable to swallow the dry bread and cold water, and consequently suffered from starvation to such a degree that he bound a rope round his waist to ease his pangs, and at times felt himself to be on the verge of madness. A scrap of meat that a warder once threw to him, as to a dog, gave him more pleasure than anything that he had ever eaten. He told the prison doctor that he was ill, but the latter, Dr. James Ridley, overestimating the strength of his constitution, judged that he could stand the punishment. The surgeon had been reproved for his leniency to former prisoners, and feared that he would lose his place if he released political prisoners from punishment without strong cause. Dr. Moorhead, the visiting justice, who found Mandeville suffering from rheumatism and exhausted from lack of nourishment, wrote protests in the prison journal, and complained to Dr. Ridley, but the latter certified that he was healthy and fit for punishment. Mandeville came out of prison on Dec. 24, 1887, pale, anæmic, emaciated, and tremulous. He partially recovered his strength, then suffered relapses, and on July 8, 1888, died of a congestive chill. A coroner's inquest was opened at Mitchelstown on the day of the funeral, which was attended by 6,000 persons. Dr. Ridley wrote a remorseful letter to the governor of the jail, and on July 20, the day on which he was summoned to give evidence before the coroner's jury, committed suicide.

Investigation of the Charges against the Parnellites.—The accusations against the Irish Land League leaders, contained in a series of articles entitled "Parnellism and Crime," published in the London "Times" in April, 1887, were met by a demand on the part of the Irish members of Parliament for an inquiry by a select committee, to which the Government would not consent. In July, 1888, the matter was brought before the public again in a suit for defamation of character, instituted against the publishers of the "Times" by Frank Hugh O'Donnell. In the trial Attorney-General Webster, who acted as counsel for the defendants, brought evidence to show that the plaintiff was not a member of the League, and thus his action failed, and instead of vindicating the reputation of the chiefs of the Irish parliamentary party, simply afforded counsel for the "Times" an opportunity to reiterate the charges of complicity in murder and outrage. Mr. Parnell, in Parliament, repeated his request for an investigation by a committee of the House of Commons. The Government at length agreed to an inquiry into the charges against members of Parliament and other persons in the action of O'Donnell vs. Walter and another by a special commission. In accordance with the proposition of W. H. Smith, the leader of the House, a commission was constituted with powers to examine witnesses under oath and to compel full disclosure of all facts and documents, and grant certificates protecting from all proceedings, except for perjury, witnesses who may have criminated themselves by their disclosures. Mr. Parnell would not positively accept the Government proposition, but left it for the House of Commons to decide. He wished to have the inquiry limited to the forged letters and other specific libels and to the actions of members of Parliament. After an excited debate, the bill was passed under application of the closure on August 3, every amendment offered by the Parnellites and Gladstonians having been rejected. Judges Hannen, Smith, and Day were appointed by the Government as members of the commission, which first met on September 17. Sir Charles Russell and Henry Asquith appeared for the Parnellites, and Mr. Graham and Attorney-General Webster for the "Times." It was decided that the commission had authority to order the production of the originals of the letters published in the "Times" and other documents, but would decide what documents Sir Charles Russell's clients could expect; also, that Mr. Dillon should be released on bail in order to appear as a witness. Instructions were given to the publishers of the "Times" to formulate the definite charges that they were prepared to prove as well as the allegations falling short of definite charges. The commission then adjourned till October 22, after issuing an order for an inspection of the bank-books of the Land League. William Redmond was also released to appear before the commission.

Dynamite Plot.—Thomas Callan and Michael Harkins, who arrived from the United States in June, 1887, were convicted on February 3, 1888, of being in the unlawful possession of dynamite and of a conspiracy to cause a dangerous explosion, and were sentenced to fifteen years' penal servitude. They had associated in London with a suspected Irish revolutionist named Melville, and received money from him, and with a certain Cohen, who, when taken seriously ill in September, 1887, before he died gave two boxes of dynamite into the charge of Harkins, one of which the latter left with Callan. Harkins was apprehended and searched by the police, without anything suspicious being found, but Callan became alarmed, and clumsily attempted to do away with the dynamite in his possession. His lodgings were searched, and both in his baggage and in that of Harkins experts discovered traces of dynamite. They asserted that they had taken the explosive from Cohen as an act of friendship in order to shield him by concealing it, but the jury were convinced from their relations with Melville, who escaped to Paris, as well as with Cohen, that all four were concerned in a dynamite plot. One of the Irish members of Parliament had introduced the two Americans to the gallery of the House of Commons, a circumstance which afforded a fresh opportunity to the Unionists to accuse the Nationalists of being in league with Fenian assassins and possibly cognizant of a plot to blow up the Houses of Parliament.

The Land Purchase Act.—Lord Ashbourne's act, which became law on Aug. 14, 1885, authorized advances of the aggregate amount of £5,000,000 to Irish tenants to enable them to become owners of their farms. At the end of three years this sum was exhausted. Under this act the state advanced the whole purchase money, but was secured by a deposit of cash equal to at least one fifth of it, which the purchasing tenant had to place in the hands of the Land Commission, and when the security seemed insufficient the commissioners called for a fourth, and in some cases even for a third of the amount of the loan. The security was usually retained from the purchase money, the selling landlord receiving 3 per cent. interest for it or causing it to be invested under the laws governing the investment of trust moneys. Under the Ashbourne act about 12,000 tenants have acquired the freehold of their farms, more than half of them being Ulster farmers, whereas in Connaught the sum applied for was only £412,687. The purchasing tenants have paid their installments with promptness and regularity, except in very few cases. Before advancing the money for the purchase of a holding, the Land Commission sends an inspector, who examines the property and reports whether the land is sufficient security for the price stated in the contract of sale between the landlord and the tenant, and whether the installments can be paid out of the profits of the farm, leaving a fair margin for the cultivator and for bad seasons. The average rate of purchase has been seventeen or eighteen times the net annual rent. The tenant pays back the entire purchase money advanced by the Government in annual installments of 4 per cent. of the loan,

3½ per cent. constituting the interest, and seven eighths of 1 per cent. a sinking-fund which will extinguish the debt in forty-nine years. The landlords have benefited by the voluntary sales through the eagerness of the tenants to acquire land, and the leaders of the Land League have advised against purchasing under the act, save in exceptional cases. Those who have purchased in the north have usually secured fair terms, and in general the new proprietors have till now shown little dissatisfaction, evincing a disposition to work harder in order to meet their installments, and many have applied for loans under the land improvement act. The installments are less than the old rent, the purchaser having in addition to assume the whole of the poor rate, and in cases where the purchase was based on rents fixed since 1870 the county taxes also, but they exceed the rents adjusted under the last land act. The peasants who have become proprietors under the act are for the most part large farmers who were well off before, while in the congested and impoverished districts there have been few sales. The most important business of the adjourned session of Parliament was the continuance of Lord Ashbourne's act, which passed the third reading on November 29. The Irish party endeavored to introduce instructions to the Land Commission to consider the question of arrears in applying the act. The sum of £5,000,000 was placed at the disposal of the commissioners for advances to purchasing tenants on the same conditions as under the original act.

Sugar Bounties.—In an international conference held in London in November, 1887, all the chief sugar-producing nations of Europe, through their representatives, agreed in principle to the total abolition of bounties on the export of sugar. In France, Germany, Austria, Belgium, and Holland the excise duty on sugar is levied on the beet-roots as they are taken in at the factory, while the manufacturer receives a drawback or bounty on all the sugar that he exports, which was intended to be exactly equal to the duty that he has already paid. After the saccharine yield had been fixed by law, the refiners had an extraordinary incentive to perfect their processes and machinery and the growers to improve the culture, in order to obtain a higher yield than the legal standard. There was a rapid development of the methods of cultivation and extraction, and the governments soon found themselves paying out more in drawbacks than they received in taxes. Under this stimulus the cultivation of the sugar-beet and the manufacture of sugar outstripped the demand. A glut in the market, a great fall in prices, and a universal crisis in the sugar industry resulted. The governments had hesitated to lower the bounties while the industry was prosperous, because none could move in the matter without placing its own producers at a disadvantage. To take away the bounties now, when the producers were embarrassed, would create a more widespread financial crisis and take away every chance for the industry to recover. A conference was held in Paris in 1877 to consider the question of abolishing bounties in all countries simultaneously, but it came to nothing, owing to the opposition of Belgium and the Netherlands. The legal yield was fixed in Germany at 8½ per cent. of the weight of the roots, but with improved processes 12½ per cent. or more of sugar was extracted, giving the manufacturer a clear bounty of $10 a ton on all the sugar that he exported. In order to make good the loss to the treasury, which was 21,000,000 marks in 1884, the Government raised the tax on consumption from 1·60 to 1·70 mark, but did not venture to disturb the export bounty. According to the latest statistics, bounties cost France $17,000,-000 a year; Germany, $16,000,000; Austria-Hungary, $5,000,000; Belgium, $4,000,000; and Holland, $3,000,000. The English, who are the greatest consumers of sugar in Europe, formerly used only cane-sugar, mainly the product of the British West Indies and Guiana. The beet-root sugar gradually displaced cane-sugar altogether. When the refiners, whose business was destroyed, called on the Government for a remedy, they were told that the people of England ought to be well content if the Continental governments chose to pay a part of the price of their sugar, and thus make them a gift of about $25,000,000 a year. The West Indian planters could not be so easily answered, for sugar is almost the only product of the British colonies in the West Indies, and, after refusing to seek for them a new market by the negotiation of a reciprocity treaty with the United States, the British Government was constrained to open negotiations with the Continental governments for the abolition of the bounty system. Belgium ranks fourth among the sugar-producing nations of Europe, and is one of the chief exporting countries, since the excise duty is fixed so high that little sugar is consumed in the country and four fifths of the product goes abroad. The Belgian representative at the London conference did not oppose the removal of export bounties, but would not accept the remedy on which all the other delegates were agreed, viz., the system of manufacturing in bond. The Belgian Government employs a machine for gauging the saccharine yield in the refineries, and proposed Government control of the legal yield and a system of equivalents in preference to the more troublesome and inquisitorial bonding system, which, it was further objected, would not prevent the covert enjoyment of bounties by means of frauds on the revenue. The other governments took the same ground in condemning the Belgian proposals. Before the second meeting of the conference at London, Baron de Worms, the English delegate, made a tour of the European capitals, seeking to bring about an agreement. The basis of a treaty on which the plenipotentiaries agreed in London on Nov. 24, 1887, was that the measures to be adopted

must give complete and absolute security that no premiums on the export of sugar, direct or indirect, should be granted, and a system of taking manufactured sugar that is destined for consumption is the only method of abolishing premiums, the taxes being extended to sirup and glucose. The conference reassembled in London on April 5, 1888. Germany, Austria, Belgium, Brazil, Denmark, Spain, France, Great Britain, Italy, the Netherlands, Russia, and Sweden, were officially represented. The United States followed the proceedings unofficially, and is expected to join a union of sugar-growing countries if one can be formed that shall embrace all those that produce beet-sugar and four fifths of the cane-producing countries. The final protocol, with a draft convention, was signed by the plenipotentiaries on May 12, with reservations on important points. In France the producers of sugar were strongly opposed to the treaty, as they consider that the conditions for production are more favorable in Germany. France and Spain raised the objection that the United States and other countries holding aloof from the convention would swamp the countries entering into the treaty with their bounty-fed sugar. In order to remove their doubts, a clause was introduced whereby the contracting powers agreed to prohibit the importation of sugar from bounty-giving countries. This, however, did not satisfy France. England, Germany, Belgium, Spain, Italy, the Netherlands, and Russia signified their acceptance of the treaty. Austria reserved its adherence until all European countries producing or consuming sugar should also adhere to the agreement. Brazil reserved her freedom; Denmark refused to exclude the produce of favored nations because it would be a breach of treaties. France reserved her adherence until all sugar-producing and sugar-consuming countries adhere and frame laws with which she is satisfied. Sweden refused to bind herself in any way. The seven countries that signed the convention agreed to appoint commissioners, who should sit at London and report what countries give bounties to sugar exporters, and to what extent, and the parties to the treaty are bound to exclude from their markets sugar that a majority of the commission decides to be bounty-fed. Before ratifying the convention, Belgium reserved the right of withdrawing her adhesion in case the treaty should be rejected by any of the signatory powers.

Colonies.—The colonial possessions of Great Britain have a total area of more than 9,000,-000 square miles and a population of 275,000,-000, but of this number 256,000,000 are found in British India and the feudatory states. The possessions in Europe are Heligoland, Gibraltar, and Malta. The Asiatic dependencies include Cyprus, Aden, India, Ceylon, Perrin, Labuan, the Straits Settlements, the Keeling Islands, the Kurea Murea Islands, and Hong-Kong, which have an aggregate area, inclusive of the feudatory states of India and the Malayan peninsula, of 1,845,366 square miles, and 261,-201,491 inhabitants. The possessions and protectorates in Africa have an area of nearly 500,000 square miles and a population of about 3,000,000. They include Gambia, the Niger Districts, Sierra Leone, Lagos, part of the Gold Coast, St. Helena and Ascension Island, Tristan d'Acunha, Socotra, Mauritius, St. Paul and Amsterdam, Cape Colony, Basutoland, Bechuanaland, Zululand, Natal, and Berbera and its vicinity. In America the colonies of Great Britain are the Dominion of Canada, Newfoundland, the Bahamas, Bermudas, and Barbadoes, Jamaica and Turk's Island, Leeward Islands, Windward Islands, Trinidad, Honduras, Guiana, Falkland Islands, and South Georgia. Their aggregate area is 3,648,140 square miles, and their population, according to the latest enumerations, is 6,215,000. In Australasia and Polynesia the colonies of Australia and New Zealand, with the Norfolk Islands, British New Guinea, the Kermadec Islands, and Auckland, Lord Howe, Caroline, Starbuck, Malden, and Fanning islands, have a total area of 3.270,232 square miles, and contain altogether 3,667,811 inhabitants.

The island of Cyprus, in the northern part of the Levant, is administered by Great Britain in behalf of the Ottoman Empire, having been ceded to England by the convention concluded on June 4, 1878. Great Britain agreed to pay a perpetual tribute of £92,800 a year, which was calculated on the net revenue derived from the island by the Porte at the time of the cession. The present High Commissioner is Sir Henry Ernest Bulwer, who carries on the Government with the aid of a Legislative Council of eighteen members, of whom six are appointed by the Government, nine are elected by the Christian inhabitants, and three are elected by the Mohammedans. The area is 3,584 square miles, and the population in 1881 was 186,173, of which number 45,458 were Mohammedans and 137,631 belonged to the Orthodox Greek Church. When Sir Garnet Wolseley took possession in the name of the Queen in July, 1878, he issued a proclamation promising great benefits to the people. None of the promised blessings have resulted from the connection with England, except a reform of the judiciary. The Government has done nothing to give the people improved roads and harbors, or to ameliorate the primitive agriculture of the country or promote education, while collecting £43.000 more taxes on the average than were paid under the Ottoman administration, and since there has been no influx of English capital the productive resources of the island have not improved. The expenses of British administration are so much greater that Parliament has been compelled each year to vote money to make up the Turkish tribute, and many people in Great Britain consider Cyprus a useless incumbrance, since its strategical value has been called in question in recent years. The grant

in aid was £78,000 in 1882, £90,000 in 1883, £30,000 in 1884, £15,000 in each of the following two years, and £18,000 in 1887. The imports have increased from £333,512 in 1883 to £355,795 in 1887, and the exports from £276,129 to £312,797. The revenue in 1886-'87 was £187,044 and the expenditure £110,-044. Of the total expenditures the sum of £66,171 was for salaries, £10,723 for police, and £10,024 for public works. The chief sources of revenue are tithes, yielding £56,159, and Verghi taxes, yielding £26,862. The tribute to the Ottoman Government was paid over at Constantinople according to the stipulation as long as Lord Beaconsfield remained in power. When the Liberal Government of 1880 came in, the covenant was broken and the tribute from that time has been detained, first to repay advances made by the English and French governments to meet the interest on the guaranteed Ottoman loan of £5,000,000 which was raised in 1855 and on which the Turkish Government defaulted in 1875, and, after these were cleared off, to provide the annual interest on that loan in excess of the Egyptian tribute. This absorbs £82,000 of the Cyprus tribute, leaving £10,800 which is also detained toward meeting the sinking-fund of 1 per cent. on the guaranteed loan. In 1887 Cyprus suffered from drought and deficient harvests, and the administration was compelled to resort to extraordinary measures to relieve famine and to expend a larger sum than usual on the police in order to check agrarian crime. Consequently the surplus revenue for 1887-'88 fell off, and the Governor informed the Colonial Secretary that a grant in aid of not less than £60,000 would be required to restore the financial equilibrium. The Chancellor of the Exchequer, however, refused to sanction a larger vote than £30,000, and suggested a temporary reduction of the salaries of the English officials. The Legislative Council had already resolved to cut down some of the higher salaries, but the proceedings were disallowed by Lord Knutsford, who announced, however, that when the next vacancy occurs the salary of the High Commissioner will be fixed at £2,000 instead of £4,000, and the salaries of other superior officials will be reduced. The people of Cyprus, groaning under the load of oppressive taxation, clamor for the repudiation of the Turkish tribute, which with the cost of the British official establishment consumes the bulk of the revenue, leaving but a fraction to be applied to public works or other useful objects. The arrangement by which the Turkish tribute has been diverted for the benefit of the British and French treasuries does not rest on a definite understanding with France, but continues only during the good pleasure of the British Government. The total sum of the grants in aid up to 1888 is £294,000, which is less by £77,-200 than the half of the eight years' tribute that has been appropriated by the British Exchequer since 1880.

New defensive works at Singapore and Hong-Kong were completed in 1888, and a part of the armament was in place. though the 10-inch guns were still wanting. The fortifications in Mauritius are to be completed in 1889. The works at Trincomalee and St. Helena were nearly finished in the middle of 1888, and those at St. Lucia were well under way. The Imperial Government has co-operated with the colonial authorities in fortifying Cape Town. The Australasian colonies have constructed forts for themselves, and armed them with guns superior to those at present available for the defense of English seaports. The imperial defense bill that was passed in the session of 1888 provides for the expense of fortifying the ports and naval stations by a loan, which is secured on the reversionary increase in value of the Suez-Canal shares held by the Government, to accrue when the existing charge is paid off. The dividends on these shares, 106,702 in number, which were purchased from the Khedive Ismail in 1875 for the sum of £3,976,582, had been pledged by him to the company till 1894.

The Queensland ministry in 1888 attempted to dictate the choice of a Governor for the colony, and thus deprive the home Government of almost the last vestige of authority and participation in the government of the colony. When Sir Anthony Musgrave, the late Governor, died suddenly in October, the Queensland ministers endeavored to obtain a promise that the name of the proposed new Governor should be communicated to them before the appointment was definitely made. Lord Knutsford declined to accede, in a dispatch dated October 19, saying that it is obvious that the officer charged with the duty of conducting the foreign relations of the Crown and of advising the Crown when any question of imperial, as distinct from colonial, interest arises must owe his appointment and be responsible to the Crown alone, and that therefore it is not possible for the responsible ministers of the colony to share the responsibility of nominating the Governor or to have a veto on his appointment. The choice of the Secretary of State for the colonies fell upon Sir Henry Blake, Governor of Newfoundland, who was obnoxious to the Queensland colonists, especially on account of his position on the Irish question. His first colonial appointment, that of Governor of the Bahamas, was given as a reward for his services to the Government as a divisional magistrate in Ireland. When this appointment was communicated to the Queensland ministers, they telegraphed a strong protest. On November 22 Sir Henry Parkes, the Premier of New South Wales, moved an address to the Queen, to which the Legislative Assembly agreed without a division, expressing the opinion that colonial governors should be selected from men who have held high office or served in the Imperial Parliament, and that a colonial Government should be informed of an intended appointment before it is actually made. South Australia and the other colonies, with the exception of Victoria, likewise supported Queensland in the position that she had taken. The incident was closed by Sir Henry Blake's asking to be relieved, and the acceptance of his resignation.

In Africa Great Britain has abandoned to Germany her claims to Damaraland and Great Namaqualand, and has contracted her sphere of interests in the region where the Germans have founded their colony of the Camaroons. In Zanzibar the Germans compete for the supremacy once held by Great Britain. Berbera and parts of the Somali coast were proclaimed British territory at various dates between July, 1884, and January, 1886, and the powers were notified, in compliance with the general act of the Berlin Conference, on July 20, 1887. The annexation of Zululand was notified on July 8, 1887. The Gold Coast protectorate has been extended so far eastward as to include the mouths of the Niger and the Calabar oil rivers. The trade of the colonies of Gambia, Sierra Leone, the Gold Coast, and Lagos is about £3,000,000 annually. The area of the Niger protectorate, extending from the mouths of the river to Yola, on the Binué, is 23,000 square miles, while the Royal Niger Company has obtained trade rights by treaty with native chiefs over 260,000 square miles more, reaching up the Binué to the German boundary, and up the Niger as far as the rapids, and including the kingdoms of Gandu and Sokoto. The protectorate over the Niger districts was notified on June 5, 1885, in the "London Gazette," and announced in diplomatic form six days later. The recent extension northward from Cape Colony into Bechuanaland and the Kalahari desert has added more than 180,000 square miles to the area of British South Africa, of which 48,000 square miles form a Crown colony, and the remainder a protectorate. According to a recent treaty with Germany, the region north of German East Africa, bounded by a line following the Sana river northwestward, across the equator, and down to Victoria Nyanza, has been allotted to England as her sphere of influence. The coast and the right of collecting transit duties have been leased by the Sultan of Zanzibar to the British East Africa Company. This acquisition is expected to give the English the control of one of the richest regions of Central Africa. The rainfall is deficient in the territory covered by the treaty, although there is good grazing country both on the coast and in the highlands of Masailand. But the chief value of the British section is that it gives access to the rich and populous countries around Lake Victoria and Lake Albert, including the Equatorial Provinces of Egypt. The total area over which Great Britain exercises a commanding influence in Africa, exclusive of Egypt, is not less than 1,000,000 square miles, with a population of 30,000,000, and a commerce of about £20,000,000 a year.

The island of Mauritius, lying in the Indian Ocean, 500 miles east of Madagascar, has an area of 708 square miles, and a population of 368,415. The present Governor is Sir John Pope Henessy. The Council of Government is composed of 10 elective, 8 official, and 9 appointed members. A new Constitution was adopted in 1885, introducing the elective principle. But few votes are cast by the Indians, who constitute two thirds of the population, and who are at present represented in the Government by one of the nominated members of the Council. The rest of the population comprises natives of African race, Chinese, French Creoles, a few English, and mixed races. The imports in 1886 were valued at 23,946,967 rupees, and the exports at 32,383,-399 rupees, of which sum 29,126,169 rupees represent the export of raw sugar.

In the beginning of 1888 the English, by means of a warlike expedition, imposed their dominion on the Yonnies and other tribes back of Sierra Leone. The Mendis and the Lok-kohs, residing within the frontiers of British Quiah, made an attack on their neighbors outside of the British protectorate. These invited the aid of the Yonnies, who in October, 1887, descended on the town of Sennehoo, and destroyed this and other places belonging to a female chief called Madame Yoko. Sir Francis de Winton was then appointed the head of an expedition into the Yonnie country, which captured Robari, the chief town, and subjugated the country, which was then placed under a chief selected by the conquerors.

The state of Sarawak, in the island of Borneo, was founded in 1841 by Sir James Brooke, who established a settled and peaceful government among the hostile races of Sulus, Malays, and Dyaks, who had previously lived by piracy and rapine. He prayed for the protection of the British Government, and even offered to transfer the dominion that he had established to the British Crown, with reservation of the rights of the natives; but was unable to obtain from his own Government the recognition of the country as an independent state until after the United States and Italy had given such recognition. After he had relinquished the government to his successor, and returned to England to end his days, he still labored to secure the protection of the Imperial Government for the state that he had created, which he feared would pass under the dominion of some other European power, and in 1864 was gratified when a British consul was appointed to Sarawak. In June, 1888, the Supreme Council of Sarawak sanctioned an agreement that the present Rajah Brooke had concluded with the British Government, which has at last decided to establish a protectorate over Sarawak, which will probably soon be extended to the recently founded state of North Borneo and the independent native state of Brunai. Sarawak will continue to be governed as an independent state by the Rajah Brooke and his successors, and the British Government acquires no right to interfere in the internal administration, but will be the arbiter in cases of disputed succession and in all disputes with foreign states, including North Borneo and Brunai, and no cession of territory to a foreign power can take place without its consent.

Labuan, an island thirty square miles in extent, off the northwest coast of Borneo, is a Crown colony. It is peopled by about 6,000 Malays from Borneo, with some Chinese traders and a score of Europeans who carry on a trade in sago, gutta-percha, India-rubber, wax, and other products of the main island with Singapore. The imports of 1887 were valued at $370,751, and the exports at $417,551. The state of North Borneo is under the direction of the proprietary British North Borneo Company, with headquarters in London, which pays over $50,000 in salaries in the colony. The area is 27,500 square miles, and the population 175,000, consisting of Mohammedan settlers on the coast and native tribes in the mountainous interior, with a few Chinese traders and artisans. Sandakan, on the east coast, is the chief port. The revenue in 1886 from licenses, duties, royalties, etc., was $127,781, and from land sales $12,034; the expenditure, $218,061. The value of the exports was $524,-724; of imports, $849,115. The convention with Sarawak is of the same form as those concluded with the sultans or rajahs of Perak, Selangore, Sungei Ujong, and other native territories around Singapore, and the acquisitions in Borneo will probably, like these, be placed under the direction of the Governor of the Straits Settlements. The last protectorate established in the Malay peninsula was over the dominions of the Rajah of Pahang, lying to the east of Perak and Selangore. The rajah, who is invested by the treaty with the title of sultan, agrees to make no concession or grant of any kind to a foreigner unless he be a British subject or a person of Chinese, Malay, or other Oriental race. The present Governor of the Straits Settlements is Sir Frederick Aloysius Weld, who received his appointment in 1880. The colony comprises the islands of Singapore and Penang, with small adjacent islands, the strips of coast on the Malayan peninsula known as Province Wellesley and the Dindings, newly acquired territory south of Krian, and Malacca, on the western coast of the peninsula. The native states under British protection occupy the whole coast line between Malacca and Province Wellesley. The British Resident in each native state, and the European officers on his staff, besides discharging executive functions reserved to them, share in the government as members of the State Council. The native rulers obtain their revenue mainly from the export duty on tin. The population of Singapore, Penang, and Malacca, in 1881, was 423,384. There were 3,483 whites, 30,985 natives of India, 174,327 Chinese, and 174,392 Malays. The chief exports are tin, sugar, pepper, nutmegs, maize, sago, tapioca, rice, buffalo-hides, rattan, gutta-percha, India-rubber, gambier, gum, coffee, and tobacco. These are mostly the products of the islands of the Malaysian Archipelago and of the peninsula outside of the Straits Settlements. The total imports in 1886 amounted to £21,776,714, and the exports to £18,655,240. The largest amount of trade is with Netherlands India, which is nearly equaled by that with Great Britain, the Malay Peninsula, and Hong-Kong coming next, and after these Siam, India, and British Burmah.

On April 3, 1888, the war-ship "Caroline" raised the British flag on Fanning, Christmas, and Penrhyn Islands in the Micronesian archipelago. The first-named was discovered in 1798 by an American sea-captain, Edmund Fanning, and has been occupied since before 1855 by an Englishman who, with native labor, cultivates the cocoanut-palm. Christmas Island, another coral lagoon island, lies near it, to the southeast, in 2° north latitude and 158° east longitude. They are about equidistant from the Samoan, the Hawaiian, and the Society groups. Large quantities of guano have been taken from both Fanning and Christmas Islands, but the old deposits are nearly exhausted. Penrhyn Island, likewise of coral formation, in 10° south latitude and 158° west longitude, is larger than the others, having a circumference of thirty-five miles, and may prove a valuable acquisition commercially and strategically, as it has a large, deep, and safe harbor, and produces considerable quantities of *bêche-de-mer* and mother-of-pearl. It is also useful as a port of refuge, as it lies in the route between Sydney and Panama, and near the course taken by mail steamers between Auckland and San Francisco.

The Hervey or Cook Islands, lying southwest of the Society group and southeast of Samoa, in 20° south latitude and 160° west longitude, were made a British protectorate in the autumn of 1838. There are seven islands, the largest of which are Rarotonga and Mangaia, each about thirty miles in circumference. Both possess a good soil and rich vegetation. On Manki, one of the smaller islands, iron-wood is found in large quantities. Hervey Island is a large atoll, covered with cocoanut-groves. The Rarotongans are governed by a queen. They are the most civilized, well-conducted, and prosperous of all the Pacific islanders. The English Government refused their prayer for a protectorate in 1864. Since then the New Zealand authorities have repeatedly recommended the annexation of the group. Rarotonga has two small, but fairly secure harbors, and its annexation, like that of Fanning and Penrhyn Islands, is due to its prospective value as a coaling station and port of safety in case the Panama Canal is completed. The population of the Hervey Islands does not exceed 8,000. The protectorate was proclaimed by the British vice-consul in Rarotonga on October 20, and afterward in the other islands.

GREECE, a constitutional monarchy in Southeastern Europe. After gaining its independence by a successful rebellion against Turkey, the kingdom was constituted in 1830 under the protection of England, France, and Russia. The present sovereign, Georgios I, born Dec. 24, 1845, a son of King Christian of Denmark, was elected King of the Hellenes in 1863, and in 1867 married Olga, daughter of the Grand-Duke Constantine, brother of the Emperor Alexander II of Russia. The heir-apparent is Prince Konstantinos, Duke of Sparta, born Aug. 2, 1868, who was betrothed in September.1888. to the Princess Sophie of Prussia. The legislative power is lodged in a single chamber. The members of the Boulé or Legislative Assembly, 150 in number, are elected for four years by universal suffrage. The ministry, constituted May 21, 1886, was composed of the following members: President of the Council and Minister of Finance and of War, C. Tricoupis; Minister of the Interior, C. Lombardos; Minister of Justice, D. S. Voulpiotis; Minister of Worship and Public Instruction, P. Manetas; Minister of Foreign Affairs, E. Dragumis; Minister of Marine, G. Theotokis. M. Lombardos died on Sept. 5, 1888, and M. Tricoupis assumed temporarily the portfolio of the Interior.

Area and Population.—The area of Greece is 25,014 square miles, including 5,073 square miles that were detached from Turkey under pressure of the great powers in 1881. The population probably exceeds 2,200,000. The capital, Athens, had 84,903 inhabitants in 1884. The vital statistics for 1882, the last year reported, were as follow: Births, 43,157; deaths, 32,194; excess of births, 10,963; marriages, 11,186. The Hellenes constitute only about one fourth of the Greek race, as there are nearly 6,000,000 Greeks in European Turkey, Asia Minor, and the Ottoman islands of the Levant, and considerable trading colonies in Northern Africa and various parts of the East.

Commerce.—The chief exports are dried currants, of which 270,000,000 pounds were produced in 1887; olive-oil; lead, of which the mines at Laurium yielded 10,147 metric tons in 1885; silver-ore; zinc; dye-stuffs; wines, the export of which is increasing; tobacco; wool; and sponges. The annexed province of Thessaly is fertile and well cultivated, and produces large quantities of wheat and barley.

A large part of the carrying-trade of the Black Sea and the eastern parts of the Mediterranean is under the Greek flag. The merchant navy at the beginning of 1886 consisted of 72 steamers, having a tonnage of 36,272, and 3,141 sailing-vessels, of 225,224 tons, not including 6,000 coasting-vessels.

There were 320 miles of railroads in operation in 1887, while 56 miles were building, 60 miles more had been authorized, and 380 miles in addition were projected. In the session of 1888-'89 the Government proposed a network in the Peloponnesus and a line to Larissa uniting the Greek system with the great European artery. The telegraph lines had in 1886 a total length of 4,128 miles, with 4,800 miles of wires. The number of internal telegrams sent in 1885 was 544,556; of international telegrams sent and received, 181,991. The Post-Office forwarded 6,182,571 letters, 167,321 postal-cards, and 4,792,522 journals, circulars, etc. The receipts were 954,477 drachmas or francs, and the expenses 802,120 drachmas.

The Army and Navy.—Universal military service was introduced by an act that was passed in 1879. The laws of 1882 and 1886 make the total period of service 19 years, namely, 2 years with the colors, 7 or 8 in the reserve, and the remainder in the militia. The term of active service is shortened by long leaves of absence. The estimates for 1888 fix the strength of the army at 26,340 officers and men.

The navy in 1887 consisted of 2 small iron-clads, 1 unarmed cruiser, 2 iron gun-boats, 3 small steamers for coast - service that were built in England in 1885, 1 corvette, 1 transport, 1 torpedo-ship, 14 small gun-boats, and 48 torpedo-boats. The Government has ordered 4 iron-clads, which are being constructed in France at a cost of 26,000,000 drachmas. In September, 1888, a squadron left the Piræus in order to re-enforce the remonstrances of the Government regarding the seizure of Greek vessels engaged in sponge - fishing in Chios and Rhodes. The Ottoman Government ultimately released the captured vessels and crews.

Finances.—The revenue in 1887 was estimated at 94,656,907 drachmas, and the expenditure at 94,269,188 drachmas. There was a deficit in 1885 that was estimated at 61,000,000 drachmas, and one of 25,000,000 drachmas in 1886, not reckoning 75,000,000 drachmas of extraordinary expenditure for mobilizing the army at the time of the Bulgaro-Servian war. These deficits compelled the Government, when it had just resumed specie payments, to re-issue a forced paper currency, causing a depreciation of 25 per cent. The budget for 1888 makes the revenue 95,306,231 drachmas, and the expenditure 92,509,705. The debt absorbs 37,409,249 drachmas of the expenditure. The salt, petroleum, and match monopolies have been pledged for the interest on a new loan of 135,000,000 drachmas, which is applied to paying off old loans bearing 7 and 9 per cent. interest, funding the floating debt, and enlarging the navy. The debt on Jan. 1, 1888, amounted to 529,921,220 drachmas, exclusive of 104,800,300 drachmas of paper notes and 6,500,000 drachmas of treasury bills.

The Macedonian Question.—Renewed activity of the Panslavist committees in the Bulgarian part of Macedonia, impelled the leaders of the Greek population of the province to prepare for a rising in case the Bulgarian agitation should lead to rebellion. Several Greek inhabitants of the district of Monastir were arrested on the charge of high treason, the bishops of Serres and Castoria were expelled by the

Turkish authorities, and the Greek Consul there, M. Panuria, was ordered to leave the country in April, 1888. In retaliation, the Greek authorities gave the Turkish Consul at Larissa notice to quit. At the close of that month the Turkish minister at Athens, Feridoun Bey, received a letter of recall; but mediation of Great Britain and Austria resulted in his being ordered to continue at his post, and the imprisoned citizens were released. The disturbances were continued by Greek brigands until they were suppressed by the energetic action of the military. On June 20 a famous robber named Nico, who some years before had captured an English officer, Col. Singer, and obtained a ransom of $75,000, was killed near Castoria, with nine of his men, and thirteen other brigands were shot at Blatza in the same week.

GREEN, SETH, pisciculturist, born in Irondequoit, N. Y., March 19, 1817; died in Rochester, N. Y., Aug. 20, 1888. He attended the district school, but spent much of his time in

SETH GREEN.

hunting and fishing, and as he grew older was noted for his knowledge of natural history. In pursuit of the white fish he became familiar with all the great northern lakes, and long before Northern New York was known to sportsmen, he had explored its woods, and in pursuit of trout had fished in the streams and lakes of the Adirondacks. His chief business for many years was the furnishing of fish and game to his patrons. In 1837 he conceived the idea of the artificial propagation of fish, and in 1838, while on a trip to Canada, studied the habits of salmon. Finding that as soon as the spawn was cast, the male salmon and other fish eat it, he devoted his attention to methods of protecting it, and increased the yield of fish until he had raised the product to ninety-five per cent. His main principle was, that in proportion as the milt of the male fish was separated from water mixed with it in a natural state, a large percentage of eggs would become inpregnated by it. In 1864 he purchased property in Caledonia, N.Y., where he began the artificial breeding of fish, and after his success with the salmon and the trout fry, continued his undertaking until he had hatched artificially whitefish; German, California, mountain, rainbow, brook, lake, and salmon trout; carp; salmon; striped and Otsego bass; sturgeon; muscalonge; grayling; herring; wall-eyed pike; mullet; creek red-side suckers; and shiners. At his shad-hatcheries, on Connecticut river, he also produced frogs and lobsters. By invitation, in 1867, of the fish commissioners of four of the New England States, he experimented on the hatching of shad at Holyoke on Connecticut river, and by his method he produced 15,000,-000 shad fry from spawn submitted to him, and in 1868 40,000,000 shad fry were hatched by his improvements. In the first-named year he devised the form of floating hatching-box, with a wire bottom, that tilted at an inclination toward the current, with which his success was so great. On the establishment of the New York Fish Commission, in 1868, he was made a member of it, and continued so until his death, having been made superintendent in 1870. In 1869 he began shad-culture in Hudson river, and in 1870 he stocked the Susquehanna, Potomac, and Savannah rivers with shad. His great triumph was the transportation, in 1871, of 10,000 young shad from Hudson river across the continent to Sacramento river, in California, as a result of which this fish is now found in almost every stream entering the Pacific Ocean. Upward of a million marketable shad are now annually sold on the Western coast. He also introduced shad into the tributaries of the Ohio and Mississippi rivers, and stocked the lakes of New York and the Great Lakes. In 1874 he visited Au Sable river, Mich., in search of the grayling, but finding the fish had spawned, he sought for fertilized eggs and finally succeeded in hatching out these fish. He hybridized striped bass with shad; shad with herrings; brook trout with salmon trout; brook trout with California salmon; salmon trout with whitefish; and European trout with American brook trout. He was one of the earliest members of the American Fish Culture Association, and his name appears as an honorary or active member on the rolls of nearly every society in this country that has for its object fishing, hunting, or the protection of fish and game. His great familiarity with trout-fishing made him famous as a fly-caster, and at one time he was the champion for long distances. The Société d'Acclimation of Paris gave him two gold medals, and his services were recognized by various foreign governments. He published

"Trout Culture"(Rochester, 1870), and "Fish-Hatching and Fish-Catching"(1879). He was called the father of American fish-culture.

GUATEMALA, a republic of Central America; area, 121,140 square kilometres; population, Jan. 1, 1887, 1,357,900. The number of deaths in 1887 was 23,401, while there were born 59,734 children, 18,020 of whom were white and 41,714 Indian. On Jan. 1, 1888, the population had increased to 1,394.233.

Government.—The President is Gen. Manuel Lisandro Barillas. The Vice-President is Gen. Calixto Mendizábal. The Cabinet is composed of the following ministers: Foreign Affairs, Don Enrique Martínez Sobral; Public Instruction, Don Francisco Muñoz; Interior and Justice, F. Anguiano; Public Works, S. Barrutia; Finance, Don Mauricio Rodriguez; War, C. Mendizábal. The Guatemalan Minister at Washington is Don Francisco Lainfiesta; the Consul-General at New York is Mr. Jacob Baiz; the Consul at New Orleans, Don Emiliano Martinez; and at San Francisco, Don José M. Romá. The U. S. Minister for all Central America. resident at Guatemala, is Henry C. Hall; and the Consul-General, James R. Hosmer.

Army.—The regular army is distributed among the capitals of departments and a few larger towns; it varies in strength, according to the exigencies of the times. It did not exceed 2,000 in number in 1888, whereas the militia, well drilled and equipped with the best of modern arms, constitutes a force of 50,000 men.

Finances.—On Dec. 31, 1887, the national indebtedness stood as follows: Home debt, $7.659,396; foreign debt, £908,292 ($4,541,-460); total, $12,200.856. The outstanding 5-per-cent. loan of 1856 and the 6-per-cent. loan of 1869 were converted. April 30, 1888, into a 4-per-cent. consolidated bonded sterling debt up to July 1, 1891, from which date the interest will be 4¼ per cent., but the arrears of interest to be paid only at the rate of 72 per cent. The income of the Government in 1887 was $6,398,727, the outlay being an equal amount. The budget for 1888 estimates the expenditure at $4,135,294. During the summer and autumn the discount rate in Guatemala ruled at 9 per cent., and only a fraction over that for advances of funds on coffee.

Postal Service.—In 1887 the home mails forwarded 4,523,385 items of mail-matter, as compared with 3,987,489 in 1886, an increase of 535,896 items. The foreign mail-matter dispatched consisted in 1887 of 186,796 ordinary letters and postal-cards, 10,683 registered letters, and 442,845 newspapers and packages; together, 640,324 items; in 1886 there were 198,168 letters and postal-cards, 8,877 registered letters, and 410,413 newspapers and packages, aggregating 617,458 items—showing an increase of 22,866 items.

Telegraphs.—The length of wire of the national telegraphic system, early in 1887, was 2,032 miles, with 89 offices, employing 259 telegraphers, and representing an investment of

$240,515. The number of messages sent in 1887 was 406,533, 152,757 being Government dispatches. The aggregate receipts were $187,712, and the expenses $180,302. The number of cablegrams sent from the central office in 1887 was 2,457.

Railroads.—There were in running order in 1888 the line connecting Guatemala with the port of San José, and the one between Retalhulen and the port of Champerico; together, 73 miles. Work was begun on the one which, starting from Puerto Barrios on the Atlantic, in the department of Livingston, is to join, at Guatemala, the line connecting the latter with the Pacific. A contract had been made for a line between Quezaltenango and the port of Ocós. A few miles were in operation between Antigua, Guatemala, and Palin, in the department of Amatitlan, as well as the branch line between Guatemala and El Guarda-Viejo.

Commerce.—The imports and exports for five years have been as follow:

YEARS.	Imports.	Exports.
1883	$2,420,569	$5,718,341
1884	3,829,651	4,937,941
1885	3,788,135	6,069,646
1886	3,587,899	6,719,508
1887	4,241,408	9,039,391
Total	$17,817,162	$32,484,822
Excess of exports over imports		14,667,660

The duties collected in the five years aggregated $8,541,960. The countries from which the goods were imported in 1887 and the amounts in thousands of dollars, were as follow:

England	1,227	China	43
United States	706	Belgium	39
South America	649	British Honduras	¼
France	376	West Indies	25
Germany	286	Italy	23
Central America	213	Mexico	19
Spain	61		
Switzerland	51	Total	3,742

In 1887 the coffee production in Guatemala was 655,075 quintals, and there were exported, between Oct. 1, 1886, and Sept. 30, 1887, 503,305 quintals. The sugar production in 1886 was 20,773,516 quintals; in 1887, 19,266,578. The molasses production in 1886 was 3,385,972 quintals; in 1887, 3,398,001. Guatemala consumed, in 1887, 72,522 head of cattle, and 85,415 hogs. The flour consumption in the same year amounted to 7,459 tons, of which there were grown in the country 4,207 tons, and 3,252 tons imported.

The banana crop excites much attention on the Atlantic coast. The export of this fruit during 1887 was 117,514 bunches. Favorable decrees on the part of the Government, by which land can be readily purchased at a low price (30 to 35 cents an acre), have stimulated this industry. Many Americans have settled in the section referred to, and either bought plantations already producing or are planting new ones. The rich alluvial lands lying along the Dulce and Sarstoon rivers and on the shores of Lake Yzabal are well adapted for

this fruit. It is estimated that 250,000 banana-plants were set out in 1888. The profits from a well-managed banana-plantation are estimated at from $75 to $100 an acre each year. Bananas will come to perfection in their production in the course of twelve to sixteen months. The average cost per acre, up to time of production, is $25. The price paid at the port per bunch is 50 cents during seven months, and 37½ cents during five months in the year.

The American trade presents these figures:

YEARS.	Imported into the United States.	Domestic export from the United States to Guatemala.
1886	$1,957,682	$528,640
1887	2,648,718	553,179
1888	2,085,467	887,771

The rise in coffee and growing prosperity in Guatemala cause a more liberal consumption of American goods. There entered the ports of the republic, in 1887, 400 steamers and 38 sailing-vessels, of an aggregate tonnage of 510,465. Among the vessels arrived, 347 carried the American flag, 39 the British, and 25 the German. By a decree of Dec. 20, 1887, an extra duty of 15 per cent. has been levied on all imported merchandise, dating from Jan. 1, 1888. The Government decreed early in 1888 that a 3-per-cent. rebate on import duties should accrue to merchandise shipped to Guatemalan ports, on board of steamers keeping up a regular service to Atlantic ports of the republic, and 2⅕-per-cent. rebate on goods arriving by steamers trading regularly to Pacific ports. Entire freedom in all commercial transactions between Guatemala and Mexico was established in 1888, and a mixed commission is to examine and adjudicate upon all claims made by Guatemalan citizens against Mexico.

Education.—The number of schools in the twenty-two departments, in 1887, was 1,027, and the number of pupils attending, 50,000. They are non-sectarian and compulsory.

Immigration.—While there arrived in 1887, through the ports and across the frontier, 4,346 individuals, 4,061 left. Among those that arrived 2,824 were Central Americans, 410 Mexicans, 177 from the United States, 118 Frenchmen, and 124 Germans. The Government is about to appoint a commission to devise plans for the encouragement of immigration.

Hospitals.—On Jan. 1, 1887, there were under treatment in the hospitals of the country 748 individuals; there were admitted during the year 13,538 sick persons, and dismissed as cured 12,212, only 727 having died. There remained under treatment on Jan. 1, 1888, 1,343 individuals. The total expenditure for the hospital service in 1887 was $108,570.

Treaty.—The treaty of commerce and navigation and consular convention, concluded on Sept. 20, 1887, between Guatemala and Germany, was ratified and exchanged at Guatemala on June 22, 1888.

H

HARRISON, BENJAMIN, twenty-third President of the United States, born in North Bend, Ohio, Aug. 20, 1833. He is the son of John Scott Harrison, who was the son of William Henry Harrison (ninth President of the United States), who was the son of Benjamin Harrison (a signer of the Declaration of Independence), whose ancestor, Thomas Harrison, became a lieutenant-general under the Protector and a member of the Parliament that tried King Charles I., as his clearly written name on the death-warrant attests, opposite to which is his seal, which bears an eagle like that on our silver dollar. On the return of the Royalists to power, Thomas Harrison was executed. Samuel Pepys records in his "Diary" that he saw the heart removed from his body and passed about among the company. It is believed that the family of the murdered Roundhead leader came to this country soon afterward. In view of questions that have recently been brought freshly into national politics, it is pertinent to quote a brief paragraph from the inaugural address of the first President Harrison:

The greatest danger to our institutions appears to me to be, not so much in a usurpation by the Government collectively of power not granted by the people, as in the accumulation in one of the departments of powers which were assigned to others. I proceed to state in as summary a manner as I can my opinion of the sources of the evils which have been so extensively complained of, and the correctives which may be applied. Some of the former are unquestionably to be found in the defects of the Constitution. Others, in my judgment, are attributable to a misconstruction of some of its provisions. Of the former is the eligibility of the same individual to a second term of the presidency. The sagacious mind of Mr. Jefferson early saw and lamented this error. It may be observed, however, as a general truth, that no republic can commit a greater error than to adopt or continue any feature in its system of government which may be calculated to create or increase the love of power in the bosoms of those to whom necessity obliges it to commit the management of its affairs; and surely nothing is more likely to produce that effect than the long continuance in the same hands of an office of high trust. Nothing can be more corrupting, nothing more dangerous to all those noble sentiments and principles which form the character of a devoted republican patriot. When this insidious passion once takes possession of the human mind, like the love of gold, it becomes insatiable. It is the never-dying worm in his bosom, which grows with his growth and strengthens with the declining years of its victim. If this be true, it is the part of wisdom for a republic to limit the service of that officer at least to whom she has intrusted the management of her foreign relations, the execution of her laws, and the command of her armies and navies, to a period so short as to prevent his forgetting that he is the accountable agent, not the principal; the servant, not the master of the people. Until an amendment to the Constitution can be effected, public opinion, if firm in its demands, may secure the desired object. I cheerfully second it by renewing the pledge heretofore given that under no circumstances will I consent to serve a second term. I consider the veto power, given by the Constitution to the Executive of the United States, solely as a conservative power to be used only to protect the Constitution from violation, the people from the effects of hasty legislation, where their will has been probably disregarded or not well understood, and to prevent the effects of combinations, violative of the rights of minorities.

William Henry Harrison, at the age of twenty-two, married Miss Anna Symmes, to whose father, Judge Symmes, had been deeded a large tract of Western land. He carried his young bride to the post of Cincinnati, and later built her a house at North Bend, on the Ohio river. The third son born to them was John Scott Harrison, father of the subject of this sketch. John Scott was the boy who stayed upon the farm. He was of quiet temperament, industrious, fond of reading, determined to educate his children, overgenerous, not a good financial manager, and almost devoid of ambition. He was twice elected to Congress. In the division of political bodies at the breaking up of the old Whig party he became an American, and supported Bell and Everett, on the Constitution-and-Union platform, in 1860. In 1861 the Democratic State Convention of Ohio nominated him for the office of Lieutenant-Governor. In his letter declining the nomination, he said:

I could not consent to be a party candidate for office in the present condition of the country. Party spirit, in my opinion, has done more than anything else to bring about the late calamities which now so seriously afflict us, and the poison which has induced this national paralysis would not prove an efficient remedy in the restoration of the patient. The time has come when we should forget party, throw off its trammels and obligations, and stand up for the country, its union, Constitution, and laws. I was not, as you know, a supporter of Mr. Lincoln for the presidency, neither do I approve of all the acts of his administration. But it seems to me that this is not the proper time to arraign the Administration for these errors of policy, and that it is neither the part of wisdom nor patriotism to assail the Government when the enemy is thundering at the gates of the capital. Let us first settle the great question of country or no country, government or no government, union or disunion; and having accomplished this great work of duty and patriotism, we will have ample time to inquire into the alleged delinquencies of our rulers, and if we find them wanting in the Jeffersonian requirements for office, let them be condemned by a verdict of the people. I certainly owe the Republicans, as a party, no debt of political obligation, and yet I do not hesitate to say that the Administration has my warmest sympathy in its effort to put down this rebellion, and I am in favor of doing this effectually and permanently—in peace if we can, in war if we must.

John Scott Harrison married Miss Elizabeth Irwin, of Mercersburg, Penn., and they made their home on a farm five miles below that of the widowed mother, at North Bend. Mrs. Harrison was a sweet-tempered, devout woman, who looked well to the ways of her home, knit endless stockings, and brought up in simple piety her six children. Of these, Benjamin was the second. When he was sixteen years old he was sent to school at an institution on College Hill, a suburb of Cincinnati. It had been called Carey's Academy, but was at this time enlarged and renamed Farmer's College. Here Harrison's literary tastes were fostered, and history and political science became his chief delights. He entered the junior class at Miami University, Oxford, Ohio; joined the literary society, and very soon distinguished himself in debate. The drill of that little rostrum was of incalculable benefit to the speaker, who during a political canvass of intense excitement was to make one, two, or three speeches a day, for which the nation was listening.

The best known of his classmates are Hon. Milton Sayler, formerly a member of Congress, and the Rev. David Swing. One who knew him in college writes:

Harrison, as I remember, was an unpretentious but courageous student. He was respectable in languages and the sciences, and excelled in political economy and history, the former being largely due to the foundations laid under the instruction of Dr. Bishop at Farmer's College. Harrison had a good voice and a pure diction. He talked easily and fluently. His manner was indicative of much earnestness of character. He never seemed to regard life as a joke, nor the opportunities for advancement as subjects for sport. During the four years that I was with him, he impressed me with the belief that he was ambitious. As a writer and speaker, he always did his best. By this I mean that he, as a rule, made special preparation, giving as much time as possible to the matter in hand. The subject of his graduating address was "The Poor of England," and his treatment of it showed that he had sounded both the depths and the causes of this poverty. He was a protectionist at the age of nineteen. He is a protectionist still. His whole career has been illustrative of his desire to save his countrymen from the poverty which oppresses "The Poor of England."

He decided to become a lawyer, and after leaving Oxford was received into the office of Storer and Gwynne, in Cincinnati, in which city he found a home with his half-sister, wife of Dr. Eaton. At the close of his second year of study he brought his young bride, Caroline Lavinia Scott (whose father was principal of a seminary in Oxford), to the homestead at North Bend, and on concluding his studies he settled in Indianapolis, Ind. He had inherited from an aunt a plot of ground in Cincinnati, on which he raised the $800 with which they began the world. John Rea, Clerk of the United States Court, gave him desk-room. There Gen. Lew Wallace (who has written his biography) first met him, and he gives this description of his personal appearance: "He was small in stature, of slender physique, and what might be called a blonde. His eyes were gray, tinged with blue, his hair light, reminding one of what in ancient days along the Wabash was more truly than poetically described as 'a tow-head.' He was plainly dressed, and in that respect gave tokens of indifference to the canons of fashion. He was modest in manner, even diffident; but he had a pleasant voice and look, and did not lack for words to express himself." He was soon

appointed crier of the Federal Court, which during term-time brought him two dollars and a half a day, the first money he had earned.

In August, 1854, a son, Russell, was born to them, and Mr. Harrison removed the little household to a home of their own. It was one story high, and had three rooms and a lean-to kitchen. Sometimes Mrs. Harrison em-

MRS. BENJAMIN HARRISON.

ployed a servant, but she was her own cook as well as nurse. Her husband filled the water-buckets and brought in the wood before he left for the office. Of these days he says: "They were close times, I tell you. A five-dollar bill was an event. There was one good friend through it all—Robert Browning, the druggist. I shall always recollect him with gratitude. He believed in me. When things were particularly tight I could go into his store and borrow five dollars from the drawer. A ticket in its place was all that was required." Not long after this, Harrison formed a law partnership with William Wallace.

In 1858 a daughter, Mary, was born. In 1860 Mr. Harrison became Republican candidate for Reporter of the Supreme Court, and he went into the canvass with his usual energy and enthusiasm, and was elected.

A year later came President Lincoln's call for troops. Business led Harrison to call upon Gov. Morton, who was found pacing gloomily up and down his room. When the matter in hand was disposed of, the never-resting subject of the state of the country was broached. Gov. Morton expressed deep anxiety and bitter mortification that there had been no response to the call for troops. Pointing to a building in process of erection, he said: "The people are following their own private affairs, so that it has come to be a serious question what I shall do next to arouse them." To the man at his side this was the final and irresistible appeal. He said, simply: "Governor, if I can be of any service, I will go." Gov. Morton replied instantly: "You can raise a regiment, but it is asking too much of you to go into the field with it; you have just been elected Reporter of the Supreme Court. But go to work and raise it, and we will find somebody to command it." Harrison replied that he could not;

that if he influenced others to go, he must be with them. "Very well, then," said the Governor, "if you want to go, you can command them." "I do not know that I want to command them." replied Harrison; "I do not know anything about military tactics. So, if you can find some suitable person of experience, I am not at all anxious to take the command." He left the court-house and, without going home, bought a military cap, engaged a fifer and drummer, returned to his office, flung out a flag from the window, and began recruiting for Company A. The regiment was soon full, and the Governor, without solicitation, commissioned him as its colonel. It was designated as the Seventieth Indiana, and was brigaded with the Seventy-ninth Ohio, the One Hundred and Second, One Hundred and Fifth, and One Hundred and Twenty-ninth Illinois, under Brig.-Gen. William T. Ward, of Kentucky. The organization of the brigade remained unchanged during the war, Harrison holding the right wing, as he held the older commission. Gen. Wallace has made a collection of letters written by various men in the regiment, some of whom are now well known. The following extracts are from these letters:

"We were encamped near Nashville, and, as all who were there at the time remember, it was one of the coldest winters on record. I remember that during one of the cold nights I was on picket, and I saw a man approaching from the direction of the officers' quarters. I halted him, and, when he gave the countersign and advanced, I saw it was Gen. (then Col.) Harrison. He had a large can filled with hot coffee, and, when I asked him what he was doing, he said he was afraid that some of the pickets would freeze to death, and he knew some hot coffee would help the men to keep alive. He was the most welcome visitor I ever met, for I really believe I would have frozen before morning had not the coffee been brought. After leaving me, the general passed on to all the other pickets."

"On the 14th of May, the day before the battle of Resaca, our regiment was ordered to advance through a strip of woodland, which ended at the foot of a hill. On the brow of an opposite hill were the rebels, and the position we were ordered to take put us in direct range of their guns. We were subjected to a terrific fire, and, as we could see no reason why we should occupy such an exposed position, many of us wanted to fall back. Gen. Harrison was with us, on foot, at the head of the column, and he said we would obey orders and stay there if we died. Our ranks were thinned by the bullets of the enemy, but we held our position, and Gen. Harrison never left his advanced post."

"No man was dearer to the boys in the line than Gen. Harrison, and it rose from one single element in the man's character—his determination to take the leading part in whatever he asked his men to do. I shall never forget the sight I had of him waving his sword and shouting, in that shrill voice for which he was noted, 'Come on, boys!' One scene has always lived in my memory. Our old chaplain, Allen, a man who was beloved by all the boys, and for whom almost every man in the regiment would have lost his life, conducted services on Sunday, with Gen. Harrison (then colonel) and Lieut.-Col. Sam Merrill assisting. I have often heard Gen. Harrison offer up the prayer for the boys' welfare and protection down there on those Southern fields, so far away from home, and many times have heard him address the boys in place of the chaplain."

"Going out a civilian and without any military training whatever, he became one of the closest students of the science and art of war there was in the army. As he does in everything else, he threw his whole heart into the work of making himself a proficient officer and his regiment a well-disciplined body of men. And he succeeded in an eminent degree in both instances. He was a very sympathetic man. Whenever a soldier was hurt in the discharge of his duty, none was readier to offer sympathy than he. And as a result of this trait of his character, he always looked after the welfare of his regiment with scrupulous care. He never went to bed at night without knowing that the boys were going to have as good a breakfast as could be secured in the morning."

"On the Atalanta campaign Harrison's regiment one day crossed a small bridge over a sluggish stream and advanced through an open field toward a neighboring crest. While they were in the field the pickets just over the hill came flying back, being driven in by the advance of the rebels in force. Harrison's regiment, and the others making up the brigade, pressed rapidly up toward the crest, and when they reached the top they met the enemy face to face. It was a fierce struggle to see who could hold the commanding position, and the fight became fierce and bloody, a hand-to-hand encounter in which soldiers on each side thrust bayonets and clubbed each other with muskets. Just at that time the rebels captured a battery on the Union right, and turned the guns on our men. It looked like disaster, indeed, and doubly so because the mule-trains, close in the rear of the troops, were filling up the road and clogging the bridge in a way that made a stampede imminent. Just then I saw Gen. Harrison riding up and down in front of the line, waving his sword and calling on the boys to stand their ground. Nothing but such an example on the part of the commander could have held the troops. They retook their battery, and prevented what looked at one time to be disaster and complete ruin."

"At Peach Tree Creek our regiment charged on their [the Confederates'] line and cleaned it out, but we lost 250 men in half an hour, so you may know we had hot work. In this fight Harrison, still a colonel, took the lead. As he swung himself into line not six feet from me he said: 'Come on, boys; we've never been licked yet, and we won't begin now. We haven't much am munition, but if necessary we can give them the cold steel, and before we get licked we can club them down; so, come on.' And we went, glad to fight by the side of 'Little Ben,' who shirked nothing, and took just the same chance of getting a bullet through the heart as we did. Not a soldier but liked Ben Harrison. We won the day after a hard fight. For his bravery on that day Harrison was promoted at the special recommendation of Gen. Hooker."

"I believe it was twenty-four years ago that Dr. Jones and myself found him alone taking care of the poor wounded boys of his regiment that suffered so severely that day. With his coat off, and sleeves rolled up, he worked far after midnight, until every wounded man was attended to."

The following is the official letter of Harrison's commander, Gen. Joseph Hooker, which was followed by his promotion:

HEADQUARTERS NORTHERN DEPARTMENT, CINCINNATI, OHIO, Oct. 31, 1864.

HON. E. M. STANTON, Secretary of War:

I desire to call the attention of the department to the claims of Col. Benjamin Harrison of the Seventieth Indiana Volunteers for the promotion to the rank of Brigadier-General of Volunteers. Col. Harrison first joined me in command of a brigade of Ward's division in Lookout valley preparative to entering upon what is called the Campaign of Atlanta. My attention was first attracted to this young officer by the superior excellence of his brigade in discipline and instruction, the result of his labor, skill, and devotion. With more foresight than I have witnessed in any officer of his experience, he seemed to act upon the principle that success depended upon the thorough preparation in discipline and *esprit* of his command for conflict, more than on any influence that could be exerted on the field itself, and when collision came his command vindicated his wisdom as much as his valor. In all of the achievements of the Twentieth Corps in that campaign Col. Harrison bore a conspicuous part. At Resaca and Peach Tree Creek the conduct of himself and command was especially distinguished. Col. Harrison is an officer of superior abilities, and of great professional and personal worth. It gives me great pleasure to commend him favorably to the Honorable Secretary, with the assurance that his preferment will be a just recognition of his services and martial accomplishments. Very respectfully, your obedient servant,

JOSEPH HOOKER, *Major-General commanding.*

When Col. Harrison had been two years continuously in the field, the War Department detailed him for special duty in Indiana. In five weeks he had completed this duty, and, hurrying back to Chattanooga, was given command of a brigade and transferred to Nashville. After Sherman reached Savannah, Harrison was ordered to join him, and was on his way when he was stricken down with scarlet fever, and lay dangerously ill for several weeks, and then rejoined Sherman at Goldsboro, N. C., in command of a brigade, where he remained until the end of the war.

Before his return he had been offered a partnership in the law-firm in Indianapolis of Porter & Fishback, which he immediately entered, the name being Porter, Harrison, & Fishback. A case of national interest was one in which Gen. Harrison, by appointment of President Grant, appeared against Thomas A. Hendricks. Gov. Hendricks appeared for Lambdin P. Milligan, who sued Gen. Hovey and others for damages sustained while working in the paint-room of the State prison, where he was placed on a charge of conspiracy against the United States Government. Harrison conducted the defence. The arguments by which he proved the fact of the conspiracy of the Sons of Liberty, or Knights of the Golden Circle, can not be given at length, but the closing paragraphs of his speech will suffice to illustrate his manner of treatment:

The nation, as the individual, through its officers, has the right to strike before it is struck. It is a right given from God. If a man is threatening my life, his hand lifted with the dagger to strike me to the heart, I am not to wait until the blow is struck. The law acquits me if I strike him dead at my feet. How much more shall these defendants stand acquit before the courts and their fellow-men who, seeing the deadliness of the peril, struck the treason before it could strike the nation? I think I have shown you now, not merely that there was peril, but that, from the information he had, Gen. Hovey was justified in arresting Milligan and bringing him to trial before the military commission. If the State had broken out in rebellion and insurrection, and your own homes been invaded by these ruthless men, your families outraged, insulted, and slain, could you have ever forgiven the recreant commander of the department, who, apprised of the danger, failed to interpose his military power? Senator Hendricks will have a great deal to say to you about the security which the Con-

stitution guarantees to life, person, and property. It is indeed a grand birthright that our fathers have given us; but, gentlemen, it was a legacy handed down to the loyal and the law-abiding. The law covers with its broad and impenetrable shield the true-hearted citizen, not the traitor and the law-breaker. Yet the gentleman comes to make appeals from a Constitution which his client would have destroyed, and in behalf of a liberty which would have been exercised for the destruction of our Government. He complains of a restraint which was in the interests of public peace. Listen to him, then, give your full accord to all he may say of the right of the citizen to be secure in person and property, but remember, those guarantees are to the loyal and the law-abiding.

If his Honor says to you that this question of the existence of war in the State is one for you, I ask you to take the definition of war given by Mr. Hendricks, and tell me on oath whether, in the summer of 1864, there was not a conflict of organized forces in the State of Indiana—whether Gen. Hovey, with home forces and the few veterans who were at home, was not arrayed upon the one hand, and if upon the other Bowles and Milligan and Horsey, with their secret legions of armed traitors, were not organized into an army within the State for the destruction of our Government. There was not more truly a state of war in Charleston harbor before the gun was fired that hurled the first shot against Sumter, than existed in the State of Indiana at the time of which I have been speaking.

And what less shall be said of the ge   m   who composed the commission that tried the plaintiff? One of them, now the marshal of this district, maimed for life, drags himself about disfigured by the loss of a left arm. Yonder, on the bloody sides of Kenesaw, he gave an arm, almost a life, for the country which he, and these his comrades, loved so well. While he lay upon the field bleeding, almost dying, here in Grand Council in the State of Indiana Milligan and his associates were plotting treason; and now they seek to rob him of the little savings from the office which a grateful country and a President who honors his valor have conferred upon him, in order to enrich traitors.

Gen. Harrison was elected United States Senator from Indiana in 1880, and filled that office for six years. His views on the political issues of the time are to be found in various speeches, some delivered from the platform and some on the floor of the Senate. On the subject of civil-service reform he said, in 1882: "I am an advocate of civil-service reform. My brief experience at Washington has led me to utter the wish, with an emphasis I do not often use, that I might be forever relieved of any connection with the distribution of public patronage. I covet for myself the free and unpurchased support of my fellow-citizens, and long to be able to give my time and energy solely to the public affairs that legitimately relate to the honorable trust which you have committed to me. It is easy for theorists to make suggestions upon this subject which in their opinion would cure all existing evils. I assure you it is more difficult to frame a law that shall be safe and practical in its application." He vigorously opposed the "green-back" theory and the demand for "fiat" money, holding that the only safe and stable currency was one based on gold and silver. In 1886, discussing the tariff question, he said: "We need not have any fear that wages will anywhere be too high. We have a common interest that a margin for comfort may be added to the necessaries of life. I am sure that none of us are so anxious for cheap goods that we would be willing to admit 'the spoils of the poor' into our houses. It seems strange that we should find a party among us opposing the protective principle when even the provinces of Great Britain are adopting it and finding increased prosperity. France and Germany still embody this idea in their legislation. There may be fair ground for debate as to the rate which particular articles of import should bear, or as to whether this or that article should not be on the free list; but that our legislation should discriminate in favor of our own country, her industries and laboring people, ought not to be questioned. I want no other evidence that wages and all the other conditions

prompt payment of wages in money. I believe that the number of working-hours can, in most of our industries, be reduced without a serious loss to production, and with great gain to the health, comfort, and contentment of our working-classes. I advocated and voted for the law of Congress prohibiting the importation of laborers under contracts made abroad, and believe that such legislation is just and wise." On the subject of the navy he declared: "I am in favor of putting upon the sea enough American ships, armed with the most improved ordnance, to enforce the just rights of our people against any foreign agressor. It is a good thing in the interests of peace and commerce to show the flag of our navy in the ports where the flag of commerce is unfurled." On the "South-

BENJAMIN HARRISON'S RESIDENCE, INDIANAPOLIS, INDIANA.

of labor are better here than in Europe than this—the laboring men and women of Europe are coming this way, and they come to stay. Millions of earnings have gone back to the old countries to pay the passage-money of friends hither, but the steerage of the returning vessel is empty." On the labor question he said: "If any railroad or other business enterprise can not earn enough to pay the labor that operates it and the interest on its bonds, no right-minded man can hesitate to say which ought to be paid first. The men who have invested money in the enterprise, or loaned money on its securities, ought to have the right to stop the business when net earnings fail; but they can not fairly appropriate the earnings of the engineer or brakeman or laborer. I believe the law should require the

ern question" he said, in February, 1888: "The truth to-day is, that the colored Republican vote of the South, and with it and by consequence the white Republican vote of the South, is deprived of all effective influence in the administration of this Government. The additional power given by the colored population of the South in the Electoral College, and in Congress, was more than enough to turn the last election for President, and more than enough to reverse, yes, largely more than reverse, the present Democratic majority of the House of Representatives. Have we the spirit to insist that everywhere, North and South, in this country of ours no man shall be deprived of his ballot by reason of his politics? There is not in all this land a place where any rebel soldier is subject to any restraint, or is denied the fullest exercise of the elective franchise. Shall we not insist that what is true of those who fought to destroy the country shall be true of every man who fought for it, or loved it, as the black man of the South did; that to belong to Abraham Lincoln's party shall be respectable and reputable everywhere in America?" In a speech delivered in Indianapolis, in June, 1884, he said: "I would not dispose of an acre of the public land otherwise than under the homestead laws." Referring to "trusts," he said: "We must find some way to stop such combinations."

In the Republican National Convention held in Chicago in June, 1888, on the first ballot fourteen candidates were voted for. John Sherman received the highest number of votes, 225; Walter Q. Gresham, 111; Chauncey M. Depew, 99; Russel A. Alger, 84; Benjamin Harrison, 83. On the eighth ballot, Sherman received 118; Alger, 100; Harrison, 544. Gen. Harrison accordingly became the party's candidate for President, and at the election in November he was elected, carrying every Northern State except New Jersey and Connecticut, and receiving 233 electoral votes, to 168 for Mr. Cleveland (see UNITED STATES).

President Harrison was inaugurated on Monday, March 4, 1889, in the midst of a rainstorm, delivering a long inaugural address, and the next day sent to the Senate the following nominations for Cabinet officers: Secretary of State, James G. Blaine, of Maine; Secretary of the Treasury, William Windom, of Minnesota; Secretary of War, Redfield Proctor, of Vermont; Secretary of the Navy, Benjamin F. Tracy, of New York; Attorney-General, William H. H. Miller, of Indiana; Postmaster-General, John Wanamaker, of Pennsylvania; Secretary of the Interior, John W. Noble, of Missouri; Secretary of Agriculture, Jeremiah M. Rusk, of Wisconsin. The Senate went into executive session, and within ten minutes confirmed all the nominations.

(See "Life of Benjamin Harrison," by Lew Wallace, Philadelphia, 1888.)

HAWAII, a constitutional kingdom occupying the Hawaiian or Sandwich Islands, in the Pacific Ocean. The reigning sovereign is Kalakaua I, born Nov. 16, 1836, who was elected by the people in 1874. The heiress presumptive to the throne is the King's eldest sister, Princess Lydia Kamaheha Liliuokalani, born Sept. 2, 1838, whose husband, John O. Dominis, is Governor of Oahu and Maui. The Legislature consists of 24 Representatives and 24 Nobles, who sit together. A new Constitution was proclaimed on July 6, 1887. The nobles, who were formerly nominated by the King, were made elective. The electoral body consists of all the adult male citizens. The nobles, in addition to the educational qualifications required in the representatives, must possess a certain amount of property. Their term is six years, while the representatives are elected for two years. The Legislative Assembly has power to amend the Constitution. The absolute veto formerly exercised by the King was changed into a conditional veto, which can be annulled by a two-third vote of the Assembly, by the Constitution of 1887, which also established the principle of ministerial responsibility. The present Cabinet is composed of the following members: Minister of Foreign Affairs, J. Anskin; Minister of the Interior, L. A. Thurston; Attorney-General, C. W. Ashford; Minister of Finance, W. L. Green.

Area and Population.—The area of the kingdom and the population of the inhabited islands on Dec. 27, 1884, when the last census was taken, were as follow:

ISLANDS.	Square miles.	Population.
Oahu	660	28,068
Hawaii	4,470	24,991
Maui	500	15,970
Kauai and Niihau	670	8,935
Molokai and Lanai	3:0	2,614
Kahulawe	60	......
Total	6,670	80,578

Honolulu, the capital, on the island of Oahu, had 20,487 inhabitants. In 1884 the natives numbered 40,014, a decrease of 4,084 since 1878. The foreign population is rapidly increasing, and the soil has passed in a large measure into the hands of Americans and other foreigners, who cultivate sugar-cane, with imported labor, Portuguese, Chinese, and latterly Japanese. The number of arrivals in 1886 was 3,725; departures, 2,189. Of the arrivals, 1,766 came from China and 929 from Japan.

Commerce.—The totals for the foreign commerce of the past three years are given in the subjoined table:

YEARS.	Imports.	Domestic exports.	Total exports.	Customs receipts.
1887	$4,944,000	$9,485,000	$9,529,000	$595,000
1886	4,875,000	10,340,000	10,457,000	580,000
1885	8,581,000	8,959,000	9,069,000	502,000

In 1862 the total imports were only $998,000 in value; the exports of domestic produce, $587,000; the total exports, $838,000; and the customs revenue, $107,000. The commerce of 1887 was distributed among the countries having commercial relations with Hawaii in the following proportions:

COUNTRIES.	Imports.	Exports.
United States	$3,648,000	$9,491,000
Great Britain	662,000	....
China and Japan	262,000	6,000
Germany	185,000	....
Australia	158,000	5,000
Other countries	29,000	27,000
Total	$4,944,000	$9,529,000

The export of sugar in 1887 was valued at $8,695,000; of rice, $554,000; of skins, $104,000; of bananas, $55,000; of molasses, $11,000; of wool, $7,000; of other products, $103,000. The imports of bullion and specie were

$900,353 in 1887, and the exports $21,276. The principal seaport is Honolulu, where in 1887 imports of the value of $4,573,196 were landed, and exports of the value of $8,216,458 were shipped.

Navigation.—The number of merchant vessels entered in 1887 was 254, of 210,703 tons, against 310, of 222,372 tons, in 1886, and 253, of 190,138 tons in 1885. The vessels and tonnage entered in 1887 were as to nationality in the following proportions:

FLAG.	Number.	Tons.
American......................	174	118,547
English......................	19	20,940
German......................	8	4,950
Hawaiian.	43	59,257
Other......................	10	7,599
Total..................	254	210,703

The mercantile marine in 1887 counted 57 vessels, including 15 steamers. The aggregate tonnage was 12,244.

Finances.—The budget is voted biennially. In that for 1886-'88 the receipts are estimated as follows: Customs, $992,066; internal commerce, $226,842; internal imposts, $766,422; fines, fees, etc., $92,299; sales of Government property, $513,732; loans, $1,-811,800; Postal savings-bank, $319,933; miscellaneous, $149,482; total, $4,812,576.

The expenditures voted under the various heads were as follow: Civil list and appanages, $137,892; Legislative Assembly and Privy Council, $60,284; Justice, $154,566; Foreign Affairs, $257,996; Interior, $1,204,214; Finances, $727,264; police, etc., $279,819; instruction, $165,913; Board of Health, $247,907; miscellaneous, $1,476,430; total, $4,712,285.

By virtue of a law signed on Sept. 1, 1886, a debt of $2,000,000 was contracted in London at 6 per cent. interest, in order to pay off anterior loans. The capital of the debt on April 1, 1888, was $1,936,500.

HAYTI, a republic in the West Indies. covering the western third of the island of Santo Domingo. (For details relating to territorial divisions, see "Annual Cyclopædia" for 1883.) The population was estimated in 1887 at 960,000.

Government.—The provisional President of the Republic is Gen. Légitime. His Cabinet was composed of the following ministers: Foreign Affairs and Justice, Eugène Margron; Interior, Gen. Isman Piquant; Finance and Commerce, Alexander Rossignol; War and Navy, Gen. Anselme Prophète; Agriculture, Dr. Roche Grellier.

The United States Minister at Port-au-Prince, is Dr. John E. W. Thompson; the Haytian Minister to the United States is Stephen Preston; the American Consul at Cape Haytien is Stanislas Gontier; the Haytian Consul-General at New York, Ebenezer D. Bassett.

Army and Navy.—The army is recruited partially through conscription, and in part by volunteers. The usual exemptions are legally admitted, the conscripts serving seven years and the volunteers four. The strength of the permanent army is 6,828. The navy consists of four war-steamers, one of which is armored, mounting four guns.

Telegraphs.—In 1888, cable communication between Hayti and Cuba was opened, the first message having been received at Mole Saint Nicolas from Aguadores, Cuba, on April 15. Mole Saint Nicolas is the Haytian landing-point of the cable with which all the towns of the republic will be connected by land wires.

Postal Service.—There were in operation, in 1886, 31 post-offices, which forwarded 233,872 letters and postal-cards, and 181,520 newspapers and sample packages; the receipts being 69,200 francs, and the expenses 137,215.

Finances.—The national indebtedness amounted in 1888 to $13,500,000, composed of a foreign debt, the loan of 1875, of $4,320,000, and the home debt of $9,180,000. The outlay in 1885-'86, amounting to $6,412,956, was met by an income of equal amount, while in 1887-'88 the expenditure was limited to $4,066,236.

Up to the year 1881 hardly any coin but Mexican and American silver was to be met with. The latter gradually became scarce, and in its stead the country was invaded by Mexican coin. The American silver dollar then commanded a premium of 10 to 15 per cent. above the Mexican. When subsequently, in 1881, the National Bank was established at Port-au-Prince, with branch banks at Aux Cayes, Jacmel, Petit Goave, and Gonaives, a newly coined Haytian silver dollar began to circulate, the "gourde," which was not worth over 80 cents in American gold. In spite of its lower intrinsic value, captains of vessels who had to collect freight in Haytian ports were frequently paid in Haytian dollars, which were charged them in account 4s. 4d. English. On refusing to submit to this unfavorable exchange, their ships' papers were simply retained. This proceeding has since become generally known, and captains usually provide themselves for ships' expenses in Hayti with the necessary silver coin abroad, and take good care to stipulate in bills of lading the coin in which they are to be paid.

Commerce.—In 1887 there were imported into Hayti $6,854,597 worth of merchandise, while the export of Haytian products reached $10,185,366. The chief exports were: Coffee, 49,811,781 pounds; logwood, 227,595,803 pounds; cocoa, 3,634,860 pounds; cotton, 2,255,540 pounds; and besides hides and skins, fustic, lignum vitæ, honey, cotton-seed, tortoise-shell, mahogany, wax, old copper, and orange-peel. The American trade with Hayti has been as follows:

FISCAL YEAR.	Import into the United States.	Domestic export to Hayti.
1885............................	$2,471,436	$3,227,059
1886............................	2,648,992	2,968,147
1887............................	1,752,587	3,059,818
1888............................	2,918,829	4,322,658

The increase both in imports and exports was due to the rise in coffee, which enabled Haytians to import American goods on a more liberal scale. From similar causes, the maritime movement in the leading ports also exhibited great activity, as represented by these figures, showing the record of vessels entered in 1887:

PORTS.	Vessels.	Tonnage.	OF WHICH WERE STEAMERS.	
			Vessels.	Tonnage.
Cape Haytien	236	239,257	163	180,651
Port-au-Prince	227	246,014	146	225,754
Gonaïves	184	111,244	83	100,116
Aux Cayes	99	94,635	71	87,777
Total	726	691,150	463	504,298

Events of 1888.—On June 2, President Salomon, then in his seventy-fifth year and with failing health, apprehending a revolutionary outbreak to upset his severe *régime*, expelled Generals Manigat and Légitime. The capital had meanwhile been put under martial law, but when the two alleged conspirators departed, it was released from it on June 4. On July 4 and 7, incendiary fires occurred at Port-au-Prince—the usual indication in Hayti that a revolution is at hand—causing the destruction of one fifth of the city and the loss of ten lives. Two rebels who tried to set fire to another quarter were summarily shot. As there was considerable discontent with Gen. Salomon's *régime*, Gen. Baibrond Canal asked the aid of the North to make an end of his rule. Gen. Thélémaque, commanding the Department of the North at Cape Haytien, responded to his summons, and arranged a general uprising there, which took place on August 5, and was quickly and willingly joined by the Departments of the Northwest and Artibonite, of which Gonaïves and St. Marc are the capitals. Salomon, seeing that resistance to such an uprising was vain, abdicated and left the country. Thereupon a general election under the supervision of a provisional government was held, and eighty-four "constituants," or electors, were chosen. Thélémaque, Boisrond, Légitime, and Hyppolite formed a part of the supervisory provisional government. When the names of the eighty-four electors became known, it was evident that Thélémaque would receive a majority of their votes. But before they could assemble at Port-au-Prince a riot occurred there on September 28, on which occasion Thélémaque met his death. Immediately thereafter, and before even a large majority of the electors could arrive at Port-au-Prince, Légitime called upon those who were present and in his interest to declare themselves a regularly constituted assembly and to vest in him supreme power. This was done by thirty three electors, little more than a third of the whole number. Seizing then upon the treasury, the arms at the capital, and the war-vessels in its harbor, Légitime assumed a dictatorship. But

the whole country was shocked at the supposed murder of Gen. Thélémaque, and another general uprising of the northern departments instantly took place. A central revolutionary committee was formed by the three protesting departments, and Jacmel, too, raised its voice in their favor. Gen. Florvil Hyppolite was named president of that committee. Thereupon Légitime, powerless to subjugate his adversaries on land, initiated a blockade, maintained only by two vessels, the "Dessalines" and "Toussaint l'Ouverture," running in and out of Port-au-Prince. Finally he got himself into trouble with the United States by capturing, on October 21, the American steamship "Haytian Republic." While she was coming out of St. Marc, she was seized by the cruiser "Dessalines," and taken to Port-au-Prince. On November 19, the Department of State at Washington received official information that the prize court, on November 3, had condemned the vessel. The United States minister immediately protested against the proceedings, alleging that the prize court was illegally constituted, and appealed to a higher court. He also advised the captain of the seized vessel to refuse to surrender the craft. The United States man-of-war "Boston" arrived on the same day, to support the protest of the United States minister. The President of the United States, in his message of December 3, made the following allusion to this case and another in which a sailing-vessel had been seized:

The tenure of power has been so unstable amid the war of factions that has ensued since the expulsion of President Salomon, that no Government constituted by the will of the Haytian people has been recognized as administering responsibly the affairs of that country. Our representative has been instructed to abstain from interference between the warring factions, and a vessel of our navy has been sent to Haytian waters to sustain our minister and for the protection of the persons and property of American citizens. Due precautions have been taken to enforce our neutrality laws and prevent our territory from becoming the base of military supplies for either of the warring factions. Under color of a blockade, of which no reasonable notice had been given, and which does not appear to have been efficiently maintained, a seizure of vessels under the American flag has been reported, and, in consequence, measures to prevent and redress any molestation of our innocent merchantmen have been adopted.

A week later, the United States war-vessels "Galena" and "Yantic" were dispatched to Port-au-Prince, arriving there on December 20, and demanding the surrender of the seized steamer. The release of the latter to Rear-Admiral Luce was not made under protest, but Gen. Légitime reserved the right to appeal to the United States courts. It was thought at Port-au-Prince that this reservation was made principally for the benefit of his followers, who were led by him and the decision of the Court of Claims to believe the seizure of the vessel lawful, and that the vessel would be held and converted into a man-of-war. An indemnity was also to be claimed in the usual form through the American minister to Gen. Légitime, the amount demanded in behalf of the owners being $200,000; that for the passengers and crew, $150,000. The "Haytian Republic" was to be formally accepted by Rear-Admiral Luce on December 24. On December 31, the Secretary of State at Washington received the copy of a decree, dated December 10, issued by the Légitime Government, closing all the northern ports— St. Marc, Gonaïves, Port de Paix, and Cape Haytien to foreign commerce provisionally.

HOLLAND. See NETHERLANDS.

HONDURAS, a republic in Central America, area, 39,600 square miles; population in 1887; 329,134.

Government.—The President is Gen. Luis Bográn, whose term will expire on Nov. 29, 1891. The Cabinet is composed of the following ministers: Foreign Affairs, Licenciado Don Jerónimo Zelaya; Justice, Public Works, and War, Señor R. Alvarado; Interior, Señor A. Gomez; Finance, Señor F. Planas; Agriculture, Señor A. Zelaya. The United States Minister is Hon. H. C. Hall, resident at Guatemala; the American Consul at Ruatan and Trujillo is William C. Burchard, at Tegucigalpa, Daniel W. Herring; the Consular Agent at Yuscaran is Theodore Koehnke. The Consul-General at New York is Jacob Baiz; at San Francisco, William V. Wells.

Finance.—The outstanding remainder of the $25,000,000 foreign debt, contracted in 1869, is gradually being canceled through the operations of the custom-houses, where 40 per cent. of the duties may be paid with such old bonds. The consolidated internal indebtedness is represented by $700,000 bonds in circulation, and there is also a floating debt of $200,000. In February the Government made a contract for the founding of a national bank at Tegucigalpa. In March a contract was made with Don Gilberto Larios for the establishment at Tegucigalpa of the Banco Centro-Americano, with a capital of $600,000, and the privilege to increase it to $1,000,000.

Treaties.—In January the Congress of Honduras ratified the treaty of commerce and navigation signed in January, 1887, at Guatemala, between Honduras and Great Britain, together with the one made with Germany, under date of Dec. 12, 1887, and also the Central American treaty of friendship agreed to between the five republics on Feb. 16, 1887.

Border Questions.—In January, commissioners delegated by the governments of Honduras and Nicaragua met on the boundary-line between the two republics, at points in dispute between the departments of Cholnteca and Nueva Segovia, in order to make the necessary surveys for the settlement of this question.

Railroads.—Construction on the Honduras North Coast Railway was begun by the contractor George E. Mansfield, of Boston, in May. The road is being built under a concession originally granted in July, 1884, by the Government of Honduras to W. Allstrom, who organized the Honduras North Coast Railway and Improvement Company in New Orleans. The concession is for 99 years, and grants nine square miles of land for each mile of line built, also exemption from taxation and the privilege of importing material for construction free of duty. The line surveyed is 150 miles long, the termini being Trujillo and Puerto Cortez, and it passes through extensive forests of mahogany, cedar, and iron-wood, and will open up the Sierra Madre mountains on their northern slopes. According to the grant, the company is obliged to have 75 miles of road in operation by July, 1889. The only railroad in Honduras at present is a line of 38 miles from Puerto Cortez, which is a portion of a projected transisthmian route to the Bay of Fonseca. The Honduras Railway Company was incorporated in London in May, with a capital of £8,000,000, to complete this enterprise, and a New York syndicate has been found to construct another line from Trujillo to the Bay of Fonseca, passing through the principal mining districts, and connecting with the capital, Tegucigalpa. The London *concessionnaire* sent in June three engineers to Puerto Cortez, for the purpose of completing the survey of the road over a track of 40 miles from Ojos de Agua toward the Atlantic, and they began their work on July 7.

New Steamship Line.—In September the Government made a contract with F. L. Philips & Co. for the establishment of regular steamship communication between the coast and bay islands, granting them certain privileges.

Mining.—Honduras is rapidly becoming an active mining country, and many miners are going there from the United States. The pay is usually $50 a month, with board and traveling expenses, for "hand-drill" men, as little machinery is used, and about $75 for mill engineers. The climate in the interior is represented as being healthful. To mining companies Honduras offers the advantages of surface mining, cheap labor, and unknown but certain mineral wealth. The Government is also willing to make liberal concessions. The New York and Honduras Rosario Mining Company, at San Jacinto, has opened tunnels driven direct on the vein down to the 650-foot level, and is producing 80 tons of ore a day. The levels are 100 feet apart, and vary in length from 600 to 1,400 feet on the vein, connected by winzes at convenient distances almost to the lowest level. The ore consists of the decomposed sulphurets of copper, iron, and some lead, carrying considerable chloride and native silver in a quartz gangue. A three-hearth roasting-furnace has been erected for chloridizing the concentrates, which consist largely of undecomposed sulphurets. The product in the summer of 1888 was from 40 to 50 bars of bullion a month, weighing 100 to 110 pounds each, and running from 600 to 800 fine in silver and 10 to 17 fine in gold. The Los Angeles Mining and Smelting Company, Valle de los Angeles, resumed ore-extraction at the Animas mine in August. The works consist of two twenty-ton water-jacket furnaces. The ore is an argentiferous galena. Many other companies have been formed.

Molybdate of lead, or wulfenite, is of frequent occurrence in Honduras, principally in the mining districts of Los Angeles and San Juancito, where limestone and slate occur.

Commerce. — The American trade shows a steady increase, and has developed as follows:

FISCAL YEAR.	Import into the United States.	Domestic export to Honduras.
1886	$780,559	$423,104
1887	857,919	425,741
1888	957,331	672,796

Condition of the Country. — One of the daily papers of Tegucigalpa drew, on August 30, the following sketch of the happy change in the republic under the present administration:

Formerly the sanguinary ground of battles and passions, we meet to-day in the new Honduras, a busy camp where foreigners and natives vie with each other to advance this country, in as short a time as possible, to the high standing which Providence and Nature have destined it to occupy in this progressive period. There are over eighteen foreign mining companies at work to explore the rich and precious veins of gold and silver which abound in this country; there are a number of improvement companies engaged to cultivate the ground and to navigate the rivers; and there are at present three important railroad lines partly under consideration and construction.

When the subject of a highway to the coast was brought to the attention of Gen. Bogran, he was found equal to the occasion. Simple as this need will appear to the reader, it must be remembered that for three hundred years this country had found in the pack-mule not merely its only means of transportation, but thereby all the requirements of the producer, merchant, and householder had been met. "All roads lead to Rome," and all highways started from the Imperial City, and thence continued to the projected point. A Latin race would naturally follow such teachings, and hence Soto had a boulevard road built from Tegucigalpa to the Cerro de Hule (which has an elevation of five thousand feet) toward the Pacific coast, extending it twenty-five miles; but as neither a wagon nor the parts of a wagon could well be carried by the pack-mule over the intervening mountains between the terminus of this boulevard and the port, it presented simply an admirable road-bed, suggesting possibilities if a connection were made with the coast. Bogran, acting under the advice of American engineers, completed a wagon-road from the Pacific road of San Lorenzo to meet this, and connect the capital with the port. A force of 175 men was employed for eleven months to build it around the mountains to the terminus of the macadamized boulevard, and from Tegucigalpa thence fifty miles to Yuscaran, which an enthusiastic expert has named the "Comstock of Central America." The work of internal improvements did not stop here. A New York company is dredging the Aguan river and building canals to connect the Olancho district with the northern ports. One of our great railway systems has recently had a survey made to determine the feasibility of building a railway from Puerto Cortez eastward, near the coast, in the interest of the fruit trade; other important internal improvements are being made in Olancho, and carbonate mines are being opened at La Union.

A Government decree, dated September 26, amplifies and modifies a good many provisions of the "Código de Minería" at the personal instigation of the President, who, during the summer, paid a visit to the mining regions.

Education. — On September 15 was founded at the capital, Tegucigalpa, in presence of the President of the Republic, the Academy of Science and Literature of Honduras, having Dr. Antonio Ramirez Fontecha for its president. Premiums of from $1,000 to $100 are to be awarded at the meeting of Sept. 14, 1889, to the best works in Spanish on primary instruction, on Central American history from the Conquest to 1842, with special reference to Honduras, and, finally, to a poem in praise of Central Union and the illustrious Gen. Francisco Morazan.

HOUSE-BOATS. It is not to be denied that the world owes very many of its most healthful and sensible out-of-door recreations to England and Englishmen. Even base-ball, now justly regarded as the American national game, is merely a scientific improvement of "rounders," known probably to English boys centuries ago. Canoeing as a civilized recreation probably originated in Canada, but it had to cross the ocean twice before it became firmly established in the United States. In like manner, the house-boat has become so thoroughly domesticated that it has ceased to be an object of curiosity on the little rivers, lakes, estuaries, and canals of the British Islands. That it is destined to a greater and more glorious career on the infinitely varied coastwise and inland waters of America, may be taken as a foregone conclusion.

We are not without our house-boats in America; but we have not passed beyond the practical and utilitarian stage. Every raft has its "head-works," rude shanties, usually, where the crew have their bunks and where the cook does his cooking. Oyster-men often keep a house-boat anchored over the beds, for protection or convenience, and floating boat-houses are common wherever boating-clubs exist. But none of these fulfill the idea of a house-boat as developed in England and as presented in Mr. Black's recent novel, "The Strange Adventures of a House-boat." Such is the present demand for this type of craft in England that there are in London several builders who devote themselves almost exclusively to their construction.

A house-boat is precisely what its name implies—a house on a boat, or at least on a float; and just as a house on land may have only one room or a score of rooms, so the house-boat may be merely a narrow cabin with the most compact arrangements for living, eating, and sleeping, or it may be a floating "establishment" with half a dozen state-rooms, dining-room, parlor, and quarters for a full corps of servants.

To the lover of out-door life, the advantages of the house-boat are at once obvious. It can be moored in any sheltered place where there is water enough to float it; it is readily supplied with provisions and other stores by means of small boats; it is easily kept clean by the simple process of throwing waste materials overboard; and it is readily moved from place to place, according to the fancy of its owner. There is no fair ground of comparison between house-boats and yachts, since they are intended for widely different purposes; but a house-boat may be built for $1,000 with better accommodations than could be secured for $10,000 in a yacht.

The first thing to be considered in planning a house-boat is the foundation or float. This may be merely a raft of logs or a frame connecting a system of water-tight pontoons, or a flat-bottomed scow of any desired dimensions or shape. Whichever form is selected, it should be covered with a slightly convex deck, so that water spilled anywhere will tend to run out-board. The raft is the cheaper form. Its advantage is, that it can never leak, and consequently requires no pumping. Its disadvantage is that it is hard to tow. The pontoon system is more costly, is also hard to tow, and is liable to leakage; but it can be so arranged that one pontoon at a time can be removed for examination or repair. The pontoons may be wooden boxes or cylinders or empty oil-barrels. By far the best float, however, is a scow or boat of some kind, such as any carpenter or amateur can build, since none of the complicated problems involving waveline theories, strains, etc., need be taken into consideration. The only elements to be considered are dimensions, strength, and tightness. In the vicinity of seaports it is often possible to purchase at a reasonable figure flat-boats that will answer every purpose; but if it is desired to build, and economy is an object, the following plan is suggested: Having decided upon the length and breadth and depth of the boat, estimate the amount of planking necessary, and buy common pine matched boards accordingly. If the boat is to be small, two thicknesses are enough; but if large, three or more are required. It is desirable to have the bottom or floor rockered or curved slightly, so that she will take the ground easily when beached; but this is not absolutely necessary. Any mechanic will know how to provide for the curve if desired. The floor is laid first on

supports, the boards running crosswise—or better, diagonally. When laid and securely nailed to temporary timbers, the ends should be sawed off along a line marking the intended shape of the bottom. This done, prepare a second course of boards of the same shape, but to be laid breaking joints with the first course, or, if diagonal, to be laid in the opposite direction. In Fig. 1 the continuous lines represent the first or lower course and the broken lines the second or upper course. Before laying the second course, a sufficient quantity of hot pitch should be prepared, and before each board is driven home and nailed, a bed of pitch should be prepared to receive it, so that all the seams and even the grooves in the edges of the boards shall be filled with pitch. Any number of courses may be laid, according to the size of the boat, but three are enough for any length less than fifty feet. Copper nails, clinched, are best but iron clinch-nails will answer very well, especially for fresh water.

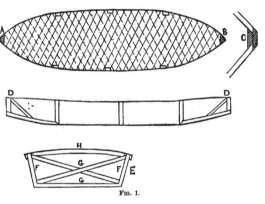

Fig. 1.

In driving them, it is desirable to set them at a slight angle and in differing directions, and all care must be taken not to split the wood. This makes a very strong and elastic bottom, absolutely water-tight.

The next step is to set up the stem and sternposts, at A and B. C shows the section of the post having a rabbet on each side deep enough to nail on the side-courses. These posts may be natural knees worked out of solid pieces, or they may be triangles built up of plank bolted together (see D, Fig. 1).

At intervals of about ten feet, transverse frames, as shown at E, should be set up, with the top piece slightly arched to make the deck shed water. The side-posts, F, should be of light stuff, only large enough to receive the nails of the first course of siding. The cross-braces, G, may be still lighter, or even ordinary

boards. The deck timbers, H, should be of
two-inch plank set on edge. All these may be
simply bolted or nailed together, no framing
or mortising being necessary.

When the bow and stern posts and the
transverse frames are in position (and there
is no reason why they should not be made
flaring outward to secure more deck-room),
the first course of matched boards is nailed on,
all abutting surfaces and edges being covered
with pitch. When the siding is nailed to the
edges of the bottom boards, use wire nails, to
avoid splitting and to secure a better hold.
Cover the first course of siding with a second
course, with pitch between, the same rules
being followed as to driving nails. Along the
outside angle formed by the meeting of the

able to mark them out before driving the deck
nails, as the saw will otherwise be pretty sure
to encounter nails. Of course, if deck-timbers
are cut through for the hatches, stanchions
must be set to take the strain ; but a two-foot
hatch is generally wide enough.

Towing-posts or bitts will be required at both
ends, and these may serve also to make fast the
cables when the boat is at anchor. They may
be placed anywhere, simply strengthening the
deck by means of stout plank bolted down, and,
in a large boat, re-enforced by carrying the posts
through the deck, down to a step on the bottom. If desired, a rudder may be hung on the
stern-post in the usual manner, but in most
cases an oar or sweep will answer quite as well.

Large vessels have been built on this plan of

Fig. 2.

sides and the bottom, fasten angle-irons wide
enough to overreach the seams, so that the
screws with which they are fastened will not
be in danger of striking the nails previously
driven.

Deck-timbers corresponding with the one
shown at E must be placed at about two-foot
intervals throughout the whole length of the
boat. The deck may be laid precisely as was
the bottom of the boat, except that care should
be taken not to allow a surplus of pitch to work
up to the surface. Before laying the deck, a
stout strip or out-wale should be spiked or
bolted along the upper edge of the siding, on
the outside, and the ends of the deck-boards
nailed to it. This out-wale affords protection
to the siding, and if payed over with pitch
makes a perfectly tight line of junction between deck and sides.

Hatches to afford access to the hold may be
cut through the deck anywhere, but it is desir-

superimposing layers, and they have proved
wonderfully strong and seaworthy, even without any interior timbers whatever. The system has never found favor with professional
builders, but for a shallow, flat-bottomed hull,
such as is required for a house-boat, it is an excellent method of construction, and is amply
strong for smooth water.

The hull being finished, nothing remains but
to build a house upon it, leaving a clear space
fore and aft and making the roof available for
a promenade or a post of observation. Any
carpenter or amateur can build such a house.
It may have only one room, with such arrangements of bunks and tables as suit the
owner, or it may have a sitting-room and
kitchen and separate sleeping-rooms to suit
either the most economical ideas of bachelors
or the more luxurious notions of those to
whom money is no object.

The illustration (Fig. 2), from a design published in "Forest and Stream," represents one of the larger and more luxurious class of boats, 95 feet long by 17 feet beam. The masts are, of course, superfluous, merely lending a somewhat nautical air to the general appearance. It may be said, however, that a mast and sail of moderate size may often prove of great convenience in changing anchorage. To effect such a change requires some practical knowledge of seamanship. In a tidal river one may easily progress up stream by the aid of a pair of sweeps or a skiff to tow the house-boat out into the current and to regain anchorage-ground just before the tide turns ebb. In a lake or an inland river some outside means of propulsion is necessary, and a sail might often prove useful. Tugs are generally available on navigable streams, and for a few dollars they will enable the house-boat owner to shift his berth a score of miles in two or three hours.

Such bodies of water as Lake George or Lake Champlain, or indeed any of the ten thousand inland lakes and rivers of North America, are lined with sheltered coves where a house-boat may lie secure from storms the summer through. She may often be moored so near the shore that a gang-plank will afford ready passage to the land. Small boats for sails or oars or both, are, of course, an indispensable adjunct for fishing, for exercise, and for the various errands necessary to a company that must depend more or less on the markets for supplies. For a large house-boat a naphtha-launch would be a great convenience. (See NAPHTHA-MOTORS, in "Annual Cyclopædia" for 1887.)

In many respects life on a house-boat is to be preferred to ordinary camp or cottage life on shore. These house-boats, with their wide variety in structure and cost, will prove a welcome addition to our American resources for out-of-door existence during the summer months, and indeed for the whole year round in some of the Southern States.

I

IDAHO. Territorial Government.—The following were the Territorial officers during the year: Governor, Edward A. Stevenson, Democrat; Secretary, Edward J. Curtis; Comptroller and Auditor, James H. Wickersham; Treasurer, Charles Himrod; Attorney-General, Richard Z. Johnson; Superintendent of Public Instruction, Silas W. Moody; Chief-Justice of the Supreme Court, James B. Hays, who died on May 31, and was succeeded by Hugh W. Weir; Associate Justices, Norman Buck and Case Broderick, succeeded by John Lee Logan and Charles H. Berry.

Population.—The following estimate of population by countries is given by the Governor in his annual report:

COUNTIES.	Population.	COUNTIES.	Population.
Ada	11,000	Latah	9,680
Alturas	16,250	Lemhi	4,500
Bear Lake	5,750	Nez Percé	5,000
Bingham	12,000	Oneida	6,500
Boisé	4,250	Owyhee	3,350
Cassia	4,500	Shoshone	8,000
Custer	4,000	Washington	5,000
Idaho	4,000		
Kootenai	1,480	Total	105,260

In this list, Latah County appears for the first time, having been created out of the northern part of Nez Percé County, by act of Congress, passed and approved May 14, 1888. A county organization was effected under this act on May 29 following.

Finances.—The receipts from all sources from Nov. 1, 1886, to Nov. 1, 1888, were $114,127.93, and the expenditures, $109,660.11; the balance on hand Nov. 1, 1888, was $4,467.82.

No change in the bonded debt of the Territory was made during the year.

Education.—From the report of the Superintendent of Education, the following comparison of the condition of the public schools for 1886 and 1888 is given:

ITEMS.	1886.	1888.
School districts	318	337
School-houses	233	268
Schools	334	365
Pupils enrolled	9,878	10,433
Libraries	7	12
Children of school age	18,555	20,180
Amount received from county tax	$78,006 05	$101,002 53
Amount received from district	48,184 76	83,810 74
Amount received from all sources	160,172 57	164,732 55
Paid teachers' salaries	85,457 97	92,910 81
Estimated value of school property		279,500 00

Of the compulsory school law, passed in 1887, the Superintendent says: "Under the exceptions in this law, many parents are avoiding its operation by setting up the excuse that their children are taught in private schools or at home, which is a valid excuse, but affords an opportunity to those whose religious belief opposes the employment of Gentile teachers to keep their children away from the public school of the district. I have not heard of a single fine being collected, and believe that such a law is of no benefit until thoroughly amended."

The act of Congress of May 20, 1886, concerning the teaching of the effects of alcoholic drinks and narcotics upon the human system, has been called to the attention of superintendents and teachers throughout the Territory, and is generally enforced. But many teachers report that they can not carry out its provisions to the letter, if strictly construed, by reason of its requiring impossibilities in the matter of using text-books.

Charities and Prisons.—In the Territorial Insane Asylum at Blackfoot, 72 patients were treated during the year ending September 15, of whom 49 were men and 23 women. At the latter date there were 48 patients—35 men and 13 women. The cost of maintaining the institution for the year was $14,827.

There were confined in the United States Penitentiary at Boisé City in October, at the expense of the Territory, 75 prisoners. The condition of this prison is characterized by Gov. Stevenson as " disgraceful." There are only 40 cells, into which are crowded 78 prisoners, three of them being United States prisoners. No provision is made for working the convicts, who are confined to their cells 20 hours each day, although a stone-quarry near at hand would afford an excellent opportunity for using their labor in enlarging the present building. The Territory pays $18,000 a year to the National Government for keeping its convicts at this place. But the crowded condition of the prison is likely to be soon relieved, Congress having this year appropriated $25,000 for its enlargement.

The Governor, in his annual report for 1888, says: " I wish particularly to call the attention of the department and Congress to the great injustice of the act of Congress of March 3, 1885. This act compels our Territorial courts to take cognizance and jurisdiction of all offenses committed by Indians against the property of another Indian or other persons, and of certain crimes committed on the Indian reservations. We have now in the Penitentiary two Indians sentenced for long terms, for which we are paying the United States $1.50 a day, besides all the expenses of their trials and convictions. Others have also been sentenced who have served out their terms and been discharged. I can not comprehend why the General Government should compel the Territory to pay for the support of a criminal class who are the wards of the Government, from whom the Territory derives no revenue, income, or support."

Statistics.—The assessed valuation of the Territory, by counties, is shown in the following table:

COUNTIES.	Valuation.	COUNTIES.	Valuation.
Ada............	$8,020,000	Latah...........	$1,668,255
Alturas........	3,787,582	Lemhi...........	768,998
Bear Lake......	580,028	Nez Percé.......	1,080,594
Bingham........	2,565,130	Oneida..........	1,018,811
Boisé..........	720,949	Owyhee..........	1,081,925
Cassia.........	919,170	Shoshone........	1,051,902
Custer.........	775,892	Washington......	917,419
Idaho..........	843,566		
Kootenai.......	548,731	Total........	$21,288,392

In this total are assessed 241,515 cattle, valued at $3,036,234; 71,984 horses, valued at $1,904,348; 1,603 mules, valued at $55,343; and 251,634 sheep, valued at $389,988.

The production of wheat for 1888 is estimated at 2,986,280 bushels; oats, 1,264,590 bushels; barley, 394,690 bushels; hay, 528,965 tons.

The mining product for 1887 is estimated by the assayer at Boisé City as follows: Gold, $2,522,209; silver, $3,422,657; gold and sil-

ver, $5,944,866; lead, $2,960,270; gold, silver, and lead, $8,905,136.

Railroads.—There were about 1,000 miles of railroad in the Territory at the close of the year. Construction has been going on during the year upon the following lines: Spokane and Palouse Railway, Oregon Railway and Navigation Company, Cœur d'Alene Railway, and Spokane and Idaho Railway.

Forests.—There are about 18,000,000 acres of timber and mineral land in the Territory, a very large portion of which is covered with timber. In some places the forests are mostly black or lodge-pole pine, which grows about 8 inches in diameter and from 60 to 100 feet high, and so thick that a person can scarcely pass between the trees. It is valuable for fuel, mining-timbers, buildings, and fencing, and is very durable. There are in other localities immense forests of the finest white and yellow pine, also spruce, fir, and cedar, suitable for manufacturing into lumber, the trees being from 2 to 4 feet in diameter and 50 to 60 feet without a limb. The lumber now manufactured in the Territory is only for home consumption.

Indians.—The extent of the various Indian agencies in the Territory and the number of Indians upon them during the year were as follow: Fort Hall or Shoshone and Bannocks, 1,700 persons, 1,202,320 acres; Lemhi, 548 persons, 105,960 acres; Cœur d'Alene, 500 persons, 598,500 acres; Western Shoshone, 400 persons, 131,300 acres; Nez Percé, 1,227 persons, 746,651 acres. No disturbances have occurred during the year. There is a doubt as to whether the valuable mineral lands near the borders of the Cœur d'Alene reservation, on which miners have made locations, are within the limits of the reservation. Dangerous complications are liable to result unless this doubt is soon settled by a resurvey of the region.

Annexation.—To any plan for dismembering the Territory, and especially to the bill before Congress creating the State of Washington out of the eastern part of that Territory with the four northern counties of Idaho attached, the people of Idaho are almost unanimously opposed. A protest against it was passed by the Territorial Legislature of last year. In June, 1888, the Democratic Territorial Convention at Boisé City adopted, by a vote of 44 to 6, the following resolution:

That we reiterate our opposition to any dismemberment of the Territory by annexation of any county or counties to any State or Territory, and that we favor at the earliest date practicable the introduction of a law in Congress for the admission of Idaho, with its present lines and boundaries, as a State of the Union.

Only one of the four northern counties, Nez Percé (with Latah, lately a part of Nez Percé), voted against the resolution. The Territorial Republican Convention, in May, included in its platform the following:

That we denounce the Stewart or any other measure for the segregation and consequent annihilation of Idaho; that while North Idaho appears before this convention through one county (Latah) and demands the annexation of North Idaho to Washington, another county (Shoshone), representing more votes, appears here with resolutions directly and absolutely opposed to any segregation of the Territory; and, further,

That the Republicans of Idaho Territory, while recognizing the sentiment as expressed by one county, and as said to exist in Nez Percé County, hereby declare for statehood for the whole Territory.

These resolutions were repeated at party conventions held in August. In his message to the Legislature, in December, the Governor says:

I would recommend that the Legislature make provision for the election and holding of a convention to form a Constitution for the State of Idaho, to be convened at an early day, and that the Constitution so formed be submitted to the people for their ratification at the next general election or at a special election to be held before that time, and that when ratified it be laid before Congress by our Delegate, with the request that Idaho be admitted a State of the Union on an equality with the original thirteen; and that the necessary appropriations to defray the expenses of such Constitutional Convention be made.

Political.—Territorial conventions to elect delegates to the national party conventions were held in May and June. On August 22 the Democrats met in convention again at Boisé City to choose a candidate for Territorial Delegate to Congress, and James H. Hawley was selected for that office. The following are some of the resolutions adopted:

That we heartily favor the filling of Territorial offices, as far as practicable, by appointments from the Territory, and we cite with pride its wisdom in the appointment of our citizen Governor, who has made us the best Governor ever appointed for the Territory.

That we favor liberal appropriations by Congress for irrigating canals and artesian wells, by which multiplied acres of our lands may be reclaimed and opened for entry and settlement.

That the settlement of our Territory is greatly retarded by the existence within our borders of large Indian reservations, useless to the Indians and of incalculable value to the whites for the valuable agricultural, mineral, and timber resources; and we earnestly recommend the opening up of the reservation to settlement having due regard to the rights of the Indians.

The second Republican Convention was in session in Hailey August 29 and 30, and nominated Delegate Dubois for re-election. The platform contains the following:

That we are unalterably opposed to any reduction of the import duties upon the product of silver, lead, and copper mines, and that any change of existing laws that shall check or hinder the prosecution and growth of this industry would be unwise and unjust; and therefore we denounce the action of the Democratic Convention of Idaho for their indorsement of the Mills Bill.

That we remain unalterably opposed to the Mormons, their priest-rule and polygamy; that we favor the Idaho test-oath, and pledge ourselves to strenuously oppose any interference with or repeal of the same, and that we view with contempt the action of the Democratic Convention at Boisé City resulting in the formation of an unholy alliance with the Mormons for political profit.

That, inasmuch as the Mormon p o have in no wise renounced polygamy and the other practices which have hitherto deprived them of their franchise, and yet defiantly declare their intention to vote at the coming election, even though they commit the crime of perjury, we call upon the Territorial administration of Idaho to see that the election laws of this Territory are sustained.

Both platforms contain also the same declarations against annexation adopted at the respective conventions in May and June. No resolution was adopted by the Democrats upon the Mormon problem. A third candidate, ex-Justice Norman Buck, was in the field as the representative of a small party in the Territory which favors division and annexation of the northern counties to Washington Territory. At the November election Buck received 1,458 votes, all but 163 of which were cast in Latah and Nez Percé counties, where he led the poll. Dubois received 8,151 votes, and Hawley 6,404 votes. A legislature was chosen, to which the Republicans elected about three fourths of the members. One Mormon was chosen, and two of the Democrats elected were supported by Mormon votes.

Legislative Session.—The Legislature chosen in November met on December 10 and sat about two weeks, adjourning until January. One of its first acts was to unseat Mr. Lamoreaux, a Democratic member of the council, on the ground that he had been elected by Mormon votes, contrary to the provisions of the Mormon test-oath. In the Lower House, Messrs. Kinport, Democrat, and Kinnersley, Mormon, were unseated for the same reason. No legislation of importance was accomplished.

IDENTIFICATION AND DESCRIPTION, PERSONAL. This has been made the subject of special study and experiment by Prof. Francis Galton, F. R. S., who detailed his results in a lecture before the Royal Institution in London on May 25. He pointed out that there is no such thing as infinite unlikeness, two profiles, or other irregular lines, for instance, differing from each other always by a finite number of least discernible differences. To illustrate, suppose two figures, A and B (Fig. 1), to be placed one on the other, and draw a third line, C, equally subdividing the interval between them. C is more like B than A was, and in like manner a line D can be drawn, still more like B. By continuing thus, a figure will be reached which, if drawn separately, is indistinguishable from B. If this is the fourth equal subdivision, there are sixteen grades of least discernible differences between A and B. This measure of resemblance is evidently applicable also to colors, sounds, tastes, and other sense indications, and may be used in personal description by first making a collection of standard profiles drawn with double lines, so that any human profile would lie entirely within some one of them. This would be quite possible; indeed, all human profile lines, taken from the brow to the lips, fall between the lines shown in Fig. 2. The measurement of profiles seems to be the best means of personal identification. Prof. Galton prefers for reference-lines B C (Fig. 3), touching the concavity above the nose and the con-

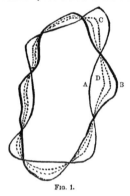

Fig. 1.

vexity of the chin, and a line parallel to this, touching the tip of the nose. From these lines various measures may be taken which are characteristic of the individual. Instead of these profile measurements, measures of the head and limbs are generally employed in prisons for purposes of identification, this idea originating in France with Alphonse Bertillon. But, whatever the system, the practical difficulty is to classify the sets of measures that are so made, so that it may be told at a glance whether any given set of measurements agrees with any or none of them within specified limits, and for this purpose Prof. Galton has devised what he calls a mechanical selector. It consists of a large number of strips of card or metal, C_1, C_2 (Fig. 4), eight or nine inches long, and having a common axis, A, passing through all their smaller ends. A tilting-frame T, turning on the same axis, has a front cross-bar, F, on which the tips of the larger ends of the cards rest when the machine is left alone, the opposite end of the frame resting on the base-board, S. When this end is raised, as in the figure, the cards descend by their own

Fig. 2.

weight. Each card has notches cut in its lower edge, whose distances from the axis represent the measurements in one of the sets. The greater the number in the set the longer the cards must be. In the figure the card has only four notches. The given set of measures that is to be compared with the sets already made is represented by the positions of movable wires, strung perpendicularly to the plane of the figure. When the cards are released, by raising the end of the tilting-frame, if the positions of all the notches in any card correspond with those of the wires, that card will fall so that a wire enters each notch; but, otherwise, the card will rest on one or more of the wires. A glance thus enables the experimenter to determine whether any sets of measurements agree with the one to be tested, and, if so, what sets so agree. In the figure, the card C_2 so agrees, and has therefore fallen lower than C_1, which rests on the second wire. By making the notches fit the wires closely or loosely, the limits within which the sets must agree may be made small or large. There is thus theoretically no limit to the number of sets of measurements that can be compared with a given set by this machine, by a single movement of the hand, and in practice the only limit is the necessity of making the machine of convenient size. It seems a valuable adjunct to the system of personal identification in prisons.

Various markings on the human body remain unchanged for years, and so afford a basis for identification, where the question is simply whether two persons are or are not identical. Those of them that admit of approximate measurement by the method of least discernible differences, described above, can also be used for the comparison of one person with a thousand others. Among them are the markings on the iris (of which there are thousands of varieties) the arrangement of the superficial veins, the shape of the ear, and the furrows on the hands and feet. The markings on the under surface of the finger-tips can be made more plainly visible by rubbing on the finger a paste of prepared chalk and water, which fills the furrows. They may be made to leave a per-

Fig. 3.

Fig. 4.

manent record by inking the finger lightly and pressing it on paper. Sir William Herschel made two such impressions in 1860 and 1888, in which the positions of the furrows and ridges remain the same, and they are probably unchanged through life. The thumb has been used as a seal that can not be counterfeited. It has been proposed to use this method for identifying Chinese immigrants, and it has been commonly supposed to be used for a like purpose in Chinese courts of justice. A large number of such thumb-impressions, taken during several generations, would doubtless enable scientists to settle interesting questions regarding heredity.

ILLINOIS. State Government.—The following were the State officers during the year: Governor, Richard J. Oglesby, Republican; Lieutenant-Governor, John C. Smith; Secretary of State, Henry D. Dement; Auditor, Charles P. Swigert; Treasurer, John R. Tanner; Attorney-General, George Hunt; Superintendent of Public Instruction, Richard Edwards; Railroad and Warehouse Commissioners, John J. Rinaker, B. F. Marsh, and W. T. Johnson; Chief-Justice of the Supreme Court, Alfred M. Craig; Associate Justices, Benjamin M. Magruder, Simeon P. Shope, David J. Baker, John Scofield, Jacob W. Wilkin, and Joseph M. Bailey.

Finances.—The amount of all funds in the State Treasury, Oct. 1, 1886, was as follows: General revenue fund, $2,663,570.01; State school fund, $218,876.23; delinquent land-tax fund, $331.06; unknown and minor heirs' fund, $10,776.19; local bond fund, $558,158.33; total, $3,451,711.82. The receipts from all sources from Oct. 1, 1886, to Sept. 30, 1888, inclusive, were as follow: General revenue fund, $5,693,563.32; State school fund, $2,196,492.36; unknown and minor heirs' fund, $3,209.80; local bond fund, $2,866,268.45; total, $10,759,533.93; grand total, $14,211,245.75. The disbursements from Oct. 1, 1886, to Sept. 30, 1888, inclusive, were as follow: General revenue fund, $5,437,843.29; State school fund, $2,109,144.16; unknown and minor heirs' fund, $153.39; local bond fund, $2,824,887.69; total, $10,372,028.53. Balance of all funds in treasury Oct. 1, 1888, $3,839,217.22. The principal of the bonded debt of the State outstanding Oct. 1, 1886, was $23,600.

Canals.—The report of the Canal Commissioners shows that the revenue derived from tolls and from other sources, during the last year, have been sufficient to keep the canal in good condition, so that it may still be utilized in connection with Illinois river. It costs the State nothing; the usual contingent appropriation of $20,000 a year is never touched by the commissioners. The affairs of the canal have been so wisely managed that the revenues collected have been sufficient, not only to keep up repairs, but to complete the system of rip-raps, which will insure the banks from waste by washing and floods. Their report shows a balance of $63,325.13 to the credit of the canal for the year ending Nov. 30, 1888, after the payments of all debts and accounts for maintenance, repairs, management, and materials and improvements thereon.

Penitentiaries.—The report of the Commissioners of the Illinois State Penitentiary, at Joliet, shows a healthy condition of that prison. The number of convicts there on Sept. 30, 1888, was 224 fewer than on Sept. 30, 1886. There was a falling off in the earnings at that institution of about $50,000 during the two years, and $35,000 was drawn from the general appropriation to make good the deficit. As the contract system has been abolished, the Governor, in his message, says: "I know of no other or better than the State-account plan. To put this into execution, so as to keep the convict employed, and not to bring his labor in conflict with free outside labor of the honest mechanic, artisan, or laboring man, will test the ingenuity of the most skilled legislator. In the mean time, under existing conditions, appropriations will be necessary for the penitentiaries of the State for the next two years. I recommend at least $100,000 for the one at Joliet." At Chester, the report shows no material change in the number of convicts confined in the prison from the two previous years. Existing contracts for the labor of about 225 convicts will expire June 30, 1890; other contracts for about 150 convicts will not expire, with the existing privilege of renewal, until several years later. The appropriation for ordinary expenses for 1887 and 1888 was $75,000 per annum. The commissioners and warden ask for $65,000 per annum for the next two years for ordinary purposes, and $15,000 for other and special purposes.

Education.—The report of the Superintendent shows that the number of children of school age in 1888 was 1,118,472; the number of pupils enrolled was 751,349; the average attendance was 518,043; the average duration of the schools was 153·3 days; the average number of days of attendance for each pupil was 105·7; the average monthly wages of male teachers was $52.93; of female teachers, $43.09. The total expenditures for public schools was $10,661,017.15. Of this amount there was paid for salaries of teachers $6,714,516.98, and the permanent productive school funds for the State, not including the university, was $10,383,132.99. The University of Illinois, the State and Southern Normal Universities, were reported as in excellent condition.

Charities.—The tenth biennial report of the State Commissioners shows that for 1886 and 1887 there was distributed $3,800,250.26 among the institutions under their jurisdiction, as follows: Northern Hospital for the Insane, $349,347.02; Eastern Hospital for the Insane, $893,511.74; Central Hospital for the Insane, $497,833.91; Southern Hospital for the Insane, $350,859.10; Institution for the Deaf and Dumb, $318,281.75; Institution for the Blind,

$111,834.80; Institution for Feeble - Minded Children, $201,261.28 ; Soldiers' Orphans' Home, $158,660.58; Charitable Eye and Ear Infirmary, $71,242.67; State Reform School, $305,933.75 ; Soldiers' and Sailors' Home, $544,453.66. The Northern Hospital is at Elgin, and from Oct. 1, 1886, till Sept. 30, 1888, 712 patients were under treatment, of whom 189 were discharged. The Eastern Hospital is at Kankakee, and during the same time 2,121 patients were at the hospital, of whom 512 received their discharges. The Central Hospital is at Jacksonville, and 1,401 persons were at that institution during the time mentioned, of whom 478 were discharged. The Southern Hospital is at Anna, where, from Oct. 1, 1887, till June 30, 1888, 732 patients were treated, of whom 102 were discharged. It is estimated that the insane increase at the rate of 1,300 to 1,500 each year in Illinois, and efforts are being made to revise the lunacy law so that greater stringency shall be used in committing those alleged to be insane. The Institution for the Deaf and Dumb is at Jacksonville. On June 30, 1888, there were 531 pupils on the rolls, and since the previous report of Sept. 30, 1886, there had been admitted 77 new students, 24 graduated, and 88 removed. At the Institution for the Blind, likewise situated at Jacksonville, there were during the nine months ending June 30, 1888, 171 persons enrolled, of whom 97 were males and 74 females. In June, 1888, six students were graduated and certificates of proficiency were issued to those who had taken the workshop course. The Soldiers' Orphans' Home is at Normal, and 611 inmates were there during the time between Oct. 1, 1886, and June 30, 1888; and 255 were for various reasons removed during that period. The other charitable institutions referred to were, according to the Governor's last message to the Legislature, "wisely, humanely, and economically managed by the various boards of trustees and superintendents charged with their care."

Railroads.—During 1887–'88 there were sixty-one railroad corporations, controlling and operating 13,000 miles of road, including 346 miles built in 1888, giving steady employment to 56,000 persons, the aggregate of whose wages exceeds $33,000,000 a year. The estimated total cost of construction and equipment of all the roads exceeded $330,000,000 ; and they carried, in 1888, 32,000,000 passengers at an average rate of 2·29 cents a mile, the total income of the passenger department of these roads for 1888 amounting to more than $17,-000,000. They transported in the same year more than 53,000,000 tons of freight, at an average charge of one and six tenths cent (1·6) a ton a mile, the total income from which was about $39,000,000. The total amount of the operating expenses of all the roads amounted to more than $38,000,000, contributing in the way of taxation for State and local purposes $2,739,612.

Live-Stock.—The acts of 1885 and 1887, creating the board of live-stock commissioners, was a timely and prudent effort upon the part of the State to protect the lives and health of domestic animals. The board appointed to carry the law into execution reports to the Legislature the complete extirpation of contagious pleuro-pneumonia in the State. The returns of local assessors show, for 1888, for purposes of taxation, the following number and value of domestic animals :

ANIMALS.	Number.	Value.
Horses...........	998,081	$24,826,145
Mules and asses..........	100,613	2,517,970
Cattle....................	2,428,484	17,229,377
Sheep....................	554,910	584,769
Hogs....................	1,966,700	2,798,326
Total................		$47,901,587

The practice of assessing all property in this State by local assessors, at one third or one fourth its actual or cash value, indicates that the real value of the domestic animals above enumerated would exceed $150,000,000.

Political.—At the presidential election there were cast 370,473 votes for Gen. Harrison; 348,278 for Mr. Cleveland ; 7,090 for Mr. Streeter ; and 21,695 for Gen. Fisk. The following Republican State officers were also chosen : Joseph W. Fifer, for Governor; Lyman B. Ray, for Lieutenant-Governor; Isaac N. Pearson, for Secretary of State ; Charles W. Parey, for Auditor; Charles Becker, for Treasurer; and George Hunt, for Attorney-General. The congressional delegation includes 13 Republicans and 7 Democrats, representing a gain of one for the Democrats over the representatives sent to the Fiftieth Congress. The Legislature includes in the Senate 35 Republicans and 16 Democrats; in the House, 80 Republicans and 72 Democrats.

IMMIGRATION, PAUPER. The war of the American Revolution virtually put an embargo upon immigration for seven years, and the European wars that immediately followed, and continued almost without interruption until 1815, checked, for a whole generation, the movement across the Atlantic. Scattered notices from shipping-lists furnish the only basis for estimates as to the number arriving previous to 1820, and investigators differ considerably in their estimates. As shrewd a guess as any seems to be that of 250,000 immigrants from 1775 to 1820, which was made by Dr. Loring, of the United States Statistical Bureau, some years ago. Since 1819 the law of Congress has required that all who come to the sea and lake ports should be registered at the custom-houses. Their names, ages, sex, nativity, occupation, and destination are ascertained and reported to the National Government. The State Department, at first, and the Treasury Department latterly, have published annual reports of the number and character of the immigrants. So far as these documents go, they may be received with confidence;

but there were manifest omissions at some ports in the earlier years, and they could give no account of foreigners who entered this country through other channels than the sea and lake ports. And yet the official returns rendered by the collectors of customs do not indicate what portion of the whole may be considered pauper immigrants. The act of Congress regulating immigration, passed Aug. 3, 1882, authorizes the Secretary of the Treasury to enter into contract with such board, commission, or officer, as may be designated by the Governor of any State, to take charge of the local affairs of immigration in the ports of such State, and to provide for the support and relief of such immigrants landing therein as may fall into distress or need public aid, to be reimbursed by the collector of the port out of the fund derived from such tax. It is made the duty of such board, commission, or officer, to examine and inquire into the condition of all passengers arriving at such ports; and if, on such examination and inquiry, there shall be found any convict, lunatic, idiot, or any person unable to care for himself, who is likely to become a public charge, this shall be reported in writing to the collector of such port, and such person shall not be permitted to land; and the expense of his return shall be borne by the vessel in which he came. Under this act the Secretary of the Treasury, soon after its passage, entered into contract with the Commissioners of Emigration of New York, with the Boards of Charities of Massachusetts and Pennsylvania, and with various local boards, commissions, and officers of other States; and the examinations, inquiries, landing, relief, and care of all immigrants arriving in the United States since then have devolved upon these local officers, commissions, and boards. A ruling of the United States Treasury Department, in September, 1885, authorized the commissioners of emigration of the State of New York, their agents or servants, to go on board of all vessels arriving from foreign ports at the port of New York; and all immigrants found thereon may be taken to Castle Garden and there examined; and if, on such examination, there shall be found any persons not entitled to land, the Collector of the Port of New York, and the owners, agents, or masters of the vessel on which such persons arrived, shall be forthwith notified in writing; and the commissioners of emigration shall detain under their custody or care, either on shipboard or elsewhere, all such persons forbidden to land by the second section of the act of 1882, except convicts, who, as provided in the fifth section of "An act supplementary to the acts in relation to immigration," approved March 3, 1875, shall be subject to the charge and direction of the collector of customs of said port; and such detention shall continue until the sailing of the vessel upon which such persons arrived, or until proper provision can be made for their return to the countries

whence they came. It was the evident intention of Congress, by these enactments, to secure ample and proper protection to immigrants arriving at our shores, and, at the same time, guard against the influx of convicts, lunatic, and otherwise infirm and chronic alien paupers. The law, as at present executed, however, is little or no barrier against the shipment of these classes, and there is no remedy after they have passed the port at which they have landed. The expenditure of a small sum for passage to any interior point generally insures the delivery of the person to the place of destination; and, though he be insane, or otherwise incapable of self support, no provision is made for his return, and he falls upon the locality where he may be as a public charge through life. The statistics of the prisons, penitentiaries, poor-houses, asylums, and other institutions of the United States, show that there are proportionately many more of the criminal, insane, pauper, and helpless alien classes in them than in former years; and the evils from these sources, apparently, are constantly and heavily increasing. These evils, it is claimed, are due largely to defects in the Federal law, in that its execution depends upon local officers, likely to be influenced by local considerations, in the generally hurried and superficial examination of immigrants at the time of their landing, in the absence of any reciprocal action between the officers of the various ports, and in the failure of the statute to prescribe any penalty for its violation. The clearest exposition of the subject ever made from the standpoint of Americans abroad was through one hundred consuls of the United States to the General Government at Washington in 1888. The consul at Palermo said: "Emigration is here considered as a mere matter of business, so far as steamship companies are concerned, and it is stimulated by them in the same sense that trade in merchandise is when they desire a cargo, or to complete one, for their vessels. Law never enters the subject, so far as emigrants are concerned. The company desire that all space in their vessels shall be occupied, and, in order to accomplish this, they employ emigrant brokers or agents, to whom they pay from three to five dollars for each emigrant obtained; sometimes even more than the latter sum is paid, the amount depending on the competition or the urgency of the case. The brokers, as may be imagined, are a low, lying, dishonorable set, who will swear to anything to induce the poor, ignorant people to emigrate, and thus earn their fees. They tell them that work is plentiful and wages very high, and that after they shall have labored for a year or two they will have saved enough to return to their homes and live without doing anything. Thus the poor, ignorant people are wheedled into selling or mortgaging what little they may have, and after the broker has received his fee from the transportation company he never thinks or cares more for the poor people whom he has swindled. Until the United States shall have arrived at some agreement with Italy in the premises, this will continue. It would be a great blessing if the class of Italians who are practically forced by the brokers to emigrate could be kept from landing on American shores." The consul at Venice wrote: "Emigrants are recruited from those people whom, as a rule, their native country does not wish to retain. They are often fugitives from justice, and, in many cases, those leaving their native countries to evade legitimate duties imposed by law—men whose stupendous ignorance is unequaled by any other class of people found in the civilized world. They are no more fitted to perform the duties of citizenship than slaves newly released from bondage. They have no intention of becoming citizens of the United States. They desire simply to get more money for their work, and to decrease as much as possible the amount of work to be done for the money received." This word came from Vienna: "I am quite positive that the intelligent classes among the emigrants are in the minority. The bulk of emigration comes from Bohemia, and it is composed of the lower classes. The educated, intelligent Bohemian remains at home. Many of the emigrants have most perverted ideas of liberty. They believe that in the United States no policeman interferes with entire freedom of action. Many of them think they have been governed too much at home, and hope to find a country where they will not be governed at all. During the last summer no fewer than eighty runners of the Hamburg-American Packet Company and of the North German Lloyd, were arrested at Oswiecine and Kraken, in the province of Galicia, on the charge of fraud and encouraging emigration. There can be no doubt that they were on the hunt for contract-laborers." The consul at Annaberg, Saxony, said: "Any one who has observed the masses of humanity crowding on board the great ocean steamers bound for the promised land, can not but be convinced of this fact. A few days ago I saw at a railway junction two common freight-cars filled with emigrants for the United States, forlorn-looking creatures, half-starved and not decently clad. In these cars were men, women, and children, with all the worldly goods they possessed, packed like sardines, to the number of sixty. There was not a seat in the car, not so much as a board on which the poor mothers with infants might rest. I have seen whole trains of just such emigrants. I have observed these people on all occasions, and I do not hesitate to say that one third of all the emigration to the United States from the Continent of Europe is not only undesirable, but positively injurious and dangerous. So much of the scum of the population of these old countries has been transferred to us, that among well-ordered people who remain it has become a

settled idea and a common expression, that America is the asylum for all the disreputable persons of Europe. The other day I had a small job for a printer. I found his door locked, and turned away, when a woman stuck her head out from a window opposite and shouted: 'He's gone to America, where all the rascals go.' I have come across direct information confirming the evidence now before the committee, to the effect that much undesirable emigration is going on to our country by way of Canada. These emigrants are dupes of rascally agents (located, as a rule, in the German shipping-ports) who, knowing that the emigrants are so poor that they might be refused a landing in New York, sell them tickets to Montreal or Quebec, representing to these ignorant creatures that passage to those points is cheaper than to New York, and that, once in Canada, they have but to step over the border and be in the United States. The transportation companies advertise extensively all over Europe, and they have innumerable agents who picture the United States and the opportunities it offers to emigrants in glowing colors; and it is common belief that they misrepresent nearly everything in connection with the United States. The character of all the emigration has lately changed for the worse, and now more than ever is decidedly injurious to our working people and our general peace and prosperity."

It has been said that to remedy these evils the execution of the law should be placed in the hands of Federal officers untrammeled by local influences and free to act in the interest of the entire country; that the examinations should be thorough and vigilant and the capacity of each immigrant for self-support be conclusively established before he is permitted to land; that the procedure at the various ports, so far as practicable, should be uniform and reciprocal; and that violations of the statute in bringing criminals, insane, and other helpless persons to the country, should subject the owners of the vessels implicated to a fine in each case, in the nature of a libel on the vessel, to be enforced in the courts. The Secretary of the Treasury, in 1886, sent to the House of Representatives a bill providing a penalty of $500 for the permanent landing of alien paupers, idiots, insane, and convicts. By it the Secretary was given power to appoint commissioners of immigration, not to exceed three in number, at Boston, New York, Philadelphia, Baltimore, Key West, New Orleans, Galveston, and San Francisco, to take exclusive charge and provide for the support and relief of such alien immigrants as may fall into distress; but this bill did not pass. Another unsuccessful bill was introduced in the Senate of the United States in December, 1887, which provided that the Secretary of State shall establish such rules and regulations, and issue from time to time such instructions to consuls of the United States, not inconsistent with law or with treaty obligations, as shall enable well-disposed and worthy persons who desire to become resident citizens of the United States to obtain certificates of character and fitness therefor from the consul of the district in which they reside without hardship or unreasonable delay, which certificate shall contain, in addition to other specifications required by this act or which may be prescribed by the Secretary of State, the full name of the individual receiving it, the place of birth, age, occupation, last legal residence, physical marks or peculiarities, and all facts necessary for identification of such individuals; that no certificate shall be granted to any convict except those convicted of political offenses, nor to any lunatic, idiot, or any person unable to take care of himself without becoming a public charge, nor to any Anarchist, Nihilist, or person hostile to the principles of the Constitution or form of Government of the United States, nor to any believer or professed believer in the Mormon religion who fails to satisfy the consul, upon examination, that he intends to and will conform to and obey the laws of the United States, nor to any person included in the prohibition in the act to prohibit the importation and immigration of foreigners and aliens under contract or agreement to perform labor in the United States, the Territories, and the District of Columbia, approved Feb. 26, 1885, or in acts amendatory to that act. In addition to this the bill provided for penalties to be imposed on any vessel violating the law by transporting uncertified persons, established machinery for enforcing the law, and created an immigration fund by imposing a per-capita tax on each immigrant, to be used in defraying the expenses incident to such regulation of immigration. These efforts led to an investigation by a committee of Congress in 1888, a part of whose work was the collection of the consular reports noted above. As the result of its labors, the committee has visited the several centers of immigration in the eastern and central parts of the United States, and it is now (January, 1889) about to report a bill providing for the appointment of consular inspectors to every foreign land that sends large numbers of immigrants to the United States, and these inspectors will be attached to the consular and ministerial services in the several countries. Those who desire to come to the United States must file applications, giving age, birthplace, occupation, purpose, pedigree, and other important or material points, thirty, sixty, or even ninety days (as may be decided upon), before taking passage; and during that time the inspectors must investigate the past lives and records of the applicants, and then act according to the finding. If the candidate for admission to the United States is honest, sober, and industrions, and desires to come over to better his condition or join those of his family who are already here, and if he gives promise by his past life to make a good citizen, he will receive

his passport. But if he is found to be a pauper, an idiot, a criminal, or insane; if he is depraved and dissolute, or wishes to come over in fulfillment of a contract, he will be rejected, and without his papers, even if he secured passage on a vessel, he will not be permitted to land. It is believed that this plan, or a modification of it, will become a law within the year.

INDIA, an empire in Southern Asia, subject to Great Britain. By act of Parliament, the British Government in 1858 assumed the administration of all the territories of the East India Company. The powers of the company and its Board of Control are now exercised by the Secretary of State for India, who is a member of the British Cabinet. The Queen of Great Britain was proclaimed Empress of India at Delhi on Jan. 1, 1877. The executive authority in India is vested in the Governor-General, commonly spoken of as the Viceroy, who acts under the orders of the Secretary of State, and has power to make laws, by the advice of his Council, for British India and for British subjects in the native states, subject to the approval of the British Government. The ordinary measures for the government of India are usually expounded by the Secretary of State at the presentation of the annual budget, and receive the approval of Parliament.

The Earl of Dufferin, who was appointed Viceroy in 1884, resigned in January, 1888, on account of the state of his wife's health, but did not hand over the administration to his successor till November. The present Viceroy is the Marquis of Lansdowne, who was transferred from the Governor-Generalship of Canada. Lord Dufferin, as a mark of honor for his annexation of the Kingdom of Ava, or Upper Burmah, was created, before his retirement, Marquis of Dufferin and Ava and Earl of Ava. The native press expressed satisfaction at his retirement, as he had disappointed all expectations, and undone much of what was done by Lord Mayo, Lord Northbrook, and Lord Ripon for the good of the people of India. His administration was marked by a vigorous foreign policy in Afghanistan and Burmah, which increased the burdens of the poor Indian taxpayers without any resulting benefits for them, but the domestic policy of progress and reform, in sympathy with the desires and aspirations of the natives, was abandoned when Lord Dufferin took the government from Lord Ripon. The Secretary of State for India is Viscount Cross.

The Council of the Governor-General consists of six ordinary members and the Commander-in-Chief. With from six to twelve additional members, appointed by the Viceroy, they constitute the Legislative Council. The Viceroy and the Governors of Bombay and of Madras, whose appointments are political, though not vacated by a change of ministry, are nominated by the home Government; and so are, sometimes, the members of the Council and the judges of the High Court, though usually the recommendations of the Government of India are followed in filling these posts. The covenanted civil service was formerly widely separated in pay, rank, and privileges from the uncovenanted, and the distinction is still officially observed, although there are numerous uncovenanted civil servants in the special departments of accounts, archæology, customs, education, forests, geological survey, jails, meteorological survey, mint, opium, pilot service, post-office, police, public works, registration, salt, surveys, and telegraphs, whose duties are more important and as highly remunerated as those of a large proportion of the covenanted officials. Among the 941 appointments of the covenanted service, ranging from an assistant-magistrate up to a lieutenant-governor in the executive branch, and up to a chief-justice of the High Court in the judicial branch, only twelve are held by natives who entered the service by competition in England under the old rules, and forty-eight by natives appointed in India direct, under the statute of 1870 and the rules made by Lord Lytton in 1879. The special services employ about 2,000 officials, of whom one quarter, mostly in the lower grades, are natives. The uncovenanted executive and judicial service, consisting of deputy-magistrates and subjudges and their subordinates, is mostly in the hands of natives, who fill 2,449 out of 2,588 posts. Of the 114,-150 posts below these, with salaries less than 1,000 rupees, 97 per cent. are held by natives. A Civil Service Commission that was appointed in October, 1886, to devise a scheme that will do justice to the claims of natives to higher and more extensive employment in the public service, has reported in favor of doing away with the names "covenanted" and "uncovenanted," and dividing the civil service into imperial and provincial. Instead of throwing the higher grades of offices wider open for the admission of natives, the commission, which was composed exclusively of officials, would abolish the appointment of natives under the statute of 1870 and Lord Lytton's rules, and compel all candidates for the imperial civil service to pass the examinations in London, which are to be open to applicants between the ages of nineteen and twenty-three, the extension of the limits of age being intended to attract more university graduates, as well as to satisfy the demands of the natives of India. The most important changes are the attaching to the provincial service of 108 offices of the covenanted service and of all of the special services, excepting some of the chief posts, which are transferred to the imperial service. By this measure the Secretary of State will be deprived of the chief part of his remaining patronage, and many offices that have heretofore been held by Europeans will fall to natives, who will receive much smaller salaries.

Area and Population.—The first complete census of British India was taken on Feb. 17, 1881, when the population was found to be 201,790,-753, inhabiting an area of 1,064,720 square miles. The feudatory native states, in which the rulers govern under the advice of the British authorities, have an aggregate area of 509,730 square miles, and in 1881 contained 55,191,742 inhabitants, making the total area of India 1,574,450 square miles, and the total population 256,982,495. The density of population for the British territories is 229, for the native states 108, and for all India 184 to the square mile. The density varies from 441 per square mile in Cochin, a native state in Madras, and 403 in the Northwest Provinces and Oudh, to 79 in Rajputana and 43 in Lower Burmah. The Christian population comprised 963,059 Roman Catholics, 353,712 Anglicans, 20,034 Scotch Presbyterians, 23,135 Episcopalians, 138,200 Baptists, Congregationalists, and other Protestants, 2,142 Greeks and Armenians, and 365,235 unspecified. The British-born population of India was returned as 89,798, divided into 77,188 males and 12,610 females. There are more than one hundred languages and dialects classed with languages spoken in India. The numbers speaking the principal languages are as follow : Hindoostani, 82,497,168; Bengali, 38,965,428; Telugu, 17,-000,358; Mahratti, 17,044,634; Punjabi, 15,-754,793; Tamil, 13,088,279; Guzarati, 9,620,-688; Canarese, 8,337,027.

Emigrant labor from India is mainly recruited in Madras. The bulk of the emigration is now directed to the Straits Settlements, to Burmah, and to Ceylon, where the tea-cultivation and the pearl-fisheries attract coolie labor. There is no emigration at present to French colonies, and very little to Natal, Mauritius, or any distant English colonies, excepting Trinidad and Demerara, a fact attributed to the decline in the sugar-trade. The number of emigrants from Madras in 1887 was 126,831. The Government, in September, 1888, prohibited further emigration to any of the French colonies, on the ground that the French authorities decline to submit to a form of procedure required for the protection of the coolies similar to that adopted in the British colonies.

The following cities contained over 150,000 inhabitants :. Calcutta, with its suburbs, 871,-504 ; Bombay, 773,196 ; Madras, 405,848 ; Hyderabad, 354,692 ; Lucknow, 261,303 ; Benares, 199,700 ; Delhi, 173,393 ; Patna, 170,-654 ; Agra, 160,203 ; Bangalore, 155,857 ; Amritsar, 151,896 ; Cawnpore, 151,444.

Education.—Education has made much progress during the past few years. English schools have been established in every district, and in each of the provinces a department of education, under a director and a staff of inspectors, has been organized. Some of the colleges and schools are entirely supported by the Government, and all the higher institutions receive some aid. In 1886 there were 16,048 Government schools of all kinds, with 863,772 pupils; 61,183 missionary and other schools, with 1,662,835 pupils, that were partly supported by Government grants; and 45,412 schools, with 812,454 pupils, that received no aid. The total expenditure on education in 1886 was 24,243,950 rupees, of which one third was paid out of governmental and provincial revenues. The universities of Calcutta, Madras, and Bombay admitted 3,802 students during the academic year 1885-'86. There are 106 other colleges for males, and two have been established for girls, which had 31 students in 1886. The technical, medical, industrial, and other special schools number 285, with 12,667 students, exclusive of 33 schools for females, with 832 students. The number of persons receiving instruction in 1886 was 3,332,851 out of a population of 32,000,000 between the ages of five and ten years and 43,000,000 between ten and twenty. Very few of the Mohammedan population have received any education, and hence they resist the demands of the National Congress for the multiplication of native employés in the civil service and the establishment of a genuine system of representative local self-government, since the Hindus who have received a European education, about 1,000,000 in number, would be the only available candidates for official places. The Government has decided to introduce stricter regulations for the discipline of the schools, by keeping pupils under constant supervision in boarding-houses, and introducing the use of the rod wherever local feeling permits, in order to curb the spirit of independence that manifests itself with adult years in demands for representative institutions and assaults on the Government by a satirical press. The institution of a homogeneous system of education under the guidance of the Government was the result of the Educational Commission, which made its report in 1883. The system of board-schools that were established are destined to cover eventually the whole of India. The natives responded quickly to the increased facilities that were afforded them. Two years after the commission made its report there were 75 per cent. more people under instruction than there were two years before it sat. The extension of education has not been equal all over India. In Bengal, lack of funds has prevented the Government from carrying out the suggestions of the commission, and in 1886-'87 there was an actual diminution in the number of pupils in the inspected elementary schools, owing to the withdrawal of subsidies from small temporary or backward schools, while in the higher educational institutions of the same Government there was a considerable increase of students. The Mohammedans of Bengal, who were originally proselytized from the ignorant peasant class of low-caste Hindoos, were slow to take advantage of the opportunities for education, but the special efforts of the Government of Lord Mayo resulted in a tenfold increase of Mohammedan pupils. Until recently they took no interest in higher education, and, al-though in the early part of the century nearly all the lawyers in Calcutta were Mussulmans, they disappeared from the professions and Government offices from the opening of the educational era till quite recently. In the Northwest Provinces and Oudh, on the contrary, the Mussulmans, who constitute only 13 per cent. of the population, but preserve the instincts of a governing aristocracy, are found in the schools and colleges considerably in excess of that ratio, and in open competition with the Hindoos secure 34 per cent. of the administrative offices and 57 per cent. of the superior judicial and executive posts to which natives are eligible. The Mussulman nobles have founded and endowed at Aligarh one of the largest and finest colleges in Islam. A prime reason for the preponderance of Hindoos in official and professional life is that they devote themselves chiefly to English, mathematics, and other studies that are of practical advantage, whereas Mohammedan youth of promise are usually sent to the religious colleges to become versed in Arabic and the theology and laws of Islam.

Commerce.—The ocean commerce of India, exclusive of Government stores and treasure, amounted in 1887 to 697,100,000 rupees of imports and 901,100,000 rupees of exports, showing an increase in ten years of 131,000,000 rupees in the imports and 228,000,000 rupees in the exports, or an expansion of 33 per cent. in the total trade. The export trade in the principal staples showed the following increase in the ten years: Raw cotton, from 93,800,000 to 134,700,000 rupees; seeds, from 73,600,000 to 92,200,000 rupees; rice, from 69,500,000 to 88,300,000 rupees; wheat, from 28,700,000 to 86,200,000 rupees; hides and skins, from 37,500,000 to 51,400,000 rupees; tea, from 30,600,000 to 48,800,000 rupees; raw jute, from 35,100,000 to 48,600,000 rupees; jute manufactures, from 7,700,000 to 11,500,000 rupees; indigo, from 34,900,000 to 36,900,000 rupees; cotton twist and yarn, 7,400,000 to 34,100,000 rupees; cotton manufactures, from 15,500,000 to 24,300,000 rupees; wool, from 9,600,000 to 13,400,000 rupees; coffee, from 13,400,000 to 15,100,000 rupees. Opium showed a falling off, the export in 1878 having been valued at 123,700,000 rupees, and in 1887 at 110,700,000 rupees. The exports of gums and resins increased each year till 1887, when they fell below the value in 1878, owing to exceptional causes. Jewelry, sugar, wood, woolen manufactures, and raw silk show a considerable and increasing decline, while the exports of hemp, ivory, and coir, and their manufactures, of the manufactures of silk, of drugs and medicines, and of oils, spices, and tobacco have grown in importance. The sea-borne imports of merchandise, exclusive of Government stores, in the year ending March 31, 1887, were valued at 586,960,710 rupees, and the imports of treasure on private account at 110,483,220 rupees, making a total of 697,-

443,930 rupees. The merchandise exports were 884,395,780 rupees in value; treasure, 16,844,210 rupees; total, 901,239,990 rupees. The imports of Government stores and treasure amounted to 31,158,890 rupees, and the exports to 774,610 rupees. The total imports of gold during the year were 28,285,610 rupees; of silver, 82,197,610 rupees; exports of gold, 6,564,920 rupees; of silver, 10,639,330 rupees. The principal countries that participated in the trade of India in 1887 and their respective shares in the imports and exports of merchandise in rupees were as follow:

COUNTRIES.	Imports.	Exports.
Great Britain	467,595,190	342,986,100
China	21,879,580	134,835,810
France	8,695,150	77,230,150
Straits Settlements	15,905,460	41,546,010
Italy	4,255,410	52,791,660
United States	11,703,810	82,481,040
Belgium	2,902,580	36,086,450
Austria-Hungary	7,238,640	26,394,820
Mauritius	16,564,550	8,815,280
Egypt	686,070	25,484,110

The imports of cotton manufactures were 291,648,850 rupees in value; of metals and hardware, 55,544,950 rupees; of silk, raw and manufactured, 21,771,111 rupees; of sugar, 20,805,390 rupees; of woolen goods, 15,288,650 rupees; of liquors, 14,597,740 rupees; of railway material and rolling-stock, 14,351,240 rupees; of oils, 14,084,300 rupees; of machinery, 13,714,590 rupees; of coal, 13,166,150 rupees. The imports by way of the land frontiers were valued for the year 1887 at 51,410,386 rupees, and the exports at 3,463,343 rupees.

Agriculture and Industry.—There are 364,051,611 acres of land in British India, exclusive of 40,185,729 acres of forests; but only 152,834,640 acres are actually cultivated, including 22,725,391 acres of fallow land. Of the 166,492,458 acres of uncultivated land, about half is fit for cultivation, affording enormous scope for the extension of the wheat, cotton, coffee, tea, indigo, and other crops of exportable produce. The distribution of the crops in 1887 was as follows: Rice, 23,114,662 acres; wheat, 19,883,040; other grains and pulse, 71,439,218; tea, 226,412; cotton, 9,852,654; oil-seeds, 7,678,382; indigo, 1,034,889. The exportation of wheat, which was always one of the principal crops of India, was rendered possible by the abolition of the export duty in 1873, and has grown to its present proportions in consequence of the development of the Indian railroads and the Suez Canal. Oil-seeds were freed from the export duty in 1875, and their exportation increased from 4,000,000 cwt. before that time to 18,000,000 cwt. in 1885. The export of indigo in 1887 showed an increase of 15½ per cent. over the preceding year in quantity, but prices fell heavily, except in the qualities demanded in the American market, owing to the competition of the Java indigo, which is said to rival the best produce of Tirhut. The pro-

duction of tea in Assam for 1886–'87 was reported as 61,719,678 pounds, which, added to 16,500,000 pounds produced in Bengal, makes the total product of India more than five times greater than in 1872. There was a failure of the wheat-crop in the Punjab and the Northwest Provinces in 1886–'87.

Cotton-weaving by hand was an important industry in India until it was crushed by the competition of the Lancashire mills. Steammills have since been established, and the manufacture is expanding with great rapidity. In 1884 there were one hundred mills for the manufacture of cotton and jute, with 22,000 looms and 2,000,000 spindles, giving employment to 110,000 people. The manufacture of iron by modern methods is a new industry that has not yet passed the experimental stage. There is an unlimited supply of iron-ore and of coal, but facilities for transportation are lacking, and new methods of smelting must be devised because the Indian coal contains from 14 to 20 per cent. of ash, six or eight times as much as English coal. This difficulty has been overcome in the application of coal to locomotives and steamboats, and partly overcome in metallurgical industry.

Gold-Mining.—Gold in Southern India is generally found only in quartz reefs at depths where the native miners have been unable to quarry, but which are accessible with the modern appliances for draining and ventilating mines. The gold-bearing rocks of India seem to be much richer on the average than those of Australia or California. In Mysore there are a large number of reefs, which even at shallow depths yield from one to two ounces per ton. The Mysore Gold Company, the first one in India to go into practical operation, has thus far worked with profit what appears to be a true fissure vein, paying twenty per cent. dividends. Other mines have been opened in the same state, and the Maharajah and his Prime Minister do all that they can to promote the industry, and have become shareholders in several of the companies. The pioneer company has now sixty stamps at work.

Navigation.—The tonnage entered and cleared at the ports of British India in 1887 was 7,172,193. The number of vessels arriving and departing by the Suez Canal was 1,671 of 2,946,650 tons. Of 5,140 vessels of 3,514,672 tons entered at all the ports, 1,903 of 2,745,162 tons belonged to England or her colonies; 1,011 of 133,865 tons were British Indian; 1,446 of 75,784 tons belonged to native states; and 780 of 359,861 tons were foreign vessels. The total number cleared was 5,444; the tonnage, 3,657,521. Coasting-vessels are not included in the foregoing figures. Of these there were entered 112,371 of 7,932,226 tons; cleared, 108,321 of 7,941,851 tons.

The Post-Office.—The number of letters, postal-cards, and money-orders that passed through the Indian Post-Office in 1886 was 216,145,796; of newspapers, 20,341,814; of parcels,

1,476,271; of packets, 5,119,335. The receipts were 11,130,860 rupees, and the expenses, 13,026,040 rupees.

Telegraphs.—The telegraph lines in 1887 had a total length of 30.034 miles, with 86,891 miles of wire. The number of messages was 2,534,685. The mileage and the business have about doubled in ten years, and the receipts also, which are not yet equal to the expenditures, although the disparity is less than in 1887, when the figures were 3,400,000 rupees for receipts, and 4,700,000 rupees for expenditure, whereas in 1887 they were respectively 6,900,000 and 7,100,000 rupees.

Railroads.—The number of miles of railroad open to traffic on March 31, 1888, was 14,383, of which 3,911 miles belonged to guaranteed companies, 654 to assisted companies, 8,994 to the Government, and 824 to native states. The mileage had increased from 13,390 miles in 1887, 12,376 in 1886, 11,983 in 1885, and 10,784 in 1884. There were 2,487 miles under construction in 1888, and 355 miles more had been sanctioned. The length of the guaranteed lines has decreased, the roads having been purchased by the state. There are 50 separate lines, of which 22 belong to the Government. The guaranteed companies have the concession of the profitable trunk lines, while the state lines serve as feeders. The total passenger traffic increased from 58,875,918 in 1882 to 95,411,779 in 1887; the freight traffic from 14,833,243 tons to 20,195,677; the receipts from 153,000,000 rupees in 1882 to 184,600,-000 rupees in 1888; and the cost of operation in the same time from 76,600,000 to 91,000,-000 rupees. The capital expended in railroad construction up to the beginning of 1887 was 1,704,989,107 rupees. The Government had expended £78,358,404 in building railroads and £35,048,368 in guaranteed interest on the subsidized lines up to March 31, 1888. The increase of capital in the guaranteed lines in five years had been £4,396,262, and in that period there had been a profit of £10,700, whereas up to 1883 there was a loss of more than £17,000. The existing railroads form five classes, viz.. state lines worked by companies, with a capital expenditure of £62,500,000; state lines worked by the Government, with £50,-000,000 of invested capital; the lines of guaranteed companies, which have invested £61,-333,000; the lines of assisted companies, which cost £3,750,000; and those owned by native states, with a capital of more than £5,000,000. The construction of military railroads in recent years has added to the annual losses of the treasury on account of railroads, the net deficit in 1886–'87 being 9,827,927 rupees, the transportation of grain having been much less than in the preceding year. The cost of the Scinde-Pishin and Bolan Pass strategic lines has been over 80,000,000 rupees.

The Army.—The strength of the British garrison in India for 1887–'88 was fixed in the army estimates at 2,551 officers and 69,240 men. Including the native army, but exclusive of artificers and followers, the Indian forces at the close of 1886 numbered 5,192 officers and 183,594 men. The Hindoo fendatory states have armies numbering 275,075 men and 3,372 guns, and the Mohammedan states 74,760 men and 865 guns. The British, after an investigation of the strength of the native armies in 1884, had in contemplation measures for the compulsory disbandment of these forces. When the Russian war-scare came two years later, the native princes, actuated partly by the old dread of a barbarian invasion from the north, and partly by the desire to prove that their military establishments are a source of strength instead of a menace to the empire, began to offer pecuniary aid and military service to the Government in case the frontier is attacked. Such offers continue to be received. In the beginning of 1888, with 60 lakhs that the Nizam of Hyderabad had promised to contribute, and 10 lakhs proffered by the Maharajah of Cashmere, the specific offers of money amounted to over a crore of rupees, or a million sterling. The princes offered troops in addition, and others of the feudatory princes, including the rulers of Bhawalpore, Patiala, Tonk, Rampore, Alwar, and Mandi, offered troops or money according to the necessities of the empire, some of them placing the entire resources of their states at the disposal of the Government.

Finances.—The revenue for the year ending March 31, 1886, was 746,641,970 rupees, and the expenditure 772,659,230 rupees, of which 598,397,530 rupees were expended in India and 184,261,700 rupees in Great Britain. The revised estimates for 1886–'87 make the revenue 760,810,000 rupees and the expenditure 760,210,000 rupees. The budget estimates for 1887–'88 calculate the total receipts at 774,-600,000 rupees, of which 229,380,000 rupees represent the land revenue, 154,320,000 rupees the road and railroad receipts, 88,930,000 rupees the revenue from the opium monopoly, 66,050,000 rupees the salt-tax, 42,250,000 rupees the excise duties, 37,160,000 rupees the stamp duties, 29,570,000 rupees the provincial rates, 20,250,000 rupees the receipts from the postal and telegraphic services and the mint, 16,880,000 rupees the irrigation rates, 14,060,-000 rupees assessed taxes, 12,330,000 rupees customs duties, 11,310,000 rupees forest receipts, and 37,870,000 rupees interest, tribute, registration duties, and other receipts. The expenditure for 1887–'88 is estimated at 774-430,000 rupees, of which 221,100,000 rupees represent expenditures on roads and railroads, 191,970,000 rupees for military purposes, 131,-800,000 rupees in the civil departments, 80,-800,000 rupees the cost of collection, 44,120,-000 rupees interest on the debt, 24,410,000 rupees irrigation expenses, 22,620,000 rupees expenses of the post-office, telegraphs, and mint, and 9,030,000 rupees for other purposes. The extraordinary expenditure on public works, fixed at 49,940,000 rupees, is not charged against the revenue. The revenue in 1887-'88 exceeded the first estimates by 15,-000,000 rupees; but there was an unexpected increase in the civil expenditures of almost that amount, while the military expenditures as usual went far beyond the estimates. To avoid a deficit, the Government raised the salt duty and imposed a new import duty on petroleum, expecting to obtain from both sources an increased income of 17,900,000 rupees. The petroleum duty is a specific duty, the rate of which is about eight per cent. The salt duty is raised to one rupee in Burmah and two and a half rupees in other parts of India per maund of eighty-two pounds. The additional tax is expected to bring in 15,000,000 rupees in India and 1,250,000 rupees in Burmah.

The National Congress.—The first Indian National Congress met in Bombay in 1885, and consisted of 50 delegates. The second was held in Calcutta in 1886, and numbered 436 delegates. A third Congress appointed by a more developed system of electoral bodies, and intended to present with the force of a general consensus the opinion of the educated native community on the political needs of the country, assembled in Madras in December, 1887. It was composed of 603 delegates, of whom 311 were appointed at public meetings and 292 were sent by organized associations. Some of the public meetings were great gatherings at the capitals of presidencies, and others concourses of representatives from the towns and villages of a province or revenue circle. The local associations represented at the Congress were of the most varied character, and included race societies of Hindoos, Mohammedans, Eurasians, native Christians, Jains, and Parsees, mercantile corporations, associations of agriculturists, landholders, tenants, and artisans, and a committee of native journalists. The Mohammedan community had taken no part in former congresses and was represented by 83 delegates in this one, which chose a Mohammedan, who had been a member of the council of the Governor of Bombay, for its president. The delegates represented widely different classes. There were Rajahs, Mohammedan nobles, members of legislative councils, officials of various grades, the prime ministers of native states, merchants, bankers, editors, professors, manufacturers, and even a Hindoo abbot, who represented his monastery, and a high-priest.

The Congress adopted resolutions for a permanent organization, providing for twelve standing committees distributed among the great territorial divisions of the Indian Empire, for the preparation of the business to be brought before the Congress at the end of each year, and for the submission of the conclusions of the Congress to the Viceroy and the Secretary of State. Four of the resolutions of the Congress relate to the expansion or modification of the existing institutions of civil government. One of these is a proposal for the separation without delay of the judicial from the executive branch of the administration. The higher judicial and executive functions were divided in the early part of the century, and the separation has been gradually carried into the lower grades until it is almost complete in some of the provinces. The collector magistrate, however, is a relic of the system preserving its faults in an obnoxious form. He is the executive head, the collector of revenue, the chief of the police administration, and the judicial magistrate for a large area embracing sometimes as many as 2,000,-000 inhabitants. As collector he must move about his district, and suitors and witnesses must follow him in his journeys, and submit often to postponements when his fiscal duties are pressing. The Government in some places has appointed a joint magistrate to hear criminal cases, with appeal to the collector. The unruly state of the country was formally pleaded as a reason for abolishing the combination of judge and executive officer in the same person, but now the main obstacle is the expense. Another subject on which the Congress laid much stress is the need of technical education to enable India to compete with Europe and America in modern industries. The 6,287 students under instruction in technical schools and colleges are confined almost exclusively to medicine and engineering, whereas schools in the mechanical arts, such as exist in European countries, and also schools of husbandry, are needed. Another proposal was to raise the limit of incomes on which the income-tax is levied from 500 to 1,000 rupees. The extortions and oppressions of subordinate officials which are mainly practiced on the poor, render the tax odious, and its severity was acknowledged by the Government, which proposed to exempt incomes of persons in public employ below 1,000 rupees, but abandoned its purpose on account of the opposition shown to such an unfair distinction. A fourth resolution suggests the expansion and reform of the legislative councils. The functions of the Viceroy's Legislative Council should embrace the examination and discussion of the budget, in the opinion of the native community, as represented in the Congress, which is sustained by the views of the Anglo-Indian community. English statesmen have often deplored the expenditure of Indian public money without criticism or control, except the farce of a discussion in Parliament before empty benches. The last new rules of parliamentary procedure deprive members of the right of raising questions of general Indian administration in the debate on the Indian budget, which must now be confined to financial and economic subjects, and consequently there is no opportunity of presenting Indian grievances. The Congress asked also for the restoration of the right of interpellation in the Legislative Council, which was conceded to the earlier body in 1854, in regard to all questions of internal civil administration. The Congress desired the increase of the non-official members from one third to one half of the Council, which would still leave the Government with a working majority, since it could never provoke the united opposition of the non-official members. The army ought, in the opinion of the Congress, to be excluded from the Council, and the introduction of the elective principle in choosing the non-official members of the councils of the Viceroy and the provincial governors was suggested. The proposition for introducing the elective method was as cautious as the other resolutions of the Congress. It is proposed that, after the electoral college has been constituted with due precautions from the municipal councils, chambers of commerce, and other representative bodies, it shall be subjected to the scrutiny and revision of the Government, which would supply the representation of classes that have been passed over or are inadequately represented by nominating additional members. The Congress reaffirmed the resolution adopted in 1886, when Russian aggression in Afghanistan drew from the leading potentates of the feudatory states the offer of a million sterling and their armies, asking the Government to authorize a system of volunteering. The Congress pointed out that the age of mercenaries is over in Europe, that England must depend in a great struggle on the fighting-men among her own subjects, and that India can furnish what England chiefly lacks, that is, numbers. The delegates were of various minds in regard to a resolution requesting the repeal of the arms act, some thinking the prohibition to carry arms a slur on the loyalty of the people, others wishing to avoid so delicate a subject, and others still insisting on the practical hardships of the people whose lives are exposed to wild beasts, whose cattle are killed by thousands, and whose crops are destroyed by wild boars, and a resolution was adopted in favor of transferring the licensing authority from the Central Government to the municipal and rural councils.

In April a meeting of Mohammedans was held at Madras to protest against the National Congress and express regret at the prospective departure of Lord Dufferin, who had shown a desire to promote the welfare of all classes and sympathy with the Moslem community. Anti-Congress meetings were held at Peshawur, Dacca, and other places, where Mohammedans condemned the movement as dangerous. The fourth National Congress met in Allahabad, the capital of the Northwest Provinces, in December, 1888.

Marriage-Reform Movement. — The movement for the reform of the Hindoo customs of infant marriage and enforced celibacy of widows is not merely an extraneous agitation carried on by Europeans, but has many adherents among educated Indians from the classes that chiefly follow these practices, viz., the higher Brahmin and Rajput castes, for neither custom is practised by the lower classes of the people. In Bengal, among every 1,000 girls between the

ages of five and nine, 271 are provided with husbands, and 11 are widows, doomed to an unhappy position of isolation and ignominy. There are about 1,000,000 girl-widows among the Hindoo population. Among the high caste every female child becomes a wife, and many are widows, before reaching their fourteenth year. The custom of enforced celibacy is closely connected with the liability of the husband's heirs to provide that no woman of the family should be without a home, and that of early marriage on the requirements of the Brahmanical religion which make it a father's duty to secure protectors for his daughters. The customs of infant marriage and perpetual celibacy in themselves have no sanction in the Veda, but they were enjoined by religious teachers of mediæval times, and are considered to have a religious sanction by the great majority of the priests. A large sect of the Brahman caste, which represents advanced thought and supplies the intellectual leaders of the people, is strongly in favor of reform, and is supported by large numbers in the lower castes. The British authorities have established by law the right of Hindoo widows to marry again and retain their property, provided they embrace some other religion. They do not venture, however, to meddle with the ecclesiastical laws and religious customs of the Hindoos.

The Government convened a meeting in March, at Ajmere, of representatives of the states of Rajputana, to consider the question of marriage reform. The representative committee adopted a set of resolutions for regulating the excessive expenses of weddings and funerals, which weigh heavily on the community, to the advantage of certain privileged classes, as well as making the marriageable age older in both sexes, to wit, fourteen years for girls and eighteen for boys. These resolutions were embodied in a decree that was issued by the princes of Rajputana, who have always held the highest rank in Hindoo society, and whose initiatory action in reforming the custom of infant marriages was, therefore, strongly desired by the British authorities.

Religious Animosities.—The religious hatred between the Hindoos and Mohammedans has been aggravated by an agitation that has sprung up among the Hindoos against cow-killing. In 1888 the Moslem festival of Mohurrum and the Hindoo festival of Ramlila, fell on the same day, with the inevitable result of sanguinary collisions and disorders. Serious disturbances at Agra, Ghazipore, and Coorg, were narrowly averted by the prompt action of the authorities in calling out the troops and volunteers to restore order. At Nujibabad a mob made an attack on a civil officer, at whose command the police fired, killing and wounding many persons.

The Hyderabad Mining Concession.—The Nizam, in January, 1886, granted a monopoly of mining rights in his dominions for ninety-nine years to two English promoters named Watson and Stewart, who undertook to form a company, primarily to work the coal-mines at Singeréni, for which purpose £150,000 shares of capital, one half paid up should be issued. The remainder of the £1,000,000 nominal capital was to be issued when new mines were opened or iron-works established, in such amounts as the needs of the company warranted. The East India Deccan Mining Company was incorporated in London, and the promoters issued to themselves the 85,000 reserve £10 shares, no part of which was paid up. The Nizam, who expected the company to aid in the material development of his country and the completion of its railroad network, authorized his Secretary of the Interior, Abdul Huk, who was in London as his representative at the Queen's Jubilee, to invest in the enterprise. Abdul Huk, who had privity of the issue of the entire stock, and received a bribe of £150,000, purchased 10,000 shares, bidding the price up to £12 per share. The Nizam, when he learned how the *concessionnaires* were swindling him and the public, in collusion with his agent, compelled the latter to disgorge the bribe, and considered how he could annul the franchise without prejudice to the rights of *bona-fide* investors. On the motion of Mr. Labouchere, the subject was investigated by a special committee of the House of Commons. Sir Salar Jung, who had innocently arranged the purchase of shares in London for the sake of aiding the credit of the company, was soon afterward succeeded as Nawab or Prime Minister by Sir Asman Jah.

The War in Sikkim.—The commercial exploitation of Tibet has been discussed by English writers for some years past, especially since the extensive travels in that country of two native Indian officials were published. The tea-planters of Assam are covetous of the Tibetan market, because the refuse of their product is superior to the article supplied at exorbitant prices by a combination of the Lama priests and Chinese merchants to the Tibetans, who would eagerly exchange their excellent wool for tea, of which they are extraordinarily fond, although so ill supplied. In 1886 a commercial mission to Lhassa was planned by the Indian Government, and an expedition was organized on a large scale, which was to start from Darjeeling, under Colman Macaulay, with an imposing military escort. The Tibetans taking alarm, occupied Sikkim, a frontier feudatory state of India, and built a fort at Lingtu to contest the advance of the English expedition from Darjeeling to the Jelapla Pass. The commercial mission was therefore abandoned, and the Tibetans were left in possession of Sikkim, the Rajah of which retired into Tibet, and made common cause with the invaders. A force was sent in 1887 to reassert British sovereignty, but it was totally inadequate, and retired on discovering the true situation. Great

Britain then made representations to the Chinese Government, considering Tibet a tributary state of China. The Chinese disclaimed any sovereignty over Lhassa, except one of a spiritual and ceremonial nature, and denied having rights of any sort over the numerous kingdoms outside of Lhassa. In the treaty concluded with the British Government on the subject of the occupation of Upper Burmah, the Pekin Government promised to exercise its good offices at Lhassa to prepare a favorable reception for a commercial mission if the English would defer the expedition till a more favorable time. The Chinese ministers in 1876, when the British Government negotiated with them for an additional article to the convention of Chefoo, explained that their authority over Lhassa was very limited, and that they could do no more than exercise their influence to assist a British mission to enter the country. In 1883, when referring to the visit of an English traveler to Yarkand, they declared that they would always issue passports to British subjects to travel in Turkistan, because that was a dominion of the empire, but were unable to issue passports for Tibet, which did not belong to the empire, and the Pekin Government could not overcome the reluctance of the lamas to admit Europeans. And again, in documents relating to the journey of Mr. Carey in Turkistan and Tibet, they made the same disclaimer of authority in Si-Tsang, or the Lhassa territory. The British have nevertheless assumed to regard Tibet as a dependency of China, and regard the two Chinese Ambans Residents at Lhassa, as the actual regents of the country. In the beginning of 1888, before taking military measures for the re-establishment of British power in Sikkim, the Government of China was called upon to secure the evacuation of the country by the Tibetans. The Lhassa authorities have heretofore given currency to the fiction that they are subject to the Chinese Emperor's rule, by pretending to have orders from Pekin whenever they refused permission to travelers to enter Tibet from India. The exclusiveness of the Mongol races is exaggerated in the Tibetans, owing to the mountainous nature of their frontiers, the character of their religion, and their dread of an influx of foreigners to contest with them the scanty food-supply of their infertile land. Formerly the Tibetans received English missions freely, and it is only since they have become afraid of British conquest that they refuse to allow Europeans to set foot on the other side of the Himalayan passes, although they admit native Indian traders.

The Indian Government made preparations to expel the Tibetans from Sikkim in August, 1887, but the Chinese Government pleaded for delay in order that it might use its influence at Lhassa. The request was granted, and the 15th of March was fixed as the last day of grace for the evacuation of Sikkim. The Rajah of Sikkim returned from Tibet to Tumlong, his capital, before the close of 1887, bringing with him a large train of Tibetan counselors. A regiment of pioneers, with two mountain-guns, was ordered to Sikkim, with the expectation that they would secure possession of the country and frighten away the Tibetans. At their approach the Rajah sent a message expressing a wish to enter into friendly negotiations, and asking for the restoration of the stipend that he received from the Indian Government before he went to Tibet. In conferences with Mr. Paul, deputy-commissioner at Darjeeling, he nevertheless showed an intractable and defiant disposition. The Viceroy addressed the lama on the subject of the violation of the Indian frontier, saying that the Indian Government desired to be on terms of friendship with Tibet; and the Chinese Government brought pressure to bear at Lhassa to secure the withdrawal of the Tibetan garrison in Sikkim. The advance of the British force of 1,300 men, whose ostensible mission was to repair the road that had been constructed by the Indian Government through Sikkim, was preceded by an ultimatum demanding the evacuation of Fort Lingtu, on the receipt of which the Tibetans strengthened their garrison. The Viceroy went to Darjeeling to hold a conference with the Rajah of Sikkim, who refused to come. The Chinese Ambans were recalled from Lhassa on account of the failure of his mediation, and others of higher rank were sent, while the Pekin Government requested a further postponement of hostile operations to allow time for one more diplomatic effort. To this the English would not accede. The expeditionary force, which was increased to 2,000 men and transformed from a pretended road-mending expedition into a regular field force, commanded by Col. Graham, halted on the border, and made preparations to march into Sikkim at the expiration of the time set. Meanwhile the Tibetans collected large bodies of troops beyond the Jelapla and Donkyla passes, ready to enter Sikkim if the British advanced. Lingtu is forty miles from Darjeeling and within seven miles of the Jelapla Pass, which is 13,700 feet above the sea-level. There are several passes connecting Sikkim with Tibet, 13,000 to 16,000 feet in height. Sikkim is the most insignificant of the Indian dependencies of Great Britain, which has no value except that it commands the principal route into Tibet. The road to the Jelapla Pass that the Tibetans seized was built by the British under a treaty made with the Rajah in 1861, giving them the right to make and maintain roads in Sikkim. The relations between the Indian Government and Sikkim began in 1814, when they entered into an alliance against Nepaul. At the close of the war the Rajah received a large accession of territory, and twenty years later he ceded to the Indian Government the district of Darjeeling, which has since become important as a sanitarium and as a tea-growing district. A few years after this the Rajah, in retaliation

for some act of the British authorities, made a captive of Dr. Joseph Hooker, the botanist, and was compelled by a military expedition to part with a section of his territory. Another expedition in 1860 extorted a treaty granting free trade, protection of foreigners, and the right of road-making. The Rajah is a Buddhist, owning the authority of the Grand Lama. and when the Macaulay expedition collected on the confines of his territory he retired to Lhassa and submitted the question to his spiritual lord to dispose of, and the latter posted a force in Sikkim to meet the invaders. The present area of Sikkim is 1,550 square miles, and the population does not exceed 7,000. The Rajah is sovereign also of a territory in the Chumbi valley across the Himalayas, where he has been accustomed to spend a portion of every year.

Col. Graham's force moved forward in two columns on March 17. On the 20th they reached the works at Lingtu under cover of a fog, and took them with a rush, the Tibetans hastily escaping into the forest. The troops advanced to Rhaderchen, where they were brought to a stand by a Tibetan force firing from a stockade. This was captured on the following day. Garrisons were posted at several points, while a Tibetan army mustered in the Chumbi valley, beyond the Jelapla Pass. The Tibetan lamas made an attack on the British at Lingtu, but were severely defeated and pursued in all directions. In the middle of April Col. Graham transferred his principal encampment from Padong to Gnatong, which commands the Tukola Pass. The Lieutenant-Governor of Bengal made an unsuccessful attempt to open peace negotiations. On May 23 the Tibetans nearly surprised the camp at Gnatong, and made a heroic effort to capture it, but were repelled after an engagement of three hours, with a loss of one hundred killed, while with their antiquated weapons they inflicted on the British a loss of only three killed and seven wounded. The European troops, who suffered severely from the cold and storms, were ordered to withdraw from Sikkim before the rainy season, being replaced by native troops in the fortified camp that was constructed at Gnatong. A campaign far away from the base, beyond the snowy mountains, was what the British desired to avoid, for if it were undertaken nothing would solve the difficulty but an expensive war for the occupation of Lhassa and the effective conquest of Tibet. They therefore preferred to remain in the awkward situation in which they had been betrayed, looking to Chinese intervention for an escape from the necessity of keeping a permanent military guard in the icy passes of the Himalayas. The Tibetans were as active as the English in the work of fortification, throwing a high stone wall across the entire width of the Jalapla Pass. Soon after the arrival of the new Chinese Residents the authorities at Lhassa sent messengers to Gnatong, but instead of making proposals for peace, they massed an army of 8,000 men that was ready to fall upon the fortifications as soon as the European forces retired to Darjeeling, and Col. Graham therefore remained at Gnatong with a part of his force. The Tibetan levies were increased to 15,000, and though they did not venture to attack the earthworks defended by mountain-guns and steel 7-pounders, they strongly held the passes. Re-enforcements of Goorkhas were sent from India, and all the British troops were ordered back to Sikkim. The lamas advanced to the foot of the Pemberingo Pass, where they threw up fortifications, and pushed forward their outposts into the Sikkim valleys, where several skirmishes took place with British troops. The threatened advance of the lamas caused consternation among the European residents of Darjeeling. By the beginning of September all the re-enforcements had arrived at Gnatong, and Col. Graham made preparations for an offensive movement against the Tibetans, who already occupied the Japhu valley in front of the Jelapla and Pemberingo passes, and were ready to take possession of the whole of Sikkim as soon as the British should retire into winter quarters at a lower level, which would tend to strengthen the endeavors of the Tibet authorities to confederate Nepaul, Bhotan, and the other frontier powers against the Indian Government. The Rajah of Sikkim was allowed to remain unmolested at Eutchi or Gantok, till now an attempt was made to seize him in the night, which resulted in his flight to the Tibetans. On September 24 the British advanced on the fortified positions. The Tibetans, who mustered in strong force on the Tukola ridge, were dislodged by artillery fire followed up by the charge of the infantry, and fled in disorder to the Jelapla and Pemberingo passes. These were also occupied, and the Tibetan levies, completely disorganized, escaped into Bhotan and northward into Tibet, while the British force crossed the mountains to Rinchigong, and on the following morning occupied Chumbi and the Rajah's palace, where his papers were seized. The Tibetan loss was 1,000, while only one Goorkha was killed on the British side, though Col. Bromhead, who commanded the left wing, was severely wounded. The troops carried only a single day's provisions, and therefore returned to Gnatong. The rout of the Tibetan army was so effectual that only 3,000 or 4,000 out of 11,000 rallied, and their magazines and commissariat supplies at Lingmutong were destroyed. The Rajah returned and yielded submission, arriving at Gantong on October 2. The Chinese Amban at Lhassa sent a letter requesting a meeting with the Lieutenant-Governor at Darjeeling to discuss terms of peace on behalf of the Tibetan Government. The Dalai Lama, whose spiritual and temporal supremacy is acknowledged by the Tibetan Buddhists, does not rule in person, but through a regent, called the Desi, being a

minor, as all his predecessors have been for nearly a hundred years. The British were anxious to make peace on any terms short of acknowledging the Tibetan claim to Sikkim, which would endanger their supremacy over the other frontier states. The government of the Dalai Lama extends over 4,000,000 people, including the monks in the monasteries, and to conquer this nation would necessitate not only the destruction of an army of 60,000 men that the lamas could immediately place in the field, but the continuous occupation of a wide country, barren of supplies, where the native Indian troops could not endure the arctic severity of the winters.

The Black Mountain Expedition.—Col. Richmond Battye and Capt. Urmston were killed in June, 1888, while making an excursion in the Hazara district, in the extreme northeastern part of the Peshawur division of the Punjab. They crossed the line into Agror, and when returning were attacked by a body of Akazais, a Black mountain tribe, against which the Indian Government had for some time maintained a blockade as a punishment for various offenses. The English officers were accompanied by a Goorkha escort of seventy men, and in defending Col. Battye, who was the commander of the blockading force stationed at Oghi, six of the sepoys were killed. In September an expedition of 8,000 fighting men was equipped to punish the mountaineers. There were five regiments of British and nine of native infantry, one regiment of native cavalry, a company of sappers, and three batteries of artillery, all under the command of Maj.-Gen. J. W. McQueen. The Government of Cashmere agreed to guard the frontier near Khagan with 1,000 men. The Hazara field force, as the expedition was called, advanced in four columns from Oghi and Darband early in October. The Hassanzais and Akazais offered a bold resistance, and were only dislodged after severe fighting. The Likariwals were the only tribe to pay their fine without fighting. Capt. C. H. H. Beley, quartermaster of one of the brigades, was killed, Col. A. Crookshank, commanding the column, received a deadly wound, and two other officers were wounded. The most desperate fighting was with the Hassanzais at Kotkai, the objective point of one of the columns, which was occupied on October 5. The villages and crops of the tribesmen were destroyed, and strategic positions were occupied, yet their resistance was not broken, and detachments sent out to scour the country were more than once defeated. The Black mountain district, which is only thirty miles long by ten in breadth, is a rugged ridge that is transected by the Indus. The Hassanzais and the Akazais together mustered only 2,000 fighting men, armed with matchlocks, and with the Chagarzais in the north, the Allaiwals, and the Pararis, the Black mountain tribes were about 6,000 strong. They all belong to the Yusufzai branch of the indomitable Pathan race and are Mohammedans in religion. When a large force of Khyber mountaineers, under Maj. Adam Khan, were sent against the Akazais, and proved a match for them in guerilla tactics, they made their submission and paid the fine after their principal villages had been burned. The Hassenzais promised to pay the fine. The Chagarzais remained neutral, but it was decided to compel them to make submission, which they did before the end of October. One of the columns advanced to Thakot on the Indus in the extreme north, and from that point invaded the Allaiwal country. The Pararis and the Allaiwals held out till early in November, and when they offered their submission the expedition returned to India.

Burmah.—The troops in Upper Burmah numbered 27,859 in February, 1887, when the army of occupation was larger than at any previous time. It was composed of 6,781 British and 21,078 Indian troops. At the end of 1887 the force had been reduced to 3,791 British and 14,275 natives, making a total of 18,066. The extra army charges were 6,050,000 rupees in 1885-'86, 11,600,000 rupees in 1886-'87, and 13,500,000 rupees in 1887-'88, making a total of 31,150,000 rupees up to March 31, 1888. The Indian Government, which formerly drew a large revenue from Burmah, but has been compelled to spend still greater sums annually on the pacification of the country since the conquest of Upper Burmah, pursues a policy that is calculated to exterminate the Burmese race, in order that their fertile country may be peopled by servile Indian ryots. The opium vice, which is singularly fatal to the Burmese, was forced upon them for the benefit of the Indian revenue, against the protests of the respectable part of the community, and the traffic in strong drink has been encouraged for the same purpose. The hatred that the conquerors provoked by suppressing the Buddhist dynasty was almost as strong in Lower Burmah, where the people had been peaceful and orderly for half a century, as in the newly annexed province; yet, instead of trying to allay this feeling and winning respect by a just and beneficent rule, the British took the course most likely to fan disaffection into rebellion. Raw and ignorant, corrupt and brutal administrators, the dregs of the Indian civil service, were placed over the country, who attempted to practice on the high-spirited Burmese the insolent tyranny to which abject Indian races are accustomed to bow their necks. A military police recruited from the treacherous and bloodthirsty tribes of northern India was let loose on the country. These Indians mutinied against their English officers, who attempted to restrain their depredations, and practiced on the unarmed inhabitants various forms of violence, oppression, and pillage. The policy of disarming the Burmese had left the industrious and honest a prey to the robbers. They asked to have a police force raised in the country, and felt it to be the harshest of their ills

that the English, whom they looked upon as their equals in intelligence and civilization, sent a horde of ferocious savages to trample upon them. The military police, in March, 1888, consisted mainly of Punjabees, and numbered 20,000 men. Dacoity, as rebellion was officially called, in order that the bold and patriotic who took up arms against the oppressors might be destroyed without quarter, spread from Upper to Lower Burmah. After the effective campaign of 1887 the chief rebel leaders had all been killed or driven out of the valley of the Irrawaddy into the outlying regions where English rule had not yet been established. Yet oppression drove others to revolt, and new bands sprang up which carried on their guerilla operations secretly, returning to their fields after tearing up the railroad or attacking a police station, or plundering the friends of the invaders. When discovered they took up their abode in the forest, and levied tribute on the villagers for their support. In order to combat the evil without the expense of hunting the dakoits the Government adopted the punitive police tax, a measure that soon reduced prosperous communities to starvation. Wherever rebellion and disorder existed the villagers, taxed already by the dakoits, are compelled to pay heavy exemplary taxes to the Government, or often to corrupt officials who use the measure as a means of extortion. The English officials have no restraints on their actions but their sense of duty, since the judicial evidence of natives against them is not admitted. An English civil officer named Powell, after two villagers who had committed no legal offense had been killed by his orders and their brother-in-law bound, was shot by the father, and Mr. Hildebrand, superintendent of the Shan states, after a thorough investigation, decided that the man was justified in avenging the butchery of his sons and attempting to rescue his son-in-law. When the Indian police had scourged the country only to produce disorder, a small Burmese force was tried, on the recommendation of Sir Frederick Roberts, with good results.

The revenue of Lower Burmah for the year 1886-'87 was 30,134,790 rupees, an increase of 4,000,000 rupees over the receipts of the previous year; and the cost of civil administration was 15,656,940 rupees, leaving a surplus for military expenditures and expenses of the Indian Government of 14,477,850 rupees. The increase of revenue was obtained by raising the salt duty and imposing an income-tax. The province of Upper Burmah yielded a revenue of about 5,200,000 rupees, while the military and police expenditure amounted to 20,000,000 rupees. The railroad between Toungboo and Mandalay, 220 miles in length, was completed in 1888, and a section of 59 miles, reaching to Pyinmana, was opened in the summer. The creditors of King Thebaw and Queen Soopyalat, 393 in number, among them three Americans, presented claims for ninety-eight lakhs.

A privileged group obtained six lakhs, and the other creditors whose claims were recognized two and a half lakhs.

The northern Shan states, as far as the Salwen river, were invaded early in 1888 by a column commanded by Maj. Yates, and most of the chiefs acknowledged allegiance to the British Government. The most powerful of these, the Tsawbwas of Thebaw, had been banished by the late King, but was restored by the British, and with their aid extended his rule over neighboring territories. Other Tsawbwas who opposed the British were deposed in favor of rivals. In April the first disturbance occurred in Arrakan, the inhabitants of which are a distinct race from the Burmese. A band of dakoits crossed the hills from the valley of the Irrawaddy, released their leader, Mikhaya Bo, who was confined in Myohoung jail, and burned the town and the neighboring village of Gmoung, where the people fired on them. Although the Arrakanese hate the Burmese and have taken no part in the insurrection, the policy of disarmament was carried out among them as elsewhere throughout Burmah. The Setkya prince in Upper Burmah defeated the military police in several encounters in the summer of 1888. The Choungwa prince, another Alompra pretender, conducted his operations with bands of Shans and Kachyens in the neighborhood of the ruby-mines. Boh Shwayan, an able dakoit chief, who led the revolt in the Tsagain district, was killed by a detachment of British soldiers on July 25. Boh Ngano kept the Minbu and Toungdwingyee districts in a state of disturbance. The Chins of the Tashon hills captured the town of Indin and held it till a force of 1,000 men, with two guns, came from Mandalay to expel them in May. The other Chins joined in the rising, and raided the Kubo and Chindwin valleys. The Shwegyobin prince led the movement, and the Tsawbwa of Kale, whom the British had deposed, planned the operations. The Chins were closely pressed by the troops that were sent out against them, and finally released the new Tsawbwa, whom they had carried off, and said that they were willing to make peace if their own plundered cattle were restored. The British refused this, and added the unacceptable condition that the Shwegyobin prince and other rebels among them should be delivered up. The military authorities contemplated an expedition into the Chin country in the winter, but this the Indian Government refused to sanction. Disturbances in the Tharawaddy and Tenasserim districts of Lower Burmah were distinctly traceable to the corruption of the officials and the cruelty and criminal excesses of the police. Arbitrary exactions under the pretext of punitive taxes caused a famine in Tharawaddy. At Tavoy, a town on the border of Siam, from which country arms were smuggled in for the rebels, the merchants, some of whom were Chinese and some natives of India, informed the Commis-

sioner of Tenasserim that his subordinates were implicated in this traffic. The commissioner took no notice of their accusations, but some time afterward a punitive tax was levied on the town. On their refusal to pay the tax, which was illegal because no dakoities had taken place in the town, the police seized the furniture, jewelry, and stock in trade of the inhabitants. The Kachyens north of Bhamo attacked the fort at Mogoung in the spring, and held the country during the summer and autumn at their mercy. In November a military expedition was sent against them. In the south the Red Karens and Shans ravaged loyal villages. The Government in June decided not to enforce strictly the disarmament decree among the Christian Karens and Burmese villagers of the lower province. On June 9 dakoits plundered and burned Yeanangyoung, the headquarters of the petroleum trade. At the time of the conquest one of the great advantages that the people were led to expect was the abolition of monopolies. The monopolies of King Thebaw were abolished, except that of the teak-forests, which was held by a British-Indian company. The British ostensibly began the war. The financial exigencies of the Government and the jobbery that prevails in the Burman administration have led to the old monopolies being reconferred and others created. The holders of the India-rubber, jade, and mineral-oil concessions are empowered to close entire districts to all enterprises except their own. The Government of India granted the monopoly of the ruby-mines to the London jewelry firm of Streeter, but, owing to the scandalous manner in which the contract was awarded, the concession was not confirmed. The Queen-mother, Princess Soopyagee, the elder sister of Soopyalat, and an Alompra prince, who were confined at Mergui, were sent to India for greater safety in June. Deportation as a precautionary measure was applied not only to members of the royal family and political personages, but to persons of all ranks and conditions, of whom 50,000 had been sent to India before the autumn of 1888. The chief commissioner, in addressing an assemblage at Myinmu, a disturbed district, accused the people of cowardice in not giving information that would lead to the capture of dakoits who plundered them and burned their town. He threatened them with hanging or imprisonment across the seas and the confiscation of all their property, so that their wives and children would have to beg if they did not give the required assistance to the Government. Burmese who could aid the police to detect dakoits very rarely gave information, even though anxious to serve the Government, because their act was sure to come to the knowledge of rebels, and would be revenged by a death of lingering torture. An emigration scheme has been devised for peopling the rich bottom lands of the Irrawaddy with Bengalee emigrants. Large tracts of land on the Mandalay Railway line are to be granted on very favorable terms to planters who undertake to cultivate indigo, sugar, or other produce, and bind themselves to employ 90 per cent. of natives of India and not more than 10 per cent. of Burmans on their plantations. The Indian emigrants are to be brought from Calcutta at greatly reduced rates. The Burmese chief priests at Mandalay visited many districts and endeavored to restore peace.

During the rainy season pursuit of the dacoits is impossible, as the whole surface of the country is covered with deep mud. When the cold season approached, the troops and police resumed active operations against the rebels who had defied them during the summer. In October, Tha-Do and Nga-Chak, two notorious *bos*, or bandit chiefs, were killed by the police in the Pakoku district, and Gna-Bo-Ka, another dakoit leader, surrendered. On the 25th of the same month the Sekya pretender was driven from a fortified position in Kyonkse after a severe fight. The Government has been accustomed to grant amnesties to dacoits who surrendered themselves, promised to remain in a particular village, and found securities for their good behavior, and in this way many dangerous marauders were induced to settle down to peaceful occupations. Before the beginning of the winter campaign, Chief-Commissioner Crosthwaite announced his determination to grant no more pardons except for special reasons.

In December an expedition was sent in two divisions, one from Upper and one from Lower Burmah, against the eastern Karennees, who invaded the land of British tributaries.

Afghanistan.—The Government of India announced the intention of sending Henry Durand, the Foreign Secretary, on a confidential mission to the Ameer of Cabul in October. 1888; but the war between Abdurrahman and his cousin, Ishak Khan, Governor of Afghan Turkistan, interfered with the plan and caused a postponement of the embassy. The war between the two grandsons of Dost Mohammed originated in Ishak's preparations to assert his right to the succession when Abdurrahman was sick and was expected to die. On recovering, the Ameer summoned Ishak to his court, and the latter, knowing that he had mortally offended his cousin, instead of accepting the invitation and going to Cabul to meet his death, prepared to fight. Gholam Haidar, the Ameer's general, led a powerful army against Ishak. The Ameer's troops had a great advantage in the rifles and artillery furnished by the Indian Government. After preliminary engagements, the two armies met in pitched battle at Tashkurgan. One of the Ameer's divisions, commanded by the Governor of Badakshan, was routed in the beginning of the fight, but the fortune of the day was retrieved by Gholam Haidar's successful attack on the main body of the enemy, and,

when it was routed, turned on the division that had driven back a section of his own troops, and made prisoners of the whole of them. Pursuing the broken army to Mazari-Sherif on the following day, Gholam completed his victory, and made a prisoner of Mohammed Hosain, commander-in-chief of the defeated army. Ishak Khan made good his escape into Russian territory. The Ameer went into Turkistan to make a final settlement of the country and inquire into the history and instigators of the revolt.

INDIANA. State Government.—The following were the State officers during the year: Governor, Isaac P. Gray, Democrat; Lieutenant-Governor, Robert S. Robertson, Republican; Secretary of State, Charles F. Griffin, Republican; Treasurer, Julius A. Lemcke, Republican; Auditor, Bruce Carr, Republican; Attorney-General, Louis T. Michener, Republican; Superintendent of Public Instruction, Harvey M. La Follette; Judges of the Supreme Court, William E. Niblack, George V. Howk, Byron K. Elliott, Allen Zollars, Joseph A. S. Mitchell.

Finances.—For the fiscal year ending October 31, the receipts of the State treasury were $3,575,091.78; cash on hand at the beginning of the year, $373,941.21; total, $3,949,035.99. The disbursements during the same period were $3,621,309.83, leaving a balance of $327,726.16 on October 31. In his message, in January, 1889, the Governor says:

The last General Assembly failed to pass the general appropriation bill for the support of the State and its institutions, or to provide for the completion of the State-house, the three additional hospitals for the insane, the institution for feeble-minded youth, the Soldiers' and Sailors' Orphans' Home, and the soldiers' monument. At first it seemed as though the failure to enact such legislation would leave the State in such a financial condition that it would be impossible to meet the current expenses of the State and the additional obligations which the State had incurred by so many public improvements, or to complete any of the new institutions; but, contrary to the most sanguine expectation, nearly all the obligations of the State have been met—the interest on the public debt paid under provisions of the act of 1852; the Soldiers' and Sailors' Orphans' Home at Knightstown rebuilt; the land for the institution for feeble-minded youth at Fort Wayne purchased and the construction of the building commenced; the Hospital for Insane at Logansport completed, equipped, and opened for reception of patients; the hospitals at Evansville and Richmond completed ready for equipment and furnishing.

During the past two fiscal years the State debt has been increased by two temporary loans of $340,000 each, bearing date of April 1, 1887, and April 2, 1888, from which the interest on the debt was paid. The total debt is now $6,770,608.84, of which the sum of $3,904,783.22 is in the form of school-fund bonds held by the State for the benefit of schools. $340,000 is held by Purdue University, and $144,000 for the benefit of the State University by the State Treasurer. The remainder of the debt, $2,381,825.12, is taken by New York banks.

Charities.—The superintendent of the Insane Hospital reports that at the beginning of the fiscal year, Oct. 31, 1886, there were 1,588 patients at the institution, 696 being men and 892 women. To this number were added during the year 697. There were discharged in the same period 387 men and 301 women, a total of 688, and there were 84 deaths, leaving 1,513 patients at the end of the year. The suit brought in 1887 by the State to oust Directors Harrison and Gapen from the governing board of the institution, failed in its object. This hospital has long been inadequate to the needs of the State, many insane persons being supported at ill-equipped county institutions. An act was passed in 1883 providing for the construction of three additional hospitals; but the failure of the last Legislature to make appropriations delayed their completion. One of these, however, the Northern Hospital at Logansport, was completed and equipped during the year, being opened for patients on June 26. It was rapidly filled from county poor-houses and jails, and contained at the end of the year 188 men and 140 women; in all 328 persons. The estimated capacity of the hospital is 366 inmates.

The Soldiers' and Sailors' Orphans' Home at Knightstown contains accommodations for only 300 children, but at the end of the fiscal year in 1888 there were 340 in the institution and 100 additional on the rolls as applicants for admission. During the year, 195 applicants were admitted and 21 inmates discharged. The receipts from the State treasury for the year were $55,530, and the disbursements $54,447.85.

The School for the Feeble-Minded, being separated from the Orphans' Home by act of the last Legislature has been temporarily domiciled at the Eastern Insane Asylum at Richmond, now in process of erection, until permanent quarters at Fort Wayne can be completed. Land has been purchased at the latter place, and buildings are in process of erection. On October 31 there were 239 pupils, an increase of 179 from the time of the passage of the law, and of 134 from Oct. 31, 1887.

The State institution for the deaf and dumb had at the close of the fiscal year an attendance of 318, and the institution for the blind 144.

Prisons.—The number of prisoners at the Northern Prison at the close of the fiscal year was 702, and at the Southern Prison 539. At the reformatory for boys there were 462 persons.

The Women's Reformatory contained in its penal department on October 31, 55 convicts, and in the girls' reformatory 153 inmates. The receipts from industries carried on at the institution last year were $3,827.50, and the managers claim that the inmates are nearly self-supporting.

Normal Schools.—The State Normal School at Terre Haute suffered the entire loss of its building and library by a fire on April 9. At that time there were 624 students at the institution, representing eighty of the ninety-two counties of the State. The Centenary Methodist Episcopal Church, of Terre Haute, offered its building, and this and a portion of the Terre Haute High-School, which was also offered, enabled the work of the schools to go on without interruption. The city of Terre Haute also gave $50,000 toward the erection of a new building, which has been completed so far as the walls, iron, and stonework are concerned.

The Capitol.—On October 22 the State Capitol building, which had been in course of construction since 1879, was completed. Later in the year the Capitol Commission rendered its final report, showing the following yearly expenditures: 1879, $132,085.69; 1880, $193,-760.47; 1881, $201,631.67; 1882, $187,066.03; 1883, $52,891.72; 1884, $286,178.97; 1885, $424,825.65; 1886, $313,510.88; 1887, $169,-082.91; 1888, $178,333.72. These amounts, with the sum of $50,491.68 expended by the commission from May 24, 1877, when it was organized, to Dec. 31, 1878, make the total expenditure $2.191,859.42. Of this amount, $1,560,658.82 were raised by taxation, $507,-500 by issuing ten-year bonds, maturing in 1895, and $200,000 by appropriation from the general fund.

Railroads.—The assessment for 1888 upon railroads in the State amounted to $64,211,717.

Live-Stock.—The following returns for 1888 are given by the Bureau of Statistics: Number of horses, 587,709; mules, 60,188; cattle (including milch cows), 1,843,473; sheep, 1,-266,109. These figures show an increase over 1887, except in the sheep industry. The wool-product has also decreased, being 3,634,159 pounds against 4,197,000 pounds in 1887.

County Statistics.—The total expenditures of ninety of the ninety-two counties of the State for 1887 was $6,110,302, and for 1888 $7,093,-645. Sixty-nine county asylums support 2,572 needy inmates, and forty-five county jails contain 7,467 convicts.

Coal and Natural Gas.—One of the most important resources of the State is its coal-deposits, which cover about 7,000 square miles. These coal-beds are found in the following counties: Warren, Fountain, Vermilion, Parke, Vigo, Clay, Sullivan, Green, Davis, Dubois, Pike, Perry, Spencer, Knox, Gibson, Vanderburg, and Posey. Clay County is the largest coal-producing county, having thirty-eight mines; Gibson County the smallest, having only three mines. During 1887 the product of 220 mines was 3,217,711 tons; during 1886 the product of 208 mines was about 3,000,000 tons. Natural gas, which has only recently been known to exist in the State, has been discovered in twenty-two counties. There are now in operation about 125 gas-wells, producing 1,000,000 cubic feet of gas a day.

Election Frauds.—Early in the year the Government succeeded in securing a new trial of the persons charged with forging tally-sheets showing false returns of the congressional election in 1886 at Indianapolis, an acquittal having been obtained in the former trial. The result of this trial was a verdict of guilty, rendered on January 28, against Simeon Coy and William F. A. Bernhamer, while Stephen J. Mattler, the third defendant, was acquitted. A motion for a new trial was denied, and the defendants were sentenced to the State Prison for eighteen months and one year respectively, with a slight fine in each case. Coy and Bernhamer then applied to Justice Harlan, of the United States Supreme Court, for a writ of error, which the latter refused by a decision rendered early in March. This decision was affirmed by the full bench of the court at Washington in May.

. **The White Caps.**—A secret organization of vigilantes by this name has existed for several years in the southern part of the State. One of its first principles is said to be that no negro shall live in the region dominated by it; but it also undertakes to drive away all persons who incur its displeasure. It proceeds by first giving a warning to leave the State, which, if disregarded, is followed by a midnight visitation from members of the order. The victim is taken from his house and severely whipped or otherwise abused; his life is in danger if he chooses to remain after this treatment. The counties of Crawford, Orange, Perry, Harrison, Spencer, and Dubois have especially suffered from these outrages by the White Caps. In the early part of the year the organization was unusually active, and the local authorities seemed powerless to bring the offenders to justice. In August, Attorney-General Michener, at the request of the Governor, made a tour of several of the southern counties for the purpose of investigating the condition of affairs. His report, especially relating to Crawford County, the center of the difficulty, was made in September, and contains the following:

The condition of affairs is not only deplorable but alarming. For at least two years past the most outrageous offenses have been committed with impunity by the "White Caps"; they have in many ways shown their entire disregard for the law and its officers; they have driven citizens out of the county and out of the State; they have cruelly whipped their victims in the villages of the county without molestation; they have dragged large numbers of persons from their beds and whipped them until the blood flowed to the ground; they have repeatedly flogged helpless women until life was nearly extinct, and they have procured the publication of their law-defying notices in the newspapers of the county. I have not given a detailed statement of these outrages, for they have long been so notorious that you are, doubtless, well informed concerning them. From the organization of one band of "White Caps" others sprung into existence, and now it is generally believed that all these bands are confederated together in one grand organization, covering portions of three or four counties. The number and the character of the violations of law to which I have briefly alluded, and the general belief that all these bands are combined in an organization of offense and defense, have brought about a reign of terror in the localities infested by the "White Caps," which can only be fully understood by those who have conversed with the people there. Property has been so depreciated that it can not be sold at half of its value. No one has that confidence

in his neighbor which is so essential to a good state of society. All is doubt, distrust, and confusion. The result is, that some who are considered good citizens openly applaud the doings of the "White Caps," and others are silent who should be loud in condemnation. The newspapers have said but little in disapproval, and of those who have openly stood for the enforcement of law, a number have been threatened with violence. As one result of such a state of affairs, there has been recently organized there, as I am informed, a body known as "Black Caps"; and it is said that they place armed men each night on the roads in the region most infested by the "White Caps," with instructions to fire upon any band of the latter which they may find. This is the inevitable result of a long and widely spread defiance and violation of the law without punishment.

The State authorities at once took active measures to destroy the organization, if possible, and to bring the members to justice. At the end of the year the Governor says, in his message:

Evidence was finally procured against the principal participants, who were indicted and their trials set for Dec. 24, 1888. The defendants have taken a change of venue, and the time of trial is now fixed for March 26. Additional evidence has been obtained, which will lead to the indictment of several others, and some who would have been arrested have fled from the State. The lawlessness has been completely suppressed.

Political.—The State campaign was opened on March 15, when the Prohibitionists met in convention at Indianapolis and nominated the following ticket: For Governor, J. S. Hughes; Lieutenant-Governor, John W. Baxter; Secretary of State, Dr. W. A. Spurgeon; Auditor, Thomas Marvel; Treasurer, Allen Furnas; Superintendent of Public Instruction, C. H. Kiracofe; Reporter of the Supreme Court, T. C. Barnes; Attorney-General, Elwood Hunt; Judges of the Supreme Court, First District, W. N. Land; Second, W. R. Coffey; Third, Newton Burrell. The resolutions adopted include the following:

We present to our fellow-citizens the one overshadowing crime—the liquor traffic. We are unalterably opposed to the enactment of laws that propose to license, tax, or otherwise to regulate the drink traffic, because they provide for its continuance.

We believe in a free and carefully-protected ballot, unrestricted by sex.

We favor applying the golden rule to the relations of capital and labor, and arbitration in cases of conflict, but the best interests of both capital and labor demand the prohibition of the liquor traffic.

We view with alarm the growing desecration of the Lord's day and the efforts making by the liquor power to repeal the laws protecting it, and we call upon all good citizens to join us in maintaining these laws.

The Democratic State Convention met at Indianapolis on April 26, and made the following nominations: For Governor, Courtland C. Matson; Lieutenant-Governor, William R. Myers; Secretary of State, R. W. Miers; Auditor, Charles A. Munson; Treasurer, Thomas Byrnes; Reporter of Supreme Court. John W. Kern; Attorney-General, John R. Wilson; Superintendent of Public Instruction, E. E. Griffith; Supreme Judges, First District, William E. Niblack; Second District, George V.

Howk; Third District, Allen Zollars. A platform was adopted, commending the administration of President Cleveland, demanding a reduction of the tariff as recommended in the President's message, favoring liberal pensions, and approving Gov. Gray's administration and his candidacy for the vice-presidential nomination. Its other declarations were as follow:

The Democratic party, being of the people and for the people, favors such legislation as will guarantee the broadest protection to the interests and welfare of the industrial masses; it recognizes the fact that labor is the producer of the wealth of a nation, and that laws should be so framed as to encourage and promote the interest, progress, and prosperity of all classes, and especially of all laboring people.

We recognize the right of all men to organize for social or material advancement; the right of wage-workers to use all lawful means to protect themselves against the encroachments of moneyed monopolists, and the right to fix a price for their labor commensurate with the work required of them, and we hold that every man has the right to dispose of his own labor upon such terms as he may think will best promote his interests. In relations between capital and labor the Democratic party favors such measures and policies as will promote harmony between them, and will adequately protect the rights and interests of both. We freely indorse and approve the laws passed pursuant to the demands of former Democratic conventions making provision for the safety and protection of laborers and miners, and providing for the collection of their wages, and are in favor of all other enactments to that end which may be necessary and proper.

It is provided by the Constitution of this State that the liberty of the people should be protected, and that their private property should not be taken without just compensation, and we are opposed to any change in the Constitution tending to weaken these safeguards, or to any legislation which asserts the power to take or destroy the private property of any portion of the people of this State without compensation or which unjustly interferes with their personal liberty as to what they shall eat or drink, or as to the kind of clothing they shall wear, believing that the government should be administered in that way best calculated to confer the greatest good upon the greatest number, without sacrificing the rights of person or of property, and leaving the innocent creeds, habits, customs, and business of the people unfettered by sumptuary laws, class legislation, or extortionate monopolies. While standing faithfully by the rights of property and personal liberty guaranteed to the people by the Constitution, we distinctly declare that we are in favor of sobriety and temperance, and all proper means for the promotion of these virtues, but we believe that a well-regulated license system and reasonable and just laws upon the subject, faithfully enforced, would be better than extreme measures, which, being subversive of personal liberty and in conflict with public sentiment, would never be effectively executed, thus bringing law into disrepute and tending to make sneaks and hypocrites of our people.

The Republican State Convention met on August 8, at Indianapolis. Strenuous efforts were made to induce Ex-Gov. Albert G. Porter to accept the gubernatorial nomination, but upon being assured of his absolute refusal, the convention nominated Congressman Alvin P. Hovey, on the second ballot. The remainder of the ticket was completed as follows: Lieutenant-Governor, Ira J. Chase; Secretary of State, Charles P. Griffin; Auditor, Bruce Carr; Treasurer, Julius A. Lemcke; Superin-

tendent of Public Instruction, R. M. La Follette; Judges of the Supreme Court, First District, S. D. Coffey; Second District, John G. Berkshire; Fourth District, Walter Olds; Reporter of the Supreme Court, John L. Griffiths. The resolutions commend the work of the National Convention, especially the nomination of Gen. Harrison, and treat at length of State and local issues as follows:

Crimes against an equal ballot and equal representation are destructive of free government. The iniquitous and unfair apportionment for congressional and legislative purposes, made at the behest of the liquor league of Indiana, followed by conspiracy and forgery upon the election returns of 1886, in Marion County, for which a number of prominent Democratic leaders were indicted and tried, two of whom are now suffering the deserved penalty of their acts, demand the rebuke of every patriotic citizen. The gerrymander, by which more than half of the people of the State are shorn of their just rights, must be repealed and constitutional apportionments made, whereby the votes of members of all political parties shall be given equal force and effect, equal political rights to be the only basis of a truly democratic and republican form of government.

The action of the Democrats in the last General Assembly was revolutionary and criminal. The will of the people expressed in a peaceable and lawful election, advised and participated in by the Democratic party, was set at defiance, and the Constitution and laws as expounded by the Supreme Court of the United States disregarded and nullified. Public and private rights were subverted and destroyed, and the Capitol of the State disgraced by violence and brutality. The alleged election of a United States Senator was accomplished by fraud and forced by high-handed usurpation of power, the overthrow of constitutional and legal forms, the setting aside of the results of a popular election, and the theft of the prerogatives of duly elected and qualified members of the Legislature. That stolen senatorship is part of the Democratic administration at Washington, now in power by virtue of public crimes and the nullification of Constitution and laws.

We favor placing all public institutions under a wisely conceived and honestly administered civil-service law.

In the interests of labor we favor the establishment and permanent maintenance of a bureau of labor statistics. We favor the passage and strict enforcement of laws which will absolutely prevent the competition of imported servile, convict, or contract labor of all kinds with free labor; prohibit the employment of young children in factories and mines; guarantee to workingmen the most favorable conditions for their service, especially proper safeguards for life and comfort in mines and factories, on railways and in all hazardous occupations; to secure which the duties and powers of the State Mine-Inspector should be enlarged, and provision made whereby only skilled and competent men can be placed in positions where they may be in control of the lives and safety of others; enforce the certain and frequent payment of wages; abridge the hours of labor wherever practicable; and provide for the submission to just and impartial arbitration, under regulations that will make the arbitration effective, all controversies between workingmen and their employers. The right of wage-workers to organize for the legitimate promotion of their mutual good can not be questioned.

The amendments to the State Constitution making the terms of county officers four years, and striking out the word "white" from section 1, Article XII, so that colored men may become a part of the regular militia force for the defense of the State, should be renewed.

Politics and legislation should be kept free from the

influence of the saloon. The liquor traffic must obey the law. We favor legislation upon the principle of local option, whereby the various communities throughout the State may be as they deem best—either control or suppress the traffic in intoxicating liquors.

Democratic filibustering in the national House of Representatives prevented the return to the treasury of the State of Indiana the sum of $904,875.33, the justice of which claim against the General Government has been officially acknowledged and its repayment provided for. Like hostile Democratic action has also prevented the return to our State treasury of $606,979.41 discount and interest on war-loan bonds, rendered necessary to equip and maintain the volunteer soldiers who went out under the first call for troops in 1861. More than a million and a half of dollars, justly due the State, are thus withheld in the presence of an increasing Federal surplus and of a practically bankrupt State treasury caused by the incompetence of the Democratic State administration.

There was also a Union Labor ticket in the field, headed by John B. Milroy. The canvass was one of great interest and excitement. Strenuous efforts were made by the Republicans to take the State from Democratic control, especially in view of the fact that the presidential candidate of their party was from Indiana. These efforts, aided by the popularity of Gen. Harrison, were successful in securing the election of the entire State and National ticket. Gen. Harrison obtained 263,361 votes; Mr. Cleveland, 261,013; Mr. Fisk, 9,801; and Mr. Streeter about 2,700. For Governor, Hovey obtained 263,194 votes; Matson, 260,994; Hughes, 9,920; and Milroy, 2,702. The Republicans elected only three out of thirteen Congressmen, a loss of four seats.

IOWA. State Government.—The following were the State officers during the year: Governor, William Larrabee, Republican; Lieutenant-Governor, John A. T. Hull; Secretary of State, Frank D. Jackson; Auditor, James A. Lyons; Treasurer, Voltaire P. Twombley; Attorney-General, A. J. Baker; Superintendent of Public Instruction, Henry Sabin; Railroad Commissioners, Peter A. Dey, Lorenzo S. Coffin, succeeded by ex-Lieutenant-Governor Frank T. Campbell, and Spencer Smith; Chief-Justice of the Supreme Court, William H. Seevers; Judges, James H. Rothrock, Joseph R. Reed, Joseph M. Beck, and Gifford S. Robinson.

Finances.—During the past fiscal year the State debt has been gradually diminishing. On June 30, 1887, the amount of outstanding warrants was $455,987.30, which had been reduced on May 25 of this year to $324,772.60, and was still further diminished before the end of the year. A part of this debt, $245,435.19, represents an indebtedness of the State to the school fund. By the so-called Hutchison law of the Legislature this year, the direct war-tax, if refunded to the State by the General Government, is to be applied, first to the payment of this debt to the school fund, the remainder, if any, being added to the general revenue. It is believed that this tax, if refunded, would be sufficient to wipe out the entire State debt. The receipts of the treasury

for the fiscal year 1888 largely exceeded the expenditures.

Legislative Session.—The Twenty-second General Assembly convened on January 9, and was in session three months. United States Senator James F. Wilson, who received the Republican nomination, was re-elected for a second term. The Democratic candidate was T. J. Anderson, and the Labor candidate Daniel Campbell. By far the most important feature of the session was its legislation affecting railroads, which is discussed below. A new pharmacy law was passed which forbids the sale of intoxicating liquor by any manufacturer or dealer other than a registered pharmacist. It amends the former law so that a person manufacturing lawfully in the State may not sell to persons outside the State for purposes other than medicinal. The act also provides additional requirements to be observed in order to obtain permits to sell liquors for medicinal purposes, and imposes severer penalties on pharmacists convicted of illegal selling. Evasion of the prohibitory law is thereby made more difficult and dangerous. The so-called "trusts" are made unlawful by the following act:

SECTION 1. If any corporation organized under the laws of this State or any other State or country for transacting or conducting any kind of business in this State, or any partnership or individual shall create, enter into, become a member of or a party to any pool, trust, agreement, combination, or confederation with any other corporation, partnership, or individual to regulate or fix the price of oil, lumber, coal, grain, flour, provisions, or any other commodity or article whatever; or shall create, enter into, become a member of or a party to any pool, agreement, combination, or confederation to fix or limit the amount or quantity of any commodity or article to be manufactured, mined, produced, or sold in this State, shall be deemed guilty of a conspiracy to defraud, and be subject to indictment and punishment as provided in the next section.

SEC. 2. Any person or corporation found guilty of a violation of this act shall be punished by a fine of not less than one hundred dollars, nor to exceed five thousand dollars, and stand committed until such fine is paid.

Another act provides for the levy of an additional property tax of three tenths of a mill, the proceeds of which shall be expended for the relief and for the funeral expenses of indigent soldiers and sailors and their families. A "Soldier's Relief Commmission" is created for each county, with power to award the money raised under this act, and to distribute it according to such award. The State was redistricted for members of the Lower House, one hundred representatives being apportioned to ninety-four districts. A tax of half a mill was levied for the years 1888 and 1889 to provide funds for paying the State debt. Among the special appropriations were $17,000 for improvements on the State Capitol; $5,000 for the site and foundation of a State soldiers' monument; $102,000 for furnishing and equipment of the Hospital for the Insane at Clarinda; $58,000 for additional lands, a new building, and other improvements at the Mount Pleasant Hospital; $28,750 for improvements at the Independence Hospital; $30,000 for the State Normal School; $17,034.80 for the College for the Blind; $21,850 for the Boys' Industrial School; $17,400 for the Girls' Industrial School; $24,300 for the Soldiers' Orphans' Home; $44,000 for the Institution for the Feeble-Minded; $52,000 for the State University; $32,900 to the two State Penitentiaries. Other acts of the session are as follow:

Creating in cities of over 30,000 inhabitants a board of public works.

Empowering cities of certain grades to fund their indebtedness.

Authorizing incorporated towns to refund their outstanding bonded debt.

Providing for the reassessment and relevy of special taxes and assessments when the first assessment or levy is for any cause invalid.

Amending the law relative to registration of voters in cities.

Providing a court for the trial of contested cases arising out of the election of presidential electors.

Creating a State board of examiners for mine inspectors, and requiring an examination of such board of all candidates for the office of mine inspector.

To establish a uniform system of weighing coal at the mines of the State, and to punish certain irregularities connected therewith.

To provide for the payment of wages of workingmen employed in mines in lawful money of the United States, and to forbid any dictation on the part of any person, firm, or corporation, as to where any employé shall purchase his goods or supplies.

To punish blacklisting of employés, or any attempt on the part of a former employer to prevent a discharged employé from obtaining employment other than by furnishing on request a truthful statement concerning such discharge.

To provide for the formation of independent school districts, and authorizing changes of boundaries in the same.

To prevent diseased swine from running at large.

Imposing a penalty on the sale of grain, seed, or other cereals at a fictitious price, and prohibiting any bond or other contract to sell at such price, or the procuring of any valuable consideration for such bond or contract.

To prevent fraud in the sale of lard by requiring all adulterations thereof to be labeled "compound lard."

To prevent fraud in the weight of flour and other mill-products.

To punish bribe-taking by State, county, township, city, school, or other municipal officers, and to punish the bribery of or the attempt or conspiracy to bribe such officers.

Restricting non-resident aliens in their right to acquire and hold real estate in the State.

To prevent persons unlawfully using or wearing badges of the Grand Army of the Republic or of the Military Order of the Loyal Legion of the United States.

Appropriating $1,500 for the aiding of discharged convicts.

Giving legislative assent to the purposes of the congressional act of March 2, 1887, in regard to the establishment of agricultural experiment stations in connection with agricultural colleges.

Authorizing the trustees of the insane hospital at Independence to purchase one hundred and eighty acres of land adjoining that now owned by the State.

Relinquishing to the United States all right and title to the so-called river lands except such as were granted to the State by resolution of Congress of March 2, 1861.

Railroads.—In his message to the Legislature, in January, Gov. Larrabee suggested several measures restrictive of railroads. A few days later, in his second inaugural address, he dwelt at length, and with considerable severity, upon the alleged tyranny and oppression of the railroads. The keynote thus struck was taken up by the Legislature, and during the session much bitterness was at times shown against railroad corporations. Numerous measures extremely radical and unjust were proposed and supported by a large minority of the members, but cooler heads finally won, although the legislation of the session is much more oppressive to railroads than that in any other State. The railroad act as passed at this session requires railroad charges to be just and reasonable; prohibits discrimination in charges for transportation either by special rate, rebate, drawback or other device; makes it unlawful for a common carrier to give preference or advantage to any particular parties, locality, or kind of traffic, except in the shipment of perishable property, or to subject to any prejudice or disadvantage any party, locality, or kind of traffic; requires all such carriers to afford reasonable, proper, and equal facilities for interchange of traffic between their respective lines and for receiving, forwarding, and delivering passengers, freight, and cars received from each other; forbids a greater charge for a short than for a long haul, or the pooling of freights between competing lines; requires printed schedules of rates for transportation of passengers and freight to be published and posted; prescribes in detail what such schedules shall contain, and how they shall be changed, and gives the railroad commissioners power to apply for and obtain a writ of mandamus for refusal to file and publish such schedules, whereupon a fine of $500 a day shall be laid upon the company disobeying the mandamus. Every carrier must adhere strictly to its published rates; it is made unlawful to prevent, by combinations or other devices, the continuous and uninterrupted carriage of freight; and for any violation of this act the common carrier is made liable to the person or persons injured thereby for three times the amount of damages sustained, with costs and a reasonable attorney's fee for the complainant, unless restitution is made within fifteen days after demand.

Penalties are also imposed, varying from $500 to $10,000, for violations of the various sections of the statute. It is the duty of the railroad commissioners, and they have authority, to inquire into the management of the business of all common carriers and for that purpose to require the attendance and testimony of officers and other witnesses and the production of books, papers, etc. They are directed to investigate and report upon all complaints made to them by individuals or others against common carriers, and their findings are *prima-facie* evidence of the facts found. It is also provided—

that whenever any common carrier shall violate or refuse or neglect to obey any lawful order or requirement of the said Board of Railroad Commissioners, it shall be the duty of said commissioners, and lawful for any company or person interested in such order or requirement, to apply in a summary way, by petition to the District or Superior Court . . . alleging such violation or disobedience as the case may be ; and the said court shall have power to hear and determine the matter, on such short notice to the common carrier complained of as the court shall deem reasonable . . . and said court shall proceed to hear and determine the matter speedily as a court of equity and without the formal pleadings and proceedings applicable to ordinary suits in equity, but in such manner as to do justice in the premises ; . . . and on such hearing the report of said commissioners shall be *prima-facie* evidence of the matter therein, or in any order made by them stated ; and if it be made to appear . . . that the order or requirement of said commissioners in question has been violated or disobeyed, it shall be lawful for such court to issue a writ of injunction, or other proper process mandatory or otherwise, to restrain such common carrier from further continuing such violation or disobedience ; . . . and in case of any disobedience of any such writ, it shall be lawful for such courts to issue writs of attachment, or any other process of said court incident or applicable to writs of injunction or other proper process, and said court may, if it shall think fit, make an order directing such common carrier or other person so disobeying . . . to pay such sum of money not exceeding for each carrier or person in default the sum of one thousand ($1,000) dollars for every day after a day to be named in the order that such carrier or other person shall fail to obey such injunction or other proper process mandatory or otherwise . . . and the payment thereof may without prejudice to any other mode of recovering the same be enforced by attachment or order, in the nature of a writ of execution, in like manner as if the same had been recovered by a final decree *in personam* in such court.

Another section provides as follows:

The Board of Railroad Commissioners of this State are hereby empowered and directed to make for each of the railroad corporations doing business in this State, as soon as practicable, a schedule of reasonable maximum rates of charges for the transportation of freight and cars on each of said railroads, and said power to make schedules shall include the power of classification of all such freights, and it shall be the duty of said commissioners to make such classification ; provided, that the said rates of charges to be so fixed by said commissioners shall not in any case exceed the rates which are or may hereafter be established by law ; and said schedules so made by said commissioners shall in all suits brought against any such railroad corporations, wherein is in any way involved the charges of any such railroad corporation for the transportation of any freight or cars or unjust discrimination in relation thereto be deemed and taken in all courts of this State as *prima-facie* evidence that the rates therein fixed are reasonable and just maximum rates of charges for the transportation of freight and cars upon the railroads for which said schedules may have been respectively prepared.

Said commissioners shall from time to time, and as often as circumstances may require, change and revise said schedules, subject to the same provision that the rates fixed are not to be higher than now or hereafter established by law.

Annual reports from the various railroad companies are also required.

Another act requires all railroads in the State to be fenced, and a third makes the Board of Railroad Commissioners more directly responsible to the people by providing that the members shall be chosen by popular election. A full board shall be chosen in November, 1888, and one member thereof each year subsequently.

The new railroad act went into effect on May 10, and in accordance with its provisions the commissioners soon thereafter prepared and published a schedule of maximum freight rates, which should go into effect on July 10. These rates, being on an average over 20 per cent. below the previous schedule rates, were strenuously opposed by the railroads. Immediately upon their publication, certain of the roads applied to Judge Brewer, of the United States Circuit Court, for a temporary injunction against their enforcement by the commission. This was granted, and July 5 was set as the day for a hearing upon the matter. On that day the question of the reasonableness of the rates and the constitutionality of the new act was argued before Judge Brewer, who, on July 26, decided to continue the temporary injunction till a further hearing and more extended evidence should be given as to the reasonableness of the schedule. Meanwhile, the Chicago, Rock Island and Pacific Railroad had applied to Judge Fairall, of the district court at Iowa City, for an injunction on the same ground, that the rates fixed were unreasonably low. The judge granted a temporary injunction, which the commissioners moved to have dissolved. The hearing and arguments on this motion consumed nearly a week. Late in August, Judge Fairall rendered his decision, denying the motion, whereupon the commissioners appealed to the State Supreme Court, where the case was argued in October. Early in September the opponents of the railroads, anticipating that the commissioners would not be able to enforce their schedule until after a long litigation, if at all, adopted a new method of securing a reduction of rates, under a section of the same act, which provides that on complaint of a person or class of persons that the charges of any common carrier are too high, the commissioners shall investigate, hear all parties interested, and fix a reasonable rate. The shippers of Davenport, Dubuque, and Burlington entered complaints under this section with the commissioners ; these complaints were heard separately, and the decision, signed by two of the three commissioners, was published a few days before the November election. The rates established were somewhat higher than the corresponding rates of the July schedule. No sooner had the commissioners announced their decision than the Chicago, Burlington and Quincy Railroad, and one other road interested, obtained from Judge Brewer a temporary injunction against the enforcement of these new rates. The hearing upon the continuance of this injunction was set for December 11 at Minneapolis, at which time the various questions involved were argued ; but no decision had been made by Judge Brewer before the end of the year.

Meanwhile, the plaintiff in the suit before Judge Fairall, from whose decision the commissioners had appealed, applied to Judge Fairall and had the suit withdrawn, on the ground that the question in controversy had actually been settled by the abandonment of the schedule by the commissioners in making and adopting another and higher schedule of rates in the Dubuque, Davenport, and Burlington jobbers' decisions. This withdrawal left nothing for the Supreme Court to decide on appeal, and it, therefore, in December, dismissed the case before it.

By the report of the commissioners it appears that during the fiscal year ending June 30, 349 miles of new railroad were constructed, making the total mileage in the State 8,436 miles; but of this new construction only four miles were built since January, when the Legislature began to discuss the railroad problem. The assessed valuation of all roads in the State for 1888 was about $42,500,000, against $38,-250,000 in 1887.

Education.—The annual report of the State Superintendent of Education for 1888 shows that there are 12,752 school-houses in the State, valued at $12,007,340; as against 12,444, valued at $11,860,472, at the close of the fiscal year 1887. The average school year in months is 7·7, against 7·4 in 1887. The number of female teachers has increased largely during the year, while the number of male teachers has decreased. The whole number of male teachers employed in the State is given as 5,595, and of female teachers 19,578. The average compensation of male teachers has decreased from $38 per month in 1887 to $36.44 in 1888. The average compensation of female teachers has increased from $29.50 in 1887 to $30.05 in 1888. The number of pupils between five and twenty-one returned is, males 325,741, females 313,507, total 639,248. The number of pupils actually enrolled in the schools of the State is 477,184, and the total average attendance only 281,070.

Prisons.—Reports from the two State Penitentiaries show a marked decrease in the number of convicts during the past fiscal year. At Anamosa there were 259 convicts on July 1, against 313 one year previous; while at Fort Madison the decrease has been from 360 on July 1, 1887, to 330 on the same day in 1888. It is claimed that this diminution is due to the enforcement of the prohibitory law.

Coal.—The coal-product of the State for the year ending June 30 is reported by the State mine inspectors as follows: District No. 1, 1,528,967 bushels; district No. 2, 1,663,206 bushels; district No. 3, 913,185 bushels; total, 4,105,558 bushels.

Prohibition.—The prohibitory law received this year a serious blow by a decision of the United States Supreme Court, rendered on March 19, in the case of Bowman vs. The Chicago and Northwestern Railroad Company. The question at issue turned upon the validity of the law enacted in 1886, prohibiting the transportation of liquors on railways from without the State, unless accompanied by a certificate from the officials of the county to which it was assigned attesting its importation for legal purposes. This enactment was held to be an interference with interstate commerce, and therefore unconstitutional. The difficulties of enforcing prohibition were multiplied by this decision, which removed all restraint upon importation. In October the same court rendered a decision affirming the rulings of the State Supreme Court in the case of Pearson vs. The International Distillery, by which the manufacture of liquors for export was declared to be forbidden by the statute. Reports during the year showed that prohibition was well enforced in 60 counties, reasonably well enforced in 28, and disregarded in 11.

Political.—The Republican State Convention was held at Des Moines on August 22, and nominated the following candidates: for Secretary of State, Frank D. Jackson; Auditor, James A. Lyons; Treasurer, Voltaire P. Twombley; Judge of the Supreme Court, Charles T. Granger; Attorney-General, John Y. Stone; Railroad Commissioners, Frank T. Campbell, Spencer Smith, and John Mahin. The platform contained the following:

We declare our firm adherence to the principle of legislative control of railways and other corporations. Having been created by the Government, they are of right subject to such just laws as may be enacted for their control and must obey the same. We would deal as justly with corporate as with individual interests. But we demand that the people shall be fully protected in all directions from corporate rapacity, whether arising from discriminations, trusts, combines, railways, or other aggregated capital. We commend the general railway legislation of the last General Assembly and demand that all just proceedings and rates thereunder shall be promptly, impartially, and vigorously enforced.

We repudiate the imputation that the people of Iowa are antagonistic to the rights of capital or desire to oppress any corporation, but we demand such legislation as will develop the agricultural, industrial, and manufacturing interests of our State and at the same time render a just equivalent for capital and labor employed.

We congratulate the people of our State on the temperance legislation inaugurated in the Eighteenth General Assembly and on the faithful obedience of all subsequent General Assemblies to the expressed will of the majority of the people, which has given to Iowa the best prohibitory law in the United States. To the credit of the Republican party, for its unselfish and non-partisan respect for the will of the people, no backward step in Iowa has been taken and none will be taken on this question, so vital to the moral welfare of all our communities. In this connection we refer with satisfaction to the large decrease in the population of our State prisons, the empty jails in so many of our counties, and the decreasing costs and expenses upon the criminal dockets of the courts.

We declare that the Democratic majority in the Lower House of Congress has shown its injustice in defeating the Senate bill, which directed the refunding to the Northern States the direct war-tax, and remitting the same which was unpaid to the United States. This tax would have placed in the treasury of Iowa about $400,000, and to that extent would have relieved Iowa tax-payers.

At the Democratic State Convention the following nominations were made: for Secretary of State, Walter McHenry; Auditor, Daniel J. Okerson; Treasurer, Amos Case; Judge of the Supreme Court, P. Henry Smythe; Attorney-General, Joseph C. Mitchell; Railroad Commissioners, Peter A. Dey, Christian L. Lund, and Herman E. Wills.

The Union Labor party nominated for Secretary of State, J. B. Van Court; Auditor, C. M. Farnsworth; Treasurer, James Rice; Judge of the Supreme Court, M. H. Jones; Attorney-General, D. H. Williamson. It adopted the Republican candidates for Railroad Commissioners. A Prohibition ticket was also in the field, presenting James Micklewait for Secretary of State; Malcolm Smith for Auditor; and E. O. Sharpe for Treasurer. For other places on the ticket the Republican nominees were generally adopted.

At the November election the vote for Secretary of State was as follows: Jackson, 211,-577 votes; McHenry, 180,455; Van Court, 9,005; Micklewait, 2,690. The vote for Auditor, Treasurer, Supreme Judge, and Attorney-General was substantially the same as for Secretary of State. For Railroad Commissioner, Smith received 225,928 votes: Campbell, 224,800; Dey, 201,265; Lund, 176,327; Wills, 175,049.

Candidate Dey ran over 21,000 votes ahead of his ticket, and is the only Democrat that has been elected to a State office in many years. The Republicans carried 10 of the 11 congressional districts, gaining two seats from the Democrats, one of them being the seat of Gen. Weaver.

ITALY, a constitutional monarchy in southern Europe. The reigning sovereign is Umberto I, born March 14, 1844, the eldest son of Vittorio Emanuele II, and Archduchess Adelaide of Austria, who succeeded to the throne on the death of his father, Jan. 9, 1878. The heir to the throne is Vittorio Emanuele, Prince of Naples, born Nov. 11, 1869. The King's only brother, Amadeo, Duke of Aosta, who was elected King of Spain in 1870, abdicated three years later, and has since been a lieutenant-general in the Italian army, married, on Sept. 11, 1888, for his second wife, his niece, the Princess Letitia Bonaparte, daughter of Prince Napoleon and the Princess Clotilde of Savoy, and sister of Prince Napoleon Victor Bonaparte, the French pretender.

The Constitution of the kingdom of Italy is contained in the fundamental statute granted by King Carlo Alberto to the people of Sardinia in 1848, and extended to the whole of Italy when Vittorio Emanuele was proclaimed King of the united nation on March 17, 1861. The legislative powers are vested in a Senate and Chamber of Deputies. The Senators are nominated by the King from among the persons above forty years of age who have held high posts in the public service, or gained fame in science, literature, or other pursuits, or pay

3,000 lire in taxes. The Deputies, 508 in number, are elected by *scrutin de liste*, every citizen having a vote who can read and write and pays 19 lire per annum in taxes, as well as members of academies, professors, and all who have served two years in the active army. The legislative period is five years, but the King can dissolve the Chamber at any time, in which case new elections must be held within four months. The executive power is exercised by the King under the advice of a cabinet of ministers responsible to the Parliament. The present Cabinet, which was constituted on Aug. 7, 1887, is composed of the following members: President of the Council and Minister of the Interior, Francesco Crispi, who has also been Minister of Foreign Affairs *ad interim* since the transfer of Count Robilant to the London Embassy in the spring of 1888; Minister of Public Instruction, P. Boselli, who succeeded Michele Coppino in February, 1888; Minister of Finance and of the Treasury, Agostino Magliani, appointed Nov. 26, 1887; Minister of War, Gen. Ettore Bertolè Viale; Minister of Marine, Benedetto Brin; Minister of Justice and Public Worship, Giuseppe Zanardelli; Minster of Commerce, Industry, and Agriculture, Bernardino Grimaldi; Minister of Public Works, Giuseppe Sarracco.

Area and Population.—The area of the kingdom, as estimated by the Military Geographical Institute of Florence, is 286,588 square kilometres or 110,620 square miles, of which 25,740 square kilometres or 9,935 square miles constitute the area of the island of Sicily, and 24,-077 square kilometres or 9,293 square miles belong to Sardinia and adjacent islands. The total population on Dec. 31, 1887, was computed to be 30,260,065. The number of Protestants in Italy is about 62,000, of whom 22,000 are in the valleys of the Vaud. The Israelitish population is estimated at 38,000. The number of marriages in 1887 was 233,338; of births, 1,194,700; of deaths, 876,777; excess of births over deaths, 317,923. The emigration to European countries in 1887 was 82,474; to Egypt, 867; to Tunis, 633; to Algeria, 1,375; to the United States and Canada, 38,-853; to the Argentine Republic, Uruguay, and Paraguay, 54,499; to Brazil and other South American countries, Mexico, and Central America, 33,003; to South America, without declared destination, 3,108; to Asia, Africa, and Oceanica, 853; total emigration. 215,665, as compared with 167,829 in 1886, 157,193 in 1885, 147,017 in 1884, and 169,101 in 1883. An act for the protection of emigrants was passed in 1888. Domiciled residents who desire to act as emigration agents must obtain a license from the Minister of the Interior, for which the recommendation of the police prefect of the province is necessary, and must deposit from 1,000 to 3,000 lire as a guarantee fund to secure emigrants against losses incurred through the fault or negligence of the agent. The agents are forbidden to receive compensation from emigrants, or to counsel, induce, or incite emigration, or to furnish emigrants with their passage, or mediate between them and the shipping company. Clergymen and local officials are likewise prohibited from advising or promoting emigration, even without hope of gain. The spreading of false information with the object of encouraging emigration is punishable as swindling.

Commerce.—The total value of the special imports in 1887 was 1,690,500,000 lire or francs, and of the exports 1,109,700,000 francs. The value of the imports and exports of the various classes of commodities were as follow:

CLASSES.	Imports.	Exports.
Articles of consumption......	487,500,000	801,900,000
Raw materials.........	522,400,000	393,200,000
Manufactures...............	478,700,000	143,400,000
Waste materials	1,800,000	700,000
Drugs, dyes, and chemicals..	48,000,000	70,900,000
Gums, fats, and oils..........	63,100,000	89,100,000
Total merchandise........	1,601,500,000	999,200,000
Precious metals..............	89,000,000	110,500,000
Total special commerce..	1,690,500,000	1,109,700,000

The transit trade in 1887 amounted to 50,046,819 lire. The imports of cereals in 1887 were valued at 232,600,000 lire; exports, 31,200,000 lire; imports of wines and liquors, 16,600,000 lire; exports, 111,200,000 lire; imports of tobacco, 19,000,000 lire; imports of fruits, vegetables, etc., 25,300,000 lire; exports, 79,700,000 lire; imports of animal food products, 104,100,000 lire; exports, 73,800,000 lire. The imports of coal amounted to 86,600,000 lire; imports of metals, 113,000,000 lire; imports of textile materials, 180,100,000 lire; exports, 327,700,000 lire; imports of timber, 81,800,000 lire; exports, 11,800,000 lire. The imports of machines and vehicles were valued at 78,900,000 lire; imports of textile yarns, 126,100,000 lire; exports, 21,900,000 lire; imports of tissues and garments, 141,500,000 lire; exports, 27,600,000 lire; imports of jewelry and art objects, 50,300,000 lire; exports, 40,600,000 lire. The value of the commerce with each of the principal foreign countries for 1887 is given in francs in the following table:

COUNTRIES.	Imports.	Exports.
France......................	404,600,000	496,900,000
Austria.................... ..	250,800,000	95,800,000
England....	306,500,000	78,900,000
Germany...................	165,800,000	115,200,000
Switzerland...............	69,600,000	100,500,000
Russia....................	121,800,000	18,500,000
Turkey, Servia, and Roumania	51,700,000	10,500,000
Other European countries,....	79,200,000	58,800,000
United States and Canada....	64,200,000	85,800,000
Other American countries....	24,500,000	73,000,000
Asia	127,300,000	16,100,000
Africa...................	23,500,000	19,800,000
Australia..................	700,000	800,000
Total	1,690,500,000	1,109,700,000

Navigation.—The number of vessels engaged in foreign trade entered at the ports of Italy in 1887 was 17,552, of 7,052,659 tons, of which 10,016, of 1,680,927 tons, were Italian. The

number of steamers among all the vessels entered was 6,584, of 6,040,586 tons, of which 1,201, of 987,364 tons, were Italian. The number of vessels entered with cargoes was 15,605, of 6,521,638 tons. The total number of vessels cleared for long voyages was 17,431, of 6,742,191 tons, of which 9,515, of 3,547,886 tons, were laden. The vessels in the coasting trade entered were 93,399 in number, of the aggregate tonnage of 13,258,643, of which all were Italian excepting 3,299 vessels, of 2,854,080 tons. The fishing-vessels entered at the ports numbered 1,367, of 10,945 tons.

The merchant navy on Jan. 1, 1887, consisted of 6,992 sailing-vessels, of 801,349 tons, and 237 steamers, of 144,328 tons, making a total of 7,229 vessels, of 945,677 tons, as compared with 7,336 vessels, of 953,419 tons, on Jan. 1, 1886. There was a decrease of 119 in the number of sailing-vessels and of 27,470 tons in the sail tonnage, while the steam-vessels increased by 12 in number and the steam tonnage by 19,728 tons.

Finances.—The treasury accounts for the financial year 1886–'87 give the total receipts as 1,801,185,804 lire and the total expenditures as 1,789,413,851 lire, showing a surplus of 11,771,953 lire. The ordinary receipts for 1886–'87 were estimated at 1,543,789,972 lire, including receipts *d'ordre*, and the extraordinary receipts at 215,028,272 lire; total, 1,758,818,244 lire. The total expenditures were set down at 1,801,757,180 lire, of which 315,695,059 lire were for extraordinary purposes. The budget for the year ending June 30, 1889, makes the ordinary receipts 1,550,535,015 lire, of which 84,618,643 lire represent revenues from railroads and other state property; 394,207,684 lire the taxes on land, houses, and incomes from personal property; 212,723,000 lire the succession, registration, stamp, and railroad taxes; 667,377,245 lire the revenue tax on imports, *octrois*, profits of the tobacco and salt monopolies, and duties on beer, alcohol, powder, sugar, etc.; 76,302,000 lire profits of the state lottery; and 77,612,985 lire revenue from the post-office, telegraph, and other public services. Including 93,688,409 lire representing the expenses of working the domains, the interest on bonds deposited as reserve against paper money, and the funds for the payment of pensions, which items are entered on both sides of the account, the total ordinary revenue amounts to 1,644,223,424 lire. The extraordinary receipts are 246,461,967 lire, of which 195,399,734 lire constitute the sum set aside for the construction of railroads. On capital account the receipts are 38,845,860 lire, of which 14,450,446 lire are derived from sales of public lands and 21,334,000 lire from loans for the improvement of the Tiber, public works in Naples, and other purposes. The ordinary disbursements are estimated at the sum of 1,538,868,599 lire, showing a surplus in the ordinary budget of 105,354,825 lire. The extraordinary disbursements, amounting to 388,801,115 lire, or 142,339,148 lire more than the extraordinary receipts, convert this surplus into a deficit of 36,984,323 lire, the total receipts of the Government from all sources being 1,890,685,391 lire and the total expenditures 1,927,669,714 lire. The ordinary expenditures of the Ministry of Finance are fixed at 188,693,997 lire; of the Ministry of Grace, Justice, and Worship, 33,775,891 lire; of the Ministry of Foreign Affairs, 7,790,-710 lire; of the Ministry of Public Instruction, 40,116,414 lire; of the Ministry of the Interior, 61,736,320 lire; of the Ministry of Public Works, 82.433,635 lire; of the Ministry of War, 247,-479,368 lire; of the Ministry of Marine, 94,-366,494 lire; of the Ministry of Agriculture, 13,665,256 lire. Of the extraordinary expenditures 222,168,759 lire are allocated to the Ministry of Public Works, 62,750,000 lire to the Ministry of War, 28,646,500 lire to the Ministry of Marine, and small sums to each of the other ministries. The interest on the consolidated debt, most of which bears 5-per-cent. interest, was 448,748,332 lire for the year ending June 30, 1888; the perpetual *rente* due to the Holy See, 3,225,000 lire; the interest on special loans, 22,178,495 lire; the interest on various other debts assumed by the state, 73,898,473 lire; and the interest on the floating debt, 14,553,635 lire, making the total interest charge of the debt 562,603,935 lire, besides 906,926 lire paid for extinction of debts.

The Army.—The war strength of the Italian army on June 1, 1888, was, according to the official statement, 2,595,637 men. The number of officers and men under arms was 253,-000. The entire war effective was composed as follows:

DESCRIPTION OF TROOPS.	PERMANENT ARMY.		MILITIA.	
	With the colors.	On leave.	Mobile.	Territorial.
Officers.				
Active	14,359	.....	533	5,394
Complementary	.....	8,872	2,744	.....
Auxiliary	.....	2,310	.....	.....
Reserve	.....	3,996	.....	.....
Total officers	14,359	10,178	3,277	5,394
Rank and file:				
Carbineers	22,995	3,047	134	8,225
Infantry	111,315	197,106	287,761	490,659
Bersaglieri	13,569	29,950	24,593	33,750
Alpine troops	9,204	17,890	25,368	15,607
Military districts	9,845	23,877	.....	695,982
Cavalry	27,014	9,596	479	26,947
Artillery	28,124	60,208	28,691	42,489
Engineers	7,542	14,465	7,017	5,767
Military schools	1,496	.....	.....	.....
Sanitary corps	2,177	7,982	6,199	8,855
Commissariat	2,113	2,768	1,174	2,739
Invalid corps	865	.....	.....	.....
Complementary troops	.....	249,223	.....	.....
Penal establishments	2,882	.....	.....	.....
Total troops	236,641	615,912	352,316	1,325,560
Total	253,000	626,090	385,593	1,380,954

The Navy.—The Italian fleet of war on Jan. 1, 1888, consisted of 175 steam-vessels of all descriptions, of 188,551 tons displacement, armed with 369 cannon. The 12 iron-clads of

the first class comprise some of the most powerful vessels afloat. Of these great iron-clads 7 were ready for service in the summer of 1888. The battle-ships of the second class number 13, of which 3 are armor-clad; and of the third class there are 16, none of them armored. The rest of the navy consists of 21 transports, 3 school-ships, 23 vessels for post service, 6 paddle-wheel gun-boats, 1 torpedo dispatch-boat, 15 sea-going torpedo-boats, 36 torpedo-boats of the first class, 21 of the second class, and 8 torpedo-vessels. There were under construction 6 iron-clad battle-ships of the first class, of a total displacement of 73,456 tons, 3 unarmored cruisers of the second class, 7 of the third class, 1 torpedo dispatch-boat, 32 sea-going torpedo-boats, 2 torpedo-boats for coast defense, 1 transport, and 1 propeller. Among the vessels lately acquired, the "Dogali," first christened "Angelo Emo," is a fast protected cruiser, carries six 4-ton guns, and the "America" is a converted merchant steamer. The value of the 102 vessels and 108 torpedo-boats comprising the Italian navy is 360,000,000 lire. The naval manœuvres of 1888 proved that Italy could arm a considerable part of her fleet without having recourse to extraordinary means for recruiting officers and sailors. The "Re Umberto," "Sicilia," and "Sardegna," have been built in the national dockyards and are being fitted mainly with domestic material. These sister vessels are equal in size to the "Italia" and "Lepanto," previously the largest war-ships in existence, and will carry four 104-ton Armstrong breech-loading guns each. The "Re Umberto," launched in October, 1888, is a twin-screw, steel, barbette ship of 13,298 tons displacement. Without side-armor, she is protected by a curved steel deck extending below the water-line, while her bottom is enveloped by a double layer of water-tight compartments, which have been proved by experiment to be a sufficient protection against torpedoes charged with 75 pounds of gun-cotton. The two barbettes are plated with inclined 19-inch compound armor. The compound triple-expansion engines are designed to be of 19,500 indicated horse-power and capable of propelling the ship at a maximum speed of 18 knots. The projectiles weigh 2,000 pounds each, and in weight of shot and energy of discharge she greatly excels any battle ship in the French, British, or other navies. In addition to her ram and heavy guns she will be armed with twelve 6-inch guns, six 3-inch guns, ten machine and quick-firing guns, and torpedo tubes. She will be ready for commission in 1892. The "Fiera Mosca," a new cruiser, was launched at Leghorn on August 30. The Gruson turret has been adopted for sea-coast batteries at Spezia, after experiments that proved that the hardness of the chilled cast-iron at the surface, the toughness of the mixture of which it is made, and the angles presented by its mushroom-like shape, are sufficient to resist the heaviest projectiles. The revolving turrets, each mounting 2 Armstrong 105-ton guns, are composed of sections of 80 tons weight, the whole weighing 1,800 tons. The same system has been adopted for coast defenses in Germany, Belgium, Holland, and Austria.

Railroads.—The length of railroad lines open to traffic on June 30, 1888, was 11,800 kilometres or 6,375 miles. The receipts for the preceding year amounted to 240,021,076 lire.

The Post-Office.—The number of letters, postal-cards, and manuscripts, forwarded in 1886 was 203,635,675; of circulars and printed matter, 170,094,704; of postal money-orders, 4,752,-363 for the aggregate sum of 491,389,758 lire. The receipts of the post-office were 40,112,477 lire, and the expenses 34,068,912 lire.

Telegraphs.—The length of lines on June 30, 1886, was 30,573 kilometres, that of wires 108,908 kilometres, exclusive of 184 kilometres of submarine cables. The number of dispatches in 1885 was 7,321,357, of which 5,896,-306 were paid internal messages, 581,657 private foreign dispatches, and 179,036 transit dispatches. The receipts were 12,826,438 lire, the expenses for service 10,213,159 lire, for material and maintenance 184,470 lire, for extraordinary purposes 553,820 lire.

Church and State.—The conflict between the Vatican and the Italian Government has become more acute since the Government has been dominated by the democratic element, and Pope Leo has put forth positive assertions of the temporal sovereignty, called on the clergy to repeat and maintain his protest against the usurpation of his kingdom, and striven to obtain the intervention of external powers. The new Italian law of communal and provincial reform says that public officers, agents, and others who, directly or through persons dependent on them, officially attempt to control the votes of electors for or against formal candidatures, or to induce them to abstain from voting, are punished by fines of from 500 to 1,000 lire, or according to the gravity of the case, by imprisonment for from three months to one year. The fine or imprisonment is applied to ministers of religion who attempt to control the votes of electors in favor of or against certain candidates, or to induce them to abstain, by allusions or discourses in places designed for worship, or in meetings of a religious character, with spiritual promises or menaces, or with instructions. The new penal code, in which for the first time an attempt is made to assimilate the penal procedure of all the provinces of Italy and make a common criminal law for all the kingdom, has the same provisions, intended to punish the assertion of the Pope's right to Rome as a crime. As it passed the Chamber of Deputies in the session of 1888, it applied special and aggravated penalties to this offense when committed by the priesthood. This drew out many protests, on the ground that it made a discrimination against the priest which was not justified by the recog-

nition of the priest in his clerical capacity, he being in the eyes of the law a simple citizen. These protests were taken into account by the Senate, and the bill was altered so as to read as follows:

The religious minister who, abusing his position, provokes contempt or disobedience of the institutions or laws of the state, or the acts of the authorities, or even the transgression of the duties inherent in a public office or service, is punished by from six months' to three years' imprisonment, with a fine of from 500 lire to 3,000 lire, with temporary or perpetual interdiction from the benefice.

Subject to the same penalty is the minister of any religion who urges or instigates anybody to acts or declarations against the laws of the state, or in prejudice of rights acquired by the state.

These stringent laws prevented the Italian clergy from instituting public demonstrations in favor of the restoration of the temporal power of the Pope such as took place during 1888 in Germany, Switzerland, Belgium, and France. The tension between the Government and the Vatican was partly due to the aggressive attitude of the clericals in connection with the fiftieth anniversary of Pope Leo's entrance into the priesthood. The congratulations and homage from sovereigns and peoples of which he was the recipient were interpreted as demonstrations of sympathy for the sorrows and wrongs of the "prisoner of the Vatican." The Pope himself raised the question in replying to various deputations, especially in addressing the Italian bishops, to whom he said, "You are among those who desire to see the Papacy restored to that condition of true sovereignty and independence which is in every way its due." The Duke of Torlonia, Syndic or Mayor of Rome, who requested the Cardinal Vicar to present the congratulations of the city to the Pope on the occasion of his jubilee, was dismissed from his post by the Government. The Syndic was governed in his action by the sentiments of the Municipal Council, in which the clericals have a majority, although they hold aloof from parliamentary elections.

Disputes with France.—Questions relating to ex-territorial jurisdiction under the capitulations in portions of the Turkish Empire that have virtually been annexed by France and Italy, arose several times between the two governments and were the subject of spirited diplomatic controversies in 1888. In January an incident occurred in Florence which was the subject of considerable correspondence. When Italy made a treaty with France in 1884, by which she consented to the suspension of the consular privileges in Tunis, France agreed that Italy's previous conventions with the Bey of Tunis should remain in force. The convention of 1868 provides that the estates of Tunisian subjects who die in Italy shall be settled according to Italian law. The French consul in Florence took possession of the property and papers of a Tunisian general, Hussein Pasha, who died in that city, leaving a large fortune, against which certain Italian creditors had claims. The Italian judicial authorities summoned the consul, who had gone so far as to break the seals placed on the property by the Italian court and to sell part of the effects, to deliver up the property in his possession, and invited him to assist in the proceedings connected with the administration of the estate. The French consul paid no attention to the order of the court, and when the pretor went to the consulate he was compelled to break a door, as the French officials would yield only to force. The French Government complained of a violation of the consulate, and the Italian Government removed the pretor to another district in the same city as a disciplinary punishment for discourtesy, but maintained the entire legality of the proceedings, and demanded that the consul should be censured. In the end the French Minister for Foreign Affairs acknowledged that the consul's conduct was illegal, and the inheritance was returned to the Florentine tribunal for adjudication.

The dismissal of Count Corti, Italian Ambassador at London, who died soon after his disgrace, was an indication of the strong feeling on the Mediterranean question of the Italian Premier, whose antipathy to Count Corti dated from the time when the latter, while Minister for Foreign Affairs at the time of the Berlin Congress, would not press the Italian claims to Tunis, although overtures were made on the part of Germany, saying that Italy, when taking her seat for the first time among the great powers, would not appear as a supplicant for favors. In regard to the supposed French aspirations toward Tripoli, Italy has assumed a determined attitude. In fortifying Tunis, the French are said to have carried the frontier line into Tripolitan territory. In the summer the French Cabinet raised a troublesome question regarding the abolition of the capitulations in Massowah before the powers had been duly notified of the Italian annexation. After making good the omission, Signor Crispi retorted by raising a point in connection with the Suez Canal convention proposed by France, which was intended to draw from Turkey a declaration regarding her sovereignty, not merely in Massowah, where Italy claimed that it had lapsed, but in Tunis, where it was still nominally in force. The interpretation put by Italy on the Suez convention led the Sultan at the last moment to withhold his signature. In regard to Massowah, Italy was supported by the majority of the powers in the contention that the Turkish sovereignty was non-effective, and that the territory was *res nullius* at the time of the Italian occupation. The school question in Tunis was the subject of representations in consequence of which the Tunisian authorities, without foregoing their purpose to introduce the French educational system, modified their rules so as not to interfere with the missionary schools of Italian monks.

Tariff Negotiations with France.—The commercial treaty with France expired in 1887. During negotiations for a new treaty it was prolonged until March 1, 1888, as were also the treaties with Spain and Switzerland. These were renewed, but the French ministers and legislators were too much under the dominion of protectionist interests to agree to a treaty that would be acceptable to Italy. The negotiations were broken off in the beginning of February, 1888, and MM. Teisserenc de Bort and Marie, the French plenipotentiaries, were recalled from Rome. The Italian representatives asked for reductions in the French duties on cattle, cereals, and the produce of the vine. On February 21 M. Flourens communicated to Count Manabrea, the Italian Ambassador in Paris, the final proposals of the French Government, and on February 27 the French Senate passed a bill authorizing reprisals against Italy in case the commercial treaty should lapse. The Senate bill contained a clause taxing raw silk, for which the Lyons manufacturers have largely depended on Italy. The Italian Government gave notice that it intended to present counter-proposals, and requested the suspension of the new tariff, but to this the French Cabinet would not accede. On March 10 Count Manabrea presented new proposals as a basis for reopening negotiations. In the mean time the reprisals were carried out. The Italian Government was armed with the necessary powers by an act that was passed on February 8, in accordance with which it declared that certain specified French imports would come under the general tariff on and after the 1st of March. Among the articles so treated were wine, spirits, coffee, sugar, chocolate, oils, soap, perfumery, dye-stuffs, furniture, toys, fire-arms, flour, preserved fruits, etc. The duty on textile fabrics, skins, railroad-cars, pottery, glass, and copper manufactures was raised to 50 per cent.; that on iron manufactures to 20 per cent.; and that on machinery to 30 per cent. The French and Italian merchants, however, very generally evaded the new tariffs by organizing a systematic smuggling trade. Goods were shipped into Switzerland, and from there invoiced to their destination in France and Italy, until persons who practiced this trick were punished for making false declarations. After that an extensive smuggling trade sprang up. The risks and cost of smuggling enhanced the prices of the goods only about 15 per cent., which nearly corresponded to the average rate of duties under the old tariff. The trade in Italian straw-goods, raw silk, and other valuable wares and in fine French manufactures was as brisk as before, but the large export of grapes and must from the Italian vineyards for the manufacture of wine was interrupted.

The Premier's Journey to Friedrichsruhe.—In the summer of 1888 Signor Crispi went to Germany in order to pay a second visit to Prince Birmarck at Friedrichsruhe, where he arrived on August 22. The meeting had the effect of dispelling Clerical expectations of an intervention of Germany in the Roman question. The Italian Ambassador at Berlin, Count de Launay, was present at Signor Crispi's interviews with the German Chancellor. On his homeward journey the Premier had a conference with Count Kálnoky at Eger.

Colonial Possessions.—Italy has occupied or extended a protectorate over about 500 kilometres of the western coast of the Red Sea, extending from the village of Emberemi, in 16° of north latitude, a short distance north of the island of Massowah, to the southern limit of the territory of Raheita, in 12° of north latitude, situated on the Bay of Assab, inclusive of the small islands adjacent to the coast and the Archipelago of Dahlak. Italian sovereignty has been declared over Assab and its territory, extending from Ras Dermah to Ras Sinthiar in the south, a distance of about 60 kilometres; over Massowah and adjacent islands, and the coast from Emberemi to the peninsula of Buri; and over the Dahlak Islands. The island and town of Massowah, according to an enumeration made in September, 1885, contains 5,000 inhabitants; Emberemi, 1,000; the Dahlak Islands, 2,000; and Assab, 1,000. The extent and population of the protected territories between Massowah and Assab, and south of Assab, are not known. By a law enacted on July 10, 1887, a special corps of African troops was created, numbering 5,000 men, of whom 238 are officers, with 492 horses. It is composed of volunteers from the regular army. The commerce of the African possessions of Italy amounted in 1887 to 158,920 lire by land, and 12,614,447 lire by sea. There is a railroad in operation between Massowah and Saati, having a length of 27 kilometres.

In the summer of 1888 Italy took possession of Zulla, in the Egyptian Soudan, and notified the powers of the step, declaring that it was taken in response to an urgent request of the natives. The Egyptian Government, acting under directions from the Porte, protested against the occupation on August 16. About the same time the Italian Government asked of the Sultan of Zanzibar the grant of the Kismaya Juba river, which flows into the Indian Ocean a few miles south of the equator, and affords a route of doubtful value to Shoa and southern Abyssinia.

J

JAPAN. The chief ruler of the Japanese Empire is Mutsuhito, born Nov. 3, 1852. The heir-apparent, Haru, was born Aug. 31, 1877. The Tenno or Mikado is assisted in his government by the Privy Council of 13 members; the Cabinet, consisting of the heads of the eight executive departments and a Minister-President ot State; the Senate, or Genro In, of 60 members; and a Supreme Court of Justice, or Dai Shin In, consisting of 24 superior judges. For administrative purposes, the empire is divided into 44 ken, or prefectures, and 3 fu, or imperial cities. Each ken has a local assembly with limited powers, the members of which are elected by ballot. The number of persons that pay land-tax of over $5 per annum is 1,581,726, of whom 1,488,700 have the right of voting. The number of persons who pay over $10 tax is 882,517, of whom 802,975 have the right both of voting and of being elected to the local assemblies. In these petty legislative bodies 2,172 members sit, and the number of standing committees is 292. The Riu Kiu (Loo Choo) islands, formerly semi-independent, now form the Okinawa ken, but Yezo and the islands of Hokkaido are governed as a colony.

Population.—By the enumeration completed Jan. 1, 1887, the native population numbered 38,507,177, of whom 19,451,491 were males and 19,055,686 were females. These are divided by law into three classes, nobles, gentry, and common people, which numbered 3,430, 1,940,271, and 36,563,476 respectively. In 1886 there were 355,311 marriages, 1,050,617 births, and 938,343 deaths. The Central Sanitary Bureau of Tokio reported that, as the result of the violation of the quarantine by an infected vessel convoyed into Yokohama by a foreign man-of-war, the cases of cholera in 1886 numbered 155,474, of which 110,086 were fatal. Only 17 days of the year presented no cases. Of the cities having over 100,000 inhabitants, Tokio has 1,552,457; Ozaka, 353,970; Kioto, 255,403; Nagoya, 126,898; and Kanazawa, 104,320. There are 30 cities having a population of between 30,000 and 100,000. Foreigners residing in Japan number 6,807, of whom 4,071 are Chinese, 1,200 British, 621 Americans, 318 Germans, 220 French, and 371 of various nationalities. Yokohama is the main seaport, and here 3,837 foreigners live, of whom 2,359 are Chinese. Of the foreign mercantile firms in Japan, 103 are British, 39 American, 42 German, 35 French, and 255 Chinese. Over 400 adult persons are connected with missionary operations. In 1887 5,489 passports were issued to Japanese to travel or live abroad, no native being exempt, by reason of absence, from the military laws.

Army and Navy.—The army consists of 43,897 privates, 7,189 non-commissioned officers, and 3,302 commissioned officers, of whom 41 are generals. There are also 2,057 pupils in the military schools, and 15,000 police, who are drilled to act as a reserve in time of war. In September, 1888, there were in the standing squadron of the navy 8, and in the reserve 21 vessels of war; besides two vessels for coast defense building in France, one first-class man-of-war in England, and three wooden ships at

Yokoska, near Yokohama; total, 35, of which 24 were true modern fighting ships. The Naval Construction Board have decided to build 25 more ships during the next five years. The facilities for ship-building at Yokoska are first class, and in addition to the finest wooden vessels of the latest approved types, iron and steel ships are in course of construction. Most of the steel plates used for the iron-clads come from England. About 35,000 sailors and officers comprise the personal equipment of the Japanese navy. For the construction of forts at Tsushima, Shimonoséki, and in Tokio Bay, the manufacture of heavy guns, torpedoes, and other items of coast defense, $2,204.742 are appropriated for the present year. The War and the Navy Departments cost respectively $12,156,474 and $11,256,555, or $25,617,771, or five sixteenths or nearly one third of the total revenue of the empire, according to the estimates of 1888–'89. Both army and navy are kept to the highest degree of efficiency.

Finance.—According to the budget of Count Matsukata for the twenty-first year of Meiji (1888–'89), the total annual revenue amounts to $80,755,923; of which internal revenue yielded $66,289,576; sale or rent of various Government properties, $8,572,472; subscription to navy and coast defense, 5,893,874. The chief item of income is the land-tax, $42,089,-149; after which is saké-brewing, which yields $14,226,680. The chief expenditures are: Redemption of the national debt, $20,000,000; administrative expenses of the Department of the Interior, including public improvements, $8,481,315; Finance Department, $10,143,825; military and naval administration, $25,617,-771; Justice, $3,167,636; communications, $4,411,597; Foreign Affairs, $833,854; Education, 854,835; colonization of Yezo, $2,066,-149, etc., the total being $80,747,853. The national debt is now $245,921,207. Japan is prevented by her treaty obligations from attempting to increase her revenue by increasing the tax on imports, which now scarcely more than pay their collection.

Mint and Coinage.—One of the most satisfactory, in its workings, of the Government industries, is the mint at Ozaka, which is equipped with the best modern 'machinery and supervised by Englishmen. During the year ending March 31, 1888, the amount of bullion imported into the mint was 134,436·86 ounces of gold; 9,702,703·47 ounces of silver; 11,846,223 ounces of copper; the coinage being 87,016,448 pieces, valued at $11,660,141.97, in denominations of gold 5 yen, silver 1 yen, and 20 and 10 sen, and copper 1 and 1½ sen, besides 250 ingots for the imperial treasury valued at $2,587,871.87. The total coinage since 1870 has amounted in value to $149,713,-992.69. The annual expense of administration is $226,411.43. The employés number 473, of whom 13 are in Tokio. Of Corean gold in small bars and disk-shaped lumps, 547 ingots and 6 parcels of gold-dust were last year re-ceived and refined, and 260·47 tons of copper were obtained by calling in and melting up the large oval copper coin called "tempo." Gas is now replacing coke as a fuel.

Communications. — A distinct department of the Government, with bureaus, has charge of light-houses, telegraphs, nautical schools, Government subsidies to steamship companies, and postal service at home and abroad. There are now 59 light-houses and light-ships, 12 of the lights being of the first order. In the telegraph service, 2,298 miles of wire are in operation, and the business is conducted by 2,569 operators, of whom 20 are women. The school of telegraphy is in Tokio. The approximate annual postal and telegraphic receipts amount to $3,217,548, the net profits in 1887 being apparently $251,168. The nautical school for the commercial marine is in Ozaka, conducted at an annual expense of $30,000. In addition to the Nippon Yusen Kaisha, or Ocean Transportation Company, with its large fleet of steamers, the newly formed Ozaka Sho Sen Kaisha, or coast-trade company, is also subsidized by the Government, the former to the extent of $880,000, and the latter $52,000. The general post-office building in Tokio was burned during 1888, but statistics preserved show that during the year 35,307,658 covers were received, of which 23,091,091 were distributed in Tokio. The new line of postage-stamps as now issued is in sen (cents) as follows: 100, scarlet; 50, brick red; 25, pale green; 20, red; 15, purple; 10, dark orange; 8, violet; 4, brown. Of railways, in March, 1887, 431 miles were open, of which 266¼ were Government property.

Industries and Wages.—Returns from all except two provinces show that the acreage of cereal crops is steadily increasing, as well as pasturage for the enlarged numbers of live-stock rendered necessary by the prevailing fashion of eating meat, in which the city people are far ahead of the country folks. In 1887 there were housed 1,482,642,658 bushels of grain of all kinds, which exceeded the total crop of the previous year by over 1,000,000 bushels. As an index of the amount of animal food consumed in the two largest cities, in which butcher's meat was almost unknown thirty years ago, there were slaughtered in one month, February, 1888, in Tokio, 2,281 animals, and in Ozaka, 772. The use of milk and ice is now quite general in the cities. Whereas coal was popularly unknown as fuel three decades ago, there were consumed in Tokio in 1887 18,000,000 tons of coal, most of which, however, went to supply the furnaces of steam-boilers in the manufactories. Despite the increasing number of brick buildings, fires are still numerous in the capital, there being 806 fires in 1886, consuming 3,491 houses. In 1887 there were 867 fires. In the central district, Nippon Bashi, in Tokio, the wages of carpenters, roofers, wood-sawyers, paper-hangers, and shipbuilders, average from 50 to 40 cents a day; plasterers and masons, 70 to 50 cents; bricklayers, matmakers, lacquerers, 55 to 40 cents; joiners, tailors, screen and door makers, 75 to 50 cents; laborers, 35 to 25 cents. As a rule, skilled workmen engaged in making articles of foreign wear, equipment, or furniture modeled on Western patterns receive higher wages than these, the native houses being increasingly furnished after European fashions.

Meteorology.—The Meteorological Office, established in 1888, is on the elevated ground within the walls of the old castle in the heart of the city. It is one of the best equipped in the world, the apparatus being both imported from Europe and the United States, and of native invention and manufacture. Reports are received by telegraph thrice daily from 30 stations in the Japanese archipelago and from Corea. Three forecasts of the weather are issued daily in telegraphic bulletins, at 6 A. M., and 2 and 9 P. M. The phenomena studied and recorded are earthquakes, typhoons, wind, temperature, and moisture. The theories of weather as formulated in other parts of the world and largely based on local phenomena, which have been assumed to be of general application, are only of moderate value here, and much of the utility of the forecasts made in Tokio depend upon the individual skill of the superintendent. Thus far it has been proved that 70 per cent. of the predictions accord with the facts as subsequently recorded. It is noteworthy that the success is far greater concerning rain than wind. There are 47 stations from which vessels may be warned of coming typhoons. The apparatus for the recording of earth-tremors has been largely invented in Japan, and is much more delicate than the Italian seismographs. A flourishing seismological society is established in Tokio, issuing regular accounts of proceedings and results. On the 1st of January, 1888, a standard meridian was officially declared, and a national system of standard time went into operation throughout the empire. The year 1888 has been noted for the number and violence of cyclonic storms, those of August and September causing the loss of nearly 300 human lives besides much cattle and shipping. On the 15th of July, at 7.30 A. M., the fire-peaked mountain Bandai san, in Fukushima ken, whose history as a volcano and the eruption of three hundred years ago had been popularly forgotten, blew up amid thunderous noises, sending out vast masses of ashes which fell like rain during four hours. Of two hot springs, around which were houses filled with people, and of three villages, not a vestige was left. Besides the many square miles covered with lumps of mud and ashes, 108,000 square feet of valuable land was spoiled and 476 persons were killed. Steam escaped daily for weeks. The people driven from their homes were fed by the Government and a thorough scientific investigation was ordered.

Literature and Art.—Since the revolution of 1868 the thought of the nation has been turned almost entirely away from Chinese ideas, traditions, and literature, to the knowledge, languages, and general literature of the nations of Christendom. In all the large cities there are shops for the sale of foreign books, several native firms in Tokio carrying notably large stocks. The majority of works imported treat of scientific subjects and the modern arts and handicrafts. Most of the copyrights issued by the Department of Education are for translations of Western books, or for treatises based on knowledge gained directly from Europe or America. The increased literary activity shown in all departments of inquiry may be seen from the statistical report published in Tokio, which shows that the books used during the years from 1881 to 1887 numbered in each year respectively as follows: 5,973, 9,648, 9,462, 9,893, 8,507, 8,105, 9,547. During the same years the newspapers and magazines published in the empire numbered respectively 252, 244, 199, 269, 321, 403, 497; and in the first half of the year 1888, 550; of which there were in Tokio 203, and in Ozaka 43. Many of these periodicals are devoted to specialties in art and science. Among the books treating of Japanese themes, there are, besides solid reference-books of sterling value, notable essays in an almost entirely new branch of philosophical and critical literature. In these books the statements handed down from the past are sifted and appraised. Public libraries are increasing, and graduates of the university are being trained to the Western library methods. A special commission has been sent by the Government to study the American system of handling books and preserving archives. In the Tokio Library there were, at the end of 1886, 86,118,234 volumes, during which year 90,013 Japanese and Chinese volumes had been consulted by 4,852 readers, and 19,800 books read by 3,569 readers. In 322 days there were 42,826 visitors. A Japanese or Chinese book is usually divided into many volumes, the standard reference-works often including hundreds of lightly but durably bound fasciculi. European methods of print, binding, and general procedure in book publishing and manufacture are becoming yearly more general. A literary event of prime importance during 1888 was the issue of the complete translation of the Bible, made directly from the Hebrew and Greek original Scriptures by the American missionaries.

Religion.—Shintō (god-doctrine), the ancient state religion, re-promulgated in 1868, has now sunk to a merely nominal existence; the only public recognition, apart from the services in the imperial palace, being an annual grant of money, which keeps in repair the tombs of the Mikado's ancestors and the memorial shrines of patriots, together with the payment of "salaries to sinecure officials," amounting in all this year to $305,451. Of Buddhist sects there are 11, with 29 subdivisions, the temples and shrines belonging to which number 71,234, with 73,759 priests. Christianity makes steady progress, nearly all restrictions having been removed. Connected with the Reformed or Protestant churches there are 28,000 communicant members, and with the Roman and Greek Catholic a still larger number of Christians. The usual appurtenances of Christian work, propaganda, and education are established in the various towns and cities, such as churches, preaching-halls, Sunday-schools, orphan asylums, convents, theological seminaries, young men's Christian associations, religious newspapers. The first consecration in Japan of a Roman Catholic bishop took place at Yokohama, June 19, 1888.

Foreign Trade.—The summary of foreign trade for the year 1887 shows an increase of $12,-540,835 over that of 1886, the imports for the former year amounting to $44,526,600, and the exports to 40,901,610. The trade movement at the chief ports was as follows: Yokohama, $54,581,880; Kobe, $25,873,165; Nagasaki, $4,424,215; Hakodate, $593,950. With Great Britain and her colonies, the trade amounted to $23,227,735; with the United States, $20,401,920; with China and Hong-Kong, $16,571,495; with the East Indies, $5,777,705; with France, $9,903,265; with Germany, $4,839,885. Of imports, Great Britain and her colonies sold goods to the amount of $19,491,585; and the United States, $3,353,690; while of exports Great Britain and her colonies took but $3,745,395, while the United States took $17,038,230. The American imports were petroleum, clocks, flour, books, leather, and manufactured tobacco, while the exports were silk, tea, camphor, sulphur, rice, rags, porcelain, plaited straw, and fancy wares. The ocean commerce was performed in 1,256 foreign vessels and 13,883 Japanese vessels of Western build, the former having a tonnage of 1,669,186, and the latter of 3,498,517, with totals of 15,139 ships and 5,167,703 tonnage. Most of the entries of Japanese steamers were those of the Nippon Yusen Kaisha, and belonged to the company's fleet of over sixty vessels which now control the trade with China, Corea, as well as the coast trade of Japan.

JEWS. The Jewish record of events, abroad and at home, is gratifying in every department. In education, religious progress, and literature, there has been a marked advance, while in philanthropy and general participation in the march of humanity the year shows its usual favorable exhibit. Happily, there has been no set-back in the form of persecutions—no anti-Semitic excesses of any magnitude—but a practical determination of the Jews in all lands to face the problems of the time.

In January, 1888, Baron de Hirsch, of Paris, gave 50,000,000 francs for the education of the Jews of Russia. Such a practical solution of a harassing problem was greeted with satisfaction throughout the globe. The fund is to be deposited with the Government, and devoted to the technical education of Jewish youth and their training in science. But not satisfied with such a donation, Baron de Hirsch commemorated the jubilee of the Emperor of Austria, in the latter part of the year, by a gift of 12,000,000 francs for the benefit of the needy population of the kingdoms of Galicia and Lodomerea, the Grand Duchy of Cracow, and the Duchy of Bukovina. While the main features of the trust are unsectarian, there are special provisions for the Jews, who, besides, will share largely in its benefits, because they form so large a portion of the population to be aided. The objects are "the spread of secular education and the promotion of handicrafts and agriculture." It is to establish schools, promote technical training, supplement the salaries of underpaid teachers, aid school-children with clothing, food, and books, apprentice boys and girls to remunerative trades, and grant subsidies and loans free of interest to Jewish artisans and agriculturists. One of the conditions is, that German must be taught in the schools, but in Galicia Polish may be employed. Baron de Hirsch's educational plans run in direct parallel lines with the efforts of the Alliance Israelite, whose schools in the East afford instruction to 10,000 Jewish children of the poor and neglected classes, and constitute what may be termed Jewish Foreign Missions. These have made steady progress during the year, and flourish in Asia Minor, Morocco, India, and Turkey. Similar bodies in England, Austria, Germany, and America co-operate with the Alliance Israelite Universelle, of Paris. A gift, in spirit equaling Baron de Hirsch's was the bequest of 800,000 lire, on March 16, by the late Guiseppe Giganto, of Alberto, Italy, toward the foundation of an agricultural school, open to all confessions. Baron Edmond de Rothschild continued to give large sums in aid of the struggling Jewish colonies of Palestine.

The anti-Semitic movement in Germany has been checked. In Roumania, the condition of the Jews has improved, thanks to a more liberal ministry. In Austria, Ritter von Schoenerer, the leader of the anti-Semites, was arrested. In Prague, anti-Jewish pamphlets were confiscated. In Hungary, the firm attitude of the Government prevented any riotous demonstrations. On March 8, the Jews of Cork, Ireland, were made the subject of harsh invective by the labor union. In Paris, Drumont's scurrilous work was followed by discussions in the press, but without any outbreaks. No further steps were taken to facilitate Jewish emigration to Spain. The sweating-system (see GREAT BRITAIN, page 391) caused much excitement in London and throughout England, and Lord Rothschild was appointed a member of the House of Lords committee. The investigation was favorable, on the whole, to the character of foreign Jewish immigrants in England; but no effective remedy was proposed to relieve the great poverty of the working-classes in the

East End of London. The first number of the "Jewish Quarterly Review" was issued in London. Among the more important new works by Anglo-Jewish writers were: "Jewish Portraits," by Lady Magnus; "Fables of Bidpai," edited by Joseph Jacobs; and "Anecdota Oxoniensia," by Dr. Neubauer. Among the noteworthy books by Jewish authors on the Continent were: L. Kahn's "History of the Jews of France"; Wogue's "Cours de Theologie Juive: Principes Generaux"; "Reime und Gedichte des Abraham Ibn Ezra," by Dr. D. Rosin; "Life of Ludwig Börne," by Dr. M. Holzmann; translations of Graetz's "History of the Jews" into French, Russian, Hebrew, and Judeo-Polish, together with a large number of *brochures* and essays on Jewish and Oriental subjects, showing the interest manifested by scholars in biblical and rabbinical literature.

Signor Maurogonato was re-elected Vice-President of the Italian Parliament. Baron Henry de Worms was appointed Under-Secretary for the Colonies of Great Britain. M. Lisbonne was elected a member of the French Senate. Isidore Gunzberg won the first prize at the International Chess Tournament in Bradford, England. Alderman Benjamin was re-elected Mayor of Melbourne, Australia.

The efforts to consolidate the various Russian and Polish synagogues in New York resulted in the election of Rabbi Joseph, of Wilna, as chief rabbi of a large number of congregations representing Russian orthodoxy. His arrival in New York formed the subject of much press comment, and his first series of lectures, as they were printed in the daily papers, reflected favorably on his tact and ability. The attempt to promote union among the tens of thousands who have reached New York from Russia of late years is fraught with difficulty, and it is by no means certain that Rabbi Joseph will succeed. He is without any influence on the great mass of American and German-American Jews.

The charitable activity continued unabated. The Jewish Hospital at Philadelphia laid the corner-stone of a new edifice on October 9, $75,000 being subscribed in a few weeks. The Montefiore Home for Chronic Invalids was dedicated in New York on December 18, and $30,000 was given in a few days. In May the Hebrew Technical Institute of Chicago was reorganized, Leon Mandel, of New York, giving $20,000 for that purpose; while the Touro Infirmary of New Orleans received $10,000 from Michael Frank. The Purim ball in New York, on February 28, netted $10,000 for the Home for Aged and Infirm Hebrews. On January 18 the corner-stone of the new Benai Berith Orphan Asylum at Atlanta, Ga., was laid. On January 8, the Montefiore Hebrew Free School was dedicated in Chicago, and on July 8, the new Benai Berith Orphan Asylum was formally opened in Cleveland, Ohio. The Home for Aged and Infirm Hebrews was dedi-

cated in Boston, Mass., June 20. On March 3, the semi-centennial of the Hebrew Sunday-School Society was celebrated in Philadelphia. The first biennial convention, on March 11, in New York, of the Jewish Theological Association showed a hopeful exhibit. The Jewish Ministers' Association of America held its spring conference in Washington, D. C., on May 23. The subject of a religious union formed the topic of debate; an essay by Rev. Dr. Kohler, of New York, being read, followed by general discussion. Rev. Dr. S. Mendelssohn, of Wilmington, N. C., read a paper on "Funeral Orations," Committees were appointed to prepare a plan of action for religious union and uniform burial service. At the public session Rev. Dr. Gottheil spoke on the "Moral Education of the People," and orations were made by Rev. Dr. Bettelheim, of Baltimore, and Rev. Leon Harrison, of Brooklyn. At the winter conference in Philadelphia, December 3, the religious condition of the working-classes formed the subject of an earnest debate, and a series of resolutions, advocating special evening services and visitation was proposed by the Rev. H. S. Jacobs, of New York. Statistics as to Jewish prisoners in various penal institutions were presented, showing that they were few and generally well behaved. It was resolved to supply literature for Jewish convicts and take steps to secure the services of a regular visitor. At the public session the Rev. Dr. Kohler spoke on "The Bible and Modern Research," pleading for a broader estimate of its character and a rearrangement of its contents from "a higher point of view than the narrow Jewish one." The Rev. Dr. F. De Sola Mendes delivered an address, advocating union among the opposing parties in American Judaism.

There have been erected new synagogues in Portland, Me., Boston, Mass., New York city, Chicago, St. Paul, Minn., Scranton, Pa., Albany, N. Y., and elsewhere.

After much discussion, the Jewish Publication Society of America was formally organized at Philadelphia on June 3, the meeting being largely attended by delegates from the country in general. Active measures to insure a successful result were promptly taken, and the movement appears to be making headway throughout the United States. It is proposed to establish a Heilprin Endowment Fund of $50,000 for the publication of original works in Jewish literature, and $10,000 toward this fund has already been subscribed by Messrs. Jacob H. Schiff, of New York, and M. Guggenheim, of Baltimore.

The necrology of the year embraces many eminent names. Among those abroad who have passed away may be mentioned Henry Herz, composer, of Paris; Ritter von Rosenberg, of Venice; Dr. Gustav Wertheim, physician and scientist, of Vienna; Prof. Dr. G. Levy, of Parma; the journalists and novelists Michael Klapp and Dr. Märzroth, of Vienna, and

Dr. S. Gumbinner, of Berlin; Rabbis Elias Cohn, of Mayence; Abraham Caro, of Pinne; Louis Morhange, of Metz; M. Feuchtwang, Nicolsburg; Adolph Ehrentheil, of Bohemia; M. M. Stern, of Vienna; Asher Stern, of Hamburg; Ornstein, of Lemberg; Hillesum, of Holland, Solomon Debenedetti, of Naples; Rafael Foa, of Parma; Fröhlich, of Halle; Isidor, Chief Rabbi of France; Samter, of Berlin; Max Kayser, Socialist deputy of Berlin; Dr. S. A. Belmonte, of Hamberg; Moritz Ritter von Goldschmidt, of Vienna; the Russian financiers and philanthropists Samuel Poliakoff and Israel Brodsky; Madame S. Goldschmidt, of Frankfort; Baroness Caroline de Hirsch, of Munich; and Miss Miriam Harris, of London, all noted for their piety and benevolence; Prof. Arsene Darmesteter, of Paris; Levi A. Cohen, of Tangiers; Rev. Dr. Louis Loewe, of London, the secretary and life-long friend of Sir Moses Montefiore; Alexander Blumenthal, President of the Venice Chamber of Commerce; Jacob de Neuscholz, the banker-philanthropist of Jassy; Moritz Lowenthal, of Dresden; Prof. Leone Levi, English political economist; Alexander Sidi, philanthropist of Smyrna; and Prof. L. Polizer, of Vienna. Among the more notable deaths among the Jews of the United States were Michael Heilprin, of New York, author and critic; Mrs. Henry Cohen, of Philadelphia; Alfred T. Jones, of Philadelphia, founder of the "Jewish Record"; Hon. G. N. Herrman, of New York; Col. Isaac May, of Philadelphia; and Dr. Joseph Aub, oculist, of Cincinnati.

The Rev. Dr. Isaac Schwab, of St. Joseph, published "The Sabbath in History"; Mr. Isaac Markens, of New York, "The Hebrews in America"; and the Rev. Dr. L. Grossman, of Detroit, "Judaism and the Science of Religion." A complete edition of Miss Emma Lazarus's poems was issued in two volumes. Dr. Charles Gross was appointed instructor in history at Harvard College.

K

KANSAS. State Government. — The following were the State officers during the year: Governor, John A. Martin, Republican; Lieutenant-Governor. A. P. Riddle; Secretary of State, E. B. Allen; Treasurer, James W. Hamilton; Auditor. Timothy McCarthy; Attorney-General, S. B. Bradford; Superintendent of Public Instruction, J. H. Lawhead; Superintendent of Insurance, Daniel W. Wilder; Railroad Commissioners, James Humphrey, L. L. Turner, and Almerin Gillett; Chief-Justice of the Supreme Court, Albert H. Horton; Associate Justices, William A. Johnston and Daniel M. Valentine.

Finances. — The bonded debt of the State, on Jan. 1, 1889, was $803,500, showing a reduction since Jan. 1, 1886, of $127,000, and a total reduction, during the past four years, of $132,500. Of this debt, $256,000 is in the hands of individuals or corporations, and $547,000 is held by different State funds. The permanent school fund holds $537,000; university fund, $9,000; sinking-fund, $1,000. State bonds to the amount of $86,000 will fall due on July 1, 1889, but provision has already been made for meeting them, by the issue of new 4-per-cent. twenty-year bonds, to be sold to the permanent school fund, under the terms of an act of the last Legislature.

The Legislature at its last session also enacted a law "to provide for the assumption and payment of claims for losses sustained by citizens of the State of Kansas by the invasion of the State by bands of guerrillas and marauders during the years 1861 to 1865," commonly known as the Quantrell raid claims. This law assumed the payment of a certain portion of the claims audited by a commission appointed in 1875, and imposed upon the State Auditor the duty of preparing a schedule of such claims, and issuing to each claimant "certificates of indebtedness bearing interest at 4 per cent. per annum from July 1, 1887." The auditor issued certificates of indebtedness, aggregating, up to the close of the year, $346,776.54 in payment of claims, and $98,252.90 in payment of interest; in all, $445,029.44.

The law provides that these certificates shall bear interest at 4 per cent. per annum, but the Legislature neglected to make any provision for the payment of this interest, and early last spring the State officers were confronted with a serious dilemma. The State Treasurer finally made arrangements for the money necessary to pay the coupons falling due July 1, 1888, all the State officers signing a personal note for $14,000, bearing interest at 4 per cent. per annum, and payable Jan. 31, 1889. The State's fiscal agent holds the coupons paid as security for the note.

The next installment of interest is payable on July 1, 1889. The coupons following are for one tenth of the principle, with interest, and fall due on and after Feb. 1, 1890, and on the same date of each year thereafter, until the whole of the certificate is paid.

The balance in the State treasury on June 30 was $324,882.06, against $584,273.16 two years previous. On Dec. 31 there was a balance of $243,830.75.

Municipal Debts. — On this subject the Governor says:

The steady and enormous growth of our municipal indebtedness amply justifies alarm. On July 1, 1884, the county bonds and warrants outstanding aggregated $8,065,748.29; township bonds and warrants, $2,650,030.90; city bonds and warrants, $2,487,436.17; and school-district bonds and warrants, $2,748,714.50, making an aggregate municipal indebtedness of $15,951,929.86. On July 1, 1886, the aggregate of this indebtedness had increased to $17,-779,299.42, and on July 1, 1888, it had reached the appalling sum of $31,107,646.90, with $373,712.03 in sinking funds, making the net municipal indebtedness to be yet provided for, $30,733,934.87. The county bonds outstanding on the 1st of July, 1888, aggregated $13,207,265.25; and the county warrants, $732,963.37; township bonds outstanding, $7,162,-002.65; and township warrants, $12,308.33; city bonds outstanding, $5,244,307.40; and city warrants, $164,168.66; school-district bonds outstanding, $4,-513,237.59; and school-district warrants, $41,393.65; making a total, as above stated, of $31,107,646.90. In other words, the municipal indebtedness of Kansas has been doubled since (in January, 1885) I called the attention of the Legislature to this subject, and urged that the most stringent restrictions and limitations be put upon the debt-creating and tax-levying powers of all municipalities. It seems to me, in view of the facts and figures presented, that it is the imperative duty of the Legislature to repeal at once every law authorizing the creation of municipal debts for any purpose whatever, except, perhaps, the building of school-houses.

Education.—The report of the Superintendent of Public Instruction shows the public-school system of the State to be in a condition of steady growth and improvement. The school population for the past school year numbered 532,010, an increase of 34,215 since 1886. The number of pupils enrolled during the last school year was 403,351, an increase of 38,112 over 1886. The average daily attendance was 145,881, an increase of 25,978. Number of teachers employed in 1886, 9,387; in 1888, 11,310. The average wages paid teachers, per month, were: Males, $41.01; females, $33.64. There were in the State, at the close of the fiscal year, 8,166 school-houses, having 10,142 rooms, and valued at $8,608,202 — an increase of 1,405 school-houses, 1,958 rooms, and $2,015,455 in valuation during the past two years. The receipts and expenditures during the school year ending July 31, 1888, were as follow:

Receipts.—Balance in district treasuries, Aug. 1, 1887, $533,200.10; amount received from county treasurers from district taxes, $3,075,867.81; from the State and county school funds, $553,390.28; from sale of school bonds, $900,597.83; from all other sources, $202,557.84, making a total of $5,265,613.86.

Expenditures.—Amount paid for teachers' wages and supervision, $2,677,513.29; for rents, repairs, fuel, and incidentals, $636,567; for district libraries and school apparatus, $62,893.45; for sites, buildings, and furniture, $1,051,124.94; and for all other purposes, $275,649.16—making a total of $4,703,647.84, and leaving in the hands of district treasurers, July 31, 1888, a balance of $561,966.02.

The State University comprises six departments—science, literature and arts, law, music, pharmacy, art, and medicine. The preparatory department has been recently discontinued, as the normal department was a few years ago, and advanced tests for admission have been established, so that the institution may be devoted to legitimate university work. These changes have largely reduced the number of students qualified for admission, but, notwithstanding this fact, the number in attendance shows a steady and gratifying increase. On Jan. 15, 1885, the students enrolled numbered 419; and 24 professors, assistants, and instructors were employed. On Jan. 1, 1889, 843 students were enrolled, and the corps of professors and instructors numbered 30.

During the past four years important additions have been made to the buildings of the university, including the "Snow Hall of Natural History," costing $50,000.

The State Agricultural College on Dec. 31 had 359 students enrolled, an increase of 21 since the close of the autumn term of 1884. Its instructors in all departments number 25, an increase of 4 during the past four years. The improvements in buildings and fixtures, since Jan. 1, 1885, have aggregated in value $27,-000, and the increase in the value of the farm, furniture, stock, and apparatus is over $70,000.

The State Normal School had 440 students enrolled on Jan. 1, 1885, and 660 at the close of 1888. Fourteen instructors are employed, an increase of three in four years. The expenditures during that period include $26,200 for buildings, $4,800 for museum and apparatus, and $5,000 for furniture and improvements.

Charities.—The institution for the blind had in attendance on Jan. 1, 1885, 63 pupils; at the close of 1888 it had 86. At the institution for the deaf and dumb there were 172 pupils at the beginning of 1885, and 321 on Dec. 31, 1888. Two large school-buildings and a laundry have been erected during the past four years, at a cost of $82,000. The Kansas institution for the deaf and dumb now ranks in size as the eighth in the United States.

The State Reform School had 103 pupils enrolled on Jan. 1, 1885; it now has 208.

The Soldiers' Orphans' Home, authorized by the Legislature of 1885, was opened for the reception of children on July 1, 1887. It was soon crowded beyond its capacity, and is now the home of 109 orphan children of deceased soldiers of the Union. The law authorizes the admission of children under sixteen years of age, but the board has been compelled to exclude all over ten years. Additional buildings are absolutely necessary to accommodate the demands made upon it.

The Asylum for Idiotic and Imbecile Youth was removed to Winfield in March, 1887. There are now over one hundred children cared for in this institution. The new building is well adapted for the uses of such an asylum, and was completed at a cost of $25,000.

The insane asylums at Topeka and Ossawatomie contained at the close of the year 1,203 patients. On July 1, 1882, the insane patients in these asylums numbered 548; at the same date in 1884, the number had increased to 692; on July 1, 1886, to 881; and on July 1, 1888, to 1,181.

During the past four years the State has expended for new buildings, and for permanent improvements at its insane asylums, over $353,-000. Yet to-day it is confronted with an apparent necessity of providing additional accommodations for this class of dependents.

Prisons.—The number of prisoners in the State Penitentiary, when compared with the population of the State, has been steadily decreasing for eight years past, and there has been an actual decrease in the number in confinement during the past two years. On Jan. 1, 1887, there were 895 State prisoners confined in the Penitentiary; on Jan. 1, 1888, there were 898; and on Jan. 1, 1889, there were 861.

The Legislature of 1885 directed the building of an industrial reformatory, which was located at Hutchinson. Appropriations aggregating $60,000 were made in 1885, and additional appropriations, aggregating $100,000, in 1887. The board of commissioners having the building of this institution in charge, report that a cell-house with fifty completed cells therein has been inclosed, and the foundations and one story for the office and guard-house have been completed.

State Capitol.—A contract for the foundations of the east wing of the Capitol was let on May 2, 1866, and this wing, partially completed, was occupied by the State officers on Dec. 25, 1870; but it was not finished until early in 1873. The State issued and sold bonds to the amount of $320,000, to provide means for its construction. Its total cost, however, was $480,000. In the summer of 1879 the building of the west wing was begun, and it was, though in an unfinished condition, occupied in the summer of 1881. It was completed in 1882, and cost $312,000. Work on the central building was begun in 1881, and its foundations were completed in 1884. Early in the spring of 1885, work was begun on the first story, and the walls are now finished to the height of the fourth and last story. The cost of the central building to date has been $517,000, and it is estimated that from $600,000 to $700,000 will be required to complete it. The remodeling of the east wing, including the Senate Chamber, in 1885–'86, cost $140,000; so that the Capitol, as it stands, has cost an aggregate of $1,449,000. No bonds have been issued since the west wing was finished. The half-mill tax for State-house purposes has provided a fund sufficient to meet all the expenditures made.

In western Kansas a strong feeling has been developing that these expenditures have been ill-advised, and that the interests of the State require the removal of the State Capitol to some central location. In April a convention of six hundred delegates was held at Abilene for the purpose of organizing a Capitol-removal movement, at which the following resolution was passed among others:

Resolved, By the representatives of the citizens of Abilene and western Kansas, in convention assembled, that we will now, in the future, oppose any further appropriations by the State Legislature for the erectment of the present State institutions of whatsoever kind. That we pledge ourselves to oppose further appropriations for work on the State-house; that while we favor the maintenance of our present State institutions where located, we favor and recommend the adoption of a new policy, commensurate with our new growth, present and future importance, and that in this line we ask all of central and western Kansas to unite with us in the work of duplicating every one of the present State institutions, locating the new buildings most advantageously to the interests of the State among the several towns of central and western Kansas, and the State Capitol at some suitable central point to be determined by the ballots of the people of the State.

Development.—The Governor says in his annual message:

The last two years have not been, in all portions of Kansas, seasons of plenty and prosperity. The harvests in many counties of the western half of the State have been below the average of former seasons. But, notwithstanding this, our general condition is fairly prosperous. The growth of the State has been constant and the development of her resources and industries remarkable. This fact is best shown by a comparison of the vote cast in 1884 and 1888. The total vote of 1884 was 265,379, while that of 1888 was 330,215—an increase of 64,836. A contrast of the vote of 1880 with the United States census of that year shows that the ratio of population to voters was nearly five to one. This ratio increases with the age of a State. The vote of 1888, therefore, clearly establishes the fact that the population of Kansas is fully 1,651,000—an increase since 1880 of over 654,000, and since 1885, of 392,000.

During the past four years twenty-three counties have been fully, and one partially organized, making a total of 106. These newly organized counties embrace an aggregate area of 19,932 square miles, or very nearly one fourth of the total area of the State. At the date of their organization their population aggregated 66,147, and they polled at the November election an aggregate vote of 19,428 votes, indicating a population, at that time, of 97,140. Five of these counties were organized in 1887, viz., Stanton, June 17; Haskell, July 1; Garfield, July 16; Gray, July 20; and Logan, September 17. Three have been organized during the past year, viz., Kearney, March 27; Grant, June 9; and Greeley, July 9.

The increase in the area of land cultivation during the past four years aggregates 6,756,873 acres; and of land taxable, 13,032,815 acres; while the assessed value of property has, during the same period, increased $117,227,941.

The most extraordinary growth, however, is shown in the railway system of the State. On Jan. 1, 1885, the railways of Kansas aggregated 4,064 miles of main and 459 miles of side track, or a total of 4,553 miles. On Jan. 1, 1888, they had completed and in operation 8,799 miles of main and 899 miles of side track, or a total of 9,698 miles, and an increase in four years of 5,135 miles. The assessed value of railway property in March, 1884, was $28,455,909, while on March 1, 1888 (when the assessments are made by the State board), it aggregated $52,829,664—an increase of $24,373,757 in four years, or very nearly double the valuation of 1884.

Statistics.—According to the assessor's returns for 1888, Kansas has 700,723 head of horses, 92,435 mules and asses, and 742,639 milch cows, a large increase in each class over the number reported in 1887. She has also 1,619,849 head of other cattle; 402,744 sheep, and 1,433,245 swine. The total value of the farms of the State, in 1887, was $453,220,155; of farming implements, $8,432,534.

The coal-product in 1885 was 30,001,427 bushels; in 1886, 34,750,000 bushels; and in 1887, 39,251,985 bushels. The industry gave employment during the latter year to 4,728 miners and 870 day-laborers.

The following cities had a population of over 10,000 on March 1, 1888: Leavenworth, 35,227; Topeka, 34,199; Wichita, 33,909; Kansas City, 33,110; Atchison, 17,023; Fort Scott, 16,159; Hutchinson, 13,451; Lawrence, 11,055.

Prohibition.—The Governor says in his message in January, 1889:

There is no longer any issue or controversy in Kansas concerning the results and beneficence of our temperance laws. Except in a few of the larger cities, all hostility to them has disappeared. For six years, at four exciting general elections, the questions involved in the abolition of the saloon were disturbing and prominent issues, but, at the election held in November last, this subject was rarely mentioned by partisan speakers or newspapers. The change of sentiment on this question is well grounded and natural. No observing and intelligent citizen has failed to note the beneficent results already attained. Fully nine tenths of the drinking and drunkenness prevalent in Kansas eight years ago have been abolished; and I affirm with earnestness and emphasis that this State is to-day the most temperate, orderly, sober community of people in the civilized world. The abolition of the saloon has not only promoted the personal happiness and general prosperity of our citizens, but it has enormously diminished crime; has filled thousands of homes where vice and want and wretchedness once prevailed, with peace, plenty, and contentment; and has materially increased the trade and business of those engaged in the sale of useful and wholesome articles of merchandise. Notwithstanding the fact that the population of the State is steadily increasing, the number of criminals confined in our Penitentiary is steadily decreasing. Many of our jails are empty, and all show a marked falling-off in the number of prisoners confined. The dockets of our courts are no longer burdened with long lists of criminal cases. In the capital district, containing a population of nearly 60,000, not a single criminal case was on the docket when the present term began. The business of the police courts of our larger cities has dwindled to one fourth of its former proportions, while in cities of the second and third class the occupation of police authorities is practically gone.

County Disorders.—In March, 1887, troubles were reported in Wichita County, growing out of a county-seat contest, and threatening serious consequences. Several persons had been killed and wounded, and the excitement and passion evoked by this affray were wide-spread. The Governor ordered the Adjutant-General and some other militia officers to the scene, and their presence was sufficient to restore quiet. Early in January, 1888, similar troubles were reported in Sherman County, also growing out of a county-seat controversy, and were quieted in the same manner. Of the difficulties in Stevens County, the Governor reports as follows: "Early in June, 1888, Sheriff Cross, of Stevens County, telegraphed me that he had been driven from the county-seat, and requesting the presence of a company of militia. A few days later a writ of mandamus was issued by the Supreme Court, directing the county commissioners to canvass a vote recently taken to establish a county-seat, and a special messenger was sent to serve this writ. On his arrival at Hugoton, this messenger found it necessary to request the presence of troops in

order to secure obedience to the decrees of the court, and I at once directed Gen. Myers to take two companies of the Second Regiment and proceed to Stevens County. The board of commissioners canvassed the vote, as directed by the court, and the troops were thereupon ordered to their respective homes. Late in July troubles were again reported in Stevens County, resulting in an armed expedition to No-Man's-Land by rival factions, and the brutal murder of Sheriff John Cross and three other citizens by persons from Hugoton. I requested Attorney-General Bradford and Brig.-Gen. Myers to proceed to Stevens County, make a thorough investigation, and report to me. These officers reported that there were two hostile factions of armed men in the county, and advised me that the presence of a strong military force was necessary to prevent further bloodshed, preserve the peace, and insure the orderly enforcement of law. Acting on this advice, I directed Gen. Myers to return to Stevens County, taking with him the Second Regiment, and to remain there until all danger of an armed collision was averted. The command was transported to Stevens County by the most direct routes, and remained on duty until the 14th of August."

Farmers' Conventions.—Early in May a convention of representatives from Kansas, Missouri, Nebraska, Illinois, and Indiana met at Topeka, under the name of the Farmers' Trust Association. The interests of the farmers were discussed in rather a stormy session, and measures were urged looking to "trust" combinations by the farmers themselves, in order to give them a proper price for their products. The convention adjourned without action to meet at the same place in November, at the time of the National Farmers' Congress. This congress met on November 14, and, after considerable discussion, the members voted against the proposed scheme of "farmers' trusts" and against all other "trusts." Resolutions were also adopted favoring the free coinage of silver; favoring the expansion of a medium of exchange; approving the policy of the Government in improving the rivers and harbors of the country, and urging a continuance of the policy; indorsing boards of railway commissioners; condemning the provisions of the national banking laws, which prohibit the acceptance of real-estate securities for loans, and asking Congress to amend the law so as to put real estate on an equal footing with other property; recommending the enactment of laws by legislatures regulating railroads and governing railroads; and recommending the enactment of a law favoring a home market. The congress was in session three days, and contained representatives from every part of the Union. At the same time and place the annual session of the National Grange was held.

Political.—The Democratic State Convention met at Leavenworth on July 4, and nominated for Governor Judge John Martin, of Topeka.

The other nominees were H. Miles Moore, for Lieutenant-Governor, superseded before election by F. W. Frasius; Allen G. Thurman for Secretary of State; W. H. Willhert for Auditor; William H. White for Treasurer; I. F. Differbaker for Attorney-General; A. N. Cole for Superintendent of Public Instruction; and W. P. Campbell for Associate Justice of the Supreme Court. Resolutions were adopted ratifying the work of the St. Louis National Convention, urging the necessity of tariff reform, and continuing as follow:

We are opposed to all sumptuary laws as being vicious in principle and unsuccessful in practice; also the action of the Republican party of Kansas in passing the law for the establishment of a metropolitan police system in certain cities in this State, and for its inequitable and unfair application and enforcement of the same for purely political reasons. We denounce the system as being partial, unjust, and undemocratic. It is a substantial denial of home rule and the right of local self-government. It impeaches the intelligence, challenges the integrity, and denies the patriotism of the people affected by it. It brands them individually and collectively as being ignorant, vicious, dishonest, corrupt, and wholly incapable of self-government, and we demand a repeal of the law.

We oppose any system of State policy which permits competition between convict and Chinese labor and the labor of the free American workman.

We favor the abolition of the grand-jury system as a useless and unnecessary measure, which adds greatly to the cost burdens of a tax-ridden people, and we demand its repeal as expensive and inquisitional legal machinery.

The Prohibitionist Convention was held at Hutchinson on July 18. It nominated the following ticket: Governor, Rev. J. D. Botkin, of Wichita; Lieutenant-Governor, R. J. Freeley; Secretary of State, L. K. McIntyre; Treasurer, R. M. Stonaker; Auditor, Gabriel Burdett; Attorney-General, Stanton A. Hyer; Superintendent of Public Instruction, Miss S. A. Brown; Associate Justice of the Supreme Court, J. O. Pickering. The usual prohibition resolutions were passed, woman suffrage was demanded, tariff reform was favored, and restrictions upon immigration, a liberal pension law, and arbitration between employer and employed were advocated. It was further resolved that—

We demand that the General Government shall by equitable and lawful means own and operate all railways and telegraphs in the interest of the whole people.

We demand that the interest be so regulated by national law that the average net earnings of capital shall not exceed the average net earnings of agriculture and labor.

We favor such a change in our present system as shall provide for the election of President, Vice-President, and United States Senators by a direct vote of the people.

We are opposed to the acquisition of landed estates by persons not citizens of the United States, or who have not under oath made bona-fide declaration of their intention to become such. And we believe the time has come when ownership of land should be so limited as to preserve a reasonable amount as a homestead for the citizen, and prevent the further acquisition of large bodies of land by corporations and individual speculators.

As under the Constitution and laws of the State all

errors and irregularities of the inferior courts may be corrected by proper proceedings in the Supreme Court, a tribunal composed entirely of Republicans, the action of Gov. Martin in exercising executive clemency to release convicted liquor-sellers who have not sought a review of their cases in the Supreme or other proper court for the correction of errors, is an attempt to destroy the confidence of the people in the courts, thereby inciting lawlessness and disobedience to public authority; and such conduct on the part of the Governor, under solemn oath to obey the Constitution and enforce the laws, merits and deserves the condemnation of all citizens, irrespective of party affiliation and regardless of personal views as to the policy of prohibition.

The Republicans held their State Convention at Topeka on July 26, and on the third ballot nominated Lyman U. Humphrey for Governor. The remainder of the ticket was as follows: Lieutenant-Governor, A. J. Felt; Secretary of State, Williams Higgins; Auditor, Timothy McCarthy; Treasurer, James W. Hamilton; Attorney-General, L. B. Kellogg; Superintendent of Public Instruction, G. W. Winans; Associate Justice, W. A. Johnston. After approving the work of the Chicago convention, and the character of the present State administration, the platform continues as follow:

We believe in the protection of the home against the saloon. We demand the complete execution of the prohibitory laws in every part of the State, including the vigorous prosecution of officers who fail to perform their duties under the law. The Republican party of Kansas is convinced that prohibition is right, and is a success, and we assert that those who seek a refuge in the third, or Prohibition, party, blindly seek a revolution in our Government for that which a revolution can not give.

We demand stringent laws to protect our workingmen against contract, pauper, or Chinese immigrants, and every class who would drag down by mere cheapness the standard which American workingmen are struggling to maintain. We favor American markets for American products, and American wages for the workingmen of America. And we favor such additional legislation as will secure weekly payments of wages to employés of municipal and private corporations, and also a practical apprenticeship law, so that our handicraftsmen may have additional protection against foreign labor.

All so-called "trusts" or combinations to monopolize food-supplies or control productions are dangerous to the interests of the people, and should be prohibited under the severest penalties of law. The "trust" or combination of the packing-houses to drive out of business all other butchers, and thus control the cattle markets, as well as the supply and prices of dressed meats, is especially obnoxious and destructive to the interests of all classes of the people, and particularly to those in Western States.

The Republican party will ever retain a sense of gratitude to those through whose valor Kansas and the nation became free, and the union of our States preserved. We especially commend the action of the Legislature in making provision for the maintenance of orphans of soldiers in a soldiers' orphans' home, and we heartily indorse the resolutions adopted by the Grand Army of the Republic at its last State encampment at Winfield on the subject of pensions.

We request our railroad commissioners to do all in their power to protect the farmers of this State against the excessive charges in the removal of the vast crops assured to Kansas this year.

We favor legislation reducing the legal rate of interest upon money to six per cent., reducing the maximum contract rate to ten per cent., prohibiting usury, and providing penalties for violations thereof.

There was also a Union Labor ticket in the field, headed by P. P. Elder.

At the November election the Republican State and National tickets were successful, receiving a large majority of the vote cast. For Governor, Humphrey received 180,841 votes; Martin, 107,480; Botkin, 6,439; and Elder, 35,837. The State Legislature, chosen at the same time, is overwhelmingly Republican, only four Democrats being elected to the House and one to the Senate. Seven Republican Congressmen, the entire State delegation, were chosen.

Two amendments to the State Constitution were voted upon at the same election—one permitting colored citizens to join the State militia, the other giving the Legislature power to regulate the rights of aliens to the ownership of land in the State. Both amendments were adopted, the former by a vote of 223,474 in favor and 22,251 against; the latter by a vote of 220,419 in favor and 16,611 against.

KENTUCKY. State Government.—The following were the State officers during the year: Governor, Simon B. Buckner, Democrat; Lieutenant-Governor, James W. Bryan; Secretary of State, George M. Adams; Auditor, Fayette Hewitt; Treasurer, James W. Tate, succeeded by Stephen G. Sharp; Attorney-General, P. W. Hardin; Superintendent of Public Instruction, Joseph D. Pickett; Register of the Land Office, Thomas H. Corbett; Railroad Commissioners, J. P. Thompson, A. R. Boone, John D. Young; Chief-Justice of the Court of Appeals, William S. Pryor; Associate Justices, William H. Holt, Joseph H. Lewis, Caswell Bennett.

Legislative Session.—The General Assembly, which met at Frankfort on the last day of 1887, remained in session over four months, adjourning on May 4. Early in January James B. Beck was nominated by the Democratic caucus and re-elected United States Senator for a third term, beginning in March, 1889. No fewer than 1,571 acts and 86 resolutions, covering nearly 3,400 printed pages, were passed during the session, of which only 168 acts, covering 216 pages, are of a general nature. Aside from legislation growing out of the defalcation of Treasurer Tate, an important act of the session provides for a second election by the people in August, 1889, on the question of calling a convention to revise the Constitution, the first election, in August of last year, having been favorable to such a convention. Another act amends, revises, and codifies the common-school laws. It was also enacted that no juror should be challenged for having read newspaper accounts of a crime, or for having formed an opinion or impression therefrom, provided he shall declare upon oath that he believes he can render an impartial verdict according to the law and the evidence. An appropriation of $150,000 was made for the completion of the Eddyville Penitentiary to the extent of accommodating at least 418 convicts; and, in order to forward the work so

that convicts now leased outside the prison-walls may be employed within the prison, in labor not competing with free labor, a further sum of $50,000 was placed at the disposal of the Governor, if he should find it necessary. Improvements at the Institute for Deaf Mutes and at the Eastern Lunatic Asylum were provided for. Other acts of the session were as follow:

Requiring all buildings of three or more stories, in cities of more than 10,000 inhabitants, in which over 20 persons are employed, to be provided with fire-escapes.

Accepting the provisions of the act of Congress providing for the establishment of agricultural experiment stations in connection with the agricultural colleges.

Making actual possession unnecessary in order that an owner may maintain an action of trespass.

Establishing a State Board of Pharmacy, defining its duties and powers, and regulating the practice of pharmacy in the State.

Making May 30 a legal holiday.

Providing for the continuation of the geological survey of the State.

Requiring all teachers in the State to obtain certificates of qualification from the county board of examiners.

Creating a lien on canals, railroads, and other public improvements, in favor of persons furnishing labor or materials therefor.

Providing for the parole of prisoners confined in the State Penitentiary under the direction of the commissioners of the sinking fund.

Establishing a State Board of Equalization of Assessments.

Providing for the care and custody of vagrant and destitute children in the city of Louisville.

Regulating the conduct of municipal elections in the city of Louisville.

Treasurer Tate's Defalcation.—On March 20 a message was sent to the Legislature by Gov. Buckner announcing that he had suspended the State Treasurer from office, and conveying the information that a large deficit had been found in his accounts. As no intimation had before been received by the Legislature or the public of any irregularities, none in fact being known to exist until the day preceding, this announcement created great surprise. Tate, generally called "Honest Dick Tate," had been universally trusted and popular, having been renominated without opposition by his party at each biennial convention for twenty years, his term of service dating from 1868. At the same time it was discovered that he had been missing from the capital for several days and had escaped from the country. The Legislature at once adopted a resolution offering a reward of $5,000 for his capture, and by another resolution confirmed the act of the Governor in suspending the defaulting official and authorized him to appoint a successor until Tate should be restored to his office or a successor should be regularly elected. Under this act the Governor appointed Stephen G. Sharp on March 27. The Senate then resolved itself into a court of impeachment, summoned the various State officers as witnesses, and on March 30, after a formal trial, found the missing Treasurer guilty of misappropriating the public funds, whereupon he was deposed from office. On March 31 the Governor appointed a commission to examine the accounts of the late Treasurer and ascertain the exact liability of his sureties. The report of this commission, laid before the Legislature by the Governor on April 24, shows that Tate's defalcations had extended over a term of years, beginning with 1876, and that the total amount missing was $229,009.21. To offset this sum there were found in the treasury vaults due-bills and other evidences of indebtedness to the late Treasurer amounting to $59,782.80, showing that he had not only used the funds of the State himself, but had lent them freely to others. For the purpose of making a settlement with these debtors of Tate, the Legislature created a commission, to be filled by appointment of the Governor, which entered upon its duties in May, and before the end of the year had made terms with nearly all persons indebted to the late Treasurer. The proceeds derived from these assets, and from other property left behind by Tate, reduced the liability of his bondsmen below $200,000. In June criminal proceedings were begun against him in Franklin County, where he was indicted under several counts for embezzlement. To guard against similar episodes in the future, the Legislature passed an act creating the office of State Inspector and Examiner. This officer is appointed and removable by the Governor, and is required to examine annually the management of the Auditor's and Treasurer's office, all the public institutions, and all other officers intrusted with property of the State, to be present at each monthly settlement between the Auditor and the Treasurer, and to report to the Governor his findings in all investigations.

Assessments.—The following table shows the assessed value of property in the State for 1888 and the changes made by the State Board of Equalization recently created:

PROPERTY.	Assessed value.	Equalized value.
Lands	$227,379,166	$227,481,085
Town lots	133,660,825	133,987,643
Personalty	77,964,416	78,634,622
Personalty not subject to equalization	52,549,782	52,549,782
Total	$491,554,189	$492,653,132

The total assessed valuation for 1887 was $483,491,690.

The Insane.—The State supports three asylums for the benefit of the insane. During 1887 the daily average number of patients at the Western Asylum was 580; at the Central, 738; and at the Eastern, 635. The steward's expenses at the Western Asylum amounted to $94,282.95, or an average of $162.55 for each patient; at the Central the expenses were $135,744.99, or an average of $183.93; and at the Eastern the amount was $106,325.98, or an average of $167.35.

Political.—On August 6 elections for county officers were held throughout the State. In the Second Appellate District an election for Judge of the Court of Appeals was also held, at which Judge William S. Pryor was reelected without opposition. No general election for State officers was held. In November the Democratic National ticket was successful. Democratic Congressmen were elected in nine districts, and Republicans in two.

Rowan County.—The Legislature, early in its session, appointed a committee to investigate the disturbances occurring in this county in 1887 and previously, and to report upon the conduct of Judge Cole in his administration of justice there. This committee visited Rowan County, and, after taking much testimony, made a report in March, censuring Judge Cole and recommending the abolition of the county courts. The Legislature passed an act removing it from the fourteenth and annexing it to the thirteenth judicial district, thus taking it from the jurisdiction of Judge Cole, who was permitted to retain his office.

Pike County Disorders.—Early in January the inhabitants of Pike County petitioned the Governor for arms and ammunition to defend themselves against threatened attacks from West Virginia. The difficulties grew out of a feud between the family of McCoys in this county and the Hatfield family of Logan County, West Virginia. This feud originated in 1882, when, in an election dispute, one of the McCoys shot and killed a Hatfield. Four McCoys were arrested for this act, captured by a Hatfield mob, carried into West Virginia, and then secretly taken back to Kentucky and shot. The matter had rested since that time till September, 1887, when Gov. Buckner offered $500 reward for the murderers of the McCoys, and at the same time made a requisition for them upon the Governor of West Virginia, which the latter refused. Later in the year the sheriff of Pike County, induced by this reward, entered Logan County, captured three of the Hatfield party, and lodged them in the Pike County jail. The remaining Hatfields retaliated on New Year's eve by burning the house of the elder McCoy and killing his wife, daughter, and son. The father escaped, and at once organized a party of about thirty men, who invaded Logan County, killed two of the Hatfields in an encounter, and later captured six others, who were also lodged in the Pikeville jail. About the middle of January another party from Kentucky made a second attack and killed another of the Hatfields. Late in the month the Governor of West Virginia sent a special agent to Gov. Buckner asking for the surrender of the captured Hatfields; but his mission was fruitless. The Governor then appealed to Judge Barr, of the United States Circuit Court, for a writ of habeas corpus; but Judge Barr, after a hearing on February 20, decided that the prisoners were properly in the custody of Kentucky authorities. During July and August, and later still, encounters took place upon the border between the two clans, and other murders were committed. The Governor also increased his reward for the Hatfield leaders to $5,000, and early in the year stationed a company of Kentucky State troops at Pikeville to prevent a rescue of the Hatfields. At the close of the year the difficulties were still unsettled.

KING'S DAUGHTERS. An incorporated society, having its headquarters in New York city, chapters in the different States, and circles in numerous localities. The society grew from the meetings of a few charitably inclined women in January, 1886, at the house of Mrs. F. Bottome, in New York city. It was first intended to put into practice the system of working by means of clubs of ten, as recommended by Edward Everett Hale; but as the organization grew, this system of tens was found to be impracticable if closely adhered to, and the local clubs are permitted to consist of any number of members. The organization has now over 50,000 members. The object of the society is to promote the association of women into small clubs for the development of spiritual life and charitable activity. Any person that claims to be a Christian may become a member. The members wear as a badge a silver Maltese cross, engraved with the initials I. H. N., and bearing the date 1886. The yearly membership fee is ten cents; a payment of $25 constitutes a contributor; and the payment of $100 a donor. The motto of the society is "In His Name."

The management of the affairs of the society is vested in a Central Council consisting of not fewer than ten women, who must be members of the society and pay a yearly fee of one dollar. Vacancies in this council are filled by the remaining councilors. The officers are a president, vice-president, treasurer, general secretary, corresponding secretary, and recording secretary. No salaries are paid to any of the officers or councilors. The business of the society was at first attended to at the homes of the officers; but as the membership grew it was found necessary to procure separate quarters and employ clerks. The business headquarters are now at No. 47 West Twenty-Second Street, New York city. Each circle usually devotes itself to some special phase of work; for example:

To visit the sick, poor, and aged; to clothe them, and to write letters for those unable to do it themselves.

To visit strangers, and welcome them to the church and prayer-meeting. To take active part in the latter, and to be punctual and regular in attendance at all church services.

Work in hospitals, orphan asylums, nurseries, poorhouses.

Indian mission in Indian Territory. Assisting home missionary in southern Virginia.

To raise money for sending poor girls to the seashore.

To raise money for Sunday-school building.

To be ready to speak and work for the Master; to live close to him.

To follow out the Golden Rule.

Bible study, with hope of outcome in practical work in many fields.

Letters for Christmas-letter mission.

Collecting pictures and cards, and making scrapbooks for children in hospitals.

Making garments, towels, bibs, etc., to start day nursery.

Appointed one to sing, another to read to old lady almost blind.

Helping mothers who have to work with their sewing.

To indulge in no gossip. Object of circle to "make sunshine."

To teach Chinese.

To gather flowers and send in to city hospitals.

To help motherless children.

To read for inmates of Old Ladies' Home.

To sing at stated times in hospital wards.

To collect papers, magazines, etc., for Sailors' Mission.

To "keep the wrinkles from our mothers' brows."

To increase purity of life.

Each circle is known by a separate name, for example: Thoughtful Ten, Willing Ten, Clothing Ten, Children's Ten, Knitting Ten, "Inasmuch" Ten, Truthful Ten, Considerate Ten, Charity Ten, Visiting-Sick Ten, Fancy-Work Ten, Widows' Ten, Helping Ten, "Withhold not" Ten, Peacemakers, Memorial Circle. Each circle also has its separate motto, usually a text from the New Testament. The existence of one hundred members of the order in any State entitles the State to a State secretary, appointed by the Central Council, for one year. The State secretary has the appointment of county secretaries. The circles in each county report the work done by them to the county secretaries, who in turn report to their State secretary, and the State secretaries report to the Central Council. These secretaries receive no pay, but are not infrequently furnished by the circles over which they have supervision with funds to pay office-rent and clerk-hire.

The King's Sons is an organization for men and boys, similar in purpose to the King's Daughters and managed by that society.

L

LABRADOR, a country between the fiftieth and sixty-second parallels of north latitude, which forms a peninsula in the extreme northeastern part of North America; area, about 420,000 square miles. The south coast extends from the small Salmon river, which flows into the Strait of Belle Isle, opposite Newfoundland, northeastward on the Atlantic Ocean, presenting a large mass of high rocks, a barrier against the Arctic icebergs. In the north the country borders on Hudson Strait and Ungava Bay; in the west, on Hudson Bay. The inland boundary, toward Canada, is not established.

THE EXPLORED PART

OF

LABRADOR

H. B. C.—Hudson Bay Company.

SCALE OF ENGLISH MILES

The summer of Labrador corresponds almost with the English summer, from the middle of June (when snow disappears) to the middle of September. The arctic current freezes the coast, but has little effect inland. Twelve miles from the coast begins a luxurious forest-growth. Toward the north are barren moors, the homes of large herds of caribou. Randle F. Holme says: "A journey of twenty or thirty miles inland in summer-time, up the country from the sea, is like passing from winter to summer. The southern coast rises abrupt from the water's edge 200 feet, increasing to 500, and on the eastern coast to 1,400, until it reaches nearly 6,000, then diminishing in height until we reach the northern Cape Chidley, which is about 1,500 feet high. The mountains consist chiefly of Laurentian gneiss and red syenite, with characteristic scenery.

The greater part of the interior is table-land over 2,000 feet high, slowly falling toward the northwest until it reaches Hudson and Ungava Bays. Most of the streams are formed by a chain of ponds, connected by rapids and waterfalls, in an uncommon way. The southern part is especially well watered, and the whole interior is dotted with large lakes. The Indians are acquainted with a system of internal navigation joining the Seven Islands, Mingan, and the mouth of St. Augustine river, on the south coast, with Northwest river on the east, and Ungava on the north. The largest stream is South river, which flows into Ungava Bay the harbor resembling very much that of London. In consequence of the mountainous and broken features of the southern and eastern coast, there are innumerable good harbors.

The Government is represented by the Hudson Bay Company only. In summer there is mail communication from Newfoundland as far as Nain, but only once in winter. There is an English mission-house in Cartwright, and farther northward are several Moravian mission and trading settlements.

The accompanying map was compiled for the "Annual Cyclopædia" by Frederick Leuthner, according to the latest explorations. The hydrographic charts, a map of the Moravian Brethren, and the explorations of Hind, Randle F. Holme, and A. S. Packard furnished the material.

From Hamilton inlet along the coast live a large number of Eskimo and half-breeds, in scattered homesteads, who are occupied in salmon-fishing, trapping in winter, and hunting seal in spring. They are civilized, and have received Christian education by the Moravian Brethren; but those toward the north are pagan and uncivilized, and live in snow-houses. In the interior live a considerable number of Red Indians of the Cree nation, in families. They are nomadic, and in spring camp near the Hudson Bay Company's posts for trading. Their tents and canoes are very light, made of birch-bark or deer-hide, and they walk long distances over the snow. Newfoundlanders

visit the coast in spring, returning home at the close of the fishing-season.

The most common birds are wild geese, black ducks, shell-birds, divers, loons, and plover. Salmon, trout, and white fish are very common. No cattle can be kept. Iron is plentiful, and a beautiful stone called "Labradorite" may be seen about the beach of Hamilton inlet. Eskimo dogs are kept in large quantities. Mosquitoes and black flies are said to be worse than anywhere else.

LANDS, PUBLIC. The public lands of the United States lie within the boundaries of sixteen States—Alabama, Arkansas, California, Colorado, Florida, Iowa, Kansas, Louisiana, Michigan, Minnesota, Mississippi, Missouri, Nebraska, Nevada, Oregon, and Wisconsin—and eight Territories—Arizona, Dakota, Idaho, Montana, New Mexico, Utah, Washington, and Wyoming—which are known as "Land States and Territories." A few isolated tracts remain also in Ohio, Indiana, and Illinois. The estimated area of the public lands, exclusive of Alaska, is 603,448,145·40 acres, of which, 83,-158,990·51 acres have been restored to the public domain since March 4, 1885. The recovery of 148,179,528·84 additional acres has been recommended to Congress. The only States that have not, at some time, contained public lands, are the thirteen original colonies, and Kentucky, Vermont, Maine, West Virginia, Tennessee, and Texas. Maps of the public-land States and Territories are prepared by the General Land Office at Washington.

History.—The public domain, as distinguished from and included within the national domain, of 4,000,000 square miles, embraces all lands acquired by the United States Government by treaty, conquest, cession of States and purchase, which are disposed of under and by its authority. (Article IV of the Constitution, section 3). It contained 2,843,575·91 square miles. The nucleus of this domain was an area of 404,955·91 square miles, ceded by seven of the original thirteen States to the General Government under the Articles of Confederation and the Constitution, after the definitive treaty of Sept. 3, 1783. These cessions of unoccupied chartered territory, extending to the Mississippi river, claimed often under conflicting grants, were made respectively by the States of New York, Virginia, Massachusetts, Connecticut, North and South Carolina, and Georgia, at intervals between March 1, 1781, and April 24, 1802. The first was volunteered by the State of New York, after previous discussion of expediency in Congress, and the passage of a resolution, Oct. 30, 1779, disapproving of the disposal of Western lands by States holding them. The total number of acres disposed of by State authority prior to June 30, 1796, was 1,484,047. Receipts, $1,201,725.68.

A peculiar feature of the cession by North Carolina of the territory now constituting the State of Tennessee (45,600 square miles) was an incumbrance of reservations, which was equivalent to adding nothing to the public domain. To the State of Georgia was paid, in all, $6,200,000 in settlement of all claims, and a strip of land from the United States containing 1,500 square miles was added to her northern boundary. The reservation of "Virginia Military Lands" in the State of Ohio, an area of 6,570 square miles, occasioned much litigation and legislation by Congress prior to 1871. From the territory thus ceded by States were formed the present States of Ohio, Indiana, Illinois, Michigan, Wisconsin, and Tennessee, that part of Minnesota lying east of the Mississippi river, and all of Alabama and Mississippi lying north of the thirty-first parallel of latitude.

The following are purchases of the United States: From France, April 30, 1803. 1,182,-752 square miles, at a cost of $27,267,621.98. From this was formed the remaining portion of the States of Alabama and Mississippi south of the thirty-first parallel, Louisiana, Arkansas, Missouri, Iowa, Nebraska, and Oregon, all of Minnesota west of the Mississippi river; almost all of Kansas, and Dakota, Montana, Idaho, Washington, and Indian Territories, with a part of Wyoming and Colorado. From Spain, Feb. 22, 1819, the provinces of East and West Florida, an area of 59,268 square miles, costing $6,489,768. The province of East Florida constitutes the present State of that name. West Florida (including the territory of Alabama and Mississippi south of the thirty-first parallel, with parishes in Louisiana) revolting from Spain in 1810, declared itself an independent State and framed a constitution, desiring annexation by the United States. It was occupied and held by proclamation of the President under the treaty of 1803, but the claim of Spain was recognized by purchase of 1819. From Mexico, Feb. 2, 1848, by treaty stipulation (at a cost of $15,000,000) 522,568 square miles. On Dec. 30, 1853 (the Gadsden purchase) the Mesilla valley, 45,535 square miles, at a cost of $10,000,000. The States formed are California, Nevada, and part of Colorado; Territories, Arizona, Utah, and New Mexico. From the State of Texas. Sept. 9, 1850, 96,707 square miles, at a cost of $16,-000,000. These lands are included in Kansas, Colorado, and New Mexico, in addition to the "Public Land Strip." From Russia, March 30, 1867, Alaska, containing 577,390 square miles, for $7,200,000. The sum total paid by the United States for purchased territory, including the Georgia cession, is $38,157,389.38.

The ordnance of July 13, 1787 (Congress of the Confederation), provided for the government of the territory northwest of the Ohio river (bounded by the Mississippi river), with provisions for the formation of States, and also with exclusion of slavery. On May 26, 1790, an act of Congress made similar provision for the territory south of the Ohio river (also bounded by the Mississippi), with the condition

"that no regulations made or to be made by Congress shall tend to emancipate slaves." Both acts became obsolete by the absorption of territory into States. The territory west of the Mississippi river was explored, settled, and organized into States and Territories by successive legislation. All business of administration and survey of the public lands is performed by the Secretary of the Interior, through the General Land Office.

Surveys.—The first surveys of public lands were conducted by the Geographer of the United States, appointed by ordinance of May 20, 1785. Thomas Hutchins was the first and only incumbent of that office. The act of May 18, 1796, for the sale of lands in the Northwest Territory, created the office of Surveyor-General. Surveying districts, under the control of surveyors-general, were created from May 7, 1822. Surveys within these are executed by contract, the surveyors-general employing deputies, with compensation fixed by Congress. A State, a Territory, or two or more of any of them joined together, constitute a surveying district. Mineral lands are surveyed by deputy mineral surveyors. There are fifteen surveying districts at present, and sixteen surveyors-general, one *ex officio* of Alaska.

When all lands within a surveying district have been surveyed, the office of the Surveyor-General is closed by act of Congress, the archives, plats, field-notes, etc., being transferred to the State authorities. Surveys of islands and keys on the sea-coast are made, under special laws, by the Coast Survey. Indian Reservations, by act of April 8, 1864, are surveyed under direction of the General Land Office.

Surveys of public lands in the United States have been uniform under the "Rectangular System," reported to Congress May 7, 1784, from a committee headed by Thomas Jefferson. By this system lands are divided into townships six miles square, and subdivided into sections one mile square, or 640 acres. These sections are again subdivided into half, quarter, and quarter-quarter sections, of 320, 160, and 40 acres. The number of principal surveying meridians and base lines intersecting at an equal number of initial points is thirty—viz., First, Second, Third, Fourth, Fifth, and Sixth Principal, Michigan, Tallahassee, St. Stephens, Huntsville, Choctaw, Washington, St. Helena, Louisiana, New Mexico, Great Salt Lake, Boisé, Mt. Diablo, San Bernardino, Humboldt, Willamette, Montana, Gila and Salt River, Indian, Wind River, Uinta (special), Navajoe (special), Black Hills, Grand River, and Cimarron. Townships are numbered north and south of the principal base lines, and ranges, or series of contiguous townships, are reckoned east and west from the surveying meridians. The necessity for enduring monuments of iron or stone to mark corners and lines of public surveys is obvious, and has been repeatedly urged upon Congress. The deficiency is serious. Plats of surveys are prepared in triplicate, and filed respectively in the offices of surveyors-general, in local land-offices, and in the General Land-Office at Washington.

Surveys are made under appropriations of Congress and under what is known as the individual deposit system. Prior to July 31, 1876, appropriations were made by separate item for the several surveying districts; subsequently a gross sum was apportioned, to be used at the discretion of the Secretary of the Interior. The annual appropriations for the years 1880 to 1886 were $300,000 and upward. Since that date they have been $50,000. The actual available appropriation of the fiscal year 1888 was $40,000, an item of appropriations for surveys and resurveys being devoted to examinations of work in the field before approval of contracts. An additional $10,000 was allowed on March 30, 1888, for deficiencies. Thirty-five contracts for the year were approved. The appropriations for surveys of Indian lands for the fiscal year 1888 were $135,000.

The system of deposits by individual settlers in payment for desired surveys of lands, certificates of deposit to be received in payment for lands by act of 1871, within township surveyed, and by act of March, 1879, for any lands in the possession of the Government under the pre-emption and homestead laws, has been the occasion of serious abuse. The act of Aug. 7, 1882, restricted receipt of certificates in payment of lands to the district within which surveys were made. The amounts of deposits have largely exceeded the appropriations of Congress, and vast arid tracts, undisposable, the subdivision of which is undesirable, have been surveyed at heavy expense and without reference to the judgment of surveyors-general. From 1880 to 1885 the amount of special deposits for surveys was $5,813,368.58, against $2,093,000 appropriated by Congress, and during this period alleged fraudulent returns were made of surveys unattempted or egregiously performed. Among these are the "Benson cases," or "California syndicate," still under prosecution. In 1885 numerous contracts were suspended and ultimately disapproved. None were approved for 1886 and 1887. The amount deposited for surveys under this system during 1888 was $68,578.50, and five contracts were awarded and approved. Surveys of railroad lands are made under deposits from companies.

The total number of acres of public domain surveyed to June 30, 1887, was 973,723,495. During 1888, 2,912,342.32 acres were surveyed. Surveys have not been extended over Alaska and the public-land strip. The highest prices paid per linear mile for surveying have been $75 for State and Territorial boundaries astronomically determined; for outboundaries of Indian reservation, $25; for principal bases and meridians, standard parallels, $20; for township lines, $18; section lines, $12. The rates prescribed by law per linear mile for surveys of public lands have ranged at various times

from $3 to $20. The present mileage allowed for public surveys—$5, $7, and $9 for section, township, and meander lines—is below statutory rate, and reported inadequate by the Commissioner of the General Land-Office. The estimated cost per acre of surveys from the beginning of the system to June 30, 1880, was three and a quarter cents. The estimated cost to Dec. 1, 1883, was from two and a half to three cents and a half per acre.

Disposal.—The authority to dispose of public lands, vested in Congress was first exercised through the Board of Treasury (three commissioners), which made sales and gave certificates from May 20, 1785. The first patent, or deed in fee-simple, for land from the Government was authorized to be issued by the President, April 21, 1792. This title is purely allodial, and deprived of the last vestige of feudal import. There are fifty-seven forms of land patent in present use by the United States. The number of acres patented or otherwise passed title to or conveyed during 1888 is 8,605,194.29. The General Land-Office, under direction of a commissioner, was created April 25, 1812, subordinate to the Treasury Department. It was reorganized July 4, 1836, and on March 3, 1849, was transferred to the Interior Department. It is at present organized in fourteen divisions. The first patents for land were signed by the President, upon recommendation of the Secretary of the Treasury, countersigned by the Secretary of State, and recorded in his office. Mineral lands were disposed of by the Secretary of War prior to 1849.

A plan for the disposition of the public lands, submitted to Congress July 20, 1790, by Alexander Hamilton, Secretary of the Treasury, is the basis of the prior and existing land service of the Government. The act of March 3, 1795, provided for the application of net proceeds of sales of public lands to the payment of the national debt. They were to create a portion of the sinking-fund, and sales were ordered in the Northwest Territory, May 18, 1796. All sales were made under the credit system, on deposit of one-twentieth of the purchase-money. The total amount of sales under this system was 13,642,536 acres, for which $27,900,379.29 were received. Cash payment for lands was ordered in 1806, and the credit system was finally abolished in 1820. The act of May 10, 1800, created defined districts of public lands open to disposal at local offices in charge of registers and receivers of public moneys. The first land-offices were within the Northwest Territory. But little change of organization has taken place to the present day. Registers and receivers are bonded officers, who make disposals of public lands, transmitting accounts to the General Land Office, and returns to the Treasury. Their salary is fixed at $500, with receipts from fees not to exceed $3,000. There are at present 111 local land-offices, with an equal number of registers and receivers. Vacant tracts of public lands in States containing no land-offices are entered under act of March 3, 1877, at the General Land-Office. Land districts are made, abolished, consolidated, or reduced in area by Congress; mineral districts by the President. They are in nowise connected in boundary with surveying districts. Prior to April 20, 1820, all sales of public land were ordered by special acts of Congress, and the minimum price, except under contracts, was $2 an acre. By act of that date the minimum price was fixed at $1.25 an acre (except in cases of alternate sections reserved on line of railroads, by later provision); public lands were to be offered for sale by proclamation of the President, and those remaining unsold were to be opened to private entry at the minimum rate. Lands at present are disposed of by public sale and private entry, and under the pre-emption, homestead, and timber-culture laws. The following are the characters of lands disposable: agricultural; mineral; coal; desert, or lands requiring irrigation to produce crops; saline, or those containing salt springs; and timber and stone. There are special laws relating to each.

Sale.—By the policy of the Government all Western lands are held for settlement. Lands within the five Southern States of Alabama, Arkansas, Florida, Louisiana, and Mississippi, reserved for settlement under the homestead act of May 20, 1862, were by act of June 22, 1876, brought into market by proclamation. These lands, containing timber, coal, iron, and other valuable deposits, having been technically offered for sale, are entered at minimum rates, and are the only public lands of moment that can be purchased for cash without settlement. The act of March 3, 1881, excluded public lands in Alabama from operation of laws relating to mineral lands. Lands such as are valuable in Western States and Territories at $2.50, $5, $10, and $20 an acre, are sold in this State in unlimited quantities for $1.25. The area of public lands within the five Southern States, June 30, 1883, was 18,620,645·93 acres. Of these there had been disposed of by public sale and private entry to June 30, 1887, 2,136,640·92 acres, for $2,695,541.

Settlement.—Those only are legal settlers upon the public lands, male or female, who are citizens of the United States, or who have declared their intention to become such, who are heads of families, or are over twenty-one years of age. Proclamation of Congress in 1785 forbade settlement upon the public lands. Authority to remove settlers by force of arms was granted to the President at that time and later. The first pre-emption or preference right to purchase land, in view of prior settlement and improvement, was accorded March 3, 1801, to contractors for lands included in the purchase of John Cleves Symmes, but outlying the patent obtained by him. Subsequent legislation culminated, Sept. 4, 1841, in the passage of the act allowing pre-emption of 160 acres with credit of from 12 to 33 months, to be paid for

at the minimum rate of $1.25 an acre. No person is allowed to pre-empt land who owns 320 acres of land within the United States, or who has removed from land of his own. The number of patents issued for pre-empted lands during 1888 is 12,403. Pre-emption filings are merged into cash sales upon making of final proof and payment, so that it is impossible to give the number or acreage of such filings for extensive periods. The filings so merged in 1887 numbered 23,151. The amount of land disposed of by pre-emption to June 30, 1887, is estimated at 185,969,023 acres. Pre-emption is allowed upon unsurveyed as surveyed lands, where not reserved or selected for town-site purposes, and where not saline or mineral.

The homestead law of May 20, 1862, originated in the Free-Soil movement ten years previous, and was the subject of animated discussion in Congress from that date. A bill passed by both Houses was vetoed by President Buchanan, June 23, 1860, but the measure finally received Executive sanction at the hands of President Lincoln. By its provisions, a home of 160 acres of the public lands is secured, without payment, upon condition of residence and improvement for a period of five years. Land thus acquired is not liable for debt contracted prior to the issuance of patent. Full citizenship is requisite for final title. Section 8 of the act allows commutation of homestead, or payment for the land as in pre-emption entry at any period within the term of five years after six months' settlement. This feature is open to the same objections as the pre-emption laws, and its repeal has been advised. Amendment to the homestead law provide for entries of homes of 160 acres by soldiers and sailors honorably discharged, their term of service in the civil war to be deducted from the five years of residence required by law. Actual residence for one year, however, is required. A claim may be filed by an agent or attorney, but entry can be made only by the soldier or sailor. Additional homestead and adjoining farm provisions are for entry of land to fill the limit of 160 acres, in cases where the right has been exercised for a smaller amount. Non-mineral affidavits are required previous to entry of lands within mineral districts. The total number of entries under the homestead law, to June 30, 1888, is 874,501, covering 113,878,601·43 acres. Of these 319,030 were final, covering 38,483,434·22 acres; and 16,077 homesteads were patented for the year 1888. Commutations of homesteads are merged in cash sales in the keeping of Government accounts; 5,835 homesteads were commuted during 1888. The act of March 3, 1875, extended the homestead privilege to Indian settlers. But commutation is denied them, nor are their titles subject to alienation or incumbrance for a period of twenty years. Commissions and fees are payable at times of making entry and final proof under homestead laws, and vary according to States, and number and value of acres.

On the Pacific slope they are advanced. The highest amount payable is $34. By the act of June 14, 1878, pre-emption entries are convertible into homesteads, to date from original settlement.

Legislation to "encourage the growth of timber on Western prairies" was begun March 3, 1873. By amendatory act of March 13, 1874, settlers are allowed entry of 160 acres of public land, on condition that one fourth of it be devoted to raising timber for a period of eight years. Upon final proof at the end of that time, or within five years thereafter, a patent issues. Agricultural as well as timber-land is thus secured by what is in reality a bounty-act for raising timber. Timber-culture entries are not liable for debt contracted prior to issue of patent. The total amount of commissions and fees, payable at making of entry and final proof, is $18. Serious objections to the timber-culture laws, as encouraging frauds upon the public domain, are urged upon the attention of Congress. The number of timber-culture entries patented for 1888 was 754. The total number of entries made from March 3, 1873, to June 30, 1888, was 246,449, covering 39,958,558·45 acres, and 5,466 entries have been perfected. Oaths of settlers under all laws, in making final proof, when not taken by registers and receivers, are made before designated judicial officers. Acts of relief to settlers suffering under drouth, incursions of grasshoppers, etc., have been passed from time to time.

The act of Aug. 4, 1854, graduated prices of public lands to actual settlers from $1 to twelve and a half cents an acre, according to the length of time the land had remained unsold in market. Entries under this act were original and for adjoining farms. It was repealed June 2, 1862. The total number of acres disposed of under the graduation act was 25,696,419·73.

Agricultural lands are obtainable under the above-mentioned laws, and 47,180 agricultural patents were issued for 1888, against 24,558 for the year previous. Mineral lands are patented or held under possessory title. They are not subject to pre-emption or homestead laws. The ordinance of May 20, 1785, for sale of lands, reserved one third part of all gold, silver, lead, and copper mined. The act of March 3, 1807, authorized lease of lands containing lead by the War Department in the Indian Territory. Lands containing lead and copper in Arkansas, Missouri, Iowa, Michigan, Minnesota, and Wisconsin were sold from March 3, 1829, under special laws, the mineral being conveyed with the soil. The area of the precious-metal bearing region of the United States is estimated at 65,000,000 acres. Iron is reckoned as among valuable deposits. The precious-metal bearing States and Territories are California, Colorado, Oregon, Nevada, Idaho, Montana, Wyoming, Utah, New Mexico, Arizona, Dakota, and Washington. (See MINING LAWS IN THE UNITED STATES.) One thousand and

thirty-four mineral patents were issued for 1888; 1,314 entries were made, for 31,734 acres, realizing $117,996.85; 13,433 claims were patented to June 30, 1887.

Coal-lands, by act of July 1, 1864, were authorized for sale, and opened to pre-emption at $20 an acre. The act of March 3, 1873, gave pre-emption right to 160 acres of coal-lands at $10 an acre fifteen miles from a completed railroad, and $20 within less distance. Entry of 320 acres is allowed to associations of persons. An additional entry of 640 acres is allowed to associations of not fewer than four persons who have expended $5,000 in improvements. The number of coal entries patented for 1888 was 114, and 152 entries were made, realizing $342,849.40. The total number of entries of coal-lands to present date cover 93,612·64 acres.

Desert lands, by act of March 3, 1877, may be entered to the amount of 640 acres, three years being given from date of entry to conduct water; twenty-five cents an acre is paid at filing of application, and the remaining $1 an acre at any time within three years. The number of desert entries patented for 1888 was 1,187. The total number of entries to date under this act is 16,821, covering 5,564,727 acres. Of these 7,156 have been perfected.

Saline lands are disposed of by public sale and private entry at $1.25 an acre, by act of Jan. 12, 1877. The act of May 18, 1796, reserved such lands to the United States. They were leased by the Surveyor-General. Grants not to exceed 12 in number, with 6 sections of land for each spring, for school purposes and public improvements, were made to each public-land State up to Nevada, upon admission into the Union; and 559,965 acres cover these grants. No saline lands are sold in the Territories nor in States with grants unsatisfied.

The act of June 3, 1878, authorized sale of lands, containing timber and stone, unfit for cultivation, at $2.50 an acre in California, Oregon, Nevada, and Washington Territory. The fee for entry of such lands is $5, and 1,063,-781·54 acres have been disposed of. The protection of timber on public lands from fire and depredation has occupied the serious attention of Congress from the origin of the Government. Appropriations for the purpose were made in 1878. Forty-one special agents were employed by the General Land-Office for 1887, under an appropriation of $75,000. The receipts for timber depredations for the fiscal year 1888 were $13,320.65. The act of June 3, 1878, allowed cutting and removal of timber for mining and domestic purposes from mineral lands in certain States and Territories. Railroads were exempt.

Town sites are entered on the public domain by three methods, under sections 2,380 to 2,390, inclusive, of the Revised Statutes. Seventeen town-site patents were issued for 1888; the total number to date is 556. The town-site and town-lot entries under all laws to date cover 163,818·12 acres. The act of May 26, 1824, authorized pre-emption of county-seats. About nine entries have been made. Mineral rights are reserved in town-site patents. Eleven hundred and twenty acres of public land may be legally obtained by any one person under the settlement and occupation laws, although contrary to their theory.

Reservations.—Lands reserved from the public domain are for Indians and for military purposes, and no settlement is allowed upon either. There are 147 Indian reservations, covering 136,394,985 acres. Surveys of these are made for definition of boundary, and for allotments in severalty to Indians under the act of Feb. 8, 1887. The receipts from Indian lands disposed of by the General Land-Office under special laws of Congress are deposited in the United States Treasury to the credit of the several Indian trust funds. The amount from lands so disposed of during 1888 was $821,-113.77.—Military reservations on the public lands cover, approximately, 2,477,378·60 acres. Abandoned military reservations are restored to the public domain by act of Congress, and disposed of by sale in Florida (act of Aug. 18, 1856) as other public lands.

Donations.—Miscellaneous donations of public lands and special grants have been made by Congress at various periods, to the number of perhaps a thousand. The latest were for reservoir purposes in Wisconsin and Minnesota, and for artesian wells east of the Rocky mountains, in charge of the Department of Agriculture (act of May 19, 1882). Two reservations for this purpose have been abandoned, the third still exists.

The grants of public lands to States are as follow: By State selection act of Sept. 4, 1841, to each State named and each one to be admitted, 500,000 acres for internal improvements, including the quantity granted for the purpose under the Territorial Government. By successive acts from March 2 1849, swamp and overflowed lands, unfit for cultivation, have been granted to States "to aid in constructing necessary levees and drains to reclaim such lands." The number of acres claimed for 1888 was 781,857·59, making the total amount 78,189,130·65 acres. The number of acres patented to all States is 56,840,-251·09; for 1888, 96,515·19 acres. The Swamp Land grant has not been extended to the States of Kansas, Nebraska, Nevada, and Colorado, nor to the Territories. Under the acts of 1855 and 1857, more than $1,500,000 have been paid from the Treasury, and 600,000 acres of agricultural land have been patented as indemnity for swamp and overflowed lands disposed of by the United States for cash, warrants, or scrip.

For educational purposes the following grants of public lands have been made in States and reserved in Territories at various periods from 1785: For public schools, in States admitted prior to 1848, every sixteenth section of public land; for States and Territories organized since that period, every sixteenth and thirty-sixth section; to the State of Nevada, 2,000,000 acres, in lieu of school selection. For seminaries and universities, the quantity of two townships in each State or Territory containing public land, and in some instances a larger quantity in proportion to grade of institution. The act of July 2, 1862, granted to each State 30,000 acres of public land for each Representative and Senator in Congress, for agricultural and mechanical colleges, "in place," where the States contained public land, and scrip representing an equal number of acres locatable in other States or Territories. Lands thus ceded for educational purposes were disposed of or are held disposable, the proceeds constituting endowments for common-school funds. The estimated total is 78,659,439 acres. Indemnity selections are made for deficiencies in school grants.

Under the distribution act of Sept. 4, 1841, the net proceeds of sales of lands to Aug. 29, 1842, were divided as therein provided among States and Territories and the District of Columbia. Amount, $691,117.05.

Acts giving lands to induce settlement in dangerous or distant portions of the nation have been passed at divers periods as follows: For East Florida (armed occupation act), Aug. 4, 1842, with amendments, total amount 200,000 acres; for Oregon Territory, Sept. 27, 1850, expiring Dec. 1, 1855; for Washington Territory, March 2, 1853, expiring Dec. 1, 1855; for New Mexico, July 22, 1854, still in force. The total amount of land covered by donation entries is 3,133.640 acres.

Grants of public land for public improvements are as follow: For canals, 4,424,073·06 acres. Grants from 1824, in Indiana, Ohio, Illinois, Wisconsin, and Michigan. Alternate sections were reserved in grant of May 24, 1828, for Miami Canal in State of Ohio, inaugurating system as pursued in other grants. For river improvements, 1,406,210·80 acres. Grants from 1828 to 1846 in Alabama, Wisconsin, and Iowa. For railroads, amount estimated to fill railroad grants, June 30, 1880, 155,504,994·59 acres; estimated value, $391,-804,610·16. There have been patented 49,-907,135·96 acres; selections pending and undisposed of, 25,429,866·11 acres. Grants are made to States and corporations direct. To States from Sept. 20, 1850; to corporations from July 1, 1862, date of grant to Union Pacific Railroad Company. Lands withdrawn from settlement for indemnity purposes have been restored since March 4, 1885, to the amount of 21,322,600 acres. The grants forfeited for non-completion of roads, and lands granted in limits restored in the same period, amount to 30,361,764·33 acres.

The alternate (odd and even numbered) sections of land reserved within railroad limits are valued at the "double-minimum" rate of $2.50 an acre. A homestead entry of but 80 acres of such land was allowed prior to the acts of 1879 and 1880. Cost of survey, selection, and conveyance of public land for railroad purposes must be paid by companies preceding issue of patent (act of July 31, 1876). For this purpose $92,617.50 were deposited in 1888. The railroad patents issued during the year were to four States, and covered 829,-162·45 acres. The selections made during the year were for 6,525,300·09 acres. Settlements upon lands granted or withdrawn for railroads have given rise to much litigation. The case of Guilford Miller, settler upon lands withdrawn for definition of limit, but not selected, was decided in his favor by the President April 28, 1887. The act of March 3, 1887, ordered immediate adjustment of all railroad grants by the Secretary of the Interior. Rights of way through public land in States and Territories have been granted (June 30, 1887) to 254 railroad companies. under the act of March 3, 1875. For wagon-roads, grants, from 1863 to 1869, were made in Wisconsin, Michigan, and Oregon, covering 1,301,040·47 acres.

Private Land-Claims.—These are numerous, and have their origin in titles to land granted by governments preceding the United States in sovereignty. They have been in process of adjustment and confirmation by Congress from the earliest days. The most important are included in the French and Mexican purchases. Many are fabulous in extent, and many probably fraudulent. The area of land embraced in private land-claims, patented and unpatented, is estimated at 80,000,000 acres.

Bounties have been granted by the Government for military and naval services in the Revolution, the War of 1812, and the Mexican War. For the first two classes military districts were set apart to fill warrants, and subsequently commutations into scrip were allowed. Under the acts of 1847, 1850, 1852, and 1855, 551,644 warrants had been issued to June 30, 1887, covering 61,096,790 acres. Of these, 20,467 are still outstanding, embracing 2,321,440 acres.

Scrip.—The total amount of scrip issued by the Government in satisfaction of private land and other claims, to June 30, 1887, is for 79,-365,716·66 acres. Of this, 76,540,675·42 acres have been located.

The gross receipts of the public domain to June 30, 1888, are $289,786,496.42. This amount includes sale of Indian lands, of which the fee-simple title lies in the Government. The total cost of the public domain to June 30, 1883, was $351,981,160.32, or nineteen cents an acre.

Taxation.—Public-land states, on admission to the Union, renounce the right to tax the public domain. In lieu thereof, by a series of acts from 1802, two, three, and five per cent. of the net proceeds of sales of public lands within their boundaries have been allowed, with the exception of California. Upward of $8,000,-000 have so accrued. Lands disposed of are taxed after entry and payment, and before issue of patent. Railroad lands are not taxed before segregation from the public domain.

Unlawful Inclosure.—To June 30, 1887, 465 unlawful inclosures had been brought to the attention of the General Land-Office, aggregating nearly 7,000,000 acres. Proceedings to compel removal have been instituted, and the practice has been largely broken up.

LEBŒUF, EDMOND, a French general, born in Paris, Nov. 5, 1809 ; died near Argentan, Orne, June 7, 1888. He was educated for the military profession at the École Polytechnique and at École d'Application at Metz, where he was graduated and commissioned lieutenant of artillery in 1833. He was ordered to Algeria, where he obtained a captaincy in 1837 for brilliant services at the Iron Gates, and distinguished himself at the siege of Constantine.

EDMOND LEBŒUF.

His skill and coolness in protecting the retreat of a column of troops that was in danger of being cut off by the Kabyles, gained him the higher grade of the Legion of Honor in 1840, and two years later he was promoted colonel. In the Crimean campaign he was chief of the artillery staff, with the rank of major-general. He took part in the battle of Alma, and at the siege of Sebastopol commanded the artillery on the left. He was advanced to the grade of lieutenant-general in 1857, and in 1859 commanded the entire artillery of the French army in Italy. At Solferino he brought up his guns just in time to stay the advance of Gen. Benedek. who with the right wing of the Austrian army threatened to crush the forces of Vittorio Emanuele and render precarious the French position. In January, 1869, he succeeded Gen. de Goyon in command of the Sixth Corps at Toulouse, and in August, on the death of Marshal Niel, he was called to the head of the Ministry of War. He remodeled the War Department and the administrative services of the army, changed the *personnel* of the bureaus, and won general approbation by his energy in improving the efficiency and readiness of the military establishment. When the Ollivier ministry was constituted under the new parliamentary system, he was invited to retain his portfolio. On March 24 he was made a marshal of France and nominated a senator. Relying on reports from all the bureaus, Marshal Lebœuf told the Emperor, when war with Prussia seemed imminent, that the army was perfectly prepared for war in every particular, down to the buttons on the gaiters. When war was declared, he took command of the Army of the Rhine as major-general, and accompanied the Emperor to the field. The reverses at Wissembourg and Woerth revealed a state of disorganization, a lack of necessary materials, gaps in the ranks, and imperfections in the transport and auxiliary services, that surprised and grieved no one so keenly as the Minister of War. The Ollivier Cabinet resigned, and Marshal Lebœuf was compelled to give up his command. He was assigned to a subordinate command under Marshal Bazaine, and was shut up with him in Metz, after fighting with desperate valor in the hope of death at Gravelotte and St. Privat. After the surrender of the fortress of Metz, he was sent to Germany as a prisoner, and when peace was concluded he retired into Switzerland. In December, 1871, he appeared before the committee of the National Assembly that was appointed to investigate the action of the Government of National Defense in signing the treaty of peace. He testified that there were 567,000 men under arms at the mobilization, and attributed the disastrous issue of the campaign to Bazaine's. unmilitary and disloyal conduct. Thenceforth he lived in retirement. Excepting Canrobert and MacMahon, he was the last surviving marshal of the French army.

LITERATURE, AMERICAN, IN 1888. A review of our literature during the year proves hardly more encouraging than did that of 1887. If possible, even fewer works of worth appeared, while book-production increased largely, reaching (from the figures of the "Publishers' Weekly") 4,631 volumes. Of these, at least, it may be said that 3,520 were produced within our own country, and but 590 from foreign sources, showing a tendency toward greater honesty on the part of native publishers and a development of fertility in native genius, but the majority were evanescent. It is surprising, in view of the efforts of specialists in some directions, to note the absolute paucity of American works in the higher regions of science and mental philosophy.

Fiction.—Of this class, 1,284 books, including juvenile books, produced in 1888, show a marked decrease from the 1,509 of 1887, which may perhaps be accounted for by the reduced issues of cheap libraries. The most widely circulated novels were "John Ward, Preacher," by Mrs. Margaret Deland, author of a volume of poems, a book somewhat similar in tone to "Robert Elsmere," and "The Quick or the Dead," by Miss Amélie Rives (now Mrs. Chanler). The latter has been mercilessly criticised and travestied. Two other works by the same writer, "Virginia of Virginia " and "A Brother to Dragons and other Old-Time Tales," while less extravagant, exhibit the same peculiarities. "Annie Kilburn" was the single production in fiction of William Dean Howells, and, though entertaining, fell below his highest efforts. Henry James, published "The Reverberator" and a volume containing three short stories, entitled "The Aspern Papers," "Louisa Palland," and "The Modern Warning." Mrs. Poultney Bigelow published "Beautiful Mrs. Thorndyke." F. Marion Crawford wrote "With the Immortals," and Frank R. Stockton "The Dusantes," a sequel to "The Casting Away of Mrs. Aleshine and Mrs. Lecks," and "Amos Kilbright, his Adscititious Experiences, with other Stories." Edgar Saltus appeared with "Eden" and "The Truth About Tristrem Varick," and Edgar Fawcett with "Olivia Delaplaine," "Divided Lives," and "A Man's Will," the last a temperance story. "The Despot of Broomsedge Cove," by Charles Egbert Craddock (Miss Murfree), "Bonaventure, a Prose Pastoral of Acadian Louisiana," by George W. Cable, and "The Graysons, a Story of Illinois," by Edward Eggleston, were portrayals of locality and of character as influenced by it. "Queen Money," by the author of "Margaret Kent" (Mrs. Ellen W. O. Kirk), is a vigorous protest against one of the most deplorable tendencies of the age, and indicated growth of experience and power. "Better-Time Stories," collected from magazine sources, being the product of earlier days, "Mr. Tangier's Vacations," and "My Friend the Boss, a Story of To-day," by Edward Everett Hale, belong of right to the year, and it is impossible to omit mention of a new and illustrated edition of "The Man Without a Country," first published twenty-five years ago. Another old favorite of the same age, which was revived, was "Two Men," by Elizabeth Stoddard. Bret Harte produced two volumes, "The Argonauts of North Liberty," and "A Phyllis of the Sierras" and "A Drift from Red-Wood Camp." The latter two are short stories, of no particular merit. "The World's Verdict," by Mark Hopkins, Jr., was the promising first attempt of a new writer of fiction. Arlo Bates wrote a continuation of his "Pagans," entitled "The Philistines," who proved hardly more attractive than their predecessors. E. W. Howe's "A Man Story" was inferior to none of his former work in power, and C. M. Newell made an addition of "The Isle of Palms" to the "Fleetwing Series." "Our Phil and other Stories," by Katharine Floyd Dana, consisted of three clever sketches of negro life; and "Two Little Confederates," by Thomas Nelson Page, author of "Marse Chan and other Stories," is a capital book for boys. Mrs. Frances Hodgson-Burnett's "Sara Crewe" is a companion-piece to "Little Lord

Fauntleroy," and her "Editha's Burglar" was reprinted in book-form from "St. Nicholas." Sidney Luska (Henry Harland) wrote "My Uncle Florimond," and Joseph Kirkland "The McVeys, an Episode." Edward Bellamy, in "Looking Backward," aimed at rather more than success as a novelist, and produced one of the most suggestive books of the year. "A Nymph of the West," by Howard Seely, is a bright story with an unconventional heroine. Archibald C. Gunter followed "Mr. Barnes of New York" with "Mr. Potter of Texas," and Gay Parker has attempted an imitation, if not of style, of title, in "Mr. Perkins of New Jersey," having written also "Playing with Fire." Julian Hawthorne, on his own account, was responsible for "The Professor's Sister" and "The Disappearance of David Poindexter, with other Stories," and, in collaboration with Inspector Byrnes, for "Section 558, or the Fatal Letter," and "Another's Crime." "The Peckster Professorship," by J. P. Quincy; "The Veiled Beyond," by Sigmund B. Alexander; "Ilian, or the Curse of the Old South Church of Boston," by Chaplain James J. Kane, U.S.N.; and "An Unlaid Ghost," anonymous, were psychological in tendency. "The Doctor's Mistake," by C. H. Montague and C. M. Hammond, being "An Experiment With Life," dealt also with abstruse questions. J. S. of Dale (Frederick J. Stimson) published "First Harvests" and "The Residuary Legatee," and Gen. Lloyd S. Brice published "Paradise." "Aristocracy" was an anonymous answer to the many recent books that have reflected upon democracy, and "De Molai," an historical novel by Edmund Flagg, contained much information with regard to the Military Order of Templar Knights, from the last Grand Master of whom the book is named. "The Lone Grave of the Shenandoah, and other Stories," by Donn Piatt, brought that journalist forward in a new light as a *raconteur*. Sarah Orne Jewett wrote "The King of Folly Island"; William L. Alden, "A New Robinson Crusoe"; William H. Bishop, "The Brown Stone Boy and other Queer People"; Robert Timsol, "A Pessimist in Theory and Practice"; and T. S. Denison, "The Man behind." Susan Coolidge (Miss Sarah C. Woolsey) completed the "Katy Stories" with "Clover"; Albion W. Tourgee published "Black Ice" and "Letters to a King"; and Howard Pyle a boys' story of mediæval Germany, entitled "Otto of the Silver Hand." "The Spell of Ashtaroth," also an historical novel, by Duffield Osborne; "Miss Hildreth," by A. De Grasse Stevens; and "The Secret of Fontaine La Croix," by Margaret Field, received commendable notices, as did "Under the Maples," by Walter N. Hinman; "In War Times at La Rose Blanche," by M. E M. Davis; and "The Youngest Miss Lorton and other Stories," by Nora Perry. "Miss Lou," the last novel of E. P. Roe, was left incomplete as to the final chapter at his death, but a note found among his papers supplied the defi-

ciency. His "Found yet Lost" was also published during the year. From Nora Helen Warddell we have "The Romance of a Quiet Watering-Place," and from One in the Swim "Society Rapids, High Life in Washington, Saratoga, and Bar Harbor." Edmund Pendleton was the author of "A Virginia Inheritance"; Gen. Hugh Ewing of "A Castle in the Air"; and Capt. Charles King of "A War-Time Wooing," "The Deserter," and "From the Ranks"—the last two included in a single volume. Lucretia P. Hale, in collaboration with Edwin B. Lasseter, wrote "An Unclosed Skeleton," and "The Story of a Débutante in New York Society" was told by Rachel Buchanan in a series of letters. F. Thickstun brought out "A Mexican Girl"; and Mrs. Amelia E. Barr "Remember the Alamo," "Master of his Fate," and "Christopher and other Stories." "Wyoming" was the first volume of a series of tales of that valley, by E. S. Ellis, who also wrote "The Star of India," and "The Doom of Mamelons." "A Legend of the Saguenay," was told by W. H. H. Murray. "Uncle Tom's Tenement," by Alice W. Rollins, a book more creditable in aim than in execution, dealt with the question of possible morality in that abode. "His Broken Sword," by Winnie L. Taylor, was written in the interests of penal reform. "The Gallery of a Random Collector" was the somewhat misleading title given by Clinton Ross to several short stories, and the history of "Yone Santo, a Child of Japan," was feelingly narrated by Edward H. House. "A Strange Narrative found in a Copper Cylinder" was an exciting tale of supernatural adventure, from the pen of the late Prof. James De Mille, written, though unpublished, twenty years before the advent of "She." "Napoleon Smith," a pure extravaganza, was said to have been written by a well-known New-Yorker. "Tilting at Windmills" was "A Story of the Blue-Grass Country," told by Emma M. Connelly; and among Southern stories may be mentioned also "Monsieur Motté," by Grace King; "A Blockaded Family," by Parthenia A. Hague; "Pleasant Waters," by Graham Claytor; and "Kenneth Cameron," by L. Q. C. Brown. "Isidra," by Willis Steell; "Mrs. Lord's Moonstone and other Stories," by Stokes C. Wayne; "The Silent Witness," by Mrs. J. H. Walworth; and "Montezuma's Gold," by F. A. Ober, held their own, as did "Roger Berkley's Probation," by Helen Campbell, and "A Blind Lead," by Josephine W. Bates. "The Case of Mohammed Benani" was an exciting story of wrongs in Morocco, published anonymously. "Glorinda," by Anna Bowman Dodd; "Young Maids and Old," by Clara Louise Burnham; "A Little Maid of Acadie," by Marion C. L. Reeves; and "Odds against her," by Margaret R. McFarlane—were all exceptionally good of their kind; and "Agatha Page," by Isaac Henderson, found many readers. Kirk Munroe wrote "Derrick Sterling" and "Chrystal, Jack & Co."; the Rev. E. A. Rand, "Making the best of it" and "When the War broke out"; J. S. Shriver, "Almost"; and G. T. Kercheval, "Lorin Mooruck and other Indian Stories." "Renée" was a romance by Marian C. Wilson; "Bryan Maurice," a semireligious novel, by the Rev. Walter Mitchell; and "Esther, the Gentile," a story of Mormon life, by Mrs. Mary W. Hudson. Miss M. G. McClelland sent forth "Madame Silva," mystical and occult; and "Eros," by Laura Daintrey, had a temporary vogue. Ernest de L. Pierson wrote "A Slave of Circumstances," a story of New York life, full of humorous situations; and Harry Castlemon (C. A. Fostick) "Snagged and Sunk, or the Adventures of a Canvas Canoe." From May Agnes Fleming we have two novels, "The Midnight Queen" and "The Virginia Heiress"; from Mary T. Palmer, "The Doctor of Deane"; and from W. F. Kip, "Would you have left her?" The latest novel of Marion Harland (Mrs. Terhune) was entitled "A Gallant Fight." Hester Stuart, in "A Modern Jacob," made a study of heredity. Mrs. Isabella M. Alden (Pansy) wrote "Judge Burnham's Daughters," and, with Mrs. C. M. Livingstone, "Profiles, and a Dozen of them," for children. Interesting stories were "Miss Merley," in the American Tauchnitz edition, by J. Elliot Curran; "Maurice Rossman's Leading," by Mary R. Baldwin; "Kesa and Saijiro, or Lights and Shades of Life in Japan," by Mrs. J. D. Carrothers; and "Judge Havisham's Will," by Miss I. T. Hopkins. "The Septameron" was a sportive imitation of the "Decameron" of Boccaccio, by seven authors leaving town to avoid the heat, who combined to produce a volume of light summer literature. Neither "The Gambler," by Franc B. Wilkie, nor "Len Gansett," by Opie P. Read, can be regarded as elevated in tone; while, on the other hand, "Mr. Absalom Billingslea" and "Other Georgia Folks" are specimens of the genial humor and quick characterization of Richard M. Johnston. Mary E. Bamford wrote "Marie's Story" and "Father Lambert's Family"; Maria McIntosh Cox, "Raymond Kershaw"; E. R. Roe (who must not be confounded with E. P. Roe), "May and June"; and E. Willett, "The Search for the Star"; while a rapid summary includes "Miss Middleton's Lover," by Laura J. Libbey; "The Major's Love," by Ellen Price Brown; "The Jolly Ten and their Year of Stories," by Agnes C. Sage; "In Safe Hands," by Mary Hubbard Howell; and "What Dreams may come" and "The Princess Daphne," by Mrs. G. F. Atherton. Among books more or less sensational are "The Great Amherst Mystery," by Walter Hubbell, who also wrote "The Curse of Marriage"; "Brinka, an American Countess," by Mary C. Spenser; "Cell 13," by Edwin H. Trafton, purporting to be "A Nihilist Episode in the Secret History of New York and St. Petersburg"; "Orion, the Gold-Beater," and "Karmel, the Scout," both by Syl-

vanus Cobb, Jr. (W. D. Dunlop). "Mr. Darwing's Daughter," by Helen B. Williams, and "How Tom and Dorothy made and kept a Christian Home," by Margaret Sidney (Mrs. H. M. Lothrop), belong to the practical religious department of fiction, as "A Modern Adam and Eve in a Garden," by Amanda M. Douglas, "A Young Prince of Commerce," by S. R. Hopkins, and "The Boy Broker," by Frank A. Munsey, to the purely utilitarian.

In the line of children's stories we have, in addition to those already referred to: "Uncle Rutherford's Nieces," by Joanna M. Matthews, author of the "Bessie Books"; "Scotch Caps," by J. A. K.; "Sparrow, the Tramp," by Lily F. Wesselhoeft; "Margareta Regis and other Girls," by Annie H. Ryder; "Kelp, a Story of the Isles of Shoals," in the "Pine Cone Series," by W. B. Allen; and "Bob Burton," by Horatio Alger. "Taken by the Enemy," opened a new "Blue-and-Gray Series," by Oliver Optic (William T. Adams). J. T. Trowbridge wrote "Biding his Time" and "A Start in Life"; Mrs. Lucy G. Morse, "The Chezzles"; Mrs. L. C. Lillie, "My Mother's Enemy" and "The Household of Glen Holly." "Tales of King Arthur and his Knights of the Round Table," by Margaret Vere Farrington, and "St. George and the Dragon" and "Kensington Junior," by Margaret Sidney, found deserved favor with young folks.

Among translations received with favor may be mentioned "The Court of Charles IV" and "Leon Roch," from the Spanish of Perez-Galdós, as also the "Maximina," of Don Armando Palacio Valdes. The rage for Russian realism apparently expired in 1887. But few of the works of Tolstoi were translated, and those were of minor importance. Among them were "Family Happiness." From the German we have "Picked up in the Streets," by H. Schobert, and "The Owl's Nest," by E. Marlitt, both adapted by Mrs. Wister, and "For the Right," by K. E. Franzos; while French literature was represented by "The Dream," "The Soil," and "The Jolly Parisiennes," of Zola; "The Magic Skin," "Modeste Mignon," and "Cousin Bette," of Balzac; and several charming stories. Among these were "The History of Nicholas Muss," by C. du Bois-Melly; "The Story of Colette" and "An Iceland Fisherman," by Pierre Loti. "The Steel Hammer" of Louis Ulbach, translated by E. W. Latimer, formed the first volume of "Appleton's Town and Country Library," and was followed by its sequel, "For Fifteen Years." "The Story of Jewäd," by Ali Aziz Effendi, The Cretan, was a novel contribution from the Turkish. Last, but not least, came "Lalja, a Tale of Finmark," from the Norwegian of J. A. Friis.

History.—This department is, perhaps, the richest, although fewer works than usual were produced. "The Critical Period of American History" was supposed by John Fiske to lie between the years 1783 and 1789, to which he devoted much research. Other important works bearing on the subject are: "Seven Conventions," by A. W. Clason; "Pamphlets on the Constitution of the United States, published during its Discussion by the People, 1787–1788," edited with notes and a bibliography by Paul Leicester Ford; "Pennsylvania and the Federal Constitution, 1787–1788," edited by John B. McMaster and Fred D. Stone; and a new edition of "The Federalist, a Commentary on the Constitution of the United States, being a Collection of Essays written in Support of the Constitution agreed upon Sept. 17, 1787," edited by Henry Cabot Lodge. "A Guide to the Study of the History and Constitution of the United States," by W. W. Rupert, should be mentioned in this connection, as also, "Civil Government," being studies of the Federal Constitution, arranged for use in public schools, by R. E. Clement. Edward Eggleston wrote "The Household History of the United States and its People, for Young Americans," with an edition for schools, both of which are beautifully illustrated in a novel style; G. B. Hall, "Historical Sketches and Events in the Colonization of America"; and Moncure D. Conway supplied "Omitted Chapters of History disclosed in the Life and Papers of Edmund Randolph, Governor of Virginia." Vol. II of "Franklin in France," edited by Edward Everett Hale, was issued. Anna M. Juliand presented "Brief Views of United States History, for the Use of High-Schools and Academies," and Eben N. Horsford printed an "Address on the Discovery of America by Northmen," delivered in Faneuil Hall, Boston, Oct. 29, 1887, at the unvailing of the statue of Lief Ericksen. "The United States of Yesterday and To-morrow," by William Barrows, and "Natural Resources of the United States," by J. H. Patton, treat of our country as a whole, while Burke A. Hinsdale, in "The Old Northwest," made a valuable contribution to sectional literature. Edmund Kirke (James R. Gilmore) supplemented "The Rear-Guard of the Revolution" and "John Sevier" with "The Advance-Guard of Western Civilization." In "The Commonwealth Series" we have: "Ohio, First Fruits of the Ordinance of 1787," by Rufus King; "Missouri, a Bone of Contention," by Lucien Carr"; and "Indiana, a Redemption from Slavery," by J. P. Dunn. D. J. Ryan furnished also a "History of Ohio, with Biographical Sketches of her Governors and the Ordinance of 1787." From James Phelan we have a "History of Tennessee, the Making of a State"; and "The Loyal Mountaineers of East Tennessee" found a eulogist in Thomas W. Humes. "The Story of Ohio" was again told by Alexander Black in "The Story-of-the-States Series"; G. J. Varney wrote "A Brief History of Maine," and E. B. Sanford a "History of Connecticut." "The Pilgrim Republic" of John A. Goodwin furnished "An Historical Review of the Colony of New Plymouth" and "Ten Years

of Massachusetts, 1878–1888" were treated by Raymond L. Bridgman, who assigns reason for laws passed during that period, with their place in State records. "Pilgrims and Puritans" was "The Story of the Planting of Plymouth and Boston," told by N. Moore, for children. "Colonial Times on Buzzard's Bay" was from the pen of W. R. Bliss, and George E. Ellis wrote on "The Puritan Age and Rule." "Blue Jackets of '76," by Willis J. Abbot, and "The Boston Tea-Party," by H. C. Watson, dwell particularly on Revolutionary days, and Lieut. W. Digby's journal of 1776–'77 furnished the material for "The British Invasion from the North." Thomas W. Higginson, in "Travelers and Outlaws," narrated "Episodes in American History." "The Republic" of John R. Irelan, M. D., reached completion in its eighteenth volume, and Hubert H. Bancroft added four volumes to his "History of the Pacific States of North America," viz., Vol. VI of "History of Mexico," Vol. VI of "California, 1848–1859," "California Pastoral" and "California Inter-Pocula." "The Narrative and Critical History of America," edited by Justin Winsor, was continued in Vols. V and VI. Among books relating to the civil war, we have "A Short History of the War of Secession," by Rossiter Johnson, which presents all information necessary to the general reader in a concise yet comprehensive manner; "France and the Confederate Navy, an International Episode," by John Bigelow; and, from the French, Vol. IV of "The History of the Civil War in America," by the Comte de Paris, and "Four Years with the Army of the Potomac," by Gen. Regis de Trobriand. "Marching to Victory," by C. C. Coffin, covers the second period of the civil war. Joseph T. Wilson (colored), in "The Black Phalanx," gives a history of negro soldiers of the United States in the wars of 1775 and 1812, as well as in that of 1861–'65, which is as creditable to the author as its incidents are to the race. Walter Allen's "Governor Chamberlain's Administration in South Carolina" presents an interesting chapter of reconstruction in the Southern States. Alfred E. Lee again fought "The Battle of Gettysburg"; and "The Volunteer Soldier in America," by the late Gen. John A. Logan, was published. "The Sailor Boys of 1861," by James R. Soley, a "History of the Corn Exchange Regiment, 118th Penn. Vols.," and S. Millet Thompson's "Thirteenth Regiment of New Hampshire Volunteer Infantry," with "Charleston in the Rebellion," by A. C. Voris, were all of interest, as were also "Incidents of the Civil War," by Mrs. Mary B. Herrick, "My Story of the War," by Mrs. Mary A. Livermore, and "The Other Side of War," by Katherine P. Wormley, which latter gives an account of the origin and work of the United States Sanitary Commission. "A Century of Town Life, A History of Charlestown, Mass., 1775–1887," by J. F. Hunnewell,

"Salem Sketches," by H. R. Blaney, and "A History of Essex County, Mass.," by D. F. Hurd, are purely local. "The Story of the City of New York," by Charles B. Todd, opened a new series of "Great Cities of the Republic"; "A History of the New York Ministerium" was written by Rev. John Nicum; and "Representative Methodists," by R. R. Doherty. Prohibition literature added to its annals "A History of the Temperance Reform in Massachusetts," by G. Faber Clark, and "Mother Stewart's Memories of the Crusade." "The Early Days of Mormonism" were traced by J. H. Kennedy. Elbridge S. Brooks wrote "The Story of the American Sailor." Histories of foreign lands, written by Americans, include the "History of Prussia under Frederick the Great," by Prof. Herbert Tuttle, "The Causes of the French Revolution," by R. Heath Dabney, "An Introduction to the Study of the Middle Ages," by Ephraim Emerton; "A Sketch of the Germanic Constitution, from Early Times to the Dissolution of the Empire," by Samuel E. Turner; and "Charles the Great," by J. I. Mombert.

Biography.—In general biography, no work extant can compare favorably with the "Cyclopædia of American Biography" (six volumes, 8 vo), just completed. One of the most valuable contributions to individual American biography is "The Diary and Letters of Gouverneur Morris," edited by his granddaughter, Anne Carey Morris. "Men and Measures of Half a Century" were studied by Hugh McCulloch from a high vantage-ground of observation, though with some astonishing blunders of fact, and "The Life and Times of Young Sir Henry Vane," by Prof. James K. Hosmer, was a work of rare interest. Lydia Hoyt Farmer wrote a "Life of Lafayette." The contributions of W. O. Stoddard to the "Lives of the Presidents" include "William Henry Harrison," "John Tyler," "James K. Polk," "Abraham Lincoln," and "Grover Cleveland." From Sarah K. Bolton we have two volumes of "Famous American Statesmen" and "Successful Women." John Frost published "The Presidents of the United States, from Washington to Cleveland"; Noah Brooks, "Abraham Lincoln, a Biography for Young People"; and Edward M. Shepard, "Martin Van Buren," in "The Statesmen Series," a carefully written and scholarly production. To strictly war biography belong the "Personal Memoirs of General Philip H. Sheridan"; "A Life of Matthew Fontaine Maury, U. S. N. and C. S. N.," by Diana Fontaine Maury Corbin; "John Brown," by H. Von Holst; and "The Antobiography of Private Dalzell." James P. Boyd wrote "Roscoe Conkling, the Distinguished American Statesman and Brilliant Advocate." "The Life of Thomas Hopkins Gallaudet," founder of deaf-mute instruction in America, as detailed by his son, E. M. Gallaudet, is of deep interest; and "A Biography of Henry Ward Beecher" was written by H. W. Beech-

er, Rev. S. Scoville, and Mrs. Beecher. A valuable and interesting book is "The Life and Letters of George Perkins Marsh," the first volume of which by Caroline C. Marsh appeared. "Harvard Reminiscences," by Andrew P. Peabody, recalled fifty-six years of college life. "The Life, Journals, and Correspondence of the Rev. Manasseh Cutler," by his grandchildren, is an interesting record of a varied career in the early days of the nation; and "The Life of Amos Lawrence," by his son, is also closely connected with historical events. "John B. Finch, his Life and Work," by Frances E. Finch and Frank J. Sibley, and "The Autobiography and Memorials of Samuel Irenæus Prime," edited by his son, possess more than ordinary interest; and this same may also be said of "Incidents in a Busy Life," by the Rev. Asa Bullard, an autobiography. In the literary world we have a "Life of James Russell Lowell," by E. E. Brown, and "Delia Bacon," a biographical sketch, by Theodore Bacon, of the remarkable woman who devoted herself to a theory. Louisa May Alcott was the subject of two brief biographies, one a "Souvenir," by Miss Lurabel liarlow, and another which Edna H. Cheney does not proffer as a substitute for the full story that it is hoped will one day be given to the world. "Amos Bronson Alcott, his Character," formed the groundwork of a sermon by Cyrus A. Bartol. "The Memorial of Sarah Pugh" and "The Life of Dr. Anandabai Joshee," by Caroline Healey Dall, were tributes to the memory of two remarkable women. R. H. Clarke wrote "Lives of Deceased Bishops of the Catholic Church in the United States." "The Nun of Kenmare," an autobiography of Sister Mary Frances Clare Cusack, details at length her reasons for resigning the office conferred upon her by the Holy Father. "From Flag to Flag," by Eliza McHatton Ripley, told "A Woman's Adventures and Experiences in the South during the War, in Mexico, and in Cuba"; and "A Business Woman's Journal" was a sequel to "Twelve Years of My Life," by Mrs. B. Beaumont. The Mapleson Memoirs, 1848–1888," possess amusing interest. "Henry Hobart Richardson and his Works," by Mrs. Schuyler Van Rensselaer, is the biography of the man characterized by Matthew Arnold as "the one architect of genius they had" in America. The electoral year called forth, among other publications, a "Life of Gen. Benjamin Harrison," by the author of "Ben Hur"; "Lives of Benjamin Harrison and Levi P. Morton," by Rev. Gilbert L. Harney; and "The President and his Cabinet," by C. B. Norton, "Indicating the Progress of the Government of the United States under the Administration of Grover Cleveland." "The Life of Clinton Bowen Fisk," the Prohibition candidate, was written by A. A. Hopkins. "A Soldier of Fortune," by J. W. McDonald, narrates the life and adventures of Gen. Henry R. Maciver. Herman Lieb wrote

"Emperor William I." Translations from the "Great French Writers Series" include "George Sand," by E. Caro; "Madame de Sévigné," by Gaston Boissier; "Montesquieu," by Albert Sorel; "Turgot," by Leon Say; and "Victor Cousin," by Jules Simon.

Poetry.—A *résumé* of the poetry of 1888 is somewhat discouraging. Neither "Heartsease and Rue," a collection of poems by James Russell Lowell, nor "Before the Curfew," by Oliver Wendell Holmes, nor "November Boughs," by Walt Whitman, offers much that is new or particularly striking; while the sadness aroused by the significant titles of the two last-named volumes of aged authors finds little alleviation. There seem to be no younger ones aspiring to the foremost rank of poets, to whom crudity might be forgiven in consideration of genius, and the poverty of effort is but too obvious. Miss Amélie Rives, it is true, astonished the literary world with "Herod and Mariamne, a Tragedy," which called forth much comment and criticism not altogether favorable. The translation of the "Kalevala," the epic poem of Finland, by J. Martin Crawford, deserves high commendation, and is, moreover, the first full rendering into English that the poem has received. Another translation of special interest is that of the Norwegian dramatic trilogy, "Sigurd Slembe," by Björnstjerne Björnson, made by William Morton Payne. J. Leslie Garner rendered "The Strophes of Omar Khayyam," from the Persian; and F. H. Hedge and Mrs. A. L. Wister published a collection of "Metrical Translations and Poems," from the German. G. E. Vincent's "Eight Songs from Horace" is a handsome attempt at reproduction of the poet in the style of his day.

To return to American poetry, we have "Forest Echoes," by G. E. Cole; and "The Witch in the Glass," which Mrs. Piatt has added to her former volumes of tender verse. "Changing Moods in Verse and Rhyme" is by W. Hunter Birckhead, and "Along the Shore" is Rose Hawthorne Lathrop's. A collection of the "Poems of Frank Forrester" (Henry W. Herbert), a novelist and writer of sporting sketches thirty years ago, was made for the first time and handsomely illustrated. Clinton Scollard wrote "Old and New World Lyrics," and Madison J. Cawein, "The Triumph of Music and other Lyrics." The "Poems" of Irwin Russell, mostly in negro dialect, were collected into a memorial volume from five years of "Century" Brie-a-Brac, and A. G. Gordon and Thomas Nelson Page were joint authors of "Befo' de War." "Some Dainty Poems," by Waldo Messaros; "Beyond the Shadow," by Stuart Sterne; "Joy, and other Poems," by Danske Dandridge; "Idylls of Israel," by D. J. Donahue; and "A Little Brother of the Rich," by E. S. Martin, offer no especial features for criticism. The same is true of "Madeleine," by D. C. Brewer; "Maurine," by Mrs. E. Wheeler Wilcox; "Tan-

cred's Daughter," by O. G. Blanden; "The Siege of Newport," by T. C. Amory; "Immortelles," by Cora M. A. Davis; and "Wanderers," by W. Winters. E. L. M. Bristol wrote "A Story of the Sands," and John Vance Cheney, "Wood-Blooms." "Judith," an English epic fragment, was edited with a translation and glossary by Prof. A. S. Cook, and "Favorite Folk-Ballads" was the product of several authors. "In the Name of the King" is the title of semi-religious poems by G. Klingle, and "The Inn of Rest," of later poems by May Riley Smith. Tracy Robinson published "The Song of the Palm and other Poems, mostly Tropical," and "The Poems of Emma Lazarus" were issued in two volumes. William D. Howells's lyrical farce, "A Sea Change, or Love's Stowaway," was welcomed by his admirers, and Harry L. Koopman wrote "Woman's Will" and "Orestes." The anthologies include "After Noontide," by Margaret E. White; "Ballads and Rondeaus," by Gleeson White; "Sundry Rhymes from the Days of our Grandmothers," by George W. Edwards; and "The Book of Latter-Day Ballads, 1858–1888," by Henry F-Randolph. From Mr. Randolph we have also "Fifty Years of English Song, Selections from the Poets of the Reign of Victoria," in four volumes.

Criticism and General Literature.—Of criticism proper there was but little, "Studies in Criticism," by Florence Trail, and "A Critical Exposition of the New Essays of Leibnitz," by J. Dewey, being perhaps the only professedly critical books. The critical element enters largely into others included under general literature, but discrimination is difficult. Prof. Henry W. Parker wrote "The Spirit of Beauty," and E. D. Walker "Reincarnation, a Study of Forgotten Truth," which presents evidence in verse and prose corroborative of the doctrine of pre-existence of souls. "Social Life and Literature Fifty Years Ago" is a spicy anonymous reply to the critical tone indulged in by prominent authors of the modern school toward that period, satirical and brief. "Books and Men" was a series of essays by Agnes Repplier, and "Poetry, Comedy, and Duty" were handled separately and relatively by C. C. Everett. "Books that have helped me," as discoursed upon by several authors in "The Forum," were collected into a volume. "Martin Luther and other Essays" is by F. H. Hedge, and "Practical Occultism" by J. J. Morse. "Master Virgil, the Author of the Æneid, as he seemed in the Middle Ages," is a novel study by J. S. Tunison, and "Irish Wonders," by D. R. McAnally, a popular and entertaining work on the superstitions of that race. Palmer Cox also treated of "Queer People, such as Goblins, Giants, Merrymen, etc." "Some Thoughts on Life's Battle," by Mark Levy, and "Your Forces, and how to use them," by Prentice Mulford, may be classed together, and supplemented by "Great Thoughts for Little Thinkers," by Lucia T. Ames. "The Great

Cryptogram" of Ignatius Donnelly by no means diminished his reputation as an enthusiast of sensational novelty, if it did not materially establish his theory as to the authorship of the plays of Shakespeare. Other Shakespearean studies include "The Human Mystery in Hamlet," by Martin W. Cooke; "William Shakespeare portrayed by himself," by Robert Watters; "Shakespeare and the Bible," by G. Q. Colton; and "Shakespeare *versus* Ingersoll," by J. G. Hall. G. Theodore Dippold devoted himself to a solution of Richard Wagner's poem, "The Ring of the Nibelung," and C. Morris to "The Aryan Race, its Origin and Achievements." Brander Matthews wrote "Pen and Ink," William S. Walsh "Paradoxes of a Philistine," and Harold Van Sant "Half-Holidays," a bizarre collection of "Elysian Dreams and Sober Realities." Eugene M. Camp, in "Journalists born or made," brought forward the suggestion of adding journalism to the curriculum of our colleges; and "Pen and Powder," by Franc B. Wilkie, detailed the difficulties of field correspondence during the civil war. "Andersonville Violets," by Herbert W. Collingwood, deals impartially with one of the saddest pages of war history. H. M. Sylvester wrote "Homestead Highways," Margaret Sidney "Old Concord," and "Negro Myths from the Georgia Coast" were told in the vernacular by C. C. Jones. "Outlooks on Society, Literature, and Politics" is the title of a volume of previously uncollected essays by Edwin P. Whipple. "Fifteenth-Century Bibles" was the subject of a book by Wendell Prime. B. C. Burt wrote "A Brief History of Greek Philosophy," and "The Poetry of the Future" was handled by James W. Davidson. Austin Bierbower wrote "The Virtues, and their Reasons," and M. J. Barnett "Justice, a Healing Power." "Of Thoughts about Women, and other things," was the title of essays by S. R. Reed. "The Mind of the Child" was translated from the German of Prof. W. Preyer by H. B. Brown; and J. H. W. Stuckenberg wrote an "Introduction to the Study of Philosophy. The second volume of "American Literature, 1607–1885," by Charles F. Richardson, is devoted to "American Poetry and Fiction." Prof. Herbert B. Adams wrote on "The Study of American History in American Colleges and Universities." Abbie H. Fairfield culled "Flowers and Fruit from the Writings of Harriet Beecher Stowe." Rose Porter wrote "Rest Awhile," and the Rev. F. S. Child, "Be strong to hope." "Chapters from Jane Austen" by Oscar Fay Adams, and "Readings from the Waverley Novels," by Alfred F. Blaisdell, belong to the "Cambridge Series of English Classics," and "First Steps with American and British Authors" was also from the pen of the latter writer. Edwin Ginn made "Selections from Ruskin on Reading and other Subjects," and "Bits of Burnished Gold" was a compilation by Rose Porter in four volumes. "Letters,

Poems, and Selected Prose Writings of David Gray" were edited by J. N. Larned, and "British Letters illustrative of Character and Social Life" by E. T. Mason. "Partial Portraits," by Henry James, is one of the most delightful and characteristic of that author's productions. "The Young Idea, or Common-School Culture" is from the pen of Caroline B. Le Row. "Word English" was a proposition to secure "The Universal Language, based upon English, as Volapük on German," made by Alexander M. Bell, and Elias Molee made "A Plea for an American Language or Germanic English." "A Short Grammar of Volapük" was compiled by J. Hanno Deiler. "Success in Society," by Lydia E. White, "Manners," by A Woman of Society, and "Good Form in England," by An American Resident in the United Kingdom, were the principal books on etiquette.

Political, Social, and Moral Science.—During the exitement of a presidential year, problems of government and social life were discussed naturally in a concrete way, and with more or less partisan feeling, but attempts were also made at higher conceptions. James Russell Lowell published "Political Essays"; Theodore Roosevelt, "Essays on Practical Politics"; Edward Payson, "The Law of Equivalents, in its Relation to Political and Social Ethics"; and W. P. Atkinson, "The Study of Politics, an Introductory Lecture. "Problems of American Civilization" were discussed by Presidents McCosh and Gates, Bishop Coxe, and others. "Selections illustrating Economic History since the Seven-Years' War" is by Benjamin Reed; and "Industrial Liberty," by John M. Bonham, investigated the tendencies of modern civilization in a broad and hopeful spirit. Edwin Cannan wrote "An Elementary Political Economy," and Richard T. Ely and John H. Finley "Taxation in American States and Cities," and Horace White translated from the Italian of Dr. Luigi Cossa "Taxation, its Principles and Methods." "How they lived in Hampton" was "A Study of Practical Christianity applied in the Manufacture of Woolens" by Edward Everett Hale. "Large Fortunes, or Christianity and Labor Problems," were handled by C. Richardson, and John Gibbons wrote "Tenure and Toil." "Property in Land," by Henry Winn, was an argument against the theories of Herbert Spencer and Henry George. "The Christian Unity of Capital and Labor," by H. W. Cadmon, gained the $1,000 prize of the John C. Green income fund. Rabbi H. Berkowitz published "Judaism on the Social Question," and Frank G. Ruffin "The Negro as a Political and Social Factor." Alfred Shaw made a collection of papers by American economists on "The National Revenues," J. B. Clark wrote on "Capital and its Earnings," Prof. P. P. Hotchkiss on "Banks and Banking, 1171–1888," and a series of articles by different authors in the "Johns Hopkins University Series" were combined into "A History of Co-operation in the United States." "Ultimate Finance" purported to be "A True Theory of Co-operation," by W. Nelson Black, and "The Stability of Prices" was discussed by Simon N. Patten. "True or False Finance the Issue of 1888" was anonymous, and from J. B. Clark and F. H. Giddings we have "The Modern Distributive Process." Of books relating to the question of the tariff, there was apparently no end. R. W. Thompson was author of "A History of Protective Tariff Laws," and Prof. Taussig, of Harvard University, of "The Tariff History of the United States." "Protection Echoes from the Capitol" were edited by Thomas H. McKee, Assistant Librarian of the United States Senate, assisted by W. W. Curry; and "Principles of the Economic Philosophy of Society, Government, and Industry" were laid down by Van Buren Denslow, with a leaning toward protective doctrines in his treatment of the last subject. Edward Everett Hale published "Tom Torey's Tariff Talks," Richard T. Ely "Problems of the Day," and Horace Castle "The Doctrine of Protection to Domestic Industries examined." "Is Protection a Benefit?" was asked by E. Taylor; "The Relation of the Tariff to Wages" was the work of David A. Wells, and "What shall we do with it?" (meaning the surplus), consisted of protective articles from various sources. "Protection *versus* Free Trade" was by Henry M. Hoyt, "Twenty-Two Years of Protection" by Henry V. Poor, "The Tariff and its Evils" by J. H. Allen, and "Tariff Chats" by H. J. Philpot. "Friendly Letters to American Farmers and others" were edited by J. S. Moore, and R. R. Bowker annotated "The President's Message, 1887." "The Civil-Service Law" was treated by W. Harrison Clarke. A "Citizen's Atlas of American Politics, 1789-1888," was prepared by F. W. Hewes, and a "Handbook of Politics for 1888" by Edward McPherson. E. Brown and A. Strauss furnished a "Dictionary of American Politics," and campaign text-books of both the Democratic and Republican parties of course appeared. John D. Long edited "The Republican Party," William L. Wilson "The National Democratic Party," and "Letters to a King," by Albion W. Tourgee, gave advice to young men about to cast their first vote. "The Ethics of Marriage" were treated by H. S. Pomeroy; "Inebriety, its Causes, its Results, its Remedy," by F. D. Clum, M. D.; and H. W. Blair wrote "The Temperance Movement." Henry Van Dyke wrote on "The National Sin of Literary Piracy," and Brander Matthews published "Cheap Books and Good Books." "The Third Annual Report of the Commissioner of Labor," on the subject of strikes and lockouts, was issued, and F. Howard Wines was responsible for "American Prisons, in the Tenth United States Census."

Theology.—Religious books, as usual, were numerous. The Rev. James McCosh published a volume of "Gospel Sermons" and "The Religious Aspect of Evolution," a subject that was also treated by Prof. Joseph Le Conte in "Evolution and its Relation to Religious Thought." "The Credentials of Science the Warrant of Faith," was from the pen of Josiah P. Cooke, and C. M. Stockwell wrote on "The Evolution of Immortality." "The Field-Ingersoll Discussion, Faith or Agnosticism," carried on in a series of articles in the "North American Review," was printed in pamphlet form. "Philosophy and Religion" was a rather voluminous but exceedingly earnest work, by Augustus H. Strong, D. D., and "Harvard Vespers" was a collection of addresses to students, by F. G. Peabody, P. Brooks, E. E. Hale, and others. "The Heart of the Creeds," by Arthur Wentworth Eaton, was a clear, concise exposition of "Historical Religion in the Light of Modern Thought," and "What is the Bible?" by G. T. Ladd, D. D., made an "Inquiry into the Origin and Nature of the Old and New Testaments in the Light of Modern Biblical Study." "Living Religions" was a presentation in popular form of "The Great Religions of the East," with the truths underlying each, and "Biblical Antiquities" a handbook for students of the Bible. David J. Burrell, D. D., in ten essays on "The Religions of the World," gave an outline of the great religious systems, and O. S. Stearns wrote an "Introduction to the Books of the Old Testament." "Some Chapters on Judaism and the Science of Religion" were furnished by Rabbi L. Grossman, and "Dissolving Views in the History of Judaism" by Rabbi Solomon Schindler. "Religious Reconstruction" was considered by M. J. Savage, and "Christian Science, its Truths and Errors," by the Rev. H. M. Tenney. "Co-operation in Christian Work" was the collected experience of Bishop Harris and Rev. Drs. Storrs, Gladden, and others. "The Best Method of Working a Parish" was set forth by the Rev. J. F. Spalding, Missionary Bishop of Colorado, and Rev. Charles F. Thwing discussed "The Working Church." Vol. VI of "The History of the Christian Church," by Philip Schaff, D. D., was issued, covering the period of the Reformation, and from the same author we have "Church and State in the United States." His "Select Library of the Nicene and Post-Nicene Fathers" was also increased by four volumes (vii-x). "The History of the Inquisition of the Middle Ages," by H. C. Lea, was completed in its second and third volumes, and from the Rev. George Park Fisher we have a "History of the Christian Church," which has received high commendation for its learning and strict impartiality. From the same source also appeared a "Manual of Christian Evidences." R. P. Kerr wrote "The People's History of Presbyterianism in all Ages," and the Rev. A. H. Lewis "A Critical History of Sunday Legislation." G. E. Ackerman, D. D., was the author of "Man a Revelation of God," W. A. Snively of "Testimonies to the Supernatural" and "Parish Lectures on the Prayer-book," C. Quick of "Mysticism unmasked, or Ministration of the Holy Spirit," and "Long Ago, as interpreted by the XIX Century," was by E. F. Burr, D. D. "The Bible Doctrine of Inspiration" was explained and vindicated by Basil Manly, D. D., and A. T. Pierson edited "The Inspired Word," a series of papers and addresses delivered at the Bible Inspiration Conference in Philadelphia, 1887. John Williams, Bishop of Connecticut, published "Studies in the Book of Acts," and from Lyman Abbott, D. D., we have a work on "The Epistle of Paul the Apostle to the Romans." "The Talmud, what it is, and what it knows about Jesus," was told by the Rev. Bernhard Pick. Hiram Orcutt was a layman "Among the Theologians." The Baldwin Lectures of 1887, delivered by the Rev. William Clark, are entitled "Witnesses to Christ." The Bishop-Paddock Lectures for 1888, on "The World and the Kingdom," were from Bishop Hugh Miller Thompson. The Rev. T. B. Neely wrote on "The Evolution of Episcopacy and Organic Methodism," Bishop W. L. Harris on "The Relations of Episcopacy to the General Conference," and C. W. Bennett on "Christian Archæology." "The Bible a Workingman's Book," is from the pen of Francis N. Zabriskie. The Rev. Daniel Dorchester wrote "Christianity in the United States, from the First Settlement down to the Present Time," and also "Romanism versus the Public School System," and H. S. Burrage "Baptist Hymn-Writers and their Hymns." From James J. Treacy we have "Conquests of our Holy Faith," from the Rev. I. T. Hecker "The Church and the Age," and from J. Waterworth a translation of "The Canons and Decrees of the Sacred and Œcumenical Council of Trent under the Sovereign Pontiffs Paul III, Julius III, and Pius IV. Abraham Coles made "A New Rendering of the Hebrew Psalms into English Verse." Wolcott Calkins wrote "Keystones of Faith." The "Sermons on the International Sunday-School Lessons" were published for 1888 and 1889, and other sermons include: "The Heath in the Wilderness, or Sermons to the People," of R. Newton, D. D., posthumously published; "Eternal Atonement," nineteen selected sermons of Dr. Roswell D. Hitchcock; "Spirit and Life Thoughts for To-Day," by Dr. Amory H. Bradford; and "The Transfiguration of Life," by Dr. E. S. Atwood. "The Seven Deadly Sins," inveighed against by the Rev. Morgan Dix in his Lenten sermons in Trinity Church, New York, form the subject of a volume, and from the Rev. J. W. Lowber we have "The Struggles and Triumphs of the Truth" and "The Devil in Modern Society." The Rev. W. Wright published eight lectures on "The Realities of Heaven"; Jermain G. Porter, Director of the Cincinnati Observatory, "Our Celestial Home"; J. S. Barlow, "Endless Being"; C. F. Dole, "Jesus and the Men about Him"; and James H. Potts,

"Faith made easy." "Christianity in the Daily Conduct of Life," was anonymous. Mrs. T. S. Childs wrote "The Altar of Earth," the Rev. E. P. Humphrey "Sacred History from the Creation to the Giving of the Law," the Rev. A. McCullagh "The Peerless Prophet," and the Rev. J. W. Jones "Christ in the Camp." "Atonement and Law" were reviewed by S. G. Burney, and "Endless Opportunity for All Souls" was advanced as a creed by the Rev. James Gorton. For children we have "A Father's Blessing and other Sermons," by the Rev. W. W. Newton, and the "Story of Moses," by Mrs. M. A. Hallock. "Missionary Enterprises in the South Sea Islands," by J. Williams, is unusually interesting.

Jurisprudence.—The yearly average of State and Federal Reports has been placed at one hundred volumes. In 1888 Myer's "Federal Decisions" reached Vol. XXVIII, and "U. S. Digests," new series, Vol. XVIII. A series of "American State Reports" was initiated by A. C. Freeman, and two volumes were published, beginning at the period where "American Reports" were discontinued, and Vol. I of the "American Digest (Annual)" was issued by the West Publishing Company, of St. Paul, Minn. Vol. I of "Interstate Commerce Reports" also appeared, and a "Digest of Decisions of the Department of the Interior and General Land-Office" was made by W. B. Matthews and W. O. Conway. Joel P. Bishop wrote on "Common Law and Codification, or the Common Law a System of Reasoning"; G. W. Field on "The Legal Relations of Infants, Parent and Child, and Guardian and Ward"; and M. M. Bigelow published "A Treatise on the Law of Fraud on its Civil Side." "A Practical Treatise on Criminal Law and Procedure in Criminal Cases" was from the pen of J. H. Gillett; and Vol. III of "Essentials of the Law," by Marshall D. Ewell, contained "Essential Parts of Pollock on Torts, Williams on Real Property, and Best on Evidence." F. Sackett prepared "Instructions and Requests for Instructions in Jury Trials," and Edwin Baylies a "Supplement to Wait's Actions and Defenses." Leonard A. Jones was an authority in "A Treatise on the Law of Liens," Joseph F. Randolph wrote "A Treatise on the Law of Commercial Paper" (Vol. III), and G. A. Finkelnburg "The Negotiability of Promissory Notes." "Commentaries on the Interpretation of Statutes, Founded on the Treatise of Sir P. B. Maxwell," were written by G. A. Endlich, and "A Brief Comparison of the most Important Statutes of the Codes of Virginia, 1873–1887," was made by C. W. Sams. F. H. Mackey set forth "The Practice and Procedure of the Supreme Court of the District of Columbia," and Morris Cooper "The Law and Practice of Referees and References under the Code of Civil Procedure and Statutes of New York." Corporations were extensively treated. T. W. Waterman published "A Treatise on the Law of

Corporations other than Municipal," F. S. Wait "A Practical Treatise on Insolvent Corporations," and H. Binmore "A Digest of the American Corporation Cases." "American and English Corporation Cases," by W. M. McKinney, reached Vol. XX, and "American and English Railroad Cases," by the same author, Vol. XXXIII. A. S. Bolles wrote on "The National Bank Act and its Judicial Meaning," and Nathan Newmark on "The Laws Relating to Bank Deposits." "A Treatise on the Law of Benefit Societies, and, Incidentally, of Life Insurance," by F. H. Bacon, "The Law of Voluntary Societies and Mutual Benefit Insurance," by W. C. Niblack, and "A Digest of the Law of Insurance," by J. R. Berryman, practically exhaust this subject. J. Lewis wrote "A Treatise on the Law of Eminent Domain in the United States," and W. H. Manier "The Law of Eminent Domain and of Railroads and Warehouses." "A Selection of Cases in the Law of Quasi-Contracts" was begun by W. Albert Keener, and the first volume completed. Clifford Boese wrote "A Hand-book on Naturalization," and B. K. and W. F. Elliott were jointly engaged on "The Work of the Advocate." "The Law in Pennsylvania of Voluntary Assignment in Trust for the Benefit of Creditors" was handled by W. Trickett, "The Law of Partnership," by Clement Bates, and J. C. Fowler published a "Supplement to the Revised Statutes of New York." M. H. Throop brought out "The Code of Civil Procedure of New York" and "The New York Justices' Manual," and G. C. Clemens "Powers and Duties of Constables, a Constable's Guide for use in the State of Kansas." "The Fish and Game Laws of the State of New York," also "The Laws for the Preservation of the Forests," were arranged by G. E. Kent, as were "The Excise Laws of New York in Chronological Order," by G. B. Colby. "Commissioners in Chancery in Virginia" was by A. Meade Smith, and "A Chromatic Chart and Manual of Parliamentary Law" was prepared by J. Ross Lee. "General Assignments for Benefit of Creditors" was a "Complete Digest of Decisions, the Rules and Practice and Statutes of New York," from J. S. Derby, and E. S. More collected "The Laws of New York relating to Villages." T. B. Hall wrote "A Treatise on Patent Estate," W. H. Bailey "The Conflict of Judicial Decisions," and I. F. Redfield "The Law of Railways." "Removal of Causes from the State to Federal Courts" was treated by Emory Speer. "A Treatise on the Law of Building and Buildings," by A. P. Lloyd, supplies a want long felt. "The American and English Encyclopædia of Law," by J. H. Merrill, reached its sixth volume, and "Hubbell's Legal Directory" was issued for the year beginning Oct. 1, 1887.

Medicine and Surgery.—While no leading book appeared during the year in either of the departments under this head, most of the work

done was creditable. Eustace Smith wrote on "The Wasting Diseases of Women and Children"; A. J. C. Skene on "Diseases of Women"; J. V. Shoemaker, on the "Diseases of the Skin"; and H. R. Crocker, "Diseases of the Skin." From Allan McLane Hamilton we have "The Modern Treatment of Headaches"; from Thomas J. Mayo, "Theine in the Treatment of Neuralgia"; from J. L. Corning, "A Treatise on Hysteria and Epilepsy"; and from Mary Putnam Jacobi, "Essays on Hysteria, Brain Tumor, etc." O. A. Wall published "The Prescription Therapeutically, Pharmaceutically, and Grammatically Considered"; S. Weir-Mitchell, "Doctor and Patient"; and D. W. Buxton, "Anæsthetics, their Uses and Administration." Vincent D. Harris handled "Diseases of the Chest"; Norman Kerr, "Inebriety, its Etiology, Pathology, Treatment, and Jurisprudence"; and T. C. Van Nuys made "A Chemical Analysis of Healthy and Diseased Urine." Vol. V of the "Cyclopædia of Obstetrics and Gynecology" appeared. A. H. N. Lewers wrote "A Practical Text-Book of the Diseases of Women," and Vol. XI of "A System of Gynecology by American Authors," edited by M. D. Mann, was issued. Nathan Allen wrote on "Physical Development," J. H. Salisbury on "The Relation of Alimentation and Disease," and W. H. Welch on "The General Pathology of Fever." "Ptomaines and Leucomaines, or the Putrefactive and Physiological Alkaloids" was by V. C. Vaughan and F. G. Noyes; "Clinical Lectures on Albuminuria," by T. G. Stewart; and an "Atlas of Venereal and Skin Diseases" was prepared by Prince A. Morrow. From Austin Flint we have "A Text-Book of Human Physiology"; from William Sterling, "Outlines of Practical Physiology"; and from J. F. Payne, "A Manual of General Pathology," designed as an introduction to the practice of medicine. L. A. Stimon published "A Treatise on Dislocations," and to surgery belong: "The Rules of Aseptic and Antiseptic Surgery," by A. G. Gerster; "Rectal and Anal Surgery," by Edmund and E. W. Andrews; "Surgery of the Abdomen," by J. E. Mears; "Abdominal Surgery," by H. C. Wyman; and "Ophthalmic Surgery," by R. B. Carter and W. A. Frost. "The Surgical Diseases of the Genito-Urinary Organs" was a revision by E. L. Keyes of the text-book by Van Buren and Keyes. R. B. Bontecou considered "What Class of Gun-shot Wounds justify Excision or Resection in Modern Warfare," and O. K. Newell, "The Best Surgical Dressing; how to prepare it, etc." "An Illustrated Encyclopædic Medical Dictionary," by Frank P. Foster; F. R. Campbell's "Language of Medicine"; and A. L. Ranney's "Applied Anatomy," were useful contributions, as were also "An Annual of the Universal Medical Science," edited by Charles E. Sajous, and a "Physician's Interpreter in Four Languages," the work of F. A. Davis. George A. Evans issued a "Hand-book of Historical and

Geographical Phthisiology, with Special Reference to the Distribution of Consumption in the United States." Valuable translations from the French were: "Animal Magnetism," by Alfred Binet and Charles Féré; "Clinical Lectures on Certain Diseases of the Nervous System," by J. M. Charcot; and, from the German, we have "The Pathology and Treatment of Displacements of the Uterus," by B. S. Schultze. "The Dispensatory of the United States of America" (sixteenth edition), by George B. Wood and Franklin Bache, was rearranged, thoroughly revised, and largely rewritten by H. C. Wood, J. P. Remington, and S. P. Sadtler.

General Science.—Works of this class were mostly popular in form. From Gen. A. W. Greely, Chief Signal Officer, U. S. A., we have "American Weather, a Popular Exposition of its Phenomena, with Numerous Illustrations and Charts," and from Mrs. Sophie B. Herrick, "The Earth in Past Ages," an elementary treatise. "Three Cruises of the United States Coast and Geodetic Survey Steamer Blake," in two volumes, by Alexander Agassiz, was a "Contribution to American Thalassography," being a study of deep-sea formations. T. K. Abbot published "An Elementary Theory of the Tides." "Astronomy with an Opera-Glass," by Garrett P. Serviss, was intended as a popular introduction to the science. "Great-Circle Sailing" and "Old and New Astronomy," by R. A. Proctor, were published; and from J. Haywood we have "The Earth, its Chief Motions and the Tangent Index"; and from Edward S. Holden, Director of the Lick Observatory, a "Handbook" of the same. "The New Agriculture," by A. N. Cole, sets forth an original theory of subterranean irrigation; and "Trees and Tree-Planting," by Gen. James S. Brisbin, was a vigorous and passionate plea for protection of American forests. "The Animal Life of Our Sea-Shore" was studied by Angelo Heilprin, with special reference to the New Jersey coast. The third series of "Butterflies of North America," by W. H. Edwards, appeared; and A. S. Packard, M. D., wrote an "Entomology for Beginners," which by intent should prove of use to fruit-growers and gardeners also. "A Frozen Dragon, and other Tales," was in reality a story-book of natural history by C. F. Holder, who published also "A Strange Company." "In Nesting-Time," was from Olive Thorne Miller, and "Three Kingdoms," a hand-book of the Agassiz Association, by H. H. Ballard. Two volumes of "Queer People," with "Paws and Claws," and "Wings and Stings," by Palmer Cox, author of "The Brownies"; "Little People and their Homes in Meadows, Woods, and Waters," by Stella Louise Hook; and "The Stories Mother Nature told her Children," by Jane Andrews, were books for children. R. P. Williams wrote a "Laboratory Manual of General Chemistry," and Annie Chambers Ketchum a "Botany for Academies and Colleges." Linus Faunce was the author

of "Descriptive Geometry," W. Wells of "The Essentials of Trigonometry," and C. W. McCord furnished "Practical Hints for Draughtsmen." "Numbers Symbolized" was an elementary algebra by M. D. Sensenig. Hand-books of practical application of scientific principles were unusually numerous. From Philip Atkinson we have "The Elements of Electric Lighting"; from Emory Edwards, "The American Steam-Engineer"; from E. D. Peters, "American Methods of Copper-Smelting"; and from A. W. Wright, "American Street Railways, their Construction, Equipment, and Maintenance." James H. Monckton wrote a work on "Stair Building," and W. F. M. Goss "A Course of Study and Practice of Bench-Work in Wood." "All Matter tends to Rotation," was a theory advanced by L. LeC. Hamilton.

Fine Arts.—The first volume of a "Cyclopædia of Music and Musicians," by John Denison Champlin, Jr., was published. "The Standard Symphonies" were added by George P. Upton to his former series of "Standard Operas" and "Oratorios," and James E. Matthew wrote "A Popular History of Music, Musical Instruments, Ballet, and Opera." G. H. Wilson edited "The Musical Year-Book of the United States"; and "Presto! from the Singing School to the May Musical Festival," was a short sketch of musical development in Ohio, by F. E. Tunison. Vol. II of "New Musical Miscellanies," by W. S. B. Matthews, told "How to understand Music." J. C. Fillmore was the author of "Lessons in Musical History," and L. O. Emerson of "Song Harmony." "How to Judge of a Picture" was told by J. C. Van Dyke, and W. H. Goodyear wrote a "History of Art," intended for the schoolroom. "Living New-England Artists," by Frank T. Robinson, contained biographical sketches with reproductions of original drawings and paintings of each, and Mrs. C. H. Stranahan compiled a valuable "History of French Painting, from its Earliest to its Latest Practice." Exquisite specimens of illustration were "Days Serene," by Margaret McDonald Pullman; "Favorite Birds," by Fidelia Bridges; "The Cathedrals of England and Wales," by Charles Whibley; and "The Home of Shakespeare," by Louisa K. Harlow, in water-color sketches. From Alice M. Baumgrass we have "By Lawn and Lea." "Baby's Lullaby-Book of Mother-Songs," was the work of several artists. "The Story of Mary the Mother," compiled by Rose Porter from various sources, was illustrated by photogravures from celebrated paintings, as was "The Boyhood of Christ," by Gen. Lew Wallace. Reproductions by the photogravure process include: "Recent Italian Art," "Rembrandt's Etchings," "European Etchings," "Madonnas by Old Masters," "Important New Etchings by American Artists," "Gems of French Art," and "The Goupil Gallery," with texts illustrative and descriptive, by Ripley Hitchcock, Walter Rowlands, and "Recent Ideals of American Art," by G. W. Sheldon. "A Portfolio of Players," was a memorial of the Augustin Daly comic troupe, and "The Napoleon Gallery" was a collection of one hundred outline proofs from foreign paintings. "Old Songs, with Drawings," by Edwin A. Abbey and Alfred Parsons, formed a dainty volume. "The New York Mirror Annual and Directory of the Theatrical Profession for 1888," was edited by H. G. Fiske; "The Dramatic Year, 1887-'88," by E. Fuller; and N. Helmer published "The Actor's Make-up Book." N. Earle composed "The Gipsy's Festival, a Musical Entertainment for Young People"; and "How to shade Embroidered Flowers and Leaves," as "Studies in Needlework," by Ellen G. Smith, will perhaps be admitted to this category. The production of "Souvenirs" and booklets increased largely during the year.

Voyages and Travels.—These were extensive. William D. Howells and T. Sergeant Perry compiled a "Library of Universal Adventure by Sea and Land"; and beginning with the cradle of humanity, Percival Lowell, author of "Chosŏn," has given us a study of Japan in "The Soul of the Far East." William E. Griffis issued a new edition of "Corea," with a chapter on Corea in 1888. The Rev. V. C. Hart described "Western China," and Simon Adler Stern made "Jottings of Travel in China and Japan." Mrs. Helen H. Holcomb wrote "Bits about India," and O. W. Wight told of "People and Countries visited in a Winding Journey around the World." Vol. II of "Around the World on a Bicycle," by T. Stephens, covered the distance "From Teheran to Yokohama." From Mrs. Susan E. Wallace we have "The Repose in Egypt," as well as "The Land of the Pueblos." The Rev. H. F. Fairbanks made "A Visit to Europe and the Holy Land," which he viewed with the eyes of a Catholic clergyman. The Rev. H. M. Field added "Old Spain and New Spain" and "Gibraltar" to his numerous delightful studies of other lands, and E. P. Thwing, M. D., wrote on "Out-Door Life in Europe." Curtis Guild produced a bright book on "Britons and Muscovites," Edwin O. Kimball wrote "Midnight Sunbeams," of course seen in the land of the Norsemen, and from Mr. and Mrs. Joseph Pennell we have "Our Sentimental Journey through France and Italy," performed on wheels. The enterprise of young ladies of the present day is shown by "Yankee Girls in Zululand," by Louise Vescelius Sheldon; "Two Girls Abroad," by Nellie M. Carter; "Three Vassar Girls in France," by Elizabeth W. Champney; and "Great Grandmother's Girls in New Mexico," by the same author. "Mexico" has been written about as "Picturesque, Political, and Progressive" by Mary Elizabeth Blake and Margaret F. Sullivan, and as "Our Neighbor" by J. H. Rice, while Fanny Chambers Gooch brings us "Face to Face with the Mexicans." F. A. Ober chronicles "The Knock-about Club in the Antilles," and William Elroy Cur-

tis, late United States Commissioner to the Governments of Central and South America, describes "The Capitals of Spanish America." W. H. Hurlbert presents his view of "Ireland under Coercion," G. Pellew treats of the same country in "Castle and Cabin," and Mrs. J. Ellen Foster in "The Crime against Ireland" found home rule the only remedy. W. F. Warren traversed Holland "In the Footsteps of Arminius." From Charles Nordhoff we have "Peninsular California," and Walter Lindley and J. P. Widney give us "The California of the South." "Sketches of the Old Santa Barbara Missions" comes from K. S. Torrey, "The Florida of To-Day" from James Wood Davidson, and "South Dakota" from Frank S. Child. Charles Dudley Warner, in "On Horseback," describes a tour of three States, and W. H. H. Murray, in "Daylight Land," furnishes a novel and interesting account of a journey from Montreal to Vancouver City. A. R. Calhoun wrote "Lost in the Cañon"; Edwards Roberts, "Shoshone and other Western Wonders"; Mrs. Elizabeth B. Custer, "Tenting on the Plains"; and Buffalo Bill (W. F. Cody) told the story of "The Wild West" in his own way. "Ranch Life and the Hunting-Trail" were described by Theodore Roosevelt, "Historic Waterways" by Reuben Gold Thwaite, and "Sketches from the Saddle" were made by John Codman, a septuagenarian. "A Summer Cruise on the Coast of New England," by Robert Carter, was republished; and Wallace P. Stanley tells the story of "Our Week Afloat." "Up the North Branch" was by Charles A. J. Farrar, and "Tenting at Stony Beach" by Maria L. Pool. "A Winter Picnic" by J. and E. Dickinson and S. E. Dowd took place in the Bahama Islands, and James H. Stark prepared "A Bermuda Guide" and "Antique Views of ye Town of Boston." The "Narrative of a Journey down the Ohio and Mississippi in 1789-'90," by Maj. S. S. Forman, was edited with a memoir and illustrative notes by L. C. Draper. "Wrecked on Labrador" was a boy's book, by W. A. Stearns. From Thomas W. Knox we have "The Boy Travelers in Australasia," and from Hezekiah Butterworth, "Zigzag Journeys in the Antipodes."

Educational.—The works of the year on the art of teaching include "Contributions to American Educational History," by Herbert B. Adams; "Industrial Education in the South," by the Rev. A. D. Mayo; and "Aims and Methods of Classical Study," by W. G. Hale. Part I of "Technical Education in Europe," by J. Schoenhof, treated of "Industrial Education in France," and W. H. Carpenter translated from the German of Otto Solomon "The Slöjd in the Service of the School." "Methods and Aids in Geography" was from the pen of Charles F. King, and Clara Conklin wrote "Topics of Recitation in Ancient Geography." "The Orbis Pictus of Comenius," reproduced, is an imitation of that first child's picture-book and first illustration of object-teaching. Levi Seeley explained and illustrated "Grube's Method of teaching Arithmetic"; R. P. Harrington prepared "Helps to the Intelligent Study of College Preparatory Latin"; and Robert Hoentz "Historical Tables; a Condensed Key to Universal History." Frank H. Foster illustrated, from Church history, "The Seminary Methods of Original Study in the Historical Sciences." "Our Language," by G. A. Southworth and B. F. Goddard, dwells upon "Its Use and Structure taught by Practice and Example," and Sarah E. H. Lockwood's "Lessons in English adapted to the Study of American Classics" is a text-book for high-schools and academies. "Arithmetic Exercises and Examination - Papers" were arranged by H. S. Hall and S. R. Knight, and Lamont Stilwell published "Practical Exercises in Analysis and Parsing." Virgil A. Pinkley's "Essentials of Elocution and Oratory," "Excellent Quotations for Home and School," by Julia B. Hoitt, and "The Patriotic Reader," by H. Carrington, were perhaps the most noticeable books of elocution. "Suggestions for Gymnastic Exercises for Schools" were made by Helen Clark Swazey.

Sports and Pastimes.—Books of special interest to sportsmen were "Wild-Fowl Shooting," by William Bruce Leffingwell, a work almost scientific, and "Names and Portraits of Birds which interest Gunners, with Descriptions understanded of the People," by Gordon Trumbull. S. Brown Goode treated the subject of "American Fishes," with special reference to their habits and to methods of capture. J. Montgomery Ward published "Base Ball; how to become a Player, with the Origin, History, and Explanation of the Game"; R. M. Hurd "A History of Yale Athletics"; and F. W. Janssen "A History of American Amateur Athletics and Aquatics, with the Records." John Boyle O'Reilly wrote "The Ethics of Boxing and Manly Sport"; T. Robinson Warren, in "On Deck," gave "Advice to a Young Corinthian Yachtsman"; Howard Patterson issued a new and enlarged edition of "The Yachtsman's Guide," and also a "Canal Guide" for pleasure-seekers. "Official Lawn-Tennis Rules" were drawn up by the United States National Lawn Tennis Association, and Valentine G. Hall wrote on "Lawn Tennis in America." H. C. Leeds and James Dwight laid down the "Laws of Euchre as adopted by the Somerset Club of Boston, March 1, 1888," and Junius explained the intricacies of "The Game of Solo-Sixty." "Pranks and Pastimes" were devised by Mary J. Jacques; Lucretia Peabody Hale collected "Fagots for the Fireside," and L. A. Higgins was author of "A Christmas Entertainment for Young People at the Court of King Christmas."

Housekeeping.—About the usual number of books on this subject appeared during the year. Sallie Joy White published "Housekeepers and Home-Makers, a Housekeeping Manual"; Mrs.

E. R. Parker, "Mrs. Parker's Complete Housekeeper"; and Christine Terhune Herrick, "Housekeeping made Easy." Flora Haines Longhead wrote "Quick Cooking," and T. J. Murrey gave recipes for and made remarks upon "Luncheon," besides writing upon "Oysters and Fish." Mrs. E. T. Rover treated of "Hot-Weather Dishes," and H. C. Davidson of "Entrées and Table Dainties for the Epicure." M. L. Holbrook, M. D., in a work on "Eating for Strength," furnished 500 recipes for wholesome food and drinks. "How she did it, or Comfort on $150 a Year," by Mary Cruger, and "Molly Bishop's Family," by Catherine Owen, deal principally with housekeeping details.

Miscellaneous.—Books not included in the classifications before given may be briefly enumerated as follow: "Our Fishery Rights in the North Atlantic," by Joseph K. Doran; "The Defense of the Sea-Coast of the United States," by Prof. H. L. Abbot; "Patriotic Addresses" of the late Henry Ward Beecher, edited by John R. Howard; and a "Tabulated Roster of the Army of the Potomac at Gettysburg," by James Beale. "The Lobby and Public Men, from Thurlow Weed's Time," by H. C. Tanner, was avowedly an attack upon the Bribery act of the State of New York; and "'89, Edited from the Original Manuscript in 1891," by Edgar Henry, essentially a sectional production. H. S. Rosenthal drew up a "Manual for Building and Loan Associations"; P. T. Barnum wrote "The Wild Beasts, Birds, and Reptiles of the World, the Story of their Capture"; Helen A. Smith told "Stories of Persons and Places in America;" and Rosa Hartwick Thorpe published "The Year's Best Days for Boys and Girls." "Children's Stories of the Great Scientists" was a most instructive and interesting volume by Henrietta C. Wright, and Esther Gracie Wheeler wrote "Stray Leaves from Newport." "Success in Speculation" was anonymous, as was also "American Ancestry." C. F. Pidgin made a useful contribution in "Practical Statistics," and J. H. Cromwell devised a "System of Easy Lettering." "Hints about Men's Dress" were given by a New York Clubman, and "Dress Cutting Out" was scientifically explained by Mrs. H. Grenfell and Miss Baker and "Minor Tactics," by Lieut. J. P. Wisser. "How Men propose" was shown by Agnes Stevens in a collection of love-scenes from popular works of fiction. J. P. Johnston wrote "Twenty Years of Hus'lin"; Wallace Peck, "The Golden Age of Patents"; H. Liddell, "The Evolution of a Democrat"; and W. J. Florence "Fables." Other humorous works include: "The Battle of the Swash and the Capture of Canada," by S. Barton; "Chip's Un-natural History," by F. P. W. Bellew; and "Nye and Riley's Railway Guide." S. Merrill wrote "Newspaper Libel"; J. D. Billings, "Hard Tack and Coffee"; and Anna E. Hahn, "Summer Assembly Days, or what was seen, heard, and felt at the Nebraska Chatauqua." "What shall make us whole?" was asked by

Helen B. Merriman; "Christian-Science Healing" was from Frances Lord; and "Ruth, the Christian Scientist, or the New Hygeia," was from the pen of Rev. John Chester. Henry Clews wrote "Twenty-eight Years in Wall Street," and a New York Broker, "The Art of Investing." "How to get rich in the South" was told by W. H. Harrison, Jr., and George W. Walling furnished "Recollections of a New York Chief of Police." "The Death-Blow to Spiritualism," by Reuben Briggs Davenport, gave "The True Story of the Fox Sisters"; and "Physical Proofs of Another Life" were proffered by F. J. Lippit, in "Letters to the Seybert Commission." Among books of reference, Vol. XII of "Appletons' Annual Cyclopædia" appeared, as also an "Index" to the series from 1876 to 1887, inclusive; a new "Cyclopædia of Universal Literature," by J. B. Alden, reached eleven, and a "Manifold Cyclopædia," from the same source, twelve volumes; and the "Library of American Literature," edited by Edmund C. Stedman and Ellen Mackay Hutchinson, was continued in four volumes. William Cushing issued a second series of "Initials and Pseudonyms." Ainsworth R. Spofford compiled "The American Almanac for 1888," and Carroll D. Wright published "Statistics of Colleges." The tenth number of "The Statistical Abstract of the United States for 1887" was issued by the Bureau of Statistics of the Treasury Department at Washington. "Ancient Rome in the Light of Recent Discoveries," by Prof. Rodolfo Lanciani, containing an account of excavations made by the Italian Government under his observation, while not, properly speaking, an American work, nevertheless made its appearance among us, and owed its existence largely to American resources.

The, following are the figures given by the "Publishers' Weekly," as representing the issues of the year:

CLASS.	1887.	1888.	No. of books made in the United States.	No. Imported.
Fiction	1,022	874	808	66
Theology and religion	358	482	p 339	143
Education and language	283	413	306	107
Juvenile books	487	410	298	112
Law	438	335	829	6
Literary history and miscellany	251	291	199	92
Poetry and the drama	221	280	165	115
Fine art and illustrated books	175	250	143	107
Biography, memoirs	201	247	145	102
Political and social science	148	227	200	27
Description, travel	180	197	144	53
Medical science, hygiene	171	151	95	56
History	157	141	110	84
Useful arts	128	124	74	50
Physical and mathematic'l science	76	56	43	13
Humor and satire	26	47	44	3
Sports and amusements	48	46	36	10
Domestic and rural	61	39	30	9
Mental and moral philosophy	21	18	12	6
Totals	4,437	4,631	3,520	1,111 3,520
Grand total				4,681

LITERATURE, BRITISH, IN 1888. Book-production in England increased largely in 1888; 4,960 new books were published, an advance of 550 over those of 1887, and of new editions there were 1,631. The increase is especially to be noted in fiction, in theology, and in poetry and the drama; though, particularly in the last instance, there was no perceptible improvement in character. Voyages and travels, with biography and history, present nearly the same number of volumes recorded in 1887, and the activity in these departments aroused during the Jubilee year appears to have extended its influence over not only the quantity but the quality of the work. On the whole, but few books of enduring merit are to be expected from a single twelvemonth, and these are no doubt to be found amid the multitude that serve the purpose of their issue.

Fine Arts.—Foremost among works on the subject of art are to be mentioned "Imagination in Landscape Painting," by Philip Gilbert Hamerton, and a "Popular Handbook to the National Gallery," prepared by E. T. Cook, to which a preface was furnished by John Ruskin. W. W. May wrote on "Marine Painting," Lady Dilke on "Art in the Modern School," and Wilfrid Meynell on "Modern Art and Artists." Margaret Stokes made a study of "Early Christian Art in Ireland," and E. Sharpe of "The Seven Periods of English Architecture." "Our Recent Actors," by Westland Marston, and "The Prima Donna, Her History and Surroundings from the Seventeenth to the Nineteenth Century," by H. Sutherland Edwards, are the leading works relating to the stage. In music we have a "Manual of Orchestration," by H. Clarke. Among illustrated works the most prominent are "Sketches of North Italian Folk," from Randolph Caldecott, in a limited edition, with text by Mrs. Comyns Carr; "Pictures of East-Anglian Life," in photogravure and small drawings, descriptive text by P. H. Emerson; and "The Pied Piper of Hamelin," by Kate Greenaway.

History.—An event of the literary year was the completion, in two volumes (V and VI), of "The Invasion of the Crimea," by Alexander William Kinglake, bringing the narrative down, as set forth in the full title, to the death of Lord Raglan. Another important work was also finished in "A History of England: Period IV," by the Rev. J. F. Bright. "Two Centuries of Irish History, 1691–1870," were edited by James Bryce, whose "American Commonwealth" at last appeared in the closing days of the year. H. W. Dulcken wrote "A Popular History of England, from the Earliest Period to the Jubilee of Victoria, Queen and Empress, 1887," and from J. A. Doyle we have "The Puritan Colonies." "A History of Scotland," chiefly in its ecclesiastical aspect, was written by M. G. J. Kinloch. Mrs. Green published a revised edition of her husband's famous "Short History of the English People," with an interesting and valuable introduction;

and Walter Besant's "Fifty Years Ago," gave a graphic picture of life and times at the date of the accession of Victoria. "Fifty Years of European History," by Edward A. Freeman, covers "Teutonic Conquests in Gaul." F. A. Gasquet wrote "Henry VIII and the English Monasteries," and the Rev. A. Jessopp "The Coming of the Friars and other Historic Essays." "The Last of the Valois and Accession of Henry of Navarre," by Catharine Charlotte (Lady Jackson), and "The Bastille," by Capt. D. Bingham, were studies in French history. From W. H. D. Adams we have "The Makers of British India"; from Col. G. B. Matheson, "Decisive Battles of India, 1746–1849"; and "Two Chapters of Irish History" were written by T. Dunbar Ingram. R. Hassencamp also published "The History of Ireland, from the Restoration to the Union." To history properly belong: "Hildebrand and his Times," by W. R. W. Stephens; "Simon de Montford and his Cause," by the Rev. W. H. Hutton; "Stronghow's Conquest of Ireland," by F. P. Barnard; and, in the "Twelve English Statesmen Series," "William the Conqueror," by Edward A. Freeman; "Oliver Cromwell," by F. Harrison; "William III," by H. D. Traill; "Henry II," by Mrs. J. R. Green; and "Cardinal Wolsey," by M. Creighton. G. M. Theal wrote a "History of South Africa, 1486–1691," and "The Story of the Nations Series" contains: "The Story of Turkey," by Stanley Lane-Poole, assisted by E. J. W. Gibb and Arthur Gilman (the latter an American); "The Story of Holland," by J. F. Thorold Rogers; "The Story of Mediæval France," by G. Masson; "The Story of Media, Babylon, and Persia," by Zénaide A. Ragozin; "The Story of the Goths," by Henry Bradley; and "The Story of Ireland," by Hon. Emily Lawless. "Imperial Germany" was from the pen of Sidney Whitman, and "The Fall of New France" from that of G. E. Hart. To Epochs of Church History were added: "The English Church of the Middle Ages," by William Hunt; "The Popes and the Hohenstaufen," by Ugo Balzani; and "The History of the University of Cambridge," by J. Bass Mullinger. Vol. I of "A New English Dictionary on Historical Principles," edited by J. A. H. Murray, was completed by the issue of Part IV.

Essays.—To this class strictly belong: "Essays in Criticism: Second Series," by Matthew Arnold; "Essays on some of the Modern Guides of English Thought in Matters of Faith," by Richard H. Hutton; "Essays Chiefly on Poetry," by A. DeVere; "Ignorant Essays," by R. Dowling; and fugitive essays of Prof. Dowden, collected under the title of "Transcripts and Studies." "Roman Mosaics" were "Studies in Rome and its Neighborhood," by Hugh McMillan, D. D. Rev. Robert Burn wrote on "Roman Literature in Relation to Roman Art"; and "Society in Rome under the Caesars," by W. R. Inge, in its first essay form took the Hare prize at Cambridge Univer-

sity in 1886. J. P. Mahaffy published "Greek Life and Thought, from Alexander to the Roman Conquest," and also "The Principles of the Art of Conversation"; and from Max Müller we have "Biographies of Words, and the Home of the Aryas." S. Kydd wrote "A Sketch of the Growth of Public Opinion," and Elliot Stock "How to write the History of a Family." J. M. Barrie told "Auld Licht Idylls," Lady Wilde "Ancient Legends of Ireland," and "Coaching Days and Coaching Ways" were commemorated by W. O. Tristram. From Mrs. Oliphant came "The Makers of Venice," a companion-piece to "The Makers of Florence." G. Maspero wrote on "Egyptian Archæology"; and from A. E. Waite we have "The Real History of the Rosicrucians" and "Lives of Alchemistical Philosophers." "Studies of the Holy Grail," with reference to the hypothesis of their Celtic origin, were made by Alfred Nutt. J. T. Davidson published "Sure to Succeed"; and Samuel Smiles, "Life and Labor," a book somewhat on the same lines. E. J. Hardy, late chaplain of Her Majesty's forces, and author of "How to be happy though married," produced "The Five Talents of Woman." "The Book of Noodles," by W. H. Clouston, gave the history of "Fools and their Follies" in all times and lands.

Biography.—The leading work of this character produced during the year, and indeed one of the best that have appeared in some time, is a "Life of the Right Hon. W. E. Forster," by T. Wemyss Reid, which won earnest commendation from high authorities. From Archibald Forbes, the great war correspondent, we have a "Biography of the late William I of Germany," and from G. Barnett Smith "William I," while "Frederick, Crown Prince and Emperor," was the subject of a sketch by Rennell Rodd. "What I remember" was told by T. A. Trollope, a brother of the novelist, and proved to be much delightful literary gossip, more of which was supplied by the "Further Reminiscences" of W. P. Frith. "The Early Life of Samuel Rogers," by P. W. Clayden, covers a rich period of England's social, political, and literary life, and contains valuable correspondence, and "John Francis and the Athenæum," by J. C. Francis, is an interesting record of a literary career of fifty years. "Princetoniana; Charles and A. A. Hodge," by a Scottish Princetonian, Rev. C. A. Salmond, is of special interest to Americans as the first attempt at biography of the younger Hodge; and it is a striking fact that the "Life of Ralph Waldo Emerson," by Richard Garnett, in "The Great Writer Series," has been pronounced "the soundest biographical work on Emerson yet written." Other "Lives" in the same series, which is edited by Prof. Eric S. Robertson, are "Adam Smith" by R. B. Haldane, "Oliver Goldsmith" by Austin Dobson, "Robert Burns" by John Stuart Blackie, and "William Congreve" by Edmund Gosse. Vol. II of "English Writers," by Henry Morley, covers the period "From Cædmon to the Conquest," and Vol. III "From the Conquest to Chaucer." J. Ross wrote "Three Generations of English Women," and in "The Famous Women Series" we have "Elizabeth Barrett Browning," by John H. Ingram, the first biography of the poetess, and "Hannah More," by Charlotte M. Yonge. Adelaide Ristori published "Studies and Memoirs, an Autobiography"; and "Reminiscences of J. L. Toole, the Comedian," were told by himself and chronicled by Joseph Hatton. "The Life and Adventures of Edmund Kean" were detailed by J. Fitzgerald Molloy. C. R. Markham wrote "The Fighting Veres: Lives of Sir Francis Vere and Sir Horace Vere," Stanley Lane-Poole "A Life of the Right Honorable Stratford Canning," and T. A. Nash a "Life of Richard, Lord Westbury, Lord High Chancellor of England." "The International Statesmen Series" contain: "Lord Beaconsfield" by T. E. Kebble, "Prince Metternich" by G. B. Malleson, and "Lord Palmerston" by Lloyd C. Sanders. "Daniell O'Connell" was written by J. A. Hamilton, and "The Correspondence of Daniel O'Connell, the Liberator," was edited by W. J. Fitzpatrick. W. Dillon was the author of a "Life of John Mitchell." Dean Burgon wrote "Lives of Twelve Good Men," who were influential though comparatively unknown; and "Christopher Wordsworth, Bishop of Lincoln" was the joint work of Canon Overton and Miss Elizabeth Wordsworth. The "Life of Bishop Colenso' was written by the Rev. Sir G. W. Cox, and "Richard Chenevix Trench, Archbishop," is the title of a volume of letters and memorials. The "Correspondence of Sir Henry Taylor" was edited by Edward Dowden, "The Letters from and to Charles Kirkpatrick Sharpe" by A. Allardyce, and other valuable "Letters" were those of "General C. G. Gordon to his Sister," and from "Dorothy Osborne to Sir William Temple," the story of a seven years' courtship. Mrs. Oliphant wrote "The Life of Principal Tulloch"; W. Knight, "John Campbell Sharp and his Friends"; Robert Louis Stevenson, a "Memoir of Fleeming Jenkin," which accompanied "Papers Literary, Scientific, etc.," of that professor, edited by Dr. Colvin and J. A. Ewing; and Walter Besant, "The Eulogy of Richard Jefferies." "Monarchs I have met" is the title of a book by W. Beatty Kingston, and "Life in the Confederate Army" was described by W. Watson from experience. "Reminiscences of W. Rogers," by R. W. Hadden, appeared, as did the "Recollections" of Dr. Westland Marston. "Robert Southey, the Story of his Life written in his Letters" was edited by John Dennis, and "The Letters of Charles Lamb" were newly arranged by Canon Ainger, with additions. "Emin Pasha in Central Africa: a Collection of his Letters and Journals," was translated from the German by Mrs. R. W. Felkin, and "The Correspondence between Liszt and Wagner, 1841-1861," by Dr.

F. Hueffer. In the philosophical classics appeared "Francis Bacon," by John Nichol, and "Spinoza," by John Caird; the latter, however, is rather a discussion of the "Ethics" of that author than a life. "Elizabeth Gilbert and her Work for the Blind" was told by F. Martin, and "The Fatal Illness of Frederick the Noble," by Sir Morell Mackenzie, was the reply to the report of the German doctors. Vol. XVII of the "Dictionary of National Biography," edited by Leslie Stephen, was reached.

Poetry.—Robert Browning made no contribution to the poetry of 1888, but a popular edition of his works was begun, showing the increasing interest that his genius has steadily excited. The "Complete Poetical Works" of William Wordsworth, including a hitherto unpublished poem entitled "The Recluse," which was also published separately, were edited with an introduction by John Morley, and "Glen Desseray, and other Poems, Lyric and Elegiac," of the late Principal Shairp, by his successor in the Oxford chair of Poetry, Prof. Palgrave. "The Marriage of Shadows and other Poems," by Margaret Veley, were also posthumously published and warmly received. Edwin Arnold wrote "With Sa'di in the Garden," in part a translation from the Persian poet, and thoroughly Oriental, and "Lotus and Jewel." From Robert Buchanan we have "The City of Dream, an Epic." Andrew Lang wrote "The Gold of Fairnilee" and "Grass of Parnassus"; W. E. Henley, "A Book of Verses," all of which possessed merit, and other authors who attained some prominence were May Kendall in "Dreams to sell," E. Nesbit in "Leaves of Life," and R. St. John Tyrwhitt in "Free-Field Lyrics." Miss A. M. F. Robinson wrote "Songs, Ballads, and a Garden Play," and Rennell Rodd, "The Unknown Madonna and other Poems." The chief collections of merit are: "More Lyrics from the Song-Books of the Elizabethan Age," by A. H. Bullen; "The Music of the Waters," a collection of sailor songs, by Laura Smith; and "In Praise of Ale," a specimen of curious research by W. T. Marchant. Plays of the old English dramatists were edited in "The Mermaid Series."

Fiction.—Mrs. Humphry Ward (a granddaughter of Dr. Arnold, of Rugby) has the credit of producing in "Robert Elsmere" the most widely read and variously discussed novel of recent years, the circulation of which in America has reached nearly 150,000 copies. "A Counsel of Perfection," by Lucas Malet (Mrs. Harrison), ranks perhaps next in power. The work done by familiar authors was of the usual average. William Black wrote "In Far Lochaber" and "The Strange Adventures of a House-boat"; Walter Besant, "Herr Paulus" and "The Inner House," both occult; and George MacDonald, "The Elect Lady." W. E. Norris wrote "Chris" and "The Rogue"; J. H. Shorthouse, "The Countess Eve" and "A Teacher of the Violin and other Tales"; and Thomas Hardy, "Wessex Tales." From Grant

Allen we have "This Mortal Coil" and "The Devil's Die"; from Frank Barrett, "A Recoiling Vengeance" and "The Admirable Lady Biddy Fane"; and from G. Mannville Fenn, "One Maid's Mischief," "The Story of Anthony Grace," and "Dick o' the Fens." H. Rider Haggard's three stories, "Mr. Meeson's Will," "Maiwa's Revenge," and "Colonel Quaritch, V. C.," achieved nothing of the popularity enjoyed by "She," but were nevertheless widely read. Mrs. Oliphant produced "The Second Son" and "Joyce"; Mrs. Louisa Parr, "Loyalty George"; and Jessie Fothergill, "The Lasses of Leverhouse" and "From Moor Isles." James Payn wrote "The Eavesdropper" and "The Mystery of Mirbridge"; Mrs. Alexander, "A Life Interest" and "Mona's Choice"; Rosa N. Carey, "Only a Governess" and "Aunt Diana"; and Miss Braddon, "The Fatal Three." Two anonymous works of unusual interest were "Fraternity" and "Nobody knows," and three of The Duchess were received by her admirers, "Marvel," "Undercurrents," and "The Hon. Mrs. Vereker." "The Happy Prince and other Tales," by Oscar Wilde, were handsomely illustrated.

Voyages and Travels.—Much of the work in this class was excellent. "The Early Adventures of Sir Henry Layard in Persia" were given to the world for the first time, and proved exciting and full of interest. Henry Drummond wrote on "Tropical Africa"; and "Incwadi Yami" was the record of twenty years' experience of Dr. J. W. Matthews in the southern part of that continent. "India, Pictorial and Descriptive," was anonymous. H. E. M. James described "The Long White Mountain, or a Journey in Manchuria"; C. M. Doughty, "Travels in Arabia Deserta"; and W. R. Carles, "Life in Corea." "Picturesque New Guinea" was from the pen of J. W. Lindt, Capt. J. Strachan published "Explorations and Adventures in New Guinea," and the Rev. S. MacFarlane "Among the Cannibals of New Guinea." W. B. Churchward was the author of "Blackbirding in the South Pacific," and James Inglis of "Tent-Life in Tiger Land." A most fascinating book is that of Mrs. Emily de Laszowska Gerard, "The Land beyond the Forest" (Transylvania). W. S. Caine wrote "A Trip Around the World in 1887–'8," and James A. Froude, "The English in the West Indies," mingling the discussion of political questions with much pleasant reading. "The Land of the Pink Pearl" is the title bestowed by L. D. Powles on the Bahama Islands, which were also visited, as well as numerous other places, by J. J. Aubertin in "A Fight with Distances." Count Gleichen went "With the Camel Corps up the Nile," and Isaac Taylor published "Leaves from an Egyptian Note-Book." A. J. C. Hare wrote "Walks in Paris" and "Days in and near Paris." Harold Brydges gave his impressions of "Uncle Sam at Home." J. C. Firth was "A New-Zealander in America," and D. J. Bannatyne

studied "Republican Institutions in the United States" for the benefit of his countrymen. "B. C. 1887, a Ramble in British Columbia," was made by J. A. Lees and W. J. Clutterbuck; and studies nearer home include: "Irish Pictures," by R. Lovett; "A Season in Sutherland," by J. E. Edwards Moss; "Old Chelsea," by B. Ellis Martin; and "De Omnibus Rebus," by the author of "Flemish Interiors." "Historic Towns," edited by Edward A. Freeman and the Rev. W. Hunt, reached "Colchester" in the sixth series; and "The Brontë Country" was made the object of special study by J. A. E. Stuart. "England as she seems, being Selections from the Notes of an Arab Hadji," though constructed on an old and somewhat trite idea, was a clever sketch by Edwin L. Arnold, son of the poet, of his native country under a disguise.

Physical, Moral, and Intellectual Science.—Of the scientific works issued during the year, to physical science belong: "The Story of Creation," by Edward Clodd; "The Building of the British Isles, a Study in Geographical Evolution," by A. J. Jukes; and an "Introduction to a Historical Geography of the British Colonies," by C. B. Lucas. In the "International Scientific Series" Sir John Lubbock wrote "On the Senses, Instincts, and Intelligence of Animals"; Sir J. W. Dawson, "A Geographical History of Plants"; the Rev. George Henslow, "The Origin of Floral Structures through Insects and other Agencies"; and the Hon. Ralph Abercrombie, "The Weather." Part XVI of the "Coleoptera of the British Isles," by Canon Fowler, was reached; and W. Swaysland, "Familiar Wild Birds"; "The Severn Tunnel, its Construction and Difficulties, 1872–1887," was described by T. A. Walker; and "Marvels under our Feet," by G. Hartwig. "The Economic Interpretation of History" was considered by J. E. Thorold Rogers, in a series of lectures; and "A History of Political Economy," J. K. Ingram, was reprinted in book-form, having been first published in the "Encyclopædia Britannica"; W. J. Ashley wrote an "Introduction to Economic History and Theory"; Wilfrid Richmond, "Christian Economics"; and L. L. F. R. Price, "Industrial Peace." "Guilds, their Origin, Constitution, Objects, and Later History," were treated by the late Cornelius Walford; and "London Government under the Local Government Act, 1888," by J. F. B. Firth and E. R. Simpson. A "Handbook to the Land-Charters and other Saxonic Documents" was drawn up by J. Earle; and W. Easterly wrote a "History of the Law of Tithes." "Tariffs and Trade of the British Empire" were discussed by Sir R. Rawson; "Capital and Wages," by F. Minton; and a "History and Criticism of Wages" was furnished by W. D. McDonnell. J. H. de Ricci wrote on "The Fisheries Dispute." "The Morality of Nations," by H. Taylor, was a "A Study on the Evolution of Ethics." "Tempted London: Young Men," was the title of a collected series of papers, which, first published in the "British Weekly," excited universal comment from the pulpits of the United Kingdom. "Savage London: Lights and Shadows of Riverside Characters," was from the pen of H. King. "The Fleet, its River, Prison, and Marriages," was the subject of a similar study by John Ashton; and "The Chronicles of Bow-Street Police Court" were opened by Percy Fitzgerald. The "Circuit Journeys," of Lord Cockburn, also belong to this class. G. Dawson wrote on "German Socialism"; and the last socialistic effort of William Morris was entitled "A Dream of John Bull and a King's Lesson," with a frontispiece by E. Burne-Jones. On the subject of Ireland we have "Gladstone and the Great Irish Struggle," by T. P. O'Conner and Robert McWade; "Ireland's Cause in England's Parliament," by Justin McCarthy, for Americans; "Ireland, the Causes of its Present Condition," by Earl Grey; "Ireland, Part II," by C. S. Ward; and a "Truthful Historie of the Settlement of Ireland by Cromwell," by Ethne. "Facts about Ireland" were told by A. B. Macdowall; and "Irish Union, before and after" was written by A. K. Connell. Sir Charles Dilke reviewed "The British Army" in an unsatisfactory mood; and Col. Maurice replied in "The Balance of Military Power in Europe." W. T. Stead advanced "The Truth about Russia"; and Stepniak treated "The Russian Peasantry, their Agrarian Condition, Social Life, and Religion." "Educational Ends, or the Idea of Personal Development," were dwelt upon by Sophie Brydges, and Laurence Oliphant, who died last year, wrote on "Scientific Religion, or Higher Possibilities of Life and Practice through the Operation of Natural Forces." "The Religion of Humanity" was the subject of an address by A. J. Balfour before the Church Congress at Manchester, and Karl Pearson discussed "The Ethics of Free Thought." The Hibbert Lectures for 1888, delivered by John Rhys, were on "The Origin and Growth of Religion as illustrated by Celtic Heathendom," and Dr. J. W. Taylor wrote on "Scotland's Strength in the Past and Scotland's Hope in the Future." James Martineau made "A Study of Religion," and A. Jukes of "The Names of God in Holy Scriptures." From E. M. Goulburn we have "Three Counsels of the Divine Master." Canon Farrar, with others, wrote on "Non-Biblical Systems of Religion," and, alone, published sermons on "Every-Day Christian Life." Dr. G. Matheson, with others, discoursed on "Christianity and Evolution," and the Rev. C. H. Spurgeon gave us "The Check-Book of the Bank of Faith." Six volumes of the "Expositor's Bible" appeared, Vol. I of the "Sermon Bible," and three additional volumes of the "People's Bible," by Joseph Parker, D. D. Spence, Exell, and Neil's "Thirty Thousand Thoughts" were completed in the sixth volume. "Kant's Critical Philosophy," Vol. III, by John P. Mahaffy, was issued, and in the "International Education Series" we have "Memory," by David Kay. "The Secret Doctrine," by Madame Blavatsky, was set forth in two volumes.

During the year the "Encyclopædia Britannica," of which the first volume appeared in 1875, was completed, as was also "Cassell's Encyclopædic Dictionary"; and a revised and enlarged edition of "Chambers's Encyclopædia" was begun, of which Vols. I and II were issued. "Cassell's Miniature Cyclopædia," convenient for very brief reference, was compiled by W. Laird Clowes.

The summary of British books issued during the year is as follows:

CLASSIFICATION.	New books.	New editions
Theology, sermons, biblical, etc...............	748	164
Educational, classical, and philological........	680	149
Juvenile works and tales..................	837	118
Novels, tales, and other fiction	929	885
Law, jurisprudence, etc....................	115	57
Political and social economy and commerce....	111	24
Arts, sciences, and illustrated works..........	184	69
Voyages, travels, geographical research	224	73
History, biography, etc	377	109
Poetry and the drama	168	68
Year-books and serials in volumes............	824	8
Medicine, surgery, etc	126	73
Belles-letters, essays, monographs, etc........	165	224
Miscellaneous, including pamphlets, not sermons......	507	120
Totals......................	4,960	1,631
		4,960
Grand total		6,591

LITERATURE, CONTINENTAL, IN 1888. On the whole, notwithstanding various disturbing causes, continental literature about held its own during the year. Authors and publishers have found occupation and profit in their vocations, and have not been disappointed with the results. Following our usual plan, we give the record in the alphabetical order of countries on the Continent of Europe.

Belgium.—Historical research has been prosecuted with spirit and industry. M. Namèche, of the University of Louvain, has published three new volumes (nineteenth, twentieth, and twenty-first) of his "Cours d'Histoire Nationale," comprising the last years of the reign of Philip II in the Netherlands, and the opening years of Albert and Isabella. The learned Bollandists are steadily working on the "Acta Sanctorum," which serves as an offset to M. Vander Haeghen's "Protestant Martyrology during the Sixteenth Century" (noted last year). M. Daris has supplied a "History of the Principality and Diocese of Liège to the Fifteenth Century," and M. H. Lonchay has dealt with a portion of the same subject in a volume that was crowned by the Royal Academy of Brussels. M. A. Wauters furnishes another volume of his "Ancient and Modern Belgium." Collections of important documents have been brought out, for the period between 1570 and 1750, by Baron de Lettenhove, M. Ch. Piot, and M. de Marneffe. The great work of M. Ch. Moeller, of the University of Louvain, "Traité des Études Historiques," has been revised and brought out by his son, in parts, and is an admirable guide for those who wish to study history on sure and sound principles. A Monograph on Tilly and the Thirty Years' War, from 1618–'32, has been written by Count de Villermont, and M. Ch. Woeste has given the views of a Roman Catholic on the History of the Culturkampf in Switzerland, 1871–'86. A number of interesting volumes on "Belgic Congo," and kindred topics in regard to African relations, have attracted much attention. Several excellent books of travel have appeared during the year, treating of Texas, China, Germany, Spain, etc. The history of the fine arts has not been neglected, and social science has been freely discussed by L. Dupriez, Ch. Lagasse, L. Halleux, Ch. Horion, Baron Colins, M. Heins, and M. E. de Laveleye. In poetry, too, both in Flemish and French, the yield has been creditable to Belgium. M. E. Verhaeren's "Les Soirs," G. Rodenbach's "Du Silence," and Ch. Potvin's "Nos Poëtes Flamands," are well spoken of. Pure literature, in the hands of the school of "Young Belgium," seems to flourish, and promises better results than were looked for last year. Prof. Stecher's "History of Flemish Literature" is pronounced to be the best work that exists on this subject. M. F. de Potter continues to work on his great history of the monuments and institutions of the City of Ghent, which is not yet completed. Various local histories of more or less merit have also appeared. Folk-lore attracts much notice, due chiefly to the poet Pol de Mont and to Prof. A. Gittée. The latter has issued an excellent manual for the use of students of Flemish folk-lore. Of old Flemish popular tales two volumes may be noted, viz., "Grandmother's Book of Stories," and "Stories of John Everyman." The drama has not been neglected, and several creditable productions have appeared. A curious posthumous work of the famous novelist Hendrik Conscience, entitled "History of my Youth," has been published, and is highly praised for its truthfulness and sincerity. Light literature holds its place as usual, and the crop of novels is not inferior to that of last year. A brilliant work by M. J. de Geyter, entitled "The Emperor Charles V and the Kingdom of the Netherlands," written in Flemish meter of the middle ages, is highly praised by the critics. It produced also a great sensation in Holland.

Denmark.—The Northern Exhibition of Industry, Agriculture, and Art in Copenhagen, which was a great success, diverted attention to some extent from literature this year, as did also the jubilee of the Danish Society of Artisans, celebrated in July; the centenary of the emancipation from villanage, held in June; and the commemoration of the twenty-fifth year of the King's reign on November 15. Several historical works relating to the emancipation of the peasantry a hundred years ago have been published. Among these Prof. E. Holm's "The Struggle for Agricultural Reforms, 1773–'91," is prominent; and Jörgensen's collection of memorials and documents, J. Steenstrup's "The Danish Peasant and Liberty," and Fredericia's "The Liberation of the Danish Peasant," are well worth consulting. In general and political history there is hardly anything worth mentioning. In literary history the first volume of J. Paludan's "Renaissence of the Literature of Denmark" has appeared; also, a small volume by R. Schröder, entitled "Œhlenschläger and the Romantic School." A considerable number of biographies have been published, of which we may name here a compendious account of the life and works of R. Kr. Rask, the eminent philologist (born one hundred years ago); a "Sketch of the Life and Times of Knud Lavard in the Middle Ages," by H. Olrik; and "The History of the Family of Bille," conspicuous in Danish annals, by Mollerup and Meidell. The great "Danish Biographical Dictionary" is being pushed forward as rapidly as possible. S. K. Sorensen has published a small volume about "The Arabs and their Civilization in the Middle Ages"; and Thor Lange, a professor at Moscow, has brought out an interesting book of travels, "A Month in the Orient." Philosophy has received only a moderate share of attention this year. In this connection may be named Wilkens's "Outlines of Æsthetics"; a treatise on "Oriental Mystics," by H. Ramussen; "The Religion of the Future," by A. C. Larsen; and a volume "On Temper," by F. Holberg. The death of M. A. Goldschmidt and of T. Lange (noted in last year's record) deprived Denmark of two of its best novelists. Posthumous novels, however, of both have appeared. H. P. Holst, the Nestor of living poets, has brought out the best of his writings as "Selected Works," and C. Hostrup has written a play, 'Under Snefog," which is praised by the critics. Younger authors have made numerous efforts in light literature, and with fair success. A few of these may be noted here; as, "The Polar Bear," by H. Pontoppidan; "The Consul's Wife," by Miss Levison; "A Purgatory," by P. Möller; "La Grande Demoiselle" (of the time of Louis XIV), by S. Schandorph; and "Stuk" ("hollow splendor"), by H. Bang. K. Gjellerup, who has abandoned realistic poetry, has brought out a great dramatic poem in two parts, "The Struggle with the Muses" and "Helicon," together with a comedy, "The Wedding Present." A. Ipsen's "Mephistopheles," a kind of Faust, is moderately praised by the critics. Several of the younger novelists are striving to portray life nowadays. V. Stuckenberg is one of these, and gives promise also of progress. The critics, however, have nothing favorable to say of the younger dramatic and lyric poets, such as E. Gad, N. Larsen, Sophus Clausen, and J. Becker.

France.—Political excitements and uncertainties as to the future have hindered the progress of literature in France this year in various ways. Nevertheless, authors have written and publishers have brought out books in poetry, history, the drama, fiction, etc. M. Sully-Prudhomme's "Le Bonheur," is a didactic poem of more than average merit, but not of the highest order. M. André Lemoyne, in his "Fleurs des Ruines," is sharply criticised by reviewers. The work of Jean Rameau, "The Song of the Stars," is pronounced the most interesting volume of verse published this year, though the critics find in it much to condemn. Numerous other contributions in verse have appeared, such as M. C. Fuster's "Les Tendresses," Eugène Manuel's "Poésies du Foyer et de l'École," Émile Peyrefort's "La Vision," and G. Khan's "Les Palais Nomades"; but these are not reckoned to be of the first, perhaps hardly of the second quality. M. d'Hérison undertakes to defend Marshal Bazaine in his "Legend of Metz," not very successfully, and M. Darimon gives valuable information and judicious criticisms in his "Notes on the War of 1870," on the responsibility attaching to the chief actors in a disastrous drama, viz., Prince Napoleon and the Empress Eugénie. This so-called prince has entered the field against M. Taine, who published last year "Studies respecting Napoleon I," by putting forth a volume entitled "Napoleon and his Slanderers." Several monographs are worthy of mention: M. Welschinger's "Le Duc d'Enghien" is exhaustive and impartial; E. Lockroy's "Ahmed Le Boucher," better known as Djezzar Pasha, presents a lively picture; and the feats of arms of French soldiers in Africa, is the theme of M. Camille Ronsset's work, "L'Algérie de 1830 à 1840," not yet completed. Germany fills considerable space in the thought of France, as is shown by various publications, such as M. E. Lavisse's "Essay on Germany under the Empire"; M. C. Grad's "The German People, their Forces, and their Resources"; M. Grand-Carteret's "France judged by Germany," an ably arranged compilation; and a translation of M. J. Janssen's excellent work, "Germany at the End of the Middle Ages." Renan is as busy as ever, and his peculiar mode of dealing with Scripture history is exhibited in his "History of the People of Israel," of which Vol. I. was published last year. His skeptical proclivities fully display themselves in all that he does. M. J. Menant has published an excellent, conscientious work on "Nineveh and Babylon." In the history of manners and ideas, two books of M. Alfred Rambaud are particularly noticeable The one is "The History of Civilization in France, from its Origin to the Present Day"; the other is "The History of Contemporary Civilization in France"; both are able and well-timed contributions. In the drama there is little worth noting. "Much Ado About Nothing," has been adapted to the French stage, with success. M. Ludovic Halévy brought out a charming comedy, "The

Abbé Constantin," and Zola dramatized one of his novels called "Germinal." This latter was a failure, and the critics predict that Zola and his school, with their so-called naturalism and its abominations, have reached the end of their popularity. Just now there is a strong disposition to furnish psychological and analytical novels, of the former of which style Madame Malot's "Folie d'Amour," M. Hector Malot's "Conscience," and M. P. Bourget's "Mensonges," are good specimens, and much praised. M. O. Mirbeau's "L'Abbé Jules," and M. E. Gondeau's "Le Froc," profess to portray the French clergy; but they are pronounced to be one-sided and unfair. M. G. Ohnet is the author of "Volonté," which has reached its hundredth edition, and he has had equal success on the stage with his "Grande Marnière." Other amusing novels are "Vaillante," by J. Vincent; "Chonchette," by M. Prévost; "La Petite Fée," by M. A. Cim; "Les Fantaisies d'une Amazone," by M. J. Chassa; and "Les Seducteurs," by Gyp. The journals of Michelet, the well-known historian, have been published by his widow, and are very instructive and useful. A work entitled "The Great French Writers," is under way, and promises to be a gratifying success. M. E. Des Essarts's "Portraits de Maitres" is highly spoken of as an excellent work. A capital biography of Victor Cousin is contained in it. In philosophy, M. Paul Janet's contributions are valuable, as set forth in "Les Passions et les Caractères dans la Litterature du XVIIᵉ Siècle," and "Les Lettres de Madame de Grignan." The critics speak of these books in the very highest terms. In biography M. E. Sergy's book on Fanny Mendelssohn, is admirably done, and M. Gabriel Ferry's "Balzac et des Amies," is said to be very agreeable and successful. Social and moral science has received considerable attention in Arsène Houssaye's "Le Livre de Minuit," M. du Camp's "Paris Bienfaisant" and "La Vertu en France," M. C. Féré's "Dégénérescence et Criminalité," and Dr. A. Piéchaud's "Les Misère du Siècle." Lack of moral training is noted as something greatly needing a speedy remedy. Books of travel are, for the most part, written in healthy tone and spirit, calculated to benefit as well as instruct and amuse, such as Guillaumet's illustrated volume on Algiers; M. H. France's work about Spain, and M. H. Imbert's conscientions "Quatre Mois au Sahel." There seems to be a disposition to have regard to English works in the way of education, if one may judge from the titles of a number of books published this year, e. g., M. L. Carrau's work on religious philosophy in England from the time of John Locke to the present day; M. P. de Coubertin's "L'Education en Angleterre," and M. O. Gérard's series of papers on "Education and Instruction." Posthumous works of Victor Hugo continue to be issued, and the "Memoires," of M. Désiré Nisard (recently deceased) well deserve to be consulted. Jurisprudence is but slightly represented this year. One solid work may here be mentioned, viz., M. E. Beaussire's "Les Principes du Droit," which is supplementary to previous publications on this subject.

Germany.—Political changes and probable or possible results have had considerable influence upon the course and progress of literature in Germany during the year. Poetical contributions have been quite numerous, chiefly in the line of lyrical sentiment, bursts of socialism, and sturdy intolerance of authority. The names of A. Formey, Fr. Beck, and Marie Janitschek, occur in this connection, but their productions do not need special mention. In honor of Walther von der Vogelweide, the greatest lyric poet of the middle ages, a volume of poems has appeared (edited by A. Mayer) on the unveiling of the poet's statue at Botzen, his supposed birthplace. The "Tirolersagen," by the Countess Wilhelmine, and the powerful ballads on the struggle for freedom, by Count A. Wickenburg, form part of the book just named. "The Song of Humanity," by Heinrich Hart, claims to be an epic in the loftiest style, like the "Nibelungenlied" and Klopstock's "Messias." Judging from the first canto, which is all that has yet appeared, the critics give praise to the conception and optimistic views of the author, but doubt as to the ultimate result. R. Hamerling's "Homunculus" is said to combine universal mockery and burlesque satire. The form and meter of the poem remind one of Heine's "Atta Troll," only the satire is social instead of literary. Plutocracy and Judaism in its several forms are mercilessly chastised, and the poem ends, the critics tell us, "in shrill discord." The aged A. F. von Schack, the translator of Firdusi, though nearly blind and almost threescore years and ten, retains his mental vigor, as is shown in an attractive volume of memoirs entitled "Half a Century." George Ebers, the novelist, also appears for the first time as a poet in a romance entitled "Elifûn"; but the critics do not find much in it to praise. The dramatic results of the year are inconsiderable, though coming from the pens of Anzengruber, R. Voss, M. Greif, P. Heyse, and H. Lingg. Anzengruber's play, "Stahl und Stein," is a national drama well wrought out; R. Voss's "Bregitta" is remarkable for delineation of character; and M. Greif's "Die Pfalz am Rhein," Paul Heyse's "Die Weisheit Salomonis," and H. Lingg's "Die Bregenzer Klause" (a subject taken from the Thirty Years' War), are duly praised by the critics. Novels of the year have shown about the usual tendencies in the way of pessimism, realism, and discussions of social and psychological problems. There is a pessimistic tendency in Marie von Ebner-Eschenbach's "Das Gemeindekind," while C. Schwarzkopf's "Lebenskünstler" and H. Heiberg's "Der Januskopf" are expressly directed against pessimism. K. Fränzel's novel, "Dunst,"

is devoted to socialistic matters. F. Spielhagen has brought out a new story, "Noblesse Oblige"; T. Storm, the Nestor of German novelists, shows in his latest productions, "Es waren zwei Königskinder" and "Bei kleinen Leuten," incomparable freshness; and the pleasant story-teller Hans Hoffman gives some "Neue Corfugeschichten," which well deserve commendation. In the literature of "memoirs" special mention is to be made of the work of Duke Ernst II, of Saxe-Coburg-Gotha, who has played an important part in German politics and prefers to be his own biographer. The work is highly commended by the critics. Montgelas, a former Bavarian minister, and Gen. von Natzmer, military instructor of the late Emperor William, have added their contributions to this department. To these may be added Jakob Ph. Fallmerayer's letters and memoirs, as showing a man who was the friend of light and high principle in knowledge and religion. Schmeding has produced an excellent work on "Victor Hugo," which is of the nature of a message of peace from Germany to France. German art has received due attention in A. Rosenberg's "Die Münchner Malerschule seit 1871," in R. Dohme's encyclopædic book, "Geschichte der Deutschen Kunst," and in A. and F. Eggers's biography of Rauch, the sculptor of the Friedrichsdenkmal. Note also is made of the issue of the fourteenth and last volume of the "Fall of the House of Stuart," by Onno Klopp, a very able writer. Ranke's "Universal History" is continued by the hand of A. Dove, and will soon reach its end. In philosophy, the centenary of Schopenhauer has given rise to a number of publications relating to his rank and position as well as the true worth and value of his contributions to philosophic literature. Activity in this department is very considerable, and displays the usual drift of German writers and thinkers on questions of psychology, religion, morals, etc. We may mention, in conclusion, Roeber's "Die Philosophie Schopenhauer's"; Nietzsche's "Genealogie der Moral," according to which mankind is "wholly sunk in the mire"; Dilthey's "Einleitung in das Studium der Geisteswissenschaften"; and R. Encken's "Einheit des Geisteslebens in Bewusstsein und That der Menschheit," both directed against materialism; and, finally, J. H. Witte's "Das Wesen der Seele," which controverts earnestly the materialistic tendency toward "psychology without a soul."

Greece.—Literature, on the whole, is well represented in Greece this year. In theology Nicephorus Calogeras has printed from a Roman MS. a work of Euthymius Zygabenus, i. e., a commentary on the "Letters in the New Testament." Prof. A. D. Kyriakos has issued a collection of "Studies of Church History"; the orator Moschakis has published a series of "Ecclesiastical Speeches," delivered on various occasions; and Bishop Dorotheus has brought out Part I of the "Treasury of

Patrology," which promises to be useful as well as important. Love of philosophy is shown in bringing out editions of ancient Greek writers, by D. Semitelos and Dr. Bernardakis. The editorial work is said to be excellent. A good contribution to the study of the dialects of modern Greece has been made by A. Paspatis, favorably known by his studies on the gypsies, etc. The glossology and folk-lore of the Morea are treated of in the "Collection of Linguistic Material and Usages of the Greek People," by S. Papazapheiropulos. A lecture by J. Balabanis gives an interesting sketch of the dialect and customs of the Greeks of Pontus. An excellent report, by A. P. Kerameus, has been printed respecting palæographic and philological researches in Thrace and Macedonia. In history and biography the contributions have been few, and of no great moment. Two works relating to the history of Cephalonia have appeared, originally written in Italian, but translated into Greek, with annotations. M. Dimitsas has published an elaborate biography of Olympias, the mother of Alexander the Great. Dr. A. Kephallinos, Sanskrit instructor in the University of Athens, has undertaken to prove the strong influence of the Greek drama on the Indian, and N. Parissis has published an interesting book on Abyssinia. Dr. D. Chassiotis, in his "Essays and Addresses on Epirus," deals with politics and statistics. A. P. Kerameus (named above), in his "Contributions to the History of Neo-Hellenic Literature," has printed valuable epistles from Greek men of letters of the sixteenth and seventeenth centuries. Archæology occupies much attention, as is shown by Dr. Th. Sophulis, in a volume on "The Ancient Athenian School," and by Dr. P. G. Papandreu, in a work entitled "Azanias, an Account of the Ancient Cities of the Arcadian Azanias." The venerable A. Rhangabé, Nestor of Neo-Hellenic literature, has brought out the first parts of an "Archæological Dictionary," and Dr. Costomoiris has devoted a monograph to the ancient Greeks as aurists and oculists. Fiction holds its own in the newspapers, but only a few stories and tales appear in book-form. The drama and poetry are but poorly represented this year. The satirist, G. Suris, has published two new volumes of "Poems." Some good verse is found in J. Polemis's "Winter Blossoms"; and the poems of Marietta Betsu, now collected in a volume, "Laurels and Myrtles," are touching and impressive.

Holland.—There has been a large production of novels and novelettes in Holland this year; only a few, however, deserve mention here. Nessuno's "Jonkheer Beemsen" is of the psychological type: "Neven en Nichten," by the brothers Van Duyl, is remarkably free from conventionality; Van Loghem's "Victor" deals with idealism and realism in a rather unsatisfactory way; and L. Van Deysel, in his "Eene Liefde," follows the Frenchman

Zola's offensive naturalism. A fairy tale, "Kleine Johannes," comes from Frederik Van Eeden; it abounds in poetic sentiment and is well worked out. In poetry little has been done worth mentioning. Beets's "Winterloof" is amusing; W. Prius's poetry, "Liefde's Erinnering," is good in parts, but unequal; and Marie Bodaert's "Aquarellen," evince feeling and taste. A translation of Shakespeare, by Burgersdyk, is now nearly completed, and is much praised by the critics. Translations from the English and Hungarian have met with favor. In the drama, Van Meerbeke's little comedy, "Eene Ministerieele Crisis" is amusing, as is also Van Maurik's "Françoise's Opstel"; but neither is of a very high order. Mr. Emant's tragedy, "Adolf van Gelre," is in blank verse, and is highly spoken of by the critics. This same Adolf is the hero of a historical novel by Mr. Huf van Buren. Colonial history has been well cultivated this year by several good writers. We may name Annie Foore's sketches, "Uit het Indisch Familie-leven"; Eckart's "Indische Brieven aan een Staatsraad"; and Van Deventer's instructive "History of the Dutch in Java," which is now complete. Various registers and documents from archives have been brought out, and P. M. Netscher has written a good history of the Dutch colonies in the West Indies. The history of Holland itself in the latter half of the seventeenth century is well illustrated by Dutch writers, specially Sypestein and the author of the "Journalen Van C. Huygens," the younger, the secretary of William III. The fourth volume of G. K. Van Hogendorp's letters and memoirs (during 1787) has appeared; and the memoirs of his brother, Gen. Dirk Van Hogendorp, which are full of interesting adventures, have been published. Prof. Ten Brink is bringing out a new series of biographies, which are well written and valuable. Prof. Pierson has published the first of a series of essays, "Geestelyke Voorouders," the purpose of which is to illustrate the chief sources of civilization and spiritual life. Dr. Kuiper's "Euripides" is an earnest effort to defend that poet against Aristophanes's charge of atheism. He holds that the author of "Alcestis" was an honest skeptic, if nothing more. Two notable scholars, Mr. Rau and Mr. Vosmaer, have died during the year.

Hungary.—Literary production this year in Hungary offers a similar record to that of 1887. The Crown Prince has acquired reputation in ethnography and natural philosophy, and the Archduke Joseph has shown himself to be an excellent philologist, in a grammar of the gypsy language, if there be really such a language. The book is spoken of in high terms by the critics, and appears to be a valuable contribution to comparative as well as special philology. Prof. E. Thewrewk has added an appendix to the grammar, giving a very full account of the origin, language, history, etc., of the gypsies. Ural-Altaic studies have met with favor, but the question is still unsettled as to the origin of the present Hungarian language; whether it be of Turco-Tartar character, or one of the Ugrian or Ugro-Finnic languages. In connection with this point it may be mentioned that able scholars are making a special study of divers dialects, such as the Lapp, the Votyak, and Vogul. Prof. I. Budenz has finished his comparative grammar of the Ugrian languages. As belonging partly to philology and partly to history, honorable mention should be made of M. L. Réthy's "Origin of the Roumanian Nation and Language," a work of undoubted merit; and of M. Fred. Pesty's book on the topographical nomenclature of Hungary. In history proper there have appeared A. Szilagyi's "Transylvanian Parliamentary Records," Vol. XII, reaching to 1661; the "Diplomatarium Ragusanum"; and Prof. Marczali's third and concluding volume of his "History of Hungary in the Time of Joseph II." This last-named work gives universal satisfaction. We may note also "Old Hungary," by M. B. Grünwald, which is said to be a really fascinating book; Prof. G. Ballagi's "Hungarian Political Literature until 1825," a mass of curious and interesting documentary matter; and a clear and satisfactory account of the war of independence in 1848-'49, wherein the somewhat famous Görgey surrendered to the Russians. The critics hold that Görgey's character is fully vindicated in the book. Memoirs and biographies have received large attention. Among the workers in this line we name M. A. Zichy, who has edited all that relates to Count Stephen Széchenyi, the real founder of modern Hungary, whose speeches have been published through the care of the academy; N. Kubinyi, who has prepared an excellent biography of Emeric Thurzó (1598-1621); and D. Angyal, whose "Life of Emeric Tököly" is learned and valuable. A history of Hungarian agriculture and a history of the Hungarian theatre have appeared. The prolific M. Jókai continues to write novels in abundance, and M. A. Várády, in his "Doctor Faust," seems to be trying to introduce what is called naturalism into Hungary. M. A. Baksay, a Protestant minister, furnishes a collection of pleasant novelettes entitled "Footpath." In lyric and epic poetry the posthumous work of the great national poet, John Arany, is specially noteworthy. Various translations have been successfully made of Tennyson's "Idylls of the King," of Burns's "Songs," of Petrarch's "Sonnets," etc., all said to be marked by fidelity and vigor of language.

Italy.—Nothing striking or out of the usual order has occurred in literary matters during the present year in Italy. The founding of a chair in Rome, in 1886, for the exposition of the "Divina Commedia" of Dante has not resulted in what was hoped for and expected, viz., an increase in the study of the great poet's works. Carducci, a distinguished poet himself, was appointed professor, and began a course of lectures; G. Bovio also lectured on Dante in Naples; a Roman priest, G. Poletto, has brought out a Dantean dictionary, in seven volumes, with notes and illustrations drawn, in part, from St. Thomas Aquinas; and a Jesuit father named Cornoldi has published a commentary on the "Divina Commedia," in which he shows much enthusiasm for his author; but, in general, the movement is regarded as a failure by those most competent to pronounce judgment on the subject. As connected with Dantean literature, mention may be made of a commentary of L. de Biase, with notes by G. da Siena, and a reprint of the commentary of Stefano Talice di Ricaldone. Failure has also attended the attempt to revive the memory of and do justice to Giordano Bruno (burned by the Inquisition in Rome in 1600). An edition of the works of the philosopher of Nola is under way, it is true, but only three volumes have been published in nine years. The period most studied just now is the fifteenth and sixteenth centuries. A. Graf's "Attraverso il Cinquecento" relates to this portion of the past, and consists of various studies on Petrarchism and anti-Petrarchism, on Pietro Aretino, on Veronica Franco, etc. C. Gioda's book on Girolamo Morone (1470-1529) is well worth reading. A book by Salvagnini on St. Anthony of Padna has met with warm appreciation. E. Musatti is reprinting his work on Venice, the Doge, etc., with additions and corrections. F. Calvi has brought out a monograph on Bianca Maria Sforza Visconti. A work of superior merit comes from the pen of L. Chiappelli, commemorating the eighth century of the Bologna University. Bartoli is working on his full and elaborate "History of Italian Literature," of which (as noted last year) the sixth volume has been published. G. Diaconis has brought out Vol. I of a new biography of Dante, and V. Crescini gives the public the benefit of his careful studies on Boccaccio. Reprints of the ancient classics meet with favor, as do also those of standard Italian authors. The "Biblioteca di Autori Italiani" is well under way, and promises well for the future. In the history of art may be named a work by Pietro Caliari on Paul Veronese. A periodical devoted to art has been begun, and it is hoped may meet with full success. The historical societies have not been idle, but have published from their archives valuable documents, such as the "Gesta" of Frederick Barbarossa, the "Secondo Registro della Curia Arcivescovile di Genova," and the "Statutum Potestatis Communis Pistorii Anni MCCLXXXVI." G. Stocchi's history of the first conquest of Britain by the Romans and Castelli's second volume of the history of the Jews are praised by the critics, as are also E. Parri's "Vittorio Amedeo II ed Eugenio di Savoia" and E. Masi's volume, containing new facts about Napoleon's two wives. The critics aver that literature in Italy, whether in poetry or novels, has not been more brilliant than in other years, but rather less so. The best novelists, Farina, Matilde Serao, and Capuana have produced nothing new or remarkable, and novels by Rovetta, Giuriati, Caponi, and Martini are hardly above the average. In poetry, Carducci brought out last year a volume of "Rime Nnove," which contains some new pieces, with others before printed. He ranks among the best of the Italian poets.

Norway.—Literature in the larger sense of the word does not seem to have flourished in Norway this year. The social and ethical questions as to the relations of the sexes have aroused much discussion, and a number of volumes have been published advocating frequently very strange and even immoral doctrines. Björnstjerne Björnson has entered the field against Bohemian doctrines and practices, and during the first half of the year he traveled over Norway, Denmark, and Sweden, lecturing on "Monogamy and Polygamy," with great success. Jonas Lie has published "Married Life," which is much praised as being, on the whole, sound in principle and capitally worked out. It abounds in genial humor, and is widely read in Norway. A. Kielland bases his stories on the newest political development, but they are not esteemed to be of much account. Other works of fiction are Amalie Skram's "Two Friends," Per Sivle's "Bundle of Stories," A. Balle's "Young Ladies," K. Janson's "Norwegians in America." Mrs. Janson's "A Young Girl," K. Winterhjelm's "Countess Sissi," and Kristofer Kristofersen's new story, "Toilers of the Soil." He is now settled in Copenhagen, and in this story describes the hard conditions of life under which the crofters labor. Numerous tales and sketches have been published, mostly relating to home topics and of average merit. A few poems have been published, viz., K. Rander's "Norwegian Scenery, Impressions, and Pictures," N. C. Vogt's "Poems," and Sigurd Bödker's erotic verse, entitled "Elskov"—i. e., "Love." These two latter have made promising *débuts*, and it is hoped that they will in time enrich the scanty lyric poetry of Norway. Several important historical works have appeared, among which we note Prof. Ernst Sars's "History of Norway" (1319–1532), interesting and well written, and valuable ; and Prof. A. C. Bang's "History of the Norwegian Church under Catholicism," instructive and fairly wrought out. J. B. Halvorsen's excellent "Dictionary of Norwegian Authors" is making steady progress, and has reached half-way into the letter H. · Art criticism has been enriched by Prof. L. Dietrichsen's history of the origin and growth of the National Picture Gallery, and literary history has been increased by H. Jaeger's pleasant picture of the literary life and work of "Henrik Ibsen," on the sixtieth anniversary of the poet's birth. This distinguished son of Norway, Björnson's twin-brother, stands in the very front rank of the authors of his native

land. A cheap popular series of standard authors has recently appeared under the title "Library for the Thousand Homes." Periodical literature does not flourish in Norway, two of its chief representatives having failed for want of support.

Poland.—Polish literature has suffered much during the past year and a half by death among men of letters. The great humorist, Jan Lam, has passed away, as have also the historian, W. Kalinka, leaving his masterpiece, "The Diet of Four Years," incomplete, and J. L. Kraszewski, renowned as a voluminous writer of romances, poems, dramas, etc. A number of books, novels, a sort of autobiography, and a popular history of Poland, by the aged writer, have been published since his death. T. T. Jez, a contemporary of Kraszewski, still remains, and is very industrious. Madame Orzesko, H. Sienkiewicz, and B. Prus are in their prime, and are expected to do good service to literature. A new writer, Adam Szymanski, gives promise of large success, judging from his "Sketches," which are taken from the life of the Polish exiles in Siberia. Two historical novels have appeared, viz., "The Knights of King Albert," by S. Kaczkowski, and "M. Wolodyjowski," by Sienkiewicz. Humorous literature seems to flourish in Poland in the hands of Jordan, Junosza, Wilczynski, and Balucki. Historical stories and tales have been published by Bykowski, Rawita, and Rapacki. Rogosz's stories, "Upon the Waves of Destiny" and "Richard Gozdawa," are well written and interesting ; Gawalewicz's tales are much admired, as are also Dygasinski's studies, in story form, of the character of the Polish peasantry. Madame Orzesko's new novel, "On the Niemen," is pronounced to be one of her very best. A few other contributions in this line may here be named : "By Sunlight and Gaslight," by W. Gomulicki ; "Heroes of To-day," by F. Lentowski ; and "The Mistake," by B. Prus. In the drama something, but not much, has been done. K. Zalewski's comedy, "Apfel, the Wedded Couple," is very popular ; Mankowski's comedy, "The Eccentric," has been applauded ; and J. Blizinski's two farces are very laughable. In poetry Madame Maria Konopnicka has published a third series of "Poems," and Gomulicki has made his first collection on an important scale. Some new names may be mentioned : Otawa, Orlowski, and Londynski, men of ability, the critics say. The fine productions of Adam Asnyk, the first lyric poet of the day, have been translated into German. Historical studies have been prosecuted with zeal. T. Korzon has brought out the concluding volume of his monumental work on the internal condition of Poland under its last kings. M. Semkowicz obtained a prize from the Polish Society of Paris for a monograph subjecting J. Dlugosz's "History of Poland" to a thorough critical analysis. Several other volumes have been published, among which may be named here W. Zakrzewski's work on the reign of King Stephen Bathory. The critical "Essays" of P. Chmielowski deserve mention, as do also the lectures, delivered in Florence, by the distinguished poet, T. Lenartowicz, on "The Character of Slavo-Polish Poetry." Translations also, into German and Spanish, of eminent writers are worthy of record. In conclusion, note must be made of a volume of economics, entitled "Galicia's Poverty," by S. Szczepanowski. It is very able, and the sad story told in it has made a profound impression in Poland.

Russia.—Death has left its mark on Russian literature this year in the removal from earth of V. Garshin, only thirty-three, and yet a writer worthy of being ranked with Tourguéneff and Tolstoi. He put an end to his own life, in a state of partial insanity, and his literary remains consist of two small volumes of "Tales." These are mournful records of what he saw, felt, and suffered. In this connection we may note also the death of Rosenheim, eminent as a writer of satirical and other poetry. In the way of novels, tales, and sketches of various sorts, the production has been quite abundant, and in the main satisfactory. Korolenko, who excels in drawing the Siberian runaway, presents another picture, in his latest novel, "During the Journey"; it is highly praised for its power and skill. A lady, signing herself Krestovski, furnishes a new novel, "The Duties," which belongs to the order of psychical analysis, and has met with much favor. Another novel has appeared from the same author, entitled "After the Deluge." Madame Shabelskaya, called the poet of the peasant life of Little Russia, published a novel, entitled "Three Currents," describing in one the new religion of Count Tolstoi, under the name of "Religion of Buddha." Matchtett has brought out a volume of "Silhouettes," which have been well received. Other novels and stories that may be named here, are: Karonin's "My World," Mrs. Dmitrieva's "The Prison," Shiloff's "After a Long Separation," Muravlin's "Not Quite Love," Volski's "The Wife," and Tchehoff's "Steppe." Several interesting books have appeared, undertaking to discuss important topics among the peasantry, like the "Woman Question," and various economical conditions of affairs. X. G. Uspenski's "A Ticket" and "Figures in Life" are of this kind. Engelhardt's "Letters from the Country" and Lineff's descriptions of prison-life are good specimens of what the critics call "artistic ethnography." Nadson, the poet, died last year (as noted); the posthumous edition of his verses is very popular. In the field of memoirs the crop is rich. Gontcharoff's "In the Mother Country" takes the lead in giving various types from Russian provincial life half a century ago. Antokolski's "Memoirs," though deficient in literary form, furnish a heartrending picture of the great sculptor's sad and deplorable career. The memoirs of Count Sollogub, Danilevski, Polevoi, Ghilaroff-Platonoff, may be noted.

Literary criticism is well illustrated in Orest Miller's "Russian Authors since Gogol"; the third volume is taken up with Aksakoff, Melnikoff, and Ostrovski, with articles on modern authors. Arsenieff has brought out two volumes of "Critical Studies of Russian Life," and Skabitchevski deals with "The Folk Novelists." Pypin continues his studies of Russian literature before Pushkin and in Pushkin's time, and Timoféeff has published a volume on the undeniable "Influence of Shakespeare on the Russian Drama." Tolstoi's "War and Peace" is discussed by Prof. Karyéeff very ably. Other publications in this line are valuable. In history, Stasulevitch's "History of Mediæval Times," Vol. III, brings the story down to the end of the thirteenth century. Mention also is proper here of Prof. Bulitch's "History of the Earlier Years of the Kazan University," of Vol. IV, of Andrievitch's "History of Siberia," in time of Catherine II; and the "Exterior Policy of Nicholas I" during the Crimean War. Sukhomlinoff has finished his "History of the Russian Academy." In philosophy, P. Lavroff has begun the publication of his "History of Thought." It is the life-work of a veteran laborer and very able expositor of the subject, and is to be published in four volumes. Kavelin's "Problems of Ethics" have appeared in a separate volume, and are remarkably well written. In archæology, Count Bobrinsky has published "The Kurgans around Smyela," and Ptashitski has brought out a "Description of the Lithuanian State Archives." Prof. Tagantseff makes public his "Lectures on Criminal Law," which contain among other things Drill's exhaustive study of "Juvenile Offenders in Russia and Western Europe." In natural science great interest is manifested, and scientific periodicals are flourishing.

Spain.—Progress in science and letters continues unchecked in Spain, and education and culture are spreading throughout the kingdom. The number of books published in 1888 exceeds by far the sum total of other years. Poetry of every description, lyric, epic, or dramatic, including works of fiction in prose, is being abundantly supplied. Although the master poets, Nuñez de Arce, Camposmor, and Zorilla, have done little or nothing this year, yet there is a large number of younger and enthusiastic men striving to supply the deficiency. Among these may be named J. de las Cuevas, in his "El Espejo del Alma"; Cubillo, in his "Ensayos Poeticos"; Iglesias, in his "Al Fin de la Jornada"; and Bustillo, in a collection of satirical romances revealing superior talent, entitled "El Ciego de Buenavista." In the drama light, short pieces, or *sainetes*, operettas, and the like, are more popular than the classical tragedy or modern melodrama. Novel-writing keeps pace with the progress noted last year, as is shown by publications of Garcia Nieto, Palacio Valdés, Emilio de la Cerda, Ramon Ortega, Gabriel Moreno, and Carlos

Maria Ocantos. Angelon has brought out a charming novel, "Espinas de una Flor" (Part II of "Flor de un Dia"), and Doña E. P. Bazan sustains her high reputation (noted last year) in her " Los Pazos de Ulloa," Vol. II, and " Mi Romeria," or pilgrimage. Several other ladies are active in this line. In general literature, criticism, and bibliography, improvement is visible. Juan Valera shows this plainly in his "Apuntes sobre el Nuevo Arte de Escribir Novelas," as do also Miguel Alvarez, in " Tentativas Literarias," and Leopoldo Alas, in " Folletos Literarios." Historical science is also making rapid advance, and numerous students and explorers are busily occupied in searching old libraries for rare manuscripts, unpublished documents, etc. M. Fuente's general History of Spain (1850-'62) in twenty-six volumes, is being reprinted, with a continuation by Juan Valera. Balaguer, whose "History of Catalonia" was noted last year, has brought out the eleventh, twelfth, and thirteenth volumes of his complete works; V. Lafuente is steadily occupied in critical studies of the history of Aragon ; and Pella y Forgas has reached the seventh volume of his archæological and topographical description of Ampurdan in Catalonia. Provincial and local history is cultivated with spirit and success. The number of publications is too great to allow of naming them here, save only Ciriaco Vigil's " Asturias Monumental, Epigráfica y Diplomática," three large volumes, with illustrations; O. y Rubio's " Investigaciones sobre la Historia de Valladolid"; and Vol. XV of the richly illustrated work, "España y sus Monumentos." The Geographical Society's "Boletin," two volumes, shows that considerable impulse has been given to this study. Two works on Morocco have appeared; the Philippine Islands have been described by Captain Moreno, and " La Isla de la Paragua," by Captain Oanga-Arguelles, both of the royal navy. A volume on the Nicaragua Interoceanic Canal by Sepulveda, and further " Noticias de Christoval Colon," by Fernandez Duro, are worthy of note here, as of special interest to Americans. In the way of reprints, or continuations of important works, much has been done, such as Lopez de Gomara's " Conquest of Mexico," M. Pelayo's " La Ciencia Española," Vols. I and II; Arteche's " War of Independence," and Bethencur's " Anales de la Nobleza Española," Vol. VIII. On the whole, the outlook in regard to Spanish literature is decidedly encouraging.

Sweden.—As noted last year, women in Sweden continue to occupy a foremost place in literature. Mrs. Benedictson's " Fru Marianne" was noted in the record of 1887 as one of the best novels published. We may add that it carried off a prize from the Swedish Academy and attained great popularity. Mrs. Benedictson writes under the pen-name Ernst Ahlgren. Another lady, Madame A. Agrell, furnishes a collection of tales, " In the Country," which are pleasing and have been well

received. A. Strindberg, the Zola representative in Sweden, writes with his usual vigor and ability in " The Inhabitants of Hemsö " ; but his invectives against family life, and his attacks on the female sex, especially married women, are offensive and discreditable in a high degree. Two of Strindberg's adherents have written comedies, viz., Per Staaff and G. af Geijerstam. The former's, entitled "Svea's Banner," is severe on what is called the boulevard press, and the latter's, named " Father-in-law," ridicules young officers' intrusions into families to catch prizes in marriage. The drama is weak this year. Fiction, on the other hand, is flourishing. This is shown by the large number of novels and tales published in 1888, among which we may name Ernst Arpi's "From a Plebeian Borough," Anna Wahlenberg's " With our Neighbors," Hilma Strandberg's " Westward," i. e., life on the west coast, and a new series of tales by Tor Hedberg, son of the veteran Frans Hedberg. C. D. af Wirsén, both rival and once friend of Count Snoilsky, and champion of the altar and the throne, has published a volume of poetry displaying much ability ; and A. U. Bååth has given a long description in verse of persecutions for witchcraft and sorcery in Sweden in the seventeenth century. A work on sociology, entitled "Om Nationernas Sammanvåxning," by G. Björklund, has attracted much attention, especially with reference to the dispute between free trade and protection. Political history has been enriched by a new volume of O. S. Rydberg's " Sweden's Treaties with Foreign Powers," 1534 to 1560. The same writer has brought out an essay on the meeting at Kalmar, 1397. A. Blomberg supplies a popular work on Charles XIV (Bernadotte). A. Nyström is very busy on his work (noted in last year's record) respecting the history of civilization and culture. S. J. Boëthius has completed his history of the French Revolution; and J. Thyrén gives a documentary history of the armed neutrality and the peace under Napoleon, including also the European policy from the peace of Amiens (1802) to the rupture between France and England (1803). Prof. G. Ljunggren has added a new volume to his great work, " The Annals of the Polite Literature of Sweden (1809-'14) "; and H. Schück is continuing his history of Swedish literature. The distinguished poetess, Anna Maria Lenngren, is handsomely dealt with in a monograph by Karl Warburg; and L. Luoström's " The Swedish Academy of Art during the First Century of its Existence," is much praised by the critics. A few volumes in general literature may be noted in conclusion. Dictionaries in that phenomenon of the day, Volapük, have been published by G. Liedbeck. C. Lundin has brought out a description (splendidly illustrated) of modern Stockholm. In a volume for young people the historian Victor Rydberg tells the story of " The Myths of our Fathers." E. Dahlgren addresses booklovers in a volume entitled "The Public Libraries of Sweden"; the Norwegian professor L. Dietrichsen, after lecturing on the subject, has published a book on "Fashions and the Reform of Dress"; and the writer whose pseudonym is Sigurd, has issued a new volume of his popular humorous tales.

LOUISIANA. State Government.—The following were the State officers during the year: Governor, Francis T. Nicholls, Democrat; Lieutenant-Governor, James Jeffries; Secretary of State, Leonard F. Mason; Treasurer, William H. Pipes; Auditor, Ollie B. Steele; Superintendent of Public Education, Joseph A. Breaux; Attorney-General, Walter H. Rogers; Chief-Justice of the Supreme Court, Edward Bermudez; Associate Justices, Felix P. Poché, Samuel D. McEnery, Charles E. Fenner, and Lynn B. Watkins.

Finances.—The following statement exhibits the condition of the State treasury during the years 1887 and 1888, till April 30:

GENERAL FUND, 1887.

Receipts during 1887	$347,965 40
Receipts during 1888	158,950 16
Total revenue tax and licenses	$506,915 56
Expenditures in 1887	$320,313 17
Expenditures in 1888	198,263 96
	518,577 13
Amount overdrawn, April 30	$11,661 57

The overdraft was caused by taking up loans of various public institutions in anticipation of settlements of tax-collectors that were expected to reach the treasury in April. There remained but $32,264.56 of warrants against the general fund of 1887 unpaid May 1, 1888, and about twenty settlements to be completed. All the loans made by public institutions for the year 1887 have been paid, except that of the State Normal School.

CURRENT SCHOOL FUND, 1887.

Receipts during 1887	$34,301 04
Receipts during 1888	160,356 01
Total receipts	$194,657 05
Expenditures during 1887	$10,391 16
Expenditures during 1888	147,299 15
	$157,690 31
Cash balance, April 30, 1888	$36,966 74

INTEREST TAX FUND, 1887.

Receipts during 1887	$82,632 33
Receipts during 1888	381,560 57
Total receipts	$464,192 90
Expenditures during 1887	$82,307 46
Expenditures during 1888	372,398 10
	454,705 56
Cash balance, April 30, 1888	$9,487 34

All advances made by the banks on coupon account have been repaid, except about $30,000. The State can secure any advances required for cashing coupons promptly at a rate not exceeding four per cent. a year, and arrangements can be made for loans to public institutions as required at a rate not exceeding five per cent. a year, provided the tax levy is adequate for interest requirements, and the general fund appropriations are confined strictly within the estimated revenues.

GENERAL ENGINEERS' FUND.

Receipts during 1887	$163,825 63
Receipts during 1888	102,154 22
Total receipts	$265,979 85
Expenditures during 1887	$162,565 10
Expenditures during 1888	86,630 10
	249,195 20
Cash balance, April 30, 1888	$16,784 65

GENERAL FUND, 1888.

Receipts to April 30, inclusive	$229,106 49
Expenditures to April 30, inclusive	169,722 79
Cash balance, April 30, 1888	$59,373 70

The total amount of general fund warrants outstanding May 1 for 1888, was $26,331.64.

Legislative Session.—The Legislature was convened at Baton Rouge on May 14, and adjourned on July 11. The Governor-elect, Gen. Francis T. Nicholls, was inaugurated on May 21. Randall L. Gilson was elected by the Legislature on May 22 to succeed himself, and on May 29 Edward D. White was chosen U. S. Senator to succeed James B. Eustis.

Revision of the Laws.—In pursuance of an act of 1884, authorizing a committee selected by the General Assembly to revise the general statutes of the State, and to incorporate them into the Revised Statutes, and to complete and arrange a code of criminal practice and a penal code, the committee arranged the laws into one volume. No arrangement or codification of the code of criminal practice and a penal code was made. The Revised Statutes were presented to the General Assembly at its session in 1886, but no action was then taken on the report of the committee. The revision will be continued so as to include the civil code and code of criminal practice and penal code.

The Swamp-Land Decision.—The Court of Claims in Washington, D. C., on January 30, rendered a judgment in favor of the State of Louisiana for about $43,000, being the five-per-cent. funds and swamp-land indemnities that had been applied as a credit by the U. S. Treasury Department on the interest on Louisiana bonds held by the U. S. Treasurer as part of the Indian trust funds.

The court held that the United States was a trustee to ascertain and pay over to Louisiana the amount of both funds, and it is also held that Louisiana then became a trustee of the fund to apply it to the building of post-roads and redemption of swamp-lands in accordance with the acts of Congress, and, therefore, it was not applicable to any State debt. The interest that had accrued was not equal to the amount of the fund due the State, and the Treasury Department had, therefore, credited a part which would not mature till 1894, and held about $12,700 until interest should accrue. It is presumed that this decision will not be appealed from by the United States, since this is the logical outcome of a former decision for $71,000 which was affirmed by the United States Supreme Court, and this case turned on that decision.

Levees.—During 1886–'88 there were 118 contracts for levee work, involving 69 miles of new levee, and the enlargement and raising of 49½ of old levee, at a cost of from ten to twenty-nine and a half cents a cubic yard, averaging eighteen and a half cents a cubic yard. The total quantity of earth-work under these contracts amounts to 3,372,828 cubic yards, at a cost of $618,622. Besides this work the Fifth Levee District has constructed 15½ miles of new levee, and has raised and enlarged 30 miles of old levee, amounting to 1,655,000 cubic yards, at a cost of $362,590. The Fifth Levee District has also contributed $9,500 for levee work in the lower part of Chicot County, Ark. The Tensas Basin Levee District has also contracted for work in Desha and Chicot Counties, Ark., involving the building of 6 miles of new levee, and 8½ miles of old levee, amounting to 592,134 cubic yards of earth at a cost of $150,000. The Mississippi River Commission, in consideration of the work done in Arkansas by Louisiana, consented to close all gaps between Amos Bayou and the Louisiana line, that had not been provided for. The work is nearly complete. It involves the raising and enlargement of 20 miles of old levee and the building of 17 miles of new levee, 1,500,000 cubic yards, at an expenditure of $320,000.

The work thus accomplished and in progress, with that done by the local levee boards, should, before another high-water season, give a continuous line of levees from the highlands south of Arkansas river to the upper limits of this State, and cut off the overflow from this source that has heretofore inundated the parishes lying between the Ouachita and the Mississippi rivers, and that was without remedy by any work possible within the boundaries of the State. The creation of the corporations of the Fifth Louisiana and the Tensas Basin Levee Districts by the General Assembly in 1886, has been the most important levee legislation of recent years. It enabled the districts to do essential work outside of the State's boundaries. The Tensas Basin Levee District has entered into agreement with the Louisiana, Arkansas and Missouri Railroad Company to construct an embankment on the west side of Bayou Macon and across the streams and lowlands known as Bœuff Cut-off. The construction of this work, if it has the proper height and strength to confine the floods, will cost a large sum. It will give additional security against overflow, and protect a greater portion of the district independently of levees on the front. The commission has also assisted, within the past two years, in the construction of the Kemp and Deer Park Levees in the Fifth District, and allowed $40,000 for the construction of the Morganza in consideration of Louisiana contributing the balance

necessary to the completion of the levee, and has also expended $75,000 in the repair of other levees. The aggregate work undertaken by the State, the Fifth District, the Tensas District, and the levee districts in the State in the past two years, is 90 miles of new levee, and 70½ miles of old levee raised and enlarged, requiring 5,684,126 cubic yards at a cost of about $1,162,696.

Sugar.—Efforts have been made to secure the location of the sugar-experimental station at Audubon Park. If successful, it is intended to devote fifty acres for a model sugar-farm, where a laboratory will be fitted up and all improvements in sugar-culture and methods in agriculture will be demonstrated. The experiments on the diffusion process conducted by the Department of Agriculture created considerable interest and were closely watched by the planters. The proposed reduction of 50 per cent. in the tariff of sugar by Congress, led to a delegation being sent to present the claims of sugar before the Finance Committee of the United States Senate, and protest against the proposed reduction, claiming that the sugar-producing and refining interests of the country give employment to several millions of our population, hence they should not ruthlessly be destroyed, particularly as they are rapidly progressing and promise to supply a large portion of the entire needs of the United States.

Against the claim that the sugar industry was non-progressive, and that, as the sugar-cane had never become thoroughly acclimated in this country, the domestic product could never be raised to a plane of successful competition with that of foreign countries, it was shown that, in spite of the destruction of the sugar industry by war, it was promptly rehabilitated, and from 5,000 tons at the date of resumption, the production has been increased to nearly 200,000 tons. This great progress has been made in the face of extreme depression in prices, lack of adequate capital, and frequent disasters from riverfloods. That sugar-cane had not become adapted to the climate, was also conclusively denied by the recital of the fact that the sugar-crop has never failed, while nearly every other crop in the country has frequently met with disaster. Besides, the productiveness of the cane has been steadily increased by careful cultivation, and has been demonstrated to be susceptible of still greater improvement. The progressive spirit of the sugar-planters was proved by the fact that, in spite of scant means, such improvements have been made in extracting machinery as have up to date resulted in almost doubling the output of many sugar-houses. The planters' memorial sets forth the fact that many millions of capital were invested in sugar-culture, and that the annual output averaged in value fully $20,000,000. Of the proceeds of the crop, fully 70 per cent. is consumed by labor, about 500,000 persons, more than half the population of Louisiana, being supported by the industry.

Political.—The Democratic State Convention was held in Baton Rouge on January 10, and the following ticket was nominated: For Governor, Francis T. Nicholls; Lieutenant-Governor, James Jeffries; Auditor, O. B. Steele; Treasurer, W. H. Pipes; Secretary of State, L. F. Mason; Attorney-General, W. H. Rogers; Superintendent of Education, Joseph A. Breaux. The platform included the following:

That the levee system of the State is a necessity for the protection of the lives and property of our citizens, and we pledge ourselves to develop, maintain, and protect the same to the fullest extent consistent with the finances of the State as absolutely essential to the happiness and prosperity of our people.

We are opposed to the employment of the penitentiary convicts of the State in such manner as to bring the convict labor in competition with free labor.

We invite to the fertile fields of Louisiana immigrants from all lands, with the assurance that they shall find here a hearty welcome and a happy home.

The Republican State Convention was held in New Orleans on January 23. The following ticket was nominated: For Governor, H. C. Warmoth; Lieutenant-Governor, Andrew Hero, Jr.; Secretary of State, John F. Patty; Treasurer, B. F. Flanders; Attorney-General, Robert Ray; Auditor, James Forsythe. The platform contained the following:

We condemn the free-trade tendencies of President Cleveland's Administration and the organization of the House of Representatives at Washington, whereby a free-trader was made Speaker, who has in turn constituted the committee of ways and means in such manner as to insure an attack upon all the protected industries of the country, and especially those of our State—sugar and rice; and we see with amazement that our representatives in Congress consorted with and voted for the organization which we condemn.

Believing it to be the duty of the National and State governments to foster and protect the agricultural and manufacturing interests and industries of the State, we pledge our cordial endeavors to assist in adequate legislation for the safety and security of the American principle of protection to all of our industries, without regard to time, place, or location, to the end that labor and capital shall be secure in their rights and privileges from foreign competition and interference.

We declare our approbation of the legislation of Congress, wherein appropriation of $15,000 per annum is made for agricultural stations in the different States; and we recommend our Legislature to supplement said appropriation, so that we may have the intent of the law carried out, to the end that we may ascertain the best practice of agriculture for our various products.

We invite *bona-fide* immigration to our State, but we condemn the importation of contract labor, which tends to debase the labor of our own people and deprive them of the employment which they would otherwise enjoy.

We condemn the use of convict labor outside of public works, and demand that it shall not be allowed to come in competition with free labor.

The Young Men's Democratic Association held a meeting in New Orleans on March 28, and adopted the following platform:

That we call on the citizens of New Orleans to assist this association in its honest endeavors to bring about an era of good government, and we declare our principles to be that we pledge ourselves to have clean streets, good drainage, better pavements, and the best of levee and shipping facilities; to insist that proper drainage-machines, with a full supply of coal and

faithful and skilled men to work them, shall save this city from such overflows as have lately made lakes of the lands in the rear parts of this city, and have brought desolation to these districts and bred pestilence and fever among the dwellers therein. To strike from the pay-rolls political dead-heads, and give employment to those who can and are willing to work, so that for each dollar spent there shall be a dollar's work done, and that those who do a dollar's work shall get a dollar's pay, and that no city official shall draw two salaries. To have the police force purged and remodeled and so fairly paid that proper men may be induced to serve. To have good schools provided and competent teachers given full pay. To insist that the taxes shall be honestly and closely collected, but fairly and without oppression; and to see that the public funds derived therefrom shall be so appropriated to legitimate expenditures and within legal limits that city warrants shall be worth par, and city employés be enabled to cash their warrants every month without discount. To insist that the taxes we pay shall be applied to giving us that protection to life and property to which we are entitled, and that they shall be expended in making this city a clean, healthy, and attractive abode, where real estate shall be worth owning, and where for every store, office, or residence there shall be a satisfied tenant and a contented landlord; and where for twelve months of the year those seeking employment may find it at remunerative wages or salaries. To have vice and corruption suppressed and all legitimate enterprises fostered and encouraged; and to have that efficient and honest administration of public affairs that will engender confidence in the community and bring capital and immigration to this locality. To have the polls so guarded that good citizens will be afforded every facility to cast their votes, and that they will be protected from any indignity or molestation while so doing; to have as our commissioners at the ballot-boxes to represent this association men of integrity and force, who will see that all fair ballots are counted and all fraudulent votes rejected, and to insist that in the exercise of their duties they will receive proper protection.

They also issued the following ticket: For Mayor, Joseph A. Shakspeare; Treasurer, Joseph N. Hardy; Comptroller, Otto Thomann; Commissioner of Public Works, Gen. G. T. Beauregard; Commissioner of Police and Public Buildings, Thomas Agnew.

The election was held on April 18, and Gen. Nicholls and the other candidates on the Democratic ticket were elected by a majority of 85,786 in a total vote of 188,728.

The Reform ticket in New Orleans received the support of the Republicans, and defeated the regular Democratic ticket by 7,000 majority. Gen. Beauregard resigned his office on July 23, and was succeeded by E. T. Leche.

In the presidential election, Mr. Cleveland received 85,032 votes; Gen. Harrison, 30,484; Gen. Fisk, 160; and Mr. Streeter, 39—a Democratic majority of 54,548. A Republican Congressman was returned from New Orleans. The five other members of the Congressional delegation are Democrats. The State Legislature contains 38 Democrats and 2 Republicans in the Senate, and 86 Democrats and 12 Republicans in the House.

LOZIER, CLEMENCE SOPHIA, physician, born in Plainfield, N. J., Dec. 11, 1813; died in New York city, April 26, 1888. She was the youngest daughter of David Harned, and was educated at Plainfield Academy. Subsequently she removed with her parents to New York city, and in 1829 married Abraham W. Lozier, an architect. Her husband's health soon began to fail, and she established a school for young ladies, which she conducted for eleven years. During this time she was associated with Mrs. Margaret Pryor in visiting the poor

CLEMENCE SOPHIA LOZIER.

and abandoned under the auspices of the Moral Reform Society. From her mother she had inherited a strong liking for medicine, and, under the direction of her brother, Dr. William Harned, introduced into her school studies on physiology, anatomy, and hygiene. Five years after the death of her husband she went to Albany, and for a time was at the head of a private school. She then determined to study medicine, and in 1849 attended lectures at the Rochester Eclectic Medical College. Subsequently she entered the Syracuse Medical College, where she received her degree in 1853 with the highest honors. Dr. Lozier then returned to New York city and at once began to practice as a homœopathist. Her success was unusual, and her income is said to have exceeded $20,000 a year in her best days. In the surgery required by the diseases of women she showed remarkable skill, and performed many capital operations. In 1860 she began a course of lectures on medical subjects in her own parlors, the outcome of which was the formation of a ladies' medical library association, and this in 1863 was merged into a medical college association. The latter through her efforts became the New York Medical College and Hospital for Women, of which she was clinical professor of diseases of women and children and also for more than twenty years dean of the faculty. This institution was the first distinctively woman's medical college established in New York State. She took an active inter-

est in all that pertained to the elevation of her sex, and was an intimate friend of Susan B. Anthony, Elizabeth Cady Stanton, and other well-known woman-suffragists. For thirteen years she was President of the New York City Woman - Suffrage Association, and for four years of the National Woman's Suffrage Association. She also held office in other reform and philanthropic associations, and was an occasional contributor to medical journals.

LUTHERANS. The year 1888 was memorable to Lutherans in the United States, since it was the two hundred and fiftieth anniversary of the organization of the first Lutheran congregation among the Swedes at Christina (now Wilmington), Del. In 1638 there were on the shores of the Delaware fifty Swedish and Finnish Lutherans, with one pastor, using Fort Christina as their church, and a few Dutch Lutherans, without pastor or church, on Manhattan Island (New York); in 1888 there were more than 1,033,000 Lutherans scattered throughout every State and Territory of the United States and the provinces of Canada, having 57 synodical organizations, more than 7,500 properly organized congregations, ministered to by more than 4,000 pastors, supporting numerous educational and benevolent institutions, and carrying on extensive home, foreign, and immigrant missions.

The statistics for 1888 show a large increase, as well in the number of ministers as in congregations and members. According to the best authorities, the Lutheran Church now numbers 4,426 clergymen, 7,415 congregations, and 1,033,846 communicants, a net increase over the figures of last year of 204 clergymen, 250 congregations, and 38,872 communicants. The membership here given does not include the baptized membership of the church, which, if given, would increase the aggregate to nearly 4,000,000. The various institutions are: Twenty-three theological seminaries or theological departments in colleges, 25 colleges, 28 academies, 10 ladies' seminaries, and 48 benevolent institutions. More than a hundred periodicals are published, in the English, German, Norwegian, Danish, Icelandic, and Finnish languages. The following is a brief *résumé* of the more important events during the year within the general bodies, and of matters that deserve to be put on record. Only two of the general bodies held conventions—the general council and the synodical conference.

General Synod.—This body, organized in 1821, embraces the following 23 district synods (almost exclusively English): Maryland, West Pennsylvania, Hartwick (N. Y.), East Ohio, Franckean (N. Y.), Allegheny, East Pennsylvania, Miami (Ohio), Wittenburg (Ohio), Olive Branch (Ind.), Northern Illinois, Central Pennsylvania, Iowa, Northern Indiana, Southern Illinois, Central Illinois, New York and New Jersey, Susquehanna, Pittsburg, Kansas, Nebraska, German Wartburg, and Middle Tennessee, numbering 957 clergymen, 1,346 congregations, and 146,871 members. There are within its bounds 5 theological seminaries, 4 colleges, 3 academies, 2 ladies' seminaries, and 2 orphans' homes. The thirty-fourth biennial convention of this body will be held at Allegheny, Pa., June 12, 1889. For the report of the last convention see "Annual Cyclopædia" for 1887, p. 447.

General Council.—This body, organized in 1867, is composed of ten district synods (English, German, and Scandinavian), as follows: Ministerium of Pennsylvania, ministerium of New York, synods of Pittsburg, Ohio, Swedish Augustana, Canada, Texas, Indiana, Norwegian Augustana, and Iowa (the two latter being merely advisory members), embracing a membership of 1,120 clergymen, 1,949 congregations, and 292,964 members. The Michigan synod severed its connection with the Council, and the Danish synod, a body consisting of 38 ministers, 88 congregations, and 5,200 members, made overtures for membership in the near future. The educational and benevolent institutions within the bounds of this general body may be summarized as follows: Four theological seminaries, 7 colleges, 6 classical seminaries, 1 ladies' seminary, 2 conservatories of music, 15 orphans' homes, 9 hospitals, 1 deaconess institution at Philadelphia, and 1 immigrant mission (Swedish, German, and Danish) at New York. The General Council held its twenty-first annual convention for the first time west of the Mississippi river, in St. John's English Lutheran Church, Minneapolis, Minn. The convention was opened with the full communion service of the Lutheran Church. The opening sermon was delivered by the president, the Rev. A. Spaeth, D. D., of the theological seminary at Philadelphia, based on Gal. iii, 9, "The nations and the Gospel." After the close of divine service the council was organized for the transaction of business. The district synods were represented by 64 clerical and 39 lay delegates, the Texas synod not being represented by delegates. The Rev. Joseph A. Seiss, D. D., LL. D., pastor of the Church of the Holy Communion, Philadelphia, was elected president. The work of the convention consisted of the consideration and action on the reports of standing committees on missions, education, liturgics, etc.

Home Missions.—This work is intrusted to three committees—English, German, and Scandinavian—which have charge of mission stations and missionaries, independent of the district synods. The English committee reported 5 missionaries and 10 missions, as follows: Illinois, 2; Ohio, 1; Minnesota, 6; Dakota, 1. The receipts for the year were $4,763.64; the expenditures, $3.892.50. The German committee reported 6 missionaries in their employ in Texas, Nebraska, and Dakota. Seven young men have been received from Kropp, Germany, and 27 students in the same institution have received aid from the committee. The receipts were $4,364.30, of which $1,225 were spent for missionary work in America, the remainder for the institution at Kropp. The Council decided that it was impracticable to enter into organic connection with the Rev. J. Paulsen's institution at Kropp. The following action was taken:

1. That it is not expedient for the General Council to have a theological seminary in Germany to which the entire theological education of our future German pastors should be committed.

2. That the chief source of supply of laborers in the German, as in our other mission fields, should be found in our own congregations; and that such persons should be trained, as far as possible, in our own institutions.

3. That, for this end, our pastors should be delegated to find devout young men in their congregations who are willing to enter the ministry; and that Wagner College, in Rochester, be strongly recommended as a proper institution to prepare them for the seminary in Philadelphia.

4. That, nevertheless, under the present circumstances it is highly desirable and necessary that young men should be secured from Germany, and that for this end the committee shall be empowered to enter into arrangements with one or more institutions in Germany; provided, first, that these arrangements receive the approval of the General Council; and, second, that such institutions have only a preparatory character.

The Swedish committee's report was read by the Rev. S. P. Lindahl. The work is chiefly carried on by the conferences of the Swedish synod, and this committee has charge of the territory outside of these. The committee reported missionaries and missions in nearly all the States and Territories of the United States, as well as in Canada. The receipts of the general committee amounted to $5.977.79; those of the entire synod for its numerous missions, $14,538.22; and for the Utah mission, $2,914.70; an aggregate of $18, 822. The report was so full of interesting and gratifying facts, that it called forth the following action:

Resolved, That we have heard with great gratification the report of the Swedish Augustana synod's missionary work, and express our gratitude to God for the marked blessing he has laid upon its faithful efforts and the honor he has conferred upon it in calling it to a task so great in its proportions and so rich in its promises.

Efforts were made at this convention to centralize all the missionary operations of the General Council and appoint one or more missionary secretaries, who shall devote their whole time to this important and ever-increasing work. The following is a summary of all the home missionary operations in the Council— English, German, and Swedish—not including, however, a number of important missions carried on and entirely supported by individual congregations: 270 missionaries and 392 congregations, for which were contributed $48,686.98.

Foreign Missions.—The report, read by the secretary of the committee, gave the following as to the affairs of the mission among the Telugus, in India: The mission, which has Rajahmundry for its principal station, has 5 foreign missionaries, 4 wives of missionaries, 2 native pastors, 7 evangelists, 10 teachers at Rajahmundry and

52 at the other stations. The pupils in the various districts number 525. There were baptized during the year, 235; the number of Christians is 2,037. The receipts for the year amounted to $10,288.20; the expenditures were $10,307.89. The Rev. I. K. Poulsen, who had been laboring in India since January, 1871, returned to his home in Denmark, on account of impaired health. The missionary operations are extending so widely and rapidly that missionaries are needed at once. The mission now has a printing-press, which is doing excellent work in disseminating religious tracts and books. A Telugu edition of "Bible History," with illustrations, is shortly to be issued.

Immigrant Mission.—The annual reports of the Rev. W. Berkenmeyer and Mr. A. B. Lilja, the German and Swedish missionaries at New York, showed that 59,248 Swedish and 11,771 German emigrants passed through the Emigrant House, at 26 State Street, New York. Of Germans, 1,192 were aided out of the benevolent funds of the mission. The receipts for the year were $17,285.11; the expenditures, $16,034.66; and for the chaplain on Ward's Island, $408.50. The money deposited for emigrants amounted to $84,612.94.

Church-Book Committee.—The committee's report embraced: 1. The remainder of ministerial acts not completed last year, i. e., forms for the visitation of the sick, communion of the sick, commendation of the dying, and burial of the dead. 2. The common service for the use of all English-speaking Lutherans, prepared by the joint committee of the General Council, the General Synod, the United Synod of the South. It has already been published by the latter two bodies, and the edition of the Council is to be published as soon as possible. 3. The standard English translation of the "Augsburg Confession," and Luther's "Small Catechism." For the former, the Latin *editio princeps* of 1530 has been made the basis, and Richard Taverner's English translation of 1536 the standard of the English edition. For the use of the committee, the English edition of 1536 has been republished by the Lutheran Publication Society, Philadelphia, under the title "The Augsburg Confession, translated from the Latin, in 1536, by Richard Taverner, edited by Henry E. Jacobs, D. D." Richard Taverner, the translator, was a celebrated lawyer and classical scholar, educated at Oxford and Cambridge. He was chief clerk to Thomas Cromwell, the distinguished minister of Henry VIII, who was a faithful and zealous Lutheran. All of Taverner's fine attainments were devoted to the cause of the restored Gospel. In 1552 he was licensed to preach, and in this capacity did good service. He will always be remembered for his excellent and idiomatic translation of the Bible in 1539. He also supplied the people with "postils" or sermons to be used in churches where no other provision could be made for the preaching of the Gospel, and in many ways rendered efficient service in bringing before the people the writings of the reformers. For the standard English translation of the catechism, Luther's last edition of 1542 has been adopted, and Dr. Philip F. Mayer's translation has been made the basis of the new translation. In addition to the three general bodies uniting in securing a uniform English edition of these Lutheran standards, the Joint Synod of Ohio has decided to take part. Closely allied to the Church-book Committee are the Committee on Sunday-School Work, who presented an elaborate schedule for a seven years' course of lessons, covering the infant, intermediate, and advanced departments in Sunday-schools, and furnishing lessons from the Old and New Testaments, from the latter for the festival, and from the former for the non-festival portion of the Church year. The committee was instructed to issue a graded series of lessons for the schools, and have it ready for use as soon as possible. During this convention, services were held in the interest of home and foreign missions, education, benevolent operations, and the work of deaconesses, besides a special service, in the Exposition Buildings, on Friday, Sept. 14, in honor of the quarto-millennial anniversary of the settlement (in 1638) of the Swedes on Delaware river. The next convention of this body will be held in Pittsburg, Pa., Oct. 12, 1889.

Synodical Conference.—This general body, organized in 1872, embraces the following four, exclusively German, district synods: Joint Synod of Missouri and other States, Wisconsin Synod, Minnesota Synod, and English Conference of Missouri—numbering 1,238 clergymen, 1,740 congregations, and 341,337 members. There are within its bounds 3 theological seminaries, 3 colleges, 7 academies, and 14 orphans' homes, hospitals, and immigrant missions. This general body held its twelfth convention in Trinity (German) Lutheran Church, Milwaukee, Wis. The opening sermon was delivered by the Rev. A. Ernst, Professor in the Northwestern University, based on Eph. iv, 3–6. Nine sessions were held, of which five were devoted to the discussion of the doctrinal subject unity of faith, and four to the transaction of business. The following officers were elected: President, Rev. John Bading; Vice-president, Rev. M. Tirmenstein; Secretary, Rev. C. Gausewitz; Treasurer, H. A. Christiansen. The home missionary work of the body is carried on by the district synods. Missionary work is carried on by the conference among the colored people of the South, seven missionaries being located in Arkansas, Louisiana, Virginia, and Illinois. The contributions for this work for two years amounted to $21,308.02, and the expenditures to $20,722.21. The next convention will be held in St. Paul, Minn., in 1890.

United Synod in the South.—This general body, organized in 1886, held its second convention in Savannah, Ga., Nov. 24–29, 1887. (See "Annual Cyclopædia" for 1887, p. 449.) It embraces the following eight district (exclusively English) synods: North Carolina, Tennessee, South Carolina, Virginia, West Virginia, Mississippi, Holston (Tenn.), and Georgia, numbering 186 clergymen, 373 congregations, and 33,641 members. There are within the bounds of this general body, 1 theological seminary, 5 colleges, 13 academies and ladies' seminaries, and 1 orphans' home. The next convention will be held in Wilmington, N. C., Nov. 14, 1889.

Independent Synods.—The following twelve synods carry on their church, educational, mis-

wife of John D. Lankenau and the daughter of the late Francis M. Drexel and sister of Francis A. Drexel. The building, erected on the grounds of the German Hospital, at Girard and Corinthian Avenues, was begun Sept. 20, 1886, and the corner-stone was laid Nov. 11, 1887. It has a frontage on Girard Avenue of 250 feet, with wings running south 300 feet, and an open court between the wings of 120 and 140 feet. The main entrance is in the center of the Girard Avenue front, having an archway 15 feet high directly under the chapel, which forms the center of the building and is

THE MARY J. DREXEL HOME, PHILADELPHIA.

sionary, and benevolent operations independent of the four general bodies and of each other: Joint Synod of Ohio, Buffalo, Norwegian, Michigan, Norwegian-Danish Conference, Hauge's Norwegian Synod, German Augsburg, Maryland (German), Danish, Danish Lutheran Union, Icelandic Synod, Immanuel's Synod, numbering 925 clergymen, 2,007 congregations, and 219,133 members, 9 theological seminaries, 4 colleges, 8 academies, and 4 benevolent institutions.

Deaconess Institution.—A notable event in the history of the Lutheran Church in America was the erection and dedication of the Mary J. Drexel Home and Mother-House of Deaconesses in Philadelphia. This is a memorial of the lady whose name it bears, who was the

surmounted by a steeple 175 feet high. The building is of brick, with cut-stone trimmings, and is three stories high. It cost $500,000, and is the gift of Mr. Lankenau to the Lutheran Church. It is to serve a threefold purpose: 1. As the mother-house for and the training-school of Lutheran deaconesses, where Christian women will be trained for hospital, school, and parish work as deaconesses, an office of high repute in the Lutheran Church of Europe, which has been adopted by the various denominations in Europe and America; 2. A well-equipped children's hospital; 3. An asylum for the aged and infirm. On Dec. 6, 1888, this building was formally consecrated, according to the liturgical form of the Lutheran Church, and set apart for its special mission of benevolence. Mr. Lankenau, the founder of this institution and of the German Hospital, in a few well-chosen words presented the building to the trustees. The following are the concluding words of his address: "I hereby surrender into your hands the building in which we are here assembled. I do this from my own free will and without any other wish or influence than the desire to be of service to my adopted country and for the good and benefit of mankind. A deed I have none to give you. Be satisfied with my word and this hand for the seal. I hope the many witnesses before you will not object to testify to these proceedings and approve my act. I do not wish you to become alarmed at the magnitude of the trust. I will therefore promise you that I will maintain the institution as long as I live; then let the institution take care of itself." The solemn service was concluded with the formal installation of the Rev. Augustus Cordes, the new rector of the Mother-House of Deaconesses, by the Rev. Dr. Spaeth.

Union among Norwegians.—For several years the Norwegian Lutherans in the United States have been divided into parties, so that hitherto there have been four separate synods carrying on their works independently and not unfrequently in opposition to each other and maintaining separate educational institutions. Conferences have been held from time to time with a view of effecting harmony of thought and union of action, and these conferences brought about a better understanding among the majority of the synods and made a union of the conflicting elements possible. In February, 1888, a meeting was held by representatives from four of the different synods, and an overture was made to the Norwegian Augustana Synod (organized in 1860), Norwegian-Danish Conference (1870), Hauge's Norwegian Synod (1875), and the Anti-Missourians of the Norwegian Synod (1853), the oldest and strongest Norwegian body, with a view of merging all the synods into one body; and a joint committee of seven members from each synod was appointed to formulate a basis of union. The committee met in August at Eau Claire, Wis., and prepared the following plan of union for adoption by the respective synods: 1. A doctrinal basis, having special regard to their previous disagreements; 2. A new synodical constitution, to take the place of existing synodical constitutions; 3. A plan for the consolidation of institutions, periodicals, and publication interests. The plan includes the consolidation of the four seminaries—two at Minneapolis, Minn., one at Beloit, Iowa, and one at Red Wing, Minn., and the raising of an endowment fund of $135,000 for the support of the six theological professors of the institutions as at present existing. A joint meeting of these synods was held at Scandinavia, Wis., Nov. 15 to 22, 1888. About 300 members were present. The threefold report of the joint committee was ratified in all its essential

features; but before the union can be finally consummated it must be ratified by the respective synods at their conventions in 1889. The prospects are very promising for a new united body in 1890 under the adopted title, "The United Norwegian Lutheran Church in America." The various synods concerned in this movement now number 250 clergymen, 800 congregations, and 70,000 members.

Swedish Quarto-Millennial.—The two hundred and fiftieth anniversary of the Swedes was celebrated on Sept. 14, 1888, in the Exposition Buildings at Minneapolis, Minn. The audience, which numbered more than 20,000 Scandinavians, was addressed by Hans Mattson, Secretary of State of Minnesota, Hon. W. W. Thomas, of Maine, late United States Minister to Norway and Sweden, J. A. Enander, editor of "Hemlandet," of Chicago, and others. The kingdom of Sweden was represented by Consul Sahlgaard. In May, 1638, two vessels sailed up the Delaware, bringing the first Swedish colony to America. The Swedes purchased from the Indians a large tract of land on the west bank of the river, extending from Cape Henlopen to the falls near Trenton, and westward without any bound or limit, embracing nearly the whole of the present State of Delaware and a large portion of Pennsylvania. The colonists immediately built a fort, to which they gave the name Christina, in honor of their queen, and erected their church and their humble dwellings in its immediate vicinity. The city of Wilmington now occupies the site of the ancient fort. The Swedes prospered and established new settlements along the Delaware. The fertile soil returned to them its increase in bountiful measure, and they lived in peace and friendship with the Indians, whom they endeavored to convert to Christianity. They came with their pastor, Reorus Torkillus, and one of these earliest pastors, John Campanius (Holm), was the first Protestant missionary among the Indians, antedating John Eliot by several years. Before long they had flourishing congregations in various parts of their territory; but the Dutch at New Amsterdam (New York) looked with jealousy upon this thriving colony, and in various ways sought to subjugate or drive away their neighbors. In 1655 the Dutch suddenly appeared in Delaware Bay with a large force, surprised the Swedes, and subjugated the colony. Many of the settlers were sent back to Sweden and the rest were held as subjects of Holland. This continued for nine years, when New Netherland, with all its possessions, passed under the control of the English crown. As a distinct political organization under the Swedish flag the colony continued only seventeen years; but its influence for good has continued down to the present through the descendants of those pioneers, many of whom are among the most honored citizens of Pennsylvania, New Jersey, and Delaware, and some of whom have occupied high places in the Church and state. Said Hon. W. W. Thomas, in his historical address:

The man who, as a member of the Continental Congress, gave the casting vote of Pennsylvania in favor of the Declaration of Independence, was a Swede of the old Delaware stock, John Morton, the worthy ancestor of the great war Governor, Morton, of Indiana; and when civil war burst upon the land it was a descendant of New Sweden, the gallant Gen. Robert Anderson, who with but a handful of men calmly and bravely met the first shock of the rebellion at Fort Sumter. And New Sweden will ever be illustrious from the principles of true humanity which distinguish its founding. The idea of New Sweden originated in the mind of Gustavus Adolphus, although it was not until after his death that the plan was carried out by his great chancellor, Oxenstjernu. It was the intention of the Swedish King that this colony should be an asylum for the oppressed of all nations—a free State where all would have equal rights and enjoy to the fullest extent the fruits of their own labor. Slavery should never exist within its borders, for, said Gustavus, "Slaves cost a great deal, labor with reluctance, and soon perish with hard usage." William Penn arrived on this continent in 1682, forty-four years after the Swedes, and landed within the limits of New Sweden. It was the Swedish settlers and their children who received the good Quaker, welcomed him to the New World, and entertained him with kindness and hospitality. It was the Swedes also who acted as Penn's interpreters with the Indians. How could it be otherwise than that so keen an observer as Penn should learn from his hosts and interpreters their manner of dealing with the red man and be impressed with its success? Precisely as the Swedes had done before him, Penn acquired land of the Indians by purchase, treated them kindly, and kept faith with them. Penn has been justl praised for his peaceful and humane policy toward the red man. I would not pluck a leaf from the laurels with which America has crowned the great Quaker; but, honor to whom honor is due. Impartial history records that the honor of originating this policy on this continent is due not to William Penn, but to the Swedes of New Sweden. Penn, in a letter, mentions his kind reception by the Swedes, and praises their industry and their respect for authority. He says: "As they are a people proper and strong of body, so they have fine children, and almost every house full; rare to find one of them without three or four boys and as many girls, some six, seven, and eight souls. And I must do them right, I see few young men more sober and industrious."

With the acquisition of the country by the English, Swedish immigration began to diminish, and for nearly two centuries was insignificant; but about twenty-five years ago it took a fresh start, and since then immigration from Sweden has assumed immense proportions and constitutes one of the marvels in the migration of nations. Taking into consideration only the later years, we note that in 1880 there arrived on these shores more than 40,000 Swedes; in 1881, 50,000; and in 1882 more than 64,000; and, during the first half of the year 1887, more than 30,000 at the port of New York alone. The great majority of these have settled in the West and Northwest. Minnesota has a Swedish population of nearly 200,000, and may justly be called the New Sweden of the great Northwest.

M

MAINE. The following were the State officers during the year: Governor, Sebastian S. Marble (Republican); Secretary of State, Oramandal Smith; Treasurer, Edwin C. Burleigh, who resigned on July 14 and was succeeded by George L. Beal; Attorney-General, Orville D. Baker; Superintendent of Public Schools, Nelson A. Luce; Railroad Commissioners, Asa W. Wildes, Roscoe L. Bowers, and David N. Mortland; Chief-Justice of the Supreme Court, John A. Peters; Associate Justices, Charles W. Walton, Charles Danforth, William W. Virgin, Artemus Libbey, Lucilius A. Emery, Enoch Foster, and Thomas H. Haskell.

Finances.—The following is a summary of the receipts and disbursements of the State during the year:

Cash in treasury, Jan. 1, 1888................	$312,288 03
Total receipts for 1888.........................	1,087,388 90
Total...	$1,399,676 93
Total expenditures for 1888....	$1,127,393 52
Cash in treasury, Dec. 31, 1888................	272,283 41
Total....................................	$1,399,676 93

The resources of the State, Jan. 1, 1889, are $2,289,073.88; liabilities, $5,381,502. Of this last-named amount $1,748,000 is war-loan bonds due Jan. 1, 1889; and $2,187,400 is bonds of loan for the assumption of municipal war debts, due Oct. 1, 1889. Expenditures under the different departments of the State have exceeded the appropriations by $104,025.62.

The fifty-six savings-banks in the State have paid a State tax of $272,128.42; the different railroads of $109,760.66, the telegraph companies of $6,350, the telephone companies of $1,387.50, the express companies of $1,293, and the insurance companies of $22,883.57, making a total from these sources of $412,803.15.

The condition of the sinking-fund of the State is shown by the following detailed exhibit:

Creditor, by balance, Jan. 1, 1888...............	$949,660 64
Amount received for interest on funds invested in securities outside the State of Maine.......	40,030 00
Total................................	$989,690 64

Debtor to amount State of Maine bonds purchased during the year 1888, and canceled as follows:

Issue, June 1, 1864 (registered).......	$10,000 00
" " " (coupon)...............	4,000 00
" Oct. 1, 1869 (registered)................	1,000 00
" " " (coupon)...............	8,600 00
To amount paid for premiums on same........	584 50
" " accrued interest on same...	209 81
Balance, sinking fund, Dec. 31, 1888, par value..	965,296 33
Total..................................	$989,690 64

Concerning the bonded debt, the Treasurer says: "The refunding of our public debt between this date (Jan. 1, 1889) and the 1st of October is an imperative duty and of the amount now outstanding, $1.748,000 fall due on the first day of June and $2,187,400 on the first of October: against this aggregate amount of $3,935,400 and available for its payment, we have securities in the sinking-fund whose market value is about $1,200,000 ; there is to be paid from the estate of Hon. Abner Coburn $150,000, of which the State has accepted the trust, and we may possibly have an additional sum of $357,702 from the National Government as a refund of the direct tax of August, 1861. The debt to be refunded can not, I think, exceed $2,600,000 in amount, and may possibly be as low as $2,200,000."

The sinking-fund is wholly composed of United States 4 and 4½ per cent. bonds, and Massachusetts and New Hampshire 5 and 6 per cent. bonds. More than 70 per cent. of the fund is invested in United States bonds; these securities will not shrink in value and they bear an average interest in excess of 4 per cent., and can profitably be maintained for the last payment. The refunding act of 1887 fixes the date for the issue of the new bonds at Oct. 1, 1889.

The State College has on deposit with the State Treasurer. under the provisions of certain resolves and acts of the Legislature, various State bonds, amounting to $118,300. This whole sum now stands in bonds which become due in 1889, and for the purpose of refunding them the Treasurer suggests that he be authorized to issue a registered bond for the full amount in favor of the State College of Agriculture and Mechanic Arts bearing interest at the rate of 5 per cent. per annum.

The Maine Insane Hospital fund has been increased by the trustees paying into the treasury $50,000 which they received from the estate of Hon. Abner Coburn. This has been accepted in trust, for which the annual interest is to be paid as authorized by resolve of the Legislature of 1887, which directed the Treasurer to issue to the hospital an unnegotiable registered bond for $50,000, bearing interest at the rate of 4 per cent. per annum, payable semi-annually.

Savings-Banks.—The fifty-five savings-banks in Maine have assets amounting to $5,031,-497.44 in excess of all liabilities, and during 1888 paid a State tax of $268,868.06. The total number of depositors on Nov. 1, 1888, was 124,562, of which number 99,293 represent a deposit of less than $500 each. During the year there has been an increase of 5,333 in the number of depositors, with an average balance to each of $328.91, an increase over that of 1887. The amount deposited Nov. 1, 1888, was $40,969,663.05—a total increase for the year of $2,150,019.83. Every bank in the State has paid its regular semi-annual dividend, the total amount of dividends paid being $1,479,785.68, and at the close of the year there remained in the banks $1,024,867.61 of undivided profits. There are in Maine also six trust companies and fifteen loan and building associations, which are represented in a most healthy, prosperous condition.

Education.—The Maine State College has continued to flourish. The State experimental station at the college was abolished on Oct. 1, 1887, and was then transferred to and became the property of the college. Meteorological observations are regularly made there. A new building for the use of the department of agriculture and natural history was completed during the year. The State apportionment of the school-fund and mill-tax amounted to $372,703.89, which was divided among the different counties according to the number of pupils in each. The total number of pupils was 211,968, a decrease of 590 for the year. The report of the State Superintendent of Schools indicates that there are fewer pupils in the State than in 1886, yet there were 444 more attending school; the registered attendance in the summer and autumn terms was increased by 1,807 and the average daily attendance by 1,844; the registered and average daily attendance for the winter and spring terms was increased by the numbers 1,315 and 632 respectively.

The reports of the Madawaska Training School, normal department of the Maine Central Institute, and Lee Normal Academy, are very satisfactory, as are also the reports of the trustees of the three State institutions.

Railroads.—The commissioners report that during 1887 the York Harbor and Beach Railroad has been wholly constructed and was opened to public travel on August 8. This railroad extends from the Boston and Maine Railroad depot in Kittery to York Beach, about 11 2/10 miles.

The Penobscot and Lake Megantic Railroad, now known as the International Railroad, is being constructed from the west line of the State easterly by the southern side of Moosehead Lake to a connection with the European and North American Railroad at Mattawamkeag station.

The Somerset Railroad Company contemplates the extension of its railroad from the present terminus at North Anson, northerly and easterly to the village of Bingham, about sixteen miles. and has graded a large portion of the road-bed.

Notwithstanding the multiplicity of railroad charters granted by the Legislature during the last session, three railroad corporations have been organized under the general law, viz.: Harmony and Wellington Railroad Company; Rumford Falls, Andover and Rangeley Lake Railroad Company; and Boston and Quebec Air Line Railroad Company.

There is at the present time (January, 1889) a total of 1,182·22 miles of railroad in the State of Maine.

Labor Statistics.—In May, 1887, Samuel W. Matthews was appointed labor commissioner, and his first report was not issued until 1888. He finds the average rates of wages derived in twenty Maine towns: Agricultural laborers, a month, $18.37 and board; in haying season, with board, $1.75 a day; barbers, $1.50; blacksmiths, $1.75; boiler-makers, $2.15; cabinet-makers, $1.75; carpenters (house), $1.75; carriage-makers, $1.50; coopers, $1 50; engineers (stationary), $1.75; engineers (locomotive), $2.43; harness-makers, $1.60; laborers (common), $1.40; masons, $2.75; machinists, $2.50; millers, $1.65; painters (house), $2.00; plumbers, $3.50; printers (male), $1.62; printers (female), $1.10; shoemakers, $1.62; teamsters, $1.60; teachers, $1.41; wheelwrights, $2.00.

The fishing industry is represented as being in a very depressed condition. The following table shows the number and tonnage of vessels engaged in the cod and mackerel fisheries in Maine as compared with other States in 1885:

STATES.	Number.	Tons.
Maine....................	596	20,785·18
New Hampshire...........	18	614·75
Massachusetts............	840	49,402·92
Rhode Island.............	60	1,946·06
Connecticut...............	112	3,196·50
New York................	103	4,202·89
New Jersey...............	1	17·23
Virginia..................	1	22·26
North Carolina............	1	33·22
Florida...................	13	391·10
California....	6	61·96
Oregon...................	1	20·70
Total..................	1,739	80,704·81

Complete returns for 1887 show the number of vessels in Maine engaged in the fisheries to be 448; tonnage, 15,857·64; a decrease of about 25 per cent. since 1885. Fifteen factories have been engaged in lobster-canning during the season, putting up from eight to ten million pounds. Each factory employs from 40 to 50 hands, about one half men and boys and the other half women and girls. The price paid for lobsters has been $1.25 per one hundred pounds.

Returns are compiled from 72 manufacturing establishments, covering 29 industries. Though few compared with the whole number in the State, and defective in many particulars, yet they are among the most important. Those reporting employ 14,695 hands. Sixty-five establishments report capital invested, $16,367,900, and 7,578 male employés over 15 years of age; 17 report 412 male employés under 15 years; 31 report 6,529 female employés over 15 years, and 12 report 176 female employés under 15 years. Twenty-five industries report the average weekly wages paid men, $10.27; 16 industries the average annual earnings of men, $477.81; and 8 the average annual earnings of women, $336.96. Forty-four establishments report their "gross product," $11,273,514.

Holidays.—In Maine, the first observance of Labor Day occurred Sept. 5, 1887. In Portland, the city Government officially recognized the day by hoisting the national colors on the City Hall, closing the city offices, and suspending public work. A large meeting of working men and women was presided over by the Mayor. The day was observed in other cities and towns in the State.

The Legislature passed the following act, approved March 10, 1887:

That the Governor shall annually set apart a day in the spring as Arbor Day, and shall issue a proclamation recommending that it be observed by the people of this State in the planting of trees, shrubs, and vines, in the adornment of public and private grounds, places, and ways, and in such other efforts and undertakings as shall be in harmony with the general character of a day so established.

In accordance with this the Governor designated May 1 as the Arbor Day.

Indians.—The annual report of John H. Stowe, agent of the Penobscot Indians, gives the annual census of the tribe as 385, an increase of five over the report of 1887. The appropriations for the year were $8,319.70. Twelve deaths occurred during the year. A. C. Munson, agent of the Passamaquoddy Indians, gives the population of that tribe as 525, against 515 last year. During the year there have been twenty deaths, including three members of the tribe who died at an age exceeding one hundred years, the oldest being one hundred and seven.

Prisons.—The prison inspectors report 150 convicts in confinement, of whom five were women, in the Maine State Prison. They find that the act of March 17, 1887, abolishing the death penalty and providing that those convicted of murder in the first degree shall not be associated or employed with other convicts, can not be carried out without incurring great or continued expense for buildings and disciplinarians. Those who have been so committed since the passage of the act, have been kept locked in the cells, deprived of the privilege of attending divine service or working at a trade, through lack of means to carry out the provisions of the law. The jails were also inspected, and several were found that were badly kept and in need of repairs. The report of the Industrial School for Girls and that of the State Reform School at Cape Elizabeth, showed that these institutions were in a satisfactory condition. Twenty-three girls were committed at the former during the year, while at the Reform School the number of boys increased from 113 at the beginning of the year to 133 at its close. The adoption of the "family system" was recommended, on the ground that it admits of more thorough classification and separation of juvenile offenders according to their ages, character, and conduct. The boys are separated into families of about fifty each, who eat, sleep, attend school, work, and play in a college by themselves. Each family is in charge of a man and his wife and a teacher.

By this system the worst boys, brought under the influence of the family, are educated and taught habits of industry.

Fisheries and Game.—The biennial report for 1887-'88 of the State commissioners shows that the game has exhibited an almost phenomenal increase. while by fish-planting and protection a bountiful return of resources that had been crippled is assured. The run of salmon in Penobscot river has been large in both years, but in 1888 it far exceeded that of 1887, both in size and numbers. It is deemed necessary for the protection of the fisheries to have the river patrolled. In 1887, 104,000 sea-salmon eggs were sent to Grand Lake and put into St. Croix waters. There were hatched at Orland and put into Craig's brook 25,000. These eggs were presented to Maine by the United States Fish Commission in 1888. In 1888 Maine purchased 232,000 eggs; and the United State Commission presented the State with 148,000. Of this number 60,000 were put into the St. Croix at Vanceboro, and 320,000 into the Penobscot and Mattawamkeag rivers.

The introduction of landlocked salmon has been advanced in 1888; 50,000 were hatched at Orland and distributed.

A wonderful increase of venison game animals is reported. Moose have been more numerous than can be accounted for, unless by immigration from the provinces. This has likewise been the case with deer. Wherever the law against dogs has been enforced, deer, moose, and caribou have made their appearance.

The commissioner of sea and shore fisheries finds that, owing to the protective law, lobsters have been cheaper and more plentiful than before in ten years. The yearly catch is estimated at 25,000,000. Mackerel have been scarce, and the yield was only 25,511 barrels in 1888, against 56,919 in 1887, which is the lowest catch in fifty years. The menhaden or porgy, which disappeared ten years ago, reappeared in 1888, and one or two menhaden-oil factories started up. Alewives are diminishing, and the herring-sardine business is on the increase. The product of 1888 was 450,000 cases, each case containing 100 boxes, and each box ten or twelve little fish. The commissioners have control of 35,000 square miles of territory, to cover which is an appropriation of 18¼ cents per square mile, or a total of $6,500. From this sum has to be paid $2,000 for sea and land-locked salmon eggs.

Ship-Building.—During 1888 this branch of industry steadily improved and was better than it had been for years. There were built 18 schooners, 1 bark, 1 steam-bark, 2 steam-yachts, 1 steamboat, and 1 steam-tug—24 vessels; total tonnage, 10,035·82. Perhaps the two most notable craft constructed during the year were the five-masted schooner "Gov. Ames" and the steam-tug "H. F. Morse"—the former the largest and only five-masted schooner on salt water, and the latter the largest tug-boat in this country. There is one larger schooner than the "Gov. Ames"—"The Golden Age," king of the Great Lakes.

Political.—The Republican State Convention was held in Portland on June 12, and Edwin C. Burleigh, then State Treasurer, was nominated for Governor. The following are the chief declarations of the platform:

That free trade as taught by the British Cobden Club and supported by Grover Cleveland and the Democratic party, is hostile to the industrial and business interests of the United States, and that the Mills Tariff Bill should be opposed by all the honorable and effective influences which the friends of American labor can exert, both in Congress and among the people.

That it is the duty of Congress to reduce the national revenue to the amount which shall equal, as nearly as possible, the annual expenditures of the Government, including therein a liberal provision for our veteran soldiers and a proper means of national defense, and that this should be done in a way not to impair our Republican protective system, which has proved of inestimable value to American labor and our home markets.

That, for its surrender of American rights and interests in the recently negotiated fishery treaty, the present national Administration deserves the emphatic censure of all patriotic Americans, and that the Republican Senators are entitled to the thanks of their countrymen for their able and effective efforts against its ratification.

That the prohibitory law against the terrible evils of the liquor traffic, after many years of trial, has become the fixed policy of the State, to which the Republicans of Maine are firmly pledged, and we demand that its provisions shall be faithfully enforced according to their terms and spirit.

The Democratic State Convention was held in Augusta on May 22, and nominated William L. Putnam, who was Mayor of Portland in 1869, for the governorship. These are the principal declarations of the platform adopted:

That unnecessary taxation is unjust extortion, and that the immediate and constantly increasing surplus now accumulating in the United States Treasury is a menace to the business interests of the country and to economical government. We believe that our tariff is so arranged as to foster wealthy monopolies at the expense of the common people, and we sincerely approve of the Democrats in Congress to pass a bill which will, in the language of President Cleveland, "relieve the people from unnecessary taxation, having a due regard to the interests of capital invested, and workingmen employed in American industries." We do not advocate free trade, but favor and desire a revision of the present unjust and burdensome tariff laws.

That reform in the administration of the affairs of the State is urgently demanded. Needless and extravagant expenditures have come largely to absorb our State revenues, thus postponing the payment of the State debt, upon which more than the original amount has already been paid for interest. Salaries have been unnecessarily increased, in some cases at their request and with a population nearly stationary, with no State enterprises requiring outlay, the expenditures for State purposes have nearly quadrupled under the rule of the Republicans.

That we view with alarm the growing evil of intemperance in our State, and in the interest of good society and temperance demand the repeal of the prohibitory liquor law, and the enactment of a stringent high-license law.

The official count of the presidential election showed a Republican majority of 23,253 votes, as follows: Gen. Harrison, 73,734; Mr.Cleveland, 50.481; Gen. Fisk, 2,691; and Mr. Sweeter, 1,344. Four Republican Congressmen were re-elected. In the Legislature the Republicans elected every one of the 31 members of the Senate, and 125 members of the House, leaving the Democrats 26. Of 99 county officers, sheriffs, probate judges, county attorneys, etc., the Republicans have elected 96 and the Democrats 3.

The official count of the votes on the two amendments at the September election resulted as follows: For lengthening the term of the State Treasurer, yes, 12.974; no, 10,249. For annual sessions of the Legislature, yes, 5,776; no, 39,320.

MANITOBA. The agitation in the province on the question of railway monopoly (see "Annual Cyclopædia" for 1887, page 455) brought about the downfall of the Norquay Government in January, 1888. An attempt by the Conservatives to retain power by forming a ministry under the leadership of the Hon. Thomas Harrison, failed. The Hon. Thomas Greenway then formed a Government, which is composed as follows: Premier and Minister of Agriculture, Thomas Greenway; Attorney-General and Railway Commissioner, Joseph Martin; Provincial Treasurer, Lyman M. Jones; Minister of Public Works, James S. Martin; Provincial Secretary, J. E. Prendergast. On July 2, John Schultz was sworn in as Lieutenant-Governor. At the general elections, July 11, the Greenway Government (Liberal) carried 34 out of 38 constituencies.

Railway Monopoly.—In March, Messrs. Greenway and Martin went to Ottawa to consult the Dominion Government with reference to the abandonment of its policy of disallowance. The deputation at first met with no encouragement, the attitude of the Dominion Government on this question being defined in a memorandum, prepared by a sub-committee composed of the Ministers of the Interior and of Justice, which was transmitted to London on January 4. But finally Mr. Greenway obtained a promise that the disallowance policy should be abandoned, and the Dominion Government entered into an agreement with the Canadian Pacific Railway for the abandonment of the monopoly clause of its charter, in consideration of the Government guaranteeing three and one half per cent. interest on its land-grant bonds to the extent of $15,000,000 for fifty years. Sir Charles Tupper, on May 11, moved resolutions in the House of Commons sanctioning this agreement, which was carried. The Government justified its change of base, on the ground that the enormous wheat-crop of 1888, resulting in a blockade of the Canadian Pacific Railway, had wrought a material change in the condition of affairs. The Opposition insisted that the conversion of the Government was due to the threatening attitude of the people of Manitoba, and to the growing sympathy with them in other parts of the Dominion.

Although the Canadian Pacific Railway had relinquished its monopoly privilege in May, it contrived, by a process of systematic obstruction and litigation, to prevent the construction of the Red River Valley Railway during 1888.

Grain-Crop.—The annual report of the Winnipeg Board of Trade for 1888 gives the following particulars of the grain crop of the Province in 1887:

The returns show an aggregate of 2,600,000 bushels reduced to flour, of which nearly 2,000,000 left the province. In wheat 8,500,000 bushels were exported. The refusal of the Canadian Pacific Railway Company to give traffic figures made it impossible to obtain close returns of the barley and oats sent out, but it is established that not less than 350,000 bushels of the first and 1,000,000 bushels of the last named were exported. The exports of flax, oatmeal, potatoes, vegetables, wool, hides, fish, and dairy products were large. The total value of the farm produce and fish sent out of the province was over $7,000,000 at local market prices to the producer. The census shows that 16,000 farmers cultivated the soil in 1887. These farmers raised 14,000,000 bushels of wheat. The wheat-land area under crop was 432,000 acres.

MARS, RECENT STUDIES OF. The map of the planet Mars accompanying this article is a reproduction of that presented by Prof. Edward S. Holden in the New York "Herald" of Nov. 28, 1888, entitled "Mars as seen through the Lick Telescope." The canals it represents are either natural or artificial, due, upon the one hand, to the forces that accompanied the geological formations of the surface, or, upon the other, to a system of engineering projected by beings like ourselves and designed for the purpose of establishing a means of communication between the inhabitants of the entire planet. If they are due to the latter cause, then a discovery has been made of the highest importance to the development of cosmical science; and for this reason it would seem wise on our part to pass it carefully in review before the best efforts of logic we can summon to our assistance. The writer, therefore, submits for consideration the conclusions he has drawn from a careful study of the map, and begs to explain that his earliest experience in the science of engineering was the construction of "water-ways" in the primitive forest for the purpose of making every available stream navigable for floating down timber and for passing small vessels up and down stream. To one having such experience the markings on the map of Mars present peculiar analogies.

One of the prominent features of our system of engineering was to avail ourselves of every natural water-way that would save labor and expense, such as lakes, long, deep stretches of streams, rivers, etc. If the reader will look on the map at a place on the thirtieth parallel of north latitude, named Lake Nillacus, he will observe that six of those canals enter this sheet of water from different directions. The lake is nearly as broad as it is long, and covers more than eighteen degrees of both latitude and longitude, which, at the thirtieth parallel of latitude upon Mars, means that the lake is about 612 miles across. · Therefore, if this is a system of Martial engineering, here is a case where the engineers gained 612 miles of natural water-way for each canal. This is just what terrestrial engineers would have done under the same circumstances. Look again at a place marked A, between the fortieth and fiftieth parallels of north latitude. It is about three degrees of latitude in width and sixteen of longitude in length, which makes it about 90 miles broad and 500 miles long. Four canals, from different directions, enter the western end of this long, narrow sheet of water; and three, from different directions also, enter its eastern end; none enter upon its sides. Lake Nillacus is practically a round lake, and its canals enter on all of its sides; but this is a long, narrow lake, and its canals enter its ends. Here, then, is another example of what a skillful engineer upon our own world would have

extremity it is entered by two canals, at its eastern end by two (here we encounter a little uncertainty, growing out of the fact that the original draughtsman was not sufficiently skilled in map-drawing to make the verges of the two hemispheres coincide), on its southern shore by the canal that we followed from B to C. This canal trends nearly due north, and a continuation of its course would carry a vessel through the western strait between the island and the mainland into the extension of the polar sea, still keeping up the character of engineering design hitherto referred to; and it is curiously corroborative of design when we find by the maps given that this system of canals has been pushed as ·far north as the eightieth parallel; for, as the axis of Mars is inclined to the plane of its orbit seven degrees more than that of our earth to its orbit, it follows that the sun moves seven degrees farther poleward

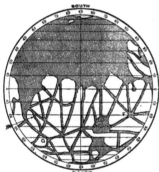 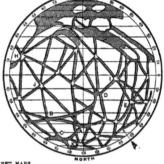

MAP OF THE PLANET MARS.

done under like circumstances, simply because, by entering a long stretch of water-way at its ends, he gains both the water-way of its length and breadth. If he entered at its sides he would only gain the water-way of its width, 90 miles. The true engineer enters at the ends, because he gains 500 miles of water-way and the 90 besides.

Moving eastward from A to the position B, we come to what is either a section of a widening of the canal system or a natural water-way about 300 miles in length; but, whichever it may be, the same order is observed; it is entered at one end by two canals coming from different directions, and at the other by four, all of which have the same divergent character. Moving northward along one of those canals that lead from its eastward end, we come to a sound of the northern sea formed by the coast of the mainland and that of a large island. This sound, or long, narrow sea, has a length of somewhat over 600 miles and an average width of about 100. At its western

in the summer than on our planet, from which fact there is due to the eightieth parallel of latitude on Mars a mean temperature equivalent to the seventy-third degree on our world, or about the latitude of the North Cape of Norway, which is inhabited to its extreme point. In other words, the canal system of Mars seems to come to an end where the population begins to grow sparse before the influence of polar desolation.

In a general way, we invite attention to the points of convergence D and E on the western hemisphere, near the twentieth degree of north latitude, as they seem to partake of the nature of the water-ways we have been considering, and also F on the eastern hemisphere and the same latitude. But let us take a glance at that great estuary running northward up into the land from the southern ocean, lying near the eastern verge of the eastern hemisphere. Its mouth opens southward at the tenth degree of south latitude, and it penetrates above the fortieth parallel of north latitude; at the point

G, which is suggestive of a possible terminus of its navigable waters, it is entered by three canals coming, as usual, from different directions, one of them suggesting by its crookedness that it may have been a river flowing into the estuary and forming its head-waters. Following this great water-course about 300 miles southward, we see two canals converging to a point on its southern bank; and, directly opposite, a single one, pursuing the general direction of both, starts from its northern bank, as if there were design in securing a continuous direction of the canal-journey on both sides of the great estuary. Some hundreds of miles still farther southward, we find two other canals entering on the northeastern shore; that at the tenth degree of north latitude being remarkable for first entering a lake from the northward and then, by a short canal, entering the gulf of the estuary from the lake.

If we now follow the coast-line, examining carefully as we go, we shall find many of the water-ways that enter the ocean growing wider as they approach the coast-line, precisely as do our own rivers, great and small, and that every one of those natural water-ways has been connected with the canal system. We again find examples of two canals converging to a place of junction and then continuing, in the general course of both, toward an objective point farther on, as pointed out by the arrows. This is so striking a feature of the economy of skillful engineering that it is very difficult to reconcile it with any other origin. If now we retrace our wanderings over the land, we can hardly help noticing that several canals radiate from common centers, some of those centers having as many as seven radiating water-ways, others six, others five, and so on, down to three. But it is also obvious, so far as we can read from the map, that they are not the locations of lakes or other natural water-ways to which an engineer might be induced to converge a system of canals for the purpose of economizing labor by gain of water-way, as in the cases already examined, and we are left to the conclusion that they are centers of population. Of this character is the point marked H, about thirteen degrees south of the equator, near the verge of the western hemisphere, and also I and J, lying between the equator and ten degrees north; and with those as guides others of similar character may be readily distinguished. Let us direct our attention to one of them, K, at the sixty-seventh parallel of north latitude, on the western hemisphere; then let us recall the fact that the sun moves seven degrees farther poleward on Mars in its summer-time than it does on our earth; then, in relation to the climatic condition of these two planets, the assumed center of population at the sixty-seventh parallel of north latitude on Mars is exactly the same as that of St. Petersburg at the sixtieth parallel on our earth, so that, assuming this point of convergence of this canal system to be a populous center upon Mars, is merely suggesting that

there may be a large city on that world bearing the same relations to its climatic conditions that St. Petersburg does to ours, and that it also is the most northerly of the great cities.

Having then passed in review this canal system of our neighboring planet, and found it replete with evidences of design, such as characterize the science of skillful engineering on our own planet, let us assume. for the sake of argument, that we have overdrawn the testimony, and that the markings have resulted from forces that accompanied the creative events of that globe. These two planets have their axis of rotation so inclined to the planes of their orbits about the sun that the alternations of their seasons are practically alike. When the sun moves northward on one or the other, the snow-line recedes toward the north pole. When the sun retires from its northern summer solstice, the snow-line advances down the northern latitudes, just in proportion as the source of heat recedes. The analogy between these concurrent phenomena of the two worlds is complete, and both, also, are divided into land and sea. So far, then, as the logic of facts can reach, the links of analogy are unbroken. This warrants us in assuming that the creative events of both worlds were equally analogous, for "like causes produce like effects," from which it follows that the primal waters of Mars came down upon that globe from an enveloping cloud of vapor covering its molten mineral substances, and thereby hardening them into the rock forms due to their composition, as the granite of our world hardened into its present form under like conditions. But whatever may be the mineral composition that assumes upon Mars the same geological relations that the granite does to our world, it was the primal sea-bottom of that globe, and, as sea-bottom, was covered with water long before its upheaval above the surface occurred, as in the case of our own primal sea-bottom. That this underlying Martial sea-bottom was genuine rock-formation, a glance at the facts will demonstrate. Rocks and clays are all combinations of metallic elementary matter with oxygen and the other five elementary forms of "the oxygen group," but the oxygen far exceeds in the quantity of its combinations all the other four. The presence of water on Mars proves the abundant presence of oxygen, for it is an oxide of hydrogen. Metals are all forms of matter in its elementary condition. and most, if not all of them, will decompose water by setting the hydrogen free and combining with the oxygen it contains; therefore the metallic elementary forms of matter upon Mars must have entered into combination with oxygen, even if no oxidizing agent were present but water. Hence the crust of the planet Mars is rock. The cooling of this rock sea-bottom, as in the case of our own world, caused it to contract or expand, as the case may have been, and therefore to wrinkle; the portions that bent upward rose above the surface of the overlying sea, and those that bent downward drained the displaced waters into the depressions thus formed, and they became seas, and the mandate was fulfilled in that world also, "Let the waters under the heaven be gathered together unto one place, and let the dry land appear." Forces so generated could not act with equal potency at every point, and there must be locations of greater and less resistance; therefore parts of the wrinkling rock sea-bottom would sink deeper than others beneath the normal level, while other parts would be elevated above it to a correspondingly unequal altitude. Hence Mars has its deep and shallow seas, its sea-level marshes, and mountains, with all sorts of intermediate relations, and the curves in several of the canals indicate that the engineers were flanking the difficulties that interposed between them and their objective point. There is nothing in the nature of the forces that upheave the land of a world from its waters that could leave such markings on its surface as those shown by the map; nor is it conceivable that Nature, in her methods of world-making, could leave upon her land-surfaces such markings as would bear the interpretation of engineering economy without a broken link in the chain of evidence.

It has already been asserted that these assumed canals can not be artificial, because they are eighty miles wide; but it is equally inconceivable that the forces of nature could, by the laws of accident, have constructed such an intricate system of markings, and observed an equal width in every case. The map given with the report has reduced them to forty-three miles wide, and a little investigation will show that this is still greatly in excess. If, when our observer is measuring their width with his micrometer, the water should be disturbed by the slightest breeze, the light would be reflected from them at all sorts of angles, and therefore it would be spread over the micrometer-lines to a much greater extent than the real width of the object under observation. But let us assume that no breeze is stirring the water. The surface then becomes a section of a polished ball, analogous to a polished glass ball, and as such its action upon light is dispersive; it therefore arrives at the earth in the character of divergent light, and must consequently occupy a width upon the micrometer greater than that actually due to an object at that distance. Hence we have probably not yet obtained the actual width of these canals.

Assuming that the weight of the evidence is in favor of the belief that the markings on the maps show a great system of engineering which connects by water-ways every part of the continent of the planet with its ocean-navigation, let us glance at the logical significance of such a state of things. Those who produced such a comprehensive system were not merely great designers, but they must have had instrumental means of "running their lines," "making and plotting field-notes," "taking levels on the surface of a globe," and "correcting them," as we do; which implies that they are familiar with the science of mathematics. The construction of those canals implies the necessity of locks. Locks could not be constructed without a knowledge of architecture, which, of course, would not be confined within the limits of lock-building. We have an axiom that architecture is the mother of art; both architecture and engineering require the most absolute accuracy of drawing, and merge too naturally into art to permit us to doubt that a people who could conceive such a comprehensive system of engineering would neglect the cultivation of the picturesque. That they are navigators is proved by the fact that their entire canal system is interoceanic; for nowhere do we find a single instance of a canal that is not in direct communication with its great southern ocean or the less expansive seas of its northern hemisphere. Look at Lake Nillaens, three of its six canals run southward, one taking the most direct route to the ocean, and two diverging to the right and left, on their way there, just enough to serve the economic purposes of the great sections of country that they traverse. Two others run direct from the lake to popular centers, one of which is in direct canal communication with the northern sea, while the sixth canal from the lake makes a long stretch westward, but a few hundred miles from the lake forms a junction with another canal, which thence proceeds in the most direct route to the northern sea. It is also worth our while to observe the fact that the system is not based on financial economy. A glance at the map will show that the original engineering scheme was the interpenetration of their entire circumplanetary continent with navigable water-ways, swerving from an equal division of land-sections only where they could utilize natural water-ways or communicate with populous centers, which seems to prove that Mammon is not worshiped on that planet, but has been banished to this. For this great system of navigable water-ways interpenetrates every part of their world alike, making a unit of the social relations of its entire people and precluding the possibility of barbaric conditions existing on any part of their planet. Let us change its name, for it is evidently a world where "Peace on earth, good will to men " is a realization, and it should no longer be called after the God of War.

MARYLAND. State Government.—The following were the State officers during the year. Governor, Elihu E Jackson, Democrat; Secretary of State, E. W. Le Compte; Treasurer, Stevenson Archer; Comptroller, L. Victor Baughman; Attorney - General, William P. Whyte; Secretary of State Board of Education, M. A. Newell; Tax Commissioner, Levin Woodford; Chief-Justice of the Court of Appeals, Richard A. Alvey; Associate Justices,

James M. Robinson, James McSherry, Lewis T. H. Irving, William S. Bryan, Frederick Stone, George Yellott, and Oliver Miller.

Finances.—The following statement exhibits the condition of the treasury during the year:

Total receipts for year ending Sept. 30, 1887...	$1,860,106 50
Balance Sept. 30, 1887........................	682,028 20
Total	$2,542,129 70
Disbursements for the fiscal year	2,010,060 24
Balance Sept. 30, 1887.....................	$532,069 46

The reduction of the receipts, as compared with the previous year, is due to the apparent increase of that year by the operation of the refunding act of 1886 and the reduction of the State levy in 1888.

The receipts on account of the free-school fund during the fiscal year were $69,860.63. This sum added to the balance standing to the credit of the fund Sept. 30, 1887, $8,836.81, makes an aggregate to the credit of the fund during the fiscal year 1888, of $78,697.44. The disbursements from the fund during the same time were $67,080.29, leaving a balance to the credit of the fund, Sept. 30, 1888, of $11,617.15.

The receipts of the several sinking-funds for the fiscal year were as follow:

To the general fund	$8,239 14
To treasury relief loan fund....................	12,793 85
To the fund for redemption of defense redemption loan	421,773 88
Making an aggregate of....................	442,806 87

In this aggregate is included the sum of $366,000 received from the Baltimore and Ohio Railroad Company for the bonds of the company held by the State to the credit of the sinking-fund for redemption of the defense redemption loan. There was invested on account of these sinking-funds during the past fiscal year the sum of $310,127.13, and there remains to the credit of the several sinking-funds in cash the sum of $132,679.74. The bonds of the State bearing 3·65 interest were quoted as high as 110 on the market in the month of December, 1888.

The total indebtedness of the State at the close of the fiscal year 1888 was $10,370,535.56, being less than the amount at the end of the fiscal year 1887, by the sum of $590,000, that amount of debt having been canceled during 1888. The State holds productive assets and cash to the credit of the sinking-funds to the amount of $4,715,181.34. There are also unproductive assets to the amount of upward of $28,000,000, investments authorized by the Legislature from time to time by way of experiment in works of internal improvement, and the interest thereon for many years, some of the items of which perhaps still have a possibility, but the majority of such investments are simply wrecks strewed along the pathway of the State's progress and prosperity.

The receipts from the oyster fund amounted to $53,236.69, and the expenditures were $67,913.13, which included the purchase of two new sailing-vessels for $6,000. The amount

standing to the credit of the oyster fund at the close of the fiscal year 1888 was $115,627.49. The receipts of the State school-tax during the fiscal year was $526,993.98, and the disbursements $520,200.37. The receipts during the fiscal year 1888 from State tobacco inspections were $82,414.70, and the disbursements $74,365.35, showing net receipts to the amount of $8,049.35, which, added to the balance to the credit of tobacco inspections at the close of the fiscal year 1887, made a total of $13,721.91.

Legislative Session.—The Legislature met on January 4, and adjourned on August 3. The Senate consisted of 21 Democrats and 4 Republicans, and the Lower House contained 68 Democrats and 23 Republicans. One of the most important measures passed was the abolition of compulsory inspection of tobacco. This restriction, it was contended, had long kept down the price of tobacco, especially in southern Maryland. The following are among the important bills that were passed during the session:

To authorize the Baltimore and Powhatan Railroad Company to use storage electricity as a motive power.

To protect diamond-back terrapin, and regulate the catching of the same.

To protect wild turkeys in Frederick County.

To protect fish in Blackwater river, Dorchester County.

Relating to jurisdiction liens of execution by justices of the peace.

To incorporate the town of Barnesville, Montgomery County.

To sanction bequests of various persons to societies.

To incorporate the village of La Plata, Charles County.

For the reorganization of the Board or Managers of the Agricultural College.

To incorporate the Industrial Educational Society of Baltimore.

To regulate fishing in Patuxent river with trap and purse seines.

Amending the charter of the Emettsburg Railroad Company.

To amend the oyster law in Somerset County.

Amending the law relating to husband and wife.

To incorporate the town of Stevensville, Queen Anne's County.

To change the name of Broad creek, Queen Anne's County, to Broad Harbor.

To authorize the Downsville and Hagerstown Turnpike Company to construct a turnpike.

For the protection of fish in Howard County.

For the protection of game and water-fowl in Charles County.

To define the oyster-grounds in the Choptank river in which scraping shall be allowed.

To prevent fishing with nets and seines in the waters of Cecil and Harford Counties.

For the catching of water-fowl.

Prohibiting the use of any other instrument than rakes or tongs by tongmen in Talbot, Queen Anne's, Anne Arundel, and Dorchester Counties.

To incorporate the town of Hampden, Carroll County.

Granting a new charter to the town of Port Tobacco.

To amend acts relating to larceny.

To amend general laws relating to proof of open accounts.

To incorporate Loudon County and Frederick County Bridge Company.

For building a bridge across the Potomac at Point of Rocks.

To add a new section to the code relating to pleading, practice, and process.

To add a section to the general laws relating to specific enforcements of contracts.

Relating to setting of pound nets in Elk, Sassafras, and Bohemia rivers and their tributaries, in Cecil County.

To add a section to the general laws. title, "Pleadings," sub-title "Judgments in detinue and replevin."

To amend general laws relating to insolvents.

To provide for the further publication of the archives of Maryland by the Maryland Historical Society.

Relating to compensation of witnesses.

To add a new section to the general law relating to crimes and punishment.

To amend charter of Agricultural and Mechanical Association of Washington County.

To protect game in Cecil County.

To provide for payments of wages and salaries due employés of insolvent employers.

To protect pheasants and partridges in Frederick County.

To incorporate the Church of the United Brethren in Christ.

Amending and re-enacting the liquor-law relating to licenses.

To prohibit the use of car-stoves on steam railroads after May, 1890.

To incorporate the town of Berlin, Worcester County.

Authorizing Dorchester County Commissioners to build a bridge on Transquekin river.

Abolishing distress for rent in Baltimore city, and substituting ejectment in lieu thereof.

To make valid deeds, mortgages, bonds of conveyances, and bills of sale.

Providing for punishment of minors guilty of felony.

Regulating the practice of medicine.

Requiring insurance companies to have $5,000 stock and to bond financial officers.

To permit creditors of insolvents to be represented by attorneys at creditors' meetings.

To punish false pretenses in obtaining certificates of registration of cattle and other animals.

To protect fish in the waters of Washington County.

To repeal the charter of the Baltimore and Ohio Relief Association.

To authorize the Mayor and City Council of Baltimore to subscribe to the erection of a monument to Francis Scott Key.

To incorporate the Cremation Company of Baltimore.

Appropriations.—Among the items in the general appropriation bill are the following: Militia, 1889, $50,000; 1890, $40,000; pensions, $520; schools, $500,000; school fund, $34,069; schools, academies, and colleges, $44,500; Deaf and Dumb Asylum at Frederick, $25,000; St. Mary's Industrial School, $15,000; Female House of Refuge, $3,000; Maryland Institute for Deaf, Dumb, and Blind, $7,000; Maryland Agricultural College, $5 (equal to no appropriation); indigent blind, $15,000; House of Correction, $25,000; House of Refuge, $15,000; House of Reformation and Institution (colored children), $10,000; Insane Hospital, $20,000; additional buildings for same, $7,500. Total for 1889, $1,535,917; for 1890, $1,670,692, against $1,607,582 for 1887 and $1,711,392 for 1888, which shows a reduction of $112,365 in the appropriations for 1889 and 1890 compared with 1887 and 1888. The

militia, which received $50,000 in 1887 and $30,000 in 1888, will receive in 1889 $50,000, and in 1890 $40,000. The interest on the public debt in 1887 and 1888 was $600,000 each year, while in 1889 and 1890 it will be but $575,000 each year.

Changes in Tax-Laws.—The Maryland Tax Commission, in its report to the General Assembly, says:

The most undue burden and severest inequality suffered by the people of this State are those which arise from the unjust discrimination made in favor of the railroad corporations. Unfortunately, $250,000 of the $400,000 a year which the railroads ought justly to pay to the State, are intrenched behind charter and contract exemptions claimed to be irrepealable. The charter of the Baltimore and Ohio Railroad Company provided that "the shares of capital stock of the said company shall be deemed and considered personal estate, and shall be exempt from the imposition of any tax or burden by the State assenting to this law." Our Court of Appeals subsequently enlarged this exemption by holding that the exemption of the shares of stock from taxation carried with it the exemption of the property and franchises of the company, and that, under the Constitution of the United States, this exemption is irrepealable. It seems peculiarly unfortunate that an exemption which, by its terms, applied to the shares of stock in the hands of the individual stockholders was thus held to extend to the franchises and property, including real estate, held by the corporation in its capacity as a legal entity. The case of the exemption of the Northern Central Railway is still more flagrant than that of the Baltimore and Ohio, and has less show of legality or right. The part of this road which lies in Maryland was formerly the Baltimore and Susquehanna Railroad, which was chartered in 1827, with the same exemption, word for word, as that contained in the charter of the Baltimore and Ohio. We recommend that a gross-receipts tax be imposed upon telegraph companies at the rate of 2 per cent.; and 3 per cent. upon telephone, express, title-insurance, safety deposit and trust companies, parlor-car and sleeping-car companies; and 1 per cent. on domestic insurance companies, leaving the tax as at present, 1½ per cent. on the gross receipts of foreign insurance companies. These taxes will, of course, be in addition to the tax measured by the companies' dividend.

A new bill, drawn by Prof. Richard T. Ely, was submitted with this report to the Legislature.

Chesapeake and Ohio Canal.—The management of this canal was the subject of much discussion in the Legislature. A delegation from Baltimore, including representatives from the commercial organizations, urged the passage of a bill permitting its lease. The Western Maryland Railroad Company has offered to take it at a rental of $45,000, and a bill was presented to the Legislature to that effect, but it failed to pass.

Political.—The Democratic State Convention was held in Baltimore on May 11, and after choosing electors adopted a platform, of which the following are important items:

National taxation ought to be limited to the aggregate annual sum needed for the following purposes, namely: The interest on the public debt, with adequate annual provision for the payment of the principal of that debt at maturity; for the payment of pensions granted by the United States, and to provide the means for all necessary expenses of an economically administered government.

The accumulation each year of a large surplus in the National Treasury, after the payment of all such charges, is in itself conclusive proof that the taxing system fastened upon the country by the Republican party requires complete revision. The resolutions of the Democratic National Convention in 1884 clearly indicate the principles upon which such revision ought to be made.

The Republican Convention was held at Easton on May 17, and the platform adopted contained the following resolutions:

That in the free-trade movement inaugurated by the Democratic party, we recognize a renewed effort to aid foreign manufacturers to displace the products of American workmen with those of pauperized labor. We believe that the protective system, which has made this nation great and its people prosperous, is the best means for maintaining that greatness and prosperity, and denounce and oppose the unpatriotic assault upon the independence and prosperity of the American workingmen.

That, recognizing the undesirability of a large surplus revenue, we favor the abolition of the internal taxes on tobacco and alcohol used in the arts and sciences, and the modification of the duty on sugar, and we declare that, in justice to the American interests involved, any necessary readjustment of the tariff should be made by its friends, and not by its enemies.

That we commend the course of the Republican Senate in the matter of pensioning the disabled veterans of the Union armies and those dependent on them. We urge the representatives of this State in the National Convention to favor greater liberality in dealing with the just claims of these defenders of the Union.

That we are in favor of an unqualified franchise and equality of men before the law.

The presidential election resulted in the easting of the following votes: Cleveland, 106,172; Harrison, 99,761; and Fisk, 5,858, which shows a plurality of 6,411 for Cleveland, against 11,118 in 1884. Two Republican and four Democratic Congressmen were elected, and one seat is to be contested—a gain of at least one Republican. In Baltimore the City Council, by Republican gains, became tied. The Legislature contains 22 Democrats and 4 Republicans in the Senate, and 68 Democrats and 23 Republicans in the Lower House

MASSACHUSETTS. State Government.—The following were the State officers during the year: Governor, Oliver Ames, Republican; Lieutenant-Governor, John Q. A. Brackett; Secretary of State, Henry B. Pierce; Auditor, Charles R. Ladd; Treasurer, Alanson W. Beard; Attorney-General, Andrew J. Waterman; Railroad Commissioners, George G. Crocker, Edward W. Kinsley, and Everett A. Stevens; Chief-Justice of the Supreme Court, Marcus Morton; Associate Justices, Walbridge A. Field, Charles Devens, William Allen, Charles Allen, Oliver W. Holmes, Jr., and Marcus P. Knowlton.

Legislative Session.—The Legislature met on January 4, and adjourned on May 29. The question of dividing the town of Beverly was again a prominent subject of discussion; but the bill for division, after passing the Senate, failed in the Lower House. Several acts restricting the liquor traffic were among the note-

worthy features of the session. One of these defines intoxicating liquor to be any beverage containing more than 1 per cent. of alcohol (instead of 3 per cent. as formerly), the object of the bill being to render easier a conviction for illegal selling. Another act forbids the sale of liquor on Fast Day, Memorial and Thanksgiving Days, and Christmas. Still another limits the number of places that may be licensed to sell liquor, to one for each one thousand of population, except in the city of Boston, where there may be one for every five hundred people, and another raises the fees to $1,000 for first-class licenses, $250 for second and third class, $200 for fourth-class, and $150 for fifth-class licenses. Lastly, the following amendment to the State Constitution was proposed and referred to the next Legislature: "The manufacture and sale of intoxicating liquors to be used as a beverage are prohibited. The General Court shall enact suitable legislation to enforce the provisions of this article."

An act regulating child labor, provides that no child under thirteen years of age shall be employed at any time in any factory, workshop, or mercantile establishment, and no such child be employed in any other indoor labor for wages during the sessions of the public schools, unless during the year preceding he has attended school for at least twenty weeks. No child under fourteen years of age shall be employed in any factory, workshop, or mercantile establishment, except during the vacation of the public schools, unless a certificate is obtained from school officials stating that the child can read and write, and has attended school twenty weeks during the preceding year, or is attending the public evening schools; and no such child shall be employed in any other indoor work for wages, except as aforesaid. No child who has been continuously a resident of a city or town, since reaching the age of thirteen years, shall be entitled to receive a certificate that he has reached fourteen years until he has attended school twenty weeks in such town or city since reaching the age of thirteen, unless exempted by law from such attendance. Truant officers are charged with the enforcement of the law, and fines are imposed on parents or guardians that disobey.

A new ballot act, modeled on the Australian system, provides for the printing and distribution of ballots at the public expense, and regulates the form of such ballots, the method of voting, and the arrangement of polling-places. Entire secrecy is secured to the voter by this method, and the possibility of fraudulent balloting reduced to a minimum.

More efficient supervision of schools in the smaller towns is secured by permitting two or more towns to unite in obtaining the services of a trained and salaried superintendent.

In order to provide for contemplated addition to the State House, which for a long time has been unable to accommodate all departments of the State Government, it was voted to take a parcel of land adjoining, known as the "Reservoir" lot, and a sum not exceeding $500,000 was appropriated for payment of damages to the owners. This sum is to be raised by an issue of four-per-cent. scrip, payable in July, 1901.

Two new cities, Quincy and Woburn, were incorporated at this session. The population of the former, by the census of 1885, was 12,-145; of the latter, 11,750.

A woman-suffrage bill and a resolution for biennial elections of State officers were defeated in the Lower House.

The following general laws were also passed:

Authorizing the Boston and Providence Railroad corporation to lease its road to the Old Colony Railroad Company.

Erecting the town of Avon out of a part of the town of Stoughton.

Increasing the number of associate justices of the Superior Court from eleven to thirteen.

Increasing the range of legal investments for savings-banks.

Providing for the registration and licensing of plumbers.

To authorize the incorporation of labor or trade organizations.

To cause proper sanitary provisions and proper ventilation in public buildings and school-houses.

Prohibiting railroad corporations from requiring women and children to ride in smoking-cars.

Extending to the first day of October the time in which persons may apply for assessment of taxes, and providing for evening sessions of the assessors.

Regulating the sale and purchase of poisons.

Providing for the free instruction of deaf mutes or deaf children.

Authorizing the Boston and Maine Railroad to purchase the franchise and property of the Eastern Railroad Company, and the Eastern Railroad in New Hampshire, and the Portsmouth, Great Falls, and Conway Railroad.

Providing a bounty of one dollar each for the destruction of seals.

To regulate the sale of commercial fertilizers.

Requiring the equipment of fire departments with apparatus for the saving of life at fires.

To punish the sending of women and girls to houses of ill-fame and their detention therein.

Requiring the plans of all public buildings, and of private buildings more than two stories in height, having above the second story accommodations for ten or more employés, or having ten or more rooms for guests above the second story, to be submitted to the inspector of factories and buildings of the district and approved by him, and making certain rules to be observed in the construction of such buildings.

To prevent encroachment upon or obstruction of the waters of great ponds.

Authorizing towns to regulate the catching of pickerel.

To establish a naval battalion to be attached to the volunteer militia.

To protect the purity of inland waters, and to require consultation with the State Board of Health regarding the establishment of systems of water-supply, drainage, and sewerage.

Authorizing cities to indemnify police officers for injuries received or expenses incurred in the discharge of their duties.

To provide for the final determination of contests concerning the election of electors of President and Vice-President of the United States.

To provide armories for the State volunteer militia.

Regulating mortgage, loan, and investment companies.

Amending and codifying the statutes relative to the collection of taxes.

Raising the age of consent in females from thirteen to fourteen years.

To prevent the desecration of graves by the removal therefrom of flowers, flags, or other memorial tokens.

Providing for the appointment of a State agent whose duty shall be to assist citizens of the State in the presentation and settlement of pension, bounty, or back-pay claims against the Federal Government.

Defining the duties and liabilities and regulating the business of safe-deposit, loan, and trust companies.

Regulating the weight and measure of cider-apples, beans, and peas.

Making an appropriation to be expended in aiding discharged female prisoners.

Changing the procedure in poor-debtor matters.

Making further regulations as to means of egress and of escape from fire in buildings.

Providing for the organization of fraternal beneficiary organizations.

Providing for a new division of wards in cities.

Providing for the public support, in cases of necessity, of soldiers or sailors of the late war and their dependent families, without requiring them to go to an almshouse.

To regulate the holding of caucuses or public meetings of voters in cities or towns for political purposes.

Finances.—The general financial statement of the Treasurer for the year is as follows: Cash on hand Jan. 1, 1888, $3,743,536.59; securities on hand, $27,845,153.35; receipts, $23,546,-078.11; securities purchased, $2,496,225.15; total, $57,630,993.20; payments, $22,970,003.-17; securities withdrawn and sold or paid, $4,-468,931.95; cash on hand, $4,319,611.53; securities on hand, $25,872,446.55; total, $57,-630,993.20.

On Dec. 31, 1887, the funded debt was $31,-429,680.90; the reduction for the year amounted to $2,578,061.25, leaving $28,851,619.65 on Dec. 31, 1888. During the same period the sinking-fund was reduced from $25,151,516.78 to $23,235,608.84, a decrease of $1,915,907.94. The following loans composed this debt at the close of the year: Boston, Hartford, and Erie loan, $3,618,729.40; county fund loan, $8,-402,148.90; coast-defense loan, $6,000; Danvers Hospital loan, $1,500,000; harbor improvement loan, $800,000; State House loan, $500,000; State Prison loan, $1,299,355.50; Troy and Greenfield loan, $11,219,966.95; war loan, $1,505,418.90; Worcester Hospital loan, $1,100,000. The total amount paid for interest on these loans was $1,458,729.46.

During the year the United States Supreme Court decided the law of the State taxing the stock of national banks to be constitutional, and the sum of $465,131.41, which had been paid by the banks under protest and was held by the Treasurer to await the decision, was distributed to the various cities and towns entitled thereto.

The actual expenses of the State Government for 1887 were $5,028,385.98; for 1888, $4,-985,135.47. For 1889 the estimated revenue is $5,087,606.82, and the expenditures $5,930,-606.16, leaving a deficit of nearly $850,000.

The limitation of time for the payment of

State aid to invalid pensioners and their dependent relatives will expire on Jan. 1, 1890. The payment of State aid began with the civil war, and has continued without interruption ever since. During 1887 the sum of $391,678.02 was expended by the State on this account for the relief of 6,650 beneficiaries.

Assessments.—For 1888 the total assessed valuation of property in the State was $1,992,804,101, of which $532,284,079 was the assessment of personal property, and $1,460,520,022 of real estate. The total assessed valuation of 1887 was $1,932,548,807; of 1886, $1,847,531,422. In this valuation are included 4,497,123 acres of land and 330,541 dwelling-houses. There were also assessed in 1888, 166,152 horses, 51,539 sheep, 187,994 cows, 65,609 of other neat cattle, and 34,749 swine.

Education.—The following summary of public-school statistics is given for the year 1887-'88: Number of public schools, 6,918; children of school age, 359,504; number of all ages enrolled, 358,000; average attendance, 264,723; number of male teachers, 1,010; number of female teachers, 8,887; average monthly pay of male teachers, $119.34; average monthly pay of female teachers, $44.88; average school year in months, 8-9. All these figures exhibit an increase over the previous year.

The high-schools, numbering 230, exhibit an increase on school, 36 teachers, and 379 pupils. These schools were materially aided by the passage of the free text-book law, which was immediately followed by a large increase in attendance. In the past five years the number attending the high-schools has increased by 3,362. Evening schools have been maintained in 50 cities and towns. The number of schools is 214, an increase of 60; the number of teachers 919, an increase of 289; the number of pupils 24,725, an increase of 9,044; the average attendance 12,823, an increase of 4,837. This large increase is due to the act of 1887, which prohibits the employment of illiterate minors unless they are regular attendants of day or evening schools. The whole amount of money raised by taxation for the support of schools, this including only wages of teachers, fuel, care of fires and school-rooms, was $5,114,402.41, an increase of $54,462.98. The amount received from all sources and expended for the schools, exclusive of money spent for building and repairing school-houses, was $5,934,195.59, an increase of $76,877.59, and equal to $16.50 for each child in the State between 5 and 15 years of age. The whole amount expended for all public-school purposes was $7,087,206.42, an increase of $87,222.90, and equal to $19.71 for each child of school age.

At the various normal schools the attendance during the year was as follows: At Bridgewater, 419; at Framingham, 155; at Salem, 274; at Westfield, 250; at Worcester, 198; at the Normal Art School, 187; total, 1,403. The school at Framingham suffered the loss of its main building by a fire on Dec. 24, 1887.

Charities.—For the fiscal year ending September 30, the Danvers Lunatic Hospital received 402 patients, and discharged 427, having at the close of the year 715 remaining. Of those discharged, 121 were transferred to other hospitals. The receipts for the year were $145,611.08; payments, $151,637.65. At the Northampton Hospital there were 469 patients at the beginning of the fiscal year, and 481 at its close, 166 persons having been admitted and 154 discharged. The receipts for the year were $97,873.46; payments, $87,522.13. At the Worcester Hospital there were 694 patients on Sept. 30, 1887; there were admitted during the year 389, discharged 313, leaving 770 patients on September 30 of this year. The receipts were $166,570.86; expenses, $147,445.68. At the Worcester Asylum for the Chronic Insane, the statistics are as follow: Patients at the beginning of the fiscal year, 392; admitted, 59; discharged, 56; remaining on September 30 of this year, 395; receipts, $79,977.93; expenses, $72,466.83. At the Westborough Hospital 333 persons were admitted and 236 discharged during the year, leaving 406 inmates on September 30. At the same date in 1887, there were 309 patients. The receipts were $93,886.61; expenses, $92,171.70. The Taunton Hospital had 634 patients at the beginning of the year; 260 were received, and 270 discharged, leaving 624 at the close of the year. The receipts were $125,180.65; expenditures, $125,605.97.

There were also 352 insane patients at the State almshouse at the close of the fiscal year. The total number of persons admitted to this institution during the year was 2,006; discharged, 2,018. On Sept. 30, 1887, there were 877 inmates; on Sept. 30, 1888, 865. The school for the feeble-minded had 195 pupils at the close of the fiscal year; 38 were admitted during the year, and 86 discharged. The present buildings in South Boston are inadequate, and the Legislature has made provision for better accommodations. An act passed in 1887 enabled the trustees to purchase a tract of land in Waltham, and another act, passed this year, appropriates $200,000 for buildings thereon.

Prisons and Reformatories.—The average number of prisoners at the State penal institutions for the year ending Sept. 30, 1888, was as follows: State Prison, 556; Massachusetts Reformatory, 792; Reformatory Prison for Women, 21. The cost per week per capita was: Massachusetts Reformatory, $3.30; State Prison, $2.52; Reformatory Prison for Women, $4.25.

The State Prison at Boston is the only State institution in which the prisoners have been employed under the act of 1887, requiring all prison labor to be done upon the account of the State, and not under contract with individuals. The results shown during the year to December 31 are as follow: Expenses of the business, $116,516.72; salary of general superintendent and other necessary expenses for the work, $20,645.26; total, $137,161.98. Receipts from the industries, $71,698.24; excess of expenditures, $65,463.74. The Governor says upon this topic:

The only difficulty in the practical working of the law governing prison labor is that of establishing industries. It is provided by section 5 of chapter 447 of the acts of the year 1887 that "no new machinery to be propelled by other than hand or foot power shall be used in any institution." This provision prevents the maintenance of the varied and improved conditions of employment which the future advantage, if not the present well-being, of the prisoners would seem to require. The law should be so amended that the prisoners may have the advantage of employment with such improved machinery as the nature of the business in which they are engaged may demand. Satisfactory pecuniary returns are not to be expected from prison labor, but the "public-account" plan gives to the prison officials more complete control of those who are committed to their charge, and in this way it is to the community a decided gain.

At the State Primary School at Monson there were 316 inmates on Oct. 1, 1887, and 314 at the same date this year. The total number in the school during the year was 538. The Westborough Reform School contained 118 boys at the beginning of the fiscal year, and 142 at its close. The Industrial School for Girls at Lancaster cared for 157 girls during the year, of whom 58 were in the school at the beginning of the year, and 63 at its close.

Savings-Banks.—In the saving-banks and institutions for savings there were, in deposits, at the end of their fiscal year, $315,185,070.57, an increase for the year of $12,236,446.49, the number of open accounts being 983,202.

The Public-School Controversy and Woman Suffrage.—Early in May, the Rev. Father Metcalf, of Boston, in a public letter, complained that a teacher of history in the city high-school, Charles B. Travis, was misrepresenting in his instruction the position of the Catholic Church with reference to the sale of indulgences, and that William Swinton's history, the text-book used in the schools, unfairly stated the facts of history in this regard, inasmuch as it did not give the whole truth. After consideration of this complaint, the school board, which was largely composed of Catholics, voted, on June 19, to dispense with the obnoxious text-book, and, after censuring Mr. Travis, transferred him to another department of history in the same school. This proceeding was looked upon by many Protestants as an attempt of the Catholics to control the public schools in the interest of their Church. They argued that the objections to the book were unfounded, that the history was truthful, even if the facts stated were unpleasant, and they considered such interference of the Church in temporal affairs as unjustifiable. A large indignation meeting was held in Faneuil Hall, on July 18, at which the action of the school committee was denounced in strong terms, stirring resolutions were adopted, and a committee was appointed to protect the interests of the public schools. The whole subject of the attitude of the Catholic Church toward the State and of parochial schools vs. public schools was a matter of earnest discussion throughout the summer and autumn, during which efforts were undertaken to defeat all retiring members of the school board who had voted in favor of the Catholics. For this purpose the aid of a law passed a few years before, permitting women to be assessed and to vote for members of the school committee, was invoked by the Protestants. Hitherto only a handful of women had exercised their right under the law, but, so great was the feeling aroused by this question, that in Boston not far from 23,000 women applied for assessment, while in the adjacent cities, to which the discussion had found its way, there was a female registration of from 1,000 to 2,000 or more, Catholics as well as Protestants being among the applicants. The result was that in Boston, at the December municipal election, every candidate suspected of favoring the Catholic side of the controversy was defeated, and in the adjacent cities the same result was reached. It is estimated that in Boston nearly 17,000 women went to the polls, of whom the majority were Protestants.

Political.—The State Democratic Convention met at Springfield on September 5, and nominated without a contest the following ticket: For Governor, William E. Russell; Lieutenant-Governor, John W. Corcoran; Secretary of State, William N. Osgood; Treasurer and Receiver-General, Henry C. Thatcher; Attorney-General, Samuel O. Lamb; Auditor, William A. Williams. The platform adopted ratified the nominations of the St. Louis Convention, commended the national Administration, and contained also the following:

Believing that all unnecessary taxation is simply robbery from the people under the forms of law, we desire and demand the reduction of the present war rates of taxation to such a point as will leave in the pockets of the people over $100,000,000 per year that is now being taken therefrom without reason or justice and locked up in idleness in the Treasury vaults at Washington.

We cordially approve the provisions of the Mills Bill as well adapted to promote industry, to protect labor, and particularly benefit the manufacturing interests of this commonwealth. The placing of wool on the free list will unquestionably give a valuable stimulus to the woolen-mills of this State, and, by reducing the cost of materials, will enable the woolen-manufacturer to compete with all foreign rivals for the trade of the world, and thus give more work and better wages to woolen-workers.

Believing that taxes should be lifted first from the common articles of necessary consumption, and last from the articles of luxury, we indorse and commend President Cleveland's proposition to take the duty off wool, salt, lumber, and such staples as, being thus made cheaper, will make lighter the task of every workingman who has a family to provide for; and we denounce the policy proposed by the Republican party of abolishing the internal-revenue taxes which bear on liquors and tobacco, thus offering the people cheap whisky instead of cheaper necessaries of life.

Believing that trusts, those creatures of the exorbitant war tariff, are iniquitous combinations, hostile alike to the legitimately employed capital and the honest labor of the country, we demand such tariff legislation by Congress and such other legislation, by the General Court of this State, as will effectually curb the power and arrest the growth of these dangerous monopolies.

We demand now, as always, the most liberal treatment of Union veterans, and of the widows and families of those of them who are dead; and promise our support to all well-considered laws for the promotion of temperance, and announce our hostility at the same time to prohibitory legislation as violating the cardinal democratic doctrine of personal liberty.

The Republican Convention met in Boston one week later, and renominated the existing State officials, except Treasurer Beard, who had refused to be a candidate for re-election. George A. Marden was nominated as his successor.

Resolutions were adopted favoring protection, condemning the system of undervaluation and false invoicing of imported goods, and recommending, as a means of checking this evil, the imposition of specific duties wherever practicable, instead of the present ad-valorem duty. Other resolutions were as follow:

We approve the action of the Legislature, and repeat the resolution of the Republican Convention of last year, "That, believing that the great question has reached a position where it demands settlement, we favor the submission to the people of an amendment to our Constitution prohibiting the manufacture and sale of alcoholic liquors as a beverage," and, in order to accomplish this, we call upon all who are opposed to the political control of the grog-shop to unite with the Republican party in securing the election of Senators and Representatives who will vote for the submission of this amendment, and further legislation in accord with this declaration of principles.

We pledge ourselves to such wise expenditures for the public schools as to render them the best places for the instruction of our youth, and to steady resistance to any plan of public aid to sectarian schools. We believe in the equal rights of all men under the law; in the same restrictive legislation for monopolies, corporations, and trusts of every description as govern and control the humblest citizen; in the immediate reform and better enforcement of the immigration and naturalization laws; in an honest ballot the country over, as the only interpretation of the popular will; in an impartial suffrage; in the payment of every honest debt of the Government, wherever contracted; in an honest, liberal, and just pension law, embodying in statute the generous gratitude of a warm-hearted people to the veteran soldier; in the exemption of the civil service from partisan spoliation. To the solution of these great questions, in which they will bear so large a part, we welcome the young men of this State to an increasing share in the honors and responsibilities which citizenship ought to confer.

We thus heartily approve and most cordially commend the platform adopted by the national Republican party at its national convention in Chicago, in June of this year, and pledge our earnest support to the national candidates of the party.

The nominees of the Prohibition party, which held its convention at Worcester, on the same date as that of its Republican opponents, were: For Governor, William H. Earle; Lieutenant-Governor, John Bascom; Secretary of State, Henry C. Smith; Treasurer and Receiver-General, John M. Fisher; Auditor, Edmund M. Stowe; Attorney-General, Allen Coffin. The most important portion of its platform is as follows:

It has been found in the experience of our courts that the mingling of civil and criminal business in the hands of district attorneys, and the making of these offices elective, operate to the disadvantage of the commonwealth. We therefore demand that said officers be appointed by the judges of the Supreme Court, and be required on entering upon duty to relinquish all civil business and devote themselves exclusively to the interests of the State.

We demand the unconditional abandonment of revenue, municipal, State, and national, from the manufacture and sale of intoxicating drinks, not with reference to the surplus in the Treasury, nor for the relief of the liquor manufacturer, dealer, or drinker, but for the readier suppression of the traffic, and to put an end to the political scandal of deriving a revenue from the poverty, degradation, and vices of the people.

We demand the preservation of our free public-school system in all its integrity; reform in the civil service; suppression of polygamy; the establishment of uniform laws governing marriage and divorce; a more generous and just distribution of the products of labor; arbitration as a means of settling international strife and local business difficulties between employers and employed; the preservation and defense of one day in seven as a day of worship and spiritual elevation; the improvement and better enforcement of our immigration laws; just and liberal provision for our surviving soldiers and families; the penalty of disfranchisement for buying or selling votes; the reservation of the public lands for actual settlers; the sacred fulfillment of our treaty stipulations with the Indian races; equal wages to men and women for equal service; the prohibition of trusts and combinations of capital to enhance prices on articles of popular consumption; and more than all, and above all, the utter destruction of the saloon, by which the laborer is robbed of his earnings, and is morally, physically, and socially burdened.

There was also a Labor ticket, with Charles E. Marks, the candidate of last year, at its head. At the election in November Ames received for Governor 180,849 votes; Russell, 152,780; Earle, 9,374; Marks and others, 111. Russell ran about 3,000 votes ahead of his ticket. There were 33 Republicans and 7 Democrats elected to the State Senate, and 181 Republicans, 58 Democrats, and 1 Independent to the House. Ten Republican and 2 Democratic Congressmen were chosen.

Municipal Elections.—Nineteen of the twenty-five cities of the State held their annual election on Tuesday, December 4. Party lines were not strictly drawn in most cases, the license question being of paramount interest. Twelve cities voted in favor of license, and seven against it. In 1887 ten voted for license and nine against it. One week later Boston and the five remaining cities held their election, all of them voting for license, as in 1887. In Boston, Thomas N. Hart, the nominee of the Republicans, was elected over Mayor O'Brien by a majority of 1,876, in a total vote of 63,548. The majority for license was 17,915.

MELIKOFF, Count **LORIS,** a Russian general born in 1826; died in Nice, France, Dec. 24, 1888. He was one of the numerous Armenians that joined Gen. Paskievich's army in the Caucasus, obtaining his first commission in 1843. He participated in several expeditions against the mountain tribes, and gained his first decoration for gallantry in 1848. He rose rapidly, served under Gen. Mouravieff in the Crimean war, and attained the rank of major-general on being appointed Russian Governor of Kars, having taken part in the capture of that stronghold. In 1865, when the pacification of the Caucasus was completed, he was appointed aid-de-camp to the Emperor, and after ten years of further service in the Caucasus was made a general. He was the trusted 'lieutenant of the Grand Duke Michael, Prince-Governor of the Caucasus, and when the Turkish war began he assumed the chief command of the army that was raised to invade the Asiatic provinces of Turkey. He crossed the frontier with a smaller force than he expected to mobilize, and, although he displayed great energy, he was unable to cope with the active strategy of Mukhtar Pasha, who, fighting on the inside line and resting on his fortresses, checked the Russian advance. Gen. Melikoff, understanding the risk of attempting to hold the extended position in the face of the victorious Turkish army, retired within the Russian frontier in order to restore his troops and receive supplies before resuming the offensive. By the middle of August, 1877, he was able to take the field with a stronger and better prepared army. Mukhtar Pasha, whose forces had been reduced by disease, forced on a general engagement at Aladja Dagh. Failing to make the most advantageous dispositions, he was defeated by Melikoff after eleven hours' fighting, notwithstanding the desperate courage of the Turkish soldiers. Gen. Melikoff waited for re-enforcements, and in October resumed the advance, and after several stubbornly fought battles, compelled the Turkish commander to evacuate his advanced line. He conducted the remaining operations of the campaign including the turning of the main position of the enemy by Gen. Lazareff's flank march on Ordok, and while the other generals pursued Mukhtar's shattered forces, he laid siege to Kars, the chief objective point of the campaign. When he had carried a part of the outer works, he concluded that the place might be captured by assault, which was accomplished on the night of November 18. For this striking feat of arms, Gen. Melikoff was decorated with the cross of St. George and at the close of the war he was made a count.

In 1879, when the Nihilists were at the height of their activity, and through the murder of Prince Krapotkine, Solovieff's attempt on the life of the Czar, and other deeds, had created a general panic, Count Melikoff was called away from Tiflis to take a place in the Central Government. The Czar had always decided to make political concessions, and Melikoff urged that these should be definite and substantial. In February, 1880, he was appointed president of a supreme executive commission, and issued a proclamation calling on all friends of order to support him in his efforts to preserve national security and tranquillity when he assumed the office, which was practically that of dictator. Alexander II was converted by him to the idea that he could win the affection of the Russian people by granting a large measure of social and individual freedom. Melikoff's relaxations of tyranical restrictions

actually caused the cessation of Nihilistic outrages for twelve months. The Czar had been persuaded by Gen. Melikoff, who was his Minister of the Interior, to sign a constitution granting representative institutions, when his assassination on March 13, 1881, put an end to all hope of liberal reforms, and caused Gen. Melikoff, who was head of the police department and was therefore held responsible for the Czar's safety, to be discarded as well as his policy. He was nevertheless retained as a member of the Council of the Empire by Alexander III. His health began to fail about 1883, and since then he has lived much of the time in the south of Europe.

METALLURGY. Iron and Steel.—In his presidential address before the Iron and Steel Institute, Mr. Daniel Adamson spoke of the falling off that had taken place in the manufacture of iron in Great Britain since 1884, and the large increase in the production of steel during the same period. Thus in 1884 about one and a quarter million tons of Bessemer steel ingots were produced, and in 1887 about two million tons, being an increase of about 60 per cent.; in 1884 nearly half a million tons of Siemen's open-hearth steel ingots were cast, and nearly a million tons in 1887, the actual increase during the period being over 106 per cent.; and a plant is in course of erection estimated to produce another quarter of a million tons annually. There has also been an enormous increase in the application of steel to ship-building purposes. Thus, whereas in 1878 less than three thousand tons of steel were employed in the manufacture of steamers and sailing-vessels built under Lloyd's survey, and over three hundred thousand tons of iron, in 1887 more than two hundred and ten thousand tons of steel were employed, and about fifty-two thousand tons of iron. The proportional increase in the use of steel in the last three years had been about cent. per cent., and the falling off in the use of iron during the same period 350 per cent.

It has been difficult to produce pig-iron with a high percentage of chromium, on account of the very high temperature that is required, for complete fusion of the metal takes place only at a temperature at which the best graphite crucibles soften—that is, probably above the melting-point of platinum. Such iron has been produced in Sweden in small quantities by modifying the composition of the slag, but at a cost too high to make it compete successfully with the poorer chrome iron produced elsewhere in blast-furnaces using coke as fuel. With regenerative crucible furnaces, this iron could not be obtained in a thoroughly fused condition, but the reduced metal is always intimately mixed with slag. A pig-iron can be produced containing 70 per cent. of chromium. It contains less carbon than the metal poorer in chromium, and acts less as a carbonizing material when added to the steel-bath than would a metal containing, say, only 45 per cent. of chromium. By the use of this chromium pig-iron and open-hearth steel can be produced which will compete in every respect with the best English crucible steel, and in many cases even excel it. Chromium steel is harder than ordinary steel with the same percentage of carbon, but it is more difficult to harden. If the carbon is kept 0·2 per cent. lower than would be used if no chromium were present, and that amount of chromium is added which will give the requisite degree of hardness, a steel can be obtained that will stand a much greater welding heat than ordinary carbon steel, and will be at the same time both tougher and harder. The percentage of carbon in a chrome steel should never exceed 0·9. The percentage of chromium need rarely exceed 1·5 per cent. If it is desired to produce a harder steel than that containing 0·9 per cent. of carbon and 2 per cent. of chromium, 0·2 per cent. of silicon must be present to insure freedom from blow-holes, and the phosphorus, on account of the presence of silicon, should be kept below 0·3 per cent.

A new direct method, applied by the Carbon Iron Company of Pittsburg, for making wrought-iron from the ore, is based upon the use, as a reducing agent, of a new kind of graphite from Rhode Island, which also protects the iron from reoxidation. This, having been ground very fine and mixed, previous to roasting, with water, is mingled with the ore in the proportion of one to four by weight.

In Huchavel's method of producing wrought-iron and steel direct from the ore, the main feature of the furnace consists of a movable hearth fitted to a blast-furnace constructed partly of cast-iron and partly of wrought-iron plates, the latter of which form a double skin to the body of the furnace, while the space between the skins is used to heat the blast. The furnace, the inventor represents, has been gradually developed from the simplest form of cold-blast furnace, under the stress of difficulties which were from time to time encountered. The fuel used is wood charcoal. From magnetic ore containing 58 per cent. of iron, the author obtains 52·4 per cent. of steel; and the loss in producing wrought-iron is said to be no greater than it is in a puddling-furnace.

In a paper on "Silicon and Sulphur in Cast-Iron," Mr. T. Turner reaches the conclusion that, in the blast-furnace, three chief agencies are at work tending to eliminate sulphur, of which in Cleveland practice not more than one twentieth passes into the iron: 1. A high temperature tends to prevent the absorption of sulphur by iron; 2. A slag rich in lime readily combines with sulphur; and 3. The amount of sulphur actually retained by the metal is influenced by the proportion of silicon, and probably certain other elements present in the iron —the more silicon the less sulphur.

The "rapid" steel-making process of B. H. Thwaite and A. Stewart is intended to combine the best features and avoid the defects of the Bessemer and Siemens–Martin processes. The pig-metal is melted in a "rapid" cupola and collected in a receiver, from which it is run into a vertical converter, and thence drawn off in the ladle. In its passage through the converter the mass is subjected to the blast from the cupola-blower. As soon as the iron is collected in the ladle, the latter is raised from its trunnions and rapidly revolved. Stirrers effectually mix the metal, and the steel is then ready for the mold. The system can be applied to existing open-hearth furnaces.

A practical demonstration has been given at the Lambeth works of Messrs. Brin of the direct conversion, by a new process, of iron into steel containing two per cent. of aluminum. The charge consisted of about forty pounds of broken cast-iron, which was smeared with clay —the source of the aluminum—and a special flux. This charge was placed in a small foundry-furnace, and was speedily transformed into excellent steel. Other metals can be similarly treated, and any percentage of aluminum can be alloyed with them. The plating of iron with aluminum by means of the blow-pipe was shown on the same occasion.

A second report has been made by the committee appointed by the British Association to investigate the influence of silicon on the properties of steel. While in the series of experiments previously reported upon the committee had used specially pure iron, in the present series it had taken ordinary basic iron, in the condition in which it would be sent into commerce, added definite quantities of silicon, and examined the product chemically and mechanically. The general results of the investigation are summarized as follow: On adding silicon to ingot iron containing manganese the metal rolls well, and does not show any signs of red-shortness; it welds perfectly well with all proportions of silicon, and (with one somewhat doubtful exception containing 0·5 per cent.) is not brittle when cold. With less than about 0·15 per cent. of silicon, the limit of elasticity, the breaking load, the extension, and reduction of area are but little, if at all, appreciably affected by the presence of silicon; but with more than 0·15 per cent. of silicon the limit of elasticity and breaking load are increased, while the extension and reduction of area are distinctly decreased by the presence of silicon. The effect exerted by silicon in increasing the tenacity of ingot iron is not nearly so great as that of carbon. The relative hardness is very slightly affected by the proportions of silicon used in these experiments. On account of the small scale on which the experiments were conducted, it was not practicable to perform tests with reference to resistance to shock.

The Carlsson modification of the Bessemer process is employed in Sweden in the treatment of a charcoal pig-iron—about 1·5 per cent. of silicon, 0·1 to 0·15 of manganese, 3·9 of graphite, and 0·1 of combined carbon. The slag resultant from the production of this pig-iron approximates more closely to a tri-silicate than to a bi-silicate, alumina being regarded as a base. After the pig-iron has been charged into the converter, it is blown for a few minutes, till the blue flame appears that marks the beginning of the combustion of the carbon. The blow is then stopped, and a definite proportion of the charge—the slag being removed, containing usually 4·15 per cent. of carbon, 0·05 of silicon, and 0·07 of manganese—is poured into a measured ladle. The portion of metal remaining in the converter is then blown until most of the carbon has been eliminated and the bath converted into malleable iron. The metal previously removed, and what more may be needed, is then added to the bath. When the reaction that ensues is ended, the metal is ready for pouring.

A number of improvements, designed to secure increased economy and greater efficiency in working, in the production of basic Siemens steel, have been introduced in a new furnace recently erected at Bilston, South Staffordshire. A rectangular furnace with rounded ends takes the place of the old round furnace, producing a longer flame, which seems to have a less destructive cutting power upon the lining and upon the gas and air ports. The roof and part of the internal side-walls are built of silica bricks, and the bottom is lined with basic bricks of exceptional density, which are separated from the silica work with a chrome brick. The roof is fixed instead of being movable as before, the movable roof having been designed, in the first place, to enable the repairs to the interior of the furnace to be more easily made; but it was found in practice that this advantage was more than lost by the destruction that ensued to the roof by removals. The repairs are now provided for by building the case of the furnace, instead of solid steel plates, of lattice-work, with silica brick-work inside, which can be removed when repairs are necessary. Three doors are provided in front, and one at the back, over the tapping-hole. The regenerative capacity of the furnace is doubled, in the same space, by making the regenerators rectangular, with rounded ends. This is effected by the lengthening of the flame, whereby the heat that formerly passed into the chimney and was lost, is now all absorbed; besides which, it is possible to work with less gas while obtaining a greater amount of heat.

Mr. W. Shimer, of Easton, Pa., uses for determining phosphorus in steel the filtrate obtained in the nitric and sulphuric method for determining silicon; it has the desirable qualities of being easily and quickly obtained and always free from silica. In order, however, to get all the phosphorus in a precipitable form, the solution must be made under conditions more strongly oxidizing than simple solution in boiling nitric acid. It is found that in a solution thus made the presence of a moderate amount of free sulphuric acid does not prevent complete precipitation of the phosphorus.

In H. Haupt's process for protecting iron against corrosion, the pipes having been lowered into the retorts, the retorts are closed until the contents are heated to a proper temperature. Steam from a boiler at 60 pounds pressure is then introduced into the superheater, which it traverses, and from which it escapes at the temperature of the iron upon which it acts for about one hour. A measured quantity of some hydrocarbon is then admitted with a jet of steam, which completes the process. The protection afforded by this method is not a mere coating, like paint, but is said to be an actual conversion, to a greater or less depth, into a new material. When properly treated, this material does not seem to be detachable by pounding, bending, rolling, or heating. The process is claimed to possess advantages over the Bower-Barff process in that it makes a coating that does not crack, and is more resisting.

Prof. A. Ledebur has made a series of experiments upon the effect of acidulated waters in producing brittleness in malleable iron. The brittleness arises from the absorption of hydrogen by the iron causing a change in its mechanical properties, whereby, while the modulus of tensile strength remains unaltered so long as the metal is not sensibly corroded, the extension under stress and the capacity of resisting bending strains are notably diminished. The author also finds that an action similar to that of weak acid is produced by the atmosphere when iron is exposed to it in an unprotected condition. Contact of the iron with zinc, which renders the former electro-negative, proved to have a notable effect in increasing the influence of the acid on the unprotected portion of the surface, so that a very much shorter time sufficed to produce brittleness than without such contact. The brittleness produced by pickling or rusting is removed by annealing, and also disappears, or is considerably diminished, by allowing the brittle metal to rest for some time in a perfectly dry place. It can not, however, be removed by mechanical treatment in the cold. Cast-iron is not sensibly, or is only slightly, affected by pickling. Some direct determinations were made of the hydrogen present in the brittle wires. It was found to be so very minute as to raise a possible question whether it was sufficient to produce the remarkable changes in mechanical qualities demonstrated by the experiments. In considering this point, the author suggests that the influence of a foreign substance upon iron may be determined not so much by the weight as by the number of the atoms present, and therefore that hydrogen, whose atomic weight is only $\frac{1}{31}$ that of phosphorus, the element which it most nearly simulates in effect, may be sufficient to produce very decided brittleness, even when present in scarcely appreciable quantity.

Aluminum.—Comparative tests of aluminum and magnesium have been made at the laboratory of the Charlottenburg High-School, Berlin. The physical properties determined were:

PROPERTIES.	Aluminum.	Magnesium.
Specific gravity..................	2·67	1·75
Tensile strength, pounds per sq. inch...........................	271 to 286	331
Expansion, per cent..............	2·5	1

Magnesium can be best worked when heated to 212° Fahr., at which temperature it can be easily pressed, rolled, and drawn. More difficulty is encountered with this metal when casting or soldering, as the melting and boiling points are only a few degrees apart, and the loss by oxidation is large. The molten metal does not fill the molds so perfectly as aluminum, and the castings obtained are always rough-surfaced, and have air-holes. The difficulty in soldering magnesium comes from the fact that it can not be easily kept free from oxidizing, and even the slightest layer of oxide renders the soldering more difficult. The same difficulty is also encountered, and has not yet been wholly surmounted in the case of aluminum. The two metals show little dissimilarity in their susceptibility to atmospheric influence —provided the magnesium is pure. Magnesium can be easily worked in the lathe. It can be engraved and polished, and rolled in complicated sections. The alloys of magnesium are beautifully bright and of fine color, but are easily affected by atmospheric influences, and brittle. Hence they are ill-adapted for technical purposes.

The experiments of W. J. Keep upon the influence of aluminum on cast-iron have determined several important points. It is known that fused iron of any kind that would make castings that would be full of blow-holes, will make solid homogeneous castings if as small a quantity of aluminum as 0·1 per cent. is added just before pouring, and that such addition causes the iron to remain fluid long enough to allow of its being cast into molds. The measure of the improvement is represented by a gain of about 44 per cent. in resistance to weight, and of 6 per cent. in resistance to impact. The castings appear of slightly finer grain, and the character of the crystallization is somewhat different, but "the secret of the strength lies in the closing of the spaces between the grains —or, in other words, in the increased solidity of the casting." It had been a question whether the aluminum remains in the iron to exert an influence when the iron is remelted. To this the experiments gave an affirmative answer. As to the effect upon the grain of the changing of the carbon from the combined to the graphitic state, "aluminum allows most of the carbon to retain its natural combined form until the metal is too thick for the separated carbon to escape, but at the instant of solidifying aluminum causes the iron to drop a portion of its carbon from the combined state. This liberated carbon takes the graphitic form, and is imprisoned in the otherwise solid iron. The advantages arising from a change of carbon from the combined to the graphitic state, at the instant of crystallization, are that all of the carbon thus liberated is imprisoned uniformly throughout the casting, and is not accumulated in pockets, forming soft and hollow spots, as would be the case if liberated while the casting was yet fluid. Aluminum, more than any known element, accomplishes this. Aluminum takes away the tendency to chill, prevents the formation of sand-scale, and modifies the hardness of the iron by refining its grain so that it may be more easily cut than iron of coarser grain. It increases the resistance, or strength to sustain a constant load, and in a greater degree the resistance to impact. A gain is observed in elasticity, while the fineness and compactness of iron alloyed with aluminum gives less permanent set than iron equally soft when such softness is produced by silicon. Aluminum—when a sufficient quantity is added—takes off or reduces shrinkage; but the first additions of it seem to cause shrinkage, through the closing of the blow-holes. The tests for influence upon fluidity gave less definite results. The experiments were made separately with a white iron, in which the carbon is combined, and with a Swedish gray iron, in which the carbon is in the form of graphite. The results were modified according as these different qualities of iron were dealt with, but mostly in degree, and not essentially in nature.

Copper.—For extracting copper from its pyrites, Mr. M. J. Pering dispenses with the unpleasant and tedious roasting of the pyrites, and finds an excellent substitute for it in the property possessed by ferric nitrate of oxidizing, at temperatures between 122° and 302° Fahr., the copper sulphide of the ores direct to copper sulphate. The pulverized copper pyrites is intimately mixed with ferric nitrate, and the mixture is exposed to a temperature of 105° Fahr. Nitrous fumes at once begin to be evolved, and copper sulphate to be formed. When the temperature is gradually increased to 212° and 302°, there results, after washing with water, pure copper sulphate, without a trace of iron, while the residue consists of unaltered iron sulphide, silver sulphide, and the ferric oxide produced from the ferric nitrate. From this the silver may be extracted by means of Russell's process, and the subsequent residue used for sulphuric-acid manufacture, and finally for iron-smelting.

Copper-wire has special adaptations for telegraphic service in its great mechanical strength when it is hard drawn and pure and its virtual freedom from those effects of electro-magnetic inertia that tend to throttle the flow of electricity through iron-wires. Several wires have been put up on the line from London to Dublin, with results that exceed the most sanguine expectations of the projectors. So m$_u$c$_h$ depends on the care and accuracy with which copper-wire is erected, that an entirely new mode of putting it up has been adopted, in which the tension is exactly measured by means of specially designed dynamometers or draw-vices. Copper-wire requires very careful handling. Flaws, indentations, scratches, and kinks, act very much in the same way as diamond scratches on glass. The continued application of heat must be avoided, for it softens and weakens the wire; therefore, quick soldering is essential. In consequence of its freedom from magneto-electric inertia, or self-induction, the speed on a copper aërial line should be at least three times that on an iron one. The phosphor and silicon bronzes, also, when of high conductivity, are nearly pure copper, and may be classed with copper.

The Sudbury copper-deposits in Canada occur, according to Mr. J. H. Collins, in Huronian rocks. The ore exists in three distinct forms, viz., as local impregnations of siliceous and feldspathic beds of clastic origin, in the form of patches and strings of cupreous pyrrhotite; as contact-deposits of the same material lying between the impregnated beds and large masses of diorite; as segregated veins of chalcopyrite and of nickeliferous pyrrhotite, filling fissures and shrinkage-cracks in the ore-masses of the second class. The author considers the first original, or of high antiquity, while the latter two are due to segregation, produced either by intrusion of diorite or by internal movements. The copper can not be extracted so cheaply by the wet method as from the Rio Tinto ore, and the ore is of no avail as a source of sulphur. Nickel is everywhere present in the cupreous pyrrhotite, and is of no advantage to the smelter.

Tin.—The tin-mines of Kwala Kawsar, the capital of Perak, cover an area of several square miles, and are worked wholly by Cantonese in the most primitive manner. After washing the sand, one man takes up the minute portions of tin, which have the appearance of points of black-lead, and which sink at once to the bottom of the trough; others pick out stones from the gravelly mixture; others, again, push up the heavier portion of the mud from which the lead is not yet completely separated, so that it may pass through the water again and nothing be lost. The ore is then washed once more in special washing-houses, and is thrown, with charcoal, into a simple furnace like a barrel standing on end, and made chiefly of clay. The molten lead oozes down through the charcoal and escapes through a hole in the bottom into a pit hollowed out of the ground, while the tin is left. The tin-molds are simply holes pressed into the sandy floor by circular wooden rollers, each consisting of half a section, with broad, wooden lips, which have indentations similar in shape to to the blocks of tin shipped abroad. The tin is left here for several days to cool, when it is hauled out with a long iron rod and dashed with water. It is curious that the only tin-mine in Perak supplied with adequate machinery and worked by Europeans fails to give

a profit, while the Chinese, with their primitive methods, can turn the most unpromising mine to advantage.

In a recently patented process for the manufacture of tin plates of great length, the substratum is of steel, which, first rolled hot and then cold, is gradually reduced to the required thickness. The surface of the metal is next scoured, and then, in the form of a continuous plate, it is fed into a bath of molten tin. After the metal has in this way received a coating of tin on both sides it is passed between highly polished rolls under immense pressure, by which means the tin and steel are so consolidated together that the finished plate is superior in every respect to the ordinary article.

Argentine is a name given to tin precipitated by galvanic action from its solution. It is usually obtained by immersing plates of zinc in a solution of tin containing six grammes of the metal to the litre. In this way tin-scrap can be utilized. To apply the argentine a bath is prepared from argentine and acid tartrate of potash rendered soluble by boracic acid. Pyrophosphate of soda, chloride of ammonium, or caustic soda may be substituted for the acid tartrate. The bath being prepared, the objects to be coated are plunged therein, having first been suitably pickled and scoured, and they may be subjected to the action of an electric current; but a simple immersion is enough. The bath for this must be brought to boiling, and objects of copper or brass, or coated with those substances, may be immersed in it.

Gold.—A specimen of the mineral called "black gold" or maldonite, from the "Nuggety Reef," Maldon, Victoria, has been analyzed by R. W. MacIvor. It is described as being without crystalline character and malleable, and having a bright silvery white luster when freshly broken, which slowly tarnishes on exposure to the air till it ultimately becomes nearly black. The composition of the mineral was found to be:

Gold	64·211
Bismuth	34·398
Siliceous matter	1·891
Total	100·000

If the silica be omitted and the metals calculated to make 100, the results would indicate for the mineral the formula Au_2Bi.

Several advantages are gained by extracting gold from its ore with a dilute solution of calcium chloride mixed with an equal amount of dilute acid, instead of with chlorine gas, as in Plattner's process. The chlorine apparatus and the labor employed for generating the gas are dispensed with. The solutions employed being much diluted, there are no noxious fumes to affect the health of the workmen. The gold is dissolved uniformly and completely. The method is applicable when the ore contains silver in addition to the gold. It has been in use since 1885 at the Falun copper-works in Sweden.

The special feature of Mr. J. Holme Pollok's process for the extraction of gold is the manner of chlorinating under hydraulic pressure, which, it is represented, enables the chlorine to extract the gold more completely, in a shorter time, and at less expense than by any other mode of treatment. In trials with refractory ores and tailings which, when treated by the ordinary processes, have yielded only a small proportion of their gold, almost the whole of the gold is said to have been extracted in nearly every case. The earliest attempt to use chlorine in gold extraction, about 1864, was found to be so expensive that the process never came into use. An improvement on this was made by Mr. Mears, of America, who pumped chlorine gas into the cylinder. A later invention is that of Messrs. Newbery and Vantin.

Gold is described by Mr. R. W. MacIvor as occurring in quantities in a matrix of serpentine at Gumdagai, in New South Wales, where it exists as fine flakes distributed irregularly through the rock. The appearance is as if the metal had been painted on the rock-surfaces by the hand. The yield of gold ranges from a few pennyweights to several ounces per ton.

Ores of auriferous tellurium are analyzed by F. M. Horn by gently heating them, finely powdered, in a current of dry chlorine. The author succeeded equally well by treating the mineral with hydrochloric acid, with the addition of a little nitric acid. Besides silver, gold, arsenic, antimony, tellurium, copper, and lead, there are generally quantities of iron, zinc, lime, magnesia, sulphur, and sulphuric acid, which are determined by the usual methods.

Silver.—In a paper at the Australasian Association on silver-smelting, rich silver mattes and their treatment, and on "kernel roasting," Mr. Edgar Hall showed that the main object of the smelter was to get clean slags. He did not consider that the dissemination of matte globules satisfactorily explained the losses of silver; for he had detached perfectly pure crystals from the very heart of the pot from slags of every kind, which yet often contained more silver than the main body of the slags. He thought that "high" silver slags might be due to the property possessed by silver of passing from already solidified portions of a body in which it is present into any portions which still remain liquid.

Silver has been detected by J. W. Mallet in the ash of the volcano of Cotopaxi, in the proportion of one part in 83,600 of the ash, or about two fifths of a troy ounce per ton of 2,240 pounds. This seems a small proportion, but it must represent a very large quantity of silver ejected during the eruption (July 22, 1885), when ash fell at Bahia de Caraguez to the depth of several inches.

Mr. Gowland, of the Japanese mint, has found that when small quantities of bismuth are present in silver, as is often the case when silver is obtained from copper containing bismuth, the metal is brittle and lacks uniformity, the parts which solidify last being richer in silver. The coinage bars prepared from this silver can not be rolled without special treatment, and even then are hard and unsuitable for mintage.

Alloys.—The following results were reached in Prof. E. J. Houston's experiments on the magnetic relations of palladium alloys in watches: A watch whose balance-wheel, hair-spring, and escapement are made of the Paillard palladium alloys can not have its weight sensibly affected by the influence of any magnetic field into which it is possible to bring it while on the person of its wearer. Experiments showed that the palladium alloys are destitute of paramagnetic properties. As far as the amount of the alloys at the author's disposal permitted, experiments failed to show that they possessed any diamagnetic properties. In four of the alloys described by Mr. Paillard the complete masking of the paramagnetic properties of some of the ingredients would seem to indicate a true chemical union of their constituents. The most interesting results of these experiments, however, were those in which it was established that no matter of what materials the balance-wheel or hair-spring may be made, provided they are conductors of electricity, their movements through a magnetic field, when the moving masses properly cut the lines of force, must result in a change in the rate of their movement, and consequently in a change in the rate of the watch; or, briefly, it was established that a watch placed in a magnetic field acts like a dynamo-electric machine. The fact that the watch subjected to this experiment, after its removal from this powerful field, did not manifest any sensible change in its rate, shows the extent of the protection the palladium alloys give it against the effects of external magnetism.

The experiments of T. H. Norton and E. H. Twitchell with alloys of calcium and zinc had in view a clear examination of the alloys and an inquiry into their availability for the production of metallic calcium. Some of them were made with the proportions indicated by Caron, who claims to have made alloys containing from 10 to 15 per cent. of calcium; and in others the amount of zinc was reduced by one half. An alloy containing 2·28 per cent. of calcium was very hard to distinguish from pure zinc. Two alloys formed from preparations containing half of Caron's proportions of zinc, contained respectively 5·44 and 6·06 per cent. of calcium. In the two succeeding experiments, Caron's proportions were restored, and the resulting alloys contained 4·97 and 6·36 per cent. of calcium. In all efforts to obtain alloys richer in calcium, although zinc was driven off in notable amounts, there was still a proportionate loss of calcium. The residual alloy rich in calcium was left in so spongy a condition that it oxidized immediately in contact with the air, and the crucibles showed traces of being attacked. The results of the experiments tend to show that it is exceedingly difficult, if not impossible, to obtain by Caron's method zinc-calcium alloys containing more than from 6 to 7 per cent. of the latter metal.

It has been shown in papers read at the Institution of Civil Engineers that whereas from 2·5 to 7·5 per cent. of manganese in steel makes it as brittle as glass, so that it will break under a much less transverse load than iron, from 12 to 14 per cent. of manganese in the metal secures high carrying power with great elongation. Thus, a bar of the composition, carbon, 0·85 per cent.; silicon, 0·23 per cent.; sulphur, 0·08 per cent.; phosphorus, 0·09 per cent.; and manganese, 13·5 per cent., carried a load of 57·02 tons to the square inch, and took a permanent set at 29½ tons, with an elongation of 39·8 per cent. This metal is toughened by heating it to a high temperature and plunging it into water at a temperature of 72° Fahr., but it is difficult to machine.

In the process of R. N. P. Richardson, of Pittsburg, for coating iron or other metallic surface with lead, the sheets, having been pickled and cleaned, are placed in the solution-vat containing various chemicals in dilute hydrochloric acid. They are then passed through the molten lead, from which they come out the first time with a clean, bright, even, and pure coating of lead. The secret of the process, according to the author, after the pickling and washing of the sheets, is simply in the solution to which the sheet is subjected before its immersion in the molten lead. The solution also forms the flux for the sheet, bone-ash mixed with charcoal being used to prevent the oxidation of the metal.

Processes.—The process of electric welding discovered by Prof. Thomson several years ago has recently been greatly developed. Having started with the welding together of small wires of iron and copper, the operators are now able to weld bars of a very large size and of almost any shape or size. The principle of the process is that of forcing through a conductor an amount of current that it will not carry without heating. The resistance in conductors being greatest at their point of abutment or contact, heat is first generated, and this heat increases the resistance at that point so greatly that more heat is developed at a remarkably rapid rate. A great advantage of the method arises out of the localization of the heat at the points or point where it is desired, whereby an enormous amount of energy is saved which is usually wasted in welding with the forge or flame. It is possible by it to weld any metal, including both those that melt at very low temperatures—such as lead, zinc, and tin—and those that melt at enormously high temperatures, as iridium, platinum, etc. Almost absolutely perfect automatic control of the current is obtained. The time required to weld metals depends upon the power of the apparatus and the skill of the operator. Strong and practically perfect welds have been made in one-half-inch round wrought-iron in six seconds; in inch round wrought-iron in forty-five seconds. The power required to weld appears to be nearly proportional to the cross-section of the piece. The authors are able, by the same process, to solder, braze, anneal, temper, and do other heating that can not be done economically by present methods.

A mixture of compressed oxygen, as prepared by Brin's cheap process with coal-gas, has been successfully applied by Thomas Fletcher to brazing and welding. With a half-inch gas-supply, a joint could be brazed in a two-inch wrought-iron pipe in about a minute, and without heating to redness more than one inch on each side of the joint. A good weld was obtained on an iron wire one eighth of an inch in diameter with a blow-pipe having an air-jet of about one thirty-second of an inch in diameter. The surface of iron heated to welding-heat by this means comes out clean and free from scale.

Carbon in steel, pig-iron, and other ferro-carbon alloys is usually determined by methods in which the carbon is first separated in a state of proximate purity, and afterward burned in a current of oxygen. To effect the separation, the particular ferro-carbon alloy is treated with some salt, whose base can either be substituted entirely, or which can be reduced to some lower compound by the iron that is present in the alloy, the carbon not taking any part in the reaction. For this purpose a neutral solution of cupric chloride has hitherto given the most satisfaction; but its use is attended by the inconvenience that the cupreous chloride that is produced is comparatively insoluble, and its precipitation has to be provided against. This inconvenience is entirely obviated in the new mixture proposed by Mr. T. W. Hogg—of a solution of ferric chloride and cupric chloride. When these substances are brought together an immediate change takes place, and cupric chloride and ferrous chloride are formed.

In M. A. Levy's process for depositing thin sheets of metal upon other metals, batteries and dynamos are dispensed with, and a double decomposition is depended upon. In depositing a layer of nickel upon either copper or iron, a solution of salt of the metal is prepared — preferably the acidulated chloride — and, after the object has been scoured, it is suspended in the solution at the extremity of a zinc wire, which partially enters the bath. The zinc is attacked by the salt, and it replaces the nickel in the chemical constitution of the solution, whereby the object is covered with a layer of nickel. In copper-plating cast-iron, an alkaline bath is employed in place of the acidulated one.

A process for tempering spring wire and ribbon, by introducing a current of electricity as the heating power, has been invented by Mr. Frederick Sedgwick, of Chicago. The greatest difficulties met with in tempering a fine piece of steel by any other process are the oxidation of the surface of the metal by contact when heated with the air, and the buckling and twisting of the ribbon in the oil-bath. Both of these troubles are avoided in Mr. Sedgwick's process.

Apparatus.—The advantages of magnesite as a refractory material in furnace-linings are thus summarized by Herr K. Sorge: The charge may be dephosphorized without difficulty to the extent of 98 per cent. of its total phosphorus; magnesite bottoms allow of the addition to the charge of 30 per cent. and upward of iron-ore, and thereby facilitate the use of every kind of said material; magnesite bricks may be made of very regular shape, so that the building of the hearth in an accurate and durable form is much facilitated; magnesite may be built up in direct contact with silica brick-work, which is not possible with any other basic material; the durability of a magnesia lining far exceeds that of any other basic substance, and it is therefore less costly for repairs; magnesite, when exposed to the action of the basic slags and metallic oxides, resists corrosion better than any other known substance; the absolute indifference of bricks and burned magnesite to the action of the air makes it possible to preserve them in quantity for any time without fear of alteration. The danger of using a partially altered material, and therefore one of small durability, as may happen with dolomite, is completely avoided with magnesite.

The difficulty of supporting the ore and fuel in the furnace, as is done in ordinary furnaces by the coke, which was the chief obstacle to the making of pig-iron by natural gas, is met in Mr. J. T. Wainwright's furnace by a series of pipes protected with fire-clay tiles. The pipes are kept cool by turning a portion of the blast into the space between them and the tiles. The furnace is fitted with a combination chamber, into which the gas and air furnished from an ordinary cupola are admitted through separate pipes. Ordinary cupolas may be easily altered to use the new fuel.

A naphtha refuse-burning furnace, acting both as a calciner and a smelting-furnace, has been introduced at the Radabeksky Copper Smelting Works of Messrs. Siemens Brothers. In a thirty-days' run it smelted 2,076,911 pounds of 7-per-cent. ore, consuming 408,-835 pounds of naphtha refuse, at 42s. per ton, and yielded 810,737 pounds of regulus, containing 25 per cent. of copper; or to produce 2,000 pounds of regulus required 1,008 pounds of refuse, costing 21s. 3d. This is said to work 3·5 times faster than the ordinary ore-furnace, and to be cheaper at these works than when wood is used.

An important improvement in puddling, introduced by the North Chicago Rolling Mill Company, includes taking the molten iron directly from the blast-furnace to the puddling-furnace. The results are very satisfactory,

both as to the quality of the puddled bar and in a considerable saving that is effected in fuel, time, and other items.

The composition of the Dinas fire-bricks and cement, which have gained an excellent reputation, is shown by the analysis of Mr. James S. Merry to be silica, 98·10; alumina, 1·04; oxide of iron, 0·56; lime, 0.53; magnesia, a trace; and water, 0·1.

The Lash open-hearth furnace, which is peculiarly adapted to the use of gas, is largely employed at Pittsburg, where twelve furnaces, varying in capacity from 40 to 15 tons, are actually at work and four others are building.

By the use of the new foundry ladle of Goodwin & How, Westminster, the ordinary method of skimming molten metal by hand is dispensed with, scoria and ashes are prevented from entering the mold, the densest and cleanest metal can be poured from the bottom, and the metal can be kept hot in the body of the ladle by the usual covering of sand while pouring.

Miscellaneous.—The Director of the United States Mint, in his report on the production of the precious metals in the United States during 1887, states that the production of gold amounted to 1,596,500 fine ounces, of the value of $33,000,000. The production of silver amounted to 41,269,240 fine ounces, of commercial value about $40,450,000, and of the coining value of $53,357,000. The gold production fell off from that of the preceding year, when it was $35,000,000. The production of silver increased over that of the preceding year, when at coining value it was $51,-000,000. The production was contributed by States and Territories as follows, in coining values:

STATE OR TERRITORY.	Gold.	Silver.	Total.
Alaska	$675,000	$300	$675,300
Arizona	880,000	3,800,000	4,680,000
California	18,400,000	1,500,000	14,900,000
Colorado	4,000,000	15,000,000	19,000,000
Dakota	2,400,000	40,000	2,440,000
Georgia	110,000	500	110,500
Idaho	1,900,000	3,000,000	4,900,000
Montana	5,230,000	15,500,000	20,730,000
Nevada	2,500,000	4,900,000	7,400,000
New Mexico	500,000	2,300,000	2,800,000
North Carolina	225,000	5,000	280,000
Oregon	900,000	10,000	910,000
South Carolina	50,000	500	50,500
Utah	220,000	7,000,000	7,220,000
Washington	150,000	100,000	250,000
Texas		250,000	250,000
Alabama, Tennessee, Virginia, Vermont, Michigan, and Wyoming	8,000	2,500	5,500
Total	$33,093,000	$53,408,800	$86,501,800

The property which the electric current possesses, said Mr. W. H. Preece, in the British Association, of doing work upon the chemical constitution of bodies so as to break up certain liquid compounds into their constituent parts, and marshal these disunited molecules in regular order, according to a definite law upon the surfaces of metals in contact with the liquid where the current enters and exists, has led to immense industries in electro-metallurgy and electro-plating. The extent of them may be gathered from the fact that there are 172 electro-platers in Sheffield and 99 in Birmingham. The term electro-metallurgy was originally applied to the electro-deposition of a thin layer of one metal on another; but this is now known as electro-plating. In 1839, Jacobi in St. Petersburg and Spencer in Liverpool laid the foundation of all we know of these interesting arts. Copper was deposited by them so as to obtain exact reproductions of coins, metals, and engraved plates. The fine metals, gold and silver, are deposited in thin layers on coarser metals, such as German silver, in immense quantities. Christofle, in Paris, deposits annually six tons of silver upon articles of use and of art. The whole of the copper-plates used in Southampton for the production of the Ordnance Survey maps are deposited by current on matrices taken from the original engraved plates, which are thus never injured or worn and are always ready for addition or correction, while the copies may be multiplied at pleasure and renewed at will. Nickel-plating, by which the readily oxidizable metals like iron are coated with a thin layer of the more durable material, nickel, is becoming a great industry. The electro-deposition of iron, as devised by Jacobi and Klein, in the hands of Prof. Roberts-Austen, is giving very interesting results. The designs for the coins which were struck at the mint on the occasion of the Jubilee of the Queen, were modeled in plaster, reproduced in intaglio by the electro-deposition of copper, and on these copper molds hard, excellent iron in layers of nearly one tenth of an inch was deposited.

Attention has been given by Prof. W. Chandler Roberts-Austen to the allotropic states of metals. Joule and Lyon Playfair showed, in 1846, that metals in different allotropic conditions possessed different atomic volumes. Matthiessen came to the view in 1860 that in certain cases when metals were alloyed they underwent allotropic changes. Instances of allotropy are observed in Bolley's lead, which oxidizes readily in air; Schutzenberger's copper; Fritsche's tin, which falls to powder when exposed to an exceptionally cold winter; Gore's antimony; Graham's palladium; and allotropic nickel. Joule proved that when iron is released from its amalgam by distilling away the mercury, the metallic iron takes fire on exposure to the air, and is therefore clearly different from ordinary iron or an allotropic form of the metal. Moissan has shown that similar effects are produced in the case of chromium and manganese, cobalt, and nickel, when released from their amalgams. Allotropy also appears in metals released from solid alloys. Certain alloys may be viewed as solidified solutions, and when they are treated with a suitable solvent it often happens that one constituent metal is dissolved and the other is released in

an insoluble form. If a certain alloy of potassium and 10 per cent. of gold is thrown upon water, the potassium takes fire, decomposing the water, and the gold is released as a dark powder. One form of this black or dark-brown gold appears to be an allotropic modification of the metal as it combines with water to form auric hydride. If this dark gold be heated to dull redness it readily assumes the ordinary golden color. The Japanese produce with this gold, by the aid of certain pickling solutions, a beautiful patina on copper which contains only 2 per cent. of gold, while even a trace of the latter metal is sufficient to alter the tint of the patina. An alloy of zinc and rhodium is described by Debray in which a simple elevation of temperature induces allotropic change in the constituent metals. This property of metals and alloys of passing into allotropic states and the possibility of changing the mechanical properties of metals by apparently slight influences may have considerable industrial importance.

A new mineral, an arsenide of platinum, $PtAs_2$, discovered by Mr. Sperry at Sudbury, Ontario, and named Sperrylite by Prof. Wells, is of interest as being the first mineral other than natural alloys with metals of the platinum group of which platinum is an important constituent. It occurs in the form of a heavy, brilliant sand composed of minute well-defined crystals. After removing impurities, the Sperrylite sand appears of a remarkably increased brilliancy, with every grain showing extremely bright crystal faces of a tin-white color, resembling that of metallic platinum itself. It is very heavy, possessing a specific gravity of 10·6. Yet, although it is so heavy, the sand shows a marked tendency to float on water owing to its not being easily wet, and even when the grains do sink they almost invariably carry down bubbles of air with them. A certain similarity in behavior when treated with *aqua regia* with that of pyrites is rendered all the more important in view of the fact that the platinum and iron groups both occur in the same vertical row (the eighth) in Mendelejeff's periodic classification.

A process by which wood is made to take on some of the special characteristics of metal has been turned to practical account in Germany. By this process the surface becomes so hard and smooth as to be susceptible of a high degree of polish, and it may be treated with a burnisher of either glass or porcelain. The wood then presents the appearance of polished metal and has the semblance of a metallic mirror, with the advantage that it is not affected by moisture. To produce this property the wood is steeped in a bath of caustic alkali for two or three days, according to its degree of permeability, at a temperature of between 164° and 197° Fahr. It is then placed in a bath of hyposulphite of calcium, to which, after some twenty-four or thirty-six hours, a concentrated solution of sulphur is added. It is then treated for from thirty to fifty hours in a bath of ace-tate of lead at a temperature of from 95° to 120° Fahr. After being thoroughly dried it is in a condition for being polished with lead, tin, or zinc, as may be desired, and finished with a burnisher.

METEOROLOGY. Temperature.—The distribu-tion of heat over the surface of the earth has been studied by Dr. Zenker. The amount of heat that reaches the earth's surface is dependent on the distance of the sun, and is greater at perihelion than at aphelion in the inverse ratio of the square of the sun's dis-tance. The varying ellipticity in outline of the earth in its various positions is not of enough extent to have an influence on the amount of heat received. If any one point of the earth's surface is alone considered, then the heat re-ceived is determined by the sine of the sun's altitude or the cosine of its zenith distance. From these relations it follows, leaving the air out of account, that the heat received by the pole on a summer day is greater than that which falls on a point at the equator. Thus taking as unit the heat received during twenty-four hours by a place at which the sun is in the zenith, the north pole receives an amount of heat represented by 0·397, and a point on the equator an amount represented by 0·292. But the air absorbs a large part of the sun's heat. The estimation of the height of the atmosphere from the amount of heat absorption can not be relied upon, because the chief ab-sorption takes place in the deeper layers of the air. For the determination of the coefficient of absorption, the author accepts the values obtained by Langley from his bolometric ex-periments, with a reservation regarding the absorption taking place in its highest layers, which he does not admit. One factor of great importance is the diffusion of heat, already described by Clausius, from the small particles of water, dust, and air in the atmosphere, which are calculated under other definite as-sumptions. Another factor that must not be lost sight of is the reflection of heat at the earth's surface. This is calculated for the three cases of a surface of land, water, and snow. In his calculations for the sea, Dr. Zenker started with the temperature of a point on its surface which was quite uninfluenced by the neighboring continents, and unaffected by warm or cold currents. In basing the cal-culations for the land surface, the conditions were first determined under which the influ-ence of the neighboring sea is either noth-ing or minim in amount. A region of purely continental conditions was found in the neigh-borhood of the east coast of Asia; while all other points were affected to a greater or less extent by the neighboring sea. The observed temperature on the land was therefore only partly dependent upon the position of the place on any given parallel, for other influences make themselves felt. Hence the real and "ac-cessory" temperature can be calculated for

each parallel. The amount of heat radiated from the sun, when compared with these tem-peratures, was about the same for each 10° C. of difference. Comparison of the tempera-tures that really exist with those thus deduced showed that the climate on the sea of the south-ern hemisphere is colder than calculation would make it—a result attributable to the oceanic currents of cold water; while, in consequence of the disturbance introduced by the Gulf Stream, the continental climate in the north-ern hemisphere is slightly too warm.

Data regarding the average time of the first killing frost in the United States have been published in the "Monthly Weather Review." They were collected from four hundred and thirty-two rural stations, and embody the re-sults of observations ranging in duration from two to forty-nine years, of which thirty-six stations have records of fifteen years or more. From them it appears that killing frosts oc-cur throughout the year along the northern border of Minnesota and Dakota. In Cali-fornia they are very unusual in the eastern and northeastern parts, but light frosts occasion-ally occur in the western part. Hard frosts come about the first of September, in the mid-dle of the upper lake region; September 15 in the lower lakes and the south end of Lake Michigan; October 1 along the New England sea-coast and southern Ohio; October 15 in the Carolinas; and from November 1 to De-cember 15 in the States farther south, to cen-tral Florida. The observations involve an average error of about eighteen days; and will therefore have to be continued through many years to obtain an approach to reasonable ac-curacy in fixing the date.

According to Von Tillo's "Researches upon the Distribution of Air-Pressure and Tempera-ture over the Earth," the mean temperatures, centigrade, of the continents are as follow:

CONTINENTS.	Year.	January.	July.
Asia and Europe	10·0	− 8·0	23·1
North America	4·7	− 8·7	19·7
South America	23·0	25·1	20·9
Africa	26·4	23·7	27·1
Australia	22·3	29·4	16·4
Continents altogether	15·0	7·3	22·9

The mean of the air-pressure of the whole northern hemisphere is, in January, 761·7 mm.; in July, 758·5 mm.; or about 3·2 mm. less. The corresponding values for temperature are 8·3° and 22·6°; difference, 14·3°; so that a change of 1 mm. in pressure is equivalent to one of 4·5° in temperature.

The greatest winter cold known to exist upon the globe prevails at Werkojansk, in Siberia, which is situated in the valley of the Jana, about nine feet above the level of the river, in latitude 67° 34′ N., longitude 133° 51′ E., and at a height of about 350 feet above the sea. Monthly means of −58° Fahr. occur in Decem-ber, and minima of −76° are usual for the three winter months, December to February. In

1886 March had also a minimum of −77°, while in January, 1885, the temperature of −89° was recorded. The yearly range of cloud is characteristic of the climate ; in the winter season the mean amounts only to about three tenths in each month.

The results of studies concerning the relations of pressure and temperature in high and low conditions of the barometer, and at different elevations, have not been harmonious. M. Dechevrens concludes that, while a high temperature accompanies a low pressure at sea-level, the fluctuations are reversed at some height above. Mr. H. Allen has arrived at a nearly opposite result. He tries to remove the disagreement by showing that the minimum pressure on a mountain does not coincide with the passage of a storm-center over the station, but lags behind it to an extent that corresponds with the height of the mountain and the surrounding topography, and which, on the summit of Mount Washington, 6,279 feet, is from ten to eleven hours. A like rule prevails with the maximum. He also concludes that the temperature change at the base precedes very slightly the pressure change, but at the summit the change occurs nearly twenty-four hours earlier; that the temperature change appears to be a very little earlier at the summit than at the base, and varies much more rapidly at the former; that in a low, the difference in temperature between base and summit is less than the mean before the storm, but that it rapidly increases after the center has passed. Just the contrary is true in a high.

A research by Supan on the mean duration of the principal temperature periods in Europe is based on observations at four hundred and seventy-one stations of the length of the frost-period (temperature of 0° C., or below), the warm period (10° C. and above), and the hot period (20° C. and upward), the results of which are presented graphically. The lines sharply mark the contrast between ocean and continental climates. The lines of equal duration of the frost-periods, like the winter isotherms, run northward into the interior of the continent in the eastern part, sometimes inclining to the south and southeast; those of the warm periods usually keep to the parallels of latitude; while those of the hot periods run decidedly to the northeast.

Hans Fischer's charts of the equatorial limits of snowfall of the northern hemisphere likewise bring out the difference between land and sea climates. The limit on the land runs nearly along the thirtieth degree of latitude, while on the sea it recedes to the thirty-fifth degree.

The question of aperiodic variations of temperature has been investigated by Dr. Perlewitz, on the basis of observations made during the forty years 1848–1887, at Berlin, and during the ninety-three years 1790–1883, at Breslau. If a year is divided into halves, the first half is characterized by a normal curve of rising temperature, and the second half by a similarly normal curve of falling temperature. Both curves, however, show negative irregularities, the number of which may be very considerable in any one month. On the whole, the number of these irregularities is greater in the first half of the year than in the second, so that the heat of the second half is greater than that of the first.

Clouds.—The British Association's Committee on the Ben Nevis Observatory reported that the work done there during the year had been mostly directed toward obtaining a wider knowledge of halos on clouds, St. Elmo's fires, and other natural phenomena. St. Elmo's fire was observable at definite phases of the weather. The usual difference in temperature between the summit and base of Ben Nevis is about 16° Fahr., but in the driest season of 1887 it was as low as 7° Fahr. It appears that when a cloud is resting upon the mountain the telegraphic wire which makes communication between the base and summit has an earth-current passing through it in one direction, but that after the cloud has passed over, the direction of the earth-current changes. "Sky-colored" or illuminated clouds have been remarked by several observers in the northern sky at night, during about six weeks near the summer solstice — from June 2 to July 20. They are not usually colored, but shine with a pearly or silvery luster. They have been seen at midnight at an altitude of about 30°, but are more usually confined to about the first 10° above the northern horizon. They are supposed to be very high cirrus clouds illuminated by the sun; or, by Jesse, as consisting of small crystals, originating from the condensation of gases under the low temperature of the upper regions of the air.

Some light may possibly be cast upon the method of formation of hail, by Mr. C. C. Wilson's observation of the drops that fell from a pine-tree during a cold fog. A part of them reached the ground in a liquid state, while another part had been converted into pellets of ice. The author believes that the ice-drops came from the upper part of the tree, having been frozen during their traverse of the greater distance by the greater loss of heat which they suffered from the more rapid and longer-continued evaporation. An instance is mentioned in which a railway-train became coated with ice, in traveling through an atmosphere above the freezing-point, and laden with mist.

After continued studies of the "red sunsets" which were prominent features of the skies from the end of August, 1883, to June, 1886, Kiessling has concluded that they were due to no other cause than the vapors mingled with combustion-products which were thrown up into the atmosphere by the volcanic explosion of Krakatoa on the 27th of August of the former year. He is convinced, from experiments with mechanically produced dust, that the solid ejecta—the finely powdered pumice-stone, constituting a large part of the volcanic ash—had no part in intensifying the coloring. The long continuance of the matter in the atmosphere agrees with experimental determinations of the rate at which smoke settles in atmospheric air. This conclusion is in substantial harmony with the conviction expressed by Mr. A. W. Claydon in the "Journal of the Royal Meteorological Society," that vapor played the principal part, and the other eruption-products only a subordinate one, in the coloration. The phenomenon called Bishop's Ring (see "Annual Cyclopædia," 1885, article "Meteorology") is also ascribed by Ricco to the eruption of Krakatoa. He supposes that it was caused by the refraction produced by a peculiar condensation of vapors into extremely minute particles. The red twilight phenomena differ from this ring in that they were not the effect of refraction, but of a selective transmission, by a well-known and common property of the atmosphere, of the less refrangible rays.

Storms.—The storm of the 11th, 12th, and 13th of March, commonly known as the "New York Blizzard," was one of the most severe ever experienced on the Atlantic coast of the United States. As described by Prof. Winslow Upton, in the "American Meteorological Journal," it was peculiarly characterized by the rapidity with which its energy was developed, and by the extreme precipitation that accompanied it, principally as snow. West of the seventy-second meridian, the precipitation was almost wholly snow, piled up in immense drifts, while east of this meridian it was rain and snow mixed. The region in which it prevailed extended, on land, from the neighborhood of Cape Hatteras to the southern part of Massachusetts. The district in which it raged with unmitigated violence included New Jersey, southeastern New York, Block Island, and southern New England. Through the latter territory snow fell to an estimated average depth of forty inches, while it was massed so irregularly in immense drifts that it was almost impossible to measure it; railroads were blockaded; telegraphic communication was stopped; shipping along the coast was exposed to great danger; many lives were lost from exposure; and the city of New York was cut off from all communication with other places, except through the Atlantic cables. According to Gen. Greely's summary of the history of the storm, the storm-center was first noticed in the North Pacific on March 6, whence it passed southeast from the Oregon coast to northern Texas by the 9th. An extended trough of low pressure, having two distinct centers, was gradually formed, which covered the Mississippi and Ohio valleys on the 10th; and on the 11th, according to Prof. Hayden, extended from the west coast of Florida up past the eastern shore of Lake Huron, and far northward toward the southern limits of Hudson Bay. The northern center moved northeastward and disappeared, while the southern center moved slowly eastward, passing off the Atlantic coast near Cape Hatteras. The "cold wave," which followed upon the track of the great trough, as it approached the coast, as explained by Prof. Hayden after examining the reports of sailing-vessels on the ocean at the time, met the warm currents of air from the south, and that accompanying the Gulf Stream, now trending northwardly after a winter interval of comparative quiet; and the difference in temperature of the two air-streams being very great, excessive precipitation was the result. The storm, Prof. Hayden says, so far as it has been possible to study it from the data at hand (which need to be re-enforced by fuller ocean reports), furnished a striking and instructive example of a somewhat unusual class of storms. Instead of a more or less circular area of low barometer at the storm-center, there was here a great trough of "low" between two ridges of "high," the whole system moving rapidly eastward, and including within the arc of its sweep almost the entire width of the temperate zone. "The trough phenomena, as an eminent meteorologist has called the violent squalls with shifts of wind and change of conditions at about the time of lowest barometer, are here illustrated most impressively." One thing to which attention is particularly called is the fact that storms of only ordinary severity are likely, upon reaching the coast, to develop increased energy. This is especially so in a storm of this kind, where the isobars are elongated in a north and south direction.

A relation between the velocity of a storm's progress and the extent of the accompanying rain area has been established by Loomis, who found also that the chief part of the rain area was in advance of the storm-center. His observations are confirmed, as to their principal features, by Ley and Abercromby. The last author has shown that the heaviest rain and cloud areas are massed toward the front of rapidly advancing cyclones, while immediately after the passage of the line of minimum pressure the sky begins to show signs of clearing. It is remarked that in the United States, when the cyclones are moving with unusual rapidity, all the rain and almost all of the cloud area are confined to the front half of the cyclone. Loomis first regarded the rapid advance of cyclones as the effect of excessive rain, but later investigations have shown that the rainfall is not an essential feature; and certain European observations recorded by Hann suggest that unequal distribution of rain around rapidly moving cyclones is not the cause but the result of the cyclone's advance. H. Helm Clayton supposes that, in cyclones which move very slowly, the air ascends almost uniformly around the center; but when the storms have a more rapid progressive motion, the air in the rear, which has not only to enter but to follow the cyclone, is more retarded by friction than the air in front, and hence does not enter the cyclone so freely, so that the formation of cloud and rain in the rear is retarded; while a larger volume of new air enters the progressing cyclone in front, and increases the amount of precipitation. Espy showed many years ago that, on account of mechanical heating by compression, no descending air can be accompanied by precipitation; and an explanation is thus afforded why there are no, or but little, cloud and precipitation in the rear of rapidly moving cyclones. On the other hand, in order that a cyclone may advance rapidly, there must be a rapid decrease in pressure, and consequently a rapid removal of the air, in front of the advancing depression. Since, according to the normal circulation of a cyclone, there are an inward movement near the earth's surface, and an upward and outward movement near the top, the upward and outward movement is necessarily increased in unusually rapidly moving cyclones, and with it also the cloudiness and precipitation are increased. Observations at Blue Hill Observatory indicate that velocity of storm movement, and especially variability of weather, are intimately connected with the velocity of movement of the general atmosphere. Hence, the author concludes that the main cause of rapid cyclone progression is an unusually rapid drifting of the atmosphere over large regions; and the unequal distribution of rain around the cyclone is due to its rapid progress.

An attempt has been made by Mr. E. Douglas Archibald, to find a basis of reconciliation between Faye's theory of storms and the theory to which it is thought to be opposed. M. Faye's theory, to express it in brief, considers that air-whirls around a vertical axis, including cyclones, typhoons, tornadoes, and waterspouts, originate in the upper currents of the atmosphere, and are propagated downward by a descending motion, accompanied by gyration round a vertical axis. The opposite theory is not, as M. Faye describes it, that the movements rise from the ground in an ascending current that borrows a gyration from that of the earth itself; but, as developed by Ferrel and Sprung, it makes the action begin in a slight upward motion in unstable air, usually near the lowest cloud-stratum, and possessing a gentle gyratory motion relative to some central point, "which is never wanting in a cyclonic area." Once the motion is started, and the air that feeds it is nearly or quite saturated, the action will go on and be propagated downward, not by a descent of the *air*, but by the transference of the physical conditions which favor the continuance and maximum development of the ascending current. The increasing rapidity of gyration of the air as it approaches the axis, however gentle it may be at starting, only allows it partially to feed the initial and continuously reproduced vacuum, which is thus compelled to draw its supplies chiefly from the non-gyrating air at the lower end of the aërial shaft. As this is drawn upward, the centrally aspiring surrounding air is made to gyrate more rapidly

(partly by the friction of the superjacent rotating layer), and thus the gyratory and other conditions are propagated downward until a balance is struck between supply and demand.

Thunder-Storms.—The Council of the Royal Meteorological Society has appointed a committee to collect volunteer observations on British hail- and thunder-storms. The objects sought are: A knowledge of the nature and causes of the different kinds of thunder-storms; a discovery of the localities where hail and thunder are most frequent and destructive; and, if possible, to obtain an increased power of forecasting hail and thunder, whereby it is hoped that eventually damage to persons, stock, and property may be lessened.

As one of the most certain prognostics of thunder, Mr. B. Woodd-Smith mentions the formation of parallel streaks or bars, in cirrus and cirro-stratus, and on the surface, apparently, of nimbus clouds. In cirrus they give often almost the first intimation of coming change after settled weather, and are most usually followed within twenty-four or thirty-six hours by thunder. When they appear on nimbus the interval is much less, but they have not been seen on the thunder-cloud itself. These small patches of definitely marked "parallel bars" should be distinguished from the more general parallel arrangement which is often seen on a much larger scale, but is not known to have any very distinct value as a weather prognostic.

The typical course of the meteorological instruments at the advent of a thunder-storm has been studied by Ferrari on the basis of the records at Bern, Santis, and Rome. Previous to the storm, the pressure and relative moisture diminish, while the temperature increases, so that, at the outbreak, the first two have reached a minimum and the last a maximum. At this moment pressure and moisture increase very rapidly, and the temperature falls at a corresponding rate, so that at the end of the storm the first two elements have reached a maximum and the last a minimum. The force of the wind, which was slight before the storm, augments very speedily when it begins, and is quickly stilled after it. The minimum of pressure and relative moisture and the maximum of temperature are thus simultaneous with the beginning of the storm, and the course of the temperature is opposite to that of the two other elements. The same course continues in the after-storm, but is less pronounced. The force of the accompanying wind and the violence of the shower increase with the velocity of advance. The storms seem to originate in a limited region, whence they spread on one side. The ordinary form of the depression is an ellipse, the major axis of which is perpendicular to the axis of the shower. The same is the case with the depression of temperature that follows the storm. Storms of short course, or local showers, are accompanied by light winds, extensive storms usually by stronger winds. The rain-tract is nearly parallel to the line of progress of the storm, as is also the narrow hail-tract.

Rainfall.—The results of investigations into the influence of forests on rainfall are thus far adverse to the supposition that, in respect to the yearly average, it is material. But the records are still too limited and imperfect, and the conditions are too complicated, to allow a final conclusion to be drawn. Prof. George F. Swain describes the present condition of the question as one in which the assumption is not proved, but observes that practically, in considering the effects of a removal of the woods, we have not to compare regions where they are replaced by bare ground, but by growths of underbrush, second growths, or fields of grain or grass, the influence of which, as regards rainfall, may be like that of the forest itself. A gradual increase in the tillable quality of the soil and in capacity to hold moisture in the plain regions west of the Mississippi river, which has been observed since the lands came under cultivation, has been assumed to indicate an increase of rainfall. The most direct evidence on the subject should be sought in the meteorological records, where they have been kept, at military posts. Some of these extend for many years back previous to the settlement of the country—they having been kept at Fort Leavenworth and Leavenworth City, for instance, since 1837. Prof. Harrington has concluded, from the comparison of the rainfall charts, based on the recent Signal Service observations, with the charts contained in Blodgett's "Climatology of the United States," that the isohyetal lines have advanced westward over the plains. Gen. Greely has expressed the opinion that the rainfall has increased in this region; while, on the other hand, it is claimed that the records at certain military posts within it or near it, going back in some cases as far as 1847, show that there has been no increase. A comparison of the records kept at Fort Leavenworth from 1837 to 1873, with those of the Signal Service at Leavenworth City since 1873, shows an apparent average increase of seven inches during the past twenty years; but the observations, having been made upon different systems, are hardly commensurable. Mr. Henry Gannett has compared the observations from twenty-six stations, covering a large part of the region in question, for periods ranging from six to twenty-six years, and giving a total of three hundred and ten years of record. Cutting the series for each station in the middle, he has added the earlier halves and the later halves separately, assuming that the totals would represent respectively the rainfall of an earlier and later term. The footings thus made show an apparent increase of sixty inches, or a mean of 0·4 inch per year for the later term—a difference that is hardly appreciable. Other series of observations compared by Mr. Gannett—in the prairie regions of the central States, where the forest area has been

considerably increased, running from ten to forty years back; in Ohio, where most of the forests have been removed, ten to forty-eight years; and in New England, where the forests having been removed, have been restored over nearly half of the territory—concur in indicating that if there be any difference in the amount of rainfall, as affected by the forests, it is too slight to be of material importance.

H. F. Blanford's observations in India indicate that the forests, particularly in the hot zone, promote an increase of rainfall.

The observations of Studinka upon the effects of altitude and other conditions, made at seven hundred stations in Bohemia, in which the amount of rain that should be expected at each step of altitude has been computed, apparently point to an excess over the theoretical amount in the neighborhood of densely wooded regions. In Australia, where the soil in the forests is bare and hard in dry weather, it has been observed by Lendenfeld that the cutting down of the trees is followed by a growth of permanent grass that holds the water and renders the soil permeable, and by an increase of humidity in the air.

While the average yearly amount of rainfall may not be visibly affected by the presence or absence of forests, there is still room for the inquiry whether the distribution of precipitation through the year may not be affected by it. Forests tend to equalize the temperature, making the air cool and moist in summer, and warding off extremes of cold in winter. What influence this fact may exert upon the relative amounts of rain in summer and winter remains to be investigated. Some light is thrown on this subject by Hann's comparisons of the mean temperature of the environs of Vienna, in the open country, with that of the forest station of Hadersdorf, in the *Wiener Wald*. They indicate that the temperature in the *Wald* is very sensibly lower than in the open country around the forest. The difference is, in January, 0°·5 C.; in April, 0°·9; in July, 1°·3; in October, 0°·8; and for the whole year, 0°·9. The influence of the forest is therefore at its minimum in winter, and at its maximum in summer. In the daily course, the cooling effect of the forest is at the maximum in the evening and early morning, and at the minimum during the warmer hours.

According to W. C. Dolberck's comparisons, the rainfall on Victoria Peak, Hong-Kong, for the past ten years, exceeds the record at the observatory, about 1,700 feet below it, by about one sixth. The fact seems to be the result of the mountain presenting an obstacle to the wind from whatever side it blows, in consequence of which the air is forced to rise, and, being thereby cooled, precipitates more moisture. Even when the air is moderately dry at sea-level, its temperature may, in rising, be brought below the dew-point. The comparatively greater rainfall in hilly districts may be similarly accounted for.

The relations of variations of underground water to precipitation and to fires caused by lightning have been studied in Bavaria by C. Lang. He finds that the height of the water underground varies according to the amount of precipitation. This influence is somewhat obscured by the fact that the increase corresponding to a certain increase of precipitation is greater in the spring and autumn than it is in summer. When the number of recorded fires caused by lightning was plotted together with the record of the variation of underground water, the maximum of one curve was found to coincide with the minimum of the other.

Mr. Blanford has found indications of a periodical recurrence of droughts since 1799, at intervals, in southern India, of from nine to twelve years, but usually about a year before the sun-spot minimum. In northern India they sometimes occur in years of maximum sun-spots.

A study of the rainfall of Paris for the last two hundred years has been made by M. Renou, beginning with observations made by Lahine in 1688. At the time of Lahine there was a maximum in July; now there are two less marked maxima in June and September. The average number of rainy days per year is 169. Snow occurs very irregularly, but is never entirely absent in any winter. During the period covered by the observations the character of the situation has essentially changed; and what was a suburban tract some distance south of the city is now in the midst of a district surrounded by high buildings.

Electricity.—In the observations upon the aurora borealis made by Mr. Carlheim-Gyllenskiold at the Swedish station in Spitzbergen, 1882 -'83, the diversion of the culminating point of the auroral arch from the magnetic meridian was found to be 11° 27′ W., while the corona was nearly in the magnetic zenith. The breadth of the arches varies with their elevation above the horizon; and they consist of rays running in the direction of the breadth, and converging toward the magnetic zenith. The greatest breadth appears to be at a height of 45°, while in the neighborhood of the zenith the arches are very narrow, stretching as a luminous band across the heavens. Sometimes the light also formed a spherical zone parallel with the earth, floating in space as a horizontal ray of light. Sometimes the zone was broken, with dark spots or irregular spaces. The movements of the arches did not prove to be subject to as regular laws as had been supposed: the phenomena of the waves of light running along the arches—"the merry dancers"—took place nearly equally in the west to east and reverse directions. The light of the aurora was yellow, monochromatic, showing in the spectrum the yellow lines of Angström; or crimson or violet, resolvable into several rays and bands. No sound was ever heard from the light, or "smell of sulphur" observed. The light was never seen to descend below the mountains or the lower clouds. Measurements by parallax gave average heights of from about 55 to 60 kilometres. No annual variation in the frequency of the auroras could be detected, but daily ranges in frequency and form were observed.

It was shown, by a collection of more than fifty photographs of flashes, from different parts of the world, at the Royal Meteorological Society's exhibition in March, that lightning does not take the zigzag path depicted by artists, but usually a sinuous and often erratic one. Sometimes it had a perceptible breadth, and resembled a piece of tape waved in the air. One photograph illustrated a dark flash. According to the committee's report, the evidence is to the effect that lightning assumes various typical forms, under conditions at present unknown. These forms may be classified provisionally, as stream, sinuous, ramified, meandering, beaded, or chapleted, and ribbon lightning. Inviting photographs to be sent to the society, the committee explains that the taking of them does not present any peculiar difficulties. "If a rapid plate, and an ordinary rapid lens with full aperture, be left uncovered at night during a thunder-storm, flashes of lightning will, after development, be found in some cases to have impressed themselves upon the plate. The only difficulty is the uncertainty whether any particular flash will happen to have been in the field of view. A rapid single lens is much more suitable than a rapid doublet; and it is believed that films on paper would effectually prevent reflection from the back. The focus should be that for a distant object, and, if possible, some point of landscape should be included to give the position of the horizon. If the latter is impossible, then the top of the picture should be distinctly marked. Any additional information, as to the time, direction in which the camera was pointed, and the state of the weather, would be very desirable."

A periodicity has been remarked by M. Moureaux in the disturbances of magnetic declination and horizontal force at Parc Saint-Maur Observatory during the years from 1883 to 1888. The monthly values of both these elements exhibit two maxima at the equinoxes, and two minima at the solstices. While monthly variation of the number of disturbances appeared to follow a general law, the diurnal variation seems to be subject to complex laws.

In his observations on English thunderstorms, which, though made in 1857 to 1859, were only reported upon to the Royal Meteorological Society in 1888, Mr. G. J. Symons found that in sheet-lightning the most prevalent color is white, and after it follow yellow,. blue, and red. In forked lightning the order is nearly reversed, blue being more than twice as frequent as any other color, then red, white, and, most rarely, yellow. Sheet-lightning was seen about twice as often as forked.

Winds.—The results of observations on the daily periodicity in the velocity of the wind extending over two years have been communicated by Dr. Vettin. From direct determination of the movement of smoke coming from a chimney and from observations with a home-made anemometer, the author found that, in addition to the well-known maximum velocity of the wind which occurs at midday, there is a second maximum just after midnight. The latter maximum is very small in summer, but in winter it is much greater. It is, however, not very marked as an average over the whole year.

Falling winds—that is, winds that blow down from the heights of mountain-crests into the valleys and depressions—may evidently have different characters. Two classes of them are usually distinguished, warm and cold falling winds. To the former class belongs the Föhn of the Alps, on the northern slopes of the Pyrenees, of the Ferral in Spain, etc.; to the latter the Mistral of the French Mediterranean coast and the Bora of Istria and Dalmatia. H. Meyer has shown, from the labors of Hann and Von Wrangell, that these winds are not intrinsically different from one another. A vapor-bearing mass of air is warmed by compression about 0·97° C. for every hundred metres of descent, while the temperature of the still atmosphere descends about 0·5° for every hundred metres of ascent.

The phenomenon of the Föhn is supposed by Hann and Wild to be simply a kind of gust or eddy which, blowing down from mountain-heights, is warmed by compression. This explanation is confirmed in a popular essay published by Erk in a Bavarian journal by descriptions of certain marked examples of Föhns that had been observed in 1885 and 1888. On two of these occasions a marked east Föhn blowing over the southern side of the Alps was regarded as the effect of a high pressure in Eastern and a low in Western Europe.

Prof. F. Waldo has determined that too high a factor of multiplication—3, when it should be 2·15—has been used in deducing wind-pressures from velocity-anemometers; and, consequently, that the pressures thus deduced have been greatly exaggerated.

Salke's observations at Tarnople on the daily periods of wind-velocity indicate, in harmony with the theory of Espy and Koppen, that the period is more sharply defined according as the conditions are favorable to a vertical circulation of air, and, consequently, to its descent from above to the surface of the earth. The difference between maxima and minima velocities diminishes with increasing strength of wind, and the daily period becomes indistinct in very strong winds. The duration as well as the velocity is influenced by the temperature; and the maxima of frequency swerve around the horizon, following the sun at a distance of about 90°, with a regularity corresponding with the warmth of the periods.

The records of the stations of the English Royal Meteorological Society for the eight years 1878–'85 show that the southwest wind is the most prevalent, and blows on the average seventy-four days in the year, while the west wind occurs almost as frequently, blowing for sixty-five days. The least dominant winds are the southeast and north, which occur on twenty-seven days, and the northeast on thirty-two days. Thunder-storms are most frequent in the eastern and midland counties, and least frequent in the north of Wales.

The name *derecho*, or "straight blow," has been proposed by Dr. Gustavus Hinrichs, of the Iowa Weather Service, to designate a kind of storm on the prairies which has been classed with tornadoes, but is distinguished from them by the absence of spirality in the motion. It is described by him as "a powerfully depressing and violently progressing mass of cold air, moving destructively onward in slightly diverging straight lines (in Iowa), generally toward the southeast, with its storm-cloud front curving as the storm-lines diverge. The barometer bounds upward and the thermometer falls greatly under the blow of this cold air of the upper strata suddenly striking the ground. The *derecho* will blow a train of cars from its track, unroof, overturn, and destroy houses; but it does not twist the timbers into splinters and drive these firmly into the hard soil of the prairie," as does the tornado. The latter is described as "a powerfully lifting column of violently revolving air, describing a narrow path of destruction as it moves along the earth's surface in a northeasterly direction; it is surmounted by a cloud from which the column seems to hang down. Its track is generally marked by stakes driven into the ground beyond where it has destroyed buildings, these stakes being the longer fragments into which the tornado has torn such buildings." As the storm-front of the *derecho* sweeps onward and spreads laterally over the prairies, it is plainly the more extensive of the two storms; but the tornado in its narrow track is by far the more destructive. The annual period of the two storms is very marked. Neither of them occurs in the cold months. In Iowa, the rising tornado season, beginning with the sudden heated and moist spells in April, continues for three months, till early in July, and is most intense in June. *Derechos* may also occur at this season, and in midsummer are the only storm forms by which the unstable equilibrium of the atmosphere is suddenly restored to stable equilibrium. Tornadoes may again occur in September and October, but have not been observed from November till April. While the *blizzard* is a winter storm, bringing the surface air of colder regions. the *derecho* is a summer storm, in its mode of progress and in some other features resembling the blizzard, but more restricted in extent, confined to definite limits, and supplied with cold air coming down from higher strata of the atmosphere.

In preparing a paper on "Synoptic Charts" for the French Meteorological "Annales," M. G. Rollin has examined day by day the movements of the atmosphere, with the view of determining the possibility of predicting the arrival of storms reaching France from the Atlantic. He has found, as has also been the case in England, that the American telegrams can not at present be turned to practical use in weather prediction. He has, however, attempted to make them useful in the future, by establishing certain types which connect the weather of the Atlantic with that of adjacent continents; and he finds that many conditions, without being actually identical, are sufficiently alike to be classified together. But he shows that much further investigation is necessary before any definite rules can be laid down, and that the atmospheric changes are often so rapid that the difficulties of weather prediction on the exposed coasts of Europe are likely to remain very great for a long time to come.

Apparatus.—The maximum pressure anemometer of W. H. Dines is so arranged that a quantity of shot equivalent in weight to the whole pressure upon the wind-receiving disk falls from the upper to the lower part of a vessel, after which the machinery is automatically readjusted.

W. N. Shaw has described an apparatus for determining the temperature by the variation of electrical resistance, which, it is claimed, will measure to within one three-hundredth of a degree centigrade.

M. Brassard has devised a recording rain-gauge, by which the fall of each tenth of a millimetre of water is registered.

M. Bertelli, of Florence, has described an apparatus for the protection of telephones from lightning.

The spring vane attached to the window of Dr. Vettin's house in Berlin indicates the direction of a wind blowing up or down the street, or over the house at right angles to this, or at any other angle. It is specially adapted for observations in narrow mountain valleys, where the direction of the wind can not be ascertained by any other means. It is observed that the wind that blows over the houses gives rise to ascending and descending currents along their walls.

Bibliography.—A selected list is appended of the more important and those possessing a more general interest among the numerous meteorological publications of the year:

Abercromby, Ralph, "On the Relations between Tropical and Extra-Tropical Cyclones." London.

Berg, E., "The Significance of Absolute Moisture in the Origin and Propagation of Storms." German.

Berghofer, R., "Wind and Weather as Motors, Pola."

Biedermann, Detler Frh. v., "Weather Indications by Animals, and their Basis." Leipsic.

Birkinbane, D., "Rainfall and Water." Franklin Institute. Philadelphia.

Buys Ballot, "Distribution of Temperature over the Earth."

Chiminelli, "On the First International Congress of Medical Hydrology and Climatology, held at Biarritz, October, 1887." Florence.

Cruls, L., "Dictionary of Universal Climatology."

De Marchi, L., "On the Influence of Mountain-Chains on the General Circulation of the Atmosphere." Turin.

Deutsche Seewarte, "Transoceanic Weather Observations."

Diercks, "Aërial Navigation and Electricity." Ghent.

Elstner and Geitel, "On the Development of Electricity by the Friction of Water-Drops" (in German).

Exner, F., "On Transportable Apparatus for the Observation of Atmospheric Electricity." Vienna.

"Dependence of Atmospheric Electricity on the Moisture in the Air." Vienna.

Findley, A. G., "Text-Book of Ocean Meteorology." London.

Flammarion, Camille, "The Atmosphere; Popular Meteorology." Paris.

Folié, F., "Annual of the Observatory of Brussels, 1888, Fifty-fifth Year." Brussels.

Fritz, H., "Relations of Terrestrial Phenomena and Solar Activity." Zurich.

Gordon, A. R., "Report of the Hudson Bay Expedition of 1886, with Isothermal Atlas." Ottawa.

Guist, Moritz, "On the Atmospheric Ebb and Flood." Hermannstadt.

Hazen, H. A., "Hand-Book of Meteorological Tables."

Hinrich, Gustavus, "The Climate of Southern Russia and Iowa compared." Ann Arbor.

Italian Meteorological Society, Annuario for 188?."

Kiessling, "Contribution to the Annals of Unusual Sun- and Sky-Colors." Hamburg.

Larroque, F., "On the Origin of Electricity in the Atmosphere and of the greater Electrical Phenomena" (in French).

Liebenow, C., "A Contribution to the Theory of the Distribution of Air-Pressure over the Earth's Surface." German.

Luvini, Jean, "Contributions to Electric Meteorology." Turin.

Millot, C., "Course of Meteorology in the Faculty of Natural Sciences at Nancy;" begun in 1884.

Mohn, "Year-Book of the Norwegian Meteorological Institute for 1886." Christiania.

Müttrich, "Annual Report of Results of Forest-Experiment Stations, etc., 1886." Berlin.

Oberbeck, "On the Phenomena of Atmospheric Movements." Berlin.

Planté, Gustav, "Electrical Phenomena of the Atmosphere." Paris.

Ricco, "Observations and Studies of the Red Twilights." Rome.

Rotch, A. Lawrence, and Upton, Winslow, "Meteorological Observations during the Solar Eclipse, Aug. 19, 1887, made at Chlamostino, Russia." Ann Arbor.

Saxony, "Year-Book of the Royal Saxon Meteorological Institute, 1886." Chemnitz.

Stoney, G. Johnston, "On the Causes of the Iridescence of Clouds." Dublin.

Toronto, Ont. "General Meteorological Register for 1887."

Upton, Winslow, "The Storm of March 11-14, 1888." Ann Arbor.

Van Bebber, J., "Typical Thunder-Storm Phenomena." Hamburg.

Velschow, Franz A., "The Natural Law of Relation between Rainfall and Vegetable Life, and its Application to Australia." London.

Von Bezold, "Thermodynamics of the Atmosphere." Berlin.

Wagner, "The Cold Climate from the Point of View of Human Life." Lille.

Zenker, Wilhelm, "Distribution of Heat over the Earth's Surface." Berlin.

METHODISTS. I. Methodist Episcopal Church.—The following is a summary of the statistics of this Church as they are tabulated in the minutes of the annual conferences for 1888: Number of annual conferences, 110; of itinerant preachers, 12,832; of preachers "on trial," 1,734; of local preachers, 14,032; of lay members (including probationers), 2,154,349; of Sunday-schools, 24,941, with 277,764 officers and teachers and 2,060,080 pupils; of churches, 21,361, having a probable total value of $84,-979,481; of parsonages, 7,853, having a probable value of $12,567,034; of baptisms, 72,305 of children, and 91,506 of adults.

Book Concern.—The Book Committee, which has the charge of the publishing interests of the Church, reported to the General Conference that the net capital of the two "book concerns" and the depositories connected with them was $2,392,366, of which $1,653,197 were accredited to the New York house and its depositories, and $739,169 to the house in Cincinnati and its depositories, the whole showing a total increase of $774,916 in four years. The total sales (net) of publications had been $6,577,525. Dividends from the profits of the business had been made to the annual conferences of $85,000. The receipts and expenditures on account of the Episcopal fund had been balanced at $252,602.

Sunday-School Union.—The board of managers of the Sunday-School Union reported to the General Conference that there were in the Church 24,225 Sunday-schools, with 268,391 officers and teachers, and 2,006,328 pupils, showing an increase during four years of 2,772 schools, 38,826 officers and teachers, and 312,-708 pupils. There were in foreign fields: In Europe, 710 schools, with 4,354 pupils; in Asia, 835 schools, with 31,752 pupils; and in Mexico and South America, 61 schools, with 2,784 pupils. Sunday-schools had been established among German and Scandinavian immigrants, of which 1,030 were returned, with 11,089 officers and teachers, and 57,733 pupils. The receipts of the union during the past four years from collections in the churches had been $73,714. Grants of aid had been made to 3,500 schools, and grants of money to foreign mission fields for Sunday-schools amounting to $10,000. The total circulation of the publications of the union (journals and "helps" for Sunday-schools) for the year 1887 had been, of English publications, 24,-910,547, and of German, 1,237,550 copies. In Sweden, Germany, Italy, Switzerland, India, Japan, and Mexico, 1,109,363 volumes had been published. The report of the union gives as the statistics of Sunday-schools connected with the German conferences (aside from the schools among immigrants already mentioned) 1,288 schools, with 11,403 officers and teachers, and 72,195 pupils.

Church Extension.—The General Committee of Church Extension met in Philadelphia, November 22. The report showed that 507 churches had been aided during the year. The receipts had been: To the general fund, $163,-657; to the loan fund, $103,239; giving for use, $206,896. Fifty special gifts of $250 each for frontier churches had been available during the year, of which forty-three had been placed, accompanied with loans of $9,400. The full number (400) of such gifts contemplated in the original call for them had been received and placed. The continuance of the system was recommended. The churches were asked to contribute the sum of $245,600 for the purposes of Church extension during the ensuing year.

Board of Education.—The receipts of the Board of Education for four years had been $228,516, and the disbursements $199,569. The market value of its endowment investments on the 1st of April, 1888, was $196,000. The educational institutions of the Church, as reported to the General Conference, include 12 theological institutions, 56 colleges and universities, 54 classical seminaries, 9 colleges and seminaries for young women, and 66 foreign mission schools, with which are connected 1,595 teachers and 32,277 pupils. They possess buildings and grounds that were valued at $10,083,725, and endowments to the amount of $11,079,682.

Freedmen's Aid.—The Freedmen's Aid Society—now the Freedmen's Aid and Southern Education Society—reported to the General Conference that it had received during the past four years $610,647, and had expended $639,-362. Its total receipts since its organization had been $2,013,082, in addition to which its endowment fund had been increased by $180,-000. The institutions aided by the society include 7 universities and colleges, 13 normal schools and seminaries, 1 theological school, 4 biblical departments, and 1 medical college, with which were connected 127 teachers and 4,632 pupils.

Missionary Society.—The General Missionary Committee met in the city of New York, November 14. The treasurer reported that the cash receipts of the society for the year ending October 31 had been $1,000,581, of which $935,121 were from conference collections, $41,984 from legacies, and $23,476 from other sources. Appropriations were made for the support of missionary work for the ensuing year as follow:

I. FOREIGN MISSIONS:	
1. Africa	$4,800
2. South America	52,960
3. China (four missions)	10,019
4. Germany	80,800
5. Switzerland	9,840
6. Scandinavia (3 missions)	47,480
7. India (3 missions)	110,500
8. Malaysia	6,500
9. Bulgaria and Turkey	19,220
10. Italy	47,000
11. Mexico	52,000
12. Japan	60,166
13. Korea	16,104
14. Lower California	1,000
Total for Foreign Missions	$566,189

Total for Foreign Missions......	$566,189

II. Missions in the United States, not in Annual Conferences, to be administered as Foreign Missions 81,722

III. Domestic Missions :

Welsh missions	$1,500
Scandinavian missions..................	37,470
German missions.......................	89,869
French missions	7,550
Chinese missions	9,500
Japanese missions.....................	5,545
American Indian.......................	4,500
Bohemian and others...................	9,450
English-speaking.	268,064
Total	379,448

IV. Miscellaneous 96,000

V. For outstanding drafts 77,691

Grand total $1,200,000

The foreign missions returned in 1887, 135 American missionaries, 130 assistant missionaries (wives of missionaries), and 62 missionaries of the Women's Foreign Missionary Society; 2,257 native agents, of all kinds, male and female; 44,255 members, 16,013 probationers, and 50,742 adherents; 5,223 conversions during the year ; 2,409 adults, and 3,099 children baptized ; 15 theological schools, 32 high-schools, and 647 other day schools, with a total of 22,458 pupils, and 1,712 Sunday-schools, with 83,945 pupils. The domestic missions returned 2,898 missionaries, 2,259 assistant missionaries, 5 agents of the Women's Foreign Missionary Society, 60 other agents, 3,442 local preachers, 250,787 members, 44,644 probationers, 15,289 adults, and 16,172 children, baptized ; 34 day-schools (in New Mexico and Utah), with 1,613 pupils; and 5,067 Sunday-schools, with 250,304 pupils.

General Conference.—The General Conference of the Methodist Episcopal Church met in the city of New York, May 1. The quadrennial address of the bishops, after reviewing the growth of the Church and its interests during the past four years, called attention to some important questions that had never been decided, which would come before the Conference for solution. One of these questions was, whether a lay electoral conference has the right to send as its representative a person who has no membership in the bounds of the conference represented. A second was, whether women were eligible as lay delegates to the General Conference. Five women had been chosen by as many lay electoral conferences to represent them, and were expected to be present to claim their seats. In view of the novelty of the question which this action raised, and of the reception of protests against the admission of the women-delegates, it had been determined not to place their names upon the roll until the validity of their claims could be decided upon by an organized conference composed of delegates whose titles were not questioned. The Conference decided that lay delegates must be members within the conference which they represent; and that "under the constitution and laws of the Church as they now are, women are not eligible as lay delegates in the General Conference." It ordered,

however, that a vote be taken in November, 1890, at every place of public worship, and in 1891 at all the annual conferences upon an amendment to the restrictive rules, providing that the lay delegates "may be men or women." The term for which a preacher may be allowed to remain in the same station (previously three years) was extended to "not more than five years, after which he shall not be appointed to the same place for five years"; and the presiding elder's term was extended to six years, with a similar interval of six years before he can be appointed again to the same district. The status of a missionary bishop was defined as that of an officer having full episcopal powers, but with jurisdiction limited to the foreign field to which he was elected; not subordinate to the general superintendents, but co-ordinate with them in authority there; and receiving his support from the episcopal fund. Provision was made for the recognition and administration of self-supporting missions, of which two have been organized—in South America and Africa—and defining their relations to the Church and the Missionary Society. Consent was given to the organization of an autonomous Methodist Church in Japan, by the union of Methodist missions in that country, whenever the missions concerned shall determine to take the step. An article concerning deaconesses defines their duties and the form of Christian labor to which they may devote themselves; declares that no vow shall be exacted from them, and that "any one of their number shall be at liberty to relinquish her position as a deaconess at any time"; institutes a board for the control of their work, which is empowered to issue licenses to them. A constitutional commission of seven ministers and seven laymen was appointed to revise certain paragraphs in the discipline, in such a way that they shall define and determine the constitution of the General Conference; state of whom it shall be composed and by what method it shall be organized; declare its powers and how they shall be exercised; provide the process by which the constitution may be amended; and report to the next General Conference. Provision was made for holding in the United States an Œcumenical Conference of Methodism in 1891, the particular arrangements for which were intrusted to a committee of five ministers, five laymen, and three bishops. It was ordered that no annual conference should be organized with less than twenty effective members. A Board of Conference Claimants was instituted, to have charge of funds contributed for the benefit of superannuated preachers, and the widows and orphans of preachers; auxiliary to which boards may be organized in the annual conferences. Five new bishops were elected, to wit: The Rev. John H. Vincent, D. D., LL. D.; the Rev. James N. Fitzgerald, D. D.; the Rev. Isaac W. Joyce, D. D.; the Rev. John P. Newman, D. D., LL. D.; the Rev. Daniel A. Goosell, D. D.;

together with the Rev. James M. Thoburn, D. D., as missionary bishop in India. An invitation was offered to other evangelical denominations to co-operate in the formation of a National Sabbath Committee. In response to the resolutions of the House of Bishops and the House of Deputies of the Protestant Episcopal Church on the subject of the organic unity of the Church, the Conference expressed itself ready to fraternize and co-operate with that Church as with all other churches of the Lord Jesus Christ, and to extend to it and accept from it Christian courtesies; and appointed a commission of three persons—one bishop, one member of an annual conference, and one layman to confer with other bodies on the increase of Christian and Church fraternity.

II. Methodist Episcopal Church South.—The whole number of traveling preachers in this Church on May 1, 1888 was 4,530; whole number of preachers and members, 1,107,456, showing an increase of 41,079 from the previous year; number of churches, 11,364, having a total probable value of $15,204,883; of parsonages, 2,199, valued at $1,269,734. The year's receipts for home missions had been $92,426; for foreign missions, $219,649. Appropriations were made for missions for 1888–'89, of $208,820, with $25,610 additional as contingent. The receipts of the Woman's Foreign Missionary Society for the year ending April 1 had been $69,729, and its expenditures $63,088. The Colored Methodist Episcopal Church has, by the last published reports, 1,729 itinerant ministers, 4,024 local preachers, and 165,000 lay members.

III. African Methodist Episcopal Church.—The Church includes, according to its latest published statistical reports, 2,550 itinerant ministers, 9,760 local preachers, and 405,000 lay members.

The report of the Publishing House to the General Conference showed that the business of the quadrennial had amounted to $229,014, or $49,159 more than the business of the previous quadrennial. The indebtedness had been diminished by more than $5,000; and the house made a return of $23,033 of assets, against which were $3,946 of liabilities.

The quadrennial educational report represented that the educational institutions of the Church were increasing in number and power. Wilberforce University had been granted by the Legislature of Ohio an appropriation of $10,000 for an industrial department. Allen University, Columbia, S. C., returned 200 students, and a debt of $4,000. Paul Quinn College, Waco, Tex., had in four years enrolled 272 students. It had a fine industrial school. Morris Brown College, Atlanta, Ga., a young institution, had made a fine start, and now registered 200 students. Funds had been raised for it to the amount of $13,000.

The collections and contributions for the Missionary Society in four years since the last General Conference were nearly $40,000.

General Conference.—The General Conference of the African Methodist Episcopal Church met at Indianapolis, Ind., May 7. The proclamation which had been made since the last General Conference of the accomplishment of a union between the African Methodist Episcopal Church in the United States and the British Methodist Episcopal Church in Canada and the West Indies, was ratified and confirmed; and the present Conference was declared to be the legitimate successor of both the uniting bodies. Delegates from the conferences of the British Methodist Episcopal Church were present and were received as members of the General Conference. Questions relating to property and the state of individual churches were referred to the annual and quarterly conferences. Bishop Payne announced that the church history authorized by the General Conference of 1848, upon which he had been engaged for forty years was completed. Four new bishops were elected, viz., W. J. Gaines, B. W. Arnett, D. D., B. T. Tanner, D. D., and A. Grant.

IV. African Methodist Episcopal Zion Church.—The latest published statistics of this Church give the number of itinerant ministers as 2,110; of local preachers, 7,710; and of lay members, 314,000.

The expenditures of the Book Concern during the past four years were reported to the General Conference to have been $8,363. The amount of its indebtedness was returned at $3,980.

A rapid growth was reported for Livingstone College, Salisbury, N. C. While six years previously it had had only three teachers and the same number of students, it had been attended during the term just closed by 210 students, in whose instruction 11 professors were employed. The institution occupies an estate of 50 acres, with several buildings, and returns a total valuation of property and funds of $100,000.

The African Mission returned—at Brewerville, Liberia, 1 elder, 3 deacons, 1 exhorter, 100 members, 67 pupils in the Sunday-school, and church property valued at $800; at Cape Palmas 50 persons, with 2 local preachers, who have called upon the missionary superintendent to be admitted into the connection. The missionary, the Rev. Andrew Cartwright, was empowered by the General Conference, to select six native African boys and girls to be educated at Livingstone College at the expense of the conferences. A plan was approved by the General Conference for sustaining one or more woman teachers in connection with the African missions by means of contributions to be taken in the Sunday-schools. The Ladies' Home and Foreign Missionary Society returned to the General Conference receipts amounting to $914.

General Conference.—The General Conference of the African Methodist Episcopal Zion Church met in Newbern, N. C., May 2. The bishops in their quadrennial address, reviewing the condition and growth of the Church during the past four years, represented the progress of the conferences and churches in the United States and Ontario as having been very encouraging. Two new conferences—the Texas and South Georgia—had been added. A still more favorable report was made of the improvement in the spiritual and temporal interests of the churches. There had been a marked advance in the addition of energetic and working young men to the ministry; also in the increase and improvement of places of worship and a manifestly greater interest in the collection of the general fund. The ministers seemed to be seeking the fullest qualification for their offices. A special report was made by the bishops on the subject of the negotiations for union with the African Methodist Episcopal Church, lamenting that the scheme had received a serious check, and that the basis that had been agreed upon by the committees at Washington had gone no further than to receive their approval. But the Church could wait till its sister-church should be ready to consummate a union. The report was adopted.

A board of commissioners having been appointed by the Colored Methodist Episcopal Church on the organic union of the two churches, a like board was appointed to meet them and arrange terms. A provision was made, for the first time in the history of the churches, for sending fraternal delegates to the General Conference of the Methodist Episcopal Church South. The bishops were authorized to appoint delegates to the Œcumenical Conference of Methodist Churches, which is to be held in the United States in 1891.

Resolutions were passed approving the action of various temperance societies and urging ministers to organize local societies and in every way to practice and teach temperance in the communities where they may be called upon to labor ; and to preach several sermons on the subject during each year. A financial plan was adopted, which is based upon the assessment of fifty cents a year upon adult members, with encouragement to children under fifteen years of age to contribute according to their ability to the general fund. The "Handbook of the Discipline," which the General Conference had authorized Bishop Jones to prepare, being submitted, was approved, and an edition of it was ordered published. A course of study for candidates for the ministry, to occupy four years, was adopted. A committee was appointed to visit the Book-Rooms in New York and select the best and cheapest works on theology, church history, and other subjects pertaining to the work and qualifications of the ministry. To the question presented to it, whether a class-leader, conductor of a prayer-meeting, or a superintendent in the Sunday-school may, in the absence of the minister, pronounce the benediction, the Conference replied "Yes; if he is fit to

open the meeting, he is fit to close it." The bishops were made a committee on criticism to pass upon all literary work intended for publication by the Church, their decision to be final. Two additional bishops were elected—the Rev. Charles Calvin Pettey, who was General Secretary of the Connection, and the Rev. Prof. C. R. Harris, of Salisbury, N. C. A collection was called for of one cent from each member in the several pastoral charges, for the support of the General Conferences.

V. Methodist Protestant Church.—The statistics of this Church, as returned to the General Conference in May, show the whole number of members to be 145,500 ; value of church property, $3,342,500 ; net increase of members during four years, 12 per cent.; of property, 13 per cent.

The Book Directory at Pittsburg returned the net value of its assets as $31,492. The receipts for the last four years had been $133,703, and the disbursements $127,116. The periodical publications include the "Methodist Recorder" (weekly) and six papers for children and Sunday-schools. The "Methodist Protestant," Baltimore, is also under the control of the Board of Publication.

Adrian College reported to the General Conference that it had been attended during the last four years by an average of 200 students ; that its endowment funds amounted to $97,500; that its property was valued at $118,000 ; its museum, at $15,000 ; and that its indebtedness was $21,765.

Missions—The receipts of the Board of Missions for the year ending April 30 had been $14,900, and the expenditures $12,158. The receipts for the four years had been $34,130, and the disbursements $29,388. Eight home missionaries had been employed; seven missionaries had been sent abroad ; three churches were returned in Japan, having in all 159 members, with 565 pupils in day and Sunday schools. The property of the mission was valued at $12,000, while $30,000 had been spent upon it. A chapel was in course of erection at Yokohama.

General Conference.—The fifteenth quadrennial General Conference of the Methodist Protestant Church met in Adrian, Mich., May 18. The Rev. David Jones, of Pittsburg, Pa., was chosen president. The commission appointed at a previous General Conference to confer with a similar commission of the Cumberland Presbyterian Church, reported that no difference of creed or polity stood in the way of the organic union of the two bodies. A report was also presented of a conference that had been held with the Congregational Methodists of Alabama, on the subject of union, which had been attended with no practical result. Both reports were referred to a special committee, which subsequently made an adverse report on the subject, in which, while recognizing the fraternal character of the communications as a favorable indication, it affirmed that the Methodist Protestant Church claims, as a reason for distinct denominational existence, "certain distinct fundamental principles, from which a departure in the least degree would involve interests and questions of vital importance, not only within our denominational lines but also with our common Methodism throughout the world. To abandon, or even to show a want of confidence in these principles, at a time when there is a strong sentiment in the Methodist Episcopal Church now leading them to the adoption of the views of our fathers upon the subject of church polity, would be to commit a grievous blunder, that in effect would be equivalent to blotting out our history in the past, and a tacit acknowledgement that the early reformers were in part mistaken, if not entirely wrong, in the position they had announced and defended." The committee was further of the opinion that, so long as the question of organic union was under the consideration of the General Conference, the Church would be in continual confusion and unrest, and the church-work would be hindered; and that, in case any changes in the fundamental laws or doctrines of the Church should be required and attempted for the sake of union, causes would be opened for litigation in regard to Church property and the disposition of trust funds, which would be destructive of the very object for which organic union is proposed. It therefore recommended that further overtures on the subject should cease. The report was adopted by the Conference. A proposition to authorize women to preach was disposed of by declaring that the proposed action involved a change in the constitution of the Church which the General Conference had no power to make. Ministers were forbidden to celebrate the marriage of divorced persons who had violated their marriage vows. The marriage ritual was amended by inserting provisions for the use of rings, and for responses by the parties. It was ordered that transfers of ministers, though signed by the president, should not entitle the person transferred to membership in another annual conference without a vote of that body accepting the transfer. The phraseology of the Apostles' Creed was modified by striking out the words "Holy Catholic Church," and inserting in their place "Universal Christian Church." A Board of Home Missions was constituted, with a traveling secretary to be supported by the conferences, for the purpose of assisting in the support of weak churches and founding new ones. On the subject of temperance, the Conference resolved: "That we are unalterably opposed to any form of license, high or low, as being wrong in principle and pernicious in practice; that any minister or any member who makes, buys, sells, or signs a petition for license to sell, or gives to others as a beverage any spirituous or malt liquor, is guilty of immorality, and shall be dealt with accordingly. We believe that the time has fully come when

Christian men should rise above party prejudices and sectional jealousy, and give their suffrage to any party which has for its object the protection of our homes by the destruction of the unholy traffic." The Conference refused to empower pastors of churches when unordained to administer the ordinances, and to allow supernumerary and superanuated ministers to be represented by laymen in the annual conferences. A committee was appointed to formulate from the articles of religion, as found in the "Discipline" of the Methodist Protestant Church for 1880, and from the recognized standards of doctrine known as Wesleyan Arminianism, articles of faith, its work to be completed by June 1. 1890, referred to the annual conferences at their next ensuing meetings for acceptance or rejection, with criticisms by the rejecting conferences; returned to the committee for revision and perfecting; and referred to the ensuing General Conference. A cheap edition of the "Discipline" was ordered printed, copies of it to be given to members when they join the Church. Arrangements were ordered for the representation of the Methodist Protestant Church in the "Œcumenical Conference of Methodists," to be held in the United States in 1891. The Conference resolved to be represented in the National Convention on Sabbath Observance which was proposed by the General Conference of the Methodist Episcopal Church. An overture was approved, to be sent to the annual conferences, contemplating such a change in the constitution as would grant the power to the annual conferences to license women to preach.

VI. Primitive Methodists in the United States.—The Primitive Methodists are represented in the United States by two conferences—the Eastern and the Western Conferences—which maintain fraternal relations with each other, and with other Primitive Methodist bodies, but are substantially independent. The Eastern Conference met in its sixteenth session at Tamaqua, Pa., May 1, the Rev. J. A. McGreaham presiding. Its statistical report gave the following numbers: Ministers, 35; local preachers, 110; full members, 2,626; probationers, 477; class-leaders, 69; Sunday-schools, 53, with 940 officers and teachers, and 6,607 pupils; valuation of church property, $195,215; debt on church property, $54,573; valuation of Sunday-school property, $4,006; amounts raised toward improvements, etc., $13,913. The business of the Book-Room was balanced at $4,247. The Western Conference met at Dodgeville, Wis., May 23, the Rev. John Ralph presiding. The following is a summary of the statistics: Number of ministers, 20, with 1 superannuate; of local preachers, 64; of class-leaders, 73; of approved members, 1,707, with 140 on trial; of churches, 40, with 25 other preaching-places; of Sunday-schools, 40, with 389 teachers and 2,820 pupils; value of church property, $62,620; indebtedness on the same, $3,112; contributions for mission fund, $752.

VII. Methodist Church of Canada.—This Church comprises a General Conference, which meets every three years, and eleven annual conferences. The statistics for 1887 gave it 1,558 traveling preachers, 1,162 local preachers, 194,761 members, and 16,847 probationers. The statistics of 1888, not completed in time for this publication, indicated, so far as they had been made up, an increase of more than 15,000 members, and a total of 2,871 Sunday-schools, with 27,209 officers and teachers, and 197,538 pupils.

VIII. Wesleyan Connection.—The summaries published with the minutes of the Conference for 1888 give the following totals of members (including those on trial) and ministers (including probationers and supernumeraries) in the British and affiliated Conferences:

CONFERENCES.	Members.	Ministers.
Great Britain	448,056	1,982
Ireland	25,951	284
France	1,541	80
South Africa	34,929	166
West Indies	46,538	87
Foreign mission stations	37,176	353
Total	594,341	2,852

The numbers of ministers and members in the Australasian Wesleyan Methodist Church and the Methodist Church of Canada are given in the minutes of their respective conferences. The whole number of declared Wesleyans in the regular army, militia, and Royal Navy, at home and abroad, is given at 16,660. The whole number of day scholars in 843 school departments was 178,918, with an average attendance of 138,813; total income of day schools (from school-pence, Government grants, subscriptions, etc.), £240,760; total expenditure, £246,377. There were also 223 students in the two training colleges, the Westminster for young men (114) and the Shortlands for young women (109). The number of Sunday-schools in Great Britain was 6,851, with 128,752 officers and teachers and 908,719 pupils. The whole number of children received at the Children's Home and Orphanage up to the end of March, 1888 was 2,300, of whom 1,472 had been provided for and 64 had died. The Temperance Committee returned 3,344 Bands of Hope, with 339,065 enrolled members, and 520 adult temperance societies, with 32,389 members.

A tendency was, however, noticed to ignore the principle on which the Wesleyan Methodist Temperance Society is founded—the co-operation of abstainers and non-abstainers.

Missionary Society.—The annual meeting of the Wesleyan Missionary Society was held in London, April 30. Mr. Isaac Hoyle, M. P., presided. The total income of the society for the year had been £131,867, and the total expenditure, £137,967. The reports from the mission fields showed that the increase in the number of chapels had been 114; of missionaries, 9; of paid agents, 175; of unpaid agents,

208; of full members, 1,037; of members on trial, 577; and of pupils, 1,508. Favorable accounts were given in the report of the European missions—in France, Germany, Bavaria, Bohemia, Italy, Spain, Portugal, and Malta. A Moslem mission had been established in Cairo, Egypt. Reviews of the missionary work in Ceylon, India, China, the Transvaal, the west coast of Africa, and the West Indies, were also given in the report.

The following general summary was given of the missions under the immediate direction of the Wesleyan Missionary Committee and British Conference, in Europe, India, China, West Africa, the Transvaal, British Honduras, and the Bahamas:

Central or principal stations, called circuits	336
Chapels and other preaching-places	1,883
Missionaries and assistant missionaries, including supernumeraries	388
Other paid agents (catechists, interpreters, day-school teachers, etc.)	2,000
Unpaid agents (local preachers, Sunday-school teachers, etc.)	8,859
Full and accredited church-members	32,825
On trial for church membership	4,674
Pupils attending either the Sunday or day schools	59,388

Conference.—The Wesleyan Conference met in its one hundred and fifteenth session at Camborne, July 24. The Rev. Joseph Bush was chosen president. A committee to which the subject had been referred by the previous Conference made a report in which it recognized that various causes, some of them pertaining to social life, militated against enforcing the rule making attendance upon class-meetings a test of membership, and suggested certain modifications in the system. A committee was appointed to continue the inquiry during the year. A proposition was discussed for changing the order of the sessions of the Conference, so that the "representative session," in which lay members participate, and which has charge of the general business, shall precede the "pastoral session," which is composed wholly of ministers, and conducts the ecclesiastical and disciplinary proceedings. The subject was referred to a committee representing the two orders, and to the district meetings of ministers and laymen. The reports from the district meetings held in May showed that the greater number of the thirty-five districts had united in protest against the "compensation clauses" of the local government bill. The committee of the Conference had united with the "Central Committee for the Prevention of the Demoralization of the Native Races by the Liquor Traffic" in inviting the attention of Parliament to the "persistent efforts made by civilized countries to introduce the sale of vile and pernicious spirits and intoxicating liquors, under Government sanction, into our colonies and dependencies." The Conference referred back to the Committee of Privileges the question of the introduction into Parliament of a bill to relieve non-conformists from the presence of the registrar at marriages celebrated in their places, with instructions to consider the whole question and act accordingly. The committee was further authorized to secure the introduction of a bill to enable non-conformists to acquire sites for places for worship where such sites can not be obtained otherwise than by the exercise of compulsory powers. The principle was approved of that all needful facilities should be given for the compulsory enfranchisement of chapels erected on leasehold sites. The committee was further directed to take the necessary steps to secure an alteration of the burial laws amendment act, 1880, by which the length of the necessary notice of intention to bury may be reduced, if possible, to twelve hours. It was also authorized to seek such an amendment in the law, or in its administration, as shall secure, within reasonable limits, the uninterrupted right of preaching in public thoroughfares and open spaces. Provision was made for considering, during the year, the electoral disadvantages to which Wesleyan ministers are subject in consequence of the itinerancy, and for taking such action as may be advisable for having them removed. A committee was appointed to consider general legislative measures affecting Wesleyan day-school education, and to take such action as may be deemed desirable. Favorable reports were received from several "middle-class" schools, and efforts were decided upon to increase the number of such schools.

IX. Primitive Methodist Church.—The statistical reports of this Church in 1888 give it 1,041 itinerant ministers, 16,219 local preachers, and 192.874 members.

The whole amount of gifts for the year to the Connectional funds, was returned to the conferences as £9,000. The Book-Room returned a year's business of nearly £41,500, with clear profits of more than £9,000. The Connectional Insurance Society had invested £12,794.

The Primitive Methodist Conference met in Liverpool, June 6. The Rev. Thomas Whittaker was chosen president. The subject of Methodist union was favorably considered, and the Conference decided to inquire whether organic union could not be secured with one or the other Methodist bodies. The General Connectional Committee was instructed to appoint representatives to assist in arranging for the "Œcumenical Methodist Conference" which it is proposed to hold in the United States in 1891. The Committee of Privileges reported upon the steps which it had taken to arrange with other Methodist bodies to secure co-operative action on public questions in which their common rights and privileges should be involved. The care of the Connectional missionary enterprises was taken from the General Connectional Committee and given to a distinct committee of fifty members, which will hold meetings fortnightly in London and quarterly in such large towns as may be appointed from time to time, with local district committees. Steps were taken for the preparation of a systematic method for training native missionaries in Africa, and for the definition of their relation to the Conference.

X. United Methodist Free Churches.—The following is a summary of the statistics of this Church as they were reported to the Annual Assembly in June, 1888 ; number of ministers, 374 ; of local preachers, 3,346; of class-leaders, 4,014; of members, 76,786 ; of persons on trial for membership, 8,476 ; of chapels, 1,371 ; of Sunday-schools, 1,358. The income of the Chapel Relief fund had been £841, and its expenditure £470. During the past twelve months 18 chapels had been completed, 75 enlarged, and 15 school-rooms has been built: while debts had been reduced by £23,606. The receipts from the Commemorative fund for the year had been £3,723, making the total raised by this fund for Connectional and local objects of £26,422. The sales from the Book-Room had amounted to £6,062, and its profits to £340.

The Annual Assembly met at Manchester, July 10. The Rev. Thomas Wakefield was chosen president. A resolution was adopted expressing a desire that the question of union might still engage the attention of the various Methodist bodies, and that friendly feeling might be cultivated in every way. The Connectional Committee was authorized to take such steps as might seem expedient to give effect to the resolution. A scheme was adopted for the organization of a Connectional fire-insurance society. A resolution bearing upon the report of the Royal Commission on Education deprecated sectarianism in the schools supported from national funds, and expressed the opinion that all public elementary schools should be under the control of the parents and rate-payers.

The annual meeting in behalf of the United Methodist Free Churches' Home and Foreign Mission was held in London, April 23. The income of the missions for the year had been £21,876, and the expenditures, £21,498. Report was made of the condition of the missionary work in East and West Africa, Jamaica, China, and the colonies.

The Rev. T. Wakefield was present, after having served for twenty-five years in the East African missions, and reviewed their progress during the seven years since he had last visited England. Three new mission-stations had been opened in East Africa, and the number of adherents had been more than doubled. A printing-office had been established, and a book containing three hundred hymns had been translated into one of the African dialects. The gospel of St. Matthew had been translated into the Kanika language. Most important of all, the original purpose of the society had been carried out in the founding of a mission to the Gallas.

XI. Methodist New Connection.—The statistical reports of this body, as presented to the Conference in June, show that, without the Australian churches, it has 512 chapels, 189 ministers, 1,270 local preachers, 30,378 members, with 5,096 persons on trial for membership, and 475 Sunday-schools, with 11,321 teachers and 85,872 pupils.

The income of the Mission fund was £5,873, or £225 less than the income of the previous year, while the expenditure had been £6,405. The receipts of the Paternal fund had been £3,189. The capital of the Trustees Mutual Insurance fund stood at £3,138; that of the Chapel and Loan fund, at £6,855. The receipts for the Beneficent fund had been £2,478; for the College, £778; for the Contingent fund, £665; and the total net amount raised for Connectional funds was £13,383.

The ninety-second Methodist.New Connection Conference, met in Hanley, June 11. The Rev. T. T. Rushworth was chosen president. A scheme was approved for establishing a General Committee of Privileges, representing all the Methodist bodies in the country, for the purpose of watching over the interests of Methodism as they are affected by social and political influences and events; of taking common counsel; and of acting, when desirable, with combined authority with reference to such matters. Provision was made for having the Connection represented in such a committee, should it be formed. In reply to a communication from the United Methodist Free Churches, the Conference expressed its desire to co-operate in every possible form of recognition and action that can strengthen the bonds of brotherhood, and recommended joint celebration of ordinances, interchange of pulpits, and the improvement of other opportunities of intercourse and fraternal greeting. A proposition submitted by the previous conference for setting apart a minister as an evangelist had been approved by a majority of the circuits, and was carried into effect. The approval of the Conference was given to the Non-Conformist Marriage Bill; and its objections were expressed against any recommendations of the Royal Commission on Education that would strengthen the denominational use of public moneys, or weaken the " Conscience Clause " in public elementary schools. A resolution was passed remonstrating against the publication of sporting reports and demoralizing serial stories by the newspapers. The committee of the Connectional Temperance Union reported that it included 268 bands, with nearly 40,000 members.

XII. Bible Christian Connection.—The statistics of this denomination, as presented to the Conference in July, showed that there were on the home stations, 145 itinerant preachers, 1,471 local preachers, 583 chapels, 41 preaching-places, 24,574 full members, 574 members on trial, 248 juvenile members, 7,191 Sunday-school teachers and 38,525 pupils in Sunday-schools, and that 3,496 members had been added during the year. The receipts of the chapel fund had been £24,695. The receipts for missions had been £7,012, and the expen-

ditures £7,539. A favorable report was received from the missions in Australia, where the first conference in Victoria had been held in February. The missions in China were prosecuted vigorously.

The seventy-ninth Conference met in London, July 31. The Rev. J. O. Keen, D. D., was chosen president. A motion relaxing certain limitations by which the power of the Conference to appoint a minister for more than four years to the same circuit was now restricted, was defeated, and the Conference decided that it would be unwise to interfere with the existing rule in view of the recent decision of the whole denomination against the " extension of the time limit."

XIII. Wesleyan Reform Union.—This body has 18 itinerant ministers and 8,574 members. The Conference met at Bakewell, July 21. A net increase of 237 members and 714 pupils in Sunday-schools was reported.

XIV. Australasian Methodist General Conference. —This body, which is composed of the New South Wales, Victoria and Tasmania, and New Zealand Conferences, returned for 1888, a total of 580 ministers and 79,477 lay members, of whom 7,692 were " on trial." The General Conference met in Melbourne, May 9. The Rev. J. C. Symons was chosen president. The most urgent question to be considered was that of the difficulties in Tonga. In consequence of certain personal and political difficulties, the Church in Tonga had been divided about three years before, and an independent church had been formed, still Methodist in doctrine and policy, but rejecting the control of the Australian (New South Wales) Conference, carrying with it about 16,000 members of the original body, and having the royal influence on its side. The separation had been accompanied by a serious persecution of the adherents of the original organization. In all attempts to negotiate for a settlement of the difficulty, the Government had insisted upon the removal of the official representative of the Conference, the Rev. J. A. Moulton. Compliance with this condition had been refused. The debate in the General Conference showed that a considerable difference concerning the proper course to be adopted existed within that body. A decision was reached to send the Rev. George Brown as a commissioner to Tonga, with instructions to inquire and report upon the best means of securing honorable and lasting reunion with the " Free Church," and generally to draw up a scheme for the permanent settlement of affairs there; the result of his efforts to be submitted to a committee on Tongan affairs, and through it, " and with such modifications as it may deem necessary," to the annual conferences next ensuing, and, if approved by a majority of them, to be accepted by the General Conference. Application by the New Zealand Conference for an independent organization was refused. The law with reference to attending class-meetings was amended by substituting the words "are strongly advised" for "are required" in the direction of the discipline upon the subject.

XV. West Indian (Wesleyan) General Conference. —This body is composed of the Eastern and Western Annual Conferences. The reports presented to the General Conference showed that it included 52,593 members, of whom 6,005 are junior members, and 2,087 are "on trial," the rest being "full members." The triennial session of the General Conference was held beginning March 20.

XVI. South African Conference (Wesleyan).—This Conference met at King William's Town, in April. The Rev. William Tyndall presided. The statistics for the year showed the number of itinerant preachers to be 89; of local preachers, 560; and of members, 45,124.

MEXICO, a confederated republic of North America; area, 761,640 square miles. It is divided into twenty-seven States, one Federal District, and one Territory (Lower California). The population is about 11,000,000, 19 per cent. being whites, 38 pure Indians, and 43 per cent. of mixed races. The cities of over 20,000 inhabitants were in 1888: Mexico, 350,-000; Puebla, 112,000; Guadalajara, 95,000; Leon, 60,000; Guanajuato, 52,000; Mérida, 40,000; San Luis Potosi, 35,000; Zacatecas, 30,000; Querétaro, 30,000; Oajaca, 28,000; Colima, 26,251; Saltillo, 26,000; Morelia, 25,-000; Aguas Calientes, 22,000; Vera Cruz, 21,-000; Orizaba, 20,500; Pachuca, 20,200; and Durango, 20,100.

Government.—The President is Don Porfirio Diaz, whose term of office will expire on Dec. 1, 1892. His Cabinet is composed of the following ministers: Foreign Relations, Señor Ignacio Mariscal; War, Gen. Pedro Hinojosa; Public Works, Gen. Pacheco; Justice, Señor Joaquin Baranda; Finance, Señor Manuel Dublan; Interior, Señor Manuel Romero Rubio. Congress will be called upon at its next session to establish a new Cabinet office, that of Minister of Posts and Telegraphs. The Minister to the United States is Señor Matias Romero: the United States Minister at Mexico is Edward S. Bragg; the Consul-General at Mexico Elawson C. More; at Matamoras, Warner P. Sutton; the Mexican Vice-Consul at New York is Don Antonio Laviada y Peon; the Consul at Brownsville, Don Manuel Treviño; the Consul-General at San Francisco, Don Alejandro K. Couey; at New Orleans, Don Manuel G. Zamora.

Proposed American Acquisition of Lower California.—Mr. Vanderveer, of California, introduced, on Jan. 21, 1889, a joint resolution in the House of Representatives at Washington, requesting the President to open negotiations with Mexico for the cession of Lower California to the United States. When asked about the chances of consummating such cession, Mr. Romero, the Mexican minister, replied that his Government had no disposition or inclination to sell any portion of Mexican territory, and

that, even if it should be inclined to do so, the transaction could not be carried out, because there is no power under the Constitution authorizing the transfer of national property.

Treaty.—The Japanese minister, Mr. Mutsu, and the Mexican minister, Señor Romero, signed, at Washington, early in December, 1888, a treaty of amity and commerce between their respective countries, subject to ratification by their governments. Heretofore there have been no diplomatic relations between the two countries.

Finance.—The proceeds of the £10,500,000 6-per-cent. loan, negotiated at Berlin, have been applied in part to buying up, at 40 per cent., the bonds issued under the English conversion debt arrangement, the remainder, over $16,-000,000 in gold, being applied to canceling the debt the Government owed the National Bank. The American debt has meanwhile been canceled, so as to leave only $300,000 unpaid. The consolidated internal debt, on June 30, 1888, amounted to $16,052,000. The floating debt was of equal amount, bearing no interest. The budget for 1888–'89 estimated the income at $37,900,000, and the outlay at $38,537,239.

The report of the Minister of Finance for the fiscal year ended June 30, 1887, was published on Feb. 18, 1888, and reads as follows:

The Federal revenues were $32,126,509. Deducting $958,156 of the part collected in credits of the public debt through the purchase of waste lands and nationalized properties, there results as the net amount received $31,168,352, or $3,357,443 more than the collection of the previous year, when the net income only reached $27,810,909; and, even comparing this product with the most favorable one of the last quinquennium, which was the fiscal year 1882–'83, it still exceeds that by $332,873. The principal causes of this increase of receipts may be found (1) in the collection of import duties, which in this fiscal year rose to $17,268,650, while in the previous year they did not exceed $14,852,980; (2) in the receipts from stamps, which reached $7,538,150, when in the previous year they only produced $5,877,458; (3) in the new tax on salaries, which yielded $885,560.

The official Government organ, in its issue of Dec. 5, 1888, contained a decree of November 30, through which the import duties were to be raised 2 per cent., the proceeds to be set aside toward defraying the cost of harbor improvements.

A 7-per-cent. £400,000 loan was floated in London for account of the city of Mexico, to provide means for the finishing of the Tesquisquiac tunnel for draining the valley of Mexico. The net profits realized by the National Bank in 1887 were $1,238,364, against $1,123,758 netted in 1886, the dividends declared being $880,000, against $800,000.

Army and Navy.—The army of the republic consisted, on June 30, 1888, of 19,466 infantry, with 1,110 officers; 6,095 cavalry, with 465 officers; 1,688 artillery, with 128 officers; and 2,768 gendarmes, with 247 officers—together, 31,967. The navy consisted of five gun-boats.

Postal Service.—The number of post-offices of the first class in 1877 was 300; minor ones,

724. In the interior 22,885,092 letters and postal-cards were handled in that year, while the number of international letters forwarded was 1,345,720. The service employed during the year 1,528 persons, the receipts amounting to $749,967, and the expenses $857,424. Arrangements were nearly completed in January, 1889, for a packet-post between France and Mexico.

About the success of the foreign parcel-post between the United States, Mexico, and other American countries, Mr. Bell, the Superintendent of Foreign Mails in the United States, reports as follows: "The effect of these conventions has been to remove the restrictions which previously existed; and there can be no doubt that it will continue to augment largely the trade relations with those countries without imposing additional burdens on the postal revenue of the United States. The conclusion of the parcel-post convention with Mexico is of special importance, as that country, with its large population and with rapidly developing industries, naturally looks to the United States for every possible aid in strengthening the bonds of commercial relations between the two great sister republics whose interests are the same; and it will be found that new and hitherto almost inaccessible markets have been opened to American merchants."

Commerce.—During the fiscal year 1886–'87 exportation was distributed as follows, reduced to thousands of dollars:

COUNTRIES.	Merchandise.	Silver.	Total.
United States	11,007	16,576	27,588
England	2,397	11,122	13,519
France	717	4,401	5,118
Germany	891	1,290	2,181
Spain	499	104	603
Other countries	125	68	198
Total	15,636	33,561	49,197

The products shipped during the year were (in thousands of dollars): Sisal hemp, 3,901; coffee, 2,627; hides and skins, 2,211; cabinet and dyewoods, 1,849; tobacco, 851; vanilla, 694; istle-fiber, 349; cattle, 471; argentiferous lead bullion, 323; other merchandise, 2,360; silver, 33,561.

The export of merchandise from Mexico from January 1 to June 30, 1888, reached the sum of $10,169,485, showing an increase of $1,146,192 over the corresponding period of the previous year, or 11 per cent. The United States' share therein was 63 per cent.; that of England, 21; that of France, 9; and that of Germany, 5 per cent.

The American trade (merchandise) with Mexico exhibits these figures:

FISCAL YEAR.	Imports into the United States.	Domestic exports from the United States.
1886	$10,687,972	$6,856,077
1887	14,719,840	7,267,129
1888	17,329,889	9,242,188

Mexican spinners imported, in 1888, 33,203 bales of cotton from the United States against 40,774 in 1887.

Vanilla.—Mexican vanilla chiefly grows in the vicinity of Misantia and Papantia, in the State of Vera Cruz. Papantia has a population of 10,000, and is in the Indian District of Toconaso. The vanilla is a creeping plant, growing on trees and shrubs in the forests. The pods mature in November and December, and are gathered by women and children, who carry them to market, where American and Mexican dealers buy them, paying from $10 to $12 a pound for them. About 1,000 green pods weigh 60 pounds, reduced to 10 pounds by drying. In 1887 the price for select pods was $15, but an abundant crop brought the price down to $10 and $12 in 1888. Papantia exports on an average 60,000,000 pods annually.

Competition in Mexican Trade.—German houses, which nearly control the wholesale trade of Mexico, owe their supremacy to the system of long credits given to customers in the interior of the country, and to economical management. They have driven out the English houses, with only two or three exceptions. Failures are very rare, although large amounts are constantly due. The French have monopolized the dry-goods trade in the larger cities. Both the German and the French houses, in their operations in Mexico, have their rights clearly and particularly defined in commercial treaties. The English are endeavoring to bring about negotiations for a comprehensive commercial treaty, and hope to gain a foothold. American interests, although now amounting to $200,000,000, are without treaty protection, as the treaty defining the status of Americans in business in Mexico has lapsed.

VESSELS ENTERED IN 1886–'87.

CLASS.	Steamers.	Tonnage.	Sailing-vessels.	Tonnage.
Sea-going	658	877,518	587	155,207
Coastwise	1,680	680,714	4,897	163,886
Total in 1885–'86	2,333	1,558,282	5,484	319,043
	1,904	1,548,557	4,975	277,847
Increase	429	14,675	509	41,696

The maritime movement increased during the fiscal year 1886–'87. The Mexican merchant marine was composed, in 1888, of 421 sea-going vessels and 847 coasting-craft.

Railroads.—The Mexican Central Railroad threw open to traffic, on May 21, the line from Irapuato to Guadalajara, 259 kilometres in length. On the line from Tampico to San Luis Potosi, 188 kilometres were put in running order, up to the banks of the Gallinas river, where a bridge is being built, and beyond which the embankments have been finished a distance of 232 kilometres. On the Aguas Calientes, San Luis Potosi line, the locomotive reached Salinas del Peñon on September 9, 110 kilometres distant from Aguas Calientes, being half the distance intervening between the two cities. The National Mexican Company was actively at work in 1888 to finish the section of the line that separates Saltillo from San Miguel Allende, a distance of 565 kilometres, and on August 31 the portion of the track coming from the north reached San Luis Potosi; the junction of the two portions of the track took place at the Boquillas Viaduct, thus linking together two important cities, and opening a third line of railway from the capital to the American frontier. The Hidalgo Railroad Company finished five kilometres on the Tepa–Tulancingo line, and the thirty kilometres, which complete the line from San Augustin to Teoloyucan; these works constitute a new track connecting Pachusa with the capital on the one hand, while joining the Central and National Railroads on the other Of the Interoceanic Railroad, twenty kilometres were finished of the Yautepec and Amacusac section, and twenty kilometres of the one between Mazapa and San Martin Texmelucan. The Yucatan lines have not been behind hand in completing their system. Between Mérida and Calkini, six kilometres have gone into operation, and between Mérida and Valladolid seven. The aggregate length of lines of railway in running order in Mexico was 7,500 kilometres on Sept. 16, 1888.

Tehuantepec Ship-Railway.—A meeting was held on June 7, 1888, at Jersey City, of those interested in the project to build a ship-railway across the Isthmus of Tehuantepec. The Eads Concession Company is the organization that secured possession of all rights in the concessions made to Capt. Eads by the Mexican Government in 1881. About six months prior to the date of this meeting a construction company was organized in New York, under the title of "Atlantic and Pacific Ship-Railway Company." The English civil engineer Benjamin Blake, is to superintend the construction, and it is believed it will not be difficult to procure the $50,000,000 of capital that will be necessary. The contract stipulates that the work shall begin within a year, dating from June, and be completed in five years. The scheme is to carry loaded ships across the isthmus in cradles. The distance is about one hundred and fifty miles.

Telegraphs.—During 1888 there were in operation 21,453 kilometres of Government lines, 6,887 kilometres of lines belonging to individual States of the confederation, 6,143 the property of railroad companies, 4,098 of private lines, and 2,926 of Mexican cable; a grand total of 41,507 kilometres. The Federal Government had 339 offices in operation. In December, 1888, the Mexican Telegraph Company declared a quarterly dividend of 2½ per cent. The Government has declared free of duty everything entering into the construction of telegraph and telephone lines.

The steamer "Faraday" arrived at Coatzacoalcos on Jan. 18, 1889, having on board over 900 miles of the most improved heavy cable, which was to be laid immediately between that port and Galveston, Tex., for the Mexican and Central and South American Telegraph Companies. This will duplicate the Gulf systems of these two companies, providing increased facilities, and insuring rapid communication by the American route via Galveston, with Valparaiso, Buenos Ayres, and other places in South America.

American Steamship-Line.—The sale of the entire plant of the Alexandre line to the New York and Cuba Mail Steamship Company, in the spring, increased the number of steamers running between New York and Mexico via Havana to five, so that since then a steamer has left New York every Wednesday.

Land Purchases.—In January, 1888, Señor M. Gonzalez, agent for several residents of Coahuila, closed the sale of 500,000 acres in the State of Coahuila to the representatives of an English syndicate, which already owns 2,000,000 acres in that State. The consideration was $125,000, or twenty-five cents an acre. The purchase comprises much mountain land. English capitalists now own one quarter of the State of Coahuila. A large tract in northern Chihuahua, known as "Las Palomas," owned by George H. Sisson, of New York, and Louis Huller, of Mexico, was sold in January, 1889, to a syndicate of Chicago and Nebraska capitalists. The consideration was $1,000,000. These lands are to be colonized with Germans, under the Huller colonization concession from the Mexican Government. George Hearst, a California capitalist, while in the city of Mexico in May, bought over 2,000,000 acres in the State of Vera Cruz, all lying in the "Tierra Caliente," and adapted to the raising of coffee, sugar, and tobacco.

In July it transpired that a French company had purchased the San Lorenzo estate, one of the best known in northern Mexico. The business will be managed in Paris and by two directors in the city of Mexico.

The Mormons have for some years past been quietly buying large tracts of agricultural lands in northern Chihuahua, principally in the valley of the Casas Grandes river, and in 1888 they were negotiating for more. There are several flourishing villages in that neighborhood, the principal one being called Porfirio Diaz; the colonists (who are probably precursors of much greater bodies in the future) are very quiet and unobtrusive.

American Enterprise.—Before the Mexican Congress adjourned, on Dec. 15, 1888, the Union Light, Fuel, and Gas Company, of America, organized under the laws of Illinois, in which St. Louis, Chicago, New York, and Detroit capitalists are largely interested, obtained a concession from the Mexican Government for the introduction of water, fuel, and gas into the cities and Government buildings throughout the republic. Among the items mentioned in the concession is the free importation for fifteen years of all materials necessary for the plant.

Mining.—There were being worked in Mexico, at the close of 1888, 324 silver-mines, employing over 100,000 miners. Eleven of the mines produced in 1888 $25,000,000 of pure silver. Mexico produced, between 1821 and 1880, $900,000,000 in silver, and only $4,800,-000 in gold. A rich pocket of silver was discovered in August, in the Concepcion, one of the Matchuala mines. Reports were received on July 24 at Mexico from Las Cruces, Lower California, that gold was being found in excellent ore-bodies. Fourteen ounces of amalgam gold were taken from a ton and a half of rock at the Santa Clara mine, in Las Cruces Cañon. The vein at this mine is reported to be four feet in width, and a true fissure vein. There were, at last accounts, thirty tons of ore on the dump. This mine is owned at Ensenada. The vein at the Bonanza mine, in the Valladores district, has widened from eight inches to two feet six inches. Expensive machinery had been erected at the Fronteriza, whence they were to begin shipping the metal in pigs about January 1. The nearest shipping-point to the mines is Baratorano station, on the Mexican International Railroad. An influx of miners in great numbers and prospectors had begun. Many of these mines were originally worked by the Spaniards, and were destroyed and filled up by them when they were driven off by the native Mexicans during the revolution of 1810. News was received on September 20 from the Santa Rosa mining region in Mexico to the effect that a great mining excitement had set in. Persons who own the larger mines, like the Cedral, the Fronteriza, and the San Juan, were said to be trying to keep the richness of the ore from the knowledge of the public; but it transpired that these and others were taking ore that yields $105 of silver to the ton, besides a large percentage of lead. The rapid rise of quicksilver in London has given an impetus to the working of quicksilver mines in Mexico, and efforts have been made to work several newly discovered deposits in the northern States. The Government is about to assume the control of all its mints, which are now under lease.

Ascent of the Iztaccihuatl Volcano.—In April two German travelers, Lenk and Topf, undertook the ascent of the volcano Iztaccihuatl, the neighbor of Popocatepetl, whose summit has an elevation of about 17,000 feet. They failed to reach the very top, but the expedition fully rewarded their efforts, as they report the existence of a glacier. It has not been supposed hitherto that there were any glaciers in this part of the American continent.

Earthquakes.—On Jan. 2, 1888, a sharp shock of earthquake was felt in the city of Mexico, at 7.30 A. M. During the last quarter of 1887 there had been seismic disturbances throughout the country. A slight shock was felt there on July 18, about midnight, and a high wind sprang up simultaneously. Another slight earthquake visited the capital at 16 minutes to

9 P. M., on September 6. The oscillations were from the northeast to southwest, and lasted 24 seconds; at Orizaba 9 seconds; and in the State of Guerrero 15 seconds, the oscillations being from west to east.

Education.—A bill was introduced in the Mexican Chamber of Deputies to make gratuitous elementary school instruction compulsory throughout the republic. For every 20,000 inhabitants, two schools are to be founded, one for boys and one for girls, and parents that do not send their children to school are to be punished with fine or imprisonment. Higher education is to be at the expense of the Federal Government.

MICHIGAN. State Government.—The following were the State officers during the year, all being Republican: Governor, Cyrus G. Luce; Lieutenant-Governor, James H. Macdonald; Secretary of State, Gilbert R. Osmun; Auditor-General, Henry H. Aplin; State Treasurer, George L. Maltz; Attorney-General, Moses Taggert; Superintendent of Public Instruction, Joseph Estabrook; Member State Board of Education, Bela W. Jenks; Commissioner of State Land-Office, Roscoe D. Dix; Chief-Justice of the Supreme Court, Thomas R. Sherwood; Associate Justices James V. Campbell, John W. Champlin, Allen B. Morse, and Charles D. Long. The principal appointees of the Governor were: Private Secretary, Milo D. Campbell; Commissioner of Railroads, John T. Rich; Commissioner of Insurance, Henry S. Raymond; Labor Commissioner, Alfred H. Heath; Commissioner of Mineral Statistics, Charles D. Lawton; State Librarian, Harriet A. Tenney; Oil Inspector, H. D. Platt; Salt Inspector, George W. Hill; Game Warden, William Alden Smith; Adjutant-General, D. B. Ainger; Quartermaster-General, S. B. Daboll; Inspector-General, F. D. Newberry.

Political.—The State officers were chosen at the general election in November for the two years beginning Jan. 1, 1889. There were four parties in the field: Republican, Democratic-Greenback (Fusion), Prohibition, and Labor. For Governor the Republicans renominated Cyrus G. Luce; the Democratic-Greenback party, Wellington R. Burt; Prohibition, Amherst B. Cheney; Labor, Wildman Mills. The officers above named were re-elected, except in two instances where the incumbents had served two terms. The new officers elected were: Stephen V. R. Trowbridge, Attorney-General, and Perry F. Powers, member State Board of Education (Republicans). The votes cast for the respective candidates for Governor were as follow: Cyrus G. Luce, Republican, 233,595; Wellington R. Burt, Fusion, 216,450; Amherst B. Cheney, Prohibition, 20,342; Wildman Mills, Labor, 4,388.

The principal State issues in the campaign were upon questions of temperance and increasing taxation. The last Legislature passed a local-option law permitting the several counties, by a vote of their electors, to prohibit the manufacture and sale of liquor within their limits. The Supreme Court of the State declared the law unconstitutional by reason of defective title, after thirty-five counties had voted for prohibition and two counties had given a majority against it. Certain provisions also of the high-license law passed by the last Legislature had been declared unconstitutional by the Supreme Court.

The Republican platform included the following:

We cordially indorse the progressive temperance legislation enacted by the last Legislature, and regret that its full fruits were not realized, owing to the technical defects in the law held by the Supreme Court to be in conflict with the Constitution. We record ourselves as in favor of an impartial enforcement of the temperance laws of the State, and recommend to the next Legislature the re-enactment of a local-option law that shall be free from constitutional objections.

The Democratic platform included the following:

That the multiplication in this State of petty boards, commissions, and officials, with such powers and surroundings as insure neither official responsibility nor the respect of the Legislature or the people, leaves the matter of appropriations for State institutions to be largely controlled by log-rolling combinations; and to this, as well as to the lack of system, we attribute great and constant increase of appropriation. Therefore we submit that the case is one demanding the election of a Legislature and State officials free to make the changes which economy and good business methods may dictate.

These two planks presented the principal State issues during the canvass. The fight centered mainly upon the Legislature and Governor. Governor Luce, being an uncompromising temperance man, was opposed, for this reason, by some within his party, but he gained strength from other sources. As a result of the election, 24 Republicans and 8 Democrats were chosen to the Senate, and 70 Republicans and 30 Democrats to the House of Representatives.

On the assembling of the Legislature, Hon. James McMillan, of Detroit, was elected to represent the State in the United States Senate for six years from March 4, 1889, receiving the unanimous support of the Republicans in both houses, in his nomination and election.

Educational.—The Superintendent of Public Instruction, in his forthcoming report, will show the school population of the State to be 629,923, between five and twenty years of age, and the enrollment for the year to have been 425,218. The total number of districts in the State is 7,087, and the average length of school taught in them 7·6 months. There are 7,428 school-houses, and the estimated value of school property is $12,857,103. The whole number of districts not having school during the year, from various causes, was only 81, being 37 fewer than during the previous year. The State has now four strictly educational colleges. The State University at Ann Arbor, during 1887-'88 enrolled 1,675 in its various departments. The State Normal School at Ypsilanti enrolled 948, the Agricultural College

at Lansing, 312, and the Michigan Mining-School at Houghton about 100. The colleges of the State were flourishing in 1888.

The principal educational questions being agitated in the State, other than those affecting the institutions, are: Uniformity of text-books, free text-books for public schools, and a change from the school-district plan to the township-unit system. These questions are not new in the State, but bills are being introduced in the Legislature, and their enactment vigorously urged.

Prisons.—The State has two prisons completed and in operation, and a third one, costing about $300,000, is being finished at Marquette, in the upper peninsula. On Dec. 1, 1888, the total prison population of the State was as follows: State House of Correction and Reformatory at Ionia, 332; State Prison at Jackson, 754. The prison population of the State decreased since Dec. 1, 1884, from 1,354 to 1,086, Dec. 1, 1888, while the population increased about 350,000 during the same period. Most of the labor performed in the two prisons is under the contract system, although during the past two or three years the State-account system has been in operation, to a certain extent, in the House of Correction at Ionia. The manufacture of furniture and knit goods is under the State-account plan there, and all contracts with outside parties have expired, except one for the manufacture of cigars. Although the State-account system can not be said to have proved a failure, yet it has failed to meet the most sanguine expectations of those who advocated the change from the contract plan. Four pardons were granted during the year and two sentences commuted by the Governor.

Insane Asylums.—The State has four asylums for the insane, in which are 2,400 patients. During the past two years it has been deemed the better policy to meet the increasing demands for asylum room by the erection of cottages, instead of establishing new plants. During the year five cottages were thus erected, with a capacity to accommodate fifty patients each, and the plan seems to give general satisfaction, at a much less expense per patient than by the establishment of new institutions.

Other State Institutions.—The Reform School for boys, at Lansing, had an average attendance during the year of 444; the Industrial Home for girls, at Adrian, 213. The State also has a blind school at Lansing, in which it cares for 88; and the deaf and dumb school at Flint, 298. These two institutions are entirely free in board, care, and instruction. The Soldiers' Home at Grand Rapids is entirely free to dependent soldiers. During the year, 450 dependent soldiers of the State were supported and cared for.

The State Public School at Coldwater, a home for dependent children and orphans established many years since, has for its object the taking of children out of poor-houses and other places where they are dependent upon the public for support, and caring for them, securing homes, and exercising guardianship over them until they become of age. During the year, 194 children were thus received into the school, and as many found homes. Since the school was established in 1874, 2,512 children have thus been cared for and educated while in the school, indentured into homes, and otherwise received the guardianship of the State during their minority.

Mineral Resources.—During the year the State produced 4,243,264 barrels of salt. The number of tons of iron shipped from the mines of Michigan during the year was 3,934,339 tons. The land-plaster produced during the year was 28,794 tons; stucco, 170,145 barrels. The amount of gold produced was $32,338; silver, $2,592.03. Valuable deposits of gold were discovered at and near Ishpeming, in the northern peninsula. The total number of tons of refined copper produced in the State during the year was 38,112.

Militia.—The State militia consists of 2,376 men. An encampment was held for two weeks in the summer of 1888 at Mackinac Island, with an enrollment of 2,062. The militia is supported by a tax that is levied upon the property of the State, and is equal to three and a half cents for each person in the State according to the last census.

Railroads.—Of the 85 counties in the State, only five are now without railway connections. During the year, 275 miles of road were completed and put in operation. The State now has 6,043 miles of railway, and 24,057,-719 passenger fares were paid during the year, at an average rate per mile of 2·39 cents. Freight to the amount of 41,209,880 tons was moved, and the average charge for carrying a ton a mile was 1·09 cent, the rates being higher than at any time since 1875. By accidents to passengers during the year, two persons were killed and 32 injured. In accordance with the law of 1887, many of the roads have put in steam-heaters connected with the engine, and others are complying with the statute as rapidly as possible. The total tax paid by the railway companies of the State during the year was $715,680.24. The total costs of railroads in the State, as reported to the present time, has been $240,000,000.

Insurance.—The Legislature of 1887, by statute, prohibited the contract system of fire insurance in the State. During the year the Supreme Court declared the law constitutional. But in effect the contract system of rating remains intact, and the old rates are virtually unchanged. A commission, appointed by the Governor for the purpose, has established a uniform policy for all fire companies doing business in the State. The so-called grave-yard insurance companies were also, by the Legislature of 1887, prohibited from doing business in this State, and during the year Michigan has been freed from them.

Crops and Stock.—The principal crops in 1888 are shown by the following table:

CROPS.	Acres.	Bushels.	Average.
Wheat	1,504,411	23,581,504	15·67
Corn	839,646	26,029,026	31·00
Oats	858,818	31,346,674	31·50
Barley	40,850	1,168,310	28·60
Hay	1,350,000	......	.....

The number of horses was 365,300; milch cows, 389,405; other cattle, 410,611; hogs, 456,436; sheep, 1,975,562; pounds of wool, 11,898,047.

The average rainfall in the State during the year was 28·68 inches.

MINING LAW. Under the common law of England, the owner of the surface of land under which minerals existed was entitled, *ex jure naturæ*, to everything beneath it, down to the center of the earth, except the minerals of gold and silver. In the case of mines under highways and non-navigable streams, the minerals belonged, as a matter of right, to the owner of the adjacent soil. All mines subjacent to navigable streams, and all gold and silver mines, belonged, by *prima-facie* right, to the crown. Where the precious metals were intermingled with a baser metal, if the gold and silver were worth more than the cost of extracting them, the mine belonged to the crown. But in certain cases the owner was permitted to work the mine on payment of a royalty. The thirteen States that formed the original Federal Union adopted the English common law, as a body, as a part of their inorganic law. But the greater part of the lands in all of the Eastern States were patented to settlers at an early period, and all minerals passed as a matter of right to the owners of the surface or soil, as the doctrine of crown reservations did not obtain in this country except in the State of New York. Such questions as have arisen in the various Eastern States in relation to mines and mining concern chiefly title-deeds, rights of support, drainage, administration, transfer of mining properties, etc., and have nothing to do with what is technically known as mining law. By virtue of title xi, chapter 9, of Part I of the Revised Statutes of New York, certain mines of gold and silver are, under certain conditions, reserved to the people of the State. In the States and Territories that are of Spanish origin the law is different. At the time of the cession to the United States of the territory originally Spanish or Mexican the Spanish or Mexican law as to mines was in force with the same, and became a part of the inorganic law of the United States, so far as that territory was concerned. The Mexican law was naturally of Spanish origin, and found its root in the code of Francisco Gamboa (1761). This code was modified in 1783, by the so-called code of Galvez, entitled "Mining Ordinance of New Spain," which left all parts of the code of Gamboa still in force, except where it was expressly repealed. These codes were elaborate and voluminous. The code of Gamboa allowed to the discoverer of mineral lands a length of 160 varas or yards, and 80 varas in width on the vein, and upon relocation of a previously discovered mine, 120 varas in length and 60 varas in width on the vein. In the case of mines or "streamworks" of gold, original locators were allowed 80 varas in length and 40 varas in width; and in case of a second location 60 varas in length and 30 in width on the vein. This code required denunciation, working, and registry of the claim, in order to perfect title. The code of Galvez treated, among other subjects, judges and deputies of mining districts, jurisdiction of mining causes, ownership of mines, drainage, laborers, and mining generally. It created a fund and bank of supplies, and provided for the establishment of mining-schools. It contained many curious provisions, among others the privilege of nobility to the scientific profession of mining, relieved mine-owners and many of their subordinates from imprisonment for debt, and created a preference in favor of mining laborers as against other persons for their wages. It allowed the original discoverer 200 varas or yards in length on the length of the vein, and a hundred level yards measured on either side of or divided on both sides of the vein. Where the vein was inclined, an increase in width was allowed, in proportion to the degree of inclination. Under this code, minerals of every sort belonged to the crown, but could be acquired by any person other than aliens, members of religious orders, and certain high civic dignitaries, upon discovery followed by location, denunciation, and working in the manner prescribed.

The Mexican statutes modified certain provisions of the code of Galvez, and extended certain privileges to miners of quicksilver, and by decree of Oct. 7, 1823, the disabilities of foreigners were removed so far as to enable them to contract with mine-owners needing capital, and as a consequence to hold shares in such mines.

On March 16, 1848, the treaty of Guadalupe Hidalgo was ratified, by virtue of which California, Arizona, New Mexico, Texas, and a part of Colorado were ceded to the United States. That year gold was discovered in California, and the law that sprang up and grew to be the inorganic law of the self-constituted mining districts of these newly acquired Territories was a fusion of the old Spanish law as modified by Mexican decrees, and the common law of England as it existed in the Eastern United States. For a review of the mining law of foreign countries, see article by R. W. Raymond in Williams's "Mineral Resources of the United States, 1883 and 1884" (Washington, 1885.)

Federal Legislation.—From 1795 to 1865 the United States Government adhered to the policy of reserving the public mineral lands from sale. In 1805 an act was passed authorizing the President to lease lead-mines for a limited period. Throughout the East there were, even at the time of the Federal Union, practically no public lands, and in the West few or no lands had been occupied by miners. Nevertheless, at an early period Congress discussed the question of the undivided public lands, and even in 1785 it passed an act by which it reserved one third of all gold, silver, lead, and copper mines. In many instances thereafter, lead-mines were reserved from the sale of certain portions of the public domain, and the general pre-emption law excludes from its provisions "all lands on which are situated any known salines or minerals." In the various acts admitting the later States to the Union, mineral lands were not expressly reserved, except so far as they were included in what are termed "lands generally reserved." The reservation of lead-mines under certain local acts relating to pre-emption has led to at least one important case in the Supreme Court.

In the Eastern States the English doctrine of royal mines has never been established, with the single exception of the State of New York. The States granted their public lands to settlers at an early date, and there never was any reservation of the minerals; hence the title to all mines became inseparably vested in the owner of the soil, and the ordinary rules of the law of real property have always applied to them. No record is found of litigation on any questions growing out of location of mines in the Eastern States, by virtue of any State or Federal laws, except in so far as the cases are found in Morrison's "Mining Reports."

From 1849 until 1866 Congress did practically nothing toward the promotion of mines and mining, and the seekers for precious metals in the new West were left to their own devices. The result was a rapid encroachment upon the public domain, and the passage of a vast number of statutes and regulations by the local legislatures and tribunals of the mining districts of the Territories, based upon the local mining code of old Spain, if the Territory was of Spanish origin, or upon the common law of England if it was of British origin.

Recent Legislation.—After the civil war it was proposed to promote the sale of the public domain then undisposed of, with a view to diminishing the public debt. In 1865 a joint resolution of Congress was passed, reserving all mineral lands from any grants made by them in the previous cessions to States or corporations. On July 26, 1866, Congress passed the first federal mining law which conceded to first discoverers of mineral deposits most of the privileges granted by the Spanish codes, and by the earlier district laws. This act was the first attempt of Congress to deal practically with the question of mining-titles on the public domain. It recognized many of the local mining customs to an extent that made it full of uncertainties. Under it the discovery of any part of the lode was made a basis for a claim.

The lode was what was claimed and subsequently acquired by patent. The locator was entitled to claim along the lode the number of feet that the local laws permitted. The surface was not conveyed to the locator; he merely acquired an easement to occupy it with structures necessary for the working of his mine.

On July 9, 1870 a new act was passed relating more particularly to water-rights and placer claims; and on March 3, 1873, one relating to coal-lands. On May 10, 1872, the general mining act was passed, which repealed sections 1, 2, 3, 4, and 6 of the act of 1866, and was subsequently codified as title xxxii, chapter 6, of the Revised Statues of the United States. But a single act of any importance has been passed since then, and this is the act of Feb. 11, 1875, relating to tunnels on mining-claims.

The Existing Law.—The act of 1872 is now a part of the organic law of the United States, and is the only specific mining law existing therein. It supersedes all local customs, rules, and regulations, and all State or Territorial laws in conflict with it, but is expressly limited to claims located after May 10, 1872, and makes no attempt to interfere with any mining claims theretofore granted. It ingrafted upon the jurisprudence of the country the so-called "doctrine of the apex," which is totally foreign to all known systems of jurisprudence and of doubtful expediency. This innovation has led to much litigation and uncertainty and has made the working of the law generally unsatisfactory. The following are some of the more important provisions of the law:

Title xxxii of chapter 6 of the Revised Statutes of the United States contains twenty-eight sections, and embodies parts of the acts of 1866 and 1872, chiefly the latter. The first section expressly reserves mineral lands from sale under pre-emption, and the second gives all citizens of the United States, or those intending to become citizens, full privilege of free and open exploration and purchase of mineral lands belonging to the Federal Government under the rules prescribed by law and the local rules and customs of the mining districts not inconsistent with the laws of the United States. The third section limits the size of the claim to 1,500 feet along the vein or lode, and prohibits the location until a "discovery" of the vein or lode is made within the limits of the claim located, and it limits the width to 300 feet on each side of the middle of the vein at the surface. It also provides that no mining regulation shall so limit any claim as to be less than twenty-five feet on each side of the middle of the vein at the surface except where adverse rights existing at that date render such limitation necessary. The fourth section defines what is proper proof of citizenship. The fifth provides that locators shall have the right of possession and enjoyment "of all the surface included between the lines of their location, and of all veins, lodes, and ledges, throughout their entire depth, the top or apex of which lies inside of such surface lines extended downward vertically, although such veins, lodes, or ledges may so far depart from a perpendicular in their course downward as to extend outside the vertical side-lines of such surface locations." It confines the right of possession of such extra-lateral portions to such parts of the vein or lode as lie between vertical lines drawn downward through the end-lines of the location so continued in their own direction that such planes will intersect such exterior parts of such veins or ledges. This is the famous

"apex" section, and is a departure from the rule of the common law and of the Spanish codes. By it the lode is made the principal thing; hence, as the location seldom covers the apex from one end-line to the other, and as deposits constantly vary in character, and are seldom or never continuous, the uncertainty of this section is obvious. For a full discussion of the legal aspect of this section, see Dr. Raymond's "Law of the Apex" ("Transactions: American Institute of Mining Engineers," vol. xii), various articles by the author of this article, in the "School of Mines Quarterly," vols. vii and viii, and Morrison's "Mining Rights in Colorado" (Denver, 1887). The sixth section regulates the location of tunnels, and the seventh provides for the location of mining claims and the annual labor necessary to hold them, defining certain specific prerequisites, such as distinctly marking the location on the ground, what the record shall contain, reference to some natural object or permanent monument, etc. It provides that one hundred dollars' worth of annual labor must be expended upon each claim for each 100 feet along the vein until the patent is issued. It allows the various mining districts to make further rules and regulations not in conflict therewith, and it gives a remedy to one co-owner for the failure of another to contribute his proportion of the expenses required by the act.

The eighth section concerns the formalities necessary for obtaining a patent, and vests the administration of the law, so far as the granting of patents is concerned, in the hands of the General Land-Office. An appeal lies therefrom to the Secretary of the Interior (see LANDS, PUBLIC).

The ninth section relates to adverse claims to a particular location, and defines what proceedings are necessary for an adverse claimant to take, in order to determine his claim. It requires the adverse claimant, within thirty days after filing his claim with the register of the particular mining-district in which it is situated, to begin proceedings in a court of competent jurisdiction to determine the right of possession. Failure to do this works a forfeiture of the adverse right. After judgment, the law provides for the issue of the patent or patents to the proper party (or parties, if there be such who are entitled to separate and different portions of the claim), on their filing with the register of the Land Office a certified copy of the judgment-roll of the court, and a certificate of the Surveyor-General, that the requisite amount of work has been done upon the claim, and upon payment of five dollars per acre, as required by law. The tenth and eleventh sections refer respectively to the way in which vein or lode claims shall be described, and to the prosecution to final decisions of applications made prior to the act, provided no adverse rights then existed. The next five sections, taken partly from the act of July 9, 1870, and partly from that of May 10, 1872, relate solely to placer mines. The first of these sections, No. 2,329, defines placers, and subjects them to entry and patent as other mineral lands. The next, No. 2,330, limits all placer claims to 160 acres, to two or more persons or associations of persons, and provides for subdivision of legal subdivisions of forty acres, into ten-acre tracts, and permits joint entry to two or more persons or associations having contiguous claims of any size, reserving all rights of *bona-fide* pre-emption or homestead claims upon agricultural lands. The next section, No. 2,331, requires that, where placer claims are located upon unsurveyed lands, they shall be located as nearly as possible in conformity with the general system of public lands, and shall not include more than 20 acres for each individual claim, and provides also certain limitations in cases where the claim can not be laid out to conform to the legal surveys. Section 2,332 is in effect a statute of limitations in favor of such persons or associations as have held and worked their claims prior to the act, and gives them the benefit of the local statute of limitation of the State or Territory where the claim is situated on giving evidence of their possession, but without prejudice to any liens that have already attached prior to the issue of the patent. The last of the five sections, No. 2,333, refers to the patenting of placer claims where a lode or vein is found within the boundaries. If the application for the patent includes this vein or lode, then the applicant must pay five dollars an acre for such vein or lode claim, and twenty-five feet of surface on each side thereof; the remainder of the placer claim to be paid for at the rate of two dollars and a half an acre, together with all costs of the proceeding. It also provides, that, where a vein or lode is known to exist within the bounds of a placer claim, an application for a patent not including the vein or lode claim is construed to amount to a waiver of all right to possession of the lode claim. The rule is otherwise if the lode claim is not known to exist. In such case, the placer claim carries with it all subsequently discovered valuable mineral deposits. The remaining sections of the title other than sections 2,336, 2,337, and 2,338 refer to the appointment, duties, and fees of deputy surveyors, the form of affidavits and proofs, reservation of homesteads, segregation of agricultural lands, creation of land districts by the President, and exemption of minerals from all State and railroad grants, and all vested rights then existing. Section 2,336 provides that priority of title shall govern when two or more veins intersect or cross each other, and gives the prior locator all ore or mineral contained within the space of intersection, but grants sublocators a right of way for exploitation, and where two veins unite, the vein below the point of union is given to the prior locator. Section 2,337 provides for the acquisition by the owner of a claim in a manner similar to that provided for the location of the claim of adjacent lands not to exceed five acres for the purposes of a mill-site, at the same price per acre that was paid for his claim, and gives owners of quartz-mills or reduction-works not owning a mine in connection therewith, a similar privilege. Section 2,338 provides that the local legislatures, in the absence of Federal legislation, may provide suitable regulations for working-mines, involving easements, drainage, and other means for their development to be fully expressed in the patent.

State Legislation.—After the incorporation of the mining laws into the Revised Statutes, various States and Territories, in conformity with the privilege granted them by section 2,338, passed laws relating to the working and drainage of mines, and also to such matters as are necessary to their complete development and preservation. Laws were also passed relating to the management of mines, transfer and mortgage of mining rights, formation of mining companies, etc. So far as the location of mines is concerned, most of the acts are mere re-enactments of the Federal statutes. Among the States and Territories that possess such local legislation are Arizona, California, Colorado, Dakota, Idaho, Minnesota, Montana, Nevada, New Mexico, Oregon, Utah, Washington, and Wyoming. A convenient compilation of these laws is found in Copp's "American Mining Code" (Washington, 1886) and in Wade's "American Mining Law" (St. Louis, 1882). A complete compilation, by Clarence King, is found in vol. xiv of the tenth census (Washington, 1885). Certain of the States have appointed executive officers or commissioners to look after the mining interests in those States, and the Constitutions and revised statutes of certain States provide for the exercise of the general police power of the

State over all mines. Pennsylvania has a general regulative act, passed in 1870. But all acts of Congress are of paramount authority, supersede local laws and regulations upon the same subject, and abrogate all those in conflict therewith, so far as they concern mineral lands upon the public domain. This has been distinctly held by the United States Supreme Court, in Basey vs. Gallaghear, 20 Wallace's Reports, 670. Miners' customs and regulations, once adopted, are presumed to be in force until the contrary is proved. A compilation of the various laws of eastern States relative to mines and mining is found in Day's "Mineral Resources of the United States for 1886," published by the U. S. Geological Survey (Washington, 1887).

Construction of the Law.—The principal sections of the existing laws under which controversies have arisen, calling for a construction of the same by the courts, are as follow: 1. Section 2,320, relating to the dimensions of claims. 2. Section 2,322, the apex section. 3. Section 2,324, relating to location and annual labor. 4. Section 2,333, relating to placer claims containing veins or lodes within their boundaries. The remaining sections have received judicial interpretation.

Location and Discovery.—The status of locators and patentees of lodes, as far as their rights of possession and enjoyment are concerned, is practically the same that it was formerly, with all claims other than placer claims. The law requires locations to be made along the lode or vein lengthwise of its course, at or near the surface. Each locator is entitled to follow the dip of the lode or vein to an infinite depth, within the planes passing vertically downward through his end-lines, provided his claim contain the apex of the lode or vein. These end-lines must necessarily be parallel to each other.

A location of a mining claim can not be made by a discovery shaft upon another claim that has been previously located and is a valid location. The weight of Federal and State authority is in favor of the validity of locations where the work required by statute has been performed, even if there are irregularities in the location papers, and actual possession is not essential to the validity of the title obtained by a valid location; and until such location is terminated by abandonment and forfeiture, no right or claim to the property can be acquired by an adverse entry thereon with a view to the relocation thereof. Mere possession, however, not based upon a valid location is valueless as against a subsequent valid location. Where a location notice fails to state the number of feet claimed on each side of the lode, the location is limited to an equal number of feet on each side of the discovery, and to an equal number of feet on the course of the lode or vein in each direction from that point. A failure to record a certificate of location of a mining claim within the time prescribed by law will not render the location invalid, provided the other necessary steps be complied with. The tendency of the decisions of the Federal courts has been to support, as far as possible, locations made in good faith, notwithstanding existing informalities; and hence claims for more than the statutory length upon the lode have been held good to the extent of the number of feet allowed by law, but void as to the remainder; but the location of a mining claim upon a lode or vein of ore should always be made lengthwise of the course of the apex, at or near the surface; otherwise, it will only secure so much of the lode or vein as it actually covers. Thus, where a location is laid crosswise of a lode or vein, so that its greatest length crosses the lode, instead of following the course thereof, it will secure only such surface as lies within it, and its side-lines will become its end-lines for the purposes of defining the rights of the owner.

The Apex Section and Rights under it.—The law of 1872 ingrafted upon the old common-law right, which included primarily the surface and everything beneath it, the additional right of following certain viens, under certain conditions and limitations, into adjacent territory. This is the so-called right of "extra-lateral pursuit," which is met with only in American jurisprudence. This right carried with it the liability of being intruded upon by an adjoining owner in the exercise of the same right. The old right of discovery, which was originally the foundation of the miner's title, is no longer of importance; for the right to follow a vein outside of the side-lines of the claim depends solely upon the possession of the apex within the surface survey. Thus the original discovery may prove valueless; but the right of extra-lateral pursuit may make a claim of extreme value. This has several times occurred in the mining-camps of the West. For full explanation of this, see "The Emma-Durant Case," "School of Mines Quarterly," vol. viii. The terms "veins," "lode," and "ledge," and the expressions, "top of the vein," and "apex of the vein," appear to be synonymous, but they have not yet been judicially settled. A vein or lode, in order to be followed outside of the side-lines of the claim, must be continuous. Continuity is a question of fact, but as yet there is no case that squarely defines the evidence of continuity. In one case, however, it has been held that a vein or lode must be a continuous body of mineralized rock, lying within any well-defined boundaries on the earth's surface or under it. Each locator is entitled to follow the dip of the lode or vein to an indefinite depth, though it carries him beyond the side-line of his claim, provided that these side-lines substantially correspond with the course of the vein at the surface. A locator working subterraneously into the dip of the vein belonging to another who is in possession of his location, is a trespasser; and, as between two locators, the boundaries of whose respective claims include common territories, priority of location confers the better title, provided a vein

in place was discovered in the discovery shaft, and provided also that it extended to the ground in controversy. No location can be made upon the middle part of a vein, or otherwise than at the top or apex, which will enable the locator to go beyond his line. While the common law never recognized extra-lateral rights as they exist to-day, it did provide, under certain conditions, for the separation of the minerals from the surface under which they lay.

Annual Labor.—The law requires, as above stated, a certain amount of work to be done annually upon each claim, in order to preserve the location. As a rule, the law in this particular has been strictly construed, and financial embarrassment and threats to deter resumption of labor, have been held not to be sufficient excuses for non-performance of the work. It has also been held that, where work was done upon one of several adjoining claims held in common, it could only count for the other claims within the meaning of the statute where it actually inured to the benefit of all of them, and was of equal beneficial value to all.

Placer Claims.—In the case of placer claims, the owner of the claim holds everything covered by his patent, except such lodes as were known to exist within the placer claim, prior to the granting of the patent. In this respect, placer claims differ from lode claims. The courts have held that by "known to exist" is meant a vein duly located or recorded and owned by a third party before the placer claimant applied for the patent, and that the mere existence of the lode by geological inference, general rumor, or belief, did not serve to exempt it from the placer claim. The requirements of the Federal statute in regard to labor performed have been held to apply to placer claims also. There are no extra-lateral rights in connection with placer claims.

Bibliography.—The literature of mining law is not large. All mining cases of general importance, both English and American, are reported in Morrison's "Mining Reports" (Chicago, fourteen volumes). This series contains reports of many cases that in no wise form a part of the general body of the American mining law. Morrison's "Digest of American and English Decisions," found in the reports from the earliest times to the year 1875 (San Francisco, 1875) is of great value to the practitioner and is the best book for the practical wants of attorneys. For definitions of technical terms, see Rossiter W. Raymond's "Glossary of Mining Terms," in vol. ix of "Transactions of the American Institute of Mining Engineers." Rockwell's "Spanish and Mexican Mining Law" (New York, 1851) is a most learned and valuable treatise, but is now antiquated. Blanchard and Weekes on "Mines, Minerals, and Mining Water-Rights" (1887) is valuable, but is no longer up to date. So are also Sickles's "United States Mining Laws and Decisions" (1881), and Wade's "American Mining Law" (Denver, 1882). A convenient work is Harris's "Titles to Mines in the United States " (London, 1877), which is to be particularly recommended to laymen on account of its briefness and thoroughness. The principle English text-book is MacSwinney s "Mines and Minerals," and the American is Bainbridge, on the "Law of Mines and Minerals " (First American Edition from Third London Edition, 1878).

MINNESOTA. State Government.—The following were the State officers during the year: Governor, Andrew R. McGill, Republican; Lieutenant-Governor, Albert E. Rice; Secretary of State, Hans Mattson; Auditor, W. W. Braden; Treasurer, Joseph Bobleter; Attorney-General, Moses E. Clapp; Superintendent of Public Instruction, D. L. Kiehle; Railroad and Warehouse Commissioners, Horace Austin, John L. Gibbs, George L. Becker; Chief-Justice of the Supreme Court, James Gilfillan; Associate Justices, John M. Berry, William Mitchell, Daniel A. Dickenson, and Charles E. Vanderburgh.

Finances.—The report of the State Treasurer for 1888 gives the following statement of finances for the year ending July 31, 1888: Receipts, $3,097,610.25; balance in treasury Aug. 1, 1887, $648,860.66; total, $3,746,470.91. Disbursements, $2,404,108.42; balance in treasury July 31, 1888, $1,342,362.67; total, $3,746,470.91. Of this balance, only $139,990.72 stands to the credit of the revenue fund available for general expenses. The estimated receipts and disbursements for such expenses for the ensuing three years are as follow:

FISCAL YEAR.	Receipts.	Disbursements.
1889	$1,854,690 72	$2,175,249 66
1890	1,747,500 00	1,313,850 00
1891	1,818,000 00	1,614,350 00
Total	$5,420,190 72	$5,103,449 66
Estimated surplus		$316,741 06

The deficiency for 1889 is thus $320,558.94. The State debt consists of but one class of bonds, viz., Minnesota, 4½-per-cent. adjustment bonds, bearing date July 1, 1881, due in twenty years, and redeemable at the State's option after ten years. The amount outstanding is $3,965,000; the State holds of her own bonds as follows: Invested school fund, $1,981,000; invested university fund, $288,000; total, $2,269,000. It will be noted that the total debt is $3,965,000; from this should be deducted $1,994,209, which represents the accumulation in the internal improvement land fund, which is by law set apart as a sinking-fund. The State debt, less the available sinking-fund, is then reduced to $1,970,791.

Education.—The permanent school fund now amounts to $8,258,096.70, having increased from sales of land $954,930.56 during 1887 and 1888. It is expected that this fund will eventually amount to $18,000,000 or $20,000,000. The whole amount expended on the public schools for the year ending June 30, 1888, including new buildings, was $4,333,695.41. The number of enrolled pupils, high and normal schools included, for the year 1888, was 259,335, and the number of persons in the State between the ages of five and twenty-one is estimated at 416,550. The average daily attendance has been 126,468, and the average length of school during the year has been 6·1 months. There have been 1,884 male teachers employed at an average monthly salary of $40.10, and 5,671 female teachers at an average monthly salary of $30.52. The number of teachers that have taught in the same district three or more years is 727 for 1888, which is an increase of 46 per cent. over 1887, and 120 per cent. over 1886. The number of normal graduates teaching in 1888 was 571, an increase of 60 per cent. over 1886; while that of teachers attending normal school in 1888 was 1,427, an increase of 40 per cent. over 1886. The amount paid to teachers in wages for the year was $1,942,665.73, and $1,121,304.83 was paid for new school houses and sites. The law requiring the teaching of temperance hygiene in the public schools has been generally complied with. Under a recent law granting aid to schools in purchasing libraries, there have been furnished by the State 311 of these libraries. "The growth of the schools has been further enhanced," says the Governor, "by the recent amendment to the State Constitution permitting the State school funds to be loaned to school districts for building purposes in providing new and better school-houses. The amount so loaned in the twenty-one months the law has been in operation is $291,124.91. One of the greatest stimulants and benefits ever received by our common schools comes through the law of 1887, which levies a straight one-mill tax annually on the taxable property of the State and devotes the proceeds, based on the enrollments of the schools, to the various school districts of the State. This levy, as extended on the tax rolls of 1888, amounted to $486,670.03."

Through an appropriation made by the last Legislature, a handsome new building has been erected at Moorhead for the fourth normal school, which is now in operation. The establishment of this school probably supplies the last demand in the State, in the way of new normal schools, for many years to come.

During the year schools of law and medicine have been organized in the State university. The school of medicine embraces a college of medicine, a college of homœpathic medicine, and a college of dentistry. The course of instruction covers three years. The schools will use the medical college building in St. Paul, and the hospital college building in Minneapolis. A school of agriculture with a two-years' course has also been opened for practical instruction in farming. The president of the university reports that the large science hall and museum, which were begun in 1887, are nearly completed.

Soldiers' Home.—The last Legislature made provision for the establishment of a home for honorably discharged soldiers and sailors, and appropriated $50,000 for that purpose. The city of Minneapolis gave a site therefor, consisting of fifty-one acres of land at Minnehaha Falls, to be eventually connected with the park system of that city. Temporary quarters were rented on grounds adjacent, and in November, 1887, the home was opened. The full capacity of these quarters was soon reached, and at the date of the annual report of the trustees (August 12), 81 soldiers had been admitted, and 65 others had applied. During the present winter fully 200 will have to be provided for. The appropriation of $50,000 for purchasing a site and erecting new buildings did not become available until 1888. This appropriation has been expended in the erection of two commodious and comfortable dwellings and it is expected that with these buildings and the temporary quarters all applicants now entitled to admission will be accommodated. But this number is constantly increasing.

State Prison.—The last Legislature abolished the contract-labor system, and appropriated $25,000 to put in motion the public-account system. This amount was considered by the prison inspectors too small to warrant them in undertaking the work, and nothing has been

Aid to Settlers.—The Legislature of 1887 appropriated $40,000 for the relief of farmers whose crops had been destroyed by hail in 1886. The cities of St. Paul and Minneapolis were repaid $10,000 advanced by them for distribution in Marshall County. Of the balance, $20,315.59 was distributed, more than half of which went to Marshall County where the greatest loss occurred. The sum of $25,-177.60 was also loaned to these farmers, to purchase seed-grain. Under the first appropriation much actual want was relieved and suffering averted, and when the season of 1887 opened, farmers who had lost their all by hail the previous year, and but for the aid extended by the State would have been in absolute want, were ready with their teams for work. Good crops were raised where, but for the means furnished by the State to purchase seed, nothing could have been planted. The benefits conferred under this law are well illustrated in the case of Marshall County, which, although the most impoverished by the losses inflicted, has already paid back $5,534.91 of the $11,625 apportioned it, besides providing comfort and plenty in the homes of a desolated portion of the State.

Valuation.—The following table shows the increase in value of the taxable property of the State in 1888:

ITEMS.	1888.	1887.	Increase.
Acres of land assessed	27,260,821	23,820,691	3,439,630
Value of land with structures	$188,614,809	$190,883,543	$2,268,784*
Value of city property	261,455,567	200,939,817	60,515,750
Value of taxable personal property	106,126,015	94,846,604	11,279,411
Total	$556,196,491	$486,669,964	$63,526,527

* Decrease.

done. The prisoners have been idle, and the inspectors recommend the repeal of the law.

High License.—Gov. McGill says in his message to the Legislature:

While no official data have been gathered, information of a character to be relied upon shows a decrease of fully one third in the number of saloons, and an increase of one quarter in the revenue derived from licenses. The consumption of liquor has been lessened, and the cause of temperance materially promoted. There is not so much intoxication as existed before the law was enacted; the saloon is no longer a dominant power in the politics of the State; public opinion for a thorough control of the liquor traffic has strengthened, and in many ways, directly and indirectly, good has resulted to our State and its people from the high-license law of 1887.

From unofficial statistics gathered by a State journal in August, at the beginning of the second year of the law, the reduction in the total number of saloons appears to be from 2,806 under the old, to 1,597 under the new system. In Hennepin County the reduction is from 346 to 242; in Ramsey County, from 688 to 352; in Winona County, from 165 to 40; in St. Louis County, from 113 to 72; and in Stearns County, from 109 to 51.

Agriculture.—The Commissioner of Statistics reports for 1887 a total product of 39,070,159 bushels of wheat, raised on 3,053,887 acres; 37,659,199 bushels of oats, on 1,325,810 acres; 17,234,422 bushels of corn, on 642,477 acres; 5,216,391 bushels of barley, on 322,612 acres; and 1,318,121 bushels of flax, on 167,264 acres. The amount of wheat for 1888 is estimated at 3,019,919 acres; oats, 1,538,134 acres; corn, 687,069 acres; barley, 370,075 acres; flax, 166,206 acres.

Decisions.—On November 22 the State Supreme Court rendered an important decision, annulling the mechanics' lien law of the last Legislature, on the ground that many of its provisions were unconstitutional. The act aimed to give labor a first lien upon property created by it, and the furnisher of materials a second lien; but its provisions were so unskillfully drawn that procedure under it was impossible. As a result, men could not appeal to the old law, for that was presumptively superseded, nor could they appeal to the new, for the ablest lawyer whom they might employ could make nothing of it. The only effect of the new law has been to suspend for a year the operation and safeguards of the former act of 1870, which by this decision is now restored.

The Legislature of 1885 passed a law regulating the removal of county seats, which provided among other things for the removal by a majority vote of the electors, excepting in counties where the question had previously been submitted to a vote, and the county seats therein had been fixed by such vote, and in this class of counties a three-fifth vote should be required. In the case of Nichols *vs.* Walter this act was declared by the Supreme Court to be contrary to that part of the Constitution which requires all laws to be uniform in their operation throughout the State. There is, therefore, no law at present providing for county-seat removals.

Political.—The Prohibitionists met in State Convention at St. Paul on July 25, and nominated the following ticket: For Governor, Hugh Harrison; Lieutenant-Governor, Theodore S. Reimstad; Secretary of State, Peter Thompson; State Treasurer, John H. Allen; Attorney-General, Charles E. Shannon. The platform contains the usual prohibitory resolutions, demands a law of Congress prohibiting the importation of liquor into those States that forbid liquor-selling, and concludes with the following resolution:

That it is the duty of the State Legislature to require each railway company doing business in the State to provide suitable and adequate stock-yards, at such stations as may be designated by the railroad commissioners, for the handling and shipping of grain, cattle, and other products, under such rules and regulations as will insure to every shipper equal rights, facilities, and privileges.

The Chief-Justice of the Supreme Court, F. L. Claffey, was later placed in nomination, and for Associate Justice, George S. Livermore.

On August 15 the Democratic State Convention was held at St. Paul, and nominated the following candidates: For Governor, Eugene M. Wilson; Lieutenant-Governor, Daniel Buck; Secretary of State, W. C. Bredenhagen; Treasurer, Hans Nelson; Attorney-General, C. D'-Autremont; Chief Justice of the Supreme Court, Seagrave Smith; Associate Judge of the Supreme Court, George W. Batchelder.

In addition to commending the National Administration and policy, the resolutions denounce the grain-inspection laws of the State, deprecate the multiplicity of offices, accuse the State Government of extravagance, and reflect upon the State Executive in the following language:

We particularly arraign the present Executive of the State, for he has persistently refused to interpose his veto for the protection of the public treasury against the extravagant schemes of an extravagant Legislature. We commend to his consideration the example of Grover Cleveland, as evidence of the wholesome influence upon vicious legislation which an intelligent Executive can exercise by a judicious and resolute exercise of the veto power. He has debased the civil service of the State by removing officers of mature experience in order to pay the debts and discharge the obligations of a political campaign. Under him the judiciary of this State, for the first time in our history, has been prostituted for the purposes of factional partisanship, and men of acknowledged incompetency have been clothed with the judge's ermine as a compensation for their political services in the caucus and upon the stump. We submit that the time has come for the decisive overthrow of the politicians who have so long directed the affairs of our State.

On August 28 a conference of farmers and labor organizations, under the name of the "Farm and Labor Party," met at St. Paul for the purpose of nominating a State ticket to represent the interests of organized labor. This conference nominated: For Governor, Ignatius Donnelly; Lieutenant-Governor, James McGaughy; Attorney-General, William Welch; State Treasurer, W. G. Jebb; Secretary of State, J. P. Schonbeck. The platform favors a revision of the tariff, governmental control of telegraphs, and further restriction of railroads, and also demands:

That the money needed for exchanges be issued direct to the people, without the intervention of banks.

The adoption of a system of voting embodying the principle of the Australian law, which abolishes the caucus system and secures to each voter an opportunity to cast a free and untrammeled ballot.

That the right to vote is inherent in citizenship, without regard to sex.

The reduction of freight and passenger rates on railroads to a sum sufficient to pay only the operating and maintaining expenses, when economically administered, and a fair rate of interest on the actual cost of the roads, thus saving to the producers of the State several millions now wrung from them to pay interest on fictitious stock.

The enactment of a law allowing the mortgagor to deduct from the amount due the mortgagee, the amount of all taxes paid upon that part of the assessed valuation of the estate taxed, represented by the mortgage.

The enactment of a factory-inspection law for the protection of the health and safety of employés in mines, factories, workshops, and places of business.

The enactment of a law defining the liability of employers for injuries sustained by employés in cases where proper safeguards have not been used, in occupations dangerous to life, limb, or health.

That eight hours shall constitute a day's work in all towns and cities on State and municipal work, and all such work shall be done by the day, and not by contract.

The enactment of a law regulating the employment of detectives and peace-officers, and forbidding the employment of secret or private detectives by other than the State or municipal governments.

The enactment of a law to enforce the payment of weekly wages in lawful money by the employers of labor in cities, and by railroad companies and other corporations, and at the hands of Congress.

Whereas, Any rate of interest above the average increase of wealth of the nation is robbery, therefore we demand a reduction of interest in this State to a reasonable rate.

A few weeks later, Mr. Donnelly, the gubernatorial candidate, announced his refusal to accept the nomination and his purpose of supporting the Republican ticket as the surest way of securing the demands of the laboring man. J. H. Paul was then nominated to fill the vacancy.

The Republicans met in convention on September 5, and after four formal ballots nominated William R. Merriam for Governor. The other principal candidates before the convention were Gov. McGill and Arthur Scheffer. The Secretary of State, Auditor, Treasurer, and Attorney-General were renominated. For the Supreme Court, Chief-Justice Gilfillan was renominated, and L. W. Collins was made the candidate for Associate Justice. The platform pledges the party to maintain the high-license system, commends the administration of Gov. McGill, approves civil-service reform, the interstate commerce law, and liberal pensions, and condemns the fishery treaty and the refusal of Democrats to admit Dakota as a State. It further declares that the party adheres to the repeated declaration of State and National platforms, in favor of the modification, readjustment and reduction of the tariff. It declares that all measures of tariff adjustment should be framed and conceived in a cautious and conservative spirit, so as not to disturb and impair interests which have grown up under existing revenue laws, and, as far as possible, to relieve the people from unnecessary taxation upon articles which do not enter into competition with American industry. It declares its hostility to trusts so called, and to all monopolistic combinations, of every form that seek to limit the production or the price, or in any way control the commodities of the country. It approves the reform of the voting system called the Australian system. In view of the recent revelations showing the abuses to which the immigration and naturalization laws have been subject, it demanded of the National Congress a thorough revision of those laws; and, in the mean time, a more efficient execution by the National Administration of such laws as we have, especially that prohibiting the importation of contract labor.

At the November election, Merriam received 134,355 votes for Governor; Wilson, 110,251; Harrison, 17,150; and Paul, 385. Merriam ran over 5,000 votes behind his ticket. Of the legislative candidates, 31 Republicans and 16 Democrats were elected to the Senate; and 89 Republicans, 9 Democrats, and 5 Independents to the Lower House. Five Republican Congressmen were chosen, and the National Republican ticket received a large majority.

At the same election, a constitutional amendment declaring combinations to monopolize or restrict the market for food-products to be criminal conspiracy, was adopted by a vote of 104,932 in its favor, to 13,064 against. Another amendment adding to section 12 of Article I the following words:

Provided, however, that all property so exempted shall be liable to seizure and sale for any debts incurred to any person for work done or materials furnished in the construction, repair, or improvement of the same. And, provided further, that such liability to seizure and sale shall also extend to all real property, for any debt incurred to any laborer or servant for labor or service performed,

was adopted by the following vote: Yeas, 153,908; nays, 48,649. A third amendment, extending the legislative session to ninety days, new bills not to be introduced in the last twenty days, was also adopted by a vote of 150,003 yeas to 52,946 nays.

MISSIONS, PROTESTANT, INTERNATIONAL CONFERENCE OF. An International Conference of Foreign Missions was held in London in June. It has become usual to hold such conferences once in ten years; and the present meeting was also associated with the centenary of the institution of missionary work. The call for the Conference was addressed to Christians of all Protestant communions engaged in missionary service of whatever kind, "to confer with one another on those many and important and delicate questions which the progress of civilization and the large expansion of missionary work have brought into prominence, with a view to develop the agencies employed for the spread of the Gospel of the grace of God." One hundred and twenty-nine societies were represented in the Conference; fifty-four British societies, by 1,254 delegates; fifty-two societies in the United States, by 140 delegates; six in Canada, by 27 delegates; and seventeen on the Continent of Europe, by 22 delegates. Of the whole number of societies, twenty-two were women's societies or boards. The opening meeting, for the reception of delegates and interchange of greetings, was held June 9, under the presidency of the Earl of Aberdeen. It was addressed by the Rev. Dr. Underhill, chairman of the Executive Committee, who gave an outline of the history of the missionary conferences, from the first, which was held by the Rev. Dr. Duff, in New York, in 1854; by the Rev. Dr. Thompson, of the American Board, who spoke of the work of the women's boards, of which there were, he said, thirty-five in the United States, with thousands of auxiliaries; and by speakers representing societies of Continental Europe. Forty-five meetings were held, which are described as sectional meetings, for members only; open meetings for conference; and public meetings in the afternoons and evenings. At the sectional meetings were discussed such topics as missionary methods and agencies, medical missions, women's work; the place of education in mission work; the organization and government of native churches, their training and support; the missionary and his relation to literature, Bible and tract societies; homework for missions; missionary comity, union, and co-operation; and commerce and diplomacy in relation to missions. The purpose of the open conferences was described to be not so much to awaken sympathy for any particular branch of mission work, as to inquire into the weak points of missionary labor with a view to future improvements. The subject of the first one was "The Increase of Islam, and the Social, Political, and Religious Influences of Mohammedanism." The chairman, Sir William W. Hunter, remarked that, after carefully going over the figures, he was convinced that while during the past ten years Islam had increased 10½ per cent., Christianity had gained 64 per cent. Another like session was devoted to the discussion of "Buddhism and other Kindred Heathen Systems; their Character and Influence, compared with those of Christianity." The subject of a third session was "The Missions of the Roman Catholic Church to Heathen Lands; their Character, Extent, Influence, and Lessons." On this subject the Rev. Principal MacVicar, of Montreal, represented that while the increase of Roman Catholic converts in India was 3½ per cent., the United Protestant missions were able to show an increase of 9 per cent. The fourth subject was "Missions and Commerce." The fifth and last open conference was devoted to the discussion of "The Intimate Relations between Home and Foreign Missions and the Reaction of the Foreign Missionary Spirit on the Life and Unity of the Church." Among the subjects considered at the public meetings were "Christianizing China," "Japan and China," "Missions One Hundred Years Ago," "Medical Missions," "Missions in Turkey," "The Nile and the Niger," "The Work in Oceania," "East and Central Africa," "Women's Mission to Women," "North and Central India," "South India and Burmah," "Missions and Bible Societies," "Material Agencies at Home," "The Church's Duty," "The Missionary in Relation to Literature," and "Missionary Comity."

Resolutions were passed denouncing the opium-trade in China—which, it was asserted, had prejudiced the people of that country against all missionary efforts—and the manufacture of opium in India; demanding the entire suppression of the trade; condemning the carrying on of the traffic in strong drink by merchants belonging to Christian nations among native races, especially in Africa; expressing "grateful appreciation" of what His Majesty, the King of the Belgians had done in the cause of humanity and religion in Central Africa, especially in founding the Congo Free State; and deploring the extension of "state-licensed vice" in India. A committee was appointed to present a memorial to the King of the Belgians, urging him to use his influence in the Congo Free State to secure the suppression of the liquor-traffic there.

Protestant Missionary Assembly in Mexico.—A General Assembly of Protestant Missionary Workers in Mexico was held in the city of Mexico, beginning January 31, at which the missions of the Methodist Episcopal, Methodist Episcopal South, Northern Presbyterian, Southern Presbyterian, Cumberland Presbyterian, Baptist, Congregational, and Episcopal Churches and the Society of Friends were represented. Discussions were held upon the questions of the attitude to be borne toward the Roman Catholic Church, a revision of the Spanish version of the Scriptures and translation into the Indian dialect, the means of combating skepticism in Mexico, comity and co-operation be-

tween the different missions, and special topics of ministerial qualification and agencies. An agreement was adopted for the purpose of securing harmony in the workings of the several missions and avoiding interferences between them; and a committee was constituted with authority to provide for another assembly at some suitable time in the future.

MISSISSIPPI. State Government.—The following were the State officers during the year: Governor, Robert Lowry, Democrat; Lieutenant-Governor, G. D. Shands; Secretary of State, George M. Govan; Auditor, W. W. Stone; Treasurer, W. L. Hemingway; Attorney-General, T. M. Miller; Superintendent of Public Instruction, J. R. Preston; Chief-Justice of the Supreme Court, J. A. P. Campbell; Associate Justices. J. M. Arnold and Timothy E. Cooper. In January, the Legislature in joint session chose J. F. Sessions, J. C. Kyle, and Walter McLaurin, to be Railroad Commissioners, to succeed J. F. Sessions, J. C. Kyle, and William McWillie.

Legislative Session.—The regular biennial session of the Legislature began on January 3, and ended March 8. Early in the session Edward C. Walthall was re-elected, without opposition, to the United States Senate, for the term beginning in March, 1889. The most important legislation of the session relates to the State finances. An act was passed authorizing the issue of $500,000 of bonds payable in thirty years, and bearing 4 per cent. interest, the proceeds to be applied to the payment of $80,000 deposited by insurance companies with the State under an act of March 14, 1884; to the payment of bonds issued in March, 1880, to the amount of $246,000; and of bonds issued in March, 1884, to the value of $153,500. Another act provides that the rate of interest payable by the State upon the Chickasaw school fund shall be 7 instead of 8 per cent. after May 1. Over $8,000 will annually be saved to the State by this reduction. The former railroad law was amended by giving the railroad commissioners additional power, and an act was passed requiring all steam railroads to provide equal but separate accommodations on each train for the two races, giving conductors power to eject passengers who refuse to ride in the car provided for their race, and imposing a fine on roads that do not comply with the act. Another law provides for the organization and equipment of an active militia of the State, to be known as the Mississippi National Guard. An act for equalizing assessments separates the counties into classes, and fixes the valuation of different qualities of land in each class. In a majority of counties, popular election of county superintendents of education is provided for, instead of appointment by the State Board of Education. The sum of $30,000 is appropriated annually for the relief of disabled Confederate soldiers and of the widows of those who were killed in the war. Payments from this sum are awarded by a State board of inquiry to such as it shall select from those certified to it by county boards of inquiry as needing assistance. Refusal to pay the poll-tax was made a misdemeanor, punishable by fine and imprisonment. In accordance with the recommendation of the Governor, it was enacted that the trial of misdemeanors may be assigned by the grand jury to justices of the peace, by directing them on information to inquire into them. This will relieve the State circuit courts of a large number of small cases which hitherto have occupied much of their time at great expense to the State and to the exclusion of more important business. The State tax for 1888–'89 was fixed at 3½ mills for the general fund, and ⅛ mill for the payment of interest on the bonds of 1886. A resolution for submitting to the people the question of calling a constitutional convention passed both Houses, but was vetoed by the Governor. An attempt to pass the bill over the veto failed to secure the necessary two-third vote in the Senate, the vote standing 19 to 16 in its favor. Other acts passed at the session were as follow :

Repealing the act of 1886 imposing a tax upon commercial travelers.

To provide for obtaining and publishing reports of banking institutions doing business in the State.

To abolish the present boards of trustees of the several charitable institutions of the State, and to provide for the appointment of new boards.

Providing for the assessment and collection of past due and unpaid taxes on railroads that have escaped payment thereof.

Authorizing the State Board of Health to purchase and distribute vaccine virus free to regular practicing physicians during 1888, and every three years thereafter.

To provide for the prevention and suppression of contagious and infectious diseases among live-stock.

Accepting the provision of the act of Congress contemplating the establishment of agricultural experiment stations in the several States.

Apportioning to the counties the number of free students allowed each at the State Agricultural and Mechanical College and at the Industrial Institute and College.

To prohibit and prevent the sale of liquor to minors.

To punish false pretenses in obtaining the registration of cattle and other animals.

To prevent purchasers of cotton from deducting two or any number of pounds, known as scalage, from the actual weight.

Appointing commissioners to readjust the boundary-line between the State and Arkansas.

Authorizing the payment of salaries to superintendents of education in certain counties.

Authorizing the Board of Mississippi Levee Commissioners to issue $200,000 of its bonds.

To remove obstructions to free navigation of the Big Black river.

Setting apart a portion of the Capitol grounds as a site for a monument to the Confederate dead.

Authorizing the city of Natchez to issue bonds not exceeding $100,000 for public improvements.

Revoking the charters of corporations that have not organized or shall not organize within one year from the date of this enactment.

Finances.—The receipts from all sources for the year 1887 amounted to $1,069,568.38, of which the sum of $215,782 was realized from the sale of bonds, leaving as the total receipts from usual sources $853,786.38. The disbursements on all accounts for the same time were $1,029,638.06. Deducting from this money borrowed and returned with interest, the disbursements on ordinary accounts for 1887 were $844,575.42, the receipts on usual accounts thus exceeding the disbursements by $9,210.06. The Treasurer gives the entire indebtedness of the State on Jan. 1, 1888, at $3,752,904.01, of which the sum of $1,083,266.40 is a floating debt, paying no interest. This part of the debt was increased during 1886 and 1887 by $317,560.17. A part of this deficiency is due to the diminution of revenue by reason of the operation of the local-option law, by which, from 1883 to 1887, there was an aggregate decrease in the receipts from liquor licenses to the amount of $178,795.88, an average of $35,759.13 per annum. Another cause was the low tax-rate that was in force up to 1887. The Legislature in 1886 raised the rate from 2½ to 3 mills, and in the present year from 3 to 3½ mills, for general purposes.

Charities.—At the Jackson Insane Asylum, at the close of the fiscal year, there were 459 patients; at the East Mississippi Asylum, 230; and at the Asylum for the Deaf and Dumb, 76. These institutions are supported by a liberal annual appropriation from the State.

Convicts.—A special report was made to the Lower House of the Legislature in February by a committee appointed to examine the prison system of the State. Of the lease system generally, and of the treatment of prisoners by the lessees, the Gulf and Ship Island Railroad Company, the report says :

The system of leasing convicts to individuals or corporations, to be worked by them for profit, simply restores a state of servitude worse than slavery, in this, that it is without any of the safeguards resulting from ownership of the slave ; and if the leasing system is objectionable, that of sub-leasing is doubly so. The treatment of convicts under sub-lessees we find to have been generally harsh, if not positively cruel, and this is shown by the evidence taken by the Board of Control. The average number of convicts for 1886 and 1887 was 738 ; of these 67 died in 1886, showing a death-rate of 9·08 per cent. The number of deaths in 1887 was 114, a death-rate of 15·44 per cent. Statistics also show that the average death-rate for six years among the negroes is more than double that of whites, and, as there is no special reason why negroes should die faster than whites, the fact is significant of different and worse treatment suffered by them. We find that the condition of convicts is improved since they were remanded to the immediate control of the railroad company and placed under the supervision of the State Board of Control and the superintendent. Within the Penitentiary we find, after diligent inquiry, no cause of complaint. The walls are the refuge for all cases of chronic disease, and for enfeebled and disabled convicts, and the death-rate is very low under the circumstances. In 1886 there were treated in the walls 567 convicts, of whom 12 died. This is a death-rate of about 2 per cent. In 1887 there were treated 671 convicts, of whom 16 died, a death-rate of 2·03 per cent. These deaths are included in the aggregate number of deaths for the two years, and, if the rate in the walls is deducted from the average death-rate, we find the death-rate in the camps for 1886 about 7 per cent., and in 1887 12·4 per cent. Such a low rate in the general hospital of the

Penitentiary, where convicts are usually sick, as compared with that in the camps, where convicts are supposed to be well, is very significant of the treatment of prisoners in the latter.

The work of the State Board of Control and Supervision, created by the Legislature of 1886, was found by the committee to be altogether beneficial. Several important recommendations were made by this committee, but the Legislature took no action upon the subject.

Later in the year complaints were made of further ill-treatment of the convicts, and on July 1 the lessees failed to pay to the State the salary and expenses of the superintendent of the Penitentiary, according to their contract. In fact, the lessees were themselves dissatisfied, and wished to cancel their agreement. The Board of Control investigated various complaints, and early in December found sufficient cause to declare the contract forfeited. The reasons given were non-payment of money, inhuman treatment, subletting without authority of the board, failure to make monthly reports, failing to care for sick convicts, and other offenses. By this order 248 men were released and brought back to the Penitentiary on December 15; 155 others, having been sublet by the lessees on a contract expiring January 1, were allowed to remain. Before the end of the year the board had negotiated a new lease of 170 of the returned men. The total number of State convicts was 526.

State Capitol.—The Legislature provided for a committee to examine the Capitol building and report upon its condition. In May this committee published its findings, which showed the building to be insecure and in need of immediate repairs to render it safe. For these repairs the sum of $4,650 was needed, and for other necessary repairs the sum of $112,300 was deemed requisite.

Immigration.—Pursuant to a proclamation of Gov. Lowry, a large number of citizens met in convention at Jackson on May 24 for the purpose of organizing a movement to attract settlers to the State. The convention organized itself into an immigration association, whose objects were stated as follow:

The objects of this association shall be to collect and disseminate accurate and reliable information as to the soil, climate, and resources of our State, to the end that immigration may be fostered and encouraged and good people of our own and all other countries induced to identify themselves with us and contribute their capital, labor, and enterprise to swell the tide of the returning prosperity of our great State; and we hereby extend a cordial invitation to all such persons to cast in their lot with us, with the assurance that they will be treated justly and fairly and on a perfect equality in all respects with our own people.

Officers were chosen and an executive committee appointed to put in operation the proper machinery to secure these results. The formation of subordinate associations in the various towns and counties was recommended, and such associations were formed in many places.

Confederate Monument.—A bill was introduced into the Legislature in January, appropriating $10,000 to the Confederate Monumental Association, for aiding in the erection of a monument to the Confederate dead, and also setting apart a portion of the Capitol grounds as a site therefor. The Legislature granted the site, but refused an appropriation, whereupon the association determined to raise the necessary amount by popular subscription. Largely through the efforts of women, the sum of $10,000 had been raised before the end of May, and on the 25th of that month the corner-stone was laid at Jackson. A letter of regret was read from Jefferson Davis, who had been invited to be present, and a notable feature of the occasion was the presentation to Miss Winnie Davis, his daughter, who was present, of a silver crown for her father. The monument is designed to be forty-five feet in height, and will cost $14,000. A statue of Jefferson Davis is to form a part of the memorial.

Yellow Fever.—On September 20 three well-defined cases of yellow fever were discovered at Jackson, among laborers engaged upon a new passenger-station of the Illinois Central Railroad. On the following day four additional cases were found, and one death occurred from the disease. An exodus from the city began at once, and in a few days only a small portion of the population, consisting largely of negroes, was left. Quarantine regulations were speedily established at all points. The Howard Citizens' Association, which had taken control of a former epidemic, was revived, and arrangements were made for a long struggle with the disease. Largely through these efforts, the infected area was confined to its original limits. Up to September 27, there were fifteen cases and five deaths. No new cases occurring after that date the excitement gradually subsided, and before the middle of October many refugees had returned and business was resumed.

Political.—Party conventions for the selection of delegates to the National Conventions were held early in the year. At the Republican Convention, in Jackson, April 4, the following arraignment of the State Government was embodied in the resolutions passed:

The present State Government, according to reports made by legislative committees, is not only weak, inefficient, and incompetent, but extravagant. It is well known that our present State Government was brought into existence through a fraudulent and violent suppression of free suffrage. Popular elections are nothing more than farcical formalities. Those who are in control of the State machinery seem to have no regard for laws and no respect for the rights of citizens.

When the city of Jackson, just preceding the last municipal election, was taken possession of by an armed mob, "for the open and avowed purpose of suppressing free suffrage and preventing a free and fair election," the State Administration was as dumb as an oyster, and could not be induced to take any notice of what was going on. Whenever mob law breaks out in any part of the State, even if it results in the death of innocent persons, as at Carrollton, Copiah, and Yazoo City, the State Administration takes no more notice of them than if they occurred in Germany or Great Britain.

Our penitentiary system is a disgrace to the State and to the civilization of the age.

The Legislature recently assembled in this State did nothing that deserves commendation ; on the contrary, it passed a number of bills which merit the condemnation of every one.

The act in relation to poll-taxes is not only cruel and unjust, crudely and carelessly drawn, evidently the product of incompetent persons, but is clearly and unmistakably unconstitutional.

The act making it obligatory upon railroad companies to provide separate accommodation for white and colored persons is one of the most barbarous and disgraceful acts of that extraordinary Legislature. We believe it to be unconstitutional and void, and that the enforcement of it should be resisted by the public in every lawful way that is possible.

The Judicial District bill is also crude and carelessly drawn.

The privilege-tax law is one of the most unjust and oppressive that could be conceived.

Under the hollow pretense of economy and reform, it has crippled the humane institutions of the State, and sought to destroy the higher institutions of learning by withholding pro e appropriations for their support while expending large sums on other and less important objects, and has been so unmindful of its duties to the citizens and the public of the State as to adjourn and leave the Capitol building in which it assembled in such an unsafe condition as to be now unfit for occupation, and pronounced so, in less than one month after they adjourned, by a competent and experienced architect.

There was no election for State officers or members of the Legislature during the year. At the presidential election in November, the Democrats were successful by the usual large majority. Seven Democratic Congressmen were elected at the same time.

MISSOURI. State Government.—The following were the State officers during the year: Governor, Albert G. Morehouse, Democrat, elected Lieutenant-Governor, but succeeding the late Governor Marmaduke in December, 1887; Secretary of State, Michael K. McGrath; Treasurer, James M. Seibert; Auditor, John Walker; Attorney-General, D. G. Boone; Superintendent of Public Schools, William E. Coleman; Register of Lands, Robert Mc Culloch; Railroad Commissioners, John B. Breathitt, James Harding, William G. Downing; Chief-Justice of the Supreme Court, Elijah H. Norton; Associate Justices, Thomas A. Sherwood, Robert D. Ray, Francis M. Black, Theodore Brace.

Finances.—On Jan. 1, 1885, the bonded State debt, not including the common - school and seminary indebtedness, amounted to $11,803,-000; on Jan. 1, 1889, it was $9,525,000. The reduction of $2,278,000 in four years. The debt in 1885 was drawing interest at 6 per cent per annum, amounting to $708,180. Since Jan. 1, 1885, $9,278,000 of this debt has matured, of which $7,000,000 has been funded in 5-20 bonds bearing interest at 3½ per cent., and the remainder has been paid.

The $7,000,000 in bonds sold for a premium of $86,321.43. The interest on the public debt proper is now $396,500 per annum, or nearly one half less than it was four years ago. The school-fund indebtedness consists of one 6-per-cent. certificate of $2,909,000 and three 5-per-cent. certificates aggregating $225,000. The seminary fund consists of one 6-per-cent. certificate for $122,000 and one 5-per-cent. certificate for $407,000. The annual interest payable on these certificates is $213,460. The Governor says in his annual message : " Missouri needs no financial policy in the future. If the present rate of taxation is maintained, of 20 cents on the $100 valuation for the purpose of paying the public debt and the interest thereon, the State debt proper will be paid in eight or nine years. Every obligation will be paid at or before maturity. There was in the treasury to the credit of the interest fund on the first day of the present year, after paying all interest and due obligations, the sum of $325,000. The net receipts to this fund the present year will be at least $1,450,000, which, with the amount in the treasury, will make $1,775,000 applicable to the payment of interest and principal of the public debt for the year 1889. Our public debt may be reduced the present year $1,100,000. The next general assessment of taxable property in the State will probably aggregate $900,000,000, when by provisions of the Constitution the tax levy for the purpose of paying the public debt and the interest thereon will be reduced to fifteen cents on the $100, which will be ample to meet all obligations of the State for this purpose. In fact, within the next four years the State interest tax can be reduced to ten cents on the $100, and meet every obligation at maturity."

Education.—The Governor says upon this subject, in his annual message : "During the past four years more than 100,000 children have been added to our public schools, and the number is now 865,750. Our permanent interest-bearing school fund on July 1, 1888, was $10,538,125.08, and the sum actually paid out by our people in the support of our public schools for the year ending June 30, 1888, was $4,843,323.15. The thirty-fourth General Assembly appropriated to the common schools one third instead of one fourth of the general revenue as had been done by former legislatures. This cost the State over $50,000 and only benefited the school - children 7½ cents each. It is doubtful if this small amount benefited the schools as much as it depressed the finances of the State."

Charities.—The State supports three asylums for the insane—one at Fulton, one at St. Joseph, and one at Nevada. The construction of the last named was authorized by the Legislature of 1885, which appropriated $200,000 therefor, to which the Legislature of 1887 added $150,000. A further appropriation will be needed to finish and furnish the building. The State institute for the deaf and dumb at Fulton suffered the destruction of its building by fire in February, causing a loss to the State of over $100,000, partially covered by an insurance of $65,000. There were 185 pupils in the institution, who were accomodated temporarily in the town, so that the work of the school was not seriously interrupted. The trustees expended the insurance in beginning the erection of a new building, which the State will be asked to finish.

Militia.—The strength of the State militia aggregates 24 companies with 1,800 men of all arms.

State Banks.—The following is a financial statement of the State banks and bankers at the close of business, April 30, 1888. The statement shows an increase of $1,500,000 over the statement on Dec. 31, 1887, as returned to the Secretary of State:

RESOURCES.

Loans on personal securities	$49,184,739
Loans on real estate	8,578,588
Overdrafts	941,109
United States bonds	623,980
Other bonds and stocks	4,135,561
Due from banks	12,882,707
Real estate	2,407,959
Furniture and fixtures	408,172
Checks and cash items	2,112,629
Currency	7,741,943
Gold coin	1,587,628
Silver coin	363,701
Exchange	8,187,802
Total	$89,704,818

LIABILITIES.

Capital	$13,566,295
Surplus	7,845,038
Undivided dividends	110,113
Deposits, sight	47,799,758
Deposits, time	11,544,658
Bills payable	446,697
Due banks	8,088,184
Expenses	8,580
Total	$89,704,818

Prisons.—The cost of the Penitentiary for the past two years to the State has been $167,000, but if credit is given for the increased value of the property by way of new buildings, it will not exceed $50,000 or $25,000 a year. The actual cash earnings for the past two years have been nearly $350,000. The average number of prisoners worked by contractors during this time has been about 950, while the average number confined has been over 1,600.

By acts of the thirty-fourth General Assembly, in 1887, much needed and long delayed legislation was begun looking toward the restraining, reforming, and educating juvenile offenders. By the provisions of those acts, an industrial home for girls has been established at Chillicothe, and a reform school for boys at Boonville. For the Chillicothe institution the Legislature appropriated $5,000 for the purchase of grounds, $30,000 for the erection of suitable buildings, $5,000 for furnishing such buildings and incidental expenses, and $10,000 for current expenses. Besides the appropriations by the State, the citizens of Chillicothe contributed $5,000 to secure the location of the home at that place. The board of control adopted the cottage or family plan, and have erected and completed beautiful and substantial buildings west of and adjoining the city of Chillicothe at a cost of $30,025. The buildings will accommodate fifty inmates.

For the location of the reform school, the city of Boonville offered the best inducements, and a tract of 165 acres, adjoining the city proper, was secured. The Legislature appropriated $5,000 for the purchase of grounds, for erection of buildings $40,000, for furnishing building $2,000, for maintenance and incidental expenses $5,000. A building four stories high, and an attached boiler-house, kitchen, dining-room, and laundry, have been erected at a total cost of $31,525. When completely furnished these buildings will accommodate from 180 to 200 boys. The committee has furnished them for the occupancy of 75 boys, within the appropriations allowed to them.

Liquor Laws.—The Governor says in his message to the Legislature: "At present we have the 'Downing law,' fixing the maximum State and county tax on license for dramshops at $1,200 per annum. The law also requires a petition signed by two thirds of the tax-paying citizens of cities, towns, and townships before it is mandatory on the county court to issue license. We have also the 'Wood local-option law,' under which elections have been held in eighty-seven counties 'submitting the question of prohibiting the sale of intoxicating liquors.' Fifty counties have adopted this law, which is virtually prohibition in those counties. The laws of the State are such that any county or any city of 2,500 inhabitants may have prohibition or they can tax the license of the liquor-dealer as high as they please, so that it does not amount to absolute prohibition, as a majority of the voters may prefer. In fact, the liquor-traffic is left to the control of the citizens of each county and city. Some communities are opposed to prohibition or high license and only collect the minimum State, county, and municipal tax on license. In such places saloons are more numerous and not as respectable as where high license prevails."

In April the State Supreme Court rendered an important decision on the question of Sunday liquor-selling. A State law forbade the sale of liquor on Sundays and closed all saloons on that day. There was opposition to the enforcement of the law in St. Louis, which claimed exemption by reason of an old city ordinance that allowed the sale of wine and beer on Sunday. A local judge sustained the ordinance when a test case was brought before him; but the Supreme Court held that the city government had no authority to pass such an ordinance, and that therefore St. Louis must obey the law in common with all other cities in the State.

The Bald-Knobbers.—The trial of the leaders of this organization for the murder of William Edens and Charles Green in March, 1887, was not held in August following, at the time when their followers were brought before the Christian County Circuit Court and fined or imprisoned for their connection with the organization, but was postponed until March and April of the present year. William Walker, son of David Walker, the chief, and two men named Matthews were first tried and convicted, receiving the death sentence on March 28. The Knobber chief was tried early in April, and was sentenced to death on April 12, at which time three other leaders, having confessed their guilt, were sentenced to prison, one for twelve years and two for twenty-one years each. The execution of the four condemned men was set for May 18; but, an appeal being taken to the State Supreme Court, the date was postponed to December 28. In October the Supreme Court affirmed the decision of the lower court. Seeing that no hope was left, the Bald-Knobber friends of the condemned leaders determined to have vengeance, and on the night of November 14 visited the homes of five of the witnesses against the prisoners, seized them, and hanged them together. A large number of men were engaged in this raid, none of whom were discovered. Emboldened by this, on December 28 (a second postponement of the execution having been had) they attempted a rescue of their friends from the county jail. The two Matthews and other prisoners escaped; the Walkers refused to accept the opportunity. Two days later one of the Matthews was captured.

Bevier Troubles.—The Governor says in his message: "There has been for several years a bad state of affairs existing at Bevier, in Macon County, where are located some of the best coal-mines in the State. Labor strikes have been frequent, riots have occurred, and deaths and murders have been the result. The civic authorities have been unsuccessful in bringing the offenders to justice, although strenuous efforts have been made in that direction. The last strike at Bevier occurred the last of September. The mine-owners brought in new men to take the place of strikers. One of the operators, Thomas Wardell, was killed, it is to be supposed, by the miners on the night of December 7. The strikers and the employés of Messrs. Loomis & Snively's mine engaged in a fusillade of firearms, in which several hundred shots were fired, endangering the lives of the citizens of Bevier. One of Loomis & Snively's men was wounded, from the effects of which he died. On December 9 I visited Bevier and found a deplorable state of affairs. The people were alarmed, fearing that at any time the town would be the scene of riot and bloodshed. I therefore ordered some forty members of the National Guard at Kansas City to Bevier. I believed that all parties feared that they would be injured in their person or property by the other side, and that if they were afforded protection for a short time they would adjust their difficulties; but I am not prepared to say that my hopes have been realized or that the feeling is much better between the contending elements than before the troops were ordered there." Before the end of the year, by order of the Governor, the troops were withdrawn.

Political.—The Republican Convention was held at Sedalia on May 15, and the following State ticket was nominated without a contest: For Governor, E. E. Kimball; Lieutenant-Governor, George H. Wallace; Secretary of State F. W. Mott; State Treasurer, A. P. Frowein; State Auditor, George W. Martin; Attorney-General, L. L. Bridges; Register of Lands, John H. Chase; Railroad Commissioner, B. W. Vedder; Supreme Judge, J. S. Botsford. Delegates to the National Republican Convention and State electors at large were chosen at the same time. The following is from the platform adopted:

Monopolies and trusts oppressing the people, or unfairly discriminating against local interests, are wrong in principle, and should be restrained by law.

We demand a free vote and an honest count of every legal ballot; that one vote in the South should count as much as one vote in the North, East, or West, and no more; that one vote in the North, East, or West should count as much as one vote in the South, and no more. And we do especially denounce the frauds in the ballot-box in the Southern States as publicly admitted by the leaders of the Democratic party.

While we at all times favor a proper revision and adjustment of the tariff so as to give legitimate encouragement to commerce, we demand that such revision shall be made on the basis of protecting American industries and labor and of preserving the home market to the home producer, and we are unalterably opposed to the doctrine proclaimed by President Cleveland in his annual message and to the fruit thereof, known as the Mills Tariff Bill.

The placing of wool, lead, zinc, and iron on the free list is a direct blow at the material interests and prosperity of the State of Missouri.

The Union soldiers are entitled to the gratitude of the nation. It was their heroic services that made freedom national and preserved the Government. Relief for disabled veterans should be extended, not as alms to paupers, but as a partial compensation for services rendered, and we condemn the action of President Cleveland in indiscriminately vetoing the pension bills passed by Congress.

We approve of equitable taxation, reaching corporations as well as individuals, as a correct system which should be perfected and enforced throughout the State.

We arraign the Democratic party of Missouri for its refusal to adopt means whereby litigants in the Supreme Court may have a speedy determination of their case. Delays for years are suffered by them, which work great hardships upon the people, and in many instances amount to a denial of justice.

A Democratic convention for the nomination of a candidate for Supreme Judge and for district judges met at Springfield on August 15. Judge Shepard Barclay was nominated for the former office after eighteen ballots. One week later a second convention met at Jefferson City, and nominated the following Democratic candidates for executive offices: For Governor, David R. Francis; Lieutenant-Governor, Stephen H. Claycomb; Secretary of State, Alexander A. Lesueur; Auditor, James M. Seibert; Treasurer, Edward T. Noland; Attorney-General, John M. Wood; Register of Lands, Robert McCulloch; Railroad Commissioner, James Hennessy. The platform contains the following:

Confident of the integrity and wisdom of the Democratic party in conducting the affairs of this State, we invite the closest scrutiny, and we congratulate the people upon the prospect of an overwhelming approval of the State and National administrations as conducted by the servants of the people and the representatives of the Democratic party.

We approve the action of the Democratic House of Representatives of the present Congress in passing the Mills Bill, and declare it to be in obedience to the terms of the Constitution, limiting taxation to the purpose of raising the revenue for the payment of the necessary expenses and obligations of the Government.

The Democratic party, as the special champion of the people, condemns all trusts and rings, and favors such wise legislation as will secure to both producers and consumers prices based on the laws of supply and demand.

The Union Labor Party placed in the field the following candidates: for Governor, ——— Manning; Lieutenant-Governor, J. C. Seabourn; Secretary of State, Boswell Fox; Auditor, William H. Noerr; Treasurer, Warren Vertrees; Attorney-General, L. L. Bridges (the Republican candidate); Register of Lands, G. B. De Bernardi; Railroad Commissioner, William H. Bell; Judge of the Supreme Court, Corbin D. Jones. The nominees of the Probibition party were: for Governor, Frank M. Lowe; Lieutenant-Governor, William C. Wilson; Secretary of State, Herman P. Farris; Auditor, James S. Cobban; Treasurer, William H. Craig; Attorney-General, George T. Bowling; Register of Lands, John F. McMurray; Railroad Commissioner, D. H. Lancy; Judge of the Supreme Court, Loren G. Rowell. At the election in November, the Democratic State and national tickets were successful, after a spirited canvass. For Governor, Francis received 255,764 votes; Kimball, 242,531; Manning, 15,438; and Lowe, 4,389. But Francis ran about 5,000 behind his ticket. On the basis of the vote for Auditor, the party strength was as follows: Seibert, 261,775 votes; Martin, 236,696; Noerr, 19,069; Cobban, 4,385. The Legislature of 1889, elected at the same time, will stand: In the Senate, Democrats, 24; Republicans, 9; Labor, 1; in the House, Democrats, 78; Republicans, 51; Labor, 11. Democratic Congressmen were elected in the first seven and in the Eleventh, Twelfth, and Fourteenth Districts. A Republican was elected in the Thirteenth District, and the fusion candidates of the Republican and Union Labor parties in the other three districts.

MOHAMMEDANS. The Faith of Islam. — The reign of Sultan Abdul Hamid has been marked by considerably more zeal in spreading the creed of Mohammed than was exhibited under those of any of his immediate predecessors, and, according to the lists published in the journals of Constantinople, an unusually large number of accessions from among Christians and Jews to the Mohammedan faith occurred during 1887. For the most part the converts were men of little note; but among the number were Chaphaz Effendi, a judge and member of an old Armenian family, and a foreigner who was identified with Mr. Schumann, a man of letters residing in Hanover, the latter gentleman having applied to the Sheik-ul-Islam, Ahmed Ersead Effendi, for a statement of the conditions on which he could be received as a Mussulman. The reply of this officer, which was published in French in the "Levant Herald," may be accepted as a clear statement for foreigners of the orthodox Mohammedan faith. It points out, first, that it is not necessary to ask permission to become a Mussulman, "for Islam does not admit of any mediators like the clergy between God and his servants," and consequently conversion to its faith entails neither religious formality nor any person's authority.

In short [it continues] the basis of the religion of Islam is belief in the unity of God and in the mission of his servant, the most beloved Mohammed (upon whom may God confer his blessings and grant salvation!), and only requires that one confirm that belief in his heart and avow it in word, as is expressed by the phrase (written in Arabic), "There is but one God, and Mohammed is his prophet." Whoever makes this profession of faith becomes a Mussulman without having to obtain the consent and approbation of any one. If, as you premise in your letter, you so make this profession of faith—that is, if you declare that there is but one God and Mohammed is his prophet—you become a Mussulman without needing any acceptation by us; and we shall proudly and joyfully felicitate you on your having been touched with divine grace, and we shall bear witness in this world as in the next that you are our brother in religion (the faithful are all brothers).

Concerning the mission of Mohammed and the inspired character of the Koran, the Sheik declared:

Man, who is superior to the other animals by reason of his intelligence, was produced from nothing to adore his Creator. His adoration may be described as obeying the commands of God and having compassion on his creatures. This double adoration exists in all religions. In its practice, religions differ in regard to the regulation, the form and number, whether it be large or small, of the rites, the times, places, and conditions of performing them, and with regard to their ministers; but human intelligence is not adequate to knowing the manner of praying most worthy of the divine glory. Hence God, in his clemency, by granting to some human beings the gift of prophecy, by sending to them through the angels and inspiration writings and books, and thus revealing the true religion to them, has loaded his servants with his benefactions. The book of God which came down last from Heaven is the Holy Koran, whose invariable precepts, preserved from the first day in written volumes and in the memory of thousands of reciters, shall endure till the day of final judgment. The first of the prophets was Adam and the last Mohammed (to whom may God grant salvation!). Between these two prophets many others have passed over the earth; the number of whom is known by God alone. The greatest of all is Mohammed. After him come Jesus, Moses, Abraham, and then Noah and Adam (to whom may God grant salvation!).

Concerning the future state and the day of judgment:

All the actions of every one in this world shall be on that day examined one by one, and while all the acts of soldiers who have fought in the holy war, even their sleep, are considered as a prayer, they also will be obliged, on the day of the last judgment, to render account of themselves. There are no exceptions except in the case of those who die for the holy cause;

that is, the martyrs, who will go into paradise without being questioned.

Of the origin of good and evil :

It is required, as an article of faith, to attribute good and evil to the providence of God. To say that the creator of good is the angel, and the author of evil the devil, is one of those prejudices that must be avoided. Consequently, the believer should have faith in God, in his angels, in his books, in his prophets, and in the last judgment, and should attribute both good and evil to the divine will. Whoever professes these truths is a true believer. But to be a perfect believer, it is necessary to perform one's duties, to pray to God, and to avoid falling into such sins as assassination, theft, adultery, and sodomy.

After describing the religious duties of prayer, charity, fasting, and pilgrimage, the paper continues:

If a believer does not conform to these commands of God and avoid the acts which he forbids, he does not thereby become an infidel; but he will be regarded as a sinner, that is, as a believer who has gone astray, and he will merit a provisional punishment in the other world. He remains at the divine disposal. God pardons him or condemns him to pass in hell a lapse of time proportioned to his sins. Faith annuls all sin. Whoever is converted to Islam becomes as innocent as one newly born, and is responsible only for the sins which he commits after his conversion.

Islam, the Sheik explains, has no clergy, the doctors of the faith being simply instructors and guides; for it holds that a man does not need the priest's aid to approach God in prayer, nor his presence at social duties—the naming of children, burial, and the like:

In a word, in all religious acts, there is no intermediary between God and his servants. It is necessary to learn the dispositions revealed on the part of the Creator by the Prophet, and to act in conformity with them. Only the performance of certain ceremonies, like the prayers of Friday and the Baïram, is subordinated to the permission of the Khalif of the Prophet and Sultan of the Mussulmans, because the keeping of the ceremonies of Islam is one of his holy attributes. Obedience to his orders is one of the most important religious duties.

MONTANA. Territorial Government.—The following were the Territorial officers during the year: Governor, Preston H. Leslie; Secretary, William B. Webb; Treasurer, William G. Preuitt; Auditor, James Sullivan; Superintendent of Public Instruction, Arthur C. Logan; Chief-Justice of the Supreme Court, N. W. McConnell; Associate Justices, Thomas C. Bach, W. J. Galbraith, succeeded by Stephen De Wolfe, and James H. McLeary, succeeded Moses B. Liddell. Chief-Justice McConnell resigned at the close of the year. The office of Attorney-General was created by the Legislature at its extra session in 1887, and a nomination was made thereto by the Governor, but the nominee was rejected by the Council, and the session adjourned without filling the vacancy. On December 31 the Governor appointed William E. Cullen to hold the office during 1888 and until the close of the next Legislative session.

Finances.—The following is a statement of the finances of the Territory for 1887: Balance in the general fund on Jan. 1, 1887, $57,-269.18; licenses and property tax, $182,-642.53; from insurance companies, etc., $3,-743.77; total, $243,655.48. Disbursements for the year, $207,628.61. Balance on Jan. 1, 1888, $36,026.87. Of the disbursements, about $60,000 was for the care of the insane, and $40,000 for maintenance of convicts. The unfortunate bounty law passed by the Legislature of 1887 cost the Territory, during the few months of its existence, $61,721. Its prompt repeal at the extra session of that year saved the treasury from bankruptcy. In the various stock funds, the balances on Jan. 1, 1887, were $17,657.97; the revenue for the year was $18,084.87; and the balances on Dec. 31, 1887, were $12,389.65. At the close of 1888 the balance in the general fund had risen to $114,340,48, and in the stock funds to $15,852.28. There is no Territorial debt.

General Development.—The Governor says in his annual report:

This Territory, containing more than 143,000 square miles, is divided into sixteen counties, and in each of fourteen of these there is a good court-house, and the necessary public buildings to facilitate the transaction of all public business. The city of Helena is the central point of legislative, judicial, financial, commercial, and educational affairs in the Territory, and is also the railroad center. This city has a population of more than 15,000, and is rapidly growing. The city of Butte, in Silver Bow County, is the largest and most populous city west of Denver, between the Mississippi river and the Pacific coast, and is the largest mining-camp in the world. The annual output of the mines ten years ago was estimated at $7,000,000; now it is over $31,000,000. The total value of taxable property in the Territory then was $12,000,000; now it is $69,-600,000 (not counting the value of the mining property). The number of cattle in the Territory then was 220,000, now it is 1,500,000; the number of sheep then was 120,000, now it is over 2,000,000; the number of horses then was 40,000, now it is 200,000; the number of acres of land then under cultivation was 265,000, now there are over 2,000,000 acres appropriated and settled for farming purposes; then the commerce of the whole Territory was $20,000,000, now it is $40,000,000; then there were but a dozen miles of railroad, now there are over 2,000; then the population was 30,000, now it is 140,000; then the Territory was in debt $112,000, now it is out of debt, and there is plenty of money in the treasury.

Mining.—This industry continues to be the leading pursuit of the people of Montana. The mines are more productive than ever. Improved methods in working and the better order of machinery used enable men to prosecute this branch of industry to a greater extent and with more success. Many mines that would not pay twenty years ago, on account of the primitive mode of working, together with the high price of labor, are now being worked at good profit. The amount of dividends declared by mining companies during 1888 was greater than ever. The product of gold and silver in 1887 was: Gold, $5,778,-536.28; silver, $17,817,548.95; total, $23,796,-085.23.

Convicts.—The Governor says in his message:

The Territory has never ye built or owned a State prison. The United States has a Penitentiary at Deer Lodge, and ever since the beginning of 1874 the Ter-

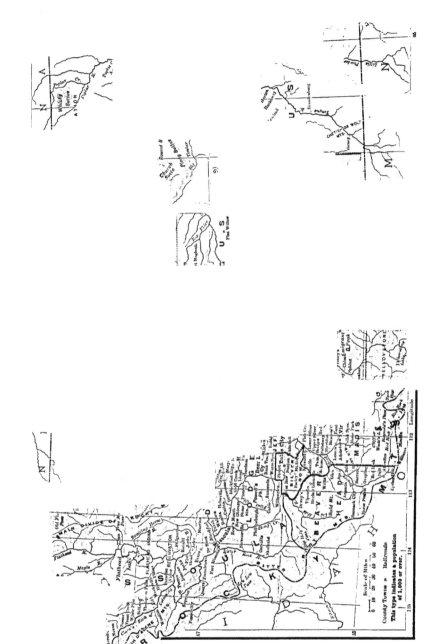

ritory has secured the confinement, care, and support of its convicted criminals in that prison. No prisoner is required to work one hour of the time for which he is there confined. The institution is a sightly, well-provided, and well-kept home. There are but seventy cells, and this limited provision has necessitated the putting of two convicts in each cell, and in addition to that number, there are periods of time when ten to fifteen others have to be accommodated and guarded. The Territory has thus paid for boarding in idleness the convicted criminals since January, 1874, $270,000, and the Auditor's office shows that these annual outlays are increasing from $3,000 to $7,000 every year.

Mineral-Land Convention.—Early in February a Territorial convention of citizens interested in mining met at Helena to devise means for preventing the mineral lands of the Territory from being taken by the Northern Pacific Railroad Company under its grant from the Government of certain sections of the public lands. Although the railroad was obliged to make its selections out of non-mineral surveyed lands, yet, by procuring surveyors to make return of mineral land as non-mineral, it might acquire title to very valuable property. Cases had already happened in Deer Lodge County and Silver Bow County, near the city of Butte, in the richest mineral region of the Territory, where land returned as non-mineral had been certified to the company, which, in fact, contained valuable deposits of metals. The means adopted by the convention to prevent the company from acquiring full title to such land consisted in the appointment of a central executive committee of five persons, with power to appoint sub-committees and employ professional assistance, to forward to the Department of the Interior, with the least possible delay, proofs setting forth the mineral character of the lands heretofore designated and selected by the Northern Pacific Railroad Company in the Territory of Montana, and likewise of all other lands included within the land-grant to said railroad company. Means were also taken to bring the subject before Congress.

Indian Reservation.—By an act of Congress, passed and approved in the early months of this year, a large tract of land, covering more than 20,000,000 acres, heretofore reserved and set apart to the use of the Piegan and other Indians, was redeemed from Indian ownership, and is soon to be surveyed and offered for purchase and occupancy.

Political.—On April 19 a mass-meeting of Prohibitionists of the Territory was held at Helena to form a Territorial Prohibition party. An organization was duly effected and delegates chosen to the National Prohibition Convention. The Democratic Convention to nominate a candidate for Territorial delegate was held at Butte on September 11, and resulted in the choice of William A. Clarke. A platform was adopted approving of the St. Louis platform, the President's message, and the Mill's Bill, favoring free coinage of silver, opposing Chinese immigration, demanding the admission of the Territory, urging a diminution of Indian reservations, and favoring the

allowance to citizens of the Territory of the free use of timber on the public domain. The Republican Convention was held at Helena on September 17, and nominated Thomas H. Carter for delegate. The resolutions contain the protectionist doctrines of the National party, whose platform and nominees they ratify, complain of the non-admission of the Territory, attack the Canadian fishery negotiations, and repeat the Democratic declaration against Chinese immigration. The Prohibition party placed in the field, as its first candidate for delegate, Davis Willson. At the November election the Republican ticket was successful, poling 22,482 votes, to 17,360 for the Democratic nominee, and 148 votes for the Prohibition candidate. At the election in 1886, Toole (Democrat) was chosen delegate by 3,718 plurality. Seven Republicans and 5 Democrats were elected to the Council, and 19 Republicans and 5 Democrats to the Lower House of the Legislature.

MONTENEGRO, a principality in Southeastern Europe. The reigning Prince is Nicholas I, born Oct. 7, 1841. (For description of the Government see "Annual Cyclopædia" for 1884, page 536). The area, including the distriet of Dulcigno, ceded by Turkey in 1880, is about 3,630 square miles, and the population 236,000. The boundaries on the south and east of the annexed district were agreed upon in November, 1887, and the delimitation was not completed till August, 1888. The uncertainty as to the boundary has led to frequent fights between the Kutchi tribe on the Montenegrin side and the Albanian tribes of Hoti and Grudi. Prince Nicholas receives subsidies from the Russian Government, and endeavors to promote Russian policy in the Balkan Peninsula. Montenegrins have taken part in all the revolutionary attempts in Bulgaria and in the guerilla warfare against the Austrians in Herzegovina. On the occasion of the promulgation of the new civil code, Prince Nicholas issued a ukase in which he expressed deep gratitude to the Czar as the " protector of all Slavs," an expression against which the official organs of Austria strongly protested.

The Montenegrins live to a great extent under the communistic and patriarchal institutions of the early Slavs. The inhabitants are divided into forty tribes, each governed by elders, who are elected. The Prince is represented in each of the eighty districts by a kujas or captain, who acts as a magistrate in time of peace, and a military commander in war. The inhabitants raise live-stock of all kinds, and export hides, cattle, goats, smoked mutton, and cheese, besides smoked sardines, skins and furs, sumac, and insect-powder. Grain is grown in insufficient quantities, and much of the food must be imported from Russia. When the crops fail, there is much suffering, as was the case in the Zeta valley in the winter of 1887-'88. The Government owes 700,000 florins to Russia for grain supplied in 1879, besides 1,000,000 florins borrowed in Vienna at 6½ per cent. in 1881.

The Civil Code.—The Montenegrins, like the rest of the Balkan Slavs, have heretofore contented themselves with laws adopted from European jurisprudence that often conflict with their traditional customary 'law. Balthazar Bogishich, a scholar and jurist, who is widely known in Slavic countries, was commissioned by Prince Nicholas to elaborate a body of laws in which the peculiar institutions and customs of the land should be confirmed as they could be brought into harmony with modern jurisprudence. The civil code was promulgated by the Prince with great ceremony on May 8, 1888, and went into force on July 1. It is the first attempt to formulate in scientific terms the customs and conceptions of justice existing among the South Slavs. The collective family, with the principle of the solidarity of all the family members, is preserved from extinction; though in certain cases the responsibility of individuals is affirmed. Since many Montenegrins now seek their fortunes abroad, it was found necessary to modify the old law by relieving families of responsibility for the debts and taxes of absent members, which in the past has brought financial ruin on many families. Several paragraphs are devoted to international private laws, regulating and limiting the operation of the laws of other states within the principality. In order to preserve the land of the people from falling into the hands of usurers, restrictions are placed on the acquisition of real estate. Land can be alienated, but the new owner only acquires the right to the commons in wood, water, and pasture, belonging to the property, in case he cultivates it himself, a restriction which is expected to prevent the acquisition of large estates. Foreigners are not permitted to own real estate, except by gift of the Prince. The law of contracts is worked out with careful application of legal theories to the conditions of the people. Definitions and elucidations are given at the end of the code. Prof. Bogishich has published in Paris a *brochure* explaining his method of codification, and is writing a work on the principles of the system of laws that he has collected.

MORAVIANS. The following are the general statistics of the Church of the United Brethren, commonly known as the Moravian Church:

PROVINCES.	Communicants.	Total members.
American Northern, 60 congregations.	9,819	15,054
American Southern, 6 congregations..	1,647	2,513
British, 38 congregations, including home missions	3,211	5,647
German, 27 congregations, including Bethel..........................	6,141	8,874
German Diaspora laborers	115	150
Bohemia....................	256	400
Missions, 107 stations................	29,707	84,201
Missionaries and their families, about.	336	430
Total	50,732	116,769

Whole number of teachers in Sunday-schools, 2,748; of pupils in the same, 26,687; number of boarding-schools, 41, with 1,842 pupils; of day-schools, 253, with 21,477 pupils. The Moravian Church throughout the world is under a single organization, which is called the Unity's Elders' Conference, and forms also the Provincial Elders' Conference for Germany. The other provincial synods are responsible to it, and are dependent upon it for the ratification of their principal acts. Its residence and offices are at Herrnhut, Saxony.

The American Province comprises a northern and a southern division, each of which has its separate synod, and the northern division is divided into five districts, each including a convenient number of congregations geographically related to one another. In the ecclesiastical nomenclature, the congregations comprise, generally speaking, the older settlements, to which are added from time to time the new flocks resulting from home missionary labors. This happens whenever a home mission is able to satisfy the conditions required for the support of a regular ministry; and then, and not till then, it is entitled to representation in the Provincial Synod. The four schools of the American Province, at Bethlehem, Litiz, and Nazareth, Pa., and Salem, N. C., date from toward the close of the last or the beginning of the present century, and return, in all, 50 teachers and 500 boarding pupils. The Moravian College and Theological Seminary, at Bethlehem, Pa., includes three classes, provides a six years' course of study, and returns about 40 students. The Theological Seminary has an endowment fund of about $75,000. The annual expenses of sustentation (of retired ministers and the widows of ministers) in the Northern Province average about $9,000. The "Malin Library" at Bethlehem, Pa., possesses the most valuable collection of Moravian literature that exists. The synod of the northern division of the American Province met in Bethlehem Pa., September 19; Bishop A. A. Reinke was chosen president. The most important business was the designation of three bishops; six candidates were nominated. Their names were submitted by ocean telegraph to the Unity's Elders' Conference in Herrnhut, Saxony, with the request that in making the selection the "apostolic lot" be used. Brethren H. T. Bachman, J. M. Levering, and A. A. Reinke were thus chosen, and were duly consecrated during the session of the synod. Resolutions were adopted welcoming any effort put forth in good faith to secure closer fellowship and communion between the churches; and a committee was appointed to confer with committees of other bodies on this subject.

The peculiar European home mission called the Diaspora has been carried on under the direction of the German Provincial Elders' Conference since 1729. It seeks not to make proselytes, or to draw members from other Protestant communities, but to excite and foster spiritual life by means additional to those provided by the established churches. Its agents are itinerant in wide circuits and hold meetings in their chapels at hours not interfering with those of the parish church; and they form societies of persons who incline toward Moravian views, but do not feel called upon to leave the established church. The Diaspora work is carried on in Germany, Russia (chiefly the Baltic Provinces and Poland), Switzerland, and Palestine.

The Unity's work in Bohemia is carried on around two centers—Pottenstein Landskron, the northeastern district, among the Bohemian speaking population; and Dauba, the northern district, among people speaking German.

The Church has sustained a mission among lepers for sixty-seven years. It was begun in 1822, at the hospital erected by the Cape Colony, which remained under the care or partial care of the Moravians till 1867, when the Government's chaplain took charge of it In the same year the Moravian missionaries assumed the care of the asylum for lepers that had been established by the Baroness von Keffenbrinck Ascheraden, at Jerusalem, where three agents are now stationed.

The income for missions among the heathen during 1887 was $84,015, and the expenditures were $100,966. The sum raised annually at the various stations toward the support of this work is estimated at about $125,000; and including the interest of capitals left for the support of particular missions, Government aid, etc., the actual expenditure for the whole mission work reaches a total of about $250,000. The number of brethren and sisters employed in this service from its beginning, in 1732, is about 2,300. The missions, which constitute by far the most important division of the Moravian Church work, are conducted in Greenland, Labrador, Alaska, among the North American Indians, in the West Indies, the Mosquito Coast, Surinam, South Africa, Australia, and Central Asia (British Tibet). They are served by 356 missionaries, of whom 48 are natives, and 1,613 native assistants, and return, besides communicants and members, already enumerated, 223 day-schools, with 18,280 pupils, and 98 Sunday-schools, with 14,099 pupils.

MOROCCO, an empire in Northern Africa. The Sultan is the unrestricted spiritual ruler, having no Ulema to guide him, such as exists in other Mohammedan states, and the absolute head of the state, although, in civil affairs, the predecessors of the present Sultan have usually taken the advice of the Vizier and other ministers. The reigning Sultan is Muley-Hassan, belonging to the Hachan family, Sherifs of the Tafilali tribe, of the Aliweein branch of the Shereefian family, being the direct descendant, in the thirty-fifth generation, of Ali, uncle of the Prophet, and of Fatima, the Prophet's daughter. He succeeded his father, Sidi-Mohammed, in 1873, at the age of forty-two. He holds his court alternately at Fez and Morocco,

and sometimes resides for a few months at Mequinez, Marakish, or Rabat. He has an army of 10,000 infantry and 2,400 cavalry, which is quartered in the city where he happens to reside. The present Grand Vizier is Mohammed el Arbi ben el Moghtar, whose brother is Minister of War. The Vizier for Foreign Affairs is Mohammed el Mofdel Garrit, while Mohammed ben el Arbi el Torres is the minister charged with the foreign relations of the Sultan at Tangier. Muley-Hassan, a more energetic ruler than his ancestors, decides all matters of policy without consultation.

Area and Population.—The area of the empire is estimated at 812,300 square kilometres or 260,000 square miles, of which 197,100 square kilometres consist of mountainous districts and large, fertile plains, 67,700 square kilometres are poorly watered tablelands, and 547,500 square kilometres, including the province of Twat. lie within the borders of the Great Sahara Desert. The population has been variously estimated at from 6,000,000 to 10,000,000, and by Dr. Gerhard Rholfs as low as 2,750,000. Two thirds of the people belong to the Moorish or Berber race, while the remainder are Bedouin Arabs, negroes, and Jews, of whom there are 340,000. About 50,000 of the people are slaves.

Commerce.—The total value of the imports in 1885, exclusive of specie, was 33,724,000 francs, against 21,432,000 francs in 1884; of the exports, 30,015,000 francs, against 19,211,000 francs. In 1886, the cargoes landed at the ports were valued at 36,418,000 francs, and those taken away at 32,316,000 francs. The imports of cotton and cotton goods in that year were valued at 15,593,000 francs; of sugar, 5,793,000 francs; of silver money, 3,153,000 francs. The chief exports were beans and peas of the value of 5,465,000 francs; maize, 4,084,000 francs; olive-oil, 3,855,000 francs; wool, 2,756,000 francs; goatskins, 2,648,000 francs; cattle, 2,450,000 francs; almonds, 1,361,000 francs. The export of silver coin was 1,573,000 francs. Of the total imports in 1885 Great Britain furnished 21,630,000 francs worth, and the exports to that country were 14,582,000 francs in value, while the share of France in the imports was 8,293,000 francs, and in the exports, 6,675,000 francs. The trade in cotton cloths has, till recently, belonged exclusively to England, but Swiss muslins and grenadines are replacing Manchester goods. Belgium supplies iron goods, Germany and Austria cloths, and France loaf-sugar, which is the usual article sent in Morocco as a complimentary present. Chemicals and matches also come from France, and candles and various other manufactures that Great Britain used exclusively to furnish are imported in increasing quantities by the Germans. The total number of vessels entered at all ports in 1886 was 1,989, of 567,619 tons, of which 854, of 256,062 tons were English, and 363, of 238,126 tons were French.

Natural Resources.—Morocco has been always closed to European commerce, except the port of Tangier, owing to the jealousy of its rulers and the fanaticism of the inhabitants. Even travelers and explorers have been excluded, and not till recently have the great natural resources of the country been even suspected. The climate, cooled by the snow-capped Atlas in the south and by the breezes of the Atlantic, is mild and genial. The soil, especially in the southern part of the country, is exceedingly fertile. Large navigable rivers flow through the land, the Azamoor and the river of Rabat being the most important.

Political and Economic Conditions. — Although descended from the Moors, who for four centuries governed Spain and built the cities of Cordova, Seville, and Granada, and although possessing now one of the finest countries in the world, the inhabitants of Morocco have been reduced to misery and barbarism by oppression. The Sultan, as the successor of the Caliphs of Cordova, does not acknowledge the superiority of the Sultan of Turkey, but considers himself the head of the faithful. His spiritual character enables him to exercise absolute despotic power over the Berbers and Arabs, which the present Sultan and his predecessors have so abused that the laws are simply instruments of pillage and oppression, and every person seeks to hide his property lest he should lose both it and his life or liberty. The authorities of the state, from the Sultan down, plunder those beneath them. Muley Hassan is said to have amassed enormous wealth. There is no Minister of Finance or Treasurer, and the key of the treasury, which is supposed to be in Mequinez, is kept by the Sultan. It often happens that the meanest slave is raised to the highest office of state, and as often that the most upright official is ordered to execution. The Sultan is consecrated by the Grand Sherif of Wazan, who exercises a power only second to that of the Sultan, and is held in such fear and veneration that his mere presence in battle has often decided the fortunes of the day. Education in Morocco is usually confined to learning by rote a few chapters of the Koran. Justice is administered daily in the residence of the pasha of each province. Stealing is punished by cutting off the hands or feet. The officials receive no pay, but are at liberty to extort as much as they like from those under them, while they are obliged to deliver large sums to the Sultan. Every officer, from the Minister of State down to the sheikh of a village, pays for his appointment, and must pay to continue in office. Their exactions and arbitrary assessments are the cause of frequent revolts. No one takes pains to make the ground more productive, because its produce would be seized by the Government. The merchants are compelled to carry on their trade secretly, to conceal their stock, and to bury their savings. When a pasha is suspected of having amassed great wealth, it is no uncommon occurrence for the Sultan to invite him to the capital and after his arrival cast him into prison and load him with chains until he parts with his gains. The inmates of the prisons die in great numbers, from foul air, cruel treatment, and starvation. The law requires every man to give a tenth part of his goods to the poor, but the tithes are collected by the Sultan's officers, and the greater part of them is retained in their hands or diverted into the imperial treasury. Slavery exists without restrictions, and slave markets are held in the public streets. The slaves are brought from the Soudan, having originally been kidnapped or taken in war. They are well treated by their masters as a rule, and some are set free. There are no roads in Morocco. Wheat is often sold in the interior for one fifth of the price that it would bring at the seaboard. The difficulties of transportation are such that only one half of the land is cultivated, and even under these circumstances the grain is often left to rot in the fields. The Sultan sometimes forbids the exportation of grain, even in years of abundance. The regular sources of the public revenue are the tithe on agricultural produce, a tax of 2 per cent. on domestic animals, a tax on *shebbel* (a kind of fish caught in the rivers), the monopoly of tobacco and hasheesh, a poll-tax on Jews, and 10 per cent. duty on all goods imported or exported, and on all produce brought to the towns. Fines are levied on every pretext, and the scale of the regular imposts is frequently raised or lowered according to the impulse of the Sultan. Fines are simply a method of extortion. A quarrel between two members of a kabyla may deprive both of half their possessions, and when a robbery is committed it is a common thing to fine every inhabitant of the village double the amount of the stolen property. Besides beating and imprisonment many forms of torture are used. The Sultan alone can condemn a criminal to death; yet the pashas order punishments that result in more cruel forms of death than decapitation by the Sultan's decree. The tobacco and hasheesh monopolies were recently abolished by a Shereefian decree forbidding the use of those narcotics, to which the Moors were greatly addicted, and are still, for notwithstanding the severe punishments inflicted they continue to indulge their habit of smoking, and now the officials have become less vigilant in enforcing the decree. In 1888 the Sultan issued a decree against intoxicants of all kinds. The Jews in Morocco are objects of detestation and contempt, and are subject on all hands to indignities and cruelties, such as the fanatical Moors would inflict as eagerly on Nazarenes or Christians if they were not restrained by the Government.

Treaty Negotiations.—The Sultan has been able to persevere in his policy of isolation and nonintercourse only through the jealousy of the European powers. Great Britain, being in possession of two thirds of the existing foreign trade, has been anxious to prevent any power from gaining a commercial footing, which might lead to political ascendancy, and thus weaken her position at Gibraltar. The power most distrusted by others has been France. She was the first to establish her rule on the Mediterranean coast of Africa, and is the only land neighbor of Morocco, and in recent years has attempted to push the frontiers of her West-African colonial possessions northward so as to inclose Morocco on every side. Italy feels the deepest interest in preventing France from realizing her dreams of an African empire that would in the natural course of events swallow up Tripoli, the special object of Italian ambition. Austria, as a Mediterranean power, also takes a watchful interest in Morocco, and is encouraged by Germany, which has an eye on the commercial possibilities of the country. Spain is the only power that has definite and acknowledged aspirations toward Morocco, which she regards as her heritage, not only on account of geographical proximity, but by reason of a historical title based on the expulsion of the Moors from Spanish ground.

In 1884 the intrigues of the Frenchman De Chavagnac, who endeavored to stir up rebellion in Morocco, and secure a footing for France in Riff, aided as they were by the French minister in Tangier, Ordéga, aroused alarm in Madrid, and were regarded with anxiety in the foreign offices of other capitals. The French Government manifested the loyalty of its intentions by recalling M. Ordéga after he had attempted to extract a secret treaty from the Sultan. Germany began to cultivate relations with Morocco about 1876, and gradually obtained such influence that, in 1885, she pressed for a revision of the commercial treaties on the basis of a considerable reduction of the import and export duties, the opening of the whole country to the free circulation of foreigners, and the right of foreigners to acquire lands and to engage in commercial, mining, and railroad enterprises. The proposals were rejected by the Sultan, but they were renewed when England, and later France, joined in the demands. The existing treaty was made in 1856 by Sir John Drummond Hay, who still represented Great Britain at Tangier, and had undergone no alteration except the addition of stipulations of minor importance at the conclusion of the Spanish war against the Moors in 1860 and changes in the port dues made at the Madrid Convention of 1880. France endeavored to remove the obstacles to a new arrangement by sending M. Ferraud as minister to Tangier with directions to reform the abuses connected with the French consular service, of which the Sultan had often complained. Neither the Sultan nor his subjects could expect any advantage from throwing open the country to European enterprise, for it would not only hasten the day of political annexation, but would raise the prices of the means of life to the natives, while the profits arising from the development of the resources of the country would all accrue to strangers, who would eventually become the owners of the land.

Foreign Protection.—The principal objection of the Sultan to enlarging the commercial privileges of foreigners was, that under the existing arrangements the allegiance of a considerable section of his subjects was alienated, and that with closer commercial relations with European countries he would be deprived of his power over the rest. The legations have the right in Morocco, as in several other Mohammedan countries, of granting protection to persons employed in any capacity in the consular service, or acting as commercial agents for firms belonging to the country giving protection. Such *protégés* are no longer subject to the jurisdiction of Moorish courts. All complaints or suits against them, or that they bring against others, are adjudicated in the consular courts of the country of which they become *quasi*-subjects. They not only escape taxation and the exactions of native officials, but are able to practice extortions themselves by making false claims or accusations, which will lead to imprisonment by order of the consuls if their blackmailing demands are not satisfied. The incumbents of diplomatic and consular posts in Morocco are often men who are open to the temptations of the great bribes that are offered for consular protection and for the support of the *protégés* in their dishonest schemes; and even those who are honorable, being usually ignorant of the language of the country, are easily misled by dragomans and interpreters. The Madrid Convention limited the number of *protégés* to two for each commercial house; yet some of the diplomatic representatives issued fifteen and twenty protections to pretended agents of the same firm, and the Moorish authorities allowed the others to do the same for the sake of avoiding disputes under the most-favored-nation clause. So great is the fear of the Moorish Government of foreign complications, leading possibly to the annexation of the country, that the authorities were ordered to obey implicitly all foreigners or persons protected by foreigners. For many years the French Government more than the others laid itself open to blame for protecting unworthy persons and supporting fraudulent claims. Afterward the representatives of the United States were the chief offenders. A wealthy American citizen, Ion Perdicaris, with the assistance of his secretary, Captain Rolleston, an Englishman, made it his task to unearth consular abuses and defend the victims of revenge or cupidity who were chained in dungeons, and often allowed to die of starvation, on account of debts that they had never owed, or had already paid in full or in part. There were more than 150 native Jews or Moors who enjoyed the protection of the United States flag, and who claimed debts amounting to $100,000, for which many un-protected natives were cast into prison and were unable to obtain a trial in order to prove the fraudulent character of the claims against them. A Jew money-lender named Reuben Tergeman, enjoying American protection, pro-cured the imprisonment of nearly a score of persons in one province alone, some of whom were kept in chains for two years, although they had paid their debts two or three times over. Mr. Perdicaris, in attempting to right such wrongs, came into conflict with the Amer-ican consul, and by the latter's order was him-self committed to prison. He succeeded in bringing the matter to the attention of the United States Government, which recalled the consul and sent out Reed Lewis, who dismissed all the old employés of the consulate. The evidence that Mr. Perdicaris had collected con-demned the system of consular protection so thoroughly in the eyes of Congress, that it passed an act in the early part of 1887 abolish-ing the extension of American protection for commercial purposes to natives in Morocco and in other countries. All persons incarcerated for debts due to American citizens and protégés were released by order of Mr. Lewis, and usu-rers suspected of having made false claims were arrested.

The present system of foreign protection has existed since 1767, when it was secured in a treaty of peace and commerce with France for persons in the service of consuls, secretaries of political agents, interpreters, and represen-tatives of foreign commercial establishments. The Madrid Convention of 1880 contained pro-visions that were intended to restrict the number of protections, while it added to the privileges and immunities of those who were protected. The restrictions were evaded, and the traffic in protections, which were made more valuable by the convention, was conducted on a larger scale. Every wealthy Moor sought the protection of a foreign power. Even the Sheriff of Wazan became a French protégé, and by that act sacrificed a great part of his pres-tige, which was already impaired through his marriage to an English woman. The conven-tion of Madrid limits the number of protected persons to the employés of the legations and consulates, simsars or commercial agents of for-eign traders, two being allowed for each firm, and Moorish subjects who accept foreign alle-giance. The powers claimed the right to protect the last-named class by right of custom, but agreed to limit the number to twelve for each of the thirteen signatory powers. The pro-tection extends, however, to all the children and the numerous dependents of the protected persons. The representatives of the powers were desirous of securing as protégés the wealth-iest and most powerful of the Sultan's subjects as a means of extending their own influence. The Moors whose wealth was sufficient to attract the cupidity of the Sultan or his officers sought foreign protection as a means of self-

preservation, and were willing to pay high premiums for the appointment of simsar to a foreign commercial firm. Many of them es-tablished Europeans in some ostensible com-mercial business in Tangier, really paying them salaries for the privilege of acting as their pre-tended agents. The latter arrangement was more secure and permanent, since the immuni-ties of the simsar terminate with the agency. M. Ferraud reduced the number of Moors claiming French protection from 800 to 60. There is, however, a large number of French subjects, born in Algeria, who practice usury and extortion under cover of their French pro-tection, while the British Government is called upon to protect the misdeeds of many Barbary Jews whose birthplace was Gibraltar. The Sultan is led to believe that the number of protected Moors is much greater than it really is, because often when he gives directions to confiscate the property of some person of whose wealth he hears, the kaid of the district is bribed by the man to report that he is under foreign protection.

The Submarine Cable.—The British Govern-ment has for twelve years past sought the per-mission of the Sultan to lay a cable from Tan-gier to connect with the European telegraph system at Gibralter. The French and Spanish governments objected to the concession being granted unless they too should have the privi-lege of laying cables. Sir William Kirby Green, who succeeded Sir John Drummond Hay as British minister at Tangier in 1886, wrote to the Sultan for his final consent. The British legation is the only one that communicates directly with the court by means of couriers, the other ministers being compelled to present their communications through the Moorish Foreign Minister in Tangier. When no answer came to the letter of the British representative, he wrote again, saying, that if the Sultan did not reply within a certain time he would take his consent for granted. This and a third letter remained unanswered, and at the time indicated the cable was put down, in February, 1887. Then the Sultan sent word that he would pay all expenses if it were taken up again. This the British Government refused to do, and when the Sultan, in a communication conveyed through the Foreign Minister to the diplomatic body at Tangier, formally protested against the cable, and demanded the suspension of its use until the matter was diplomatically regulated, no attention was paid to his remonstrances.

Rebellion of the Beni Zemour.—In 1887 the Beni Zemour, a powerful tribe dwelling between Marakish and Mequinez rebelled against the exactions of the Sultan, who was then at Mara-kish, where his presence was manifested as usual by wholesale pillage. Muley Hassan sent word that if they would submit themselves and bring tribute in token of subjection, he would pardon them and leave their territory in peace. The Beni Zemour complied at once, and more than 70,000 men and women carried baskets of supplies on their heads to Marakish. The Sultan, after he had received their offerings, turned his soldiers loose on the tribe to plunder and murder as they pleased for two days, in order, he said, to teach the rebels to respect his authority. The Beni Zemour in retaliation poisoned all the wells, with the result that the Sultan's favorite wife and many members of his household died. He himself was taken very ill, it was supposed from the same cause.

Naval Demonstration.—The prospect of a change of rulers is regarded with consternation by all the inhabitants of Morocco, the foreigners doing business there not excepted. The death of Muley Hassan would be followed inevitably by a conflict among all the tribes, each of which would fight for the candidate for the throne with whom it is most nearly connected. A new Sultan is supposed to be selected by his predecessor, but he must be accepted by the majority of the people before he is permitted to take his seat under the Shereefian Umbrella. The present Sultan, in the beginning of his reign, killed off his two uncles and the most prominent member of the Drissian branch of the Shereefian family, and then banished all his male relatives to the oasis of Tafilet, where they have been kept in penury and solitude. His sons are so young that none of them is likely to be accepted as his successor. There are, however, several descendants of both the Aliweein and the Drissian dynasties who have powerful tribes at their back, ready to defend their claims to the succession. The jealous powers, whose mutual distrust has prevented the introduction of civilizing agencies, regard the situation with watchful anxiety. In September, 1887, when the news of the probably fatal sickness of Muley Hassan was brought to Madrid, the Spanish Government at once got its fleet ready and moved an army corps to the ports nearest the Moorish coast. On October 1 Señor Moret advised the governments of Germany, England, Austria, France, and Italy of Spain's intention to send troops to the Spanish fortresses on the coast of Morocco. Great Britain was prompted by the Spanish armaments to dispatch a naval force to Morocco, and France and Italy were equally alert. These powers, in their replies to the Spanish dispatch, which was amplified on October 5 in a circular to all the signatories of the Madrid Convention, expressed approval of the steps taken by Spain, and declared their intention of sending ships to Tangier to protect the lives and property of their subjects. A few weeks later, powerful war-ships of the various nations anchored in the bay of Tangier, and remained to watch events until the recovery of the Sultan and the progress of diplomatic negotiations removed the cause of their presence there.

Proposed Morocco Conference.—The Morocco crisis impelled the Spanish Cabinet to urge the elevation of the representatives of the great powers at Madrid to ambassadorial rank, in the hope that Spain as a great power would be able to press her historical claims to Morocco with more weight. When the Madrid statesmen perceived that the right of their country to dispose of the fortunes of the Moorish empire was disputed by all the powers, they resorted to another method of placing Spain in the lead. On October 2 Señor Moret suggested the advisability of reassembling the conference of 1880. In the note of October 5 he dwelt upon the reasons for Spain's taking the initiative and uniting with the powers in demanding in Morocco the reforms demanded by civilization, declaring that the policy of Spain is opposed to any idea of territorial aggrandizement. The Spanish interest in the fate of Morocco was recognized in 1880 by the powers to the extent of an understanding that the views of Spain should be heard in the first instance on all questions affecting Morocco. The powers assented in principle to the proposed conference. France, however, in order to close the way to any further assertion of the pretensions of Spain, insisted that the business of the conference should be restricted to the revision of the Madrid Convention. This limitation, which was supported by Great Britain, Spain was finally forced to accept. The English Government made the suggestion that the powers should guarantee the integrity of the Sultan's dominions in return for concessions of facilities for commerce and of improved government. The various cabinets accepted the invitation to take part in the conference, which was to meet at Madrid before the end of January, 1888. The countries represented in the Madrid Conference of 1880 were Germany, Great Britain, Austria, Belgium, the United States, France, Italy, Holland, Portugal, Sweden and Norway, and Morocco itself. The Spanish minister resident at Tangier, Señor Diosdado, was instructed to inform the Sultan of the circumstances that had occurred in consequence of his illness, and to urge upon him the necessity of granting the commercial rights demanded by the powers. Muley Hassan had himself requested the Spanish Government in August to reopen some of the questions that were discussed, but not finally settled, at the previous international conference. The Spanish minister at Paris sounded the French Government, and found it willing to consider the subject, whereas in 1880 it had categorically refused to acquiesce in a modification of the rights of protection. At the suggestion of M. Flourens, the Spanish Government directed its political representatives in Morocco to collect evidence regarding the inconveniences and abuses of the protection system. The Sultan had reason to suspect the French of aggressive designs on his western frontier, because they had very recently engaged in expeditions against the Figuig and Twat tribes, whose lands lie within the borders of Morocco, and had established military posts and fortifications close to the boundary, if they did not encroach upon the Sultan's dominions. The Spanish Government was the only one whose dealings with the Sultan had been marked throughout with sincerity and justice. The conference at Madrid was rendered practically abortive by France's refusal to accede to the proposals on behalf of Morocco made by Spain, and then supported by Great Britain. The Spanish legation at Tangier is the only one that has kept itself entirely clean from the illegitimate use of the right of protection, and the Spanish Government has consistently urged the justice of the Sultan's demand that foreign protection should be done away with. England acknowledged the evils of the system, but refused to consider proposals for remedying them, except in return for substantial commercial concessions, and in this position was supported by several other powers. The Spanish minister to Morocco then endeavored to persuade Muley Hassan to concede the demands of the powers, the meeting of the proposed conference being postponed from time to time, but could not induce him to throw the country open to foreign capital and enterprise. A new rebellion of more formidable dimensions than that of 1887, followed by a recurrence of the Sultan's sickness, interrupted the negotiations, and caused the conference to be indefinitely postponed.

Outrages on Europeans.—Owing to the failure of the conference negotiations and the exhibition of discord among the Christian powers, or to the unsettled condition of the country resulting from rebellions and the precarious health of the Sultan, the Moors were more insolent toward Christians in 1888 than they had been for many years. British *protégés* were stripped of their possessions, imprisoned, and tortured by order of the kaids. An American *protégé* was arrested at Rabat, and the American Consul-General demanded his release, which the Moorish authorities refused to grant, on the ground that a suit was pending against him when the protection was issued. The matter was finally submitted to the decision of arbitrators. Numerous other outrages were reported.

Revolt of Berber Tribes.—The warlike mountaineers inhabiting the Beni M'Gilol hills on the northern slope of the Atlas, have never been subdued. They boast that eleven sultans have entered their territory, and that only two of them returned alive. The Sultan Muley Hassan, who had extended the boundaries of his dominions in some directions, and aims at a confederation of the Mohammedan states of the Western Soudan as far as Timbuctoo, resolved to conquer this troublesome tribe, which still clings to the Drissian dynasty, having in its midst a pretender, and became aggressive when the ferment pervaded Morocco that was caused by the Sultan's illness. Muley Hassan, who was at Mequinez, took the field with his army in the summer, and after two months of almost daily fighting, during which his army was twice nearly cut in two, he succeeded, as

he supposed, in putting down the revolt, visited cruel vengeance on the kabylas that were reduced to submission, placed governors over the conquered districts, and marched toward the seacoast with the intention of making a promised visit to Tangier, which he had never seen. Kaid Maclean, the English officer who instructs his troops and commands the cavalry, was left at Fez with a part of the army, in order to quell any fresh outbreak. In September the Sultan, who had reached the borders of the Zimouri and Beni Hassan country, received intelligence of a fresh rising of the tribes, and of the massacre of his cousin Muley Souro, who had been entrapped in an ambush and, with 300 of his followers, was put to the sword. Muley Hassan immediately set out upon an expedition to avenge his cousin's death. The tribes rose in the rear of the Sultan's army, exasperated by the taxes he had levied on them to maintain his army of 70,000 men, the troops, perishing of starvation, deserted in large numbers, the enemy attacked him in front, and at last Muley Hassan found himself far in the hills, with neither food nor ammunition. Kaid Maclean was shut up in Fez by the Beni M'Gilol tribe, who were joined by others in that region. The Sultan had excited general indignation by ordering all the members of a certain tribe to be beheaded, on the mistaken supposition that they were concerned in the massacre of his cousin's force. Messengers reached Tangier at last, and Sir William Kirby Green, the British minister, obtained from the Governor of Gibraltar 150 rounds of ammunition, which he sent to Fez. Kaid Maclean broke through the Beni M'Gilol tribe who besieged Fez, and reached the Sultan's camp with the ammunition. Muley Hassan then abandoned the expedition.

MORTON, LEVI PARSONS, Vice-President of the United States, born in Shoreham, Vt., May 16, 1824. His first ancestor was George Morton, who came in the ship "Ann" from England, and landed at Plymouth in 1623. The Morton family afterward settled at Middleborough, Mass. Mr. Morton's father, the Rev. Daniel Oliver Morton, was a Congregational minister, and his mother, Lucretia Parsons, was the daughter of the Rev. Justin Parsons, while her brother, for whom the Vice-President was named, was the first American missionary to Palestine. The Rev. Mr. Morton sent his eldest son to college, but even the marvelous economy of a New England minister's family could not make the few hundred dollars of salary stretch far enough to cover the second boy's expenses, and after partly preparing Levi for Middlebury College, the father reluctantly consented to let him go as clerk into a store at Enfield, Mass., where he remained for two years. He was then sixteen years old, and returning to his home, which had been removed to Bristol, N. H., he taught a district school for a while, and then, at the age of seventeen, entered the store of a Mr. Esterbrook, in Concord. His employer was so pleased with his aptitude for business that he established him in a branch store in Hanover, N. H. (the seat of Dartmouth College), giving the young proprietor an interest in the business. He soon became a favorite with the students, and remained there six years, and then went to Boston, where, in 1849, he entered the house of James M. Beebe

of L. P. Morton & Co., one member of which was Charles W. McCune, afterward of the Buffalo "Courier." In 1863 Mr. McCune withdrew, while the remaining partners established the banking-house of L. P. Morton & Co., at No. 35 Wall Street. A London branch was soon established under the title, L. P. Morton, Burns & Co., but in 1869 that firm was dissolved, Sir

LEVI PARSONS MORTON.

& Co. Two years later, the firm made him a partner, opened a branch in New York known as J. M. Beebe, Morgan & Co., and placed him in it. In 1854 Mr. Morgan (father of Pierpont Morgan, of Morgan, Drexel & Co.) went to London, and Mr. Morton soon afterward organized the firm of Morton & Grinnell, which continued in business until the beginning of the civil war. · In 1856 Mr. Morton had married Miss Lucy Kimball, daughter of Elijah H. Kimball, of Flatlands, Long Island. Late in 1861 Mr. Morton founded the mercantile firm

VOL. XXVIII.—37 A

John Rose, Finance Minister of Canada, becoming Mr. Morton's partner in London, under der the firm-name of Morton, Rose & Co. At the same time George Bliss entered the New York firm. At home the house of Morton, Bliss & Co. rendered material aid to the Government; and abroad, Morton, Rose & Co. became the fiscal agents of the United States, and were active in the negotiations that ended in the Geneva and Halifax fisheries awards. In 1876 Mr. Morton was nominated for Congress by the Republicans of the Eleventh New

York District. In accepting the nomination he wrote: "It is a distinction which I have not solicited, and I am not sure of my fitness for the place. I have never been a politician, have never sought or contemplated holding office, and am by training and tastes simply a man of business. If, however, in your judgment, I can serve the district and protect its interest in Congress, I shall feel constrained to regard your nomination as a plain call to public duty, which I have no right to shirk. I believe the Republic has a right to command the services of its humblest citizen, and in obedience to that conviction I accept the nomination." His opponent was Col. Benjamin A. Willis, a forcible speaker and able politician. Mr. Morton, although defeated, reduced Willis's majority from 2,500 to 400. In 1878 he was renominated, and defeated Col. Willis by 7,000 majority. In 1880 he was again successful against James W. Gerard, Jr. The New York "World," opposed to him in politics, said: "Against Mr. Morton's individual character and his fitness to represent his district in Congress, no one who knows him can have a word to say."

In 1881 President Garfield appointed Mr. Morton minister to France, and he remained such under President Arthur. In 1871 Mrs. Morton had died in their country home, Fairlawn, Newport, R. I. She was noted for her benevolent nature, and, carrying out her feeling, as well as his own, Mr. Morton gave a park of twelve acres to the people of Newport, and built in her memory in Fourth Avenue, New York, contiguous to Grace Church, the beautiful building known as Grace Memorial Chapel. Among his other benefactions was the first contribution of one quarter of the cargo for the ship "Constellation," which was sent by our Government to the sufferers from the Irish famine.

In 1878 Mr. Morton was honorary commissioner to the Paris Exposition, and he was American commissioner-general to the Paris Electrical Exposition, and representative of the United States at the Submarine-Cable Convention. He publicly received, in the name of the people of the United States, the Bartholdi statue of "Liberty enlightening the World." In 1882 and 1887 he was candidate for a United States Senatorship, from New York. Middlebury College, where he has recently founded a professorship, and Dartmouth, conferred upon him the degree of LL. D. He married Miss Street, of Poughkeepsie, whose accomplishments and amiability did much to render his foreign mission successful and his home memorable for its hospitality. They have five children, and a few years ago selected as their summer home a beautiful place called Ellerslie, at Rhinebeck, on the Hudson.

In July, 1888, Mr. Morton was unanimously nominated for Vice-President by the Republican National Convention, on the ticket with Gen. Harrison, which was successful, and he was inaugurated March 4, 1889.

MUSIC, PROGRESS OF, IN 1888. To the novel productions brought out on the operatic stage in 1887 are to be added: "Faust," a musical drama, in a prelude and four acts, by Heinrich Zöllner (Cologne, Stadttheater, December 14), *succès d'estime;* the third act found the most favor. "Die Camisarden" (formerly "Jean Cavalier"), by Anton Langert, entirely rewritten (Coburg, Hoftheater, December 15), conducted by the composer, and received with great applause. "Per Svinaherde" (Peter, the Swineherd), in three acts, by Ivar Hallström; libretto by Christiernson (Stockholm, December 29); with success, repeated to full houses eleven times. The music is graceful, at times characteristic, the libretto contains several striking scenes, and the *mise-en-scène* was magnificent. "Don Pedro dei Medina," an operetta by Lanzini, libretto by Ovidi (Rome, Teatro Costanzi. October), with great success, in which the libretto has no small share, being one of the happiest conceptions of its kind.

During 1888 the dramatic-musical movement did not rise above the average. No great accomplishment is to be recorded, no event of significant augury fell to its share. The number of new grand operas produced in France, Belgium, and Germany was scant; England furnished only one; and even Italy was more reserved than usual. Nor was the field of comic opera worked very extensively. On the other hand, the production of new operettas was fairly overwhelming. In the following we record the facts in chronological order, grouped according to their national origin:

Operas.—"La Dame de Monsoreau," in five acts, by Gaston Salvayre, libretto by Auguste Maquet, Paris, Opéra. January 30, was a complete failure, in spite of the gorgeous *mise-en-scène,* and the creditable performance on the part of the artists; the displeasure of the public was aroused as much by the libretto as by the music. "Jocelyn," in four acts, by Benjamin Godard, libretto by Armand Silvestre and Victor Capoul (Brussels, Théâtre de la Monnaie, February 25), obtained a brilliant success on this occasion, but it remains to be seen how much of it was due to the influence of the friends of the composer and the librettists, who had flocked over from Paris; to the impartial, the weaknesses of both the musical score and the libretto are evident; the representation, including the *mise-en-scène,* was excellent. The opera was subsequently given in Paris, at the Théâtre Lyrique du Château-d'Eau, October 13, with no particular effect; the representation was insufficient, and the *mise-en-scène* paltry. "Le Roi d'Ys," in three acts, by Edouard Lalo, libretto by Eduard Blau (Paris, Opéra-Comique, May 7), was given with decided success; singers, orchestra, and stage-managers deserved great credit. "Le Roi Lear," in four acts, by Armand Raynaud, text by Henri Lapierre (Toulouse, Théâtre du Capitole, June 1), met with a favorable reception. "Renaud," by Gilbert des Roches—Baroness Legoux (Boulogne-sur-Mer, during the summer). "Richilde," in four acts and ten tableaus, by Émile Matthieu, who also wrote the libretto (Brussels, Théâtre de la Monnaie, December 19), was given with great success; the work, whose subject is from the mediæval history of Flanders, shows dramatic skill and much inventive power; the instrumentation is excellent, and a gorgeous *mise-en-scène* contributed to the result. "Hertha," a romantic opera in four acts, by Franz Curti (Altenburg, in February). "Aphrodite," by Nicolaus Milan (Agram, Croatia, in February), with considerable success. "König Arpad," by Verhey, libretto by Van Loghem (Rotterdam, German Opera, end of February). "Dido," in three acts, by Otto Neitzel (Weimar, March 18), obtained a fair success. "Harold," by Eduard Nápravnik, the first time outside of Russia (Prague, National Theatre, in April), was well received; the music is not very original, but appears throughout to be the product of a refined musician. "Satanella," by Reznicek. (Prague, Deutsches Landestheater, May 13), met with a very favorable reception. "Der Sturm," in three acts, by Anton Urspruch, text by Emil Pirazzi, freely after Shakespeare's "Tempest" (Frankfort, Stadttheater, May 17), was rewarded with great applause. "Murillo," in three acts, by Ferdinand Langer, libretto by E. Henle (Mannheim, Hoftheater, September 16); the opera had been given last year, but appeared entirely remodeled, and obtained a complete and well-deserved success. "De Geuzenbruid," by Melos, libretto by Marnix (Amsterdam, in October); "Katherine und Lambert," by Van der Linden (Amsterdam, in November). "Nelly," in three acts, by Carl Bouman (Dordrecht, in November). "Aladdin," by Emil Horneman, who also wrote the libretto, after the "Arabian Nights" (Copenhagen, Royal Theatre, November 19). "Eugen Onégin," in three acts, by Tschaikowsky, the first time outside of Russia (Prague, National Theatre, early in December), conducted by the composer, and very successful. "Die Gletscherjungfrau," by Franz Curti (Altenburg, Hoftheater, December 25). "Das steinerne Herz," a romantic opera, in four acts, by Ignaz Brüll, libretto by J. V. Widmann, after Hauff's tale (Prague, Deutsches Landestheater, December 19), was brought out with signal success, taking immediate hold with its popular strains and dance rhythms, which never fall below the high standard of the composer's refinement; the first and third acts are the most attractive. It is a genuine example of the good old-time folk-opera, as produced by Dittersdorf and Weigl, modernized. "The Corsican Brothers," by George Fox, libretto by Charles Bradberry (London, Crystal Palace, September 25). Among Italian operas may be mentioned Verdi's "Otello," as having been produced for the first time on this side of the Atlantic, in New York, Academy of Music, April 16, by the Campanini troupe, with great artistic success. The novelties in Italy were: "Asraël," by Alberto Franchetti, libretto by Fontana (Reggio d'Emilia, Teatro Municipale, in February, with brilliant success. "Diana d'Almeida," by Raffaele Ronco (Genoa, Teatro Carlo Felice, February 22), met with a favorable reception. "Il Saggio," by Alfredo Soffredini (Lucera, Collegio Reale, February) had great success. "Nestorio," by Galignani (Milan, Scala, April 3), with indifferent result. "Carmosina," by João Gomes de Aranjo, a Brazilian composer, libretto by Ghislanzoni (Milan, Teatro Del Verme, in April), was received with applause. "Don Pedro," by Castegnaro (Vicenza, June 21), was very successful. "Ivanhoe," by Ciardi (Prato, Teatro Metastasio). "Don Prospero," by Garzia (Naples, Teatro Rossini, in September). "Bice di Roccaforte," by Giacomo Medini (Savona, Politeama, in October). "Medgè," by Spiro Samara (Rome, Teatro Costanzi, December 12), met with a most favorable reception. There were also two Italian operas given in Portugal: "La Donna Bianca," by Alfredo Keil, and "Ribelli," by Marino Mancinelli (both at Lisbon, Teatro San Carlos).

Comic Operas.—"Die Drei Pintos," in three acts, by Carl Maria von Weber (Leipsic, Stadttheater, January 20), based upon the sketches and manuscripts left by the composer and upon the libretto by Theodor Hell, the opera was compiled and finished, the musical part by Kapellmeister Gustav Mahler, the dramatic part by Capt. Carl von Weber, grandson of the composer. This work occupied the master before the composition of the "Freischütz" was completed, and as late as the end of 1824 he had not given up his intention to finish it, although the last note of the existing sketches was written in November, 1821. Meyerbeer proposed to complete the opera, but desisted; Jules Benedict, Weber's pupil and biographer, declined to undertake the task, which has now been very creditably achieved by the able orchestra leader of the Leipsic Stadt-theater and Capt. Weber. Both were recipients of ovations on the night of the first performance, which was unusually brilliant, the house being crowded to its utmost capacity by a most enthusiastic audience, among whom were to be seen many foreign musical and dramatic celebrities. The director, Herr Stägemann, who had taken charge of the entire *mise en scène*, and the artists, shared largely in the generous applause. The opera was subsequently given at Hamburg (April 5), Munich (April 10), Dresden (May 10), Prague (August 18), Coburg (November 6), Breslau and Bremen (also in November). "Turandot," by Theobald Rehbaum, text freely after Gozzi's tale (Berlin, Royal Opera House, April 11). The work, which was very favorably received, contains many pleasing melodies; composer and performers were called after each act. "Im Namen des Gesetzes," in three acts, text and music by Siegfried Ochs (Hamburg, Stadt-theater, November 3), met with a kindly re-ception. "Die Königin von Leon," romantic-comic opera, by V. E. Becker (Nuremberg, November 15), obtained a fair success. "Le Diable à Yvetot," by Gessler, libretto by Paul Stark (Rouen, Théâtre des Arts). "La Fau-vette du Temple," by André Messager (Brus-sels, Alhambra, January 26); the work is very attractive, and received much applause for its *mise en scène* as well as its clever interpreta-tion. "La Perle de Brimborio," by Castelain and Coupin (Marseilles, in February), with great success. "Les Réservistes," by Félix Boisson, libretto by E. Le Roy (Châlons-sur-Marne, in February). "Le Dîner de Madelon," by Maurice Lefèvre, libretto by Désaugiers (Brussels, Théâtre de la Monnaie, March 6); the audience found the "*diner*" much to its taste, especially as it was extremely well served by the artist waiters. "Le Bossu," in four acts, by Charles Grisart, libretto by Bocage and Livrat, after Paul Féval's novel (Paris, Théâtre de Gaîté, in March), was a fair suc-cess. "Le Puits qui parle," by Edmond Au-dran, libretto by Nuitter, Beaumont, and Bu-rani (Paris, Théâtre des Nouveautés, middle of March), found great favor, and will probably continue on the repertory. "Une Aventure d'Arlequin," by Paul and Lucien Hillemacher, libretto by Judicis (Brussels, Théâtre de la Monnaie, March 22), was fairly successful, the music being line and spirited, while the libretto proved rather dull, and the performance was only moderately good. "Le Dragon de la Reine," by Leopold Wenzel, libretto by Pierre Decourcelle and François Beauvallet (Brussels, Alhambra, March 23), was given with signal success, well deserved by the attractive music and the interesting libretto, which is fre-quently amusing; the time of action is 1736; *mise en scène* and ballet were above reproach. "Le Baiser de Suzon," by Herman Bemberg, text by Pierre Barbier (Paris, Opéra-Comique, June 4), *succès d'estime.* "L'Amour au Vil-lage," by Émile Camys, libretto by Albert Réandel (Paris, Menus-Plaisirs, in July). "Le Bouquet," by Chaulier, libretto by V. Duleron (Boulogne-sur-Mer, in August) was well re-ceived. "L'Héritage de Chaudebec," by Bag-gers, libretto by Riesse (Vichy, in August), with fair success. "Nella," by Sudessi (Bag-nères-de-Luchon, Théâtre du Casino, in Au-gust). "L'Escadron volant de la Reine," by Henry Litolff, libretto by D'Ennery and Bré-sil (Paris, Opéra-Comique, December 14), had only a *succès d'estime.* "Isline," fairy opera, by André Messager, libretto by Catulle Men-dès (Paris, Théâtre de la Renaissance, last week in December). afforded much pleasure to connoisseurs. "The Yeomen of the Guard," in two acts, by Arthur Sullivan, libretto by Gil-bert, after Victor Hugo (London, Savoy The-atre, October 4), conducted by the composer, who, with the librettist and the representatives of the principal *rôles*, was called at the close of the performance and overwhelmed with applause. As the work was soon after given in this city at the Casino, and held that stage for several months, New Yorkers are suffi-ciently familiar with its subject and music to need no commentary. "Babette," by Gustave Michiels, libretto by Ordonneau and Verneuil (London, Strand Theatre, Jan. 26). "Carina," by Julia Woolf, libretto by F. L. Blanchard (London, Opéra-Comique, in October), met with a friendly reception. "La Sérénade," by J. Batchelor and O. Gaggs, libretto by Lucke M'Hale (Manchester, Prince's Theatre). "The Grand Duke," by Tito Mattei, libretto by Far-ney and Murray (London, Avenue Theatre). In Italy appeared "Il Grembiulino rosa," by Dr. Azzo Albertoni, who also wrote the libretto (Castelfranco, Venetia, in spring), with great success; "I Cerretani," in three acts, by Ri-naldo Caffi (Cremona, Teatro Ricci); "Papà Martin," by Cagnoni (Rome, Teatro Nazionale, in June); "Gli Studenti," by Rota (Bologna, Teatro Contavalli, in October) was very favor-ably received; "Una Tazza di Tè," by Sca, rano, libretto by Ugo Flores (Turin, Circolo Artistico), met with considerable applause.

Operettas.—"Mam'zelle Crénom," by Léon Vasseur. libretto by Jaime Duval (Paris, Bouffes-Parisiens, January 19), pleased particularly because of its amusing subject. "La Volière," by Charles Lecocq (Paris, Théâtre des Nou-veautés, February 8). "La Belle Sophie," by Edmond Missa, libretto by Paul Burani and Eugène Adenis (Paris, Menus-Plaisirs, April 11), with moderate success. "Le Valet de Cœur," by Raoul Pugno, libretto by Paul Ferrier and Charles Clairville (Paris, Bouffes-Parisiens, between April 15 and 22), was much applauded. "Le Masque de Velours," text and music by Prosper Morton (Laval, May 18). "Miette," in three acts, by Edmond Audran, libretto by Maurice Ordonneau (Paris, Théâtre de la Renaissance, in September), with an indifferent result. "Oscarine," by Victor Roger, text by Nuitter and Albert Guinon (Paris, Bouffes-Parisiens, October 16), with fair result. "La Gardeuse d'Oies," by Paul Lacome, text by Leterrier and Vanloo (Paris, Théâtre de la Renaissance, October 26), was well received. "La Petite Froude," by Au-dran, libretto by Bisson and Duru (Paris, Folies-Dramatiques, middle of November). "La Veillée des Noces," by Frédéric Toulmouche, libretto by Bisson and Bureau-Jettiot (Paris, Menus-Plaisirs, end of November), earned much applause. "Le Mariage avant la Lettre," by Olivier Métra, libretto by Jaime and Duval (Paris, Bouffes-Parisiens, December 5), was given with doubtful success; the music of the popular dance composer, to which the Paris-ians had looked forward with great expecta-tions, pleased only partially and was powerless to elevate the disreputable libretto. "L'En-tr'acte," by André Martinet, libretto by Ma-xime Boucheron (Paris, Cercle de la Presse, last week in December), was received with applause. "Der Königspage," by Franz Soucoup (Baden, near Vienna, February 4), was favorably received. "Der Sänger von Palermo," by Alfred Zamara, Jr., text by Bernhard Buchbinder (Vienna, Carl-Theater, February 14), with signal success; composer and librettist were repeatedly called before the footlights; the music is distinguished by great wealth of melody and a certain bearing of dignity; a charming love-duet, a terzet in waltz form, and a Sicilian folk song, were particularly applauded. "Der Fürst von Sevilla," by Fritz Baselt, text by Mordtmann (Nuremberg, Stadttheater, April 8), met with a very favorable reception; the music is full of life and melody. "Pagenstreiche," by Carl Weinberger, text by Hugo Wittmann, after Kotzebue's comedy (Vienna, Theater an der Wien, April 28), was very successful, and bore testimony to the young composer's talent and skill. "Der Feldwebel," in three acts, by J. Bartz, text by H. Rockstroh (Moscow, German Club, April 19), conducted by the composer, who received much applause for his skillful production. "Marràzevi," text and music by Adolf Wilt (Hamburg, Carl-Schultze Theater, May 15), met with success. "Der Savoyarde," by Ottokar Feyth, text by Franz Josef Brackl and Victor Léon (Munich, Gärtnerplatz-Theater, June 9), was kindly received. "Madelaine," by Ludwig Engländer, text by Carl Hauser (Hamburg, Carl-Schultze Theater, June 26). "Liebesdiplomaten," in three acts, by Carl Dibbern, text by Heinrich Kadelburg and the composer (Carlsbad, Stadttheater, August 1), was received with applause. "Der Freibeuter" (first given in Paris under the title "Robert Surcouf"), by Planquette, libretto by Chivot and Duru (Vienna, Carl-Theater, September 1), had decided success. "Der Schelm von Bergen," by Alfred Oehlschlegel, libretto by Conrad Loewe and Carl Lindau, freely after Julius von der Traun's tale of the same title (Vienna, Theater an der Wien, September 29), met with a mild reception. "Gräfin Wildfang," by Wilhelm Behre, text by Ludwig Ordemann (Berlin, Friedrich-Wilhelmstädtisches Theater, October 5), received only limited applause. "Sataniel," in three acts, by Adolph Ferron (Brünn, Stadttheater, October 26), was successful. "Die Jagd nach dem Glück," by Suppé, text by Richard Genée and Zappert (Vienna, Carl-Theater, October 27), conducted by the composer, with brilliant success, fully deserved by the melodious music and the amusing libretto; the performance was admirable, and composer and actors were repeatedly called before the footlights. "Simplicius," by Johann Strauss (first given in Vienna last year), completely remodeled (Prague, Deutsches Landestheater, November 10), conducted with great success by the composer. "Der Liebeshof," by Adolf Müller, Jr., text by Hugo Wittmann and Oscar Blumenthal (Vienna, Theater an der Wien, November 14), obtained a fair success. "Der Zaunkönig," by Bernhard

Triebel, libretto by Sigurd Ring and Sigward Roche (Frankfort, Stadttheater, November 16), was received with much applause. "Mirolan," by M. Fall, libretto by M. Heldern (Olmütz, Stadttheater, in November), won a complete success in spite of the deficient performance. "Ein Deutschmeister," romantic-comic operetta, by Carl M. Ziehrer, libretto by Genée and Zappert (Vienna, Carl-Theater, November 30), was given with brilliant success. The truly Viennese dance and march rhythms of the music electrified the public, whose merriment was roused at the same time by the amusing libretto. "Karin," by Hermann Zumpe, text by Fr. Wilibald Wulff and Eduard Pochmann (Hamburg, Carl-Schultze Theater, December 1), conducted by the composer, who was rewarded with generous applause; most of the musical numbers had to be repeated, and the interesting subject, based upon historical facts, contributed essentially to the effectiveness of the skillfully elaborated libretto. "Die Bonifaciusnacht," a romantic-comic operetta, by Friedrich von Thul, text by Ludwig Sendlach (Prague, Deutsches Landestheater, December 8), was very successful. "Der Posaunist von Scherkingen," by Franz Beier, text by Otto Ewald (Cassel, Hoftheater, December 17), a parody of Nessler's "Trompeter von Säkkingen," which put the audience in the merriest frame of mind. "Die Royalisten," by Manas, text by A. Philipp (Magdeburg, Wilhelm-Theater, December 27), was given with fair success. In England we find only "Quits," by John Crook, libretto by Hugues (London, Avenue Theatre); and in Italy we gather from among a score the following, which were reported as having won fair success: "Le Nozze sospirate," by Oreste Carlini (Florence, Teatro Alfieri, in January). "Ercole ed Euristeo," by Virgilio Galleani (Milan, Teatro Foscati). "Lorenzino," by Lanzini (Rome, Teatro Metastasio, in June), "La Mandragola," by Achille Graffigna, and "Raffaelo e la Fornarina," by Maggi (both at Turin, Teatro d'Alfieri). In Spain and Portugal appeared a few operettas and zarzuelas, among which may be mentioned, for the sake of the curious title more than for any other reason, "O Imperador Alchim Fá XVIII," by Rio de Carvalho (Lisbon, Teatro do Rato).

The Ballet. — No notice has hitherto been taken of a theatrical composition closely connected with the operatic stage which, if answering the proper artistic conditions, may possess as much merit and claim as great prominence as any drama or opera—the scenic representation, through pantomime and dance, of a dramatic or comic action, accompanied by music—the ballet. Although its origin may be traced back to the pantomimes of the ancient Romans, it was developed, in its modern form, in Italy, toward the end of the fifteenth century, when it appears as a theatrical performance, enacted by dancing, but accompanied by speech and often also by singing. These entertainments were devised in the service and for the pleasure of the courts; and princes, princesses, and courtiers took part in the performances, which from that time forth counted among the most brilliant festivities of the splendor-loving courts of Europe, and often were executed with an extravagance surpassing all reasonable limits. The ballet reached its true artistic development at the court of France, for which Baltazarini, one of the foremost violinists of his time, composed his famous "Ballet Comique de la Reine," in 1581, for the wedding of the Duc de Joyeuse. More than eighty grand ballets were performed at court during the reign of Henry IV, and in the beginning of the seventeenth century the ballet was essentially improved by Ottavio Rinuncini, whom Maria de Medici patronized with royal liberality. Under Louis XIV, who often, and as late as 1699 took part, with his courtiers, in the performances, the ballet attained to great perfection. A new epoch began for it with the foundation of the grand opera through Lully and Quinault, when dance and pantomime were required to heighten the sumptuousness of their operas. The first attempt of this kind, which the author called a pastorale, was "Les Fêtes de Bacchus et de l'Amour," given with extraordinary success in 1671, and these ballet-operas, in which the dance was entirely subordinate to the lyric part, were much admired, until Antoine Houdart de la Motte reformed it in 1697, by expressing the dramatic action through the ballet itself. The first work of this kind was "L'Europe Galante," which, with the music by Campra, was performed in 1697, and served as a model for the time following. Through several modifications, the most important of which was made by Cabussac in 1747, the ballet reached its dramatic independence about the middle of the eighteenth century, when Jean Georges Noverre became its true creator as a special branch of histrionic art, by separating it entirely from the opera, and raising it to an independent performance enacted by dance, pantomime, and music, divided into several acts. A most peculiar and brilliant feature were, in the beginning of this century, the great pantomimic ballets of Vicenzo Galeotti, royal ballet-master at Copenhagen, who, following in Noverre's path, went a step further, subordinating the dance to the dramatic-plastic principle, in the spirit of the antique pantomime. These gorgeous and ingenious creations became very little known outside of Denmark, and ceased there with Galeotti's death in 1817. In a similar manner they were continued longest in Milan, which in the representation of the grandest tableaux and the daring attempts in pantomimic expression had no equal. As regards the music to the ballet, its function is not merely that of ordinary dance music, to support the rhythmical motions, but it has to interpret situations, and

lends a sort of language to the mimic and pantomimic exhibition; ample scope is therefore given it for characteristic instrumentation, and the description of various sentiments, and even great musicians, like Gluck, Cherubini, and Beethoven, have not deemed it beneath their dignity to write ballet music, and have achieved important results in this field. In the following we enumerate the new ballets that have made their appearance since 1876:

1876: "Sylvia ou La Nymphe de Diane," mythological ballet in three acts (four tableaux), by Jules Barbier and Louis Mérante, music by Léo Delibes (Paris, Opéra, June 14); the fundamental idea of this work is borrowed from Tasso's pastoral "Aminta," which in the Italian poet's florid language created such a sensation (1572), but whose barren subject, transformed and amplified in "Sylvia," could scarcely have aroused great interest in its stale mythological apparatus, if the composer had not succeeded in producing such music as would not only assume a more prominent part than usual in the ballet, but hold its own even if severed from the latter. Among the numbers that pleased particularly were the waltz in the first act, the introduction to the second, and the pizzicato polka in the third act. "Madeleine," pantomimic ballet by Taglioni, music by Peter Ludwig Hertel (Berlin, Royal Opera House, in March); there is much dramatic life and action in this ballet, which in scenic effects, ensembledances, and grouping must satisfy the most fastidious taste. The music contributed much to the success of the new work. "Les Fumeurs de Kiff," by Gaston Berardi, music by Émile Matthieu (Brussels, Théâtre de la Monnaie).

1877: "Loreley," by Monplaisir, music by Dall'Argine (Milan, Teatro della Scala, in January), won great applause. "Le Fandango," by Meilhac and Halévy, music by Salvayre (Paris, Opéra, November 26).

1878: "La Stella di Granata," by Marzagora (Rome, Teatro Apollo, in March). "Ein glückliches Ereigniss," by Taglioni, music by Hertel (Berlin, Royal Theatre, in October), introduces us to the circle of the famous Dutch artists Jan Steen, Jan van Goyen, Rembrandt, Hals, and Van der Helst, telling of merry and interesting episodes in their lives; the composer has again successfully displayed his charming talent as the great ballet-master's musical accompanist.

1879: "Yedda," music by Metra (Paris, Opéra, January 17). "Djellah oder die Touristen in Indien" (Vienna, Opera House).

1880: "Morgano," by Taglioni, music by Hertel (Milan, Teatro della Scala). "Sieba," in twelve tableaux, by Manzotti, music by Venanzi and Marcuso (Trieste, Teatro Communale, in March); the subject is taken from the Edda; Sieba is a Valkyria who falls in love with Arnoldo, the young king of Thule, and in consequence is renounced by Odin and loses her immortality, but in the end finds her earthly happiness in the union with Arnoldo. "Der Stock im Eisen," in three acts, by Pasquale Borri, after an old Vienna legend, music by Franz Doppler (Vienna, Opera House, in October); the extremely popular subject of the old mysterious Vienna landmark secured at the outset a favorable reception for this choreographic product, successfully accompanied by the composer's music, which reaches its climax in a waltz in the first act, and in the spirited march of the finale. "La Korrigane," a fantastic ballet in two acts, by François Coppée, music by Charles Widor (Paris, Opéra, December 1); the libretto is based upon a popular legend of Brittany, where Korrigane is the name of some fairies who compel the belated wanderer to dance with them in the moonlight, and otherwise exert great magic power. The *mise-en-scène* by Louis Mérante, deserves much credit, but the great success is mainly due to the composer's poetic score, which rises far above the level of ordinary ballet music.

1881: "Excelsior," a fantastic-allegorical ballet, in six acts (eleven tableaux), by Manzotti (Milan, Scala, in January), was greeted with enthusiastic applause by the Milanese public and critics; the fundamental idea of the contest between the spirit of light and that of darkness runs through the six acts of this spectacular curiosity, in which several modern inventions and discoveries play a part, carrying the spectator into various countries, and ending in a most brilliant apotheosis, intended to represent the union of all nations through modern science. "In Versailles," a lyric-choreographic tableau in one act, by Louis Frappart, music by Franz Doppler (Vienna, Opera House, March 9); the scene of this charming conception being the court of Louis XIV, ample opportunity was offered for the display of gorgeous costumes, which, added to the pretty dances and the graceful music, secured for the novelty, a most favorable reception. "Der Spielmann," by Telle, after a sketch of Gauthier, music by J. Forster (Vienna, Opera House, in June): the subject is modeled partially after the well-known legend of the rat-catcher, the music, especially of the first part, has a good deal of merit, and was much applauded. "Pygmalion," in three acts, libretto and music by Prince J. Trubetzkoi (Vienna, Opera House, November 22); the end of the pretty fable in Ovid's narrative is the starting-point in the ballet. The sculptor is given a palm-branch, whose touch imparts life to his creation, but which, when broken, changes the living again into a statue; an Egyptian king, who is present at the miracle falls in love with the maiden, and carries her off to make her his queen, but Pygmalion appears with the palm-branch, breaks it, and life vanishes from the blooming form. She is revived by the goddess, who, rejecting the cruel artist, ascends heavenward with the beauty; the music, though pleasing, can hardly be called original.

1882: "Namouna," by Nuitter and Petipa, music by Edouard Lalo (Paris, Opéra, March 6); the subject is borrowed from the charming poem of Alfred de Musset, in which the beautiful slave Namouna appears repeatedly as the guardian angel of her benefactor Ottavio, who had given her her freedom; neither libretto nor music did justice to the poet's conception. "Melusine," by Carl Telle, after Moritz von Schwind's well-known pictorial cycle, set to music by Franz Doppler (Vienna, Opera House, October 4), met with immediate and great success. The music of this composition is very attractive and melodious, including many spirited dances, and describing the situations very characteristically.

"1883: Les Poupées Électriques," music by Frédéric Barbier (Paris, Palace Théâtre, middle of March). "La Vague," by Justament, music by Victor Roger (Paris, Palace Théâtre, April 9). "Endymion," by Louis Gallet, music by Albert Cohen (Paris, Cirque d'Hiver). "Die Assassinen," by Archduke Johann, music by J. Forster (Vienna, Opera House, November 19); the scene is laid in the time of Frederick II of Hohenstaufen, and the whole work, for which the royal author had even made the drawings for all the decorations, was greeted with unanimous applause. "La Farandole," music by Théodore Dubois (Paris, Opéra, early in December), obtained full and well-deserved success; the action is simple and easily comprehensible, at the same time having its poetic charm, and the music contains much that is fine and ingenious.

1884: "Nurjahd," in two acts, by Ch. Guillemin, music by Eichelberg (Berlin, Royal Opera House, end of February). "Der Vater der Debûtantin," anonymous, after the farce with the same title, music by A. M. Willmer (Vienna, Opera House, March 26). "Harlekin als Elektriker," by Julius Price, music by Josef Hellmesberger, Jr., (ibid). "Die Rheinnixe," by Annetta Balbo, music by Josef Miroslav Weber (Wiesbaden). "Un'Avventura di Carnevale," by Borri, music by Giorza (Milan, Teatro dal Verme). "Sakuntala," by Friedrich Uhl, after Kalidasa's drama, music by S. Bachrich (Vienna, Opera House, in October), met with tolerable success; the music, abounding in reminiscences, offers here and there an independent trait, moving in piquant rhythms. In the waltz and csárdás the composer is at his best, and it was altogether a happy thought to associate the gypsy music, on this occasion, with its Indian home.

1885: "Wiener Walzer," in three tableaux, by Louis Frappart and Franz Gaul, the music adapted by Josef Bayer (Vienna, Opera House, January 10), was a successful attempt to give in these tableaux a sketch of the history of the Vienna waltz; the intermediate music consisted of waltzes by Schubert, Josef Lanner, and Johann Strauss (father and son), and the public greeted its old favorites with enthusiastic applause. "Messalina," by Luigi

Danesi, music by Giaquinta (Milan, Scala, in January), was given with great success. "La Tzigane," by Edmond Cattier, music by Stoumon (Brussels, Théâtre de la Monnaie.

1886: "Amor," by Manzotti, music by Marenco (Milan, Scala, in February), had great success, and was immediately accepted for performance at the Opera House of Vienna, the Théâtre Eden of Paris, the Victoria Theatre in Berlin, the Teatro Costanzi of Rome, and the National Theatre in Prague. "Uriella," a fantastic *ballet-divertissement* after Mazielier (Frankfort, Stadttheater, March 16). "Pierrot Macabre," by Hannot and Hansen, music by Lanciani (Brussels, Théâtre de la Monnaie, in March). "Fata Morgana," lyric-choreographic drama in four acts, by Mosenthal, music by Josef Hellmesberger, Jr. (Vienna, Opera House, March 30), an attempt to blend opera and ballet; the work is well equipped musically, and was heartily applauded. "Les Deux Pigeons," in two acts (three tableaux), by Henry Régnier and L. Mérante, after La Fontaine's fable, music by André Messager (Paris, Opéra, October 18), was eminently successful; the scene is on the coast of Thessaly, and presents a series of brilliant pictures and surprising effects, well accompanied by the composer's easily flowing music. "Deutsche Märsche," in three acts (four tableaux), by Alfred Holzbock and Louis Frappart, music by Josef Bayer (Berlin, Royal Opera House, October 23), received cordial applause. "Viviane," by Gondinet, music by Raoul Pugno and Clément Lippacher (Paris, Théâtre Éden, October 28), met with decided success. "Dresdina," by Hansen, music by M. Jacobi (London, Alhambra Theatre, in November), in which the finest products of German ceramic art in the last century are impersonated on the stage; the exquisite figures, created by the industry of Dresden, Meissen, and Ludwigsburg were represented faithfully after the models, the unique combination of colors of that art period producing a dazzling effect. "Myosotis," by Saracco, music by Flon (Brussels, Théâtre de la Monnaie, December 11). "Ein Märchen aus der Champagne," an allegorical-fantastic ballet, by Willmer, music by Ignaz Brüll (Vienna, Opera House, December 14), met with a complimentary reception; the music, without showing prominently characteristic qualities, is pleasing and elegant.

1887: "Der Blumen Rache," by August Reissmann (Weisbaden, Hoftheater, February 5); the subject is borrowed from the well-known poem by Freiligrath, and was most skillfully interpreted by the composer. "Nedjira," by Nuitter, music by Paul Gennevray (Monte Carlo, Monaco, in February), was given with great success. "Die verwandelte Katze," by Zell, music by Josef Hellmesberger, Jr. (Vienna, Opera House, February 14), earned cordial applause, especially for the composer's refined music, which includes several charming dances. "Orphée et les Bacchantes," by D'Alexandri and Felix Galey, music by the latter (Toulouse, Théâtre du Capitole, in March), was successful. "Les Gitanos," by G. Adrien, music by Marius Carman (Paris, Folies-Bergères, in March). "Narenta," by Manzotti, music by De Giorza (Milan, Scala, in March). "Le Lion amoureux," in one act, with choruses, by Cosseret and Agoust, after La Fontaine, music by Felix Pardon (Brussels, Théâtre de la Monnaie, about the middle of March). "Lauretta," comic ballet by Ginghini, music by Bernhard Triebel (Frankfort, Opera House, April 21). "Le Château de Mac-Arrot," music by Cieutat (Paris, Folies-Bergères, in April). "Les Constellations," music by Laffont (Marseilles, Grand-Théâtre, in April), met with decided success. "Die Harlemer Tulpe," music by Scheel (St. Petersburg, in October).

1888: "Teodora," by Grassi, music by Marenco (Naples, Teatro San Carlo, in January). "Au fond des Bois," by Léopold Roux, music by Gustave Mack (Nantes, in March). "Calirrhoë," by Elzéar Rougier, music by Mlle. Chaminade (Marseilles, Grand Théâtre, in March). "Fleur de Neiges," by Ricard, music by Albert Cahen (Geneva, Grand Théâtre, April 6). "Rolla," by Manzotti, music by Angeli (Paris, Théâtre Eden, May 24). "La Rose d'Amour," by Kathi Lanner, music by Hervé, and "Diana," by the same authors (London, Empire Theatre, the first in July, the second in December). "Antiope," by Casati, music by Georges Jacobi (London, Alhambra Theatre, in July). "La Recluta," comic ballet, by Le Grassi, music by Herbin (Palermo, Circo Universale, in July or August). "Die Puppenfee," pantomimic *divertissement*, in one act, by J. Hassreiter and Franz Gaul, music by Josef Baier (Vienna, Opera House, October 4). "Il Saltimbanco," by Pogna, music by Bonicioli (Milan, Teatro dal Verme, in October). "Milenka," music by Jan Blockx (Brussels, Théâtre de la Monnaie, first week in November).

N

NAZARENES. The Nazarenes are a denomination composed of persons who seceded from the Christadelphians in 1873, on account of dissent from the doctrines of that sect on the depravity of the human race and their ascription to Christ of a share and inheritance in that depravity, as expressed in the article of the Christadelphian "Statement of First Principles," "He (Christ) inherited the consequences of Adam's sin, including the sentence of death." This doctrine the Nazarenes vigorously oppose, and teach that Jesus Christ was God's only begotten son, that he was "holy, harmless, undefiled, and separate from sinners," by virtue of this divine begetting; and thus possessing an unforfeited life, he was in a position to give that life as a ransom for the race of which he was not a member. The Nazarenes are looking for the early second coming of Christ, when he and "his immortal brethren" will rule the whole earth in righteousness from Jerusalem. They are believers in conditional immortality, regard sin as the only devil, hold that the fourth commandment is abrogated, and disbelieve in the unity of God and Christ. Their churches are in England.

NEBRASKA. State Government.—The following were the State officers during the year: Governor, John M. Thayer, Republican; Lieutenant-Governor, H. H. Shedd; Secretary of State, George L. Laws; Treasurer, Charles H. Willard; Auditor of Public Accounts, H. A. Babcock; Attorney-General, William Leese; Superintendent of Public Instruction, George B. Lane; Commissioner of Public Lands and Buildings, Joseph Scott; Chief-Justice of the Supreme Court, M. B. Reese; Associate Justices, Samuel Maxwell, Amasa Cobb.

Finances.—The financial condition of the State is highly satisfactory. The receipts and expenditures of the treasury for the past two years are as follow: Balance in treasury, Nov. 30, 1886, $944,352.76; receipts, Dec. 1, 1886, to Nov. 30, 1888, $4,236,528.94; total receipts, $5,180,881.70; disbursements, Dec. 1, 1886, to Nov. 30, 1888, $4,244,582.98; balance in treasury, Nov. 30, 1888, $936,298.72. Of the total receipts, $2,287,093.43 was raised by taxation, and $1,681,136.45 was revenue from land and other sources. The levy of 1888 will yield the following amounts: General fund, $871,668.63; school fund, $66,004.80; capitol fund, $132,009.60; sinking fund, $27,596.49; with other funds making a total of $1,325,887.79.

For the next two years the Legislature is asked to appropriate $2,890,294.57 for the expenses of the State Government and public institutions. This is an increase of $846,725.84 over the estimates of two years ago. The assessment of 1888 gave the value of the property of the State for taxation at $176,012,820.45, a total increase for two years of $32,080,249.94. The rate of taxation for State purposes for 1887 was 8¼ mills, and for 1888, 7¼ mills on each dollar valuation. The Governor, in his message, says the valuation rests on a fictitious basis, and, if property had been assessed at its true value, the amount given above would have been ten times as large. This seems to be due to a desire of the counties to escape taxation for State purposes. The Governor gives the following table, compiled from official sources, showing the assessment value of the principal kinds of property in Nebraska and the adjoining States to prove that the assessment valuation in Nebraska is far below the actual value.

PROPERTY.	Minnesota.	Kansas.	Iowa.	Nebraska.
Land, per acre.......	$7 46	$4 24	$7 98	$3 53
Horses...............	67 30	31 61	31 56	19 67
Cattle...............	22 21	9 50	10 97	5 53
Mules................	63 53	....	36 07	23 01
Hogs.................	2 47	1 60	1 91	1 07

Education.—The report of the State Superintendent of Public Instruction shows the schools to be in a prosperous condition. The total amount contributed for public education for the year just closed was $4,057,274.66, an increase of $934,659.84 over the amount of the previous year. The value of school property is reported at $5,123,179 for 1888, $4,779,116.22 for 1887, and $3,821,317 for 1886. The total number of school-children is 298,006. Of these, 215,889 are enrolled as pupils in the schools. This is an increase of nearly 50,000 children in two years. The total number in average attendance for the year was 129,623. The following table, giving the number of teachers employed and the amounts paid in salaries to teachers, shows the rapid increase in school accomodations:

ITEMS.	1886.	1888.
Number of males..............	2,605	2,753
Number of females............	5,984	7,184
Days employed, males.........	217,741	258,152
Days employed, females.......	494,766	642,886
Wages paid, males............	$464,652 78	$557,118 87
Wages paid, females..........	$858,644 46	$1,142,670 74
Average monthly wages, males.	$42 68	$43 18
Average monthly wages, females	$34 70	$35 54

One of the most striking features of the growth in education is the increase in graded schools. In 1888 there were 243 such schools in the State, while two years before there were but 188. The schools in the rural districts are making progress, and a united effort is being made to bring a large percentage of all children into the schools and give them a systematic course of instruction. The State University has grown rapidly in all departments except the medical course, which was suspended in 1887. There were, in the autumn term of 1888, 186 students in the colleges, 126 in the preparatory department, and 94 in the School of Fine Arts. Graduates of high-schools in the State are admitted to the university on the presentation of their diplomas.

The tabulated statement shows that the number of acres granted and confirmed to the State for educational purposes is 2,884,398 acres; 162,051·66 have been deeded, leaving 2,722,346·34 acres, title to which is still vested in the State. There are now under contract of sale 639,454·16 acres, and under lease contract, 1,427,460·19 acres, and 655,431·99 acres that have not been leased or sold. The increase in the permanent school fund in the past two years has been about 13½ per cent. There is now invested $1,807,142.35; unpaid principal on sales, $4,432,048.51, and cash on hand in the treasury, $293,602.10, making a grand total of the permanent fund of $6,532,792.96.

Pursuant to an act of the Legislature approved March 31, 1887, the Board of Educational Lands ordered a reappraisement of the unsold educational lands in about thirty counties. More than double the value by the former appraisement is shown.

Soldiers' Home.—The main building in this institution was completed in July, 1888, and opened for the reception of inmates, 52 in number. The home is on a tract of 640 acres given by the citizens of Grand Island. The main building is to be occupied by unmarried men, as the plan contemplates the erection of cottages on tracts of from two to five acres each, where soldiers having families may live. Nebraska is one of the first States to establish a home for soldiers where families are not separated. The Legislature is asked to appropriate $189,500 for the home during the ensuing two years.

Insane Asylums.—The hospital at Lincoln has been overcrowded during the year, its accommodations being only for 300 patients. There were in the hospital, Nov. 30, 1888, 392, and there have been present at one time as many as 414. A new asylum at Norfolk was opened in February, 1888, and a portion of the patients were transferred from Lincoln, but already this is filled. Two new wings are being built to the latter hospital, and an asylum for incurables is approaching completion at Hastings; but even after these buildings are completed and filled there will be a large number of insane in poor-houses and jails.

The institution for feeble-minded children, at Beatrice, was opened in May 1887, and the capacity of the building has already been reached, 70 pupils being accommodated. A large addition to the building has just been completed; but this will not provide for all the applicants. The superintendent estimates that there are over 700 feeble-minded children in the State. The law gives a preference for admission to the institution to the "most improvable cases," thus practically debarring the most helpless and unfortunate.

Other Charities.—In the Institute for the Deaf and Dumb at Omaha during the past two years, 150 children have been cared for and instructed. There have been admitted to the blind institute during the biennial term ending Nov. 30, 1888, 31 blind children, and the total enrollment has reached 56. The number remaining at the close of the period was 41.

At the State Home for the Friendless there were 72 inmates in December, 1888. Since that time 375 have been admitted and 331 have been surrendered to friends, placed in homes, or otherwise cared for, leaving at the close of this year 116 inmates.

Penitentiary.—There have been received into the Penitentiary since its establishment 1,465 convicts. The number of those discharged or pardoned is 1,118, and the number of deaths 9, leaving in prison, Nov. 30, 1888, 338, an increase of ten in two years. The number received by commitment during the two years ending Nov. 30, 1888, was 816. The number discharged in the same period under the good-time act was 269.

Reform School.—This institution is now known as the Industrial School, and is operated on the open or family system as distinguished from the prison system. There are no high walls or fences or grated windows, but the school, reading-room, and workshops are resorted to as aids in the work of reformation. The attendance of 184 boys and 61 girls shows an increase of 109 over that in 1886.

Normal School.—The aggregate attendance for the past two years at the State Normal School at Peru was 645. There were graduated 111 teachers, nearly all of whom are now engaged in the schools. The attendance for 1887 was 458, and for 1888 492. There were 310 students in the normal classes at the end of this year, besides 40 in the training classes.

Cattle Diseases.—Thorough quarantine regulations have been established and efforts have been made by the live-stock agents and veterinarians to stamp out all cattle diseases. Eight hundred and thirty horses and mules were destroyed by the Live-Stock Commission from Nov. 30, 1886, to Dec. 1, 1888. The indemnity allowed was $36,071.50, averaging $43.50 a head. At the present, forty counties report freedom from disease among cattle.

National Guard.—Since July 1, 1887, one regiment of infantry and one troop of cavalry have been organized, so that the militia of the State now numbers 1,200. New uniforms have been purchased for the whole command, with new arms and equipments. An encampment was held in Lincoln in 1887, and in Wahoo in 1888.

New Counties.—During the past two years five new counties have been organized—Box, Butte, Thomas, Grant, Perkins, and Rock. Four more will complete their organization early in 1889—Banner, Deuel, Scotts Bluffs, and Kimball. The last four are being organized out of Cheyenne County.

New State Buildings.—The following is a list of the State buildings erected by virtue of appropriations made by the last Legislature and the cost of each, most of them being additions to buildings previously erected: Asylum for Incurable Insane at Hastings $63,900; Industrial Home at Milford, $13,700; Soldiers' and Sailors' Home at Grand Island, $28,000; Institute for Deaf and Dumb at Omaha, $10,000; Industrial School at Kearney, $29,975; Hospital for Insane at Norfolk, $84,292; Home for the Friendless, $5,651.20; Penitentiary, $39,200; Feeble-Minded Institute at Beatrice, $18,218; Institute for Blind, $30.700; Grant Memorial Hall, $19,100; Industrial College building (Nebraska Hall), $41,000.

Political.—A full set of State officers and members of the Legislature and of Congressmen, as well as presidential electors, were to be chosen at the election this year. The first ticket for State officers in the field was nominated by the Prohibitionists in convention at Omaha on August 16, and was as follows: For Governor, George E. Bigelow; Lieutenant-Governor, John Dale: Secretary of State. John E. Hopper; Auditor, John F. Holin; Treasurer, James H. Stewart; Attorney-General, John Barud; Commissioner of Public Lands, Artemas Roberts; Superintendent of Public Instruction, Horatio S. Hilton. The usual prohibitory resolutions were adopted.

A week later the Republicans met at Omaha and renominated Governor Thayer, Secretary of State Laws, Attorney-General Leese, and Superintendent of Public Instruction Lane. For Lieutenant-Governor, George D. Meiklejohn was nominated: for Auditor, T. H. Benton; for Treasurer, J. E. Hill; and for Commissioner of Public Lands, J. Steen.

The Democrats nominated the following ticket: For Governor, John A. McShane; Lieutenant-Governor, Frank Folda; Secretary of State, Patrick A. Hines; Auditor, W. A. Poynter; Treasurer, James M. Patterson; Attorney-General, W. H. Munger; Commissioner of Public Lands, P. H. Jussen; Superintendent of Public Instruction, Marion Thrasher.

The Union Labor party held its convention at Hastings on September 4 and nominated: For Governor, David Butler; Lieutenant-Governor, C. W. Potter: Secretary of State, I. Henthern; Auditor, H. S. Alley; Treasurer, D. C. Nash; Attorney-General, M. F. Knox; Commissioner of Public Lands and Buildings, W. F. Wright; Superintendent of Public Instruction, Mrs. M. F. Wood. The resolutions denounce the national banking system, call for free sugar, free wool, and free woolen goods, free lumber, coal, and salt; favor the fixing of local freight-rates on the same scale with through rates, with proper allowance for terminal facilities; demand the suppression of trusts; and condemn the Chicago, Burlington and Quincy road in its action toward the Brotherhood of Engineers.

The canvass was unmarked by features of special note. At the November election the Republican national ticket was successful, and Gov. Thayer was re-elected, receiving 103.983 votes to 85.420 for McShane, 9,511 for Bigelow, and 3,941 for Butler; but Gov. Thayer ran about 4,000 votes behind the rest of his ticket. The Legislature, elected at the same time, will contain 27 Republicans and 6 Democrats in the Senate, and 76 Republicans, 22 Democrats, 1 Union Labor, and 1 Independent in the House. Republicans were elected in the three congressional districts.

NETHERLANDS, a constitutional monarchy in western Europe. The Constitution adopted on the re-establishment of the kingdom in 1815 was revised in 1848. and in 1887 it was amended by a law extending the right of suffrage to all male citizens, twenty-three years of age, who pay ten guilders in taxes on real estate or a personal tax of similar amount, that passed the Second Chamber on October 14, and was

proclaimed on November 30. The States-General, as the national legislature is called, consists of a First Chamber of 50 members elected by the provincial states for nine years, one third retiring every three years, and a Second Chamber of 104 deputies elected directly by the people for four years. The Government and the Second Chamber have the right of introducing legislation. but the First Chamber possesses only a veto power.

The reigning sovereign is Willem III, born Feb. 19, 1817, whose second wife is Queen Emma, daughter of Georg Victor, the reigning Prince of Waldeck-Pyrmont. Their only child is the Princess Wilhelmina, born Aug. 31, 1880, who will succeed her father under the Netherlands law of succession which admits female heirs in default of males. In case there is no legal heir the King can appoint his successor with the consent of a specially elected legislature, and if he dies without an heir being nominated the States-General, consisting of twice the usual number of members, elects a king by a joint vote of both Chambers.

The following ministers were in office at the beginning of 1888: President of the Council and Minister of the Interior, Dr. J. Heemskerk Az, appointed April 22, 1883; Minister of Foreign Affairs. Jonkheer A. P. C. van Karnebeek; Minister of Finance, J. C. Bloem; Minister of Justice, Baron du Tour de Bellinchave; Minister of the Colonies, J. P. Sprenger van Eyk; Minister of Marine, F. C. Tromp; Minister of War, General A. W. P. Weitzel; Minister of Commerce, J. N. Bastert.

Area and Population.—The area of the kingdom is 33,000 square kilometres or 12,648 square miles. The population on Dec. 31, 1887, was computed to be 4,450,870, as compared with 4,012,693 in 1879, when a census was taken. The population of 1887 was divided into 2,204,259 males and 2,246,611 females. The number of marriages in 1887 was 30,924; births, 156,906; deaths, 94.842; excess of births, 62.064. The largest cities are Amsterdam, having 390,016 inhabitants on December 31, 1887; Rotterdam, with 193,658; and the Hague, with 149,447.

Finance.—The revenue is estimated in the budget of 1888 at 118,966,686 guilders, of which 26,705,100 guilders are derived from direct taxes; 42,725,000 guilders from excise duties; 22,-003,500 guilders from stamps, registration, and succession duties: 5.010,500 guilders from customs; 5,850.000 guilders from the post-office; 2,210,000 guilders from railroads; 2.585.000 guilders from domains; 1,120.800 guilders from the telegraphs; 1,050,000 guilders from pilotage dues; and 9,726,786 guilders from other sources. The total expenditures are estimated at 136,-039,594 guilders, of which 36.353.966 guilders are for the debt; 24.048,701 guilders for the expenses of the ministry of Waterstaat. commerce, and industry; 24,045,212 guilders for financial administration and worship: 20,274,391 guilders for military expenses; 12,656,786 guilders for the navy; 10,237,497 guilders for the Department of the Interior; 5,108,789 guilders for the Department of Justice; 1,269,691 guilders for the central administration of the colonies; 692,766 guilders for the diplomatic service; 651,795 guilders for the Cabinet; and 650,000 guilders for the civil list of the King. The Government has authority, when the expenditures exceed the revenue, to emit treasury bills for not more than 18,000,000 guilders.

The capital of the public debt in 1888 amounted to 1,072,021,650 guilders, including 15,000,-000 guilders of paper money, showing a reduction in twelve months of 2,110,700 guilders. The expenses of the debt in 1888 were 30,589,-555 guilders for interest and 5,164,400 guilders for amortization.

Change of Ministry.—The first elections for the Second Chamber under the new Constitution took place on March 6, 1888, and those for the First Chamber a few days later. The new Second Chamber was composed of 45 Liberals, 27 Anti-Revolutionaries or Calvinist Clericals, 26 Roman Catholics, 1 Conservative, and 1 Socialist. The Socialist member is Nieuwenhuis, the leader of the party, who was elected in Schoterland by 1,167 out of 2,203 votes. The members of the First Chamber were divided into 35 Liberals, 10 Ultramontanes, 4 Conservatives, and 1 Calvinist. Since the Liberal ministry was left without a majority in the Lower House, Heemskerk and his colleagues handed in their resignations to the King. The new Cabinet was not constituted till April 19. It is composed of the following members: Minister of the Interior, Baron A. E. Mackay; Minister of Justice, Jonkheer G. L. M. H. Ruys van Beerenbeck; Minister of Finance, Jonkheer K. A. Godin de Beaufort; Minister of Foreign Affairs, Jonkheer C. Hartsen; Minister of the Colonies, Dr. L. W. C. Keuchenius; Minister of War, Col. J. W. Bergansius; Minister of Waterstaat, Commerce, and Industry, J. P. Havelaar; Minister of Marine, Capt. H. Dyserinck. The new ministers, of whom Hartsen and Ruys van Beerenbeck were High Conservatives, the former being a Protestant and the latter a Catholic, Dyserinck a Liberal, and Keuchinius a Radical, were pledged to the principle of confessional education. They were in favor of introducing universal obligatory military service, of which Col. Bergensius was an advocate, and the Minister of the Colonies was anxious to purify and reform the colonial administration. Otto van Rees, the Governor-General of India, resigned at once, anticipating removal. The Minister of the Interior unfolded the ministerial programme in the States-General on May 1, the opening day, the chief feature of which was the removal of hindrances to the development of denominational schools. The inquiry regarding social reform in both the agricultural and the industrial branches of labor was to be pursued further, and a commission was appointed with instructions to prepare new laws for the national defense.

Legislative Session.—The serious illness of the King made it necessary for the States-General to come together on July 12 for the purpose of considering the question of the guardianship of the Princess Wilhelmine. Queen Emma is made guardian of her daughter, but in respect to her sojourn at any time outside the country, as also in respect to the persons to whom her education shall be confided, the advice of a council, consisting of five high officials, designated in the law, and four persons nominated by the King, must be followed. If the Queen marries again her guardianship ceases, unless it is continued by a special law. The regular session began on September 18. Baron Mackay read the speech from the throne, in which an amendment to the Constitution, a new law on elementary education, the division of the large cities into separate electoral districts, an act to restrict child labor in factories, and a change in the sugar-tax summed up the ministerial programme.

Commerce.—The total value of the special imports in 1886, inclusive of the precious metals, was 1,091,488,000 guilders, and that of the special exports 949,489,000 guilders. The imports from Dutch colonies amounted to 92,-490,000 guilders, the share of Java being 90,-188,000 guilders and that of the Dutch West Indies 2,302,000 guilders, while the value of the exports to the colonies was 47,624,000 guilders, 44,826,000 guilders representing the exports to the East Indies and 2,798,000 guilders those to the West Indian possessions. The commerce with foreign countries in 1886 is shown in the following table, which gives the value in guilders:

COUNTRIES.	Imports.	Exports.
Germany Zollverein.	295,318,000	396,768,000
Great Britain	262,138,000	255,406,000
Belgium	157,960,000	187,589,000
United States	66,978,000	45,756,000
Russia	74,715,000	4,896,000
Hanse Towns	20,160,000	17,545,000
British India	86,423,000	39,000
France	17,975,000	10,811,000
Sweden and Norway	10,894,000	7,666,000
Spain	15,819,000	577,000
Italy	4,575,000	10,364,000
Peru	8,127,000	....
Denmark	984,000	4,952,000
Japan	4,762,000	328,000
Portugal	1,454,000	1,876,000
Austria	542,000	1,442,000
Other countries	81,089,000	6,848,000
Total	1,102,698,000	949,489,000

Navigation.—The number of sailing-vessels entered at Dutch ports in 1887 was 2,302, of 1,799,181 metric tons, of which 2,060, of 1,751,858 tons, had cargoes. The total number cleared was 2,327, of 1,833,616 tons, and of these 1,481, of 956,354 tons, shipped cargoes. Of the total number entered 883, of 538,676 tons, and of those cleared 911, of 582,710 tons, were registered in the Netherlands. The steam-vessels entered numbered 6,340, of 11,667,436 tons, of which 6,029, of 11,269,718 tons, were with cargoes; the number cleared was 6,296, of 11,451,874, of which 4,232, of 7,130,327 tons shipped cargoes. Of the steamers entered 1,657, of 3,423,661 tons, carried the Dutch flag, and of those cleared 1,734, of 3.567,297 tons. The mercantile navy of the Netherlands on Jan. 1, 1888, comprised 516 sailing-vessels, of 440,430 metric tons, and 105 steamers, of 284,927 metric tons.

Railroads.—There were 2,550 kilometres or 1,584 miles of railroads in operation on Jan. 1, 1887. The state owned 1,390 kilometres. The earnings of all the lines in 1885 amounted to 25,319.000 guilders, and the expenses were 14,466,000 guilders. The earnings of the State railroads were 11,876,000 guilders, and the expenses 7,210,000 guilders. The capital invested in railroad construction up to 1885 was 213,651,089 guilders.

Telegraphs.—The State had 4,903 kilometres of telegraph lines and 17.233 kilometres of wires on Jan. 1, 1888. Of 657 stations in the country 358 belonged to the State and 299 to companies. The number of messages that passed over the wires in 1887 was 3,734,065, of which 1,996,628 were internal, 1,706,396 international, and 31,041 official. The receipts were 1,176,146 guilders; the expenses, 1,519,028 guilders for ordinary, and 28,639 guilders for extraordinary purposes.

The Army.—The war strength of the European army in 1887 was 2,342 officers and 63,391 men, exclusive of the active schutteryen, numbering 41,217 men, and the territorial militia, numbering 76,467 men. The Vitali system of converted rifle has been adopted for the infantry.

The Navy.—The fleet of war in July, 1888, consisted of 24 iron-clads, 12 monitors, 6 river gun-boats, 28 cruisers, 8 paddle-wheel gun-boats, 30 coast-guard gun-boats, 31 torpedo-boats, 5 batteries, and 21 other vessels.

Colonies.—The Dutch possessions in the East Indies are divided into the colony of Java and Madura, where there is a settled government, and the so called outposts, which include Sumatra, Borneo, the Riouw-Lingga Archipelago, Banka, Billiton, Celebes, the Molucca Archipelago, and the Sunda Islands. Java has been governed since 1832 on the culture system, under which the labor of the natives is officially superintended and directed so as to produce food crops sufficient for the population and as much colonial produce for the European market as is possible. Under this system coffee, indigo, sugar, pepper, tea, tobacco, and other articles have been cultivated for the Government by the forced labor of the natives. Forced labor has been abolished except in the cultivation of coffee and sugar, and will cease in connection with the latter crop after 1890 in accordance with a law that was passed in 1870. The culture system has not been introduced in the outposts except in the tobacco districts of the west coast of Sumatra and in the residency of Menado on the island of Celebes, where it is applied to the cultivation of coffee. The Government, by monopolizing the trade, derives a large profit from the privately grown tobacco of Java, which is purchased at one fifth or one sixth of the price for which it is sold in the auction sale at Amsterdam. The opium monopoly adds to the revenue of the Government, although the introduction of the narcotic has tended to impoverish the people. The natives of Java were formerly submissive and satisfied, but of late years the failures of the coffee-crop, the crises in the sugar and indigo trades, and the irregularities that have crept into the colonial administration have produced widespread discontent. In 1888 an insurrection took place in the spring in the district of Bantam, which was put down with difficulty by the prompt and energetic action of the military authorities, who sent a large force into the disturbed district. A pretender appeared who falsely claimed to be a descendant of the former sultans. and obtained a large following, but was finally arrested and proved to be an impostor, and was condemned to four years' imprisonment. In the summer the rumor of a general insurrection spread through the eastern part of the island, and the Europeans were plunged into a state of extreme anxiety. At Soerabaya the civic guard had orders to take up arms at the first alarm, and the whites who lived outside brought their families into the town. The expected uprising was prevented by the timely action of the police. There was a conspiracy extending through central and eastern Java. In Surakarta, where nightly meetings took place in various places, the authorities seized the principal ringleaders, who confessed that their object was to establish a new Javan empire. In the residencies of Kediri, Madiun, and Pasuruan the head conspirators were caught in time and brought behind bars. In Vorstenlanden a nocturnal assembly was surprised by the police, and in the house of one of the leaders was found a seal of state on which was engraved the name Mangku Negoro IV, as the prospective ruler of the restored empire was called.

The island of Sumatra is divided into a number of districts, provinces. or kingdoms, some of which are directly under Dutch rule, whereas others continue under the native rulers aided by Dutch advisers. The latest official statements give the population at 2,792,561 natives, 105,823 Chinese, and 3,847 Europeans.

The military authorities were no nearer mastering the rebellion in 1888 than they had been in previous years. A falling out between the Sultan and one of his vassals, who was a formidable enemy of the Dutch, was a favorable circumstance. Yet the strongest foe that they had to encounter, the berri-berri disease, was worse than ever before. It attacked European women, who had previously been spared. A medical commission that was sent to study the nature of the plague and means of prevention, suggested preventive measures that reduced the ravages among the soldiers. The hospital doctor made the discovery that the soldiers were able to simulate the disease very perfectly in order to be transferred and thus escape the real sickness. In the budget for 1888-'89 a sum is appropriated for a body of troops composed of the soldiers who are sent back to Holland on account of temporary sickness, and who will serve as *cadres* of instruction for the new troops that are raised for India. The Government is now attempting to bribe the Acheenese chiefs into submission. In the Indian budget the sum of 45,000 guilders is set down for pensions to those who have ceased their hostilities. The plan of restoring the Sultanate, evacuating Aeheen and retiring to Oleh-leh is contemplated by the present Government.

NEVADA. State Government.—The following were the State officers during the year: Governor, Christopher C. Stevenson, Republican; Lieutenant-Governor, Henry C. Davis; Secretary of State, John M. Dormer; Treasurer, George Tufly; Comptroller, J. F. Hallock; Attorney-General, John F. Alexander; Superintendent of Public Instruction, W. C. Dovey; Chief-Justice, of the Supreme Court, Orville R. Leonard; Associate Justices, Charles H. Belknap, Thomas P. Howley.

Finances.—The total State expenditures for 1887 were $523,412.84, of which $130,980 represents interchanges between the various State funds, leaving the actual State expenses $392,532.84. These expenditures exceeded the income for the year by about $50,000. Of the above amount $41,498.07 was expended for the support of the State Prison, $50,933.44 for the State Insane Asylum, $13,022.90 for the Orphan's Home, $13.164.25 for completion and improvements of the State University, and $11,112.55 for its support. The legislative session cost $52,487.84, and $53,682.37 was paid for the support of schools.

Concerning the State debt, the Comptroller says in his report at the close of 1888: "The reduction of the rate of taxation in 1879, from ninety cents to fifty-five cents on each $100 of property valuation and the net proceeds of mines, resulted in a loss of revenue of about $240,000 for the years 1879-'80, and was the means of creating a bonded debt for general expenses, the interest on which has already amounted to $39,688.55, and will probably amount to much more before the debt can be disposed of, as $106,000 of the principal is still unpaid, and the necessities of this year will probably increase this amount by $80,000 or more. In view of these facts, and with the knowledge that the revenue has fallen off·in the last two years in the sum of about $16,000 a year, through loss of the drummer tax and the reduction of poll taxes; that the State is now almost entirely dependent upon the tax on property, for revenue; and of the strong probability that appropriations from the general fund, largely in excess of those for past years, will be found necessary for the ensuing

two years for exigencies that have arisen; it is hoped that the Legislature at this session will not make the mistake of reducing the tax rate, without discovering some compensating source or sources of revenue."

In addition to the debt above mentioned, the State holds in the school fund an irredeemable bond for $380,000, on which it pays 5 per cent. interest annually.

Education.—The number of children of school age in the State for the school year 1887-'88 was 9,716, a decrease of 112 from the previous year. The amount apportioned by the State from its school funds to the public schools was about $63,000.

The second year of the State University since its removal to Reno has proved prosperous. At its opening in the autumn of 1887, after being closed six months for extensive repairs, the number of students in attendance was only 36; but before the close of 1888 there were 115 on the rolls, outside of the normal course. An agricultural experiment station is established in connection with the University, which receives annually $15,000 from the General Government for its support. A school of mines, a school of agriculture, a school of liberal arts, a business department, and a normal school are all organized under the university.

The Insane.—By an act of 1887 the Governor, Comptroller, and Treasurer were created a board of commissioners for the care of the indigent insane. The board at once took control of the State asylum, and made a thorough examination of its condition. Grave charges having been made against the superintendent, the board in May instituted an investigation, which resulted in the exoneration of that official. An attempt to provide a supply of water for the asylum from Truckee river, has led the board into an expensive litigation, not yet ended. The number of inmates during the year has averaged 162.

Mining.—The bullion-product of Nevada for 1888 amounted to about $12,305,603; for 1887 it was $10,232,453; for 1886, $9,169,920.

Silver Coinage.—The Governor says in his annual message: "This question is one of the most important to the people of Nevada, and it may be said to be paramount to all others. The difference in the price paid for silver by the Government and the price at which it pays it out would make a good profit for the miner. For the past year the price paid for silver has averaged about ninty-three cents a fine ounce, while it is paid out at $1.2928. Thus the Government makes in seigniorage about thirty-six cents on every ounce of silver purchased, and this is taken from the comparatively small number of miners in the United States, compared with the entire population interested in silver money. The low price paid by the Government for silver has closed down hundreds of mines that would to-day be in active operation, giving employment to thousands of men, if silver were on the same footing in regard to coinage at our mints as gold. The gold-miner can take his gold to the mint and receive the coin value in gold, which is virtually free coinage to him; but the silver-miner must sell to the mint at a price regulated by the London market. It is believed, as the silver question is better understood, we shall have free coinage of the white metal. When that is brought about this State will become prosperous."

Decisions.—The Legislature of 1887 passed an act making it necessary to subscribe to an oath against Mormonism, in order to qualify as a voter. By a decision of the State Supreme Court, early in October, this act was found to be unconstitutional.

Political.—The Republican State Convention was called to meet at Winnemucca on May 15. It selected delegates to the National Convention and presidential electors, and the following ticket for State officers: For Justice of the Supreme Court, M. A. Murphy; Regents of the State University, T. H. Wells, H. L. Fish, and E. T. George. As candidate for Congress, H. F. Bartine was selected. The platform adopted contains the following:

A financial policy whereby both gold and silver shall form the basis of circulation, whether the money used by the people be coin, or in certificates redeemable in coin, or both, as convenience may require, is imperatively demanded.

The attempt to substitute National bank-notes, costing the Government millions of dollars annually, for free silver, costing nothing, is an outrage upon the people: that the money ring or trust, which has usurped the sovereign power of the Government to issue money, and which has fraudulently demonetized silver and seized the revenues of the Government for private speculation, shocks the moral sense of the people and destroys respect for Government and law.

We are in favor of the protection of home industry, and that the laborers of this country have a right to all the work required to supply the people of the United States, and that we are in favor of high wages in this country, and to that end will protect the wage-workers' competition with the cheap labor of other lands.

We are in favor of the absolute exclusion of Chinese, and the restriction of immigration, by which the present overcharged condition of the labor market is made worse, and also favor legislation by which a revision of our naturalization and land laws may be accomplished.

We demand, in behalf of our various industries, the retention of the duties on lead, borax, soda, hides, and leather, and to restore the tariff of 1867 on wool.

We recognize the right of labor to organize for its lawful protection.

We favor the submission by the Legislature to the people of an amendment to the Constitution giving the Legislature the power to regulate the liquor-traffic.

We favor liberal appropriations by Congress for hydrographical and topographical surveys in this State to the end that the waste waters may be preserved for the purpose of irrigation.

We favor the reduction of the Treasury surplus by the payment of pensions to Union soldiers, their widows and orphans, the improvement of rivers and harbors, the building of defenses for our sea-coasts, the erection of public buildings, the creation of a navy, the purchase of bonds, and the repeal of the internal-revenue laws taxing tobacco.

It is the duty of the State to maintain free non-sectarian schools in the rural and sparsely settled districts as well as in towns and thickly settled sections, and such a division of the school money should be made as will furnish the means of education to all children in the State.

We are in favor of reopening the Carson Mint for coinage, and raising the wages of its employés to the standard paid by the last Republican Administration.

The Democratic State Convention met on May 16, at Reno, and nominated for Congress, George W. Cassidy; for Justice of the Supreme Court, William M. Sewell; for Regents of the State University, M. S. Bonnifield, S. D. King, and F. M. Edmunds. Presidential electors and delegates to the National Convention were also chosen. The platform adopted strongly urges the free coinage of silver, opposes Chinese immigration, and approves civil-service reform. The National Administration is commended. At the election in November, the Republican State and National tickets were successful. For Congressman, Bartine received 6,921 votes, and Cassidy 5,682. The vote for Justice of the Supreme Court was: Murphy, 6,467; Sewell, 6,122. The State Legislature, elected at the same time, will stand 15 Republicans and 5 Democrats in the Senate, and 26 Republicans and 14 Democrats in the House.

At the same election a vote was taken on the question whether a convention to revise the State Constitution should be called, and also on eleven proposed constitutional amendments. The proposition for a constitutional convention was rejected by a vote of 1,644 in its favor to 2,740 against. Of the amendments, ten were adopted and one, which had been irregularly adopted two years before, providing that constitutional amendments may be submitted to the people after passage by one Legislature, was rejected. The successful amendments change the time of meeting for the Legislature from the first to the third Monday of January; empower each branch of the Legislature to expel a member for disorderly conduct; enable the Legislature to establish and regulate the compensation and fees of county and township officers, and to regulate the rates of freight on railroads incorporated within the State; prohibit "salary-grab" bills; abolish the office of Lieutenant-Governor; provide that the President of the Senate shall be elected by its members and succeed to the governorship in case of vacancy, and that in case of his death or disability the Speaker of the House shall succeed to the governorship; regulate the impeachment of public officers by the Legislature; regulate the revenues for educational purposes and prohibit the transfer of school moneys to any other fund; authorize the levy of a special tax for the maintenance of the State University; and make it obligatory upon the State, instead of the counties, to support indigent infirm or otherwise unfortunate citizens needing aid. A question, however, soon arose as to the legality of the procedure by which these amendments were adopted. An act of the Legislature of 1897 upon this point provided that publication of proposed amendments should be made " for a period of ninety days next preceding any general election held in this State, when any proposed amendments are pending." There had been publication of the amendments two years before prior to a general election, and through a misapprehension of the terms of the new act, a second publication this year was not deemed necessary ; but the State Supreme Court, by a decision rendered late in December, decided that such publication should not have been omitted, and that the election was therefore illegal and of no effect.

NEW BRUNSWICK. There were no changes in the Executive Government of the Province of New Brunswick in 1888. Three members of the Legislative Council died during the year, viz., Hon. William Hamilton, who was the last surviving member of the Council appointed directly by the Crown, Hon. John Lewis, and Hon. W. M. Kelly. Dr. Lewis, a member of the Assembly, resigned during the year, and H. R. Emmerson was elected in his stead.

Agriculture.—The year was remarkable for excessive rainfall and early frosts. At St. John the rainfall during the twelve months was 55·675 inches, against an average of 41·959 inches for the preceding eight years. The autumn freshets were unusually high, and considerable damage was done to bridges and to the crops stored on low lands. Nearly all crops were below an average, owing to the wet harvest and early frost.

In 1886 the Provincial Government imported from Europe and the United States a number of pure bred stallions, retaining the ownership and leasing the animals at public competition annually. In 1888 a further importation was made, and, in order to encourage the raising of pure bred stock, an importation of pure bred mares was also made. The latter were sold at public auction, subject to the restriction that they should be kept in the province and bred to pure bred sires of their respective breeds. The sale was very successful. An importation of pure bred sheep was made at the same time, and the animals were sold under restrictions.

The Legislature in 1888 passed an important act relating to agriculture. The Board of Agriculture, which formerly supervised the expenditures for this service, was abolished, and a Department of Agriculture was created, presided over by a member of the Executive Government, who is known as the Commissioner for Agriculture. Hon. David McLellan was appointed commissioner. Under the new law the province is divided into sixty districts, and in each district an agricultural society may be established. A membership of fifty and a subscription list of $100 is necessary to constitute a society, which will receive a charter and also an annual appropriation from the provincial treasury. The object of establishing this new department is the promotion of improved husbandry and stock-raising, the holding of exhibitions, and the dissemination of information in regard to agriculture.

Legislation.—The principal other acts of general interest passed by the Legislature in the session of 1888 were : An act relating to mines and mining-leases, providing for the forfeiture of leases under which no minerals have been raised for twelve months continuously, or in case of breach of conditions, and exempting limestone and gypsum from crown royalty. An act prohibiting the killing of moose, deer, or red deer for three years.

Shipping.—The following shows the number, description, and tonnage of vessels registered in New Brunswick on Dec. 31, 1880 :

CLASS OF VESSELS.	Number.	Tonnage.
Ships	146	66,844
Barks	182	109,819
Barkentines	13	5,843
Brigs	2	492
Brigantines	32	10,086
Schooners	605	83,025
Wood-boats	88	5,345
Sloops	6	116
Steamers	85	6,058
Total	1,109	237,678

There was a loss on tonnage of 31,796 tons from the previous year.

Commerce.—The foreign trade of New Brunswick during the year ending June 30, 1888, was as follows :

MOVEMENT.	Dutiable goods.	Free goods.	Total.
Imports	$3,783,828	$2,274,261	$6,058,084
Exports			6,929,563
Total foreign trade			$12,987,647

The principal countries with which this trade was carried on and the value of the trade with each were as follow :

Imports from Great Britain	$2,142,694
Exports to Great Britain	2,709,529
Imports from the United States	3,022,221
Exports to the United States	2,648,855
Imports from the West Indies	305,775
Exports to the West Indies	24,095

The largest item in the export trade is composed of products of the forest, which were valued at $4,891,832, of which a little more than half was sent to Great Britain. The United States imported $981,235 worth of provincial lumber, and $1,209,538 worth cut in the United States was manufactured in and exported from the province to the United States.

Railways.—The following new lines of railway, in whole or in part in New Brunswick, were opened for traffic during the year : The Riviere du Loup and Temiscouata Railway, from Edmundston on the New Brunswick Railway to Riviere du Loup on the Intercolonial Railway, 90 miles, of which 13 miles are in New Brunswick; the Fredericton Railway, connecting the Northern and Western and New Brunswick Railways, 1 mile long. The following lines were under construction during the year : The Central Railway, from Norton on the Intercolonial Railway to the head of Grand Lake, 40 miles ; the Albert Southern Railway, 12 miles; the Fredericton and Woodstock Railway, 66 miles; the Tobique Railway, 28 miles. The following is the mileage of railway in operation in the province during the year: Intercolonial and branches, 374 miles; New Brunswick, 443 miles; Northern and Western, 121 miles; Grand Southern, 80 miles; Albert, 48 miles; Kent Northern and St. Louis, 33 miles; Elgin, 14 miles; Chatham, 9 miles; St. Martin's and Upham, 30 miles; Havelock, Elgin, and Petitcodiac, 12 miles; Caraquet, 66 miles; New Brunswick and Prince Edward Island, 30 miles; Mondon and Buctouche, 40 miles; St. John Bridge and Railway, 2 miles; Riviere du Loup and Temiscouata, 13 miles; Fredericton Bridge, 1 mile—total, 1,317 miles. The increase since 1886 is 297.

Finances.—The revenue of the province during the year was as follows: From Dominion subsidies, $487,306.53; territorial revenue, $134,604.17; other sources, $67,968.98—total, $689,879.68. The principal items of expenditure were: Education, $165,676.38; roads, bridges, and public buildings, $218,432.81; interest, $95,187.50; agriculture, $30,599.17; executive and legislative expenses, $50,042.70; care of the insane, $35,000. The minor items swell the expenditure for the year to $676,-093.22. The provincial debt on Dec. 31, 1888, was $768,000 at 6 per cent.; $148,200 at 5 per cent.; $280,000 at 4½ per cent.; $910,000 at 4 per cent.—total, $2,106,200. The average interest is 4·86¼ per cent., entailing a future charge of $102,490.

Ship-building was at a comparatively low ebb in New Brunswick in 1888; only 2 steamers and 20 schooners, aggregating 1,967 tons, were built in the province during the year ending June 30, 1888. The additions to the shipping register of the province in the same period included 39 vessels, aggregating 3,865 tons, and there were sold to other countries 5 vessels, aggregating 4,638 tons and valued at $55,643.

The arrivals and departures at New Brunswick ports during the same period including vessels engaged in the foreign and coasting trade were:

MOVEMENT.	Number.	Tonnage.
Arrivals.		
Steamers..........................	739	252,017
Sailing-vessels	4,808	263,767
Departures:		
Steamers..........................	565	235,969
Sailing-vessels....................	4,723	210,876

NEW HAMPSHIRE. State Government. — The following were the State officers during the year: Governor, Charles Henry Sawyer (Republican); Secretary of State, Ai B. Thompson; Treasurer, Solon A. Carter; Attorney-General, Daniel Barnard; Superintendent of Public Instruction, James W. Patterson; Insurance Commissioner, Oliver Pillsbury, who died on February 22, and was succeeded by Henry H. Huse; Railroad Commissioners, Henry M. Putney, Edward B. S. Sanborn, Benjamin F. Prescott; Chief-Justice of the Supreme Court, Charles Doe; Associate Justices, Isaac W.

Smith, William H. H. Allen, Lewis W. Clark, Isaac N. Blodgett, Alonzo P. Carpenter, and George A. Bingham.

Finances.—The annual report of the State Treasurer, for the fiscal year ending May 31, 1888, shows the following facts:

RECEIPTS.

Cash on hand, June 1, 1887..................	$240,616 11
Total receipts during the year...............	1,170.990 48
Total.......	$1,411,606 59

DISBURSEMENTS.

Total disbursements during the year.........	$1,310,850 67
Cash on hand, June 1, 1888..................	100,755 92
Total....................................	$1,411,606 59

STATE DEBT.

Liabilities, June 1, 1888......................	$2,966,363 24
Assets, June 1, 1888...........	107,702 67
Net indebtedness......................	$2,858,660 57
Liabilities, June 1, 1887......................	$3,079,161 80
Assets, June 1, 1887..........................	247,860 51
Net indebtedness...............	$2,831,300 79
Increase of debt during the year..............	27,359 78

The total receipts of the Treasury from ordinary revenue were $534,523.36, and the total State expenses $561,883.14. Among the larger receipts were: From State tax, $400,000; from railroad tax, $99,757.61; from insurance tax, $6,930.22; and from charter fees, $15,088.50. The disbursements include $322,288 for ordinary State expenses, $63,998.24 for extraordinary charges, and $175,596.90 for interest on the State debt.

Education.—The report of the State Superintendent for the school year of 1887 shows that, under the recent law permitting town management of schools, five school districts gave up their special organization during the year, and went into the town system, leaving only 270 districts reported in the State.

The average length of the schools in weeks, for the whole State, was 22·9. For 1885, under the old system, it was only 19·95. Thus the new law gives on the average three weeks additional to every school of the State. The whole number of enrolled scholars for 1887 was 61,826. The whole number in 1877 was 68,-035. This is a decrease of 6,209 in ten years. The whole number reported in private schools in 1887 was 7,652. The number reported in 1877 was 1,493. This shows an increase of 6,159 in ten years, and measurably to what extent children have been drawn into parochial schools in that time. It does not vary materially from one tenth of the entire school population of the State. As yet this movement has been confined to the cities and larger towns.

There has been an increase of twenty-two graded schools resulting from a union of small schools. Twenty-eight new school-houses have been built, and the average attendance upon the schools was 45,877·72, an increase of 2,738·-72 over the previous year. Of the town system, the Superintendent says:

Towns that have abolished their unnecessary schools have given to the children more schooling than ever before for the same money, and in towns that have not the only practical effect of the law has been to give an improved system of supervision, a less burdensome method of providing and maintaining school property, and more equitable educational privileges. In putting the system into operation there may have been cases of hardship. There were under the old law, and will be under any system in a sparsely settled locality.

State Prison.—The report of the warden of the State Prison for the year ending May 1 contains the following statistics: Number of prisoners, May 1, 1887, 121; committed during the year, 38; discharged, etc., during the year, 44; number in prison, May 1, 1888, 115; earnings for the year, $15,190.98; expenses for the year, $19,450.30; deficit, $4,259.32.

Savings-Banks.—The total number of depositors in the savings-banks on April I was 139,-967—an increase of more than 7,000 within the year. The average amount due each depositor was $385.36, and the average to each person in the State, estimating the population at 355,000, was $151.94. The total number of savings-banks was 69—an increase of three. Three trust companies were reported, and one additional has been organized since April. Twenty-five of the banks paid a 5-per-cent. dividend in 1887, thirty-two paid 4 per cent., five paid 4½ per cent., two paid 4 per cent. and an extra, one paid 3½ per cent., one paid 3 per cent., and three were recently organized. The total earnings of the banks for the year 1887 was $3,645,504.71, and the total amount of dividend paid was $2,361,888.95.

Insurance.—The annual report of the Insurance Commissioner for 1887 shows the following facts with reference to the business of the fire-insurance companies of the State: Cash capital, $1,255,000.70; gross assets, $2,-595,067.87; liabilities, except capital, $1,351,-303.91; net assets as to policy-holders, $3,850,-067.97; surplus as to capital, $304,044.28; cash income, $1,544,369.95; cash expenditures, $1,314,074.66; dividends paid stock-holders, $49,350; fire risks written, $133,088,758.86; premiums received, $1,710,804.32; fire losses paid, $809,568.09.

There are twenty-three life-insurance companies doing business in the State.

Statistics.—According to the report of the State Board of Equalization for 1887 there were in the State 59,285 horses, 22,419 oxen, 94,329 cows, 47,476 other cattle, 155,685 sheep. Comparison with the report for the previous year shows a gain of 2,445 horses, 862 oxen, 3,866 cows, 2,474 other cattle, and 5,172 sheep—increasing the value of the live-stock of the State $499,606.

Political.—A State convention of the Prohibition party met at Concord, on June 19, and nominated Edgar L. Carr, for Governor. The convention adopted resolutions, of which the following are the more important:

We regard the system of taxation by which the traffic in liquors is used to support the revenues of the Government as a virtual partnership of the United States in the crime and iniquity of that traffic. We believe that the Government is thus made a bulwark to protect and perpetuate it, and we therefore demand the abolition of the system.

We approve the enactment by the Legislature of this State of the so-called nuisance law, calculated to make prohibition more effective, and we call upon the officials elected for that purpose to continue the enforcement of this and other features of the prohibitory law, until the liquor-traffic is exterminated in New Hampshire. We hold that the party in power in the legislative and executive departments of the State is responsible for the making and execution of the laws; and we therefore affirm that the Republican party of New Hampshire is guilty of the evils of the liquor-traffic in this State. With an efficient law on the statute books, with all the executive and judicial force of the State in their control, they have suffered the existence among us of a lawless institution, which they might at any hour overthrow. We arraign that party as faithless to the interests of the people, and unworthy to be continued in power. We also affirm that the record of the Democratic party in this State is a record of opposition to temperance in legislation and in practice, and that it is equally unworthy the suffrages of temperance men.

We believe in the right of the people to the enjoyment of a quiet Sabbath, and we request the railroad companies of the State to discontinue the running of Sunday trains. We oppose the publication and circulation of Sunday newspapers, and we call upon the Legislature to pass such laws as shall be best adapted to secure the people of the State from all forms of Sabbath desecration.

The Republican State Convention met at Concord, on September 4. Several candidates for gubernatorial nomination were before the convention, receiving upon the first ballot the following support: Hiram A. Tuttle, 209 votes; John B. Smith, 187; David H. Goodell, 121; Woodbury L. Melcher, 68; Albert S. Twitchell, 28; John A. Spalding, 14. Six ballots were taken without a choice, although on the fourth Tuttle received 306 votes, or within seven votes of the number necessary for the nomination. On the seventh ballot Goodell received 355 votes; Tuttle, 205; Melcher, 22; Smith, 17; and Goodell was declared the nominee. The platform contained the following:

We heartily approve of the declaration in the National Republican platform in favor of temperance and morality; of such laws as will best protect our people from the evils of strong drink, and of the suppression of its illegal sale.

We invite the co-operation of all who believe in the enactment of laws for the protection of our industries from the competition incident to the free importation of the products of the pauper labor of the Old World; of our laborers, from unjust exactions of employers; of our property-owners, from the attacks of anarchy and communism, and of all classes from the evils of illiteracy and immorality.

Two days later, the Democratic State Convention met at Concord, and, on the first ballot, nominated Charles H. Amsden for Governor. At the November election, the Republican National ticket was successful, but there was no election of Governor by the people. Goodell received 44,809 votes; Amsden, 44,093; Carr, 1,567. A majority of all the votes cast being necessary to elect, the choice of Governor will fall upon the next Legislature, which will meet in June, 1889. In this Legislature, as chosen at the same election, the Republicans will have 18 Senators and 169 Representatives, and the Democrats 6 Senators and 144 Representatives. Republican Congressmen were elected by narrow majorities in both of the congressional districts, a gain of one seat for that party. At the same election, delegates were chosen by the people to a constitutional convention appointed by the Legislature to meet on Jan. 2, 1889. This, the sixth constitutional convention in the history of the State, will consist of 321 members, of which the Republicans elected 180 members and the Democrats 140, one member being ranked as Independent.

NEW JERSEY. State Government.—The following were the State officers during the year: Governor, Robert S. Green (Democrat); Secretary of State and Insurance Commissioner, Henry C. Kelsey; Treasurer, John J. Toffey; Comptroller, Edward L. Anderson; Attorney-General, John P. Stockton; Superintendent of Public Instruction, Edwin O. Chapman, succeeded by Charles W. Fuller; Chief-Justice of the Supreme Court, Mercer Beasley; Associate Justices, Manning M. Knapp, Alfred Reed, Edward W. Scudder, Bennet Van Syckel, David A. Depue, Jonathan Dixon, William J. Magie, and Charles G. Garrison. Judge Garrison succeeded Joel Parker, deceased, being nominated by the Governor and confirmed by the Legislature in January. Chancellor, Alexander T. McGill, Jr.; Vice-Chancellors, Abraham V. Van Fleet and John T. Bird.

Legislative Session.—The one hundred and twelfth Legislature was in session from January 10 to March 30. Its action on the liquor question was noteworthy. A local-option law was passed, providing for special elections as often as once in three years, if desired, in any county, on petition of one-tenth of the legal voters, and by the same act the license fees of inn-holders were increased to $100 in places of fewer than 3,000 inhabitants, $150 in places of from 3,000 to 10,000, and $250 in places of over 10,000. This act was vetoed by Gov. Green, and passed again over the veto by a vote in the House of 34 to 24, and in the Senate of 13 to 8. The governing boards of incorporated towns were also given power to license, regulate, or prohibit liquor-selling within their jurisdiction. Another act provides that no honorably discharged soldier or sailor holding a salaried place under any city or county, whose term of office is not fixed by law, shall be removed from office for political reasons, but only for good cause shown after a hearing.

A new election law was passed, requiring, among other things, the closing of the polls at sunset and personal registration in Newark and Jersey City. The welfare of convicts is provided for by an act requiring persons under sixteen years of age, confined in county institutions, to be kept separate from older prisoners. The sum of $15,000 was appropriated for the erection of a monument at the Princeton battle-ground, provided an equal sum be raised by private subscription, and a commission was created to erect such monument. A home for the care and training of feeble-minded women was established, and the sum of $10,000 appropriated for the purchase of buildings. An appropriation of $50,000 was made for the construction and equipment of buildings for the Soldiers' Home, as provided by an act of 1886, and $30,000 was devoted to additions and improvements at the asylum for the insane at Morristown. Other acts of the session, which exceeded the work of its predecessors by passing 336 general measures, were as follow :

Providing a penalty for mutilating books, magazines, etc., in an incorporated library.

Providing for the appointment of a vice-ordinary or vice-surrogate general of the prerogative court.

Authorizing incorporated towns and township committees to borrow money and issue bonds to provide for the construction of sewers or drains.

Authorizing towns to widen private streets in certain cases.

Regulating the construction, care, and improvement of the public ways, parks, and sewers in all cities except those of the first class, and providing for a street commissioner therein.

Enabling cities to purchase lands for public parks or squares, and to improve the same, and to issue bonds for the cost of such purchase and improvement.

Empowering corporations to diminish the number of their directors.

Providing for the further relief of the poor in cities.

Providing a penalty for selling liquors in a boarding-house without license.

Providing for the condemnation of lands held by any school district the title to which is defective.

To provide for the erection of armories for the National Guard in incorporated towns, boroughs, etc.

To promote manual training by contributing to every school district that maintains a manual-training school a sum equal to the amount raised by such district for such purpose.

To secure the certification of births, marriages, and deaths, and of the vital facts relating thereto, and to provide for the record thereof.

To take for public use a tract of land at Sea Girt, in the county of Monmouth, to vacate the streets and ways thereon and certain easements therein.

For the better protection of homing pigeons.

Authorizing the abolishment of the office of surveyor of highways in cities.

Ratifying and confirming the agreement made between the commissioners of the State of New York and those of New Jersey locating and marking the boundary-line between the two States in lands under the waters of Raritan Bay.

Providing that taxes and assessments levied by boards of trustees shall be a first lien on real estate, and that the same may be sold to pay such taxes and assessments.

Authorizing cities and township committees to borrow money in anticipation of taxes.

Requiring savings-banks not having a capital stock to pay an annual tax of one half of one per cent. on the amount of their deposits not otherwise taxed or exempt.

Increasing the salaries of the State Treasurer and the Comptroller to $6,000 each.

Declaring that if any person in possession of a building or buildings, and not the owner thereof, shall burn or cause to be burned, or aid, counsel, or procure the burning of such buildings, whereby a dwelling-house is burned, such person shall be guilty of arson.

Providing that tangible personal property used in any business shall be taxed at the place where such business is carried on, shipping excepted.

Empowering assignees to sell land of their insolvent assignor at private sale, on obtaining leave of the court.

To enable the boards of commissions and improvement commissions in towns and villages, or within townships, to employ police.

Permitting registered physicians to practice in any part of the State.

Providing for the election of an assessor, collector, and commissioners of appeals at each annual borough election.

Proving for the support of certain indigent and feeble-minded women in suitable homes selected by the Governor.

Authorizing the issue of bonds for building public bridges in counties.

Enabling counties to acquire and improve lands for public parks,

To provide for vacating dedicated streets, roads, and alleys.

Regulating the procedure in selling lands for unpaid taxes or assessments.

Providing for the extension of borough boundaries.

Punishing the sale or circulation of obscene papers, books, or periodicals, or those having indecent pictures therein, or three or more pictures purporting to illustrate criminal acts.

Declaring bicycles and tricycles to be carriages, and regulating their use on public ways.

To provide for the preservation and protection of State boundary marks and monuments.

To prevent the shooting, trapping, or hunting of English hare for three years.

Authorizing any city, town, or borough to establish and maintain a fire department.

To provide for the temporary custody of dangerous lunatics.

Giving dyers a lien upon goods dyed by them.

Proivding for armories in cities of the first and second class.

Providing for the retirement and pensioning of firemen.

To establish standard packages for cranberries.

Making valid instruments in which a scroll or ink or other device is used instead of a seal.

Providing for the appointment by the Legislature of commissioners of juries for each county.

Providing for descriptive indexes of land-records in counties having over 200,000 inhabitants.

Regulating the consolidation of any city with another city, or with a borough, town, or township, or any portion thereof.

To prevent persons from unlawfully wearing the insignia of the Military Order of the Loyal Legion of the United States.

To provide for the support of the New Jersey School for Deaf Mutes.

To prevent adulteration of vinegar and deception in its sale, and providing for the appointment of inspectors of vinegar.

Authorizing any municipal corporation to contract for a supply of water, or for a further or other supply of water therefor.

Dividing the counties of the State into sections, known as game-sections, and fixing the time for shooting certain game birds and animals therein.

Appropriating $2,000 for stocking the waters of the State with food-fishes.

Authorizing the board of chosen freeholders of any county, upon the approval of the electors thereof, to lay out, construct, and maintain a public road therein.

Requiring savings-banks to report and publish lists of unclaimed deposits.

Authorizing cities to construct public docks and piers, and to purchase necessary land under and near thereto.

Providing for the incorporation of library associations.

To provide for the construction of a State laboratory for the Agricultural Experiment Station.

To encourage the formation of associations for the improvement of public grounds in any city, town, township, in borough in the State.

Providing for the formation and government of towns.

Enabling cities to pay past due improvement certificates out of their general funds.

Authorizing the appointment of a commission to locate and mark out the boundary between the State and New York, in Hudson River, New York Bay, Kill von Kull, and Arthur Kill or Staten Island Sounds.

Consolidating with the city of Trenton the borough of Chambersburg and the township of Millham.

Finances.—Of the bonded State debt, the sum of $100,000 becomes due and payable by law on January 1 of each year, but the reduction of the debt for the fiscal year ending October 31 was but $98,000, as $2,000 of bonds becoming due were not presented for redemption. The total bonded debt on the latter date was $1,298,800. The total receipts of the sinking-fund for the last fiscal year were $206,960.31, and the payments $179,635.57. The fund itself on October 31 amounted to $645,385.98. The revenue and expenses of the State for general purposes for the fiscal year were as follow:

RECEIPTS.

State tax on railroad corporations	$980,263 86
Tax on miscellaneous corporations	209,874 08
State Prison receipts	57,284 48
From other sources	106,596 85
Total revenue	$1,353,518 77
Balance on hand Oct. 31, 1887	208,429 43
	$1,561,948 20

EXPENDITURES.

On account of public debt	$90,000 00
Charitable and reformatory institutions	421,408 91
Courts, State Prison, etc	334,216 27
State Government, including Legislature	285,951 72
Military	114,963 41
Printing laws, etc., in newspapers	72,779 55
Printing and binding reports, etc	80,994 57
Blind, Deaf-Mute School, feeble-minded	58,086 86
Scientific, sanitary, etc	76,028 80
Miscellaneous	55,588 18
Total disbursements	$1,542,007 72
Balance on Oct. 31, 1888	$19,940 48

During the year, in order to meet urgent demands, the Treasurer was obliged to obtain a temporary loan of $150,000, so that the actual cash in the treasury on October 31 was $169,940.48. It will be seen from the above statement that the expenses of the year exceeded the actual income, exclusive of the balance on hand at the beginning, by nearly $200,000, and in consequence the balance of $208,429.43 existing on Oct. 31, 1887, was nearly wiped out. In addition, there remained unpaid on Oct. 31, 1888, of appropriations already made, which are a charge on the general receipts, $352,775.16. Before the end of December the demands upon the treasury were such that a second temporary loan, of $100,000, was necessary. The estimated receipts for 1889 are $1,478,161, and the estimated expenses for ordinary purposes $1,250,000, leaving a balance of $228,161, to apply to the temporary indebtedness of $250,000. This estimate omits extraordinary expenses, which may be incurred by the Legislature of 1889, and which will materially reduce the amount applicable to payment of the temporary debt. The Governor says in his message, in January, 1889: "The restoration of the State Capitol and the addition to the Trenton asylum have made imperative demands upon the treasury during the last two years, and the amounts paid for these purposes, as well as the appropriations and payments for the Soldiers' Home, Gettysburg Monuments, Reform and Industrial School, Home for Feeble-Minded Women, and State Prison improvements, all extraordinary expenditures, have not only exhausted the annual revenues for those years, but some of the anticipated receipts of the next."

Education.—The amount raised by State tax and appropriated to the public schools during the year was $1,870,055, to which was added the $100,000 annual appropriation from the school fund, making an increase of $413,395 of receipts over those of the preceding year. The operation of the law of last winter, raising the State school-tax from four to five dollars to each child, has proved satisfactory. The amount of township school-tax ordered to be raised was $48,992.01. The amount received from the interest of the surplus revenue fund was $32,084.49. The amount of district and city tax for teachers' salaries was $474,293.45. The total amount devoted during the year to the maintenance of the schools was $2,525,424.95. In addition to this amount $590,016.46 was ordered to be raised for building and repairing school-houses. The school accommodation has been increased, and the buildings improved; there were 30 new school-houses erected and 45 enlarged or remodeled. The total value of the school property in the State is $7,837,706, an increase of $351,500 during the year. Nine hundred schools have established libraries. There were at the close of the school year 1,615 public schools, employing 4,121 teachers, and giving instruction to 387,847 pupils. There have been in attendance at the Normal School during the school year ending in 1888, 241 pupils. The average attendance was 189. The number graduated from the advance course, 22; the number graduated from the elementary course, 13; total graduates, 35. The whole number in attendance at the Model School during the year was 471, and the average attendance, 390; graduates, 18. The attendance at the Farnum School, Beverly, amounted to 139; the average attendance, 129.

Charities. — The number of patients under treatment at the Trenton Insane Asylum during the year was 905, and there remained there on October 31, 761. The total amount of receipts, including balance on hand, Oct. 31, 1887, was $219,908.29. The amount disbursed was $186,954.43. At the Morristown asylum there were 1,111 patients, of whom 904 remained on Oct. 31, 772 being public, and 131 private. The receipts for the year were $241,494.86, and the expenditures, $229,764.08.

The Legislature at its session this year appropriated $10,000 to the establishment of a home for feeble-minded women, with an additional $2,000 for its maintenance. The managers purchased a property in Vineland, and report that they require additional accommodation.

There were under instruction at the School for Deaf Mutes during the year 117 pupils, with an average daily attendance of 96. The amount expended in the maintenance of the school has been for the fiscal year $26,162; for improvements and repairs, $5,000. This school is in that part of the city of Trenton which was formerly Chambersburg, and consists of a large building which was erected for other purposes, and is not especially well adapted to the use of this institution.

The blind children who are supported at the expense of the State are placed in institutions in the city of New York and Philadelphia, 31 being in New York and 8 in Philadelphia. The amount paid during the year for the former was $8,704.73; for the latter, $2,410.83.

There have been 108 feeble-minded children provided for by the State during the year, 82 of these being at the Pennsylvania Training-School for Feeble-minded Children at Elwyn; 5 at the Connecticut Institution for Imbeciles, and 21 at the Educational Home for Feeble-minded Children at Vineland, N. J. The amount expended for the maintenance and support of these children was $24,821.87.

By the report of the managers of the Soldiers' Home, it appears that there were 367 inmates on Oct. 31, 1888. There were admitted during the year, 266; discharged, 190; expelled, 11; died, 26. The average number of inmates was 349 per day. Since the home was opened there have been 15,318 inmates cared for by the institution. The total receipts for the year, including the balance on hand Oct. 31, 1887, was $37,769.58. The expenses for the same time were $36,837.73. The balance on hand Oct. 31, 1888, $931.85.

The commissioners appointed to erect a suitable home for the disabled soldiers, report that their work has been substantially completed, and that in October the inmates of the old home were removed to their new quarters.

Prisons.—There were in confinement at the State Prison on Oct. 31, 1888, 881 prisoners. The total number during the year was 1,305, and the daily average 874, of whom 835 were males and 39 females. There was expended for maintenance the sum of $67,000.76, and the total expenditures were $151,048.81, a per capita cost of $47\frac{44}{100}$ cents per diem and $172.82 per annum. The earnings for the year were $57,287.13.

Concerning prison labor the Governor says: "The contracts made to put the piece-price system in operation will expire during the year 1889. The supervisor reports that, in his opinion, the trial of the system has not been encouraging. I can not but think that these contracts were made under disadvantageous circumstances. It is difficult to understand why, under a system which throws the whole risk on the State and none on the contractor, contracts less advantageous to the State were secured than under a system which reverses the conditions and the liabilities of loss, and throws the risk upon the contractor."

At the State Reform School the whole number of persons confined during the year was 424. There remained, Oct. 31, 1888, 298. There were received during the year, on account of maintenance, $42,317.24 from the State; from the farm and other works, $7,-028.60, which, with a balance on account Oct. 31, 1887, of $2,088.37, in all amounting to $51,488.20 received, is chargeable to the maintenance account during the fiscal year. The amount of expenditures and expenses during the same period was $50,664.49, leaving a balance on hand, Oct. 31, 1888, of $823.72.

The State Industrial School for Girls had, at the close of the fiscal year, 76 girls under its charge, an increase of 9 over the number one year previous. Of these, 26 are out at service and 50 at the home. As this institution was intended to provide for only thirty-five girls, an enlargement of its buildings is needed.

The Governor, in his message, strongly urges the need of a State reformatory to secure the separation of young offenders from the class of old and hardened criminals. The Legislature of 1888 made a step forward in prison management by enacting a law requiring those in charge of the jails to keep all persons under the age of sixteen, who are sent to such jails for any purpose whatever, separate and apart, so that no communication can take place between them and other persons above such age; but reports at the close of the year showed that in only two counties had the law been fully complied with, while four counties had entirely disregarded it.

Militia.—From the report of the Inspector-General of the last annual muster and inspection, the strength of the National Guard is shown to be 316 commissioned officers and 3,719 enlisted men, a total of 4,035. Two new companies have been added, the force now consisting of 55 companies of infantry and 2 Gatling-gun companies. Negotiations to secure a tract of land at Sea Girt, Monmouth County, for the use of the militia have not yet met with success.

Riparian Commissioners.—The grants, leases, and leases converted into grants during the year, amount to $104,479.89. The rentals paid to the State during the past year on leases heretofore made by legislative acts and by the commissioners amount to $59,754.43. The amount, which represents the principal for land disposed of by grants or leases from April 4, 1884, to Oct. 31, 1888, is $3,182,347.56.

Railroad Taxation.—The Attorney-General reports that the formidable combination, embracing over thirty-five corporations, which has contested every point from the constitutionality of the law to the minutest element which constitutes valuation, has entirely disappeared during the past year, and that the representatives of the various railroad companies now manifest a desire to assist in the arduous labor of settling up the arrears of taxation, as well as aiding the Board of Assessors in arriving at proper results in its valuation. Of the State tax payable in 1888, nearly 97 per cent. has been collected, and of the State tax payable in 1887, nearly 95 per cent. has been received.

Decision.—The local-option and high-license act of the Legislature this year was speedily brought before the State Court of Errors and Appeals in order to test the constitutionality of its provisions. In the two test cases brought before it, the court rendered a decision about August 1, by which the high-license features of the act were unanimously sustained, and the local-option portion upheld by a majority of the court, eight judges being in favor of, and seven against its constitutionality.

Political.—On May 9 a Republican State Convention was held at Trenton for the selection of delegates to the National Convention of the party. A platform was adopted, of which only the following portion refers directly to State questions:

We favor protection to the homes of the people by the due restriction of vice and intemperance, and we congratulate the Legislature of this State on their honest, earnest, and courageous efforts to restrain the evils of the liquor-traffic, and indorse their action.

On the following day a Democratic Convention for the same purpose was held at the same place. The platform adopted contains the following:

The party confidently directs the attention of the people of the State to the administration of State affairs by Governor Green. The system of railroad taxation devised and inaugurated by his Democratic predecessor has been placed upon a firm foundation and given the authority of Executive and judicial approval; the dignity of the Executive has been zealously defended against the most bitter and dangerous encroachments ; the qualified power of the veto has been exercised against legislation, which, in its extravagance, attacked alike economical government and the inherent and constitutional rights of the people.
It denounces as subversive of the principle of our representative government the caucus legislation practiced by the Republican Legislature at its last session, by which the votes of the Republican members of each House were massed, directed, and controlled by the decision of a secret caucus, for or against laws of general import upon which the individual judgment and responsibility of each member was due to the State.
It demands such legislation as will check the growing evil of combined corporate power, and that shall make it unlawful to maintain an armed band or drilled and uniformed army in private hands for hire as a menace to the people.

On September 27 another Democratic Convention was held to nominate presidential electors, and on October 4 the Republicans in convention nominated their candidates for the same office. Similar conventions of the Prohibition party were also held. There was no general election for State officers this year, but six members of the State Senate and all members of the Lower House of the Legislature were chosen. The Democratic National ticket was successful at the November election. Four of the six State Senators elected were Democrats (there will consequently be 10 Republicans and 11 Democrats in that body in 1889), and the Assembly will have 32 Democrats to 28 Republicans, giving the Democrats a majority of 5 on joint ballot. In the Legislature of 1888 the Republicans had a majority of 17 on joint ballot. For members of Congress, Republicans were elected in the First, Second, Fifth, and Sixth Districts, and Democrats in the Third, Fourth, and Seventh, the Democrats gaining a member in the Third District.

NEW JERUSALEM CHURCH. The General Convention of this body is composed of the Canada Association, 7 societies; the Illinois Association, 11 societies; the Maine Association, 5 societies; the Maryland Association, 5 societies, and individual members; the Massachusetts Association, 19 societies; the Michigan Association, 5 societies; the Minnesota Association, 2 societies; the New York Association, 14 societies; the Ohio Association, 12 societies; the General Conference of Pennsylvania, 12 societies; 8 single societies; and four members by election. The list of ministers of the General Conference includes the names of 8 "general pastors"; 100 "pastors and ministers"; and 9 "authorized candidates and preachers." The number of members is not given in the reports.

The General Convention of the New Jerusalem Church in the United States met in Boston, Mass., May 19. The Rev. Chauncey Giles presided. The treasurer gave the amounts of the capital investments of the funds of the General Convention as follow: Simpkins fund, $20,000 ; Wales fund, $5,000; Jenkins fund, $2,000 ; Wilkins fund, $3,750 ; White fund, $4,500; Richards fund, $1,000; in all, $36,250. The Board of Publication reported that the collections for the "Fifty-Thousand-Dollar fund" to date amounted to $42,065, $421 having been added during the year. The property of the publishing house was valued at $9,274. The year's business showed a net loss of $1,009. The Endowment fund of the Theological School was returned at $31,370 ; and the whole amount of funds the income of which is applicable to the support of the institution was $99,310. Eight students for the ministry had attended the school during the year. The course of instruction includes Latin, Greek, and Hebrew, Swedenborgian theology, Church history, and homiletics and pastoral duties, the younger pupils beginning with the "Athanasian Creed." The New Church Building fund amounted to $1,269. The amounts of other special funds and legacies were returned as follow: Rice legacy, $8,519 ; Rotch legacy, $24,-364, with $8,507 invested in plates, books, etc. ;

Iungerich fund, $36,696 ; fund for photo-lithographing Swedenborg's manuscripts, $2,400 subscribed, $191 paid. The committee of this fund was authorized by the Convention to make arrangements for the publication of the manuscripts as soon as the amount raised in the United States and in England for the work should warrant beginning it. The trustees of the Iungerich fund had distributed during the year 5,508 copies of Swedenborg's works, making the whole number of copies distributed under this fund since its institution 88,816. The receipts of the Board of Home and Foreign Missions had been $3,883, and its expenditures $3,304. It expected also to receive a legacy of $1,000. Report was made of mission work in Nova Scotia, Canada, Southern and Western States and Territories of the United States, Sweden, Denmark, Italy, France, and Switzerland. The Swiss Union of the New Church having indicated a desire to be received into the Convention as an association, the Convention responded, that on account of the inconvenience with which such a position would be attended by reason of distance, it seemed better that the Union should act as a sister body, having a position in Switzerland corresponding with that of the Convention in America, with which annual messages should be exchanged, "to be conveyed personally whenever it can be done." In the address adopted by the General Convention to the General Conference in Great Britain, reference is made to the growing strength of the State Associations, which were becoming less dependent upon the general body. With some of them there was a desire for more latitude in the choice of a General Pastor and in the rules in regard to his continuance in office. The general body had shown a willingness to leave to the State associations the particular arrangement and classification of their ministers, so far as their rules did not conflict with the order of the general body. By the observance of this principle the freedom of the local bodies would be recognized, and the general order of the Church at the same time preserved. The relation between the organized bodies of the New Church and those of other churches had engaged the attention of a portion of the New Church people in the United States. How much, if any, affiliation and co-operation could or ought to exist could not well be determined by any formal action ; and only a single instance of such action—in which members of the New Church were excluded because they were not regarded as orthodox—was mentioned. An address was received from the Australian Conference.

The British Church.—The whole number of New Church societies in association in Great Britain was reported to the Conference in August to be 70, and the whole number of members 5,920. The number of churches had increased by three, and the number of members by 200, during the year.

The British Annual Conference met at Accrington, August 14. About 120 delegates were present. The Rev. Richard Sterry presided. Reports were received from the Students' and Ministers Aid Committee, of New Church work on the Continent, and concerning the support of " Weak Societies."

The seventy-eighth annual meeting of the Swedenborgian Society was held in London, June 12. Mr. Samuel Teed presided. The income for the year had been £1,155. The report of the committee represented that 2,854 volumes of the society's publications had been delivered during the year, and 700 volumes had been presented to free libraries and other institutions and individuals.

NEW MEXICO. Territorial Government.—The following were the Territorial officers during the year: Governor, Edmund G. Ross; Secretary, George W. Lane; Treasurer, Antonio Ortiz y Salazar; Auditor, Trinidad Alarid; Attorney-General, William Breeden; Commissioner of Immigration, Henry C. Burnett; Chief-Justice of the Supreme Court, Elisha Van Long; Associate Justices, William H. Brinker, William F. Henderson, and Reuben A. Reeves.

Population.—As estimated by the Governor in his annual report, the number of people in the Territory in October was about 175,000, an increase of 10,000 or 12,000 during the year preceding. Fully one quarter of the immigration has been to the southeast portion of the Territory, and largely from Texas.

Finances.—At the convening of the twenty-seventh Legislative Assembly, Dec. 27, 1887, the funded debt of the Territory was $350,000, and the amount of outstanding warrants or floating debt $203,117.92, making a total of $553,117.92. Since that date the public debt has increased to $762,192. The face value of warrants issued during the same time was $512,162.72, and the cash receipts of the Treasurer (general fund) $357,162.72, leaving a deficit of $155,631.09.

In 1887 the total expenses of the Territory were $265,255.42, of which the expenses for courts alone amounted to $164,384 25. In 1888 the expenses, up to Dec. 15, 1888, were $247,538.39, and the expenses at the courts amounted to $156,042.64.

Assessments.—The rate of taxation prescribed by law for Territorial revenue is one half of 1 per cent. for ordinary revenue, one fourth of 1 per cent. for county revenue, and for school purposes three mills on the dollar. The assessments for 1838 show an aggregate valuation of taxable property of $43,151,920. Of this amount $15,370,960 is on live-stock, $7,-466,869 on lands, and $6,858,350 on houses and improvements. These amounts are exclusive of $300 exemption to each property owner, of poll-taxes, and of a specified extent of tree-culture. The proper aggregate of taxation is greatly diminished by the ineffectiveness of the revenue system. Large areas of land pay little or no taxes for lack of proper definition. Another serious source of loss of revenue is in the fact that 7,000,000 acres of taxable lands are included in Spanish and Mexican grants, patented and unconfirmed. If these lands were assessed, the tax rolls would be increased by several million dollars.

Penitentiary.—The only public building of the Territory, besides the Capitol, is the Penitentiary, constructed in 1884–'85. The number of prisoners confined there has steadily increased since its opening, and in March of this year had reached 114. In consequence of defeets in its construction a large number of guards are needed, thereby increasing the cost of its maintenance.

Railroads.—The only railway construction during the year was the Denver and Fort Worth, about eighty miles across the northeast corner of the Territory. The construction of this line has been the means of establishing three thriving towns in eastern Colfax County —Folsom, Clayton, and Texline. The addition of this line makes the aggregate mileage of railway in operation in the Territory 1,130 miles, 182 of which is narrow-gauge.

Stock-Raising.—This industry was not as prosperous during the year as previously, losses of cattle during the winter and low prices contributing to this condition. As a result of low prices, the appraisement for taxation was reduced, at the request of cattle owners, from $12 to $10 a head for the year; so that, though the assessment rolls for 1888 show an increase of 135,000 head over the rolls of 1887, the assessments show a diminution of $1,200,-000. The assessment rolls of the sheep-stock of the Territory show 1,750,000 for 1887, and 1,500,000 for 1888, a loss of 250,000, with a corresponding reduction on the tax rolls, they being uniformly assessed for taxation at $1 a head each year.

Mining.—The gold-product of the Territory was greater during 1888 than in any previous year. In addition to the old mines, an important gold deposit recently discovered is being operated at Elizabethtown, in the mountains of Colfax County, with a fair output; another valuable lead in central Santa Fé County is developing into a producing mine; while in the Jicarilla mountains in Lincoln County, in the Organ mountains in Doña Ana County, and other portions of the Territory, gold finds have been numerous.

Iron-ore has lately been discovered in large quantities in the Guadaloupe and Sacramento mountains, in Lincoln County. It is found in considerable quantities in different portions of the Territory; but this latter discovery is very extensive. The total mineral product of the Territory for 1886 is estimated at $3,821,871, and for 1887 at $4,229,234.

An indication that the great mineral wealth of this district was known to the early Spanish colonists is the discovery within the last few years of fully developed silver-mines containing many hundred feet of drifts, tunnels, and shafts, but the openings of which had been filled up and all surface trace of them obliterated at the time of the Pueblo Indian insurrection two hundred years ago, when the Spanish residents were all slaughtered or driven out of the country and permitted to return several years later only on condition that the mines should never again be worked. Several of these have been rediscovered, and some of them are being redeveloped with profit.

Coal.—The Gallup mines, in the western part of Bernalillo County, on the line of the Atlantic and Pacific Railroad, are the most extensive coal-mines in the Territory. These mines are supposed to be on the southern point of a coal deposit about 10 miles wide from east to west, and widening northward into Colorado, a distance of 200 miles. The output for the year was 300,000 tons. The Monero and Amargo mines, in Rio Arriba County, on the Colorado border and near the Denver and Rio Grande Railroad, also produce an excellent quality of coal. Excellent bituminous coal is also found in Lincoln County, in the vicinity of White Oaks. The output of the Blossburg mines, near the Colorado border, was 156.000 tons, and of the San Pedro Coal and Coke Company in Socorro County, 59,000 tons the latter rendered into 14,000 tons of coke. Coal has been found also in other portions of the Territory.

Irrigation.—The Governor, in his last annual report, says it has become evident that the present system of independent ditching must be abandoned, and that in its stead the State must assume jurisdiction of the water-supply and its distribution by a carefully devised and adjusted system that shall economize the water-supply and guarantee equal rights in it.

Political.—On May 7 a Democratic Territorial Convention met at Santa Fé and nominated delegates to the National Convention. The platform adopted at that time, after approving of the administration of President Cleveland, continues as follows:

That we approve of that portion of the Democratic platform which promised that Territorial offices should be filled by *bona-fide* residents of the Territories, and believe that the only method of securing Democratic success is by a fair, honest, and manly fulfillment of that promise.

That we feel that no prosperity can come to this people until the titles to our lands are finally settled and determined, and that we approve the bill introduced by our delegate for that purpose, and most respectfully request all of our friends in Congress to aid him in the passage thereof, calling to their attention the fact that under the existing laws, which have now been in force for forty years, not one twentieth of the claims presented have been passed upon, and there are now unsettled and undetermined more than 1,000 claims, the greater number of which, though small and insignificant as to the quantity of land claimed, constitute the homesteads of fully 10,000 of our people, not one of whom can sell or dispose of his land at its reasonable value on account of the uncertainty of the tenure of title which has during all of this time rested upon it, and that there is a multitude of small

claims involving from twenty to forty acres that have never been presented, owing to the fact that the prosecution thereof under the present law involves the expenditure in costs and fees of more than the value of the land, thereby virtually working a confiscation thereof.

The Republican Territorial Convention met at Santa Fé, on May 15, to elect delegates to the Chicago Convention, and adopted a long series of resolutions, of which the following are the more important:

We earnestly denounce the wholesale and unwarranted action of the Administration in procuring to be brought hundreds of indictments against respectable and honest citizens of this Territory for alleged violations of the land and timber laws, and assert that such action was taken for political purposes, and for the obtaining of fees by the different court officials and the smirching for political effect of the characters of good and reputable citizens.

That we denounce the administration of the Governor of this Territory, Edmund G. Ross, appointed by President Cleveland, as characterized by corruption, imbecility, and a total disregard of the laws of the Territory of New Mexico.

That, it being the plain intent of the act of Congress creating the office of surveyor-general to submit the inquiry as to the existence, validity, nature, and extent of our Mexican land-titles to a learned, honest, and impartial tribunal, we view with indignation and disgust the action of the President in forcing upon our Territory as surveyor-general such an embodiment of stilted vanity and mendacious partisanship as George W. Julian, who, coming hither in the guise of a fair-minded judge, has devoted himself to the vandal work of overturning long-settled titles granted by Spain and Mexico, fully recognized by those Governments and guaranteed by the treaty of Guadalupe Hidalgo, and in this criminal work of destruction has prostituted an office judicial in nature to personal and political ends.

That we condemn the action of Gov. Ross in the exercise of the pardoning power, by which he has released from the Territorial Penitentiary large numbers of the most atrocious criminals, who had been convicted at great expense.

Early in July the Prohibitionists placed in nomination J. C. Tiffany as delegate to Congress, and, a few weeks later, a Republican convention nominated M. S. Otero for the same office. The Democrats renominated Delegate Joseph. At the November election Joseph received 17,525 votes, and Otero 15,775. But the Republicans elected a majority of the Legislature for 1889, which will stand: Senate—Republicans, 6; Democrats, 5; House—Republicans, 14; Democrats, 9.

NEW YORK (STATE). State Government.—The following were the State officers during the year: Governor, David B. Hill, Democrat; Lieutenant-Governor, Edward F. Jones; Secretary of State, Frederick Cook; Comptroller, Edward Wemple; Treasurer, Lawrence J. Fitzgerald; State Engineer and Surveyor, John Bogart; Attorney-General, Charles F. Tabor; Superintendent of Public Instruction, Andrew S. Draper; Superintendent of Prisons, Austin Lathrop; Superintendent of Insurance Department, Robert A. Maxwell; Superintendent of Bank Department, Willis S. Paine; Superintendent of Public Works, James Shanahan; Chief-Judge of the Court of Appeals, William C. Ruger; Associate Judges, Charles Andrews, Robert Earl, George F. Danforth, Rufus W. Peckham, Francis M. Finch, and John Clinton Gray. Judge Gray was appointed by the Governor on January 22 to fill the vacancy caused by the death of Judge Rapallo in 1887 until his successor should be elected.

Legislative Session.—Laws were passed amending the Revised Statutes so that inventories shall be filed more accurately; authorizing a compromise by executors and administrators of debts due their testators relative to the sale of doubtful claims; extending the time for the payment of capital stock in certain corporations; providing that in making assignments the nature and place of business shall be stated; providing that dealers in grave-stones shall have a lien upon the property; exempting railroad equipment or rolling-stock, sold, leased, or loaned under a contract, from the law requiring the filing of contracts for the conditional sale of personal property on credit. The Legislature made scant appropriations for the State prisons, which will probably result in keeping the prisoners in idleness for a part of the year. A law was passed providing that, whenever it can be so arranged, the sentences of convicts shall expire during the summer months. Several bills were introduced as the result of an investigation by the Senate Committee on General Laws into the working of those combinations known as "trusts." But none of these bills were passed.

The Governor vetoed a bill for the prevention of bribery at elections; also a bill, based upon the Australian system, providing that ballots shall be printed at the expense of the city or county; that voters shall have separate compartments in which to prepare their ballots; and that no electioneering shall take place within one hundred feet of the polls. The factory-inspectors were required to see that the obligations of employers to their apprentices are enforced; and mechanics' liens were extended to cover gas and electric fixtures.

A bill passed the Senate, but was adversely reported in the Assembly, providing that every adult citizen, irrespective of sex, shall hereafter be entitled to vote at any municipal election, or at any election for supervisor or excise officers; and that no poll-clerk or inspector of election shall refuse to register or receive the vote of any adult citizen at such election on account of sex. Another bill providing that there shall be no discrimination on account of sex at any election was not reported from the Senate Committee. A third bill, killed in the Committee of the Assembly, provided that at all municipal elections, for five years and no longer, all females who pay taxes on property, or lease a whole building or premises in which they reside or carry on business, may vote for municipal officers; and that at elections where only male tax-payers can now vote, female tax-payers can vote under the act; and that, if

registered, every female voter shall describe the property which she leases for business. The Governor vetoed a bill to amend the act of 1887 so as to give half-holidays during only June, July, August, and September.

A law was passed providing that, instead of taking fees variously estimated at from $50,000 to $100,000, the health officer of the port of New York should hereafter give the fees to the State, and receive a salary of $10,000. The Governor vetoed a bill providing that quarantine commissioners should be elected by a joint ballot of the two Houses of the Legislature, instead of being nominated by the Governor and confirmed by the Senate, as at present.

A concurrent resolution for amending the Constitution was passed, and, having passed a previous Legislature, will now be submitted to the people, which provides that the Governor shall select seven justices of the Supreme Court to act as associate justices, and to form a second division of the Court of Appeals, for the relief of the latter. Another concurrent resolution was passed (but must pass another Legislature before it is submitted to the people), which prohibits the manufacture and sale of intoxicating liquors as beverages. A bill was introduced (but not passed) providing for a convention to revise and amend the Constitution of the State. It was similar to the bill vetoed by the Governor the year before.

A law was passed appointing a committee of five assemblymen to investigate all the reservations within the State, and report to the next Legislature what should be done in regard to civilizing the Indians. Another bill was passed allowing a commissioner to investigate the claims of that branch of the Cayuga Indians which has lived in Canada since the war of 1812 because it fought against the United States at that time. The Canadian Cayugas claim a portion of the annuity that is paid by the State to the nation.

A bill was passed appropriating $570,000 to continue the work of lengthening the locks and improving the canals. A law was passed providing that in New York, Brooklyn, and Buffalo, the charges for elevating, receiving, weighing, and discharging grain shall be five eighths of one cent a bushel. The former rate, including five days' storage, was three fourths of a cent.

A bill was passed appropriating $143,260 to finish the State Library and the Law Library, and to remove the books, the work to be in charge of the Capitol commissioner and three of the officers of the Senate and Assembly. Another bill appropriates $287,000 to repair the Assembly staircase, and to replace the stone ceiling of the Assembly Chamber with a ceiling of wood, the work to be in charge of a committee composed of the speaker and four members of the Assembly whom he should appoint; $20,000 was appropriated to lay out the park in front of the Capitol.

Laws were enacted amending former acts

to facilitate the formation of agricultural and horticultural societies; amending the acts relating to contagious diseases among animals; incorporating the Western New York Horticultural Society; authorizing the State Agricultural Society to borrow money for the erection of new buildings; for the destruction, at the expense of the State, of animals afflicted with glanders; appropriating $2,500 to extend dairy knowledge throughout the State; allowing the State dairy commissioner to appoint five extra butter-and-cheese-makers to inspect butter and cheese throughout the State.

A bill was passed which substitutes electricity for hanging, to take effect in the execution of sentences for crimes committed after Jan. 1, 1889.

It was provided that the thin paper used on type-writers shall hereafter be classed as legal paper.

The following became laws: For the incorporation of societies for providing play-grounds for children; providing for police matrons in cities of the State, who shall serve in places of detention, no more than two to be appointed in any city; permitting the burial without a coroner's inquest of persons dying suddenly without medical attendance, in case of accident or organic diseases, where no suspicion of foul play can exist; requiring all plumbers in Albany to be registered; providing schools for nurses; providing that the remains of persons dying at the Quarantine Hospital in New York shall be cremated unless taken away by relatives; amending the act to protect owners of bottles by including those used for medical preparations, perfumery, etc. Provision was made for supplying water to Albany, Syracuse, Schenectady, Watkins, and Little Falls.

An extra session was held on July 17-20. The Governor did not give his reasons for calling the session, as had been the custom heretofore. When the Legislature convened, his first message said that the convicts in the State prisons were in idleness, and recommended legislation applying to all State institutions. The Legislature passed a bill the main points of which were as follow: No motive-power machinery for manufacturing shall be placed or used in any of the penal institutions of the State; and no person in such institutions shall be required or allowed to work, while under sentence thereto, at any trade or industry where his labor, or the production or profit of his labor, is farmed out, contracted, given, or sold to any person or persons whomsoever: the Superintendent of State Prisons, and all other officers having in charge the management of the penal institutions of the State, shall hereafter cause to be manufactured therein, by the inmates thereof, such articles only as are commonly needed and used in the public institutions of this State, for clothing and other necessary supplies of such institutions and the inmates thereof; and all the articles manufactured in such penal institutions, not required for use therein, shall be furnished to the several institutions, supported in whole or in part by the State, for the use of their inmates, upon the requisitions of the trustees or managers thereof upon the Superintendent of State Prisons, and no article so manufactured shall be purchased for the use of such inmates unless the same can not be furnished upon such requisitions. The Comptroller, the Superintendent of State Prisons, and the President of the State Board of Charities shall constitute a board whose duties shall be to determine the price at which all articles manufactured in such penal institutions, and furnished for use in the several institutions of the State, shall be so furnished, which price shall be uniform to all institutions; the comptroller shall devise and furnish to the several institutions a proper form for such requisitions, and also a proper system of accounts to be kept for all such transactions. All moneys received for such articles so furnished upon requisition shall be paid into the treasury, as now required by law in case of sales of the products of State prisons. There was appropriated $250,000 to purchase materials and to carry out the provisions of the act. The Governor signed the bill. The Governor sent in a message advising that the conspiracy laws of the State be so amended that workingmen might gather for peaceful discussion with less embarrassment than at present; but the recommendation was not acted upon. Another message by the Governor called attention to alleged irregularities in the work of the commission appointed to construct the new aqueduct for New York city. The Legislature immediately passed a bill legislating the old commissioners out of office and making the new commissioners the Mayor, the Comptroller, and the Commissioner of Public Works, together with four citizens (two Democrats and two Republicans), to be appointed by the Mayor. The Governor signed the bill, and the board was appointed.

Finances.—The State debt was reduced $601,-650 during the year by the payment at maturity of $100,000 Niagara reservation bonds; by the purchase and cancellation of canal stock, forming part of the canal debt, to the amount of $403,250; and by the redemption of canal stock that matured on July 1, 1887, amounting to $98,400. On Sept. 30, 1888, the total funded debt was $6,965,354.87, classified as follows: Indian annuities (general fund), $122,-694.87; canal debt, $6,142,660; Niagara reservation bonds, $700,000; canal debt sinking-fund, $4,076,289.39. Total debt unprovided for but not yet due, $2,889,065.48. The latter sum is about one twelfth of 1 per cent. of the valuation of the State. On Sept. 30, 1887, the total debt was $7,567,004.87, and the sinking-fund $4,061,188.84, leaving as the net debt $3,505,816.03. The increase of the sinking-fund during the year was $15,100.55. Valuing investments at par, the capital of the more important trust funds held by the State on Sept. 30, 1888, was as follows:

FUNDS.	Securities.	Money in the treasury.	Total.
Common-school fund.............	$3,957,176 69	$16,464 08	$3,973,640 77
United States deposit fund........	3,979,476 73	37,743 98	4,017,220 71
Literature fund.....	280,000 00	4,201 36	284,201 30
College land-scrip fund.............	415,400 00	59,009 12	474,409 12
Total..........	$8,632,053 42	$117,418 48	$8,749,471 90

The capital of the same funds on Sept. 30, 1887, was: Securities, $8,498,045.49; money in treasury, $208,445.23; total, $8,706,488.52.

The canal debt sinking-fund, as above stated, contained on Sept. 30, 1888, securities and cash to the amount of $4,076,289.39. The total amount, therefore, of cash and securities held by the Comptroller for the principal funds, Sept. 30, 1888, was $12,825,761.29.

For the current year the State tax is $9,089,-303.86, the rate being two and sixty-two one hundredths mills, and the valuation $3,469,-199.945, the tax to be devoted as follows: School purposes, $3,469,199.95; canals, including canal debt, $2,254,979.96; general purposes, $3,365,123.95. The direct school-tax for the last fiscal year produced $3,697,240.99. The total expenditure from the State treasury for education was $4,192,314.92. The total expenditure, State and local, for the maintenance of schools was $15,696,012.39.

The balance in the treasury on Oct. 1, 1887, amounted to $5,222,256.68. There was paid into the treasury from all sources during the fiscal year $17,800,755.42. There was drawn therefrom for all purposes $17,626,557.35, leaving on Oct. 1, 1888, a balance of $5,396,-454.75. The balance in the general fund on Oct. 1, 1887, was $3,326,127.06; the receipts for the year were $9,855,472.75, and the payments $10,061,718.49, leaving $3,119,881.32. Among the receipts of the general fund were: From State tax, 1887, $5,005,500.78; from tax on corporations, $993,677.82; from tax on organization of corporations, $181,838.27; from tax on collateral inheritances, $736,084.88; from salt duty, $52,115.69; and from State-Prison earnings, $2,110,042.84. Among the expenses of the same time are: For the State Capitol, $167,957.60; for normal schools, $71,-481.24; for legislative expenses, $410,981.07; for the militia, $546,105.67; for the Utica Lunatic Asylum, $57,373.20; Willard Asylum, $47,425; Buffalo Asylum, $92,414.33; Homœopathic Asylum, $35,729.20; Hudson River Asylum, $173,747.78; St. Lawrence Asylum, $133,338.10; Binghampton Asylum, $101,-358.20; institutions for the blind, $87,812.61; institutions for deaf and dumb, $265,369.05; Soldiers' and Sailors' Home, $143,000; State Reformatory, $195,000; State Industrial School, $217,300; Asylum for Insane Criminals, $161,516.63; State prisons, $1,967,315.-74; for canal purposes (canal tax), $2,305,-

733.93. The canal receipts for the year were $3,246,552.68; expenditures, $2,788,046.71.

Assessments.—The Comptroller says in his annual report: "Our taxing system is in many respects glaringly defective. Real estate is overburdened, while personal property escapes its due proportion of liability. The total assessed valuation of the property of the people of the State for the purpose of taxation for 1887 was:

Personal....................................	$335,898,859
Real..	3,025,229,758
Total..................................	$3,361,128,177

"The assessed valuation of the same for 1888 was:

Personal....................................	$346,611,861
Real..	3,122,588,084
Total..................................	$3,469,199,945

" This shows an increase in one year on

Real estate..................................	$97,358,296
Personal estate.............................	10,713,472
Total increase............................	$108,071,768

"These valuations clearly exhibit the unjust proportion of the burdens of taxation borne by the real over the personal property. It can not be that the personal property amounts to less in value than the real, and in that case we have within the State to-day over $2,500,000,-000 of personal property that is not but ought to be subject to taxation."

Education.—For the school year ending Aug. 20, 1887, the total amount expended for public education was $14,461,774.94, which was greater than ever before by nearly half a million dollars. Of this sum, the amount paid directly for common schools was $13,760,669.-57, an increase of $475,682.93 over the preceding year. The sum expended in the cities was $8,340,117.77, and in the towns $5,420,-551.80. The total valuation of school buildings and sites is reported at $36,376,553, of which $24,217,240 is in the cities and $12,159,313 in the towns; in this item the increase was $714,-469, of which $708,729 were in the cities and but $5,740 in the towns. There were paid for teachers' wages during the year, $9,306,425.88; for libraries, $39,722.45; for apparatus, $360,-208.08: for new buildings, sites, repairs, etc., $2,394,004.35. The total number of teachers employed during the year was 31,318, and the number employed for terms of twenty-eight weeks or more, 22,708. Of the whole number of teachers employed, 5,821 were males and 25,497 females. The average annual salary paid was $687.12 in the cities, and $262.44 in the towns. The amount paid for teachers' wages was greater last year than ever before by $204,157.11. The number of children of school age (between five and twenty-one years) was 1,763,115. There are 173,178 more children of school age resident in the cities than in the towns. The total number enrolled in the schools during the year was 1,037,812, and the average daily attendance 625,610. For the year ending Aug. 30, 1888, out of a total of $15,686,012.39 expended for education, the sum of $14,980,841.47 was paid for support of common schools, which is an increase of over $1,000,000 over 1887. Of this sum, $9,209,-464.14 was expended in cities and $5,771,-377.33 in towns. The total number of teachers employed during the year was 31,726, of whom 5,651 were males and 26,075 females. Their average annual salary in cities was $702.92, and in towns $266.75. The total amount paid for teachers' wages was $9,676,-091.93. There were 1,772,958 children of school age, 997,155 in the cities, and 775,803 in the towns. Of these 1,033,269 were enrolled, and 630,595 were in average daily attendance. The State Superintendent says in his annual report : " We have a compulsory education law upon our statute books, but it is a law which does not compel. It has never been acted under to any considerable extent, and, this being so after fourteen years of trial, it is fair to presume that it never will be."

Normal Schools.—In the nine normal schools of the State there was a total enrollment during the school year 1887 of 5,995 pupils, and during 1888 of 6,328. The total enrollment in the normal departments proper for 1887 was 2,884; for 1888, 3,012. The value of normal-school property is estimated at $1,327,775.84. The cost of the schools for 1888 was $243,-131.71. A tenth school, at Oneonta, established in 1887, will be opened in 1889.

For many years the State has recognized that these schools would not be able to train teachers in sufficient numbers to meet the needs of the common schools. It has undertaken therefore to supply the deficiency by organizing teachers' classes in the academies and union schools. During the school year 1887-'88 there were 195 of these classes organized in 142 different schools. The number of students that received instruction for ten consecutive weeks or more, was 3,258. The number completing the course of study, and for whom tuition was allowed from the State appropriation, was 2.676.

Prisons.—Superintendent Lathrop, in his report for the year ending Sept. 30, 1888, announces that " the prisons have distinctly and positively receded in condition and in their tendency during the last year. In the previous year there had been much difficulty and embarrassment, which were incident to the change of the labor system in the prisons and the establishment of new industries, or the change from the contract system to public account of the same industries formerly pursued. But at the opening of the last fiscal year these changes had become far advanced, the system of public account had been generally introduced and put into practical operation, and any other change w as not anticipated, at least until the new system had had a fair trial. The prime factor on which the solution of the problem of successful operations in the prisons then depended, so far

as the public-account system was concerned, was the sufficient appropriation of money to carry on that system, which was the only system then permitted by statute, in an effective way. This was withheld, and the effect has been in every sense discouraging and detrimental, in spite of the greatest diligence and most assiduous energy of the officers who have conducted the prisons."

The report attributes the causes of the change to the legislation of 1888. The million-dollar prison appropriation bill, introduced early in the session, was reduced to $250,000 and passed. In a month this sum was exhausted, and a further appeal was made, which procured $500,-000 additional. The Legislature thus appropriated in all only $750,000 to provide for the employment of 2,600 men, when during the previous year the preceding Legislature had furnished $1,300,000 for the employment of an average number of 1,300 men, then engaged on the prison industries. Before the year was half completed the money was exhausted, and on July 1 the superintendent looked forward to six months or more of idleness and the attendant evils. At his request the Governor convened the Legislature in July to provide for the emergency. The passage of the Yates bill at that session overthrew the public-account system, as well as every other system of productive labor. It introduced idleness instead of industry, withdrew the convicts from the shops and put them into their cells. The change in the law wrought a great decline in the material and moral conditions that have existed in the State prisons. As a result, the deficit is more than twice as large as in any other year since the reform prison system was established. In 1888 the cost of maintenance was $404,509.94 and the deficit $153,924.46.

On September 30 the number of convicts in the prisons was as follows: at Auburn, 1,248; at Clinton, 755; at Sing Sing, 1,405; total, 3,408. This total is an increase of 129 over 1887. At the same date there were confined in the several penitentiaries in the State 622 State convicts, 828 in the State Reformatory at Elmira, and 108 in the House of Refuge for Women at Hudson.

The Insane.—The following was the number of patients in the several asylums at the close of the fiscal years ending Sept. 30, 1887 and 1888 :

LOCATION.	1887.	1888.
Utica	578	611
Willard	1,512	1,962
Poughkeepsie	419	476
Middletown	455	459
Buffalo	356	868
Binghamton	1,039	1,077
Total	4,659	4,958

On September 30 there were 450 patients in the Idiot Asylum at Syracuse, and 194 in the Custodial Asylum at Newark.

Banks.—On October 1 there were 130 banks of deposit and discount in active operation, an increase of 25 banks and $2,235,000 capital in one year. The aggregate resources of the State banks on September 22 were $217,398,717, an increase over 1887 of $26,440,170. Of the 25 new banks, 2 were converts from the national system and 7 are in New York city and have a capital amounting to $950,000. Of the total increase in banking capital, $250,000 represents the increase of existing institutions and $1,-985,000 the capital of new associations. As evidence of the prosperous condition of the State banks, it is noted that there has been no reduction in the capital of any of the number during the year, and not a single suspension or failure has occurred in that period. There are 25 trust, loan, and mortgage companies in operation, which show total resources of $224,-018,183.68 and liabilities amounting to $224,-554,324.51. The total amount of interest-bearing deposits was $165,317,364.07, an increase of $18,685,900.50. Three new trust companies, with a capital of $1,500,000, were organized during the year. The total capital employed by the trust companies operating under the State laws shows an increase of $3,498,000 in the same period. At the close of the fiscal year there were 17 safe-deposit companies in operation in this State, with an aggregate capital of $3,123,900, an increase during the year of $294,000.

Railroads.—The following statistics show the work of the railroads of the State during the past two years: Gross earnings, 1888, $152,-122,705.73 ; 1887, $143,724,490.62. Net earnings, 1888, $50,517,643.94 ; 1887, $51,284,-516.02. Taxes, 1888, $5.252,224.10 ; 1887, $5,018,907.21. Surplus, 1888, $5,362,202.58 ; 1887, $8,284,403.60. Miles of road built in New York State, 1888, 7,437.85 ; 1887, 7,-383.38. The increase in tons of freight carried one mile is 5·27 per cent. It will be seen that there has been a distinct reduction in the net earnings, although a greater amount of business has been done than previously. This result is attributed by the railroad commissioners to several causes, among them the clause in the Interstate Commerce act prohibiting pooling; the reckless efforts of some railroad managers to procure business at any rates, however unprofitable ; the building of new roads in advance of any necessity ; strikes, and the deliberate reduction of rates to unprofitable points for stock-jobbing purposes.

The Indians.—From a report of a committee appointed by the Legislature of this year, it appears that there are still in the State tribal reservations having the following population : Onondaga, 450 ; Oneida, 178 ; Tuscarora, 439 ; Tonawanda, 500 ; Shinnecock, 150 ; St. Regis, 1,044 ; Cattaraugus, 1,305 ; Allegany, 834 ; total, 4,900. The Onondaga reservation, near Syracuse, is reported to be in a deplorable condition, the Indians defying all attempts to educate them or to induce them to till the soil.

Similar reports come from nearly all the other tribes, except the Oneidas, Tuscaroras, and St. Regis, where the land is generally held in severalty. The committee recommend that all lands of the Indians be allotted in severalty, and that they be admitted to the rights of citizenship and subjected to the general laws of the State. On the several reservations there are 1,546 Indian children of school age. Of these, 1,082 were enrolled in the 30 reservation schools during the school year 1887-'88, but the average daily attendance was only 420.

The Erie Canal.—In 1888 the number of tons of freight carried was 4,942,948, or a decrease of 610,857 over 1887. The figure for 1888, however, is somewhat in excess of the average for the past five years. Among the reasons assigned for the falling off are these: 1. The contracts made with railroads centering at Buffalo with vessels of deep draught loaded with coal and other freight for the ports of the northern lakes, their return cargoes being in grain (the chief reliance of the boats on the Erie Canal), which is turned over by the large vessels to the railroads that furnish the western-bound freight; 2. Short crops, causing a decreased export trade ; 3. The corner in grain, which overturned the markets in Chicago and New York for several weeks ; 4. The insistance of the canal boatmen for higher rates, in consequence of which much of the freight was sent by rail. During the past year the work of lengthening the locks so as to allow the passage of two boats tandem has progressed until now there are only fifty-one miles on the Erie Canal containing single-tiered locks to interfere with the navigation of "doubleheaders." Other locks are now in process of lengthening, and many of them will be completed before the season of 1889 opens.

The Erie Canal was completed in 1825. Its dimensions were 40 feet wide on the surface, 28 feet wide at the bottom, with single locks 90 feet long and 12 feet wide, and a waterway at the aqueducts of 19 feet. The capacity of boats was 100 tons. In 1833 the increased business on the canals exceeded all public expectation, and the Legislature of 1834 passed an act authorizing the construction of a second set of locks to increase the facility of transportation. This was supplemented in 1835 by the passage of an act directing the canal commissioners to enlarge and improve the canal, giving them discretionary powers as to its dimensions, location, etc., to alter, arrange, and construct new feeders and other works, as they might deem necessary, for supplying the enlarged canal with an additional supply of water. At a meeting of the canal board, June 30, 1835, it was resolved to make the canal 60 feet wide, with 6 feet depth of water. At a subsequent meeting, in October, the board decided to increase its capacity to 70 feet wide and 7 feet depth of water, to build the locks 110 feet long and 18 feet wide, thus giving boats a carrying capacity of 240 tons. The engineers made a survey for the enlargement, following, or using, as far as practicable, the line of the old canal, and in many places building a portion of it new, or on a more direct line than the old canal. The work was immediately put under contract, thousands of men were employed, and the Legislature of 1838 authorized the commissioners of the canal fund to borrow $4,000,000 to carry on the work. The canal commissioners were directed to prepare and put under contract, with as little delay as possible, such portions of the work as would complete the entire enlargement. The work progressed rapidly until 1842, when what is known as the "stop law" was enacted, suspending further expense on public works. The canal remained in an unfinished condition for five years following, until 1847, when the Legislature made an appropriation to continue the work. Other annual appropriations were made up to 1862, when the enlargement was completed.

Insurance.—The latest reports of the insurance department show that the aggregate assets of the fire and fire marine companies of this country doing business in the State of New York is $163,041,841.32, classified as follow: New York joint-stock companies, $60,-929,147.70; joint-stock companies of other States, $99,645,876.33; New York mutuals, $1,961,934.53; mutuals of other States, $504,-882.76. Compared with 1886, these figures show an aggregate decrease of $1,372,808.66. Excepting scrip and capital, their liabilities are: New York joint-stock companies, $24,-945,447.25; other State joint-stock companies, $35,573,822.53; New York mutuals, $668,994.39; other State mutuals, 286,646.19; total, $61,474,910.36, an increase of $3,159,-661.65. The total amount of scrip liabilities is $701,017, and of capital, $60,542,620. The fire premiums received were $18,425,955.69; fire losses paid, $13,419,011.99; fire losses incurred, $13,937,470.98. The estimated amount of expense for the transaction of this business is $5,527,786.72, which, if added to the incurred losses, make a total of $19,465,257.70; showing, as compared with the premium receipts, an apparent loss of $1,039,302.01. At the close of 1887 the marine and fire insurance companies doing business in the State of New York were possessed of $227,702,823 of admitted assets, not including assets held abroad or premium notes of mutual companies, a loss of $146,222 as compared with 1886. The liabilities of these companies, excepting scrip and capital, were $90,263,202, an increase of $4,-861,148 over the return of the preceding year. The income was $444,506 and the expenditures were $103,957,528, an increase, as compared with 1886, of $1,504,841 in income and $5,534,517 in expenditures. The whole number of companies reporting in 1887 was 182, being four less than in 1886. In the last annual report there were pointed out some of the objectionable features of the statute, which provides for licensing agents to do fire-insurance business in this State, through unadmitted companies of other States or countries. The experience of one more year in observing its practical operation confirms the impression, on the part of the insurance department, that the incorporating of this act into the insurance laws of the State, makes them, in a very material respect, anomalous, illogical, inconsistent, and radically bad. The theory on which the law was enacted, that the insurance thus authorized could be kept strictly within the limit of "surplus line"—in other words, could be confined to such insurance only as could not be obtained from duly authorized companies—has proved fallacious, and the superintendent is disposed to think that most of the insurance written under the provisions of this statute could have been obtained in duly authorized companies if the policy-holders had made reasonably diligent efforts to obtain it, which, however, the statute does not require them to make. He thinks the statute ought to be repealed, and that the penal provisions of the statutes enacted with special reference to the prevention of unauthorized fire insurance need some material amendments to give them wider scope and practical effect.

In March, 1888, an important decision was made in regard to insurance law in the State of New York. It was on an appeal taken by defendant from an order of the Supreme Court, sustaining plaintiff's exceptions, taken at the trial in the Monroe circuit, and ordered to be heard in the first instance at General Term and directing a new trial. The trial justice had directed a verdict for the defendant. The property insured was a merchant's stock of goods in Phelps, Ontario Co., and it was destroyed by fire May 3, 1884. The policy was for $1,500, and plaintiff asserted a loss value of over $3,000. The answer was that plaintiff had effected subsequent insurance without notifying defendant's agent, in violation of the terms of his policy. The trial justice held that this vitiated the policy, and directed a verdict for defendant, to which ruling plaintiff excepted. On the hearing of the exceptions at the General Term the Supreme Court held that the clause in the policy reading: "If the assured shall have, or shall hereafter make, any other insurance on the property hereby assured, or on any part thereof, without the consent of the company written thereon, then the policy shall be void," is a part of a contract that requires the written consent of the assured to render valid and obligatory, and that, as no written indorsement to that effect appears on the policy the clause is of no binding effect. It was, therefore, held that the question of fact for a jury to pass upon was whether the defendant's agent had or had not orally consented to the subsequent insurance. The defendant, instead of going back to the circuit for a new trial, took a direct appeal to the court of last resort, to have the matter fully and finally determined, stipulating, as the rule requires, that if the principle was found against the defendant judgment absolute should be rendered for plaintiff. It was accordingly argued in the Court of Appeals, and the court handed down its decision, unanimously affirming the judgment of the General Term, and ordering judgment absolute for plaintiff with costs. No opinion was written, that of the justice in the Supreme Court being adopted as fully covering and deciding every point at issue.

New Cities.—In 1888 Hornellsville, Ithaca, and Middletown were incorporated as cities. This makes the total number of cities in the State 30. The other 27 are Albany, Amsterdam, Auburn, Binghamton, Brooklyn, Buffalo, Cohoes, Dunkirk, Elmira, Hudson, Jamestown, Kingston, Lockport, Long Island City, Newburg, New York, Ogdensburg, Oswego, Poughkeepsie, Rochester, Rome, Schenectady, Syracuse, Troy, Utica, Watertown, and Yonkers.

Hornellsville, in Steuben County, secured a charter on March 2, 1888. The city is divided into six wards. The mayor, chamberlain, overseer of the poor, recorder, sealer, game-constable, and three commissioners of excise are to be elected on the general ticket. All other officers are elected on ward tickets. The city contains about 12,000 inhabitants. It is on Canisteo river which runs southward into the Alleghany. Hornellsville is at the junction of several railroads. A short railroad to Bath, in the same county, connects that village with Hornellsville and with the Delaware, Lackawanna and Western Railroad. There are planing-mills and shoe-factories; but the chief industry is in the shops of the New York, Lake Erie and Western Railroad, and its employés form a large part of the population. There are six churches, five schools, and a free public library. The city is known as a tri-shire town, the remaining public buildings of the county being in the villages of Bath and Corning. Hornellsville is the center of a large agricultural interest which is shown in the farmers' clubs and in what are claimed to be the largest county fairs in any rural city of the State.

Ithaca became a city by an act of the Legislature on March 2, 1888. The city is divided into four wards. The mayor, recorder, and two supervisors are the only officers elected on a general ticket. The charter is considered a marvel of brevity and thoroughness, by those who have paid attention to the charters of cities. This city is at the southern end of Cayuga Lake. As a village it was founded in 1796 by Simeon De Witt, who was then surveyor-general of the State of New York. The opening of the Erie Canal and the second railroad built and operated in the State from Ithaca to Owego, connecting the waters of Cayuga Lake with Susquehanna river, gave a rapid growth to the village, and it became an important distributing point. The lower tier of counties in New York and the northern tier in Pennsylvania brought many of their

supplies through the Erie Canal, Cayuga Lake, and Ithaca. Binghamton and Elmira were tributaries to Ithaca at that time; but they have since distanced her, owing to largely improved railroad facilities. It was necessary in the early days to reach Ithaca in order to take steamboats on Cayuga Lake to go to Albany or to the West, and a large territory was dependent upon Ithaca for cheap and rapid transportation. The turnpike was used by early stages to Catskill, Geneva, and Buffalo. A ship-canal was devised to Lake Ontario; and the price of property in Ithaca rose very high. But when the Erie Railway was constructed, in 1849, the whole territory southward of Ithaca became tributary to Elmira and Binghamton. The late Ezra Cornell removed to the village in its day of distress, and by his wealth and enterprise restored much of its former prosperity. The university bearing his name was but a part of the great work that he accomplished. The city has 12,000 inhabitants. The railroad connections are the Delaware, Lackawanna and Western, the Utica, Ithaca and Elmira, and two smaller roads. There are many factories producing clocks, stoves, agricultural implements, steam-engines, organs, and rifles. The city is an important center for the distribution of coal from the mines of Pennsylvania. There are 14 churches, 8 schools, a public library, 3 banks, 8 hotels, 2 daily and 4 weekly newspapers. The city is lighted by the electric light and by gas; and it has a fine system of water-works.

Middletown became a city on June 9, 1888. The number of wards is four. The officers elected on the general ticket are the mayor, treasurer, alderman-at-large, recorder, two justices of the peace, two constables, nine members of the board of education, three excise commissioners, five water commissioners, and three assessors. The city lies on Walkill river, nearly seventy miles northwest of New York city. The New Jersey Midland Railroad, the New York, Lake Ontario, and Western, the New York, Lake Erie, and Western, the Susquehanna and Western, and the Middletown and Crawford Railroads, all center at this point. The population is about 15,000. The city is a large manufacturing center, more especially for nails, files, farming-implements, saws, condensed milk, and iron castings. It is also the center of a large dairy and agricultural interest. It has water-works and gas-works. There are twelve churches and a graded high school, with twelve other public schools. Middletown is the site of the Homœopathic Asylum for the Insane. The buildings have been erected on what is known as the hospital system of treatment; but new ones will be erected according to the cottage system.

Political.—On May 15 a Democratic State Convention met in New York city and elected delegates to the St. Louis convention, who were instructed to vote for the renomination of President Cleveland. Presidential electors were also selected. The resolutions of the convention approve the National and State Administrations, and strongly condemn trusts. The Saxton electoral-reform bill, which was passed by the Legislature but vetoed by the Governor, was also condemned. The Republican Convention met at Buffalo on May 16, and chose as delegates at large to the Chicago convention the four leaders of the party in the State, Senator Hiscock, ex-Senators Piatt and Miller, and Chauncey M. Depew. The delegation was uninstructed. Resolutions on State and National issues, as well as the nomination of electors at large, were referred to a subsequent convention for the nomination of State officers. This latter convention was held at Saratoga on August 28. It nominated ex-Senator Warner Miller for Governor by acclamation, and selected as candidates for Lieutenant-Governor and for Judge of the Court of Appeals, to fill the vacancy caused by the death of Judge Rapallo, S. V. R. Cruger and William Rumsey, respectively. The platform included the following:

The Legislature of 1888 gave proof of the purpose and effort of the Republican party to enact laws for the best interests of the people. The reduction in the rate of State taxation bears witness to the spirit which guided legislation. The investigation into trusts and combinations, by making their evils known, points the way to effectual remedies. The examination into the conduct of affairs in connection with the New York aqueduct, still in progress, has already exposed abuses which call for reparation, and has given warning how the campaign expenses of a Democratic governor may be met out of contracts paid by the taxpayers.

The Republican party favor the payment by the State of the legitimate expenses for ballots and their distribution, and the punishment, by disfranchisement and other severe penalties, of bribery and fraud at election. The efforts of the last Legislature in this direction deserve commendation, while Gov. Hill merits censure and rebuke for his veto of a measure aiming to purify the ballot and to assure absolute independence to vote at the polls.

In view of the recent revelations, showing the abuse of our naturalization and immigration laws, we desire and urge a thorough revision of said laws, in order that our country and fellow-citizens may be protected from the pauper and criminal classes of other countries.

The Democratic convention for nominating State officers met at Buffalo on September 12, and renominated Gov. Hill and Lieut.-Gov. Jones by acclamation. For Judge of the Court of Appeals John Clinton Gray was nominated. The platform contained the following:

We oppose all sumptuary laws, needlessly interfering with the personal liberties and reasonable habits and customs of any part of our citizens. We believe in the regulation and restriction of the liquor-traffic by just and equitable excise laws rigorously enforced, without unjust discrimination, throughout the State. Local excise revenues raised by State law, like other proper local revenue laws, should be applied in lessening the burdens of local taxation. We favor a revision of the excise laws and approve the recommendation of a Democratic governor to that effect, made to the last Legislature, and adopted by it, whereby a commission was appointed to make such revision, and we trust that the work of the commission will be such as

to merit the approval of the people of the State. We denounce the variable, defective, and hypocritical legislation of the Republican Legislature upon the liquor question in the last few years, much of which was clearly inconsistent, not honestly designed or calculated to aid the cause of temperance, but intended only to mislead the people and for political effect.

The Democratic party, now as ever, earnestly favors the presentation of the purity of elections, the protection of the ballot, and of honest returns. It believes that these conditions are the safeguards of our free institutions, and that all good citizens should cordially unite in promoting such conditions and in promoting all adverse and fraudulent influences. We favor all reasonable and practical measures which may conduce to these ends, and of all changes in our election laws which will then more effectually preserve to every citizen the right of free ballot, fairly counted and honestly returned. We favor any practical and properly framed measure, however stringent and severe, which will more surely prevent and punish bribery and fraud, as well as intimidation and coercion at elections. We approve the veto of the so-called Saxton electoral bill, because it contained provisions which were unconstitutional, grossly defective, clearly impracticable, and otherwise objectionable, and which would, therefore, have failed to accomplish the reforms desired.

The Prohibitionists, at their State convention held in Syracuse, June 27, nominated W. Martin Jones for Governor, George F. Powell for Lieutenant-Governor, and Charles W. Stephens for Judge of the Court of Appeals. The United Labor party, at their convention in New York city, September 20, accepted Warner Miller, the Republican nominee, as its candidate for Governor, and nominated John H. Blakeney for Lieutenant-Governor, and Lawrence J. McParlin for Judge of the Court of Appeals.

On September 23 the Socialists of New York city, at a public meeting, resolved to nominate candidates for national, State, and municipal offices, and at a subsequent meeting Edward Hall was made a candidate for Governor, Christian Pattberg for Lieutenant-Governor, and Francis Gerau for Judge of the Court of Appeals. The canvass was one of great interest, but of no unusual excitement. As in 1884, the decision of the national contest was considered to depend on the vote of New York, and largely also upon the vote of New York city. At the election in November, while the Republicans carried the State on the national ticket, their candidates on the State ticket were defeated. For Governor, Hill received 650,464 votes; Miller, 631,293; Jones, 30,215; and Hall, 3,348. Gray, for Judge of the Court of Appeals, was elected by only 3,425 plurality, receiving 634,878 votes to 631,453 for Rumsey, 31,178 for Stephens, 3,841 for McParlin, and 3,523 for Gerau. The Republicans elected 20 members of the State Senate, and 79 members of the House; the Democrats securing 11 Senators and 49 members of the House. Democratic Congressmen were elected in the first fourteen congressional districts (except the Third), and in the Nineteenth and Thirty-third Districts; the remaining nineteen districts elected Republicans. At the same election an amendment to the State Constitution, providing that the Governor may select seven Supreme Court judges for service at Albany as a second court of appeals, to visit the regular court, was adopted by a vote of 498,114 yeas to 55,822 nays.

NEW YORK (CITY). Government.—The following is the list of officers during the year: Mayor, Abram S. Hewitt, Democrat; President of the Board of Aldermen, George H. Forster; Register, James J. Slevin; Sheriff, Hugh J. Grant.

Debt.—The following table gives the condition of the finances:

FUNDED DEBT.	Outstanding Dec. 31, 1887.	Issued during 1888.	Redeemed during 1888.	Outstanding Dec. 31, 1888.
1. Payable from the sinking-fund, under ordinances of the Common Council	$4,671,900 00	....	$78,500 00	$4,593,400 00
2. Payable from the sinking-fund, under provisions of chapter 388, section 6, Laws of 1878, and section 176, New York City Consolidation act of 1882	9,700,000 00	....		9,700,000 00
3. Payable from the sinking-fund, under provisions of chapter 388, section 8, Laws of 1878, and section 192, New York City Consolidation act of 1882	19,960,337 96	$3,707,215 15	....	23,667,553 11
4. Payable from taxation, under provisions of chapter 490, Laws of 1883	445,000 00	....		445,000 00
5. Payable from the sinking-fund, under provisions of the constitutional amendment adopted Nov. 4, 1884	16,750,000 00	4,150,000 00	....	20,900,000 00
6. Payable from taxation, under the several statutes authorizing their issue	72,258,481 49	....	8,900,339 14	63,388,142 35
7. Bonds issued for local improvements after June 9, 1880	3,768,000 00	380,000 00	....	4,098,000 00
8 Debt of the annexed territory of Westchester County	690,000 00	....	32,000 00	658,000 00
Total funded debt	$128,268,719 45	$8,187,215 15	$4,010,889 14	$182,445,095 46
TEMPORARY DEBT—*Revenue Bonds.*				
1. Issued under special laws	196,746 70	395,180 49	196,746 70	395,180 49
2. Issued in anticipation of taxes of 1887	4,357,600 00	....	4,357,600 00	....
3. Issued in anticipation of taxes of 1888	....	17,210,475 00	14,302,875 00	2,907,600 00
Total amounts	$132,823,066 15	$25,792,820 64	$22,868,060 84	$135,747,825 95

Total funded debt............................... $182,445,095 46
Less amount held by commissioners of the sinking fund
as investments............ $38,806,425 95
Cash (includes Marine Bank, $110,000)................... 6,088,264 17
　　　　　　　　　　　　　　　　44,484,690 12
Net funded debt, Dec. 31, 1888............. $88,010,405 34
Revenue bonds......................... 3,302,730 49
Debt including revenue bonds, Dec. 31, 1888............................. $91,313,135 83

By the new constitutional amendment, the city is forbidden to increase its indebtedness beyond an amount equal to ten per cent. of the valuation of the real estate within its limits. The assessed valuation for 1888 was $1,302,-818,879. An examination of the above statement will show that the gross bonded indebtedness is $132,445,095.46, while the amount held by the sinking-fund for the redemption of the city's debt is $44,434,690.12. The net indebtedness of the city, therefore, amounts to $88,010,405.34. For the purchase of new parks, for the improvement of the river-front, and for the discharge of other obligations already imposed upon it, says the Mayor, the city will be compelled to issue additional bonds amounting to about $19,561,000. The city's net income accruing to the sinking-fund for 1889 is estimated at over $9,000,000. It is fair, therefore, to assume that during the current year the city will be compelled to increase its indebtedness by about $10,000,000. As by the provisions of the constitutional enactment the borrowing capacity of the corporation is limited to about $130,000,000, and as the liabilities which it has already incurred amount to over $98,000,000, it follows that the amount of money which the city may raise by pledging its credit for further improvements can not exceed the sum of $32,000,000.

Schools.—The president of the Board of Education is J. Edward Simmons, and the superintendent is John Jasper. There are 84 grammar schools and 39 primary schools and also a school-ship, the "St Mary's." The average attendance at the grammar schools during the year was 114,710; at the primary schools, 19,-538; total 134,248. The total number taught at the grammar schools during the year was 214,461; at the primary schools, 40,328; total, 254,789. At the evening schools the average attendance was 7,357, and the total number taught was 21,839. According to the financial statement of funds down to Jan. 1, 1889, the total resources were $5,589,525.59; total expenditure, $4,503,797.71; total sum relinquished, $18,503.55; total balance of all funds, Dec. 31, 1888, $1,067,224.33. The chief details of the expenditures were: Salaries of teachers in grammar and primary schools, $2,824,327.69; salaries of janitors in grammar and primary schools, $124,232.68; salaries of professors et al. in Normal College, $74,468.94; salaries of teachers in training department, $19,185.62; salaries of janitor and engineer in Normal College, etc., $3,999.99; salaries of teachers and janitors in evening schools, $109,661.69; salaries of officers and clerks of Board of Education, $39,490.56; salary of counsel to the board, $3,000; salaries of city superintendent and assistants, $34,558.47; salaries of truant agents, $11,781.79; support of nautical school, $27,-541.86; depository—books, maps, supplies, etc., $144,709.19; rents of school-buildings, $40,-664.24; fuel, $93,021.84; gas, $18,381.89.

Vital Statistics.—The president of the Board of Health is James C. Bayles. According to the report made under his direction, the total number of deaths during the year was 40,175; of these, 17,360 were of children under five years of age. Classified according to diseases, the more important were: Small-pox, 81; typhoid fever, 438; whooping-cough, 573; scarlet fever, 1,361; diphtheria, 1,914; diarrhœal diseases, 3,489; pneumonia, 4,288; consumption, 5,260. The death-rate was 26·33 in a thousand. There were 36,136 births during the year, including 3,239 that were reported as still-births; 14,533 marriages were recorded, and 4,390 coroners' certificates were issued, indicating the necessity of an inquest. The statistics of the deaths are very perfect, as no burial can take place without a permit; but the information concerning the marriages and births is necessarily defective. The estimated population of New York city on July 1 was 1,526,081. This was determined from the proportional increase between the State census taken in 1875 and the national census of 1880. Prior to July 1, the weekly increase of the population was estimated at 845, and since that time at 872.

Police.—This department is controlled by four commissioners, of whom Stephen B. French is president. The superintendent is William Murray, and the force under his command numbered on Jan. 1, 1889, 3,351, of whom 2,253 are patrolmen. These were distributed among 35 precincts and 1 sub-precinct, each of which was under the special supervision of a captain. There were 85,049 arrests during the year, for the following offenses: Assault and battery, male, 4,709, female, 521; disorderly conduct, male, 40,350, female, 7,180; intoxication, male, 14,282, female, 6,461; petty larceny, male, 2,843, female, 418; suspicious persons, male, 3,279, female, 298; violations of corporation ordinances, male, 4,942, female, 77; violations of health law, male, 14,040, female, 150; violation of excise law, male, 5,810, female, 120.

Fires—The fire department is managed by a board of three commissioners, of which Henry D. Purroy is president. Charles O. Shay is chief of the department, and the force includes 1,028 men. During 1888 there were 3,422 alarms of fire, and 3,217 actual fires. Of the latter, 2,888 were confined to the point of starting, 200 were confined to the building where the fire originated, 49 extended to other buildings, 28 were vessels, and 54 were of places other than buildings or vessels; 2,078 fires were extinguished without an engine-stream; 686 with one engine-stream; 347 with two or three engine-streams; and 106 required more than three engine-streams. The following table gives the damage to structures:

STRUCTURES.	Slight.	Consid-erable.	De-stroyed.
Brick, iron, or stone	562	72	9
Wooden..................	142	84	9

Political.—In addition to the excitement incidental to a presidential canvass, the local politics were somewhat complicated by the nomination by Tammany Hall of Hugh J. Grant for Mayor. Abram S. Hewitt two years previously had been the nominee of Tammany, but by his independence while in office he incurred the ill-will of the politicians and consequent repudiation by that local faction of the Democratic party. But he was promptly nominated by an independent convention, and his candidacy was accepted by the County Democracy. At the election, Hugh J. Grant (Tammany) received 114,111 votes; Joel B. Erhardt (Republican), 73,037; Abram S. Hewitt (County Democracy), 71,979; James J. Coogan (United Labor), 9,809; William T. Wardwell (Prohibition), 832. George H. Forster (Tammany) was elected President of the Board of Aldermen, but his death before his inauguration led to the selection of John H. V. Arnold for that place. The Board of Aldermen consists of 16 Tammany, 2 County Democrats, and 7 Republicans. Besides the foregoing, James A. Flack was elected sheriff, Edward F. Reilly county clerk, and Ferdinand Levy, Daniel Hanly, and Louis W. Schultze coroners. The presidential vote in New York city was: Mr. Cleveland, 162,735; Gen. Harrison, 106,-922; Gen. Fisk, 1,343.

Mayor's Message.—This document contained the following paragraphs of general interest:

The parks of the city have been established for the use and enjoyment of the whole people. Everything that they contain should therefore be freely accessible to the citizens. The closing of the Museums of Art and Natural History on Sundays is a practical exclusion of the industrial masses from all opportunity to visit them. I hope that some means will soon be devised by which these museums will be made accessible to the public on Sunday.

At present there is little or no classification of shipping at our docks. Ferry-boats, sea-going vessels, and the smaller craft which ply between this city and adjacent towns are crowded indiscriminately together. Passenger-boats and freight-vessels sail from the same piers. Lines of trucks laden with merchandise render the streets in the neighborhood of the freight depots impassable to foot-passengers. The pavements along the streets fronting on the river are in such wretched condition that travel upon them is dangerous to vehicles. Great ruts and holes act as traps for heavily laden trucks, and it is no uncommon sight to see the entire traffic of the street suspended while a driver vainly urges his team to pull from a break in the street-bed a load which would tax the full strength of his horses to draw upon an even pavement.

The pavements of the city are in such pressing need of repair and improvement that attention should be immediately devoted to them. I have already mentioned the inexcusable condition in which I have found the streets fronting on the rivers, and I venture to say that there are few thoroughfares which are in the condition that befits the trade and commerce of this city. Under the law the public authorities are limited to an expenditure of $500,000 annually for the repavement of the highways, which sum is utterly inadequate to the extensive alterations and improvements which are now absolutely essential.

With proper pavements an effective system of street-cleaning could be easily maintained. At present it is generally conceded that our street-cleaning system fails properly to provide for the public comfort. Substantial sums are appropriated annually from the public treasury for the cleaning of the streets, but their filthy condition is the cause of universal and well-founded complaint.

For many years this city has been compelled to pay an unjust proportion of the expenses of the State Government. The State Board of Assessors has fixed the valuation of taxable property within this city at a sum almost equal to 45 per cent. of the entire valuation of the State, and the city is consequently compelled to bear 45 per cent. of the entire State taxa-

the harbor, telegraph lines were torn down, for two days an almost total suspension of business occurred, and for a week from the beginning of the storm its effects were still felt in the stagnation of business interests. Articles of food became scarce, milk was not to be had in the city, and condensed milk had to be used by all. The price of all provisions began to rise, notably that of meat and poultry.

WEST ELEVENTH STREET, AFTER THE BLIZZARD.

tion. The injustice of this distribution of the burden of government between this and other counties is apparent from the mere statement of it. Notwithstanding the unjust proportion of State taxation which is imposed upon us, the city has no representation in the Board of State Assessors. Were such representation afforded it is probable that the injustice from which we now suffer would be to some extent lessened, and the burden of our taxation sensibly reduced.

Notwithstanding the general demand for the burial of electric wires and for the removal of the poles which disfigure our streets, the nuisance remains unabated. Laws have been enacted which were intended to afford the city relief from this imposition, but either on account of imperfections in the law or remissness of the officers charged with its execution, the poles and wires continue to obstruct our thoroughfares. All the provisions of the existing law should be invoked to remedy this evil; and, if they prove inadequate, we should ask the Legislature for additional powers.

The Blizzard.—A snow-storm of great severity, preceded by rain, visited New York city and vicinity on March 11, 12, and 13. For over forty-eight hours a very heavy northwest wind prevailed and caused the snow to drift in all directions. Railroad communication was cut off, vessels were detained from reaching

In the suburbs, where many business men reside, thousands were detained either in their houses or on trains of cars. On all the roads the morning trains of the 12th were stopped by the storm, and in some cases two nights were spent by passengers on board the trains. The New Jersey railroads, and those running from the Grand Central Depot toward the north and east, suffered greatly. Where the trains were delayed at stations the capacity of the neighboring country was taxed to its utmost to provide food for the passengers. At some places long lines of cars and engines, representing ten or more separate trains, were snow-bound. The suspension of mail facilities was absolute for over forty-eight hours.

The immediate effect of the storm was to suspend all traffic on the surface street-roads. The elevated roads, it would be supposed, would be free from trouble; but, owing to the position of their rails, on each side of which two heavy wooden guard-rails are bolted down, they experienced much difficulty. The rain coated the rails with ice, snow was deposited upon the ice, and the increasing fall of snow rapidly filled up the space, burying the rail completely, and preventing transit over the road. In some instances the cars were all day in going the length of the road. The people, in many cases, came down on ladders, the trains being detained between stations.

The fire department set to work to build sleighs and hire all suitable ones in order to use them for the transportation of engines, hose, and ladders to fires. The telephone company, finding its wires were in many instances crossed by the electric-light wires, it became necessary as a precaution against conflagration to shut off the light currents, so that the city was for one or two nights practically without illumination. Coal was delivered with great difficulty to many private residences. The Steam Supply Company supplied steam without interruption to all its customers. The gas companies supplied gas without trouble, while coal and all objects that had to be transported on the surface were only with great delay and at the cost of great efforts delivered to those requiring them.

To dispose of the masses of snow, fires were built against the heaps, and in other places jets of steam were used to melt the accumulation. Carting the snow to the docks and dumping it into the river was the most efficient of the methods adopted. The East River Bridge was operated at a disadvantage, the cable transport having stopped. In the midst of the blockade thus occasioned an ice bridge formed across the East river, and several thousand people crossed upon it. A very sad feature was the loss of life. Owing to the exposure, several persons perished in the city and suburbs.

NICARAGUA, a republic in Central America; area, 51,600 square miles; population in 1886, 262,372. The capital is Managua, population, 18,000.

Government.—The President is Don Evaristo Carazo, whose term of office will expire on March 1, 1891. The Cabinet is composed of the following ministers: Foreign Affairs, Don Adrian Zavala; Finance, Don Bernabé Portocarrero; Interior, Don David Osorno; Public Works, Don Chosé Chamorro; War, Gen. J. Elizondo. The Nicaraguan Minister at Washington is Don Horacio Guzman; the Consul-General at New York, Alexander Cotheal; the American Consul at Managua is Charles H. Wills.

Finances.—The income in 1885 was $1,479,-093; the outlay, $2,191,076; in 1886 the former was $1,594,236, and the latter, $1,998,667. The foreign debt is represented by £285,000, bearing 6 per cent. interest, and the home debt, including paper money in circulation, amounted to $491,123 on Oct. 31, 1886. In September, 1888, the Minister of Finance made a contract with the Banco de Nicaragua by virtue of which the Government engaged to withdraw and cancel all the paper money in circulation on November 15 of that year, with the exception of $200,000, which are to be withdrawn gradually; to provide for which, 10 per cent. of the duties on imports at the seaports are to be set aside until the amount is canceled. The bank bound itself to take at par in silver coin all such paper money on presentation. In this manner specie payment has virtually been resumed.

Army.—The effective strength of the permanent army is 1,258 men, commanded by 83 officers; and of the militia 14,000, officered by 581.

American Arbitration.—The President of the United States, in his message of December 3, expressed himself in the following terms: "The long-pending boundary dispute between Costa Rica and Nicaragua was referred to my arbitration; and by an award made on March 22 last, the question has been finally settled to the expressed satisfaction of both of the parties in interest." A dispute having arisen afterward between the two republics, in relation to the site of the proposed Nicaraguan Canal, the American minister to Guatemala was instructed to use his good offices to bring about an understanding between the two governments. The following dispatch from him was received at the Department of State on Jan. 17, 1889: "The convention between Nicaragua and Costa Rica to arbitrate questions affecting the Nicaraguan Canal was signed on the 10th instant. The President of the United States is named the arbitrator."

Annexation of Corn Island.—The "Gaceta Oficial" of Sept. 22, 1888, announced the taking possession of Corn Island by the Government on August 30. This small island lies off the Nicaraguan coast, on the Atlantic side, thirty-six miles east of Bluefields. It has a population of 500, and a good port with a depth of forty feet. The island is fertile. and exports a large amount of cocoanuts. There is also a ship-yard, where sloops of twenty tons capacity are built.

Postal Service.—During 1885-'86 the number of items of mail matter handled was 2,480,153, while the expense involved was $71,406; the receipts did not exceed $22,717.

Telegraphs.—The number of telegrams sent during 1885-'86 was 261,116, 87,010 being Government dispatches and 174,106 private messages. The latter were 91,607 in 1884, 88,580 in 1885, and 85,526 in 1886; the cablegrams numbered 9,267. The receipts during 1886 were $49,101, and the expenses $83,300. There were in operation in 1887 808 miles of telegraph and 32 of telephone. In October several new telegraph offices were opened. A line went into operation a distance of forty miles between Eteli and Sauce, to be soon followed by one between Matagalpa and Juigalpa, which will connect the former with the Department of Chontales.

Electric Light.—The municipality of Leon made a contract in October for the lighting of the city during twenty-five years, at the end of which time the city has the option of buying the plant or extending the privilege for another equal period, on the expiration of which the plant becomes city property without compensation.

Railroads.—There are in operation two lines of railway, one between Corinto and Momotombo via Chinandega and Leon, and one between Managua and Granada via Masaya, measuring together 159 kilometres in length.

Lake Navigation.—In July the Government made a contract for the establishment of a new line of steamboats to ply on the lake between Managua and Momotombo; the first steamer to begin its trips in eighteen months, and no steamer of the line to register less than 150 tons burden.

Commerce.—During four biennial periods the total foreign trade of Nicaragua was as follows:

187)-'80.......... $6,644,816 | 1883-'84 .... $8,699,680
1881-'82.......... 7,381,662 | 1885-'86 8,410,188

The imports and exports during the last two were distributed as follow:

MOVEMENT.	1883-'84.	1885-'86.
Import.........................	$3,794,981	$3,684,173
Export.........................	4,904,649	4,726,015
Total trade.	$8,699,680	$8,410,188

During the last two years the products exported were: India-rubber, 23,007 quintals; gold, 19,785 ounces; coffee, 142,472 quintals; cattle, 406 head.

The American trade with Nicaragua has been as follows:

FISCAL YEARS.	Import into the United States.	Domestic export to Nicaragua.
1888.........................	$1,496,171	$561,156
1887.........................	1,664,169	701,151
1886.........................	1,067,902	471,671

Education.—In 1887 there were 233 common schools, attended by 9,033 pupils, who were taught by 256 teachers, and 10 colleges, attended by 998 students, taught by 64 professors. The painter, Don José Maria Ibarra, is about to open a school of arts at the capital; simultaneously a young ladies' educational institute is to be established. Dating from May 1, the academies at Leon and Granada were changed to national universities. The Government in 1888 spent $1,940 monthly in aid extended to colleges and universities, and $5,362 per month for common schools; adding thereto other subsidies for education, the monthly state aid aggregated during the year $14,046.

Nicaragua Canal.—The apparent collapse of the Panama Canal and the slight interest taken in the Tehauntepec Ship-Canal, bring into prominence the Nicaragua Canal. The Maritime Canal Company of Nicaragua, which had already received a charter from the State of Vermont, received also a charter from the Congress of the United States in February, 1889. After debates and investigations in both houses of Congress, of the most exhaust-

ive nature, continued at intervals throughout a period of more than a year, this act of incorporation was signed by President Cleveland in the same month, after careful examination by himself and cabinet of the constitutionality of the measure, and of the claims and objections of previous concessions. This measure is in line with the joint resolution of the Senate Committee on Foreign Affairs that the ship-canal should not be under European control. It requires the president, vice-president, and a majority of the directors of the company to be citizens of the United States.

The first concession to build a ship-canal by the route now proposed was granted by Nicaragua in 1849 to the Atlantic and Pacific Ship-Canal Company. The original company was succeeded by the Central American Transit Company. This organization is still in existence, and its members claim that it has rights prior to those of any other concern, which must be respected by any company that attempts to construct a canal on the route covered by the concessions. These claims have been frequently denied by the Government of Nicaragua, and the action of the United States Congress and President in granting national approval to the present company confirms this denial. A report was made giving the cost and description of the route of a ship-canal from the harbor of San Juan Del Norte, or Greytown, on the Atlantic, to the harbor of Brito on the Pacific, in Nicaragua. Two other lines were surveyed, but were deemed impracticable. The estimated cost of the entire work was $31,500,000. The undertaking was carried on for several years with considerable energy. It was purely an American enterprise; and it therefore encountered considerable opposition through representatives of foreign governments. Complications with political intriguers led to assurances by the Government at Washington, in 1858-'59, that the interests of citizens of the United States would be protected. The Bulwer and Clayton treaty was negotiated partially in behalf of the company's interests. In 1862 the Government of Nicaragua confiscated the property of the company. Through the intervention of the United States minister, the property was returned. Owing to the civil war in this country the company was left to protect its own interests, and in 1863 the Government of Nicaragua took away the exclusive privileges held by the company, and ratified a contract with Capt. Pim, who represented an English company that proposed building a railroad across the Isthmus. After the exclusive right had been taken away and the charter of the company modified, it made a new contract with Nicaragua, and proceeded with its work. In 1868 the company's steamer on Lake Nicaragua was seized by the troops of the Government, the franchises of the company were declared forfeited, and all its property was seized for debt and sold. This last act drove the company's employés out of the coun-

INTEROCEANIC CANAL OF NICARAGUA.

try, and as further work was impossible, it was decided that the aid of the United States Government should be invoked. Accordingly, on Nov. 5, 1869, the company made a formal request to President Grant for intervention. Claims against Nicaragua for the amount of property seized and destroyed and the damages incurred, were filed with the Secretary of State.

In March, 1887, a contract was signed with Nicaragua, securing to the New York Association exclusive right of way through the territory of the republic, for the construction of a ship-canal between the Atlantic and the Pacific Ocean. The route chosen has been surveyed several times—twice by expeditions sent out by the United States Navy Department. During Gen. Grant's presidency it was approved as the most practicable and feasible route for a ship-canal through the American Isthmus, by a Government commission consisting of the Chief of Engineers of the Army, the Chief of the Bureau of Navigation, and the Superintendent of the Coast Survey, after a technical examination, extending over several years, of the whole subject of interoceanic communication. The detailed estimates of the cost of construction, amounting to $65,000,000, were examined and accepted by eminent engineers in this country and Europe. Engineers and surveyors were sent to Nicaragua in 1887, and the work of survey has been carried on until the present time. The route is 169·8 miles in length, but only 28·9 miles can really be called a canal. It begins at Greytown, on the eastern side, follows the course of the San Juan river above Ochoa, through Lake Nicaragua, a distance of 129 miles, and thence to the harbor of Brito, the Pacific terminus. The surface of the lake, 110 feet above the sea, is the summit level. At the eastern end of the lake the San Juan river will be backed up and kept at the lake level by a dam for a distance of 64 miles, thus forming an extension of the lake, which will have a width of 1,000 feet and a depth of from

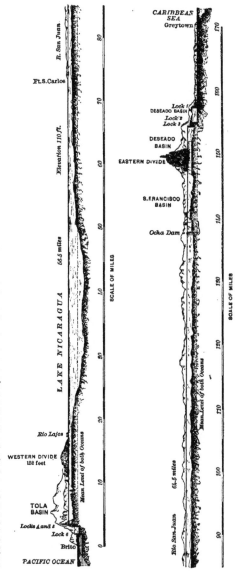

28 to 130 feet. There are 90 miles of lake-navigation, very wide and deep. From the point where the canal leaves the lake on the west to Brito, 17 miles, three locks are proposed. Over this portion of the route some rock-cutting and dredging will be necessary, though the difficulties are not formidable. The canal itself is to be 80 feet wide at the bottom in the deep cuts, and 120 feet wide in the enlarged sections. It is also proposed to enlarge the canal between the last lock and the sea at each terminus, so as to form extensions of the harbors at Greytown and Brito. It is further proposed to overcome the natural difficulties presented in the two harbors by the fluctuations and accumulations of sand by dredging and the use of jetties. The estimated cost of the canal, according to civil engineer Menocal's figures, is $64,000,000, which includes also electric lighting and railroads for the transportation of canal supplies; and the time for its completion is fixed at six years. The probabilities as to business are estimated as follow by the projectors: " According to reports of the Bureau of Statistics, United States Treasury Department, prepared from official data, the vessels that would have made use of the canal if there had been one were, in 1879, of 2,771,886 tons, and in 1885 of 4,252,434, showing an increase in six years of 1,480,548 tons. From this it is estimated that at least 5,000,000 tons of shipping would be ready to seek transit through the canal by 1892. With a toll of $2.50 a ton, this would yield a gross income of $12,500,-000. It is believed that $500,000 will cover ordinary operating expenses, as those of the Suez, with much longer actual canal, are only about $1,000,000 per annum. This would leave net receipts of $12,000,000, or 6 per cent. on $200,000,000." The length of the lock-chambers is 650 feet, and the width 70 feet—dimensions capable of admitting every ship afloat. Lock No. 3, which may be divided into two locks, will be cut out of solid rock, but the others are to have timber and concrete foundations, and the cavities as they may occur will be filled with concrete. The question to solve in regard to these locks is the gates, which are of exceptional size. Civil engineer Peary has invented a rolling gate, combining strength with lightness, as well as facility in opening and shutting. The lower part of the gate consists of a water-tight compartment, in which shifting water-ballast aids both in raising and lowering the gate, while the moving force employed is hydraulic. The gate moves on rails above the floor of the lock.

In May, 1887, the Government of Nicaragua granted important concessions. for which the company paid $100,000 in American gold to bind the bargain. The Government binds itself, for a period of ninety-nine years, not to make any subsequent concession for the opening of a canal between the two oceans, and also to abstain from granting a concession for a railroad, such as might compete with the

canal for the transportation of merchandise during the same period. The canal is declared neutral during the term of the concession, and the transit through the canal in case of war between two powers. or between one or more and Nicaragua, shall not be interrupted for such cause. The transit of foreign troops and vessels of war will be subjected to the prescriptions established by treaties between Nicaragua and other powers or by international law; but entrance to the canal will be rigorously prohibited to vessels of war of such powers as may be at war with Nicaragua or with any other of the Central American republics. The Government of Nicaragua places at the disposal of the company all the lands that may be required, as well as the materials found thereon; and, in case of the appropriation of property, the company shall enjoy the same privileges as the State. Alternating plots of land will be deeded to the company as the work progresses. It is required that at least $2,000,000 must be expended during the first year of construction. In consideration of the valuable privileges, franchises, and concessions granted to the company by this contract, it is provided that the republic shall receive in shares, bonds, certificates, or other securities which the company may issue, 6 per cent. of the total amount of the issue. The Government's share shall in no event be less than $4,000,000. The Government, in its capacity of shareholder, shall have the right to appoint one director. From the receipts of the enterprise the company shall take, in the first place, the amount necessary to cover all the expenses for maintenance, operation, and administration; all the sums necessary to secure the interest, which shall not exceed 6 per cent., and the amortization of the obligations and of the shares; and what remains shall form the net profits, of which at least 80 per cent. shall be divided among the shareholders. It is agreed that, after the lapse of ten years after the completion of the canal, the company shall not divide among the shareholders in payment of dividends, directly or indirectly, by issue of shares or otherwise, more than 15 per cent. annually, or, in this proportion, from dues collected from the canal; and, when it shall appear that these dues yield a greater profit, they shall be reduced to the fixed limit of 15 per cent. per annum. On the expiration of the ninety-nine years stipulated in the concession, it is provided that the republic shall enter upon possession in perpetuity of the canal and all establishments used in its administration, with the exception of vessels, stores of coal, and other materials and mechanical works belonging to the company, its floating capital and reserve fund, as also the lands ceded to it by the State. But the company shall have the right, at the expiration of the ninety-nine years, to the full enjoyment of the free use and control of the canal in the capacity of lessee, with all the privileges and advantages granted by the said concession, for another term of ninety-nine years, on condition of paying 25 per cent. of the annual net profits of the enterprise to the Government of the republic, beside the dividends due to it for its shares in the capital stock. All misunderstandings that may arise between the state of Nicaragua and the company will be submitted to arbitration. A valuable concession has also been obtained by the canal association from Costa Rica, on a basis similar to that mentioned above.

It is claimed that there are many points of advantage for the Nicaragua Canal. In the first place, it has no such bar to its way as the Culebra mountain, the cutting through of which, from the fact that there is danger of one side of the mountain sliding into the cut, is said to be a doubtful task. It has no such formidable difficulty to contend against as the Chagres river, the controlling of which for the rainy season is an unsolved problem. The San Juan river at Nicaragua is not comparable to it, for that river is known as the only river in the tropics not subject to sudden rises, and floods never occur either in the lake or in the San Juan for the first sixty-four miles of its course. At that point (San Carlos) a dam is proposed, which is said to be practicable. The river flows through a narrow valley, and has no large tributaries, and the heavy rains that fall on the Isthmus at Panama are unknown in this locality. The Chagres river runs beside the Panama Canal, and, though it is nothing more than a slow stream in the dry season, yet in the flood season it is 1,560 feet wide, 28 feet deep, and very rapid. Still another advantage claimed for the Nicaragua is, that the climate is much more healthful than on the Panama route.

NORTH CAROLINA. State Government. — The following were the State officers during the year: Governor, Alfred M. Scales (Democrat); Lieutenant-Governor, Charles M. Stedman; Secretary of State, William L. Saunders; Treasurer, Donald W. Bain; Auditor, William P. Roberts; Attorney-General, Theodore F. Davidson; Superintendent of Public Instruction, Sidney M. Finger; Commissioner of Agriculture, John Robinson; Chief-Justice of the Supreme Court, William N. H. Smith; Associate Justices, Augustus S. Merrimon and Joseph J. Davis.

Finances.—The receipts for 1888, including balance brought over, were $897,644.09; the expenditures, $824,611.88; balance, $73,032.21. Of this balance, $13,450.38 was deposited in the State National Bank of Raleigh, which suspended in March, 1888. The revenues applicable to general purposes were $515,693.78 for 1888, a decrease of $140,000 from 1887. This decrease is partly due to a lower rate of taxation in 1888, being twenty cents on $100, against twenty-five cents in 1887, and to the suspension of the collection of the tax on commercial travelers, in consequence of a decision of the Supreme Court of the United States declaring the

tax an interference with interstate commerce. This tax had yielded an annual average of $83,000. The Auditor and Treasurer concur in the opinion that, in order to meet the expenditures of the next two years, it will be necessary to raise the general tax rate to thirty cents on each $100 worth of property. The chief items of expenditure for 1888 were: Departments of the State Government, $22,607.84; judiciary, $46.721.82; agricultural department, $24,500; asylums and institutions, $197,400; interest on State debt, $267,687; Penitentiary, $100,000; pensions to Confederate soldiers, $29,583.80; university, $27,500; public printing, $13,189.16; State guard, $4.583.82. The estimated resources for the same time are $702,395. These estimates are based on a tax levy of thirty cents on $100, on the assessed valuation of $211,700,000.

The principal of the bonded debt recognized in the act of 1879 was as follows: Bonds issued before May, 1861, $5,477,400; issued during and since the late war, by authority of acts passed prior thereto, $3.261,045; issued in pursuance of the funding acts of March 10, 1866, and Aug. 20, 1868, $3,888,600; total recognized debt, $12,627,045. By that act this sum was to be refunded in 4-per-cent. bonds at a discount, and bonds have been surrendered and exchanged as follow: Class 1, at 40 per cent., $4,925,900; class 2, at 25 per cent., $2, 591,045; class 3, at 15 per cent., $3,197,-000. Total exchanged, $10.753,945. New 4-per-cent. bonds have been issued for these redeemed bonds as follow: Bonds at 40 per cent., $1,970,360; bonds at 25 per cent., $647,-761.25; bonds at 15 per cent., $479,550. Total new bonds issued, $3,097,671.25. There is still outstanding of the old bonds, $1,913,100; when the exchange is completed, the amount of the 4-per-cent. bonds will be $3,613,511.25.

Exchanges have continued under the act of March 14, 1879, to adjust and renew that portion of the State debt incurred in aid of the construction of the North Carolina Railroad. The commissioners have received $2,606,000 of the old bonds, and new bonds of the same amount, bearing 6 per cent. interest, maturing April 1, 1919, have been issued, and there remain $189,000 outstanding, the larger part being held by the United States Treasury. The total debt of the State will thus be funded at $6,408,511.25.

At the last session of the Legislature, the Treasurer was authorized, with the sanction of Governor and Auditor, to sell 4-per-cent. bonds, as many as may be necessary, at not less than par value, and to apply the proceeds to the payment of the 6-per-cent. construction bonds, wherever found. At the passage of the act, these 4-per-cent. bonds were at par, but they soon began to fall, and now command in the market about ninety-one cents.

Education.—The whole number of white and colored children between the ages of six and twenty-one years in 1887 was 566,270. The white children, during the four years ending in 1887, increased from 321,561 to 353,481; the colored children from 193,843 to 212,789.

During 1887 there were enrolled in the white schools 57·2 per cent.; in the colored schools 57·8 per cent. The average daily attendance in white schools was 35·2 per cent., and in the colored schools 33·5 per cent. The total expenditure for schools in 1887 was $653,037.33, and the average length of the school year sixty days.

For 1888, the average length of the school year was sixty-three days, the amount of money spent $729,388.02, and the number of children of school age 580,810—whites, 363,982; colored, 216,837. The total enrollment in the schools was 58 per cent., the average attendance about 35 per cent. At the State University, owing to the reductions in the income made by the last Legislature, it has been found necessary to diminish the number of teachers. The new building for the College of Agriculture, at Raleigh, begun in 1888, is approaching completion. It is built of brick made at the Penitentiary.

State Institutions.—Over 400 convicts have been employed on the railroads and in the swamps, and have done much work also upon the Supreme Court room and other public buildings. There are 400 convicts under the age of twenty years.

The State asylums are insufficient for the accommodation of the insane patients. A large number are now confined in poor-houses and jails, and there are many others in private families. The State Asylum at Raleigh has 292 patients, and there is accommodation at the Morganton Asylum for about 500.

The Institution for the Deaf, Dumb, and Blind is well managed, and its pupils now number 287, an increase of 47 in two years.

Militia.—The State Guard, organized in March, 1877, began its existence without State aid, and continued to be supported by private individuals till 1883, when the Legislature granted an appropriation of $150 a year to each company, limiting the number of companies to twenty-five. In 1887 this was increased to $300. With this aid, and the Federal appropriation of $10,000 per annum in arms, ammunition, equipment, and clothing, etc., the Guard is now on a good financial basis. It has increased from 1,043 officers and men in 1886 to 1,192 in 1887 and 1,459 in 1888.

Railroads.—There are 2,550 miles of railroad in the State owned by fifty-one companies. Two railroads are in great part owned by the State—the North Carolina and the Atlantic and North Carolina. The former is leased at a yearly rental of $260,000, and the State is thus enabled to pay the interest on its 6-per-cent. bonds issued in aid of the construction of the road. The other road was built as an extension of the former road to the sea. The State is contemplating building branch lines as feeders to the roads thus owned.

Manufacturing.—During the past two years twenty factories have been established for canning fruit and vegetables, and have been uniformly successful. There is a marked activity in cotton and wool manufacture, forty-one new factories having been established in 1888. The only silk-factory in the Southern States has been established in North Carolina during the past twelve months by Northern capitalists, and is highly successful. A large amount of machinery has been put into the Sam Christian gold-mine. Water is conveyed five miles, and is forced by a 500-horse-power engine against the hill-sides.

Crops. — Unfavorable weather during the spring and summer injured the crops; the corn-crop is unusually short, and the cotton is below the average; so, also, the tobacco-crop is shorter than for several years. The culture of sorghum cane is increasing, and three times as much land is devoted to grape-culture as there was two years ago.

Oyster-Survey.—The oyster-survey has been completed with the aid of the Federal Government. An area of over 1,000,000 acres has been examined, and 583,000 acres are reported suitable for oyster-culture. Since May 1, 1888, 472 entries of oyster-ground have been made in Hyde, Carteret, and Dare Counties; the total area entered is about 53,000 acres.

Boundary-Lines.—The survey between North Carolina and Virginia, in the counties of Currituck, Camden, and Gates, has been completed, and the line permanently marked with stones. The line between North Carolina and Tennessee and South Carolina is in dispute, and reference to arbitration is proposed.

Pensions.—By the acts and amendments of 1885 and 1887, $30,000 was appropriated to a certain defined class of soldiers and widows of deceased soldiers, in the expectation that each entitled would receive the sum of thirty dollars. So great has been the number of applications under these acts that the amount received by each applicant has been reduced to a mere pittance. The number of soldiers drawing pensions during the year was 1,083, and the number of widows, 2,625; total, 3,708; making the allowance for each soldier and widow, $8.25.

Immigration.—A convention of delegates from nearly all the Southern States east of the Mississippi river met at Hot Springs on April 25, under the auspices of the Southern railroad and steamship companies, to promote immigration into these States. The Governors of Virginia, South Carolina, and Georgia were present. After a discussion it was resolved that an immigration association be established with headquarters in the city of New York, to be styled the Southern Immigration Association. The object of the association is to direct immigrants, immediately upon their landing in New York, to homes in the South.

Farmers' Convention.—The annual meeting of the Interstate Farmers' Association was held this year at Raleigh, August 21. It brought together over one hundred delegates, representing nearly all the Southern States. Resolutions denouncing "trusts," asking for a repeal of the tariff on jute, and bespeaking encouragement for sheep-raising, were discussed and passed.

Political.—The Republican State Convention met at Raleigh on May 23, and nominated a complete State ticket as follows: For Governor, Oliver H. Dockery; Lieutenant-Governor, J. C. Pritchard; Secretary of State, George W. Staunton; Treasurer, G. A. Bingham; Auditor, C. F. McKesson; Attorney-General, Thomas P. Devereux; Superintendent of Public Instruction, James D. Mason; Judges of the Supreme Court, D. L. Russell, to succeed to the vacancy caused by the death of Judge Ashe, and Ralph B. Buxton and David M. Furches as the two Associate Judges provided for by the proposed constitutional amendment to be submitted to the people at the November election. The following resolutions, among others, were adopted:

We look upon the purity of the ballot-box as the best possible security against threatening evils, and we demand such reasonable State legislation as will fully protect the elector in the exercise of the elective franchise. Any denial of the free and just exercise of the elective franchise by fraud or violence poisons the springs of power.

As the means of preventing any further accumulation [of surplus in the United States Treasury] we demand the repeal of the internal-revenue system of taxation, and the passage of the Blair educational bill, as the best method of public education and of distributing the already accumulated surplus in the Treasury.

We are opposed to the present system of county government, and we demand the election of all county and township officers by the people.

We oppose the present system of hiring out convicts by the State, so as to bring other labor in competition with free labor.

The Democratic State Convention convened at Raleigh on May 30. There were three principal candidates for the gubernatorial nomination, Lieut.-Gov. Stedman, Daniel G. Fowle, and S. B. Alexander, each of whom received on the first ballot the following vote: Fowle, 374; Stedman, 331; Alexander, 245. Fowle was nominated on the twenty-third ballot by a vote of 523 to 435 for Stedman. The convention thereupon nominated Alexander for Lieutenant-Governor, but, upon his declining to accept the nomination, chose Thomas M. Holt. Secretary of State Saunders, Treasurer Bain, Attorney-General Davidson, and Superintendent of Public Instruction Finger were renominated. For Auditor, George W. Sanderlin was nominated; for Judge of the Supreme Court, to succeed Judge Ashe, Joseph J. Davis, and as additional judges, in case the constitutional amendment should be adopted, James E. Shepherd and Alphonso C. Avery. The platform approves the administration of Gov. Scales and President Cleveland, favors a tariff for revenue only, and contains the following:

That we, as heretofore, favor, and will never cease to demand, the unconditional abolition of the whole internal-revenue system as a war tax not to be justified in times of peace, as a grievous burden to our people and a source of annoyance in its practical operations. We call the attention of the people of the State to the hypocritical pretensions of the Republican party in their platforms that they are in favor of the repeal of this onerous system of taxation enacted by their party while the Republicans in Congress are taxing their energies to obstruct all legislation inaugurated by the representatives of the Democratic party to relieve the people of all or a part of this odious system.

That to meet an existing evil we will accept for educational purposes from the Federal Government our *pro-rata* share of the surplus in its Treasury; *Provided*, that it be disbursed through State agents and the bill for the distribution be free from objectionable features.

That it is due to the people of our eastern counties, who have so cheerfully borne their share of our common burdens, that the present or some equally effective system of county government shall be maintained.

The Prohibition party also nominated a State ticket, with William T. Walker for Governor, Moses Hammond for Secretary of State, Hugh W. Dixon for Treasurer, James W. Winstead for Auditor, John W. Moody for Attorney-General, and Robert T. Bonner for Superintendent of Public Instruction. Before the election the name of W. A. Guthrie was substituted on the Republican ticket for that of D. L. Russell, the latter having declined the nomination. The November election resulted in the usual Democratic victory for both State and national tickets. For Governor, Fowle received 147,925 votes; Dockery, 133,475; and Walker, 3,116. Members of the Legislature of 1889 were elected as follow: Senate—Democrats, 37; Republicans, 13. House—Democrats, 83; Republicans, 35; Independents, 2. Democratic Congressmen were elected in the First, Third, Fourth, Sixth, Seventh, and Eighth Districts, and Republicans in the Second, Fifth, and Ninth, a gain of one seat by the Republicans. At the same election the constitutional amendment increasing the number of judges of the Supreme Court from three to five was adopted by 121,961 to 29,393.

NOVA SCOTIA. There were no changes in the Executive Government of the Province of Nova Scotia during 1888.

Legislation.—The session of the Provincial Legislature in 1888 was characterized by the passage of several statutes of great local importance. The Towns Incorporation act is a measure to provide for the local government of all towns already incorporated within the province, and for the incorporation of other towns, without necessity for special legislation. Its principal provisions are as follows: When fifty of the rate-payers of any unincorporated district desire incorporation, they may hand to the sheriff of the county a requisition for an election to test the sentiment of the district. On receipt of this, the sheriff shall proceed to define the boundaries of the proposed town; but on the application of ten rate-payers in the district the sheriff's conclusions in this regard will be reviewed by the Lieutenant-

Governor in Council, and altered by that body in its discretion. After twenty days' notice, the election is held, at which all persons entitled to vote in the district for members of the provincial Legislature may vote, and if the decision is in the affirmative, or if half of the votes are in the affirmative, the Lieutenant-Governor issues a proclamation declaring the town incorporated. The sheriff is the officer to hold the election. Every town already incorporated within the province, or becoming incorporated under the act, is declared to be a separate school district, and the schools are under the control of a board of five commissioners, two of whom are appointed by the Lieutenant-Governor in Council, and three by the town council. This board determines what amount shall be assessed upon the town for school purposes, and under certain conditions may pledge the credit of the towns for school loans. The towns are made distinct from the municipalities in which they are situated, but their liability for indebtedness incurred by the municipality previous to the incorporation of the town continues. Full provisions are made for the assessment and collection of taxes, the laying out of streets, the establishment of local courts of civil and criminal jurisdiction, the regulation of the procedure in such courts, the establishment of a local police force, and in general to meet all probable exigencies likely to arise in a town corporation. The Assessment act of 1888 consolidates and amends all previous statutes on the same subject, and is very full in its provisions. Under it the incidence of taxation falls upon real and personal property and income. One fourth of the taxes in any year may be raised by a poll-tax, provided each individual poll-tax does not exceed fifty cents; but a municipal council may omit to levy a poll-tax if it deems it expedient to do so.

The Miners' Arbitration act, 1888, provides for the appointment of a board of arbitration to settle disputes between persons employed in mines and their employers. This board consists of five persons; two are appointed by the Lieutenant-Governor in Council, each of the parties to the dispute appoints one, and the two so appointed choose the fifth. The arbitrators are sworn, and have full powers to compel the attendance of witnesses, to administer oaths, and to examine documents. Their award may be made a rule of the Supreme Court on motion, and be enforced in the same manner as other rules of court.

The Public Health act, 1888, authorizes the Governor in Council to make all necessary orders to promote sanitary precautions, including such steps as are needed to prevent the spread of infectious diseases; to regulate burials; and to supply medical aid, medicine, and hospital accommodation in cases of epidemic, endemic, or contagious diseases. It provides for the annual appointment of boards of health in all the cities, towns, and municipalities, the ap-

pointment being vested in the city, town, or municipal councils, as the case may be; but in case the councils do not appoint, the Lieutenant-Governor in Council may do so. Each city, town, or municipality is made a health-district, and a sanitary inspector is to be appointed in each, whose salary and expenses, as well as all the necessary expenses of the board of health, are to be borne by the district. Provision is made for compulsory vaccination, which is to be gratuitous in the case of indigent persons. Houses in which persons are sick from any infectious disease are to be quarantined; children of families so inflicted must be detained from school. Heavy penalties are imposed for violation of the act or any of the regulations made under it.

Many important amendments were made in the details of the Liquor-License act, 1886; also in the County Courts act. All the statutes relating to trustees were consolidated and amended, and an act was passed to provide for the compulsory attendance of children at school; but the provisions of the latter statute only apply to Halifax.

Shipping.—Five steamers, aggregating 397 tons, and 101 sailing-vessels, aggregating 13,976 tons, were built in Nova Scotia during the year ending June 30, 1888. There were added to the Provincial Registry of Shipping during the same period, 126 vessels, aggregating 16,231 tons, and there were sold to other countries 13 vessels, aggregating 3,633 tons and valued at $59,150. The arrivals and departures from Nova Scotia ports during the year ending June 30, 1888, were as follow:

MOVEMENT.	Number.	Tons.
Arrivals:		
Steamers......................	3,073	956,652
Sailing-vessels...............	14,227	749,165
Departures:		
Steamers......................	3,021	952,787
Sailing-vessels...............	13,855	798,928

Provincial Revenue and Expenditure.—The revenue of Nova Scotia for the year ending Dec. 31, 1888, was as follows: From dominion subsidies, $504,382.32; mines, $151,208.72; crown lands, $14,258.15; other sources, $53,002.30; total, $712,951.49. The principal items of expenditure were: For education, $212,000; road surplus, $113,829; interest, $49,377; agriculture, $21,283; subsidies to steamers, $36,923; legislative expenses, $40,620; salaries, $17,658; hospital maintenance, $20,048; railway subsidies, $28,038. A balance of $44,551 was carried over to 1889.

Railways.—Following is a statement of the railways in operation in Nova Scotia in 1888: Intercolonial, 251 miles; Windsor and Annapolis, 84; Western Counties, 67; Eastern Extension, 80; Joggins, 14: Springhill and Parrsboro, 32; Sydney and Louisburg, 32.

The following roads were under construction during the year: Oxford and New Glasgow, 72 miles; Cape Breton, 98; Nictaux and Atlantic, 75.

O

OBITUARIES, AMERICAN. Sketches of some of the more noted Americans that died in 1888 will be found in their alphabetical places in this volume, accompanied by portraits.

Abell, Arunah Shepherdson, publisher, born in East Providence, R. I., Aug. 10, 1806; died in Baltimore, Md., April 19, 1888. He learned the printer's trade, and, with two partners, issued the first number of the Philadelphia "Public Ledger," on March 25, 1836. In 1837 he went to Baltimore, and on May 17 brought out the first number of the "Sun." He retained his interest in the Philadelphia "Public Ledger" till 1864, and in the Baltimore "Sun" till death. Mr. Abell was associated with Prof. Morse in establishing the magnetic telegraph, published the first message sent over the wires between Washington and Baltimore in 1844, and received for publication the first presidential message ever transmitted by wire, May 11, 1846. At the time of his death he was believed to be the wealthiest citizen of Baltimore, and had an estate near the city that originally cost him $500,000, and on which he subsequently expended $1,000,000 in improvements.

Adam, John Johnston, railroad official, born in Paisley, Scotland, Oct. 30, 1807; died in Tecumseh, Mich., July 4, 1888. He was graduated at the University of Glasgow in 1826, removed to the United States, and was soon afterward appointed principal of Meadville, Pa., academy. In 1831 he removed to Michigan; in 1835 was a member of the convention that framed the first Constitution of the State; in 1836-'40 was Secretary of the State Senate; and, after a service in the State House of Representatives, was elected State Treasurer. He was appointed Auditor-General of Michigan in 1845, and in January, 1851, resigned the office to accept one with the Michigan Central Railroad. Two years afterward he became auditor of the Michigan Southern Railroad Company, with which he remained until 1863. Mr. Adam was a member of the two first boards of regents, under which the State University was reorganized.

Agnew, Cornelius Rea, surgeon, born in New York, Aug. 8, 1830; died there, April 18, 1888. He was graduated at Columbia College in 1849, and at the College of Physicians and Surgeons in 1852, and became connected with the New York Hospital. Subsequently he studied at the Lying-in Asylum in Dublin, attended Prof. Ferguson's Clinical Lectures in London, and applied himself to the study of diseases of the eye and skin in Paris. On his return to New York, he assumed the duties of surgeon to the Eye and Ear Infirmary and engaged in private practice. In 1858 Gov. Morgan appointed him Surgeon-General of the State of New York, and shortly after his re-election in 1860 made him Medical Director of the State Volunteer Hospital. He was one of the founders of the United States Sanitary Commission, and as a commissioner devoted his entire time to its service during the civil war. He joined three other gentlemen in establishing the Union League Club of New York. In 1866 he established ophthalmia clinics in the College of Physicians and Surgeons, and three years later was elected Clinical Professor of diseases of the Eye and Ear. In 1870 he organized the Brooklyn Eye and Ear Hospital, and the Manhattan Eye and Ear Hospital in New York; and he was one of the organizers of the School of Mines in Columbia College, and became a trustee of the college in 1874. He was a manager of the State Lunatic Asylum at Poughkeepsie, and secretary of the executive committee of its board; president of the Board of Education of New York; a governor of the New York Women's

Medical College; secretary of the first sanitary reform association organized in New York; and president of the New York State Medical Society in 1872. He was a popular and effective lecturer, and published, among many works, "A Contribution to the Surgery of Divergent Squint," "Trephining the Cornea to Remove a Foreign Body," and "Authoplasty as a Remedy in Certain Diseases of the Eye."

Alexander, Edmund Brooke, soldier, born in Haymarket, Va., Oct. 6, 1802; died in Washington, D. C., Jan. 3, 1888. He was graduated at the United States Military Academy in 1823, assigned to the Sixth Infantry as brevet second lieutenant, promoted captain, and appointed assistant quartermaster in 1838, and transferred to the general staff. He resigned his staff appointment, and, as senior captain, commanded the Third Infantry through the Mexican War. His regiment carried the enemy's breastworks with the bayonet at Cerro Gordo; and he was brevetted major for this action, and lieutenant-colonel for gallantry at Contreras and Churubusko. After the war he served in New Mexico, was promoted major and assigned to the Eighth Infantry, and was selected by President Pierce for one of the new colonelcies on the enlargement of the army in 1855. He was in command at Fort Laramie at the beginning of the civil war, and was kept at remote frontier posts as chief mustering officer; was brevetted brigadier-general for faithful services; and retired, after forty-nine years of continuous service, in 1872.

Ayres, Romeyn Beck, soldier, born in East Creek, Montgomery County, N. Y., Dec. 20, 1825; died in Fort Hamilton, New York harbor, Dec. 4, 1888. He was graduated at the United States Military Academy in 1847, served in the Mexican War as second lieutenant in the Third United States Artillery, and after its close was on garrison duty at Fort Preble, Mexico, and on similar and frontier duty in the United States till 1859, when he was ordered to the Artillery School at Fort Monroe. With the exception of a three months' sick-leave, he was actively engaged through the civil war. He was promoted first lieutenant in March, 1852; captain in May, 1861; brevet-major, July 2, 1863; lieutenant-colonel, May 5, 1864; colonel, Aug. 18, 1864; brigadier-general and major-general, March 13, 1865; was mustered out the volunteer service as full major-general, April 30, 1866, and was promoted lieutenant-colonel, Twenty-eighth United States Infantry, July 28, 1866; transferred to Third United States Artillery, Dec. 15, 1870, and promoted colonel, Second United States Artillery, July 18, 1879. His brevets were conferred for gallant and meritorious services in the battle of Gettysburg, in the Wilderness, on the Weldon Railroad, at Five Forks, and during the war, and for conspicuous gallantry in the Wilderness, at Spottsylvania Court-House, Jericho Mills, Bethesda Church, Petersburg, and Globe Tavern.

Bacon, John William, jurist, born in Natick, Mass., in 1818; died in Taunton Mass., March 21, 1888. He was graduated at Harvard in 1843, admitted to the bar in 1846, elected a State Senator in 1859 and 1862, appointed chief-justice of the municipal court of Boston in 1866, and elevated to the bench of the Superior Court in 1871. He was suddenly taken ill while holding court. In the evening he was stricken with apoplexy, and died in a few minutes.

Baker, William Emerson, manufacturer, born in Boston, Mass., April 16, 1828; died there, Jan. 5, 1888. He began business life in a dry-goods store, and subsequently joined W. O. Grover in forming the Grover & Baker Sewing-Machine Company. Mr. Baker spent several years abroad, contesting patent suits, and on returning to the United States bought Ridge Hill farm at Wellesley, Mass., and spent the remainder of his life in gratifying an extreme eccentricity for curious buildings, fantastic decorations, and mirth-provoking apparatus. His farm comprised over 500 acres, and on it he erected an immense stable which he decorated within and without with extraordinary paintings; a tall tower, whose successive floors constituted a combined museum, zoölogical cabinet, and kindergarten; several pavilions from the Centennial grounds; a chapel in which he placed a huge bronzed Buddha; a pig-pen of vast proportions and regal splendor, its interior covered with large oil paintings; numerous costly mausoleums in which favorite departed pigs, restored by a taxidermist, were exhibited on magnificent pedestals; and many grotesque edifices, all gaudily painted. He constructed an artificial lake, and placed in it a curious steamboat that would go equally well on land or in water; tunneled a subterranean labyrinth through the rock; and filled his grounds with stuffed animals and all the extravagant, odd, and nondescript things he could make or buy. He was fond of entertaining distinguished people, and opened his grounds to the public every day but Sunday.

Baldwin, Charles H., naval officer, born in New York city, Dec. 23, 1822; died there, Nov. 17, 1888. He entered the United States Navy as a midshipman, April 24, 1839, was promoted passed midshipman July 2, 1845, was engaged in the operations in the vicinity of Mazatlan, from November, 1847, till June, 1848, was commissioned lieutenant in November, 1853, and resigned Feb. 23, 1854. At the outbreak of the civil war in 1861 he was appointed acting lieutenant. During Farragut's passage of Forts Jackson and St. Philip below New Orleans and the capture of the city he was in command of the steamer "Clifton," and at the first attack on Vicksburg in 1862 he rendered important service on the same vessel. He was commissioned commander Nov. 18, 1862, was on special service in command of the "Vanderbilt" in 1863–'64, was in charge of the ordnance bureau at Mare Island Navy Yard, San Francisco in 1864–'67, was fleet captain of the North Pacific squadron in 1868–'69, was commissioned captain June 12, 1869, commodore Aug. 8, 1876, and rear-admiral Jan. 31, 1883, and was retired Sept. 3, 1884. In the interval of his naval service he was captain of a mail steamship plying between New York and San Francisco. As commander of the "Vanderbilt," he chased the Confederate privateer "Alabama" half-way round the world, and as commander of the European squadron after his promotion to rear-admiral he represented the United States at the coronation of the present Emperor of Russia.

Barnard, Daniel P., lawyer, born in Hudson, N. Y., in 1812; died in Brooklyn, N. Y., Feb. 18, 1888. He removed to New York in 1824, and for a time was engaged in a banking-house. Subsequently he was admitted to the Baltimore bar, and became a Democratic member of the city council. In 1842 he settled in Brooklyn, in 1852 was elected a member of the council, and in 1855 was chosen president of the board of aldermen, to which office were then added the duties of city judge. He was one of the foremost advocates of the consolidation of Williamsburgh with Brooklyn, and of the introduction of water into the city, was a member of the Constitutional convention of 1867–'68, settled the famous Jackson Hollow litigation, and successfully defended Cortland Sprague, city treasurer, Isaac Badeau, collector, and Evan M. Johnson, comptroller, on charges of malfeasance.

Barnes, Alfred Smith, publisher, born in New Haven, Conn., Jan. 28, 1817; died in Brooklyn, N. Y., Feb. 17, 1888. He entered the bookstore of D. F. Robinson & Co. in Hartford, removed with the firm to New York, and in his twenty-first year associated himself with Prof. Charles Davies and began publishing his mathematical works. He personally canvassed every section of the country with their first publication, and pursued the same course for several years with subsequent ones. The firm opened a book-store in Philadelphia in 1840, and removed their manufactory to that city in 1842; but Prof. Davies soon after-

ward retired, and Mr. Barnes returned to New York in 1855. In 1868 the firm erected the building on the corner of John and William Streets, New York, and in 1880 put up another large one on the corner of Liberty and Nassau Streets. Brooklyn, where all the manufacturing is done. The firm has confined itself almost exclusively to school-books. Mr. Barnes retired from the active management in 1880, leaving five sons in charge. He was president of the Brooklyn City Mission Society, and a director in several financial corporations. He gave the Faith Home $25,000, and the Young Men's Christian Association of Cornell University, $40,000; and bequeathed $50,000 to various charities, churches, and schools.

Barnes, Demas, manufacturer, born in Gorham, Ontario County, N. Y., April 4, 1827; died in New York city May 1, 1888. He removed to New York when fourteen years old, learned the drug business, and established a store of his own four years afterward. At one time he had branch stores in San Francisco, New Orleans, and Montreal. In 1866 he was elected to Congress as a Democrat from the second Congressional District, which included the greater part of the city of Brooklyn, and in that body served as a member of the committees on banking and currency, education, and labor. He aided in procuring legislation for the construction of the East River Bridge, and became one of its first trustees, and ably supported the demand for a new post-office building in New York city. He was one of the founders of the Brooklyn "Eagle," but withdrew from it in 1873 and established the Brooklyn "Argus," from which he retired in February, 1877. Afterward he joined the independent movement in Brooklyn, and was appointed a member of the committee of one hundred citizens, who undertook to check municipal abuses. Mr. Barnes moved to New York city in 1882, but continued his relations with various financial, educational, and charitable institutions of Brooklyn till his death.

Barron, Samuel, naval officer, born in Hampton, Va., in 1802; died in Essex County, Va., Feb. 26, 1888. He was commissioned mid-shipman in the United States Navy when only three years old, being the youngest Government officer ever known in any country, except the scions of royalty, and when eight years old made his first sea-cruise, up the Mediterranean. He served with honor in various parts of the world, rendered efficient aid through the Mexican War, was commandant of the naval station at Norfolk during the yellow-fever epidemic, and was in command of the United States frigate "Wabash" at the beginning of the civil war. When his State seceded he resigned his commission in the United States Navy, entered that of the Confederacy, with the rank of commodore, and while on his first service, as commander of Fort Hatteras, at Hatteras Inlet, was captured with his entire command by the National forces. After a confinement of about a year in Fort Warren he was exchanged, and during the remainder of the war served the Confederacy in London, superintending the equipment of cruisers.

Belden, David, lawyer, born in Newtown, Fairfield County, Conn., Aug. 14, 1832; died in San José, Cal., May 14, 1888. He was apprenticed to a carpenter, and on attaining his majority removed to Marysville, Cal., where he worked at his trade. He there attracted the attention of James Churchman, a lawyer of Nevada City, who induced him to remove to that city and study law. In 1856 he was admitted to the bar of the Supreme Court; in 1858 was elected judge of Nevada County, and at the expiration of his term declined a re-election; and in 1865 was elected a State senator and served four years, during which he was first a member and then chairman of the judiciary committee. He settled in San José, and in 1871 was appointed judge of the newly created Twentieth Judicial District of the State, and on the expiration of his first term was unanimously re-elected. Under the new Constitution the judiciary system of the State was reorganized, and at the first election, in 1880, he was chosen a judge of the Supreme Court, and was re-elected in 1884. Judge Belden was a Democrat until the civil war, and then became a strong Union man. He was an enthusiastic meteorologist, established an experimental horticultural garden on his estate, and constructed an instrument that registered automatically all the details of an earthquake.

Bellew, Francis Henry Temple, artist, born in Cawnpore, Hindostan, April 18, 1828; died on Long Island, N. Y., June 29, 1888. He was the son of a British officer, studied art in France, and in 1850 came to this country, where his immediate success as a caricaturist in John Brougham's "Lantern" led him to devote himself entirely to drawing. When this venture failed, he joined Thomas Strong in founding "Yankee Notions," and later joined William Levison in the "Picayune." He also wrote and drew for "Harper's Magazine" and "Harper's Weekly," and afterward founded various papers, among which were "John Donkey" and "Vanity Fair." In 1860 he returned to England, where, with George Augustus Sala and Blanchard Jerrold, he founded "Temple Bar," and also drew sketches for "Punch" and American scenes for the "Illustrated London News." He returned to New York in 1861, resumed work for publishers, and was correspondent for the New York "Tribune" and the "Illustrated London News" at the battle of Gettysburg. His later sketches and writings appeared in "Harper's Magazine," "Harper's Young People," "St. Nicholas," "Texas Siftings," and similar publications. He established a daily called "Dawn" in 1885, but it failed. His forte was writing and sketching stories for children. He published "The Characteristics of the Three Kingdoms" (1850) and "The Art of Amusing" (New York, 1865).

Bergh, Henry, born in New York city in 1823; died there, March 12, 1888. He was of German and English Puritan lineage, and the son of Christian Bergh, a ship-builder. Henry received a collegiate education, and began studying law in Columbia College, but before completing the course went to Europe. He married Matilda, daughter of Thomas Taylor, in 1848, and then traveled in almost every part of the Continent and in the East. In 1861 President Lincoln appointed him Secretary of the American Legation in Russia, and soon afterward United States consul at St. Petersburg. The failing health of his wife led him to resign in 1864 and return to New York. In London he made the acquaintance of the Earl of Harrowby, president of the Royal Society for the Prevention of Cruelty to Animals, became intensely interested in the work of that organization, studied its details thoroughly, and formulated a plan for a similar society in New York. In 1865 he founded the American Society for the Prevention of Cruelty to Animals, was chosen its president, and in 1866 secured the passage of an act giving the society, through its officers, the power of making arrests and carrying on prosecutions for violations of the statute on which the organization was instituted. From the day the society was formed until his death he remained its president and guiding spirit, living wholly in its work, and serving without salary. Through its efforts dog-fighting, cock-fighting, and rat-baiting were almost entirely suppressed, and branch societies were organized in thirty-six States. Mr. Bergh was an enthusiastic student of geology, and author of a drama, "Love's Alternative," produced at the Union League Theatre, Baltimore, in 1881, and several poems.

Bessels, Emil, naturalist, born in Heidelberg, Germany, June 2, 1847; died in Stuttgart, Germany, March 30, 1888. He was educated at the university of his native place, where he received the degree of M. D. He was made an assistant at the Royal Museum in Stuttgart, and there became interested in Arctic discovery. In 1869 he made the voyage into sea between Spitzbergen and Nova Zembla. By his observations on this journey he traced the influence of the gulf stream east of Spitzbergen, and added much to the scanty knowledge of that region. He was called to the field as a military surgeon in 1870, and for his services in hospitals received public commendation from the Grand Duke of Baden. In 1871 he came to this country at August Petermann's suggestion, and was made naturalist and surgeon to the expedition sent to the polar regions under Capt. Charles F. Hall. Most of the scientific results of this voyage were the fruit of his personal efforts, and, after the rescue of the survivors, he was occupied for several years at the Smithsonian Institution preparing for publication the scientific results of the voyage, one of which was the proof, just advanced by him, of the insularity of Greenland, which he deduced from the tidal observations secured on the expedition. This work he issued as "Report on the Scientific Results of the Polaris Expedition" (Washington, 1876). In 1879 he published a German narrative of the expedition, illustrated with his own sketches. Subsequently he undertook an ethnological voyage to the northwest coast of America, but it was terminated prematurely by the wreck of the vessel in Seymour Narrows, British Columbia. He returned to Washington, where he prepared several contributions to Arctic and zoölogical literature and projected a work on the Eskimo, but his material was destroyed by a fire at his residence in 1885. Dr. Bessels then went to Germany and settled in Stuttgart, where he was engaged in literary pursuits, the study of art, and geographical instruction until his death.

Birge, Henry Warner, soldier, born in Hartford, Conn., Aug. 25, 1825; died in New York city, June 1, 1888. He received a classical education, and at the beginning of the civil war organized the Fourth Regiment of Connecticut Volunteers, and was commissioned its major on May 23, 1861. After service in Maryland and Virginia, he was recalled by his uncle Gov. Buckingham and appointed colonel of the Thirteenth Regiment in November. In March, 1862, he took this regiment by sea to join Gen. Butler's army in New Orleans, and on reaching that city was placed in charge of its defenses. In December he accompanied the army up the Mississippi to co-operate with Gen. Grant in the siege of Vicksburg, was appointed to the command of a brigade, which he held through the first Red River campaign and the siege of Port Hudson, and volunteered to lead a storming party against the works of the latter stronghold. He was promoted brigadier-general in September, 1863. During Gen. Grant's Virginia campaign he was assigned to the command of a division in the Nineteenth Corps, and was with Gen. Sheridan in his most brilliant movements in the Shenandoah valley. In February, 1865, he was placed in command of the defenses of Savannah, and held that post until the following November, when he resigned with the rank of brevet major-general. After the war he traveled considerably in the Southwest and on the Pacific coast.

Bittinger, William, merchant, born near Hanover, Pa., Nov. 21, 1820; died in Abbottstown, Adams County, Pa., March 3, 1888. He became a clerk in a store in Abbottstown when fifteen years old, and, with the exception of one year spent in teaching, was in mercantile business all his life. His will disposed of an estate valued at $225,000, of which a farm worth $45,000 was given to Pennsylvania College, in Gettysburg, which also was made residuary legatee to found the William Bittinger professorship of Intellectual and Moral Science; another farm, valued at $40,000, to Lebanon Valley College, in Annville, to endow the Josephine Bittinger-Eberly professorship in that institution; and $3,000 to the Lutheran congregation in Abbottstown for a new church-building.

Bobbett, Albert, wood-engraver, born in London, England, in 1813; died in New York city, Aug. 6, 1888. He learned to engrave on wood in London, removed to New York city about 1843, and was connected with nearly every effort to establish illustrated periodicals in this country. He engraved illustrations for P. T. Barnum, in Boston, for Gleason's "Pictorial," for Frank Leslie's early publications, for the first issues of Harper's "Magazine" and "Weekly," and for publishers of educational works, and continued work till his death. He was a member of the American Water-Color Society, a man of extensive reading and artistic taste, and the instructor of many of the best engravers on wood of the present day.

Bodley, Rachel Littner, physician, born in Cincinnati, Ohio, Dec. 7, 1831; died in Philadelphia, Pa., June 15, 1888. She was educated at Wesleyan College in Cincinnati, and in 1860 was appointed preceptor in the higher collegiate branches in that institution. Subsequently she entered the Polytechnic College in Philadelphia as a special student in chemistry and physics, and after a two years' course was appointed Professor of Natural Sciences in the Cincinnati Female Seminary, and held the chair three years. In 1865 she was elected Professor of Chemistry and Toxicology in the Woman's Medical College of Pennsylvania, Philadelphia, being the first woman professor of chemistry on record. She was elected dean of the faculty in 1877, and held both offices till her death. In 1864 she became a corresponding member of the State Historical Society of Wisconsin; 1871 a member of the Academy of Natural Sciences of Philadelphia, and received the degree of M. A. from her *alma mater;* 1879 received the degree of M. D. from the Woman's Medical College of Pennsylvania; in 1882 was elected a school director in Philadelphia, and received many similar honors.

Bogart, William Henry, journalist, born in Albany, N. Y., in 1810; died in Aurora, N. Y., Aug. 21, 1888. He was graduated at the Albany Law School in 1831, but after practicing his profession a short time abandoned it for journalism. His first permanent employment was as legislative correspondent for the New York "Courier and Enquirer," then edited by Gen. James Watson Webb. He remained with that paper till it was merged into the New York "World," and then severed his connection with it, and established in Albany a legislative corresponding bureau for supplying newspapers with political news from the capital. While so employed he contributed to the "Atlantic Monthly" and other periodicals, and became clerk to the Senate, member of the Albany Institute, and one of the first trustees of Wells College. He traveled extensively in early life, and was well known as an accomplished after-dinner speaker.

Boggs, Charles Stuart, naval officer, born in New Brunswick, N. J., Jan. 28, 1810; died there, April 22, 1888. He was appointed midshipman in the United States Navy in 1826, and served in the Mediterranean squadron till 1830, was attached to the East India squadron from 1830 till 1832, was promoted passed midshipman in 1832, and was commissioned lieutenant on Sept. 6, 1837. While attached to the "Princeton," during the Mexican War, he took part in the siege of Vera Cruz, and commanded the boat expedition that destroyed the United States brig "Truxton" after her surrender to the Mexicans. He was executive officer of the frigate "Lawrence" at the World's Fair in London in 1848, served as light-house inspector on the Pacific coast, and was promoted commander in 1855. Assigned to command the "Varuna," of Farragut's fleet, in 1862, he distinguished himself in the attack on Forts Jackson and St. Philip, below New Orleans, by running ahead of the other vessels, attacking the Confederate squadron above the fort, and destroying six of its gunboats before his own vessel was sunk by two rams. The "Varuna" set both rams on fire, and discharged a parting shot when the water was nearly on a level with her last serviceable gun. He was made bearer of dispatches to Washington, promoted captain, and given command of the "Juniata." During 1864-'65 he was on duty at the Brooklyn Navy-Yard, superintending the construction of steam picket-boats, and there designed and fitted out the torpedo-boat with which the Confederate ram "Albemarle" was destroyed. He was promoted commodore in July, 1866, commanded the "De Soto," of the North Atlantic

squadron, in 1867-'68, was on special duty in 1869-'70, and in July of the latter year was promoted rear-admiral. In 1871-'72 he commanded the European squadron, and then served as light-house inspector till 1873, when he was retired.

Booth, James Curtis, chemist, born in Philadelphia, Pa., July 28, 1810; died in West Haverford, Pa., March 21, 1888. He was educated at Hartsville Seminary and was graduated at the University of Pennsylvania in 1829, after which he spent a year at the Rensselaer Polytechnic Institute. During the winter of 1831-'32 he delivered a course of lectures on chemistry in Flushing, L. I., and in December, 1832, he went to Germany, where he entered the private laboratory of Prof. Friedrich Wöhler in Cassel. It is believed that he was the first American to study analytical chemistry in Germany. A year later he went to Berlin, and there studied under Gustav Magnus for a year, after which he devoted some time to the practical study of chemistry applied to the arts in the manufacturing centers of Europe. In 1836 he returned to Philadelphia and established a laboratory for instruction in chemical analysis and applied chemistry. This soon acquired considerable reputation, and students from various parts of the country came to him for instruction. His analytical practice increased, and he was assisted by Dr. Martin H. Boyé until 1845. Three years later, Thomas H. Garrett became his associate, and in 1881 the firm became Booth, Garrett, and Blair. He was made Professor of Chemistry Applied to the Arts in the Franklin Institute in 1836, and for nine successive winters he continued his lectures, making three full courses of three years each; also in 1842-'45 he was Professor of Chemistry in the Central High-School of Philadelphia. Soon after his return from Europe he was called on to take part in the geological survey of Pennsylvania, and during 1837-'38 he had charge of the geological survey of Delaware, in connection with which he issued the first and second "Annual Report of the Delaware Geological Survey" (Dover, 1839) and "Memoirs of the Geological Survey of Delaware" (1841). In 1849 he was appointed melter and refiner at the United States Mint in Philadelphia, which office he held until Jan. 7, 1888, when his resignation was accepted, to take effect on the qualification of his successor. In his official capacity Mr. Booth was frequently consulted by the Government on questions pertaining to chemistry, and his studies of the nickel ores of Pennsylvania led, in 1856, to the adoption of nickel as one of the components of the alloys used in the coinage of the cent issued in 1857. The degree of LL. D. was conferred upon him by the University of Lewisburg in 1867, and that of Ph. D. by the Rensselaer Polytechnic Institute in 1884. He was a member of the American Philosophical Society, and of other scientific associations, and in 1883-'84 was president of the American Chemical Society. In addition to scientific papers, he published "Encyclopedia of Chemistry, Practical and Theoretical," in the preparation of which he was assisted by Martin H. Boyé, Richard S. McCulloh, and Campbell Morfit (Philadelphia, 1850), and "Recent Improvements in the Chemical Arts," issued by the Smithsonian Institution (Washington, 1852). He edited, with notes, a translation from the French of Regnault's "Elements of Chemistry" (2 vols., Philadelphia, 1853).

Bovee, Marvin H., reformer, born in Amsterdam, N. Y., in 1827; died in Whitewater, Wis., May 7, 1888. He removed with his parents to Wisconsin in 1843, and after teaching for several years was elected State Senator from Waukesha County. As chairman of the select committee, one of his first acts was to report a bill for the abolition of capital punishment, which became a law. At the close of his term he delivered over 1,200 addresses to the Legislatures and people of half the States in the Union, and in several of them secured the passage of laws making the punishment for murder life imprisonment as well as death. His labors were self-imposed, and cost him many thousands of dollars, besides his time and labor, as he would never accept money for his efforts or even hall-hire. About 1860 he established a State reformatory for boys at Waukesha on original plans. He believed that the only way to effect a permanent reform was to surround the youthful criminal with wholesome influences, treat him kindly, and teach him to be industrious. Accordingly he placed the boys in home-like cottages, gave them all judicious liberty, taught them trades, and sought to encourage a pride in elevated manhood. Mr. Bovee was an active Democrat, and spoke in the presidential canvass of 1884.

Boyce, James Petigru, educator, born in Greenville, S. C., Jan. 11, 1827; died in Pau, France, Dec. 28, 1888. He was graduated at Brown University in 1847 and at Princeton Seminary in 1851, and was ordained pastor of a Baptist church in Columbia, S. C. In 1855 he became Professor of Theology in Furman University, Greenville, S. C., and three years afterward was called to the same chair in the Southern Baptist Theological Seminary, then also in Greenville. In 1873, through the endowments of friends in Kentucky and a large donation from Prof. Boyce, the seminary was removed to Louisville, and he was chosen president, which office he filled until his death. He was a trustee of the John F. Slater educational fund, published numerous sermons, addresses, and periodical articles, and had received the degrees of D. D. and LL. D.

Brenner, Carl, artist, born in Lautereicken, Bavaria, in 1838; died in Louisville, Ky., July 22, 1888. He removed to the United States when a boy, settled in Louisville, and became a sign-painter. He studied drawing and landscape-painting, and soon obtained high proficiency. His first notable exhibition was at Philadelphia in 1876, and from that time his paintings were to be found in most of the large exhibitions in the country. He was very industrious, and found his favorite subjects in glimpses of scenery in which the beech-tree was conspicuous.

Brewster, Benjamin Harris, lawyer, born in Salem County, N. J., Oct. 13, 1816; died in Philadelphia, Pa., April 4, 1888. He was graduated at Princeton College in 1834, and admitted to the bar in Philadelphia in 1838. In 1846 he was appointed a commissioner to adjudicate the claims of the Cherokee Indians against the United States; in 1867 was appointed Attorney-General of Pennsylvania; and in December, 1881, was appointed Attorney-General of the United States by President Arthur. These were all the public offices he ever held, though he was twice a candidate for the United States Senate, and came very near election each time. He was wedded to his profession, and practiced it with great assiduity and success. Shortly after the death of President Garfield, he was formally retained by United States Attorney-General MacVeagh to assist in the prosecution of the Star Route conspirators. Prior to the civil war Mr. Brewster was a Democrat, but when Fort Sumter was fired upon he became one of the most zealous supporters of the Administration. He was widely esteemed for his literary and scholarly attainments; and was an impressive orator. He received the degrees of A. B., A. M., and LL. D. from Princeton College, and the latter also from Dickinson College. The disfigurement of his face was caused by burns received in early youth in attempting to rescue his sister from a fire into which she had fallen. (See portrait in "Annual Cyclopædia" for 1882, page 812.)

Brigham, David, abolitionist, born in Westborough, Mass., Sept. 2, 1794; died in Bridgewater, Mass., April 18, 1888. He was graduated at Union College in 1818, took a private course in theology, was ordained a Congregational clergyman, and settled over the church at East Randolph, Mass., Dec. 29, 1819. Subsequently he held pastorates in Framingham, Bridgewater, Falmouth, and South Plymouth, Mass., and elsewhere. For many years he was a zealous friend and colaborer of Wendell Phillips and William Lloyd Garrison in the abolition movement, and was so outspoken in his

denunciation of slavery that he not only incurred the animosity of many people who otherwise admired him, but was subjected to insult and personal violence. His extreme language nearly cost him the fellowship of his Church twice. He was also an equally aggressive prohibitionist.

Brightly, Frederick Charles, author, born in Bungay, Suffolk County, England, Aug. 20, 1812; died in Germantown, Pa., Jan. 24, 1888. He passed his youth in the marine service of the East India Company, came to the United States in 1831, and was admitted to the bar in 1838. He practiced in Germantown and Philadelphia about fifteen years, and then applied himself exclusively to legal writing. He accumulated the most complete and valuable collection of works relating to the laws of Pennsylvania extant. His first work was a treatise on "Costs" (1852), which was followed by a treatise on "Equity," "Digest of United States Statutes," "Digest of New York Reports," "Federal Digest," "Digest of Pennsylvania Reports," "Digest of Forty Volumes of United States Reports," "Reports" (select cases), "On Bankruptcy," "On Nisi Prius Reports," "Election Cases," and editions of Binn's "Justice," Perdeu's "Digest of Pennsylvania Statutes," and Troubat and Halley's "Practice."

Brown, John Henry Hobart, clergyman, born in New York city, Dec. 1, 1831; died in Fond du Lac, Wis., May 2, 1888. He was graduated at the General Theological Seminary, New York, in 1854, was ordained deacon in the Protestant Episcopal Church, and priest on Dec. 1, 1855. He became assistant minister in Grace Church, Brooklyn, in 1854; and while there organized the Church of the Good Angels (now Emmanuel), of which he was appointed rector in 1855. In 1856 he became rector of the Church of the Evangelists (Old St. George's Chapel, in Beckman Street), New York, and he was actively engaged in the large missionary work of that parish several years. In 1863 he was chosen rector of St. John's Church at Cohoes, N. Y., in 1868 secretary to the Diocesan Convention of Albany, and in 1870 archdeacon of the Albany Convocation. While stationed at Cohoes he rendered efficient service in promoting the missionary work of the northern part of the diocese of New York, and in organizing the diocese of Albany. He was consecrated first Bishop of Fond du Lac on Dec. 15, 1875. Racine College gave him the degree of S. T. D. in 1874.

Bruce, Benjamin Franklin, born in Lenox, Madison County, N. Y., in 1811; died there, Dec. 20, 1888. He was a farmer, and an influential member of the Whig party. He was a member of the State Constitutional Convention in 1846; was brigade-major and inspector of the Thirty-fifth Brigade of New York State militia under Gov. Marcy, and Inspector-General under Govs. Hunt, Clark, and King; was appointed Canal Commissioner to succeed William H. Barnes in January, 1861, and elected to the office for a full term in November, 1863; was elected a member of the Assembly in 1867, and served as chairman of the Committee on Federal Relations. Through his efforts while Inspector-General New York city secured possession of the old Arsenal Building and ten acres of ground, all of which are now within Central Park.

Buddington, Sidney Oxias, explorer, born in Groton, Conn., Sept. 16, 1823; died there, June 13, 1888. He became a fisherman at an early age, and in his sixteenth year went into the whaling business and followed it with success till June, 1871. His skill as a navigator and his familiarity with the extreme northern waters led to his selection as sailing and ice master of the polar expedition fitted out for Capt. Charles F. Hall. The instructions provided that in the event of Capt. Hall's death or disability, Capt. Buddington should continue as the sailing and ice master, and control the movements of the vessel, with Dr. Emil Bessels (see page 623 of this volume) as chief of the scientific department. Also, that in the emergency of their non-agreement as to the course to be pursued, Capt. Buddington should assume sole charge and return with the expedition to the United States.

The disasters that overtook the "Polaris" expedition, the death of Capt. Hall, the crushing of the vessel in the ice, and the dispersion of the crew, have been described already. The emergencies for which Secretary Robeson made provision occurred, and Capt. Buddington succeeded to the sole command. Capt. Buddington and Mate Tyson reached home in 1872, and delivered all the books and papers belonging to Capt. Hall to the naval authorities. After the official investigation, Capt. Buddington returned to his home in Groton, and spent the remainder of his life there. Among several natives he brought to the United States at various times, was the late Eskimo Joe, who was pilot on the "Polaris" and "Era," and accompanied the Greely expedition.

Bulkley, John Williams, educator, born in Fairfield, Conn., Nov. 3, 1802; died in Brooklyn, N. Y., June 19, 1888. He became a teacher in his native place, removed to Troy, N. Y., in 1832, and taught there till 1851, when he settled in Brooklyn, and was appointed principal of public school No. 19, in the Williamsburgh district. On the consolidation of Williamsburgh with Brooklyn in 1855, he was appointed Assistant Superintendent of Public Schools, and held the office till 1885. He was the first President of the New York State Teachers' Association, and a founder of the National Teachers' Association.

Bullard, Asa, clergyman, born in Northbridge, Mass., March 26, 1804; died in Cambridge, Mass., April 5, 1888. He was graduated at Amherst in 1828, and, after studying at the Andover Theological School, was ordained a Congregational clergyman at Portland, Me., in 1832. During 1831-'34 he was agent of the Maine Sunday-School Union, and in the latter year became Secretary of the Massachusetts Sunday-School Society, which was subsequently reorganized as the Congregational Publishing Society. He was editor of the "Congregational Visitor" three years; of the "Sunday - School Visitor" ten years; and of the "Wellspring" thirty-one years, and edited and published many books that have been familiar to Sunday-school children.

Bureau, Achille, foundryman, born in Lille, France, Dec. 3, 1835; died in Philadelphia, Pa., Feb. 2, 1888. He served an apprenticeship and worked several years in his uncle's foundry in Brussels, came to the United States previous to the civil war, was a private in the Eighteenth Pennsylvania Volunteers during the greater part of the war, established a foundry in Philadelphia in 1878, and was the first to engage in the casting of large statuary in bronze in the United States. Among his best-known castings are the statue of Gen. Thomas, in Washington, and Gen. Reynolds, in Philadelphia, the Indian group in Chicago, and the Shakespeare, in Central Park, New York.

Campbell, Bartley, dramatist, born in Allegheny City, Pa., Aug. 12, 1843; died in Middletown, N. Y., July 30, 1888. While following journalism in Pittsburg, he attained repute as a Democratic political speaker. In 1868 he established the "Evening Mail" in Pittsburg, in 1869 the "Southern Magazine" in New Orleans, in 1870 was elected official reporter of the Louisiana House of Representatives, and in 1871, on the suspension of his magazine, he returned to Pittsburg, and was appointed editor-in-chief of "The Paper." While so employed he wrote his first play, for J. Newton Gotthold, entitled "Through Fire," which was received with favor and had a run of four weeks. Under this encouragement he began writing plays regularly, producing about one every two years. He considered "Clio" his best composition, but "The Galley Slave" was the most successful financially. In 1885 he leased the Fourteenth Street Theatre, New York, and produced his "Paquita." Early in 1886 he developed signs of insanity, and on September 28 he was pronounced insane by a sheriff's jury and removed to Bloomingdale Asylum, whence, November 30, he was taken to the State Homœopathic Insane Asylum at Middletown, N. Y. His plays include "Peril," "Fate," "Risks," "The Virginian,"

"On the Rhine," "Heroine in Rags," "How Women Love," "The Vigilantes," "Fairfax, or Life in the Sunny South," "My Partner," "Matrimony," "My Geraldine," and "Siberia."

Campbell, Jacob Miller, legislator, born in Allegheny Township, Somerset County, Pa., Nov. 20, 1821; died in Johnstown, Pa., Sept. 27, 1888. He learned the printer's trade, was employed on a Mississippi river steamboat 1841-'47, and in gold-mining in California in 1850, removed to Johnstown in 1853, assisted in building the Cambria iron-works, and remained in the employ of that company till the outbreak of the civil war. In April, 1861, he became first lieutenant in the Third Pennsylvania Volunteers, and at the close of that year recruited the Fifty-fourth Regiment of three years' men, and was elected its colonel. He served meritoriously through the war, being promoted brigadier-general by brevet, June 5, 1864. In 1865 he was elected Surveyor-General of Pennsylvania (the office now known as Secretary of Internal Affairs) for three years; and at the expiration of the first term was re-elected. He was elected a member of Congress as a Republican from the Seventeenth Congressional District in 1876, 1880, and 1882, and served on the Committees on Manufactures and on the Alcoholic-Liquor Traffic. He was a delegate to the first National Republican Convention in 1856, was chairman of the Republican State Convention in 1887, and a trustee of the Pennsylvania State College many years.

Carll, David, ship-builder, born in New York city in 1826; died near Crescent City, Fla., Dec. 27, 1888. He learned the ship-building trade when a boy, and followed it all his life. In 1861 he removed from New York city to Long Island and established a ship-yard of his own on City Island. In 1870 he bought the old United States line-of-battle ship "North Carolina" at public auction, and from her timbers built the schooner yacht "Resolute" for A. S. Hatch, the yacht "Atalanta" for William Astor, and the bridge from City Island to Pelham. Subsequently he rebuilt the famous racing schooner "Sappho" and the "Magic," and built the "Ambassadress," "Nervana," "Vega," "Vesta," "Phœbe," and "Lurline," beside many smaller vessels. Some years before his death he bought a large estate, including many acres in orange-groves, in Florida.

Carney, Thomas, merchant, born in Delaware County, Ohio, Aug. 10, 1824; died in Leavenworth, Kan., July 28, 1888. He worked several years on a farm, studied in the evenings, and when eighteen years old attended a school in Berkshire, Ohio, six months. Soon afterward he went to Columbus and worked in a dry-goods store, then removed to Cincinnati, where he was employed by a firm that admitted him to partnership after six years, and in 1858 settled in Leavenworth. In 1861 he was elected to the Legislature, in 1862 became the second Governor of the State, and in 1864 United States Senator. Owing to a doubt as to the legality of the time of the election, he declined the seat in the Senate, and was chosen Mayor of Leavenworth. He rendered the national cause effective service during his gubernatorial term.

Cass, George W., engineer, born in Muskingum County, Ohio, in 1810; died in New York city, March 21, 1888. He was a nephew of Gen. Lewis Cass, was graduated at the United States Military Academy with special honor as a mathematician in 1832, and was assigned to the Corps of Military Engineers. After serving four years on topographical and engineering duty on the Northwestern frontier, he resigned from the army, and was shortly afterward appointed one of the engineers in charge of the construction of the Great National Road through Maryland, Pennsylvania, and Virginia. He held this office till the completion of the road, and during his service constructed over Dunlap's creek, a tributary of Monongahela river, the first cast-iron bridge ever built in the United States. On the organization of a company for improving the navigation of the Monongahela, he became first its engineer and afterward one of its managers, and completed the work in 1844. He then organized the first steamboat-line on that river, and the first transportation-line across the mountains; consolidated all the Adams Express lines between Boston, Richmond, and St. Louis, and was elected president of the consolidated company in 1850; was elected President of the Ohio and Pennsylvania Railroad Company in 1856, and of the organizations that consolidated under the name of the Pittsburg, Fort Wayne, and Chicago Railway Company in 1857, holding the latter office twenty-six years; and was President of the Northern Pacific Railroad Company from 1872 till 1877.

Cathcart, Charles W., farmer, born in the Island of Madeira, in 1809; died in Michigan City, Ind., Aug. 22, 1888. He followed the sea for several years, studied mechanics, settled in La Porte, Ind., in 1831, became a Government land-surveyor, and engaged in farming. After serving two terms in the State Legislature, he was elected a member of Congress in 1844 and 1846, and in 1849 was appointed United States Senator. He retained the office till 1853, and then resumed farming.

Cheever, Byron William, scientist, born in Ellisburg, Jefferson County, N. Y., Sept. 17, 1841; died in Ann Arbor, Mich., March 6, 1888. He was graduated at the University of Michigan with the degree of A. B. in 1863, and with that of M. D. in 1867. During the interval of his courses in arts and medicine, he applied himself to chemical work, partly in Philadelphia and partly in the West Indies. After receiving his medical diploma, he was engaged as an analytical and consulting chemist in Philadelphia two years, and was then employed in professional work in the Rocky mountain mining-region till 1872. He then returned to Ann Arbor, somewhat broken in health. Fearing the effects of further work in a chemical laboratory, he studied law, but still applied the greater part of his time to chemical work till 1878, when he became instructor in quantitative analysis in the chemical laboratory of the University of Michigan. In 1881 his duties were enlarged, and he was appointed to the chair of Metallurgy.

Chouteau, Berenice, pioneer, born in Kaskaskia, Ill., in 1801; died in Kansas city, Mo., Nov. 20, 1888. She was a daughter of Col. Peter Menard, first Territorial Governor of Illinois, received a good education, and when eighteen years old married Francis F. Chouteau, whose family were noted French fur-traders, and founded and managed for many years the American Fur Company. She made her wedding-journey on a flat-boat up the Missouri river to Black Snake Hills, afterward the site of the city of St. Joseph, and after living there two years accompanied her husband to the present Kansas City, where he established the first trading-post in that section and built a log-house in the woods where the Union Railroad station now stands. In 1826, and again in 1844, her husband lost nearly all his land and property, but, acquiring most of the valuable farming-land in the vicinity of the mouth of the Kansas river, he subsequently became wealthy. She was very liberal with the large fortune given her by her husband, was a devout Roman Catholic, and built the first church in Kansas City. The city is built upon a portion of her property, and other large tracts are occupied by people who derive their title from squatter settlers. A few years ago she brought suits of dispossession, involving more than $5,000,000, and two weeks before her death the courts decided that she had lost all claim to the property, through the statute of limitation.

Christman, Joseph Alonzo, lawyer, born in Evansburg, Montgomery County, Pa., Sept. 1, 1838; died in Paris, France, April 5, 1888. He was graduated at Yale in 1857, and afterward taught in the South till the beginning of the civil war. He served during the war on the staff of Gen. Samuel R. Curtis, and at the battle of Pea Ridge, Ark., was severely wounded. At the close of the war he removed to Louisville, Ky., was admitted to the bar, and began practice in St. Louis.

In 1867 he was appointed United States District-Attorney for California. He resumed practice in St. Louis at the expiration of his term, and remained there till 1876, when his health gave way. He then went to Paris, and with several acquaintances established a banking-house, with which he was connected till death. He left a valuable estate, out of which he bequeathed $60,000 to Yale University, and $10,000 to St. James's Church at Evansburg.

Clarke, James Freeman, an American clergyman, born in Hanover, N. H., April 4, 1810; died in Jamaica Plain, Mass., June 8, 1888. He was a grandson of the Rev. James Freeman, the first clergyman in the United States that preached Unitarian doctrines, with whom he spent the first ten years of his life. He was graduated at Harvard in 1829, at the Cambridge Divinity School, in 1833, and accepted a call from the Unitarian Church in Louisville, Ky., where he preached till 1840, and edited the "Western Messenger." He returned to Boston in 1841, and became a founder and the pastor of the Church of the Disciples in April of that year, and (excepting an interval, 1850-'53) held that office continuously till his death. The pastor and his congregation made the church absolutely free to all, and combined in their service the forms of worship in the Protestant Episcopal and Congregational Churches with those of the Friends. Mr. Clarke was an intimate friend of Margaret Fuller, Ralph Waldo Emerson, and William Ellery Channing, an overseer of Harvard University for many years, and one of the first advocates of the movement for the admission of women to the full privileges of study there; an early promoter of the anti-slavery cause; a friend of every practical scheme to advance the moral and material welfare of humanity; a voluminous writer, apart from his sermons; and an eloquent pulpit and platform orator. During his long pastorate he also held the offices of Secretary of the American Unitarian Association, 1859-'62; Professor of Natural Theology and Christian Doctrine in Harvard, 1867-'71; lecturer on ethnic religion in Cambridge Divinity School, 1876-'77; and State Commissioner of Education, 1863-'70. His published works embrace a translation of De Wette's "Theodore" (Louisville, 1840); "Service and Hymn Book for the Church of the Disciples" (Boston, 1844); "History of the Campaign of 1812, and Defense of Gen. William Hull for the Surrender of Detroit" (New York, 1848); "Christian Doctrine of Forgiveness of Sin" (1852); "Christian Doctrine of Prayer" (1854); "Orthodoxy: its Truths and Errors" (1866); "Steps of Belief, or Rational Christianity maintained against Atheism, Free Religion, and Romanism" (1870); "Ten Great Religions" (1871-'83); "Exotics: Attempts to domesticate them" (1876); "Essentials and Non-Essentials in Religion" (1878); "Memorial and Biographical Sketches" (1878); "Common Sense in Religion" (1879); "Events and Epochs in Religious History" (1881); "Anti-Slavery Days in New York" (1884); "Manual of Unitarian Belief" (1884); "Every-day Religion" (1886); and "Vexed Questions" (1886). He received the degree D. D. from Harvard in 1863.

Coffin, Roland Folger, journalist, born in Brooklyn, N. Y., March 8, 1826; died at Prospect, Shelter Island Heights, July 16, 1888. He came of old English, sea-faring stock, and for more than two centuries his family had lived on Nantucket Island. At the time of his birth his father was captain of a large merchantman plying between Liverpool and New York. He became a clerk in New York; in 1846 he shipped before the mast, and after making several voyages was taken by his father aboard his own vessel, on which he became first mate. When the elder Coffin retired, the son took command of a merchantman and handled it so skillfully that he found steady employment afterward and succeeded his father as captain. At the outbreak of the civil war he enlisted in the United States Navy, served on the "Monitor" in her famous fight with the Merrimac, and was subsequently master of the "Ericsson." He returned to the mercantile navy at the close of the war, and in 1869 retired to become a short hand reporter and engage in journalism. In the following year he was appointed nautical editor of the New York "World," and held that place till death. Besides special reports on yachting events, he published "The Queen's Cup," "Old Sailors' Yarns," and "Archibald the Cat."

Collins, Richard Henry, historian, born in Maysville, Ky., in 1824; died in Louisville, Ky., Jan. 1, 1888. He was son of Judge Lewis Collins, the first historian of Kentucky, and was editor and publisher of the Maysville "Eagle" for many years. He revised and greatly enlarged his father's history of Kentucky. He led a very secluded life, if not one of actual want. He was an accomplished writer, excessively modest, and had received the degree of LL. D.

Colyer, Vincent, artist, born in Bloomingdale, N. Y., in 1825; died on Contentment Island, Conn., July 12, 1888. He studied painting with J. R. Smith, and in the school of the National Academy of Design, and began exhibiting at the Academy in 1848. His early work was on portraits and ideal heads in crayon, but these were soon superseded by portraits in oil. He remained in New York city till the outbreak of the civil war, then removed to Rowayton, Conn., originated the Christian Commission, and rendered valuable services to the soldiers at home, in hospitals, and on the field, till the close of the war. He was afterward appointed a member of the Board of Indian Commissioners, and elected a member of the Connecticut Legislature. He was elected an associate of the National Academy of Design in 1849, and was a founder of the Artists' Fund Society, and its first secretary. His paintings include "A Loyal Refugee" (1863); "A Soldier's Widow," "Darienshire, Conn.," "A Rainy Day on the Connecticut Shore," and "Winter on the Connecticut Shore" (1867); "Johnson Straits, British Columbia"; "Home of the Yalhamas, Oregon"; "Spring Flowers" (1885); "Moonlight on the Grand Canal, Venice," and "Valley of the Lauterbrunnen, Bridal Veil Fall, Switzerland" (1886); and "Lake Maggiore, Italy" (1888).

Corcoran, William Wilson, philanthropist, born in Georgetown, D. C., Dec. 27, 1798; died in Washington, D. C., Feb. 24, 1888. He received a collegiate education in his native place, and carried on a combined dry-goods, auction, and commission business, with two brothers from 1815 till 1823, when the stringency of the financial market led to their suspension. He then became a clerk first in a local bank of which Gen. John Mason was president, and in the Washington branch of the United States Bank, where he was placed in charge of its real estate. He began the banking business for himself in 1837, and formed a partnership with George W. Riggs, whose father, Elisha Riggs, had greatly aided both Mr. Corcoran and George Peabody in their first business efforts in 1837. In the following year he was appointed financial agent of the State Department, and laid the foundation of his great wealth by taking $5,000,000 of Government bonds at 101 and floating them after other agents had failed to secure the money the Government then greatly needed. His success in this operation induced the Government to offer him the first opportunity to negotiate the bonds issued at the beginning of the Mexican War, and he quickly disposed of from $45,000,000 to $50,000,000 of them, in London. In 1848 he again went to London, and placed a large block of a further loan, and on his return was given a great reception by the bankers and capitalists of New York. In 1854 he retired from the banking business, with a large fortune, which was subsequently augmented by investments in real estate. In 1857 he conceived the idea of his first great and enduring public benefaction. He had presented to his native city a plot of ten acres on the Heights for the now beautiful Oak Hill Cemetery, together with a liberal endowment; had sent $5,000 to Ireland to relieve sufferers by famine; and had furnished the means of transporting a large body of Hungarians from New York to homes in the West. He

now began erecting the grand art gallery bearing his name, and had scarcely finished the exterior when the civil war broke out, and the Government took the elegant building for military purposes, and converted his suburban residence into a hospital. After the war he resumed work on the art gallery, and it was opened to the public in 1874. The building cost him $200,000; be endowed it with $900,000, and began its priceless collections with statuary and paintings from his Washington mansion, worth $100,000. His next work was the erection of a memorial to his dead wife and daughter, which took the form of the Louise Home for Indigent Gentlewomen, and cost him $200,000 for the building and $250,000 for an endowment, besides the ground. He gave $250,000 to Columbian University, of Washington, richly endowed several chairs in the University of Virginia, and put William and Mary College on a solid financial basis; and had the remains of John Howard Payne, author of "Home, Sweet Home," transferred from Tunis to Oak Hill Cemetery, and erected a suitable monument over them. The value of his public, educational, and charitable benefactions was estimated at from $3,000,000 to $5,000,000; and he bequeathed $100,000 to the art gallery, to which he had already given $1,500,000; $50,000 to the Louise Home, which had had $500,000; $5,000 each to three orphan asylums in the District of Columbia; and $3,000 to the Little Sisters of the Poor.

Corliss, George Henry, inventor, born in Easton, N. Y., July 2, 1817; died in Providence, R. I., Feb. 21, 1888. He was the son of Dr. Hiram Corliss, and in 1825 removed to Greenwich, N. Y., where he attended school. After serving for several years as clerk in a cotton-factory he spent three years in the academy at Castleton, Vt., and in 1838 he opened a store in Greenwich. His mechanical skill was first shown in temporarily rebuilding a bridge that had been washed away by a freshet, after it had been decided that such a structure was impracticable; and soon afterward he devised a machine for stitching leather, before the invention of the original Howe sewing-machine. In 1844 he removed to Providence, R. I., where he organized the firm of Corliss, Nightingale & Co., and in 1846 began his improvements in steam-engines which he patented in 1849. In these inventions, uniformity of motion was secured by connecting the governor with the cut-off. The governor had previously been made to do the work of moving the throttle-valve, the result being an imperfect response and a great loss of power. By his improvement, the governor did no work, but simply indicated to the valves the work to be done. This arrangement also prevented waste of steam, and rendered the working of the engine so uniform that if all but one of a hundred looms in a factory were suddenly stopped, that one would continue working at the same rate. It is said that his improvements revolutionized the construction of the steam-engine. In introducing the new engines, the inventor and manufacturers adopted the plan of offering to take as their pay the saving of fuel for a given time. In one case, the saving in a year is said to have been $4,000. It required a legal contest extending over fifteen years, and an expense of over $100,000, to obtain a declaration that this invention was new and patentable. In 1856 the Corliss Steam-Engine Company was incorporated, and he became its president. The works erected during 1848–'50 occupy nine acres, and are the most extensive of the kind in the world. An order for an engine of 350 horse-power, including boilers and all the appurtenances, has been executed in sixty days. During the past twenty years Mr. Corliss patented many other important inventions connected with the steam-engine, including an improved boiler with an apparatus for condensing and using over again the waste steam, thus obviating the necessity of employing salt-water in marine engines. His greatest achievement was the mammoth steam-engine used in Machinery Hall at the World's Fair held in Philadelphia in 1876, of which he was the designer and builder. It was of 1,400 horse-power, and, although used with entire success as the single propelling power of all the machinery of the exhibition, was furnished as a voluntary contribution by Mr. Corliss and as an exhibit from Rhode Island. The cylinders were forty-four inches in diameter, with a ten-foot stroke ; the gear-wheel was thirty feet in diameter ; and the whole engine weighed 700 tons. It was removed to the town of Pullman, near Chicago, and now drives the machinery in the Pullman Car-Works. Bartholdi, in his report to the French Government, said that "it belonged to the category of works of art, by the general beauty of its effect, and its perfect balance to the eye." Mr. Corliss was a member of the State Legislature in 1868–'70, and was a Republican presidential elector in 1876. He was appointed Centennial Commissioner from Rhode Island in 1872, and was one of the executive committee of seven to whom the responsibility of the preliminary work was intrusted. At the World's Fair held in Paris in 1867 he received a medal, and at the one held in Vienna in 1873 he received a grand diploma of honor. The Rumford medal of the American Academy of Arts and Sciences was given him in 1870 ; the Institute of France gave him the Montyon prize in 1878, its highest honor for mechanical achievement, and in 1886 the King of the Belgians made him an officer of the Order of Leopold.

Craig, James, lawyer, born in Pennsylvania, May 7, 1820 ; died in St. Joseph, Mo., Oct. 21, 1888. After his admission to the bar he removed to St. Joseph to practice. He was a member of the Missouri Legislature in 1846–'47, was captain of a volunteer company in the Mexican War, was Attorney for the Twelfth Judicial District of Missouri from 1852 till 1856, was a member of Congress from Dec. 7, 1857, till March 3, 1861, and served on the Committee on Post-Offices and Post-Roads. On March 21, 1862, he was commissioned brigadier-general of volunteers, and he had command of the Union forces at St. Joseph during the war. He was a friend and admirer of President Lincoln, though opposed to him politically. He negotiated the Platt purchase, which comprised all of northwest Missouri, and was the first President of the Hannibal and St. Joseph Railroad, the first line built across the State, and the first Comptroller of the city of St. Joseph.

Crane, Benjamin Franklin, civil engineer, born in Saratoga, N. Y., in 1817 ; died in New York city, Jan. 16, 1888. He removed to New York city in early life, studied civil engineering, and was subsequently connected with several noted public works, including the construction of the Croton Aqueduct, the Erie Canal, and the New York Central Railroad. The work of which he was always the most proud, however, was his large share in laying out Central Park, according to the plans of Frederick Law Olmsted and Calvert Vaux. He was admirably suited for this service. When the work was sufficiently advanced to permit its dedication to public use, he was appointed its first superintendent, and held the office many years. He retired from the public service in 1877.

Crocker, Charles, financier, born in Troy, N. Y., Sept. 16. 1822 ; died in Monterey, Cal., Aug. 14, 1888. He began selling newspapers for a living when twelve years old, removed with the family to northern Indiana in 1836, was turned out-of-doors by his father in 1839, became an apprentice in a forge in 1840, discovered a bed of iron-ore in Marshall County, Ind., 1845, and with the aid of his employer established a forge there soon afterward. In 1850 he crossed the Plains with two brothers ; but, not meeting with the success he had anticipated in placer-mining, he abandoned it and opened a store for the sale of mining-supplies. In 1852 he established a similar store in Sacramento, and in two years was considered rich. He was elected a member of the Common Council in 1855, and of the Legislature in 1860, as a Republican. Associated with Leland Stanford, Mark Hopkins, and Collis P. Huntington, he furnished the means for a survey by Theodore D. Judah of a railway route across the Sierra Nevada Mountains, at a time when no bank or capitalist would risk a dollar on such an apparently chi-

merical scheme. On the passage of the Union Pacific Railroad bill by Congress, these four men constructed the Central Pacific Division, and he personally the most difficult section. He became General Superintendent of the Central Pacific Railroad in 1862, President of the Southern Pacific Railroad and second Vice-President of the Central Pacific Company in 1871, and superintended the construction of the Arizona, New Mexico, and Texas Divisions. In 1884 the two railroads, several laterals, and some coastwise and ocean steamship lines were consolidated under the management of a single company—the Southern Pacific—and of this he was elected second vice-president. He also acquired large banking and industrial interests. In 1885 he removed to New York city, and in 1886 met with an accident that indirectly caused his death.

Crosby, George Avery, physician, born in Lowell, Mass., Dec. 27, 1831 ; died in Manchester, N. H., Jan. 30, 1888. He came from a family of eminent physicians, and was gradusted at Dartmouth in 1852, and in the Medical Department in 1855. In 1857 he went to Peru and practiced there till 1864, when he returned to the United States and settled in Manchester. He married a daughter of Hon. A. J. Bryant, of San Francisco, in 1877, was President of the New Hampshire Medical Society in 1886, spent 1886–'87 in hospitals on Deer Island and in New York city, and at the time of his death was a member of the Manchester Board of Health.

Curtis, Samuel Johnson, philanthropist, born in Meriden, Conn., Jan. 15, 1814 ; died there, Jan. 10, 1888. He was a director and stockholder in nearly every manufacturing company in Meriden, and was also interested to a large extent in the local fire-insurance, street-railroad, and other companies. He accumulated a large fortune, and gave liberally to charitable objects. A few years before his death he founded the Curtis Home for Aged and Indigent Women and Destitute Children, erected a building at an expense of $40,000, and supported it until his death. He made this home the residuary legatee of all his property, which, it is believed, will amount to $500,000.

Dahlgren, Charles G., lawyer, born in Philadelphia, Pa., in 1809 ; died in Brooklyn, N. Y., Dec. 18, 1888. He was a brother of the late Admiral John A. Dahlgren, United States Navy, removed to Natchez, Miss., to become cashier of a branch of the Bank of the United States in 1830, held the office till the liquidation of the bank in 1848, and then engaged in cotton-planting and acquired a large fortune. At the outbreak of the civil war he raised and equipped the Third Mississippi Regiment for the Confederate service, and received a brigadier-general's commission. During the first two days of the defense of Vicksburg he was virtually in command, and on the third day was incapacitated for service by a bullet-wound. Subsequently he took part in the battles of Iuka, Corinth, Chickamauga, Atlanta, and the operations of Gen. Hood's army against Gen. Sherman, and was promoted major-general. After the war he lived in New Orleans till 1870, when he removed to Brooklyn.

Darley, Felix Octavius Carr, artist, born in Philadelphia, Pa., June 23, 1822 ; died near Claymount, Del., March 27, 1888. He received a public-school education, and in 1836 was placed in a counting-house, but his taste for art led him to apply all his leisure to drawing. When eighteen years old he offered a collection of original sketches of city life and scenes to the "Saturday Museum," of Philadelphia, and when they were published and paid for he determined to become an artist. His first collection of sketches attracted the attention of New York and Philadelphia publishers. In 1848 he was engaged by the American Art Union to design a series of illustrations for Washington Irving's works, and, removing to New York city, he produced the familiar designs in the "Sketch-Book," "Rip Van Winkle," the "Knickerbocker History of New York," the "Life of Washington," and others. He also illustrated several of William Gilmore Simms's novels, and about this time completed the outline drawings to Judd's "Margaret," which was published in 1856. On the completion of the Irving series of illustrations, he received flattering offers from publishers to go to London, but declined on account of his many home engagements. His next great work was the series of five hundred sketches drawn to illustrate James Fenimore Cooper's novels, a series noted for originality, power of expression, and quaint humor. During the civil war he designed historical sketches in water-color, which were reproduced by the Government on the greenback bills, and at the close of the war went to Europe. On his return in 1868 he published "Sketches Abroad with Pen and Pencil." For several years thereafter he executed orders for book illustrations, but gave the

larger part of his time to work in water-color, and in 1879 produced what his admirers claim to be the crowning achievement of his career—a series of twelve "Compositions in Outline from Hawthorne's 'Scarlet Letter.'" These were followed by similar series illustrating Longfellow's "Evangeline" (1883), and Shakespeare's plays (1886). He was a member of the National Academy of Design, the American Water-Color Society, and the Artists' Fund Society.

Davidge, William Pleater, actor, born in London, England, April 17, 1814; died in Cheyenne, Wyoming Territory, Aug. 7, 1888. He appeared on the stage, when sixteen years old, at Drury-Lane Theatre, London, as James in "The Miller's Maid," and his first professional appearance was at Nottingham, on June 20, 1836, as Adam Winterton in "The Iron Chest." In September following he achieved success at the Queen's Theatre, London, as Baron Oakland in "The Haunted Tower," and afterward played in the chief theatres in London and in the provinces. In 1850 he made his first American appearance at the old Broadway Theatre, New York, on August 19, as Sir Peter Teazle. He followed that with the performance of Caliban in "The Tempest," and then for five years supported Edwin Forrest, Gustavus V. Brooke, Julia Dean, Mme. Celeste, Lola Montez, and other star actors. In 1855 he was attached to the Cleveland Athenæum, and at the close of his engagement made a professional tour of the country. His next engagement was with the Wallack company in 1861. From that he went to Mrs. John Wood's company, and played at the Olympic Theatre in 1863–'64, and in 1869 he began an engagement with Augustin Daly at the Fifth Avenue Theatre, which continued eight years. He traveled with Fanny Davenport and Margaret Mather; in 1879 became the American originator of the part of Dick Dead-Eye in "Pinafore"; and in 1885 began an engagement with the Madison Square company, which lasted till his death. He had played more than one thousand parts, and was a founder of the American Dramatic fund.

Davis, Edwin Hamilton, archæologist, born in Ross County, Ohio, Jan. 22, 1811; died in New York city, May 15, 1888. He was educated at Kenyon College, and was graduated at Cincinnati Medical College in 1838. While at Kenyon, he conducted a series of explorations among the mounds of the Scioto valley, and his work coming to the notice of Daniel Webster —then traveling through the West—he was urged to continue his researches. Mr. Webster, who regretted

the rapid disappearance of these antiquities, suggested the formation of a society to purchase and preserve some of the most remarkable works of the mound-builders. In 1836 he aided Charles Whittlesey in his explorations, and from 1845 till 1847, assisted by Ephraim G. Squier, he surveyed nearly one hundred groups of works, and opened two hundred mounds at his own expense. He gathered the largest collection of mound-relics ever made in this country, which, failing an American purchaser, was taken to England, where it now forms part of Blackmore's Museum in Saulsbury. A second collection, consisting of duplicates and the results of subsequent collections, is at the American Museum of Natural History, New York city. The fruits of his extensive explorations are embodied in "Ancient Monuments of the Mississippi Valley" (Washington, 1848), which formed the first volume of the "Smithsonian Contributions to Knowledge." This work was characterized by A. Morlot, the distinguished Swiss archæologist, in a paper before the American Philosophical Society, in 1862, as being as "glorious a monument to American science as Bunker Hill is of American bravery." Dr. Davis followed the practice of medicine in Chillicothe, Ohio, until 1850, when he was called to the chair of Materia Medica and Therapeutics in the New York Medical College, and continued there for ten years. During the spring of 1854 he delivered a course of lectures on archæology before the Lowell Institute, Boston, and subsequently repeated them in Brooklyn and New York. He was for a time one of the conductors of the "American Medical Monthly."

Davis, George Turnbull Moore, lawyer, born in the island of Malta, May 24, 1810; died in New York city, Dec. 20, 1888. He was a son of George Davis, a surgeon and naval officer, who was United States Consul-General to the Barbary States, at the time of his son's birth; came to the United States when a boy; was admitted to the bar in Syracuse, N. Y., in 1831; and settled in Alton, Ill., where he practiced until the opening of the Mexican War. He became intimate with Lincoln, Douglas, Trumbull, Baker, Singleton, and other well-known men of the State, and gained a wide reputation by his spirited prosecution of the murderers of Lovejoy, the abolitionist, in 1837. At the beginning of the Mexican War he entered the army as a private, rose to the rank of colonel, served on the staffs of Generals Shields and Quitman, and while Gen. Scott remained in command of the city of Mexico he was his secretary. At the close of the war he was appointed chief clerk in the War Department at Washington, and introduced woman clerks into the department. On resigning the office he removed to New York city, became an iron merchant, engaged in importing iron and building locomotives, and was elected to the directory of several railroads. He completed an autobiography a few months before his death for posthumous publication.

Dawson, Benjamin Frederick, physician, born in New York city, June 28, 1847; died there, April 3, 1888. He began studying medicine in the early part of the civil war, served as acting assistant surgeon in the national army during 1865, and was g a a c at the New York College of Physicians and Surgeons in 1866. He settled in New York, and made a specialty of surgery, gynæcology and the diseases of children; established the "American Journal of Obstetrics," in 1868, and edited it till 1874; invented a galvanic battery for galvano-caustic surgery; held the offices of assistant surgeon of the Woman's Hospital, attending physician of the New York Foundling Asylum, and Professor of Gynæcology in the New York Post-Graduate Medical School; and was a member of the New York Obstetric Society.

Ditson, Oliver, publisher, born in Boston, Mass., Oct. 20, 1811; died there, Dec. 21, 1888. He received a grammar-school education, served an apprenticeship at the printer's trade, entered the employ of Col. Samuel Parker, the music publisher, and on attaining his majority formed a partnership first with Mr. Morrisey and afterward with Mr. Parker, under the firm name of Parker & Ditson. In 1840 Mr. Parker retired, and Mr. Ditson carried on the business alone till 1857, when he took Joseph C. Haynes, a clerk, as a partner, forming the firm of Oliver Ditson & Co. Branch houses were established by Mr. Ditson's sons in New York city (C. H. Ditson & Co.), 1867, and Philadelphia (J. E. Ditson & Co.), 1876, the father remaining in Boston. His was by far the largest music-publishing business that ever existed in the United States. Mr. Ditson was for twenty-two years president of the Continental Bank of Boston, and was also a director of the Boston Safe-Deposit Company, the Franklin Savings-Bank, and the Old Men's Home. He bequeathed $25,000 to be expended under the direction of trustees for the benefit of poor musicians.

Dorsheimer, William, lawyer and journalist, born in Lyons, N. Y., Feb. 5, 1832; died in Savannah, Ga., March 26, 1888. He was educated at Phillips Academy, Andover, Mass., and spent two years at Harvard. He then settled in Buffalo, N. Y., and was admitted to the bar in 1854. Early in his legal career he attained considerable influence by winning a very complicated case, and became actively interested in politics. His first votes were cast for the Democratic ticket, but in 1856 he affiliated with the Republican party. At the opening of the civil war he offered his services to the Government, was appointed on the staff of Gen. John C. Frémont, with the rank of major, and served through the three months' campaign in Missouri. He then returned to Buffalo, and formed a law partnership with Spencer Clinton. In April, 1867, he was appointed United States District Attorney for the Northern District of New York, and at the expiration of his term, he reunited with the Democratic party, after a brief adhesion to the Liberal Republican party. In 1874 he was elected Lieutenant-Governor of New York on the ticket with Samuel J. Tilden, and in 1876 was re-elected. Between these periods he took an active part in the prosecution of Gov. Tilden's measures against the canal ring. At the expiration of his second term, he removed to New York city, whence he was elected to Congress in 1882, and served as a member of the Judiciary Committee. He supported Grover Cleveland for President in 1884, was appointed United States District Attorney for the Southern District of New York in July, 1885, but resigned in March, 1886, to assume control of the New York "Star," in which relation he continued till death. In 1858 he contributed two papers to the "Atlantic Monthly," a review of Parton's "Life of Aaron Burr" and one on a "Life of Jefferson"; in 1861 published a series of articles in the same magazine on "Frémont's Hundred Days in Missouri"; and in 1884 published a biography of Grover Cleveland. He received the degree of M. A. from Harvard in 1859.

Douai, Carl Daniel Adolf, educator, born in Altenburg, Germany, Feb. 22, 1819; died in Brooklyn., N. Y., Jan. 21, 1888. He studied in the Dresden Gymnasium, and was graduated at the University of Leipsic. Soon afterward he was appointed a lecturer in the University of Jena, and after two years' service there took a professorship in the Russo-German University at Dorpat. At the outbreak of the revolution of 1848, he returned to Germany to take part in it, proclaimed the republic in his native city, and aided in successfully defending the city against the assaults of a full brigade of the army. He was an active member of the diet called to institute a reform government, and was elected a member of the provisional Landtag; but on the suppression of the new government he with others was arrested for high treason, imprisoned till 1852, and then pardoned and released. In that year he settled in San Antonio, Tex., and established the "Zeitung," a social-democratic paper. In May, 1854, he was one of the signers to a call for a convention, which declared that slavery was a political and moral evil, and shortly afterward he was compelled to give up his paper and leave the city. He then taught in Philadelphia and Boston till 1860, when he was a delegate to the National Republican Convention that nominated Abraham Lincoln, and an active speaker in the ensuing canvass. The same year he became editor of the "New Yorker Demokrat," but gave up that office to accept the principalship of the Hoboken, N. J., Academy. In 1866 he established another school of his own in New York city; in 1871 was appointed editor of the "Arbeiter Union," an organ of the German trades-unions in New York city, and espoused the French cause in the Franco-Prussian War; and in 1878 became editor of the "Volks Zeitung." He introduced Froebel's kindergarten system of instruction into the United States, and wrote numerous philosophical articles and treatises from a social-democratic and free-thinker standpoint.

Drew, Thomas, abolitionist, born in Plymouth, Mass., in 1819; died in Dorchester, Mass., Nov. 12, 1888. He entered journalism in Philadelphia, became associated with Elihu Burritt in publishing the "Christian Citizen" in Worcester, and afterward with John Milton Earle, and was editor and proprietor of the Worcester "Spy" for several years preceding the civil war. He had been an active anti-slavery advocate many years, and at the time of the Anthony Burns riot in Boston (1854), went there at the head of a train-load of Worcester friends and made a vain attempt to rescue him. After the inauguration of Gov. Andrew and the opening of the civil war, he was appointed military secretary to the Governor, and besides the duties of this office was frequently sent to the field to look after the sick and wounded soldiers of Massachusetts. For several years he was an editorial writer on the Boston "Herald."

Drexel, Joseph Wilhelm, banker, born in Philadelphia, Pa., Jan. 24, 1833; died in New York city, March 25, 1888. He was one of the three sons of Francis Martin Drexel, a native of the Austrian Tyrol, who established a banking-house in Philadelphia in 1837. Joseph entered his father's-banking house as a clerk, and afterward was admitted to partnership. The firm established branch houses in several large cities, and Joseph became manager of the German branch. During his residence abroad he traveled extensively. In 1861 he returned to the United States and opened a banking-house in Chicago, where he attained such a degree of popularity that the authorities named two of the handsomest boulevards after him and his wife. On the death of his father, in 1863, he returned to Philadelphia. In 1871 he came to New York city, and with J. S. Morgan, of London, and his brother, Anthony Joseph Drexel, established the firm of Drexel, Morgan & Co. He retired from active business in 1876, but retained his interest in the houses of Drexel & Co., of Philadelphia; J. S. Morgan & Co., of London; Drexel, Harjies & Co., of Paris; and Drexel, Morgan & Co., of New York; besides a third interest, with George W. Childs and Anthony J. Drexel, in the Philadelphia "Ledger." He was also a trustee of the Knickerbocker Trust Company and of the American Bank-note Company, and a director in eleven national banks, including the Garfield, of New York city, of which he was a founder. After his retirement from business, he devoted his time and means to the advancement of the various literary, philanthropic, scientific, and musical organizations with which he was connected, and was particularly interested in an original scheme for assisting the worthy and industrious poor. He bought 13,000 acres of choice land in Maryland

and Michigan, divided it into farms of 100 acres, erected comfortable five-room dwellings, and sold them at cost, on twelve years' time, to people whom he thought worthy of such assistance. He offered Gen. Grant the use of his furnished cottage on Mount MacGregor, and after his death therein presented the building and grounds to the Grand Army of the Republic as a memorial of the great soldier. In 1887 he presented a $2,000 oil-painting by Edward Gay to the State of New York, for the adornment of the new Executive mansion at Albany. It is estimated that he spent an average of $50,000 a year in charitable work; and it was not known until his death that he had kept an agent at the city prison (Tombs) for many years to investigate the condition of the families of criminals confined there and relieve deserving ones. Mr. Drexel was a director of the Metropolitan Museum of Art, and gave it some early Italian paintings, a collection of Egyptian casts, and another of coins, the painting "Harpsichord," and a cabinet of ancient musical instruments. He also was president of the New York Philharmonic Society and of the Sanitary League, a director of the Metropolitan Opera House, treasurer of the Cancer Hospital Society, and a member of the Philadelphia Academy of Natural Sciences, the Society for the Improvement of the Condition of the Poor, the American Geographical Society, and the New York and Saratoga Historical Societies.

Drumgoole, John C., clergyman, born in County Longford, Ireland, in 1828; died in New York city, March 28, 1888. He came to the United States with his parents when eight years old, entered St. John's College, Fordham, N. Y., in 1848, and studied there till obliged to leave to help support the family, and then became sexton of St. Mary's Church. While filling this office he made a vow to consecrate himself to the physical and spiritual improvement of the poor. He resumed his studies in St. Francis Xavier College, took the theological course in the Seminary of Our Lady of Angels, Niagara Falls, and was ordained a priest on May 24, 1865. For a time he was curate at his old church, St. Mary's, when he applied to Archbishop McCloskey for permission to establish a mission for the protection of homeless and destitute children. His plans were approved, and he was appointed director of St. Vincent de Paul's Newsboys' Lodging-house, and under his administration the enterprise soon attained prosperity. He took charge in 1871, was obliged to rent the adjoining building in 1872, and after ten years of devoted labor erected a large fire-proof building on the corner of Great Jones Street and Lafayette Place, which occupies four city lots and cost, with the ground, $300,000. In 1883, the accommodations again proving insufficient, he purchased over 500 acres on Prince's Bay, Staten Island, and erected buildings there. The property represents over $700,000, and when each part was opened it was free from debt. Nearly 1,500 children are housed, fed, clothed, and educated in the institution, the name of which was changed to Mission of the Immaculate Virgin for Homeless and Destitute Children.

Duffield, George, hymnologist, born in Carlisle, Pa., Sept. 12, 1818; died in Bloomfield, N. J., July 7, 1888. He was graduated at Yale College in 1837, and after a three years' course in Union Theological Seminary, New York city, was ordained a Presbyterian minister, Dec., 27, 1840. He held pastorates in Brooklyn, 1840; Bloomfield, N. J., 1847; Philadelphia, 1852; Adrian, Mich., 1861; Galesburg, Ill., 1865; Saginaw city, Mich., 1869; and Lansing, Mich., 1877–'80; and resided in Detroit, Mich., without a charge in 1884–'87, when he removed to Bloomfield. He was author of many hymns, of which "Blessed Saviour, thee I love" (1851); and "Stand up, stand up for Jesus" (1858), are the most widely known. The latter has been translated into French, German, and Chinese, and was written as the concluding exhortation of a sermon delivered by him on the death of the Rev. Dudley S. Tyng. He received the degree of D. D., from Knox College, Illinois, in 1872.

Dunkel, Aaron Kline, printer, born in Lancaster, Pa., May 20, 1837; died in Philadelphia, Pa., May 31, 1888. He learned the printer's trade in the office of the "Lancasterian," and removing to Philadelphia in 1856, was employed as a compositor on the old "Pennsylvanian." In 1861 he enlisted in the second company of the State Fencibles, under the three-months' call, and on the expiration of this service re-enlisted in the Zouaves d'Afrique (Gen. N. P. Banks's body-guard), afterward attached to the Fourteenth Pennsylvania Volunteers. He attained the rank of captain, was wounded at Chancellorsville, in May, 1863, recovered, and commanded his company at Gettysburg, where he was taken prisoner in the second day's fight. He was confined in Libby Prison nine months, made his escape with others through the famous tunnel, and was recaptured three days afterward. After being exchanged he served on the staff of Gen. Patrick, as assistant adjutant-general. During his service he took part in the battles of Winchester, Cedar Mountain, Fredericksburg, Chancellorsville, Gettysburg, and the siege of Petersburg. After the war he resumed his occupation as a printer, and was employed on "The Press" till 1868, when, in association with three other printers, he established the "Sunday Republic," which he conducted successfully till 1886, and then retired on account of failing health. He was twice elected State Senator from Philadelphia, and was elected Secretary of Internal Affairs on the ticket with ex-Gov. Henry M. Hoyt. b

Dunlop, George Kelly, clergyman, orn in County Tyrone. Ireland, Nov. 10, 1830; died in Las Cruces, New Mexico, March 13, 1888. He was educated at the Royal College of Dungannon and at Queen's University, and came to the United States in 1852. He was ordained deacon in the Protestant Episcopal Church, Dec. 3, 1854, and priest, Aug. 7, 1856, and accepted a charge in St. Charles, Mo. Two years later he became rector of Christ Church, Lexington, Ky., and after a service of seven years, resigned to take charge of Grace Church, Kirkwood, Mo., which he held for sixteen years. He was a deputy from his diocese to the General Conventions of 1871, 1877, and 1880, a member of the standing committee, an examining chaplain, and dean of the St. Louis Convocation, and was consecrated second Missionary Bishop of New Mexico and Arizona, in St. Louis, Mo., on Nov. 21, 1880. He received the degree of S. T. D. from Racine College in 1880.

Dunster, Edward Swift, physician, born in Springville, York County, Me., Sept. 2, 1834; died in Ann Arbor, Mich., May 3, 1888. He was graduated at Harvard in 1856, and at the New York College of Physicians and Surgeons in 1859, and began practice in New York in 1860. At the beginning of the civil war he entered the national army as an assistant surgeon, and served continuously on the field and in hospitals till February, 1866. He was appointed a medical inspector by Gen. Rosecrans, and the greater part of his service was in connection with that office. At the close of the war he returned to New York, where he edited the "New York Medical Journal" from 1866 till 1872, and was physician in charge of the Randall's Island Hospital from 1869 till 1873, in the mean time occupying the chair of Obstetrics and Diseases of Women and Children in the University of Vermont for three years, and the same chair in the Long Island Medical College for two years. In 1873 he became Professor of Gynæcology in the medical department of the University of Michigan, at Ann Arbor, and held this office at the time of his death. He was the author of several works in his special branch.

Dwight, William, soldier, born in Springfield, Mass., July 14, 1831; died in Boston, Mass., April 21, 1888. He was appointed a cadet in the United States Military Academy, but resigned before graduation, and engaged in business. On May, 14, 1861, he was commissioned a captain in the Thirteenth United States Infantry, and in the following month lieutenant-colonel of the Seventieth Regiment of New York Volunteers, under command of Col. Daniel E. Sickles. He participated in the early movements in Virginia, and at the battle of Williamsburg was wounded three times and left on the field as dead. After a brief confinement he was released, and, on rejoining the army, was promoted brigadier-general for his gallantry in that battle, Nov. 29, 1862. In the final attack on Port Hudson, he led the advance troops, and so distinguished himself that he was appointed a member of the commission to arrange the terms of surrender. In May, 1864, when Gen. Banks set out on his Red river expedition, he was appointed chief of staff to that officer; in July he became commander of the First Division, Nineteenth Army Corps, and rendered efficient services in the campaign in the Shenandoah valley; and on Jan. 15, 1866, he resigned from the army.

Eckles, Delano R., lawyer, born in Kentucky in 1806; died in Greencastle, Ind., Oct. 29, 1888. He removed to Greencastle in 1838, studied law, and was admitted to the bar; was the first mayor of the city, served through the Mexican War, and reached the rank of captain; was a circuit court judge sixteen years, and was chief-justice of the United States courts in the Territory of Utah during the administration of President Buchanan, 1857-'61.

Eggleston, Benjamin, merchant, born in Corinth, N. Y., Jan. 3, 1816; died in Cincinnati, Ohio, Feb. 9, 1888. He removed to Cincinnati when quite young, engaged in mercantile business, and became interested in public affairs. He was a member and president of the city council for several years, member of the State Senate from 1862 till 1866, and member of Congress from the First Congressional District from 1865 till 1869. Subsequently he was president of the Cincinnati Chamber of Commerce, and proprietor of the "Cincinnati Times" for several years.

Elliott, Ezekiel Brown, statistician, born in Sweden, Monroe County, N. Y., July 16, 1823; died in Washington, D. C., May 24, 1888. He was graduated at Hamilton in 1844, and then taught for some years. On the development of telegraphy in New York State, he was called to its service, but soon resigned to become actuary of a life-insurance company in Boston. In 1861 he was invited to a similar office on the United States Sanitary Commission, which he held until the completion of its labors. He then entered the Government service, and in 1865 was secretary of the commission for revising the United States revenue laws. In 1871 he was associated with the civil-service reform commission, and later became Government actuary in the United States Treasury Department, which office he held until his death. Mr. Elliott was a member of the International Statistical Congress that met in Berlin in 1863, and 1882 was vice-president of the American Association for the Advancement of Science, presiding over the section of economic science and statistics. He was also a member of other scientific societies. He published papers on mathematical physics, but attained his highest reputation in connection with the many valuable statistical reports on coinage, weights and measures, and similar topics that he prepared for the United States Government. Several of these have appeared in the reports of United States census, especially in the volume on "Vital Statistics."

Elliott, Washington Lafayette, soldier, born in Carlisle, Cumberland County, Pa., March 31, 1821; died in San Francisco, Cal., June 29, 1888. He was a son of Capt. Jesse Duncan Elliott, United States Navy, accompanied his father on several long cruises, was educated at Dickinson Academy and the United States Military Academy, and became second lieutenant of United States mounted rifles in 1846. At the outbreak of the Mexican War he accompanied his regiment to the field, and served until the surrender of Vera Cruz, gaining a first lieutenancy in July, 1847. He afterward served on the frontier and in Texas and New Mexico, and took part in the campaign against the Navajo Indians in 1858. He was promoted captain in July, 1854. His first service in the civil war was in the engagements at Springfield and Wilson's Creek, Mo., and from that time till the close of the war he was constantly on duty. He became colonel of the Second Iowa Cavalry in September, 1861; major in the regular army in November, 1861; brigadier-general of volunteers in June, 1862; chief of cavalry in the Army of Virginia in August, 1862; commander of the Department of the Northwest and of a division in the Army of the Potomac in 1863; commander of the Army of the Cumberland, chief of cavalry in the Army of the Cumberland, commander of a division in the Fourth Army Corps in 1865; brevet major-general of volunteers and brevet brigadier-general in the regular army; lieutenant-colonel in August, 1866; and colonel in April, 1878. He took part in the capture of Madrid and Island No. 10, the siege of Corinth, second battle of Bull Run, the Atlanta campaign, pursuit of Gen. Hood, and the battles around Nashville, and was retired at his own request on March 20, 1879.

Fairbanks, Horace, manufacturer, born in Barnet, Vt., March 23, 1820; died in New York city, March 17, 1888. He was the second son of Erastus Fairbanks, war Governor of Vermont, and the sixth in descent from Jonathan Fairbanks, who came from England and settled in Dedham, Mass., in 1633. His father was the senior member of the firm of E. & T. Fairbanks, of St. Johnsbury, Vt., scale manufacturers. Shortly after attaining his majority Horace and his brother Franklin were admitted to the firm, which became E. & T. Fairbanks & Co. In 1874 it was incorporated under the same name and Horace became its president, and held that office till his death. In 1876 he was elected Governor. In early life he built the St. Johnsbury Athenæum, and provided it with a library of 10,000 volumes and an art gallery, which contains among other treasures Bierstadt's painting of the Yosemite valley, and presented the whole to the city. Afterward, in connection with his brother Franklin, he built the North Congregational Church and gave it to the congregation. He was president of the Portland and Ogdensburg Railroad and of the St. Johnsbury and Lake Champlain Railroad till it became a part of the Boston and Lowell system, was a director of the American Board of Commissioners for Foreign Missions, a trustee of the Fairbanks Educational Board, founded by his father and himself for educating young men for the ministry, and of the St. Johnsbury Academy and the University of Vermont.

Ferrer, Martha W., philanthropist, born in South Britain, Conn., in 1824; died in New York city, May 2, 1888. She was a sister of the late Ann S. Stephens, the author, and married Don Fermin Ferrer, ex-President of Nicaragua, in 1858. On the organization of the Workingwomen's Protective Union of New York, for the primary purpose of aiding and protecting women and girls who had been thrown upon their own exertions for support during the civil war, she was appointed its superintendent. She held this office continuously till her death, and proved an admirable executive and a sympathetic friend to all who came under her charge.

Fisher, Charles Henry, engineer, born in Lansingburg, N. Y., in 1835; died in New York city, Jan. 18, 1888. He was educated for the profession of civil engineering, and began railroad work when seventeen years old on the Racine and Janesville road, in Wisconsin. Afterward he was engaged for several years in repairing the Erie Canal. In 1860 he was attached to the engineering staff of the New York Central and Hudson River Railroad, and during the ensuing eight years rose through the various grades to the office of first assistant engineer. He resigned this office in 1868 to accept that of chief engineer of the projected Lake Ontario Shore road, and made the surveys and laid the lines on which it was built. On Jan. 1, 1869, he was appointed chief engineer of the New York Central and Hudson River road, and held the office till within three years, when he resigned.

Among his most noted works were the two additional tracks, the stations at Albany, Syracuse, and Buffalo, several costly bridges, and the elevation of the tracks and the new station in Rochester.

Foster, Joshua, educator, born near Holmesburg, Philadelphia County, Pa., July 10, 1813; died in New Brunswick, N. J., Nov. 20, 1888. He was educated at the University of the City of New York; in October, 1838, became a teacher in the Pennsylvania Institution for the Deaf and Dumb, and held that place till September, 1870, when he was appointed principal. After a service of forty six years as teacher and principal, he withdrew from active labor in the institution in October, 1884, and took up his residence in New Brunswick, N. J. Before leaving the scene of his long labor he presented his large and valuable library and extensive and choice collection of pictures to the institution. He ranked high among the instructors of deaf mutes in the United States, was an enthusiastic student of, and lecturer on zoölogy, botany, ornithology, and English history. and had every available space in his school-room occupied with cages filled with singing-birds.

Foster, Melvin, billiard-player, born in Cavendish, Vt., Sept. 12, 1844; died in New York city, July 6, 1888. He was educated in Rutland, became interested in billiards in 1858, and played his first public match, in which he defeated the late Robert E. Wilmarth by 1,000 to 821 points, in a full American game, in Boston, Mass., May 13, 1863. On April 6, 1864, he made his first appearance in New York city at Irving Hall, in a tournament for the benefit of the United States Sanitary Commission, in which he made the best average in a 500-point game of caroms, 15 20-32, against Dudley Kavanagh. In the same year he gained wide repute by defeating John Decry in a home-and-home game, his majority in New York city being 376 in 1,500, and in Washington, D. C., 55. His next great contest was in Montreal, Canada, July 19, 1865, when he was matched against Joseph Dion for $2,000 a side in gold, and was defeated by Dion, who scored 1,500 points to Foster's 1,108. He then won the Memphis tournament, and followed it with a similar victory at Cincinnati in 1867, but in his first championship match at Chicago, April 8, 1868, he lost the game to John McDevitt, by a score of 1,268 to 1,262. On Dec. 23, 1868, he defeated Joseph Dion by 300 to 296, three-ball caroms, for $2,000, in New York city. Jan. 28, 1869, Dion defeated him, 1,500 to 1,116, at the four-ball game in Montreal. April 23, Foster defeated Deery, 300 to 153, at the three-ball game in New York city; and June 19, 1871, he played his third championship match for the diamond cue, in New York city, and lost to Cyrille Dion, by 1,500 to 616. He introduced several novel features in playing, which others used to better advantage than he.

Fourat, Enos, soldier, born in Piscataway, N. J., Sept. 19, 1827; died in New Brunswick, N. J., July 22, 1888. In 1861 he was chosen a captain in the First New Jersey Volunteers, and afterward became Colonel of the Thirty-third New Jersey Regiment. He was wounded in the head during the battle of Antietam, and lett on the field for dead nearly two days. He was on court-martial duty in Nashville, Tenn., in 1864; accompanied Gen. Sherman's army on its march to the sea; and was mustered out of the service, after having taken part in twenty-six battles, in 1865. He then engaged in railroad business for several years, and in 1885 was appointed chief of police of New Brunswick, N. J.

Fullerton, William, Jr., composer, born in Newburg, N. Y., in 1854; died in London, England, Aug. 25, 1888. He was a son of ex-Judge William Fullerton, received his early education in Newburg Academy, studied music in Germany and England, and settled in London. Under the patronage of the Prince and Princess of Wales he was the author of many musical compositions, notably "The Lady of the Locket," and the opera "Waldemar," which he was preparing

to bring out at the Prince of Wales Theatre at the time of his fatal illness.

Gardner, William Sewall, lawyer, born in Hallowell, Me., Oct. 1, 1827; died in Newton, Mass., April 4, 1888. He was graduated at Bowdoin College in 1850, studied law in Lowell, and was admitted to the Middlesex bar in 1852. In February, 1855, he formed a partnership with Hon. Theodore H. Sweetser, and maintained this connection in Lowell and Boston till his appointment to the bench of the Superior Court in 1875. He held his judicial office till August, 1887, when failing health caused his resignation. Judge Gardner was an active member of the masonic fraternity, and a voluminous writer on freemasonry.

Garfield, Eliza Ballou, an American pioneer, born in Richmond, Chester County, N. H., Sept. 25, 1801; died in Mentor, Ohio, Jan 21, 1888. She was a descendant of Maturin Ballou, who fled from France on the revocation of the edict of Nantes and joined Roger Williams's colony in Rhode Island, and a niece of the Universalist clergyman, Hosea Ballou. In 1819 she married, while living in Watertown, Mass., Abram Garfield, son of a farmer of Otsego County, N. Y., and soon afterward they removed to "The Wilderness" of Ohio, and settled on a farm in Newburg, now a part of Cleveland. They built a log-cabin, twenty by thirty feet, in which three children—Mehetabel, Thomas, and Mary—were born. The family removed to New Philadelphia, Ohio, in 1826, but returned to the lake country four years later, settled on a farm in Orange township, Cuyahoga County, and erected another log-cabin. In this humble dwelling a fourth child, James Abram Garfield, who became teacher, soldier, congressman. United States Senator, and twentieth President of the United States, was born on Nov. 19, 1831. Two years afterward the father died, and Mrs. Garfield was left with the farm and four children to care for. When President Garfield was shot, with his own hand he traced an almost illegible letter to his mother. She bore up bravely after his death, till a month before her own, and her last words were a wish to see "my boy Jimmy."

Garnett, Alexander Yelverton Peyton, physician, born in Essex County, Va., Sept. 20, 1820; died at Rehoboth Beach, Del., July 11, 1888. In 1841 he was graduated at the medical department of the University of Pennsylvania, and commissioned an assistant surgeon in the United States Navy. In 1848 he was promoted surgeon, and in 1850 resigned to become Professor of Clinical Medicine in the National Medical College, in Washington, D. C. At the outbreak of the civil war he resigned his professorship, removed to Richmond, was appointed a member of the Confederate board of examining surgeons for the army, and afterward surgeon in charge of the military hospitals in that city, and as family physician of Jefferson Davis, accompanied him after the evacuation of the capital. He returned to Washington after the war, resumed his professorship in the medical college, and held it till 1870, when, on his resignation, he was elected professor emeritus. In 1886 he was vice-president of the American Medical Association. Among his numerous medical papers were: "Condurango as a Cure for Cancer," "The Potomac Marshes and their Influence as a Pathogenic Agent," "Epidemic Jaundice among Children," "The Sorghum Vulgare, or Broom-Corn Seed in Cystitis," "Nélaton's Probe in Gunshot Wounds," and "Coloproctitis treated by Hot-Water Douche and Dilatation or Division of the Sphincters."

Gay, Sydney Howard, author, born in Hingham, Mass., in 1814; died in New Brighton, Staten Island, N. Y., June 25, 1888. When fifteen years old, he entered Harvard University, but was compelled by failing health to give up his studies while in his junior year. He then spent some time traveling in China and the East Indies, and, settling in Boston, entered on a mercantile career, but soon afterward abandoned it to study law. Having conscientious scruples against taking the oath to support the Constitution of the United States, on account of his strong anti-slavery principles, he became an ardent abolitionist instead of a lawyer, and was appointed lecturing-agent of the American Anti-Slavery Society, in 1842.

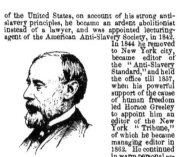

In 1844 he removed to New York city, became editor of the "Anti-Slavery Standard," and held the office till 1857, when his powerful support of the cause of human freedom led Horace Greeley to appoint him an editor of the New York "Tribune," of which he became managing editor in 1862. He continued in warm personal as-sociation with Mr. Greeley and in editorial connection with his paper till 1868, and then removed to Chicago, and assumed the managing editorship of the "Tribune" of that city. Immediately after the great fire in 1871 he re-signed this office, and became one of the most effective members of the relief committee; and on the comple-tion of this work returned to New York, and spent two years on the editorial staff of the "Evening Post." In conjunction with William Cullen Bryant he wrote and published an illustrated "History of the United States" (4 vols., New York, 1876–'81). He also wrote a life of James Madison (Boston, 1884), and was at work on a life of Edmund Quincy.

Gibson, George, soldier, born in Carlisle, Pa., April 4, 1826; died in Las Vegas, New Mexico, Aug. 5, 1888. He entered the United States Army as military store-keeper in the quartermaster's department on April 9, 1853, was appointed captain in the Eleventh regiment of United States Infantry on May 14, 1861, and was brevetted major for gallant conduct in the battle of Gettysburg on March 13, 1865, and lieutenant-colonel for meritorious services in the operations resulting in the fall of Richmond and the surrender of Gen. Lee on April 9, 1865. He was promoted major of the First United States Infantry, Jan. 12, 1868; assigned to the Fifth United States Infantry June 9, 1869, pro-moted lieutenant-colonel Third United States Infant-ry March 20, 1879, and colonel Fifth United States Infantry Aug. 1, 1886. At the time of his death he was commandant at Fort Bliss, El Paso, Tex., but was on a brief leave of absence.

Gibson, Walter Murray, adventurer, born at sea, in 1823; died in San Francisco, Cal., Jan. 21, 1888. He was the son of a merchant of Newcastle-on-Tyne, England, who removed to Montreal, Canada, in 1829, and was educated in the College of St. Sulpice there. When fourteen years old he went to New York, and engaged with a wealthy Southern planter, then on his wedding-trip, to drive his coach to his estate in An-derson County, S. C. On the way South he aston-ished his employer with his proficiency in the Ger-man and French languages and his general culture. He remained in Anderson County several years, taught school, and married; then became restless, searched the hills for the silver-mines of the Indians, ran a passenger steamer on Savannah river, tried journalism in New York, took advantage of the Cali-fornia gold-fever and made a fortune by speculating in cheap mining-apparatus; went to Mexico with De Cramer, the Russian envoy, with the intention of try-ing Daniel Webster's plan of centralizing the several States, and joined the fortunes of Gen. Carrera, of Guatemala, in his endeavor to effect the centraliza-tion of the Central American republics. He then fitted out a war-vessel in New York, from which the United States Government removed the guns and ammunition, sailed to the island of Sumatra, con-tracted with a native prince for the sale of forty square miles of land, on which he proposed to settle an American colony, and was arrested by the Dutch colonial authorities and imprisoned nearly two years. He returned to the United States in 1853, went to Salt Lake City, and in 1861 was appointed an agent of the Mormon Church, to establish a colony on the Hawai-ian Islands. At first he confined his operations to Lahaina, capital of the Island of Maui, and then aban-doning his Mormon colonization scheme, removed to the island of Lanai, leased a large tract, and raised wheat and sheep. In 1867 he settled in Honolulu, established the "News," advocated the claims of Prince Lunalilo to the throne, and, in 1869, was sent to the United States, where he negotiated a reci-procity treaty. On the accession of Prince Kalakaua he was offered a cabinet appointment, and for sev-eral years had great influence with the King. In 1878 he was elected a member of the Legislature, and in 1882 was appointed Premier and Minister of For-eign Affairs. He held these offices till the revolution of 1887, when, with the other ministers, he was de-posed, a price was set upon his head, and he fled to San Francisco, leaving interests aggregating $1,000,-000 in value.

Gilbert, Addison, philanthropist, born in Gloucester, Mass., in 1809; died there, July 2, 1888. He had been actively connected with the business interests of the city for fifty years, accumulated property valued at over $500,000, and for many years before his death was president of the City, National, and Cape Ann Savings-Banks. He bequeathed $100,000 to a board of trustees for a public hospital, $75,000 for an old folks' home, $10,000 to the Widows' and Orphans' Aid Society, $5,000 to the Firemen's Relief Asso-ciation, $4,000 to the Cape Ann Scientific and Lit-erary Association, and $3,000 to the Female Charita-ble Society.

Gillmore, Quincy Adams, soldier, born in Black River, Lorain Co., Ohio, Feb. 28, 1825; died in Brooklyn, N. Y., April 7, 1888. He was graduated at the United States Military Academy, first in a class of forty-three, in 1849, and was assigned to the corps of engineers with the rank of second lieutenant. In 1852 he was ap-pointed assistant instructor in practical military engi-neering in the United States Military Academy, and held the office till Sept. 15, 1856, and was promoted first lieutenant in July of the latter year. Between 1856 and the opening of the civil war he was treasurer and quartermaster at West Point, in charge of the New York agency for the purchase and shipment of material used in the construction of fortifications, and in charge of the fortifications in New York harbor. In August, 1861, he was promoted captain, and in October was appointed chief of engineers of the Port Royal expedition. He took an active part in the op-erations at Hilton Head, S. C., on Nov.

7, 1861, rebuilt the forts after their re-duction, and super-intended the erec-tion of new ones. In 1862 he erected the fortifications for the attack on Fort Pu-laski, at the mouth of Savannah river, and commanded the troops in the suc-cessful engagement in April. A few days after the capt-ure he was brev-etted lieutenant-colonel. Failing health then compelled him to take a brief leave of absence, during which he was appointed brigadier-general of volunteers, and assisted in organizing and forwarding to the field sixty regiments of volunteers from New York State. He reported for duty in August, was in command of the division that operated before Covington, Ky., September 18-28, and of a division in western Virginia from September 28 till October 14, was then appointed to command the first division of the Army of Kentucky, and subsequently the division of Central Kentucky. While holding this command, he defeated the Confederates under Gen. Pegram in the battle of Somerset, for which he was brevetted colonel. After another sick-leave, he was appointed commander of the Department of the South, and, in July, 1863, of the Tenth Army Corps. He directed the operations against Charleston, S. C., captured Morris Island on July 10, for which he was brevetted brigadier-general, bombarded Fort Sumter, besieged and captured Fort Wagner and Battery Gregg, and for planting and operating the famous "Swamp Angel" gun on Morris Island, seven miles form Charleston, received this commendation from Gen. Henry W. Halleck: "He has overcome difficulties almost unknown in modern sieges. Indeed, his operations on Morris Island constitute a new era in the science of engineering and gunnery." For his services at Charleston he was promoted major-general of volunteers. In 1864, at the head of the Tenth Corps, he commanded on the James river, Va., captured the line in front of Drewry's Bluff, covered Gen. B. F. Butler's retreat at Bermuda Hundred, and joined in the pursuit of the Confederates under Gen. Jubal Early. He was assigned to the defense of Washington with two divisions of the Nineteenth Corps. He commanded the Department of the South from Feb 9 till Nov. 17, 1865, resigned his volunteer commission in December, and was appointed engineer-in-chief of all the fortifications on the Atlantic coast south of New York city. In the regular army he was promoted major in June, 1863, lieutenant-colonel in 1874, and colonel on Feb. 20, 1874. As one of the judges of the Centennial Exhibition in 1876, he made elaborate reports on "Brick-making Machinery, Brick-Kilns, Perforated and Enameled Bricks and Pavements," and on "Portland, Roman, and other Cements and Artificial Stones." He also wrote "The Siege and Reduction of Fort Pulaski" (New York, 1862); "Limes, Hydraulic Cements, and Mortars" (1863); "Engineering and Artillery Operations against Charleston in 1863" (1865); "Beton, Coignet, and other Artificial Stones" (1871); "The Strength of the Building Stones of the United States" (1874); and "Roads, Streets, and Pavements" (1876).

Goldsmith, Oliver B., educator, born in Cutchogue, L. I., in 1815; died in New York city, April 28, 1888. When fifteen years old he removed to New York city, became a clerk in a dry-goods store, was established in the same line of business, and in 1837 owned the largest dry-goods store on the east side of the city, and was the chief rival of Lord & Taylor. The financial crisis of that year reduced him to poverty. While seeking other means of employment he was shown a specimen of artistic penmanship written by Isaac F. Bragg, and immediately afterward took a course of instruction in Mr. Bragg's school. Within a year he took the first prize of the American Institute for off-hand penmanship. In 1838 he opened a school in Brooklyn, and subsequently one in New city, which he conducted for forty years, and became known as the best off-hand penman in the United States. A few years ago he made a tour of the principal cities with his six-year old son, who had developed an extraordinary talent for Shakespearean recitations. In 1877 he was accidentally shot in the shoulder, and a few weeks afterward broke several bones in a fall. These injuries resulted in paralysis, from which he never recovered.

Gray, David, journalist, born in Edinburgh, Scotland, Nov. 9, 1836; died in Binghamton, N. Y., March 18, 1888. He settled in Buffalo, N. Y., about 1857, was successively a contributor, reporter, and editor of the Buffalo "Courier," and became its editor-in-chief in 1876. He held this office till 1882, and was then obliged to resign it on account of feeble health. In 1886 he was appointed secretary and treasurer of the New York State Niagara Park Commission, and held the offices till three months prior to his death, when he became secretary of the Buffalo Park Commission. He was on his way to Nassau, for his health, when he sustained injuries in a railroad accident at Vestal, N. Y., which caused his death. Mr. Gray, aside from his high reputation as a journalist, was known as a man of fine literary tastes and the author of a few exquisite fugitive poems. His writings, including essays, letters, and poems, with a sketch of his life, have been published (2 vols., Buffalo, 1888).

Greey, Edward, author, born in Sandwich, Kent, England, Dec. 1, 1835; died in New York city, Oct. 1, 1888. He received a private and a military education, accompanied the English naval expedition to China, and as captain of a company of marines was among the foremost in the storming of Pekin. After the war he was appointed to an office in the British Legation in Japan, and during his residence in that country studied its language, literature, art, customs, and form of government. In 1868 he removed to the United States, passed several years in commercial pursuits in New York city, went to Manchester, Mass., and during a season of disability began his series of Japanese historical, discriptive, and story books. On his recovery he made several trips to Japan, and opened a store for the sale of Japanese curios and works of art in New York. His English translation of the great historical work of Japan, "The Loyal Ronins" (1880), elicited the commendation of the imperial authorities, and prompted a banquet to him on his next visit to that country. He was a member of the Zoölogical and Anthropological Societies of London, and of the Authors', Lotus, and other clubs of New York. He published the plays: "Vendome," "Mirah," "The Third Estate," "The College Belles," and "Uncle Abner," and the following works on Japanese history, manners, and customs: "Blue Jackets" (1871); "Young Americans in Japan" (1881); "The Wonderful City of Tokio" (1882); "The Golden Lotus" (1883); "Bear-Worshipers of Yezo" (1884); and "A Captive of Love" (1885).

Grefin, Henriette Augusta, Baroness de, educator, born in Paris, France, in 1819; died in Orange, N. J., July 25, 1888. She married at an early age Baron Charles de Grefin, a captain in the Chasseurs d'Afrique, accompanied her husband to the United States in 1855, and lived in the South till the close of the civil war, in which they lost all their property. Her husband died soon after the peace, and the widow, who was an accomplished musician and linguist, came north and supported herself by teaching. For several years she was Professor of Languages in Vassar College.

Gunning, William D., scientist, born in Bloomingburg, Ohio, in 1830; died in Greeley, Col., March 8, 1888. He was graduated at Oberlin College, pursued a course in comparative anatomy in New York city, and in biology under Prof. Agassiz at Cambridge, Mass., held lectureships in Hillsdale College, Mich., and in Pittsburg, Pa., was a contributor to "The Index" and "The Open Court," and published a "Life History of our Planet." For some time previous to his death he was pastor of the Unitarian Society in Greeley.

Hager, Albert David, geologist, born in Chester, Vt., Nov. 1, 1817; died in Chicago, Ill., July 29, 1888. He was educated in the public schools of his native town, and in 1856 became assistant State naturalist of Vermont. During 1857-'61 he served under Edward Hitchcock as assistant geologist of Vermont, and from 1862 till 1870 was curator of the State cabinet of natural history. He then became geologist of Missouri, but in 1872 settled in Chicago, where, in 1877, he became librarian of the Historical Society, which place he held until his death. In 1867 he was appointed State commissioner from Vermont to the World's Fair in Paris. He contributed to the "Report on the Geology of Vermont" (2 vols., Claremont, N. H., 1861); "Annual Reports of Vermont

Fish Commission" (Montpelier, Vt., 1866–'69); and "Annual Report of the State Geologist for the State of Missouri" (Jefferson City, 1871).

Hamilton, Peter, lawyer, born in Pennsylvania in 1811; died in Mobile, Ala., Nov. 22, 1888. He was graduated at Princeton, removed to Mobile, and was admitted to the bar in 1838. He was vice-president and general manager of the Mobile and Ohio Railroad Company during the civil war; served in both branches of the State Legislature; was a special commissioner to Washington, D. C., in 1875, to arrange the political troubles in the State, and effected a consolidation of two legislatures then sitting in Montgomery. He assisted in the adjustment of the State debt and the drafting of the revenue law, and was a member of the commission to codify the laws of the State in 1886.

Hamilton, William J., lawyer, born in Washington County, Md., Sept. 8, 1820; died in Hagerstown, Md., Oct. 26, 1888. He studied in Jefferson College, Pa., was admitted to the bar of his native county in 1843, was elected to the State Assembly as a Democrat in 1846, was a Cass presidential elector in 1848, and in 1849 was elected to Congress. By re-elections he served from 1849 till 1855, was then defeated, and retired from political life till after the civil war. In 1867 he was defeated for Governor by Oden Bowie, by a majority of one; in 1868 was elected United States Senator for the term beginning March 4, 1869; and in 1879 was elected Governor by a majority of 22,000. Shortly after his inauguration he became involved in a conflict with the most active members of his own party, especially those constituting the board of public works, and his administration closed without a restoration of harmony. At his death he was the wealthiest person in Washington County.

Harris, Samuel Smith, clergyman, born in Autauga County, Ga., Sept. 14, 1841; died in London, England, Aug. 21, 1888. He was graduated at the University of Alabama in 1859, studied law, and, by special act of the Legislature, was admitted to the bar in 1860. He began practice in Montgomery, but on the outbreak of the civil war joined the Third Alabama Regiment, and served in the Confederate army till the close of the war. He became adjutant-general on the staff of Gen. Bragg with the rank of major. After the war he resumed his practice in Montgomery, but soon afterward removed to New York city, where he practiced three years. He studied theology, and was ordained deacon in Montgomery on Feb. 10, 1869, and priest on June 30 following. As deacon, he had charge of St. John's Church, Montgomery, and as priest he was rector of Trinity Church, Columbus, Ga., Trinity Church, New Orleans, and from 1875 till 1879 of St. James's Church, Chicago. He was elected Bishop of Quincy in 1878, but declined the office, and was elected Bishop of Michigan, and consecrated in Detroit on Sept. 17, 1879. He was a founder of "The Living Church," and received the degree of D. D. from the college of William and Mary in 1874, and that of LL. D. from the university of Alabama in 1879.

Hassard, John Rose Greene, journalist, born in New York city, Sept. 4, 1836; died there, April 18, 1888. He was graduated at St. John's (R. C.) College, Fordham, N. Y., in 1855, intending to enter the priesthood, but a season of delicate health interposed, and he engaged in literary work. He was an assistant editor of the "New American Cyclopædia" from 1857 till 1863; took George Ripley's place as literary editor of the New York "Tribune," while the latter was on a vacation in Europe; was appointed editor of the "Catholic World" in 1865, but soon afterward went to Chicago with Charles A. Dana, who there founded the "Republican"; returned to New York on the discontinuance of the "Republican," and joined the editorial staff of the "Tribune," and on the death of Mr. Ripley succeeded to the literary editorship. Subsequently he was also musical critic for many years. In 1878, in conjunction with William M. Grosvenor, he translated, after many persons had tried and failed, a large number of cipher telegrams

that had been sent by the Democratic National Committee to various persons in the Southern States concerning the presidential election returns of 1876. He passed the summer of 1879 in England and the winter of 1880 in Nassau and Bermuda, in the hope of regaining his health, and afterward traveled and lived in France, Southern California, and the Adirondacks, but never regained his strength. Besides his literary and musical criticisms and correspondence with the "Tribune," he was the author of a "Life of Archbishop Hughes" (1866); "The Ring of the Nibelung" (1877); "Life of Pius IX" (1878); a school "History of the United States" (1878); and "A Pickwickian Pilgrimage" (1881).

Hastings, Alice, actress, born in Ireland in 1856; died in New York city, Dec. 1, 1888. She came to the United States with her parents when a child, made her first appearance on the stage when sixteen years old at Wood's Museum, Philadelphia, in "Man and Wife," and after two successful seasons in that city played at the Academy of Music in Cleveland as Susan Nipper in "Dombey and Son," Tidy in "Lost in London," and Audrey in "As you like it." Two seasons at the Grand Opera House in Pittsburg followed. She was then engaged by James McVicker for his Chicago theatre, and made a notable success there as Mrs. Brown in "The Banker's Daughter." In 1881 she played male parts at the Fourteenth Street Theatre in New York city, starred with Augustin Daly's company as the Wild Rose in "An Arabian Night," and in 1882 became leading lady in Roland Reed's company, holding the place till her death. She created the parts of the Adventuress in "Cheek" and Mrs. Ponsby in "Humbug." Her last appearance was in "The Woman Hater," at the Fourteenth Street Theatre. New York city, a week before her death.

Hays, James Buchanan, lawyer, born in Crawford County, Pa., Sept. 10, 1838; died in Boisé City, Idaho, May 31, 1888. He removed with his parents to Ashippun, Dodge County, Wis., in 1847, and re-educated his education in the University of Wisconsin. In 1863 he was admitted to the bar of Dodge County, in 1867 to the bar of the Wisconsin Supreme Court, and in 1870 to that of the United States Circuit Court for Wisconsin. He was elected clerk of the circuit court of Dodge County for the term beginning Jan. 1, 1863, was re-elected in 1865, was elected member of the Assembly for the session of 1867, was Democratic candidate for county judge in 1869, and was elected district attorney for the county in 1874, 1876, 1878, and 1880. For several years he was president of the village of Haricon, and in 1877 was a candidate for Secretary of State of Wisconsin. In the early part of 1885 he was appointed Chief-Justice of Idaho Territory, and immediately assumed the duties of the office, which he continued to discharge till his death.

Hazard, Rowland Gibson, manufacturer and author, born in South Kingston, R. I., Oct. 9, 1801; died in Peacedale, R. I. June 24, 1888. He was engaged in the woolen business all his life. He was known throughout the United States for his philanthropy, literary work, and political services. In 1841 he was called to New Orleans, and during that and the following year he effected the release from the chain-gang of many free Northern negroes employed in the commercial marine service. His efforts were made with great pertinacity and in the face of frequent threats of personal violence. He served two terms in the Rhode Island Assembly, 1851–'52 and 1854–'55, and one term in the State Senate, 1866–'67. His publications comprise: "Language; its Connection with the Constitution and Prospects of Man" (1836); "Lectures on the Adaptation of the Universe to the Cultivation of the Mind" (1840); "Lecture on the Causes of Decline of Political and National Morality" (1841); "Essay on the Philosophical Character of Channing" (1844); "Essay on the Duty of Individuals to support Science and Literature" (1855); "Essays on the Resources of the United States" (1864); "Freedom of the Mind in Willing" (1864); "Essays on Finance and Hours of Labor" (1868); and letters on "Causation and Freedom in Willing," addressed to John Stuart Mill (1869). He received the degree of LL. D. in 1869 from Brown University.

Hecker, Isaac Thomas, clergyman, born in New York city, Dec. 18, 1819; died there, Dec. 22, 1888. He received a meager education, was compelled to support himself from an early age, and became connected with his two brothers in the flour business. While so engaged, he was led to the study of metaphysics and theology by reading Kant, and, withdrawing from business life, joined the Brook Farm Community. He soon be-

came dissatisfied with that life, and on attaining his majority returned to mercantile pursuits with his brothers. Up to his twenty - second year he had been a Protestant in religious belief and association. At that time he was drawn to a study of the Roman Catholic faith, and a year later became a convert. He again relinquished his business interests, went to Germany, studied for the priesthood, was ordained in 1849, passed two years as a novitiate at the retreat of the Redemptorist Fathers at St. Troud, Belgium, performed missionary service in England, and returned to the United States in 1851. After continuing his missionary labors here several years, he came to the belief that the United States and Canada offered a good field for a new society which should be wholly American and composed of converts from Protestantism. In 1857 he went to Rome, laid his plans before the Pope, was released from the Redemptorist Order, and received authority to organize his projected society, to which the name of " The Congregation of St. Paul the Apostle" was given. The founder was appointed Superior of the Paulist Fathers, returned to New York city, collected funds, and erected a church, home, and cluster of schools. In 1865 he founded " The Catholic World," which has since been conducted by members of the congregation; in 1869 was a member of the Roman Catholic Congress at Malines; in 1870–'71 attended the Vatican Council as theologian to Archbishop Spalding; in 1871–'75 traveled through Europe, Egypt, and the Holy Land; and in 1875 returned to New York city, and was elected superior of the congregation for a term of nine years. Besides his editorial writings and an article in the " Revue Générale," of Brussels (1869), setting forth the relations that should and did exist between the Roman Catholic Church and democracy in the United States, he published " Questions of the Soul " (New York, 1855); " Aspirations of Nature " (1857); " Catholicity in the United States " (1879); and " Catholics and Protestants agreeing on the School Question " (1881).

Heilprin, Michael, born in Piotrkow, Poland, in 1823; died in Summit, N. J., May 10, 1888. He was a son of Phineas Mendel Heilprin, an eminent scholar and native of Russian Poland, removed to Hungary early in life, received a classical education, and became an active member of the revolutionary party in 1848. During the brief provisional governorship of Louis Kossuth, he was on the literary staff in the interior department. He settled in the United States in 1856, and soon attracted attention by his literary abilities, his scholarship, and his linguistic accomplishments. He was a contributor to the " Nation," of New York, from its fourth number, and to other literary periodicals, and did a large amount of work on the " American Cyclopædia " from its second

volume. It is believed that his death was hastened by his untiring labor in behalf of the Russian Jows, whose attempts at colonization in the United States he very materially promoted. He published " The Historical Poetry of the Ancient Hebrews " (2 vols., New York, 1879–'80).

Herreshoff, Charles Frederick, ship-builder, born in Providence, R. I., July 26, 1809; died in Bristol, R. I., Sept. 8, 1888. He was graduated at Brown University in 1828, and in 1833 settled in Bristol, on the Point Pleasant farm. Though he was ostensibly engaged in farming, his real energies were applied to naval construction. In 1856 he removed to Bristol, where shortly afterward his son, John Herreshoff, began boat-building. Within a short time John lost his eyesight, and his father took a more active interest in the business, and as the other sons grew up, all with the father's skill in naval architecture, the Herreshoff Manufacturing Company was established. For many years the business was confined to building sailing-vessels, and a number of remarkably fast boats, like the " Qui Vive " and the " Sadie," were constructed. But about 1875 the company began building steam-vessels, and afterward steel yachts, torpedo-boats, and war-vessels. John Herreshoff, now (1889) known as the " blind boat-builder," became president of the company, designed the coil-boiler and the fast steam-launch " Stiletto," which was bought by the Navy Department, and by the aid of his father's eyes planned outlines and details with astonishing accuracy.

Hickok, Laurens Perseus, educator, born in Bethel, Conn., Dec. 29, 1798; died in Amherst, Mass., May 6, 1888. He was graduated at Union College in 1820, licensed to preach in 1822, and from that time till 1836 held pastorates in Newtown, Kent, and Litchfield, Conn. In 1836 he was elected Professor of Theology in Western Reserve College, Ohio, and served till 1844, when he was chosen to the similar chair in Auburn Theological Seminary. In 1852 he was elected Professor of Mental and Moral Science, and vice-president of Union College. He assisted the venerable Dr. Nott in the government of the college till 1860, had sole charge till March 1, 1866, and was then elected president, but only served two years, resigning when seventy years of age, and retiring to Amherst, Mass. Of his numerous works, which have been adopted as text-books in many of the higher institutions of learning in the United States, and translated into several foreign languages, the best known are: " Rational Psychology, or the Subjective Idea and Objective Laws of all Intelligence " (1848); " System of Moral Science " (1853); " Rational Cosmology " (1858); " Humanity Immortal " (1872); and " Rational Logic " (1875).

Hinckley, Isaac, railroad president, born in Hingham, Mass., Oct. 28, 1815; died in Philadelphia, Pa., March 28, 1888. He was graduated at Harvard in 1834, and in 1846 was appointed superintendent of transportation of the Boston and Providence Railroad, holding the office two years. From January, 1848, till April 1, 1865, he was employed on various railroads in New England, and on the latter date was elected president of the Philadelphia, Wilmington and Baltimore Company. During the first eleven years of the existence of the Eastern Railroad Association he was its president, and for many years occupied the same office in the Junction Railroad Company, owned jointly by the Philadelphia, Wilmington and Baltimore, the Pennsylvania, and the Reading Railroad Companies.

Hitchcock, Robert B., naval officer, born in Cheshire, Conn., Sept. 25, 1803; died in New York city, March 24, 1888. He was appointed midshipman in the United States Navy on Jan. 1, 1825; on March 3, 1835, was commissioned lieutenant; and, after serving in the Pacific squadrons, was ordered on ordnance duty in 1846, and given command of the storeship " Relief " in 1853. On Sept. 14, 1855, he was commissioned commander. He was on ordnance duty 1855–'58; commanded the steam-frigate " Merrimac " 1858–'60; became captain and inspector of ordnance in 1861, and commodore and commander of the steam-sloop "Susquehanna" on July 16, 1862, and was senior officer of the fleet that blockaded Mobile. In 1866 he was appointed commandant of the navy-yard at Norfolk, Va., on Sept. 25 of that year was retired, and in 1870–'72 was on duty in the Ordnance Department at Washington.

Hoffman, John Thompson, lawyer, born in Sing Sing, N. Y., Jan. 10, 1828; died in Wiesbaden, Germany, March 24, 1888. He was graduated at Union College in 1846, removed to New York city, and was admitted to the bar in January, 1849. Soon afterward he became a member of the law firm of Woodruff, Leonard and Hoffman. He was chosen a member of the Democratic State Central Committee when only twenty years old, and gave an active "stump" support to Lewis Cass in the presidential canvass. By 1854 he had firmly established himself in practice, and attained a reputation as an orator. He then joined Tammany Hall, took sides against Fernando Wood in the contest for the control of that organization, applied to President Buchanan for the office of United States District Attorney of New York, and was refused on the ground that he was too young. In 1860, after formally declining to become the candidate of Tammany Hall for the office of recorder of New York, he was put in nomination and elected, receiving twice the number of votes for Abraham D. Russell, the Mozart Hall candidate, and four thousand more than Thomas B. Van Buren, Republican. During his first term three events gave him a high reputation: his charge to the jury in the Jafford murder case, his charge to the grand jury on the occasion of the riots of July, 1863, and his imposition of sentences on the convicted rioters. His fearlessness in the two last acts led to his unanimous re-election, the Republican judiciary convention warmly approving both his official conduct and his renomination. He was elected Mayor in 1865 and 1867, and defeated for Governor by Reuben E. Fenton in 1866. He was elected Governor over John A. Griswold in 1868 (though the opposing party claimed that the State was carried for him by frauds in New York city), and re-elected over Gen. Stewart L. Woodford in 1870. In 1871 the exposures of the Tweed ring were made, and the charges against the political organization that had been the means of his rapid official advancement, reacted against him personally. On Feb. 7, 1876, he delivered a lecture on "Liberty and Order—the Limits of Government," under the auspices of the New York Association for the Advancement of Science and Art, before a large audience in New York city.

Holder, Joseph Bassett, naturalist, born in Lynn, Mass., Oct. 26, 1824; died in New York city, Feb. 28, 1888. He studied at the Friends' School in Providence, R. I., and at the Harvard Medical College. After practicing medicine for several years in Lynn, he was sent to the Dry Tortugas in the capacity of physician and naturalist, and there began his study of invertebrate zoölogy. From 1860 till 1867 he was surgeon in charge of the United States military prison in Tortugas, Fla., and then was assistant post-surgeon at Fort Monroe, Va. He came to New York city in 1870, and was appointed curator of invertebrate zoölogy, ichthyology, and herpetology in the American Museum of Natural History, which post he held until his death. Dr. Holder was a fellow of the New York Academy of Sciences, a member of the American Ornithological Union, and of various other scientific societies. Besides papers on his specialty, contributed to technical journals, he wrote for the popular magazines, and published "History of the North American Fauna" (New York, 1882); "History of the Atlantic Right Whales" (1883); and "The Living World" (1884).

Hunn, David Lathrop, clergyman, born in Colerain, Mass., Nov. 5, 1789; died in Buffalo, N. Y., Jan. 29, 1888. He entered Yale University in 1809, and after being graduated took the theological course at Andover, and was ordained a Congregational clergyman.

He held pastorates at Greenfield, Mass., Sandwich, on Cape Cod, Vernon, Conn., and East Windsor and North Hadley, Mass., and on removing from the latter place to Rochester, N. Y., left the Congregational Church and was received into the Presbyterian. After a long residence in Rochester, where he was an editor of the "Genesee Evangelist," he settled in Buffalo, and preached at irregular intervals until his ninetieth year. He was a member of the local Yale Association, and spoke at its meetings till within a short time of his death. He was the oldest graduate of Yale, and the oldest clergyman in the United States.

Ibach, Lawrence J., astronomer, born in Allentown, Pa., Jan. 17, 1816; died in Newmanstown, Lebanon County, Pa., Oct. 9, 1888. His father was a blacksmith, who brought him up to the same trade, and throughout his life he stuck to his forge, making horse-shoes, iron barrel-hoops, wheel-tires, smoothing-irons, shovels, and a variety of kitchen utensils. He received his first instructions in mathematics and astronomy from a French gentleman, and when nineteen years old he accompanied the family to Sheridan, Lebanon County, Pa., where his father died three years afterward. He carried on the blacksmithing business there till 1849, when he rented a forge near Reading. While working there he became acquainted with Charles F. Engleman, the astronomer, and with him began studying astronomy systematically. In 1852 he returned to Sheridan, and in 1860, on the death of Mr. Engleman, found himself heir to all his friend's books, charts, and instruments. About the same time he was called upon to make several series of astronomical calculations for almanacs that had been promised by his benefactor. He filled this first order in 1863, and from that time till his death the "blacksmith-astronomer" made annual calculations for almanacs published in the United States, Canada, Cuba, and South America. In 1875 he translated his calculations into four different languages. He was a member of astronomical and scientific societies, and after working at the forge all day was accustomed to spend a part of the night in studying the heavens.

Irving, Roland Duer, geologist, born in New York city, April 27, 1847; died in Madison, Wis., May 30, 1888. He was a son of the Rev. Pierre P. Irving, and a grand-nephew of Washington Irving. In 1869 he was graduated at the Columbia College School of Mines, and ten years later he received the degree of Ph. D. from that institution. Soon after graduating he became assistant to John S. Newberry, on the Ohio State Geological Survey, and in 1870 was elected Professor of Geology, Mining, and Metallurgy in the University of Wisconsin, which chair in 1879 became that of Geology and Mineralogy and was filled by him until his death. Prof. Irving became an assistant geologist on the survey of Wisconsin—authorized by the State in 1873—and continued so until 1879. During 1880–'82 he was one of the experts engaged on the work of the United States census, and in 1882 was appointed by the United States Geological Survey geologist in charge of the Lake Superior Division. He made a specialty of the micro-petrography of the fragmental rocks and crystalline schists, and his best work was accomplished in the direction of the pre-Cambrian stratigraphy and the genesis of some of the so-called crystalline rocks, particularly of the quartzites and ferruginous rocks of the Lake Superior region. He was a Fellow of the American Association for the Advancement of Science, a member of the American Institute of Mining Engineers, and of other scientific bodies, whose proceedings he enriched with contributions on his specialties. His publications under the auspices of the Wisconsin Geological Survey include "Geology of Western Wisconsin" (Madison, 1877); "Geology of the Lake Superior Region" (1880); "Crystalline Rocks of the Wisconsin Valley" (1882); and "Mineralogy and Lithology of Wisconsin" (1883). He contributed to the reports of the United States Geological Survey "The Copper-Bearing Rocks of Lake Superior"

(Washington, 1883); "On Secondary Enlargements of Mineral Fragments in Certain Rocks" (1884); with Charles R. Vanhise "The Archæan Formation of the Northwestern States" (1885); with Thomas C. Chamberlain "The Junction between the Eastern Sandstone and the Keweenaw Series, Keweenaw Point, Lake Superior" (1885); and "The Classification of the Early Cambrian and Pre-Cambrian Formations" (1886). He gained "the reputation of being one of the world's best geologists."

Jarves, James Jackson, author, born in Boston, Mass., Aug. 20, 1818; died in Tarasp, Switzerland, June 28, 1888. He prepared for college, but a weakness of the eyes caused a change in his plans, and in 1837 he set out on a journey that embraced California, Mexico, Central America, and South America, and concluded with his settling in Honolulu. He established the first newspaper published in the Sandwich Islands, the "Polynesian," in 1840; became director of the Government press in 1844; was appointed special commissioner of Hawaii to negotiate commercial treaties with the United States, Great Britain, and France in 1848; and after concluding his official duties spent several years in Paris, Florence, and Rome, applying himself to literary work and the collection of art-treasures. He made four notable collections—a gallery of masters illustrating the history and showing the development of Italian art, now belonging to Yale University; a joint collection of old paintings and sculptures, now in Cleveland, Ohio; a collection illustrating the ancient and modern glass-work of Venice, now in the Metropolitan Museum of Art, New York; and unique specimens of laces, embroideries, costumes, and various fabrics, dating from the twelfth century, which he sold in New York in 1886. He was United States vice-consul and acting consul in Florence in 1879–'82, and Italian Commissioner to the Boston Exhibition in 1882–'83; was an honorary member of the Academy of Fine Arts in Florence; and had received the decoration of a Chevalier of the Crown of Italy for his services in the interest of Italian art, and that of a Knight-Commander of the Royal Order of Kamehameha I, for diplomatic services to Hawaii. Mr. Jarves corresponded regularly with journals and periodicals for many years, and published a "History of the Hawaiian or Sandwich Islands" (Boston and London, 1843); "Scenes and Scenery in the Sandwich Islands" (1844); "Parisian Sights and French Principles, seen through American Spectacles" (New York, 1853); "Art Hints, Architecture, Sculpture, and Painting" (1855); "Kiana, a Tradition of Hawaii" (Boston, 1855); "Italian Sights and Papal Principles, seen through American Spectacles" (New York, 1855); "The Confessions of an Inquirer" (3 parts, Boston, 1857–'69); "Art Studies; The Old Masters of Italy" (New York, 1861); "The Art Idea, Sculpture, Painting, and Architecture in America" (Boston, 1866); "Art Thoughts; The Experiences and Observations of an American Amateur in Europe" (1869); "Glimpses at the Art of Japan" (New York, 1876); and "Italian Rambles" (1884).

Jenks, Francis H., founder of the American safe-deposit business, born in Boston, Mass., July 3, 1812; died in Worcester, Mass., Dec. 19, 1888. He was a son of the Rev. William Jenks, a distinguished Orientalist, author of "The Comprehensive Commentary." He was educated in the Boston Latin School, was employed in a mercantile house in Boston, removed to Baltimore in 1832, and was engaged in business there with George H. Weld under the name of Jenks & Weld until 1856, and then settled in New York city. Soon afterward he originated and entered upon the safe-deposit business. In 1861 he obtained a charter from the New York Legislature for the Safe-Deposit Company of New York, which he organized in 1865. He was elected president of the company, and held the office till 1885.

Jennings, Russell, philanthropist, born in Weston (now Easton), Fairfield County, Conn., Feb. 22, 1800; died in Deep River, Conn., March 8, 1888. He was educated at what is now Madison University, was ordained a minister of the Baptist Church while a student, and completed his studies in Newton Theological Institution. For some years he was a missionary of the Connecticut Baptist Convention, and afterward held pastorates in Saybrook, Meriden, Waterbury, Norwich, Deep River, and Haddam. When compelled by his health to decline a further settled charge, he acted as supply to destitute churches, and continued to officiate to within a year and a half of his death. In 1855 he invented the extension-lip bit, and then spent ten years in inventing and making the machinery for its economical manufacture, after which he derived a large income from its sale. Before he had acquired any considerable wealth, he made it a rule to give a portion of his income annually to the support of struggling Baptist churches, and at the beginning of his more prosperous days he established a domestic mission of his own, assuming the care of several churches that were unable to support a pastor. By his aid each of these was soon able to maintain a settled pastor. At the same time he was one of the largest contributors to the funds of the Connecticut Baptist Convention for domestic missions and of the Baptist home and foreign missions. He continued his private domestic mission nearly twenty years, and then gave to each of the churches a fund producing a handsome annual interest. In 1870 he bought ground in Chester, Conn., built and furnished a church for the congregation at a cost of over $16,000 and a parsonage valued at $2,500, and presented the congregation a fund of $5,000. In South Windsor he bought property at a cost of over $7,000, built a church at a little more cost than the Chester edifice, and presented the whole to the congregation. He made further cash donations of $2,000 to the Moodus, $4,000 and a parsonage to the Haddam, $5,000 to the Easton, $5,000 to the Winthrop, $10,000 to the Deep River, $3,000 to the Rowayton, $3,000 to the New Canaan, $4,000 to the Stepney, $3,000 to the White Hills, $3,000 to the Shelton, $3,000 to the Clinton, $3,000 to the Lyme, $3,000 to the Cromwell, $3,000 to the Plainville, and $3,000 to the Rainbow Baptist churches. In addition he gave large sums to other churches to aid them in erecting new edifices and parsonages and paying off debts. His private charities were said to be on a correspondingly liberal scale.

Jerome, Lawrence Roscoe, broker, born in Pompey, Onondaga County, N. Y., Feb. 20, 1820; died in Sharon, Conn., Aug. 12, 1888. He was a son of Thomas Jerome and a brother of Leonard and Addison Jerome. He worked some years on his father's farm, was then placed with a Presbyterian clergyman in Palmyra, N. Y., to be prepared for a theological education, studied Greek and Latin, decided that he was better fitted to be a physician, studied medicine in his native village, and after a few months returned to farm-work. In 1842 he removed to New York city, spent several years in mercantile business, assisted his brother Leonard in establishing the "Rochester American," which the brothers conducted for two years as a Whig journal, and in 1854 returned to New York city and with Leonard established a brokerage business in Wall Street. He continued this till about 1879. In 1870 he was elected a member of the Board of Aldermen, and in 1878 was defeated as Tammany candidate for Congress by Gen. Anson G. McCook. He was one of the best known and most popular club-men in New York city and London, a liberal promoter of gentlemanly sports, a capital story-teller, and man of ready wit.

Johonnot, James, educator, born in Bethel, Vt., in 1823; died in Tarpon Springs, Fla., June 18, 1888. He received a common-school education, and when sixteen years old began his special educational work that was continued with few interruptions for almost half a century. He taught for many years, compiled a large number of text-books, began organizing teachers' institutes through New York State in 1850, and became State-Institute instructor, to which office he gave all his time and energy till 1885, when failing health compelled him to resign. Besides the text-books he wrote "Principles and Practice of Teaching," which had a large circulation in the United States, and in a translation is now the principal guide of the native teachers of Japan.

Judd, David Wright, publisher, born in Lewiston, Niagara County, N. Y., Sept. 1, 1838; died in New York city, Feb. 6, 1888. He was a son of Ozias Judd, a well-known advocate of anti-slavery measures, who allowed his enthusiasm such wide scope that he emigrated to Kansas, though well advanced in years, to take part in the agitation that disturbed that region in 1855–'60. David was graduated at Williams College in 1860. At the beginning of the civil war he accompanied the Twenty-second Regiment of New York Volunteers to the field as press correspondent, and remained with the army till 1864, when he joined the editorial staff of the New York "Commercial Advertiser." During his service in the field he was taken prisoner at Harper's Ferry and at Chancellorsville, but escaped both times, and was commissioned captain in the First New York Cavalry. He remained with the "Commercial Advertiser" about seven years, then became editor and part proprietor of "Hearth and Home," and in 1883 was elected president of the Orange Judd Company and took charge of the editorial and business departments of the "American Agriculturist." In 1871 he was elected a member of the State Legislature from Richmond County (Staten Island), served on the Committees on Cities (chairman), Commerce and Navigation, Libraries and Apportionment, and introduced the "Judd Jury Bill" and the bill for the establishment of free libraries. He was appointed a quarantine commissioner in 1873, and was reappointed three times. He was a director of the National Rifle Association, to which he gave a costly prize for annual competition, and an active member of the Union League and New York Republican Clubs.

Kelly, William, inventor, born in Pittsburg, Pa., Aug. 22, 1811; died in Louisville, Ky., Feb. 11, 1888. When quite young he built a tin steam engine and boiler. When he was eighteen he made a propelling water-wheel and, four years later, a rotary steam-engine. He engaged in the commission and transportation business in Pittsburg, and owned interests in steamboats. In 1845 his warehouse was burned, and he removed to Kentucky. He purchased the Eddyville Iron Works on Cumberland river, in Lyon County, and with his brother, John F. Kelly, began the manufacture of iron. The plant included the Suwanee furnace and the Union forge. At the former about half of the metal produced was converted into large iron sugar-kettles, made in cast-iron elastic molds of his own invention, which he sold to the sugar-planters of Louisiana and Cuba, while the remainder of the metal was worked into charcoal blooms by the knobbling process. The latter was held in high reputation, and were almost entirely used for making boiler-plates. He began experimenting in 1847 in the direction of decarbonizing the iron by the introduction of a current of air. Concerning this, he wrote: "I conceived the idea that, after the metal was melted, the use of fuel would be unnecessary—that the heat generated by the union of the oxygen of the air with the carbon of the metal would be sufficient to accomplish the refining and decarbonizing of the iron." After devising several plans for testing this idea, he began experimenting with a small blast-furnace having a hearth and bosh similar to the ordinary type. Into this he introduced two tuyeres, one above the other, the upper one for the purpose of melting the stock, while the lower one, fixed near the bottom of the hearth, was intended to conduct the air into the hearth. He continued these experiments until 1851, when, on the completion of a new blast-furnace, he tried various improvements

with considerable success. The melting and decarbonizing departments were separated, so that the crude metal as it came from the blast-furnace was run into a converter, which was provided with three tuyeres. A powerful blast of air was then turned on through the tuyeres and the fluid metal run into the converter, which immediately began to boil violently. The blast was allowed to act on the metal for fifteen or twenty minutes, until the carbon of the metal was oxidized, when the converter was tapped and the metal run out into molds. Zerah Colburn, in his history of the Bessemer process of refining iron, says: "The first experiments in the conversion of melted cast-iron into malleable steel, by blowing air in jets through the mass in fusion, appear to have been made by William Kelly, an iron-master at the Suwanee furnaces, Lyon County, Kentucky, United States." This method, long known as "Kelly's air-boiling process," was used for the manufacture of boiler-plates before Sir Henry Bessemer was known. When Bessemer brought out his process in England, application was at once made by Mr. Kelly for a patent in the United States, and after considerable delay, during which time the English applicant appeared in the Patent-Office, the commissioner decided that Mr. Kelly was entitled to the patent, which he at once issued to him. In 1863 a syndicate of iron-masters organized the Kelly Process Company, for the purpose of controlling the Kelly patents, and erected experimental works at Wyandotte, Mich., where steel was first made under these patents in the United States months before the similar production under Bessemer's patents at Troy by Alexander L. Holley. The interests of the several patentees were consolidated in 1866 under the title of the Pneumatic Steel Association. In 1871 application was made for the renewal of the Bessemer, Mushet, and Kelly patents, and the claims of the two former were rejected, while a renewal of seven years was granted to Mr. Kelly.

Kelso, James J., police officer, born in New York city, Oct. 31, 1838; died there, Nov. 26, 1888. He was graduated at the College of the City of New York, then held a mercantile clerkship a short time, and in 1858 was appointed clerk in the office of the chief clerk of the New York Police Department. In January, 1861, he was made a patrolman and detailed to the detective squad, and during the following eight years made a wide-spread reputation by his detective skill and personal bravery. In 1869 he was promoted sergeant on March 29, captain on October 14, and chief of detectives on December 28. On July 28, 1870, the mysterious and still unexplained murder of Benjamin Nathan, a wealthy and highly esteemed Jewish citizen, occurred. The skill of the detectives was apparently baffled, and John Jourdan, Superintendent of Police, died three months after the murder from worry over the inability of the police authorities to fasten the crime upon the perpetrator. On October 17 following Captain Kelso was appointed superintendent to fill the vacancy. On the reorganization of the police department in 1873, he was removed from command by the new board of commissioners. He then engaged in the coal business till 1885, when he was appointed collector of city revenue and superintendent of markets.

Kennedy, Hugh, physician, born in Belfast, Ireland, in 1810; died in Louisville, Ky., May 19, 1888. He engaged in the drug business in New Orleans in 1833, and was an active worker during the severe epidemic of cholera mixed with cases of yellow fever of that year. He conducted the drug business for twenty years, and in the mean time became proprietor of the "New Delta," a Democratic organ that opposed the Slidell wing of the party. During 1860 and the early part of 1861 the paper was strongly anti-secession. In 1864 he was appointed by the military and civil authority Mayor of New Orleans, but was afterward removed by Gen. Banks and replaced by Col. Samuel Quincy, of Boston. An appeal to President Johnson led to the removal of Col. Quincy and the reinstatement of Dr. Kennedy. In 1868 he removed to Louisville, Ky., and became proprietor of the celebrated cannel-coal mine in Breckenridge County.

King, John H., soldier, born in Michigan, about 1818; died in Washington, D. C., April 7, 1888. He was appointed a second lieutenant in the United States Army, Dec. 2, 1837, promoted first lieutenant March 2, 1839, and captain Oct. 31, 1846; was on duty on the Western frontier till the Mexican War, and served with distinction at Vera Cruz in 1847. On May 14, 1861, he was promoted major and assigned to the Fifteenth United States Infantry; Nov. 29, 1862, was commissioned brigadier-general of volunteers; May 31, 1865, was brevetted major-general; July 30, 1865, was commissioned colonel in the permanent establishment; and Feb. 6, 1882, was retired. During the civil war he was engaged in the battles of Shiloh, Murfreesborough, Chickamauga, Resaca, New Hope Church, Kenesaw Mountain, Peach Tree and Utoy Creeks. He received brevets in the regular army of colonel for services at Chickamauga, brigadier-general for Ruff's station, and major-general for gallantry in the field through the war. He had lived quietly in Washington since his retirement.

King, John Pendleton, lawyer, born in Glasgow, Barren County, Ky., April 3, 1799; died in Augusta, Ga., March 19, 1888. In 1815 his parents settled in Augusta, where he resided until his death. He was graduated at Richmond Academy, Augusta, and was admitted to the bar in 1819. On Nov. 21, 1833, he was elected United States Senator to fill the vacancy caused by the resignation of George M. Troup, and took his seat in the following month. In November, 1834, he was re-elected for a full term, but only served two years, his opposition to certain measures of the Administration leading the press of his State to criticise him severely. He served one year as judge of the Court of Common Pleas, was president of the Georgia Railroad and Banking Company from 1841 till 1878, and also, for some years, president of the Atlanta and West Point Railroad, which he planned and completed. He was a member of the State Convention of 1865, which repealed the ordinance of secession, repudiated the Confederate war debt, and abolished slavery.

Kissam, Agnes Allen, centenarian, born in New York city, March 4, 1788; died in Brooklyn, N. Y., March 25, 1888. She was born in Greenwich Street, and when a young lady passed the summers in her father's country-house just above the present Canal Street, and for some years had a city residence on Bowling Green. On her hundredth birthday she received several hundred relatives and family friends for six hours, without being fatigued, and showed that she retained her faculties. She had been a widow fifty years.

Krekel, Arnold, lawyer, born in Germany, March 12, 1815; died in Kansas City, Mo., July 15, 1888. He came to the United States in 1832, attended St. Charles College, Missouri, and was admitted to the bar in 1841. In 1852 he was elected to the State Legislature, and in 1865 was president of the State Constitutional Convention. In the latter year he was appointed United States District Judge for the Western District of Missouri, and he held the office till his death.

Lamy, John Baptist, clergyman, born in Auvergne, France, in 1814; died in Santa Fé, New Mexico, Feb. 13, 1883. He was educated and ordained a priest of the Roman Catholic Church in France, came to the United States as a missionary, and filled his first pastorate in Danville, Ohio, in 1839. He labored in that immediate field till 1848, when he was appointed pastor of a church in Covington, Ky., then in the Cincinnati diocese. Soon after the acquisition by the United States of the province of New Mexico, the Pope erected the territory into a vicariate-apostolic, and appointed Father Lamy to that change. He was consecrated Bishop of Agathonica and vicar-apostolic on Nov. 24, 1850. The see of Santa Fé was erected in July, 1863, and Dr. Lamy was elected its first bishop; and in 1875 the see was made archiepiscopal, with Bishop Lamy as archbishop. In 1885 he resigned on account of feeble health. When he went to New Mexico he was the first Roman Catholic bishop that had visited it in eighty years, and when he resigned the diocese contained 34 parish churches, 203 chapels, 56 priests, 110,000 Catholics of Spanish origin, 3,000 English-speaking Catholics, 12,000 Pueblo Indians under Catholic instruction, and colleges, academies, hospitals, and asylums.

Lane, Harvey Bradburn, bibliophilist, born in Plymouth, Wyoming valley, Pa., Jan. 10, 1813; died in Saratoga Springs, N. Y., Aug. 28, 1888. He was graduated at Wesleyan University in 1835, spent a year in European travel, taught for a year in Wilbraham Academy, and in 1838 removed to Georgia. He was a civil engineer in the survey for the first railroad constructed across that State, and, after eighteen months' service, was Professor of Mathematics successively in Oxford College, Georgia; Dickinson College, Carlisle, Pa.; and Wesleyan University, Middletown, Conn. In the latter institution he was Professor of Greek from 1844 till 1860, when he removed to New York city to become assistant editor of the "American Agriculturist." About 1868 he established himself as a collector of rare and valuable books for private and public libraries, and continued in this business until his death.

Lane, James C., civil engineer, born in New York city, July 23, 1823; died there, Dec. 13, 1888. He was graduated at Poultney Academy, Vt., in 1841, engaged in business as an architect and civil engineer till 1851, aided in the construction of the Illinois Central Railroad, entered the United States Coast Survey in 1852, and was employed in exploring in New Granada for an interoceanic canal company, and in mineralogical surveying in Santo Domingo, Porto Rico, and Cuba till the outbreak of the civil war. Returning to New York city, he was commissioned major of the the One Hundred and Second New York Volunteers, and assigned to the command of McCall's camp at Dranesville. In April and May, 1862, he was in command of the defenses of Harper's Ferry, Va., and in July was promoted lieutenant-colonel. He commanded his regiment at Cedar Mountain, the second Bull Run, Chantilly, and Antietam, in 1862. In December, 1862, he was promoted colonel. At the battle of Chancellorsville his regiment captured sixty-two Confederate officers and men and a flag. At Gettysburg he had command of a brigade, and was wounded. On being transferred to the West, he led the advance on Lookout mountain, was conspicuous at Mission Ridge and in the Georgia campaign, and was brevetted brigadier and major general of volunteers. He was mustered out July 12, 1864. Subsequently he was engaged in mineralogical surveys in California, Arizona, and Nevada; in archaeological surveys in Palestine and the Jordan region; in railroad construction on Long Island, and since 1884 in surveying for the new parks beyond Harlem river, New York city.

Lassalle, Charles, journalist, born in Liege, Belgium, in Oct., 1817; died in Green Cove, Fla., Jan. 28, 1888. He accompanied Sir John Ross on his arctic expedition in the "Victory" in 1829-'33, and on his return settled first in Canada and then in New York city. After serving an apprenticeship as a compositor, he established a printing-office of his own, in which the French newspaper, the "Courrier des Etats-Unis," conducted by Frederick Gaillardet, was printed. In 1851, on the retirement of the proprietor, Mr. Lassalle became owner of the paper and conducted its editorial and business departments till 1882, when he retired from active business. He was a keen journalist, a man of quick perceptions, and sterling integrity. His paper was a steadfast promoter of the interests of his adopted country and city. He was a liberal patron of art.

Lecompte, Samuel Dexter, lawyer, born in Maryland in 1814; died in Leavenworth, Kan., April 24, 1888. He was admitted to the bar in his native State, and appointed chief-justice of the Territory of Kansas in 1854, and held the office during all the excitement attending the legislation for the admission of the Territory into the Union as a State. He presided over the first constitutional convention, in October, 1856, and the first capital of the State was named in his honor. During his term of office, which expired on the admission of the Territory as a State, J. H. Gihon, in "Governor Geary's Administration in Kansas," says: "Judge Lecompte immediately affiliated with the most ultra of the pro-slavery men; declared himself warmly attached to their peculiar institutions; received their unqualified approbation; applauded their acts; addressed their meetings; and went quite as far as the most exacting could possibly expect or desire." Judge Lecompte was bitterly assailed for a charge he delivered to the grand jury of Douglas County, in May, 1856, in which he gave instructions concerning the extraordinary conditions and responsibilities under which they met, and an exposition of the nature of treason, holding that treason could be committed against the Federal Government by levying war upon the Territorial Government. This decision, Judge Lecompte claimed, led to a misconstruction of his motives and words that obtained circulation as late as December, 1884, when he wrote a long letter recalling the circumstances of 1856, reiterating his repudiation of the doctrine of constructive treason.

Le Roy, William Edgar, naval officer, born in New York city, March 24, 1818; died there, Dec. 10, 1888. He was appointed a midshipman in the United States Navy in 1832, was commissioned lieutenant July 13, 1843, took part in the engagement with Mexican soldiers at Rio Aribiqua in 1847, and was promoted commander July 1, 1861. In 1862, while in command of the "Keystone State," he took part in the capture of Fernandina, Fla., and in 1863 in the bombardment in Charleston harbor. During this action, after the boilers of his vessel had burst through by Confederate cannon-balls, and twenty-four of his men had been killed, he hauled down his flag to surrender, but a moment later manned his only remaining gun, ran up his flag, and kept on firing till other vessels in the fleet came to his relief. In 1864 he took part in the battle of Mobile Bay, in command of the steam-sloop "Ossipee," and received the surrender of the Confederate ram "Tennessee." On July 25, 1866, he was promoted captain, July 3, 1870, commodore, and April 5, 1874, rear-admiral. On March 24, 1880, he was placed on the retired list.

Lewis, Henry Carvil, geologist, born in Philadelphia, Pa., Nov. 16, 1853; died in Manchester, England, July 21, 1888. He was graduated at the University of Pennsylvania in 1873, and after several years spent in special studies, he joined, in 1879, the Pennsylvania Geological Survey as a volunteer. At first he investigated the surface geology of Southern Pennsylvania, after which he studied the glacial phenomena of the northern part of the State, and traced the great terminal moraine from New Jersey to the Ohio frontier. His report on this subject was issued in 1884 by the survey as "Z" in its series of volumes. He was elected Professor of Mineralogy in the Academy of Natural Sciences in 1880, and to the chair of Geology in Haverford College in 1883. These places he retained until his death, although after 1885 he resided in Europe. During 1885–'86 he investigated glacial action in Great Britain, and completed a map of the separate ancient glaciers and ice-sheets of England, Wales, and Ireland. He was also engaged in studying microscopic petrology at the University of Heidelberg. Prof. Lewis furnished numerous papers on the geology and mineralogy of Pennsylvania to the "Proceedings of the Philadelphia Academy of Natural Sciences." He was also a zealous mineralogist, and for a time was editor of the mineralogical department of the "American Naturalist." He published "Notes on the Zodiacal Light" (1880), and "Genesis of the Diamond" (1886).

Lincoln, Thomas Blodgett, farmer, born in Philadelphia, Pa., April 27, 1813; died near Elkton, Md., June 28, 1888. About the time of the annexation of Texas, he went there as agent of the New York syndicate to purchase scrip and head-right land. While living in Texas he became acquainted with its leading politicians and with members of the order of Knights of the Golden Circle, and for some time after the beginning of the civil war was an agent of that organization in the Northwestern States. In August, 1861, while so engaged, he was arrested in Cincinnati, and subsequently tried for treason in the United States Circuit Court there. United States Senator Jesse D. Bright had written a letter introducing him to Jefferson Davis, and the production of this letter in court was not only the most damaging evidence against him, but it led to Mr. Bright's expulsion from the Senate. Mr. Lincoln's counsel succeeded in having the indictment quashed, and he was allowed to return to the South. He was the only person tried for treason during the civil war. It is said that, at the instigation of Alexander H. Stephens, Vice-President of the Confederacy, he came North early in 1865, and furnished the authorities in Washington with information upon which they acted promptly, with the effect of bringing the war to a close within a few weeks. At the close of the war Mr. Lincoln received a custom-house appointment in New York. In 1872 he purchased a farm near Elkton, Md.

Linen, George, artist, born in Greenlaw, Scotland, April 29, 1802; died in Bloomingdale, N. J., Sept. 27, 1888. He was educated at the Royal Scottish Academy in Edinburgh, spent several years in England painting portraits and landscapes, and opened a studio in New York city in 1834. He began his career in the United States as a painter of cabinet portraits, and Henry Clay and Daniel Webster were among his patrons. In 1839 he was awarded by the National Academy of Design the medal for the best specimen of portrait-painting by American artists. He retired from studio work about 1868, bought a farm near Bloomingdale, N. J., gave it the Scottish name "Glenburn," and passed the remainder of his days there.

Lippe, Adolph, physician, born in Berlin, Germany, in 1814; died in Philadelphia, Pa., Jan. 23, 1888. He was a son of Count Ludwig and Countess Augusta zur Lippe, received a legal education in Berlin, but removed to the United States in 1839 without being admitted to practice, and was graduated at the Homœopathic Medical College in Allentown, Pa., in 1841. From that date till within a week of his death he practiced in Carlisle and Philadelphia with a success that made him well known throughout the country. He was for many years a lecturer on materia medica in the old Homœopathic Medical College of Pennsylvania, published a standard treatise on that subject, and contributed frequently to the periodical literature of his school of medicine.

Locke, David Ross, journalist, born in Vestal, Broome County, N. Y., Sept. 20, 1833; died in Toledo, Ohio, Feb. 15, 1888. He was apprenticed to the printer's trade in the office of the "Cortland Democrat" when ten years old, remained there seven years, and then set out on a journey over the United States, working as printer, reporter, and miscellaneous writer on various newspapers, as circumstances required. In 1852 he joined James G. Robinson in establishing "The Advertiser" in Plymouth, Ohio; in 1856 he began "The Journal" in Bucyrus, Ohio; and soon afterward wrote a series of stories for the paper. These attracted wide interest, and were extensively republished. After conducting in turn the Mansfield "Herald" and the Bellefontaine "Republican," he became editor and proprietor of "The Jeffersonian," a weekly newspaper of Findlay, Ohio, in 1861. The manifestation of disloyalty in Wingert's Corners, a small hamlet in Crawford County, Ohio, after the secession of South Carolina, and the circulation of a petition there asking the Legislature to remove all the colored people from the State and to forbid any others coming into it, suggested to him the publication of that inimitable series of patriotic satires which will ever remain an important feature of the literature of the civil war. His first letter, announcing that this hamlet had declared itself free and independent of the State, was dated "Wingert's Corners, March the 21st, 1861," and signed "Petroleum V. Nasby." But he soon changed the location to "Confedrit X Roads, Ky.," and all his war letters were dated from that imaginary place. The early letters appeared in his Findlay "Jeffersonian"; but when he bought an interest in and took editorial charge of the "Toledo Blade" the letters were transferred to that paper. The influence of these letters for the national cause was incalculable. They were eagerly looked for and read by President Lincoln, who conceded their value; and that his opinion was shared by others high in authority is attested by the fact that ex-Secretary George S. Boutwell, in a public address in New York city, attributed the crushing of the rebellion to "three forces—the army, the navy, and the Nasby letters." After the close of the war, Mr. Locke dealt with President Johnson's administration and the reconstruction measures of Congress in the same manner. In 1871 he removed to New York city, and was for some years managing editor of the "Evening Mail," and subsequently established himself there as an advertising agent. He retained his interest in the "Toledo Blade" until his death. Besides his "Nasby" letters, numerous lectures, which he delivered through the Northern States after the war, and several plays, he wrote "Divers Views, Opinions, and Prophecies of Yours Truly," "Swingin' Round the Cirkle," "Ekkoes from Kentucky," "The Moral History of America's Life-Struggle," "The Struggles of P. V. Nasby," "The Morals of Abou Ben Adhem; or, Eastern Fruit in Western Dishes," "A Paper City," "Hannah Jane," a poem, and "Nasby in Exile."

Loring, Edward Greely, physician, born in Boston, Mass., Sept. 28, 1837; died in New York city, April 23, 1888. He was a son of Judge Edward Greely Loring, was a member of the class of 1861 of Harvard University a short time, went abroad, and studied in Italy. He returned to the United States in 1862, was graduated at Harvard Medical School in 1864, won the Boylston prize with an essay, and applied himself to the special study of ophthalmology under Dr. Hasket Derby in Boston. After holding brief appointments in the City Hospital and the Massachusetts Eye and Ear Infirmary, he removed to Baltimore in 1865, and a year later settled in New York city and became associated with the late Dr. C. R. Agnew. About 1870 this partnership was dissolved, and thence till his death he practiced alone. In 1874 he was appointed an ophthalmic surgeon in the New York Eye and Ear Infirmary, and held a similar office in St. Luke's Hospital, besides being a surgeon of the Manhattan and Brooklyn Eye and Ear Hospitals and consulting surgeon of the latter institution. He was a skillful surgeon and a thoroughly trained physician, while as an author he was widely known for his original contributions to medical and scientific literature, especially in the line of ophthalmology. He published a "Text-book of Ophthalmology," Part I (New York, 1886), and was completing the second part at the time of his death. He also invented the refraction ophthalmoscope that bears his name. Among his published papers are "Relative Accommodation" (1869); "Some Remarks on Cataract" (1871); "Is the Human Eye changing its Form under the Influence of Modern Education?" (1878); "Conjunctivitis from Impure Dust of the Streets" (1881); "An Improved Operation for New Pupil after Cataract Operation" (1881); "The Effect of the Optical Condition of the Eye on the Development of Character," "Hypermetropia in Public-School Children" (1882); "Premature Delivery for the Prevention of Blindness" (1883); and "An Improved Means of Oblique Illumination: a Corneal Condenser." Dr. Loring fell dead in the street.

McAllister, William K., lawyer, born in Salem, Washington County, N. Y., Aug. 5, 1818; died in Ravens-

wood, Ill.. Oct. 29, 1888. He lived in Illinois many years, served as judge of the State Supreme Court from 1870 till 1875, and then resigned to accept an election to the circuit bench of Cook County.

McCarter, Ludlow, lawyer, born in Green Valley, Morris County, N. J., Oct. 23, 1844; died in Newark, N. J., Sept. 23, 1888. He was graduated at Newton Collegiate Institute, New Jersey, was admitted to the bar in February, 1869, and after practicing in Newton, N. J., two years, removed to Newark. In 1879 he was appointed president judge of the Court of Common Pleas for Essex County, and held the office till 1885. He was considered a sound lawyer, an able pleader, and a judge of great firmness and independence. By the severity of his sentences he became a terror to law-breakers.

McElrath, Thomas, lawyer, born in Williamsport, Pa., May 1, 1807; died in New York city, June 6, 1888. He learned the printer's trade in Harrisburg and Philadelphia, returned home and studied law, and then, removing to New York, became connected with the Methodist Book Concern. In 1825 he engaged in the publication of school and religious books. After a while he abandoned that business, renewed the study of law, was admitted to the bar, and, with William Bloomfield and Charles P. Daly, established the firm of McElrath, Bloomfield & Daly. In 1834 he was elected a trustee of the Public School Society; in 1838 one of the thirteen representatives of New York city in the Legislature, and in 1840 was appointed one of the ten masters in chancery for New York city. The next year he retired from the law, formed a partnership with Horace Greeley, and when the latter founded the New York "Tribune," became its business manager. He was elected alderman in 1845 and corresponding secretary of the American Institute in 1857; edited its annual reports till 1861; was appointed appraiser-general for the New York district, which comprised all the custom-houses in the State and those in the South below Virginia, in 1861; resigned, and resumed the management of the "Tribune" in 1864; was appointed chief appraiser of foreign merchandise at the port of New York under the act of Congress reorganizing that department in 1866, and became a commissioner to the Paris Exposition in 1867. On his return from France he applied himself to the completion of a cyclopædic work which he had projected while appraiser, "A Dictionary of Words and Phrases used in Commerce, with Explanatory and Practical Remarks" (New York, 1872). The high executive ability he had shown at Paris led to his appointment as one of the United States commissioners to the Vienna Exposition in 1873, and his selection as secretary and general executive manager of the New York State Commission at the Centennial Exhibition of 1876. The act of Congress providing for the World's Fair (1881) named him as one of the commissioners, and at the first meeting of all the commissioners in New York in 1884 he called the convention to order, and was elected secretary, with Gen. Grant as president.

McIntosh, John Baillie, soldier, born in Tampa Bay, Fla., June 6, 1829; died in New Brunswick, N. J., June 29, 1888. He was a son of Lieut.-Col. James Simmons McIntosh, United States Army, who commanded a brigade in the Mexican War, was educated by his uncle, Commodore McIntosh of the United States Navy, and served as a midshipman two years. At the beginning of the civil war he was appointed a lieutenant in the Second United States Cavalry, and a year later became first lieutenant of the Fifth Cavalry. He served through the Peninsula campaign, was appointed colonel of the Third Pennsylvania Cavalry, commanded a brigade at Chancellorsville and Gettysburg, was engaged in the Wilderness campaign and the battles around Richmond, led a brigade of cavalry at Winchester, and lost a leg at Opequan. He was commissioned brigadier-general of volunteers in July, 1864; brevetted major in the regular army for gallantry at Fair Oaks, lieutenant-colonel for Gettysburg, colonel for Ashland, and brigadier-general for Winchester; brevetted major-general of volunteers for bravery and skill at Opequan, and promoted to the full rank for services during the war. He was commissioned colonel of the Forty-second United States Infantry in 1866, and retired with the rank of brigadier-general, United States Army, in 1870.

Markland, Absalom Hanks, postal executive, born in Clarke County, Ky., Feb. 18, 1825; died in Washington, D. C., May 25, 1888. He was educated at Augusta College, and first went to Washington with Henry Clay in 1849. He served as a clerk in the Indian Office, and then in the Post-Office Department, and at the beginning of the civil war was in business for himself. In 1861 Gen. Grant, who knew of his large experience in the Western steamboat service, selected him to take charge of the mails of his army, and appointed him a member of his staff, with the rank of colonel. This office he held until the general disbanding of the army in 1865. He was invested with full authority, and by Gen. Grant's express command had the entire army co-operating with him in his difficult and important duty. Though nominally under the orders of the Post-Office Department and reporting regularly and directly to it, he was without a superior officer in his service in the field, and was appropriately called the postmaster-general of the army. Under the system that he organized, every regiment and every isolated command had its postmaster; all these reported to brigade postmasters; they in turn to division postmasters, and they, again, to Col. Markland. The advantage, if not the necessity, of maintaining as regular communication between the field and the home as the exigencies of the service would permit, was apparent; but few, even to-day, can appreciate the immense amount of detailed work, the executive ability, and the personal dangers involved in the task. The effort to keep track of every regiment and every detached company, officer, and man amid the intricacies of army movements seemed almost beyond possibility; yet, under the direction of Col. Markland, the soldiers' letters were handled with surprising promptness, regularity, and care. At the close of the war among the earliest appointmentments made by President Grant was that of Col. Markland to be third Assistant Postmaster-General and special agent for Ohio, Indiana, and Kentucky, which office he held from 1869 till 1873.

Matthews, James Newson, journalist, born in Bungay, Suffolk, England, Nov. 21, 1828; died in Buffalo, N. Y., Dec. 20, 1888. He learned the printer's trade in England, came to the United States in 1846, and settling in Buffalo obtained work as foreman in the printing-office of Jewett, Thomas & Co. In 1850 he established the "Journal of Commerce," and on its suspension within a few months became foreman of the job office connected with the "Express," then owned by A. M. Clapp and Rufus Wheeler. After a year's service, he was admitted to partnership in the job-printing business, and the new firm of Clapp, Matthews & Co. soon became known throughout the country as railroad printers. In 1860 he joined Rufus Wheeler and James D. Warren to acquire and conduct the "Commercial Advertiser"; in 1862 Mr. Wheeler retired, and thence till 1877 Messrs. Matthews and Warren were the sole proprietors of the establishment, and Mr. Matthews the editor. On Oct. 29, 1877, Mr. Matthews announced his retirement from the firm and paper as a result of a disagreement with his partner on local political matters, and early in 1878 he bought the Buffalo "Express" and established the art-printing firm of Matthews, Northrup & Co., both of which interests grew rapidly under his management. In 1883 he added a Sunday edition to his paper, which was prosperous from the start. He supported the Republican party editorially till 1882, then supported Mr. Cleveland's candidacy for Governor, but opposed him in the presidential canvass of 1884, and afterward adhered to the Repub-

lican party. He was a delegate-at-large from New York to the Republican National Conventions of 1872 and 1876.

Mauran, James Eddy, book-collector, born in New York city in 1817; died in Newport, R. I., Nov. 28, 1888. His father was a merchant, owning a large number of ships and doing business with all parts of the world. The son was well educated, and spent several years in foreign travel. By the time he was twenty-two years old he had formed an ambition to collect all available books illustrating and relating to the literature of the fourteenth century. For fifty years he collected, illuminated, and annotated rare and costly books, beginning with Froissart's "Chronicles," and extending his researches both to earlier and later periods. In 1866 he built an attractive home and a storehouse for his treasures in Newport, and resided there till his death, though conducting a book business in New York city. He restored and became president of Redwood Library in Newport, was a founder of the Newport Historical Society, was a voluminous writer on the history of Rhode Island affairs and people, had collected a large quantity of manuscript books and pamphlets relating to the history of Newport, and in his travels had gathered a rich museum of Indian relics, articles of colonial dress, ornament, and implement, and a great variety of curious Americana.

Maverick, Augustus, journalist, born in New York city in 1828; died in Brooklyn, N. Y., June 1, 1888. He began his newspaper career as a reporter on the New York "Tribune," under Horace Greeley, and was subsequently connected as reporter and editor with the "Times," "Evening Post," and "Brooklyn Advertiser." "Brooklyn Argus," and "Brooklyn Eagle." His last engagement was on "Munsey's Weekly," where, as well as on the rostrum, he was an enthusiastic worker for the Republican presidential candidates in 1884.

May, Abby Williams, philanthropist, born in Boston, Mass., in 1829; died there, Nov. 30, 1888. She was a daughter of the Rev. Samuel May, of the old Hollis Street Church, and an early abolitionist, and from an early age was engaged in philanthropic and educational work. She was one of the organizers and became president of the woman's branch of the United States Sanitary Commission in Boston, and discharged the duties of that office with great zeal till the close of the civil war. Subsequently she was elected president of the Woman's Auxiliary of the American Unitarian Association, and one of the founders of the New England Hospital for Women and Children, vice-president of the Society for the Advancement of Women and of the New England Woman Suffrage Association, and treasurer of the Improved Dwelling-House Society, and was a founder of the New England Woman's Club and of the Horticultural School for Women. In 1873 she was one of the four women elected for the first time to membership in the Boston School Board. A dispute as to the eligibility of the woman members led the Legislature in 1874 to pass a law giving women the right to vote for members of the school board, and, after a second election, she was one of the three women to serve on the board. In 1875 she was appointed a commissioner of the State Board of Education, and she served as such till within a few months of her death.

Meany, Stephen Joseph, journalist, born in Ennis, County Clare, Ireland, in December, 1825; died in Waterbury, Conn., Feb. 8, 1888. He received a collegiate and classical education, studied stenography, became a member of the Dublin police force before he was eighteen years old, and for some time was employed by the Government to follow Daniel O'Connell and report his speeches. Unwilling to act the part of a spy, he resigned from the force, and was continued as O'Connell's reporter by the "Freeman's Journal"; and on one occasion, when the London "Times" sent a reporter to Dublin to report a speech at a monster meeting, and O'Connell spoke wholly in pure Irish, Mr. Meany was the only reporter able to follow him and write out the speech. He joined the "Young Ireland" movement of 1848, and was imprisoned three months in consequence. On his release, he went to England, and was employed first on the "Post," and then the "Mercury" in Liverpool. He was one of the organizers of the Fenian brotherhood, and, after the events of 1866 in London and on the Canadian border of the United States, was arrested and sentenced to fifteen years of penal servitude, but was pardoned after a year's imprisonment. In 1868 he settled in the United States, and established the "Commercial" in Toledo, Ohio. In 1869 he removed to New York city, was admitted to the bar, and was employed as editorial writer and Irish correspondent on the "Irish Democrat," "World," and "Star." He was an active member of the Land League, and took part in the defense of Burton and Cunningham, accused of attempting to blow up the Tower of London with dynamite in 1885. While he was employed on the "Star" an accident compelled him to abandon work for some time, and, on his partial recovery, he accepted editorial charge of the "Evening Democrat," in Waterbury, Conn., where he remained from Dec. 1, 1887, till his death.

Mell, Patrick Hues, educator, born in Walthourville, Liberty County, Ga., July 19, 1814; died in Athens, Ga., Jan. 26, 1888. He was left a penniless orphan when fourteen years old, and when seventeen began supporting himself by teaching. Soon afterward he had an opportunity for attending Walthourville Academy by teaching some of the subordinate classes, and thence went to Amherst College, where he studied two years. Before he completed the regular course there he was appointed teacher in the academy in West Springfield, Mass., and, after an engagement of one year, became associate principal of the high-school in East Hartford, Conn. He held this office one year, then returned to Georgia, 1838, and taught in various places till February, 1842, when, on the recommendation of Gov. Troup, he was elected Professor of Ancient Languages in Mercer University. In November, 1855, he resigned, and in 1856 was elected Professor of Ancient Languages in the University of Georgia. He occupied this chair till the resignation of Rev. Dr. Church, president of the university, in 1880, and was then elected Professor of Metaphysics and Ethics. This chair, in conjunction with the chancellorship of the university, to which he was elected in 1878, and the *ex-officio* presidency of the State College of Agriculture and Mechanic Arts he held until his death. With one exception, he was moderator of the Georgia Baptist Association for twenty-four years; excepting four years, was elected president of the Georgia Baptist conventions for twenty-two years; and was president of the Southern Baptist Convention for eight years. He was the author of "Parliamentary Practice," and of several religious works.

Merrick, Priscilla Braislin, educator, born in Burlington, N. J., in July, 1838; died in Holyoke, Mass., Dec. 15, 1888. She was educated and for several years taught in her native city. On the opening of Vassar College in 1865, she was appointed tutor in mathematics and chemistry, subsequently became the head of that department, and held the chair till the spring of 1887, when she resigned, and in November married Timothy Merrick, a manufacturer. As Prof. Braislin she was well known in American educational circles.

Middleton, John Cavarly, clergyman, born in New London, Conn., in February, 1833; died in New York city, July 7, 1888. He was graduated at Yale in 1859, studied theology, and was ordained deacon in the Protestant Episcopal Church in 1860. His first appointment was that of assistant to Bishop Littlejohn, then rector of the Church of the Holy Trinity, Brooklyn. after which he was rector at Stonington and New Britain, Conn., and from 1874 till his death at Glen Cove, Long Island. He was principal of St. Paul's School at Glen Cove from 1874 till 1878, warden of the Cathedral schools at Garden City in 1877–

'79, editor for several years of "The Teachers' Helper" and the Protestant Episcopal Sunday-school lesson leaflets, author of several hymns, and composer of the Christmas and Easter carols for his own church and school. At the time of his death he was archdeacon of the diocese of Queens County, N. Y.

Mills, Robert, pioneer, born in Todd County, Ky., in 1809; died in Galveston, Tex., April 13, 1888. He was graduated at Nashville University, and removed to Texas in 1830. He established himself as a cotton-planter in Brazoria County, and became owner of a dozen of the largest plantations in the South and 1,000 slaves. He shipped the first bale of cotton from Texas to Europe in 1839, and afterward employed vessels of his own to carry his cotton and sugar abroad. During the war for Texan independence he bought and equipped the Texas navy and furnished the means to carry on the war. In addition to his great plantations, he engaged in commercial pursuits, supplied the entire Southwest of early days with its currency, and after the panic of 1857, his credit was so high that his private notes of issue were the only currency that was taken at par. He was known through Texas and the South as the "Duke of Brazoria." At the beginning of the civil war, he was considered the richest man in the South, his estates and slaves representing an aggregate of $3,000,000. He contributed freely to the Confederate cause, and was ruined by the results of the war. With a brother he resumed business, but his losses had been so heavy that in 1867 he was compelled to give up.

Mitchell, Lucy Myers, archæologist, born in Oroomiah, Persia, in 1845; died in Berlin, Germany, March 10, 1888. She was a daughter of Rev. Austin H. Wright, a missionary and physician among the Nestorians at the time of her birth, was educated in the United States chiefly at Mount Holyoke Seminary, returned to Persia in 1864, married Samuel S. Mitchell, an artist, in 1867, and subsequently spent the greater part of her time in Europe. In 1872–'73, while living in Leipsic, she became deeply interested in classical archæology, and published a series of letters on recent archæological researches and discoveries and several illustrated articles on Greek sculpture. She published her "History of Ancient Sculpture" (New York, 1883), established herself in Berlin and began collecting materials for a history of Greek vases and vase paintings in 1884, was taken sick while collecting, and spent the last year of her life in a vain search of health in Switzerland.

Morford, James Chamberlain, patriot, born in Baltimore, Md., in 1795; died there, Dec. 17, 1888. He was the last member of the Old Defenders' Association, which originally had 1,259 members, and was formed in 1844 by the survivors of the citizens who had taken part in the defense of Baltimore, when the British attacked North Point and Fort McHenry in 1814. The members had met annually on Sept. 12, dined, and marched twice around the battle monument. On anniversary day, 1888, but two members were left, and the death of Nathaniel Watts, on Oct. 30, left Mr. Morford the sole survivor.

Morgan, William Ferdinand, clergyman, born in Hartford, Conn., Dec. 21, 1818; died in New York city, May 19, 1888. He was graduated at Union College in 1837, and at the General Theological Seminary of the Protestant Episcopal Church in 1840, was consecrated deacon in 1841, and ordained priest in 1842. He remained in New Haven three years, and then for fourteen years was rector of Christ Church, Norwich, Conn. At the end of this period he was called to the rectorship of St. Thomas's Church, New York city, and with this parish he continued till his death. During his pastorate the membership of families increased from 200 to 500, and of communicants from 350 to over 1,000, and the church built a free chapel that cost $40,000. A few weeks before his death he resigned his charge, and was chosen rector emeritus.

Moulton, Charles William, lawyer, born near Cleveland, Ohio, Dec. 16, 1830; died in New York city,

Jan. 24. 1888. He studied law, and at Mansfield, Richland County, where he settled to begin practice, he became acquainted with the Sherman family, and married Frances, sister of Gen. William T. and Senator John Sherman. From Mansfield he went to Toledo, and formed a partnership with George R. Hayes. In June, 1861, he was commissioned a captain and quartermaster of Ohio Volunteers, and assigned to duty under Gen. McClellan in western Virginia. He also served there under Gens. Reynolds, Frémont, and Pope. In March, 1863, he was appointed lieutenant-colonel in the regular army, and ordered to Cincinnati as assistant to Quartermaster-General Swords, where he had charge of the purchasing of all the supplies for the armies then operating under Gens. Grant and Sherman. He was promoted colonel in 1864, and had charge of the depot, where his expenditures averaged $5,000,000 a month the year round, and frequently amounted to $10,000,000 in a single month, till the close of the war. He then resigned, and resumed the practice of law, first in Cincinnati, and afterward in New York city. He was well versed in revenue, insurance, and admiralty laws, and was counsel for the Government in cases in Louisiana based on infractions of the revenue statutes.

Mulford, Joseph L., physician, born in Pemberton, N. J., in 1830; died in New Brunswick, N. J., Feb. 5, 1888. He was graduated at the Homœopathic Medical College, Philadelphia, commissioned surgeon of the Forty-eighth New York Volunteers in October, 1861, and served till the autumn of 1864. He was engaged in the Port Royal expedition, was assigned to the staff of the brigade commander, and was promoted to division surgeon. Most of the desperately wounded men at Morris Island, Fort Wagner, and Cold Harbor were placed under his charge, owing to his great skill as an operator. In the autumn of 1864 he was assigned to duty at the hospitals of the general army corps; in the following May he took charge of the Foster general hospital at Newbern, N. C., and was thence transferred to Queensborough, N. C., where he was discharged Aug. 25, 1865. After the war he practiced in New Brunswick till 1880, when he was appointed acting assistant surgeon in the army. He spent three years with the army in Texas, then resigned, and was then appointed surgeon for the Metropolitan Life-Insurance Company, New York.

Neilson, Joseph, lawyer, born in Argyle, N. Y., in 1813; died in Brooklyn, N. Y., Jan. 26, 1888. He was of Scotch-Irish lineage, studied law, and practiced in Oswego, N. Y., till 1844, when he removed to New York city, and five years afterward to Brooklyn. He was chairman of the bar convention that drew up the plan of reorganization of the city court, embodied in the constitutional amendment which became law in 1869–'70, increasing the number of judges of the court to three, was elected a judge of the court, as a Democrat, for fourteen years in 1869, and was chosen Chief-Justice by his associates on the retirement of Judge Thompson in 1873. On Dec. 31, 1882, having reached the constitutional limit of age, he retired. He published "Reminiscences of Rufus Choate," and was a contributor to periodicals.

Nichols, James Robinson, inventor, born in West Amesbury (now Merrimac), Mass., July 18, 1819; died in Haverhill, Mass., Jan. 2, 1888. In 1836 he became a clerk in his uncle's drug-store in Haverhill, and while so employed devoted considerable attention to scientific reading, and in 1842 attended lectures at the medical department of Dartmouth College. He never practiced his profession, but in 1843 established a drug-store in Haverhill, and spent his leisure in studying chemistry. In 1857, having disposed of his retail business, he removed to Boston, where he began the manufacture of chemical and medical preparations, then a comparatively new industry in this country. In 1872 he retired, and in 1873 was chosen president of the Vermont and Canada Railroad, holding that place until 1878. He introduced new and improved chemical and pharmaceutical compounds,

and devised simple and economical methods and machinery for their manufacture. His inventions in other fields were numerous. All the modern forms of soda-water apparatus, portable gas-machines, and carbonic-acid fire-extinguishers, as well as the leather-board industry, are based either upon his original patents or inventions. An improved form of hot-air furnace was devised by him in later years, and is extensively used. As an agricultural chemist he gained a high reputation in consequence of his investigations at Lakeside Farm, which he purchased in 1865, and which was one of the earliest experimental farms in the United States. He established the "Boston Journal of Chemistry" in 1866, which, in 1883, became "The Popular Science News," and was its senior editor. Besides many scientific papers, notably those on agriculture, he published "Chemistry of the Farm and the Sea" (Boston, 1867); "Fireside Science" (1869); and "Whence, What, Where? a View of the Origin, Nature, and Destiny of Man" (1882). He also issued Dr. James Hinton's "Mystery of Pain," with an introduction (1886).

Noble, Samuel, pioneer, born in Pennsylvania; died in Anniston, Ala., Aug. 14, 1888. He was the son of an iron-founder and machinery manufacturer, was apprenticed to that trade, and after serving his time, became his father's assistant. While the Kansas-Nebraska troubles were at their height, the business was removed to Rome, Ga. When the civil war broke out, the Noble factories were the most extensive of their kind south of Richmond, and during the war they produced a vast quantity of material for the Confederate Government. In 1872 Gen. Daniel Tyler, a veteran of the regular army, while visiting his son in Charleston, became acquainted with Samuel Noble, and expressed a desire to engage in his old business, iron-manufacturing, if he could find a suitable location. Mr. Noble informed him of a place in Alabama that answered all the conditions. The locality was visited, the two men formed a company, purchased land, and erected a charcoal-furnace at a cost of $300,000, and then began building a town. In 1879 the town was incorporated, and in 1888 the worn-out farm of 1872 had been transformed into the city of Anniston. (See ANNISTON, page 153.)

Norris, A. Wilson, lawyer, born in Lewiston, Pa., in 1841; died in Philadelphia, Pa., May 21, 1888. He was educated at Georgetown College, D. C., and intended studying law, but in November, 1861, he joined the army as a lieutenant in the One Hundred and Seventh Regiment of Pennsylvania Volunteers. During the battle of Gettysburg, July, 1863, he was taken prisoner, and afterward was confined in Libby Prison nearly two years. After the war he studied law, was graduated at the law-school of the University of Pennsylvania in 1867, and practiced in Philadelphia till 1872, when Gov. John F. Hartranft appointed him his private secretary. In 1876 he was appointed official reporter of the Supreme Court of Pennsylvania, and held the office till January, 1881, and then was elected State Senator from the Sixth District. He was appointed United States pension agent at Philadelphia in 1884, held the office till after the accession of President Cleveland, and was elected Auditor-General of Pennsylvania as a Republican in 1886.

Oakley, Lewis Williams, physician, born in New York city, Nov. 22, 1823; died in Elizabeth, N. J., March 3, 1888. He was graduated at Princeton in 1849, and at the New York College of Physicians and Surgeons in 1852. At the outbreak of the civil war he was appointed assistant surgeon of the Second New Jersey Infantry, May 21, 1861, commissioned surgeon of the Fourth Infantry in October following, transferred to his former regiment in 1862, and retained his commission there till mustered out of the service in June, 1864. In January, 1862, he was appointed surgeon of the New Jersey Brigade in the first division of the Sixth Army Corps, and served upon the staffs of Gens. Kearny and Tarbert. He was detailed to the general hospital at Harrison's Landing later in the year, and after the army moved from that place was almost continuously in charge of the Sixth Corps hospital in the field. After the war he practiced in Elizabeth till his death.

Palmer, Courtlandt, founder of the Nineteenth Century Club, born in New York city, March 25, 1843; died at Lake Dunmore. Vt., July 23, 1888. He was educated at Columbia and Williams Colleges, and was graduated a Columbia Law School in 1869, but never practiced. He inherited a fourth part of his father's estate of $4,000,000, and had a private fortune of $250,000. In 1880 he organized the Nineteenth Century Club, which for three years held its meetings at his residence. Of this organization he was president until his death. On religious and social questions he entertained what are known as extreme liberal views. He made occasional contributions to current literature, and left an unpublished volume.

Parker, Joel, lawyer, born near Freehold, N. J., Nov. 24, 1816; died in Philadelphia, Pa., Jan. 2, 1888. He was graduated at Princeton in 1839, was admitted to the bar in 1842, and began practicing in Freehold, where he resided until death. Directly after graduation he entered political life, and through the presidential canvass of 1840 worked for the election of Martin Van Buren. During the succeeding four years he attained reputation as a Democratic speaker, and in 1844 canvassed the State. In 1847 he entered the Legislature, being the youngest member and the only lawyer on the Democratic side at that session. He represented the minority on the judiciary and other committees, and introduced various reform bills. He was prosecuting attorney of Monmouth County from 1852 till 1857, and was a Democratic presidential elector in 1860. He was commissioned brigadier-general of State militia in 1857, and major-general in 1861, gave a vigorous support to the national Administration from the beginning of the civil war, and was elected Governor in 1862. He served in that office till 1866, and was a third time elected Governor in 1870. In 1868 and 1876 the New Jersey delegation supported him for the presidential nomination, and in 1872 the National Labor Reform Convention nominated him for Vice-President on the ticket headed by Judge David Davis. In 1880 and 1887 he was appointed a judge of the Supreme Court of the State, and in 1883 declined a fourth nomination for Governor.

Parker, Peter, physician and clergyman, born in Framingham, Mass., June 18, 1804; died in Washington, D. C., Jan. 10, 1888. He took the academic, medical, and theological courses at Yale, and in 1834 was ordained a Congregational clergyman and appointed a missionary to China. Soon after his arrival at Canton, he combined both professions, established a hospital for the special treatment of diseases of the eye, which he was shortly obliged to throw open for general practice, and preached regularly to his patients. His success as a physician was so large that within the first year he treated over 2,000 persons, and formed a class of native students in medicine and surgery to aid him in his work. In 1840, in consequence of the war with England, he closed his hospital and returned to the United States. In 1842 he returned to Canton, and reopened his hospital; in 1845 he was appointed secretary and interpreter to the United States embassy; was acting United States minister several times; and in 1855 was appointed United States Commissioner to China to revise the treaty of 1844. On the completion of this service in 1857, he returned permanently to the United States. Among his publications are "Journal of an Expedition from Singapore to Japan" (London, 1838); "A Statement respecting Hospitals in China" (1841); and "Eulogy on Henry Wilson" (Washington, 1876).

Patrick, Marsena R., soldier, born near Watertown, Jefferson County, N. Y., March 15, 1811; died in Dayton, Ohio, July 27, 1888. He was graduated at the United States Military Academy in 1835, served through the Mexican War, became captain in 1847,

and major in 1849, and, resigning from the army, engaged in farming in his native county in 1850. He followed this pursuit till 1859, when he was appointed president of the New York State Agricultural College, and held the office till the outbreak of the civil war. Entering the military service, he was appointed inspector-general of State militia, and in March, 1862, was commissioned brigadier-general of volunteers. Subsequently he was appointed provost-marshal general of the Army of the Potomac, of the combined forces operating against Richmond, and of the military Department of Virginia. He resigned his commission June 12, 1865, and on Sept. 23, 1880, was appointed governor of the Central Branch, National Home for Disabled Volunteer Soldiers, at Dayton, Ohio, in which office he served until his death.

Patton, Alfred Spencer, clergyman, born in Suffolk, England, Dec. 25, 1825; died in Brooklyn, N. Y., Jan. 12, 1888. He came to the United States with his parents when a child, was educated at Columbian University, Washington, D. C., and Madison University, Hamilton, N. Y., studied for the Baptist ministry, and held his first pastorate in West Chester, Pa. After a brief service there, he went to Haddonfield, N. J., and thence to the First Baptist Church in Hoboken, N. J., where he remained five years. In 1859 he accepted a call from Watertown, Mass., preached there five years, and was chaplain of the State Senate in 1862-'63, and went to the old Broad Street Church in Utica, N. Y., in 1864. He remained with the latter congregation till 1872, and built the Tabernacle Baptist Church. In 1872 he removed to New York city, bought the "American Baptist," changed its name to the "Baptist Weekly," and edited it until his death. His published works comprise "Light in the Valley" (Philadelphia, 1852); "My Joy and Crown" (1855); "Kincaid, the Hero Missionary" (New York, 1868); "The Losing and Taking of Mansoul, or Lectures on the Holy War" (1859); "Live for Jesus" (Philadelphia, 1861); and numerous pamphlets.

Pearson, John James, lawyer, born in Delaware County, Pa., Oct. 25, 1800; died in Harrisburg, Pa., May 30, 1888. He was educated and admitted to the bar in Mercer County, began practice in Franklin, Venango County, in 1822, and returned to Mercer County in 1830. In 1835 he was elected to Congress, and on the expiration of his term was sent to the State Senate. In 1849 he was appointed judge of the Twelfth Judicial District, and in 1851, under a change in the State Constitution, was elected to the office for ten years. He was re-elected in 1861 and 1871, and declined the nomination in 1881. He became president judge of the district, and retired from service in January, 1882.

Perkins, George Leonard, treasurer, born in Norwich, Conn., Aug. 5, 1788; died there, Sept. 5, 1888. He was educated in public schools, and in 1807 he walked to Poughkeepsie to embark in the "Clermont" for New York city. The steamer trip lasted a day and a night, and he then returned home on foot by way of New Haven. During the war with Great Britain he was paymaster of the United States Military District No. 2, including Rhode Island, Connecticut, and Massachusetts, and was several times in service as major of brigade. He was one of the committee appointed to receive Lafayette in 1824. At the age of forty-seven he became a director in the Norwich and Worcester Railroad, of which he was one of the incorporators, and in 1838 was elected treasurer of the road, which office he then held until his death. He outlived eight of the nine presidents and more than ninety directors of the company. Mr. Perkins voted at eighteen presidential elections, and was introduced to twelve of the Presidents. He continued in the full possession of his faculties until his death, and his one hundredth birthday was celebrated.

Phelps, George May, inventor, born in Watervliet, Albany County, N. Y., March 19, 1820; died in Brooklyn, N. Y., May 18, 1888. In early life he became a manufacturer of mathematical instruments, and afterward of light machinery. Soon after Samuel B. F. Morse had demonstrated the practicability of the magnetic telegraph, Mr. Phelps engaged in the manufacture of telegraphic instruments and the invention of new apparatus, as the service was developed. On the organization of the American Telegraph Company he sold out his manufacturing business and entered the employ of that corporation. He had charge of the factory till the company was merged with the Western Union, and then remained in the latter's service till 1884, when he was retired. His inventions include the electro-magnetic speed governor (1858); printing telegraphs (1869–'78); electrical railroad-signal (1869); magnetic motor (1874); printing telegraph-transmitter (1877); polarized electro-magnet (1878); speaking telephone (1878); switch for electric speaking telephones (1879); carbon telephone (1879); signal-box for district and alarm telegraphs (1882); rotating type-wheels of printing telegraph (1884); and microphone transmitter (1888).

Pickering, Charles W., naval officer, born in New Hampshire in 1806; died in St. Augustine, Fla., Feb. 29, 1888. He was appointed a midshipman in the United States Navy, May 1, 1822, was commissioned lieutenant, Dec. 8, 1838, commander, Sept. 14, 1855, captain, July 16, 1862, placed on the retired list, Feb. 1, 1867, and promoted commodore, Dec. 8, 1867. During his naval service he was on sea duty eighteen years and seven months, on shore and other duty eleven years and six months, and was unemployed nearly thirty-seven years. He was the executive officer of the "Cyane," which took out the Darien Exploring Expedition in 1854, and immediately afterward sailed to Greytown, Nicaragua, and bombarded the place in consequence of outrages committed on American citizens, and was the first commander of the "Kearsarge," but before her fight with the "Alabama" was transferred to the "Housatonic."

Pierrepont, Henry Evelyn, philanthropist, born in Brooklyn, N. Y., Aug. 8, 1808; died there, March 28, 1888. He received an academic education, assisted his father in managing his vast estate in Brooklyn, went abroad in 1833, and in his absence was appointed one of the commissioners to prepare plans for laying out the public grounds and streets of the newly chartered city of Brooklyn, and prepared the plans, after a personal inspection of all the large cities in Europe, that were in substance adopted in 1835. While abroad he also studied the principal rural cemeteries, and on his return drew plans for converting the Gowanus hills into a city of the dead. He employed Maj. David B. Douglas to elaborate his scheme, and in 1838 obtained a charter for the Greenwood Cemetery Company. In that year, on the death of his father, he inherited the greater part of the Brooklyn estate and a portion of that in the northern counties, and his subsequent life was occupied with the improvement of his property and the promotion of benevolent and ecclesiastical enterprises.

Pinkney, Howard, surgeon, born in New York city, Jan. 9, 1837; died near London, England, May 14, 1888. He was graduated at the New York Free Academy in 1856, and at the College of Physicians and Surgeons in 1860, and immediately went on duty as house-surgeon in Bellevue Hospital. At the beginning of the civil war he went to the field as surgeon of the Ninth Militia Regiment (the Eighty-third New York Volunteers), took part in the battles of Ball's Bluff, Harper's Ferry, South Mountain, and Antietam, was several times assigned to special hospital duty, and was forced by an attack of typhoid fever to resign in 1863. On his recovery he was appointed an assistant surgeon, United States Army, with the rank of major, and p ac in charge of the hospital in Frederick City, Md1 After the war, he returned to New York city, and practiced. He was one of the first physicians in the United States to make a specialty of the study of the ear, was senior surgeon of the New York Eye and Ear Infirmary for twenty years, founded and conducted an unsectarian dispensary in

connection with the Church of the Holy Trinity for nine years, discovered the method of discoloring iodine, was a delegate to the International Medical Congress in London in 1881, and published many articles and pamphlets on the treatment of the ear.

Porter, Elbert S., clergyman, born in Hillsborough, N. J., Oct. 23, 1820; died in Claverack, Columbia County, N. Y., Feb. 26, 1888. He was graduated at Princeton in 1839, studied law, but gave it up to prepare for the ministry, and was graduated at the Theological Seminary in New Brunswick, N. J., in 1842. The same year he entered the New Brunswick Classis of the Reformed Church. In 1843 he was called by a missionary congregation in Chatham, N. Y., with whom he remained seven years; in 1849 he went to the First Reformed Dutch Church of Williamsburgh (now a part of Brooklyn), and held its pastorate thirty-four years, resigning in 1883 on account of impaired health. In 1852 he became editor of the "Christian Intelligencer," the organ of his denomination, and remained in charge of it sixteen years. Though he retired from editorial work to give his whole time to his church in 1868, he continued to write for the "Intelligencer," and also contributed to the "Christian at Work," the "Christian Weekly," and other periodicals. He was president of the first General Synod held after the name of the denomination was changed to Reformed Church of North America, and published "A History of the Reformed Dutch Church in the United States," "The Pastor's Guide," and tracts and hymns.

Porter, James, clergyman, born in Middleborough, Mass., March 21, 1808; died in Brooklyn, N. Y., April 16, 1888. He was prepared at Kent's Hill Seminary, Readfield, Me, and received into the New England Conference; was president of the board of trustees of the Conference; a delegate to the General Conference from 1844 till 1872; an overseer of Harvard University (the first Methodist clergyman chosen to that office), from 1852 till 1855; a trustee of Wesleyan University from 1855 till 1871; a trustee for several years of the Concord, N. H., Biblical Institute; Manager of the Methodist Book Concern in New York city from 1856 till 1868; and secretary of the National Temperance Society from 1868 till 1882. Dr. Porter was a contributer to numerous periodicals, and published "Camp-Meetings considered" (New York, 1849); "Chart of Life" (1855); "The True Evangelist" (1860); "The Winning Worker" (1874); "Compendium of Methodism" (1876); "Revival of Religion" (1877); "Hints to Self-Educated Ministers" (1879); "Christianity demonstrated by Experience" (1882); "History of Spirit Rappings;" and "Common-Place Book."

Potts, Frederick A., financier, born in Pottsville, Pa., April 4, 1836; died in New York city, Nov. 9, 1888. He was a son of George H. Potts, for many years president of the National Park Bank of New York city, and one of the first shippers of coal by canal to the seaboard. He became a clerk in the coal firm of Louis Audenried & Co. in 1855, was admitted to the firm in 1865, and formed the coal firm of F, A. Potts & Co. in 1870. In 1872 he was defeated as Republican candidate for Congress in the Fourth District of New Jersey; but in 1874 was elected to the New Jersey State Senate. He served for several years as chairman of the Republican State Committee, and in 1880 was defeated as candidate for Governor. In 1877 he made a director of the Central Railroad of New Jersey; and in June, 1881, on the consolidation of the New Jersey Midland and other smaller lines, and the formation of the New York, Susquehanna and Western Railroad Company, he was elected president. He was one of the largest shippers of coal in the world.

Pulsifer, Royal Mackintosh, publisher, born in Newton, Mass., June 2, 1843; died in Islington, Mass., Oct. 18, 1888. He received a common-school education, and at the age of eighteen entered the counting-room of the Boston "Herald," where at the end of four years, he had risen to a partnership, and in 1869 he became head of the firm. He was foremost in procuring a city charter for Newton, and in the building of the water-works there; and in 1879 he was elected Mayor without opposition. He was the first secretary and treasurer of the New England Associated Press, and a director in several business corporations, and in 1886 became president of the Marietta and Georgia Railroad.

Rafferty, Thomas, soldier, born in Londonderry, Ireland, April 10, 1823; died in Plainfield, N. J. Feb. 21, 1888. He came to the United States in 1834, and when fourteen years old was apprenticed to the hatter's trade. On attaining his majority he began manufacturing hats on his own account, and in 1849 went to California. Subsequently settling in New York city, he was brought under the influence of Elder Jacob Knapp, withdrew from the Roman Catholic Church, and united with the Tabernacle Baptist Church, with which he held membership till within a short time of his death. On July 7, 1861, he was appointed captain of a Brooklyn regiment; July 31, 1862, was promoted major; May 1, 1863, became lieutenant-colonel, and with that rank, though he had long been in command of his regiment, was mustered out on July 30, 1864. During this service he participated in the battles of Fair Oaks, Fredericksburg, Chancellorsville, Gettysburg, Wapping Heights, the Wilderness, Cold Harbor, Petersburg, where he was wounded, and elsewhere, and was brevetted brigadier-general for gallantry in the field, but declined the promotion. He believed that he had been unfairly treated through motives of jealousy, and claimed that, as he had long been colonel of his regiment in fact, he should have received that rank. He was a member of the New York Produce Exchange, and retired from business in January, 1887.

Ray, John, lawyer, born in Washington County, Mo., Oct. 14, 1816; died in New New Orleans, La., March 4, 1888. He was graduated at Transylvania University, Lexington, Ky., in 1835, removed to Monroe, La., the same year, and was admitted to the bar in 1839. In 1844 he was elected to the lower branch of the State Legislature; in 1850 to the State Senate; in 1854 and 1858 was defeated as Whig candidate for Lieutenant-Governor; in 1860 was a presidential elector on the Bell and Everett ticket; and through the civil war was a strong Unionist. He gave his support to the reconstruction plan of Congress, and was elected to that body in 1865, but was not seated. During 1868–'72 he served as State Senator, and also as commissioner to revise the civil code, the code of procedure, and the statutes of the State. He removed to New Orleans in 1872; was elected United States Senator in 1873 by the Kellogg Legislature when William L. McMillen, the choice of the McEnery Legislature, contested the election, with the result that neither was seated; was registrar of the State Land-Office in 1873–'77; and was appointed special attorney for the Federal Government to prosecute the local whisky cases in 1878. He was also an attorney for Mrs. Myra Clark Gaines, and for the French citizens of New Orleans who had claims against the Government for losses sustained during the civil war by the operations of the national army in Louisiana. He was author of a "Digest of the Laws of Louisiana" (2 vols., New Orleans, 1870).

Raymond, Robert Raikes, educator, born in New York city, Nov. 2, 1817; died in Brooklyn, N. Y., Nov. 16, 1888. He was graduated at Union College in 1837, studied law in Cincinnati with Salmon P. Chase, abandoned it for theology, took the full course in Madison University, and was ordained to the ministry of the Baptist Church. After preaching ten years, he applied himself to teaching, literary pursuits, and the study of Shakespeare. In 1856 he was appointed Professor of English Literature in Brooklyn Polytechnic Institute, in 1876 removed to Boston to teach Shakespeare in the School of Oratory there, in 1879 became president of that institution, and in 1884 returned to Brooklyn. He was a brother of Dr. John H. Raymond, president of Vassar College.

Redfield, Justus Starr, publisher, born in Wallingford, Conn., Jan. 2, 1810; died near Florence, N. J., March 24, 1888. He was apprenticed to the printer's trade, and also learned stereotyping. When twenty-one years old he opened a publishing-office in New York city, and brought out the first illustrated monthly periodical in the United States, "The Family Magazine." He published this, under the editorship of Benson J. Lossing and A. Sidney Doane, eight years, and on the death of his brother, who managed the pictorial department, discontinued it, and established himself as a bookseller, printer, and publisher. He carried on this business till 1860, was appointed United States consul at Otranto, Italy, in 1861, was transferred to the consulate at Brindisi in 1864, and resigned that year. Mr. Redfield was the original American publisher of the collected writings of Edgar Allan Poe, William Maginn, and John Doran; brought out "Noctes Ambrosianæ," the revised works of William Gilmore Simms, and numerous miscellaneous works; edited Jean Macé's "Histoire d'une Bouchée de Pain" (Paris, 1861); and translated "The Mysteries of Neapolitan Convents," from the Italian of Henrietta Caracciolo (Hartford, 1867).

Riley, Henry Hiram, lawyer, born in Great Barrington, Mass., Sept. 1, 1813; died in Constantine, Mich., Feb. 8, 1888. He was apprenticed to the printer's trade in the office of the "Columbia Republican," Hudson, N. Y., and afterward worked in the office of the "New York Gazette and Commercial Advertiser." In 1837 he went to Waterloo, N. Y., and was editor and publisher of the "Seneca Observer" five years; and in 1842 removed to Kalamazoo, Mich., studied law, and was admitted to the bar. He then made his permanent residence in Constantine. He was prosecuting attorney of St. Joseph County in 1846–'50; State Senator in 1850, 1851, and 1862; was appointed one of the commissioners to revise the State Constitution in 1873; and became a trustee of the Northern Asylum for the Insane in Travers City and district court judge. He was a frequent contributor to the "Knickerbocker Magazine," and published several editions of his papers in that periodical, under the title of "Puddleford and its people."

Robinson, John, showman, born in Utica, N. Y., July 22, 1802; died in Cincinnati, Ohio, Aug. 4, 1888. He ran away from home when a boy to ship as a sailor, but a shipwreck satisfied this ambition, and he spent several years working as a driver on the Erie Canal, and in a Newport hotel. While at Newport he made his first visit to a circus, and then resolved to seek employment in that line. An opportunity was soon afforded him to travel with Col. Page's menagerie. In four years he became a skillful and daring performer, and for twenty years he was a popular favorite. From Page's menagerie he went with Page & McCracken's circus, and then with Turner's circus, Stewart's Amphitheatre, Hawkins's circus, Benedict & Haddock's circus, and the Zoölogical Institute. He first visited Cincinnati in 1820, and thirty years afterward built an elegant mansion there, which he ever afterward occupied. At St. Louis he organized a circus, and, under a contract with the American Theatre of New Orleans, took it to Havana and then exhibited throughout the United States. With the proceeds of this venture he was able to travel wholly on his own account, and made money rapidly. He built the National Theatre in New Orleans in 1840, made a business connection with Dan Rice in 1845, and built Robinson's Opera House in Cincinnati.

Rockwell, Julius, lawyer, born in Colebrook, Conn., April 26, 1805; died in Lenox, Mass., May 19, 1888. He was graduated at Yale in 1826, studied in the New Haven Law School, was admitted to the bar in 1829, and began practicing in Pittsfield, Mass., in 1830. He was a member of the Massachusetts Legislature as a Whig from 1834 till 1838, was Speaker from 1835 till 1838, and in the latter year was appointed State Bank

Commissioner. In 1846 he was elected to Congress; served till 1852; succeeded Edward Everett as United States Senator in 1854; was a member of the convention to revise the Constitution of Massachusetts in 1853; was the first candidate of the Republican party for Governor; and was again elected to the Legislature in 1858. In 1859 the State Superior Court was organized, and he was appointed its first judge; he held this office till 1886, when he resigned.

Roe, Edward Payson, author, born in New Windsor, N. Y., March 7, 1838; died in Cornwall, N. Y., July 19, 1888. He was graduated at Williams College and Auburn Theological Seminary, and ordained to the Presbyterian ministry. In 1862 he was appointed chaplain of the Second New York Regiment, the Harris Light Cavalry, and served with the army till the close of the war, taking part in the raid upon Richmond, in which Col. Ulric Dahlgren was killed in 1864, and receiving from President Lincoln the appointment of chaplain of the hospitals at Fort Monroe, Va. From the close of the war till 1874 he was pastor of the Presbyterian church at Highland Falls, N. Y. In 1874 he resigned his pastorate, bought a farm at Cornwall, and, removing thither, engaged in the cultivation of fruit and plants and in authorship. The Chicago fire of 1871 first inspired him to become an author. He spent several days amid the ruins, studied the topography of the city, and as the story grew upon him, he "merely let the characters do as they pleased, and work out their own destiny." This story, "Barriers burned away," was published in 1872, and within a few years had a sale of 69,000 copies. All his stories were founded upon American events or phases of American life. "Without a Home" deals with New York tenement-house and retail-store life; "An Original Belle" derives its action from the civil war and the draft riots in New York city; "Nature's Serial Story" describes country life and work and the scenery of the Hudson Highlands; and "The Earth trembled" is a reflex of the Charleston earthquakes. At the time of his death the sale of his works of fiction was thus estimated: "Barriers burned away" (1872), 69,000; "What can she do?" (1873), 44,000; "Opening a Chestnut Burr" (1874), 66,000; "Near to Nature's Heart" (1876), 53,000; "From Jest to Earnest" (1875), 61,000; "A Knight of the Nineteenth Century" (1877), 54,000; "A Face Illumined" (1878), 52,000; "A Day of Fate" (1880), 50,000; "Without a Home" (1880), 60,000; "His Somber Rivals" (1883), 47,000; "A Young Girl's Wooing" (1884), 42,000; "An Original Belle" (1885), 35,000; "Driven back to Eden" (1885), 20,000; "Nature's Serial Story" (1884), 24,000; "The Earth trembled" (1887), 34,000; and "He fell in Love with his Wife" (1886), 38,000. His "Miss Lou," a story of Southern life after the close of the war, was completed after his death, by means of an extract from his diary. Besides these works he published "Culture of Small Fruits," "Success with Small Fruits," and "Play and Profit in the Garden."

Rollins, James Sidney, lawyer, born in Madison County, Ky., April 19, 1812; died in Columbia, Mo., Jan. 9, 1888. He was graduated at the State University of Indiana in 1830; and at the Transylvania Law School, Kentucky, in 1833; and settled in Boone County, Mo. In 1838, 1840, and 1842 he was elected member of the State Assembly; in 1846 was elected State Senator, and served four years; in 1854 was again elected to the Assembly; in 1857 was defeated as Whig candidate for Governor by 230 votes out of 100,000; and in 1860 was elected to Congress. During his first service he was a member of the Committees on Commerce and on Expenditures in the War Department, and after his re-election in 1862 served on the Committee on Naval Affairs. He was author of the bill that led to the construction of the Union Pacific, the Kansas Pacific, and the Central Pacific Railroads; and in 1867 was appointed one of the directors of the former. In 1868 he was again elected State Senator, and after a fruitful service there withdrew from political life. On the dissolution of the Whig party he joined the American, and after that the Democratic, with which he affiliated till 1880, when he became a Republican. Mr. Rollins was the father of the State University of Missouri.

Schmucker, Beale Melanchthon, theologian, born in Gettysburg, Pa., Aug. 26, 1827; died in Pottstown, Pa., Oct. 18, 1888. He belonged to the third generation of distinguished Lutheran clergymen, was graduated at Pennsylvania College in 1844, and studied theology. In 1847 he was licensed to preach by the West Pennsylvania Synod, and in 1849 ordained by the Synod of Virginia. He held the following pastorates: At Martinsburg, Va., 1848-'51; Allentown, Pa., 1842-'62; Easton, Pa., 1862-'67; Reading, Pa., 1867-'80; Pottstown, Pa., 1880-'88. He was secretary of the Committee for Foreign Missions of the General Council in 1869-'88; secretary of the executive committee of the Ministerium of Pennsylvania for many years; corresponding secretary of the General Council from its organization, in 1867, until his death; and secretary of the board of directors of the Theological Seminary, at Philadelphia, 1864-'88. He was one of the founders of the Theological Seminary at Philadelphia in 1864; of Muhlenberg College, Allentown, Pa., in 1867; and of the General Council in 1867. He was recognized as one of the best liturgical scholars and hymnologists in America. Most of his leisure time was devoted to these studies, and most of his contributions to Lutheran literature were in that line. As co-editor he furnished valuable material for the new edition of "Hallesche Nachrichten" (Allentown, Pa., and Halle; English edition, Reading, Pa.), the primary source of information concerning the early history of the Lutheran Church in America. He edited "Liturgy of the Ministerium of Pennsylvania" (Philadelphia, 1860); "Collection of Hymns" (1865); "Church-Book of the General Council" (1868); "Ministerial Acts of the General Council" (1887). The Common Service is based on the liturgies of the sixteenth century, and may be regarded as the result of Dr. Schmucker's research. He took a leading part in the preparation of the service, and with the complete manuscript in his satchel he died on the way to the printer.

Seawell, Washington, soldier, born in Virginia in 1802; died in San Francisco, Cal., Jan. 9, 1888. He was graduated at the United States Military Academy in 1825, and commissioned brevet second lieutenant of the Seventh United States Infantry, served with that regiment and on engineering duty till 1829, was appointed disbursing agent of Indian affairs in 1832, and became adjutant-general and side-de-camp on the staff of Gen. Matthew Arbuckle in 1834. After a meritorious service among the Indians on the Western frontier, he was promoted captain in July, 1836, was brevetted major for gallantry in the Seminole War in Florida, took part in the operations of the Army of Occupation in Texas in 1845-'46, distinguished himself at Fort Brown, Tex., at the beginning of Gen. Taylor's campaign, and was promoted major of the Second Infantry, March 3, 1847. In 1849 he accompanied his regiment to Monterey, Cal. Subsequently he was on duty at Jefferson Barracks, Mo., Fort Hamilton, N. Y., and Benicia, Cal. In 1852 he was promoted lieutenant-colonel, and served in Texas till 1860; in October, 1860, was promoted colonel and as-

signed to the Sixth Infantry at Benicia, Cal. ; and on Feb. 20, 1862, was placed on the retired list in consequence of disabilities incurred in the service. Though unable to perform field duty, he was anxious for military employment during the civil war, and after his official retirement was chief mustering and disbursing officer of Kentucky 1862-'63, and of the Department of the Pacific 1863-'64, was acting assistant provost-marshal in San Francisco 1865-'66, was brevetted brigadier-general, United States Army, March 13, 1865, and was fully retired in March, 1869.

Seay, William A., lawyer, born in Burkville, Va., in 1831 ; died at Shreveport, La., Dec. 21, 1888. He was graduated at Princeton College in 1850, subsequently went to St. Louis, became editor of the "Journal," a Democratic paper, and joined the "Kaw" Society during the Kansas troubles. Removing to Louisiana, he became a teacher in the State Military Academy, and during the civil war was a staff officer, and subsequently lieutenant of engineers. He was admitted to the bar, removed to Rapides, and entered upon practice. He served as a Democratic presidential elector in 1876, and as district judge and member of the Legislature. He was appointed chairman of the commission to revise the statutes of the State, and soon after the completion of this work, he was sent as minister resident to Bolivia. The climate disagreeing with him, he resigned, and returning to Louisiana, resumed the practice of his profession at Shreveport.

Settle, Thomas, jurist, born in Rockingham County, N. C., Jan. 23, 1831 ; died in Raleigh, N. C., Dec. 1, 1883. He was graduated at the University of North Carolina in 1850, and soon afterward began the study of law. He became in 1854 a member of the State Legislature, in which he served till 1859, being Speaker of the House during the latter year. He opposed the secession movement, but entered the Confederate Army as captain in the Third North Carolina Regiment, and having served one year, returned to the practice of his profession. In 1865 he joined the Republican party, and was that year elected to the State Senate, over which he was called to preside. From 1868 till 1871 he was a judge of the Supreme Court of North Carolina, and from that place was called by President Grant to be United States minister to Peru, in which country he remained but a few months on account of feeble health. In June, 1872, he presided over the National Republican Convention. In 1877 he was appointed United States District Judge for the Northern District of Florida.

Sewall, Samuel Edmand, lawyer, born in Boston, Nov. 9, 1799 ; died there Dec. 20, 1888. He was graduated at Harvard in 1817, and at the Law School in 1821, and was admitted to the bar. The anti-slavery cause received from its infancy his most active support, and he was frequently called upon to defend fugitive slaves who were arrested, and threatened with a return to captivity. He was himself once arrested for the part he took in rescuing one of these unfortunates. William Lloyd Garrison early enlisted him as a supporter, and his pecuniary aid enabled Garrison to establish the "Liberator" and continue it through the first year, and even up to its last volume. He p are the arguments and assisted by his counsel and suggestions at the trial of John Brown. For several years he was the Liberty party's candidate for Governor of Massachusetts. He is said to have introduced and secured the passage of more bills for the benefit of women than any other man in Massachusetts. Grateful women placed a marble bust of him in Memorial Hall, at Lexington, and a marble tablet beneath it bears a poetic tribute from his intimate friend, John G. Whittier.

Sheridan, Mary Minar, pioneer, born in Cavan County, Ireland, April 16, 1801 ; died in Somerset, Ohio, June 12, 1888. She married John Sheridan, a native of the same county, in 1824 ; removed to Quebec, Canada, in 1829 ; to Albany, N. Y., in 1830 ; and to Somerset a few years afterward. While she was living in Albany, her oldest child, Philip Henry Sheridan, the future General of the Army of the United States, was born, March 6, 1831. She was a woman of remarkable courage, pertinacity, and benevolence, was greatly attached to her children, and after their happiness and the discharge of her household duties, found her greatest delight in ministering to the sick and needy of her neighborhood. She became a widow in 1875.

Sheridan, Philip Henry, soldier, died in Nonquitt, Mass., Aug. 5, 1888. His birthplace has been supposed to be Somerset, Ohio, but it was recently ascertained to be Albany, N. Y. (For a full sketch of his career, with a portrait on steel, see the "Annual Cyclopædia" for 1883, page 497.) During his last illness, a bill was passed by Congress and signed by the President, restoring the grade of full general in the United States Army, and Gen. Sheridan was appointed to that rank and immediately confirmed.

Sibley, Hiram, financier, born in North Adams, Mass., Feb. 6, 1807 ; died in Rochester, N. Y., July 12, 1888. At an early age he was apprenticed to a shoemaker, but the trade was displeasing to him, and he set out, on completing his seventeenth year, for Lima, N. Y., where he found employment in a cotton-factory. Here he remained until the age of twenty-one, when he established a machine-shop at a place now called Sibleyville, in Monroe County. At the end of ten years he had established a business which he sold out for a sum that enabled him to remove to Rochester and there open a banking-house. Within five years he was elected sheriff of Monroe County. In 1854 he became associated with Ezra Cornell, and with him was largely interested in telegraph companies and grants under the Morse patent. Together they absorbed and brought into one large company twenty others, in which about $7,000,000 had been invested, and thus organized the Western Union Telegraph Company, which was chartered by the Legislatures of Wisconsin and New York in 1856. Of this company he was the first president, and so remained till 1866, when failing health compelled him to retire. In 1860 he undertook his transcontinental telegraph, for the promotion of which Congress passed an act granting an annual subsidy for ten years of $40,000. Soon afterward the Overland Telegraph Company was organized in San Francisco, and subsequently the Sibley and Overland interests were united under the name of the Pacific Telegraph Company. Five years afterward telegraphic communication from ocean to ocean was at the service of the public. Mr. Sibley's next project was to establish telegraphic communication with Europe by way of Asia, across Behring Strait. Wires were actually strung in Siberia and in Alaska, but the successful laying of the Atlantic cable put an end to this enterprise. After retiring from the Western Union Company, he established a seed and nursery business in Rochester, for which he bought, in various parts of the country, 57,000 acres of land. He entered also into mining operations. Notwithstanding all his business cares he was public spirited, and spent large sums of money in philanthropic and charitable objects. He founded the Sibley College of Mechanical Arts at Cornell University, built and presented Sibley Hall to the University of Rochester; built a church in his native town, North Adams; contributed largely to the charitable institutions of Rochester; and performed a thousand charitable deeds that will never be publicly known.

Simpson, Edward, naval officer, born in New York city, March 3, 1824 ; died in Washington, D. C., Dec. 2, 1888. He entered the naval service Feb. 11, 1840, and was in the steamer "Vixen," on the coast of Mexico, during the Mexican War, taking part in the attacks upon the forts of Alvarado and Tabasco, and in the capture of Tampico. In 1856 he joined the sloop "Portsmouth," and was engaged in the bombardment and capture of the Barrier Forts in Canton river, China. Returning home, he entered upon duty at the Naval Academy as instructor in naval gunnery and commandant of midshipmen. In 1862 he was commissioned lieutenant-commander, and while in command of the iron-clad "Passaic" in 1863, took part in the attacks on Fort Wagner, Fort Sumter, and Fort Moultrie. He was fleet-captain of the blockading squadron before Mobile when that city capitulated. He was promoted commander in 1835, and captain in 1870. In 1877 he was detailed at the Brooklyn Navy-Yard as captain, and having been promoted in 1878 to commodore, he was placed in charge of the New London Naval Station, where he remained till 1881, when he took command of League Island Navy-Yard. There he remained till his promotion to rear-admiral in January, 1884, when he was appointed president of the Gun-Foundry Board. From this service he was transferred to the advisory board, and from this to the board of inspection, on which duty he was engaged when he was retired, March 3, 1886.

Sliver, William A., playwright, born in Baltimore, Md., April 10, 1843; died in New York city, May 19, 1888. He was graduated at Dickinson College in 1862, studied law, and was admitted to the bar in Philadelphia, Pa., in 1865. He practiced for several years, wrote a successful comedy in 1871, followed it with an adaptation from one of Ouida's novels, "Alma," adopted the name of Frederick Marsden, and thereafter applied himself wholly to dramatic work. His most ambitious play was "Clouds," an American society drama, for which he received $8,000. At the time of his death he was under contract to write plays for which he was to receive $38,000, and it was estimated that he had made over $100,000 by his dramatic compositions and adaptations. After "Clouds," his best known pieces are "Zip," "Musette," "Bob," "Humbug," "Cheek," "Quack," "The Donagh," "Shaun Rhue," "The Kerry Gow," "The Irish Minstrel," "Zara," "Eily," "Otto," "Yule," "Nemesis," and "Called to account."

Spofford, Richard S., lawyer, born in Newburyport, Mass., in 1832; died on Deer Island, Amesbury, Mass., Dec. 11, 1888. He was graduated at Dummer Academy, studied law, and opened an office in Boston. During the administration of President Pierce, he was sent to Mexico on a diplomatic service for the Government. In 1858 he was a member of the Massachusetts Legislature. He was on several occasions a delegate to national and State conventions, and was president of the Democratic State Convention that nominated Gen. Butler the last time. In 1884 he was the Democratic candidate for Congress from his district. In 1866 he married Harriet Prescott, the well-known author, who survives him.

Squier, Ephraim George, author, born in Bethlehem, N. Y., June 17, 1821; died in Brooklyn, N. Y., April 17, 1888. He was the son of a Methodist clergyman, and was brought up to work on a farm. He became

connected with the village newspaper, and studied engineering. In 1841 he was associated in the publication of the "New York State Mechanic," in Albany, and in 1843 served on the Hartford "Journal." He then went to Chillicothe, Ohio, where he was employed on the "Scioto Gazette," and also served as clerk of the Ohio Legislature. In the mean time he became associated with Dr. Edwin H. Davis, who was engaged in exploring the mounds in the vicinity, and for several years he investigated these prehistoric remains under the direction of Dr. Davis. The results were published in "Ancient Monuments of the Mississippi Valley" (Washington, 1848), and formed the first volume of the "Smithsonian Contributions

to Knowledge." During 1848 Mr. Squier examined the ancient deposits of New York State, under the auspices of the New York Historical Society, publishing his report through the Smithsonian Institution, as "Aboriginal Monuments of the State of New York" (1850). He was appointed special *chargé d'affaires* to all the Central American States in 1849, and negotiated treaties with Nicaragua, Honduras, and San Salvador. In 1853 he returned to Central America as secretary of the Honduras Interoceanic Railway Company, and he subsequently visited Europe in behalf of that enterprise. He was appointed United States commissioner to settle claims in Peru, where for two years (1863-'65) he made exhaustive researches concerning the remains of the Incas, and took numerous photographs. On his return to New York he was for a time chief editor of Frank Leslie's publications; but in 1874 his mind became so seriously impaired that he was obliged to relinquish all original work. Subsequently he recovered sufficiently to direct the final preparation and revision of his work on Peru, but he never entirely regained his strength. The medal of the French Geographical Society was given him in 1856. He was a member of various scientific and historical societies, and in 1871 was chosen first president of the American Anthropological Institute of New York. Besides official reports, scientific papers, magazine articles, and contributions to the "Encyclopædia Britannica" and foreign periodicals, he published "The Serpent Symbol, or Worship of Reciprocal Principles of Nature in America" (New York, 1852); "Nicaragua: its People, Scenery, Ancient Monuments, and Proposed Interoceanic Canal" (1852); "Notes on Central America" (1854); "Waikua, or Adventures on the Mosquito Shore" (1855); "Question Anglo-Américaine" (Paris, 1856); "The States of Central America" (New York, 1857); "Report of the Survey of the Honduras Interoceanic Railway" (London, 1859); "Translation, with Notes, of the Letter of Don Diego de Palacio (1571) to the Crown of Spain, on the Provinces of Guatemala and San Salvador" (New York, 1860); "Monographs of Authors who have written on the Aboriginal Languages of Central America" (1861); "Tropical Fibers, and their Economic Extraction" (1861); "Is Cotton King? Sources of Cotton Supply" (1861); "Honduras, Descriptive, Historical, and Statistical" (1870); and "Peru: Incidents of Travel and Exploration in the Land of the Incas" (1876). Many of his works were translated into German, French, and Spanish.

Stearns, Silas, ichthyologist, born in Bath, Me., May 13, 1859; died in Asheville, N. C., Aug. 2, 1888. In 1875 he engaged in business in Pensacola, Fla., and began to study the fauns of the surrounding waters, becoming familiar with the coast from Pensacola to Key West. In 1878 he visited the Smithsonian Institution, and by his thorough and exact knowledge with regard to the fishes of the Gulf of Mexico, he attracted the special attention of Spencer F. Baird and others. He then spent a year at Waterville, Me., where he engaged in classical studies, in order to acquire a knowledge of scientific nomenclature. Failing health compelled his return to Florida, but in 1880 he became a special agent of the United States Fish Commission and also of the United States Census Bureau in charge of investigations of the marine industries of the Gulf of Mexico. From this time his contributions to the Fish Commission were numerous and large. Upward of fifty new species of fishes were discovered by him, or through his aid, embracing many of what are known as the deep-sea fishes of those waters; and four species of the genera *Lutjanus, Scorpæna, Blennius,* and *Prionotus,* bear his name.

Stevenson, James, ethnologist, born in Maysville, Ky., Dec. 24, 1840; died in New York city, July 25, 1888. He showed great fondness for ethnology when he was a boy, and as early as 1855 went beyond the frontiers in pursuit of information concerning the habits of Indian tribes. In 1856 he entered the national service, and engaged under Prof. F. V. Hayden, who was then making geological investigations in the Northwest with Lieut. G. K. Warren. Acting on the advice of Prof. Hayden, he spent several winters among the Blackfoot and Sioux Indians, studying their languages, customs, and traditions; and then made an exploration of the Yellowstone country. His researches were interrupted by the civil war, and he joined the National army, served as a staff officer in the Army of the Potomac under Gen. Fitz John Porter, and after that officer's retirement, continued with the army until the close of the war, attaining the rank of colonel. He then resumed his explorations in the Northwest with Prof. Hayden and with the United States Engineers. During the winter of 1866–'67, largely through his influence, Congress appropriated $5,000 for geological work in the West. The Geological Survey of the Territories then came into existence, and Prof. Hayden was made its chief, and Mr. Stevenson became its executive officer. Continuing his explorations, he followed the Columbia and Snake rivers to their sources, making maps and correcting the supposed geography of those sections of the country. This work accomplished, he ascended the Great Teton mountain, being the only white man ever known to have reached its summit. On repeating the ascent, he succeeded in reaching the peak of the mountain, and there found a traditional Indian altar of stone. His next work was the blazing of a road over the Rocky mountains near this point. He then joined Prof. Hayden at the Yellowstone Lake, where further explorations were conducted. On the organization of the present United States Geological Survey in 1879, his services were continued as executive officer of the bureau, which place he held until his death. In the same year, with Maj. John W. Powell, he succeeded in obtaining an appropriation from Congress for ethnological research, and the Bureau of Ethnology was established under the Smithsonian Institution. He was detailed to this bureau by Maj. Powell, and directed to explore the ruins of the Southwest. Assisted by his wife, he investigated the habits, history, and religious myths of the Zuni, Moqui, and other Pueblo Indians, also of the Navajos of New Mexico and Arizona, and the Mission Indians of California. The extensive and valuable collections made by him in this field, as well as large fossil, ethnological, and ornithological collections made in the early years of his explorations, are deposited in the United States National Museum and in the Smithsonian Institution. He was a Fellow of the American Association for the Advancement of Science, and a member of other scientific societies, to whose "Proceedings" and to Government publications he contributed.

Stone, James Andrus Blinn, educator, born in Piermont, N. H., Oct. 28, 1810; died in Detroit, Mich., May 19, 1888. He was graduated at Middlebury College in 1834, and at Andover Theological Seminary in 1838. After his ordination he held a pastorate in Gloucester, Mass., was Professor of Biblical Literature and Interpretation in Newton Theological Seminary, and edited a missionary periodical in Boston. In May, 1843, he removed to Kalamazoo, Mich., to assume the presidency of the Literary Institute, which has since become Kalamazoo College. He resigned the presidency in 1863, was editor and publisher of the Kalamazoo "Telegraph" several years, was postmaster four years under President Grant's administration, and was president of the Michigan State Teachers' and the Michigan Publishers' Associations.

Stoughton, William Lewis, lawyer, born in New York, March 20, 1827; died in Sturgis, Mich., June 6, 1888. He received an academic education, removed to Michigan early in life, and was admitted to the bar in 1851. In 1855–'60 he was prosecuting attorney of his county, was appointed United States Attorney for the District of Michigan in March, 1861, and resigned a few months afterward to enter the national army. He

went to the field as second lieutenant of the Eleventh Michigan Volunteers, was rapidly promoted for meritorious services, lost a leg at Stone River, commanded a brigade in the battles of Chickamauga and Mission Ridge and the Atlanta campaign, and was mustered out with the brevet rank of major-general of volunteers. He resumed his law practice till 1867, when he was elected Attorney-General of Michigan, and in 1868 was re-elected, and also elected to Congress as a Republican. In 1870 he was re-elected.

Strother, David Hunter, author, born in Martinsburg, W. Va., Sept. 16, 1816; died in Charleston, W. Va., March 8, 1888. He developed strong artistic abilities in early youth, studied drawing, and traveled in Europe from 1840 till 1846. On his return he spent two years studying drawing on wood for engraving,  then traveled through the West and South, and, establishing himself in his native place, contributed the first of his series of illustrated articles, under the pen name of Porte Crayon, to Harper's "Magazine" in 1852. When John Brown made his attack upon Harper's Ferry, the artist, who lived near by, hastened to the scene of action, made sketches and wrote descriptions. He opposed the secession agitation in Virginia, and organized and equipped, at his own expense, a company of his townsmen. When the State seceded, his company deserted him and joined the Confederate army, while he hurried to Washington and offered the Government his services. He was appointed captain and assistant adjutant-general, assigned to duty on Gen. McClellan's staff, and subsequently served on the staffs of Generals Pope and Banks (at New Orleans and on the Red River expedition), and his cousin, Gen. David Hunter. He became colonel of the Third West Virginia Cavalry; resigned in September, 1864; and was brevetted brigadier-general of volunteers in 1865. After the war he resumed his literary and art work, and was United States consul-general to Mexico from 1877 till 1885. He published "The Blackwater Chronicle" (New York, 1853), and "Virginia Illustrated" (1857); and in later years illustrated the works of other authors.

Sweitzer, J. Bowman, soldier, born in Brownsville, Fayette County, Pa., July 4, 1821; died in Pittsburg, Pa., Dec. 12, 1888. He was graduated at Jefferson College, studied law, and was admitted to the bar. During the administration of President Taylor he was appointed United States Attorney for the Western District of Pennsylvania. In 1861 he became major of the Sixty-second Pennsylvania Volunteers, succeeded to the command of the regiment during the battle of Gaines's Mills, June 27, 1862, but before the battle had ended was himself made a prisoner, and sent to Libby Prison. He was exchanged in August, resumed his command, and was mustered out in July, 1864. On March 13, 1865, he was made brigadier-general "for gallant and meritorious conduct on the field of battle." Soon after the close of the war he was appointed Supervisor of Internal Revenue in Pennsylvania, and subsequently prothonotary of the Supreme Court of the Western District.

Tarbox, Increase Niles, clergyman, born in East Windsor, Conn., Feb. 11, 1815; died in Newton, Mass., May 3, 1888. He was graduated at Yale in 1839, and at Yale Theological Seminary in 1844, was tutor there from 1842 till 1844, pastor of Plymouth Congregational Church in Framingham, Mass., from 1844 till 1851, and secretary of the American Educational Society and American College and Educational Society from 1851 till 1884. For some time he was associate editor of the "Congregationalist" and a contributor to the "New Englander." He published "Winnie-and-Walter Stories" (4 vols., Boston, 1860·: "When I was a Boy" (1862); "The Curse. or the Position occupied in History by the Race of Ham" (1864); "Nineveh, or the Buried City" (1864); "Tyre and Alexandria" (1865); "Uncle George's Stories" (4 vols., 1868); "Life of Israel Putnam" (1876); "Sir Walter Raleigh and his Colony in America" (1884); "Songs and Hymns for Common Life" (1885); and "Diary of Thomas Robbins, D. D." (1886).

Terry, William, soldier, born in Amherst County, Va., Aug. 14, 1824; died near Wytheville, Va., Sept. 5. 1888. He was graduated at the University of Virginia, and was admitted to the bar in 1851. He practiced in Wytheville till the beginning of the civil war, when he entered the Confederate army as a lieutenant. In 1862 he was promoted major of the Fourth Virginia Regiment; in February, 1864, colonel; and in May following brigadier-general. In 1868 he was nominated for representative in Congress from the Eighth Congressional District of Virginia as a Conservative, and was elected, but was declared ineligible. In 1870 he was re-elected and admitted. He was drowned while trying to ford Reed creek, near his home.

Thieblin, Napoleon L., journalist, born in St. Petersburg, Russia, June 6, 1834.; died in New York city, Nov. 1, 1888. He was graduated at the Russian Imperial Academy of Artillery in 1853, entered the Russian army at the outbreak of the Crimean War, and was in command of forty pieces of artillery at the siege of Sebastopol. He was decorated for his services, withdrew from the army in 1857, removed to London, and became foreign correspondent of the "Pall Mall Gazette." He also contributed to British magazines, and translated the works of Macaulay and Darwin into Russian. He followed the French army during the Franco-German War as correspondent for the "Pall Mall Gazette," described the atrocities of the Commune, wrote for the "Gazette" over the signature Azamet Batuk," and reported the Carlist War in Spain for the New York "Herald." In 1875 he came to the United States to lecture, but re-entered journalism, wrote the articles entitled "A Stranger's Note-Book" for the New York "Sun," and subsequently the Wall Street letters signed Rigolo, and contributed to various newspapers and magazines.

Thompson, Cephas Giovanni, artist, born in Middleborough, Mass., in 1809; died in New York city, Jan. 5, 1888. He was a son of Cephas Thompson, a well-known portrait-painter, studied with his father, and when eighteen years old removed to Plymouth, Mass., where he spent two years painting portraits, chiefly of sea-captains and their families. From Plymouth he went to Boston, and in 1837 removed to New York city, where for ten years he was busily employed in portrait painting. He then spent five years in New Bedford and Boston, went abroad in 1852, visited London, Paris, Florence, and Rome, and resided in the latter city seven years. In 1860 he established himself permanently in New York city. In 1885 he was appointed a clerk in the Treasury Department. While in Rome he copied the Staffa "Madonna" of Raphael and the "Beatrice Cenci." His ideal paintings include "The Guardiau Angel," "Prospero and Miranda," or "St. Peter delivered from Prison," and "The Angel of Truth."

Tilton, John Rollin, artist, born in Loudon, N. H., in 1833; died in Rome, Italy, March 22, 1888. He studied landscape painting without a teacher, following the style of the Venetian school, and particularly that of Titian, and spent his professional life almost entirely in Italy. He traveled extensively through Europe, Egypt, and the Holy Land, and had exhibited frequently at the Royal Academy, London, the National Academy, New York, and the Athenæum, Boston. Among his paintings, mostly in private galleries in England, are "Rome from the Aventine," "The Palace of Thebes," "Como," "Venice," "Venetian Fishing-Boats," and "Kern Ombres."

Trimble, Isaac R., soldier, born in Culpeper County, Va., in 1802; died in Baltimore, Md., Jan. 2, 1888. He was graduated at the United States Military Academy in 1822, and was assigned to survey the military road from Washington to the Ohio river. In 1832 he resigned from the army and engaged in civil engineering, was chief engineer of the Northern Central, the Philadelphia, Wilmington and Baltimore, and the Boston and Providence Railroads, and was engaged in large railroad operations in the West Indies when the civil war began. He hastened to Baltimore, was placed in command of the uniformed volunteers mustered to protect the city, and on the dispersion of the Maryland Legislature in May, 1861, went South and joined the Confederate army, in which he attained the rank of major-general. He erected the batteries that closed the Potomac river in 1861, took part in the battle of Bull Run, commanded the Stonewall division after Gen. Jackson's promotion, was in charge of the fortifications in the valley of Virginia, and commanded Pender's division at Gettysburg, where he lost a leg and was captured during the third day's fight.

Tryon, George Washington, naturalist, born in Philadelphia, Pa., May 20, 1835; died there, Feb. 5, 1888. He was educated at the Friends' School in his native city, and then entered business, from which he retired in 1868. His attention was early directed to conchology, and his reputation in that specialty became world-wide. He was active in the Philadelphia Academy of Natural Sciences, of which he became a member in 1859, and in 1865 organized the movement to consider methods for the erection of its present building. Through his efforts the conchological section contributed three thousand dollars to the work, and he added an equal sum. In 1869 he was chosen curator of the Academy, and under his direction the library and collections were arranged in the new building in 1876. He was elected conservator of the conchological section of the Academy in 1875, and held that office until his death. The present condition of this collection, which is said to outrank even that of the British Museum, is due to his skill and labor, and he bequeathed funds for the preservation of the conchological specimens of the Academy. He was a member of scientific societies, and in 1865–'71 edited the "American Journal of Conchology," of which he was one of the founders. Mr. Tryon was a prolific writer on his specialty, and prepared numerous memoirs, including "On the Mollusca of Harper's Ferry" (1861); "Synopsis of the Recent Species of Gastrochænidæ" (1861); "Monograph of the Order of Pholadoœa" (1862); and "Monograph of the Terrestrial Mollusks of the United States" (1865); "List of American Writers on Conchology" (New York, 1861); "Synopsis of the Species Strepomatidæ" (1865). His larger works comprise "Land and Fresh-Water Shells of North America," including monograph on the genus Strepomatidæ (4 vols., Washington, 1873); "American Marine Conchology" (Philadelphia, 1873); "Structural and Systematic Conchology" (3 vols., 1882); and "Manual of Conchology," including "Marine Shells," 9 vols., and "Land Shells," 3 vols. (1879–'85). With William D. Binney he edited "The Complete Writings of Constantine S. Rafinesque on Recent and Fossil Conchology" (Philadelphia, 1864).

Underwood, Adin Ballou, lawyer, born in Milford, Mass., May 19, 1828; died in Boston, Mass., Jan. 14, 1888. He was graduated at Brown University in 1849, was admitted to the bar in 1853, and practiced in Milford and Boston till the outbreak of the civil war. At the first call for troops he raised a company for the Second Massachusetts Infantry, was elected captain, and joined Gen. Patterson's division in the advance toward Winchester. He bore a conspicuous part in the rear-guard fight during Gen. Banks's retreat, May

24, 25, 1862, was appointed major of the Thirty-third Massachusetts Regiment in July, 1862, was soon afterward promoted lieutenant-colonel, became colonel in April, 1863, and commanded his regiment at Chancellorsville, Gettysburg, and other engagements. On the night of Oct. 28, 1863, while leading a successful charge at Wauhatchie, in the movement to relieve the beleaguered army at Chattanooga, he received a wound, at first supposed to be mortal, which prostrated him for over a year. For his gallantry on this occasion, Gen. Hooker solicited for him promotion to brigadier-general, which was granted November 6; and on Aug. 13, 1865, he was brevetted major-general of volunteers for services during the war. Gen. Underwood was appointed surveyor of the port of Boston, Aug. 20, 1865, and held the office till July, 1886. He published a "History of the Thirty-third Massachusetts Regiment" (Boston, 1881).

Underwood, John William Henry, lawyer, born in Elbert County, Ga., Nov. 20, 1816; died in Floyd County, Ga., July 18, 1888. He received a classical education, studied law, and was admitted to the bar in 1834. From 1843 till 1847 he was solicitor-general for the Western Circuit, in 1850 was a member of the Constitutional Convention of Georgia, in 1857 was a member and Speaker of the Georgia Legislature, in 1859 was elected a representative in Congress, in which he served on the committee on expenses in the Navy Department, and in February, 1861, resigned his seat and returned to Georgia. He served for several years after the war as a judge of the Superior and Supreme Courts of Georgia, and was a member of President Arthur's tariff commission.

Van Wickle, Simon, merchant, born in Jamesburg, N. J., in March, 1820; died in New Brunswick, N. J., May 15, 1888. He received a district-school education, removed to New Brunswick after attaining his majority, became a marine captain, and obtained wide notoriety about 1844 as commander of the steamer "Antelope," which was run in opposition to Commodore Vanderbilt's vessels. Afterward he was a conductor of the New Jersey Railroad and Transportation Company, and then engaged in the coal business, subsequently establishing the present New York firm of Van Wickle & Stout. He became a member of the Baptist Church in 1851, and for sixteen years he was superintendent of a Sabbath-school. In 1873 he was elected treasurer of the New Jersey Central Baptist Association, and in 1887 vice-president of the State Baptist Convention. He was also a member of the board of managers of the Peddie Institute at Hightstown, N. J., and gave it at one time $15,000. He erected a church for the colored Baptists of New Brunswick, gave $10,000 to another, and various sums to struggling congregations through the State, supposed to aggregate $100,000.

Vassar, John Guy, born in Poughkeepsie, N. Y., in 1811; died there, Oct. 27, 1888. He was a nephew of Matthew Vassar, Sr., founder of Vassar College, and on attaining his majority was admitted to partnership in his uncle's brewing firm. He was actively engaged in the business from 1832 till 1839, when ill health caused him to retire and seek restoration in foreign travel. He acquired great wealth by fortunate investments and inheritance. He gave an equal sum with Matthew Vassar to the Vassar College Laboratory, and, after Matthew's death, a handsome endowment; to the Vassar Home for Old Men, $15,000; and to Vassar Institute, $65,000, and an endowment. He bequeathed to Vassar College, $130,000 in securities—$40,000 for a chair of Modern Languages, $40,000 for a chair of Natural History, $10,000 for materials and apparatus for the laboratory, $20,000 for a department of music, and $20,000 for a department of art; $25,000 for the completion of the Vassar Brothers' Hospital, and $200,000 toward its permanent maintenance fund; $17,000 for special hospital purposes; his College Hill property and $18,000 for the establishment of an orphan asylum, and $100,000 for a permanent fund; $70,000 and two valuable pieces of real estate to the Vassar Brothers' Home for Old Men; $25,000, besides the property and $30,000 previously transferred, to the Vassar Brothers' Institute; $10,000 to the Baptist church of Poughkeepsie, and $5,000 as an endowment fund; $5,000 to the American Seamen's Friend Society of New York; $1,000 each to the Young Men's Christian Association, Woman's Christian Association, Old Ladies' Home, House of Industry, Society for the Prevention of Cruelty to Animals, and the Associated Fire Department, all of Poughkeepsie; and $500 each to fourteen churches, irrespective of denomination, in the city. Vassar College, Vassar Hospital, and Vassar Orphan Asylum are his residuary legatees, each of which will receive about $500,000.

Wadleigh, Lydia F., educator, born in Sutton, N. H., in 1818; died in Brooklyn, N. Y., Oct. 27, 1888. She became so widely known as a teacher of girls and young ladies, that when the Twelfth Street Advanced School for Girls was organized in New York city, in 1856, she was summoned to take charge of it. In the face of bitter opposition, she agitated the establishment of a free normal school for girls, and by her work as a teacher showed the public that such an institution would be practical, effective, and appreciated. When she had accomplished her project, she took possession of the Normal College of New York with her 300 girl pupils, and entered upon a new career of usefulness, which terminated only with her death. During the summer she had made a tour of England, Scotland, and Wales. She was an exceptionally good classical scholar.

Walker, George, lawyer, born in Peterborough, N. H., in 1824; died in Washington, D. C., Jan. 15, 1888. He was graduated at Dartmouth College in 1842, studied law in the Harvard Law School, and was admitted to the bar in Springfield, Mass., in 1847. In 1857 he was elected to the State Senate, and gave special attention to banking and financial legislation during two terms. On his retirement he was appointed bank commissioner of Massachusetts. At the expiration of his term he resumed his legal practice, and in addition engaged in the banking business, becoming president of the Third National Bank in Springfield. In 1865 he went to Europe on a confidential mission for Hugh McCulloch, Secretary of the United States Treasury, and while there prepared an article on the public debt and resources of the United States, which was published in the principal newspapers of the financial centers. He was chairman of the finance committee of the Massachusetts Legislature in 1868, and in the following year went to Europe on business for his State. After this service he gave up law practice and removed to New York city. In 1879 he was sent to Europe by Secretary Evarts of the State Department, to investigate the subject of bimetallism, and in 1880 was appointed United States Consul-General in Paris, where he served till June, 1887.

Wallack, John Lester, actor, born in New York city Jan. 1, 1820; died near Stamford, Conn., Sept. 6, 1888. His grandfather, William Wallack, was a noted English actor, as was also his father, James William Wallack, who, two years before the birth of Lester, as he was commonly called, became a resident of New York. From early childhood, young Lester was destined by his parents for the British army, and to this end he was taken to England to be educated. His examination was passed, and a commission granted to him; but he soon left the army for the stage. His first appearance in London was at the Haymarket Theatre, Nov. 26, 1846, where he was discovered by John Barnett, an American *impresario*, in 1847. "He is too good for London, and I'll take him over the pond," said Barnett, who at once offered him a large sum for a season in New York. He appeared at the New Broadway Theatre under the name of Mr. John Lester, and under this name he played till 1861, when he resumed his patronymic. Business at the New Broadway was beginning to languish, when the manager announced his intention to produce "Monte Cristo" with Lester in the principal *rôle*. Lester objected strongly, saying: "I have never played a melodrama in my life." But remonstrances were useless, and he prepared himself for an effort which he feared would be a ridiculous failure. When, however, the ordeal came, he was so thoroughly himself

that the vast audience was completely carried away, and "Monte Cristo" created a *furor* that continued for a hundred nights, and made Mr. John Lester a popular favorite. The following season he went to the Bowery Theatre, where he brought out his own versions of the "Three Guardsmen" and the sequel to it, based on the novels of the author of "Monte Cristo." He became a member of Burton's Company at the Chambers Street Theatre, where he began the performances of the old comedies with which his name and fame are associated. In 1851 he went to London for the purpose of inducing his father, then in feeble health, to come back to America. Regaining his health, the father in 1852 secured a lease of Brougham's Lyceum, on the corner of Broome Street and Broadway, and opened it as Wallack's Theatre. Into this enterprise young Lester threw his whole soul, figuring on the bills as Mr. John Lester, stage manager, and for nine years it was conducted with uniform success. In 1861 the senior Wallack established the theatre known then as Wallack's (now as the Star), on the corner of Broadway and Thirteenth Street. In 1864 the elder Wallack died. Lester, adopting his father's policy, gathered around him actors of acknowledged ability and good repute, and by his considerate treatment of every one in his employ won the esteem of the whole profession. Perceiving, in 1880, that the demand for a theatre farther up-town could be no longer resisted, he leased ground on the corner of Broadway and Thirtieth Street, and built a splendid play-house, said to be the most perfect in the world. This was opened on Jan. 4, 1882, and continued under his control till 1887. Early in the spring of 1888 Mr. Wallack, who had not appeared on the stage for several years, suffered very much from rheumatic gout, but in May of that year he was present at the most brilliant performance ever given in the city of New York, known as the "Wallack Testimonial." On that occasion he made a speech full of hope that he might again be able to tread the boards with those who had that evening done him so much honor, but that speech was his farewell to public life. Mr. Wallack married at an early age Miss Millais, a sister of John Everett Millais, the English painter. She, with three sons and one daughter, survived him. He was the author of eight plays: "The Three Guardsmen" (1849); "The Four Musketeers" (1849); "The Fortunes of War" (1851); "Two to One, or, The King's Visit" (1854); "First Impressions" (1856); "The Veteran" (1859); "Central Park" (1862); and "Rosedale" (1863).

Warren, William, actor, born in Philadelphia, Pa., Nov. 17, 1812; died in Boston, Mass., Sept. 21, 1888. He was the son of an English comedian of the same name, who came to the United States in 1796, and made his reputation as an actor mainly in Washington, Baltimore, and Philadelphia, becoming the manager of the Chestnut Street Theatre, in Philadelphia, and of the Holiday Street Theatre, in Baltimore. William Warren, the younger, was trained for a mercantile life. By the death of his father, in 1832, his mother was left in straitened circumstances; a benefit for her was arranged at the Arch Street

Theatre, and her son made his *debut* as young Norval, the character in which his father, forty-eight years before, had first appeared before an audience. After acting for a time in Philadelphia, he joined a traveling troupe, managed by Joseph Jefferson, father of the comedian of Rip-Van-Winkle fame. In this troupe he played all kinds of parts, and sometimes two or three characters in the same piece, the circuit of the troupe being through the rough regions of the West and Southwest, and their theatre very frequently a barn, a log-cabin, or a deserted storehouse. In 1841 he made his first appearance in New York, at the old Park Theatre, and for more than four years played in that city and other places in the State of New York. In 1845 he appeared at the Strand Theatre, London, in Logan's farce "The Vermonter." This was his first and last appearance on the boards of any European theatre. On his return to America in 1846, he was engaged for the stock company of the Howard Athenæum, Boston, and from that time Boston was his home, and he the favorite actor of the town. From the Athenæum he went to the Boston Museum, where he remained, except during a starring tour in 1865, until he retired. The fiftieth anniversary of his entrance upon the stage occurred on Oct. 28, 1882, and in celebration of it a benefit was g at the Museum, on the stage of which he had appeared in 577 different parts, the total number of performances being 13,345. At this time he was seventy years of age, but still vigorous and pleasing. After the evening performance he was escorted to his home in Bulfinch Place, where a party of his friends awaited him. A superb "loving-cup," the offering of Joseph Jefferson, John McCullough, Lawrence Barrett, Edwin Booth, and Mary Anderson, was presented to him. From other sources came costly gifts of various kinds. Shortly after this benefit he retired with an ample fortune. Mr. Warren never married.

Weisse, John Adam, philologist, born in Ropperviller, canton of Bitche, Lorraine, Dec. 3, 1810; died in New York city, Jan. 12, 1888. He was graduated in classics and natural sciences at Bitche College, and in chemistry and philosophy at Metz Seminary, became a Professor of French at the Imperial School in Vienna, and came to the United States in 1840, settling in Boston. In 1848 he went abroad to study medicine, in 1849 was graduated at the University of Brussels, and in 1850 settled in New York city, where he built up a lucrative practice. During his active professional career of thirty-eight years, he applied considerable time to literary and philological labor, became president of the American Philological Society, and published "Progress, Future, and Destiny of the English Language" and a book on obelisks. He was the author of the elaborate article on "Obelisks," in the "Annual Cyclopædia" for 1884. At the time of his death he had in hand a work on medical practice, for which he had made extensive researches.

Wells, Clarke H., naval officer, born in Reading, Pa., Sept. 22, 1822; died in Washington, D. C., Jan. 28, 1888. He was appointed a midshipman in the United States Navy in 1840, served on the home and Mediterranean squadrons, entered the Naval Academy in 1845, and was graduated in 1846. During the Mexican War he took part in the attack on the castle of San Juan d'Ulloa at Vera Cruz, and the capture of Tampico and Tuspan. He then made a voyage round the world, was promoted master, March 1, and commissioned lieutenant in September, 1855, and was on duty on the "Niagara" when she assisted in laying the first Atlantic cable. At the outbreak of the civil war he was executive officer of the "Susquehanna," and with that vessel took part in the battle of Port Royal, S. C., and the occupation of Fernandina, Fla. He was then transferred to the "Vandalia," in which he was engaged on blockade duty at Warsaw Sound and Charleston several months; was commissioned lieutenant-commander on July 16, 1862; was executive officer at the Philadelphia Navy-Yard in 1863; and commanded the "Galena" in the Gulf squadron under Farragut, having the "Oneida" also under his orders at the battle of Mobile Bay in 1864. Subsequently he was attached to Admiral Porter's fleet in the James river till the close of the war. He was commissioned commander July 25, 1866, captain June 19, 1871, commodore Jan. 22, 1880, and rear-admiral April 1, 1884. He was authorized to accept the French decoration of the Legion of Honor from President Thiers, by act of Congress March 3, 1875.

Welles, Edward Randolph, clergyman, born in Waterloo, N. Y., Jan. 10, 1830; died there, Oct. 19, 1888. He was graduated at Hobart College in 1850, was ordained deacon in the Protestant Episcopal Church, Dec. 20, 1857, taught in De Veaux College, and was ordained priest Sept. 12, 1858. In the following month he entered upon pastoral work at Red Wing, Minn., organized the parish of Christ Church there, and was its rector till his elevation to the episcopate in 1874. He was consecrated in New York city, Oct. 24, 1874, and received the degree of S. T. D. from Racine College, Wisconsin, the same year. In 1875, when the diocese of Fond du Lac was erected from the northern portion of his jurisdiction, he was continued in his old field by his own choice.

Wentworth, John, lawyer, born in Sandwich, N. H., March 5, 1815; died in Chicago, Ill., Oct. 16, 1888. He was graduated at Dartmouth College in 1836, settled in Chicago, studied law, and in 1841 was admitted to the bar. He was elected to Congress in 1843, and was re-elected four times. In 1857 and 1860 he was elected Mayor of Chicago. In 1861 he was a member of the board of education and of the committee to revise the State Constitution; in 1863 -'64 was a police commissioner; in 1865-'67 was again a representative in Congress; and in 1880 was a vice-president of the Republican National Convention, but was declared ineligible by the majority report, which confirmed the rule of representation by congressional districts. He gave Dartmouth College $10,000, received the degree of LL. D. from it in 1867, and was elected president of its alumni association in 1882 and 1883. His height, six and a half feet, made him a conspicuous figure in Chicago, and he was familiarly spoken of as "Long John Wentworth."

Westcott, Thompson, journalist, born in Philadelphia, Pa., June 5, 1820; died there, May 9, 1888. He began his career as law reporter on the "Public Ledger," where he remained until May, 1851; was editor-in-chief of the "Philadelphia Inquirer" from December, 1863, till May, 1869; was contributing editor of the same paper from May, 1869, till September, 1876; and was an editorial writer on the "Philadelphia Record" from 1884 till within a few months of his death. He was the oldest journalist in continuous work in Philadelphia, and was the author of a popular history of that city and other works.

Wight, Orlando Williams, physician, born in Centerville, N. Y., Feb. 19, 1824; died in Detroit, Mich., Oct. 19, 1888. He was educated at the Westfield Academy and the Rochester Collegiate Institute, taught Latin and Greek in Genoa Academy, and mathematics and languages in Aurora Academy, and when twenty-three years old removed to New York city. There he studied theology and was ordained,

but never connected himself with any religious denomination. He afterward studied medicine and qualified to practice. He removed to Milwaukee, Mich., became health officer of that city in 1877, and, on the reorganization of the health board of Detroit in 1882, accepted a similar office there, serving till 1888. He was an accomplished linguist, received the degree of LL. D. from Yale University, and published a large number of works, including "Lives and Letters of Abélard and Héloïse," "The Philosophy of Sir William Hamilton," translations of Cousin's "Course of the History of Modern Philosophy" and "Lectures on the True, the Beautiful, and the Good," and twelve volumes of "Standard French Classics." He was also associated with Mary L. Booth in translating Henri Martin's "History of France."

Wilson, Allen Benjamin, inventor, born in Willett, Cortland County, N. Y., Oct. 18, 1824; died in Woodmont, Conn., April 29, 1888. He learned the cabinet-making trade, and while working in Pittsfield, Mass., perfected the sewing-machine that was afterward known as the Wheeler and Wilson. The most important of his inventions were the rotary hook and bobbin and the four-motion feed, and the latter has since been adopted in some form in all sewing-machines. His principal patents were granted Nov. 12, 1850; Aug. 12, 1851; June 15, 1852; and Dec. 19, 1854. While perfecting his machine in Pittsfield, he had a small workshop in a room that he and the late William D. Axtell used jointly. Mr. Axtell was his only confidant during his experimenting days and an important witness in court in the case subsequently brought to establish the validity of his claim to the invention. Mr. Wilson proposed locating in Pittsfield to manufacture the machine, but, as the town would render him no assistance by abatement of taxes, he removed to Bridgeport, Conn., where the Wheeler and Wilson Manufacturing Company was organized and began working under his patents.

Wister, Casper, physician, born in Germantown, Pa., in 1817; died in Philadelphia, Pa., Dec. 20, 1888. He was a great-grandson of John Wister, who emigrated from Heidelberg, Germany, and built the old Wister homestead in Germantown. While still a minor, he went to Texas and served under Samuel Houston in the State's war for independence. In 1847 he was graduated at the Medical Department of the University of Pennsylvania, and had since practiced with success in Philadelphia. His widow, the daughter of William H. Furness, has attained wide repute by her translations of popular German novels.

Worthen, Amos Henry, geologist, born in Bradford, Vt., Oct. 31, 1813; died in Warsaw, Ill., May 6, 1888. He was educated at common schools and at Bradford Academy. In 1834 he went to Harrison County, Ky., where he taught for a year, and in June, 1836, settled in Warsaw, Ill., which thereafter became his permanent home. At first he engaged in the forwarding and commission business, but subsequently became a dry-goods merchant. The Mormon difficulties of 1842 caused a depression of business, and, disposing of his interests, he went to Boston where he remained until 1844, when he returned to Warsaw. Meanwhile his attention had been directed to the geological features of the country in the vicinity of his home, and he studied especially the fossil remains preserved in the sedimentary rocks, and he also investigated the geode-beds in that vicinity. When he removed to Boston he took with him several barrels of specimens, chiefly geodes, which he exchanged there for a cabinet of sea-shells that he carried back to Warsaw. He found similar forms to these shells everywhere preserved in the limestone rocks of that locality, and he devoted his leisure to the exploration of the ravines and bluffs and every exposure of the subjacent rocks that could be reached. His collection grew rapidly, and he soon began that system of exchanges that made his cabinet of such value as to command the attention of James Hall, who secured from him many of the specimens with which he illustrated the first volume of his reports on the geology of Iowa. The palæontology of that State was subsequently placed in Mr. Worthen's hands, by Prof. Hall, for description. On the organization of the geological survey of Illinois in 1851, he was appointed assistant in the work and served actively for three years. In 1855 he was assistant State geologist of Iowa, but in 1858 he became State geologist of Illinois, which place he then held until 1877, when the office was abolished. He devoted himself largely to active work in the field,

and engaged the services of eminent specialists in the different lines of science to work up the material collected; thus he assigned the mineralogy to Josiah D. Whitney, the description of plants to Leo Lesquereux, the vertebrate palæontology to John S. Newberry, the invertebrate palæontology to Fielding B. Meek, and the geology to Garland C. Broadhead and Edward T. Cox. This resulted in the publication of his reports on the "Geological Survey of Illinois" (8 vols., quarto, Springfield, 1866–'88). In 1877 he was appointed curator of the State Historical Library and Natural History Museum, which place he held until his death. During his term of office he gathered an extensive collection of minerals and fossils, which were arranged by him in the Natural History Museum, now in the State Capitol, and also furnished numerous collections to different colleges in the State. Mr. Worthen was a member of scientific societies, and in 1874 was elected a fellow of the American Association for the Advancement of Science. In 1872 he was chosen a member of the National Academy of Sciences. The value of his reports was widely recognized, and besides a few professional papers was his only literary work.

Wotherspoon, William Wallace, merchant, born in New York city in 1821; died there, Oct. 11, 1888. He received a collegiate education, studied painting in Rome, took part in the Italian revolution of 1848, and, returning to New York city in 1849, established himself as a painter. He became a founder of the Artists' Fund and the Sketch Club, and was an active member of the National Academy of Design. On the death of his father, a well-to-do merchant with a fondness for art, he relinquished his art career and applied himself to his father's large business. For over twenty years he had painted only for pleasure, yet in that time he lost none of his enthusiasm for art, and delighted in quietly extending pecuniary and other encouragement to struggling artists of merit.

Wyckoff, William C., journalist, born in New York city, May 28, 1832; died in Brooklyn, N. Y., May 2, 1888. He was educated at Forrest's Collegiate School, in 1854 was appointed corresponding clerk and mathematician to Beebe & Co., who were at that time the largest specie and bullion dealers in the United States.

From 1861 till 1866 he was chief clerk of the National Bank-Note Company, and in 1869 became day and scientific editor of the New York "Tribune." He was secretary of the Silk Association of America from 1878 till his death, and during that period was associate editor of the "Science News"; 1879–'80, special agent and expert of the United States Government for the statistics of the American silk industry for the census, 1880–'83; and editor-in-chief of the "American Magazine" from the latter part of 1886 till March, 1888. He published "The Silk Goods of America" (New York, 1879); "Silk Manufacture in the United States" (1883); and "American Silk Manufacture" (1887); and he had nearly completed a curious work on "Silk Legends."

Young, Thomas L., lawyer, born in Killyleagh, County Down, Ireland. Dec. 14, 1832; died in Cincinnati, Ohio, July 20, 1888. He came to the United States when a boy, entered the United States Army by enlistment in the last year of the Mexican War, served till 1857, settled in Cincinnati, and was graduated at the Law School. In 1861, after the firing on Fort Sumter, he entered the army as a lieutenant of volunteers, was appointed captain in Frémont's bodyguard in August, and assisted in raising the One Hundred and Eighteenth Ohio Regiment, of which he was appointed major and promoted colonel in 1862. He was brevetted brigadier-general for gallantry at Resaca in 1865. Returning to Cincinnati, he was admitted to the bar, appointed assistant auditor of the city, and elected a member of the Legislature in 1865, was elected recorder of Hamilton County in 1867, appointed supervisor of internal revenue in 1868, elected State Senator in 1871, Lieutenant-Governor of Ohio in 1875, and succeeded Gov. Rutherford B. Hayes in 1877. He was elected to Congress as a Republican in 1878 and 1880, and was appointed a member of the board of public affairs of Cincinnati in 1886, holding the office till his death.

Zerega, Augustus, merchant, born in Martinique, Dec. 4, 1803; died in New York city, Dec. 23, 1888. He was the son of a wealthy ship-owner, was educated in London, England, and Balbec, France, returned to the West Indies in 1818, studied navigation on his father's vessels, and became a ship-owner and captain in 1820. During the next fifteen years he was engaged in the West India and South American trade, sailing his vessels himself, and making and losing three fortunes. While temporarily living in La Guayra, he became intimate with Gen. Simon Bolivar, encouraged his scheme for liberating the South American states from Spanish rule, and in 1831 made a voyage to the United States to procure munitions of war for him. In 1835 he established himself as a coffee-merchant in New York city, and owned and managed a fleet of thirty vessels, noted in their day as the "Z" line, till 1855, when he retired from business and sold his vessels. One of his ships, the "Antartic," rescued over 300 United States soldiers from the "San Francisco" when she foundered at sea, in 1854. He lived in retirement at Throgg's Neck from 1855 till 1863, and after that spent his winters in New York.

OBITUARIES, FOREIGN. Sketches of a few of the most eminent foreigners that died in 1888 will be found in their own alphabetical places in this volume, accompanied with portraits.

Arnason, Jon, an Icelandic scholar, born Aug. 17, 1819; died in Reykjavik, Iceland, Nov. 13, 1888. He was for many years librarian of the public library of Iceland, which was largely increased under his direction, and did much to preserve the memorials of the early history of Iceland. Dr. Arnason was famous for his great collection of Icelandic sagas. He published, with Grimson, a collection of Icelandic tales, followed by a larger one of "Popular Legends of Iceland" (Leipsic, 1862–'64).

Baden, Prince Ludwig Wilhelm, second son of the Grand-Duke and of Princess Louise of Prussia, born in Baden, June 12, 1865; died in Freiburg, Feb. 23, 1888. He was a lieutenant of the Uhlan Guards at Potsdam, and a favorite grandson of the Emperor Wilhelm. Leaving active service to pursue his studies at Freiburg, he was attacked by inflammation of the lungs, and died unexpectedly.

Bagallay, Sir Richard, an English lawyer, born in Stockwell (now a part of London), May 13, 1816; died in Brighton, Nov. 13, 1888. He was educated at Oxford, becoming a fellow of Caius College in 1839, and was called to the bar in 1843. He entered Parliament in 1865, was appointed Solicitor-General under Mr. Disraeli in August, 1868, was knighted, and went out of office with his party in December of the same year. When the Conservatives defeated Mr. Gladstone in 1874, on the issue of the abolition of the income-tax, Sir Richard Bagallay resumed the office he had held, but before the end of the year he succeeded the retiring Attorney-General, Sir John Karslake, and in the autumn of 1875 was appointed a judge of the Court of Appeal. He retired in 1885, having for some years taken the lead as senior justice in the chancery division.

Bargash ben Said, Sultan or Seyyid of Zanzibar, born in 1835; died in Zanzibar, March 27, 1888. He succeeded his elder brother, Majid, Oct. 7, 1870. Formerly he administered an extensive range of coast extending northward and southward from the island of Zanzibar, where he had his residence, and maintained an army to guard the caravan-routes into the interior. Great Britain compelled him to sign a treaty in 1873, pledging himself to suppress the slave-trade in his dominions. A few months before his death Germany obtained a lease or cession of the coast-line lying in front of the territory of the East African Company, and England obtained the grant of the coast giving access to her newly acquired possessions, leaving the Sultan only a fraction of his former dominion on the mainland. He was succeeded by his brother, who rules under the title of Seyyid Khalifa.

Bartsch, Karl Friedrich Adolf Konrad, a German philologist, born in Sprottau, Silesia, Feb. 25, 1832; died in Heidelberg, Feb. 20, 1888. He practiced poetical composition in German and Latin while at the gymnasium, and studied Germanic philology at Breslau and Berlin. Taking his doctor's degree in 1853, he went to Paris to study the poetry of the Troubadours, which he was one of the earliest to introduce to the attention of German students. In 1855 he became librarian of the German Museum in Nuremberg, and in the same year published a reading-book of Provençal literature, which was followed by a chrestomathy of Troubadour poetry and an edition of the songs of Pierre Vidal. He also edited " Karl," an epic poem by Stricker, an Austrian poet of the Thirteenth century. In 1858 Bartsch was called to the professorship of Modern and German Literature at Rostock, where he established a Seminary of German Philology. He became editor of " Germania," the periodical devoted to German antiquities, in 1869, and in 1871 went to Heidelberg as Professor of Early German Literature. His voluminous published works include critical editions of Old and Middle High German poets, many of whose works were first issued in print by him, and of old French romances, pastorals, and popular songs, poetry of his own, of which a collected edition has been published, and lectures and essays, some of which were republished in 1883.

Beard Charles, an English divine, born in 1828; died at Liverpool, March 9, 1888. He became a minister of the Unitarian church at Hyde, removing subsequently to Liverpool. In 1861 was published his " Port Royal, a Contribution to the History of Religion and Literature in France." He founded the " Theological Review," in 1864. His other important works were, " Outlines of Christian Doctrine " and a translation of M. Renan's " Lectures on the Influence of the Institutions, Thought, and Culture of Rome on Christianity " (1880). In 1883 he delivered the Hibbert Lectures in London and Oxford, taking for his subject " The Reformation of the Sixteenth Century in its Relation to Modern Thought and Knowledge."

Bergaigne, Abel, a French Orientalist, died in Paris Aug. 20, 1888. He held the chair of Sanskrit at the Sorbonne. His translation of the gnomic poem, " Le Bhāminīvilāsa," was published in 1872. In 1879 he published a translation of the Buddhist drama, " Nāgānanda " with the Sanskrit text, and from 1878 to 1883, he issued three volumes entitled " The Vedic Religion, after the Hymns of the Rig-Veda." He translated into French the drama, " Sacountala," in 1884, and during the same year began the issue of " Etudes sur le Lexique du Rig-Veda," which was still in progress at the time of his death.

Brand, Sir Johannes Henricus, President of the Orange Free State, born in Cape Town, Dec. 6, 1823; died July 15, 1888. He was the son of the Speaker of the Cape House of Representatives, studied law in Leyden, and in 1849 began practice in the Supreme Court in Cape Town. In 1863 he became Professor of Law in the South African College, and in 1863 he was elected President of the Orange River Free State, to which post he was re-elected every five years until his death. It was owing to his influence that the Free State held aloof from the Transvaal war and has declined to enter into the plans of the Transvaal Republic for a union of the three South African republics, accepting in preference the railroad and tariff proposals of Cape Colony. In recognition of his friendly services to England, the Queen knighted him.

Cameron, Sir Duncan Alexander, a Scottish soldier, born in 1808; died at Blackheath, June 7, 1888. He entered the army at the age of seventeen; became a captain in 1833, major in 1839, colonel in 1854, major-general in 1859, and general in 1873. In the Crimean War he was present at the battle of Alma, and commanded the Highland Brigade at the battle of Balaklava. He was also actively engaged in the siege of Sebastopol, and on the assault on the Redan. He commanded the forces in the New Zealand war of 1863-'65, in the battles of Kalikara, Kohasoa, Tangiriri, and Gate Pah. From 1868 to 1875 he was governor of the Military College at Sandhurst. In 1878 he was retired.

Carnot, Lazare Hippolyte, a French statesman, father of the President of the French Republic, born in St. Omer, April 6, 1801; died in Paris, March 16, 1888. He was the son of the War Minister of the Revolution, and at the restoration accompanied his father into exile. Returning to France in 1823, he studied law, and became a supporter of the St. Simon sect, but seceded when Enfantin introduced the doctrine of free love. He was elected deputy in 1839, and after the revolution of 1848 became Minister of Education. He was forced to retire from this office in consequence of a circular that he addressed to schoolmasters, enjoining on them activity at elections. He was one of the three Republican deputies that refused to take the oath of allegiance after the coup d'état, and was unseated. He entered the Chamber again in 1863, but was defeated by Gambetta in 1869. In 1871 he was again elected deputy, and on the formation of the Senate in 1875 was elected a life member. He published biographies of his father and of Bishop Grégoire, and edited the memoirs of Barère.

Correnti, Cesare, an Italian statesman, born in 1815; died in Meina, Oct. 4, 1888. He took part in the conflicts for the deliverance and unification of Italy, and was Minister of Education in 1867 and again from 1869 till 1872, when he prepared and carried through Parliament the laws for pensioning elementary schoolteachers and abolishing the theological faculties in the universities.

Corti Luigi, an Italian diplomatist, died in Rome, Feb. 18, 1888. He studied mathematics in Padua, took part in the Revolution of 1848, filling an office in the Sardinian Ministry for Foreign Affairs, and afterward serving in the ranks against Austria. In 1850 he entered the diplomatic service as secretary of legation at London. He rose to be councilor in 1862, and filled in rapid succession the posts of *chargé d'affaires*, minister resident, and minister plenipotentiary in Brussels, Stockholm, Madrid, and Washington. In 1873 he presided over the Alabama Commission, and two years later he went to Constantinople as ambassador, where he so skillfully asserted the position of Italy in the complicated Eastern question that from that time forth he was the chief diplomatic authority in Italy in Oriental affairs. When the center of gravity in European diplomacy shifted in the direction of Constantinople. Carioli, in 1878, called Corti into his Cabinet as Minister of Foreign Affairs, and, when the Congress of Berlin was convened, while retaining his post in the Cabinet, he went as the Italian representative. Soon after the work of the Congress was finished he resigned on account of a ministerial crisis, having been severely attacked by Crispi and others of the Opposition, because he had secured no territorial advantage for Italy, and went to London as ambassador, in which post he remained until he was removed by the Crispi ministry. He was a member of the Italian Senate.

Crampton, Thomas Russell, an English engineer, born in Broadstairs, Kent, in 1816; died in April, 1888. After receiving a liberal education he became the pupil of an eminent mechanical engineer in London. He designed the first locomotive for the Great Western Railway, and between 1842 and 1847 he perfected the type of locomotive that bears his name, in which a long boiler, outside cylinders, and a low center of gravity are the essential features. In 1851 his locomotives won for him the grand medal in the Great Exhibition. He laid the first submarine cable between Dover and Calais in 1851.

Debray, Jules Henri, French chemist, born in France, July 26, 1827; died in Paris, July 19, 1888. He was educated in Paris, and received the degree of Doctor of Sciences in 1855. Subsequently he was called to the chair of Chemistry at the Charlemagne Lyceum, and was assistant at the Normal School. In 1868 he was advanced to the rank of Maitre de Conférences. He was also assayer at the testing department of the mint. In 1877 he was chosen a member of the French Academy of Sciences, and was vice-president of the Society of Encouragement for National Industry. Prof. Debray was a member of the Higher Council of Public Instruction, and of the Consulting Committee of Arts and Manufactures. The greater part of his original work was performed in association with Henri Sainte-Claire Deville, notably, the investigation of the properties of the rarer platinum metals, such as osmium and iridium, which at that time were but little known, also in the difficult construction of the standard metre of platinum alloyed with iridium, adopted by the International Metric Commission, and in the development of Salute-Claire Deville's ideas on dissociation. His publications include, besides his thesis for the doctorate on " Glucinum and its Compounds " (1855), " Des Principales Sources de Lumière " (1863); " Métallurgie du Platine et des Metaux qui l'Accompagnent " (2 vols., 1863); and " Cours Élémentaire de Chemie " (2 vols., 1865).

Delius, Nikolaus, a German Shakespearian commentator, born in Bremen, Oct. 19, 1813; died in Berlin, Nov. 18, 1888. He studied at Bonn and Berlin, acquired a name as a scholar in Sanskrit and in the Provençal and English languages and literature, and was professor of those subjects at Bonn from 1855 until his death. Besides notes on the Romance literature, he published " The Shakespeare Myth " (1851); an edition of Shakespeare's " Works " (7 vols., 1854–'61); a volume on the English theatre in Shakespeare's time (1853); and a " Shakespeare Lexicon " (1854).

Devon, William Reginald Courtenay, Earl of, an English nobleman, born April 14, 1807; died at Powderham Castle, near Exeter, Nov. 18, 1888. He was graduated at Oxford in 1828, entered the House of Commons in 1841 as a Conservative, became a Peelite, and was secretary to the Poor Law Board from 1852 till 1858. Subsequently rejoining the Conservatives, he entered Lord Derby's Cabinet in July, 1866, as Chancellor of the Duchy of Lancaster, exchanging that office in May, 1867, for that of president of the Poor Law Board, which he held until December, 1868. He was a promoter of railroad enterprises in Devonshire and in Ireland, and was a supporter of religious, educational, and philanthropic societies.

Doyle, Sir Francis Hastings, Bart., an English poet, born in Yorkshire, Aug. 22, 1810; died in London, June 8, 1888. He was graduated with honor at Oxford in 1832, was called to the bar shortly afterward, succeeded to a baronetcy in 1839, and was appointed receiver-general of customs in 1846. He was elected Professor of Poetry at Oxford in 1867, and in 1872 was re-elected. He published ballads and other poetical pieces, and in 1886 a volume of " Reminiscences and Opinions."

Duclerc, Charles Théodore Eugène, a French statesman, born in Bagnères-de-Bigorre, Nov. 9, 1812; died in July, 1888. He was a prominent Republican in 1848, a frequent speaker in the Constituent Assembly, and for a time Minister of Finance. During the time of the empire he devoted himself to private business. He was a member of the National Assembly that was summoned to make peace with Germany, was made President of the Republican Left, was regarded as an authority on financial questions, was elected Vice-President of the Chamber, and in 1875 was chosen a Senator for life, and was looked upon in the Senate as a leader of the Moderate Left. In 1882, after M. de Freycinet's defeat, on the proposal of a joint expedition to Egypt with England, M. Grévy invited him, after the other Republican leaders had declined, to form a working ministry, which he successfully accomplished by inducing several Gambettists to accept portfolios.

Duncan, Francis, a British artillery officer, born in Aberdeen, Scotland, in 1835; died in London, Nov. 16, 1888. He was graduated at the University of Aberdeen, passed the artillery examination at the head of all competitors, rose rapidly in the army, and after holding several staff appointments was selected by Sir Evelyn Wood, in 1883, to reorganize the Egyptian artillery. He commanded the outpost at Wady Halfa in 1884–'85, and rendered important services in caring for the refugees that Gen. Gordon sent down the Nile from Khartoum. Col. Duncan was a Fellow of the Geological and other learned societies, author of " The English in Spain " and " History of the Royal Artillery," a founder of the St. John's Ambulance Association, and a prime mover in the establishment of coffee-palaces in garrison towns. He was elected to Parliament as a Conservative after his return from Egypt in 1885.

Eassie, William, an English sanitarian, born in Lochee, Forfarshire, Scotland, in 1832; died in South Hampstead, England, Aug. 16, 1888. He was a civil engineer by training, was one of the designers of the Renkioi Hospital during the Crimean War, and made the first excavations on the site of Troy after the conclusion of hostilities. He was one of the founders of the Sanitary Institute of Great Britain, and in 1874 of the Cremation Society, the " Transactions " of which he edited. He published " Healthy Houses," a work that gave an impetus to sanitary reform, and subsequently a maturer work on " Sanitary Arrangements for Dwellings." In 1874 he published " Cremation of the Dead," a standard work on the subject.

Etex, Antoine, a French sculptor, born in Paris March 20, 1808; died there, July 8, 1888. He belonged to a family of artists, and in 1828 gained the prize of Rome with his " Hyacinth slain by Apollo." He exhibited the colossal group of " Cain " in 1833. The power and originality displayed in this work caused M. Thiers to commission the sculptor to execute the groups representing " 1814 " and " 1815 " on the Arc de l'Étoile. He would not exhibit again at the Salon, because some of his works were rejected, until 1841, when he appeared with the " Tomb of

Géricault." Étex was distinguished as a painter, engraver, and architect, as well as in sculpture. His most important statues are "Léda," "Olympia," "Rossini," "The Cholera," "Blanche de Castille," "Charlemagne," "St. Augustine," and "Gen. Lecourbe." He executed busts of Émile de Girardin, Delacroix, and M. de Lesseps, and many medallions and portraits. In 1868 he was commissioned with the execution of the monument to Ingres at Montauban. His most famous paintings are "Christ Preaching," "Sappho," "Dante and Beatrice," "Jacob Blessing the Sons of Joseph," "The Flight into Egypt," "Romeo and Juliet," and "The Great Men of the United States (for the City Hall, New York). He drew the plans for a fountain and swimming-schools in the woods of Boulogne and Vincennes and for several monuments and tombs. He published an "Essay on the Beautiful" (1851) and a volume of art studies on "Pradier and Scheffer" (1859).

Eversley, Charles Shaw-Lefevre, Viscount, an English statesman, born in London Feb. 22, 1794; died at Heckfield Place, his seat in Hampshire, Dec. 28, 1888. He was graduated at Cambridge in 1815, and in 1819 was called to the bar. He married a daughter of Samuel Whitbread and niece of Earl Grey in 1817. In 1830 he entered Parliament, and in 1831 was returned as a Liberal for his own county, the northern division of which he represented after the passage of the reform act of 1832. His tact, courtesy, fine presence, and knowledge of business made him the choice of his party and of the country gentlemen for the Speaker's chair when it was vacated in 1839, and on May 27 he was elected by a majority of eighteen over the Tory candidate. The fairness, firmness, readiness, and good temper with which he directed the stormy debates of the period, with the aid of new forms of procedure of his own suggestion, led to his retention in the chair, on the motion of Sir Robert Peel in 1841. Mr. Shaw-Lefevre governed the proceedings of the House during the embittered contest over free trade, was continued in the chair as a matter of course when a general election placed Lord John Russell at the head of the Government in 1847. And when the Tories again came in to power in 1852, Mr. Disraeli, as leader of the House, followed the precedent set by Sir Robert Peel, and Mr. Shaw-Lefevre was re-elected by acclamation. He resigned when the fourth Parliament over which he had presided was dissolved by Lord Palmerston in 1857, having served longer than any of his predecessors except Arthur Onslow. He was created Viscount Eversley, of Heckfield, in the county of Southampton, and devoted himself to farming and horticulture and to his duties as chairman of quarter sessions, colonel of Yeomanry, Governor of the Isle of Wight, and ecclesiastical commissioner.

Feyen-Perrin, François, a French artist, born in Bey-sur-Seille in 1829, died Oct. 14, 1888. He studied in the École des Beaux Arts, and relinquished the contest for the prize of Rome on receiving the commission to paint the curtain for the Théâtre des Italiens, which still remains one of the most beautiful designs of its kind. He devoted himself at first to historical painting, which brought him prizes, but only small pecuniary rewards. His best works of this period are "La Barque de Caron" (1857), "Le Cercle des Voluptueux de Dante" (1859), "Fête Venetienne" (1861), "La Muse de Boulanger" (1863), and "Charles le Téméraire retrouvé après la Bataille de Nanez" (1865). At the time when this last was painted he had already begun to search for a more popular class of subjects. In 1864 he exhibited the "Gréve," which was followed by "La Vanneuse," a work that was much admired. A painting representing oyster-dredgers returning from fishing hangs in the Luxembourg Palace. Others of his works of the later period are "Naufrage de l'Evening Star" (1868), "Melancholie" (1870), "Le Printemps" (1872), and "La Rosée" (1874). He was one of the Society of Ten, the members of which each year exposed their new works at the Hôtel Drouot.

Fleischer, Heinrich Leberecht, a German philologist, born in Schandau, Saxony, Feb. 21, 1801; died in Leipsic, Feb. 15. 1888. He was a pupil of De Sacy's, and became the head of a large school of Arabic scholars in Germany. He began lecturing on Arabic at Leipsic in 1835. His most important works were editions of Abulfeda's "Historia ante-Islamica" and Beidhawi's "Commentary on the Koran." He was a foreign member of the French Institute.

Galliera, Duchess of, an Italian benefactress, born in Paris; died in Genoa, Dec. 10, 1888. She was the daughter of the Marquis de Brignole-Sall, who represented Peidmont in Paris for many years under Carlo Alberto, and married the Duke de Galliera-Ferrari, the wealthiest of Italian speculators, who acquired ducal and princely rank by the purchase of the estate of Galliera, near Bologua, and that of Lucedio, in the vicinity of Turin. After his death his widow carried out his wish to give 20,000,000 lire toward the harbor improvements of the city of Genoa and 6,000,000 lire for laborers' dwellings. Their son, renouncing the titles and wealth that his father had won by reprehensible practices, induced a Frenchman to adopt him under the French law, in order that he might take the name De la Renaudière-Ferrari, and became a Professor of German History at Brussels. The duchess gave the Palazzo Rosso, with its library and picture-gallery and a fund for their maintenance, to the city of Genoa, and founded there the San Andrea Hospital, at a cost of 18,000,000 lire, and the Hospital della Coronata, which cost 5,000,000 lire, besides charitable institutions of lesser importance. She provided a great number of dowerless girls, in all ranks of life, with the means of marriage. In her will she endowed orphan asylums and made bequests for numerous charitable institutions. The Galliera property, valued at 80,000,000 lire, she willed to the Duke de Montpensier. Large legacies that were destined for other members of the Orleans family are said to have been stricken from the will, owing to her dissatisfaction with the political course of the Comte de Paris. Her palace in Paris, worth 5,000,000 francs, she bequeathed to the Austro-Hungarian Government, on condition that it shall be maintained as the Embassy forever. The residuary estate was left to be divided in equal parts between her son and the Empress Friedrich of Germany.

Gleig, George Robert, an English author, born in Stirling, Scotland, April 20, 1796; died near Winchfield, England, July 9, 1888. He was the son of a Scottish bishop, was educated at Glasgow and entered Oxford, but left in 1812 to join the army, and served in the Peninsular campaign, and afterward in the American war. Returning to Balliol College, he took his degree, and was ordained in 1820. He was rector of a church in Kent, became chaplain of Chelsea in 1844, and two years later was appointed chaplain-general of the forces, a post that he held for nearly thirty years. He devised a scheme for the education of soldiers, and was appointed inspector-general of military schools soon after he became chaplain-general. Among his numerous published works are, "The Subaltern"; "Campaigns at Washington and New Orleans"; "Lives of Military Commanders"; "History of India"; "History of the Bible"; "The Story of the Battle of Waterloo"; "Lives of Lord Clive, Warren, Hastings, and the Duke of Wellingtou"; "Memoirs of Sir Thomas Monro"; "Traditions of Chelsea Hospital"; "Chronicles of Waltham"; "The Country Curate"; "Military History of Great Britain"; and "The Great Problem."

Godin, St. Jean Baptiste André, a French philanthropist, born in 1817; died in Guise, Jan. 17, 1888. He was the son of a locksmith, and was a workingman in early life. In 1846 he established an iron-foundry at Guise. He rapidly became wealthy, and in 1859 he erected a *familistière*, with co-operative shops, a club, a theatre, and other institutions for his workmen. He was elected a deputy in 1871, but withdrew from political life in 1875.

Godwin, George, an English author, born in London, Jan. 28, 1815; died there. Jan. 27, 1888. He was the son of an architect and practiced the same profession, but devoted himself also to art journalism and literature. He became editor of the "Builder" in 1844. He published a standard treatise on "Concrete" (1835), which was translated into various languages; "The Churches of London" (2 vols., 1838-'39); "Buildings and Monuments, Modern and Mediæval" (1848); "History in Ruins" (1853); "London Shadows" (1854); "Town Swamps and Social Bridges" (1855); "Memorials of Workers"; and "Another Blow for Life." His later works dealt with sanitary and social reforms. He was the designer of St. Mary's Church, West Brompton, and other ecclesiastical and public buildings.

Gondinet, Edmond, a French dramatist, born in Lauriére, March 7, 1829; died in Paris, Nov. 10, 1888. He was the author of "Lakmé," "Le Roi l'a dit," "Le Panache," "Gavand," "Minard et Compagnie," "Le Plus Heureux des Trois," "Le Parisien," and other successful comedies. His co-operation and advice were sought by authors and managers, and made successes of many unpresentable plays, such as "Le Club," which would never have been performed but for his assistance. His works are distinguished for wit and refined humor.

Gosse, Philip Henry, an English naturalist, born in Worcester in 1810; died in Torquay, Aug. 23, 1888. In 1827 he went as a merchant's clerk to Newfoundland, where he spent his leisure in collecting insects and making colored drawings of them and their transformations. He removed to Lower Canada in 1835, studied zoölogy and entomology three years, afterward traveled in the United States, and passed a year in Alabama in making drawings of insects. He returned to England in 1839, and prepared for publication the results of his investigations, visited Jamaica in 1844-'45, and from that time forward resided in England, and devoted himself chiefly to the microscopic study of the *Rotifera* and to collecting shells for public and private cabinets. He also pursued a series of investigations into the characters of the *Papilionidæ*. Besides his works on natural history, both scientific and popular, he published several volumes of sacred and ancient history. Among his books are "The Canadian Naturalist" (London, 1840); "Birds of Jamaica" (with an atlas) and "A Naturalist's Sojourn in Jamaica"; "Introduction to Zoölogy"; "Monuments of Egypt" (1847); "Sacred Streams" (1850); "History of the Jews" (1851); "Assyria" (1852); "The Aquarium" (1854); "Manual of Marine Zoölogy" (1855); "Life in its Lower, Intermediate, and Higher Forms" (1857); "Actinologia Britannica: a History of British Sea Anemones and Corals" (1860); "The Romance of Natural History" (1860-'62); "A Year at the Shore" (1865); "Land and Sea" (1865); "Wonders of the Great Deep" (Philadelphia, 1874); and "The Mysteries of God: a Series of Expositions of Holy Scripture" (London, 1884).

Gregory, F. T., an Australian explorer, born in England; died in Brisbane, Queensland, Nov. 10, 1888. He accompanied his father to Western Australia in 1829, on the second ship that sailed from England with that destination. In 1857 he traced the Murchison river, and in 1860 was intrusted by the Government with an expedition from the northwest coast of Australia in search of cotton-lands, which led to the discovery of the pearl-fisheries of Western Australia, of rich pastoral lands, and of Ashburton and Fortescue rivers. He made a geological map of Western Australia, and was the first to call attention to the coal-mines of the colony. Settling in Queensland, he became Commissioner of Crown Lands and Postmaster-General, and was a member of the Legislative Council.

Heller, Stephen, a Hungarian musician, born in Pesth, May 15, 1815; died in Paris, Jan. 14, 1888. He studied in Vienna, and remained for a few years in Augsburg, but settled in Paris in 1838, and remained there during the rest of his life. He was a composer of pieces for the pianoforte, which are distinguished for tenderness of sentiment and artistic finish. One of his collections is called "Promenades d'un Solitaire," referring to Rousseau, and another is "Blumen, Frucht, und Dornen Stücke," supposed to have been inspired by the works of Richter. He rarely appeared in concerts, and as a player he was only heard to advantage in the inspiring presence of his pupils and admirers.

Hesse, Prince Alexander, of, a general in the Austrian army, born in Darmstadt, Germany, July 15, 1823; died near Jugenheim, Dec. 16, 1888. He was the third son of the Grand Duke Ludwig. Entering the Hessian service as lieutenant in 1833, he joined the Russian army as colonel, in 1840, after his sister's marriage to the future Czar Alexander II, rose to be a major-general, and took service in the Austrian army in 1852, a year after his marriage to Julie, daughter of Count Maurice Haucke. The ability and decision that he displayed on the field of Montebello in 1859 led to his promotion to the rank of lieutenant field-marshal. He distinguished himself likewise at Solferino, and was intrusted later with the command of the Seventh Corps. He returned to his home in 1863, and devoted himself to the education of his children and the gratification of scientific and artistic tastes till the war of 1866 called him to the head of the Eighth Army Corps of the German Federation. He has shared with Field-Marshal Benedek the blame for the defeat of Austria and the South German States, although tardy mobilization and incoherent organization, sufficiently explained the failure of his corps, made up as it was of six contingents of troops all trained on different systems, commanded by generals who were strangers to him. After the close of the campaign he returned to his country-seat, called Heiligenberg, where he spent the rest of his life. His eldest son, Prince Alexander of Battenburg, filled for seven years the Bulgarian throne, and his second son, Prince Henry, married in 1885 the Princess Beatrice, daughter of Queen Victoria of England.

Hesse, Friedrich Wilhelm, Landgrave of, born in Copenhagen. Oct. 15, 1854; died at sea, Oct. 14, 1888. He was traveling in the tropics, and while sailing from Batavia to Singapore he disappeared from his cabin in the night, and is supposed to have committed suicide. His successor as chief of the electoral or elder line of the house of Hesse is his brother Alexander Friedrich.

Holl, Frank, an English artist, born in London, July 4, 1845; died there, July 31, 1888. He was the son of Francis Holl, the engraver, studied painting in London, and in 1864 began to exhibit pictures on sentimental subjects in the Royal Academy. A portrait of Samuel Cousins, the engraver, was so strongly handled that the artist was at once overwhelmed with commissions, and for the last ten years of his life painted nothing but portraits. Among his sitters were Lord Spencer, John Bright, Mr. Chamberlain, Sir Frederick Roberts, Lord Wolseley, Mr. Gladstone, the Prince of Wales, and the Duke of Cambridge. His last work was a portrait of Cornelius Vanderbilt. He was made an Academician in 1884.

Houzeau, Jean Charles, a Belgian astronomer, born in Mons, Oct. 7, 1820; died in Schârbeck, July 12, 1888. He succeeded Quetelet as director of the Brussels Observatory, which he thoroughly reorganized and kept up to the requirements of modern science. His "Uranométrie Générale," containing all the stars of both hemispheres that are visible to the naked eye, was based on observations that he made for several years near the equator. A second great undertaking was the "Bibliographie Générale de l'Astronomie," of which only two volumes have appeared, containing a methodically arranged catalogue of all treatises, works, and published observations in the field of astronomy, from the invention of printing to the year 1880. He also published a "Vademecum de Al'stronomie."

Hewitt, Mary, an English author, born in Uttoxeter in 1799 ; died in Rome, Italy, Jan. 30, 1888. She was the daughter of a Quaker named Botham, and married William Howitt in 1823. In the same year they published a volume of verse, beginning a career of joint authorship that made their names widely known. In 1834 she issued a dramatic poem called " The Seven Temptations," which was followed by " Wood Leighton," a story. She wrote largely for young people, and while residing in Germany translated from the Danish and Swedish, and first made the works of Fredrika Bremer known to English readers. In 1851 she produced with her husband " The Literature and Romance of Northern Europe." Besides the works that they jointly wrote and her books for children, Mrs. Howitt produced a novel entitled " The Cost of Caergwyn " and a " Popular History of the United States." They settled in Italy in 1872.

Jellett, John Hewitt, Irish mathematician, born in Cashel, Dec. 25, 1817 ; died in Dublin, Feb. 20, 1888. He was educated at Trinity College, Dublin, became a fellow in 1840, was appointed to the chair of Natural Philosophy in 1848, received the appointment of commissioner of national education in 1868, and in 1881 was appointed provost of Trinity College. He wrote a " Treatise on the Calculus of Variations " (1850) ; a " Treatise on the Theory of Friction " (1872) ; and several theological essays, of which the principal ones are " The Moral Difficulties of the Old Testament " and " The Efficacy of Prayer."

Juste, Theodore, a Belgian historian, born in Brussels, Jan. 11, 1818 ; died there, Aug. 12, 1888. He did much to popularize the history of his own country and of France, publishing more than fifty volumes. Among his most important works were a " History of the French Revolution, the Consulate, and the Empire " (1839-'40) ; " Charlemagne " (1849) ; " Charles V and Margaret of Austria " (1858) ; " History of the Revolt of the Low Countries " (1862-'63) ; " History of the States-General in the Low Countries " (1864) ; " The Belgian Revolution of 1830 " (1873) ; and " Founders of the Belgian Monarchy " (20 vols., 1865-'74).

Key, Sir Astley Cooper, an English naval officer, born in 1821 ; died in Maidenhead, March 3, 1888. He distinguished himself in the Naval College, and obtained a lieutenant's commission, rescued the stranded " Gorgon " off Montevideo in 1844, was wounded in action and made a commander in 1845, became a captain in 1850, and took part in the capture of the forts of Bomarsund and the other operations of the Baltic campaign in 1855. In 1857 he commanded a fleet of gunboats at Calcutta during the Indian mutiny, and in 1858 he commanded a battalion of seamen at the capture of Canton. On returning to England, he served on the board to consider the state of the defenses that was called into existence on account of the building of the French iron-clad " Gloire." When the British Government began to build iron-plated vessels and to make heavy guns, Captain Key was made director-general of naval ordnance. In 1869 he was appointed superintendent of Portsmouth dockyard. In 1873-'76 he was president of the Naval College at Greenwich, holding the rank of vice-admiral. He was promoted admiral in 1878, and held the office of Principal Naval Lord of the Admiralty under two successive administrations.

Labiche, Eugène Marin, a French dramatist, born in Paris, May 5, 1815 ; died there, Jan. 23, 1888. He was educated at the Bourbon College, and entered the Law School, wrote *feuilletons* for the Paris papers, and in 1838 published a romance entitled " La Clef des Champs." His first attempt at dramatic authorship, the play of " M. de Coylin," in which he had the assistance of two other writers, was not a success. He applied himself, however, to the work, and developed a new kind of vaudeville farce, in which the central character is involved in a constant succession of laughable complications caused by the eccentric actions of the persons of the drama, producing absurdly improbable situations. His plays became ex-

ceedingly popular, keeping the stage at the Gymnase, the Palais Royal, and the Variétés longer than any contemporaneous works. In 1880 he was elected to the Academy. Among his more popular works were " Frisette " (1846) ; " Madame Lariffa " (1849) ; " Un Garçon de chez Véry " (1850) ; " Une Femme qui perd ses Jarretières " (1851) ; " Le Chapeau de Paille d'Italy," Ravel's favorite piece (1851) ; " Otez votre Fille, s'il vous plais " (1854) ; " L'Affaire de la Rue de Lourcine " (1857) ; " Le Voyage de M. Perrichon," a comedy of superior merit, written in collaboration with Édouard Martin (1860) ; " La Poudre aux Yeux " (1861) ; " Moi " (1864) ; " La Gagnotte " (1864) ; " Madame est trop Belle " (1874) ; " Un Mouton à l'Entresol," with M. Second (1875) ; and " La Charge de Cavallerie," his last piece (1876). He published a complete edition of his works in 1878.

Latham, Robert Gordon, an English ethnologist, born in 1812 ; died in London, March 9, 1888. He was educated at Eton and King's College, Cambridge, of which he became a fellow, studied medicine, and for some years lectured on materia medica and medical jurisprudence at Middlesex Hospital. Before 1840 he had published books on Norway, and translated Tegner's " Frithiof Saga." Many ethnological and philological works followed, of which the most successful were " The Ethnology of Europe " (1852) ; and " The English Language " (1855). He prepared a revised edition of Johnson's " Dictionary " (1870).

Lee, Henry, an English naturalist, born in 1827 ; died in London in 1888. As naturalist to the Brighton aquarium he carried out experiments regarding the habits of the herring, the natural history and classification of white bait, and the migration of smolts. He published " Aquarium Notes," describing the life history of the fish under his care ; " Sea Fables explained," " The Octopus," and " The Cuttle-Fish of Fact and Fiction."

Levi, Leone, an English statistician, born in Ancona, Italy, July 6, 1821 ; died in London, May 9, 1888. He went to England when a young man on a commercial enterprise, and finding difficulties in the commercial laws, he studied law, obtained admission to the bar, organized the Liverpool Chamber of Commerce in 1849, and similar institutions elsewhere, and by agitation secured the removal of some of the obstructions to foreign trade. He published a treatise on " The Commercial Law of the World " in 1850, and in 1852 was called to the chair of Commercial Law in King's College, London, which he filled for many years. He was the author of " Taxation : how it is raised, and how expended " (London, 1860) ; " History of British Commerce and of the Economic Progress of the British Nation, 1863-'78 " ; and " Work and Pay " ; " War and its Consequences " ; and other published lectures.

Levy, Joseph M., an English journalist, born in London in 1812 ; died in Ramsgate, Oct. 12, 1888. In the earlier period of his life he was engaged in various mercantile pursuits. He purchased the London " Daily Telegraph " about 1857, when it was a small sheet with insignificant circulation. Through his enterprise in obtaining interesting news and in engaging vigorous writers, he gained a circle of readers, especially among the Dissenters and Liberals of England, as large as any newspaper in the world commanded.

Lucan, George Charles Bingham, Earl of, an English general, born April 16, 1800 ; died Nov. 10, 1888. He entered the army in 1816, and while holding the rank of lieutenant-colonel volunteered to serve on the staff of Gen. Diebitsch in the Russian campaign against Turkey in 1828. He succeeded to the earldom in 1839, and was elected an Irish representative peer. When the war with Russia began, in 1854, Lord Lucan was a major-general, having reached that rank in 1851. He was placed in command of the cavalry, took part in the battles of Alma and Inkerman and the covering operations intrusted to the cavalry during the siege of Sebastopol, and was wounded at Balaklava ; he and his brother-in-law, Lord Cardigan, being chiefly responsible for the sacrifice of the Light Brigade on that day. He was made a major-general in 1858, and a field-marshal the year before his death.

Lupton, Bey, an English officer in the Egyptian service, died in Khartoum, in June, 1888. He went to Khartoum with Gen. Gordon, and when the place was taken by the Mahdi he was made a prisoner and put at menial tasks, but subsequently was given the technical direction of the arsenal.

Maclay, Mikuloho, a Russian explorer, born in 1846; died in St. Petersburg, April 15, 1888. He came of half Scotch and half Cossack parentage, was educated at the University of St. Petersburg and in Germany, went to the Pacific in 1866, and settled in an unexplored part of the coast of Papua, where he investigated the natural history and ethnology of the island, and acquired great influence over the natives. He endeavored to induce the Russian Government to annex the country of his adherents when New Guinea was divided between Germany and Great Britain, and returned to Russia with the object of founding a Russian colony among the Papuans and of composing an account of his travels. He had only half completed this work when he died.

Maine, Sir Henry James Sumner, an English jurist, born in 1822; died in Cannes, France, Feb. 3, 1858. He distinguished himself at Cambridge in classics and mathematics, became a tutor in Trinity College, of which he was afterward master, and in 1847 was elected Regius Professor of Civil Law. He published in 1856 an essay on "Roman Law and Legal Education," and contributed frequently to periodical literature, but published no important work till 1861, when his "Ancient Law" was issued. This work was based on the earlier labors of Savigny and other German jurists, but it was the first presentation in the English language of the study of early institutions by the method of comparative Jurisprudence, and as such produced a profound effect in England and America. A year after its publication the author was appointed legal member of the Council of the Governor-General of India. He was the chief author of the reform of land tenures in India that was carried out under Lord Lawrence's administration. The understanding and respect for indigenous institutions which have been the aim of recent Indian administrations are largely attributable to the influence of Sir Henry Maine. After his return to England in 1871 he was appointed a member of the Council of the Secretary of State for India, and created a knight of the Star of India. He held the Corpus professorship of Jurisprudence which was created for him at the University of Oxford from 1871 till 1878, and from 1877 till his death filled the post of Master of Trinity, although his duties at the Indian Council, of which he was one of the most influential members, made it necessary for him to continue his residence in London. In 1885 he was offered the post of permanent Under-Secretary of State for the Home Department, but declined the appointment. Sir Henry Maine's experience in India enabled him to bring valuable original contributions to the science of the evolution of laws and political institutions. Soon after his return he published the first series of his "Village Communities in the East and West," embodying and supplementing the researches of Maurer, Nasse, and others. In 1875 appeared "Lectures on the Early History of Institutions," which was followed in 1883 by "Dissertations on Early Law and Customs." He delivered a lecture at Cambridge in 1875 on "The Effects of Observation of India on Modern European Thought," and in 1878 lectured at Oxford on "Modern Theories of Succession to Property after Death, and the Correctness of them suggested by Recent Researches." His latest work was "Popular Government," which originally appeared as a series of articles in the "Quarterly Review." The Whewell Lectures on "International Law" delivered at Cambridge in 1887 were published after his death.

Mancini, Pasquale Stanislas, an Italian statesman, born in Castel-Baronia, near Ariano, in 1817; died in Na-

ples, Dec. 26, 1888. He studied law in Naples, becoming a professor of the University. When the revolution of 1848 broke out, he espoused the side of the Parliament, and after the suppression of the disturbances went into exile. He settled at Turin, where he became Professor of International Law. He was one of the most earnest pioneers in the cause of Italian unity, and on the constitution of the kingdom he was elected to represent the circle of Ariano in Parliament. Taking his seat among the Left, he became one of the leaders of the party. When the Liberals gained the ascendancy, two years later, and the Ratazzi Cabinet was formed in 1862, Mancini was appointed to the Department of Public Instruction. The measure with which his name is identified is the abolition of capital punishment, which he carried in 1865, after having gained the reluctant consent of his political associates. Public opinion in Italy is not yet settled as to the expediency of this measure, which did away with the death penalty for all crimes except parricide and regicide. There was an apparent increase of crimes of violence, causing Parliament to repeal the law in 1874; yet it was again enacted in March, 1876, when Mancini was Minister of Justice in the Depretis Cabinet. He retired from office in 1878. He filled the chair of Criminal Jurisprudence in the University of Rome from 1872 till his death, and was the author of many legal treatises, one of which was a "Projet de Code Pénal Unique," the first part of which was presented to the French Academy of Moral Sciences in 1877.

Martinelli, Tommaso Maria, an Italian prelate, born in 1827; died in Rome, March 30, 1888. He was a member of the Augustinian order and one of the most learned theologians of the Catholic Church. He was created a cardinal in 1873, becoming Bishop of Sabina and one of the six cardinal-bishops, and was made Prefect of the Congregation of the Index. He received the largest number of votes at the first ballot for a successor to Pius IX, but exerted his influence in favor of Cardinal Pecci, who became Leo XIII.

Matout, Louis, a French painter, born in Charleville, Ardennes, in 1813; died in Paris, Jan. 30, 1888. He studied architecture at the École des Beaux Arts, but afterward turned his attention to historical painting. He was commissioned by the Government in 1846 to paint pictures representing the "Five Senses," and was sent to Rome for the purpose. Two of these he completed, which were exhibited in the Salon of 1848, together with "Le Dieu Pan au Milieu des Nymphes." He passed several years in Algiers, and on his return decorated the Paris Medical School, for which he was given the Legion of Honor in 1857. Among his works are "Minerve," "Danse Antique," "Ariane endormie" (1874), "Vénus Pandemos" (1876), "Saint Jacques le Majeur" (1877), "Jésus chez Simon le Pharisien" (1879), and "St. Louis" (1880).

Molbech, Christian Knut Friedrich, a Danish poet, born in Copenhagen, July 21, 1821; died there, May 20, 1888. He published a succession of lyric and dramatic works, among which were a series of poems on "The Life of Jesus," "Barbarossa," "Dante," and other dramas, a collection of sonnets called "Madonna," another of lyrics, and a highly commended translation of Dante. In 1864 he became Professor of Danish Literature in the University of Kiel. Subsequently he was the literary critic of the "Dagblad" of Copenhagen, and in 1871 he became censor of the Royal Theatre, for which he composed "Ambrosius," "Pharaoh's Ring," and other plays, besides translations and adaptations. He was also the author of a biographical study on Ludvig Holberg, the Danish dramatist, and of a comedy that was written for the unveiling of a statue to that poet.

Mongredien, Augustus, an English economist, born in 1807; died near London, March 30, 1888. He was the author of "Free Trade and English Commerce," "History of the Free-Trade Movement," "Wealth Creation," "Trade Depression, Recent and Present," "The Western Farmer of America," and "England's Foreign Policy."

Monselet, Charles, a French author, born in Nantes, April 30, 1825; died in Paris, May 22, 1888. When seventeen years old he published "Marie et Ferdinand," a poem that was much admired, then wrote several pieces for the stage, and in 1846 settled in Paris, where he wrote romances, sketches, and critical articles for newspapers, was dramatic critic for the "Figaro" for some time, and edited a short-lived weekly called "Le Gourmet." In the long list of his books the most important are "Histoire du Tribunal Révolutionaire" (1850); "Les Vignes du Seigneur," a volume of poems (1854); "La Lorgnette Litteraire," sketches of contemporary writers (1857); "Les Oubliés et les Dédaignés," portraits from the last century (1857); "La Franc-Maçonnerie des Femmes" (1861); "Les Frères Chantemesse" (1872); "Les Amours des Temps Passé" (1875); "Lettres Gourmandes" (1877); and "Le Petit Paris" (1879).

Morison, James Cotter, an English author, born in London, April 30, 1831; died in London, Feb. 26, 1888. He spent several years in France before he entered Oxford University. With some of his associates, he identified himself with the Positivist Society after settling in London, where he contributed frequently to reviews and magazines. His longest work was "Life and Times of St. Bernard" (1863). He published a pamphlet on "Irish Grievances" in 1868; the lives of "Gibbon" and "Macaulay" to the "English Men of Letters" series: "Madame de Maintenon, an Étude" (London, 1885); and "Service of Man," a polemical statement of the Positivist arguments against Christianity (1886). Mr. Morison projected a great work on French history, and spent many years in study and preparation, but died before he could carry out his plan.

Mount-Temple, William Francis Cowper-Temple, Baron, an English official, born Dec. 13, 1811; died at Broadlands, near Romsey, Oct. 16, 1888. He was the second son of the fifth Earl Cowper. After serving a short time in the army, he became secretary to Lord Melbourne, then Prime Minister, was elected to Parliament for Hertford as a Liberal in 1834, and continued to sit for that borough till 1838. From 1846 till 1852 he was Lord of the Admiralty in Lord John Russell's administration, and in 1853 he resumed that office, which he exchanged in 1855 for that of president of the Board of Health. In 1857 he became the first vice president of the Committee on Education, and held that office in conjunction with the other till the ministry resigned in the following year. In August, 1859, he became vice-president of the Board of Trade, and in the following February was appointed Commissioner of Public Works. In this post, which he held until 1866, he carried through the Thames-Embankment bill and made many improvements in public parks and buildings. He was member of Parliament for South Hampshire from 1868 till 1880, when he was created Lord Mount-Temple, having assumed the additional name of Temple in 1869 on inheriting the estate of Broadlands from his step-father, Lord Palmerston.

Musgrave, Sir Anthony, Governor of Queensland, born in Antigua in 1823; died in Brisbane, Oct. 9, 1888. He studied law in London, and returned in 1852 to Antigua to take a clerical appointment under his father, who was colonial treasurer. He became colonial secretary in 1854, filled a succession of posts in the colonial administrative service, became Governor of Newfoundland in 1864, and of British Columbia in 1869, was nominated Lieutenant-Governor of Natal in 1872 and Governor of South Australia in 1873, was thence transferred to Jamaica in 1877, and in March, 1883, succeeded Sir A. J. Kennedy as Governor of Queensland. He married in 1870 a daughter of David Dudley Field, of New York, who survives him.

Oliphant, Laurence, an English author, born in 1829; died in London, Dec. 23, 1888. He was the son of the chief-justice of Ceylon, who sent him home with a tutor at the age of twelve, and five years later set out on a tour through Europe with his son, who was moved by his adventurous spirit to participate in the Italian revolutionary uprising, helping to burn the Austrian arms at Rome, and recklessly exposing his life at the bombardment of Messina. Returning to Ceylon as his father's private secretary, he made the acquaintance of Jung Bahadoor, and accompanied him on a journey to Nepaul, which afforded material for a very successful book entitled "Katmandu." He practiced for a short time at the Ceylon bar, but his passion for travel and literary ambition brought him back to Europe. He set out for Lapland, and when the authorities objected to his scheme of exploration, made a journey in the south of Russia, which he described in "Crimea and the Shores of the Black Sea." He was invited to accompany the British army to the Crimea; but he yielded to the requests of Lord Elgin to go with him on his special mission to Washington, where his social charms were of service in bringing about the Canadian reciprocity treaty that was "floated in a sea of champagne." He then accompanied Lord Elgin to Canada, and was sent on a diplomatic tour along the Red river settlements as civil secretary and commissioner for Indian affairs, recording his experiences in "Minnesota and the Far West." After his return to England he published a pamphlet on the Crimean campaign, suggesting a diversion in the Caucasus, and offered to undertake a mission to Schamyl in Daghestan. Lord Stratford de Redcliffe, whom he accompanied to Sebastopol, would not countenance so perilous an undertaking. Oliphant was with Omar Pasha on his Transcaucasian operations, which he reported in a series of letters to the London "Times." When Lord Elgin went out as special ambassador to China he was accompanied by his former secretary, who was present at the exciting scenes of the mutiny when the expeditionary force tarried to aid the British in India, and in the Chinese war took an active part in the capture of Canton and other military operations besides assisting in the diplomatic negotiations. He went to Japan as *chargé d'affaires* in 1860, and in the attack on the British embassy was severely wounded. He published a "Narrative of Lord Elgin's Mission to China and Japan," and recounted other episodes of his adventurous life, such as his experiences with the filibusters of Central America and with Garibaldi and the Sicilian legion on the expedition to Montenegro, Albania, and the camps of the Polish insurgents, in his volumes entitled "Patriots and Filibusters" and "Incidents of Travel." In 1865 he entered Parliament, but attained no prominence as a legislator, and in 1868 resigned his seat. He was a contributor to "Blackwood's Magazine" while living in London, and mingled much in society, satirizing its follies and vices in the novel of "Piccadilly." Withdrawing to a peaceful retreat in the United States, he lost himself in spiritual speculations, and became a disciple of Thomas Lake Harris, submissively yielding to the religious direction of that enthusiast. He acted for some time as an agent and promoter of the Transatlantic Telegraph Company. He was in France during the war of 1870 as a correspondent of the "Times," and remained in Paris in the same capacity after the peace, until he was summoned to America by Harris. Embracing the chance that was opened by the Treaty of Berlin, permitting the interposition of Christian powers in Turkish affairs, for the realization of a cherished scheme for the colonization of Jews in Palestine, especially the impoverished and persecuted Jews of Roumania whom he had materially aided, he visited southern Gilead and the land of Moab, which he described as eminently suited for settlement in "The Land of Gilead." He resided for a long time at Haifa, where he befriended the Druses and dispensed justice as an Oriental magistrate. Among his later publications are "Traits and Travesties" (1882); "Altiora Peto," a novel (1883); "Irene McGillicuddy," a satire on American manners; "Masullam," a mystical novel (1886); and "Scientific Religion," an exposition of his spiritualistic faith.

Paley, Frederick Apthorpe, an English commentator, born near York in 1816; died at Bournemouth, Dec. 11, 1888. He was graduated at Cambridge in 1838, and continued to reside there till 1846, when he joined the Roman Catholic Church. In 1860, the religious disabilities of nonconformists having been partially removed, he returned to Cambridge, and was a tutor there till 1874, when he accepted the chair of Classical Literature in the Catholic University College at Kensington. He edited Homer, Hesiod, Theocritus, Demosthenes, and the Greek tragic writers for the "Bibliotheca Classica" and other series of classics, prepared the text of the Greek tragedies for the "Cambridge Texts," translated Æschylus, Pindar, and some of the works of Plato a d Aristotle, and wrote many papers on archæology and botany.

Palgrave, William Gifford, an English traveler, born in London, Jan. 24, 1826; died in Montevideo, Uruguay, Oct. 1, 1888. He was the son of Sir Francis Palgrave, the historian, and brother of Reginald F. D. Palgrave, clerk of the House of Commons. He left Cambridge University after a brilliant academic course, to serve with the army in Bombay, but resigned his commission after a short time, and a few years later entered the Jesuit order, and in due time became a priest. In this capacity he was engaged in southern India, in Rome, and in Palestine and Syria, where he acquired such mastery of the Arabic language and manners that he was able to pass himself off as a Mohammedan. He was summoned to France in 1860 to report to the Emperor Napoleon concerning the Syrian massacres, and was then commissioned by the French Government to penetrate into central Arabia, where he had many narrow escapes from death. An account of his journeyings in the disguise of an Arabian physician he published under the title "Narrative of a Year's Journey through Central and Eastern Arabia, 1862-'63" (London, 1865). He was employed in 1865 by the English Government to negotiate for the release of prisoners in Abyssinia, afterward held consulships in various Oriental cities, was consul-general to Bulgaria in 1878, and thence transferred to Bangkok in 1879, and from 1884 till his death was British minister to Uruguay. His other literary works were "Essays on Eastern Questions" (1872); "Hermann Agha, an Eastern Narrative" (1872); and "Dutch Guiana" (1876).

Palizzi, Joseph, Italian artist, born in Lanciano, Italy, in 1813; died in Paris, Jan. 7, 1888. He studied art in his native city, and in 1844 went to Paris. He was eminent as a landscape painter, and was also successful in his representations of animals. His principal works are "Storm in the Abruzzi" (1845); "Shepherd guarding his Flock" (1848); "Goats ravaging the Vines" (1855); "Cattle in the Valley of the Tonque" (1859); "Drove of Oxen in a Storm" (1864); "Souvenir of the Landes" (1872); and "In the Vicinity of Pæstum" (1873).

Péne, Henri de, a French journalist, born in Paris, April 25, 1830; died there, Jan. 27, 1888. He came from a noble Bearn family possessing a castle near Pau. He was educated at the Collège Rollin, became a writer for the "Evénement" and other papers. In 1858, for a paragraph in the "Figaro" reflecting on the ball-manners of the military, he was overwhelmed with challenges, which he offered to accept in alphabetical order. He was wounded severely by his second adversary, and went to Mannheim for surgical treatment, publishing on his return "Une Mois en Allemagne," which had been preceded by a similar volume of Portuguese sketches. Piquant sketches of Parisian life that he wrote for the "Indépendance Belge" were reproduced in book-form under the titles of "Paris Aventureux," "Paris Viveur," etc. He founded the "Paris," and when it expired the "Paris Journal," which was merged in the "Gaulois." In 1871 he was wounded in a manifestation of Friends of Order who had organized with the intention of disarming the Commune. He was the editor-in-chief of the "Gaulois" and always an ardent Royalist. He wrote a life of the Comte de Chambord under the title of "Henri de France." In 1886 he published a novel called "Trop Belle," and in 1887 "Rose Michon," which has been dramatized.

Planchon, Jules Émile, French botanist, born in Ganges, France, March 21, 1823; died in Montpelier, April 2, 1888. He was educated at Montpelier, studied botany under Auguste Saint-Hilaire, and received the degree of doctor of sciences in 1844. To perfect his botanical knowledge, he went to England, where until 1849 he was officially connected with the botanical garden at Kew. In 1845-'51 he was connected with the faculty of the Horticultural Institute at Ghent, in Belgium. He then received the degree of doctor of medicine, and was professor at the College of Medicine and Pharmacy in Nancy until 1853, when he became Professor of Botany in the scientific faculty at Montpelier and also of the Pharmaceutical College in that place, of which he subsequently became president. He had charge in 1873 of the scientific mission to America to study the disease that was threatening the extinction of the grape-plant. Corroborating his previous observations, he demonstrated that the trouble sprang from an insect, *Phylloxera vastatrix*, which he had discovered in 1868, a native of this country, which preyed upon the root. He also found that some varieties of the vine in America were not subject to the attacks of the insect. In addition to many papers in scientific journals, he contributed to the "Revue des Deux Mondes," and he published "Le Phylloxera de 1854 à 1873" (Paris, 1874); "Les Vignes Américaines" (1875); "La Truffe et les Truffières Artificielles" (1875); and "L'Eucalyptus Globus" (1875).

Poliakoff, Samuel, a Russian financier, born in Orscha, Lithuania; died in St. Petersburg in April, 1888. He was the son of poor Jewish parents, was a butcher, then clerk to a wood-seller, learned Russian, went to St. Petersburg in 1850, and in ten years became very wealthy. Before he died he was the owner of five great railroads, constituting a fourth of the entire Russian system. In 1885 he elaborated a plan for consolidating the railroads under the direction of the state, and was sworn a member of the Czar's Privy Council. He founded the first school of railroad engineering and the Russian School of Mines, the Alexander II College and dormitories for students at the University of St. Petersburg, a large hospital at Moscow, technical schools for women, and many other institutions. His public benefactions before 1882 amounted to 6,000,000 rubles.

Price, Bonamy, an English economist, born in Guernsey, May 22, 1807; died in London, Jan. 8, 1888. He obtained a double first in classics and mathematics and was graduated at Oxford in 1829, became master of mathematics at Rugby, and was a teacher in that school till 1850, when he removed to London and devoted his attention to business. In 1868 he was elected Professor of Political Economy at Oxford as the successor of Thorold Rogers, whose theories were condemned by the Conservative majority. He published a course of lectures on "The Principles of Currency" (1869); a work entitled "Of Currency and Banking" (1876); and a course of his lectures entitled "Chapters on Practical Political Economy" (1878), besides several that preceded it. As a member of the Duke of Richmond's Royal Commission on Agriculture he appended to the minority report some remarks which called forth Mr. Gladstone's comment that he alone "had the resolution to apply, in all their unmitigated authority, the principles of abstract political economy to the people and circumstances of Ireland, exactly as if he had been proposing to legislate for the inhabitants of Saturn."

Prjevalsky, Nicholas M., a Russian traveler, born in the district of Smolensk in March, 1839; died in Central Asia between Tashkend and Vernoje in October, 1888. He entered the Russian army, and in 1867 volunteered for service in eastern Siberia, where he spent two years in exploring the Ussuri valley, publishing on his return to St. Petersburg a volume of "Notes on the Ussuri." In 1870–'73 he traveled in western China, and in 1876 left Russia for the purpose of determining the position of Lob Nor. He was absent a year, during which he explored the Tarim valley, discovered the true Lob Nor, and reached the Altyn Tagh mountains. In April, 1879, he undertook a journey to Tibet, but was deserted by his guides after having penetrated to the Tsaidam steppe and the region of the Koko Nor, and made his way back amid extreme perils and hardships. In 1885 he made another unsuccessful attempt to reach Lhassa, and on his return traversed Chinese Turkistan. When the British began their war against the Tibetans in Sikkim, Gen. Prjevalsky was placed at the head of a strong expedition, and ordered to reach Lhassa at all hazards. Already weakened by years of hardship, he was unable to endure the fatigues and exposure of another journey, and died on the route to Vernoje, where he intended to equip his party.

Questel, Charles Auguste, a French architect, born in Paris, Sept. 18, 1807; died Feb. 15, 1888. He received his artistic training at the École des Beaux Arts. His first great work was the cathedral at Nîmes, which was begun in 1838 and completed in 1849. He designed an elaborate fountain in the same city. The library and museum at Grenoble were built after his plans. He was the architect of the Historical Monuments Commission who directed the restorations of the amphitheatre at Arles and the Pont du Gard. He was architect to the palaces of Versailles and Trianon under the Empire, served as a member of the Council on Public Buildings, and was a professor in the École des Beaux Arts.

Richthofen, Baron Ferdinand von, a German geographer, born in Karlsruhe in May, 1833; died May 8, 1888. He studied at Breslau and Berlin, was attached for some years to the Geological Survey of Austria, and in 1860 accompanied Count Eulenberg's Prussian expedition to Eastern Asia as geologist, visiting Formosa, the Philippine Islands, Java, Celebes, Siam, and Indo-China. He then crossed the Pacific, and traveled through California and the Sierra Nevada. In August, 1868, he returned to China, which he traversed in various directions during the next four years, studying the orography and geology of the country, and also its productions and commercial possibilities. Returning to Germany after twelve years of absence, he spent the remainder of his life in working out the results of his researches in China. He was appointed Professor of Geography at Bonn in 1879, and in 1883 was transferred to Leipsic, which he quitted in 1886 to accept the same chair at Berlin. Of his great work on "China" three volumes have been issued. His atlas, in which he reconstructed the map of China from his own observations and from the best native information, is not completed.

Rose, Sir John, a British financier, born in Aberdeenshire, Scotland, in 1820; died in Caithness-shire, Aug. 26, 1888. He emigrated to Canada at the age of sixteen, served as a volunteer during the rebellion, studied law, and in 1842 was admitted to the bar of Lower Canada. He became Solicitor-General in 1857, and entered Parliament as a member for Montreal. In 1859 he was Minister of Public Works. He took part in the Canadian conference in London as the representative of the Protestants of Lower Canada, and assisted in framing the act of federation. In the Government of the new Dominion he was appointed Minister of Finance, and during the three years that he held the office he prepared measures providing for the defense of the Dominion and assimilating the fiscal laws. He was intrusted with several diplomatic missions to settle difficulties that arose with the United States between 1860 and 1870 on the Oregon boundary question, reciprocity, the fisheries, copyright, and extradition. In 1870 he resigned his post in the ministry, and went to England to engage in commercial business. He was at once sent to Washington by the English Government on a confidential mission in connection with the "Alabama" and fishery disputes, and assisted in negotiating the Washington Treaty, receiving the honor of a baronetcy for his services. He has since served on several commissions dealing with affairs relating to British America. On his return to England he promoted Canadian railroad enterprises, became a partner in the banking firm of Morton, Rose, & Co., and when he left it connected himself with the London and Westminster Bank enterprise and with an insurance company. He died suddenly while out hunting deer.

Rousseau, Émile, French chemist, born in Clamency, France, April 4, 1815; died in Paris, Feb. 4, 1888. He came to Paris when he was twenty-three years old, and became assistant to Mateo José Bonaventura Orfila, of the medical faculty. Subsequently he assisted Jean Baptiste Dumas, and also taught in several of the public colleges. In 1843 he resigned his appointments and entered upon the manufacture of chemical products. At his laboratory, and with his aid, Henri Sainte-Clair Deville and Jules Henri Debray developed the industrial production of aluminium. He made investigations on the use of pyrites for the manufacture of sulphuric acid, introduced a new method for the production of charcoal, and devised the sugar process known by his name.

Rutland, Charles Cecil John Manners, Duke of, born May 16, 1815; died at Belvoir Castle, March 4, 1888. He was elected to Parliament in 1837, after receiving his education at Cambridge, and represented Stamford for fifteen years. He became one of the principal members of the Protectionist party, and in February, 1848, was chosen to succeed Lord George Bentinck as its leader. He only held the place till the former leader was willing to resume it, and when Lord George Bentinck died in September, 1848, the Marquis of Granby was unwilling to take on himself again the onerous duties, which Mr. Disraeli then assumed. From 1852 till he succeeded to the dukedom in 1857, Lord Granby represented North Leicestershire. He had no sympathy with the progressive Toryism of the Young England party, and did not scruple to criticise the Government when Mr. Disraeli and his own brother, Lord John Manners, were in office. He clung to the principle of protection when Lord Derby and Disraeli abandoned it, and even to the end of his life he lost no opportunity to advocate it, more than once drawing upon himself the sarcastic rebukes of Lord Beaconsfield. The Duke of Rutland was a courageous defender also of the most extreme and unpopular Conservative views regarding land, the ballot, and all other subjects. His successor in the title is Lord John Manners, Chancellor of the Duchy of Lancaster in Lord Salisbury's Cabinet.

Salomon, Louis E. F., ex-President of Hayti, born in 1815; died in Paris, Oct. 19, 1888. He was of pure negro blood, and long occupied a prominent place in Haytian politics. The revolution of 1879 resulted in his election to the presidency for seven years, at the end of which he was re-elected; but the revolution of August, 1888, drove him into exile.

Sarmiento, Domingo F., an Argentine statesman, born in 1811; died in Asuncion, Nov. 2, 1888. He was first director of a school in the province of San Luis, went to Chili in 1831, returned in 1836 and founded a female school at San Juan, but settled in Chili in 1840, where he greatly promoted education, publishing many school-books, editing educational periodicals, and founding schools and colleges, one of these being the normal school at Santiago. He also established a daily newspaper, the first one published in Santiago. In 1845 the Chilian Government sent him to the United States and Europe to study the common-school systems of those countries, and on his return he published a work on "Popular Education." Returning to the Argentine Republic, he became Minister of the Interior, then colonel commanding the military forces, afterward governor of the province of San Juan, and from that post was transferred to the Ministry of Public Instruction. In 1864–'68 he was Minister to the United States. His election to the presidency of the republic recalled him to Buenos Ayres. During his administration, which lasted until October, 1874, the war with Paraguay was brought to a successful termination, several insurrections were quelled, railroads and telegraphs were constructed, immigration was promoted, foreign trade was developed, a national college was established in every province, the National Observatory was founded, and many institutions were introduced, mainly modeled after those of the United States. Among his literary works the principal were "Manual of the History of Ancient Peoples," "Civilization in Barbary," "Travels in Europe, Africa, and America," and a "Life of Abraham Lincoln."

Schleyer, Johann Martin, the inventor of Volapük, born in Constance, Baden, in 1831; died there, Oct. 10, 1888. He was a priest of the Catholic Church. His successor as chief of the Volapük Society is M. Kerckhoffs, teacher of languages in the Commercial High-School at Paris. (See VOLAPÜK, in the "Annual Cyclopædia" for 1887, page 794.)

Storm, Theodor, a German novelist, born in Husum, Holstein, Sept. 14, 1817; died in Hadamarsch, July 4, 1888. He left Schleswig-Holstein in consequence of the revolt of the Holsteiners against Denmark in 1853, in which he took part, entered the Prussian service, became a district judge in Potsdam and Heiligenstadt, and returned in later years to practice law in his native town. He was the author of many tales characterized by dreamy melancholy and love of nature. He also wrote lyric poetry that was equally expressive of North German thought and sentiment.

Tommasi, Salvatore, an Italian physician, born in 1814; died in Naples, July 14, 1888. He took part in political movements while yet a schoolboy, and was obliged to flee from the Romagna, began his medical studies in Aquila, was appointed Professor of Pathology in the University of Naples at the age of thirty-three, and in a few years he reached a pre-eminent position in his profession as physician, university teacher, and medical author. The half-dozen warring schools or tendencies in medicine then existing in Italy were harmonized under his lead. His works contain the germs of many discoveries and theories that have been developed later by other men in other countries. In 1846 he published "Fisiologia Umana," a work that had a great influence on medical thought in Italy. Taking part in the revolution of 1848, he was elected to the Neapolitan House of Deputies and twice condemned to prison in that year, and finally exiled. He lived in poverty at Turin with other political refugees, whom he served as physician, until after the deliverance of Lombardy he was appointed a professor at Pavia. When the Bourbon monarchy was overthrown and the clinical hospital that he had suggested was established in Naples, he returned thither in 1863, and continued to work indefatigably during the remaining years of his life, devoting his remarkable skill to the good of the poor, and imparting his knowledge and enthusiasm to thousands of students.

Tuson, Richard Vine, English chemist, born in England in 1832; died near London, Oct. 31, 1888. He received his scientific training at University College, London, where he made a specialty of chemistry. Subsequently he served as assistant in chemistry at Galway, and later at St. Bartholomew's Hospital in London. He was afterward elected lecturer on chemistry at the Medical School of Charing Cross Hospital, where he continued until 1860, when he was chosen Professor of Chemistry at the Royal Veterinary College in London, which place he held until his death. Besides various scientific papers in technical journals, he edited and partly rewrote the sixth edition of Cooley's "Cyclopædia of Practical Receipts" (2 vols., New York, 1879).

Walsh, John Henry, an English author, born in 1810; died in London, Feb. 12, 1888. He was originally a physician practicing in Worcestershire, and settled in London in 1855, when he wrote a book on "The Greyhound," and shortly after its appearance published under the pen-name of Stonehenge the first edition of "British Rural Sports," which has obtained great popularity. From 1857 until his death he was the editor of the "Field." He published among other works "The Dog in Health and Disease" (1858); "Dogs of the British Islands," which passed through several editions, and "The Modern Sportsman's Gun and Rifle" (2 vols., 1882-'84).

Weber, Georg, a German historian, born in Bergzabern, Feb. 10, 1808; died Aug. 19, 1888. He studied theology at Erlangen, left that university to devote himself to history and ancient literature at Heidelberg, and after residing in Switzerland, Italy, and France, where he engaged in historical researches, he became a teacher in 1839 of the Bürgerschule at Heidelberg, of which he was afterward principal till 1872. His principal works are: "Calvinism in its Relations to the State" (1836); "History of the English Reformation" (1853); "History of German Literature" (1855); "Germany in the First Stages of its Historical Existence" (1862); "Manual of Universal History" (1865); "Survey of the World's History" (1866); "History of the People of Israel and of the Birth of Christianity," with Dr. Holtzmann (1867); and "Universal History of the Peoples of the World" (15 vols., 1857-'84).

Wroblewski, Sigismund, a Russian chemist, born in 1848; died in Cracow, Austrian Poland, April 10, 1888. He was educated at the Universities of St. Petersburg and Strasburg, and in 1882 became Professor of Experimental Physics at the University of Cracow. This place he held until his death, which was the result of an explosion in his laboratory. He became noted for his experiments on the so-called permanent gases, and with his colleague, Dr. Z. Olozewiski, he determined the critical temperatures and pressures of oxygen and nitrogen. From similar researches, he proved that carbonic acid did not form the hydrate, and he succeeded in solidifying both carbon bisulphide and alcohol. The insulating properties of liquid oxygen and nitrogen were determined by him in 1885, and in 1886 he determined the density and properties of liquefied air, and established the fact that atmospheric air, when in a liquid state, behaves as a mixture. The atomic volumes of these gases were also first accurately determined by him, and his results have been confirmed. In 1887 he proposed that the relations of the physical properties of gases be represented by curves showing the rate of change of pressure with temperature for different densities, instead of by isothermal lines. These curves he called "isopyknics," and from the inspection of them new and important conclusions were deduced.

Zuckertort, J. H., a German chess-player, born in Riga in 1842; died in London, England, June 20, 1888. He studied in Berlin, settled in London in 1872, devoting himself to the game of chess, and in 1880 became editor of the "Chess Monthly." In the international tournament at Paris in 1878 he took the first prize, and in 1883 he defeated Steinitz in the international tournament at London, and was accounted the champion of the world until the same player won a match of a series of games played in New York, St. Louis, and New Orleans in 1886. Dr. Zuckertort was unequaled as a blindfold player.

OHIO.

OHIO. The State Government in 1888 was: Governor, Joseph B. Foraker (Republican); Lieut.-Governor, William C. Lyon; Secretary of State, James S. Robinson; Auditor, Ebenezer W. Poe; Treasurer of State, John C. Brown; Attorney-General, David K. Watson; Board of Public Works, William M. Hahn, C. A. Flickinger, Wells S. Jones; Commissioner of Common Schools, Eli T. Tappan; Judges of the Supreme Court, Selwyn N. Owen, Marshall J. Williams, William T. Spear, Thaddeus A. Minshall, Franklin J. Dickman ; Clerk of the Supreme Court, Urban H. Hester.

Finances.—The report of the Auditor shows the balance to the credit of the general revenue fund, Nov. 15, 1887, to have been $65,364 ; receipts during 1888, $3,310,716.75, this amount including $100,000 advance draft drawn on the taxes collected for the fiscal year 1889 ; disbursements, $3,349.328.13 ; balance in treasury, Nov. 15, 1888, $26,752.71. The sinking-fund began the fiscal year with $102,294.08 ; receipts, $894,511.77, this amount including $10,000 advance draft drawn on the taxes collected for 1889 ; disbursements, $995,357.16 ; leaving balance $1,448.69. The State common-school fund had on hand $54,620.56 ; receipts, $1,690,961.04 ; disbursements, $1,654,057.50 ; balance, $91,524.10. During the year the public funded debt of the State was reduced by the payment of loans to the amount of $619,-800. On Nov. 15, 1888, the public funded debt of the State was $3.046,665, of which $5,000 was foreign loan not bearing interest, $1,665 domestic debt, and the remainder 3-per-cent. loans payable July 1 yearly in sums of $250,-000, except in 1899, $240,000, and 1890, $300,-000. The irreducible State debt (trust funds) was $45,638,127. The aggregate of local debts in the State was $56,780,024.40, divided as follows : Counties, $7,110,343.24 ; cities, $44,-831,672.15 ; incorporated villages, $1,937,403.-24 ; townships, $451,734.76 ; special school districts, $2.448,871.01. There has been a steady annual increase of local indebtedness, mostly in counties and cities.

Property and Taxation.—The value of all taxable real estate and personal property in the State, according to the consolidated tax-duplicate of 1888, is as follows: Real estate in cities, towns, and villages, $477,604,587 ; real estate not in cities, towns, or villages, $722,459,608 ; chattel property, $531,994,601 ; total taxable values, $1,732,058,796. The taxes levied for 1889 on that basis are : Total State purposes (2 9-10 mills), $5,020,384.81 ; county purposes, $8,594,293.55 ; township, city, school, and special taxes, $19,318,687.33 ; levies for all purposes, $32,933,365.69 ; per-capita tax on dogs —for the sheep fund, $203,840 ; total taxes, including all the delinquinces of former years, $35,481,758.62.

Railroads.—The Commissioner of Railroads, in his annual report, gives the railroad mileage of entire lines that pass through Ohio, and places the Ohio mileage at about 10,227½ miles ; of this amount about 467¼ miles are in the hands of receivers, and of this total amount of track 6,960½ miles are laid with steel rail and 2,059¼ miles with iron. The total train mileage was 91,420,208, and of cars 1,489,572,169. The total tonnage of freight yielding revenue was 87,-030,555 ; total number of cars, 136,531. The average of passengers killed to number carried is 1 to 3,334,196. The number injured was 1,453, an average of one to 582,161 carried.

Centennial Celebrations.—The centennial of the settlement of Ohio and organization of the Territory of the Northwest was celebrated on four different occasions during the year. The first was at Marietta, to commemorate the landing at that place of the first colony, April 7, 1788. A second celebration was held in July at the same place to commemorate the organization of civil government in the new territory. Each celebration occupied several days and was participated in by representatives of other States, orations being delivered by Hon. George F. Hoar, of Massachusetts, Hon. John Randolph Tucker, of Virginia, Hon. William M. Evarts, of New York, and Hon. John W. Daniel, of Virginia, in addition to a number of speeches by eminent citizens of Ohio. The centennial celebration of the Ohio valley and Central States was held at Cincinnati and took the form of an exhibition showing the progress and present prosperity of those States. The exhibition was opened July 4 with exercises in which the States of Kentucky, Pennsylvania, Indiana, and Nebraska were represented by their respective executives and other officials and distinguished citizens. The Ohio Centennial celebration was at Columbus, taking the place of the annual State fair. It was opened September 4 with speeches by State and visiting officials, the States of Massachusetts and Connecticut being officially represented, and continued to October 19.

White Caps.—Ohio had been free from organized bands of outlaws that under various names had troubled neighboring States, but on the night of November 17 there suddenly appeared in the town of Sardinia, Brown County, a band of from thirty to fifty horsemen, wearing masks and calling themselves "White Caps," who went to the house of Adam Berkes, dragged him from his bed and severely whipped him, on the ground of immoral conduct. The local authorities failing to take cognizance of the crime, appeal was made to the Governor. In a message to the Legislature, the Governor said an investigation was immediately instituted, by which it was disclosed that a regular organization had been formed of a secret, oath-bound character, with a growing membership, including some prominent respectable and responsible citizens ; and that they were proceeding upon the theory that they would be strong enough to take the law into their own hands, defy the local authorities, and bring prosecutions against their members to naught if attempted. The declared purpose of the order was to protect society from petty crimes and misdemeanors for which, it was alleged, the tedious and expensive processes of the law afforded no adequate relief. It was manifest that the organization must be broken up at once. But it was difficult to ascertain who its members were, and to command the evidence necessary to support a prosecution and secure a conviction. No one that belonged to the organization could be found who could be, under any circumstances, induced to give testimony that would implicate a fellow-member. It was finally determined to accept as better than the uncertainty of waiting for testimony, which otherwise might never be obtained, and then resorting to legal proceedings, with the uncertainties, delays, and expenses always attendant thereon, the following agreement, which was signed by members of the order as settlement of the whole matter, viz.:

We, the undersigned, members of the organization known as White Caps, do hereby agree and bind ourselves to procure the immediate disbanding of said organization; and we do further promise and agree that there shall be no more raids, whippings, threatenings, intimidations, terrorizing, or other violation of law of any kind whatsoever by said organization or the members thereof, acting either together or separately; and we further agree that if this stipulation on our part be violated by any members of said organization who may refuse to be controlled by us we will, in such event, do all in our power to give information and to aid the officers of the law in bringing them to justice.

To all who in good faith sign and keep the above agreement the State hereby promises immunity from further proceedings against them.

The Governor informed the Legislature that "in pursuance of this agreement, the organization has been permanently disbanded and the State has been put in possession of all the evidence necessary to secure convictions should there be any necessity to resort to the courts."

The Legislature.—The sixty-eighth General Assembly began its session on January 2, with a Republican majority of 14 in the Senate and 20 in the House. The proceedings were more than ordinarily devoid of interest although a large number of laws were enacted, most of them of a local or minor character. The adjournment took place April 16. The liquor-tax law was amended by increasing the annual tax to $250. A board of pardons to advise with the Governor was created. Instruction as to the effect of alcoholic drinks and narcotics on the human system was ordered to be made part of the common-school course.

Political.—The Republican State Convention was held at Dayton, April 18, 19, and the Democratic at the same place, May 15, 16. The platforms of both parties were of the usual character. Prohibition and Union Labor Conventions were also held, and full State tickets placed in the field. There were but three State offices to be filled. The result of the election, November 6, was as follows: For Secretary of State, Daniel J. Ryan (Republican), 417,510; Boston G. Young (Democrat), 395,522; Walter S. Payne (Prohibition), 24,618; George F. Ebner (Union Labor), 3,452. For Judge of Supreme Court, Joseph P. Bradbury (Republican), 415,862; Lyman R. Critchfield (Democrat), 396,236; John T. Moore (Prohibition), 24,569; Grandison N. Tuttle (Union Labor), 3,422. For member of Board of Public Works, Wells S. Jones (Republican), 416,243; James Emmitt (Democrat), 395,869; James W. Penfield (Prohibition). 24,532; William W. Dunipace (Union Labor), 3,435.

ONTARIO, PROVINCE OF. By the retirement, through ill health, of the Hon. T. B. Pardee, Hon. A. S. Hardy became Commissioner of Crown Lands, and J. M. Gibson, of Hamilton, took his place as Provincial Secretary. A new portfolio of Agriculture was created, and Charles Drury was appointed minister. The reconstructed ministry is as follows: Lieutenant-Governor, Sir Alexander Campbell; Attorney-General, Oliver Mowatt; Commissioner of Public Works, C. F. Fraser; Commissioner of Crown Lands. A. S. Hardy; Provincial Treasurer, A. M. Ross; Minister of Education, G. W. Ross; Provincial Secretary, J. M. Gibson; Minister of Agriculture, Charles A. Drury.

Finances.—The financial statement for the year ending Dec. 31, 1888, showed a total expenditure of $3,536,248, and a total revenue of $3,589,423, leaving a surplus on the year's operations of $51,172. The surplus assets of the province over all liabilities are estimated at $6,734,649.

Dairy Industry.—The latest statistical abstract issued by the Provincial Bureau of Industries gives figures connected with the dairy industry of Ontario. The approximate product of cheese for three years was:

YEARS.	Pounds.	Value.
1885	71,209,719	$5,751,569
1886	63,721,621	5,898,818
1887	65,688,656	6,918,918

The quantity of milk used and the number of cheese-factories are given as follow for the same period:

YEARS.	Milk used.	No. of factories.
	Lbs.	
1885	733,497,254	752
1886	654,708,243	770
1887	691,934,579	737

The returns for butter are approximately as follow: 1885, 353.347 pounds, valued at $69,583; 1886, 823.853 pounds, at $160,797; 1887, 1,136,576 pounds, at $230,022.

Legislation.—The second session of the fifth Legislature opened Jan. 25, 1888. The principal measures adopted were: An act establishing manhood suffrage in provincial elections, doing away with property qualification, and granting the voting privilege to every male citizen twenty-one years of age, a British subject by birth or naturalization, and not disqualified by having been a criminal undergoing sentence in jail, or a lunatic, or receiving state aid as a pauper; an act creating a new Cabinet office, that of Minister of Agriculture; a measure giving municipalities the power to pass by-laws regulating the hours at which shops shall be closed, the by-law to be passed on application of three fourths of the occupiers of shops, the hour of closing in the evening to be not earlier than seven o'clock, and providing a system of penalties for violation of the law; a series of resolutions adopted at a conference in Quebec, in 1887, of representatives of the provinces of Canada, suggesting amendments to the Federal Constitution, assented to by the British Parliament in July, 1867.

Miscellaneous.—The public events of 1888 included the formal opening, on May 24, of the Canadian Park at Niagara Falls; the election of four members to the Legislature, through the deaths of the sitting members, the result being a net loss of one seat to the Government, which is sustained in the Legislature by a majority of 25 in a house of 91 members; the decision by the Imperial Privy Council of Great Britain, in a lawsuit appealed from the Supreme Court of Canada, awarding to Ontario a large tract of timber-lands, the ownership of which was in dispute, owing to their being Indian lands.

OREGON. State Government.—The following were the State officers during the year: Governor, Sylvester Pennoyer (Democrat); Secretary of State, George W. McBride; Treasurer, George W. Webb; Superintendent of Public Instruction, E. B. McElroy; Chief-Justice of the Supreme Court, William P. Lord; Associate Justices, William W. Thayer, and Reuben S. Strahan.

Finances.—The following is a statement of the indebtedness of Oregon on Jan. 1, 1889: Principal, $35,705.96; interest, $25,058.24; less funds applicable to its payment, $31,351.54; net indebtedness, $29,411.66. All other indebtedness is nominal and fully provided for. It is expected that the debt will have been extinguished before the year is over.

The expenditures in 1887–'88 were as follow:

Total amount of warrants drawn during term for expenditures during term	$763,656 53	
Deficiencies Jan. 1, 1889, for which warrants are yet to be drawn....	16,372 66	
		$777,029 19
Deduct expenses previously incurred	$45,740 70	
Expenditures for public buildings..	85,629 66	
Expenditures on account of trust funds and funds arising from special tax	65,466 99	
		196,837 35
Ordinary expenses	$580,191 84	

The expenditures for 1887–'88 were swollen by the outlay of about $25,000 on account of the Railroad Commission and the Fish Commission, with the outlay thereunder, to which the previous term was not subjected.

Education.—The following is a statement of the total amounts of the common-school funds on January 1 of each year: 1885, $868,735.16; 1887, $1,059,409.01; 1889, $1,756,700.90; increase of funds in 1885–'86, $190,637.85; and increase of funds in 1887–'88, $697,291.89. The interest arising from the fund during the past few years has been distributed as follows:

YEAR.	Per capita.	Total.
1885	$0 75	$50,046 75
1886	90	74,571 30
1887	1 00	87,217 00
1888	1 25	108,217 50

There were also on Jan. 1, 1889, in the other trust funds, the following amounts: Agricultural College fund, notes and cash, $100,511.80; Agricultural College fund, due on certificates of sale, $12,627.57; total, $113,139.37; University fund, notes and cash, $80,733.71; University fund, due on certificates, $1,472.32; total, $82,206.93. The money belonging to the foregoing trust funds is loaned on land at one third of its appraised value.

Agricultural College.—This institution has an endowment of upward of $100,000, the proceeds of the sale of the Agricultural College lands given by the General Government to the State. It also receives $15,000 a year from the Federal Government under the Hatch act. It has a commodious building, erected by the citizens of Corvallis. All that is needed to give it a fair start is to furnish it with the necessary land for a farm for which the Legislature has been asked to appropriate $10,000. When this shall have been received and the free scholarships abolished, the Agricultural College at Corvallis, like the State University at Eugene, will be able with frugal management to enjoy a prosperous existence without being a pensioner upon the tax-payers of the State. By authority of law, the Governor has accepted the college buildings and grounds for and in behalf of the State, and as such property is under State control, and in the peaceable possession of the State by virtue of deeds of title and possession, no suit can be maintained against the State in regard to it.

State University.—From the report of the president of the regents of the State University it appears that the institution now has, besides the Villard fund of $50,000, an endowment of over $80,000 arising from the sales of University lands, and that over 15,000 acres of such lands remain unsold. Of the 110 pupils in attendance at the university during the present year, 56 paid tuition and 54 had free scholarships. With its present endowment, and with the abolition of free scholarship, says the Governor, the State University can now prosper without imposing any further tax upon the people. Certain funds belonging to the State University at Eugene have been diverted for the support of a law school at Portland; but there is no authority of law for such diversion of the funds of the State University. It is suggested that the State should provide funds for the support of a school of medicine at Portland; but there is now in that city a college of medicine, built by private individuals, at a cost of $25,000.

The Salmon-Fishery.—Concerning these interests, the Governor in his message says:

Positive prohibitory enactments should be made against the taking of salmon in the Columbia river and its tributaries by either fish-traps or fish-wheels. There ought to be but one mode provided by law for the taking of salmon, and that mode should be the one open to all classes, and by which no monopoly or undue advantage can be had. It is due to those who will come after us that the fishing interest of our State should not be entirely destroyed by the greed and avarice of those now engaged in it. The records of the Supreme Court of our State disclose the fact that a paid lobby was employed by those interested in the monopolies of traps and fish-wheels during the last Legislature, and although such a lobby may again be employed, it is to be hoped that the Legislature will change the law by which the monopoly of the men owning fish-traps and fish-wheels may be destroyed. The last Legislature created a board of three fish commissioners, one of whom is denominated president, and the law creating such board declared that "it shall be the duty of the president to see that all laws for the propagation, protection, and preservation of food fishes in the public waters in the State of Oregon, whether entirely or partially within the State boundaries, are enforced." The Constitution of the State declares one of the prerogatives of the Governor to be that "he shall take care that the laws are faithfully executed." If the Legislature can thus rightfully invest a commission of its own creation and selection with the powers conferred upon the Governor by the fundamental law of the land, then our Constitution is a mere wanton fraud, and your supporting oaths a hollow mockery. The commission has been rather a detriment than an aid in the enforcement of the law. No further need for its existence remains since the Clackamas hatchery has passed under the control of the Federal Government, and no other suitable location in Oregon, as the board asserts, can be found. Besides, it can be questioned if it is any more just for the State to expend money in the establishment of fish-hatcheries in order that cannery men may have plenty of fish for future use than it would be to furnish seed wheat to the farmer in order to insure him future great harvests.

Political.—In June, 1888, a State election was held for the Chief-Justice of the Supreme Court, and William P. Lord was elected by 33,008 votes, against 26,336 for John Burnet. At the same time, Binger Herman was chosen, as a Republican, to Congress. The Legislature consists of twenty-one Republicans and nine Democrats in the Senate, and fifty-one Republicans and nine Democrats in the lower branch. The vote in the Presidential election was as follows: Gen. Harrison, 33,291; Mr. Cleveland, 26,522; Gen. Fisk, 1,677; Mr. Streeter, 363.

P

PARAGUAY, a republic in South America. (For details of the census taken in 1886, see "Annual Cyclopædia" for 1887.)

Government.—The President is Gen. Patricio Escobar, whose term of office will expire on Nov. 25, 1890. His Cabinet is composed of the following ministers: Interior, Col. Meza; Foreign Affairs, J. S. Decoud; Finances, H. Uriarte; Justice and Public Worship, M. Maciel; War, Col. Duarte. The United States Minister for Paraguay and Uruguay, resident at Montevideo, is John E. Bacon; the American Consul at Asuncion is Frank D. Hill. The Paraguayan Consul-General in the United States is John Stewart.

Army.—All citizens capable of bearing arms between the ages of twenty and thirty-five are liable to be enrolled in the army, but the strength of the latter has for economical reasons been reduced to 623 men. In case of war the National Guard is mobilized.

Navy.—The fleet consists of a screw-steamer registering 440 tons, carrying 4 guns, having 6 officers, and manned by 36 sailors, and of two small steamers doing river service.

Finances.—The foreign debt, contracted in 1871–'72, amounted in 1888 to $4,250,000, bearing 2 per cent. interest. After Jan. 1, 1892, the interest is to be 3 per cent., and after Jan. 1, 1897, 4 per cent. The home debt amounts to $1,068,250, the sinking-fund having canceled $398,000 in 1887. The revenue collected in 1887 was $1,609,030; money collected for land sales effected $329,146; total, $1,938,176; deducting therefrom the expenditure, which, together with the interest on the foreign and home debt, did not exceed $1,400,-503, there remained a surplus of $537,673. The Government still owed the National Bank $47,-200 in 1886; this money has been refunded, VOL. XXVIII.—43 A

and a total internal debt reduction effected in 1887 of $293,200.

Communications.—The number of items of mail matter in 1887 reached 438,846, the receipts amounting to $9,695. Aside from the 72 kilometres of telegraph running parallel with the Paraguari Railroad, there is the one from Paso de la Patria to Asuncion, which communicates with the world's cable system. The number of messages forwarded in 1887 was 31,857, the receipts aggregating $22,511.

The telephone service at Asuncion has been in operation since 1884, when a seven years' privilege was extended to the company. The lines measure 1,000 kilometres, the number of subscribers being 175.

There is in running order the line from Asuncion to Paraguari, 72 kilometres, and building the line from Paraguari to Villa Rica, 80 kilometres. There were 257,668 passengers in 1887, the expenses being $111,337, and the receipts $161,550. Some 25 kilometres of tramway are in operation at the capital.

Commerce.—The imports increased from $1,-805,741 in 1886 to $2,221,750 in 1887, and the exports from $1,620,779 to $1,715,853. The number of vessels that entered the ports of Montevideo and Buenos Ayres with cargoes intended for Paraguay was 320 in 1886, of which 223 were steamers; the tonnage being 60,408.

Education.—Besides the National College at Asuncion, attended by 209 students, there are 9 schools for boys in the capital and 7 for girls, attended respectively by 1,148 and 792 pupils. The number of professors at the National College is 21. The library contains 2,538 volumes, and had 2,626 readers in 1886.

Government Land Sales.—The proceeds of public lands during 1887 were $1,408,123, of which $485,489 were for cash and the remainder payable in installments between 1888 and 1891, both inclusive. The sale of Paraguay tea lands produced $73,938, of which $18,900 cash; the Government also collected $19,465 from renting tea-lands which it owns. The Government granted in 1888 to a Netherland society extensive concessions for the creation of tobacco-plantations.

Colonies. — The Government possesses two colonies, San Bernardino and Villa Hayes. The first-named extends along the shore of Lake Ipacaraí near the Aregua Railroad depot, and comprises 25 square leagues of exuberantly fertile land. The number of colonists was 384 in 1886, 69 new comers having arrived in that year. The second is in the Chaco, on the banks of the river, five miles from the capital, and the number of families composing the colony in 1886 was 31, only a dozen settlers having joined it during the year. Government agricultural lands are worth $2 to $4 the "cuadra"; private lands, $10 to $12.

German-Paraguayan Treaty. — The treaty of commerce and navigation, signed between Germany and Paraguay on July 21, 1887, was ratified and exchanged on May 18, 1888.

PATENTS. General Statistics.—The statement of the work of the United States Patent-Office for the year ending Dec. 31, 1888, will be found in the following summary:

Applications for patents for inventions	84,718
Applications for patents for designs	971
Applications for reissues of patents	113
Total number of applications relating to patents	85,797
Caveats filed	2,251
Applications for registration of trade-marks	1,814
Applications for registration of labels	729
Disclaimers filed	8
Appeals on the merits	1,252
Total	6,054
Total number of applications requiring investigation and action	41,351
Patents issued, including designs	20,420
Patents reissued	86
Trade-marks registered	1,059
Labels registered	327
Total	21,892
Patents expired during the year	11,687
Patents withheld for non-payment of final fee	2,881

In inventiveness the State of Connecticut led the list with one patent for every 820 inhabitants; the District of Columbia came next, with one for every 830 inhabitants; and Massachusetts was third with one for every 944 inhabitants. North Carolina was least inventive, only one inhabitant out of 25,450 securing a patent. In total patents issued New York was first with 3,634, however, only representing one to 1,398 inhabitants, giving her the eighth place in inventiveness. Among foreign countries England as usual has the best record, 523 American patents being issued to her citizens; Germany is next with 355 patents; and France is third with 131 patents; Brazil, the Canary Islands, China, Newfoundland, Queensland, Turkey, and Wales have one patent apiece.

The year 1888 in number of patents issued ranks fifth; it is surpassed in numbers by the years 1885 (24,233 patents), 1886 (22,508 patents), 1883 (22,383 patents), and 1887 (21,477 patents). The immense increase in business is shown by an examination of the records of past years. In 1837 only 436 patents were issued, and in 1855 for the first time the number exceeded two thousand (2,012 patents).

Commissioner's Report.—This document, dated Jan. 31, 1889, is published in the "Official Gazette" of the United States Patent-Office of Feb. 12, 1889. In addition to the usual interesting statistical tables, it contains various recommendations for legislation, among other changes suggesting the repeal of section 4887 of the patent laws. This is the section limiting the duration of an American patent to the shortest term of a foreign patent granted for the same invention to the same inventor. In the decision of the United States Supreme Court in "Bate *vs.* Hammond" noted below, some limitation of the scope of this statute was laid down.

Proposed Legislation.—One most important modification in the operation of the patent laws has been the subject of much agitation among those interested in patents, and involves the establishment of a new court, to be termed the Court of Patent Appeals. The fact is undoubted that the docket of the United States Supreme Court is overloaded with matter, much of which is appealed patent suits, in which the action is carried up from the United States circuit courts. The Supreme Court of the District of Columbia is the recipient of appeals from the Commissioner of Patents. The new body is to take the place of both these courts to a certain extent. It is to have jurisdiction over appellate cases coming from the circuit courts, the Supreme Court of the District, and the Commissioner of Patents. It is not proposed to make it of last resort. If a sufficient amount is involved cases can be carried up from it to the United States Supreme Court.

Litigation.—An important decision was rendered by Judge Kekewich, of London, in the English suit brought to annul the Ganlard and Gibbs patent on transformers; it declared the patent to be invalid. He so decided, concluding that the invention was not a fitting subject for a patent, as well as that the parties named were not the first inventors. The "transformer" as essential to the newly developed system of alternate current lighting has within the last year acquired much importance. Attention is called to a corresponding American decision (Westinghouse *vs.* Sun Electrical Company, see below). In England also Justice Kay declared the Edison "carbon filament," patent 4,576 of 1879, invalid, this being one of the basic patents on incandescent electric lamps.

One of the great patent suits reached an accounting during the last part of the year. It was brought by the Webster Loom Company against the Higgins Carpet Company. It referred to the famous Webster patent upon one feature of weaving Brussels carpet. The patent was granted in 1872, and a special company with a capital of $200,000 was formed to litigate it. The present suit occupied four years, 1874 to 1878, before the final hearing in the United States Circuit Court was reached, where the patent was decided to be invalid. On appeal the United States Supreme Court upheld the patent and ordered an accounting. Two years were devoted to it, and two tons of books and documents were eventually produced. The claim presented by the Webster Loom Company was $28,750,000. On cross-examination of the president of the company the claim was reduced to $1,500,000. His testimony embraced nearly 6,300 questions and extended over two years. In the final argument before the master eleven days were occupied and over 1,000 pages of briefs were handed him. His decision practically threw out the patent in suit as an element of damages. The Webster Company were awarded nothing. The most eminent counsel were retained in the case, which passes into history as one of the most famous patent litigations of America.

The Bell telephone patent at last reached the Supreme Court on appeal, five cases being consolidated into one for the purposes of the bearing. The court upheld the patent in its broadest scope, so that all electric speaking telephones are covered by it. A minority opinion representing the views of three out of seven judges was delivered as against the patent, in favor of the claims of priority of Daniel Drawbaugh. Meanwhile the suit brought by the Government for the cancellation of the Bell telephone patent of 1876 is slowly progressing. On a demurrer it reached the Supreme Court, and the Government's right to bring such a suit was upheld (see "Official Gazette" of the United States Patent-Office" xlv, 1,311).

A very important decision of the U. S. Supreme Court was rendered in the suit entitled Bate Refrigerating Company against George H. Hammond & Co. A United States patent had been awarded to John J. Bate for a process of preserving meat, and previous to the issue of his American patent he had taken out a Canadian patent for five years. Although by due payment of fees he had kept the Canadian patent alive for fifteen years, it not having as yet expired, it was claimed that the American patent was limited in duration to the first period of five years of the Canadian patent. The Supreme Court decided otherwise, and held that as long as the Canadian patent was extended it was without effect upon the American franchise. It did not state, however, that if the Canadian fees had not been paid, and the foreign patent had expired after five years, that such expiration would not have limited the American patent. It left it to be inferred that it would have had that effect.

Foreign Laws.—For changes or new legislation in, or recent publication of foreign patent laws, the following references to the "Official Gazette" of the United States Patent-Office are given: The Congo Free State, xlii, 202; Guatemala, xlii, 830; Germany, xliii, 889; British India, xliii, 1,588; South African Republic, xliv, 1,507; South Australia, xliv, 1,510; Switzerland, xlv, 233 and 1,070; New South Wales, xlv, 128.

Court Decisions.—Abstracts of some of the more important points decided in the Federal courts are given below, the references being to volume and page of the "Official Gazette."

The mere fact that a person sells an article to which a patented device may be attached does not make him an infringer, provided the article is not so constructed that the patented device and no other can be used with it. Bliss *et al. vs.* Merrill *et al.*, xlii, 97.

Where one patentee has invented a combination for a particular purpose, the field is open to another to invent a combination of the same parts differently arranged and affecting the same result by a different mode of operation. Railway Register Manufacturing Company *vs.* Third Avenue Railway Company *et al.*, xlii, 379.

The omission of one step of an old process with an improved result constitutes a new process. Lawther *vs.* Hamilton *et al.*, xlii, 487.

Where the new process requires greater care, or even greater skill, on the part of the workmen than formerly, it does not change its character as a process or materially affect its utility. Ibid.

A patent sufficiently describes a process when by the aid of the knowledge derived from the state of the art the same may be carried out from the description in the patent by those skilled in the particular manufacture. Ibid.

A claim for a process consisting of several steps may be limited by the state of the art and the description in the patent to the instrumentalities or their equivalents as thus described, which are essential in the carrying out of the process claimed. Ibid.

In claims for combinations it is unnecessary to include any element except such as are essential to the peculiar combination and affected by the invention. Rapid Service Store Railway Company *vs.* Taylor *et al.*, xlii, 721.

A reconstruction of a machine so that a less number of parts will perform all the functions of the greater may be invention of a high order; but the omission of a part with a corresponding omission in function, so that the retained parts do just what they did before in the combination, can not be other than a mere matter of judgment, depending upon whether it is desirable to have the machine do all or less than it did before. McClain *vs.* A. Ortmayer & Sons *et al.*, xlii, 724.

Where notice is not given in the answer of a specified prior use of the invention described in the patent, it can not be set up as an anticipation of such invention; but, as exhibiting the state of the art, the evidence is competent to aid the court in putting a proper construction on the patent. Stevenson *vs.* Magowan *et al.*, xlii, 1,063.

A fraudulent surreptitious purchase or construction or use of an invention prior to the application for a patent probably would not affect the rights of the patentee under this section of the act of 1839. Andrews *et al. vs.* Hovey, xlii, 1,285.

After a patent has been granted for an article described or made in a certain way the inventor can not afterward obtain a valid patent on an independent application for the method or process of making the article in the way described in the earlier patent. The Mosler Safe and Lock Company *vs.* Mosler, Bahmann & Company, xliii, 1,115.

It is not material whether the foreign patent is granted to the inventor who made the application in this country or to some other person to whom he has caused the invention to be patented, nor that the inventor who makes the application here is one of our citizens. Edison Electric Light Company *vs.* United States Electric Lighting Company, xliii, 1,456.

It is difficult to find invention in mixing or putting together, in a dry state, two materials, it being old to mix the same materials during the process of manufacturing or brewing. Geis *vs.* Kimber, xliv, 108.

Where a patent has been found to be valid by a circuit court at an earlier date upon the same evidence as now exhibited, and since that date the Supreme Court has defined more strictly the line between mere mechanical skill and the exercise of invention, it is no longer the duty of the last circuit court to follow and adopt the adjudication of the former court. The Rubber and Celluloid Harness Trimming Company *vs.* The India-Rubber Comb Company, xliv, 343.

For several important points in this connection, see Russia Cement Company *vs.* Le Page, xliv, 833.

The inventor's consent to or allowance of the public use or sale of his invention is not requisite to invalidate a patent. Campbell *vs.* The Mayor, etc. of New York, xliv, 1,185.

Three things are requisite to the acquisition of a title to a trade-mark. First, the person desiring to acquire the title must adopt some mark not in use to distinguish goods of the same class or kind already on the market; second, he must apply his mark to some article of traffic; third, he must put his article marked with his mark on the market. Mere adoption of the mark and a public declaration that the mark so adopted will be used to distinguish goods to be put on the market at a future time, create no right, no title arises until the thing is actually on the market marked with the particular mark. Schneider *et al. vs.* Williams xlv, 1,400.

A "sale," to invalidate a patent, must have been completely effected more than two years before the application for the patent. Campbell *vs.* The Mayor, etc. of New York, xlv, 345.

For limitation of the Ganlard and Gibbs converter system of distributing electric energy, see Westinghouse Electric Company *vs.* The Sun Electric Company, xlv, 710.

PECULIAR PEOPLE. The sect of Peculiar People was established in Essex, England, about half a century ago; and, while members of the body have removed to London and other parts of the United Kingdom, and some have emigrated to the colonies, it still exists in its greatest strength in that county, and chiefly at Prittlewell. The name of the body is taken from the Scripture, and the particular tenet for which they are principally known is founded on these words of St. James: "Is any sick among you? let him call for the elders of the Church; and let them pray over him, anointing him with oil in the name of the Lord: and the prayer of faith shall save the sick, and the Lord shall raise him up." They argue that this text proves that medical aid is needless, and when a member of the body falls sick, the elders pray over him and anoint him, and then leave nature to take its course. Their steadfast adherence to this belief and practice has many times brought them in conflict with the laws which require a certain amount of care and attention to be given to children and the sick. Members of the sect have been prosecuted for neglect of those dependent upon them in not calling medical aid to their relief; and, in cases where the patients died, prosecutions for manslaughter have been instituted

against those responsible for their care. Conviction in the latter kind of cases is, however, difficult, because medical men are not able or willing to declare positively that if called in they would have advised measures that would have saved life. Hence only one conviction is recorded against them for this offense. Aside from this idiosyncrasy the Peculiar People are reputed to be exemplary in the social virtues. While none among them are wealthy and few are above the condition of laborers, they never permit one of the "brethren" to become chargeable to the poor-rates. They are faithful and careful in their family relations, always make full provision of wholesome food, are strict abstainers from intoxicating drinks, are neat and cleanly, and are orderly citizens, no instance being known of any of them having been brought before the courts, except in connection with their single peculiarity. Their Church polity is of a very simple character. They recognize a single head or bishop, who is at present Mr. Samuel Harrod, from whose decisions there is no appeal. Their worship is marked by earnest singing of easy tunes, usually without the aid of musical instruments. For the most part their meetings are held in barns and other buildings of that character; but they have erected a few special places of worship, to which members of congregations are often drawn from considerable distances.

PENNSYLVANIA. State Government.—The following were the State officers during the year Governor, James A. Beaver, Republican; Lieutenant-Governor, William T. Davies; Secretary of State, Charles W. Stone; Treasurer, William B. Hart; Auditor-General, A. Wilson Norris (who died on May 21); Secretary of Internal Affairs, Thomas J. Stewart; Attorney-General, W. S. Kirkpatrick; Superintendent of Public Instruction, E. E. Higbee; Insurance Commissioner, J. M. Forster; Chief-Justice of the Supreme Court, Isaac G. Gordon; Justices, Edward M. Paxson, John Trunkey, James P. Sterrett, Henry Green, Silas M. Clark, and Henry W. Williams. Justice Trunkey died on June 24, and the Governor appointed Alfred Hand to fill the vacancy, his commission dating from July 31 and continuing till the first Monday of January, 1889.

Finances.—The Legislature of 1887 made appropriations amounting to nearly $17,000,000, but the revenues were about two millions less, and several important public works were necessarily postponed, including the remodeling of the legislative building, and the enlargement of the House of Refuge in Philadelphia. The revenues have also been crippled by the decision of the Supreme Court of the United States, that what was known as the "gross-receipts tax" is unconstitutional so far as it is a tax on interstate commerce. The loss in revenue from this source in 1888 was about $800,000, but owing to the thorough collection of claims due the State, little embarrassment was experienced. The receipts for the year amount to $8,694,060.42, of which $5,-920,504.06 belong to the general fund and $2,-773,556.36 to the sinking-fund, the former being applicable to general purposes, and the latter to the redemption of the principal and the payment of the interest on the public debt. The principal items of the receipts were: Taxes on corporations, $2,398,405.44; tax on bank stock, $456,102.76; tax on personal property, $1,014,823.20; tax on collateral inheritances, $713,434.11; tavern and liquor licenses, $1,-017,807.57; tax on foreign insurance companies, $428,816.41; commutation of tonnage tax, $460,000. The principal items of disbursement during 1888 were: Expenses of State Government, $790,535.30; judiciary, $560,611.01; payment of loans and interest, $1,884,322.26; charitable institutions, $1,063,-077.91; penitentiaries, $244,686.25; reform schools, $226,242.16; common schools, $1,-614,276.58; National Guard, $354,446.37; Soldiers' Home, $151,850; soldiers' orphans' schools, $336,419.22; second geological survey, $50,000; State College, $59,500. The balance in the treasury Dec. 1, 1888, was $3,-687,035.65, against $2,380,841.47 on the same date in 1887. Of this balance, only $1,318,-691.92 is applicable to general expenses, the sinking-fund absorbing the rest.

The State debt on Nov. 30, 1888, was as follows: Non-interest bearing debt, $134,621.28; 3½-per-cent. bonds, $1,857,900; 4-per-cent. bonds, $7,798,700; 5-per-cent. bonds, $4,430,-500; 6-per-cent. Agricultural College bond, $500,000; 6 per cent. on proceeds of sale of experimental farms, $17,000; making an aggregate indebtedness of $14,738,921.28.

The 5-per-cent. loan may be paid in accordance with its terms in 1892. The available funds are more than sufficient to pay this balance now, and the commissioners have endeavored to purchase these bonds at a reasonable premium, but many holders refuse to sell. The larger part of the balance of the debt, funded at 3½ and 4 per cent., is not due until 1912. The net reduction in the debt for 1888 was $496,794.90.

Education.—The State is divided into thirteen normal-school districts. There are normal schools in eleven districts, and a twelfth has recently been erected at Centerville, leaving only one district (the fourth) without a school. The Central State Normal-School buildings at Lock Haven have recently been burned. There has been a strong movement to secure industrial training as part of the public-school system, and in 1887 the Legislature authorized the Governor to appoint a commission to investigate the subject. The commission report strongly in favor of the system. Isaiah V. Williamson, a wealthy citizen of Philadelphia, toward the end of 1888, conveyed to trustees property valued at several million dollars for the establishment of a "Free School of Mechanical Trades." The State College has had a year of prosperity, there being ninety students

in the college and seventy-seven in the preparatory department, with nineteen professors.

Soldiers' Orphans' Schools.—The Legislature of 1887 provided for the closing of these schools on June 1, 1890. The Governor recommends the repeal of this law, and calls attention to the fact that, at the time set for closing the schools, there will be 1,549 children in them under the age of sixteen, all orphan children of deceased soldiers of the Union. There are at present in these schools 2,249 children, the schools having been established in 1864. By the same act, the schools were closed to further applicants June 1, 1887, yet many applications have been made.

Insurance.—The last annual report of the insurance commissioner gives the following statement of the business done in the State in 1887: Premiums for life insurance, $10,855,-456.37; premiums for fire and marine insurance, $9,305,172.21; total paid for insurance, $20,160,628.58. This aggregate is $1,880,-550.16 greater than the total sum paid for insurance in 1886. The total losses paid in 1887 were as follow: Paid by fire and marine companies, $5,400,637.34; paid by life companies, $4,357,188.36; total losses paid, $9,757,825.70.

National Guard.—The last annual report of the adjutant-general gives the total strength of the guard at 7,788 enlisted men and 601 officers. In twenty-three counties no military organization exists, while in the two counties of Allegheny and Philadelphia there are fifty-four companies. The annual appropriation for the guard has been increased from $220,000 to 300,000, and the term of enlistment reduced from five to three years.

State Institutions.—The last Legislature provided for the erection of an Industrial Reformatory at Huntington. The buildings have been erected and equipped, but, owing to the fact that no appropriation had been made for maintenance, the institution is not open. The courts have discretion to send convicts to this reformatory instead of to the State penitentiaries. Work on the Western Penitentiary approaches completion. The Eastern Penitentiary continues what is known as the solitary or confinement plan. The House of Refuge in Philadelphia is about to make an important departure. Through the liberality of two individuals, large funds have been given for the purchase of a farm and the erection of new buildings. The five insane asylums of the State contain 4,265 inmates, of whom 1,568 are at Norristown, 676 at Warren, 843 at Danville, 618 at Dixmont, and 560 at Harrisburg. The number has largely increased by reason of the legislation requiring the removal of insane in county homes to the State institutions.

Decision.—Late in December the State Supreme Court rendered a decision declaring the act of 1887, dividing the cities of the State into seven classes, unconstitutional and void, on the ground that the act was in the nature of local and special legislation. This decision brings into force again the act of 1874, dividing cities into three classes, which the same court has already decided to be valid.

Harbor at Philadelphia.—The Governor says in his message to the Legislature in January, 1889:

Smith's and Windmill Islands, which constitute a formidable obstacle to navigation and lie directly in the harbor, must be purchased and entirely removed, and 140 acres of Petty's Island cut away. It is proposed to give to the harbor of Philadelphia a channel from the upper part of the city to Delaware Bay 600 feet wide and 26 feet deep at mean low water. The entire cost of this work, when completed, will exceed $6,000,000. An appropriation for $500,000 for beginning the work has already been made by Congress with this proviso: "That no part of this sum shall be expended until the title to the lands forming said islands shall be acquired and vested in the United States without charge to the latter, beyond $300,000 of the sum herein appropriated." Proceedings to condemn these islands for public use have been already commenced. It is believed that the amount necessary to pay for them will equal $700,000 to $800,000.

Political.—The Republican State Convention met at Harrisburg on April 25, and nominated delegates to the National Convention and a candidate for Judge of the Supreme Court to succeed Chief-Justice Gordon. For the latter office James T. Mitchell secured the nomination, after several ballots, over the Chief-Justice and several other contestants. Resolutions were passed demanding legislation by Congress to secure fair elections, protesting against placing wool on the free list, reiterating the doctrine of protection and continuing:

We recognize the strength of the sentiment in this commonwealth relative to the evils and abuses of the sale of liquor; and we favor all laws looking in this respect to the elevation of the moral condition of the people. We, therefore, repeat our pledge to submit the question of prohibition to a popular vote.

We earnestly protest against the passage by Congress of the "Dunn Free-Ship Bill" which has been reported to the House by the Democratic majority of the Committee on Merchant Marine, or any other similar measure, as calculated to work an injustice to American labor by imperiling the livelihood of the large number of workers in wood, metals, and other materials, who are engaged in American ship-building industries and who should have home protection the same as other wage-workers.

We have the enactment of a law that will allow the laborer an exemption to the amount of $300 from levy and sale upon execution.

We recommend such a revision of the revenue laws of the State as will impose upon corporations taxation equal in amount to that from which they have been exempted by judicial decisions recently rendered.

On May 23 the Democratic Convention at Harrisburg nominated J. B. McCollum for Judge of the Supreme Court, and selected delegates to the National Convention and electors-at-large for the State. The delegates to the National Convention were instructed to vote for the renomination of President Cleveland. The platform included the following:

We denounce the prevalent abuse of corporate power, the formation and operation of trusts, combinations, and monopolies, all of which interfere with and limit the natural and inalienable rights of the individual; and we pledge ourselves to secure remedies and to apply the same, with due regard for all interests of the people.

The Republican party is justly responsible for the failure of the late Legislature to give relief to the tax-payers by the enactment of an equitable and judicious revenue law; and the scandal connected with the failure of the revenue bill to become a law should work a forfeiture of all claims of that party to legislate for the people of the commonwealth.

The present State administration is to be condemned for its failure to enforce the provisions of the Constitution against the consolidation of corporations and other encroachments and abuses of corporate power; it has failed and refused to redeem the pledges of its own party; and the action of the last Republican Legislature in the defeat of the bill for the relief of the producers and refiners of oil, known as the Billingsley Bill, was in the interest of monopoly and opposed to the interests of the people of that large section of the State for whose relief the bill was intended.

On May 3, the Prohibitionists at Harrisburg selected delegates to their National Convention, and nominated James Black for Supreme Judge. The Union Labor party nominated John B. Young for the same office.

The death of Auditor-General Norris, on May 21, rendered necessary the election of a successor at the November election, and candidates were nominated by the executive committees of the various parties. By the Republicans, Thomas McCamant was made the candidate; by the Democrats, Henry Meyer; by the Prohibitionists, Milton S. Marquis; by the Union Labor party, J. M. Green. A vacancy on the Supreme Court bench, caused by the death of Judge Trunkey, on June 24, made it necessary to choose two judges of that court in November; but, in consequence of a peculiar provision of the State Constitution, that when two judges are to be chosen at one election, each voter is limited to vote for only one, no further party nominations were necessary. At the November election, therefore, both the Republican and Democratic nominees for this office were elected, being the two highest candidates. Mitchell received 523,585 votes; McCollum, 444,327; Black, 20,708; and Young 3,877. For Auditor-General, McCamant received 523,581 votes; Meyer, 443,438; Marquis, 20,262; and Green, 3,575. The Republicans elected 34 members of the State Senate, and the Democrats 16; of the Lower House, 114 members are Republican, and 60 Democratic. In the Third, Eighth, Ninth, Thirteenth, Seventeenth, Nineteenth, and Twenty-eighth Congressional Districts, Democratic candidates were elected; in the remaining 21 districts the Republicans were successful. This is a gain of one district for the Republicans.

PERSIA, an empire in Central Asia. The government is an unlimited monarchy. The present ruler is Nassreddin, who was born July 18, 1831, and succeeded his father Mohammed Shah, in September, 1848. The heir-apparent, called Valiahd, is his son Muzaffereddin, born March 25, 1853. The Shah has the entire revenue of the country at his disposal, and has amassed a private fortune said to amount to $35,000,000, most of it in the form of precious stones. The governors-general of the provinces, who possess a large measure of authority, are mostly sons or relatives of the Shah. The priests are a powerful body, exercising a strong restraining influence over the acts of the Shah, and opposing all ideas of progress coming from Europe. The chief priest is the Mujtahad, who resides at Kerbela, near Bagdad.

Legal Reform.—Justice is administered by the governors and their representatives, who follow the *Urf* or common law, and by the priests and Sheikhs-el-Islam, who are guided by the *Shar*, or sacred written law. The Shah and his governors are unrestricted in their powers, and have abused their authority to enrich themselves in a way to check production and material progress. In May, 1888, the Shah issued an edict promising to the people equal justice and protection against extortion and oppression. He declared that henceforward every Persian shall have the complete disposal of his property, and shall be at liberty to enter into financial associations for the construction of public works, or for other purposes.

Russian and English Rivalry.—Russian influence has for a long period been preponderant at the Persian court, more especially since the Russian possessions in Turkistan have been extended so as to encompass Persian territory on the northeast and east. A Belgian company has recently begun, under Russian auspices, a railroad 200 miles long, connecting Teheran, the Persian capital, with Resht, near the Caspian Sea, which will probably be extended to Baku, where it will join the Russian system of railroads. The first section of the railroad was opened in June, 1888. Sir Henry Drummond Wolff, the present English Minister to Persia, has endeavored to regain the influence that Great Britain formerly had in Teheran, and has encouraged the Shah to take a more independent stand in dealing with Russian demands, by holding out hopes of the political and financial support of Great Britain. The edict promising protection to companies was suggested by the British representative, who pressed for a concession to a British company to construct a railroad from Teheran to the Persian Gulf, as a counterpoise to the Russian railroad. Instead of this, he obtained for foreign merchant steamers of all nations the right to navigate Karun river as far as Ahvaz, 125 miles from its mouth. This river, which enters the estuary of the Euphrates after many windings, is one of the few navigable waterways in a country devoid of roads. The Russian Government assumed a threatening attitude toward Persia on account of this concession and other anti-Russian proceedings that took place during the absence of Prince Dolgorouky, the Czar's representative in Teheran. The Shah's proclamation was communicated to the powers in a circular note dated Oct. 30, 1888. Sir H. Drummond Wolff, the son of a German missionary who once visited Persia and Turkistan, found the Shah fully alive to the danger of Russian proximity on the east, especially to the rich province of Khorassan, whose inhabitants have twice rebelled. En-

couraged by signs of English support, the Shah refused the Russian application for the right to establish a consulate at Meshed, and forbade the exportation of grain from Khorassan into Turkistan at Lutfabad. The vigorous representations of the Russian Government led the Shah afterward to retreat from the bold position he had been encouraged to take, and to undo most of the advantages that England had gained while the Russian minister was away from his post. The refusal of the *exequatur* to the Russian consul at Meshed was held by Russia to be a violation of the treaties of peace, commerce, and navigation; and when the Persian Government replied that no other power had a consul in that place, it was pointed out that Gen. Macleod, the British agent to supervise the Afghan frontier, has his headquarters at Meshed. The Shah not only gave way on this point, but issued in December a second note as an appendix to his circular throwing open the Karun to international navigation, in which he greatly limited the privileges to British commerce and enterprise that were supposed to have been granted. The later note forbids Persian subjects to undertake works of any kind with the help of foreign capital, declaring that all irrigation-works, roads, and other undertakings must be carried out by Persian subjects with Persian capital. The proclamation that Sir Henry Drummond Wolff induced the Shah to issue in May, encouraging the formation of companies and promising them protection, was supposed to grant to foreigners the right to embark in speculations in Persia, and to give foreign governments a claim to interfere in behalf of companies or capitalists, and it was so construed by the British Under-Secretary for Foreign Affairs, who affirmed in Parliament the right to appeal to the proclamation, since it had been formally communicated to the foreign representatives in Teheran, as well as to the most-favored-nation clause as a guarantee of the rights of British companies for the construction of railroads and carriage-roads from the Persian Gulf.

PERU, a republic in South America. (For details relating to area, population, etc., see "Annual Cyclopædia" for 1883.)

Government. — The President (since June 3, 1886) is Gen. Andres Avelino Cáceres. The Cabinet is composed of the following ministers: President of the Council and Minister of the Interior, Don Pedro A. del Solar; Minister of Justice, Señor Zegarra; Minister of Foreign Affairs, Don Isaac Alzamora; Minister of Finance, Señor Urigoyen; Minister of War, Señor Torrico. The United States Minister at Lima is Charles W. Buck. The American Consul at Callao is Henry May Brent. The Peruvian Minister at Washington is Don Felix Cipriano C. Zegarra. The Peruvian Consul at New York is Don Francisco Perez de Vilasco.

Finances.—The home debt of Peru included, October, 1888, $39,235,947 of bonded debt, inclusive of accumulated interest; $10,000,000 of floating debt; $77,469,923 of paper money in circulation ($1,530,077 having been burned and replaced by silver coin in April, 1888); and $9,541,000 of Inca notes outstanding; together, $136,246,870. Of the proceeds of the alcohol tax, 70 per cent. are to be applied to paying the interest on the bonded debt, and 30 per cent. to the gradual withdrawal of the paper money.

As a measure of economy, the salaries of Peruvian consuls have been discontinued by decree of Aug. 23, 1887; by way of compensation, they are to be allowed to retain a part of the consular fees.

Army and Navy.—The strength of the permanent army, rank and file, is 7,371 men, including a police force of 3,371, of whom 843 are mounted. The fleet has been reduced to two steam transports, registering 1,300 tons each. In January, 1888, it was resolved to reorganize the national forces by enrolling all Peruvians between the ages of twenty-one to thirty years in the active National Guard, in which they are to serve for five consecutive years, and a sufficient number of them drawn annually to be incorporated in the permanent army for the remainder of their term of service.

In May a decree was issued organizing the naval militia, under the law of Oct. 30, 1886. A naval school was founded at Callao in February, 1888.

New Treaty.—A treaty of amity and commerce between the United States and Peru was proclaimed on Nov. 7, 1888.

Communications.—The number of post-offices in 1886 was 230, which forwarded during the year 2,254,434 items of mail matter, the receipts being 741,551 francs, and the expenses 798,976 francs.

In addition to the 2,600 kilometres in running order, the Government, by decree, in November, invited tenders for the construction and exploitation of a line from Lima to Pisco. This line will open communication between the capital and the fertile region extending between Ica and Islay, and will also intersect the nitrate fields. A branch line is to connect Islay with Arequipa.

A decree of January 26 invited tenders for the organization of communication by telephone throughout the republic, the exclusive privilege to extend fifteen years.

In May, 1888, a new steamship line was established between Antwerp and Chilian and Peruvian ports. It is called the "Anglo-Belgian Pacific Line."

Commerce.—The trade between Peru and the leading maritime nations has of late years been as follows:

COUNTRIES.	Import from Peru.	Export to Peru.
United States (fiscal year 1887).	$461,726	$717,968
England (calendar year 1886)....	8,108,311	4,204,983
France (calendar year 1885)	4,155,708	1,890,492
Germany (calendar year 1885)..	1,408,484	298,090
Spain (calendar year 1885)......	147,425	15,250

The American trade with Peru presents these figures:

FISCAL YEAR.	Import from Peru.	Domestic export to Peru.
1886..........................	$961,480	$798,577
1887..........................	461,726	717,968
1888..........................	809,040	865,180

Before the war, Peru produced annually 60,000 tons of sugar; in 1888 the production had decreased to 30,000 tons, half of the fine machinery on the sugar-estates having been destroyed during the war, and little of it replaced for lack of funds in the present impoverished condition of the country. The export of silver from Callao during the first six months of 1888 amounted to 4,936,876 kilogrammes, the bulk of which was shipped to Hamburg. Hitherto argentiferous lead bullion has been shipped to Germany, but now a German company is smelting on the spot.

A decree was issued in September, by virtue of which coal is to enter Peru duty free. The same privilege is extended to personal effects the property of foreign diplomatic agents; steam fire-engines and all fire-extinguishing apparatus; articles imported for hospital use and asylums; clerical church garments and sacred vessels; school and university books and apparatus.

PETROLEUM (Latin, *petra*, a rock, and *oleum*, oil), rock-oil, is that form of bitumen which has an oily or etherial consistence. The lighter varieties are sometimes called naphtha (Persian, *nafta*). It rises with the water of springs and through artesian borings. (The history of the petroleum industry, down to 1875, is given in the "American Cyclopædia," vol. xiii.)

An examination of the relative position of many of the most successful wells led C. D. Angell to the opinion that the strata of sandrock in Pennsylvania, from which the oil issued, extended northeast and southwest on certain parallel lines of moderate lateral extent. This led to the sinking of "wild-cat" or prospective wells upon such lines, run by compass for long distances in both directions over the hills of that region, and resulted in the discovery and development, about 1875, of the Butler and Clarion County fields; later, in an opposite direction, to the Bradford or McKean County field; still later, to that of Warren County, Pa., and Allegany County, N. Y. The enormous volumes of inflammable gas that often accompanied petroleum led, in 1885, to the drilling of wells for natural gas over an area extending from Michigan to Alabama, and from the Alleghany to the Rocky mountains. Not only gas but petroleum was discovered in several localities where it had not been known to exist. Most notable among these is the region around Washington, in southwestern Pennsylvania; and in northwestern Ohio, around Lima, Findlay, and North Baltimore, in Hancock, Wood, and Auglaise Counties. Attempts had been made as early as 1860, and again in

1865, to obtain oil in commercial quantities in southern California. But little success attended these efforts until about 1880. Several wells have been successful at or near Los Angeles, also near Newhall and in the Sespé Cañon, and on the Ojai Ranch. These last-mentioned localities lie along the Santa Clara valley, east of San Buenaventura, in Ventura County. The oil is chiefly used as fuel.

Distribution. — Petroleum, as well as other forms of bitumen, is one of the most widely distributed substances in nature; but its occurrence in commercial quantities is limited to comparatively small areas. Besides the petroleum regions of the United States, the only region that furnishes petroleum to commerce is Galicia and Roumania and the Apsheron peninsula of the Caspian Sea, which really form one region, extending from central Austria along the line of the Transylvanian Alps and the Caucasus to the shores of the Caspian and farther east into Central Asia. Other localities of less importance, together with the " oil regions " of the United States, form an ellipse around the Cincinnati anticlinal, which is in general an uplift of Silurian rocks sloping in all directions, and extends from central Kentucky to Lake Erie. Starting at Great Manitoulin Island, in the northern part of Lake Huron, and passing southwesterly to Chicago, petroleum is encountered at several points in eastern Michigan, near Chicago in limestone, in northwestern Ohio, at Lima, rarely in Indiana, and in Illinois, Kentucky, and Tennessee, as far south and east as Chattanooga, where the line of outcrop turns north and appears in Cumberland and Johnson Counties, Kentucky, and in West Virginia, southeastern Ohio, Greene and Washington Counties, Pa., and all through the valley of the Alleghany into New York. The oil-fields of Canada complete the ellipse. In Kansas, Missouri, Lousiana, and Texas, springs of petroleum occur, but few wells have proved productive, Farther west, in Wyoming, Utah, and Colorado, several localities produce petroleum for local uses. Along the mountain-range from Alaska to Patagonia petroleum has been found at intervals, and it has been produced in commercial quantities in California and Peru. In Cuba and the Windward Islands, including Trinidad, and on the mainland in Venezuela, and southward into Bolivia, the outcrops of bitumen of various forms are of marvelous extent, especially the famous Pitch Lake of Trinidad. An area fifteen hundred miles long and of unknown breadth extends from the Saskatchewan northward along the valley of the Mackenzie river to its mouth.. On the Eastern Continent petroleum has been observed in insignificant quantities in the British Islands, along the Pyrennees, in central France, in the valley of the Rhône, in the Tyrol, Italy, Sicily, Dalmatia, and the Ionian Islands; in Egypt along the Red Sea; in Morocco. At various points in China, and in Japan, oil-springs have been known from time immemorial, and oil-wells have occasionally been productive.

Beginning on the Lüneburger heath, south of Hamburg, a line of outcrops extends through Germany and Austria-Hungary, through the principalities north of the Danube, the Crimea, Kertch, the Caucasus, through Armenia and the mountains that surround the plateau of Iran, along the valleys of the Euphrates and the Tigris, eastward through the Punjab, through the Burman peninsula, and into Java. In Austria-Hungary the production has been of moderate commercial importance for many years. In the Caucasus and at Baku wells have poured forth enormous quantities and are now rivaling those of the United States. In Armenia and Persia, the Punjab and Burmah, and the Assyrian valley, the use of petroleum and other forms of bitumen for local purposes has been continuous from remote antiquity, but the amount produced is nowhere of commercial importance. A careful study of all the localities mentioned will show them to be intimately connected with the principal mountain-chains of the world.

Geological Relations. — Petroleum occurs in, or issues from all geological formations, but this statement alone would be misleading. There have been two bitumen-producing eras in geological history, viz., the series older than the carboniferous, especially the Silurian, and the older Tertiary. The vast accumulations along the principal axis of occurrence in North America are found in Silurian and Devonian rocks; the most productive axis of occurrence in the Eastern Hemisphere lies in the Eocene and Miocene of the Carpathians, Transylvanian Alps, and the Caucasus. In England the small quantities obtained have sprung from the Coal-Measures; in the valley of the Rhône from Jurassic limestones. The little that is known concerning the geology of the oil-bearing strata in Persia, the Punjab, and Burmah, leads to the conclusion that they are of the same age. At Great Manitoulin Island, in Canada, and in northwestern Ohio the oil is found in the Trenton limestone; at Chicago and Terre Haute, Ind., in the Niagara limestone; both of which are Silurian. The Great Devonian black shale is considered to be the source of the oil in Kentucky. At Glasgow the oil is found saturating sandstone; near Burkesville in crevices in a sort of marble; near Nashville, Tenn., it is often found in geodes in the Silurian rocks of that region; in Johnson County, Ky., it lies in the Subcarboniferous sandstones, often above the drainage-level of the country. In West Virginia the so-called " oil-break " yields oil from several strata of sandstone that lie within the Coal-Measures. Throughout the oil regions of Pennsylvania and New York the " oil-sands " are found beneath the Coal-Measures, in the Upper Devonian. "Petroleum exists in the Cretaceous rocks which extend along the eastern slope of the Rocky mountains from British Columbia to Mexico, and in many of the interior valleys." The bitumen of California is Miocene, while that of Mexico, the West India Islands, and Peru, is Eocene.

It will be seen that there is an area, estimated at 200,000 square miles in the Mississippi valley, the formations of which are nowhere later than the Coal-Measures, which yields petroleum at many points and often in vast quantities. Another area yielding bitumen, of vast extent, reaching from California to Bolivia is everywhere Tertiary; while on the Eastern Continent a belt of corresponding age, so far as is known, extends from the North Sea to Java. At present, the greatest volume of petroleum issues from rocks older than the Carboniferous, while the greater number of localities producing bitumen are Eocene. In Canada and West Virginia it rises from sandstone strata beneath the crowns of anticlinals, as also in northwestern Ohio, where the rock is the Trenton limestone. In Pennsylvania the so-called "oil-sands" appear to lie in the inclosing rocks in long narrow belts or sheets, far beneath superficial erosion, like sand-bars in a flowing stream. They run through a vast accumulation of sediments, from the lower Devonian to the Upper Carboniferous, and lie conformably with the inclosing rocks dipping gently to the southwest. The Bradford field—at a depth of about 1,800 feet, 100 square miles in extent, by from 20 to 80 feet in thickness—lies with its lowest southwestern edge submerged in salt water, and its northeastern edge filled with gas, originally under an enormous pressure. In Galicia the sandstones that hold the oil are implicated in the folds of the Carpathians and much distorted; while at Baku the sands appear to be lenticular masses inclosed in a stiff blue clay.

Chemistry.—The first analyses of petroleum were ultimate, and showed that it consists of carbon and hydrogen, with occasional small quantities of sulphur and nitrogen appearing as impurities. There are, however, several varieties of petroleum, to some extent dependent upon the age of the rocks from which they issue. All, or nearly all, Trenton limestone petroleum contains sulphur and more or less nitrogen. The Upper Devonian and Subcarboniferous petroleum of Pennsylvania is a very pure hydrocarbon, and, along with the Eocene petroleum of Galicia, contains paraffine. The Miocene petroleum of California appears to be a mixture of unstable fluids, compounds of carbon and hydrogen, containing a notable amount of nitrogen. These, with the Mexican and South American oils, do not contain paraffine, and readily oxidize into asphaltum. There are many other petroleums of this class, and others still have been little examined chemically. The proximate examinations that have been made show that petroleums from different localities are quite unlike. The petroleum of Pennsylvania, eastern Ohio, and West Virginia, contains a large number of the paraffine series in varying proportion, in mixture with a smaller

and indefinite proportion of the olefine series. Other petroleums of nearly identical composition contain small quantities of the benzole series with an increasingly large proportion of unstable compounds that oxidize into asphaltum. Those of Galicia are of this description. Those of California have been little examined, but appear to be almost entirely confined to unstable, easily oxidized oils. The Russian oils from Baku consist of the additive compounds of the benzole series, which have the same percentage composition as the olefines, and contain less hydrogen than the paraffines. Burmese petroleum contains a notable proportion of the benzole series. All of the compounds derived from petroleum absorb oxygen when exposed to light, and become colored and viscid. The residues from the distillation of petroleum have remarkable fluorescence. It is not supposed that these substances are present in the natural oil, although it is not impossible that they are.

Origin.—The theory that petroleum is the product of chemical reactions still in progress in the earth's crust was originally put forward by Bertholet, and has since been continued on the same line by Mendeljeff, the eminent Russian chemist. Their theories are based on the results of laboratory experiments, and assume the existence in the earth's crust of powerful deoxidizing agents, such as the alkali metals, cast-iron, spiegeleisen, etc., which in contact with steam and carbonic acid set free the hydrogen and carbon, causing them to unite in the nascent state and produce mixtures of hydrocarbons resembling petroleum. These theories require conditions nowhere proved to exist in nature.

Petroleum is, without a reasonable doubt, primarily derived from a partial decomposition of animal or vegetable remains. In the Trenton limestone and other Silurian rocks it has probably been produced by the transformation of low forms of animal life. The petroleum issuing from the Miocene shales of southern California is also of animal origin. The first of these oils is often found hermetically sealed in the cavities of large fossils and in geodes in limestones rich in animal remains. These older oils are rich in sulphur, and those of California are comparatively rich in nitrogen also. They are dark, fetid, and in many instances, particularly those of California, they rapidly change on exposure to the air to a black, viscid mass, which finally becomes solid asphaltum. The California oils undergo changes due to a sort of putrefactive process, as pools of oil have there been observed to become infested with maggots, like a pool of blood when similarly exposed. These fetid animal oils are difficult to refine, and are chiefly used as fuel.

The Devonian oils of eastern Ohio, Pennsylvania, New York, and West Virginia are with equal certainty derived by spontaneous distillation from the deposits of shales that underlie the oil-sands, and, where exposed along the shores of Lake Erie, exhibit such an extraordinary accumulation of fucoids as to suggest to Dr. J. S. Newberry the idea that a "sargasso sea" existed at that point in the primeval ocean. The oil-sands overlie more than 1,000 feet of the Devonian shales, and are themselves overlaid by beds of shale containing so much silica as to form an impervious shell that holds down the oil and gas under such a pressure that much of the material that is gaseous when it reaches the surface, is doubtless liquid while within the oil-sand. These "shells," being impervious over wide areas, prevent the escape of the oil except from minute fissures, where oil or gas springs are produced. This fucoidal shale has been subjected to destructive distillation at a low temperature, and has yielded fifty gallons to the ton of an oil resembling petroleum. In like manner, other shales, coal, peat, wood, or animal matter, either recent or fossil, will yield petroleum-like oils, and the lower the temperature and slower the distillation the more nearly will the product resemble the natural oil. In the light of these facts, with the added weight of laboratory experiments that have confirmed them, the French chemical geologists have maintained that all forms of bitumen are the product of metamorphism, or of those physical agencies that, through the combined action of heat, steam, and pressure exerted through indefinite periods of time, have produced such changes as those that have converted the sedimentary rocks of the Eastern States, New York, and Pennsylvania into crystalline schists, and the coal into anthracite. These agencies, acting with less violence upon the strata forming the gentle western slope of the Alleghanies, have left in undisturbed repose the strata that underlay and inclosed the oil-sands, while the superficial have been subject to erosion through immense cycles of geological time. Under these conditions, no arbitrary line could mark the point at which such agencies ceased to act, and the natural process of distillation going forward through indefinite periods of time and of necessity at the lowest possible temperature, must result in the accumulation of distillates in any overlying strata porous enough to act as a reservoir. No additional evidence seems to be required to render this an adequate origin for petroleum as it occurs in Pennsylvania and Galicia. Petroleum occurs at many points along the entire western slope of the Appalachian System, from Point Gaspie on the St. Lawrence river to northern Alabama, and is most abundant where there is the greatest accumulation of organic remains. These sediments were deposited in a current whose course was from northeast to southwest. The facts that concern petroleum are found in the undisturbed and nearly level position in which the rocks containing it lie like sand-bars in a flowing stream, and the further evidence they afford that the metamorphic action that has altered nearly all the formations of the eastern border of the Appalachian System became extinct along a plane that descended deeper and deeper, in many instances far below the surface formations and the coal that they inclose. In Galicia and Transylvania, the metamorphic core of the Carpathians is flanked by beds of fucoidal shale rich in the remains of marine animals, intercalated with the sandstone strata holding the oil. If petroleum is a product of metamorphism, the production is long since completed, and the vast natural reservoirs, when once emptied of their contents, are as completely removed from future consideration as a worked out bed of coal.

Throughout the world petroleum is obtained by means of artesian wells. Dug wells were used in Japan for many centuries, and other primitive methods were employed in other regions; but the so-called American method is now employed universally where petroleum is handled in commercial quantities. The wells are drilled like other artesian wells. Sometimes the oil pours forth in an artesian torrent that flows without control until partial exhaustion renders it possible to stop the flow. Such wells have been of frequent occurrence in the United States and at Baku. When brought within control, the oil is conducted into a tank. Here it accumulates until the tank is nearly filled when an agent of the pipe-line appears and gauges the tank. The oil is then run from the tank into the pipes of a pipe-line, and the tank is gauged again. The difference between the first and second gauging is the measure of the oil run. When a well ceases to flow, a pump is introduced. Often several wells are so connected as to be pumped by one power. At present it is usual to stimulate the flow of wells of moderate productiveness by torpedoes. The torpedo consists of several long cylinders of tin, into which nitro-glycerin is poured, and the whole is carefully lowered to that point in the well at which it is desired to quicken the flow of oil. To the last section a cap is attached, upon which a mass of iron, called a "go-devil," is allowed to descend. The charge is from twenty-five to one hundred quarts of nitroglycerin, and the result of its explosion is usually the projection of a column of oil, resembling a geyser, above the top of the derrick, often one hundred feet in height. After a few minutes, the fountain gradually subsides, and the flow continues uninterruptedly in increased volume until the well is exhausted. The effect upon the oil-sand is, first, an enormous pressure in all directions, driving the oil and gas back into the rock until a point of maximum tension is reached, when the reaction sends everything before it out of the rock and into the air. The oil-rock is thus effectually cleared, and the flow of the oil unimpeded.

As soon as the flow of oil is established and connection has been made with the pipe-line, the action of the well goes on uninterruptedly, often for months. The pipe-lines converge from many wells to trunk-lines which have pumping-stations at which powerful pumps force the oil through sections of pipe about forty miles long. Trunk-lines of six-inch pipe run out of the oil regions to Baltimore, Philadelphia, and New York, Buffalo, Cleveland, and Pittsburg. Small quantities of crude oil are transported in tank-cars, and a very little is still transported in barrels, from localities of small production that are remote from the trunk pipe-lines.

The methods employed in transporting oil in pipe-lines have made possible a vast amount of speculation in crude petroleum. When a run of oil is made from a well-tank to a trunk-line, the owner of the oil receives a certificate for each 1,000 barrels run, which, when properly indorsed by the officers of the pipe-line, becomes negotiable paper, after the manner of an accepted draft or a certified check. These certificates may be sold and resold many times daily without any reference to the oil that they represent. But if a person wishes to use the oil, he purchases the certificates and, taking them to the nearest pipe-line station, demands the delivery of the oil. From 1870 until 1884 the production of oil was each year greatly in excess of its use for all purposes; consequently, oil accumulated above-ground. In August, 1884, this accumulated oil reached the enormous maximum amount of 39,083,464 barrels, since which period it has been reduced to less than 30,000,000 barrels. The storage of these vast accumulations of inflammable material was at first managed by private individuals and corporations; but it was finally undertaken by the pipe-lines acting together as the United Pipe-Lines. In the hands of this great corporation the storage of oil has been carried on with remarkable success and safety. Besides the vast quantity of oil required to fill the nearly 1,000 miles of six-inch pipe of which the trunk-pipe lines consist, the United Lines provide storage-tanks. The usual size of these tanks is ninety-five feet in diameter and twenty-nine feet high, having a working capacity of 35,000 barrels. They are constantly menaced with destruction from lightning, and are occasionally struck and fired. In the Caucasus a pipe-line extends from Batoum to Poti on the Black Sea, 600 miles.

Transportation of both crude and refined oil across the ocean has been carried on in barrels, for northern ports, and in cases, each containing two tin cans holding five gallons. This case oil goes to all equatorial countries and the far East. Since 1880 experiments have been in progress for carrying bulk cargoes of oil across the ocean. Steamers fitted with tanks in such a manner that the liquid cargo is comparatively motionless have successfully transported Russian oil from ports on the Black Sea to England, Adriatic ports, Germany, and Russian ports on the Baltic. Such cargoes have also been carried from Philadelphia to English ports.

Statistics.—The following table shows the amount of oil exported from 1864 to 1887:

YEAR.	Gallons.	Value.
1864	12,791,518	$6,764,411
1865	12,722,005	9,520,957
1866	84,255,921	18,626,141
1867	62,686,657	22,509,468
1868	67,969,961	19,977,870
1869	84,408,892	27,686,187
1870	97,902,505	29,864,198
1871	102,608,955	34,188,736
1872	122,589,575	30,506,108
1873	158,102,414	37,195,735
1874	217,220,504	37,560,995
1875	191,551,933	27,080,861
1876	204,814,673	28,755,638
1877	262,441,844	55,401,132
1878	289,214,541	41,518,676
1879	381,586,442	35,999,862
1880	367,325,823	31,783,575
1881	332,288,015	34,317,695
1882	488,218,633	41,588,854
1883	419,821,018	36,926,574
1884	415,615,639	38,195,349
1885	458,243,192	40,074,827
1886	469,471,451	40,684,331
1887	480,845,811	37,303,907

The following table shows the amount of oil produced from 1859 to 1886 inclusive, with the average price per barrel for each year. The apparently large price in 1864 was due to the condition of the currency, a paper dollar being worth less than fifty cents in gold:

YEAR.	Barrels.	Price.
1859	2,000	$20 00
1860	200,000	9 60
1861	2,110,000	2 73
1862	3,055,000	1 05
1863	2,610,000	3 15
1864	2,180,000	9 87½
1865	2,721,000	6 59
1866	3,732,000	3 74
1867	3,583,000	2 41
1868	3,716,000	3 62½
1869	4,351,000	5 62¾
1870	5,371,000	3 89
1871	5,531,000	4 34
1872	6,357,000	3 64
1873	9,932,000	1 83
1874	10,883,000	1 17
1875	8,800,000	1 35
1876	9,015,000	2 56½
1877	13,043,000	2 42
1878	15,367,000	1 19
1879	19,827,000	85⅞
1880	26,048,000	94½
1881	27,238,000	85⅞
1882	30,460,000	78⅞
1883	24,300,000	1 05⅜
1884	23,500,000	83⅞
1885	20,900,000	88
1886	26,150,000	71⅜
Total	310,942,000	....

With the consumption of Galician oil confined to Austria-Hungary, Russian oil is the only competitor with the United States in the markets of the world. From insignificant proportions, this competition has grown year by year until all Europe and Eastern Asia are feeling its influence. The low price and superlative quality of American petroleum alone permit it to maintain its superiority in many localities not yet seriously invaded by Russian oil. For the past ten years oil at one dollar or more a barrel has been predicted along with the partial exhaustion of every new pool that has been opened and gradually declined in production; yet, during that period, prices have been for the most part much below that figure. While it can not be disputed that the present production is less than the consumption, it is equally true that a permanent advance in price from present prices to one dollar a barrel would lead to an abandonment of the use of petroleum for many purposes, and, at the same time, would stimulate production in many localities where oil is known to exist over a very wide area.

Petroleum Products.—The extent to which substances manufactured from petroleum have become necessities places them among the most important products of modern technology. First in importance among these products is illuminating oil or kerosene, both in respect to the vast bulk of the commodity and also the large proportion of the human race dependent upon it for artificial light. When compared with the methods in use half a century ago, illumination by means of this material has prolonged human life over half the habitable globe, and it is the cheapest and most perfect illuminating agent yet discovered.

Next in importance in the list of products are lubricating oils, which, when prepared of various grades and qualities for different purposes, have nearly superseded all other oils devoted to similar uses.

The lighter products begin with righolene, which boils at 65° Fahr., and is the lightest of all known fluids. This is prepared by condensing in a mixture of ice and salt that portion of the distillate from petroleum that at ordinary temperatures would be gaseous. It evaporates so rapidly that it will reduce the temperature to −19° Fahr. in twenty seconds. It was originally prepared, and is still used for producing local anæsthesia in surgical operations. A similar but not so volatile fluid has been prepared in commercial quantities under the name of cymogene. It has been used in ice-machines to produce a very low temperature by its evaporation. The next least volatile product is gasolene, the most volatile commercial product of petroleum when no unusual means are taken to condense the vapors. It is used in automatic gas-machines to saturate air with the volatile vapor, and, by thus carburetting the air, to produce an inflammable gas. It has been found extremely useful for this purpose, and is also used as a fuel in a so-called "gasolene-stove"—a very dangerous utensil. A, B, and C naphthas are fluids of different volatilities, taken off between gasolene and illuminating oil. They are used in mixing paint, printing oil-cloths, dissolving resins, and for other similar uses. Illuminating oils are of different grades and qualities. Lubricating oils are also of very various quality, from the most delicate strained oils used on spindles to heavy mixtures of residuum and crude oil used on railroad axles. Filtered petroleum residues, under the name of petroleum oint-

ment, cosmoline, vaseline, etc., have been widely introduced into medicine, having been admitted to the United States Pharmacopœia, and very extensively used as a domestic remedy. Lastly, the solid product of petroleum, paraffine, has become of immense importance in the arts, for candles, water-proofing cloth and paper, insulating electrical conductors, and many other uses.

Technology.—The general technology of petroleum is simple in its details, and is adapted to the handling of vast quantities of material in the most rapid and economical manner. The oil is received at the refineries from the wells through one of the trunk-pipe lines, and is allowed to settle in huge tanks, in order that the small amount of water that invariably accompanies the oil, with any other impurities, may be completely separated. From these storage-tanks the oil is thrown by powerful steam-pumps into the stills, at the rate of 2,000 to 3,000 barrels an hour. The stills are either low, upright cylinders, heated by several fires around their circumference, or plain cylinders set horizontally in banks, similarly to steam-boilers. The stills hold about 1,200 barrels each. In the refineries recently constructed they are not inclosed in a building, but are entirely exposed to the atmosphere, excepting a sheet-iron jacket, which prevents too great radiation. The vapors from the stills are conducted through a series of pipes immersed in cold water, in which they are condensed. The distillates at first are gaseous, but they gradually increase in density and pass through a great variety of fluids, from cymogene to solid paraffine. The fluids are separated and discharged into different tanks by means of a complicated system of stop-cocks. A system of traps in these discharge-pipes also enables the operator to send the gaseous distillates beneath the stills, where the gas may be consumed as fuel.

The crude naphtha is first run off, and in a subsequent operation, often at another establishment, is by redistillation converted by fractionation into gasolene and A, B, and C naphthas. From crude naphtha the distillate is run off until it becomes too dense for the preparation of illuminating oil. This distillate forms the "high-test" illuminating oil, having a fire-test of 120° to 150° Fahr. The residue in the still is then in a condition for "cracking." This process consists of a slow distillation, during which the vapors are constantly being condensed upon the upper portion of the still, from which they flow or drop down upon the heated oil. The oils are thus repeatedly heated to a temperature above their boiling-points, producing destructive distillation, and resulting in the disengagement of a permanent gas, the deposition of carbon in the still, and the production of an oil of a specific gravity suitable for illumination. But this so-called "cracked oil," is not identical in quality or in composition with the illuminating oil first distilled from the crude petroleum. There are, therefore, three distillates possible and in a general way three qualities of illuminating oil. They consist of oils that are pure distillates, oils that are cracked, and mixtures of the two. Whatever the distillate may be, about 1,200 barrels are pumped into a tank 40 feet high and 12 feet in diameter, called an agitator, which rests upon a base of timber; 6,600 pounds of strong oil of vitriol are then forced into the tank from a closed cistern into which the carboys are emptied. The cistern is closed, and air is forced into it until the pressure is sufficient to drive the acid into the tank. The distillate and acid are then thoroughly mixed by air forced into the bottom of the tank. After the acid has been drawn off, the oil is washed with water, then with a solution of caustic soda, again with water, and lastly with caustic ammonia, which is supposed to remove the last traces of sulphur compounds. The oil is then discharged into settling-tanks through a perforated perpendicular pipe, in a fine spray, which causes any remnant of very volatile oil to be evaporated and removed. In these settling-tanks, beneath skylights, the last traces of water settle and leave the oil clear and almost colorless. It is then pumped into tank-cars or into storage tanks.

The residue in the still is worked over by distillation and mixture into lubricating oils and paraffine. Lubricating oils are prepared by a great variety of processes for as great a variety of purposes. For lubricating the interiors of steam cylinders oils are deprived of their more volatile constituents by exposing them to the sun on the surface of water in shallow tanks. Sometimes the water is heated by a steam-coil. For the same purpose, oils are deprived of their naphtha and illuminating oil in a still, and the residue, called "reduced oil," is then run out of the still. Sometimes the reduced oil is filtered through animal charcoal or other material, and deprived of much of its odor and color. Other oils of less density—which in the ordinary distillation of petroleum "without cracking" come off between illuminating oil and the heavy oils next to residuum—are treated in a still by means of superheated steam in such a manner as to remove the volatile cracked products invariably resulting from the first distillation, leaving in the still an oil of high boiling-point, almost entirely without taste or odor. These oils are called "neutral lubricating oils." The oils that are distilled from them after treatment have been called "mineral sperm," and are distinguished from ordinary illuminating oils by their very high boiling-point and fire-test.

Another class of petroleum products of superior quality has been prepared by distilling the crude oil in a vacuum apparatus, by which the effects of cracking are prevented. These oils have been largely used in treating leather. When crude petroleum is carefully distilled without cracking until the residue in the still has the consistence of jelly at ordinary temperatures, and the residue while hot filtered through animal charcoal, the product is an amorphous paraffine of a semi-transparent pale-brown color. This substance has been widely introduced into pharmacy as petroleum ointment, and is used as a basis for medicated ointments, being found greatly superior to preparations of lard and spermaceti on account of its freedom from rancidity. The same preparation is also widely consumed under the names of cosmoline, vaseline, petrolina, etc.

The use of petroleum prior to the past thirty years for illuminating, though centuries old, was confined to various rude attempts to burn the crude oil in the regions in which oil-springs occurred in greatest abundance. In Burmah, the Rangoon tar was burned in earthen lamps of the simplest construction possible. In Persia pencils of dried camel's dung, which served as a wick, were immersed in the oil, in vessels that were placed in niches in the houses, the niches communicating with the open air. In Italy the fluidity of the oil made possible its combustion in street-lamps. In the valley of Oil Creek in Pennsylvania the crude petroleum was used in a vessel resembling a tea-kettle, the wick protruding from the nozzle, for lighting salt-well derricks and saw-mills, long before the introduction of coal-oil had suggested the refining of the crude oil.

Since 1854, when petroleum was first refined in Pittsburg, Pa., refined petroleum has penetrated the most remote regions of the habitable globe, until it has superseded almost every other illuminating agent except coal-gas and electricity. Under many conditions of place and purpose, one serious objection lies against its use, which has been found to require constant legal and sanitary supervision. The vapors of the more volatile constituents of petroleum, when mingled with air in proper proportion, form mixtures that burn with great explosive violence. If these light oils, even in very small proportion, are allowed to mingle with illuminating oil, the mixture becomes unsafe under the ordinary conditions of domestic life, and frightful disasters have followed a careless disregard of these facts. To insure public safety, nearly all civilized countries and most of the States of the American Union have enacted laws intended to compel the use of oils properly prepared. Their safety is determined through tests designed to ascertain the temperature at which any given specimen of oil will give off a sufficient amount of vapor to burn explosively when mingled with air. The instruments and methods vary, but a sufficient uniformity follows their use to insure a generally uniform result, and in the main protect the public from unsafe oils.

For many and obvious reasons, petroleum can not generally compete with coal as a fuel. There are localities, notably the Caspian region and the Pacific Coast of North America, where petroleum of inferior quality is abundant and cheap, while other fuel is scarce and dear, and large quantities of petroleum are consumed as fuel. Elaborate experiments have been made, not only by private individuals but by the governments of the United States, Great Britian, and other countries, to ascertain the most practical methods of burning petroleum as a steam fuel. The result has been in every respect satisfactory, especially in the Caspian region, where stationary, marine, and locomotive engines are being run, not only by means of the crude oil, but also by means of the "astalki" or residuum that results in much larger proportion from the manufacture of Russian than American petroleum. Crude petroleum and naphtha have been successfully used in the manufacture of iron, and one of the purposes for which the fetid oils of northwestern Ohio have been lately introduced by pipe-line to Chicago is to provide fuel for the extensive steel-works in the southern suburb of that city. High-test oils are largely used as a fuel in so-called kerosene-stoves.

PHARMACY. The advance in this art has been manifested by the recognition that it has received from the proposed formation of a section on pharmacy and materia medica by the American Medical Association. This was suggested early in the year, and at the subsequent meeting of that association an amendment to its constitution providing for such a section was introduced, but, according to the rules, an amendment can not be acted on till the next annual meeting. At the meeting of the International Medical Conference in Washington Dr. F. E. Stewart, of Wilmington, Del., in a paper that he read before the section on therapeutics and materia medica, advocated the establishment of a national laboratory for pharmacological investigation. The duties of such an institution would include the scientific examination of new therapeutic agents, with an expression of opinion as to their value. With such a bureau, the public would no longer be at the mercy of dealers of nostrums who widely advertise their preparations, claiming that they contain new drugs having wonderful curative properties. A bill was introduced into Congress by Samuel J. Randall providing that the Government undertake the preparation of a national pharmacopœia, its execution to be charged on a detail of officers from the various governmental medical departments, who are to invite three representatives from the American Medical Association, and a like number from the American Pharmaceutical Association, to aid in the work. This bill has not as yet become a law. According to a recent compilation, there are in the United States and the Dominion of Canada 32,244 druggists (proprietors of stores) and drug firms. Of this number there are 315 strictly wholesale, 310 wholesale and retail, and 31,619 retail drug establishments in the two countries. In the Dominion the number of establishments of all kinds is placed at 1,199. New York contains

2,897 drug-stores, and leads the list in this country, which ends with Nevada, that contains only 80. The other States that contain over 1,000 drug-stores are Pennsylvania, 2,536; Illinois, 2,284; Ohio, 1,902; Missouri, 1,753; Indiana, 1,549; Kansas, 1.442; Massachusetts, 1,388; Iowa, 1,372; Maryland, 1,219; and Texas, 1,156.

Colleges.—The faculty of the Michigan College of Medicine in Detroit have organized a school of pharmacy in connection with their college. Two lectures each on chemistry, materia medica, and practical pharmacy are delivered every week, in the evening. It is reported that a department in pharmacy had been organized at the Denver University, Col., the first session of which was to take place in September.

Legislation.—In Louisiana an act was passed, on July 11, to regulate the practice of pharmacy; the sale of compounded medicines and drugs, preparations and prescriptions; the sale of poisons; to create a State board of pharmacy, and to regulate the fees and emoluments thereof; to prevent the practice of pharmacy by unauthorized persons; and to provide for the trial and punishment of violators of the provisions of this act by fine or imprisonment. The amendment to the Kentucky law, that went into effect on March 3, requiring druggists to obtain certificates, has given general satisfaction, and it is the desire of the pharmacists that it be extended so as to include those doing business in cities of less than one thousand inhabitants. In Massachusetts, the law concerning the sale of poisons has been amplified so as to include some thirty more substances. The new law provides that whoever sells any of the poisonous articles named without the written prescription of a physician, shall affix to the bottle, box, or wrapper containing the article sold a label of red paper upon which shall be printed in large black letters the word "poison," and also the word "antidote," if there be one, and the name and place of business of the vender. The States of Arkansas, California, Florida, Indiana, Mississippi, Nevada, Oregon, Tennessee, Texas, and Vermont still lack proper legislative measures to regulate the practice of pharmacy. An interesting legal decision was rendered during the year to the effect that "acid phosphate," claimed by the Rumford Chemical Works as a trade-mark, was decided against that corporation. The matter is now before the higher courts, and a definite decision has not yet been reached.

Pharmacopœial Revision.—During the coming year delegates for this purpose will be chosen, and the present committee have issued an appeal to the several State pharmaceutical associations for aid in gathering information concerning the drugs and preparations actually in use by physicians in this country. They desire that analyses of the prescriptions of physicians in all parts of the United States be made by any who have the time and inclination, and offer to supply to societies, at cost price, printed blanks to facilitate the work. This will be a collective investigation of great importance. The committee also desire to obtain from societies, and presumably also from individuals, expressions regarding the question of weights or measures in the pharmacopœial formulas.

Associations.—The thirty-sixth annual meeting of the American Pharmaceutical Association was held in Detroit, Mich., on September 3–7, under the presidency of John U. Lloyd. Delegates from five alumni associations, eight colleges, and five local and twenty State associations were formally recognized. The scientific section was presided over by James M. Good, and the following papers were presented: "Artificial Salicylic Acid," by Albert B. Prescott and Erwin E. Ewell; "Calycanthus Seed," by R. G. Eccles; "The Masking of Quinine," by Luther F. Stevens; "Adulterating Peppermint Oil," by Alviso C. Stevens; "Acacia Catechu and Uncaria Gambier," by Henry Trimble; "Nomenclature of Pharmaceutical Preparations," by C. S. Hallberg; "The Loco Weed," by L. E. Sayre; "Artificial and Natural Mineral Waters," by Enno Sanders; "Phosphomolybdic Acid for the Quantitative Estimation of Alkaloids," by H. W. Snow; "Is the Precipitated Sulphate of Iron of Constant Composition? and does it contain the same Proportion of Water of Crystallization as the Large Crystals," by Henry Trimble; "Pepsin Testing," by Frank A. Thompson; "Notes on the Morphiometric Assay of Opium," by Joseph F. Geisler; "Sponges," by Rosa Upson; "Assay of Powdered Ipecacuanha," by John E. Pennington; "A New Method of preparing Mercurous Iodide," by Edward Soetje; "Arsenic in Medicinal Bismuth Salts," by R. E. Hawkes; and "Cream of Tartar," by Charles V. Boetcher. This section discussed very fully the recently issued "National Formulary" published under the auspices of the association. It was the result of the labors of a committee appointed in 1885 to prepare a list of unofficial preparations, so that when a prescription calling for a compound generally recognized but not in the "United States Pharmacopœia," was presented to the druggist a reliable and uniform article of standard quality could be made. The volume which contains 435 titles was published in July, and means tending toward its periodical revision were discussed, but it was decided to leave the matter open.

The commercial section discussed, under the chairmanship of A. H. Hollister, various trade measures, notably a resolution calling on the National Wholesale Druggists' Association to abolish the rebate system, and the questions "Is substitution going on?" and "Should we practice substitution?" referring to the treatment of drugs by the jobbers, also the very important "liquor question." Earnest protest was made against the present laws which, it was claimed, "placed the pharmacy and the grog-shop on the same level." The education

and legislative sections held brief meetings at which pertinent topics were considered. The special object of the legislative section was to consider how best "to secure a uniform standard of requirement for graduation through the States, so that the certificates of all State boards of pharmacy will be received as *prima-facie* evidence of competency."

At the business meeting 154 new members were admitted, and at the close of the sessions the total membership was 1,411. The financial condition of the Association was found to be excellent. The receipts were $12,656.49 and expenditures $10,280.42, showing a cash balance, and $11,347.82 were invested in United States bonds. Considerable discussion as to the next place of meeting prevailed, but ultimately San Francisco, Cal., was chosen and the date left to the council. Maurice W. Alexander, of St. Louis, Mo., was elected president, and John M. Maisch, of Philadelphia, Pa., continued as secretary. Various local associations were organized during the year, among which was that of the drug clerks of Newark.

Trade Associations.—The fourteenth annual meeting of the National Wholesale Druggists' Association, under the presidency of E. Waldo Cutter, was held at Saratoga Springs, N. Y., beginning on September 11 and continued for three days. The proposition of extending the rebate plan to the retailers was discussed and its impracticability decided upon. The committee on legislation reported its failure to secure the repeal of the excise tax on all spirits, and urged that efforts be made toward the total repeal of all revenue taxes; also the repeal of the tax on spirits to 50 per cent. and the removal of the druggists' license tax. The committee on proprietary goods reported that the annual sales of these goods by the members of the association was estimated at $37,500,-000. Reports of the committees on fraternal relations; on paints, oils, and glass; on Paris green; on transportation; on boxes and cartage; and on commercial travelers were presented and referred to the board of control. A deficiency of $465.93 in the Druggists' Mutual Fire Insurance Company was shown, and concerning it a resolution was passed from which the following is taken:

"An important feature of this company is its advance premium fund. This fund, of $100,000, is intended to furnish the company with substantial assets; and in addition to the premiums paid on policies, it is fair to suppose, with the care exercised in the selection of risks, that prosperity will follow.

"Of this fund $55,000 has been subscribed and paid. It is earnestly hoped that the members of the National Wholesale Druggists' Association, who have not already subscribed to this fund, will avail themselves of the opportunity now offered. These certificates are issued in sums of $500 or more—30 per cent. payable at time of subscription, and the balance payable in monthly installments of 10 per cent. for seven months. Six per cent. interest per annum is allowed on installments until all are paid; and after that, 6 per cent. per annum on amount of certificate; and in addition thereto a further participation in the profits of the company, at the rate of 10 per cent. per annum. After the expiration of one year from the date of the certificate, the amount subscribed may be used in the payment of premiums on accepted insurance.

"The policies of insurance of the company are not assessable."

The secretary reported a total membership of 341, and the treasurer showed a balance of $1,639.50 on hand. George A. Kelly, of Pittsburg, Pa., was chosen president, and A. B. Merriam, of Indianapolis, Ind., continued as secretary. The next annual meeting will be held, beginning on September 10, at Indianapolis. A supplementary meeting was held of the Western members in St. Louis, Mo., on October 18 to consider various trade matters in which they dissented from the resolutions adopted at the Saratoga meeting. The wholesale druggists of Chicago, St. Louis, Peoria, and Indianapolis met in Chicago on December 4 and organized a "Central Drug Exchange," having for its object the promotion of friendly relations, the correction of any mercantile abuses in the trade, and the maintenance of the high standard in the quality of goods handled. P. Singer, of Peoria, was elected president; Peter Van Schaak, of Chicago, vice-president; and C. Walbridge, of St. Louis, treasurer and secretary.

The Association of Manufacturers and Dealers in Proprietary Articles held its annual meeting at Saratoga Springs, N. Y., on September 14. About twenty members were present. Several communications were received and referred to committees for consideration, after which R. V. Pierce, of Buffalo, N. Y., was elected president, and Henry E. Bowen, of New York city, as secretary. The Association then adjourned subject to the call of the president. A National Paint, Oil, and Varnish Association was organized at Saratoga Springs on September 11, and Charles Richardson, of Boston, Mass., was chosen president, and G. H. Vrooman, of Chicago, Ill., secretary.

Literature.—The books of the year include: "The Art of Dispensing" (London); "The National Formulary" (Philadelphia); "Pictorial History of Ancient Pharmacy," translated from the German by Dr. William Netter (Chicago); "Organic Analysis," by Prof. Albert B. Prescott (New York); "The Beginnings in Pharmacy," by R. Rother (Detroit); "An Introductory Treatise on the Practical Manipulation of Drugs," by R. Rother (Detroit); "The Prescription, Therapeutically. Pharmaceutically, and Grammatically Considered," by Otto A. Wall (St. Louis); "Price and Dose Labels," by Hans M. Wilder (New York); "Toilet Medicine," by Edwin Wooton (New York); also new editions of "The Dispensatory of the

United States," 16th edition (Philadelphia); "Pharmacology, Therapeutics, and Materia Medica," by T. Lauder Brunton (Philadelphia); "Prescription Writing," by Frederick H. Gerrish (Portland, Me.); "Chemical Lecture Notes," by H. M. Whelpey (St. Louis); "Therapeutics: its Principles and Practice," by Dr. Horatio C. Wood (Philadelphia). The pharmaceutical journals have been active in the exposure of the objectionable character of various proprietary medicines. "The Druggists Circular" deserves credit for its analysis of "Scotch Oats Essence," which it showed to be a preparation of morphine. Samples of the widely advertised "Recamier Balm" proved on analysis to consist of one drachm of oxide of zinc and two grains and a quarter of corrosive sublimate in four ounces of water. The original cost of the mixture could hardly have exceeded three cents yet it finds a ready sale at $1.50 a bottle. The "Vita Nuova" owes, according to the same journal, its wonderful properties to a small quantity of cocaine dissolved in alcohol; still it is advertised as "free from alcohol" and as not being a "wine of coca."

"The Rocky Mountain Druggist," edited by J. L. T. Davidson, made its appearance in Denver, Col., in June, and is the first distinctively pharmaceutical journal to be issued west of the Mississippi. "The New England Druggist," of Boston, Mass., edited by J. W. Colcord, began publication later in the year.

PHYSIOLOGY. The Nervous System.—The researches of Profs. Victor Horsley and Schäfer go to show that, as the result both of ablation and excitation, the motor region of the brain cortex may be mapped out into a series of main areas, each being connected with the movements of a particular part—such as the head, trunk, leg, arm, and face areas—and these, again, present subdivisions concerned with more specialized movements; there are, however, no sharp lines of demarkation between the several areas, but they overlap one another. Brown-Sequard has made another contribution to the discussion of this subject, in which he suggests that each function, each property of the central-nerve system, is strongly localized in certain nerve-cells, but these cells are not localized in restricted areas or microscopic centers, but are distributed through many parts of the central nervous system. This dissemination, he considers, explains the fact that there is no single spot or region in the whole of the central nervous system the destruction of which is followed with absolute certainty by either paralysis or anæsthesia.

A distinction has been made by some writers between cranial and spinal nerves; and, although efforts have not been wanting to bring both groups under the same system, they have failed, on account of some misconceptions and confusions that are pointed out in a paper by W. H. Gaskell. This author has made a new study of the subject, from the results of which he concludes that both of the groups to which he assigns these nerves—a foremost, which in man are entirely efferent, and a hindmost group of nerves of a mixed character—are built upon the same plan as the spinal nerves, both with respect to the structure, function, and distribution of their nerve-fibers, and as far as the arrangement of the centers of origin of those nerve-fibers in the central nervous system is concerned; and he thinks it probable that the reason for the deviation of the cranial nerves from the spinal-nerve type is bound up with the changes which occurred at the time when a large portion of the fibers of the foremost group of cranial nerves lost their functional activity.

Dr. Marckwald has brought forward evidence to show that, although the respiratory centers in the medulla oblongata are automatically active, as well as excitable by reflex action, yet the automatically active center can only liberate respiratory spasms, but no regular rhythmic respiratory movements.

Dr. Gersung, of Vienna, has successfully performed the novel operation of transplanting a portion of the nerve of a rabbit to the thumb of a patient, Prof. Von Fleischl. The transplanted nerve not only united with the human nerve upon which it was ingrafted and performed its functions normally, but the operation resulted in curing a tendency to neuromatous degeneration with which the original thumb nerve had been affected. The case is further interesting from the light which it casts upon the existence of a practical identity between the nerves of different species of animals.

A remarkable case is described by Mr. Sutton in which the divided ends of a median nerve that had been severed ten weeks previously were dissected out, revivified, and after five days began to recover function. Mr. Barwell, discussing Mr. Sutton's paper, mentioned a case in which recovery of a function occurred when the parts were brought together six months after division.

Special Senses.—The experiments of Herr Urbanschitsch, of Vienna, on the reciprocal influence of organs of sense lead to the general conclusion that any sense-excitation results in an increase of the acuteness of other senses. Thus, sensations of hearing sharpen the visual perceptions. If colored plates are placed at such a distance that one can hardly distinguish the colors, and various sounds are then produced, the colors become generally more distinct the higher the sounds. Similarly, one can, while a sound affects the ear, read words which he could not read before. The ticking of a watch is better heard when the eyes are open than when they are closed. Red and green increase the auditive perceptions, while blue and yellow weaken them. Several musicians, however, were agreed that red, green, yellow, and blue caused an intensification of sound of about one eighth, while violet had a weakening effect. Taste, smell, and touch are

under like laws. Light and red and green colors increase their delicacy, while darkness, blue, and yellow diminish it. Under the influence of red and green, taste extends from the anterior border of the tongue to the whole surface; on the other hand, a strengthening of smell, taste, or touch, exalts the other sensitive perceptions. The reciprocal influence of touch and the sense of temperature is specially interesting. If we tickle the skin with a hair, and plunge the hand in hot water, the tickling ceases; but, if the hand be placed in cold water and a part of the body is tickled, the temperature is felt more vividly.

From a purely physical point of view, Prof. S. P. Langley has concluded that the time required for the distinct perception of an excessively faint light is about half a second. A relatively very long time is, however, needed for the recovery of sensitiveness after exposure to a bright light, and the time demanded for this restoration of complete visual power appears to be the greatest when the light to be perceived is of a violet color. The visual effect produced by any given constant amount of energy varies enormously according to the color of the light in question. It varies considerably between eyes which may ordinarily be called normal ones; but, letting 1 represent the amount of energy required to make us see light in the crimson of the spectrum near A, the average will give the following proportionate results for the wave-lengths corresponding approximately to the six colors: Violet, 1,600; blue, 62,000; green, 100,-000; yellow, 28,000; orange, 14,000; red, 1,200. Since we can recognize color still deeper than crimson, it appears that the same amount of energy may produce at least 100,000 times the visual effect in one color of the spectrum that it does in another. The absolute measure of energy represented by the sensation of crimson light is $0.000,000,000,000,3$ horse-power.

Dr. Kœnig has made some experiments for testing Holmgren's statement that very small colored dots can be seen only of one of the primary colors of Young and Helmholtz's theory—red, green, or violet. The statement was not confirmed when the necessary precautions were taken, and it was found that small dots of any color, even yellow and blue, were perceived as possessing their own objective color. This had also been observed by Hering. Isaacksen had, further, investigated the power which the eye possesses of distinguishing between minute dot-like lights which are so small that their image on the retina only falls on one cone, and found that it was as fully developed as for the colors of large surfaces.

The attention of anatomists was first directed to the papilla foliata of mammals as an organ of taste by Van Wyss in 1869-'70, and Engelmann in 1872. The investigations have been carried on by other observers—as to man, by Krause, Ajtai, and Lustig. Boulart and Pilliet examined the tongues of a large number of mammals with special reference to the presence or absence of the papillæ foliatæ. They found them existing in marsupials, edentates, insectivora, rodents, proboscidæ, and swine; and wanting in cetacea, chiroptera, perissodactyla, ruminantia, and many carnivora. Frederick Tuckerman observes that there are probably many groups of existing animals whose remote ancestors possessed foliate areas, which have long since disappeared from their present representatives. An exception is met in the swine, which have undergone fewer structural modifications from the primitive type than most of the other mammals since the Eocene period. According to this author, this organ in the pig is now and then rudimentary, is usually more or less atrophied, and very frequently shows a want of symmetry between the two papillæ. With a single exception all the specimens of swine's tongues examined had well-developed foliate areas. The papilla foliata consists of four or five rather irregular folds, with slightly rounded crests, separated by furrows varying much in breadth, and slightly in depth. Occasionally the bottom of a furrow is invaginated upward into a ridge, which may or may not bear taste-bulbs. Serous glands and ducts are very abundant at the base of the folds and occupy a large space within them. Some of the ducts of these glands are very tortuous, and several millimetres in length. They usually open between the folds at the bottom of the furrows. Glands of the mucous type are sparingly scattered through this region. Each fold carries at its upper part many secondary papillæ, the depressions between which are filled by the epithelium. The taste-bulbs of this gustatory region are a little smaller on the average than those of the circumvallate area, and are estimated to number 2,400 for each papilla. Dr. Tuckerman quotes from Dr. Luigi Griffini, of Modena, on his experimental study of the reproduction of the gustatory papillæ and regeneration of the taste-bulbs in the rabbit and dog. Destruction, partial or complete, of the organs of taste appears to be effected by the direct removal from the animal of the papillæ themselves, or by division of the glosso-pharyngeal nerves. The process of reproduction is described in the memoir. Griffini rejects the theory of direct continuity between nerve-fibers and epithelial cells, and asserts that reproduction of the papillæ after their partial or complete removal always takes place. He has also made an experimental study of the organ of smell, the motorial end-plate of the muscle-fiber, and the retina of the lower animals, the results of which have not been published. Dr. Tuckerman has added to his contributions in this branch studies of the tongue and gustatory organs of *Fiber Zibetheeus*, and of the gustatory organs of *Putorius Vison*.

In the experiments of E. H. S. Bailey and E. L. Nichols upon the delicacy of the sense of taste as to different classes of substances, quinine, cane-sugar, sulphuric acid, sodium bicarbonate, and common salt were employed as severally representing, typically, the bitter, sweet, acid, alkaline, and saline tastes. The tests were made upon 82 men and 46 women. The average results were as follow :

I. Quinine:
  Male observers detected 1 part in 390,000 parts of water.
  Female observers detected 1 part in 456,000 parts of water.
II. Cane-sugar :
  Male observers detected 1 part in 199 parts of water.
  Female observers detected 1 part in 204 parts of water.
III. Sulphuric acid :
  Male observers detected 1 part in 2,080 parts of water.
  Female observers detected 1 part in 8,250 parts of water.
IV. Bicarbonate of soda :
  Male observers detected 1 part in 98 parts of water.
  Female observers detected 1 part in 126 parts of water.
V. Common salt:
  Male observers detected 1 part in 2,240 parts of water.
  Female observers detected 1 part in 1,980 parts of water.

The authors conclude that the sense of taste is much more delicate for bitter substances than for the others included in the list (the relative delicacy for quinine and sugar being very nearly 2,000 : 1); that, taken in the order of their effect upon the organs of taste, the classes of substances must stand in the order — bitters, acids, saline substances, sweets, and alkalies ; that the sense of taste is, as a rule, more delicate in women than in men (in the case of all the substances tried excepting salt); that the ability to detect a dilute bitter is very generally accompanied by inability to detect a dilute sweet, and *vice versa ;* and that the long-continued habitual use of a substance does not seem to influence in any marked way the delicacy of the sense of taste for that substance. While these conclusions represent the average results, the tests brought out some astonishing individual peculiarities. Thus there were persons who could detect with certainty 1 part of quinine in 5,120,000, while others failed to notice 1 part in 160,000.

A device for measuring the acuteness of the sense of smell has been invented by M. Zwaardemaker, of Utrecht. It consists of two tubes, a smaller one of glass and a larger one of India-rubber or gutta-percha, sliding over the former in such a way that the air breathed in by the nostrils at the free end of the glass tube may pass through a desired length—short or long—of the odor-bearing tube. The length is read off in centimetres, which it is required to give to the passage in the odor-bearing tube to produce a definite olfactory impression upon the nose.

Circulation.—The changes in the volume of the heart and the amount of blood propelled by it under varying conditions of pressure have been studied by Prof. Roy and J. G. Adami. A slight compression of the abdomen of a dog caused an increase in the volume of the heart and in the amount of blood passing through it in a given time. The phenomenon is explained by the fact that the abdominal vessels are capable of containing more than all the blood in the body. Slight compression of the abdomen will, without disturbing the arterial supply, drive out a large amount of blood which will be of use for other regions of the body, where it may be applied to the augmentation of their functional activity. The front and side abdominal walls are, furthermore, formed of soft, elastic tissues, which, in health, exert an adequate pressure upon the abdominal contents and blood-vessels. If, however, the muscles lose their tone, the walls become flaccid, the veins dilate and become reservoirs for more blood than is needed there, depriving the rest of the body of a part of the fluid requisite for its due nutrition. Here, then, we have an explanation of the office of the waist-belts worn by active peoples and athletes. They help to maintain a due pressure on the abdominal vessels to prevent a useless storing of the blood there, and to secure an adequate supply for the parts of the body where it will be demanded. Hence some form of moderate pressure upon the abdomen may be beneficial to persons leading sedentary lives and to women. But if the pressure is made extreme, it will prevent instead of aiding exercise and activity, will affect the arteries also, and disturb the blood-supply of the abdomen and lower extremities.

Dr. John A. McWilliam has found that the rule of behavior of the cardiac muscle of cold-blooded animals under the influence of single stimuli—that the minimum stimulation is at the same time maximal—holds also with the mammalian heart. There occurs a rhythmic rise and fall in the excitability of the organ; a fall immediately succeeding the occurrence of an effective stimulation, followed by a gradual rise, and this again by subsidence into the phase of quiescence. The facts indicate that all parts of the organ are endowed with independent rhythmic power, but not in equal degree; and if one portion of the heart possesses a higher power of spontaneous rhythm than the rest of the organ, its rhythm will supersede the inherent rhythm of the other parts, and determine the rate of contraction in the whole organ. The causes determining rhythm are to be sought for at the venous end of the organ, and ultimately in the molecular changes occurring deep in the tissue. The propagation of the contraction from auricles to ventricles is mainly effected through the nerves that pass between those parts.

Dr. E. W. Carlier has explained a method by which human blood may be withdrawn from the body and its fluidity preserved. The finger from which the blood is obtained is greased and plunged into castor-oil before the puncture is made, while every precaution is taken to prevent the blood coming in contact with the air or with solid matter. In this way the blood may be preserved in a fluid state for a considerable time. As the drops of blood settle slowly in the oil, the corpuscles are seen to fall to the lower part of the drops, while the clear plasma remains above. Prof. Haycraft and Dr.

Carlier believe that the human blood plasma has never before been demonstrated in an unaltered condition, except microscopically. Coagulation eventually occurs, because the blood necessarily comes in contact with the sides of the wound made in the finger.

Continuing his researches on the coagulation of the blood, Dr. Wooldridge endeavors to show that the antecedents of the fibrin are not pure albumens, but fibrinogens consisting of albumen and lecithin; and he attributes great importance to lecithin in the process of coagulation. The experiments of Prof. Haycraft and Dr. Carlier in the same line tend to show that the white corpuscles play an important part in the process.

The distribution of the blood-vessels in the valves of the heart has been investigated by M. Darier, who finds that both in the fœtus and the adult, in health, there are no vessels in the purely fibro-elastic portion of the auriculo-ventricular valves, and that there are none in the chordæ tendinæ attached to these valves. The aortic segment of the mitral valve, however, presents at its upper part a vascular area of small extent, not exceeding one sixth of the whole height of the valve; and in the fœtus a few muscular fibers accompanied by vessels penetrate the auriculo-ventricular valves, but never extend to the lower fourth of these valves. The semi-lunar valves of the aorta and pulmonary arteries are always destitute of vessels; when vessels are found, therefore, in those non-vascular parts, they may always be regarded as pathological.

Researches on the blood-vessels of the carnivora, made by Bellarminoff under the direction of Dr. H. Virchow, show that the blood-vessels of the eye have a tendency to form rings, from which a large number of fine branches pass posteriorly, and that the arrangement is very different in different classes of animals; thus, for instance, the course of the arteries in the eye of a dog, as compared with that of a rabbit, is such that the dog's eye must be turned through an angle of 180° in order to make the course of its arteries correspond with that of the rabbit's eye.

Respiration.—A simplified method of measuring the gaseous interchange during respiration is described by Prof. Zuntz. In it breathing is carried on, the nose being closed, through a mouth-piece, which is connected by very mobile valves with gasometers, which thus measure the volume of the inspired as well as of the expired air. Samples of the expired air can be collected at any desired intervals of time, and the amount of oxygen and carbonic acid in them determined. Dr. Loewy has carried out some experiments with this apparatus in order to determine the influence of digestive activity on the process. The respiratory interchange of the patients was determined in the morning, while they were fasting and in a quiescent condition; they were then given Glaubers'-salt; as soon as the action of the salt had manifested itself painfully, and increased peristaltic action had set in, the respiratory interchange was again determined. In all cases the gaseous interchange was increased by from 7 to 30 per cent. more than the normal. The several persons behaved very differently in this respect, and the same person showed marked differences in the increase of respiratory interchange at different times, after equal doses of salt. As a rule, the increase was proportional to the amount of discomfort experienced by the patient in the lower parts of the body.

Dr. Marcet, in the investigation of normal respiration, directs attention to the occlusion of a proportion of the air inspired, and insists on the importance of considering the proportion of it to the carbonic acid expired. ·

Digestive System.—Later studies by Dr. J. N. Langley on the physiology of the salivary secretion relate to the effect of atropine upon the supposed varieties of secretory nerve-fibers. Heidenhain supposes that there are two kinds of secretory fibers, one proper secretory causing a flow of liquid, and the other trophic causing an increase in solubility in the stored-up gland substance. The author had already shown that on the assumption of the existence of different kinds of secretory fibers, there is ground for supposing that there is a third variety—anabolic fibers—causing the formation of fresh substance by the cells. The effects of atropine having been observed only on the proper secretory fibers, Dr. Langley's observations were extended to the other fibers, with the result that the drug was found to paralyze the trophic, anabolic, and secretory fibers simultaneously. Hence, the author concludes, the various changes caused in the gland-cells by nerve stimulation are all affected by atropine, and to approximately equal extents. When paralysis of the chorda occurs, it is a paralysis of the whole of its function with regard to the gland-cells. In other words, the phenomena of atropine poisoning give no indication of the existence of more than one kind of secretory nerve-fiber in the chorda tympani.

G. Sticker concludes, from his observations, among which were special experiments upon living persons, that the supposition that the salivary secretion plays no part in gastric digestion is erroneous; and that, on the contrary, the presence of saliva in the stomach has a direct effect in promoting the secretion of gastric juice.

Dr. Poulet has found evidence that the acid of the gastric juice in man, as ascertained by the process of dialysis during the first period of digestion, is exclusively the hippuric, while during the close of digestion there is a mixture of hippuric and tartaric acids. In the fasting state tartaric acid is alone present.

In experiments to determine the effect of cooking on the digestibility of starchy foods, Dr. N. Butiagin, of St. Petersburg, found that the activity of the saliva does not differ much among healthy persons, but that when people are badly nourished and weak, and especially when they are also suffering from disease, their saliva has a diminished power of dissolving starch. When starchy substances are subjected to prolonged cooking they become more easily digestible; and in this way compensation may be provided for the inactivity of the saliva of weakly persons. Thus, rice and peas were found to require three hours' cooking in order to render them as easily digested in the saliva, possessing only 88 per cent. of the normal activity, of a badly nourished, hysterical woman, as they were with a single hour's cooking by the saliva of healthy persons; and generally it was found that in the case of weakly or diseased persons starchy food must be cooked twice or thrice as long, in order that it may be equally acted upon, as in the case of healthy persons. Again, when starch has been cooked for a long time there is less difference between the effects of healthy and unhealthy saliva upon it; this is especially remarkable in the case of millet, which after one hour's cooking showed a difference of 12·89 per cent. in favor of the saliva of healthy as against that of diseased persons, but after three hours' cooking a difference of only 5·77 per cent.

From a series of experiments still going on, Drs. Vincent D. Harris and Howard H. Tooth have obtained evidence in support of the generally accepted belief that micro-organisms need not take any part in gastric digestion. In regard to the formation of leucin and tyrosin in pancreatic digestions, although their experiments were inconclusive, they have been led to believe that the formation of these substances depends, in part at all events, on bacteria. It seems to them likely that the formation of indol and its allies in the alimentary canal below the stomach is a mode of excreting nitrogen, like the production of leucin and tyrosin, and that the former substances are not formed from the latter, but directly from peptone.

The researches of Drs. Henry Leffmann and William Beam on the action of antiseptics in perishable articles of food upon the organism and their effect on the nutritive or medicinal value of any articles with which they may be associated were based on the estimation of the sugar formed in presence of a large excess of starch, arrow-root starch being selected for the purpose of the experiments. It was found that salicylic acid prevents the conversion of starch into sugar under the influence of either diastase or pancreatic extract, but does not seriously interfere with peptic or pancreatic digestion of albumen. Saccharin holds about the same relation as salicylic acid. Sodium acid, sulphite, and boric acid are practically without retarding effect. Beta-naphthol interferes decidedly with the formation of sugar by diastase, but not with the action of pancreatic extract on starch. Peptic and pancreatic digestions of albuminoids were almost prevented by this agent. The authors conclude that the indiscriminate use of these agents is to be regarded as objectionable and a proper subject of sanitary inspection.

Nutrition.—The results of an investigation of the effect of the Russian bath on nitrogenous metabolism have been published by Dr. Makovetski, of St. Petersburg. The subjects were four student friends in perfect health. The baths were given daily for five days; perspiration in a hot chamber was induced with the usual amount of shampooing, but without the use of steam. It was found that the assimilation of the nitrogenous parts of the food was diminished, while the nitrogenous metabolism was increased. The loss by the lungs and skin was increased to a marked degree, but the urine was diminished.; and the uric acid was diminished during the days when the baths were given. The baths have the effect of strengthening the muscular and nervous systems, and of increasing secretion when there is much muscular work, especially when the food is deficient in nitrogen, when there is a large amount of nervous and mental activity, and when there is deficient action of the secretory organs in consequence of preceding hypersecretion, or morbid conditions, such as chronic catarrh of the bronchi, stomach, intestines, or genito-urinary tract, chronic hepatic, renal, or splenic affections. In these cases, together with the baths, fat and hydrocarbons are required in the food. As contra-indications, theory would lead us to conclude all conditions where the nitrogenous metabolism is diminished, and also those where artificially induced diminution of it appears to act prejudicially.

After an investigation of the qualities of vegetable albumens, Dr. Rutgers concludes, in the "Zeitschrift für Biologie," that they are capable of supplying the place of the ordinary albumens which we are accustomed to consume as food, without causing any disturbance in the nitrogenous balance of the economy; that beans and peas overcharge the alimentary tract, because both of their solids and of their disposition to develop gas, while meat and rice cause no disturbance. There are consequently various contra-indications as to an exclusively vegetable diet. The acidity of the stomach and of the urine are much less upon a wholly vegetable than upon an ordinary mixed diet.

Dr. R. Schneider has experimented upon the absorption of iron and on its occurrence as oxide in the organs and tissues of animals. All the animals examined—whether living in water, mud, or underground—contained oxide of iron. It was detected by employing ferrocyanide of potassium and dilute hydrochloric acid. Among vertebrates, oxide of iron was found in the alimentary canal, in the liver and spleen, occasionally in the kidneys and teeth; and in the proteus it occurred throughout the whole skeleton. Among the invertebrates it was found in the cells of the liver and intestine, in the respiratory organs, the shells, and the chitinous envelopes. It occurred chiefly in the protoplasm of the cells, but also frequently in the nuclei.

Muscular System.—The researches of Profs. Horsley and Schäfer (see "Annual Cyclopædia," for 1886) on the character of certain muscular contractions are supplemented by observations of Mr. W. Griffiths, to determine the influence of strain in modifying the number and character of the waves seen in the myogram of a voluntarily contracting muscle. The author concludes that the waves seen in the myogram represent contraction and not vibration waves; that the number of these per second varies in different individuals; that the number of muscular responses per second in a voluntarily contracting muscle varies with the weight lifted, increasing with the weight up to a certain maximum, beyond which a decrease takes place; that the number of responses varies with the time during which the muscle is made to contract; a similar course is observed with increased activity to that described in connection with increased weight; and that the number of responses per second presented by an unweighted muscle and the same muscle in a state of dead strain is fairly constant, and is the lowest number of muscular responses obtained from a voluntarily contracting muscle.

The experiments of Horsley and Schäfer have led them to conclude that the normal muscular rhythm is about ten per second. Charcot, studying the differences in the rates of muscular movements in different forms of tremor, has determined tremors of slow rhythm —four or five per second—in paralysis agitans and multiple sclerosis; and of rapid rhythm—eight or nine per second—in alcoholic and mercurial tremors and the tremor of exophthalmic goitre. Drs. R. N. Wolfenden and Dawson Williams urge that these distinctions must be taken with reserve, and maintain that the rate of the normal tremor is preserved in pathological conditions, but with variations in amplitude. While the apparent rate is five or six per second in the tremors of old age, a careful study of the curves will show that the apparent single vibrations are really made up of two, and that the slow tremor is therefore one of normal rate in which every other vibration is imperfect.

An attempt has been made by Dr. G. F. Yeo to settle the doubt which had arisen in regard to the duration and significance of the latent period of excitation in muscle contraction. He finds that as the intensity of stimulation increases up to the injurious point, the duration of latency decreases, but beyond this point the latent period becomes longer. Also that if the weight with which the muscle is loaded be suspended by an elastic band from the axle of the lever belonging to the apparatus, difference of tension no longer seems to influence the duration of latency. He has not recorded less than ·004 of a second as the normal time of latency, and no reliable measurement (without heating) of a less duration can be found in ordinary records. From these and other results he concludes that there is a period of some ·005 of a second (net latency) during which certain molecular changes, necessary for its energy to become visible, take place in muscle. The influence of the elasticity of muscle or the rate of propagation of the wave of contraction can only come into operation after this period.

The study of the action of caffeine upon voluntary muscle is one of especial interest, because different observers have often obtained very different results. In taking the subject up again for investigation, Drs. T. Lauder Brunton and J. Theodore Cash have kept in view the facts that the action which a substance is alleged to have upon a living organism may vary according to the nature of the drug; according to the nature of the organism; and according to the conditions (of temperature, duration of observation, dose, etc.) under which the experiments are made. So far as described in their paper, the experiments of the authors have been directed to the amount of caffeine producing rigor, and to the effect of certain acids and alkalies on caffeine rigor.

Whatever view may be entertained as to the nature of the electric currents present in an injured muscle or nerve, whether they be regarded as pre-existing in the uninjured condition or as being developed through injury, such currents exist in the injured condition. They have been made the subject of investigations, with improved apparatus, by Drs. Henry C. Chapman and Albert P. Brubaker, who have sought to demonstrate their presence in muscle and nerve, and to determine their electro-motive force. The method of these authors has been applied to the gastrocnemius muscle and the sciatic nerve of the frog, and they have determined that the electro-motive force of the muscle is more than three times as great as that of the nerve.

John Campbell, of Johns Hopkins University, has found that when curarized muscles are moderately weighted and stimulated with electricity, the stimulus starts from only one electrode—viz., the cathode on closing and the anode on opening the current; while with insignificant weights the muscle is stimulated at both anode and cathode, with equal and simultaneous stimuli.

Poisons.—An investigation has been undertaken by Dr. Weyl of the toxic or non-toxic properties of the coloring matters derived from coal-tar, including especially those that might be employed for the coloration of food-materials. The author first tested the nitroso and nitro derivatives of benzol and phenol, and, taking phenyl green as a typical representative, found the first to be non-poisonous. The nitro-derivatives which he examined—namely, picric acid, dinitro-kresol, and Martin's yellow —he found to be poisonous; the sulpho-compounds of the last-named matter were harmless; two of these—naphthol yellow and brilliant yellow—are articles of commerce. The difference points to a relationship between the chemical constitution and physiological action of these bodies.

The general physiological action of carbonic monoxide was well illustrated in a case of fatal poisoning by that gas at Troy, N. Y., of which Prof. W. P. Mason gave an account before the American Association. Owing to a break in the mains, a quantity of fuel-gas passed beneath the frozen crest of the earth and escaped into the adjoining houses. Three deaths and a number of serious illnesses resulted. The fuel-gas contained about 40 per cent. of carbon monoxide and was practically odorless. Very searching autopsies were made with the result of finding nothing abnormal except the bright, cherry-red color of the tissues and the vivid redness of the blood. The physician making the autopsies was seized with giddiness and great oppression in the chest, calling strongly to mind the symptoms described by Sir Humphry Davy when he so rashly experimented upon himself with carbon monoxide. The presence of carbon monoxide in the blood was shown by the spectroscope, the characteristic absorption bands being strongly marked. Although now twenty months since the time of its removal from the body, the blood still preserves its brilliant redness and gives the carbon monoxide bands as distinctly as ever.

The toxic milk ptomaine, tyrotoxicon, according to Braithwaite's "Retrospect," is, chemically speaking, diazo-benzole. It is developed in milk by the growth of a micro-organism which multiplies rapidly under favorable conditions. These are principally the exclusion of air, entirely or to a great extent, and a temperature approaching 36°. It is observed under these conditions if milk, as it is drawn from the cow, is placed in cans and they are tightly closed.

It is shown in a memoir by MM. Roux, and Chamberland, to which M. Pasteur has called attention in the French Academy of Sciences, that the septic vibrion, a living ferment analogous to the butyric vibrion, develops soluble chemical products, which gradually act as an antiseptic on the organism itself. These products, introduced in sufficient quantities into the body of the guinea-pig, confer absolute immunity from the attacks of the virus, to which that animal is specially susceptible.

Experiments by Dr. R. H. Chittenden have shown that uranium is an irritant poison tending to destroy the life of the intestinal and renal tissues. Enteritis, or acute catarrhal inflammation, was easily induced by the administration of small doses of its salts. In toxic doses it causes absolute anuria; in smaller doses, merely acute parenchymatous nephritis; in minute doses it has a diuretic effect. Oxalate of lime crystals in the urine, and glycosuria were constantly noted in cases of poisoning by uranium.

There are a number of substances, according to Prof. Liebriech, which, when injected subcutaneously, give rise to anæsthesia in the immediate neighborhood of the place where they are injected. Antipyrine, sal-ammoniac, salts of tannin, resorcin, chloride of iron, and other substances have this action, although there is no chemical or physiological similarity between them. They possess, however, the property in common that they all have a corrosive action on the tissues—the expression being understood to imply any kind of alteration of molecular structure. The alkaloids, in the cases where they possess a local anæsthetic action, act in the same way, as, for instance, erythrophœin. Cocaine alone is an exception to the rule, inasmuch as it is a local anæsthetic, but does not corrode the tissues. When applied subcutaneously to man, the substances named produce either no localized anæsthesia, or one which is very imperfect. When testing the action of anæsthetics on the eye, it is essential to take into account the difference in sensitiveness of the conjunctiva and cornea, as Claude Bernard has pointed out.

PORTUGAL, a constitutional monarchy in Southwestern Europe. The crown is hereditary to both sexes in the house of Braganza. The present sovereign is Luis I, born Oct. 31, 1838, the son of Queen Maria II and Prince Ferdinand of Saxe-Coburg, who succeeded his brother Pedro V, Nov. 11, 1861, and married in 1862, Pia, youngest daughter of King Vittorio Emanuele of Italy.

The *Carta de Ley*, or Constitution, granted in 1826, and altered in 1852, was further modified by the law of July 24, 1885, which abolishes hereditary peerages by a gradual process. These become extinct on the death of the immediate successors of the peers now living. In the place of the hereditary peers, there will be 100 peers appointed for life by the King, and 50 elective peers. The Chamber of Peers consists of 162 members, and the Chamber of Deputies since 1884 has had 173 members. The present Cabinet, constituted on Feb. 20, 1886, is composed as follows: President of the Council and Minister of the Interior, Lucianno de Castro Pereira Corte Real; Minister of Justice, F. A. da Veiga Beirao; Minister of Public Works, E. J. Navarro; Minister of Finance, M. Cyrillo de Carvalho; Minister of War, Col. Viscount San Januario; Minister of Marine and the Colonies, H. de Barros Gomes, who is also Minister of Foreign Affairs *ad interim*.

Finances.—The public debt on June 30, 1887, amounted to 490,493,599 milreis. The interest discharged during the year was 14,907,479 milreis, and the interest in default that was added to the debt was 5,237,420 milreis.

Communications.—The main lines in 1888 had the total length of 1,761 kilometres, while 382 kilometres were in course of construction. Of subsidiary railroads, there were 144 kilometres completed and 109 kilometres building. The number of letters sent through the mails

in 1887 was 20,219,712; post-cards, 3,056,279; circulars and newspapers, 16,944,182. The length of the Government lines at the beginning of 1885 was 4,978 kilometres, with 11,732 kilometres of wire. The receipts were 220,684 milreis.

Commerce.—The values of the imports and exports of the various classes in 1887 are given, in milreis, in the following table:

CLASSES.	Imports.	Exports.
Cereals........................	6,199,000	317,000
Fruits and vegetables........	1,058,000	1,714,000
Colonial produce..............	3,363,000	90,000
Wines and spirits.............	162,000	11,422,000
Animals and animal products.	4,614,000	2,521,000
Minerals......................	2,468,000	1,063,000
Metals........................	7,765,000	161,000
Hides and leather.............	2,844,000	232,000
Timber........................	1,177,000	17,900
Textiles......................	6,805,000	140,000
Various manufactures.........	5,246,000	373,000
Drugs and chemicals..........	400,000	468,000
Total merchandise........	42,018,000	21,244,000

The imports of precious metals amounted to 4,771,000 milreis, and the exports to 5,000 milreis.

The countries participating in the foreign commerce of Portugal in 1886 and the value of the trade with each, in milreis, are given in the following table:

COUNTRIES.	Imports.	Exports.
Great Britain................	12,174,000	6,722,000
France	5,130,000	9,491,000
Brazil.......................	2,014,000	4,575,000
Germany	4,635,000	1,318,000
United States................	4,978,000	647,000
Spain........................	2,504,000	1,155,000
Portuguese possessions.......	1,582,000	557,000
Belgium......................	1,537,000	849,000
Italy........................	799,000	164,000
Sweden and Norway........	741,000	218,000
Russia.......................	471,000	296,000
Other countries..............	238,000	430,000
Total............	37,326,000	26,123,000

The merchant marine in 1888 consisted of 48 steam-vessels of the aggregate capacity of 16,260 cubic metres, and 421 sailing-vessels of 32,310 cubic metres.

The Army.—The effective strength of the army on the peace footing, Aug. 31, 1888, was 2,073 officers and 28,534 men, with 2,852 horses and 768 mules. The war strength was 3,862 officers and 125,057 men, with 7,821 horses, 4,870 mules, and 264 guns. These figures do not include the colonial forces, consisting of a regiment of infantry 1,193 strong, and 7,633 colonial troops of the first line, besides numerous native troops of the second and third lines.

The Navy.—The fleet in 1888 numbered 42 steamers with 126 guns, and 13 sailing-vessels with 41 guns. The steam navy included 1 iron-clad corvette, the "Vasco de Gamo"; 6 other corvettes; 18 gun-boats; 7 other steamers; and 6 torpedo-vessels.

Colonies.—In Macao, Portuguese sovereignty over which has recently been acknowledged by China in return for the co-operation of the colonial authorities in suppressing opium-smuggling, great excitement was produced in September by the conduct of the Governor in dissolving the Senado or municipal council, owing to a difference of opinion between himself and its members. This body has existed for three hundred years, managing all the internal affairs of the colony, regulating trade, administering finances, and performing all duties of an administration except the control of troops. The Portuguese Government notified to the powers in 1888 the abandonment of the protectorate that it assumed over the Kingdom of Dahomey in August, 1885, being unwilling to bear the international responsibility for the actions of the Sultan. On the African coast farther south the Government has made extraordinary efforts to extend and consolidate its authority. The Governor of the Congo territory, in February, 1888, took peaceable possession of Ambrizette. New export duties for the Portuguese Congo, copied from those of the Congo Free State, went into force on March 1. The Portuguese occupation interfered in no way with trade, though the natives complained of having to pay duties to the native chief in addition to the new import duties imposed by the Portuguese authorities. Kinsembo was also occupied, but not without a struggle. The Portuguese military posts have been advanced into the interior, and Portuguese emissaries and traders have penetrated toward Kassai river and into the Congo Free State. In East Africa the colonial authorities have been active in extending Portuguese influence, though with less success. The cause of this unusual activity is the desire to preserve the regions where Portugal has her colonies and the belt extending through the interior from shore to shore, as a field for colonization and a commercial outlet for Portuguese manufactures. Portugal obtained from France, in her treaty of May 12, 1886, an acknowledgement that the territories between Angola and Mozambique were within her sphere of influence. Germany, in the treaty signed on December 30 of the same year, likewise promised not to encroach upon this territory. Great Britain, however, made no such agreement, but in 1888, in order more especially to hem in the Transvaal Boers, announced that the country of Lobengula and all the territory west of the Portuguese possessions and south of the Zambesi river, would henceforth be regarded as within the sphere of British influence. This includes Mashonaland, where the most important of the gold-fields are situated. An English company having obtained from Lobengula the exclusive right to mine for gold in Mashonaland, the Portuguese consul at Cape Town, in the name of his Government, repudiated the pretended rights of Lobengula to Mashonaland and the adjacent territories, over which Portugal claims sovereignty. A project for a transcontinental railroad has been adopted, and the first section of two hundred miles from the west coast has been begun. In order to link the two colonies together, a line of steamers between Loango and Mozambique has been established, while the Portuguese subsidy has been withdrawn from the British line running between Mozambique and Bombay, which is the chief outlet for the products of the Portuguese possessions on the east coast. Portugal has undertaken to preserve peace and order on the shores of Lake Nyassa, where English missionaries and traders are established, having abolished the transit-dues for goods passing to Lake Nyassa in 1884, thus making a financial sacrifice in order to obviate any claim of Great Britain to interfere in that region.

PRESBYTERIANS. I. Presbyterian Church in the United States of America.—The following is the General Summary of the statistics of this Church, as they are published with the "Journal" of the General Assembly for 1888. The statistics for 1874, 1880, and 1887 are also given for comparison, and to show the growth of the Church during the past fifteen years:

ITEMS.	1874.	1880.	1887.	1888.
Synods........	85	88	28	28
Presbyteries...	174	177	201	202
Candidates.....	767	600	986	997
Licentiates	809	294	857	814
Ministers......	4,597	5,044	5,654	5,789
Elders.........	....	....	21,885	22,434
Deacons.......	....	....	7,085	7,210
Churches......	4,946	5,489	6,487	6,543
Churches organized..........	174	159	225	206
Added on examination....	86,971	26,588	53,587	51,062
Communicants.	495,684	578,671	696,827	722,071
Baptisms, adults	11,682	9,232	20,115	18,799
Baptisms, infants	18,808	18,960	28,470	28,869
Sunday-school members	516,971	631,952	771,869	793,442
Contributions:				
Home missions.	$416.067	$429,769	$785,075	$844,695
Foreign miss'ns	508,520	420,427	669,903	748,495
Education.....	248,952	109,066	117,900	152,820
Publication*...	61,605	27,688	39,439	78,182
Church erection	145,068	151,815	256,690	225,864
Relief fund	78,927	57 750	110,942	†525,555
Freedmen	47,419	48,497	108,406	106,647
Sustentation ..	68,115	20,849	26,419	215,009
General Assembly..........	86,485	42,044	62,880	87,026
Aid for colleges	....	....	127,627	68,125
Congregational.	6.642,108	6,098,150	7,902,485	8,808,502
Miscellaneous..	882,576	954,943	860,762	1,014,863
Total......	$9,120,792	$8,861,028	$11,092,728	$12,817,758

* To be known hereafter as Sunday-school work.
† Includes part of Centenary fund.

The receipts of the Board of Home Missions for the year had been $783,627, the largest ever returned, and also the largest, it was claimed, that had ever been contributed to this cause in a single year by any evangelical denomination in America. Fourteen hundred and eighty-six missionaries had been employed, in all but six States, in the Union; under whose labors 170 churches had been organized, 371 Sabbath-schools established, 119 houses of worship built, and 10,182 church-members added on profession of faith. The Woman's Board had maintained 29 schools, with 115 teachers, among the Indians; 24 schools, with 48 teachers, among the Mexicans; and 38 schools, with 81 teachers, among the Mormon population. Its receipts of money for the year had been $226,092. The committee of the Centenary fund reported that the receipts from less than one half of the churches of the denomination to May 19 had been $419,000 in cash and $140,000 in pledges. The Board of Aid for Colleges and Academies had received $40,000. The General Assembly invited contributions for it for the coming year of $100,000. The Committee on Theological Seminaries, of which there are eight, returned the aggregate value of the property of those institutions as $7,216,000, and the whole number of students attending them as 607. The contributions of the churches to the funds of the Board of Publication had amounted to $73,000, giving an increase from the previous year more than sufficient to pay off its debt. Twenty-three new volumes and eleven tracts had been added to its book-list; 10,000 books and 3,000,000 lesson helps and papers had been granted; and 73 mission schools had been organized during the year. The debt of the Board of Education had been reduced from $15,000 to $3,800, and the number of students for the ministry had increased. The trustees of the General Assembly returned the whole amount of its trust funds on the 31st of March, 1888, at $467,390. The treasurer of the General Assembly had received $62,986, and had expended $44,324. The Board of Missions for Freedmen reported that its receipts for the year had been $131,653 or $35,132 more than for the previous year. It had employed 26 white and 81 colored missionaries, 48 white and 106 colored teachers, and 10 catechists, and sustained 235 churches, with 16,661 members, and 226 Sabbath-schools, with 14,555 members. Thirteen churches had been organized, and 1,210 members added on examination.

The total receipts of the Board of Foreign Missions had been $901,181, or $117,023 more than those of the previous year.

The one hundredth General Assembly met in Philadelphia, May 17. The Rev. Charles L. Thompson, D. D., was chosen moderator. The Committee of Conference with the Southern Presbyterian Church presented its report, relating the correspondence and negotiations that had passed between it and the similar committee of the Southern Church in relation to organic union. The committees had held a conference in Louisville, Ky., in December, 1887. The Southern committee indicated four points on which it desired to know the mind of the Northern Church. These points were: 1. The spirituality of the Church, referring especially to its attitude in regard to "political deliverances"—concerning which the declaration of the previous Northern General Assembly would be satisfactory if the Southern Church was assured its interpretation of it was correct. 2. The relation of the Church in the Southern States to the colored people—a matter concern-

ing which the alternative plans were suggested of organizing these people into churches of an entirely separate existence, or into separate churches, presbyteries, and synods, with representation in the General Assembly, and in the expectation that an independent organization would ultimately be effected. 3. The powers and responsibilities of the various boards of the Northern Church and to what extent they are under the control of the General Assembly. 4. "Touching those portions of the Confession of Faith which more specifically involve the great system of truth known as the Calvinistic, and particularly whether there is traceable any distinct tincture of such Pelagian and semi-Pelagian heresies as were matters of controversy in 1837." The Northern committee replied to these questions, February 2, that the reunited General Assembly has no other doctrine on the subject of political deliverances than is declared in its expression of May, 1887 (see "Annual Cyclopædia" for 1887), which is in the language of the Confession of Faith and is equally binding on both Churches. Having asserted that the Northern Church is not in favor of setting off its colored members into a separate organization, the committee expressed the belief that the religious work to be done among this people could only be fully done by the Church reunited as one; that a careful supervision of their churches and a well-defined system of moral and scriptural education of them was demanded; that while their evangelization should be continued under the direction of the General Assembly, the General Assembly had recognized that it was best accomplished by the education of colored ministers and the organization of churches composed of colored members and of those connected with this work, and had organized such churches with presbyteries and synods, with representation in the General Assembly. The committee added, on this point:

We are of the opinion that our Assembly will agree to a basis of organic union, by which the present boundaries and constituencies of presbyteries and synods in the South shall remain *in statu quo*, to be changed only with the consent of the parties interested; and that all the new churches and all new presbyteries hereafter established, shall be organized by and received into connection with presbyteries and synods respectively, as the interested parties may mutually agree.

The ecclesiastical boards were described to be agents of the General Assembly and subject to the government and control of the Church. On the fourth point, the committee declared that no heresy existed in the Northern Church and no doctrinal question was agitating it. In conclusion, while it was hoped that such substantial unity of belief was disclosed as would encourage the continuance of the committees with powers for a full conference on organic union, and such union was favored by the Northern Church, it would not be desirable unless it could be consummated with mutual confidence in the doctrinal soundness of both parties.

The Assembly, while declaring that it would be premature and improper to consider the report as furnishing a definite and formal basis of union, inasmuch as that subject was not properly before it, approved of the general principles enunciated in the replies of the committee to the inquiries of the Southern brethren, as furnishing substantially a reflection of its views touching the subjects to which they relate; expressed the conviction that the most effective form of co-operation could be secured only by an organic union of the two Churches; and declared itself ready to enter upon negotiations looking to that result whenever in the judgment of the Southern Assembly it might be deemed desirable. The committee was continued and enlarged, with instructions to confer with a committee of the Southern General Assembly, if one should be appointed, in devising such methods for conducting the common work as should "open the door to the fullest and heartiest co-operation." A committee was appointed to visit the Presbytery of Rio Janeiro and be present at the organization of the Synod of Brazil. A conference was held by his desire with President Cleveland, by a committee of the Assembly, on Indian affairs, particularly with reference to the modification of certain orders affecting missionary work among the tribes. A committee was appointed to act with committees of other evangelical church organizations in the United States as a National Sabbath Committee. A committee was appointed to inquire into the duties of the Presbyterian Church toward the immigrant population, with special reference to the Germans, Scandinavians, Bohemians, and French. Provision was made for the revision of the proof texts of the Church standards, and the suggestion of such changes as may be found desirable; also for drawing up a plan for the systematic instruction and training of young persons and others, with a view to their admission to the Lord's table. A resolution was passed deprecating the prevalence of improper advertisements in religious newspapers, and particularly disapproving all such advertising "as involves the essential principle of a lottery"; as promises or encourages investors to expect improbable returns from capital invested; and "all those advertisements of patent medicines which are prejudicial to the refinement, modesty, and purity of home life." In view of "the unsettled condition of public opinion" regarding the Revised Version of the Scriptures, it was decided to be inexpedient to authorize its use in public worship. A plan was ordered prepared for bringing together unemployed ministers and vacant churches. The Assembly, "while disclaiming all connection with or relation to political action or measures," declared itself "unequivocally in favor of the entire suppression of the traffic in intoxicating liquors as a beverage"; and cautioned the sessions against admitting as members persons who are engaged in it. It also, regarding the introduc-

tion of the traffic by civilized nations into heathen lands with "shame, horror, and apprehension," declared itself ready to unite with other Churches in an effort to induce Christian governments to abolish and prevent it. A resolution recognizing "Decoration Day," and the value of the services of Union soldiers, was supplemented by a declaration that it was not intended to contradict the great principles of the spirituality of the Church as laid down in the Confession of Faith. A case of discipline came before the Assembly in which the question of the legality of responsive services in the Presbyterian Church was involved. The action of the Assembly, without deciding the issue, virtually reiterated the decision of the Assembly of 1876, which declined to make responsive readings a subject of discipline.

II. Presbyterian Church in the United States (Southern).—The following is a summary of the statistics of this Church as they were reported to the General Assembly in May:

Number of synods	12
Number of presbyteries	68
Number of candidates	285
Number of licentiates	55
Number of ministers	1,129
Number of churches	2,250
Number of churches organized	47
Number of ruling elders	7,310
Number of deacons	5,228
Number added on examination	10,173
Number of communicants	156,249
Number of adults baptized	3,482
Number of infants baptized	5,155
Number of baptized non-communicants	83,444
Number of teachers in Sunday-schools and Bible-classes	12,201
Number of pupils in Sunday-schools and Bible-classes	101,700

Amount of contributions:

For sustentation	$47,291
For evangelistic fund	48,388
For invalid fund	12,687
For foreign missions	72,859
For education	35,296
For publication	9,092
For Tuscaloosa Institute	6,028
Presbyterial	13,581
For pastors' salaries	625,921
Congregational	765,658
Miscellaneous	97,826

The Executive Committee of Education had received during the year $15,879, and had aided 150 candidates in the total sum of $13,887.

The Committee of Publication had received from churches, Sabbath-schools, and individuals, $8,119; and from royalties, $2,824. The whole amount of its grants had been $3,494. The business of the Book Depository had increased by nearly 20 per cent. The balance-sheet of the Publishing House showed an excess of arrests amounting to $73,243. All of the 4-per-cent. bonds issued by the concern had been redeemed except four representing $300. The Tuscaloosa Institute for colored ministers had been attended by 26 students.

The receipts of the Committee of Home Missions had been $64,455; of which $28,406 were in the Department of Sustentation, $14,769 for the Evangelistic fund, $15,117 for the Invalid fund, and $6,105 for the Colored Evangelistic fund. From the Sustentation fund $2,595 had been appropriated in aid of the erection of 20 church-buildings, and $19,509 in aid of 122 ministers supplying 500 feeble churches; from the Evangelistic fund, $12,387 in aid of the support of 61 evangelists; from the Invalid fund, $11,957 in aid of 109 ministers and widows and children of ministers; and from the Colored Evangelistic fund, $3,446 for Tuscaloosa Institute, and $2,689 in the support of 22 ministers. Loans of $650 had been made in aid of the erection of 6 church-buildings.

The Committee of Foreign Missions had received $88,040, or $3,967 more than in any previous year. The missions—in Brazil, China, Mexico, Greece, Italy, Japan, and among the American Indians—returned 66 missionaries, men and women; 38 stations; 89 out-stations; 897 communicants, of whom 423 had been added during the year; 15 ministers, ordained or licensed; 29 other native helpers; 1,238 pupils in Sunday-schools; 891 pupils in day schools; and $5,087 of contributions by the native churches. Nine missionaries had been added to the number in the field, and 4 new stations opened.

The General Assembly met in Baltimore, May 17. The Rev. J. J. Bullock, D. D., was chosen moderator. The "Committee of Inquiry," which had been appointed to confer with a committee of the Northern General Assembly with reference to organic union, made its report relating to the conferences and correspondence which it had held with the committee of the Northern General Assembly.

On consideration of this report, the Assembly declared itself unable to discover that the obstacles to organic union heretofore existing between the two General Assemblies had been to any considerable extent removed; therefore, in view of all the interests involved, it continued established in the conviction that it would be best for it to remain distinct. In reply to the communications of the Northern General Assembly, it declared a desire to forget as far as possible all past dissensions and to cultivate the most friendly relations. A committee was appointed to confer with a committee of the Northern General Assembly "in reference to all such modes of fraternal co-operation in Christian work, both at home and abroad, as may be considered practicable and edifying," and report to the next General Assembly. The case of the Rev. James Woodrow, D. D., against the Synod of Georgia, came up for adjudication. This case has been, in one shape or another, before the Presbyterian courts for several years. It originated in the removal of Dr. Woodrow from his professorship in Columbia Theological Seminary for holding and teaching the doctrine of evolution. In 1886 charges were presented against him before the Presbytery of Augusta for holding and teaching views contrary to the word of God as interpreted in the standards of the Church in respect to the probable animal origin of Adam's body. The

Presbytery found a verdict of "not guilty." A complaint was made to the Synod of Georgia against this verdict as contrary to the law and evidence. The synod sustained the complaint and annulled the verdict. Dr. Woodrow complained to the General Assembly against this action, and it decided not to sustain the complaint. The minute formally expressing the action of the Assembly declared that:

It is the judgment of this General Assembly that Adam's body was directly fashioned by Almighty God of the dust of the ground, without any natural animal parentage of any kind. The wisdom of God prompted him to reveal the fact while the inscrutable words of his action therein he has not revealed.

Therefore the Church does not propose to teach, handle, or conclude any question of science which belongs to God's kingdom of nature; she must by her divine constitution see that these questions are not thrust upon her to break the silence of Scripture and supplement it by any scientific hypothesis concerning the mode of God's being or acts in creation which are inscrutable to us. It is, therefore, ordered that this complaint in this case be not sustained and the judgment of the Synod of Georgia be, and the same is hereby, in all things, affirmed.

The Rev. T. C. Whaling, of the Synod of South Carolina, then offered the following protest, which is to go on record alongside the minute presented by Dr. Smoot:

We, whose names are undersigned, desire to enter our solemn protest against the decision of this General Assembly refusing to sustain the complaint of the Rev. James Woodrow, D. D., against the Synod of Georgia, for the following reasons:

1. The second specification in the indictment against the Rev. James Woodrow, D. D., is expressly excluded by the constitution of our Church, inasmuch as "nothing ought to be considered by any court as an offense, or admitted as a matter of accusation, which can not be proved to be such from Scripture as interpreted in the standards."

2. In the view of your protestants, the Holy Bible does not reveal the form or the mode of the matter out of which, the time in which, or the mode by which God created the body of Adam, and therefore the hypothesis of evolution as believed by Dr. Woodrow can not be regarded as in conflict with teachings of the Sacred Scriptures.

3. The Westminster Standards simply reproduce, without interpretation, the statements of the Scriptures in reference to the creation of Adam's body, and as the views of the complainant are not in conflict with the statements of the Scripture, so neither can they be with the teachings of the standards.

4. The action of the Assembly in refusing to sustain this complaint is equivalent to pronouncing as certainly false the theory of evolution as applied by Dr. Woodrow to Adam's body, which is a purely scientific question entirely foreign to the legitimate sphere of ecclesiastical action. Your protestants, therefore, are unwilling that this General Assembly should express any opinion whatever respecting the hypothesis of evolution or any other scientific question.

A committee was appointed to prepare and report to the next General Assembly on the intemperate use of intoxicating drinks, for the instruction of the churches respecting their duty in suppressing the evil, with the reservation by the Assembly that it was to decide no political question connected with the subject. Provision was made for the representation of the General Assembly on the National Sabbath Committee proposed by the General Conference of the Methodist Episcopal Church.

Centennial of the General Assembly.—The centennial anniversary of the organization of the General Assembly in America was celebrated in Philadelphia during the session of the Northern General Assembly by special popular meetings in behalf of the several benevolent enterprises of the Church and by a series of meetings throughout the day of May 24, in which both the Northern and Southern General Assemblies participated. The Southern General Assembly had been invited by the Northern body to join with it in the celebration, and was met by it May 23 at Overbrook, on the Baltimore Railroad, where both bodies were addressed by President Cleveland. The meetings of May 24 were held in the morning, afternoon, and evening at the Academy of Music and Horticultural Hall, and were presided over severally by the Moderator of the Southern General Assembly, Justice William Strong, of the United States Supreme Court, Gov. A. M. Scales, of North Carolina, the Moderator of the Northern General Assembly, the Hon. J. L. Marye, of Fredericksburg, Va., and Gov. J. A. Beaver, of Pennsylvania. Addresses were delivered by the Rev. T. L. Cuyler, D. D., on the "History of Presbyterianism"; Rev. T. D. Witherspoon, D. D., on "The Work of Presbyterianism for the Future"; Hon. J. R. Tucker, on "The Adaptation of Presbyterianism to the Masses"; Rev. S. J. McPherson, D. D., on "Presbyterianism and Education"; Hon. J. S. Cothran, M. C., on "Calvinism and Human Progress"; Hon. S. J. McMillan, on "Presbyterianism and Republican Government"; Rev. G. P. Hays, D. D., LL. D., on "Home Missions"; Rev. M. H. Houston, D. D., on "Foreign Missions"; Rev. C. J. Thompson, D. D., on "Historic Presbyterian Characters"; Rev. W. C. P. Breckinridge, on "Calvinism"; Rev. Howard Crosby. D. D., LL. D., on "Presbyterianism and Biblical Scholarship"; Rev. John Hall, D. D., and Mr. M. K. Jessup, on "The Necessity of City Evangelization"; Rev. M. O. Hodge, D. D., on "The Methods of City Evangelization"; Rev. Samuel J. Niccolls, D. D., on "Preaching to the Masses"; Hon. B. H. Young, on "Lay Effort among the Masses"; Rev. W. W. Moore, D. D., on "Home Missions"; Rev. C. S. Pomeroy, D. D., on "The Work of the Presbyterian Church in Foreign Fields"; and the Rev. W. P. Breed, D. D., closing the proceedings.

Committees on Organic Union.—The committees appointed by the Northern and Southern General Assemblies of 1888 to consider the question of fraternal co-operation in Christian work met in New York city, December 28, and, after several conferences, they adjourned to meet again in Atlanta, Ga., April 24, 1889.

Presbyterian Synod of Brazil.—A Synod of Brazil was organized at a meeting of the three missionary presbyteries of the Presbyterian Church in the United States, which was held in Rio Janeiro for that purpose, in the last week in August and the first week in September. The Rev. Dr. Alexander L. Blackford, the oldest missionary, was chosen moderator, and a native minister was made stated clerk. The Westminster Confession and Catechism and the Book of Order of the Southern Presbyterian Church, with slight modifications, were adopted as standards. Fraternal delegates from the Northern Presbyterian Church were present, and greetings were received from the Council of the Presbyterian Alliance in London and the General Synod of the Reformed Church in America. The subjects of revising the Portuguese translation of the Scriptures and of forming an alliance with all other English-speaking missionary churches were referred to special committees. The new synod has 50 churches, 19 missionaries, 12 native ministers, 22 church schools, 2 high-schools, 13 women teachers and missionaries, 30 native assistants, and 3,000 communicants. A society of national missions already existed in two of the presbyteries. The next meeting of the Synod was appointed to be held in 1891.

United Christian Church of Japan.—Negotiations have been conducted for the constitution of the "United Christian Church of Japan," by the union of the Presbyterian, Reformed, and Congregational Mission Churches in that country. The doctrinal basis of this Church will consist of the Apostles' Creed and the Nicene Creed, with which are associated the special Confessions of the Presbyterian, Reformed, and Congregational Churches, all being held subordinate to the Bible. In the system of government the Presbyterian elder and the Congregational committee-man are equally recognized, to be ordained for a definite time as the congregation may designate; the elders recommend candidates for admission, who are to be received or dismissed by a vote of the Church; and specified powers are delegated to bodies corresponding with the presbytery and assembly or conference and national council. The new Church organization will include about 11,000 members.

III. United Presbyterian Church in North America. —The statistics of this Church, presented to the General Assembly in May, show that it includes 10 synods, 61 presbyteries, 753 ministers, 3,580 elders, and 98,992 members. The contributions of Sunday-school and missionary societies for the year amounted to $1,019,937.

The General Assembly met in Cedar Rapids, Iowa, May 23. The Rev. Dr. W. T. Maloney was chosen moderator. The Committee on Union with the Reformed Presbyterian Church reported that the negotiations on that subject had been without result, and that union as yet appeared impracticable. The point of difference on which the negotiations broke was the toleration of participation by members of the Church in political action under a government which does not recognize the headship of Christ—to which the Reformed Presbyterian Church is opposed, while the United Presbyterian Church leaves it to the individual member to determine conscientiously what his action shall be. A proposition to instruct presbyteries to refuse to license candidates for the ministry who are addicted to the use of tobacco was rejected, on the ground that the Assembly has no right to make such a rule.

IV. Reformed Presbyterian Church (Synod).— This body includes eleven presbyteries, with 121 congregations, 116 ministers, 503 elders, 325 deacons, 10,970 communicants, and 12,574 members of Sabbath-schools. The number of baptisms returned during the year was 462. The contributions were: For foreign missions, $18,247; for home missions, $3,767; for the Southern mission, $3,632; for the Chinese mission, $1,493; for the Theological Seminary, $8,222; for education, $5,177; for sustentation, $2,156; for church erection, $21,648; for pastors' salaries, $78,190; for national reform, $4,650.

The Central Board of Missions, besides "domestic missions" in the States and Territories, supports a school at Selma, Ala., and a mission among the Chinese of the Pacific coast, and contemplates a mission among the Indians. The Board of Foreign Missions returns at Latakiyeh and Tarsus, in Syria, 11 missionaries, 57 teachers and other agents, 209 native communicants, 1,165 pupils in schools, 23 baptisms during the year, and $465 of contributions.

The Synod met at Allegheny City, Pa., May 29. The Rev. J. W. Sproull was chosen moderator. The Committee on Union with the United Presbyterian Church reported as the result of its conferences with the committee of that Church that the difference between the bodies in their doctrines and practices on the subject of civil government and their attitude toward the Government of the United States had proved to be irreconcilable, although the two bodies were in full accord on other fundamental principles. The Synod, approving the course of its committee, reaffirmed its conviction that—

The Constitution of the United States is a virtual agreement or compact to administer the Government without reference to Christ or the Christian religion, and that incorporation with the Government on the basis of this Constitution is therefore an act of disloyalty to Christ. With this conviction in our hearts, we can not do otherwise than maintain to the end the discipline we have maintained in the past.

While expressing itself desirous for the restoration of the unity of the Church, it declared that—

Partial unions on the basis of compromise, for the purpose simply of forming a larger sect, involves for us the abandonment of our testimony and unfaithfulness to the special work which the Lord, as we believe, has called us to do.

The Synod resolved, on the subject of jury-service that it recognized—

But one supreme law in civil and in ecclesiastical courts, and this is God's revealed Word. If any of our members be summoned to serve on juries, it shall be the duty of such member to state in open court his determination to make God's law, as we understand it, the basis of all decisions involving moral considerations, and that he shall take the juror's oath—such oath being otherwise unobjectionable—only on this condition being definitely accepted by the court. In such case there shall be no censure visited on a member sitting on a jury, since the court, in accepting him on this condition, has, so far as he is concerned, accepted God's law as the basis of judicial action. In case any member acts as a juror, he may be required, by the session of the congregation to which he belongs, to furnish proof that he has complied with the conditions laid down above.

A special service was held in commemoration of the second century after the revolution of 1688, when addresses were made upon the principles for which the Covenanters contended, the character and spirit and the influence of the Covenanters and their struggles on American history.

V. Cumberland Presbyterian Church.— The following is a summary of the statistical reports that were made to the General Assembly in May: Number of ministers, 1,584; of licentiates, 246; of candidates, 262; of congregations, 2,648; of communicants, 151,929; of members of Sunday-schools, 85,890. These statistics do not include the Colored Cumberland Presbyterian Church, which numbers about 15,000 communicants.

The Publishing House returned a profit of $8,272 on the business of the year. It had freed itself from debt, and had declared a dividend of $5,000 in favor of the Board of Ministerial Relief. The latter board had received $5,826, and had relieved 59 families of ministers. The Board of Missions had received $13,071 for home, and $9,418 for foreign missions; while the Woman's Board of Foreign Missions returned an income of $11,212.

The fifty-eighth General Assembly met at Waco, Tex., May 17. The Rev. W. H. Black was chosen moderator. The Board of Missions was directed to take immediate steps toward establishing a theological training-school in Japan. Satisfaction was expressed at the movement toward organic union among the mission forces and native Christians of different denominations of Christians in that country, and a willingness that the Cumberland Presbyterian Missions should enter the "United Christian Church" upon the basis of the exceptions to the Westminster Confession that are set forth in the Declaratory Act of the United Presbyterian Church of Scotland.

VI. Presbyterian Church in Canada.— This Church comprises 5 synods, 43 presbyteries, 783 pastoral charges, with 1,831 churches and stations supplied, 145,640 communicants, 78,649 families and 1,326 single persons connected with the Church, and 12,976 teachers and 112,940 pupils in Sabbath-schools and Bible-classes. The number of members admitted during the year on profession of faith was 12,471; number of baptisms, 10,144 of infants and 1,148 of adults. Amount of contributions to the schemes of the Church, $22,490; amount raised for all purposes, $1,730,252. The

Church and Manse Building scheme, which was started to raise a fund of $100,000 for the purposes implied in its name, had received in 1888, $115,499. Under it, 109 buildings, valued at $127,700, had been aided to the extent of $48,897. A large increase was reported in the income for Foreign Missions. One hundred and sixty-nine missionaries and assistants were laboring in Central India, Formosa, Trinidad, Demarara, the New Hebrides, and among the Indians of the Northwest. A new mission was to be begun in the province of Honan, China.

The General Assembly met at Halifax, N. S., June 13. The Rev. W. T. McMullen was chosen moderator. An *ad-interim* act, passed at the previous General Assembly, on marriage with a deceased wife's sister was re-enacted, and the proposal to alter that part of the Confession of Faith bearing on the subject, was sent down to the presbyteries.

VII. Church of Scotland.—The report to the General Assembly of the Committee on Presbyterial Superintendence gave the total number of communicants in 1887 as 579,002, showing an increase of 7,973. Since 1873, communicants had been added to the roll of the Church at the rate of 1·8 per cent., while the annual increase of the population was only 1·1 per cent.

The income of the Colonial Committee had risen from £4,176 in 1886 to £4,859 in 1887, the increase being solely due to legacies. The income of the Jewish Mission Committee had been £6,400, and the expenditure £5,045, while the adverse balance had been reduced to £1,323. There were 1,792 children in the schools, 950 of whom were Jewish. Four baptisms had taken place. The contributions to the Aged and Infirm Ministers' fund had been £2,737,836 parishes contributing. The capital now stood at £24,182, showing an increase of £2,213. The sum of £1,362 had been dispensed on nine grants.

The total revenue of the Committee on Home Missions had been £10,395 or £1,855 more than the revenue of the previous year. Seventy-two mission churches were returned, with 15,124 worshipers, of whom 10,263 were communicants. The total of collections and contributions reported for 1887 to the Committee on Statistics of Christian Liberality amounted to £385,506 as compared with £407,212 in 1886.

The receipts of the Committee on Foreign Missions had been £24,481, while a deficit of nearly £1,500 had been incurred. Toward the special fund of £10,000, £4,700 had been received. Fifteen mission stations were returned in Africa and India, with, in Africa, 30 European missionaries and 110 native agents, and 2,932 native Christians, 733 of whom were communicants; while in India there were about 8,000 baptized Christians connected with the mission, and 827 had been baptized during the year.

The General Assembly met in Edinburgh, May 24. The Rev. Dr. W. H. Gray was chosen moderator. A question arose concerning the commissioners from Edinburgh, whose town council had refused by a majority to send representatives to the Assembly, leaving action on the subject to be taken by the minority. A legal opinion having been read, to the effect that it was the duty of the town council to send representatives to the Assembly, the commissioners were received. A hearing was given in the case of an appeal concerning a petition which had been refused by the Committee on Bills for the removal of certain "images" from St. Giles's Cathedral. The petitioners complained that the laws of the Church of Scotland were being set at defiance, and that "the superstitions of Rome" were being brought in again. If they were true to the historic teaching of their Church, they would see that the "images" were swept away. It was argued against the petition that the time had passed for occupying attention with such matters; and that hardly any persons now seriously believed that there was anything superstitious or idolatrous in the erection and maintenance of such images. The Assembly refused to sustain the appeal. An overture declaring that any person found guilty of carrying on simoniacal practices to procure a benefice or office should be deprived of his license if a probationer, and deposed if a minister, having been approved by a majority of the presbyteries, was converted into a law of the Church. A resolution was passed approving the leading features of the "Universities Scotland Bill" which was then pending in Parliament. The report of the Committee on Church Interests represented that the course of events had afforded proof of the artificial character of the agitation which had been "created from time to time" against the connection between Church and State in Scotland, and intimated that the agitation might have had no existence except where it had been created or stimulated for sectarian purposes. There was no evidence that the majority of the people of Scotland were opposed to the Established Church. With the report was adopted a renewed expression of the desire of the Assembly to maintain toward the other Churches of Scotland an attitude of earnest watchfulness for any opportunity for kindly co-operation and intercourse. The report of the Committee on the Subscription of Office-Bearers of the Churh suggested that it was desirable that in the case of ministers and licentiates, the Church should revert to the formula contained in the act of Parliament of 1693, entitled "An act for settling the quiet and peace of the Church"; and in the case of elders to an act of 1690 requiring simply approbation of the Confession of Faith. The report was adopted as an overture to be sent down to the presbyteries. Sunday, the 4th, and Monday, the 5th, of November, were appointed as days for celebrating throughout the Church the bicentenary of the revolution of 1688. The employment of deaconesses and the opening of city churches on week days were approved. Satisfaction was expressed at the results of the bill for the early closing of liquor-saloons in Scotland; and the committee of the Assembly was authorized to approach the Government with reference to the drink-traffic among native races.

VIII. Free Church of Scotland.—The total contributions of the year for the Sustentation fund of this Church had been £168,657, showing a decrease from the previous year of £3,-476. In the report on colonial missions it was claimed that some of the most prosperous settlements in the colonies had originated through the efforts of these missions. A favorable report was made of the condition of the Jewish missions. The financial statement of the Foreign Mission Committee showed a charge amounting to £51,908. The discharge showed a balance in favor of the scheme of £8,674. The increase in contributions from associations had been higher than ever before in the history of the Church. It was reported that the desire had spread among the Hindoo population at Madras, India, for the foundation of a national Hindoo college, in which religion should be taught as an inseparable portion of the curriculum.

The General Assembly met at Inverness, May 24. The Rev. Dr. Gustavus Aird, was chosen moderator. The report on the state of religion and morals, represented that while peculiar hardships affected some of the Highland ministers, in general adequate organization existed among the churches. The belief was expressed that intemperance was on the decrease; but in many places tourists were doing much to lower the tone of Sabbath observance. A congratulatory address was voted to the Presbyterian Churches of the United States on the occasion of their friendly meeting in Philadelphia, and of the centenary of Presbyterianism in the United States. An active debate on the question of disestablishment terminated in the adoption of a resolution declaring that the maintenance of a Church Establishment in Scotland was unjust, inexpedient, and a hinderance to the welfare of the Presbyterian churches of the land. A resolution was adopted recognizing the grievances of the crofters, and asking for suitable legislation for the relief of their distress. An overture, concerning federal relations with the Presbyterian Church in England, having been approved by a majority of the presbyteries, was passed into a standing order of the Church. A petition to Parliament was approved against the bill for legalizing marriage with a deceased wife's sister, otherwise known as the marriage affinity bill. A committee was directed to consider whether the benefits of the Widow's fund may not be extended to the widows and orphans of missionaries.

IX. United Presbyterian Church (Scotland).—The statistical reports of this Church, made to the Synod in May, gave the following results:

Number of congregations, 565; of members, 182,170, showing an increase during the year of 107; number of baptisms, 9,374; of Sabbath-schools, 887, with 12,075 teachers and 97,-475 pupils. The total congregational income amounted to £320,698.

The income for foreign-mission purposes had been £56,534, the largest amount ever received in one year. The eight mission fields returned 60 ordained European missionaries, with 56 other trained agents, 95 native evangelists, 301 native teachers, and 100 other native helpers. The 87 congregations and 155 out-stations had an aggregate membership of 13,497, with 2,074 candidates for admission. The Sabbath-schools, exclusive of those in China and Japan, returned 11,418 pupils, and the day-schools 13,676 pupils. The Board of Missions was empowered by the Synod to discontinue the Spanish mission, and to take steps to form, along with other Protestant agencies in Spain, a native Spanish Protestant Church.

X. Presbyterian Church in England.—The entire income of this Church for the year was returned at £219,585. The Home Mission reported that two congregations had been added. The Jewish Mission reported concerning its labors in London. The receipts for foreign missions had been £15,800. The Synod had in China 15 European ordained missionaries, 6 medical missionaries, 13 women missionaries, supported by the Women's Association, and a number of native evangelists and pastors. Some of the native churches were self-supporting, and were themselves undertaking mission work. The income of the Women's Missionary Association had been £2,336, showing an increase during the year of £600. Additions having been made to the capital of the Aged and Infirm Ministers fund, the minimum annuity had been raised from £45 to £50. The minimum ministerial dividend had been retained at £200 a year.

The Synod met in Newcastle-on-Tyne, April 30. The Rev. Dr. Oswald Dykes was chosen moderator. The Committee on the Church's Relations to the Confession of Faith, which had been engaged for three years in the revision of the creed, reported; the declaratory statement, setting forth the sense in which the Church received the Westminster Catechism, was held in abeyance, as legal difficulties might arise in view of certain clauses in the trust-deeds, were it adopted. The new articles were to be regarded in the light of a summary of the Confession in which the language of that document was simplified, while the Confession itself would remain the standard by which they held their respective properties. To the new creed as reported was appended a list of illustrative passages in support of the various clauses, drawn from the Apostle's and Nicene Creeds, and various confessions of the Reformation period. The creed consists of twenty-three articles, of which the article on the creation declares:

We believe that Almighty God for his own holy and loving ends was pleased at the beginning to create the heaven and the earth, through the Son, the eternal Word, and through progressive stages to fashion and order this world, giving life to every creature, and to make man after his own image, that he might glorify and enjoy God, occupying and subduing the earth, and having dominion over the creatures, to the praise of his Maker's name.

That on the fall of man:

We believe and confess that our first father Adam, the representative head as well as common ancestor of mankind, transgressed the commandment of God through temptation of the devil, by which transgression he fell, and all mankind in him, from his original state of innocence and communion with God; and so all men have come under just condemnation, are subject to the penalty of death, and inherit a sinful nature, degenerate in every part, estranged from God, and prone to evil; out of which condition we acknowledge that no man is able by any means to deliver himself.

Concerning the salvation of men, the belief is avowed

In the Holy Spirit, the Lord and Giver of life, who worketh freely as he will, without whose gracious influence there is no salvation, and who is never withheld from any who truly ask for him;

and

That every one who, through the quickening grace of the Holy Spirit, repents and believes the Gospel, confessing and forsaking his sins, and humbly relying upon Christ alone for salvation, is freely pardoned and accepted as righteous in the sight of God, solely on the ground of Christ's perfect obedience and atoning sacrifice.

The doctrine of election is also reiterated in the article:

We humbly own and believe that God the Father, before the foundation of the world, was pleased of his sovereign grace to choose a people unto himself in Christ, whom he gave to the Son that he might bring them unto glory; and to those who were thus chosen we believe that the Holy Spirit imparts spiritual life by a secret and wonderful operation of his power, using, as his ordinary means, where years of understanding have been reached, the truths of his Word in ways agreeable to the nature of man; so that, being born from above, they are the children of God, and his new creation in Christ Jesus.

Concerning the Holy Scriptures, it is declared:

We believe that it has pleased God, in addition to the manifestation of his glory in creation and providence, and especially in the spirit of man, to reveal his mind and will to man at successive periods and in various ways; and that this revelation has been, so far as needful, committed to writing by men inspired of the Holy Spirit, and is contained in the Scriptures of the Old and New Testaments, which are therefore to be devoutly studied by all; and we reverently acknowledge the Holy Spirit speaking in the Scriptures as the Supreme Judge in questions of faith and duty;

and concerning the final judgment:

We believe the Lord will judge the world in righteousness by Jesus Christ, before whom we must all appear, who shall separate the righteous from the wicked, make manifest the secrets of the heart, and render to every man according to the deeds which he hath done in the body, whether good or evil, when the wicked shall go away into eternal punishment, but the righteous into eternal life.

VOL. XXVIII.—45 A

The document was accepted by the Synod, and sent down by it to the presbyteries for consideration.

The Committee on the Revision of the Westminster Directory of Worship reported progress, having completed the morning service and the evening service, and the service of the administration of baptism. The last will be in two parts, the first for the baptism of adults, of which no notice is taken in the Westminster Directory, and the second for the baptism of children. The committee adheres to the plan of a directory as against a prescribed liturgy.

XI. Presbyterian Church in Ireland.—The statistical reports of this Church, made to the General Assembly in June, give the number of congregations as 557; of families, 79,971; of communicants, 103,499; of stipend-payers, 67,965; and of Sabbath schools, 1,099, with 9,119 teachers and 103,607 pupils.

The General Assembly met at Belfast, in June. The Rev. R. J. Lynd was chosen moderator. The amount of capital invested in the various departments of the work of the Church was represented in the reports on the subject to be £893,640. The proceeds of the invested funds for the year had been £35,542. The donations and bequests had been for missions, £6,808; for the Orphan Society, £1,508; for the Sustentation fund, £767; making in all, £9,083. The annual income of the Church from all sources was therefore £205,106. The Sustentation fund had made substantial progress, the total increase being £768, and the dividend having increased by £1 to each minister. In the mission in India, the first two native pastors had been ordained over congregations of converts from heathenism. The report of the Jewish Mission showed progress in Syria. The report of the Committee in Correspondence with the Government showed that, while the claims of Presbyterians for civil appointments had in some measure been successful, they were still suffering from religious disabilities. Resolutions were adopted approving of the most decided legislation in behalf of temperance.

XII. Welsh Calvinistic Methodist Church.—The General Assembly of the Welsh Calvinistic Methodists met at Merthyr Tydvil, June 4. The Rev. Owen Thomas, D. D., served as moderator. The statistical reports showed that the number of members in Wales and England was 130,617, or 1,159 more than in the previous year, and the highest number ever reached by the denomination; the number of hearers was 281,073. The whole amount of collections was returned at £198,948. Eight foreign missionaries had gone out during the year from South Wales. There were 119 churches and preaching-stations in the mission on the Khassia Hills, India, with 4,401 members, 5,899 children in the Sunday-schools, and 6,499 in the day schools.

XIII. Presbyterian Alliance.—The fourth General Council of the Alliance of Reformed Churches holding the Presbyterian system, met in London, July 3. About three hundred delegates were present, representing more than twenty-five countries and colonies in all the quarters of the earth. Statistical reports were presented showing that the family of churches represented in the definition of the Alliance represented 78 branches, having 1,392 presbyteries, 209 synods, 3,603,209 communicants; with 500 brethren at work in the missionary field, and more than 60,000 communicants gathered from among the heathen; that the aggregate contributions of free-will offerings in these churches amounted to $30,000,000 a year; that the newly organized women's associations had been the means, during the past year, of contributing nearly $500,000 to the cause of missions. A different chairman was chosen for each of the several sessions of the Council. The following topics were discussed during the meetings of the Council, which continued through nine days: "How to work the Presbyterian System—as directing the Eldership and the Deaconship in their Various Lines of Influence and Work, and as promoting Co-operation and fostering Activity, Harmony, and Spiritual Life in Congregations," by Drs. Andrew Thomson and J. B. Drury and Principals Rainy and Caven; "Some Elements of Congregational Prosperity," "Prayerfulness," "Self-sacrifice," and "Organized Christian Work," by Pastor Theodore Monod, E. R. Craven, D. D., A. T. Pierson, D. D., and Principal Cairns; "The Duties of the Church with Reference to Present Tendencies of a more Intellectual Kind, bearing on Faith and Life," the subject comprehending the "Originality of Christianity," "The Speculative Tendencies of the Age," "How Far is the Church responsible for Present Unbelief?" "Responsibility for Belief," and "Historical Research and Christian Faith," by Rev. E. de Presseuse, D. D., Rev. Dr. Ellinwood, Rev. Marcus Dods, D. D., Pastor Monod, Rev. G. F. Moore, D. D., and Principal Edwards; "The Duty of the Church with Reference to Social and other Tendencies bearing on Faith and Life," including "The Pressure of Commercial Life," "Rich and Poor," "The Church in Relation to the Socialistic Drift of the Times," and "Christ's Method of reconciling Social Antagonisms," by Dr. Marshall Lang, Principal McVicar, Prof. W. S. Emslie, and Rev. Dr. Moses Hoge; "Co-operation in Foreign-Mission Work," after the discussion of which the Council approved of measures for the union of mission churches in heathen lands, such as is proposed in Japan; "Woman's Work," by Dr. Charteris, at whose suggestion a resolution was passed favoring organizations of women for Christian work; "Church Worship," "Aggressive Work in Cities," "Church Work on the European Continent and the Progress of the Colonial Churches," "The Desiderata of Presbyterian History," by Prof. Mitchell; "Commemoration of the Revolution of 1688," by Rev. Dr. Philip Schaff; "Sabbath-schools and the Church's Duty to the Young," by Rev. Dr. Horton, of California,

Prof. Ellis Edwards, Rev. Dr. John Hall, Rev. J. M. C. Holmes, D. D., and Rev. John McNeil. A resolution was adopted urging international action to repress the liquor-traffic in Western Africa, and to prevent the sale of fire-arms to uncivilized peoples. The next meeting of the Council was appointed to be held in Toronto, Ont., in 1892.

PRINCE EDWARD ISLAND, PROVINCE OF. The estimated population in 1888 was 120,000. The Lieutenant-Governor is Andrew A. Macdonald; Executive Council, W. W. Sullivan, Premier and Attorney-General; D. Ferguson, Provincial Secretary, Treasurer, and Commissioner of Public Lands; G. W. W. Bentley, Commissioners of Public Works; John Lefurgey, Neil McLeod, Samuel Prowse, I. O. Arsenault, Archibald J. Macdonald, and James Nicholson. Thomas W. Dodd is President of the Legislative Council; John A. Macdonald, Speaker of the House of Assembly; Edward Palmer, Chief-Justice of the Supreme Court; I. H. Peters and Joseph Hensley, Assistant Judges.

Finances.—In Prince Edward Island the Provincial Government defrays the cost of education, the maintenance of public works, the expense of local legislation, and the administration of justice. The revenue in 1887 was $241,637.26; the expenditure, $287,700.17. On July 1, 1887, $20,000 was added to the annual subsidy paid to Prince Edward Island by the Dominion Government, which now amounts to $193,537.20. There is no provincial taxation. The school system is non-sectarian. The Provincial Government is Liberal-Conservative.

Communications.—The want of winter communication, hitherto one of the most serious disadvantages of this province, has to some extent been supplied by the steel steamship "Stanley," built in 1888. This steamship has been procured by the Dominion Government at a cost of $150,000, and is especially designed for the arduous service of navigating the Strait of Northumberland in winter. The hull and engines are of superior strength and power; the registered tonnage is 1,000 tons. In open water she can steam twenty knots an hour, and she has been known to go through ice from two to four feet thick, at the rate of five miles an hour.

Summer.—As a summer resort, Prince Edward Island is rapidly gaining favor. Visitors are pleased with the delightful, clear, sunny atmosphere. Fair hotel accommodation is provided at Rustico, Malpeque, Tracadie, and on the north side of the island, and also in several towns throughout the province. The farmers have comfortable homes, where many tourists find accommodation.

Fisheries.—The north shore of Prince Edward Island is one of the best fishing-grounds in North America. Here mackerel of the finest quality are caught. Eighty-six American fishing-vessels visited those waters in 1888, and hundreds of Canadian fishermen also were employed in this business. The coast-line was patrolled by Canadian cutters, but no seizures were made.

PROCTOR, RICHARD ANTHONY, astronomer, born in Chelsea, England, March 23, 1837; died in New York city, Sept. 12, 1888. He received his early education at home, being a sickly child, and then attended the academy in Wilton-on-Thames. The death of his father unsettled his school life, the patrimony became involved in

RICHARD ANTHONY PROCTOR.

a chancery suit, and in 1854 he entered the London Joint-Stock Bank as a clerk. In 1855 he began studying at King's College, London, and a year later went to St. John's, Cambridge, where he took a high stand in mathematics, and was graduated in 1860 among the wranglers. For three years he devoted his time to historical and literary studies, when the bank in which his money was deposited failed. He had begun the study of astronomy, and in December, 1863, published in the "Cornhill Magazine" a paper on "Double Stars." In 1864 he began a series of investigations in regard to the great ringed planet of the solar system, the fruits of which were ultimately embodied in his treatise of "Saturn and its System" (London, 1865). In preparing this work he had to make many maps, and from these grew his "Gnomonic Star Atlas" (1866). which in turn suggested his "Hand-Book of the Stars" (1866). Thereafter his literary industry was very great, and he published in quick succession "Constellation Seasons, Sun-Views of the Earth" (1867); "Half-hours with the Telescope" (1868); "Half-hours with Stars" (1869); and "Other Worlds than ours; the Plurality of Worlds, studied under the Light of Recent Scientific Researches," with a

large star-atlas (1870). The last-named was one of the most popular works ever published on astronomy, and after its publication he was regarded as perhaps the most fertile popular writer on astronomical subjects of his day. His original work included numerous researches on the stellar system, the law of distribution of stars and the nebulæ, and the general constitution of the heavens. In 1869 he advanced a theory of the solar corona, which has since been generally accepted, and also that of the inner complex solar atmosphere, which was afterward advanced by Prof. Charles A. Young. He was active in the transit-of-Venus expeditions of 1874 and 1882, and became involved in a dispute with the Astronomer Royal of England as to the best methods of observation. In 1873-'74 he visited the United States and lectured on popular phases of astronomy. Again, in 1875, he came to this country, and during a stay of seven months delivered 142 lectures. In 1879 he left England for America and Australia, and lectured in all of the principal towns of Victoria, New South Wales, South Australia, and New Zealand. His first wife died in 1879, and in 1881 he married Mrs. Robert J. Crawley, of St. Joseph, Mo , and for some years made that city his home. In October, 1887, he removed to Orange Lake, Fla.. and there established his residence and observatory; but, early in September, 1888, he set out for London to fill a lecture engagement. On reaching New York he was taken ill and died of hemorrhagic malarial fever. Prof. Proctor was appointed an Honorary Fellow of King's College, London, in 1873, and became a Fellow of the Royal Astronomical Society in 1866. He was appointed honorary secretary of that society and editor of its proceedings in February, 1872, but resigned these offices in November, 1873. In 1881 he founded "Knowledge," a weekly scientific journal, but changed it to a monthly in 1885, and continued its editor until his death. His productiveness and versatility were remarkable. In the same issue of his journal he would appear in several *rôles* at once: as the editor and as Richard A. Proctor, writing on astronomy and mathematics; as Thomas Foster, criticising and carrying to its logical conclusions Dickens's unfinished novel of "Edwin Drood"; and then anonymously criticising and refuting the said Thomas Foster; as the whist editor and the chess editor and every other sort of editor demanded by the occasion. At the same time he was writing articles for other periodicals and newspapers, and he wrote well on every subject he handled. Besides those already mentioned, he published "Light Science for Leisure Hours" (three series, 1871, 1873, and 1883); "Elementary Astronomy"(1871); "Orbs around us" (1872); "Elementary Geography" (1872); "School Atlas of Astronomy" (1872); "Essays on Astronomy" (1872); "Familiar Science Studies" (1872); "The Moon" (1873); "Borderland of Science" (1873); "Expanse of Heaven" (1873); "The Universe and Coming Transits " (1874); "Transits of Venus" (1874); "A Treatise on the Cycloid " (1878). He edited the "Knowledge Library," consisting of a series of works made up of papers that appeared in his own journal, among which were several of his own, notably "How to Play Whist " (1885) "and "Home Whist" (1885). After becoming an American citizen, he published "Chance and Luck" (1887); "First Steps in Geometry " (1887); "Easy Lessons in Differential Calculus" (1887) ; and "Old and New Astronomy," which at the time of his death was being issued in parts.

PROTESTANT EPISCOPAL CHURCH IN THE UNITED STATES. This Church has moved on steadily in its appointed course during 1888. It is true, it has been roused to more than ordinary effort in order to test and examine its liturgy and services by the proposed plan for enrichment and flexibility, whereby congregations are urged to use fully and freely the Church's provisions for worship and growth in spirituality and the higher Christian life. This matter will come up for final adjustment at the General Convention in October, 1889. The sources of information in preparing this article are the published journals of conventions, reports and documents of Church societies and corporations, Pott's "Church Almanac," and Whittaker's "Protestant Episcopal Almanac." The following table presents a summary of statistics of the Church during 1888:

DIOCESES AND MISSIONS.

DIOCESES.	Clergy.	Parishes.	Baptisms.	Confirmations.	Communicants.
Alabama	83	42	490	483	4,885
Albany	126	100	1,723	1,296	15,702
Arkansas	19	21	216	168	1,599
California	83	85	1,058	407	6,747
Central New York	99	106	1,498	1,118	14,820
Central Pennsylvania	108	92	1,397	1,119	9,383
Chicago	72	49	1,838	978	11,343
Colorado	83	25	856	825	2,400
Connecticut	193	145	1,966	1,284	28,848
Delaware	27	24	247	143	2,2.9
East Carolina	28	35	339	150	3,015
Easton	36	38	394	131	2,499
Florida	52	37	579	862	3,047
Fond du Lac	33	18	341	270	2,982
Georgia	41	38	572	408	5,350
Indiana	33	41	681	510	5,2.5
Iowa	54	49	686	448	5,661
Kansas	33	26	886	279	2,498
Kentucky	42	28	617	533	6,173
Long Island	113	80	2,586	1,642	20,011
Louisiana	36	42	568	367	4,488
Maine	25	22	330	185	2,982
Maryland	171	127	2,674	1,991	25,125
Massachusetts	181	110	2,718	1,784	25,029
Michigan	76	69	1,482	1,066	12,314
Milwaukee	67	88	650	519	5,500
Minnesota	91	71	980	738	7,360
Mississippi	81	85	352	264	2,756
Missouri	70	52	964	886	7,615
Nebraska	45	25	513	430	2,804
Newark	98	77	1,779	1,051	13,491
New Hampshire	36	28	321	257	2,635
New Jersey	109	75	1,445	906	10,587
New York	342	200	6,339	3,665	47,690
North Carolina	58	47	728	599	4,109
Ohio	62	73	789	826	6,218
Pennsylvania	210	123	4,254	2,487	33,700
Pittsburg	58	47	1,156	853	5,968
Quincy	24	28	190	160	2,080
Rhode Island	57	44	1,012	561	8,488
South Carolina	48	54	441	385	4,267

DIOCESES.	Clergy.	Parishes.	Baptisms.	Confirmations.	Communicants.
Southern Ohio	54	48	637	584	7,218
Springfield	40	50	405	496	3,192
Tennessee	46	32	539	507	3,879
Texas	28	40	484	337	3,834
Vermont	37	46	340	266	3,851
Virginia	152	166	1,690	1,382	16,512
Western Michigan	26	27	456	270	2,576
Western New York	118	100	1,609	1,264	18,647
West Virginia	25	27	214	218	2,775
MISSIONARY JURISDICTIONS.					
Oregon	17	24	220	184	1,824
North Dakota	16	88	154	81	683
Utah	6	7	149	45	518
Nevada	4	9	128	57	416
South Dakota	82	50	818	388	1,628
Northern Texas	14	25	140	101	1,715
Western Texas	14	40	229	117	1,429
Northern California	13	19	282	268	976
New Mexico and Arizona	6	21	106	84	192
Montana	12	20	218	115	1,081
Washington	18	15	185	71	507
Wyoming and Idaho	16	20	256	119	577
Alaska	2				
Western Africa	14		154	99	576
China	24		157	127	874
Japan	11		494	242	673
Total	3,950	3,250	56,709	39,590	455,729

Number of dioceses 50
Number of missionary jurisdictions 16
Bishops 68
Candidates for orders....................... 248
Deacons ordained.......................... 140
Priests ordained 110
Priests and deacons 3,950
Whole number of clergy...................... 4,018
Whole number of parishes (including 400 mission stations), about......................... 3,650
Baptisms, infant.......................... 44,500
Baptisms, adult.......................... 11,440
Baptisms, not specified..................... 76)
Total.................. 56,709
Confirmed, number of....................... 39,590
Communicants.... 455,729
Marriages.................................. 15,297
Burials 29,706
Sunday-school teachers 29,818
Sunday-school scholars 362,700
Contributions for church purposes............. $11,483,598

Missionary Society.—In accordance with the canon, this society comprehends all persons who are members of the Protestant Episcopal Church. The Board of Missions consists of all the bishops of this Church, the members for the time being of the House of Deputies of the General Convention, the delegates from the missionary jurisdictions, and the Board of Managers. The Missionary Council comprises all the bishops, an equal number of presbyters, and an equal number of laymen. It meets annually (except in the years when the Board of Missions meets), and is charged with taking all necessary action in regard to the missionary work of the Church which shall not conflict with the general policy of the board. The Council met in Washington, D. C., November 13, and continued in session for two days. It was largely attended by bishops, clergy, and laity, and disposed of its work with promptitude and hearty zeal. The annual report of the Board of Managers was received, with accompanying documents; careful attention was given to the Commission for Work among the Colored People; also to the Woman's Auxiliary, and to the important work of the Church Building-Fund Commission. Appropriate action was freely discussed and tolerably clearly outlined, and the subject of increasing the interest of Church people in behalf of missions was urgently pressed upon all who were present. The Board of Missions divides its work between a domestic committee and a foreign committee, which have headquarters in New York city.

Domestic Missions.—From Sept. 1, 1887, to Sept. 1, 1888, there were: Missionaries (16 missionary jurisdictions and 30 dioceses): Bishops, 13; other clergy (white, colored, Indian), 490; teachers, other helpers, etc., 75; total, 578. The financial condition was as follows: Cash in hand (September, 1887), $25,468.92; offerings, etc., $156,240; legacies for domestic missions, $51,009.43; legacies for investment, $53,-500; legacy for endowment of missionary episcopate, $100,000; specials, $23,478.01. Total, $409,691.36. Expenditures (16 missionary jurisdictions and 32 dioceses), $108,658.98; missions among Indians and colored people, $62,-059.41; specials, $27,905.80; missionary episcopate endowment (paid over), $100,000; legacies, etc. (paid over), $55,127.80; office and other expenses, $17,732.23; balance in hand, $38,207.14. Total, $409,691.36.

Foreign Missions.—From Sept. 1, 1887, to Sept. 1, 1888, the number of missionary bishops was 3; the number of other clergy (white and native) 50; teachers, physicians, helpers, etc., 173; total, 223. The financial condition was as follows: Cash in hand (September, 1888), $44.974.38; offerings, legacies, general fund, $163,519.45; legacy for investment, $9,550; specials for China, Japan, etc., $16,-863.22; total, $234,907.05. Expenditures on account of missions, etc., in West Africa, China, and Japan (including Hayti and Mexico), $132,795.12; legacies, etc. (paid over), $10,169.63; specials, $21,209.99; salaries, rent, printing, etc., $17,732.22; balance in hand, $53,-001.09; total, $234,907.05. The mission property at foreign stations is estimated to be worth much the same as last year, viz., in Africa (about), $22,000; in China (about), $170,000; in Japan (about), $50,000; and others making nearly half a million dollars.

Woman's Auxiliary to the Board of Missions renders important and efficient aid in all the departments by means of parochial, city, county, and diocesan associations of ladies, formed for the purpose of raising money, preparing and forwarding boxes to missionaries and mission stations, and in various other ways giving help to the missionary work of the Church. Money raised for domestic, foreign, and other mission work, $100,985.33; boxes for the same (3,246 in number), value, $175,-168.77; total, $276,154.10.

American Church Missionary Society (also auxiliary to the Board of Missions) has employed during the year in 17 dioceses and missionary jurisdictions 38 missionaries. The financial condition was as follows: For general work, domestic missions, $33,456.91; for general work, foreign missions, $680.05; specials, $5,958.85; Ely professorship, Griswold College, $7,000; balance to new account ($7,350 being trust fund not yet invested), $31,873.33; total, $78 969.14. The society holds in securities, property, etc., $102,675. Boxes of clothing were sent to the missionaries, in value about $4,000.

Church Work in Mexico.—Aid in this work was continued by the reappointment for another year of the presbyter sent out in 1887. His duty remains the same, viz., that of "counseling and guiding presbyters and readers in Mexico who have asked for the fostering care of this Church to be extended to them as a mission." An advisory committee for the work in Mexico has in charge all offerings made through the Board of Missions. "The Mexican League" is still actively at work as an independent association, consisting of ladies, for aid in missionary work in Mexico. It has no further connection with the Board of Missions.

Church in Hayti.—This Church, though independent, is not strong, and seeks aid from the Protestant Episcopal Church in the United States. A commission of bishops has it in charge, and it receives help from the Domestic and Foreign Missionary Society. Aid was extended to the amount of $6,551.73. Statistics: Bishop, 1; other clergy, 13; teachers, 2; catechists, 16; mission stations, 23; baptisms, 58; communicants, 370; day scholars, 552; Sunday-school scholars, 221; contributions, $647; mission property, estimated value, $17,470.

Protestant Episcopal Churches in Europe, under the charge of a bishop of the American Church: In France, 2; in Germany, 1; in Italy, 2; in Switzerland, 1.

American Church Building-Fund Commission, established in 1880, continues its very useful and important work. It aims to create a fund of not less than $1,000,000, so as to be enabled to give effective aid in all parts of the United States toward building chapels and new churches. Thus far the permanent fund has reached to $103,408.83; but, as the matter becomes better understood, there is good reason to expect that the fund will be raised to the desired amount. During the year forty-seven applications for aid were responded to and loans were voted in sums from $200 to $3,000, the average being about $1,000 to each church. The total amount was $46,500.

Society for Promoting Christianity among the Jews (auxiliary to the Board of Missions) reports quiet and steady progress. The society has missionaries in seven of the large cities as well as in numerous large towns. There are five missionary schools, five industrial schools, and two branch schools, and 252 of the parochial clergy kindly co-operate in local activities. The entire work is such as to reach the Jews in 254 cities and towns in the United States.

Of publications 35,556 copies have been issued, and Bibles, Testaments, Scripture portions, and prayer-books have been distributed in the English, German, and Hebrew tongues. Balance in hand (Sept. 1, 1887), $7,846.95; contributions, specials, etc., $12,188.43; total, $20,035.38. Expenditures for schools, salaries, publications, etc., $12,752.52; real-estate account, $518.20; balance to new account, $6,764.66; total, $20,035.38.

Changes in the Clergy.—During the year four of the bishops have died, viz., Bishop Edward R. Welles, of Milwaukee, Bishop J. H. H. Brown, of Fond du Lac, Bishop S. S. Harris, of Michigan, and Bishop G. K. Dunlop, Missionary Bishop of New Mexico and Arizona. Three presbyters have been consecrated bishops, viz., J. S. Johnston, Missionary Bishop of Western Texas; A. Leonard, Missionary Bishop of Nevada and Utah; and L. Coleman, Bishop of Delaware. Three are on the list of retired bishops, viz., H. Southgate, C. C. Penick, and S. I. J. Schereschewsky. Over seventy of the clergy died in 1888.

Q

QUEBEC, PROVINCE OF. Finances.—The Treasurer of the province, in his budget speech on June 18, 1888, shortly before the close of the fiscal year, announced that the ordinary receipts up to April 1 amounted to $3,024,981.65, and the ordinary expenses to $2,259,960.14.

An act was passed authorizing the Government to issue debentures bearing interest at not more than 4 per cent. to the amount of the whole existing debt of the province. As the act left the creditors of the province no option but to accept the lower rate of interest or to terminate their debentures, it was severely criticised in London as well as in Canada, as amounting to a partial repudiation of the province's liability to its creditors. Presumably in deference to freely expressed public opinion, the Government refrained from carrying out the scheme of conversion.

District Magistrates Act.—This act, of little importance in itself, gave rise to no little public excitement through being disallowed by the Dominion Government as *ultra vires* of the Quebec Legislature. The purport of the act was to abolish the Circuit Court of Montreal and substitute therefor a court with practically the same jurisdiction, to be called the District Magistrates Court. Under the British North America Act, the provincial legislatures enjoy the power to make laws in relation to the administration of justice in the province, including the Constitution, maintenance, and organization of provincial courts both of civil and criminal jurisdiction; but the appointment of judges to the superior, district, and county courts in each province appertains to the Governor-General in Council. The appointment of magistrates rests with the provincial governments. Consequently, the practical effect of the act was simply to change the name of the court and of its presiding officer, and to confer upon the Quebec Government the power of appointing that presiding officer, which power of appointment is by the British North America act of the Imperial Parliament expressly conferred upon the Dominion Government. The Quebec Government appointed two district magistrates under the act, and the friends of the local government, in mass meeting assembled, protested against the disallowance as an unwarrantable interference with provincial rights. Some justification for the Quebec Legislature straining the interpretation of the British North America Act in order to authorize the appointment of the judges by the Provincial Government, is to be found in the persistent neglect of the Dominion Government to appoint new judges, although the work in the courts was notoriously in arrears.

The Jesuits' Estates Settlement.—An act passed by the Legislature during the session of 1888, destined to arouse considerable dissension throughout the Dominion, was the act respecting the settlement of the Jesuits' estates. At the time of the suppression of the Society of Jesus throughout the world by the Pope in 1774, the Jesuits owned large estates in Canada, which had been bestowed upon them chiefly for educational purposes. According to a schedule made in 1787, their properties included: 1, Six superficial arpents, on which the Quebec college and church are erected, given for the instruction of the inhabitants; 2, the two Lorettes or Seigniory of St. Gabriel; 3, the peninsula of Lavacherie; 4, Sillery, near Cape Rouge; 5, Belair; 6, Cap de la Magdelaine, near Three Rivers; 7, Batiscan; 8, the Island of St. Christophe, near Three Rivers; 9, Laprairie de la Magdelaine; 10, a piece of ground at St. Nicholas; 11, eleven arpents of ground at Pointe Levis; 12, the Isle of Reaux, below the Island of Orleans; 13, six arpents at Tadousac; 14, the Fief Pacherigny, near Three Rivers; 15, another lot at' the same place; 16, a remnant of ground extending to a small river near Lake St. Peter; 17, a number of lots in Quebec city, now built upon, and many used as public streets; 18, the ground used by the church and mission house of Montreal, etc. Altogether the Jesuits owned 48,-000 acres in the district of Montreal, 439,000 in the district of Three Rivers, and 129,500 in the district of Quebec—valued at from $2,000,-000 to $3,000,000. In 1791 the society was suppressed as a body corporate by King George III, and all its lands were declared to be vested in the crown. Provision was made out of the revenues of the property for the surviving members of the order, the last of whom died in 1800. It is contended that, even if the lands had not been already confiscated, they would then have escheated to the crown for want of other heirs. The revenues of the estates were applied to educational purposes. The estates were transferred to the old Province of Canada, and at the time of confederation (1867) a large portion of them was ceded to the Province of Quebec. From time to time the ecclesiastical authorities have demanded the transfer of the Jesuits' estates to the Roman Catholic Church. In 1878 it was claimed that the bishops were the rightful heirs to the suppressed order. In 1887 the Quebec Legislature passed an act incorporating the Jesuits, and the Quebec Government entered into negotiations with the Jesuits and with the Holy See for a settlement of the long-disputed claims. In these negotiations the Premier, the Hon. Honoré Mercier, refused to recognize any civil obligation, but merely "a moral obligation," on the part of the Government. The Jesuit fathers were authorized by the Pope to treat with the Government, on condition that the money received be deposited and left at the free disposal of the Holy See. Finally an agreement was made and ratified by the Legislature, at this session, in the act respecting the settlement of the Jesuits' estates. Under this act the Government of the Province pays $400,000 to the Society of Jesus, and also transfers Laprarie Common to it, and pays $60,000 to the Protestant Committee of the Council of Public Instruction for the purposes of higher education. The society —in its own behalf, for its suppressed predecessor, for the Pope, and for the Roman Catholic Church generally—accepts the grant as a full settlement.

The passage of the act gave great offense to Protestants, and the Dominion Government was urged to exercise its power of disallowance; but the Dominion Government took the ground that, wise or unwise, the legislation was within the competence of the Provincial Legislature. Some politicians were unkind enough to say that the act was passed in the hope that it would be disallowed, in which case the Quebec ministry would have appealed to the electorate upon an issue that would have greatly strengthened their weak majority.

R

REFORMED CHURCHES. The following table of comparative statistics of the Reformed Churches is published in the "Almanac for the Reformed Church in the United States" for 1889:

No.	NAMES OF CHURCHES AND COUNTRIES.	Synods.	Ministers.	Congregations.	Communicants.	Adherents.
*1	Reformed Church in the Province of Austria	1	4	4	6,889	8,144
*2	Reformed Church in the Province of Bohemia	1	56	58	4,548	6,250
*3	Reformed Church in the Province of Moravia	1	25	34	2,200	3,900
*4	Reformed Church of the Helvetic Confession of Hungary	5	1,909	3,261	200,000	80,000
5	Union of Evangelical Churches, Belgium				3,923	8,000
6	Missionary Christian Reformed Church, Belgium	1	19	88	4,896	5,100
7	Walloon Churches, Belgium and Netherlands		24			10,000
8	Reformed Church of France	21	814		86,000	101,000†
9	Free Reformed Church of France	4	44	50	8,272	4,800
10	Old Reformed Church of Bertheln, Germany	1	7	9	2,400	4,000
11	Free (Dutch) Church, Elberfeld		5	3	440	1,000†
12	Reformed Church East of the Rhine, Germany	1	7	9	2,598	3,000†
13	Reformed Churches (Separatists), Germany				30,000†	20,000†
14	Reformed Churches (in the Union), Germany				500,000†	1,000,000†
15	Reformed Church in the Netherlands, including Dutch Colonies	10	1,611	1,349	200,000	850,000†
16	Christian Reformed Churches in the Netherlands	10	821	415	70,000	100,000†
17	Reformed (Cantonal) Churches of Switzerland				1,200,000†	1,500,000†
18	Free Church of Geneva	1	8	4	478	600
19	Free Reformed Evangelical Church of Neufchâtel		78	27	8,128	10,000†
20	National Evangelical Reformed Church of the Canton of Vaud	1	78		8,128	10,000†
21	Free Evangelical Reformed Church of the Canton of Vaud	1	127	59	4,000	6,270†
22	Waldensian Evangelical Church		77	44	17,335	25,000
23	Free Christian Church of Italy	1	13	42	1,480	2,000
24	Spanish Christian Church		16	21	840	1,500
25	Reformed Church in Russia	1			7,000	10,000†
26	United Hanoverian Reformed Church				14,608	20,000†
27	Reformed Church in Algiers				150,000†	150,000†
28	Dutch Reformed Church in South Africa	2	158	140	30,600	50,000†
29	Dutch Reformed Church in Orange Free State	1	25	27	8,000	15,000†
30	Christian Reformed Church in South Africa	1	16	34	6,095	9,000†
31	Dutch Reformed Church in Natal and Transvaal	2	17	25	6,445	9,000†
32	Reformed Church in America (Dutch)	4	566	547	85,548	200,000
33	Free Reformed Dutch Church	1	10	13	317	500
34	Christian Reformed Church in America	1	44	70	8,157	15,000
35	Dutch Reformed Church, Surinam		6	6	1,120	1,500†
36	Reformed Church in United States (German)	8	822	1,312	190,527	500,000†
37	Reformed Church (German), Japan ‡	1	11	8	1,202	....

* These four organizations compose the General Synod of the Reformed Church in Austria.
† Estimated.   ‡ In United Church of Japan.

I. Reformed Church in the United States.— "The Almanac of the Reformed Church in the United States" for 1887 gives the following statistics of this denomination: Number of districts synods, 8; of classes, 54; of ministers, 823; of congregations, 1,512; of members, 190,527; of unconfirmed members, 111,-416; of persons communing during the year, 152,274; of baptisms, 13,743 of infants and 1,500 of adults; of confirmations, 10,542; of Sunday-schools, 1,464, with 129,713 pupils; of students for the ministry, 207. Amount of contributions for benevolent purposes, $147,-297; for congregational purposes, $841,291.

Eight colleges and universities, 9 academical schools and institutes, and 2 theological seminaries are conducted and 4 orphan homes are maintained under the patronage of the Church. The publishing enterprises passed into private hands on the last day of 1887, and are now carried on at Philadelphia under the style of the " Reformed Church Publication House." Home missions are carried on under the care of Boards of the General Synod and of three district synods. Fifty-six missions are returned, with 5,430 communicants, who contributed during the year $38,724 for congregational, and $3,500 for benevolent purposes. The General Board had received during the fiscal year 1887-'88, $16,738, and asked for $20,000 for the ensuing year. The Board of Foreign Missions received $20,000. The missions of the Tokio and Sendai districts in Japan returned 8 organized churches, 4 of which were self-supporting; 7 preaching-stations; 482 baptisms of adult converts; 8 baptisms of children; 1,202 members; 3 schools, with 209 pupils; 16 Sunday-schools, with 719 pupils; 1 theological school, with 9 pupils; 7 native ministers; 4 other agents; and $1,950 of contributions.

II. Reformed Church in America.—The following is a summary of the statistics of this Church as they were reported to the General Synod in June, 1888 : Number of classes, 34; of churches, 546; of ministers, 555; of licentiates, 9; of families, 47,520; of communicants, 87,015; of baptisms during the year, 4,751 of infants and 1,230 of adults; of members admitted on confession, 4,949; of baptized non-communicants 34,070; of catechumens, 31,814; of Sunday - schools, 750, with 96,019 members. Amount of contributions for religious and benevolent purposes, $284,902; for congregational purposes, $970,856.

The Board of Education reported to the General Synod that it had received $9,070, while its debt had been increased by $450; had 80 students under its care; and had aided 5 parochial schools. Its permanent funds amounted to $41,665. The Widows' fund had been increased by $3,000, and was now $73,971. It had aided 31 annuitants in the amount of $4,661. It was, however, able to pay only 75 per cent. of the maximum annuity. The income of the Disabled Ministers' fund had been $9,199.

Appropriations had been made on its account to 16 ministers, 21 ministers' widows, and to guardians of ministers' children. The investments in its behalf were returned at $53,817. The Theological Seminary at New Brunswick possessed scholarship endowments amounting to $113,110. The treasurer of the General Synod gave the whole amount of its funds in his hands as $768,173.

The receipts of the Board of Domestic Missions for the year had been for the Missionary Department, $47,472 ; for the Church Building fund, $19,584. The expenditures had been in the Missionary Department, $32,-293 ; from the Church Building fund, $16,-255. The board had aided 108 churches and stations, served by 90 pastors, and comprising 4,802 families and 6,947 members, in which 756 members had been received on confession ; with 108 Sunday-schools having an average attendance of 9,349 pupils. These stations had contributed $1,672 to home missions and $4,474 to other objects.

The Board of Foreign Missions had received $109,946. From the missions—in China, India, and Japan—were returned 11 stations; 123 out-stations and preaching-places ; 25 ordained and 3 unordained missionaries; 30 assistant - missionaries ; 26 native ordained missionaries; 220 native helpers; 4,559 communicants; 7 seminaries for boys, with 308 pupils; 5 seminaries for girls, with 300 pupils; 4 theological schools or classes, with 32 students; and 106 day schools, with 2,612 pupils. The contributions of the native churches amounted to $8.324. One ordained missionary and one assistant missionary were under appointment.

The eighty-second General Synod met in Catskill, N. Y., June 3. The Rev. M. H. Hutton, D. D., was chosen moderator. The Committee on Conference with the Reformed Church in the United States presented a report of progress, and was continued. The committees had held a preliminary joint meeting in the city of New York, in December, 1887, and a meeting and conference of ministers and laymen in Philadelphia, April 3 and 4, 1888. At the latter meeting, papers which had been previously arranged for were read, on " The Historical and Doctrinal Relations of the Two Churches," by Dr. E. T. Corwin and Prof. J. H. Dubbs; "The Canons of Dort," by Dr. Van Gieson; " The Present Condition of the Two Denominations," by Dr. Van Horne; " Church Union for the Evangelization of the World," by Dr. E. B. Coe; "The Obstacles to Union, and Methods of overcoming them," by Profs. Mabon and Williams; and "The Advantages of Union," by the Rev. Messrs. C. Cleaver and Peter Moerdyke. Three alternative forms of union were suggested : 1. the return of the Reformed Church in the United States to the articles of the Synod of Dort which conform to the Heidelberg standard catechism ; 2, with the retention by each body of its own standard; or, 3, on the basis of a common formula in which both Churches could unite. The Conference expressed its judgment that "a closer union between these two bodies, the only ecclesiastical organizations of the Reformed Church, of Continental origin, in America, is desirable, and at this juncture of the religious issues of our land specially important and, if the object is pursued in Christian wisdom and love, undoubtedly practicable. Besides, there is good reason for the opinion that, if judicious efforts in behalf of a closer union be conducted by the two committees, present obstacles will gradually disappear, and the end in some form just and acceptable to both branches may, without much delay, be attained." The ministers of the two organizations were advised to inform themselves more fully on the history of the Reformed Churches in Europe and in this country, "particularly in its bearing on the present movement, and, as occasion may arise, to promote, by preaching and otherwise, among all our congregations better knowledge of the Christian propriety and practical worth of the proposed union." Whatever action may be taken on the subject will have to wait for ratification by the General Synod of the Reformed Church in the United States, which will not meet till 1890.

A committee was appointed to make such additions to the liturgy of the Church "as may make it more available and comprehensive for service and worship," and report at the next meeting of the General Synod. A resolution protesting against the toleration of the traffic in intoxicating liquors on the Congo was passed and telegraphed by cable to the International Missionary Conference sitting in London. The Synod also recorded its pleasure at the growing public interest in efforts that are being made to diminish the evils growing out of the liquor-traffic, and declared that these evils constitute one of the greatest obstacles to the religious progress of the nation, and should be "energetically opposed" by all who love the Lord Jesus Christ. The Committee on Systematic Benevolence recommended the substitution of the term "offering" for "collection" in ordinary usage, and the revival of the idea of worship in making offerings of money to the Church. A minute was adopted recognizing the efforts of the Evangelical Alliance, particularly as they are directed to the preservation of the public schools in their integrity, and against efforts to divert public moneys to the advantage of particular denominations. The committee appointed to prepare a manual of instruction for young children presented a catechism which, after examination, was recommitted to a committee enlarged by the appointment of two women upon it.

III. Reformed Churches in the Netherlands.—The Christian Reformed Church of the Netherlands originated in a secession in 1835 from the state Church as established by the law of 1815. It consists of eleven provincial synods, each of which sends four delegates to the General Synod meeting every three years.

A more recent movement within the state Church has resulted in the organization of an orthodox or conservative party, strictly adhering to the old ways and faith, as distinct from the other parties which are more ready to follow the modern tendencies of criticism and questioning thought, under the lead of Dr. A. Kuyper, of the Free University of Amsterdam. This party came to an issue with the authorities of the state Church in 1886, on a question of the admission of persons denying the divinity of Christ to full membership in the Church at Amsterdam. The Consistory refusing to consent to their admission, the orthodox majority —being eighty in number, and including Dr. Kuyper—were suspended, and afterward deposed. After this exclusion, a correspondence was begun with reference to a union with the Christian Reformed Church, and two meetings of a satisfactory character were held between representatives of the two parties. The General Synod of the Christian Reformed Church, at its meeting held at Assen in August, took action demanding that the orthodox party recognize that Church as the real Church of the Netherlands, and declare more openly than it had done that it had broken with the established Church and its representative bodies.

The first synodical meeting of the orthodox body was also held in August at Utrecht, when 180 churches, forming twelve classes, were represented by twenty-four delegates, besides five general advisers of the Synod.

RHODE ISLAND. State Government.—The following were the State officers during the year: Governor, John W. Davis, Democrat, succeeded by Royal C. Taft, Republican; Lieutenant-Governor, Samuel R. Honey, succeeded by Enos Lapham; Secretary of State, Edwin D. McGuinness, succeeded by Samuel H. Cross; General Treasurer, John G. Perry, succeeded by Samuel Clark; State Auditor and Insurance Commissioner, Elisha W. Bucklin, succeeded by Almon K. Goodwin; Attorney-General, Ziba O. Slocum, succeeded by Horatio Rogers; Railroad Commissioner, James H. Anderson; Commissioner of Public Schools, Thomas B. Stockwell; Chief-Justice of the Supreme Court, Thomas Durfee; Associate Justices, Pardon E. Tillinghast, Charles Matteson, John H. Stiness, and George A. Wilbur.

Legislative Sessions.—The General Assembly met at Providence on January 17, and remained in session till March 23, adjourning on that day to meet at Newport on May 29. The most important work of the session was the passage of the so-called Bourn amendment to the State Constitution, abolishing the property qualification for electors, which had been approved by the preceding Legislature. The proposed amendment provides that—

Every male citizen of the United States of the age of twenty-one years who has had his residence and home in this State for two years and in the town or city in which he may offer to vote six months next preceding the time of his voting, and whose name shall be registered in the town or city where he resides on or before the last day of December in the year next preceding the time of his voting, shall have a right to vote in the election of all civil officers and on all questions in all legally organized town or ward meetings; provided, that no person shall at any time be allowed to vote in the election of the city council of any city, or upon any proposition to impose a tax or for the expenditure of money in any town or city, unless he shall within the year next preceding have paid a tax assessed upon his property therein, valued at least at $134.

Section 2 provides that—

The assessors of each town and city shall annually assess upon every person, who, if registered, would be qualified to vote a tax of one dollar, or such sum as with his other taxes shall amount to one dollar, which tax shall be paid into the treasury of such town or city and be applied to the support of public schools therein; provided that such tax, assessed upon any person who has performed military duty, shall be remitted for the year he shall perform such duty; and said tax, assessed upon any mariner for any year while he is at sea, or upon any person who, by reason of extreme poverty, is unable to pay said tax, shall upon application of such mariner or person be remitted. The General Assembly shall have power to provide by law for the collection and remission of this tax.

Provision was made for the submission of this amendment to the electors at the April election.

Another act provides for the establishment of a State Agricultural School, and appropriates $5,000 therefor. Any sums received from the Federal Government under the Hatch act, for the aid of agriculture, are placed at the disposal of the governing board of the school. The sum of $26,000 was appropriated for enlarging and improving the Hospital for the Insane.

Other acts of the session were as follow:

To prevent discriminations by life-insurance companies.

Providing for an examination, by the State Board of Health, of the sanitary condition of hotels and boarding-houses.

Requiring savings institutions to report to the State Auditor every five years a list of unclaimed deposits remaining in such banks for twenty years, and to publish said list.

Requiring railroad corporations to draw cars, passenger and merchandise, of any other railroad corporation connecting with it over its road, for a reasonable compensation, and to furnish suitable depot accommodations therefor; in case of failure to agree upon a compensation, commissioners appointed by the Supreme Court shall decide.

The General Assembly elected in April convened at Newport on May 29, and after a session of four days adjourned to June 12. The following acts were passed during the session:

To establish a board of registration in dentistry.

Authorizing the city of Pawtucket to issue $300,000 of bonds to obtain money for public improvements.

Authorizing the redemption of the franchise and property of railroad corporations from sale on execution.

Approving and confirming the lease of the Boston and Providence Railroad to the Old Colony Railroad Company.

Appropriating $50,000 for a new almshouse at the State farm in Cranston.

At the adjourned session, which occupied only two days, United States Senator Jonathan Chace was re-elected, receiving 29 votes in the Senate and 59 in the House. Ex-Gov. John W. Davis received 4 votes in the Senate and 8 in the House, and Charles H. Page 1 vote in each body.

The most important act of Legislation provides for the incorporation and establishment of the city of Woonsocket.

Finances.—The State debt on the last day of the year consisted of bonds of 1863, payable in 1893, to the value of $584,000; and bonds of 1864, payable in 1894, to the value of $699,000; total, $1,283,000. This is a reduction in the total debt during the year of $58,000. At the same time the securities in the sinking-fund have increased by $66,192.69, and now amount to $757,641.18, reckoning these securities at par. The net debt, less the sinking-fund, on December 31 was therefore $525,358.82. One year before it was $639,495.60. The treasury statement for the year is as follows: Balance in the treasury, Jan. 1, 1888, $135,458.16; receipts for the year ending Dec. 31, 1888, $822,903.74; payments for year ending Dec. 31, 1888, $895,648.22; balance in treasury Jan. 1, 1889, $62,713.68.

The excess of expenditure over the revenue for 1888 was only about half that of the preceding year, in consequence of an act of March, 1888, increasing the tax on ratable property of the State from twelve to fourteen cents on each $100 of valuation. By this increase the treasury received $65,703.11 above that received from taxes the previous year. For 1889 the excess will be still further reduced by an act, also of March, 1888, reducing for 1889 and subsequent years the amount of annual payment into the sinking-fund from $100,000 to $50,000.

Banks.—The deposits in savings-banks of the State amounted on December 31, to $57,699,884.94, an increase of $2,336,601.61 for the past year. The number of depositors is 123,102, an increase of 2,958, being an average of $468.07 to each depositor.

Education.—The last report of the Commissioner of Public Schools, covering the school year ending in April, 1887, presents the following statistics: Number of children of school age, 63,199; number attending public schools, 42,798; number attending Catholic schools, 6,852; number attending select schools, 1,745; total registration in public schools, 49,507; average attendance, 32,632; length of school year in months, 9¼; male teachers employed, 190; female teachers employed, 1,120; average wages per month, male teachers, $82.67; average wages per month, female teachers, $44.38; number of evening schools, 38; number of public-school houses, 465; value of public-school property, $2,404,031; total school expenditures for the year, $798,465. These figures show a slight decrease in the average attendance over the preceding year, but an increase in the total enrollment, in the number and salary of teachers, in the number of school-houses, and in the value of school-property.

The number of students enrolled in the Normal School since its reorganization in 1871 is 1,226. A large proportion of these have taught in the schools of Rhode Island. The whole number of graduates, including the latest class, is 446. The attendance during the second half of the year was 149, the largest in the history of the institution.

Charities.—The State Home and School, providing a home and education for homeless children, had an average attendance for 1887 of 57; and for 1888 of 80; there were remaining in the Home at the close of the year 87 children, an increase of 9 over that of a year ago. This increase in members calls for an increase in the annual appropriations. The expenses for conducting the Home and School for the year were $12,179.94, against $9,816.32 for 1887. At the beginning of 1888 there were 28 pupils at the State School for the Deaf, supported at the expense of the State.

Prohibition.—The Governor said in his annual message in January, 1889: "The operation of the laws prohibiting the manufacture and sale of intoxicating liquors is, as yet, very far from being satisfactory. Until the advent to office of the present Attorney-General, the litigation arising under the law had not been prosecuted with the zeal and energy necessary to demonstrate whether the system itself, properly administered, was effective or not."

The opponents of the law introduced a measure into the Legislature during the year providing for the resubmission of the prohibitory amendment to the people, while its friends urged the passage of a bill similar to the Kansas injunction law to secure a more effective enforcement. The sentiment of the Legislature was in favor of a further trial of prohibition, but action upon the injunction bill was deferred from the May and June sessions to the following January. The Chief of State Police, who is charged with the duty of enforcing the law, reports that great difficulty is found in the failure of the local police, especially in Providence, to co-operate with him. The former, with only ten men at his command at any one time, made during the first four months of the year 465 seizures of liquors, entered 13 complaints for illegal keeping, 22 for illegal selling, and 8 for common nuisances; while in the same time the Providence Chief of Police, with 200 men under him, made only 165 seizures, 78 complaints for illegal selling, and 8 for common nuisances. During the remaining eight months of the year the State police made 1,258 seizures, 26 complaints for illegal selling, 141 for illegal keeping, and 30 for common nuisances. In the same period the Providence police made only 241 seizures and 3 complaints for illegal keeping.

The total number of seizures by local officers as distinct from the State police during the first four months of the year were 325, complaints for illegal keeping 123, for illegal selling 26, for common nuisances 16; during the remaining eight months the seizures were 535, complaints for illegal selling 42, for illegal keeping 16, and for common nuisances 15.

The Bourn Amendment.—The vote cast for this amendment in April was not opened and officially counted till late in November, when the announcement of its adoption was made by the Governor's proclamation. Questions at once arose as to the validity of the existing registry acts under the new provision of the Constitution, and these questions were submitted by the Governor to the Supreme Court. The Court decided that such parts of those acts as were not inconsistent with the amended Constitution should be allowed to stand; that the statutory provisions relating to the assessment and payment of a registry tax must be considered as null and void; but that the method of registration by town and ward clerks was still in force as before. It is estimated that the increase of the voting-lists under this amendment will be over twenty thousand names.

Political.—On February 22 a State Convention of Prohibitionists met at Providence and nominated a ticket as follows: For Governor, George W. Gould; Lieutenant-Governor, H. D. Scott; Secretary of State, F. A. Warner; General Treasurer, A. B. Chadsey; Attorney-General, John T. Blodgett. The usual prohibitory resolutions were adopted, and also the following:

We declare our belief that the laws governing the right of suffrage in our State should be so amended as to bring them into harmony with the laws of other States upon this subject. We further believe that the registry tax has been a great source of corruption and that it should be abolished.

We believe that gross corruption prevails through the use of open ballots, and we declare ourselves in favor of a secret ballot, as most likely to prevent intimidation of voters, and some adaptation of the "Australian system," as providing best against facilities for bribery.

The Republicans met in State Convention at Providence, March 15, and nominated: For Governor, Royal C. Taft; Lieutenant-Governor, Enos Lapham; Secretary of State, Samuel H. Cross; General Treasurer, Samuel Clark; Attorney-General, Horatio Rogers. The platform includes the following:

We believe that all proposals to divide the present surplus among the States or to distribute it by extraordinary expenditures are indefensible, but we favor sufficient appropriations for building the navy, for constructing coast-defenses adequate for the protection of our homes and property, which are now exposed to the attacks of a foreign enemy, and for pensions.

We heartily indorse the action of the Republican members of the General Assembly in securing the submission to the people of the State of a proposition for an extension of the right of suffrage, and we again express ourselves in favor of the abolition of the registry tax as a prerequisite for voting.

On March 19 the Democratic State Convention met at Providence, and renominated Governor Davis, Secretary of State McGuinness,

Treasurer Perry, and Attorney-General Slocum. Lieutenant-Governor Honey declined a
renomination. and was succeeded on the ticket
by Howard Smith. The resolutions included
the following:

The constantly increasing surplus in the National
Treasury (estimated at nearly $100,000,000 annually)
which arises from unjust and unnecessary taxation
of the people, threatens to paralyze trade and commerce by the withdrawal from their channels of the
money which is needed in their operations; reduction of taxation is therefore an imperative duty, and
should be made first upon those articles which can be
classed as necessaries to the whole people—men, wom-
en, and children. The industries of Rhode Island will
be most efficiently fostered and protected by the introduction into our ports free of duty of such raw
materials as enter into or are used in connection with
our manufactures; we designate wool, lumber, and
coal as among the most important of such raw materials.

We pledge ourselves:
1. To secure for the people of this State a constitutional convention, to the end that the many reforms
needed may be accomplished and that the abuses and
irregularities now existing, which have been bred and
fostered by the ruling element of the Republican party
of this State, may be abolished.
2. To abolish the registry tax, which has for another year continued to be a source of unmitigated
evil and fraud on the native-born voters of this State,
and again making money instead of intelligence and
capacity a qualification for office.
3. To abolish the property qualification which is
unjustly imposed upon naturalized citizens of the
United States as a prerequisite for voting.

At the election, in April, the Republican
ticket was elected by a plurality of over 3,000
votes. For Governor, Taft received 20,744
votes; Davis, 17,556; Gould, 1,326. The Legislature elected at the same time was composed
of 31 Republicans and 8 Democrats in the Senate, and 61 Republicans, 10 Democrats, and 1
Prohibitionist in the House. At the same
time the Bourn amendment to the State Constitution, passed by the Legislature in January,
was submitted to the people and approved by
a vote of 20,068 in its favor and 12,193 against
it. Three fifths of the total vote cast being
necessary for its adoption, it secured only 711
votes more than the requisite number.

ROMAN CATHOLIC CHURCH. The two most
important events in the history of the Catholic Church during the past year were the
celebration of the Papal Jubilee—the fiftieth
anniversary of the ordination of Leo XIII to
the priesthood—and the visit of the Emperor
William to the Sovereign Pontiff. The first
event, which occupied the end of 1887 and the
first days of 1888 was most elaborately celebrated. All the rulers of the world, including
the Sultan, sent gifts to the Pope. King Hum-
bert was the only exception. The gift of
President Cleveland was particularly appropriate. It was a copy of the Constitution of
the United States. Brazil, in honor of the
festival, freed several thousand slaves. Later
in the year the Pope issued an encyclical to
the bishops of Brazil on the subject of slavery, one of the most remarkable documents of
his pontificate. In connection with this unre-

served throwing of the influence of the Church
against the owning of human beings, the cordial approval of the Holy Father to Cardinal
Lavigerie's project for the suppression of the
African slave-trade makes in itself an epoch
in the annals of the Church which has from
the beginning regarded liberty as the most
beautiful of all things. The visit of the Emperor William to the Sovereign Pontiff, though
apparently deprived of all political significance
by the rules of papal and royal etiquette, had
no effect in clarifying the Roman question.
The Emperor seems to have avoided committing himself by any verbal promise to the
amelioration of the Pope's position. Mr.
Gladstone's letter to the Marquis de Riso,
quoted in the "Osservaton Romano," which
created a sensation during his visit to Naples,
seems to show that public opinion in Europe
was, late in 1888, not averse to the submission
of the Roman question to an international
tribunal. But, taking Mr. Gladstone's later
explanation of that letter, it becomes evident
that the Marquis de Riso was mistaken. The
position of the Pope still remains, in his own
phrase, "intolerable."

The abolition of slavery in Brazil, brought
about by the entire sympathy of Dom Pedro
and his people on the subject and the counsels
of the bishops of Brazil, urged on by the
Pope, occasioned His Holiness to send the golden
rose—sent to some royal personage each year
on Lætare Sunday—to the Princess-Regent of
Brazil. The new Archbishop of Carthage—a
see created by the Pope to revive the past
glory of the African Church is Cardinal Lavigerie. The cardinal is nearly sixty-four
years of age, but he believes that he will be
enabled to lead a new crusade against the
slave-trade in Africa with as much success as
if he were half his present age. In London,
Paris, Naples, Madrid, and Brussels, he has
gained the enthusiastic sympathy of all who
heard him. At Rome, he aroused the intensest
interest in the heart of Leo XIII. He is forming a defensive force for the protection of defenseless tribes against the slave-traders. He
believes that less than a thousand well-drilled
soldiers would be sufficient to abolish slavery
from Albert Nyanza to the south of Tanganika;
with an American regiment at his command,
he would guarantee to wipe out the bloody
marks which the Arabs and mulattoes make
each recurring year. It is computed that, out
of the five hundred thousand men, women, and
children stolen and sold every year, fifty
thousand die under the oppression of their
captors. Human life is held very cheap in the
interior of Africa.

The deaths during 1887–'88 were unusually
numerous in ecclesiastical circles. The Most
Rev. Francis X. Leray died Sept. 23, 1887.
The death of the Rev. John Bapst, S. J., occurred on November 4 of the same year; Father Bapst was the hero of an outburst of un-
American fanaticism in 1854, and of Miss

Tincker's well-known novel "Grapes and Thorns." The death of the Rev. John J. Riordan, the rector of the Irish Emigrants' Mission at Castle Garden, a great loss to the poor, was followed by that of Dom Bosco in Italy, who died on March 28, and that of Father Drumgoole, in New York—both apostles of poor boys of the streets. On February 13, the Most Rev. John B. Lamy, the first Bishop of Santa Fé, departed this life; he had resigned his see in 1885; March 9, Cardinal Czacki died; March 31, Cardinal Martinelli; April 14, the Most. Rev. Joseph Sadoc Alemany, O. P., first Archbishop of San Francisco, who had resigned his see to spend his last days with the Brothers of his Orders in Valencia, Spain; May 10, Archbishop Lynch, of Toronto; and on June 29, the Rev. Francis X. Weninger, S. J., famous as a preacher of missions.

The death of the Very Rev. I. T. Hecker, C. S. P., took place on December 20. Father Hecker, born in 1819 and received into the Church in 1845, had long been a prominent figure in the annals of the Catholic Church. The conversion of Father Hecker, who had been seeking in various religious organizations the peace he desired, introduced a new element into the Church in this country. He saw the necessity of making, as he himself expressed it, the synthesis between the Catholic Church and the American Republic more apparent. He had been a member of the Brook Farm Community, he had studied for the Protestant Episcopal ministry, he had paused awhile in Congregationalism. Entering the Catholic Church, he brought with him a great experience, gained entirely from contact with American social life. He became a Redemptorist in Belgium. As one of this famous religious congregation, which in this country devotes itself to the preaching of missions, he performed his priestly duties scrupulously for several years. It then occurred to him that a similar association, composed of American priests, might be very useful in the United States. He went to Rome and secured the approbation of the Pope for his project. The Congregation of St. Paul (C. S. P.) was founded and reached a class of Catholics and searching non-Catholics more effectually than any other organization within the Church. Father Hecker's "Aspirations of Nature" and "Questions of the Soul," are in every complete religious library. He founded "The Catholic World," now conducted by the Rev. Walter Elliott, and justly regarded a foremost exposition of Catholic thought. He was succeeded by the Very Rev. Augustine Hewit, C. S. P., the present Superior of the Congregation.

On May 24, the corner-stone of the Divinity Building, near Washington, D. C., was laid by Cardinal Gibbons. The sermon was delivered by the Right Rev. J. Lancaster Spalding, Bishop of Peoria. A gold medal sent by the Pope was presented to Miss Mary G. Caldwell, whose generous contribution has made the university possible. Among those present were the Misses Drexel, who had founded a chair of Divinity. The Right Rev. Bishop Keane, having resigned the see of Richmond, was made Titular Bishop of Jasso and rector of the new university. Having formulated the statutes he departed for Rome to consult the Holy Father further on the affairs of the great school.

The University of Notre Dame, Indiana, celebrated on Aug. 15, 1888, the fiftieth anniversary of the ordination of the Very Rev. Edward Sorin, its founder, to the priesthood. The Very Rev. E. Sorin is the founder of the university and the Superior-General of the Congregation of the Holy Cross. His Eminence Cardinal Gibbons, several archbishops, many priests, and a great assemblage of other distinguished gentlemen visited Notre Dame on this occasion. The Very Rev. Father Sorin was born in France, Feb. 6, 1814; he came to this country in 1844. Notre Dame did not exist then; Indians lived in the wilderness of wood and prairie which then occupied its site; now magnificent buildings containing over five hundred students give the place the appearance of a large and handsome university town.

Another important celebration occurred on September 20, in honor of the twenty-fifth anniversary of the ordination of the Most Rev. Archbishop Corrigan. The ceremony, at which were present all the priests of his diocese not on duty and an immense congregation, was one of the most imposing ever held within the cathedral. The principal episcopal sees filled during the year were that of New Orleans by the Most Rev. Francis Janssens; that of Belleville, Ill. (newly created); and that of Alton, Ill., filled by the Right Rev. John Janssen and the Right Rev. James P. Ryan.; Vancouver Island by the Rev. John N. Lemmens, succeeding Archbishop Seghers; Detroit by the Rev. Dr. John S. Foley, who succeeded Bishop Borgess, resigned. The Right Rev. Leo Haid. O. S. B., was consecrated Vicar Apostolic of North Carolina, and Rev. Andrea Hintenbach, O. S. B., made Archabbot of St. Vincents, in Westmoreland County, Pa.

At Rome, in March, 1888, the Pope made a vigorous speech to the cardinals on the necessity of his temporal independence and a pronouncement on the attitude of the Church toward the Knights of Labor, whose association is not condemned, provided their statutes contain nothing communistic or tending to oppose the right of holding property. In Prussia a law was passed restoring to a large number of religious orders the rights abrogated by the Kulturkampf. At Baden, the Chambers refused to admit the excluded religious congregations.

At Rome, in May, the Pope received a great crowd of Spanish Catholics headed by Mgr. Catala. Arrangements were made with Prussia on the question of the veto—the Government agreeing not to oppose for political reasons a nomination of a bishop by the Pope. The new Italian penal laws were protested against by the Neapolitan episcopate. Herr Windhorst's jubilee was celebrated.

In June, at Rome, a *triduum* was held in honor of the Blessed de la Salle, founder of the Institute of the Christian Brothers. The success of the Catholic Belgians in the legislative elections gave great pleasure to the Holy Father. Cardinal Manning, in London, issued a pastoral letter on the progress of the Church in England.

The Holy Father issued an encyclical on liberty and license.

At Rome, in July, the Italian Counsel of State explained that the law of the guarantees did not confer on the Pope extraterritorial rights or privileges. The Pope protested. An encyclical letter to the bishops of Ireland was issued which had a good effect on the minds of the Irish people, made anxious by the exaggerated rumors about the Papal rescript condemning the Plan of Campaign and boycotting. The schism of the Armenians ended; an encyclical letter was addressed by the Pope to Mgr. Azarian and the other Armenian bishops.

In September the Prussian bishops met at Fulda and expressed their loyalty to the Pope and their desire for the restoration of Rome. The Catholic Congress of Fribourg, which expressed similar sentiments, was held.

In October the Pope gave the decree *Tolerari posse* on the Knights of Labor; this decree was interpreted by Cardinal Gibbons in a letter printed in the Baltimore "Mirror."

The Holy Father ordered a universal mass of requiem on the last Sunday in October for the repose of the souls of all the faithful departed. The Italian penal laws which force students studying for the priesthood into the army were protested against by assemblages held in nearly every city of the Continent. An important encyclical letter *exeunte jam anno* appeared in December as the finish of the jubilee. It is a protest against unbelief and the ostentation of the rich. In France Mgr. Treppel made an attempt to revive the French laws against dueling. The year was closed by a universal mass, ordered by the Pope in thanksgiving for the graces of the jubilee.

ROUMANIA, a constitutional monarchy in Eastern Europe. The reigning sovereign is Carol I, born April 20, 1839, of the family of Hohenzollern, being the brother of the present Prince of Hohenzollern-Sigmaringen. He was elected Domnul or Lord of Roumania by a Constituent Assembly on April 20, 1866, and proclaimed King on March 26, 1881. The heir-presumptive is his nephew Prince Leopold of Hohenzollern-Sigmaringen. The Constitution voted by the Constituent Assembly of 1866 was amended in 1879 and 1884. The Senate consists of 112 members elected for eight years and 8 bishops. The Chamber of Deputies numbers 185 members elected for four years.

Finances.—The financial accounts for the year ending March 31, 1887, show 131,329,693 lei of receipts and 127,045,614 lei of expenditures.

The capital of the public debt at the close of the fiscal year 1888-'89 is 788,732,489 lei. It was increased by the emission of new bonds for 100,000,000 lei in July, 1888. In a period of seven years the funded debt has been increased by the sum of 218,000,000 lei, and the annual charge of the debt has grown from 41,000,000 to 54,500,000 lei.

The Army.—The effective strength of the permanent army in time of peace is 1,430 officers and 33,714 rank and file, with 6,969 horses and 370 guns. The strength of the active territorial army is 1,350 officers and 29,679 men, with 11,742 horses. The country is divided into 4 territorial districts, each of which can furnish a *corps d'armée* of 28,000 troops, not reckoning the active division of troops belonging to the separate territorial division of the Dobrudja. The Government possesses 1 torpedo-cruiser, 6 gun-boats, and 5 torpedo-boats for the defense of the Danube. The Prime Minister declared in Parliament, in March, 1888, that Roumania in case of war could put 300,000 soldiers into the field. Fortifications at Focshani, commanding the river Sereth and the railways leading to Galatz and Bucharest, and at Barbosh, near Galatz, where the largest bridge spans the Sereth, were completed in 1888, and others were begun on the Russian frontier that are designed to bar the passage of Russian troops toward the lower Danube.

Commerce.—The values of the imports and exports in 1886, in lei or francs, and their distribution among commercial nations are given in the following table:

COUNTRIES.	Imports.	Exports.
Great Britain	71,407,000	116,627,000
Austria-Hungary	93,518,000	84,678,000
Germany	78,340,000	2,618,000
France	14,495,000	29,184,000
Belgium	14,496,000	15,240,000
Russia	9,645,000	12,897,000
Italy	3,153,000	16,668,000
Turkey and Bulgaria	8,985,000	5,998,000
Greece	3,400,000	2,718,000
Switzerland	2,559,000	68,000
Other countries	1,499,000	18,916,000
Total	296,497,000	255,547,000

The imports of textiles amounted to 117,000,000 lei; metals and metal goods, 53,800,000 lei; hides and leather, 23,200,000 lei; timber, 12,000,000 lei. The exports of cereals were valued at 184,200,000 lei; fruits, pulse, etc., 21,000,000 lei; wines, 12,800,000 lei.

Railroads.—The state lines in 1888 had a total length of 2,235 kilometres, or 1,390 miles. There were 224 kilometres, or 140 miles, belonging to companies. The railroads in course of construction or in contemplation will add 457 kilometres, or 287 miles, to the network.

Post-Office.—The number of letters and postal-cards, circulars, and newspapers carried in the mails during 1887 was 19,084,914; the number of packets, 533,556.

Telegraphs.—The length of the telegraph lines in 1887 was 5,396 kilometres, or 3,350 miles, with 11,911 kilometres, or 7,397 miles, of wire. The paid internal messages transmitted in 1887 numbered 830,829; private international messages, 281,264; total number of dispatches, private and official, 1,256,696. The receipts from the postal and telegraph service amounted to 5,049,218 francs, and the expenses to 3,702,-567 francs.

The European Commission of the Danube.—The International Danube Commission, created by the Treaty of Paris in 1856 and confirmed by the Treaty of Berlin in 1878, exercises certain sovereign powers over the Danube river below Galatz. When the powers deputed to the commission expired by limitation of time, on March 13, 1883, a new commission was constituted. The financial statement for 1885 shows a total expenditure for the year of 1,805,824 francs, and receipts amounting to 2,627,358 francs, of which 1,430,958 francs were obtained from tolls, and the remainder from special sources. The number of steamers that passed the Sulina mouth of the Danube on the outward voyage in 1886 was 872, of 866,763 tons, of which 564, of 622,201 tons, were British; 61, of 63,140 tons, Greek; 81, of 62.826 tons, Austrian; 49, of 55,772 tons, French; 26, of 20,585 tons, Italian; 60, of 19,736 tons, Russian; and 28, of 22,493 tons, were Norwegian, German, Dutch, and 1 of them Spanish. The Greek sailing-vessels numbered 201, of 39,459 tons, and the Turkish 257, of 33,001 tons, while 49, of 11,-344 tons, belonged to other countries. The grain exports from the ports of the lower Danube in 1886 were 6,461,889 quarters, as against 6.070,157 quarters in 1885, and 4,441,-039 quarters in 1884.

Political Crisis.—The Conservative ministry of Lascar Catargio, constituted in 1871, made the first attempt to create a Government party and set the national needs and interests above personal and sectional rivalries. Lacking the courage of an energetic initiative, Catargio failed to unlock new financial resources for the growing requirements of the state until he was confronted by a deficit of 80,000,000 lei, and had no money in the treasury to pay salaries and other current expenses. The Conservatives succumbed to the attacks of the Liberals, who, owing to their French sympathies, had been under a shadow since the Franco-German War. Joan Bratiano, the most prominent among those Liberals to whom the King would intrust the Government, formed a ministry in 1876, and with the exception of a few weeks in the spring of 1881, he has guided the policy of the Government for twelve years with the aid of his colleague, Demeter Sturdza. By securing to the state the revenues of the salt and tobacco monopolies, establishing the banking and credit system of Roumania, and completing the railroads, he placed the finances on a solid basis, and developed the economical resources of the country. On the eve of the Russo-Turkish conflict he obtained from Russia the recognition of Roumanian independence, telling

Gortchakoff that without a treaty Russian troops could not march through Roumania except over the bodies of the Roumanians, and in May, 1876, he issued the proclamation of Roumanian independence. He adopted, in opposition to the Radical section of his party, the policy of subservience to German and Austrian wishes to gain protection against Russian aggression, and through this course and the successes of his internal administration drew to his side some of the ablest of the Moderate Conservatives, and built up the National Liberal party, which was supported by the great majority of the voting population. Gradually, however, the reluctance of Bratiano to embrace new reforms, and still more the dictatorial methods of personal government into which his energetic character betrayed him, alienated the strongest men in the Liberal party. Some retired from public life and others formed a Liberal Opposition, of which the brother of the Prime Minister was one of the leaders. These politicians joined forces with the Junimini or Young Conservatives, a group that sprang from a literary society founded in 1867 by Theodor Rosetti, P. Carp, and T. Majoresco, which had for its object the cultivation of German ideas in opposition to the French tendencies of the Liberals. The Young Conservatives were equally removed from the ideas of class rule represented by the Old Conservative or Boyar party, which disappeared from the political field to a great extent after the advent of the Liberal Cabinet. They contributed their money and efforts when the United Opposition was formed, and to their aid was added that of Russian intriguers, who paid liberally for assaults on the German prince and his Philo-German Cabinet. Such was the unbridled license of the Opposition press and orators that a revolutionary spirit pervaded the community in the early part of 1888. There were strong grounds for the charges made against Bratiano's administration that undermined his popularity. Deserted by the best of his fellow-workers, he was obliged to rely more and more on servile and selfish instruments, with no one to aid him in watching and checking abuses and corruption. When the Opposition grew strong enough to threaten the continuance of the ministry, the officials resorted to oppressive expedients to control the elections. The attacks of the press led them to take unusual measures for silencing criticism. Thus the editor of the "Lupta" was sentenced and imprisoned for *lèse majesté* until the Government was constrained by popular clamor to pardon him in February, 1888. The chief accusation against the official clique that Bratiano had gathered about him, with more regard to ability than to uprightness, was that they enriched themselves at the public expense by all kinds of corrupt methods. No suspicion of personal dishonesty attached to Bratiano himself; but against officers, high and low, in various departments charges were made in the press, and were generally believed. At length Col. Maican-Dumitresco, director of the Military School and president of a commission for the trial of weapons, was arraigned before a court-martial for demanding a bribe of 40,-000 lei for recommending a revolver from Capt. Dimancea, its inventor. As the investigation proceeded it was found that the go-between in this transaction, the English commercial agent Broadwell, who represented the firm of Sir William Armstrong, had paid the brother of the culprit, Gen. Maican, commander of the flotilla, a heavy bribe while he was secretary of the Ministry of War, and thus induced him to reveal the sealed bids for two new cruisers. While the trial of the two officers was pending, the Chambers met in February, 1888, and members of the United Opposition gave notice of interpellations affecting the personal character of many men connected with the Government. Bratiano had emerged from the parliamentary elections with a majority of full two thirds. The new Chamber of Deputies was composed of 126 Ministerialists, 49 members of the United Opposition, 7 Independents, and 1 Socialist. Although Bratiano obtained a vote of confidence of two to one, the situation was such that he offered his resignation on March 2, 1888, and Prince Ghika attempted to form a coalition Cabinet. He failed because the leaders of the Opposition imposed unacceptable conditions, and the Bratiano Cabinet was reconstructed, Ministers Raduchihai, Statesco, and Gheorghian, of the Departments of the Interior, Justice, and Domains and Commerce, retiring. The Cabinet as reconstituted was composed as follows: President of the Council and Minister of War, Joan C. Bratiano; Minister of Foreign Affairs, M. Pherekyde; Minister of Public Instruction and Worship, C. Naku, who assumed provisionally the portfolio of the Interior; Minister of Public Works, P. S. Aurelian ; Minister of Commerce, M. Gane; Minister of Justice, M. Giani. The troubles of the Bratiano-Sturdza ministry were precipitated by the revelations of bribery in the War Department, from which Gen. Angelesco had retired some time before the attacks in the Chamber impelled Bratiano to carry out his frequently declared intention of resigning. When he was, nevertheless, induced to resume the helm, and the same ministry, with slight changes, returned to power, the Opposition redoubled its attacks, and in the press wholesale charges of maladministration and corruption were brought. The Russian minister at Bucharest, Hitrovo, spurred on the malcontents. The Opposition, not content with the violent scenes that they enacted in the Chambers, arranged popular demonstrations and mass meetings. The Government attempted to put a stop to these by issuing a police regulation forbidding public gatherings. Several meetings were broken up by the military, who wounded many persons. This suppression of the right of assemblage was the occasion of a stormy sitting in the Chamber on March 26. It had the

approval, however, of a large section of the trading community of Bucharest, and they offered a dinner to the Prime Minister, who was hooted by the people on his way to the saloon. In the evening the deputies of the Opposition went to the royal palace, and, while a mob gathered in front shouting for the dismissal of the ministry, they demanded an audience with the King in order to lay before him the wishes of the people. King Carol sent word to the spokesman, Lascar Catargio, the ex-Premier and leader of the Old Conservative party, that he would not receive him before morning. The street before the palace was cleared by the military, and finally the deputation of legislators left the palace. On the following day an appeal that was signed by all the Opposition members of the Senate and Chamber was distributed from the office of the "Epoca" newspaper, and in accordance therewith the members marched with bared heads through the streets to the legislative hall, in order thus to express their grief at the bloodshed that had occurred. The guards were unable to keep out the crowd that followed, and in the struggle many revolver-shots were fired, some of them by deputies. One of the doorkeepers was killed. Troops were sent on the demand of Gen. Lecca, President of the Chamber, and many persons were arrested, among them two deputies, Nicholas Fleva, ex-Mayor of Bucharest, and M. Philipesco, and the editors of the "Epoca" and the "Indépendance Roumaine." Opposition politicians meanwhile made incendiary addresses to the people on the streets. In the judicial inquiry evidence was brought to show that many of the Radical deputies were armed, and that from the direction of the shots the intention was to kill Bratiano, who happened to be absent in audience with the King. On the 31st a vote of want of confidence in the ministry, coupled with a demand for the liberation of the imprisoned deputies, was lost by 90 against 42 votes, and a simple motion for the release of the deputies by 83 against 45 votes, after which the Government party carried, by a majority of 87 against 36, a vote of confidence based on the charges against the Opposition of disturbing the peace of the land and jeopardizing its political position by intemperate speeches and shameless newspaper attacks, and finally violating the privacy of the King and the independence of Parliament, when every member was free to exercise the fullest liberty of criticism. The personal questions that had been brought up made it impossible for the Cabinet to remain in office, and Bratiano was determined not to head another ministry, whatever might be its composition. The King appealed to Prince Demeter Ghika, the President of the Senate, and when he for the second time declined, turned to the Young Conservatives because the leaders of the Liberal Opposition and of the Old Conservatives had made themselves impossible by their connection with the recent disturbances. Theodor

Rosetti, President of the Court of Cassation and a member of the Senate, was invited to form a Cabinet, which was constituted on April 2 as follows: President of the Council and Minister of the Interior, T. Rosetti; Minister of Foreign Affairs, P. P. Carp, formerly Minister Plenipotentiary to Vienna; Minister of Education and Provisional Minister of Commerce, J. Majoresco; Minister of Justice, A. Marghiloman; Minister of Finance, M. Ghermani; Minister of Public Works, Prince A. B. Stirbey; Minister of War, Gen. C. Barossi, Adjutant-General of the King. Prince Stirbey and Ghermani belong to the Old Conservative party. The first act of the new ministry was to release the imprisoned deputies and journalists. The majority promised to vote the budget and observe an expectant attitude if the new elections were postponed till the autumn, whereas the minority demanded that they should take place soon. The ministry promised to hold the elections as soon as the agitated state of public feeling subsided, and on April 15 the regular session was closed.

Peasant Insurrection.—Just before the closing of Parliament the new Cabinet had to deal with an outbreak of agrarian discontent which began in the sub-prefecture of Urticeni in the Jalomitza district, and spread into the neighboring districts of Prahova and Iloof. In the sub-prefecture of Panteleimon in the Iloof district, which reaches to the city-bounds of Bucharest, the entire peasantry rose against the local authorities, the landlords, and the tenant farmers, and stoned the military that were sent out to restore order, but commanded not to use their weapons. In the village of Stefanesci, near the capital, the mayor was shot by the insurgents. In many places they attacked unpopular estate stewards and extortionate farmers, and in others the local officials, whom they accused of keeping back the money that the Government had given to relieve their distress. The occurrence of disturbances in various other sections of the country showed that agencies had been at work to foment trouble, and the fact that hawkers of Russian pictures of saints and of the Czar had told the peasants of many villages to demand land of the Government, and said that if it were refused Russian troops would come to their aid, as well as the story of large sums left for each village by the Russians, which was spread among the gypsy communes of Shindrelita, indicated the source of the agitation. Premier Rosetti declared in the Chamber that the instigators of the disturbance were not Roumanians. The Government adopted severe measures to put down the disturbances. Bands of peasants who were marching to Bucharest to present their grievances to the Government were fired into by detachments of soldiers, and many were shot. The territorial militia was first called out, but it showed open sympathy with the rioters, and was replaced by regular soldiery. The important town of Kalarasch

was on April 17 entirely in the power of the insurgents, until a detachment of troops arrived, and in the encounter that took place killed a large number of peasants. At Perish, north of Bucharest, the insurgents attacked the railroad station. At Budescht the troops killed or wounded more than 100 peasants.

The troubles had their root in the same conditions that have caused uprisings in the Russian peasantry. When serfdom was abolished there were 72,108 peasants possessing two yoke of oxen, to whom were alloted 11 *pogon*, or 13¼ acres, each; 199,791 who had a single team, and received 7 *pogon*, or 8⅔ acres; and 134,995 without draught-animals, whose share was 4 *pogon*, or 5 acres, for each family. The right to pasturage and wood, which they had enjoyed as serfs, was taken away from them, and the land that was assigned to them was usually selected by the land-owner from the poorest or the most inaccessible part of his estate. The peasants, who were made to pay in installments the price of good land, often found their allotments measured out in worthless bogs or rocky hills. The boyars have always lived away from their estates as a rule, the smaller landlords entering the professions or the Government service. Since the emancipation of the serfs they have been accustomed to lease their estates, usually for three or five years, to speculative farmers, Jews, Greeks, and Bulgarians, whose rent depends not so much on the extent or quality of the land as on the number of peasants living on the property. The peasants are kept in a condition of practical serfdom by these tenant farmers, who exact so many days' labor for fuel and fodder that the peasants are compelled to purchase on the farmers' terms. Advances of money the peasants likewise contract to repay in work. The peasants are forbidden by law to alienate their allotments, and are thus prevented from acquiring one from another enough land to make them independent of the land-owners and farmers. The boyars will not sell land to peasants on any terms, although a considerable part of their estates must remain idle for want of labor to cultivate it. The peasants' allotments, originally much too small because the villages possess no common pastures, have been divided by inheritance. In the gypsy villages there are large numbers of cottiers who have no land. The peasants often rent land, usually the poorest that there is, from the farmers or landlords, paying a third of the produce crop and in addition agreeing to work for their landlords, who often exact so much labor that the peasants are unable to attend to their own crops. A deficient maize and fodder crop in 1887 was followed by a severe winter. The peasants were compelled to sell the cattle that they could not feed, and were in consequence reduced to extreme misery. The Government took measures to relieve distress, but the aid did not reach the sufferers soon enough, and was altogether insufficient. The insurrection was put down in a few weeks, and the peasantry were appeased by promises. The plan of distributing crown lands among them was taken into consideration. When no effective practical measures were taken to relieve the distress, new outbreaks occurred sporadically during the summer and autumn. An attempt on the life of the King, although without serious political significance, was a sequel of the peasant uprising. In the evening of May 7 a former police-officer named Preda Fóntanaro fired two shots at the palace, one of which entered the window next to the room where the King was. The perpetrator of the murderous attempt, a dissipated man, was clothed in the dress of the peasantry, and, when questioned as to his motive, said that he desired to avenge the many peasants who had been shot by the military during the disturbances. The total area of Roumania is about 30,000,000 acres, of which 5,000,000 acres are forest. The emancipated serfs received something over 3,250,000 acres, and the free communes, which always existed in the mountainous part of the country, possess an equal amount. The remaining 18,500,000 acres are divided between the state, which has confiscated the extensive possessions of the monasteries, charitable corporations, and the landed nobility. Some of the boyars own 25,000 acres. Yet as a rule the large estates range from 1,250 to 4,000 acres, and the small ones from 125 to 625 acres.

General Election.—The ministry, refusing the demand of the Radicals for speedy elections on the ground of the excited state of the country, did not dissolve the Chamber and order new elections till September 20. The old Conservative or Boyar party profited by the delay and put forth its whole strength, while attempts to reunite the party of Demeter Bratiano with the Liberals who had adhered to his brother came to naught. The Old Conservatives were victorious in the elections, returning a clear majority that was able to dictate the policy of the Junimist ministry, or to overturn it at any time. The ministry was reconstituted on November 24, after the election of Lascar Catargio to the presidency of the Chamber. Rosetti remained Minister President, but without a portfolio, while the Conservative Prince Stirbey, son of a former hospodar of Wallachia, succeeded him as Minister of the Interior, giving up the portfolio of Public Works to Marghilo- man, who gave place in the Ministry of Justice to a new member of the Cabinet, Vernesca, the possessor of great wealth, and one of the leaders of the Conservative party. Gen. Barossi, who owned no party ties, was succeeded in the Ministry of War by a Conservative, Gen. Mano. The portfolio of Agriculture, Commerce, and Domains, which was held *ad interim* by Carp, was intrusted to Alexander Lahovary, one of the bitterest of the assailants of Bratiano's Cabinet and the leader of a movement to protest against the crown domains, which

were declared to be a robbery of state property. With others of his family, he has taken the lead in the pro-Russian and anti-dynastic opposition within the Conservative party. The results of the general election were the return of 51 Conservatives, 39 Junimists, 31 Independent Liberals, 5 partisans of Joan Bratiano, 4 Socialists, and 42 Ministerialists. Ex-Premier Bratiano lost his seat. The success of the Boyar party compelled the Government to abandon its project of dividing a part of the public domains among the landless peasantry in lots of from four to eight acres. The Conservatives, under threats of a dissolution, agreed to allow the ministry to proceed with its bills for establishing a national bank and a gold currency, and making the higher judiciary irremovable except for cause, and promised not to oppose the foreign policy of the Cabinet. The compromise ministry, nevertheless, could not stand, and on December 31 the Parliament was dissolved, and new elections were appointed for Feb. 4, 1889.

ROUTLEDGE, GEORGE, an English publisher, born in Brampton, Cumberland, Sept. 23, 1812; died in London, Dec. 13, 1888. He served as an apprentice to Charles Thurnam, in Carlisle, in

GEORGE ROUTLEDGE.

1827-'33, and then entered the employ of Baldwin and Cradock, at a salary of £60 a year. At first his special duty was to collect books from other publishers for the country booksellers for whom that house was agent, and later he was given charge of the bindery. In September, 1836, he began business on his own account in Ryder's Court, Leicester Square, as a retail bookseller and purchaser of books at sales, supplying new books as they were ordered. His first book, "The Beauties of Gilsland Spa" (1836), proved a failure, as it depended upon local sale entirely. In November, 1837, he was given charge of the documents in the Tithe-Office, where he remained for four years, beginning with a salary of £80 a year. Meanwhile he continued his publishing-house, also doing some stationery business, which proved profitable and increased his capital for other ventures. He removed to Soho Square in 1843, and began the publication of Barnes's "Notes on the Old and New Testaments," in twenty-one volumes. In 1848 he began the "Railway Library," with "The Pilot," by J. Fenimore Cooper, and the series is still continued, now numbering upward of a thousand volumes. It includes the "Colleen Bawn," of which 30,000 copies were sold, and "The Romance of War," of which more than 100,000 copies have been sold. Another series, called the "Popular Library," comprising travels, biography, and miscellaneous works, was begun about the same time. In 1852 he removed to Farringdon Street, and there published an edition of "Uncle Tom's Cabin," of which over 500,000 copies were sold, also a companion volume, called "The White Slave," of which 100,000 copies were sold. Of Miss Warner's "Wide, Wide World" and "Queechy" enormous editions were disposed of. These editions of American books were all "pirated," no compensation being given to the authors. In 1853 Mr. Routledge entered into an engagement with Sir Edward Bulwer, to pay him a sum of £20,000 for a term of ten years, to republish nineteen of his novels in the "Railway Library." Ultimately he paid this author in all £40,000 for his works. Mr. Routledge came to New York in 1854, and established an agency. Later, he was the first to publish an edition of Oliver Wendell Holmes's poems in England, and in 1855 issued Longfellow's poetical works, illustrated by John Gilbert, whose drawings were engraved by Dalziel Brothers. In 1857 he began the publication of Shakespeare's works in monthly parts, illustrated by Gilbert. This edition was edited by Howard Staunton, and the outlay, exclusive of printing and binding, was £10,000. Another important work issued by him was the Rev. J. G. Wood's "Natural History," for which the plant cost £16,000. In 1868 he issued Longfellow's "New England Tragedy," and later his translation of Dante. He began in 1883 the "Universal Library," edited by Henry Morley, comprising standard works of the best old authors. In all, Mr. Routledge published more than 5,000 volumes during the fifty years that he was in business, an average of two a week. He retired from business in 1887, and at that time a public dinner was given him. Mr. Routledge was a justice of the peace in Carlisle, and deputy lieutenant of Cumberland County.

RUSSIA, an empire in Northeastern Europe. The supreme legislative, executive, and judicial authority resides in the Emperor, who is assisted by the Council of the Empire, which examines every project of law; the Senate, which promulgates every new law and is the high court of justice for the empire; the Holy Synod, which superintends ecclesiastical affairs and decides religious questions; and the Committee of Ministers.

The reigning Emperor is Alexander III, born Feb. 26, 1845, who succeeded to the throne at his father's death by assassination, March 13, 1881. The heir-apparent is the Grand Duke Nicholas, born May 18, 1868, eldest son of the Czar and of the Czarina Maria Dagmar, a daughter of King Christian IX of Denmark. The Czar's Cabinet of Ministers is composed as follows: Minister of the Imperial Household, Gen. Count Vorontzoff-Dashkoff; Minister of Foreign Affairs, Nicholas Carlovich de Giers; Minister of War, Gen. Vannofsky; Minister of Marine, Vice-Admiral Shestakoff; Minister of the Interior, Count Tolstoi; Minister of Public Instruction, M. Delyanoff; Minister of Finance. M. Vyshnegradsky; Minister of Justice, M. Manasein; Minister of Domains, M. Ostrofsky; Minister of Public Works and Railroads, Admiral Possiet; Comptroller-General of the Treasury, M. Solsky. The Grand Dukes Michael and Constantine are also members of the Committee of Ministers, the President of which is M. Bunge, ex-Minister of Finance.

Area and Population.—The area of the geographical divisions of the Russian Empire, in square miles, and their population in 1885 are given in the following table:

DIVISIONS.	Area.	Population.
Russia in Europe.................	1,902,092	81,725,185
Kingdom of Poland...............	49,157	7,960,804
Grand Duchy of Finland.........	144,255	2,232,578
Caucasus........................	152,565	7,284,547
Siberia.........................	4,524,570	4,313,650
Central Asia....................	1,320,387	5,327,098
Sea of Aral................	25,768	....
Caspian Sea..................	169,670	....
Sea of Azov.....................	14,421	....
Total.......................	**8,682,925**	**108,548,192**

The population of Russia in Europe and Poland together is 89,685,480, consisting of 44,524,239 males and 45,161,250 females. The population of the Caucasus consists of 3,876,868 males and 3,407,679 females; that of Siberia of 2,146,411 males and 2,002,879 females; that of Central Asia into 2,448,085 males and 2,207,563 females. The following cities in European Russia contained more than 100,000 inhabitants in 1885: St. Petersburg, 861,303; Moscow, 753,469; Warsaw, 454,298; Odessa, 240,000; Riga, 175,332; Kharkov, 171,416; Kiev, 165,561; Kasan, 139,915; Saratov, 122,829; Kishinev, 120,074; Lodz, 113,413; Vilna, 102,845. The largest cities of Russia in Asia are Tashkend, with 121,410 inhabitants, and Tiflis, the capital of the Caucasus, with a population of 89,551. The population of St. Petersburg on June 27, 1888, was 842,583, of which number 488,990 were males. This shows a falling off of 85,133 as compared with 1881, and even this does not measure the entire decline, because the former census was taken in the winter, and does not include workmen from the provinces engaged in building, who figure for 41,696 in the returns for 1888.

Finances.—The financial account for 1887 makes the total ordinary receipts 829,661.000 rubles, and the extraordinary receipts 144,-543,000 rubles. Of the ordinary receipts 41,-102,000 rubles were derived from the land and forest taxes, 28,862,000 rubles from patents, 11,677,000 rubles from the income-tax, 257,624,000 rubles from the tax on drink, 24,-093,000 rubles from the tobacco-tax, 23,162,-000 rubles from the sugar-duty, 107,425,000 rubles from customs duties, 18,242,000 rubles from stamps, 10,282,000 rubles from registration fees, 24,417,000 rubles from various indirect imposts, 29,397,000 rubles from the post-office, telegraphs, and royalties, 51,298.000 rubles from railroads, forests, and mines, 88,-937,000 rubles from payments for land redemption, and 108,727,000 rubles from other sources. The total expenditures for ordinary purposes in 1887 amounted to 835,850,000 rubles, and the extraordinary expenditures to 95,093,000 rubles. Of the ordinary expenditures, 280,-908,000 rubles were for the public debt, 210,-953,000 rubles for military purposes, 109,067,-000 rubles for financial administration, 40,359,-000 rubles for the navy, 72,576,000 rubles for the Interior Department, 25,834,000 rubles for highways, 20,684,000 rubles for public instruction, 20,443,000 rubles for the judiciary, 22,350,000 rubles for domains, 10,999,000 rubles for the Holy Synod, and 10,560,000 rubles for the court.

The gold value of the paper ruble in the spring of 1888 fell to 45 per cent. below par, a lower point than it had yet reached. Only 20 per cent. of the depreciation is due to inflation, the remaining 25 per cent. being accounted for by the fall in silver. The exchange market for the ruble is in Berlin, where Russian currency has become an object of speculative manipulation, which interferes seriously with the foreign trade of Russia, and has lately caused distrust of the paper ruble in Russia, although it has hitherto passed freely from hand to hand amid all fluctuations. The exchange rates are raised or lowered on the Berlin Bourse by corners and false rumors in connection with enormous speculative dealings in the Russian internal loans. The metallic ruble in March was worth 1·80 paper ruble, against 1·67 in 1887, and 1·50 in 1886. The Government in 1881, and again in 1887, decreed the redemption of all paper currency not guaranteed by a metallic reserve, and has repeatedly declared its intention to redeem and destroy the 266,000,000 rubles of paper money that were issued during the Turkish war. In February, 1888, the new Minister of Finance presented a project for establishing a metallic standard. On July 20 the minister was empowered by an imperial ukase to issue 15,000,-000 rubles of additional paper currency against deposits of gold, merely as a temporary measure to facilitate the large export movement of grain. Another issue of credit-notes of the same amount was decreed in October.

The internal debt, payable in paper rubles, amounted on Jan. 1, 1888, to 3,104,899,764 rubles. In addition, the Government owed at that date 391,505,969 metallic rubles, 66,068,-000 Dutch florins, £122,271,720, and 552,081,-000 francs. There were in circulation 780,032,-238 rubles of paper money, of which 211,472,-495 rubles were protected by a reserve. A new loan contracted in 1887 yielded 81,068,000 rubles, of which 45,093,000 rubles were applied to the construction of railroads and harbors. A 4-per-cent gold loan of 500,000,000 francs for the conversion of old 5-per-cent. debts was offered in Paris on December 10, and found subscribers for six times the required sum.

The Army.—The peace strength. of the Russian army in the beginning of 1887 was 659,274 men. The war effective of the regular army is about 1,689,000 combatants, including 36,600 officers, with 3,776 guns and 204,390 horses. The Cossack troops, a great part of which have been incorporated in the regular army, have a peace strength of 47,150 men, and a war strength of 140,033 men, inclusive of 3,644 officers. The irregular forces, comprising Tartars, Georgians, and Turkomans, number 5,769 men, of whom 1,420 are infantry and 4,349 cavalry. The *opoltchenïe* or militia, which is about equal in numbers to the rest of the armed forces, brings up the total military strength of the empire to nearly 4,000,000 men.

In accordance with an imperial ukase published on July 13, the recruit of the army for 1888 was 250,000 men, an increase of 15.000 over the previous year. A second law fixes the duration of military service at eighteen years, of which five are spent in the active army, and the remainder in the two classes of the Landwehr, the second of which can only be called into active service by a proclamation of the Czar. Although the legal period of service in the active army is shortened by a year, the actual term of service with the colors will probably be a year longer than under the old law, when the men were furloughed on the average two years out of the six. The entire period of military service is made three years longer, increasing the strength of the regular army on the war footing by 750,000 men nominally, and in reality by not less than 400,000.

In the latter part of 1887 the movement of Russian troops toward the western frontiers and unprecedented activity in building barracks, fortifications, and military railroads created alarm in Austria and Germany, and necessitated the strengthening of the frontier garrisons in Prussia and Galicia. The Russian Government explained the dislocation of troops as the execution of a plan that had been in existence for a long time, and while Prince Bismarck accepted this assurance with equanimity, M. Tisza declared in the Hungarian Chamber in January, 1888, that measures would be taken by the Austro-Hungarian Government for contingencies that might imperil the security of the frontiers. The Russian forces on the western frontier at that time numbered 123,275 men, with 24,198 horses and 274 field-cannon. In March re-enforcements of about 100,000 men arrived. Works were begun at Libau which will transform it by 1890 into a military port, with a harbor formed by two breakwaters. There were 96 barracks erected along the frontier of Austria and Germany, and about 100,000 cavalry were held in readiness to cross the frontier at a moment's notice Two branch lines of the Ivangorod-Dabrova Railroad running to the Austrian and Prussian frontiers were opened in the spring. At Rovno, Ivangorod, and other places in the western districts new fortifications were constructed.

The Navy.—Russia in 1888 had 32 iron-clads, 39 armed steamers, 59 other steamers, 8 sailing-vessels, and 95 torpedo-boats in the Baltic Sea ; 7 iron-clads, 27 armed steamers, 59 unarmed steamers, and 16 torpedo-boats in the Black Sea; 12 armed and 4 unarmed steamers in the Caspian Sea; 6 steamers in the Lake of Aral; and 8 armed steamers, 13 unarmed steamers, and 6 torpedo-boats on the Pacific coast. The most powerful vessels are the "Tchesma" and "Catherine II," which were launched in the Black Sea in 1886, and the "Sinope," which was launched in June, 1887, each of which has a displacement of 10,180 tons, and carries six 12-inch and seven 6-inch guns. The armor at the water-line is 16 inches thick. The guns are mounted in a casemated, pear-shaped redoubt. The "Alexander II" and the "Nicholas I," 2 barbette cruisers of 8,440 tons, have 14 inches of armor above the belt, and are armed with two 12-inch, four 9-inch, and eight 6-inch guns. These vessels—the latter of which was launched on the Neva in October, 1888—are of the same type as the English "Imperieuse," but heavier and more powerfully armed. The "Pamiat Azoff," which was launched in the Baltic on June 1, 1888, is an iron-clad frigate of 6,000 tons displacement, carrying 14 heavy long-range guns, 15 machine-guns, and 3 torpedo-guns.

Commerce.—The values in rubles of the imports and exports of merchandise in 1886 and the shares of the different countries in the foreign commerce of Russia are exhibited in the following table :

COUNTRIES.	Imports.	Exports.
Germany	135,854,000	119,210,000
Great Britain	110,071,000	143,984,000
France	12,274,000	30,292,000
Austria-Hungary	16,996,000	25,316,000
Netherlands	3,995,000	36,795,000
Turkey	16,901,000	16,583,000
China	30,016,000	1,615,000
Italy	7,781,000	21,947,000
Belgium	8,884,000	18,190,000
United States	26,774,000	332,000
Sweden and Norway	5,632,000	14,569,000
Persia	10,256,000	6,129,000
Greece	845,000	9,108,000
Denmark	1,175,000	5,378,000
Roumania	2,461,000	4,014,000
Other countries	48,888,000	35,077,000
Total	433,206,000	488,484,000

The imports by way of the Baltic ports in 1886 were of the value of 152,400,000 rubles; the exports, 144,500,000 rubles. The value of the imports from European countries brought by railroad was 150,400,000 rubles, and that of the exports by way of the land frontiers was 114,100,000 rubles. The imports at the ports of the Black Sea were valued at 78,800,000 rubles, and the exports at 172,300,000 rubles. The imports passing by way of the White Sea were 1,300,000 rubles in value, and the exports 5,600,000 rubles. The imports from Finland amounted to 9,900,000 rubles, and the exports to Finland to 16,600,000 rubles. The imports across the Asiatic frontiers amounted to 45,400,000 rubles, and the exports to 35,400,000 rubles.

The imports of alimentary products in 1887 across the European frontiers were valued at 50,397,000 rubles; exports, 350,640,000 rubles; imports of materials, raw or partly manufactured, 224,404,000 rubles; exports, 193,262,000 rubles; imports of live animals, 498,000 rubles; exports, 11,991,000 rubles; imports of manufactured articles, 57,940,000 rubles; exports, 12,627,000 rubles; total merchandise imports in 1887, 333,239,000 rubles; total exports, 568,520,000 rubles.

The overland exports to China in 1887 consisted of 2,353,502 rubles worth of Russian merchandise, 251,914 rubles worth of other European products, 2,924,085 rubles of the precious metals, and 309,860 rubles of paper currency. The principal articles of Russian produce were grain, hogs, sugar, cotton goods, Russia leather, sheepskins, and furs. During the same year China exported to Russia 26,456,557 rubles worth of merchandise, in which total the single article tea stands for 24,097,679 rubles.

Agriculture.—The grain belt in European Russia stretches from the government of Tchernigoff, on the middle Dnieper, to the Ural mountains. North of it is the zone containing the industrial cities, between which and the tundras of the Arctic Circle the great forests extend from Poland and the western governments northeastward to the Ural. In the southern part of the wheat belt is the "black-earth" country, a vast plain extending from Krementchug on the Dnieper to the other side of the Volga. Herds of horses and sheep cover the steppes farther south. The productive land in Russia amounts to 70·4 per cent. of the entire surface, 20·4 per cent. being occupied by farms and gardens, 11·9 per cent. by pastures, and 38·1 per cent. by forests. The number of persons employed in agriculture in Russia, exclusive of Poland, is about 48,000,000. The economical condition of this population has in some respects become worse since the emancipation of the peasants from serfdom. The insufficiency of the land transferred to the peasants, their drunkenness, which has been actually fostered by the Government in order to swell the revenue from excise duties, and their indolence, which is a consequence of the communistic *mir* system, have reducèd the whole class to poverty and debt. The nobility, owing to their lavish way of living and their ignorance of practical affairs, are in still worse case. Russians say that there is hardly an estate outside of the " black-earth " region that is not mortgaged for its full value. More blighting even than the vices of the people is the corruption of the officials, who embezzle the funds that are raised for public improvements and draw blackmail from every private enterprise. The grain-crop in 1886 was poor, and in 1887, though the harvest was abundant, prices were very low. Protective duties in Germany and other countries have seriously injured the export trade in Russian cereals. In 1888 the reported yield of autumn wheat, excluding Poland, was 11,445,-000 quarters, being 39 per cent. above the average; of spring wheat, 18,480,000 quarters, or 3 per cent. better than the average; of rye, 85,-400,000 quarters, 9 per cent. more than a normal crop; of oats, 63,160,000 quarters, exceeding the average by 4 per cent.; of barley, 16,-284,000 quarters, which was 6 per cent. above the average. Count Tolstoi in 1888 proposed a bill prohibiting peasant proprietors from selling their land. The peasants have in recent years purchased largely of the nobles, whose land was unremunerative in their own hands. The transfers have been facilitated by the Peasants' Credit Bank, established under Government patronage, which during 1887 made 5,000 loans, 4,300 of them to *mirs* or rural associations containing in all 590,000 members. The sum of the loans was 50,000,000 rubles, with which 3,400,000 acres were bought. More recently the Government has founded a Nobles' Bank to prevent the lands of the hereditary proprietors from passing into the hands of commercial men and usurers. The question of constructing grain-elevators was considered in 1888 by a special commission, which recommended building with Government means elevators at the export ports and on the lines of railroad with capacity for 600,000,000 kilogrammes, the amortization of the required capital of 20,000,000 rubles being provided for by an export tax of half a copeck per pood, yielding 1,500,000 rubles on a minimum export of 300,000,000 poods. This improvement will tend to place it out of the power of traders to control and dictate prices as they do, paying sometimes only half as much for one farmer's grain as for that of his astuter neighbor.

Navigation.—There were 5,373 vessels entered and 5,329 cleared at the ports of the Baltic during 1886; 647 entered and 625 cleared at Archangel, on the White Sea; 4,483 entered and 4,481 cleared in the ports of the Black Sea and the Sea of Azov; and 1,087 entered and 1,005 cleared at the ports of the Caspian Sea. Of the 11,590 vessels entered at all ports, 7,204 were steamers; and of 11,440 cleared, 7,122 were steamers. Of the total number, 2,485 were Russian vessels, 2,828 English, 1,439 German, 1,397 Swedish and Norwegian, 757 Greek, 637

Turkish, 776 Danish, 639 Austrian, and 185 Dutch. The number of coasting-vessels entered was 37,656, of which 14,708 were steamers. The merchant navy in 1886 numbered 2,157 sailing-vessels of 469,098 tons, and 218 steamers of 108,295 tons. The Russian marine in the Caspian is rapidly increasing, 10 new iron steamboats having been finished in 1888, making a total of 70 steamers, besides many sailing-vessels. The Government has granted an annual subsidy of 111,000 rubles to a new line of steamers between the Russian Pacific ports and the ports of Corea, Japan, and China, which in time of war will be at the disposal of the Government.

Railroads.—The railroad network completed at the beginning of 1888 had a total length of 26,964 kilometres, or 16,745 miles, exclusive of the railroads of Finland and the Transcaspian line of 660 miles. The amount invested in railroads at the end of 1885 was 2,800,000,000 rubles, and the net revenue they produced was 87,400,000 rubles. The Transcaspian Railroad to Samarcand was opened with public ceremonies on May 27, the anniversary of the Czar's coronation. When Gen. Skobeleff took command of the Transcaspian territory in 1880 it was with the condition that Kysil Arvat should be connected with the Caspian Sea by a narrow-gauge railroad. After the conquest of Merv the railroad, on which camels were used instead of locomotives, was extended to the Akhal-Tekke oasis. Gradually the plan expanded, and the tramway was converted into a broad-gauge steam-railway, and carried across the newly acquired Turkoman districts into the Turanian khanates on the other side of the Oxus. The ukase authorizing this railroad was issued on May 20, 1885, and within three years the line was built to Samarcand which is destined to play an important part in the commercial development of Central Asia, as well as in furthering the political and strategical plans of Russia by enabling the Government to store reserves and supplies at Merv, Sarakhs, Penjdeh, Chardjui, and Kerki, and in a short space of time to concentrate an army of 100,000 men on the Asiatic frontier. The railroad is expected to give Russian manufacturers a great advantage over their English and French competitors in the markets of Central Asia, and to lead to a large development of the material resources of the Russian dominions in that part of the world, especially of the cotton-culture in Turkistan, Ferghana, and Samarcand. The cost of the line, which has a total length of about 1,000 miles, was $43,000,000 rubles. The embankments and stations are nearly all, however, of a temporary character, and must be replaced by permanent works at a cost of many more millions. The Transcaspian line connects all the trade-routes converging in the Black Sea with Central Asia, and will be joined with the Indian system if English fears will allow. A new railroad from the Vladikavkas line through the Kuban valley to Novoroskoi, on the Black Sea. was opened to traffic on March 27, 1888. The communications of the Transcaucasus will be greatly improved by the Suram Tunnel, which is nearly completed between Tsipa and Malita. The route of the projected Siberian railroad has been surveyed as far as Irkutsk. It will start from Tomsk, and pass through Marjinsk, Krasnojarsk, Irkutsk, Verkne, Oudinsk, Chita, Stretensk, and Nikolskoi, to Vladivostock, on the Pacific coast. A branch line will be constructed to the Transbaikal province between Lake Baikal and the Chinese frontier. The European connection of the Siberian line will be with a railroad from Samara running through Omsk, which was completed as far as Ufa, in Astrakhan, in September, 1888, and is being extended to Statusk. A private capitalist has undertaken to build a railroad from the river Obi to the Bay of Chainuder, an accessible port in the Arctic Ocean, in order to compete in the wheat, cattle, fish, fur, and timber trades of western Siberia, with the English company that made an unsuccessful attempt in 1888 to take a freighted steamer through the Sea of Kara.

Post-Office.—The number of ordinary letters forwarded in 1886 was 150,348,689 ; of postal-cards, 15,333,686 ; of registered letters, 13,-087,881 ; of letters containing valuables, 11,-017,635 ; of journals, 106,100,275 ; of sealed packets, 20,986,078. The receipts in 1886 were 67,694,516 francs, and the expenses of the postal and telegraph service 99,852,560 francs.

Telegraphs.—The length of the state telegraph lines in 1886 was 107,574 kilometres ; length of wires, 204,043 kilometres. Including railroad and private lines, the Anglo-Indian line, and military and police lines, there were 116,692 kilometres of telegraph lines in the empire, with 267,414 kilometres of wire. The number of internal dispatches in 1886 was 8,371,187 ; international dispatches sent, 559,-754 ; received, 568,815 ; dispatches in transit, 130,202 ; official dispatches, 660,833 ; total, 10,290,791. The receipts in 1886 were 35,869,-680 francs.

Foreigners in Russia.—Statistics compiled by the Ministry of the Interior show that the yearly average of foreigners arriving in Russia has been 800,000, and of those who leave the country 750,000. During the ten years ending with 1881 there were 9,458,132 arrivals and 8,025,198 departures. Among the number entering the country were 4,871,571 Germans, 1,305,133 Austrians, 255,207 Persians, 122,-771 French, 70,387 Turks, 41,878 Roumanians, Bulgarians, and Servians, 20,691 English, 17,-359 Italians, 14,885 Greeks, and 120,638 of other nationalities. Stringent passport regulations and restrictions on the enterprise of foreigners have been the rule during the past three years. In 1887 all foreigners were prohibited by an imperial ukase from holding or leasing lands. This is a reversal of the policy the Government has followed steadily since the year 1815.

Russification of the Baltic Provinces.—The Government has ordained that instruction in the gymnasia and secondary schools in Revel, Dorpat, Goldingen, Libau, Birkenruh, and Fellin shall henceforth be given in the Russian, instead of in the German language. When the Esthonian and Livonian nobility protested against the banishment of their mother-tongue from the schools in which their sons are educated the Minister of Education replied that the only alternative would be to abolish the schools and demand the restitution of the sums contributed by the Government to their erection and endowment. The Directing Senate in April rejected a complaint against a decree of the Governor of Livonia according to which no report or document in the German language will be received by the courts or the municipal authorities. The Senate also decided that no part of the local revenues of the Baltic provinces can henceforth be diverted to ecclesiastical purposes, which will deprive many Protestant religious institutions of a considerable portion of their income. A proposition of Count Tolstoi, made at the suggestion of the Procurator of the Holy Synod, whereby the Minister of the Interior shall have the power to remove Evangelical pastors in the Baltic provinces after they have been suspended by the Governor, was approved by the Council of the Empire, but encountered such opposition on the part of influential statesmen that the Czar ordered the matter to be reconsidered, with the result that a majority of 28 against 16 voted against the proposition. Afterward the Czar, yielding to Panslavist arguments, changed his own mind, and confirmed the decision of the minority. The Swiss branch of the Evangelical Alliance addressed a petition to the Emperor which was answered by Procurator-General Pobedonostzeff. The reason for clothing the Minister of the Interior with powers that the Czars never assumed in former times is found in the return to the Protestant faith of many of the Letts and Esths who have lately been induced to enter the Orthodox Church. This movement the Russian Panslavists expect to check by deposing every Protestant pastor who exerts himself to undo the extrordinary proselyting work of the Russian clergy among the Slav peasantry of the German provinces of Russia.

Closing of the Universities.—Toward the close of 1887 students' riots occurred in many of the universities and other educational institutes. The disturbances began in Moscow, where the inspector of the university excited the ill-will of the students, who became so disorderly that the troops were called out. There were similar occurrences at Kiev, Odessa, Kasan, and other universities, all of which were closed. The students hoped by uproarious demonstrations to compel the Government to rescind the recent regulations which curtail the liberty of students by various vexations restrictions, limit the period in which they are allowed to remain at the universities, and exclude whole classes from the gymnasia and universities on account of lack of means or social station. In St. Petersburg the arrest of many of the students who engaged in a demonstration against the rector was followed by a stormier outbreak, during which the authorities shut the rioters in the building. In January the Minister of Education announced that the universities of St. Petersburg, Moscow, Kasan, Kharkov, and Odessa would not be opened at the beginning of the term. The Kiev and Moscow universities were the first ones reopened, before the end of January. Several hundred students were sent to Siberia or to prison; but eventually some of the obnoxious university statutes were altered, and complaints of the students ceased. A Siberian university was opened in August at Tomsk with the establishment of a faculty of medicine to supply the need of doctors, who now number only twenty-two for the whole of Siberia.

Commemoration of the Introduction of Christianity. —The nine hundredth anniversary of the adoption of Christianity under Vladimir the Great was celebrated throughout Russia on July 27, 1888. The principal festivities were held at Kiev, the mother of Russian cities and the first seat of the Russian Church.

The Political Situation.—With Count Tolstoi at the head of the Ministry of the Interior, Pobedonostzeff in charge of ecclesiastical affairs, and a high Protectionist directing the finances, the Nationalists, Panslavists, and Old Conservatives have controlled the internal politics of Russia during the reign of Alexander III, and have even influenced the Czar to sometimes act in foreign affairs at variance with the officially declared policy of his Government, although they have not succeeded in displacing M. de Giers from the Foreign Office. The Greek Orthodox propaganda has been carried on by the aid of Government encouragement and intervention. Poland is governed as though it were a part of Old Russia. The state schools of the Baltic provinces have been Russified, and the separate police system of Livonia, Esthonia, and Courland has given place to Russian institutions conducted by Russians. The provincial and district autonomy granted by Alexander II has been shorn of one feature after another, the independence of the courts has been reduced to the smallest limits, and ecclesiastical and civil bureaucrats rule with power as unrestricted as in the time of the Emperor Nicholas. Early in 1888 Count Tolstoi brought forward a project for the transformation of the Semstvos or representative bodies of the governments and districts established by the law of January 13, 1864. These councils, in which land-owners, manufacturers, merchants, and rural communes are proportionally represented, have the disposal of the local revenues and of a part of the imperial revenue that is devoted to local purposes, and are empowered to legislate in matters relating to the erection and maintenance

of schools, churches, poor-houses, jails, roads, and bridges; to sanitation, and the prevention of epidemics and cattle-plagues; to public charities, mutual insurance, and the encouragement of commerce and industry; and to satisfying the requirements of the civil and military authorities and the post-office. The governor can protest against acts of the Semstvo; but the decision rests with the Directing Senate. The Semstvo elects an executive committee from among its members, and fixes the salaries of the committeemen. Tolstoi proposed to change the basis of representation by having each 8,000 acres of land held by the nobility, each 450,000 rubles of commercial capital, and each 4,000 adult male peasants represented by one delegate in the council, thus giving the nobles a great preponderance. Even then he would give the governor an absolute veto over the decisions of the Semstvo, while the standing committee which prepares the legislation would be appointed by the Government, not necessarily from the members of the Semstvo, and the rate of salary would be determined by the Government. There was much opposition in several of the ministries to this plan, which practically extinguishes the right of local self-government, and the question was therefore postponed till another year. A proof of the strength of Panslavism was the appointment in April, 1888, to the chief place in the Department of the Interior, next to that of the minister, of Gen. Bogdanovich, whom a year before the Czar had dismissed from the army in disgrace because he had entered into secret dealings with Gen. Boulanger with the object of bringing about an alliance between Russia and France. Gen. Ignatieff was elected president of the Slavonic Benevolent Society, which is the chief agency of Panslavic agitation in the Balkan Peninsula on the eve of the anniversary of Russia's conversion to Christianity. The organs of Liberal opinion and Western ideas have all been suppressed in Russia, except one monthly.

Central Asia.—Col. Alikhanoff on the Afghan frontier has succeeded in bringing nearly all the Turkomans under the Russian ægis. The Afghan authorities at the instigation of Col. Maclean, the British political agent in that region, have sought to prevent by force the migration of Turkomans into Russian dominions, and on April 15, 1888, a collision took place between Afghan troops and Salor Turkomans. According to the British account, Alikhanoff entered Afghan territory, as he had done before, in order to protect a band of 168 emigrant Salors in their flight over the border, while the Russians say that the Afghan troops pursued the fleeing Salors 36 versts (about 20 miles) on Russian territory; and on overtaking them fired at them and received their fire in return, which caused them to recross the frontier, carrying with them their dead and wounded comrades before Alikhanoff and his cavalry appeared on the scene.

S

SALVADOR, a republic in Central America. Area, 18,720 square miles; population, Jan. 1, 1888, 664,513, an increase for 1887 of 13,383.

Government.—The President is Gen. Francisco Menendez, whose term of office will expire in 1891. In April, 1888, the Legislative Assembly appointed vice-presidents, and to succeed one another in the order in which their names are given: Don José Larreynaga, Don Manuel Delgado, and Don José Antonio Quirós. The President's Cabinet is composed of the following ministers: Public Instruction and Charitable Institutions, Dr. Hermogenes Alvarado; Finance, Señor E. Perez; Foreign Affairs, Justice, and Public Worship, Dr. Manuel Delgado; Interior, Dr. Rafael Reyes; and War, Señor Arriola. The United States Minister to the Central American republics is Hon. Henry C. Hall, residing at Guatemala. The American Consul at Salvador is Thomas T. Tunstall; the Salvadorian Consul at New York is Don Mariano Pomáres.

Finances.—Instead of owing any money abroad, Salvador has lodged money in London for the completion of its railroad. The home indebtedness of $5,000,000 involves an annual interest charge of $369,777. The Government's expenditure in 1887 of $2,106,508 was met by an income of equal amount. The liquor-tax produced $818,040 in 1887.

Army.—A decree issued in August fixed the strength of the military forces at 24,000, including the militia, to be drawn by lot, all Salvadorians between the ages of eighteen and forty-five capable of bearing arms to be subject to enrollment, with the exception of the clergy. The Minister of War has procured several infantry and artillery officers from the Spanish army to drill the national recruits and instruct Salvadorian cadets.

Communications.—In addition to the 1,231 miles of wire that were in operation in Salvador prior to 1888, there were laid 180 miles during the year, the number of offices being increased from 68 to 74.

In July, 1888, the Government made a contract with Stanley McNider for the establishment of a telephone plant and service in the cities of San Salvador and Santa Tecla. The concession covers a term of twenty-five years.

Commerce.—The trade of Salvador has developed of late years as follows:

MOVEMENT.	1883-'84.	1884-'85.	1885-'86.
Imports	$2,646,628	$2,184,005	$3,460,047
Exports	6,065,799	5,716,428	7,597,688

During the last fiscal year named the trade was distributed as follows, reduced to thousands of dollars:

COUNTRIES.	Import.	Export.
England	1,524	1,578
France	441	1,198
Germany	209	1,101
Italy	48	909
Spain	49	517
United States	781	1,929
Central America	848	863
Total	3,460	7,597

The chief products exported were as follow: Coffee, $5,024,283; indigo, $1,603,952; silver, in bars, $263,457; Peruvian balsam, $115,856; sugar, $108,139; brown sugar, $107,356. There entered Salvadorian ports in 1886, 380 vessels, 317 being steamers.

The American trade exhibits these figures:

FISCAL YEAR.	Import into the United States.	Domestic export to Salvador.
1855-'56	$1,261,275	$470,541
1886-'57	1,050,841	477,125
1857-'58	1,478,430	645,802

The increase during the last fiscal year is due to the advance in coffee.

Mining.—The Chamber of Deputies, in their last session, made a decision of great importance to mine-owners, by abolishing the taxes upon transfers of mine property, which formerly amounted to five per cent. of the purchase price. They have also removed the duties upon all kinds of imported mining machinery and implements.

Education.—On July 1 was inaugurated, at the University of Salvador, the Academy of Sciences and Fine Arts, Don José María Francés y Rosillo occupying the chair, and Don David Guzman delivering the inaugural address. The National Library was inaugurated on March 15 at the capital.

Agriculture.—In April an agricultural school was created in Salvador, with a model farm and experimental station, to which are to be admitted, at the expense of the state and municipalities, at least two apprentices for every department into which the republic is divided, and as many paying pupils as may apply.

Waterworks.—The Government has made a contract with Señor Patricio Branon to provide the city of San Salvador with drinking-water, by means of steam machinery, at the rate of 2,500 gallons an hour. The Government contributes toward the work the sum of $15,000, advancing the *concessionnaire* $6,000.

Charitable Institutions.—During the fiscal year ended June 30, 1888, the expenditure in Salvador toward entertaining hospitals, workhouses, and orphan asylums, and for pensions, reached the sum of $142,217, toward which the Government contributed direct $41,915.

SAMOA, a kingdom in the western Pacific, occupying the Samoan Islands, formerly known as the Navigator Islands.* The group of twelve islands, two of which are uninhabited, has an area of 1,000 square miles, and contained in 1874 a population of 34.265 natives, of whom 16,568 lived on the island of Upolu, 12,530 on Savaii, 3,746 on Tutuila, and 1,431 on the other islands. There are about 300 whites and 1,000 imported Polynesian laborers employed on the plantations. The cocoanut plantations, the incipient cotton and coffee cultures, and the trade in copra, which is the chief article of export, are conducted mainly by Germans, who have their commercial headquarters in this part of the Pacific at Apia. The principal imports are cotton goods, hardware, arms, ammunition, building-material, coal for steamers, provisions, beer, and tobacco. The total value of the imports in 1885 was $468,000; of exports, $369,000. The share of Germany in the imports was $355,000, and in the exports $295,-000. Of 88 vessels, with an aggregate tonnage of 22,003, that were engaged in 1886 in the foreign and coastwise trade, 37, of 14,588, carried the German flag. The house of Godeffroi and Son, Hamburg merchants, since succeeded by the German Trading and Plantation Company, took the lead in developing the copra-trade in the Samoan Islands. The imports of this company in 1885 were valued at $306,000, and its exports at $532,000.

History.—Formerly there were ten independent chiefs on the island of Tutuila, while the remaining islands were governed from time immemorial by the two royal houses of Malletoa and Tupua. In 1873, at the suggestion of foreign residents, a House of Nobles and a House of Representatives were established, with Malietoa Laupepa and the chief of the royal house of Tupua as joint Kings. The islanders had been converted to Christianity by American and French missionaries, and the commerce was divided between the Americans and the English until the cocoanut culture and the exportation of copra grew to large proportions in the hands of the Germans. Steinberger, who went to Samoa in 1875, nominally as a special agent of the United States Government, but in reality as the secret agent of the

Godeffrois in a scheme to acquire the administration of the finances and the political control of the country, instigated Malietoa to make war on Tupua, and by means of fire-arms supplied by the German company in exchange for grants of land the former made himself sole King, and chose Steinberger for his Prime Minister, dismissing and banishing him, however, as soon as he discovered his real purposes. The Germans then furnished the adherents of the rival dynasty with war material, and Malietoa was forced to abdicate; but the majority of the people remained true to him, and he fought his way back to power. His position was strengthened by the official recognition of the United States Government, which was anxious to secure the confirmation of the cession of the port of Pango Pango for a naval and coaling station, which had been made in 1872 by the then sovereign chief of the part of Tutuila in which it is situate. A treaty was signed at Washington on Jan. 17, 1878, and the ratifications exchanged on February 13, by which the right to establish at Pango Pango a

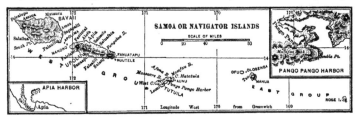

SAMOA OR NAVIGATOR ISLANDS

station for coal and naval supplies, freedom of trade, commercial treatment as a favored nation, and extra-territorial consular jurisdiction were secured to the United States. On Jan. 24, 1879, King Malietoa made a perpetual treaty of amity and commerce with Germany, and by a special clause confirmed the grants of all lands acquired by Germans, and debarred himself from future interference with regard to their lands, plantations, wharves, and houses. Soon afterward civil war broke out again, and at the end of the fighting Malietoa was firmly established upon the throne. This fact was recognized in a proclamation that was signed by the American, British, and German consuls, which was issued by the British Commissioner for the Western Pacific. Sir Arthur Gordon, who, on Aug. 27, 1879, made a treaty with Malietoa securing to England most-favored-nation treatment, extra-territorial jurisdiction, and the right to select a harbor for a naval station and coaling depot. On Sept. 2, 1879, a convention was agreed upon between the United States, Germany, Great Britain, and Samoa, by the terms of which the administration of the town and district of Apia was assumed by the consular authorities for three years, at the end of which

* For another map, showing some of the islands on a larger scale, see the "Annual Cyclopædia" for 1836, page 798.

it should revert to Malietoa's government. Malietoa Laupepa a few days later was succeeded by his nephew Teiavao. The new Malietoa refused to ratify the treaty with Germany, in the belief that it confirmed land titles that were in dispute, and acknowledged all kinds of land transfers made to Germans, and maintained his objections until the British Commissioner for the Western Pacific assured him a year later that this was not the case. In July, 1881, in order to put an end to the warfare that continued between the two dynastic parties, an agreement was made between the United States, Great Britain, and Germany, whereby it was arranged that all Samoa should be ruled by Malietoa as King, and Tupua as Vice-King. In 1882 the joint administration of the three foreign powers in Apia was continued by a new convention until such time as the internal state of the island should admit of the district being placed again under the native government. Germans continued to barter rifles and powder for land at the price of about thirty-seven cents and a half an acre, and on Nov. 10, 1884, Dr. Stübel, the acting German consul, by threats compelled Malietoa to sign a treaty creating a State Council consisting of the German consul, two Germans designated by him, and two Samoans, one to be appointed by the King and the other by the Vice-King. This Council should have power to make laws on all subjects affecting the interests of Germans or persons in their employ, and especially laws in regard to crimes committed by Samoans against the persons or property of Germans. The King bound himself furthermore to appoint a German of the consul's selection who should advise him on all subjects relating to German residents and their interests, and act as judge in cases in which Germans were interested. The German officer in the Samoan Government should also have supervision of the prisons, and command of a police force for the prison service and for the security of the German plantations. On Dec. 29, 1884, Malietoa sent a protest to the German Kaiser, complaining that the treaty was wrung from him by intimidation, and that the former German consul, Weber, was continually stirring up rebellion, giving arms and money to Samoan chiefs, and encouraging them to rise against their sovereign. Soon after this Malietoa, Tupua, and fifty-two chiefs petitioned for British annexation. The King had offered the sovereignty of the islands to Great Britain about a year previously, and also offered it to the United States, in order to escape German domination. The British Government supported German encroachments, in accordance with a secret understanding, and the municipal administration at Apia passed entirely into the control of the Germans.

Tamasese, before he was set up as King by Germany, never had a large party at his back. Malietoa had been able to crush the rebellion at any time, but did not, because he knew that any attempt to enforce his authority against Tamasese would be resented by the Germans, and probably treated as a *casus belli.* The Hamburg Commercial and Plantation Company was the earliest of the enterprises that have led to the formation of a German colonial empire. Prince Bismarck was willing to extend financial Government aid when the company had become embarrassed through interfering with Samoan politics, but the opposition in the Reichstag was too strong. The naval forces, however, were employed to further the political purposes of the company, in which some of the Chancellor's personal friends were interested. In the spring of 1886 Admiral Knorr went with a squadron to Samoa, with the evident intention of creating a state of affairs that would lead to German annexation. He treated Malietoa, the King, with open contempt and indignity, visited the camp of Tamasese in his flagship, landed with his officers and band of music, and feasted with the rebel chief. The flag that the Germans had given Tamasese was saluted, instead of the royal ensign. Malietoa consulted with his English and American friends, and, by their advice, appealed to Consul Greenebaum to proclaim an American protectorate temporarily by virtue of the supposed promise of the United States to extend protection in the event of difficulties with foreign powers. The fifth article of the American treaty was so construed by the consul, who acted on this supposition, although, whatever its covert intent, it did not indeed promise more than the good offices of the United States. The bold action of Greenebaum and the attitude of the English deterred the German admiral from carrying out his intentions. He held no further communication with the rebels, and in a few days left Apia just as a British war-ship entered the harbor. Malietoa had been assured by English consuls and by the captains of English men-of-war that, if he refrained from putting down the rebellion by force, England would not only give him advice but protection. At length the German Government determined to depose Malietoa, and notified the English and American Governments that, since the German representatives in Apia did not enjoy the expected support from their colleagues, it would be obliged to protect German interests by independent action, and therefore found it necessary to declare war and refuse to recognize Malietoa. In a dispatch to the German minister at Washington, dated Aug. 7, 1887, the German Chancellor wrote that Germany was unable to renounce her demand for immediate reparation for the insults to the Emperor and to the national honor of which the partisans of King Malietoa had been guilty, and must obtain a guarantee that German interests would be protected.

In August, 1887, four German war-vessels arrived at Apia, and on the 23d, after the mail-steamers had left, the German consul made a demand on the King for the immediate payment of $12,000 as damages for cocoanuts that had been stolen during the previous four years and $1,000 for an injury sustained by a German in a street fight. King Malietoa asked for three days to consult with his chiefs; but on the next morning a detachment of marines seized the Government House, affixed a declaration of war signed by Heusner, the German commodore, raised the German flag, and searched the town for Malietoa, who had escaped to his residence at Afanga, eight miles distant, from which he fled just before the arrival of a German man-of-war. On the 25th the Germans proclaimed as King the rebel chief, Tamasese, who took possession of the Government House and hoisted his flag. Once before the Germans had raised the rebel flag of their *protégé*, but had been obliged to take it down again. The American consul - general, Harold M. Sewall, who had succeeded Greenebaum when the latter was recalled for proclaiming on his own authority an American protectorate over Samoa on the occasion of the former German attempt to depose Malietoa, now was joined by the British pro-consul in a declaration that the American and British Governments would not recognize Tamasese, but would continue as heretofore to recognize Malietoa as King. Malietoa was hunted by the Germans until he finally gave himself up, on the promise that his life would be spared, and was taken as a state prisoner first to German New Guinea, then to Cameroons, and in August, 1888, to Hamburg. A large number of his chiefs and principal followers were likewise banished to distant islands. When the German squadron was sent to carry out this intention, Malietoa was disposed to resist, and was only deterred by the proclamation of the British and American consuls advising submission to the inevitable, and declaring that their Governments would never acknowledge Tamasese as King.

The Germans, on landing from their warvessels, endeavored to provoke disturbances that would afford a pretext for carrying out the warlike intentions that Germany had notified to the other interested powers through diplomatic channels. They first set up a target for rifle-practice, and fired through the principal street of Apia. When this arrogant proceeding led to no result, they regaled the natives with intoxicants, which was a breach of the law, and bullied them into a fight in which a German's nose was broken. This also led to nothing, because the German magistrate before whom the matter was taken refused to hold the accused persons, for lack of evidence. It was only then that they fell back upon the thefts of cocoanuts, for which the courts created under German auspicies had failed to bring the guilty parties to justice, and, proceeding on the novel theory that the King was responsible for the pilferings of his subjects,

made a sudden demand for a money indemnity, which Malietoa could not at once satisfy, or would not without a decent interval for consideration.

The German naval authorities declared and enforced martial law. Some natives tore down the proclamations to this effect, whereupon the village of Sapapaha was bombarded and burned. The German consul refused to recognize the municipality of Apia, which, under the convention of 1879, had been administered by the foreign consuls. The American consul protested. The British consul issued a proclamation to British residents saying that he had received no instructions to recognize the existing Government, and that British subjects would be under the jurisdiction and protection of the consulate. The British Government took no action until Feb. 24, 1888, when orders were sent to the acting British consul that since the continuance of the municipal board had been found impracticable, the convention should be considered as suspended and the district as having passed under the control of the *de facto* Samoan Government as provided by the terms of the convention in case of its termination. The Government of the United States refrained from any official communications with Tamasese's Government, and would not recognize him. The English Government, however, in spite of the pledges made to Malietoa by the British consul, recognized Tamasese as the King *de facto*, and entered into diplomatic relations with his Government.

The Samoan Conference.—The convention of 1879, the renewal of it in 1883, and the previous acts of the three foreign powers in relation to Samoa, were based on a definite understanding and express assurances of a mutual guarantee of its neutrality and independence. In 1884 a treaty was entered into between Germany and Great Britain to respect the independence of Samoa. The action of the German consul in forcing Malietoa in November of that year to sign a treaty giving Germany a virtual protectorate, and the events of 1886, made it desirable for the United States Government to have the diplomatic understanding attested in a solemn treaty. The powers were therefore invited to a conference, which was held at Washington in the summer of 1887. At the conference the German minister proposed to commit the actual control of the islands for a term of five years to a foreign adviser of the King, who should be appointed by the power having the preponderant commercial interests in the islands, the other powers having the right to approve or disapprove the nominee. At the end of the quinquennial term the control should be renewed on the same conditions. Mr. Bayard proposed, instead, to place the executive authority in the hands of a council composed of the King and Vice-King of Samoa and three foreigners designated respectively by the three treaty powers, but under the commission and pay of the native Government, which would make them as free as possible from the control of the Governments to which they owed their original appointment. In a dispatch to Minister Pendleton at Berlin, the Secretary of State afterward explained that his opposition to the German plan was not due to the fact that under it the appointment of the actual governor of the islands would be given to Germany, but to the union of complete political control with commercial preponderance supplanting instead of aiding the native Government, and tending to diminish rather than to develop the capacity of the natives to manage their own affairs.

In 1886 the British Government, following Prince Bismarck's principle of *quid pro quo*, which had previously led to the clandestine surrender of the best shores of Papua behind the backs of the Australians, and which involved the Samoan question in combinations affecting European politics and the British position in Egypt, in South Africa, on the Niger, in Zanzibar, and in other parts of the world, had entered into a secret bargain with the German Government to give it practically a free hand in its dealings with Samoa. The United States Government has for a long period regarded Samoa, as well as Hawaii, as a country possessing a frame of government admitting of permanent treaty relations, and in whose independence the United States have for military reasons a supreme interest. In 1877 Secretary Evarts declared that the desire of the United States in respect to Samoa was to see a stable, independent native Government established. In 1880 President Hayes, in his annual message, spoke of the diplomatic agreement subsisting between the three treaty powers as the best security for harmony in their relations to the native Government. When the rumor was circulated that in May, 1886, Germany intended to annex Samoa, as well as the Marshall and Gilbert Islands, Secretary Bayard, in communicating his views of the policy of the United States in the Pacific for the guidance of the ministers at London and Berlin, said that the concern of the United States Government in Samoa differs from that in regard to distant groups of islands, and that we have established treaty relations with Samoa, with which relations Germany disclaims any intention to interfere.

Mr. Bayard refused to consent to the German proposals, and, when it became evident that the English minister had entered the conference instructed to support the scheme of the German Government implicitly, he broke off the negotiations. The conference was not concluded, but suspended. The question passed out of the diplomatic stage when, ten days after the adjournment, the German fleet sailed for Samoa to carry out the purposes to which the American Government had refused its consent. The correspondence with the German Government was closed by a letter from Mr. Bayard in January, 1888, in which he declares that, while willing to accept the explanation that the action of the German Government in Samoa was influenced by a desire to protect the people, he can not bring himself to believe that its course has been proper.

Tamasese's Government.—No sooner had the German forces overthrown the legitimate King than they began to compel the puppet whom they had placed on the throne to carry out the scheme of transferring into German possession all the productive resources of the islands. Through land titles and mortgages the German speculators, with the aid of the new Government, held the natives entirely under their control. Herr Brandeis, who had been connected with the German consulate, was made the chief adviser of Tamasese, and practically directed all acts of government. The German squadron, which consisted of the flagship "Bismarck," the "Olga," the "Carola," and the "Sophie," sailed away as soon as the new Government seemed to be established. Yet, when the war-vessels left, the position of the usurper at once became precarious. He deeply offended the people when, at the suggestion of his German Prime Minister, he assumed the hereditary name of Malietoa. When he was further misled into imposing a poll-tax, his followers dwindled to a mere handful of men, and the country openly rebelled against the tax, which he was unable to collect. Influential chiefs called the people together and urged them to resist the tax; and, when Tamasese was induced by the German agent to propose the suppression of these assemblages, chiefs of his own party grew angry and threatening. Many of the influential men of the islands remained away from the Legislature when it met, and many who attended were hostile to the Government. The Germans introduced the registration of title-deeds and mortgages, an elaborate judicial system, and regulations for village councils and assemblies of chieftains. The authority of the Government was recognized in parts of the districts of Aana and Atua at the western and eastern extremities of Upolu, while the middle district of Tuamasanga, the birthplace of the Malietoas, as well as the other islands, were hostile. The American gunboat "Adams" arrived at Apia on Oct. 19, 1887, before the departure of the German squadron. The German cruiser "Adler" and the gunboat "Eber" were subsequently stationed in Samoa. An English war-vessel, the "Lizard," was also sent to observe. Mr. Sewall, the American consul, returned to the United States on leave, a deputy, Mr. Blacklock, being left to look after American interests. The Germans in Apia subjected Americans to injustice and hostility, and American and British trade suffered greatly. The American residents, and some of the English, encouraged the spirit of resistance, which became so strong and determined that the entire country, except his own clan and political dependents, was ready to rise against Tamasese.

Civil War.—Mataafa, a near relative of Malietoa, was the chief of the loyalist party, and its candidate for the throne as the legitimate successor of the exiled King. The enemies of Tamasese were supplied with arms by American and English traders. The crisis was precipitated by a conflict, on August 31, between Tamasese's people and five chiefs of the Tuamasanga district, which occurred on the occasion of a division of mats. The chiefs were summoned on the following day to appear before the royal court of justice at Matianu. Refusing to obey, they raised the flag of revolt, and called on Mataafa, who was chief of Faleula, fifteen miles from Apia, to lead them against Tamasese. The King gathered his military forces, fortified Matianu, a point of land jutting into the Bay of Apia, where the kings had from ancient times held their court, and occupied two forts at Matantu. Warriors from Upolu and Savaii streamed into Mataafa's camp at Faleula. On Sept. 9 the representative of the old dynasty proclaimed himself King of all Samoa, under the title Mataafa Malietoa II. On Sept. 12 Mataafa led his forces around Apia to the neighborhood of Matantu, where a battle took place that lasted from noon till evening. There were about two thousand combatants on either side, Tamasese's men having the greater number of breech-loading rifles. According to their wont, the Samoans fired without aim, discharging about thirty thousand shots, many of which passed through the houses of Europeans and struck the shipping, killing Capt. Bisset, of an English merchant-schooner, who was in the English consulate, and wounding a sailor on the "Adler." The killed on neither side numbered more than half a dozen; but after the battle many heads were cut off from the wounded as trophies of victory. Conquered by noise and the consciousness of a failing cause, the soldiers of Tamasese fled from their forts, and escaped by swimming to Matianu, while Mataafa took up his position in Matantu. On the morning after the battle an officer of the "Adler," with forty men, occupied the strip of land giving access to Matianu, to prevent the victors from attacking Tamasese's demoralized army.

At the proposal of the German and English consuls, Mataafa declared the neutrality of Apia. The conqueror was elected King in meetings that were held all over the country, and was proclaimed as such in Apia, where he took possession of the Government property. The English and American consuls were anxious to have the foreign parts of the district of Apia declared neutral, but the German consul insisted on extending neutrality to all German land throughout the island, including the promontory where Tamasese's army lay encamped, and similar places of refuge everywhere, in which he could gather his forces and prepare his attacks without molestation. Mataafa would not agree to this, and, in order to remove the scene of conflict from the vicinity of the

Europeans, Tamasese established himself at Saluafata, where he was supplied with arms and ammunition by a German schooner which made many trips between Apia and his camp. Brandeis, who had served in the German artillery, became his military adviser. An English merchant named McArthur and an American named Moores supplied Mataafa with munitions of war. Mataafa's authority as King was acknowledged all over the islands, except in a few villages. The American vice-consul, Blacklock, in replying to the notification of Mataafa's election by the people, said that he thought it was in accordance with the wishes of the three powers. The English consul simply informed Mataafa that the party of Tamasese, as he was assured by the German consul, would respect the territory declared neutral if Mataafa would also do so.

Mataafa gathered together an army of five thousand men, while Tamasese's force at Saluafata did not exceed seventeen hundred warriors from the Ituatane district of Savaii and the Aana and Atua tribes. The main body of all these tribes, with the Tumasasas and the Mononos who fight in canoes joined Mataafa's standard. On Nov. 5 Mataafa moved from the village of Laulii on the formidable works at Saluafata. These consisted of stockades in the forest, parapets on the mountain-side leading up to the fort, from which the timber had been cleared to afford a free rifle-range, and the big fort built of stones and baskets filled with sand, in three sections, with narrow passage-ways between them. The fort stood on a hill at the eastern extremity of the Bay of Apia. Mataafa's position was likewise fortified. The fighting lasted many days. About one hundred and twenty men were killed, and one hundred and fifty wounded. Both parties took the heads of their enemies. Tamasese's outposts in the bush were driven from their principal stockade on Nov. 6, and retreated up the side of a steep hill, where they hastily made a clearing and threw up a stockade. The Tumasaga warriors of Mataafa's army stormed the height, pulling themselves up by bushes in the face of the enemy's fire, drove the Tamasesans from the stockade, and forced them to retire farther up the mountain, where they made another stand. By Nov. 9 the Tumasaga men had fought their way to a good position in the mountains, and built a stockade within twenty-five yards of a Tamasese stockade. The wounded of Mataafa's army were taken to Apia, where they were bandaged by the surgeons of the "Adams" and "Lizard," and cared for under the directions of Col. H. de Coëtlogon, the British consul, Vice-Consul Blacklock, and the commanders of the American and British men-of-war. The German naval surgeons dressed the wounds of Tamasese's men. On Nov. 10 the German steamer "Lübeck" arrived with Dr. Knappe, who relieved Consul Becker.

The new German consul, on the arrival of the "Adler," ordered Mataafa to leave his encampment, on account of alleged violations of German neutral territory and depredations on the plantations, which Mataafa denied, saying that he would not stop fighting nor forego the advantage that he had gained, and only desired foreigners to leave the Samoans to settle the war for themselves. The second day after this the three consuls held a meeting, at which Vice-Consul Blacklock proposed that the three consuls should assume the government jointly, until they received definite instructions from their Governments. The British consul said that the only peaceable solution was to deprive Tamasese and Brandeis of all power; but Dr. Knappe replied that he must continue to recognize Tamasese. On the next day, Nov. 16, the British consul issued a proclamation, assuming jurisdiction over British subjects, and directing them to pay taxes to him in trust for the Samoan Government, whenever it should be properly established.

On Nov. 19 the Monono and Savaii men of Mataafa's army made an attack by water on Saluafata in thirty-eight canoes and three of the Samoan naval vessels, which consist simply of two large canoes lashed together, holding a stockade, on which small ancient cannon are mounted. Two other ports were taken. The German gunboat "Eber" and the "Nipsic," which had come to relieve the "Adams," anchored off Saluafata. The German authorities warned Mataafa to keep away from German ground. They obtained an agreement from him to this effect, but he renounced it when he learned that international law imposed no such obligation, ascertaining that such was the view of the American and British consuls, and made his military dispositions without regard to the ownership of the soil.

On the arrival of the "Olga" the Germans decided to make an attempt to disarm the natives. Marines were landed from the "Olga" on Dec. 17 and 18. An American newspaper correspondent, John C. Klein, acted as military adviser to Mataafa. The Samoans fired at the German boats, but a landing was made, and the party already on shore cut their way through the natives and joined the others at Bailele. The Germans, one hundred and fifty in number, took their position in the houses on the plantation and held their own against thousands of natives for two hours, at the end of which they were re-enforced by a detachment from the "Eber." The Germans then advanced and drove the Samoans before them, burning their villages. Several hundred natives were killed, while the German losses were fifteen killed and thirty-seven wounded. The Germans bombarded and destroyed eighteen villages.

After these events the German authorities proclaimed martial law, and assumed complete authority in Apia. All vessels were searched, American goods were not allowed to land unless sent to German warehouses for examination, the English newspaper was suppressed,

the confiscation of all fire-arms was ordered, houses were searched, and several English and American residents were roughly handled. Capt. Mullan, of the "Nipsic," received Klein on board, and refused to give him up to be tried before a military tribunal on the demand of Capt. Fritze, the German naval commander. These events led to fresh correspondence between the Governments of Germany and the United States. The firmness of the latter caused the Berlin authorities to check the high-handed proceedings, which could only lead to German annexation. Consul Knappe and Vice-Consul Brandeis were recalled, while the State Department at Washington ordered Consul Sewall not to return to Samoa. At the proposal of Prince Bismarck it was decided to re-open in Berlin the conference that was suspended at Washington on July 26, 1887.

SANDS, HENRY BERTON, surgeon, born in New York city, Sept. 27, 1830; died there, Nov. 18, 1888. He was graduated at the College of Physicians and Surgeons in 1856, and then studied abroad. On his return he became demonstrator of anatomy in that college until

HENRY BERTON SANDS.

1866, and in 1869 he was called to the chair of Anatomy, which he held for ten years, when he accepted that of the Practice of Surgery, which he filled until his death. Dr. Sands had been connected with various hospitals as consulting and attending surgeon, but had gradually withdrawn from such relations to devote his entire time to private practice. From 1860 till 1870 he was in partnership with Dr. Willard Parker. He was a member of many medical societies, including the New York Academy of Medicine, and in 1883 was chosen a corresponding member of the Society of Surgery of Paris. In 1866–'67 he was President of the New York County Pathological Society, in 1874–'76 of the County Medical Society, and in 1883 of the New York County Surgical Society. For many years he had been recognized as the foremost surgeon in New York city, astute in diagnosis, sound in judgment, and dextrous as an operator. He was called for consultation in President Garfield's case, and also in ex-President Grant's illness, and he attended Roscoe Conkling in his last illness, performing the operation on his head. Dr. Sands was too busy to devote much time to publishing his results, but among the descriptions of operations that he contributed to medical literature are "Case of Cancer of the Larynx successfully removed by Laryngotomy" (1865); "Aneurism of the Sub-Clavian, treated by Galvano-Puncture" (1869); "Case of Traumatic Brachial Neuralgia, treated by the Excision of the Cords which go to form the Brachial Plexus" (1873); "Case of Bony Anchylosis of the Hip-Joint, successfully treated by Subcutaneous Division of the Neck of the Femur" (1873); "Esmarch's Bloodless Method" (1875); "Treatment of Intussusception by Abdominal Section" (1877); "The Question of Trephining in Injuries of the Head" (1883); and "Rupture of the Ligamentum Patellæ and its Treatment by Operation" (1885).

SANTO DOMINGO, a republic, occupying the eastern portion of the West Indian island of that name, the western portion being Hayti. The population of the republic, by the census of 1887, is 504,000.

Government.—The President is Gen. Ulysses Heureaux. His Cabinet is composed of the following ministers: Interior and Police, Gen. Wenceslao Figueredo; Foreign Affairs, Don Manuel Maria Gautier; War and Navy, Gen. Miguel A. P. Pichardo; Finance and Commerce, Gen. Julio J. Juliá; Justice, Public Works, and Instruction, Don Juan Tomás Mejía; Public Works, Señor P. M. Garrido. The United States *Chargé d'Affaires* is John E. W. Thompson, resident at Port-au-Prince, Hayti. The American Consul at Puerto Plata is Thomas Simpson. The Dominican Consul at New York is Don Leoncio Juliá.

Finances.—The public indebtedness on July 1, 1888, included an internal debt of $1,650,-000, a balance of $234,250 of foreign debt (which is being paid off by an extra 2-percent. import duty), and the old 6-per cent. English-Santo Domingo loan of 1869, of which £750,700 is still held in London. The republic in July, 1888, made a loan in London and on the Continent to the amount of £770,000, bearing 6 per cent. interest, to be paid off within thirty years, the amount to be applied as follows: First, £142,860 for canceling the Hartmont loan of 1869; second, £151,660 toward canceling the internal debt, the remaining £475,480 to bear interest dating from July 1, 1888. This debt is to be paid off at par by sixty half-yearly drawings, the first of which is to be made on June 15, 1889. This loan was placed at 83½.

Communications.—There is in operation a line from Sanchez to La Vega, 115 kilometres. Besides the telegraph running along the San-

chez and La Vega Railroad, there is one connecting the capital with Puerto Plata. Santo Domingo has been connected with the world's telegraph system since April, 1888, by the submarine cable connecting Mole St. Nicolas (Hayti), Puerto Plata, and Santo Domingo with Santiago de Cuba.

Commerce.—The imports in 1887 amounted to $2,057,928, and the exports to $2,660,471. The chief articles of export were tobacco, sugar, coffee, honey, wax, mahogany, and cabinet and dye woods. Guano exportation has been resumed on a large scale. The American trade exhibits the following figures:

FISCAL YEAR.	Import from Santo Domingo.	Domestic export to Santo Domingo.
1886	$1,656,131	$1,017,285
1887	1,380,126	1,014,414
1888	1,459,392	792,560

SAVAGE, JOHN, author, born in Dublin, Ireland, Dec. 13, 1828; died in Spragueville, Pa., Oct. 9, 1888. He was educated in the Jesuit college at Colougoues, and took a course in the art school of the Dublin Society, where he gained several prizes. While studying art he began to contribute patriotic articles and poems to John Mitchell's Dublin newspaper, and when that was seized by the British Government, and its editor sent to Australia, he joined several friends in establishing another

JOHN SAVAGE.

newspaper devoted to the popular cause. He gave much aid with his pen to the revolutionary movement of 1848, and the suppression of his newspaper led him to undertake more active and personal work. At the outbreak of the revolt he organized and commanded a body of armed peasantry in the south of Ireland, and at their head captured several British garrisons. On the failure of the movement, he came to New York city and secured employment as a proof-reader in the "Tribune" office. While so engaged he contributed frequently to newspapers and periodicals, wrote several dramas and poems, planned historical works, and painted pictures. Subsequently he held editorial appointments on the New York "Citizen" and on newspapers in New Orleans and Washington, besides writing regularly for the "Democratic Review" and the "American Review." While in Washington he became editor-in-chief of Stephen A. Douglas's political organ "The States," and afterward its proprietor. When the civil war broke out he was assistant editor of the New York "Irish News," but he resigned his appointment, aided Gen. Thomas Francis Meagher in organizing the famous Irish brigade, and served in the war as his aide, though on the roll of the Sixty-ninth New York Regiment. He first became connected with Irish politics in the United States in 1868, when he was chosen head center of the Fenian Brotherhood, and through the solicitations of John O'Mahony, his friend and the founder of the order, reluctantly accepted the office. He applied himself with vigor to the reconciliation of the antagonistic factions within the order, and, though a man of great popularity and influence in Irish and Roman Catholic circles, was unsuccessful. During the presidential canvass of 1864 he had rendered the Republican party much service as an orator, and on the conclusion of peace his friends urged upon President Johnson the propriety of appointing him to a foreign office, and the President tendered him the United States consulship at Leeds, England. He felt deeply grieved at this action, because he was widely known as an expatriated man, and was convinced that the British Government would never recognize him officially. Still, believing he might be of some service to the Fenian prisoners confined in England, he went to Paris, and there, through the aid of Gen. John A. Dix, the American minister to France, began negotiations with the British Government which resulted in the release of some of the prisoners. Returning to New York city, he engaged in literary work, bought a summer home, "Laurelside," at Spragueville, Pa., and made his winter quarters in Fordham, N. Y. He was an accomplished scholar, and as an orator and lecturer was in great demand with Roman Catholic colleges and societies. St. John's College, Fordham, N. Y., gave him the degree of LL. D. in 1875. His published works include "Lays of the Fatherland" (1850); "Ninety-eight and Forty-eight; the Modern Revolutionary History and Literature of Ireland" (1856); "Our Living Representative Men" (1860); "Faith and Fancy," poems (1863); "Campaign Life of Andrew Johnson" (1864); "Life and Public Services of Andrew Johnson" (1868); "Fenian Heroes and Martyrs" (1868); "Poems; Lyrical, Dramatic, and Romantic" (1870); and "Picturesque Ireland" (1878–'83).

SCHOFIELD, JOHN McALLISTER, an American soldier, born in Chautauqua County, N. Y., Sept. 29, 1831. He was graduated at West Point Military Academy in 1853, Philip H.

Sheridan, James B. McPherson, and John B. Hood, being among his classmates. McPherson was at the head of the class, Schofield was No. 7, Sheridan No. 34, and Hood No. 44. The whole number was 52. On his

JOHN McALLISTER SCHOFIELD.

graduation, Schofield was assigned to the First United States Artillery, and served for two years in South Carolina and Florida; and from 1855 to 1860 he was Assistant Professor of Natural Philosophy at West Point, after which, on leave of absence, he was for one year Professor of Physics in Washington University, St. Louis, Mo. He had been commissioned first lieutenant, United States Army, in August, 1855, and captain, in May, 1861. At the outbreak of the civil war he became major of the First Regiment of Missouri Volunteers, and on April 26, 1861, was made chief-of-staff to Gen. Nathaniel Lyon, with whom he served in the Missouri campaign. He was appointed brigadier-general of volunteers in November, 1861, and soon afterward brigadier-general of Missouri militia, and he commanded in that State until April, 1863. He was made major-general of volunteers in November, 1862, and from May, 1863, till February, 1864, he commanded the Department of the Missouri. He was next assigned to the command of the Department and Army of the Ohio, which formed a part of the army that Gen. William T. Sherman organized for his Georgia campaign against the Confederate army under Gen. Joseph E. Johnston.

In that great campaign, Gen. Schofield participated in the battles of Resaca, Dallas, Kenesaw mountain, and Atlanta. After the capture of Atlanta, when Sherman was preparing for his march to the sea, Schofield, in command of the Twenty-third Corps, was sent back to Nashville, where he joined the army of Gen. George H. Thomas. When the Confederate army, of about 40,000 men, under Hood, defeated by Sherman at Atlanta, turned back to attack Thomas, it was first confronted by Schofield's force of about 25,000. Schofield made a skillful retreat as far as Franklin, on the Harpeth river, eighteen miles from Nashville, where he intrenched a line with both flanks resting on the stream. Here he was attacked on the afternoon of Nov. 30, 1864. The brigade forming Schofield's rear guard, instead of falling back quickly to the main line as ordered, so as to permit the whole fire to be directed on the advancing enemy, attempted to withstand the onset alone. It was soon borne back in confusion, and the enemy followed it over a part of the intrenchments. A portion of the line thus seized was recaptured after hard fighting; but the remainder could not be retaken, and Schofield established a new line a few rods in the rear, where the battle was continued until dark. Meanwhile he had got his artillery and trains across the stream, and at midnight he followed with his whole force and retreated to Nashville. In the battle of Franklin, Schofield lost 2,500 men; Hood, about 6,000. For this action, Schofield was made brigadier-general and brevet major-general in the regular army. He participated with his corps in the battle of Nashville, Dec. 15 and 16, 1864, in which Thomas destroyed Hood's army.

In January, 1865, Gen. Schofield, with 15,-000 men, was detached from Thomas's army and sent by rail to Washington, and thence by transports to the mouth of Cape Fear river, when Schofield was given command of the Department of North Carolina. He captured Wilmington on Feb. 22, 1865, fought the battle of Kinston on March 8–10, and on March 22 joined at Goldsborough the army of Gen. Sherman as it moved northward after its march to the sea. When Gen. Johnston's army surrendered to Sherman's, April 26, Gen. Schofield had charge of the details.

In June, 1865, he was sent to Europe on a mission relating to the French occupation of Mexico, whence he returned in May, 1866; and in August of that year he was assigned to the command of the Department of the Potomac. From June 2, 1868, till March 12, 1869, he was Secretary of War. He was then commissioned major-general in the United States Army and ordered to the Department of the Missouri. He commanded the Division of the Pacific from 1870 till 1876, and again in 1882-'83. He was superintendent of the Military Academy at West Point from 1876 till 1881, commanded the Division of the Missouri from 1883 till 1886, and was then transferred to the Division of the Atlantic. On the death of Gen. Philip H. Sheridan, in August, 1888, Gen. Schofield became the ranking officer of the United States Army. He was president of the board that in 1870 adopted the system of tactics now in use in the army, and was also president of the board that investigated the Fitz John Porter case in 1878.

SERVIA, a monarchy in Southeastern Europe, which gained its independence in 1829, after a war with Turkey lasting fourteen years, and was erected into a kingdom in 1882. The executive authority is vested in the King, who is assisted by a council of eight ministers. The legislative body is the Narodna Skupshtina, or National Assembly, a single house composed of 208 members, of whom one fourth have been nominated hitherto by the King. No member of the legal or the military profession is eligible. A Great National Assembly of four times the number of members in the ordinary Skupshtina is sometimes convoked to consider matters of vital national importance.

The Radical Ministry.—The Radicals in Servia, whose opinions coincide with the ideas of constitutional liberty prevalent in Europe, with a tincture of the socialistic theories of Russian nihilism, have for many years represented the prevailing sentiment of the Servian people. The official class and the merchants are, to a great extent, Progressists or Conservatives, and the liberal professions contain many Liberals; but the peasantry, almost to a man, belong to the Radical party. The King, sustained by the pro-Russian Liberals under Ristich or the pro-Austrian Progressists who followed the lead of Garashanin, has repressed the demand for a more popular form of government, annulled the victories of the Radicals at the polls, and imprisoned or banished their leaders, who were driven by persecution to conspire the violent overthrow of despotic power. The Bulgarian war was a desperate resort to restore the King's prestige, and when this failed, and Garashanin retired, King Milan called Ristich to the head of the Administration in June, 1887, and attempted to govern with a coalition Cabinet. The Radicals gained another victory in the autumn elections. The King was constrained to accept their programme. A commission was appointed to devise a scheme of constitutional revision. He was unwilling to intrust the Government to a party which had been hostile to him and was distrusted abroad on account of its revolutionary tendencies. The Radicals had, however, a majority of four over the elected and appointed ministerial deputies, and after a preliminary agreement on their part to continue the foreign policy of the King, and to accept the financial programme of the retiring ministry, at least in regard to the issuance of a loan of 20,000,000 dinars for the payment of the floating debt, the King sent for Col. Gruich, who, on Jan. 1, 1888, formed a new ministry of Radical complexion, made up as follows: Premier and Minister of War, Sava Gruich; Minister of Foreign Affairs, Franassovich; Minister of Communications, Velimirovich; Minister of Finance, Vujich; Minister of the Interior, Milosavlyevich; Minister of Commerce, Stefan Popovich; Minister of Justice and Education, Gershich. Col. Gruich had been Minister of War under Ristich. Col. Franassovich was Minister of Foreign Affairs in Garashanin's Cabinet. The new Minister of Justice was a Professor of International Law who was sentenced to death in 1883 for participating in the revolution of Alexinatz, and Dr. Vujich, the Minister of Finance, was expelled from Russia in 1884 for suspected complicity in the Nihilistic conspiracies.

After voting the new loan, which was raised in Vienna at 6 per cent., the Skupshtina, on January 3, adjourned till the end of the month. The chiefs of the Radical party, whose demand for a general amnesty to political offenders was granted, sent an address expressing fidelity to the King. In a circular note to the powers the Minister of Foreign Affairs unfolded the scheme of political reforms. Personal and civil liberties should be extended, though not at the expense of order, by enlarging the self-government of the communes, restricting official interference in elections, liberalizing the laws governing the press, associations, and public meetings, and modifying the criminal code and laws relating to security of person and property, and the civil service.

The Radical Cabinet, existing only by the King's sufferance, endeavored to carry out their pact, and to prove the capability of their party to conduct the Government. But in the new Chamber elected in February and convened on March 31, in which the Radicals secured 129 seats out of 142, the Prime Minister was unable to control the majority, which was composed largely of men educated in France, holding Republican and Socialistic opinions. King Milan, in an angry message to the Chamber, warned the ministers that they could not continue in office if they allowed the Radical Club to control their decisions, and if they could not forward legislative business within acceptable lines. Resolutions of revolutionary tendency were voted, such as one in favor of taxing luxuries, another to make 3,000 dinars the uniform salary of officials of all grades, a third abolishing bishoprics, and others reducing the pay of military officers, making officers of the militia elective, and introducing new direct and indirect taxes, some of which were contrary to existing treaties. One deputy proposed to dismiss all foreigners employed in the railroad service, and another demanded to know if there was a secret treaty with Austria. The bill on the government of communes took away from the central authorities the right to interfere with the ordinances or the acts of the local authorities within their province, and the powers to remove mayors and to dissolve communal councils. The only other act that was passed, a bill on the reorganization of the army, contained provisions for abolishing about half of the standing army, and replacing it with a militia. Both these bills the King refused to sanction. At a conference with the ministers on April 26, he persisted in his refusal to sign the bill on communal representation, and said that he considered the agreement which he had made with the Radical majority in the winter no longer binding for either party, whereupon the ministry resigned in obedience to the demand of the Radical Club. The King determined to call to his aid the moderate men of the Conservative party, and therefore invited Nikola Christich, who had thrice performed a similar task, to select a neutral ministry.

The Christich Ministry.—The new Council of Ministers, constituted on April 27, was made up as follows: Premier and Minister of the Interior, Christich; Minister of Foreign Affairs, Miyatovich; Minister of Public Instruction and Ecclesiastical Affairs, Vladan Djorjevich; Minister of Justice, Georg Pantelich; Minister of Agriculture and Commerce ad interim, Vladan Djorjevich; Minister of Finance, Dimitrije Rakich; Minister of Public Works, Michael Bogitchevich; Minister of War, Costa Protich. The new Minister of Foreign Affairs held the same portfolio in the Pirotshanatz Cabinet, which first entered into the Austrian alliance, and has since been several times Minister of Finance. The present Minister of Finance is a young man prominent in the councils of the Progressist party, who has been chief of sections in the department over which he was called to preside and in the Ministry of Foreign Affairs. The Minister of Justice, an eminent jurist who was a member of the Christich Cabinet in 1883 is free from party ties, as are also Dr. Djorjevich, an author and scientist who has done much for sanitary reform, and Gen. Protich, a distinguished military administrator. The Minister of Public Works held the same office in Garashanin's last Cabinet, and in 1883 under Christich.

The Skupshtina was dissolved on April 29 without having voted the budget. The leaders of the Radicals published assurances that they would countenance no revolutionary disturbances, and would act within constitutional limits. Gen. Gruich, on account of a statement made to a foreign newspaper correspondent, in which he ascribed the dismissal of the Radical Cabinet to Austrian pressure, was placed on the retired list of the army. The arrears of taxes were collected more strictly than under Ristich and Gruich, who spared their party followers. The Government attempted again to break the spirit of Radicalism by tyrannical repression. Many politicians were arrested and thrown into jail. The financial situation was difficult, but, by means of the new loan, the Government in June redeemed the tobacco régie, which had been sold to a foreign corporation. Besides suppressing insurrectionary movements in Servia, especially in the Saitchar department, the authorities, after a frontier raid of political brigands into Bulgaria had taken place in the Trn district, dismissed the prefects of Pirot and Nish, and took measures to prevent the recurrence of such disturbances.

The Royal Divorce.—King Milan married Natalie, Princess Sturdza, born May 14, 1859, daughter of a Russian nobleman, Col. de Keshko de Pulcherie, on Oct. 17, 1875. Their only child, the Crown-Prince, was born in 1876. Domestic differences arose between them; the opponents of the King all sympathized with Queen Natalie, and even those who plotted to overthrow Milan desired to preserve the throne for her son, except some of the Panslavist Liberals, who dreamed of the restoration of the Servian Empire, embracing all the South Slavs, under Russian auspices, with Prince Karageorgevich or Prince Nikola of Montenegro on the throne. The Queen thus became identified with the party having Russian leanings. In 1887 the King insisted on Natalie's leaving Servia, and compelled her to sign articles of separation and take up her residence abroad. The Queen under this arrangement was given the custody of her son. In May, 1888, Natalie announced her intention to return to Belgrade. The King forbade her to do so, and, meeting her at Vienna, directed her to go to Wiesbaden. While she was there, he sent a proposal for a new agreement, declaring that the former one was impracticable. She rejected the new proposition, whereupon King Milan applied to the Synod of the Servian Church for a divorce. The Queen made a compromise more difficult by addressing indignant protests to the Synod, the Consistory, and the Council of Ministers. Ex-Minister Pirotshanatz became her advocate. She denied the competence of the Synod to try the case. The Synod, consisting of the Metropolitan, three bishops, and seven clergymen, asserted its jurisdiction; but, after the King had transferred the case to the Belgrade Consistorial Court, consisting of three delegates of the Consistory, the bishop agreed that this was the proper tribunal. The Queen purposed appearing in person before the Consistory, but was forbidden by the King, who demanded that the Crown-Prince be given into his custody, and sent Gen. Protich to Wiesbaden to bring him to Belgrade. Queen Natalie refused to give up her child, but the German authorities interfered, and took him by force from his mother.

The ground given for the petition of divorce was "irreconcilable mutual antipathy." The Servian law gives to the ecclesiastical authorities alone the power of divorce, which can only be granted after the parties have been brought face to face and a formal attempt has been made to reconcile their differences. Bishop Dimitrije, of Nish, a friend of the Queen, was sent by the Synod to Wiesbaden to arrange a reconciliation, if possible, on the terms proposed by the King, allowing Natalie to retain all the rights and privileges of Queen on condition that she should not return to Servia except at the King's invitation. The Queen scornfully refused to accede to these conditions, but afterward, when Milan showed a determination to proceed with his application for an absolute divorce, she pressed for a compromise on these very terms. After being robbed of her child and expelled from Wiesbaden by order of the German Government, she demonstratively identified her cause with the political designs of Russia by going to that country in order to interest the people and the Czar in her wrongs. Subsequently she went to the house of her brother-in-law, Prince

Ghika, in Bucharest, and waited for permission to answer the summons of the ecclesiastical tribunal in Belgrade. Her cause was espoused by the Liberal and Radical Opposition, and even the leaders of the Progressist party disapproved the divorce proceedings. Gen. Horvatovich, for championing the Queen, was placed on the retired list. The Cabinet could not approve the King's course, and the ministers wished to retire. So determined was Milan to punish his consort that he contemplated recalling the Russian party to power on condition of its upholding the divorce proceedings; but Ristich declined to take office if the suit were not dropped. Milan's temper became so moody and violent that he sent into exile his old and devoted friend Garashanin for advising him to withdraw his application for absolute divorce.

The Court of the Consistory ruled that the King and Queen must both be heard in person. The ministers decided that there was no law to prevent the Queen from entering Servia, yet held that they could prohibit her sojourn in any particular town as likely to produce political disorders. When King Milan found the Consistorial Court determined to treat him as a private person, he suspended its action, requesting an adjournment for three months to allow the Queen time to prepare an answer. While the matter remained in abeyance in the Consistorial Court and before the Holy Synod, Milan applied to the Metropolitan Theodosije, and on Oct. 24 obtained from him a decree of absolute divorce, granted in his capacity as autonomous head of the Servian Church. The law gives the Metropolitan no authority to grant divorces independently of the Synod; and, even if he had the right, the title of Archbishop Theodosije to his office is doubtful, since many religious persons look upon the deposed Metropolitan Michael as the rightful head of the Church. Milan took this irregular way to accomplish his purpose, because he expected an adverse decision in the Consistorial Court. To prevent hostile action of the Synod, the King suspended Bishops Dimitrije and Nicato, on the ground of contumacy.

Revision of the Constitution.—King Milan followed up his divorce with a bid for popular favor, ordering elections for a Grand Skupshtina, to be held on December 2, and summoning the Assembly for December 25. The manifesto ends with an assurance that the elections should be free. A commission for the revision of the Constitution, consisting of 85 members, chosen from the three political parties, met in Belgrade, under the presidency of the King, on November 3. The King brought about a fusion in the revision commission between the Progressists and the Liberals, whose political alliances have heretofore been made only with the Radicals. The preliminary elections were by no means free. The police interfered everywhere, and a great many persons were arrested or maltreated.

Notwithstanding this, the Radicals were generally victorious. The King then annulled the elections, and ordered new ones to be held, under the supervision of three royal commissioners in each of the 430 circumscriptions. In these the Radicals achieved still greater successes. The Liberals did not maintain the alliance with the Progressists at the polls, but aided the Radicals. In the final elections, which were postponed till December 16, nearly three quarters of the seats went to Radicals. The Liberals elected about 100 of the 628 members of the Great Assembly, and the Progressists not more than 60. Before convoking the Assembly, the King required every member to give a written promise that he would vote for the Constitution as drafted by the commission. The Radicals, under the lead of Gen. Gruich, stood out especially for the relinquishment by the King of the right to conclude alliances and military conventions without the consent of the Skupshtina, and when he yielded on this and some other points, the bulk of the party agreed to accept the compromise Constitution. The session of the Grand Skupshtina was opened on December 30. A royal ukase declared that no discussion would be allowed, and no amendment proposed, but that the Constitution must be accepted or rejected as a whole. The Radicals were inclined to insist on having the Skupshtina meet annually, without requiring the King's summons. They also wished to take away from the King the power to declare war, and many were pledged to vote for the abolition of the standing army, and wished at least to obtain a considerable reduction in the military establishment. The King had already surrendered the right to allow foreign armies to cross Servian territory without the consent of the Assembly. The limitation of the time that was allowed to the King to continue provisionally the budget of the previous year without convoking the Skupshtina to three months, was likewise a concession on the King's part, as the old Constitution allowed a full year. The Radicals objected particularly to the electoral system in the new Constitution, which provides that in the 10 *zupanias* into which the country is divided the deputies shall be elected by *scrutin de liste*, in the proportion of one to every 4,500 tax-payers, that voting shall be by ballot, and that three members from each *zupania* must be graduates of universities. Notwithstanding the objectionable features, fewer than 100 of the Radical deputies proved irreconcilable, and voted against the Constitution, which was adopted.

The direct active franchise under the new Constitution is given to all citizens paying 15 dinars in direct taxes, and the passive franchise to persons whose taxes amounted to 30 dinars. Every elector is eligible to the Skupshtina. All parties approved the removal of the disqualifications of advocates and state pensioners, including ex-ministers who, under the old Constitution, were not allowed to sit in the Chamber. In the place of deputies appointed by the King, a class of official deputies is created, consisting of the members of the Council of State, the bishops, generals on the retired list, and the presidents of the Courts of Cassation and Appeal. The Skupshtina has the initiative in legislation. A significant article provides for a regency of the King's selection in case of his abdication, showing the earnestness of King Milan's desire to retire from his difficult position before involving his dynasty in his fall. The Great Skupshtina will hereafter consist of double the number of deputies in the ordinary Assembly, and its functions will comprise the consideration of questions affecting the throne, the election of a regent in a case of its vacancy, and constitutional revision. The Council of State will consist of eight members nominated by the King and an equal number chosen by the Skupshtina for life, whose duties will be to draw up bills and administrative decrees, and nominate candidates for judges of the Supreme Court and the Courts of Cassation and Appeal. Courts are declared absolutely independent, and judges irremovable. The *zupanias* are to have autonomous organization for matters relating to roads and communications, sanitary and financial requirements, and schools. The Servian Church is declared independent and autocephalous, and its head shall bear the title of Patriarch. All religions are free. The liberty of the press is guaranteed, and newspapers may be founded without a deposit of caution money. No citizen shall be arrested or have his house searched without a warrant. Foreigners may possess any kind of property in Servia and may be employed in the state service. Public instruction is gratuitous and compulsory. No titles of nobility may be borne by Servian citizens. No pensions may be granted without a special act of the Skupshtina. While he retains the right of declaring war and making peace, the King can not conclude negotiations involving the payment or exaction of a war indemnity or the cession or acquisition of territory without summoning the Skupshtina.

SEVENTH-DAY BAPTIST CHURCH. The statistics of this Church as presented to the General Conference in August were incomplete. They gave the whole number of members as 8,337, but the returns of the contributions for the several purposes of the Church were defective and unsatisfactory. Seventy-five Sabbath-schools returned 5,754 members, including officers and teachers and pupils. The revenue and expenditure of the Education Society were balanced at $46,557. It received reports from Albion (Wisconsin) Academy and Normal Institute; Milton (Wisconsin) College, and Alfred (New York) University. The last two of these institutions have endowment funds amounting together to $148,000. Young men and young women are admitted on an equal footing to all the institutions. The society at its meeting recommended that the English language and literature should hold a more prominent place in both preparatory and higher courses of instruction. The American Sabbath Tract Society had received $6,543. Three journals in the English language, one in Dutch (in Holland), one in Swedish (in Sweden), and one Hebrew journal are published under its care. The receipts of the Missionary Society had been, from all sources, $12,039. The society had supported a mission in China, with three American missionaries, two native preachers, and eight other native laborers, with which a dispensary was connected; a mission in Holland; a mission to the Jews, home missions, and a Scandinavian mission, in the United States, in which twenty-six laborers were employed. The whole number of additions by baptism during the year in all the missions was ninety-one.

The Seventh-Day Baptist General Conference met at Leonardsville. N. Y., August 22. The Rev. L. A. Platts presided. A record was entered of the organization of a new association—the South Western—of eight churches at Texarkana, Ark. Four other churches in the South were admitted to the Conference. The Memorial Board reported that the amount of the memorial fund, excluding original notes for $14,148 and certain real estate not estimated, was $111,924. Provision was made for the more complete collection of materials for the history of the denomination and its churches through the action of individual churches, pastors, and families. In view of the movement of the Women's Christian Temperance Union for promoting the observance of Sunday as the Sabbath, the Woman's Executive Board was authorized to present a memorial to that body explaining the reasons why the women of this Church could not join in its effort; and a resolution adopted by the Conference declared all legislation "against rightful business on Sunday" unwarrantable from a religious point of view, and protested, "in the name of religious liberty, against all infringement upon the rights and duties of Sabbath-keepers by such legislation." Another resolution declared that "total abstinence from the use of all intoxicating beverages is the imperative duty of every individual, and the suppression of the manufacture and sale of such beverages, by law, is the duty of the state." A committee was appointed to consider and develop a proper method for bringing about united action by the young people of the denomination in denominational work.

SOUTH CAROLINA. State Government.—The following were the State officers during the year: Governor, John P. Richardson, Democrat; Lieutenant-Governor, William L. Mauldin; Secretary of State, William Z. Leitner, who died early in the year and was succeeded by J. F. Marshall by appointment of the Governor; Treasurer, Isaac S. Bamberg; Comptroller-General, J. S. Verner, elected by the Legislature in December, 1887, to fill out the unexpired term of William E. Stoney, who resigned; Attorney-General, Joseph H. Earle; Superintendent of Education, James H. Rice; Commissioner of Agriculture, A. P. Butler; Chief-Justice of the Supreme Court, W. D. Simpson; Associate Justices, Henry McIver and Samuel McGowan.

Finance.—The revenues for the year ending Oct. 31, 1888, amounted to $1,163,218.21, not including the balance from the previous year of $104,385.05, and were derived from the following sources: Direct taxes, $582,611.78; phosphate royalty, $187,064.12; deficiency bonds and stock, $322,367.46: Department of Agriculture, $31,562.14; railroad assessment, $8,139.62. The annual interest charge on the State debt was $356,126.81. For all purposes the total expenditures were $1,190,482.63, leaving a balance in the treasury, Nov. 1, 1888, of $77,120.63. The personal property in the State was assessed for the year at $41,407,412, the real estate at $84,261,348, and railroad property at $16,317,394, aggregating $141,986,154. The State tax of five mills on this valuation yielded $709,784.91. The poll-tax is not uniformly collected, as the returns show only 1,576 polls in Charleston, while there were 6,089 in Spartansburg.

State Debt.—The deficiency bonds and stocks, which became due and payable on July 1 and amounted to $420,692.26, have been settled as follow: $20,962.26 were bought up and canceled by the Sinking-Fund Commission; $177,913.79 were exchanged for 4½-per-cent. bonds, under the act of the last General Assembly; and $216,898.48 was redeemed for cash realized from the sale of the 4½-per-cent. bonds, as authorized by the act, leaving a balance of $5,187.73 of bonds and stock yet to be redeemed in cash. The remaining portion of the State debt, which has been funded under the consolidation acts of 1873, 1878, and 1879, consists of consol. stocks, $2,161,140.26: consol. bonds, $3,841,000; and the Agricultural College stock, a permanent fund of $191,800. These amounts added to the 4½-per-cent. stock of $183,000 and 4½-per-cent. bonds of $217,000, together with the $5,187.73 deficiency bonds and stocks to be redeemed, makes the total funded debt $6,599,127.99. The 4½-per-cent. bonds, known in the State as "blue bonds," were advertised for sale in New York and London, but no bid having been received, the entire issue was purchased, in some cases at a premium, by citizens of South Carolina. The bonds redeemable in 1893 are selling at a premium.

Legislative Session.—The Legislature elected in November met on the 27th of that month. On Dec. 12 it re-elected United States Senator Matthew C. Butler. The pension act of 1887, which had proved so expensive to the State, was revised and amended, the annual sum available for pensions was limited to $50,000, and each pensioner allowed only $3 a month. An act to establish a home for disabled soldiers was defeated.

The railroad law was amended so as to give the railroad commissioners power to establish fares and rates, under certain limitations.

The State tax for general purposes was fixed at 5¼ mills for the ensuing year; a regular 2-mill tax for schools is also levied.

Almost contemporaneously with the opening of the session, the State Supreme Court, in the case of Floyd *vs.* Perrin, rendered an important decision, which nullified all acts theretofore done by townships in issuing bonds and assessing taxes for their payment to aid in the construction of railroads. The court decided that the act of 1882, and acts amendatory thereto, by which counties and townships were authorized to subscribe to the stock of railroad corporations, and for that purpose were declared to be bodies politic and corporate with necessary powers to carry out the provisions of the act, were in violation of that clause of the State Constitution which permits the grant to the corporate authorities of townships of the authority to assess taxes for corporate purposes. By this decision the liability of townships for over $900,000 of bonds issued by them was destroyed. As it was evidently unjust that these bonds, purchased in good faith by the bondholders, should be repudiated, several measures were introduced into the Legislature to restore the liability of the townships. After considerable discussion and much opposition, the Legislature finally passed an act declaring that where the railroad had already been constructed, the principal sum of the township bonds issued should be a debt of the township issuing them, for the payment of which with interest a tax might be levied. An important act to regulate and protect primary elections, based upon the New York law, was passed. The sum of $77,250, received from the United States for rent of and damage to the State Military Academy building by United States troops, was appropriated to public uses.

Education.—The total enrollment of school children for 1887-'88 was 193,434, an increase of 18,417 over the previous year. Of these children 103,334 were colored and 90,100 were white. The average attendance for the year was 139,557, an increase of 14,036 over 1886-'87. There were 4,203 teachers employed, receiving $381,837.31 in salaries—a gain of 209 in the number of teachers over the previous year, but a decrease of $3,419.41 in salaries; 2,611 teachers were white and 1,592 were colored; 2,242 were men and 1,961 women. In one county, Georgetown, there were no public schools during the year; twenty-one counties report an increase in the number of public schools and ten report a decrease. Eighty-six new school-houses were erected during the year at a cost of $31,486.22, so that the total number of school-houses is 3,280, valued at $435,455.36; 757 are log buildings, 1,856 frame buildings, and 33 brick or stone. The statement of receipts for school purposes dur-

ing the year were $466,619.78; the expenditures, $430,669.28.

The last session of the university was the first under the new system requiring payment of tuition fees. The attendance was large (170), and the number withdrawing during the year was smaller than ever before. At the end of the year 221 students were enrolled. Sixty-eight have asked for a remission of tuition fees. The university has 28 teachers. The expenses for 1887-'88 amounted to $50,230, of which $41,500 was paid in salaries.

Claflin College, devoted to the education of colored people, had an enrollment of 946, a large gain over any previous year, with 55 teachers and superintendents. The State appropriates $5,000 annually to this institution.

Militia.—Companies have been organized in every county in the State but three, and interest in military affairs is everywhere increasing. There are now 92 companies in the State, with 341 officers and 4,743 men. A movement has been made to uniform the troops with the regular United States Army uniform, which is furnished free by the General Government. Twelve companies have been so uniformed.

State Institutions.—The Penitentiary contained at the close of the year 894 convicts, of whom 843 were colored and 51 white. Of these 217 are at work on phosphate-mines near Summerville, 199 are employed on shoe and hosiery contracts inside the prison, and the others are at work on the farms connected with the institution. All the convicts are now being worked under the sole control and supervision of the officers of the Penitentiary, and are paid for by the contractors at a stated price per capita per day. The prison is on a self-supporting basis, and there was an excess of receipts over expenditures for the year of $3,444.23.

The State Lunatic Asylum has 680 inmates, an increase of 31 over 1887, of which 393 are white and 287 are colored. The present buildings are crowded. It is proposed to build a separate hospital for the colored insane.

There are 102 pupils in the Institution for the Deaf, Dumb, and Blind. Here, too, a separate school for colored children is proposed.

Pensions.—Under the act of 1887, providing a pension of five dollars a month for disabled Confederate soldiers and the widows of those killed in the Confederate service, an unexpectedly large number of claimants appeared. Up to September 30, 2,623 applications had been filed, of which the pension-board had approved 2,025, 1,492 being in favor of widows and 533 in favor of soldiers. In the payment of these approved claims the annual appropriation of $50,000 was not only expended, but the Governor, in accordance with the law, borrowed $50,000 additional, which was nearly exhausted at the close of the year.

Political.—A Republican State Convention met at Columbia on May 1, nominated delegates to the National Convention, and adopted a platform containing the following:

We declare the work and achievements of the Republican party are such as to commend it to the continued favor of the nation, and its mission will not be completed until all American citizens are protected at home as well as abroad, and a full ballot and a fair count make a solid South no longer possible.

We denounce the methods employed by the Democratic party in carrying elections in this State, and charge them as being responsible for the violence and intimidation which has suppressed the Republican vote.

While registration laws are usually intended to prevent fraud and to secure the free expression of the will of the people, the registration law of this State is plainly designed to facilitate fraud and suppress the will of the majority, and is on its face one of the most disgraceful acts ever placed upon the statutes of this or any other State.

We invoke the aid of the National Government to relieve us of this obnoxious law and demand of Congress to enact such legislation as shall secure a fair election at least for members of Congress and presidential electors.

On May 17, at the same place, the Democrats elected delegates to the St. Louis Convention, and adopted a short series of resolutions, approving the National Administration, the renomination of President Cleveland, tariff reform, and the message of the President on that subject, but omitting any reference to the Mill's Bill, the provisions of which relative to rice were not approved. A second Democratic State Convention met at Columbia on September 6 to nominate candidates for State officers. The renomination of Gov. Richardson was opposed by a considerable number of delegates, who united upon Attorney-General Joseph H. Earle as a candidate, but the Governor obtained nearly two thirds of the convention on the first ballot, and his nomination was made unanimous. The other State officers were also renominated. The resolutions reaffirm the National Democratic platforms of 1884 and 1888, without adverting to State issues. No nominating convention was held by the Republicans, and no State ticket supported by them, so that the Democratic ticket received the entire vote cast at the election in November. The Democrats elected every member of the State Senate (35 in all) and 121 out of 124 members of the Lower House, the three remaining members being Republicans. The Democratic national ticket was successful, and Democrats were elected in the seven congressional districts. In the Third, Fourth, and Fifth Districts there was no opposition to the Democratic candidate; in the First District the vote stood, Democratic 8,540, Republican 1,296; in the Second District, Democratic 10,704, Republican 1,405; in the Sixth District, Democratic 8,586, Republican 327; and in the Seventh District, Democratic 8,358, Republican 7,003.

The people voted at the same election upon two constitutional amendments—one extending the term of probate judges from two to four years, which was adopted by a vote of 26,806 yeas to 20,543 nays; the other abolishing the election of county school commissioners, which was rejected by a vote of 15,125 yeas to 33,457 nays.

SPAIN, a constitutional monarchy in Southwestern Europe. The present King is Alfonso XIII, posthumous son of Alfonso XII, born May 17, 1886. Queen Maria Christina, mother of the King, is Regent during the minority of her son. She was an Austrian princess, daughter of the late Archduke Karl Ferdinand.

The following ministers were in office at the beginning of 1888, having been appointed Nov. 27, 1885: Prime-Minister and President of the Council, Praxedes Mateo Sagasta; Minister of Foreign Affairs, Segismundo Moret; Minister of Finance, Joaquin Lopez Puigcerver; Minister of the Interior, José L. Albareda; Minister of Justice, Manuel Alonso Martinez; Minister of Agriculture and Public Works, Carlos Navarro Rodrigo; Minister of War, Manuel Cassola; Minister of Marine, Rafael Rodriguez de Arias; Minister of Colonies, Victor Balaguer.

The Army.—The peace establishment of the Spanish army was fixed by the resolution of the Cortes of April 14, 1887, at 131,400 men, of whom 100,000 were for service in the peninsula, 19,000 for Cuba, 8,700 for the Philippine Islands, and 3,700 for Porto Rico. The number of horses provided for is 16,495; the number of guns, 416. The war effective is 869,353 men, with 23,467 horses and 484 guns.

The Navy.—The fleet on Jan. 1, 1888, comprised 3 iron-clad frigates, 9 unarmored frigates and cruisers, 12 gun-boats, 6 avisos, 1 torpedo-catcher, 12 torpedo-boats, and 71 other vessels. There were under construction 1 armored frigate, 3 belted cruisers, 3 unarmored cruisers of the first class, 8 of the third class, and 2 torpedo-boats. A credit of 171,000,000 pesetas to be spent on the navy in the space of nine years was made conditional on all the ships being built in Spain from Spanish material. The Government in 1888 ordered 3 armored cruisers, of 7,000 tons each, and 3 torpedo gun-boats.

Commerce.—The total value of the imports in 1886 was 855,206,950 pesetas, against 764,758,000 pesetas in 1885; the value of the exports was 727,349,885 pesetas, against a total of 698,003,000 pesetas for the preceding year. The principal articles of import and their values were the following: Cotton and cotton goods, 73,136,042 pesetas; spirits, 63,614,684 pesetas; cereals and flour, 53,233,645 pesetas; tobacco, 48,133,521 pesetas; timber, 37,625,930 pesetas; sugar, 32,625,930 pesetas; wool and woolen goods, 27,606,381 pesetas; fish, 27,520,010 pesetas; hides and skins, 26,061,640 pesetas; coal, 26,033,681 pesetas; machinery, 20,902,194 pesetas; cattle, 20,409,521 pesetas; silk and silk goods, 18,186,885 pesetas; iron and manufactures of iron, 17,290,616 pesetas; hemp and flax, and their manufactures, 17,888,335 pesetas; chemicals, 15,851,813 pesetas; cocoa, 14,023,433 pesetas; all other articles, 320,629,218 pesetas. The principal exports and their values in 1886 were as follow: Wine, 334,816,652 pesetas; minerals, 61,849,023 pesetas; fruits, 59,520,923 pesetas; lead, copper, iron, and zinc

48,194,270 pesetas; cattle, 22,069,928 pesetas; cork, 17,671,091 pesetas; wool, 16,094,946 pesetas; oil, 14,358,312 pesetas; all other articles, 152,774,740 pesetas. Of 162,623,472 gallons of wine exported, 130,313,000 gallons went to France and 4,785,800 to England.

Railroads, Posts, and Telegraphs. — The total length of the railroads open to traffic at the beginning of 1887 was 9,309 kilometres, or 5,780 miles.

The number of letters forwarded in 1886 was 90,345,607; postal-cards, 332,054; samples and printed inclosures, 10,054,974; registered articles and letters, 1,243,537; money letters, 62,148. These figures do not include the international service, in which 11,955,213 letters, 38,461 postal-cards, 7,794,370 registered letters, and 13,356 money letters were sent or received. The receipts of the post-office were 16,577,417 francs; expenses, 9,515.468 francs.

The length of telegraph lines in 1887 was 18,419 kilometres, or 11,512 miles; length of wires, 46,187 kilometres, or 28,870 miles. The number of dispatches in 1886 was 3,549,860, of which one fourth were international.

Political Crisis. — The Sagasta ministry found itself compelled in 1888, to do something to redeem its pledges in regard to the long-promised political reforms, lest it should be overturned by the Democrats, although at the imminent risk of defeat through the defection of the Ministerial Right. The Minister of Justice accordingly brought in a bill to introduce trial by jury. Canovas del Castillo met it with a proposition to raise the grain duties, asserting that the agricultural crisis demanded the first attention. The Conservative bill to impose a supplementary duty on cereals was defeated in Congress on January 9, by 133 votes against 60. In February the party in power was upheld by Castelar, the leader of the Possibilists or Conservative Republicans, in a great speech in which, without formally renouncing Republicanism, he accepted the existing frame of government, including the union of Church and state, as the most suitable for Spain, and declared that as soon as the ministry had carried out its scheme of Democratic reforms he would bid farewell to public life and devote his remaining years to a "History of Spain." The official corruption and despotic misrule of the colonies, especially Cuba and Porto Rico, afforded Gen. Salamanca—whose appointment as Governor-General of Cuba had been canceled—and the opponents of the Government an opportunity to charge the ministers with apathy, weakness, and indifference to official immorality, and to condemn as futile a commission that was appointed to investigate colonial administrations; yet the discussion of colonial wrongs awakened, as ever, very little interest. The Protectionist agitation caused the greatest difficulties that the ministry had to contend with. The commercial and agricultural crisis was made use of by politicians, who organized an Agrarian League, at the head of which stood the Liberal ex-Minister of the Colonies Gamazo. This movement divided the ministerial majority, attracted Reformists like Romero y Robledo and Montillo, was supported by Canovas, Villaverde, and the rest of the Conservatives, and even obtained the support of Muro and other Republicans. The Cabinet met the demands of the Agrarian League with partial concessions, agreeing to take off 18,000,000 pesetas of the land-taxes, whereas the agriculturists asked for a reduction of 50,000,000 pesetas, promising to secure lower rates on the railroads for agricultural and mineral produce, and accepting the proposition to spend large sums on public works. The main demand for higher duties, however, the Premier declared, could not be granted without a violation of national faith, because the slight reductions of which Spanish manufacturers and farmers complained were made in pursuance of treaty obligations entered into with twenty different nations in the course of the last twenty years. The Reformist party which contested the succession to the tottering Sagasta ministry with the Conservatives, was disrupted in the spring by the secession of Lopez Dominguez, the founder of the party, and of his powerful military following, leaving its parliamentary leader, Romero y Robledo, at the head of a remnant that was no better than a political group. Gen. Lopez Dominguez organized a new group, called by the name of Monarchical Democrats, to advocate the old programme which Romero y Robledo had not faithfully observed.

The ministerial crisis had lasted almost a year when the resignation of the Cabinet took place as the result of a trivial question of military etiquette. The Queen had left Madrid for an excursion to Valencia, which the Minister of Justice insisted on her making according to the published arrangement, lest the postponement should be construed as a sign of fear of the Zorillist Republicans, who had convoked a mass meeting in the same city. The Infanta Isabel, who was left to represent her, decided to take a journey also, and informed Gen. Martinez Campos that her sister, the Infanta Eulalie, would give out the military watchword. The Military Governor of Madrid replied that the married infanta was not legally competent to perform that office, and that it was impossible, according to military rules, for him to receive the parole from her husband, Prince Antonio, Duc de Montpensier, who was only a captain in rank. The Minister of War, who was not on good terms with the Captain-General, sent a brusque telegram ordering him to receive the pass-word from the Princess Eulalie, whereupon Gen. Campos offered his resignation. All attempts to accommodate the quarrel failed, and as the majority of the Cabinet sided with the Captain-General, Gen. Cassola and the ministers who had supported his view resigned their portfolios. Señor Sagasta handed in the resignation of the entire Cabinet to the Queen Regent, who requested him to form a new ministry. In the reconstructed Cabinet the Marques de la Vega de Armijo, who was Minister of the Exterior in 1881-'83, resumed that office, Señor Moret, who had held the portfolio, exchanging it for that of the Interior. Señores Puigcerver, Martinez, and Rodriguez, remained at the head of the Ministries of Finance, Justice, and Marine. Señor Ruiz Capdepon entered the Cabinet as Minister of the Colonies, and Señor Canalejas y Mendez as Minister of Commerce. Gen. Cassola was succeeded as Minister of War by Gen. O'Ryan, the director of infantry, who had never before held a political office.

The question of military reform brought the generals again to the front in Spanish politics, destroying the discipline which had been cultivated since the accession of Alfonso XII. A Democratic reform of the army was the demand of the progressive wing of the Ministerial party, which was led by Martos, President of the Chamber, and represented in the Cabinet by Moret, Puigcerver, Capdepon, and Canalejas. For fiscal, as well as for political and military reasons, it was desirable to reduce the peace establishment which has an officer for every half-dozen soldiers. Gen. Cassola elaborated a plan which was under discussion for a full year. It met with such opposition that he was driven from office before the Cortes could come to a decision. Gen. Lopez Dominguez and Gen. Martinez Campos had other plans of reform. The Government created a dangerous situation by announcing just before the separation of the Cortes in July the intention of enacting reforms by royal decree during the recess. Gen. O'Ryan who was expected to carry out Cassola's scheme, inclined rather to that of Martinez Campos, which was a virtual abandonment of army regeneration. The army officers divided into parties supporting Cassola, Campos, Lopez Dominguez, and the Government respectively. The friends of Gen. Cassola, who had never led a political group before his dismissal, subscribed money to have his reform project printed as a testimonial, and arranged political demonstrations which the Government attempted to suppress, placing officers under arrest for such breaches of discipline. Gen. Cassola entered into a coalition with Gen. Lopez Dominguez, whose persistent agitation for army reform had compelled Sagasta to promise such a measure, and who had demanded a more radical reform than was embodied in the bills of Gen. Cassola and his predecessor, Gen. Castillo. The Democratic members of the Cabinet urged the promulgation of reform measures by Executive orders, but were defeated in a Cabinet council on October 21, when it was decided to call the Cortes together in November, and re-submit the project for legislative action. After the opening of the Cortes, a conference was held with all interested parties, at which it was decided to withdraw the military reform bill,

and bring the matter before the Cortes in a revised form. But immediately afterward the Premier was goaded by the Opposition into an announcement that Cassola's bill and all other unfinished legislation would be revised. Gen. O'Ryan tendered his resignation. At the election of the Budget Committee, the dissentient Liberals and Protectionists who follow the lead of Gamazo and Montero Rios, carried two fifths of the seats, and were only prevented from gaining a majority by groups of the regular Opposition, notably the followers of Castelar and Romero y Robledo, who came to the support of the ministry. Señor Sagasta, in consequence of this moral defeat, on December 8 placed the resignations of all the members of the Cabinet in the hands of the Queen, who invited him to constitute another ministry. Gen. O'Ryan and Señores Moret, Alonso Martinez, and Puigcerver, were determined not to resume office. The Minister of Marine, who had sustained the course of Gen. O'Ryan, also retired. The list of the new ministry was published on December 10. The Marques de la Vega de Armijo, retained the portfolio of Foreign Affairs, and Señor Canalejas remained Minister of Commerce. Señor Ruiz Capdepon took the portfolio of the Interior, being succeeded as Minister of the Colonies by Señor Becerra. The other new Ministers were Venancio Gonzalez, of the Department of Finance; Count Xiquena, Minister of War; Gen. Chinchilla, Minister of War; and Admiral Arias, Minister of Marine.

Legislation.—Among the reforms promised by the Sagasta ministry were trial by jury, civil marriage, and universal military service. The bill introducing jury trials was passed, and was signed by the Queen-Regent in March, 1888. The civil-marriage law, which was framed with the design of meeting all the objections of the Clericals, fails entirely to satisfy the Radicals. The sanction of the clergy is as necessary as before for mixed marriages, and free-thinkers of Catholic birth are still required to go through the religious ceremony in order to be legally married, since the new law prescribes that every Catholic must be married in church, and that this marriage is valid in all civil relations. The latter provision annuls the only innovation in the new law, which provides that a Government official shall be present at the ceremony, whose duty it is to have the marriage properly registered, because the marriage is legal even if the registration is for any reason evaded. The principle of the bill was agreed upon in negotiations between the Government and the Vatican before it was presented to the Cortes, and when a paragraph was added to the effect that marriages of Spanish subjects abroad could be contracted according to the custom of the country in which they take place the Vatican objected, and it was stricken out.

The bill introducing trial by jury was agreed to by both Houses on March 26. The jury law withholds for the present from the juries about thirty crimes and punishable offenses, or two thirds of the entire number on the statute-books. The election of jurors was fixed for January, 1889, and the juries will begin their functions throughout the kingdom in the following April. The establishment of trial by jury is regarded with great satisfaction by the majority of Spaniards because the administration of justice by judges who are the creatures of politicians has been often scandalously partial and has brought the law and the courts into contempt.

In the financial legislation for 1888, Señor Puigcerver was called upon to obtain a larger revenue, and at the same time to remit a part of the land-tax in order to relieve the agricultural depression caused by the fall in the prices of grain and diminished exports of cattle. Heavy taxes on imported spirits met the approval of all the chambers of commerce, as they served the double purpose of increasing the receipts of the treasury and of discouraging the manufacture of artificial wine, and thus promoting vine-culture. The spirits used in imitation and fortified wines are mostly German potato brandy. The new tax is a consumption duty on all spirits, foreign and domestic, ranging from 80 pesetas per hectolitre for qualities containing less than 60 per cent. of pure alcohol to 120 pesetas for these above 80 per cent. The wine-growers demanded the prohibition of imports, and in their interest the Cortes passed a law against the manufacture of spurious wines, in pursuance of which many factories were closed and the manufactured stock was destroyed. In attempting to collect the new tax on spirits the revenue officials encountered in all the large towns the resistance of the distillers, who organized indignation meetings and appointed a committee to arrange with the Government for changes in the law. At Tarragona, where there are large distilleries, the populace rose against the police and revenue collectors, stoned them, and raised barricades. To prevent serious disturbances the Government suspended the collection of the duties. The largest distillery in that town is a Swedish concern on behalf of which the Swedish Government raised a protest. In Saragossa, Barcelona, and Madrid, the manufacturers, liquor merchants, and retailers refused to pay the tax on their stock in trade, and threatened to close up their establishments if the Government insisted on the payment. The Minister of Finance finally yielded and agreed with the deputations from Tarragona, Barcelona, Reus, and other cities that the tax on pure alcohol should be collected, but not on manufactured wines; that the tax on spirits of all kinds should be remitted if the municipal authorities of any town demand it; and that the cost of excise licenses should be graduated according to the density of population.

Elevation to a Great Power.—Germany has gone out of her way to show diplomatic courtesies to monarchical Spain, and aimed to be the sponsor who would help Spain to regain her former place in the European councils, partly with the object of attracting the good will of Spain and of gaining her moral support or definite adhesion to the Central European league, and partly in order to enable her to assert her pretensions to Morocco, and thus prevent the French and English from establishing themselves in that country, and gaining control of the road to the Suez Canal. In 1881 Germany invited Spain to take part in the conference of the great powers for the regulation of the Suez Canal. Spanish pride and antipathy, especially on the part of the Liberals, toward the "hereditary foe of the Latin nations" defeated the purpose of the patronizing courtesies. The consequences of the indiscreet nomination of Alfonso XII to the colonelcy of the Uhlan regiment in Strasburg, and, the feeling roused by the Caroline Islands dispute, caused the Government to abandon the purpose of raising the Berlin legation to the rank of an embassy after the visit of the German Crown-Prince in 1885, although the permission of the Cortes had been obtained, lest it should be construed as a sign of a political treaty. The allied monarchical powers are especially interested in preventing the establishment of a republic in Spain, and since 1885 a secret agreement for this end has subsisted between them. The matter of raising the rank of ministers to that of ambassadors was allowed to rest until 1887, when Spain called the Morocco conference, where it was desirable that she should appear as a great power. The authorization of the Cortes was obtained, and by the royal decree of Dec. 27, 1887. the ministries at Berlin, London, Vienna, and Rome were changed into embassies. In January, 1888, the representatives of these four great powers at Madrid presented their credentials as ambassadors.

It was the opposite of a *rapprochement* with Germany that Señor Moret and his colleagues had in view when they invested Spain with the outward rank of a great power. They hoped to see their country take the lead in the Latin League, comprising Spain, France, Belgium, and Italy, with the Spanish republics of South and Central America, over which the supremacy of the mother-country would again be asserted when Spain, strengthened by the acquisition of Morocco, should be restored to a leading position among the powers of Europe. The alliance, which is the dream of Spanish statesmen, is to be directed against Germany's predominance in Europe and the expansion of the Germanic races in all parts of the world. Count Benomar, the Spanish ambassador at Berlin, disclosed to Prince Bismarck communications of Anti-German tenor, intended only for his own instruction, revealing this secret aim of Spanish policy, and for this offense was abruptly recalled in the autumn of 1888.

Labor-Riots.—The farmers and land-owners in the province of Huelva, adjacent to the mining district of Rio Tinto, complained that the process of roasting copper-ore in the open air was injurious to the health of the people, as the sulphurous fumes poisoned the air for a wide distance. The mines had been sold in 1873 for 92,800,000 pesetas by the Government to an English company, which had developed an industry that gave employment to 12,000 work - people. The Government appointed a commission, and at the request of the local officials issued a provisional edict forbidding the open-air process of calcination pending the investigation. The mining company entered a protest, which was supported by the English ambassador, and when the Government declined to rescind the order the managers cut down wages and discharged a part of the force of laborers. This led to a general strike and tumultuous demonstrations. The miners demanded not only the restoration of the old scale of wages, but the shortening of the hours of work in their deadly occupation as a preventive of mortality. The Government ordered out the military, and in a collision on February 4 the troops were ordered to fire, and poured a volley into the unarmed crowd. There were 230 persons hit, and 50 were killed, whose blood "sprinkled the ministerial bench." Romero Robledo declared in moving a vote of censure, which received only 19 votes against 176. A royal decree was issued in accordance with the conclusions of the commission on March 1 for the gradual abolition before 1891 of open-air calcinations. This decision, contravening the contract with the company and the law of Dec. 17, 1873, it is feared will ruin the industry and give cause for claims against the Government.

The Barcelona Exhibition.—An international industrial exhibition, opened on April 7, 1888, was planned on a large scale, and proved moderately successful notwithstanding the large number of similar exhibitions that were held in Europe, and the critical economical and political conditions existing in Spain.

When Queen Christina visited the National Exhibition at Barcelona in May, the naval powers of Europe united in a demonstration in her honor in the harbor, where the greater part of the Spanish fleet was also assembled. The Italian navy was represented by the "Italia," " Duilio," and other great ships; the French by the "Colbert," "Amiral Dupret," "Courbet," and other formidable iron-clads; Great Britain by the Mediterranean squadron under the command of the Duke of Edinburgh; Austria-Hungary by an imposing detachment; Germany by the "Kaiser"; and the United States, Russia, the Netherlands, and Portugal by representatives from their respective fleets.

Colonies.—The colonial possessions of Spain comprise Cuba, with 118,833 square kilometres of territory and 1,521,684 inhabitants; Porto Rico, with an area of 9,620 square kilometres and 754,313 inhabitants in 1880; the Philippine Islands, having an area of 293,726 square kilometres and 5,559,020 inhabitants; the Sulu Islands, 2,456 square kilometres in extent, and

containing a population of about 75,000; the Mariana Islands, with an area of 1,140 square kilometres and a population of 8,665; the Carolines, 700 square kilometres in extent, with 22,000 inhabitants; the Palaos Islands, 750 square kilometres in extent, with a population of about 14,000 souls; Fernando Po, Elobey, Annobom, and the territory of San Juan, on the coast of Guinea, having an aggregate area of 2,203 square kilometres and 68,656 inhabitants; and the Western Sahara, between Cape Bojador and Cape Blanco, with the territory of Ifni and other districts on the west coast of Africa. The extent and population of these latter possessions are not known, except in the case of the barren Saharan, where her coast-line is 1,300 kilometres, and her claim extends 400 kilometres into the interior. The territory at Coresco Bay, on the French Gaboon, is 24,-960 square kilometres in extent. Spain also claims the little district of Spri, at Cape Nun. The strip of coast in Assab Bay, between Ras Garibal and Ras Macama, on which there is a commodious harbor, has been leased from Italy as a coaling-station for fifteen years.

In March extensive districts in the Sulu Archipelago were occupied, but not without a sharp conflict, during which many of the natives and several Spaniards were slain.

SUNDAY LEGISLATION. The Roman Empire established religion by entering into a contract with the gods through its official representatives. Worship, therefore, consisted of ceremonies, prayers, sacrifices, and games, through which the people fulfilled their part of this contract. The state maintained colleges of sacred lore, which determined all matters connected with religion. The most important of these was the College of Pontifices. The Emperor stood at the head of this as *Pontifex Maximus*, and had full power to decide "what days were suitable for the transaction of business, public or private, and what were not." The Oriental sun-worship cultus, Mithraicism, was widely prevalent and extremely popular in the Roman Empire about the beginning of the Christian era. It was for a long time a dangerous and a well-nigh successful competitor for the controlling religious influence throughout the empire. The evidences of this worship are still associated with the ruins of all the principal military stations that sprung up in the course of the Roman conquest of Europe. The division of days into judicial and non-judicial was an established custom under the original pagan cultus of the empire. This custom was enlarged and intensified by the influence of Mithraicism, in which the sun's day occupied a prominent place. Even before the age of Augustus the number of days on which no trials could take place at Rome, because of reverence to the gods to whom these days were consecrated, had become a means by which wealthy criminals evaded justice; and Suetonius sets it down as a praiseworthy act on the part of Augustus that he rejected thirty days from that number in order that business might not be impeded and crime might not go unpunished. The ferial system also included the forbidding of various kinds of labor on the days consecrated by religious observances. This system and these practices antedate Christianity.

Constantine, like his predecessors, was a devotee of the sun god, and he favored all influences and used all measures to establish himself as supreme ruler. While he was thus struggling for the supremacy, Sunday legislation first appeared (321 A. D.). The pagan character of this first legislation is shown by the law and its associations. There is nothing in contemporaneous history to indicate that such legislation was desired or sought by the people of the empire or by any class thereof. On the contrary, everything shows that these edicts sprung from the will of the Emperor alone. In 386 A. D. legislation was renewed, forbidding shows and litigation on Sunday, and then, for the first time, the term "Lord's Day," was used as the counterpart of Sunday.

In the middle ages almost all questions of religious duty and of ecclesiastical organization were subject to civil control. The ecclesiastico-civil authority claimed the prerogative of legislating on religious questions, after the manner of the Jewish theocracy. Hence there are several points of analogy between the Sunday legislation of the middle ages and the Sabbath legislation of the Mosaic period. Legislation fixed sacred time from noon on Saturday until sunrise on Monday; and during the latter part of the middle-age period those who dared to disobey such requirements were coerced by additional commands, which, it was claimed, were furnished by direct interposition of Heaven.

The Saxon legislation was much like the middle-age legislation of Southern Europe. It began as early as 688 A. D. under Ina, King of Wessex. It divided the punishment for working on Sunday between the slave, the master who required work of him, and the freeman who worked from his own choice. The sacred time sometimes began with sunset on Saturday and ended with sunset on Sunday, known as "Monday eve." In some instances, as under Edgar, 959–975 A. D., it extended from noon on Saturday until daylight on Monday.

The English Sunday laws were a continuation and expansion of the Saxon laws, and, like these, were the product of the original Roman legislation. In 1281, under Edward I, an attempt was made to eliminate the Jewish theocratic idea. The showing of wool in the market was forbidden under Edward III in 1354. Islip, Archbishop of Canterbury, in 1359 enlarged the prohibitions and requirements with reference to Sunday and other church-appointed days. Marketing, and fairs for the sale of goods, which seem to have been held in and about church-buildings and cemeteries, were forbidden on Sunday and other

festivals, under Thorsby, Archbishop of York, in 1357 A. D.; while "unlawful games on Sundays and other festivals" were prohibited under Henry IV in 1409 A. D. Fairs and markets, which evidently increased rather than diminished, were especially inveighed against under Henry VI in 1448. The sale of goods by "cobblers and cordwainers in the city of London," excepting in certain localities, was forbidden "on Sunday and other festivals," in 1464. In 1547, under Edward VI, more stringent regulations concerning religious worship on Sunday were introduced. In 1552 he issued "an act for the keeping holy days and fast days," which included a large number of days and made many strict prohibitions. The "Injunctions of Elizabeth" created a stricter legislation, and made special provision for the appointment of "discreet men to see that all the parishioners duly resort to their churches upon Sundays and all holy days," and to punish neglect thereof. The spread of the Puritanic element in England, which urged this stricter legislation, was opposed by the "Book of Sports," first published by James I in 1618, and republished by Charles I in 1633. This declaration set aside much of the stricter legislation that preceded it, and favored the ruder and irreligious habits of the masses.

The Sunday legislation in England that was peculiarly Puritanic, dates from 1640 to 1660. The Sunday laws passed during the Puritan supremacy, were at once civil enactments and theological treatises. In strictness of requirement, extent of application, special features, regulations, and provisions, these laws are in strong contrast with nearly all that preceded them. They form a curious and interesting epoch in the history of Sunday legislation. They were prefaced by the complaint that Sunday was little regarded as a sacred day, and was wickedly desecrated by business and recreation. They forbade all secular business, traveling, and recreation, in careful detail. They specified minutely in all particulars, and instituted a rigid system of police supervision and of punishment. The dates of the long and prominent laws under Cromwell are 1644, 1650, and 1656. In connection with these laws, and in the more stringent laws enacted before and after the Cromwellian supremacy, excise regulations concerning drinking-shops were prominent.

Sunday legislation in Scotland appeared under James I in 1424; the main feature of the first law being a requirement that all men practice themselves in archery in connection with their attendance upon parish churches on "holy days," under penalty of fine. This was in the interest of military service. In 1469, under James III, special legislation forbade moving, collecting of rents, etc., on holy days. Next came the forbidding of fairs and markets, in 1503. From this time Sunday legislation increased in strictness, being in its general characteristics like that of England, and allied to that of the Cromwellian period. This legislation also included "legal fast days," as early as 1693. Many of these Scotch laws are still in force.

The first Sunday law in America was enacted in Virginia, previous to 1623. It punished absence from church service on Sunday, without excuse, by the forfeiture of fifty pounds of tobacco. But the representative and most important type of Sunday legislation during the colonial period, appeared in the New England colonies. The early government of these colonies was theocratic, after the Jewish model; and all Sunday legislation was analogous to, or identical with, the Mosaic legislation concerning the Sabbath (Saturday). This legislation began in the Plymouth Colony as early as 1650, previous to which time the common law of England was regnant in the colonies. All this colonial legislation was emphatically religious. The usual punishments were fine, imprisonment, whipping, caging, and setting in the stocks. This legislation forbade servile work, and even the simplest forms of recreation, not excepting "walking in the streets or fields after sunset on Saturday night, and before sunset on Sunday." It also required attendance on such public worship as was legally established, and forbade all other. Police regulations were rigidly enforced. Sunday excise legislation began in the Plymouth Colony as early as 1662. By a law enacted in that year at Plymouth, those having occasion to travel, "in case of danger of death, or such necessitous occasion," were to receive a ticket from one appointed for that purpose, without which the traveler was liable to arrest by any person. Servile work and sports were also forbidden on days of public fasting, prayer, and thanksgiving. In 1665, in the Plymouth Colony, sleeping in church was forbidden, under penalty of being admonished for the first offense, set in the stocks for the second, and being reported to the court for further punishment if this did not reclaim. In 1669 sleeping and playing outside the building, and near the meeting-house, were also forbidden, under penalty. A fine of twelve-pence was inflicted upon "any person or persons that shall be found smoking of tobacco on the Lord's Day, going to or coming from the meetings, within two miles of the meeting-house."

The first Sunday legislation in the Massachusetts Bay Colony was in 1629. This ordered the cessation of all labor on "every Saturday throughout the year, at three of the clock in the afternoon," and the spending of the rest of that day in "catechizing and preparation for the Sabbath, as the ministers shall direct." In 1644, among the answers of the reverend elders to certain questions propounded to them, they agreed that "any sin committed with a high hand, as the gathering of sticks on the Sabbath-day, may be punished with death, when a lesser punishment might serve for gathering sticks privily and in some need."

The first draft of certain laws for this colony made "profaning the Lord's Day, in a careless or scornful neglect or contempt thereof," a capital crime. This form of the law was erased from the code as finally adopted. In 1679 the General Court at Boston set a special guard "from sunset on Saturday night until nine of the clock or after, between the fortification and the town's end," with instructions not to permit any cart, footman, or horseman to pass out of the town, except upon such necessity as the guard deemed sufficient. Those who disregarded the challenge of the guard were proceeded against as "Sabbath-breakers."

Sunday legislation in the New Haven Colony began in 1647. It forbade all work from sunset to sunset, with punishment according to the judgment of the court. About this time, also, profaning Sunday, "either by sinful, servile work, unlawful sports, or careless neglect, was punished by fine, imprisonment, or whipping," and upon evidence that the "sin was proudly, presumptuously, and with a high hand committed, against the known authority of the blessed God, such a person therein disobeying and reproaching the Lord shall be put to death, that all others may fear and shun such provoking and rebellious courses." In the colony of Connecticut there were at first no special statutes concerning Sunday. The code of 1650 punished burglary or theft, "in the fields or in the house, on the Lord's Day," by the loss of one ear for the first offense, and the second ear for the second offense. For the third offense, "he shall be put to death." These requirements were often repeated, being enlarged or changed in minor particulars.

Sunday legislation in the colony of Rhode Island was less severe than in those already noticed; but there was a general prohibition of labor, gaming, shooting, drinking, etc. In the colony of New Netherlands (New York) in 1647, the dictator issued a proclamation against "Sabbath-breaking, brawling, and drunkenness." In the colony of Pennsylvania the early Sunday legislation was much more lenient than in New England. Virginia led in Sunday legislation, although that legislation never reached such extreme features as were common in New England. The Sunday laws of New England were not a dead letter; many examples of punishment for "Sabbath-breaking" are on record, while the majority of cases were tried in the lower courts, concerning which no record remains.

The Sunday laws of the colonial period passed into the legislation of the States, but in most instances were considerably modified. Naturally the Eastern States, where colonial influences had been strongest, retained more of the rigid features of the earlier laws. The influences connected with the Revolutionary War diminished religious regard for Sunday in no small degree, and the stricter features were gradually eliminated from subsequent legislation. The Sunday laws of the Western and

Southwestern States are slight in extent and mild in requirements, when compared with earlier legislation. This is still more marked in the Territories. Arizona has no Sunday laws, and Colorado and Wyoming scarcely more than fragments; while the former law of California, though mild, was wholly repealed in 1883. Louisiana had no Sunday law until 1886, and the original law of Massachusetts was so amended in 1887 as to make it extremely liberal. In general, the Sunday laws forbid ordinary employment—works of necessity and mercy excepted—and in a greater or less degree, sporting, gaming, fishing, and hunting. But the legal status of Sunday in the States is very different from the actual. For many years past, the Sunday laws have been nearly or quite inoperative. Aside from excise legislation, little is done to enforce existing laws. All serious efforts to do so, even against liquor-selling, have, in most instances, been checkmated by the attempt to enforce the provisions against traveling, and other secular occupations that have become almost universal. Thus opposed, those who have sought to enforce the law in one particular have soon desisted, and the execution of the law has failed. The history of this practical decline in the execution of our Sunday laws shows a marked change in the public opinion concerning the religious status of the Sunday; nor can any one seeking to analyze the causes that have produced the history here outlined, make such analysis successfully without a careful and extended consideration of the religious features of the case.

For more than twenty years past preparation has been made for an epoch in the history of Sunday legislation in the United States, which has appeared, definitely, within the current year. The National Reform Association, organized to secure a recognition of the name and authority of God and Christ in the national Constitution, has included in its mission the work of reviving and securing the better enforcement of existing Sunday laws, and the enactment of more stringent ones. The National Women's Christian Temperance Union has lately entered into this movement with great zeal; and, still later, individuals in religious circles have joined in the movement, by organizing "The American Sabbath Union." In May, 1888, a bill was introduced into Congress by Senator Blair, of New Hampshire, proposing national legislation which forbids all secular business and work on Sunday, in all places under the control of Congress, such as the postal service, the army and navy, the Territories, and in interstate commerce. At the present writing this bill is in the hands of a committee which has granted two public hearings to the advocates of the bill, in one of which the opponents of the bill were also recognized. This movement is a radical departure from the historical policy of the United States concerning Sunday legislation. The friends of the bill claim that it is necessary,

since State legislation is of little value, while the nation, in its corporate capacity through the Post-Office Department and otherwise, continues "to be the greatest Sabbath-breaker"; that State laws against commerce and traveling are insufficient, and hence Sunday legislation must continue to be a failure, unless Congress assumes control of all such matters, under the general provisions of the interstate commerce act. The history of this movement includes two prominent features. It involves more extended efforts, and more nearly national organization in its favor, among the religious people of the United States than any similar movement in the history of the nation. Through their efforts, the "the workingmen," so-called, and especially representative organizations in which these are combined, are petitioning Congress for the passage of the bill. The friends of this movement claim that the Roman Catholics of the United States have united with Protestants in support of the Blair Bill. Those who advocate its passage on religious grounds, insist that they do not wish to deal with religion directly, but desire the passage of the law for its indirect effect. Nevertheless, the bill avows a distinctly religious character, as is shown by its title: "A bill to secure to the people the enjoyment of the first day of the week, commonly known as the Lord's Day, as a day of rest, and to promote its observance as a day of religious worship." The history of this movement also includes an unprecedented interest and agitation on the part of the people in the various phases of the Sunday question. The Blair Sunday-Rest bill expired in the hands of the Committee, in March, 1889.

It is impossible to trace the results of Sunday legislation in detail in different periods; but some general results appear in the successive laws. Prominent among these is the fact that legislation has not secured religious regard for Sunday. Neither has legislation been strictly enforced and sustained in any period when there was not high religious regard for Sunday. The general effect has been, rather, the development of Sunday as a holiday; the character of this holiday varying with the state of civilization, refinement, and general culture. The verdict on this point, as shown in the results connected with the stringent legislation of the Puritan period, both in Great Britain and in the United States, is emphatic and important. Such legislation has always been lightly regarded by the irreligious. In spite of all stringent legislation, the strictness required under the Puritan régime declined rapidly in England, and steadily, though perhaps a little less rapidly, in the New England colonies, where such legislation passed through a searching historic test. In many instances the history of Sunday legislation shows that enforced abstinence from legitimate business has increased objectionable holidayism on the part of the irreligious. Another fact is clearly set forth in the history of this legislation, especially in modern times, viz., that the more carefully men have studied the history of such legislation and its philosophy, the less eager have they been in its support; if, indeed, they have not wholly discarded it. The discussions of the past few years, and in some instances the decisions of courts, have sought a new basis for Sunday legislation in the needs of society and of individuals, apart from religious considerations. Many now deny the right of the civil law to touch Sunday in any way as a religious institution, and admit only the right to consider it as a legal holiday, on hygienic and economic grounds. See Irmischer's "State and Church Ordinances concerning the Christian Observances of Sunday" (Erlangen, 1839), and Lewis's "Critical History of Sunday Legislation from 321 to 1888" (New York, 1888).

SURGERY. While the advance in the science of surgery during the past three years has been great, it has not been due to the addition of many new ideas, but rather to the development of some already suggested and partly tested.

Bacteriology.—The study of bacteria, or the germs of disease, has been pursued vigorously. Many troubles belonging to the domain of surgery are directly caused by these organisms, and by their exclusion or destruction prevention or cure is accomplished. The following surgical diseases are proved to be due to microbes, and their peculiar forms of bacteria are so well known that the diagnosis can be made from them alone: The various forms of tuberculosis or scrofula, septicæmia or pyæmia, anthrax or malignant pustule, suppurative inflammation (abscess), gonorrhœa, glanders, and hydrophobia. Many other diseases are presumed to have the same origin, but we must wait for proof positive. Cancer and syphilis are among these latter. While there can be little doubt that their peculiar bacteria have been discovered, that fact has not yet been placed beyond a question. The antiseptic method is founded on the germ theory, and neglect of it on the one hand, or strict observance on the other, will furnish ample proof of the correctness of the theory.

Anæsthetics.—Many new substances have been tested, but a good anæsthetic has not been added to the list. Cocaine has been extensively experimented with, and has proved very valuable. It has aided greatly in the study and treatment of diseases of the eye and the throat. It is extremely useful in small surgical operations and in dressings. For instance, abscesses, felons, small tumors, etc., may be operated upon painlessly by its aid, and irritable wounds may be dressed without discomfort. When it can be employed it possesses a great advantage, as its effect is local and transient, and we can have the intelligent co-operation of the patient.

Antiseptics.—In general, our methods of securing an aseptic condition have not changed. By aseptic is understood freedom from germs of disease that cause inflammation, blood-poisoning, and similar conditions. It is chemical and microscopic cleanliness. The weak solution of corrosive sublimate ($\frac{1}{2000}$), carbolic acid, and heat (for the instruments and dressings), are the chief agents employed. A new substance called creoline is being tested, and has shown excellent results. It is a coal-tar product. The advance in this connection has been a more general knowledge of its importance and a more universal adoption of its use.

Abdomen.—In surgery of the abdomen the greatest advance in medical science has been made. By the careful use of antiseptic measures the operation known as laparotomy, or opening the abdominal cavity, is so free from danger that the patient is put to scarcely any risk, and we are therefore able to treat successfully and safely many diseases and accidents that formerly would have been hopeless. The past three years have added little that is entirely new in this connection, but there has been great improvement in operative technique, and consequently much better statistics as to results.

The most important operations are: 1. Gastrotomy, or opening the stomach for the removal of foreign bodies. 2. Gastrorrhaphy, or sewing wounds of the stomach-wall. 3. Digital dilatation of the intestinal end of the stomach, done by forcing the finger through the opening to the intestine without cutting (except the laparotomy). The intestine is inverted over the end of the finger, and the constriction is dilated. This is done in cases of stricture due to cancer or to scar following ulceration. 4. Gastro-enterostomy, or joining the intestine to the side of the stomach and making a communication between them, so that the food shall pass through the new opening. This is done for cancer at the lower end of the stomach or at the upper end of the bowel. 5. Removing intestinal obstruction, which may be due to any one of several causes, such as twisting or knotting of the bowel, telescoping of a portion of the intestine within itself, constriction due to matting together of the bowels by inflammation, impaction of foreign bodies, often gall-stones, etc. 6. Resection or removal of a diseased portion of the intestine in cases of cancer, gangrene, extensive wound, typhoidal ulceration causing peritonitis, etc. 7. Enterorrhaphy, or sewing of wounds of intestine. 8. Entero-enterostomy, or making a direct communication between two portions of the intestine, so that their contents shall pass through the new opening and avoid the intervening diseased part of the bowel. This is done in case of cancer. 9. Abscesses or cystic tumors of the liver may be opened and cured. The laparotomy is done, and the wall of the abscess or cyst is sewed to the abdominal wall, and not opened till the third day. By that time firm union takes place, and there can be no leakage into the abdominal cavity. 10. The gall-bladder may be opened (cholecystotomy), and accumulated gall - stones removed. Peritonitis is treated surgically. Laparotomy is performed, and the cause removed. A frequent cause of peritonitis, and one that is often cured, is perforation of the vermiform appendix, due to ulceration or gangrene. The diseased appendix is removed, then the abdominal cavity is disinfected by washing, carefully dried, and closed. This is also done in peritonitis from other causes. Hæmorrhage from an abdominal organ, following disease or accident, may be arrested. Laparotomy is performed, and the bleeding vessel ligated. Tumors of many of the organs may be removed, especially those of the uterus and ovaries. The uterus and ovaries may be removed when diseased. All the above-named operations are done frequently and with good results. An important innovation in this connection is the device known as Senn's absorbable plates, used for the various sewing operations on the intestines. They consist of flat rings of bone, from which the mineral elements have been removed by acid and are used as follows: To each circular plate four threads are attached and passed through needles. One plate is then placed in each end of the intestine that is to be united, and the needles passed through the intestine from the interior about a quarter of an inch from the margin. The corresponding threads are then tied tightly together, bringing the outer layer of the intestines firmly in contact, pressed together between the two rings of bone. Nature causes adhesion to take place in a few hours, which gradually becomes a complete union. The bone plates are softened, and, after a few days, are discharged through the bowels. This is a complete and rapid method of connecting the parts. The old method of sewing the ends together required from one to two and a half hours, while this process can be completed in about half an hour.

Hernia is cured by operation, with little or no risk. The proportion of permanent cures has greatly improved, owing to better methods and to the increased experience of individual surgeons.

But little has been added to our possibilities in surgery of the kidneys and bladder. An ingenious instrument has been perfected, known as the cystoscope, which enables us to explore the interior of the bladder visually and renders our means of diagnosis much more perfect and extended. It consists of a tube, at the end of which is a small but powerful electric lamp which illuminates the bladder. The tube is passed into the bladder, as a catheter would be, and the current turned on, the bladder having first been filled with water. The entire interior of the bladder is seen, part at a time, in a small mirror at the end of the tube. A telescope in the tube magnifies the image to about the actual size. Tumors, ulcerations, encysted stones, etc., can be seen, which could not be detected otherwise without opening the bladder. By watch-

ing the urine enter the bladder, we can tell which kidney is the source of hæmorrhage or of pus.

Enlargement of the prostate gland, obstructing the flow of urine from the bladder, has of late been successfully treated by operation. Operations on the kidney are not new, but the results are much better than formerly. The removal of a stone from the kidney has become a comparatively common operation, and is quite free from danger. Floating or movable kidneys are replaced and retained by sutures; and in case of destruction of a kidney by disease, as diffuse abscess or cystic degeneration or tubercular disease, the unhealthy organ may be removed, the other kidney carrying on the work.

The Brain and the Nervous System.—The brain has become much more a field for operative surgery, and mortality from its diseases and injuries has been diminished considerably, many cases being saved by an operation which formerly would have been lost. A most important advance in this direction is our enlarged and improved knowledge of what is known as cerebral localization, i. e., determining, by paralysis and other nervous phenomena in a given part of the body, exactly what part of the brain or spinal cord is affected, and to about what extent. So exact has our knowledge become that abscesses, tumors, inflammatory changes, bullets, hæmorrhage, old fractures causing pressure on the brain, etc., can be successfully located and operated upon. Many parts of the brain may be cut into quite freely without producing ill effects. This has been shown by experiments on animals and by some remarkable cases of head-injury. By removing diseased conditions, many cases of epilepsy, constant headache, neuralgia, and paralysis have been cured. The interior of the skull is reached by removing a button-shaped piece of bone with a trephine. Tumors have been removed from the spinal cord, and some cases have been successfully treated where the bone has been pressed upon the nerve substance by fracture of the spinal column. It has been known for a long time that a nerve accidentally divided may be sewed together and regain its full power. This practice was at first confined to recent cases, but lately cases of local paralysis of long standing are cured by this operation.

Respiratory Organs.—The most important addition to the treatment of diseases of the larynx is known as intubation of the larynx (O'Dwyer). It is especially useful in cases of obstruction of the larynx due to diphtheria and membranous croup. It is now universally employed, and has greatly reduced the death-rate. It is a substitute for the operation of tracheotomy, consisting in placing a very perfectly shaped and sized tube in the larynx, through the natural opening. This forms a metallic lining to the larynx, through which the patient breathes. The tube can be retained several days, and is not removed until the disease has subsided.

Tumors of the larynx are frequently removed by making an incision through the front of the organ, which is afterward closed. Complete removal of the larynx for cancer has been done successfully in a sufficient number of instances to prove it to be a justifiable operation in exceptionally favorable cases. The death-rate from the operation is very high, but in considering this point we must remember that the disease is fatal, and that, without the operation, the patient's life can be but short. We are limited in our ability to operate on the lungs. The attempt has been made to cure localized consumption by excision; but, with our present skill, the undertaking is too dangerous. Some very brilliant results, however, have been obtained in the treatment of abscess of the lungs by surgical means.

The Eye.—Here, also, has been a steady advance, though little that is entirely new has been done. Since the last writing some successful transplantations of animals' eyes have been made on human subjects. The object is to furnish a living artificial eye. It is hoped, in young patients, that the eye (of a young animal) will cause the orbital cavity to continue to grow as does the unaffected one, so that there shall be but little difference in size at the time of maturity.

SWEDEN AND NORWAY, two kingdoms in the north of Europe united in one sovereignty by the act promulgated Aug. 6, 1815. They have a common diplomacy, which is directed by a Council of State composed of Swedes and Norwegians. The reigning sovereign is Oscar II, born Jan. 21, 1829, who succeeded to the throne in 1872.

SWEDEN.—The Diet consists of two chambers, both elective. The First Chamber has 143 members, elected by the provincial and municipal bodies for nine years. The Second Chamber contains 222 members, of whom 76 represent the towns and 146 the rural districts, elected for three years. The King, in the exercise of the executive power, in making appointments to office, in concluding treaties, and in legislating on matters of political administration, acts under the advice of a Council of State, which was composed, in 1888, of the following members: Oskar R. Themptander, Minister of State; Count Albert Carl Lars Ehrensvärd, Minister of Foreign Affairs; Nils Henrik Vult von Steyern, Minister of Justice; Gen. Knut Axel Ryding, Minister of War; Baron Carl Gustaf von Otter, Minister of Marine; Julius Edvard von Krusenstjerna, Minister of the Interior; Baron Claes Gustaf Adolf Tamm, Minister of Finance; Carl Gustaf Hammarskjöld, Minister of Education and Ecclesiastical Affairs; Johan Henrik Lovén; and Johan Christer Emil Richert.

Finances.—The budget for 1889 makes the ordinary receipts 18,929,000 kronor, and the extraordinary receipts 65,280,000 kronor, giving a total sum, with 3,472,000 kronor remaining in the treasury from the previous year, of 87,681,000 kronor. The ordinary receipts are made up of 4,435,000 kronor from land-taxes, 2,700,000 kronor from farmed domains, 1,600,000 kronor from forests, 1,200,000 kronor from tonnage dues, 6,000,000 kronor net receipts from railways, 1,200,000 kronor from telegraphs, and 1,794,000 kronor from other sources. The customs revenue, amounting to 36,000,000 kronor, the postal receipts of 6,580,000, the stamp-tax, yielding 3,500,000 kronor, the spirit duty, amounting to 15,000,000 kronor, the income-tax, reckoned at 3,600,000 kronor, and the sugar duty and other receipts, amounting to 600,000 kronor, constitute the extraordinary receipts. The ordinary expenditures are estimated at 65,493,411 kronor. The capital of the public debt, which was contracted exclusively for the construction of railways, was 245,967,703 kronor on Jan. 1, 1888.

The Army.—The Swedish army in 1888 numbered 9 general officers, 38 officers on the staff, 974 officers and men in the engineer corps, 4,520 in the artillery, 4,974 in the cavalry, 27,468 in the infantry, and 303 in the transport service, making a total of 38,289 inclusive of civil employés. The enlisted troops, counting only rank and file, numbered 9,423, and the cantoned troops 26,657. Including the *beväring*, or militia, the forces of the kingdom had a total strength of 194,577 officers and men, with 246 cannon and 6,178 horses.

The Navy.—The naval force in 1887 comprised 15 armored gunboats, 16 sloop gunboats, 1 school-ship, 1 frigate, 3 corvettes, 3 avisos, 1 torpedo school-ship, 18 torpedo-boats, 6 transports, and 6 sailing-vessels.

Commerce.—The imports in 1886 were of the total value of 301,366,000, kronor as compared with 340,003,000 kronor in 1885 and 325,817,000 kronor in 1884. The value of the exports was 228,398,000 kronor, as compared with 246,271,000 kronor in 1885 and 238,612,000 kronor in 1884 (1 krona = 27 cents). Nearly one third of the imports in 1886 came from Germany, one fourth from Great Britain, and one seventh from Denmark, while of the exports nearly one half went to Great Britain, and one third were divided between Denmark, Germany, and France. The imports of textile manufactures in 1885 were valued at 53,929,186 kronor, and those of textile materials and yarn at 29,686,080 kronor. Grain and flour were imported to the amount of 46,813,719 kronor, while the exports amounted to 28,544,414 kronor. The imports of groceries amounted to 41,535,545 kronor; of coal, 25,000,000 kronor; of metal goods and machinery, 28,682,618 kronor. The imports of live animals and animal food-products were valued at 22,490,777 kronor, and the exports at 33,772,438 kronor. The timber exports were 107,215,793 kronor in value, and those of raw metals 34,751,320 kronor.

Communications.—There were in operation at the end of 1887 2,496 kilometres of state railroads and 2,892 kilometres of lines belonging to companies, making altogether 7,388 kilometres, or 4,588 miles.

The Post-Office in 1886 forwarded 52,022,-864 letters and postal-cards, 9,462,185 circulars and samples, and 39,664,046 journals. The receipts were 6,106,476 kronor, and the expenses 5,896,960 kronor.

The state telegraph lines in 1887 had a total length of 8,345 kilometres, with 21,304 kilometres of wires. The dispatches sent during the year numbered 539,273 for the interior and 489,146 in the international service, besides 161,287 in transit. The receipts were 1,229,-860 kronor, and the expenses 1,241,978 kronor.

Politics.—The old Agrarian party gave place to a new one of protectionist leanings, which achieved an unexpected victory in the elections for the Rigsdag that met in January, 1888. In Stockholm there was a disputed election, which was decided by awarding the 22 seats to the Protectionist candidates, giving the party a majority in the House of 112 against 110. Prime Minister Themptander offered his resignation to the King, and advised him to send for Archbishop Sundberg; but the latter was unwilling to take the responsibility of broaching a decided protective policy with a chance majority that was not proved to represent the actual majority of electors in the country. As the King would not agree to an immediate dissolution of the Diet, the ministers retained their portfolios until, on February 6, a compromise Cabinet was formed by Baron D. A. G. Bildt, in which Count Ehrensvärd, J. von Krusentsjerna, and Baron Otter, the Ministers of Foreign Affairs, the Interior, and Marine, were retained in office. The new members of the Cabinet were as follow: Bergström, Minister of Justice; Maj.-Gen. Baron N. A. H. Palmstjerna, Minister of War; Baron F. von Essen, Minister of Finance; and Dr. G. Wennerberg, Minister of Ecclesiastical Affairs. Of the two Associate Ministers, Lovén and Lönegren, the former served in the Themptander Cabinet. The elections for the First Chamber in September placed beyond a doubt the preponderance of the protectionist sentiment in the country. The Chief of the Department of Justice retired from the ministry, and was replaced on September 28 by C. G. A. Orbom, and on the same date Baron A. L. E. Akerhielm succeeded State Councilor Lönegren. Krusenstjerna and Count Ehrensvärd, two pronounced Free-Traders, offered their resignations, but were induced to withdraw them.

The grain tariff was passed by a majority of 117 against 96 in the Second Chamber and 73 against 42 in the First Chamber, and went into force on February 14. The duties are 2·50 kronor per 100 kilogrammes on wheat, rye, barley, maize, peas, and beans; 4·30 kronor on flour; 3 kronor on malt; and 1 kronor on oats. The import duties on spirits were made much higher, although the budget committee

considered that the grain duties would add enough to the revenue to make the accounts balance. The Diet, which had a considerable Protectionist majority even in the joint session of both houses, proceeded to impose a series of protective duties calculated to yield 15,000,000 kronor annually, while the ministers remained entirely neutral. The new tariff went into force on July 1, except the duties on raw iron, which were postponed, pending negotiations with France in regard to the free importation of Swedish iron. Ships were declared free of duty if purchased by Swedes before July 1 and brought into the country before the end of the year. The surplus revenue obtained by the new duties is to be applied, in accordance with the desire of the King, in establishing accident insurance and old-age pensions for workingmen; for the reduction of local taxes, especially those for the support of churches and public charities; for the reduction of the land-tax; for the equipment and maintenance of the military forces; and for the encouragement of the shipping industry. In accordance with King Oscar's suggestion, a commission was appointed to draw up plans for the application of the surplus revenue from the protective duties in the manner proposed for the relief of the working and farming classes. The increased revenue for 1889 and 1890 will be required to cover the deficits for 1886 and 1887, so that three years must pass before there will be means available for these objects.

The new tariff places a duty on raw iron, in which there is no foreign competition, but could not be made to protect manufacturers of machinery and iron wares, because these articles are embraced in the commercial treaty with France, which will not expire till Feb. 1, 1892. The treaty of 1874 with Norway renders illusory many of the new duties, and diverts the benefit to Norwegian producers. This treaty provides for free trade between the two countries, not only in the products of the countries themselves, but in all articles that have been subjected to a manufacturing process made from materials imported in a raw or partly finished state from other countries. The Norwegians, in competing with Swedish manufacturers, have the advantage of free materials for iron manufactures and ship-building. The Swedish duties on live animals, in like manner, benefit Norwegian stock-raisers, who can abundantly supply the demand for sheep, hogs, cattle, and horses.

The new ministry was attacked by the Advanced Liberals not only for its protective policy, which threatened to shut out foreign commerce with tariff barriers, but for its reactionary political tendencies, manifested especially in an administrative order to the police to watch and, if necessary, to close political meetings. This was designed to put an end to the meetings of Social Democrats and their agitation for universal suffrage. The Themptander Cabinet appointed a commission after the first manifestations of Socialistic activity in Sweden to consider measures for improving the condition of the working-classes. This commission, in September, 1888, reported projects of laws embracing measures for the protection of the life and health of workmen, the insurance of laborers and seamen against accidents, and a state insurance establishment.

NORWAY.—The legislative power is vested in the Storthing, consisting of 114 members, which, on assembling, divides itself into the Odelsthing and the Lagthing. All legislation originates in the Odelsthing, which is thrice as numerous as the Lagthing. The smaller body adopts or rejects the bills that come from the other House. Bills that are rejected by the Lagthing can be passed by a vote of two thirds of the entire Storthing sitting together. The King can veto a measure twice, but, if it is passed by three successive Storthings, it becomes law. The executive authority is exercised by the King through a Council of State, consisting of a Minister of State in Christiania, another minister residing in Stockholm near the King, and at least seven Councilors of State, of whom two reside in Stockholm. The Council of State at Christiania in the beginning of 1888 was composed as follows: Minister of State, Johan Sverdrup; Department of Education and Ecclesiastical Affairs, Dr. Elias Blix; Department of Justice, Hans Georg Jakob Stang; Department of the Interior, Sofus Anton Birger Arctander; Department of Public Works, Birger Kildal; Department of Finance and Customs, Baard Madsen Haugland; Department of Defense, Johan Sverdrup; Department of the Revision of Accounts, Jakob Liv Rosted Sverdrup. The delegation of the Council of State at Stockholm was composed of Ole Richter, Minister of State, and Aimar August Sörenssen and Hans Rasmus Astrup, Councilors of State.

Finances.—The receipts of the treasury for the year ending June 30, 1887, were 42,977,-000 kronor, of which sum 19,495,600 kronor were derived from customs, 6,038,400 kronor from railways, 2,594,400 kronor from the brandy-tax, 2,276,700 kronor from the postal service, 2,165,700 kronor from invested capital, and smaller amounts from the malt duty, domains and forests, and other sources. The total expenditure was 43,145,400 kronor, of which 7,951,300 kronor were for railroads, bridges, and other public works, 9,026,800 kronor for the administration of the finances, 5,280,100 kronor for posts, telegraphs, and other services under the charge of the Interior Department, 4,310,300 kronor for education and worship, 4,131,400 kronor for sanitary service, police, and prisons, 6,654,100 kronor for the army, and 2,601,900 kronor for the navy. The amount of the state debt on June 30, 1887, was 108,427,600 kronor, and of active capital 139,207,700 kronor.

The Army.—By virtue of the laws of 1866, 1876, and 1885, the military forces are divided into troops of the line, *landværn*, and *landstorm*. The troops of the line are limited to 800 officers and 18,000 men. The other bodies are destined for the defense of the country within its borders.

The Navy.—The fleet of war in 1887 consisted of 4 monitors, 2 frigates, 2 corvettes, 30 gunboats, 9 torpedo-boats, and 7 other vessels, having a total armament of 163 guns.

Commerce.—The total value of the imports in 1887 was 133,691,000 kronor, as compared with 135,169,000 kronor in 1886; the value of the exports was 106,628,000 kronor, as compared with 102,844,000 kronor. The average value of the imports for the five years preceding was 152,272,000 kronor, and of the exports 111,215,000 kronor. The imports from Great Britain in 1887 were 35,368,000 kronor in value; from Germany, 34,950,000 kronor; from Sweden, 16,873,000 kronor; from Russia, 14,873,000 kronor. The exports to Great Britain were valued at 34,588,000 kronor; to Sweden, 14,455,000 kronor; to Germany, 13,-817,000 kronor. The value of the imports from the United States was 7,185,000 kronor, and of the exports to the United States 1,108,-000 kronor. The imports of cereals and flour in 1886 were of the value of 26,891,000 kronor, the most important article being wool, of the value of 9,328,000 kronor, after which came coffee, coal, sugar, butter and cheese, and cotton goods. Fish was exported of the value of 31,153,000 kronor, and timber of the value of 29,275,000 kronor. Other articles of export are wood-pulp, train-oil, butter, woolen and cotton goods, skins and hides, and matches.

Communications.—The length of railroads open to traffic in 1888 was 1,562 kilometres, or 970 miles.

There were 21,722,315 letters and 21,332,664 newspapers carried in the mails during 1887. The receipts of the Post-Office were 2,366,288 kronor; expenses, 2,439,355 kronor.

The state telegraph lines at the end of 1887 had a length of 7,494 kilometres, with 13,087 kilometres of wires. The number of internal dispatches was 442,660 in 1887; of foreign dispatches, 172,621 sent and 214,215 received. The receipts were 838,528 kronor; expenses, 1,030,487 kronor.

Politics.—The dissatisfaction of the Radicals with the Cabinet led to their secession from the party in the beginning of the year on the refusal of the Premier to dismiss his nephew, Jakob Sverdrup, and admit the Democratic leaders, Steen and Qvam, into the ministry. The Storthing was opened on February 2. The Odelsthing did not re-elect Qvam as president, but Daae, a Moderate. The left formally dissolved itself, and a group of the Pure Left was constituted under the leadership of Rector Steen. The Radical ministers, Arctander, Astrup, and Kildal, retired, and their resignations were accepted on February 16 by the King, whom the crisis brought to Christiania. Two weeks later the Minister of Education and

Worship, Dr. Elias Blix, resigned. The Opposition mustered 51 in the Storthing on a vote of censure emanating from the Radical Left, the Government being supported by 30 Moderates and 31 men of the Right. In June Ole Richter, the Minister of State, representing the Government at Stockholm, and Aimar A. Sörenssen, of the same section of the ministry, handed in their resignations, and Hans G. J. Stang and Baard M. Haugland were transferred to their posts. Richter's resignation was the consequence of an attack on the Prime Minister by Björnson Björnstierna, the real leader of the Radical party, who accused Sverdrup of falsehood and violation of his word on the authority of his colleague in Stockholm. Richter denied having made the accusation, but the evidence was so strong that, after his return to Stockholm, he shot himself in despair on June 15. The ministry as finally reconstituted was made up as follows; Minister of State at Christiania and Minister of National Defense, Johan Sverdrup; Chief of the Department of Justice and Police, W. S. Dahl, appointed March 5, 1888; Chief of the Department of Revision of Accounts, L. K. Liestöl, appointed March 5, 1838; Chief of the Department of Education and Ecclesiastical Affairs, Jakob Liv Rosted Sverdrup; Chief of the Department of Public Works, O. Jakobsen, appointed March 5, 1888; Chief of the Department of Finance and Customs, O. J. Olsen, appointed July 19, 1888; Minister of State at Stockholm, Hans Georg Jakob Stang; Councilors of State at Stockholm, Baard Madsen Haugland, previously Chief of the Department of Finance. and P. O. Schjött, appointed March 5, 1888. The Ministry of the Interior, formerly held by Sofus A. B. Arctander, was left vacant.

The Storthing rejected a scheme of protective duties on wheat, butter, and other agricultural products, agreeing only to an impost of 4 öre per kilogramme, equal to $\frac{1}{4}$ cent a pound, on oleomargarine, and to duties on fresh fruit ranging from 4 to 7 öre per kilogramme. On June 25 an act was passed reducing the salaries of members of the State Council from 12,000 to 10,000 kronor, and taking away the additional allowances of the councilors residing in Stockholm. The Storthing separated on July 7, after rejecting, by 64 against 50 votes, a motion of the Radicals declaring want of confidence in the ministry.

A law was passed on April 21, 1888, in relation to state citizenship, declaring that Norwegians who become citizens of foreign states lose their rights of citizenship in Norway, and likewise those who reside permanently abroad, unless they record their intention to remain as such in the Norwegian consulate within a year, and renew the declaration every ten years.

General Election.—Johan Sverdrup, when he formed a Radical ministry, was regarded as a true representative of the Norwegian Democracy, of which party he was a leader of many years' standing. In office, however, he abandoned the principles of popular sovereignty and national independence, and made one compromise after another with the monarchist reaction that has spread through the Scandinavian lands, owing to the example and influence of Germany, until he stood on the platform of the Constitutional Right, from which his chief support now came, and was surrounded by ministerial colleagues taken from that party. The electoral contest that took place in the autumn of 1888 was embittered by the accusations of faithlessness brought against the minister. The suicide of Richter was laid to his door. Councilor Stang, the leader of the Constitutionalists, sought to make the issue one of principles, asserting that his party was the defender of the historic rights of the crown, of the connection between Church and state, and of the Union against destructive "European" innovations, foreign to the national character. The Conservatives and Ministerialists, while preserving separate party organizations, formed an electoral alliance against the Radicals. The Radical leaders, Qvam, Steen, and Konow, lost their seats, and were shut out from the next Storthing, as the law requires every candidate to be a resident of the district that he seeks to represent. The new Storthing consists of 54 members belonging to the Right, 38 adherents of the Pure Left, and 22 who belong to the ministerial group.

SWITZERLAND, a federal republic in Central Europe. The central Legislature is composed of the State Council, in which each of the twenty-two cantons is represented by two members, and the National Council, containing one deputy for every twenty thousand of the population, elected by direct universal suffrage. The executive body is the Federal Council, which was composed, in 1888, of the following members: President, W. F. Hertenstein; Vice-President, B. Hammer; members, Dr. A. Schenck, Dr. E. Welti, L. Ruchonnet, Dr. N. Droz, and Dr. A. Deucher. (For area and population, see the "Annual Cyclopædia" for 1887.)

Finances.—The federal revenue in 1887 amounted to 59,586,972 francs, of which 24,632,285 francs were derived from customs and 21,103,869 francs from the Post-Office. The expenditures amounted to 56,829,996 francs, the principal items being 21,157,204 francs for military administration and 19,571,324 francs for the post-office. The debt of the federation on Jan. 1, 1888, was 38,984,982 francs, and the capital assets were 78,002,798 francs.

The Army.—The Swiss army consists of the regulars, called Bundesauszug, and the Landwehr. Men between the ages of seventeen and fifty, not belonging to either of these forces, are enrolled in the Landstrum. The strength of the regular army in 1888 was 123,031 officers and men, and that of the Landwehr 80,248. The Landstrum comprises 4,922 former officers, 5,652 non-commissioned officers, and 287,069 men, of whom 40,247 have served in the regular army. The Federal Council has divided the Landsturm into the armed and the auxiliary forces. The active army has 20,000 horses, and is armed with the Vetterli repeating rifle with ten charges, 280 Krupp field-guns, and 22 mountain-guns. The cost of the army has nearly doubled in ten years. The Swiss Government has fortified the entrances to the St. Gothard Tunnel, and to other tunnels of the international railroad lines, and has prepared the means of blocking them instantly by filling them with stones precipitated with the aid of electricity.

Commerce.—The special imports in 1887 were valued at 792,284,000 francs; the exports at 641,918,000 francs. The imports of precious metals were 44,751,000 francs, and the exports 29,175,000 francs. Switzerland has a foreign trade of 510 francs *per capita*, which exceeds that of every other country except Holland. The commerce for three years past has increased 3 per cent. per annum, almost the entire growth having been in imports.

Railroads.—The railroads in operation in 1886 had a total length of 2,912 kilometres, exclusive of 63 kilometres belonging to foreign companies. The total capital was 1,050,608,170 francs. The receipts were 75,392,588 francs, and the expenses 41,084,353 francs. A mountain railroad over the Brünig Pass, connecting Lucerne with the Bernese Oberland, was opened in June, 1888.

The Post-Office.—The number of domestic letters and postal-cards forwarded in 1887 was 61,001,268, exclusive of 6,880,115 official letters; the number of printed inclosures, 16,-292,656 ; of packets, 8,828,127 ; of postal money-orders, 2,488,221, of the total value of 275,410,943 francs. The number of international letters and postal-cards was 30,651,127; of printed inclosures, 13,576,430; of journals, 65,805,033 ; of packets, 2,649,474; the value of money-orders, 33,653,038 francs.

Telegraphs.—The length of the telegraph lines in 1887 was 7,060 kilometres; the length of wires, 17,102 kilometres. The number of dispatches was 3,331,155, of which 1,816,524 were internal, 1,008,097 international, 396,037 in transit, and 110,497 official. The receipts were 3,531,598 francs; expenses, 2,893,992 francs.

The Alcohol Law.—In order to check the spread of drunkenness, the Swiss Legislature made the sale of spirits a state monopoly in 1887, except such as are used in industrial processes, which must be rendered unfit for drinking. A commission of experts decided what substances should be used in denaturalizing alcohol to be used in the various industries, and fixed the proportions of the admixture in each case.

Emigration.—In 1886 the National Council passed an act to license and supervise emigration-agents, the provisions of which were made stricter by a bill approved in April, 1888. Agencies are required to give bonds in the sum of forty thousand francs, and to pay an annual license-fee of fifty francs. Sub-agents can be employed on conditions subject to the investigation of the cantonal authorities, but an additional bond of three thousand francs is required for each. No colonial enterprise can be undertaken by companies, individuals, or agencies, without the approval of the Federal Government. When agencies undertake to forward money to emigrants in foreign lands they must deliver the full sum without deduction. A special bureau was created for the purpose of supervising emigration-agencies and furnishing information to intending emigrants, and protection to Swiss citizens in foreign countries.

Anti-Socialist Proceedings.—The German Government has brought pressure to bear on the Federal authorities continuously for several years past, to secure the suppression of the German Socialists who make Zürich their headquarters, and the Swiss rulers have done everything to please Germany except abrogating the right of asylum. Four German Anarchists, named Schopen, Metzler, Haupt, and Von Ehrenberg, were expelled from Zürich in January, 1888. Against a German, named Bürger, who had become a naturalized Swiss citizen, and acted as a spy and *agent provocateur* in the pay of the Berlin police, the cantonal authorities brought criminal proceedings. On March 20 the Bundesrath voted a credit for the establishment of a political police, which was asked for on the ground that the relations with Germany necessitated measures to prevent a disturbance of the friendship between the two countries and abuse of the right of asylum. In introducing the bill, Federal Councilor Droz said : "The majority of the Swiss people are determined that our house shall be respected by all who dwell in it. The air we breathe is the air of healthy liberty. We will not allow it to be vitiated by the miasma of anarchism. Neither shall our house be a refuge whence assaults can be directed with impunity against the repose of other countries." The chief object of the German Government was to suppress the Socialistic journals and pamphlets that are smuggled into Germany, notwithstanding the vigilance of the post-office police authorities, and, especially the "Social Demokrat" newspaper, which is the organ of the German Parliamentary Socialist party, and has a circulation of from 10,000 to 12,000 copies. Several urgent notes from the German Government demanded the suppression of this organ of moderate Socialism, which continued to spread through Germany the views that no one there dared to utter except from the tribune of the Reichstag, and was more obnoxious to the German Chancellor than the revolutionary "Rothe Teufel" and the Anarchistic *brochures* that were also issued by thousands in Zürich for circulation in Germany, because it helped to keep alive the Parliamentary party. The Federal authorities sent a warning to the editor, to which he replied in the next issue of the paper, "*Sit aut est, aut non sit.*" Yet he was careful not to print anything that could give occasion for interference. The German authorities were not satisfied, and fresh representations from Berlin made it a point that Switzerland should prevent Germans from using the right of asylum to carry on a political agitation in their own country. At length the Federal Council decided on April 16 to issue a decree of expulsion against four Germans connected with the paper: Bernstein, the editor, who came from Berlin; Schlütter, the publisher, a native of Schleswig-Holstein; Tauscher, the business manager, a naturalized American, who once lived in Chicago; and Motteler, formerly editor of a journal in Saxony, and an ex-member of the German Parliament, who was the agent for circulating the paper. The printing-office was not suppressed, because it was carried on under the firm name of a Swiss citizen, although the managers and the printers were all Germans. New editors and business agents at once stepped into the places of those who were expelled, and the journal continued to appear and to find its way into Germany just as before. In the beginning of June the Bundesrath ordered the expulsion of Ulrich Wübbeler and Martin Eller, two Germans who had been enticed into sending a box of dynamite to an agent of the Berlin police named Schröder, in Zürich. In July the Bundesrath directed the cantonal authorities to have all Socialistic meetings watched by the police. The Swiss Socialists united into a single Social-Democratic party, and arranged to hold a Labor Assembly in October. The Swiss Government was at last induced to take measures to suppress the exportation of forbidden literature into Germany. The Bavarian, Franz Troppmann, a correspondent of the Chicago Anarchists, was expelled in September, and the evidence taken in the case of ex-Captain von Ehrenberg, of the German army, was delivered up to a military tribunal in Baden. Many Socialists joined the Swiss Grütli Association, which rejected a proposition to exclude foreigners from membership. The "Social Demokrat" was finally driven in September to change its place of publication to London. A Swiss "Social Demokrat" was established during the summer, and announced the programme of a Swiss Socialistic party, embracing obligatory education up to the age of fifteen; assistance for capable poor students who wish to complete their education in the highers institutions of learning; election of the Bundesrath by the people; a Federal code of criminal law; obligatory sick and accident insurance, gratuitous medical service, and Federal trade laws; the acquisition by the state of railroads, and management by the Government of banking and the grain-trade; the recognition in the Constitution of the right of all citizens to labor, and of the duty of the authorities to provide every one who asks, with work corresponding to his abilities and justly compensated either in the service of the public or of private persons who are willing to furnish the employment; and the gradual naturalization of commerce, transportation, industry, and agriculture, with the distribution among the producers, as equally as is expedient, of the proceeds over and above the working expenses, and a sum was set aside for insurance, justice, military, civil administration, etc.

Commercial Treaties.—Negotiations for a new commercial treaty with Germany were suspended, pending the settlement of commercial and railroad regulations between Germany and Austria. The German treaty with the Swiss Confederation was concluded on Nov. 15, 1888, and a Swiss-Austrian treaty on November 23. The latter embodies substantial reductions in the tariff on both sides. Switzerland obtained the same duties as Italy on silks, machinery, and other manufactures, and in return lowered the duties on grain, flour, cattle, and timber.

The Institute of International Law.—The annual meeting of the Institute of International Law was opened at Lausanne on Sept. 3, 1888. The principal subjects of discussion were the exceptions to the rule determining the capacity of persons for entering into binding contracts on foreign soil or with foreigners; the law of collisions at sea; extra-territoriality of consulates; and the obligations toward neutral powers incurred through territorial annexations. The Institute in its meeting at Oxford decided that the nationality of parties entering into contracts ought to be the test of their capacity. At Lausanne a resolution was adopted to the effect that in commercial matters, if the person seeking to escape the obligations of his contract on the ground of legal incapacity had deceived the other party in this particular, or if there were a combination of grave circumstances showing fraudulent intent, the judge should follow the law of the country in which the contract was made. The liability for negligence in maritime collisions the Institute would place upon the vessel that was the cause of the accident, except where both ships were negligent, in which case the one chiefly offending should pay its just share of the loss to the other vessel, while damages to passengers and cargoes should be divided between them. The question of the inviolability of consulates was brought up by a French member, in connection with the seizure of papers relating to a will case, by order of an Italian magistrate, in the French consulate at Florence. The consul had placed the documents among the consular archives, and warned the Italian authorities not to search the consulate, as a special article in the Treaty of 1862 between France and Italy guarantees the inviolability of the archives. The Institute decided to deal with the subject of extra-territoriality as a whole, and appointed a committee to report on the subject comprehensively. Among the other questions discussed were conflicts of law in connection with public companies; the limitations of the right of Governments to expel foreigners; railways, telegraphs, and telephones in time of war; and the theory of the Berlin Conference on the occupation of territory. The Institute adopted resolutions in respect to the assertion of properly asserted rights in newly annexed territory in the uncivilized parts of the globe; to the protection of vested interests of citizens of civilized nations; to freedom of access and settlement without regard to nationality; to the prohibition of slavery; and to the proper treatment of natives.

T

TEACHERS' ASSOCIATIONS. The oldest living educational association in this country is the American Institute of Instruction, organized in Boston, in 1830. The earliest educational association in this country was formed at Middletown, Conn., in 1799, under the name of "Middlesex County Association for the Improvement of Common Schools." The existence of this society was due to the efforts of the Rev. William Woodbridge, of Middletown, Conn., a famous teacher. Although this effort was premature, it gave a great impulse to the cause of education, and its recommendation was considered one of a teacher's best testimonials. There is no record of any other continuous associated movement until 1826, when Josiah Holbrook organized in Connecticut the "lyceum," which had for its main object "the association of teachers for mutual improvement." One of the first societies of this kind was organized in Windsor County, Conn., by Mr. Holbrook himself, assisted by the Rev. Samuel J. May. Twenty of these lyceums were in active operation as late as 1838. In 1827, a "Society for the Improvement of Common Schools" was formed in Hartford, and in 1830 a general convention of teachers and friends of education was held in that city, of which Noah Webster was president. This meeting was largely attended, and addresses were delivered by President Humphrey, of Amherst College, Noah Webster, and W. A. Alcott. In 1839 a State convention was held at Hartford, at which addresses were delivered by Prof. Calvin E. Stowe, Thomas Cushing, Alexander H. Everett, and Mrs. Lydia H. Sigourney. In the autumn of the same year the first teachers' institute in this country was held at Hartford, under the invitation and arrangement of the secretary of the Connecticut Board of Education. The expenses of this institute were paid by the Hon. Henry Barnard. During the same year, a plan for a State association was drawn up by Dr. Barnard, which was the first decisive movement of this kind in Connecticut, and, perhaps, in the country, although there were voluntary conferences in Massachusetts for discussing educational questions at a much earlier date. For instance, in August, 1636, "a general meeting of the registered inhabitants of the town of Boston" was convened, and money was subscribed " toward maintaining a free schoolmaster for the youth with us." This was not distinctively an association of teachers, but it was the beginning of conferences that led to the formation of organized efforts, as well as teachers' associations at a later date. These voluntary meetings led to the general organization of the State, and afterward to the formation of Bible, Educational, Tract, and Sunday-school societies. In 1812 the first successful effort was made to bring the teachers of Boston and vicinity into an association for their own professional improvement. The name of this was "The Associated Instructors of Youth in the Town of Boston and its Vicinity." Meetings were held for several years, and in 1835 it was reorganized under the name of "The Association of the Masters of Boston Grammar-Schools," and came before the public in the memorable controversy of the "thirty-one Boston masters" with Horace Mann, in 1844-'45. The lyceum movement mentioned above, led to the formation of the Boston Mechanics' Institute in 1827, the Boston Infant-School Society in 1828, and the Boston Society for the Diffusion of Useful Knowledge the same year, and to State educational conventions in 1829 and 1830. One result was the organization of the American Institute of Instruction, Aug. 21, 1830, annual meetings of which have been held until the present time. It was proposed to call this society "The New England Association of Teachers"; but as several of the Middle, Southern, and Western States were represented in its first conventions, and many persons not teachers were desirous of membership, a more comprehensive name and plan were adopted, although it has continued to be an association of New England teachers. Its presidents from 1830 to 1856 were Francis Wayland, William B. Calhoun, James G. Carter, George B. Emerson, Gideon F. Thayer, Thomas Sherman, and John Kingsbury. Through the efforts of James G. Carter in 1835, then a member of the Massachusetts Legislature, an appropriation of $300 a year, for five successive years, was made in aid of the association, and this grant was from time to time renewed. Year after year the institute has held its meetings, usually in one of the principal cities or towns of New England, each session occupying three or four days in lectures, reports, and discussions. The day meetings have been attended by hundreds of teachers, school-officers, and friends of education, and the evening sessions by thousands of people.

The first national educational association was the American Association for the Advancement of Education, organized in Philadelphia in December 1849, under the leadership of Horace Mann, Alonzo Potter, Joseph Henry, Henry Barnard, Charles Northend, John S. Hart, John Griscom, Joseph Chandler, Nathan Bishop, Alexander D. Bache, Samuel S. Randall, and others. The early presidents were Horace Mann (1849), Eliphalet Nott (1850), Right Rev. Alonzo Potter (1851-'52), Joseph Henry (1853), Alexander D. Bache (1854), and Henry Barnard (1855). The credit of suggesting and originating the formation of the present National Educational Association is probably due to William Russell, who was born in Glasgow, Scotland, in 1798, and was educated in the Latin School and University of that city. He began his life work as a teacher in Georgia, and was the author of an admirable address setting forth the nature and objects of an organization that should include all the professional teachers in this country. This address was read to a convention held in Philadelphia, Aug. 27, 1857, and resulted in a formal organization of the National Teachers' Association, with Zalmon Richards as president. The first anniversary of the association was held in Cincinnati on Aug. 11-13, 1858. Its successive presidents were: Andrew J. Rickoff, J. W. Bulkley, John D. Philbrick, W. H. Wells, S. S. Green, J. P. Wickersham, J. M. Gregory, L. VanBokelen, and Daniel B. Hagar. This association was merged into the National Educational Association, at Albany, N. Y., in 1870. The successive presidents have been: J. L. Pickard (1871), E. E. White (1872), B. G. Northrop (1873), S. H. White (1874), W. T. Harris (1875), W. F. Phelps (1876), M. A. Newell (1877), John Hancock (1879), J. Ormond Wilson (1880), John H. Smart (1881), G. J. Orr (1882), E. T. Tappan (1883), Thomas W. Bicknell (1884), F. Louis Soldan (1885), N. A. Calkins (1886), W. E. Sheldon (1887), Aaron Gove (1888), and A. P. Marble (1889). These meetings have been held in most of the principal cities of our country, the last being in San Francisco. The meeting for 1889 is to be held in Nashville, Tenn. An historical sketch of the organization of the associations in each of the States would fill a large volume, but the following outline will indicate a few facts concerning their early history. In some instances the records of the first meetings have been lost, but the dates as given below are thought to be correct:

Arkansas—Teachers' Association, 1860.
Alabama—State Educational Association, 1856.
California—Education Society, 1854.
Connecticut—State Association, 1839.
District of Columbia—Association of Teachers, 1849.
Delaware—State Convention, 1853-'56.
Florida—Education Society, Tallahassee, 1831.
Georgia—Teachers' Society, 1831.
Iowa—State Teachers' Association, 1854.
Indiana—State Teachers' Association, 1854.
Illinois—State Education Society, 1841.
Kansas—State Teachers' Association, 1863.

Kentucky—State Teachers' Association, 1857.
Louisiana—Institute for the Promotion of Education, 1838.
Mississippi—Teachers' Association, 1858.
Maine—State Teachers' Association, 1846.
Maryland—Institute of Education, 1843.
Massachusetts—State Association, 1835.
Michigan—State Education Society, 1852.
Minnesota—State Teachers' Association, 1853.
Missouri—Teachers' Association, 1848.
New York—State Teachers' Association, 1845.
New Jersey—State Teachers' Association, 1853.
New Hampshire—State Teachers' Association, 1843.
North Carolina—Institute of Education, 1830.
Oregon—State Educational Association, 1863.
Ohio—State Teachers' Association, 1853.
Pennsylvania—State Teachers' Association, 1852.
Rhode Island—Institute of Instruction, 1844.
South Carolina—State Teachers' Association, 1849.
Texas—Literary Institute, 1846.
Tennessee—Association of Professional Teachers, 1837.
Vermont—State Teachers' Association, 1850.
Virginia—State Teachers' Association, 1856.
West Virginia—State Teachers' Association, 1865.
Wisconsin—Teachers' Association, 1853.

The National Educational Association, as now organized, is divided into the following departments: General Association; National Council of Education; and Departments of Kindergarten Work, Elementary Education, Secondary Education, Higher Education, Normal Education, Superintendence, Industrial Education, Art, and Music. The National Council of Education holds its meetings the week previous to the sessions of the General Association. During its meetings, the General Association occupies the forenoon and evening of each day, while the departments meet at assigned places in the afternoons.

Questions bearing directly upon the work of education in all parts of our country, and in all its relations, are discussed by able educators, whose papers and remarks are published in an annual volume of "Proceedings." The volume for 1888 contains 944 pages; that of 1887, 829 pages; and the volumes of several years preceding 1887 contained from 400 to 550 pages. The attendance at these meetings during the past few years has been very large. The membership attendance at Madison, 1884, was over 8,000; at Topeka, 1886, 5,000; at Chicago, 1887, about 10,500; at San Francisco, 1888, about 4,500.

Among the principal subjects discussed at the San Francisco meeting were: "The Place of Literature in Common-School Education," "The Best Discipline to Prepare Law-Abiding Citizens," "Current Criticism of Public Schools," "The Relation of the State to School Supplies," "The American Schools and the American Library," "Waste in Elementary Education," "The Business Side of City School Systems," "The University and the High-School," "The Normal School and the Academy," "The Ethics of School Management," "Industrial Training and General Culture," "Elementary Music in Public Schools." As an example of the scope and value of these discussions, we refer to the papers on the relation of the State to school-supplies. This subject, during the past few years, has been exciting considerable attention, and it was given a large place in the discussions of the California meeting. The question at issue was, Should the State raise by taxation a fund sufficient to furnish to all pupils in the public schools text-books and other supplies free of cost? In other words, should the State become a public corporation, publishing text-books and manufacturing supplies for the schools under its care? Superintendent R. W. Stevenson, of Columbus, Ohio, in discussing this question, said: "The principle underlying free text-books is wrong, and must result in evil. That government is the best which gives the people the power and the opportunity to do the most for themselves. There can be no co-operation without interest. To be interested in anything, the person must have a share in its use that costs something to secure—even in education. There are, therefore, limitations beyond which the State, for its own safety, should not go. The State that supplies those wants of its people which, by common industry and economy they can supply for themselves, encourages idleness and dependence. No good will come from a system of free text-books, but, on the contrary, great dangers. The taxation of the Northern States for school purposes is now as heavy as the people will bear. The plan of free text-books means higher taxes, or the attraction of the money now raised from more useful purposes."

Hon. L. S. Cornell, of Denver, Col., in discussing this question, said: "The members of the State board of education and text-book commissions, however constituted, are usually men whose time is fully occupied with official and private duties. They are not, as a rule, connected with the work of the common schools, and are unable to make the best selections. Books that have been adopted by such persons with the greatest confidence in their merits, have frequently been found very defective when practically tested in the school-room. The power to decide what books should be used by every child in the State, and to give some publishing-house or dealer a monopoly of the school-book trade, is too great to place in the hands of any board or commission. The record of the past in many States will testify to great danger in this direction. It is not desirable for the State to enter the field as a publisher or manufacturer on the ground of economy. No one will claim that the State will make better books than those issued by some private houses, nor that it can do the work more cheaply than they. A first-class book is a thing of growth; it can not be made to order in a few weeks or a month." The testimony of the superintendent of a Western State was given in the following words: "It has been the misfortune of our common schools that they have been forced to use books, by authority of law, which none would

prefer, while independent and special districts have been at liberty to choose for their children the best and freshest in the markets."

It was urged during the discussion that the tendency of our school systems is to make them machines that grind out all the individuality from children; that the manufacture of text-books by State authority, and the forcing of these books upon the districts, is a species of literary tyranny that is contrary to the free character of our institutions, and would intensify the "machine" in education; that there is no more sense in requiring all schools to use the same geography or history or grammar than there would be in requiring all farmers' wives to use the same kind of flour or sugar or potatoes. It was urged with great force that States attempting to adopt the system of manufacturing school-books had failed to carry with them the sympathy of the people, and thus the plan had fallen into disrepute from the evident unfairness of its requirements. It was also said by the Hon. E. E. Higbee, of Pennsylvania, that a legalized State monopoly and a uniform system of text-books by State authority would create a tyranny; that the large publishing-houses command the best skill in workmanship and the best experience of learned men and professional teachers, which the State would fail to do; that the competition now existing is itself a guarantee that prices will not be excessive, and that also the highest degree of perfection will be obtained.

In opposition to these arguments it was urged by Thomas Tash, of Portland, Maine, that it is wise to furnish text-books at public expense on account of convenience and economy. Much confusion, especially in rural districts, results from the ownership of wrong and unsuitable books. In such schools pupils do not pursue all the studies they should, or such as they ought, on the plea that they have not the books. With an ample supply of books a school can be more easily and promptly classified. There is no waiting for slow-moving fathers. Reducing the grade of scholars or loss of time or neglect of study vanish when text-books are furnished by the State. Parents criticise the classification of their children far less than under the old voluntary system. Where text-books are supplied by the State, supplementary books may be furnished in any study without increase of cost—two sets of readers lasting six years costing no more than one set lasting three years.

The picture of the State establishing its own shops, gathering its material, constructing its various machines, fixing prices, enforcing the use of its books, establishing its depots of supplies and its numerous agents of distribution, its collectors, and accounts, were presented in such a forcible manner as to lead to the general verdict that such a course would be the death-knell of our inventive genius in the direction of text-book making; would cripple all self-developing enterprise on the part of the people, and tend to destroy the chief inducements to individual impulse and activity.

The discussion of this question gives a fair example of the subjects considered by the National Association from year to year. In State and county meetings the topics discussed are generally more technical, relating to subjects usually taught in elementary village and country schools. Teachers' institutes are in some respects modified teachers' associations.

TENNESSEE. State Government.—The following were the State officers during the year: Governor, Robert L. Taylor, Democrat; Secretary of State, John Allison; Treasurer and Insurance Commissioner, Atha Thomas; Comptroller, P. P. Pickard; Attorney-General, B. J. Lea; Superintendent of Public Instruction, Frank M. Smith; Commissioner of Agriculture, Statistics, and Mines, B. M. Hord; Chief-Justice of the Supreme Court, Peter Turney; Associate Justices, W. C. Folkes, W. C. Caldwell, B. L. Snodgrass, and W. H. Lurton.

Finances.—The receipts of the State Treasury for the biennial period ending Dec. 20, 1888, were $3,694,996.37, of which $916,002.10 is a temporary loan. Deducting this and $22,942.50 for accidental receipts, there remains $2,756,-052.13. The total disbursements during the two years were $3,408,761.69, of which $373,-114.43 represents Bank of Tennessee certificates paid by the State, and $262,500 of the temporary loan repaid, leaving $2,773,147.26 as the actual expense for ordinary purposes. This is greater than the ordinary revenue by $17,095.33.

The assessed valuation of the State for 1888 was $297,205,054, divided as follows: Land, $165,479,717; town lots, $88,646,633; personal property, $43,078,704. The increase in valuation over 1887 is $57,654,973. Railroad property is assessed for the year at $32,290,-302.10. There are 2,224 miles of railroad in the State.

Education.—The last annual report of the State Superintendent, for the year ending June 30, 1887, presents the following public-school statistics: Scholastic population between six and twenty-one years, white males, 248,112; white females, 230,509; total white, 478,621; colored males, 81,006; colored females, 80,-387; total colored, 161,393; grand total, 640,-014. Number of teachers employed: White males, 3,906; white females, 1,833; colored males, 1,075; colored females, 565; total, 7,-379. Number of schools: White, 5,101; colored, 1,506; total, 6,607. Number of pupils enrolled during the year, 380,625; average daily attendance, 252,248.

The State University has undergone, during the year, a thorough reorganization; a new president and almost an entirely new faculty have been selected. Commodious buildings have been erected and the older ones improved.

Charities.—The School for the Blind, on December 20, had 84 pupils, 73 being white and 11 colored, an increase of 13 since December,

1886. The total number in the school during the past two years was 120, and the expenditures during that period were $31,906.62.

At the School for the Deaf and Dumb the attendance at the close of the year had increased to 115.

Mills and Manufactories.—The following figures for 1888 are taken from the annual report of the State Commissioner of Statistics: Woolen-mills, 19; pounds of scoured wool used, 2,113,-000; of which 837,500 pounds were Tennessee wool; hands employed, 879; cotton-mills, 23; spindles, 100,161; bales of cotton consumed, 37,610; hands employed, 2,677; iron manufactories, 13; hands employed, 5,510.

Coal.—The product for 1886 in short tons was as follows: First District, coal, 188,424; coal coked, 260.082; total, 448,506. Second District, coal, 438,917; coal coked, 311,259; total, 750,176. Third District, coal, 515,608. Total, 1,714,290 tons. The product for 1888 in short tons was: First District, coal, 332,715; coal coked, 304,700; total, 637,415. Second District, coal, 309,973; coal coked, 374,000; total, 683,973. Third District, coal, 645,909. Total for the three districts, 1,967.297 tons.

Political.—A Democratic State Convention met at Nashville on May 9, for the purpose of electing delegates at large to the St. Louis Convention, nominating presidential electors, and selecting a candidate for Governor. The two former objects were easily accomplished, but a prolonged contest arose over the gubernatorial nomination, which required a session of four days and forty ballots. Gov. Taylor was a candidate for renomination, but was opposed by a large minority of the delegates, whose support was divided between four aspirants—T. M. McConnell, W. M. Daniel, Julius A. Trousdale, and W. P. Caldwell. On the first ballot, Taylor received 649 votes, McConnell 241, Daniel 226, Trousdale 100, and Caldwell 114. A two-third vote of the 1,334 delegates was necessary for a choice. The contest was marked with so great excitement and bitterness that more than one third of the minority refused to vote at all on the decisive ballot, in which 1,081 votes were cast for Taylor, with 214 scattering votes. The nomination was then made unanimous. The resolutions included the following:

We favor such reform in our penal system as will separate minor convicts and offenders of low grade from hardened criminals, and will reduce to a minimum the competition between convict and free labor.

We are opposed to all monopolies and "trusts."

On May 16 the Republicans met at Nashville and selected delegates to the Chicago Convention, but postponed the nomination of a gubernatorial candidate till the meeting of a subsequent convention on July 18. This convention selected Samuel W. Hawkins. The platform included the following:

We favor an exemption from taxation of $1,000 worth of property in the hands of every head of a family who is a citizen of the State, without regard to its character, in lieu of the present law exempting $1,000 worth of personal property.

We oppose the present system of assessing and equalization of values of the taxable property of the State, and favor such revision of the assessment laws as will secure a more just and equal assessment and equalization, to the end that the burdens of taxation will fall equally upon all the tax-payers of the entire State.

We are opposed to the taxation of the agents of the agricultural organizations of our State, and will favor the enactment of such laws as will secure to the farmers equal rights and privileges with all other secular occupations and professions in the State.

We again denounce the system of leasing the convicts in our Penitentiary to be worked in the mines in competition with the free labor engaged in developing our wonderful mineral resources.

Late in July the Prohibitionist State Executive Committee announced the name of J. C. Johnson as the candidate of its party. At the November election, Taylor received 156,799 votes, Hawkins 139,014, Johnson 6,893. The Legislature elected at the same time will contain 23 Democrats and 10 Republicans in the Senate, and 73 Democrats and 26 Republicans in the House. Cleveland electors were chosen, and Democratic Congressmen elected in all of the ten districts except the First, Second, and Third. In the Third District the contest was close. Upon the face of the returns, it appeared that Evans, the Republican candidate, had a majority of 228 votes; but the friends of Creed F. Bates, the Democratic candidate, claimed that fraud in two of the election districts could be shown, sufficient to justify the canvassing board in rejecting the returns from those districts. In the event of such rejection, the Democratic candidate would have a majority of one vote. On the representation of these facts, the Governor, as the head of the board of canvassers, prepared, at the suggestion of Bates's friends, a certificate of his election prior to the meeting of the board, in order that, if it should find that he had been duly elected, the certificate might be instantly issued before an injunction could be obtained by the Republican candidate. The certificate was signed and sealed and delivered by the Governor to the Secretary of State, with orders that it was not to be considered as issued, and was not to be entered or copied into the records, until further directions were given. When the canvassing board met, it was found that the facts would not justify the exclusion of the votes in the two districts referred to, and the Governor destroyed the first certificate and prepared another in favor of Evans. But the Secretary of State disagreed with him in his conclusions regarding the frauds, and refused to attest his signature to the second certificate. He was also enjoined from issuing and delivering the certificate to Evans. The investigation of the returns not only showed that Evans was elected, but, even if the amended returns were accepted and the two districts thrown out, still Evans was elected, because an amendment from Bradley County increased his majority by four votes, thus overcoming Bates's majority of one and leaving Evans a clear majority of three.

Arguments in the injunction case were made before Chancellor Allison in December, the Governor appearing by counsel and denying that the court had any jurisdiction to control the Executive in the exercise of what he claimed was the discretionary power of his office. The Chancellor decided in favor of the Governor, and an appeal was taken to the State Supreme Court.

TEXAS. State Government.—The following were the State officers during the year: Governor, Lawrence S. Ross, Democrat; Lieutenant-Governor, T. B Wheeler; Secretary of State, J. M. Moore; Treasurer, Frank R. Lubbock; Comptroller, John D. McCall; Attorney-General, James S. Hogg; Superintendent of Public Instruction, Oscar H. Cooper; Commissioner of the General Land-Office, R. M. Hall; Chief-Justice of the Supreme Court, Asa H. Willie, who offered his resignation, to take effect March 3, and was succeeded by Associate Justice John W. Stayton; Associate Justices, John W. Stayton, promoted as above, R. R. Gaines, and Alexander H. Walker, appointed in March to succeed Justice Stayton.

Legislative Session.—A special session of the Legislature was called to meet on April 16. The more important reasons for this were, first, the existence of a large and growing surplus in the revenue account of the treasury, amounting at that time to over $1,500,000, exclusive of the net indemnity claim of $922,541.52, recently received from the General Government; second, a large deficiency in the school revenues, amounting to $400,000 for the year 1886–'87 and $250,000 for 1887–'88; third, the completion of the new State Capitol. The existence of a large surplus revenue gave rise to various extravagant measures for its expenditure, but the action of the Legislature in making appropriations was on the whole moderate, though its reduction of the tax-rate from 25 cents to 10 cents for 1888, and 20 cents for each year thereafter, proved to be ill-advised. For the purpose of reducing the school-revenue deficiency a bill was passed transferring $254,000, or so much of it as should be needed, to pay outstanding warrants held by the counties against the available school-fund, from the general revenue fund to the school-fund; and the further sum of $250,000, which was appropriated out of the treasury as a sinking-fund to pay such part of the bonded debt payable in 1890 and 1891 as should be held by individuals, was loaned to the school-fund without interest till the maturity of said bonds. The sum of $504,000 was thus made available for the use of the school-fund. Among the other appropriations of the season was $150,000 for the erection of two wings, for the accommodation of 400 patients, at the North Texas Insane Asylum, in Terrell; $140,000 for furnishing the State Capitol and grading and fencing the grounds; $50,000 for the expenses of the session; $125,000 as a loan to the University of Texas, without interest, payable in 1910, of which $50,000 is to be used in the construction of a medical department at Galveston; $18,500 for enlarging the Asylum for the Blind; $20,000 for a new dormitory and hall at the Agricultural and Mechanical College; $25,890 for additions and improvements at the State Reformatory; $18,-000, $25,000, and $15,000 for similar purposes at the Deaf and Dumb Asylum, Prairie View Normal School, and State Orphan Asylum at Corsicana, respectively. The total appropriations of the session amounted to $1,241,471.17.

With regard to the State Capitol, the Legislature passed a bill appointing the Governor, Treasurer, Comptroller, and Commissioner of the General Land-Office, a board for the purpose of accepting or rejecting the building, and another bill creating a Capitol-furnishing board of three members, appointed by the Governor, to superintend the expenditure of the above-named appropriation for furnishing and grading the grounds. Other acts were

Providing that the Commissioner of Agriculture shall cause a geological and mineralogical survey of the State to be made, and appropriating $15,000 therefor.

Amending the general incorporation law so as to permit the incorporation of mercantile companies to purchase and sell goods, wares, and merchandise, and agricultural and farm products.

Requiring the assessment of property for taxes that may be removed from the State before January 1 to evade taxation, provided it be returned to the State before the tax-rolls are completed for the year.

To establish a tax-lien upon property assigned or levied upon by creditors.

Providing that the county or district attorney or Attorney-General may procure issuance of the writ of injunction to prohibit, prevent, or restrain the violation of any revenue or penal law of the State.

Requiring suits to be instituted by order of commissioners' courts to recover taxes due on unrendered personal property.

The session adjourned on May 15.

Finances.—At the close of the fiscal year, August 31, there was a balance in the treasury of $1,261,000 to the available school fund. The general revenue surplus, one year previously, was $888,-970.44. By the reduction of the tax-rate at the special session to 10 cents, it is estimated $750,000 of annual revenue will be cut off, while the extraordinary appropriations of the special session will further reduce the surplus, so that, according to the Comptroller's estimate, only about $70,000 will remain in the treasury on Aug. 31, 1889. The balance of $83,000 in the school-fund is produced by addition to the fund of $504,000 loaned to it by act of the special session. The actual deficiency of the fund is, therefore, about $420,000.

The total bonded debt of the State, on August 31, was $4,237,730, of which $3,017,100 is held by the State in its various special funds, and $1,220,630 by individuals. The only bonds falling due in 1890 and 1891 are $200,000, of revenue 6-per-cent. deficiency bonds, none of which are held by individuals.

Education.—The report of the State Superintendent shows the total scholastic population of the State, for the school year 1886–'87, to have been 489,795, an increase of 37.117 in one year; 364,953 being white and 124,842 colored. Of this number, 295,510 white and 113,150 colored children, or 408,660 in all, were enrolled in the public schools, an increase of 5,349 over 1885–'86. There were 6,911 schools for white children and 2,076 for colored children maintained during the year, a total increase of 267. In the white schools 8,232 teachers were employed at an average monthly salary of $43.27 in the counties and $69.32 in the cities; in the colored schools 2,891 teachers were employed at a monthly salary of $38.65 in the counties and $49.78 in the cities. The average school term in the counties was 5·07 months; in cities, 7·92 months. During the year the amount of the school-fund apportioned to counties was $2,362,226.25 or $4.75 per capita. This apportionment was $400,000 in excess of the school-fund revenue for the year. For 1887–'88 the total school apportionment was $2,285,551, $4.50 for each child.

Charities.—The State Orphan Asylum established by the Legislature in 1887 was located by commissioners at Corsicana, on a tract given by that city. Buildings were in process of erection at the close of the year for the accommodation of 200 children.

The Institute for Deaf, Dumb, and Blind Colored Youth, established at Austin by the same Legislature, was completed during the year, and many of beneficiaries were received.

Prisons.—The report of the State Penitentiary for the two years ending in November is as follows: Convicts, Nov. 1, 1886, 2,859; convicts, Nov. 1, 1888, 3,302; increase 442. Highest number at any time, on July 25, 1888, 3,396; average number daily, 3,129. Cash receipts, $1,256,795.44; cash disbursements, $1,226,-212.10; cash balance, $30,583.34. The number of deaths for the period, 223, is high.

The State Reformatory, established by the Legislature of 1887, was located by commissioners in Coryell County, near Gatesville, on a farm of 696 acres purchased for $10,000. They expended $62,157 for buildings, which were completed and transferred to the State on November 10. The institution was opened, and the youthful prisoners transferred thereto by proclamation of the Governor of Jan. 1, 1889.

Statistics.—The following figures for the year ending Jan. 1, 1888, are taken from the annual report of the Commissioner of Agriculture:

Population........................	2,015,632
Cotton: Acres planted..........................	3,239,972
Bales made..........................	1,123,237
Value of crop..........................	$45,127,676
Wheat: Acres planted..........................	520,219
Bushels made..........................	5,174,454
Value of crop..........................	$3,765,672
Corn: Acres planted..........................	2,929,267
Bushels made..........................	53,775,745
Value of crop..........................	$25,849,652
Oats: Acres planted..........................	561,021
Bushels made..........................	13,490,925
Value of crop..........................	$4,453,682

There are 422 saw-mills, with a capital of $3,147,633; 17 cotton-seed oil-mills, with a capital of $12,045,000; 36 marble-shops, with a capital of $123,360; 76 carriage and wagon factories, with a capital of $336,988; 136 flour-mills, with a capital of $1,316,110; 8 coal-mines, with a capital of $135,840; the woolen-mills, with a capital of $650,000; and 40 foundries and machine-shops, with a capital of $702,760.

Decision.—On October 29 the United States Supreme Court rendered a decision declaring unconstitutional the State law making it a misdemeanor for any person to do business as a commercial traveler without having first paid an occupation-tax. The law was held to be a regulation of interstate commerce by the State.

State Capitol.—This building was so far completed in May that the government occupied it early in the month, and the closing meetings of the special session were held in it. On May 16, the day following the adjournment of the session, exercises in dedication of the building were held. At this time it had been accepted by the construction commission only conditionally. Some further improvements were made, and it was finally accepted by that commission on September 20 and delivered over as complete to the receiving commission created at the special session to receive the property in behalf of the State. But, finding manifest defects in the roof and elsewhere, this commission refused to accept the report of the construction commission or to receive the building. It was then agreed that an expert be engaged to examine the work; the contractors made such changes as he suggested, and it finally became the property of the State late in the year.

Political.—A Republican State Convention met at Fort Worth on April 24, and selected delegates to the Chicago Convention, and appointed a committee of thirty-three, who should meet at Austin, on August 28, and nominate a State ticket. Among the resolutions were the following:

We recognize the importance of sheep husbandry in this State, and the danger threatening its future prosperity, and we therefore repeat the demands of this important agricultural interest for a full and adequate protection of her product.

We demand of our General Government at Washington to make ample provision for the construction of a first-class deep-water harbor on our Gulf coast, at such point as may be designated by the Government engineers, and that Congress concentrate the appropriations of money for that purpose.

On the following day the Prohibitionists met in convention at Waco, selected delegates to their National Convention, and nominated the following ticket: For Governor, Marian Martin; Lieutenant-Governor, F. E. Yoakum; Superintendent of Public Instruction, F. O. McKinzey; Treasurer, W. D. Jackson; Comptroller, C. R. King; Commissioner of the General Land-Office, J. C. Rathburn; Attorney-General, J. B. Goff. The resolutions included the following:

We favor the repeal of the United States internal revenue laws, and the repeal of all revenue laws, State and national, by which taxes are collected on the manufacture or sale of intoxicating liquors.

That such public lands as remain to the State of Texas be reserved as homesteads for citizens, and the school lands be sold only to actual settlers in quantities not exceeding 320 acres.

That the State convicts should be confined within prison walls, and the contract system abolished.

On May 15, delegates from the State Alliance, Knights of Labor, and Union Labor party met at Waco in a semi-political convention. Their common interests were discussed, and a platform adopted which included these paragraphs:

The national banks should be abolished and their bank-notes retired from circulation, and in lieu thereof we advocate a legal-tender money and a direct loan of the same to the people at a low rate of interest on real-estate security.

The means of transportation and communication should be owned or controlled by the people, as is the United States Post-Office, and equitable rates everywhere established.

No aliens should be permitted to hold or own real estate in the United States, and that no further grant of public lands be made to corporations.

We demand that an amendment be submitted to Congress making the President and Vice-President eligible by a direct vote of the people.

We demand a free ballot and a fair count, and that tampering with the ballot-box shall constitute one of the greatest of crimes.

The Democrats selected delegates to their National Convention on May 22, at Fort Worth. At the same place, on July 3, the Independent party, organized at Waco on May 15, held a second State Convention, and nominated a State ticket as follows: Evan Jones for Governor; H. S. Broiles for Lieutenant-Governor; Ward Taylor for Superintendent of Public Instruction; C. W. Geers for Comptroller; J. M. McFadin for Treasurer; J. P. Philpot for Land Commissioner; William Chambers for Attorney-General; J. C. Kearby for Chief-Justice; J. T. Nugent and W. K. Homan for Associates; Hal. W. Greer and William H. Burkhardt for Court of Appeals. The resolutions included these:

We demand the immediate payment of the national debt at its face value.

We are in favor of free and unlimited coinage of silver.

We demand a graduated income-tax.

We favor the passage of compulsory arbitration laws by which a just and speedy settlement of differences can be had between corporations and their employés.

We demand that all real estate held for speculative purposes be taxed to the full amount at which it is offered to purchasers.

A committee was appointed to confer with a State Convention distinctively of the Union Labor party, which should meet on the following day at the same place, and to secure its adoption of the Independent ticket. In this object they were successful, and the two parties were practically united. But the ticket was unfortunately constructed. The candidates for Governor, Lieutenant-Governor, Chief-Justice, and one of the Associate Justices, soon sent in their declinations. On August 24 the committee selected in their places Marion Martin as its candidate for Governor, W. A. Moers for Lieutenant-Governor, and H. F. O'Neal for Chief-Justice.

The Democratic State nominating convention met at Dallas on August 15, and renominated Gov. Ross by acclamation. The Lieutenant-Governor, Treasurer, Comptroller. Attorney-General, Superintendent of Public Instruction, and Superintendent of the General Land-Office were also renominated. For Chief-Justice of the Supreme Court, John W. Stayton of that court was nominated, and R. R. Gaines was renominated as Associate Justice. For the third member of the court John T. Henry was selected. For Judges of the Court of Appeals, John P. White, J. M. Hurt, and Samuel A. Wilson were the nominees. The platform includes the following:

We favor the enactment of prudent and efficient mining and irrigation laws to develop the agricultural and mineral resources of our State.

We favor the enactment of such laws as shall restrict the freight charges of railway and express companies, so that they may only yield a fair interest on the money actually invested in them, and at the same time to prevent discrimination in charges against any points within the State.

That the next Legislature shall pass laws defining trusts, pools, and all illegal combinations in restraint of trade, and imposing severe penalties.

The Republican Executive Committee, instead of nominating a State ticket, according to the vote of the Fort Worth Convention of April 24, called a second convention at the same place for September 20, at which the question of nominating a ticket was earnestly discussed, and where it was finally determined to support the Prohibition-Independent-Union-Labor ticket headed by Marion Martin. At the November election the Democratic national ticket was successful by a large majority, and Gov. Ross was re-elected.

TURKEY, an empire in eastern Europe and western Asia. The Government is an absolute monarchy. The Sultan is recognized as Khalif or Vicar of the Prophet in most Mohammedan lands. The legislative and executive power is exercised, under the direction of the Sultan, by the Sheikh-ul-Islam, who is the head of the religious and judicial departments of the Government, and the Grand Vizier, who is the chief in civil and administrative affairs. With these are associated heads of departments corresponding to ministers of state in European Governments. The present Sheikh-ul-Islam is Ahmed Essad Effendi. The Grand Vizier is Kiamel Pasha. The Cabinet in 1888 was as follows: President of the Council, Aarifi Pasha; Minister of Foreign Affairs, Said Pasha; Minister of War and Grand Master of Artillery, Ali Saib Pasha; Minister of Marine, Hassan Pasha; Minister of the Interior, Munir Pasha; Minister of Justice, Djevdet Pasha; Minister of Finance, Zihni Pasha; Minister of Public Works, Commerce, and Agriculture, Agob Pasha Kaziazin; Minister of

Public Instruction, Munif Pasha; Ekvaf-Naziri or Intendant of Religious Property and Revenues, Mustafa Pasha. The reigning Sultan is Abdul Hamid Khan, born Sept. 21, 1841, the thirty-fourth sovereign of the family of Osman. He succeeded his brother Murad V on Aug. 31, 1876. (For area and population see "Annual Cyclopædia" for 1887.)

Finances.—The receipts of the Sultan's treasury for the year 1887-'88 are estimated at 17,-500,000 Turkish liras. The debt, on March 13, 1887, amounted to 104,458,706 pounds sterling. Agob Pasha gave place in the Ministry of Finance, in the beginning of 1888, to Mahmoud Djelal-ed-Din Pasha, who promised to extricate the Government from its financial difficulties by an extensive scheme of improvements, and especially by unlocking new sources of revenue through the development of fisheries, mines, forests, and new industries. German capital was embarked in these enterprises, but the minister failed in accomplishing his task. The salaries of officials remained, and only at the Bairam festival was the Sultan able to pay an installment of the sums due to civil and military officers. The Minister of Finance was detected in discounting the salaries of the suffering officials at 60 per cent., and in the summer was dismissed from his post. Agob Pasha, an Armenian Christian, would not undertake the task of establishing the finances of the Empire on a sound basis, but was induced to resume the administration of the department provisionally. Eventually Zihni Pasha was appointed to the post. The Deutsche Bank, representing the group of German financiers who obtained the concession for the Asiatic Railroad to the Euphrates, negotiated a loan of 1,350,000 Turkish pounds. The unpaid creditors of the Porte clamored for the payment of their claims out of this sum, which the Minister of Finance reserved to carry out his projected reforms. The Ottoman Bank, which encashes the funds for the payment of the public debt, objected to the infringement of the monopoly of all loan transactions given to it by law. The Government, having been unable to obtain a loan from this institution except on exorbitant terms, answered that it had failed to fulfill its part of the bargain. The Russian Government made a pressing demand in June, 1888, for the payment of the arrears for two years of the war indemnity. The amount that Turkey undertook to pay was fixed by the treaty of February, 1879, at 802,-500,000 francs. By a subsequent convention, dated May 14, 1882, it was settled that the payments should be effected in annual installments of 350,000 Turkish pounds, the proceeds of the sheep-tax and the tithes of certain vilayets being assigned for that purpose. The revenues on which the payment of the indemnity was secured failed owing to a famine in these districts. In November the Minister of Finance reported a deficit in the treasury of 1,500,000 liras, and informed the Sultan that no means would be available to provide against it without severe economy and the reorganization of certain departments. By an imperial irade, promulgated on November 6, machinery and apparatus of public utility imported into Turkey were declared free of duty for ten years. A commercial treaty was negotiated with Germany in the autumn.

The Navy.—The Turkish naval force, at the beginning of 1887, comprised 15 iron-clads, of which 7 were frigates and 8 corvettes; 50 wooden vessels—viz., 3 frigates, 8 corvettes, 18 gun-boats and avisos, 3 imperial yachts, and 18 transports; and 12 torpedo-boats, including 2 submarine boats of the Nordenfeldt pattern.

Commerce.—The value of the imports into Turkey for the year ending March 12, 1888, was 21,025,953 Turkish pounds (equal to $91,-988,000), against 20,703,231 pounds for the previous year. The exports were valued at 11,287,300 Turkish pounds, against 12,707.295 in 1886–'87. The trade in tobacco, which is administered by the Régie, is not included in these figures, nor are articles free of duty. The exports of tobacco amount to about 10,-000,000 kilogrammes per annum. The values of the principal imports in 1886–'87 were, in Turkish pounds, as follow : Sugar, 1,473,226; cotton thread, 1,278,312; cotton prints, 1,171,-217; linen goods, 441,177; cotton and linen stuffs, 288,361; sheeting, 533,253; cashmere, 242,717; cloth, 463,990; muslin, 296,688; coffee, 768,045; flour, 693,506; wheat, 529,538; live animals, 447,961; petroleum, 429,744; leather, 340,386; iron, 314,581; carpets, 278,-458; skins, 255,932; chemicals and drugs, 203,266; butter, 192,346; coal, 178,574; glass, 127,895; timber, 177,408. The principal exports were of the following values: Raisins, 1,828,895; other fruits, 844,190; opium, 798,-181; raw silk, 792,233; cocoons, 338,896; wheat, 765,447; cotton, 528,911; valonia, 512,-660; wool, 500,280; coffee, 490,067; skins, 366,913; wines, 311,509; chemicals and drugs, 274,996; sesame, 272,614; olive-oil, 266,949; beans and lentils, 191,606; carpets, 145,930; soap, 138,761; minerals, 121,391; seeds, 109,-217; confectionery, 108,264; gum tragacanth, 49,042.

The merchant navy in 1886 numbered 416 vessels of over 50 tons burden, with an aggregate tonnage of 69,627, and 17 steamers of 100 ton or above, having an aggregate tonnage of 7,297.

Railroads.—The length of railroads open to traffic in 1888 was 788 kilometres in European Turkey, and in Asia Minor 660 kilometres, viz., four lines in the vicinity of Smyrna of the total length of 462 kilometres, the line from Scutari to Ismid, 93 kilometres in length, the line of 38 kilometres from Modania to Brussa, and one of 67 kilometres between Mersina and Tarsus. The international railroads of European Turkey, which have been in contemplation for twenty years, were completed in 1888. The line from the Servian frontier to Larissa

was opened to traffic in the spring, and the line through Servia and Bulgaria to Constantinople by way of Adrianople, affording rail communication with all the capitals of Europe, was opened on August 12. A concession, which English and French applicants have sought, was given to a German syndicate in September, 1888, to extend the Scutari-Ismid line to Angora, and eventually to Bagdad.

Posts and Telegraphs.—There were 408 post-offices in European Turkey in 1886 and 746 in Asiatic. The state telegraph stations numbered 233 in Europe, 438 in Asia, and 12 in Africa. The European governments have maintained separate post-offices for their citizens doing business in Turkey. The arrangement was not protected by treaty, and when the international railroad was completed the Turkish Government determined to suppress the foreign post-offices. Although prompt and efficient service was promised, the governments refused to part with the privilege that had grown up by custom, and which yielded some profit in addition to the power and prestige connected with it. The Austrian Government took the lead, and was able to compel the Turkish authorities to abandon the system of an international postal service that they had carefully organized, by refusing to deliver or forward official correspondence of the Ottoman Government.

Fortifications.—To supply the loss of Kars, the Turkish engineer, Gen. Chahab Pasha, has converted Erzerum into a fortress of the first rank, by building fifteen forts on the side fronting the road from the Russian frontier. The Russian Government, supported by the English, remonstrated with the Porte in August, 1888, against the erection of fortifications at El Arab, near the confluence of the Tigris and the Euphrates. Adrianople has been fortified, and the Government has decided to establish a military port at Chinkin or St. Juan de Medua on the Albanian coast. opposite Italy. The defenses of the Bosporus and the Dardanelles have been strengthened since the war under the superintendence of German officers.

The Macedonian Question.—Jealousies between the Christian nationalities inhabiting European Turkey involved Turkey, in 1888, in a dispute with Greece, and created a ferment throughout the peninsula. The Greeks once counted all the Christians as of their nationality, and confidently expected to extend the limits of the Hellenic kingdom to the Danube. The language of the Church, of the schools, of business, and of educated society was Greek. The rise of the Balkan nationalities and their development as independent states has destroyed this dream of a greater Greece, and now the only hope the Hellenes have of advancing their boundaries into Macedonia is in preserving the predominance of the Greek language with the help of the Phanariot in Constantinople. The creation of the independent Exarchy of Bulgaria made this difficult in respect to the Bulgarians of Macedonia. Very recently the Roumanians and Albanians on the borders of the Greek kingdom have begun to cultivate their separate nationalities, encouraged probably by Austria. The Roumanian Government and an educational society founded for the purpose in Bucharest have aided the Wallachian peasantry of Epirus to maintain schools in their own language. In the districts of Salonica and Clissura the Greeks used every means to check the Roumanian nationalist movement, and began to form political conspiracies for the annexation of these districts to Greece. The Patriarch refused the request of the Roumanians for a liturgy in their national language, and when the Bulgarian Exarch requested the Turkish Government to install Bulgarian bishops in certain districts of Macedonia, the Porte refused, acting at the instigation of the Russian ambassador. Many Bulgarians were arrested in the autumn for refusing to recognize the jurisdiction of the Greek clergy.

The Armenian Agitation.—The Turkish authorities took vigorous measures in 1888 to suppress the national movement that has for its object the re-establishment of the ancient Kingdom of Armenia. The local authorities searched the houses, and even the churches and convents, in the districts of Van, Harpoot, Diabebir, and Erzerum. In Van a great number of persons who possessed arms or compromising documents were imprisoned, and some were subjected to torture in order to extort confessions. Armenian teachers and merchants in Constantinople were placed in confinement or banished to Tripoli. Sir William White, the English ambassador at Constantinople, addressed an inquiry to the Grand Vizier concerning the arrests, and was informed that the Government possessed documentary proofs of an insurrectionary conspiracy. The British Government, which the Armenians have considered their special protector, refused to interfere, saying it had no right to do so under the Treaty of Berlin, unless it did so in conjunction with the other signatory powers. The Armenian Patriarch, Harioutioun Vehabedian, who had sought in vain to allay the revolutionary spirit, was forced to resign by his compatriots.

U

UNITARIANS. The "Year-Book of the Unitarian Congregational Churches" for 1889 gives lists of 392 Unitarian Societies and 488 ministers in the United States and Canada, and 365 Unitarian churches and others in fellowship and habitual association with them in Great Britain, Ireland, and Australia.

American Unitarians.—The American Unitarian churches and their associations and benevolent societies are represented in the National Conference of Unitarian and other Christian churches, a body that imposes no authoritative tests of membership, which meets for consultation and discussion every two years. The American Unitarian Association, organized in 1825, is the most active agency through which work for the extension of the principles of the societies is carried on. Its objects are to collect and diffuse information respecting the state of Unitarian Christianity in America; to promote union, sympathy, and co-operation, publish and distribute books and tracts, supply missionaries when they are needed, and to promote its purposes by such other measures as may be expedient. These purposes are also furthered by a number of local organizations in virtual co-operation or affiliation with this society. The sixty-third annual meeting of the American Unitarian Association was held in Boston, Mass., May 29. The Hon. George S. Hale presided. The receipts for the year had been, from societies and individuals, $50,291, and from the income of invested funds and all other sources, except legacies, $28,922. The expenditures had amounted to $103,989 showing a deficiency of $24,775, the amount of which

had to be withdrawn from the general fund. The general fund, after accounting for the addition of $69,000 to it from legacies and for the amounts that had been withdrawn from it, stood at $139,609. The trustees of the Church-Building Loan·fund had received $3,650 in contributions and $3,075 from payments on loans, and had on hand $5,266. The association gives aid in Southern education at the Hampton Institute, Va., Tuskegee, Ala., Palatka, Fla., and the Highland Academy, N. C., and supports an industrial school for Indian children at the Crow Reservation, Montana. The mission in Hindustan has been discontinued since the death of the Rev. C. H. A. Dall. A mission has been begun in Japan, in the conduct of which the British and Foreign Unitarian Association co-operates. The Woman's Auxiliary Conference, which was formed in 1880 to aid the Association and supplement its work, had, since that time collected and applied $31,887, the contributions of its last financial year having amounted to $6,000.

The Unitarian Sunday-School Society, incorporated in 1885, seeks to promote moral and religious instruction in Sunday-schools. It publishes text-books and "Lesson-Helps for Sunday-Schools," and an illustrated Sunday-school paper, and has a missionary work of increasing scope and importance. The Meadville Theological School, Meadville, Pa., and the Divinity School of Harvard University are under Unitarian influence.

Unitarians in Great Britain.—The third Triennial National Conference of Unitarian and other non-subscribing or kindred congregations met at Leeds, April 24. Papers were read by the Rev. T. W. Freckelton and Mr. John Dendy, Jr., on the best means of commending free Christianity to public favor. Propositions were made for building chapels at Oxford and Cambridge to hold Unitarian students to their faith. An address on "The Organization of our Churches," by Dr. Martineau, attracted much attention. The speaker was not satisfied with the Congregational system, or with the Unitarian name. He proposed a Presbyterian organization, and the name English Presbyterian. A committee was appointed to consider the questions raised, and call a special conference to consider its report.

The British and Foreign Unitarian Association met in London, May 23, and was opened with a sermon by Prof. Estlin Carpenter, who urged that theology be based on the broadest human experience. The Unitarian churches of the United States, the Reformed Church of France, and the Sadharan Brahmo Somaj of India were represented by visiting delegates. Mr. Harry Rawson, J. P., of Manchester, presided. A diminished income was reported. Papers were read on "Some Special Difficulties of Unitarianism To-day, and how to overcome them," in which the character of the religious services in the chapels was discussed. The autumnal meeting of the association was held in Newcastle in October. A paper unfavorable to the scheme of church organization which had been presented by Dr. Martineau, was read by Dr. Glendining.

The council of the Association issued a protest against the proposals of the Education Commission, in which it was affirmed that the only satisfactory scheme of national education is one placing the management of the schools under the control of those who are compelled to contribute to their support. Since the last report till October, 1888, 12,000 tracts had been sent out, and 86 copies of Channing's works, with other books, had been presented in answer to applications.

The Unitarian Sunday-School Association in Great Britain includes 251 schools, with 32,244 pupils and 3,989 teachers. It returned an income for the year of £1,067.

Unitarians in Continental Europe.—The number of Unitarian churches in Hungary — where Unitarianism was introduced into Transylvania in 1563—is 110, and the number of registered Unitarians is 57,000. The head of the organization is Bishop Joseph Ferencz, who has under him eight rural deans and an ecclesiastical council of 350 members. The higher education is provided for by the college at Klausenburg, where there are five theological and nine ordinary professors, with assistant professors and teachers; and the middle schools at Thorda and Szekely Keresztur. The Church has a considerable religious literature, including a periodical organ, "The Christian Seed-Sower."

The American "Year-Book" mentions several organizations in other European countries

outside of the British Empire and Hungary, which, without taking the Unitarian name, are in substantial agreement with the Unitarian faith. A considerable number of the 225 Protestant churches in Austria are liberal in their theology. The Protestanten Verein of Germany has about 40 branches and 27,000 members, and supports two missionaries in Japan. The Free Christian Association in Switzerland is active in the Protestant cantons. The Protestant Union of Holland has 13,000 members. A minority of the Protestants of France hold liberal views. The Spanish Evangelical Church includes a few liberal congregations. The Liberals in Sweden, while having societies similar to the Protestant unions, retain their membership in the state church. Services of a Unitarian type are held in Rome and Brussels. The Unitarian faith is represented in Salem, Madras, and Calcutta, India. A missionary is supported in Tokio, Japan, by the American Unitarian Association, the British and Foreign Unitarian Association co-operating.

UNITED BRETHREN IN CHRIST. The following is a summary of the statistics of this Church, as they are given in the "United Brethren Year-Book" for 1889: Number of bishops, 6; of organized churches, 445; of itinerant preachers, 1,490; of local preachers, 560; of members, 204,517; of Sunday-schools, 3,509, with 32,026 officers and teachers and 219,846 pupils; of church edifices, 2,609, having a total value of $3,757,161; of parsonages, 493, valued at $401,959. Total amount of contributions, $1,036,086; of which $474,591 were for preachers' salaries, $366,258 for church expenses, $3,566 for bishops, $3,566 for preachers' aid, $91,134 for missions, $1,964 for church erection, and the remainder for Sunday-school and educational purposes. The property of the Publishing-House at Dayton, Ohio, is valued at $252,987 above indebtedness; its receipts from business for the year ending April 1, 1888, were $156,198. The educational institutions include 9 colleges, 6 academies and seminaries, and 1 Biblical seminary. The United Brethren Home, Frontier, and Foreign Missionary Society received during its fiscal year $66,238. It operates missions in West Africa, Germany, Canada, and the United States, with a station among the Chinese at Walla Walla, Washington Territory, and gives aid to eighteen conferences. The two missions in Africa returned 27 stations, reaching 328 towns; 12 organized churches, 6 American and 25 native missionaries; 4 ordained and 25 unordained preachers; 4,105 members; 14 Sunday-schools, with 33 teachers and officers and 564 pupils; 12 day schools, with 12 teachers and 500 pupils; 11 church-houses, 8 mission residences, and property valued at $66,000. The German mission returned 720 members and 345 pupils in Sunday-schools. The society has an interest-bearing fund of $85,264, and has expended since its organization in 1853, $2,301,908.

UNITED STATES. The Administration.—On January 16 the United States Senate, after much discussion and delay, confirmed the nomination, made by the President, in December, of Lucius Q. C. Lamar to be a Justice of the United States Supreme Court, the vote standing 32 for confirmation and 28 against. Three Republican Senators (Stanford, Stewart, and Riddleberger) voted with the majority. The Republicans that voted against confirmation, based their objections upon the record of Mr. Lamar in the Confederacy. At the same time, the nominations of William F. Vilas to be Secretary of the Interior and D. M. Dickinson to be Postmaster-General were confirmed, and these officers qualified on the following day. On January 19 the appointments of the President to the Interstate Commerce Commission, made in the preceding March, were approved.

The most important change in the Government during the year was caused by the death of Chief-Justice Morrison R. Waite on March 23 (for sketch of Chief-Justice Waite see page 836; for portrait see the "Annual Cyclopædia" for 1882, page 126). The President made no appointment of his successor till April 30, when the name of Melville W. Fuller, of Chicago, was sent to the Senate (see page 359). This appointment was confirmed on July 20, by a vote of 41 to 20; but the new Chief-Justice did not take his seat until the October term of the court.

Strother M. Stockslager, of Indiana, was nominated on March 20, to be Commissioner of the General Land-Office, *vice* William J. Sparks, resigned; and Thomas J. Anderson, of Iowa, to be Assistant Commissioner, a former nomination by the President to the commissionership having been annulled. On May 21, Thomas J. Smith, of New Hampshire, was nominated as Solicitor of Internal Revenue, *vice* Charles Chesley. The resignation of Commissioner of Indian Affairs Atkins, in June, caused a vacancy, which was filled by the nomination of Civil-Service Commissioner John H. Oberly. Other nominations were: Carroll D. Wright, of Massachusetts, to be Commissioner of Labor for a second term; William L. Bancroft, of Michigan, to be General Superintendent of the Railway-Mail Service; John S. Bell, of New Jersey, to be Chief of the Secret Service Division of the Treasury Department; and Charles Cary, of New York, to be Soliciter of the Treasury Department. All of these nominations were confirmed. The President, on July 17, nominated as envoys extraordinary and ministers plenipotentiary: Lambert Tree, of Illinois, to Belgium; Robert B. Roosevelt, of New York, to the Netherlands; Rufus Magee, of Indiana, to Sweden and Norway; and Charles L. Scott, of Alabama, to Venezuela; also John E. Bacon, of South Carolina, to be Minister Resident at Paraguay and Uruguay. The Senate confirmed these nominations on August 14. Soon thereafter the resignation of George V. N. Lothrop from the Russian mission was received, and

the President, on September 11, nominated Lambert Tree, the recently confirmed Belgian minister, to the vacancy. Ten days later he nominated John G. Parkhurst, of Michigan, to the Belgian mission. These nominations, as also that of Perry Belmont, of New York, in December, to be minister to Spain, were confirmed. Ezekiel E. Smith, of North Carolina, was nominated and confirmed as Minister Resident and Consul-General in Liberia. On January 12 Edward S. Bragg, of Wisconsin, was confirmed as minister to Mexico.

On August 5 Gen. Philip H. Sheridan died, and on August 14 the President promoted Maj.-Gen. John M. Schofield to the command of the army (see page 737).

The Army.—At the date of the last consolidated returns, the army consisted of 2,188 officers and 24,549 enlisted men. The actual expenditures of the War Department for the fiscal year ended June 30, 1888, amounted to $41,-165,107.07, of which $9,158,516.68 was expended for public works, including river and harbor improvements, and $23,337,245.11 for the actual support of the army and the Military Academy. The only difficulty with the Indians that occurred was upon the Crow Reservation in Dakota, where a threatened outbreak was promptly suppressed by Gen. Ruger, and the ringleaders arrested and punished. All the States and Territories now have an active militia sufficient under the regulations to entitle them to receive ordnance and quartermaster's stores' from the United States, excepting Arkansas, Arizona, Idaho, and Utah.

Postal Service.—For the fiscal year ending June 30, 1888, the total revenue was $52,695,-176.79, while the actual and estimated expenses were $56,885,403.84, leaving an estimated deficiency of $4,190,227.05. The actual deficiency for the fiscal year preceding was $4,-297,238.31, the total expenses $53,134,847.70, and the total revenue $48,837,609.39.

The number of post-offices on June 30, 1888, was 57,376; there were established during the year preceding 3,864 offices, and 1,645 were discontinued. The number of postmasters appointed during the year ended June 30, 1888, was 12,288, of which 6,521 were upon resignations and commissions expired, 1,244 upon removals, 659 to fill vacancies by death, and 3,-864 on establishment of new post-offices. The free-delivery service was extended to 169 additional places, under the act of Jan. 3, 1887, making a total of 358 free-delivery cities. The volume of ordinary mail has largely increased, as shown by the increased revenue of the department from the sale of postage-stamps. The total number of pieces handled has doubled since 1883.

The number of money-order offices at the close of the year was 8,241, and the number of postal-note offices 311. The domestic orders issued numbered 9,959,207, of the aggregate amount of $119,649,064.98, while the orders paid and repaid were in excess of that sum by $94,280.27. There were issued 6,668,-006 postal notes, amounting to $12,134,459.04, and the notes paid were only $29,577.49 less in value. There were 759,636 orders drawn for payment in foreign countries, reaching the large total of $11,293,870.05, while 236,992 orders of the value of $1,169,675.64 were transmitted from abroad for payment in the United States.

Pensions.—The number of pensioners added to the rolls during the fiscal year ended June 30, 1888, is 60,252, and increase of pensions was granted in 45,716 cases. The names of 15,730 pensioners were dropped from the rolls during the year, and at the close of the year the number of persons of all classes receiving pensions was 452,557.

The Civil Service.—The fourth annual report of the Civil-Service Commission, covering the period between Jan. 16, 1886, and July 1, 1887, was transmitted to Congress in July. During the time covered by the report, 15,852 persons were examined for admission in the classified civil service of the Government in all its branches, of whom 10,746 passed the examination and 5,106 failed. Of those who passed the examination 2,977 were applicants for admission to the departmental service at Washington, 2,547 were examined for admission to the customs service, and 5,222 for admission to the postal service. During the same period 547 appointments were made from the eligible lists to the departmental service, 641 to the customs service, and 3,254 to the postal service. Since the period covered by the report, the rules and regulations governing the violations of the law upon the subject have been completely remodeled in such a manner as to render the enforcement of the statute more effective and greatly increase its usefulness.

Indians.—Reports of Indian agents show that the total Indian population for the fiscal year 1887-'88 was 246,095, not including the Indians of Alaska. The entire extent of territory now in reservation for Indian purposes, including all portions of the Indian Territory, is 112,413,440 acres, being an average of 456 acres for each Indian, computed on the last reported number of the total population. The work of allotting lands in severalty which was begun in 1887 on seven reservations, the Yankton and Lake Traverse Reservations in Dakota Territory, the Winnebago Reservation in Nebraska, the Pottawatomie Reservation in the Indian Territory, the Crow Reservation in Montana, the Fon du Lac Reservation in Minnesota, and the Siletz Reservation in Oregon, was suspended early in 1888, because the funds had been exhausted.

In June Congress appropriated $10,000, and with this money the work was resumed on three reservations, the Winnebago Reservation in Nebraska, the Crow Reservation in Montana, and the Fond du Lac Reservation in Minnesota. The allotment on the Lake Traverse Reservation is complete.

Alaska.—The Governor estimates the population of Alaska as follows: Whites, 6,500; creoles, 1,900; Aleuts, 2,950; civilized natives, 3,500; uncivilized natives, 35,000—a total of 49,850. The town of Juneau has doubled in population during the past year, owing to the development of valuable mining properties, and most of the towns in the southeastern section of the Territory show an increase. During the past year considerable progress was made in mining; the great stamp-mill on Douglas Island has now two hundred and forty stamps in operation, and it is the largest mill of the kind in the world, its output being at least $150,000 a month. The ore at this mine is improving, and four undeveloped claims on this island were recently sold to Eastern and European capitalists for $1,500,000. Mines are being opened and new discoveries made of promising ore-beds.

Coal seems to abound in the explored parts of the Territory. During the last year cannel coal was found. The United States steamer "Thetis" replenished her bunkers from a vein that measured thirty-two feet in thickness, and while on a cruise with this vessel the Governor saw all along the coast coal-veins from one to fifteen feet thick.

The following is a careful estimate of the market value of Alaskan products for the year: Furs, $3,000,000; fish, oil, bone, and ivory, $4,000,000; gold (bullion and dust), $2,000,-000; silver, $50,000; lumber, $50,000—total, $9,100,000.

Foreign Relations.—On February 15 the commissioners appointed to negotiate a treaty between Great Britain and the United States with respect to the Canadian fisheries completed their work at Washington, and signed a proposed treaty, which was transmitted to the Senate, which on August 21 rejected the treaty by a strict party vote of 30 Republicans against 27 Democrats. The President thereupon sent a warlike message to Congress, saying that retaliatory measures were now the only ones to be adopted, and asking for greater powers to carry them into effect. The Republicans in Congress claimed that he already had sufficient authority for that purpose, and, regarding the message as an attempt to attract supporters in the pending political canvass, refused to take any action thereon.

On March 12 a treaty with China was signed at Washington. It provides for the absolute exclusion of Chinese laborers from this country for twenty years, and for a second period of twenty years unless notice to the contrary should be given by either party. The Senate ratified this treaty with some amendments on May 7, but it was rejected by the Chinese Government, whereupon a Chinese exclusion bill, having already passed the House, was adopted by the Senate on September 7 and signed by the President. Differences existing between the United States and Morocco were settled by an agreement made in May.

In November difficulties arose with Hayti in consequence of the seizure and detention of American vessels, especially the steamer "Haytian Republic," by the authorities temporarily in power in that island. A strife of factions had existed there for several months, and the President, without recognizing any settled government, had sent to Haytian waters a war-vessel for the protection of American people and interests. On being satisfied that the seizure of the "Haytian Republic" was wrongful, he dispatched Admiral Luce with the ships "Galena" and "Yantic" to demand a return of the vessel. The demand was promptly acceded to, the steamer was surrendered on December 22, and the former amicable relations between the two countries were restored.

A comprehensive treaty of amity and commerce with Peru was completed and ratified during the year, and became effective by proclamation of the President dated November 7.

Democratic Convention.—At a meeting of the Democratic National Committee in Washington, on February 23, it was voted to call the National Convention to meet at St. Louis on June 5. Some time before the date of the convention, President Cleveland's renomination was universally conceded; the only question was regarding the second place on the ticket. The convention organized by the choice of S. M. White, of California, as temporary chairman, and Congressman Patrick A. Collins, of Massachusetts, as permanent chairman. The name of President Cleveland was presented to the convention by Daniel Dougherty, of New York, and his nomination unanimously carried amid great enthusiasm. For the Vice-Presidency, Gov. Isaac P. Gray, of Indiana, and Ex-Senator Allen G. Thurman, of Ohio, were the only candidates formally before the convention.

Before the first ballot was completed, it was evident that Mr. Thurman would easily obtain a majority. The name of Gov. Gray was then withdrawn, and the Ex-Senator was unanimously nominated. Of the votes cast on this ballot, 690 were for Thurman, 105 for Gray, and 25 for John C. Black, of Illinois.

The platform is as follows:

The Democratic party of the United States in national convention assembled renews the pledge of its fidelity to Democratic faith and reaffirms the platform adopted by its representatives in the convention of 1884, and indorses the views expressed by President Cleveland in his last earnest message to Congress as the correct interpretation of that platform upon the question of tariff reduction, and also indorses the efforts of our Democratic representatives in Congress to secure a reduction of excessive taxation. Chief among its principles of party faith are the maintenance of the indissoluble union of free and indestructible States, now about to enter upon its second century of unexampled progress and renown; devotion to a plan of Government regulated by a written constitution strictly specifying every granted power and expressly reserving to the States or people the entire ungranted residue of power; the encouragement of jealous, popular vigilance directed to all who have been chosen for brief terms to enact and execute the laws and are charged with the duty of preserving peace, insuring equality, and establishing justice.

The Democratic party welcomes an exacting scrutiny of the administration of the Executive power which four years ago was committed to its trust in the selection of Grover Cleveland as President of the United States, but it challenges the most searching scrutiny concerning its fidelity and devotion to the pledges which then invited the suffrages of the people. During a most critical period of our financial affairs, resulting from overtaxation, the anomalous condition of our currency, and a public debt unmatured, it has, by the adoption of a wise and conservative course, not only averted disaster, but greatly promoted the prosperity of the people.

It has reversed the improvident and unwise policy of the Republican party touching the public domain, and has reclaimed from corporations and syndicates, alien and domestic, and restored to the people nearly 100,000,000 acres of valuable land to be sacredly held as homesteads for our citizens.

While carefully guarding the interests of the tax-payers and conforming strictly to the principles of justice and equity, it has paid out more for pensions and bounties to the soldiers and sailors of the republic than was ever paid before during an equal period.

It has adopted and consistently pursued a firm and prudent foreign policy, preserving peace with all nations while scrupulously maintaining all the rights and interests of our own Government and people at home and abroad.

The exclusion from our shores of Chinese laborers has been effectually secured under the provisions of a treaty, the operation of which has been postponed by the action of a Republican majority in the Senate.

Honest reform in the civil service has been inaugurated and maintained by President Cleveland, and he has brought the public service to the highest standard of efficiency, not only by rule and precept, but by the example of his own untiring and unselfish administration of public affairs.

In every branch and department of the Government under Democratic control the rights and the welfare of all the people have been guarded and defended; every public interest has been protected, and the equality of all our citizens before the law, without regard to race or color, has been steadfastly maintained. Upon its record thus exhibited and upon a pledge of a continuance to the people of these benefits, the Democracy invokes a renewal of popular trust by the re-election of a Chief Magistrate who has been faithful, able, and prudent. We invoke in addition to that trust the transfer also to the Democracy of the entire legislative power.

The Republican party, controlling the Senate and resisting in both Houses of Congress a reformation of unjust and unequal tax laws which have outlasted the necessities of war and are now undermining the abundance of a long peace, deny to the people equality before the law and the fairness and the justice which are their right. Thus the cry of American labor for a better share in the rewards of industry is stifled with false pretenses, enterprise is fettered and bound down to home markets, capital is discouraged with doubt, and unequal, unjust laws can neither be properly amended nor repealed. The Democratic party will continue with all the power confided to it the struggle to reform these laws in accordance with the pledges of its last platform, indorsed at the ballot-box by the suffrages of the people.

Of all the industrious freemen of our land the immense majority, including every tiller of the soil, gain no advantage from excessive tax laws, but the price of nearly everything they buy is increased by the favoritism of an unequal system of tax legislation. All unnecessary taxation is unjust taxation. It is repugnant to the creed of Democracy that by such taxation the cost of the necessaries of life should be unjustifiably increased to all our people. Judged by Democratic principles, the interests of the people are betrayed when, by unnecessary taxation, trusts and combinations are permitted to exist, which, while unduly enriching the few that combine, rob the body of our citizens by depriving them of the benefits of natural competition.

Every Democratic rule of governmental action is violated when, through unnecessary taxation, a vast sum of money far beyond the needs of an economical administration is drawn from the people and the channels of trade, and accumulated as a demoralizing surplus in the national Treasury. The money now lying idle in the General Treasury, resulting from superfluous taxation, amounts to more than $125,000,000, and the surplus collected is reaching the sum of more than $60,000,000 annually. Debauched by this immense temptation, the remedy of the Republican party is to meet and exhaust by extravagant appropriation and expenses, whether constitutional or not, the accumulation of extravagant taxation. The Democratic policy is to enforce frugality in public expense and abolish unnecessary taxation.

Our established domestic industries and enterprises should not and need not be endangered by the reduction and correction of the burdens of taxation. On the contrary, a fair and careful revision of our tax laws, with due allowance for the difference between the wages of American and foreign labor, must promote and encourage every branch of such industries and enterprises by giving them assurance of an extended market and steady and continuous operations. In the interests of American labor, which should in no event be neglected, the revision of our tax laws contemplated by the Democratic party should promote the advantage of such labor by cheapening the cost of necessaries of life in the home of every workingman, and at the same time securing to him steady and remunerative employment. Upon this question of tariff reform, so closely concerning every phase of our national life, and upon every question involved in the problem of good government the Democratic party submits its principles and professions to the intelligent suffrages of the American people.

Resolution presented by Mr. Scott, of Pennsylvania:
"*Resolved*, That this convention hereby indorses and recommends the early passage of the Mill for the reduction of the revenue now pending in the House of Representatives."

Resolution presented by Mr. Lehmann, of Iowa:
"*Resolved*, That a just and liberal policy should be pursued in reference to the Territories; that right of self-government is inherent in the people and guaranteed under the Constitution; that the Territories of Washington, Dakota, Montana, and New Mexico are by virtue of population and development entitled to admission into the Union as States, and we unqualifiedly condemn the course of the Republican party in refusing Statehood and self-government to their people."

Resolution presented by ex-Governor Abbett, of New Jersey:
"*Resolved*, That we express our cordial sympathy with the struggling people of all nations in their effort to secure for themselves the inestimable blessings of self-government and civil and religious liberty, and we especially declare our sympathy with the efforts of those noble patriots who, led by Gladstone and Parnell, have conducted their grand and peaceful contest for home rule in Ireland."

Republican Convention.—The place and date of the Republican National Convention were fixed at a meeting of the National Committee held late in 1887, Chicago being the choice of a majority of the committee, and June 19 the time agreed upon. On February 12 a letter of James G. Blaine, from Florence, Italy, to Chairman B. F. Jones, of the committee, was published, in which Mr. Blaine said that, as personal reasons would prevent him from entering the contest, his name "would not be presented to the convention." No serious efforts in behalf of any candidate had hitherto been made, except for Senator John Sherman, of Ohio, who had been recommended for the nomination by the Ohio State Convention in July, 1887, and who, during the autumn of that year, had delivered speeches in Southern cities. Other names were now mentioned, and as the various State conventions were held, in April and May, to select delegates to the National Convention, candidates were formally presented. The Indiana Convention recommended ex-Senator Benjamin Harrison; Iowa recommended Senator William B. Allison; Michigan, ex-Gov. Russell A. Alger; Wisconsin, Gov. Jeremiah M. Rusk. Judge Walter Q. Gresham, of Indiana, attracted earnest supporters in many parts of the country, and the Republican Convention of Illinois instructed its delegates to vote in his favor. In New York, Chauncey M. Depew was a popular candidate, although the delegation from that State was unpledged. Senator Joseph R. Hawley was the favorite of Connecticut, Congressman William Walter Phelps of New Jersey, and Senator John J. Ingalls of Kansas. The possibility that Mr. Blaine might finally be induced to accept the nomination was a disturbing element, which apparently prevented many of the delegates from earnestly supporting any other candidate. On May 30 a second letter from him was published, which set at rest all reasonable doubts. In this letter, dated at Paris, France, he said, unequivocally, that he could not accept a nomination without showing bad faith toward those candidates who, relying on his former letter, were already in the field, and therefore he could not accept at all. No one of the candidates was assured of the support even of one third of the delegates. The convention organized by choosing John M. Thurston, of Kansas, for temporary chairman and M. Estee, of California, for permanent chairman. Three days were occupied in the work of organization, in the preparation and adoption of a platform, and in the presentation of candidates. Nominating speeches were made in favor of Gresham by Leonard Swett, of Illinois; in favor of Harrison by ex-Gov. Albert G. Porter, of Indiana; for Allison by William P. Hepburn, of Iowa; for Alger by R. E. Frazier, of Michigan; for Depew by Senator Hiscock, of New York; for Sherman by Gen. Hastings, of Pennsylvania; for Rusk by Senator Spooner, of Wisconsin. The names of Senator Hawley and ex-Mayor Edwin H. Fitler, of Philadelphia, were also presented in brief speeches. On the first ballot 830 votes were cast, a majority being 416. Of these, Sherman had 229, Gresham 111, Depew 99, Alger 84, Harrison 80, Allison 72, Blaine 35, Ingalls 28, Rusk 25, Phelps 25, Fitler 24, Hawley 13, ex-Secretary Robert T. Lincoln 3, and Congressman William McKinley, of Ohio, 2. The vote of Senator Ingalls came from Kansas and Arkansas, and sixteen of the Pennsylvania delegation voted for Fitler. The New York delegates voted unitedly for Depew, according to an agreement made in caucus on the preceding day. The State delegations not having favorites were very much divided.

Upon the second ballot, after the names of ex-Mayor Fitler and Senator Hawley had been withdrawn, the following vote was cast: Sherman 249 votes, Alger 116, Gresham 108, Depew 99, Harrison 91, Allison 75, Blaine 33, Rusk 20, Phelps 18, Ingalls 16, McKinley 3, Lincoln 2. On the third ballot Kansas ceased to vote for Ingalls, and nearly all the New Jersey delegates abandoned Phelps. Sherman received on this ballot 244 votes, Gresham 123, Alger 122, Harrison 94, Depew 91, Allison 88, Blaine 35, Rusk 16, McKinley 8, Phelps 5, Lincoln 2, and Mr. Justice Miller 2. The convention adjourned after this ballot, and on its reassembling, Mr. Depew made an address, withdrawing his name. Col. Robert G. Ingersoll, then being asked to address the convention, attempted to advocate the nomination of Gresham, but the convention refused to hear him. The convention again adjourned without balloting. When it reassembled on the fifth day Congressman McKinley protested against the use of his name, but without effect. On the fourth ballot Wisconsin transferred her vote from Rusk to Harrison, and 59 votes from New York went to the same candidate. Sherman received 235 votes, Harrison 217, Alger 135, Gresham 98, Allison 88, Blaine 42, McKinley 11, Gov. Foraker, Lincoln, and Fred. Douglas one each. The fifth ballot resulted as follows: Sherman 224, Harrison 213, Alger 142, Allison 99, Gresham 87, Blaine 48, McKinley 14. The convention then adjourned to the following Monday.

It had become evident that Sherman, although still leading, could not command a following sufficient to nominate him, and the strength of Harrison appeared to have reached its highest point. A conference committee of friends of the various candidates met on Saturday evening and during Sunday, but without uniting upon a candidate. When the convention came together, Congressman Boutelle, of Maine, announced the receipt of two telegrams from Mr. Blaine, at Edinburgh, in which he earnestly requested his friends to respect his Paris letter and to refrain from voting for him. This was accepted as a finality, although the California delegation and a few others still voted for their favorite. On the sixth ballot Sherman received 244 votes, Harrison 231, Alger 137, Gresham 91, Allison 73, Blaine 40, and McKinley 12. The seventh ballot resulted as follows: Harrison 278, Sherman 231, Alger 120, Gresham 91, Allison 76, McKinley 16, Blaine 15, Lincoln 2, Foraker 1. The decisive point was now reached, when Congressman Henderson, of Iowa, arose and withdrew the name of Senator Allison, whose strength was at once transferred to Harrison. Friends of the other candidates joined to swell the winning column, and at the end of roll-call, on the eighth ballot, Harrison had obtained 544 votes, or over 100 more than were necessary for a choice. Sherman received on this ballot 118 votes, Alger 100, Gresham 59, Blaine 5, McKinley 4. The nomination was then made unanimous.

For Vice-President, William O. Bradley, of Kentucky; William Walter Phelps, of New Jersey; and Levi P. Morton, of New York, were placed in nomination. Mr. Morton was nominated on the first ballot by the following vote: Morton 561, Phelps 119, Bradley 93, Blanche K. Bruce, of Mississippi, 11. The nomination was made unanimous.

The platform adopted by the convention is as follows:

The Republicans of the United States, assembled by their delegates in National Convention, pause on the threshold of their proceedings to honor the memory of their first great leader, the immortal champion of liberty and the rights of the people—Abraham Lincoln—and to cover also with wreaths of imperishable remembrance and gratitude the heroic names of our later leaders who have been more recently called away from our councils—Grant, Garfield, Arthur, Logan, Conkling. May their memories be faithfully cherished!

We also recall with our greetings and with prayer for his recovery the name of one of our living heroes, whose memory will be treasured in the history both of the Republicans and the republic, the name of that noble soldier and favorite child of victory, Philip H. Sheridan.

In the spirit of those great leaders and of our own devotion to human liberty, and with that hostility to all forms of despotism and oppression which is the fundamental idea of the Republican party, we send fraternal congratulations to our fellow Americans of Brazil upon their great act of emancipation which completed the abolition of slavery throughout the two American continents.

We earnestly hope we may soon congratulate our fellow-citizens of Irish birth upon the peaceful recovery of home rule for Ireland.

We reaffirm our unswerving devotion to the national Constitution and to the indissoluble union of the States, to the autonomy reserved to the States under the Constitution, to the personal rights and liberties of citizens in all the States and Territories of the Union, and especially to the supreme and sovereign right of every lawful citizen, rich or poor, native or foreign born, white or black, to cast one free ballot in public elections and to have that ballot duly counted.

We hold a free and honest popular ballot and just and equal representation of all the people to be the foundation of our republican Government, and demand effective legislation to secure the integrity and purity of elections, which are the fountains of all public authority.

We charge that the present Administration and Democratic majority in Congress owe their existence to the suppression of the ballot by a criminal nullification of the Constitution and the laws of the United States.

We are uncompromisingly in favor of the American system of protection; we protest against its destruction as proposed by the President and his party. They serve the interests of Europe; we will support the interests of America. We accept the issue and confidently appeal to the people for their judgment. The protective system must be maintained. Its abandonment has always been followed by general disaster to all interests except those of the usurer and the sheriff.

We denounce the Mills Bill as destructive to the general business, the labor, and the farming interests of the country, and we heartily indorse the consistent and patriotic action of the Republican representatives in Congress in opposition to its passage.

We condemn the proposition of the Democratic party to place wool on the free list, and we insist that the duties thereon shall be adjusted and maintained so as to furnish full and adequate protection to that industry.

The Republican party would effect all needed reduction of the national revenue by repealing the taxes upon tobacco, which are an annoyance and burden to agriculture, and the taxes upon spirits used in the arts and for mechanical purposes, and by such revision of the tariff laws as will tend to check imports of such articles as are produced by our people, the production of which gives employment to our labor, and release from import duties those articles of foreign production except luxuries the like of which can not be produced at home. If there shall still remain a larger revenue than is requisite for the wants of the Government, we favor the entire repeal of internal taxes rather than the surrender of any part of our protective system at a joint behest of whisky trusts and agents of foreign manufacturers.

We declare our hostility to the introduction into this country of foreign contract labor and of Chinese labor alien to our civilization and our Constitution, and we demand the rigid enforcement of existing laws against it and favor such immediate legislation as will exclude such labor from our shores.

We declare our opposition to all combinations of capital organized in trusts or otherwise to control arbitrarily the condition of trade among our citizens, and we recommend to Congress and State legislatures in their respective jurisdictions, such legislation as will prevent the execution of all schemes to oppress the people by undue charges on their supplies or by unjust rates for the transportation of their products to market. We approve the legislation by Congress to prevent alike unjust burdens and unfair discriminations between States.

We reaffirm the policy of appropriating the public lands of the United States to be homesteads for American citizens and settlers not aliens which the Republican party established in 1862 against the persistent opposition of the Democrats in Congress, and which has brought our great Western domain into such magnificent development. The restoration of unearned railroad land grants to public domain for the use of actual settlers which was begun under the administration of President Arthur should be continued. We deny that the Democratic party has ever restored one acre to the people, but declare that by joint action of Republicans and Democrats about fifty million acres of unearned lands, originally granted for the construction of railroads, have been restored to the public domain in pursuance of the conditions inserted by the Republican party in the original grant.

We charge the Democratic Administration with failure to execute the laws securing to settlers titles to their homesteads and with using appropriations made for that purpose to harrass the innocent settlers with spies and prosecutions under the false pretense of exposing frauds and vindicating law.

The government by Congress of the Territories is based upon necessity only to the end that they may become States in the Union ; therefore, whenever the conditions of population, material resources, public intelligence, and morality are such as to insure stable local government therein, the people of such Territories should be permitted as a right inherent in them to form for themselves constitutions and State governments and be admitted into the Union. Pending the preparation for statehood, all officers thereof should be selected from *bona-fide* residents and citizens of the Territory wherein they are to serve. South Dakota should of right be immediately admitted as a State in the Union under the Constitution framed and adopted by her people, and we heartily indorse the action of the Republican Senate in twice passing bills for her admission. The refusal of the Democratic House of Representatives, for partisan purposes, to favorably consider these bills is a willful violation of the sacred American principle of local self-government, and merits the condemnation of all just men. The pending bills in the Senate for acts to enable the people of Washington, North Dakota, and Montana Territories to form constitutions and establish State governments should be passed without unnecessary delay. The Republican party pledges itself to do all in its power to facilitate the admission of the Territories of New Mexico, Wyoming, Idaho, and Arizona to the enjoyment of self-government as States ; such of them as are now qualified as soon as possible, and the others as soon as they become so.

The political power of the Mormon Church in the Territories as exercised in the past is a menace to free institutions too dangerous to be long suffered. Therefore we pledge the Republican party to appropriate legislation asserting the sovereignty of the nation in all Territories where the same is questioned, and, in furtherance of that end, to place upon the statute-books legislation stringent enough to divorce the political from the ecclesiastical power and thus stamp out the attendant wickedness of polygamy.

The Republican party is in favor of the use of both gold and silver as money, and condemns the policy of the Democratic Administration in its efforts to demonetize silver.

We demand the reduction of letter postage to one cent per ounce.

In a republic like ours, where the citizen is sovereign and the official the servant, where no power is exercised except by the will of the people, it is important that the sovereign—the people—should possess intelligence. The free school is a promoter of that intelligence which is to preserve us a free nation. Therefore the State or nation, or both combined, should support free institutions of learning sufficient to afford to every child growing up in the land the opportunity of a good common-school education.

We earnestly recommend that prompt action be taken by Congress in the enactment of such legislation as will best secure the rehabilitation of our American merchant marine, and we protest against the passage by Congress of a free ship bill, as calculated to work injustice to labor by lessening the wages of those engaged in preparing materials as well as those directly employed in our ship-yards.

We demand appropriations for the early rebuilding of our navy ; for the construction of coast fortifications and modern ordnance, and other approved modern means of defense for the protection of our defenseless harbors and cities ; for the payment of just pensions to our soldiers ; for necessary works of national importance in the improvement of harbors and the channels of internal, coastwise, and foreign commerce ; for the encouragement of the shipping interests of the Atlantic, Gulf, and Pacific States, as well as for the payment of the maturing public debt. This policy will give employment to our labor, activity to our various industries, increase security of our country, promote trade, open new and direct markets for our produce, and cheapen the cost of transportation. We affirm this to be far better for our country than the Democratic policy of loaning the Government's money without interest to "pet banks."

The conduct of foreign affairs by the present Administration has been distinguished by its inefficiency and its cowardice. Having withdrawn from the Senate all pending treaties effected by Republican Administrations for the removal of foreign burdens and restrictions upon our commerce and for its extension into better markets, it has neither effected nor proposed any others in their stead. Professing adherence to the Monroe doctrine, it has seen with idle complacency the extension of foreign influence in Central America and of foreign trade everywhere among our neighbors. It has refused to charter, sanction, or encourage any American organization for constructing the Nicaragua Canal, a work of vital importance to the maintenance of the Monroe doctrine and of our national influence in Central and South America, and necessary for the development of trade with our Pacific territory, with South America, and with the islands and further coasts of the Pacific Ocean.

We arraign the present Democratic Administration for its weak and unpatriotic treatment of the fisheries question, and its pusillanimous surrender of the essential privileges to which our fishing-vessels are entitled in Canadian ports under the treaty of 1818, the reciprocal maritime legislation of 1830 and the comity of the nations, and which Canadian fishing-vessels receive in the ports of the United States. We condemn the policy of the present Administration and the Democratic majority in Congress toward our fisheries as unfriendly and conspicuously unpatriotic, and as tending to destroy a valuable national industry and an indispensible resource of defense against a foreign enemy. The name of American applies alike to all citizens of the republic and imposes upon all alike the same obligation of obedience to the laws. At the same time that citizenship is and must be the panoply and safeguard of him who wears it and protect him, whether high or low, rich or p   , in all his civil rights. It should and must afford him protection at home and follow and protect him abroad in whatever land he may be on a lawful errand.

The men who abandoned the Republican party in 1834, and continue to adhere to the Democratic party, have deserted not only the cause of honest government, of sound finance, of freedom, of purity of the ballot, but especially have deserted the cause of reform in the civil service. We will not fail to keep our pledges because they have broken theirs, or because their candidate has broken his. We therefore repeat our declaration of 1884, to wit: The reform of the civil service, auspiciously begun under the Republican Administration, should be completed by the further extension of the reform system already established by law to all the grades of the service to which it is applicable. The spirit and purpose of the reform should be observed in all Executive appointments, and all laws at variance with the object of existing reform legislation should be repealed, to the end that the dangers to free institutions which lurk in the power of official patronage may be wisely and effectively avoided.

The gratitude of the nation to the defenders of the Union can not be measured by laws. The legislation of Congress should conform to the pledge made by a loyal people and be so enlarged and extended as to provide against the possibility that any man who honorably wore the Federal uniform shall become an inmate of an almshouse or dependent upon private charity. In the presence of an overflowing Treasury, it would be a public scandal to do less for those whose valorous service preserved the Government. We denounce the hostile spirit shown by President Cleveland in his numerous vetoes of measures for pension relief, and the action of the Democratic House of Representatives in refusing even a consideration of general pension legislation.

In support of the principles herewith enunciated we invite the co-operation of patriotic men of all parties, and especially of all workingmen, whose prosperity is seriously threatened by the free-trade policy of the present Administration.

The following addendum was adopted in the closing hours of the convention:

The first concern of all good government is the virtue and sobriety of the people and the purity of their homes. The Republican party cordially sympathizes with all wise and well directed efforts for the promotion of temperance and morality.

Prohibition Convention.—The Prohibition National Convention met at Indianapolis on May 30, and organized by choosing H. C. Delano, of Connecticut, to be temporary chairman. The permanent chairman was Ex-Gov. John P. St. John, of Kansas. Gen. Clinton B. Fisk, of New Jersey, was nominated by acclamation for President, and John A. Brooks, of Missouri, for Vice-President. Considerable discussion arose regarding the platform, especially upon the subject of woman suffrage. The report of the majority of the Platform Committee was finally adopted in the following form:

The Prohibition party, in national convention assembled, acknowledging Almighty God as the source of all power in government, do hereby declare:

1. That the manufacture, importation, exportation, transportation, and sale of alcoholic beverages shall be made public crimes, and punished as such.

2. That such prohibition must be secured through amendments of our national and State constitutions, enforced by adequate laws adequately supported by administrative authority; and to this end the organization of the Prohibition party is imperatively demanded in State and nation.

3. That any form of license, taxation, or regulation of the liquor-traffic is contrary to good government; that any party which supports regulation, license, or tax enters into alliance with such traffic and becomes the actual foe of the State's welfare, and that we arraign the Republican and Democratic parties for their persistent attitude in favor of the licensed iniquity, whereby they oppose the demand of the people for prohibition, and, through open complicity with the liquor cause, defeat the enforcement of law.

4. For the immediate abolition of the internal revenue system, whereby our national Government is deriving support from our greatest national vice.

5. That, an adequate public revenue being necessary, it may properly be raised by impost duties and by an equitable assessment upon the property and the legitimate business of the country, but import duties should be so reduced that no surplus shall be accumulated in the Treasury, and that the burdens of taxation shall be removed from foods, clothing, and other comforts and necessaries of life.

6. That civil-service appointments for all civil offices, chiefly clerical in their duties, should be based upon moral, intellectual, and physical qualifications, and not upon party service or party necessity.

7. That the right of suffrage rests on no mere circumstance of race, color, sex, or nationality, and that where, from any cause, it has been held from citizens who are of suitable age and mentally and morally qualified for the exercise of an intelligent ballot, it should be restored by the people through the Legislatures of the several States, on such educational basis as they may deem wise.

8. For the abolition of polygamy and the establishment of uniform laws governing marriage and divorce.

9. For prohibiting all combinations of capital to control and to increase the cost of products for popular consumption.

10. For the preservation and defense of the Sabbath as a civil institution without oppressing any who religiously observe the same on any other day than the first day of the week.

That arbitration is the Christian, wise, and economic method of settling national differences, and the same method should, by judicious legislation, be applied to the settlement of disputes between large bodies of employés and employers; that the abolition of the saloon would remove the burdens, moral, physical, pecuniary, and social, which now oppress labor and rob it of its earnings, and would prove to be the wise and success-ful way of promoting labor reform; and we invite labor and capital to unite with us for the accomplishment thereof; that monopoly in land is a wrong to the people, and the public land should be reserved to actual settlers, and that men and women should receive equal wages for equal work.

That our immigration laws should be so enforced as to prevent the introduction into our country of all convicts, inmates of other dependent institutions, and of others physically incapacitated for self-support, and that no person should have the ballot in any State who is not a citizen of the United States.

Recognizing and declaring that prohibition of the liquor-traffic has become the dominant issue in national politics, we invite to full party fellowship all those who, on this one dominant issue, are with us agreed, in the full belief that this party can and will remove sectional differences, promote national unity, and insure the best welfare of our entire land.

Union Labor and United Labor Conventions.—On May 15 a national convention of the Union Labor party, consisting of two hundred and seventy-four delegates, from twenty-five States, met at Cincinnati for the purpose of nominating presidential candidates. This party was formed on Feb. 22, 1887, at a convention held in the same city, to which delegates had been invited from the labor and farmers' organizations, including the Knights of Labor, the Agricultural Wheelers, the Corn-growers, the Homesteadry, Farmers' Alliances, Greenbackers, and Grangers. The party thus formed placed a State ticket in the field, in Ohio, in the autumn of 1887, and in Arkansas, Missouri, and nearly all the Western States during the canvass of this year. The convention nominated for President, Alson J. Streeter, of Illinois; and for Vice-President, Charles E. Cunningham, of Arkansas. The platform, after reciting the existing hardships of farmers and laborers, contains the following declarations:

We oppose land monopoly in every form, demand the forfeiture of unearned grants, the limitation of land ownership, and such other legislation as will stop speculation in lands and holding it unused from those whose necessities require it. A homestead should be exempt, to a limited extent, from execution or taxation.

The means of communication and transportation shall be owned by the people, as is the United States postal system.

The establishment of a national monetary system in the interest of the producer, instead of the speculator and usurer, by which the circulating medium in necessary quantity shall be issued directly to the people, without the intervention of banks, and loaned to citizens upon land security, at a low rate of interest, so as to relieve them from the extortion of usury, and enable them to control the money supply. Postal savings banks should be established, and while we have free coinage of gold we should have free coinage of silver. We demand the immediate application of all the money in the United States Treasury to the payment of the bonded debt, and condemn the further issue of interest-bearing bonds, either by the national Government or by States, Territories, or municipalities.

Arbitration should take the place of strikes and other injurious methods of settling labor disputes. The letting of convict labor to contractors should be prohibited, the contract system be abolished on public works, the hours of labor in industrial establishments be reduced commensurate with the increased produc-tion by labor-saving machinery, employés protected from bodily injury, equal pay for equal work for both sexes, and labor, agricultural, and co-operative associations be fostered and encouraged by law.

We demand the passage of a service pension bill to every honorably discharged soldier and sailor of the United States.

A graduated income-tax is the most equitable system of taxation.

We demand a constitutional amendment making United States Senators elective by a direct vote of the people.

We demand the strict enforcement of laws prohibiting the importation of subjects of foreign countries under contracts.

We demand the passage and enforcement of such legislation as will absolutely exclude the Chinese from the United States.

The right to vote is inherent in citizenship, irrespective of sex, and is properly within the province of State legislation.

The paramount issues to be solved in the interests of humanity are the abolition of usury, monopoly, and trusts, and we denounce the Democratic and Republican parties for creating and perpetuating these monstrous evils.

The Union Labor party drew its support from the Greenbackers, the farmer organizations, and the older labor-reformers. In this it differed from the United Labor party, which was an outgrowth of the Henry George movement of two years ago in New York city. This latter organization supported Henry George in the canvass of 1887 for Secretary of State in New York, and, with the opening of the national canvass, placed in nomination its first national ticket. The National Convention, consisting of ninety delegates, representing nine States, was held at Cincinnati on May 16, one day after the Union Labor Convention, and nominated Robert H. Cowdrey, of Illinois, for President; and William H. T. Wakefield, of Kansas, for Vice-President. The national platform contains the following declarations:

We, the delegates of the United Labor party of the United States, in national convention assembled, hold that the corruptions of government and the impoverishment of the masses result from neglect of the self-evident truths proclaimed by the founders of this republic, that all men are created equal and are endowed with inalienable rights. We aim at the abolition of the system which compels men to pay their fellow-creatures for the use of the common bounties of nature, and permits monopolizers to deprive labor of natural opportunities for employment.

We see access to farming-land denied to labor, except on payment of exorbitant rent or the acceptance of mortgage-burdens, and labor, thus forbidden to employ itself driven into the cities. We see the wage-workers of the cities subjected to this unnatural competition, and forced to pay an exorbitant share of their scanty earnings for cramped and unhealthful lodgings. We see the same intense competition condemning the great majority of business and professional men to a bitter and often unavailing struggle to avoid bankruptcy, and that while the price of all that labor produces ever falls, the price of land ever rises.

We trace these evils to a fundamental wrong—the making of the land on which all must live the exclusive property of but a portion of the community. To this denial of natural rights are due want of employment, low wages, business depressions, that intense competition which makes it so difficult for the majority of men to get a comfortable living, and that wrongful distribution of wealth which is producing the millionaire on one side and the tramp on the other.

To give all men an interest in the land of their country; to enable all to share in the benefits of social growth and improvement; to prevent the shutting out of labor from employment by the monopolization of natural opportunities; to do away with the one-sided competition which cuts down wages to starvation rates; to restore life to business and prevent periodical depressions; to do away with that monstrous injustice which deprives producers of the fruits of their toil while idlers grow rich; to prevent the conflicts which are arraying class against class, and which are fraught with menacing dangers to society—we propose so to change the existing system of taxation that no one shall be taxed on the wealth he produces, nor any one suffered to appropriate wealth he does not produce by taking to himself the increasing values which the growth of society adds to land.

What we propose is not the disturbing of any man in his holding or title; but, by taxation of land according to its value and not according to its area, to devote to common use and benefit those values which arise not from the exertion of the individual, but from the growth of society, and to abolish all taxes on industry and its products. This increased taxation of land-values must, while relieving the working farmer and small homestead owner of the undue burdens now imposed upon them, make it unprofitable to hold land for speculation, and thus throw open abundant opportunities for the employment of labor and the building up of homes.

We would do away with the present unjust and wasteful system of finance, which piles up hundreds of millions of dollars in treasury vaults while we are paying interest on an enormous debt; and we would establish in its stead a monetary system in which a legal-tender circulating medium should be used by the Government without the intervention of banks.

We wish to abolish the present unjust and wasteful system of ownership of railroads and telegraphs by private corporations—a system which, while failing to supply adequately public needs, impoverishes the farmer, oppresses the manufacturer, hampers the merchant, impedes travel and communication, and builds up enormous fortunes and corrupting monopolies that are becoming more powerful than the Government itself. For this system we would substitute Government ownership and control for the benefit of the whole people instead of private profit.

While declaring the foregoing to be the fundamental principles and aims of the United Labor Party, and while conscious that no reform can give effectual and permanent relief to labor that does not involve the legal recognition of equal rights to natural opportunities, we, nevertheless, as measures of relief from some of the evil effects of ignoring those rights, favor such legislation as may tend to reduce the hours of labor, to prevent the employment of children of tender years, to avoid the competition of convict labor with honest industry, to secure the sanitary inspection of tenements, factories, and mines, and to put an end to the conspiracy laws.

We desire also to so simplify the procedure of our courts, and diminish the expense of legal proceedings, that the poor may therein be placed on an equality with the rich, and the long delays which now result in scandalous miscarriages of justice may be prevented.

Since the ballot is the only means by which in our republic the redress of political and social grievances is to be sought, we especially and emphatically declare for the adoption of what is known as the Australian system of voting, in order that the effectual secrecy of the ballot, and the relief of candidates for public office from the heavy expenses now imposed upon them, may prevent bribery and intimidation, do away with practical discriminations in favor of the rich and unscrupulous, and lessen the pernicious influence of money in politics.

We denounce the Democratic and Republican parties as hopelessly and shamelessly corrupt, and by reason of their affiliation with monopolies, equally unworthy of the suffrages of those who do not live upon public plunder; we therefore require of those who would act with us that they sever all connection with both.

Unsuccessful attempts were made at this time to unite these two labor parties in the support of a single ticket, and on August 2 a conference of their leaders was held at Chicago for the purpose; but as the Union Labor representatives demanded the entire withdrawal of the United Labor ticket, no agreement was reached. The canvass of the latter party was, however, not pushed with enthusiasm, and except in New York and Illinois it polled only a scattering vote.

American Party Convention.—The National Convention of the American party was held at Washington, D. C., on August 14 and 15, delegates to the number of 126 being present. More than half of these were from the State of New York, and their disposition to rule the convention in their own interest early led to a withdrawal of about 25 members from other States, and a consequent division in the party councils. James L. Curtis, of New York, was nominated for President, receiving 45 to 15 for Abram S. Hewitt. The nominee for Vice-President was James R. Greer, of Tennessee, who later declined the honor. The resolutions adopted include the following:

Resolved, That all law-abiding citizens of the United States of America, whether native or foreign born, are politically equals (except as provided by the Constitution), and all are entitled to and should receive the full protection of the laws.

Resolved, That the Constitution of the United States should be so amended as to prohibit the Federal and State Governments from conferring upon any person the right to vote unless such person be a citizen of the United States.

Resolved, That we are in favor of fostering and encouraging American industries of every class and kind, and declare that the assumed issue "Protection" *vs.* "Free Trade" is a fraud and a snare. The best "protection" is that which protects the labor and life blood of the republic from the degrading competition with and contaminations by imported foreigners; and the most dangerous "free trade" is that in paupers, criminals, communists, and anarchists, in which the balance has always been against the United States.

Whereas, One of the greatest evils of unrestricted foreign immigration is the reduction of the wages of the American workingman and workingwoman to the level of the underfed and underpaid labor of foreign countries; therefore,

Resolved, That we demand that no immigrant shall be admitted into the United States without a passport obtained from the American Consul at the port from which he sails; that no passport shall be issued to any pauper, criminal, or insane person, or to any person who, in the judgment of the consul, is not likely to become a desirable citizen of the United States; and that for each immigrant passport there shall be collected by the consul issuing the same the sum of one hundred dollars ($100), to be by him paid into the Treasury of the United States.

Resolved, That the present naturalization laws of the United States should be unconditionally repealed.

Resolved, That the soil of America should belong to Americans; that no alien non-resident should be permitted to own real estate in the United States, and that the realty possessions of the resident alien should be limited in value and area.

Resolved, That no flag shall float on any public buildings, municipal, State, or national, in the United States, except the municipal, State, or national flag of the United States—the flag of the stars and stripes.

Resolved, That we reassert the American principles of absolute freedom of religious worship and belief, the permanent separation of Church and state; and we oppose the appropriation of public money or property to any church or institution administered by a church. We maintain that all church property should be subject to taxation.

Other Conventions. — The first presidential ticket of the year was nominated by a convention of the Industrial Reform party, at Washington, D. C., on February 22, and contained the names of Albert E. Redstone, of California, for President, and John Colvin, of Kansas, for Vice-President. The new party found only a few supporters, and had no appreciable influence in the election. Another ticket, equally without support at the polls, was nominated by the National Equal Rights party at Des Moines, Iowa, on May 15, bearing the names of Belva Lockwood, of Washington, D. C., for President, and Alfred H. Love, of Philadelphia, for Vice-President. The latter declined the nomination, and the name of Charles Stuart Wells was substituted. A demand for woman suffrage and equal rights of man and woman constituted the most important portion of the platform. On July 16 the Grand Council of the Independent Labor party met at Detroit, and, after discussion of the different parties and candidates, voted to support the Republican candidates. A call issued on August 16 for a national convention of the Greenback party, brought together only eight delegates at Cincinnati on September 12, who issued an address proclaiming the Greenback principles, but made no nominations. On July 25 a convention of colored Democrats was called to meet at Indianapolis to organize a movement to divide the negro vote. There were 64 delegates divided into two factions, each of which strove for control of the convention, and their quarrels tended largely to destroy the influence and effect of the movement. Resolutions supporting the Democratic ticket and approving Democratic principles were adopted. A large and enthusiastic conference of anti-saloon Republicans was held at New York on May 2 and the day following. Representatives were present from nearly every State, and the necessity of solving the liquor problem through the agency of the Republican party was discussed. Resolutions were adopted and a movement organized intended to arrest the growing defection of Prohibitionists from the Republican party.

Political Clubs.—An important feature of the political canvass of this year was the rapid growth of the political club system. Two powerful organizations, the Republican League of the United States and the National Association of Democratic Clubs, were formed, whose influence stimulated the formation of clubs over the whole country, supplementing and in some cases practically superseding the regular party machinery.

Early in 1887 the Republican Club of New York city began the work of enlisting the Republican clubs already in existence into one compact body, and, by means of circulars and letters, the existence of about three hundred clubs was discovered, A national convention of these organizations was held in New York city, Dec. 15-17, 1887, with about 1,500 delegates in attendance from twenty-three States and Territories. Daniel J. Ryan, of Ohio, was temporary, and William M. Evarts permanent, chairman. A National Republican League was there organized, to be composed of State leagues, which in turn were to be made up of local clubs. James P. Foster, of New York, was elected president; Andrew B. Humphrey secretary; and J. S. Clarkson, of Iowa, chairman of the executive committee; the headquarters being in New York city. New clubs sprung up everywhere, and by August, 1888, 6,500 clubs were reported, with an estimated membership of one million voters. The work of forming clubs in the doubtful States was pushed rapidly. In West Virginia the number increased in six weeks from 4 to 118, and there were over 300 clubs in November. Before the election there were 1,100 clubs in Indiana, with a membership of 80,000, and 1,400 clubs in New York. State leagues were formed and State conventions of Republican clubs were held during the campaign in nearly all the Northern States. A great work was done by these organizations in the distribution of campaign documents, and especially in the enrollment of Republican voters.

The former work was aided and extended by the Home Market Club, of Boston, Mass., which was formed to spread the doctrine of protection. Its work was largely confined to the circulation of documents, nearly thirteen million being issued and distributed, to a great extent, by the local clubs of the Republican League.

In this movement the Democrats were scarcely less active than their opponents. The National Association of Democratic Clubs grew out of a suggestion of the Young Men's Democratic Club of New York to form a league of Democratic clubs to secure the adoption of the principles of tariff and civil-service reform. After much correspondence, several clubs united in a call for a conference, which was held in New York city, April 21, 1888, and was participated in by delegates from twenty-one clubs from fourteen States. This conference called a convention of Democratic clubs, which was held in Baltimore, July 4, 1888, and was attended by 2,400 delegates from 500 clubs. W. E. Russell, of Massachusetts, was chosen temporary, and John Winans permanent, chairman of the convention. The principles of the association were adopted, which henceforth became an organization for the success of the party. Chauncey F. Black, of Pennsylvania, was elected president; Edward B. Whitney, of New York, secretary; and Robert Grier, of New York, chairman of the executive committee; and headquarters were opened in New York city. State organizations were formed in twelve States, and by November 3,009 clubs were reported from forty-two States and Territories, with an aggregate membership of 300,-000. New York led the list with 480 clubs; Kentucky had 301; West Virginia, Pennsylvania, and Illinois more than 200 each; and seven other States more than 100 each. The National Association distributed about one million documents during the canvass, and the State leagues many times that number. The New York State League undertook a unique work in chartering a canal-boat, the "Thomas Jefferson," which, under the command of President Thatcher of the League, with a crew of speakers and a cargo of tariff documents, made a three weeks' voyage across the State, through the Erie and Champlin Canals, holding meetings and distributing documents. The State League of Pennsylvania opened the canvass with a thousand simultaneous meetings in all parts of the State.

Besides these party organizations, the tariff reform clubs throughout the country were active in the canvass, notably the Reform Club of New York, the Massachusetts Tariff Reform League, the New Haven Reform Club, and the American Tariff Reform League of Chicago.

The Presidential Canvass.—On August 6 the candidates of the Prohibition party made public their letters of acceptance. President Cleveland's letter accepting the Democratic nomination was published on September 10, and on the following day that of ex-Senator Harrison appeared. Mr. Morton's letter accepting the vice-presidential nomination appeared on October 2, and ex Senator Thurman's on October 14. President Cleveland reiterated in his letter the strong views in favor of tariff reduction, and the danger of a surplus in the national Treasury, expressed by him in his message to Congress in December, 1887. The Republicans were not slow in taking up the tariff issue thereby presented, and that question became the absorbing topic of discussion in the canvass. The controversy became largely one between protection and free trade, the Republicans striving to show that the President's utterances and the Mills Bill committed their opponents to a free-trade policy, while they were themselves pledged to abolish the entire internal revenue system before destroying protective tariff rates. Civil-service reform, the Southern problem, the sonal record of the candidates, and all other questions dwindled into comparative insignificance.

An incident of the later days of the canvass was the publication on Oct. 24 of a letter purporting to be written by one Charles F. Murchison, of Pomona, Cal., to the British minister at Washington, asking advice in regard to the political situation, and of the reply of Minister West thereto. The writer said he was a naturalized citizen of the United States of English birth, but he still considered England the mother-land. He further said that the information he sought was not for himself alone, but to enable him to give assurances to many other persons in the same situation as himself, for the purpose of influencing their political action as citizens of the United States of English birth. The letter also contained gross reflections upon the conduct of the United States Government in respect to questions in controversy and unsettled between the United States and Great Britain, and both directly and indirectly imputed insincerity in such conduct. The British minister replied that "any political party which openly favored the mother-country at the present moment would lose popularity, and that the party in power is fully aware of that fact"; and that in respect to the "questions with Canada which have been unfortunately reopened since the rejection of the (fisheries) treaty by the Republican majority in the Senate, and by the President's message to which you allude, . . . allowances must be made for the political situation as regards the presidential election."

The President regarded this reply as an interference of Minister West in the politics of this country by giving political advice to American citizens, and notified the British Government of his conduct. No action being taken by that Government for his recall, the President, on Oct. 30, notified him that his presence as the representative of Great Britain was no longer agreeable to this Government, and his passports were delivered to him. The British Government, regarding this action as unduly hasty and discourteous, refused to fill the vacant mission during the remaining months of the Administration. The incident acquired unusual importance from the circumstance that it was a part of the Republican argument throughout the campaign to show that the Democratic party, in its tariff-reform and free-trade views, was adopting a course that would open our markets to British manufacturers, and was hostile to American interests.

The efforts of both parties were directed mainly to the doubtful States of Indiana, New York, New Jersey, and Connecticut. President Cleveland took no active part in the canvass, and Gen. Harrison confined his efforts to short addresses made to the numerous delegations that came to pay their respects to him at his home. Ex-Senator Thurman delivered a series of addresses in the West, and spoke also in New York city and at Newark, N. J. The central figure of the canvass on the Republican side, was Mr. Blaine, whose return in August from his European trip was signalized by a great demonstration in his honor in New York city. He took an active part in the Maine

STATES.	Cleveland, Dem.	Harrison, Rep.	Fisk, Pro.	Streeter, Union Labor.	Cowdry, United Labor.	Curtis, Amer.	Cleveland's pluralities.	Harrison's pluralities.	Total vote.
Alabama................	117,320	56,197	588				61,123		174,100
Arkansas...............	85,962	58,752	641	10,613			27,210		155,968
California..............	117,729	124,816	5,761			1,591		7,087	251,839
Colorado...............	37,567	50,774	2,191	1,266				13,207	91,798
Connecticut............	74,920	74,584	4,234	240			336		158,978
Delaware...............	16,414	12,973	400				3,441		29,787
Florida................	39,561	26,657	423				12,904		66,641
Georgia................	100,499	40,496	1,803	136			60,003		142,989
Illinois................	348,278	370,473	21,695	7,090	150			22,195	747,686
Indiana................	261,013	263,361	9,881	2,694				2,848	536,949
Iowa..................	179,887	211,598	8,550	9,105				31,711	404,140
Kansas................	103,744	182,934	6,768	37,726				79,190	331,172
Kentucky..............	183,800	155,134	5,225	622			28,666		344,781
Louisiana..............	85,032	30,484	160	39			54,548		115,744
Maine.................	50,481	73,734	2,691	1,344				23,253	128,250
Maryland..............	106,168	99,986	4,767				6,182		210,921
Massachusetts..........	151,855	183,892	8,701					32,037	344,443
Michigan..............	213,459	236,370	20,942	4,542				22,911	475,313
Minnesota.............	104,385	142,492	15,311	1,094				38,106	263,306
Mississippi............	85,471	80,096	218	22			55,375		115,807
Missouri...............	261,974	236,257	4,539	18,632			25,717		528,198
Nebraska..............	80,552	108,425	9,429	4,226				27,873	202,622
Nevada................	5,362	7,229	41					1,867	12,682
New Hampshire........	43,456	45,722	1,593	13				2,272	90,683
New Jersey............	151,493	144,344	7,904				7,149		303,741
New York..............	635,757	648,759	30,231	626	2,668			13,002	1,320,109
North Carolina.........	147,902	134,784	2,787	32			13,118		285,473
Ohio..................	396,455	416,054	24,356	3,496				19,599	841,941
Oregon................	26,522	33,291	1,677	363				6,769	61,911
Pennsylvania...........	446,693	526,091	20,947	3,873				79,452	997,568
Rhode Island...........	17,530	21,968	1,250	18				4,438	40,766
South Carolina.........	65,825	13,736					52,089		79,561
Tennessee.............	158,779	138,988	5,969	48			19,791		303,736
Texas.................	234,883	88,422	4,749	29,459			146,461		357,513
Vermont...............	16,788	45,192	1,460					28,404	63,440
Virginia...............	151,977	150,439	1,678				1,539		304,093
West Virginia..........	79,664	77,791	669	1,064			1,873		159,188
Wisconsin.............	155,232	176,553	14,277	8,552				21,321	354,614
Total..............	**5,540,329**	**5,439,853**	**249,506**	**146,985**	**2,818**	**1,591**	**577,518**	**477,042**	**11,888,085**
Plurality............	**100,476**								

canvass before the September election, and afterward made a tour of the West, speaking to large audiences.

At the election in November the Democrats carried all the Southern States, as usual, and the Northern States of New Jersey and Connecticut. In New York, while the State Democratic ticket was elected, their National ticket was nearly 15,000 votes behind the Republican ticket. Gen. Harrison was thus assured of 233 electoral votes, while Mr. Cleveland had 168. The popular vote, by counties, may be found in the article UNITED STATES, PRESIDENTIAL ELECTIONS IN. The accompanying table gives it by States.

A presidential candidate nominated by the Socialists of New York city received 2,068 votes.

The result of the Congressional elections was to give control of the popular branch of Congress to the Republicans by a small majority. The Governor of West Virginia denied certificates of election to two Republicans who were elected to Congress upon the face of the returns and gave them to their Democratic opponents. Should the Republicans be finally seated, the Republican majority in the Fifty-first Congress will be increased from 3 to 7. The Democratic majority in the Fiftieth Congress was 19.

UNITED STATES, FINANCES OF THE. During the fiscal year ended June 30, 1888, the reve-

nues collected by the United States Government averaged more than $1,000,000 a day, including all Sundays and holidays, or about $379,000,000 for the twelve months. This aggregate is more by about eight million than for the preceding year, and is at the rate of a little more than six dollars per capita of population, about the average rate of the past fifteen years, and less than half the highest rate of Federal taxation per capita per annum of which the Government has record ($15.73 per capita in 1866).

The expenditures for the year have been about $268,000,000, or about the same as in 1887, and greater than in any previous year since 1875.

The surplus in the Treasury at the close of the fiscal year, over and above all accrued liabilities, was about $103,000,000. It was about $41,000,000 when the year began.

The average monthly surplus has been twice as great during 1888 as during 1887, and the highest amount has been nearly double the highest aggregate of the preceding year. The surplus at one time during the past year was greater by $53,487,000 than the highest point previously reached, and has since declined to little less than half its greatest aggregate.

The National Bank depositary system, which has been the subject of much recent discussion, has just rounded out a quarter of a century of its existence. From the beginning of the fiscal year 1864 to the close of the fiscal year 1888, it has been maintained by each successive Secretary of the Treasury under the discretionary authority conferred by law. The aggregate amount of public funds handled during the twenty-five years by this important adjunct to the Treasury has been nearly $5,000,-000,000, and the balance held has varied at different dates from $6,000,000 to $62,000,000. At the close of 1864 the balance was about $40,000,000, and during the four years following declined steadily to $23,000,000 in 1868. Since that year it has never risen to the latter figure except in 1873, when it exceeded $62,-000,000, and during the past fiscal year, when it again rose to this high sum, and has been maintained for several months at about $60,-000,000. From 1874 to 1887 the balance never exceeded $15,000,000, and it is to-day nearly three times as large as it was two years ago. During the entire period the Government has never been subjected to the slightest loss except during the earliest stages, when the system was imperfect and the necessary safeguards had not yet been applied.

During the year just closed the number of depositaries was increased more rapidly than ever before. The system has proved itself to be an important monetary agency of the Government—safe, economical, efficient, and expeditious in the discharge of public business. The important changes of policy toward the depositaries during the past year have relieved the system of the suspicion of favoritism and have placed it upon a basis of better business principles. The undue expansion of the balance far beyond the amount necessary for the true scope and purpose of the depositary system is due exclusively to the present excessive tax laws, and whatever objection is justly made to this large balance will apply with greater force to any other disposition which the Treasury could have made of the money.

The holdings of public money by depositary banks were almost exactly the same at the close of the year as at its beginning, or about $52,000,000.

The following tables exhibit in detail the revenue and expenditures of the Government for the fiscal year ending June 30, 1888:

REVENUE.

Customs	$219,091,173 63
Internal revenue	124,296,571 98
Sales of public lands	11,202,017 23
Profits on coinage	9,387,634 48
Consular, letters patent, and land fees	3,433,443 99
Tax on national banks	1,748,566 85
Customs fees, fines, etc	1,097,448 20
Pacific Railroad sinking-fund	1,170,831 43
Pacific Railroad interest	681,696 95
Sales of Indian lands	680,057 43
Soldiers' Home fund	483,189 29
Sales of Government property	365,877 26
Tax on seal-skins	317,500 00
Immigrant fund	291,189 50
Surveying public lands	161,890 76
Deductions on mutilated notes, etc	112,422 05
Sale of naval vessels	105,665 88
Revenues of District of Columbia	2,650,350 31
Miscellaneous	1,838,712 54
Total	$379,266,074 76

EXPENDITURES.

Civil list	$22,552,834 08
Foreign intercourse	1,503,461 40
Indian service	6,249,307 87
Pensions	80,288,508 77
Military establishment	38,522,436 11
Naval establishment	16,926,437 65
Miscellaneous, including public buildings, lighthouses, and collecting the revenue	44,223,351 89
District of Columbia	4,278,113 48
Interest on the public debt	44,715,007 47
Total	$259,653,958 67
Leaving a surplus of	$119,612,116 09

Which was applied as follows :

Purchase of bonds for the sinking-fund, including $2,552,015.88 paid for premium	$46,577,165 88
Purchase of 4 and 4½ per-cent. bonds other than for the sinking-fund, including $5,418,-826.58 for premium	$1,990,826 58
Redemption of 3-per-cent. loan of 1882	4,175,750 00
Redemption of other loans, fractional currency, etc	841,163 05
Total	$53,084,465 51
Leaving a balance added to the cash in the Treasury of	86,527,710 58
Total	$119,612,116 09

It will be seen from the foregoing that, of all the items in the national expenditure, pensions constitute much the largest, and exceed the total cost of administering the legislative, executive, and judicial branches of the Government, as well as the Indian and diplomatic and consular branches. The pension-roll costs the Government more than twice as much as its military establishment and engineering-works, and more than four times as much as the navy, even during these days of increased expenditure in naval construction. This item of pension payments is the only one that is growing in amount. It was $5,000,000 more in 1888 than in 1887, and $12,000,000 increase in 1887 over 1886, while the aggregate of other expenditures was no greater for 1888 than for 1887.

As compared with the fiscal year 1887, the revenues for 1888 increased $11,041,749.38 in the following items : Internal revenue, $5,473,-480.76 ; customs, $1,804,280.50 ; sales of public lands, $1,947,730.81 ; profits on coinage, $458,-381,65 ; consular fees, $161,426.40 ; deduction on mutilated notes, etc., $112,422.05 ; sale of naval vessels, $105,665.88 ; sale of Government property, $103,044.94 ; customs fees, $97,871.-98 ; surveying public lands, $67,601 ; immigrant fund, $32,787 ; fees on letters patent, $14,487.36 ; revenues of the District of Columbia, $323,290.13 ; and miscellaneous items, $339,278.92. There was a decrease of $3,178,-952.28, as follows : Soldiers' Home fund, $793,070.18 ; tax on national banks, $637,284.-33 ; sales of old public buildings, $624,882.20 ; sales of Indian lands, $598,941.38 ; Pacific Railroad interest, $233,096.18 ; Pacific Railroad sinking-fund, $194,104.44 ; customs fees, $50,-373 ; land fees, $44,111.93 ; and customs fines, penalties, and forfeitures, $3,088.64 ; making a net increase of revenue for the year of $7,862,-797.10. There was a decrease in the expenditures of $15,377,724.31, as follows : Civil expenses, $12,312,564.79 ; interest on the public debt, $3,026,569.78; military establishment, $38,589.74. There was an increase in the following: Pensions, $5,259,406.98; naval establishment, $1,785,310.85; Indian service, $54,-785.18; making a net decrease in expenditures of $8,278,221.30.

The revenue derived from the various objects of internal taxation during the past two fiscal years is shown in the following table:

OBJECT.	1887.	1888.
Spirits....................	$65,829,321 71	$69,306,166 41
Tobacco...................	30,108,067 13	30,662,431 52
Fermented liquors........	21,922,187 49	23,324,218 43
State banks and bankers..	4,288 37	4,202 55
Oleomargarine............	723,948 04	864,139 88
Miscellaneous............	249,483 32	165,316 48
Total...................	$118,837,801 06	$124,326,475 32

In 1888 the receipts from customs were $219,091,173.63; from internal revenue, $124,296,871.98.

State of the Treasury.—The following is a statement of the condition of the public Treasury on Dec. 31, 1887, and Dec. 31, 1888:

ITEMS.	Dec. 31, 1887.	Dec. 31, 1888.
Assets:		
Gold coin.................	$182,618,963 66	$227,854,212 88
Gold bullion..............	122,723,223 19	96,919,453 63
Standard silver dollars.....	218,917,539 00	254,406,869 00
Silver bullion............	3,232,686 66	4,774,441 16
Trade-dollar bullion.......	6,729,229 54	6,090,795 61
United States notes........	22,409,424 94	41,125,859 86
National-bank notes... ...	164,093 00	343,323 00
Deposits in national banking depositaries	52,199,917 54	52,890,163 79
Fractional and minor coin..	24,383,289 70	23,733,796 19
National-bank notes in process of redemption.......	4,755,340 74	3,724,728 12
Miscellaneous items	4,506,542 09	286,998 95
Total.................	$642,640,200 28	$711,650,637 24
Liabilities:		
Gold certificates outstanding.................	$96,734,057 00	$120,888,443 00
Silver certificates outstanding.................	176,855,423 00	246,219,999 00
Currency certificates outstanding.................	6,985,000 00	10,250,000 00
Reserve for redemption of United States notes......	100,000,000 00	100,000,000 00
Funds for retirement of bank circulation	102,534,767 50	86,279,471 50
Five-per-cent. redemption fund...................	7,878,699 48	6,583,079 92
Disbursing-officers'balances	32,766,835 79	32,991,569 62
Transfer checks and drafts.	2,819,738 88	4,120,075 64
Post-Office Department account........	4,248,473 83	4,291,860 97
Matured debt and interest..	15,344,944 50	13,306,302 26
Miscellaneous items	2,246,092 04	2,344,770 01
Balance...................	94,226,168 81	84,870,060 32
Total.................	$642,640,200 28	$711,650,637 24

In the judicious management of the silver coinage and the careful fostering of gold resources, the administration of the Treasury Department has achieved greatest credit and accomplished the most important results. In March, 1885, the Treasury silver holdings, unrepresented by silver certificates in circulation, amounted to $48,000,000, and in July, 1886, they had risen to $97,000,000 ($185,000,000 of standard dollars and bullion in the vaults being

offset by only $87,500,000 of certificates outstanding). At the close of December, 1888, the net silver holdings were only $12,900,000 ($260,000,000 of dollars and bullion being offset by more than $246,000,000 of outstanding silver certificates).

While thus successful in putting out silver, the Treasury has achieved equally good results in accumulating gold. The net gold fund when the administration began was $125,700,000, and it soon fell to about $110,000,000, a dangerously narrow margin, if gold payments were to continue. In little more than two years from that date it was nearly doubled. Three years from the beginning of the administration it reached $218,800,000, and at the close of 1888 it was $203,800,000, having doubled during the past decade. In 1878 the Government gold fund was $100,000,000, and in October, 1887, it reached $200,000,000. Since the latter date its highest amount has been $218,-000,000, and its lowest $186,000,000; both extremes having been touched within the past year—the highest in March and the lowest in October. On Jan. 1, 1888, the gold fund was $208,000,000. Since the amount of $100,000,000 was reached in 1878, the Government gold holdings have never declined nearly to that limit, except in May, 1885, when the Treasurer resorted to the expedient of borrowing gold from the banks.

The Public Debt.—Two of the most striking features of our recent history have been the increase of population and the decrease of public debt, and these have operated together to cause a reduction of the debt per capita at a rate more rapid than is generally known. When our public debt was at its highest aggregate of nearly $3,000,000,000, in 1865, and the population fewer than 35,000,000, the debt amounted to more than $80 for each individual. At the close of the fiscal year 1888 the public debt unpaid and unprovided for, less cash in the Treasury, was about $1,165,000,000, while the population was 61,394,000. The amount of debt per capita has thus been reduced from over $80 to less than $19. The period of less than a quarter of a century has witnessed a reduction of the debt by nearly $2,000,000,000, and an increase of population by more than 26,000,000. In 1865, when the public debt per capita was over $80, the Government revenues collected amounted to $9.60 per capita. In 1888, with the debt at less than $19 per capita, the revenues amounted to $6.18 from each individual.

The operation of the present revenue laws, if all the collections could be applied to the payment of the public debt at par value, would cancel the entire amount in less than three years.

The following is a statement of the principal and interest of the national debt at the close of the calendar years 1887 and 1888. But this statement is exclusive of cash applicable to payment of the debt and of cash held by the

Treasury to offset outstanding gold, silver, and currency certificates:

CHARACTER OF DEBT.	Dec. 31, 1887.	Dec. 31, 1888.
Bonds at 4½ per cent.....	$230,544,600 00	$181,152,800 00
Bonds at 4 per cent......	732,442,100 00	681,187,600 00
Refunding certificates at 4 per cent.............	151,580 00	128,240 00
Navy pension fund at 3 per cent.............	14,000,000 00	14,000,000 00
Interest accrued on the above loans	10,053,105 86	9,102,128 19
Matured debt	8,163,955 26	2,094,695 26
Interest on matured debt.	178,392 04	160,788 64
Bonds issued to Pacific Railway companies	64,628,512 00	64,628,512 00
Interest unpaid thereon..	1,948,695 32	1,948,215 32
Demand and United States notes...........	346,738,121 00	346,737,528 50
Gold certificates........	96,784,057 00	120,888,443 00
Silver certificates.......	176,555,423 00	246,219,999 00
Currency certificates:....	6,985,000 00	10,250,000 00
Fractional currency.....	6,942,214 12	6,919,526 47
Total debt..	$1,691,360,705 60	$1,685,368,271 88

Currency Circulation.—The tendency of national financial operations for some time past has been to bring the legal-tender notes to a metallic basis, despite the fact that Congress has not apparently had that end in view, and to prepare the way for their cancellation, although their retirement has not yet been authorized. When the anxiety and apprehension with which these notes have at times been regarded are recalled and the doubts as to the ability of the Government to maintain their credit are remembered, it seems wonderful that, with little aid from statesmanship and financiering, the great problem has solved itself, and this legal-tender currency has been

brought to such a basis as no longer to present a practical question or difficulty as to the means of redemption on the one hand, nor to threaten any financial disturbance as a consequence of the eventual retirement and cancellation of these notes on the other.

Such are the daily operations of the coinage and currency laws that the Treasury could now, without the slightest difficulty, redeem and cancel the greenbacks as rapidly as they would be voluntarily surrendered. At the same time the increase in metallic money has been so rapid and so great, and the expansion of circulation of other forms of paper money has been so large that the greenbacks are no longer essential for the purposes of a convenient currency, and could be withdrawn and canceled in accordance with a conservative plan of gradual retirement without causing any popular inconvenience or injuriously affecting the circulating medium. A statement is given below of the actual paper-money circulation of the United States on Dec. 31, 1887 and Dec. 31, 1888, showing the year's changes in the four forms of note circulation.

The National Banks.—Although a contraction of $27,700,000 has occurred during the past fiscal year in the national bank-note circulation, only $11,800,000 of this amount has been due to the withdrawal during that period of bonds deposited with the Treasury as security. The larger amount, or $15,900,000, came from the fund for the redemption of notes of banks that had before the beginning of the year surrendered this part of their circulation. In other words, the contraction of note-circula-

COMPARATIVE STATEMENT, BY DENOMINATIONS, OF UNITED STATES CURRENCY AND BANK-NOTE CIRCULATION.

DENOMINATIONS.	NATIONAL BANK-NOTES.		UNITED STATES NOTES.	
	Dec. 31, 1887.	Dec. 31, 1888.	Dec. 31, 1887.	Dec. 31, 1888.
One dollar....................	$389,514	$379,463	$6,783,495 90	$4,328,349 90
Two dollars...................................	200,084	192,874	6,698,134 60	4,024,964 60
Five dollars...................................	75,738,320	65,590,695	93,448,519 50	70,691,085 50
Ten dollars...................................	88,416,040	76,095,830	87,985,822 00	83,060,524 00
Twenty dollars...............................	68,462,220	56,014,860	72,346,119 00	56,233,632 00
Fifty dollars.	13,440,450	18,814,900	20,554,405 00	23,940,520 00
One hundred dollars..........................	24,356,800	21,771,900	28,665,820 00	32,905,140 00
Five hundred dollars..........................	307,500	258,500	8,068,500 00	13,142,500 00
One thousand dollars..........................	55,000	47,000	23,095,500 00	29,309,000 00
Five thousand dollars.........................	....	....	85,000 00	85,000 00
Ten thousand dollars..........................	....	....	10,000 00	10,000 00
Total.................................	$268,898,878	$283,660,027	$347,651,016 00	$347,651,016 00

DENOMINATIONS.	SILVER CERTIFICATES.		GOLD CERTIFICATES.	
	Dec. 31, 1887.	Dec. 31, 1888.	Dec. 31, 1887.	Dec. 31, 1888.
One dollar....................................	$17,692,298 80	$27,253,687 90	....	....
Two dollars...................................	10,891,154 20	19,230,672 60	... .	....
Five dollars...................................	32,482,485 50	71,452,982 50	....	....
Ten dollars...................................	64,560,947 00	84,698,879 00	....	....
Twenty dollars................................	48,158,128 00	40,192,624 00	$14,080,846	$12,187,250
Fifty dollars.	4,921,450 00	2,935,500 00	10,999,825	9,488,250
One hundred dollars..........................	8,478,030 00	2,727,720 00	14,850,600	12,698,200
Five hundred dollars	555,500 00	409,500 00	18,028,500	12,552,000
One thousand dollars..........................	425,000 00	267,000 00	22,905,000	25,654,000
Five thousand dollars.......	....	....	14,055,000	21,915,000
Ten thousand dollars..........	....	....	36,020,000	30,950,000
Total....................................	$183,194,993 00	$250,175,566 00	$125,392,671	$126,854,710

tion has been much more largely due to the continued retirement of the notes originally based upon the 3-per-cent. bonds, for the redemption of which the banks furnished funds when the 3 per cents were redeemed than from the voluntary surrender of 4 or 4½ per cent. bonds. Expensive as these bonds have become, and slight as is the inducement for holding them as a basis of note-circulation, here is another evidence that the banks surrender their circulation very slowly, and that the contraction which is in progress is more largely due to the compulsory surrender of the 3-per-cent. bonds, when they were being called, than to the subsequent voluntary sale of the high-priced bonds now held as the basis of circulation.

Despite the heavy burden that is now imposed upon bank-note circulation, and the unjust and illogical requirements of law, the banks adhere tenaciously to their bonds, and are making a desperate struggle for existence. The vitality of the system and the strength of its popular support are shown by the pertinacity with which the banks maintain their charters and continue to comply with the requirements, which are steadily becoming more severe as the prices of bonds advance. The analysis of the year's returns shows clearly that scarcely a bond has been surrendered except under the pressure of absolute necessity, and yet the relinquishment has proceeded more rapidly than it can continue without forcing many banks out of the national system.

Public sentiment has demanded the maintenance of the national banks in the great cities and small towns throughout the country, no matter how well established State or private banks may be. The returns show a steady reduction of the bond-deposits to the amounts which the law makes compulsory, and that the new banks organized have deposited less bonds for circulation than a similar number of banks have ever done before. The action of the old banks and the continued admission of new ones show the earnestness of the battle that the banking-system will make for self-preservation; but the returns show, in a manner equally conclusive, the necessity for a prompt reduction in the compulsory amount of bond-deposits.

One respect in which the year's returns will be disappointing is the failure of the banks to make any progress in the substitution of 4 for 4½ per cent. bonds. As the former have several years longer to run, there has been general recognition among bankers of the importance of substituting the long-term for the short-term bonds, and thus securing the maintenance of the bank charters at least as long as the lease of life of the 4-per-cent. bonds. The two classes of bonds are nearly at a par when interest worth is computed; but the past two years have not witnessed any progress in this direction. Two years ago the national banks had on deposit, as security for circulation, about $315,000,000 of 4-per-cent. bonds, and about $57,000,000 of 4½ per cents;

one year ago they had about $116,000,000 4s and about $70,000,000 4½s; and now they have about $105,000,000 of 4s and $69,000,000 4½s. It will thus be seen that the proportion of 4-per-cent. bonds has fallen instead of rising. This is partially offset by the fact that the national bank depositaries have furnished over $37,000,000 of 4s and less than $18,000,000 of 4½s as security for deposits; and this amount of 4-per-cents is, to some extent, owned by national banks, which can substitute these bonds for the 4½s now held as security for circulation.

The Comptroller has matured an elaborate plan for the issue of circulation based upon commercial paper and a small cash reserve, and regulated by national-bank unions in various cities, in which the banks as well as the Government will be represented.

The following statement shows the condition of the national banks on Dec. 12, 1888, as shown by reports from 3,150 banks then in operation:

RESOURCES.

Loans and discounts	$1,665,573,386 48
Overdrafts	10,981,527 24
United States bonds to secure circulation	162,820,650 00
United States bonds to secure deposits	48,949,000 00
United States bonds on hand	6,874,400 00
Other stocks, bonds, and mortgages	102,276,898 17
Due from approved reserve agents	156,587,199 27
Due from other national banks	107,175,402 59
Due from State banks and bankers	24,217,165 51
Real estate, furniture, and fixtures	68,486,066 74
Current expenses and taxes paid	11,342,192 45
Premiums paid	16,681,256 56
Checks and other cash items	14,140,853 12
Exchanges for Clearing-House	91,765,292 99
Bills of other banks	21,723,238 00
Fractional currency	628,337 42
Trade-dollars	786 56
Specie, viz.:	
Gold coin	$70,825,187 96
Gold Treasury certificates	75,834,420 00
Gold Clearing-House certificates	7,899,000 00
Silver coin, dollars	7,096,626 00
Silver coin, fractional	3,276,200 54
Silver Treasury certificates	8,812,844 00
	172,784,278 50
Legal-tender notes	82,585,060 00
United States certificates of deposit for legal-tender notes	9,220,000 00
Five-per-cent. redemption fund with Treasurer of the United States	7,141,434 41
Due from Treasurer of the United States other than redemption fund	1,246,391 04
Aggregate	$2,777,575,799 00

LIABILITIES.

Capital stock paid in	$593,848,247 29
Surplus fund	187,292,469 97
Other undivided profits	88,802,689 01
National-bank notes issued	$146,033,429 00
Amount on hand	2,484,132 50
Amount outstanding	143,549,296 50
State-bank notes outstanding	82,354 50
Dividends unpaid	1,267,980 19
Individual deposits	1,381,265,617 08
United States deposits	46,707,010 88
Deposits of United States disbursing officers	4,415,608 41
Due to other national banks	252,291,184 80
Due to State banks and bankers	108,001,606 46
Notes and bills re-discounted	14,844,803 00
Bills payable	5,707,581 41
Aggregate	$2,777,575,799 00

The Coinage.—The gold deposited at the mints and assay-offices during the fiscal year 1888, not including re-deposits, was 3,882,120·497 standard ounces, of the value of $72,225,497.56 in the preceding year, an excess of $4,002,424.69 over the fiscal year 1887. In addition there were re-deposits of the value of $8,668,959.11. Of the re-deposits of gold, $4,395,315.84 represents the value of imported bars, and $4,273,-643.27 of fine bars bearing the stamp of the assay-office at New York, sent in for coinage. The total deposits of gold during the fiscal year 1888, including re-deposits as above cited, were 4,348,077·049 standard ounces, of the value of $80,894,456.67. The deposits and purchases of silver, not including re-deposits, were 35,518,-839·97 standard ounces, of the coining value of $41,331,014.66, against $47,756,918.75 in the preceding year. In addition there were re-deposits of silver of the coining value of $491,-831.79, of which $275,189.75 consisted of imported bars, principally of the minor assay-offices, and $216,642.04 of fine bars. The total deposits and purchases of silver were 35,941,-507·92 standard ounces, of the value (calculated at coining rate in standard silver dollars) of $41,822,846.45. The value of both the gold and silver deposited and purchased at the mints and assay-offices during the fiscal year, not including re-deposits, was $113,556,512.22, and including re-deposits, $122,717,303.12. Of the gold received at the mints and assay-offices during the year, $32,406,306.59 was classified as of domestic production, against $32,973,-027.41 in the preceding year. A reduction of a little over $500,000 in the production of the United States is thus indicated. The foreign gold bullion deposited aggregated $21,741,-042.44, and the foreign gold coin $14,596,-885.03; a total of $36,337,927.47, against $32,467,840.98 in the year preceding. The value of the United States light-weight gold coin deposited for re-coinage, was $492,512.60. Old material was deposited in the form of jewelry, bars, plate, etc., containing gold of the value of $2,988,750.90.

Of the silver bullion deposited and purchased, 32,135,165·79 standard ounces, valued at $37,-393,648.34, was classified as of domestic production; and 29,671,470·54 standard ounces of the coining value of $34,526,803.02, consisted of fine bars bearing the stamp of well known private refineries in the United States, but the classification at the mints of silver bullion is inexact, for the reason that fine silver bars purchased from private refineries are all necessarily classified as of domestic production, while as a matter of fact they are to a large extent composed, as for several years they have been, of silver obtained from ore and bullion imported from Mexico. The silver bullion classified as foreign bullion received at the mints during the year was $1,668,384.25. Foreign silver coins of the value of $87,336 were melted during the year. United States silver coins, consisting almost entirely of worn and uncurrent subsidiary coins and old silver dollars, were melted, of the value, at coining rate in

standard silver dollars, of $494,155.64. In addition, trade-dollars were received and melted of the coining value in silver dollars of $1,060,-174.11 (911,087·13 standard ounces). Old material, consisting of plate, jewelry, etc., was deposited, containing silver of the value of $627,316.32.

The coinage during the fiscal year 1888 consisted of 109,030,547 pieces, of the value of $63,719,242.32. The gold consisted of 2,350,-534 pieces, of the value of $28,364,170.50, of which $16,301,740 was in double-eagles; $8,-998,260 in eagles; $2,995,510 in half-eagles; $34,098 in three-dollar pieces; $15,682.50 in quarter-eagles; and 18,880 gold dollars. The silver coinage consisted of $32,717,673; $2,-836.50 in half-dollars; $194,668.25 in quarter-dollars; and $1,219,917.50 in dimes. The subsidiary coinage amounted to 12,983,521 pieces, of the value of $1,417,422.25. The minor coinage consisted of 15,207,173 five-cent nickel pieces, of the nominal value of $760,-358.65; 45,573 three-cent nickel pieces, of the nominal value of $1,367.19; and 45,725,073 one-cent bronze pieces, of the nominal value of $457,250.73; the total minor coinage amounting to 60,977,819 pieces, of the nominal value of $1,218,976.57. The coinage of the fiscal year exceeded in number of pieces even the large coinage executed the preceding year, being 109,030,547 pieces in 1888 against 98,-122,517 in 1887.

UNITED STATES NAVY. Since 1881, when the United States Navy had fallen into a condition of material decay, a great and successful effort has been made to restore the fleet to the position it occupied prior to 1861, when its ships were in general the best of their classes in the world. The movement began with the appointment, by Secretary William H. Hunt, of the first advisory board, in 1881, to determine the composition of the fleet required by the necessities of national policy. This board was composed of able officers, presided over by Rear-Admiral John Rodgers. Its report commanded general attention, and is still quoted in debates relating to naval construction. It reported that the fleet should be composed of twenty-one armored vessels, seventy unarmored cruisers of different types, five rams, five torpedo-gunboats, and twenty torpedo-boats, and that steel should be the material of which they should be built. The adoption by Congress, at the instance of Secretary William E. Chandler, of the principle that obsolete ships should not be rebuilt or repaired when the expenditure exceeded 20 per cent. of the original cost, was an important step in preparing the way for reconstruction. During Secretary Chandler's administration the "Chicago," "Boston," "Atlanta," and "Dolphin" were built by John Roach, on designs furnished by the second advisory board. In 1885, at a critical time in our naval reconstruction, the Navy Department came under the administration of William C. Whitney. During his administra-

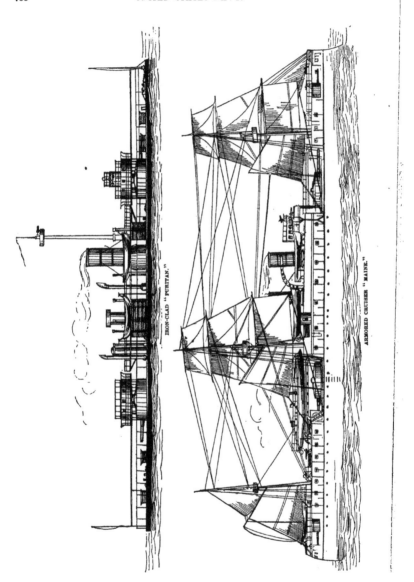

IRON-CLAD "PURITAN."

ARMORED CRUISER "MAINE."

tion the department has maintained an intimate relation with the mechanical industries and ingenuity of the country; its requirements for vessels, guns, armor, torpedoes, and the munitions of war have been of the highest standard, and every suitable encouragement has been given to all ship-builders, manufacturers, and inventors whose efforts promised success. In 1885, forgings for guns of more than 6-inch caliber, armor, steel shafting, rapid-fire and machine guns, torpedoes, and torpedo-boats, could be procured only from abroad. Before the end of the present year (1889) the domestic manufacture of guns of 8-inch, 10-inch, 12-inch, and 16-inch caliber, steel armor of the highest character and greatest thickness, steel shafting for engines of enormous power, rapid-fire and machine guns and ammunition, dynamite-guns, torpedoes, torpedo-boats, and submarine boats will be fully established. As a result of Secretary Whitney's policy, the United States will soon be absolutely independent of foreign aid for the production of every component part of the modern war-ship.

The modern war-ship represents the highest effort of mechanical skill and ingenuity, and has become a machine of the costliest production—high-power guns, armor, machinery of the greatest power, torpedoes, torpedo-boats, and electric lights, all find places in its construction, and the battle-ship of to-day is, under the most favorable conditions, from three to five years in building, while its cost is more than double that of its prototype of twenty years ago. The sentiment throughout the country seems to be decidedly in favor of building a fleet capable of efficiently aiding in the defense of our coasts, and of maintaining our rights and interests abroad. Such a fleet must be composed of a variety of vessels, armored and unarmored, and can be created only at considerable expense, and the appropriations must be continuous and liberal if the object is to be speedily and economically accomplished.

The development of the fleet by new constructions authorized since 1882 is shown in the tables on pages 790 and 791, indicating the principal characteristics of each vessel.

Notes to the Tables.—In all cases, unless noted, boilers and machinery are placed in water-tight compartments; the material of which the vessels are built is steel, except the monitors, which are built of iron; the armor is steel, and will be furnished by the Bethlehem Iron Company, except that for the "Miantonomoh," which is compound armor, purchased in England; the hulls are divided into numerous water-tight compartments, and the bottoms of the larger vessels are double. All are twin-screw vessels, so far as designed, except the "Boston," "Atlanta," "Dolphin," and "Petrel." Rapid-fire and machine guns, forming what is known as the secondary battery, are mounted about the upper and superstructure decks, and in military tops. The main and secondary batteries are placed so as to secure all-round fire. Trial speeds given are for vessels at load draught. Where two amounts are given in the column "Coal Capacity," the first is the normal supply: the second the total bunker capacity. Coal is placed about machinery and boilers for additional protection against gun-fire. Boilers are of the horizontal tubular type, single or double ended.

The "Puritan" is a low free-board, double-turreted monitor, built of iron; armored with a steel belt extending the entire length of the vessel; and carrying four 10-inch breech-loading guns in two armored turrets, besides an efficient secondary battery. The motive power is furnished by two direct-acting horizontal engines. The armor on the turrets is 11½ inches thick. The side armor is 12 inches thick amidships, reduced to 8 inches at the ends. The conning-tower is 12 inches thick.

The "Miantonomoh," "Terror," "Amphitrite," and "Monadnock" are of similar type, though smaller than the "Puritan," but carry the same battery. The machinery of this class, except the "Monadnock," is of the compound type. The machinery of the "Monadnock" is of the triple-expansion type, of recent design, and of much greater power than that of the other vessels of this class. The armor on the turrets of the "Terror," "Amphitrite," and "Monadnock" is 11½ inches thick, and on the sides the armor-belt varies in thickness from 7 inches amidships to 5 inches at the extremities. The conning-tower is 9 inches thick. The "Miantonomoh" is similarly protected by compound armor, purchased in England in 1884.

The "Maine" is an armored cruiser, designed by the Navy Department, building at the Brooklyn Navy-Yard. The material for her construction is on hand, the keel has been laid, and several of the frames placed. The 10-inch guns are mounted in pairs, in two turrets placed *en échelon* on upper deck; two 6-inch guns are mounted in recessed bow ports; two are similarly placed in quarter ports, and two are on the superstructure deck in broadside. The engines are of the vertical triple-expansion type. The protection of the "Maine" consists of an armor-belt 180 feet long and 11 inches thick; the two forward ends are joined by a 6-inch armored athwartship bulkhead. Above the belt and below turret, oval redoubts carrying 10-inch armor protect turret-bases, loading-tubes, machinery, etc.; the turret-armor varies from 10·5 inches to 11·5 inches in thickness. The conning-tower is 10 inches thick, and a 4·5-inch tube runs down from it to the protective deck. The armored deck is 2 inches thick, except on the slope at the after end of the belt, where it is 4 inches.

The "Texas" is an armored battle-ship building at the Norfolk Navy-Yard on designs by William John, of England, submitted in competition in reply to proposals issued by the Navy Department. The material for its construction is now being received. The 12-inch guns are mounted singly in turrets placed *en échelon* on the upper deck. Four 6-inch guns are mounted on the lower deck, and two on the upper deck, near the 12-inch guns. The engines, driving twin screws, are triple expansion. For defense, the vessel has a water-line belt of 12-inch steel armor in wake of magazines, engines, and boilers. The ends are connected by athwart-ship <>-shaped, 6-inch armored bulkheads. An armored redoubt runs diagonally across the vessel on the main deck, inclosing and protecting bases of turrets and their machinery; this, as well as the turret and conning-tower, carries 12-inch armor. The ammunition-tubes and the tube from conning-tower down to protective deck carry 6-inch and 3-inch armor, respectively. The protective deck, 3 inches thick, covers the armor-belt and curves down forward and abaft it to stem and stern.

The Coast-Defense Vessel No. 1 is a formidable low free board, barbette, twin-screw vessel. The main battery assigned consists of one 16-inch 110-ton breach-loader in forward barbette; one 12-inch in after barbette; one 15-inch pneumatic dynamite-gun in bow; and six 33-pounder rapid-fire guns mounted on the light superstructure that joins the barbettes. The protection consists of an armor-belt extending the entire length of the vessel, sixteen inches thick along vital parts, reduced to six inches at the extremi-

UNARMORED VESSELS.

Name or designation	Type and rig	Date of act authorizing building	Keel laid	Length bet. perpendic'rs. (Ft. In.)	Breadth extreme (Ft. In.)	Mean draught (Ft. In.)	Displacement (Tons)	I. H. P.	Maximum speed (Knots)	Fuel endurance	Coal capacity (Tons)	Weight of machinery (Tons)	Main battery	Secondary battery	Torpedo tubes	Total cost of hull and machinery	Where built or building	Condition
Dolphin	Dispatch-vessel, fore and aft, 3 masts.	Aug. 5, '82; Mar. 3, '83.	'83	240 0	32 0	14 3	1485	2,240	15	2,338 kts. at 13·6 kts. speed. 4,556 kts. at 10 kts. speed.	310	411	I 6-in. B. L. R.	II 6-pdr. R. P. IV 47 mm. R. C. II Gatlings.	No.	$315,000	Roach's, Chester, Pa.	In commission.
Boston	Partially protected cruiser, brig.	Aug. 5, '82; Mar. 3, '83.	'83	270 3	42 0	17 0	3189	3,789	16	2,845 kts. at 18·9 kts. speed. 4,968 kts. at 10 kts. speed.	480	690	II 8-in. B. L. R. VI 6-in. B. L. R.	II 6-pdr. R. F. II 3-pdr. R. F. II 1-pdr. R. F. II 47 mm. R. C. II 37 mm. R. C. II Gatlings.	No.	619,000	Roach's.	In commission.
Atlanta *	Partially prot'ctd cruiser, brig.	Aug. 5, '82; Mar. 3, '83.	'83	270 3	42 0	17 0	3189	3,856	16	Same as Boston.	480	690	Same as Boston.	Boston.	No.	617,000	Roach's.	In commission.
Chicago	Partially prot'ctd cruiser, bark.	Aug. 5, '82; Mar. 3, '83.	'83	315 0	48 0	19 0	4500	5,084	16·8	2,800 kts. at 14·8 kts. speed. 8,000 kts. at 10 kts. speed.	940	1007	IV 8-in. B. L. R. VIII 6-in. B. L. R. II 5-in. B. L. R.	II 6-pdr. R. F. II 1-pdr. R. F. IV 47 mm. R. C. II 37 mm. R. C. II Gatlings.	No.	889,000	Roach's.	Ready for commission.
Charleston	Protected cruiser, fore and aft, 2 masts.	Mar. 3, '85.	1887	300 0	46 0	18	3730	7,000	18-19	2,800 kts. at 16·5 kts. speed. 6,800 kts. at 10 kts. speed.	839 to 800	710	Same as Boston.	II 6-pdr. R. F. II 3-pdr. R. F. II 1-pdr. R. F. IV 37 mm. R. C. II Gatlings.	Yes	1,017,000	Union Iron Works, San Francisco.	Ready for steam trial.
Newark	Protected cruiser, bark.	Mar. 3, '85.	1888	310 0	49 2	18	4083	8,500	18-19	3,100 kts. at 17 kts. speed. 10,700 kts. at 10 kts. speed.	400 to 830	830	XII 6-in. B. L. R.	IV 6-pdr. R. F. II 3-pdr. R. F. II 1-pdr. R. F. III 37 mm. R. C. IV Gatlings.	Yes	1,248,000	Cramps', Philadelphia.	Building.
York'wn	Partially prot'ctd cruiser, fore and aft, 3 masts.	Mar. 3, '85.	1887	280 0	36 0	14	1700	3,400	16-17	2,800 kts. at 15 kts. speed. 6,000 kts. at 10 kts. speed.	200 to 808	825	VI 6-in. B. L. R.	II 6-pdr. R. F. II 3-pdr. R. F. I 1-pdr. R. F. II 37 mm. R. C. II Gatlings.	Yes	445,000	Cramps'.	Ready for commission sheathing.
Petrel	Partially prot'ctd cruiser, fore and aft, barkentine.	Mar. 3, '85.	1887	175 0	31 0	11 7	890	1,350	18	1,700 kts. at 11·5 kts. speed. 2,300 kts. at 10 kts. speed.	100 to 168	130	IV 6-in. B. L. R.	II 6-pdr. R. F. I 1-pdr. R. F. II 37 mm. R. C. II Gatlings.	.....	247,000	Columbia Iron W'rks, Baltimore.	Ready for steam trial.
Baltimore	Protected cruiser, fore and aft, 2 m.	Aug. 3, '86.	1887	315 0	48 6	19 9	4413	10,500	19-20	8,300 kts. at 17 kts. speed. 11,500 kts. at 10 kts. speed.	400 to 900	900	IV 8-in. B. L. R.	Same as Charleston.	Yes	1,325,000	Cramps'.	Receiving machin'ry.
Philadelphia	Protected cruiser, fore and aft, 3 m.	Mar. 3, '87.	1888	315 0	48 6	19 9¼	4324	10,500	19-20	8,500 kts. at 11 kts. speed. 11,600 kts. at 10 kts. speed.	400 to 900	900	XII 6-in. B. L. R.	Same as Newark.	Yes	1,350,000	Cramps'.	Building.
San Francisco	Protected cruiser, fore and aft, 3 m.	Mar. 3, '87.	1888	310 0	49 2	13	4083	10,000	19-20	11,600 kts. at 10 kts. speed. 10,100 kts. at 10 kts. speed.	400 to 900	900	Same as Philad'lphia.		Yes	1,425,000	Union Iron Works.	Building.
Concord	Same as Yorktown.	Mar. 3, '87.	1888	230 0	36 0	14	1700	3,400	16-17	2,800 kts. at 15 kts. speed. 5,300 kts. at 10 kts. speed.	200 to 850	825	Same as Yorktown.	Yorktown.	Yes	490,000	Palmer & Co., Chester, Pa.	Building.
Bennington	Same as Yorktown.	Mar. 3, '87.	1888	230 0	36 0	14	1700	3,400	16-17	2,800 kts. at 15 kts. speed. 5,300 kts. at 10 kts. speed.	200 to 893	825	Same as Yorktown.	Yorktown.	Yes	490,000	Palmer & Co. Cramps'.	Building.
Vesuvius	Dynamite cruiser.	Aug. 3, '86.	1887	246 8	26 5	9	800	4,366	21·6	1,400 kts. at 20 kts. speed. 5,800 kts. at 10 kts. speed.	140	256	III 15-in. dynamite guns.	II 8-pdr. R. F. I 1-pdr. R. F. II 37 mm. R. C. II Gatlings.	No.	350,000	Cramps'.	Ready for commission sheathing.
First-class	Torpedo-boat.	Aug. 3, '86.	1888	138 0	14 6	8 7	99	1,500	23	....	......	47	Torpedoes.	II 6-pdr. R. F.	Yes	82,750	Herreshoff & Co., Bristol, R. I.	Building.

UNARMORED VESSELS (*Continued*).

Cruiser No. 6, protected cruiser, authorized Sept. 8, 1888, displacement 5,300, speed 20–21. Cruisers Nos 7 and 8, protected cruisers, authorized Sept. 8, 1888, displacement 3,000, speed 19–20. Cruisers Nos. 9, 10, and 11, protected cruisers, authorized Sept. 8, 1888, displacement 2,000, speed 18. Practice-vessel, authorized Sept. 8, 1888, displacement 800. Cruisers Nos. 12 and 13, authorized March 1, 1889, displacement 800 to 1200. In these cruisers, rapid fire guns of 4-inch caliber, about 33-pounder, will be largely used in the main battery.

ARMORED VESSELS.

Name or designation.	Type.	Date of act authorizing building.	Dimensions. Length bet. perpendic'rs.	Dimensions. Breadth, extreme.	Dimensions. Mean draught.	Displacement.	I. H. P.	Maximum speed.	Armor. Side.	Armor. Turret or barbette.	Fuel endurance.	Coal capacity.	Weight of machinery.	Battery. Main.	Battery. Secondary.	Total cost of hull and machinery.	Where built.	Condition.
			Ft.	Ft. in.	Ft. in.	Tons		Knots.				Tons.	Tons					
Puritan...	Two turrets, low foreboard monitor.	Complet'n authorized Aug., '86.	280	60 1½	18 2	6060	3058	13·0	12	11¼	About 2,00 knots.	400	1260	IV 10-in. B. L. R.	II 6-pdr. R. F. II 3-pdr. R. F. II 37 mm. R. C. II Gatlings.	....	Roach's, Chester.	Awaiting armor.
Terror....	do.	... .	250	55 6¼	14 1¼	3815	888	10·0	7	11¼	About [illegible]0 knots.	830	546	Same as	Puritan.	....	Cramps', Phila.	Awaiting armor.
Miantonomoh.	do.	....	250	55 6¼	14 1¼	3815	1030	10·5	7	11¼	About 1,800 knots.	830	569	Same as	Puritan.	....	Roach's.	Ready within year.
Amphitrite.	do.	....	250	55 6¼	14 1¼	3815	1000	10·2	7	11¼	About 1,80 knots.	830	560	Same as	Puritan.	....	Harlan, Hollingsw'rth, Wilmington.	Awaiting armor.
Monadnock.	do.	....	250	55 6¼	14 1¼	3815	3000	14·0	7	11¼	About 3,00 knots.	830	351	Same as	Puritan.	....	Vallejo, Cal.	Awaiting armor.
Maine....	Armored cruiser.	Aug., '86.	310	57 0	21 6	6648	9000	17·0	11	10½	2,770 kts. at 14·8 kts. speed. 7,000 kts. at 10 kts. speed.	400 to 822	890	IV 10-in. B. L. R. VI 6-in. B. L. R. VII torpedo-tubes.	IV 6-pdr. R. F. VIII 3-pdr. R. F. II 1-pdr. R. F. IV 37 mm. R. C. IV Gatlings.	Not to exceed $2,500,000	Navy Yard, New York	Keel laid.
Texas....	Battle-ship.	Aug., '86.	290	64 1	21 6	6300	8600	17·0	12	12	3,117 kts. at 15·2 kts. speed. 8,592 kts. at 10 kts. speed.	500 to 950	816	II 12-in. B. L. R. VI 6 in. B. L. R. IV torpedo-tubes.	IV 6-pdr. R. F. VIII 3-pdr. R. F. IV 1-pdr. R. F. IV 37 mm. R. C. II Gatlings.	Not to exceed $2,500,000	Navy Yard, Norfolk.	Material being received.
Coast-defense, No. 1.	Two barbettes, low freeboard.	Mar. 3, '87.	250	59 0	14 6	4000	5400	16·0	16	16–14	1,000 kts. at 14 kts. speed. 2,200 kts. at 10 kts. speed.	200	430	I 16-in. 115-ton B. L. R. I 12-in. 48-ton B. L. R. I 15-in. dynamite gun.	IV 33-pdr. R. F. III 9-pdr. R. F. II 6-pdr. R. F. IV 3-pdr. R. F.	Not to exceed $2,000,000	....	Bids to be received Apr., '89.
Armored cruiser.	Not yet designed.	Sept., '88.	....	......	.....	7500	....	17·0	....	.....	....	......	....	....	....	Not to exceed $3,500,000	....	Designs not yet determined.
Coast-defense, No. 2.	Single turret, monitor, submergible by water-ballast.	Mar., '89.	235	55 0	14 6	3030 cruising	7500	17·0	5	10	8,500 kts. at 10 kts. speed.	550	....	II 10-in. B. L. R. I 6-in. B. L. R. I 15-in. dynamite gun.	III 3-pdr. R. F. I 37 mm. R. C.	Not to exceed $1,500,000		
Ram.....	Not determined	Mar., '89.																

ties; a complete armored deck three inches thick over the magazines, boilers, and all machinery, and two inches at the extremities; armor on barbettes, sixteen and fourteen inches, and on conning-tower ten inches. The shields over the barbettes are three inches thick. The engines are of the most approved triple-expansion type. The designs were made in the Navy Department, in conformity with conditions prescribed by Secretary Whitney.

The designs for the armored cruiser of 7,500 tons displacement are in preparation in the Navy Department. The vessel will be an important and formidable addition to the fleet.

Coast-Defense Vessel No. 2 is a vessel of novel type, capable of being submerged on going into action, by means of water-ballast admitted, three feet beyond the ordinary cruising-line of flotation, for the purpose of diminishing the target exposed and increasing the protection to vital parts. Two 12-inch breech-loading guns are mounted in a turret, at a height of eleven feet above the fighting water-line, one 6-inch breech-loader on the deck near the stern, one 15-inch dynamite-gun in the bow. Two torpedo-tubes in the bow. The armor on the turret is ten inches thick, and on the curved upper deck three inches on the crown and five inches on the sides, which extend four feet below the fighting water-line. On top of this armored deck, and between the turret and the stern gun, is a light superstructure, which affords quarters and a convenient working-deck.

The "Dolphin" is a single-screw dispatch-vessel, carrying but a light battery. The engine is of the compound vertical type. The design of the "Dolphin" affords no protection to either and machinery.

The "Boston" and the "Atlanta" are central superstructure, single-deck, partially protected cruisers. They are unquestionably very efficient. The design is a modification of the "Esmeralda" type, of which examples are found in several navies. The steel protective deck, over engines and boilers only, is 1½ inch thick. The main battery is mounted as follows: The 8-inch guns, in barbettes on main deck, are placed *en échelon* forward and abaft the superstructure; the 6-inch guns and rapid-fire and heavier machine guns are mounted within the central superstructure. The engines are three-cylinder, compound, horizontal, back-acting, driving a single screw. The "Atlanta" during a six-hour trial developed a mean speed of 15·43 knots and an indicated horse-power of 3,356. The maximum speed was 16·33 knots. The "Boston" during a six-hour trial developed a mean speed of 13·8 knots with a mean indicated horse-power of 3,780; but at this time the bottom was very foul, and under favorable conditions her speed should be greater than that of the "Atlanta."

The "Chicago" is a double-deck, partially protected cruiser. The protective deck is of the same thickness and extent as in the "Boston" and the "Atlanta." The main battery is thus distributed: Four 8-inch guns are mounted in sponsons on the spar-deck, twenty-four feet above the water-line; the eight 6-inch and two 5-inch guns are mounted on the gun-deck. There are two sets of two-cylinder, compound, overhead-beam engines, and fourteen cylindrical return-tubular boilers, fitted with exterior furnaces lined with firebrick. These boilers and engines are altogether unique in war-ships. During a continuous six-hour trial the ship developed a mean speed of 15·3 knots and a mean indicated horse-power of 5,083. The maximum speed for one hour was 16·3 knots. The bottom was foul, and the fire-rooms were not closed for forcing the draught.

The "Charleston" is a protected cruiser of an improved Esmeralda type. The protective deck extends the entire length of the vessel, two inches thick on flat, and three inches on inclined parts. The battery is distributed as in the "Atlanta," except that the 8-inch guns are on the middle line of the ship. The engines are of the two-cylinder compound horizontal type.

The "Newark" is a protected cruiser, designed in the Navy Department to meet the requirements of the Naval Board. The protective deck is complete, two to two and a half inches thick on flat, and three inches on inclined parts. The conning-tower is three inches thick. The battery is mounted on the spar-deck. The engines are of horizontal triple-expansion type, designed by Cramp & Sons.

The "Yorktown," "Concord," and "Bennington," are poop-and-forecastle, partially protected cruisers; designs from same source as those of the "Newark." The protective deck is complete, but only three eighths inch thick. The conning-tower is two inches thick. Two 6-inch guns are mounted on the forecastle, two on the poop, and two amidships on the main deck. The engines are of the horizontal triple-expansion type.

The "Petrel" is a single-screw, poop-and-forecastle, partially p o c e cruiser or gun-vessel; designs of hull and machinery made in the Navy Department. The protective deck extends over the boilers and machinery only, and is but three eighths to five sixteenths inch thick. There are two guns on each side, mounted in sponsons about four feet above the main deck and ten feet above the water-line, just abaft the forecastle and forward of the poop.

The "Baltimore" is a poop-and-forecastle protected cruiser. The protective deck is complete, two and a half inches thick on flat, and four inches on inclined sides. The 8-inch guns are mounted on forecastle and poop, and the 6-inch guns on the spar-deck. The designs for the "Baltimore" and "Charleston" and their machinery were purchased of Sir William Armstrong & Co., of England.

The "San Francisco" is like the "Newark," with the following modifications: Rig, fore and aft, three masts; the 6-inch guns nearest the extremities are mounted on forecastle and poop; the engines are horizontal triple-expansion, designed in the Navy Department.

The "Philadelphia" is like the "Baltimore," modified as follows: Rig and distribution of battery same as in the "San Francisco"; the engines of the same type, but designed by Cramp & Sons.

The "Vesuvius" is a vessel of altogether novel type, of high speed, armed with three 15-inch pneumatic dynamite-guns placed abreast at a fixed angle of 16°, the muzzles projecting through the deck about thirty-seven feet from the bow. Thirty full-caliber projectiles are carried. The engines are of the four-cylinder triple-expansion type. On trial, in January, 1889, she ran twice over a measured course of 2·54 knots at a mean speed of 21·64 knots, developing 4,366 indicated horse-power. (For remarks concerning guns, see the following sections.)

For the Cruisers No. 6, 7, 8, 9, 10, 11, 12, 14, the designs are not yet completed. The table indicates the general character for each class.

Guns and Armor.—In 1885 the armament of United States war-ships consisted of smooth-bore guns, principally of 9-inch caliber, supplemented by a few converted 8-inch muzzle-loading rifles and converted 80 and 60 pounder breech-loading rifles. The 8-inch converted muzzle-loading rifles were 11-inch cast-iron, smooth-bore Dahlgrens, converted into rifles by the introduction of a wrought-iron tube (which was afterward rifled) into the cast-iron body, the latter being expanded by heat sufficiently to permit the tough wrought-iron tube to be pushed into place. On cooling, the cast-iron body held the tube securely in place. The 100-pounder and 60-pounder Parrotts were converted into 80 and 60 pounder breech-loaders in a similar manner by the introduction into the bore of a steel tube extending from

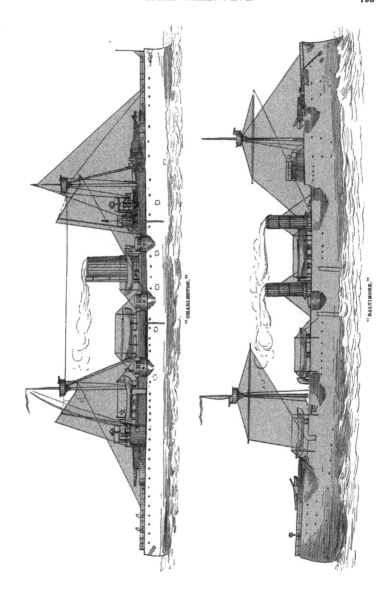

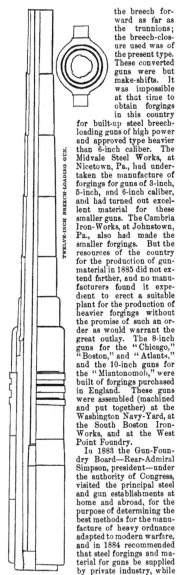

TWELVE-INCH BREECH-LOADING GUN.

the breech forward as far as the trunnions; the breech-closure used was of the present type. These converted guns were but make-shifts. It was impossible at that time to obtain forgings in this country for built-up steel breech-loading guns of high power and approved type heavier than 6-inch caliber. The Midvale Steel Works, at Nicetown, Pa., had undertaken the manufacture of forgings for guns of 3-inch, 5-inch, and 6-inch caliber, and had turned out excellent material for these smaller guns. The Cambria Iron-Works, at Johnstown, Pa., also had made the smaller forgings. But the resources of the country for the production of gun-material in 1885 did not extend farther, and no manufacturers found it expedient to erect a suitable plant for the production of heavier forgings without the promise of such an order as would warrant the great outlay. The 8-inch guns for the "Chicago," "Boston," and "Atlanta," and the 10-inch guns for the "Miantonomoh," were built of forgings purchased in England. These guns were assembled (machined and put together) at the Washington Navy-Yard, at the South Boston Iron-Works, and at the West Point Foundry. In 1883 the Gun-Foundry Board—Rear-Admiral Simpson, president—under the authority of Congress, visited the principal steel and gun establishments at home and abroad, for the purpose of determining the best methods for the manufacture of heavy ordnance adapted to modern warfare, and in 1884 recommended that steel forgings and material for guns be supplied by private industry, while the Government should maintain gun-factories in which the material delivered by steel-works should be machined and assembled. The sites chosen for these Government factories were the Washington Navy-Yard for the naval gun-factory, and the Watervliet Arsenal (Troy, N. Y.) for the army. The report also urged an appropriation of $15,000,000 for forgings, and $2,000,000 for the plant of the two factories.

Up to this time the question of producing armor of domestic manufacture had received little consideration. In May, 1885, the Board on Fortifications, composed of civilians and officers of the army and navy, was convened, and in January, 1886, renewed the recommendations of the Gun-Foundry Board, and suggested steel as the preferable material for armor-plates. These suggestions and recommendations were also supported by Senator Hawley's select committee in February, 1886. Steel armor and gun-forgings are most economically produced if manufactured in a single establishment, much of the plant for the production of each being common to both, but the creation of such a plant involves an expenditure of about $3,000,000. In order to make the creation of such an establishment practicable, Secretary Whitney secured, in August, 1886, an appropriation of $4,000,000 for armor, and $2,128,000 for guns for the vessels authorized, and immediately invited proposals for the supply of 6,700 tons of steel armor, and 1,220 tons of gun-forgings. In May, 1887, the contract for this was awarded to the Bethlehem Iron Company. The terms of the contract required the company to establish its plant within two and a half years, and begin the delivery of gun-forgings and armor-plates by February, 1890. The contract price of 1,221 tons of gun-forgings was $851,513, and of 6,700 tons of steel armor-plates, $3,610,707. The gun-plant is now in working order and producing forgings, and the armor-plates will be forthcoming within the year. When completed, the Bethlehem will be the finest establishment of its kind in the world; its plant includes Whitworth's liquid compression for making ingots; two hydraulic forging-presses, capable of forging the parts of guns up to 16-inch caliber; the heaviest steam-hammer in the world; and tools of the most approved type for machining armor-plates and rough-boring and turning gun-forgings.

The naval gun-factory has been in process of reconstruction since 1887; buildings have been erected, and contracts have been made for the supply of the necessary tools, cranes, etc. Since 1884 the old establishment has turned out two 5-inch, twenty-two 6-inch, four 8-inch, and three 10-inch guns. The yearly capacity of the enlarged factory will in another year be twenty-five 6-inch, four 8-inch, six 10-inch, and four 12-inch guns.

The high-power guns of all nations at the present day are of steel. In all the principle of initial tension is employed, which consists in giving the exterior portion of the gun a certain initial tension, gradually decreasing toward the interior, and giving to the interior parts a certain normal state of compression by the shrinkage of the outer jacket and hoops. The tube or body of the gun is a single forging, extending almost the entire length of the gun. Over the rear portion of the tube is shrunk a jacket extending about two fifths of the length, and over the remainder of the tube and over the jacket is shrunk a series of hoops, all the parts being locked together so as to form an extremely strong structure. The breech-closure screws into the jacket. The tube and jackets are made from solid steel ingots, forged, tempered in oil, annealed, and bored and machined to the required dimensions. The hoops are forged upon a mandrel, and subsequently treated in the same manner as other forgings. To shrink the jacket on the tube, the latter is placed vertically in a pit, breech end up, and after heating the jacket to a temperature sufficient to expand its interior diameter to the required amount, it is lifted by a crane and dropped over the tube. The hoops are then shrunk on, and finally the trunnion-band is screwed on in place, which also assists in locking the parts together. The gun is then ready to be rifled, and afterward to have the breech-closure and sights fitted. The following are the requirements for material for 6-inch and 8-inch guns: ·

ELEMENTS.	Tubes.	Jackets.	Hoops.	Remarks.
Tensile strength....lbs.	80,000	85,000	100,000	Test-pieces
Elastic limit.........“	38,000	40,000	50,000	2 inches
Elongation....per cent.	22	20	18	long, ½ inch
Contraction of area..“	35	30	30	diameter.

The powder-pressure is usually about 15 tons to the square inch, but the guns may be safely fired under a pressure of 22 tons.

Recently manufacturers of steel have claimed that solid steel-cast guns are preferable to the built-up gun before described. In order to test the claims of these, Congress authorized the construction of three steel-cast guns—the first to be made of Bessemer, the second of open-hearth, and the third of crucible steel. Proposals were received from two firms—the Pittsburg Steel-Casting Company for the Bessemer gun, and the Standard Steel-Casting Company, of Thurlow, Pa., for the open-hearth gun. No proposals were received for the gun of crucible steel. The Pittsburg gun exploded on firing the first round under service conditions; the Thurlow gun successfully underwent the trial of ten service-rounds, fired as rapidly as possible. The test of material for the Pittsburg guns showed very poor characteristics; that of the Thurlow gun very fair characteristics. But a comparison of the weights of the steel-cast gun and the built-up gun shows their relative weight at 13,000 to 11,000 pounds. No nation has yet adopted the steel-cast gun for the armament of vessels or forts, the material be-

ing considered too uncertain, and the increased weight objectionable.

Gunpowder.—In the improvement of gunpowder probably lies the principal field of development of gun-power. Great improvements have already been made, and study and experiment are being devoted to this question. The initial velocities of projectiles in 1870 ranged between 1,100 feet and 1,300 feet a second, while at present initial velocities of guns in service rise to 2,000 and 2,100 feet with a pressure of but 15 tons to the square inch, and powders recently fired in Germany and France have again raised this velocity to 2,400 and even 2,600 feet with the moderate pressure of 15 to 16 tons. Much attention is being directed to the production of a powder that shall give a high initial velocity with low pressure, and yet be comparatively smokeless. By the employment of gun-cotton and picric powders, much has been accomplished in Europe in this direction. But the new powders are less stable than the old, and doubtless deteriorate under influences of heat or moisture. The powders for United States naval guns (and each caliber has a powder whose exact quality is peculiar to itself) have been developed and manufactured by the Messrs. Dupont, near Wilmington, Del.

Projectiles.—Ordinary shells are still made of cast-iron, but armor-piercing projectiles are made of steel, forged and highly tempered. The manufacture of armor-piercing projectiles has been developed chiefly in France, and has introduced another important element in the relation between the resistance of armor and the capacity of the gun for penetration. So perfect is the manufacture of these projectiles that, when fired under service conditions, they perforate the best armor-plate of a thickness 30 per cent. greater than the caliber of the projectile, and remain practically undeformed. The bursting-charge even in ordinary shells is comparatively small—for 6-inch, 5 to 10 pounds; for the 16-inch (weighing 1,800 pounds), 179 pounds. This has given rise to a further development of the destructiveness of shellfire by introducing high-explosive shells, whose bursting-charges are dynamite, explosive gelatine, gun-cotton, or melinite. Shells loaded with 500 pounds of dynamite and explosive gelatine are safely fired from the Zalinski dynamite-gun. Gun-cotton is used as a bursting-charge in Germany, while the French use melinite as a burster for shells fired from service-guns under service conditions. High-explosive shells, however, are quickly detonated if the surface hit offers fair resistance, and for this reason armor is coming much more into vogue and is being more distributed over the sides of vessels than has recently been the practice. Four inches of armor are said to be sufficient to cause the detonation of high-explosive shells. The ordinary side-plating of ships is not sufficient to detonate these, and the destructive effects of their explosion within a ship are appalling.

Rapid-Fire Guns.—Rapid-fire guns and revolving cannon have hitherto been procurable only from abroad, the principal type—that of the American inventor and manufacturer Hotchkiss—being made in Europe. In 1887 the Navy Department contracted with the Hotchkiss Ordnance Company for the supply of ninety-four rapid-fire guns and revolving cannon of domestic manufacture, at a cost of $121,400, to include thirty 6-pounder rapid-fire guns, twenty-two 3-pounder rapid-fire guns, ten 1-pounder rapid-fire guns, thirty-two 37-millimetre revolving cannon. The material for these guns has been supplied by the Midvale Steel Company; the guns are made by Pratt & Whitney, Hartford, Conn.; and the ammunition by the Winchester Arms Company.

A new type of rapid-fire gun, the invention of two naval officers, known as the Driggs-Schrœder gun, has been designed and manufactured in this country. It has been tried and favorably reported upon.

Rapid-fire guns are light guns using metallic ammunition, in which the operation of loading is performed wholly or in part by hand, although the empty cartridge is mechanically extracted, and the gun recovers automatically from recoil, if any is permitted. Aiming is done from the shoulder, and the guns, up to 6-pounder caliber, may fire about fifteen aimed shots in a minute. The largest gun of this type adopted for service is the 36-pounder (4·72 inches caliber), which in England has fired ten carefully aimed shots in a minute and thirty-eight seconds; its penetration in wrought-iron is seven inches. In machine-guns the operation of feeding, loading, and extracting the metallic ammunition are successively performed by a continuous action of the breech mechanism; no recoil is permitted. The rapidity of fire is great—60 rounds from Hotchkiss revolving cannon and up to 1,000 rounds from the Gatling gun.

GUNS IN SERVICE IN 1884.

CALIBER.	Type.	Weight of gun.	Length of gun.	Powder charge.	Projectile.	Energy at muzzle.	Penetration in wrought-iron at muzzle.
		Tons	Ins.	Lbs.	Lbs.	Ft. tons	Ins.
9-inch.......	Smooth bore.	4	132	10	70	847	....
8-inch.......	Convert'd M. L. R.	7·8	160	35	180	2,481	10·8
80-pdr...;...	Convert'd B L. R.	4·5	139	8	80	696	6·2
60-pdr.......	Convert'd B. L. R.	2·4	112	8	48	562	6·1
NEW GUNS IN SERVICE, OR UNDER CONTRACT, 1889.							
12-inch......	B. L. R	45·2	441	425	850	25,990	26·7
10-inch......	B L. R.	24·1	329	250	500	13,870	21·5
8-inch.......	B. L. R.	12·3	258	125	250	6,984	17·0
6-inch.......	B L. R.	4·9	196	50	100	2,774	12·5
5-inch.......	B. L. R.	2·8	162	30	60	1,564	10·6
		Lbs.	Ons.				
6-pdr.......	R. F. G.	605	97·6	31·5	6·90	187	4·9
3-p'r.......	R. F. G.	507	80·6	27·5	3·82	94	4·4
1-pdr.......	R. F. G.	73	33·1	2·5	1·11	....	1·2
47-mm.......	R. C.	1268	....	7·1	2 4	....	1·7
37-mm.......	R. C.	441	....	2·8	1·1	....	·75

M. L. R., muzzle-loading rifle ; B. L. R., breech-loading rifle ; R. F. G., rapid-fire gun ; R. C., revolving cannon.

Dynamite-Gun.—The dynamite-gun is the invention of Mr. Mefford, of Ohio, developed and made practicable by Capt. Edmund L. G. Zalinski, of the United States Army, and produced as a marketable weapon by the Pneumatic Gun Company, of New York. The original gun of this system was of 2-inch caliber (see "Annual Cyclopædia" for 1884, page 273). After experimenting with other guns of 4 and 8 inch caliber, the Pneumatic Gun Company has produced 15-inch guns for the "Vesuvius." These are 55 feet long, placed at a fixed angle of 16°, and throw projectiles containing from 500 to 600 pounds of explosive gelatine and dynamite one mile, or sub-caliber projectiles containing 100 or 200 pounds of explosive up to 4,000 yards. The projectiles are discharged by compressed air, at a pressure of about 1,000 pounds, which gives an initial velocity of about 800 feet a second. The trajectory is of course very much curved. The most valuable feature of the system is the electric fuse, which is entirely the invention of Capt. Zalinski, so constructed that the projectile may be exploded upon entering the water or by delayed action explode at any desired depth beneath the surface. The dynamite-gun is not intended to replace the service powder-guns; it is really a torpedo-gun affording a safe means of throwing shells, which are virtually torpedoes charged with a large amount of the highest explosives, through the air to a considerable range and with accuracy. If the chances of dropping its projectile at the desired spot are only fair, this, when successfully placed, will secure results that no other single projectile or torpedo can produce—the probable destruction of any vessel yet built.

Torpedoes.—There are no automobile torpedoes in the United States service. We here occupy an entirely unique position, and have been far in the rear in this, as in many other respects, of Brazil, Chili, Japan, and China. But contracts have been made with the Hotchkiss Ordnance Company to supply the Howell torpedo. This torpedo, the invention of Capt. J. A. Howell, of the United States Navy, is thought to be superior in most respects to the celebrated Whitehead. Its advantages over the Whitehead are comparative smallness, inherent directive force derived from the gyroscopic properties of its fly-wheel, and large explosive capacity. Its disadvantage lies in the fact that it requires an appreciable time to prepare it for discharge. Power is stored in a heavy fly-wheel, in the middle of the torpedo, which, in about thirty seconds, is spun up to a velocity of 10,000 turns a minute by means of a motor. This fly-wheel imparts its power to two propellers, which drive the torpedo. The submersion is automatically controlled by a horizontal rudder, actuated by a hydro-pneumatic cylinder, the piston of which moves with the varying pressures at different depths.

The contractors will furnish a torpedo whose size and performance are guaranteed to be within the following prescribed limits :

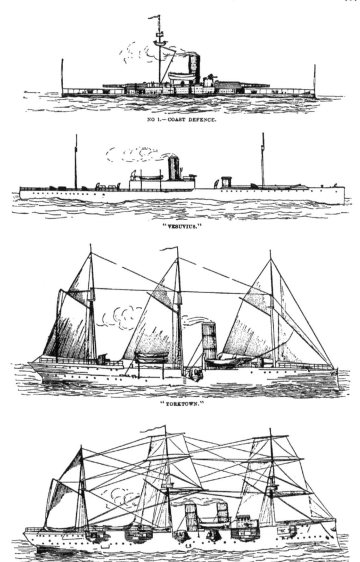

NO 1.—COAST DEFENCE.

" VESUVIUS."

" YORKTOWN."

" NEWARK."

Length.	Diameter.	Total weight.	Least weight of explosive charge.	Least speed for 400 yards	Total range.
12 ft.	14·2 in.	458 lbs.	80 lbs.	22¼ knots.	1,000 yds
9 ft. 6 in.	14·2 in.	428 lbs.	75 lbs.	2.¼ knots.	800 yds

The Patrick torpedo, of the controllable type, is made of copper, fusiform, 40 feet long and 24 inches in greatest diameter. It is held at a depth of nearly 4 feet by means of a float 46 feet long and 18 inches in diameter, filled with cotton or lamp-black. The motive power is carbonic-acid gas, contained in liquid form in a flask near the center of the torpedo. From the flask the gas passes through pipes about which an intense heat is obtained by the action of sulphuric acid on quick-lime. The gas thus expanded passes to a six-cylinder engine, which drives the propeller. The range is one mile, and the explosive charge carried 200 pounds. The torpedo is controlled by an electric cable paid out as it runs. It has been tried by a naval board, and upon its report three torpedoes have been ordered by the Navy Department, at a cost of $55,000. The contractor guarantees a speed of 20 knots. This torpedo is intended for harbor-defense, and is operated from the shore or from a stationary vessel. Undoubtedly it is the best of the controllable type. The French Navy Department has purchased it for coast-defense.

Torpedo-Boats.—The United States occupies a most singular position in regard to torpedo-boats. All nations agree that these are most efficient for coast and harbor defense, and all possess them in large numbers. England has 145; France, 131; Germany, 75; Italy, 120; Spain, 13; Brazil, 15; Chili, 10; Japan, 12; China, 26; the United States, 2.

The "Stiletto" is the single torpedo-boat (unworthy of the title) yet possessed by the United States, although a new first-class boat is being built by Messrs. Herreshoff, at Bristol, R. I. This boat will compare favorably, it is thought, with those built abroad (see table of ships for description). The Fortification Board placed the number of torpedo-boats at 150.

Submarine Boat.—The latest device in naval warfare is the submarine boat, intended to dive beneath the surface, to be there manœuvred and discharge torpedoes. Submarine boats have been used in naval warfare since 1776, but with unsatisfactory results. Recently they have again come into notice in Europe, and several have been built there. In 1888, the Navy Department published a circular containing its views of the requirements for a submarine boat, and invited proposals for the construction of such a boat under guarantees. After considerable delay in finding any one to undertake this, bids were received in February, 1889, from the Columbia Iron-Works, of Baltimore, in which a very good performance is guaranteed. The dimensions of the boat are: Length, 85 feet; greatest diameter, 10·9 feet; displacement, submerged, 120 tons, with compartments empty, 98 tons. The hull is to be of steel; the engine, triple-expansion, driving a single screw; the fuel, petroleum. Diving is to be effected by horizontal rudders. The greatest surface-speed guaranteed is 12 knots, and the speed submerged, 9 knots. The boat is cigar-shaped, and is capable of being operated under three different conditions; first, above the surface, with nearly half of the boat above water; second, awash, with only a few inches of the upper deck exposed; third, completely submerged. The armament consists of a tube placed in a horizontal axis, from which are discharged, either by pneumatic power or powder, 8-inch projectiles, giving a range of several hundred feet, or, if desired, some form of automobile torpedo may be used. In addition to this, there is another 8-inch tube fixed at an angle for over-water fire to a range of about 1,000 yards. The contract for the boat has not yet been awarded.

Personnel.—The *personnel* of the United States Navy consists of 7,500 enlisted men, 750 apprentices, and the following officers: Admiral, 1; vice-admiral, 1; rear-admirals, 6; commodores, 10; captains, 45; commanders, 85; lieutenant-commanders, 74; lieutenants, 250; lieutenants (J. G.), 75; ensigns, 181; medical directors, 15; medical inspectors, 15; surgeons, 50; passed assistant surgeons, 55; assistant surgeons, 23; constructors, 7; assistant constructors, 14; professors of mathematics, 12; civil engineers, 10; pay-directors, 13; pay-inspectors, 18; paymasters, 43; passed assistant paymasters, 23; assistant paymasters, 14; chief engineers, 70; passed assistant engineers, 78; assistant engineers, 68.

Besides these, there are allowed one naval cadet for each congressional district, and ten at large. The course for naval cadets is four years at the Naval Academy, Annapolis, and two years in cruising-ships. At the end of the six years a number of cadets pass into the service, equal to the number of vacancies in the line, engineer and marine corps; usually from 20 to 25, never fewer than 10. The marine corps is composed of 82 officers and about 1,900 enlisted men, under regimental organization, a colonel-commandant commanding. The number of enlisted men and apprentices allowed in the navy is too small, in view of the fact that the fleet is being rapidly increased.

Not more than 50 per cent. of the enlisted men are native or naturalized Americans, and the present small number of apprentices, who are American boys, is not sufficient to give the desired tone to ships' companies. The officers, as a body, are highly educated, well trained, and efficient; but slowness of promotion, by keeping them in subordinate grades to an advanced age, threatens seriously to impair their efficiency. Promotion in the navy is altogether by seniority. The system presents few advantages and affords no incentive to energetic effort and no reward for hard work or distinguished service.

UNITED STATES, PRESIDENTIAL ELECTIONS IN. The following tables, referring to presidential contests, include every county in each State of the Union, and reveal the political history of all sections during the past twenty years. Results are shown from 1872 to the election of 1838, the year in which each contest took place being indicated at the top of the column. The figures opposite each county represent the total vote and the plurality, and the capital letter R or D denotes whether the county plurality was Republican or Democratic. By this arrangement not only can the political history of every county be ascertained without difficulty, but increases and decreases can be readily observed and easily noted. Those interested in the political affairs of each State can ascertain, by running the eye down the columns or across the lines, how many counties were carried at each election during the past twenty years by each of the great political parties, and also how many counties have recorded an unwavering allegiance to one party or the other:

ALABAMA.

COUNTY.	1872.	1876.	1880.	1884.	1888.
Autauga	2,262 / 924R	2,580 / 772R	1,967 / 4D	1,788 / 34D	1,412 / 374D
Baker	712 / 298D				
Baldwin	1,256 / 158R	1,451 / 127D	1,453 / 104D	1,478 / 74D	1,271 / 177D
Barbour	5,076 / 436R	3,756 / 3,432D	3,974 / 1,573D	2,822 / 1,422D	3,962 / 3,078D
Bibb	1,222 / 356D	1,223 / 557D	843 / 631D	897 / 347D	1,626 / 303D
Blount	825 / 273D	1,749 / 1,065D	1,558 / 1,058D	1,953 / 1,027D	2,255 / 1,496D
Bullock	4,326 / 1,876R	2,526 / 606D	780 / 582R	876 / 384D	1,181 / 351D
Butler	2,589 / 387D	2,961 / 951D	2,880 / 1,165D	2,804 / 644D	3,277 / 558D
Calhoun	2,164 / 1,364D	2,461 / 1,619D	2,505 / 1,475D	3,101 / 969D	3,628 / 1,742D
Chambers	3,062 / 456D	3,335 / 1,289D	2,830 / 1,084D	2,934 / 796D	3,708 / 622D
Cherokee	1,453 / 997D	1,959 / 1,373D	1,570 / 1,210D	1,824 / 970D	2,038 / 1,353D
Chilton	......	879 / 577D	845 / 583D	1,136 / 546D	1,588 / 664D
Choctaw	1,796 / 506D	1,902 / 516D	2,272 / 530D	1,331 / 597D	2,018 / 760D
Clarke	2,542 / 352D	2,526 / 296D	1,913 / 433D	1,933 / 157D	2,801 / 731D
Clay	1,335 / 533D	1,374 / 1,002D	1,228 / 950D	1,421 / 873D	1,658 / 902D
Cleburne	928 / 96D	1,271 / 833D	1,021 / 787D	1,290 / 650D	1,217 / 664D
Coffee	839 / 643D	859 / 811D	827 / 701D	914 / 836D	1,131 / 1,117D
Colbert	1,863 / 151D	2,160 / 604D	2,376 / 165D	2,294 / 106R	2,596 / 41R
Conecuh	1,853 / 49R	1,944 / 390D	1,997 / 311D	2,008 / 64D	2,095 / 599D
Coosa	1,918 / 138D	2,082 / 616D	2,122 / 484D	2,178 / 544D	2,068 / 506D
Covington	670 / 530D	851 / 789D	946 / 815D	830 / 653D	1,108 / 1,060D
Crenshaw	1,328 / 710D	1,801 / 1,253D	2,005 / 1,543D	1,846 / 1,354D	2,120 / 1,726D
Cullman	......	......	499 / 173D	738 / 274D	1,272 / 570D
Dale	1,333 / 689D	1,412 / 874D	1,508 / 940D	1,125 / 835D	1,281 / 1,251D
Dallas	9,015 / 5,147R	5,539 / 3,321R	2,902 / 686D	5,049 / 1,053D	7,396 / 3,312D
De Kalb	1,161 / 9R	1,464 / 510D	1,102 / 507D	1,542 / 612D	1,937 / 734D
Elmore	2,872 / 255R	2,648 / 150D	2,869 / 78D	2,593 / 311D	3,252 / 182D

COUNTY.	1872.	1876.	1880.	1884.	1888.
Escambia	815 / 383D	982 / 586D	1,119 / 527D	1,049 / 315D	1,187 / 210D
Etowah	996 / 420D	1,471 / 925D	1,568 / 870D	2,126 / 800D	2,808 / 1,071D
Fayette	832 / 162D	1,202 / 668D	876 / 429D	1,069 / 405D	1,186 / 549D
Franklin	871 / 21D	917 / 645D	1,004 / 545D	1,131 / 395D	420 / 52R
Geneva	316 / 206D	3,741 / 1,631R	466 / 454D	488 / 488D	799 / 789D
Greene	3,711 / 1,321R	410 / 406D	2,406 / 520R	1,929 / 879R	2,181 / 623D
Hale	4,467 / 2,863R	4,585 / 211R	3,285 / 187D	4,128 / 278R	4,400 / 1,436D
Henry	2,271 / 1,475D	2,020 / 1,154D	2,002 / 1,456D	1,849 / 1,437D	1,970 / 1,925D
Jackson	2,287 / 987D	3,383 / 1,995D	3,614 / 1,460D	3,269 / 1,165D	3,366 / 1,282D
Jefferson	2,257 / 151D	2,792 /	2,669 / 931D	4,301 / 165D	8,613 / 2,507D
Lamar	......	......	1,028 / 684D	1,062 / 594D	1,377 / 890D
Lauderdale	2,275 / 408D	2,764 / 676D	3,059 / 515D	2,327 / 1,009D	2,758 / 517D
Lawrence	2,669 / 267R	3,143 / 211R	3,557 / 141D	2,987 / 178R	2,925 / 8R
Lee	4,531 / 207R	3,990 / 1,780D	3,517 / 374D	3,587 / 227D	3,496 / 559D
Limestone	1,719 / 67R	3,027 / 341D	3,279 / 23R	2,880 / 20R	2,698 / 306D
Lowndes	4,864 / 3,054R	5,461 / 2,843R	3,813 / 985R	4,398 / 1,526D	3,573 / 637D
Macon	3,021 / 1,125R	2,374 / 612D	729 / 347D	408 / 243D	1,199 / 663D
Madison	5,457 / 525R	6,300 / 646D	6,359 / 254R	5,955 / 355R	4,737 / 429R
Marengo	3,276 / 36D	4,737 / 773D	4,184 / 534D	3,980 / 984D	5,359 / 1,493D
Marion	533 / 39R	844 / 622D	541 / 455D	471 / 421D	994 / 448D
Marshall	912 / 316D	1,234 / 900D	1,081 / 856D	1,060 / 914D	1,434 / 918D
Mobile	12,468 / 576D	9,602 / 1,058D	7,224 / 545D	5,603 / 9D	5,661 / 577D
Monroe	1,920 / 958D	2,138 / 926D	1,908 / 266D	1,905 / 317D	2,212 / 678D
Montgomery	10,075 / 4,117R	8,540 / 3,878R	8,479 / 2,498R	7,797 / 2,623R	6,678 / 746D
Morgan	2,024 / 12R	2,305 / 659D	2,339 / 776D	2,426 / 720D	2,227 / 1,200D
Perry	5,527 / 2,759R	4,995 / 2,061R	4,358 / 198D	4,587 / 2,429D	3,519 / 1,939D
Pickens	1,923 / 1,036D	2,206 / 2,110D	1,776 / 1,348D	1,116 / 1,054D	1,344 / 1,309D
Pike	2,394 / 1,288D	2,575 / 1,647D	3,071 / 1,586D	3,277 / 1,711D	3,513 / 1,733D
Randolph	1,839 / 117R	2,044 / 314D	1,318 / 346D	1,782 / 116D	1,764 / 230D
Russell	4,202 / 860R	3,073 / 1,029D	3,018 / 276D	3,345 / 651D	3,058 / 882D
Sanford	859 / 303D	1,399 / 1,008D			
Shelby	1,966 / 172D	2,245 / 705D	2,303 / 615D	2,512 / 266D	2,681 / 589D
St. Clair	1,301 / 299D	1,569 / 699D	1,443 / 451D	1,562 / 240D	2,150 / 849D
Sumter	4,141 / 841R	3,604 / 864D	3,124 / 450D	2,488 / 562D	2,890 / 1,241D
Talladega	3,495 / 391R	3,323 / 705D	3,478 / 98R	3,057 / 501R	4,252 / 196R
Tallapoosa	2,826 / 1,576D	3,603 / 2,181D	3,450 / 1,897D	2,996 / 1,586D	3,136 / 1,614D
Tuscaloosa	3,014 / 288D	3,172 / 1,196D	2,662 / 1,048D	2,583 / 969D	3,299 / 1,157D
Walker	870 / 30R	1,304 / 294D	812 / 319D	1,313 / 27D	2,173 / 79D
Washington	574 / 416D	649 / 457D	775 / 436D	612 / 326D	725 / 291D
Wilcox	5,294 / 2,662R	5,089 / 2,109R	3,124 / 596D	3,915 / 943D	5,418 / 4,304D
Winston	538 / 325R	691 / 217R	275 / 23D	315 / 53R	543 / 103R

ARKANSAS.

COUNTY.	1872.	1876.	1880.	1884.	1888.
Arkansas	1,271 / 19R	1,666 / 192D	1,577 / 145D	1,375 / 65R	1,997 / 40R
Ashley	1,544 / 42D	1,572 / 242D	1,399 / 55D	1,546 / 100R	1,889 / 289D
Baxter	......	440 / 302D	763 / 451D	741 / 379D	1,072 / 399D

COUNTY	1872	1876	1880	1884	1888
Benton	1,385 / 915D	2,294 / 1,542D	2,262 / 1,666D	3,121 / 1,835D	4,301 / 2,051D
Boone	926 / 508D	1,226 / 790D	1,459 / 809D	1,524 / 676D	2,048 / 764D
Bradley	1,049 / 269D	783 / 365D	753 / 387D	917 / 389D	1,008 / 605D
Calhoun	641 / 231D	749 / 169D	741 / 201D	755 / 137D	991 / 254D
Carroll	602 / 48D	1,016 / 308D	1,286 / 488D	1,995 / 462D	2,820 / 456D
Chicot	1,932 / 1,384R	2,002 / 1,034R	1,818 / 1,286R	1,324 / 1,018R	1,832 / 1,410R
Clark	2,120 / 528R	2,153 / 561D	2,143 / 383D	2,628 / 424D	3,063 / 575D
Clay		525 / 473D	663 / 517D	992 / 652D	1,424 / 622D
Cleburne				590 / 470D	770 / 461D
Cleveland					1,345 / 602D
Columbia	1,944 / 432D	2,000 / 550D	1,755 / 591D	2,242 / 709D	2,342 / 948D
Conway	291 / 191D	1,328 / 215D	1,928 / 112R	2,551 / 315R	2,705 / 80D
Craighead	648 / 375D	550 / 416D	657 / 491D	1,180 / 842D	1,576 / 995D
Crawford	1,507 / 329R	1,617 / 291D	2,112 / 164D	2,033 / 247D	3,615 / 233D
Crittenden	2,187 / 1,587R	1,336 / 782R	1,152 / 674R	946 / 690R	1,365 / 745R
Cross	856 / 242D	601 / 197D	763 / 165D	955 / 377D	1,086 / 150D
Dallas	1,010 / 428D	799 / 337D	791 / 199D	1,015 / 322D	1,136 / 251D
Desha	1,158 / 332R	881 / 469R	1,061 / 489D	865 / 405R	1,653 / 909R
Drew	1,742 / 790D	1,811 / 361D	1,441 / 335D	2,112 / 47R	2,276 / 146D
Dorsey		1,091 / 517D	795 / 284D	1,059 / 345D	No vote recorded.
Faulkner		920 / 588D	1,556 / 638D	1,972 / 494D	2,505 / 479D
Franklin	780 / 278R	1,384 / 838D	2,051 / 1,115D	2,597 / 1,249D	3,022 / 1,348D
Fulton	541 / 301D	381 / 267D	636 / 480D	888 / 365D	1,340 / 601D
Garland		1,202 / 244D	1,380 / 248D	1,942 / 64D	2,243 / 209D
Grant	633 / 263D	455 / 289D	583 / 373D	718 / 414D	919 / 550D
Greene		570 / 570D	538 / 492D	1,113 / 901D	1,620 / 939D
Hempstead	2,021 / 718R	2,923 / 213D	3,091 / 191R	3,478 / 22D	3,897 / 155R
Hot Spring	978 / 474D	518 / 256D	817 / 401D	1,109 / 503D	1,374 / 670D
Howard		1,012 / 508D	1,337 / 431D	1,401 / 544D	1,944 / 882D
Independence	1,441 / 179R	1,742 / 870D	1,958 / 968D	2,608 / 1,310D	3,333 / 1,465D
Izard	794 / 482D	1,068 / 760R	1,228 / 782D	1,092 / 586D	1,633 / 809D
Jackson		1,345 / 589D	1,383 / 383D	2,116 / 447D	2,479 / 718D
Jefferson	3,890 / 1,804R	3,946 / 2,300R	4,081 / 2,311R	4,357 / 2,431R	7,286 / 3,508R
Johnson		1,200 / 818D	1,377 / 819D	1,871 / 965D	2,296 / 916D
Lafayette	2,176 / 674R	970 / 192R	859 / 229R	882 / 265R	838 / 169R
Lawrence	701 / 501R	727 / 719D	904 / 696D	1,842 / 890D	1,097 / 989D
Lee		1,519 / 233R	1,534 / 456R	2,578 / 494D	2,514 / 577R
Lincoln	1,906 / 110R	1,603 / 259R	1,316 / 380R	1,883 / 304R	1,947 / 434R
Little River	778 / 228R	752 / 78R	1,088 / 56R	996 / 216R	1,262 / 25R
Logan		1,419 / 329D	1,982 / 328D	2,536 / 620D	2,053 / 765D
Lonoke		1,843 / 547D	1,600 / 402D	2,275 / 488D	2,596 / 426D
Madison	648 / 467D	1,190 / 280D	1,149 / 821D	1,754 / 218D	2,590 / 174D
Marion	818 / 528D	869 / 508D	774 / 534D	810 / 404D	1,308 / 542D
Miller		1,298 / 25D	934 / 149D	1,619 / 79D	2,244 / 149D
Mississippi	575 / 223R	892 / 288D	934 / 138D	1,169 / 175R	1,137 / 74R

COUNTY	1872	1876	1880	1884	1888
Monroe	1,566 / 24R	1,395 / 121R	1,678 / 248R	2,073 / 123R	1,971 / 378R
Montgomery	548 / 170D	387 / 159D	587 / 308D	555 / 247D	969 / 645D
Nevada	1,413 / 383D	1,546 / 762D	1,308 / 564D	2,185 / 406D	2,258 / 416D
Newton	496 / 152R	597 / 61R	660 / 20R	582 / 108R	932 / 192R
Ouachita	2,127 / 17R	2,008 / 4D	1,787 / 71R	2,145 / 157R	2,535 / 138D
Perry	247 / 111R	296 / 56D	362 / 12D	594 / 130D	680 / 204D
Phillips	4,922 / 3,042R	3,849 / 1,865R	3,291 / 1,448R	2,583 / 911R	2,912 / 1,334R
Pike	349 / 133R	541 / 107D	498 / 194D	682 / 215D	1,081 / 581D
Poinsett		268 / 178D	288 / 242D	402 / 338D	523 / 283D
Polk	457 / 219D	399 / 327D	382 / 266D	525 / 406D	984 / 659D
Pope	847 / 213R	1,488 / 760D	1,532 / 780D	2,139 / 922D	2,672 / 1,320D
Prairie	708 / 481R	1,150 / 306D	1,253 / 245D	1,340 / 150D	1,529 / 158D
Pulaski	5,311 / 1,227R	5,415 / 1,075R	5,322 / 1,380R	6,583 / 1,692R	7,343 / 1,578R
Randolph	495 / 95R	897D	1,052 / 758D	1,868 / 1,064D	1,900 / 1,357D
Saline	765 / 749D	993 / 531D	985 / 453D	1,376 / 612D	1,410 / 590D
Scott		806 / 402D	814 / 404D	1,119 / 594D	1,578 / 584D
Searcy	487 / 268R	585 / 127R	1,018 / 114R	770 / 53R	1,023 / 38R
Sebastian	1,604 / 464R	2,312 / 492D	2,704 / 556D	3,871 / 906D	4,125 / 1,025D
Sevier	691 / 157D	623 / 385D	732 / 450D	935 / 605D	1,308 / 789D
Sharp	649 / 413D	786 / 504D	967 / 619D	1,021 / 601D	1,435 / 798D
St. Francis	1,043 / 73D	1,464 / 374D	1,187 / 119D	1,593 / 237D	2,009 / 85R
Stone		386 / 297D	477 / 357D	474 / 314D	620 / 348D
Union	2,179 / 479R	1,838 / 346D	1,885 / 305D	1,996 / 232D	1,549 / 177D
Van Buren	246 / 28R	584 / 466D	1,035 / 711D	626 / 344D	840 / 338D
Washington	1,966 / 464D	2,705 / 1,071D	2,725 / 1,149D	3,773 / 1,149D	5,212 / 1,230D
White	2,001 / 1,375D	1,922 / 1,458D	2,223 / 1,621D	2,538 / 1,524D	2,747 / 1,392D
Woodruff	1,205 / 168R	1,676 / 154D	1,406 / 70R	1,647 / Tie vote.	3,449 / 215D
Yell		1,472 / 478D	2,000 / 602D	2,162 / 813D	2,532 / 1,192D
CALIFORNIA.					
Alameda	3,793 / 1,337R	8,297 / 1,601R	9,795 / 1,999R	12,401 / 2,739R	15,461 / 3,147R
Alpina	127 / 51R	175 / 45R	107 / 25R	130 / 40R	80 / 26R
Amador	1,760 / 228R	2,487 / 143D	2,756 / 66D	2,760 / 41D	2,892 / 56D
Butte	2,019 / 387R	3,300 / 30R	3,644 / 16D	4,430 / 57R	4,541 / 34D
Calaveras	1,659 / 157R	1,822 / 520D	2,295 / 19R	2,400 / 70R	2,762 / 136R
Colusa	989 / 9D	2,235 / 703D	2,490 / 736D	2,899 / 774D	3,176 / 894D
Contra Costa	308 / 497R	441 / 346R	560 / 293R	622 / 382R	577 / 341R
Del Norte	308 / 30R	441 / 42D	560 / 16R	622 / 34D	577 / 16R
El Dorado	2,402 / 216R	2,772 / 110D	2,938 / 100D	2,837 / 180D	2,871 / 106D
Fresno	848 / 126D	1,296 / 620D	1,748 / 522D	3,105 / 390D	5,492 / 361D
Humboldt	1,396 / 590R	2,764 / 510R	2,225 / 755R	4,053 / 734R	4,956 / 758R
Inyo	382 / 30R	718 / 83D	595 / 47R	623 / 65R	745 / 164R
Kern	450 / 111D	1,400 / 288D	1,125 / 199D	1,423 / 200D	2,195 / 319D
Lake	557 / 153D	1,092 / 314D	1,181 / 223D	1,386 / 210D	1,629 / 186D
Lassen	272 / 90R	483 / 29R	624 / 22R	821 / 31D	1,043 / 47D
Los Angeles	2,529 / 81R	6,658 / 574D	5,766 / 62R	10,881 / 912R	25,264 / 3,695R

COUNTY.	1872.	1876.	1880.	1884.	1888.
Marin	819 / 381R	1,270 / 32R	1,321 / 199R	1,587 / 123R	1,774 / 134R
Mariposa	763 / 35R	919 / 189D	1,030 / 166D	1,107 / 144D	1,308 / 138D
Mendocino	1,387 / 63D	2,212 / 354D	2,283 / 345D	3,013 / 272D	3,821 / 295D
Merced	643 / 117D	1,362 / 248D	1,283 / 221D	1,762 / 144D	1,796 / 199D
Modoc	205 / 39D	530 / 114D	833 / 93D	1,120 / 131D	1,278 / 127D
Mono	138 / 38R	278 / 28R	1,735 / 91R	795 / 171R	581 / 132R
Monterey	2,131 / 179R	2,195 / 171R	2,470 / 50R	2,910 / 95R	3,862 / 9R
Napa	1,449 / 345R	2,118 / 188R	2,283 / 115R	2,881 / 337R	3,314 / 267R
Nevada	3,473 / 599R	4,305 / 395R	4,269 / 213R	4,199 / 577R	4,192 / 244R
Placer	2,255 / 579R	2,888 / 332R	3,059 / 227R	3,307 / 266R	3,364 / 214R
Plumas	792 / 232R	1,086 / 82R	1,343 / 53R	907 / 157D	1,233 / 78R
Sacramento	4,862 / 1,924R	6,324 / 1,354R	6,609 / 979R	7,266 / 1,704R	8,460 / 1,322R
San Benito	.....	1,099 / 229D	1,074 / 216D	1,300 / 98D	1,553 / 133D
San Bernardino	509 / 129R	1,281 / 67R	1,441 / 19R	2,974 / 329R	5,718 / 671R
San Diego	873 / 158R	1,462 / 126R	1,288 / 198R	1,861 / 332R	8,194 / 1,472R
San Francisco	22,969 / 599R	41,571 / 773R	40,557 / 2,897D	47,440 / 4,315R	55,717 / 2,991D
San Joaquin	3,095 / 471R	4,129 / 422R	4,977 / 159R	6,114 / 174R	5,981 / 7R
San Luis Obispo	782 / 140R	1,716 / 172D	1,560 / 100R	2,027 / 257R	3,400 / 104R
San Mateo	951 / 345R	1,567 / 175R	1,479 / 41R	1,722 / 201R	2,117 / 141R
Santa Barbara	1,172 / 212R	1,918 / 430R	1,610 / 204R	2,443 / 194R	3,423 / 119R
Santa Clara	3,889 / 549R	6,401 / 271R	5,983 / 293R	7,276 / 652R	8,924 / 485R
Santa Cruz	1,499 / 559R	2,669 / 405R	2,336 / 136R	3,106 / 302R	3,940 / 246R
Shasta	821 / 257R	1,266 / 16D	1,746 / 10D	2,214 / 130R	2,989 / 96R
Sierra	1,300 / 552R	1,428 / 406R	1,557 / 437R	1,619 / 509R	1,695 / 315R
Siskiyou	1,372 / 46R	1,579 / 143D	1,700 / 100D	1,955 / 152D	2,845 / 98D
Solano	3,670 / 1,156R	3,705 / 199R	3,922 / 4R	4,443 / 404R	4,492 / 73R
Sonoma	3,304 / 102R	5,339 / 475D	4,918 / 338D	6,147 / 100R	7,011 / 101D
Stanislaus	1,130 / 202D	1,899 / 295D	1,913 / 409D	2,479 / 445D	2,314 / 412D
Sutter	772 / 220R	1,108 / 8D	1,194 / 10R	1,387 / 40R	1,475 / 24R
Tehama	635 / 165R	1,321 / 29D	1,822 / 86D	2,243 / 71D	2,508 / 109D
Trinity	652 / 88R	796 / 20D	1,122 / 206R	886 / 16R	985 / 1D
Tulare	893 / 103D	2,356 / 384D	2,925 / 391D	3,158 / 423D	5,192 / 362D
Tuolumne	1,536 / 84R	1,726 / 108D	1,922 / 78D	1,917 / 230D	2,075 / 305D
Ventura	.....	1,199 / 17R	1,105 / 93R	1,388 / 146R	2,056 / 201R
Yolo	1,553 / 131R	2,602 / 135D	2,628 / 116D	1,575 / 49D	3,023 / 230D
Yuba	2,015 / 311R	2,327 / 175R	2,350 / 20D	1,843 / 222R	2,487 / 40D
COLORADO.					
Arapahoe	.....	.....	7,898 / 632R	13,030 / 1,803R	20,412 / 3,225R
Archuleta	.....	.....	.....	.....	204 / 50R
Bent	.....	.....	422 / 68D	863 / 64D	2,994 / 264R
Boulder	.....	.....	2,402 / 576R	2,690 / 489R	2,978 / 462R
Chaffee	.....	.....	2,340 / 53D	2,180 / 155R	2,272 / 336R
Clear Creek	.....	.....	2,611 / 606R	2,212 / 343R	2,044 / 540R
Conejos	.....	.....	1,219 / 8D	1,309 / 197R	1,656 / 313R
Costilla	.....	.....	713 / 45D	975 / 89R	898 / 124R

COUNTY.	1872.	1876.	1880.	1884.	1888.
Custer	.....	.....	2,394 / 236R	1,480 / 143D	955 / 200R
Delta	.....	.....	.....	411 / 56R	584 / 18R
Dolores	.....	.....	.....	846 / 36R	243 / 27R
Douglas	.....	.....	614 / 49R	534 / 42R	731 / 78R
Eagle	.....	.....	.....	497 / 116R	1,007 / 204R
Elbert	.....	.....	377 / 19D	518 / 63D	1,378 / 306R
El Paso	.....	.....	1,761 / 571R	1,746 / 675R	3,672 / 883R
Fremont	.....	.....	1,201 / 76R	1,640 / 331R	2,252 / 356R
Garfield	.....	.....	.....	385 / 106R	1,960 / 290R
Gilpin	.....	.....	2,067 / 431R	2,267 / 218R	1,794 / 265R
Grand	.....	.....	212 / 34R	427 / 65R	247 / 80R
Gunnison	.....	.....	2,079 / 48D	2,294 / 232R	1,622 / 287R
Hillsdale	.....	.....	782 / 60R	425 / 65R	272 / 40R
Huerfano	.....	.....	1,013 / 66D	1,197 / 207D	1,452 / 76R
Jefferson	.....	.....	1,679 / 42R	1,594 / 108R	1,834 / 202R
Lake	.....	.....	8,140 / 396D	6,150 / 747R	5,373 / 486R
La Plata	.....	.....	604 / 86D	1,416 / 90R	1,661 / 75R
Larimer	.....	.....	1,212 / 258R	1,770 / 393R	2,268 / 554R
Las Animas	.....	.....	1,944 / 728D	2,492 / 812D	5,505 / 180D
Logan	.....	.....	.....	.....	1,893 / 417R
Mesa	.....	.....	.....	665 / 25R	589 / 58R
Montrose	.....	.....	.....	671 / 191R	916 / 136R
Ouray	.....	.....	903 / 61R	889 / 109R	1,739 / 227R
Park	.....	.....	1,327 / 100R	1,427 / 148R	1,357 / 776R
Pitkin	.....	.....	.....	1,084 / 126R	2,781 / 308R
Pueblo	.....	.....	1,684 / 36D	3,269 / 354R	4,458 / 242R
Rio Grande	.....	.....	496 / 100R	735 / 187R	737 / 192R
Routt	.....	.....	58 / 20R	179 / 33R	587 / 147R
Saguache	.....	.....	884 / 138R	991 / 107R	1,030 / 164R
San Juan	.....	.....	425 / 28R	1,159 / 191R	710 / 105R
San Miguel	.....	.....	.....	789 / 60R	937 / 102R
Summit	.....	.....	2,617 / 99R	1,174 / 54R	1,260 / 144R
Washington	.....	.....	.....	.....	1,370 / 305R
Weld	.....	.....	1,428 / 431R	2,403 / 564R	3,374 / 906R
CONNECTICUT.					
Fairfield	16,917 / 115D	21,620 / 1,800D	24,148 / 68D	25,939 / 677D	20,848 / 217D
Hartford	20,822 / 425R	25,848 / 1,226D	27,141 / 931R	28,480 / 271D	31,381 / 565R
Litchfield	8,970 / 160R	11,158 / 684D	11,937 / 58R	11,819 / 470D	12,354 / 290R
Middlesex	6,047 / 849R	7,522 / 208R	7,923 / 453R	7,707 / 437R	8,251 / 750R
New Haven	22,472 / 226R	29,509 / 1,749D	33,818 / 2,180D	36,716 / 3,016D	42,189 / 3,110D
New London	11,107 / 1,109R	13,793 / 553R	14,552 / 1,124R	14,589 / 813R	15,911 / 144R
Tolland	4,331 / 379R	5,072 / 396R	5,317 / 622R	5,063 / 519R	5,371 / 332R
Windham	5,853 / 1,725R	7,146 / 1,502R	7,484 / 1,716R	7,099 / 1,389R	7,073 / 1,010R
DELAWARE.					
Kent	5,297 / 429D	5,213 / 1,343D	6,695 / 625D	6,092 / 1,840D	6,872 / 1,170D

COUNTY.	1872.	1876.	1880.	1884.	1888.
New Castle...	10,410 1,280R	12,667 559D	15,347 103R	16,363 745D	14,786 2,332D
Sussex.......	5,614 58R	6,253 727D	7,366 030D	7,460 1,428D	8,136 63R

FLORIDA.

COUNTY.	1872.	1876.	1880.	1884.	1888.
Alachua......	2,275 739R	3,244 746R	3,364 326R	3,828 354R	3,446 616D
Baker........	217 43D	381 95D	373 109D	513 161D	530 220D
Bradford.....	639 249D	905 501D	1,226 620D	1,288 634D	1,370 640D
Brevard......		169 53D	297 145D	416 196D	722 210D
Calhoun......	191 117D	279 151D	292 114D	338 62D	368 300D
Citrus........					618 372D
Clay.........	346 114D	437 185D	558 144D	815 185D	1,042 74D
Columbia	1,250 46R	1,621 185D	1,831 195D	2,014 88D	2,018 61D
Dade.........	27 3R	14 4R	55 9D	67 13D	139 49D
De Soto					893 473D
Duval........	2,513 731R	3,804 980R	4,120 1,102R	5,276 1,498R	4,095 1,318R
Escambia	1,503 93R	3,028 170R	2,764 160D	3,757 35D	3,586 326D
Franklin	293 47D	248 66D	331 87D	492 60D	682 12D
Gadsden	1,983 459R	2,135 465R	2,293 159D	1,931 169D	1,732 1,254D
Hamilton	460 424D	308 114D	1,236 260D	1,219 99D	1,096 386D
Hernando....	182 166D	718 430D	819 485D	1,310 770D	621 163D
Hillsborough.	457 41D	976 604D	1,157 717D	1,609 905D	2,374 1,018D
Holmes	218 210D	316 284D	344 338R	473 825D	581 519D
Jackson......	2,029 217R	2,139 217R	2,658 292D	2,556 284D	2,994 756D
Jefferson.....	2,834 1,636R	3,336 1,864R	2,499 863R	2,269 781R	2,383 11D
Lafayette....	221 101D	371 247D	427 277D	431 335D	593 537D
Lake.........					2,232 368D
Lee..........					313 173D
Leon........	3,071 1,723R	4,086 2,030R	3,817 1,837R	3,032 1,364R	1,502 1,126D
Levy........	452 196D	695 281D	1,258 310D	991 317D	1,116 201D
Liberty	168 76D	230 64D	235 27D	256 68D	241 85D
Madison......	1,986 604R	2,602 446R	2,067 89D	1,148 32R	902 544D
Manatee.....	277 119D		766 442D	896 454R	595 250D
Marion.......	1,716 424R	2,514 590R	2,600 460R	3,501 513R	3,755 70D
Monroe	906 332D	1,567 275R	2,045 311D	1,794 18R	2,285 35R
Nassau.......	1,039 121R	1,460 135R	1,476 246R	1,663 141R	1,869 47D
Orange.......	332 264D	1,109 693D	1,452 680D	3,028 706D	3,423 298D
Osceola					653 193D
Pasco					706 523D
Polk.........	362 362D	462 450D	517 499D	816 669D	1,073 958D
Putnam	803 15D	1,191 19D	1,499 1R	2,262 74R	2,513 190R
St. John's ...	554 188D	839 163D	962 254D	1,240 212D	2,070 14D
Santa Rosa..	927 213D	1,177 263D	1,012 232D	1,275 333D	1,233 376D
Sumter	433 157D	679 383D	984 448D	1,649 601D	1,691 473D
Suwanee	849 131D	1,084 168D	1,308 280D	1,754 202D	1,791 213D
Taylor	252 62D	315 169D	370 254D	323 95D	365 287D
Volusia	310 94D	645 273D	814 158D	1,691 65D	2,158 145R

COUNTY.	1872.	1876.	1880.	1884.	1888.
Wakulla	436 76D	543 179D	557 205D	544 206D	590 108D
Walton.......	441 297D	674 582D	716 574D	786 178D	987 111D
Washington .	348 288D	526 291D	281D	549 89D	740 278D

GEORGIA.

COUNTY.	1872.	1876.	1880.	1884.	1888.
Appling......	147 129D	545 281D	417 163D	848 158D	755 312D
Baker...... ..	828 424D	1,025 615D	875 193D	424 424D	380 303D
Baldwin......	1,270 614D	905 805D	1,177 543D	641 425D	681 188D
Banks........	310 178D	717 551D	765 525D	664 336D	1,031 597D
Bartow.......	1,879 493D	3,389 1,555D	2,744 1,090D	1,619 451D	1,290 626D
Berrien	456 448D	931 861D	891 799D	745 601D	736 710D
Bibb........	5,164 388D	4,698 2,136D	2,496 680D	2,584 870D	3,455 1,094D
Brooks.......	1,463 61D	1,285 935D	1,728 245D	1,481 55D	1,421 248D
Bryan.......	472 72R	1,130 426R	344 102D	492 14D	227 202D
Bullock......	563 563D	1,006 1,006D	1,007 977D	848 698D	1,105 1,019D
Burke........	2,147 25R	1,299 753D	3,097 1,311R	558 558D	962 436D
Butts........	608 44R	1,110 376D	1,075 209D	1,175 101D	875 358D
Calhoun......	1,284 186R	1,177 65D	776 20R	643 17D	451 451D
Camden......	598 240R	740 166R	1,266 4R	533 198R	510 129R
Campbell.....	1,063 11R	1,227 489D	922 230D	1,000 330D	1,100 457D
Carroll.......	1,290 428D	2,177 1,435D	1,569 911D	2,557 1,559D	2,114 1,361D
Catoosa......	380 54D	799 577D	553 423D	557 329D	555 322D
Charlton.....	200 96R	262 244D	187 95D	221 167D	173 55D
Chatham.....	5,617 947D	3,774 670D	5,564 1,244D	4,861 1,387D	5,372 2,565D
Chattahoochee.	700 76D	826 450D	682 14D	773 117D	167 123D
Chattooga....	601 205D	1,386 924D	1,372 960D	984 602D	820 458D
Cherokee.....	1,091 865D	1,817 1,598D	1,938 1,668D	1,005 795D	2,053 1,116D
Clarke.......	2,279 107R	2,340 46D	1,565 35D	1,553 8D	1,467 141D
Clay.........	732 130R	1,004 390D	896 184D	663 72D	839 270D
Clayton......	734 30D	1,277 499D	550 234D	784 226D	828 880D
Clinch.......	817 265D	665 433D	551 185D	487 361D	554 320D
Cobb	1,701 509D	3,209 1,708D	2,589 1,431D	1,908 836D	1,562 752D
Coffee........	66 44D	388 362D	235 235D	255 195D	408 184D
Colquitt......	322 296D	253 181D	220 134D	190 113D	261 251D
Columbia	100 Tie.	526 526D	244 244D	402 402D	408 391D
Coweta.......	2,815 267R	2,734 168D	2,666 96D	2,815 163D	2,472 486D
Crawford....	1,012 40D	1,194 1,004D	543 198D	463 145D	469 416D
Dade.........	269 269D	516 472D	542 376D	609 291D	557 876D
Dawson.......	386 30R	557 283D	548 292D	346 228D	864 178D
Decatur......	2,290 556R	3,136 186R	2,104 94D	1,708 76R	1,780 805D
De Kalb......	1,172 826D	1,807 987D	1,208 548D	1,475 575D	1,347 708D
Dodge........	156 138D	626 286D	428 296D	910 42D	914 90D
Dooly	397 203D	1,754 1,166D	1,084 586D	1,037 721D	1,174 401D
Dougherty ...	2,195 309R	942 114D	1,308 674R	417 217D	1,042 593D
Douglas......	425 57D	762 458D	606 358D	663 253D	708 842D
Early	801 73D	743 541D	986 488D	657 163D	755 179D

COUNTY	1872.	1876.	1880.	1884.	1888.
Echols	120 / 80D	107 / 43D	225 / 145D	277 / 95D	198 / 107D
Effingham	470 / 56D	769 / 495D	571 / 159D	517 / 221D	565 / 173D
Elbert	491 / 239D	871 / 871D	855 / 799D	924 / 846D	809 / 763D
Emanuel	333 / 333D	808 / 650D	946 / 592D	965 / 603D	689 / 628D
Fannin	467 / 165R	466 / 106D	645 / 41D	724 / 160R	1,072 / 318R
Fayette	655 / 111R	1,094 / 242D	682 / 316D	824 / 332D	895 / 486D
Floyd	2,128 / 326D	3,542 / 1,090D	3,143 / 1,359D	2,517 / 791D	1,748 / 560D
Forsyth	424 / 146D	1,022 / 820D	1,039 / 1,259D	694 / 420D	1,800 / 1,370D
Franklin	484 / 478D	990 / 974D	1,324 / 1,032D	880 / 438D	733 / 485D
Fulton	4,636 / 1,032R	6,518 / 1,950D	5,374 / 816D	2,864 / 1,014D	5,147 / 586D
Gilmer	514 / 86R	625 / 397D	719 / 269D	530 / 226D	1,121 / 13D
Glascock	312 / 280D	408 / 348D	213 / 197D	280 / 222D	835 / 345D
Glynn	801 / 321R	854 / 300R	660 / 76R	1,096 / 222R	1,212 / 19D
Gordon	866 / 408D	1,976 / 1,624D	1,411 / 1,085D	1,011 / 759D	1,007 / 733D
Greene	1,743 / 747R	1,200 / 1,000D	1,712 / 202R	1,587 / 77R	1,533 / 69D
Gwinnett	1,010 / 616D	1,763 / 1,427D	2,056 / 1,568D	1,940 / 948D	2,213 / 1,818D
Habersham	229 / 145D	1,054 / 990D	1,181 / 1,061D	660 / 410D	1,027 / 642D
Hall	814 / 474D	1,108 / 778D	2,013 / 1,475D	1,501 / 988D	2,486 / 1,806D
Hancock	1,100 / 165D	1,292 / 538D	966 / 200D	766 / 318D	774 / 419D
Haralson	235 / 7R	541 / 356D	481 / 317D	530 / 530D	595 / 400D
Harris	2,235 / 171R	2,136 / 658D	1,929 / 143D	2,056 / 338D	1,666 / 387D
Hart	605 / 41D	868 / 658D	624 / 296D	822 / 530D	775 / 594D
Heard	873 / 308D	1,006 / 470D	881 / 353D	1,148 / 403D	823 / 441D
Henry	1,268 / 58D	2,124 / 300D	1,197 / 185D	1,627 / 239D	1,673 / 624D
Houston	3,205 / 1,313R	4,027 / 265D	2,291 / 473D	1,733 / 867D	1,418 / 483D
Irwin	136 / 102D	305 / 305D	676 / 206R	416 / 344D	276 / 214D
Jackson	967 / 387D	1,683 / 309D	1,712 / 630D	1,493 / 671D	2,698 / 1,674D
Jasper	451 / 381D	1,204 / 480D	791 / 257D	864 / 8R	765 / 411D
Jefferson	950 / 298D	1,725 / 213D	933 / 317D	1,087 / 133D	976 / 686D
Johnson	347 / 347D	448 / 289D	263 / 235D	289 / 279D	516 / 255D
Jones	1,160 / 518D	1,290 / 250D	1,024 / 16R	817 / 179D	976 / 88D
Laurens	629 / 629D	1,082 / 520D	679 / 369D	847 / 395D	1,070 / 617D
Lee	702 / 164R	1,124 / 328R	978 / 452D	934 / 64R	584 / 227R
Liberty	808 / 395R	1,238 / 224R	1,139 / 301R	1,313 / 369R	1,200 / 231R
Lincoln	286 / 286D	546 / 546D	275 / 275D	385 / 385D	447 / 446D
Lowndes	1,239 / 11R	1,442 / 270D	1,406 / 86D	1,246 / 50D	1,427 / 124D
Lumpkin	289 / 63D	594 / 538D	650 / 522D	511 / 211D	770 / 129D
Macon	1,302 / 64D	1,654 / 250D	1,451 / 45R	1,211 / 11D	1,004 / 363D
Madison	263 / 109D	599 / 599D	1,696 / 488D	848 / 330D	727 / 439D
Marion	682 / 182D	919 / 243D	703 / 231D	1,089 / 415D	638 / 449D
McDuffie	328 / 316D	664 / 656D	411 / 291D	613 / 228D	692 / 386D
McIntosh	662 / 426R	980 / 300R	801 / 433R	973 / 565R	865 / 481R
Meriwether	1,842 / 88R	2,101 / 673D	1,916 / 140D	2,571 / 357D	1,454 / 539D
Miller	254 / 102D	427 / 365D	259 / 223D	115 / 115D	179 / 161D
Milton	245 / 173D	736 / 694D	506 / 414D	554 / 440D	958 / 839D
Mitchell	1,040 / 18R	1,165 / 83D	1,306 / 92R	761 / 109D	1,084 / 217D
Monroe	2,287 / 607D	2,910 / 864D	2,335 / 280D	1,743 / 743D	1,897 / 954D
Montgomery	195 / 195D	518 / 488D	318 / 144D	646 / 208D	671 / 302D
Morgan	1,283 / 201R	1,163 / 481D	1,933 / 277R	1,278 / 74D	730 / 296D
Murray	491 / 249D	1,111 / 961D	1,018 / 828D	908 / 428D	738 / 325D
Muscogee	2,520 / 106D	2,292 / 1,364D	2,441 / 581D	2,541 / 1,361D	1,724 / 496D
Newton	1,428 / 312R	2,043 / 159D	1,324 / 162D	1,506 / 12D	1,219 / 290D
Oconee		723	787 / 101D	749 / 129D	537 / 224D
Oglethorpe	862 / 28D	1,186 / 726D	805 / 489D	552 / 422D	556 / 546D
Paulding	423 / 71D	1,276 / 800D	1,212 / 694D	910 / 468D	785 / 407D
Pickens	566 / 132R	572 / 174D	545 / 93R	636 / 40R	1,158 / 420R
Pierce	312 / 14D	600 / 64D	470 / 80D	657 / 263D	566 / 168D
Pike	1,452 / 162R	2,236 / 870D	1,803 / 337D	1,592 / 224D	1,589 / 516D
Polk	911 / 117R	1,672 / 612D	1,574 / 558D	1,024 / 184D	1,064 / 137D
Pulaski	948 / 446D	1,546 / 1,162D	1,271 / 375D	1,271 / 695D	1,407 / 809D
Putnam	1,112 / 18R	950 / 870D	628 / 626D	519 / 519D	512 / 511D
Quitman	560 / 64D	512 / 416D	464 / 108D	201 / 117D	450 / 205D
Rabun	183 / 171D	482 / 482D	534 / 530D	234 / 224D	488 / 348D
Randolph	1,771 / 69D	2,064 / 782D	2,512 / 1,740D	1,116 / 222D	940 / 207D
Richmond	5,090 / 436D	4,457 / 2,397D	3,097 / 933D	5,238 / 1,348D	949 / 665D
Rockdale	634 / 62D	1,029 / 457D	707 / 221D	733 / 283D	588 / 588D
Schley	508 / 20D	689 / 111D	444 / 156D	707 / 105D	588 / 122D
Scriven	758 / 348D	1,194 / 606D	1,449 / 818D	1,288 / 791D	1,409 / 918D
Spalding	2,030 / 408R	1,710 / 490D	1,668 / 119R	1,314 / 68D	1,507 / 591D
Stewart	1,631 / 255D	1,236 / 618D	708 / 512D	891 / 477D	823 / 523D
Sumter	2,441 / 617R	2,515 / 625D	2,153 / 181R	1,912 / 460D	1,595 / 288D
Talbot	1,471 / 117D	1,510 / 488D	1,482 / 6D	672 / 424R	595 / 186D
Taliaferro	279 / 71R	667 / 241D	745 / 35R	681 / 155D	595 / 191D
Tatnall	397 / 95D	545 / 485D	675 / 449D	897 / 393D	647 / 647D
Taylor	1,048 / 296D	1,122 / 282D	896 / 248D	1,213 / 833D	606 / 436D
Telfair	228 / 228D	475 / 401D	330 / 204D	597 / 357D	739 / 259D
Terrell	1,352 / 394D	1,217 / 495D	1,063 / 409D	819 / 263D	902 / 445D
Thomas	2,488 / 802R	2,805 / 875D	2,529 / 103D	579 / 1D	2,320 / 627D
Towns	308 / 308D	434 / 189D	432 / 76D	312 / 18D	/ 2R
Troup	2,046 / 384D	2,354 / 1,750D	1,937 / 341D	1,672 / 746D	1,684 / 807D
Twiggs	871 / 257R	955 / 21D	568 / 166R	432 / 104D	460 / 142D
Union	420 / 96D	631 / 465D	691 / 507D	553 / 201D	988 / 107D
Upson	1,679 / 117D	1,854 / 356D	1,386 / 192D	1,152 / 404D	1,323 / 632D
Walker	756 / 108D	1,602 / 810D	1,535 / 853D	1,018 / 522D	990 / 458D
Walton	1,002 / 352D	1,395 / 1,391D	1,134 / 576D	1,341 / 693D	1,023 / 532D
Ware	246 / 14D	627 / 163D	554 / 231D	544 / 156D	572 / 183D
Warren	892 / 90D	1,063 / 363D	888 / 306D	668 / 379D	648 / 435D
Washington	1,692 / 818D	1,229 / 419D	2,010 / 132D	2,022 / 144D	1,926 / 779D
Wayne	197 / 79D	712 / 380D	475 / 231D	648 / 250D	467 / 180D
Webster	636 / 54D	772 / 162D	465 / 137D	614 / 92D	514 / 66D

COUNTY.	1872.	1876.	1880.	1884.	1888.
White	394 / 274D	498 / 441D	700 / 580D	370 / 264D	639 / 355D
Whitfield	807 / 105D	1,772 / 962D	1,075 / 735D	1,453 / 313D	1,320 / 416D
Wilcox	193 / 97D	361 / 309D	310 / 278D	440 / 354D	435 / 284D
Wilkes	734 / 450D	1,141 / 1,137D	920 / 534D	785 / 785D	696 / 668D
Wilkinson	1,073 / 863D	1,261 / 1,047D	629 / 485D	914 / 336D	411 / 270D
Worth	374 / 198D	808 / 450D	623 / 359D	598 / 242D	757 / 368D

ILLINOIS.

COUNTY.	1872.	1876.	1880.	1884.	1888.
Adams	9,520 / 834D	11,302 / 1,355D	11,708 / 1,126D	12,068 / 1,712D	13,643 / 1,108D
Alexander	2,271 / 191R	2,499 / 61D	2,978 / 226R	3,168 / 347R	3,643 / 470R
Bond	2,260 / 438R	2,679 / 378R	3,092 / 338R	3,197 / 266R	3,181 / 400R
Boone	1,938 / 1,446R	2,371 / 1,602R	2,443 / 1,717R	2,576 / 1,557R	2,783 / 1,605R
Brown	2,135 / 509D	2,622 / 551D	2,816 / 647D	2,739 / 687D	2,836 / 671D
Bureau	5,053 / 1,413R	6,082 / 1,501R	7,063 / 1,444R	6,843 / 1,948R	7,993 / 583R
Calhoun	1,006 / 154D	1,341 / 459D	1,473 / 441D	1,481 / 433D	1,581 / 350D
Carroll	2,582 / 1,354R	3,260 / 1,313R	3,490 / 1,456R	3,706 / 1,345R	4,153 / 1,305R
Cass	2,301 / 7D	2,901 / 409D	3,264 / 516D	3,585 / 651D	3,736 / 540D
Champaign	5,719 / 1,827R	8,237 / 1,427R	8,758 / 1,248R	9,054 / 1,052R	9,621 / 1,001R
Christian	4,873 / 393D	5,995 / 786D	6,227 / 650D	6,127 / 647D	6,688 / 497D
Clark	3,426 / Tie vote.	4,247 / 383D	4,710 / 375D	4,861 / 291D	5,220 / 268D
Clay	2,928 / 208R	3,069 / 125D	3,350 / 105D	3,585 / 17R	3,498 / 59R
Clinton	3,063 / 430D	3,430 / 660D	3,936 / 664D	3,842 / 1,064D	3,669 / 774D
Coles	5,053 / 236R	5,881 / 135R	6,037 / 86R	6,509 / 41D	6,883 / 138D
Cook	50,253 / 12,379R	76,502 / 2,402D	100,286 / 10,514R	131,692 / 8,618R	172,839 / 804R
Crawford	2,238 / 74R	3,036 / 288D	3,482 / 376D	3,563 / 264D	3,832 / 206D
Cumberland	2,262 / 50D	2,681 / 262D	3,020 / 198D	3,250 / 321D	3,438 / 237D
De Kalb	3,576 / 2,382R	5,157 / 2,266R	5,806 / 2,546R	5,908 / 2,367R	6,162 / 2,178R
De Witt	3,239 / 129R	3,848 / 754R	4,024 / 166R	4,080 / 6R	4,186 / 66R
Douglas	2,674 / 1,426R	3,082 / 274R	3,672 / 229R	3,737 / 230R	4,208 / 268R
Du Page	2,876 / 982D	3,430 / 853R	3,572 / 1,008R	3,912 / 685R	4,166 / 742R
Edgar	4,474 / 114R	5,759 / 168D	5,830 / 155D	6,246 / 283D	6,452 / 62D
Edwards	1,282 / 460R	1,497 / 504R	1,762 / 602R	1,937 / 608R	2,006 / 633R
Effingham	2,721 / 515D	3,453 / 1,120D	3,013 / 1,091D	4,061 / 1,276D	4,120 / 1,055D
Fayette	3,438 / 17R	4,359 / 540D	4,976 / 497D	5,054 / 443D	5,184 / 496D
Ford	1,733 / 753R	2,367 / 859R	3,002 / 1,077R	3,129 / 948R	3,519 / 905R
Franklin	2,031 / 125D	2,659 / 336D	3,179 / 324D	3,264 / 280D	3,396 / 91D
Fulton	7,206 / 202D	8,945 / 482D	9,489 / 550D	9,747 / 301D	10,315 / 17D
Gallatin	2,009 / 249D	2,125 / 437D	2,644 / 524D	2,707 / 417D	3,262 / 421D
Greene	3,568 / 826D	4,856 / 1,465D	5,074 / 1,195D	5,317 / 1,195D	5,537 / 1,165D
Grundy	2,308 / 874R	3,246 / 854R	3,424 / 952R	3,666 / 953R	4,051 / 636R
Hamilton	2,053 / 313D	2,830 / 806D	3,261 / 758D	3,372 / 684D	3,549 / 546D
Hancock	6,469 / 187D	7,742 / 711D	7,841 / 347D	7,388 / 603D	7,777 / 342D
Hardin	870 / 16D	1,075 / 281D	1,259 / 281D	1,286 / 160D	1,408 / 138D
Henderson	1,996 / 408R	2,331 / 300R	2,354 / 356R	2,218 / 321R	2,330 / 445R
Henry	5,304 / 2,004R	6,445 / 2,349R	7,266 / 2,408R	8,041 / 2,041R	7,208 / 2,067R
Iroquois	4,841 / 1,321R	6,590 / 1,190R	7,307 / 1,380R	7,175 / 747R	7,780 / 751R

COUNTY.	1872.	1876.	1880.	1884.	1888.
Jackson	3,367 / 347D	4,217 / 31D	4,805 / 8D	5,164 / 202R	5,800 / 65D
Jasper	1,982 / 148D	2,485 / 543D	3,043 / 567D	3,506 / 574D	3,813 / 581D
Jefferson	3,104 / 422D	3,660 / 321D	4,315 / 604D	4,877 / 542D	4,584 / 397D
Jersey	2,636 / 226D	3,511 / 821D	4,078 / 250D	3,330 / 707D	3,469 / 572D
Jo Daviess	4,654 / 750R	5,323 / 631R	5,525 / 651R	5,487 / 288R	5,696 / 8R
Johnson	1,681 / 611R	2,821 / 474R	2,584 / 628R	2,660 / 796R	2,929 / 810R
Kane	6,263 / 3,051R	8,420 / 2,548R	9,421 / 3,349R	11,031 / 3,585R	12,684 / 3,186R
Kankakee	3,497 / 1,585R	4,116 / 1,264R	4,948 / 1,561R	5,194 / 1,111R	5,596 / 1,118R
Kendall	1,982 / 1,244R	2,702 / 1,345R	2,866 / 1,275R	2,809 / 1,166R	2,814 / 1,085R
Knox	6,169 / 2,461R	8,008 / 2,603R	8,124 / 2,471R	8,060 / 2,560R	8,844 / 2,565R
Lake	3,065 / 1,423R	4,321 / 972R	4,437 / 1,890R	4,514 / 1,139R	4,717 / 1,072R
La Salle	9,003 / 1,089R	12,793 / 277R	14,141 / 633R	14,744 / 247D	17,010 / 307D
Lawrence	2,199 / 21R	2,554 / 131D	3,028 / 5D	3,121 / 57D	3,369 / 26R
Lee	3,252 / 1,452R	5,267 / 1,007R	5,996 / 1,317R	5,873 / 816R	6,044 / 876R
Livingston	2,996 / 1,222R	6,854 / 1,416R	7,497 / 910R	7,664 / 381R	8,057 / 223R
Logan	4,260 / 632R	5,420 / 193R	5,537 / 42R	5,782 / 256D	5,792 / 315D
Macon	5,084 / 418R	6,170 / 338R	6,701 / 378R	7,856 / 311R	8,529 / 295R
Macoupin	6,316 / 154D	7,757 / 509D	8,358 / 437D	8,708 / 612D	9,240 / 633D
Madison	7,236 / 106R	9,393 / 176D	9,814 / 347R	10,584 / 252D	10,960 / 310R
Marion	4,359 / 223D	4,662 / 435D	5,088 / 447D	5,349 / 507D	5,168 / 327D
Marshall	2,663 / 985R	3,118 / 123R	3,394 / 81R	3,471 / 28R	3,416 / 84D
Mason	2,970 / 198D	3,581 / 383D	3,690 / 310D	3,607 / 531D	3,797 / 558D
Massac	1,685 / 349R	2,044 / 438R	2,276 / 706R	2,261 / 637R	2,355 / 731R
McDonough	5,397 / 197R	6,110 / 141R	6,359 / 187R	6,434 / 1D	6,634 / 51R
McHenry	3,074 / 1,814R	5,373 / 1,591R	5,509 / 1,717R	5,087 / 1,027R	5,888 / 1,561R
McLean	9,180 / 2,510R	11,291 / 1,053R	12,886 / 2,115R	13,513 / 1,868R	14,373 / 1,773R
Menard	2,084 / 214D	2,782 / 542D	2,987 / 479D	2,961 / 445D	3,126 / 356D
Mercer	3,085 / 935R	3,727 / 781R	4,283 / 861R	4,221 / 639R	4,339 / 545R
Monroe	2,105 / 1,061D	2,508 / 806D	2,884 / 540D	2,964 / 767D	2,944 / 461D
Montgomery	4,736 / 300D	5,700 / 527D	6,076 / 471D	6,257 / 578D	6,800 / 733D
Morgan	5,198 / 314R	6,352 / 500D	6,948 / 253D	7,163 / 431D	7,377 / 217D
Moultrie	2,172 / 162D	2,945 / 427D	3,023 / 360D	3,116 / 415D	3,260 / 322D
Ogle	4,346 / 1,848R	5,858 / 1,912R	6,388 / 1,969R	6,413 / 1,644R	6,704 / 1,880R
Peoria	7,622 / 304D	10,203 / 778D	11,520 / 600D	13,304 / 705D	14,487 / 799D
Perry	2,522 / 456R	2,972 / 158R	3,350 / 216R	3,506 / 2R	3,602 / 15D
Piatt	2,356 / 510R	3,240 / 491R	3,529 / 337R	3,928 / 259R	4,226 / 295R
Pike	5,461 / 193D	7,190 / 985D	6,557 / 156D	7,191 / 971D	7,267 / 772D
Pope	1,781 / 591R	2,124 / 519R	2,514 / 647R	2,552 / 742R	2,698 / 735R
Pulaski	1,739 / 351R	1,815 / 271R	1,953 / 432R	2,190 / 177R	2,370 / 703R
Putnam	911 / 291R	1,119 / 187R	1,200 / 201R	1,194 / 72R	1,161 / 64R
Randolph	3,746 / 14R	4,948 / 232D	5,360 / 91R	5,257 / 222D	5,398 / 152D
Richland	2,660 / 26D	3,017 / 142D	3,366 / 108D	3,281 / 153D	3,257 / 84D
Rock Island	4,732 / 1,078R	6,777 / 1,874R	7,591 / 1,460R	7,629 / 1,039R	8,571 / 940R
Saline	2,156 / 60R	2,709 / 101D	3,121 / 1,300D	3,515 / 145R	4,066 / 145R
Sangamon	8,530 / 232D	10,777 / 996D	11,910 / 730D	13,114 / 833D	14,321 / 712D

COUNTY	1872.	1876.	1880.	1884.	1888.
Schuyler	3,007 147D	3,441 282D	3,526 417D	3,538 423D	3,714 384D
Scott	2,003 141D	2,361 359D	2,452 253D	2,437 297D	2,598 283D
Shelby	4,565 763D	5,963 1,484D	6,362 1,311D	6,544 1,512D	6,936 1,467D
Stark	1,824 612R	2,322 654R	2,443 701D	2,460 581R	2,351 533R
St. Clair	8,314 116R	10,698 1,183D	11,975 30D	12,421 1,592D	12,936 256D
Stephenson	4,969 723R	5,982 440R	6,717 510R	6,858 198D	7,231 55R
Tazewell	4,452 268R	6,065 321D	6,439 448D	6,192 715D	6,532 500D
Union	2,592 868D	3,136 1,177D	3,413 1,125D	3,527 994D	3,800 1,021D
Vermilion	5,080 1,606R	7,091 1,341R	8,856 1,561R	10,118 1,539R	11,292 1,626R
Wabash	1,666 72D	1,793 286D	2,120 203D	2,348 1,579D	2,530 252D
Warren	4,105 883R	4,917 811R	5,157 846R	5,114 697R	5,047 693R
Washington	2,982 502R	3,621 245R	4,236 368R	4,219 167R	3,952 242R
Wayne	3,288 40D	3,803 181D	4,426 141D	4,828 218D	4,882 60D
White	2,982 534D	3,832 769D	4,667 780D	4,775 805D	5,243 659D
Whitesides	4,460 1,926R	6,115 1,720R	6,536 1,708R	6,392 1,409R	6,714 1,390R
Will	7,149 1,275R	9,446 771R	10,461 1,973R	11,007 1,070R	11,952 1,100R
Williamson	2,646 18R	3,357 28R	3,819 28R	4,297 272R	4,493 327R
Winnebago	4,860 2,758R	6,143 2,937R	6,406 3,106R	7,285 3,153R	8,959 1,910R
Woodford	3,277 187D	4,075 312D	4,479 357D	4,341 606D	4,447 598D

INDIANA.

COUNTY	1872.	1876.	1880.	1884.	1888.
Adams	1,977 531D	2,902 1,165D	3,621 1,212D	3,854 1,502D	4,363 1,650D
Allen	8,710 1,638D	11,762 3,719D	12,690 2,976D	14,025 3,972D	15,406 4,237D
Bartholomew	4,457 47D	5,277 484D	5,568 355D	5,542 305D	5,927 968D
Benton	1,480 246R	2,550 171R	2,856 250R	2,966 283R	3,116 201R
Blackford	1,418 26D	1,602 126D	1,937 248D	2,122 194D	2,450 91D
Boone	5,272 454R	5,709 170R	6,202 28R	6,325 199D	7,029 117R
Brown	1,419 495D	1,851 766D	2,217 977D	2,218 914D	2,873 877D
Carroll	3,328 364D	3,186 10D	4,481 122D	4,787 122D	5,326 48R
Cass	4,841 609R	6,601 466D	7,085 192D	7,748 487D	8,248 399D
Clarke	5,101 365D	5,780 1,079D	6,559 760D	6,654 810D	7,045 580D
Clay	4,096 642R	5,065 340D	6,107 42D	6,545 111D	7,712 62D
Clinton	3,800 186R	4,941 320D	5,690 450D	6,355 243D	6,968 241D
Crawford	2,059 5D	2,192 181D	2,557 234D	2,938 314D	3,105 188D
Daviess	3,533 297R	4,400 330R	4,692 67D	4,873 202D	5,426 8R
Dearborn	4,782 802D	5,508 1,286D	6,189 1,068D	6,130 1,039D	6,268 883D
Decatur	4,233 209R	4,846 69R	4,984 308R	4,930 211R	5,140 269R
De Kalb	3,305 317R	4,971 171D	5,133 141D	5,404 340D	6,221 281D
Delaware	4,212 1,314R	4,970 1,514R	5,568 1,857R	5,674 1,529R	6,794 1,860R
Dubois	2,366 1,186D	3,040 1,631D	3,413 1,598D	3,726 1,685D	4,226 1,765D
Elkart	5,342 654R	7,175 352R	7,850 719R	8,677 823R	9,789 492R
Fayette	2,430 302R	2,899 330R	3,001 530R	3,621 549R	3,448 482R
Floyd	4,300 934D	4,903 1,165D	5,450 1,046D	5,922 1,150D	6,872 877D
Fountain	3,636 342R	4,658 84R	5,072 4D	4,897 205D	5,278 88R
Franklin	4,069 1,147D	4,645 1,374D	4,836 1,468D	4,585 1,343D	4,622 1,159D
Fulton	2,403 133R	3,285 133D	3,612 47D	4,052 167D	4,297 110D

COUNTY	1872.	1876.	1880.	1884.	1888.
Gibson	4,002 128R	4,673 43D	5,213 185R	5,490 125R	5,937 232R
Grant	4,212 904R	5,122 704R	5,669 755R	6,243 748R	7,293 939R
Greene	3,643 363R	4,579 104R	4,894 210R	4,937 184R	5,647 275R
Hamilton	4,642 1,718R	5,342 1,362R	5,897 1,545R	6,230 1,208R	6,423 1,186R
Hancock		3,703 550D	4,120 550D	4,276 686D	4,448 890D
Harrison	3,776 364D	4,228 677D	4,562 531D	4,572 623D	4,765 396D
Hendricks	4,460 1,208R	5,156 1,095R	5,408 1,202R	5,321 934R	5,624 1,214R
Henry	4,970 1,840R	4,678 1,697R	6,067 1,753R	5,886 1,571R	6,414 1,570R
Howard	4,571 1,193R	4,560 1,179R	4,917 1,304R	5,188 1,045R	6,122 1,402R
Huntington	4,089 289R	4,935 12D	5,430 19D	6,349 19D	7,229 78R
Jackson	3,900 754D	4,501 1,109D	5,202 1,141D	5,207 1,088D	5,535 972D
Jasper	1,408 488R	2,093 511R	2,259 472R	2,318 368R	2,706 601R
Jay	3,177 287R	3,998 20D	4,560 82R	5,253 25R	5,807 69R
Jefferson	4,949 547R	5,795 294R	6,003 649R	5,983 462R	6,057 630R
Jennings	3,295 152R	3,699 358R	3,834 267R	3,728	3,703 459R
Johnson	3,806 409D	4,527 503D	4,768 441D	4,731 495D	4,990 426D
Knox	4,632 522D	5,370 770D	6,160 750D	6,296 884D	6,708 698D
Kosciusko	4,500 806R	5,927 514R	6,501 734R	6,971 834R	7,430 1,065R
Lagrange	2,693 1,083R	3,524 940R	3,926 974R	3,749 869R	3,946 746R
Lake	2,103 731R	3,148 512R	3,539 1,004R	4,152 307R	4,693 474R
Laporte	5,686 120R	7,085 411D	7,632 249D	8,069 898D	8,437 884D
Lawrence	3,346 380R	3,689 268R	3,904 356R	3,993 520R	4,084 442R
Madison	5,069 521D	6,042 771D	6,513 284D	6,813 783D	7,592 492D
Marion	17,015 2,117R	24,669 1,302R	25,873 2,441R	18,994 226R	35,113 379D
Marshall	3,522 20R	4,981 568D	5,370 543D	5,491 762D	5,910 600D
Martin	2,054 114D	2,695 454D	2,969 310D	3,849 256D	2,902 165D
Miami	4,654 416R	4,681 123D	6,189 50D	6,432 314D	6,714 449D
Monroe	2,956 228R	3,351 108R	3,627 98R	3,738 164R	3,090 241R
Montgomery	5,326 142R	6,434 242D	7,211 238R	7,501 61R	7,892 248R
Morgan	3,733 467R	4,191 268R	4,570 345R	4,443 267R	4,668 423R
Newton	1,357 271R	1,955 370R	2,021 486R	1,966 413R	2,225 423R
Noble	4,119 407R	5,324 34D	5,787 Tie.	5,912 74R	6,155 46R
Ohio	1,047 135R	1,237 50R	1,333 139R	1,273 104R	1,315 140R
Orange	2,426 76D	2,880 334D	3,038 100D	3,077 23D	3,444 125R
Owen	2,891 127D	3,401 522D	3,569 491D	3,522 496D	3,620 286D
Parke	3,449 987R	4,532 679R	4,783 797R	4,577 633R	5,189 605R
Perry	2,618 100R	3,101 388D	3,553 206D	3,793 33D	3,985 33D
Pike	2,666 88R	2,281 182D	3,607 141D	3,847 56D	4,392 99R
Porter	2,655 715R	3,629 493R	3,938 665R	4,460 613R	4,597 411R
Posey	3,701 405D	4,087 698D	4,765 488D	4,961 616D	5,184 315D
Pulaski	1,274 426R	2,032 290D	2,190 207D	2,534 442D	2,721 233D
Putnam	4,459 397D	5,184 519D	5,508 311D	5,598 377D	5,696 446D
Randolph	4,843 1,829R	5,933 1,019R	6,397 2,237R	6,551 2,097R	7,109 2,372R
Ripley	3,911 83D	4,480 213D	4,881 71D	4,749 122D	4,829 24R
Rush	3,992 324R	4,680 265R	5,053 353R	5,091 348R	5,172 421R

COUNTY.	1872.	1876.	1880.	1884.	1888.
Scott	1,477 115D	1,852 300D	1,887 320D	1,738 305D	1,800 287D
Shelby	4,811 517D	5,627 796D	6,271 907D	6,347 581D	6,478 532D
Spencer	4,102 148R	4,458 415D	4,917 112D	4,090 122D	5,442 48R
Starke	727 41D	974 139D	1,022 182D	1,363 274D	1,766 70D
Steuben	2,591 1,163R	3,563 1,342R	3,714 1,042R	3,694 907R	3,848 1,004R
St. Joseph	5,829 1,023R	7,073 72R	8,159 465R	9,578 490D	10,401 320D
Sullivan	3,498 740D	4,516 1,348D	4,796 1,442D	4,613 1,550D	5,348 1,480D
Switzerland	2,559 327R	3,013 99R	3,138 120R	3,807 10R	3,259 77D
Tippecanoe	7,278 1,058R	8,453 599R	9,017 1,241D	9,342 643R	9,500 701R
Tipton	2,586 68D	3,145 362D	3,436 338D	3,976 450D	4,548 328D
Union	1,555 391R	1,840 239R	1,904 269R	1,970 295R	2,024 240R
Vanderburg	7,375 631R	8,500 56D	9,625 428R	11,074 63D	11,909 137R
Vermilion	1,962 664R	2,600 263R	2,946 327R	3,011 271R	3,304 202R
Vigo	7,006 814R	8,515 178D	10,340 407R	11,329 144R	12,586 171R
Wabash	4,740 1,236R	5,765 1,272R	6,134 1,400R	6,507 1,302R	6,824 1,431R
Warren	2,288 735R	2,659 908R	2,875 949R	2,886 818R	2,919 828R
Warrick	3,518 73D	4,145 473D	4,424 336D	4,706 35D	5,818 196D
Washington	3,519 351D	3,955 719D	4,134 691D	4,050 588D	4,260 540D
Wayne	7,524 1,712R	9,002 2,396R	9,715 2,937R	10,045 2,565R	10,079 2,483R
Wells	2,846 252D	3,866 837D	4,428 880D	4,745 1,146D	5,182 1,016D
White	2,363 257R	3,002 52R	3,325 109R	3,627 106D	4,045 75D
Whitley	3,051 249D	3,721 391D	4,263 258D	4,436 358D	4,619 192D

IOWA.

COUNTY.	1872.	1876.	1880.	1884.	1888.
Adair	968 546R	2,489 1,241R	2,642 1,092R	3,134 443R	3,178 705R
Adams	1,120 620R	2,097 750R	2,451 757R	2,725 13R	2,608 241R
Allamakee	2,837 73R	3,394 63R	3,701 307R	3,729 263D	3,970 120D
Appanoose	2,455 661R	3,343 292R	3,621 361R	3,522 68D	4,043 266R
Audubon	830 38R	779 75R	1,676 326R	2,438 6R	2,860 156R
Benton	3,419 1,601R	4,527 1,545R	4,609 1,576R	5,093 221R	5,485 122R
Black Hawk	3,285 1,609R	4,612 1,388R	4,641 1,455R	5,237 1,069R	5,307 979R
Boone	2,204 694R	3,501 713R	3,919 983R	4,834 411R	4,786 241R
Bremer	1,932 1,028R	2,507 978R	2,567 841R	3,199 206R	3,401 115D
Buchanan	2,740 1,014R	3,845 810R	3,807 948R	4,155 293R	4,309 468R
Buena Vista	572 454R	1,083 570R	1,426 740R	2,276 559R	2,603 836R
Butler	1,864 1,002R	2,631 1,049R	3,046 1,135R	3,281 755R	3,840 747R
Calhoun	435 245R	796 453R	1,179 558R	2,139 742R	2,589 901R
Carroll	526 294R	1,570 28R	2,452 20R	3,560 572D	3,723 459D
Cass	1,229 767R	2,916 897R	3,725 1,043R	4,268 133R	4,329 651R
Cedar	3,152 1,298R	3,589 883R	3,934 957R	4,165 239R	4,344 3R
Cerro Gordo	1,084 726R	1,737 825R	2,301 927R	2,643 762R	2,948 802R
Cherokee	573 353R	1,191 689R	1,620 706R	2,561 753R	3,265 798R
Chickasaw	1,621 619R	2,686 484R	2,776 296R	3,062 196D	3,230 43D
Clarke	1,517 553R	2,342 589R	2,398 769R	2,517 1,108R	2,488 485R
Clay	626 522R	671 473R	919 642R	1,397 668R	1,968 944R
Clayton	4,395 201R	5,306 40R	5,635 679R	5,768 683D	5,964 735D
Clinton	5,460 732R	7,090 257R	6,680 599R	7,828 1,342D	8,792 1,509D
Crawford	649 191R	1,681 405R	2,537 643R	3,295 283D	3,800 465D
Dallas	2,184 1,056R	3,306 1,411R	4,119 1,794R	4,670 602R	4,383 959R
Davis	2,838 326R	3,356 44D	3,565 64D	3,284 904D	3,436 198D
Decatur	2,168 308R	2,718 335R	3,151 682R	3,354 152R	3,481 256R
Delaware	2,863 897R	3,660 806R	3,944 907R	3,984 502R	3,887 677R
Des Moines	4,538 464R	6,241 407R	6,320 601R	6,907 1,021D	7,716 923D
Dickinson	368 266R	808 213R	371 279R	756 230R	906 447R
Dubuque	5,804 1,046D	7,814 2,179D	7,840 1,569D	9,285 2,787D	9,451 2,888D
Emmett	276 140R	282 210R	315 252R	486 285R	799 367R
Fayette	3,256 1,246R	4,763 1,319R	4,621 1,377R	5,074 186R	5,309 599R
Floyd	2,026 1,214R	2,910 1,282R	*2,868 1,305R	3,889 6R	3,362 694R
Franklin	1,016 714R	1,552 807R	1,986 1,091R	2,336 864R	2,452 767R
Fremont	2,553 31D	3,488 22D	3,909 280R	3,836 180D	3,840 15D
Greene	852 628R	1,974 801R	2,501 1,188R	3,472 394R	3,510 813R
Grundy	869 645R	1,517 682R	2,091 917R	2,524 414R	2,535 940R
Guthrie	1,346 626R	1,872 195D	2,957 1,072R	3,711 658R	3,802 813R
Hamilton	1,081 643R	1,655 762R	1,920 973R	2,710 596R	2,807 771R
Hancock	239 133R	380 182R	689 349R	1,054 330R	1,467 331R
Hardin	2,291 1,287R	3,301 1,192R	3,150 1,411R	3,851 1,237R	3,873 1,253R
Harrison	1,773 527R	3,070 171R	3,905 581R	4,699 101R	4,918 134R
Henry	3,749 1,265R	4,405 1,321R	4,170 1,316R	4,194 580R	4,322 757R
Howard	904 640R	1,815 549R	1,514 781R	1,998 171R	2,268 221R
Humboldt	518 288R	709 340R	945 410R	1,608 484R	1,915 506R
Ida	95 69R	302 158R	1,033 359R	2,182 340R	2,380 182R
Iowa	2,309 587R	3,370 523R	3,108 501R	3,701 481D	8,709 314D
Jackson	3,741 27R	4,712 350D	4,924 372D	5,047 1,119D	5,132 1,000D
Jasper	3,798 1,908R	5,297 1,571R	5,713 1,755R	5,789 263R	5,901 796R
Jefferson	2,900 630R	3,733 718R	3,676 744R	3,756 305R	3,722 458R
Johnson	3,998 229D	4,916 222D	5,292 366D	5,183 1,132D	5,108 987D
Jones	3,522 1,048R	4,358 828R	4,259 990R	4,628 394R	4,665 341R
Keokuk	3,213 491R	4,328 501R	4,530 564R	5,305 219D	5,450 55R
Kossuth	638 400R	865<>411R	1,099 504R	1,775 316R	2,519 425R
Lee	5,757 57R	6,814 550D	7,056 366D	7,499 919D	8,505 890D
Linn	4,818 579R	7,255 1,405R	7,679 1,628R	9,223 534R	9,664 874R
Louisa	2,218 788R	2,988 922R	2,665 1,025R	2,870 638R	2,949 824R
Lucas	1,807 429R	2,530 484R	2,934 579R	3,192 418R	3,226 666R
Lyon	88 86R	308 216R	475 273R	865 360R	1,634 276R
Madison	2,704 812R	3,944 708R	3,750 986R	3,749 121R	3,612 524R
Mahaska	3,707 1,357R	5,557 1,517R	5,477 1,871R	6,254 572R	6,707 997R
Marion	4,052 430R	5,040 432R	5,163 932R	4,984 237D	5,019 52R
Marshall	2,614 1,878R	4,368 1,661R	4,590 1,850R	5,544 1,279R	5,448 1,422R
Mills	1,852 486R	2,694 288R	3,025 617R	3,230 612R	3,320 162R
Mitchell	1,584 808R	2,399 992R	2,580 833R	2,501 432R	2,757 655R
Monona	747 395R	1,317 409R	1,684 612R	2,548 122R	2,988 502R

COUNTY.	1872.	1876.	1880.	1884.	1888.
Monroe	2,061 / 349R	2,665 / 172R	2,547 / 514R	2,785 / 32D	2,866 / 209R
Montgomery	1,440 / 534R	2,707 / 990R	2,693 / 1,289R	3,521 / 747R	3,340 / 1,032R
Muscatine	3,566 / 724R	4,674 / 499R	4,912 / 698R	5,391 / 241D	5,496 / 113D
O'Brien	305 / 271R	605 / 347R	899 / 400R	1,839 / 555R	2,762 / 586R
Osceola	211 / 193R	386 / 268R	523 / 341R	883 / 397R	1,055 / 341R
Page	2,125 / 691R	3,821 / 1,382R	4,020 / 1,737R	4,409 / 1,090R	4,422 / 1,108R
Palo Alto	445 / 53R	676 / 10R	869 / 23R	1,322 / 21D	1,762 / 10D
Plymouth	610 / 328R	1,349 / 333R	1,700 / 728R	3,870 / 62D	4,014 / 385D
Pocahontas	341 / 195R	527 / 234R	686 / 247R	1,271 / 277R	1,786 / 253R
Polk	4,524 / 1,578R	7,088 / 1,942R	8,146 / 2,620R	10,920 / 1,354R	12,955 / 2,083R
Pottawatta-mie	2,604 / 298R	7,021 / 2,151R	6,564 / 894R	8,784 / 88D	9,603 / 290D
Poweshiek	2,515 / 1,397R	3,637 / 1,435R	3,962 / 1,504R	4,187 / 434R	4,827 / 568R
Ringgold	1,019 / 589R	2,912 / 1,823R	2,411 / 1,014R	2,789 / 581R	3,650 / 26R
Sac	353 / 257R	1,951 / 1,475R	1,888 / 901R	2,894 / 672R	2,996 / 730R
Scott	5,017 / 279D	3,702 / 2,086D	7,066 / 1,728R	7,987 / 2,460D	8,628 / 2,860D
Shelby	517 / 241R	4,527 / 3,365R	2,567 / 536R	3,546 / 61R	3,654 / 48D
Sioux	427 / 193R	659 / 219R	1,089 / 326R	2,262 / 446R	3,339 / 497R
Story	1,735 / 1,043R	1,724 / 269R	3,049 / 1,497R	3,537 / 1,102R	3,605 / 1,370R
Tama	2,663 / 1,203R	2,737 / 21R	3,995 / 1,622R	4,643 / 331R	4,726 / 112R
Taylor	1,554 / 690R	2,851 / 1,051R	3,327 / 1,200R	3,586 / 499R	3,596 / 693R
Union	1,091 / 501R	2,460 / 444R	3,127 / 784R	3,589 / 80R	3,731 / 419R
Van Buren	3,214 / 518R	3,790 / 449R	3,704 / 347R	3,835 / 131R	3,895 / 253R
Wapello	3,778 / 484R	5,053 / 169R	5,488 / 501R	5,942 / 26R	6,730 / 181R
Warren	2,918 / 1,336R	4,999 / 23R	4,176 / 1,186R	4,013 / 348D	4,090 / 766R
Washington	3,361 / 919R	4,205 / 959R	4,233 / 1,146R	4,497 / 378R	4,444 / 355R
Wayne	2,052 / 376R	3,042 / 342R	3,401 / 963R	3,880 / 9D	3,441 / 211R
Webster	1,856 / 296R	2,684 / 312R	2,962 / 777R	4,003 / 43R	4,410 / 544R
Winnebago	286 / 254R	537 / 449R	803 / 636R	911 / 474R	1,135 / 676R
Winneshiek	2,996 / 1,142R	4,496 / 1,142R	4,101 / 1,059R	4,437 / 479R	4,651 / 516R
Woodbury	1,229 / 351R	2,143 / 31R	2,583 / 458R	5,186 / 409R	7,886 / 581R
Worth	489 / 311R	857 / 554R	1,241 / 643R	1,391 / 412R	1,684 / 521R
Wright	509 / 339R	755 / 393R	971 / 576R	2,001 / 625R	2,528 / 846R

KANSAS.

COUNTY.	1872.	1876.	1880.	1884.	1888.
Allen	1,673 / 641R	2,012 / 208R	2,423 / 773R	3,168 / 836R	3,331 / 850R
Anderson	1,280 / 613R	1,269 / 515R	1,994 / 630R	2,935 / 846R	3,343 / 883R
Atchison	3,312 / 596R	3,377 / 355R	5,097 / 762R	6,015 / 702R	6,179 / 616R
Barbour		170 / 24D	530 / 87R	1,747 / 180R	2,002 / 267R
Barton	224 / 96R	936 / 315R	1,948 / 458R	2,194 / 21R	2,752 / 125R
Bourbon	3,394 / 626R	3,473 / 1,149R	3,845 / 1,159R	4,917 / 1,303R	6,254 / 1,738R
Brown	1,513 / 751R	2,078 / 662R	2,854 / 953R	3,819 / 954R	4,851 / 803R
Butler	1,920 / 981R	2,275 / 851R	3,950 / 1,279R	5,442 / 1,380R	5,730 / 1,534R
Chase	669 / 295R	1,381 / 832R	1,449 / 392R	1,853 / 317R	2,061 / 524R
Chautauqua		1,300 / 57R	2,309 / 666R	3,169 / 700R	2,762 / 896R
Cherokee	2,079 / 295D	2,608 / 296R	4,910 / 693R	5,633 / 662R	6,434 / 897R
Cheyenne					1,235 / 859R

COUNTY.	1872.	1876.	1880.	1884.	1888.
Clark					922 / 124R
Clay	932 / 556R	1,409 / 873R	2,665 / 1,234R	3,291 / 1,192R	3,768 / 994R
Cloud	1,180 / 660R	1,680 / 695R	3,109 / 1,268R	4,158 / 1,534R	4,269 / 1,490R
Coffey	1,505 / 565R	1,564 / 305R	2,462 / 571R	3,467 / 730R	3,746 / 743R
Comanche					967 / 106R
Cowley	1,758 / 724R	2,620 / 714R	4,390 / 1,060R	6,524 / 1,435R	7,609 / 2,179R
Crawford	1,613 / 443D	2,400 / 395R	3,708 / 546R	5,313 / 964R	6,513 / 1,281R
Davis	988 / 106R	939 / 152R	1,436 / 303R	1,659 / 241R	1,890 / 271R
Decatur			408 / 144R	702 / 255R	2,132 / 493R
Dickinson	1,068 / 624R	1,861 / 873R	3,132 / 1,068R	4,202 / 1,019R	5,071 / 1,051R
Doniphan	2,881 / 693R	3,683 / 620R	3,261 / 924R	3,314 / 1,043R	3,375 / 1,136R
Douglas	4,385 / 1,731R	3,720 / 1,388R	4,737 / 1,585R	5,532 / 1,680R	5,313 / 1,520R
Edwards		338 / 28R	414 / 210R	810 / 139R	1,009 / 207R
Elk		1,473 / 578R	2,218 / 816R	3,027 / 877R	2,912 / 870R
Ellis	277 / 49R	352 / 68R	1,154 / 260R	1,077 / 96D	1,553 / 66D
Ellsworth	473 / 5D	599 / 237R	1,592 / 594R	1,875 / 327R	2,051 / 328R
Finney				889 / 59R	1,102 / 846R
Ford		812 / 48D	658 / 82R	1,308 / 119R	1,681 / 252R
Franklin	1,812 / 1,504R	2,431 / 986R	3,734 / 1,380R	4,342 / 1,363R	4,799 / 1,309R
Garfield					302 / 96R
Gove					890 / 308R
Graham			808 / 390R	580 / 289R	1,194 / 455R
Grant					886 / 145R
Gray					766 / 149R
Greeley					715 / 242R
Greenwood	1,308 / 511R	1,449 / 506R	2,325 / 644R	3,369 / 933R	3,941 / 1,132R
Hamilton					812 / 180R
Harper			1,010 / 232R	2,937 / 615R	3,054 / 550R
Harvey	750 / 376R	1,857 / 655R	2,275 / 969R	3,553 / 971R	3,944 / 1,000R
Haskell					509 / 94R
Hodgeman			241 / 124R	419 / 138R	880 / 343R
Jackson	1,366 / 454R	1,486 / 293R	2,371 / 651R	3,050 / 711R	3,304 / 750R
Jefferson	2,636 / 814R	2,477 / 526R	3,451 / 570R	3,982 / 595R	3,979 / 667R
Jewell	799 / 560R	1,859 / 833R	3,481 / 1,316R	4,034 / 1,394R	4,169 / 1,286R
Johnson	3,030 / 644R	3,062 / 929R	3,698 / 950R	3,991 / 718R	4,073 / 729R
Kearney					618 / 119R
Kingman		20 / 14R	721 / 256R	2,347 / 433R	2,815 / 791R
Kiova					1,043 / 148R
Labette	2,792 / 764R	3,473 / 719R	4,603 / 1,259R	6,084 / 1,381R	6,057 / 1,894R
Lane					795 / 192R
Leavenworth	5,445 / 413R	5,443 / 257R	5,848 / 699R	7,251 / 108R	7,194 / 244D
Lincoln	435 / 207R	690 / 218R	1,330 / 581R	1,686 / 524R	2,004 / 452R
Linn	2,336 / 1,072R	2,413 / 1,102R	3,312 / 1,245R	3,807 / 1,189R	4,125 / 1,364R
Logan					925 / 326R
Lyon	2,041 / 1,205R	2,076 / 1,149R	3,669 / 1,529R	4,999 / 1,557R	5,015 / 1,637R

COUNTY.	1872.	1876.	1880.	1884.	1888.
Marion	825 / 529R	1,253 / 491R	2,049 / 700R	2,921 / 785R	3,948 / 1,092R
Marshall	2,000 / 756R	2,565 / 815R	3,700 / 1,279R	4,873 / 785R	5,270 / 732R
McPherson	491 / 395R	1,728 / 1,060R	3,334 / 1,661R	4,092 / 1,593R	4,406 / 1,450R
Meade					1,018 / 236R
Miami	2,414 / 676R	2,745 / 745R	3,788 / 686R	4,178 / 359R	4,229 / 570R
Mitchell	901 / 535R	1,405 / 615R	2,780 / 931R	2,984 / 950R	2,998 / 796R
Montgomery	3,194 / 400R	3,354 / 647R	3,760 / 479R	5,662 / 860R	5,476 / 1,008R
Morris	464 / 194R	1,101 / 387R	2,010 / 731R	2,439 / 745R	2,745 / 201R
Morton					574 / 128R
Nemaha	1,551 / 668R	1,786 / 498R	2,694 / 821R	3,964 / 666R	4,371 / 833R
Neosho	2,727 / 77R	2,493 / 415R	2,880 / 523R	4,061 / 578R	4,297 / 990R
Ness			444 / 186R	660 / 200R	1,556 / 421R
Norton	34 / 34R	245 / 146R	1,296 / 426R	1,224 / 457R	2,359 / 540R
Osage	2,342 / 1,284R	1,895 / 564R	4,404 / 1,797R	5,462 / 2,006R	5,987 / 2,002R
Osborne	461 / 385R	850 / 473R	2,096 / 857R	2,409 / 969R	2,593 / 994R
Ottawa	732 / 478R	1,094 / 591R	2,300 / 919R	2,790 / 759R	2,798 / 800R
Pawnee		407 / 250R	649 / 462R	1,102 / 460R	1,445 / 592R
Phillips	179 / 115R	676 / 282R	2,035 / 708R	1,807 / 587R	3,071 / 918R
Pottawatomie	1,999 / 615R	2,118 / 615R	3,541 / 959R	4,272 / 705R	4,104 / 948R
Pratt			327 / 99R	1,840 / 805R	2,222 / 465R
Rawlins				363 / 23R	1,785 / 390R
Reno	356 / 176R	1,460 / 774R	2,172 / 848R	3,477 / 913R	5,763 / 1,557R
Republic	1,076 / 980R	1,509 / 982R	2,697 / 1,214R	3,545 / 1,377R	4,069 / 1,390R
Rice	232 / 160R	750 / 481R	1,917 / 610R	2,754 / 705R	3,203 / 917R
Riley	1,393 / 717R	1,421 / 910R	2,207 / 1,108R	2,621 / 1,042R	2,970 / 1,084R
Rooks		172	1,469 / 67R	1,614 / 467R	1,907 / 600R
Rush		151	804 / 131R	793 / 304R	1,160 / 187R
Russell	162 / 130R	408 / 253R	1,359 / 615R	1,269 / 314R	1,563 / 257R
Saline	1,437 / 725R	1,713 / 954R	2,883 / 1,112R	3,535 / 1,331R	3,904 / 1,077R
Scott					538 / 112R
Sedgwick	1,476 / 508R	2,753 / 799R	4,006 / 934R	6,461 / 997R	10,937 / 2,046R
Seward					654 / 198R
Shawnee	3,500 / 1,542R	3,622 / 1,505R	6,074 / 2,855R	8,752 / 3,505R	11,203 / 4,529R
Sheridan			209	144 / 41R	1,005 / 286R
Sherman					1,442 / 322R
Smith	441 / 291R	1,084 / 455R	2,447 / 1,007R	2,882 / 1,019R	3,273 / 949R
Stafford			782 / 338R	1,160 / 461R	2,052 / 492R
Stanton					548 / 101R
Stevens					657 / 39R
St. John					
Sumner	1,190 / 326R	1,802 / 243R	4,021 / 654R	7,088 / 941R	1,360R
Thomas					1,364 / 205R
Trego			467 / 225R	571 / 270R	746 / 257R
Wabaunsee	817 / 445R	1,007 / 454R	1,838 / 769R	2,396 / 739R	2,732 / 748R
Wallace	98 / 10R				624 / 214R

COUNTY.	1872.	1876.	1880.	1884.	1888.
Washington	1,430 / 588R	1,724 / 697R	3,014 / 1,130R	4,296 / 1,355R	4,815 / 1,488R
Wichita					738 / 231R
Wilson	1,882 / 834R	2,297 / 737R	2,876 / 905R	3,337 / 881R	3,944 / 1,156R
Woodson	1,020 / 544R	.979 / 367R	1,344 / 461R	1,963 / 507R	2,211 / 554R
Wyandotte	2,460 / 148R	2,496 / 267R	4,179 / 677R	5,733 / 931R	9,801 / 1,276R

KENTUCKY.

COUNTY.	1872.	1876.	1880.	1884.	1888.
Adair	1,485 / 91R	2,238 / 144D	2,150 / 156D	2,059 / 70D	2,446 / 155R
Allen	955 / 71R	1,713 / 415D	1,698 / 261D	1,830 / 285D	2,898 / 201D
Anderson	1,090 / 362D	1,663 / 645D	1,753 / 523D	1,753 / 507D	2,085 / 492D
Ballard	1,500 / 952D	2,404 / 1,718D	2,051 / 1,188D	2,478 / 1,340D	1,294 / 640D
Barren	2,198 / 14D	3,494 / 876D	3,609 / 782D	3,308 / 908D	4,681 / 958D
Bath	1,508 / 66R	1,954 / 292D	2,005 / 254D	2,400 / 128D	2,947 / 188D
Bell	602 / 308R	692 / 224R	795 / 272R	787 / 299R	1,308 / 649R
Boone	1,024 / 844D	2,210 / 1,394D	2,153 / 1,318D	2,252 / 1,165D	2,769 / 1,481D
Bourbon	2,985 / 109R	3,376 / 176D	3,355 / 18D	3,669 / 8D	4,082 / 62R
Boyd	1,044 / 252R	1,943 / 165D	1,969 / 168R	2,457 / 229R	2,850 / 229R
Boyle	1,963 / 29R	2,610 / 258D	2,479 / 98D	2,546 / 19D	2,823 / 32D
Bracken	1,619 / 287D	2,209 / 941D	2,301 / 725D	2,712 / 814D	2,851 / 636D
Breathitt	787 / 319D	1,038 / 336D	1,129 / 467D	1,347 / 412D	1,158 / 131D
Breckenridge	1,801 / 297R	2,157 / 557D	2,750 / 464D	2,570 / 162D	3,608 / 57D
Bullitt	791 / 233D	1,279 / 755D	1,106 / 513D	954 / 330D	1,448 / 567D
Butler	1,100 / 258R	1,006 / 108R	1,805 / 188R	1,922 / 236R	2,688 / 664R
Caldwell	1,408 / 32D	1,951 / 447D	2,066 / 261D	2,004 / 304D	2,204 / 18D
Calloway	1,331 / 935D	1,893 / 1,401D	1,711 / 930D	1,784 / 1,007D	1,376 / 655D
Campbell	3,291 / 351D	5,253 / 645D	6,006 / 160D	6,486 / 206R	8,369 / 19D
Carroll	1,068 / 710D	1,564 / 1,014D	1,832 / 1,088D	1,849 / 915D	2,228 / 1,009D
Carter	967 / 175R	1,476 / 50D	1,547 / 118D	2,529 / 205R	3,183 / 408R
Carlisle					1,146 / 577D
Casey	946 / 6D	1,010 / 72D	1,624 / 184D	1,530 / 6D	2,800 / 79R
Christian	3,970 / 970R	4,904 / 780R	5,183 / 991R	5,021 / 817R	5,954 / 1,284R
Clark	1,686 / 80R	2,381 / 341D	2,339 / 204D	2,749 / 249D	3,356 / 368D
Clay	1,140 / 980R	1,731 / 89R	1,596 / 246R	1,022 / 249R	2,043 / 738R
Clinton	556 / 184R	840 / 156R	1,008 / 272R	817 / 271R	1,326 / 494R
Crittenden	1,500 / 212R	1,875 / 13D	1,814 / 41D	1,849 / 55R	2,564 / 182R
Cumberland	777 / 361R	1,210 / 18R	1,342 / 131R	1,215 / 146R	1,696 / 389R
Daviess	3,121 / 949D	4,395 / 2,235D	4,564 / 1,782D	4,773 / 1,508D	6,124 / 1,580D
Edmonson	653 / 143R	875 / 83D	983 / 52D	1,184 / 88D	1,538 / 2D
Elliott	506 / 258D	880 / 598D	801 / 513D	1,184 / 612D	1,520 / 664D
Estill	1,106 / 62R	1,553 / 89R	1,587 / 27D	1,525 / 48D	1,762 / 82D
Fayette	5,405 / 807R	6,048 / 122R	5,318 / 381R	5,640 / 407R	6,858 / 134D
Fleming	2,020 / 86R	2,646 / 422D	2,909 / 224D	3,259 / 135D	3,625 / 102D
Floyd	920 / 466D	1,209 / 645D	1,845 / 528D	1,745 / 528D	1,819 / 482D
Franklin	2,342 / 294D	3,073 / 905D	2,903 / 617D	3,060 / 598D	3,792 / 600D
Fulton	711 / 537D	1,185 / 889D	912 / 528D	1,814 / 680D	1,306 / 600D
Gallatin	733 / 281D	916 / 440D	957 / 409D	1,015 / 499D	1,160 / 508D

COUNTY.	1872.	1876.	1880.	1884.	1888.
Garrard	1,879 263R	2,271 1D	2,283 121R	2,196 77R	2,384 96R
Grant	1,393 111D	2,016 578D	2,302 464D	2,198 541D	2,792 478D
Graves	2,429 875D	3,911 2,059D	3,513 1,513D	3,901 1,673D	3,699 1,250D
Grayson	1,204 128R	1,681 455D	2,019 288D	2,279 146D	3,032 52R
Green	1,218 308R	1,692 210D	1,525 41R	1,477 102R	2,268 134R
Greenup	1,398 406R	1,909 41D	2,081 202R	2,198 198D	2,598 124R
Hancock	879 303D	1,015 605D	1,347 290D	1,299 124D	1,793 19D
Hardin	2,066 388D	2,948 1,823D	2,949 715D	2,481 630D	3,672 754D
Harlan	561 367R	787 431R	875 538R	867 433R	1,065 626R
Harrison	2,374 384D	2,903 927D	2,970 763D	3,024 741D	3,624 806D
Hart	1,599 123R	2,615 553D	2,672 380D	2,287 479D	3,197 129D
Henderson	2,950 384D	4,116 1,068D	3,966 713D	4,429 409D	5,544 630D
Henry	2,023 448D	2,682 1,042D	2,757 778D	2,572 600D	3,290 780D
Hickman	1,188 376D	1,698 936D	1,484 683D	1,724 715D	1,513 670D
Hopkins	1,705 129D	2,811 907D	2,929 621D	2,973 508D	3,703 313D
Jackson	645 353R	857 295R	1,040 486R	957 376R	1,270 788R
Jefferson	16,725 2,895D	20,561 8,751D	23,238 5,224D	20,399 2,557D	30,590 4,672D
Jessamine	1,851 285R	2,228 56D	2,040 78R	2,111 163D	2,480 200D
Johnson	806 206R	1,266 148D	1,161 131R	1,917 376R	2,232 503R
Josh Bell	602 308R	....	849 332D	702 329D	....
Kenton	4,855 1,083D	6,635 1,745D	7,363 1,390D	8,059 1,030D	9,991 1,885D
Knox	1,216 324R	1,540 238R	1,581 353R	1,541 313R	2,079 778R
Knott	....	....	....	584 334D	633 304D
La Rue	837 157D	1,400 556D	1,541 563D	1,227 404D	1,748 278D
Laurel	989 247R	1,230 100R	1,533 283R	1,890 221R	2,405 409R
Lawrence	849 21D	1,663 433D	1,696 210D	2,052 188D	3,378 62R
Lee	560 20R	719 15R	813 24R	795 25R	948 82R
Leslie	....	....	575 461R	594 442R	726 594R
Letcher	585 47R	....	679 79D	654 61R	902 335R
Lewis	1,596 308R	2,281 13D	2,557 313R	2,078 346R	3,297 501R
Lincoln	1,911 217D	2,594 500D	2,715 375D	2,520 305D	3,143 290D
Livingston	1,004 500D	1,328 818D	1,131 646D	1,302 552D	1,594 488D
Logan	2,635 349D	3,799 685D	4,000 930R	4,210 456D	5,302 762D
Lyon	911 81R	1,205 297D	1,153 203D	1,378 177D	1,252 67D
Madison	3,341 243R	4,203 269D	4,063 53D	4,437 189D	4,508 63D
Magoffin	643 13R	925	1,172 66R	1,409 98R	1,528 205R
Marion	1,674 64D	2,459 805D	2,559 502D	2,452 545D	2,634 591D
Marshall	1,148 658D	1,528 1,094D	1,354 789D	1,561 634D	1,391 634D
Martin	204 148D	329 141R	425 183D	561 223D	744 307R
Mason	3,108 288D	3,882 844D	4,179 896D	4,813 526D	5,077 513D
McCracken	1,825 147D	2,699 813D	2,600 492D	3,272 780D	3,426 277D
McLean	998 246D	1,085 473D	1,422 418D	1,355 340D	1,703 230D
Meade	997 478D	1,485 969D	1,584 750D	1,380 566D	1,946 755D
Menifee	270 144D	510 292D	649 332D	702 329D	814 340D
Mercer	2,272 114D	2,790 528D	2,760 433D	2,728 335D	3,200 350D

COUNTY.	1872.	1876.	1880.	1884.	1888.
Metcalfe	742 240R	1,387 49D	1,534 36R	1,369 40R	1,952 137R
Monroe	866 394R	1,254 74R	1,446 61R	1,366 252R	2,163 474R
Montgomery	1,631 121D	2,082 345D	2,109 254D	2,460 203D	2,768 329D
Morgan	902 394D	1,357 087D	1,582 696D	1,913 693D	2,035 659D
Muhlenburg	1,536 324R	2,109 209D	2,313 140D	2,303 287D	3,634 49R
Nelson	1,711 189D	2,597 907D	2,794 809D	2,451 657D	3,022 774D
Nicholas	1,644 242D	2,077 553D	2,316 515D	2,271 469D	2,551 542D
Ohio	2,158 184R	2,703 475D	2,683 943D	3,070 174D	4,211 34R
Oldham	1,108 248D	1,880 522D	1,445 399D	1,096 304D	1,332 366D
Owen	2,139 1,544D	3,098 2,303D	3,278 2,014D	3,028 1,822D	3,909 2,088D
Owsley	584 282R	741 311R	885 441R	817 364R	950 451R
Pendleton	1,968 32D	2,606 766D	2,967 593D	2,850 226D	3,387D 498D
Perry	610 150D	930 284R	877 241R	240 234D	997 403R
Pike	787 179D	1,376 518D	1,829 302D	2,217 69D	2,521 17R
Powell	429 136D	594 94D	654 85D	688 85D	851 38D
Pulaski	2,320 606R	3,633 329R	3,348 401R	3,505 757R	4,822 1,172R
Robertson	814 168D	1,048 330D	1,093 301D	736 235D	1,021 311D
Rockcastle	1,146 6D	1,600 48D	1,518 49R	1,603 207R	1,869 273R
Rowan	434 136R	545 51R	597 8D	873 47R	799 28R
Russell	788 2R	1,175 119D	1,030 175D	1,029 58D	1,522 107R
Scott	2,465 229D	3,149 505D	2,985 384D	3,184 461D	3,691 506D
Shelby	2,543 273D	3,345 925D	2,996 810D	3,258 755D	3,687 783D
Simpson	1,497 217D	1,869 675D	1,579 575D	1,701 390D	2,443 666D
Spencer	785 299D	1,201 561D	1,209 492D	1,284 512D	1,424 599D
Taylor	927 27D	1,461 519D	1,416 342D	1,390 274D	1,914 267D
Todd	1,729 488R	2,610 180D	2,653 40D	2,188 146D	3,215 67D
Trigg	1,905 49D	2,502 514D	2,144 3c8D	2,367 416D	2,000 50R
Trimble	781 533D	1,162 944D	1,244 931D	1,148 769D	1,465 948D
Union	1,978 896D	2,854 1,546D	2,854 1,317D	2,558 1,287D	3,217 1,289D
Warren	3,435 171R	4,551 753D	4,195 550D	4,869 1,071D	6,276 997D
Washington	1,795 253R	2,442 414D	2,529 147D	2,284 11D	2,710 87R
Wayne	1,245 632D	1,744 356D	1,369 180D	1,452 121D	2,243 1D
Webster	1,277 265D	1,761 789D	1,904 553D	2,027 628D	2,084 592D
Whitley	1,036 430R	1,476 500R	1,448 483R	1,610 626R	2,917 1,521R
Wolfe	537 167D	801 261D	920 224D	1,095 285D	1,263 301D
Woodford	2,109 19R	2,430 260D	2,333 124D	2,421 141D	2,327 170D

LOUISIANA.

COUNTY.	1872.	1876.	1880.	1884.	1888.
Acadia	....	....	....	....	611 03D
Ascension	2,492 1,168R	3,268 874R	2,054 1,252R	2,855 1,213R	2,935 1,075D
Assumption	3,190 434D	2,377 5R	2,254 662R	2,950 558R	3,284 1,194D
Avoyelles	3,166 426D	2,975 33R	2,599 21D	2,273 73R	2,114 900D
Baton Rouge (East)	2,189 487D	2,252 670R	2,211 95D	2,480 40R	3,105 565R
Baton Rouge (West)	1,187 613R	1,353 471R	691 31R	1,100 440D	1,002 144D
Bienville	1,207 53°D	1,183 729D	1,564 80D	912 714D	990 987D
Bossier	1,504 396D	2,228 1,022R	2,329 1,959D	2,175 1,825D	2,327 1,983D

COUNTY	1872.	1876.	1880.	1884.	1888.
Caddo	3,384 / 236D	4,343 / 1,031R	2,486 / 2,470D	2,439 / 1,715D	2,666 / 2,416D
Calcasieu	652 / 528D	1,336 / 1,336D	883 / 685D	1,744 / 1,076D	1,700 / 1,147D
Caldwell	829 / 31D	692 / 270D	669 / 389D	810 / 508D	904 / 860D
Cameron	214 / 134D	298 / 194D	222 / 108D	257 / 147D	215 / 191D
Carroll (East)	1,854 / 1,110R	3,024 / 1,840R	1,497 / 1,078R	1,431 / 1,027R	2,370 / 1,622D
Carroll (West)	……	……	289 / 205D	371 / 59D	563 / 563D
Catahoula	1,543 / 103D	1,641 / 37D	774 / 458D	981 / 35D	1,061 / 405D
Claiborne	2,197 / 313D	1,824 / 960D	1,513 / 1,193D	2,063 / 1,263D	1,695 / 1,637D
Concordia	1,788 / 1,490R	2,832 / 1,200D	1,690 /	2,048 / 1,384R	2,943 / 2,011D
De Soto	1,873 / 985D	1,330 / 104R	955 / 635D	841 / 817D	1,022 / 1,018D
Feliciana (East)	2,314 / 1,020R	……	879 / 647D	1,194 / 726D	884 / 819D
Feliciana (West)	1,077 / 1,229R	862 / 386R	1,302 / 1,034D	1,202 / 720D	1,841 / 1,749D
Franklin	785 / 205D	838 / 614D	571 / 571D	796 / 734D	592 / 540D
Grant	905 / 95D	……	412 / 240D	336 / 146D	679 / 489D
Iberia	1,572 / 320R	2,366 / 516R	1,715 / 515R	2,833 / 167D	1,619 / 1,585D
Iberville	2,943 / 1,555R	3,251 / 1,343R	2,735 / 1,687R	3,275 / 1,931R	3,187 / 955D
Jackson	1,273 / 71D	485 / 439D	382 / 382D	630 / 650D	520 / 519D
Jefferson	3,262 / 190R	……	1,419 / 543D	1,276 / 730R	1,653 / 465R
Jefferson (R. B.)	……	1,715 / 433R			
Jefferson (L. B.)	……	828 / 546R			
Lafayette	1,347 / 395D	1,287 / 21R	1,027 / 153D	1,907 / 309D	1,405 / 1,341D
La Fourche	3,462 / 78D	3,555 / 179R	1,864 / 992D	3,579 / 50D	3,067 / 1,603D
Lincoln	……	1,401 / 739D	2,813 / 583D	1,184 / 1,176D	883 / 842D
Livingston	679 / 381D	512 / 270D	342 / 198D	438 / 212D	570 / 261D
Madison	2,055 / 1,009R	2,912 / 2,256R	1,382 / 470D	1,232 / 470R	2,680 / 2,357D
Morehouse	1,295 / 833R	821 / 33R	1,082 / 930D	1,490 / 1,074D	1,292 / 1,282D
Natchitoches	1,795 / 699D	3,510 / 674R	2,158 / 1,105D	2,159 / 1,227D	1,937 / 1,261D
Orleans	36,221 / 9,933D	38,889 / 8,947D	24,312 / 10,356D	21,164 / 7,506D	22,312 / 6,858D
Ouachita	2,305 / 825R	1,094 / 396R	2,243 / 2,207D	1,982 / 1,810D	2,710 / 2,698D
Plaquemines	1,499 / 579R	2,466 / 1,042R	1,715 / 245R	2,062 / 756D	2,075 / 669R
Point Coupée	2,551 / 355R	3,070 / 904R	1,650 / 132D	1,118 / 230R	1,669 / 87D
Rapides	3,132 / 780D	3,376 / 137R	2,328 / 1,168D	2,627 / 869D	3,802 / 2,995D
Red River	1,272 / 554R	1,245 / 421R	675 / 505D	509 / 403D	1,352 / 1,406D
Richland	970 / 322D	314 / 74D	1,164 / 1,100D	955 / 591D	1,098 / 1,090D
Sabine	808 / 688D	929 / 883D	432 / 432D	563 / 563D	642 / 642D
St. Bernard	773 /	1,027 / 355R	731 / 49D	594 / 102R	911 / 211D
St. Charles	1,373 / 1,083R	1,458 / 1,000R	1,138 / 922R	989 / 885R	1,333 / 1,148R
St. Helena	979 / 425D	1,169 / 149D	612 / 124D	563 / 115D	470 / 316D
St. James	……	2,963 / 1,005R	2,143 / 945R	1,823 / 1,081R	2,374 / 1,288R
St. John Baptist	1,705 / 627R	2,031 / 545R	1,441 / 675R	1,347 / 705R	1,493 / 695R
St. Landry	4,250 / 1,484D	6,020 / 1,232D	3,221 / 797D	3,558 / 198D	2,305 / 1,057D
St. Martin's	1,354 / 50R	2,122 / 76R	1,570 / 316R	1,760 / 452R	1,013 / 1,005D
St. Mary's	2,603 / 459R	3,864 / 946R	2,752 / 1,610R	4,072 / 2,066R	3,225 / 336D
St. Tammany	1,200 / 773D	788 / 98D	702 / 74D	660 / 66D	80D
Tangipahoa	1,382 / 164D	1,420 / 290D	1,053 / 375D	1,106 / 416D	1,298 / 511D

COUNTY	1872.	1876.	1880.	1884.	1888.
Tensas	2,466 / 2,164R	3,671 / 2,743R	2,671 / 1,478D	2,772 / 1,378D	2,151 / 1,494D
Terre Bonne	……	3,358 / 580R	2,701 / 691R	3,385 / 629R	2,560 / 410D
Union	1,730 / 754D	1,586 / 1,398D	1,214 / 1,110D	1,441 / 1,061D	2,087 / 2,033D
Vermilion	908 / 447D	1,186 / 632D	490 / 258D	1,129 / 495D	1,178 / 817D
Vernon	718 / 608D	647 / 291D	372 / 372D	472 / 472D	588 / 588D
Washington	584 / 250D	679 / 349D	390 / 302D	450 / 300D	496 / 328D
Webster	1,578 / 330D	1,091 / 189R	1,049 / 673D	1,271 / 85D	1,353 / 1,208D
Winn	657 / 417D	626 / 474D	320 / 320D	421 / 320D	599 / 537D

MAINE.

COUNTY	1872.	1876.	1880.	1884.	1888.
Androscoggin	5,777 / 2,597R	7,370 / 1,218R	9,396 / 759R	6,855 / 1,276R	6,898 / 1,308R
Aroostook	2,236 / 1,278R	3,101 / 577R	5,385 / 178D	5,492 / 836R	5,541 / 1,557R
Cumberland	12,022 / 2,960R	16,287 / 1,375R	19,998 / 1,828R	18,292 / 1,340R	18,363 / 1,905R
Franklin	3,111 / 1,369R	3,675 / 557R	4,690 / 212R	4,015 / 1,012R	4,077 / 967R
Hancock	4,510 / 1,432R	6,159 / 603R	8,149 / 616R	7,251 / 1,029R	7,058 / 1,388R
Kennebec	8,459 / 4,005R	10,844 / 2,658R	13,157 / 2,770R	12,012 / 3,666R	11,932 / 3,314R
Knox	3,868 / 1,304R	5,992 / 306R	6,954 / 779D	5,895 / 455R	5,071 / 675R
Lincoln	3,187 / 863R	4,219 / 807R	5,657 / 221D	4,746 / 410R	4,381 / 635R
Oxford	5,806 / 1,542R	6,788 / 620R	8,574 / 385R	7,642 / 1,323R	7,521 / 1,398R
Penobscot	10,726 / 5,112R	13,917 / 3,495R	15,650 / 1,879R	13,869 / 2,703R	13,580 / 2,581R
Piscataquis	2,326 / 1,110R	2,815 / 783R	3,418 / 618R	3,312 / 807R	3,465 / 794R
Sagadahoc	2,887 / 1,363R	3,020 / 1,078R	4,724 / 1,171R	4,148 / 1,452R	4,010 / 1,290R
Somerset	5,777 / 1,715R	7,067 / 771R	8,056 / 564R	7,518 / 1,185R	7,580 / 1,721R
Waldo	4,844 / 1,576R	6,072 / 858R	6,816 / 1,100D	6,123 / 484R	5,783 / 619R
Washington	5,478 / 1,432R	6,815 / 501R	8,081 / 789R	7,666 / 901R	7,298 / 1,422R
York	9,485 / 2,773R	12,181 / 1,061R	15,018 / 610R	13,587 / 1,188R	13,142 / 1,679R

MARYLAND.

COUNTY	1872.	1876.	1880.	1884.	1888.
Allegany	5,896 / 1,206R	6,520 / 86D	6,421 / 255R	6,208 / 448D	7,538 / 773R
Anne Arundel	4,795 / 297R	5,375 / 885D	5,204 / 804D	5,865 / 239D	6,085 / 13R
Baltimore city	42,398 / 3,354D	54,257 / 10,141D	56,010 / 9,534D	61,952 / 6,796D	85,415 / 5,045D
Baltimore Co.	7,917 / 309D	12,304 / 2,802D	12,672 / 1,970D	14,113 / 1,599D	12,131 / 1,240D
Calvert	1,762 / 378R	2,008 / 42R	2,012 / 188D	2,019 / 167R	2,149 / 230R
Caroline	2,144 / 72R	2,325 / 173D	2,638 / 220D	2,830 / 34D	3,023 / 70R
Carroll	5,092 / 82R	4,207 / 2,409D	6,680 / 354D	6,705 / 383D	7,616 / 96D
Cecil	4,650 / 444R	5,492 / 450D	5,657 / 311D	5,657 / 232D	5,939 / 91D
Charles	2,791 / 391R	3,308 / 11D	3,575 / 203D	3,391 / 259R	2,873 / 1R
Dorchester	3,607 / 97R	3,901 / 263D	4,374 / 108R	4,626 / 166R	4,851 / 578D
Frederick	9,251 / 1,121R	10,281 / 289R	11,042 / 480R	10,701 / 293R	11,440 / 437R
Garrett	……	1,973 / 17R	2,334 / 86R	2,541 / 197R	2,792 / 294R
Harford	4,072 / 162R	5,078 / 974D	5,492 / 540D	5,832 / 647D	6,413 / 578D
Howard	2,506 / 113R	2,880 / 452D	3,152 / 482D	3,125 / 341D	3,360 / 253D
Kent	3,281 / 35R	3,622 / 252D	3,880 / 114D	4,199 / 103D	4,188 / 25D
Montgomery	4,070 / 172D	4,949 / 781D	5,623 / 629D	5,689 / 649D	6,124 / 558D
Prince George's	3,895 / 633R	5,047 / 187D	5,885 / 41D	5,821 / 121D	6,121 / 882D
Queen Anne	3,458 / 150D	3,625 / 673D	3,973 / 641D	4,054 / 634D	4,197 / 548D
Somerset	2,737 / 493R	3,700 / 128D	3,598 / 173R	3,756 / 288R	4,071 / 447R

COUNTY.	1872.	1876.	1880.	1884.	1888.
St. Mary's...	2,675 / 397R	3,042 / 88R	3,302 / 242R	3,312 / 234R	3,357 / 221R
Talbot......	3,184 / 142R	3,620 / 4D	4,136 / 160D	4,421 / 7D	4,510 / 162R
Washington..	6,868 / 460R	7,905 / 133D	8,110 / 50R	8,579 / 201R	9,107 / 394R
Wicomico....	2,551 / 389D	3,153 / 993D	3,406 / 710D	3,616 / 908D	3,887 / 769D
Worcester....	2,900 / 568D	3,892 / 1,494D	3,658 / 854D	3,705 / 737D	3,732 / 443D
MASSACHUSETTS.					
Barnstable...	3,056 / 2,350R	4,278 / 2,708R	4,429 / 2,517R	4,625 / 2,207R	4,596 / 2,326R
Berkshire...	9,435 / 2,650R	11,493 / 532R	11,420 / 1,354R	11,865 / 382R	13,302 / 753R
Bristol	12,601 / 7,317R	17,390 / 5,762R	19,594 / 7,242R	19,876 / 5,816R	24,139 / 5,585R
Duke's.....	672 / 440R	548 / 250R	750 / 402R	839 / 366R	888 / 371R
Essex.......	27,575 / 9,571R	36,581 / 6,791R	38,978 / 6,122R	42,570 / 5,156R	48,684 / 7,670R
Franklin...	5,368 / 3,302R	6,329 / 1,815R	6,120 / 1,926R	6,882 / 1,099R	7,337 / 1,246R
Hampden...	10,605 / 2,405R	14,568 / 1,358R	18,868 / 2,478R	16,536 / 652R	19,269 / 3,196R
Hampshire..	6,318 / 3,069R	7,555 / 2,511R	7,186 / 2,914R	7,433 / 1,283R	8,461 / 1,326R
Middlesex...	39,051 / 14,099R	46,862 / 7,740R	50,138 / 10,540R	57,017 / 5,448R	63,911 / 7,144R
Nantucket...	338 / 294R	482 / 276R	503 / 287R	551 / 124R	715 / 272R
Norfolk....	12,654 / 4,402R	15,648 / 2,278R	16,530 / 3,506R	17,723 / 1,030R	19,948 / 2,041R
Plymouth ..	9,024 / 4,998R	12,838 / 3,792R	13,602 / 4,282R	14,518 / 3,198R	16,077 / 3,273R
Suffolk......	28,936 / 6,602R	47,938 / 2,264D	57,206 / 518D	62,682 / 11,338D	70,735 / 7,482D
Worcester....	27,042 / 12,614R	36,370 / 7,732R	35,891 / 10,193R	39,154 / 8,949R	44,446 / 7,066R
MICHIGAN.					
Alcona...	127 / 103R	317 / 7D	647 / 134R	895 / 206R	1,160 / 143R
Alger...					456 / 122R
Allegan.....	5,071 / 1,875R	7,724 / 1,112R	8,548 / 2,587R	8,452 / 635R	9,763 / 1,249R
Alpena......	810 / 209R	1,364 / 6D	1,832 / 126R	2,113 / 200D	3,152 / 18D
Antrim......	354 / 214R	756 / 195R	968 / 447R	1,924 / 845R	2,300 / 424R
Arenac......				974 / 284D	1,121 / 96R
Baraga......			450 / 14D	703 / 51D	799 / 89R / 17D
Barry	3,373 / 875R	5,471 / 1,064R	6,232 / 2,003R	6,087 / 238D	6,613 / 586R
Bay	3,218 / 678R	5,348 / 432D	6,306 / 336R	8,040 / 2,047D	10,012 / 1,008D
Benzie.......	507 / 398R	667 / 288R	761 / 279R	1,013 / 176R	1,246 / 298R
Berrien......	6,176 / 1,628R	8,171 / 509R	8,611 / 999R	9,248 / 13D	10,314 / 439R
Branch......	4,624 / 2,362R	6,834 / 1,622R	6,942 / 2,926R	7,048 / 713R	7,403 / 1,359R
Calhoun.....	6,836 / 2,136R	12,136 / 1,718D	9,174 / 2,044R	9,286 / 804R	10,862 / 1,374R
Cass........	4,262 / 602R	5,259 / 414R	5,454 / 679R	5,724 / 20R	5,786 / 365R
Charlevoix..	275 / 255R	1,166 / 209R	/ 480R	1,924 / 218R	2,249 / 306R
Cheboygan..	410 / 38R	707 / 183D	1,246 / 65R	1,714 / 120D	2,431 / 127D
Chippewa...	225 / 117R	367 / 23D	745 / 49R	1,342 / 51R	2,046 / 146R
Clare........	320 / 112R	508 / 36R	902 / 118R	1,341 / 63D	1,886 / 7D
Clinton......	4,339 / 771R	6,348 / 173R	6,802 / 502R	6,317 / 438D	7,180 / 245R
Crawford ...			345 / 41R	536 / 81R	925 / 43D
Delta........	559 / 219R	957 / 53R	1,155 / 267R	1,816 / 592R	2,980 / 255R
Eaton........	4,837 / 1,567R	6,978 / 1,107R	7,685 / 1,514R	8,317 / 369R	8,873 / 1,358R
Emmett......	202 / 76R	746 / 111D	1,227 / 319R	1,779 / 116D	2,108 / 110D
Genesee.....	5,949 / 2,025R	8,787 / 1,308R	8,945 / 1,848R	8,990 / 671R	10,165 / 1,500R

COUNTY.	1872.	1876.	1880.	1884.	1888.
Gladwin....		246 / 78D	410 / 83D	501 / 75R	893 / 168R
Gogebic.....					2,515 / 255R
Grand Traverse.	853 / 555R	1,353 / 670R	1,854 / 928R	2,547 / 887R	2,946 / 934R
Gratiot......	2,059 / 905R	3,605 / 838R	5,002 / 1,059R	5,015 / 60D	7,005 / 813R
Hillsdale....	6,099 / 3,059R	7,900 / 1,758R	8,235 / 2,958R	8,166 / 1,093R	8,700 / 1,924R
Houghton...	2,284 / 428R	3,705 / 827R	3,441 / 789R	4,116 / 689R	5,892 / 316R
Huron......	1,215 / 529R	2,305 / 233R	3,000 / 468R	3,432 / 543D	4,659 / 380D
Ingham.....	5,715 / 1,185R	8,063 / 64R	8,410 / 572R	8,743 / 853D	9,948 / 235D
Ionia.......	5,028 / 1,624R	7,606 / 1,078R	8,009 / 1,668R	7,869 / 262D	8,706 / 657R
Iosco.......	587 / 253R	836 / 98R	1,327 / 296R	1,923 / 152R	3,311 / 184D
Iron........					1,263 / 78R
Isabella.....	978 / 458R	1,814 / 301R	2,563 / 442R	3,310 / 7R	4,186 / 313R
Jackson.....	7,578 / 608R	10,214 / 314D	10,089 / 743R	10,901 / 648D	11,566 / 476R
Kalamazoo..	6,410 / 1,604R	8,169 / 913R	8,072 / 1,484R	8,720 / 765R	9,959 / 1,487R
Kalkaska...	106 / 100R	524 / 254R	607 / 326R	1,034 / 261R	1,282 / 398R
Kent........	9,006 / 2,828R	15,136 / 1,725R	16,465 / 3,198R	19,686 / 682D	25,931 / 947R
Keweenaw..		1,149 / 321R	853 / 220R	833 / 419R	600 / 220R
Lake.......		242 / 202R	631 / 205R	851 / 318R	1,956 / 254R
Lapeer......	3,853 / 1,119R	5,729 / 732R	6,317 / 834R	6,079 / 321R	6,863 / 748R
Leelenaw....	688 / 320R	1,046 / 222R	1,222 / 49R	1,403 / 240R	1,620 / 226R
Lenawee.....	9,131 / 2,445R	12,110 / 976R	12,099 / 1,205R	12,496 / 255R	13,083 / 804R
Livingston..	4,247 / 423R	5,665 / 194R	5,929 / 60R	5,807 / 341D	6,015 / 196D
Luce........					395 / 40R
Mackinac ...	172 / 26D	278 / 130D	442 / 150D	1,040 / 79D	1,553 / 288D
Macomb.....	4,606 / 286R	6,480 / 444D	6,556 / 81D	6,469 / 682D	7,173 / 463D
Manistee....	1,209 / 301R	1,783 / 85R	2,299 / 319R	3,393 / 621D	4,402 / 660D
Manitou....	75 / 75R	134 / 54D	173 / 105D	166 / 130D	144 / 138D
Marquette...	2,652 / 1,166R	4,058 / 558R	3,719 / 1,163R	5,756 / 2,752R	6,861 / 2,407R
Mason......	947 / 411R	1,057 / 253R	2,109 / 501R	2,573 / 82R	3,842 / 124R
Mecosta....	1,422 / 784R	2,309 / 416R	2,748 / 769R	4,399 / 518R	4,740 / 811R
Menominee..	557 / 313R	744 / 42R	2,264 / 500R	3,575 / 1,578R	5,698 / 928R
Midland....	1,012 / 506R	1,139 / 171R	1,571 / 356R	1,908 / 188R	2,694 / 188R
Missaukee..	119 / 108R	267 / 51R	424 / 145R	869 / 97R	1,253 / 60R
Monroe......	4,837 / 453R	6,948 / 861D	7,108 / 523D	7,169 / 895D	7,568 / 510D
Montcalm...	2,760 / 1,200R	5,628 / 661R	7,696 / 1,393R	7,818 / 69R	8,437 / 985R
Montmorency				239 / 44D	481 / 2D
Muskegon...	2,458 / 1,086R	3,929 / 744R	4,795 / 1,177R	6,971 / 312R	8,622 / 1,007R
Newaygo....	969 / 615R	2,351 / 514R	3,111 / 867R	4,225 / 80D	4,721 / 516R
Oakland....	7,816 / 1,164R	10,417 / 290D	10,838 / 220R	10,750 / 544R	11,390 / 21D
Oceana......	1,854 / 962R	1,993 / 766R	2,464 / 999R	3,207 / 424R	3,609 / 300R
Ogemaw....		188 / 14R	513 / 78R	966 / 6R	1,280 / 41R
Ontonagon...	379 / 57R	525 / 120D	471 / 10R	558 / 68R	852 / 234R
Osceola.....	721 / 371R	1,721 / 184R	1,829 / 644R	2,562 / 705R	3,301 / 792R
Oscoda......				290 / 112R	587 / 22D
Otsego		329 / 39R	626 / 111R	916 / 75R	1,085 / 139R

COUNTY	1872	1876	1880	1884	1888
Ottawa	3,733 1,527R	7,091 1,781R	6,087 1,265R	7,038 709R	7,818 1,111R
Presque Isle	132 132R	321 15D	361 71R	619 160R	905 76D
Roscommon		238 130D	1,021 261D	864 8D	730 2R
Saginaw	7,327 21R	9,037 668D	11,120 97D	13,191 1,108D	16,025 2,200D
Sanilac	1,733 937R	3,791 67R	3,720 942R	3,905 106R	5,691 506R
Schoolcraft	293 261R	224 18R	198 116R	829 229R	1,234 1R
Shiawassee	4,299 1,255R	5,667 723R	6,486 1,375R	6,469 436D	7,719 820R
St. Clair	5,556 1,088D	7,890 357R	8,416 780R	9,033 651D	11,051 183R
St. Joseph	4,945 1,363R	6,403 675R	6,477 1,042R	6,948 293R	7,171 155R
Tuscola	2,395 1,245R	3,892 1,179R	4,874 1,482R	5,860 290R	7,357 776R
Van Buren	5,354 1,744R	7,146 1,447R	7,197 2,127R	7,513 1,286R	8,340 1,797R
Washtenaw	7,135 1,077R	9,690 552D	9,919 328D	9,981 1,266D	10,588 983D
Wayne	21,475 2,897R	28,718 2,498D	31,939 1,093R	38,948 3,015R	48,215 4,660D
Wexford	351 203R	937 300R	1,645 705R	2,226 344R	2,663 372R
MINNESOTA.					
Aitkin	09 45R	54 20R	69 21R	435 7R	627 223R
Anoka	433 183R	1,222 238R	1,498 452R	1,934 870R	2,306 515R
Becker	170 58R	589 391R	831 555R	1,273 567R	2,174 850R
Beltrami				19 7R	
Benton	314 8R	436 108D	586 84D	871 169D	1,324 235D
Big Stone	32 32R	106 102R	704 196R	759 345R	1,196 195R
Blue Earth	3,523 280R	4,448 870R	4,550 908R	4,506 452R	6,479 546R
Brown	1,239 305R	1,637 150R	2,001 585R	2,326 110D	2,933 204D
Carlton	194 78R	284 28R	445 13D	934 404R	1,417 486R
Carver	1,957 331D	2,309 441D	2,442 146R	2,777 408D	3,433 400D
Cass	28 6R	38 12R	199 63R	150 140R	716 238R
Chippewa	434 378R	701 551R	1,021 690R	1,151 437R	1,514 314R
Chisago	888 664R	1,263 775R	1,498 994R	1,798 1,186R	2,073 1,061R
Clay	412 276R	504 276R	1,269 571R	1,908 449R	2,717 575R
Cook				54 38R	53 5D
Cottonwood	488 388R	467 310R	845 589R	736 462R	1,123 487R
Crow Wing	788 128R	261 143R	555 101R	1,468 466R	1,908 445R
Dakota	2,827 77D	3,883 573D	3,852 132D	3,347 301D	4,254 709D
Dodge	1,453 449R	2,350 998R	2,302 1,102R	1,655 693R	2,557 725R
Douglas	1,260 820R	1,406 796R	1,738 1,143R	2,302 1,084R	2,825 1,063R
Faribault	2,135 1,117R	2,259 986R	2,597 1,129R	2,322 1,044R	3,527 1,122R
Fillmore	4,213 1,653R	5,605 2,073R	6,002 2,370R	3,940 1,914R	5,623 1,869R
Freeborn	2,267 1,179R	2,745 1,660R	3,086 1,836R	2,837 1,371R	3,776 1,442R
Goodhue	4,006 1,812R	5,697 2,850R	5,394 2,686R	5,542 2,272R	5,898 2,099R
Grant	197 175R	304 241R	639 553R	948 672R	1,385 583R
Hennepin	7,063 1,069R	10,600 769R	12,141 3,931R	23,654 6,538R	38,038 6,170R
Houston	2,777 637R	3,434 542R	3,204 610R	2,797 431R	3,103 248R
Hubbard				176 26R	378 12D
Isanti		835 641R	903 775R	1,356 1,130R	1,403 765R
Itasca					173 47D

COUNTY	1872	1876	1880	1884	1888
Jackson	650 508R	592 453R	893 641R	798 506R	1,580 542R
Kanabec	35 9R	138 80R	149 53R	320 240R	358 80R
Kandiyohi	1,240 956R	1,696 1,300R	1,758 1,458R	2,070 1,646R	2,809 1,464R
Kittson			231 85R	501 125R	1,040 247R
Lac qui Parle	243 229R	372 331R	925 831R	1,186 746R	1,926 758R
Lake		17 17R	20 20R	80 68R	313 138R
Le Sueur	2,101 448D	2,680 598D	3,265 499D	3,479 243D	4,133 304D
Lincoln		106 70R	580 350R	758 445R	1,071 194R
Lyon		606 447R	1,336 981R	1,465 741R	1,820 668R
Marshall			215 39R	741 427R	1,709 740R
Martin	841 529R	794 474R	950 773R	996 476R	1,831 685R
McLeod	1,099 183R	1,700 17D	2,142 50R	2,649 507D	3,255 504D
Meeker	1,283 431R	2,028 728R	1,898 770R	2,815 597R	3,272 506R
Mille Lacs	257 105R	285 103R	366 164R	441 161R	606 185R
Morrison	401 79D	598 166D	1,126 208D	1,697 323D	2,490 362D
Mower	2,070 900R	2,999 1,014R	2,941 1,219R	2,446 856R	3,887 1,080R
Murray		275 191R	741 373R	871 383R	1,378 290R
Nicollet	1,541 131R	828 561D	2,007 539R	1,880 428R	2,704 182R
Nobles		542 416R	920 466R	737 245R	1,754 214R
Norman				1,211 621R	1,979 806R
Olmsted	3,180 922R	4,424 980R	4,044 928R	3,666 588R	4,675 338R
Otter Tail	1,313 809R	2,091 1,167R	3,400 1,856R	4,935 1,915R	6,378 2,104R
Pembina	40 40R	26 26R			
Pine	295 75R	291 13D	156 114D	666 72R	981 56R
Pipestone			355 167R	864 342R	1,385 363R
Polk	609 41R	554 191R	1,035 971R	1,518 663R	1,900 1,385R
Pope		606 558R	813 608R	1,098 878R	1,286 813R
Ramsey	5,336 30D	6,496 1,158D	9,920 252D	14,681 1,203R	26,190 932D
Redwood	247 40R	329 26R	649 493R	973 493R	1,768 478R
Renville	1,011 577R	1,270 646R	2,050 854R	2,281 753R	3,164 833R
Rice	3,110 730R	4,241 833R	4,254 732R	4,264 622R	5,102 317R
Rock	185 153R	587 449R	818 488R	903 579R	1,422 676R
Scott	2,030 854D	2,396 1,076D	2,610 942D	2,534 1,150D	2,948 1,287D
Sherburne	484 194R	657 224R	643 219R	990 298R	1,286 358R
Sibley		1,707 242D	2,031 91D	2,162 82D	2,880 48D
Stearns	3,053 790D	3,536 1,395D	3,864 1,054D	4,453 1,691D	7,115 2,574D
Steele	1,680 406R	2,542 640R	2,586 698R	2,279 287R	2,832 281R
Stevens	149 57R	301 98R	1,151 125R	1,012 214R	1,232 204R
St. Louis	1,175 641R	743 225R	1,116 280R	3,193 1,539R	7,875 3,004R
Swift		229 213R	757 441R	1,465 538R	1,498 490R
Todd	560 178R	673 169R	1,005 323R	1,307 209R	2,481 638R
Traverse			203 33R	664 158R	1,040 92R
Wabasha	2,794 112R	3,949 335R	3,907 173R	3,564 344R	3,681 365D
Wadena			74 38R	259 250R	627 141R
Waseca	1,572 274R	1,926 385R	2,344 418R	2,056 322R	2,839 328R

COUNTY.	1872.	1876.	1880.	1884.	1888.
Washington..	2,050 / 390R	3,075 / 354R	3,575 / 559R	4,406 / 1,002R	4,904 / 747R
Watonwan..	811 / 345R	751 / 353R	965 / 525R	818 / 434R	1,334 / 602R
Wilkin	100 / 26R	132 / 48R	355 / 167R	604 / 196R	955 / 187R
Winona	4,027 / 195R	5,579 / 291R	5,127 / 17R	5,967 / 630D	7,058 / 568D
Wright	2,065 / 207R	2,762 / 202R	3,427 / 793R	3,992 / 774R	5,355 / 744R
Yellow Medicine.	330 / 238R	573 / 493R	920 / 780R	1,305 / 919R	1,600 / 829R

MISSISSIPPI.

COUNTY.	1872.	1876.	1880.	1884.	1888.
Adams	3,754 / 2,190R	3,955 / 701R	2,284 / 354D	2,609 / 1,235R	2,774 / 1,188R
Alcorn	1,374 / 424D	2,269 / 943D	1,776 / 553D	1,862 / 612D	1,544 / 647D
Amite	1,573 / 417R	1,544 / 1,396D	870 / 262D	1,713 / 873D	1,777 / 1,024D
Attala	1,871 / 281R	3,043 / 899D	2,212 / 450D	2,181 / 53R	2,651 / 997D
Benton	1,080 / 270D	1,904 / 396D	1,733 / 16D	1,483 / 89D	1,294 / 335D
Bolivar	1,568 / 1,322R	3,383 / 793R	1,299 / 737R	2,077 / 1,448R	2,633 / 819R
Calhoun	672 / 544D	1,972 / 1,630D	1,573 / 976D	1,407 / 1,005D	1,276 / 1,055D
Carroll	2,006 / 212R	3,010 / 976D	1,533 / 1,019D	2,171 / 897D	1,116 / 992D
Chickasaw	2,400 / 304R	2,897 / 885D	2,303 / 838D	1,757 / 129D	1,698 / 832D
Choctaw	725 / 69D	1,121 / 815D	659 / 593D	743 / 680D	746 / 740D
Claiborne	2,679 / 1,801R	1,927 / 1,081D	1,349 / 765D	1,243 / 761D	613 / 585D
Clarke	1,999 / 243R	2,248 / 654D	1,416 / 725D	1,448 / 588D	2,018 / 1,014D
Clay	2,561 / 1,143R	2,771 / 1,133D	1,654 / 914D	1,394 / 852D	1,742 / 1,274D
Coahoma	1,404 / 1,100R	2,235 / 637R	573 / 155R	1,481 / 618R	2,203 / 979R
Copiah	3,608 / 283R	4,238 / 975D	3,446 / 692D	2,954 / 1,416D	2,728 / 1,806D
Covington	611 / 71D	903 / 337D	636 / 237D	547 / 297D	642 / 634D
De Soto	5,145 / 796R	4,212 / 615D	3,405 / 816D	3,314 / 1,123D	3,043
Franklin	926 / 10D	1,258 / 480D	712 / 186D	840 / 310D	988 / 573D
Greene	219 / 143D	437 / 325D	251 / 150D	496 / 294D	444 / 318D
Grenada	1,811 / 709R	1,927 / 655D	1,036 / 463D	1,086 / 117R	961 / 455D
Hancock	529 / 5R	856 / 238D	630 / 236D	959 / 177D	1,071 / 412D
Harrison	809 / 137D	1,035 / 461D	750 / 248D	1,279 / 383D	1,350 / 372D
Hinds	5,554 / 2,476R	5,977 / 3,029D	3,481 / 1,381D	3,899 / 461D	3,169 / 1,245D
Holmes	3,003 / 1,757R	3,765 / 1,463D	3,007 / 590D	1,956 / 386D	2,383 / 947D
Issaquena	1,623 / 1,365R	1,697 / 121R	392 / 278R	1,290 / 900R	1,055 / 81R
Itawamba	583 / 487D	1,451 / 1,369D	1,303 / 1,198D	1,307 / 1,137D	1,410 / 1,310D
Jackson	805 / 180D	1,230 / 544D	858 / 262D	1,656 / 346D	1,457 / 217D
Jasper	1,449 / 103D	2,020 / 622D	1,255 / 577D	1,392 / 302D	1,660 / 434D
Jefferson	2,087 / 1,381R	1,966 / 1,128D	1,068 / 808D	1,399 / 681D	1,046 / 320D
Jones	328 / 184D	337 / 329D	295 / 295D	412 / 376D	671 / 671D
Kemper	2,030 / 526R	2,483 / 675D	1,694 / 525D	1,500 / 394D	1,588 / 888D
Lafayette	2,557 / 85R	4,006 / 942D	3,622 / 917D	3,217 / 621D	2,174 / 1,200D
Lauderdale	2,789 / 215R	2,627 / 1,433D	1,964 / 995D	1,534 / 1,160D	2,495 / 1,818D
Lawrence	954 / 140R	1,475 / 219D	1,198 / 39D	1,458 / 338D	839 / 835D
Leake	1,263 / 93D	1,916 / 1,082D	1,692 / 984D	1,295 / 959D	1,409 / 991D
Lee	1,685 / 895D	2,931 / 2,925D	1,902 / 1,555D	1,936 / 525D	1,535 / 1,481D
Leflore	1,220 / 610R	2,058 / 662D	918 / 366D	1,116 / 592D	828 / 834D
Lincoln	1,447 / 249R	2,150 / 400D	1,539 / 70R	1,520 / 126D	1,728 / 466D

COUNTY.	1872.	1876.	1880.	1884.	1888.
Lowndes	3,915 / 2,519R	2,075 / 2,071D	1,533 / 873D	2,335 / 1,829D	1,141 / 1,105D
Madison	3,277 / 1,747R	1,486 / 1,460D	2,176 / 820D	1,929 / 559D	2,377 / 1,688D
Marion	457 / 5R	698 / 218D	518 / 116D	952 / 414D	836 / 821D
Marshall	4,739 / 971R	6,328 / 228D	5,170 / 56D	3,990 / 242D	3,684 / 844D
Monroe	3,962 / 1,194R	4,628 / 894D	2,810 / 1,406D	3,002 / 1,910D	3,375 / 2,549D
Montgomery	1,665 / 187R	1,965 / 1,063D	1,521 / 1,229D	1,367 / 981D	1,107 / 871D
Neshoba	497 / 127D	1,235 / 997D	882 / 652D	604 / 522D	887 / 581D
Newton	1,065 / 289D	1,943 / 1,341D	1,026 / 1,026D	1,119 / 869D	2,011 / 1,740D
Noxubee	3,844 / 2,272R	3,059 / 201D	1,661 / 807D	1,956 / 1,090D	846 / 846D
Oktibbeha	1,678 / 1,088R	2,396 / 350D	1,609 / 844D	1,547 / 597D	1,732 / 943D
Panola	3,196 / 1,234R	5,307 / 283D	4,266 / 10R	3,797 / 849R	2,771 / 529D
Pearl	70 / 48D	193 / 171D			
Perry	213 / 163D	363 / 301D	278 / 166D	613 / 257D	598 / 530D
Pike	1,578 / 82R	2,398 / 650D	1,550 / 270D	2,635 / 432D	2,109 / 923D
Pontotoc	1,549 / 533D	2,194 / 1,076D	1,840 / 680D	1,423 / 403D	1,480 / 458D
Prentiss	1,040 / 674D	2,044 / 1,718D	1,698 / 373D	1,747 / 1,209D	1,512 / 950D
Quitman			236 / 8D	9 / 68R	272 / 62R
Rankin	2,152 / 50R	2,577 / 1,003D	1,767 / 647D	1,896 / 302D	2,049 / 1,041D
Scott	1,129 / 209D	1,432 / 1,334D	793 / 793D	680 / 530D	1,133 / 904D
Sharkey		683 / 490D	660 / 304D	795 / 161R	831 / 371R
Simpson	805 / 159D	1,129 / 447D	745 / 293D	948 / 720D	944 / 557D
Smith	550 / 354D	1,125 / 1,105D	968 / 966D	772 / 708D	1,086 / 1,080D
Sumner		1,397 / 581D	1,086 / 522D		
Sunflower	317 / 117R	750 / 282D	816 / 16D	734 / 156D	379 / 351D
Tallahatchee	1,219 / 563R	1,145 / 1,143D	1,188 / 945D	1,302 / 208D	1,049 / 993D
Tate	3,456 / 438D	3,261 / 191D	3,040 / 64D	2,368 / 1,494D	
Tippah	720 / 334D	1,865 / 1,231D	1,708 / 919D	1,995 / 845D	1,785 / 818D
Tishemingo	514 / 348D	948 / 900D	945 / 745D	989 / 597D	959 / 666D
Tunica	1,121 / 949R	1,626 / 1,168R	734 / 838R	508 / 316R	1,463 / 447R
Union	1,115 / 363D	2,008 / 1,213D	1,937 / 1,098D	2,092 / 1,256D	1,450 / 652D
Warren	5,993 / 3,425R	2,659 / 1,413D	1,108 / 960D	2,995 / 667D	3,322 / 1,406D
Washington	3,164 / 2,774R	4,499 / 1,303D	2,379 / 95R	2,702 / 874R	3,181 / 528D
Wayne	696 / 26R	1,046 / 155D	971 / 113D	1,025 / 137D	1,188 / 196D
Webster				972 / 424D	910 / 564D
Wilkinson	2,589 / 1,663R	2,687 / 163R	2,510 / 366D	1,457 / 621D	532 / 458D
Winston	968 / 900D	1,476 / 870D	1,241 / 600D	905 / 550D	710 / 706D
Yalabusha	1,510 / 54D	2,705 / 1,043D	2,482 / 1,079D	2,000 / 316D	1,357 / 835D
Yazoo	3,345 / 1,501R	3,674 / 3,670D	2,288 / 1,973D	1,336 / 1,324D	1,203 / 1,189D

MISSOURI.

COUNTY.	1872.	1876.	1880.	1884.	1888.
Adair	2,380 / 446R	2,820 / 415R	3,255 / 388R	3,518 / 898R	3,850 / 697R
Andrew	2,987 / 221R	3,149 / 87R	3,483 / 210R	3,733 / 278R	3,737 / 285R
Atchison	1,913 / 89R	2,416 / 39R	2,979 / 33D	3,063 / 335R	3,366 / 89R
Audrain	2,248 / 902D	3,104 / 1,432D	3,355 / 1,839D	4,616 / 1,480D	4,784 / 1,616D
Barry	1,446 / 72D	2,014 / 1D	2,460 / 193D	3,248 / 76R	4,225 / 76R
Barton	1,173 / 33R	1,511 / 50D	2,173 / 423D	3,553 / 122D	3,954 / 340D

COUNTY.	1872.	1876.	1880.	1884.	1888.
Bates.........	3,245 / 247D	3,551 / 503D	5,091 / 1,052D	6,892 / 781D	7,024 / 882D
Benton.......	1,719 / 105R	1,947 / 245R	2,330 / 242R	2,823 / 232R	3,140 / 330R
Bollinger.....	1,070 / 252D	1,570 / 426D	1,814 / 439D	2,107 / 323D	2,402 / 213D
Boone........	4,192 / 2,206D	5,030 / 2,664D	4,857 / 2,099D	4,945 / 2,305D	5,645 / 2,557D
Buchanan....	6,123 / 081D	6,700 / 1,040D	8,401 / 1,376D	9,115 / 1,357D	11,509 / 1,358D
Butler......	592 / 216D	926 / 466D	1,117 / 471D	1,391 / 409D	2,089 / 332D
Caldwell.....	2,205 / 455R	2,556 / 325R	2,880 / 230R	3,211 / 507R	3,501 / 325R
Callaway....	3,439 / 1,997D	4,473 / 2,517D	4,664 / 2,185D	4,770 / 2,073D	5,565 / 2,288D
Camden......	967 / 161R	1,178 / 08R	1,240 / 29R	1,410 / 200R	1,950 / 381R
Cape Girardeau.	2,387 / 179D	3,260 / 419D	3,612 / 228D	4,174 / 6D	4,308 / 304R
Carroll.......	3,179 / 219D	4,408 / 426D	4,852 / 365D	5,670 / 119D	6,140 / 24R
Carter........	156 / 96D	306 / 129D	368 / 158D	416 / 152D	748 / 163D
Cass.........	3,465 / 559D	3,721 / 837D	4,695 / 1,000D	5,232 / 950D	5,234 / 920D
Cedar........	1,615 / 20R	1,825 / 17R	2,084 / 26R	3,019 / 113D	3,306 / 10D
Chariton.....	3,684 / 1,000D	4,012 / 1,416D	5,064 / 1,282D	5,481 / 1,093D	5,908 / 1,107D
Christian.....	916 / 410R	1,427 / 435R	1,758 / 353R	2,242 / 896R	2,802 / 746R
Clarke.......	2,542 / 34R	3,083 / 87D	3,198 / 67D	3,254 / 53D	3,552 / 67D
Clay.........	2,795 / 1,679D	3,409 / 2,335D	3,751 / 2,380D	4,157 / 2,263D	4,877 / 2,525D
Clinton.......	2,393 / 443D	2,856 / 737D	3,485 / 824D	3,878 / 528D	3,960 / 535D
Cole..........	2,468 / 176D	2,628 / 430D	2,777 / 46D	3,044 / 13D	3,550 / 115D
Cooper.......	3,611 / 747D	4,101 / 561D	4,291 / 459D	4,758 / 252D	5,138 / 209D
Crawford	1,201 / 153D	1,790 / 282D	1,973 / 294D	2,170 / 53D	2,438 / 83R
Dade.........	1,068 / 261R	2,236 / 412R	2,307 / 325R	3,048 / 424R	3,530 / 262R
Dallas........	1,242 / 340R	1,446 / 109R	1,696 / 167R	2,050 / 676R	2,368 / 463R
Daviess	2,754 / 56R	3,515 / 185D	4,126 / 249D	4,896 / 33R	4,635 / 271D
De Kalb......	1,858 / 176R	2,355 / 27R	2,764 / 07D	3,154 / 144R	3,290 / 25R
Dent.........	909 / 121D	1,266 / 374D	1,815 / 306D	1,969 / 373D	2,202 / 217D
Douglas......		927 / 608R	1,216 / 334R	1,570 / 794R	2,417 / 829R
Dunklin.. ...	919 / 695D	1,241 / 1,055D	1,515 / 1,151D	1,909 / 1,145D	2,557 / 1,119D
Franklin.....	3,307 / 143R	4,445 / 145D	4,965 / 387R	5,221 / 641R	5,881 / 682R
Gasconade...	1,154 / 602R	1,716 / 600R	1,909 / 1,025R	2,072 / 975R	2,309 / 1,179R
Gentry	2,210 / 152D	2,554 / 263D	3,698 / 605D	4,015 / 355D	3,870 / 419D
Greene.......	3,748 / 416R	5,026 / 250R	5,396 / 286R	7,182 / 603R	9,737 / 949R
Grundy	2,197 / 649R	2,923 / 697R	3,143 / 815R	3,341 / 923R	3,778 / 981R
Harrison.....	2,865 / 635R	3,390 / 640R	3,922 / 511R	4,195 / 722R	4,301 / 006R
Henry........	3,650 / 508D	3,880 / 581D	4,821 / 1,127D	5,628 / 1,012D	5,307 / 655D
Hickory......	904 / 406R	1,021 / 241R	1,363 / 239R	1,696 / 487R	1,868 / 448R
Holt.........	2,221 / 533R	2,961 / 313R	3,114 / 308R	3,496 / 482R	3,891 / 398R
Howard......	2,845 / 1,099D	3,420 / 1,323D	3,726 / 887D	3,552 / 1,089D	3,933 / 1,300D
Howell.......	739 / 27R	953 / 87D	1,388 / 209D	2,487 / 253D	3,208 / 136D
Iron..........	977 / 223D	1,197 / 419D	1,419 / 280D	1,336 / 241D	1,768 / 342D
Jackson......	7,289 / 1,661D	8,837 / 2,529D	12,558 / 1,580D	18,900 / 270D	30,765 / 1,313D
Jasper.......	3,430 / 784R	6,563 / 283R	652 / 341R	7,442 / 806R	2,949 / 887R
Jefferson.....	2,118 / 362D	3,010 / 696D	3,582 / 511D	4,178 / 434D	4,709 / 210D
Johnson......	4,803 / 205D	4,923 / 551D	5,513 / 395D	6,429 / 272D	6,249 / 288D

COUNTY.	1872.	1876.	1880.	1884.	1888.
Knox.........	2,011 / 311D	2,708 / 373D	2,807 / 894D	2,970 / 300D	3,110 / 280D
Laclede......	1,381 / 269D	1,751 / 278D	2,099 / 595D	2,511 / 80R	2,843 / 244R
Lafayette....	4,507 / 1,461D	5,015 / 1,547D	5,087 / 1,341D	6,293 / 1,111D	6,880 / 1,046D
Lawrence....	2,297 / 101R	2,656 / 43R	3,380 / 91R	4,118 / 156R	5,183 / 279R
Lewis........	2,812 / 594D	3,379 / 780D	3,232 / 776D	3,492 / 706D	3,703 / 856D
Lincoln......	2,182 / 892D	3,308 / 1,290D	3,463 / 1,349D	3,567 / 922D	4,013 / 752D
Linn	3,164 / 206R	3,806 / 36D	4,222 / 58D	4,425 / 111R	5,421 / 83D
Livingston...	3,316 / 174D	3,779 / 397D	4,292 / 694D	4,288 / 197R	4,753 / 51D
Macon.......	4,080 / 590D	4,816 / 1,024D	5,450 / 1,154D	5,728 / 481D	6,378 / 443D
Madison.....	1,064 / 384D	1,727 / 830D	1,844 / 561D	1,417 / 458D	1,872 / 433D
Maries	692 / 186D	1,091 / 589D	1,270 / 636D	1,300 / 532D	1,637 / 516D
Marion.......	4,278 / 908D	4,825 / 1,376D	4,984 / 1,275D	5,482 / 1,085D	5,879 / 1,071D
McDonald....	294 / 8D	1,117 / 315D	1,890 / 498D	1,750 / 380D	2,111 / 267D
Mercer.......	1,728 / 674R	2,483 / 541R	2,794 / 583R	2,794 / 847R	3,053 / 824R
Miller........	1,581 / 149R	1,507 / 174R	1,894 / 213R	2,407 / 318R	2,847 / 401R
Mississippi...	1,033 / 417D	1,653 / 737D	1,775 / 612D	1,946 / 500D	2,129 / 525D
Moniteau.....	2,361 / 289D	2,740 / 465D	2,819 / 470D	2,881 / 40R	3,301 / 12R
Monroe	3,012 / 391D	4,011 / 593D	4,279 / 724D	4,299 / 828D	4,893 / 797D
Montgomery.	2,351 / 227D	3,249 / 398D	3,396 / 302D	3,590 / 289D	3,953 / 83D
Morgan.......	1,552 / 238D	1,786 / 290D	1,805 / 152D	2,157 / 127D	2,632 / 102D
New Madrid..	1,089 / 553D	1,825 / 759D	1,418 / 736D	1,551 / 625D	1,466 / 762D
Newton	2,194 / 122R	3,333 / 186D	3,467 / 582D	3,983 / 104D	4,329 / 182D
Nodaway	3,186 / 180R	4,083 / 198D	5,729 / 162D	6,859 / 310R	6,548 / 27R
Oregon	499 / 391D	719 / 593D	917 / 734D	1,400 / 828D	1,525 / 797D
Osage........	423 / 561R	1,990 / 187D	2,264 / 20D	2,317 / 123R	2,676 / 256R
Ozark........	423 / 153R	658 / 196R	855 / 95R	978 / 290R	1,495 / 450R
Pemiscot.....	486 / 466D	754 / 737D	834 / 664D	803 / 568D	768 / 481D
Perry........	1,346 / 104R	1,884 / 467D	2,068 / 223D	2,218 / 237D	2,582 / 86D
Pettis.......	3,640 / 290D	4,984 / 735D	5,671 / 451D	6,644 / 410D	6,938 / 27R
Phelps.......	1,602 / 210D	1,971 / 466D	2,096 / 716D	2,167 / 498D	2,186 / 498D
Pike.........	4,318 / 838D	5,354 / 1,045D	5,676 / 1,085D	5,874 / 968D	6,306 / 764D
Platte.......	3,084 / 1,212D	3,512 / 1,784D	3,687 / 1,748D	3,753 / 1,646D	3,775 / 1,717D
Polk.........	2,170 / 174R	2,505 / 176R	3,116 / 146R	3,487 / 391R	4,288 / 306R
Pulaski......	858 / 210D	1,157 / 340D	1,253 / 310D	1,571 / 383D	1,769 / 386D
Putnam.........		2,318 / 669R	2,662 / 788R	2,773 / 901R	3,104 / 940R
Ralls........	1,568 / 786D	2,198 / 1,176D	2,417 / 1,197D	2,470 / 1,042D	2,774 / 1,126D
Randolph....	3,082 / 1,342D	4,820 / 2,269D	4,609 / 1,876D	5,011 / 1,375D	5,527 / 1,591D
Ray.	3,412 / 1,090D	3,627 / 1,385D	4,090 / 1,706D	4,504 / 1,287D	5,106 / 1,386D
Reynolds.....	525 / 275D	737 / 507D	786 / 708D	996 / 592D	123 / 603D
Ripley........	411 / 217R	552 / 324D	768 / 464D	1,195 / 448D	1,393 / 298D
Saline........	4,073 / 1,507D	5,670 / 2,214D	6,117 / 1,944D	6,668 / 1,462D	7,324 / 1,703D
Schuyler.....	1,580 / 4R	2,042 / 209D	2,092 / 495D	2,224 / 198D	2,398 / 287D
Scotland	2,004 / 256D	2,526 / 404D	2,573 / 716D	2,630 / 449D	2,989 / 454D
Scott........	1,248 / 360D	1,469 / 857D	1,789 / 871D	1,846 / 816D	2,011 / 758D
Shannon	262 / 222D	515 / 323D	541 / 402D	729 / 415D	1,281 / 405D

COUNTY.	1872.	1876.	1880.	1884.	1888.
Shelby	2,165 397D	2,643 715D	2,907 1,430D	3,056 782D	3,315 1,003D
St. Charles	3,231 113D	3,571 1,447D	4,447 32R	4,452 216R	5,067 287R
St. Clair	2,186 132D	2,121 259D	2,781 198D	3,352 56D	3,692 63D
St. François	1,470 586D	2,102 970D	2,588 972D	2,882 874D	3,759 769D
St. Genevieve	1,018 250D	1,692 626D	2,771 431D	1,709 431D	1,995 301D
St. Louis city	....	48,380 2,469D	47,715 831D	42,925 577D	63,026 6,255D
St. Louis Co.	....	....	5,496 504R	6,077 1,034R	7,176 1,709R
Stoddard	979 341D	1,811 997D	2,223 051D	2,488 957D	3,005 855D
Stone	470 226R	591 273R	711 295R	905 439R	1,262 551R
Sullivan	2,252 14R	2,935 41R	3,597 24D	3,658 114R	3,996 73R
Taney	540 138R	719 17R	1,857 976D	1,106 186R	1,401 356R
Texas	1,319 357D	1,708 581D	2,012 773D	2,663 682D	3,321 652D
Vernon	1,945 743D	2,674 1,100D	3,638 1,898D	5,826 1,774D	6,627 1,805D
Warren	1,573 440R	2,083 450R	2,208 681R	1,955 753R	2,146 800R
Washington	1,519 237D	2,866 848D	2,342 714D	2,451 455D	2,560 114D
Wayne	919 211D	1,509 719D	1,758 576D	2,151 523D	2,434 427D
Webster	1,571 45D	2,087 73D	1,701 463D	2,549 87R	3,003 155D
Worth	977 85R	1,357 34D	1,571 94D	1,673 126R	1,736 18D
Wright	1,087 69R	1,110 107R	1,415 232R	2,217 292R	2,692 601R
NEBRASKA.					
Adams	133 115R	971 563R	2,048 897R	3,076 744R	3,816 647R
Antelope	97 81R	271 141R	770 432R	1,603 657R	2,284 828R
Blaine	....	....	....	....	270 50R
Boone	63 63R	307 217R	807 445R	1,641 540R	1,844 590R
Box Butte	....	....	....	....	1,323 162R
Brown	....	....	....	1,689 559R	1,800 533R
Buffalo	245 179R	651 331R	1,623 805R	2,796 465R	3,926 949R
Burt	503 183R	984 364R	1,487 630R	2,012 921R	2,388 1,014R
Butler	488 400R	1,001 165R	1,788 242R	2,540 73D	3,246 17D
Cass	1,735 345R	2,298 496R	3,356 558R	4,112 430R	6,214 128R
Cedar	149 7R	431 143D	544 108D	827 160D	1,305 54D
Chase	....	....	....	....	1,212 317R
Cherry	....	....	....	497 23R	1,388 209R
Cheyenne	106 2D	303 97D	554 90D	765 35R	2,946 575R
Clay	286 224R	1,378 696R	2,096 997R	2,589 873R	3,400 1,095R
Colfax	318 128R	923 7R	1,080 286R	1,596 16D	1,958 211D
Cuming	594 4D	904 88D	1,192 61R	1,805 49D	2,472 278D
Custer	....	....	439 169R	1,931 582R	4,678 1,277R
Dakota	319 111R	....	714 58D	989 18R	1,616 190D
Dawes	....	....	....	....	1,784 472R
Dawson	27 7R	247 95R	526 198R	1,085 902R	1,773 473R
Dixon	346 160R	657 69R	790 144R	1,260 363R	1,628 261R
Dodge	960 146R	1,940 28R	2,530 360R	3,395 67D	4,282 392D
Douglas	3,078 706R	4,612 72R	5,589 883R	9,497 802R	21,540 573D
Dundy	....	....	....	104 2R	922 256R

COUNTY.	1872.	1876.	1880.	1884.	1888.
Fillmore	457 367R	1,090 588R	2,016 954R	2,674 622R	2,791 610R
Franklin	115 50R	514 200R	880 837R	1,215 208R	1,563 332R
Frontier	17 5R	....	175 91R	400 174R	1,706 456R
Furnas	....	265 137R	861 405R	1,229 452R	2,100 670R
Gage	756 492R	1,089 605R	2,714 937R	5,126 1,071R	6,579 922R
Garfield	....	....	....	256 40R	397 113R
Gosper	....	32 14R	237 86R	538 110R	1,062 96
Grant	....	....	....	....	96 7D
Greeley	....	41 35R	315 55R	693 19D	1,093 50D
Hall	444 212R	1,015 425R	1,711 603R	2,693 251R	3,548 398R
Hamilton	139 107R	608 609R	1,644 651R	2,287 456R	2,860 742R
Harlan	72 88R	457 227R	530 430R	1,137 430R	1,799 599R
Hayes	....	....	....	....	878 196R
Hitchcock	....	26 6R	184 80R	248 72R	1,344 390R
Holt	....	22 22R	718 26R	2,906 472R	3,742 458R
Howard	92 72R	376 208R	992 285R	1,441 6D	1,909 47D
Jefferson	445 289R	688 394R	1,653 668R	2,147 554R	2,883 741R
Johnson	743 385R	1,073 321R	1,649 489R	2,381 370R	2,393 305R
Kearney	51 39R	228 144R	798 208R	1,589 360R	1,933 389R
Keith	....	71 39D	93 19D	140 5D	637 56R
Keya Paha	....	....	....	....	1,069 298R
Knox	....	266 160R	802 326R	1,400 410R	1,897 332R
Lancaster	1,028 945R	2,692 1,240R	4,888 2,016R	6,368 1,831R	9,980 2,169R
Lincoln	227 61R	490 12R	638 116R	880 144R	1,909 429R
Logan	....	....	....	....	358 57R
Loup	....	....	....	206 126R	270 146R
Madison	....	665 67R	1,154 244R	1,796 158R	2,715 238R
Merrick	429 251R	769 350R	1,128 544R	1,562 386R	2,055 497R
Nance	....	....	283 115R	732 250R	1,127 276R
Nemaha	1,395 477R	1,600 484R	2,338 616R	2,926 482R	2,766 333R
Nuckolls	69 43R	307 119R	931 263R	1,542 400R	2,202 509R
Otoe	1,545 243R	2,343 169R	3,193 692R	4,070 84R	4,544 98D
Pawnee	726 514R	896 566R	1,589 855R	2,063 600R	2,229 652R
Perkins	....	....	....	....	1,132 243R
Phelps	....	69 53R	493 300R	1,064 618R	1,851 883R
Pierce	45 43D	121 81D	195 43D	620 47R	917 19D
Platte	403 69R	1,044 100	1,608 22R	2,430 168D	2,958 387D
Polk	183 149R	627 460R	1,190 707R	1,811 162R	2,072 471R
Red Willow	....	102 62R	479 137R	897 327R	2,072 590R
Richardson	1,854 342R	2,340 188R	3,380 272R	4,143 55R	4,145 196R
Saline	917 487R	1,522 584R	2,944 844R	3,867 860R	4,149 363R
Sarpy	406 124R	512 30D	1,026 25D	1,249 6R	1,605 217D
Saunders	1,106 652R	1,570 642R	2,970 1,161R	3,659 152R	4,373 333R
Seward	775 449R	1,280 580R	2,279 655R	3,028 297R	3,578 146R
Sheridan	....	....	....	....	1,852 309R

COUNTY.	1872.	1876.	1880.	1884.	1888.
Sherman	....	100 / 22R	397 / 228R	867 / 153R	1,310 / 145R
Sioux	....	....	....	....	618 / 6D
Stanton	145 / 19R	257 / 5D	354 / 20R	667 / 31D	989 / 25D
Thayer	229 / 197R	521 / 275R	1,244 / 486R	2,093 / 361R	2,607 / 331R
Thomas	....	....	....	....	166 / 2R
Valley	....	188 / 176R	485 / 299R	1,170 / 350R	1,534 / 304D
Washington	872 / 374R	1,439 / 515R	1,730 / 691R	2,392 / 495R	2,475 / 331R
Wayne	33 / 33R	62 / 36R	161 / 75R	637 / 208R	1,230 / 173R
Webster	191 / 149R	625 / 393R	1,397 / 617R	1,985 / 645R	2,304 / 567R
Wheeler	....	....	....	205 / 84R	430 / 107R
York	124 / 48D	1,197 / 611R	2,108 / 914R	2,973 / 1,007R	3,608 / 1,142R

NEVADA.

COUNTY.	1872.	1876.	1880.	1884.	1888.
Churchill	94 / 12D	80 / 12D	181 / 17D	184 / 8R	175 / 3D
Douglas	336 / 126R	511 / 153R	522 / 28D	382 / 48R	419 / 125R
Elko	1,169 / 53R	1,583 / 57D	1,668 / 104D	1,306 / 78R	1,494 / 98R
Esmeralda	474 / 60R	743 / 3D	1,280 / 66D	841 / 277R	680 / 148R
Eureka	....	1,548 / 10R	1,917 / 135R	1,271 / 280R	964 / 251R
Humboldt	750 / 34R	804 / 106D	970 / 226D	957 / 101D	908 / 37D
Lander	1,800 / 54R	905 / 145D	1,090 / 60D	948 / 146R	644 / 104R
Lincoln	1,894 / 196D	752 / 84D	674 / 160D	455 / 65D	322 / 27D
Lyon	638 / 276R	838 / 228R	648 / 61R	644 / 76R	712 / 186R
Nye	45R / 45R	865 / 7D	757 / 69D	403 / 11R	335 / 61R
Ormsby	824 / 204R	1,350 / 338R	1,076 / 172R	872 / 202R	924 / 216R
Storey	4,074 / 1,132R	6,918 / 466R	5,138 / 392D	2,609 / 367R	2,852 / 370R
Washoe	761 / 193R	1,568 / 244R	1,583 / 73D	1,209 / 227R	1,571 / 247R
White Pine	1,112 / 208R	1,136 / Tie vote.	838 / 42D	630 / 60R	600 / 173R

NEW HAMPSHIRE.

COUNTY.	1872.	1876.	1880.	1884.	1888.
Belknap	3,958 / 110D	4,335 / 281D	4,888 / 133D	4,889 / 9D	5,337 / 150R
Carroll	3,675 / 5R	4,490 / 458D	5,089 / 213D	4,869 / 157D	4,984 / 96D
Cheshire	6,328 / 1,428R	7,146 / 1,178R	7,386 / 1,361R	7,153 / 907R	7,416 / 953R
Coos	3,146 / 308D	3,809 / 451D	4,260 / 558D	4,568 / 310D	5,074 / 132D
Grafton	8,989 / 99D	9,854 / 828D	10,396 / 336D	10,276 / 255R	10,570 / 39R
Hillsborough	12,569 / 1,811R	14,980 / 1,400R	15,744 / 1,690R	16,017 / 1,467R	18,166 / 1,021R
Merrimack	9,556 / 24R	11,347 / 27D	11,866 / 13R	11,867 / 493R	13,467 / 118D
Rockingham	10,201 / 1,341R	11,998 / 846R	13,036 / 967R	12,170 / 480R	13,229 / 103D
Strafford	5,801 / 1,185R	7,415 / 689R	8,593 / 713R	8,276 / 591R	8,932 / 310R
Sullivan	4,369 / 467R	4,674 / 402R	4,916 / 554R	4,591 / 446R	4,710 / 548R

NEW JERSEY.

COUNTY.	1872.	1876.	1880.	1884.	1888.
Atlantic	2,285 / 381R	3,134 / 237R	4,251 / 768R	4,594 / 585R	5,847 / 476R
Bergen	6,050 / 70D	7,610 / 1,104D	7,942 / 562D	8,151 / 639D	9,240 / 658D
Burlington	10,924 / 1,464R	12,878 / 60D	13,707 / 467R	13,616 / 378R	15,009 / 510R
Camden	7,517 / 2,877R	11,796 / 1,352R	13,784 / 2,063R	15,581 / 1,903R	18,867 / 2,592R
Cape May	1,314 / 484R	1,921 / 189R	3,240 / 685D	2,399 / 231R	2,728 / 363R
Cumberland	6,133 / 1,437R	7,654 / 545R	8,600 / 906R	8,805 / 1,081R	10,735 / 1,189R
Essex	26,035 / 5,021R	34,308 / 1,905R	38,968 / 2,912R	42,818 / 1,215R	51,236 / 116R

COUNTY.	1872.	1876.	1880.	1884.	1888.
Gloucester	4,316 / 1,138R	5,701 / 449R	6,180 / 687R	6,587 / 626R	7,377 / 877R
Hudson	19,555 / 1,447D	28,750 / 6,826D	34,371 / 4,954D	38,820 / 5,825D	47,839 / 8,169D
Hunterdon	7,562 / 676D	9,488 / 2,081D	9,574 / 1,897D	9,299 / 2,007D	9,625 / 1,075D
Mercer	9,548 / 354R	12,125 / 53R	13,960 / 575R	15,108 / 613R	18,042 / 1,241R
Middlesex	9,088 / 816R	11,097 / 603D	12,041 / 1,187D	11,944 / 587D	13,538 / 1,148D
Monmouth	8,974 / 474D	11,652 / 2,233D	13,354 / 1,921D	14,502 / 1,106D	16,511 / 1,153D
Morris	7,959 / 1,353R	10,301 / 65R	10,902 / 683R	10,707 / 377R	11,927 / 246R
Ocean	2,811 / 689R	3,405 / 271R	3,604 / 244R	3,774 / 496R	3,893 / 850R
Passaic	8,631 / 1,665R	11,012 / 407R	13,424 / 1,800R	14,780 / 1,873R	19,215 / 1,034R
Salem	4,838 / 506R	5,806 / 109R	6,233 / 148R	6,166 / 158R	6,760 / 217R
Somerset	4,955 / 475R	6,187 / 16D	6,415 / 60R	6,189 / 189D	6,629 / 159D
Sussex	4,913 / 719D	5,743 / 1,609D	5,892 / 834D	5,851 / 1,240D	5,813 / 967D
Union	9,079 / 175R	11,160 / 560D	11,719 / 119D	12,218 / 730D	14,469 / 919D
Warren	6,668 / 1,102D	8,461 / 2,426D	8,576 / 2,109D	8,772 / 2,140D	8,941 / 1,719D

NEW YORK.

COUNTY.	1872.	1876.	1880.	1884.	1888.
Albany	28,207 / 621R	34,194 / 1,180D	36,542 / 646D	37,337 /	40,806 / 1,675D
Allegany	9,131 / 3,169R	10,707 / 2,998R	11,805 / 3,345R	12,470 / 2,782R	11,866 / 3,442R
Broome	10,041 / 1,367R	12,219 / 1,842R	12,826 / 1,723R	13,564 / 1,402R	15,649 / 1,909R
Cattaraugus	9,221 / 2,009R	11,891 / 1,664R	13,582 / 1,935R	14,880 / 1,898R	15,616 / 2,413R
Cayuga	12,771 / 3,207R	15,211 / 2,837R	15,912 / 3,396R	16,258 / 2,984R	16,692 / 3,266R
Chautauqua	13,025 / 3,265R	15,871 / 4,371R	16,543 / 4,950R	17,512 / 4,809R	19,179 / 5,683R
Chemung	8,078 / 622R	9,992 / 498D	10,421 / 570D	10,715 / 479R	10,880 / 570D
Chenango	9,856 / 1,296R	11,156 / 1,348R	11,043 / 1,210R	10,710 / 1,052R	11,043 / 1,158R
Clinton	8,651 / 481R	10,298 / 706R	10,404 / 1,880R	11,177 / 825R	11,055 / 1,547R
Columbia	11,509 / 585D	12,210 / 510D	12,497 / 494R	12,487 / 570R	12,776 / 410R
Cortland	5,928 / 1,229R	6,722 / 1,396R	6,964 / 1,375R	7,307 / 1,268R	8,455 / 1,609R
Delaware	9,680 / 1,018R	11,128 / 640R	11,392 / 974R	11,439 / 978R	12,617 / 1,270R
Dutchess	16,872 / 402D	18,697 / 899R	19,641 / 2,570R	18,974 / 1,024R	20,148 / 1,016R
Erie	30,299 / 5,363R	39,872 / 765R	45,480 / 835R	51,992 / 1,490R	61,889 / 2,069R
Essex	5,667 / 1,780R	7,502 / 1,522R	7,721 / 2,001R	7,453 / 1,775R	8,007 / 2,113R
Franklin	5,447 / 1,295R	7,055 / 1,158R	7,083 / 1,586R	7,723 / 1,690R	8,886 / 2,729R
Fulton	6,478 / 624R	7,627 / 278R	7,906 / 1,252R	8,406 / 1,923R	9,678 / 1,211R
Genesee	6,634 / 1,454R	7,668 / 1,001R	8,378 / 1,334R	8,701 / 988R	8,995 / 1,319R
Greene	7,145 / 263D	8,503 / 1,093D	8,493 / 520D	8,701 / 45D	9,238 / 34D
Hamilton	845 / 139D	891 / 247D	1,019 / 146D	1,112 / 46D	1,244 / 47R
Herkimer	9,561 / 1,447R	11,381 / 754D	11,531 / 1,261R	11,880 / 810R	12,635 / 1,072R
Jefferson	14,250 / 2,712R	16,360 / 2,733R	16,704 / 3,223R	16,773 / 1,954R	18,125 / 2,390R
Kings	71,477 / 4,739D	96,684 / 18,400D	113,829 / 9,311D	126,299 / 15,729D	153,676 / 12,457D
Lewis	6,485 / 369R	7,325 / 98D	7,723 / 362R	7,759 / 77R	8,348 / 562R
Livingston	8,103 / 1,403R	9,540 / 1,023R	9,945 / 1,280R	9,622 / 1,153R	10,182 / 1,517R
Madison	9,994 / 2,198R	11,506 / 1,922R	11,718 / 2,110R	12,066 / 1,743R	10,182 / 2,560R
Monroe	22,294 / 3,772R	27,958 / 1,661R	31,153 / 3,378R	33,384 / 5,080R	39,686 / 4,973R
Montgomery	7,855 / 371R	9,849 / 209D	10,112 / 283R	11,100 / 92R	12,198 / 688R
New York	132,481 / 28,147D	171,380 / 53,969D	205,381 / 41,285D	227,780 / 43,064D	270,789 / 55,813D
Niagara	9,798 / 1,006R	11,950 / 316D	12,519 / 541R	12,637 / 316D	13,697 / 457R

COUNTY.	1872.	1876.	1880.	1884.	1888.
Oneida	23,462 / 3,306R	27,010 / 1,175R	27,539 / 1,946R	28,693 / 30D	31,363 / 1,965R
Onondaga	22,457 / 2,959R	26,158 / 3,706R	28,072 / 4,422R	30,748 / 3,736R	34,864 / 6,115R
Ontario	9,625 / 1,531R	11,917 / 807R	12,700 / 1,107R	12,385 / 739R	13,086 / 1,214R
Orange	16,180 / 756R	19,262 / 346D	19,926 / 416R	20,630 / 128R	22,750 / 409R
Orleans	6,248 / 1,466R	7,396 / 1,135R	7,778 / 1,477R	7,641 / 1,090R	8,326 / 1,063R
Oswego	16,001 / 3,115R	17,645 / 3,811R	17,487 / 3,490R	18,235 / 2,542R	19,350 / 3,867R
Otsego	12,510 / 40D	13,886 / 168D	14,575 / 28D	14,694 / 436D	15,364 / 857R
Putnam	3,043 / 369R	3,754 / 144R	3,824 / 406R	3,723 / 577R	3,722 / 583R
Queens	11,732 / 422R	17,005 / 3,024D	18,641 / 2,240D	19,283 / 1,922D	23,943 / 1,666D
Rensselaer	20,607 / 3,265R	25,245 / 672D	27,043 / 641R	28,302 / 318R	31,678 / 309R
Richmond	5,269 / 187R	7,222 / 1,455D	8,116 / 1,524D	8,462 / 1,970D	10,033 / 1,664D
Rockland	4,653 / 211D	5,663 / 1,145D	6,114 / 727D	6,441 / 1,104D	7,230 / 926D
St. Lawrence	15,730 / 6,940R	19,281 / 7,677R	19,617 / 7,913R	19,807 / 7,406R	21,627 / 8,101R
Saratoga	11,689 / 2,221R	14,026 / 991R	13,992 / 2,308R	14,553 / 2,344R	15,810 / 2,024R
Schenectady	5,050 / 567R	5,649 / 257D	5,956 / 622R	6,383 / 283R	7,120 / 304R
Schoharie	7,479 / 913D	8,887 / 1,775D	8,965 / 1,616D	9,261 / 1,867D	8,825 / 1,310D
Schuyler	4,474 / 482R	5,263 / 605R	5,230 / 497R	4,920 / 577R	4,898 / 729R
Seneca	5,773 / 33R	6,723 / 537D	7,243 / 406D	7,094 / 298D	7,437 / 129D
Steuben	15,491 / 1,611R	18,646 / 959R	19,825 / 1,253R	20,599 / 988R	21,897 / 2,483R
Suffolk	7,997 / 1,677R	11,529 / 215D	12,641 / 455R	11,351 / 553D	14,259 / 567R
Sullivan	6,321 / 199R	7,670 / 1,140D	7,491 / 379D	7,354 / 275D	7,773 / 103R
Tioga	7,292 / 870R	8,641 / 769R	8,614 / 1,123R	8,351 / 988R	8,842 / 1,243R
Tompkins	7,687 / 949R	9,191 / 1,004R	9,232 / 940R	9,052 / 428R	9,363 / 1,164R
Ulster	16,432 / 912R	19,625 / 1,722D	19,926 / 124R	20,385 / 59R	21,835 / 338R
Warren	4,704 / 1,098R	5,855 / 472R	6,334 / 712R	6,672 / 784R	7,332 / 1,252R
Washington	10,300 / 2,770R	12,218 / 2,488R	11,980 / 3,684R	11,929 / 3,115R	12,692 / 3,739R
Wayne	9,932 / 2,396R	12,360 / 1,882R	13,062 / 2,393R	12,447 / 2,213R	13,583 / 2,729R
Westchester	21,345 / 879D	21,650 / 2,476D	23,316 / 491D	24,493 / 1,238D	29,447 / 1,148D
Wyoming	6,211 / 1,609R	7,712 / 1,162R	8,071 / 1,386R	8,166 / 1,252R	8,589 / 1,733R
Yates	4,568 / 952R	5,293 / 1,181R	5,740 / 1,235R	5,439 / 1,273R	5,836 / 1,271R

NORTH CAROLINA.

COUNTY.	1872.	1876.	1880.	1884.	1888.
Alamance	1,775 / 75R	2,837 / 55R	2,710 / 216D	2,866 / 348D	3,408 / 172D
Alexander	680 / 54D	1,190 / 502D	1,190 / 458D	1,247 / 579D	1,523 / 400D
Alleghany	362 / 78D	677 / 377D	808 / 290D	979 / 269D	1,094 / 280D
Anson	1,993 / 41R	2,916 / 282D	2,627 / 607D	2,935 / 775D	3,212 / 1,102D
Ashe	854 / 230R	1,899 / 255D	2,786 / 648D	2,435 / 53D	2,934 / 102R
Beaufort	2,478 / 440R	3,266 / 180D	3,480 / 43D	3,708 / 282D	3,992 / 200D
Bertie	2,307 / 887R	2,781 / 529R	2,351 / 613R	3,459 / 369R	2,332 / 109D
Bladen	2,167 / 651R	2,787 / 7D	2,815 / 259R	2,542 / 122R	2,895 / 145D
Brunswick	1,347 / 367R	2,046 / 42R	1,635 / 143R	1,864 / 8R	1,992 / 58D
Buncombe	2,079 / 139D	3,177 / 905D	3,586 / 404D	4,636 / 642D	5,050 / 88D
Burke	1,109 / 21D	1,793 / 687D	1,915 / 335D	2,246 / 300D	2,418 / 87D
Cabarrus	1,741 / 149D	2,568 / 714D	2,553 / 445D	2,883 / 903D	2,673 / 726D
Caldwell	846 / 202D	1,479 / 907D	1,430 / 546D	1,683 / 881D	1,981 / 534D
Camden	979 / 111R	1,239 / 127D	1,166 / 118D	1,277 / 135D	1,202 / 26R

COUNTY.	1872.	1876.	1880.	1884.	1888.
Carteret	1,396 / 92D	1,860 / 440D	1,727 / 325D	1,778 / 554D	1,829 / 368D
Caswell	2,813 / 293R	3,125 / 139R	3,244 / 330R	3,163 / 67R	2,969 / 276R
Catawba	1,693 / 811D	2,320 / 1,428D	2,507 / 1,259D	2,969 / 1,645D	3,208 / 1,584D
Chatham	2,886 / 286R	4,011 / 271D	4,090 / 322D	4,169 / 733D	4,738 / 554D
Cherokee	656 / 88R	1,212 / 148D	1,371 / 73D	1,195 / 161R	1,561 / 215R
Chowan	1,137 / 277R	1,435 / 177R	1,482 / 222R	1,528 / 130R	1,550 / 70R
Clay	329 / 79D	499 / 131D	552 / 178D	569 / 149D	700 / 111D
Cleveland	1,004 / 102R	2,252 / 1,286D	2,271 / 1,301D	2,658 / 1,426D	3,058 / 1,502D
Columbus	1,507 / 47R	2,201 / 660D	2,519 / 675D	2,815 / 919D	2,996 / 1,185D
Craven	3,713 / 1,805R	4,016 / 1,438R	3,989 / 1,629R	3,869 / 1,209R	3,983 / 1,259R
Cumberland	3,288 / 404R	4,353 / 107D	4,246 / 28R	4,661 / 277D	4,551 / 495D
Currituck	....	1,890 / 594D	1,338 / 610D	1,408 / 558D	1,468 / 549D
Dare	361 / 73R	542 / 68D	562 / 14D	546 / 36R	658 / 16R
Davidson	2,195 / 713R	2,955 / 609D	3,646 / 84R	3,997 / 197R	4,466 / 323R
Davie	1,147 / 127R	1,708 / 304D	1,741 / 209D	2,162 / 46R	2,234 / 191R
Duplin	2,250 / 172D	3,448 / 942D	3,243 / 787D	3,428 / 1,066D	3,347 / 1,074D
Durham	....	....	....	2,768 / 382D	3,535 / 217D
Edgecombe	4,657 / 2,215R	5,493 / 2,189R	5,201 / 1,749R	4,978 / 1,608R	3,878 / 1,211R
Forsyth	1,858 / 342R	3,025 / 33R	3,569 / 138R	4,001 / 119D	4,851 / 375R
Franklin	2,740 / 346R	3,798 / 47R	4,044 / 20D	4,118 / 124D	4,238 / 190D
Gaston	1,448 / 168D	2,065 / 435D	2,246 / 32R	2,334 / 378D	2,926 / 329D
Gates	1,065 / 135D	1,430 / 398D	1,533 / 487D	1,882 / 408D	1,957 / 335D
Graham	117 / 43D	....	420	429 / 132D	479 / 89D
Granville	4,843 / 963R	4,141 / 47R	6,006 / 850R	4,294 / 74D	5,032 / 228R
Greene	1,395 / 445R	1,963 / 171R	1,823 / 63R	2,139 / 55R	2,072 / 84R
Guilford	3,116 / 356R	4,302 / 866D	4,518 / 47D	4,684 / 160D	5,544 / 259R
Halifax	5,270 / 2,309R	4,909 / 1,543R	4,221 / 733R	6,445 / 1,597R	5,355 / 379R
Harnett	1,326 / 12R	1,806 / 334D	1,732 / 324D	1,908 / 510D	2,598 / 398D
Haywood	1,009 / 327D	1,437 / 563D	1,439 / 425D	1,946 / 416D	2,341 / 387D
Henderson	905 / 167R	1,539 / 29D	1,510 / 162D	1,774 / 218R	2,220 / 382R
Hertford	1,523 / 407R	2,101 / 61R	2,123 / 157R	2,449 / 215R	2,162 / 52D
Hyde	948 / 108D	1,554 / 242D	1,428 / 410D	1,552 / 210D	1,614 / 72D
Iredell	2,139 / 179D	3,649 / 1,165D	4,005 / 773D	4,380 / 908D	4,087 / 826D
Jackson	568 / 287D	913 / 391D	938 / 416D	1,085 / 859D	1,532 / 290D
Johnston	2,177 / 559R	3,876 / 492D	3,890 / 428D	4,693 / 974D	5,128 / 863D
Jones	1,029 / 279R	1,396 / 204R	1,374 / 226R	1,501 / 7D	1,322 / 90D
Lenoir	2,005 / 603R	2,720 / 292R	2,485 / 221R	3,017 / 201R	3,065 / 171D
Lincoln	1,361 / 113D	1,787 / 463D	1,699 / 127D	1,930 / 412D	2,138 / 283D
Macon	652 / 334D	1,052 / 488D	1,081 / 411D	1,244 / 168D	1,600 / 51D
Madison	797 / 37R	1,707 / 83D	2,075 / 178R	2,500 / 370R	3,063 / 743R
Martin	2,250 / 332R	2,484 / 181D	2,695 / 121R	2,814 / 314D	2,971 / 335D
McDowell	903 / 21D	1,506 / 420D	1,372 / 262D	1,591 / 280D	1,887 / 128D
Mecklenburg	4,383 / 21D	6,006 / 768D	6,606 / 116D	6,767 / 565D	7,552 / 953D
Mitchell	532 / 404R	1,305 / 180D	1,502 / 474R	1,717 / 567R	2,265 / 907R
Montgomery	861 / 379R	1,399 / 103R	1,581 / 143R	1,831 / 59R	2,202 / 215R

COUNTY.	1872.	1876.	1880.	1884.	1888.
Moore	1,445 17R	2,568 162D	2,843 109D	3,237 301D	3,823 129D
Nash	2,218 212R	3,058 374D	3,018 206D	1,401 289D	3,900 462D
New Hanover	5,322 1,568R	4,618 1,370R	3,638 762D	4,639 1,149R	4,726 986R
Northampton	2,750 1,246R	3,615 787D	3,599 571R	4,115 653R	3,686 312R
Onslow	1,349 191D	1,807 767D	1,615 555D	1,796 788D	1,630 734D
Orange	2,750 216D	4,006 760D	4,439 635D	2,732 604D	2,947 314D
Pamlico	648 68R	1,258 232D	944 220D	1,356 150D	1,344 125D
Pasquotank	1,400 698R	2,073 375R	1,634 484R	2,149 361R	2,072 395R
Pender	......	2,424 80R	2,241 227R	2,453 39R	1,483 33R
Perquimans	1,299 495R	1,852 188R	1,750 284R	1,761 213R	1,785 203R
Person	1,734 134D	2,200 222D	2,467 221D	2,580 390D	2,661 77D
Pitt	3,163 305R	4,031 241D	4,016 324D	4,711 145D	4,995 211D
Polk	363 165D	750 66D	755 85R	933 47R	800 18D
Randolph	2,274 308D	3,345 205D	3,816 194D	3,658 78D	4,720 218R
Richmond	1,916 456D	2,806 106R	3,106 390R	3,051 241D	3,481 14R
Robeson	2,554 452D	3,856 378D	4,195 275D	4,781 225D	4,890 900D
Rockingham	2,786 46R	3,643 657D	3,942 864D	4,171 877D	4,571 175D
Rowan	1,938 14D	3,415 963D	3,352 718D	4,014 1,270D	4,064 1,458D
Rutherford	1,327 529D	2,386 168D	2,443 29D	2,769 243D	3,371 9D
Samson	2,359 581D	3,767 433D	3,748 496D	4,142 960D	4,005 782D
Stanley	861 95R	1,384 530D	1,462 312D	1,704 526D	1,813 245D
Stokes	1,664 14R	2,202 242D	2,247 241D	2,390 292D	2,812 79D
Surry	1,768 6D	2,364 340D	2,470 354D	2,815 111R	3,298 61D
Swain	298 228R	432 306D	409 207D	648 314D	1,003 74D
Transylvania	380 80R	695 223D	745 177D	782 122D	1,088 42R
Tyrrel	556 86D	805 298D	786 164D	844 98D	847
Union	1,140 238R	2,280 832D	2,340 692D	2,473 1,219D	2,962 1,188D
Vance				2,776 490R	3,314 544R
Wake	6,112 1,298D	8,756 126R	8,961 203R	9,041 459D	9,628 518R
Warren	3,463 1,447D	3,819 1,179R	4,047 1,315R	3,286 990R	1,429 330R
Washington	1,325 545D	1,697 313R	1,584 380R	1,745 427R	1,837 275R
Watauga	984 610R	994 430D	1,257 167D	1,398 128D	1,887 68R
Wayne	3,245 623D	4,472 96D	4,684 170D	5,286 202D	5,419 119D
Wilkes	1,817 539D	2,880 121R	3,098 73R	3,369 687R	3,999 601R
Wilson	2,177 71D	2,933 609D	3,020 284D	3,643 639D	3,710 550D
Yadkin	1,335 209D	1,991 181R	2,109 227R	2,208 272R	2,541 366R
Yancey	651 37R	1,081 411D	1,155 269D	1,401 85D	1,734 124D

OHIO.

COUNTY.	1872.	1876.	1880.	1884.	1888.
Adams	3,849 95D	4,687 405D	5,288 162D	5,776 58D	6,015 152D
Allen	4,473 453D	5,999 1,087D	6,844 984D	7,908 1,070D	9,158 1,362D
Ashland	4,551 185D	5,804 684D	5,969 465D	6,104 759D	5,782 707D
Ashtabula	7,442 4,086R	9,066 4,477R	9,486 4,640R	10,472 4,626R	10,081 4,480R
Athens	4,423 1,627R	5,806 1,818R	5,966 1,411R	6,465 1,576R	6,568 2,958R
Auglaize	3,715 1,855D	5,081 2,089D	5,451 1,762D	5,922 1,856D	6,223 1,716D
Belmont	7,914 620R	10,000 48D	11,088 160D	12,180 423R	12,832 837R

COUNTY.	1872.	1876.	1880.	1884.	1888.
Brown	5,930 744D	7,094 1,112D	7,516 1,140D	7,547 1,046D	7,461 1,184D
Butler	7,919 1,933D	9,380 2,678D	10,008 2,435D	10,829 2,775D	11,916 3,811D
Carroll	3,100 534R	3,614 506R	3,855 672R	4,141 649R	4,309 659R
Champaign	5,244 874R	6,400 656R	6,969 1,235R	7,379 1,079R	7,341 884R
Clark	6,707 1,483R	8,672 1,600R	10,461 2,050R	13,129 2,313R	13,762 1,268R
Clermont	7,066 250D	8,168 467D	8,694 389D	8,612 49R	8,505 83D
Clinton	4,891 1,319R	5,548 1,452R	6,110 1,770R	6,313 1,580R	6,410 1,511R
Columbiana	7,670 1,876R	9,417 1,417R	11,184 2,272R	12,061 2,523R	13,491 2,546R
Coshocton	4,908 404D	5,830 794D	6,282 609D	6,353 630D	6,558 799D
Crawford	5,676 1,514D	6,677 2,053D	7,217 1,945D	7,715 2,120D	7,985 2,404D
Cuyahoga	22,484	32,623	37,612	48,613	51,052 2,045R
Darke	5,829 309R	8,244 1,090D	9,287 1,121D	9,911 1,052D	10,199 1,228D
Defiance	2,813 627D	4,408 1,368D	5,142 1,163D	5,519 1,104D	6,080 1,322D
Delaware	4,726 700R	6,046 428D	6,481 540R	6,950 435R	6,911 428R
Erie	5,192 618R	6,270 46R	7,058 356R	7,706 537D	8,179 601D
Fairfield	6,428 1,348D	7,907 1,827D	7,958 1,739D	8,244 1,712D	8,124 1,788D
Fayette	3,685 595R	4,310 562R	4,954 719R	5,386 1,011R	5,674 1,124R
Franklin	13,121 1,569D	16,940 1,826D	19,398 425D	23,477 648D	28,271 673D
Fulton	3,086 1,384R	4,294 1,100R	4,784 1,125R	5,005 944R	5,307 904R
Gallia	4,409 1,301R	5,504 900R	5,805 1,178R	6,082 1,357R	5,958 1,435R
Geauga	3,311 2,111R	3,812 2,196R	3,920 2,238R	3,968 2,136R	3,777 1,669R
Greene	6,030 2,108R	6,982 1,994R	7,391 2,472R	7,762 2,296R	7,930 2,211R
Guernsey	4,530 728R	5,566 646R	5,912 750R	6,178 839R	6,544 1,040R
Hamilton	45,024 4,858D	58,320 582D	65,297 5,051R	72,486 5,496R	80,587 3,846R
Hancock	4,760 138D	6,026 404D	6,507 226D	6,858 252D	9,557 95R
Hardin	4,208	5,532 164D	6,505 440R	7,139 274R	7,288 272R
Harrison	3,908 608R	4,584 544R	4,870 665R	4,992 686R	5,080 838R
Henry	2,670 350D	3,972 918D	4,625 1,138D	5,235 1,214D	5,801 1,586D
Highland	6,104 228R	6,664 18R	7,138 158R	7,245 245R	7,357 87R
Hocking	3,210 510D	3,784 784D	4,340 509D	4,416 657D	4,861 428D
Holmes	3,619 1,441D	4,412 1,930D	4,656 1,911D	4,782 2,002D	4,809 2,147D
Huron	5,994 1,620R	7,518 1,490R	7,786 1,526R	8,302 1,339R	8,282 954R
Jackson	3,813 708R	4,476 568R	4,829 732R	6,123 852R	6,652 942R
Jefferson	5,878 1,674R	6,989 1,145R	7,456 1,489R	8,321 1,551R	8,791 1,631R
Knox	5,503 48R	6,452 150D	6,965 43D	7,288 48R	7,871 60R
Lake	3,730 1,772R	4,082 1,800R	4,190 1,874R	4,200 1,805R	4,369 1,880R
Lawrence	5,261 1,987R	6,994 1,026R	7,506 1,765R	8,508 1,193R	7,916 1,645R
Licking	8,055 1,069D	9,585 1,511D	9,850 1,365D	10,702 1,359D	11,307 1,332D
Logan	4,750 840D	5,545 973R	6,328 1,271R	6,796 1,373R	6,835 1,582R
Lorain	6,529 2,335R	7,907 2,467R	8,428 2,857R	9,085 2,279R	9,133 1,924R
Lucas	8,335 2,171R	11,679 1,869R	13,568 1,172R	16,085 987R	18,412 805R
Madison	4,336 309R	5,000 46R	5,516 373R	5,840 315R	332R
Mahoning	6,275 1,239R	7,612 230R	9,219 890R	10,806 1,575R	12,011 825R
Marion	3,182 502D	4,521 685D	5,131 740D	5,657 679D	6,092 776D
Medina	4,489 1,099R	5,311 927R	5,519 1,182R	5,758 1,298R	5,789 1,152R

COUNTY.	1872.	1876.	1880.	1884.	1888.
Meigs	5,313 / 1,689R	6,735 / 1,180R	6,862 / 1,354R	6,917 / 1,547R	6,603 / 1,576R
Mercer	3,116 / 1,064D	3,963 / 1,712D	4,853 / 1,894D	5,136 / 2,344D	6,135 / 2,305D
Miami	6,663 / 843R	7,897 / 879R	8,572 / 1,324R	9,491 / 1,189R	10,016 / 1,054R
Monroe	4,185 / 1,571D	5,267 / 2,343D	5,457 / 2,151D	5,675 / 2,365D	5,581 / 2,265D
Montgomery	14,181 / 185D	16,892 / 1,050D	20,112 / 600D	22,993 / 198R	26,085 / 651D
Morgan	3,890 / 788R	4,484 / 268R	4,627 / 419R	4,636 / 584R	4,690 / 557R
Morrow	3,886 / 508R	4,496 / 404R	4,766 / 488R	4,986 / 452R	4,927 / 446R
Muskingum	8,862 / 254R	10,639 / 225D	11,208 / 468R	11,734 / 200R	12,474 / 350R
Noble	3,643 / 389R	4,321 / 129R	4,548 / 272R	4,563 / 334R	4,729 / 428R
Ottawa	2,561 / 317D	3,544 / 872D	4,128 / 1,049D	4,366 / 1,167D	4,842 / 1,335D
Paulding	1,616 / 342R	2,493 / 133R	2,963 / 96R	4,283 / 100R	5,890 / 194R
Perry	4,079 / 265D	4,894 / 736D	6,240 / 511D	6,686 / 106R	7,177 / 54R
Pickaway	5,013 / 307D	5,954 / 824D	6,667 / 843D	6,871 / 958D	7,019 / 785D
Pike	2,852 / 284D	3,561 / 631D	3,973 / 436D	4,093 / 446D	4,030 / 393D
Portage	5,916 / 1,040R	6,718 / 706R	7,223 / 843R	7,543 / 658R	7,410 / 620R
Preble	4,816 / 614R	5,555 / 453R	5,898 / 472R	6,206 / 361R	6,435 / 191R
Putnam	3,406 / 856D	4,780 / 1,568D	5,292 / 1,566D	6,349 / 1,815D	6,805 / 1,906D
Richland	7,041 / 303D	8,056 / 758D	8,923 / 853D	9,359 / 1,173D	9,644 / 1,010D
Ross	7,361 / 61D	8,608 / 234D	9,313 / 183R	9,603 / 107R	9,747 / 358R
Sandusky	5,107 / 349D	6,362 / 376D	6,847 / 581D	6,940 / 554D	7,297 / 699D
Scioto	4,970 / 797R	6,384 / 334R	6,612 / 727R	7,233 / 1,165R	7,396 / 995R
Seneca	6,590 / 384D	8,308 / 722D	8,962 / 837D	9,159 / 946D	9,668 / 1,067D
Shelby	4,028 / 504D	5,126 / 1,566D	5,602 / 1,046D	5,955 / 1,076D	6,108 / 1,150D
Stark	11,007 / 567R	13,182 / 962D	14,492 / 299R	16,797 / 320R	18,520 / 331D
Summit	7,272 / 1,796R	8,859 / 1,251R	10,153 / 1,819R	11,771 / 2,002R	12,553 / 960R
Trumbull	8,180 / 3,548R	9,163 / 3,103R	10,188 / 3,612R	9,978 / 3,521R	10,082 / 3,122R
Tuscarawas	6,764 / 408D	8,119 / 971D	9,011 / 748D	9,774 / 821D	10,457 / 754D
Union	4,014 / 886R	5,008 / 857R	5,540 / 1,066R	5,907 / 1,273R	5,925 / 1,244R
Van Wert	3,492 / 118D	4,700 / 120D	5,210 / 63R	6,052 / 112R	7,079 / 13R
Vinton	2,654 / 63R	3,350 / 284D	3,697 / 292D	3,598 / 127D	3,744 / 38D
Warren	5,931 / 1,595R	6,705 / 1,357R	7,134 / 2,001R	6,883 / 1,837R	6,981 / 1,575R
Washington	7,911 / 551R	8,353 / 131D	9,275 / 259R	9,593 / 123R	9,604 / 475R
Wayne	7,301 / 235R	8,607 / 589D	9,266 / 395D	9,557 / 321D	9,507 / 727D
Williams	3,632 / 794R	5,247 / 155R	5,653 / 285R	5,979 / 10R	6,268 / 94R
Wood	4,890 / 1,098R	7,824 / 834R	8,573 / 961R	10,060, / 796R	768R
Wyandot	3,911 / 279D	4,698 / 540D	5,381 / 583D	5,520 / 694D	5,418 / 725D

OREGON.

COUNTY.	1872.	1876.	1880.	1884.	1888.
Baker	590 / 26D	869 / 230D	1,118 / 132D	1,794 / 156D	1,607 / 96R
Benton	905 / 189R	1,359 / 48R	1,551 / 126R	2,068 / 16R	2,200 / 237R
Clackamas	1,116 / 238R	1,691 / 226R	2,043 / 294R	2,496 / 366R	2,708 / 522R
Clatsop	209 / 127R	817 / 47R	970 / 102R	1,551 / 202R	1,759 / 413R
Columbia	193 / 36R	357 / 83D	550 / 54R	762 / 153R	963 / 272R
Coos	507 / 135R	1,086 / 56R	1,162 / 54R	1,445 / 120R	1,797 / 127R
Crook				742 / 111D	977 / 84D
Curry	161 / 55R	258 / 7R	298 / 6R	335 / 43R	877 / 91R

COUNTY.	1872.	1876.	1880.	1884.	1888.
Douglas	1,277 / 265R	1,802 / 155R	2,379 / 151R	2,375 / 91R	2,523 / 148R
Gilliam					1,055 / 161R
Grant	376 / 90R	594 / 37R	940 / 68R	1,334 / 34D	1,937 / 38R
Jackson	1,096 / 44D	1,430 / 255D	1,808 / 319D	2,275 / 304D	2,580 / 139D
Josephine	232 / 12R	465 / 43D	500 / 80D	550 / 80D	1,068 / 7R
Klamath				332 / 22D	732 / 90D
Lake		431 / 85D	600 / 152D	387 / 60D	737 / 13D
Lane	1,384 / 246R	1,928 / 3R	2,151 / 80D	2,557 / 19R	3,087 / 225R
Linn	1,808 / 83R	2,869 / 80D	3,114 / 260D	3,167 / 197D	3,385 / 3D
Malheur					668 / 27R
Marion	2,037 / 825R	2,960 / 628R	3,451 / 666R	3,910 / 556R	4,133 / 668R
Morrow					1,119 / 119R
Multnomah	2,741 / 919R	3,649 / 597R	5,930 / 492R	9,023 / 1,173R	10,456 / 2,252R
Polk	791 / 185R	1,204 / 66R	1,491 / 59R	1,572 / 11R	1,585 / 56R
Tillamook	114 / 70R	196 / 43R	218 / 50R	377 / 47R	631 / 173R
Umatilla	768 / 8D	1,270 / 256D	2,787 / 285D	3,928 / 142D	3,205 / 25D
Union	738 / 92R	923 / 159D	1,583 / 235D	2,538 / 70D	2,550 / 80R
Walloma					775 / 149R
Wasco	706 / 78R	1,112 / 130D	2,840 / 180D	3,043 / 274R	2,725 / 541R
Washington	728 / 332R	1,115 / 269R	1,458 / 302R	1,847 / 180R	2,156 / 411R
Yamhill	1,012 / 190R	1,490 / 136R	1,999 / 115R	2,267 / 150R	2,380 / 205R

PENNSYLVANIA.

COUNTY.	1872.	1876.	1880.	1884.	1888.
Adams	5,313 / 158R	6,379 / 518D	6,958 / 515D	6,674 / 450D	7,243 / 425D
Allegheny	34,901 / 16,791R	48,862 / 9,482R	59,271 / 13,443R	61,106 / 18,396R	70,966 / 20,408R
Armstrong	4,575 / 419R	7,454 / 1,782D	9,067 / 736R	8,707 / 1,094R	9,000 / 1,267R
Beaver	5,315 / 1,719R	7,274 / 1,033R	8,322 / 1,200R	8,981 / 1,529R	9,534 / 1,846R
Bedford	5,066 / 736R	6,743 / 332D	7,414 / 85D	7,873 / 170R	8,215 / 465R
Berks	17,943 / 2,450D	23,961 / 7,589D	26,363 / 7,734D	26,297 / 6,897D	28,932 / 7,479D
Blair	6,434 / 2,068R	8,720 / 819R	10,731 / 1,080R	11,430 / 1,747R	12,837 / 2,136R
Bradford	11,015 / 3,889R	15,094 / 1,019R	13,598 / 3,302R	13,446 / 4,189R	13,908 / 4,210R
Bucks	12,358 / 1,468R	15,758 / 301D	17,035 / 242D	16,898 / 413D	17,479 / 58D
Butler	6,549 / 1,481R	10,551 / 813R	10,243 / 591R	9,950 / 981R	9,951 / 1,372R
Cambria	*5,388 / 294R	7,351 / 1,268D	8,667 / 598D	9,567 / 563D	11,711 / 431D
Cameron	*892 / 212R	1,125 / 29R	1,256 / 65R	1,354 / 167R	1,845 / 281R
Carbon	4,398 / 506R	5,959 / 348D	6,406 / 607D	6,815 / 142D	7,177 / 386D
Centre	5,837 / 447R	7,356 / 799D	8,299 / 108D	8,695 / 438D	9,471 / 18D
Chester	13,051 / 544R	16,893 / 3,088R	18,912 / 3,774R	18,579 / 3,793R	19,788 / 4,037R
Clarion	4,860 / 232R	7,244 / 1,107D	7,088 / 1,500D	7,084 / 1,143D	7,073 / 930D
Clearfield	4,299 / 359D	6,564 / 1,902D	8,322 / 1,823D	9,763 / 898D	11,900 / 969D
Clinton	3,761 / 245R	4,842 / 1,164D	5,438 / 833D	6,353 / 1,000D	6,073 / 448D
Columbia	5,010 / 992D	6,483 / 2,321D	7,026 / 2,362D	7,056 / 1,805D	7,441 / 2,192D
Crawford	11,825 / 2,051R	14,051 / 808R	14,798 / 1,345R	14,730 / 1,600R	15,003 / 2,076R
Cumberland	7,452 / 338R	9,263 / 912D	10,012 / 100D	10,185 / 716D	10,347 / 693D
Dauphin	10,285 / 3,623R	13,368 / 2,090R	15,507 / 1,954R	16,070 / 3,016R	18,822 / 3,168R
Delaware	5,397 / 3,065R	8,736 / 2,234R	11,483 / 2,535R	12,261 / 2,974R	14,170 / 3,763R

COUNTY.	1872.	1876.	1880.	1884.	1888.
Elk.........	1,482 / 74D	1,914 / 796D	2,342 / 814D	2,687 / 365D	3,215 / 503D
Erie.........	11,287 / 3,715R	14,988 / 2,545R	15,864 / 2,281R	16,951 / 2,005R	17,281 / 2,261R
Fayette	6,544 / 1,318R	10,224 / 1,215D	11,779 / 1,330D	13,121 / 779D	14,306 / 89D
Forest........	515 / 205R	849 / 79R	976 / 45R	1,447 / 268R	1,602 / 305R
Franklin	7,447 / 1,155R	9,526 / 277R	10,847 / 415R	10,961 / 309R	11,042 / 600R
Fulton	1,545 / 71D	2,011 / 369D	2,105 / 399D	2,197 / 328D	2,215 / 279D
Greene......	4,681 / 977D	5,675 / 1,763D	6,513 / 2,061D	6,650 / 1,980D	6,630 / 1,749D
Huntingdon..	4,904 / 1,294R	6,525 / 511R	7,219 / 748R	7,194 / 1,005R	7,201 / 1,428R
Indiana	5,652 / 3,120R	7,227 / 2,686R	8,224 / 2,498R	8,157 / 2,628R	8,092 / 2,853R
Jefferson....	3,409 / 1,097R	4,863 / 109D	5,522 / 115R	6,639 / 440R	7,648 / 833R
Juniata	2,571 / 41R	3,564 / 463D	3,686 / 374D	3,671 / 189D	3,699 / 82D
Lackawanna.	......	......	14,686 / 179R	16,511 / 3,485R	21,195 / 421R
Lancaster....	20,005 / 8,571R	27,106 / 7,787R	30,317 / 8,700R	30,141 / 9,895R	33,016 / 11,481R
Lawrence....	4,374 / 2,484R	5,475 / 1,666R	6,575 / 2,313R	6,916 / 2,174R	6,941 / 2,229R
Lebanon.....	6,247 / 2,095R	7,585 / 1,524R	7,277 / 834R	8,506 / 2,530R	9,895 / 9,429R
Lehigh	10,964 / 280D	13,346 / 2,173D	14,453 / 2,148D	14,540 / 1,738D	16,094 / 1,950D
Luzerne.....	23,870 / 2,062R	24,022 / 3,475D	24,375 / 1,147D	27,252 / 952D	31,558 / 925R
Lycoming....	8,260 / 586R	10,252 / 1,313D	11,931 / 1,461D	11,834 / 545D	14,536 / 876D
McKean......	1,658 / 422R	2,739 / 107R	7,161 / 521R	7,647 / 840R	7,709 / 1,144R
Mercer	8,928 / 2,106R	10,645 / 922R	11,598 / 1,050R	12,270 / 1,496R	11,923 / 162R
Mifflin.......	2,812 / 558R	3,614 / 175D	4,095 / 120R	4,233 / 3D	4,510 / 237R
Monroe......	2,992 / 1,418D	4,056 / 2,504D	4,813 / 2,372D	4,278 / 2,233D	4,437 / 2,167D
Montgomery.	13,193 / 2,967R	19,133 / 268D	22,129 / 1R	22,936 / 529R	26,417 / 863R
Montour.....	2,717 / 51R	2,916 / 591D	3,207 / 597D	3,045 / 590D	3,230 / 576D
Northampt'n.	10,996 / 1,314D	14,597 / 3,960D	15,717 / 3,692D	16,051 / 8,164D	17,103 / 3,242D
Northumberland.	7,627 / 915R	9,427 / 792D	10,087 / 1,084D	11,933 / 117D	12,841 / 81R
Perry	4,307 / 819R	5,478 / 125D	5,926 / 188R	6,051 / 223R	5,973 / 490R
Philadelphia.	92,199 / 45,385R	139,218 / 14,965R	173,787 / 20,890R	174,683 / 30,000R	205,444 / 18,572R
Pike........	1,136 / 437D	1,831 / 944D	1,879 / 795D	1,673 / 829D	1,840 / 706D
Potter......	2,017 / 909R	2,919 / 341R	3,162 / 639R	3,637 / 637R	4,616 / 878R
Schuylkill...	15,640 / 1,674R	20,381 / 1,777D	23,336 / 2,174D	24,047 / 72R	25,980 / 532D
Snyder......	1,998 / 160R	3,462 / 383R	3,712 / 541R	3,686 / 726R	3,910 / 867R
Somerset....	4,858 / 2,132R	6,129 / 1,448R	6,705 / 1,650R	7,391 / 2,343R	7,882 / 2,506R
Sullivan....	1,011 / 131D	1,408 / 377D	1,691 / 369D	1,921 / 888D	2,310 / 314D
Susquehanna.	7,443 / 1,629R	8,762 / 938R	9,089 / 1,229R	8,804 / 1,321R	9,076 / 1,691R
Tioga	7,507 / 3,953R	8,802 / 3,163R	9,684 / 3,203R	10,310 / 4,033R	11,279 / 4,830R
Union	2,913 / 1,081R	3,652 / 664R	3,767 / 752R	3,670 / 814R	4,000 / 866R
Venango ...	7,766 / 1,794R	7,627 / 371R	8,347 / 516R	8,518 / 529R	8,762 / 949R
Warren	4,628 / 1,552R	5,617 / 786R	6,009 / 1,089R	7,528 / 1,257R	7,764 / 1,689R
Washington..	8,357 / 1,181R	11,330 / 483R	12,631 / 601R	13,341 / 850R	14,227 / 1,954R
Wayne......	4,615 / 311R	6,450 / 920D	6,556 / 229D	6,042 / 65D	6,324 / 71D
Westmoreland.	10,131 / 693R	13,958 / 1,249D	15,957 / 832D	17,549 / 7D	20,105 / 324R
Wyoming....	2,951 / 153R	3,702 / 341D	3,806 / 196D	3,996 / 67D	3,996 / 185R
York........	13,052 / 454D	17,230 / 3,576D	19,460 / 3,711D	19,698 / 3,538D	21,707 / 3,812D

RHODE ISLAND.

COUNTY.	1872.	1876.	1880.	1884.	1888.
Bristol	1,004 / 596R	1,639 / 405R	1,494 / 596R	1,784 / 333R	1,765 / 278R
Kent.........	1,608 / 834R	2,393 / 465R	2,931 / 606R	2,577 / 716R	3,314 / 727R
Newport	1,958 / 1,140R	2,876 / 786R	3,048 / 1,085R	3,416 / 835R	4,160 / 818R
Providence...	11,984 / 4,860R	17,165 / 2,757R	18,487 / 4,341R	21,702 / 3,896R	27,430 / 1,767R
Washington..	2,433 / 899R	2,426 / 602R	3,250 / 788R	3,352 / 859R	4,076 / 854R
SOUTH CAROLINA.					
Abbeville.....	4,184 / 2,502R	7,516 / 92D	8,057 / 4,905D	3,714 / 3,562D	3,065 / 2,911D
Aiken.......	2,958 / 1,660R	5,119 / 683D	6,438 / 3, D	3,316 / 2,394D	2,936 / 2,128D
Anderson....	2,057 / 81R	5,211 / R	5, /	2,856 / 2,582D	2,189 / 1,921D
Barnwell....	2,868 / 1,698R	6,730 / 1,060D	8,606 / 3,1 D	4,281 / 2,213D	3,700 / 2,252D
Beaufort....	5,003 / 4,013R	9,803 / 5,308R	6, 55 / 5,632R	2,895 / 2,393R	2,278 / 1,260R
Berkeley....				3,106 / 646R	2,929 / 293D
Charleston...	18,400 / 6,370R	23,864 / 6,308R	19,602 / 3,278D	3,949 / 2,067D	3,114 / 3,217D
Chester	3, /	4,414 / 468R	4,037 / 1,809D	2,214 / 1,502D	1,781 / 1,698D
Chesterfield..	1,036 / 189R	2,614 / 638D	2,998 / 852D	1,924 / 1,212D	2,048 / 1,694D
Clarendon...	1, 1 / 1,1R	3,319 / 469R	3,986 /	1,829 / 697D	1,783 / 1,121D
Colleton....	2,493 / 1,581R	7,152 / 1,310R	3, /	2,739 / 1,103D	3,509 / 2,101D
Darlington...	3,348 / 2,418R	6,258 / 784R	6, / 2, D	3,419 / 1,919D	2,146 / 1,558D
Edgefield....	4,863 / 2,637R	9,1 D /	7,900 / 5,884D	3, /	3,196 / 3,088D
Fairfield....	3,224 / 1,906R	3, R /	5,417 / 2,057D	1, D /	1,402 / 1,384D
Georgetown..	2,305 / 1, R	3, /	785 / 461R	1, D /	1,831 / 750
Greenville...	2,581 / 475R	5,380 / 2,668D	6,329 / 2,153D	3,896 / 3 D	3,776 / 2,849D
Hampton....				2, / 1,017D	1,753 / 1,074D
Horry.......	767 / 83R	2,538 / 1,350D	2,781 / 1, R	1,898 / 982D	1,604 / 876D
Kershaw....	1,783 / 1,051R	3,822 / 818R	4, / 1, D	1, /	1,428 / 1,088D
Lancaster...	1,519 / 418R	2,778 / 260D	1, / 1, D	2 /	1,969 / 1,519D
Laurens.....	2,845 / 1,157R	4,721 / 1,093D	4,555 / 3,088D	2, D /	1,502 / 1,415D
Lexington...	1,035 / 553R	3,392 / 798D	3,182 / 840D	2, D /	2,008 / 1,812D
Marion.....	2,875 / 2,019R	5,648 / 644D	6,462 / 1,556D	3,807D / 1,999D	3,168 / 1,712D
Marlborough.	1,717 / 1,508R	3,539 / 825D	3,906 / 950D	2,162 / 1 D	1,343 / 1,219D
Newberry...	3,673 / 2,061R	4,964 / 724R	5,791 / 326R	2, / 1,252D	1,789 / 1,671D
Oconee.....	904 / 118R	2,636 / 1,560R	2,449 / 1,417D	1,594 / 970D	1,445 / 981D
Orangeburg..	3,884 / 2,344R	7,321 / 1,651R	6,349 / 901D	4,704 / 1,296D	4,209 / 1,879D
Pickens	903 / 85R	2,417 / 1,571D	2,186 / 1,204D	1,424 / 1,216D	953 / 763D
Richland....	3 /	6 / 1, R	6,291 /	2,637 /	2,360 / 1,469D
Spartanburg.	2 R /	1, R /	6,787 / 377D	885D / 361	3,861 / 1,469D
Sumter.....	3,322 / 2,450R	6 /	3,980 / 724D	3,610 / 760D	2,679 / 791D
Union......	3,121 / 4. D	4, /	3,741 /	2,426 / 2,178D	1,950 / 1,890D
Williamsburg	2, / 1, R	4,666 / 706R	2,771 / 785D	1,733 / 251D	2,447 /
York.......	3, 33 / 860R	5,683 / 751D	6,144 / 1,444D	3,321 / 1,657D	2,410 / 2,300D
TENNESSEE.					
Anderson	1,001 / 315R	1,425 / 139R	1,582 / 484R	2,060 / 852R	2,473 / 1,007R
Bedford.....	3,397 / 127D	4,302 / 634D	4,387 / 738D	3,935 / 171D	4,463 / 487D
Benton......	1,003 / 493D	1,325 / 717D	1,358 / 988D	1,653 / 455D	715 / 435D

COUNTY	1872.	1876.	1880.	1884.	1888.	COUNTY	1872.	1876.	1880.	1884.	1888.
Bledsoe	624, 50R	754, 78D	807, 112R	988, 156R	1,135, 171R	Lauderdale	1,587, 381D	1,946, 582D	2,205, 176D	2,818, 158D	3,271, 401D
Blount	1,754, 614R	2,114, 382R	2,485, 714R	2,672, 974R	3,246, 1,228R	Lawrence	677, 199D	1,146, 612D	1,290, 506D	1,504, 342D	1,722, 456D
Bradley	1,359, 199R	1,727, 147R	1,738, 267R	2,196, 412R	2,509, 527R	Lewis	167, 99D	218, 194D	238, 163D	273, 145D	386, 122D
Campbell	746, 462R	1,088, 330R	1,397, 769R	1,793, 995R	2,404, 1,286R	Lincoln	3,191, 2,245D	4,618, 3,422D	4,632, 2,750D	3,729, 1,831D	4,367, 2,203D
Cannon	1,238, 648D	1,456, 770D	1,528, 735D	1,526, 496D	1,852, 536D	Loudon	1,169, 443R	1,610, 404R	1,554, 488R	1,470, 522R	1,756, 606R
Carroll	3,113, 443R	3,973, 283R	4,053, 388R	4,169, 469R	4,231, 481R	Macon	835, 23R	969, 198D	1,306, 154D	1,429, 191R	1,999, 241R
Carter	1,339, 1,009R	1,545, 867R	2,049, 1,339R	1,982, 1,168R	2,250, 1,344R	Madison	3,643, 549D	4,680, 1,518D	5,213, 611D	4,294, 482D	4,685, 1,727D
Cheatham	987, 419D	1,166, 632D	1,172, 502D	1,294, 624D	1,868, 758D	Marion	790, 222R	1,297, 139R	1,626, 146R	2,003, 206R	2,681, 288R
Claiborne	1,155, 305R	1,710, 186R	2,179, 245R	2,311, 469R	2,351, 433R	Marshall	2,041, 801D	2,844, 1,474D	2,698, 1,518D	2,812, 1,356D	3,077, 1,505D
Clay	557, 221D	744, 484D	802, 390D	961, 295D	1,228, 270D	Maury	5,201, 325R	6,418, 844D	6,048, 564D	5,966, 330D	6,494, 822D
Cocke	1,300, 586R	1,812, 562R	2,514, 702R	2,462, 712R	2,789, 1,105R	McMinn	2,231, 333R	2,694, 196R	2,672, 254R	2,956, 370R	3,205, 537R
Coffee	1,250, 804D	1,527, 1,183D	2,079, 1,568D	1,973, 1,221D	2,357, 1,270D	McNairy	1,899, 31D	2,310, 362D	2,483, 186D	2,748, 124D	3,086, 4D
Crockett	......	......	......	1,788, 1,028D	2,333, 173D	Meigs	692, 120D	949, 289D	1,002, 212D	1,203, 155D	1,329, 151D
Cumberland	366, 60R	492, 6D	678, 84R	800, 176R	1,054, 210R	Monroe	1,487, 253D	2,033, 567D	2,102, 262D	2,378, 138D	2,850, 58D
Davidson	11,303, 9D	13,009, 2,115D	14,440, 1,094D	16,276, 54D	19,036, 894D	Montgomery	4,220, 92D	4,935, 741D	4,961, 807D	4,538, 694D	4,792, 464D
Decatur	843, 213D	1,144, 496D	1,259, 342D	1,387, 81D	1,691, 105D	Moore	......	......	......	959, 853D	1,062, 878D
De Kalb	1,377, 101D	1,441, 659D	2,192, 458D	2,526, 292D	2,772, 152D	Morgan	338, 110R	729, 179R	679, 189R	907, 307R	1,229, 491R
Dickson	1,266, 568D	1,787, 895D	1,868, 672D	1,900, 778D	2,276, 746D	Obion	2,814, 1,552D	2,868, 1,988D	2,783, 1,399D	3,448, 1,570D	4,154, 1,820D
Dyer	1,600, 939D	1,513, 1,293D	1,573, 812D	2,151, 933D	2,938, 1,068D	Overton	863, 589D	1,296, 738D	1,587, 722D	1,600, 758D	1,802, 574D
Fayette	4,767, 1,917R	5,295, 137R	5,329, 835R	4,366, 908R	4,793, 2,833D	Perry	778, 404D	936, 678D	907, 381D	1,162, 268D	1,376, 322D
Fentress	433, 79R	563, 161R	825, 197R	674, 234R	851, 358R	Pickett	......	......	......	559, 9R	771, 47R
Franklin	2,016, 1,478D	2,551, 1,999D	2,550, 1,890D	2,736, 1,446D	3,036, 1,688D	Polk	815, 61D	1,140, 260D	1,020, 291D	1,237, 171D	1,314, 44D
Gibson	3,853, 1,281D	4,497, 2,201D	4,808, 991D	5,209, 1,211D	5,636, 1,870D	Putnam	850, 384D	1,113, 747D	1,509, 573D	1,614, 512D	2,178, 544D
Giles	3,963, 115R	5,143, 1,409D	5,016, 859D	5,053, 497D	5,281, 1,081D	Rhea	672, 198D	898, 836D	1,095, 241D	1,667, 157D	2,591, 237R
Grainger	1,229, 149R	1,827, 263R	2,102, 327R	2,143, 463R	2,347, 485R	Roane	1,552, 782R	2,369, 801R	2,438, 823R	2,651, 1,035R	2,896, 1,198R
Greene	2,617, 99R	3,545, 27R	4,504, 243R	4,618, 396R	4,917, 527R	Robertson	2,479, 705D	3,368, 1,368D	3,119, 1,350D	2,771, 1,189D	3,155, 1,251D
Grundy	386, 262D	575, 465D	533, 308D	773, 397D	1,117, 685D	Rutherford	4,829, 177D	4,986, 1,058D	6,414, 1,373D	4,868, 788D	5,781, 823D
Hamblen	1,241, 235R	1,742, 142R	1,955, 247R	1,947, 197R	2,110, 328R	Scott	308, 354D	377, 239R	709, 455R	1,099, 839R	1,582, 1,254R
Hamilton	2,728, 532R	3,501, 275R	4,172, 865R	6,266, 1,388R	10,170, 2,358R	Sequatchie	249, 83D	367, 111D	345, 105D	426, 142D	530, 170D
Hancock	789, 247R	1,036, 252R	1,441, 455R	1,474, 624R	1,696, 736R	Sevier	1,314, 1,088R	1,888, 1,204R	2,476, 1,014R	2,710, 1,774R	3,311, 2,341R
Hardeman	2,642, 126D	3,302, 466D	3,150, 157D	3,166, 714D	3,012, 814D	Shelby	14,801, 2,089R	16,666, 412D	14,979, 801R	16,791, 1,539R	20,209, 3,655D
Hardin	1,668, 278R	2,059, 83R	2,323, 373R	2,633, 459R	2,953, 537R	Smith	1,840, 558D	2,378, 1,088D	2,524, 864D	2,472, 712D	3,210, 1,006D
Hawkins	2,047, 179R	2,810, 144R	3,549, 353R	3,502, 444R	3,884, 636R	Stewart	1,308, 672D	1,742, 1,054D	1,820, 861D	1,866, 806D	1,813, 741D
Haywood	4,337, 1,647R	4,912, 1,134R	5,454, 1,791R	4,110, 1,426R	3,686, 238D	Sullivan	2,222, 822D	2,922, 926D	3,471, 1,057D	3,474, 878D	3,768, 742D
Henderson	1,671, 81D	2,356, 353D	2,736, 111R	3,107, 151R	3,284, 260R	Sumner	3,300, 918D	3,452, 1,460D	3,999, 1,802D	3,170, 1,280D	4,006, 1,550D
Henry	2,594, 1,298D	3,425, 1,825D	3,483, 1,292D	3,080, 802D	3,300, 906D	Tipton	2,470, 98D	2,723, 171D	3,520, 289D	3,790, 54D	3,837, 865D
Hickman	1,126, 636D	1,452, 1,094D	1,611, 705D	1,844, 426D	2,616, 372D	Trousdale	881, 525D	827, 509D	1,058, 546D	810, 588D	1,108, 476D
Houston	533, 365D	602, 402D	649, 395D	804, 456D	1,004, 486D	Unicoi	......	......	......	650, 468R	780, 560R
Humphreys	1,186, 836D	1,612, 1,218D	1,642, 1,080D	1,769, 1,199D	1,838, 1,048D	Union	852, 348R	1,348, 320R	1,630, 660R	1,851, 791R	2,024, 978R
Jackson	909, 793D	1,380, 1,334D	1,462, 1,163D	1,661, 1,099D	2,130, 1,040D	Van Buren	203, 131D	269, 207D	341, 221D	407, 289D	526, 320D
James	547, 231R	637, 71R	630, 194R	758, 250R	895, 270R	Warren	1,837, 679D	2,120, 818D	2,145, 1,095D	2,286, 1,220D	2,611, 1,339D
Jefferson	1,864, 960R	2,483, 923R	2,538, 1,114R	2,645, 1,173R	3,154, 1,542R	Washington	2,295, 621R	3,160, 318R	3,680, 528R	3,374, 256R	3,582, 484R
Johnson	835, 721R	922, 512R	1,295, 889R	1,280, 922R	1,527, 1,167R	Wayne	1,353, 127R	1,381, 43D	1,554, 256R	1,792, 456R	1,976
Knox	5,089, 1,699R	6,601, 745R	7,496, 1,242D	8,729, 1,767R	10,052, 2,194R	Weakley	2,381, 969D	3,106, 1,424D	3,996, 1,050D	3,899, 687D	4,528, 1,000D
Lake	292, 292D	411, 411D	399, 309D	375, 359D	509, 391D	White	1,026, 788D	1,362, 1,118D	1,557, 1,135D	1,680, 1,050D	2,133, 1,135D

COUNTY.	1872.	1876.	1880.	1884.	1888.
Williamson...	3,403 / 313D	4,196 / 932D	4,389 / 1,182D	3,486 / 564D	3,849 / 867D
Wilson......	3,686 / 1,238D	3,934 / 1,774D	4,145 / 1,601D	3,425 / 957D	4,194 / 842D

TEXAS.

COUNTY.	1872.	1876.	1880.	1884.	1888.
Anderson	2,002 / 182D	2,258 / 172D	2,595 / 341D	3,644 / 345D	3,200 / 267D
Angelina....	433 / 193D	273 / 103D	771 / 770D	1,008 / 894D	1,236 / 908D
Aransas.....	177 / 105D	141 / 113D	217 / 102D	186 / 130D	200 / 138D
Archer.....			114 / 82D	127 / 46D	167 / 57D
Atascosa.....	175 / 111D	193 / 161D	407 / 328D	750 / 670D	660 / 643D
Austin......	2,100 / 206D	1,811 / 361D	1,308 / 160R	2,021 / 217R	3,251 / 917D
Bandera.....	130 / 88D	119 / 111D	375 / 345D	552 / 376D	673 / 249D
Bastrop.....	1,995 / 113D	2,116 / 118D	2,446 / 17D	3,311 / 143D	3,630 / 671D
Baylor.....			148 / 148D	308 / 291D	241 / 237D
Bee........	83 / 83D	166 / 166D	329 / 295D	244 / 315D	515 / 540D
Bell........	592 / 284D	2,214 / 1,916D	3,385 / 2,749D	5,697 / 4,009D	5,617 / 4,130D
Bexar.......	1,558 / 194D	2,047 / 521D	4,174 / 1,060D	6,656 / 1,329D	7,228 / 1,578D
Blanco......	196 / 124D	303 / 201D	135 / 65D	843 / 388D	812 / 457D
Bosque.....	484 / 406D	780 / 682D	1,695 / 1,413D	2,147 / 1,658D	2,420 / 1,671D
Bowie.......	661 / 43D	792 / 412D	1,979 / 301D	2,141 / 385D	3,504 / 813D
Brazoria....	1,263 / 775R	1,240 / 600R	1,468 / 820R	1,560 / 698R	1,750 / 846R
Brazos.....	1,893 / 145D	2,096 / 168D	2,397 / 269D	2,828 / 125D	3,081 / 19D
Brewster....					274 / 172D
Brown......	12 / 12D	546 / 544D	1,232 / 822D	1,783 / 1,574D	1,680 / 1,160D
Burleson....	928 / 714D	1,090 / 214D	1,330 / 281D	2,094 / 122D	2,307 / 173D
Burnet.....	231 / 131D	505 / 483D	1,050 / 599D	1,276 / 1,010D	1,479 / 1,082D
Caldwell....	1,080 / 110D	866 / 234D	2,152 / 715D	2,360 / 613D	2,677 / 754D
Calhoun....	387 / 11R	307 / 83D	321 / 59D	294 / 64D	166 / 72D
Callahan....			441 / 412D	862 / 816D	784 / 561D
Cameron....	419 / 93D	1,017 / 171D	2,119 / 1,685D	3,160 / 618D	1,856 / 1,008D
Camp.......		702 / 64D	1,067 / 158D	1,146 / 62D	1,233 / 89D
Carson.....					74 / 42D
Cass........	1,348 / 324D	1,714 / 784D	2,115 / 633D	3,257 / 1,031D	3,863 / 964D
Chambers...	203 / 65D	161 / 139D	883 / 176D	416 / 182D	410 / 131D
Cherokee...	1,340 / 596D	1,554 / 648D	2,296 / 882D	3,039 / 1,253D	3,542 / 1,317D
Chilbress...					80 / 80D
Clay........		50 / 34D	893 / 688D	1,039 / 623D	1,000 / 604D
Coleman....		123 / 123D	488 / 414D	727 / 705D	941 / 558D
Collin......	837 / 497D	2,369 / 1,909D	4,062 / 3,061D	5,693 / 4,908D	6,705 / 5,091D
Colorado....	2,325 / 25R	2,358 / 286R	2,912 / 635R	3,059 / 341R	3,641 / 226D
Comal......	568 / 194D	442 / 90R	843 / 169R	969 / 63R	1,127 / 257D
Comanche...	265 / 263D		1,382 / 1,181D	1,924 / 1,736D	2,226 / 1,981D
Concho.,....			145 / 132D	302 / 204D	239 / 147D
Cooke... ...	419 / 355D	1,504 / 1,432D	3,777 / 2,921D	4,151 / 3,138D	4,324 / 2,768D
Coryell.....	576 / 534D	1,065 / 1,058D	1,770 / 1,665D	2,487 / 2,339D	2,541 / 1,622D
Crosby.....					241 / 228D
Dallas.......	1,500 / 694D	3,837 / 2,221D	6,109 / 2,605D	8,520 / 3,845D	10,990 / 4,030D

COUNTY.	1872.	1876.	1880.	1884.	1888.
Delta........	288 / 170D	538 / 416D	968 / 647D	1,207 / 866D	1,708 / 1,312D
Denton......	559 / 447D	1,576 / 1,426D		3,943 / 2,546D	3,773 / 2,202D
De Witt.....	644 / 128D	957 / 493D	1,392 / 95D	1,682 / 151D	2,055 / 273D
Dimmitt			49 / 49D	240 / 174D	195 / 97D
Donley.....				137 / 113D	339 / 222D
Duval......			532 / 471D	491 / 235D	740 / 2R
Eastland....			175 / 175D	397 / 367D	1,471 / 1,089D
Edwards....				67 / 63D	363 / 148D
Ellis........	605 / 543D	1,787 / 1,781D	3,821 / 2,731D	5,151 / 3,681D	6,030 / 4,631D
El Paso....		177 / 65D	490 / 122R	1,972 / 302D	2,472 / 890D
Erath........	262 / 230D	896 / 888D	2,005 / 1,083D	2,569 / 2,008D	2,877 / 1,770D
Falls........	1,708 / 24R	1,513 / 059D	2,069 / 1,036D	3,603 / 749D	3,742 / 594D
Fannin.....	970 / 268D	2,015 / 1,225D	4,491 / 2,501D	4,802 / 2,881D	6,687 / 3,939D
Fayette.....	2,338 / 50D	2,923 / 107D	4,295 / 381R	4,789 / 660D	5,171 / 1,594D
Fisher......					215 / 212D
Fort Bend...	1,222 / 790R	1,234 / 840R	1,184 / 652R	1,905 / 127R	2,523 / 1,419R
Franklin....		478 / 466D	894 / 639D	1,002 / 901D	1,184 / 921D
Freestone...	1,484 / 218D		2,333 / 846D	2,556 / 568D	2,859 / 681D
Frio.........	48 / 48D	49 / 35D	230 / 165D	359 / 219D	421 / 265D
Galveston...	3,665 / 1,010D	3,943 / 1,835D		6,391 / 2,181D	6,101 / 1,660D
Gillespie...	398 / 32D	265 / 1D	707 / 65R	948 / 10R	1,152 / 866D
Goliad......					912 / 87D
Gonzales...	1,344 / 308D	1,519 / 739D	2,258 / 1,076D	2,805 / 1,011D	3,225 / 1,342D
Grayson.. ..	1,081 / 391D	3,837 / 2,319D	7,020 / 3,511D	8,358 / 3,509D	8,589 / 3,525D
Greer......					957 / 249D
Gregg......		1,307 / 175D	1,623 / 334R	1,648 / 113R	1,372 / 162D
Grimes.....	2,557 / 463R	1,907 / 461R	3,282 / 395R	3,527 / 170R	No vote recorded.
Guadalupe..	1,310 / 132D	1,042 / 152D	1,734 / 283D	2,238 / 237D	2,536 / 358D
Hale........					81 / 81D
Hamilton...	122 / 118D	409 / 460D	817 / 765D	1,461 / 1,395D	1,436 / 1,171D
Hardeman..					818 / 291D
Hardin.....	51 / 17D	36 / 36D	214 / 210D	376 / 272D	697 / 192D
Harris......	4,089 / 261R	4,050 / 697D	5,257 / 944D	6,558 / 448D	6,615 / 780D
Harrison....	3,149 / 1,599R	4,246 / 1,648R	4,827 / 297R	2,770 / 435R	2,723 / 1,151D
Haskell.....					179 / 179D
Hays........	598 / 216D	675 / 345D	1,404 / 748D	1,681 / 790D	1,891 / 911D
Henderson..	948 / 484D	872 / 384D	1,363 / 736D	1,801 / 899D	2,184 / 900D
Hidalgo.....	136 / 22D	135 / 65D	545 / 379D	319 / 317D	558 / 468D
Hill........	937 / 633D	1,633 / 1,625D	2,386 / 2,489D	4,028 / 3,296D	4,826 / 3,022D
Hood.......	442 / 442D	574 / 568D	1,146 / 1,099D	1,250 / 1,084D	1,130 / 946D
Hopkins....	753 / 431D	1,592 / 1,188D	2,600 / 1,876D	2,568 / 1,732D	3,861 / 2,681D
Howard.....				310 / 186D	267 / 107D
Houston....	1,563 / 49D	1,995 / 70D	2,367 / 235D	3,003 / 515D	3,019 / 456D
Hunt.......	569 / 421D	1,706 / 1,518D	3,140 / 2,388D	4,055 / 3,269D	5,521 / 3,817D
Jack........	201 / 1R	140 / 54D	1,136 / 682D	1,498 / 1,091D	1,387 / 724D

COUNTY.	1872.	1876.	1880.	1884.	1888.
Jackson	316 / 86R	346 / 26R	474 / 20R	529 / 13R	616 / 8D
Jasper	551 / 69D	365 / 365D	672 / 582D	799 / 307D	782 / 254D
Jeff Davis					358 / 54R
Jefferson	191 / 63D	230 / 110D	561 / 185D	902 / 264D	941 / 121D
Johnson	922 / 920D	1,734 / 1,668D	3,506 / 2,967D	3,585 / 2,968D	4,251 / 2,851D
Jones				515 / 302D	423 / 349D
Karnes	201 / 145D	278 / 276D	316 / 316D	431 / 278D	508 / 405D
Kaufman	812 / 438D	1,505 / 1,531D	3,107 / 1,909D	4,084 / 2,785D	4,909 / 3,925D
Kendall	162 / 26R	214 / 92R	473 / 190R	582 / 214R	697 / 195R
Kerr	182 / 75D	160 / 48D	357 / 125D	516 / 224D	626 / 120D
Kimble		9 / 9D	175 / 88D	303 / 265D	349 / 319D
Kinney	202 / 92R	172 / 116D	559 / 313D	733 / 143D	606 / 120R
Knox					157 / 157D
Lamar	1,342 / 432D	3,043 / 1,309D	4,104 / 1,825D	4,925 / 2,193D	5,401 / 2,130D
Lampasas	169 / 153D	479 / 469D	841 / 547D	1,469 / 1,071D	1,302 / 670D
La Salle				373 / 226D	430 / 136R
Lavaca	1,158 / 447D	1,382 / 648D	2,018 / 893D	2,109 / 1,105D	3,029 / 1,890D
Lee		998 / 688D	1,561 / 319D	1,837 / 270D	2,029 / 908D
Leon	1,413 / 443D	1,135 / 767D	1,417 / 992D	2,411 / 749D	2,335 / 693D
Liberty	542 / 6R	503 / 159D	747 / 121D	845 / 107D	677 / 107D
Limestone	1,464 / 574D	1,740 / 1,258D	2,326 / 1,022D	2,958 / 1,740D	3,495 / 1,545D
Limpscomb					212 / 56D
Live Oak	122 / 120D	158 / 154D	269 / 255D	809 / 292D	331 / 322D
Llano	150 / 144D	116 / 116D	696 / 468D	1,019 / 950D	952 / 863D
Madison	601 / 157D	580 / 456D	988 / 300D	1,160 / 594D	1,337 / 546D
Marion	1,819 / 263R	1,671 / 367R	1,834 / 661R	1,803 / 731R	
Martin					155 / 39D
Mason	156 / 34D	98 / 54D	430 / 271D	823 / 532D	804 / 433D
Matagorda	500 / 230R	375 / 43D	679 / 109R	724 / 228R	756 / 255R
Maverick	204 / 16D	142 / 30D	430 / 154D	423 / 109R	715 / 47R
McCulloch		121 / 121D	210 / 169D	409 / 305D	532 / 375D
McLennan	2,469 / 237D	2,853 / 1,201D	3,986 / 1,726D	4,692 / 1,760D	7,016 / 2,234D
McMullen				178 / 136D	194 / 173D
Medina	184 / 104R	180 / 48D	616 / 114R	811 / 69D	1,083 / 370D
Menard			179 / 141D	244 / 158D	276 / 224D
Midland					168 / 88D
Milam	1,017 / 653D	1,912 / 1,328D	2,223 / 1,120D	3,891 / 1,912D	4,026 / 1,937D
Mitchell				675 / 185D	415 / 183D
Montague	152 / 96D	472 / 456D	2,076 / 1,658D	2,743 / 2,570D	766 / 589D
Montgomery	1,148 / 96R	1,082 / 70D	1,805 / 449D	2,025 / 50D	2,136 / 159D
Morris		510 / 174D	834 / 236D	974 / 184D	1,261 / 274D
Nacogdoches	1,191 / 353D	1,311 / 405D	1,805 / 1,903D	2,180 / 1,170D	2,662 / 1,473D
Navarro	1,562 / 684D	2,255 / 1,099D	3,191 / 1,707D	4,681 / 2,294D	5,896 / 2,545D
Newton	247 / 67D	268 / 268D	485 / 485D	747 / 369D	620 / 440D
Nolan				389 / 318D	263 / 209D

COUNTY.	1872.	1876.	1880.	1884.	1888.
Nueces	645 / 101D	772 / 434D	1,059 / 721D	1,194 / 756D	1,438 / 744D
Oldham				159 / 159D	441 / 122D
Orange	137 / 27D	108 / 50D	352 / 145D	697 / 383D	
Palo Pinto	142 / 132D	204 / 204D	901 / 779D	1,250 / 1,188D	925 / 925D
Panola	896 / 890D	1,227 / 1,169D	1,501 / 1,281D	2,080 / 1,212D	2,453 / 899D
Parker	579 / 356D	1,097 / 943D	2,564 / 1,655D	3,231 / 2,361D	3,108 / 2,043D
Pecos		141 / 103D	209 / 193D	297 / 157D	178 / 139D
Polk	392 / 124D	275 / 275D	953 / 500D	1,462 / 390D	1,821 / 364D
Potter					72 / 66D
Presidio				704 / 218D	456 / 296D
Rains	845 / 295D	313 / 295D	515 / 365D	585 / 499D	897 / 490D
Red River	1,551 / 29R	2,090 / 356D	2,321 / 535D	3,061 / 841D	3,887 / 1,291D
Reeves					322 / 294D
Refugio	184 / 168D	166 / 160D	198 / 162D	127 / 53D	229 / 93D
Robertson	2,272 / 104D	2,919 / 1R	4,063 / 310R	4,150 / 6R	4,517 / 274R
Rockwall		244 / 200D	617 / 518D	724 / 660D	1,132 / 979D
Runnels			176 / 176D	308 / 296D	37 / 28R
Rusk	2,709 / 39D	2,658 / 607D	2,292 / 445D	3,587 / 657D	3,719 / 739D
Sabine	379 / 79D	341 / 341D	571 / 429D	632 / 458D	680 / 680D
San Augustine	647 / 107R	629 / 7R	890 / 234D	963 / 261D	803 / 802D
San Jacinto	748 / 132R	488 / 196R	951 / 133R	997 / 215R	1,167 / 226R
San Patricio	87 / 71D	47 / 45D	163 / 157D	137 / 111D	149 / 149D
San Saba	148 / 136D	289 / 287D	661 / 425D	1,088 / 336D	910 / 687D
Scurry				129 / 93D	140 / 115D
Shackelford		138 / 131D	350 / 224D	496 / 279D	371 / 159D
Shelby	725 / 245D	758 / 674D	1,348 / 1,308D	1,556 / 1,485D	2,161 / 1,732D
Smith	2,530 / 74R	3,234 / 242D	3,865 / 187D	4,626 / 723D	4,917 / 737D
Somerville		209 / 209D	472 / 332D	539 / 471D	436 / 292D
Starr	277 / 21R	111 / 19R	569 / 69R	639 / 131D	481 / 477D
Stephens		2 / 2R	745 / 680D	793 / 768D	755 / 676D
Tarrant	689 / 469D	1,771 / 1,495D	4,644 / 2,978D	6,504 / 3,748D	6,939 / 3,064D
Taylor			302 / 260D	986 / 730D	826 / 570D
Throckmorton			129 / 125D	244 / 206D	171 / 101D
Titus	967 / 513D	638 / 386D	915 / 869D	1,200 / 794D	1,538 / 925D
Tom Green			828 / 192D	1,216 / 313D	1,296 / 460D
Travis	2,477 / 87D	3,256 / 698D	4,042 / 291D	5,714 / 587D	6,083 / 443D
Trinity	440 / 214D	289 / 175D	715 / 489D	1,144 / 688D	1,126 / 894D
Tyler	431 / 131D	374 / 318D	818 / 767D	1,299 / 658D	2,228 / 500D
Upshur	1,404 / 212D	1,042 / 314D	1,777 / 861D	1,892 / 888D	2,071 / 727D
Uvalde	101 / 89D	160 / 138D	312 / 268D	680 / 414D	665 / 357D
Van Zandt	796 / 290D	891 / 579D	2,218 / 1,204D	2,608 / 1,801D	3,136 / 1,854D
Val Verde					516 / 120D
Victoria	890 / 62D	575 / 180D	1,140 / 16D	1,738 / 121R	1,569 / 121R
Walker	1,753 / 205R	398 / 396D	1,450 / 551D	1,929 / 133R	1,919 / 390D
Waller		1,530 / 330R	1,717 / 570R	2,007 / 367R	2,141 / 562R

COUNTY.	1872.	1876.	1880.	1884.	1888.
Washington..	4,171 547R	3,945 567R	4,988 866R	5,411 609R	4,851 357D
Webb	....	283 205D	1,448 1,230D	1,767 985D	904 628D
Wharton.....	837 619R	448 365R	733 523R	930 592R	1,488 821R
Wheeler.....	....	....	81 65D	400 298D	447 267D
Wichita	....	....	....	509 255D	439 240D
Wilbarger...	....	....	....	241 195D	434 185D
Williamson..	665 835D	1,336 994D	2,675 1,498D	3,474 1,909D	3,835 1,809D
Wilson	....	805 205D	259 213D	1,390 1,416D	1,779
Wise	208 125D	610 556D	2,884 1,865D	4,202 3,194D	3,186 2,055D
Wood	864 358D	1,049 601D	1,862 952D	2,316 1,265D	2,876 1,096D
Young	....	274 230D	800 684D	842 687D	765 595D
Zapata......	99 23R	110 18R	111 9D	169 37R	196 196D
Zavala......	....	....	....	145 141D	175 151D
VERMONT.					
Addison.....	4,103 3,069R	4,622 2,952R	4,482 3,257R	4,282 3,418R	4,819
Bennington .	3,340 1,606R	4,161 695R	4,081 1,301R	3,731 909R	3,716 1,369R
Caledonia ..	3,554 2,128R	4,443 1,327R	4,535 1,762R	4,249 1,317R	4,499
Chittenden..	4,908 2,214R	6,249 1,675R	6,016 1,882R	5,620 2,754R	6,201 2,205R
Essex	1,100 548R	1,222 288R	1,330 381R	1,461 398R	1,435 405R
Franklin	3,945 2,113R	5,047 1,257R	5,024 1,366R	5,385 1,223R	4,635 1,778R
Grand Isle..	571 225R	695 153R	653 158R	648 200R	648 295R
Lamoille....	2,157 1,355R	2,548 1,134R	2,557 1,115R	2,435 936R	2,435 1,254R
Orange......	3,616 1,936R	4,807 1,353R	4,770 1,476R	3,886 959R	4,183 1,515R
Orleans	2,937 2,231R	3,657 1,987R	3,742 2,107R	3,384 1,795R	3,864 2,312R
Rutland.....	6,460 3,332R	7,717 2,757R	8,153 3,269R	7,643 2,843R	8,658 3,671R
Washington..	4,553 2,107R	5,899 1,407R	5,762 1,684R	5,215 1,317R	5,712 1,829R
Windham....	4,562 3,344R	5,698 3,097R	6,072 3,211R	5,643 2,085R	5,084 2,826R
Windsor.....	6,532 4,294R	7,586 3,756R	7,921 4,382R	6,884 3,509R	6,697 3,706R
VIRGINIA.					
Accomack ...	2,405 283D	3,691 1,263D	3,018 708D	4,646 1,252D	5,333 1,191D
Albemarle ..	4,894 16D	5,049 563D	3,459 171D	5,528 354D	4,752 407D
Alexandria..	580 330R	824 350R	715 227R	773 245R	726 207R
Alleghany...	259 140D	639 54D	406 114D	1,663 201R	1,760 396R
Amelia......	1,446 692R	1,128 220R	1,345 667R	1,688 458R	1,740 332R
Amherst	2,507 63D	3,164 418D	2,879 703R	3,332 606D	3,188 366D
Appomattox .	1,510 42D	1,755 187D	1,040 120D	1,729 31R	1,490 98R
Augusta.....	2,005 798D	4,279 2,435D	3,689 1,600D	5,304 860D	5,979 846D
Bath	418 286D	645 481D	285 113D	841 123D	889 771D
Bedford.....	3,921 657D	4,787 1,061D	4,793 1,017D	5,404 1,390D	5,198 1,213D
Bland	431 245D	629 497D	1,173 1,053D	966 36D	1,046 28D
Botetourt ...	1,623 445D	2,093 369D	2,024 832D	2,687 541D	2,902 342D
Brunswick ..	1,964 694R	2,738 44D	1,368 952R	2,673 459R	2,815 232R
Buchanan...	267 161D	1,332 1,328D	143 77D	530 44D	919 65D
Buckingham.	2,318 440R	2,521 200R	1,418 269R	2,832 470R	2,711 396R
Campbell	2,562 240D	6,327 447D	2,919 437D	7,471 795D	3,665 585D

COUNTY.	1872.	1876.	1880.	1884.	1888.
Caroline......	2,579 23R	2,916 72D	2,354 10D	3,053 41R	3,082 146R
Carroll.......	1,043 357D	1,498 1,047D	1,537 861D	2,232 296D	2,486 175D
Charles City..	541 185R	1,051 257R	697 231R	1,024 324R	988 381R
Charlotte. ...	1,382 490R	1,964 130R	1,905 475R	2,620 588D	2,757 684D
Chesterfield..	3,168 8D	3,340 82D	1,975 65D	3,662 198D	3,175 13D
Clarke	973 229D	1,234 510D	1,375 651D	1,661 705D	1,740 675D
Craig.........	376 242D	460 352D	379 285D	655 433D	731 378D
Culpeper	2,042 Tie vote.	2,229 295D	2,020 868D	2,520 270D	2,585 223D
Cumberland .	1,472 522R	1,861 413R	1,323	1,680	1,623 467R
Dickenson ...	....	....	58 27R	522 54D	896 67D
Dinwiddie...	1,812 572R	1,648 60R	1,470 678R	2,287 548R	2,487 345R
Elizabeth City	1,519 929R	1,788 834R	1,650 714R	2,006 956R	1,818 769R
Essex	1,620 324R	1,651 185R	1,627 243R	1,958 202D	1,862 814R
Fairfax	2,135 129R	3,042 262D	2,910 114D	3,564	3,850 160D
Fauquier....	2,876 388D	3,545 1,007D	3,607 1,233D	4,106 1,152D	4,439 888D
Floyd........	957 133R	1,481 601D	1,055 365D	1,959 235R	2,455 530R
Fluvanna ...	832 84R	1,668 264D	689 95D	1,873 221D	2,752 735R
Franklin	2,109 91D	3,366 1,392D	2,478 1,356D	4,116 1,118D	4,164 646D
Frederick	1,376 488D	1,905 1,133D	2,560 1,028D	3,490 1,025D	2,746 961D
Giles	730 322D	879 645D	804 374D	1,499 301D	1,646 337D
Gloucester ...	1,530 202R	2,020 42D	1,580 134R	2,341 191R	2,442 295R
Goochland ...	1,335 175R	755 71D	732 228R	1,792 288R	1,659 311R
Grayson.....	1,065 629D	1,409 1,171D	873 559D	1,906 304D	2,552 29D
Greene......	625 84R	758 416D	471 79D	959 141D	1,052 12D
Greenville ..	1,086 364R	1,060 16D	1,032 618R	1,828 548R	1,610 179R
Halifax......	3,185 571R	5,354 486R	3,825 149R	6,347 439D	6,078 1,097D
Hanover	2,820 286D	3,138 846D	2,065 293D	3,804 328D	3,284 210D
Henrico.....	2,807 178R	3,281 11R	2,055 9R	3,929 419R	4,088 614R
Henry.......	1,854 22R	2,528 172D	1,630 248R	2,767 55R	3,027 99R
Highland....	478 858D	684 584D	294 144D	967 45D	898 14D
Isle of Wight.	1,575 295D	2,144 754D	1,671 205D	2,020 76R	2,316 84D
James City..	537 267R	667 201R	455 257R	852 368R	826 388R
King George.	777 19R	1,070 90D	850 178R	1,374 186R	1,262 178R
King and Queen.	1,588 136R	1,678 71R	1,237 125R	1,859 7D	1,787 129D
King William	1,335 139R	1,386 166R	1,328 261R	1,815 251R	1,839 347R
Lancaster...	573 109R	1,139 133R	1,112 188R	1,526 192R	1,773 89R
Lee	1,339 763D	1,603 1,023D	952 416D	2,354 314D	2,798 184D
Loudoun....	2,901 1D	4,126 824D	4,427 843D	4,773 817D	5,090 652D
Louisa	2,551 525R	2,902 130R	2,059 401R	2,959 215R	2,843 530R
Lunenburg ..	1,577 333R	2,025 88R	1,101 579R	1,825 301R	2,031 399D
Madison.....	1,298 396D	1,192 1,004D	1,219 261D	1,834 182D	542 84D
Matthews ...	983 177D	1,063 421D	970 308D	1,487 439D	1,652 406D
Mecklenburg.	3,551 1,108R	4,288 733R	2,984 1,374R	4,063 693R	4,383 843R
Middlesex ...	879 137R	1,137 11R	1,181 105R	1,410 150R	1,556 132R
Montgomery.	1,659 93R	2,307 687D	1,499 297D	2,724 108D	2,999 181R

COUNTY.	1872.	1876.	1880.	1884.	1888.
Nansemond..	2,505 47R	2,808 482D	1,472 444R	3,373 667R	3,468 704R
Nelson	2,147 65D	2,692 574D	2,327 507D	2,905 411D	2,778 330D
New Kent..	837 113R	1,010 70R	468 254R	1,181 251R	1,074 314R
Norfolk	3,546 1,296R	4,612 490R	3,494 600R	4,731 1,095R	5,722 1,771R
Northampton	1,317 407R	1,705 147D	1,668 224R	2,003 193R	2,201 241R
Northumberland	963 109R	887 99D	1,275 93D	1,755 31D	1,458 354R
Nottoway...	1,583 688R	1,291 5D	1,172 914R	1,730 824R	1,731 505R
Orange	1,650 62D	2,074 152D	1,838 228D	2,290 228D	2,288 27R
Page	654 242D	1,398 1,120D	466 165D	2,246 68D	2,540 138R
Patrick	1,150 46R	1,564 778D	1,085 449D	1,692 292D	2,274 216D
Pittsylvania..	3,945 173R	6,331 691D	6,009 557D	7,947 1,007D	8,138 414D
Powhatan...	1,318 460R	1,411 271R	888 448R	1,392 416R	1,328 206R
Prince Edward.	1,768 602R	2,738 464R	1,624 388R	2,177 457R	2,703 437R
Prince George.	1,348 512R	1,820 160R	1,945 677R	1,729 609R	1,679 357R
Prince William.	1,227 245D	1,582 556D	1,554 636D	1,819 667D	2,055 571D
Princess Anne	1,255 327R	1,885 165D	1,260 52D	1,857 15D	1,854 160R
Pulaski	787 105D	1,179 405D	1,046 112D	1,671 111D	2,079 77D
Rappahannock.	1,169 143D	1,406 476D	1,315 557D	1,498 501D	1,587 481D
Richmond....	952 294R	1,082 84R	1,165 137R	1,878 154R	1,298 188R
Roanoke....	1,304 70R	1,926 378D	1,293 97D	2,122 110R	
Rockbridge...	2,321 419D	3,408 1,602D	2,598 686D	4,042 102D	4,124 44R
Rockingham..	2,869 1,395D	3,988 2,872D	2,502 1,129D	5,528 1D	6,186 280R
Russell	1,105 379D	1,168 934D	513 132D	2,301 143D	2,952 268D
Scott	1,952 82D	1,698 686D	903 135D	2,949 301R	3,350 250R
Shenandoah..	1,983 1,265D	2,958 2,428D	1,783 1,083D	3,848 104D	4,259 101D
Smyth	1,192 438D	1,597 1,047D	743 339D	2,250 94D	2,540 82D
Southampton	2,390 278R	3,168 650D	2,698 740R	3,310 212R	3,731 557R
Spottsylvania	1,342 150D	1,833 361D	1,082 70R	1,664 24D	1,800 46R
Stafford	1,023 501D	1,256 788D	755 219D	1,406 118R	1,478 288R
Surry	711 215R	1,232 40D	1,118 246R	1,541 319R	1,768 440R
Sussex	1,511 603R	1,854 434R	1,593 813R	2,192 632R	2,484 686R
Tazewell....	932 504D	1,389 1,105D	826 530D	2,142 426R	3,600 938R
Warren	815 515D	1,068 794D	1,064 776D	1,471 839D	1,690 784D
Warwick....	400 196R	444 134D	402 172R	957 331R	1,148 378R
Washington..	1,539 661D	2,947 1,500D	1,705 539D	4,578 576D	5,588 382D
Westmoreland.	993 225R	1,279 39D	1,081 125R	1,671 235R	1,637 383R
Wise	603 245D	649 373D	594 91D	971 49D	1,469 20R
Wythe	1,315 535D	2,041 1,181D	1,910 509D	2,620 8D	3,121 181R
York	1,106 390R	1,357 279R	1,154 278R	1,497 341R	1,494 477R
CITIES.					
Danville....	880 48R	1,517 103R	1,316 166D	1,885 109D	1,886 258D
Alexandria city.		2,960 274D	2,452 464D	3,003 457D	3,205 142D
Fredericksburg.	708 192D	798 300D	756 212D	964 160D	1,004 186D
Norfolk city..	3,675 1D	3,826 958D	2,831 65D	5,187 403R	5,837 586R
North Danville.			235 43D	396 74D	560 114D

COUNTY.	1872.	1876.	1880.	1884.	1888.
Manchester..		1,065 285D	689 237D	1,457 271D	1,640 161D
Petersburg...	3,799 743R	3,431 765R	2,659 569R	4,377 1,153R	4,235 161R
Portsmouth city.	2,011 343R	2,337 1,023D	2,802 754D	2,656 32R	2,566 336D
Richmond....		12,495 1,605D	7,104 2,786D	13,315 1,883D	14,474 1,938D
Roanoke city.				1,189 53D	98R
WEST VIRGINIA.					
Barbour.....	1,355 99R	2,121 335D	2,110 175D	2,529 22D	2,992 35D
Berkeley....	2,594 28R	3,460 334D	3,360 130D	3,646 77D	4,199 172R
Boone........	328 20D	705 350D	838 294D	837 106D	1,264 221D
Braxton.....	821 301D	1,312 570D	1,615 515D	2,274 610D	2,755 626D
Brooke......	849 81R	1,138 146D	1,237 74D	1,476 5D	1,602 17D
Cabell......	1,922 268D	2,101 613D	2,470 557D	3,334 430D	4,412 480D
Calhoun.....	284 38D	783 267D	1,018 253D	1,258 254D	1,570 312D
Clay........	196 18D	284 13D	423 68D	596 30D	888 50R
Doddridge...	985 269R	1,463 61D	1,831 73R	2,229 219R	2,553 242R
Fayette.....	722 42D	1,616 350D	2,400 301D	3,332 198R	4,754 693R
Gilmer......	442 54D	859 307D	1,379 371D	1,710 353D	2,018 346D
Grant.......	617 269R	1,422 210D	931 291R	1,160 486R	1,416 649R
Greenbrier...	1,248 429D	2,288 1,050D	2,329 897D	2,987 809D	3,522 728D
Hampshire...	639 197D	1,937 1,379D	1,831 1,173D	2,154 1,344D	2,433 1,386D
Hancock.....	708 198R	946 90R	1,028 140R	1,119 200R	1,209 156R
Hardy.......	550 321D	1,024 730D	1,046 640D	1,390 842D	1,597 714D
Harrison....	2,322 574R	3,768 247D	4,118 150D	4,660 234R	4,929 467R
Jackson.....	1,446 34R	2,537 59D	3,097 28R	3,527 118R	4,196 292R
Jefferson....	2,456 486D	2,999 1,047D	3,088 1,007D	3,309 1,212D	3,512 1,225D
Kanawha	2,976 300R	5,458 712D	6,094 266D	7,188 1,420R	8,307 1,452R
Lewis.......	1,216 98R	2,031 365D	2,377 236D	2,849 169D	3,195 115D
Lincoln	470 90D	908 326D	1,106 384D	1,623 46R	2,106 197D
Logan.......	196 98D	744 622D	927 743D	1,184 862D	1,926 1,140D
Marion......	2,380 114R	3,341 175D	3,515 241D	4,008 2R	4,608 23D
Marshall....	2,430 630R	3,470 472D	3,810 590R	4,134 618R	4,604 433R
Mason.......	2,489 265R	3,810 10D	4,066 7R	4,465 398R	5,014 325R
McDowell ...		157 121D	202 192D	389 17D	991 178R
Mercer......	576 316D	899 577D	1,025 425D	1,410 486D	2,789 28R
Mineral.....	894 162R	1,668 274D	1,840 150D	2,111 192D	2,500 478R
Monongalia..	2,337 723R	2,716 436R	3,078 512R	3,312 690R	3,509 847R
Monroe......	950 256D	1,844 634D	1,980 356D	2,178 203D	2,587 116D
Morgan......	588 212R	941 97R	1,049 261R	1,220 302R	1,439 348R
Nicholas	419 53D	605 251D	977 304D	1,271 147D	1,848 257D
Ohio	4,845 89R	7,071 591D	8,116 165D	8,869 125D	9,696 106D
Pendleton...	566 71D	1,154 462D	1,176 344D	1,444 245D	1,792 283D
Pleasants ...		902 121D	1,166 171D	1,217 153D	1,510 110D
Pocahontas..	520 164D	896 388D	845 317D	1,066 278D	1,484 304D
Preston.....	2,434 1,006R	3,407 959R	3,838 1,012R	3,995 1,309R	4,480 1,595R
Putnam......	965 63D	1,731 373D	2,000 377D	2,394 181D	3,049 131R

COUNTY.	1872.	1876.	1880.	1884.	1888.
Raleigh	306 / 28D	839 / 211D	927 / 254D	1,366 / 185D	1,750 / 118D
Randolph	567 / 109D	1,244 / 644D	1,282 / 508D	1,680 / 565D	2,198 / 654D
Ritchie	1,512 / 216R	2,097 / 122R	2,621 / 230R	3,105 / 437R	3,500 / 552R
Roane	902 / 118D	1,607 / 276D	1,835 / 542D	2,487 / 224D	3,091 / 187D
Summers	496 / 84D	1,365 / 373D	1,624 / 232D	1,957 / 187D	2,640 / 81D
Taylor	1,600 / 286R	2,349 / 205R	2,409 / 195R	2,578 / 274R	2,831 / 261R
Tucker	210 / 32D	446 / 186D	533 / 151D	725 / 146D	1,320 / 52D
Tyler	1,251 / 329R	1,804 / 175R	2,174 / 195R	2,454 / 362R	2,714 / 425R
Upshur	1,134 / 536R	1,611 / 447R	1,785 / 400R	1,980 / 585R	2,602 / 873R
Wayne	865 / 271D	1,893 / 831D	1,964 / 633D	2,817 / 744D	3,473 / 640D
Webster	124 / 82D	367 / 281D	305 / 234D	598 / 256D	953 / 363D
Wetzel	1,053 / 159D	2,072 / 778D	2,619 / 834D	3,008 / 889D	3,721 / 910D
Wirt	672 / 28R	1,045 / 164D	1,342 / 235D	1,593 / 152D	1,988 / 133D
Wood	3,152 / 436R	4,632 / 180D	5,087 / 129R	5,441 / 381R	6,254 / 452R
Wyoming	252 / 54R	427 / 51R	456 / 44D	555 / 20D	1,068 / 125R
WISCONSIN.					
Adams	1,118 / 652R	1,428 / 539R	1,387 / 651R	1,470 / 548R	1,549 / 678R
Ashland	129 / 43R	298 / 80D	425 / 23D	1,772 / 412R	5,157 / 635R
Barron	158 / 82R	901 / 387R	1,430 / 633R	2,576 / 908R	2,974 / 915R
Bayfield	131 / 47R	160 / 2R	164 / 8D	675 / 188R	1,940 / 497R
Brown	4,880 / 508R	6,352 / 942D	5,825 / 852D	6,705 / 730D	6,438 / 890D
Buffalo	1,725 / 19D	2,348 / 24R	2,426 / 751R	2,803 / 319R	3,174 / 423R
Burnett	167 / 153R	313 / 257R	426 / 312R	635 / 574R	789 / 421R
Calumet	2,070 / 556D	3,158 / 1,135D	3,245 / 843D	3,284 / 1,182D	3,124 / 1,082D
Chippewa	1,775 / 275R	3,370 / 178D	3,194 / 27D	5,149 / 45R	5,474 / 179R
Clark	920 / 682R	1,855 / 655R	2,251 / 871R	3,860 / 708R	3,723 / 963R
Columbia	4,905 / 1,235R	6,025 / 1,080R	5,919 / 1,261R	6,355 / 840R	6,565 / 859R
Crawford	2,313 / 11R	2,959 / 249D	3,046 / 44D	3,233 / 75D	3,467 / 562D
Dane	9,924 / 360R	11,161 / 291D	11,215 / 1,017R	13,247 / 1,890R	14,341 / 401R
Dodge	8,673 / 2,571D	9,042 / 3,078D	9,499 / 2,085D	9,501 / 3,000D	9,484 / 2,800D
Door	1,687 / 59R	1,691 / 499R	2,158 / 722R	3,050 / 72R	2,763 / 670R
Douglas	168 / 24D	117 / 25D	117 / 33D	525 / 26R	1,983 / 405R
Dunn	1,888 / 892R	2,927 / 1,139R	3,444 / 1,429R	3,874 / 1,334R	3,971 / 1,282R
Eau Claire	2,434 / 798R	4,251 / 681R	4,009 / 816R	4,788 / 673R	6,270 / 791R
Florence				508 / 230R	562 / 94R
Fond du Lac	8,722 / 138D	10,504 / 814D	10,005 / 170D	9,638 / 177D	9,819 / 399D
Forest					460 / 17R
Grant	6,626 / 1,988R	7,521 / 1,525R	7,871 / 1,616R	7,808 / 887R	8,199 / 828R
Green	3,636 / 1,204R	4,335 / 896R	4,550 / 214R	5,609 / 674R	5,414 / 561R
Green Lake	2,596 / 496R	3,252 / 234R	3,439 / 194R	2,925 / 233R	3,247 / 287R
Iowa	4,056 / 100R	4,999 / 303R	5,063 / 364R	5,148 / 167R	5,202 / 227R
Jackson	1,314 / 598R	2,219 / 783R	2,575 / 1,168R	3,145 / 1,095R	3,331 / 1,104R
Jefferson	6,189 / 979D	7,006 / 1,260D	7,063 / 863D	7,363 / 1,313D	7,493 / 1,288D
Juneau	2,489 / 353R	3,182 / 256R	3,309 / 369R	3,873 / 302R	3,926 / 400R
Kenosha	2,628 / 193R	3,045 / 179R	3,086 / 264R	3,232 / 748R	3,408 / 8R

COUNTY.	1872.	1876.	1880.	1884.	1888.
Kewaunee	1,515 / 509D	2,215 / 1,093D	2,362 / 772D	2,761 / 1,260D	2,927 / 1,228D
La Crosse	4,140 / 214R	5,126 / 168R	4,857 / 734R	7,363 / 338R	8,556 / 227R
Lafayette	3,969 / 173R	4,828 / 125R	4,730 / 358R	4,365 / 293R	5,112 / 280R
Langlade				1,238 / 69D	2,062 / 418D
Lincoln		246 / 102D	708 / 108R	2,106 / 88R	2,390 / 106R
Manitowoc	4,966 / 388D	6,608 / 1,308D	6,605 / 689D	6,768 / 1,678D	7,067 / 1,516D
Marathon	1,402 / 420D	2,464 / 1,128D	3,315 / 952D	5,589 / 1,214D	5,833 / 1,243D
Marinette			1,911 / 753R	3,052 / 1,102R	3,893 / 425R
Marquette	1,553 / 267D	1,200 / 417D	1,908 / 79D	2,068 / 138D	2,154 / 114R
Milwaukee	14,346 / 2,675D	22,026 / 2,026D	25,161 / 3,091R	34,363 / 555R	43,529 / 4,092R
Monroe	3,542 / 692R	4,288 / 228R	4,638 / 514R	5,052 / 426R	5,099 / 557R
Oconto	1,473 / 681R	2,987 / 639R	1,866 / 214R	2,582 / 461R	2,507 / 167R
Oneida					1,645 / 97D
Outagamie	3,505 / 435D	5,467 / 1,749D	5,662 / 1,136D	7,075 / 1,525D	7,064 / 1,241D
Ozaukee	2,168 / 1,020D	3,063 / 1,897D	2,946 / 1,257D	2,912 / 1,455D	2,866 / 1,276D
Pepin	936 / 392R	1,230 / 442R	1,340 / 643R	1,389 / 544R	1,562 / 465R
Pierce	2,094 / 826R	3,130 / 1,150R	3,308 / 1,467R	3,792 / 1,358R	4,223 / 1,319R
Polk	848 / 470R	1,391 / 657R	1,893 / 966R	2,515 / 1,711R	2,666 / 1,072R
Portage	2,332 / 7R	3,645 / 61R	3,555 / 418R	4,695 / 65R	5,114 / 281R
Price			336 / 52R	1,125 / 465R	1,634 / 295R
Racine	4,320 / 780R	6,440 / 680R	6,884 / 1,029R	7,848 / 607R	8,092 / 621R
Richland	2,674 / 676R	3,629 / 447R	4,045 / 625R	4,498 / 674R	4,520 / 727R
Rock	6,873 / 3,398R	8,521 / 2,803R	8,550 / 3,395R	10,447 / 2,818R	10,217 / 2,734R
St. Croix	2,563 / 183R	3,511 / 678R	4,141 / 263R	4,851 / 762R	6,628 / 629R
Sauk	4,056 / 1,348R	5,596 / 1,194R	5,888 / 1,551R	6,253 / 1,576R	1,054 / 81R
Sawyer				412 / 189R	3,465 / 139R
Shawano	880 / 48D	1,455 / 291D	1,940 / 36D	2,926 / 6D	8,571 / 591D
Sheboygan	5,633 / 261D	6,358 / 470D	6,787 / 292R	7,792 / 475D	5,467 / 629R
Taylor			485 / 5D	574 / 26R	1,394 / 185R	1,526 / 78R
Trempealeau	1,274 / 1,040R	3,150 / 1,570R	3,317 / 1,627R	3,502 / 881R	4,068 / 690R
Vernon	2,987 / 1,903R	3,880 / 1,646R	4,313 / 1,760R	4,866 / 134R	5,169 / 1,776R
Walworth	5,011 / 2,013R	6,182 / 2,242R	6,386 / 2,475R	6,806 / 2,208R	7,157 / 2,445R
Washburn				465 / 144R	983 / 151R
Washington	3,674 / 1,780D	4,368 / 1,726D	4,798 / 332D	4,595 / 1,380D	4,753 / 1,008D
Waukesha	5,391 / 49D	6,464 / 206D	6,312 / 251R	6,899 / 57D	7,625 / 382R
Waupaca	2,995 / 1,105R	4,234 / 1,050R	4,368 / 1,207R	5,049 / 1,270R	5,374 / 1,616R
Waushara	2,097 / 1,319R	2,628 / 1,582R	2,763 / 1,668R	2,872 / 1,541R	3,100 / 1,582R
Winnebago	7,249 / 1,311R	3,518 / 666R	5,078 / 980R	10,258 / 205R	10,633 / 327R
Wood	1,080 / 90R	1,404 / 150R	2,098 / 150R	3,258 / 244D	4,002 / 80D

Summary.—The increase in the popular vote since 1872 is 4,921,873. The total vote cast in 1872 was 6,466,165; in 1888, 11,388,038. The increase in the electoral vote since 1872 is 35. Electoral vote in 1872, 366; in 1888, 401. The Republican party carried the States by a majority of .25 States in 1872, 4 States in 1876, a tie (of 19 States each), with majority of popular vote, in 1880, and 2 States in 1888. The Democratic party carried the States by a majority of

2 States in 1884. The Republican party obtained a plurality of the popular vote as follows: 1872, 762,991; 1880, 7,018. The Democratic party obtained a plurality of the popular vote as follows: 1876, 250,935; 1884, 62,683; 1888, 100,476.

One new State (Colorado) has been admitted to the Union since 1872; 91 counties voted for the first time in 1876; 65 counties voted for the first time in 1880; 47 counties voted for the first time in 1884; 69 counties voted for the first time in 1888; 230 counties "changed sides" in 1888, placing a Republican plurality on record, against a Democratic plurality in 1884, or *vice versa*.

Alabama.—There has been an increase of 4,384 in the popular vote since 1872; the total vote in that year being 169,716, and, in 1888, 174,100. In the interval there was a falling off of nearly 20,000, the vote in 1880 being only 151,507, and 153,489 in 1884. The Republican party carried the State by a plurality of 10,828 in 1872. Since that time the record shows Democratic pluralities—1876, 33,772; 1880, 34,509; 1884, 33,829; 1888, 61,123. Three new counties have been formed, according to the returns, since 1872. There is no record of Baker County after 1872, nor of Sanford County after 1876. Five counties changed sides in 1888.

Arkansas.—The increase in the popular vote since 1872 is 76,668. Total vote in 1872, 79,300; in 1888, 155,968. The Republican party carried the State by a plurality of 3,446 in 1872. Since that time the record shows Democratic pluralities—1876, 19,113; 1880, 18,828; 1884, 22,032; 1888, 27,210. Eighteen new counties have been formed since 1872. Eight counties changed sides in 1888.

California.—The increase in the popular vote since 1872 is 155,533. Total vote cast in 1872, 95,806; in 1888, 251,339. The Republican party carried the State in every election except that of 1880, when the Democratic nominee received a plurality of 78. Eleven new counties have been formed since 1872. Seven counties changed sides in 1888.

Colorado.—The increase in the popular vote since 1880 is 38,266. Total vote in 1880, 53,532; in 1888, 91,798. The Republican party carried the State at every election—in 1880, plurality 2,803; 1884, 8,563; 1888, 13,207. Eleven new counties have been formed since 1880. Three counties changed sides in 1888.

Connecticut.—The increase in the popular vote since 1872 is 57,050. Total vote in 1872, 96,928; in 1888, 153,978. The Republican party carried the State by a plurality of 4,348 in 1872, and 2,656 in 1880; the Democratic party by a plurality of 1,712 in 1876; 1,284 in 1884, and 336 in 1888. Two counties changed sides in 1888.

Delaware.—The increase in the popular vote since 1872 is 7,979. Total vote in 1872, 21,808; in 1888, 29,787. The Republican party carried the State by a plurality of 422 in 1872. Since that time the Democratic pluralities have been—1876, 2,629; 1880, 1,033; 1884, 3,923; 1888, 3,441. One county changed sides in 1888.

Florida.—The increase in the popular vote since 1872 is 33,451. Total vote in 1872, 33,190; in 1888, 66,641. The Republican party carried the State by a plurality of 2,336 in 1872, and 926 in 1876. Since that time the Democratic pluralities have been—1880, 4,310; 1884, 3,738; 1888,12,904. Six new counties have been formed since 1872. Eight counties changed sides in 1888.

Georgia.—A notable increase in the popular vote has been recorded twice since 1872, i. e., in 1876, when the total vote was 180,534 (increase over that of 1872, 37,628), and in 1880, when the total was 155,651 (increase over that of 1872, 12,745). The record for 1884 gives 143,543 (decrease since 1880, 12,108), and the figures given for 1888 show 142,939 (decrease since 1884, 604). The Democratic party carried the State at every election, the plurality being—in 1872, 9,806; 1876, 79,642; 1880, 49,874; 1884, 46,961; 1888, 60,003. One new county has been formed since 1872. Six counties changed sides in 1888.

Illinois.—The increase in the popular vote since 1872 is 317,746. Total vote in 1872, 429,940; in 1888, 747,686. The Republican party carried the State at every election, the pluralities being—in 1872, 53,948; 1876, 1,971; 1880, 40,716; 1884, 24,827; 1888, 22,195. Eight counties changed sides in 1888.

Indiana.—The increase in the popular vote since 1872 is 185,753. Total vote in 1872, 351,196; in 1888, 536,949. The Republican party carried the State by a plurality of 21,098 in 1872; 6,636 in 1880; and 2,348 in 1888. The Democratic party had a plurality of 5,505 in 1876, and 6,512 in 1884. One new county has been formed since 1872. Thirteen counties changed sides in 1888.

Iowa.—The increase in the popular vote since 1872 is 199,157. Total vote in 1872, 204,983; in 1888, 404,140. The Republican party carried the State at every election, the pluralities being—in 1872, 58,149; 1876, 50,191; 1880, 78,059; 1884, 19,773; 1888, 31,711. Eight counties changed sides in 1888.

Kansas.—The increase in the popular vote since 1872 is 230,558. Total vote in 1872, 100,614; in 1888, 331,172. The Republican party carried the State at every election, the pluralities being—in 1872, 33,482; 1876, 32,511; 1880, 61,731; 1884, 64,274; 1888, 79,190. Forty-four counties have been formed since 1872. One county changed sides in 1888.

Kentucky.—The increase in the popular vote since 1872 is 153,646. Total vote in 1872, 191,135; in 1888, 344,781. The Democratic party carried the State at every election, the pluralities being—in 1872, 8,855; 1876, 59,772; 1880, 43,449; 1884, 34,839; 1888, 26,666. Three new counties have been formed since 1872. Sixteen counties changed sides in 1888. There is no record of a vote in Josh Bell County in 1888.

Louisiana.—An increase of importance in the popular vote has only been recorded once since 1872, i. e., in 1876, when the record showed 145,643 (increase over that of 1872, 16,951). The vote of 1880 was 97,201 (decrease from that of 1876, 48,442), and that of 1884 was 109,234. The vote of 1888 was 115,744, an increase of 6,510 over that of 1884, but a decrease of 12,948 as compared with 1872. The Republican party carried the State by a plurality of 14,634 in 1872, and 4,627 in 1876. Since that time the Democratic pluralities have been—in 1880, 27,316; 1884, 16,199; 1888, 54,548. Eight counties have been formed since 1872. Twelve counties changed sides in 1888.

Maine.—The increase in the popular vote since 1872 is 37,741. Total vote in 1872, 90,509; in 1888, 128,250. The Republican party carried the State at every election, the pluralities being—in 1872, 32,335; 1876, 15,814; 1880, 8,868; 1884, 20,060; 1888, 23,253. Every county has recorded a Republican plurality since 1872.

Maryland.—The increase in the popular vote since 1872 is 76,455. Total vote in 1872, 134,466; in 1888, 210,921. The Democratic party carried the State at every election, the pluralities being—in 1872, 908; 1876, 19,756; 1880, 15,191; 1884, 11,118; 1888, 6,182. One new county has been formed since 1872. Three counties changed sides in 1888.

Massachusetts.—The increase in the popular vote since 1872 is 151,716. Total vote in 1872, 192,732; in 1888, 344,448. The Republican party carried the State at every election, the pluralities being—in 1872, 74,-212; 1876, 40,423; 1880, 53,215; 1884, 24,372; 1888, 32,037. With one exception (Suffolk County, 1876-'88), every county has recorded a Republican plurality since 1872.

Michigan.—The increase in the popular vote since 1872 is 254,371. Total vote in 1872, 220,942; in 1888, 475,313. The Republican party carried the State at every election, the pluralities being—in 1872, 55,968; 1876, 15,542; 1880, 53,890; 1884, 3,308; 1888, 22,911. Fourteen counties have been formed since 1872. Nineteen counties changed sides in 1888.

Minnesota.—The increase in the popular vote since 1872 is 173,766. Total vote in 1872, 89,540; in 1888, 263,306. The Republican party carried the State at every election, the pluralities being—in 1872, 20,694; 1876, 21,780; 1880, 40,588; 1884, 41,620; 1888, 33,-106. Seventeen new counties have been formed in Minnesota since 1872. Three counties changed sides in 1888.

Mississippi.—The decrease in the popular vote since 1872 is 13,656. There was a conspicuous increase in 1876, when the total vote was 164,778 (increase over 1872, 35,315). The vote in 1880 (117,078) and in 1884 (120,019), compared with that of 1888 (115,807), shows a considerable decrease. The Republican party carried the State by a plurality of 34,837 in 1872. Since that time the Democratic pluralities have been—in 1876, 59,568; 1880, 40,896; 1884, 33,001; 1888, 55,375. Five new counties have been formed since 1872. Five counties changed sides in 1888.

Missouri.—The increase in the popular vote since 1872 is 250,148. Total vote in 1872, 273,050; in 1888, 523,198. The Democratic party carried the State at every election, the pluralities being—in 1872, 29,809; 1876, 54,389; 1880, 55,042; 1884, 33,059; 1888, 25,717. Four new counties have been formed since 1872. Ten counties changed sides in 1888.

Nebraska.—The increase in the popular vote since 1872 is 176,481. Total vote in 1872, 26,141; in 1888, 202,622. The Republican party carried the State at every election, the pluralities being—in 1872, 10,517; 1876, 10,326; 1880, 26,458; 1884, 22,512; 1888, 27,873. Thirty-two counties changed sides in 1888. Six counties changed sides in 1888.

Nevada.—The decrease in the popular vote since 1872 is 2,017. Total vote in 1872, 14,649. There was an increase in 1876, when the total vote was 19,691; but the total fell to 18,343 in 1880, again, to 12,797 in 1884, and again to 12,632 in 1888. The Republican party carried the State at every election except that of 1880, its pluralities being—in 1872, 2,177; 1876, 1,075; 1884, 1,615; 1888, 1,867. The Democratic plurality was 879 in 1880. One county has been formed since 1872. One county changed sides in 1888.

New Hampshire.—The increase in the popular vote since 1872 is 21,941. Total vote in 1872, 68,892; in 1888, 90,833. The Republican party carried the State at every election, the pluralities being—in 1872, 5,444; 1876, 2,954; 1880, 4,058; 1884, 4,063; 1888, 2,272. Three counties changed sides in 1888.

New Jersey.—The increase in the popular vote since 1872 is 134,999. Total vote in 1872, 148,742; in 1888, 303,741. The Republican party carried the State by a plurality of 14,570 in 1872. Since that time the Democratic pluralities have been—in 1876, 11,690; 1880, 2,010; 1884, 4,412; 1888, 7,149.

New York.—The increase in the popular vote since 1872 is 490,437. Total vote in 1872, 829,672; in 1888, 1,320,109. The Republican party carried the State by a plurality of 51,800 in 1872, 21,033 in 1880, and 13,-002 in 1888. The Democratic party carried the State by a plurality of 26,568 in 1876, and 1,047 in 1884. Seven counties changed sides in 1888.

North Carolina.—The increase in the popular vote since 1872 is 120,610. Total vote in 1872, 164,863; in 1888, 285,473. The Republican party carried the State by a plurality of 24,675 in 1872. Since that time the Democratic pluralities have been—in 1876, 17,010; 1880, 8,326; 1884, 17,884; 1888, 13,118. Four new counties have been formed since 1872. Sixteen counties changed sides in 1888.

Ohio.—The increase in the popular vote since 1872 is 312,505. Total vote in 1872, 529,436; in 1888, 841,941. The Republican party carried the State at every election, the pluralities being—in 1872, 34,268; 1876, 2,747; 1880, 34,227.; 1884, 31,796; 1888, 19,599. Four counties changed sides in 1888.

Oregon.—The increase in the popular vote since 1872 is 41,790. Total vote in 1872, 20,121; in 1888, 61,911. The Republican party carried the State at every election, the pluralities being—in 1872, 3,517; 1876, 547; 1880, 671; 1884, 2,256; 1888, 6,769. Seven new counties have been formed since 1872. Four counties changed sides in 1888.

Pennsylvania.—The increase in the popular vote since 1872 is 434,308. Total vote in 1872, 563,260; in 1888, 997,568. The Republican party carried the State at every election, the pluralities being—in 1872, 135,913; 1876, 17,964; 1880, 37,276; 1884, 81,019; 1888, 79,452. One new county has been formed since 1872. Seven counties changed sides in 1888.

Rhode Island.—The increase in the popular vote since 1872 is 21,772. Total vote in 1872, 18,994; in 1888, 40,766. The Republican party carried the State at every election, the pluralities being—in 1872, 8,336; 1876, 5,075; 1880, 7,410.; 1884, 6,489; 1888, 4,438.

South Carolina.—The decrease in the popular vote since 1872 is 15,619. In 1876 the total vote was 182,-776 (increase over that of 1872, 87,596). This total was reduced to 91,578 in 1884, and a great falling off was again apparent in 1888, the total for that year being only 79,561 (decrease, compared with the vote of 1884, 12,017). The Republican party carried the State by a plurality of 49,400 in 1872, and 964 in 1876. Since that time, the Democratic pluralities have been—in 1880, 54,241; 1884, 48,031; 1888, 52,089. Two new counties have been formed since 1872. Two counties changed sides in 1888.

Tennessee.—The increase in the popular vote since 1872 is 123,690. Total vote in 1872, 180,046; in 1888, 303,736. The Democratic party carried the State at every election, the pluralities being—in 1872, 8,736; 1876, 43,600; 1880, 20,514; 1884, 9,180; 1888, 19,791. Four new counties have been formed since 1872. Four counties changed sides in 1888.

Texas.—The increase in the popular vote since 1872 is 241,108. Total vote in 1872, 116,405; in 1888, 357,513. The Democratic party carried the State at every election, the pluralities being—in 1872, 16,595; 1876, 59,955; 1880, 98,383; 1884, 131,978; 1888, 146,-461. Thirty-three counties have been formed since 1872. Nine counties changed sides in 1888.

Vermont.—The increase in the popular vote since 1872 is 10,439. Total vote in 1872, 53,001; in 1888, 63,440. The Republican party carried the State at every election, the pluralities being—in 1872, 29,961; 1876, 23,838; 1880, 26,909; 1884, 22,183; 1888, 28,404.

Virginia.—The increase in the popular vote since 1872 is 118,929. Total vote in 1872, 185,164; in 1888, 304,093. The Republican party carried the State by a plurality of 1,772 in 1872. Since that time the Democratic pluralities have been—in 1876, 44,112; 1880, 43,956; 1884, 6,141; 1888, 1,539. Six new counties have been formed since 1872. Fifteen counties changed sides in 1888.

West Virginia.—The increase in the popular vote since 1872 is 96,822. Total vote in 1872, 82,366; in 1888, 159,188. The Republican party carried the State by a plurality of 2,264 in 1872. Since that time the Democratic pluralities have been—in 1876, 12,384; 1880, 11,148; 1884, 4,221; 1888, 1,873. Two new counties have been formed since 1872. Seven counties changed sides in 1888.

Wisconsin.—The increase in the popular vote since 1872 is 162,306. Total vote in 1872, 192,308; in 1888, 354,614. The Republican party carried the State at every election, the pluralities being—in 1872, 17,686; 1876, 5,205; 1880, 29,763; 1884, 14,698; 1888, 21,321. Ten counties have been formed since 1872. Seven counties changed sides in 1888.

UNIVERSALISTS. The "Universalist Register" for 1889 gives statistics of this denomination of which the following is a summary: Number of parishes, 971; of families, 41,474; of preachers, 711; of churches, 721; of members, 38,780; of Sunday-schools, 657, with 53,-205 members; of church edifices, 816; value of church property, $7,915,756. The figures show an apparent loss from the previous year of 17 parishes, 9 church organizations, and 1,431 members of Sunday-schools. The loss is partly accounted for by the dropping from the roll, by order of one of the State conventions, of 28 parishes which had long been inactive. Gains appear of 2,136 families, 973 communicants, 20 church edifices, and $324,206 in valuation of church property. The twelve schools—four colleges and universities, three theological schools and departments, and five academical institutions—returned 114 teachers and professors, 1,284 students, and $2,716,500 of property. The Universalist Publishing-House reports net assets of about $70,000, and publishes and owns the copyrights of 150 volumes and six periodicals.

The funds of the General Convention, as reported upon at its meeting in October, 1888, amount in all to $193,559, distributed as follows: Murray Centenary fund (in aid of theological students, the distribution of Universalist literature, Church extension, and missions), $129,549; Theological Scholarship fund (for loans to theological students), $29,925; Church Extension fund, $4,149; Gunn Ministerial Relief fund, $11,213; Ada Tibbetts Memorial fund (valuable property over and above the liens), $9,500; three other special funds, $13,223. The aggregate increase of these funds during the convention year 1887–'88 was $15,833.

The Chapin Home, New York, has an endowment of $145,000, and returns 56 inmates.

The Woman's Centenary Association reported to the General Convention that its receipts for the year had been $3,147, and its expenditures $2,240; and that it had a permanent fund of $7,647.

The Universalist General Convention met in Chicago, Ill., October 24. The Hon. Hosea Parker presided. The resolution adopted by the General Convention of 1887 providing for holding the meetings of the body biennially instead of annually, was ratified as required by the provisions of the Constitution, to become operative from and after 1889. In connection with this action a proposition was considered for authorizing the trustees to call a Universalist Church Conference to be held in the years intervening between the sessions of the General Convention, for the discussion of questions relating to religion, morals, and education. The discussion of the creed which was proposed for adoption at the General Convention held in New York in 1887 was continued, and the subject was referred to a new committee which is expected to report upon it at a subsequent session of the General Convention. The publishers of the Sunday-school-lesson papers were requested to furnish, in connection with the ordinary papers, a serial exposition of the leading features of Christian doctrine as held by the Universalist Church. A resolution providing for calling an International Conference of Sunday-school workers was referred to a committee to report upon at the next meeting of the General Convention.

URUGUAY, a republic in South America. Area, 69,835 square miles. In 1886 the population was 596,463; that of the city of Montevideo was 115,462 in 1885.

Government.—The President is Gen. Máximo Tajes. The Cabinet is composed of the following ministers: Prime Minister and Interior, Dr. Herrera y Obes; Foreign Affairs, Dr. J. García Lagos; Finance, Dr. N. M. Marquez; Justice, Public Worship, and Instruction, Dr. M. Berinduague; War and Navy, Col. P. de Leon. The American Consul at Montevideo is Edward J. Hill. The Uruguayan Consul-General at New York is Don Enrique Estrázulas.

Army and Navy.—The standing army was increased in 1887 to about 4,000 men. There is also a police force of 3,200 men, and a National Guard of 20,000. The navy is composed of five small steamers and three gun-boats.

Finances.—On Dec. 1, 1887, the national indebtedness amounted to $71,000,000, of which $17,000,000 constituted the home debt and $54,000,000 the foreign debt, the latter being represented by £10,865,300 five-per-cent. bonds and £4,255,360 six-per-cent. bonds. The conversion of the latter amount into four-per-cent. bonds was effected by issuing in London $20,-000,000 at 82½ per cent., in August, 1888.

South American Congress.—On July 18, 1888, at the invitation of the Argentine Republic and Uruguay, a congress of delegates from South American nations assembled at Montevideo for the purpose of forming a treaty to determine questions of international rights pending between South American nations. This congress is the first of its kind that ever assembled in South America.

Railroads.—On July 1, 1888, there were 553 kilometres of railway in operation. Early in 1888 a Government decree announced the intention of building a railway embracing the following lines: 1. From Montevideo to Rivera, with branch lines to Paysandú and Salto. 2. From Montevideo to Colonia. 3. From Agosto to Carmelo and Nueva Palmira. 4. From Montevideo to the northern frontier and Bazé. 5. From Montevideo eastward to Laguna and Merino. 6. From Salto to Santa Rosa, with a branch line from Peballo to San Eugenio. The Government offers to guarantee seven per cent. interest for forty years on a capital of £5,000 per kilometre.

In October the Central Uruguayan Extension Railway Company (limited) was formed, with a capital of £1,000,000, to build a line of railway from Paso de los Toros to Rivera (Santa Una) on the Brazilian frontier, 288 kilometres, the Government guaranteeing seven per cent. interest for forty years on a capital of £5,000 per kilometre.

Telegraphs.—The length of lines in operation in 1888 was 2,789 kilometres. The first submarine cable for telephone use was laid between Montevideo and Buenos Ayres in the autumn, and it does better service than the overland lines.

Commerce.—Uruguayan foreign commerce has developed as follows, reduced to millions of dollars:

	Imports.	Exports.
1883	20.3	25.2
1884	24.6	24.3
1885	25.3	25.3
1886	20.2	23.8

The following Uruguayan products were exports: Cattle, $800,000; jerked beef, $2,858,-000; preserved beef in tins, $37,000; extract of beef, $894,000; hides, $4,842,000; skins, $816,000; tallow, $1,237,000; wool, $4,998,-000; horse-hair, $185,000; bones and bone-ashes, $110,000; fertilizers, $316,000; ostrich-feathers, $54,000; grain, $712,000.

The American trade exhibits the following figures:

FISCAL YEAR.	Imports into the United States.	Domestic export to Uruguay.
1886	$4,925,848	$1,110,545
1887	2,818,761	1,393,725
1888	2,711,521	1,837,430

Tariff Changes.—The revised customs-tariff became operative on April 1, 1888, the modifications being slight, ad valorem duties being raised from 30½ per cent. to 31 per cent.; goods under schedule No. 2, from 47 per cent. to 48 per cent.; and No. 3, from 43 to 44. On the other hand, the 6½ per mille was abolished, and the number of articles entering duty free notably increased.

Viticulture.—Under the provision of an act of the Uruguayan Congress of 1889, gold medals were awarded to Pascal Harriague, a Frenchman, and F. Vidiella, a Uruguayan, as the first and most successful viticulturists in the republic. The growing of vines has been extending rapidly during late years in Uruguay, and is giving the best results. The Viticultural Society, founded in 1887, with a capital of $100,000, has acquired lands along the Central Railway; vineyards have been laid out, and 100,000 vines were planted in 1888.

Earthquake.—During the night of July 4–5, 1888, there were, for the first time in forty years, two violent shocks of earthquake at Montevideo, the direction being from northwest to southeast, the shocks extending over fifty seconds. The shocks were felt at sea, the phenomenon coinciding with great cold and a terrific snow-storm in the Cordillera, at Uzpalata, and at Bahia Blanca in the province of Buenos Ayres, Argentine Republic, 39° south latitude, where for the first time a heavy snow-storm occurred.

UTAH. Territorial Government.—The following were the Territorial officers during the year: Governor, Caleb W. West; Secretary, William C. Hall; Treasurer *de facto*, James Jack; Auditor *de facto*, Nephi W. Clayton. (In January the Governor sent to the Council of the Legislature the nomination of Bolivar Roberts to be Territorial Treasurer, and Arthur Pratt to be Territorial Auditor; but that body refused confirmation, on the ground that the Governor's right of appointment was in dispute in a case pending before the United States Supreme Court. Late in March, after the adjournment of the Legislature, the Governor again made the same nominations, he then having full power of appointment till the next meeting of the Legislature in 1890. The Governor had previously, in March, 1886, appointed the same persons to the same positions; but Treasurer Jack and Auditor Clayton, holding by election of the people, had refused to yield up their offices, and the litigation, which has not yet reached its end in the Supreme Court of the United States, resulted. The appointees of March, 1888, were again refused their offices by the *de facto* officials as before. About the same time they brought suit against the latter, demanding payment of salary from March, 1886, out of the appropriation made by the Legislature in January for the salaries of the Treasurer and Auditor. The determination of this suit will depend upon the decision of the United States Supreme Court case.) Commissioner of Schools, P. L. Williams; Chief-Justice of the Supreme Court, Charles S. Zane, succeeded by Elliott Sandford; Associate Justices, Jacob S. Boreman, and H. P. Henderson. During the year the Territory was allowed, by act of Congress, an additional judge, and John W. Judd was appointed to that position.

Legislative Session.—The Twenty-eighth Territorial Legislature assembled on January 9, and remained in session two months. One of the earliest measures passed was a deficiency appropriation bill, to meet expenses of the Government, for several years unpaid, owing to the veto of appropriation bills passed by the previous Legislature. Several new institutions were provided for—a Territorial Reform School in Weber County at a cost of $75,000, an Agricultural College, and an agricultural experiment station in connection therewith, in Cache County, to cost $25,000, and an Institution for Deaf-Mutes, in connection with the University of Deseret, to cost $20,000. The sum of $85,451 was appropriated for the completion of buildings at the University of Deseret and to pay debts of the institution previously incurred. For the purpose of meeting these extraordinary expenditures a board of commissioners was established and directed to negotiate a loan not exceeding $150,000. The bonds for this loan were all taken by a Denver bank at a small premium.

A gift of land from Salt Lake City as a site for Capitol buildings was accepted at this session, and a commission appointed to submit to the next Legislature plans and estimates for a new Capitol building.

The general election for members of the Legislature was fixed in August, 1889, and biennially thereafter, the first meeting of the

Legislature to be on the second Monday of the following January.

An act to prevent crimes against the elective franchise provides penalties for fraudulent registration, fraudulent voting or attempts to vote, tampering with ballot-boxes, forgery or alteration of election returns, or other means used to defeat the purpose of the voter.

Other acts of the session were as follow :

Providing for a compilation of the laws of the Territory.

Raising the age of consent to thirteen years.

Providing that a married woman may join in a deed by her husband, and release her right of dower in the property therein conveyed or encumbered.

Designating May 31 as the time at which new laws shall go into effect, unless otherwise provided in such laws.

Exempting from taxation for six years the property, capital stock, and bonds or mortgages of any company in the Territory engaged in the production and manufacture of sugar from products raised in the Territory.

To prevent the sale or giving away of intoxicating beverages on election-days.

Regulating the business of life insurance.

Regulating marriage in the Territory, prohibiting, among other things, marriage between a negro and a white person, or between a Mongolian and a white person.

Providing that occupying claimants shall not be evicted by process of law till they have been paid the full value of improvements made by them, or unless they refuse to pay upon demand to the successful claimant the full value of his share or claim in the property.

Establishing a uniform system of county governments.

Accepting from Salt Lake City a gift of lands for Agricultural Fair Grounds, and appropriating $20,000 for the erection of suitable fair buildings.

Railroads.—The railroad system of the Territory at the beginning of the year was as follows: Union Pacific Railroad and branches, 581 miles; Denver and Rio Grande Western and branches, 368 miles; Central Pacific, 154 miles; and San Pete Valley, 34 miles; total, 1,140 miles. Two new roads were in course of construction during the year—the Salt Lake and Fort Douglas and the Salt Lake and Eastern. The former of these, 24 miles in length, was practically completed at the end of the year; on the latter, construction was not far advanced.

Agriculture.—The wheat-crop of the Territory for 1888 is estimated at 3,000,000 bushels; oats, 1,500,000 bushels; barley, 750,000 bushels; rye, 50,000 bushels; corn, 750,000 bushels. There were also produced about 200,000 bushels of apples, 150,000 bushels of peaches, and 75,000 bushels of pears. The hay-crop is estimated at 500,000 tons.

Mining.—Mining for the precious metals began about twenty-five years ago, but was carried on only in a small way until after the completion of the first Pacific Railroad. This gave a market, and from 1871 to 1887, both inclusive, the value of the output was as follows: Gold, $3,065,692.72; silver, $73,201,-966.51; lead, $33,799,599.17; copper, $3,003,-889.21; total, $113,071,147.61. The product

for 1887 is summarized as follows: Copper, $124,566; refined lead, $111,750; unrefined lead, $1,196,788.77; fine silver, $5,976,884.89; fine gold, $227,740; total export value, $7,637,-729.66.

Prison.—The report of the United States Penitentiary at Salt Lake City, for the year ending June 30, is as follows: Number in prison July 1, 1887, 197; number received from July 1, 1887, to June 30, 1888, 299; total number in prison during the year, 496; number discharged from July 1, 1887, to June 30, 1888, 315; number remaining in prison July 1, 1888, 181. The Forty-eighth Congress appropriated $50,000 for the construction of a new prison building, which was completed early in the year, and will accommodate 240 prisoners, by placing two in a cell.

Confiscation of Church Property.—In the suits begun in 1887, under the provisions of the Edmunds-Tucker act, to secure the forfeiture of the property held by the Mormon Church corporation and by the Perpetual Emigrating Fund Company, in which suits a receiver had been appointed to collect and take possession of such property pending the suit, an appeal from the order of the court making such appointment was prayed for by the defendants late in that year, but refused by the Territorial Supreme Court in January, on the ground that the order was merely interlocutory and not final. The receiver during the year instituted numerous investigations and heard witnesses with the view of ascertaining property of the Church and company, took possession of such personal and real property as he could find, and began suits for the rest. The real estate received by him during the year included the Temple Block in Salt Lake City, the Gardo House and grounds, the Tithing-Office and grounds, the Historian's Office and grounds, the Church farm of 1,108 acres, and one undivided half of the Church coal-mines in Summit County. For the escheat and forfeiture of this property, except the Temple Block, a proceeding was begun during the year by information in the Third District Court of the Territory. Before October the receiver had also secured possession of money of the defendants, amounting to $237,666.15; about 30,000 head of sheep, 4,732 shares of the Deseret Telegraph Company, 300 shares of the Salt Lake City Gas Company, and a few other securities. As to this personalty, and on the legal standing of the defendants generally since the Edmunds-Tucker act, the Supreme Court of the Territory rendered a final decree on October 9, a part of which is as follows:

That on the 3d day of March, 1887, the corporation of the Church of Jesus Christ of Latter-Day Saints became and the same was dissolved; and that since said date it has had no legal corporate existence. And it is furthermore adjudged that all and entire the personal property set out in this decree as having belonged to said corporation has, by reason of the dissolution of said corporation as aforesaid, on account of the failure or illegality of the trusts to which it was dedicated at its acquisition, and for which it has been used by said late corporation and by operation of law, become escheated to and the property of the United States of America, subject to the costs and expenses of this proceeding, and of the receivership by this court instituted and ordered. It is furthermore ordered and adjudged that there is not now, and has not been, since the 3d day of March, 1887, any person legally authorized to take charge of, manage, preserve, and control the personal and real property hereinbefore set out, except the receiver appointed by this court; and it is therefore ordered that the receivership hereinbefore established by this court is continued in full force and effect, and that the said receiver shall continue to exercise all and entire the powers and authority conferred upon him by the decree appointing him.

The Temple Block was excepted from this decree, and the receiver was ordered to surrender possession of it to trustees already appointed for the use of the Mormon Church as a house of worship. An appeal from this decree was taken to the United States Supreme Court, the principal ground therefor being the constitutionality of the act under which the decision was rendered. No decree had been made at the close of the year by the District Court as to the escheat of the other realty.

. **Political.**—Late in September a call was issued by the Utah Democratic Club for a meeting of representatives at Salt Lake City, on October 6, to form an independent Democratic Territorial organization, the object being to include in the organization all anti-Mormon Democrats of the Territory. This convention accomplished the object for which it was called, and nominated S. R. Thurman as its candidate for delegate to Congress. The People's party (Mormon) held its Territorial Convention at Salt Lake City on October 8, and renominated Delegate John T. Caine. The Republicans, Labor men, and other opponents of Mormonism, joined in supporting Mr. Baskin for delegate. At the November election Caine received 10,127 votes, Baskin 3,484, and Thurman 511.

V

VENEZUELA, a republic in South America. Area, 1,539,398 square kilometres; population in 1886, 2,198,320.

Government.—The President, elected on July 5, 1888, is Don Pablo Rojas Paúl. His term will expire on Feb. 20, 1890. The Vice-President is Dr. S. Pacheco. The Cabinet was formed of the following ministers: Interior, Dr. Nicanor Borges; Treasury, Don Vicente Coronado; Public Credit, Don Bermudes Grau; Public Instruction, Don Santiago Gonzalez Guinan; Public Improvements, Don Nicolas Gil; Public Works, Señor Muñoz Lebar; and Foreign Affairs, Don Agustin Toturiz. The United States Minister Resident at Carácas is Charles L. Scott; the American Consul at Ciudad Bolivar is George F. Underhill. The Venezuelan *chargé d'affaires* at Washington is Don Francisco Antonio Silva. The Consul-General at New York is Dr. Pedro Vicente Mijares.

Finances.—By virtue of a convention concluded on Nov. 24, 1888, between the financial agent of the republic in Europe and the council of foreign bondholders, the debt of the republic was consolidated, making £3,753,420, for which amount 4-per-cent. bonds were issued, bearing interest from Jan. 1, 1889. Part of the customs receipts is to be regularly set aside in pledge for payment of both the principal and the interest. Aside from this conversion, the Government floated an additional loan for £457,000, to which a similar pledge of duties for payment attaches.

Army and Navy.—The effective strength of the permanent army is 2,000 men. The navy is composed of 3 steamers, 1 schooner, and 1 school-ship.

Postal Service.—There are 162 post-offices, which forwarded 2,734,576 items of mail-matter during the fiscal year 1885-'86.

Railroads.—There were in operation, on Jan. 1, 1888, 286 kilometres of railway; in course of construction, 353; authorized, 1,982. Since that time several other lines have been chartered. The railway between Puerto Cabello and Valencia was opened in February, 1888.

Telegraphs.—The length of telegraph lines in Venezuela is 4,462 kilometres, with 80 offices. Communication was opened in 1888 between Carácas, La Guayra, and Colombia, and simultaneously by cable with Hayti.

Steamship Line.—In May, 1888, a new line of steamers was established, the Royal Dutch West Indian Mail Steamship Company, whose steamers ply between New York, Port-au-Prince, Curaçoa, Puerto Cabello, La Guayra, Trinidad, Demerara, and other West Indian ports. Three steamers were placed on the line to begin with.

Commerce.—Venezuela imported in 1887 from England $2,194,237 worth of merchandise; from France, $678,441; from Spain, $148,267. She exported to those countries in the same year goods to the amount of $705,044, $3,500,421, and $707,016, respectively. The American trade was as follows:

FISCAL YEAR.	Import into the United States.	Domestic export to Venezuela.
1886	$5,791,621	$2,695,488
1887	8,261,236	2,827,010
1888	10,051,250	3,008,836

The Anglo-Venezuelan Imbroglio.—Early in 1888 there was excitement once more about the frontier dispute between Venezuela and British

Guiana, and the United States was appealed to not to allow Great Britain and her colony to retain Barimas Point, together with the disputed territory in the gold-mines. The Venezuelans insisted that the Monroe doctrine was opposed to such encroachments. The matter was rather coolly received in the United States, both in and out of Congress, in view of the long-pending claim against Venezuela for the seizure of the Venezuelan Steam Transportation Company's steamers in 1871, when there chanced to be a revolution in that country. Meanwhile this dispute about the Guiana border remains in abeyance, England declining to submit to international arbitration.

VERMONT. State Government.—The following were the State officers during the year: Governor, Ebenezer J. Ormsbee (Republican), succeeded by William P. Dillingham (Republican); Lieutenant-Governor, Levi K. Fuller, succeeded by Urban A. Woodbury; Secretary of State, Charles W. Porter; Treasurer, William H. Dubois; Auditor, E. Henry Powell; Superintendent of Education, Justus Dartt; Inspector of Finance, Savings-Banks, and Trust Companies, Carroll S. Page, succeeded by L. O. Greene; Chief Judge of the Supreme Court, Homer E. Royce; Assistant Judges, Jonathan Ross, Wheelock G. Veazey, H. Henry Powers, John W. Rowell, Russell S. Taft, and James M. Tyler, appointed in September, 1887, to succeed William H. Walker, resigned. The Secretary of State and Treasurer are, *ex officio*, Insurance Commissioners.

Legislative Session.—The Legislature met at Montpelier on October 3, and remained in session till November 28. One of the most important acts of the session was the passage of a new law for the government of the public schools. It provides for a State Superintendent of Education, to be chosen by the Legislature; for a County Board of Education, composed of one member from each town, chosen at its annual meeting; and for a County Supervisor of Schools, to be chosen every two years, in May, by the County Board of Education. These county boards have cognizance of all matters of education in their respective counties, including the selection of text-books. The Supervisor is a salaried administrative officer, who examines teachers, grants certificates, visits the schools, advises school-district officers, gives instruction to teachers, and otherwise stimulates the interests of education. The school-district system is still maintained, and the Prudential Committee of the district has still the financial management of the schools in his district, and the selection or dismissal of teachers therefor. Women have the same right to vote as men in school-district meetings. Numerous changes in the details of school management were made.

The Legislature was more liberal than many of its predecessors in the matter of appropriations. The sum of $1,125,000 was appropriated for 1889 and 1890, for State expenses, and the

Treasurer was authorized to borrow $500,000 in addition, if necessary. The construction of a State Insane Asylum was authorized, and $100,000 was appropriated for that purpose. Liberal provision was also made for the Burlington and Middlebury Colleges, and for the Soldiers' Home. In consequence of these appropriations, it became necessary to levy a State tax for 1889 of twenty cents on each $100 of taxable property in the State.

Amendments to the prohibitory acts were made, in order to secure better enforcement of prohibition, and an act making the payment of a United States special tax as a liquor-seller *prima facie* evidence of liquor-selling was passed. The existing status of the Normal Schools was continued till 1900. Other acts of the session were as follow:

Providing for the sale of leased property for taxes.

Empowering the Railroad Commissioners to authorize the running of through trains on Sunday.

Giving the Railroad Commissioners the power to prescribe the method of heating cars, provided that they shall not prohibit the heating by steam from the engine.

Requiring all railroads to issue uniform mileage-tickets in books containing coupons for not more than one thousand miles.

Providing that no personal property shall be exempt from attachment on a suit brought to recover the purchase-money for the same.

Creating a Board of Supervisors of the Insane.

Providing for the care of habitual drunkards at institutions in the State established for their treatment.

To prevent the adulteration of milk and the false branding of butter and cheese.

Providing for the appointment of a commissioner to investigate the agricultural and manufacturing interests of the State, and to devise means for developing the same.

To prohibit discrimination in life or endowment insurance policies.

Fixing the standard weight for a bushel of salt at seventy pounds.

Prohibiting the sale or gift of tobacco to persons under sixteen years of age.

Providing that every person who shall make, alter, or repair any article of personal property, shall have a lien thereon for his just and reasonable charges therefor, and may retain possession of such property till the charges are paid, and may sell the same at public auction after three months, if the value of the article is not over $100.

To suppress "bucket-shops" and gambling in stocks, bonds, petroleum, cotton, grain, and provisions.

Punishing, by a fine, persons who bet on the result of any election.

Changing the fiscal year so that it shall end on June 30.

Finances.—For the year ending July 31, the State Treasurer reports receipts amounting to $710,052.20; cash on hand at the beginning of the year, $21,476.77; total, $731,528.97. The expenditures during the same period were $643,466.67, leaving a balance of $88,062.30 on July 31. The assessment of a special property-tax of twelve cents on each $100 increased the revenue for the year by $210,017.84, and enabled the Treasurer to pay off a floating debt of $225,165. The tax on corporations yielded a revenue of $239,003.61. From convict-labor the sum of $13,037.50 was derived, and $61,-

027.83 from the courts and Judges of Probate. Regarding expenditures the Auditor says in his report: "A comparison of the figures for some years back will show a steady increase in State expenses, and that, as a whole, they exceed for the last biennial term the expenses of any two years preceding. This change is wrought principally by more liberal legislation of late years in the matter of special appropriations, increase of salaries and fees, and the transfer to the State of expenses heretofore borne by the counties and towns." The funded debt of the State remains unchanged, consisting of $135,500 of 6-per-cent. bonds, held by the State Agricultural College fund.

Education.—The following statistics exhibit the condition of the public schools for the school year ending March 31, 1888: Districts, 2,144; schools, 2,547; pupils enrolled, 68,453; average daily attendance, 46,061; male teachers, 479; female teachers, 3,517; total revenue for school purposes, $628,157.47; total expenditure, not including supervision, $640,274.07. The enrollment of pupils shows a decrease of nearly 3,000 from the figures of the previous year, and is smaller than has been reported for ten years. The percentage of attendance, based upon the number enrolled, is smaller in Vermont than in any other New England State. "Another two years of experience in the common schools of the State," says the State Superintendent, "has still more fully convinced me of the utter inefficiency of our plan of district management."

At the State Normal School, in Castleton, there were 185 students in attendance during the school year, against 217 for the year 1886-'87; at the Randolph Normal School there were 115; and at the Johnson School about the same number.

Savings-Banks.—The whole number of depositors in all the savings banks and trust companies in the State, June 30, 1888, was 57,520, an increase during the year of 3,710. There was to the credit of such depositors $16,602,067.76, showing an increase during the year of $1,015,016.83. Of the total amount of deposits in the different savings-banks and trust companies, $13,888,186.65 belong to depositors living in the State, being an increase of $885,642.96 as compared with 1887. The average amount of each deposit is $288.63, a decrease of $1.04 as compared with 1887.

Railroads.—There are now 932 miles of railroad in the State. During the year there were constructed and put in operation 12.8 miles of new road—viz., by the Central Vermont Railroad, from Barre to Williamstown, 7.8 miles; by the Clarendon and Pittsford Railroad Company, in Rutland, West Rutland, and Proctor, 5 miles. The Montpelier and Wells River Railroad Company has begun the construction of a road from Montpelier to Barre, which will be completed early in 1889. Returns made to the Railroad Commissioners and the Commissioner of State Taxes for 1888 show the following railroad earnings for the year ending June 30, 1888: Gross income, $4,884,372; operating expenses, $3,319,964; net income, $1,564,408.

Political.—A Democratic State Convention met at Montpelier on May 10, and nominated the following candidates for State offices: For Governor, Stephen C. Shurtleff; Lieutenant-Governor, Thomas C. O'Sullivan; Treasurer, William E. Peck; Secretary of State, William B. Mayo; Auditor. George M. Dearborn. The platform contained the following:

We reassert our belief that property should be the principal subject of taxation, and that this burden should fall proportionately upon the property taxed, and we demand such legislation as will make the list of each taxable poll one dollar instead of two dollars, and will adjust taxes upon mortgaged property equitably between mortgagor and mortgagee.

We recognize the necessity of controlling by law the traffic in intoxicating liquors, and are in favor of the enforcement of existing laws enacted for that purpose while they remain in force. But we believe a stringent license law with local option would produce better results than the present law, and would increase the revenue rather than burden taxation.

The Republican party in the State has repeatedly professed itself to be in favor of prohibition, and has enacted prohibitory laws; but, although in power, it has neglected to enforce those laws and has left them mainly to such enforcement as has been prompted by greed of gain, revenge, or malice.

Candidates of the Prohibition party were nominated at a convention held at Montpelier on June 12. They were: For Governor, Henry M. Seeley; Lieutenant-Governor, George E. Crowell; Secretary of State, Archibald O. Ferguson; Treasurer, Armentus B. Bixbey; Auditor, Charles S. Parker.

The Republicans held a State Convention on April 4 for the choice of delegates to the Chicago Convention, and a second convention on June 27, at which William P. Dillingham was nominated for Governor and Urban A. Woodbury for Lieutenant-Governor. The Secretary of State, Treasurer, and Auditor were renominated. The following are the more important resolutions adopted:

That the railroads of Vermont were chartered and endowed with certain powers and privileges, primarily for the benefit of all the people, and that their services should be open to all upon the same relative terms and conditions, without discriminations or favoritism in any form or degree; that, in justice to their owners and paying patrons, the practice of issuing free passes to persons other than their officers, employés, and officers and employés of other railroads, ought to be promptly discontinued. We especially deprecate the issuing to and acceptance for use of free passes by State officers, members of the Legislature, and all others whose official acts may concern the rights and interests of the railroads as demoralizing in intent and tendency, and demand that such practices be prohibited by law. We believe that justice between man and man, as well as the obvious interests of the State, require that the principles embodied in what are known as the "long- and short-haul" provisions of the interstate commerce law and the laws of several of our sister States should find a place in the Statutes of Vermont, and that our State Railroad Commission should be clothed with ample power to exact obedience to such laws and to their own judgments and decrees.

This convention reaffirms the devotion of the Republican party to the temperance legislation of the State as enacted by the Republican party, and its determination that no retrograde steps shall be taken, but that the lines shall be advanced until the saloon shall cease to be a power in the land.

The election occurred early in September, and resulted in an unusually large majority for the Republican ticket. For Governor, Dillingham received 48,522 votes; Shurtleff, 19,-527; Seeley, 1,372. Of the Legislature chosen at the same time, the Republicans elected the entire 30 members of the Senate, and 219 members of the House; of the remaining 21 members of the House, 19 were Democrats and 2 Independents. At the national election in November, Republican presidential electors were chosen and two Republican Congressmen elected.

VIRGINIA. State Government.—The following were the State officers during the year: Governor, Fitzhugh Lee, Democrat; Lieutenant-Governor, John E. Massey; Secretary of State, H. W. Flournoy; Treasurer, A. W. Harmon; Auditor, Morton Marye; Second Auditor, Frank G. Ruffin; Attorney-General, Rufus A. Ayers; Superintendent of Public Instruction, James L. Buchanan; Commissioner of Agriculture, Thomas Whitehead; Railroad Commissioner, James C. Hill; President of the Supreme Court, Lunsford L. Lewis; Judges, T. T. Fauntleroy, Robert A. Richardson, Benjamin T. Lacy, and Drury A. Hinton.

Legislative Session.—The Legislature, which was in session at the beginning of the year, adjourned on March 5. Among the important bills that became laws were those providing for the establishment of a board of agriculture and further defining and enlarging the duties of the Commissioner of Agriculture; abolishing the compulsory inspection of flour and fish; and inaugurating a system of pensions for Confederate soldiers and appropriating therefor $65,000 per annum. The pension act is a substitute for a law that has been in force for several years, appropriating $70,000 annually "for the relief of Confederate soldiers," and establishes a better method of distributing the appropriation than that therein provided. About February 1 a fire at the State Penitentiary in Richmond destroyed the shoe-shops, involving a loss of $20,000 to the State. To restore this building an appropriation of $30,000 was made. The appropriation for the State University was reduced from $40,000 to $35,000, and that of the Virginia Military Institute from $35,000 to $30,000. On the question of selling the State's interest in the Chesapeake and Ohio Railroad, amounting to about 17,621 shares, of the par value of $100 a share, it was decided to authorize the sale, although the present value of shares was but $2.50 or $3. An act was also passed providing for submitting to the voters, at the November election, the question whether a convention should be called to revise the State Constitution. A memorial to Congress was adopted, asking the Federal Government to assist the State in paying its debt. Other acts of the session were:

To provide for the removal of obstructions from Chickahominy river.

Appropriating money for furnishing the new addition to the Central Lunatic Asylum, and for the support of more inmates.

To prevent the pollution of drinking-water.

To incorporate the Foreign Mission Board of the Southern Baptist Convention.

Authorizing the Governor to hire convicts to the Abingdon Coal and Iron Railroad Company.

To provide for the purchase of certain property, an additional improvement for the State Normal School, and to make appropriation therefor.

To give the assent of the State of Virginia to the provisions of an act of Congress approved March 2, 1887, in relation to an agricultural experiment station.

To authorize clerks of circuit courts to take acknowledgments to deeds and other writings and to certify the same.

Amending the oyster laws and further protecting the oyster interest of the State.

The State Debt.—No settlement of the controversy between the State and its foreign bondholders regarding the State debt was reached during the year. When the conference of 1887, between representatives of the Legislature and of the bondholders, failed to agree upon a compromise adjustment of the liability of the State, the contest reverted again to the courts where the question regarding the right of the State to refuse debt-coupons in payment of taxes was at issue. The act requiring persons offering coupons for taxes to surrender them, file a petition to prove their genuineness, and produce in court the original bond from which they were taken as proof, before such coupons would be received, had been made practically non-enforceable by the decision of the United States Supreme Court declaring the tender of genuine coupons for taxes to be payment, without further proceedings by the tax-payer. The Legislature of 1887 then passed the "coupon-crusher" act, by which, on tender of the coupons, the State was to take the initiative by bringing suit against the tax-payer to compel him to prove his coupons, requiring as proof the production of the original bond. In all these cases the production of the original bond, which was held by the owner in Europe, was of course impossible. The action of the bondholders in obtaining from the Federal Circuit Court an injunction against the State officers from enforcing this act proved abortive, as the United States Supreme Court, late in 1887, declared such a proceeding to be contrary to that clause of the Constitution which forbids suits against a State by foreign citizens. The constitutionality of the "coupon-crusher" act itself was not in issue in this case; but the counsel of the bondholders at once took measures to bring that question before the State courts, to secure a decision, and to obtain an appeal therefrom to the United States Supreme Court. Early in December, 1888, this preliminary procedure had been completed and writs of error were obtained from the State Supreme

Court in four cases, involving all the mooted questions. Later, the United States Supreme Court fixed the second Monday of October, 1889, for a hearing of the cases.

The bondholders adopted another method of forcing coupons upon the State, believing that if they overwhelmed the treasury with these, the State, in order to escape bankruptcy, would be compelled to meet the terms offered by them for settling the debt. They decided to take as much advantage as possible of the existing legislation of the State, and established a central agency at Richmond, with subagencies throughout the State, for the purpose of facilitating and stimulating the use of coupons in paying taxes. Bondholders were urged to send over their bonds to these agencies, that they might be produced in court under the requirements of the "verification" and "coupon-crusher" acts. Tax-payers were urged to file petitions under the former act for verification of their coupons, although it had been decided that the State could not compel them to do so; the bonds were produced in court by the agents of the bondholders, and in this way a large and constantly increasing number of coupons were forced upon the State. In Richmond alone, the number of tax-payers filing petitions for verification increased from 231 in 1887 to 720 in 1888. So numerous had these petitions become, that early in 1889 Gov. Lee and others organized a movement to rouse popular sentiment upon the matter and, by holding public meetings in the six cities and seven counties from which the tender of coupons exclusively came, urged the citizens, as a matter of patriotic duty, to sign resolutions pledging themselves to pay all their taxes hereafter in money, in order to save the State from bankruptcy. Many signatures to such resolutions were obtained.

Political.—There was no election for State officers during the year. State conventions of the various political parties were held, to select delegates to the national nominating conventions and to nominate presidential electors. The Democratic Convention met at Norfolk on May 16, and the Republicans at Petersburg on the following day. The Petersburg Convention witnessed a factional contest between followers of ex-Senator William Mahone and John S. Wise, which resulted in the withdrawal of the latter and the holding of a second convention by his followers. Each faction selected delegates to the Chicago Convention. A resolution was passed by the Mahone Convention, opposing the proposed constitutional convention. At the November election the Democratic presidential electors were chosen. Republican congressmen were elected in the First and Second Congressional Districts, and Democrats in the remaining eight districts.

On the question whether a convention should be called to revise the Constitution, the vote was overwhelmingly in the negative—3,698 yeas to 63,125 nays.

W

WAITE, MORRISON REMICK, jurist, born in Lynn, Conn., Nov. 29, 1816; died in Washington, D. C., March 23, 1888. He was the eldest of eight children of Henry Matson Waite, Chief-Justice of Connecticut, was graduated at Yale College in 1837, in the class that also included William M. Evarts, Edwards Pierrepont, Daniel B. Coe, and Benjamin Silliman, Jr., and immediately began studying law with his father. Soon afterward he removed to Maumee City, Ohio, where he finished his studies, was admitted to the bar in 1839 and began practicing in partnership with Samuel Young. In 1850 the firm removed to Toledo, and in 1854 a new partnership was formed by Mr. Waite and his brother Robert. Though a Whig till 1856 and a Republican thereafter, and possessing wide repute for his legal acumen and success at the bar, he was loath to accept public office based on politics. In 1849 he was elected a member of the State Legislature, and in 1862 was an unwilling and defeated candidate for Congress. He was frequently tendered but always declined a seat on the bench of the Supreme Court of Ohio, preferring to remain at the bar. The office of member of the Legislature was the only one to which he was ever elected as a political preferment. In 1871 he was appointed by President Grant one of the three counsel of the United States before the Geneva Court of Arbitration which passed upon the "Alabama" claims, his associates being his old classmate, William M. Evarts, and Caleb Cushing. Besides his general arguments before that court, he made a special one, on the liability of the British Government for permitting the Confederate steamers to take in supplies of coal in British ports, which attracted much attention in legal and diplomatic circles. He returned to Toledo in November, 1872, and resumed his practice. In 1873 he was unanimously elected by both parties as a member of the Ohio Constitutional Convention, and at its organization was chosen president. On Jan. 19, 1874, he was nominated by President Grant to be the seventh Chief-Justice of the United States, to succeed Salmon Portland Chase, after the United States Senate had rejected the nominations of George H. Williams and Caleb Cushing. After a discussion of one hour the Senate indorsed the nomination, and two days afterward confirmed it, every Senator present, 62, voting in his favor. For his share of circuit labor he took the States of Maryland, West Virginia, Virginia, North Carolina, and South Carolina. In 1876 he was

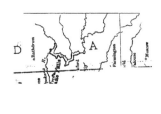

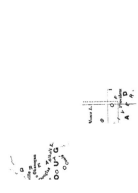

Scale of Miles

County Towns ⊛ Railroads
This type indicates a population
of 1,000 or over.

Greenwich

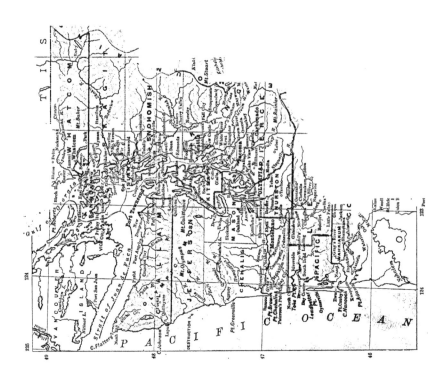

urged by many friends to permit the use of his name as a candidate for the presidency, but declined in a characteristic letter, in which he declared that no man ought to accept the chief-justiceship unless he took a vow to leave it as honorable as he found it, and expressed the opinion that in the interest of impartial justice the Constitution might wisely have prohibited the election of a Chief-Justice to the presidency. He received the degree of LL. D. from Yale in 1872. (For a portrait of Chief-Justice Waite, see "Annual Cyclopædia" for 1882, page 126.)

WASHINGTON TERRITORY. Territorial Government.—The following were the Territorial officers during the year: Governor, Eugene Semple; Secretary, N. H. Owings; Treasurer, T. M. Ford, succeeded by Frank I. Blodgett; Auditor, T. M. Reed, succeeded by J. M. Murphy; Superintendent of Public Instruction, J. C. Lawrence, succeeded by J. H. Morgan; Chief-Justice of the Supreme Court, Richard A. Jones, who died on August 19, and was succeeded by Charles E. Boyle, by appointment of the President. Chief-Justice Boyle entered upon his duties in November, but died on December 15, after scarcely a month's service. Thomas Burke was then appointed Chief-Justice, entering upon his duties in the last week of the year. Associate Justices, Frank Allyn, William G. Langford, and George Turner, succeeded by Lucius B. Nash. The office of Attorney-General, created by the Legislature in January, was filled by the appointment of J. B. Metcalfe.

Legislative Session.—The Legislature, which was in session at the beginning of the year, adjourned on February 2. An important feature of its work was the passage of an act granting to women over twenty-one years old, otherwise qualified by residence, etc., the right of suffrage in all elections for Territorial or local offices. It is substantially the same act that was passed in 1886 and declared unconstitutional by the Territorial Supreme Court. The law that imposes a tax on the gross earnings of railroads was repealed, and an act taxing railroad property was substituted therefor. A new organization and new rules for the militia were adopted. An annual tax of one fifth of a mill is to be levied for its support, to be kept as a separate fund for militia purposes exclusively. At each general election a brigadier-general and adjutant-general are to be elected. In time of peace the National Guard shall consist of not more than twelve companies of infantry and one company of cavalry, the infantry companies to consist of not fewer than twenty-four or more than sixty men. License-fees for the sale of liquors were fixed at not less than ·$300 and not more than $1,000, 10 per cent. of the fee to be paid into the Territorial treasury, the remainder to be applied for school and local purposes. The county commissioners in counties outside of cities, and the governing authorities in cities,

have sole power to grant licenses and to fix the amount of the fee. The appropriations include $173,490 for a new building at the Penitentiary and for the purchase of machinery to manufacture grain-sacks therein; $30,000 for buildings at the School for Defective Youth at Vancouver; $60,000 for erecting a new hospital for the insane at Medical Lake; $10,600 for the Territorial University; and $75,000 for the support of the Insane Asylum for two years. Congress was memorialized to admit the Territory into the Union with North Idaho annexed. Other acts of the session were as follow:

Changing the time of meeting of the Legislature, so that the next session shall begin on the second Monday of January, 1889.

Providing for the commutation of the sentence of prisoners as a reward for good behavior.

Directing the Governor to appoint four lawyers, two from each of the great political parties, as commissioners to codify the laws.

Authorizing organized counties to issue bonds to refund their indebtedness.

An elaborate act in relation to coal-mines, providing for their inspection, regulation, and ventilation, and for escapement-shafts and other appliances for the safety and health of miners.

Regulating the location and recording of quartz-mining claims, and providing for assessment-work done thereon.

Providing a mode of garnishment in civil actions.

Regulating the practice of dentistry by requiring every practitioner to obtain a diploma from some regularly chartered dental college, or a certificate from the Territorial Board of Dentistry created by this act.

Declaring Sundays, New-Year's Day, Fourth of July, Twenty-second of February, Christmas, Thanksgiving, Memorial Day, and days on which general or special elections for delegate or county officers are held, legal holidays.

Abolishing the use of seals upon deeds, and providing that the word "heirs," or other technical terms, shall not be necessary to convey an estate in fee simple.

Providing a penalty for the careless use of firearms.

Prescribing a short form of mortgage and acknowledgment.

Authorizing telegraph and telephone companies to exercise the right of eminent domain in constructing their lines.

A new fish and game law.

To punish the giving of false pedigrees of animals.

Revising the procedure in civil actions.

Making it larceny for a bailee to appropriate goods of another in his possession.

To prevent the introduction or spread of contagious diseases among sheep, and providing for the appointment of a county inspector of sheep.

Prohibiting corporations from paying their employés otherwise than in lawful money of the United States.

Authorizing a married man to deed property directly to his wife, and the wife to her husband.

Creating the county of Okanagan out of the western half of Stevens County.

Authorizing county commissioners to levy a tax not exceeding three tenths of a mill to create a fund for the relief of indigent soldiers and sailors and their families, to be expended under the direction of the Grand Army posts.

Declaring it arson for the owner to set fire to an unoccupied building.

Development.—Estimates made by the Governor place the population of the Territory, on Sept. 30, 1888, at 167,982 persons, an increase of 24,213 over the census returns of 1887. The assessed valuation of the Territory for 1888 exhibits an increase of $23,058,443 over 1887, the total valuation being $84,621,182. This large increase is partially due to the assessment of railroad property for *ad-valorem* taxation for the first time. During the year 137 miles of new railroad have been constructed, the total mileage in October being 1,197 miles.

Coal.—For the year ending Sept. 30, the total coal-product of the Territory is estimated at 1,133,801 tons, against 525,705 tons for the year preceding. The mines having the largest yield are as follow: Roslyn, 234,201 tons; Carbon Hill, 203,702 tons; Black Diamond, 186,-522 tons; Franklin, 182,921 tons; Newcastle, 158,134 tons.

Charities.—A small appropriation was made by the Legislature of 1885–'86 for the maintenance of a school for defective youth, and a small class of unfortunates that had been assembled at Tacoma were removed to Vancouver and adopted as wards of the Territory. Through the liberality of citizens of Vancouver, a farm was purchased and some buildings erected thereon for the accommodation of this school, and the small appropriation was made to serve. By a bill approved Jan. 26, 1888, an appropriation of $30,000 was made for a building for this school, and an act approved Jan. 28, 1888, appropriated $12,000 for maintenance. The building was in process of construction during the year.

Militia.—By the militia act of this year, above referred to, the National Guard of the Territory was placed upon a secure basis. The troops have been provided with uniforms and armories, and the regiments with colors, and the service thus being made more attractive, the companies were immediately recruited up to the maximum. The force now consists of two regiments of infantry and a troop of cavalry, in all 750 officers and men.

The Chinese.—How strong a feeling exists in the Territory against Chinese labor was shown by an incident in Pierce County. The hop-fields in this county are extensive, and when the season for gathering the crop came, it was found that the labor of Indians and others heretofore employed in this work could not be obtained. It was proposed by some of the hop-growers to import Chinese laborers from Portland, Oregon. Rumors of the fact at once created excitement, especially in the city of Tacoma, where a large public meeting was held to consider the situation. Among the resolutions adopted by this meeting were the following:

That the public-school board is most respectfully requested to grant applicant children leave of absence to enable them to go to the hop-fields.

That a committee of five members be appointed in each ward and precinct to take applications, both from employers and employes, to facilitate exchange between both parties.

That under no consideration nor in any emergency will we consent to the reintroduction of Chinese into Pierce County, and that we will use every legal means to prevent the same.

The immediate result was that white people, who had hitherto considered hop-picking as fit only for Indians and foreigners, readily offered their services to the growers, and the crop was gathered without the aid of Chinese.

Local Option.—The Supreme Court of the Territory rendered a decision in January, declaring that the local-option law passed in 1886 was unconstitutional and void. Two of the judges based their opinion on the ground that it delegated legislative power to local bodies, while a third, rejecting this reason, decided that the authority given by the act had by its terms been granted to no legally constituted local officials or bodies. The fourth judge dissented from these views.

Woman Suffrage.—In August the Territorial Supreme Court unanimously decided that the woman-suffrage law of 1888 was unconstitutional, as it had two years before decided regarding a similar law of the Legislature of 1886. The decision recites that the Legislature of the Territory has only such power as is given it by the organic act and other acts of Congress, and the question, therefore, turns upon the construction of the word "citizen" in that act. The court finds that the use of that term was to indicate males only. Section 1,859 refers to "male citizens" and the court reasons that in all places where the mere word citizen is used it means "male citizen." They find that the Constitution of the United States and all laws of Congress were made with the purpose and intention of males alone exercising the right of franchise.

Political.—On Sept. 4 a Democratic Territorial Convention met at Spokane Falls, and renominated Delegate Charles S. Voorhees for Congress. J. J. Hunt was nominated for Brigadier-General of the Territorial militia, and Hillory Butler for Adjutant-General. The platform adopted contains the following:

That we are opposed to the un-American policy of interfering with or destroying any now legally existing private or public business interests, by sumptuary laws or otherwise, without just compensation and due process of law.

The Republican Territorial Convention met at Ellensburg on Sept. 11, and nominated John B. Allen for Delegate, A. P. Curry for Brigadier-General, and R. G. OBrien for Adjutant-General. Its platform contains the following:

We arraign the Democratic Administration for its failure to place an adequate force on the frontier of Washington Territory to prevent the unlawful entry of Chinese.

We heartily advocate the forfeiture of all unearned land grants within our Territory, and their restriction to the use of actual settlers, and we demand the immediate passage of the Dolph Bill declaring forfeiture of that portion of the grant to the Northern Pacific Railway Company between Wallula and Portland.

We are in favor of legislation establishing the eight-hour system for the working of mines, and prohibiting the employment of child labor therein, and we disapprove of the introduction of armed men for the purpose of intimidating and humiliating laborers in mines, mills, etc.

We believe that the charges of transportation, warehouse, and elevator companies are subjects to be regulated by law, and we favor the enactment of such laws as, while assuring to capital a fair return for its use, will fully protect the people from unjust or discriminating charges or tariffs.

When the Territory of Washington is admitted into the Union, we ask that the boundaries be extended to include North Idaho.

A Prohibition ticket was also in the field. At the November election the Republican candidates were successful, changing a Democratic plurality of 2,200 in 1886 to a Republican plurality of over 7,300. For Delegates, Allen received 26,291 votes; Voorhees, 18,920; and Roger S. Greene (Prohibition), 1,137. At the same election, members of the Territorial Legislature for 1889 were chosen. The Republicans elected 11 of the 12 members of the Council, and 21 of the 24 members of the Lower House.

WEST INDIES. British. *Bahamas.*—The Bahamas are a chain of islands lying between 20° 42' and 27° 34' north latitude, and 72° 40' and 79° 5' west longitude, composed of about twenty inhabited islands and an immense number of islets and rocks, comprising altogether 4,466 square miles. The principal island is New Providence. The population in 1886 was 47,278. The town of Nassau has about 5,000 inhabitants. The Governor is H. A. Blake. The commercial relations of the colony are mainly with the United States. Considerable quantities of pineapples, oranges, and bananas are exported. The public debt amounts to £83,126. The revenue in 1886 was £43,920; the expenditure, £44,629. The imports in 1886 were valued at £189,410, and the exports at £150,390. The total tonnage entered and cleared in the same year was 209,996.

Barbadoes is in latitude 13° 4' north, longitude 59° 7' west, and is the most windward of the Caribbee Islands. It is nearly 21 English miles long by 14 in breadth. The population of the island is 180,000. The Governor is Sir Charles C. Lees. Almost the sole productions are sugar and molasses. In 1886 the island exported 45,768 hogsheads of the former and 33,218 puncheons of the latter. The public debt does not exceed £29,800. The revenue in 1886 was £136,286, and the expenditure £136,628. The total imports reached £863,491; the exports, £739,911. The aggregate tonnage of vessels entered and cleared in 1886 was 916,242.

Bermuda.—The "Bermudas" form a group of about 300 small islands in the western Atlantic Ocean, in latitude 32° 15' north and longitude 64° 51' west. The Governor is Lieut.-Gen. Thomas Lionel John Gallwey. The population in 1886 was 15,177; that of Hamilton, the capital, 2,100. The public debt in 1886 was £2,714; the revenue, £30,518; and the expenditure £28,432. The chief products are early potatoes, onions, tomatoes, and beets, which are sent to New York. The imports in 1886 were valued at £279,190; the exports, £78,546. The total tonnage entered and cleared in the same year was 281,528.

British Guiana.—This colony is on the South American Continent, extending from east to west about 200 miles. It includes the settlements of Demerara, Essequibo, and Berbice. Its area is about 109,000 square miles. About 130 square miles are under cultivation. The Governor is Charles Bruce. The capital is Georgetown, with 52,000 inhabitants. The chief product is sugar, there being, in 1886, in active operation, 105 sugar-estates, cultivating 76,203 acres. The population of the colony in 1886 was 274,311, of whom 74,026 were aborigines; 94,782 East Indians; 3,346 Chinese; 11,847 Portuguese; and 4,231 negroes. The public debt, on Dec. 31, 1886, was £446,700. The revenue in 1886 was £446,025 and the expenditure £476,964. The imports in 1886 were valued at £1,436,297; exports, £1,812,585. The tonnage of shipping entered and cleared in 1886 was 627,845.

Jamaica, an island in the Caribbean Sea, southward of the eastern extremity of Cuba. The Cayman Islands are dependencies of Jamaica, and have an area of 89 miles. The population of Jamaica in 1886 was 620,000, the number of whites not exceeding 15,000. The population of Kingston, the capital, is 38,566. The Governor is Gen. Sir H. W. Norman. The chief crops are sugar, coffee, ginger, and pimento; and the exports comprise, in addition to those products, rum, dyewoods, and fruit. There are 150 acres of Government cinchona-plantations. The number of sugar-estates in operation is 198. The public debt amounts to £1,552,543. The revenue in 1886 was £564,375; the expenditure, £582,735. The imports in 1886 were valued at £1,325,603; the exports at £1,280,118. The amount of shipping entered and cleared in 1886 was 881,516 tons.

Trinidad.—This island is about sixteen miles eastward of Venezuela, and is separated from the continent by the Gulf of Paria, into which fall the northern mouths of the Orinoco. The colony will henceforth include Tobago. The population in 1886 was 178,270; that of Port of Spain, the capital, being 31,858; of San Fernando, 6,335. The total length of railroads in operation, all Government property, is 51¼ miles. There are 63 miles of telegraph. The public debt amounts to £571,880. The revenue in 1886 was £453,407; the expenditure, £443,503. The imports in the same year were valued at £2,503,514; the exports at £2,509,140. The amount of shipping entered and cleared in 1886 was 1,196,076 tons.

British Honduras, a colony on the eastern coast of Central America, bounded north by Yucatan, west by a straight line drawn from the rapids of Gracias-á-Dios on the river Sarstoon to Garbutt's Falls on the river Belize, and thence due north to the Mexican frontier. The area is 7,562 square miles. The population does not exceed 30,000; that of the chief port, Belize, being 5,767. The Governor is K. T. Goldsworthy. The public debt amounts to $268,750. The revenue in 1886 was $271,-810; the expenditure, $302,775. In the forests and wilds are found the cedar, rose-wood, bullet-tree, faustic, lignum-vitæ, sapodilla, Santa Maria, iron-wood, red and white pine, India-rubber, and gutta-percha trees. The cocoanut flourishes, as do also the cahoon-plant and the ground-nut. The cultivation of fruit (bananas and plantains) and its shipment to New Orleans, are extending and proving remunerative. Arrangements are being made to ship fruit to the European markets, in steamers fitted with refrigerating apparatus. The chief industry is wood-cutting, now 200 years old; 3,000,000 feet of mahogany and 17,000 tons of logwood are on an average exported annually. There are 61 sugar-mills and large fruit-plantations. The chief exports are logwood, mahogany, sugar, fruit, India-rubber, tortoise-shell, and sarsaparilla. The imports in 1886 were valued at $1,179,813; the exports at $1,400,-234. The shipping entered and cleared in 1886 was 237,254 tons.

French.—*Guadeloupe* and its dependencies have an area of 1,870 square kilometres; the population numbering 182,619. The Governor is M. Le Boucher. The public indebtedness is 1,001,000 francs; the budget for 1886 estimated the income at 4,158,000 francs, and the outlay at the same sum. The home Government spent on the colony, in the same year, 2,118,000 francs. The imports of merchandise in 1886 amounted to 17,500,000 francs; the exports to 16,300,000. There entered the harbors 417 sea-going vessels. During the fiscal year 1887 the colony exported 45,646 tons of sugar in crystals, and 2,269 tons of brown sugar; during 1888 the amounts were respectively 40,878 and 1,690 tons. The rum exportation was 2,904,166 litres in 1887, declining to 2,636,322 in 1888. The molasses importation declined from 832,280 litres in 1887 to 184,926 in 1888. In January, 1889, the General Council of Guadeloupe passed a law favoring importation into the colony of certain manufactures of the mother-country, by fixing higher duties on articles made outside of France. Thus the duty on foreign cotton goods is doubled, the duties on shoe-leather and boots and shoes are materially raised, as are also those on butter, wines, and codfish. By way of reciprocity, the home Government is urged to reduce the duties now levied in France on coffee, cocoa, vanilla-beans, and pimento, of colonial growth.

Martinique covers 988 square kilometres, and the population is 175,755. The Governor is Albert Grodet. The island chiefly produces sugar, the yield of which in 1888 was 50,000 tons. The public debt does not exceed 435,000 francs; the budget for 1886 showed expenditures to the amount of 4,584,000 francs. The home Government, in 1886, spent on the colony 2,187,000 francs. The import of merchandise reached 23,700,000 francs in 1886, while the export amounted to 20,400,000 francs. The

number of sea-going vessels entering in the same year was 897.

French Guiana is still a penal colony. The climate being considered unhealthful, it attracts but little immigration, in spite of its exuberantly fertile soil and manifold resources, among which placer and quartz gold are prominent. The population (exclusive of the wild Indians) is only 26,905. The Governor is M. Gerville-Réaché. The colony has no public debt. The budget for 1886 showed an outlay of 2,123,000 francs, the home Government at the same time spending on the colony 3,266,000 francs. The import of merchandise was 7,200,000 francs; the export, 4,700,000 francs. There entered, in the same year, the port of Cayenne, 86 sea-going vessels.

Spanish.—*Porto Rico* is the lesser of the Spanish Antilles. (For area and population, see "Annual Cyclopædia" for 1885.) The Governor and Captain-General is L. Tabán. The American Consul at St. Johns is Edward Conroy. The island is in a remarkably prosperous condition, and continually attracts immigration from Spain, the Canary Islands, and the other West Indies. The population of the leading cities is as follows: Ponce, 37,-545; San German, 30,146; Mayagüez, 26,446; Arecibo, 25,457; Naguabo, 24,912; St. Johns (the capital), 23,414. A railroad is to be built to connect the above-named ports and thus encircle the entire island. It will measure 546 kilometres. The cost is estimated at 50,000,-000 francs, on which the Government guarantees an annual interest of 8 per cent. In 1888 there were in operation 833 kilometres of telegraph, the number of offices being 35. The colonial budget for 1888–'89 fixes the expenditure at $3,973,491, and the revenue at $3,863,-100. The peninsula and foreign trade movement in 1886 was: Imports, $11,116,543; exports, $10,293,544. The chief articles exported were: Sugar, 59,333 tons; coffee, 16,761 tons; molasses, 20,086 tons; tobacco, 2,053 tons. In 1887 the export of sugar increased to 81,-355 tons. The number of vessels entered Portorican ports in 1886 was 1,374, with a tonnage of 96,855. The American trade with Porto Rico has been as follows:

FISCAL YEAR.	Imports into the United States.	Domestic exports from the United States
1886	$4,594,544	$1,676,929
1887	4,661,690	1,701,241
1888	4,412,488	1,920,358

The Spanish Transatlantic Steamship Company began on Oct. 30, 1888, a new steamship service between New York and Porto Rico.

WEST VIRGINIA. State Government.—The following were the State officers during the year: Governor, E. Willis Wilson, Democrat; Secretary of State, Henry S. Walker; Treasurer, William T. Thompson; Auditor, Patrick F. Duffey; Attorney-General, Alfred Caldwell; Superintendent of Free Schools, Benjamin S. Morgan; President of the Supreme

Court of Appeals, Okey Johnson; Judges, Thomas C. Green, Adam C. Snyder, and Samuel Woods.

Finances.—The following statement shows the operations of the State treasury for the biennial period ending Sept. 30, 1888; Receipts for the fiscal year ended Sept. 30, 1887, $1,316,020.58; balance at the end of the preceding year, $368,001.80; making a total of $1,684,022.38; disbursements during the same period, $1,324,116.55; balance at the end of 1887, $359,905.83. Receipts during the year ended Sept. 30, 1888, $1,205,119.71; balance at the end of preceding year, $359,905.83; making a total of $1,565,025.54; disbursements during the same period, $1,227,288.98; balance at the end of 1888, $337,736.56.

The balance in the State fund on Sept. 30, 1888, was $52,974,80; in the general school fund, $279,811.16; and in the school fund, $4,950.60.

During the two years 1887 and 1888 it became necessary, in order to meet unusually large appropriations, to borrow $143,000, of which sum $125,000 was borrowed from banks and $18,000 from the board of the school fund, all of which amounts have since been paid, and in addition thereto the sum of $67,545.46, on account of claims filed by sheriffs prior to 1885. There has also been paid $7,000 on account of the $59,000, which was borrowed from the board of the school fund during 1885 and 1886.

There was expended on account of criminal charges during the fiscal year ending in September, 1887, $117,632.46, and for the year ending in September, 1888, $65,882.87.

The assessment of property in the State for 1887, was as follows: Real property, $118,181,936; personal property, $43,978,803; railroad property, $15,185,650. For 1888 the assessment was: Real property, $119,414,434; personal property, $44,469,225; railroad property, $15,501,670. The past six years have shown an increase in the wealth of the State, especially in railroad property, which has grown in value from $8,458,904 to $15,501,670. Real property has increased from $106,958,137, and personal property from $39,637,735.

Education.—The number of youth in the State between six and twenty-one years, according to the enumeration of 1887, was 249,178; according to that of 1888, 256,360. The number enrolled in the free schools for 1887 was 179,507; for 1888, 189,251. For 1887 the average daily attendance was 108,293, and for 1888 122,020. There were 4,603 schools of all grades in 1887, and 4,816 in 1888, an increase of 216; 5,089 teachers were employed in 1887, and 5,238 in 1888. The number of school-houses in 1887 was 4,465; in 1888, 4,567. The average length of the school year increased from four months and nineteen days in 1887 to five months and two days in 1888. The average salary per month paid teachers holding number one certificates for 1887 was $31.52; for 1888 it was

$33. The same salary was paid males and females for the same grade of work. The State also supports six normal schools and a State University.

Immigration.—The first organized movement to promote immigration to the State was begun during the year. On February 29, at the invitation of the Chamber of Commerce of Wheeling, about 1,000 business men of the State met in that city and organized the West Virginia Immigration and Development Association, said association to have in each county a county auxiliary, to be organized as soon as practicable by the representatives of each county in this convention, the necessary steps to be taken to organize the counties not here represented.

Election Frauds.—The Governor says, in his biennial message to the Legislature, in 1889:

Reproach has been cast upon our State as never before by illegal, fraudulent, and corrupt voting in almost every county within its borders. This is so palpable that "he who runs may read." The capitations of 1884 were 133,522, and the entire vote, after the most active political campaign ever made in the State, 137,527. The capitations of 1888 were 147,408, and the vote 159,440. The difference in the capitations and the vote in 1884 was 4,065, in 1888 it was 12,032. This shows an increase of votes in four years of 21,853, which, if legitimate, would indicate a population of 900,000, and an increase in four years of much more than 100,000. It is certain that no such increase has taken place.

The Governor advises, among other remedies, the passage of a registration act, although its operation would seem to be limited, if not destroyed, by the following provisions of the State Constitution:

No citizen shall ever be denied or refused the right or privilege of voting at an election, because his name is not, or has not been registered or listed as a qualified voter.

The Legislature shall never authorize or establish any board or court of registration of voters.

Freshets.—On July 11 and 12, in consequence of heavy rains, an unusual rise and overflow of many of the rivers of the State occurred, inundating a large territory and sweeping away bridges, buildings, crops, and other property. The rise of the waters was in many streams greater than ever before known. Scarcely a week later, on July 19, the city of Wheeling and vicinity was visited by a storm of great fury, though scarcely of an hour's duration, which destroyed bridges in the city limits, eight people thereon being drowned, and caused great loss of property. On August 21, another destructive storm swelled the rivers and swept away bridges and property in the northern portion of the State. The homes and entire property of many were swept away, and whole villages were for a time dependent on the charity of their neighbors.

Political.—The earliest nominations for State officers were made by the Union Labor party, which met in convention at Charleston on May 3, and selected as candidates, S. H. Piersol for Governor; J. H. Burtt for Auditor, who later withdrew from the ticket and gave his support to the Republicans; S. P. Hawver for Treasurer; D. D. T. Farnsworth for Attorney-General; and O. D. Hill for Superintendent of Free Schools. The platform included the following:

We favor the enactment of such laws as will cause the operator to pay the miner for all merchantable coal.

In releasing the revenues necessary to carry on the State Government the property of corporations shall have no advantage over property owned by individuals.

We favor the enactment of such laws in general as shall so change our laws as to place them abreast of those of the most populous and prosperous States of the Union; that shall remove the last vestige of antiquated mossback laws that hamper commerce, retard development, depreciate capital, stand as a menace to immigration, and chain West Virginia and her destiny to the past, not the future.

The passage of the miners' bill at the last session of the Legislature, containing the conspiracy feature, is a blow to organized labor, and passed designedly for the purpose of overawing those who are connected therewith.

On July 31, the Prohibitionists met at Parkersburg and nominated a State ticket headed by Thomas R. Carskadon for Governor.

The Democratic State Convention was held at Huntington on August 16. Its nominees were: A. B. Fleming for Governor, Patrick F. Duffy for Auditor, W. T. Thompson for Treasurer, Alfred Caldwell for Attorney-General, B. S. Morgan for Superintendent of Free Schools, and Henry Brannon and J. T. English for Judges of the Supreme Court of Appeals.

The platform approved President Cleveland's message, and the Mills Bill, the present State Administration, and that of the United States; denied that the Democratic party was for free trade, and declared for the St. Louis platform.

On August 22, the Republicans held their State Convention at Charleston, and nominated Gen. Nathan Goff for Governor by acclamation. Other candidates upon the ticket were: For Auditor, George M. Bowers; for Treasurer, Hiram Lewis; for Attorney-General, William P. Hubbard; for Superintendent of Schools, F. B. McLure; for Judges of the Supreme Court of Appeals, John W. Mason and H. C. McWharter. The resolutions approve the Chicago platform, demand protection not only for manufactures but for raw materials and for all farm-products, demand a tax of $200 or more on immigrants for the protection of American labor, and oppose the importation of contract or pauper labor.

The following were also a part of the platform:

Whereas, The passage of the miners' bill by the Democratic Legislature of 1887, containing the conspiracy feature, was a direct blow at organized labor, and was passed with the design and purpose of overawing those who are connected therewith; Therefore, be it resolved, We pledge our party to repeal so much of Chapter 50 of the Acts of 1887 as refers to conspiracy, and also provide that the inspector shall be a practical miner instead of a civil engineer, as is now required by law.

On September 12 a convention of about fifty delegates, calling themselves the "Colored Independents," met at Charleston and placed in nomination presidential electors and a State ticket containing the following names: For Governor, W. H. Davis; Auditor, E. A. Turner; Treasurer, Alfred Whiting. The resolutions adopted denounce the Republican party, ask the Legislature to prevent discriminating branches of study in the public schools; oppose monopolies, corporations, trusts; oppose taking the revenue off whisky and tobacco, and ask that all necessaries be placed upon the free list and that the tariff be reduced to prevent a surplus.

An address was issued to the colored voters, urging them to desert the Republican party and to stand together.

At the November election the contest was close, and the result remained in doubt until returns were received from the last election district. It then appeared that, while the Democrats had elected their candidates for presidential electors and nearly all their State ticket, the Republican candidate for Governor had a plurality of 106 votes on the face of the returns. As certified by the local officials, the vote stood: Goff, 78,904; Fleming, 78,798; Carskadon, about 1,000; and Piersol, about 1,400. The official vote for Treasurer was: Thompson, 78,969; Lewis, 78,127; Hawver, 1,399; and Bodley, 1,035. For Auditor: Duffey, 78,855; Bowers, 78,201; Sayre, 1,438; Bains, 1,027. For Attorney-General: Caldwell, 78,687; Hubbard, 78,520; Farnsworth, 1,579; Myers, 935. The Democratic candidates for Superintendent of Free Schools and for Supreme Judges were also elected. The Legislature chosen at the same time will contain in the Senate, 12 Democrats, 12 Republicans, and 1 Union Labor man, and in the House, 34 Democrats and 31 Republicans, giving the Democrats on joint ballot a majority of one vote. On the face of the returns, Democratic Congressmen were elected in the First and Second districts, and Republicans in the Third and Fourth, in each case by narrow pluralities. The Democratic candidate in the First District was elected by 16 votes, while in the Third the Republicans claimed only 13 more votes than their opponents. On December 26, Gov. Wilson issued certificates of election to the Democratic candidates in the First and Second districts, but refused to issue any for the other districts, alleging that, as there was a contest over the returns in those districts, he could not legally do so.

At the same election, three constitutional amendments were submitted to the people, and all of them were rejected. The most important one, prohibiting the manufacture and sale of liquor, failed of adoption by about 35,000 votes.

WILHELM I, Emperor of Germany, born in Potsdam, Prussia, March 22, 1797; died in Berlin, March 9, 1888. He was the second son of Friedrich Wilhelm, Crown-Prince of Prussia, and his wife Princess Luise, daughter of the Grand Duke of Mecklenburg-Strelitz.

Prince Wilhelm, as he was called (his full name being Friedrich Wilhelm Ludwig) was pronounced a weakly child by the physicians, and until he grew to manhood his health was a subject of solicitude. His father ascended the Prussian throne as Friedrich Wilhelm III when the prince was six months old. In his parents' retreat, at Paretz, Wilhelm was accustomed to simple living, and from the teachings of his philosophical father and the Rev. Dr. Delbrück, his tutor, he imbibed high notions of duty. In Berlin he was made familiar with another life, that of a luxurious and profligate aristocracy, inflated with pride and arrogance. After the defeat at Jena, on Oct. 14, 1806, the King and his family became exiles from Prussia. The two princes were taken to their mother at Schwedt, in Pomerania, and with her took their flight in an open carriage along the sea-shore in mid-winter to Stettin, Königsberg, and Memel. Wilhelm and the Queen both sickened with typhus fever before reaching Memel, whence they were obliged, six months later, to emigrate to Tilsit, where the unfortunate Queen, when forced to receive Napoleon, replied to his taunts that it was a pardonable error in the descendants of Frederick the Great to overrate their strength. From the day when the Prussian and Austrian armies were defeated by the "upstart" till she died of a broken heart in 1810, when the foe was still unexpelled, the proud and patriotic Luise never ceased to admonish her sons to revenge the humiliation of Jena when the opportunity came, and redeem the glory of Prussian arms. Friedrich Wilhelm III was restored

against his inclination. In 1840 Friedrich Wilhelm IV came to the throne, and his soldierly brother, who was popular only among military men, was acknowledged as his heir.

As Prince of Prussia Wilhelm was accorded an important influence on the decisions of Government. He strengthened the Conservative resolutions of the King, but could not withhold him from granting a constitution in 1847. The irresolute monarch was induced by his brother and other Absolutist advisers to nullify the charter that he had signed, and to declare at the opening of the Diet that no sheet of paper should stand between him and his subjects. The revolution of 1848 followed, and the ruthless action of the military under Prince Wilhelm's orders could not avert the enactment of a genuine constitution. He would have "riddled Berlin with bullets" before yielding had he been king. The "cartridge prince," as he was nicknamed for that expression, was the special object of popular hatred and fury. "The Prince of Prussia was his murderer," cried a woman whose son had fallen at the barricades, walking through the streets beside the litter on which the corpse was borne to the burial-ground. "I will remember that," threatened the prince, when a stone aimed at his head crashed through his palace-window. The King left Berlin, against the strenuous protests of his brother, and the troops were then withdrawn. "No music while our sons are dying!" shouted the populace, when the band of the guards struck up a martial strain. The mob hunted the prince in his palace, and hung from the balcony the black, red, and gold the conferring of any share in legislation on an assembly elected by universal male suffrage, and finally placed himself at the head of the Prussian army that was sent to disperse the Frankfort Parliament and put an end to popular government by defeating the national army in Baden. But the police *régime* under the Manteuffel, Westphalen, and Hinckeldey ministries found no favor in the eyes of the upright prince, and the abasement of Prussia before Russia and Austria so incensed him that he would have gone to war with Russia, though the Emperor Nicholas was his brother-in-law and the guardian of monarchical principles in Europe, rather than renounce Prussian supremacy in Germany and accede to the resuscitation of the old Bund, as was done in the treaty of Olmütz. When the Crimean War broke out, in 1854, he dissuaded his brother from making an alliance with the power that had so humiliated Prussia.

After the peace of Paris was signed in 1856, King Friedrich Wilhelm, who began to show symptoms of insanity, resigned the direction of public business into the hands of the Prince of Prussia. The decree was twice renewed, and when the King's condition grew worse, Prince Wilhelm was appointed Regent on Oct. 9, 1858. Disgusted with the "white terror," the Prince Regent determined to create a Liberal administration, to the head of which he called Prince Hohenzollern - Sigmaringen, by whom, with the aid of his colleague Rudolf von Auerswald and others of like opinions, police espionage and repression were abolished. When Napoleon III made war on Austria in 1859 the Emperor Franz Josef gave up the Italian provinces and hastened to conclude peace as soon as he heard of the proposal of Prussia in the Diet to mobilize the German armies and send them to the Rhine, preferring to suffer the diminution of his own territory rather than aid in the aggrandizement of his rival for military supremacy in Germany. On the death of Friedrich Wilhelm the Prince-Regent succeeded to the throne as William I, Jan. 2, 1861. He had already begun to prepare for the struggle with Austria, being aided in the development of his policy by the genius of Otto von Bismarck. The German people had no predilection for a military state, and in the Prussian and German Parliaments it was proposed to convert the armies into a militia with elective officers following civil occupations in time of peace, a scheme which the Prince of Prussia had opposed in an anonymous pamphlet. In 1860 Bismarck brought in a budget authorizing the doubling of the army. The minister had incurred great unpopularity by aiding Russia to suppress the Polish insurrection, and the Assembly rejected the military bill by a large majority, whereupon Bismarck declared that, as the House of Lords had accepted the budget rejected by the Chamber, there was no properly authorized budget, and the Government must therefore frame one to suit the exigencies of the case. This singular interpretation of the Constitution was sustained by the supreme tribunal, packed for the purpose, and for four years the administration was carried on without a properly voted budget. The people protested against the collection of taxes, but did not openly resist the despotism of the Hohenzollern and his Prime Minister. The terror and dismay that hung over the country in this period was not dispelled by the successes of the Danish war and the acquisition of Schleswig-Holstein in 1864, and when Prussia went to war with Austria in 1866 for the retention of the duchies, the Prussian people mistrusted their rulers and feared a bargain with Napoleon for the cession of the Rhine frontier. The sudden and complete victory of the North German armies, paving the way to German unity, dissipated all doubts, and nearly reconciled the people to the usurpation of their liberties, since it had led to the triumph of their national ambition. Parliament at once voted an indemnity for all military expenditure. King Wilhelm and his counselors began forthwith to prepare for the greater war that must ensue from the refusal of the Emperor Napoleon's demand for the cession of Mayence and the Rhine frontier of 1814, as compensation for German unity and the baffling of his subsequent designs on Belgium and Luxemburg. King Wilhelm concluded secret offensive and defensive alliances with each of the South German states after the campaign of 1866, and therefore acceded without demur to the article placed in the Treaty of Prague to appease French susceptibilities, to the effect that those states should maintain " an international and independent position." The Franco-Prussian War of 1870 was planned by King Wilhelm, under the guidance of Count Bismarck, as the means of consolidating the power of Prussia and completing the political unification of Germany. Count Moltke, as early as the winter of 1868, elaborated a complete scheme for the invasion of France. Napoleon III more confidently and more hastily rushed into the war in the expectation of crushing the military power of Prussia and retrieving his political position at home. Both governments were eager to seize on the dispute about the candidacy of Prince Leopold of Hohenzollern for the Spanish throne, as a device for kindling popular enthusiasm in the war. King Wilhelm, accustomed from his youth to a soldier's fare, marched across the frontier with his armies at the age of 73, frequently exposed himself to the enemy's fire in the hottest battles, and by his presence inspired his troops with irresistible courage.

On Jan. 18, 1871, the 170th anniversary of the coronation of the first King of Prussia, the victorious monarch was acclaimed German Emperor by the princes of the German states and the commanders of the army, in the Hall of Mirrors at Versailles. As soon as the war was over, and the German Empire established

Eng⁴ by BB Hall Jr New York.

WILLIAM II. EMPEROR OF GERMANY.

D APPLETON & CO.

... rm foundation, Prince ...
... in a conflict with ...
... dering the lately ...
... papal ... libility a men ...
... and the attitude of the clerg ...
... being an op ... le ... the amal ...
the various elements composing the ...
When the era of the Kulturkampf ...
and the force of his ... st resistan ...
itself, the republic ... and socialist ...
were an important ... in the ...
ary movement of 1848 ... the ...
the Social-Democra... ... ...
named ... del, inflamed ... ...
sion and desire for no... ... ...
peror as he was passing ... ...
ter den Linden, on May ... ...
try presented a bill to ... ...
movement, which the ... ...
majority of nearly 200 ... ...
an educated Socialist, ... by ... ...
pulses that actuated ... ...
with buckshot at ... ...
on June 2, and a ... ...
Reichstag was at ... ...
one passed Pr ... ...
bill. The ... ...
repea... ... the ...

Of ... ... was disso ...
not ... ... At length the ...
his Chancellor turned to conser ...
tion, in order to promote ... ...
avert the danger of revolut ...
scheme of social reform that ...
make the lot of the laborin ...
... are less against want. ...
... ... been developed and ...
have approved by Wilhelm I. ...
the Prussian army he considered ...
of his life. His foreign policy ... ...
as to retain the acquisitions of t... ...
and, to guard against a combin ...
France and Russia, a military ... and ...
tered into with Austria-Hungary ... on ...
The Emperor Wilhelm w... s r...
his habits. He slept on a hard ...
simple food, drank sparingly of w...
no tobacco. He was pious and ...
his religious faith.
WILHELM II, Emperor of Germa...
Berlin, Jan. 27, 1859. He is th...
Frederick III of Prussia, the ...
of Germany, and of his w... ...
Princess Royal of England ...
oped a liking for military ... ...
couraged in such taste ... ...
learning many details of ... ...
cipline before he could ... ...
the old Emperor's m... ... ...
ernment and his ... ...
tative government ... ...
an English g ... ...
to study po... ...
mathematics ... ...
directions w...

... ...
... the fiscal year
... and the disburse-
... for the year 1887-'88
... $2,284,513.26, and the dis-
... $4.90. The receipts from
... the former year were $...
... latter year, $996,504.41. The
... yielded in the f...
... in the latter, $1,608 s...
... debt on September ...
... and all of which is for ...
... —The assess... ...
... follows: Personal ...
... and village lots, $... 4... ...
tate, $302,996,10... ...
... ...
... $540,231 ...
... ... of ... ...
... of four and ... ...
... $567 ... ...
were ... ...
The t... ... amounts
... State for educational pur-
... support of university, $218,808-
... schools, $99,999.58; common and
... $3,509,746.75.
... the Legislature passed an act giving
... women the right of suffrage in mun...
... ctions, on all matters relating to sc...

... ... burg, to
... ... stra-
... had

... ...
... ...

on a firm foundation, Prince Bismarck engaged his master in a conflict with the Catholic Church, considering the lately promulgated doctrine of papal infallibility a menace to the state, and the attitude of the clericals in the Reichstag an obstacle to the amalgamation of the various elements composing the Empire. When the era of the Kulturkampf was ended, and the force of Separatist resistance had spent itself, the republican and socialistic·ideas that were an important element in the revolutionary movement of 1848 asserted themselves in the Social-Democratic agitation. A desperado named Hödel, inflamed with revolutionary passion and desire for notoriety, fired at the Emperor as he was passing along the avenue Unter den Linden, on May 11, 1878. The ministry presented a bill to suppress the Socialist movement, which the Reichstag rejected by a majority of nearly 200 votes. Dr. Nobiling, an educated Socialist, moved by the same impulses that actuated Hödel's attempt, fired with buckshot at the Emperor in his carriage on June 2, and wounded him severely. The Reichstag was at once dissolved, and a new one passed Prince Bismarck's anti-Socialist bill. The law expired in 1881, and has been repeatedly renewed and strengthened. The Social-Democratic party, by the unsparing use of repressive powers, was disorganized, but not destroyed. At length the Emperor and his Chancellor turned to constructive legislation, in order to promote contentment and avert the danger of revolution, devising a scheme of social reform that is intended to make the lot of the laboring-man easier and to secure him against want. The military system has been developed and extended on the lines approved by Wilhelm I. The creation of the Prussian army he considered the chief task of his life. His foreign policy was shaped so as to retain the acquisitions of the French war, and, to guard against a combined attack from France and Russia, a military alliance was entered into with Austria-Hungary and Italy.

The Emperor Wilhelm was a soldier in all his habits. He slept on a hard couch, ate simple food, drank sparingly of wine, and used no tobacco. He was pious and orthodox in his religious faith.

WILHELM II, Emperor of Germany, born in Berlin, Jan. 27, 1859. He is the eldest son of Frederich III of Prussia, the second Emperor of Germany, and of his wife Victoria, the Princess Royal of England. He early developed a liking for military affairs, and was encouraged in such tastes by his grandfather, learning many details of tactics, drill, and discipline before he could read. He imbibed also the old Emperor's monarchical ideas of government and his dislike for popular representative government. His earliest teacher was an English governess. He was sent to Bonn to study political science, jurisprudence, and mathematics, and in 1882, by his grandfather's directions, was placed with Dr. Aschenbusch,

president of the province of Brandenburg, to learn the practical details and the administrative routine of the civil service. He also had instruction from Prince Bismarck, whom he visited once a fortnight. In military matters he became as proficient as his grandfather. Prince Wilhelm (whose full name is Friedrich Wilhelm Victor Albrecht), married the Princess Augusta Victoria, daughter of Friedrich, Duke of Schleswig-Holstein, on Feb. 27, 1881. The family consists of five sons, of whom the eldest, the Crown-Prince Friedrich Wilhelm Victor August Ernst, was born on May 6, 1882. For portraits of the Emperor Wilhelm II and the Crown-Prince, see the "Annual Cyclopædia" for 1887, page 321.

WISCONSIN. State Government.—The following were the State officers during the year: Governor, Jeremiah M. Rusk, Republican; Lieutenant-Governor, George W. Ryland; Secretary of State, Ernst G. Timme; Treasurer, Henry B. Harshaw; Attorney-General, Charles E. Estabrook; Superintendent of Public Schools, Jesse B. Thayer; Insurance Commissioner, Philip Cheek; Railroad Commissioner, Atley Peterson; Chief-Justice of the Supreme Court, Orsamus Cole; Associate Justices, William P. Lyon, David Taylor, John B. Cassoday, and Harlow S. Orton.

Finances.—On Oct. 1, 1886, the balance in the treasury aggregated $736,720.24; the total receipts for the succeeding biennial period were $5,469,996.10, and the disbursements $5.447,-072.82, leaving a balance in the treasury on Sept. 30, 1888, of $750,702.44. Of this balance, there was in the general fund $304,139.-09 and in the school fund $151.241.85. The receipts of the general fund for the fiscal year 1886–'87 were $1,805,122.76; and the disbursements $2,171,201.79; for the year 1887–'88 the receipts were $2,284,513.26, and the disbursements $2,099,984.99. The receipts from the State tax for the former year were $902,-484.88; for the latter year, $996,504.41. The tax on railroads yielded in the former year $763,994.56; in the latter, $1,068,632.96. The State debt on September 30 amounted to $2,251,000, all of which is held by State funds.

Statistics.—The assessed valuation for 1888 is as follows: Personal property, $125,922.683; city and village lots, $152,345,964; other real estate, $302,996,102; total, $581,264,749. There were assessed 404,036 horses, 1.236,452 cattle, 723,639 sheep and lambs, and 540,231 swine.

Education.—The whole number of persons enrolled between the ages of four and twenty years, June 30, 1888, was 567,702, and of this number only 265,477 were reported as attending the public schools. The following amounts were paid by the State for educational purposes in 1888: Support of university, $218.856-.71; normal schools, $99,229.58; common and high schools, $3,509,786.75.

In 1885 the Legislature passed an act giving ing to women the right of suffrage in municipal elections, on all matters relating to schools.

The State Supreme Court, in January, interpreted this to allow women to vote for school-officers, but not for such other municipal officers, like the mayor, as only indirectly controlled educational matters.

Charities.—Wisconsin has a peculiar system for the maintenance and care of its insane. This system includes two exclusively State institutions and the Milwaukee County Asylum, which is both governed and maintained in part by the State. These institutions have a normal capacity for the care of 1,370 patients, and at the close of the fiscal year had 1,425 inmates.

In addition to these hospitals proper there are now 16 county asylums for the care of the chronic insane, with two others in process of erection. The combined capacity of these asylums will be sufficient to accommodate 1,505 inmates. These asylums, while they are maintained and managed by the counties exclusively in which they are situated, yet when conducted in a manner satisfactory to the State Board of Charities and Reform, become entitled to assistance from the State at the rate of $1.50 a week for each inmate.

The School for the Deaf cost the State $35,515.30 for 1887, and $37,609.29 for 1888. The number of pupils in attendance in 1887 was 198; in 1888, 206. The School for the Blind maintained 73 pupils in 1887 at a cost of $19,630.52, and 84 pupils in 1888 at a cost of $20,365.41.

The last two Legislatures made provision for the establishment and maintenance of a State public school at Sparta. There has been expended for that institution $95,000 for lands and buildings—$30,000 in 1885, and $65,000 in 1887. Five substantial cottages and one large main building have been erected, and surrounding these is a farm of 165 acres, nearly all under cultivation. The cost for current expenses in 1888 was $20,128.48. The school was opened Nov. 13, 1886, and from that time to Sept. 30, 1888, 301 children were received. At the close of the present year there were 184 remaining in the school.

Prisons.—The average number of prisoners confined in the State prison in 1887 was 448; in 1888, 441. The total expense for the support of the prison for the past two years was $59,325.53 for 1887, and $61,073.87 for the fiscal year ending Sept. 30, 1888. Total for the two years, $120,399.40. Of this amount $99,187.96 was received from the prison-labor contractor. This leaves the net cost of the prison to the State for the two years, $21,-211.44.

The Industrial School for Boys cost the State for 1887, $45,583.12; and for 1888, $49,104.25. The average population of the school in 1887 was 334, and in 1888, 359.

Railroads.—At the close of 1888 the entire mileage of the State was 5,178 miles, an increase in two years of 400 miles. Of this, 340 miles were built in 1887 and 60 miles in 1888. The entire cost of the railroads of Wisconsin,

as reported on June 30, 1888, was $208,867,-606.27. The capital stock at the same date was $97,393,515.86. The amount of debt, funded or unfunded, was $117,547,909.35, or a total of capital stock and debt of $214,941,425.21. There was earned on Wisconsin railroads for the year ending June 30, 1888, $24,891,619.06, of which $6,266,259.35 was for transportation of passengers, and $17,165,959.24 for freight, and $1,459,400.47 for mails, express, etc. There has been a decrease in the cost of freight carriage in ten years of over 50 per cent.

Fisheries.—The value of the catch of Wisconsin fishermen on the Great Lakes in 1888 was $270,595.06; value of property, $337,706; number of persons employed, 628. Fishing is assuming an important place among the State industries.

Militia.—The National Guard consists of three regiments, one battalion of infantry, one troop of cavalry, and one light battery, aggregating 2,282 officers and enlisted men. The expenses for 1887 were $54,990.14, and for 1888, $56,-927.37.

Political.—Democratic and Republican State Conventions for the choice of delegates to the National Conventions were held on May 1 and 9 respectively. On May 23 the Prohibitionists, in State Convention at Madison, selected delegates to the Indianapolis Convention and nominated the following candidates for State offices: for Governor, E. G. Durant; Lieutenant-Governor, Christopher Carlson; Secretary of State, Nelson La Due; Treasurer, L. W. Hoyt; Attorney-General, Charles E. Pike; Superintendent of Public Schools, J. H. Gould; Railroad Commissioner, E. W. Drake; Insurance Commissioner, S. M. Bixby.

On July 24 a State Convention of the Union Labor party met at Oshkosh and nominated the following ticket: For Governor, D. Frank Powell; Lieutenant-Governor, Nelson E. Allen; Secretary of State, William M. Lockwood; Treasurer, Alfred Manheimer; Attorney-General, T. E. Ryan; Superintendent of Public Schools, E. W. Krackowitzer; Railroad Commissioner, John E. Thomas; Insurance Commissioner, Rittner Stephens. This ticket was changed before the election by the substitution of Kerellio Shawoan for Attorney-General, Joseph W. Stewart for Superintendent of Public Schools, and Frank J. Heines for Railroad Commissioner. Resolutions were adopted, demanding:

Taxation of all notes and mortgages:
All laws should be simplified so that there is but one law on one subject, and that worded in plain language, which will enable the people to understand the law without paying enormous fees to lawyers.
The one-man power has no place in a republic; hence all public officials, as far as practicable, should be elected by a direct vote of the people, and the voters be allowed to recall all unfaithful, inefficient, and dishonest officials.
A revision of the patent laws giving inventors a premium for their inventions and then giving the free use of such inventions to all the people, which will prevent the system of monopoly now existing, and

stop the robbery of both inventors and the people by heartless and greedy capitalists.

The Republican Convention for the nomination of State officers met at Milwaukee on Aug. 22, and on the first formal ballot chose William D. Hoard as candidate for Governor. All the other State officers were renominated. A very short platform was adopted, including the following:

With regard to the affairs of the State, they [the Republicans of Wisconsin] offer as the best guarantee of the future and the strongest claim to the continued confidence of the people, the record of the present Republican Administration and its predecessors. It is a record of the honest, economical, impartial and judicious application of sound business methods to the conduct of the various departments of the State Government.

The Democratic State Convention met at Milwaukee Sept. 5, and nominated James Morgan for Governor, Andrew Kull for Lieutenant-Governor, August C. Larson for Secretary of State, Theodore Kersten for Treasurer, Timothy E. Ryan for Attorney - General, Amos Squire for Superintendent of Schools, Herman Naber for Railroad Commissioner, and Evan W. Evans for Insurance Commissioner.

At the November election, Hoard received for Governor 155,690 votes; Morgan, 155,423 votes; Durant, 14,373; Powell, 9,196. The other candidates on the Republican ticket were also elected. The Legislature chosen at the same time will be composed as follows: Senate—Republicans 24, Democrats 6, Union Labor men 2, Independent 1; House — Republicans 70, Democrats 18, Independent 1. Democratic Congressmen were chosen in the Second and Fifth Districts, and Republicans in the remaining seven districts.

A proposed amendment to the Constitution, giving the Legislature power to prescribe the powers, duties, and compensation of the State Superintendent of Schools, was defeated, 12,-967 votes in favor of it and 18,342 against it.

WYOMING TERRITORY. Territorial Government.—The following were the Territorial officers during the year: Governor, Thomas Moonlight; Secretary of Territory, Samuel D. Shannon; Auditor, Mortimer N. Grant; Treasurer, William P. Gannett, succeeded by Luke Voorhees; Attorney - General, Hugo Douzelman; Superintendent of Education, John Slaughter; Chief-Justice of the Supreme Court, William L. Maginnis; Associates, Samuel T. Corn and Jacob P. Blair, succeeded by M. C. Saufley.

Legislative Session.—The tenth Territorial Legislature was in session from Jan. 10 to March 9. Its most important legislation relative to public institutions and the Territorial finances is discussed above. The so-called "maverick" stock-law was repealed at this session, and in its stead an act was passed creating a board of live - stock commissioners, consisting of one member from each county, appointed by the Governor for two years. This board has the appointment of local stock-inspectors, who are to take up and sell estrays, mavericks, and oth-

erwise to carry out the provisions of the law, and has control of the funds derived from such sales. A law providing for a more strict observance of the Sabbath was passed. Three new counties were created—Converse from portions of Laramie and Albany Counties, Sheridan from a portion of Johnson County, and Natrona out of a portion of Carbon County. The two former were organized during the year. A law for the promotion of immigration makes the Secretary of the Territory a commissioner of immigration, and provides a small appropriation for his use in making known the advantages of the Territory. A rearrangement of legislative districts and a reapportionment of members of the Legislature was made necessary by the creation of new counties. Congress was memorialized to provide for the early admission of the Territory as a State. The bounty laws were repealed. Other acts of the session were as follow:

Authorizing the Governor to designate Arbor Day, and to encourage tree-planting.

Regulating the business of foreign mutual life-insurance companies in the Territory.

Requiring all banks (except national banks) to publish sworn statements once each quarter, regarding their financial condition, and providing penalties for receiving deposits when the bank is in an insolvent condition.

Describing lawful fences in the Territory, and providing for penalties when the provisions of the act are violated.

Making it a felony to sign any false certificate of acknowledgment or jurat.

Authorizing the semi-annual payment of interest on bonds.

Prohibiting the unauthorized wearing of the Grand Army badge and using the letters "G. A. R." for business purposes.

Requiring owners and operators of oil-lands to plug their wells so as to shut off all water from the oil-bearing rock, and to exclude the oil and gas from the water before abandonment.

Providing for the exercise of the right of eminent domain by railroad companies.

Providing for reports of Territorial officers and boards of public institutions.

Providing for the organization, management, and control of banks, banking institutions, savings-banks, and trust and loan companies.

To protect grazing lands of Wyoming from livestock brought temporarily into the Territory from other States and Territories.

Creating the office of Territorial Engineer, and concerning appropriation of water.

Regulating the practice of pharmacy.

Providing for the release of dower by married women.

To make the mechanics' lien laws of Laramie County applicable to all parts of the Territory.

Providing a method for the taxation of live-stock on the open range.

Providing for the bonding of school districts.

Finances.—The Territorial debt at the beginning of the year was $230, in the form of 6-per-cent bonds, issued to raise funds for the construction of necessary public buildings. It was increased to $320,000 by the Legislature of this year, which authorized the issue of $90,000 in 6-per-cent bonds payable in forty years. These bonds were sold at an average premium of 12 per cent.

The assessed valuation of the Territory is about $31,000,000, or over $1,000,000 less than in 1887. As the Legislature increased the bonded debt up to the prescribed limit of one per cent. of the valuation on the basis of the assessment for 1887, which was the latest then available, it follows that the Territorial indebtedness of $320,000 now exceeds the one per cent. limit. The valuation of railroad property, included in the above total, was $5,908,-984, an increase of over $150,000 above 1887. The tax-levy for Territorial purposes was increased this year from slightly over 3 mills in 1887 to $6\frac{71}{100}$ mills, apportioned as follows: General fund, $2\frac{1}{2}$ mills; Capitol-building fund,

$30,000 this year for its completion and enlargement. For finishing and enlarging the new University building $25,000 was appropriated. A Penitentiary building at Rawlins was also provided for by the Legislature of this year, $30,000 being appropriated. The sum of $5,000 was appropriated for a Poor Asylum building at Lander, which shall cost, when completed, not more than $25,000. A building for the Deaf, Dumb, and Blind Asylum at Cheyenne has been erected, with the appropriation of $8,000 made by the Legislature of 1886 for that purpose, but no provision has yet been made for the support or management of the institution, and the building is unused.

STATE HOUSE AT CHEYENNE.

$2\frac{1}{2}$ mills; university income-tax, $\frac{1}{2}$ mill; Territorial bond-tax, $\frac{7}{10}$ of a mill; insane asylum bond-tax, $\frac{1}{10}$ of a mill; stock indemnity fund, $\frac{1}{100}$ of a mill.

Public Buildings.—Prior to 1886 the Territory was almost without public buildings, but the Legislatures of that and the present year have provided liberally therefor. The Capitol-building, begun in 1886, was so far completed in January as to be occupied by the Legislature during the session, the sum of $150,000 being expended in its erection. A further appropriation of $125,000 was made this year for enlarging the building by the addition of wings, and an extra tax of $2\frac{1}{2}$ mills was imposed for 1888 and 1889 to raise this sum. The building already completed is a substantial structure of cut and dressed stone, provided with the latest modern conveniences.

The Insane Asylum building, for which $30,-000 was appropriated in 1886, received another

Education.—The latest report of the Territorial Superintendent, for the year ending with October, 1887, presents the following statistics: Number of school-houses, 124; schools, 197; male pupils, 2,890; female pupils, 2,732; teachers, 231. The average monthly salary of teachers was $59.90. The first year of the University of Wyoming, which began on Sept. 1, 1887, was considered successful. An additional appropriation of $25.000 for the completion of the University building at Laramie City was made by the Legislature this year, and the annual levy for its support was increased from one fourth to one half of a mill, providing an income for 1888-'89 of about $15,500. The school and university public lands given by the Federal Government to the various States and Territories for educational purposes, do not by law become available until Statehood is attained, but, by a special law passed by Congress in August, the Territory of Wyoming is authorized to lease these lands for a term not exceeding five years, and a considerable increased revenue to both the school and university funds is expected from these leases.

Settlement.—The total number of acres of the public domain taken up in Wyoming, up to and inclusive of June 30, 1887, was 2,041,730; during the year ending June 30, 1888, 317,356; total, 2,359,086. This is scarcely one thirtieth of the area of the Territory.

Railroads.—The report of the Governor, dated in September, shows that 139 miles of new road were constructed during the preceding twelve months, making the total length of railroads 891 miles. The Wyoming Central has extended its road as far west as Fort Casper, or the old Platte Bridge, a distance of about 132 miles in the Territory, and for the present seems to rest there. The Cheyenne and Northern has completed the road to the Platte river in a northwesterly direction from Cheyenne, 125 miles. The Burlington and Missouri Railroad has in operation a line to Cheyenne from Sterling, on the South Platte river, 29 miles.

Coal.—Every county in the Territory has its deposits of coal, which are nowhere at such depth as to make mining expensive. No anthracite coal has been discovered. The largest mines are those operated by the Union Pacific Railroad Company. Returns from all the large companies show that the total product for 1887 was about 1,170,318 tons.

Political.—The Democratic Territorial Convention met at Cheyenne, on October 6, and nominated Caleb Perry Organ for delegate to Congress. The resolutions include the following:

The Democrats heartily favor the appointment of residents of the Territory to the Federal offices.

We desire to place ourselves on record as being emphatically opposed to the lavish use of money in our Territorial and local elections.

We believe the people of this Territory are law-abiding, and their sense of justice is sufficiently strong, with the aid of their local government, not only to maintain the public peace but to protect public and private property, and are therefore opposed to the importation of foreign police mercenaries.

On October 10 the Republican Territorial Convention met at Cheyenne, and renominated Delegate Joseph M. Carey. The platform contains the following:

The Republicans of Wyoming favor home rule, and will hail with delight the era of self-government. We now have the taxable wealth and the population necessary to support a State government, and, being therefore entitled to admission into the Union, we earnestly favor such Congressional legislation as will enable us to adopt a Constitution and secure the rights of Statehood.

We favor the adoption and enforcement of a liberal and honest policy relating to the deposition of the public lands, and we further urge the importance of securing Government aid in the construction of reservoirs in which the waters of Wyoming may be stored for the use of the people.

The Republican party is strenuously opposed to the use of money for the purpose of influencing votes, and heartily condemns this outrageous practice, which was so early introduced into our Territorial elections by the Democracy.

Both parties declare their strong opposition to Chinese immigration. At the November election, Carey received 10,451 votes, and Organ, 7,557. Members of the next Territorial Legislature were chosen as follow: Senate, Republicans, 5; Democrats, 7; House, Republicans, 17; Democrats, 7.

Y

YOUNG MEN'S CHRISTIAN ASSOCIATION. The "Year-Book" of the Young Men's Christian Association for 1888 gives lists of 1,250 associations in America, and 3,840 in the world. Of the American associations, 77 are engaged specially in work among railroad men, 10 among German-speaking young men, 273 in colleges, 29 among colored men, and 18 among Indians; 226 make mention in their reports of classes in from one to fifteen branches of study, 287 of special attention to physical culture through gymnasiums and other sports, 63 of special work among commercial travelers, 158 of organized boys' departments, and 435 of woman's auxiliaries. Among other special services spoken of are 398 Bible-classes, 367 Bible training classes, and 661 weekly prayer-meetings. The associations employ 752 men for their entire time as secretaries and assistant secretaries. The whole number of members in the American associations is 175,000, the buildings owned by them are valued at $5,609,265, and their entire property at $7,261,658. The expenditure in 1887 was $1,181,338 in local work, and $104,949 in general work. From other countries there were reported to the International Conference at Stockholm:

COUNTRIES.	Associations.	Members.
Great Britain and Ireland	601	51,513
Germany....................	673	35,732
Holland....................	505	7,409
Switzerland................	362	5,000
France.....................	93	550
Sweden....................	17	800
Belgium	23	415
Denmark...................	78	1,667
Spain	10	150
Italy......................	27	480
Turkey....................	1	25
Austria-Hungary..........	9	95
Russia....................	9	230
Norway...................	43	690
Asia......................	43	450
Africa....................	12	580
Australia and New Zealand ..	25	5,500

The associations of the world are represented in an International Union, which has a Central Executive Committee composed of delegates from each nationality, with a president, secretary, and offices at Geneva. Through this committee are arranged the triennial World's Conferences, of which the eleventh, in Stockholm, was opened Aug. 15. About 400 delegates attended; Bishop K. H. Gez von Scheele, of Visby, Sweden, was president. The review of the association work showed that it had increased largely in Germany, Switzerland, Holland, Norway, Sweden, and Paris. The following subjects were considered in formal written papers, with general discussions following them; "What the Bible says to the Young Men of Our Day," "What Means ought to be employed for the Spiritual Development of the Members and for the Conversion of Young Men in general," "The Mutual Duties of Members of the Young Men's Christian Association," "The Means which ought to be employed by the Association for the Moral Development of their Members," "Creation

and Organization of Associations," "Different Kinds of Young Men's Christian Associations," "The Real Source of Life for our Associations," "The Different Means employed for the Physical Development of Young Men," "The Young Men's Christian Association as compared with the True and False Socialism," and "The Association's Work in Non-Protestant Countries." Public meetings, held in the afternoon of each of the five days of the session of the Conference, were addressed by Messrs. Gustave Topfel, President of the Executive Central Committee; Krummacher, of Elberfeld; Soholt, of Drammen; Williams, of London; Frommel, court chaplain at Berlin; Hoskins, of London; Beck, of Denmark; Lyons, of France; Favre, of Geneva; Morse, of New York; Farwell, of Chicago, and others.

Z

ZANZIBAR, a monarchy on the eastern coast of Africa. The reigning Sultan or Seyyid is Khalifa, who succeeded his brother, Bargash ben-Said, on March 27, 1888. The island of Zanzibar has an area of 1,590 square kilometres, or 625 square miles. The Sultan's authority formerly extended along the coast of the mainland from Warsheikh to Delgado Bay, about 900 miles. In 1886 Germany established a protectorate over the interior, from the river Rovuma northward to Kilimandjaro. North of that mountain, as far as Tana river, England's sphere of influence extends, in accordance with an agreement between the two powers. Zanzibar's sovereign rights were limited to the coast between Kipini on the Ozi river and Cape Delgado, and to the garrisoned stations of Lamoo, Kismayu, Brava, Merka, Mukdusha, and Warsheikh. The population of the island of Zanzibar is about 200,000, half of whom live in the city of Zanzibar. The rulers are Arabs, and the subject population mostly negroes. The entire Arab population on the eastern coast of Africa and in the island of Zanzibar does not exceed 2,500; yet they own all the valuable soil, hold the bulk of the population in slavery, and monopolize the slave-trade. There are about 6,000 Indian traders and slave-owners in Zanzibar and on the coast, and 150 Europeans who reside in the towns.

War against Europeans.—The Arabs of Zanzibar and the interior of Africa, who, in spite of the convention made in 1873 between the Sultan of Zanzibar and the English Government, continue to supply Asia with negro slaves, organized an attack on the European settlements in the autumn of 1888, with the object of driving away the Germans, in order to keep open the caravan routes to the sea and avert the suppression of the slave-traffic. The Arab slave-traders in the vicinity of Lake Nyassa beleaguered the British missionary stations, which were on ground claimed by Portugal.

Soon afterward the Yaos, the northernmost branch of the Kaffirs, began to pour into the German settlements. On September 20, thousands of armed men from the south bank of the Rovuma appeared before Mikandini. At some of the harbors the natives refused to receive the German officials. The inhabitants finally took up arms and drove the Germans from all their establishments on the coast. When Ernst Vohsen, the chief director of the German East African Company, attempted to land at Pangani on September 5, a line of Arabs along the shore fired at the Germans, declaring that they were banded together to make a stand against the oppression and insults of the company's officials. Herr Michahelles, the German consul-general, and Herr Vohsen, in an interview with the Sultan, contradicted the stories of German violence and tyranny. They admitted that they could not return to Pangani and Tanga for some time, and accepted the arrangement proposed by Seyyid Khalifa, to the effect that the Sultan was to appoint his own governors and garrisons, and administer justice; and that the Germans were to nominate natives to superintend customs, and not to attempt to land at the ports until the population was willing to receive them. The German flag was not to be re-hoisted. The coast population would not accept an arrangement that contemplated the reinstatement of the Germans. Gen. Matthews, commanding the troops of the Sultan, who was sent to reassert the Sultan's authority in Pangani, was defeated and driven away by the rebels. The German gun-boats thereupon shelled Pangani and other places.

Blockade of the Coast.—The English colonial project, which had been begun in order to prevent the Germans from acquiring dominion over all the lake-region and the trade-routes, suffered likewise. The Sultan had lost all authority on the mainland. More than 1,000

ZANZIBAR.

Indian subjects of Great Britain, engaged in trading and agriculture, had abandoned their possessions and fled to Zanzibar. British missionary settlements had been destroyed, and some of the missionaries who could not escape were besieged in their stations. Lord Salisbury, who had made the British Government a partner in the German scheme for the conquest of the most productive regions of the African Continent, accepted Prince Bismarck's proposal to fight the slave-traders and restore European prestige by blockading the coast. Portugal, having important colonial interests to conserve, and Italy, ambitious of extending her influence in East Africa, were induced to promise assistance with their war-vessels in the naval blockade. France has no important colonial interests in this part of the continent, but she has some commerce with the African tribes, which must suffer by a blockade. The Arab dhows, when chased, have been accustomed to display the French flag, which usually has saved them from capture.

The slave trade fell away in consequence of the abolition of slavery in American countries, the co-operation of the Sultan of Zanzibar in the efforts to suppress the traffic, and the vigilance of the English patrol off the eastern coast of Africa. Recently, however, there has been an increase in the traffic. This fact has been ascribed to the establishments of the French in Madagascar and the Comoro Islands, owing to the increase of French shipping in these seas, and the facility thus given to slavers to escape under false colors. The slave-raids are now attended with more cruelty, destruction of life, and desolation than they were when the supply of slaves was more abundant and not so remote from the sea-coast. The export of slaves is variously estimated from 60,000 to 180,000 a year. At least ten lives are sacrificed in bringing one slave to market. A large proportion of the slaves that are taken die on the march or on shipboard, and the people who are not fit for slaves—the aged, the women, and the children—are either butchered by the raiders or left to starve. Large areas, once populous, have been stripped of inhabitants.

The English were not entirely sincere in their efforts to uproot slavery and put an end to the traffic in men, and the Germans were still less so, for the laws that the British Government had compelled the Sultan to enact, prohibiting the holding or hiring of slaves in the Zanzibar dominions, had, in the interest of Indian and British capitalists, been suffered to fall into desuetude, while the enterprise of the German East Africa Company was based upon slave-labor. The Belgian Government, through its consul at Zanzibar, recruited slaves for the Congo Free State, paying their masters their market value, while the slaves received an equal sum for the term of their indentures. The French Government refused the request of the German and English Governments for

liberty to search French vessels, adhering to the principle of international law that the right of search can be exercised only in case of an effective blockade, which would require three times the naval force that the parties to the blockade were disposed to employ. M. Goblet subsequently yielded when the suppression of the slave-trade was represented to him as the object of the blockade, conceding the right to search ships and boats flying French colors that were suspected of carrying slaves, but still insisted that the search for contraband of war and its seizure should be conditional on the blockade being made effective. To show its sincerity in desiring to stop the slave-traffic, the French Government sent a vessel to co-operate in the blockade.

Admiral Deinhard, of the German blockading fleet, and Admiral Fremantle, of the co-operating English squadron, declared the blockade of the coast for the purpose of preventing the exportation of slaves and the importation of arms and munitions of war in a proclamation issued on December 2. The German fleet undertook to watch the coast south of the Wanga to Lindi, and the English fleet from the Wanga northward to the island of Lamu. The English East Africa Company conciliated the Arabs in Mombassa by paying for 1,500 runaway slaves who had been harbored by the missionaries. The German squadron, which bombarded the coast opposite Zanzibar before the vessels took up their stations in the blockade, consisted of the frigate "Leipzig," the corvettes "Carola" and "Sophie," the cruisers "Möwe" and "Schwalbe," and the dispatch-boat "Pfeil." The German land force at Bagamoyo was besieged by the Arab leader, Bushire. The Germans strengthened their position at that point and at Dar-es-Salaam by building stone forts, and prepared to recover the other harbors by force of arms under protection of the blockade. They recruited native soldiers, who were employed in ineffectual operations against the coast tribes at Sadani and elsewhere, thereby closing the caravan routes and bringing ruin upon the British Indians that they had induced to resume trade, many of whom were plundered by the black soldiers in the employ of the German company. Bushire, who had 2,500 men armed with breech-loaders, captured Bagamoyo, and cut off the retreat of the Germans, who were besieged in their block-houses till December 7, when the shells of the war-vessels compelled the Arabs to withdraw. The town was laid in ruins. The German vessels bombarded Lindi, Mikandini, Tanga, Pangani, and other coast towns, destroying much property belonging to East Indians, and causing the owners to be detained as prisoners by the Arabs. The Portuguese authorities on December 10 announced the extension of the blockade and the prohibition of the importation of arms from the Rovuma to Pomba Bay, in 13° of south latitude.

INDEX TO THIS VOLUME.

A complete index to the preceding twelve volumes is issued separately.

END OF VOLUME XIII.